Pygmalion P. 98–137

Modern Drama

Selected Plays from 1879 to the Present

Edited by

Walter Levy
Pace University

PRENTICE HALL
Upper Saddle River, New Jersey 07458

Library of Congress Cataloging-in-Publication Data

Modern drama: selected plays from 1879 to the present / edited by Walter Levy.
p. cm.
Includes a selection of previously published critical essays in the appendix.
ISBN 0-13-226721-7 (pbk.)
1. Drama—19th century. 2. Drama—20th century. I. Levy, Walter.
PN6112.M537 1999
808.82'034—dc21 98-4292
CIP

Editorial Director: Charlyce Jones-Owen
Editor-in-Chief: Leah Jewell
Acquisitions Editor: Carrie Brandon
Editorial Assistant: Gianna Caradonna
AVP, Director of Production and Manufacturing: Barbara Kittle
Senior Managing Editor: Bonnie Biller
Production Liaison: Fran Russello
Editorial/Production Supervision and Interior Design: Joseph Barron/P. M. Gordon Associates, Inc.
Permissions Editor: Frederick Courtright
Manufacturing Manager: Nick Sklitsis
Prepress and Manufacturing Buyer: Mary Ann Gloriande
Cover Director: Jayne Conte
Cover Design: Kiwi Design
Director, Image Resource Center: Lori Morris–Nantz
Photo Research Supervisor: Melinda Reo
Image Permission Supervisor: Kay Dellosa
Photo Researcher: Linda Sykes
Copy Editor: Sabina Vanish

This book was set in 9/10 Palatino by Lithokraft II
and was printed and bound by Courier Companies, Inc.
The cover was printed by Phoenix Color Corp.

Printed in the United States of America
10 9 8 7 6 5 4 3 2

ISBN 0-13-226721-7

Prentice-Hall International (UK) Limited, London
Prentice-Hall of Australia Pty. Limited, Sydney
Prentice-Hall Canada Inc., Toronto
Prentice-Hall Hispanoamericana, S.A., Mexico
Prentice-Hall of India Private Limited, New Delhi
Prentice-Hall of Japan, Inc., Tokyo
Pearson Education Asia Pte. Ltd., Singapore
Editora Prentice-Hall do Brasil, Ltda., Rio de Janeiro

Contents

Acknowledgments

My sincerest appreciation to everyone who helped me bring this project to completion: Carrie Brandon, whose kindness, thoroughness, and brisk enthusiasm kept me moving forward; Tony English, who initiated this project and provided me with the initial guidance for selecting texts; and Nancy Perry, who pushed me along and set the production course of this book. Special appreciation is extended to Fred Courtright for obtaining permissions, Joe Barron for his service as production editor, and Mark Gallaher and Sabina A. Vanish, whose expert editorial skills and patience helped make my prose readable and the content accurate.

I am grateful to William A. Clary, who listened, edited, and criticized (always gently and firmly). My thanks to Joshua and Jennifer Starbuck, who make their living in the theater and were kind enough to talk me through the initial selections of the text. Seymour Hutner, whose memory for long forgotten plays is the subject for another anthology, was always ready with new suggestions. Karen Malpede kindly helped me with information about modern women playwrights. Elaine Portnow gave me some basic insight about feminism in the modern theater. Sheri Goldhirsch, artistic director of Young Playwrights, showed me the virtues of young playwrights (though I was unable to include any of them in this text).

Among my colleagues at Pace University, I am grateful to Sherman Raskin, who provided me with support, counsel, and the time I needed to complete my research and writing; Abraham Silverstein, who helped out with his knowledge of art history; and the staff at the Henry Birnbaum Library, especially Elizabeth Birnbaum, Michelle Fanelli, Luce Gonzalez, and William McBride.

I also extend my sincere appreciation to those who reviewed the book for Prentice Hall: Gene Barnett, Department of English, Farleigh Dickinson University, Teaneck, New Jersey, campus; George L. Meshke, Drama Director, Yakima Valley Community College, Yakima, Washington; Howard L. McMillen, Department of English, Indiana State University, Terre Haute; Evelyn S. Newlyn, Department of English, State University of New York, Brockport campus; and D. Douglas Waters, Department of English, University of Wisconsin, Eau Claire campus.

My thanks to my children, Alexander Levy, Mathew Levy, Katherine Freitag, and Kristina Wronski, who think that writing a book is fun and get pleasure from reading their names in the preface and my name on the title page. My thanks to Jerrold Freitag, Matthew Stark, Christopher and Willa Hallowell, and Robert and Karin Gettings, all of whom listened kindly. Mitchell and Skit Rabbino, whose love of Broadway is boundless, kept me in touch with what it means to be a devoted theatergoer. For companionship, there was Rex the

Wonder Dog, who sat alongside my chair and knew that when the computer was turned off, and the buzzer sounded, it was time for a well-deserved walk.

Most of all, I appreciate Gene Lovelace Moncrief, my wife, who lovingly endured my quirkiness and the time spent compiling this text. I wish the hours spent elsewhere might have been with you.

Introduction

Disciples and Descendants of Ibsen and Strindberg, 1879–1992

What is called "contemporary drama" is descended from two nineteenth-century Scandinavians, Henrik Ibsen (1828–1906), a Norwegian, and August Strindberg (1849–1912), a Swede. It is to them we owe the profound change from a drama that was aristocratic to a drama that is primarily middle class. There are many influences leading to Ibsen and Strindberg, but in the final years of the twentieth century, we view these two playwrights as the central axis for the past 125 years of drama. Their influence is so pervasive that the playwrights represented in this anthology, whatever their affiliation, label, or school, are their disciples or descendants.

Separated by a generation in age, and very different in temperament, Ibsen and Strindberg never met, but they watched each other warily at a distance. Ibsen was contemptuous of Strindberg's scandalous personal life; Strindberg admired Ibsen's plays but did not like the man, whom he considered old-fashioned. Ibsen and Strindberg, however, share many of the characteristics they incorporated into their plays. By birth, both were essentially middle class: Ibsen's father was a successful merchant who went bust; Strindberg's father was a minor aristocrat who married a barmaid. Both failed at university education: Ibsen because he could not pass the entrance examinations, Strindberg because he was too impatient with going to classes. Both rebelled against oppressive social decorum and refused to be compliant or accommodating. Both lived as expatriates: Ibsen for seventeen years in Denmark, Germany, and Italy, and Strindberg for fifteen years in France, Germany, Denmark, and Italy. As dramatic craftsmen, each disdained the fashion of artificiality and made his plays seem real. They drew on contemporary situations that were readily known to audiences, who were often shocked to recognize conflicts (personal, familial, political, or social) that they considered unpleasant to behold in public. Ibsen and Strindberg each portrayed the struggles of individuals trying to come to terms with themselves in a society they found neither congenial nor compliant. They often used their own experience (Ibsen) or personal demons (Strindberg) as the source of inspiration. Both began as traditionalists but shifted to the avant-garde. With success, they became idols of the mainstream theater, and in their turn, targets for criticism by newer playwrights. For example, Sam Shepard observes in "Language, Visualization and the Inner Library" (1977) that he needs to be an experimental playwright unhampered by convention: "I'm talking now about an open-ended structure where anything could happen as opposed to a carefully planned and regurgitated event which, for me, has always been as painful as pissing nickels. There are writers who work this way successfully, and I admire them and all, but I don't see the point exactly."

Ibsenism

Ibsen's early and mid-career were dedicated to writing history and traditional drawing room drama. Then he found his true voice and turned to realism. His brilliant innovation was to revise the familiar well-made play used by the French playwright Augustin Eugène Scribe (1791–1861) as a vehicle for entertainment and comedy and make it into a discussion of social ideas. Beginning with *A Doll's House,* which he wrote in Rome, Ibsen presents contemporary middle-class characters in a realistic setting, usually a parlor or drawing room, where they discuss personal and social problems, such as marriage, morality, and venereal disease. By turning frivolous domestic melodrama on its head, Ibsen caused *A Doll's House* and subsequent plays to become known as "problem plays," a term still in currency. By centering plot and character among the middle class, Ibsen sidestepped the issue of classical tragedy, which is concerned with nobility and aristocrats. In effect, he conspicuously created serious bourgeois drama that is still the main concern of contemporary plays.

Ibsen's most important disciple was George Bernard Shaw (1856–1950), whose collection of essays *Quintessence of Ibsenism* (1891, rev. 1913) rallied support for Ibsen in England and the United States. Shaw tirelessly defended Ibsen's plays and in "The Problem Play—A Symposium" (1895) argued that "the material of the dramatist is always some conflict of human feeling with circumstances; so that, since institutions are circumstances, every social question furnishes material for drama. But every drama does not involve a social question, because human feeling may be in conflict with circumstances which are not institutions, which raise no question at all, which are part of human destiny." Ibsen was not a political activist. Shaw, however, seized on the problem play as a vehicle for social satire, class conflict, and political reform. He was so taken with this form that he began writing his own plays, beginning with *Widowers' Houses* (1892), in which the poor and slum lords conflict. Over the next decade Shaw followed with *Arms and the Man* (1894), *Major Barbara* (1905), and *Pygmalion* (1913), all of which are problem plays based on sociopolitical events of Victorian and Edwardian England.

Ibsen's problem plays find variations not only in Shaw but also in the work of such playwrights as Oscar Wilde, John Millington Synge, Anton Chekhov, Lillian Hellman, Arthur Miller, Lorraine Hansberry, Tom Stoppard, Marsha Norman, and Wendy Wasserstein. These playwrights have their own characteristics, but they share Ibsen's structural and technical aspects of realism: setting action in a specific locality with true-to-life detail, linking of time and place to the characters, and portraying of middle-class characters in conflict with social and political decorum, threatening to thwart self-expression or fulfillment of codes of ethical conduct.

Arthur Miller's homage to Ibsen is seen in his revision of the problem play, first in *All My Sons* (1947) and then *Death of a Salesman* (1949). In the introduction to his adaptation of Ibsen's *An Enemy of the People* (1950), Miller said, "Every Ibsen play begins with the unwritten words: 'Now listen here!' And these words have shown me a path through the wall of 'entertainment,' a pretense fraud, of the business of the stage. Whatever else Ibsen has to teach, this is his first and greatest contribution." Like Ibsen, Miller contends that his fictional character's ability to face his personal failures makes him a hero. Unlike Ibsen, Miller argues that the hero's struggle raises him above the local problem, and so makes him a tragic hero in search of his universal destiny.

Less complimentary to Ibsen is Edward Albee, who takes Ibsenism to task. When asked by interviewer Walter Wager if his play *Who's Afraid of Virginia Woolf?* (1962) is something that Ibsen might have written, Albee responded, "More Strindberg than Ibsen. Ibsen approached things from a much more sociological point of view, rather than psychological. . . . I'm glad Ibsen happened because he helped free a lot of playwrights from artificial convention. But I do think too many of our playwrights are limited by imitation of Ibsen."

Albee's distinction—that Ibsen is sociological while Strindberg is psychological—highlights the division of influence between these playwrights. August Strindberg's innovations began when he gave up writing traditional history plays and found his métier analyzing the psychological motives and actions of dramatic characters. As with Ibsen's, Strindberg's plays are about middle-class people. But his characters are more volatile and are deeply involved in a mordant battle between the sexes and constant class struggle. These conflicts mirrored Strindberg's own life, something that he was not embarrassed to showcase, even if it proved scandalous. Ibsen's problem plays had aroused strong passions because he dared to discuss marriage from a woman's point of view, women's rights, divorce, and venereal disease, but about his private life he was socially reserved. Alternately, Strindberg never avoided scandal if one could be found.

Strindberg

By the time Strindberg began to write, realism had been superseded by naturalism, and he was most influenced by the French novelist Émile Zola (1840–1902), who attempted to use scientific factualness (truth) and psychological analysis to probe motivations and actions. Zola wanted an antiromantic literature based on realistic observation and scientific fact. He argued that characters must withstand the scrutiny of psychological analysis and that scenery, approximating real living space, should define and suggest mood and atmosphere. Strindberg too was infused with the desire to deromanticize literature, and he adopted Zola's stern verisimilitude and made it his own.

Strindberg's characters derive motivation from their inner lives; character is more important than plot and motivation more important than action. This is so in *The Father* (1887) and in *Miss Julie* (1888), probably Strindberg's best expositions of naturalism, which offended the smug aristocratic and middle-class Swedish theatergoers, who expected a well-made play. Seeking to explain *his* sense of drama, Strindberg's "Preface" to *Miss Julie* was intended as a manifesto for naturalism and a warning that he had broken with established conventions of literature and drama: "If my tragedy depresses many people, it is their own fault. When we become as strong as the first French revolutionaries, it will afford nothing but pleasure and relief to witness the thinning out in royal parks of overage, decaying trees that have long stood in the way of others equally entitled to their time in the sun, the kind of relief we feel when we see someone incurably ill die!"

Always restless and always searching for new venues, Strindberg continued to innovate until he carried his art beyond naturalism to a realm of ordered chaos called expressionism, an art theory whose proponents exalt the inner state of mind and, most importantly, defy verisimilitude. Strindberg was drawn to expressionism because of its heavy reliance on the exploration of ego. Nevertheless, he saw no contradiction between the two theories, and depending on his creative mood and emotional needs, he could write as either a naturalist or an expressionist. Paradoxically, expressionism is a kind of romanticism centering on analysis of one's ego, but Strindberg was capable of being contrary, and he understood the need for the flexibility of romantic vision.

Like many romantic artists, Strindberg used his personal life as the main source of his art, recasting events and conflicts. In *A Dream Play* (1902), he attempted to recreate the logic of a dream: events are loosely connected and relationships are deliberately ambiguous, even absurd. This line of artistic expression was enormously influential and is still a major resource for the avant-garde. Strindberg's many descendants include Luigi Pirandello, Eugene O'Neill, Susan Glaspell, Thornton Wilder, Tennessee Williams, Samuel Beckett, Eugène Ionesco, Harold Pinter, Edward Albee, Sam Shepard, and August Wilson. Each occupies a niche in the dramatic repertoire. Tennessee Williams, for instance, called *The Glass Menagerie* (1944) a memory play, and in his "Production Notes," he divulged his debt to Strindberg:

> Expressionism and all other unconventional techniques in drama have only one valid aim, and that is a closer approach to the truth. When a play employs unconventional techniques, it is not, or certainly shouldn't be, trying to escape its responsibility of dealing with reality, or interpreting existence, but is actually or should be attempting to find a closer approach, a more penetrating and vivid expression of things as they are. The straight realistic play with its genuine Frigidaire and authentic ice-cubes, its characters who speak exactly as its audience speaks, corresponds to the academic landscape and has the same virtue as a photographic likeness. Everyone should know nowadays the unimportance of the photographic in art: that truth, life, or reality is an organic thing which the poetic imagination can represent or suggest, in essence, only through transformation, through changing into other forms than those which were merely present in appearance.

The Theater of the Absurd

Out of the dark age of social and philosophical dislocation following World War II came a group of playwrights linked by their belief that modern life was without harmony or hope. The term "Theater of the Absurd" was coined by drama critic Martin Esslin in *The Theatre of the Absurd* (1961):

> The hallmark of this attitude is its sense that the certitudes and unshakable basic assumptions of former ages have been swept away, that they have been tested and found wanting, that they have been discredited as cheap and somewhat childish illusions. The decline of religious faith was masked until the end of the Second World War by the substitute religions of faith in progress, nationalism, and various totalitarian fallacies. All this was shattered by the war.

The chief playwrights of the Absurdists are Eugène Ionesco (1912–1994) and Samuel Beckett (1906–1989), who recognized in Strindberg's expressionist plays the means for defining their characters: unrealistic and incomprehensible situations, incongruous action, repetitive dialogue, illogical reasoning, and bitter humor. Beginning in the early 1950s, these playwrights pushed the limits of expressionism and created an illusion of unreality so that their plays appear chaotic and meaningless. What Ionesco did in his plays was to create a *different* reality based on imagined truth that he said is "more profound, more loaded with significance, than everyday reality." In the "Preface" (1960) to his most important play, *Rhinoceros* (1954), Ionesco wrote,

> *Rhinoceros* is certainly an anti-Nazi play, yet it is also and mainly an attack on collective hysteria and the epidemics that lurk beneath the surface of reason and ideas but are none the less serious collective diseases passed off as ideologies: once we realize that History has lost its reason, that lying propaganda masks a contradiction between the facts and the ideologies that explain them, once we cast a lucid eye on the world as it is today, this is enough to stop us being taken in by irrational reasons and so help us not to lose our heads.

In contrast to problem plays such as Ibsen's, absurd plays do not tell a story in a traditional way but present scenes that are often plotless. Scenes are meant to convey images of situations, portraying the complexity and disparity of a chaotic world, as the world appears to playwrights at the time of writing the play. Realism, or verisimilitude, is abandoned in favor of symbolism and abstraction. Playwrights first confuse in order to enlighten, and they make a deliberate attempt to break down conventions. Edward Albee, a second-generation Absurdist in the United States, defined this outlook in his essay "Which Theatre Is Absurd" (1962) by suggesting that the realistic theater is absurd because it pretends to be self-congratulatory and reassuring. Albee proclaimed that the Theater of the Absurd does not pretend because it shows the world as it is—bereft of moral, religious, and social structures that make sense. In England, Harold Pinter is the chief disciple of Beckett. Since the late 1960s, his plays have been central to the English theater. Critics and audiences are still baffled by a Pinter play, but the British establishment now embraces him. In the United States, Sam Shepard's plays that intentionally blur thought and action are still among the avant-garde, though many of them date back to the late 1960s.

Brecht's Epic Theater

Bertolt Brecht (1898–1956) was influenced by both Ibsen and Strindberg, but his sense of the theater was unromantic and political. Like Zola, he used the play as a means for political action and social awareness after the chaos of World War I. But unlike Ibsen or Strindberg, Brecht created a politically based theater, Epic Theater, specifically designed to satirize middle-class values, capitalism in particular. Brecht found his milieu with *The Threepenny Opera* (1928), a modern satire of John Gay's ballad-opera, *The Beggar's Opera* (1728). Together with his collaborator Kurt Weill, who wrote the music, Brecht aimed at lowering opera, making it a tool for sociopolitical criticism.

Brecht's dramatic theory borrowed a little from Ibsen, more from Strindberg, and most of all from his own belief that his drama should exemplify the tenets of Marxism and Communist socialism. Along with his theatrical collaborator Erwin Piscator, Brecht revised the traditional act and scene structure of drama and replaced it with a series of episodes, something on the order of a vaudeville show or cinematic montage. The illusion of reality is discarded, and the stage becomes a platform for ideas. Scenery is reduced to essentials, often just a stage with the stage workings—scaffolds, ropes, and so on—left open for scrutiny. The actors are meant to be seen and understood by the audience not as persons observed in activities but as actors acting. The audience is supposed to think about what the actors say and to be moved more by intellect than by emotion, which according to Brecht is romantic and unreliable. In Epic Theater, the message is more important than the production, which is often purposely crude and blatantly artificial.

Chekhov, Pirandello, and Wilder

As a realist, Anton Chekhov (1860–1904) is Ibsen's descendant. He explored social and domestic problems, but unlike lbsen's, his plays are essentially plotless. For Chekhov, the action of the characters is secondary to their psychological lives, an outlook that links him to Strindberg but without Strindberg's ferocity. Chekhov's characters bemoan the passing of the old regime and the supplanting of their own aristocracy by middle-class nouveaux riches. Much of the mood in his plays is nostalgia for a past that has just about faded from memory. At first, Chekhov's plays left his audiences baffled because neither the directors nor the actors understood the psychology of the characters. Under the direction of Konstantin Stanislavsky, however, Chekhov's genius was realized on stage, first with *The Seagull* (1896), but also more particularly with *The Cherry Orchard* (1904). Stanislavsky's understanding of psychological realism provided the right approach to Chekhov's characters and their largely passive turmoil. Stanislavsky took issue with Ibsen's accentuation of realistic situations, and in *My Life in Art* (1925) he explained that a new method of production and acting was required because realism and local color were passé.

The influence of Chekhov's psychological realism became pervasive. It is found in Luigi Pirandello's *Six Characters in Search of an Author* (1921), Eugene O'Neill's *Desire Under the Elms* (1924), Tennessee Williams's *The Glass Menagerie*, Arthur Miller's *All My Sons* (1947), Edward Albee's *Zoo Story* (1959), and Sam Shepard's *Buried Child* (1978). It is not what happens in *Zoo Story* that matters, for example, but the examination of character. And Shepherd's *Buried Child* may be scanty in plot, but it is strong on portrayal of the psychological life of the characters.

Overall, modern theater is varied. It ranges to extremes, from realism and naturalism to expressionism and absurdism. It has no absolute pattern but reveals competing styles and competing philosophical, social, spiritual, and political points of view. These elements coexist and cross-fertilize each other, but they have also caused fierce conflicts that have never been entirely resolved. Luigi Pirandello (1867–1936), for example, like Ibsen and Shaw, seized on the ambiguities of middle-class morality and exposed its superficiality and personal tragedies. On the other hand, like Strindberg, Pirandello applied many aspects of expressionism in his plays, especially the interaction of illusion and reality, which he said creates a drama carried along by the actions that confuse the planes of reality, making action like a dream that intrudes into waking life. Having revealed his dramatic precursor in his "Preface to *Six Characters in Search of an Author*" (1921), Pirandello said that his plays, like Strindberg's dream plays, were intended to be chaotic—a romantic mix of the realistic and the fantastic.

Thornton Wilder (1894–1976) is a curious mixture. His plays seem traditional, but he was especially influenced by Strindberg's expressionist plays. Wilder was also deeply inspired by Gertrude Stein's minimalism and by the idea of hiding metaphor and making the characters and actions seem flat. The simplicity of *Our Town*, his most influential play, is undercut by the nonrealistic staging and setting and by the use of a narrator. The action is so smoothly jointed that it moves from reality to unreality, as if this is a matter of course. Wilder is neither exuberant like Eugene O'Neill, nor flamboyant like Tennessee Williams, nor a social moralist like Arthur Miller. Contrary to the dreamy chaos of Strindberg's dream plays or Pirandello's planned confusion, Wilder makes the case for strong narration, characters defined by action, and action measured against a Christian moralism, positions that leave him open to the accusation of being "old-fashioned."

The Efficacy of Labels

According to the fashion of the era, playwrights are often associated with artistic movements. The exactitude of labeling is sometimes misleading, however. Eugene O'Neill praised Strindberg as his master when he received the Nobel Prize for Literature, but he complained that he was confounded by labels. In 1925, in a personal letter to critic A. H. Quinn, O'Neill wrote,

> It's not in me to pose much as a "misunderstood" one, but it does seem discouragingly (that is, if one lacked a sense of ironic humor!) evident to me that most of my critics don't want to see what I am trying to do or how I'm trying to do it, although I flatter myself that end and means are characteristic, individual, and positive enough not to be mistaken for anyone's else or for those of any "modern" or "pre-modern" school. To be called a "sordid Realist" one day, a "grim pessimistic Naturalist" the next, a "lying Moral Romanticist" the next, a "violent Expressionist" the next, etc., etc., is quite perplexing—not to add the [*New York*] *Times* editorial that settled *Desire* [*Under the Elms*] once and for all by calling it a "Neo-Primitive," a Matisse of the drama, as it were! So I'm really longing to explain and try and convince some sympathetic ear that I've tried to make myself a melting pot for all these methods, seeing some virtues for my ends in each of them, and thereby, if there is enough real fire in me, boil down to *my own* technique.

Although in their time, Ibsen and Strindberg were both avant-garde, they are now the Old Masters. As this century ends, Ibsen, Strindberg, and Chekhov are being rediscovered by contemporary playwrights eager to revise the plays and make them modern and fashionable. Some critics may be bothered by tampering with "sacred texts," but these new revisions show how important they have become to contemporary theater.

HENRIK IBSEN

Henrik Ibsen (1828–1906) was prickly, combative, and probably manic-depressive. At the time of his birth his family was financially successful and Ibsen received a good education. But when the family fell on hard times, Ibsen lost his place in the society of the small Norwegian town of Skien where he had been born. He seems always to have suffered from a kind of social inferiority, which was manifest in his disdain for Norwegian middle-class values. He eventually turned away from his parents and family, did not communicate with his father for twenty-five years, and resolutely followed his own path.

At sixteen, Ibsen was apprenticed to a pharmacist and worked with him until he was twenty-two, when he left to study for matriculation at the university in Christiania (Oslo, the big town mentioned in *A Doll's House*). To his chagrin, Ibsen failed his examinations, but undaunted, and already the author of three unsuccessful plays, he decided on a literary career as a poet and playwright. By 1851 he was working as dramatist for the Bergen Theater, and in 1857 he was appointed director of the Norwegian National Theater in Christiania. His work as a director added new dimensions to theatrical productions because he tended to stage plays from a playwright's point of view. Among his plays of this period are *The Warriors of Helgeland* (1857) and *The Pretenders* (1864).

Love's Comedy (1862), Ibsen's only comedy, is about the incompatibility of love and marriage. It was obvious to many at the time, but generally unsaid, that this was an autobiographical play. Henrik and his wife Suzannah had only one child, a son named Sigurd, and their marriage was successful but perhaps loveless. Though he was devoted to and dependent on Suzannah and Sigurd, Ibsen's art came first. Ibsen's nickname for Suzannah was "eagle"; her nickname for him was "tiger" or "bear." Even in their private correspondence, Suzannah refers to him in the third person as "Ibsen."

The National Theater failed when Ibsen was thirty-six. He had a wife and child, no job prospects, and little money. Searching for a way out, Ibsen decided to leave Norway for a more congenial environment. So with a small grant from the Norwegian government, borrowed money, and financial assistance from a friend, he left Norway to go south. From 1864 to 1891 he lived as an expatriate among Scandinavians, mainly in Germany and Italy. During this time, Norway was establishing its independence from Sweden, but Ibsen preferred Norwegian life from a distance, and being an expatriate gave him the room he needed to write about subjects and themes that he held dear. *The League of Youth* (1869), a satire of Norwegian politics and petty-mindedness, was written in Dresden, Germany.

Ibsen was pragmatic about his financial arrangements (usually he was just on the edge of economic solvency), and until *A Doll's House* brought him success, he generally published his plays as texts before they were produced. In this way he could earn income from books sold as well as from play productions. *Brand*

(1866) and *Peer Gynt* (1867), his major efforts in mid-career, were conceived as dramatic or epic poems before they became plays.

Brand was a success, but it only temporarily staved off Ibsen's economic troubles. In it, Brand, a young priest, denounces modern hedonism, but the play may also be understood as a commentary on Ibsen's life at age forty-eight: for Brand read Ibsen; for Brand's wife, Agnes, read Suzannah. When Agnes and their child are told to leave for a warmer climate to restore their health, Brand chooses not to heed this advice. Agnes and the child die, and Brand is distraught. He leads his parishioners up the mountain in order to find God. Unsuccessful, they turn on Brand and stone him. Bloody and in pain, he is mistaken for Christ by Gerd, a mad woman whom he meets high on the mountain in a place called the Ice Church. When Gerd shoots a rifle at an imaginary hawk that she believes torments her, both she and Brand are killed by an avalanche. In the thunder of the avalanche, Brand asks who will save mankind, and a voice answers "the God of Love." In real life, Ibsen was not so sanguine, and he waited for success, angry with his critics for not appreciating his genius.

Peer Gynt was written as a dramatic poem in five acts. It was not produced until 1876, when the production was accompanied by a musical score by Edvard Grieg (1843–1907), Norway's most prominent composer. *Peer Gynt* is based on the adventures of a picaresque folk hero confronted by the ethical dilemma of whether to live an ordinary life or the life of a wandering egocentric. The play shows the influence of Søren Kierkegaard (1813–1855), the Danish philosopher whom Ibsen studied during this period. The poem received a very mixed response but has become a Norwegian national epic.

In 1873 Ibsen completed *Emperor and Galilean*, the last of his epic historical dramas about the Roman emperor Julian. He had been working on this play for nine years, and he expected that it would be hailed as a great work, but it was only moderately successful. However, with the play finished, he began to work out a concept for a new drama that was not historical but emphatically current, dealing with problems of modern living. He made the characters more realistic by allowing them to converse in ordinary daily language. This shift in style now seems commonplace, but in the 1870s it provided startling and effective theater. The plays of this period include *A Doll's House* (1879) and *Ghosts* (1881), both of which deal with the problem of a bad marriage, venereal disease, and the struggle of women to achieve independent identities.

The plot of *Ghosts* (1881) inverts the story of *A Doll's House*, which ends with a wife leaving her husband. In *Ghosts*, Mrs. Alving leaves her husband but is persuaded to return by Pastor Manders, the man she really loves. She has a child by her husband and is then tormented when she learns that the boy has inherited his father's syphilis. The play antagonized Scandinavian audiences, and Ibsen was vilified by critics.

His next play, *An Enemy of the People* (1882), focuses on ethics and idealism. It is about Stockmann, an idealistic doctor and scientist, who calls attention to the adulterated water in the spa that is the chief economic resource in his town. Stockmann's moral rectitude and inflexibility lead to his vilification. At the end of the final act, he and his family huddle in their parlor while the townspeople pelt the house with stones.

The Wild Duck (1885) is about a man whose zealous pursuit of truth leads to disaster. *Rosmersholm* (1886) concerns Rebecca West's marital triangle, which ultimately results in three suicides. In *The Lady from the Sea* (1888), Ibsen again reverses the plot and conflict of *A Doll's House*. In this instance, the heroine, Ellida Wangel, refuses to go away with a mysterious stranger when her husband offers her the freedom of choice. Ellida accepts the role of wife and stepmother because she has the free will to choose. The fact that she chooses to stay clearly demonstrates the priority of social obligation over personal emotional needs.

In *Hedda Gabler* (1890), a woman's passionate desires are repressed by her almost neurotic sense of propriety. Hedda Gabler marries the mousy George Tesman because the marriage provides her with wealth and social stability. She repels Eilert Løvborg, a bohemian poet for whom she has a passion, because her inhibitions make her incapable of returning his amorous advances. In a fit of jealousy, she destroys Løvborg's manuscript, and at the play's climax she realizes that she is implicated in his suicide. Unable to face scandal, Hedda kills herself with her father's pistol.

During the last period of his career, Ibsen moved toward an examination of problems that are more symbolic in theme and content. Plays of this period concern older men (like Ibsen himself) who must reconcile their art and life's work with vitality and passion. *The Master Builder* (1892), which is about ego, sexuality, and old age, depicts an architect who falls from a tower in an attempt to impress a young woman. *John Gabriel Borkman* (1896) is a play with a Faustian theme that deals with a man who gives up love for power. Borkman fails at love, suffers the indignity of serving a jail sentence for fraud, and, incapable of redemption, dies unrepentant.

A Doll's House was produced when Ibsen was fifty-one, and its success provided most of his income for the remainder of his career. As a text it became a best-seller; and in the theater it played to sold-out audiences. It was also his first play to gain critical popularity outside of Scandinavia and Germany, and it brought him wider recognition.

It is based on the experiences of an acquaintance of Ibsen's named Laura Keeler, who borrowed money from a friend in order to take her sick husband to Italy to improve his health. When the friend needed immediate repayment of the loan, Keeler was unable to pay him. Ibsen, who did not know the whole story, could have helped Keeler by endorsing a novel that she had written, but he would not because he didn't think it worthy of praise. Desperate, Keeler forged a check. When she was found out, her husband repudiated her as his wife and the mother of their children. Keeler went mad, and when she recovered, abjectly asked for forgiveness.

The Keeler incident occurred at a time when Ibsen was looking for a new plot for his next play. He worked out the story and the problem in Munich, where he was living, and then completed the play during a stay in Rome and Amalfi in 1878. Ibsen's "Note for a Modern Tragedy," written at this time, shows him working out the problem:

> There are two kinds of moral laws, two kinds of conscience, one for men, and one, quite different, for women. They don't understand each other; but in

> practical life, the woman is judged by masculine law, as though she weren't a woman but a man. . . . She has committed a forgery, and is proud of it; for she has done it out of love for her husband, to save his life. But this husband of hers takes his standpoint, conventionally honorable, on the side of the law, and sees the situation with masculine eyes.

Ibsen rearranged the real personal events to suit his moral theme: rather than with Keeler's abject contrition, he concludes the play by presenting a woman on the verge of commanding her own destiny, even if it means abandoning her husband and children.

Like his previous plays, *A Doll's House* is carefully constructed as a traditional narrative leading to a climax and resolution. By a stroke of genius, however, Ibsen reinterpreted the "well-made play" that French playwright Eugène Scribe (1791–1861) developed for comedy and farce. As a dour Scandinavian, Ibsen disdained comedy, and he made serious social issues the center of the action, essentially inventing the "problem play," so-called because the plot's conflict poses a problem of ethical or conscientious behavior that the characters have to resolve. Ibsen's well-made play, like Scribe's, reveals the characters, the setting, and the conflict in the first act, shows the increasing tension caused by the conflict in the second act, and leads directly to an intense climax and resolution in the third act. The play ends with characters either overcoming obstacles that before seemed insurmountable or being trapped by their fate succumbing to spiritual or physical death.

In *A Doll's House*, Torvald Helmer's ego and puritan rigidity render him incapable of sympathy for his own wife's transgressions. He loves honor too much and his wife too little. When his wife, Nora, forces him to see the harshness of his behavior, it is too late for reconciliation, and she leaves home, husband, and children. Through this act of defiance, Nora achieves a personal freedom and a sense of victory when she overcomes her fear of scandal and personal shame to break her ties with her husband Torvald.

Having raised the issues of women's rights in marriage and divorce, the play caused a sensation. It was all the more sensational because it is the woman who leaves the man and because Ibsen defends Nora's actions and moral integrity. Ibsen seems to not have intended it, but the play precipitated a fierce public discussion of the social and moral aspects of marriage. It established Ibsen as a defender of women's rights, something that he was uncomfortable about outside of the realm of drama.

Ibsen's plays were slow to be produced in England. It took ten years for *A Doll's House* to be staged in London, and *Ghosts* was not presented until 1891. English Victorians and Edwardians were uncomfortable with subjects such as women's rights, divorce, venereal disease, and adultery being portrayed in household parlors similar to their own. Despite their controversy, the plays found an approving audience, especially through the support of William Archer, who first translated Ibsen into English, and George Bernard Shaw, then a leading drama critic. Shaw was so impressed that he became a leader of the Ibsenites, a group dedicated to supporting Ibsen's drama. In *The Quintessence of Ibsenism* (1891, rev. 1913), Shaw explained that Ibsen's drama had forever changed the technique of constructing plays. Inspired, Shaw began his own career as a dramatist by writing problem plays that deal with important social issues. The line of influence from Ibsen to Shaw greatly affected modern and contemporary dramatists who work in the style of the well-made play, especially Eugene O'Neill, Susan Glaspell, Lillian Hellman, Arthur Miller, and Lorraine Hansberry.

Film

A Doll's House (1959), with Julie Harris, Christopher Plummer, Jason Robards, Jr., Hume Cronyn, Eileen Heckart, and Richard Thomas. MGM.

A Doll's House (1973), directed by Joseph Losey, with Jane Fonda, Edward Fox, Trevor Howard, David Warner, and Delphine Syrig. World Film Services/Films de la Boétie.

A Doll's House (1989), directed by Patrick Garland, with Claire Bloom, Anthony Hopkins, Ralph Richardson, Denholm Elliot, Anna Massey, and Edith Evans. Elkins/Freeward.

A Doll's House

TRANSLATED BY OTTO REINERT

CHARACTERS

TORVALD HELMER, a lawyer
NORA, his wife
DR. RANK
MRS. LINDE
KROGSTAD
THE HELMERS' THREE SMALL CHILDREN
ANNE-MARIE, the children's nurse
A HOUSEMAID
A PORTER

SCENE. *The Helmers' living room.*

ACT I

A pleasant, tastefully but not expensively furnished, living room. A door on the rear wall, right, leads to the front hall, another door, left, to HELMER*'s study. Between the two doors a piano. A third door in the middle of the left wall; further front a window. Near the window a round table and a small couch. Towards the rear of the right wall a fourth door; further front a tile stove with a rocking chair and a couple of armchairs in front of it. Between the stove and the door a small table. Copperplate etchings on the walls. A whatnot with porcelain figurines and other small objects. A small bookcase with de luxe editions. A rug on the floor; fire in the stove. Winter day.*

The doorbell rings, then the sound of the front door opening. NORA, *dressed for outdoors, enters, humming cheerfully. She carries several packages, which she puts down on the table, right. She leaves the door to the front hall open; there a* PORTER *is seen holding a Christmas tree and a basket. He gives them to the* MAID *who has let them in.*

NORA: Be sure to hide the Christmas tree, Helene. The children mustn't see it before tonight when we've trimmed it. [*Opens her purse; to the* PORTER.] How much?

PORTER: Fifty ore.

NORA: Here's a crown. No, keep the change. [*The* PORTER *thanks her, leaves.* NORA *closes the door. She keeps laughing quietly to herself as she takes off her coat, etc. She takes a bag of macaroons from her pocket and eats a couple. She walks cautiously over to the door to the study and listens.*] Yes, he's home. [*Resumes her humming, walks over to the table, right.*]

HELMER [*in his study*]: Is that my little lark twittering out there?

NORA [*opening some packages*]: That's right.

HELMER: My squirrel bustling about?

NORA: Yes.

HELMER: When did squirrel come home?

NORA: Just now. [*Puts the bag of macaroons back in her pocket, wipes her mouth.*] Come out here, Torvald. I want to show you what I've bought.

HELMER: I'm busy! [*After a little while he opens the door and looks in, pen in hand.*] Bought, eh? All that? So little wastrel has been throwing money around again?

NORA: Oh but Torvald, this Christmas we can be a little extravagant, can't we? It's the first Christmas we don't have to scrimp.

HELMER: I don't know about that. We certainly don't have money to waste.

NORA: Yes, Torvald, we do. A little, anyway. Just a tiny little bit? Now that you're going to get that big salary and make lots and lots of money.

HELMER: Starting at New Year's, yes. But payday isn't till the end of the quarter.

NORA: That doesn't matter. We can always borrow.

HELMER: Nora! [*Goes over to her and playfully pulls her ear.*] There you go being irresponsible again. Suppose I borrowed a thousand crowns today and you spent it all for Christmas and on New Year's Eve a tile hit me in the head and laid me out cold.

NORA [*putting her hand over his mouth*]: I won't have you say such horrid things.

HELMER: But suppose it happened. Then what?

NORA: If it did, I wouldn't care whether we owed money or not.

HELMER: But what about the people I had borrowed from?

NORA: Who cares about them! They are strangers.

HELMER: Nora, Nora, you *are* a woman! No, really! You know how I feel about that. No debts! A home in debt isn't a free home, and if it isn't free it isn't beautiful. We've managed nicely so far, you and I, and that's the way we'll go on. It won't be for much longer.

NORA [*walks over toward the stove*]: All right, Torvald. Whatever you say.

HELMER [*follows her*]: Come, come, my little songbird mustn't droop her wings. What's this? Can't have a pouty squirrel in the house, you know. [*Takes out his wallet.*] Nora, what do you think I have here?

NORA [*turns around quickly*]: Money!

HELMER: Here. [*Gives her some bills.*] Don't you think I know Christmas is expensive?

NORA [*counting*]: Ten—twenty—thirty—forty. Thank you, thank you, Torvald. This helps a lot.

HELMER: I certainly hope so.

NORA: It does, it does. But I want to show you what I got. It was cheap, too. Look. New clothes for Ivar. And a sword. And a horse and trumpet for Bob. And a doll and a little bed for Emmy. It isn't any good, but it wouldn't last, anyway. And here's some dress material and scarves for the maids. I feel bad about old Anne-Marie, though. She really should be getting much more.

Donald Madden, Patricia Elliott, and Claire Bloom in A Doll's House, *directed by Patrick Garland, the Playhouse Theatre, 1971.*

HELMER: And what's in here?

NORA [*cries*]: Not till tonight!

HELMER: I see. But now what does my little prodigal have in mind for herself?

NORA: Oh, nothing. I really don't care.

HELMER: Of course you do. Tell me what you'd like. Within reason.

NORA: Oh, I don't know. Really, I don't. The only thing—

HELMER: Well?

NORA [*fiddling with his buttons, without looking at him*]: If you really want to give me something, you might—you could—

HELMER: All right, let's have it.

NORA [*quickly*]: Some money, Torvald. Just as much as you think you can spare. Then I'll buy myself something one of these days.

HELMER: No, really Nora—

NORA: Oh yes, please, Torvald. Please? I'll wrap the money in pretty gold paper and hang it on the tree. Won't that be nice?

HELMER: What's the name for little birds that are always spending money?

NORA: Wastrels, I know. But please let's do it my way, Torvald. Then I'll have time to decide what I need most. Now that's sensible, isn't it?

HELMER [*smiling*]: Oh, very sensible. That is, if you really bought yourself something you could use. But it all disappears in the household expenses or you buy things you don't need. And then you come back to me for more.

NORA: Oh, but Torvald—

HELMER: That's the truth, dear little Nora, and you know it. [*Puts his arm around her.*] My wastrel is a little sweetheart, but she *does* go through an awful lot of money awfully fast. You've no idea how expensive it is for a man to keep a wastrel.

NORA: That's not fair, Torvald. I really save all I can.

HELMER [*laughs*]: Oh, I believe that. All you can. Meaning, exactly nothing!

NORA [*hums, smiles mysteriously*]: You don't know all the things we songbirds and squirrels need money for, Torvald.

HELMER: You know, you're funny. Just like your father. You're always looking for ways to get money, but as soon as you do it runs through your fingers and you can never say what you spent it for. Well, I guess I'll just have to take you the way you are. It's in your blood. Yes, that sort of thing is hereditary, Nora.

NORA: In that case, I wish I had inherited many of Daddy's qualities.

HELMER: And I don't want you any different from just what you are—my own sweet little songbird. Hey!—I think I just noticed something. Aren't you looking—what's the word?—a little—sly—?

NORA: I am?

HELMER: You definitely are. Look at me.

NORA [*looks at him*]: Well?

HELMER [*wagging a finger*]: Little sweet-tooth hasn't by any chance been on a rampage today, has she?

NORA: Of course not. Whatever makes you think that?

HELMER: A little detour by the pastryshop maybe?

NORA: No, I assure you, Torvald—

HELMER: Nibbled a little jam?

NORA: Certainly not!

HELMER: Munched a macaroon or two?

NORA: No, really, Torvald, I honestly—

HELMER: All right. Of course I was only joking.

NORA [*walks toward the table, right*]: You know I wouldn't do anything to displease you.

HELMER: I know. And I have your promise. [*Over to her.*] All right, keep your little Christmas secrets to yourself, Nora darling. They'll all come out tonight, I suppose, when we light the tree.

NORA: Did you remember to invite Rank?

HELMER: No, but there's no need to. He knows he'll have dinner with us. Anyway, I'll see him later this morning. I'll ask him then. I did order some good wine. Oh Nora, you've no idea how much I'm looking forward to tonight!

NORA: Me, too. And the children Torvald! They'll have such a good time!

HELMER: You know, it *is* nice to have a good, safe job and a comfortable income. Feels good just thinking about it. Don't you agree?

NORA: Oh, it's wonderful!

HELMER: Remember last Christmas? For three whole weeks you shut yourself up every evening till long after midnight making ornaments for the Christmas tree and I don't know what else. Some big surprise for all of us, anyway. I'll be damned if I've ever been so bored in my whole life!

NORA: I wasn't bored at all!

HELMER [*smiling*]: But you've got to admit you didn't have much to show for it in the end.

NORA: Oh, don't tease me again about that! Could I help it that the cat got in and tore up everything?

HELMER: Of course you couldn't, my poor little Nora. You just wanted to please the rest of us, and that's the important thing. But I *am* glad the hard times are behind us. Aren't you?

NORA: Oh yes. I think it's just wonderful.

HELMER: This year, I won't be bored and lonely. And you won't have to strain your dear eyes and your delicate little hands—

NORA [*claps her hands*]: No I won't, will I Torvald? Oh, how wonderful, how lovely, to hear you say that! [*Puts her arm under his.*] Let me tell you how I think we should arrange things, Torvald. Soon as Christmas is over— [*The doorbell rings.*] Someone's at the door. [*Straightens things up a bit.*] A caller, I suppose. Bother!

HELMER: Remember, I'm not home for visitors.

THE MAID [*in the door to the front hall*]: Ma'am, there's a lady here—

NORA: All right. Ask her to come in.

THE MAID [*to* HELMER]: And the Doctor just arrived.

HELMER: Is he in the study?

THE MAID: Yes, sir.

[HELMER *exits into his study.* THE MAID *shows* MRS. LINDE *in and closes the door behind her as she leaves.* MRS. LINDE *is in travel dress.*]

MRS. LINDE [*timid and a little hesitant*]: Good morning, Nora.

NORA [*uncertainly*]: Good morning.

MRS. LINDE: I don't believe you know who I am.

NORA: No—I'm not sure—Though I know I should—Of course! Kristine! It's you!

MRS. LINDE: Yes, it's me.

NORA: And I didn't even recognize you! I had no idea [*In a lower voice.*] You've changed, Kristine.

MRS. LINDE: I'm sure I have. It's been nine or ten long years.

NORA: Has it really been that long? Yes, you're right. I've been so happy these last eight years. And now you're here. Such a long trip in the middle of winter. How brave!

MRS. LINDE: I got in on the steamer this morning.

NORA: To have some fun over the holidays, of course. That's lovely. For we are going to have fun. But take off your coat! You aren't cold, are you? [*Helps her.*] There, now! Let's sit down here by the fire and just relax and talk. No, you sit there. I want the rocking chair. [*Takes her hands.*] And now you've got your old face back. It was just for a minute, right at first—Though you are a little more pale, Kristine. And maybe a little thinner.

MRS. LINDE: And much, much older, Nora.

NORA: Maybe a little older. Just a teeny-weeny bit, not much. [*Interrupts herself, serious.*] Oh, but how thoughtless of me, chatting away like this! Sweet, good Kristine, can you forgive me?

MRS. LINDE: Forgive you what, Nora?

NORA [*in a low voice*]: You poor dear, you lost your husband, didn't you?

MRS. LINDE: Three years ago, yes.

NORA: I know. I saw it in the paper. Oh please believe me, Kristine. I really meant to write you, but I never got around to it. Something was always coming up.

MRS. LINDE: Of course, Nora. I understand.

NORA: No, that wasn't very nice of me. You poor thing, all you must have been through. And he didn't leave you much, either, did he?

MRS. LINDE: No.

NORA: And no children?

MRS. LINDE: No.

NORA: Nothing at all, in other words?

MRS. LINDE: Not so much as a sense of loss—a grief to live on—

NORA [*incredulous*]: But Kristine, how can that *be?*

MRS. LINDE [*with a sad smile, strokes* NORA's *hair*]: That's the way it sometimes is, Nora.

NORA: All alone. How awful for you. I have three darling children. You can't see them right now, though; they're out with their nurse. But now you must tell me everything—

MRS. LINDE: No, no; I'd rather listen to you.

NORA: No, you begin. Today I won't be selfish. Today I'll think only of you. Except there's one thing I've just got to tell you first. Something marvelous that's happened to us just these last few days. You haven't heard, have you?

MRS. LINDE: No; tell me.

NORA: Just think. My husband's been made manager of the Mutual Bank.

MRS. LINDE: Your husband—! Oh, I'm so glad!

NORA: Yes, isn't that great? You see, private law practice is so uncertain, especially when you won't have anything to do with cases that aren't—you know—quite nice. And of course Torvald won't do that and I quite agree with him. Oh, you've no idea how delighted we are! He takes over at New Year's, and he'll be getting a big salary and all sorts of extras. From now on we'll be able to live in quite a different way—exactly as we like. Oh, Kristine! I feel so carefree and happy! It's lovely to have lots and lots of money and not have to worry about a thing! Don't you agree?

MRS. LINDE: It would be nice to have enough at any rate.

NORA: No, I don't mean just enough. I mean lots and lots!

MRS. LINDE [*smiles*]: Nora, Nora, when are you going to be sensible? In school you spent a great deal of money.

NORA [*quietly laughing*]: Yes, and Torvald says I still do. [*Raises her finger at* MRS. LINDE.] But "Nora, Nora" isn't so crazy as you all think. Believe me, we've had nothing to be extravagant with. We've both had to work.

MRS. LINDE: You too?

NORA: Yes. Oh, it's been little things, mostly—sewing, crocheting, embroidery—that sort of thing. [*Casually.*] And other things too. You know, of course, that Torvald left government service when we got married? There was no chance of promotion in his department, and of course he had to make more money than he had been making. So for the first few years he worked altogether too hard. He had to take jobs on the side and work night and day. It turned out to be too much for him. He became seriously ill. The doctors told him he needed to go south.

MRS. LINDE: That s right; you spent a year in Italy, didn't you?

NORA: Yes, we did. But you won't believe how hard it was to get away. Ivar had just been born. But of course we had to go. Oh, it was a wonderful trip. And it saved Torvald's life. But it took a lot of money, Kristine.

MRS. LINDE: I'm sure it did.

NORA: Twelve hundred specie dollars. Four thousand eight hundred crowns. That's a lot of money.

MRS. LINDE: Yes. So it's lucky you have it when something like that happens.

NORA: Well, actually we got the money from Daddy.

MRS. LINDE: I see. That was about the time your father died, I believe.

NORA: Yes, just about then. And I couldn't even go and take care of him. I was expecting little Ivar any day. And I had poor Torvald to look after, desperately sick and all. My dear, good Daddy! I never saw him again, Kristine. That's the saddest thing that's happened to me since I got married.

MRS. LINDE: I know you were very fond of him. But then you went to Italy?

NORA: Yes, for now we had the money, and the doctors urged us to go. So we left about a month later.

MRS. LINDE: And when you came back your husband was well again?

NORA: Healthy as a horse!

MRS. LINDE: But—the doctor?

NORA: What do you mean?

MRS. LINDE: I thought the maid said it was the doctor, that gentleman who came the same time I did.

NORA: Oh, that's Dr. Rank. He doesn't come as a doctor. He's our closest friend. He looks in at least once every day. No, Torvald hasn't been sick once since then. And the children are strong and healthy, too, and so am I. [*Jumps up and claps her hands.*] Oh God, Kristine! Isn't it wonderful to be alive and happy! Isn't it just lovely!—But now I'm being mean again, talking only about myself and my things. [*Sits down on a footstool close to* MRS. LINDE *and puts her arm on her lap.*] Please don't be angry with me! Tell me, is it really true that you didn't care for your husband? Then why did you marry him?

MRS. LINDE: Mother was still alive then, but she was bedridden and helpless. And I had my two younger brothers to look after. I didn't think I had the right to turn him down.

NORA: No, I suppose not. So he had money then?

MRS. LINDE: He was quite well off, I think. But it was an uncertain business, Nora. When he died, the whole thing collapsed and there was nothing left.

NORA: And then—?

MRS. LINDE: Well, I had to manage as best I could. With a little store and a little school and anything else I could think of. The last three years have been one long work day for me, Nora, without any rest. But now it's over. My poor mother doesn't need me any more. She's passed away. And the boys are on their own too. They've both got jobs and support themselves.

NORA: What a relief for you—

MRS. LINDE: No, not relief. Just a great emptiness. Nobody to live for any more. [*Gets up restlessly.*] That's why I couldn't stand it any longer in that little hole. Here in town it has to be easier to find something to keep me busy and occupy my thoughts. With a little luck I should be able to find a permanent job, something in an office—

NORA: Oh but Kristine, that's exhausting work, and you look worn out already. It would be much better for you to go to a resort.

MRS. LINDE [*walks over to the window*]: I don't have a Daddy who can give me the money, Nora.

NORA [*getting up*]: Oh, don't be angry with me.

MRS. LINDE [*over to her*]: Dear Nora, don't *you* be angry with *me*. That's the worst thing about my kind of situation: you become so bitter. You've nobody to work for, and yet you have to look out for yourself, somehow. You've got to keep on living, and so you become selfish. Do you know—when you told me about your husband's new position I was delighted not so much for your sake as for my own.

NORA: Why was that? Oh, I see. You think maybe Torvald can give you a job?

MRS. LINDE: That's what I had in mind.

NORA: And he will too, Kristine. Just leave it to me. I'll be ever so subtle about it. I'll think of something nice to tell him, something he'll like. Oh I so much want to help you.

MRS. LINDE: That's very good of you, Nora—making an effort like that for me. Especially since you've known so little trouble and hardship in your own life.

NORA: I—?—have known so little—?

MRS. LINDE [*smiling*]: Oh well, a little sewing or whatever it was. You're still a child, Nora.

NORA [*with a toss of her head, walks away*]: You shouldn't sound so superior.

MRS. LINDE: I shouldn't?

NORA: You're just like all the others. None of you think I'm good for anything really serious.

MRS. LINDE: Well, now—

NORA: That I've never been through anything difficult.

MRS. LINDE: But Nora! You just told me all your troubles!

NORA: That's nothing! [*Lowers her voice.*] I haven't told you about *it*.

MRS. LINDE: It? What's that? What do you mean?

NORA: You patronize me, Kristine, and that's not fair. You're proud that you worked so long and so hard for your mother.

MRS. LINDE: I don't think I patronize anyone. But it *is* true that I'm both proud and happy that I could make mother's last years comparatively easy.

NORA: And you're proud of all you did for your brothers.

MRS. LINDE: I think I have the right to be.

NORA: And so do I. But now I want to tell you something, Kristine. I have something to be proud and happy about too.

MRS. LINDE: I don't doubt that for a moment. But what exactly do you mean?

NORA: Not so loud! Torvald mustn't hear—not for anything in the world. Nobody must know about this, Kristine. Nobody but you.

MRS. LINDE: But what is it?

NORA: Come here. [*Pulls her down on the couch beside her.*] You see, I *do* have something to be proud and happy about. I've saved Torvald's life.

MRS. LINDE: Saved—? How do you mean—"saved"?

NORA: I told you about our trip to Italy. Torvald would have died if he hadn't gone.

MRS. LINDE: I understand that. And so your father gave you the money you needed.

NORA [*smiles*]: Yes, that's what Torvald and all the others think. But—

MRS. LINDE: But what?

NORA: Daddy didn't give us a penny. *I* raised that money.

MRS. LINDE: *You* did? That whole big amount?

NORA: Twelve hundred specie dollars. Four thousand eight hundred crowns. *Now* what do you say?

MRS. LINDE: But Nora, how could you? Did you win in the state lottery?

NORA [*contemptuously*]: State lottery! [*Snorts.*] What is so great about that?

MRS. LINDE: Where did it come from then?

NORA [*humming and smiling, enjoying her secret*]: Hmmm. Tra-la-la-la-la!

MRS. LINDE: You certainly couldn't have borrowed it.

NORA: Oh? And why not?

MRS. LINDE: A wife can't borrow money without her husband's consent.

NORA [*with a toss of her head*]: Oh, I don't know—take a wife with a little bit of a head for business—a wife who knows how to manage things—

MRS. LINDE: But Nora, I don't understand at all—

NORA: You don't have to. I didn't say I borrowed the money, did I? I could have gotten it some other way. [*Leans back.*] An admirer may have given it to me. When you're as tolerably good-looking as I am—

MRS. LINDE: Oh, you're crazy.

NORA: I think you're dying from curiosity, Kristine.

MRS. LINDE: I'm beginning to think you've done something very foolish, Nora.

NORA [*sits up*]: Is it foolish to save your husband's life?

MRS. LINDE: I say it's foolish to act behind his back.

NORA: But don't you see: he couldn't be told! You're missing the whole point, Kristine. We couldn't even let him know how seriously ill he was. The doctors came to *me* and told me his life was in danger, that nothing could save him but a stay in the south. Don't you think I tried to work on him? I told him how lovely it would be if I could go abroad like other young wives. I cried and begged. I said he'd better remember what condition I was in, that he had to be nice to me and do what I wanted. I even hinted he could borrow the money. But that almost made him angry with me. He told me I was being irresponsible and that it was his duty as my husband not to give in to my moods and whims—I think that's what he called it. All right, I said to myself, you've got to be saved somehow, and so I found a way—

MRS. LINDE: And your husband never learned from your father that the money didn't come from him?

NORA: Never. Daddy died that same week. I thought of telling him all about it and ask him not to say anything. But since he was so sick—It turned out I didn't have to—

MRS. LINDE: And you've never told your husband?

NORA: Of course not! Good heavens, how could I? He, with his strict principles! Besides, you know how men are. Torvald would find it embarrassing and humiliating to learn that he owed me anything. It would upset our whole relationship. Our happy, beautiful home would no longer be what it is.

MRS. LINDE: Aren't you ever going to tell him?

NORA [*reflectively, half smiling*]: Yes—one day, maybe. Many, many years from now, when I'm no longer young and pretty. Don't laugh! I mean when Torvald no longer feels about me the way he does now, when he no longer thinks it's fun when I dance for him and put on costumes and recite for him. Then it will be good to have something in reserve— [*Interrupts herself.*] Oh, I'm just being silly! That day will never come.—Well, now, Kristine, what do you think of my great secret? Don't you think I'm good for something too?—By the way, you wouldn't believe all the worry I've had because of it. It's been very hard to meet my obligations on schedule. You see, in business there's something called quarterly interest and something called installments on the principal, and those are terribly hard to come up with. I've had to save a little here and a little there, whenever I could. I couldn't use much of the housekeeping money, for Torvald has to eat well. And I couldn't use what I got for clothes for the children. They have to look nice, and I didn't think it would be right to spend less than I got—the sweet little things!

MRS. LINDE: Poor Nora! So you had to take it from your own allowance!

NORA: Yes, of course. After all, it was my affair. Every time Torvald gave me money for a new dress and things like that, I never used more than half of it. I always bought the cheapest, simplest things for myself. Thank God, everything looks good on me, so Torvald never noticed. But it was hard many times, Kristine, for it's fun to have pretty clothes. Don't you think?

MRS. LINDE: Certainly.

NORA: Anyway, I had other ways of making money too. Last winter I was lucky enough to get some copying work. So I locked the door and sat up writing every night till quite late. God! I often got so tired—! But it was great fun, too, working and making money. It was almost like being a man.

MRS. LINDE: But how much have you been able to pay off this way?

NORA: I couldn't tell you exactly. You see, it's very difficult to keep track of business like that. All I know is I have been paying off as much as I've been able to scrape together. Many times I just didn't know what to do. [*Smiles.*] Then I used to imagine a rich old gentleman had fallen in love with me—

MRS. LINDE: What! What old gentleman?

NORA: Phooey! And now he was dead and they were reading his will, and there it said in big letters, "All my money is to be paid in cash immediately to the charming Mrs. Nora Helmer."

MRS. LINDE: But dearest Nora—who *was* this old gentleman?

NORA: For heaven's sake, Kristine, don't you see? There *was* no old gentleman. He was just somebody I made up when I couldn't think of any way to raise the money. But never mind him. The old bore can be anyone he likes to for all I care. I have no use for him or his last will, for now I don't have a single worry in the world. [*Jumps up.*] Dear God, what a lovely thought this is! To be able to play and have fun with the children, to have everything nice and pretty in the house, just the way Torvald likes it! Not a care! And soon spring will be here, and the air will be blue and high. Maybe we can travel again. Maybe I'll see the ocean again! Oh yes, yes!—it's wonderful to be alive and happy!

The doorbell rings.

MRS. LINDE [*getting up*]: There's the doorbell. Maybe I better be going.

NORA: No, please stay. I'm sure it's just someone for Torvald—

THE MAID [*in the hall door*]: Excuse me, ma'am. There's a gentleman here who'd like to see Mr. Helmer.

NORA: You mean the bank manager.

THE MAID: Sorry, ma'am; the bank manager. But I didn't know—since the Doctor is with him—

NORA: Who is the gentleman?

KROGSTAD [*appearing in the door*]: It's just me, Mrs. Helmer.

MRS. LINDE *starts, looks, turns away toward the window.*

NORA [*takes a step toward him, tense, in a low voice*]: You? What do you want? What do you want with my husband?

KROGSTAD: Bank business—in a way. I have a small job in the Mutual, and I understand your husband is going to be our new boss—

NORA: So it's just—

KROGSTAD: Just routine business, ma'am. Nothing else.

NORA: All right. In that case, why don't you go through the door to the office.

Dismisses him casually as she closes the door. Walks over to the stove and tends the fire.

MRS. LINDE: Nora—who was that man?

NORA: His name's Krogstad. He's a lawyer.

MRS. LINDE: So it *was* him.

NORA: Do you know him?

MRS. LINDE: I used to—many years ago. For a while he clerked in our part of the country.

NORA: Right. He did.

MRS. LINDE: He has changed a great deal.

NORA: I believe he had a very unhappy marriage.

MRS. LINDE: And now he's a widower, isn't he?

NORA: With many children. There now; it's burning nicely again. [*Closes the stove and moves the rocking chair a little to the side.*]

MRS. LINDE: They say he's into all sorts of business.

NORA: Really? Maybe so. I wouldn't know. But let's not think about business. It's such a bore.

DR. RANK [*appears in the door to* HELMER'*s study*]: No. I don't want to be in the way. I'd rather talk to your wife a bit. [*Closes the door and notices* MRS. LINDE.] Oh, I beg your pardon. I believe I'm in the way here too.

NORA: No, not at all. [*Introduces them.*] Dr. Rank. Mrs. Linde.

RANK: Aha. A name often heard in this house. I believe I passed you on the stairs coming up.

MRS. LINDE: Yes. I'm afraid I climb stairs very slowly. They aren't good for me.

RANK: I see. A slight case of inner decay, perhaps?

MRS. LINDE: Overwork, rather.

RANK: Oh, is that all? And now you've come to town to relax at all the parties?

MRS. LINDE: I have come to look for a job.

RANK: A proven cure for overwork, I take it?

MRS. LINDE: One has to live, Doctor.

RANK: Yes, that seems to be the common opinion.

NORA: Come on, Dr. Rank—you want to live just as much as the rest of us.

RANK: Of course I do. Miserable as I am, I prefer to go on being tortured as long as possible. All my patients feel the same way. And that's true of the moral invalids too. Helmer is talking with a specimen right this minute.

MRS. LINDE [*in a low voice*]: Ah!

NORA: What do you mean?

RANK: Oh, this lawyer, Krogstad. You don't know him. The roots of his character are decayed. But even he began by saying something about having *to live*—as if it were a matter of the highest importance.

NORA: Oh? What did he want with Torvald?

RANK: I don't really know. All I heard was something about the bank.

NORA: I didn't know that Krog—that this Krogstad had anything to do with the Mutual Bank.

RANK: Yes, he seems to have some kind of job there. [*To* MRS. LINDE.] I don't know if you are familiar in your part of the country with the kind of person who is always running around trying to sniff out cases of moral decrepitude and as soon as he finds one puts the individual under observation in some excellent position or other. All the healthy ones are left out in the cold.

MRS. LINDE: I should think it's the sick who need looking after the most.

RANK [*shrugs his shoulders*]: There we are. That's the attitude that turns society into a hospital.

[NORA, *absorbed in her own thoughts, suddenly starts giggling and clapping her hands.*]

RANK: What's so funny about that? Do you even know what society is?

NORA: What do I care about your stupid society! I laughed at something entirely different—something terribly amusing. Tell me, Dr. Rank—all the employees in the Mutual Bank, from now on they'll all be dependent on Torvald, right?

RANK: Is that what you find so enormously amusing?

NORA [*smiles and hums*]: That's my business, that's my business! [*Walks around.*] Yes, I do think it's fun that we—that Torvald is going to have so much influence on so many people's lives. [*Brings out the bag of macaroons.*] Have a macaroon, Dr. Rank.

RANK: Well, well—macaroons. I thought they were banned around here.

NORA: Yes, but these were some that Kristine gave me.

MRS. LINDE: What! I?

NORA: That's all right. Don't look so scared. You couldn't know that Torvald won't let me have them. He's afraid they'll ruin my teeth. But who cares! Just once in a while—! Right, Dr. Rank? Have one! [*Puts a macaroon into his mouth.*] You too, Kristine. And one for me. A very small one. Or at most two. [*Walks around again.*] Yes, I really feel very, very happy. Now there's just one thing I'm dying to do.

RANK: Oh, and what's that?

NORA: Something I'm dying to say so Torvald could hear.

RANK: And why can't you?

NORA: I don't dare to, for it's not nice.

MRS. LINDE: Not nice?

RANK: In that case, I guess you'd better not. But surely to the two of us—? What is it you'd like to say for Helmer to hear?

NORA: I want to say, "Goddammit!"

RANK: Are you out of your mind!

MRS. LINDE: For heaven's sake, Nora!

RANK: Say it. Here he comes.

NORA [*hiding the macaroons*]: Shhh!

[HELMER *enters from his study, carrying his hat and overcoat.*]

NORA [*going to him*]: Well, dear, did you get rid of him?

HELMER: Yes, he just left.

NORA: Torvald, I want you to meet Kristine. She's just come to town.

HELMER: Kristine—? I'm sorry; I don't think—

NORA: Mrs. Linde, Torvald dear. Mrs. Kristine Linde.

HELMER: Ah, yes. A childhood friend of my wife's, I suppose.

MRS. LINDE: Yes, we've known each other for a long time.

NORA: Just think; she has come all this way just to see you.

HELMER: I'm not sure I understand—

MRS. LINDE: Well, not really—

NORA: You see, Kristine is an absolutely fantastic secretary, and she would so much like to work for a competent executive and learn more than she knows already—

HELMER: Very sensible, I'm sure, Mrs. Linde.

NORA: So when she heard about your appointment—there was a wire—she came here as fast as she could. How about it, Torvald? Couldn't you do something for Kristine? For my sake. Please?

HELMER: Quite possibly. I take it you're a widow, Mrs. Linde?

MRS. LINDE: Yes.

HELMER: And you've had office experience?

MRS. LINDE: Some—yes.

HELMER: In that case I think it's quite likely that I'll be able to find you a position.

NORA [*claps her hands*]: I knew it! I knew it!

HELMER: You've arrived at a most opportune time, Mrs. Linde.

MRS. LINDE: Oh, how can I ever thank you—

HELMER: Not at all, not at all. [*Puts his coat on.*] But today you'll have to excuse me—

RANK: Wait a minute; I'll come with you. [*Gets his fur coat from the front hall, warms it by the stove.*]

NORA: Don't be long, Torvald.

HELMER: An hour or so; no more.

NORA: Are you leaving, too, Kristine?

MRS. LINDE [*putting on her things*]: Yes, I'd better go and find a place to stay.

HELMER: Good. Then we'll be going the same way.

NORA [*helping her*]: I'm sorry this place is so small, but I don't think we very well could—

MRS. LINDE: Of course! Don't be silly, Nora. Goodbye, and thank you for everything.

NORA: Goodbye. We'll see you soon. You'll be back this evening, of course. And you too, Dr. Rank; right? If you feel well enough? Of course you will. Just wrap yourself up.

[*General small talk as all exit into the hall. Children's voices are heard on the stairs.*]

NORA: There they are! There they are! [*She runs and opens the door. The nurse* ANNE-MARIE *enters with the children.*]

NORA: Come in! Come in! [*Bends over and kisses them.*] Oh, you sweet, sweet darlings! Look at them, Kristine! Aren't they beautiful?

RANK: No standing around in the draft!

HELMER: Come along, Mrs. Linde. This place isn't fit for anyone but mothers right now.

[DR. RANK, HELMER, *and* MRS. LINDE *go down the stairs. The* NURSE *enters the living room with the children.* NORA *follows, closing the door behind her.*]

NORA: My, how nice you all look! Such red cheeks! Like apples and roses. [*The children all talk at the same time.*] You've had so much fun? I bet you have. Oh, isn't that nice! You pulled both Emmy and Bob on your sleigh? Both at the same time? That's very good, Ivar. Oh, let me hold her for a minute, Anne-Marie. My sweet little doll baby! [*Takes the smallest of the children from the* NURSE *and dances with her.*] Yes, yes, of course; Mama'll dance with you too, Bob. What? You threw snowballs? Oh, I wish I'd been there! No, no; *I* want to take their clothes off, Anne-Marie. Please let me; I think it's so much fun. You go on in. You look frozen. There's hot coffee on the stove.

[*The* NURSE *exits into the room to the left.* NORA *takes the children's wraps off and throws them all around. They all keep telling her things at the same time.*]

NORA: Oh, really? A big dog ran after you? But it didn't bite you. Of course not. Dogs don't bite sweet little doll babies. Don't peek at the packages, Ivar! What's in them? Wouldn't you like to know! No, no; that's something terrible! Play? You want to play? What do you want to play? Okay, let's play hide-and-seek. Bob hides first. You want *me* to? All right. I'll go first.

[*Laughing and shouting,* NORA *and the children play in the living room and in the adjacent room, right. Finally,* NORA *hides herself under the table; the children rush in, look for her, can't find her. They hear her low giggle, run to the table, lift the rug that covers it, see her. General hilarity. She crawls out, pretends to scare them. New delight. In the meantime there has been a knock on the door between the living room and the front hall, but nobody has noticed. Now the door is opened half-way;* KROGSTAD *appears. He waits a little. The play goes on.*]

KROGSTAD: Pardon me, Mrs. Helmer—

NORA [*with a muted cry turns around, jumps up*]: Ah! What do you want?

KROGSTAD: I'm sorry. The front door was open. Somebody must have forgotten to close it—

NORA [*standing up*]: My husband isn't here, Mr. Krogstad.

KROGSTAD: I know.

NORA: So what do you want?

KROGSTAD: I'd like a word with you.

NORA: With—? [To *the children.*] Go in to Anne-Marie. What? No, the strange man won't do anything bad to Mama. When he's gone we'll play some more.

[*She takes the children into the room to the left and closes the door.*]

NORA [*tense, troubled*]: You want to speak with me?

KROGSTAD: Yes I do.

NORA: Today—? It isn't the first of the month yet.

KROGSTAD: No, it's Christmas Eve. It's up to you what kind of holiday you'll have.

NORA: What do you want? I can't possibly—

KROGSTAD: Let's not talk about that just yet. There's something else. You do have a few minutes, don't you?

NORA: Yes. Yes, of course. That is,—

KROGSTAD: Good. I was sitting in Olsen's restaurant when I saw your husband go by.

NORA: Yes—?

KROGSTAD: —with a lady.

NORA: What of it?

KROGSTAD: May I be so free as to ask: wasn't that lady Mrs. Linde?

NORA: Yes.

KROGSTAD: Just arrived in town?

NORA: Yes, today.

KROGSTAD: She's a good friend of yours, I understand?

NORA: Yes, she is. But I fail to see—

KROGSTAD: I used to know her myself.

NORA: I know that.

KROGSTAD: So you know about that. I thought as much. In that case, let me ask you a simple question. Is Mrs. Linde going to be employed in the bank?

NORA: What makes you think you have the right to cross-examine me like this, Mr. Krogstad—you, one of my husband's employees? But since you ask, I'll tell you. Yes, Mrs. Linde is going to be working in the bank. And it was I who recommended her, Mr. Krogstad. Now you know.

KROGSTAD: So, I was right.

NORA [*walks up and down*]: After all, one does have a little influence, you know. Just because you're a woman, it doesn't mean that—Really, Mr. Krogstad, people in a subordinate position should be careful not to offend someone who—oh well—

KROGSTAD: —has influence?

NORA: Exactly.

KROGSTAD [*changing his tone*]: Mrs. Helmer, I must ask you to be good enough to use your influence on my behalf.

NORA: What do you mean?

KROGSTAD: I want you to make sure that I am going to keep my subordinate position in the bank.

NORA: I don't understand. Who is going to take your position away from you?

KROGSTAD: There's no point in playing ignorant with me, Mrs. Helmer. I can very well appreciate that your friend would find it unpleasant to run into me. So now I know who I can thank for my dismissal.

NORA: But I assure you—

KROGSTAD: Never mind. Just want to say you still have time. I advise you to use your influence to prevent it.

NORA: But Mr. Krogstad, I don't have any influence—none at all.

KROGSTAD: No? I thought you just said—

NORA: Of course I didn't mean it that way. I! Whatever makes you think that I have any influence of that kind on my husband?

KROGSTAD: I went to law school with your husband. I have no reason to think that the bank manager is less susceptible than other husbands.

NORA: If you're going to insult my husband, I'll ask you to leave.

KROGSTAD: You're brave, Mrs. Helmer.

NORA: I'm not afraid of you any more. After New Year's I'll be out of this thing with you.

KROGSTAD [*more controlled*]: Listen, Mrs. Helmer. If necessary I'll fight as for my life to keep my little job in the bank.

NORA: So it seems.

KROGSTAD: It isn't just the money; that's really the smallest part of it. There is something else—Well, I guess I might as well tell you. It's like this. I'm sure you know, like everybody else, that some years ago I committed—an impropriety.

NORA: I believe I've heard it mentioned.

KROGSTAD: The case never came to court, but from that moment all doors were closed to me. So I took up the kind of business you know about. I had to do something, and I think I can say about myself that I have not been among the worst. But now I want to get out of all that. My sons are growing up. For their sake I must get back as much of my good name as I can. This job in the bank was like the first rung on the ladder. And now your husband wants to kick me down and leave me back in the mud again.

NORA: But I swear to you, Mr. Krogstad; it's not at all in my power to help you.

KROGSTAD: That's because you don't want to. But I have the means to force you.

NORA: You don't mean you're going to tell my husband I owe you money?

KROGSTAD: And if I did?

NORA: That would be a mean thing to do. [*Almost crying.*] That secret, which is my joy and my pride—for him to learn about it in such a coarse and ugly manner—to learn it from *you*—! It would be terribly unpleasant for me.

KROGSTAD: Just unpleasant?

NORA [*heatedly*]: But go ahead! Do it! It will be worse for you than for me. When my husband realizes what a bad person you are, you'll be sure to lose your job.

KROGSTAD: I asked you if it was just domestic unpleasantness you were afraid of?

NORA: When my husband finds out, of course he'll pay off the loan, and then we won't have anything more to do with you.

KROGSTAD [*stepping closer*]: Listen, Mrs. Helmer—either you have a very bad memory, or you don't know much about business. I think I had better straighten you out on a few things.

NORA: What do you mean?

KROGSTAD: When your husband was ill, you came to me to borrow twelve hundred dollars.

NORA: I knew nobody else.

KROGSTAD: I promised to get you the money—

NORA: And you did.

KROGSTAD: I promised to get you the money on certain conditions. At the time you were so anxious about your husband's health and so set on getting him away that I doubt very much that you paid much attention to the details of our transaction. That's why I remind you of them now. Anyway, I promised to get you the money if you would sign an I.O.U., which I drafted.

NORA: And which I signed.

KROGSTAD: Good. But below your signature I added a few lines, making your father security for the loan. Your father was supposed to put his signature to those lines.

NORA: Supposed to—? He did.

KROGSTAD: I had left the date blank. That is, your father was to date his own signature. You recall that, don't you, Mrs. Helmer?

NORA: I guess so—

KROGSTAD: I gave the note to you. You were to mail it to your father. Am I correct?

NORA: Yes.

KROGSTAD: And of course you did so right away, for no more than five or six days later you brought the paper back to me, signed by your father. Then I paid you the money.

NORA: Well? And haven't I been keeping up with the payments?

KROGSTAD: Fairly well, yes. But to get back to what we were talking about—those were difficult days for you, weren't they, Mrs. Helmer?

NORA: Yes, they were.

KROGSTAD: Your father was quite ill, I believe.

NORA: He was dying.

KROGSTAD: And died shortly afterwards?

NORA: That's right.

KROGSTAD: Tell me, Mrs. Helmer; do you happen to remember the date of your father's death? I mean the exact day of the month?

NORA: Daddy died on September 29.

KROGSTAD: Quite correct. I have ascertained that fact. That's why there is something peculiar about this [*takes out a piece of paper*], which I can't account for.

NORA: Peculiar? How? I don't understand—

KROGSTAD: It seems very peculiar, Mrs. Helmer, that your father signed this promissory note three days after his death.

NORA: How so? I don't see what—

KROGSTAD: Your father died on September 29. Now look. He has dated his signature October 2. Isn't that odd?

[NORA *remains silent.*]

KROGSTAD: Can you explain it?

[NORA *is still silent.*]

KROGSTAD: I also find it striking that the date and the month and the year are not in your father's handwriting but in a hand I think I recognize. Well, that might be explained. Your father may have forgotten to date his signature and somebody else may have done it here, guessing at the date before he had learned of your father's death. That's all right. It's only the signature itself that matters. And that is genuine, isn't it, Mrs. Helmer? Your father *did* put his name to this note?

NORA [*after a brief silence tosses her head back and looks defiantly at him*]: No, he didn't. *I* wrote Daddy's name.

KROGSTAD: Mrs. Helmer—do you realize what a dangerous admission you just made?

NORA: Why? You'll get your money soon.

KROGSTAD: Let me ask you something. Why didn't you mail this note to your father?

NORA: Because it was impossible. Daddy was sick—you know that. If I had asked him to sign it, I would have had to tell him what the money was for. But I couldn't tell him, as sick as he was, that my husband's life was in danger. That was impossible. Surely you can see that.

KROGSTAD: Then it would have been better for you if you had given up your trip abroad.

NORA: No, that was impossible! That trip was to save my husband's life. I couldn't give it up.

KROGSTAD: But didn't you realize that what you did amounted to fraud against me?

NORA: I couldn't let that make any difference. I didn't care about you at all. I hated the way you made all those difficulties for me, even though you knew the danger my husband was in. I thought you were cold and unfeeling.

KROGSTAD: Mrs. Helmer, obviously you have no clear idea of what you have done. Let me tell you that what I did that time was no more and no worse. And it ruined my name and reputation.

NORA: You! Are you trying to tell me that you did something brave once in order to save your wife's life?

KROGSTAD: The law doesn't ask about motives.

NORA: Then it's a bad law.

KROGSTAD: Bad or not—if I produce this note in court you'll be judged according to the law.

NORA: I refuse to believe you. A daughter shouldn't have the right to spare her dying old father worry and anxiety? A wife shouldn't have the right to save her husband's life? I don't know the laws very well, but I'm sure that somewhere they make allowance for cases like that. And you, a lawyer, don't know that? I think you must be a bad lawyer, Mr. Krogstad.

KROGSTAD: That may be. But business—the kind of business you and I have with one another—don't you think I know something about that? Very well. Do what you like. But let me tell you this: if I'm going to be kicked out again, you'll keep me company. [*He bows and exits through the front hall.*]

NORA [*pauses thoughtfully; then, with a defiant toss of her head*]: Oh, nonsense! Trying to scare me like that! I'm not all that silly. [*Starts picking up the children's clothes; soon stops.*] But—? No! That's impossible! I did it for love!

THE CHILDREN [*in the door to the left*]: Mama, the strange man just left. We saw him.

NORA: Yes, yes; I know. But don't tell anybody about the strange man. Do you hear? Not even Daddy.

THE CHILDREN: We won't. But now you'll play with us again, won't you, Mama?

NORA: No, not right now.

THE CHILDREN: But Mama—you promised.

NORA: I know, but I can't just now. Go to your own room. I've so much to do. Be nice now, my little darlings. Do as I say. [*She nudges them gently into the other room and closes the door. She sits down on the couch, picks up a piece of embroidery, makes a few stitches, then stops.*] No! [*Throws the embroidery down, goes to the hall door and calls out.*] Helene! Bring the Christmas tree in here, please! [*Goes to the table, left, opens the drawer, halts.*] No—that's impossible!

THE MAID [*with the Christmas tree*]: Where do you want it, ma'am?

NORA: There. The middle of the floor.

THE MAID: You want anything else?

NORA: No, thanks. I have everything I need. [THE MAID *goes out.* NORA *starts trimming the tree.*] I want candles—and flowers—That awful man! Oh, nonsense! There's nothing wrong. This will be a lovely tree. I'll do everything you want me to, Torvald. I'll sing for you—dance for you—

[HELMER, *a bundle of papers under his arm, enters from outside.*]

NORA: Ah—you're back already?

HELMER: Yes. Has anybody been here?

NORA: Here? No.

HELMER: That's funny. I saw Krogstad leaving just now.

NORA: Oh? Oh yes, that's right. Krogstad was here for just a moment.

HELMER: I can tell from your face that he came to ask you to put in a word for him.

NORA: Yes.

HELMER: And it was supposed to be your own idea, wasn't it? You were not to tell me he'd been here. He asked you that too, didn't he?

NORA: Yes, Torvald, but—

HELMER: Nora, Nora, how could you! Talk to a man like that and make him promises! And lying to me about it afterwards—!

NORA: Lying—?

HELMER: Didn't you say nobody had been here? [*Shakes his finger at her.*] My little songbird must never do that again. Songbirds are supposed to have clean beaks to chirp with—no false notes. [*Puts his arms around her waist.*] Isn't that so? Of course it is. [*Lets her go.*] And that's enough about that. [*Sits down in front of the fireplace.*] Ah, it's nice and warm in here. [*Begins to leaf through his papers.*]

NORA [*busy with the tree; after a brief pause*]: Torvald.

HELMER: Yes.

NORA: I'm looking forward so much to the Stenborgs' costume party day after tomorrow.

HELMER: And I can't wait to find out what you're going to surprise me with.

NORA: Oh, that silly idea!

HELMER: Oh?

NORA: I can't think of anything. It all seems so foolish and pointless.

HELMER: Ah, my little Nora admits that?

NORA [*behind his chair, her arms on the back of the chair*]: Are you very busy, Torvald?

HELMER: Well—

NORA: What are all those papers?

HELMER: Bank business.

NORA: Already?

HELMER: I've asked the board to give me the authority to make certain changes in organization and personnel. That's what I'll be doing over the holidays. I want it all settled before New Year's.

NORA: So that's why this poor Krogstad—

HELMER: Hm.

NORA [*leisurely playing with the hair on his neck*]: If you weren't so busy, Torvald, I'd ask you for a great big favor.

HELMER: Let's hear it, anyway.

NORA: I don't know anyone with better taste than you, and I want so much to look nice at the party. Couldn't you sort of take charge of me, Torvald, and decide what I'll wear—Help me with my costume?

HELMER: Aha! Little Lady Obstinate is looking for someone to rescue her?

NORA: Yes, Torvald. I won't get anywhere without your help.

HELMER: All right. I'll think about it. We'll come up with something.

NORA: Oh, you *are* nice! [*Goes back to the Christmas tree. A pause.*] Those red flowers look so pretty.—Tell me, was it really all that bad what this Krogstad fellow did?

HELMER: He forged signatures. Do you have any idea what that means?

NORA: Couldn't it have been because he felt he had to?

HELMER: Yes, or like so many others he may simply have been thoughtless. I'm not so heartless as to condemn a man absolutely because of a single imprudent act.

NORA: Of course not, Torvald!

HELMER: People like him can redeem themselves morally by openly confessing their crime and taking their punishment.

NORA: Punishment—?

HELMER: But that was not the way Krogstad chose. He got out of it with tricks and evasions. That's what has corrupted him.

NORA: So you think that if—?

HELMER: Can't you imagine how a guilty person like that has to lie and fake and dissemble wherever he goes—putting on a mask before everybody he's close to, even his own wife and children. It's this thing with the children that's the worst part of it, Nora.

NORA: Why is that?

HELMER: Because when a man lives inside such a circle of stinking lies he brings infection into his own home and contaminates his whole family. With every breath of air his children inhale the germs of something ugly.

NORA [*moving closer behind him*]: Are you so sure of that?

HELMER: Of course I am. I have seen enough examples of that in my work. Nearly all young criminals have had mothers who lied.

NORA: Why mothers—particularly?

HELMER: Most often mothers. But of course fathers tend to have the same influence. Every lawyer knows that. And yet, for years this Krogstad has been poisoning his own children in an atmosphere of lies and deceit. That's why I call him a lost soul morally. [*Reaches out for her hands.*] And that's why my sweet little Nora must promise me never to take his side again. Let's shake on that.—What? What's this? Give me your hand. There! Now that's settled. I assure you, I would find it impossible to work in the same room with that man. I feel literally sick when I'm around people like that.

NORA [*withdraws her hand and goes to the other side of the Christmas tree*]: It's so hot in here. And I have so much to do.

HELMER [*gets up and collects his papers*]: Yes, and I really should try to get some of this reading done before dinner. I must think about your costume too. And maybe just possibly I'll have something to wrap in gilt paper and hang on the Christmas tree. [*Puts his hand on her head.*] Oh my adorable little songbird! [*Enters his study and closes the door.*]

NORA [*after a pause, in a low voice*]: It's all a lot of nonsense. It's not that way at all. It's impossible. It has to be impossible.

THE NURSE [*in the door, left*]: The little ones are asking ever so nicely if they can't come in and be with their mama.

NORA: No, no no! Don't let them in here! You stay with them, Anne-Marie.

THE NURSE: If you say so, ma'am. [*Closes the door.*]

NORA [*pale with terror*]: Corrupt my little children—! Poison my home—? [*Brief pause; she lifts her head.*] That's not true. Never. Never in a million years.

ACT II

The same room. The Christmas tree is in the corner by the piano, stripped, shabby-looking, with burnt-down candles. NORA*'s outside clothes are on the couch.* NORA *is alone. She walks around restlessly. She stops by the couch and picks up her coat.*

NORA [*drops the coat again*]: There's somebody now! [*Goes to the door, listens.*] No. Nobody. Of course not —not on Christmas. And not tomorrow either.—But perhaps— [*Opens the door and looks.*] No, nothing in the mailbox. All empty. [*Comes forward.*] How silly I am! Of course he isn't serious. Nothing like that could happen. After all, I have three small children.

[*The* NURSE *enters from the room, left, carrying a big carton.*]

THE NURSE: Well, at last I found it—the box with your costume.

NORA: Thanks. Just put it on the table.

NURSE [*does so*]: But it's all a big mess, I'm afraid.

NORA: Oh, I wish I could tear the whole thing to little pieces!

NURSE: Heavens! It's not as bad as all that. It can be fixed all right. All it takes is a little patience.

NORA: I'll go over and get Mrs. Linde to help me.

NURSE: Going out again? In this awful weather? You'll catch a cold.

NORA: That might not be such a bad thing. How are the children?

NURSE: The poor little dears are playing with their presents, but—

NORA: Do they keep asking for me?

NURSE: Well, you know, they're used to being with their mamma.

NORA: I know. But Anne-Marie, from now on I can't be with them as much as before.

NURSE: Oh well. Little children get used to everything.

NORA: You think so? Do you think they'll forget their mamma if I were gone altogether?

NURSE: Goodness me—gone altogether?

NORA: Listen, Anne-Marie—something I've wondered about. How could you bring yourself to leave your child with strangers?

NURSE: But I had to, if I were to nurse you.

NORA: Yes, but how could you *want* to?

NURSE: When I could get such a nice place? When something like that happens to a poor young girl, she'd better be grateful for whatever she gets. For *he* didn't do a thing for me—the louse!

NORA: But your daughter has forgotten all about you, hasn't she?

NURSE: Oh no! Not at all! She wrote to me both when she was confirmed and when she got married.

NORA [*putting her arms around her neck*]: You dear old thing—you were a good mother to me when I was little.

NURSE: Poor little Nora had no one else, you know.

NORA: And if my little ones didn't, I know you'd—oh, I'm being silly! [*Opens the carton.*] Go in to them, please. I really should—. Tomorrow you'll see how pretty I'll be.

NURSE: I know. There won't be anybody at that party half as pretty as you, ma'am. [*Goes out, left.*]

NORA [*begins to take clothes out of the carton; in a moment she throws it all down*]: If only I dared to go out. If only I knew nobody would come. That nothing would happen while I was gone.—How silly! Nobody'll come. Just don't think about it. Brush the muff. Beautiful gloves. Beautiful gloves. Forget it. Forget it. One, two, three, four, five, six—[*Cries out.*] There they are! [*Moves toward the door, stops irresolutely.*]

[MRS. LINDE *enters from the hall. She has already taken off her coat.*]

NORA: Oh, it's you, Kristine. There's no one else out there, is there? I'm so glad you're here.

MRS. LINDE: They told me you'd asked for me.

NORA: I just happened to walk by. I need your help with something—badly. Let's sit here on the couch. Look. Torvald and I are going to a costume party tomorrow night—at Consul Stenborg's upstairs—and Torvald wants me to go as a Neapolitan fisher girl and dance the tarantella. I learned it when we were on Capri.

MRS. LINDE: Well, well! So you'll be putting on a whole show?

NORA: Yes. Torvald thinks I should. Look, here's the costume. Torvald had it made for me while we were there. But it's all so torn and everything. I just don't know—

MRS. LINDE: Oh, that can be fixed. It's not that much. The trimmings have come loose in a few places. Do you have needle and thread? Ah, here we are. All set.

NORA: I really appreciate it, Kristine.

MRS. LINDE [*sewing*]: So you'll be in disguise tomorrow night, eh? You know—I may come by for just a moment, just to look at you.—Oh dear. I haven't even thanked you for the nice evening last night.

NORA [*gets up, moves around*]: Oh, I don't know. I don't think last night was as nice as it usually is.—You should have come to town a little earlier, Kristine.—Yes, Torvald knows how to make it nice and pretty around here.

MRS. LINDE: You too, I should think. After all, you're your father's daughter. By the way, is Dr. Rank always as depressed as he was last night?

NORA: No, last night was unusual. He's a very sick man, you know—very sick. Poor Rank, his spine is rotting away. Tuberculosis, I think. You see, his father was a nasty old man with mistresses and all that sort of thing. Rank has been sickly ever since he was a little boy.

MRS. LINDE [*dropping her sewing to her lap*]: But dearest, Nora, where have you learned about things like that?

NORA [*still walking about*]: Oh, you know—with three children you sometimes get to talk with—other wives. Some of them know quite a bit about medicine. So you pick up a few things.

MRS. LINDE [*resumes her sewing; after a brief pause*]: Does Dr. Rank come here every day?

NORA: Every single day. He's Torvald's oldest and best friend, after all. And my friend too, for that matter. He's part of the family, almost.

MRS. LINDE: But tell me, is he quite sincere? I mean, isn't he the kind of man who likes to say nice things to people?

NORA: No, not at all. Rather the opposite, in fact. What makes you say that?

MRS. LINDE: When you introduced us yesterday, he told me he'd often heard my name mentioned in this house. But later on it was quite obvious that your husband really had no idea who I was. So how could Dr. Rank—?

NORA: You're right, Kristine, but I can explain that. You see, Torvald loves me so very much that he wants me all to himself. That's what he says. When we were first married he got almost jealous when I as much as mentioned anybody from back home that I was fond of. So of course I soon stopped doing that. But with Dr. Rank I often talk about home. You see, he likes to listen to me.

MRS. LINDE: Look here, Nora. In many ways you're still a child. After all, I'm quite a bit older than you and have had more experience. I want to give you a piece of advice. I think you should get out of this thing with Dr. Rank.

NORA: Get out of what thing?

MRS. LINDE: Several things in fact, if you want my opinion. Yesterday you said something about a rich admirer who was going to give you money—

NORA: One who doesn't exist, unfortunately. What of it?

MRS. LINDE: Does Dr. Rank have money?

NORA: Yes, he does.

MRS. LINDE: And no dependents?

NORA: No. But—?

MRS. LINDE: And he comes here every day?

NORA: Yes, I told you that already.

MRS. LINDE: But how can that sensitive man be so tactless?

NORA: I haven't the slightest idea what you're talking about.

MRS. LINDE: Don't play games with me, Nora. Don't you think I know who you borrowed the twelve hundred dollars from?

NORA: Are you out of your mind! The very idea—! A friend of both of us who sees us every day—! What a dreadfully uncomfortable position that would be!

MRS. LINDE: So it really isn't Dr. Rank?

NORA: Most certainly not! I would never have dreamed of asking him—not for a moment. Anyway, he didn't have any money then. He inherited it afterwards.

MRS. LINDE: Well, I still think it may have been lucky for you, Nora dear.

NORA: The idea! It would never have occurred to me to ask Dr. Rank—. Though I'm sure that if I *did* ask him—

MRS. LINDE: But of course you wouldn't.

NORA: Of course not. I can't imagine that that would ever be necessary. But I am quite sure that if I told Dr. Rank—

MRS. LINDE: Behind your husband's back?

NORA: I must get out of—this other thing. That's also behind his back. I *must* get out of it.

MRS. LINDE: That's what I told you yesterday. But—

NORA [*walking up and down*]: A man manages these things so much better than a woman—

MRS. LINDE: One's husband, yes.

NORA: Silly, silly! [*Stops.*] When you've paid off all you owe, you get your I.O.U. back; right?

MRS. LINDE: Yes, of course.

NORA: And you can tear it into a hundred thousand little pieces and burn it—that dirty, filthy, paper!

MRS. LINDE [*looks hard at her, puts down her sewing, rises slowly*]: Nora—you're hiding something from me.

NORA: Can you tell?

MRS. LINDE: Something's happened to you, Nora, since yesterday morning. What is it?

NORA [*going to her*]: Kristine! [*Listens.*] Shhh. Torvald just came back. Listen. Why don't you go in to the children for a while. Torvald can't stand having sewing around. Get Anne-Marie to help you.

MRS. LINDE [*gathers some of the sewing things together*]: All right, but I'm not leaving here till you and I have talked.

[*She goes out left, as* HELMER *enters from the front hall.*]

NORA [*towards him*]: I have been waiting and waiting for you, Torvald.

HELMER: Was that the dressmaker?

NORA: No, it was Kristine. She's helping me with my costume. Oh Torvald, just wait till you see how nice I'll look!

HELMER: I told you. Pretty good idea I had, wasn't it?

NORA: Lovely! And wasn't it nice of me to go along with it?

HELMER [*his hands under her chin*]: Nice? To do what your husband tells you? All right, you little rascal; I know you didn't mean it that way. But don't let me interrupt you. I suppose you want to try it on.

NORA: And you'll be working?

HELMER: Yes. [*Shows her a pile of papers.*] Look. I've been down to the bank. [*Is about to enter his study.*]

NORA: Torvald.

HELMER [*halts*]: Yes?

NORA: What if your little squirrel asked you ever so nicely—

HELMER: For what?

NORA: Would you do it?

HELMER: Depends on what it is.

NORA: Squirrel would run around and do all sorts of fun tricks if you'd be nice and agreeable.

HELMER: All right. What is it?

NORA: Lark would chirp and twitter in all the rooms, up and down—

HELMER: So what? Lark does that anyway.

NORA: I'll be your elfmaid and dance for you in the moonlight, Torvald.

HELMER: Nora, don't tell me it's the same thing you mentioned this morning?

NORA [*closer to him*]: Yes, Torvald. I beg you!

HELMER: You really have the nerve to bring that up again?

NORA: Yes. You've just got to do as I say. You *must* let Krogstad keep his job.

HELMER: My dear Nora. It's his job I intend to give to Mrs. Linde.

NORA: I know. And that's ever so nice of you. But can't you just fire somebody else?

HELMER: This is incredible! You just don't give up do you? Because you make some foolish promise, *I* am supposed to—!

NORA: That's not the reason, Torvald. It's for your own sake. That man writes for the worst newspapers. You've said so yourself. There's no telling what he may do to you. I'm scared to death of him.

HELMER: Ah, I understand. You're afraid because of what happened before.

NORA: What do you mean?

HELMER: You're thinking of your father, of course.

NORA: Yes. Yes, you're right. Remember the awful things they wrote about Daddy in the newspapers. I really think they might have forced him to resign if the ministry hadn't sent you to look into the charges and if you hadn't been so helpful and understanding.

HELMER: My dear little Nora, there is a world of difference between your father and me. Your father's official conduct was not above reproach. Mine is, and I intend for it to remain that way as long as I hold my position.

NORA: Oh, but you don't know what vicious people like that may think of. Oh, Torvald! Now all of us could be so happy together here in our own home, peaceful and carefree. Such a good life, Torvald, for you and me and the children! That's why I implore you—

HELMER: And it's exactly because you plead for him that you make it impossible for me to keep him. It's already common knowledge in the bank that I intend to let Krogstad go. If it gets out that the new manager has changed his mind because of his wife—

NORA: Yes? What then?

HELMER: No, of course, that wouldn't matter at all as long as little Mrs. Pighead here got her way! Do you want me to make myself look ridiculous before my whole staff—make people think I can be swayed by just anybody—by outsiders? Believe me, I would soon enough find out what the consequences would be! Besides, there's another thing that makes it absolutely impossible for Krogstad to stay on in the bank now that I'm in charge.

NORA: What's that?

HELMER: I suppose in a pinch I could overlook his moral shortcomings—

NORA: Yes, you could; couldn't you, Torvald?

HELMER: And I understand he's quite a good worker, too. But we've known each other for a long time. It's one of those imprudent relationships you get into when you're young that embarrass you for the rest of your life. I guess I might as well be frank with you: he and I are on a first name basis. And that tactless fellow never hides the fact even when other people are around. Rather, he seems to think it entitles him to be familiar with me. Every chance he gets he comes out with his damn "Torvald, Torvald." I'm telling you, I find it most awkward. He would make my position in the bank intolerable.

NORA: You don't really mean any of this, Torvald.

HELMER: Oh? I don't? And why not?

NORA: No, for it's all so petty.

HELMER: What! Petty? You think I'm being petty!

NORA: No, I *don't* think you are petty, Torvald dear. That's exactly why I—

HELMER: Never mind. You think my reasons are petty, so it follows that I must be petty too. Petty! Indeed! By God, I'll put an end to this right now! [*Opens the door to the front hall and calls out.*] Helene!

NORA: What are you doing?

HELMER [*searching among his papers*]: Making a decision. [THE MAID *enters.*] Here. Take this letter. Go out with it right away. Find somebody to deliver it. But quick. The address is on the envelope. Wait. Here's money.

THE MAID: Very good sir. [*She takes the letter and goes out.*]

HELMER [*collecting his papers*]: There now, little Mrs. Obstinate!

NORA [*breathless*]: Torvald—what was that letter?

HELMER: Krogstad's dismissal.

NORA: Call it back, Torvald! There's still time! Oh Torvald, please—call it back! For my sake, for your own sake, for the sake of the children! Listen to me, Torvald! Do it! You don't know what you're doing to all of us!

HELMER: Too late.

NORA: Yes. Too late.

HELMER: Dear Nora, I forgive you this fear you're in, although it really is an insult to me. Yes, it is! It's an insult to think that I am scared of a shabby scrivener's revenge. But I forgive you, for it's such a beautiful proof how much you love me. [*Takes her in his arms.*] And that's the way it should be, my sweet darling. Whatever happens, you'll see that when things get really rough I have both strength and courage. You'll find out that I am man enough to shoulder the whole burden.

NORA [*terrified*]: What do you mean by that?

HELMER: All of it, I tell you—

NORA [*composed*]: You'll never have to do that.

HELMER: Good. Then we'll share the burden, Nora—like husband and wife, the way it ought to be. [*Caresses her.*] Now are you satisfied? There, there, there. Not that look in your eyes—like a frightened dove. It's all your own foolish imagination.—Why don't you practice the tarantella—and your tambourine, too. I'll be in the inner office and close both doors, so I won't hear you. You can make as much noise as you like. [*Turning in the doorway.*] And when Rank comes, tell him where to find me. [*He nods to her, enters his study carrying his papers, and closes the door.*]

NORA [*transfixed by terror, whispers*]: He would do it. He'll do it. He'll do it in spite of the whole world.—No, this mustn't happen. Anything rather than that! There must be a way—! [*The doorbell rings.*] Dr. Rank! Anything rather than that! Anything—anything at all!

[*She passes her hand over her face, pulls herself together, and opens the door to the hall.* DR. RANK *is out there, hanging up his coat. Darkness begins to fall during the following scene.*]

NORA: Hello there, Dr. Rank. I recognized your ringing. Don't go in to Torvald yet. I think he's busy.

RANK: And you?

NORA [*as he enters and she closes the door behind him*]: You know I always have time for you.

RANK: Thanks. I'll make use of that as long as I can.

NORA: What do you mean by that—As long as you can?

RANK: Does that frighten you?

NORA: Well, it's a funny expression. As if something was going to happen.

RANK: Something is going to happen that I've long been expecting. But I admit I hadn't thought it would come quite so soon.

NORA [*seizes his arm*]: What is it you've found out? Dr. Rank—tell me!

RANK [*sits down by the stove*]: I'm going downhill fast. There's nothing to do about that.

NORA [*with audible relief*]: So it's *you*—

RANK: Who else? No point in lying to myself. I'm in worse shape than any of my other patients, Mrs. Helmer. These last few days I've been making up my inner status. Bankrupt. Chances are that within a month I'll be rotting up in the cemetery.

NORA: Shame on you! Talking that horrid way!

RANK: The thing itself is horrid—damn horrid. The worst of it, though, is all that other horror that comes first. There is only one more test I need to make. After that I'll have a pretty good idea when I'll start coming apart. There is something I want to say to you. Helmer's refined nature can't stand anything hideous. I don't want him in my sick room.

NORA: Oh, but Dr. Rank—

RANK: I don't want him there. Under no circumstances. I'll close my door to him. As soon as I have full certainty that the worst is about to begin I'll give you my card with a black cross on it. Then you'll know the last horror of destruction has started.

NORA: Today you're really quite impossible. And I had hoped you'd be in a particularly good mood.

RANK: With death on my hands? Paying for someone else's sins? Is there justice in that? And yet there isn't a single family that isn't ruled by the same law of ruthless retribution, in one way or another.

NORA [*puts her hands over her ears*]: Poppycock! Be fun! Be fun!

RANK: Well, yes. You may just as well laugh at the whole thing. My poor, innocent spine is suffering from my father's frolics as a young lieutenant.

NORA [*over by the table, left*]: Right. He was addicted to asparagus and goose liver paté, wasn't he?

RANK: And truffles.

NORA: Of course. Truffles. And oysters too, I think.

RANK: And oysters. Obviously.

NORA: And all the port and champagne that go with it. It's really too bad that goodies like that ruin your backbone.

RANK: Particularly an unfortunate backbone that never enjoyed any of it.

NORA: Ah yes, that's the saddest part of it all.

RANK [*looks searchingly at her*]: Hm—

NORA [*after a brief pause*]: Why did you smile just then?

RANK: No, it was you that laughed.

NORA: No, it was you that smiled, Dr. Rank!

RANK [*gets up*]: You're more of a mischief-maker than I thought.

NORA: I feel in the mood for mischief today.

RANK: So it seems.

NORA [*with both her hands on his shoulders*]: Dear, dear Dr. Rank, don't you go and die and leave Torvald and me.

RANK: Oh, you won't miss me for very long. Those who go away are soon forgotten.

NORA [*with an anxious look*]: Do you believe that?

RANK: You'll make new friends, and then—

NORA: Who'll make new friends?

RANK: Both you and Helmer, once I'm gone. You yourself seem to have made a good start already. What was this Mrs. Linde doing here last night?

NORA: Aha—Don't tell me you're jealous of poor Kristine?

RANK: Yes, I am. She'll be my successor in this house. As soon as I have made my excuses, that woman is likely to—

NORA: Shh—not so loud. She's in there.
RANK: Today too? There you are!
NORA: She's mending my costume. My God, you really *are* unreasonable. [*Sits down on the couch.*] Now be nice, Dr. Rank. Tomorrow you'll see how beautifully I'll dance, and then you are to pretend I'm dancing just for you—and for Torvald too, of course. [*Takes several items out of the carton.*] Sit down, Dr. Rank; I want to show you something.
RANK [*sitting down*]: What?
NORA: Look.
RANK: Silk stockings.
NORA: Flesh-colored. Aren't they lovely? Now it's getting dark in here, but tomorrow—No, no. You only get to see the foot. Oh well, you might as well see all of it.
RANK: Hmm.
NORA: Why do you look so critical? Don't you think they'll fit?
RANK: That's something I can't possibly have a reasoned opinion about.
NORA [*looks at him for a moment*]: Shame on you. [*Slaps his ear lightly with the stocking.*] That's what you get. [*Puts the things back in the carton.*]
RANK: And what other treasures are you going to show me?
NORA: Nothing at all, because you're naughty. [*She hums a little and rummages in the carton.*]
RANK [*after a brief silence*]: When I sit here like this, talking confidently with you, I can't imagine—I can't possibly imagine what would have become of me if I hadn't had you and Helmer.
NORA [*smiles*]: Well, yes—I do believe you like being with us.
RANK [*in a lower voice, lost in thought*]: And then to have to go away from it all—
NORA: Nonsense. You are not going anywhere.
RANK [*as before*]: —and not to leave behind as much as a poor little token of gratitude, hardly a brief memory of someone missed, nothing but a vacant place that anyone can fill.
NORA: And what if I were to ask you—? No—
RANK: Ask me what?
NORA: For a great proof of your friendship—
RANK: Yes, yes—?
NORA: No, I mean—for an enormous favor—
RANK: Would you really for once make me as happy as all that?
NORA: But you don't even know what it is.
RANK: Well, then; tell me.
NORA: Oh, but I can't, Dr. Rank. It's altogether too much to ask—It's advice and help and a favor—
RANK: So much the better. I can't even begin to guess what it is you have in mind. So for heaven's sake tell me! Don't you trust me?
NORA: Yes, I trust you more than anyone else I know. You are my best and most faithful friend. I know that. So I will tell you. All right, Dr. Rank. There is something you can help me prevent. You know how much Torvald loves me—beyond all words. Never for a moment would he hesitate to give his life for me.
RANK [*leaning over to her*]: Nora—do you really think he's the only one—?
NORA [*with a slight start*]: Who—?
RANK: —would gladly give his life for you.
NORA [*heavily*]: I see.
RANK: I have sworn an oath to myself to tell you before I go. I'll never find a better occasion.—All right, Nora; now you know. And now you also know that you can confide in me more than in anyone else.
NORA [*gets up; in a calm, steady voice*]: Let me get by.
RANK [*makes room for her but remains seated*]: Nora—
NORA [*in the door to the front hall*]: Helene, bring the lamp in here, please. [*Walks over to the stove.*] Oh, dear Dr. Rank. That really wasn't very nice of you.
RANK [*gets up*]: That I have loved you as much as anybody—was that not nice?
NORA: No; not that. But that you told me. There was no need for that.
RANK: What do you mean? Have you known—?

[THE MAID *enters with the lamp, puts it on the table, and goes out.*]

RANK: Nora—Mrs. Helmer—I'm asking you: did you know?
NORA: Oh, how can I tell what I knew and didn't know! I really can't say—But that you could be so awkward, Dr. Rank! Just when everything was so comfortable.
RANK: Well, anyway, now you know that I'm at your service with my life and soul. And now you must speak.
NORA [*looks at him*]: After what just happened?
RANK: I beg of you—let me know what it is.
NORA: There is nothing I can tell you now.
RANK: Yes, yes. You mustn't punish me this way. Please let me do for you whatever anyone *can* do.
NORA: Now there is nothing you can do. Besides, I don't think I really need any help, anyway. It's probably just my imagination. Of course that's all it is. I'm sure of it! [*Sits down in the rocking chair, looks at him, smiles.*] Well, well, well, Dr. Rank! What a fine gentleman you turned out to be! Aren't you ashamed of yourself, now that we have light?
RANK: No, not really. But perhaps I ought to leave—and not come back?
NORA: Don't be silly; of course not! You'll come here exactly as you have been doing. You know

perfectly well that Torvald can't do without you.

RANK: Yes, but what about you?

NORA: Oh, I always think it's perfectly delightful when you come.

RANK: That's the very thing that misled me. You are a riddle to me. It has often seemed to me that you'd just as soon be with me as with Helmer.

NORA: Well, you see, there are people you love, and then there are other people you'd almost rather be with.

RANK: Yes, there is something in that.

NORA: When I lived at home with Daddy, of course I loved him most. But I always thought it was so much fun to sneak off down to the maids' room, for they never gave me good advice and they always talked about such fun things.

RANK: Aha! So it's *their* place I have taken.

NORA [*jumps up and goes over to him*]: Oh dear, kind Dr. Rank, you know very well I didn't mean it that way. Can't you see that with Torvald it is the way it used to be with Daddy?

[THE MAID *enters from the front hall.*]

THE MAID: Ma'am! [*Whispers to her and gives her a caller's card.*]

NORA [*glances at the card*]: Ah! [*Puts it in her pocket.*]

RANK: Anything wrong?

NORA: No, no; not at all. It's nothing—just my new costume—

RANK: But your costume is lying right there!

NORA: Oh yes, that one. But this is another one. I ordered it. Torvald mustn't know—

RANK: Aha. So that's the great secret.

NORA: That's it. Why don't you go in to him, please. He's in the inner office. And keep him there for a while—

RANK: Don't worry. He won't get away. [*Enters* HELMER's *study.*]

NORA [*to* THE MAID]: You say he's waiting in the kitchen?

THE MAID: Yes. He came up the back stairs.

NORA: But didn't you tell him there was somebody with me?

THE MAID: Yes, but he wouldn't listen.

NORA: He won't leave?

THE MAID: No, not till he's had a word with you, ma'am.

NORA: All right. But try not to make any noise. And, Helene—don't tell anyone he's here. It's supposed to be a surprise for my husband.

THE MAID: I understand, ma'am—[*She leaves.*]

NORA: The terrible is happening. It's happening, after all. No, no, no. It can't happen. It won't happen. [*She bolts the study door.*]

[THE MAID *opens the front hall door for* KROGSTAD *and closes the door behind him. He wears a fur coat for traveling, boots, and a fur hat.*]

NORA [*toward him*]: Keep your voice down. My husband's home.

KROGSTAD: That's all right.

NORA: What do you want?

KROGSTAD: To find out something.

NORA: Be quick, then. What is it?

KROGSTAD: I expect you know I've been fired.

NORA: I couldn't prevent it, Mr. Krogstad. I fought for you as long and as hard as I could but it didn't do any good.

KROGSTAD: Your husband doesn't love you any more than that? He knows what I can do to you, and yet he runs the risk—

NORA: Surely you didn't think I'd tell him?

KROGSTAD: No, I really didn't. It wouldn't be like Torvald Helmer to show that kind of guts—

NORA: Mr. Krogstad, I insist that you show respect for my husband.

KROGSTAD: By all means. All due respect. But since you're so anxious to keep this a secret, may I assume that you are a little better informed than yesterday about exactly what you have done?

NORA: Better than *you* could ever teach me.

KROGSTAD: Of course. Such a bad lawyer as I am—

NORA: What do you want of me?

KROGSTAD: I just wanted to find out how you are, Mrs. Helmer. I've been thinking about you all day. You see, even a bill collector, a pen pusher, a—anyway, someone like me—even he has a little of what they call a heart.

NORA: Then show it. Think of my little children.

KROGSTAD: Have you and your husband thought of mine? Never mind. All I want to tell you is that you don't need to take this business too seriously. I have no intention of bringing charges right away.

NORA: Oh no, you wouldn't; would you? I knew you wouldn't.

KROGSTAD: The whole thing can be settled quite amiably. Nobody else needs to know anything. It will be between the three of us.

NORA: My husband must never find out about this.

KROGSTAD: How are you going to prevent that? Maybe you can pay me the balance on the loan?

NORA: No, not right now.

KROGSTAD: Or do you have a way of raising the money one of these next few days?

NORA: None I intend to make use of.

KROGSTAD: It wouldn't do you any good, anyway. Even if you had the cash in your hand right this minute, I wouldn't give you your note back. It wouldn't make any difference *how* much money you offered me.

NORA: Then you'll have to tell me what you plan to use the note *for.*

KROGSTAD: Just keep it; that's all. Have it on hand, so to speak. I won't say a word to anybody else. So if you've been thinking about doing something desperate—

NORA: I have.

KROGSTAD: —like leaving house and home—

NORA: I have!

KROGSTAD: —or even something worse—

NORA: How did you know?

KROGSTAD: —then: don't.

NORA: How did you know I was thinking of *that?*

KROGSTAD: Most of us do, right at first. I did, too, but when it came down to it I didn't have the courage—

NORA [*tonelessly*]: Nor do I.

KROGSTAD [*relieved*]: See what I mean? I thought so. You don't either.

NORA: I don't. I don't.

KROGSTAD: Besides, it would be very silly of you. Once that first domestic blowup is behind you—. Here in my pocket is a letter for your husband.

NORA: Telling him everything?

KROGSTAD: As delicately as possible.

NORA [*quickly*]: He mustn't get that letter. Tear it up. I'll get you the money somehow.

KROGSTAD: Excuse me, Mrs. Helmer, I thought I just told you—

NORA: I'm not talking about the money I owe you. Just let me know how much money you want from my husband, and I'll get it for you.

KROGSTAD: I want no money from your husband.

NORA: Then, what *do* you want?

KROGSTAD: I'll tell you, Mrs. Helmer. I want to rehabilitate myself; I want to get up in the world; and your husband is going to help me. For a year and a half I haven't done anything disreputable. All that time I have been struggling with the most miserable circumstances. I was content to work my way up step by step. Now I've been kicked out, and I'm no longer satisfied just getting my old job back. I want more than that; I want to get to the top. I'm being quite serious. I want the bank to take me back but in a higher position. I want your husband to create a new job for me—

NORA: He'll never do that!

KROGSTAD: He will. I know him. He won't dare not to. And once I'm back inside and he and I are working together, you'll see! Within a year I'll be the manager's right hand. It will be Nils Krogstad and not Torvald Helmer who'll be running the Mutual Bank!

NORA: You'll never see that happen!

KROGSTAD: Are you thinking of—?

NORA: Now I *do* have the courage.

KROGSTAD: You can't scare me. A fine, spoiled lady like you—

NORA: You'll see, you'll see!

KROGSTAD: Under the ice, perhaps? Down into that cold, black water? Then spring comes, and you float up again—hideous, can't be identified, hair all gone—

NORA: You don't frighten me.

KROGSTAD: Nor you me. One doesn't do that sort of thing, Mrs. Helmer. Besides, what good would it do? He'd still be in my power.

NORA: Afterwards? When I'm no longer—?

KROGSTAD: Aren't you forgetting that your reputation would be in my hands?

[NORA *stares at him, speechless.*]

KROGSTAD: All right; now I've told you what to expect. So don't do anything foolish. When Helmer gets my letter I expect to hear from him. And don't you forget that it's your husband himself who forces me to use such means again. That I'll never forgive him. Goodbye, Mrs. Helmer. [*Goes out through the hall.*]

NORA [*at the door, opens it a little, listens*]: He's going. And no letter. Of course not! That would be impossible. [*Opens the door more.*] What's he doing? He's still there. Doesn't go down. Having second thoughts—? Will he—?

[*The sound of a letter dropping into the mailbox. Then* KROGSTAD'*s steps are heard going down the stairs, gradually dying away.*]

NORA [*with a muted cry runs forward to the table by the couch; brief pause*]: In the mailbox. [*Tiptoes back to the door to the front hall.*] There it is. Torvald, Torvald—now we're lost!

MRS. LINDE [*enters from the left, carrying* NORA'*s Capri costume*]: There now. I think it's all fixed. Why don't we try it on you—

NORA [*in a low, hoarse voice*]: Kristine, come here.

MRS. LINDE: What's wrong with you? You look quite beside yourself.

NORA: Come over here. Do you see that letter? There, look—through the glass in the mailbox.

MRS. LINDE: Yes, yes; I see it.

NORA: That letter is from Krogstad.

MRS. LINDE: Nora—it was Krogstad who lent you the money!

NORA: Yes, and now Torvald will find out about it.

MRS. LINDE: Oh believe me, Nora. That's the best thing for both of you.

NORA: There's more to it than you know. I forged a signature—

MRS. LINDE: Oh my God—!

NORA: I just want to tell you this, Kristine, that you must be my witness.

MRS. LINDE: Witness? How? Witness to what?

NORA: If I lose my mind—and that could very well happen—

MRS. LINDE: Nora!

NORA: —or if something were to happen to me—something that made it impossible for me to be here—

MRS. LINDE: Nora, Nora! You're not yourself!

NORA: —and if someone were to take all the blame, assume the whole responsibility—Do you understand—?

MRS. LINDE: Yes, yes; but how can you think—!

NORA: Then you are to witness that that's not so, Kristine. I am not beside myself. I am perfectly rational, and what I'm telling you is that nobody else has known about this. I've done it all by myself, the whole thing. Just remember that.

MRS. LINDE: I will. But I don't understand any of it.

NORA: Oh, how could you! For it's the wonderful that's about to happen.

MRS. LINDE: The wonderful?

NORA: Yes, the wonderful. But it's so terrible, Kristine. It mustn't happen for anything in the whole world!

MRS. LINDE: I'm going over to talk to Krogstad right now.

NORA: No, don't. Don't go to him. He'll do something bad to you.

MRS. LINDE: There was a time when he would have done anything for me.

NORA: He!

MRS. LINDE: Where does he live?

NORA: Oh, I don't know—Yes, wait a minute—[*Reaches into her pocket.*] here's his card.—But the letter, the letter—!

HELMER [*in his study, knocks on the door*]: Nora!

NORA [*cries out in fear*]: Oh, what is it? What do you want?

HELMER: That's all right. Nothing to be scared about. We're not coming in. For one thing, you've bolted the door, you know. Are you modeling your costume?

NORA: Yes, yes; I am. I'm going to be so pretty, Torvald.

MRS. LINDE [*having looked at the card*]: He lives just around the corner.

NORA: Yes, but it's no use. Nothing can save us now. The letter is in the mailbox.

MRS. LINDE: And your husband has the key?

NORA: Yes. He always keeps it with him.

MRS. LINDE: Krogstad must ask for his letter back, unread. He's got to think up some pretext or other—

NORA: But this is just the time of day when Torvald—

MRS. LINDE: Delay him. Go in to him. I'll be back as soon as I can. [*She hurries out through the hall door.*]

NORA [*walks over to* HELMER*'s door, opens it, and peeks in*]: Torvald.

HELMER [*still offstage*]: Well, well! So now one's allowed in one's own living room again. Come on, Rank. Now we'll see— [*In the doorway.*] But what's this?

NORA: What, Torvald dear?

HELMER: Rank prepared me for a splendid metamorphosis.

RANK [*in the doorway*]: That's how I understood it. Evidently I was mistaken.

NORA: Nobody gets to admire me in my costume before tomorrow.

HELMER: But, dearest Nora—you look all done in. Have you been practicing too hard?

NORA: No, I haven't practiced at all.

HELMER: But you'll have to, you know.

NORA: I know it, Torvald. I simply must. But I can't do a thing unless you help me. I have forgotten everything.

HELMER: Oh it will all come back. We'll work on it.

NORA: Oh yes, please, Torvald. You just have to help me. Promise? I am so nervous. That big party—. You mustn't do anything else tonight. Not a bit of business. Don't even touch a pen. Will you promise, Torvald?

HELMER: I promise. Tonight I'll be entirely at your service—you helpless little thing.—Just a moment, though. First I want to— [*Goes to the door to the front hall.*]

NORA: What are you doing out there?

HELMER: Just looking to see if there's any mail.

NORA: No, no! Don't, Torvald!

HELMER: Why not?

NORA: Torvald, I beg you. There is no mail.

HELMER: Let me just look, anyway. [*Is about to go out.*]

[NORA *by the piano, plays the first bars of the tarantella dance.*]

HELMER [*halts at the door*]: Aha!

NORA: I won't be able to dance tomorrow if I don't get to practice with you.

HELMER [*goes to her*]: Are you really all that scared, Nora dear?

NORA: Yes, so terribly scared. Let's try it right now. There's still time before we eat. Oh please, sit down and play for me, Torvald. Teach me, coach me, the way you always do.

HELMER: Of course I will, my darling, if that's what you want. [*Sits down at the piano.*]

[NORA *takes the tambourine out of the carton, as well as a long, many-colored shawl. She quickly drapes the shawl around herself, then leaps into the middle of the floor.*]

NORA: Play for me! I want to dance!

[HELMER *plays and* NORA *dances.* DR. RANK *stands by the piano behind* HELMER *and watches.*]

HELMER [*playing*]: Slow down, slow down!
NORA: Can't!
HELMER: Not so violent, Nora!
NORA: It has to be this way.
HELMER [*stops playing*]: No, no. This won't do at all.
NORA [*laughing, swinging her tambourine*]: What did I tell you?
RANK: Why don't you let me play?
HELMER [*getting up*]: Good idea. Then I can direct her better.

[RANK *sits down at the piano and starts playing.* NORA *dances more and more wildly.* HELMER *stands over by the stove, repeatedly correcting her. She doesn't seem to hear. Her hair comes loose and falls down over her shoulders. She doesn't notice but keeps on dancing.* MRS. LINDE *enters.*]

MRS. LINDE [*stops by the door, dumbfounded*]: Ah—!
NORA [*dancing*]: We're having such fun, Kristine!
HELMER: My dearest Nora, you're dancing as if it were a matter of life and death!
NORA: It is! It is!
HELMER: Rank, stop. This is sheer madness. Stop, I say!

[RANK *stops playing;* NORA *suddenly stops dancing.*]

HELMER [*goes over to her*]: If I hadn't seen it I wouldn't have believed it. You've forgotten every single thing I ever taught you.
NORA [*tosses away the tambourine*]: See? I told you.
HELMER: Well! You certainly need coaching.
NORA: Didn't I tell you I did? Now you've seen for yourself. I'll need your help till the very minute we're leaving for the party. Will you promise, Torvald?
HELMER: You can count on it.
NORA: You're not to think of anything except me—not tonight and not tomorrow. You're not to read any letters—not to look in the mailbox—
HELMER: Ah, I see. You're still afraid of that man.
NORA: Yes—yes, that too.
HELMER: Nora, I can tell from looking at you. There's a letter from him out there.
NORA: I don't know. I think so. But you're not to read it now. I don't want anything ugly to come between us before it's all over.
RANK [*to* HELMER *in a low voice*]: Better not argue with her.
HELMER [*throws his arm around her*]: The child shall have her way. But tomorrow night, when you've done your dance—
NORA: Then you'll be free.
THE MAID [*in the door, right*]: Dinner can be served any time, ma'am.
NORA: We want champagne, Helene.
THE MAID: Very good, ma'am. [*Goes out.*]
HELMER: Aha! Having a party, eh?
NORA: Champagne from now till sunrise! [*Calls out.*] And some macaroons, Helene. Lots!—just this once.
HELMER [*taking her hands*]: There, there—I don't like this wild—frenzy—Be my own sweet little lark again, the way you always are.
NORA: Oh, I will. But you go on in. You too, Dr. Rank. Kristine, please help me put up my hair.
RANK [*in a low voice to* HELMER *as they go out*]: You don't think she is—you know—expecting—?
HELMER: Oh no. Nothing like that. It's just this childish fear I was telling you about. [*They go out, right.*]
NORA: Well?
MRS. LINDE: Left town.
NORA: I saw it in your face.
MRS. LINDE: He'll be back tomorrow night. I left him a note.
NORA: You shouldn't have. I don't want you to try to stop anything. You see, it's a kind of ecstasy, too, this waiting for the wonderful.
MRS. LINDE: But what is it you're waiting *for?*
NORA: You wouldn't understand. Why don't you go in to the others. I'll be there in a minute.

[MRS. LINDE *enters the dining room, right.*]

NORA [*stands still for a little while, as if collecting herself; she looks at her watch*]: Five o'clock. Seven hours till midnight. Twenty-four more hours till next midnight. Then the tarantella is over. Twenty-four plus seven—thirty-one more hours to live.
HELMER [*in the door, right*]: What's happening to my little lark?
NORA [*to him, with open arms*]: Here's your lark!

ACT III

The same room. The table by the couch and the chairs around it have been moved to the middle of the floor. A lighted lamp is on the table. The door to the front hall is open. Dance music is heard from upstairs.

MRS. LINDE *is seated by the table, idly leafing through the pages of a book. She tries to read but seems unable to concentrate. Once or twice she turns her head in the direction of the door, anxiously listening.*

MRS. LINDE [*looks at her watch*]: Not yet. It's almost too late. If only he hasn't— [*Listens again.*] Ah! There he is. [*She goes to the hall and opens the front door carefully. Quiet footsteps on the stairs. She whispers.*] Come in. There's nobody here.

KROGSTAD [*in the door*]: I found your note when I got home. What's this all about?

MRS. LINDE: I've got to talk to you.

KROGSTAD: Oh? And it has to be here?

MRS. LINDE: It couldn't be at my place. My room doesn't have a separate entrance. Come in. We're quite alone. The maid is asleep and the Helmers are at a party upstairs.

KROGSTAD [*entering*]: Really? The Helmers are dancing tonight, are they?

MRS. LINDE: And why not?

KROGSTAD: You're right. Why not, indeed.

MRS. LINDE: All right, Krogstad. Let's talk, you and I.

KROGSTAD: I didn't know we had anything to talk about.

MRS. LINDE: We have much to talk about.

KROGSTAD: I didn't think so.

MRS. LINDE: No, because you've never really understood me.

KROGSTAD: What was there to understand? What happened was perfectly commonplace. A heartless woman jilts a man when she gets a more attractive offer.

MRS. LINDE: Do you think I'm all that heartless? And do you think it was easy for me to break with you?

KROGSTAD: No?

MRS. LINDE: You really thought it was?

KROGSTAD: If it wasn't, why did you write the way you did that time?

MRS. LINDE: What else could I do? If I had to make a break, I also had the duty to destroy whatever feelings you had for me.

KROGSTAD [*clenching his hands*]: So that's the way it was. And you did—*that*—just for money!

MRS. LINDE: Don't forget I had a helpless mother and two small brothers. We couldn't wait for you, Krogstad. You know yourself how uncertain your prospects were then.

KROGSTAD: All right. But you still didn't have the right to throw me over for somebody else.

MRS. LINDE: I don't know. I have asked myself that question many times. Did I have that right?

KROGSTAD [*in a lower voice*]: When I lost you I lost my footing. Look at me now. A shipwrecked man on a raft.

MRS. LINDE: Rescue may be near.

KROGSTAD: It *was* near. Then you came between.

MRS. LINDE: I didn't know that, Krogstad. Only today did I find out it's your job I'm taking over in the bank.

KROGSTAD: I believe you when you say so. But now that you *do* know, aren't you going to step aside?

MRS. LINDE: No, for it wouldn't do you any good.

KROGSTAD: Whether it would or not—*I* would do it.

MRS. LINDE: I have learned common sense. Life and hard necessity have taught me that.

KROGSTAD: And life has taught me not to believe in pretty speeches.

MRS. LINDE: Then life has taught you a very sensible thing. But you do believe in actions, don't you?

KROGSTAD: How do you mean?

MRS. LINDE: You referred to yourself just now as a shipwrecked man.

KROGSTAD: It seems to me I had every reason to do so.

MRS. LINDE: And I am a shipwrecked woman. No one to grieve for, no one to care for.

KROGSTAD: You made your choice.

MRS. LINDE: I had no other choice that time.

KROGSTAD: Let's say you didn't. What then?

MRS. LINDE: Krogstad, how would it be if we two shipwrecked people got together?

KROGSTAD: What's this!

MRS. LINDE: Two on one wreck are better off than each on his own.

KROGSTAD: Kristine!

MRS. LINDE: Why do you think I came to town?

KROGSTAD: Surely not because of me?

MRS. LINDE: If I'm going to live at all I must work. All my life, for as long as I can remember, I have worked. That's been my one and only pleasure. But now that I'm all alone in the world I feel nothing but this terrible emptiness and desolation. There is no joy in working just for yourself. Krogstad—give me someone and something to work for.

KROGSTAD: I don't believe this. Only hysterical females go in for that kind of high-minded self-sacrifice.

MRS. LINDE: Did you ever know me to be hysterical?

KROGSTAD: You really could do this? Listen—do you know about my past? All of it?

MRS. LINDE: Yes, I do.

KROGSTAD: Do you also know what people think of me around here?

MRS. LINDE: A little while ago you sounded as if you thought that together with me you might have become a different person.

KROGSTAD: I'm sure of it.

MRS. LINDE: Couldn't that still be?

KROGSTAD: Kristine—do you know what you are doing? Yes, I see you do. And you think you have the courage—?

MRS. LINDE: I need someone to be a mother to, and your children need a mother. You and I need one another. Nils, I believe in you—in the real you. Together with you I dare to do anything.

KROGSTAD [*seizes her hands*]: Thanks, thanks, Kristine—Now I know I'll raise myself in the eyes of others—Ah, but I forget—!

MRS. LINDE [*listening*]: Shh!—there's the tarantella. You must go; hurry!

KROGSTAD: Why? What is it?

MRS. LINDE: Do you hear what they're playing up there? When that dance is over they'll be down.

KROGSTAD: All right. I'm leaving. The whole thing is pointless, anyway. Of course you don't know what I'm doing to the Helmers.

MRS. LINDE: Yes, Krogstad; I do know.

KROGSTAD: Still, you're brave enough—?

MRS. LINDE: I very well understand to what extremes despair can drive a man like you.

KROGSTAD: If only it could be undone!

MRS. LINDE: It could, for your letter is still out there in the mailbox.

KROGSTAD: Are you sure?

MRS. LINDE: Quite sure. But—

KROGSTAD [*looks searchingly at her*]: Maybe I'm beginning to understand. You want to save your friend at any cost. Be honest with me. That's it, isn't it?

MRS. LINDE: Krogstad, you may sell yourself once for somebody else's sake, but you don't do it twice.

KROGSTAD: I'll demand my letter back.

MRS. LINDE: No, no.

KROGSTAD: Yes, of course. I'll wait here till Helmer comes down. Then I'll ask him for my letter. I'll tell him it's just about my dismissal—that he shouldn't read it.

MRS. LINDE: No, Krogstad. You are not to ask for that letter back.

KROGSTAD: But tell me—wasn't that the real reason you wanted to meet me here?

MRS. LINDE: At first it was, because I was so frightened. But that was yesterday. Since then I have seen the most incredible things going on in this house. Helmer must learn the whole truth. This miserable secret must come out in the open; those two must come to a full understanding. They simply can't continue with all this concealment and evasion.

KROGSTAD: All right; if you want to take that chance. But there is one thing I *can* do, and I'll do that right now.

MRS. LINDE [*listening*]: But hurry! Go! The dance is over. We aren't safe another minute.

KROGSTAD: I'll be waiting for you downstairs.

MRS. LINDE: Yes, do. You must see me home.

KROGSTAD: I've never been so happy in my whole life. [*He leaves through the front door. The door between the living room and the front hall remains open.*]

MRS. LINDE [*straightens up the room a little and gets her things ready*]: What a change! Oh yes!—what a change! People to work for—to live for—a home to bring happiness to. I can't wait to get to work—! If only they'd come soon— [*Listens.*] Ah, there they are. Get my coat on— [*Puts on her coat and hat.*]

[HELMER'*s and* NORA'*s voices are heard outside. A key is turned in the lock, and* HELMER *almost forces* NORA *into the hall. She is dressed in her Italian costume, with a big black shawl over her shoulders. He is in evening dress under an open black cloak.*]

NORA [*in the door, still resisting*]: No, no, no! I don't want to! I want to go back upstairs. I don't want to leave so early.

HELMER: But dearest Nora—

NORA: Oh please, Torvald—please! I'm asking you as nicely as I can—just another hour!

HELMER: Not another minute, sweet. You know we agreed. There now. Get inside. You'll catch a cold out here. [*She still resists, but he guides her gently into the room.*]

MRS. LINDE: Good evening.

NORA: Kristine!

HELMER: Ah, Mrs. Linde. Still here?

MRS. LINDE: I know. I really should apologize, but I so much wanted to see Nora in her costume.

NORA: You've been waiting up for me?

MRS. LINDE: Yes, unfortunately I didn't get here in time. You were already upstairs, but I just didn't feel like leaving till I had seen you.

HELMER [*removing* NORA'*s shawl*]: Yes, do take a good look at her, Mrs. Linde. I think I may say she's worth looking at. Isn't she lovely?

MRS. LINDE: She certainly is—

HELMER: Isn't she a miracle of loveliness, though? That was the general opinion at the party, too. But dreadfully obstinate—that she is, the sweet little thing. What can we do about that? Will you believe it—I practically had to use force to get her away.

NORA: Oh Torvald, you're going to be sorry you didn't give me even half an hour more.

HELMER: See what I mean, Mrs. Linde? She dances the tarantella—she is a tremendous success—quite deservedly so, though perhaps her performance was a little too natural—I mean, more than could be reconciled with the rules of art. But all right! The point is: she's a success, a tremendous success. So should I let her stay after that? Weaken the effect? Of course not. So I take my lovely little Capri girl—I might say, my capricious little Capri girl—under my arm—a quick turn around the room—a graceful bow in all directions, and—as they say in the novels—the beautiful apparition is gone. A finale should always be done for effect, Mrs. Linde, but there doesn't seem to be any way of getting that into Nora's head. Poooh—! It's hot in here. [*Throws his cloak down on a chair and opens the door to his room.*] Why, it's dark in here! Of course. Excuse me— [*Goes inside and lights a couple of candles.*]

NORA [*in a hurried, breathless whisper*]: Well?

MRS. LINDE [*in a low voice*]: I have talked to him.

NORA: And—?

MRS. LINDE: Nora—you've got to tell your husband everything.

NORA [*no expression in her voice*]: I knew it.

MRS. LINDE: You have nothing to fear from Krogstad. But you must speak.

NORA: I'll say nothing.

MRS. LINDE: Then the letter will.

NORA: Thank you, Kristine. Now I know what I have to do. Shh!

HELMER [*returning*]: Well, Mrs. Linde, have you looked your fill?

MRS. LINDE: Yes. And now I'll say goodnight.

HELMER: So soon? Is that your knitting?

MRS. LINDE [*takes it*]: Yes, thank you. I almost forgot.

HELMER: So you knit, do you?

MRS. LINDE: Oh yes.

HELMER: You know—you ought to take up embroidery instead.

MRS. LINDE: Oh? Why?

HELMER: Because it's so much more beautiful. Look. You hold the embroidery so—in your left hand. Then with your right you move the needle—like this—in an easy, elongated arc—you see?

MRS. LINDE: Maybe you're right—

HELMER: Knitting, on the other hand, can never be anything but ugly. Look here: arms pressed close to the sides—the needles going up and down—there's something Chinese about it somehow—. That really was an excellent champagne they served us tonight.

MRS. LINDE: Well, goodnight! Nora. And don't be obstinate any more.

HELMER: Well said, Mrs. Linde!

MRS. LINDE: Goodnight, sir.

HELMER [*sees her to the front door*]: Goodnight, goodnight. I hope you'll get home all right? I'd be very glad to—but of course you don't have far to walk, do you? Goodnight, goodnight. [*She leaves. He closes the door behind her and returns to the living room.*] There! At last we got rid of her. She really is an incredible bore, that woman.

NORA: Aren't you very tired, Torvald?

HELMER: No, not in the least.

NORA: Not sleepy either?

HELMER: Not at all. Quite the opposite. I feel enormously—animated. How about you? Yes, you do look tired and sleepy.

NORA: Yes, I am very tired. Soon I'll be asleep.

HELMER: What did I tell you? I was right, wasn't I? Good thing I didn't let you stay any longer.

NORA: Everything you do is right.

HELMER [*kissing her forehead*]: Now my little lark is talking like a human being. But did you notice what splendid spirits Rank was in tonight?

NORA: Was he? I didn't notice. I didn't get to talk with him.

HELMER: Nor did I—hardly. But I haven't seen him in such a good mood for a long time. [*Looks at her, comes closer to her.*] Ah! It does feel good to be back in our own home again, to be quite alone with you—my young, lovely, ravishing woman!

NORA: Don't look at me like that, Torvald!

HELMER: Am I not to look at my most precious possession? All that loveliness that is mine, nobody's but mine, all of it mine.

NORA [*walks to the other side of the table*]: I won't have you talk to me like that tonight.

HELMER [*follows her*]: The Tarantella is still in your blood. I can tell. That only makes you all the more alluring. Listen! The guests are beginning to leave. [*Softly.*] Nora—soon the whole house will be quiet.

NORA: Yes, I hope so.

HELMER: Yes, don't you, my darling? Do you know—when I'm at a party with you, like tonight—do you know why I hardly ever talk to you, why I keep away from you, only look at you once in a while—a few stolen glances—do you know why I do that? It's because I pretend that you are my secret love, my young, secret bride-to-be, and nobody has the slightest suspicion that there is anything between us.

NORA: Yes, I know. All your thoughts are with me.

HELMER: Then when we're leaving and I lay your shawl around your delicate young shoulders—around that wonderful curve of your neck—then I imagine you're my young bride, that we're coming away from the wedding, that I am taking you to my home for the first time—that I am alone with you for the first time—quite alone with you, you young, trembling beauty! I have desired you all evening—there hasn't been a longing in me that hasn't been for you. When you were dancing the tarantella, chasing, inviting—my blood was on fire; I couldn't stand it any longer—that's why I brought you down so early—

NORA: Leave me now, Torvald. Please! I don't want all this.

HELMER: What do you mean? You're only playing your little teasing bird game with me; aren't you, Nora? Don't want to? I'm your husband, aren't I?

[*There is a knock on the front door.*]

NORA [*with a start*]: Did you hear that—?

HELMER [*on his way to the hall*]: Who is it?

RANK [*outside*]: It's me. May I come in for a moment?

HELMER [*in a low voice, annoyed*]: Oh, what does he want now? [*Aloud.*] Just a minute. [*Opens the door.*] Well! How good of you not to pass by our door.

RANK: I thought I heard your voice, so I felt like saying hello. [*Looks around.*] Ah yes—this dear, familiar room. What a cozy, comfortable place you have here, you two.

HELMER: Looked to me as if you were quite comfortable upstairs too.
RANK: I certainly was. Why not? Why not enjoy all you can in this world? As much as you can for as long as you can, anyway. Excellent wine.
HELMER: The champagne, particularly.
RANK: You noticed that too? Incredible how much I managed to put away.
NORA: Torvald drank a lot of champagne tonight, too.
RANK: Did he?
NORA: Yes, he did, and then he's always so much fun afterwards.
RANK: Well, why not have some fun in the evening after a well spent day?
HELMER: Well spent? I'm afraid I can't claim that.
RANK [*slapping him lightly on the shoulder*]: But you see, I can!
NORA: Dr. Rank, I believe you must have been conducting a scientific test today.
RANK: Exactly.
HELMER: What do you know—little Nora talking about scientific tests!
NORA: May I congratulate you on the result?
RANK: You may indeed.
NORA: It was a good one?
RANK: The best possible for both doctor and patient—certainty.
NORA [*a quick query*]: Certainty?
RANK: Absolute certainty. So why shouldn't I have myself an enjoyable evening afterwards?
NORA: I quite agree with you, Dr. Rank. You should.
HELMER: And so do I. If only you don't pay for it tomorrow.
RANK: Oh well—you get nothing for nothing in this world.
NORA: Dr. Rank—you are fond of costume parties, aren't you?
RANK: Yes, particularly when there is a reasonable number of amusing disguises.
NORA: Listen—what are the two of us going to be the next time?
HELMER: You frivolous little thing! Already thinking about the next party!
RANK: You and I? That's easy. You'll be Fortune's Child.
HELMER: Yes, but what is a fitting costume for that?
RANK: Let your wife appear just the way she always is.
HELMER: Beautiful. Very good indeed. But how about yourself? Don't you know what you'll go as?
RANK: Yes, my friend. I know precisely what I'll be.
HELMER: Yes?
RANK: At the next masquerade I'll be invisible.
HELMER: That's a funny idea.
RANK: There's a certain black hat—you've heard about the hat that makes you invisible, haven't you? You put that on, and nobody can see you.
HELMER [*suppressing a smile*]: I guess that's right.
RANK: But I'm forgetting what I came for. Helmer, give me a cigar—one of your dark Havanas.
HELMER: With the greatest pleasure. [*Offers him his case.*]
RANK [*takes one and cuts off the tip*]: Thanks.
NORA [*striking a match*]: Let me give you a light.
RANK: Thanks. [*She holds the match; he lights his cigar.*] And now goodbye!
HELMER: Goodbye, goodbye, my friend.
NORA: Sleep well, Dr. Rank.
RANK: I thank you.
NORA: Wish me the same.
RANK: You? Well, if you really want me to—. Sleep well. And thanks for the light. [*He nods to both of them and goes out.*]
HELMER [*in a low voice*]: He had had quite a bit to drink.
NORA [*absently*]: Maybe so.

[HELMER *takes out his keys and goes out into the hall.*]

NORA: Torvald—what are you doing out there?
HELMER: Emptying the mailbox. It is quite full. There wouldn't be room for the newspapers in the morning—
NORA: Are you going to work tonight?
HELMER: You know very well I won't.—Say! What's this? Somebody's been at the lock.
NORA: The lock—?
HELMER: Yes. Why, I wonder. I hate to think that any of the maids—. Here's a broken hairpin. It's one of yours. Nora.
NORA [*quickly*]: Then it must be one of the children.
HELMER: You better make damn sure they stop that. Hm, hm.— There! I got it open, finally. [*Gathers up the mail, calls out to the kitchen.*] Helene?—Oh Helene—turn out the light here in the hall, will you? [*He comes back into the living room and closes the door.*] Look how it's been piling up. [*Shows her the bundle of letters. Starts leafing through it.*] What's this?
NORA [*by the window*]: The letter! Oh no, no, Torvald!
HELMER: Two calling cards—from Rank.
NORA: From Dr. Rank?
HELMER [*looking at them*]: "Doctor medicinae Rank." They were on top. He must have put them there when he left just now.
NORA: Anything written on them?
HELMER: A black cross above the name. What a macabre idea. Like announcing his own death.
NORA: That's what it is.
HELMER: Hm? You know about this? Has he said anything to you?
NORA: That card means he has said goodbye to us. He'll lock himself up to die.
HELMER: My poor friend. I knew of course he wouldn't be with me very long. But so soon—. And hiding himself away like a wounded animal—

NORA: When it has to be, it's better it happens without words. Don't you think so, Torvald?

HELMER [*walking up and down*]: He'd grown so close to us. I find it hard to think of him as gone. With his suffering and loneliness he was like a clouded background for our happy sunshine. Well, it may be better this way. For him, at any rate. [*Stops.*] And perhaps for us, too, Nora. For now we have nobody but each other. [*Embraces her.*] Oh you—my beloved wife! I feel I just can't hold you close enough. Do you know, Nora—many times I have wished some great danger threatened you, so I could risk my life and blood and everything—everything, for your sake.

NORA [*frees herself and says in a strong and firm voice*]: I think you should go and read your letters now, Torvald.

HELMER: No, no—not tonight. I want to be with you, my darling.

NORA: With the thought of your dying friend—?

HELMER: You are right. This has shaken both of us. Something not beautiful has come between us. Thoughts of death and dissolution. We must try to get over it—out of it. Till then—we'll each go to our own room.

NORA [*her arms around his neck*]: Torvald—goodnight! Goodnight!

HELMER [*kisses her forehead*]: Goodnight, my little songbird. Sleep well, Nora. Now I'll read my letters. [*He goes into his room, carrying the mail. Closes the door.*]

NORA [*her eyes desperate, her hands groping, finds* HELMER*'s black cloak and throws it around her; she whispers, quickly, brokenly, hoarsely*]: Never see him again. Never. Never. Never. [*Puts her shawl over her head.*] And never see the children again, either. Never; never.—The black, icy water—fathomless—this—! If only it was all over.—Now he has it. Now he's reading it. No, no; not yet. Torvald—goodbye—you—the children—

[*She is about to hurry through the hall, when* HELMER *flings open the door to his room and stands there with an open letter in his hand.*]

HELMER: Nora!

NORA [*cries out*]: Ah—!

HELMER: What is it? You know what's in this letter?

NORA: Yes, I do! Let me go! Let me out!

HELMER [*holds her back*]: Where do you think you're going?

NORA [*trying to tear herself loose from him*]: I won't let you save me, Torvald!

HELMER [*tumbles back*]: True! Is it true what he writes? Oh my God! No, no—this can't possibly be true.

NORA: It is true. I have loved you more than anything else in the whole world.

HELMER: Oh, don't give me any silly excuses.

NORA [*taking a step towards him*]: Torvald—!

HELMER: You wretch! What have you done!

NORA: Let me go. You are not to sacrifice yourself for me. You are not to take the blame.

HELMER: No more playacting. [*Locks the door to the front hall.*] You'll stay here and answer me. Do you understand what you have done? Answer me! Do you understand?

NORA [*gazes steadily at him with an increasingly frozen expression*]: Yes. Now I'm beginning to understand.

HELMER [*walking up and down*]: What a dreadful awakening. All these years—all these eight years—she, my pride and my joy—a hypocrite, a liar—oh worse! worse!—a criminal! Oh, the bottomless ugliness in all this! Damn! Damn! Damn!

[NORA, *silent, keeps gazing at him.*]

HELMER [*stops in front of her*]: I ought to have guessed that something like this would happen. I should have expected it. All your father's loose principles—Silence! You have inherited every one of your father's loose principles. No religion, no morals, no sense of duty—. Now I am being punished for my leniency with him. I did it for your sake, and this is how you pay me back.

NORA: Yes. This is how.

HELMER: You have ruined all my happiness. My whole future—that's what you have destroyed. Oh, it's terrible to think about. I am at the mercy of an unscrupulous man. He can do with me whatever he likes, demand anything of me, command me and dispose of me just as he pleases—I dare not say a word! To go down so miserably, to be destroyed—all because of an irresponsible woman!

NORA: When I am gone from the world, you'll be free.

HELMER: No noble gestures, please. Your father was always full of such phrases too. What good would it do me if you were gone from the world, as you put it? Not the slightest good at all. He could still make the whole thing public, and if he did, people would be likely to think I had been your accomplice. They might even think it was my idea—that it was I who urged you to do it! And for all this I have you to thank—you, whom I've borne on my hands through all the years of our marriage. *Now* do you understand what you've done to me?

NORA [*with cold calm*]: Yes.

HELMER: I just can't get it into my head that this is happening; it's all so incredible. But we have to come to terms with it somehow. Take your shawl off. Take it off, I say! I have to satisfy him one way or another. The whole affair must be kept quiet at whatever cost.—And as far as you and I are concerned, nothing must seem to have changed. I'm talking about appearances, of course. You'll go on living here; that goes without saying. But I won't let you bring up the children; I dare not trust you with them.—Oh! Having to say this to one I have loved so much, and whom I still—! But all that is past. It's not a question of happiness any more but of hanging on to what can be salvaged—pieces, appearances— [*The doorbell rings.*]

HELMER [*jumps*]: What's that? So late. Is the worst—? Has he—! Hide, Nora! Say you're sick.

NORA *doesn't move.* HELMER *opens the door to the hall.*

THE MAID [*half dressed, out in the hall*]: A letter for your wife, sir.

HELMER: Give it to me. [*Takes the letter and closes the door.*] Yes, it's from him. But I won't let you have it. I'll read it myself.

NORA: Yes, you read it.

HELMER [*by the lamp*]: I hardly dare. Perhaps we're lost, both you and I. No; I've got to know. [*Tears the letter open, glances through it, looks at an enclosure; a cry of joy.*] Nora!

[NORA *looks at him with a question in her eyes.*]

HELMER: Nora!—No, I must read it again.—Yes, yes; it is so! I'm saved! Nora, I'm saved!

NORA: And I?

HELMER: You too, of course; we're both saved, both you and I. Look! He's returning your note. He writes that he's sorry, he regrets, a happy turn in his life—oh, it doesn't matter what he writes. We're saved, Nora! Nobody can do anything to you now. Oh Nora, Nora—. No, I want to get rid of this disgusting thing first. Let me see— [*Looks at the signature.*] No, I don't want to see it. I don't want it to be more than a bad dream, the whole thing. [*Tears up the note and both letters, throws the pieces in the stove, and watches them burn.*] There! Now it's gone.—He wrote that ever since Christmas Eve—. Good God, Nora, these must have been three terrible days for you.

NORA: I have fought a hard fight these last three days.

HELMER: And been in agony and seen no other way out than—. No, we won't think of all that ugliness. We'll just rejoice and tell ourselves it's over, it's all over! Oh, listen to me, Nora. You don't seem to understand. It's over. What *is* it? Why do you look like that—that frozen expression on your face? Oh my poor little Nora, don't you think I know what it is? You can't make yourself believe that I have forgiven you. But I have, Nora; I swear to you, I have forgiven you for everything. Of course I know that what you did was for love of me.

NORA: That is true.

HELMER: You have loved me the way a wife ought to love her husband. You just didn't have the wisdom to judge the means. But do you think I love you any less because you don't know how to act on your own? Of course not. Just lean on me. I'll advise you; I'll guide you. I wouldn't be a man if I didn't find you twice as attractive because of your womanly helplessness. You mustn't pay any attention to the hard words I said to you right at first. It was just that first shock when I thought everything was collapsing all around me. I have forgiven you, Nora. I swear to you—I really have forgiven you.

NORA: I thank you for your forgiveness. [*She goes out through the door, right.*]

HELMER: No, stay— [*Looks into the room she entered.*] What are you doing in there?

NORA [*within*]: Getting out of my costume.

HELMER [*by the open door*]: Good, good. Try to calm down and compose yourself, my poor little frightened songbird. Rest safely; I have broad wings to cover you with. [*Walks around near the door.*] What a nice and cozy home we have, Nora. Here's shelter for you. Here I'll keep you safe like a hunted dove I have rescued from the hawk's talons. Believe me: I'll know how to quiet your beating heart. It will happen by and by, Nora; you'll see. Why, tomorrow you'll look at all this in quite a different light. And soon everything will be just the way it was before. I won't need to keep reassuring you that I have forgiven you; you'll feel it yourself. Did you really think I could have abandoned you, or even reproached you? Oh, you don't know a real man's heart, Nora. There is something unspeakably sweet and satisfactory for a man to know deep in himself that he has forgiven his wife—forgiven her in all the fullness of his honest heart. You see, that way she becomes his very own all over again—in a double sense, you might say. He has, so to speak, given her a second birth; it is as if she had become his wife and his child, both. From now on that's what you'll be to me, you lost and helpless creature. Don't worry about a thing, Nora. Only be frank with me, and I'll be your will and your conscience.—What's this? You're not in bed? You've changed your dress—!

NORA [*in an everyday dress*]: Yes, Torvald. I have changed my dress.

HELMER: But why—now—this late?

NORA: I'm not going to sleep tonight.

HELMER: But my dear Nora—

NORA [*looks at her watch*]: It isn't all that late. Sit down here with, me, Torvald. You and I have much to talk about. [*Sits down at the table.*]

HELMER: Nora—what is this all about? That rigid face—

NORA: Sit down. This will take a while. I have much to say to you.

HELMER [*sits down, facing her across the table*]: You worry me, Nora. I don't understand you.

NORA: No, that's just it. You don't understand me. And I have never understood you—not till tonight. No, don't interrupt me. Just listen to what I have to say.—This is a settling of accounts, Torvald.

HELMER: What do you mean by that?

NORA [*after a brief silence*]: Doesn't one thing strike you, now that we are sitting together like this?

HELMER: What would that be?

NORA: We have been married for eight years. Doesn't it occur to you that this is the first time that you and I, husband and wife, are having a serious talk?

HELMER: Well—serious—. What do you mean by that?

NORA: For eight whole years—longer, in fact—ever since we first met, we have never talked seriously to each other about a single serious thing.

HELMER: You mean I should forever have been telling you about worries you couldn't have helped me with anyway?

NORA: I am not talking about worries. I'm saying we have never tried seriously to get to the bottom of anything together.

HELMER: But dearest Nora, I hardly think that would have been something *you*—

NORA: That's the whole point. You have never understood me. Great wrong has been done to me, Torvald. First by Daddy and then by you.

HELMER: What! By us two? We who have loved you more deeply than anyone else?

NORA [*shakes her head*]: You never loved me—neither Daddy nor you. You only thought it was fun to be in love with me.

HELMER: But, Nora—what an expression to use!

NORA: That's the way it has been, Torvald. When I was home with Daddy, he told me all his opinions, and so they became my opinions too. If I disagreed with him I kept it to myself, for he wouldn't have liked that. He called me his little doll baby, and he played with me the way I played with my dolls. Then I came to your house—

HELMER: What a way to talk about our marriage!

NORA [*imperturbably*]: I mean that I passed from Daddy's hands into yours. You arranged everything according to your taste, and so I came to share it—or I pretended to; I'm not sure which. I think it was a little of both, now one and now the other. When I look back on it now, it seems to me I've been living here like a pauper—just a hand-to-mouth kind of existence. I have earned my keep by doing tricks for you, Torvald. But that's the way you wanted it. You have great sins against me to answer for, Daddy and you. It's your fault that nothing has become of me.

HELMER: Nora, you're being both unreasonable and ungrateful. Haven't you been happy here?

NORA: No, never. I thought I was, but I wasn't.

HELMER: Not—not happy!

NORA: No; just having fun. And you have always been very good to me. But our home has never been more than a playroom. I have been your doll wife here, just the way I used to be Daddy's doll child. And the children have been my dolls. I thought it was fun when you played with me, just as they thought it was fun when I played with them. That's been our marriage, Torvald.

HELMER: There is something in what you are saying—exaggerated and hysterical though it is. But from now on things will be different. Playtime is over; it's time for growing up.

NORA: Whose growing up—mine or the children's?

HELMER: Both yours and the children's, Nora darling.

NORA: Oh Torvald, you're not the man to bring me up to be the right kind of wife for you.

HELMER: How can you say that?

NORA: And I—? What qualifications do I have for bringing up the children?

HELMER: Nora!

NORA: You said so yourself a minute ago—that you didn't dare to trust me with them.

HELMER: In the first flush of anger, yes. Surely, you're not going to count that.

NORA: But you were quite right. I am *not* qualified. Something else has to come first. Somehow I have to grow up myself. And you are not the man to help me do that. That's a job I have to do by myself. And that's why I'm leaving you.

HELMER [*jumps up*]: What did you say!

NORA: I have to be by myself if I am to find out about myself and about all the other things too. So I can't stay here with you any longer.

HELMER: Nora, Nora!

NORA: I'm leaving now. I'm sure Kristine will put me up for tonight.

HELMER: You're out of your mind! I won't let you! I forbid you!

NORA: You can't forbid me anything any more; it won't do any good. I'm taking my own things with me. I won't accept anything from you, either now or later.

HELMER: But this is madness!

NORA: Tomorrow I'm going home—I mean back to my old home town. It will be easier for me to find some kind of job there.

HELMER: Oh, you blind, inexperienced creature—!

NORA: I must see to it that I get experience, Torvald.

HELMER: Leaving your home, your husband, your children! Not a thought of what people will say!

NORA: I can't worry about that. All I know is that I have to leave.

HELMER: Oh, this is shocking! Betraying your most sacred duties like this!

NORA: And what do you consider my most sacred duties?

HELMER: Do I need to tell you that? They are your duties to your husband and your children.

NORA: I have other duties equally sacred.

HELMER: You do not. What duties would they be?

NORA: My duties to myself.

HELMER: You are a wife and a mother before you are anything else.

NORA: I don't believe that any more. I believe I am first of all a human being, just as much as you—or at any rate that I must try to become one. Oh, I know very well that most people agree with you, Torvald, and that it says something like that in all the books. But what people say and what the books say is no longer enough for me. I have to think about these things myself and see if I can't find the answers.

HELMER: You mean to tell me you don't know what your proper place in your own home is? Don't you have a reliable guide in such matters? Don't you have religion?

NORA: Oh but Torvald—I don't really know what religion is.

HELMER: What are you saying!

NORA: All I know is what the Reverend Hansen told me when he prepared me for confirmation. He said that religion was *this* and it was *that*. When I get by myself, away from here, I'll have to look into that, too. I have to decide if what the Reverend Hansen said was right, or anyway if it is right for *me*.

HELMER: Oh, this is unheard of in a young woman! If religion can't guide you, let me appeal to your conscience. For surely you have moral feelings? Or—answer me—maybe you don't?

NORA: Well, you see, Torvald, I don't really know what to say. I just don't know. I am confused about these things. All I know is that my ideas are quite different from yours. I have just found out that the laws are different from what I thought they were, but in no way can I get it into my head that those laws are right. A woman shouldn't have the right to spare her dying old father or save her husband's life! I just can't believe that.

HELMER: You speak like a child. You don't understand the society you live in.

NORA: No, I don't. But I want to find out about it. I have to make up my mind who is right, society or I.

HELMER: You are sick, Nora; you have a fever. I really don't think you are in your right mind.

NORA: I have never felt so clearheaded and sure of myself as I do tonight.

HELMER: And clearheaded and sure of yourself you're leaving your husband and children?

NORA: Yes.

HELMER: Then there is only one possible explanation.

NORA: What?

HELMER: You don't love me any more.

NORA: No, that's just it.

HELMER: Nora! Can you say that?

NORA: I am sorry, Torvald, for you have always been so good to me. But I can't help it. I don't love you any more.

HELMER [*with forced composure*]: And this too is a clear and sure conviction?

NORA: Completely clear and sure. That's why I don't want to stay here any more.

HELMER: And are you ready to explain to me how I came to forfeit your love?

NORA: Certainly I am. It was tonight, when the wonderful didn't happen. That was when I realized you were not the man I thought you were.

HELMER: You have to explain. I don't understand.

NORA: I have waited patiently for eight years, for I wasn't such a fool that I thought the wonderful is something that happens any old day. Then this—thing—came crashing in on me, and then there wasn't a doubt in my mind that now—now comes the wonderful. When Krogstad's letter was in that mailbox, never for a moment did it even occur to me that you would submit to his conditions. I was so absolutely certain that you would say to him: make the whole thing public—tell everybody. And when that had happened—

HELMER: Yes, then what? When I had surrendered my wife to shame and disgrace—!

NORA: When that had happened, I was absolutely certain that you would stand up and take the blame and say, "I'm the guilty one."

HELMER: Nora!

NORA: You mean I never would have accepted such a sacrifice from you? Of course not. But what would my protests have counted against yours. *That* was the wonderful I was hoping for in terror. And to prevent that I was going to kill myself.

HELMER: I'd gladly work nights and days for you, Nora—endure sorrow and want for your sake. But nobody sacrifices his *honor* for his love.

NORA: A hundred thousand women have done so.

HELMER: Oh, you think and talk like a silly child.

NORA: All right. But you don't think and talk like the man I can live with. When you had gotten over your fright—not because of what threatened *me* but because of the risk to *you*—and the whole danger was past, then you acted as if nothing at all had happened. Once again I was your little songbird, your doll, just as before, only now you had to handle her even more carefully, because she was so frail and weak. [*Rises.*] Torvald—that moment I realized that I had been living here for eight years with a stranger and had borne him three children—Oh, I can't stand thinking about it! I feel like tearing myself to pieces!

HELMER [*heavily*]: I see it, I see it. An abyss has opened up between us.—Oh but Nora—surely it can be filled?

NORA: The way I am now I am no wife for you.

HELMER: I have it in me to change.

NORA: Perhaps—if your doll is taken from you.

HELMER: To part—to part from you! No, no, Nora! I can't grasp that thought!

NORA [*goes out, right*]: All the more reason why it has to be. [*She returns with her outdoor clothes and a small bag, which she sets down on the chair by the table.*]

HELMER: Nora, Nora! Not now! Wait till tomorrow.

NORA [*putting on her coat*]: I can't spend the night in a stranger's rooms.

HELMER: But couldn't we live here together like brother and sister—?

NORA [*tying on her hat*]: You know very well that wouldn't last long—. [*Wraps her shawl around her.*] Goodbye, Torvald. I don't want to see the children. I know I leave them in better hands than mine. The way I am now I can't be anything to them.

HELMER: But some day, Nora—some day—?

NORA: How can I tell? I have no idea what's going to become of me.

HELMER: But you're still my wife, both as you are now and as you will be.

NORA: Listen, Torvald—when a wife leaves her husband's house, the way I am doing now, I have heard he has no more legal responsibilities for her. At any rate, I now release you from all responsibility. You are not to feel yourself obliged to me for anything, and I have no obligations to you. There has to be full freedom on both sides. Here is your ring back. Now give me mine.

HELMER: Even this?

NORA: Even this.

HELMER: Here it is.

NORA: There. So now it's over. I'm putting the keys here. The maids know everything about the house—better than I. Tomorrow, after I'm gone, Kristine will come over and pack my things from home. I want them sent after me.

HELMER: Over! It's all over! Nora, will you never think of me?

NORA: I'm sure I'll often think of you and the children and this house.

HELMER: May I write to you, Nora?

NORA: No—never. I won't have that.

HELMER: But send you things—? You must let me.

NORA: Nothing, nothing.

HELMER: —help you, when you need help—?

NORA: I told you, no; I won't have it. I'll accept nothing from strangers.

HELMER: Nora—can I never again be more to you than a stranger?

NORA [*picks up her bag*]: Oh Torvald—then the most wonderful of all would have to happen—

HELMER: Tell me what that would be—!

NORA: For that to happen, both you and I would have to change so that—Oh Torvald, I no longer believe in the wonderful.

HELMER: But I *will* believe. Tell me! Change, so that—?

NORA: So that our living together would become a true marriage. Goodbye. [*She goes out through the hall.*]

HELMER [*sinks down on a chair near the door and covers his face with his hands*]: Nora! Nora! [*Looks around him and gets up.*] All empty. She's gone. [*With sudden hope.*] The most wonderful—?!

[*From downstairs comes the sound of a heavy door slamming shut.*]

AUGUST STRINDBERG

August Strindberg (1849–1912) was born in Stockholm, Sweden, into a family of social unequals: His father was an aristocrat disowned by his family for marrying a barmaid. In the tightly controlled Swedish social establishment, Strindberg was an outsider, which was a source of bitterness, and he took issues of class struggle as a theme throughout his writing. It appears strongly in the biographical novel *Son of a Servant* (1886), in which he documents the Strindberg family's squalid living conditions and his own attempts to overcome them. The plight of the working class was an enduring social cause for Strindberg, and he criticized the aristocracy and the middle classes with passion.

Strindberg's education was spotty. He was a brilliant and irascible student, accepted to study at Uppsala University, but he never completed his courses. He thought he would study medicine but failed at it. He tried acting, but failed at that too. He left the university dissatisfied with formal learning but with a desire to become a writer. During a period of eight years, Strindberg received some small success as a writer, and he supported himself by working in the Royal Library. Strindberg wrote prose and poetry, but his major effort was *Master Olaf,* a historical drama about the Protestant Reformation in Sweden, which he continually revised until it was finished in 1881. His luck changed at age thirty, when *The Red Room* (1879), a satirical novel about bohemian life (his own) in Stockholm, successfully launched his career.

Strindberg's nearly sixty plays show an extensive range of subjects and an eclectic mind able to interweave history, science, politics, and religion. He was particularly interested in history, and twenty-four of his plays are concerned with Swedish history, all written more or less in a conventional manner. Most of all, he was interested in using his own personal life as a source for literature. Like many artists, his creative genius was driven by the psychological crises in his life, particularly his three unhappy marriages: to Siri Wrangel (1877–1891), Frida Uhl (1893–1894), and Harriet Bosse (1901–1904). The relationship with Wrangel, in particular, is indicative of the conflicting forces in his character. Wrangel was an actress of small talent who was married to a Swedish baron when Strindberg began an affair with her. When she divorced Baron Wrangel they married, and over the next fourteen years they lived in increasing disharmony. Toward the end of this bitter relationship Strindberg suffered from a pathological belief that he was being betrayed by an unfaithful wife, and he cracked up. Divorce proceedings drained him, and he was left in despair when the court deprived him of parental rights over his children. Driven to make his voice heard, Strindberg wrote *Married* (1884), a collection of stories about the unhappiness of marriage that reveals a deep-seated misogyny, which periodically surfaced throughout his life. The stories were considered so scandalous by the staid society of Sweden that he was charged with blasphemy and brought to trial, but ultimately acquitted. This personal attack on his character and his literature added to Strindberg's sense of alienation from his homeland.

By the late 1880s, Strindberg entered his most intense phase of writing, working particularly on autobiographical works, especially the novel *Son of a Servant* (1886) and the fictional memoir *A Madman's Defense* (1888), which starkly reveal his social biases and neuroses. He admitted that *A Madman's Defense* was an "analysis of the soul, or psychological anatomy," probably of his own, and he ended it with a discussion of marriage paranoia. It was during his work on *A Madman's Defense* that he wrote *The Father* (1887), a play that vents his frustration in the character of a man who cannot face the relentless power and sexual demands of his wife, and so goes mad. As with the best of Strindberg's works, characters in *The Father* transcend his personal life history. The Captain and his crushing defeat by his wife, Laura, may bear autobiographical scrutiny, but this disastrous conflict is meant to rival that of Agamemnon and Clytemnestra in Aeschylus's *Agamemnon* or Othello and Desdemona in Shakespeare's *Othello.* On another level, Strindberg may have been slyly responding to Henrik Ibsen's *A Doll's House,* which had become a rallying point for advocates of divorce and women's rights. Strindberg was opposed to such advocacy and was disdainful of the play. In addition, Strindberg disliked Ibsen, whom he viewed as a defender of the middle class.

Greatly disaffected by life in Sweden, Strindberg became an expatriate at the age of thirty-two. For fifteen years he moved about, living mainly in France, Germany, Austria, Switzerland, Denmark, and occasionally Sweden, but without roots. When he finally resettled in Sweden in 1897, his spiritual and personal life was chaotic. His love life was unhappy, his marriage to Frida Uhl had ended in another divorce, and he was on the verge of a mental collapse. Still, he recorded all of this in *Inferno* (1897), a book about his life in Paris.

At home in Sweden, critics remained unfriendly to Strindberg and his work. But with a new vigor, Strindberg's imagination took a different turn, and he began to explore spiritual and religious themes through the outlets of historical drama and expressionist works. Important plays of this period include *To Damascus* (1898–1904), *Erik XIV* (1899), *Crimes and Crimes* (1899), *The Dance of Death* (1900), *Gustav Adolf* (1900), and *Carl XII* (1901). His greatest success came with the production of *Easter* (1901), about a young man's despair and eventual social and spiritual reconciliation. *Easter*'s popularity rests on its sentimentality and optimism. Harriet Bosse, then his third wife, acted the female lead. Strindberg was at ease at the time, and the play shows an uncharacteristic side of the playwright's search for spiritual redemption. It is also a well-made play of the kind that Strindberg criticized as being old-fashioned.

Strindberg's last plays suggest his antithetical states of mind: drawing on the conventions of myth and melodrama, on one hand, but, on the other, creating works of great abstraction that break down traditional forms. *A Dream Play* (1902) and *The Ghost Sonata* (1907), in particular, show an imagination in flux and creative agitation. The latter play, which takes its name from the musical form of the sonata, perhaps inspired by the second movement of Ludwig van Beethoven's Opus 70 in D Major, is abstract in form and highly symbolic. It is a bleak vision of the cruelty of modern society. *A Dream Play* is expressionistic and has the unpredictability and heightened unreality of a dream. These plays go well beyond the conventional aspects of theater that Strindberg advocates in the "Preface" to *Miss Julie*. But even while he was writing in an avant-garde vein, he was also writing fairy-tale plays, such as *The Bridal Crown* (1900) and *Swanwhite* (1901), and more conventional plays, such as *Storm Weather* (1907) and *The Pelican* (1907).

Eleven years after returning to Sweden, stomach cancer eroded Strindberg's health. He persevered, but in *The Great Highway* he wrote verses that might have been his epitaph:

> Bless me, your human creature,
> Who suffers from the life you gave;
> Me first, who suffered most,
> Suffered most the pain of not being
> the human being I wanted to be.

Though he was, by then, secure and a powerful literary presence in Scandinavia and Europe, he was still an outsider in the artistic establishment. The Swedish Academy snubbed him by not awarding him the Nobel Prize for Literature. But as an act of homage, the workingmen of Sweden took up a public subscription in his honor, and Strindberg accepted the award and its cash prize as his due. Four years later he was dead at sixty-three.

Of all his plays, *Miss Julie* (1888) best demonstrates Strindberg's advocacy of the new naturalism in the theater. Written in Paris when Strindberg was thirty-seven, it was rejected by his Swedish publisher because it was too risky. When it was finally published by another house in 1888, it was condemned by critics as being immoral. Its first scheduled performance in 1889 in Copenhagen was banned, and a private production had to be arranged in order to avoid censorship by the police.

Miss Julie presents a harsh portrait of the relationship between a servant and an aristocratic young woman who is destroyed by her sexual passion. It is a penetrating psychological examination filled with artful allusions to the magic associated with Midsummer's Night (the summer solstice) and the biblical story of Salomé and John the Baptist. The action takes place in the course of an evening ending with a sunrise that ironically brings death rather than new life. Middle-class audiences squirmed as they saw Miss Julie, an aristocrat and daughter of a count, seduce her father's valet.

Equally disturbing was Julie's confession of her sordid family relationships—her mother's insistence that she would never be a wife and that she married only after Julie was born; that the mother has been unfaithful to her husband, the count; and that Julie, like her mother, hates men. And finally, the audience was left ill at ease as Julie realizes her mistake and says to Jean: "Oh, I'm so tired. I'm not able to do anything. I can't repent, can't run away, can't stay, can't live—can't die! Help me! Order me, and I'll obey like a dog! Do me this last service, save my honor, save his name! You know what I *should* do, but don't have the will to . . . You will it, you order me to do it!" When Jean cannot act, Julie takes action; when the count arrives, Jean says to her finally, "It's horrible! But there's no other way!" and she "*walks firmly out through the door.*"

Julie's decision to kill herself rather than face the shame of succumbing to a man beneath her social class reflected Strindberg's hostility towards the aristocracy. Working-class audiences who shared Strindberg's opinions saw in the play the downfall of their oppressors and understood Strindberg's social purposes.

For contemporary audiences with knowledge of Strindberg's personal life, it is possible to see more clearly how he interweaves life and art, making use of his family situation. Miss Julie, the count's daughter, suggests Strindberg's wife, Siri Wrangel Strindberg, who had been married to an aristocrat. Jean, the valet, suggests Strindberg, the son of a servant. In life, Strindberg suffered from slights of the establishment and his experience with women. The play gave him the opportunity to rewrite events and settle his scores. Jean's sexual triumph represents a victory for the working class over the aristocracy. Miss Julie's anguish and suicide served as a wish fulfillment, a sort of revenge for Strindberg's messy divorce from Siri.

In the "Preface" to *Miss Julie,* which appeared with the published version of the text, Strindberg expounded ideas of theatrical naturalism on the stage, which he adapted from his literary mentor Émile Zola (1840–1902), the French novelist. Zola wanted an antiromantic literature based on realistic observation and scientific fact. He argued that characters must withstand the scrutiny of psychological analysis, and that scenery, approximating real living space, should define and suggest mood and atmosphere. Strindberg, too, was infused with the desire to deromanticize literature, and he adopted Zola's stern verisimilitude and made it his own.

Strindberg explained: "In the following play, instead of trying to do anything new—which is impossible—I have simply modernized the form in accordance with demands I think contemporary audiences make upon this art." Of course, he has made something profoundly new, and his suggestion that characters should be developed in depth psychologically to correct the notion that life is not "idiotically mathematical" shocked audiences and critics. "Every event in life," said Strindberg, "—and this is rather a new discovery!—is ordinarily the result of a whole series of more or less deep-lying motives. . . . Therefore, I do not believe in simple theatrical characters. And an author's summary judgements of people—this one is stupid, that one brutal, this one jealous, that one stingy—should be challenged by naturalists, who know how rich the soul-complex is and realize that 'vice' has a reverse side closely resembling virtue. . . . Our inquisitive souls are not satisfied just to see something happen; we want to know how it happened."

Among his other revisions for a new theater, Strindberg called for integrating monologue, mime, and ballet in drama to provide momentary interludes for the audience and the actors. These additions would allow the audience a rest from the intensity of the performance without losing the illusion that the play has created. Strindberg called for using realistic makeup for actors, for abandoning footlights, and for providing lighting from the sides and from above. Criticizing the arbitrary division of a play into acts, Strindberg asserted that in *Miss Julie,* he experimented with eliminating act divisions because of the dwindling capacity for accepting illusion is possibly further disturbed by intermissions, during which the spectator has time to reflect and thereby escape the suggestive influence of the author-hypnotist. He said that "a ninety-minute theatre piece will not be too tiring."

Curiously, Strindberg insisted on applying techniques of impressionism and realism for setting, and he wanted the stage to be viewed as a room where the fourth wall is removed. "As for the scenery," he wrote, "I have borrowed from impressionist painting the device of making a setting appear cut off and asymmetrical, thus strengthening the illusion. . . . With only one setting we should be able to demand that it be realistic. . . . Even if the walls must be of canvas, it is surely time to stop painting shelves and kitchen utensils on them. We have so many other stage conventions in which we are asked to believe, we should not have to strain ourselves trying to believe painted pots and pans." Thus Strindberg's stage directions for *Miss Julie* call for a realistic kitchen in which the props are required to be off-center and the rear wall set diagonally to right so that it provides an exaggerated and asymmetrical sense of proportion. Seen through the window at the right is a garden and a fountain with a statue of Cupid. The opposition of kitchen and Cupid, obvious symbolism, is intended to amplify the contrast of Jean and Miss Julie.

Though the changes Strindberg advocated are now taken for granted, they were at the time avant-garde. His challenges to the traditional "bourgeois" portrayal of character and the ornamental theatrical techniques of the last decade of the nineteenth century have proved to be most influential, especially in the American theater, where Strindberg is the acknowledged master of playwright Eugene O'Neill and an inspiration for Tennessee Williams and Arthur Miller.

Film

Miss Julie (1950), directed by Alf Sjöberg, with Anita Björk, Ulf Palme, and Anders Henrikson. Swedish with English subtitles. Sandrew.

Miss Julie

TRANSLATED BY HARRY G. CARLSON

CHARACTERS

MISS JULIE, 25 years old
JEAN, her father's valet, 30 years old
KRISTINE, her father's cook, 35 years old

The action takes place in the count's kitchen on midsummer eve.

SETTING. *A large kitchen, the ceiling and side walls of which are hidden by draperies. The rear wall runs diagonally from down left to up right. On the wall down left are two shelves with copper, iron, and pewter utensils; the shelves are lined with scalloped paper. Visible to the right is most of a set of large, arched glass doors, through which can be seen a fountain with a statue of Cupid, lilac bushes in bloom, and the tops of some Lombardy poplars. At down left is the corner of a large tiled stove; a portion of its hood is showing. At right, one end of the servants' white pine dining table juts out; several chairs stand around it. The stove is decorated with birch branches; juniper twigs are strewn on the floor. On the end of the table stands a large Japanese spice jar, filled with lilac blossoms. An ice-box, a sink, and a washstand. Above the door is an old-fashioned bell on a spring; to the left of the door, the mouthpiece of a speaking tube is visible.*

KRISTINE *is frying something on the stove. She is wearing a light-colored cotton dress and an apron.* JEAN *enters. He is wearing livery and carries a pair of high riding-boots with spurs, which he puts down on the floor where they can be seen by the audience.*

JEAN: Miss Julie's crazy again tonight; absolutely crazy!

KRISTINE: So you finally came back?

JEAN: I took the Count to the station and when I returned past the barn I stopped in for a dance. Who do I see but Miss Julie leading off the dance with the gamekeeper! But as soon as she saw me she rushed over to ask me for the next waltz. And she's been waltzing ever since—I've never seen anything like it. She's crazy!

KRISTINE: She always has been, but never as bad as the last two weeks since her engagement was broken off.

JEAN: Yes, I wonder what the real story was there. He was a gentleman, even if he wasn't rich. Ah! These people have such romantic ideas. [*sits at the end of the table*] Still, it's strange, isn't it? I mean that she'd rather stay home with the servants on midsummer eve instead of going with her father to visit relatives?

KRISTINE: She's probably embarrassed after that row with her fiancé.

JEAN: Probably! He gave a good account of himself, though. Do you know how it happened, Kristine? I saw it, you know, though I didn't let on I had.

KRISTINE: No! You saw it?

JEAN: Yes, I did.——That evening they were out near the stable, and she was "training" him—as she called it. Do you know what she did? She made him jump over her riding crop, the way you'd teach a dog to jump. He jumped twice and she hit him each time. But the third time he grabbed the crop out of her hand, hit her with it across the cheek, and broke it in pieces. Then he left.

KRISTINE: So, that's what happened! I can't believe it!

JEAN: Yes, that's the way it went!——What have you got for me that's tasty, Kristine?

KRISTINE [*serving him from the pan*]: Oh, it's only a piece of kidney I cut from the veal roast.

JEAN [*smelling the food*]: Beautiful! That's my favorite *délice*. [*feeling the plate*] But you could have warmed the plate!

KRISTINE: You're fussier than the Count himself, once you start! [*She pulls his hair affectionately.*]

JEAN [*angry*]: Stop it, leave my hair alone! You know I'm touchy about that.

KRISTINE: Now, now, it's only love, you know that. [JEAN *eats.* KRISTINE *opens a bottle of beer.*]

JEAN: Beer? On midsummer eve? No thank you! I can do better than that. [*opens a drawer in the table and takes out a bottle of red wine with yellow sealing wax*] See that? Yellow seal! Give me a glass! A wine glass! I'm drinking this *pur.*

KRISTINE [*returns to the stove and puts on a small saucepan*]: God help the woman who gets you for a husband! What a fuss-budget.

JEAN: Nonsense! You'd be damned lucky to get a man like me. It certainly hasn't done you any harm to have people call me your sweetheart. [*tastes the wine*] Good! Very good! Just needs a little warming. [*warms the glass between his hands*] We bought this in Dijon. Four francs a liter, not counting the cost of the bottle, or the customs duty.——What are you cooking now? It stinks like hell!

KRISTINE: Oh, some slop Miss Julie wants to give her dog Diana.

JEAN: Watch your language, Kristine. But why should you have to cook for that damn mutt on midsummer eve? Is she sick?

KRISTINE: Yes, she's sick! She sneaked out with the gatekeeper's dog—and now there's hell to pay. Miss Julie won't have it!

JEAN: Miss Julie has too much pride about some things and not enough about others, just like her mother was. The Countess was most at home in the kitchen and the cowshed, but a *one*-horse carriage wasn't elegant enough for her. The cuffs of her blouse were dirty, but she had to have her coat of arms on her cufflinks.——And Miss Julie won't take proper care of herself either. If you ask me, she just isn't refined. Just now, when she was dancing in the barn, she pulled the gamekeeper away from Anna and made him dance with her. *We* wouldn't behave like that, but that's what happens when aristocrats pretend they're common people—they get *common!*——But she is quite a woman! Magnificent! What shoulders, and what—et cetera!

KRISTINE: Oh, don't overdo it! I've heard what Clara says, and she dresses her.

JEAN: Ha, Clara! You're all jealous of each other! I've been out riding with her . . . And the way she dances!

KRISTINE: Listen, Jean! You're going to dance with me, when I'm finished here, aren't you?

JEAN: Of course I will.

KRISTINE: Promise?

JEAN: Promise? When I say I'll do something, I do it! By the way, the kidney was very good. [*corks the bottle*]

JULIE [*in the doorway to someone outside*]: I'll be right back! You go ahead for now! [JEAN *sneaks the bottle back into the table drawer and gets up respectfully.* MISS JULIE *enters and crosses to* KRISTINE *by the stove.*] Well? Is it ready? [KRISTINE *indicates that* JEAN *is present.*]

JEAN [*gallantly*]: Are you ladies up to something secret?

JULIE [*flicking her handkerchief in his face*]: None of your business!

JEAN: Hmm! I like the smell of violets!

JULIE [*coquettishly*]: Shame on you! So you know about perfumes, too? You certainly know how to dance. Ah, ah! No peeking! Go away.

JEAN [*boldly but respectfully*]: Are you brewing up a magic potion for midsummer eve? Something to prophesy by under a lucky star, so you'll catch a glimpse of your future husband!

JULIE [*caustically*]: You'd need sharp eyes to see him! [*to* KRISTINE] Pour out half a bottle and cork it well.——Come and dance a schottische with me, Jean . . .

JEAN [*hesitating*]: I don't want to be impolite to anyone, and I've already promised this dance to Kristine . . .

JULIE: Oh, she can have another one—can't you Kristine? Won't you lend me Jean?

KRISTINE: It's not up to me, ma'am. [*to* JEAN] If the mistress is so generous, it wouldn't do for you to say no. Go on, Jean, and thank her for the honor.

JEAN: To be honest, and no offense intended, I wonder whether it's wise for you to dance twice running with the same partner, especially since these people are quick to jump to conclusions.

JULIE [*flaring up*]: What's that? What sort of conclusions? What do you mean?

JEAN [*submissively*]: If you don't understand, ma'am, I must speak more plainly. It doesn't look good to play favorites with your servants . . .

JULIE: Play favorites! What an idea! I'm astonished! As mistress of the house, I honor your dance with my presence. And when I dance, I want to dance with someone who can lead, so I won't look ridiculous.

JEAN: As you order, ma'am! I'm at your service!

JULIE [*gently*]: Don't take it as an order! On a night like this we're all just ordinary people having fun, so we'll forget about rank. Now, take my arm!——Don't worry, Kristine! I won't steal your sweetheart! [JEAN *offers his arm and leads* MISS JULIE *out.*]

MIME: *The following should be played as if the actress playing* KRISTINE *were really alone. When she has to, she turns her back to the audience. She does not look toward them, nor does she hurry as if she were afraid they would grow impatient. Schottische music played on a fiddle sounds in the distance.* KRISTINE *hums along with the music. She clears the table, washes the dishes, dries them, and puts them away. She takes off her apron. From a table drawer she removes a small mirror and leans it against the bowl of lilacs on the table. She lights a candle, heats a hairpin over the flame, and uses it to set a curl on her forehead. She crosses to the door and listens, then returns to the table. She finds the handkerchief* MISS JULIE *left behind, picks it up, and smells it. Then, preoccupied, she spreads it out, stretches it, smoothes out the wrinkles, and folds it into quarters, and so forth.*

JEAN [*enters alone*]: God, she really *is* crazy! What a way to dance! Everybody's laughing at her behind her back. What do you make of it, Kristine?

KRISTINE: Ah! It's that time of the month for her, and she always gets peculiar like that. Are you going to dance with me now?

JEAN: You're not mad at me, are you, for leaving . . . ?

KRISTINE: Of course not!——Why should I be, for a little thing like that? Besides, I know my place . . .

JEAN [*puts his arm around her waist*]: You're a sensible girl, Kristine, and you'd make a good wife . . .

JULIE [*entering; uncomfortably surprised; with forced good humor*]: What a charming escort—running away from his partner.

JEAN: On the contrary, Miss Julie. Don't you see how I rushed back to the partner I abandoned!

JULIE [*changing her tone*]: You know, you're a superb dancer!——But why are you wearing livery on a holiday? Take it off at once!

JEAN: Then I must ask you to go outside for a moment. You see, my black coat is hanging over here . . . [*gestures and crosses right*]

JULIE: Are you embarrassed about changing your coat in front of me? Well, go in your room then. Either that or stay and I'll turn my back.

JEAN: With your permission, ma'am! [*He crosses right. His arm is visible as he changes his jacket.*]

JULIE [*to* KRISTINE]: Tell me, Kristine—you two are so close—. Is Jean your fiancé?

KRISTINE: Fiancé? Yes, if you wish. We can call him that.

JULIE: What do you mean?

KRISTINE: You had a fiancé yourself, didn't you? So . . .

JULIE: Well, we were properly engaged . . .

KRISTINE: But nothing came of it, did it? [JEAN *returns dressed in a frock coat and bowler hat.*]

JULIE: *Très gentil, monsieur Jean! Très gentil!*

JEAN: *Vous voulez plaisanter, madame!*

JULIE: *Et vous voulez parler français!* Where did you learn that?

JEAN: In Switzerland, when I was wine steward in one of the biggest hotels in Lucerne!

JULIE: You look like a real gentleman in that coat! *Charmant!* [*sits at the table*]

JEAN: Oh, you're flattering me!

JULIE [*offended*]: Flattering you?

JEAN: My natural modesty forbids me to believe that you would really compliment someone like me, and so I took the liberty of assuming that you were exaggerating, which polite people call flattering.

JULIE: Where did you learn to talk like that? You must have been to the theatre often.

JEAN: Of course. And I've done a lot of traveling.

JULIE: But you come from here, don't you?

JEAN: My father was a farm hand on the district attorney's estate nearby. I used to see you when you were little, but you never noticed me.

JULIE: No! really?

JEAN: Sure. I remember one time especially . . . but I can't talk about that.

JULIE: Oh, come now! Why not? Just this once!

JEAN: No, I really couldn't, not now. Some other time, perhaps.

JULIE: Why some other time? What's so dangerous about now?

JEAN: It's not dangerous, but there are obstacles.——Her, for example. [*indicates* KRISTINE, *who has fallen asleep in a chair by the stove.*]

JULIE: What a pleasant wife she'll make! She probably snores, too.

JEAN: No, she doesn't, but she talks in her sleep.

JULIE [*cynically*]: How do *you* know?

JEAN [*audaciously*]: I've heard her! [*pause, during which they stare at each other*]

JULIE: Why don't you sit down?

JEAN: I couldn't do that in your presence.

JULIE: But if I order you to?

JEAN: Then I'd obey.

JULIE: Sit down, then.——No, wait. Can you get me something to drink first?

JEAN: I don't know what we have in the ice box. I think there's only beer.

JULIE: Why do you say "only"? My tastes are so simple I prefer beer to wine. [JEAN *takes a bottle of beer from the ice box and opens it. He looks for a glass and a plate in the cupboard and serves her.*]

JEAN: Here you are, ma'am.

JULIE: Thank you. Won't you have something yourself?

JEAN: I'm not partial to beer, but if it's an order . . .

JULIE: An order?——Surely a gentleman can keep his lady company.

JEAN: You're right, of course. [*opens a bottle and gets a glass*]

JULIE: Now, drink to my health! [*He hesitates.*] What? A man of the world—and shy?

JEAN [*In mock romantic fashion, he kneels and raises his glass.*]: Skål to my mistress!

JULIE: Bravo!——Now kiss my shoe, to finish it properly. [JEAN *hesitates, then boldly seizes her foot and kisses it lightly.*] Perfect! You should have been an actor.

JEAN [*rising*]: That's enough now, Miss Julie! Someone might come in and see us.

JULIE: What of it?

JEAN: People talk, that's what! If you knew how their tongues were wagging just now at the dance, you'd . . .

JULIE: What were they saying? Tell me!——Sit down!

JEAN [*sits*]: I don't want to hurt you, but they were saying things——suggestive things, that, that . . . well, you can figure it out for yourself! You're not a child. If a woman is seen drinking alone with a man—let alone a servant—at night—then . . .

JULIE: Then what? Besides, we're not alone. Kristine is here.

JEAN: Asleep!

JULIE: Then I'll wake her up. [*rising*] Kristine! Are you asleep? [KRISTINE *mumbles in her sleep.*]

JULIE: Kristine!——She certainly can sleep!

KRISTINE [*in her sleep*]: The Count's boots are brushed—put the coffee on—right away, right away—uh, huh—oh!

JULIE [*grabbing* KRISTINE'*s nose*]: Will you wake up!

JEAN [*severely*]: Leave her alone—let her sleep!

JULIE [*sharply*]: What?

JEAN: Someone who's been standing over a stove all day has a right to be tired by now. Sleep should be respected . . .

JULIE [*changing her tone*]: What a considerate thought—it does you credit—thank you! [*offering her hand*] Come outside and pick some lilacs for me! [*During the following,* KRISTINE *awakens and shambles sleepily off right to bed.*]

JEAN: Go with you?

JULIE: With me!

JEAN: We couldn't do that! Absolutely not!

JULIE: I don't understand. Surely you don't imagine . . .

JEAN: No, I don't, but the others might.

JULIE: What? That I've fallen in love with a servant?

JEAN: I'm not a conceited man, but such things happen—and for these people, nothing is sacred.

JULIE: I do believe you're an aristocrat!

JEAN: Yes, I am.

JULIE: And I'm stepping down . . .

JEAN: Don't step down, Miss Julie, take my advice. No one'll believe you stepped down voluntarily. People will always say you fell.

JULIE: I have a higher opinion of people than you. Come and see!——Come! [*She stares at him broodingly.*]

JEAN: You're very strange, do you know that?

JULIE: Perhaps! But so are you!——For that matter, everything is strange. Life, people, everything. Like floating scum, drifting on and on across the water, until it sinks down and down! That reminds me of a dream I have now and then. I've climbed up on top of a pillar. I sit there and see no way of getting down. I get dizzy when I look down, and I must get down, but I don't have the courage to jump. I can't hold on firmly, and I long to be able to fall, but I don't fall. And yet I'll have no peace until I get down, no rest unless I get down, down on the ground! And if I did get down to the ground, I'd want to be under the earth . . . Have you ever felt anything like that?

JEAN: No. I dream that I'm lying under a high tree in a dark forest. I want to get up, up on top, and look out over the bright landscape, where the sun is shining, and plunder the bird's nest up there, where the golden eggs lie. And I climb and climb, but the trunk's so thick and smooth, and it's so far to the first branch. But I know if I just reached that first branch, I'd go right to the top, like up a ladder. I haven't reached it yet, but I will, even if it's only in a dream!

JULIE: Here I am chattering with you about dreams. Come, let's go out! Just into the park! [*She offers him her arm, and they start to leave.*]

JEAN: We'll have to sleep on nine midsummer flowers, Miss Julie, to make our dreams come true! [*They turn at the door.* JEAN *puts his hand to his eye.*]

JULIE: Did you get something in your eye?

JEAN: It's nothing—just a speck—it'll be gone in a minute.

JULIE : My sleeve must have brushed against you. Sit down and let me help you. [*She takes him by the arm and seats him. She tilts his head back and with the tip of a handkerchief tries to remove the speck.*] Sit still, absolutely still! [*She slaps his hand.*] Didn't you hear me?——Why, you're trembling; the big, strong man is trembling! [*feels his biceps*] What muscles you have!

JEAN [*warning*]: Miss Julie!

JULIE: Yes, *monsieur* Jean.

JEAN: *Attention! Je ne suis qu'un homme!*

JULIE: Will you sit still!——There! Now it's gone! Kiss my hand and thank me.

JEAN [*rising*]: Miss Julie, listen to me!——Kristine has gone to bed!——Will you listen to me!

JULIE: Kiss my hand first!

JEAN: Listen to me!

JULIE: Kiss my hand first!

JEAN: All right, but you've only yourself to blame!

JULIE: For what?

JEAN: For what? Are you still a child at twenty-five? Don't you know that it's dangerous to play with fire?

JULIE: Not for me. I'm insured.

JEAN [*boldly*]: No, you're not! But even if you were, there's combustible material close by.

JULIE: Meaning you?

JEAN: Yes! Not because it's me, but because I'm young——

JULIE: And handsome—what incredible conceit! A Don Juan perhaps! Or a Joseph! Yes, that's it, I do believe you're a Joseph!

JEAN: Do you?

JULIE: I'm almost afraid so. [JEAN *boldly tries to put his arm around her waist and kiss her. She slaps his face.*] How dare you?

JEAN: Are you serious or joking?

JULIE: Serious.

JEAN: Then so was what just happened. You play games too seriously, and that's dangerous. Well, I'm tired of games. You'll excuse me if I get back to work. I haven't done the Count's boots yet and it's long past midnight.

JULIE: Put the boots down!

JEAN: No! It's the work I have to do. I never agreed to be your playmate, and never will. It's beneath me.

JULIE: You're proud.

JEAN: In certain ways, but not in others.

JULIE: Have you ever been in love?

JEAN: We don't use that word, but I've been fond of many girls, and once I was sick because I couldn't have the one I wanted. That's right, sick, like those princes in the Arabian Nights—who couldn't eat or drink because of love.

JULIE: Who was she? [JEAN *is silent.*] Who was she?

JEAN: You can't force me to tell you that.

JULIE: But if I ask you as an equal, as a—friend! Who was she?

JEAN: You!

JULIE [*sits*]: How amusing . . .

JEAN: Yes, if you like! It was ridiculous!——You see, that was the story I didn't want to tell you earlier. Maybe I will now. Do you know how the world looks from down below?——Of course you don't. Neither do hawks and falcons, whose backs we can't see because they're usually soaring up there above us. I grew up in a shack with seven brothers and sisters and a pig, in the middle of a wasteland, where there wasn't a single tree. But from our window I could see the tops of apple trees above the wall of your father's garden. That was the Garden of Eden, guarded by angry angels with flaming swords. All the same, the other boys and I managed to find our way to the Tree of Life.——Now you think I'm contemptible, I suppose.

JULIE: Oh, all boys steal apples.

JEAN: You say that, but you think I'm contemptible anyway. Oh well! One day I went into the Garden of Eden with my mother, to weed the onion beds. Near the vegetable garden was a small Turkish pavilion in the shadow of jasmine bushes and overgrown with honeysuckle. I had no idea what it was used for, but I'd never seen such a beautiful building. People went in and came out again, and one day the door was left open. I sneaked close and saw walls covered with pictures of kings and emperors, and red curtains with fringes at the windows—now you know the place I mean. I——[*breaks off a sprig of lilac and holds it in front of* MISS JULIE*'s nose*]——I'd never been inside the manor house, never seen anything except the church—but this was more beautiful. From then on, no matter where my thoughts wandered, they returned—there. And gradually I got a longing to experience, just once, the full pleasure of—*enfin,* I sneaked in, saw, and marveled! But then I heard someone coming! There was only one exit for ladies and gentlemen, but for me there was another, and I had no choice but to take it! [MISS JULIE, *who has taken the lilac sprig, lets it fall on the table.*] Afterwards, I started running. I crashed through a raspberry bush, flew over a strawberry patch, and came up onto the rose terrace. There I caught sight of a pink dress and a pair of white stockings—it was you. I crawled under a pile of weeds and I mean under—under thistles that pricked me and wet dirt that stank. And I looked at you as you walked among the roses, and I thought; if it's true that a thief can enter heaven and be with the angels, then why can't a farmhand's son here on God's earth enter the manor house garden and play with the Count's daughter?

JULIE [*romantically*]: Do you think all poor children would have felt the way you did?

JEAN [*at first hesitant, then with conviction*]: If *all* poor—yes—of course. Of course!

JULIE: It must be terrible to be poor!

JEAN [*with exaggerated suffering*]: Oh, Miss Julie! Oh! ——A dog can lie on the Countess's sofa, a horse can have his nose patted by a young lady's hand, but a servant——[*changing his tone*]——oh, I know—now and then you find one with enough stuff in him to get ahead in the world, but how often?——Anyhow, do you know what I did then? ——I jumped in the millstream with my clothes on, was pulled out, and got a beating. But the following Sunday, when my father and all the others went to my grandmother's, I arranged to stay home. I scrubbed myself with soap and water, put on my best clothes, and went to church just to see you! I saw you and returned home, determined to die. But I wanted to die beautifully and pleasantly, without pain. And then I remembered that it was dangerous to sleep under an elder bush. We had a big one, and it was in full flower. I plundered its treasures and bedded down under them in the oat bin. Have you ever noticed how smooth oats are?—and soft to the touch, like human skin . . . ! Well, I shut the lid and closed my eyes. I fell asleep and woke up feeling very sick. But I didn't die, as you can see. What was I after?——I don't know. There was no hope of winning you, of course.——You were a symbol of the hopelessness of ever rising out of the class in which I was born.

JULIE: You're a charming storyteller. Did you ever go to school?

JEAN: A bit, but I've read lots of novels and been to the theatre often. And then I've listened to people like you talk—that's where I learned most.

JULIE: Do you listen to what we say?

JEAN: Naturally! And I've heard plenty, too, driving the carriage or rowing the boat. Once I heard you and a friend . . .

JULIE: Oh?——What did you hear?

JEAN: I'd better not say. But I was surprised a little. I couldn't imagine where you learned such words. Maybe at bottom there isn't such a great difference between people as we think.

JULIE: Shame on you! We don't act like you when we're engaged.

JEAN [*staring at her*]: Is that true?——You don't have to play innocent with me, Miss . . .

JULIE: The man I gave my love to was a swine.

JEAN: That's what you all say—afterwards.

JULIE: All?

JEAN: I think so. I know I've heard that phrase before, on similar occasions.

JULIE: What occasions?

JEAN: Like the one I'm talking about. The last time . . .

JULIE [*rising*]: Quiet! I don't want to hear any more!

JEAN: That's interesting—that's what *she* said, too. Well, if you'll excuse me, I'm going to bed.

JULIE [*gently*]: To bed? On midsummer eve?

JEAN: Yes! Dancing with the rabble out there doesn't amuse me much.

JULIE: Get the key to the boat and row me out on the lake. I want to see the sun come up.

JEAN: Is that wise?

JULIE: Are you worried about your reputation?

JEAN: Why not? Why should I risk looking ridiculous and getting fired without a reference, just when I'm trying to establish myself. Besides, I think I owe something to Kristine.

JULIE: So, now it's Kristine . . .

JEAN: Yes, but you, too.——Take my advice, go up and go to bed!

JULIE: Am I to obey you?

JEAN: Just this once—for your own good! Please! It's very late. Drowsiness makes people giddy and liable to lose their heads! Go to bed! Besides—unless I'm mistaken—I hear the others coming to look for me. And if they find us together, you'll be lost! [*The* CHORUS *approaches, singing:*]

The swineherd found his true love
a pretty girl so fair,
The swineherd found his true love
but let the girl beware.

For then he saw the princess
the princess on the golden hill,
but then saw the princess,
so much fairer still.

So the swineherd and the princess
they danced the whole night through,
and he forgot his first love,
to her he was untrue.

And when the long night ended,
and in the light of day, of day,
the dancing too was ended,
and the princess could not stay.

Then the swineherd lost his true love,
and the princess grieves him still,
and never more she'll wander
from atop the golden hill.

JULIE: I know all these people and I love them, just as they love me. Let them come in and you'll see.

JEAN: No, Miss Julie, they don't love you. They take your food, but they spit on it! Believe me! Listen to them, listen to what they're singing!——No, don't listen to them!

JULIE [*listening*]: What are they singing?

JEAN: It's a dirty song! About you and me!

JULIE: Disgusting! Oh! How deceitful! ——

JEAN: The rabble is always cowardly! And in a battle like this, you don't fight; you can only run away!

JULIE: Run away? But where? We can't go out—or into Kristine's room.

JEAN: True. But there's my room. Necessity knows no rules. Besides, you can trust me. I'm your friend and I respect you.

JULIE: But suppose—suppose they look for you in there?

JEAN: I'll bolt the door, and if anyone tries to break in, I'll shoot! ——Come! [*on his knees*] Come!

JULIE [*urgently*]: Promise me . . . ?

JEAN: I swear! [MISS JULIE *runs off right.* JEAN *hastens after her.*]

BALLET: *Led by a fiddler, the servants and farm people enter, dressed festively, with flowers in their hats. On the table they place a small barrel of beer and a keg of schnapps, both garlanded. Glasses are brought out, and the drinking starts. A dance circle is formed and "The Swineherd and the Princess" is sung. When the dance is finished, everyone leaves, singing.*

[MISS JULIE *enters alone. She notices the mess in the kitchen, wrings her hands, then takes out her powder puff and powders her nose.*]

JEAN [*enters agitated*]: There, you see? And you heard them. We can't possibly stay here now, you know that.

JULIE: Yes, I know. But what can we do?

JEAN: Leave, travel, far away from here.

JULIE: Travel? Yes, but where?

JEAN: To Switzerland, to the Italian lakes. Have you ever been there?

JULIE: No. Is it beautiful?

JEAN: Oh, an eternal summer—oranges growing everywhere, laurel trees, always green . . .

JULIE: But what'll we do there?

JEAN: I'll open a hotel—with first-class service for first-class people.

JULIE: Hotel?

JEAN: That's the life, you know. Always new faces, new languages. No time to worry or be nervous. No hunting for something to do—there's always work to be done: bells ringing night and day, train whistles blowing, carriages coming and going, and all the while gold rolling into the till! That's the life!

JULIE: Yes, it sounds wonderful. But what'll I do?

JEAN: You'll be mistress of the house: the jewel in our crown! With your looks . . . and your manner—oh—success is guaranteed! It'll be wonderful! You'll sit in your office like a queen and push an electric button to set your slaves in motion. The guests will file past your throne and timidly lay their treasures before you.——You have no idea how people tremble when they get their bill.——I'll salt the bills and you'll sweeten them with your prettiest smile.——Let's get away from here——[*takes a timetable out of his pocket*]——Right away, on the next train!——We'll be in Malmö six-thirty tomorrow morning, Hamburg at eight-forty; from Frankfort to Basel will take a day, then on to Como by way of the St. Gotthard Tunnel, in, let's see, three days. Three days!

JULIE: That's all very well! But Jean—you must give me courage!——Tell me you love me! Put your arms around me!

JEAN [*hesitating*]: I want to—but I don't dare. Not in this house, not again. I love you—never doubt that—you don't doubt it, do you, Miss Julie?

JULIE [*shy; very feminine*]: "Miss!"——Call me Julie! There are no barriers between us any more. Call me Julie!

JEAN [*tormented*]: I can't! There'll always be barriers between us as long as we stay in this house.——There's the past and there's the Count. I've never met anyone I had such respect for.——When I see his gloves lying on a chair, I feel small.——When I hear that bell up there ring, I jump like a skittish horse.——And when I look at his boots standing there so stiff and proud, I feel like bowing! [*kicking the boots*] Superstitions and prejudices we learned as children—but they can easily be forgotten. If I can just get to another country, a republic, people will bow and scrape when they see my livery—*they'll* bow and scrape, you hear, not me! I wasn't born to cringe. I've got stuff in me, I've got character, and if I can only grab on to that first branch, you watch me climb! I'm a servant today, but next year I'll own my own hotel. In ten years I'll have enough to retire. Then I'll go to Rumania and be decorated. I could—mind you I said *could*—end up a count!

JULIE: Wonderful, wonderful!

JEAN: Ah, in Rumania you just buy your title, and so you'll be countess after all. My countess!

JULIE: But I don't care about that—that's what I'm putting behind me! Show me you love me, otherwise—otherwise, what am I?

JEAN: I'll show you a thousand times—afterwards! Not here! And whatever you do, no emotional outbursts, or we'll both be lost! We must think this through coolly, like sensible people. [*He takes out a cigar, snips the end and lights it.*] You sit there, and I'll sit here. We'll talk as if nothing happened.

JULIE [*desperately*]: Oh, my God! Have you no feelings?

JEAN: Me? No one has more feelings than I do, but I know how to control them.

JULIE: A little while ago you could kiss my shoe—and now!

JEAN [*harshly*]: Yes, but that was before. Now we have other things to think about.

JULIE: Don't speak harshly to me!

JEAN: I'm not—just sensibly! We've already done one foolish thing, let's not have any more. The Count could return any minute, and by then we've got to decide what to do with our lives. What do you think of my plans for the future? Do you approve?

JULIE: They sound reasonable enough. I have only one question: for such a big undertaking you need capital—do you have it?

JEAN [*chewing on the cigar*]: Me? Certainly! I have my professional expertise, my wide experience, and my knowledge of languages. That's capital enough, I should think!

JULIE: But all that won't even buy a train ticket.

JEAN: That's true. That's why I'm looking for a partner to advance me the money.

JULIE: Where will you find one quickly enough?

JEAN: That's up to you, if you want to come with me.

JULIE: But I can't; I have no money of my own. [*pause*]

JEAN: Then it's all off . . .

JULIE: And . . .

JEAN: Things stay as they are.

JULIE: Do you think I'm going to stay in this house as your lover? With all the servants pointing their fingers at me? Do you imagine I can face my father after this? No! Take me away from here, away from shame and dishonor——Oh, what have I done! My God, my God! [*She cries.*]

JEAN: Now, don't start that old song!——What have you done? The same as many others before you.

JULIE [*screaming convulsively*]: And now you think I'm contemptible!——I'm falling, I'm falling!

JEAN: Fall down to my level and I'll lift you up again.

JULIE: What terrible power drew me to you? The attraction of the weak to the strong? The falling to the rising? Or was it love? Was this love? Do you know what love is?

JEAN: Me? What do you take me for? You don't think this was my first time, do you?

JULIE: The things you say, the thoughts you think!

JEAN: That's the way I was taught, and that's the way I am! Now don't get excited and don't play the grand lady, because we're in the same boat now! ——Come on, Julie, I'll pour you a glass of something special! [*He opens a drawer in the table, takes out a wine bottle, and fills two glasses already used.*]

JULIE: Where did you get that wine?

JEAN: From the cellar.

JULIE: My father's burgundy!

JEAN: That'll do for his son-in-law, won't it?

JULIE: And I drink beer! Beer!

JEAN: That only shows I have better taste.

JULIE: Thief!

JEAN: Planning to tell?

JULIE: Oh, oh! Accomplice of a common thief! Was I drunk? Have I been walking in a dream the whole evening? Midsummer eve! A time of innocent fun!

JEAN: Innocent, eh?

JULIE [*pacing back and forth*]: Is there anyone on earth more miserable than I am at this moment?

JEAN: Why should you be? After such a conquest? Think of Kristine in there. Don't you think she has feelings, too?

JULIE: I thought so awhile ago, but not any more. No, a servant is a servant . . .

JEAN: And a whore is a whore!

JULIE [*on her knees, her hands clasped*]: Oh, God in Heaven, end my wretched life! Take me away from the filth I'm sinking into! Save me! Save me!

JEAN: I can't deny I feel sorry for you. When I lay in that onion bed and saw you in the rose garden, well . . . I'll be frank . . . I had the same dirty thoughts all boys have.

JULIE: And you wanted to die for me!

JEAN: In the oat bin? That was just talk.

JULIE: A lie, in other words!

JEAN [*beginning to feel sleepy*]: More or less! I got the idea from a newspaper story about a chimney sweep who curled up in a firewood bin full of lilacs because he got a summons for not supporting his illegitimate child . . .

JULIE: So, that's what you're like . . .

JEAN: I had to think of something. And that's the kind of story women always go for.

JULIE: Swine!

JEAN: *Merde!*

JULIE: And now you've seen the hawk's back . . .

JEAN: Not exactly its *back* . . .

JULIE: And I was to be the first branch . . .

JEAN: But the branch was rotten . . .

JULIE: I was to be the sign on the hotel . . .

JEAN: And I the hotel . . .

JULIE: Sit at your desk, entice your customers, pad their bills . . .

JEAN: That I'd do myself . . .

JULIE: How can anyone be so thoroughly filthy?

JEAN: Better clean up then!

JULIE: You lackey, you menial, stand up, when I speak to you!

JEAN: Menial's strumpet, lackey's whore, shut up and get out of here! Who are you to lecture me on coarseness? None of my kind is ever as coarse as you were tonight. Do you think one of your maids would throw herself at a man the way you did? Have you ever seen any girl of my class offer herself like that? I've only seen it among animals and streetwalkers.

JULIE [*crushed*]: You're right. Hit me, trample on me. I don't deserve any better. I'm worthless. But help me! If you see any way out of this, help me, Jean, please!

JEAN [*more gently*]: I'd be lying if I didn't admit to a sense of triumph in all this, but do you think that a person like me would have dared even to look at someone like you if you hadn't invited it? I'm still amazed . . .

JULIE: And proud . . .

JEAN: Why not? Though I must say it was too easy to be really exciting.

JULIE: Go on, hit me, hit me harder!

JEAN [*rising*]: No! Forgive me for what I've said! I don't hit a man when he's down, let alone a woman. I can't deny though, that I'm pleased to find out that what looked so dazzling to us from below was only tinsel, that the hawk's back was only gray, after all, that the lovely complexion was only powder, that those polished fingernails had black edges, and that a dirty handkerchief is still dirty, even if it smells of perfume . . . ! On the other hand, it hurts me to find out that what I was striving for wasn't finer, more substantial. It hurts me to see you sunk so low that you're inferior to your own cook. It hurts like watching flowers beaten down by autumn rains and turned into mud.

JULIE: You talk as if you were already above me.

JEAN: I am. You see, I could make you a countess, but you could never make me a count.

JULIE: But I'm the child of a count—something you could never be!

JEAN: That's true. But I could be the father of counts—if . . .

JULIE: But you're a thief. I'm not.

JEAN: There are worse things than being a thief! Besides, when I'm working in a house, I consider myself sort of a member of the family, like one of the children. And you don't call it stealing when a child snatches a berry off a full bush. [*His passion is aroused again.*] Miss Julie, you're a glorious woman, much too good for someone like me! You were drinking and you lost your head. Now you want to cover up your mistake by telling yourself that you love me! You don't. Maybe there was a physical attraction—but then your love is no better than mine.——I could never be satisfied to be no more than an animal to you, and I could never arouse real love in you.

JULIE: Are you sure of that?

JEAN: You're suggesting it's possible——Oh, I could fall in love with you, no doubt about it. You're beautiful, you're refined——[*approaching and taking her hand*]——cultured, lovable when you want to be, and once you start a fire in a man, it never goes out. [*putting his arm around her waist*] You're like hot, spicy wine, and one kiss from you . . . [*He tries to lead her out, but she slowly frees herself.*]

JULIE: Let me go!?——You'll never win me like that.

JEAN: *How* then?——Not like that? Not with caresses and pretty speeches. Not with plans about the future or rescue from disgrace! *How* then?

JULIE: How? How? I don't know!——I have no idea!——I detest you as I detest rats, but I can't escape from you.

JEAN: Escape with me!

JULIE [*pulling herself together*]: Escape? Yes, we must escape!——But I'm so tired. Give me a glass of wine? [JEAN *pours the wine. She looks at her watch.*] But we must talk first. We still have a little time. [*She drains the glass, then holds it out for more.*]

JEAN: Don't drink so fast. It'll go to your head.

JULIE: What does it matter?

JEAN: What does it matter? It's vulgar to get drunk! What did you want to tell me?

JULIE: We must escape! But first we must talk, I mean I must talk. You've done all the talking up to now. You told about your life, now I want to tell about mine, so we'll know all about each other before we go off together.

JEAN: Just a minute! Forgive me! If you don't want to regret it afterwards, you'd better think twice before revealing any secrets about yourself.

JULIE: Aren't you my friend?

JEAN: Yes, sometimes! But don't rely on me.

JULIE: You're only saying that.——Besides, everyone already knows my secrets.——You see, my mother was a commoner—very humble background. She was brought up believing in social equality, women's rights, and all that. The idea of marriage repelled her. So, when my father proposed, she replied that she would never become his wife, but he could be her lover. He insisted that he didn't want the woman he loved to be less respected than he. But his passion ruled him, and when she explained that the world's respect meant nothing to her, he accepted her conditions.

But now his friends avoided him and his life was restricted to taking care of the estate, which couldn't satisfy him. I came into the world—against my mother's wishes, as far as I can understand. She wanted to bring me up as a child of nature, and, what's more, to learn everything a boy had to learn, so that I might be an example of how a woman can be as good as a man. I had to wear boy's clothes and learn to take care of horses, but I was never allowed in the cowshed. I had to groom and harness the horses and go hunting—and even had to watch them slaughter animals—that was disgusting! On the estate men were put on women's jobs and women on men's jobs—with the result that the property became run down and we became the laughing stock of the district. Finally, my father must have awakened from his trance because he rebelled and changed everything his way. My parents were then married quietly. Mother became ill—I don't know what illness it was—but she often had convulsions, hid in the attic and in the garden, and sometimes stayed out all night. Then came the great fire, which you've heard about. The house, the stables, and the cowshed all burned down, under very curious circumstances, suggesting arson, because the accident happened the day after the insurance had expired. The quarterly premium my father sent in was delayed because of a messenger's carelessness and didn't arrive in time. [*She fills her glass and drinks.*]

JEAN: Don't drink any more!

JULIE: Oh, what does it matter.——We were left penniless and had to sleep in the carriages. My father had no idea where to find money to rebuild the house because he had so slighted his old friends that they had forgotten him. Then my mother suggested that he borrow from a childhood friend of hers, a brick manufacturer who lived nearby. Father got the loan without having to pay interest, which surprised him. And that's how the estate was rebuilt.——[*drinks again*] Do you know who started the fire?

JEAN: The Countess, your mother.

JULIE: Do you know who the brick manufacturer was?

JEAN: Your mother's lover?

JULIE: Do you know whose money it was?

JEAN: Wait a minute—no, I don't.

JULIE: It was my mother's.

JEAN: You mean the Count's, unless they didn't sign an agreement when they were married.

JULIE: They didn't.——My mother had a small inheritance which she didn't want under my father's control, so she entrusted it to her—friend.

JEAN: Who stole it!

JULIE: Exactly! He kept it.——All this my father found out, but he couldn't bring it to court, couldn't repay his wife's lover, couldn't prove it was his wife's money! It was my mother's revenge for being forced into marriage against her will. It nearly drove him to suicide—there was a rumor that he tried with a pistol, but failed. So, he managed to live through it and my mother had to suffer for what she'd done. You can imagine that those were a terrible five years for me. I loved my father, but I sided with my mother because I didn't know the circumstances. I learned from her to hate men—you've heard how she hated the whole male sex—and I swore to her I'd never be a slave to any man.

JEAN: But you got engaged to that lawyer.

JULIE: In order to make him my slave.

JEAN: And he wasn't willing?

JULIE: He was willing, all right, but I wouldn't let him. I got tired of him.

JEAN: I saw it—out near the stable.

JULIE: What did you see?

JEAN: I saw—how he broke off the engagement.

JULIE: That's a lie! I was the one who broke it off. Has he said that he did? That swine . . .

JEAN: He was no swine, I'm sure. So, you hate men, Miss Julie?

JULIE: Yes!——Most of the time! But sometimes—when the weakness comes, when passion burns! Oh, God, will the fire never die out?

JEAN: Do you hate me, too?

JULIE: Immeasurably! I'd like to have you put to death, like an animal . . .

JEAN: I see—the penalty for bestiality—the woman gets two years at hard labor and the animal is put to death. Right?

JULIE: Exactly!

JEAN: But there's no prosecutor here—and no animal. So, what'll we do?

JULIE: Go away!

JEAN: To torment each other to death?

JULIE: No! To be happy for—two days, a week, as long as we can be happy, and then—die . . .

JEAN: Die? That's stupid! It's better to open a hotel!

JULIE [*without listening*]: ——on the shore of Lake Como, where the sun always shines, where the laurels are green at Christmas and the oranges glow.

JEAN: Lake Como is a rainy hole, and I never saw any oranges outside the stores. But tourists are attracted there because there are plenty of villas to be rented out to lovers, and that's a profitable business.——Do you know why? Because they sign a lease for six months—and then leave after three weeks!

JULIE [*naively*]: Why after three weeks?

JEAN: They quarrel, of course! But they still have to pay the rent in full! And so you rent the villas out again. And that's the way it goes, time after time. There's never a shortage of love—even if it doesn't last long!

JULIE: You don't want to die with me?

JEAN: I don't want to die at all! For one thing, I like living, and for another, I think suicide is a crime against the Providence which gave us life.

JULIE: You believe in God? *You?*

JEAN: Of course I do. And I go to church every other Sunday.——To be honest, I'm tired of all this, and I'm going to bed.

JULIE: Are you? And do you think I can let it go at that? A man owes something to the woman he's shamed.

JEAN [*taking out his purse and throwing a silver coin on the table*]: Here! I don't like owing anything to anybody.

JULIE [*pretending not to notice the insult*]: Do you know what the law states . . .

JEAN: Unfortunately the law doesn't state any punishment for the woman who seduces a man!

JULIE [*as before*]: Do you see any way out but to leave, get married, and then separate?

JEAN: Suppose I refuse such a *mésalliance?*

JULIE: *Mésalliance* . . .

JEAN: Yes, for me! You see, I come from better stock than you. There's no arsonist in my family.

JULIE: How do you know?

JEAN: You can't prove otherwise. We don't keep charts on our ancestors—there's just the police records! But I've read about your family. Do you know who the founder was? He was a miller who let the king sleep with his wife one night during the Danish War. I don't have any noble ancestors like that. I don't have any noble ancestors at all, but I could become one myself.

JULIE: This is what I get for opening my heart to someone unworthy, for giving my family's honor . . .

JEAN: Dishonor!——Well, I told you so: when people drink, they talk, and talk is dangerous!

JULIE: Oh, how I regret it!——How I regret it!——If you at least loved me.

JEAN: For the last time—what do you want? Shall I cry; shall I jump over your riding crop! Shall I kiss you and lure you off to Lake Como for three weeks, and then God knows what . . . ? What shall I do? What do you want? This is getting painfully embarrassing! But that's what happens when you stick your nose in women's business. Miss Julie! I see that you're unhappy. I know you're suffering, but I can't understand you. We don't have such romantic ideas; there's not this kind of hate between us. Love is a game we play when we get time off from work, but we don't have all day and night, like you. I think you're sick, really sick. Your mother was crazy, and her ideas have poisoned your life.

JULIE: Be kind to me. At least now you're talking like a human being.

JEAN: Be human yourself, then. You spit on me, and you won't let me wipe myself off—

JULIE: Help me! Help Me! Just tell me what to do, where to go!

JEAN: In God's name, if I only knew myself.

JULIE: I've been crazy, out of my mind, but isn't there any way out?

JEAN: Stay here and keep calm! No one knows anything!

JULIE: Impossible! The others know and Kristine knows.

JEAN: No they don't, and they'd never believe a thing like that!

JULIE [*hesitantly*]: But—it could happen again!

JEAN: That's true!

JULIE: And then?

JEAN [*frightened*]: Then?——Why didn't I think about that? Yes, there is only one thing to do—get away from here! Right away! I can't come with you, then we'd be finished, so you'll have to go alone—away—anywhere!

JULIE: Alone?——Where?——I can't do that!

JEAN: You must! And before the Count gets back! If you stay, we both know what'll happen. Once you make a mistake like this, you want to continue because the damage has already been done . . . Then you get bolder and bolder—until finally you're caught! So leave! Later you can write to the Count and confess everything—except that it was me! He'll never guess who it was, and he's not going to be eager to find out, anyway.

JULIE: I'll go if you come with me.

JEAN: Are you out of your head? Miss Julie runs away with her servant! In two days it would be in the newspapers, and that's something your father would never live through.

JULIE: I can't go and I can't stay! Help me! I'm so tired, so terribly tired.——Order me! Set me in motion—I can't think or act on my own . . .

JEAN: What miserable creatures you people are! You strut around with your noses in the air as if you were the lords of creation! All right, I'll order you. Go upstairs and get dressed! Get some money for the trip, and then come back down!

JULIE [*in a half-whisper*]: Come up with me!

JEAN: To your room?——Now you're crazy again! [*hesitates for a moment*] No! Go, at once! [*takes her hand to lead her out*]

JULIE [*as she leaves*]: Speak kindly to me, Jean!

JEAN: An order always sounds unkind—now you know how it feels. [JEAN, *alone, sighs with relief. He sits at the table, takes out a notebook and pencil, and begins adding up figures, counting aloud as he works. He continues in dumb show until* KRISTINE *enters, dressed for church. She is carrying a white tie and shirt front.*]

KRISTINE: Lord Jesus, what a mess! What have you been up to?

JEAN: Oh, Miss Julie dragged everybody in here. You mean you didn't hear anything? You must have been sleeping soundly.

KRISTINE: Like a log.

JEAN: And dressed for church already?

KRISTINE: Of course! You remember you promised to come with me to Communion today!

JEAN: Oh, yes, that's right.——And you brought my things. Come on, then! [*He sits down.* KRISTINE *starts to put on his shirt front and tie. Pause.* JEAN *begins sleepily*] What's the gospel text for today?

KRISTINE: On St. John's Day?—the beheading of John the Baptist, I should think!

JEAN: Ah, that'll be a long one, for sure.——Hey, you're choking me!——Oh, I'm sleepy, so sleepy!

KRISTINE: Yes, what have you been doing, up all night? Your face is absolutely green.

JEAN: I've been sitting here gabbing with Miss Julie.

KRISTINE: She has no idea what's proper, that one! [*pause*]

JEAN: You know, Kristine . . .

KRISTINE: What?

JEAN: It's really strange when you think about it.——Her!

KRISTINE: What's so strange?

JEAN: Everything! [*pause*]

KRISTINE [*looking at the half-empty glasses standing on the table*]: Have you been drinking together, too?

JEAN: Yes.

KRISTINE: Shame on you!——Look me in the eye!

JEAN: Well?

KRISTINE: Is it possible? Is it possible?

JEAN [*thinking it over for a moment*]: Yes, it is.

KRISTINE: Ugh! I never would have believed it! No, shame on you, shame!

JEAN: You're not jealous of her, are you?

KRISTINE: No, not of her! If it had been Clara or Sofie I'd have scratched your eyes out!——I don't know why, but that's the way I feel.——Oh, it's disgusting!

JEAN: Are you angry at her, then?

KRISTINE: No, at you! That was an awful thing to do, awful! Poor girl!——No, I don't care who knows it—I won't stay in a house where we can't respect the people we work for.

JEAN: Why should we respect them?

KRISTINE: You're so clever, you tell me! Do you want to wait on people who can't behave decently? Do you? You disgrace yourself that way, if you ask me.

JEAN: But it's a comfort to know they aren't any better than us.

KRISTINE: Not for me. If they're no better, what do we have to strive for to better ourselves.——And think of the Count! Think of him! As if he hasn't had enough misery in his life! Lord Jesus! No, I won't stay in this house any longer!——And it had to be with someone like you! If it had been that lawyer, if it had been a real gentleman . . .

JEAN: What do you mean?

KRISTINE: Oh, you're all right for what you are, but there are men and gentlemen, after all!——No, this business with Miss Julie I can never forget. She was so proud, so arrogant with men, you wouldn't have believed she could just go and give herself—and to someone like you! And she was going to have poor Diana shot for running after the gatekeeper's mutt!——Yes, I'm giving my notice, I mean it—I won't stay here any longer. On the twenty-fourth of October, I leave!

JEAN: And then?

KRISTINE: Well, since the subject has come up, it's about time you looked around for something since we're going to get married, in any case.

JEAN: Where am I going to look? I couldn't find a job like this if I was married.

KRISTINE: No, that's true. But you can find work as a porter or as a caretaker in some government office. The state doesn't pay much, I know, but it's secure, and there's a pension for the wife and children . . .

JEAN [*grimacing*]: That's all very well, but it's a bit early for me to think about dying for a wife and children. My ambitions are a little higher than that.

KRISTINE: Your ambitions, yes! Well, you have obligations, too! Think about them!

JEAN: Don't start nagging me about obligations, I know what I have to do! [*listening for something outside*] Besides, this is something we have plenty of time to think over. Go and get ready for church.

KRISTINE: Who's that walking around up there?

JEAN: I don't know, unless it's Clara.

KRISTINE [*going*]: You don't suppose it's the Count, who came home without us hearing him?

JEAN [*frightened*]: The Count? No, I don't think so. He'd have rung.

KRISTINE [*going*]: Well, God help us! I've never seen anything like this before. [*The sun has risen and shines through the treetops in the park. The light shifts gradually until it slants in through the windows.* JEAN *goes to the door and signals.* MISS JULIE *enters, dressed in travel clothes and carrying a small birdcage, covered with a cloth, which she places on a chair.*]

JULIE: I'm ready now.

JEAN: Shh! Kristine is awake.

JULIE [*very nervous during the following*]: Does she suspect something?

JEAN: She doesn't know anything. But my God, you look awful!

JULIE: Why? How do I look?

JEAN: You're pale as a ghost and—excuse me, but your face is dirty.

JULIE: Let me wash up then.——[*She goes to the basin and washes her hands and face.*] Give me a towel! ——Oh—the sun's coming up.

JEAN: Then the goblins will disappear.

JULIE: Yes, there must have been goblins out last night!——Jean, listen, come with me! I have some money now.

JEAN [*hesitantly*]: Enough?

JULIE: Enough to start with. Come with me! I just can't travel alone on a day like this—midsummer day on a stuffy train—jammed in among crowds of people staring at me. Eternal delays at every station, while I'd wish I had wings. No, I can't, I can't! And then there'll be memories, memories of midsummer days when I was little. The church—decorated with birch leaves and lilacs; dinner at the big table with relatives and friends; the afternoons in the park, dancing, music, flowers, and games. Oh, no matter how far we travel, the memories will follow in the baggage car, with remorse and guilt!

JEAN: I'll go with you——but right away, before it's too late. Right this minute!

JULIE: Get dressed, then! [*picking up the birdcage*]

JEAN: But no baggage! It would give us away!

JULIE: No, nothing! Only what we can have in the compartment with us.

JEAN [*has taken his hat*]: What've you got there? What is it?

JULIE: It's only my greenfinch. I couldn't leave her behind.

JEAN: What? Bring a birdcage with us? You're out of your head! Put it down!

JULIE: It's the only thing I'm taking from my home—the only living being that loves me, since Diana was unfaithful. Don't be cruel! Let me take her!

JEAN: Put the cage down, I said!——And don't talk so loudly—Kristine will hear us!

JULIE: No, I won't leave her in the hands of strangers! I'd rather you killed her.

JEAN: Bring the thing here, then, I'll cut its head off!

JULIE: Oh! But don't hurt her! Don't . . . no, I can't.

JEAN: Bring it here! I can!

JULIE [*taking the bird out of the cage and kissing it*]: Oh, my little Serena, must you die and leave your mistress?

JEAN: Please don't make a scene! Your whole future is at stake! Hurry up! [*He snatches the bird from her, carries it over to the chopping block, and picks up a meat cleaver.* MISS JULIE *turns away.*] You should have learned how to slaughter chickens instead of how to fire pistols. [*He chops off the bird's head.*] Then you wouldn't feel faint at the sight of blood.

JULIE [*screaming*]: Kill me, too! Kill me! You, who can slaughter an innocent animal without blinking an eye! Oh, how I hate, how I detest you! There's blood between us now! I curse the moment I set eyes on you! I curse the moment I was conceived in my mother's womb!

JEAN: What good does cursing do? Let's go!

JULIE [*approaching the chopping block, as if drawn against her will*]: No, I don't want to go yet. I can't . . . until I see . . . Shh! I hear a carriage——[*She listens, but her eyes never leave the cleaver and the chopping block.*] Do you think I can't stand the sight of blood? You think I'm so weak . . . Oh—I'd like to see your blood and your brains on a chopping block!——I'd like to see your whole sex swimming in a sea of blood, like my little bird . . . I think I could drink from your skull! I'd like to bathe my feet in your open chest and eat your heart roasted whole!——You think I'm weak. You think I love you because my womb craved your seed. You think I want to carry your spawn under my heart and nourish it with my blood—bear your child and take your name! By the way, what is your family name? I've never heard it.——Do you have one? I was to be Mrs. Bootblack—or Madame Pigsty.——You dog, who wears my collar, you lackey, who bears my coat of arms on your buttons—do I have to share you with my cook, compete with my own servant? Oh! Oh! Oh!——You think I'm a coward who wants to run away! No, now I'm staying—and let the storm break! My father will come home . . . to find his desk broken open . . . and his money gone! Then he'll ring—that bell . . . twice for his valet—and then he'll send for the police . . . and then I'll tell everything! Everything! Oh, what a relief it'll be to have it all end—if only it will end!—And then he'll have a stroke and die . . . That'll be the end of all of us—and there'll be peace . . . quiet . . . eternal rest!——And then our coat of arms will be broken against his coffin—the family title extinct—but the valet's line will go on in an orphanage . . . win laurels in the gutter, and end in jail!

JEAN: There's the blue blood talking! Very good, Miss Julie! Just don't let that miller out of the closet! [KRISTINE *enters, dressed for church, with a psalmbook in her hand.*]

JULIE [*rushing to* KRISTINE *and falling into her arms, as if seeking protection*]: Help me, Kristine! Help me against this man!

KRISTINE [*unmoved and cold*]: What a fine way to behave on a Sunday morning! [*sees the chopping block*] And look at this mess!——What does all this mean? Why all this screaming and carrying on?

JULIE: Kristine! You're a woman and my friend! Beware of this swine!

JEAN [*uncomfortable*]: While you ladies discuss this, I'll go in and shave. [*slips off right*]

JULIE: You must listen to me so you'll understand!

KRISTINE: No, I could never understand such disgusting behavior! Where are you off to in your traveling clothes?——And he had his hat on.——Well?—— Well?——

JULIE: Listen to me, Kristine! Listen, and I'll tell you everything——

KRISTINE: I don't want to hear it . . .

JULIE: But you must listen to me . . .

KRISTINE: What about? If it's about this silliness with Jean, I'm not interested, because it's none of my business. But if you're thinking of tricking him into running out, we'll soon put a stop to that!

JULIE [*extremely nervous*]: Try to be calm now, Kristine, and listen to me! I can't stay here, and neither can Jean—so we must go away . . .

KRISTINE: Hm, hm!

JULIE [*brightening*]: You see, I just had an idea.——What if all three of us go—abroad—to Switzerland and start a hotel together?——I have money, you see—and Jean and I could run it—and I thought you, you could take care of the kitchen . . . Wouldn't that be wonderful?——Say yes! And come with us, and then everything will be settled!——Oh, do say yes! [*embracing* KRISTINE *and patting her warmly*]

KRISTINE [*coolly, thoughtfully*]: Hm, hm!

JULIE [*presto tempo*]: You've never traveled, Kristine.——You must get out and see the world. You can't imagine how much fun it is to travel by train—always new faces—new countries.——And when we get to Hamburg, we'll stop off at the zoo—you'll like that.——And then we'll go to the theatre and the opera—and when we get to Munich, dear, there we have museums, with Rubens and Raphael, the great painters, as you know.——You've heard of Munich, where King Ludwig lived—the king who went mad.——And then we'll see his castles—they're still there and they're like castles in fairy tales.——And from there it isn't far to Switzerland—and the Alps.——Imagine—the Alps have snow on them even in the middle of summer!——And oranges grow there and laurel trees that are green all year round——

[JEAN *can be seen in the wings right, sharpening his razor on a strop which he holds with his teeth and his left hand. He listens to the conversation with satisfaction, nodding now and then in approval.* MISS JULIE *continues tempo prestissimo.*] And then we'll start a hotel—and I'll be at the desk, while Jean greets the guests . . . does the shopping . . . writes letters. ——You have no idea what a life it'll be—the train whistles blowing and the carriages arriving and the bells ringing in the rooms and down in the restaurant.——And I'll make out the bills—and I know how to salt them! . . . You'll never believe how timid travelers are when they have to pay their bills!——And you—you'll be in charge of the kitchen.——Naturally, you won't have to stand over the stove yourself.——And since you're going to be seen by people, you'll have to wear beautiful clothes.——And you, with your looks—no, I'm not flattering you—one fine day you'll grab yourself a husband!——You'll see!——A rich Englishman—they're so easy to——[*slowing down*]——catch—and then we'll get rich—and build ourselves a villa on Lake Como.——It's true it rains there a little now and then, but——[*dully*]——the sun has to shine sometimes—although it looks dark—and then . . . of course we could always come back home again——[*pause*]——here—or somewhere else——

KRISTINE: Listen, Miss Julie, do you believe all this?

JULIE [*crushed*]: Do I believe it?

KRISTINE: Yes!

JULIE [*wearily*]: I don't know. I don't believe in anything any more. [*She sinks down on the bench and cradles her head in her arms on the table.*] Nothing! Nothing at all!

KRISTINE [*turning right to where* JEAN *is standing*]: So, you thought you'd run out!

JEAN [*embarrassed; puts the razor on the table*]: Run out? That's no way to put it. You heard Miss Julie's plan, and even if she is tired after being up all night, it's still a practical plan.

KRISTINE: Now you listen to me! Did you think I'd work as a cook for that . . .

JEAN [*sharply*]: You watch what you say in front of your mistress! Do you understand?

KRISTINE: Mistress!

JEAN: Yes!

KRISTINE: Listen to him! Listen to him!

JEAN: Yes, you listen! It'd do you good to listen more and talk less! Miss Julie is your mistress. If you despise her, you have to despise yourself for the same reason!

KRISTINE: I've always had enough self-respect——

JEAN: ——to be able to despise other people!

KRISTINE: ——to stop me from doing anything that's beneath me. You can't say that the Count's cook has been up to something with the groom or the swineherd! Can you?

JEAN: No, you were lucky enough to get hold of a gentleman!

KRISTINE: Yes, a gentleman who sells the Count's oats from the stable.

JEAN: You should talk—taking a commission from the grocer and bribes from the butcher,

KRISTINE: What?

JEAN: And you say you can't respect your employers any longer. You, you, you!

KRISTINE: Are you coming to church with me, now? You could use a good sermon after your fine deed!

JEAN: No, I'm not going to church today. You'll have to go alone and confess what you've been up to.

KRISTINE: Yes, I'll do that, and I'll bring back enough forgiveness for you, too. The Savior suffered and died on the Cross for all our sins, and if we go to Him with faith and a penitent heart, He takes all our sins on Himself.

JEAN: Even grocery sins?

JULIE: And do you believe that, Kristine?

KRISTINE: It's my living faith, as sure as I stand here. It's the faith I learned as a child, Miss Julie, and kept ever since. "Where sin abounded, grace did much more abound!"

JULIE: Oh, if I only had your faith. If only . . .

KRISTINE: Well, you see, we can't have it without God's special grace, and that isn't given to everyone——

JULIE: Who is it given to then?

KRISTINE: That's the great secret of the workings of grace, Miss Julie, and God is no respecter of persons, for the last shall be the first . . .

JULIE: Then He does respect the last.

KRISTINE [*continuing*]: . . . and it is easier for a camel to go through the eye of a needle, than for a rich man to enter the Kingdom of God. That's how it is, Miss Julie! Anyhow, I'm going now—alone, and on the way I'm going to tell the groom not to let any horses out, in case anyone wants to leave before the Count gets back! ——Goodbye! [*leaves*]

JEAN: What a witch!——And all this because of a greenfinch!——

JULIE [*dully*]: Never mind the greenfinch!——Can you see any way out of this? Any end to it?

JEAN [*thinking*]: No!

JULIE: What would you do in my place?

JEAN: In your place? Let's see—as a person of position, as a woman who had—fallen. I don't know—wait, now I know.

JULIE [*taking the razor and making a gesture*]: You mean like this?

JEAN: Yes! But—understand—*I* wouldn't do it! That's the difference between us!

JULIE: Because you're a man and I'm a woman? What difference does that make?

JEAN: The usual difference—between a man and a woman.

JULIE [*with the razor in her hand*]: I want to, but I can't——My father couldn't either, the time he should have done it.

JEAN: No, he shouldn't have! He had to revenge himself first.

JULIE: And now my mother is revenged again, through me.

JEAN: Didn't you ever love your father, Miss Julie?

JULIE: Oh yes, deeply, but I've hated him, too. I must have done so without realizing it! It was he who brought me up to despise my own sex, making me half woman, half man. Whose fault is what's happened? My father's, my mother's, my own? My own? I don't have anything that's my own. I don't have a single thought that I didn't get from my father, not an emotion that I didn't get from my mother, and this last idea—that all people are equal—I got that from my fiancé.——That's why I called him a swine! How can it be my fault? Shall I let Jesus take on the blame, the way Kristine does?——No, I'm too proud to do that and too sensible—thanks to my father's teachings.——And as for someone rich not going to heaven, that's a lie. But Kristine won't get in—how will she explain the money she has in the savings bank? Whose fault is it?——What does it matter whose fault it is? I'm still the one who has to bear the blame, face the consequences . . .

JEAN: Yes, but . . . [*the bell rings sharply twice.* MISS JULIE *jumps up.* JEAN *changes his coat.*] The Count is back! Do you suppose Kristine—[*He goes to the speaking tube, taps the lid, and listens.*]

JULIE: He's been to his desk!

JEAN: It's Jean, sir! [*listening; the audience cannot hear the Count's voice.*] Yes, sir! [*listening*] Yes, sir! Right away! [*listening*] At once, sir! [*listening*] I see, in half an hour!

JULIE [*desperately frightened*]: What did he say? Dear Lord, what did he say?

JEAN: He wants his boots and his coffee in half an hour.

JULIE: So, in half an hour! Oh, I'm so tired. I'm not able to do anything. I can't repent, can't run away, can't stay, can't live—can't die! Help me! Order me, and I'll obey like a dog! Do me this last service, save my honor, save his name! You know what I *should* do, but don't have the will to . . . You will it, you order me to do it!

JEAN: I don't know why——but now I can't either ——I don't understand.——It's as if this coat made it impossible for me to order you to do anything.——And now, since the Count spoke to me—I—I can't really explain it—but—ah, it's the damn lackey in me!——I think if the Count came down here now—and ordered me to cut my throat, I'd do it on the spot.

JULIE: Then pretend you're he, and I'm you!——You gave such a good performance before when you knelt at my feet.——You were a real nobleman. ——Or—have you ever seen a hypnotist in the theatre? [JEAN *nods.*] He says to his subject: "Take the broom," and he takes it. He says: "Sweep," and he sweeps——

JEAN: But the subject has to be asleep.

JULIE [*ecstatically*]: I'm already asleep.——The whole room is like smoke around me . . . and you look like an iron stove . . . shaped like a man in black, with a tall hat—and your eyes glow like coals when the fire is dying—and your face is a white patch, like ashes——[*The sunlight has reached the floor and now shines on* JEAN.]——it's so warm and good——[*She rubs her hands as if warming them before a fire.*]——and bright—and so peaceful!

JEAN [*taking the razor and putting it in her hand*]: Here's the broom! The sun's almost up. Go now—out to the barn—and . . . [*whispers in her ear*]

JULIE [*awake*]: Thank you. I'm going now to rest! But just tell me—that those who are first can also receive the gift of grace. Say it, even if you don't believe it.

JEAN: The first? No, I can't!——But wait—Miss Julie—now I know! You're no longer among the first—you're now among—the last!

JULIE: That's true.——I'm among the very last. I'm the last of all! Oh!——But now I can't go!——Tell me once more to go!

JEAN: No, now I can't either! I can't!

JULIE: And the first shall be the last!

JEAN: Don't think, don't think! You're taking all my strength, making me a coward.——What was that? I thought the bell moved!——No! Shall we stuff paper in it?——To be so afraid of a bell!——But it isn't just a bell.——There's someone behind it—a hand sets it in motion—and something else sets the hand in motion.——Maybe if you cover your ears—cover your ears! But then it rings even louder! rings until someone answers.——And then it's too late! And then the police come—and—then——[*The bell rings twice loudly.* JEAN *flinches, then straightens up.*] It's horrible! But there's no other way!——Go! [MISS JULIE *walks firmly out through the door.*]

Oscar Wilde

Oscar Fingal O'Flahertie Wills Wilde (1854–1900) was born in Dublin, Ireland, the son of Sir William, a prominent surgeon, and Lady Jane, a flamboyant woman, about six feet tall, who wrote fiction and poetry under the name "Speranza." Lady Wilde's marriage was difficult, and when Sir William was accused of rape, she endured the scandal, but moved to London, where she conducted a salon for the entertainment of artists and writers that provided a stage for her adored, and adoring, son. The family scandal was never quite forgotten, and the propriety of Victorian marriage and its secrets became an enduring theme for Wilde in such plays as *Lady Windermere's Fan* and *An Ideal Husband.*

Wilde was a precocious child who won many awards as a student of the classics. After graduating Oxford University, he entered London society by advertising himself as Professor of Aesthetics. Known for his literary talent and sparkling wit, he mixed easily in high society and in the world of arts and letters, counting among his friends the actresses Sarah Bernhardt, Lillie Langtry, and Ellen Terry, and the painter James McNeill Whistler. Wilde and Whistler became so well-known for their esthetic pronouncements and generally outlandish behavior and dress that W. S. Gilbert and Arthur Sullivan satirized them in the operetta *Patience* (1881). When George Bernard Shaw first met Wilde, at the home of Lady Wilde, Oscar was dressed all in white, in a coat made in the design of a cello, and knee breeches, which Shaw said reminded him of a great white caterpillar. The meeting was not a success because Shaw was also repelled by Wilde's exhibitionism and evident, though not confirmed, homosexuality.

It was not until 1895, at the height of his career as a playwright, that Wilde's private life spilled out into public view and his reputation for homosexual liaisons was confirmed. He was brought to trial and convicted of indecent behavior and sentenced to two years of hard labor. Divorced by his wife and abandoned by family and friends, in 1897 he began a self-imposed exile from England. During this time, he wrote *De Profundis* (published posthumously in 1905) in which he excoriated himself: "The gods had given me almost everything: I had genius, a distinguished name, high social position, brilliancy, intellectual daring. . . . But I let myself be lured into long spells of senselessness and sensual ease. . . . I ended in horrible disgrace. There is only one thing for me now, absolute humility." *The Ballad of Reading Gaol* (1898) was his final serious work, based on the sad decline of his life and an account of his imprisonment. He died in Paris two years later and is buried in Père Lachaise cemetery.

Prior to his success as a playwright, Wilde was versatile and productive: author of *Poems* (1881), *The Happy Prince and Other Tales* (1888), *Lord Arthur Savile's Crime and Other Stories* (1891), critical essays "The Critic as Artist" (1891), "The Soul of Man under Socialism" (1891), and editor of *The Woman's World.* His only novel, *The Picture of Dorian Gray* (1891), is a cautionary tale of the effects of hedonism, whose protagonist is a man whose portrait ages while he remains youthful. Gray's fall from grace and suicide at thirty-seven in some ways parallel Wilde's secret life as a homosexual.

In the final analysis, Wilde is best known for his mastery of comic drama and farce. He was greatly influenced by the French playwrights Eugène Scribe (1791–1861) and Victorien Sardou (1831–1908), the masters of the well-made play that aimed to entertain rather than enlighten. On a more serious level, he was impressed by Henrik Ibsen's *A Doll's House* when it was produced in London in 1891. Wilde read George Bernard Shaw's *Quintessence of Ibsenism* carefully and admired Shaw's early comedies *Widowers' Houses* (1892) and *The Philanderer* (1893). However, Wilde's witty irreverence and sense of satirical humor set his work apart from Shaw's finely tuned social and political humor, and from Ibsen's serious ethical drama. Shaw could never fathom Wilde's wit, and he thought that *The Importance of Being Earnest, A Trivial Comedy for Serious People,* Wilde's masterpiece, was essentially hateful and heartless.

Vera, or the Nihilist (1883), Wilde's first play, was produced in New York City and failed there. He tried again with *The Duchess Of Padua* (1891), with dialogue written in blank verse, but it too was unsuccessfully produced in New York City, under the title *Guido Ferranti.* Wilde was unable to get a London production.

Wilde's first successful play that was produced in England, *Lady Windermere's Fan* (1892), was a more polished farce that took aim at Henrik Ibsen's *Ghosts,* in production in London at the time. Today's audiences are less apt to see Ibsen's influence in this play, and it stands on its own as a domestic comedy about a daughter's memory of an ideal mother. Lady Windermere, an abandoned child, has no knowledge of her mother's scandalous past life, or even that she is still alive. When that illusion is threatened, Lord Windermere very properly protects his wife and saves his marriage by expelling from their social circle the dandified Lord Darlington, a pernicious influence. He never knows that Mrs. Erlynne, a friend of Darlington's, has saved Lady Windermere from running off with Darlington. When Lord Windermere, knowing that Mrs. Erlynne is really Lady Windermere's mother, asks her to repent, he is rebuffed. The husband and wife both keep a secret, but they also keep their marriage intact.

Wilde followed *Lady Windermere's Fan* with two equally successful comedies. *A Woman of No Importance* (1893) concerns an illegitimate son, Gerald, who meets his father, Lord Illington, and then learns that his mother, Mrs. Artbuthnot, has kept a secret. Gerald rejects his father, marries an American heiress, and makes his own way. *An Ideal Husband* (1895) is another of Wilde's comedies in the style of the well-made play that gently ridicules the discrepancy between Victorian public and private morality. In this story, Robert Chiltern, a rising politician, is idealized by his puritanical wife. When it is revealed that he is not a model husband and that he used insider information to make his fortune and career, she is disillusioned and wants him to confess publicly. Turning for help to his oldest friend, Lord Goring, a dandy and seemingly frivolous man-about-town, Chiltern defends himself on the grounds that it takes great courage to commit an immoral act. Goring, ultimately, saves the day and reunites the mismatched couple. Though Chiltern will never be an "ideal" husband, his immoral behavior is pardoned because he has such a promising future. For his part, Goring renounces his frivolous ways and gets a bride worthy of his intellect and wit. They will make an "ideal couple."

Salomé, Wilde's most intense and serious play, was written in 1893 as a star vehicle for the great French actress Sarah Bernhardt (1844–1923), who enjoyed exploiting the role of a powerful and exotic woman. Bernhardt encouraged Wilde, but she never played the role; characteristically, Wilde forgave her. *Salomé* is a melodrama about the intricate and sordid relationships of Salomé and King Herod, which resulted in the death of John the Baptist. Wilde embroidered the theme of the rejected woman and characterized Salomé as a young woman who is obsessively in love with Iokanaan, Greek for John, who hates her. When she cannot seduce him, she petulantly requests that he be killed. Herod, who loves Salomé, orders her killed when she resists his sexual advances.

Sensing the inflammatory quality of *Salomé*, Wilde wrote the play in French because he hoped that the English censors would be more lenient. When they banned it, Wilde eventually arranged to have it produced in Paris, but not until 1896, by which time he was in prison. It was not fully staged in England until 1931, though dance hall versions of *Salomé* evaded censorship. *Salomé* is best known today as the basis for Richard Strauss's opera (1905), which is widely performed in international opera houses.

Wilde's calamitous fall from grace at forty-one stands in marked contrast to the effervescence of his last play, *The Importance of Being Earnest*. Subtitled *A Trivial Comedy for Serious People*, this is a brilliant farce focusing on upper-class customs of courtship and betrothal. Though it opened to great acclaim just shortly before Wilde's trial, it was withdrawn from the stage after his conviction and not revived until fifteen years later.

The Importance of Being Earnest is built on the stock concepts of farce: confusion of identity, secrets, and unknown parentage finally revealed. The characters parody an upper-class type. John Worthing and Algernon Moncrieff are dandies, cynical young gentlemen without a calling. Cecily Cardew and Gwendolen Fairfax are ambitious (and innocent) young ladies searching for proper husbands. Lady Bracknell is the imperious mother and social doyen. Reverend Chasuble is the bumbling Anglican priest, Miss Prism is the slightly dotty governess and would-be author of romantic novels, and Lane and Merriman are the perfect sangfroid servants, who always seem superior to their station. The story is purposely convoluted. John Worthing, known as Ernest in London and Jack in the country, is in love with Gwendolen, who loves the name Ernest but hates the name John or Jack. Algernon Moncrieff, known as Algy, takes the name of Ernest in order to woo Jack's ward, Cecily Cardew, who lives in the country. Lady Bracknell, Gwendolen's mother, resists approving her daughter's engagement because Ernest is an orphan and may not have suitable parentage. Algy also refuses his approval because he wants Jack to approve his own marriage to Cecily, though she thinks that Algy is Ernest, Jack's wayward brother from town. When it is finally discovered that Jack Worthing is really Ernest Moncrieff, the misplaced child of Lady Bracknell's dead sister, and Algy's older brother, he can, at last, marry Gwendolen. The secret of his mistaken identity is revealed by Miss Prism, the governess and erstwhile novelist, who had years before confused her manuscript with the baby Ernest. She had placed the manuscript in the pram and put the baby in a valise in storage at Victoria Railway Station. Once this absurd mistake is explained, Jack/Ernest approves Cecily's marriage to Algy.

Lady Bracknell, silenced for once, is pleased. When she does regain her imperious composure, she says, "My nephew, you seem to be displaying signs of triviality." Jack responds with the pun, "On the contrary, Aunt Augusta, I've now realized for the first time in my life the vital Importance of Being Earnest."

Film

The Importance of Being Earnest (1952), directed by Anthony Asquith, with Michael Redgrave, Edith Evans, Margaret Rutherford, Michael Denison, and Joan Greenwood. Paramount.

The Importance of Being Earnest

A Trivial Comedy for Serious People

THE PERSONS OF THE PLAY

JOHN WORTHING, J.P.
ALGERNON MONCRIEFF
REV. CANON CHASUBLE, D.D.
MERRIMAN, Butler
LANE, Manservant
LADY BRACKNELL
GWENDOLEN FAIRFAX
CECILY CARDEW
MISS PRISM, Governess

THE SCENES OF THE PLAY

ACT I ALGERNON MONCRIEFF's Flat in Half Moon Street, W.
ACT II The Garden at the Manor House, Woolton.
ACT III Drawing-Room at the Manor House, Woolton.
Time—The Present.

ACT I

SCENE. Morning-room in ALGERNON's *flat in Half Moon Street. The room is luxuriously and artistically furnished. The sound of a piano is heard in the adjoining room.*

[LANE *is arranging afternoon tea on the table, and after the music has ceased,* ALGERNON *enters.*]

ALGERNON: Did you hear what I was playing, Lane?

LANE: I didn't think it polite to listen, sir.

ALGERNON: I'm sorry for that, for your sake. I don't play accurately—anyone can play accurately—but I play with wonderful expression. As far as the piano is concerned, sentiment is my forte. I keep science for Life.

LANE: Yes, sir.

ALGERNON: And, speaking of the science of Life, have you got the cucumber sandwiches cut for Lady Bracknell?

LANE: Yes, sir. [*Hands them on a salver.*]

ALGERNON [*Inspects them, takes two, and sits down on the sofa.*]: Oh! . . . by the way, Lane, I see from your book that on Thursday night, when Lord Shoreham and Mr Worthing were dining with me, eight bottles of champagne are entered as having been consumed.

LANE: Yes, sir; eight bottles and a pint.

ALGERNON: Why is it that at a bachelor's establishment the servants invariably drink the champagne? I ask merely for information.

LANE: I attribute it to the superior quality of the wine, sir. I have often observed that in married households the champagne is rarely of a first-rate brand.

ALGERNON: Good Heavens! Is marriage so demoralizing as that?

LANE: I believe it *is* a very pleasant state, sir. I have had very little experience of it myself up to the present. I have only been married once. That was in consequence of a misunderstanding between myself and a young person.

ALGERNON [*Languidly.*]: I don't know that I am much interested in your family life, Lane.

LANE: No, sir; it is not a very interesting subject. I never think of it myself.

ALGERNON: Very natural, I am sure. That will do, Lane, thank you.

LANE: Thank you, sir.

[LANE *goes out.*]

ALGERNON: Lane's views on marriage seem somewhat lax. Really, if the lower orders don't set us a good example, what on earth is the use of them? They seem, as a class, to have absolutely no sense of moral responsibility.

[*Enter* LANE.]

LANE: Mr Ernest Worthing.

[*Enter* JACK.]

[LANE *goes out.*]

ALGERNON: How are you, my dear Ernest? What brings you up to town?

JACK: Oh, pleasure, pleasure! What else should bring one anywhere? Eating as usual, I see, Algy!

ALGERNON [*Stiffly.*]: I believe it is customary in good society to take some slight refreshment at five o'clock. Where have you been since last Thursday?

JACK [*Sitting down on the sofa.*]: In the country.

ALGERNON: What on earth do you do there?

JACK [*Pulling off his gloves.*]: When one is in town one amuses oneself. When one is in the country one amuses other people. It is excessively boring.

ALGERNON: And who are the people you amuse?

JACK [*Airily.*]: Oh, neighbours, neighbours.

ALGERNON: Got nice neighbours in your part of Shropshire?

JACK: Perfectly horrid! Never speak to one of them.

ALGERNON: How immensely you must amuse them! [*Goes over and takes sandwich.*] By the way, Shropshire is your county, is it not?

JACK: Eh? Shropshire? Yes, of course. Hallo! Why all these cups? Why cucumber sandwiches? Why such reckless extravagance in one so young? Who is coming to tea?

ALGERNON: Oh! merely Aunt Augusta and Gwendolen.

JACK: How perfectly delightful!

ALGERNON: Yes, that is all very well; but I am afraid Aunt Augusta won't quite approve of your being here.

JACK: May I ask why?

ALGERNON: My dear fellow, the way you flirt with Gwendolen is perfectly disgraceful. It is almost as bad as the way Gwendolen flirts with you.

JACK: I am in love with Gwendolen. I have come up to town expressly to propose to her.

The Importance of Being Earnest, *Dover Little Theatre, 1937.*

ALGERNON: I thought you had come up for pleasure? . . . I call that business.

JACK: How utterly unromantic you are!

ALGERNON: I really don't see anything romantic in proposing. It is very romantic to be in love. But there is nothing romantic about a definite proposal. Why, one may be accepted. One usually is, I believe. Then the excitement is all over. The very essence of romance is uncertainty. If ever I get married, I'll certainly try to forget the fact.

JACK: I have no doubt about that, dear Algy. The Divorce Court was specially invented for people whose memories are so curiously constituted.

ALGERNON: Oh! there is no use speculating on that subject. Divorces are made in Heaven——[JACK *puts out his hand to take a sandwich.* ALGERNON *at once interferes.*] Please don't touch the cucumber sandwiches. They are ordered specially for Aunt Augusta. [*Takes one and eats it.*]

JACK: Well, you have been eating them all the time.

ALGERNON: That is quite a different matter. She is my aunt. [*Takes plate from below.*] Have some bread and butter. The bread and butter is for Gwendolen. Gwendolen is devoted to bread and butter.

JACK [*Advancing to table and helping himself.*]: And very good bread and butter it is too.

ALGERNON: Well, my dear fellow, you need not eat as if you were going to eat it all. You behave as if you were married to her already. You are not married to her already, and I don't think you ever will be.

JACK: Why on earth do you say that?

ALGERNON: Well, in the first place girls never marry the men they flirt with. Girls don't think it right.

JACK: Oh, that is nonsense!

ALGERNON: It isn't. It is a great truth. It accounts for the extraordinary number of bachelors that one sees all over the place. In the second place, I don't give my consent.

JACK: Your consent!

ALGERNON: My dear fellow, Gwendolen is my first cousin. And before I allow you to marry her, you will have to clear up the whole question of Cecily. [*Rings bell.*]

JACK: Cecily! What on earth do you mean? What do you mean, Algy, by Cecily? I don't know anyone of the name of Cecily.

[*Enter* LANE.]

ALGERNON: Bring me that cigarette case Mr Worthing left in the smoking-room the last time he dined here.

LANE: Yes, sir.

[LANE *goes out.*]

JACK: Do you mean to say you have had my cigarette case all this time? I wish to goodness you had let me know. I have been writing frantic letters to Scotland Yard about it. I was very nearly offering a large reward.

ALGERNON: Well, I wish you would offer one. I happen to be more than usually hard up.

JACK: There is no good offering a large reward now that the thing is found.

[*Enter* LANE *with the cigarette case on a salver.* ALGERNON *takes it at once.* LANE *goes out.*]

ALGERNON: I think that is rather mean of you, Ernest, I must say. [*Opens case and examines it.*] However, it makes no matter, for, now that I look at the inscription inside, I find that the thing isn't yours after all.

JACK: Of course it's mine. [*Moving to him.*] You have seen me with it a hundred times, and you have no right whatsoever to read what is written inside. It is a very ungentlemanly thing to read a private cigarette case.

ALGERNON: Oh! it is absurd to have a hard-and-fast rule about what one should read and what one shouldn't. More than half of modern culture depends on what one shouldn't read.

JACK: I am quite aware of the fact, and I don't propose to discuss modern culture. It isn't the sort of thing one should talk of in private. I simply want my cigarette case back.

ALGERNON: Yes; but this isn't your cigarette case. This cigarette case is a present from someone of the name of Cecily, and you said you didn't know anyone of that name.

JACK: Well, if you want to know, Cecily happens to be my aunt.

ALGERNON: Your aunt!

JACK: Yes. Charming old lady she is, too. Lives at Tunbridge Wells. Just give it back to me, Algy.

ALGERNON [*Retreating to back of sofa.*]: But why does she call herself little Cecily if she is your aunt and lives at Tunbridge Wells? [*Reading.*] "From little Cecily with her fondest love."

Jack [*Moving to sofa and kneeling upon it.*]: My dear fellow, what on earth is there in that? Some aunts are tall, some aunts are not tall. That is a matter that surely an aunt may be allowed to decide for herself. You seem to think that every aunt should be exactly like your aunt! That is absurd! For Heaven's sake give me back my cigarette case. [*Follows* ALGERNON *round the room.*]

ALGERNON: Yes. But why does your aunt call you her uncle? "From little Cecily, with her fondest love to her dear Uncle Jack." There is no objection, I admit, to an aunt being a small aunt, but why an aunt, no matter what her size may be, should call her own nephew her uncle, I can't quite make out. Besides, your name isn't Jack at all; it is Ernest.

JACK: It isn't Ernest; it's Jack.

ALGERNON: You have always told me it was Ernest. I have introduced you to everyone as Ernest. You answer to the name of Ernest. You look as if your name was Ernest. You are the most earnest looking person I ever saw in my life. It is perfectly absurd your saying that your name isn't Ernest. It's on your cards. Here is one of them. [*Taking it from case.*] "Mr. Ernest Worthing, B.4, The Albany." I'll keep this as a proof that your name is Ernest if ever you attempt to deny it to me, or to Gwendolen, or to anyone else. [*Puts the card in his pocket.*]

JACK: Well, my name is Ernest in town and Jack in the country, and the cigarette case was given to me in the country.

ALGERNON: Yes, but that does not account for the fact that your small Aunt Cecily, who lives at Tunbridge Wells, calls you her dear uncle. Come, old boy, you had much better have the thing out at once.

JACK: My dear Algy, you talk exactly as if you were a dentist. It is very vulgar to talk like a dentist when one isn't a dentist. It produces a false impression.

ALGERNON: Well, that is exactly what dentists always do. Now, go on! Tell me the whole thing. I may mention that I have always suspected you of being a confirmed and secret Bunburyist, and I am quite sure of it now.

JACK: Bunburyist? What on earth do you mean by a Bunburyist?

ALGERNON: I'll reveal to you the meaning of that incomparable expression as soon as you are kind enough to inform me why you are Ernest in town and Jack in the country.

JACK: Well, produce my cigarette case first.

ALGERNON: Here it is. [*Hands cigarette case.*] Now produce your explanation, and pray make it improbable. [*Sits on sofa.*]

JACK: My dear fellow, there is nothing improbable about my explanation at all. In fact it's perfectly ordinary. Old Mr Thomas Cardew, who adopted me when I was a little boy, made me in his will guardian to his grand-daughter, Miss Cecily Cardew. Cecily who addresses me as her uncle from motives of respect that you could not possibly appreciate, lives at my place in the country under the charge of her admirable governess, Miss Prism.

ALGERNON: Where is that place in the country, by the way?

JACK: That is nothing to you, dear boy. You are not going to be invited. . . . I may tell you candidly that the place is not in Shropshire.

ALGERNON: I suspected that, my dear fellow! I have Bunburyed all over Shropshire on two separate occasions. Now, go on. Why are you Ernest in town and Jack in the country?

JACK: My dear Algy, I don't know whether you will be able to understand my real motives. You are hardly serious enough. When one is placed in the position of guardian, one has to adopt a very high moral tone on all subjects. It's one's duty to do so. And as a high moral tone can hardly be said to conduce very much to either one's health or one's happiness, in order to get up to town I have always pretended to have a younger brother of the name of Ernest, who lives in the Albany, and gets into the most dreadful scrapes. That, my dear Algy, is the whole truth pure and simple.

ALGERNON: The truth is rarely pure and never simple. Modern life would be very tedious if it were either, and modern literature a complete impossibility!

JACK: That wouldn't be at all a bad thing.

ALGERNON: Literary criticism is not your forte, my dear fellow. Don't try it. You should leave that to people who haven't been at a University. They do it so well in the daily papers. What you really are is a Bunburyist. I was quite right in saying you were a Bunburyist. You are one of the most advanced Bunburyists I know.

JACK: What on earth do you mean?

ALGERNON: You have invented a very useful younger brother called Ernest, in order that you may be able to come up to town as often as you like. I have invented an invaluable permanent invalid called Bunbury, in order that I may be able to go down into the country whenever I choose. Bunbury is perfectly invaluable. If it wasn't for Bunbury's extraordinary bad health, for instance, I wouldn't be able to dine with you at Willis's tonight, for I have been really engaged to Aunt Augusta for more than a week.

JACK: I haven't asked you to dine with me anywhere tonight.

ALGERNON: I know. You are absurdly careless about sending out invitations. It is very foolish of you. Nothing annoys people so much as not receiving invitations.

JACK: You had much better dine with your Aunt Augusta.

ALGERNON: I haven't the smallest intention of doing anything of the kind. To begin with, I dined there on Monday, and once a week is quite enough to dine with one's own relations. In the second place, whenever I do dine there I am always treated as a member of the family, and sent down with either no woman at all, or two. In the third place, I know perfectly well whom she will place me next to, tonight. She will place me next Mary Farquhar, who always flirts with her own husband across the dinner-table. That is not very pleasant. Indeed, it is not even decent . . . and that sort of thing is enormously on the increase. The amount of women in London who flirt with their own husbands is perfectly scandalous. It looks so bad. It is simply washing one's clean linen in public. Besides, now that I know you to be a confirmed Bunburyist I naturally want to talk to you about Bunburying. I want to tell you the rules.

JACK: I'm not a Bunburyist at all. If Gwendolen accepts me, I am going to kill my brother, indeed I think I'll kill him in any case. Cecily is a little too much interested in him. It is rather a bore. So I am going to get rid of Ernest. And I strongly advise you to do the same with Mr . . . with your invalid friend who has the absurd name.

ALGERNON: Nothing will induce me to part with Bunbury, and if you ever get married, which seems to me extremely problematic, you will be very glad to know Bunbury. A man who marries without knowing Bunbury has a very tedious time of it.

JACK: That is nonsense. If I marry a charming girl like Gwendolen, and she is the only girl I ever saw in my life that I would marry, I certainly won't want to know Bunbury.

ALGERNON: Then your wife will. You don't seem to realize, that in married life three is company and two is none.

JACK [*Sententiously.*]: That, my dear young friend, is the theory that the corrupt French Drama has been propounding for the last fifty years.

ALGERNON: Yes; and that the happy English home has proved in half the time.

JACK: For heaven's sake, don't try to be cynical. It's perfectly easy to be cynical.

ALGERNON: My dear fellow, it isn't easy to be anything nowadays. There's such a lot of beastly competition about. [*The sound of an electric bell is heard.*] Ah! that must be Aunt Augusta. Only relatives, or creditors, ever ring in that Wagnerian manner. Now, if I get her out of the way for ten minutes, so that you can have an opportunity for proposing to Gwendolen, may I dine with you tonight at Willis's?

JACK: I suppose so, if you want to.

ALGERNON: Yes, but you must be serious about it. I hate people who are not serious about meals. It is so shallow of them.

[*Enter* LANE.]

LANE: Lady Bracknell and Miss Fairfax.

[ALGERNON *goes forward to meet them. Enter* LADY BRACKNELL *and* GWENDOLEN.]

LADY BRACKNELL: Good afternoon, dear Algernon, I hope you are behaving very well.

ALGERNON: I'm feeling very well, Aunt Augusta.

LADY BRACKNELL: That's not quite the same thing. In fact the two things rarely go together. [*Sees* JACK *and bows to him with icy coldness.*]

ALGERNON [*To* GWENDOLEN.]: Dear me, you are smart!

GWENDOLEN: I am always smart! Aren't I, Mr Worthing?

JACK: You're quite perfect, Miss Fairfax.

GWENDOLEN: Oh! I hope I am not that. It would leave no room for developments, and I intend to develop in many directions. [GWENDOLEN *and* JACK *sit down together in the corner.*]

LADY BRACKNELL: I'm sorry if we are a little late, Algernon, but I was obliged to call on dear Lady Harbury. I hadn't been there since her poor husband's death. I never saw a woman so altered; she looks quite twenty years younger. And now I'll have a cup of tea, and one of those nice cucumber sandwiches you promised me.

ALGERNON: Certainly, Aunt Augusta. [*Goes over to tea-table.*]

LADY BRACKNELL: Won't you come and sit here, Gwendolen?

GWENDOLEN: Thanks, mamma, I'm quite comfortable where I am.

ALGERNON [*Picking up empty plate in horror.*]: Good heavens! Lane! Why are there no cucumber sandwiches? I ordered them specially.

LANE [*Gravely.*]: There were no cucumbers in the market this morning, sir. I went down twice.

ALGERNON: No cucumbers!

LANE: No, sir. Not even for ready money.

ALGERNON: That will do, Lane, thank you.

LANE: Thank you, sir.

[*Goes out.*]

ALGERNON: I am greatly distressed, Aunt Augusta, about there being no cucumbers, not even for ready money.

LADY BRACKNELL: It really makes no matter, Algernon. I had some crumpets with Lady Harbury, who seems to me to be living entirely for pleasure now.

ALGERNON: I hear her hair has turned quite gold from grief.

LADY BRACKNELL: It certainly has changed its colour. From what cause I, of course, cannot say. [ALGERNON *crosses and hands tea.*] Thank you. I've quite a treat for you tonight, Algernon. I am going to send you down with Mary Farquhar. She is such a nice woman, and so attentive to her husband. It's delightful to watch them.

ALGERNON: I am afraid, Aunt Augusta, I shall have to give up the pleasure of dining with you tonight after all.

LADY BRACKNELL [*Frowning.*]: I hope not, Algernon. It would put my table completely out. Your uncle would have to dine upstairs. Fortunately he is accustomed to that.

ALGERNON: It is a great bore, and, I need hardly say, a terrible disappointment to me, but the fact is I have just had a telegram to say that my poor friend Bunbury is very ill again. [*Exchanges glances with* JACK.] They seem to think I should be with him.

LADY BRACKNELL: It is very strange. This Mr Bunbury seems to suffer from curiously bad health.

ALGERNON: Yes; poor Bunbury is a dreadful invalid.

LADY BRACKNELL: Well, I must say, Algernon, that I think it is high time that Mr Bunbury made up his mind whether he was going to live or to die. This shilly-shallying with the question is absurd. Nor do I in any way approve of the modern sympathy with invalids. I consider it morbid. Illness of any kind is hardly a thing to be encouraged in others. Health is the primary duty of life. I am always telling that to your poor uncle, but he never seems to take much notice . . . as far as any improvement in his ailments goes. I should be much obliged if you would ask Mr Bunbury, from me, to be kind enough not to have a relapse on Saturday, for I rely on you to arrange my music for me. It is my last reception, and one wants something that will encourage conversation, particularly at the end of the season when everyone has practically said whatever they had to say, which, in most cases, was probably not much.

ALGERNON: I'll speak to Bunbury, Aunt Augusta, if he is still conscious, and I think I can promise you he'll be all right by Saturday. Of course the music is a great difficulty. You see, if one plays good music, people don't listen, and if one plays bad music people don't talk. But I'll run over the programme I've drawn out, if you will kindly come into the next room for a moment.

LADY BRACKNELL: Thank you, Algernon. It is very thoughtful of you. [*Rising, and following* ALGERNON.] I'm sure the programme will be delightful, after a few expurgations. French songs I cannot possibly allow. People always seem to think that they are improper, and either look shocked, which is vulgar, or laugh, which is worse. But German sounds a thoroughly respectable language, and indeed, I believe is so. Gwendolen, you will accompany me.

GWENDOLEN: Certainly, mamma.

[LADY BRACKNELL *and* ALGERNON *go into the music-room,* GWENDOLEN *remains behind.*]

JACK: Charming day it has been, Miss Fairfax.

GWENDOLEN: Pray don't talk to me about the weather, Mr Worthing. Whenever people talk to me about the weather, I always feel quite certain that they mean something else. And that makes me so nervous.

JACK: I do mean something else.

GWENDOLEN: I thought so. In fact, I am never wrong.

JACK: And I would like to be allowed to take advantage of Lady Bracknell's temporary absence . . .

GWENDOLEN: I would certainly advise you to do so. Mamma has a way of coming back suddenly into a room that I have often had to speak to her about.

JACK [*Nervously.*]: Miss Fairfax, ever since I met you I have admired you more than any girl . . . I have ever met since . . . I met you.

GWENDOLEN: Yes, I am quite aware of the fact. And I often wish that in public, at any rate, you had been more demonstrative. For me you have always had an irresistible fascination. Even before I met you I was far from indifferent to you. [JACK *looks at her in amazement.*] We live, as I hope you know, Mr Worthing, in an age of ideals. The fact is constantly mentioned in the more expensive monthly magazines, and has reached the provincial pulpits I am told: and my ideal has always been to love some one of the name of Ernest. There is something in that name that inspires absolute confidence. The moment Algernon first mentioned to me that he had a friend called Ernest, I knew I was destined to love you.

JACK: You really love me, Gwendolen?

GWENDOLEN: Passionately!

JACK: Darling! You don't know how happy you've made me.

GWENDOLEN: My own Ernest!

JACK: But you don't really mean to say that you couldn't love me if my name wasn't Ernest?

GWENDOLEN: But your name is Ernest.

JACK: Yes, I know it is. But supposing it was something else? Do you mean to say you couldn't love me then?

GWENDOLEN [*Glibly.*]: Ah! that is clearly a metaphysical speculation, and like most metaphysical speculations has very little reference at all to the actual facts of real life, as we know them.

JACK: Personally, darling, to speak quite candidly, I don't much care about the name of Ernest . . . I don't think the name suits me at all.

GWENDOLEN: It suits you perfectly. It is a divine name. It has a music of its own. It produces vibrations.

JACK: Well, really, Gwendolen, I must say that I think there are lots of other much nicer names. I think Jack, for instance, a charming name.

GWENDOLEN: Jack? . . . No, there is very little music in the name Jack, if any at all, indeed. It does not thrill. It produces absolutely no vibrations. . . . I have known several Jacks, and they all, without exception, were more than usually plain. Besides, Jack is a notorious domesticity for John! And I pity any woman who is married to a man called John. She would probably never be allowed to know the entrancing pleasure of a single moment's solitude. The only really safe name is Ernest.

JACK: Gwendolen, I must get christened at once—I mean we must get married at once. There is no time to be lost.

GWENDOLEN: Married, Mr Worthing?

JACK [*Astounded.*]: Well . . . surely. You know that I love you, and you led me to believe, Miss Fairfax, that you were not absolutely indifferent to me.

GWENDOLEN: I adore you. But you haven't proposed to me yet. Nothing has been said at all about marriage. The subject has not even been touched on.

JACK: Well . . . may I propose to you now?

GWENDOLEN: I think it would be an admirable opportunity. And to spare you any possible disappointment, Mr Worthing, I think it only fair to tell you quite frankly beforehand that I am fully determined to accept you.

JACK: Gwendolen!

GWENDOLEN: Yes, Mr Worthing, what have you got to say to me?

JACK: You know what I have got to say to you.

GWENDOLEN: Yes, but you don't say it.

JACK: Gwendolen, will you marry me? [*Goes on his knees.*]

GWENDOLEN: Of course I will, darling. How long you have been about it! I am afraid you have had very little experience in how to propose.

JACK: My own one, I have never loved anyone in the world but you.

GWENDOLEN: Yes, but men often propose for practice. I know my brother Gerald does. All my girl-friends tell me so. What wonderfully blue eyes you have, Ernest! They are quite, quite, blue. I hope you will always look at me just like that, especially when there are other people present.

[*Enter* LADY BRACKNELL.]

LADY BRACKNELL: Mr Worthing! Rise, sir, from this semi-recumbent posture. It is most indecorous.

GWENDOLEN: Mamma! [*He tries to rise; she restrains him.*] I must beg you to retire. This is no place for you. Besides, Mr Worthing has not quite finished yet.

LADY BRACKNELL: Finished what, may I ask?

GWENDOLEN: I am engaged to Mr Worthing, mamma. [*They rise together.*]

LADY BRACKNELL: Pardon me, you are not engaged to anyone. When you do become engaged to some one, I, or your father, should his health permit him, will inform you of the fact. An engagement should come on a young girl as a surprise, pleasant or unpleasant, as the case may be. It is hardly a matter that she could be allowed to arrange for herself. . . . And now I have a few questions to put to you, Mr Worthing. While I am making these inquiries, you, Gwendolen, will wait for me below in the carriage.

GWENDOLEN [*Reproachfully.*]: Mamma!

LADY BRACKNELL: In the carriage, Gwendolen! [GWENDOLEN *goes to the door. She and* JACK *blow kisses to each other behind* LADY BRACKNELL'*s back.* LADY BRACKNELL *looks vaguely about as if she could not understand what the noise was. Finally turns round.*] Gwendolen, the carriage!

GWENDOLEN: Yes, mamma.

[*Goes out, looking back at* JACK.]

LADY BRACKNELL [*Sitting down.*]: You can take a seat, Mr Worthing. [*Looks in her pocket for note-book and pencil.*]

JACK: Thank you, Lady Bracknell, I prefer standing.

LADY BRACKNELL [*Pencil and note-book in hand.*]: I feel bound to tell you that you are not down on my list of eligible young men, although I have the same list as the dear Duchess of Bolton has. We work together, in fact. However, I am quite ready to enter your name, should your answers be what a really affectionate mother requires. Do you smoke?

JACK: Well, yes, I must admit I smoke.

LADY BRACKNELL: I am glad to hear it. A man should always have an occupation of some kind. There are far too many idle men in London as it is. How old are you?

JACK: Twenty-nine.

LADY BRACKNELL: A very good age to be married at. I have always been of the opinion that a man who desires to get married should know either everything or nothing. Which do you know?

JACK [*After some hesitation.*]: I know nothing, Lady Bracknell.

LADY BRACKNELL: I am pleased to hear it. I do not approve of anything that tampers with natural ignorance. Ignorance is like a delicate exotic fruit; touch it and the bloom is gone. The whole theory of modern education is radically unsound. Fortunately in England, at any rate, education produces no effect whatsoever. If it did, it would prove a serious danger to the upper classes, and probably lead to acts of violence in Grosvenor Square. What is your income?

JACK: Between seven and eight thousand a year.

LADY BRACKNELL [*Makes a note in her book.*]: In land, or in investments?

JACK: In investments, chiefly.

LADY BRACKNELL: That is satisfactory. What between the duties expected of one during one's lifetime, and the duties exacted from one after one's death, land has ceased to be either a profit or a pleasure. It gives one position, and prevents one from keeping it up. That's all that can be said about land.

JACK: I have a country house with some land, of course, attached to it, about fifteen hundred acres, I believe; but I don't depend on that for my real income. In fact, as far as I can make out, the poachers are the only people who make anything out of it.

LADY BRACKNELL: A country house! How many bedrooms? Well, that point can be cleared up afterwards. You have a town house, I hope? A girl with a simple, unspoiled nature, like Gwendolen, could hardly be expected to reside in the country.

JACK: Well, I own a house in Belgrave Square, but it is let by the year to Lady Bloxham. Of course, I can get it back whenever I like, at six months' notice.

LADY BRACKNELL: Lady Bloxham? I don't know her.

JACK: Oh, she goes about very little. She is a lady considerably advanced in years.

LADY BRACKNELL: Ah, nowadays that is no guarantee of respectability of character. What number in Belgrave Square?

JACK: 149.

LADY BRACKNELL [*Shaking her head.*]: The unfashionable side. I thought there was something. However, that could easily be altered.

JACK: Do you mean the fashion, or the side?

LADY BRACKNELL [*Sternly.*]: Both, if necessary, I presume. What are your politics?

JACK: Well, I am afraid I really have none. I am a Liberal Unionist.

LADY BRACKNELL: Oh, they count as Tories. They dine with us. Or come in the evening, at any rate. Now to minor matters. Are your parents living?

JACK: I have lost both my parents.

LADY BRACKNELL: Both? To lose one parent may be regarded as a misfortune—to lose *both* seems like carelessness. Who was your father? He was evidently a man of some wealth. Was he born in what the Radical papers call the purple of commerce, or did he rise from the ranks of the aristocracy?

JACK: I am afraid I really don't know. The fact is, Lady Bracknell, I said I had lost my parents. It would be nearer the truth to say that my parents seem to have lost me . . . I don't actually know who I am by birth. I was . . . well, I was found.

LADY BRACKNELL: Found!

JACK: The late Mr Thomas Cardew, an old gentleman of a very charitable and kindly disposition, found me, and gave me the name of Worthing, because he happened to have a first-class ticket for Worthing in his pocket at the time. Worthing is a place in Sussex. It is a seaside resort.

LADY BRACKNELL: Where did the charitable gentleman who had a first-class ticket for this seaside resort find you?

JACK [*Gravely.*]: In a hand-bag.

LADY BRACKNELL: A hand-bag?

JACK [*Very seriously.*]: Yes, Lady Bracknell. I was in a hand-bag—a somewhat large, black leather hand-bag, with handles to it—an ordinary hand-bag in fact.

LADY BRACKNELL: In what locality did this Mr James, or Thomas, Cardew come across this ordinary hand-bag?

JACK: In the cloak-room at Victoria Station. It was given to him in mistake for his own.

LADY BRACKNELL: The cloak-room at Victoria Station?

JACK: Yes. The Brighton line.

LADY BRACKNELL: The line is immaterial. Mr Worthing, I confess I feel somewhat bewildered by what you have just told me. To be born, or at any rate bred, in a hand-bag, whether it had handles or not, seems to me to display a contempt for the ordinary decencies of family life that reminds one of the worst excesses of the French Revolution. And I presume you know what that unfortunate movement led to? As for the particular locality in which the hand-bag was found, a cloak-room at a railway station might serve to conceal a social indiscretion—has probably, indeed, been used for that purpose before now—but it could hardly be regarded as an assured basis for a recognized position in good society.

JACK: May I ask you then what you would advise me to do? I need hardly say I would do anything in the world to ensure Gwendolen's happiness.

LADY BRACKNELL: I would strongly advise you, Mr Worthing, to try and acquire some relations as soon as possible, and to make a definite effort to produce at any rate one parent, of either sex, before the season is quite over.

JACK: Well, I don't see how I could possibly manage to do that. I can produce the hand-bag at any moment. It is in my dressing-room at home. I really think that should satisfy you, Lady Bracknell.

LADY BRACKNELL: Me, sir! What has it to do with me? You can hardly imagine that I and Lord Bracknell would dream of allowing our only daughter—a girl brought up with the utmost care—to marry into a cloak-room, and form an alliance with a parcel? Good morning, Mr Worthing!

[LADY BRACKNELL *sweeps out in majestic indignation.*]

JACK: Good morning! [ALGERNON, *from the other room, strikes up the Wedding March.* JACK *looks perfectly furious, and goes to the door.*] For goodness' sake don't play that ghastly tune, Algy! How idiotic you are!

[*The music stops, and* ALGERNON *enters cheerily.*]

ALGERNON: Didn't it go off all right, old boy? You don't mean to say Gwendolen refused you? I know it is a way she has. She is always refusing people. I think it is most ill-natured of her.

JACK: Oh, Gwendolen is as right as a trivet. As far as she is concerned, we are engaged. Her mother is perfectly unbearable. Never met such a Gorgon . . . I don't really know what a Gorgon is like, but I am quite sure that Lady Bracknell is one. In any case, she is a monster, without being a myth, which is rather unfair . . . I beg your pardon, Algy, I suppose I shouldn't talk about your own aunt in that way before you.

ALGERNON: My dear boy, I love hearing my relations abused. It is the only thing that makes me put up with them at all. Relations are simply a tedious pack of people, who haven't got the remotest knowledge of how to live, nor the smallest instinct about when to die.

JACK: Oh, that is nonsense!

ALGERNON: It isn't!

JACK: Well, I won't argue about the matter. You always want to argue about things.

ALGERNON: That is exactly what things were originally made for.

JACK: Upon my word, if I thought that, I'd shoot myself . . . [*A pause.*] You don't think there is any chance of Gwendolen becoming like her mother in about a hundred and fifty years, do you Algy?

ALGERNON: All women become like their mothers. That is their tragedy. No man does. That's his.

JACK: Is that clever?

ALGERNON: It is perfectly phrased! and quite as true as any observation in civilized life should be.

JACK: I am sick to death of cleverness. Everybody is clever nowadays. You can't go anywhere without meeting clever people. The thing has become an absolute public nuisance. I wish to goodness we had a few fools left.

ALGERNON: We have.

JACK: I should extremely like to meet them. What do they talk about?

ALGERNON: The fools? Oh! about the clever people, of course.

JACK: What fools!

ALGERNON: By the way, did you tell Gwendolen the truth about your being Ernest in town, and Jack in the country?

JACK [*In a very patronizing manner.*]: My dear fellow, the truth isn't quite the sort of thing one tells to a nice sweet refined girl. What extraordinary ideas you have about the way to behave to a woman!

ALGERNON: The only way to behave to a woman is to make love to her, if she is pretty, and to someone else if she is plain.

JACK: Oh, that is nonsense.

ALGERNON: What about your brother? What about the profligate Ernest?

JACK: Oh, before the end of the week I shall have got rid of him. I'll say he died in Paris of apoplexy. Lots of people die of apoplexy, quite suddenly, don't they?

ALGERNON: Yes, but it's hereditary, my dear fellow. It's a sort of thing that runs in families. You had much better say a severe chill.

JACK: You are sure a severe chill isn't hereditary, or anything of that kind?

ALGERNON: Of course it isn't!

JACK: Very well, then. My poor brother Ernest is carried off suddenly in Paris, by a severe chill. That gets rid of him.

ALGERNON: But I thought you said that . . . Miss Cardew was a little too much interested in your poor brother Ernest? Won't she feel his loss a good deal?

JACK: Oh, that is all right. Cecily is not a silly romantic girl, I am glad to say. She has got a capital appetite, goes on long walks, and pays no attention at all to her lessons.

ALGERNON: I would rather like to see Cecily.

JACK: I will take very good care you never do. She is excessively pretty, and she is only just eighteen.

ALGERNON: Have you told Gwendolen yet that you have an excessively pretty ward who is only just eighteen?

JACK: Oh! one doesn't blurt these things out to people. Cecily and Gwendolen are perfectly certain to be extremely great friends. I'll bet you anything you like that half an hour after they have met, they will be calling each other sister.

ALGERNON: Women only do that when they have called each other a lot of other things first. Now, my dear boy, if we want to get a good table at Willis's, we really must go and dress. Do you know it is nearly seven?

JACK [*Irritably.*]: Oh! it always is nearly seven.

ALGERNON: Well, I'm hungry.

JACK: I never knew you when you weren't. . . .

ALGERNON: What shall we do after dinner? Go to a theatre?

JACK: Oh no! I loathe listening.
ALGERNON: Well, let us go to the Club?
JACK: Oh, no! I hate talking.
ALGERNON: Well, we might trot round to the Empire at ten?
JACK: Oh no! I can't bear looking at things. It is so silly.
ALGERNON: Well, what shall we do?
JACK: Nothing!
ALGERNON: It is awfully hard work doing nothing. However, I don't mind hard work where there is no definite object of any kind.

[*Enter* LANE.]

LANE: Miss Fairfax.

[*Enter* GWENDOLEN. LANE *goes out*.]

ALGERNON: Gwendolen, upon my word!
GWENDOLEN: Algy, kindly turn your back. I have something very particular to say to Mr Worthing.
ALGERNON: Really, Gwendolen, I don't think I can allow this at all.
GWENDOLEN: Algy, you always adopt a strictly immoral attitude towards life. You are not quite old enough to do that.

[ALGERNON *retires to the fireplace*.]

JACK: My own darling!
GWENDOLEN: Ernest, we may never be married. From the expression on mamma's face I fear we never shall. Few parents nowadays pay any regard to what their children say to them. The old-fashioned respect for the young is fast dying out. Whatever influence I ever had over mamma, I lost at the age of three. But although she may prevent us from becoming man and wife, and I may marry someone else, and marry often, nothing that she can possibly do can alter my eternal devotion to you.
JACK: Dear Gwendolen!
GWENDOLEN: The story of your romantic origin, as related to me by mamma, with unpleasing comments, has naturally stirred the deeper fibres of my nature. Your Christian name has an irresistible fascination. The simplicity of your character makes you exquisitely incomprehensible to me. Your town address at the Albany I have. What is your address in the country?
JACK: The Manor House, Woolton, Hertfordshire.

[ALGERNON, *who has been carefully listening, smiles to himself, and writes the address on his shirt-cuff. Then picks up the Railway Guide*.]

GWENDOLEN: There is a good postal service, I suppose? It may be necessary to do something desperate. That of course will require serious consideration. I will communicate with you daily.
JACK: My own one!
GWENDOLEN: How long do you remain in town?
JACK: Till Monday.
GWENDOLEN: Good! Algy, you may turn round now.
ALGERNON: Thanks, I've turned round already.
GWENDOLEN: You may also ring the bell.
JACK: You will let me see you to your carriage, my own darling?
GWENDOLEN: Certainly.
JACK [*To* LANE, *who now enters*.]: I will see Miss Fairfax out.
LANE: Yes, sir.

[JACK *and* GWENDOLEN *go off*.]

[LANE *presents several letters on a salver to* ALGERNON. *It is to be surmised that they are bills, as* ALGERNON, *after looking at the envelopes, tears them up*.]

ALGERNON: A glass of sherry, Lane.
LANE: Yes, sir.
ALGERNON: Tomorrow, Lane, I'm going Bunburying.
LANE: Yes, sir.
ALGERNON: I shall probably not be back till Monday. You can put up my dress clothes, my smoking jacket, and all the Bunbury suits . . .
LANE: Yes, sir. [*Handing sherry*.]
ALGERNON: I hope tomorrow will be a fine day, Lane.
LANE: It never is, sir.
ALGERNON: Lane, you're a perfect pessimist.
LANE: I do my best to give satisfaction, sir.

[*Enter* JACK. LANE *goes off*.]

JACK: There's a sensible, intellectual girl! the only girl I ever cared for in my life. [ALGERNON *is laughing immoderately*.] What on earth are you so amused at?
ALGERNON: Oh, I'm a little anxious about poor Bunbury, that is all.
JACK: If you don't take care, your friend Bunbury will get you into a serious scrape some day.
ALGERNON: I love scrapes. They are the only things that are never serious.
JACK: Oh, that's nonsense, Algy. You never talk anything but nonsense.
ALGERNON: Nobody ever does.

[JACK *looks indignantly at him, and leaves the room.* ALGERNON *lights a cigarette, reads his shirt-cuff, and smiles*.]

ACT DROP

ACT II

SCENE. Garden at the Manor House. A flight of gray stone steps leads up to the house. The garden, an old-fashioned one, full of roses. Time of year, July. Basket chairs, and a table covered with books, are set under a large yew tree.

[MISS PRISM *discovered seated at the table.* CECILY *is at the back watering flowers.*]

MISS PRISM [*Calling.*]: Cecily, Cecily! Surely such a utilitarian occupation as the watering of flowers is rather Moulton's duty than yours? Especially at a moment when intellectual pleasures await you. Your German grammar is on the table. Pray open it at page fifteen. We will repeat yesterday's lesson.

CECILY [*Coming over very slowly.*]: But I don't like German. It isn't at all a becoming language. I know perfectly well that I look quite plain after my German lesson.

MISS PRISM: Child, you know how anxious your guardian is that you should improve yourself in every way. He laid particular stress on your German, as he was leaving for town yesterday. Indeed, he always lays stress on your German when he is leaving for town.

CECILY: Dear Uncle Jack is so very serious! Sometimes he is so serious that I think he cannot be quite well.

MISS PRISM [*Drawing herself up.*]: Your guardian enjoys the best of health, and his gravity of demeanour is especially to be commended in one so comparatively young as he is. I know no one who has a higher sense of duty and responsibility.

CECILY: I suppose that is why he often looks a little bored when we three are together.

MISS PRISM: Cecily! I am surprised at you. Mr Worthing has many troubles in his life. Idle merriment and triviality would be out of place in his conversation. You must remember his constant anxiety about that unfortunate young man his brother.

CECILY: I wish Uncle Jack would allow that unfortunate young man, his brother, to come down here sometimes. We might have a good influence over him, Miss Prism. I am sure you certainly would. You know German, and geology, and things of that kind influence a man very much. [CECILY *begins to write in her diary.*]

MISS PRISM [*Shaking her head.*]: I do not think that even I could produce any effect on a character that according to his own brother's admission is irretrievably weak and vacillating. Indeed I am not sure that I would desire to reclaim him. I am not in favour of this modern mania for turning bad people into good people at a moment's notice. As a man sows, so let him reap. You must put away your diary, Cecily. I really don't see why you should keep a diary at all.

CECILY: I keep a diary in order to enter the wonderful secrets of my life. If I didn't write them down I should probably forget all about them.

MISS PRISM: Memory, my dear Cecily, is the diary that we all carry about with us.

CECILY: Yes, but it usually chronicles the things that have never happened, and couldn't possibly have happened. I believe that Memory is responsible for nearly all the three-volume novels that Mudie sends us.

MISS PRISM: Do not speak slightingly of the three-volume novel, Cecily. I wrote one myself in earlier days.

CECILY: Did you really, Miss Prism? How wonderfully clever you are! I hope it did not end happily? I don't like novels that end happily. They depress me so much.

MISS PRISM: The good ended happily, and the bad unhappily. That is what Fiction means.

CECILY: I suppose so. But it seems very unfair. And was your novel ever published?

MISS PRISM: Alas! no. The manuscript unfortunately was abandoned. I used the word in the sense of lost or mislaid. To your work, child, these speculations are profitless.

CECILY [*Smiling.*]: But I see dear Dr Chasuble coming up through the garden.

MISS PRISM [*Rising and advancing.*]: Dr Chasuble! This is indeed a pleasure.

[*Enter* CANON CHASUBLE.]

CHASUBLE: And how are we this morning? Miss Prism, you are, I trust, well?

CECILY: Miss Prism has just been complaining of a slight headache. I think it would do her so much good to have a short stroll with you in the Park, Dr Chasuble.

MISS PRISM: Cecily, I have not mentioned anything about a headache.

CECILY: No, dear Miss Prism, I know that, but I felt instinctively that you had a headache. Indeed I was thinking about that, and not about my German lesson, when the Rector came in.

CHASUBLE: I hope Cecily, you are not inattentive.

CECILY: Oh, I am afraid I am.

CHASUBLE: That is strange. Were I fortunate enough to be Miss Prism's pupil, I would hang upon her lips. [MISS PRISM *glares.*] I spoke metaphorically.—My metaphor was drawn from bees. Ahem! Mr

Worthing, I suppose, has not returned from town yet?

MISS PRISM: We do not expect him till Monday afternoon.

CHASUBLE: Ah yes, he usually likes to spend his Sunday in London. He is not one of those whose sole aim is enjoyment, as, by all accounts, that unfortunate young man his brother seems to be. But I must not disturb Egeria and her pupil any longer.

MISS PRISM: Egeria? My name is Lætitia, Doctor.

CHASUBLE [*Bowing.*]: A classical allusion merely, drawn from the Pagan authors. I shall see you both no doubt at Evensong?

MISS PRISM: I think, dear Doctor, I will have a stroll with you. I find I have a headache after all, and a walk might do it good.

CHASUBLE: With pleasure, Miss Prism, with pleasure. We might go as far as the schools and back.

MISS PRISM: That would be delightful. Cecily, you will read your Political Economy in my absence. The chapter on the Fall of the Rupee you may omit. It is somewhat too sensational. Even these metallic problems have their melodramatic side.

[*Goes down the garden with* DR CHASUBLE.]

CECILY [*Picks up books and throws them back on table.*]: Horrid Political Economy! Horrid Geography! Horrid, horrid German!

[*Enter* MERRIMAN *with a card on a salver.*]

MERRIMAN: Mr Ernest Worthing has just driven over from the station. He has brought his luggage with him.

CECILY [*Takes the card and reads it.*]: "Mr Ernest Worthing, B.4 The Albany, W." Uncle Jack's brother! Did you tell him Mr Worthing was in town?

MERRIMAN: Yes, Miss. He seemed very much disappointed. I mentioned that you and Miss Prism were in the garden. He said he was anxious to speak to you privately for a moment.

CECILY: Ask Mr Ernest Worthing to come here. I suppose you had better talk to the housekeeper about a room for him.

MERRIMAN: Yes, Miss.

[MERRIMAN *goes off.*]

CECILY: I have never met any really wicked person before. I feel rather frightened. I am so afraid he will look just like everyone else.

[*Enter* ALGERNON, *very gay and debonnair.*]

He does!

ALGERNON [*Raising his hat.*]: You are my little cousin Cecily, I'm sure.

CECILY: You are under some strange mistake. I am not little. In fact, I believe I am more than usually tall for my age. [ALGERNON *is rather taken aback.*] But I am your cousin Cecily. You, I see from your card, are Uncle Jack's brother, my cousin Ernest, my wicked cousin Ernest.

ALGERNON: Oh! I am not really wicked at all, cousin Cecily. You mustn't think that I am wicked.

CECILY: If you are not, then you have certainly been deceiving us all in a very inexcusable manner. I hope you have not been leading a double life, pretending to be wicked and being really good all the time. That would be hypocrisy.

ALGERNON [*Looks at her in amazement.*]: Oh! Of course I have been rather reckless.

CECILY: I am glad to hear it.

ALGERNON: In fact, now you mention the subject, I have been very bad in my own small way.

CECILY: I don't think you should be so proud of that, although I am sure it must have been very pleasant.

ALGERNON: It is much pleasanter being here with you.

CECILY: I can't understand how you are here at all. Uncle Jack won't be back till Monday afternoon.

ALGERNON: That is a great disappointment. I am obliged to go up by the first train on Monday morning. I have a business appointment that I am anxious . . . to miss.

CECILY: Couldn't you miss it anywhere but in London?

ALGERNON: No: the appointment is in London.

CECILY: Well, I know, of course, how important it is not to keep a business engagement, if one wants to retain any sense of the beauty of life, but still I think you had better wait till Uncle Jack arrives. I know he wants to speak to you about your emigrating.

ALGERNON: About my what?

CECILY: Your emigrating. He has gone up to buy your outfit.

ALGERNON: I certainly wouldn't let Jack buy my outfit. He has no taste in neckties at all.

CECILY: I don't think you will require neckties. Uncle Jack is sending you to Australia.

ALGERNON: Australia! I'd sooner die.

CECILY: Well, he said at dinner on Wednesday night, that you would have to choose between this world, the next world, and Australia.

ALGERNON: Oh, well! The accounts I have received of Australia and the next world are not particularly encouraging. This world is good enough for me, cousin Cecily.

CECILY: Yes, but are you good enough for it?

ALGERNON: I'm afraid I'm not that. That is why I want you to reform me. You might make that your mission, if you don't mind, cousin Cecily.

CECILY: I'm afraid I've no time, this afternoon.

ALGERNON: Well, would you mind my reforming myself this afternoon?

CECILY: It is rather Quixotic of you. But I think you should try.

ALGERNON: I will. I feel better already.

CECILY: You are looking a little worse.

ALGERNON: That is because I am hungry.

CECILY: How thoughtless of me. I should have remembered that when one is going to lead an entirely new life, one requires regular and wholesome meals. Won't you come in?

ALGERNON: Thank you. Might I have a buttonhole first? I never have any appetite unless I have a buttonhole first.

CECILY: A Maréchal Niel? [*Picks up scissors.*]

ALGERNON: No, I'd sooner have a pink rose.

CECILY: Why? [*Cuts a flower.*]

ALGERNON: Because you are like a pink rose, cousin Cecily.

CECILY: I don't think it can be right for you to talk to me like that. Miss Prism never says such things to me.

ALGERNON: Then Miss Prism is a short-sighted old lady. [CECILY *puts the rose in his buttonhole.*] You are the prettiest girl I ever saw.

CECILY: Miss Prism says that all good looks are a snare.

ALGERNON: They are a snare that every sensible man would like to be caught in.

CECILY: Oh! I don't think I would care to catch a sensible man. I shouldn't know what to talk to him about.

[*They pass into the house.* MISS PRISM *and* DR CHASUBLE *return.*]

MISS PRISM: You are too much alone, dear Dr Chasuble. You should get married. A misanthrope I can understand—a womanthrope, never!

CHASUBLE [*With a scholar's shudder.*]: Believe me, I do not deserve so neologistic a phrase. The precept as well as the practice of the Primitive Church was distinctly against matrimony.

MISS PRISM [*Sententiously.*]: That is obviously the reason why the Primitive Church has not lasted up to the present day. And you do not seem to realize, dear Doctor, that by persistently remaining single, a man converts himself into a permanent public temptation. Men should be more careful; this very celibacy leads weaker vessels astray.

CHASUBLE: But is a man not equally attractive when married?

MISS PRISM: No married man is ever attractive except to his wife.

CHASUBLE: And often, I've been told, not even to her.

MISS PRISM: That depends on the intellectual sympathies of the woman. Maturity can always be depended on. Ripeness can be trusted. Young women are green. [DR CHASUBLE *starts.*] I spoke horticulturally. My metaphor was drawn from fruits. But where is Cecily?

CHASUBLE: Perhaps she followed us to the schools.

[*Enter* JACK *slowly from the back of the garden. He is dressed in the deepest mourning, with crape hat-band and black gloves.*]

MISS PRISM: Mr Worthing!

CHASUBLE: Mr Worthing?

MISS PRISM: This is indeed a surprise. We did not look for you till Monday afternoon.

JACK [*Shakes* MISS PRISM*'s hand in a tragic manner.*]: I have returned sooner than I expected. Dr Chasuble, I hope you are well?

CHASUBLE: Dear Mr Worthing, I trust this garb of woe does not betoken some terrible calamity?

JACK: My brother.

MISS PRISM: More shameful debts and extravagance?

CHASUBLE: Still leading his life of pleasure?

JACK [*Shaking his head.*]: Dead!

CHASUBLE: Your brother Ernest dead?

JACK: Quite dead.

MISS PRISM: What a lesson for him! I trust he will profit by it.

CHASUBLE: Mr Worthing, I offer you my sincere condolence. You have at least the consolation of knowing that you were always the most generous and forgiving of brothers.

JACK: Poor Ernest! He had many faults, but it is a sad, sad blow.

CHASUBLE: Very sad indeed. Were you with him at the end?

JACK: No. He died abroad; in Paris, in fact. I had a telegram last night from the manager of the Grand Hotel.

CHASUBLE: Was the cause of death mentioned?

JACK: A severe chill, it seems.

MISS PRISM: As a man sows, so shall he reap.

CHASUBLE [*Raising his hand.*]: Charity, dear Miss Prism, charity! None of us are perfect. I myself am peculiarly susceptible to draughts. Will the interment take place here?

JACK: No. He seemed to have expressed a desire to be buried in Paris.

CHASUBLE: In Paris! [*Shakes his head.*] I fear that hardly points to any very serious state of mind at the last. You would no doubt wish me to make some slight allusion to this tragic domestic affliction next

Sunday. [JACK *presses his hand convulsively.*] My sermon on the meaning of the manna in the wilderness can be adapted to almost any occasion, joyful, or, as in the present case, distressing. [*All sigh.*] I have preached it at harvest celebrations, christenings, confirmations, on days of humiliation and festal days. The last time I delivered it was in the Cathedral, as a charity sermon on behalf of the Society for the Prevention of Discontent among the Upper Orders. The Bishop, who was present, was much struck by some of the analogies I drew.

JACK: Ah! that reminds me, you mentioned christenings I think, Dr Chasuble? I suppose you know how to christen all right? [DR CHASUBLE *looks astounded.*] I mean, of course, you are continually christening, aren't you?

MISS PRISM: It is, I regret to say, one of the Rector's most constant duties in this parish. I have often spoken to the poorer classes on the subject. But they don't seem to know what thrift is.

CHASUBLE: But is there any particular infant in whom you are interested, Mr Worthing? Your brother was, I believe, unmarried, was he not?

JACK: Oh, yes.

MISS PRISM [*Bitterly.*]: People who live entirely for pleasure usually are.

JACK: But it is not for any child, dear Doctor. I am very fond of children. No! the fact is, I would like to be christened myself, this afternoon, if you have nothing better to do.

CHASUBLE: But surely, Mr Worthing, you have been christened already?

JACK: I don't remember anything about it.

CHASUBLE: But have you any grave doubts on the subject?

JACK: I certainly intend to have. Of course I don't know if the thing would bother you in any way, or if you think I am a little too old now.

CHASUBLE: Not at all. The sprinkling, and, indeed, the immersion of adults is a perfectly canonical practice.

JACK: Immersion!

CHASUBLE: You need have no apprehensions. Sprinkling is all that is necessary, or indeed I think advisable. Our weather is so changeable. At what hour would you wish the ceremony performed?

JACK: Oh, I might trot round about five if that would suit you.

CHASUBLE: Perfectly, perfectly! In fact I have two similar ceremonies to perform at that time. A case of twins that occurred recently in one of the outlying cottages on your own estate. Poor Jenkins the carter, a most hard-working man.

JACK: Oh! I don't see much fun in being christened along with other babies. It would be childish. Would half-past five do?

CHASUBLE: Admirably! Admirably! [*Takes out watch.*] And now, dear Mr Worthing, I will not intrude any longer into a house of sorrow. I would merely beg you not to be too much bowed down by grief. What seem to us bitter trials are often blessings in disguise.

MISS PRISM: This seems to me a blessing of an extremely obvious kind.

[*Enter* CECILY *from the house.*]

CECILY: Uncle Jack! Oh, I am pleased to see you back. But what horrid clothes you have got on! Do go and change them.

MISS PRISM: Cecily!

CHASUBLE: My child! my child!

[CECILY *goes towards* JACK; *he kisses her brow in a melancholy manner.*]

CECILY: What is the matter, Uncle Jack? Do look happy! You look as if you had a toothache, and I have got such a surprise for you. Who do you think is in the dining-room? Your brother!

JACK: Who?

CECILY: Your brother Ernest. He arrived about half an hour ago.

JACK: What nonsense! I haven't got a brother.

CECILY: Oh, don't say that. However badly he may have behaved to you in the past he is still your brother. You couldn't be so heartless as to disown him. I'll tell him to come out. And you will shake hands with him, won't you, Uncle Jack?

[*Runs back into the house.*]

CHASUBLE: These are very joyful tidings.

MISS PRISM: After we had all been resigned to his loss, his sudden return seems to me peculiarly distressing.

JACK: My brother is in the dining-room? I don't know what it all means. I think it is perfectly absurd.

[*Enter* ALGERNON *and* CECILY *hand in hand. They come slowly up to* JACK.]

JACK: Good heavens! [*Motions* ALGERNON *away.*]

ALGERNON: Brother John, I have come down from town to tell you that I am very sorry for all the trouble I have given you, and that I intend to lead a better life in the future.

[JACK *glares at him and does not take his hand.*]

CECILY: Uncle Jack, you are not going to refuse your own brother's hand?

JACK: Nothing will induce me to take his hand. I think his coming down here disgraceful. He knows perfectly well why.

CECILY: Uncle Jack, do be nice. There is some good in everyone. Ernest has just been telling me about his poor invalid friend Mr Bunbury whom he goes to visit so often. And surely there must be much good in one who is kind to an invalid, and leaves the pleasures of London to sit by a bed of pain.

JACK: Oh! he has been talking about Bunbury has he?

CECILY: Yes, he has told me all about poor Mr Bunbury, and his terrible state of health.

JACK: Bunbury! Well, I won't have him talk to you about Bunbury or about anything else. It is enough to drive one perfectly frantic.

ALGERNON: Of course I admit that the faults were all on my side. But I must say that I think that Brother John's coldness to me is peculiarly painful. I expected a more enthusiastic welcome, especially considering it is the first time I have come here.

CECILY: Uncle Jack, if you don't shake hands with Ernest I will never forgive you.

JACK: Never forgive me?

CECILY: Never, never, never!

JACK: Well, this is the last time I shall ever do it. [*Shakes hands with* ALGERNON *and glares*.]

CHASUBLE: It's pleasant, is it not, to see so perfect a reconciliation? I think we might leave the two brothers together.

MISS PRISM: Cecily, you will come with us.

CECILY: Certainly, Miss Prism. My little task of reconciliation is over.

CHASUBLE: You have done a beautiful action today, dear child.

MISS PRISM: We must not be premature in our judgments.

CECILY: I feel very happy.

[*They all go off.*]

JACK: You young scoundrel, Algy, you must get out of this place as soon as possible. I don't allow any Bunburying here.

[*Enter* MERRIMAN.]

MERRIMAN: I have put Mr Ernest's things in the room next to yours, sir. I suppose that is all right?

JACK: What?

MERMAN: Mr Ernest's luggage, sir. I have unpacked it and put it in the room next to your own.

JACK: His luggage?

MERRIMAN: Yes, sir. Three portmanteaus, a dressing-case, two hat-boxes, and a large luncheon-basket.

ALGERNON: I am afraid I can't stay more than a week this time.

JACK: Merriman, order the dog-cart at once. Mr Ernest has been suddenly called back to town.

MERRIMAN: Yes, sir.

[*Goes back into the house.*]

ALGERNON: What a fearful liar you are, Jack. I have not been called back to town at all.

JACK: Yes, you have.

ALGERNON: I haven't heard anyone call me.

JACK: Your duty as a gentleman calls you back.

ALGERNON: My duty as a gentleman has never interfered with my pleasures in the smallest degree.

JACK: I can quite understand that.

ALGERNON: Well, Cecily is a darling.

JACK: You are not to talk of Miss Cardew like that. I don't like it.

ALGERNON: Well I don't like your clothes. You look perfectly ridiculous in them. Why on earth don't you go up and change? It is perfectly childish to be in deep mourning for a man who is actually staying for a whole week with you in your house as a guest. I call it grotesque.

JACK: You are certainly not staying with me for a whole week as a guest or anything else. You have got to leave . . . by the four-five train.

ALGERNON: I certainly won't leave you so long as you are in mourning. It would be most unfriendly. If I were in mourning you would stay with me, I suppose. I should think it very unkind if you didn't.

JACK: Well, will you go if I change my clothes?

ALGERNON: Yes, if you are not too long. I never saw anybody take so long to dress, and with such little result.

JACK: Well, at any rate, that is better than being always over-dressed as you are.

ALGERNON: If I am occasionally a little over-dressed, I make up for it by being always immensely over-educated.

JACK: Your vanity is ridiculous, your conduct an outrage, and your presence in my garden utterly absurd. However, you have got to catch the four-five, and I hope you will have a pleasant journey back to town. This Bunburying, as you call it, has not been a great success for you.

[*Goes into the house.*]

ALGERNON: I think it has been a great success. I'm in love with Cecily, and that is everything.

[*Enter* CECILY *at the back of the garden. She picks up the can and begins to water the flowers.*]

But I must see her before I go, and make arrangements for another Bunbury. Ah, there she is.

CECILY: Oh, I merely came back to water the roses. I thought you were with Uncle Jack.
ALGERNON: He's gone to order the dog-cart for me.
CECILY: Oh, is he going to take you for a nice drive?
ALGERNON: He's going to send me away.
CECILY: Then have we got to part?
ALGERNON: I am afraid so. It's a painful parting.
CECILY: It is always painful to part from people whom one has known for a very brief space of time. The absence of old friends one can endure with equanimity. But even a momentary separation from anyone to whom one has just been introduced is almost unbearable.
ALGERNON: Thank you.

[*Enter* MERRIMAN.]

MERRIMAN: The dog-cart is at the door, sir.

[ALGERNON *looks appealingly at* CECILY.]

CECILY: It can wait, Merriman . . . for . . . five minutes.
MERRIMAN: Yes, Miss.

[*Exit* MERRIMAN.]

ALGERNON: I hope, Cecily, I shall not offend you if I state quite frankly and openly that you seem to me to be in every way the visible personification of absolute perfection.
CECILY: I think your frankness does you great credit, Ernest. If you will allow me I will copy your remarks into my diary. [*Goes over to table and begins writing in diary.*]
ALGERNON: Do you really keep a diary? I'd give anything to look at it. May I?
CECILY: Oh no. [*Puts her hand over it.*] You see, it is simply a very young girl's record of her own thoughts and impressions, and consequently meant for publication. When it appears in volume form I hope you will order a copy. But pray, Ernest, don't stop. I delight in taking down from dictation. I have reached 'absolute perfection'. You can go on. I am quite ready for more.
ALGERNON [*Somewhat taken aback.*]: Ahem! Ahem!
CECILY: Oh, don't cough, Ernest. When one is dictating one should speak fluently and not cough. Besides, I don't know how to spell a cough. [*Writes as* ALGERNON *speaks.*]
ALGERNON [*Speaking very rapidly.*]: Cecily, ever since I first looked upon your wonderful and incomparable beauty, I have dared to love you wildly, passionately, devotedly, hopelessly.
CECILY: I don't think that you should tell me that you love me wildly, passionately, devotedly, hopelessly. Hopelessly doesn't seem to make much sense, does it?
ALGERNON: Cecily!

[*Enter* MERRIMAN.]

MERRIMAN: The dog-cart is waiting, sir.
ALGERNON: Tell it to come round next week, at the same hour.
MERRIMAN [*Looks at* CECILY, *who makes no sign.*]: Yes, sir.

[MERRIMAN *retires.*]

CECILY: Uncle Jack would be very much annoyed if he knew you were staying on till next week, at the same hour.
ALGERNON: Oh, I don't care about Jack. I don't care for anybody in the whole world but you. I love you, Cecily. You will marry me, won't you?
CECILY: You silly boy! Of course. Why, we have been engaged for the last three months.
ALGERNON: For the last three months?
CECILY: Yes, it will be exactly three months on Thursday.
ALGERNON: But how did we become engaged?
CECILY: Well, ever since dear Uncle Jack first confessed to us that he had a younger brother who was very wicked and bad, you of course have formed the chief topic of conversation between myself and Miss Prism. And of course a man who is much talked about is always very attractive. One feels there must be something in him after all. I daresay it was foolish of me, but I fell in love with you, Ernest.
ALGERNON: Darling! And when was the engagement actually settled?
CECILY: On the 14th of February last. Worn out by your entire ignorance of my existence, I determined to end the matter one way or the other, and after a long struggle with myself I accepted you under this dear old tree here. The next day I bought this little ring in your name, and this is the little bangle with the true lovers' knot I promised you always to wear.
ALGERNON: Did I give you this? It's very pretty, isn't it?
CECILY: Yes, you've wonderfully good taste, Ernest. It's the excuse I've always given for your leading such a bad life. And this is the box in which I keep all your dear letters. [*Kneels at table, opens box, and produces letters tied up with blue ribbon.*]
ALGERNON: My letters! But my own sweet Cecily, I have never written you any letters.
CECILY: You need hardly remind me of that, Ernest. I remember only too well that I was forced to write

your letters for you. I wrote always three times a week, and sometimes oftener.

ALGERNON: Oh, do let me read them, Cecily?

CECILY: Oh, I couldn't possibly. They would make you far too conceited. [*Replaces box.*] The three you wrote me after I had broken off the engagement are so beautiful, and so badly spelled, that even now I can hardly read them without crying a little.

ALGERNON: But was our engagement ever broken off?

CECILY: Of course it was. On the 22nd of last March. You can see the entry if you like. [*Shows diary.*] "Today I broke off my engagement with Ernest. I feel it is better to do so. The weather still continues charming."

ALGERNON: But why on earth did you break it off? What had I done? I had done nothing at all. Cecily, I am very much hurt indeed to hear you broke it off. Particularly when the weather was so charming.

CECILY: It would hardly have been a really serious engagement if it hadn't been broken off at least once. But I forgave you before the week was out.

ALGERNON [*Crossing to her, and kneeling.*]: What a perfect angel you are, Cecily.

CECILY: You dear romantic boy. [*He kisses her, she puts her fingers through his hair.*] I hope your hair curls naturally, does it?

ALGERNON: Yes, darling, with a little help from others.

CECILY: I am so glad.

ALGERNON: You'll never break off our engagement again, Cecily?

CECILY: I don't think I could break it off now that I have actually met you. Besides, of course, there is the question of your name.

ALGERNON: Yes, of course. [*Nervously.*]

CECILY: You must not laugh at me, darling, but it had always been a girlish dream of mine to love some one whose name was Ernest. [ALGERNON *rises,* CECILY *also.*] There is something in that name that seems to inspire absolute confidence. I pity any poor married woman whose husband is not called Ernest.

ALGERNON: But, my dear child, do you mean to say you could not love me if I had some other name?

CECILY: But what name?

ALGERNON: Oh, any name you like—Algernon—for instance . . .

CECILY: But I don't like the name of Algernon.

ALGERNON: Well, my own dear, sweet, loving little darling, I really can't see why you should object to the name of Algernon. It is not at all a bad name. In fact, it is rather an aristocratic name. Half of the chaps who get into the Bankruptcy Court are called Algernon. But seriously, Cecily . . . [*Moving to her*] . . . if my name was Algy, couldn't you love me?

CECILY [*Rising.*]: I might respect you, Ernest, I might admire your character, but I fear that I should not be able to give you my undivided attention.

ALGERNON: Ahem! Cecily! [*Picking up hat.*] Your Rector here is, I suppose, thoroughly experienced in the practice of all the rites and ceremonials of the Church?

CECILY: Oh yes. Dr Chasuble is a most learned man. He has never written a single book, so you can imagine how much he knows.

ALGERNON: I must see him at once on a most important christening—I mean on most important business.

CECILY: Oh!

ALGERNON: I shan't be away more than half an hour.

CECILY: Considering that we have been engaged since February the 14th, and that I only met you today for the first time, I think it is rather hard that you should leave me for so long a period as half an hour. Couldn't you make it twenty minutes?

ALGERNON: I'll be back in no time.

[*Kisses her and rushes down the garden.*]

CECILY: What an impetuous boy he is! I like his hair so much. I must enter his proposal in my diary.

[*Enter* MERRIMAN.]

MERRIMAN: A Miss Fairfax has just called to see Mr Worthing. On very important business Miss Fairfax states.

CECILY: Isn't Mr Worthing in his library?

MERRIMAN: Mr Worthing went over in the direction of the Rectory some time ago.

CECILY: Pray ask the lady to come out here; Mr Worthing is sure to be back soon. And you can bring tea.

MERRIMAN: Yes, Miss.

[*Goes out.*]

CECILY: Miss Fairfax! I suppose one of the many good elderly women who are associated with Uncle Jack in some of his philanthropic work in London. I don't quite like women who are interested in philanthropic work. I think it is so forward of them.

[*Enter* MERRIMAN.]

MERRIMAN: Miss Fairfax.

[*Enter* GWENDOLEN.]

[*Exit* MERRIMAN.]

CECILY [*Advancing to meet her.*]: Pray let me introduce myself to you. My name is Cecily Cardew.

GWENDOLEN: Cecily Cardew? [*Moving to her and shaking hands.*] What a very sweet name! Something tells me that we are going to be great friends. I like you already more than I can say. My first impressions of people are never wrong.

CECILY: How nice of you to like me so much after we have known each other such a comparatively short time. Pray sit down.

GWENDOLEN [*Still standing up.*]: I may call you Cecily, may I not?

CECILY: With pleasure!

GWENDOLEN: And you will always call me Gwendolen, won't you.

CECILY: If you wish.

GWENDOLEN: Then that is all quite settled, is it not?

CECILY: I hope so.

[*A pause. They both sit down together.*]

GWENDOLEN: Perhaps this might be a favourable opportunity for my mentioning who I am. My father is Lord Bracknell. You have never heard of papa, I suppose?

CECILY: I don't think so.

GWENDOLEN: Outside the family circle, papa, I am glad to say, is entirely unknown. I think that is quite as it should be. The home seems to me to be the proper sphere for the man. And certainly once a man begins to neglect his domestic duties he becomes painfully effeminate, does he not? And I don't like that. It makes men so very attractive. Cecily, mamma, whose views on education are remarkably strict, has brought me up to be extremely short-sighted; it is part of her system; so do you mind my looking at you through my glasses?

CECILY: Oh! not at all, Gwendolen. I am very fond of being looked at.

GWENDOLEN [*After examining* CECILY *carefully through a lorgnette.*]: You are here on a short visit I suppose.

CECILY: Oh no! I live here.

GWENDOLEN [*Severely.*]: Really? Your mother, no doubt, or some female relative of advanced years, resides here also?

CECILY: Oh no! I have no mother, nor, in fact, any relations.

GWENDOLEN: Indeed?

CECILY: My dear guardian, with the assistance of Miss Prism, has the arduous task of looking after me.

GWENDOLEN: Your guardian?

CECILY: Yes, I am Mr Worthing's ward.

GWENDOLEN: Oh! It is strange he never mentioned to me that he had a ward. How secretive of him! He grows more interesting hourly. I am not sure, however, that the news inspires me with feelings of unmixed delight. [*Rising and going to her.*] I am very fond of you, Cecily; I have liked you ever since I met you! But I am bound to state that now that I know that you are Mr Worthing's ward, I cannot help expressing a wish you were—well just a little older than you seem to be—and not quite so very alluring in appearance. In fact, if I may speak candidly—

CECILY: Pray do! I think that whenever one has anything unpleasant to say, one should always be quite candid.

GWENDOLEN: Well, to speak with perfect candour, Cecily, I wish that you were fully forty-two, and more than usually plain for your age. Ernest has a strong upright nature. He is the very soul of truth and honour. Disloyalty would be as impossible to him as deception. But even men of the noblest possible moral character are extremely susceptible to the influence of the physical charms of others. Modern, no less than Ancient History, supplies us with many most painful examples of what I refer to. If it were not so, indeed, History would be quite unreadable.

CECILY: I beg your pardon, Gwendolen, did you say Ernest?

GWENDOLEN: Yes.

CECILY: Oh, but it is not Mr Ernest Worthing who is my guardian. It is his brother—his elder brother.

GWENDOLEN [*Sitting down again.*]: Ernest never mentioned to me that he had a brother.

CECILY: I am sorry to say they have not been on good terms for a long time.

GWENDOLEN: Ah! that accounts for it. And now that I think of it I have never heard any man mention his brother. The subject seems distasteful to most men. Cecily, you have lifted a load from my mind. I was growing almost anxious. It would have been terrible if any cloud had come across a friendship like ours, would it not? Of course you are quite, quite sure that it is not Mr Ernest Worthing who is your guardian?

CECILY: Quite sure. [*A pause.*] In fact, I am going to be his.

GWENDOLEN [*Enquiringly.*]: I beg your pardon?

CECILY [*Rather shy and confidingly.*]: Dearest Gwendolen, there is no reason why I should make a secret of it to you. Our little country newspaper is sure to chronicle the fact next week. Mr Ernest Worthing and I are engaged to be married.

GWENDOLEN [*Quite politely, rising.*]: My darling Cecily, I think there must be some slight error. Mr Ernest Worthing is engaged to me. The announcement will appear in the "Morning Post" on Saturday at the latest.

CECILY [*Very politely, rising.*]: I am afraid you must be under some misconception. Ernest proposed to me exactly ten minutes ago. [*Shows diary.*]

GWENDOLEN [*Examines diary through her lorgnette carefully.*]: It is certainly very curious, for he asked me to be his wife yesterday afternoon at 5.30. If you would care to verify the incident, pray do so. [*Produces diary of her own.*] I never travel without my diary. One should always have something sensational to read in the train. I am so sorry, dear Cecily, if it is any disappointment to you, but I am afraid *I* have the prior claim.

CECILY: It would distress me more than I can tell you, dear Gwendolen, if it caused you any mental or physical anguish, but I feel bound to point out that since Ernest proposed to you he clearly has changed his mind.

GWENDOLEN [*Meditatively.*]: If the poor fellow has been entrapped into any foolish promise I shall consider it my duty to rescue him at once, and with a firm hand.

CECILY [*Thoughtfully and sadly.*]: Whatever unfortunate entanglement my dear boy may have got into, I will never reproach him with it after we are married.

GWENDOLEN: Do you allude to me, Miss Cardew, as an entanglement? You are presumptuous. On an occasion of this kind it becomes more than a moral duty to speak one's mind. It becomes a pleasure.

CECILY: Do you suggest, Miss Fairfax, that I entrapped Ernest into an engagement? How dare you? This is no time for wearing the shallow mask of manners. When I see a spade I call it a spade.

GWENDOLEN [*Satirically.*]: I am glad to say that I have never seen a spade. It is obvious that our social spheres have been widely different.

[*Enter* MERRIMAN, *followed by the footman. He carries a salver, table cloth, and plate stand.* CECILY *is about to retort. The presence of the servants exercises a restraining influence, under which both girls chafe.*]

MERRIMAN: Shall I lay tea here as usual, Miss?

CECILY [*Sternly, in a calm voice.*]: Yes, as usual.

[MERRIMAN *begins to clear table and lay cloth. A long pause.* CECILY *and* GWENDOLEN *glare at each other.*]

GWENDOLEN: Are there many interesting walks in the vicinity, Miss Cardew?

CECILY: Oh! yes! a great many. From the top of one of the hills quite close one can see five counties.

GWENDOLEN: Five counties! I don't think I should like that. I hate crowds.

CECILY [*Sweetly.*]: I suppose that is why you live in town?

[GWENDOLEN *bites her lip, and beats her foot nervously with her parasol.*]

GWENDOLEN [*Looking round.*]: Quite a well-kept garden this is, Miss Cardew.

CECILY: So glad you like it, Miss Fairfax.

GWENDOLEN: I had no idea there were any flowers in the country.

CECILY: Oh, flowers are as common here, Miss Fairfax, as people are in London.

GWENDOLEN: Personally, I cannot understand how anybody manages to exist in the country, if anybody who is anybody does. The country always bores me to death.

CECILY: Ah! This is what the newspapers call agricultural depression, is it not? I believe the aristocracy are suffering very much from it just at present. It is almost an epidemic amongst them, I have been told. May I offer you some tea, Miss Fairfax?

GWENDOLEN [*With elaborate politeness.*]: Thank you. [*Aside.*] Detestable girl! But I require tea!

CECILY [*Sweetly.*]: Sugar?

GWENDOLEN [*Superciliously.*]: No, thank you. Sugar is not fashionable any more.

[CECILY *looks angrily at her, takes up the tongs and puts four lumps of sugar into the cup.*]

CECILY [*Severely.*]: Cake or bread and butter?

GWENDOLEN [*In a bored manner.*]: Bread and butter, please. Cake is rarely seen at the best houses nowadays.

CECILY [*Cuts a very large slice of cake, and puts it on the tray.*]: Hand that to Miss Fairfax.

[MERRIMAN *does so, and goes out with footman.* GWENDOLEN *drinks the tea and makes a grimace. Puts down cup at once, reaches out her hand to the bread and butter, looks at it, and finds it is cake. Rises in indignation.*]

GWENDOLEN: You have filled my tea with lumps of sugar, and though I asked most distinctly for bread and butter, you have given me cake. I am known for the gentleness of my disposition, and the extraordinary sweetness of my nature, but I warn you, Miss Cardew, you may go too far.

CECILY [*Rising.*]: To save my poor, innocent, trusting boy from the machinations of any other girl there are no lengths to which I would not go.

GWENDOLEN: From the moment I saw you I distrusted you. I felt that you were false and deceitful. I am never deceived in such matters. My first impressions of people are invariably right.

CECILY: It seems to me, Miss Fairfax, that I am trespassing on your valuable time. No doubt you have many other calls of a similar character to make in the neighbourhood.

[*Enter* JACK.]

GWENDOLEN [*Catching sight of him.*]: Ernest! My own Ernest!
JACK: Gwendolen! Darling! [*Offers to kiss her.*]
GWENDOLEN [*Drawing back.*]: A moment! May I ask if you are engaged to be married to this young lady? [*Points to* CECILY.]
JACK [*Laughing.*]: To dear little Cecily! Of course not! What could have put such an idea into your pretty little head?
GWENDOLEN: Thank you. You may! [*Offers her cheek.*]
CECILY [*Very sweetly.*]: I knew there must be some misunderstanding, Miss Fairfax. The gentleman whose arm is at present round your waist is my dear guardian, Mr John Worthing.
GWENDOLEN: I beg your pardon?
CECILY: This is Uncle Jack.
GWENDOLEN [*Receding.*]: Jack! Oh!

[*Enter* ALGERNON.]

CECILY: Here is Ernest.
ALGERNON [*Goes straight over to* CECILY *without noticing anyone else.*]: My own love! [*Offers to kiss her.*]
CECILY [*Drawing back.*]: A moment, Ernest! May I ask you—are you engaged to be married to this young lady?
ALGERNON [*Looking round.*]: To what young lady? Good heavens! Gwendolen!
CECILY: Yes, to good heavens, Gwendolen, I mean to Gwendolen.
ALGERNON [*Laughing.*]: Of course not! What could have put such an idea into your pretty little head?
CECILY: Thank you. [*Presenting her cheek to be kissed.*] You may. [ALGERNON *kisses her.*]
GWENDOLEN: I felt there was some slight error, Miss Cardew. The gentleman who is now embracing you is my cousin, Mr Algernon Moncrieff.
CECILY [*Breaking away from* ALGERNON.]: Algernon Moncrieff! Oh!

[*The two girls move towards each other and put their arms round each other's waists as if for protection.*]

CECILY: Are you called Algernon?
ALGERNON: I cannot deny it.
CECILY: Oh!
GWENDOLEN: Is your name really John?
JACK [*Standing rather proudly.*]: I could deny it if I liked. I could deny anything if I liked. But my name certainly is John. It has been John for years.
CECILY [*To* GWENDOLEN.]: A gross deception has been practiced on both of us.
GWENDOLEN: My poor wounded Cecily!
CECILY: My sweet wronged Gwendolen!
GWENDOLEN [*Slowly and seriously.*]: You will call me sister, will you not?

[*They embrace.* JACK *and* ALGERNON *groan and walk up and down.*]

CECILY [*Rather brightly.*]: There is just one question I would like to be allowed to ask my guardian.
GWENDOLEN: An admirable idea! Mr Worthing, there is just one question I would like to be permitted to put to you. Where is your brother Ernest? We are both engaged to be married to your brother Ernest, so it is a matter of some importance to us to know where your brother Ernest is at present.
JACK [*Slowly and hesitatingly.*]: Gwendolen—Cecily—it is very painful for me to be forced to speak the truth. It is the first time in my life that I have ever been reduced to such a painful position, and I am really quite inexperienced in doing anything of the kind. However I will tell you quite frankly that I have no brother Ernest. I have no brother at all. I never had a brother in my life, and I certainly have not the smallest intention of ever having one in the future.
CECILY [*Surprised.*]: No brother at all?
JACK [*Cheerily.*]: None!
GWENDOLEN [*Severely.*]: Had you never a brother of any kind?
JACK [*Pleasantly.*]: Never. Not even of any kind.
GWENDOLEN: I am afraid it is quite clear, Cecily, that neither of us is engaged to be married to anyone.
CECILY: It is not a very pleasant position for a young girl suddenly to find herself in. Is it?
GWENDOLEN: Let us go into the house. They will hardly venture to come after us there.
CECILY: No, men are so cowardly, aren't they?

[*They retire into the house with scornful looks.*]

JACK: This ghastly state of things is what you call Bunburying, I suppose?
ALGERNON: Yes, and a perfectly wonderful Bunbury it is. The most wonderful Bunbury I have ever had in my life.
JACK: Well, you've no right whatsoever to Bunbury here.
ALGERNON: That is absurd. One has a right to Bunbury anywhere one chooses. Every serious Bunburyist knows that.
JACK: Serious Bunburyist! Good heavens!
ALGERNON: Well, one must be serious about something, if one wants to have any amusement in life.

I happen to be serious about Bunburying. What on earth you are serious about I haven't got the remotest idea. About everything, I should fancy. You have such an absolutely trivial nature.

JACK: Well, the only small satisfaction I have in the whole of this wretched business is that your friend Bunbury is quite exploded. You won't be able to run down to the country quite so often as you used to do, dear Algy. And a very good thing too.

ALGERNON: Your brother is a little off colour, isn't he, dear Jack? You won't be able to disappear to London quite so frequently as your wicked custom was. And not a bad thing either.

JACK: As for your conduct towards Miss Cardew, I must say that your taking in a sweet, simple, innocent girl like that is quite inexcusable. To say nothing of the fact that she is my ward.

ALGERNON: I can see no possible defence at all for your deceiving a brilliant, clever, thoroughly experienced young lady like Miss Fairfax. To say nothing of the fact that she is my cousin.

JACK: I wanted to be engaged to Gwendolen, that is all. I love her.

ALGERNON: Well, I simply wanted to be engaged to Cecily. I adore her.

JACK: There is certainly no chance of your marrying Miss Cardew.

ALGERNON: I don't think there is much likelihood, Jack, of you and Miss Fairfax being united.

JACK: Well, that is no business of yours.

ALGERNON: If it was my business, I wouldn't talk about it. [*Begins to eat muffins.*] It is very vulgar to talk about one's business. Only people like stockbrokers do that, and then merely at dinner parties.

JACK: How you can sit there, calmly eating muffins when we are in this horrible trouble, I can't make out. You seem to me to be perfectly heartless.

ALGERNON: Well, I can't eat muffins in an agitated manner. The butter would probably get on my cuffs. One should always eat muffins quite calmly. It is the only way to eat them.

JACK: I say it's perfectly heartless your eating muffins at all, under the circumstances.

ALGERNON: When I am in trouble, eating is the only thing that consoles me. Indeed, when I am in really great trouble, as anyone who knows me intimately will tell you, I refuse everything except food and drink. At the present moment I am eating muffins because I am unhappy. Besides, I am particularly fond of muffins. [*Rising.*]

JACK [*Rising.*]: Well, that is no reason why you should eat them all in that greedy way. [*Takes muffins from* ALGERNON.]

ALGERNON [*Offering tea-cake.*]: I wish you would have tea-cake instead. I don't like tea-cake.

JACK: Good heavens! I suppose a man may eat his own muffins in his own garden.

ALGERNON: But you have just said it was perfectly heartless to eat muffins.

JACK: I said it was perfectly heartless of you, under the circumstances. That is a very different thing.

ALGERNON: That may be. But the muffins are the same. [*He seizes the muffin-dish from* JACK.]

JACK: Algy, I wish to goodness you would go.

ALGERNON: You can't possibly ask me to go without having some dinner. It's absurd. I never go without my dinner. No one ever does, except vegetarians and people like that. Besides I have just made arrangements with Dr Chasuble to be christened at a quarter to six under the name of Ernest.

JACK: My dear fellow, the sooner you give up that nonsense the better. I made arrangements this morning with Dr Chasuble to be christened myself at 5.30, and I naturally will take the name of Ernest. Gwendolen would wish it. We can't both be christened Ernest. It's absurd. Besides, I have a perfect right to be christened if I like. There is no evidence at all that I ever have been christened by anybody. I should think it extremely probable I never was, and so does Dr Chasuble. It is entirely different in your case. You have been christened already.

ALGERNON: Yes, but I have not been christened for years.

JACK: Yes, but you have been christened. That is the important thing.

ALGERNON: Quite so. So I know my constitution can stand it. If you are not quite sure about your ever having been christened, I must say I think it rather dangerous your venturing on it now. It might make you very unwell. You can hardly have forgotten that someone very closely connected with you was very nearly carried off this week in Paris by a severe chill.

JACK: Yes, but you said yourself that a severe chill was not hereditary.

ALGERNON: It usen't to be, I know—but I daresay it is now. Science is always making wonderful improvements in things.

JACK [*Picking up the muffin-dish.*]: Oh, that is nonsense; you are always talking nonsense.

ALGERNON: Jack, you are at the muffins again! I wish you wouldn't. There are only two left. [*Takes them.*] I told you I was particularly fond of muffins.

JACK: But I hate tea-cake.

ALGERNON: Why on earth then do you allow tea-cake to be served up for your guests? What ideas you have of hospitality!

JACK: Algernon! I have already told you to go. I don't want you here. Why don't you go!

ALGERNON: I haven't quite finished my tea yet! and there is still one muffin left. [JACK *groans, and sinks into a chair.* ALGERNON *still continues eating*.]

ACT DROP

ACT III

SCENE. Morning-room at the Manor House.

[GWENDOLEN *and* CECILY *are at the window, looking out into the garden.*]

GWENDOLEN: The fact that they did not follow us at once into the house, as anyone else would have done, seems to me to show that they have some sense of shame left.

CECILY: They have been eating muffins. That looks like repentance.

GWENDOLEN [*After a pause.*]: They don't seem to notice us at all. Couldn't you cough?

CECILY: But I haven't got a cough.

GWENDOLEN: They're looking at us. What effrontery!

CECILY: They're approaching. That's very forward of them.

GWENDOLEN: Let us preserve a dignified silence.

CECILY: Certainly. It's the only thing to do now.

[*Enter* JACK *followed by* ALGERNON. *They whistle some dreadful popular air from a British Opera.*]

GWENDOLEN: This dignified silence seems to produce an unpleasant effect.

CECILY: A most distasteful one.

GWENDOLEN: But we will not be the first to speak.

CECILY: Certainly not.

GWENDOLEN: Mr Worthing, I have something very particular to ask you. Much depends on your reply.

CECILY: Gwendolen, your common sense is invaluable. Mr Moncrieff, kindly answer me the following question. Why did you pretend to be my guardian's brother?

ALGERNON: In order that I might have an opportunity of meeting you.

CECILY [*To* GWENDOLEN.]: That certainly seems a satisfactory explanation, does it not?

GWENDOLEN: Yes, dear, if you can believe him.

CECILY: I don't. But that does not affect the wonderful beauty of his answer.

GWENDOLEN: True. In matters of grave importance, style, not sincerity is the vital thing. Mr Worthing, what explanation can you offer to me for pretending to have a brother? Was it in order that you might have an opportunity of coming up to town to see me as often as possible?

JACK: Can you doubt it, Miss Fairfax?

GWENDOLEN: I have the gravest doubts upon the subject. But I intend to crush them. This is not the moment for German scepticism. [*Moving to* CECILY.] Their explanations appear to be quite satisfactory, especially Mr Worthing's. That seems to me to have the stamp of truth upon it.

CECILY: I am more than content with what Mr Moncrieff said. His voice alone inspires one with absolute credulity.

GWENDOLEN: Then you think we should forgive them?

CECILY: Yes. I mean no.

GWENDOLEN: True! I had forgotten. There are principles at stake that one cannot surrender. Which of us should tell them? The task is not a pleasant one.

CECILY: Could we not both speak at the same time?

GWENDOLEN: An excellent idea! I nearly always speak at the same time as other people. Will you take the time from me?

CECILY: Certainly.

[GWENDOLEN *beats time with uplifted finger.*]

GWENDOLEN and CECILY [*Speaking together.*]: Your Christian names are still an insuperable barrier. That is all!

JACK and ALGERNON [*Speaking together.*]: Our Christian names! Is that all? But we are going to be christened this afternoon.

GWENDOLEN [*To* JACK]: For my sake you are prepared to do this terrible thing?

JACK: I am.

CECILY [*To* ALGERNON.]: To please me you are ready to face this fearful ordeal?

ALGERNON: I am!

GWENDOLEN: How absurd to talk of the equality of the sexes! Where questions of self-sacrifice are concerned, men are infinitely beyond us.

JACK: We are. [*Clasps hands with* ALGERNON.]

CECILY: They have moments of physical courage of which we women know absolutely nothing.

GWENDOLEN [*To* JACK.]: Darling!

ALGERNON [*To* CECILY.]: Darling! [*They fall into each other's arms.*]

[*Enter* MERRIMAN. *When he enters he coughs loudly, seeing the situation.*]

MERRIMAN: Ahem! Ahem! Lady Bracknell!

JACK: Good heavens!

[*Enter* LADY BRACKNELL. *The couples separate in alarm.*]

[*Exit* MERRIMAN.]

LADY BRACKNELL: Gwendolen! What does this mean?
GWENDOLEN: Merely that I am engaged to be married to Mr Worthing, mamma.
LADY BRACKNELL: Come here. Sit down. Sit down immediately. Hesitation of any kind is a sign of mental decay in the young, of physical weakness in the old. [*Turns to* JACK.] Apprised, sir, of my daughter's sudden flight by her trusty maid, whose confidence I purchased by means of a small coin, I followed her at once by a luggage train. Her unhappy father is, I am glad to say, under the impression that she is attending a more than usually lengthy lecture by the University Extension Scheme on the Influence of a permanent income on Thought. I do not propose to undeceive him. Indeed I have never undeceived him on any question. I would consider it wrong. But of course, you will clearly understand that all communication between yourself and my daughter must cease immediately from this moment. On this point, as indeed on all points, I am firm.
JACK: I am engaged to be married to Gwendolen, Lady Bracknell!
LADY BRACKNELL: You are nothing of the kind, sir. And now, as regards Algernon! . . . Algernon!
ALGERNON: Yes, Aunt Augusta.
LADY BRACKNELL: May I ask if it is in this house that your invalid friend Mr Bunbury resides?
ALGERNON [*Stammering*.]: Oh! No! Bunbury doesn't live here. Bunbury is somewhere else at present. In fact, Bunbury is dead.
LADY BRACKNELL: Dead! When did Mr Bunbury die? His death must have been extremely sudden.
ALGERNON [*Airily*.]: Oh! I killed Bunbury this afternoon. I mean poor Bunbury died this afternoon.
LADY BRACKNELL: What did he die of?
ALGERNON: Bunbury? Oh, he was quite exploded.
LADY BRACKNELL: Exploded! Was he the victim of a revolutionary outrage? I was not aware that Mr Bunbury was interested in social legislation. If so, he is well punished for his morbidity.
ALGERNON: My dear Aunt Augusta, I mean he was found out! The doctors found out that Bunbury could not live, that is what I mean—so Bunbury died.
LADY BRACKNELL: He seems to have had great confidence in the opinion of his physicians. I am glad, however, that he made up his mind at the last to some definite course of action, and acted under proper medical advice. And now that we have finally got rid of this Mr Bunbury, may I ask, Mr Worthing, who is that young person whose hand my nephew Algernon is now holding in what seems to me a peculiarly unnecessary manner?
JACK: That lady is Miss Cecily Cardew, my ward.

[LADY BRACKNELL *bows coldly to* CECILY.]

ALGERNON: I am engaged to be married to Cecily, Aunt Augusta.
LADY BRACKNELL: I beg your pardon?
CECILY: Mr Moncrieff and I are engaged to be married, Lady Bracknell.
LADY BRACKNELL [*With a shiver, crossing to the sofa and sitting down*.]: I do not know whether there is anything peculiarly exciting in the air of this particular part of Hertfordshire, but the number of engagements that go on seems to me considerably above the proper average that statistics have laid down for our guidance. I think some preliminary enquiry on my part would not be out of place. Mr Worthing, is Miss Cardew at all connected with any of the larger railway stations in London? I merely desire information. Until yesterday I had no idea that there were any families or persons whose origin was a Terminus.

[JACK *looks perfectly furious, but restrains himself.*]

JACK [*In a clear, cold voice*.]: Miss Cardew is the granddaughter of the late Mr Thomas Cardew of 149, Belgrave Square, S.W.; Gervase Park, Dorking, Surrey; and the Sporran, Fifeshire, N.B.
LADY BRACKNELL: That sounds not unsatisfactory. Three addresses always inspire confidence, even in tradesmen. But what proof have I of their authenticity?
JACK: I have carefully preserved the Court Guides of the period. They are open to your inspection, Lady Bracknell.
LADY BRACKNELL [*Grimly*.]: I have known strange errors in that publication.
JACK: Miss Cardew's family solicitors are Messrs Markby, Markby, and Markby.
LADY BRACKNELL: Markby, Markby, and Markby? A firm of the very highest position in their profession. Indeed I am told that one of the Mr Markbys is occasionally to be seen at dinner parties. So far I am satisfied.
JACK [*Very irritably*.]: How extremely kind of you, Lady Bracknell! I have also in my possession, you will be pleased to hear, certificates of Miss Cardew's birth, baptism, whooping cough, registration, vaccination, confirmation, and the measles; both the German and the English variety.
LADY BRACKNELL: Ah! A life crowded with incident, I see; though perhaps somewhat too exciting for a young girl. I am not myself in favour of premature experiences. [*Rises, looks at her watch.*] Gwendolen! the time approaches for our departure. We have not a moment to lose. As a matter of form,

Mr Worthing, I had better ask you if Miss Cardew has any little fortune?

JACK: Oh! about a hundred and thirty thousand pounds in the Funds. That is all. Goodbye, Lady Bracknell. So pleased to have seen you.

LADY BRACKNELL [*Sitting down again.*]: A moment, Mr Worthing. A hundred and thirty thousand pounds! And in the Funds! Miss Cardew seems to me a most attractive young lady, now that I look at her. Few girls of the present day have any really solid qualities, any of the qualities that last, and improve with time. We live, I regret to say, in an age of surfaces. [*To* CECILY.] Come over here, dear. [CECILY *goes across.*] Pretty child! your dress is sadly simple, and your hair seems almost as Nature might have left it. But we can soon alter all that. A thoroughly experienced French maid produces a really marvellous result in a very brief space of time. I remember recommending one to young Lady Lancing, and after three months her own husband did not know her.

JACK [*Aside.*]: And after six months nobody knew her.

LADY BRACKNELL [*Glares at* JACK *for a few moments. Then bends, with a practised smile, to* CECILY.]: Kindly turn round, sweet child. [CECILY *turns completely round.*] No, the side view is what I want. [CECILY *presents her profile.*] Yes, quite as I expected. There are distinct social possibilities in your profile. The two weak points in our age are its want of principle and its want of profile. The chin a little higher, dear. Style largely depends on the way the chin is worn. They are worn very high, just at present. Algernon!

ALGERNON: Yes, Aunt Augusta!

LADY BRACKNELL: There are distinct social possibilities in Miss Cardew's profile.

ALGERNON: Cecily is the sweetest, dearest, prettiest girl in the whole world. And I don't care twopence about social possibilities.

LADY BRACKNELL: Never speak disrespectfully of Society, Algernon. Only people who can't get into it do that. [*To* CECILY.] Dear child, of course you know that Algernon has nothing but his debts to depend upon. But I do not approve of mercenary marriages. When I married Lord Bracknell I had no fortune of any kind. But I never dreamed for a moment of allowing that to stand in my way. Well, I suppose I must give my consent.

ALGERNON: Thank you, Aunt Augusta.

LADY BRACKNELL: Cecily, you may kiss me!

CECILY [*Kisses her.*]: Thank you, Lady Bracknell.

LADY BRACKNELL: You may also address me as Aunt Augusta for the future.

CECILY: Thank you, Aunt Augusta.

LADY BRACKNELL: The marriage, I think, had better take place quite soon.

ALGERNON: Thank you, Aunt Augusta.

CECILY: Thank you, Aunt Augusta.

LADY BRACKNELL: To speak frankly, I am not in favour of long engagements. They give people the opportunity of finding out each other's character before marriage, which I think is never advisable.

JACK: I beg your pardon for interrupting you, Lady Bracknell, but this engagement is quite out of the question. I am Miss Cardew's guardian, and she cannot marry without my consent until she comes of age. That consent I absolutely decline to give.

LADY BRACKNELL: Upon what grounds may I ask? Algernon is an extremely, I may almost say an ostentatiously, eligible young man. He has nothing, but he looks everything. What more can one desire?

JACK: It pains me very much to have to speak frankly to you, Lady Bracknell, about your nephew, but the fact is that I do not approve at all of his moral character. I suspect him of being untruthful.

[ALGERNON *and* CECILY *look at him in indignant amazement.*]

LADY BRACKNELL: Untruthful! My nephew Algernon? Impossible! He is an Oxonian.

JACK: I fear there can be no possible doubt about the matter. This afternoon, during my temporary absence in London on an important question of romance, he obtained admission to my house by means of the false pretence of being my brother. Under an assumed name he drank, I've just been informed by my butler, an entire pint bottle of my Perrier-Jouet, Brut, '89; a wine I was specially reserving for myself. Continuing his disgraceful deception, he succeeded in the course of the afternoon in alienating the affections of my only ward. He subsequently stayed to tea, and devoured every single muffin. And what makes his conduct all the more heartless is, that he was perfectly well aware from the first that I have no brother, that I never had a brother, and that I don't intend to have a brother, not even of any kind. I distinctly told him so myself yesterday afternoon.

LADY BRACKNELL: Ahem! Mr Worthing, after careful consideration I have decided entirely to overlook my nephew's conduct to you.

JACK: That is very generous of you, Lady Bracknell. My own decision, however, is unalterable. I decline to give my consent.

LADY BRACKNELL [*To* CECILY.]: Come here, sweet child. [CECILY *goes over.*] How old are you, dear?

CECILY: Well, I am really only eighteen, but I always admit to twenty when I go to evening parties.

LADY BRACKNELL: You are perfectly right in making some slight alteration. Indeed, no woman should ever be quite accurate about her age. It looks so calculating. . . . [*In a meditative manner.*] Eighteen, but admitting to twenty at evening parties. Well, it will not be very long before you are of age and free from the restraints of tutelage. So I don't think your guardian's consent is, after all, a matter of any importance.

JACK: Pray excuse me, Lady Bracknell, for interrupting you again, but it is only fair to tell you that according to the terms of her grandfather's will Miss Cardew does not come legally of age till she is thirty-five.

LADY BRACKNELL: That does not seem to me to be a grave objection. Thirty-five is a very attractive age. London society is full of women of the very highest birth who have, of their own free choice, remained thirty-five for years. Lady Dumbleton is an instance in point. To my own knowledge she has been thirty-five ever since she arrived at the age of forty, which was many years ago now. I see no reason why our dear Cecily should not be even still more attractive at the age you mention than she is at present. There will be a large accumulation of property.

CECILY: Algy, could you wait for me till I was thirty-five?

ALGERNON: Of course I could, Cecily. You know I could.

CECILY: Yes, I felt it instinctively, but I couldn't wait all that time. I hate waiting even five minutes for anybody. It always makes me rather cross. I am not punctual myself, I know, but I do like punctuality in others, and waiting, even to be married, is quite out of the question.

ALGERNON: Then what is to be done, Cecily?

CECILY: I don't know, Mr Moncrieff.

LADY BRACKNELL: My dear Mr Worthing, as Miss Cardew states positively that she cannot wait till she is thirty-five—a remark which I am bound to say seems to me to show a somewhat impatient nature—I would beg of you to reconsider your decision.

JACK: But my dear Lady Bracknell, the matter is entirely in your own hands. The moment you consent to my marriage with Gwendolen, I will most gladly allow your nephew to form an alliance with my ward.

LADY BRACKNELL [*Rising and drawing herself up.*]: You must be quite aware that what you propose is out of the question.

JACK: Then a passionate celibacy is all that any of us can look forward to.

LADY BRACKNELL: That is not the destiny I propose for Gwendolen. Algernon, of course, can choose for himself. [*Pulls out her watch.*] Come, dear; [GWENDOLEN *rises*] we have already missed five, if not six, trains. To miss any more might expose us to comment on the platform.

[*Enter* DR CHASUBLE.]

CHASUBLE: Everything is quite ready for the christenings.

LADY BRACKNELL: The christenings, sir! Is not that somewhat premature?

CHASUBLE [*Looking rather puzzled, and pointing to* JACK *and* ALGERNON.]: Both these gentlemen have expressed a desire for immediate baptism.

LADY BRACKNELL: At their age? The idea is grotesque and irreligious! Algernon, I forbid you to be baptized. I will not hear of such excesses. Lord Bracknell would be highly displeased if he learned that that was the way in which you wasted your time and money.

CHASUBLE: Am I to understand then that there are to be no christenings at all this afternoon?

JACK: I don't think that, as things are now, it would be of much practical value to either of us, Dr Chasuble.

CHASUBLE: I am grieved to hear such sentiments from you, Mr Worthing. They savour of the heretical views of the Anabaptists, views that I have completely refuted in four of my unpublished sermons. However, as your present mood seems to be one peculiarly secular, I will return to the church at once. Indeed, I have just been informed by the pew-opener that for the last hour and a half Miss Prism has been waiting for me in the vestry.

LADY BRACKNELL [*Starting.*]: Miss Prism! Did I hear you mention a Miss Prism?

CHASUBLE: Yes, Lady Bracknell. I am on my way to join her.

LADY BRACKNELL: Pray allow me to detain you for a moment. This matter may prove to be one of vital importance to Lord Bracknell and myself. Is this Miss Prism a female of repellent aspect, remotely connected with education?

CHASUBLE [*Somewhat indignantly.*]: She is the most cultivated of ladies, and the very picture of respectability.

LADY BRACKNELL: It is obviously the same person. May I ask what position she holds in your household?

CHASUBLE [*Severely.*]: I am a celibate, madam.

JACK [*Interposing.*]: Miss Prism, Lady Bracknell, has been for the last three years Miss Cardew's esteemed governess and valued companion.

LADY BRACKNELL: In spite of what I hear of her, I must see her at once. Let her be sent for.

CHASUBLE [*Looking off.*]: She approaches; she is nigh.

[*Enter* MISS PRISM *hurriedly.*]

MISS PRISM: I was told you expected me in the vestry, dear Canon. I have been waiting for you there for an hour and three quarters. [*Catches sight of* LADY BRACKNELL *who has fixed her with a stony glare.* MISS PRISM *grows pale and quails. She looks anxiously round as if desirous to escape.*]

LADY BRACKNELL [*In a severe, judicial voice.*]: Prism! [MISS PRISM *bows her head in shame.*] Come here, Prism! [MISS PRISM *approaches in a humble manner.*] Prism! Where is that baby? [*General consternation. The* CANON *starts back in horror.* ALGERNON *and* JACK *pretend to be anxious to shield* CECILY *and* GWENDOLEN *from hearing the details of a terrible public scandal.*] Twenty-eight years ago, Prism, you left Lord Bracknell's house, Number 104, Upper Grosvenor Street, in charge of a perambulator that contained a baby, of the male sex. You never returned. A few weeks later, through the elaborate investigations of the Metropolitan police, the perambulator was discovered at midnight, standing by itself in a remote corner of Bayswater. It contained the manuscript of a three-volume novel of more than usually revolting sentimentality. [MISS PRISM *starts in involuntary indignation.*] But the baby was not there! [*Everyone looks at* MISS PRISM.] Prism! Where is that baby? [*A pause.*]

MISS PRISM: Lady Bracknell, I admit with shame that I do not know. I only wish I did. The plain facts of the case are these. On the morning of the day you mention, a day that is for ever branded on my memory, I prepared as usual to take the baby out in its perambulator. I had also with me a somewhat old, but capacious hand-bag in which I had intended to place the manuscript of a work of fiction that I had written during my few unoccupied hours. In a moment of mental abstraction, for which I never can forgive myself, I deposited the manuscript in the bassinette, and placed the baby in the hand-bag.

JACK [*Who has been listening attentively.*]: But where did you deposit the hand-bag?

MISS PRISM: Do not ask me, Mr Worthing.

JACK: Miss Prism, this is a matter of no small importance to me. I insist on knowing where you deposited the hand-bag that contained that infant.

MISS PRISM: I left it in the cloak-room of one of the larger railway stations in London.

JACK: What railway station?

MISS PRISM [*Quite crushed.*]: Victoria. The Brighton line. [*Sinks into a chair.*]

JACK: I must retire to my room for a moment. Gwendolen, wait here for me.

GWENDOLEN: If you are not too long, I will wait here for you all my life.

[*Exit* JACK *in great excitement.*]

CHASUBLE: What do you think this means, Lady Bracknell?

LADY BRACKNELL: I dare not even suspect, Dr Chasuble. I need hardly tell you that in families of high position strange coincidences are not supposed to occur. They are hardly considered the thing.

[*Noises heard overhead as if someone was throwing trunks about. Everyone looks up.*]

CECILY: Uncle Jack seems strangely agitated.

CHASUBLE: Your guardian has a very emotional nature.

LADY BRACKNELL: This noise is extremely unpleasant. It sounds as if he was having an argument. I dislike arguments of any kind. They are always vulgar, and often convincing.

CHASUBLE [*Looking up.*]: It has stopped now. [*The noise is redoubled.*]

LADY BRACKNELL: I wish he would arrive at some conclusion.

GWENDOLEN: This suspense is terrible. I hope it will last.

[*Enter* JACK *with a hand-bag of black leather in his hand.*]

JACK [*Rushing over to* MISS PRISM.]: Is this the hand-bag, Miss Prism? Examine it carefully before you speak. The happiness of more than one life depends on your answer.

MISS PRISM [*Calmly.*]: It seems to be mine. Yes, here is the injury it received through the upsetting of a Gower Street omnibus in younger and happier days. Here is the stain on the lining caused by the explosion of a temperance beverage, an incident that occurred at Leamington. And here, on the lock, are my initials. I had forgotten that in an extravagant mood I had had them placed there. The bag is undoubtedly mine. I am delighted to have it so unexpectedly restored to me. It has been a great inconvenience being without it all these years.

JACK [*In a pathetic voice.*]: Miss Prism, more is restored to you than this hand-bag. I was the baby you placed in it.

MISS PRISM [*Amazed.*]: You?

Jack [*Embracing her.*]: Yes . . . mother!

MISS PRISM [*Recoiling in indignant astonishment.*]: Mr Worthing! I am unmarried!

JACK: Unmarried! I do not deny that is a serious blow. But after all, who has the right to cast a stone against one who has suffered? Cannot repentance wipe out an act of folly? Why should there be one law for men, and another for women? Mother, I forgive you. [*Tries to embrace her again.*]

MISS PRISM [*Still more indignant.*]: Mr Worthing, there is some error. [*Pointing to* LADY BRACKNELL.] There is the lady who can tell you who you really are.

JACK [*After a pause.*]: Lady Bracknell, I hate to seem inquisitive, but would you kindly inform me who I am?

LADY BRACKNELL: I am afraid that the news I have to give you will not altogether please you. You are the son of my poor sister, Mrs Moncrieff, and consequently Algernon's elder brother.

JACK: Algy's elder brother! Then I have a brother after all. I knew I had a brother! I always said I had a brother! Cecily—how could you have ever doubted that I had a brother. [*Seizes hold of* ALGERNON.] Dr Chasuble, my unfortunate brother. Miss Prism, my unfortunate brother. Gwendolen, my unfortunate brother. Algy, you young scoundrel, you will have to treat me with more respect in the future. You have never behaved to me like a brother in all your life.

ALGERNON: Well, not till today, old boy, I admit. I did my best, however, though I was out of practice. [*Shakes hands.*]

GWENDOLEN [*To* JACK.]: My own! But what own are you? What is your Christian name, now that you have become someone else?

JACK: Good heavens! . . . I had quite forgotten that point. Your decision on the subject of my name is irrevocable, I suppose?

GWENDOLEN: I never change, except in my affections.

CECILY: What a noble nature you have, Gwendolen!

JACK: Then the question had better be cleared up at once. Aunt Augusta, a moment. At the time when Miss Prism left me in the hand-bag, had I been christened already?

LADY BRACKNELL: Every luxury that money could buy, including christening, had been lavished on you by your fond and doting parents.

JACK: Then I was christened! That is settled. Now, what name was I given? Let me know the worst.

LADY BRACKNELL: Being the eldest son you were naturally christened after your father.

JACK [*Irritably.*]: Yes, but what was my father's Christian name?

LADY BRACKNELL [*Meditatively.*]: I cannot at the present moment recall what the General's Christian name was. But I have no doubt he had one. He was eccentric, I admit. But only in later years. And that was the result of the Indian climate, and marriage, and indigestion, and other things of that kind.

JACK: Algy! Can't you recollect what our father's Christian name was?

ALGERNON: My dear boy, we were never even on speaking terms. He died before I was a year old.

JACK: His name would appear in the Army Lists of the period, I suppose, Aunt Augusta?

LADY BRACKNELL: The General was essentially a man of peace, except in his domestic life. But I have no doubt his name would appear in any military directory.

JACK: The Army Lists of the last forty years are here. These delightful records should have been my constant study. [*Rushes to bookcase and tears the books out.*] M. Generals . . . Mallam, Maxbohm, Magley, what ghastly names they have—Markby, Migsby, Mobbs, Moncrieff! Lieutenant 1840, Captain, Lieutenant-Colonel, Colonel, General 1869, Christian names, Ernest John. [*Puts book very quietly down and speaks quite calmly.*] I always told you, Gwendolen, my name was Ernest, didn't I? Well, it is Ernest after all. I mean it naturally is Ernest.

LADY BRACKNELL: Yes, I remember now that the General was called Ernest. I knew I had some particular reason for disliking the name.

GWENDOLEN: Ernest! My own Ernest! I felt from the first that you could have no other name!

JACK: Gwendolen, it is a terrible thing for a man to find out suddenly that all his life he has been speaking nothing but the truth. Can you forgive me?

GWENDOLEN: I can. For I feel that you are sure to change.

JACK: My own one!

CHASUBLE [*To* MISS PRISM.]: Lætitia! [*Embraces her.*]

MISS PRISM [*Enthusiastically.*]: Frederick! At last!

ALGERNON: Cecily! [*Embraces her.*] At last!

JACK: Gwendolen! [*Embraces her.*] At last!

LADY BRACKNELL: My nephew, you seem to be displaying signs of triviality.

JACK: On the contrary, Aunt Augusta, I've now realized for the first time in my life the vital Importance of Being Earnest.

TABLEAU

CURTAIN

George Bernard Shaw

George Bernard Shaw (1856–1950) was born in Dublin into a middle-class family of modest means. He was called Sonny, a nickname that indicated his place as the only son in the family. In later life, Shaw disavowed nicknames for himself and preferred to be known by his initials, G.B.S., or by Bernard Shaw. His father, George Carr Shaw, was a gentle incompetent who suffered from alcoholism. His mother, Lucinda, called Bessie, was seventeen years her husband's junior and as energetic as he was indolent.

The Shaw household in Dublin was for many years a ménage à trois. Bessie Shaw was a rather cold and unloving mother but, nonetheless, was a passionate woman. Aspiring to be a singer, Bessie began an affair with George V. Lee, a noted voice and music teacher, and with her husband's consent, she invited her teacher and lover to live in the family home.

Lee became a second father to Sonny Shaw and eventually introduced him to the literary profession. Another father figure was Bessie Shaw's brother, Walter John Gurly, a man of great charm, who loved to tell ribald stories. A ship's surgeon, Gurly lived with the family periodically, and it is from him that Shaw developed his sense of gusto and humor. Shaw liked to say that he had three fathers, and the concept of older men passing on wisdom to younger men or women is an important theme in his plays. The family was nominally Protestant, but Shaw disavowed religion early on: He was from his teens a free thinker who substituted social reform for religious dogma.

Shaw left Dublin at twenty without having gone to college, largely because he hated school. From the age of fifteen he had worked as a financial clerk in a real estate firm, but after five years he emigrated to London, made it his permanent home, and decided on a career as a writer. He began by ghostwriting articles for George Lee and moved on to writing novels. By 1883 he had produced five unsuccessful novels, one of which, *Cashel Byron's Profession* (1882), is about prizefighting, a sport that Shaw found "noble." In fact, Shaw trained for a while as a middleweight boxer. He was just over six feet tall and weighed 140 pounds, and he was so keenly interested in physical stamina and good health that he became a lifelong vegetarian and a teetotaler. When studying the art of boxing, Shaw tried to find a scientific technique for winning, in his typical methodical way. Boxing also provided an outlet for Shaw's combative nature. He was forever verbally sparring with friends and lovers, political cronies and adversaries. He liked people generally but did not care for intimacy. He preferred his relationships with women to be intellectual rather than sexual. His plays seldom include love scenes, and while there is much discussion of love, there is never any suggestion of physical lovemaking. Shaw had many significant love interests over the course of his life, but he married only once, to Charlotte Payne-Townshend, in 1896. It was a long, difficult, and generally successful but childless marriage, which ended with Charlotte's death in 1943.

Shaw first began attending the theater on his own in Dublin, and he continued to do so in London. In 1884 he befriended William Archer, the critic and an early admirer of Henrik Ibsen. Together Shaw and Archer attempted to write a play, but the project proved abortive. Through his association with a socialist political activist group called the Fabians, Shaw achieved success as a music critic. By 1889 he was one of England's leading journalistic reviewers of music and drama, which led to his own career as a playwright.

Shaw's view of drama was deeply influenced by Henrik Ibsen, particularly by *A Doll's House* and *Ghosts,* which Shaw found congenial because of their support for social reform and women's rights. Shaw even acted the role of Nils Krogstad in an amateur production of *A Doll's House* in 1886, whose cast included Eleanor Marx, Karl Marx's daughter, as Nora Helmer. Shaw explained his affinity for the playwright in a series of essays collected as *The Quintessence of Ibsenisim* (1891, rev. 1913). In one of these essays, "The Technical Novelty in Ibsen's Plays," Shaw praised Ibsen for transforming the well-made play into a play of ideas. Shaw particularly approved of Ibsen's use of the conventions of domestic drama to discuss a social problem from differing perspectives, and he thought that after Ibsen's *A Doll's House*

> the serious playwright recognizes in the discussion not only the main test of his [Ibsen's] highest powers, but also the real centre of his play's interest. . . . In new plays, the drama arises through a conflict of unsettled ideals rather than through vulgar attachments, rapacities, generosities, resentments, ambitions, misunderstandings, oddities and so forth as to which moral question is raised. The conflict is not between clear right and wrong: the villain is as contentious as the hero, if not more so: in fact, the question which makes the play interesting (when it *is* interesting) is which is the villian and which the hero.

Shaw is generally credited with establishing Ibsen's British reputation and thereby extending his influence to the United States. In turn, Shaw's dramas show the influence of Ibsen, particularly *Widowers' Houses, Arms and the Man, Major Barbara,* and *St. Joan.*

Arms and the Man, produced in 1894, is a successful romantic comedy that is also an antimilitary drama about war in the Balkans: The hero, Bluntshli, carries chocolate candies rather than ammunition in his cartridge belt. *Candida* (1898) portrays a firm-minded woman who rules her household absolutely and whose husband does as he is told. Shaw said that the play was "a counterblast to Henrik Ibsen's *A Doll's House,* showing that in the real typical doll's house it is the man who is the doll." But the characterizations are fictionalizations of his own family life, particularly of his domineering mother.

In 1895, *The Man of Destiny* failed, but *The Devil's Disciple,* a historical drama set during the American Revolution, succeeded. In it, the protagonist, Richard Dudgeon, admits to a crime he did not commit in order to save the reputation of a young woman. Another historical drama, *Caesar and Cleopatra* (1901), contrasts a mature Caesar dealing deftly with the charms and sexual maneuvering of a much younger Cleopatra. *Man and Superman* (1903) turns the story of Wolfgang Amadeus Mozart's Don Juan into a comedy of manners. Don Juan's explanation of the vital force in life is Shaw's own, however: "To Life, the force behind the Man, intellect is a necessity, because without it he blunders into death. . . . I sing not of arms and the hero, but the philosophic man: he who seeks in contemplation to discover the inner will of the world, in invention to discover the means of fulfilling that will, and in action to do that will by the so-discovered means. Of all other sorts of men I declare myself tired."

Major Barbara (1905) describes the trials and tribulations of Barbara Undershaft, a major in the Salvation Army, who must disavow the materialism of her father, Samuel Undershaft, the millionaire munitions maker, while trying to save the soul of the reprobate, Bill Walker. *Getting Married* (1908) is another play about marriage; and its sequel, *Misalliance: A Debate in One Sitting* (1910), a discussion of marriage and the upbringing of children, became Shaw's longest running play to that date. *Androcoles and the Lion* (1912), a morality play for children, was Shaw's response to *Peter Pan* (1904), the crowd-pleaser by J. M. Barrie (1860–1937). *Back to Methuselah* (1921) is Shaw's idea of a theatrical extravaganza, a cycle of five plays discussing the playwright's perspectives on history, politics, religion, science, and the conflict of life and death. The cycle begins with Genesis and the temptation of Adam and Eve by Satan and ends with a vision of humanity in the distant future. Shaw's depiction of the year A.D. 31,920 provides a glimpse of another Pygmalion, now a scientist, who joins with a sculptor, Marcellus, to create new humans, who resemble the English circa 1920.

Saint Joan (1923), Shaw's most important historical drama, depicts the life of Joan of Arc (1412–1431) and follows the arc of her glory: She inspires the French King and leads the French to victory, until she is finally betrayed and martyred because she obeyed her vision of God rather than the church. In the epilogue of this play, a dream sequence shows Joan offering to return to Earth but being repudiated again by the same people who condemned her the first time.

Bertolt Brecht, an admirer of Shaw, was impressed with the production of *Saint Joan* in Berlin in 1924. In honor of Shaw's seventieth birthday, Brecht wrote "Three Cheers for Shaw" (1926), in which he praised Shaw and called him a terrorist, insofar as he is "of the opinion that nothing in the world need be feared so much as the ordinary man's calm and incorruptible eye, but that this must be feared without question." Shaw, he said, "claims a right for every man to act in all circumstances with decency, logic, and humour, and sees it as his duty to do so even when it creates opposition. He knows just how much courage is needed to laugh at what is amusing, and how much seriousness to pick it out."

Shaw was awarded the Nobel Prize for Literature in 1925, when he was sixty-nine, and it seemed a fitting reward for a lifetime of writing. However, he remained active and lucid, completing *Buoyant Billions* (1948) when he was ninety-two. By the time he died at age ninety-four, Shaw had written over fifty full-length plays with extensive prefaces, many volumes of criticism, five novels, scores of political tracts, and thousands of letters.

Pygmalion: A Romance in Five Acts (1913) was first produced in Vienna and Berlin because Shaw wanted the response of a Continental audience, unprejudiced by London critics. It was immediately successful in those cities and has since proved to be Shaw's most popular play. *Pygmalion* is a jab at the hollowness of the British middle class. Shaw set out to show how proper speech, cleanliness, fashionable dress, and good manners are no substitutes for the real essence and strength of character. The role of Eliza Doolittle was written for the actress Mrs. Patrick Campbell, with whom Shaw had a friendship that began in the early 1890s and ended in 1939 when he wrote his last letter to her. In 1913, Shaw was infatuated with Campbell, whom he called Stella, and he tried desperately and unsuccessfully to seduce her. She rebuffed him, and his letter of reproach says much about the man and the artist that seems to have echoes in Henry Higgins's relationship with Eliza: "I have treated you far too well, idolized you, thrown my heart & mind to you (as I throw them to all the world) to make of what you could of [sic]; and what you make of them is to run away. . . . You have wounded my vanity: an inconceivable audacity, an unpardonable crime. Farewell, wretch that I loved."

Shaw's story owes its inspiration and plot both to Ovid's "The Myth of Pygmalion and Galatea" (ca. A.D. 8) and to French writer Charles Perrault's version of the fairy tale "Cinderella" (1688), both of which are concerned with love and transformation. Pygmalion, the king of Cyprus, can find no woman worthy of his attention, and so he creates an ivory statue, which he lovingly attends. The goddess Venus takes pity on the king, and the statue is transformed into a breathing woman. Perrault's Cinderella, being a good-hearted and pious young woman, is transformed into a beautiful princess through the magic of her attentive fairy godmother. Other playwrights had mined the myth and the fairy tale, and Shaw was aware of the versions: Dion Boucicault's *Grimaldi: Or the Actress* (1862) shows the transformation of Violet, the flower girl of Covent Garden, into Violet the successful actress; W. S. Gilbert's *Pygmalion and Galatea* (1871) is a satire about Galatea, who is so ill at ease in a perilous world that she decides to return to her inanimate form, leaving Pygmalion to face the real world alone; and Israel Zangwill's *Merely Mary Ann* (1904) follows the trials of a young boardinghouse maid who falls in love, is not ruined, marries, and becomes a lady.

More a social critic than these earlier dramatists, Shaw has his protagonist, Professor Henry Higgins, painstakingly transform Eliza Doolittle, a cockney Cinderella selling flowers on the curb of Covent Garden, into a princess, through hard work. While her transformation is largely superficial (adhering to the essentials of middle-class virtues of cleanliness, proper dress, standard speech, and correct etiquette and manners), Eliza carries it off stylishly because she is good-hearted and has an indomitable spirit.

The transformation begins in Act II when Eliza visits Wimpole Street in order to ask Higgins, a linguist, to teach her to speak like a lady, something she has overheard him assert he can do. Higgins's friend Colonel Pickering challenges Higgins to prove his claim that he can teach even someone as low as Eliza to speak like a duchess. Absorbed in their wager, neither man stops to consider the housekeeper's question of what is to become of the girl when they are through with her. When Eliza's father, Alfred Doolittle, a dustman, appears, he assumes that the men are up to something sexually improper with Eliza, and he extorts £5 from them.

Eliza's first social test comes in Act III when she appears at Mrs. Higgins's home for tea. Eliza's efforts at chitchat while taking tea comically hint of her potential, but her mingling of slang and proper English, especially the expression "Not bloody likely," gives her away. Later, Eliza succeeds marvelously among the socially elite at the ambassador's party. (In the original stage production the ball scene was omitted; however, it is an obligatory scene, and in Shaw's 1938 filmscript, he rectified the omission.) She is tested not only by the occasion, but by Nepommuck, the self-proclaimed first and best of Higgins's students, who declares that Eliza is a Hungarian princess. The Cinderella story is completed when the hostess, rejecting Higgins's suggestion that Eliza is an "ordinary London girl out of the gutter," says, "She must be a princess at least."

Act IV finds Higgins and Pickering back in Wimpole Street, congratulating themselves. They ignore Eliza, who stands and smolders with anger until her fury is released and she throws Higgins's slippers at him. In the argument that follows, Eliza tries to get back at Higgins, but she has a hard time of it because he is so self-righteous. Eliza resolves to leave and finds Freddy on the doorstep and takes him off in a taxi; he hasn't the fare, but she does.

In Act V, Alfred Doolittle appears again, transformed into a gentleman of sorts, dressed in formal clothes and on his way to be married. In an offhand moment, Higgins had recommended Doolittle as a moralist, and subsequently the Wannafeller Trust engaged him as a lecturer on modern morality. Doolittle sets off for church, muttering, "Middle class morality claims its victim." Eliza's return to Wimpole Street sets up a discussion of what is to become of her: Higgins says that she'll turn out fine, but Eliza is anxious. Their final argument is a battle of wills that recalls the situation of Katherina and Petruchio in Shakespeare's *Taming of the Shrew,* or that of Beatrice and Benedict in *Much Ado About Nothing*. The ending is ambiguous. Eliza and Higgins continue sparring: She says, "Then I shall not see you again, Professor. Goodbye." He says, "Oh, by the way, Eliza, order a ham and a Stilton cheese, will you?" Eliza responds, "What you are to do without me I cannot imagine." Mrs. Higgins mistakenly suggests Higgins might be jealous of Eliza's feelings for Pickering, but Higgins retorts roaring with laughter, "Nonsense: she's going to marry Freddy."

Shaw, who detested sentimentality, settled the issue by explaining in an afterward to the play that Eliza's story is called a romance not because of its "happy ending" but because her transfiguration is real: "Eliza, in telling Higgins she would not marry him if he asked her, was not coquetting; she was announcing a well-considered decision." Though Eliza prefers to argue with Higgins, she marries Freddy, and with Pickering's generosity, they set up a flower shop.

Here, as elsewhere, Shaw's adaptation of an Ibsen problem play proved highly popular, and his success influenced other playwrights to experiment with social themes. One finds Shaw's mark in the plays of such disparate playwrights as Eugene O'Neill, Arthur Miller, John Osborne, Harold Pinter, and Wendy Wasserstein.

Film

Pygmalion (1938), co-directed by Anthony Asquithe and Leslie Howard; with Leslie Howard, Wendy Hiller, Wilfred Lawson, and Marie Lohr. Shaw wrote the screenplay and won an Oscar for best screenplay adaptation. Gabriel Pascal.

My Fair Lady (1964), directed by George Cuckor; with Rex Harrison, Audrey Hepburn, Stanley Holloway, Wilfrid Hyde-White, Theodore Bikel, Jeremy Brett, Mona Washbourne, Robert Coote, and Gladys Cooper. Lyrics by Alan Jay Lerner, musical score by Frederick Lowe, based on their 1956 theater production. CBS/Warner.

Pygmalion

A Romance in Five Acts

PREFACE

A Professor of Phonetics

As will be seen later on, Pygmalion needs, not a preface, but a sequel, which I have supplied in its due place.

The English have no respect for their language, and will not teach their children to speak it. They cannot spell it because they have nothing to spell it with but an old foreign alphabet of which only the consonants—and not all of them—have any agreed speech value. Consequently no man can teach himself what it should sound like from reading it; and it is impossible for an Englishman to open his mouth without making some other Englishman despise him. Most European languages are now accessible in black and white to foreigners: English and French are not accessible even to Englishmen and Frenchmen. The reformer we need most today is an energetic phonetic enthusiast: that is why I have made such a one the hero of a popular play.

There have been heroes of that kind crying in the wilderness for many years past. When I became interested in the subject towards the end of the eighteen-seventies, the illustrious Alexander Melville Bell, the inventor of Visible Speech, had emigrated to Canada, where his son invented the telephone; but Alexander J. Ellis was still a London patriarch, with an impressive head always covered by a velvet skull cap, for which he would apologize to public meetings in a very courtly manner. He and Tito Pagliardini, another phonetic veteran, were men whom it was impossible to dislike. Henry Sweet, then a young man, lacked their sweetness of character: he was about as conciliatory to conventional mortals as Ibsen or Samuel Butler. His great ability as a phonetician (he was, I think, the best of them all at his job) would have entitled him to high official recognition, and perhaps enabled him to popularize his subject, but for his Satanic contempt for all academic dignitaries and persons in general who thought more of Greek than of phonetics. Once, in the days when the Imperial Institute rose in South Kensington, and Joseph Chamberlain was booming the Empire, I induced the editor of a leading monthly review to commission an article from Sweet on the imperial importance of his subject. When it arrived, it contained nothing but a savagely derisive attack on a professor of language and literature whose chair Sweet regarded as proper to a phonetic expert only. The article, being libellous, had to be returned as impossible; and I had to renounce my dream of dragging its author into the limelight. When I met him afterwards, for the first time for many years, I found to my astonishment that he, who had been a quite tolerably presentable young man, had actually managed by sheer scorn to alter his personal appearance until he had become a sort of walking repudiation of Oxford and all its traditions. It must have been largely in his own despite that he was squeezed into something called a Readership of phonetics there. The future of phonetics rests probably with his pupils, who all swore by him; but nothing could bring the man himself into any sort of compliance with the university to which he nevertheless clung by divine right in an intensely Oxonian way. I daresay his papers, if he has left any, include some satires that may be published without too destructive results fifty years hence. He was, I believe, not in the least an ill-natured man: very much the opposite, I should say; but he would not suffer fools gladly; and to him all scholars who were not rabid phoneticians were fools.

Those who knew him will recognize in my third act the allusion to the Current Shorthand in which he used to write postcards. It may be acquired from a four and sixpenny manual published by the Clarendon Press. The postcards which Mrs Higgins describes are such as I have received from Sweet. I would decipher a sound which a cockney would represent by *zerr*, and a Frenchman by *seu*, and then write demanding with some heat what on earth it meant. Sweet, with boundless contempt for my stupidity, would reply that it not only meant but obviously was the word Result, as no other word containing that sound, and capable of making sense with the context, existed in any language spoken on earth. That less expert mortals should require fuller indications was beyond Sweet's patience. Therefore, though the whole point of his Current Shorthand is that it can express every sound in the language perfectly, vowels as well as consonants, and that your hand has to make no stroke except the easy and current ones with which you write m, n, and u, l, p, and q, scribbling them at whatever angle comes easiest to you, his unfortunate determination to make this remarkable and quite legible script serve also as a shorthand reduced it in his own practice to the most inscrutable of cryptograms. His true objective was the provision of a full, accurate, legible script for our language; but he was led past that by his contempt for the popular Pitman system of shorthand, which he called the Pitfall system. The triumph of Pitman was a triumph of business organization: there was a weekly paper to persuade you to learn Pitman: there were cheap textbooks and exercise books and transcripts of speeches for you to copy, and schools where experienced teachers coached you up to the necessary proficiency. Sweet could not organize his market in that fashion. He might as well have been the Sybil who tore up the leaves of prophecy that nobody would attend to. The four and sixpenny manual, mostly in his lithographed handwriting, that was never vulgarly advertized, may perhaps some day be taken up by a syndicate and pushed upon the public as The Times pushed the Encyclopædia Britannica; but until then it will certainly not prevail against Pitman. I have bought three copies of it during my lifetime; and I am informed by the publishers that its cloistered existence is still a steady and healthy one. I actually learned the system two several times; and yet the shorthand in which I am writing these lines is Pitman's. And the reason is, that my secretary cannot transcribe Sweet, having been perforce taught in the schools of Pitman. In America I could use the commercially organized Gregg shorthand, which has taken a hint from Sweet by making its letters writable (current, Sweet would have called them) instead of having to be geometrically drawn like Pitman's; but all these systems, including Sweet's, are spoilt by making them available for verbatim reporting, in which complete and exact spelling and word division are impossible. A complete and exact phonetic script is neither practicable nor necessary for ordinary use; but if we enlarge our alphabet to the Russian size, and make our spelling as phonetic as Spanish, the advance will be prodigious.

Pygmalion Higgins is not a portrait of Sweet, to whom the adventure of Eliza Doolittle would have been impossible; still, as will be seen, there are touches of Sweet in the play. With Higgins's physique and temperament Sweet might have set the Thames on fire. As it was, he impressed himself professionally on Europe to an extent that made his comparative personal obscurity, and the failure of Oxford to do justice to his eminence, a puzzle to foreign specialists in his subject. I do not blame Oxford, because I think Oxford is quite right in demanding a certain social amenity from its nurslings (heaven knows it is not exorbitant in its requirements!); for although I well know how hard it is for a man of genius with a seriously underrated subject to maintain serene and kindly relations with the men who underrate it, and who keep all the best places for less important subjects which they profess without originality and sometimes without much capacity for them, still, if he overwhelms them with wrath and disdain, he cannot expect them to heap honors on him.

Of the later generations of phoneticians I know little. Among them towered Robert Bridges, to whom perhaps Higgins may owe his Miltonic sympathies, though here again I must disclaim all portraiture. But if the play makes the public aware that there are such people as phoneticians, and that they are among the most important people in England at present, it will serve its turn.

I wish to boast that Pygmalion has been an extremely successful play, both on stage and screen, all over Europe and North America as well as at home. It is so intensely and deliberately didactic, and its subject is esteemed so dry, that I delight in throwing it at the heads of the wiseacres who repeat the parrot cry that art should never be didactic. It goes to prove my contention that great art can never be anything else.

Finally, and for the encouragement of people troubled with accents that cut them off from all high employment, I may add that the change wrought by Professor Higgins in the flower-girl is neither impossible nor uncommon. The modern concierge's daughter who fulfills her ambition by playing the Queen of Spain in Ruy Blas at the Théâtre Français is only one of many thousands of men and women who have sloughed off their native dialects and acquired a new tongue. Our West End shop assistants and domestic servants are bi-lingual. But the thing has to be done scientifically, or the last state of the aspirant may be worse than the first. An honest slum dialect is more tolerable than the attempts of phonetically untaught persons to imitate the plutocracy. Ambitious flower-girls who read this play must not imagine that they can pass themselves off as fine ladies by untutored imitation. They must learn their alphabet over again, and different, from a phonetic expert. Imitation will only make them ridiculous.

NOTE FOR TECHNICIANS. A complete representation of the play as printed for the first time in this edition is technically possible only on the cinema screen or on stages furnished with exceptionally elaborate machinery. For ordinary theatrical use the scenes separated by rows of asterisks are to be omitted.

In the dialogue an e upside down indicates the indefinite vowel, sometimes called obscure or neutral, for which, though it is one of the commonest sounds in English speech, our wretched alphabet has no letter.

ACT I

London at 11.15 p.m. Torrents of heavy summer rain. Cab whistles blowing frantically in all directions. Pedestrians running for shelter into the portico of St Paul's church (not Wren's cathedral but Inigo Jones's church in Covent Garden vegetable market), among them a lady and her daughter in evening dress. All are peering out gloomily at the rain, except one man with his back turned to the rest, wholly preoccupied with a notebook in which he is writing.

The church clock strikes the first quarter.

THE DAUGHTER [*in the space between the central pillars, close to the one on her left*]: I'm getting chilled to the bone. What can Freddy be doing all this time? He's been gone twenty minutes.

THE MOTHER [*on her daughter's right*]: Not so long. But he ought to have got us a cab by this.

A BYSTANDER [*on the lady's right*]: He wont get no cab not until half-past eleven, missus, when they come back after dropping their theatre fares.

THE MOTHER: But we must have a cab. We cant stand here until half-past eleven. It's too bad.

THE BYSTANDER: Well it aint my fault, missus.

THE DAUGHTER: If Freddy had a bit of gumption, he would have got one at the theatre door.

THE MOTHER: What could he have done, poor boy?

THE DAUGHTER: Other people get cabs. Why couldnt he?

FREDDY *rushes in out of the rain from the Southampton Street side, and comes between them closing a dripping umbrella. He is a young man of twenty, in evening dress, very wet round the ankles.*

THE DAUGHTER: Well, havnt you got a cab?

FREDDY: Theres not one to be had for love or money.

THE MOTHER: Oh, Freddy, there must be one. You cant have tried.

THE DAUGHTER: It's too tiresome. Do you expect us to go and get one ourselves?

FREDDY: I tell you theyre all engaged. The rain was so sudden: nobody was prepared; and everybody had to take a cab. Ive been to Charing Cross one way and nearly to Ludgate Circus the other; and they were all engaged.

THE MOTHER: Did you try Trafalgar Square?

FREDDY: There wasnt one at Trafalgar Square.

THE DAUGHTER: Did you try?

FREDDY: I tried as far as Charing Cross Station. Did you expect me to walk to Hammersmith?

THE DAUGHTER: You havnt tried at all.

THE MOTHER: You really are very helpless, Freddy. Go again; and dont come back until you have found a cab.

FREDDY: I shall simply get soaked for nothing.

THE DAUGHTER: And what about us? Are we to stay here all night in this draught, with next to nothing on? You selfish pig—

FREDDY: Oh, very well: I'll go, I'll go. [*He opens his umbrella and dashes off Strandwards, but comes into collision with a flower girl who is hurrying in for shelter, knocking her basket out of her hands. A blinding flash of lightning, followed instantly by a rattling peal of thunder, orchestrates the incident*].

THE FLOWER GIRL: Nah then, Freddy: look wh' y' gowin, deah.

FREDDY: Sorry [*he rushes off*].

THE FLOWER GIRL [*picking up her scattered flowers and replacing them in the basket*]: Theres menners f' yer! Tə-oo banches o voylets trod into the mad. [*She sits down on the plinth of the column, sorting her flowers, on the lady's right. She is not at all a romantic figure. She is perhaps eighteen, perhaps twenty, hardly older.*

She wears a little sailor hat of black straw that has long been exposed to the dust and soot of London and has seldom if ever been brushed. Her hair needs washing rather badly: its mousy color can hardly be natural. She wears a shoddy black coat that reaches nearly to her knees and is shaped to her waist. She has a brown skirt with a coarse apron. Her boots are much the worse for wear. She is no doubt as clean as she can afford to be; but compared to the ladies she is very dirty. Her features are no worse than theirs; but their condition leaves something to be desired; and she needs the services of a dentist].

THE MOTHER: How do you know that my son's name is Freddy, pray?

THE FLOWER GIRL: Ow, eez, yə-ooa san, is e? Wal, fewd dan y' d-ooty bawmz a mather should, eed now bettern to spawl a pore gel's flahrzn than ran awy athaht pyin. Will ye-oo py me f'them? [*Here, with apologies, this desperate attempt to represent her dialect without a phonetic alphabet must be abandoned as unintelligible outside London*].

THE DAUGHTER: Do nothing of the sort, mother. The idea!

THE MOTHER: Please allow me, Clara. Have you any pennies?

THE DAUGHTER: No. Ive nothing smaller than sixpence.

THE FLOWER GIRL [*hopefully*]: I can give you change for a tanner, kind lady.

THE MOTHER [*to* CLARA]: Give it to me. [CLARA *parts reluctantly*]. Now [*to the girl*] This is for your flowers.

THE FLOWER GIRL: Thank you kindly, lady.

THE DAUGHTER: Make her give you the change. These things are only a penny a bunch.

THE MOTHER: Do hold your tongue, Clara. [*To the girl*] You can keep the change.

THE FLOWER GIRL: Oh, thank you, lady.

THE MOTHER: Now tell me how you know that young gentleman's name.

THE FLOWER GIRL: I didnt.

THE MOTHER: I heard you call him by it. Dont try to deceive me.

THE FLOWER GIRL [*protesting*]: Who's trying to deceive you? I called him Freddy or Charlie same as you might yourself if you was talking to a stranger and wished to be pleasant.

THE DAUGHTER: Sixpence thrown away! Really, mamma, you might have spared Freddy that. [*She retreats in disgust behind the pillar*].

Peter O'Toole (right) as Henry Higgins, with (left to right) Kirstie Poolie, Osmund Bullock, Mary Peach, Amanda Plummer as Eliza, and Joyce Redman in Pygmalion, *directed by Val May, the Little Theatre, New York, 1987.*

An elderly gentleman of the amiable military type rushes into the shelter, and closes a dripping umbrella. He is in the same plight as FREDDY, *very wet about the ankles. He is in evening dress, with a light overcoat. He takes the place left vacant by the daughter.*

THE GENTLEMAN: Phew!

THE MOTHER [*to* THE GENTLEMAN]: Oh, sir, is there any sign of its stopping?

THE GENTLEMAN: I'm afraid not. It started worse than ever about two minutes ago [*he goes to the plinth beside the flower girl; puts up his foot on it; and stoops to turn down his trouser ends*].

THE MOTHER: Oh dear! [*She retires sadly and joins her daughter*].

THE FLOWER GIRL [*taking advantage of the military gentleman's proximity to establish friendly relations with him*]: If it's worse, it's a sign it's nearly over. So cheer up, Captain; and buy a flower off a poor girl.

THE GENTLEMAN: I'm sorry. I havnt any change.

THE FLOWER GIRL: I can give you change, Captain.

THE GENTLEMAN: For a sovereign? Ive nothing less.

THE FLOWER GIRL: Garn! Oh do buy a flower off me, Captain. I can change half-a-crown. Take this for tuppence.

THE GENTLEMAN: Now dont be troublesome: theres a good girl. [*Trying his pockets*] I really havnt any change—Stop: heres three hapence, if thats any use to you [*he retreats to the other pillar*].

THE FLOWER GIRL [*disappointed, but thinking three halfpence better than nothing*]: Thank you, sir.

THE BYSTANDER [*to the girl*]: You be careful: give him a flower for it. Theres a bloke here behind taking down every blessed word youre saying. [*All turn to the man who is taking notes*].

THE FLOWER GIRL [*springing up terrified*]: I aint done nothing wrong by speaking to the gentleman. Ive a right to sell flowers if I keep off the kerb. [*Hysterically*] I'm a respectable girl: so help me, I never spoke to him except to ask him to buy a flower off me.

General hubbub, mostly sympathetic to the flower girl, but deprecating her excessive sensibility. Cries of Dont start hollerin. Who's hurting you? Nobody's going to touch you. Whats the good of fussing? Steady on. Easy easy, etc., *come from the elderly staid spectators, who pat her comfortingly. Less patient ones bid her shut her head, or ask her roughly what is wrong with her. A remoter group, not knowing what the matter is, crowd in and increase the noise with question and answer:* Whats the row? What-she-do? Where is he? A tec taking her down. What! him? Yes: him over there: Took money off the gentleman, etc.

THE FLOWER GIRL [*breaking through them to the gentleman, crying wildly*]: Oh, sir, dont let him charge me. You dunno what it means to me. Theyll take away my character and drive me on the streets for speaking to gentleman. They—

THE NOTE TAKER [*coming foward on her right, the rest crowding after him*]: There! there! there! there! who's hurting you, you silly girl? What do you take me for?

THE BYSTANDER: It's aw rawt: e's a genleman: look at his bə-oots. [*Explaining to the note taker*] She thought you was a copper's nark, sir.

THE NOTE TAKER [*with quick interest*]: Whats a copper's nark?

THE BYSTANDER [*inapt at definition*]: It's a—well, it's a copper's nark, as you might say. What else would you call it? A sort of informer.

THE FLOWER GIRL [*still hysterical*]: I take my Bible oath I never said a word—

THE NOTE TAKER [*overbearing but good-humored*]: Oh, shut up, shut up. Do I look like a policeman?

THE FLOWER GIRL [*far from reassured*]: Then what did you take down my words for? How do I know whether you took me down right? You just shew me what youve wrote about me. [*The note taker opens his book and holds it steadily under her nose, though the pressure of the mob trying to read it over his shoulders would upset a weaker man*]. Whats that? That aint proper writing. I cant read that.

THE NOTE TAKER: I can. [*Reads, reproducing her pronunciation exactly*] "Cheer ap, Keptin; n' baw ya flahr orf a pore gel."

THE FLOWER GIRL [*much distressed*]: It's because I called him Captain. I meant no harm. [*To the gentleman*] Oh, sir, dont let him lay a charge agen me for a word like that. You—

THE GENTLEMAN: Charge! I make no charge. [*To the note taker*] Really, sir, if you are a detective, you need not begin protecting me against molestation by young women until I ask you. Anybody could see that the girl meant no harm.

THE BYSTANDERS GENERALLY [*demonstrating against police espionage*]: Course they could. What business is it of yours? You mind your own affairs. He wants promotion, he does. Taking down people's words! Girl never said a word to him. What harm if she did? Nice thing a girl cant shelter from the rain without being insulted, etc., etc., etc. [*She is conducted by the more sympathetic demonstrators back to her plinth, where she resumes her seat and struggles with her emotion*].

THE BYSTANDER: He aint a tec. He's a blooming busy-body: thats what he is. I tell you, look at his bə-oots.

THE NOTE TAKER [*turning on him genially*]: And how are all your people down at Selsey?

THE BYSTANDER [*suspiciously*]: Who told you my people come from Selsey?

THE NOTE TAKER: Never you mind. They did. [*To the girl*] How do you come to be up so far east? You were born in Lisson Grove.

THE FLOWER GIRL [*appalled*]: Oh, what harm is there in my leaving Lisson Grove? It wasnt fit for a pig to live in; and I had to pay four-and-six a week. [*In tears*] Oh, boo—hoo—oo—

THE NOTE TAKER: Live where you like; but stop that noise.

THE GENTLEMAN [*to the girl*]: Come, come! he cant touch you: you have a right to live where you please.

A SARCASTIC BYSTANDER [*thrusting himself between the note taker and the gentleman*]: Park Lane, for instance. I'd like to go into the Housing Question with you, I would.

THE FLOWER GIRL [*subsiding into a brooding melancholy over her basket, and talking very low-spiritedly to herself*]: I'm a good girl, I am.

THE SARCASTIC BYSTANDER [*not attending to her*]: Do you know where *I* come from?

THE NOTE TAKER [*promptly*]: Hoxton.

Titterings. Popular interest in the note taker's performance increases.

THE SARCASTIC ONE [*amazed*]: Well, who said I didnt? Bly me! you know everything, you do.

THE FLOWER GIRL [*still nursing her sense of injury*]: Aint no call to meddle with me, he aint.

THE BYSTANDER [*to her*]: Of course he aint. Dont you stand it from him. [*To the note taker*] See here: what call have you to know about people what never offered to meddle with you?

THE FLOWER GIRL: Let him say what he likes. I dont want to have no truck with him.

THE BYSTANDER: You take us for dirt under your feet, dont you? Catch you taking liberties with a gentleman!

THE SARCASTIC BYSTANDER: Yes: tell him where he come from if you want to go fortune-telling.

THE NOTE TAKER: Cheltenham, Harrow, Cambridge, and India.

THE GENTLEMAN: Quite right.

Great laughter. Reaction in the note taker's favor. Exclamations of He knows all about it. Told him proper. Hear him tell the toff where he come from? etc.

THE GENTLEMAN: May I ask, sir, do you do this for your living at a music hall?

THE NOTE TAKER: I've thought of that. Perhaps I shall some day.

The rain has stopped; and the persons on the outside of the crowd begin to drop off.

THE FLOWER GIRL [*resenting the reaction*]: He's no gentleman, he aint, to interfere with a poor girl.

THE DAUGHTER [*out of patience, pushing her way rudely to the front and displacing the gentleman, who politely retires to the other side of the pillar*]: What on earth is Freddy doing? I shall get pneumownia if I stay in this draught any longer.

THE NOTE TAKER [*to himself, hastily making a note of her pronunciation of 'monia'*]: Earlscourt.

THE DAUGHTER [*violently*]: Will you please keep your impertinent remarks to yourself.

THE NOTE TAKER: Did I say that out loud? I didnt mean to. I beg your pardon. Your mother's Epsom, unmistakeably.

THE MOTHER [*advancing between the daughter and the note taker*]: How very curious! I was brought up in Largelady Park, near Epsom.

THE NOTE TAKER [*uproariously amused*]: Ha! ha! what a devil of a name! Excuse me. [*To the daughter*] You want a cab, do you?

THE DAUGHTER: Dont dare speak to me.

THE MOTHER: Oh, please, please, Clara. [*Her daughter repudiates her with an angry shrug and retires haughtily*]. We should be so grateful to you, sir, if you found us a cab. [*The note taker produces a whistle*]. Oh, thank you. [*She joins her daughter*].

The note taker blows a piercing blast.

THE SARCASTIC BYSTANDER: There! I knowed he was a plainclothes copper.

THE BYSTANDER: That aint a police whistle: thats a sporting whistle.

THE FLOWER GIRL [*still preoccupied with her wounded feelings*]: He's no right to take away my character. My character is the same to me as any lady's.

THE NOTE TAKER: I dont know whether youve noticed it; but the rain stopped about two minutes ago.

THE BYSTANDER: So it has. Why didnt you say so before? and us losing our time listening to your silliness! [*He walks off towards the Strand*].

THE SARCASTIC BYSTANDER: I can tell where you come from. You come from Anwell. Go back there.

THE NOTE TAKER [*helpfully*]: Hanwell.

THE SARCASTIC BYSTANDER [*affecting great distinction of*

speech]: Thank you, teacher. Haw haw! So long [*he touches his hat with mock respect and strolls off*].

THE FLOWER GIRL: Frightening people like that! How would he like it himself?

THE MOTHER: It's quite fine now, Clara. We can walk to a motor bus. Come. [*She gathers her skirts above her ankles and hurries off towards the Strand*].

THE DAUGHTER: But the cab— [*her mother is out of hearing*]. Oh, how tiresome! [*She follows angrily*].

All the rest have gone except the note taker, the gentleman, and the flower girl, who sits arranging her basket, and still pitying herself in murmurs.

THE FLOWER GIRL: Poor girl! Hard enough for her to live without being worried and chivied.

THE GENTLEMAN [*returning to his former place on the note taker's left*]: How do you do it, if I may ask?

THE NOTE TAKER: Simply phonetics. The science of speech. Thats my profession: also my hobby. Happy is the man who can make a living by his hobby! You can spot an Irishman or a Yorkshireman by his brogue. *I* can place any man within six miles. I can place him within two miles in London. Sometimes within two streets.

THE FLOWER GIRL: Ought to be ashamed of himself, unmanly coward!

THE GENTLEMAN: But is there a living in that?

THE NOTE TAKER: Oh, yes. Quite a fat one. This is an age of upstarts. Men begin in Kentish Town with £80 a year, and end in Park Lane with a hundred thousand. They want to drop Kentish Town; but they give themselves away every time they open their mouths. Now I can teach them—

THE FLOWER GIRL: Let him mind his own business and leave a poor girl—

THE NOTE TAKER [*explosively*]: Woman: cease this detestable boohooing instantly; or else seek the shelter of some other place of worship.

THE FLOWER GIRL [*with feeble defiance*]: Ive a right to be here if I like, same as you.

THE NOTE TAKER: A woman who utters such depressing and disgusting sounds has no right to be anywhere—no right to live. Remember that you are a human being with a soul and the divine gift of articulate speech: that your native language is the language of Shakespear and Milton and The Bible; and dont sit there crooning like a bilious pigeon.

THE FLOWER GIRL [*quite overwhelmed, looking up at him in mingled wonder and deprecation without daring to raise her head*]: Ah-ah-ah-ow-ow-ow-oo!

THE NOTE TAKER [*whipping out his book*]: Heavens! what a sound! [*He writes; then holds out the book and reads, reproducing her vowels exactly*] Ah-ah-ah-ow-ow-ow-oo!

THE FLOWER GIRL [*tickled by the performance, and laughing in spite of herself*]: Garn!

THE NOTE TAKER: You see this creature with her kerbstone English: the English that will keep her in the gutter to the end of her days. Well, sir, in three months I could pass that girl off as a duchess at an ambassador's garden party. I could even get her a place as lady's maid or shop assistant, which requires better English.

THE FLOWER GIRL: What's that you say?

THE NOTE TAKER: Yes, you squashed cabbage leaf, you disgrace to the noble architecture of these columns, you incarnate insult to the English language: I could pass you off as the Queen of Sheba. [*To the Gentleman*] Can you believe that?

THE GENTLEMAN: Of course I can. I am myself a student of Indian dialects; and—

THE NOTE TAKER [*eagerly*]: Are you? Do you know Colonel Pickering, the author of Spoken Sanscrit?

THE GENTLEMAN: I a m Colonel Pickering. Who are you?

THE NOTE TAKER: Henry Higgins, author of Higgins's Universal Alphabet.

PICKERING [*with enthusiasm*]: I came from India to meet you.

HIGGINS: I was going to India to meet you.

PICKERING: Where do you live?

HIGGINS: 27A Wimpole Street. Come and see me tomorrow.

PICKERING: I'm at the Carlton. Come with me now and lets have a jaw over some supper.

HIGGINS: Right you are.

THE FLOWER GIRL [*to* PICKERING, *as he passes her*]: Buy a flower, kind gentleman. I'm short for my lodging.

PICKERING: I really havnt any change. I'm sorry [*he goes away*].

HIGGINS [*shocked at the girl's mendacity*]: Liar. You said you could change half-a-crown.

THE FLOWER GIRL [*rising in desperation*]: You ought to be stuffed with nails, you ought. [*Flinging the basket at his feet*] Take the whole blooming basket for sixpence.

The church clock strikes the second quarter.

HIGGINS [*hearing in it the voice of God, rebuking him for his Pharisaic want of charity to the poor girl*]: A reminder. [*He raises his hat solemnly; then throws a handful of money into the basket and follows* PICKERING].

THE FLOWER GIRL [*picking up a half-crown*]: Ah-ow-ooh! [*Picking up a couple of florins*] Aaah-ow-ooh! [*Picking up several coins*] Aaaaaah-ow-ooh! [*Picking up a half-sovereign*] Aaaaaaaaaaaah-ow-ooh!!!

FREDDY [*springing out of a taxicab*]: Got one at last. Hallo! [*To the girl*] Where are the two ladies that were here?

THE FLOWER GIRL: They walked to the bus when the rain stopped.

FREDDY: And left me with a cab on my hands! Damnation!

THE FLOWER GIRL [*with grandeur*]: Never mind, young man. I'm going home in a taxi. [*She sails off to the cab. The driver puts his hand behind him and holds the door firmly shut against her. Quite understanding his mistrust, she shews him her handful of money*]. A taxi fare aint no object to me, Charlie. [*He grins and opens the door*]. Here. What about the basket?

THE TAXIMAN: Give it here. Tuppence extra.

LIZA: No: I dont want nobody to see it. [*She crushes it into the cab and gets in, continuing the conversation through the window*] Goodbye, Freddy.

FREDDY [*dazedly raising his hat*]: Goodbye.

TAXIMAN: Where to?

LIZA: Bucknam Pellis [Buckingham Palace].

TAXIMAN: What d'ye mean—Bucknam Pellis?

LIZA: Dont you know where it is? In the Green Park, where the King lives. Goodbye, Freddy. Dont let me keep you standing there. Goodbye.

FREDDY: Goodbye. [*He goes*].

TAXIMAN: Here? Whats this about Bucknam Pellis? What business have you at Bucknam Pellis?

LIZA: Of course I havnt none. But I wasnt going to let him know that. You drive me home.

TAXIMAN: And wheres home?

LIZA: Angel Court, Drury Lane, next Meiklejohn's oil shop.

TAXIMAN: That sounds more like it, Judy. [*He drives off*].

* * *

Let us follow the taxi to the entrance to Angel Court, a narrow little archway between two shops, one of them Meiklejohn's oil shop. When it stops there, ELIZA gets out, dragging her basket with her.

LIZA: How much?

TAXIMAN [*indicating the taximeter*]: Cant you read? A shilling.

LIZA: A shilling for two minutes!!

TAXIMAN: Two minutes or ten: it's all the same.

LIZA: Well, I dont call it right.

TAXIMAN: Ever been in a taxi before?

LIZA [*with dignity*]: Hundreds and thousands of times, young man.

TAXIMAN [*laughing at her*]: Good for you, Judy. Keep the shilling, darling, with best love from all at home. Good luck! [*He drives off*].

LIZA [*humiliated*]: Impidence!

She picks up the basket and trudges up the alley with it to her lodging: a small room with very old wall paper hanging loose in the damp places. A broken pane in the window is mended with paper. A portrait of a popular actor and a fashion plate of ladies' dresses, all wildly beyond poor ELIZA'*s means, both torn from newspapers, are pinned up on the wall. A birdcage hangs in the window; but its tenant died long ago: it remains as a memorial only.*

These are the only visible luxuries: the rest is the irreducible minimum of poverty's needs: a wretched bed heaped with all sorts of coverings that have any warmth in them, a draped packing case with a basin and jug on it and a little looking glass over it, a chair and table, the refuse of some suburban kitchen, and an American alarum clock on the shelf above the unused fireplace: the whole lighted with a gas lamp with a penny in the slot meter. Rent: four shillings a week.

Here ELIZA, chronically weary, but too excited to go to bed, sits, counting her new riches and dreaming and planning what to do with them, until the gas goes out, when she enjoys for the first time the sensation of being able to put in another penny without grudging it. This prodigal mood does not extinguish her gnawing sense of the need for economy sufficiently to prevent her from calculating that she can dream and plan in bed more cheaply and warmly than sitting up without a fire. So she takes off her shawl and skirt and adds them to the miscellaneous bedclothes. Then she kicks off her shoes and gets into bed without any further change.

ACT II

Next day at 11 a.m. HIGGINS'*s laboratory in Wimpole Street. It is a room on the first floor, looking on the street, and was meant for the drawing room. The double doors are in the middle of the back wall; and persons entering find in the corner to their right two tall file cabinets at right angles to one another against the wall. In this corner stands a flat writing-table, on which are a phonograph, a laryngoscope, a row of tiny organ pipes with a bellows, a set of lamp chimneys for singing flames with burners attached to a gas plug in the wall by an indiarubber tube, several tuning-forks of different sizes, a life-size image of half a human head, shewing in section the vocal organs, and a box containing a supply of wax cylinders for the phonograph.*

Further down the room, on the same side, is a fireplace, with a comfortable leather-covered easy-chair at the side of the hearth nearest the door, and a coal-scuttle. There is a clock on the mantel-piece. Between the fireplace and the phonograph table is a stand for newspapers.

On the other side of the central door, to the left of the visitor, is a cabinet of shallow drawers. On it is a telephone and the telephone directory. The corner beyond, and most of the side wall, is occupied by a grand piano, with the keyboard at the end furthest from the door, and a bench for the player extending the full length of the keyboard. On the piano is a dessert dish heaped with fruit and sweets, mostly chocolates.

The middle of the room is clear. Besides the easy-chair, the piano bench, and two chairs at the phonograph table, there is one stray chair. It stands near the fireplace. On the walls, engravings: mostly Piranesis and mezzotint portraits. No paintings.

PICKERING *is seated at the table, putting down some cards and a tuning-fork which he has been using.* HIGGINS *is standing up near him, closing two or three file drawers which are hanging out. He appears in the morning light as a robust, vital, appetizing sort of man of forty or thereabouts, dressed in a professional-looking black frock-coat with a white linen collar and black silk tie. He is of the energetic scientific type, heartily, even violently interested in everything that can be studied as a scientific subject, and careless about himself and other people, including their feelings. He is, in fact, but for his years and size, rather like a very impetuous baby "taking notice" eagerly and loudly, and requiring almost as much watching to keep him out of unintended mischief. His manner varies from genial bullying when he is in a good humor to stormy petulance when anything goes wrong; but he is so entirely frank and void of malice that he remains likeable even in his least reasonable moments.*

HIGGINS [*as he shuts the last drawer*]: Well, I think thats the whole show.

PICKERING: It's really amazing. I havnt taken half of it in, you know.

HIGGINS: Would you like to go over any of it again?

PICKERING [*rising and coming to the fireplace, where he plants himself with his back to the fire*]: No, thank you: not now. I'm quite done up for this morning.

HIGGINS [*following him, and standing beside him on his left*]: Tired of listening to sounds?

PICKERING: Yes. It's a fearful strain. I rather fancied myself because I can pronounce twenty-four distinct vowel sounds: but your hundred and thirty beat me. I cant hear a bit of difference between most of them.

HIGGINS [*chuckling, and going over to the piano to eat sweets*]: Oh, that comes with practice. You hear no difference at first; but you keep on listening, and presently you find theyre all as different as A from B. [MRS PEARCE *looks in: she is* HIGGINS*'s housekeeper*]. Whats the matter?

MRS PEARCE [*hesitating, evidently perplexed*]: A young woman asks to see you, sir.

HIGGINS: A young woman! What does she want?

MRS PEARCE: Well, sir, she says youll be glad to see her when you know what she's come about. She's quite a common girl, sir. Very common indeed. I should have sent her away, only I thought perhaps you wanted her to talk into your machines. I hope Ive not done wrong; but really you see such queer people sometimes—youll excuse me, I'm sure, sir—

HIGGINS: Oh, thats all right. Mrs Pearce. Has she an interesting accent?

MRS PEARCE: Oh, something dreadful, sir, really. I dont know how you can take an interest in it.

HIGGINS [*to* PICKERING]: Lets have her up. Shew her up, Mrs Pearce [*he rushes across to his working table and picks out a cylinder to use on the phonograph*].

MRS PEARCE [*only half resigned to it*]: Very well, sir. It's for you to say. [*She goes downstairs*].

HIGGINS: This is rather a bit of luck. I'll shew you how I make records. We'll set her talking; and I'll take it down first in Bell's Visible Speech; then in broad Romic; and then we'll get her on the phonograph so that you can turn her on as often as you like with the written transcript before you.

MRS PEARCE [*returning*]: This is the young woman, sir.

The flower girl enters in state. She has a hat with three ostrich feathers, orange, sky-blue, and red. She has a nearly clean apron and the shoddy coat has been tidied a little. The pathos of this deplorable figure, with its innocent vanity and consequential air, touches PICKERING, *who has already straightened himself in the presence of* MRS PEARCE. *But as to* HIGGINS, *the only distinction he makes between men and women is that when he is neither bullying nor exclaiming to the heavens against some featherweight cross, he coaxes women as a child coaxes its nurse when it wants to get anything out of her.*

HIGGINS [*brusquely, recognizing her with unconcealed disappointment, and at once, babylike, making an intolerable grievance of it*]: Why, this is the girl I jotted down last night. She's no use: Ive got all the records I want of the Lisson Grove lingo; and I'm not going to waste another cylinder on it. [*To the girl*] Be off with you: I dont want you.

THE FLOWER GIRL: Dont you be so saucy. You aint heard what I come for yet. [*To* MRS PEARCE, *who is waiting at the door for further instructions*] Did you tell him I come in a taxi?

MRS PEARCE: Nonsense, girl! what do you think a gentleman like Mr Higgins cares what you came in?

THE FLOWER GIRL: Oh, we a r e proud! He aint above giving lessons, not him: I heard him say so. Well, I aint come here to ask for any compliment; and if my money's not good enough I can go elsewhere.

HIGGINS: Good enough for what?
THE FLOWER GIRL: Good enough for yə-oo. Now you know, dont you? I'm coming to have lessons, I am. And to pay for em tə-oo: make no mistake.
HIGGINS [*stupent*]: Well!!! [*Recovering his breath with a gasp*] What do you expect me to say to you?
THE FLOWER GIRL: Well, if you was a gentleman, you might ask me to sit down, I think. Dont I tell you I'm bringing you business?
HIGGINS: Pickering: shall we ask this baggage to sit down, or shall we throw her out of the window?
THE FLOWER GIRL [*running away in terror to the piano, where she turns at bay*]: Ah-ah-oh-ow-ow-ow-oo! [*Wounded and whimpering*] I wont be called a baggage when Ive offered to pay like any lady.

Motionless, the two men stare at her from the other side of the room, amazed.

PICKERING [*gently*]: But what is it you want?
THE FLOWER GIRL: I want to be a lady in a flower shop stead of sellin at the corner of Tottenham Court Road. But they wont take me unless I can talk more genteel. He said he could teach me. Well, here I am ready to pay him—not asking any favor—and he treats me zif I was dirt.
MRS PEARCE: How can you be such a foolish ignorant girl as to think you could afford to pay Mr Higgins?
THE FLOWER GIRL: Why shouldnt I? I know what lessons cost as well as you do; and I'm ready to pay.
HIGGINS: How much?
THE FLOWER GIRL [*coming back to him, triumphant*]: Now youre talking! I thought youd come off it when you saw a chance of getting back a bit of what you chucked at me last night. [*Confidentially*] Youd had a drop in, hadnt you?
HIGGINS [*peremptorily*]: Sit down.
THE FLOWER GIRL: Oh, if youre going to make a compliment of it—
HIGGINS [*thundering at her*]: Sit down.
MRS PEARCE [*severely*]: Sit down, girl. Do as youre told.
THE FLOWER GIRL: Ah-ah-ah-ow-ow-oo! [*She stands, half rebellious, half-bewildered*].
PICKERING [*very courteous*]: Wont you sit down? [*He places the stray chair near the hearthrug between himself and* HIGGINS].
LIZA [*coyly*]: Dont mind if I do. [*She sits down.* PICKERING *returns to the hearthrug*].
HIGGINS: Whats your name?
THE FLOWER GIRL: Liza Doolittle.
HIGGINS [*declaiming gravely*]:
Eliza, Elizabeth, Betsy and Bess,
They went to the woods to get a bird's nes':
PICKERING: They found a nest with four eggs in it:
HIGGINS: They took one apiece, and left three in it.

They laugh heartily at their own fun.

LIZA: Oh, dont be silly.
MRS PEARCE [*placing herself behind* ELIZA*'s chair*]: You mustnt speak to the gentleman like that.
LIZA: Well, why wont he speak sensible to me?
HIGGINS: Come back to business. How much do you propose to pay me for the lessons?
LIZA: Oh, I know whats right. A lady friend of mine gets French lessons for eighteenpence an hour from a real French gentleman. Well, you wouldnt have the face to ask me the same for teaching me my own language as you would for French; so I wont give more than a shilling. Take it or leave it.
HIGGINS [*walking up and down the room, rattling his keys and his cash in his pockets*]: You know, Pickering, if you consider a shilling, not as a simple shilling, but as a percentage of this girl's income, it works out as fully equivalent to sixty or seventy guineas from a millionaire.
PICKERING: How so?
HIGGINS: Figure it out. A millionaire has about £150 a day. She earns about half-a-crown.
LIZA [*haughtily*]: Who told you I only—
HIGGINS [*continuing*]: She offers me two-fifths of her day's income for a lesson. Two-fifths of a millionaire's income for a day would be somewhere about £60. It's handsome. By George, it's enormous! it's the biggest offer I ever had.
LIZA [*rising, terrified*]: Sixty pounds! What are you talking about? I never offered you sixty pounds. Where would I get—
HIGGINS: Hold your tongue.
LIZA [*weeping*]: But I aint got sixty pounds. Oh—
MRS PEARCE: Dont cry, you silly girl. Sit down. Nobody is going to touch your money.
HIGGINS: Somebody is going to touch you, with a broomstick, if you dont stop snivelling. Sit down.
LIZA [*obeying slowly*]: Ah-ah-ah-ow-oo-o! One would think you was my father.
HIGGINS: If I decide to teach you, I'll be worse than two fathers to you. Here [*he offers her his silk handkerchief*]!
LIZA: Whats this for?
HIGGINS: To wipe your eyes. To wipe any part of your face that feels moist. Remember: thats your handkerchief, and thats your sleeve. Dont mistake the one for the other if you wish to become a lady in a shop.

LIZA, *utterly bewildered, stares helplessly at him.*

MRS PEARCE: It's no use talking to her like that, Mr Higgins: she doesnt understand you. Besides, youre quite wrong: she doesnt do it that way at all [*she takes the handkerchief*].

LIZA [*snatching it*]: Here! You give me that handkerchief. He gev it to me, not to you.

PICKERING [*laughing*]: He did. I think it must be regarded as her property, Mrs Pearce.

MRS PEARCE [*resigning herself*]: Serve you right, Mr Higgins.

PICKERING: Higgins: I'm interested. What about the ambassador's garden party? I'll say youre the greatest teacher alive if you make that good. I'll bet you all the expenses of the experiment you cant do it. And I'll pay for the lessons.

LIZA: Oh, you are real good. Thank you, Captain.

HIGGINS [*tempted, looking at her*]: It's almost irresistible. She's so deliciously low—so horribly dirty—

LIZA [*protesting extremely*]: Ah-ah-ah-ah-ow-ow-oo-oo!!! I aint dirty: I washed my face and hands afore I come, I did.

PICKERING: Youre certainly not going to turn her head with flattery, Higgins.

MRS PEARCE [*uneasy*]: Oh, dont say that, sir: theres more ways than one of turning a girl's head; and nobody can do it better than Mr Higgins, though he may not always mean it. I do hope, sir, you wont encourage him to do anything foolish.

HIGGINS [*becoming excited as the idea grows on him*]: What is life but a series of inspired follies? The difficulty is to find them to do. Never lose a chance: it doesnt come every day. I shall make a duchess of this draggletailed guttersnipe.

LIZA [*strongly deprecating this view of her*]: Ah-ah-ah-ow-ow-oo!

HIGGINS [*carried away*]: Yes: in six months—in three if she has a good ear and a quick tongue—I'll take her anywhere and pass her off as anything. We'll start today: now! this moment! Take her away and clean her, Mrs Pearce. Monkey Brand, if it wont come off any other way. Is there a good fire in the kitchen?

MRS PEARCE [*protesting*]: Yes; but—

HIGGINS [*storming on*]: Take all her clothes off and burn them. Ring up Whiteley or somebody for new ones. Wrap her up in brown paper til they come.

LIZA: Youre no gentleman, youre not, to talk of such things. I'm a good girl, I am; and I know what the like of you are, I do.

HIGGINS: We want none of your Lisson Grove prudery here, young woman. Youve got to learn to behave like a duchess. Take her away, Mrs Pearce. If she gives you any trouble, wallop her.

LIZA [*springing up and running between* PICKERING *and* MRS PEARCE *for protection*]: No! I'll call the police, I will.

MRS PEARCE: But Ive no place to put her.

HIGGINS: Put her in the dustbin.

LIZA: Ah-ah-ah-ow-ow-oo!

PICKERING: Oh come, Higgins! be reasonable.

MRS PEARCE [*resolutely*]: You must be reasonable, Mr Higgins: really you must. You cant walk over everybody like this.

HIGGINS, *thus scolded, subsides. The hurricane is succeeded by a zephyr of amiable surprise.*

HIGGINS [*with professional exquisiteness of modulation*]: *I* walk over everybody! My dear Mrs Pearce, my dear Pickering, I never had the slightest intention of walking over anyone. All I propose is that we should be kind to this poor girl. We must help her to prepare and fit herself for her new station in life. If I did not express myself clearly it was because I did not wish to hurt her delicacy, or yours.

LIZA, *reassured, steals back to her chair.*

MRS PEARCE [*to* PICKERING]: Well, did you ever hear anything like that, sir?

PICKERING [*laughing heartily*]: Never, Mrs Pearce: never.

HIGGINS [*patiently*]: Whats the matter?

MRS PEARCE: Well, the matter is, sir, that you cant take a girl up like that as if you were picking up a pebble on the beach.

HIGGINS: Why not?

MRS PEARCE: Why not! But you dont know anything about her. What about her parents? She may be married.

LIZA: Garn!

HIGGINS: There! As the girl very properly says, Garn! Married indeed! Dont you know that a woman of that class looks a worn out drudge of fifty a year after she's married?

LIZA: Whood marry me?

HIGGINS [*suddenly resorting to the most thrillingly beautiful low tones in his best elocutionary style*]: By George, Eliza, the streets will be strewn with the bodies of men shooting themselves for your sake before Ive done with you.

MRS PEARCE: Nonsense, sir. You mustnt talk like that to her.

LIZA [*rising and squaring herself determinedly*]: I'm going away. He's off his chump, he is. I dont want no balmies teaching me.

HIGGINS [*wounded in his tenderest point by her insensibility to his elocution*]: Oh, indeed! I'm mad, am I? Very well, Mrs Pearce: you neednt order the new clothes for her. Throw her out.

LIZA [*whimpering*]: Nah-ow. You got no right to touch me.

MRS PEARCE: You see now what comes of being saucy. [*Indicating the door*] This way, please.

LIZA [*almost in tears*]: I didnt want no clothes. I wouldnt have taken them [*she throws away the handkerchief*]. I can buy my own clothes.

HIGGINS [*deftly retrieving the handkerchief and intercepting her on her reluctant way to the door*]: Youre an ungrateful wicked girl. This is my return for offering to take you out of the gutter and dress you beautifully and make a lady of you.

MRS PEARCE: Stop, Mr Higgins. I wont allow it. It's you that are wicked. Go home to your parents, girl; and tell them to take better care of you.

LIZA: I aint got no parents. They told me I was big enough to earn my own living and turned me out.

MRS PEARCE: Wheres your mother?

LIZA: I aint got no mother. Her that turned me out was my sixth stepmother. But I done without them. And I'm a good girl, I am.

HIGGINS: Very well, then, what on earth is all this fuss about? The girl doesnt belong to anybody—is no use to anybody but me. [*He goes to* MRS PEARCE *and begins coaxing*]. You can adopt her, Mrs Pearce: I'm sure a daughter would be a great amusement to you. Now dont make any more fuss. Take her downstairs; and—

MRS PEARCE: But whats to become of her? Is she to be paid anything? Do be sensible, sir.

HIGGINS: Oh, pay her whatever is necessary: put it down in the housekeeping book. [*Impatiently*] What on earth will she want with money? She'll have her food and her clothes. She'll only drink if you give her money.

LIZA [*turning on him*]: Oh you are a brute. It's a lie: nobody ever saw the sign of liquor on me. [*To* PICKERING] Oh, sir: youre a gentleman: dont let him speak to me like that.

PICKERING [*in good-humored remonstrance*]: Does it occur to you, Higgins, that the girl has some feelings?

HIGGINS [*looking critically at her*]: Oh no, I dont think so. Not any feelings that we need bother about. [*Cheerily*] Have you, Eliza?

LIZA: I got my feelings same as anyone else.

HIGGINS [*to* PICKERING, *reflectively*]: You see the difficulty?

PICKERING: Eh? What difficulty?

HIGGINS: To get her to talk grammar. The mere pronunciation is easy enough.

LIZA: I dont want to talk grammar. I want to talk like a lady in a flower shop.

MRS PEARCE: Will you please keep to the point, Mr Higgins. I want to know on what terms the girl is to be here. Is she to have any wages? And what is to become of her when youve finished your teaching? You must look ahead a little.

HIGGINS [*impatiently*]: Whats to become of her if I leave her in the gutter? Tell me that, Mrs Pearce.

MRS PEARCE: Thats her own business, not yours, Mr Higgins.

HIGGINS: Well, when Ive done with her, we can throw her back into the gutter; and then it will be her own business again; so thats all right.

LIZA: Oh, youve no feeling heart in you: you dont care for nothing but yourself. [*She rises and takes the floor resolutely*]. Here! Ive had enough of this. I'm going [*making for the door*]. You ought to be ashamed of yourself, you ought.

HIGGINS [*snatching a chocolate cream from the piano, his eyes suddenly beginning to twinkle with mischief*]: Have some chocolates, Eliza.

LIZA [*halting, tempted*]: How do I know what might be in them? Ive heard of girls being drugged by the like of you.

HIGGINS *whips out his penknife; cuts a chocolate in two; puts one half into his mouth and bolts it; and offers her the other half.*

HIGGINS: Pledge of good faith, Eliza. I eat one half: you eat the other. [LIZA *opens her mouth to retort: he pops the half chocolate into it*]. You shall have boxes of them, barrels of them, every day. You shall live on them. Eh?

LIZA [*who has disposed of the chocolate after being nearly choked by it*]: I wouldnt have ate it, only I'm too ladylike to take it out of my mouth.

HIGGINS: Listen, Eliza. I think you said you came in a taxi.

LIZA: Well, what if I did? Ive as good a right to take a taxi as anyone else.

HIGGINS: You have, Eliza; and in future you shall have as many taxis as you want. You shall go up and down and round the town in a taxi every day. Think of that, Eliza.

MRS PEARCE: Mr Higgins: youre tempting the girl. It's not right. She should think of the future.

HIGGINS: At her age! Nonsense! Time enough to think of the future when you havnt any future to think of. No, Eliza: do as this lady does: think of other people's futures; but never think of your own. Think of chocolates, and taxis, and gold, and diamonds.

LIZA: No: I dont want no gold and no diamonds. I'm a good girl, I am. [*She sits down again, with an attempt at dignity*].

HIGGINS: You shall remain so, Eliza, under the care of Mrs Pearce. And you shall marry an officer in the Guards, with a beautiful moustache: the son of a marquis, who will disinherit him for marrying you, but will relent when he sees your beauty and goodness—

PICKERING: Excuse me, Higgins; but I really must interfere. Mrs Pearce is quite right. If this girl is to put herself in your hands for six months for an experiment in teaching, she must understand thoroughly what she's doing.

HIGGINS: How can she? She's incapable of understanding anything. Besides, do any of us understand what we are doing? If we did, would we ever do it?

PICKERING: Very clever, Higgins; but not to the present point. [*To* ELIZA] Miss Doolittle—

LIZA [*overwhelmed*]: Ah-ah-ow-oo!

HIGGINS: There! Thats all youll get out of Eliza. Ah-ah-ow-oo! No use explaining. As a military man you ought to know that. Give her her orders: thats enough for her. Eliza: you are to live here for the next six months, learning how to speak beautifully, like a lady in a florist's shop. If youre good and do whatever youre told, you shall sleep in a proper bedroom, and have lots to eat, and money to buy chocolates and take rides in taxis. If youre naughty and idle you will sleep in the back kitchen among the black beetles, and be walloped by Mrs Pearce with a broomstick. At the end of six months you shall go to Buckingham Palace in a carriage, beautifully dressed. If the King finds out youre not a lady, you will be taken by the police to the Tower of London, where your head will be cut off as a warning to other presumptuous flower girls. If you are not found out, you shall have a present of seven-and-sixpence to start life with as a lady in a shop. If you refuse this offer you will be a most ungrateful wicked girl; and the angels will weep for you. [*To* PICKERING] Now are you satisfied, Pickering? [*To* MRS PEARCE] Can I put it more plainly and fairly, Mrs Pearce?

MRS PEARCE [*patiently*]: I think youd better let me speak to the girl properly in private. I dont know that I can take charge of her or consent to the arrangement at all. Of course I know you dont mean her any harm; but when you get what you call interested in people's accents, you never think or care what may happen to them or you. Come with me, Eliza.

HIGGINS: Thats all right. Thank you, Mrs Pearce. Bundle her off to the bathroom.

LIZA [*rising reluctantly and suspiciously*]: Youre a great bully, you are. I wont stay here if I dont like. I wont let nobody wallop me. I never asked to go to Bucknam Palace, I didnt. I was never in trouble with the police, not me. I'm a good girl—

MRS PEARCE: Dont answer back, girl. You dont understand the gentleman. Come with me. [*She leads the way to the door, and holds it open for* ELIZA].

LIZA [*as she goes out*]: Well, what I say is right. I wont go near the King, not if I'm going to have my head cut off. If I'd known what I was letting myself in for, I wouldnt have come here. I always been a good girl; and I never offered to say a word to him; and I dont owe him nothing; and I dont care; and I wont be put upon; and I have my feelings the same as anyone else—

MRS PEARCE shuts the door, and ELIZA's plaints are no longer audible.

* * *

ELIZA is taken upstairs to the third floor greatly to her surprise; for she expected to be taken down to the scullery. There MRS PEARCE opens a door and takes her into a spare bedroom.

MRS PEARCE: I will have to put you here. This will be your bedroom.

LIZA: O-h, I couldnt sleep here, missus. It's too good for the likes of me. I should be afraid to touch anything. I aint a duchess yet, you know.

MRS PEARCE: You have got to make yourself as clean as the room: then you wont be afraid of it. And you must call me Mrs Pearce, not missus. [*She throws open the door of the dressingroom, now modernized as a bathroom*].

LIZA: Gawd! whats this? Is this where you wash clothes? Funny sort of copper I call it.

MRS PEARCE: It is not a copper. This is where we wash ourselves, Eliza, and where I am going to wash you.

LIZA: You expect me to get into that and wet myself all over! Not me. I should catch my death. I knew a woman did it every Saturday night; and she died of it.

MRS PEARCE: Mr Higgins has the gentlemen's bathroom downstairs; and he has a bath every morning, in cold water.

LIZA: Ugh! He's made of iron, that man.

MRS PEARCE: If you are to sit with him and the Colonel and be taught you will have to do the same. They wont like the smell of you if you dont. But you can have the water as hot as you like. There are two taps: hot and cold.

LIZA [*weeping*]: I couldnt. I dursnt. Its not natural: it would kill me. Ive never had a bath in my life: not what youd call a proper one.

MRS PEARCE: Well, dont you want to be clean and sweet and decent, like a lady? You know you cant be a nice girl inside if youre a dirty slut outside.

LIZA: Boohoo!!!!

MRS PEARCE: Now stop crying and go back into your room and take off all your clothes. Then wrap yourself in this [*taking down a gown from its peg and handing it to her*] and come back to me. I will get the bath ready.

LIZA [*all tears*]: I cant. I wont. I'm not used to it. Ive never took off all my clothes before. It's not right: it's not decent.

MRS PEARCE: Nonsense, child. Dont you take off all your clothes every night when you go to bed?

LIZA [*amazed*]: No. Why should I? I should catch my death. Of course I take off my skirt.

MRS PEARCE: Do you mean that you sleep in the underclothes you wear in the daytime?

LIZA: What else have I to sleep in?

MRS PEARCE: You will never do that again as long as you live here. I will get you a proper nightdress.

LIZA: Do you mean change into cold things and lie awake shivering half the night? You want to kill me, you do.

MRS PEARCE: I want to change you from a frowzy slut to a clean respectable girl fit to sit with the gentlemen in the study. Are you going to trust me and do what I tell you or be thrown out and sent back to your flower basket?

LIZA: But you dont know what the cold is to me. You dont know how I dread it.

MRS PEARCE: Your bed wont be cold here: I will put a hot water bottle in it. [*Pushing her into the bedroom*] Off with you and undress.

LIZA: Oh, if only I'd a known what a dreadful thing it is to be clean I'd never have come. I didnt know when I was well off. I— [MRS PEARCE *pushes her through the door, but leaves it partly open lest her prisoner should take to flight*].

MRS PEARCE *puts on a pair of white rubber sleeves, and fills the bath, mixing hot and cold, and testing the result with the bath thermometer. She perfumes it with a handful of bath salts and adds a palmful of mustard. She then takes a formidable looking long handled scrubbing brush and soaps it profusely with a ball of scented soap.*

ELIZA *comes back with nothing on but the bath gown huddled tightly round her, a piteous spectacle of abject terror.*

MRS PEARCE: Now come along. Take that thing off.

LIZA: Oh I couldnt, Mrs Pearce: I reely couldnt. I never done such a thing.

MRS PEARCE: Nonsense. Here: step in and tell me whether it's hot enough for you.

LIZA: Ah-oo! Ah-oo! It's too hot.

MRS PEARCE [*deftly snatching the gown away and throwing* ELIZA *down on her back*]: It wont hurt you. [*She sets to work with the scrubbing brush*].

ELIZA's *screams are heartrending.*

* * *

Meanwhile the colonel has been having it out with HIGGINS *about* ELIZA. PICKERING *has come from the hearth to the chair and seated himself astride of it with his arms on the back to cross-examine him.*

PICKERING: Excuse the straight question, Higgins. Are you a man of good character where women are concerned?

HIGGINS [*moodily*]: Have you ever met a man of good character where women are concerned?

PICKERING: Yes: very frequently.

HIGGINS [*dogmatically, lifting himself on his hands to the level of the piano, and sitting on it with a bounce*]: Well, I havnt. I find that the moment I let a woman make friends with me, she becomes jealous, exacting, suspicious, and a damned nuisance. I find that the moment I let myself make friends with a woman, I become selfish and tyrannical. Women upset everything. When you let them into your life, you find that the woman is driving at one thing and youre driving at another.

PICKERING: At what, for example?

HIGGINS [*coming off the piano restlessly*]: Oh, Lord knows! I suppose the woman wants to live her own life; and the man wants to live his; and each tries to drag the other on to the wrong track. One wants to go north and the other south; and the result is that both have to go east, though they both hate the east wind. [*He sits down on the bench at the keyboard*]. So here I am, a confirmed old bachelor, and likely to remain so.

PICKERING [*rising and standing over him gravely*]: Come, Higgins! You know what I mean. If I'm to be in this business I shall feel responsible for that girl. I hope it's understood that no advantage is to be taken of her position.

HIGGINS: What! That thing! Sacred, I assure you. [*Rising to explain*] You see, she'll be a pupil; and teaching would be impossible unless pupils were sacred. Ive taught scores of American millionairesses how to speak English: the best looking women in the world. I'm seasoned. They might as well be blocks of wood. *I* might as well be a block of wood. It's—

MRS PEARCE *opens the door. She has* ELIZA's *hat in her hand.* PICKERING *retires to the easy-chair at the hearth and sits down.*

HIGGINS [*eagerly*]: Well, Mrs Pearce: is it all right?

MRS PEARCE [*at the door*]: I just wish to trouble you with a word, if I may, Mr Higgins.

HIGGINS: Yes, certainly. Come in. [*She comes forward*] Dont burn that, Mrs Pearce. I'll keep it as a curiosity. [*He takes the hat*].

MRS PEARCE: Handle it carefully, sir, please. I had to promise her not to burn it; but I had better put it in the oven for a while.

HIGGINS [*putting it down hastily on the piano*]: Oh! thank you. Well, what have you to say to me?

PICKERING: Am I in the way?

MRS PEARCE: Not at all, sir. Mr Higgins: will you please be very particular what you say before the girl?

HIGGINS [*sternly*]: Of course. I'm always particular about what I say. Why do you say this to me?

MRS PEARCE [*unmoved*]: No sir: youre not at all particular when youve mislaid anything or when you get a little impatient. Now it doesnt matter before me: I'm used to it. But you really must not swear before the girl.

HIGGINS [*indignantly*]: *I* swear! [*Most emphatically*] I never swear. I detest the habit. What the devil do you mean?

MRS PEARCE [*stolidly*]: Thats what I mean, sir. You swear a great deal too much. I dont mind your damning and blasting, and what the devil and where the devil and who the devil—

HIGGINS: Mrs Pearce: this language from your lips! Really!

MRS PEARCE [*not to be put off*]: —but there is a certain word I must ask you not to use. The girl used it herself when she began to enjoy the bath. It begins with the same letter as bath. She knows no better: she learnt it at her mother's knee. But she must not hear it from your lips.

HIGGINS [*loftily*]: I cannot charge myself with having ever uttered it, Mrs Pearce. [*She looks at him steadfastly. He adds, hiding an uneasy conscience with a judicial air*] Except perhaps in a moment of extreme and justifiable excitement.

MRS PEARCE: Only this morning, sir, you applied it to your boots, to the butter, and to the brown bread.

HIGGINS: Oh, that! Mere alliteration, Mrs Pearce, natural to a poet.

MRS PEARCE: Well, sir, whatever you choose to call it, I beg you not to let the girl hear you repeat it.

HIGGINS: Oh, very well, very well. Is that all?

MRS PEARCE: No, sir. We shall have to be very particular with this girl as to personal cleanliness.

HIGGINS: Certainly. Quite right. Most important.

MRS PEARCE: I mean not to be slovenly about her dress or untidy in leaving things about.

HIGGINS [*going to her solemnly*]: Just so, I intended to call your attention to that. [*He passes on to* PICKERING, *who is enjoying the conversation immensely*]. It is these little things that matter, Pickering. Take care of the pence and the pounds will take care of themselves is as true of personal habits as of money. [*He comes to anchor on the hearthrug, with the air of a man in an unassailable position*].

MRS PEARCE: Yes, sir. Then might I ask you not to come down to breakfast in your dressing-gown, or at any rate not to use it as a napkin to the extent you do, sir. And if you would be so good as not to eat everything off the same plate, and to remember not to put the porridge saucepan out of your hand on the clean tablecloth, it would be a better example to the girl. You know you nearly choked yourself with a fishbone in the jam only last week.

HIGGINS [*routed from the hearthrug and drifting back to the piano*]: I may do these things sometimes in absence of mind; but surely I dont do them habitually. [*Angrily*] By the way: my dressing-gown smells most damnably of benzine.

MRS PEARCE: No doubt it does, Mr Higgins. But if you will wipe your fingers—

HIGGINS [*yelling*]: Oh very well, very well: I'll wipe them in my hair in future.

MRS PEARCE: I hope youre not offended, Mr Higgins.

HIGGINS [*shocked at finding himself thought capable of an unamiable sentiment*]: Not at all, not at all. Youre quite right, Mrs Pearce: I shall be particularly careful before the girl. Is that all?

MRS PEARCE: No, sir. Might she use some of those Japanese dresses you brought from abroad? I really cant put her back into her old things.

HIGGINS: Certainly. Anything you like. Is that all?

MRS PEARCE: Thank you, sir. Thats all. [*She goes out*].

HIGGINS: You know, Pickering, that woman has the most extraordinary ideas about me. Here I am, a shy, diffident sort of man. Ive never been able to feel really grown-up and tremendous, like other chaps. And yet she's firmly persuaded that I'm an arbitrary overbearing bossing kind of person. I cant account for it.

MRS PEARCE *returns.*

MRS PEARCE: If you please, sir, the trouble's beginning already. Theres a dustman downstairs, Alfred Doolittle, wants to see you. He says you have his daughter here.

PICKERING [*rising*]: Phew! I say!

HIGGINS [*promptly*]: Send the blackguard up.

MRS PEARCE: Oh, very well, sir. [*She goes out*].

PICKERING: He may not be a blackguard, Higgins.

HIGGINS: Nonsense. Of course he's a blackguard.

PICKERING: Whether he is or not, I'm afraid we shall have some trouble with him.

HIGGINS [*confidently*]: Oh no: I think not. If theres any trouble he shall have it with me, not I with him.

And we are sure to get something interesting out of him.

PICKERING: About the girl?

HIGGINS: No. I mean his dialect.

PICKERING: Oh!

MRS PEARCE [*at the door*]: Doolittle, sir. [*She admits* DOOLITTLE *and retires*].

ALFRED DOOLITTLE *is an elderly but vigorous dustman, clad in the costume of his profession, including a hat with a back brim covering his neck and shoulders. He has well marked and rather interesting features, and seems equally free from fear and conscience. He has a remarkably expressive voice, the result of a habit of giving vent to his feelings without reserve. His present pose is that of wounded honor and stern resolution.*

DOOLITTLE [*at the door, uncertain which of the two gentlemen is his man*]: Professor Iggins?

HIGGINS: Here. Good morning. Sit down.

DOOLITTLE: Morning, Governor. [*He sits down magisterially*] I come about a very serious matter, Governor.

HIGGINS [*to* PICKERING]: Brought up in Hounslow. Mother Welsh, I should think. [DOOLITTLE *opens his mouth, amazed.* HIGGINS *continues*] What do you want, Doolittle?

DOOLITTLE [*menacingly*]: I want my daughter: thats what I want. See?

HIGGINS: Of course you do. Youre her father, arnt you? You dont suppose anyone else wants her, do you? I'm glad to see you have some spark of family feeling left. She's upstairs. Take her away at once.

DOOLITTLE [*rising, fearfully taken aback*]: What!

HIGGINS: Take her away. Do you suppose I'm going to keep your daughter for you?

DOOLITTLE [*remonstrating*]: Now, now, look here, Governor. Is this reasonable? Is it fairity to take advantage of a man like this? The girl belongs to me. You got her. Where do I come in? [*He sits down again*].

HIGGINS: Your daughter had the audacity to come to my house and ask me to teach her how to speak properly so that she could get a place in a flower-shop. This gentleman and my housekeeper have been here all the time. [*Bullying him*] How dare you come here and attempt to blackmail me? You sent her here on purpose.

DOOLITTLE [*protesting*]: No, Governor.

HIGGINS: You must have. How else could you possibly know that she is here?

DOOLITTLE: Dont take a man up like that, Governor.

HIGGINS: The police shall take you up. This is a plant—a plot to extort money by threats. I shall telephone for the police [*he goes resolutely to the telephone and opens the directory*].

DOOLITTLE: Have I asked you for a brass farthing? I leave it to the gentleman here: have I said a word about money?

HIGGINS [*throwing the book aside and marching down on* DOOLITTLE *with a poser*]: What else did you come for?

DOOLITTLE [*sweetly*]: Well, what w o u l d a man come for? Be human, Governor.

HIGGINS [*disarmed*]: Alfred: did you put her up to it?

DOOLITTLE: So help me, Governor, I never did. I take my Bible oath I aint seen the girl these two months past.

HIGGINS: Then how did you know she was here?

DOOLITTLE [*"most musical, most melancholy"*]: I'll tell you, Governor, if youll only let me get a word in. I'm willing to tell you. I'm wanting to tell you. I'm waiting to tell you.

HIGGINS: Pickering: this chap has a certain natural gift of rhetoric. Observe the rhythm of his native woodnotes wild. "I'm willing to tell you: I'm wanting to tell you: I'm waiting to tell you." Sentimental rhetoric! thats the Welsh strain in him. It also accounts for his mendacity and dishonesty.

PICKERING: Oh, please, Higgins: I'm west country myself. [*To* DOOLITTLE] How did you know the girl was here if you didnt send her?

DOOLITTLE: It was like this, Governor. The girl took a boy in the taxi to give him a jaunt. Son of her landlady, he is. He hung about on the chance of her giving him another ride home. Well, she sent him back for her luggage when she heard you was willing for her to stop here. I met the boy at the corner of Long Acre and Endell Street.

HIGGINS: Public house. Yes?

DOOLITTLE: The poor man's club, Governor: why shouldnt I?

PICKERING: Do let him tell his story, Higgins.

DOOLITTLE: He told me what was up. And I ask you, what was my feelings and my duty as a father? I says to the boy, "You bring me the luggage," I says—

PICKERING: Why didnt you go for it yourself?

DOOLITTLE: Landlady wouldnt have trusted me with it, Governor. She's that kind of woman: y o u know. I had to give the boy a penny afore he trusted me with it, the little swine. I brought it to her just to oblige you like, and make myself agreeable. Thats all.

HIGGINS: How much luggage?

DOOLITTLE: Musical instrument, Governor. A few pictures, a trifle of jewlery, and a bird-cage. She said she didn't want no clothes. What was I to think from that, Governor? I ask you as a parent what was I to think?

HIGGINS: So you came to rescue her from worse than death, eh?

DOOLITTLE [*appreciatively: relieved at being so well understood*]: Just so, Governor. Thats right.

PICKERING: But why did you bring her luggage if you intended to take her away?

DOOLITTLE: Have I said a word about taking her away? Have I now?

HIGGINS [*determinedly*]: Youre going to take her away, double quick. [*He crosses to the hearth and rings the bell*].

DOOLITTLE [*rising*]: No, Governor. Dont say that. I'm not the man to stand in my girl's light. Heres a career opening for her as you might say; and—

MRS PEARCE *opens the door and awaits orders.*

HIGGINS: Mrs Pearce: this is Eliza's father. He has come to take her away. Give her to him. [*He goes back to the piano, with an air of washing his hands of the whole affair*].

DOOLITTLE: No. This is a misunderstanding. Listen here—

MRS PEARCE: He cant take her away, Mr Higgins: how can he? You told me to burn her clothes.

DOOLITTLE: Thats right. I cant carry the girl through the streets like a blooming monkey, can I? I put it to you.

HIGGINS: You have put it to me that you want your daughter. Take your daughter. If she has no clothes go out and buy her some.

DOOLITTLE [*desperate*]: Wheres the clothes she come in? Did I burn them or did your missus here?

MRS PEARCE: I am the housekeeper, if you please. I have sent for some clothes for the girl. When they come you can take her away. You can wait in the kitchen. This way, please.

DOOLITTLE, *much troubled, accompanies her to the door; then hesitates: finally turns confidentially to* HIGGINS.

DOOLITTLE: Listen here, Governor. You and me is men of the world, aint we?

HIGGINS: Oh! Men of the world, are we? Youd better go, Mrs Pearce.

MRS PEARCE: I think so, indeed, sir. [*She goes, with dignity*].

PICKERING: The floor is yours, Mr Doolittle.

DOOLITTLE [*to* PICKERING]: I thank you, Governor. [*To* HIGGINS, *who takes refuge on the piano bench, a little overwhelmed by the proximity of his visitor; for* DOOLITTLE *has a professional flavor of dust about him*]. Well, the truth is, Ive taken a sort of fancy to you, Governor; and if you want the girl, I'm not so set on having her back home again but what I might be open to an arrangement. Regarded in the light of a young woman, she's a fine handsome girl. As a daughter she's not worth her keep; and so I tell you straight. All I ask is my rights as a father; and youre the last man alive to expect me to let her go for nothing; for I can see youre one of the straight sort, Governor. Well, whats a five-pound note to you? and whats Eliza to me? [*He turns to his chair and sits down judicially*].

PICKERING: I think you ought to know, Doolittle, that Mr Higgins's intentions are entirely honorable.

DOOLITTLE: Course they are, Governor. If I thought they wasn't, I'd ask fifty.

HIGGINS [*revolted*]: Do you mean to say that you would sell your daughter for £50?

DOOLITTLE: Not in a general way I wouldnt; but to oblige a gentleman like you I'd do a good deal, I do assure you.

PICKERING: Have you no morals, man?

DOOLITTLE [*unabashed*]: Cant afford them, Governor. Neither could you if you was as poor as me. Not that I mean any harm, you know. But if Liza is going to have a bit out of this, why not me too?

HIGGINS [*troubled*]: I dont know what to do, Pickering. There can be no question that as a matter of morals it's a positive crime to give this chap a farthing. And yet I feel a sort of rough justice in his claim.

DOOLITTLE: Thats it, Governor. Thats all I say. A father's heart, as it were.

PICKERING: Well, I know the feeling; but really it seems hardly right—

DOOLITTLE: Dont say that, Governor. Dont look at it that way. What am I, Governors both? I ask you, what am I? I'm one of the undeserving poor: thats what I am. Think of what that means to a man. It means that he's up agen middle class morality all the time. If theres anything going, and I put in for a bit of it, it's always the same story: "Youre undeserving so you cant have it." But my needs is as great as the most deserving widow's that ever got money out of six different charities in one week for the death of the same husband. I dont need less than a deserving man: I need more. I dont eat less hearty than him; and I drink a lot more. I want a bit of amusement, cause I'm a thinking man. I want cheerfulness and a song and a band when I feel low. Well, they charge me just the same for everything as they charge the deserving. What is middle class morality? Just an excuse for never giving me anything. Therefore, I ask you, as two gentlemen, not to play that game on me. I'm playing straight with you. I aint pretending to be deserving. I'm undeserving; and I mean to go on being undeserving. I like it; and thats the truth. Will you take advantage of a man's nature to do him out of the price of his own daughter what he's brought up and fed and clothed by the sweat of his brow until she's growed big enough to be interesting to you two gentlemen? Is five pounds unreasonable? I put it to you; and I leave it to you.

HIGGINS [*rising, and going over to* PICKERING]: Pickering: if we were to take this man in hand for three months, he could choose between a seat in the Cabinet and a popular pulpit in Wales.

PICKERING: What do you say to that, Doolittle?

DOOLITTLE: Not me, Governor, thank you kindly. Ive heard all the preachers and all the prime ministers—for I'm a thinking man and game for politics or religion or social reform same as all the other amusements—and I tell you it's a dog's life any way you look at it. Undeserving poverty is my line. Taking one station in society with another, it's—it's—well, it's the only one that has any ginger in it, to my taste.

HIGGINS: I suppose we must give him a fiver.

PICKERING: He'll make a bad use of it, I'm afraid.

DOOLITTLE: Not me, Governor, so help me I wont. Dont you be afraid that I'll save it and spare it and live idle on it. There wont be a penny of it left by Monday: I'll have to go to work same as if I'd never had it. It wont pauperize me, you bet. Just one good spree for myself and the missus, giving pleasure to ourselves and employment to others, and satisfaction to you to think it's not been throwed away. You couldnt spend it better.

HIGGINS [*taking out his pocket book and coming between* DOOLITTLE *and the piano*]: This is irresistible. Lets give him ten. [*He offers two notes to the dustman*].

DOOLITTLE: No, Governor. She wouldnt have the heart to spend ten; and perhaps I shouldnt neither. Ten pounds is a lot of money: it makes a man feel prudent like: and then goodbye to happiness. You give me what I ask you, Governor: not a penny more, and not a penny less.

PICKERING: Why dont you marry that missus of yours? I rather draw the line at encouraging that sort of immorality.

DOOLITTLE: Tell her so, Governor: tell her so. *I'm* willing. It's me that suffers by it. Ive no hold on her. I got to be agreeable to her. I got to give her presents. I got to buy her clothes something sinful. I'm a slave to that woman, Governor, just because I'm not her lawful husband. And she knows it too. Catch her marrying me! Take my advice, Governor—marry Eliza while she's young and dont know no better. If you dont youll be sorry for it after. If you do, she'll be sorry for it after; but better her than you, because youre a man, and she's only a woman and dont know how to be happy anyhow.

HIGGINS: Pickering: If we listen to this man another minute, we shall have no convictions left. [*To* DOOLITTLE] Five pounds I think you said.

DOOLITTLE: Thank you kindly, Governor.

HIGGINS: Youre sure you wont take ten?

DOOLITTLE: Not now. Another time, Governor.

HIGGINS [*handing him a five-pound note*]: Here you are.

DOOLITTLE: Thank you, Governor. Good morning. [*He hurries to the door, anxious to get away with his booty. When he opens it he is confronted with a dainty and exquisitely clean young Japanese lady in a simple blue cotton kimono printed cunningly with small white jasmine blossoms.* MRS PEARCE *is with her. He gets out of her way deferentially and apologizes*]. Beg pardon, miss.

THE JAPANESE LADY: Garn! Dont you know your own daughter?

DOOLITTLE: } *exclaiming simultaneously* { Bly me! it's Eliza!
HIGGINS: Whats that? This!
PICKERING: By Jove!

LIZA: Dont I look silly?

HIGGINS: Silly?

MRS PEARCE [*at the door*]: Now, Mr Higgins, please dont say anything to make the girl conceited about herself.

HIGGINS [*conscientiously*]: Oh! Quite right, Mrs Pearce. [*To* ELIZA] Yes: damned silly.

MRS PEARCE: Please, sir.

HIGGINS [*correcting himself*]: I mean extremely silly.

LIZA: I should look all right with my hat on. [*She takes up her hat; puts it on; and walks across the room to the fireplace with a fashionable air*].

HIGGINS: A new fashion, by George! And it ought to look horrible!

DOOLITTLE [*with fatherly pride*]: Well, I never thought she'd clean up as good looking as that, Governor. She's a credit to me, aint she?

LIZA: I tell you, it's easy to clean up here. Hot and cold water on tap, just as much as you like, there is. Woolly towels, there is; and a towel horse so hot, it burns your fingers. Soft brushes to scrub yourself, and a wooden bowl of soap smelling like primroses. Now I know why ladies is so clean. Washing's a treat for them. Wish they could see what it is for the like of me!

HIGGINS: I'm glad the bathroom met with your approval.

LIZA: It didnt: not all of it; and I dont care who hears me say it. Mrs Pearce knows.

HIGGINS: What was wrong, Mrs Pearce?

MRS PEARCE [*blandly*]: Oh, nothing, sir. It doesnt matter.

LIZA: I had a good mind to break it. I didn't know which way to look. But I hung a towel over it, I did.

HIGGINS: Over what?

MRS PEARCE: Over the looking-glass sir.

HIGGINS: Doolittle: you have brought your daughter up too strictly.

DOOLITTLE: Me! I never brought her up at all, except to give her a lick of a strap now and again. Dont put it on me, Governor. She aint accustomed to it, you see: thats all. But she'll soon pick up your free-and-easy ways.

LIZA: I'm a good girl, I am; and I wont pick up no free-and-easy ways.

HIGGINS: Eliza: if you say again that youre a good girl, your father shall take you home.

LIZA: Not him. You dont know my father. All he come here for was to touch you for some money to get drunk on.

DOOLITTLE: Well, what else would I want money for? To put into the plate in church, I suppose. [*She puts out her tongue at him. He is so incensed by this that* PICKERING *presently finds it necessary to step between them*]. Dont you give me none of your lip; and dont let me hear you giving this gentleman any of it neither, or youll hear from me about it. See?

HIGGINS: Have you any further advice to give her before you go, Doolittle? Your blessing, for instance.

DOOLITTLE: No, Governor: I aint such a mug as to put up my children to all I know myself. Hard enough to hold them in without that. If you want Eliza's mind improved, Governor, you do it yourself with a strap. So long, gentlemen. [*He turns to go*].

HIGGINS [*impressively*]: Stop. Youll come regularly to see your daughter. It's your duty, you know. My brother is a clergyman; and he could help you in your talks with her.

DOOLITTLE [*evasively*]: Certainly, I'll come, Governor. Not just this week, because I have a job at a distance. But later on you may depend on me. Afternoon, gentlemen. Afternoon, maam. [*He touches his hat to* MRS PEARCE, *who disdains the salutation and goes out. He winks at* HIGGINS, *thinking him probably a fellow-sufferer from* MRS PEARCE'*s difficult disposition, and follows her*].

LIZA: Dont you believe the old liar. He'd as soon you set a bulldog on him as a clergyman. You wont see him again in a hurry.

HIGGINS: I dont want to, Eliza. Do you?

LIZA: Not me. I dont want never to see him again, I dont. He's a disgrace to me, he is, collecting dust, instead of working at his trade.

PICKERING: What is his trade, Eliza?

LIZA: Talking money out of other people's pockets into his own. His proper trade's a navvy; and he works at it sometimes too—for exercise—and earns good money at it. Aint you going to call me Miss Doolittle any more?

PICKERING: I beg your pardon, Miss Doolittle. It was a slip of the tongue.

LIZA: Oh, I dont mind; only it sounded so genteel. I should just like to take a taxi to the corner of Tottenham Court Road and get out there and tell it to wait for me, just to put the girls in their place a bit. I wouldnt speak to them, you know.

PICKERING: Better wait til we get you something really fashionable.

HIGGINS: Besides, you shouldnt cut your old friends now that you have risen in the world. Thats what we call snobbery.

LIZA: You dont call the like of them my friends now, I should hope. Theyve took it out of me often enough with their ridicule when they had the chance; and now I mean to get a bit of my own back. But if I'm to have fashionable clothes, I'll wait. I should like to have some. Mrs Pearce says youre going to give me some to wear in bed at night different to what I wear in the daytime; but it do seem a waste of money when you could get something to shew. Besides, I never could fancy changing into cold things on a winter night.

MRS PEARCE [*coming back*]: Now, Eliza. The new things have come for you to try on.

LIZA: Ah-ow-oo-ooh! [*She rushes out*].

MRS PEARCE [*following her*]: Oh, dont rush about like that, girl. [*She shuts the door behind her*].

HIGGINS: Pickering: we have taken on a stiff job.

PICKERING [*with conviction*]: Higgins: we have.

* * *

There seems to be some curiosity as to what HIGGINS's lessons to Eliza were like. Well, here is a sample: the first one.

Picture ELIZA, in her new clothes, and feeling her inside put out of step by a lunch, dinner, and breakfast of a kind to which it is unaccustomed, seated with HIGGINS and the Colonel in the study, feeling like a hospital out-patient at a first encounter with the doctors.

HIGGINS, constitutionally unable to sit still, discomposes her still more by striding restlessly about. But for the reassuring presence and quietude of her friend the Colonel she would run for her life, even back to Drury Lane.

HIGGINS: Say your alphabet.

LIZA: I know my alphabet. Do you think I know nothing? I dont need to be taught like a child.

HIGGINS [*thundering*]: Say your alphabet.

PICKERING: Say it, Miss Doolittle. You will understand presently. Do what he tells you; and let him teach you in his own way.

LIZA: Oh well, if you put it like that—Ahyee, bəyee, cəyee, dəyee—

HIGGINS [*with the roar of a wounded lion*]: Stop. Listen to this, Pickering. This is what we pay for as elementary education. This unfortunate animal has been locked up for nine years in school at our expense to teach her to speak and read the language of Shakespear and Milton. And the result is Ahyee, Bə-yee, Cə-yee, Də-yee. [*To* ELIZA] Say A, B, C, D.

LIZA [*almost in tears*]: But I'm saying it. Ahyee, Bəyee, Cə-yee—

HIGGINS: Stop. Say a cup of tea.

LIZA: A cappətə-ee.

HIGGINS: Put your tongue forward until it squeezes against the top of your lower teeth. Now say cup.

LIZA: C-c-c—I cant. C-Cup.

PICKERING: Good. Splendid, Miss Doolittle.

HIGGINS: By Jupiter, she's done it at the first shot. Pickering: we shall make a duchess of her. [*To* ELIZA] Now do you think you could possibly say tea? Not tə-yee, mind: if you ever say bə-yee cə-yee də-yee again you shall be dragged round the room three times by the hair of your head. [*Fortissimo*] T, T, T, T.

LIZA [*weeping*]: I cant hear no difference cep that it sounds more genteel-like when you say it.

HIGGINS: Well, if you can hear that difference, what the devil are you crying for? Pickering: give her a chocolate.

PICKERING: No, no. Never mind crying a little, Miss Doolittle: you are doing very well; and the lessons wont hurt. I promise you I wont let him drag you round the room by your hair.

HIGGINS: Be off with you to Mrs Pearce and tell her about it. Think about it. Try to do it by yourself: and keep your tongue well forward in your mouth instead of trying to roll it up and swallow it. Another lesson at half-past four this afternoon. Away with you.

ELIZA, *still sobbing, rushes from the room.*

And that is the sort of ordeal poor ELIZA has to go through for months before we meet her again on her first appearance in London society of the professional class.

ACT III

It is MRS HIGGINS's *at-home day. Nobody has yet arrived. Her drawing room, in a flat on Chelsea Embankment, has three windows looking on the river; and the ceiling is not so lofty as it would be in an older house of the same pretension. The windows are open, giving access to a balcony with flowers in pots. If you stand with your face to the windows, you have the fireplace on your left and the door in the right-hand wall close to the corner nearest the windows.*

MRS HIGGINS *was brought up on Morris and Burne Jones; and her room, which is very unlike her son's room in Wimpole Street, is not crowded with furniture and little tables and nicknacks. In the middle of the room there is a big ottoman; and this, with the carpet, the Morris wallpapers, and the Morris chintz window curtains and brocade covers of the ottoman and its cushions, supply all the ornament, and are much too handsome to be hidden by odds and ends of useless things. A few good oil-paintings from the exhibitions in the Grosvenor Gallery thirty years ago (the Burne Jones, not the Whistler side of them) are on the walls. The only landscape is a Cecil Lawson on the scale of a Rubens. There is a portrait of* MRS HIGGINS *as she was when she defied the fashion in her youth in one of the beautiful Rossettian costumes which, when caricatured by people who did not understand, led to the absurdities of popular estheticism in the eighteen-seventies.*

In the corner diagonally opposite the door MRS HIGGINS, *now over sixty and long past taking the trouble to dress out of the fashion, sits writing at an elegantly simple writing-table with a bell button within reach of her hand. There is a Chippendale chair further back in the room between her and the window nearest her side. At the other side of the room, further forward, is an Elizabethan chair roughly carved in the taste of Inigo Jones. On the same side a piano in a decorated case. The corner between the fireplace and the window is occupied by a divan cushioned in Morris chintz.*

It is between four and five in the afternoon.

The door is opened violently; and HIGGINS *enters with his hat on.*

MRS HIGGINS [*dismayed*]: Henry! [*Scolding him*] What are you doing here today? It is my at-home day: you promised not to come. [*As he bends to kiss her, she takes his hat off, and presents it to him*].

HIGGINS: Oh bother! [*He throws the hat down on the table*].

MRS HIGGINS: Go home at once.

HIGGINS [*kissing her*]: I know, mother. I came on purpose.

MRS HIGGINS: But you mustnt. I'm serious, Henry. You offend all my friends: they stop coming whenever they meet you.

HIGGINS: Nonsense! I know I have no small talk; but people dont mind. [*He sits on the settee*].

MRS HIGGINS: Oh! dont they? Small talk indeed! What about your large talk? Really, dear, you mustnt stay.

HIGGINS: I must. Ive a job for you. A phonetic job.

MRS HIGGINS: No use, dear. I'm sorry; but I cant get round your vowels; and though I like to get pretty postcards in your patent shorthand, I always have to read the copies in ordinary writing you so thoughtfully send me.

HIGGINS: Well, this isnt a phonetic job.

MRS HIGGINS: You said it was.

HIGGINS: Not your part of it. Ive picked up a girl.

MRS HIGGINS: Does that mean that some girl has picked you up?

HIGGINS: Not at all. I dont mean a love affair.

MRS HIGGINS: What a pity!

HIGGINS: Why?

MRS HIGGINS: Well, you never fall in love with anyone under forty-five. When will you discover that there are some rather nice-looking young women about?

HIGGINS: Oh, I cant be bothered with young women. My idea of a lovable woman is somebody as like you as possible. I shall never get into the way of seriously liking young women: some habits lie too deep to be changed. [*Rising abruptly and walking about, jingling his money and his keys in his trouser pockets*] Besides, theyre all idiots.

MRS HIGGINS: Do you know what you would do if you really loved me, Henry?

HIGGINS: Oh bother! What? Marry, I suppose.

MRS HIGGINS: No. Stop fidgeting and take your hands out of your pockets. [*With a gesture of despair, he obeys and sits down again*]. Thats a good boy. Now tell me about the girl.

HIGGINS: She's coming to see you.

MRS HIGGINS: I dont remember asking her.

HIGGINS: You didnt. *I* asked her. If youd known her you wouldnt have asked her.

MRS HIGGINS: Indeed! Why?

HIGGINS: Well, it's like this. She's a common flower girl. I picked her off the kerbstone.

MRS HIGGINS: And invited her to my at-home!

HIGGINS [*rising and coming to her to coax her*]: Oh, thatll be all right. Ive taught her to speak properly; and she has strict orders as to her behavior. She's to keep to two subjects: the weather and everybody's health—Fine day and How do you do, you know—and not to let herself go on things in general. That will be safe.

MRS HIGGINS: Safe! To talk about our health! about our insides! perhaps about our outsides! How could you be so silly, Henry?

HIGGINS [*impatiently*]: Well, she must talk about something. [*He controls himself and sits down again*]. Oh, she'll be all right: dont you fuss. Pickering is in it with me. Ive a sort of bet on that I'll pass her off as a duchess in six months. I started on her some months ago; and she's getting on like a house on fire. I shall win my bet. She has a quick ear; and she's been easier to teach than my middle-class pupils because she's had to learn a complete new language. She talks English almost as you talk French.

MRS HIGGINS: Thats satisfactory, at all events.

HIGGINS: Well, it is and it isnt.

MRS HIGGINS: What does that mean?

HIGGINS: You see, Ive got her pronunciation all right; but you have to consider not only h o w a girl pronounces, but what she pronounces; and thats where—

They are interrupted by the parlormaid, announcing guests.

THE PARLORMAID: Mrs and Miss Eynsford Hill. [*She withdraws*].

HIGGINS: Oh Lord! [*He rises: snatches his hat from the table; and makes for the door; but before he reaches it his mother introduces him*].

MRS *and* MISS EYNSFORD HILL *are the mother and daughter who sheltered from the rain in Covent Garden. The mother is well bred, quiet, and has the habitual anxiety of straitened means. The daughter has acquired a gay air of being very much at home in society: the bravado of genteel poverty.*

MRS EYNSFORD HILL [*to* MRS HIGGINS]: How do you do? [*They shake hands*].

MISS EYNSFORD HILL: How d'you do? [*She shakes*].

MRS HIGGINS [*introducing*]: My son Henry.

MRS EYNSFORD HILL: Your celebrated son! I have so longed to meet you, Professor Higgins.

HIGGINS [*glumly, making no movement in her direction*]: Delighted. [*He backs against the piano and bows brusquely*].

MISS EYNSFORD HILL [*going to him with confident familiarity*]: How do you do?

HIGGINS [*staring at her*]: Ive seen you before somewhere. I havnt the ghost of a notion where; but Ive heard your voice. [*Drearily*] It doesnt matter. Youd better sit down.

MRS HIGGINS: I'm sorry to say that my celebrated son has no manners. You mustnt mind him.

MISS EYNSFORD HILL [*gaily*]: I dont. [*She sits in the Elizabethan chair*].

MRS EYNSFORD HILL [*a little bewildered*]: Not at all. [*She sits on the ottoman between her daughter and* MRS HIGGINS, *who has turned her chair away from the writing-table*].

HIGGINS: Oh, have I been rude? I didnt mean to be.

He goes to the central window, through which, with his back to the company, he contemplates the river and the flowers in Battersea Park on the opposite bank as if they were a frozen desert.

The parlormaid returns, ushering in PICKERING.

THE PARLORMAID: Colonel Pickering. [*She withdraws*].
PICKERING: How do you do, Mrs Higgins?
MRS HIGGINS: So glad youve come. Do you know Mrs Eynsford Hill—Miss Eynsford Hill? [*Exchange of bows. The Colonel brings the Chippendale chair a little forward between* MRS HILL *and* MRS HIGGINS, *and sits down*].
PICKERING: Has Henry told you what weve come for?
HIGGINS [*over his shoulder*]: We were interrupted: damn it!
MRS HIGGINS: Oh Henry, Henry, really!
MRS EYNSFORD HILL [*half rising*]: Are we in the way?
MRS HIGGINS [*rising and making her sit down again*]: No, no. You couldnt have come more fortunately: we want you to meet a friend of ours.
HIGGINS [*turning hopefully*]: Yes, by George! We want two or three people. Youll do as well as anybody else.

The parlormaid returns, ushering FREDDY.

THE PARLORMAID: Mr Eynsford Hill.
HIGGINS [*almost audibly, past endurance*]: God of Heaven! another of them.
FREDDY [*shaking hands with* MRS HIGGINS]: Ahdedo?
MRS HIGGINS: Very good of you to come. [*Introducing*] Colonel Pickering.
FREDDY [*bowing*]: Ahdedo?
MRS HIGGINS: I dont think you know my son, Professor Higgins.
FREDDY [*going to* HIGGINS]: Ahdedo?
HIGGINS [*looking at him much as if he were a pickpocket*]: I'll take my oath Ive met you before somewhere. Where was it?
FREDDY: I dont think so.
HIGGINS [*resignedly*]: It dont matter, anyhow. Sit down.

He shakes FREDDY'*s hand and almost slings him on to the ottoman with his face to the window; then comes round to the other side of it.*

HIGGINS: Well, here we are, anyhow! [*He sits down on the ottoman next* MRS EYNSFORD HILL, *on her left*]. And now, what the devil are we going to talk about until Eliza comes?
MRS HIGGINS: Henry: you are the life and soul of the Royal Society's soirées; but really youre rather trying on more commonplace occasions.
HIGGINS: Am I? Very sorry. [*Beaming suddenly*] I suppose I am, you know. [*Uproariously*] Ha, ha!
MISS EYNSFORD HILL [*who considers* HIGGINS *quite eligible matrimonially*]: I sympathize. *I* havnt any small talk. If people would only be frank and say what they really think!
HIGGINS [*relapsing into gloom*]: Lord forbid!
MRS EYNSFORD HILL [*taking up her daughter's cue*]: But why?
HIGGINS: What they think they ought to think is bad enough, Lord knows; but what they really think would break up the whole show. Do you suppose it would be really agreeable if I were to come out now with what *I* really think?
MRS EYNSFORD HILL [*gaily*]: Is it so very cynical?
HIGGINS: Cynical! Who the dickens said it was cynical? I mean it wouldnt be decent.
MRS EYNSFORD HILL [*seriously*]: Oh! I'm sure you dont mean that, Mr Higgins.
HIGGINS: You see, we're all savages, more or less. We're supposed to be civilized and cultured—to know all about poetry and philosophy and art and science, and so on; but how many of us know even the meanings of these names? [*To* MISS HILL] What do you know of poetry? [*To* MRS HILL] What do you know of science? [*Indicating* FREDDY] What does he know of art or science or anything else? What the devil do you imagine I know of philosophy?
MRS HIGGINS [*warningly*]: Or of manners, Henry?
THE PARLORMAID [*opening the door*]: Miss Doolittle. [*She withdraws*].
HIGGINS [*rising hastily and running to* MRS HIGGINS]: Here she is, mother. [*He stands on tiptoe and makes signs over his mother's head to* ELIZA *to indicate to her which lady is her hostess*].

ELIZA, *who is exquisitely dressed, produces an impression of such remarkable distinction and beauty as she enters that they all rise, quite fluttered. Guided by* HIGGINS'*s signals, she comes to* MRS HIGGINS *with studied grace.*

LIZA [*speaking with pedantic correctness of pronunciation and great beauty of tone*]: How do you do, Mrs Higgins? [*She gasps slightly in making sure of the H in Higgins, but is quite successful.*] Mr Higgins told me I might come.
MRS HIGGINS [*cordially*]: Quite right: I'm very glad indeed to see you.
PICKERING: How do you do, Miss Doolittle?
LIZA [*shaking hands with him*]: Colonel Pickering, is it not?
MRS EYNSFORD HILL: I feel sure we have met before Miss Doolittle. I remember your eyes.
LIZA: How do you do? [*She sits down on the ottoman gracefully in the place just left vacant by* HIGGINS].
MRS EYNSFORD HILL [*introducing*]: My daughter Clara.
LIZA: How do you do?
CLARA [*impulsively*]: How do you do? [*She sits down on the ottoman beside* ELIZA, *devouring her with her eyes*].

FREDDY [*coming to their side of the ottoman*]: Ive certainly had the pleasure.
MRS EYNSFORD HILL [*introducing*]: My son Freddy.
LIZA: How do you do?

FREDDY *bows and sits down in the Elizabethan chair, infatuated.*

HIGGINS [*suddenly*]: By George, yes: it all comes back to me! [*They stare at him*]. Covent Garden! [*Lamentably*] What a damned thing!
MRS HIGGINS: Henry, please! [*He is about to sit on the edge of the table*]. Dont sit on my writing-table: youll break it.
HIGGINS [*sulkily*]: Sorry.

He goes to the divan, stumbling into the fender and over the fire-irons on his way; extricating himself with muttered imprecations; and finishing his disastrous journey by throwing himself so impatiently on the divan that he almost breaks it. MRS HIGGINS *looks at him, but controls herself and says nothing.*

A long and painful pause ensues.

MRS HIGGINS [*at last, conversationally*]: Will it rain, do you think?
LIZA: The shallow depression in the west of these islands is likely to move slowly in an easterly direction. There are no indications of any great change in the barometrical situation.
FREDDY: Ha! ha! how awfully funny!
LIZA: What is wrong with that, young man? I bet I got it right.
FREDDY: Killing!
MRS EYNSFORD HILL: I'm sure I hope it wont turn cold. Theres so much influenza about. It runs right through our whole family regularly every spring.
LIZA [*darkly*]: My aunt died of influenza: so they said.
MRS EYNSFORD HILL: [*clicks her tongue sympathetically*]!!!
LIZA [*in the same tragic tone*]: But it's my belief they done the old woman in.
MRS HIGGINS [*puzzled*]: Done her in?
LIZA: Y-e-e-e-es, Lord love you! Why should she die of influenza? She come through diphtheria right enough the year before. I saw her with my own eyes. Fairly blue with it, she was. They all thought she was dead; but my father he kept ladling gin down her throat til she came to so sudden that she bit the bowl off the spoon.
MRS EYNSFORD HILL [*startled*]: Dear me!
LIZA [*piling up the indictment*]: What call would a woman with that strength in her have to die of influenza? What become of her new straw hat that should have come to me? Somebody pinched it: and what I say is, them as pinched it done her in.
MRS EYNSFORD HILL: What does doing her in mean?
HIGGINS [*hastily*]: Oh, thats the new small talk. To do a person in means to kill them.
MRS EYNSFORD HILL [*to* ELIZA, *horrified*]: You surely dont believe that your aunt was killed?
LIZA: Do I not! Them she lived with would have killed her for a hat-pin, let alone a hat.
MRS EYNSFORD HILL: But it cant have been right for your father to pour spirits down her throat like that. It might have killed her.
LIZA: Not her. Gin was mother's milk to her. Besides, he'd poured so much down his own throat that he knew the good of it.
MRS EYNSFORD HILL: Do you mean that he drank?
LIZA: Drank! My word! Something chronic.
MRS EYNSFORD HILL: How dreadful for you!
LIZA: Not a bit. It never did him no harm what I could see. But then he did not keep it up regular. [*Cheerfully*] On the burst, as you might say, from time to time. And always more agreeable when he had a drop in. When he was out of work, my mother used to give him fourpence and tell him to go out and not come back until he'd drunk himself cheerful and loving-like. Theres lots of women has to make their husbands drunk to make them fit to live with. [*Now quite at her ease*] You see, it's like this. If a man has a bit of a conscience, it always takes him when he's sober; and then it makes him low-spirited. A drop of booze just takes that off and makes him happy. [*To* FREDDY, *who is in convulsions of suppressed laughter*] Here! what are you sniggering at?
FREDDY: The new small talk. You do it so awfully well.
LIZA: If I was doing it proper, what was you laughing at? [*To* HIGGINS] Have I said anything I oughtnt?
MRS HIGGINS [*interposing*]: Not at all, Miss Doolittle.
LIZA: Well, thats a mercy, anyhow. [*Expansively*] What I always say is—
HIGGINS [*rising and looking at his watch*]: Ahem!
LIZA [*looking round at him; taking the hint; and rising*]: Well: I must go. [*They all rise.* FREDDY *goes to the door*]. So pleased to have met you. Goodbye. [*She shakes hands with* MRS HIGGINS].
MRS HIGGINS: Goodbye.
LIZA: Goodbye, Colonel Pickering.
PICKERING: Goodbye, Miss Doolittle. [*They shake hands*].
LIZA [*nodding to the others*]: Goodbye, all.
FREDDY [*opening the door for her*]: Are you walking across the Park, Miss Doolittle? If so—
LIZA [*perfectly elegant diction*]: Walk! Not bloody likely. [*Sensation*]. I am going in a taxi. [*She goes out*].

PICKERING *gasps and sits down.* FREDDY *goes out on the balcony to catch another glimpse of* ELIZA.

MRS EYNSFORD HILL [*suffering from shock*]: Well, I really cant get used to the new ways.

CLARA [*throwing herself discontentedly into the Elizabethan chair*]: Oh, it's all right, mamma, quite right. People will think we never go anywhere or see anybody if you are so old-fashioned.

MRS EYNSFORD HILL: I daresay I am very old-fashioned; but I do hope you wont begin using that expression, Clara. I have got accustomed to hear you talking about men as rotters, and calling everything filthy and beastly; though I do think it horrible and unladylike. But this last is really too much. Dont you think so, Colonel Pickering?

PICKERING: Dont ask me. Ive been away in India for several years; and manners have changed so much that I sometimes dont know whether I'm at a respectable dinner-table or in a ship's forecastle.

CLARA: It's all a matter of habit. Theres no right or wrong in it. Nobody means anything by it. And it's so quaint, and gives such a smart emphasis to things that are not in themselves very witty. I find the new small talk delightful and quite innocent.

MRS EYNSFORD HILL [*rising*]: Well, after that, I think it's time for us to go.

PICKERING *and* HIGGINS *rise.*

CLARA [*rising*]: Oh yes: we have three at-homes to go to still. Goodbye, Mrs Higgins. Goodbye, Colonel Pickering. Goodbye, Professor Higgins.

HIGGINS [*coming grimly at her from the divan, and accompanying her to the door*]: Goodbye. Be sure you try on that small talk at the three at-homes. Dont be nervous about it. Pitch it in strong.

CLARA [*all smiles*]: I will: Goodbye. Such nonsense, all this early Victorian prudery!

HIGGINS [*tempting her*]: Such damned nonsense!

CLARA: Such bloody nonsense!

MRS EYNSFORD HILL [*convulsively*]: Clara!

CLARA: Ha! ha! [*She goes out radiant, conscious of being thoroughly up to date, and is heard descending the stairs in a stream of silvery laughter*].

FREDDY [*to the heavens at large*]: Well, I ask you— [*He gives it up, and comes to* MRS HIGGINS]. Goodbye.

MRS HIGGINS [*shaking hands*]: Goodbye. Would you like to meet Miss Doolittle again?

FREDDY [*eagerly*]: Yes, I should, most awfully.

MRS HIGGINS: Well, you know my days.

FREDDY: Yes. Thanks awfully. Goodbye. [*He goes out*].

MRS EYNSFORD HILL: Goodbye, Mr Higgins.

HIGGINS: Goodbye. Goodbye.

MRS EYNSFORD HILL [*to* PICKERING]: It's no use. I shall never be able to bring myself to use that word.

PICKERING: Dont. It's not compulsory, you know. Youll get on quite well without it.

MRS EYNSFORD HILL: Only, Clara is so down on me if I am not positively reeking with the latest slang. Goodbye.

PICKERING: Goodbye. [*They shake hands*].

MRS EYNSFORD HILL [*to* MRS HIGGINS]: You mustnt mind Clara. [PICKERING, *catching from her lowered tone that this is not meant for him to hear, discreetly joins* HIGGINS *at the window*]. We're so poor! and she gets so few parties, poor child! She doesnt quite know. [MRS HIGGINS, *seeing that her eyes are moist, takes her hand sympathetically and goes with her to the door*]. But the boy is nice. Dont you think so?

MRS HIGGINS: Oh, quite nice. I shall always be delighted to see him.

MRS EYNSFORD HILL: Thank you, dear. Goodbye. [*She goes out*].

HIGGINS [*eagerly*]: Well? Is Eliza presentable [*he swoops on his mother and drags her to the ottoman, where she sits down in* ELIZA'S *place with her son on her left*]?

PICKERING *returns to his chair on her right.*

MRS HIGGINS: You silly boy, of course she's not presentable. She's a triumph of your art and of her dressmaker's; but if you suppose for a moment that she doesnt give herself away in every sentence she utters, you must be perfectly cracked about her.

PICKERING: But dont you think something might be done? I mean something to eliminate the sanguinary element from her conversation.

MRS HIGGINS: Not as long as she is in Henry's hands.

HIGGINS [*aggrieved*]: Do you mean that m y language is improper?

MRS HIGGINS: No, dearest: it would be quite proper—say on a canal barge; but it would not be proper for her at a garden party.

HIGGINS [*deeply injured*]: Well I must say—

PICKERING [*interrupting him*]: Come, Higgins: you must learn to know yourself. I havnt heard such language as yours since we used to review the volunteers in Hyde Park twenty years ago.

HIGGINS [*sulkily*]: Oh, well, if y o u say so, I suppose I dont always talk like a bishop.

MRS HIGGINS [*quieting* HENRY *with a touch*]: Colonel Pickering: will you tell me what is the exact state of things in Wimpole Street?

PICKERING [*cheerfully: as if this completely changed the subject*]: Well, I have come to live there with Henry. We work together at my Indian Dialects; and we think it more convenient—

MRS HIGGINS: Quite so. I know all about that: it's an excellent arrangement. But where does this girl live?
HIGGINS: With us, of course. Where should she live?
MRS HIGGINS: But on what terms? Is she a servant? If not, what is she?
PICKERING [*slowly*]: I think I know what you mean, Mrs Higgins.
HIGGINS: Well, dash me if *I* do! Ive had to work at the girl every day for months to get her to her present pitch. Besides, she's useful. She knows where my things are, and remembers my appointments and so forth.
MRS HIGGINS: How does your housekeeper get on with her?
HIGGINS: Mrs Pearce? Oh, she's jolly glad to get so much taken off her hands; for before Eliza came, she used to have to find things and remind me of my appointments. But she's got some silly bee in her bonnet about Eliza. She keeps saying "You dont think, sir": doesnt she, Pick?
PICKERING: Yes: thats the formula. "You dont think, sir." Thats the end of every conversation about Eliza.
HIGGINS: As if I ever stop thinking about the girl and her confounded vowels and consonants. I'm worn out, thinking about her, and watching her lips and her teeth and her tongue, not to mention her soul, which is the quaintest of the lot.
MRS HIGGINS: You certainly are a pretty pair of babies, playing with your live doll.
HIGGINS: Playing! The hardest job I ever tackled: make no mistake about that, mother. But you have no idea how frightfully interesting it is to take a human being and change her into a quite different human being by creating a new speech for her. It's filling up the deepest gulf that separates class from class and soul from soul.
PICKERING [*drawing his chair closer to* MRS HIGGINS *and bending over to her eagerly*]: Yes: it's enormously interesting. I assure you, Mrs Higgins, we take Eliza very seriously. Every week—every day almost—there is some new change. [*Closer again*] We keep records of every stage—dozens of gramophone disks and photographs—
HIGGINS [*assailing her at the other ear*]: Yes, by George: it's the most absorbing experiment I ever tackled. She regularly fills our lives up: doesn't she, Pick?
PICKERING: We're always talking Eliza.
HIGGINS: Teaching Eliza.
PICKERING: Dressing Eliza.
MRS HIGGINS: What!
HIGGINS: Inventing new Elizas.

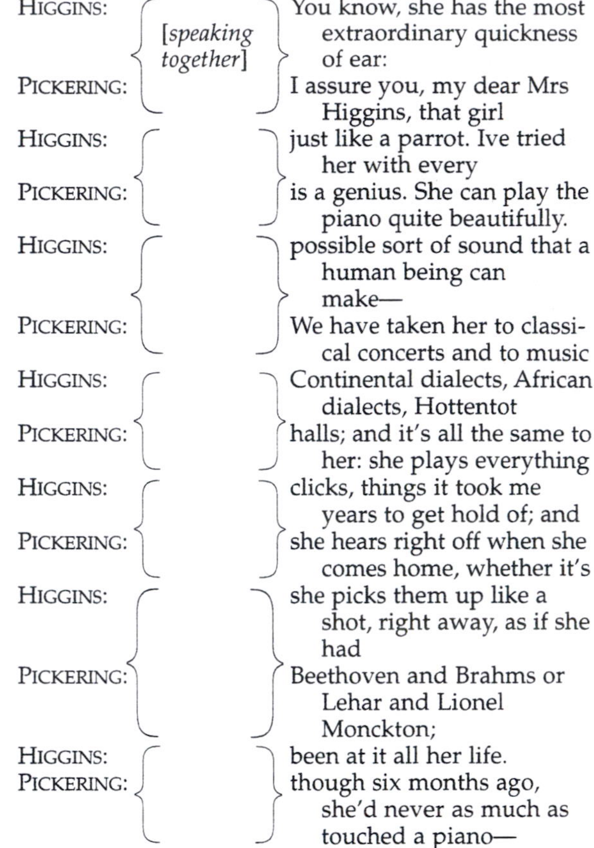

HIGGINS: [*speaking together*] You know, she has the most extraordinary quickness of ear:
PICKERING: I assure you, my dear Mrs Higgins, that girl
HIGGINS: just like a parrot. Ive tried her with every
PICKERING: is a genius. She can play the piano quite beautifully.
HIGGINS: possible sort of sound that a human being can make—
PICKERING: We have taken her to classical concerts and to music
HIGGINS: Continental dialects, African dialects, Hottentot
PICKERING: halls; and it's all the same to her: she plays everything
HIGGINS: clicks, things it took me years to get hold of; and
PICKERING: she hears right off when she comes home, whether it's
HIGGINS: she picks them up like a shot, right away, as if she had
PICKERING: Beethoven and Brahms or Lehar and Lionel Monckton;
HIGGINS: been at it all her life.
PICKERING: though six months ago, she'd never as much as touched a piano—

MRS HIGGINS [*putting her fingers in her ears, as they are by this time shouting one another down with an intolerable noise*]: Sh-sh-sh—sh!

[*They stop*].

PICKERING: I beg your pardon. [*He draws his chair back apologetically*].
HIGGINS: Sorry. When Pickering starts shouting nobody can get a word in edgeways.
MRS HIGGINS: Be quiet, Henry. Colonel Pickering: dont you realize that when Eliza walked into Wimpole Street, something walked in with her?
PICKERING: Her father did. But Henry soon got rid of him.
MRS HIGGINS: It would have been more to the point if her mother had. But as her mother didnt something else did.
PICKERING: But what?
MRS HIGGINS [*unconsciously dating herself by the word*]: A problem.
PICKERING: Oh I see. The problem of how to pass her off as a lady.

HIGGINS: I'll solve that problem. Ive half solved it already.

MRS HIGGINS: No, you two infinitely stupid male creatures: the problem of what is to be done with her afterwards.

HIGGINS: I dont see anything in that. She can go her own way, with all the advantages I have given her.

MRS HIGGINS: The advantages of that poor woman who was here just now! The manners and habits that disqualify a fine lady from earning her own living without giving her a fine lady's income! Is that what you mean?

PICKERING [*indulgently, being rather bored*]: Oh, that will be all right, Mrs Higgins. [*He rises to go*].

HIGGINS [*rising also*]: We'll find her some light employment.

PICKERING: She's happy enough. Dont you worry about her. Goodbye. [*He shakes hands as if he were consoling a frightened child, and makes for the door*].

HIGGINS: Anyhow, theres no good bothering now. The thing's done. Goodbye, mother. [*He kisses her, and follows* PICKERING].

PICKERING [*turning for a final consolation*]: There are plenty of openings. We'll do whats right. Goodbye.

HIGGINS [*to* PICKERING *as they go out together*]: Lets take her to the Shakespear exhibition at Earls Court.

PICKERING: Yes: lets. Her remarks will be delicious.

HIGGINS: She'll mimic all the people for us when we get home.

PICKERING: Ripping. [*Both are heard laughing as they go downstairs*].

MRS HIGGINS [*rises with an impatient bounce, and returns to her work at the writing-table. She sweeps a litter of disarranged papers out of the way; snatches a sheet of paper from her stationery case; and tries resolutely to write. At the third time she gives it up; flings down her pen; grips the table angrily and exclaims*]: Oh! men! men!! men!!!

* * *

Clearly ELIZA will not pass as a duchess yet; and HIGGINS's bet remains unwon. But the six months are not yet exhausted; and just in time ELIZA does actually pass as a princess. For a glimpse of how she did it imagine an Embassy in London one summer evening after dark. The hall door has an awning and a carpet across the sidewalk to the kerb, because a grand reception is in progress. A small crowd is lined up to see the guests arrive.

A Rolls-Royce car drives up. Pickering in evening dress, with medals and orders, alights, and hands out ELIZA, in opera cloak, evening dress, diamonds, fan, flowers and all accessories. HIGGINS follows. The car drives off; and the three go up the steps and into the house, the door opening for them as they approach.

Inside the house they find themselves in a spacious hall from which the grand staircase rises. On the left are the arrangements for the gentlemen's cloaks. The male guests are depositing their hats and wraps there.

On the right is a door leading to the ladies' cloakroom. Ladies are going in cloaked and coming out in splendor. PICKERING whispers to ELIZA and points out the ladies' room. She goes into it. HIGGINS and PICKERING take off their overcoats and take tickets for them from the attendant.

One of the guests, occupied in the same way, has his back turned. Having taken his ticket, he turns round and reveals himself as an important looking young man with an astonishingly hairy face. He has an enormous moustache, flowing out into luxuriant whiskers. Waves of hair cluster on his brow. His hair is cropped closely at the back, and glows with oil. Otherwise he is very smart. He wears several worthless orders. He is evidently a foreigner, guessable as a whiskered Pandour from Hungary; but in spite of the ferocity of his moustache he is amiable and genially voluble.

Recognizing HIGGINS, he flings his arms wide apart and approaches him enthusiastically.

WHISKERS: Maestro, maestro [*he embraces* HIGGINS *and kisses him on both cheeks*]. You remember me?

HIGGINS: No I dont. Who the devil are you?

WHISKERS: I am your pupil: your first pupil, your best and greatest pupil. I am little Nepommuck, the marvellous boy. I have made your name famous throughout Europe. You teach me phonetic. You cannot forget M E.

HIGGINS: Why dont you shave?

NEPOMMUCK: I have not your imposing appearance, your chin, your brow. Nobody notices me when I shave. Now I am famous: they call me Hairy Faced Dick.

HIGGINS: And what are you doing here among all these swells?

NEPOMMUCK: I am interpreter. I speak 32 languages. I am indispensable at these international parties. You are great cockney specialist: you place a man anywhere in London the moment he open his mouth. I place any man in Europe.

A footman hurries down the grand staircase and comes to NEPOMMUCK.

FOOTMAN: You are wanted upstairs. Her Excellency cannot understand the Greek gentleman.

NEPOMMUCK: Thank you, yes, immediately.

The footman goes and is lost in the crowd.

NEPOMMUCK [*to* HIGGINS]: This Greek diplomatist pretends he cannot speak nor understand English. He cannot deceive me. He is the son of a Clerkenwell watchmaker. He speaks English so villainously that he dare not utter a word of it without betraying his origin. I help him to pretend; but I make him pay through the nose. I make them all pay. Ha ha! [*He hurries upstairs*].

PICKERING: Is this fellow really an expert? Can he find out Eliza and blackmail her?

HIGGINS: We shall see. If he finds her out I lose my bet.

ELIZA *comes from the cloakroom and joins them.*

PICKERING: Well, Eliza, now for it. Are you ready?

LIZA: Are you nervous, Colonel?

PICKERING: Frightfully. I feel exactly as I felt before my first battle. It's the first time that frightens.

LIZA: It is not the first time for me, Colonel. I have done this fifty times—hundreds of times—in my little piggery in Angel Court in my day-dreams. I am in a dream now. Promise me not to let Professor Higgins wake me; for if he does I shall forget everything and talk as I used to in Drury Lane.

PICKERING: Not a word, Higgins. [*To* ELIZA] Now ready?

LIZA: Ready.

PICKERING: Go.

They mount the stairs, HIGGINS *last.* PICKERING *whispers to the footman on the first landing.*

FIRST LANDING FOOTMAN: Miss Doolittle, Colonel Pickering, Professor Higgins.

SECOND LANDING FOOTMAN: Miss Doolittle, Colonel Pickering, Professor Higgins.

At the top of the staircase the Ambassador and his wife, with NEPOMMUCK *at her elbow, are receiving.*

HOSTESS [*taking* ELIZA*'s hand*]: How d'ye do?

HOST [*same play*]: How d'ye do? How d'ye do, Pickering?

LIZA [*with a beautiful gravity that awes her hostess*]: How do you do? [*She passes on to the drawing room*].

HOSTESS: Is that your adopted daughter, Colonel Pickering? She will make a sensation.

PICKERING: Most kind of you to invite her for me. [*He passes on*].

HOSTESS [*to* NEPOMMUCK]: Find out all about her.

NEPOMMUCK [*bowing*]: Excellency— [*he goes into the crowd*].

HOST: How d'ye do, Higgins? You have a rival here tonight. He introduced himself as your pupil. Is he any good?

HIGGINS: He can learn a language in a fortnight—knows dozens of them. A sure mark of a fool. As a phonetician, no good whatever.

HOSTESS: How d'ye do, Professor?

HIGGINS: How do you do? Fearful bore for you this sort of thing. Forgive my part in it. [*He passes on*].

In the drawing room and its suite of salons the reception is in full swing. ELIZA passes through. She is so intent on her ordeal that she walks like a somnambulist in a desert instead of a débutante in a fashionable crowd. They stop talking to look at her, admiring her dress, her jewels, and her strangely attractive self. Some of the younger ones at the back stand on their chairs to see.

The HOST and HOSTESS come in from the staircase and mingle with their guests. HIGGINS, gloomy and contemptuous of the whole business, comes into the group where they are chatting.

HOSTESS: Ah, here is Professor Higgins: he will tell us. Tell us all about the wonderful young lady, Professor.

HIGGINS [*almost morosely*]: What wonderful young lady?

HOSTESS: You know very well. They tell me there has been nothing like her in London since people stood on their chairs to look at Mrs Langtry.

NEPOMMUCK *joins the group, full of news.*

HOSTESS: Ah, here you are at last, Nepommuck. Have you found out all about the Doolittle lady?

NEPOMMUCK: I have found out all about her. She is a fraud.

HOSTESS: A fraud! Oh no.

NEPOMMUCK: YES, yes. She cannot deceive me. Her name cannot be Doolittle.

HIGGINS: Why?

NEPOMMUCK: Because Doolittle is an English name. And she is not English.

HOSTESS: Oh, nonsense! She speaks English perfectly.

NEPOMMUCK: Too perfectly. Can you shew me any English woman who speaks English as it should be spoken? Only foreigners who have been taught to speak it speak it well.

HOSTESS: Certainly she terrified me by the way she said How d'ye do. I had a schoolmistress who talked like that: and I was mortally afraid of her. But if she is not English what is she?

NEPOMMUCK: Hungarian.

ALL THE REST: Hungarian!

NEPOMMUCK: Hungarian. And of royal blood. I am Hungarian. My blood is royal.

HIGGINS: Did you speak to her in Hungarian?

NEPOMMUCK: I did. She was very clever. She said "Please speak to me in English: I do not understand French." French! She pretends not to know the difference between Hungarian and French. Impossible: she knows both.

HIGGINS: And the blood royal? How did you find that out?

NEPOMUCCK: Instinct, maestro, instinct. Only the Magyar races can produce that air of the divine right, those resolute eyes. She is a princess.

HOST: What do you say, Professor?

HIGGINS: I say an ordinary London girl out of the gutter and taught to speak by an expert. I place her in Drury Lane.

NEPOMMUCK: Ha ha ha! Oh, maestro, maestro, you are mad on the subject of cockney dialects. The London gutter is the whole world for you.

HIGGINS [*to the* HOSTESS]: What does your Excellency say?

HOSTESS: Oh, of course I agree with Nepommuck. She must be a princess at least.

HOST: Not necessarily legitimate, of course. Morganatic perhaps. But that is undoubtedly her class.

HIGGINS: I stick to my opinion.

HOSTESS: Oh, you are incorrigible.

The group breaks up, leaving HIGGINS *isolated.* PICKERING *joins him.*

PICKERING: Where is Eliza? We must keep an eye on her.

ELIZA *joins them.*

LIZA: I dont think I can bear much more. The people all stare so at me. An old lady has just told me that I speak exactly like Queen Victoria. I am sorry if I have lost your bet. I have done my best; but nothing can make me the same as these people.

PICKERING: You have not lost it, my dear. You have won it ten times over.

HIGGINS: Let us get out of this. I have had enough of chattering to these fools.

PICKERING: Eliza is tired; and I am hungry. Let us clear out and have supper somewhere.

ACT IV

The Wimpole Street laboratory. Midnight. Nobody in the room. The clock on the mantelpiece strikes twelve. The fire is not alight: it is a summer night.

Presently HIGGINS *and* PICKERING *are heard on the stairs.*

HIGGINS [*calling down to* PICKERING]: I say, Pick: lock up, will you? I shant be going out again.

PICKERING: Right. Can Mrs Pearce go to bed? We dont want anything more, do we?

HIGGINS: Lord, no!

ELIZA *opens the door and is seen on the lighted landing in all the finery in which she has just won* HIGGINS*'s bet for him. She comes to the hearth, and switches on the electric lights there. She is tired: her pallor contrasts strongly with her dark eyes and hair; and her expression is almost tragic. She takes off her cloak; puts her fan and gloves on the piano; and sits down on the bench, brooding and silent.* HIGGINS, *in evening dress, with overcoat and hat, comes in, carrying a smoking jacket which he has picked up downstairs.*

He takes off the hat and overcoat; throws them carelessly on the newspaper stand; disposes of his coat in the same way; puts on the smoking jacket; and throws himself wearily into the easy-chair at the hearth. PICKERING, *similarly attired, comes in. He also takes off his hat and overcoat, and is about to throw them on* HIGGINS*'s when he hesitates.*

PICKERING: I say: Mrs Pearce will row if we leave these things lying about in the drawing room.

HIGGINS: Oh, chuck them over the bannisters into the hall. She'll find them there in the morning and put them away all right. She'll think we were drunk.

PICKERING: We are, slightly. Are there any letters?

HIGGINS: I didnt look. [PICKERING *takes the overcoats and hats and goes downstairs.* HIGGINS *begins half singing half yawning an air from La Fanciulla del Golden West. Suddenly he stops and exclaims*] I wonder where the devil my slippers are!

ELIZA *looks at him darkly; then rises suddenly and leaves the room.*

HIGGINS *yawns again, and resumes his song.*

PICKERING *returns, with the contents of the letterbox in his hand.*

PICKERING: Only circulars, and this coroneted billet-doux for you. [*He throws the circulars into the fender, and posts himself on the hearthrug, with his back to the grate*].

HIGGINS [*glancing at the billet-doux*]: Money-lender. [*He throws the letter after the circulars*].

ELIZA *returns with a pair of large down-at-heel slippers. She places them on the carpet before* HIGGINS, *and sits as before without a word.*

HIGGINS [*yawning again*]: Oh Lord! What an evening! What a crew! What a silly tomfoolery! [*He raises his shoe to unlace it, and catches sight of the slippers. He stops unlacing and looks at them as if they had appeared there of their own accord*]. Oh! theyre there, are they?

PICKERING [*stretching himself*]: Well, I feel a bit tired. It's been a long day. The garden party, a dinner party, and the reception! Rather too much of a good thing. But youve won your bet, Higgins. Eliza did the trick, and something to spare, eh?

HIGGINS [*fervently*]: Thank God it's over!

ELIZA *flinches violently; but they take no notice of her; and she recovers herself and sits stonily as before.*

PICKERING: Were you nervous at the garden party? I was. Eliza didnt seem a bit nervous.

HIGGINS: Oh, she wasnt nervous. I knew she'd be all right. No: it's the strain of putting the job through all these months that has told on me. It was interesting enough at first, while we were at the phonetics; but after that I got deadly sick of it. If I hadnt backed myself to do it I should have chucked the whole thing up two months ago. It was a silly notion: the whole thing has been a bore.

PICKERING: Oh come! the garden party was frightfully exciting. My heart began beating like anything.

HIGGINS: Yes, for the first three minutes. But when I saw we were going to win hands down, I felt like a bear in a cage, hanging about doing nothing. The dinner was worse: sitting gorging there for over an hour, with nobody but a damned fool of a fashionable woman to talk to! I tell you, Pickering, never again for me. No more artificial duchesses. The whole thing has been simple purgatory.

PICKERING: Youve never been broken in properly to the social routine. [*Strolling over to the piano*] I rather enjoy dipping into it occasionally myself: it makes me feel young again. Anyhow, it was a great success: an immense success. I was quite frightened once or twice because Eliza was doing it so well. You see, lots of the real people cant do it at all; theyre such fools that they think style comes by nature to people in their position; and so they never learn. Theres always something professional about doing a thing superlatively well.

HIGGINS: Yes: thats what drives me mad; the silly people dont know their own silly business. [*Rising*] However, it's over and done with; and now I can go to bed at last without dreading tomorrow.

ELIZA'*s beauty becomes murderous.*

PICKERING: I think I shall turn in too. Still, it's been a great occasion: a triumph for you. Goodnight. [*He goes*].

HIGGINS [*following him*]: Goodnight. [*Over his shoulder, at the door*] Put out the lights, Eliza; and tell Mrs Pearce not to make coffee for me in the morning: I'll take tea. [*He goes out*].

ELIZA *tries to control herself and feel indifferent as she rises and walks across to the hearth to switch off the lights. By the time she gets there she is on the point of screaming. She sits down in* HIGGINS'*s chair and holds on hard to the arms. Finally she gives way and flings herself furiously on the floor, raging.*

HIGGINS [*in despairing wrath outside*]: What the devil have I done with my slippers? [*He appears at the door*].

LIZA [*snatching up the slippers, and hurling them at him one after the other with all her force*]: There are your slippers. And there. Take your slippers; and may you never have a day's luck with them!

HIGGINS [*astounded*]: What on earth—! [*He comes to her*]. Whats the matter? Get up. [*He pulls her up*]. Anything wrong?

LIZA [*breathless*]: Nothing wrong—with you. Ive won your bet for you, havent I? Thats enough for you. I dont matter, I suppose.

HIGGINS: You won my bet! You! Presumptuous insect! I won it. What did you throw those slippers at me for?

LIZA: Because I wanted to smash your face. I'd like to kill you, you selfish brute. Why didnt you leave me where you picked me out of—in the gutter? You thank God it's all over, and that now you can throw me back again there, do you? [*She crisps her fingers frantically*].

HIGGINS [*looking at her in cool wonder*]: The creature is nervous, after all.

LIZA [*gives a suffocated scream of fury, and instinctively darts her nails at his face*]!!

HIGGINS [*catching her wrists*]: Ah! would you? Claws in, you cat. How dare you shew your temper to me? Sit down and be quiet. [*He throws her roughly into the easy-chair*].

LIZA [*crushed by superior strength and weight*]: Whats to become of me? Whats to become of me?

HIGGINS: How the devil do I know whats to become of you? What does it matter what becomes of you?

LIZA: You dont care, I know you dont care. You wouldnt care if I was dead. I'm nothing to you—not so much as them slippers.

HIGGINS [*thundering*]: Those slippers.

LIZA [*with bitter submission*]: Those slippers. I didnt think it made any difference now.

A pause. ELIZA *hopeless and crushed.* HIGGINS *a little uneasy.*

HIGGINS [*in his loftiest manner*]: Why have you begun going on like this? May I ask whether you complain of your treatment here?

LIZA: No.

HIGGINS: Has anybody behaved badly to you? Colonel Pickering? Mrs Pearce? Any of the servants?

LIZA: No.

HIGGINS: I presume you dont pretend that *I* have treated you badly?

LIZA: No.

HIGGINS: I am glad to hear it. [*He moderates his tone*]. Perhaps youre tired after the strain of the day. Will you have a glass of champagne? [*He moves towards the door*].

LIZA: No. [*Recollecting her manners*] Thank you.

HIGGINS [*good-humored again*]: This has been coming on you for some days. I suppose it was natural for you to be anxious about the garden party. But thats all over now. [*He pats her kindly on the shoulder. She writhes*]. Theres nothing more to worry about.

LIZA: No. Nothing more for you to worry about. [*She suddenly rises and gets away from him by going to the piano bench, where she sits and hides her face*]. Oh God! I wish I was dead.

HIGGINS [*staring after her in sincere surprise*]: Why? In heaven's name, why? [*Reasonably, going to her*] Listen to me, Eliza. All this irritation is purely subjective.

LIZA: I dont understand. I'm too ignorant.

HIGGINS: It's only imagination. Low spirits and nothing else. Nobody's hurting you. Nothing's wrong. You go to bed like a good girl and sleep it off. Have a little cry and say your prayers: that will make you comfortable.

LIZA: I heard your prayers. "Thank God it's all over!"

HIGGINS [*impatiently*]: Well, dont you thank God it's all over? Now you are free and can do what you like.

LIZA [*pulling herself together in desperation*]: What am I fit for? What have you left me fit for? Where am I to go? What am I to do? Whats to become of me?

HIGGINS [*enlightened, but not at all impressed*]: Oh, thats whats worrying you, is it? [*He thrusts his hands into his pockets, and walks about in his usual manner, rattling the contents of his pockets, as if condescending to a trivial subject out of pure kindness*]. I shouldnt bother about it if I were you. I should imagine you wont have much difficulty in settling yourself somewhere or other, though I hadnt quite realized that you were going away. [*She looks quickly at him: he does not look at her, but examines the dessert stand on the piano and decides that he will eat an apple*]. You might marry, you know. [*He bites a large piece out of the apple and munches it noisily*]. You see, Eliza, all men are not confirmed old bachelors like me and the Colonel. Most men are the marrying sort (poor devils!); and youre not bad-looking: it's quite a pleasure to look at you sometimes—not now, of course, because youre crying and looking as ugly as the very devil; but when youre all right and quite yourself, youre what I should call attractive. That is, to the people in the marrying line, you understand. You go to bed and have a good nice rest; and then get up and look at yourself in the glass; and you wont feel so cheap.

ELIZA *again looks at him, speechless, and does not stir. The look is quite lost on him: he eats his apple with a dreamy expression of happiness, as it is quite a good one.*

HIGGINS [*a genial afterthought occurring to him*]: I daresay my mother could find some chap or other who would do very well.

LIZA: We were above that at the corner of Tottenham Court Road.

HIGGINS [*waking up*]: What do you mean?

LIZA: I sold flowers. I didnt sell myself. Now youve made a lady of me I'm not fit to sell anything else. I wish youd left me where you found me.

HIGGINS [*slinging the core of the apple decisively into the grate*]: Tosh, Eliza. Dont you insult human relations by dragging all this cant about buying and selling into it. You neednt marry the fellow if you dont like him.

LIZA: What else am I to do?

HIGGINS: Oh, lots of things. What about your old idea of a florist's shop? Pickering could set you up in one: he has lots of money. [*Chuckling*] He'll have to pay for all those togs you have been wearing today; and that, with the hire of the jewellery, will make a big hole in two hundred pounds. Why, six months ago you would have thought it the millennium to have a flower shop of your own. Come! youll be all right. I must clear off to bed: I'm devilish sleepy. By the way, I came down for something: I forget what it was.

LIZA: Your slippers.

HIGGINS: Oh yes, of course. You shied them at me. [*He picks them up, and is going out when she rises and speaks to him*].

LIZA: Before you go, sir—

HIGGINS [*dropping the slippers in his surprise at her calling him Sir*]: Eh?

LIZA: Do my clothes belong to me or to Colonel Pickering?

HIGGINS [*coming back into the room as if her question were the very climax of unreason*]: What the devil use would they be to Pickering?

LIZA: He might want them for the next girl you pick up to experiment on.

HIGGINS [*shocked and hurt*]: Is that the way you feel towards us?

LIZA: I dont want to hear anything more about that. All I want to know is whether anything belongs to me. My own clothes were burnt.

HIGGINS: But what does it matter? Why need you start bothering about that in the middle of the night?

LIZA: I want to know what I may take away with me. I dont want to be accused of stealing.

HIGGINS [*now deeply wounded*]: Stealing! You shouldnt have said that, Eliza. That shews a want of feeling.

LIZA: I'm sorry. I'm only a common ignorant girl; and in my station I have to be careful. There cant be any feelings between the like of you and the like of me. Please will you tell me what belongs to me and what doesnt?

HIGGINS [*very sulky*]: You may take the whole damned houseful if you like. Except the jewels. Theyre hired. Will that satisfy you? [*He turns on his heel and is about to go in extreme dudgeon*].

LIZA [*drinking in his emotion like nectar, and nagging him to provoke a further supply*]: Stop, please. [*She takes off her jewels*]. Will you take these to your room and keep them safe? I dont want to run the risk of their being missing.

HIGGINS [*furious*]: Hand them over. [*She puts them into his hands*]. If these belonged to me instead of to the jeweller, I'd ram them down your ungrateful throat. [*He perfunctorily thrusts them into his pockets, unconsciously decorating himself with the protruding ends of the chains*].

LIZA [*taking a ring off*]: This ring isnt the jeweller's: it's the one you bought me in Brighton. I dont want it now. [HIGGINS *dashes the ring violently into the fireplace, and turns on her so threateningly that she crouches over the piano with her hands over her face, and exclaims*] Dont you hit me.

HIGGINS: Hit you! You infamous creature, how dare you accuse me of such a thing? It is you who have hit me. You have wounded me to the heart.

LIZA [*thrilling with hidden joy*]: I'm glad. Ive got a little of my own back, anyhow.

HIGGINS [*with dignity, in his finest professional style*]: You have caused me to lose my temper: a thing that has hardly ever happened to me before. I prefer to say nothing more tonight. I am going to bed.

LIZA [*pertly*]: Youd better leave a note for Mrs Pearce about the coffee; for she wont be told by me.

HIGGINS [*formally*]: Damn Mrs Pearce; and damn the coffee; and damn you; and [*wildly*] damn my own folly in having lavished my hard-earned knowledge and the treasure of my regard and intimacy on a heartless guttersnipe. [*He goes out with impressive decorum, and spoils it by slamming the door savagely*].

ELIZA *goes down on her knees on the hearthrug to look for the ring. When she finds it she considers for a moment what to do with it. Finally she flings it down on the dessert stand and goes upstairs in a tearing rage.*

* * *

The furniture of ELIZA*'s room has been increased by a big wardrobe and a sumptuous dressing-table. She comes in and switches on the electric light. She goes to the wardrobe; opens it; and pulls out a walking dress, a hat, and a pair of shoes, which she throws on the bed. She takes off her evening dress and shoes: then takes a padded hanger from the wardrobe; adjusts it carefully in the evening dress; and hangs it in the wardrobe, which she shuts with a slam. She puts on her walking shoes, her walking dress, and hat. She takes her wrist watch from the dressing-table and fastens it on. She pulls on her gloves; takes her vanity bag; and looks into it to see that her purse is there before hanging it on her wrist. She makes for the door. Every movement expresses her furious resolution.*

She takes a last look at herself in the glass.

She suddenly puts out her tongue at herself; then leaves the room, switching off the electric light at the door.

Meanwhile, in the street outside, FREDDY EYNSFORD HILL, *lovelorn, is gazing up at the second floor, in which one of the windows is still lighted.*

The light goes out.

FREDDY: Goodnight, darling, darling, darling.

ELIZA *comes out, giving the door a considerable bang behind her.*

LIZA: Whatever are you doing here?

FREDDY: Nothing. I spend most of my nights here. It's the only place where I'm happy. Dont laugh at me, Miss Doolittle.

LIZA: Dont you call me Miss Doolittle, do you hear? Liza's good enough for me. [*She breaks down and grabs him by the shoulders*] Freddy: you dont think I'm a heartless guttersnipe, do you?

FREDDY: Oh no, no, darling: how can you imagine such a thing? You are the loveliest, dearest—

He loses all self-control and smothers her with kisses. She, hungry for comfort, responds. They stand there in one another's arms.

An elderly police constable arrives.

CONSTABLE [*scandalized*]: Now then! Now then!! Now then!!!

They release one another hastily.

FREDDY: Sorry, constable. Weve only just become engaged.

They run away.

The constable shakes his head, reflecting on his own courtship and on the vanity of human hopes. He moves off in the opposite direction with slow professional steps.

The flight of the lovers takes them to Cavendish Square. There they halt to consider their next move.

LIZA [*out of breath*]: He didnt half give me a fright, that copper. But you answered him proper.
FREDDY: I hope I havnt taken you out of your way. Where were you going?
LIZA: To the river.
FREDDY: What for?
LIZA: To make a hole in it.
FREDDY [*horrified*]: Eliza, darling. What do you mean? What's the matter?
LIZA: Never mind. It doesnt matter now. Theres nobody in the world now but you and me, is there?
FREDDY: Not a soul.

They indulge in another embrace, and are again surprised by a much younger constable.

SECOND CONSTABLE: Now then, you two! What's this? Where do you think you are? Move along here, double quick.
FREDDY: As you say, sir, double quick.

They run away again, and are in Hanover Square before they stop for another conference.

FREDDY: I had no idea the police were so devilishly prudish.
LIZA: It's their business to hunt girls off the streets.
FREDDY: We must go somewhere. We cant wander about the streets all night.
LIZA: Cant we? I think it'd be lovely to wander about for ever.
FREDDY: Oh, darling.

They embrace again, oblivious of the arrival of a crawling taxi. It stops.

TAXIMAN: Can I drive you and the lady anywhere, sir?

They start asunder.

LIZA: Oh, Freddy, a taxi. The very thing.
FREDDY: But, damn it, Ive no money.
LIZA: I have plenty. The Colonel thinks you should never go out without ten pounds in your pocket. Listen. We'll drive about all night; and in the morning I'll call on old Mrs Higgins and ask her what I ought to do. I'll tell you all about it in the cab. And the police wont touch us there.
FREDDY: Righto! Ripping. [*To the* TAXIMAN] Wimbledon Common. [*They drive off*].

ACT V

MRS HIGGINS'*s drawing room. She is at her writing-table as before. The Parlormaid comes in.*

THE PARLORMAID [*at the door*]: Mr Henry, maam, is downstairs with Colonel Pickering.
MRS HIGGINS: Well, shew them up.
THE PARLORMAID: Theyre using the telephone, maam. Telephoning to the police, I think.
MRS HIGGINS: What!
THE PARLORMAID [*coming further in and lowering her voice*]: Mr Henry is in a state, maam. I thought I'd better tell you.
MRS HIGGINS: If you had told me that Mr Henry was not in a state it would have been more surprising. Tell them to come up when theyve finished with the police. I suppose he's lost something.
THE PARLORMAID: Yes, maam [*going*].
MRS HIGGINS: Go upstairs and tell Miss Doolittle that Mr Henry and the Colonel are here. Ask her not to come down til I send for her.
THE PARLORMAID: Yes, maam.

HIGGINS *bursts in. He is, as the parlormaid has said, in a state.*

HIGGINS: Look here, mother: heres a confounded thing!
MRS HIGGINS: Yes, dear. Good morning. [*He checks his impatience and kisses her, whilst the parlormaid goes out*]. What is it?
HIGGINS: Eliza's bolted.
MRS HIGGINS [*calmly continuing her writing*]: You must have frightened her.
HIGGINS: Frightened her! nonsense! She was left last night, as usual, to turn out the lights and all that; and instead of going to bed she changed her clothes and went right off: her bed wasnt slept in. She came in a cab for her things before seven this morning; and that fool Mrs Pearce let her have them without telling me a word about it. What am I to do?

MRS HIGGINS: Do without, I'm afraid, Henry. The girl has a perfect right to leave if she chooses.

HIGGINS [*wandering distractedly across the room*]: But I cant find anything. I dont know what appointments Ive got. I'm— [PICKERING *comes in,* MRS HIGGINS *puts down her pen and turns away from the writing-table*].

PICKERING [*shaking hands*]: Good morning, Mrs Higgins. Has Henry told you? [*He sits down on the ottoman*].

HIGGINS: What does that ass of an inspector say? Have you offered a reward?

MRS HIGGINS [*rising in indignant amazement*]: You dont mean to say you have set the police after Eliza?

HIGGINS: Of course. What are the police for? What else could we do? [*He sits in the Elizabethan chair*].

PICKERING: The inspector made a lot of difficulties. I really think he suspected us of some improper purpose.

MRS HIGGINS: Well, of course he did. What right have you to go to the police and give the girl's name as if she were a thief, or a lost umbrella, or something? Really! [*She sits down again, deeply vexed*].

HIGGINS: But we want to find her.

PICKERING: We cant let her go like this, you know, Mrs Higgins. What were we to do?

MRS HIGGINS: You have no more sense, either of you, than two children. Why—

The parlormaid comes in and breaks off the conversation.

THE PARLORMAID: Mr Henry: a gentleman wants to see you very particular. He's been sent on from Wimpole Street.

HIGGINS: Oh, bother! I cant see anyone now. Who is it?

THE PARLORMAID: A Mr Doolittle, sir.

PICKERING: Doolittle! Do you mean the dustman?

THE PARLORMAID: Dustman! Oh no, sir: a gentleman.

HIGGINS [*springing up excitedly*]: By George, Pick, it's some relative of hers that she's gone to. Somebody we know nothing about. [*To the parlormaid*] Send him up, quick.

THE PARLORMAID: Yes, sir. [*She goes*].

HIGGINS [*eagerly, going to his mother*]: Genteel relatives! now we shall hear something. [*He sits down in the Chippendale chair*].

MRS HIGGINS: Do you know any of her people?

PICKERING: Only her father: the fellow we told you about.

THE PARLORMAID [*announcing*]: Mr Doolittle. [*She withdraws*].

DOOLITTLE *enters. He is resplendently dressed as for a fashionable wedding, and might, in fact, be the bridegroom. A flower in his buttonhole, a dazzling silk hat, and patent leather shoes complete the effect. He is too concerned with the business he has come on to notice* MRS HIGGINS. *He walks straight to* HIGGINS, *and accosts him with vehement reproach.*

DOOLITTLE [*indicating his own person*]: See here! Do you see this? You done this.

HIGGINS: Done what, man?

DOOLITTLE: This, I tell you. Look at it. Look at this hat. Look at this coat.

PICKERING: Has Eliza been buying you clothes?

DOOLITTLE: Eliza! not she. Why would she buy me clothes?

MRS HIGGINS: Good morning, Mr Doolittle. Wont you sit down?

DOOLITTLE [*taken aback as he becomes conscious that he has forgotten his hostess*]: Asking your pardon, maam. [*He approaches her and shakes her proffered hand*]. Thank you. [*He sits down on the ottoman, on* PICKERING*'s right*]. I am that full of what has happened to me that I cant think of anything else.

HIGGINS: What the dickens has happened to you?

DOOLITTLE: I shouldnt mind if it had only happened to me: anything might happen to anybody and nobody to blame but Providence, as you might say. But this is something that you done to me: yes, you, Enry Iggins.

HIGGINS: Have you found Eliza?

DOOLITTLE: Have you lost her?

HIGGINS: Yes.

DOOLITTLE: You have all the luck, you have. I aint found her; but she'll find me quick enough now after what you done to me.

MRS HIGGINS: But what has my son done to you, Mr Doolittle?

DOOLITTLE: Done to me! Ruined me. Destroyed my happiness. Tied me up and delivered me into the hands of middle class morality.

Higgins [*rising intolerantly and standing over* DOOLITTLE]: Youre raving. Youre drunk. Youre mad. I gave you five pounds. After that I had two conversations with you, at half-a-crown an hour. Ive never seen you since.

DOOLITTLE: Oh! Drunk am I? Mad am I? Tell me this. Did you or did you not write a letter to an old blighter in America that was giving five millions to found Moral Reform Societies all over the world, and that wanted you to invent a universal language for him?

HIGGINS: What! Ezra D. Wannafeller! He's dead. [*He sits down again carelessly*].

DOOLITTLE: Yes: he's dead; and I'm done for. Now did you or did you not write a letter to him to say that the most original moralist at present in England, to the best of your knowledge, was Alfred Doolittle, a common dustman?

HIGGINS: Oh, after your first visit I remember making some silly joke of the kind.

DOOLITTLE: Ah! You may well call it a silly joke. It put the lid on me right enough. Just give him the chance he wanted to shew that Americans is not like us: that they reckonize and respect merit in every class of life, however humble. Them words is in his blooming will, in which, Henry Higgins, thanks to your silly joking, he leaves me a share in his Pre-digested Cheese Trust worth three thousand a year on condition that I lecture for his Wannafeller Moral Reform World League as often as they ask me up to six times a year.

HIGGINS: The devil he does! Whew! [*Brightening suddenly*] What a lark!

PICKERING: A safe thing for you, Doolittle. They wont ask you twice.

DOOLITTLE: It aint the lecturing I mind. I'll lecture them blue in the face, I will, and not turn a hair. It's making a gentleman of me that I object to. Who asked him to make a gentleman of me? I was happy. I was free. I touched pretty nigh everybody for money when I wanted it, same as I touched you, Enry Iggins. Now I am worrited; tied neck and heels; and everybody touches me for money. It's a fine thing for you, says my solicitor. Is it? says I. You mean it's a good thing for you, I says. When I was a poor man and had a solicitor once when they found a pram in the dust cart, he got me off, and got shut of me and got me shut of him as quick as he could. Same with the doctors: used to shove me out of the hospital before I could hardly stand on my legs, and nothing to pay. Now they finds out that I'm not a healthy man and cant live unless they looks after me twice a day. In the house I'm not let do a hand's turn for myself: somebody else must do it and touch me for it. A year ago I hadnt a relative in the world except two or three that wouldnt speak to me. Now Ive fifty, and not a decent week's wages among the lot of them. I have to live for others and not for myself: thats middle class morality. You talk of losing Eliza. Dont you be anxious: I bet she's on my doorstep by this: she that could support herself easy by selling flowers if I wasnt respectable. And the next one to touch me will be you, Enry Iggins. I'll have to learn to speak middle class language from you, instead of speaking proper English. Thats where youll come in; and I daresay thats what you done it for.

MRS HIGGINS: But, my dear Mr Doolittle, you need not suffer all this if you are really in earnest. Nobody can force you to accept this bequest. You can repudiate it. Isnt that so, Colonel Pickering?

PICKERING: I believe so.

DOOLITTLE [*softening his manner in deference to her sex*]: Thats the tragedy of it, maam. It's easy to say chuck it; but I havnt the nerve. Which of us has? We're all intimidated. Intimidated, maam: thats what we are. What is there for me if I chuck it but the workhouse in my old age? I have to dye my hair already to keep my job as a dustman. If I was one of the deserving poor, and had put by a bit, I could chuck it; but then why should I, acause the deserving poor might as well be millionaires for all the happiness they ever has. They dont know what happiness is. But I, as one of the undeserving poor, have nothing between me and the pauper's uniform but this here blasted three thousand a year that shoves me into the middle class. (Excuse the expression, maam; youd use it yourself if you had my provocation.) Theyve got you every way you turn: it's a choice between the Skilly of the workhouse and the Char Bydis of the middle class; and I havnt the nerve for the workhouse. Intimidated: thats what I am. Broke. Bought up. Happier men than me will call for my dust, and touch me for their tip; and I'll look on helpless, and envy them. And thats what your son has brought me to. [*He is overcome by emotion*].

MRS HIGGINS: Well, I'm very glad youre not going to do anything foolish, Mr Doolittle. For this solves the problem of Eliza's future. You can provide for her now.

DOOLITTLE [*with melancholy resignation*]: Yes, maam: I'm expected to provide for everyone now, out of three thousand a year.

HIGGINS [*jumping up*]: Nonsense! he cant provide for her. He shant provide for her. She doesnt belong to him. I paid him five pounds for her. Doolittle: either youre an honest man or a rogue.

DOOLITTLE [*tolerantly*]: A little of both, Henry, like the rest of us: a little of both.

HIGGINS: Well, you took that money for the girl; and you have no right to take her as well.

MRS HIGGINS: Henry: dont be absurd. If you want to know where Eliza is, she is upstairs.

HIGGINS [*amazed*]: Upstairs!!! Then I shall jolly soon fetch her downstairs. [*He makes resolutely for the door*].

MRS HIGGINS [*rising and following him*]: Be quiet, Henry. Sit down.

HIGGINS: I—

MRS HIGGINS: Sit down, dear; and listen to me.

HIGGINS: Oh very well, very well, very well. [*He throws himself ungraciously on the ottoman, with his face towards the windows*]. But I think you might have told us this half an hour ago.

MRS HIGGINS: Eliza came to me this morning. She told me of the brutal way you two treated her.

HIGGINS [*bouncing up again*]: What!

PICKERING [*rising also*]: My dear Mrs Higgins, she's been telling you stories. We didnt treat her brutally. We hardly said a word to her; and we parted on particularly good terms. [*Turning on* HIGGINS] Higgins: did you bully her after I went to bed?

HIGGINS: Just the other way about. She threw my slippers in my face. She behaved in the most outrageous way. I never gave her the slightest provocation. The slippers came bang into my face the moment I entered the room—before I had uttered a word. And used perfectly awful language.

PICKERING [*astonished*]: But why? What did we do to her?

MRS HIGGINS: I think I know pretty well what you did. The girl is naturally rather affectionate, I think. Isnt she, Mr Doolittle?

DOOLITTLE: Very tender-hearted, maam. Takes after me.

MRS HIGGINS: Just so. She had become attached to you both. She worked very hard for you, Henry. I dont think you quite realize what anything in the nature of brain work means to a girl of her class. Well, it seems that when the great day of trial came, and she did this wonderful thing for you without making a single mistake, you two sat there and never said a word to her, but talked together of how glad you were that it was all over and how you had been bored with the whole thing. And then you were surprised because she threw your slippers at you! *I* should have thrown the fire-irons at you.

HIGGINS: We said nothing except that we were tired and wanted to go to bed. Did we, Pick?

PICKERING [*shrugging his shoulders*]: That was all.

MRS HIGGINS [*ironically*]: Quite sure?

PICKERING: Absolutely. Really, that was all.

MRS HIGGINS: You didnt thank her, or pet her, or admire her, or tell her how splendid she'd been.

HIGGINS [*impatiently*]: But she knew all about that. We didnt make speeches to her, if thats what you mean.

PICKERING [*conscience stricken*]: Perhaps we were a little inconsiderate. Is she very angry?

MRS HIGGINS [*returning to her place at the writing-table*]: Well, I'm afraid she wont go back to Wimpole Street, especially now that Mr Doolittle is able to keep up the position you have thrust on her; but she says she is quite willing to meet you on friendly terms and to let bygones be bygones.

HIGGINS [*furious*]: Is she, by George? Ho!

MRS HIGGINS: If you promise to behave yourself, Henry, I'll ask her to come down. If not, go home; for you have taken up quite enough of my time.

HIGGINS: Oh, all right. Very well. Pick: you behave yourself. Let us put on our best Sunday manners for this creature that we picked out of the mud. [*He flings himself sulkily into the Elizabethan chair*].

DOOLITTLE [*remonstrating*]: Now, now, Enry Iggins! Have some consideration for my feelings as a middle class man.

MRS HIGGINS: Remember your promise, Henry. [*She presses the bell-button on the writing-table*]. Mr Doolittle: will you be so good as to step out on the balcony for a moment. I dont want Eliza to have the shock of your news until she has made it up with these two gentlemen. Would you mind?

DOOLITTLE: As you wish, lady. Anything to help Henry to keep her off my hands. [*He disappears through the window*].

The parlormaid answers the bell. PICKERING *sits down in* DOOLITTLE*'s place.*

MRS HIGGINS: Ask Miss Doolittle to come down, please.

THE PARLORMAID: Yes, maam. [*She goes out*].

MRS HIGGINS: Now, Henry: be good.

HIGGINS: I am behaving myself perfectly.

PICKERING: He is doing his best, Mrs Higgins.

A pause. HIGGINS *throws back his head; stretches out his legs; and begins to whistle.*

MRS HIGGINS: Henry, dearest, you dont look at all nice in that attitude.

HIGGINS [*pulling himself together*]: I was not trying to look nice, mother.

MRS HIGGINS: It doesnt matter, dear. I only wanted to make you speak.

HIGGINS: Why?

MRS HIGGINS: Because you cant speak and whistle at the same time.

HIGGINS *groans. Another very trying pause.*

HIGGINS [*springing up, out of patience*]: Where the devil is that girl? Are we to wait here all day?

ELIZA *enters, sunny, self-possessed, and giving a staggeringly convincing exhibition of ease of manner. She carries a little work-basket, and is very much at home.* PICKERING *is too much taken aback to rise.*

LIZA: How do you do, Professor Higgins? Are you quite well?

HIGGINS [*choking*]: Am I— [*He can say no more*].

LIZA: But of course you are: you are never ill. So glad to see you again, Colonel Pickering. [*He rises hastily; and they shake hands*]. Quite chilly this morning, isnt it? [*She sits down on his left. He sits beside her*].

HIGGINS: Dont you dare try this game on me. I taught it to you; and it doesnt take me in. Get up and come home; and dont be a fool.

ELIZA *takes a piece of needlework from her basket, and begins to stitch at it, without taking the least notice of this outburst.*

MRS HIGGINS: Very nicely put, indeed, Henry. No woman could resist such an invitation.

HIGGINS: You let her alone, mother. Let her speak for herself. You will jolly soon see whether she has an idea that I havnt put into her head or a word that I havnt put into her mouth. I tell you I have created this thing out of the squashed cabbage leaves of Covent Garden; and now she pretends to play the fine lady with me.

MRS HIGGINS [*placidly*]: Yes, dear; but youll sit down, wont you?

HIGGINS *sits down again, savagely.*

LIZA [*to* PICKERING, *taking no apparent notice of* HIGGINS, *and working away deftly*]: Will you drop me altogether now that the experiment is over, Colonel Pickering?

PICKERING: Oh dont. You mustnt think of it as an experiment. It shocks me, somehow.

LIZA: Oh, I'm only a squashed cabbage leaf—

PICKERING [*impulsively*]: No.

LIZA [*continuing quietly*]: —but I owe so much to you that I should be very unhappy if you forgot me.

PICKERING: It's very kind of you to say so, Miss Doolittle.

LIZA: It's not because you paid for my dresses. I know you are generous to everybody with money. But it was from you that I learnt really nice manners; and that is what makes one a lady, isnt it? You see it was so very difficult for me with the example of Professor Higgins always before me. I was brought up to be just like him, unable to control myself, and using bad language on the slightest provocation. And I should never have known that ladies and gentlemen didnt behave like that if you hadnt been there.

HIGGINS: Well!!

PICKERING: Oh, thats only his way, you know. He doesnt mean it.

LIZA: Oh, *I* didnt mean it either, when I was a flower girl. It was only my way. But you see I did it; and thats what makes the difference after all.

PICKERING: No doubt. Still, he taught you to speak; and I couldnt have done that, you know.

LIZA [*trivially*]: Of course: that is his profession.

HIGGINS: Damnation!

LIZA [*continuing*]: It was just like learning to dance in the fashionable way: there was nothing more than that in it. But do you know what began my real education?

PICKERING: What?

LIZA [*stopping her work for a moment*]: Your calling me Miss Doolittle that day when I first came to Wimpole Street. That was the beginning of self-respect for me. [*She resumes her stitching*]. And there were a hundred little things you never noticed, because they came naturally to you. Things about standing up and taking off your hat and opening doors—

PICKERING: Oh, that was nothing.

LIZA: Yes: things that shewed you thought and felt about me as if I were something better than a scullery-maid; though of course I know you would have been just the same to a scullery-maid if she had been let into the drawing room. You never took off your boots in the dining room when I was there.

PICKERING: You mustnt mind that. Higgins takes off his boots all over the place.

LIZA: I know. I am not blaming him. It is his way, isnt it? But it made such a difference to me that you didnt do it. You see, really and truly, apart from the things anyone can pick up (the dressing and the proper way of speaking, and so on), the difference between a lady and a flower girl is not how she behaves, but how she's treated. I shall always be a flower girl to Professor Higgins, because he always treats me as a flower girl, and always will; but I know I can be a lady to you, because you always treat me as a lady, and always will.

MRS HIGGINS: Please dont grind your teeth, Henry.

PICKERING: Well, this is really very nice of you, Miss Doolittle.

LIZA: I should like you to call me Eliza, now, if you would.

PICKERING: Thank you. Eliza, of course.

LIZA: And I should like Professor Higgins to call me Miss Doolittle.

HIGGINS: I'll see you damned first.

MRS HIGGINS: Henry! Henry!

PICKERING [*laughing*]: Why dont you slang back at him? Dont stand it. It would do him a lot of good.

LIZA: I cant. I could have done it once but now I cant go back to it. You told me, you know, that when a child is brought to a foreign country, it picks up the language in a few weeks, and forgets its own. Well, I am a child in your country. I have forgotten my own language, and can speak nothing but yours. Thats the real break-off with the corner of Tottenham Court Road. Leaving Wimpole Street finishes it.

PICKERING [*much alarmed*]: Oh! but youre coming back to Wimpole Street, arnt you? Youll forgive Higgins?

HIGGINS [*rising*]: Forgive! Will she, by George! Let her go. Let her find out how she can get on without us. She will relapse into the gutter in three weeks without me at her elbow.

DOOLITTLE *appears at the centre window. With a look of dignified reproach at* HIGGINS, *he comes slowly and silently to his daughter, who, with her back to the window, is unconscious of his approach.*

PICKERING: He's incorrigible, Eliza. You wont relapse, will you?

LIZA: No: not now. Never again. I have learnt my lesson. I dont believe I could utter one of the old sounds if I tried. [DOOLITTLE *touches her on her left shoulder. She drops her work, losing her self-possession utterly at the spectacle of her father's splendor*] A-a-a-a-a-ah-ow-ooh!

HIGGINS [*with a crow of triumph*]: Aha! Just so. A-a-a-a-ahowooh! A-a-a-a-ahowooh! A-a-a-a-ahowooh! Victory! Victory! [*He throws himself on the divan, folding his arms, and spraddling arrogantly*].

DOOLITTLE: Can you blame the girl? Dont look at me like that, Eliza. It aint my fault. Ive come into some money.

LIZA: You must have touched a millionaire this time, dad.

DOOLITTLE: I have. But I'm dressed something special today. I'm going to St. George's, Hanover Square. Your stepmother is going to marry me.

LIZA [*angrily*]: Youre going to let yourself down to marry that low common woman!

PICKERING [*quietly*]: He ought to, Eliza. [*To* DOOLITTLE] Why has she changed her mind?

DOOLITTLE [*sadly*]: Intimidated, Governor. Intimidated. Middle class morality claims its victim. Wont you put on your hat, Liza, and come and see me turned off?

LIZA: If the Colonel says I must, I—I'll [*almost sobbing*] I'll demean myself. And get insulted for my pains, like enough.

DOOLITTLE: Don't be afraid: she never comes to words with anyone now, poor woman! respectability has broke all the spirit out of her.

PICKERING [*squeezing* ELIZA'*s elbow gently*]: Be kind to them, Eliza. Make the best of it.

LIZA [*forcing a little smile for him through her vexation*]: Oh well, just to shew theres no ill feeling. I'll be back in a moment. [*She goes out*].

DOOLITTLE [*sitting down beside* PICKERING]: I feel uncommon nervous about the ceremony, Colonel. I wish youd come and see me through it.

PICKERING: But youve been through it before, man. You were married to Eliza's mother.

DOOLITTLE: Who told you that, Colonel?

PICKERING: Well, nobody told me. But I concluded—naturally—

DOOLITTLE: No: that aint the natural way, Colonel: it's only the middle class way. My way was always the undeserving way. But dont say nothing to Eliza. She dont know: I always had a delicacy about telling her.

PICKERING: Quite right. We'll leave it so, if you dont mind.

DOOLITTLE: And youll come to the church, Colonel, and put me through straight?

PICKERING: With pleasure. As far as a bachelor can.

MRS HIGGINS: May I come, Mr Doolittle? I should be very sorry to miss your wedding.

DOOLITTLE: I should indeed be honored by your condescension, maam; and my poor old woman would take it as a tremenjous compliment. She's been very low, thinking of the happy days that are no more.

MRS HIGGINS [*rising*]: I'll order the carriage and get ready. [*The men rise, except* HIGGINS]. I shant be more than fifteen minutes. [*As she goes to the door* ELIZA *comes in, hatted and buttoning her gloves*]. I'm going to the church to see your father married, Eliza. You had better come in the brougham with me. Colonel Pickering can go on with the bridegroom.

MRS HIGGINS *goes out.* ELIZA *comes to the middle of the room between the centre window and the ottoman.* PICKERING *joins her.*

DOOLITTLE: Bridegroom! What a word! It makes a man realize his position, somehow. [*He takes up his hat and goes towards the door*].

PICKERING: Before I go, Eliza, do forgive Higgins and come back to us.

LIZA: I dont think dad would allow me. Would you, dad?

DOOLITTLE [*sad but magnanimous*]: They played you off very cunning, Eliza, them two sportsmen. If it had been only one of them, you could have nailed him. But you see, there was two; and one of them chaperoned the other, as you might say. [*To* PICKERING] It was artful of you, Colonel; but I bear no malice: I should have done the same myself. I been the victim of one woman after another all my life, and I dont grudge you two getting the better of Liza. I shant interfere. It's time for us to go, Colonel. So long, Henry. See you in St. George's, Eliza. [*He goes out*].

PICKERING [*coaxing*]: Do stay with us, Eliza. [*He follows* DOOLITTLE].

ELIZA *goes out on the balcony to avoid being alone with* HIGGINS. *He rises and joins her there. She immediately comes back into the room and makes for the door; but he goes along the balcony quickly and gets his back to the door before she reaches it.*

HIGGINS: Well, Eliza, youve had a bit of your own back, as you call it. Have you had enough? and are you going to be reasonable? Or do you want any more?

LIZA: You want me back only to pick up your slippers and put up with your tempers and fetch and carry for you.

HIGGINS: I havnt said I wanted you back at all.

LIZA: Oh, indeed. Then what are we talking about?

HIGGINS: About you, not about me. If you come back I shall treat you just as I have always treated you. I cant change my nature; and I dont intend to change my manners. My manners are exactly the same as Colonel Pickering's.

LIZA: Thats not true. He treats a flower girl as if she was a duchess.

HIGGINS: And I treat a duchess as if she was a flower girl.

LIZA: I see. [*She turns away composedly, and sits on the ottoman, facing the window*]. The same to everybody.

HIGGINS: Just so.

LIZA: Like father.

HIGGINS [*grinning, a little taken down*]: Without accepting the comparison at all points, Eliza, it's quite true that your father is not a snob, and that he will be quite at home in any station of life to which his eccentric destiny may call him. [*Seriously*] The great secret, Eliza, is not having bad manners or good manners or any other particular sort of manners, but having the same manner for all human souls: in short, behaving as if you were in Heaven, where there are no third-class carriages, and one soul is as good as another.

LIZA: Amen. You are a born preacher.

HIGGINS [*irritated*]: The question is not whether I treat you rudely, but whether you ever heard me treat anyone else better.

LIZA [*with sudden sincerity*]: I dont care how you treat me. I dont mind your swearing at me. I shouldnt mind a black eye: Ive had one before this. But [*standing up and facing him*] I wont be passed over.

HIGGINS: Then get out of my way; for I wont stop for you. You talk about me as if I were a motor bus.

LIZA: So you are a motor bus: all bounce and go, and no consideration for anyone. But I can do without you: dont think I cant.

HIGGINS: I know you can. I told you you could.

LIZA [*wounded, getting away from him to the other side of the ottoman with her face to the hearth*]: I know you did, you brute. You wanted to get rid of me.

HIGGINS: Liar.

LIZA: Thank you. [*She sits down with dignity*].

HIGGINS: You never asked yourself, suppose, whether *I* could do without you.

LIZA [*earnestly*]: Dont you try to get round me. Youll have to do without me.

HIGGINS [*arrogant*]: I can do without anybody. I have my own soul: my own spark of divine fire. But [*with sudden humility*] I shall miss you, Eliza. [*He sits down near her on the ottoman*]. I have learnt something from your idiotic notions: I confess that humbly and gratefully. And I have grown accustomed to your voice and appearance. I like them, rather.

LIZA: Well, you have both of them on your gramophone and in your book of photographs. When you feel lonely without me, you can turn the machine on. It's got no feelings to hurt.

HIGGINS: I cant turn your soul on. Leave me those feelings; and you can take away the voice and the face. They are not you.

LIZA: Oh, you are a devil. You can twist the heart in a girl as easy as some could twist her arms to hurt her. Mrs Pearce warned me. Time and again she has wanted to leave you; and you always got round her at the last minute. And you dont care a bit for her. And you dont care a bit for me.

HIGGINS: I care for life, for humanity; and you are a part of it that has come my way and been built into my house. What more can you or anyone ask?

LIZA: I wont care for anybody that doesnt care for me.

HIGGINS: Commercial principles, Eliza. Like [*reproducing her Covent Garden pronunciation with professional exactness*] s'yollin voylets [*selling violets*], isnt it?

LIZA: Dont sneer at me. It's mean to sneer at me.

HIGGINS: I have never sneered in my life. Sneering doesnt become either the human face or the human soul. I am expressing my righteous contempt for Commercialism. I dont and wont trade in affection. You call me a brute because you couldnt buy a claim on me by fetching my slippers and finding my spectacles. You were a fool: I think a woman fetching a man's slippers is a disgusting sight: did I ever fetch your slippers? I think a good deal more of you for throwing them in my face. No use slaving for me and then saying you want to be cared for: who cares for a slave? If you come back, come back for the sake of good fellowship; for youll get nothing else. Youve had a thousand times as much out of me as I have out of you; and if you dare to set up your little dog's tricks of fetching and carrying slippers against my creation of a Duchess Eliza, I'll slam the door in your silly face.

LIZA: What did you do it for if you didnt care for me?

HIGGINS [*heartily*]: Why, because it was my job.

LIZA: You never thought of the trouble it would make for me.

HIGGINS: Would the world ever have been made if its maker had been afraid of making trouble? Making life means making trouble. Theres only one way of escaping trouble; and thats killing things. Cowards, you notice, are always shrieking to have troublesome people killed.

LIZA: I'm no preacher: I dont notice things like that. I notice that you dont notice me.

HIGGINS [*jumping up and walking about intolerantly*]: Eliza: youre an idiot. I waste the treasures of my Miltonic mind by spreading them before you. Once for all, understand that I go my way and do my work without caring twopence what happens to either of us. I am not intimidated, like your father and your stepmother. So you can come back or go to the devil: which you please.

LIZA: What am I to come back for?

HIGGINS [*bouncing up on his knees on the ottoman and leaning over it to her*]: For the fun of it. Thats why I took you on.

LIZA [*with averted face*]: And you may throw me out tomorrow if I dont do everything you want me to?

HIGGINS: Yes; and you may walk out tomorrow if I dont do everything you want me to.

LIZA: And live with my stepmother?

HIGGINS: Yes, or sell flowers.

LIZA: Oh! If I only could go back to my flower basket! I should be independent of both you and father and all the world! Why did you take my independence from me? Why did I give it up? I'm a slave now, for all my fine clothes.

HIGGINS: Not a bit. I'll adopt you as my daughter and settle money on you if you like. Or would you rather marry Pickering?

LIZA [*looking fiercely round at him*]: I wouldnt marry you if you asked me; and youre nearer my age than what he is.

HIGGINS [*gently*]: Than he is: not "than what he is."

LIZA [*losing her temper and rising*]: I'll talk as I like. Youre not my teacher now.

HIGGINS [*reflectively*]: I dont suppose Pickering would, though. He's as confirmed an old bachelor as I am.

LIZA: Thats not what I want; and dont you think it. Ive always had chaps enough wanting me that way. Freddy Hill writes to me twice and three times a day, sheets and sheets.

HIGGINS [*disagreeably surprised*]: Damn his impudence! [*He recoils and finds himself sitting on his heels*].

LIZA: He has a right to if he likes, poor lad. And he does love me.

HIGGINS [*getting off the ottoman*]: You have no right to encourage him.

LIZA: Every girl has a right to be loved.

HIGGINS: What! By fools like that?

LIZA: Freddy's not a fool. And if he's weak and poor and wants me, may be he'd make me happier than my betters that bully me and dont want me.

HIGGINS: Can he make anything of you? Thats the point.

LIZA: Perhaps I could make something of him. But I never thought of us making anything of one another; and you never think of anything else. I only want to be natural.

HIGGINS: In short, you want me to be as infatuated about you as Freddy? Is that it?

LIZA: No I dont. Thats not the sort of feeling I want from you. And dont you be too sure of yourself or of me. I could have been a bad girl if I'd liked. Ive seen more of some things than you, for all your learning. Girls like me can drag gentlemen down to make love to them easy enough. And they wish each other dead the next minute.

HIGGINS: Of course they do. Then what in thunder are we quarrelling about?

LIZA [*much troubled*]: I want a little kindness. I know I'm a common ignorant girl, and you a book-learned gentleman; but I'm not dirt under your feet. What I done [*correcting herself*] What I did was not for the dresses and the taxis: I did it because we were pleasant together and I come — came—to care for you; not to want you to make love to me, and not forgetting the difference between us, but more friendly like.

HIGGINS: Well, of course. Thats just how I feel. And how Pickering feels. Eliza: youre a fool.

LIZA: Thats not a proper answer to give me [*she sinks on the chair at the writing-table in tears*].

HIGGINS: It's all youll get until you stop being a common idiot. If youre going to be a lady, youll have to give up feeling neglected if the men you know dont spend half their time snivelling over you and the other half giving you black eyes. If you cant stand the coldness of my sort of life, and the strain of it, go back to the gutter. Work til youre more a brute than a human being; and then cuddle and squabble and drink til you fall asleep. Oh, it's a fine life, the life of the gutter. It's real: it's warm: it's violent: you can feel it through the thickest skin: you can taste it and smell it without any training or any work. Not like Science and Literature and Classical Music and Philosophy and Art. You find me cold, unfeeling, selfish, dont you? Very well: be off with you to the sort of people you like. Marry some sentimental hog or other with lots of money, and a thick pair of lips to kiss you with and a thick pair of boots to kick you with. If you cant appreciate what youve got, youd better get what you can appreciate.

LIZA [*desperate*]: Oh, you are a cruel tyrant. I cant talk to you: you turn everything against me: I'm always in the wrong. But you know very well all the time that youre nothing but a bully. You know I cant go back to the gutter, as you call it, and that I have no real friends in the world but you and the Colonel. You know well I couldnt bear to live with a low common man after you two; and it's wicked and cruel of you to insult me by pretending I could. You think I must go back to Wimpole Street because I have nowhere else to go but father's. But dont you be too sure that you have me under your feet to be trampled on and talked down. I'll marry Freddy, I will, as soon as I'm able to support him.

HIGGINS [*thunderstruck*]: Freddy!!! that young fool! That poor devil who couldnt get a job as an errand boy even if he had the guts to try for it! Woman: do you not understand that I have made you a consort for a king?

LIZA: Freddy loves me: that makes him king enough for me. I dont want him to work: he wasnt brought up to it as I was. I'll go and be a teacher.

HIGGINS: Whatll you teach, in heaven's name?

LIZA: What you taught me. I'll teach phonetics.

HIGGINS: Ha! ha! ha!

LIZA: I'll offer myself as an assistant to that hairyfaced Hungarian.

HIGGINS [*rising in a fury*]: What! That impostor! that humbug! that toadying ignoramus! Teach him my methods! my discoveries! You take one step in his direction and I'll wring your neck. [*He lays hands on her*]. Do you hear?

LIZA [*defiantly non-resistant*]: Wring away. What do I care? I knew youd strike me some day. [*He lets her go, stamping with rage at having forgotten himself, and recoils so hastily that he stumbles back into his seat on the ottoman*]. Aha! Now I know how to deal with you. What a fool I was not to think of it before! You cant take away the knowledge you gave me. You said I had a finer ear than you. And I can be civil and kind to people, which is more than you can. Aha! [*Purposely dropping her aitches to annoy him*] Thats done you, Enry Iggins, it az. Now I dont care that [*snapping her fingers*] for your bullying and your big talk. I'll advertize it in the papers that your duchess is only a flower girl that you taught, and that she'll teach anybody to be a duchess just the same in six months for a thousand guineas. Oh, when I think of myself crawling under your feet and being trampled on and called names, when all the time I had only to lift up my finger to be as good as you, I could just kick myself.

HIGGINS [*wondering at her*]: You damned impudent slut, you! But it's better than snivelling; better than fetching slippers and finding spectacles, isnt it? [*Rising*] By George, Eliza, I said I'd make a woman of you; and I have. I like you like this.

LIZA: Yes: you can turn round and make up to me now that I'm not afraid of you, and can do without you.

HIGGINS: Of course I do, you little fool. Five minutes ago you were like a millstone round my neck. Now youre a tower of strength: a consort battleship. You and I and Pickering will be three old bachelors instead of only two men and a silly girl.

MRS HIGGINS *returns, dressed for the wedding.* ELIZA *instantly becomes cool and elegant.*

MRS HIGGINS: The carriage is waiting, Eliza. Are you ready?

LIZA: Quite. Is the Professor coming?

MRS HIGGINS: Certainly not. He cant behave himself in church. He makes remarks out loud all the time on the clergyman's pronunciation.

LIZA: Then I shall not see you again, Professor. Goodbye. [*She goes to the door*].

MRS HIGGINS [*coming to* HIGGINS]: Goodbye, dear.

HIGGINS: Goodbye, mother. [*He is about to kiss her, when he recollects something*]. Oh, by the way, Eliza, order a ham and a Stilton cheese, will you? And buy me a pair of reindeer gloves, number eights, and a tie to match that new suit of mine. You can choose the color. [*His cheerful, careless, vigorous voice shews that he is incorrigible*].

LIZA [*disdainfully*]: Number eights are too small for you if you want them lined with lamb's wool. You have three new ties that you have forgotten in the drawer of your washstand. Colonel Pickering prefers double Gloucester to Stilton; and you dont notice the difference. I telephoned Mrs Pearce this morning not to forget the ham. What you are to do without me I cannot imagine. [*She sweeps out*].

MRS HIGGINS: I'm afraid youve spoilt that girl, Henry. I should be uneasy about you and her if she were less fond of Colonel Pickering.

HIGGINS: Pickering! Nonsense: she's going to marry Freddy. Ha ha! Freddy! Freddy!! Ha ha ha ha ha!!!!!

[*He roars with laughter as the play ends*].

Anton Chekhov

Anton Pavlovich Chekhov (1860–1904) was born in Taganrog, a provincial town of sixty thousand on the Sea of Azov in Ukraine, where his family, once serfs, had bought their freedom. Chekhov's mother seems to have been a compliant woman who dedicated her life to her family. His father, a grocer, was a devout member of the Russian Orthodox Church, whose faith bordered on fanaticism and who believed in strict discipline for his six children. The family was poor, and by the time he was sixteen, Chekhov was living on his own in Moscow. His difficult and unhappy childhood seems not to have depressed him or affected his later disposition. He was by all accounts a friendly and happy man, and he maintained good relations with all of his family. Characteristically, Chekhov tended to avoid confrontation, preferring to subdue his feelings rather than quarrel with others. He was evasive and often indirect. Chekhov's aversion to conflict may have influenced his later plays, whose characters' emotions tend to be stifled or only obliquely expressed. Many of Chekhov's characters are trapped in provincial towns, which he often characterized as suffocating places whose inhabitants, unable to seize initiative, stagnated and saw their passions die away. This emerged as a major theme in both his fiction and his drama.

While issues of religion and money abound in Chekhov's work, he shied away from political and religious arguments, focusing instead on his characters' moral and psychological states of mind. His fictional characters range the whole of Russian society, from peasants to aristocrats, though he generally took characters from the middle and upper classes for protagonists. Chekhov also had a wonderful sense of humor that pervades most of his work. Though his work is sometimes gentle, as his friend Maxim Gorky suggested, and other times ironic and tinged with despair, it is scarcely ever biting or caustic.

Chekhov followed parallel careers in medicine and literature. While attending the University of Moscow, from which he received a medical degree in 1884, he wrote for small magazines and newspapers in order to support himself and his family. An astonishingly fluid writer, he dabbled in many forms with ease, but the quality of his early work was, in his own word, "trash." He continued to divide his time between literature and medicine, working sporadically as a doctor until 1899. Being Doctor Chekhov was always his second career.

By his late twenties, Chekhov was an established writer of fiction, having developed a mastery of the short story form; he eventually wrote hundreds, among them "The Lady with the Dog," "Gooseberries," "The Darling," and "The Duel," all of which were greeted with high praise. Also during this period he wrote a number of popular short farces for the stage, many based on his short stories, the most famous of which is *The Bear* (1888).

When he was twenty-seven, Chekhov tried his hand at serious drama with *Ivanov*, his first major play. When it failed, he said he would never write another. The story concerns Ivanov, an aristocratic landowner who leads an indolent intellectual life that leaves him stagnant as well as deeply in debt. He marries Anna, a Jew who gives up her religion for him, but is disappointed that she has not brought a large dowry with her. When Anna dies of tuberculosis, Ivanov tries to revive his fortune by romancing Sasha Lebedev, the money-lender's willing daughter. But he ultimately cancels his wedding ceremony, and, declaring that he is acting according to the dictates of his conscience, he commits suicide.

The theme of alienation and boredom shows the influence of Nikolay Gogol's *Dead Souls*, but in Chekhov's drama it lacks comic flourishes. The pall that hangs over *Ivanov* is perhaps a consequence of Chekhov's foreboding sense of death from tuberculosis, which he contracted while he was studying medicine. Tuberculosis was then an incurable disease, and it killed him fourteen years later.

In 1890 Chekhov completed *The Wood Demon*, a play that was such a disaster he refused to let it reappear under his name in his lifetime. (He eventually revised the play as *Uncle Vanya*, which enjoyed greater success nine years later.) Depressed and eager to escape the literary world, Chekhov took off on a humanitarian investigation of a penal colony over three thousand miles from Moscow. The journey lasted eight months, and later he wrote a memoir, *The Island of Sakhalin* (1891), advocating penal reform and humane care for inmates. Chekhov was an inveterate traveler, and even when he was severely ill he traveled through Eastern and Middle Europe. He spent time in Nice but did not visit Paris.

After *Ivanov*, Chekhov did not complete another play for six years. This was the three-act comedy, *The Seagull* (1896), which failed in its first production in St. Petersburg. In it Treplev, an immature and unpublished writer who believes that he is avant-garde, is ridiculed by Trigorin, his mother's lover, a famous but mediocre writer. He is cast off by Nina, the young woman he loves. In anguish, Treplev shoots a seagull, an act that is meant to symbolize his unhappy love affair. Some years later, Treplev, now successful, meets Nina, who has become a mediocre provincial actress, and he woos her again. Decisively rebuffed, Treplev kills himself. Chekhov had intended Treplev's behavior to be understood ironically, but critics complained that the play was neither comic nor tragic. Chekhov was so disheartened that he decided, again, to forgo drama and concentrate on his fiction.

In 1897 Chekhov's lungs hemorrhaged, and from that point on his health declined, though he was also entering the most intense period of his career as a dramatist. He spent most of that year recuperating and writing in Nice, where the climate was mild. Besides writing short stories, he revised *The Wood Demon* as *Uncle Vanya*, but Chekhov kept the play from production until 1899.

In 1898 he revised *The Seagull* for production by the Moscow Art Theater, then under the leadership of Konstantin Stanislavsky (1863–1938) and Vladimir Nemirovich-Danchenko (1858–1943). It premiered in 1899 under the direction of Stanislavsky and was Chekhov's first theatrical success. Stanislavsky directed the play as a comedy and coached his actors in drawing out the psychological realism of Chekhov's characters. Stanislavsky's method was to explore the conflict between the outer and inner aspects of personality. This suited Chekhov's drama, which portrays people's states of mind rather than their overt actions. Stanislavsky rightly understood that one must accentuate the facets of a Chekhovian character: the foibles, the inability to communicate, the inability to take action, and the frustration of loving. In his autobiography, *My Life in Art* (1925, rev. 1936), he wrote: "In staging Chekhov's plays we should bring out his dreams, his *leit-motif.* Unfortunately, it is more difficult to do that than to depict the outer life of a play."

Since Stanislavsky demonstrated the potential and power of Chekhov's plays, they have been produced to great and lasting effect. Ironically, Chekhov and Stanislavsky were not close, and at times their relations were antagonistic. Chekhov thought that Stanislavsky tended to be overblown and that his acting often missed Chekhov's intentions. Stanislavsky caricatured Chekhov as a fussy, ailing old man with a pince-nez.

Chekhov, who most of his life delighted in being unencumbered by a wife, in 1898 met Olga Knipper. Knipper was an actress with the Moscow Art Theater, and he was introduced to her during rehearsals for *The Seagull*, in which she portrayed Irina, Madame Trepleva, the actress. After a courtship of two years, they married, though they were apart for much of the time, he recuperating in Yalta and she performing at the Moscow Art Theater. She created important roles in his plays, including Helen in *Uncle Vanya* and Lyubov in *The Cherry Orchard.* She is also probably the inspiration for his short story "The Lady with the Dog," which was composed in Yalta during their period of courtship.

Chekhov's next produced play, *Uncle Vanya* (1899), concerns Vanya (Ivan Voititsky), a kindly soul, who in order to live simply gives up his share of an inheritance. When his sister dies and her husband, Professor Serebryakov, an unbearable man, suggests selling the estate, Vanya nearly shoots him. The problem is solved when Vanya and his niece Sonia send Serebryakov away and agree to provide him with financial support. Vanya and Sonia keep the estate but little else, and they are contented.

The Three Sisters (1901) was written while Chekhov was living in Yalta, where the climate was mild and his illness would abate some. His wife was in Moscow most of the time, and her letters to him constantly asking when he would return to Moscow echo the three sisters of the play who talk endlessly about leaving their country estate and returning to Moscow. Olga, Masha, and Irina, the daughters of the dead General Prozorov, presume they would be happier in Moscow, but they have not the will to make the change. Olga, the oldest and portrayed by Knipper, is a spinster and an unhappy teacher who dreams of living in Moscow but never marries or leaves the safety of her position. Masha, the second sister, marries Kulygin, a schoolteacher whom she imagines is cultured, only to realize that she made a mistake. Bored, she has an affair with Colonel Vershinin, until he leaves with his regiment. Irina, the youngest, in order to get away from home, agrees to marry Baron Tuzenbach, but she does not love him. Her hopes are dashed when Tuzenbach is killed in a duel that could have easily been resolved if he was not so obtuse. Only Kulygin achieves a separate peace, and then only because he is too stupid to resent his wife's infidelity or realize how tedious his life is.

The Cherry Orchard (1904) was written and produced while Chekhov was dying, and this probably accounts for some of the play's wistfulness and sense of resignation. In his direction, Stanislavsky brought out the tragic aspects of the story, the lack of real communication among the characters, and the overall sense of loss. Chekhov, however, insisted that *The Cherry Orchard* was a comedy with elements of farce, and he was angered that his play was not presented this way.

The plot hinges on the fate of the Ranevskaya estate, which is encumbered with debt that must be satisfied or the estate will be sold for nonpayment of taxes. Lyubov Ranevskaya, the absentee owner, returns from Paris, where her love life has turned sour, in order to save the estate. She is well-meaning and arrives full of hope, but she is simply lacking in initiative. It is not in her nature to look after important financial matters, and what money there is gets spent foolishly. At first, Lopahin, the crafty entrepreneur, whose father was a serf on the estate, tries to help Lyubov. But when she fails to act, he buys the estate at auction. He is sympathetic for Lyubov, but he is also a practical man with the understanding that business requires action. He plans to cut down the orchard and divide the land for real estate development.

In Act IV, those who are departing the estate make their good-byes, and the house is filled with a sense of desolation, without deep sadness. The act is punctuated with concerned inquiries for Firs, the estate's ancient valet; the response is always that he has been taken care of. However, rather than being taken to the hospital, he gets lost in the shuffle. The champagne Lopahin brings is drunk without toasts. Trofimov, the eternal scholar who will never finish his studies, seriously announces to Lopahin, "Your father was a peasant, mine was a chemist—and that proves absolutely nothing whatever. . . . I am an independent man, and everything that all of you, rich and poor alike, prize so highly and hold so dear, hasn't the slightest power over me. . . . I can pass by you. I am strong and proud. Humanity is advancing towards the highest truth, the highest happiness, which is possible on earth, and I am in the front ranks." Lopahin says, "Good-bye, my dear fellow; it's time to be off. We turn up our noses at one another, but life is passing all the while. When I am working hard without resting, then my mind is more at ease, and it seems to me as though I too know what I exist for; but how many people there are in Russia, my dear boy, who exist, one doesn't know what for."

The clerk, Epihodov, puts a trunk down on a hatbox and crushes it. The young servants, Yasha and Dunyasha, talk of love, but he is off to Paris with Lyubov while she will remain. Lyubov's brother, Gaev, says that now that the cherry orchard is sold, they are happy: "Yes, really everything is all right now. Before the cherry orchard was sold, we were all worried and wretched, but afterwards, when once the question was settled conclusively, irrevocably, we all felt calm and even cheerful." He announces that now he is a bank clerk, a financier, but his new beginning seems hollow. As a matter of ingratiating himself into the household, Lopahin had promised to marry Varya, Lyubov's adopted daughter, but once the estate is his property, the promise is set aside, and Varya says that she will work as a housekeeper for a family seventy miles away.

Disappointed, Lyubov Andreyevna and Gaev stand alone, embrace each other, and "break into subdued smothered sobbing." Before she exits, Lyubov cries, "Oh, my orchard!—my sweet, beautiful orchard! My life, my youth, my happiness, good-bye! good-bye!" It is a heartfelt but ineffectual line for the departure from Russia to Paris.

Then when family and friends have gone and the sounds of the axe are heard, old Firs appears. Forgotten in the tumult, he tries the door handles, but they are locked. With resignation, he lies down and mutters to himself, "Life has slipped by as though I hadn't lived." As he lies motionless, "A sound is heard that seems to come from the sky, like a breaking harp-string, dying away mournfully." There is a silence, and then axes are heard thudding against trees in the cold late fall afternoon.

In his fiction and plays, Chekhov portrays Russia emerging from the feudalism that still characterized Russian life in the last half of the nineteenth century. Twelve years after his death, just before the Revolution of 1917, he was still the great man of Russian drama. Even during the years of the Soviet regime, the Communist government did not suppress productions of his plays, despite their aristocratic and bourgeois characters. Chekhov's work was viewed as a criticism of the old regime and thus was interpreted as being politically correct. Joseph Stalin seems to have had a fondness for Chekhov and even arranged for Chekhov's villa in Yalta to be preserved.

More important, Chekhov's works remain a powerful alternative to Henrik Ibsen's problem plays and August Strindberg's high-charged naturalism. Chekhov's complex delineation of character functioning without the crisis of action provided a platform to develop drama with fully realized characters who struggle internally with their own lack of initiative or their self-delusion. In Europe and the United States his technique and style have exerted great influence, particularly with regard to characterization. His adherents include such playwrights as George Bernard Shaw, Eugene O'Neill, Tennessee Williams, Thornton Wilder, Arthur Miller, and Wendy Wasserstein.

The Cherry Orchard

A Comedy in Four Acts

TRANSLATED BY CONSTANCE GARNETT

CHARACTERS IN THE PLAY

MADAME RANEVSKY (LYUBOV ANDREYEVNA), the owner of the Cherry Orchard
ANYA, her daughter, aged 17
VARYA, her adopted daughter, aged 24
GAEV (LEONID ANDREYEVITCH), brother of MADAME RANEVSKY
LOPAHIN (YERMOLAY ALEXEYEVITCH), a merchant
TROFIMOV (PYOTR SERGEYEVITCH), a student
SEMYONOV-PISHTCHIK, a landowner
CHARLOTTA IVANOVNA, a governess
EPIHODOV (SEMYON PANTALEYEVITCH), a clerk
DUNYASHA, a maid
FIRS, an old valet, aged 87
YASHA, a young valet
A VAGRANT
THE STATION MASTER
A POST-OFFICE CLERK
VISITORS, SERVANTS

The action takes place on the estate of MADAME RANEVSKY.

ACT I

A room, which has always been called the nursery. One of the doors leads into ANYA*'s room. Dawn, sun rises during the scene. May, the cherry trees in flower, but it is cold in the garden with the frost of early morning. Windows closed.*

Enter DUNYASHA *with a candle and* LOPAHIN *with a book in his hand.*

LOPAHIN: The train's in, thank God. What time is it?

DUNYASHA: Nearly two o'clock [*puts out the candle*]. It's daylight already.

LOPAHIN: The train's late! Two hours, at least [*yawns and stretches*]. I'm a pretty one; what a fool I've been. Came here on purpose to meet them at the station and dropped asleep. . . . Dozed off as I sat in the chair. It's annoying. . . .You might have waked me.

DUNYASHA: I thought you had gone [*listens*]. There, I do believe they're coming!

LOPAHIN [*listens*]: No, what with the luggage and one thing and another [*a pause*]. Lyubov Andreyevna has been abroad five years; I don't know what she is like now. . . . She's a splendid woman. A good-natured, kind-hearted woman. I remember when I was a lad of fifteen, my poor father—he used to keep a little shop here in the village in those days—gave me a punch in the face with his fist and made my nose bleed. We were in the yard here, I forget what we'd come about—he had had a drop. Lyubov Andreyevna—I can see her now—she was a slim young girl then—took me to wash my face, and then brought me into this very room, into the nursery. "Don't cry, little peasant," says she, "it will be well in time for your wedding day". . . [*a pause*]. Little peasant. . . . My father was a peasant, it's true, but here am I in a white waistcoat and brown shoes, like a pig in a bun shop. Yes, I'm a rich man, but for all my money, come to think, a peasant I was, and a peasant I am [*turns over the pages of the book*]. I've been reading this book and I can't make head or tail of it. I fell asleep over it [*a pause*].

DUNYASHA: The dogs have been awake all night, they feel that the mistress is coming.

LOPAHIN: Why, what's the matter with you, Dunyasha?

DUNYASHA: My hands are all of a tremble. I feel as though I should faint.

LOPAHIN: You're a spoilt soft creature, Dunyasha. And dressed like a lady too, and your hair done up. That's not the thing. One must know one's place.

[*Enter* EPIHODOV *with a nosegay; he wears a pea-jacket and highly polished creaking topboots; he drops the nosegay as he comes in.*]

EPIHODOV [*picking up the nosegay*]: Here! the gardener's sent this, says you're to put it in the dining-room [*gives* DUNYASHA *the nosegay*].

LOPAHIN: And bring me some kvass.

DUNYASHA: I will [*goes out*].

EPIHODOV: It's chilly this morning, three degrees of frost, though the cherries are all in flower. I can't say much for our climate [*sighs*]. I can't. Our climate is not often propitious to the occasion. Yermolay Alexeyevitch, permit me to call your attention to the fact that I purchased myself a pair of boots the day before yesterday, and they creak, I venture to assure you, so that there's no tolerating them. What ought I to grease them with?

LOPAHIN: Oh, shut up! Don't bother me.

EPIHODOV: Every day some misfortune befalls me. I don't complain, I'm used to it, and I wear a smiling face.

[DUNYASHA *comes in, hands* LOPAHIN *the kvass.*]

EPIHODOV: I am going [*stumbles against a chair, which falls over*]. There! [*as though triumphant*]. There you see now, excuse the expression, an accident like that among others. . . . It's positively remarkable [*goes out*].

DUNYASHA: Do you know, Yermolay Alexeyevitch, I must confess, Epihodov has made me a proposal.

LOPAHIN: Ah!

DUNYASHA: I'm sure I don't know. . . . He's a harmless fellow, but sometimes when he begins talking, there's no making anything of it. It's all very fine and expressive, only there's no understanding it. I've a sort of liking for him too. He loves me to distraction. He's an unfortunate man; every day there's something. They tease him about it—two and twenty misfortunes they call him.

LOPAHIN [*listening*]: There! I do believe they're coming.

DUNYASHA: They are coming! What's the matter with me? . . . I'm cold all over.

LOPAHIN: They really are coming. Let's go and meet them. Will she know me? It's five years since I saw her.

DUNYASHA [*in a flutter*]: I shall drop this very minute. . . . Ah, I shall drop.

[*There is a sound of two carriages driving up to the house.* LOPAHIN *and* DUNYASHA *go out quickly. The stage is left empty. A noise is heard in the adjoining rooms.* FIRS, *who has driven to meet* MADAME RANEVSKY, *crosses the stage hurriedly leaning on a stick. He is wearing old-fashioned livery and a high hat. He says something to himself, but not a word can be distinguished. The noise behind the scenes goes on increasing. A voice: "Come, let's go in here." Enter* LYUBOV ANDREYEVNA, ANYA, *and* CHARLOTTA IVANOVNA *with a pet dog on a chain, all in travelling dresses.* VARYA *in an out-door coat with a kerchief over her head,* GAEV, SEMYONOV-PISHTCHIK, LOPAHIN, DUNYASHA *with bag and parasol, servants with other articles. All walk across the room.*]

The Cherry Orchard, *directed by Eva Le Gallienne, the Lyceum Theatre, New York, 1968, with Richard Woods (far left) as Gaev and Uta Hagen, far right, as Madame Ranevsky.*

ANYA: Let's come in here. Do you remember what room this is, mamma?

LYUBOV [*joyfully, through her tears*]: The nursery!

VARYA: How cold it is, my hands are numb. [*To* LYUBOV ANDREYEVNA] Your rooms, the white room and the lavender one, are just the same as ever, mamma.

LYUBOV: My nursery, dear delightful room. . . . I used to sleep here when I was little. . . . [*cries*]. And here I am, like a little child . . . [*kisses her brother and* VARYA, *and then her brother again*]. Varya's just the same as ever, like a nun. And I knew Dunyasha [*kisses* DUNYASHA].

GAEV: The train was two hours late. What do you think of that? Is that the way to do things?

CHARLOTTA [*to* PISHTCHIK]: My dog eats nuts, too.

PISHTCHIK [*wonderingly*]: Fancy that!

[*They all go out except* ANYA *and* DUNYASHA.]

DUNYASHA: We've been expecting you so long [*takes* ANYA's *hat and coat*].

ANYA: I haven't slept for four nights on the journey. I feel dreadfully cold.

DUNYASHA: You set out in Lent, there was snow and frost, and now? My darling! [*laughs and kisses her*]. I *have* missed you, my precious, my joy. I must tell you . . . I can't put it off a minute. . . .

ANYA [*wearily*]: What now?

DUNYASHA: Epihodov, the clerk, made me a proposal just after Easter.

ANYA: It's always the same thing with you . . . [*straightening her hair*]. I've lost all my hairpins . . . [*she is staggering from exhaustion*].

DUNYASHA: I don't know what to think, really. He does love me, he does love me so!

ANYA [*looking towards her door, tenderly*]: My own room, my windows just as though I had never gone away. I'm home! To-morrow morning I shall get up and run into the garden. . . . Oh, if I could get to sleep! I haven't slept all the journey, I was so anxious and worried.

DUNYASHA: Pyotr Sergeyevitch came the day before yesterday.

DUNYASHA [*joyfully*]: Petya!

DUNYASHA: He's asleep in the bath house, he has settled in there. I'm afraid of being in their way, says he. [*Glancing at her watch*] I was to have waked him, but Varvara Mihalovna told me not to. Don't you wake him, says she.

[*Enter* VARYA *with a bunch of keys at her waist.*]

VARYA: Dunyasha, coffee and make haste. . . . Mamma's asking for coffee.

DUNYASHA: This very minute [*goes out*].

VARYA: Well, thank God, you've come. You're home again [*petting her*]. My little darling has come back! My precious beauty has come back again!

ANYA: I have had a time of it!

VARYA: I can fancy.

ANYA: We set off in Holy Week—it was so cold then, and all the way Charlotta would talk and show off her tricks. What did you want to burden me with Charlotta for?

VARYA: You couldn't have travelled all alone, darling. At seventeen!

ANYA: We got to Paris at last, it was cold there—snow. I speak French shockingly. Mamma lives on the fifth floor, I went up to her and there were a lot of French people, ladies, an old priest with a book. The place smelt of tobacco and so comfortless. I felt sorry, oh! so sorry for mamma all at once, I put my arms round her neck, and hugged her and wouldn't let her go. Mamma was as kind as she could be, and she cried. . . .

VARYA [*through her tears*]: Don't speak of it, don't speak of it!

ANYA: She had sold her villa at Mentone, she had nothing left, nothing. I hadn't a farthing left either, we only just had enough to get here. And mamma doesn't understand! When we had dinner at the stations, she always ordered the most expensive things and gave the waiters a whole rouble. Charlotta's just the same. Yasha too must have the same as we do; it's simply awful. You know Yasha is mamma's valet now, we brought him here with us.

VARYA: Yes, I've seen the young rascal.

ANYA: Well, tell me—have you paid the arrears on the mortgage?

VARYA: How could we get the money?

ANYA: Oh, dear! Oh, dear!

VARYA: In August the place will be sold.

ANYA: My goodness!

LOPAHIN [*peeps in at the door and moo's like a cow*]: Moo! [*disappears*].

VARYA [*weeping*]: There, that's what I could do to him [*shakes her fist*].

ANYA [*embracing* VARYA *softly*]: Varya, has he made you an offer? [VARYA *shakes her head.*] Why, but he loves you. Why is it you don't come to an understanding? What are you waiting for?

VARYA: I believe that there never will be anything between us. He has a lot to do, he has no time for me . . . and takes no notice of me. Bless the man, it makes me miserable to see him. . . . Everyone's talking of our being married, everyone's congratulating me, and all the while there's really nothing in it; it's all like a dream. [*In another tone*] You have a new brooch like a bee.

ANYA [*mournfully*]: Mamma bought it. [*Goes into her own room and in a light-hearted childish tone*] And you know, in Paris I went up in a balloon!

VARYA: My darling's home again! My pretty is home again!

[DUNYASHA *returns with the coffee-pot and is making the coffee.*]

VARYA [*standing at the door*]: All day long, darling, as I go about looking after the house, I keep dreaming all the time. If only we could marry you to a rich man, then I should feel more at rest. Then I would go off by myself on a pilgrimage to Kiev, to Moscow . . . and so I would spend my life going from one holy place to another. . . . I would go on and on. . . . What bliss!

ANYA: The birds are singing in the garden. What time is it?

VARYA: It must be nearly three. It's time you were asleep, darling [*going into* ANYA'*s room*]. What bliss!

[YASHA *enters with a rug and a travelling bag.*]

YASHA [*crosses the stage, mincingly*]: May one come in here, pray?

DUNYASHA: I shouldn't have known you, Yasha. How you have changed abroad.

YASHA: H'm! . . . And who are you?

DUNYASHA: When you went away, I was that high [*shows distance from floor*]. Dunyasha, Fyodor's daughter. . . . You don't remember me!

YASHA: H'm! . . . You're a peach! [*Looks round and embraces her: she shrieks and drops a saucer.* YASHA *goes out hastily.*]

VARYA [*in the doorway, in a tone of vexation*]: What now?

DUNYASHA [*through her tears*]: I have broken a saucer.

VARYA: Well, that brings good luck.

ANYA [*coming out of her room*]: We ought to prepare mamma: Petya is here.

VARYA: I told them not to wake him.

ANYA [*dreamily*]: It's six years since father died. Then only a month later little brother Grisha was drowned in the river, such a pretty boy he was, only seven. It was more than mamma could bear, so she went away, went away without looking back [*shuddering*]. . . . How well I understand her, if only she knew! [*a pause*] And Petya Trofimov was Grisha's tutor, he may remind her.

[*Enter* FIRS: *he is wearing a pea-jacket and a white waistcoat.*]

FIRS [*goes up to the coffee-pot, anxiously*]: The mistress will be served here [*puts on white gloves*]. Is the coffee ready? [*Sternly to* DUNYASHA] Girl! Where's the cream?

DUNYASHA: Ah, mercy on us! [*goes out quickly*].

FIRS [*fussing round the coffee-pot*]: Ech! you good-for-nothing! [*Muttering to himself*] Come back from Paris. And the old master used to go to Paris too . . . horses all the way [*laughs*].

VARYA: What is it, Firs?

FIRS: What is your pleasure? [*Gleefully*] My lady has come home! I have lived to see her again! Now I can die [*weeps with joy*].

[*Enter* LYUBOV ANDREYEVNA, GAEV *and* SEMYONOV-PISHTCHIK; *the latter is in a short-waisted full coat of fine cloth, and full trousers.* GAEV, *as he comes in, makes a gesture with his arms and his whole body, as though he were playing billiards.*]

LYUBOV: How does it go? Let me remember. Cannon off the red!

GAEV: That's it—in off the white! Why, once, sister, we used to sleep together in this very room, and now I'm fifty-one, strange as it seems.

LOPAHIN: Yes, time flies.

GAEV: What do you say?

LOPAHIN: Time, I say, flies.

GAEV: What a smell of patchouli!

ANYA: I'm going to bed. Good-night, mamma [*kisses her mother*].

LYUBOV: My precious darling [*kisses her hands*]. Are you glad to be home? I can't believe it.

ANYA: Good-night, uncle.

GAEV [*kissing her face and hands*]: God bless you! How like you are to your mother! [*To his sister*] At her age you were just the same, Lyuba.

[ANYA *shakes hands with* LOPAHIN *and* PISHTCHIK, *then goes out, shutting the door after her.*]

LYUBOV: She's quite worn out.

PISHTCHIK: Aye, it's a long journey, to be sure.

VARYA [*to* LOPAHIN *and* PISHTCHIK]: Well, gentlemen? It's three o'clock and time to say good-bye.

LYUBOV [*laughs*]: You're just the same as ever, Varya [*draws her to her and kisses her*]. I'll just drink my coffee and then we will all go and rest. [FIRS *puts a cushion under her feet.*] Thanks, friend. I am so fond of coffee, I drink it day and night. Thanks, dear old man [*kisses* FIRS].

VARYA: I'll just see whether all the things have been brought in [*goes out*].

LYUBOV: Can it really be me sitting here? [*laughs*]. I want to dance about and clap my hands. [*Covers her face with her hands*] And I could drop asleep in a moment! God knows I love my country, I love it tenderly; I couldn't look out of the window in the train, I kept crying so. [*Through her tears*] But I must drink my coffee, though. Thank you, Firs, thanks, dear old man. I'm so glad to find you still alive.

FIRS: The day before yesterday.

GAEV: He's rather deaf.

LOPAHIN: I have to set off for Harkov directly, at five o'clock. . . . It is annoying! I wanted to have a look at you, and a little talk. . . . You are just as splendid as ever.

PISHTCHIK [*breathing heavily*]: Handsomer, indeed. . . . Dressed in Parisian style . . . completely bowled me over.

LOPAHIN: Your brother, Leonid Andreyevitch here, is always saying that I'm a low-born knave, that I'm a money-grubber, but I don't care one straw for that. Let him talk. Only I do want you to believe in me as you used to. I do want your wonderful tender eyes to look at me as they used to in the old days. Merciful God! My father was a serf of your father and of your grandfather, but you—you—did so much for me once, that I've forgotten all that; I love you as though you were my kin . . . more than my kin.

LYUBOV: I can't sit still, I simply can't . . . [*jumps up and walks about in violent agitation*]. This happiness is too much for me. . . . You may laugh at me, I know I'm silly. . . . My own bookcase [*kisses the bookcase*]. My little table.

GAEV: Nurse died while you were away.

LYUBOV [*sits down and drinks coffee*]: Yes, the Kingdom of Heaven be hers! You wrote me of her death.

GAEV: And Anastasy is dead. Squinting Petruchka has left me and is in service now with the police captain in the town [*takes a box of caramels out of his pocket and sucks one*].

PISHTCHIK: My daughter, Dashenka, wishes to be remembered to you.

LOPAHIN: I want to tell you something very pleasant and cheering [*glancing at his watch*]. I'm going directly . . . there's no time to say much . . . well, I can say it in a couple of words. I needn't tell you your cherry orchard is to be sold to pay your debts; the 22nd of August is the date fixed for the sale; but don't you worry, dearest lady, you may sleep in peace, there is a way of saving it. . . . This is what I propose. I beg your attention! Your estate is not twenty miles from the town, the railway runs close by it, and if the cherry orchard and the land along the river bank were cut up into building plots and then let on lease for summer villas, you would make an income of at least 25,000 roubles a year out of it.

GAEV: That's all rot, if you'll excuse me.

LYUBOV: I don't quite understand you, Yermolay Alexeyevitch.

LOPAHIN: You will get a rent of at least 25 roubles a year for a three-acre plot from summer visitors, and if you say the word now, I'll bet you what you like there won't be one square foot of ground vacant by the autumn, all the plots will be taken up. I congratulate you; in fact, you are saved. It's a perfect situation with that deep river. Only, of course, it must be cleared—all the old buildings, for example, must be removed, this house too, which is really good for nothing and the old cherry orchard must be cut down.

LYUBOV: Cut down? My dear fellow, forgive me, but you don't know what you are talking about. If there is one thing interesting—remarkable indeed—in the whole province, it's just our cherry orchard.

LOPAHIN: The only thing remarkable about the orchard is that it's a very large one. There's a crop of cherries every alternate year, and then there's nothing to be done with them, no one buys them.

GAEV: This orchard is mentioned in the "Encyclopædia."

LOPAHIN [*glancing at his watch*]: If we don't decide on something and don't take some steps, on the 22nd of August the cherry orchard and the whole estate too will be sold by auction. Make up your minds! There is no other way of saving it, I'll take my oath on that. No, No!

FIRS: In old days, forty or fifty years ago, they used to dry the cherries, soak them, pickle them, make jam too, and they used——

GAEV: Be quiet, Firs.

FIRS: And they used to send the preserved cherries to Moscow and to Harkov by the waggon-load. That brought the money in! And the preserved cherries in those days were soft and juicy, sweet and fragrant. . . . They knew the way to do them then. . . .

LYUBOV: And where is the recipe now?

FIRS: It's forgotten. Nobody remembers it.

PISHTCHIK [*to* LYUBOV ANDREYEVNA]: What's it like in Paris? Did you eat frogs there?

LYUBOV: Oh, I ate crocodiles.

PISHTCHIK: Fancy that now!

LOPAHIN: There used to be only the gentlefolks and the peasants in the country, but now there are these summer visitors. All the towns, even the small ones, are surrounded nowadays by these summer villas. And one may say for sure, that in another twenty years there'll be many more of these people and that they'll be everywhere. At present the summer visitor only drinks tea in his verandah, but maybe he'll take to working his bit of land too, and then your cherry orchard would become happy, rich and prosperous. . . .

GAEV [*indignant*]: What rot!

[*Enter* VARYA *and* YASHA.]

VARYA: There are two telegrams for you, mamma [*takes out keys and opens an old-fashioned bookcase with a loud crack*]. Here they are.

LYUBOV: From Paris [*tears the telegrams, without reading them*]. I have done with Paris.

GAEV: Do you know, Lyuba, how old that bookcase is? Last week I pulled out the bottom drawer and there I found the date branded on it. The bookcase was made just a hundred years ago. What do you say to that? We might have celebrated its jubilee. Though it's an inanimate object, still it is a *book* case.

PISHTCHIK [*amazed*]: A hundred years! Fancy that now.

GAEV: Yes. . . . It is a thing . . . [*feeling the bookcase*]. Dear, honoured, bookcase! Hail to thee who for more than a hundred years hast served the pure ideals of good and justice; thy silent call to fruitful labour has never flagged in those hundred years, maintaining [*in tears*] in the generations of man, courage and faith in a brighter future and fostering in us ideals of good and social consciousness [*a pause*].

LOPAHIN: Yes. . . .

LYUBOV: You are just the same as ever, Leonid.

GAEV [*a little embarrassed*]: Cannon off the right into the pocket!

LOPAHIN [*looking at his watch*]: Well, it's time I was off.

YASHA [*handing* LYUBOV ANDREYEVNA *medicine*]: Perhaps you will take your pills now.

PISHTCHIK: You shouldn't take medicines, my dear madam . . . they do no harm and no good. Give them here . . . honoured lady [*takes the pill-box, pours the pills into the hollow of his hand, blows on them, puts them in his mouth and drinks off some kvass*]. There!

LYUBOV [*in alarm*]: Why, you must be out of your mind!

PISHTCHIK: I have taken all the pills.

LOPAHIN: What a glutton! [*All laugh.*]

FIRS: His honour stayed with us in Easter week, ate a gallon and a half of cucumbers . . . [*mutters*].

LYUBOV: What is he saying?

VARYA: He has taken to muttering like that for the last three years. We are used to it.

YASHA: His declining years!

[CHARLOTTA IVANOVNA, *a very thin, lanky figure in a white dress with a lorgnette in her belt, walks across the stage.*]

LOPAHIN: I beg your pardon, Charlotta Ivanovna, I have not had time to greet you [*tries to kiss her hand*].

CHARLOTTA [*pulling away her hand*]: If I let you kiss my hand, you'll be wanting to kiss my elbow, and then my shoulder.

LOPAHIN: I've no luck to-day! [*all laugh.*] Charlotta Ivanovna, show us some tricks!

LYUBOV: Charlotta, do show us some tricks!

CHARLOTTA: I don't want to. I'm sleepy [*goes out*].

LOPAHIN: In three weeks' time we shall meet again [*kisses* LYUBOV ANDREYEVNA'*s hand*]. Good-bye till then—I must go. [*To* GAEV] Good-bye. [*Kisses* PISHTCHIK] Good-bye. [*Gives his hand to* VARYA, *then to* FIRS *and* YASHA] I don't want to go. [*To* LYUBOV ANDREYEVNA] If you think over my plan for the villas and make up your mind, then let me know; I will lend you 50,000 roubles. Think of it seriously.

VARYA [*angrily*]: Well, do go, for goodness sake.

LOPAHIN: I'm going, I'm going [*goes out*].

GAEV: Low-born knave! I beg pardon, though . . . Varya is going to marry him, he's Varya's fiancé.

VARYA: Don't talk nonsense, uncle.

LYUBOV: Well, Varya, I shall be delighted. He's a good man.

PISHTCHIK: He is, one must acknowledge, a most worthy man. And my Dashenka . . . says too that . . . she says . . . various things [*snores, but at once wakes up*]. But all the same, honoured lady, could you oblige me . . . with a loan of 240 roubles . . . to pay the interest on my mortgage tomorrow?

VARYA [*dismayed*]: No, no.

LYUBOV: I really haven't any money.

PISHTCHIK: It will turn up [*laughs*]. I never lose hope. I thought everything was over, I was a ruined man, and lo and behold—the railway passed through my land and . . . they paid me for it. And something else will turn up again, if not to-day, then to-morrow . . . Dashenka'll win two hundred thousand . . . she's got a lottery ticket.

LYUBOV: Well, we've finished our coffee, we can go to bed.

FIRS [*brushes* GAEV, *reprovingly*]: You have got on the wrong trousers again! What am I to do with you?

VARYA [*softly*]: Anya's asleep. [*Softly opens the window*] Now the sun's risen, it's not a bit cold. Look, mamma, what exquisite trees! My goodness! And the air! The starlings are singing!

GAEV [*opens another window*]: The orchard is all white. You've not forgotten it, Lyuba? That long avenue that runs straight, straight as an arrow, how it shines on a moonlight night. You remember? You've not forgotten?

LYUBOV [*looking out of the window into the garden*]: Oh, my childhood, my innocence! It was in this nursery I used to sleep, from here I looked out into the orchard, happiness waked with me every morning and in those days the orchard was just the same, nothing has changed [*laughs with delight*]. All, all white! Oh, my orchard! After the dark gloomy autumn, and the cold winter; you are young again, and full of happiness, the heavenly angels have never left you. . . . If I could cast off the burden that weighs on my heart, if I could forget the past!

GAEV: H'm! and the orchard will be sold to pay our debts; it seems strange. . . .

LYUBOV: See, our mother walking . . . all in white, down the avenue! [*Laughs with delight.*] It is she!

GAEV: Where?

VARYA: Oh, don't, mamma!

LYUBOV: There is no one. It was my fancy. On the right there, by the path to the arbour, there is a white tree bending like a woman. . . .

[*Enter* TROFIMOV *wearing a shabby student's uniform and spectacles.*]

LYUBOV: What a ravishing orchard! White masses of blossom, blue sky. . . .

TROFIMOV: Lyubov Andreyevna! [*She looks round at him.*] I will just pay my respects to you and then leave you at once [*kisses her hand warmly*]. I was told to wait until morning, but I hadn't the patience to wait any longer. . . .

[LYUBOV ANDREYEVNA *looks at him in perplexity.*]

VARYA [*through her tears*]: This is Petya Trofimov.

TROFIMOV: Petya Trofimov, who was your Grisha's tutor. . . . Can I have changed so much?

[LYUBOV ANDREYEVNA *embraces him and weeps quietly.*]

GAEV [*in confusion*]: There, there, Lyuba.

VARYA [*crying*]: I told you, Petya, to wait till to-morrow.

LYUBOV: My Grisha . . . my boy . . . Grisha . . . my son!

VARYA: We can't help it, mamma, it is God's will.

TROFIMOV [*softly through his tears*]: There . . . there.

LYUBOV [*weeping quietly*]: My boy was lost . . . drowned. Why? Oh, why, dear Petya? [*More quietly*] Anya is asleep in there, and I'm talking loudly . . . making this noise. . . . But, Petya? Why have you grown so ugly? Why do you look so old?

TROFIMOV: A peasant-woman in the train called me a mangy-looking gentleman.

LYUBOV: You were quite a boy then, a pretty little student, and now your hair's thin—and spectacles. Are you really a student still? [*Goes towards the door.*]

TROFIMOV: I seem likely to be a perpetual student.

LYUBOV [*kisses her brother, then* VARYA]: Well, go to bed. . . . You are older too, Leonid.

PISHTCHIK [*follows her*]: I suppose it's time we were asleep. . . . Ugh! my gout. I'm staying the night! Lyubov Andreyevna, my dear soul, if you could . . . to-morrow morning . . . 240 roubles.

GAEV: That's always his story.

PISHTCHIK: 240 roubles . . . to pay the interest on my mortgage.

LYUBOV: My dear man, I have no money.

PISHTCHIK: I'll pay it back, my dear . . . a trifling sum.

LYUBOV: Oh, well, Leonid will give it you. . . . You give him the money, Leonid.

GAEV: Me give it him! Let him wait till he gets it!

LYUBOV: It can't be helped, give it him. He needs it. He'll pay it back.

[LYUBOV ANDREYEVNA, TROFIMOV, PISHTCHIK *and* FIRS *go out.* GAEV, VARYA *and* YASHA *remain.*]

GAEV: Sister hasn't got out of the habit of flinging away her money. [*To* YASHA] Get away, my good fellow, you smell of the hen-house.

YASHA [*with a grin*]: And you, Leonid Andreyevitch, are just the same as ever.

GAEV: What's that? [*To* VARYA] what did he say?

VARYA [*to* YASHA]: Your mother has come from the village; she has been sitting in the servants' room since yesterday, waiting to see you.

YASHA: Oh, bother her!

VARYA: For shame!

YASHA: What's the hurry? She might just as well have come to-morrow [*goes out*].

VARYA: Mamma's just the same as ever, she hasn't changed a bit. If she had her own way, she'd give away everything.

GAEV: Yes [*a pause*]. If a great many remedies are suggested for some disease, it means that the disease is incurable. I keep thinking and racking my brains; I have many schemes, a great many, and that really means none. If we could only come in for a legacy from somebody, or marry our Anya to a very rich man, or we might go to Yaroslavl and try our luck with our old aunt, the Countess. She's very, very rich you know.

VARYA [*weeps*]: If God would help us.

GAEV: Don't blubber. Aunt's very rich, but she doesn't like us. First, sister married a lawyer instead of a nobleman. . . .

[ANYA *appears in the doorway.*]

GAEV: And then her conduct, one can't call it virtuous. She is good, and kind, and nice, and I love her, but, however one allows for extenuating circumstances, there's no denying that she's an immoral woman. One feels it in her slightest gesture.

VARYA [*in a whisper*]: Anya's in the doorway.

GAEV: What do you say? [*a pause*]. It's queer, there seems to be something wrong with my right eye. I don't see as well as I did. And on Thursday when I was in the district Court . . .

[*Enter* ANYA.]

VARYA: Why aren't you asleep, Anya?

ANYA: I can't get to sleep.

GAEV: My pet [*kisses* ANYA*'s face and hands*]. My child [*weeps*]. You are not my niece, you are my angel, you are everything to me. Believe me, believe . . .

ANYA: I believe you, uncle. Everyone loves you and respects you . . . but, uncle dear, you must be silent . . . simply be silent. What were you saying just now about my mother, about your own sister? What made you say that?

GAEV: Yes, yes . . . [*puts his hand over his face*]. Really, that was awful! My God, save me! And to-day I made a speech to the bookcase . . . so stupid! And only when I had finished, I saw how stupid it was.

VARYA: It's true, uncle, you ought to keep quiet. Don't talk, that's all.

ANYA: If you could keep from talking, it would make things easier for you, too.

GAEV: I won't speak [*kisses* ANYA*'s and* VARYA*'s hands*]. I'll be silent. Only this is about business. On Thursday I was in the district Court; well, there was a large party of us there and we began talking of one thing and another, and this and that, and do you know, I believe that it will be possible to raise a loan on an I.O.U. to pay the arrears on the mortgage.

VARYA: If the Lord would help us!

GAEV: I'm going on Tuesday; I'll talk of it again. [*To* VARYA] Don't blubber. [*To* ANYA] Your mamma will talk to Lopahin; of course, he won't refuse her. And as soon as you're rested you shall go to Yaroslavl to the Countess, your great-aunt. So we shall all set to work in three directions at once, and the business is done. We shall pay off arrears, I'm convinced of it [*puts a caramel in his mouth*]. I swear on my honour, I swear by anything you like, the estate shan't be sold [*excitedly*]. By my own happiness, I swear it! Here's my hand on it, call me the basest, vilest of men, if I let it come to an auction! Upon my soul I swear it!

ANYA [*her equanimity has returned, she is quite happy*]: How good you are, uncle, and how clever! [*Embraces her uncle.*] I'm at peace now! Quite at peace! I'm happy!

[*Enter* FIRS.]

FIRS [*reproachfully*]: Leonid Andreyevitch, have you no fear of God? When are you going to bed?

GAEV: Directly, directly. You can go, Firs. I'll . . . yes, I will undress myself. Come, children, bye-bye. We'll go into details to-morrow, but now go to bed [*kisses* ANYA *and* VARYA]. I'm a man of the eighties. They run down that period, but still I can say I have had to suffer not a little for my convictions in my life. It's not for nothing that the peasant loves me. One must know the peasant! One must know how . . .

ANYA: At it again, uncle!

VARYA: Uncle dear, you'd better be quiet!

FIRS [*angrily*]: Leonid Andreyevitch!

GAEV: I'm coming. I'm coming. Go to bed. Potted the shot—there's a shot for you! A beauty! [*Goes out,* FIRS *hobbling after him.*]

ANYA: My mind's at rest now. I don't want to go to Yaroslavl, I don't like my great-aunt, but still my mind's at rest. Thanks to uncle [*sits down*].

VARYA: We must go to bed. I'm going. Something unpleasant happened while you were away. In the old servants' quarters there are only the old servants, as you know—Efimyushka, Polya and Yevstigney—and Karp too. They began letting stray people in to spend the night—I said nothing. But all at once I heard they had been spreading a report that I gave them nothing but pease pudding to eat. Out of stinginess, you know. . . . And it was all Yevstigney's doing. . . . Very well, I said to myself. . . . If that's how it is, I thought, wait a bit. I sent for Yevstigney . . . [*yawns*]. He comes. . . . "How's this, Yevstigney," I said, "you could be such a fool as to? . . . " [*Looking at* ANYA] Anitchka! [*a pause*]. She's asleep [*puts her arm round* ANYA]. Come to bed . . . come along! [*leads her*]. My darling has fallen asleep! Come . . . [*They go.*]

[*Far away beyond the orchard a shepherd plays on a pipe.* TROFIMOV *crosses the stage and, seeing* VARYA *and* ANYA, *stands still.*]

VARYA: 'Sh! asleep, asleep. Come, my own.

ANYA [*softly, half asleep*]: I'm so tired. Still those bells. Uncle . . . dear . . . mamma and uncle. . . .

VARYA: Come, my own, come along.

[*They go into* ANYA*'s room.*]

TROFIMOV [*tenderly*]: My sunshine! My spring.

CURTAIN

ACT II

The open country. An old shrine, long abandoned and fallen out of the perpendicular; near it a well, large stones that have apparently once been tombstones, and an old garden seat. The road to GAEV'S *house is seen. On one side rise dark poplars; and there the cherry orchard begins. In the distance a row of telegraph poles and far, far away on the horizon there is faintly outlined a great town, only visible in very fine clear weather. It is near sunset.* CHARLOTTA, YASHA *and* DUNYASHA *are sitting on the seat.* EPIHODOV *is standing near, playing something mournful on a guitar. All sit plunged in thought.* CHARLOTTA *wears an old forage cap; she has taken a gun from her shoulder and is tightening the buckle on the strap.*

CHARLOTTA [*musingly*]: I haven't a real passport of my own, and I don't know how old I am, and I always feel that I'm a young thing. When I was a little girl, my father and mother used to travel about to fairs and give performances—very good ones. And I used to dance *salto-mortale* and all sorts of things. And when papa and mamma died, a German lady took me and had me educated. And so I grew up and become a governess. But where I came from, and who I am, I don't know. . . . Who my parents were, very likely they weren't married . . . I don't know [*takes a cucumber out of her pocket and eats*]. I know nothing at all [*a pause*]. One wants to talk and has no one to talk to . . . I have nobody.

EPIHODOV [*plays on the guitar and sings*]: "What care I for the noisy world! What care I for friends or foes!" How agreeable it is to play on the mandoline!

DUNYASHA: That's a guitar, not a mandoline [*looks in a hand-mirror and powders herself*].

EPIHODOV: To a man mad with love, it's a mandoline. [*Sings*] "Were her heart but aglow with love's mutual flame." [YASHA *joins in.*]

CHARLOTTA: How shockingly these people sing! Foo! Like jackals!

DUNYASHA [*to* YASHA]: What happiness, though, to visit foreign lands.

YASHA: Ah, yes! I rather agree with you there [*yawns, then lights a cigar*].

EPIHODOV: That's comprehensible. In foreign lands everything has long since reached full complexion.

YASHA: That's so, of course.

EPIHODOV: I'm a cultivated man, I read remarkable books of all sorts, but I can never make out the tendency I am myself precisely inclined for, whether to live or to shoot myself, speaking precisely, but nevertheless I always carry a revolver. Here it is . . . [*shows revolver*].

CHARLOTTA: I've had enough, and now I'm going [*puts on the gun*]. Epihodov, you're a very clever fellow, and a very terrible one too, all the women must be wild about you. Br-r-r! [*goes*] These clever fellows are all so stupid; there's not a creature for me to speak to. . . . Always alone, alone, nobody belonging to me . . . and who I am, and why I'm on earth, I don't know [*walks away slowly*].

EPIHODOV: Speaking precisely, not touching upon other subjects, I'm bound to admit about myself, that destiny behaves mercilessly to me, as a storm to a little boat. If, let us suppose, I am mistaken, then why did I wake up this morning, to quote an example, and look round, and there on my chest was a spider of fearful magnitude . . . like this [*shows with both hands*]. And then I take up a jug of kvass, to quench my thirst, and in it there is something in the highest degree unseemly of the nature of a cockroach [*a pause*]. Have you read Buckle? [*a pause*]. I am desirous of troubling you, Dunyasha, with a couple of words.

DUNYASHA: Well, speak.

EPIHODOV: I should be desirous to speak with you alone [*sighs*].

DUNYASHA [*embarrassed*]: Well—only bring me my mantle first. It's by the cupboard. It's rather damp here.

EPIHODOV: Certainly. I will fetch it. Now I know what I must do with my revolver [*takes guitar and goes off playing on it*].

YASHA: Two and twenty misfortunes! Between ourselves, he's a fool [*yawns*].

DUNYASHA: God grant he doesn't shoot himself! [*a pause*] I am so nervous, I'm always in a flutter. I was a little girl when I was taken into our lady's house, and now I have quite grown out of peasant ways, and my hands are white, as white as a lady's. I'm such a delicate, sensitive creature, I'm afraid of everything. I'm so frightened. And if you deceive me, Yasha, I don't know what will become of my nerves.

YASHA [*kisses her*]: You're a peach! Of course a girl must never forget herself; what I dislike more than anything is a girl being flighty in her behaviour.

DUNYASHA: I'm passionately in love with you, Yasha; you are a man of culture—you can give your opinion about anything [*a pause*].

YASHA [*yawns*]: Yes, that's so. My opinion is this: if a girl loves anyone, that means that she has no principles [*a pause*]. It's pleasant smoking a cigar in the open air [*listens*]. Someone's coming this way . . . it's the gentlefolk [DUNYASHA *embraces him impulsively*]. Go home, as though you had been to the river to bathe; go by that path, or else they'll meet you and suppose I have made an appointment with you here. That I can't endure.

DUNYASHA [*coughing softly*]: The cigar has made my head ache . . . [*goes off*].

[YASHA *remains sitting near the shrine. Enter* LYUBOV ANDREYEVNA *and* LOPAHIN.]

LOPAHIN: You must make up your mind once for all—there's no time to lose. It's quite a simple question, you know. Will you consent to letting the land for building or not? One word in answer: Yes or no? Only one word!

LYUBOV: Who is smoking such horrible cigars here? [*sits down*].

GAEV: Now the railway line has been brought near, it's made things very convenient [*sits down*]. Here we have been over and lunched in town. Cannon off the white! I should like to go home and have a game.

LYUBOV: You have plenty of time.

LOPAHIN: Only one word! [*Beseechingly*]. Give me an answer!

GAEV [*yawning*]: What do you say?

LYUBOV [*looks in her purse*]: I had quite a lot of money here yesterday, and there's scarcely any left to-day. My poor Varya feeds us all on milk soup for the sake of economy; the old folks in the kitchen get nothing but pease pudding, while I waste my money in a senseless way [*drops purse, scattering gold pieces*]. There, they have all fallen out! [*annoyed*]

YASHA: Allow me, I'll soon pick them up [*collects the coins*].

LYUBOV: Pray do, Yasha. And what did I go off to the town to lunch for? Your restaurant's a wretched place with its music and the tablecloth smelling of soap. . . . Why drink so much, Leonid? And eat so much? And talk so much? To-day you talked a great deal again in the restaurant, and all so inappropriately. About the era of the 'seventies, about the decadents. And to whom? Talking to waiters about decadents!

LOPAHIN: Yes.

GAEV [*waving his hand*]: I'm incorrigible; that's evident. [*Irritably to* YASHA] Why is it you keep fidgeting about in front of us!

YASHA [*laughs*]: I can't help laughing when I hear your voice.

GAEV [*to his sister*]: Either I or he . . .

LYUBOV: Get along! Go away, Yasha.

YASHA [*gives* LYUBOV ANDREYEVNA *her purse*]: Directly [*hardly able to suppress his laughter*]. This minute . . . [*goes off*].

LOPAHIN: Deriganov, the millionaire, means to buy your estate. They say he is coming to the sale himself.

LYUBOV: Where did you hear that?

LOPAHIN: That's what they say in town.

GAEV: Our aunt in Yaroslavl has promised to send help; but when, and how much she will send, we don't know.

LOPAHIN: How much will she send? A hundred thousand? Two hundred?

LYUBOV: Oh, well! . . . Ten or fifteen thousand, and we must be thankful to get that.

LOPAHIN: Forgive me, but such reckless people as you are—such queer, unbusiness-like people—I never met in my life. One tells you in plain Russian your estate is going to be sold, and you seem not to understand it.

LYUBOV: What are we to do? Tell us what to do.

LOPAHIN: I do tell you every day. Every day I say the same thing. You absolutely must let the cherry orchard and the land on building leases; and do it at once, as quick as may be—the auction's close upon us! Do understand! Once make up your mind to build villas, and you can raise as much money as you like, and then you are saved.

LYUBOV: Villas and summer visitors—forgive me saying so—it's so vulgar.

GAEV: There I perfectly agree with you.

LOPAHIN: I shall sob, or scream, or fall into a fit. I can't stand it! You drive me mad! [*To* GAEV] You're an old woman!

GAEV: What do you say?

LOPAHIN: An old woman! [*Gets up to go.*]

LYUBOV [*in dismay*]: No, don't go! Do stay, my dear friend! Perhaps we shall think of something.

LOPAHIN: What is there to think of?

LYUBOV: Don't go, I entreat you! With you here it's more cheerful, anyway [*a pause*]. I keep expecting something, as though the house were going to fall about our ears.

GAEV [*in profound dejection*]: Potted the white! It fails—a kiss.

LYUBOV: We have been great sinners. . . .

LOPAHIN: You have no sins to repent of.

GAEV [*puts a caramel in his mouth*]: They say I've eaten up my property in caramels [*laughs*].

LYUBOV: Oh, my sins! I've always thrown my money away recklessly like a lunatic. I married a man who made nothing but debts. My husband died of champagne—he drank dreadfully. To my misery I loved another man, and immediately—it was my first punishment—the blow fell upon me, here, in the river . . . my boy was drowned and I went abroad—went away for ever, never to return, not to see that river again . . . I shut my eyes, and fled, distracted, and *he* after me . . . pitilessly, brutally. I bought a villa at Mentone, for *he* fell ill there, and for three years I had no rest day or night. His illness wore me out, my soul was dried up. And last year, when my villa was sold to pay my debts, I went to Paris and there he robbed me of everything and abandoned me for another woman; and I tried to poison myself. . . . So stupid, so shameful! . . . And suddenly I felt a yearning for Russia, for my country, for my little girl . . . [*dries her tears*]. Lord, Lord, be merciful! Forgive my sins! Do not chastise me more! [*Takes a telegram out of her pocket*] I got this to-day from Paris. He implores forgiveness, entreats me to return [*tears up the telegram*]. I fancy there is music somewhere [*listens*].

GAEV: That's our famous Jewish orchestra. You remember, four violins, a flute and a double bass.

LYUBOV: That still in existence? We ought to send for them one evening, and give a dance.

LOPAHIN [*listens*]: I can't hear. . . . [*Hums softly*] "For money the Germans will turn a Russian into a Frenchman." [*Laughs*] I did see such a piece at the theatre yesterday! It was funny!

LYUBOV: And most likely there was nothing funny in it. You shouldn't look at plays, you should look at yourselves a little oftener. How grey your lives are! How much nonsense you talk.

LOPAHIN: That's true. One may say honestly, we live a fool's life [*pause*]. My father was a peasant, an idiot; he knew nothing and taught me nothing, only beat me when he was drunk, and always with his stick. In reality I am just such another blockhead and idiot. I've learnt nothing properly. I write a wretched hand. I write so that I feel ashamed before folks, like a pig.

LYUBOV: You ought to get married, my dear fellow.

LOPAHIN: Yes . . . that's true.

LYUBOV: You should marry our Varya, she's a good girl.

LOPAHIN: Yes.

LYUBOV: She's a good-natured girl, she's busy all day long, and what's more, she loves you. And you have liked her for ever so long.

LOPAHIN: Well? I'm not against it. . . . She's a good girl [*pause*].

GAEV: I've been offered a place in the bank: 6,000 roubles a year. Did you know?

LYUBOV: You would never do for that! You must stay as you are.

[*Enter* FIRS *with overcoat.*]

FIRS: Put it on, sir, it's damp.

GAEV [*putting it on*]: You bother me, old fellow.

FIRS: You can't go on like this. You went away in the morning without leaving word [*looks him over*].

LYUBOV: You look older, Firs!

FIRS: What is your pleasure?

LOPAHIN: You look older, she said.

FIRS: I've had a long life. They were arranging my wedding before your papa was born . . . [*laughs*]. I was the head footman before the emancipation came. I wouldn't consent to be set free then; I stayed on with the old master . . . [*a pause*]. I remember what rejoicings they made and didn't know themselves what they were rejoicing over.

LOPAHIN: Those were fine old times. There was flogging anyway.

FIRS [*not hearing*]: To be sure! The peasants knew their place, and the masters knew theirs; but now they're all at sixes and sevens, there's no making it out.

GAEV: Hold your tongue, Firs. I must go to town to-morrow. I have been promised an introduction to a general, who might let us have a loan.

LOPAHIN: You won't bring that off. And you won't pay your arrears, you may rest assured of that.

LYUBOV: That's all his nonsense. There is no such general.

[*Enter* TROFIMOV, ANYA *and* VARYA.]

GAEV: Here come our girls.

ANYA: There's mamma on the seat.

LYUBOV [*tenderly*]: Come here, come along. My darlings! [*Embraces* ANYA *and* VARYA.] If you only knew how I love you both. Sit beside me, there, like that. [*All sit down.*]

LOPAHIN: Our perpetual student is always with the young ladies.

TROFIMOV: That's not your business.

LOPAHIN: He'll soon be fifty, and he's a student.

TROFIMOV: Drop your idiotic jokes.

LOPAHIN: Why are you so cross, you queer fish?

TROFIMOV: Oh, don't persist!

LOPAHIN [*laughs*]: Allow me to ask you what's your idea of me?

TROFIMOV: I'll tell you my idea of you, Yermolay Alexeyevitch: you are a rich man, you'll soon be a millionaire. Well, just as in the economy of nature a wild beast is of use, who devours everything that comes in his way, so you too have your use.

[*All laugh.*]

VARYA: Better tell us something about the planets, Petya.

LYUBOV: No, let us go on with the conversation we had yesterday.

TROFIMOV: What was it about?

GAEV: About pride.

TROFIMOV: We had a long conversation yesterday, but we came to no conclusion. In pride, in your sense of it, there is something mystical. Perhaps you are right from your point of view; but if one looks at it simply, without subtlety, what sort of pride can there be, what sense is there in it, if man in his physiological formation is very imperfect, if in the immense majority of cases he is coarse, dull-witted, profoundly unhappy? One must give up glorification of self. One should work, and nothing else.

GAEV: One must die in any case.

TROFIMOV: Who knows? And what does it mean—dying? Perhaps man has a hundred senses, and only the five we know are lost at death, while the other ninety-five remain alive.

LYUBOV: How clever you are, Petya!

LOPAHIN [*ironically*]: Fearfully clever!

TROFIMOV: Humanity progresses, perfecting its powers. Everything that is beyond its ken now will one day become familiar and comprehensible; only we must work, we must with all our powers aid the seeker after truth. Here among us in Russia the workers are few in number as yet. The vast majority of the intellectual people I know, seek nothing, do nothing, are not fit as yet for work of any kind. They call themselves intellectual, but they treat their servants as inferiors, behave to the peasants as though they were animals, learn little, read nothing seriously, do practically nothing, only talk about science and know very little about art. They are all serious people, they all have severe faces, they all talk of weighty matters and air their theories, and yet the vast majority of us—ninety-nine per cent.—live like savages, at the least thing fly to blows and abuse, eat piggishly, sleep in filth and stuffiness, bugs everywhere, stench and damp and moral impurity. And it's clear all our fine talk is only to divert our attention and other people's. Show me where to find the crèches there's so much talk about, and the reading-rooms? They only exist in novels: in real life there are none of them. There is nothing but filth and vulgarity and Asiatic apathy. I fear and dislike very serious faces. I'm afraid of serious conversations. We should do better to be silent.

LOPAHIN: You know, I get up at five o'clock in the morning, and I work from morning to night; and I've money, my own and other people's, always passing through my hands, and I see what people are made of all round me. One has only to begin to do anything to see how few honest, decent people there are. Sometimes when I lie awake at night, I think: "Oh! Lord, thou hast given us immense forests, boundless plains, the widest horizons, and living here we ourselves ought really to be giants."

LYUBOV: You ask for giants! They are no good except in story-books; in real life they frighten us.

[EPIHODOV *advances in the background, playing on the guitar.*]

LYUBOV [*dreamily*]: There goes Epihodov.

ANYA [*dreamily*]: There goes Epihodov.

GAEV: The sun has set, my friends.

TROFIMOV: Yes.

GAEV [*not loudly, but, as it were, declaiming*]: O nature, divine nature, thou art bright with eternal lustre, beautiful and indifferent! Thou, whom we call mother, thou dost unite within thee life and death! Thou dost give life and dost destroy!

VARYA [*in a tone of supplication*]: Uncle!

ANYA: Uncle, you are at it again!

TROFIMOV: You'd much better be cannoning off the red!

GAEV: I'll hold my tongue, I will.

[*All sit plunged in thought. Perfect stillness. The only thing audible is the muttering of* FIRS. *Suddenly there is a sound in the distance, as it were from the sky—the sound of a breaking harp-string, mournfully dying away.*]

LYUBOV: What is that?

LOPAHIN: I don't know. Somewhere far away a bucket fallen and broken in the pits. But somewhere very far away.

GAEV: It might be a bird of some sort—such as a heron.

TROFIMOV: Or an owl.

LYUBOV [*shudders*]: I don't know why, but it's horrid [*a pause*].

FIRS: It was the same before the calamity—the owl hooted and the samovar hissed all the time.

GAEV: Before what calamity?

FIRS: Before the emancipation [*a pause*].

LYUBOV: Come, my friends, let us be going; evening is falling. [*To* ANYA] There are tears in your eyes. What is it, darling? [*Embraces her.*]

ANYA: Nothing, mamma; it's nothing.

TROFIMOV: There is somebody coming.

[THE WAYFARER *appears in a shabby white forage cap and an overcoat; he is slightly drunk.*]

WAYFARER: Allow me to inquire, can I get to the station this way?

GAEV: Yes. Go along that road.

WAYFARER: I thank you most feelingly [*coughing*]. The weather is superb. [*Declaims*] My brother, my suffering brother! . . . Come out to the Volga! Whose groan do you hear? . . . [*To* VARYA] Mademoiselle, vouchsafe a hungry Russian thirty kopeks.

[VARYA *utters a shriek of alarm.*]

LOPAHIN [*angrily*]: There's a right and a wrong way of doing everything!

LYUBOV [*hurriedly*]: Here, take this [*looks in her purse*]. I've no silver. No matter—here's gold for you.

WAYFARER: I thank you most feelingly! [*goes off*].

[*Laughter.*]

VARYA [*frightened*]: I'm going home—I'm going . . . Oh, mamma, the servants have nothing to eat, and you gave him gold!
LYUBOV: There's no doing anything with me. I'm so silly! When we get home, I'll give you all I possess. Yermolay Alexeyevitch, you will lend me some more . . . !
LOPAHIN: I will.
LYUBOV: Come, friends, it's time to be going. And Varya, we have made a match of it for you. I congratulate you.
VARYA [*through her tears*]: Mamma, that's not a joking matter.
LOPAHIN: "Ophelia, get thee to a nunnery!"
GAEV: My hands are trembling; it's a long while since I had a game of billiards.
LOPAHIN: "Ophelia! Nymph, in thy orisons be all my sins remember'd."
LYUBOV: Come, it will soon be supper-time.
VARYA: How he frightened me! My heart's simply throbbing.
LOPAHIN: Let me remind you, ladies and gentlemen: on the 22nd of August the cherry orchard will be sold. Think about that! Think about it!

[*All go off, except* TROFIMOV *and* ANYA.]

ANYA [*laughing*]: I'm grateful to the wayfarer! He frightened Varya and we are left alone.
TROFIMOV: Varya's afraid we shall fall in love with each other, and for days together she won't leave us. With her narrow brain she can't grasp that we are above love. To eliminate the petty and transitory which hinders us from being free and happy—that is the aim and meaning of our life. Forward! We go forward irresistibly towards the bright star that shines yonder in the distance. Forward! Do not lag behind, friends.
ANYA [*claps her hands*]: How well you speak! [*a pause*]. It is divine here to-day.
TROFIMOV: Yes, it's glorious weather.
ANYA: Somehow, Petya, you've made me so that I don't love the cherry orchard as I used to. I used to love it so dearly. I used to think that there was no spot on earth like our garden.
TROFIMOV: All Russia is our garden. The earth is great and beautiful—there are many beautiful places in it [*a pause*]. Think only, Anya, your grandfather, and great-grandfather, and all your ancestors were slave-owners—the owners of living souls—and from every cherry in the orchard, from every leaf, from every trunk there are human creatures looking at you. Cannot you hear their voices? Oh, it is awful! Your orchard is a fearful thing, and when in the evening or at night one walks about the orchard, the old bark on the trees glimmers dimly in the dusk, and the old cherry trees seem to be dreaming of centuries gone by and tortured by fearful visions. Yes! We are at least two hundred years behind, we have really gained nothing yet, we have no definite attitude to the past, we do nothing but theorise or complain of depression or drink vodka. It is clear that to begin to live in the present we must first expiate our past, we must break with it; and we can expiate it only by suffering, by extraordinary unceasing labour. Understand that, Anya.
ANYA: The house we live in has long ceased to be our own, and I shall leave it, I give you my word.
TROFIMOV: If you have the house keys, fling them into the well and go away. Be free as the wind.
ANYA [*in ecstasy*]: How beautifully you said that!
TROFIMOV: Believe me, Anya, believe me! I am not thirty yet, I am young, I am still a student, but I have gone through so much already! As soon as winter comes I am hungry, sick, careworn, poor as a beggar, and what ups and downs of fortune have I not known! And my soul was always, every minute, day and night, full of inexplicable forebodings. I have a foreboding of happiness, Anya. I see glimpses of it already.
ANYA [*pensively*]: The moon is rising.

[EPIHODOV *is heard playing still the same mournful song on the guitar. The moon rises. Somewhere near the poplars* VARYA *is looking for* ANYA *and calling* "Anya! where are you?"]

TROFIMOV: Yes, the moon is rising [*a pause*]. Here is happiness—here it comes! It is coming nearer and nearer; already I can hear its footsteps. And if we never see it—if we may never know it—what does it matter? Others will see it after us.
VARYA'S VOICE: Anya! Where are you?
TROFIMOV: That Varya again! [*Angrily*] It's revolting!
ANYA: Well, let's go down to the river. It's lovely there.
TROFIMOV: Yes, let's go. [*They go.*]
VARYA'S VOICE: Anya! Anya!

CURTAIN

ACT III

A drawing-room divided by an arch from a larger drawing-room. A chandelier burning. The Jewish orchestra, the same that was mentioned in Act II, is heard playing in the ante-room. It is evening. In the larger drawing-room they are dancing the grand chain. The voice of SEMYONOV-PISHTCHIK: *"Promenade à une paire!" They enter the drawing-room in couples first* PISHTCHIK *and* CHARLOTTA IVANOVA, *then* TROFIMOV *and* LYUBOV ANDREYEVNA, *thirdly* ANYA *with the* POST-OFFICE CLERK, *fourthly* VARYA *with the* STATION MASTER, *and other guests.* VARYA *is quietly weeping and wiping away her tears as she dances. In the last couple is* DUNYASHA. *They move across the drawing-room.* PISHTCHIK *shouts: Grand rond, balancez!" and "Les Cavaliers à genou et remerciez vos dames."*

FIRS *in a swallow-tail coat brings in seltzer water on a tray.*

PISHTCHIK *and* TROFIMOV *enter the drawing-room.*

PISHTCHIK: I am a full-blooded man; I have already had two strokes. Dancing's hard work for me, but as they say, if you're in the pack, you must bark with the rest. I'm as strong, I may say, as a horse. My parent, who would have his joke—may the Kingdom of Heaven be his!—used to say about our origin that the ancient stock of the Semyonov-Pishtchiks was derived from the very horse that Caligula made a member of the senate [*sits down*]. But I've no money, that's where the mischief is. A hungry dog believes in nothing but meat . . . [*snores, but at once wakes up*]. That's like me . . . I can think of nothing but money.

TROFIMOV: There really is something horsy about your appearance.

PISHTCHIK: Well . . . a horse is a fine beast . . . a horse can be sold.

[*There is the sound of billiards being played in an adjoining room.* VARYA *appears in the arch leading to the larger drawing-room.*]

TROFIMOV [*teasing*]: Madame Lopahin! Madame Lopahin!

VARYA [*angrily*]: Mangy-looking gentleman!

TROFIMOV: Yes, I am a mangy-looking gentleman, and I'm proud of it!

VARYA [*pondering bitterly*]: Here we have hired musicians and nothing to pay them! [*Goes out.*]

TROFIMOV [*to* PISHTCHIK]: If the energy you have wasted during your lifetime in trying to find the money to pay your interest, had gone to something else, you might in the end have turned the world upside down.

PISHTCHIK: Nietzsche, the philosopher, a very great and celebrated man . . . of enormous intellect . . . says in his works, that one can make forged bank-notes.

TROFIMOV: Why, have you read Nietzsche?

PISHTCHIK: What next . . . Dashenka told me. . . . And now I am in such a position, I might just as well forge bank-notes. The day after to-morrow I must pay 310 roubles—130 I have procured [*feels in his pockets, in alarm*]. The money's gone! I have lost my money! [*Through his tears*] Where's the money? [*Gleefully*] Why, here it is behind the lining. . . . It has made me hot all over.

[*Enter* LYUBOV ANDREYEVNA *and* CHARLOTTA IVANOVNA.]

LYUBOV [*hums the Lezginka*]: Why is Leonid so long? What can he be doing in town? [*To* DUNYASHA] Offer the musicians some tea.

TROFIMOV: The sale hasn't taken place, most likely.

LYUBOV: It's the wrong time to have the orchestra, and the wrong time to give a dance. Well, never mind [*sits down and hums softly*].

CHARLOTTA [*gives* PISHTCHIK *a pack of cards*]: Here's a pack of cards. Think of any card you like.

PISHTCHIK: I've thought of one.

CHARLOTTA: Shuffle the pack now. That's right. Give it here, my dear Mr. Pishtchik. Ein, zwei, drei—now look, it's in your breast pocket.

PISHTCHIK [*taking a card out of his breast pocket*]: The eight of spades! Perfectly right! [*Wonderingly*] Fancy that now!

CHARLOTTA [*holding pack of cards in her hands, to* TROFIMOV]: Tell me quickly which is the top card.

TROFIMOV: Well, the queen of spades.

CHARLOTTA: It is! [*To* PISHTCHIK] Well, which card is uppermost?

PISHTCHIK: The ace of hearts.

CHARLOTTA: It is! [*claps her hands, pack of cards disappears*]. Ah! what lovely weather it is to-day!

[*A mysterious feminine voice which seems coming out of the floor answers her.* "Oh, yes, it's magnificent weather, madam."]

CHARLOTTA: You are my perfect ideal.

VOICE: And I greatly admire you too, madam.

STATION MASTER [*applauding*]: The lady ventriloquist—bravo!

PISHTCHIK [*wonderingly*]: Fancy that now! Most enchanting Charlotta Ivanovna. I'm simply in love with you.

CHARLOTTA: In love? [*Shrugging shoulders*] What do you know of love, guter Mensch, aber schlechter Musikant.

TROFIMOV [*pats* PISHTCHIK *on the shoulder*]: You dear old horse. . . .

CHARLOTTA: Attention, please! Another trick! [*takes a travelling rug from a chair*]. Here's a very good rug; I want to sell it [*shaking it out*]. Doesn't anyone want to buy it?

PISHTCHIK [*wonderingly*]: Fancy that!

CHARLOTTA: Ein, zwei, drei! [*quickly picks up rug she has dropped; behind the rug stands* ANYA; *she makes a curtsey, runs to her mother, embraces her and runs back into the larger drawing-room amidst general enthusiasm.*]

LYUBOV [*applauds*]: Bravo! Bravo!

CHARLOTTA: Now again! Ein, zwei, drei! [*lifts up the rug; behind the rug stands* VARYA, *bowing*].

PISHTCHIK [*wonderingly*]: Fancy that now!

CHARLOTTA: That's the end [*throws the rug at* PISHTCHIK, *makes a curtsey, runs into the larger drawing-room*].

PISHTCHIK [*hurries after her*]: Mischievous creature! Fancy! [*Goes out.*]

LYUBOV: And still Leonid doesn't come. I can't understand what he's doing in the town so long! Why, everything must be over by now. The estate is sold, or the sale has not taken place. Why keep us so long in suspense?

VARYA [*trying to console her*]: Uncle's bought it. I feel sure of that.

TROFIMOV [*ironically*]: Oh, yes!

VARYA: Great-aunt sent him an authorisation to buy it in her name, and transfer the debt. She's doing it for Anya's sake, and I'm sure God will be merciful. Uncle will buy it.

LYUBOV: My aunt in Yaroslavl sent fifteen thousand to buy the estate in her name, she doesn't trust us—but that's not enough even to pay the arrears [*hides her face in her hands*]. My fate is being sealed to-day, my fate . . .

TROFIMOV [*teasing* VARYA]: Madame Lopahin.

VARYA [*angrily*]: Perpetual student! Twice already you've been sent down from the University.

LYUBOV: Why are you angry, Varya? He's teasing you about Lopahin. Well, what of that? Marry Lopahin if you like, he's a good man, and interesting; if you don't want to, don't! Nobody compels you, darling.

VARYA: I must tell you plainly, mamma, I look at the matter seriously; he's a good man, I like him.

LYUBOV: Well, marry him. I can't see what you're waiting for.

VARYA: Mamma. I can't make him an offer myself. For the last two years, everyone's been talking to me about him. Everyone talks; but he says nothing or else makes a joke. I see what it means. He's growing rich, he's absorbed in business, he has no thoughts for me. If I had money, were it ever so little, if I had only a hundred roubles, I'd throw everything up and go far away. I would go into a nunnery.

TROFIMOV: What bliss!

VARYA [*to* TROFIMOV]: A student ought to have sense! [*In a soft tone with tears*] How ugly you've grown, Petya! How old you look! [*To* LYUBOV ANDREYEVNA, *no longer crying*] But I can't do without work, mamma; I must have something to do every minute.

[*Enter* YASHA.]

YASHA [*hardly restraining his laughter*]: Epihodov has broken a billiard cue! [*Goes out.*]

VARYA: What is Epihodov doing here? Who gave him leave to play billiards? I can't make these people out [*goes out*].

LYUBOV: Don't tease her, Petya. You see she has grief enough without that.

TROFIMOV: She is so very officious, meddling in what's not her business. All the summer she's given Anya and me no peace. She's afraid of a love affair between us. What's it to do with her? Besides, I have given no grounds for it. Such triviality is not in my line. We are above love!

LYUBOV: And I suppose I am beneath love. [*Very uneasily*] Why is it Leonid's not here? If only I could know whether the estate is sold or not! It seems such an incredible calamity that I really don't know what to think. I am distracted . . . I shall scream in a minute . . . I shall do something stupid. Save me, Petya, tell me something, talk to me!

TROFIMOV: What does it matter whether the estate is sold to-day or not? That's all done with long ago. There's no turning back, the path is overgrown. Don't worry yourself, dear Lyubov Andreyevna. You mustn't deceive yourself; for once in your life you must face the truth!

LYUBOV: What truth? You see where the truth lies, but I seem to have lost my sight, I see nothing. You settle every great problem so boldly, but tell me, my dear boy, isn't it because you're young—because you haven't yet understood one of your problems through suffering? You look forward boldly, and isn't it that you don't see and don't expect anything dreadful because life is still hidden from your young eyes? You're bolder, more honest, deeper than we are, but think, be just a little magnanimous, have pity on me. I was born here, you know, my father and mother lived here, my grandfather lived here, I love this house. I can't conceive of life without the cherry orchard, and if it really must be sold, then sell me with the orchard [*embraces* TROFIMOV, *kisses him on the forehead*]. My boy was drowned here [*weeps*]. Pity me, my dear kind fellow.

TROFIMOV: You know I feel for you with all my heart.

LYUBOV: But that should have been said differently, so differently [*takes out her handkerchief, telegram falls on the floor*]. My heart is so heavy to-day. It's so noisy here, my soul is quivering at every sound,

I'm shuddering all over, but I can't go away; I'm afraid to be quiet and alone. Don't be hard on me, Petya . . . I love you as though you were one of ourselves. I would gladly let you marry Anya—I swear I would—only, my dear boy, you must take your degree, you do nothing—you're simply tossed by fate from place to place. That's so strange. It is, isn't it? And you must do something with your beard to make it grow somehow [*laughs*]. You look so funny!

TROFIMOV [*picks up the telegram*]: I've no wish to be a beauty.

LYUBOV: That's a telegram from Paris. I get one every day. One yesterday and one to-day. That savage creature is ill again, he's in trouble again. He begs forgiveness, beseeches me to go, and really I ought to go to Paris to see him. You look shocked, Petya. What am I to do, my dear boy, what am I to do? He is ill, he is alone and unhappy, and who'll look after him, who'll keep him from doing the wrong thing, who'll give him his medicine at the right time? And why hide it or be silent? I love him, that's clear. I love him! I love him! He's a millstone about my neck, I'm going to the bottom with him, but I love that stone and can't live without it [*presses* TROFIMOV'*s hand*]. Don't think ill of me, Petya, don't tell me anything, don't tell me . . .

TROFIMOV [*through his tears*]: For God's sake forgive my frankness: why, he robbed you!

LYUBOV: No! No! No! You mustn't speak like that [*covers her ears*].

TROFIMOV: He is a wretch! You're the only person that doesn't know it! He's a worthless creature! A despicable wretch!

LYUBOV [*getting angry, but speaking with restraint*]: You're twenty-six or twenty-seven years old, but you're still a schoolboy.

TROFIMOV: Possibly.

LYUBOV: You should be a man at your age! You should understand what love means! And you ought to be in love yourself. You ought to fall in love! [*Angrily*] Yes, yes, and it's not purity in you, you're simply a prude, a comic fool, a freak.

TROFIMOV [*in horror*]: The things she's saying!

LYUBOV: I am above love! You're not above love, but simply as our Firs here says, "You are a good-for-nothing." At your age not to have a mistress!

TROFIMOV [*in horror*]: This is awful! The things she is saying! [*goes rapidly into the larger drawing-room clutching his head*]. This is awful! I can't stand it! I'm going. [*Goes off, but at once returns.*] All is over between us! [*Goes off into the ante-room.*]

LYUBOV [*shouts after him*]: Petya! Wait a minute! You funny creature! I was joking! Petya! [*There is a sound of somebody running quickly downstairs and suddenly falling with a crash.* ANYA *and* VARYA *scream, but there is a sound of laughter at once.*]

LYUBOV: What has happened?

[ANYA *runs in.*]

ANYA [*laughing*]: Petya's fallen downstairs! [*Runs out.*]

LYUBOV: What a queer fellow that Petya is!

[*The Station Master stands in the middle of the larger room and reads "The Magdalene," by Alexey Tolstoy. They listen to him, but before he has recited many lines strains of a waltz are heard from the ante-room and the reading is broken off. All dance.* TROFIMOV, ANYA, VARYA *and* LYUBOV ANDREYEVNA *come in from the ante-room.*]

LYUBOV: Come, Petya—come, pure heart! I beg your pardon. Let's have a dance! [*dances with* PETYA].

[ANYA *and* VARYA *dance.* FIRS *comes in, puts his stick down near the side door.* YASHA *also comes into the drawing-room and looks on at the dancing.*]

YASHA: What is it, old man?

FIRS: I don't feel well. In old days we used to have generals, barons and admirals dancing at our balls, and now we send for the post-office clerk and the station master and even they're not overanxious to come. I am getting feeble. The old master, the grandfather, used to give sealing-wax for all complaints. I have been taking sealing-wax for twenty years or more. Perhaps that's what's kept me alive.

YASHA: You bore me, old man! [*yawns*] It's time you were done with.

FIRS: Ach, you're a good-for-nothing! [*mutters*]

[TROFIMOV *and* LYUBOV ANDREYEVNA *dance in larger room and then on to the stage.*]

LYUBOV: *Merci.* I'll sit down a little [*sits down*]. I'm tired.

[*Enter* ANYA.]

ANYA [*excitedly*]: There's a man in the kitchen has been saying that the cherry orchard's been sold to-day.

LYUBOV: Sold to whom?

ANYA: He didn't say to whom. He's gone away.

[*She dances with* TROFIMOV, *and they go off into the larger room.*]

YASHA: There was an old man gossiping there, a stranger.

FIRS: Leonid Andreyevitch isn't here yet, he hasn't come back. He has his light overcoat on, *demi-saison*, he'll catch cold for sure. Ach! Foolish young things! !

LYUBOV: I feel as though I should die. Go, Yasha, find out to whom it has been sold.

YASHA: But he went away long ago, the old chap [*laughs*].

LYUBOV [*with slight vexation*]: What are you laughing at? What are you pleased at?

YASHA: Epihodov is so funny. He's a silly fellow, two and twenty misfortunes.

LYUBOV: Firs, if the estate is sold, where will you go?

FIRS: Where you bid me, there I'll go.

LYUBOV: Why do you look like that? Are you ill? You ought to be in bed.

FIRS: Yes [*ironically*]. Me go to bed and who's to wait here? Who's to see to things without me? I'm the only one in all the house.

YASHA [*to* LYUBOV ANDREYEVNA]: Lyubov Andreyevna, permit me to make a request of you; if you go back to Paris again, be so kind as to take me with you. It's positively impossible for me to stay here [*looking about him; in an undertone*]. There's no need to say it, you see for yourself—an uncivilised country, the people have no morals, and then the dullness! The food in the kitchen's abominable, and then Firs runs after one muttering all sorts of unsuitable words. Take me with you, please do!

[*Enter* PISHTCHIK.]

PISHTCHIK: Allow me to ask you for a waltz, my dear lady. [LYUBOV ANDREYEVNA *goes with him.*] Enchanting lady, I really must borrow of you just 180 roubles [*dances*], only 180 roubles. [*They pass into the larger room.*]

YASHA [*hums softly*]: "Knowest thou my soul's emotion."

[*In the larger drawing-room, a figure in a gray top hat and in check trousers is gesticulating and jumping about. Shouts of* "Bravo, Charlotta Ivanovna."]

DUNYASHA [*she has stopped to powder herself*]: My young lady tells me to dance. There are plenty of gentlemen, and too few ladies, but dancing makes me giddy and makes my heart beat. Firs, the post-office clerk said something to me just now that quite took my breath away.

[*Music becomes more subdued.*]

FIRS: What did he say to you?

DUNYASHA: He said I was like a flower.

YASHA [*yawns*]: What ignorance! [*Goes out.*]

DUNYASHA: Like a flower. I am a girl of such delicate feelings, I am awfully fond of soft speeches.

FIRS: Your head's being turned.

[*Enter* EPIHODOV.]

EPIHODOV: You have no desire to see me, Dunyasha. I might be an insect [*sighs*]. Ah! life!

DUNYASHA: What is it you want?

EPIHODOV: Undoubtedly you may be right [*sighs*]. But of course, if one looks at it from that point of view, if I may so express myself, you have, excuse my plain speaking, reduced me to a complete state of mind. I know my destiny. Every day some misfortune befalls me and I have long ago grown accustomed to it, so that I look upon my fate with a smile. You gave me your word, and though I—

DUNYASHA: Let us have a talk later, I entreat you, but now leave me in peace, for I am lost in reverie [*plays with her fan*].

EPIHODOV: I have a misfortune every day, and if I may venture to express myself, I merely smile at it, I even laugh.

[VARYA *enters from the larger drawing-room.*]

VARYA: You still have not gone, Epihodov. What a disrespectful creature you are, really! [*To* DUNYASHA] Go along, Dunyasha! [*To* EPIHODOV] First you play billiards and break the cue, then you go wandering about the drawing-room like a visitor!

EPIHODOV: You really cannot, if I may so express myself, call me to account like this.

VARYA: I'm not calling you to account, I'm speaking to you. You do nothing but wander from place to place and don't do your work. We keep you as a counting-house clerk, but what use you are I can't say.

EPIHODOV [*offended*]: Whether I work or whether I walk, whether I eat or whether I play billiards, is a matter to be judged by persons of understanding and my elders.

VARYA: You dare to tell me that! [*Firing up*] You dare! You mean to say I've no understanding. Begone from here! This minute!

EPIHODOV [*intimidated*]: I beg you to express yourself with delicacy.

VARYA [*beside herself with anger*]: This moment! get out! away! [*He goes towards the door, she following him.*] Two and twenty misfortunes! Take yourself off! Don't let me set eyes on you! [EPIHODOV *has gone out, behind the door his voice,* "I shall lodge a complaint against you."] What! You're coming back? [*Snatches up the stick* FIRS *has put down near the door.*] Come! Come! Come! I'll show you! What!

you're coming? Then take that! [*She swings the stick, at the very moment that* LOPAHIN *comes in.*]

LOPAHIN: Very much obliged to you!

VARYA [*angrily and ironically*]: I beg your pardon!

LOPAHIN: Not at all! I humbly thank you for your kind reception!

VARYA: No need of thanks for it. [*Moves away, then looks round and asks softly*] I haven't hurt you?

LOPAHIN: Oh, no! Not at all! There's an immense bump coming up, though!

VOICES FROM LARGER ROOM: Lopahin has come! Yermolay Alexeyevitch!

PISHTCHIK: What do I see and hear? [*Kisses* LOPAHIN.] There's a whiff of cognac about you, my dear soul, and we're making merry here too!

[*Enter* LYUBOV ANDREYEVNA.]

LYUBOV: Is it you, Yermolay Alexeyevitch? Why have you been so long? Where's Leonid?

LOPAHIN: Leonid Andreyevitch arrived with me. He is coming.

LYUBOV [*in agitation*]: Well! Well! Was there a sale? Speak!

LOPAHIN [*embarrassed, afraid of betraying his joy*]: The sale was over at four o'clock. We missed our train—had to wait till half-past nine. [*Sighing heavily*] Ugh! I feel a little giddy.

[*Enter* GAEV. *In his right hand he has purchases, with his left hand he is wiping away his tears.*]

LYUBOV: Well, Leonid? What news? [*Impatiently, with tears*] Make haste, for God's sake!

GAEV [*makes her no answer, simply waves his hand. To* FIRS, *weeping*]: Here, take them; there's anchovies, Kertch herrings. I have eaten nothing all day. What I have been through! [*Door into the billiard room is open. There is heard a knocking of balls and the voice of* YASHA *saying* "Eighty-seven." GAEV'*s expression changes, he leaves off weeping.*] I am fearfully tired. Firs, come and help me change my things [*goes to his own room across the larger drawing-room*].

PISHTCHIK: How about the sale? Tell us, do!

LYUBOV: Is the cherry orchard sold?

LOPAHIN: It is sold.

LYUBOV: Who has bought it?

LOPAHIN: I have bought it. [*A pause.* LYUBOV *is crushed; she would fall down if she were not standing near a chair and table.*]

[VARYA *takes keys from her waist-band, flings them on the floor in middle of drawing-room and goes out.*]

LOPAHIN: I have bought it! Wait a bit, ladies and gentlemen, pray. My head's a bit muddled, I can't speak [*laughs*]. We came to the auction. Deriganov was there already. Leonid Andreyevitch only had 15,000 and Deriganov bid 30,000, besides the arrears, straight off. I saw how the land lay. I bid against him. I bid 40,000, he bid 45,000, I said 55, and so he went on, adding 5 thousands and I adding 10. Well . . . So it ended. I bid 90, and it was knocked down to me. Now the cherry orchard's mine! Mine! [*chuckles*] My God, the cherry orchard's mine! Tell me that I'm drunk, that I'm out of my mind, that it's all a dream [*stamps with his feet*]. Don't laugh at me! If my father and my grandfather could rise from their graves and see all that has happened! How their Yermolay, ignorant, beaten Yermolay, who used to run about barefoot in winter, how that very Yermolay has bought the finest estate in the world! I have bought the estate where my father and grandfather were slaves, where they weren't even admitted into the kitchen. I am asleep, I am dreaming! It is all fancy, it is the work of your imagination plunged in the darkness of ignorance [*picks up keys, smiling fondly*]. She threw away the keys; she means to show she's not the housewife now [*jingles the keys*]. Well, no matter. [*The orchestra is heard tuning up.*] Hey, musicians! Play! I want to hear you. Come, all of you, and look how Yermolay Lopahin will take the axe to the cherry orchard, how the trees will fall to the ground! We will build houses on it and our grandsons and great-grandsons will see a new life springing up there. Music! Play up!

[*Music begins to play.* LYUBOV ANDREYEVNA *has sunk into a chair and is weeping bitterly.*]

LOPAHIN [*reproachfully*]: Why, why didn't you listen to me? My poor friend! Dear lady, there's no turning back now. [*With tears*] Oh, if all this could be over, oh, if our miserable disjointed life could somehow soon be changed!

PISHTCHIK [*takes him by the arm, in an undertone*]: She's weeping, let us go and leave her alone. Come [*takes him by the arm and leads him into the larger drawing-room*].

LOPAHIN: What's that? Musicians, play up! All must be as I wish it. [*With irony*] Here comes the new master, the owner of the cherry orchard! [*Accidentally tips over a little table, almost upsetting the candelabra.*] I can pay for everything! [*Goes out with* PISHTCHIK. *No one remains on the stage or in the larger drawing-room except* LYUBOV, *who sits huddled up, weeping bitterly. The music plays softly.* ANYA *and* TROFIMOV *come in quickly.* ANYA *goes up to her mother and falls on her knees before her.* TROFIMOV *stands at the entrance to the larger drawing-room.*]

ANYA: Mamma! Mamma, you're crying, dear, kind, good mamma! My precious! I love you! I bless you! The cherry orchard is sold, it is gone, that's true, that's true! But don't weep, mamma! Life is still before you, you have still your good, pure heart! Let us go, let us go, darling, away from here! We will make a new garden, more splendid than this one; you will see it, you will understand. And joy, quiet, deep joy will sink into your soul like the sun at evening! And you will smile, mamma! Come, darling, let us go!

CURTAIN

ACT IV

SCENE: *Same as in First Act. There are neither curtains on the windows nor pictures on the walls: only a little furniture remains piled up in a corner as if for sale. There is a sense of desolation; near the outer door and in the background of the scene are packed trunks, travelling bags, etc. On the left the door is open, and from here the voices of* VARYA *and* ANYA *are audible.* LOPAHIN *is standing waiting.* YASHA *is holding a tray with glasses full of champagne. In front of the stage* EPIHODOV *is tying up a box. In the background behind the scene a hum of talk from the peasants who have come to say good-bye. The voice of* GAEV: "Thanks, brothers, thanks!"

YASHA: The peasants have come to say good-bye. In my opinion, Yermolay Alexeyevitch, the peasants are good-natured, but they don't know much about things.

[*The hum of talk dies away. Enter across front of stage* LYUBOV ANDREYEVNA *and* GAEV. *She is not weeping, but is pale; her face is quivering—she cannot speak.*]

GAEV: You gave them your purse, Lyuba. That won't do—that won't do!

LYUBOV: I couldn't help it! I couldn't help it!

[*Both go out.*]

LOPAHIN [*in the doorway, calls after them*]: You will take a glass at parting? Please do. I didn't think to bring any from the town, and at the station I could only get one bottle. Please take a glass [*a pause*]. What? You don't care for any? [*Comes away from the door*] If I'd known, I wouldn't have bought it. Well, and I'm not going to drink it. [YASHA *carefully sets the tray down on a chair.*] You have a glass, Yasha, anyway.

YASHA: Good luck to the travellers, and luck to those that stay behind! [*drinks*]. This champagne isn't the real thing, I can assure you.

LOPAHIN: It cost eight roubles the bottle [*a pause*]. It's devilish cold here.

YASHA: They haven't heated the stove to-day—it's all the same since we're going [*laughs*].

LOPAHIN: What are you laughing for?

YASHA: For pleasure.

LOPAHIN: Though it's October, it's as still and sunny as though it were summer. It's just right for building! [*Looks at his watch; says in doorway*] Take note, ladies and gentlemen, the train goes in forty-seven minutes; so you ought to start for the station in twenty minutes. You must hurry up!

[TROFIMOV *comes in from out of doors wearing a great-coat.*]

TROFIMOV: I think it must be time to start, the horses are ready. The devil only knows what's become of my goloshes; they're lost. [*In the doorway*] Anya! My goloshes aren't here. I can't find them.

LOPAHIN: And I'm getting off to Harkov. I an going in the same train with you. I'm spending all the winter at Harkov. I've been wasting all my time gossiping with you and fretting with no work to do. I can't get on without work. I don't know what to do with my hands, they flap about so queerly, as if they didn't belong to me.

TROFIMOV: Well, we're just going away, and you will take up your profitable labours again.

LOPAHIN: Do take a glass.

TROFIMOV: No, thanks.

LOPAHIN: Then you're going to Moscow now?

TROFIMOV: Yes. I shall see them as far as the town, and to-morrow I shall go on to Moscow.

LOPAHIN: Yes, I daresay, the professors aren't giving any lectures, they're waiting for your arrival.

TROFIMOV: That's not your business.

LOPAHIN: How many years have you been at the University?

TROFIMOV: Do think of something newer than that—that's stale and flat [*hunts for goloshes*]. You know we shall most likely never see each other again, so let me give you one piece of advice at parting: don't wave your arms about—get out of the habit. And another thing, building villas, reckoning up that the summer visitors will in time become independent farmers—reckoning like that, that's not the thing to do either. After all, I am fond of you: you have fine delicate fingers like an artist, you've a fine delicate soul.

LOPAHIN [*embraces him*]: Good-bye, my dear fellow. Thanks for everything. Let me give you money for the journey, if you need it.

TROFIMOV: What for? I don't need it.
LOPAHIN: Why, you haven't got a halfpenny.
TROFIMOV: Yes, I have, thank you. I got some money for a translation. Here it is in my pocket, [*anxiously*] but where can my goloshes be!
VARYA [*from the next room*]: Take the nasty things! [*Flings a pair of goloshes on to the stage.*]
TROFIMOV: Why are you so cross, Varya? h'm! . . . but those aren't my goloshes.
LOPAHIN: I sowed three thousand acres with poppies in the spring, and now I have cleared forty thousand profit. And when my poppies were in flower, wasn't it a picture! So here, as I say, I made forty thousand, and I'm offering you a loan because I can afford to. Why turn up your nose? I am a peasant—I speak bluntly.
TROFIMOV: Your father was a peasant, mine was a chemist—and that proves absolutely nothing whatever. [LOPAHIN *takes out his pocket-book.*] Stop that—stop that. If you were to offer me two hundred thousand I wouldn't take it. I am an independent man, and everything that all of you, rich and poor alike, prize so highly and hold so dear, hasn't the slightest power over me—it's like so much fluff fluttering in the air. I can get on without you. I can pass by you. I am strong and proud. Humanity is advancing towards the highest truth, the highest happiness, which is possible on earth, and I am in the front ranks.
LOPAHIN: Will you get there?
TROFIMOV: I shall get there [*a pause*]. I shall get there, or I shall show others the way to get there.

[*In the distance is heard the stroke of an axe on a tree.*]

LOPAHIN: Good-bye, my dear fellow; it's time to be off. We turn up our noses at one another, but life is passing all the while. When I am working hard without resting, then my mind is more at ease, and it seems to me as though I too know what I exist for; but how many people there are in Russia, my dear boy, who exist, one doesn't know what for. Well, it doesn't matter. That's not what keeps things spinning. They tell me Leonid Andreyevitch has taken a situation. He is going to be a clerk at the bank—6,000 roubles a year. Only, of course, he won't stick to it—he's too lazy.
ANYA [*in the doorway*]: Mamma begs you not to let them chop down the orchard until she's gone.
TROFIMOV: Yes, really, you might have the tact [*walks out across the front of the stage*].
LOPAHIN: I'll see to it! I'll see to it! Stupid fellows! [*Goes out after him.*]
ANYA: Has Firs been taken to the hospital?
YASHA: I told them this morning. No doubt they have taken him.
ANYA [*to* EPIHODOV, *who passes across the drawing-room*]: Semyon Pantaleyevitch, inquire, please, if Firs has been taken to the hospital.
YASHA [*in a tone of offence]:* I told Yegor this morning—why ask a dozen times?
EPIHODOV: Firs is advanced in years. It's my conclusive opinion no treatment would do him good; it's time he was gathered to his fathers. And I can only envy him [*puts a trunk down on a cardboard hat-box and crushes it*]. There, now, of course—I knew it would be so.
YASHA [*jeeringly*]: Two and twenty misfortunes!
VARYA [*through the door*]: Has Firs been taken to the hospital?
ANYA: Yes.
VARYA: Why wasn't the note for the doctor taken too?
ANYA: Oh, then, we must send it after them [*goes out*].
VARYA [*from the adjoining room*]: Where's Yasha? Tell him his mother's come to say good-bye to him.
YASHA [*waves his hand*]: They put me out of all patience! [DUNYASHA *has all this time been busy about the luggage. Now, when* YASHA *is left alone, she goes up to him.*]
DUNYASHA: You might just give me one look, Yasha. You're going away. You're leaving me [*weeps and throws herself on his neck*].
YASHA: What are you crying for? [*drinks the champagne*]. In six days I shall be in Paris again. To-morrow we shall get into the express train and roll away in a flash. I can scarcely believe it! *Vive la France!* It doesn't suit me here—it's not the life for me; there's no doing anything. I have seen enough of the ignorance here. I have had enough of it [*drinks champagne*]. What are you crying for? Behave yourself properly, and then you won't cry.
DUNYASHA [*powders her face, looking in a pocket-mirror*]: Do send me a letter from Paris. You know how I loved you, Yasha—how I loved you! I am a tender creature, Yasha.
YASHA: Here they are coming!

[*Busies himself about the trunks, humming softly. Enter* LYUBOV ANDREYEVNA, GAEV, ANYA *and* CHARLOTTA IVANOVNA.]

GAEV: We ought to be off. There's not much time now [*looking at* YASHA]. What a smell of herrings!
LYUBOV: In ten minutes we must get into the carriage [*casts a look about the room*]. Farewell, dear house, dear old home of our fathers! Winter will pass and spring will come, and then you will be no more; they will tear you down! How much those walls have seen! [*Kisses her daughter passionately.*] My treasure, how bright you look! Your eyes are sparkling like diamonds! Are you glad? Very glad?
ANYA: Very glad! A new life is beginning, mamma.

GAEV: Yes, really, everything is all right now. Before the cherry orchard was sold, we were all worried and wretched, but afterwards, when once the question was settled conclusively, irrevocably, we all felt calm and even cheerful. I am a bank clerk now—I am a financier—cannon off the red. And you, Lyuba, after all, you are looking better; there's no question of that.

LYUBOV: Yes. My nerves are better, that's true. [*Her hat and coat are handed to her.*] I'm sleeping well. Carry out my things, Yasha. It's time. [*To* ANYA] My darling, we shall soon see each other again. I am going to Paris. I can live there on the money your Yaroslavl auntie sent us to buy the estate with—hurrah for auntie!—but that money won't last long.

ANYA: You'll come back soon, mamma, won't you? I'll be working up for my examination in the high school, and when I have passed that, I shall set to work and be a help to you. We will read all sorts of things together, mamma, won't we? [*Kisses her mother's hands.*] We will read in the autumn evenings. We'll read lots of books, and a new wonderful world will open out before us [*dreamily*]. Mamma, come soon.

LYUBOV: I shall come, my precious treasure [*embraces her*].

[*Enter* LOPAHIN. CHARLOTTA *softly hums a song.*]

GAEV: Charlotta's happy; she's singing!

CHARLOTTA [*picks up a bundle like a swaddled baby*]: Bye, bye, my baby. [*A baby is heard crying: "Ooah! ooah!"*] Hush, hush, my pretty boy! [*Ooah! ooah!*] Poor little thing! [*Throws the bundle back.*] You must please find me a situation. I can't go on like this.

LOPAHIN: We'll find you one, Charlotta Ivanovna. Don't you worry yourself.

GAEV: Everyone's leaving us. Varya's going away. We have become of no use all at once.

CHARLOTTA: There's nowhere for me to be in the town. I must go away. [*Hums*] What care I . . .

[*Enter* PISHTCHIK.]

LOPAHIN: The freak of nature!

PISHTCHIK [*gasping*]: Oh! . . . let me get my breath. . . . I'm worn out . . . my most honoured . . . Give me some water.

GAEV: Want some money, I suppose? Your humble servant! I'll go out of the way of temptation [*goes out*].

PISHTCHIK: It's a long while since I have been to see you . . . dearest lady. [*To* LOPAHIN] You are here . . . glad to see you . . . a man of immense intellect . . . take . . . here [*gives* LOPAHIN] 400 roubles. That leaves me owing 840.

LOPAHIN [*shrugging his shoulders in amazement*]: It's like a dream. Where did you get it?

PISHTCHIK: Wait a bit . . . I'm hot . . . a most extraordinary occurrence! Some Englishmen came along and found in my land some sort of white clay. [*To* LYUBOV ANDREYEVNA] And 400 for you . . . most lovely . . . wonderful [*gives money*]. The rest later [*sips water*]. A young man in the train was telling me just now that a great philosopher advises jumping off a house-top. "Jump!" says he; "the whole gist of the problem lies in that." [*Wonderingly*] Fancy that, now! Water, please!

LOPAHIN: What Englishmen?

PISHTCHIK: I have made over to them the rights to dig the clay for twenty-four years . . . and now, excuse me . . . I can't stay . . . I must be trotting on. I'm going to Znoikovo . . . to Kardamanovo. . . . I'm in debt all round [*sips*]. . . . To your very good health! . . . I'll come in on Thursday.

LYUBOV: We are just off to the town, and to-morrow I start for abroad.

PISHTCHIK: What! [*In agitation*] Why to the town? Oh, I see the furniture . . . the boxes. No matter . . . [*through his tears*] . . . no matter . . . men of enormous intellect . . . these Englishmen. . . . Never mind . . . be happy. God will succour you . . . no matter . . . everything in this world must have an end [*kisses* LYUBOV ANDREYEVNA*'s hand*]. If the rumour reaches you that my end has come, think of this . . . old horse, and say: "There once was such a man in the world . . . Semyonov-Pishtchik . . . the Kingdom of Heaven be his!" . . . most extraordinary weather . . . yes. [*Goes out in violent agitation, but at once returns and says in the doorway*] Dashenka wishes to be remembered to you [*goes out*].

LYUBOV: Now we can start. I leave with two cares in my heart. The first is leaving Firs ill. [*Looking at her watch*] We have still five minutes.

ANYA: Mamma, Firs has been taken to the hospital. Yasha sent him off this morning.

LYUBOV: My other anxiety is Varya. She is used to getting up early and working; and now, without work, she's like a fish out of water. She is thin and pale, and she's crying, poor dear! [*a pause*] You are well aware, Yermolay Alexeyevitch, I dreamed of marrying her to you, and everything seemed to show that you would get married [*whispers to* ANYA *and motions to* CHARLOTTA *and both go out*]. She loves you—she suits you. And I don't know—I don't know why it is you seem, as it were, to avoid each other. I can't understand it!

LOPAHIN: I don't understand it myself, I confess. It's queer somehow, altogether. If there's still time, I'm ready now at once. Let's settle it straight off, and go ahead; but without you, I feel I shan't make her an offer.

LYUBOV: That's excellent. Why, a single moment's all that's necessary. I'll call her at once.

LOPAHIN: And there's champagne all ready too [*looking into the glasses*]. Empty! Someone's emptied them already. [YASHA coughs.] I call that greedy.

LYUBOV [*eagerly*]: Capital! We will go out. Yasha, *allez!* I'll call her in. [*At the door*] Varya, leave all that; come here. Come along! [*goes out with* YASHA].

LOPAHIN [*looking at his watch*]: Yes.

[*A pause. Behind the door, smothered laughter and whispering, and, at last, enter* VARYA.]

VARYA [*looking a long while over the things*]: It is strange, I can't find it anywhere.

LOPAHIN: What are you looking for?

VARYA: I packed it myself, and I can't remember [*a pause*].

LOPAHIN: Where are you going now, Varvara Mihailova?

VARYA: I? To the Ragulins. I have arranged to go to them to look after the house—as a housekeeper.

LOPAHIN: That's in Yashnovo? It'll be seventy miles away [*a pause*]. So this is the end of life in this house!

VARYA [*looking among the things*]: Where is it? Perhaps I put it in the trunk. Yes, life in this house is over—there will be no more of it.

LOPAHIN: And I'm just off to Harkov—by this next train. I've a lot of business there. I'm leaving Epihodov here, and I've taken him on.

VARYA: Really!

LOPAHIN: This time last year we had snow already, if you remember; but now it's so fine and sunny. Though it's cold, to be sure—three degrees of frost.

VARYA: I haven't looked [*a pause*]. And besides, our thermometer's broken [*a pause*].

[*Voice at the door from the yard*: "Yermolay Alexeyevitch!"]

LOPAHIN [*as though he had long been expecting this summons*]: This minute!

[LOPAHIN *goes out quickly.* VARYA *sitting on the floor and laying her head on a bag full of clothes, sobs quietly. The door opens.* LYUBOV ANDREYEVNA *comes in cautiously.*]

LYUBOV: Well? [*a pause*] We must be going.

VARYA [*has wiped her eyes and is no longer crying*]: Yes, mamma, it's time to start. I shall have time to get to the Ragulins to-day, if only you're not late for the train.

LYUBOV [*in the doorway*]: Anya, put your things on.

[*Enter* ANYA, *then* GAEV *and* CHARLOTTA IVANOVNA. GAEV *has on a warm coat with a hood. Servants and cabmen come in.* EPIHODOV *bustles about the luggage.*]

LYUBOV: Now we can start on our travels.

ANYA [*joyfully*]: On our travels!

GAEV: My friends—my dear, my precious friends! Leaving this house for ever, can I be silent? Can I refrain from giving utterance at leave-taking to those emotions which now flood all my being?

ANYA [*supplicatingly*]: Uncle!

VARYA: Uncle, you mustn't!

GAEV [*dejectedly*]: Cannon and into the pocket . . . I'll be quiet. . . .

[*Enter* TROFIMOV *and afterwards* LOPAHIN.]

TROFIMOV: Well, ladies and gentlemen, we must start.

LOPAHIN: Epihodov, my coat!

LYUBOV: I'll stay just one minute. It seems as though I have never seen before what the walls, what the ceilings in this house were like, and now I look at them with greediness, with such tender love.

GAEV: I remember when I was six years old sitting in that window on Trinity Day watching my father going to church.

LYUBOV: Have all the things been taken?

LOPAHIN: I think all. [*Putting on overcoat, to* EPIHODOV] You, Epihodov, mind you see everything is right.

EPIHODOV [*in a husky voice*]: Don't you trouble, Yermolay Alexeyevitch.

LOPAHIN: Why, what's wrong with your voice?

EPIHODOV: I've just had a drink of water, and I choked over something.

YASHA [*contemptuously*]: The ignorance!

LYUBOV: We are going—and not a soul will be left here.

LOPAHIN: Not till the spring.

VARYA [*pulls a parasol out of a bundle, as though about to hit someone with it.* LOPAHIN *makes a gesture as though alarmed*]: What is it? I didn't mean anything.

TROFIMOV: Ladies and gentlemen, let us get into the carriage. It's time. The train will be in directly.

VARYA: Petya, here they are, your goloshes, by that box. [*With tears*] And what dirty old things they are!

TROFIMOV [*putting on his goloshes*]: Let us go, friends!

GAEV [*greatly agitated, afraid of weeping*]: The train—the station! Double baulk, ah!

LYUBOV: Let us go!

LOPAHIN: Are we all here? [*Locks the side-door on left.*] The things are all here. We must lock up. Let us go!
ANYA: Good-bye, home! Good-bye to the old life!
TROFIMOV: Welcome to the new life!

[TROFIMOV *goes out with* ANYA. VARYA *looks round the room and goes out slowly.* YASHA *and* CHARLOTTA IVANOVNA, *with her dog, go out.*]

LOPAHIN: Till the spring, then! Come, friends, till we meet! [*Goes out.*]

[LYUBOV ANDREYEVNA *and* GAEV *remain alone. As though they had been waiting for this, they throw themselves on each other's necks, and break into subdued smothered sobbing, afraid of being overheard.*]

GAEV [*in despair*]: Sister, my sister!
LYUBOV: Oh, my orchard!—my sweet, beautiful orchard! My life, my youth, my happiness, good-bye! good-bye!
VOICE OF ANYA [*calling gaily*]: Mamma!
VOICE OF TROFIMOV [*gaily, excitedly*]: Aa—oo!
LYUBOV: One last look at the walls, at the windows. My dear mother loved to walk about this room.
GAEV: Sister, sister!
VOICE OF ANYA: Mamma!
VOICE OF TROFIMOV: Aa-oo!
LYUBOV: We are coming. [*They go out.*]

[*The stage is empty. There is the sound of the doors being locked up, then of the carriages driving away. There is silence. In the stillness there is the dull stroke of an axe in a tree, clanging with a mournful lonely sound. Footsteps are heard.* FIRS *appears in the doorway on the right. He is dressed as always—in a pea-jacket and white waistcoat with slippers on his feet. He is ill.*]

FIRS [*goes up to the doors, and tries the handles*]: Locked! They have gone . . . [*sits down on sofa*]. They have forgotten me. . . . Never mind . . . I'll sit here a bit. . . . I'll be bound Leonid Andreyevitch hasn't put his fur coat on and has gone off in his thin overcoat [*sighs anxiously*]. I didn't see after him. . . . These young people . . . [*mutters something that can't be distinguished*]. Life has slipped by as though I hadn't lived. [*Lies down*] I'll lie down a bit. . . . There's no strength in you, nothing left you—all gone! Ech! I'm good for nothing [*lies motionless*].

[*A sound is heard that seems to come from the sky, like a breaking harp-string, dying away mournfully. All is still again, and there is heard nothing but the strokes of the axe far away in the orchard.*]

CURTAIN

Luigi Pirandello

Luigi Pirandello (1867–1936) was born in Agrigento, Sicily, the stark character of which did much to shape his work. His family was engaged in sulphur mining, and while comfortably well-off, for the most part, their financial situation fluctuated wildly. Pirandello's father was stern and unloving, and he preferred being away from home; his mother was the opposite. When he discovered that his father was involved in an adulterous affair, Pirandello never forgave him. Still, he lived on the allowance from his father that enabled him to become a professional writer. Characteristically, Pirandello repaid his father and took the old man into his care near the end of his life. Like his father, Pirandello was marked by a Sicilian temperament that alternated between quiet melancholy and the explosive, something alluded to in the title of his first book of poetry, *Troubled Joy.* Published when Pirandello was twenty-two, this book exposes his emotional dichotomy, which can be traced throughout his career.

Pirandello was educated at universities in Palermo and Rome, where he studied law because it was expected of him. Abandoning law, he earned a doctorate in Romance Philology at the University in Bonn, Germany, and then returned to Rome in 1891. Three years later, at twenty-seven, he consented to the Sicilian custom of an arranged marriage and wed Antonietta Portulano, a high-strung, argumentative, and jealous woman. The marriage was not successful from the start, and after nine years, Antonietta suffered a mental collapse. Pirandello put up with her jealousy and paranoia for fifteen years, despite the humiliation and unhappiness it caused him and their children. She was not institutionalized until 1919, and she outlived her husband.

The illogic and formlessness of insanity revealed by his wife's madness greatly affected Pirandello's creative imagination. What is perceived as real, he saw, often has less to do with some "objective" reality than with an "inner" reality that each of us creates. He called this contradiction the "idea of the opposite," and discussed it in his essay "On Humor" (1908), which is really a discussion of the artistic imagination. Pirandello said that the "work of art is created by the free movement of inner life which organizes the ideas and images into a form that often is the opposite of what was intended, and that what one sees and feels is often the opposite of what one perceives and understands." The linkage of art and life is perhaps the most important thematic element in his fiction and plays, and *Six Characters in Search of an Author* is his most successful exploration of the variations of reality and illusion.

At thirty, Pirandello began teaching at the Magistero, a school for young women in Rome, and in 1908, was appointed chair of Italian philology and Latin and Greek literature. He remained there unhappily until 1922, when his success as a dramatist finally provided him with an income that permitted him to concentrate entirely on writing. Pirandello's success ironically coincided with the rise to power of Benito Mussolini (1883–1945), the Italian fascist. Two years later, Pirandello officially joined the Fascist Party, and he was awarded financial backing for his own acting company, Teatro D'Arte, which toured extensively throughout Europe and the United States for nearly six years. Given Pirandello's inherent skepticism, his defense of artistic integrity, and his avant-garde philosophy, it is difficult to reconcile his political associations with the challenge to the authority of his art. It may be that Pirandello thought that Mussolini, whose slogan was "Our Italy," would support his personal campaign for a native Italian literature, free from external influences. It may be that Mussolini's backing for a theater allowed Pirandello the opportunity to showcase Marta Abba, an actress less than half of his age, who was also his mistress. Whatever the reasons, by 1929 Pirandello's theatrical company had failed, his romance had stuttered, and his sympathy with Italian fascism had waned. Still, he did not renounce Mussolini.

Pirandello's international reputation was secured when he received the Nobel Prize for Literature in 1934. He was cited for his accomplishments as dramatist and fiction writer, though outside of Italy his fiction is not popular or influential. He published his first novel, *The Outcast* (1893), the year he settled in Rome, and though he continued to publish, not until 1904 did he achieve fame, though not financial success, with *The Late Mattia Pascal*. Pirandello did not begin to write drama seriously until he was nearly fifty years old, and then with sustained dedication, he wrote twenty-eight plays over the next twenty-one years before his death.

Altogether he wrote forty-two plays, thirty-one of them full length. Pirandello's early plays were in the traditional style of the Sicilian theater. But later on, he abandoned traditional theater and deliberately set out to be audacious. *Right You Are, If You Think So* (1917), a dramatization of his short story "Signora Frola and Signor Ponza, Her Son-in-Law," is a comedy built on the accusations and counteraccusations of Frola and Ponza regarding each other's sanity; the interacting planes of reality and illusion serve to reveal the psychology of characters. This contrast, Pirandello's signature theme, emerges forcefully, and not unexpectedly, at a time when Pirandello's wife's sanity deteriorated.

In 1920 Pirandello achieved financial success with a traditional play, *As Before, Only Better.* Feeling liberated, he sought to concentrate now on the more experimental aspects of drama. Pirandello explained that drama should be more than a discussion of a problem, as one finds in Eugène Scribe's well-made plays or Henrik Ibsen's problem plays. In their stead, he argued for psychological realism, interwoven with a sense of life that could make the action universally meaningful. In *Six Characters in Search of an Author* (1921), the plot of the play-within-the-play deliberately distorts the traditional concept of family drama, the problem plays of Ibsen, and the traditional narrative plots Pirandello himself wrote when he began as a dramatist. Moreover, the play presents characters who wander freely between being fictional and real, although they are, of course, always characters in a play. This mixture of different states of reality infused his imagination, and after *Six Characters in Search of an Author*, he followed with plays that work out his "idea of the opposite": *Henry IV* (1922), *Tonight We Improvise* (1930), and *As You Desire Me* (1930).

The idea for *Six Characters in Search of an Author* began as a concept for a novel that Pirandello could not write. It was about six characters who follow Pirandello (the author) and beseech him to write a novel about them, and though he chases them away, they persist and follow him obsessively. When he put this conflict into the form of a play, Pirandello was able to elaborate his "idea of the opposite" by actually having actors playing characters who are *characters,* rather than naturalistic representations of reality. In doing so, he gave a different twist to some traditional questions of art: What happens to characters when art comes to life? Do characters have a life beyond the author who creates them? What happens to characters when their author abandons them?

The action begins as an acting company and its manager begin rehearsal for a Pirandello play called *Mixing It Up*. This rehearsal is abruptly interrupted when six characters enter and begin to dominate the stage. These characters, the Father, the Mother, the Step-Daughter, the Son, the Boy, and the Child, are dressed as stylized stage characters, in contrast to the actors and the Manager, who look "normal." Once onstage, the characters explain that they are searching for the author who abandoned them in a fit of despondency and disgust. Though the author may have abandoned them, they have not abandoned him. Then they begin to tell their story and act it out for the Manager, who is skeptical and annoyed. The act ends when the Manager agrees to serve as their author and write their story down.

In Act II, there is no script for the Characters, so the Manager allows them to act a scene for real actors to play. There is much arguing among the Characters, the Actors, and the Manager. The key action is the enactment of the incestuous seduction scene in which the Father and Step-Daughter meet at Madame Pace's. The Manager interferes with the re-creation of the scene by refusing to allow the Step-Daughter to remove her clothing. She argues that she is only doing what happened, but the Manager (now also the author) censors her. She responds by saying that censored theater is "crap." Still, there is psychological ambiguity about her mania for acting out this devastating scene.

Act III is set in a formal garden, in which the Characters finish acting out their functions in the plot: the young Child drowns, the Son shoots himself, and the Step-Daughter runs away. In these final moments, the interaction of reality and illusion is so jarring and disorienting that the Manager tries to restore order by shouting, "Pretense? Reality! To hell with it all!" And in a final burst of anger, he finishes with a coup de grâce: "Never in my life has such a thing happened to me. I've lost a whole day over these people, a whole day!" And the play ends abruptly.

Throughout the play, Pirandello explores complex questions regarding artistic creation, reality, and the function of art. The Father says that all of the Characters carry a painful drama, but why are they in search of an author if they already know of their painful suffering and torment? Why increase the agony of life? Indeed, the Father seems to be something more than a character because he rebels against his situation even though he has no hope of changing it. The Mother, an unfaithful wife, tries to explain that she is trapped in time because she is a character in a play who must obey the script even though she suffers to do so. In his "Preface," Pirandello said that she is "a very human figure, certainly, because mindless, that is, unaware of being what she is or caring to explain it to herself. But not knowing that she is a character doesn't prevent her from being one." The Step-Daughter, unlike the Father, is imbued with a sense of fatality. Though she is trapped in a sordid life of a prostitute and has had an incestuous encounter with the Father, she is still eager to act out her life on the stage. The Son, who stands to the side of the family group, may be crazy. Pirandello said, however, that "he is the only one who lives solely as a 'character' in search of an author." The Son's suicide is an outcome of his desire for ending his chaotic existence. Only the Manager of the production seems to have a positive character. But he is referred to in the "Preface" as being vulgar, perhaps Pirandello's way of indicating that when any manager (or director) gives a play theatrical life, the dramatist's fantasy is vulgarized, a traditional complaint of playwrights. Here, Pirandello deftly examines the relationship of text and production as if it were akin to the contrast of reality and illusion. The Manager tries to sort out the Characters, but he cannot. Since the future is proscribed but incomplete, the action ends without a satisfactory resolution for the Characters, the Actors, or the Manager.

So despite Pirandello's assurance that *Six Characters in Search of an Author* is a comedy in the making, a deep skepticism pervades this play. The shifts between comedy and stark negativism (with which the action finally ends) suggest that Pirandello is taking liberty with the traditional concept of comedy, which usually has a happy resolution. Oscar Wilde called *The Importance of Being Earnest* "a trivial comedy for serious people"; by contrast, Pirandello wrote a serious comedy for serious people.

Pirandello considered himself a philosophical author able to draw meaning from the mix of fantasy and reality. He was among the avant-garde who was able to create the illusion that characters have a life on stage and beyond. Pirandello said, "I want to make it clear that the inherent torment of my spirit is one thing, a torment which I can legitimately—provided that it be organic—reflect in a character, and that the activity of my spirit as revealed in the realized work, the activity that succeeds in forming a drama out of the six characters in search of an author is another thing." Contemporary playwright and critic Lionel Abel has called Pirandello's pretense of theatrical reality "metatheater," or the paradox that as a play presents the world as reality, life becomes less real. According to Abel, metatheater postulates that the playwright presumes the world to be a stage because human actions and emotions are theatrical and that life is dream because it cannot be understood.

Pirandello's deliberately ambiguous portrayal of the human condition and the confounding of reality and illusion greatly influenced Eugène Ionesco (reality and illusion), Samuel Beckett (complexity of inner consciousness), Eugene O'Neill (separation of inner and outer life), and Tennessee Williams and Tom Stoppard (confounding of reality and time). Though Arthur Miller is more closely linked to the theater of Ibsen, the use of time and memory in *Death of a Salesman* (1949) is particularly indebted to Pirandello.

Six Characters in Search of an Author

A Comedy in the Making

English version by Edward Storer

CHARACTERS OF THE COMEDY IN THE MAKING

The Father
The Mother
The Step-Daughter
The Son
The Boy
The Child
(The last two do not speak)
Madame Pace

ACTORS OF THE COMPANY

The Manager
Leading Lady
Leading Man
Second Lady
Lead
L'Ingénue
Juvenile Lead
Other Actors and Actresses
Property Man
Prompter
Machinist
Manager's Secretary
Door-keeper
Scene-Shifters

Daytime. The Stage of a Theatre

N. B. The Comedy is without acts or scenes. The performance is interrupted once, without the curtain being lowered, when the manager and the chief characters withdraw to arrange the scenario. A second interruption of the action takes place when, by mistake, the stage hands let the curtain down.

ACT I

The spectators will find the curtain raised and the stage as it usually is during the day time. It will be half dark, and empty, so that from the beginning the public may have the impression of an impromptu performance.

Prompter's box and a small table and chair for the manager.

Two other small tables and several chairs scattered about as during rehearsals.

The Actors *and* Actresses *of the company enter from the back of the stage: first one, then another, then two together; nine or ten in all. They are about to rehearse a Pirandello play: Mixing It Up. Some of the company move off towards their dressing rooms. The* Prompter *who has the "book" under his arm, is waiting for the manager in order to begin the rehearsal.*

The Actors *and* Actresses, *some standing, some sitting, chat and smoke. One perhaps reads a paper; another cons his part.*

Finally, the Manager *enters and goes to the table prepared for him. His* Secretary *brings him his mail, through which he glances. The* Prompter *takes his seat, turns on a light, and opens the "book."*

The Manager [*throwing a letter down on the table*]: I can't see [*To* Property Man.] Let's have a little light, please!

Property Man: Yes sir, yes, at once. [*A light comes down on to the stage.*]

The Manager [*clapping his hands*]: Come along! Come along! Second act of "Mixing It Up." [*Sits down.*]

[*The* Actors *and* Actresses *go from the front of the stage to the wings, all except the three who are to begin the rehearsal.*]

The Prompter [*reading the "book"*]: "Leo Gala's house. A curious room serving as dining-room and study."

The Manager [*to* Property Man]: Fix up the old red room.

Property Man [*noting it down*]: Red set. All right!

The Prompter [*continuing to read from the "book"*]: "Table already laid and writing desk with books and papers. Book-shelves. Exit rear to Leo's bedroom. Exit left to kitchen. Principal exit to right."

The Manager [*energetically*]: Well, you understand: The principal exit over there; here, the kitchen. [*Turning to actor who is to play the part of* Socrates.] You make your entrances and exits here. [*To* Property Man.] The baize doors at the rear, and curtains.

Property Man [*noting it down*]: Right!

PROMPTER [*reading as before*]: "When the curtain rises, Leo Gala, dressed in cook's cap and apron is busy beating an egg in a cup. Philip, also dressed as a cook, is beating another egg. Guido Venanzi is seated and listening."

LEADING MAN [*to* MANAGER]: Excuse me, but must I absolutely wear a cook's cap?

THE MANAGER [*annoyed*]: I imagine so. It says so there anyway. [*Pointing to the "book."*]

LEADING MAN: But it's ridiculous!

THE MANAGER [*jumping up in a rage*]: Ridiculous? Ridiculous? Is it my fault if France won't send us any more good comedies, and we are reduced to putting on Pirandello's works, where nobody understands anything, and where the author plays the fool with us all? [*The* ACTORS *grin. The* MANAGER *goes to* LEADING MAN *and shouts.*] Yes sir, you put on the cook's cap and beat eggs. Do you suppose that with all this egg-beating business you are on an ordinary stage? Get that out of your head. You represent the shell of the eggs you are beating! [*Laughter and comments among the* ACTORS.] Silence! and listen to my explanations, please! [*To* LEADING MAN.] "The empty form of reason without the fullness of instinct, which is blind."—You stand for reason, your wife is instinct. It's a mixing up of the parts, according to which you who act your own part become the puppet of yourself. Do you understand?

LEADING MAN: I'm hanged if I do.

THE MANAGER: Neither do I. But let's get on with it. It's sure to be a glorious failure anyway. [*Confidentially.*] But I say, please face three-quarters. Otherwise, what with the abstruseness of the dialogue, and the public that won't be able to hear you, the whole thing will go to hell. Come on! come on!

PROMPTER: Pardon sir, may I get into my box? There's a bit of a draught.

THE MANAGER: Yes, yes, of course!

At this point, the DOOR-KEEPER *has entered from the stage door and advances towards the manager's table, taking off his braided cap. During this manoeuvre, the* SIX CHARACTERS *enter, and stop by the door at back of stage, so that when the* DOOR-KEEPER *is about to announce their coming to the* MANAGER, *they are already on the stage. A tenuous light surrounds them, almost as if irradiated by them—the faint breath of their fantastic reality.*

This light will disappear when they come forward towards the actors. They preserve, however, something of the dream lightness in which they seem almost suspended; but this does not detract from the essential reality of their forms and expressions.

He who is known as THE FATHER *is a man of about 50: hair, reddish in colour, thin at the temples; he is not bald, however; thick moustaches, falling over his still fresh mouth, which often opens in an empty and uncertain smile. He is fattish, pale; with an especially wide forehead. He has blue, oval-shaped eyes, very clear and piercing. Wears light trousers and a dark jacket. He is alternatively mellifluous and violent in his manner.*

THE MOTHER *seems crushed and terrified as if by an intolerable weight of shame and abasement. She is dressed in modest black and wears a thick widow's veil of crêpe. When she lifts this, she reveals a wax-like face. She always keeps her eyes downcast.*

THE STEP-DAUGHTER *is dashing, almost impudent, beautiful. She wears mourning too, but with great elegance. She shows contempt for the timid half-frightened manner of the wretched* BOY *(14 years old, and also dressed in black); on the other hand, she displays a lively tenderness for her little sister,* THE CHILD *(about four), who is dressed in white, with a black silk sash at the waist.*

THE SON (22) *tall, severe in his attitude of contempt for* THE FATHER, *supercilious and indifferent to* THE MOTHER. *He looks as if he had come on the stage against his will.*

DOOR-KEEPER [*cap in hand*]: Excuse me, sir . . .

THE MANAGER [*rudely*]: Eh? What is it?

DOOR-KEEPER [*timidly*]: These people are asking for you, sir.

THE MANAGER [*furious*]: I am rehearsing, and you know perfectly well no one's allowed to come in during rehearsals! [*Turning to the* CHARACTERS.] Who are you, please? What do you want?

THE FATHER [*coming forward a little, followed by the others who seem embarrassed*]: As a matter of fact . . . we have come here in search of an author . . .

THE MANAGER [*half angry, half amazed*]: An author? What author?

THE FATHER: Any author, sir.

THE MANAGER: But there's no author here. We are not rehearsing a new piece.

THE STEP-DAUGHTER [*vivaciously*]: So much the better, so much the better! We can be your new piece.

AN ACTOR [*coming forward from the others*]: Oh, do you hear that?

THE FATHER [*to* STEP-DAUGHTER]: Yes, but if the author isn't here . . . [*To* MANAGER.] unless you would be willing . . .

THE MANAGER: You are trying to be funny.

THE FATHER: No, for Heaven's sake, what are you saying? We bring you a drama, sir.

THE STEP-DAUGHTER: We may be your fortune.

THE MANAGER: Will you oblige me by going away? We haven't time to waste with mad people.

THE FATHER [*mellifluously*]: Oh sir, you know well that life is full of infinite absurdities, which, strangely enough, do not even need to appear plausible, since they are true.

THE MANAGER: What the devil is he talking about?

THE FATHER: I say that to reverse the ordinary process may well be considered a madness: that is, to create credible situations, in order that they may appear true. But permit me to observe that if this be madness, it is the sole *raison d'être* of your profession, gentlemen. [*The* ACTORS *look hurt and perplexed.*]

THE MANAGER [*getting up and looking at him*]: So our profession seems to you one worthy of madmen then?

THE FATHER: Well, to make seem true that which isn't true . . . without any need . . . for a joke as it were . . . Isn't that your mission, gentlemen: to give life to fantastic characters on the stage?

THE MANAGER [*interpreting the rising anger of the* COMPANY]: But I would beg you to believe, my dear sir, that the profession of the comedian is a noble one. If today, as things go, the playwrights give us stupid comedies to play and puppets to represent instead of men, remember we are proud to have given life to immortal works here on these very boards! [*The* ACTORS, *satisfied, applaud their* MANAGER.]

THE FATHER [*interrupting furiously*]: Exactly, perfectly, to living beings more alive than those who breathe and wear clothes: beings less real perhaps, but truer! I agree with you entirely. [*The* ACTORS *look at one another in amazement.*]

THE MANAGER: But what do you mean? Before, you said . . .

THE FATHER: No, excuse me, I meant it for you, sir, who were crying out that you had no time to lose with madmen, while no one better than yourself knows that nature uses the instrument of human fantasy in order to pursue her high creative purpose.

THE MANAGER: Very well,—but where does all this take us?

THE FATHER: Nowhere! It is merely to show you that one is born to life in many forms, in many shapes, as tree, or as stone, as water, as butterfly, or as woman. So one may also be born a character in a play.

THE MANAGER [*with feigned comic dismay*]: So you and these other friends of yours have been born characters?

THE FATHER: Exactly, and alive as you see! [MANAGER *and* ACTORS *burst out laughing.*]

THE FATHER [*hurt*]: I am sorry you laugh, because we carry in us a drama, as you can guess from this woman here veiled in black.

THE MANAGER [*losing patience at last and almost indignant*]: Oh, chuck it! Get away please! Clear out of here! [*To* PROPERTY MAN.] For Heaven's sake, turn them out!

THE FATHER [*resisting*]: No, no, look here, we . . .

THE MANAGER [*roaring*]: We come here to work, you know.

LEADING ACTOR: One cannot let oneself be made such a fool of.

THE FATHER [*determined, coming forward*]: I marvel at your incredulity, gentlemen. Are you not accustomed to see the characters created by an author spring to life in yourselves and face each other? Just because there is no "book" [*Pointing to the* PROMPTER'*s box.*] which contains us, you refuse to believe . . .

THE STEP-DAUGHTER [*advances towards* MANAGER, *smiling and coquettish*]: Believe me, we are really six most interesting characters, sir; side-tracked however.

THE FATHER: Yes, that is the word! [*To* MANAGER *all at once.*] In the sense, that is, that the author who created us alive no longer wished, or was no longer able, materially to put us into a work of art. And this was a real crime, sir; because he who has had the luck to be born a character can laugh even at death. He cannot die. The man, the writer, the instrument of the creation will die, but his creation does not die. And to live for ever, it does not need to have extraordinary gifts or to be able to work wonders. Who was Sancho Panza? Who was Don Abbondio? Yet they live eternally because—live germs as they were—they had the fortune to find a fecundating matrix, a fantasy which could raise and nourish them: make them live for ever!

THE MANAGER: That is quite all right. But what do you want here, all of you?

THE FATHER: We want to live.

THE MANAGER [*ironically*]: For Eternity?

THE FATHER: No, sir, only for a moment . . . in you.

AN ACTOR: Just listen to him!

LEADING LADY: They want to live, in us . . . !

JUVENILE LEAD [*pointing to the* STEP-DAUGHTER]: I've no objection, as far as that one is concerned!

THE FATHER: Look here! look here! The comedy has to be made. [*To the* MANAGER.] But if you and your actors are willing, we can soon concert it among ourselves.

THE MANAGER [*annoyed*]: But what do you want to concert? We don't go in for concerts here. Here we play dramas and comedies!

THE FATHER: Exactly! That is just why we have come to you.

THE MANAGER: And where is the "book"?

THE FATHER: It is in us! [*The* ACTORS *laugh.*] The drama is in us, and we are the drama. We are impatient to play it. Our inner passion drives us on to this.

THE STEP-DAUGHTER [*disdainful, alluring, treacherous, full of impudence*]: My passion, sir! Ah, if you only knew! My passion for him! [*Points to the* FATHER *and makes a pretence of embracing him. Then she breaks out into a loud laugh.*]

THE FATHER [*angrily*]: Behave yourself! And please don't laugh in that fashion.

THE STEP-DAUGHTER: With your permission, gentlemen, I, who am a two months' orphan, will show you how I can dance and sing. [*Sings and then dances* Prenez garde à Tchou-Tchin-Tchou.]

Les chinois sont un peuple malin,
De Shangaî à Pekin,
Ils ont mis des écriteaux partout:
Prenez garde à Tchou-Tchin-Tchou.

ACTORS AND ACTRESSES: Bravo! Well done! Tip-top!

THE MANAGER: Silence! This isn't a café concert, you know! [*Turning to the* FATHER *in consternation.*] Is she mad?

THE FATHER: Mad? No, she's worse than mad.

THE STEP-DAUGHTER [*to* MANAGER]: Worse? Worse? Listen! Stage this drama for us at once! Then you will see that at a certain moment I . . . when this little darling here . . . [*Takes the* CHILD *by the hand and leads her to the* MANAGER.] Isn't she a dear? [*Takes her up and kisses her.*] Darling! Darling! [*Puts her down again and adds feelingly.*] Well, when God suddenly takes this dear little child away from that poor mother there; and this imbecile here [*Seizing hold of the* BOY *roughly and pushing him forward.*] does the stupidest things, like the fool he is, you will see me run away. Yes, gentlemen, I shall be off. But the moment hasn't arrived yet. After what has taken place between him and me [*indicates the* FATHER *with a horrible wink.*] I can't remain any longer in this society, to have to witness the anguish of this mother here for that fool . . . [*Indicates the* SON.] Look at him! Look at him! See how indifferent, how frigid he is, because he is the legitimate son. He despises me, despises him [*Pointing to the* BOY.], despises this baby here; because . . . we are bastards. [*Goes to the* MOTHER *and embraces her.*] And he doesn't want to recognize her as his mother—she who is the common mother of us all. He looks down upon her as if she were only the mother of us three bastards. Wretch! [*She says all this very rapidly, excitedly. At the word "bastards" she raises her voice, and almost spits out the final "'Wretch!"*]

THE MOTHER [*to the* MANAGER *in anguish*]: In the name of these two little children, I beg you . . . [*She grows faint and is about to fall.*] Oh God!

THE FATHER [*coming forward to support her as do some of the* ACTORS]: Quick, a chair, a chair for this poor widow!

THE ACTORS: Is it true? Has she really fainted?

THE MANAGER: Quick, a chair! Here!

[*One of the* ACTORS *brings a chair, the* OTHERS *proffer assistance.* THE MOTHER *tries to prevent* THE FATHER *from lifting the veil which covers her face.*]

THE FATHER: Look at her! Look at her!

THE MOTHER: No, no; stop it please!

THE FATHER [*raising her veil*]: Let them see you!

THE MOTHER [*rising and covering her face with her hands, in desperation*]: I beg you, sir, to prevent this man from carrying out his plan which is loathsome to me.

THE MANAGER [*dumbfounded*]: I don't understand at all. What is the situation? Is this lady your wife? [*To the* FATHER.]

THE FATHER: Yes, gentlemen: my wife!

THE MANAGER: But how can she be a widow if you are alive? [*The* ACTORS *find relief for their astonishment in a loud laugh.*]

THE FATHER: Don't laugh! Don't laugh like that, for Heaven's sake. Her drama lies just here in this: she has had a lover, a man who ought to be here.

THE MOTHER [*with a cry*]: No! No!

THE STEP-DAUGHTER: Fortunately for her, he is dead. Two months ago as I said. We are in mourning, as you see.

THE FATHER: He isn't here you see, not because he is dead. He isn't here—look at her a moment and you will understand—because her drama isn't a drama of the love of two men for whom she was incapable of feeling anything except possibly a little gratitude—gratitude not for me but for the other. She isn't a woman, she is a mother, and her drama—powerful sir, I assure you—lies, as a matter of fact, all in these four children she has had by two men.

THE MOTHER: I had them? Have you got the courage to say that I wanted them? [*To the* COMPANY.] It was his doing. It was he who gave me that other man, who forced me to go away with him.

THE STEP-DAUGHTER: It isn't true.

THE MOTHER [*startled*]: Not true, isn't it?

THE STEP-DAUGHTER: No, it isn't true, it just isn't true.

THE MOTHER: And what can you know about it?

THE STEP-DAUGHTER: It isn't true. Don't believe it. [*To* MANAGER.] Do you know why she says so? For that fellow there. [*Indicates the* SON.] She tortures herself, destroys herself on account of the neglect of that son there; and she wants him to believe that if she abandoned him when he was only two years old, it was because he [*Indicates the* FATHER.] made her do so.

THE MOTHER [*vigorously*]: He forced me to it, and I call God to witness it. [*To the* MANAGER.] Ask him [*Indicates* HUSBAND.] if it isn't true. Let him speak. You [*To* STEP-DAUGHTER.] are not in a position to know anything about it.

THE STEP-DAUGHTER: I know you lived in peace and happiness with my father while he lived. Can you deny it?

THE MOTHER: No, I don't deny it . . .

THE STEP-DAUGHTER: He was always full of affection and kindness for you. [*To the* BOY, *angrily.*] It's true, isn't it? Tell them! Why don't you speak, you little fool?

THE MOTHER: Leave the poor boy alone. Why do you want to make me appear ungrateful, daughter? I don't want to offend your father. I have answered him that I didn't abandon my house and my son through any fault of mine, nor from any wilful passion.

THE FATHER: It is true. It was my doing.

LEADING MAN [*to the* COMPANY]: What a spectacle!

LEADING LADY: We are the audience this time.

JUVENILE LEAD: For once, in a way.

THE MANAGER [*beginning to get really interested*]: Let's hear them out. Listen!

THE SON: Oh yes, you're going to hear a fine bit now. He will talk to you of the Demon of Experiment.

THE FATHER: You are a cynical imbecile. I've told you so already a hundred times. [*To the* MANAGER.] He tries to make fun of me on account of this expression which I have found to excuse myself with.

THE SON [*with disgust*]: Yes, phrases! phrases!

THE FATHER: Phrases! Isn't everyone consoled when faced with a trouble or fact he doesn't understand, by a word, some simple word, which tells us nothing and yet calms us?

THE STEP-DAUGHTER: Even in the case of remorse. In fact, especially then.

THE FATHER: Remorse? No, that isn't true. I've done more than use words to quieten the remorse in me.

THE STEP-DAUGHTER: Yes, there was a bit of money too. Yes, yes, a bit of money. There were the hundred lire he was about to offer me in payment, gentlemen . . . [*Sensation of horror among the* ACTORS.]

THE SON [*to the* STEP-DAUGHTER]: This is vile.

THE STEP-DAUGHTER: Vile? There they were in a pale blue envelope on a little mahogany table in the back of Madame Pace's shop. You know Madame Pace—one of those ladies who attract poor girls of good family into their ateliers, under the pretext of their selling *robes et manteaux.*

THE SON: And he thinks he has bought the right to tyrannize over us all with those hundred lire he was going to pay; but which, fortunately—note this, gentlemen—he had no chance of paying.

THE STEP-DAUGHTER: It was a near thing, though, you know! [*Laughs ironically.*]

THE MOTHER [*protesting*]: Shame, my daughter, shame!

THE STEP-DAUGHTER: Shame indeed! This is my revenge! I am dying to live that scene . . . The room . . . I see it . . . Here is the window with the mantles exposed, there the divan, the looking-glass, a screen, there in front of the window the little mahogany table with the blue envelope containing one hundred lire. I see it. I see it. I could take hold of it . . . But you, gentlemen, you ought to turn your backs now: I am almost nude, you know. But I don't blush: I leave that to him. [*Indicating* FATHER.]

THE MANAGER: I don't understand this at all.

THE FATHER: Naturally enough. I would ask you, sir, to exercise your authority a little here, and let me speak before you believe all she is trying to blame me with. Let me explain.

THE STEP-DAUGHTER: Ah yes, explain it in your own way.

THE FATHER: But don't you see that the whole trouble lies here. In words, words. Each one of us has within him a whole world of things, each man of us his own special world. And how can we ever come to an understanding if I put in the words I utter the sense and value of things as I see them; while you who listen to me must inevitably translate them according to the conception of things each one of you has within himself. We think we understand each other, but we never really do. Look here! This woman [*Indicating the* MOTHER.] takes all my pity for her as a specially ferocious form of cruelty.

THE MOTHER: But you drove me away.

THE FATHER: Do you hear her? I drove her away! She believes I really sent her away.

THE MOTHER: You know how to talk, and I don't; but, believe me, sir [*To* MANAGER.], after he had married me . . . who knows why? . . . I was a poor insignificant woman . . .

THE FATHER: But, good Heavens! it was just for your humility that I married you. I loved this simplicity in you. [*He stops when he sees she makes signs to contradict him, opens his arms wide in sign of desperation, seeing how hopeless it is to make himself understood.*] You see she denies it. Her mental deafness, believe me, is phenomenal, the limit: [*Touches his forehead.*]

deaf, deaf, mentally deaf! She has plenty of feeling. Oh yes, a good heart for the children; but the brain—deaf, to the point of desperation——!

THE STEP-DAUGHTER: Yes, but ask him how his intelligence has helped us.

THE FATHER: If we could see all the evil that may spring from good, what should we do? [*At this point the* LEADING LADY, *who is biting her lips with rage at seeing the* LEADING MAN *flirting with the* STEP-DAUGHTER, *comes forward and says to the* MANAGER.]

LEADING LADY: Excuse me, but are we going to rehearse today?

MANAGER: Of course, of course; but let's hear them out.

JUVENILE LEAD: This is something quite new.

L'INGÉNUE: Most interesting!

LEADING LADY: Yes, for the people who like that kind of thing. [*Casts a glance at* LEADING MAN.]

THE MANAGER [*to* FATHER]: You must please explain yourself quite clearly. [*Sits down.*]

THE FATHER: Very well then: listen! I had in my service a poor man, a clerk, a secretary of mine, full of devotion, who became friends with her. [*Indicating the* MOTHER.] They understood one another, were kindred souls in fact, without, however, the least suspicion of any evil existing. They were incapable even of thinking of it.

THE STEP-DAUGHTER: So he thought of it—for them!

THE FATHER: That's not true. I meant to do good to them—and to myself, I confess, at the same time. Things had come to the point that I could not say a word to either of them without their making a mute appeal, one to the other, with their eyes. I could see them silently asking each other how I was to be kept in countenance, how I was to be kept quiet. And this, believe me, was just about enough of itself to keep me in a constant rage, to exasperate me beyond measure.

THE MANAGER: And why didn't you send him away then—this secretary of yours?

THE FATHER: Precisely what I did, sir. And then I had to watch this poor woman drifting forlornly about the house like an animal without a master, like an animal one has taken in out of pity.

THE MOTHER: Ah yes . . . !

THE FATHER [*suddenly turning to the* MOTHER]: It's true about the son anyway, isn't it?

THE MOTHER: He took my son away from me first of all.

THE FATHER: But not from cruelty. I did it so that he should grow up healthy and strong by living in the country.

THE STEP-DAUGHTER [*pointing to him ironically*]: As one can see.

THE FATHER [*quickly*]: Is it my fault if he has grown up like this? I sent him to a wet nurse in the country, a peasant, as *she* did not seem to me strong enough, though she is of humble origin. That was, anyway, the reason I married her. Unpleasant all this may be, but how can it be helped? My mistake possibly, but there we are! All my life I have had these confounded aspirations towards a certain moral sanity. [*At this point the* STEP-DAUGHTER *bursts into a noisy laugh.*] Oh, stop it! Stop it! I can't stand it.

THE MANAGER: Yes, please stop it, for Heaven's sake.

THE STEP-DAUGHTER: But imagine moral sanity from him, if you please—the client of certain ateliers like that of Madame Pace!

THE FATHER: Fool! That is the proof that I am a man! This seeming contradiction, gentlemen, is the strongest proof that I stand here a live man before you. Why, it is just for this very incongruity in my nature that I have had to suffer what I have. I could not live by the side of that woman [*Indicating the* MOTHER.] any longer; but not so much for the boredom she inspired me with as for the pity I felt for her.

THE MOTHER: And so he turned me out—.

THE FATHER: —well provided for! Yes, I sent her to that man, gentlemen . . . to let her go free of me.

THE MOTHER: And to free himself.

THE FATHER: Yes, I admit it. It was also a liberation for me. But great evil has come of it. I meant well when I did it; and I did it more for her sake than mine. I swear it. [*Crosses his arms on his chest; then turns suddenly to the* MOTHER.] Did I ever lose sight of you until that other man carried you off to another town, like the angry fool he was? And on account of my pure interest in you . . . my pure interest, I repeat, that had no base motive in it . . . I watched with the tenderest concern the new family that grew up around her. She can bear witness to this. [*Points to the* STEP-DAUGHTER.]

THE STEP-DAUGHTER: Oh yes, that's true enough. When I was a kiddie, so so high, you know, with plaits over my shoulders and knickers longer than my skirts, I used to see him waiting outside the school for me to come out. He came to see how I was growing up.

THE FATHER: This is infamous, shameful!

THE STEP-DAUGHTER: No. Why?

THE FATHER: Infamous! infamous! [*Then excitedly to* MANAGER *explaining.*] After she [*Indicating* MOTHER.] went away, my house seemed suddenly empty. She was my incubus, but she filled my house. I was like a dazed fly alone in the empty rooms. This boy here [*Indicating the* SON.] was educated away from home, and when he came back, he seemed to me to be no more mine. With no mother to stand between him and me, he grew up entirely for himself, on his own, apart, with no tie of intellect or affection binding him to me. And then—strange but true—I was driven, by curiosity at first and then by some tender sentiment, towards her family, which had come into being through my will. The thought of her began gradually to fill up the emptiness I felt all around me. I wanted to know if she were happy in living out the simple daily duties of life. I wanted to think of her as fortunate and happy because far away from the complicated torments of my spirit. And so, to have proof of this, I used to watch that child coming out of school.

THE STEP-DAUGHTER: Yes, yes. True. He used to follow me in the street and smiled at me, waved his hand, like this. I would look at him with interest, wondering who he might be. I told my mother, who guessed at once. [*The* MOTHER *agrees with a nod.*] Then she didn't want to send me to school for some days; and when I finally went back, there he was again—looking so ridiculous—with a paper parcel in his hands. He came close to me, caressed me, and drew out a fine straw hat from the parcel, with a bouquet of flowers—all for me!

THE MANAGER: A bit discursive this, you know!

THE SON [*contemptuously*]: Literature! Literature!

THE FATHER: Literature indeed! This is life, this is passion!

THE MANAGER: It may be, but it won't act.

THE FATHER: I agree. This is only the part leading up. I don't suggest this should be staged. She [*Pointing to the* STEP-DAUGHTER.], as you see, is no longer the flapper with plaits down her back—.

THE STEP-DAUGHTER: —and the knickers showing below the skirt!

THE FATHER: The drama is coming now, sir; something new, complex, most interesting.

THE STEP-DAUGHTER: As soon as my father died . . .

THE FATHER: —there was absolute misery for them. They came back here, unknown to me. Through her stupidity! [*Pointing to the* MOTHER.] It is true she can barely write her own name; but she could anyhow have got her daughter to write to me that they were in need . . .

THE MOTHER: And how was I to divine all this sentiment in him?

THE FATHER: That is exactly your mistake, never to have guessed any of my sentiments.

THE MOTHER: After so many years apart, and all that had happened . . .

THE FATHER: Was it my fault if that fellow carried you away? It happened quite suddenly; for after he had obtained some job or other, I could find no trace of them; and so, not unnaturally, my interest in them dwindled. But the drama culminated unforeseen and violent on their return, when I was impelled by my miserable flesh that still lives . . . Ah! what misery, what wretchedness is that of the man who is alone and disdains debasing *liaisons!* Not old enough to do without women, and not young enough to go and look for one without shame. Misery? It's worse than misery; it's a horror; for no woman can any longer give him love; and when a man feels this . . . One ought to do without, you say? Yes, yes, I know. Each of us when he appears before his fellows is clothed in a certain dignity. But every man knows what unconfessable things pass within the secrecy of his own heart. One gives way to the temptation, only to rise from it again, afterwards, with a great eagerness to re-establish one's dignity, as if it were a tombstone to place on the grave of one's shame, and a monument to hide and sign the memory of our weaknesses. Everybody's in the same case. Some folks haven't the courage to say certain things, that's all!

THE STEP-DAUGHTER: All appear to have the courage to do them though.

THE FATHER: Yes, but in secret. Therefore, you want more courage to say these things. Let a man but speak these things out, and folks at once label him a cynic. But it isn't true. He is like all the others, better indeed, because he isn't afraid to reveal with the light of the intelligence the red shame of human bestiality on which most men close their eyes so as not to see it.

Woman—for example, look at her case! She turns tantalizing inviting glances on you. You seize her. No sooner does she feel herself in your grasp than she closes her eyes. It is the sign of her mission, the sign by which she says to man: "Blind yourself, for I am blind."

THE STEP-DAUGHTER: Sometimes she can close them no more: when she no longer feels the need of hiding her shame to herself, but dry-eyed and dispassionately, sees only that of the man who has blinded himself without love. Oh, all these intellectual complications make me sick, disgust me—all this philosophy that uncovers the beast in man, and then seeks to save him, excuse him . . . I can't stand it, sir. When a man seeks to "simplify" life bestially, throwing aside every relic of humanity, every chaste aspiration, every pure feeling, all sense of ideality, duty, modesty, shame . . . then nothing is more revolting and nauseous than a certain kind of remorse—crocodiles' tears, that's what it is..

THE MANAGER: Let's come to the point. This is only discussion.

THE FATHER: Very good, sir! But a fact is like a sack which won't stand up when it is empty. In order that it may stand up, one has to put into it the reason and sentiment which have caused it to exist. I couldn't possibly know that after the death of that man, they had decided to return here, that they were in misery, and that she [*Pointing to the* MOTHER.] had gone to work as a modiste, and at a shop of the type of that of Madame Pace.

THE STEP-DAUGHTER: A real high-class modiste, you must know, gentlemen. In appearance, she works for the leaders of the best society; but she arranges matters so that these elegant ladies serve her purpose . . . without prejudice to other ladies who are . . . well . . . only so so.

THE MOTHER: You will believe me, gentlemen, that it never entered my mind that the old hag offered me work because she had her eye on my daughter.

THE STEP-DAUGHTER: Poor mamma! Do you know, sir, what that woman did when I brought her back the work my mother had finished? She would point out to me that I had torn one of my frocks, and she would give it back to my mother to mend. It was I who paid for it, always I; while this poor creature here believed she was sacrificing herself for me and these two children here, sitting up at night sewing Madame Pace's robes.

THE MANAGER: And one day you met there . . .

THE STEP-DAUGHTER: Him, him. Yes sir, an old client. There's a scene for you to play! Superb!

THE FATHER: She, the Mother arrived just then . . .

THE STEP-DAUGHTER [*treacherously*]: Almost in time!

THE FATHER [*crying out*]: No, in time! in time! Fortunately I recognized her . . . in time. And I took them back home with me to my house. You can imagine now her position and mine; she, as you see her; and I who cannot look her in the face.

THE STEP-DAUGHTER: Absurd! How can I possibly be expected—after that—to be a modest young miss, a fit person to go with his confounded aspirations for "a solid moral sanity"?

THE FATHER: For the drama lies all in this—in the conscience that I have, that each one of us has. We believe this conscience to be a single thing, but it is many-sided. There is one for this person, and another for that. Diverse consciences. So we have this illusion of being one person for all, of having a personality that is unique in all our acts. But it isn't true. We perceive this when, tragically perhaps, in something we do, we are as it were, suspended, caught up in the air on a kind of hook. Then we perceive that all of us was not in that act, and that it would be an atrocious injustice to judge us by that action alone, as if all our existence were summed up in that one deed. Now do you understand the perfidy of this girl? She surprised me in a place, where she ought not to have known me, just as I could not exist for her; and she now seeks to attach to me a reality such as I could never suppose I should have to assume for her in a shameful and fleeting moment of my life. I feel this above all else. And the drama, you will see, acquires a tremendous value from this point. Then there is the position of the others . . . his . . . [*Indicating the* SON.]

THE SON [*shrugging his shoulders scornfully*]: Leave me alone! I don't come into this.

THE FATHER: What? You don't come into this?

THE SON: I've got nothing to do with it, and don't want to have; because you know well enough I wasn't made to be mixed up in all this with the rest of you.

THE STEP-DAUGHTER: We are only vulgar folk! He is the fine gentleman. You may have noticed, Mr. Manager, that I fix him now and again with a look of scorn while he lowers his eyes—for he knows the evil he has done me.

THE SON [*scarcely looking at her*]: I?

THE STEP-DAUGHTER: You! you! I owe my life on the streets to you. Did you or did you not deny us, with your behaviour, I won't say the intimacy of home, but even that mere hospitality which makes guests feel at their ease? We were intruders who had come to disturb the kingdom of your legitimacy. I should like to have you witness, Mr. Manager, certain scenes between him and me. He says I have tyrannized over everyone. But it was just his behaviour which made me insist on the reason for which I had come into the house,—this reason he calls "vile"—into his house, with my mother who is his mother too. And I came as mistress of the house.

THE SON: It's easy for them to put me always in the wrong. But imagine, gentlemen, the position of a son, whose fate it is to see arrive one day at his home a young woman of impudent bearing, a young woman who inquires for his father, with whom who knows what business she has. This young man has then to witness her return bolder than ever, accompanied by that child there. He is obliged to watch her treat his father in an equivocal and confidential manner. She asks money of him in a way that lets one suppose he must give it her, *must*, do you understand, because he has every obligation to do so.

THE FATHER: But I have, as a matter of fact, this obligation. I owe it to your mother.

THE SON: How should I know? When had I ever seen or heard of her? One day there arrive with her [*Indicating* STEP-DAUGHTER.] that lad and this baby here. I am told: "This is *your* mother too, you know." I divine from her manner [*Indicating* STEP-DAUGHTER *again.*] why it is they have come home. I had rather not say what I feel and think about it. I shouldn't even care to confess to myself. No action can therefore be hoped for from me in this affair. Believe me, Mr. Manager, I am an "unrealized" character, dramatically speaking; and I find myself not at all at ease in their company. Leave me out of it, I beg you.

THE FATHER: What? It is just because you are so that . . .

THE SON: How do you know what I am like? When did you ever bother your head about me?

THE FATHER: I admit it. I admit it. But isn't that a situation in itself? This aloofness of yours which is so cruel to me and to your mother, who returns home and sees you almost for the first time grown up, who doesn't recognize you but knows you are her son . . . [*Pointing out the* MOTHER *to the* MANAGER.] See, she's crying!

THE STEP-DAUGHTER [*angrily, stamping her foot*]: Like a fool!

THE FATHER [*indicating* STEP-DAUGHTER]: She can't stand him you know. [*Then referring again to the* SON.] He says he doesn't come into the affair, whereas he is really the hinge of the whole action. Look at that lad who is always clinging to his mother, frightened and humiliated. It is on account of this fellow here. Possibly his situation is the most painful of all. He feels himself a stranger more than the others. The poor little chap feels mortified, humiliated at being brought into a home out of charity as it were. [*In confidence.*] He is the image of his father. Hardly talks at all. Humble and quiet.

THE MANAGER: Oh, we'll cut him out. You've no notion what a nuisance boys are on the stage . . .

THE FATHER: He disappears soon, you know. And the baby too. She is the first to vanish from the scene. The drama consists finally in this: when that mother re-enters my house, her family born outside of it, and shall we say superimposed on the original, ends with the death of the little girl, the tragedy of the boy and the flight of the elder daughter. It cannot go on, because it is foreign to its surroundings. So after much torment, we three remain: I, the mother, that son. Then, owing to the disappearance of that extraneous family, we too find ourselves strange to one another. We find we are living in an atmosphere of mortal desolation which is the revenge, as he [*Indicating* SON.] scornfully said of the Demon of Experiment, that unfortunately hides in me. Thus, sir, you see when faith is lacking, it becomes impossible to create certain states of happiness, for we lack the necessary humility. Vaingloriously, we try to substitute ourselves for this faith, creating thus for the rest of the world a reality which we believe after their fashion, while, actually, it doesn't exist. For each one of us has his own reality to be respected before God, even when it is harmful to one's very self.

THE MANAGER: There is something in what you say. I assure you all this interests me very much. I begin to think there's the stuff for a drama in all this, and not a bad drama either.

THE STEP-DAUGHTER [*coming forward*]: When you've got a character like me.

THE FATHER [*shutting her up, all excited to learn the decision of the* MANAGER]: You be quiet!

THE MANAGER [*reflecting, heedless of interruption*]: It's new . . . hem . . . yes . . .

THE FATHER: Absolutely new!

THE MANAGER: You've got a nerve though, I must say, to come here and fling it at me like this . . .

THE FATHER: You will understand, sir, born as we are for the stage . . .

THE MANAGER: Are you amateur actors then?

THE FATHER: No. I say born for the stage because . . .

THE MANAGER: Oh, nonsense. You're an old hand, you know.

THE FATHER: No sir, no. We act that rôle for which we have been cast, that rôle which we are given in life. And in my own case, passion itself, as usually happens, becomes a trifle theatrical when it is exalted.

THE MANAGER: Well, well, that will do. But you see, without an author . . . I could give you the address of an author if you like . . .

THE FATHER: No, no. Look here! You must be the author.

THE MANAGER: I? What are you talking about?

THE FATHER: Yes, you, you! Why not?

THE MANAGER: Because I have never been an author: that's why.

THE FATHER: Then why not turn author now? Everybody does it. You don't want any special qualities. Your task is made much easier by the fact that we are all here alive before you . . .

THE MANAGER: It won't do.

THE FATHER: What? When you see us live our drama . . .

THE MANAGER: Yes, that's all right. But you want someone to write it.

THE FATHER: No, no. Someone to take it down, possibly, while we play it, scene by scene! It will be enough to sketch it out at first, and then try it over.

THE MANAGER: Well . . . I am almost tempted. It's a bit of an idea. One might have a shot at it.

THE FATHER: Of course. You'll see what scenes will come out of it. I can give you one, at once . . .

THE MANAGER: By Jove, it tempts me. I'd like to have a go at it. Let's try it out. Come with me to my office. [*Turning to the* ACTORS.] You are at liberty for a bit, but don't step out of the theatre for long.

In a quarter of an hour, twenty minutes, all back here again! [*To the* FATHER.] We'll see what can be done. Who knows if we don't get something really extraordinary out of it?

THE FATHER: There's no doubt about it. They [*Indicating the* CHARACTERS.] had better come with us too, hadn't they?

THE MANAGER: Yes, yes. Come on! come on! [*Moves away and then turning to the* ACTORS.] *Be punctual, please!* [MANAGER *and the* SIX CHARACTERS *cross the stage and go off. The other* ACTORS *remain, looking at one another in astonishment.*]

LEADING MAN: Is he serious? What the devil does he want to do?

JUVENILE LEAD: This is rank madness.

THIRD ACTOR: Does he expect to knock up a drama in five minutes?

JUVENILE LEAD: Like the improvisers!

LEADING LADY: If he thinks I'm going to take part in a joke like this . . .

JUVENILE LEAD: I'm out of it anyway.

FOURTH ACTOR: I should like to know who they are. [*Alludes to* CHARACTERS].

THIRD ACTOR: What do you suppose? Madmen or rascals!

JUVENILE LEAD: And he takes them seriously!

L'INGÉNUE: Vanity! He fancies himself as an author now.

LEADING MAN: It's absolutely unheard of. If the stage has come to this . . . well I'm . . .

FIFTH ACTOR: It's rather a joke.

THIRD ACTOR: Well, we'll see what's going to happen next.

[*Thus talking, the* ACTORS *leave the stage; some going out by the little door at the back; others retiring to their dressing-rooms.*

The curtain remains up.

The action of the play is suspended for twenty minutes].

ACT II

The stage call-bells ring to warn the company that the play it about to begin again.

The STEP-DAUGHTER *comes out of the* MANAGER'S *office along with the* CHILD *and the* BOY. *As she comes out of the office, she cries:—*

Nonsense! nonsense! Do it yourselves! I'm not going to mix myself up in this mess. [*Turning to the* CHILD *and coming quickly with her on to the stage.*] Come on, Rosetta, let's run!

[*The* BOY *follows them slowly, remaining a little behind and seeming perplexed.*]

THE STEP-DAUGHTER: [*stops, bends over the* CHILD *and takes the latter's face between her hands*]: My little darling! You're frightened, aren't you? You don't know where we are, do you? [*Pretending to reply to a question of the* CHILD.] What is the stage? It's a place, baby, you know, where people play at being serious, a place where they act comedies. We've got to act a comedy now, dead serious, you know; and you're in it also, little one. [*Embraces her, pressing the little head to her breast, and rocking the* CHILD *for a moment.*] Oh darling, darling, what a horrid comedy you've got to play! What a wretched part they've found for you! A garden . . . a fountain . . . look . . . just suppose, kiddie, it's here. Where, you say? Why, right here in the middle. It's all pretence you know. That's the trouble, my pet: it's all make-believe here. It's better to imagine it though, because if they fix it up for you, it'll only be painted cardboard, painted cardboard for the rockery, the water, the plants . . . Ah, but I think a baby like this one would sooner have a make-believe fountain than a real one, so she could play with it. What a joke it'll be for the others! But for you, alas! not quite such a joke: you who are real, baby dear, and really play by a real fountain that is big and green and beautiful, with ever so many bamboos around it that are reflected in the water, and a whole lot of little ducks swimming about . . . No, Rosetta, no, your mother doesn't bother about you on account of that wretch of a son there. I'm in the devil of a temper, and as for that lad . . . [*Seizes* BOY *by the arm to force him to take one of his hands out of his pockets.*] What have you got there? What are you hiding? [*Pulls his hand out of his pocket, looks into it and catches the glint of a revolver.*] Ah! where did you get this? [*The* BOY, *very pale in the face, looks at her, but does not answer.*] Idiot! If I'd been in your place, instead of killing myself, I'd have shot one of those two, or both of them: father and son.

[*The* FATHER *enters from the office, all excited from his work. The* MANAGER *follows him.*]

THE FATHER: Come on, come on dear! Come here for a minute! We've arranged everything. It's all fixed up.

THE MANAGER [*also excited*]: If you please, young lady, there are one or two points to settle still. Will you come along?

THE STEP-DAUGHTER [*following him towards the office*]: Ouff! what's the good, if you've arranged everything.

[*The* FATHER, MANAGER *and* STEP-DAUGHTER *go back into the office again (off) for a moment. At the same time, the* SON *followed by the* MOTHER, *comes out.*]

THE SON [*looking at the three entering office*]: Oh this is fine, fine! And to think I can't even get away!

[*The* MOTHER *attempts to look at him, but lowers her eyes immediately when* HE *turns away from her.* SHE *then sits down. The* BOY *and the* CHILD *approach her.* SHE *casts a glance again at the* SON, *and speaks with humble tones, trying to draw him into conversation.*]

THE MOTHER: And isn't my punishment the worst of all? [*Then seeing from the* SON*'s manner that he will not bother himself about her.*] My God! Why are you so cruel? Isn't it enough for one person to support all this torment? Must you then insist on others seeing it also?

THE SON [*half to himself, meaning the* MOTHER *to hear, however*]: And they want to put it on the stage! If there was at least a reason for it! He thinks he has got at the meaning of it all. Just as if each one of us in every circumstance of life couldn't find his own explanation of it! [*Pauses.*] He complains he was discovered in a place where he ought not to have been seen, in a moment of his life which ought to have remained hidden and kept out of the reach of that convention which he has to maintain for other people. And what about my case? Haven't I had to reveal what no son ought ever to reveal: how father and mother live and are man and wife for themselves quite apart from that idea of father and mother which we give them? When this idea is revealed, our life is then linked at one point only to that man and that woman; and as such it should shame them, shouldn't it?

[*The* MOTHER *hides her face in her hands. From the dressing-rooms and the little door at the back of the stage the* ACTORS *and* STAGE MANAGER *return, followed by the* PROPERTY MAN, *and the* PROMPTER. *At the same moment, the* MANAGER *comes out of his office, accompanied by the* FATHER *and the* STEP-DAUGHTER.]

THE MANAGER: Come on, come on, ladies and gentlemen! Heh! you there, machinist!

MACHINIST: Yes sir?

THE MANAGER: Fix up the white parlor with the floral decorations. Two wings and a drop with a door will do. Hurry up!

[*The* MACHINIST *runs off at once to prepare the scene, and arranges it while the* MANAGER *talks with the* STAGE MANAGER, *the* PROPERTY MAN, *and the* PROMPTER *on matters of detail.*]

THE MANAGER [*to* PROPERTY MAN]: Just have a look, and see if there isn't a sofa or divan in the wardrobe . . .

PROPERTY MAN: There's the green one.

THE STEP-DAUGHTER: No no! Green won't do. It was yellow, ornamented with flowers—very large! and most comfortable!

PROPERTY MAN: There isn't one like that.

THE MANAGER: It doesn't matter. Use the one we've got.

THE STEP-DAUGHTER: Doesn't matter? It's most important!

THE MANAGER: We're only trying it now. Please don't interfere. [*To* PROPERTY MAN.] See if we've got a shop window—long and narrowish.

THE STEP-DAUGHTER: And the little table! The little mahogany table for the pale blue envelope!

PROPERTY MAN [*to* MANAGER]: There's that little gilt one.

THE MANAGER: That'll do fine.

THE FATHER: A mirror.

THE STEP-DAUGHTER: And the screen! We must have a screen. Otherwise how can I manage?

PROPERTY MAN: That's all right, Miss. We've got any amount of them.

THE MANAGER [*to the* STEP-DAUGHTER]: We want some clothes pegs too, don't we?

THE STEP-DAUGHTER: Yes, several, several!

THE MANAGER: See how many we've got and bring them all.

PROPERTY MAN: All right!

[*The* PROPERTY MAN *hurries off to obey his orders. While he is putting the things in their places, the* MANAGER *talks to the* PROMPTER *and then with the* CHARACTERS *and the* ACTORS.]

THE MANAGER [*to* PROMPTER]: Take your seat. Look here: this is the outline of the scenes, act by act. [*Hands him some sheets of paper.*] And now I'm going to ask you to do something out of the ordinary.

PROMPTER: Take it down in shorthand?

THE MANAGER [*pleasantly surprised*]: Exactly! Can you do shorthand?

PROMPTER: Yes, a little.

THE MANAGER: Good! [*Turning to a* STAGE HAND.] Go and get some paper from my office, plenty, as much as you can find.

[*The* STAGE HAND *goes off, and soon returns with a handful of paper which he gives to the* PROMPTER.]

THE MANAGER [*to* PROMPTER]: You follow the scenes as we play them, and try and get the points down, at any rate the most important ones. [*Then addressing the* ACTORS.] Clear the stage, ladies and gentlemen! Come over here [*Pointing to the left.*] and listen attentively.

LEADING LADY: But, excuse me, we . . .

THE MANAGER [*guessing her thought*]: Don't worry! You won't have to improvise.

LEADING MAN: What have we to do then?

THE MANAGER: Nothing. For the moment you just watch and listen. Everybody will get his part written out afterwards. At present we're going to try the thing as best we can. They're going to act now.

THE FATHER [*as if fallen from the clouds into the confusion of the stage*]: We? What do you mean, if you please, by a rehearsal?

THE MANAGER: A rehearsal for them. [*Points to the* ACTORS.]

THE FATHER: But since we are the characters . . .

THE MANAGER: All right: "characters" then, if you insist on calling yourselves such. But here, my dear sir, the characters don't act. Here the actors do the acting. The characters are there, in the "book" [*Pointing towards* PROMPTER'*s box.*]—when there is a "book"!

THE FATHER: I won't contradict you; but excuse me, the actors aren't the characters. They want to be, they pretend to be, don't they? Now if these gentlemen here are fortunate enough to have us alive before them . . .

THE MANAGER: Oh this is grand! You want to come before the public yourselves then?

THE FATHER: As we are . . .

THE MANAGER: I can assure you it would be a magnificent spectacle!

LEADING MAN: What's the use of us here anyway then?

THE MANAGER: You're not going to pretend that you can act? It makes me laugh! [*The* ACTORS *laugh.*] There, you see, they are laughing at the notion. But, by the way, I must cast the parts. That won't be difficult. They cast themselves. [*To the* SECOND LADY LEAD.] You play the Mother. [*To the* FATHER.] We must find her a name.

THE FATHER: Amalia, sir.

THE MANAGER: But that is the real name of your wife. We don't want to call her by her real name.

THE FATHER: Why ever not, if it is her name? . . . Still, perhaps, if that lady must . . . [*Makes a slight motion of the hand to indicate the* SECOND LADY LEAD.] I see this woman here [*Means the* MOTHER.] as Amalia. But do as you like. [*Gets more and more confused.*] I don't know what to say to you. Already, I begin to hear my own words ring false, as if they had another sound . . .

THE MANAGER: Don't you worry about it. It'll be our job to find the right tones. And as for her name, if you want her Amalia, Amalia it shall be; and if you don't like it, we'll find another! For the moment though, we'll call the characters in this way: [*To* JUVENILE LEAD.] You are the Son. [*To the* LEADING LADY.] You naturally are the Step-Daughter . . .

THE STEP-DAUGHTER [*excitedly*]: What? what? I, that woman there? [*Bursts out laughing.*]

THE MANAGER [*angry*]: What is there to laugh at?

LEADING LADY [*indignant*]: Nobody has ever dared to laugh at me. I insist on being treated with respect; otherwise I go away.

THE STEP-DAUGHTER: No no, excuse me . . . I am not laughing at you . . .

THE MANAGER [*to* STEP-DAUGHTER]: You ought to feel honored to be played by . . .

LEADING LADY [*at once, contemptuously*]: "That woman there" . . .

THE STEP-DAUGHTER: But I wasn't speaking of you, you know. I was speaking of myself—whom I can't see at all in you! That is all. I don't know . . . but . . . you . . . aren't in the least like me . . .

THE FATHER: True. Here's the point. Look here, sir, our temperaments, our souls . . .

THE MANAGER: Temperament, soul, be hanged! Do you suppose the spirit of the piece is in you? Nothing of the kind!

THE FATHER: What, haven't we our own temperaments, our own souls?

THE MANAGER: Not at all. Your soul or whatever you like to call it takes shape here. The actors give body and form to it, voice and gesture. And my actors—I may tell you—have given expression to much more lofty material than this little drama of yours, which may or may not hold up on the stage. But if it does, the merit of it, believe me, will be due to my actors.

THE FATHER: I don't dare contradict you, sir; but, believe me, it is a terrible suffering for us who are as we are, with these bodies of ours, these features to see . . .

THE MANAGER [*cutting him short and out of patience*]: Good heavens! The make-up will remedy all that, man, the make-up . . .

THE FATHER: Maybe. But the voice, the gestures . . .

THE MANAGER: Now, look here! On the stage, you as yourself, cannot exist. The actor here acts you, and that's an end to it!

THE FATHER: I understand. And now I think I see why our author who conceived us as we are, all alive, didn't want to put us on the stage after all. I haven't the least desire to offend your actors. Far from it! But when I think that I am to be acted by . . . I don't know by whom . . .

LEADING MAN [*on his dignity*]: By me, if you've no objection!

THE FATHER [*humbly, mellifluously*]: Honored, I assure you, sir. [*Bows.*] Still, I must say that try as this gentleman may, with all his good will and wonderful art, to absorb me into himself . . .

LEADING MAN: Oh chuck it! "Wonderful art!" Withdraw that, please!

THE FATHER: The performance he will give, even doing his best with make-up to look like me . . .

LEADING MAN: It will certainly be a bit difficult! [*The* ACTORS *laugh.*]

THE FATHER: Exactly! It will be difficult to act me as I really am. The effect will be rather—apart from the make-up—according as to how he supposes I am, as he senses me—if he does sense me—and not as I inside of myself feel myself to be. It seems to me then that account should be taken of this by everyone whose duty it may become to criticize us . . .

THE MANAGER: Heavens! The man's starting to think about the critics now! Let them say what they like. It's up to us to put on the play if we can. [*Looking around.*] Come on! come on! Is the stage set? [*To the* ACTORS *and* CHARACTERS.] Stand back—stand back! Let me see, and don't let's lose any more time! [*To the* STEP-DAUGHTER.] Is it all right as it is now?

THE STEP-DAUGHTER: Well, to tell the truth, I don't recognize the scene.

THE MANAGER: My dear lady, you can't possibly suppose that we can construct that shop of Madame Pace piece by piece here? [*To the* FATHER.] You said a white room with flowered wall paper, didn't you?

THE FATHER: Yes.

THE MANAGER: Well then. We've got the furniture right more or less. Bring that little table a bit further forward. [*The* STAGE HANDS *obey the order. To* PROPERTY MAN.] You go and find an envelope, if possible, a pale blue one; and give it to that gentleman. [*Indicates* FATHER.]

PROPERTY MAN: An ordinary envelope?

MANAGER AND FATHER: Yes, yes, an ordinary envelope.

PROPERTY MAN: At once, sir. [*Exit.*]

THE MANAGER: Ready, everyone! First scene—the Young Lady. [*The* LEADING LADY *comes forward.*] No, no, you must wait. I meant her [*Indicating the* STEP-DAUGHTER.] You just watch—

THE STEP-DAUGHTER [*adding at once*]: How I shall play it, how I shall live it! . . .

LEADING LADY [*offended*]: I shall live it also, you may be sure, as soon as I begin!

THE MANAGER [*with his hands to his head*]: Ladies and gentlemen, if you please! No more useless discussions! Scene I: the young lady with Madame Pace: Oh! [*Looks around as if lost.*] And this Madame Pace, where is she?

THE FATHER: She isn't with us, sir.

THE MANAGER: Then what the devil's to be done?

THE FATHER: But she is alive too.

THE MANAGER: Yes, but where is she?

THE FATHER: One minute. Let me speak! [*Turning to the* ACTRESSES.] If these ladies would be so good as to give me their hats for a moment . . .

THE ACTRESSES [*half surprised, half laughing, in chorus*]: What?
Why?
Our hats?
What does he say?

THE MANAGER: What are you going to do with the ladies' hats? [*The* ACTORS *laugh.*]

THE FATHER: Oh nothing. I just want to put them on these pegs for a moment. And one of the ladies will be so kind as to take off her mantle . . .

THE ACTORS: Oh, what d'you think of that?
Only the mantle?
He must be mad.

SOME ACTRESSES: But why?
Mantles as well?

THE FATHER: To hang them up here for a moment. Please be so kind, will you?

THE ACTRESSES [*taking off their hats, one or two also their cloaks, and going to hang them on the racks*]: After all, why not?
There you are!
This is really funny.
We've got to put them on show.

THE FATHER: Exactly; just like that, on show.

THE MANAGER: May we know why?

THE FATHER: I'll tell you. Who knows if, by arranging the stage for her, she does not come here herself, attracted by the very articles of her trade? [*Inviting the* ACTORS *to look towards the exit at back of stage.*] Look! Look!

[*The door at the back of stage opens and* MADAME PACE *enters and takes a few steps forward. She is a fat, oldish woman with puffy oxygenated hair. She is rouged and powdered, dressed with a comical elegance in black silk. Round her waist is a long silver chain from which hangs a pair of scissors. The* STEP-DAUGHTER *runs over to her at once amid the stupor of the actors.*]

THE STEP-DAUGHTER [*turning towards her*]: There she is! There she is!

THE FATHER [*radiant*]: It's she! I said so, didn't I? There she is!

THE MANAGER [*conquering his surprise, and then becoming indignant*]: What sort of a trick is this?

LEADING MAN [*almost at the same time*]: What's going to happen next?

JUVENILE LEAD: Where does *she* come from?

L'INGÉNUE: They've been holding her in reserve, I guess.

LEADING LADY: A vulgar trick!

THE FATHER [*dominating the protests*]: Excuse me, all of you! Why are you so anxious to destroy in the name of a vulgar, commonplace sense of truth, this reality which comes to birth attracted and formed by the magic of the stage itself, which has indeed more right to live here than you, since it is much truer than you—if you don't mind my saying so? Which is the actress among you who is to play Madame Pace? Well, here is Madame Pace herself. And you will allow, I fancy, that the actress who acts her will be less true than this woman here, who is herself in person. You see my daughter recognized her and went over to her at once. Now you're going to witness the scene!

[*But the scene between the* STEP-DAUGHTER *and* MADAME PACE *has already begun despite the protest of the* ACTORS *and the reply of the* FATHER. *It has begun quietly, naturally, in a manner impossible for the stage. So when the actors, called to attention by the* FATHER, *turn round and see* MADAME PACE, *who has placed one hand under the* STEP-DAUGHTER'*s chin to raise her head, they observe her at first with great attention, but hearing her speak in an unintelligible manner their interest begins to wane.*]

THE MANAGER: Well? well?

LEADING MAN: What does she say?

LEADING LADY: One can't hear a word.

JUVENILE LEAD: Louder! Louder please!

THE STEP-DAUGHTER [*leaving* MADAME PACE, *who smiles a Sphinx-like smile, and advancing towards the* ACTORS]: Louder? Louder? What are you talking about? These aren't matters which can be shouted at the top of one's voice. If I have spoken them out loud, it was to shame him and have my revenge. [*Indicates* FATHER.] But for Madame it's quite a different matter.

THE MANAGER: Indeed? indeed? But here, you know, people have got to make themselves heard, my dear. Even we who are on the stage can't hear you. What will it be when the public's in the theatre? And anyway, you can very well speak up now among yourselves, since we shan't be present to listen to you as we are now. You've got to pretend to be alone in a room at the back of a shop where no one can hear you.

[*The* STEP-DAUGHTER *coquettishly and with a touch of malice makes a sign of disagreement two or three times with her finger.*]

THE MANAGER: What do you mean by no?

THE STEP-DAUGHTER [*sotto voce, mysteriously*]: There's someone who will hear us if she [*Indicating* MADAME PACE.] speaks out loud.

THE MANAGER [*in consternation*]: What? Have you got someone else to spring on us now? [*The* ACTORS *burst out laughing.*]

THE FATHER: No, no sir. She is alluding to me. I've got to be here—there behind that door, in waiting; and Madame Pace knows it. In fact, if you will allow me, I'll go there at once, so I can be quite ready. [*Moves away.*]

THE MANAGER [*stopping him*]: No! Wait! wait! We must observe the conventions of the theatre. Before you are ready . . .

THE STEP-DAUGHTER [*interrupting him*]: No, get on with it at once! I'm just dying, I tell you, to act this scene. If he's ready, I'm more than ready.

THE MANAGER [*shouting*]: But, my dear young lady, first of all, we must have the scene between you and this lady . . . [*Indicates* MADAME PACE.] Do you understand? . . .

THE STEP-DAUGHTER: Good Heavens! She's been telling me what you know already: that mamma's work is badly done again, that the material's ruined; and that if I want her to continue to help us in our misery I must be patient . . .

MADAME PACE [*coming forward with an air of great importance*]: Yes indeed, sir, I no wanta take advantage of her, I no wanta be hard . . .

[*Note.* MADAME PACE *is supposed to talk in a jargon half Italian, half English.*]

THE MANAGER [*alarmed*]: What? What? She talks like that? [*The* ACTORS *burst out laughing again.*]

THE STEP-DAUGHTER [*also laughing*]: Yes yes, that's the way she talks, half English, half Italian! Most comical it is!

MADAME PACE: Itta seem not verra polite gentlemen laugha atta me eef I trya best speaka English.

THE MANAGER: *Diamine!* Of course! Of course! Let her talk like that! Just what we want. Talk just like that, Madame, if you please! The effect will be certain. Exactly what was wanted to put a little comic relief into the crudity of the situation. Of course she talks like that! Magnificent!

THE STEP-DAUGHTER: Magnificent? Certainly! When certain suggestions are made to one in language of that kind, the effect is certain, since it seems almost a joke. One feels inclined to laugh when one hears her talk about an "old signore" "who wanta talka nicely with you." Nice old signore, eh, Madame?

MADAME PACE: Not so old my dear, not so old! And even if you no lika him, he won't make any scandal!

THE MOTHER [*jumping up amid the amazement and consternation of the actors who had not been noticing her.* THEY *move to restrain her*]: You old devil! You murderess!

THE STEP-DAUGHTER [*running over to calm her* MOTHER]: Calm yourself, Mother, calm yourself! Please don't . . .

THE FATHER [*going to her also at the same time*]: Calm yourself! Don't get excited! Sit down now!

THE MOTHER: Well then, take that woman away out of my sight!

THE STEP-DAUGHTER [*to* MANAGER]: It is impossible for my mother to remain here.

THE FATHER [*to* MANAGER]: They can't be here together. And for this reason, you see: that woman there was not with us when we came . . . If they are on together, the whole thing is given away inevitably, as you see.

THE MANAGER: It doesn't matter. This is only a first rough sketch—just to get an idea of the various points of the scene, even confusedly . . . [*Turning to the* MOTHER *and leading her to her chair.*] Come along, my dear lady, sit down now, and let's get on with the scene . . .

[*Meanwhile, the* STEP-DAUGHTER, *coming forward again, turns to* MADAME PACE.]

THE STEP-DAUGHTER: Come on, Madame, come on!

MADAME PACE [*offended*]: No, no, *grazie.* I not do anything witha your mother present.

THE STEP-DAUGHTER: Nonsense! Introduce this "old signore" who wants to talk nicely to me. [*Addressing the* COMPANY *imperiously.*] We've got to do this scene one way or another, haven't we? Come on! [*To* MADAME PACE.] You can go!

MADAME PACE: Ah yes! I go'way! I go'way! Certainly! [*Exits furious.*]

THE STEP-DAUGHTER [*to the* FATHER]: Now you make your entry. No, you needn't go over here. Come here. Let's suppose you've already come in. Like that, yes! I'm here with bowed head, modest like. Come on! Out with your voice! Say "Good morning, Miss" in that peculiar tone, that special tone . . .

THE MANAGER: Excuse me, but are you the Manager, or am I? [*To the* FATHER, *who looks undecided and perplexed.*] Get on with it, man! Go down there to the back of the stage. You needn't go off. Then come right forward here.

[The FATHER *does as he is told, looking troubled and perplexed at first. But as soon as he begins to move, the reality of the action affects him, and he begins to smile and to be more natural. The* ACTORS *watch intently.*]

THE MANAGER [*sotto voce, quickly to the* PROMPTER *in his box*]: Ready! ready? Get ready to write now.

THE FATHER [*coming forward and speaking in a different tone*]: Good afternoon, Miss!

THE STEP-DAUGHTER [*head bowed down slightly, with restrained disgust*]: Good afternoon!

THE FATHER [*looks under her hat which partly covers her face. Perceiving she is very young, he makes an exclamation, partly of surprise, partly of fear lest he compromise himself in a risky adventure*]: Ah . . . but . . . ah . . . I say . . . this is not the first time that you have come here, is it?

THE STEP-DAUGHTER [*modestly*]: No sir.

THE FATHER: You've been here before, eh? [*Then seeing her nod agreement.*] More than once? [*Waits for her to answer, looks under her hat, smiles, and then says.*] Well then, there's no need to be so shy, is there? May I take off your hat?

THE STEP-DAUGHTER [*anticipating him and with veiled disgust*]: No sir . . . I'll do it myself. [*Takes it off quickly.*]

[*The* MOTHER, *who watches the progress of the scene with the* SON *and the other two children who cling to her, is on thorns; and follows with varying expressions of sorrow, indignation, anxiety, and horror the words and actions of the other two. From time to time* SHE *hides her face in her hands and sobs.*]

THE MOTHER: Oh, my God, my God!

THE FATHER [*playing his part with a touch of gallantry*]: Give it to me! I'll put it down. [*Takes hat from her hands.*] But a dear little head like yours ought to have a smarter hat. Come and help me choose one from the stock, won't you?

L'INGÉNUE [*interrupting*]: I say . . . those are our hats you know.

THE MANAGER [*furious*]: Silence! silence! Don't try and be funny, if you please . . . We're playing the scene now I'd have you notice. [*To the* STEP-DAUGHTER.] Begin again, please!

THE STEP-DAUGHTER [*continuing*]: No thank you, sir.

THE FATHER: Oh, come now. Don't talk like that. You must take it. I shall be upset if you don't. There are some lovely little hats here; and then—Madame will be pleased. She expects it, anyway, you know.

THE STEP-DAUGHTER: No, no! I couldn't wear it!

THE FATHER: Oh, you're thinking about what they'd say at home if they saw you come in with a new hat? My dear girl, there's always a way round these little matters, you know.

THE STEP-DAUGHTER [*all keyed up*]: No, it's not that. I couldn't wear it because I am . . . as you see . . . you might have noticed . . . [*Showing her black dress.*]

THE FATHER: . . . in mourning! Of course: I beg your pardon: I'm frightfully sorry . . .

THE STEP-DAUGHTER [*forcing herself to conquer her indignation and nausea*]: Stop! Stop! It's I who must thank you. There's no need for you to feel mortified or specially sorry. Don't think any more of what I've said. [*Tries to smile.*] I must forget that I am dressed so . . .

THE MANAGER [*interrupting and turning to the* PROMPTER]: Stop a minute! Stop! Don't write that down. Cut out that last bit. [*Then to the* FATHER *and* STEP-DAUGHTER.] Fine! it's going fine! [*To the* FATHER *only.*] And now you can go on as we arranged. [*To the* ACTORS.] Pretty good that scene, where he offers her the hat, eh?

THE STEP-DAUGHTER: The best's coming now. Why can't we go on?

THE MANAGER: Have a little patience! [*To the* ACTORS.] Of course, it must be treated rather lightly.

LEADING MAN: Still, with a bit of go in it!

LEADING LADY: Of course! It's easy enough! [*To* LEADING MAN.] Shall you and I try it now?

LEADING MAN: Why, yes! I'll prepare my entrance. [*Exit in order to make his entrance.*]

THE MANAGER [*to* LEADING LADY]: See here! The scene between you and Madame Pace is finished. I'll have it written out properly after. You remain here . . . oh, where are you going?

LEADING LADY: One minute. I want to put my hat on again. [*Goes over to hat-rack and puts her hat on her head.*]

THE MANAGER: Good! You stay here with your head bowed down a bit.

THE STEP-DAUGHTER: But she isn't dressed in black.

LEADING LADY: But I shall be, and much more effectively than you.

THE MANAGER [*to* STEP-DAUGHTER]: Be quiet please, and watch! You'll be able to learn something. [*Clapping his hands.*] Come on! come on! Entrance, please!

[*The door at rear of stage opens, and the* LEADING MAN *enters with the lively manner of an old gallant. The rendering of the scene by the* ACTORS *from the very first words is seen to be quite a different thing, though it has not in any way the air of a parody. Naturally, the* STEP-DAUGHTER *and the* FATHER, *not being able to recognize themselves in the* LEADING LADY *and the* LEADING MAN, *who deliver their words in different tones and with a different psychology, express, sometimes with smiles, sometimes with gestures, the impression they receive.*]

LEADING MAN: Good afternoon, Miss . . .

THE FATHER [*at once unable to contain himself*]: No! no!

[*The* STEP-DAUGHTER *noticing the way the* LEADING MAN *enters, bursts out laughing.*]

THE MANAGER [*furious*]: Silence! And you please just stop that laughing. If we go on like this, we shall never finish.

THE STEP-DAUGHTER: Forgive me, sir, but it's natural enough. This lady [*Indicating* LEADING LADY.] stands there still; but if she is supposed to be me, I can assure you that if I heard anyone say "Good afternoon" in that manner and in that tone, I should burst out laughing as I did.

THE FATHER: Yes, yes, the manner, the tone . . .

THE MANAGER: Nonsense! Rubbish! Stand aside and let me see the action.

LEADING MAN: If I've got to represent an old fellow who's coming into a house of an equivocal character . . .

THE MANAGER: Don't listen to them, for Heaven's sake! Do it again! It goes fine. [*Waiting for the* ACTORS *to begin again.*] Well?

LEADING MAN: Good afternoon, Miss.

LEADING LADY: Good afternoon.

LEADING MAN [*imitating the gesture of the* FATHER *when he looked under the hat, and then expressing quite clearly first satisfaction and then fear*]: Ah, but . . . I say . . . this is not the first time that you have come here, is it?

THE MANAGER: Good, but not quite so heavily. Like this. [*Acts himself.*] "This isn't the first time that you have come here" . . . [*To* LEADING LADY.] And you say: "No, sir."

LEADING LADY: No, sir.

LEADING MAN: You've been here before, more than once.

THE MANAGER: No, no, stop! Let her nod "yes" first. "You've been here before, eh?" [*The* LEADING LADY *lifts up her head slightly and closes her eyes as though in disgust. Then* SHE *inclines her head twice.*]

THE STEP-DAUGHTER [*unable to contain herself*]: Oh my God! [*Puts a hand to her mouth to prevent herself from laughing.*]

THE MANAGER [*turning round*]: What's the matter?

THE STEP-DAUGHTER: Nothing, nothing!

THE MANAGER [*to* LEADING MAN]: Go on!

LEADING MAN: You've been here before, eh? Well then, there's no need to be so shy, is there? May I take off your hat?

[*The* LEADING MAN *says this last speech in such a tone and with such gestures that the* STEP-DAUGHTER, *though she has her hand to her mouth, cannot keep from laughing.*]

LEADING LADY [*indignant*]: I'm not going to stop here to be made a fool of by that woman there.

LEADING MAN: Neither am I! I'm through with it!

THE MANAGER [*shouting to* STEP-DAUGHTER]: Silence! for once and all, I tell you!

THE STEP-DAUGHTER: Forgive me! forgive me!

THE MANAGER: You haven't any manners: that's what it is! You go too far.

THE FATHER [*endeavouring to intervene*]: Yes, it's true, but excuse her . . .

THE MANAGER: Excuse what? It's absolutely disgusting.

THE FATHER: Yes, sir, but believe me, it has such a strange effect when . . .

THE MANAGER: Strange? Why strange? Where is it strange?

THE FATHER: No, sir; I admire your actors—this gentleman here, this lady; but they are certainly not us!

THE MANAGER: I should hope not. Evidently they cannot be you, if they are actors.

THE FATHER: Just so: actors! Both of them act our parts exceedingly well. But, believe me, it produces quite a different effect on us. They want to be us, but they aren't, all the same.

THE MANAGER: What is it then anyway?

THE FATHER: Something that is . . . that is theirs—and no longer ours . . .

THE MANAGER: But naturally, inevitably. I've told you so already.

THE FATHER: Yes, I understand . . . I understand . . .

THE MANAGER: Well then, let's have no more of it! [*Turning to the* ACTORS.] We'll have the rehearsals by ourselves, afterwards, in the ordinary way. I never could stand rehearsing with the author present. He's never satisfied! [*Turning to* FATHER *and* STEP-DAUGHTER.] Come on! Let's get on with it again; and try and see if you can't keep from laughing.

THE STEP-DAUGHTER: Oh, I shan't laugh any more. There's a nice little bit coming for me now: you'll see.

THE MANAGER: Well then: when she says "Don't think any more of what I've said. I must forget, etc.," you [*Addressing the* FATHER.] come in sharp with "I understand, I understand"; and then you ask her . . .

THE STEP-DAUGHTER [*interrupting*]: What?

THE MANAGER: Why she is in mourning.

THE STEP-DAUGHTER: Not at all! See here: when I told him that it was useless for me to be thinking about my wearing mourning, do you know how he answered me? "Ah well," he said, "then let's take off this little frock."

THE MANAGER: Great! Just what we want, to make a riot in the theatre!

THE STEP-DAUGHTER: But it's the truth!

THE MANAGER: What does that matter? Acting is our business here. Truth up to a certain point, but no further.

THE STEP-DAUGHTER: What do you want to do then?

THE MANAGER: You'll see, you'll see! Leave it to me.

THE STEP-DAUGHTER: No sir! What you want to do is to piece together a little romantic sentimental scene out of my disgust, out of all the reasons, each more cruel and viler than the other, why I am what I am. He is to ask me why I'm in mourning; and I'm to answer with tears in my eyes, that it is just two months since papa died. No sir, no! He's got to say to me; as he did say: "Well, let's take off this little dress at once." And I; with my two months' mourning in my heart, went there behind that screen, and with these fingers tingling with shame . . .

THE MANAGER [*running his hands through his hair*]: For Heaven's sake! What are you saying?

THE STEP-DAUGHTER [*crying out excitedly*]: The truth! The truth!

THE MANAGER: It may be. I don't deny it, and I can understand all your horror; but you must surely see that you can't have this kind of thing on the stage. It won't go.

THE STEP-DAUGHTER: Not possible, eh? Very well! I'm much obliged to you—but I'm off!

THE MANAGER: Now be reasonable! Don't lose your temper!

THE STEP-DAUGHTER: I won't stop here! I won't! I can see you've fixed it all up with him in your office. All this talk about what is possible for the stage . . . I understand! He wants to get at his complicated "cerebral drama," to have his famous remorses and torments acted; but I want to act my part, *my part!*

THE MANAGER [*annoyed, shaking his shoulders*]: Ah! Just *your* part! But, if you will pardon me, there are other parts than yours: His [*Indicating the* FATHER.] and hers! [*Indicating the* MOTHER.] On the stage you can't have a character becoming too prominent and overshadowing all the others. The thing is to pack them all into a neat little framework and then act what is actable. I am aware of the fact that everyone has his own interior life which he wants very much to put forward. But the difficulty lies in this fact: to set out just so much as is necessary for the stage, taking the other characters into consideration, and at the same time hint at the unrevealed interior life of each. I am willing to admit, my dear young lady, that from your point of view it would be a fine idea if each character could tell the public all his troubles in a nice monologue or a regular one hour lecture. [*Good humoredly.*] You must restrain yourself, my dear, and in your own interest, too; because this fury of yours, this exaggerated disgust you show, may make a bad impression, you know. After you have confessed to me that there were others before him at Madame Pace's and more than once . . .

THE STEP-DAUGHTER [*bowing her head, impressed*]: It's true. But remember those others mean him for me all the same.

THE MANAGER [*not understanding*]: What? The others? What do you mean?

THE STEP-DAUGHTER: For one who has gone wrong, sir, he who was responsible for the first fault is responsible for all that follow. He is responsible for my faults, was, even before I was born. Look at him, and see if it isn't true!

THE MANAGER: Well, well! And does the weight of so much responsibility seem nothing to you? Give him a chance to act it, to get it over!

THE STEP-DAUGHTER: How? How can he act all his "noble remorses," all his "moral torments," if you want to spare him the horror of being discovered one day—after he had asked her what he did ask her—in the arms of her, that already fallen woman, that child, sir, that child he used to watch come out of school! [SHE *is moved.*]

[*The* MOTHER *at this point is overcome with emotion, and breaks out into a fit of crying.* ALL *are touched. A long pause.*]

THE STEP-DAUGHTER [*as soon as the* MOTHER *becomes a little quieter, adds resolutely and gravely*]: At present, we are unknown to the public. Tomorrow, you will act us as you wish, treating us in your own manner. But do you really want to see drama, do you want to see it flash out as it really did?

THE MANAGER: Of course! That's just what I do want, so I can use as much of it as is possible.

THE STEP-DAUGHTER: Well then, ask that Mother there to leave us.

THE MOTHER [*changing her low plaint into a sharp cry*]: No! No! Don't permit it, sir, don't permit it!

THE MANAGER: But it's only to try it.

THE MOTHER: I can't bear it. I can't.

THE MANAGER: But since it has happened already . . . I don't understand!

THE MOTHER: It's taking place now. It happens all the time. My torment isn't a pretended one. I live and feel every minute of my torture. Those two children there—have you heard them speak? They can't speak any more. They cling to me to keep up my torment actual and vivid for me. But for themselves, they do not exist, they aren't any more. And she [*Indicating the* STEP-DAUGHTER.] has run away, she has left me, and is lost. If I now see her here before me, it is only to renew for me the tortures I have suffered for her too.

THE FATHER: The eternal moment! She [*Indicating the* STEP-DAUGHTER.] is here to catch me, fix me, and hold me eternally in the stocks for that one fleeting and shameful moment of my life. She can't give it up! And you sir, cannot either fairly spare me it.

THE MANAGER: I never said I didn't want to act it. It will form, as a matter of fact, the nucleus of the whole first act right up to her surprise. [*Indicates the* MOTHER.]

THE FATHER: Just so! This is my punishment: the passion in all of us that must culminate in her final cry.

THE STEP-DAUGHTER: I can hear it still in my ears. It's driven me mad, that cry!—You can put me on as you like; it doesn't matter. Fully dressed, if you like—provided I have at least the arm bare; because, standing like this [*She goes close to the* FATHER *and leans her head on his breast.*] with my head so, and my arms round his neck, I saw a vein pulsing in my arm here; and then, as if that live vein had awakened disgust in me, I closed my eyes like this, and let my head sink on his breast. [*Turning to the* MOTHER.] Cry out mother! Cry out! [*Buries head in* FATHER'*s breast, and with her shoulders raised as if to prevent her hearing the cry, adds in tones of intense emotion.*] Cry out as you did then!

THE MOTHER [*coming forward to separate them*]: No! My daughter, my daughter! [*And after having pulled her away from him.*] You brute! you brute! She is my daughter! Don't you see she's my daughter?

THE MANAGER [*walking backwards towards footlights*]: Fine! fine! Damned good! And then, of course—curtain!

THE FATHER [*going towards him excitedly*]: Yes, of course, because that's the way it really happened.

THE MANAGER [*convinced and pleased*]: Oh, yes, no doubt about it. Curtain here, curtain!

[*At the reiterated cry of the* MANAGER, *the* MACHINIST *lets the curtain down, leaving the* MANAGER *and the* FATHER *in front of it before the footlights.*]

THE MANAGER: The darned idiot! I said "curtain" to show the act should end there, and he goes and lets it down in earnest. [*To the* FATHER, *while he pulls the curtain back to go on to the stage again.*] Yes, yes, it's all right. Effect certain! That's the right ending. I'll guarantee the first act at any rate.

ACT III

When the curtain goes up again, it is seen that the stage hands have shifted the bit of scenery used in the last part, and have rigged up instead at the back of the stage a drop, with some trees, and one or two wings. A portion of a fountain basin is visible. The MOTHER *is sitting on the right with the two children by her side. The* SON *is on the same side, but away from the others. He seems bored, angry, and full of shame. The* FATHER *and the* STEP-DAUGHTER *are also seated towards the right front. On the other side (left) are the* ACTORS, *much in the positions they occupied before the curtain was lowered. Only the* MANAGER *is standing up in the middle of the stage, with his hand closed over his mouth in the act of meditating.*

THE MANAGER [*shaking his shoulders after a brief pause*]: Ah yes: the second act! Leave it to me, leave it all to me as we arranged, and you'll see! It'll go fine!

THE STEP-DAUGHTER: Our entry into his house [*Indicates* FATHER.] in spite of him . . . [*Indicates the* SON.]

THE MANAGER [*out of patience*]: Leave it to me, I tell you!

THE STEP-DAUGHTER: Do let it be clear, at any rate, that it is in spite of my wishes.

THE MOTHER [*from her corner, shaking her head*]: For all the good that's come of it . . .

THE STEP-DAUGHTER [*turning towards her quickly*]: It doesn't matter. The more harm done us, the more remorse for him.

THE MANAGER [*impatiently*]: I understand! Good Heavens! I understand! I'm taking it into account.

THE MOTHER [*supplicatingly*]: I beg you, sir, to let it appear quite plain that for conscience' sake I did try in every way . . .

THE STEP-DAUGHTER [*interrupting indignantly and continuing for the* MOTHER]: . . . to pacify me, to dissuade me from spiting him. [*To* MANAGER.] Do as she wants: satisfy her, because it is true! I enjoy it immensely. Anyhow, as you can see, the meeker she is, the more she tries to get at his heart, the more distant and aloof does be become.

THE MANAGER: Are we going to begin this second act or not?

THE STEP-DAUGHTER: I'm not going to talk any more now. But I must tell you this: you can't have the whole action take place in the garden, as you suggest. It isn't possible!

THE MANAGER: Why not?

THE STEP-DAUGHTER: Because he [*Indicates the* SON *again.*] is always shut up alone in his room. And then there's all the part of that poor dazed-looking boy there which takes place indoors.

THE MANAGER: Maybe! On the other hand, you will understand—we can't change scenes three or four times in one act.

THE LEADING MAN: They used to once.

THE MANAGER: Yes, when the public was up to the level of that child there.

THE LEADING LADY: It makes the illusion easier.

THE FATHER [*irritated*]: The illusion! For Heaven's sake, don't say illusion. Please don't use that word, which is particularly painful for us.

THE MANAGER [*astounded*]: And why, if you please?

THE FATHER: It's painful, cruel, really cruel; and you ought to understand that.

THE MANAGER: But why? What ought we to say then? The illusion, I tell you, sir, which we've got to create for the audience . . .

THE LEADING MAN: With our acting.

THE MANAGER: The illusion of a reality.

THE FATHER: I understand; but you, perhaps, do not understand us. Forgive me! You see . . . here for you and your actors, the thing is only—and rightly so . . . a kind of game . . .

THE LEADING LADY [*interrupting indignantly*]: A game! We're not children here, if you please! We are serious actors.

THE FATHER: I don't deny it. What I mean is the game, or play, of your art which has to give, as the gentleman says, a perfect illusion of reality.

THE MANAGER: Precisely—!

THE FATHER: Now, if you consider the fact that we [*Indicates himself and the other five* CHARACTERS.], as we are, have no other reality outside of this illusion . . .

THE MANAGER [*astonished, looking at his* ACTORS, *who are also amazed*]: And what does that mean?

THE FATHER [*after watching them for a moment with a wan smile*]: As I say, sir, that which is a game of art for you is our sole reality. [*Brief pause. He goes a step or two nearer the* MANAGER *and adds.*] But not only for us, you know, by the way. Just you think it over well. [*Looks him in the eyes.*] Can you tell me who you are?

THE MANAGER [*perplexed, half smiling*]: What? Who am I? I am myself.

THE FATHER: And if I were to tell you that that isn't true, because you and I . . . ?

THE MANAGER: I should say you were mad—! [*The* ACTORS *laugh.*]

THE FATHER: You're quite right to laugh: because we are all making believe here. [*To* MANAGER.] And you can therefore object that it's only for a joke that that gentleman there [*Indicates the* LEADING MAN.], who naturally is himself, has to be me, who am on the contrary myself—this thing you see here. You see I've caught you in a trap! [*The* ACTORS *laugh.*]

THE MANAGER [*annoyed*]: But we've had all this over once before. Do you want to begin again?

THE FATHER: No, no! That wasn't my meaning! In fact, I should like to request you to abandon this game of art [*Looking at the* LEADING LADY *as if anticipating her.*] which you are accustomed to play here with your actors, and to ask you seriously once again: who are you?

THE MANAGER [*astonished and irritated, turning to his* ACTORS]: If this fellow here hasn't got a nerve! A man who calls himself a character comes and asks me who I am!

THE FATHER [*with dignity, but not offended*]: A character, sir, may always ask a man who he is. Because a character has really a life of his own, marked with his especial characteristics; for which reason he is always "somebody." But a man—I'm not speaking of you now—may very well be "nobody."

THE MANAGER: Yes, but you are asking these questions of me, the boss, the manager! Do you understand?

THE FATHER: But only in order to know if you, as you really are now, see yourself as you once were with all the illusions that were yours then, with all the things both inside and outside of you as they seemed to you—as they were then indeed for you. Well, sir, if you think of all those illusions that mean nothing to you now, of all those things which don't even *seem* to you to exist any more, while once they *were* for you, don't you feel that—I won't say these boards—but the very earth under your feet is sinking away from you when you reflect that in the same way this *you* as you feel it today—all this present reality of yours—is fated to seem a mere illusion to you tomorrow?

THE MANAGER [*without having understood much, but astonished by the specious argument*]: Well, well! And where does all this take us anyway?

THE FATHER: Oh, nowhere! It's only to show you that if we [*Indicating the* CHARACTERS.] have no other reality beyond the illusion, you too must not count overmuch on your reality as you feel it today, since, like that of yesterday, it may prove an illusion for you tomorrow.

THE MANAGER [*determining to make fun of him*]: Ah, excellent! Then you'll be saying next that you, with this comedy of yours that you brought here to act, are truer and more real than I am.

THE FATHER [*with the greatest seriousness*]: But of course; without doubt!

THE MANAGER: Ah, really?

THE FATHER: Why, I though you'd understand that from the beginning.

THE MANAGER: More real than I?

THE FATHER: If your reality can change from one day to another . . .

THE MANAGER: But everyone knows it can change. It is always changing, the same as anyone else's.

THE FATHER [*with a cry*]: No, sir, not ours! Look here! That is the very difference! Our reality doesn't change: it can't change! It can't be other than what it is, because it is already fixed for ever. It's terrible. Our is an immutable reality which should make you shudder when you approach us if you are really conscious of the fact that your reality is a mere transitory and fleeting illusion, taking this form today and that tomorrow, according to the conditions, according to your will, your sentiments, which in turn are controlled by an intellect that shows them to you today in one manner and tomorrow . . . who knows how? . . . Illusions of reality represented in this fatuous comedy of life that never ends, nor can ever end! Because if tomorrow it were to end . . . then why, all would be finished.

THE MANAGER: Oh for God's sake, will you *at least* finish with this philosophizing and let us try and shape this comedy which you yourself have brought me here? You argue and philosophize a bit too much, my dear sir. You know you seem to me almost, almost . . . [*Stops and looks him over from head to foot.*] Ah, by the way, I think you introduced yourself to me as a—what shall . . . we say—a "character," created by an author who did not afterward care to make a drama of his own creations.

THE FATHER: It is the simple truth, sir.

THE MANAGER: Nonsense! Cut that out, please! None of us believes it, because it isn't a thing, as you must recognize yourself, which one can believe seriously. If you want to know, it seems to me you are trying to imitate the manner of a certain author whom I heartily detest—I warn you—although I have unfortunately bound myself to put on one of his works. As a matter of fact, I was just starting to rehearse it, when you arrived. [*Turning to the* ACTORS.] And this is what we've gained—out of the frying-pan into the fire!

THE FATHER: I don't know to what author you may be alluding, but believe me I feel what I think; and I seem to be philosophizing only for those who do not think what they feel, because they blind themselves with their own sentiment. I know that for many people this self-blinding seems much more "human"; but the contrary is really true. For man never reasons so much and becomes so introspective as when he suffers; since he is anxious to get at the cause of his sufferings, to learn who has produced them, and whether it is just or unjust that he should have to bear them. On the other hand, when he is happy, he takes his happiness as it comes and doesn't analyze it, just as if happiness were his right. The animals suffer without reasoning about their sufferings. But take the case of a man who suffers and begins to reason about it. Oh no! it can't be allowed! Let him suffer like an animal, and then—ah yet, he is "human"!

THE MANAGER: Look here! Look here! You're off again, philosophizing worse than ever.

THE FATHER: Because I suffer, sir! I'm not philosophizing: I'm crying aloud the reason of my sufferings.

THE MANAGER [*makes brusque movement as he is taken with a new idea*]: I should like to know if anyone has ever heard of a character who gets right out of his part and perorates and speechifies as you do. Have you ever heard of a case? I haven't.

THE FATHER: You have never met such a case, sir, because authors, as a rule, hide the labour of their creations. When the characters are really alive before their author, the latter does nothing but follow them in their action, in their words, in the situations which they suggest to him; and he has to will them the way they will themselves—for there's trouble if he doesn't. When a character is born, he acquires at once such an independence, even of his own author, that he can be imagined by everybody even in many other situations where the author never dreamed of placing him; and so he acquires for himself a meaning which the author never thought of giving him.

THE MANAGER: Yes, yes, I know this.

THE FATHER: What is there then to marvel at in us? Imagine such a misfortune for characters as I have described to you: to be born of an author's fantasy, and be denied life by him; and then answer me if these characters left alive, and yet without life, weren't right in doing what they did do and are doing now, after they have attempted everything in their power to persuade him to give them their stage life. We've all tried him in turn, I, she [*Indicating the* STEP-DAUGHTER.] and she. [*Indicating the* MOTHER.]

THE STEP-DAUGHTER: It's true. I too have sought to tempt him, many, many times, when he has been sitting at his writing table, feeling a bit melancholy, at the twillight hour. He would sit in his armchair too lazy to switch on the light, and all the shadows that crept into his room were full of our presence coming to tempt him. [*As if she saw herself still there by the writing table, and was annoyed by the presence of the* ACTORS.] Oh, if you would only go away, go away and leave us alone—mother here with that son of hers—I with that Child—that Boy there always alone—and then I with him [*Just hints at the* FATHER.] —and then I alone, alone . . . in those shadows! [*Makes a sudden movement as if in the vision she has of herself illuminating those shadows she wanted to seize hold of herself.*] Ah! my life! my life! Oh, what scenes we proposed to him—and I tempted him more than any of the others!

THE FATHER: Maybe. But perhaps it was your fault that he refused to give us life: because you were too insistent, too troublesome.

THE STEP-DAUGHTER: Nonsense! Didn't he make me so himself? [*Goes close to the* MANAGER *to tell him as if in confidence.*] In my opinion he abandoned us in a fit of depression, of disgust for the ordinary theatre as the public knows it and likes it.

THE SON: Exactly what it was, sir; exactly that!

THE FATHER: Not at all! Don't believe it for a minute. Listen to me! You'll be doing quite right to modify, as you suggest, the excesses both of this girl here, who wants to do too much, and of this young man, who won't do anything at all.

THE SON: No, nothing!

THE MANAGER: You too get over the mark occasionally, my dear sir, if I may say so.

THE FATHER: I? When? Where?

THE MANAGER: Always! Continuously! Then there's this insistence of yours in trying to make us believe you are a character. And then too, you must really argue and philosophize less, you know, much less.

THE FATHER: Well, if you want to take away from me the possibility of representing the torment of my sprirt which never gives me peace, you will be suppressing me: that's all. Every true man, sir, who is a little above the level of the beasts and plants does not live for the sake of living, without knowing how to live; but he lives so as to give a meaning and a value of his own to life. For me this is *everything*. I cannot give up this, just to represent a mere fact as she [*Indicating the* STEP-DAUGHTER.] wants. It's all very well for her, since her "vendetta" lies in the "fact." I'm not going to do it. It destroys my *raison d' être*.

THE MANAGER: Your *raison d'être!* Oh, we're going ahead fine! First she starts off, and then you jump in. At this rate, we'll never finish.

THE FATHER: Now, don't be offended! Have it your own way—provided, however, that within the limits of the parts you assign us each one's sacrifice isn't too great.

THE MANAGER: You've got to understand that you can't go on arguing at your own pleasure. Drama is action, sir, action and not confounded philosophy.

THE FATHER: All right. I'll do just as much arguing and philosophizing as everybody does when he is considering his own torments.

THE MANAGER: If the drama permits! But for Heaven's sake, man, let's get along and come to the scene.

THE STEP-DAUGHTER: It seems to me we've got too much action with our coming into his house. [*Indicating* FATHER.] You said, before, you couldn't change the scene every five minutes.

THE MANAGER: Of course not. What we've got to do is to combine and group up all the facts in one simultaneous, close-knit, action. We can't have it as you want, with your little brother wandering like a ghost from room to room, hiding behind doors and meditating a project which—what did you say it did to him?

THE STEP-DAUGHTER: Consumes him, sir, wastes him away!

THE MANAGER: Well, it may be. And then at the same time, you want the little girl there to be playing in the garden . . . one in the house, and the other in the garden: isn't that it?

THE STEP-DAUGHTER: Yes, in the sun, in the sun! That is my only pleasure: to see her happy and careless in the garden after the misery and squalor of the horrible room where we all four slept together. And I had to sleep with her—I, do you understand?—with my vile contaminated body next to hers; with her folding me fast in her loving little arms. In the garden, whenever she spied me, she would run to take me by the hand. She didn't care for the big flowers, only the little ones; and she loved to show me them and pet me.

THE MANAGER: Well, then, we'll have it in the garden. Everything shall happen in the garden; and we'll group the other scenes there. [*Calls a* STAGE HAND.] Here, a backcloth with trees and something to do as a fountain basin. [*Turning round to look at the back of the stage.*] Ah, you've fixed it up. Good! [*To* STEP-DAUGHTER.] This is just to give an idea, of course. The Boy, instead of hiding behind the doors, will wander about here in the garden, hiding behind the trees. But it's going to be rather difficult to find a child to do that scene with you where she shows you the flowers. [*Turning to the* BOY.] Come forward a little, will you please? Let's try it now! Come along! come along! [*Then seeing him come shyly forward, full of fear and looking lost.*] It's a nice business, this lad here. What's the matter with him? We'll have to give him a word or two to say. [*Goes close to him, puts a hand on his shoulders, and leads him behind one of the trees.*] Come on! come on! Let me see you a little! Hide here . . . yes, like that. Try and show your head just a little as if you were looking for someone . . . [*Goes back to observe the effect, when the* BOY *at once goes through the action.*] *Excellent! fine!* [*Turning to* STEP-DAUGHTER.] Suppose the little girl there were to surprise him as he looks round and run over to him, so we could give him a word or two to say?

THE STEP-DAUGHTER: It's useless to hope he will speak, as long as that fellow there is here . . . [*Indicates the* SON.] You must send him away first.

THE SON [*jumping up*]: Delighted! Delighted! I don't ask for anything better. [*Begins to move away.*]

THE MANAGER [*at once stopping him*]: No! No! Where are you going? Wait a bit!

[*The* MOTHER *gets up alarmed and terrified at the thought that he is really about to go away. Instinctively she lifts her arms to prevent him, without, however, leaving her seat.*]

THE SON [*to* MANAGER *who stops him*]: I've got nothing to do with this affair. Let me go please! Let me go!

THE MANAGER: What do you mean by saying you've got nothing to do with this?

THE STEP-DAUGHTER [*calmly, with irony*]: Don't bother to stop him: he won't go away.

THE FATHER: He has to act the terrible scene in the garden with his mother.

THE SON [*suddenly resolute and with dignity*]: I shall act nothing at all. I've said so from the very beginning. [*To the* MANAGER.] Let me go!

THE STEP-DAUGHTER [*going over to the* MANAGER]: Allow me? [*Puts down the* MANAGER'S *arm which is restraining the* SON.] Well, go away then, if you want to! [*The* SON *looks at her with contempt and hatred. She laughs and says*] You see, he can't, he can't go away! He is obliged to stay here, indissolubly bound to the chain. If I, who fly off when that happens which has to happen, because I can't bear him—if I am still here and support that face and expression of his, you can well imagine that he is unable to move. He has to remain here, has to stop with that nice father of his, and that mother whose only son he is. [*Turning to the* MOTHER.] Come on, mother, come along! [*Turning to* MANAGER *to indicate her.*] You see, she was getting up to keep him back. [*To the* MOTHER, *beckoning her with her hand.*] Come on! come on! [*Then to* MANAGER.] You can imagine how little she wants to show these actors of yours what she really feels; but so eager is she to get near him that . . . There, you see? She is willing to act her part. [*And in fact, the* MOTHER *approaches him; and as soon as the* STEP-DAUGHTER *has finished speaking, opens her arms to signify that she consents.*]

THE SON [*suddenly*]: No! no! If I can't go away, then I'll stop here; but I repeat: I act nothing!

THE FATHER [*to* MANAGER *excitedly*]: You can force him, sir.

THE SON: Nobody can force me.

THE FATHER: I can.

THE STEP-DAUGHTER: Wait a minute, wait . . . First of all, the baby has to go to the fountain . . . [*Runs to take the* CHILD *and leads her to the fountain.*]

THE MANAGER: Yes, yes of course; that's it. Both at the same time.

[*The second* LADY LEAD *and the* JUVENILE LEAD *at this point separate themselves from the group of* ACTORS. *One watches the* MOTHER *attentively; the other moves about studying the movements and manner of the* SON *whom he will have to act.*]

THE SON [*to* MANAGER]: What do you mean by both at the same time? It isn't right. There was no scene between me and her. [*Indicates the* MOTHER.] Ask her how it was!

THE MOTHER: Yes, it's true. I had come into his room . . .

THE SON: Into my room, do you understand? Nothing to do with the garden.

THE MANAGER: It doesn't matter. Haven't I told you we've got to group the action?

THE SON [*observing the* JUVENILE LEAD *studying him*]: What do you want?

THE JUVENILE LEAD: Nothing! I was just looking at you.

THE SON [*turning towards the second* LADY LEAD]: Ah! she's at it too: to re-act her part! [*Indicating the* MOTHER.]

THE MANAGER: Exactly! And it seems to me that you ought to be grateful to them for their interest.

THE SON: Yes, but haven't you yet perceived that it isn't possible to live in front of a mirror which not only freezes us with the image of ourselves, but throws our likeness back at us with a horrible grimace?

THE FATHER: That is true, absolutely true. You must see that.

THE MANAGER [*to second* LADY LEAD *and* JUVENILE LEAD]: He's right! Move away from them!

THE SON: Do as you like. I'm out of this!

THE MANAGER: Be quiet, you, will you? And let me hear your mother! [*To* MOTHER.] You were saying you had entered . . .

THE MOTHER: Yes, into his room, because I couldn't stand it any longer. I went to empty my heart to him of all the anguish that tortures me . . . But as soon as he saw me come in . . .

THE SON: Nothing happened! There was no scene. I went away, that's all! I don't care for scenes!

THE MOTHER: It's true, true. That's how it was.

THE MANAGER: Well now, we've got to do this bit between you and him. It's indispensable.

THE MOTHER: I'm ready . . . when you are ready. If you could only find a chance for me to tell him what I feel here in my heart.

THE FATHER [*going to* SON *in a great rage*]: You'll do this for your mother, for your mother, do you understand?

THE SON: [*quite determined*]: I do nothing!

THE FATHER [*taking hold of him and shaking him*]: For God's sake, do as I tell you! Don't you hear your mother asking you for a favor? Haven't you even got the guts to be a son?

THE SON [*taking hold of the* FATHER]: No! No! And for God's sake stop it, or else . . . [*General agitation. The* MOTHER, *frightened, tries to separate them.*]

THE MOTHER [*pleading*]: Please! please!

THE FATHER [*not leaving hold of the* SON]: You've got to obey, do you hear?

THE SON [*almost crying from rage*]: What does it mean, this madness you've got? [*They separate.*] Have you no decency, that you insist on showing everyone our shame? I won't do it! I won't! And I stand for the will of our author in this. He didn't want to put us on the stage, after all!

THE MANAGER: Man alive! You came here . . .

THE SON [*indicating* FATHER]: *He* did! I didn't!

THE MANAGER: Aren't you here now?

THE SON: It was his wish, and he dragged us along with him. He's told you not only the things that did happen, but also things that have never happened at all.

THE MANAGER: Well, tell me then what did happen. You went out of your room without saying a word?

THE SON: Without a word, so as to avoid a scene!

THE MANAGER: And then what did you do?

THE SON: Nothing . . . walking in the garden . . . [*Hesitates for a moment with expression of gloom.*]

THE MANAGER [*coming closer to him, interested by his extraordinary reserve*]: Well, well . . . walking in the garden . . .

THE SON [*exasperated*]: Why on earth do you insist? It's horrible! [*The* MOTHER *trembles, sobs, and looks towards the fountain.*]

THE MANAGER: [*slowly observing the glance and turning towards the* SON *with increasing apprehension*]: The baby?

THE SON: There in the fountain . . .

THE FATHER [*pointing with tender pity to the* MOTHER]: She was following him at the moment . . .

THE MANAGER [*to the* SON *anxiously*]: And then you . . .

THE SON: I ran over to her; I was jumping in to drag her out when I saw something that froze my blood . . . the boy standing stock still, with eyes like a madman's, watching his little drowned sister, in the fountain! [*The* STEP-DAUGHTER *bends over the fountain to hide the* CHILD. *She sobs.*] Then . . . [*A revolver shot rings out behind the trees where the* BOY *is hidden.*]

THE MOTHER [*with a cry of terror runs over in that direction together with several of the* ACTORS *amid general confusion*]: My son! My son! [*Then amid the cries and exclamations one hears her voice.*] Help! Help!

THE MANAGER [*pushing the* ACTORS *aside while they lift up the* BOY *and carry him off*]: Is he really wounded?

SOME ACTORS: He's dead! dead!

OTHER ACTORS: No, no, it's only make believe, it's only pretence!

THE FATHER [*with a terrible cry*]: Pretence? Reality, sir, reality!

THE MANAGER: Pretence? Reality? To hell with it all! Never in my life has such a thing happened to me. I've lost a whole day over these people, a whole day!

CURTAIN

JOHN MILLINGTON SYNGE

Edmund John Millington Synge (1871–1909) was born near Dublin into a well-to-do Anglo-Irish family. The last of five children, he was raised by his widowed mother, Kathleen Synge, a staunch Protestant, who was usually disturbed by his erratic behavior and particularly disapproving when her "poor Johnnie" rejected religion at sixteen. Synge was impressed with Darwinism and held that religion was theological mysticism; given his lifelong penchant for making shocking statements, however, Synge's rejection of religion may have been more of a rebellion against authority than a true philosophical belief. Synge's first choice for a career was to be a classical musician, which also displeased his mother, but when he turned to literature, she was even more appalled.

Synge's antipathy toward established authority sometimes caused him to be called a traitor to his class, and he felt little sympathy for the values of the middle class. He lamented the decline of values of modern Irish culture, but he found the true spirit of life, which he called "joy," in the Irish peasantry. In order to get closer to the peasantry and the old values, Synge studied Gaelic and Celtic at Trinity College and later at the Sorbonne in Paris. He had an ear for local Irish speech, but his characters generally speak a kind of earthy peasant dialect that is more poetic than accurate. With characteristic impishness, Synge made his characters converse in old-fashioned, even archaic, idioms and phrases. When he was later attacked for his depictions of the Irish peasantry, Synge defended himself by claiming that what he wrote about Irish country life was based on his own "true" observations and imbued with admiration.

After he graduated from Trinity in Dublin, Synge studied music and violin at the Royal Irish Academy and later in Germany, but he gave this up because he realized that he did not have the talent. He moved to Paris to study French literature in 1894, returned to Dublin, then traveled to Italy. Unlike James Joyce (1882–1941), his contemporary, who rebelled against the strictures of Irish life and became a writer in self-imposed exile, Synge returned to Ireland to make his reputation at a time when the Irish nationalists were fighting for independence from Britain. He briefly joined the Irish League, a nationalistic political organization, along with his compatriot William Butler Yeats (1865–1939), with whom he established a firm personal and professional friendship. Yeats, however, had a zealous interest in politics, while Synge's nationalism was primarily cultural and artistic. He was actively engaged in the Irish literary renaissance, and in 1902 he was a founder of the Irish National Theatre (now the Abbey Theatre) in Dublin, along with Yeats and with Lady Augusta Gregory (1852–1932), patron and playwright.

To understand the real Ireland and its peasantry, Synge made many visits to the isolated Aran Islands, a group of small rocky islands off the west coast of Ireland at the mouth of Galway Bay. These islands and the people who lived there are the subject of his book-length essay *The Aran Islands*, illustrated by Jack Yeats, Ireland's most renowned painter and brother of William Butler Yeats. *The Aran Islands* was completed in 1902 but not published until 1907, after Synge's reputation was established. Gathering the material for *The Aran Islands* was a seminal episode in Synge's artistic life and influenced most of his plays.

As early as his mid-twenties, Synge was suffering from Hodgkin's disease, a malignant disease of the lymph glands and spleen, which contributed to his death at age thirty-eight. This period of illness coincides with the most intense period of his creativity and professional literary life.

Synge's plays offered an unvarnished, unsentimental depiction of the Irish peasantry, and they opened to mixed praise and condemnation. Many among his nationalistic middle-class audience took criticism of Irish life, even the peasantry, as an attack on themselves. *In the Shadow of the Glen* (1902), his first play, was condemned as a universal attack on Irish women and motherhood, though it was intended as a satiric jab at the Irish middle class. It is a one-act play about Dan Burke, an old man whose attempt to test his wife's fidelity backfires. Instead of remaining true, Nora Burke runs off with a smooth-talking tramp. There is also a possibility that the play is a spoof of Henrik Ibsen's problem plays, which Synge thought were dreary. Ibsen's Nora, in *A Doll's House*, finds independence but does not betray her husband sexually. Synge's Nora is more earthy and does not suffer from Ibsen's Nordic seriousness.

Riders to the Sea (1904), a short play about the ritual of death and mourning, written when Synge was thirty-one, signified the playwright's realization of his own mortality, no doubt fueled by his Hodgkin's disease. *Riders to the Sea* portrays the hardship of peasant fishing life on the Aran Islands, a place where the men live dangerously at the mercy of the cruel sea, and the women keep home and family, tragically spending too much time mourning their dead men. Maurya mourns her husband and four dead sons. The last one alive is Bartley, but Maurya has a premonition that he will surely die soon. As Bartley leaves to sail to the mainland, news is brought that the body of his brother Michael, who was lost at sea, has been found and identified. The play is a tragedy in miniature, exalting the women of Aran, who face death with grief and nobility.

The Well of the Saints (1905) was panned by many of Synge's contemporaries as a caricature of the Irish. It is a satire about Martin and Mary Doul, two blind beggars, who are told by the cynical townspeople that they are beautiful, though they are in fact ugly. When Martin and Mary are visited by a saint and have their sight miraculously restored, they lose their happiness, for Martin now sees that he has an ugly wife, and he moves away from her. He tries to seduce the beautiful Molly Byrne, but she shames him. When the saint gives a second wish to the Douls, they prefer to become blind again. In their blindness they take solace and are relatively happy because they can imagine the world and themselves as they want them to be.

The Tinker's Wedding (1908), produced posthumously in 1909, was severely criticized because of its unflattering portrayal of a Catholic priest. The story was based on a tale that Synge heard in Aran, which he adapted for the stage, knowing that it would outrage his predominantly Irish-Catholic audience. The story is this: After many years of living together and having children, Sarah

Casey decides to have the tinker Michael Byrne marry her. Trouble comes when the mercenary priest refuses to let them marry in the church because they do not have the money to pay for it. After coming to a financial agreement, the priest marries Sarah and Michael, who promise to pay him after the ceremony. Of course, the priest is duped, and the sack containing his payment is filled with empty beer bottles. Synge's sardonic comedy was calculated to offend his Catholic audience, and he was not disappointed.

Deirdre of the Sorrows (1910) is a story taken from Irish mythology concerning Conchubor, the king of Ulster, who kills the youthful Deirdre because she leaves him for a younger man, Naisi. Conchubor commits this treacherous act of vengeance even though he knows that a prophecy tells that he will suffer for it. The name Deirdre means sorrow, or the troubler, and Synge was aware of the pun in his title. The play was unfinished at Synge's death and produced posthumously. Mollie Allgood, the great love of Synge's life and his fiancée, directed and starred as Deirdre.

The Playboy of the Western World (1907) is Synge's most accomplished play. Like the others, it satirizes the Irish character and culture, but this time in the guise of a mock Greek tragedy. In Sophocles' play, Oedipus seeks to escape his destiny of killing his father, Laius, but does so unknowingly and suffers dire consequences. Synge's story concerns Christopher (Christy) Mahon, a callow youth of twenty-one, who claims that he killed his father, Mahon, in a fit of anger. When he brags of his deed, Christy is taken up by local townspeople and treated as a celebrity. Life is so uneventful in this small village in County Mayo that even patricide makes for welcome news. In turn, Christy is fought over by Pegeen Mike, the barkeep's daughter, and the lascivious Widow Quin. Pegeen is even willing to throw over her fiancé, Shawn Keogh, for the love of this hero. As Act I ends, Christy is almost ecstatic with his good luck, and he says to Pegeen, "May God and Mary and St Patrick bless you and reward you for your kindly talk. [*She shuts the door behind her. He settles his bed slowly, feeling the quilt with immense satisfaction.*] Well, it's a clean bed and soft with it, and it's great luck and company I've won me in the end of time—two fine women fighting for the likes of me—till I'm thinking this night wasn't I a foolish fellow not to kill my father in the years gone by."

In Act II, Christy's celebrity and his romantic love life are threatened when his father, Mahon, very much alive, appears. Fearing disclosure, Christy appeals to Widow Quin for help: "Where'll I hide my poor body from that ghost of hell?" She complies, thinking that this will serve her will in the quest for marrying Christy, and sends Mahon off on a wild-goose chase. When Christy comes out from hiding, she says to him, "Well, you're the walking Playboy of the Western World, and that's the poor man you had divided to his breeches belt." In near despair, Christy listens to Widow Quin's blackmail: "If I aid you, will you swear to give me a right of way I want, and a mountainy ram, and a load of dung at Michaelmas, the time that you'll be master here?" Agreeing out of fear of disgrace, Christy is carried off by adoring girls to ride in the mule races, a sly allusion to medieval tournaments at arms and meant to remind the audience that this is humble fare.

Act III substitutes the horror of Oedipus's deed and the recognition of his guilt with satiric comedy aimed at the Irish and their fickleness of character. Instead of Oedipus's tormented search for the murderer of his father, Christy escapes confronting his father. Just as the race is about to start, Mahon returns to the pub after his unsuccessful search, and while he talks with the farmers and Widow Quin, the sounds of the crowd cheering for Christy are heard in the distance. Mahon watches with interest and for a moment thinks that the champion is Christy, but the Widow Quin holds him back and together they stand on a bench watching the race and cheering until Christy wins.

When Christy is carried in triumph to the pub, Mahon recognizes him, but Widow Quin gets him to believe that he is seeing things:

> MAHON: Then the blight of the sacred drouth upon myself and him, for I never went mad to this day. . . . Is my visage astray?
> WIDOW QUIN: It is then. You're a sniggering maniac, a child could see.

So, taking his leave without making a scene, Mahon departs. Flushed with pride and bravado, Christy asks Pegeen to marry him, even though she is engaged to Shawn. She radiantly replies, "If that's the truth I'll be burning candles from this out to the miracles of God that have brought you from the south to-day, and I with my gowns bought ready, the way that I can wed you, and not wait at all." When Michael, Pegeen's father, supports her fiancé, Pegeen urges Shawn to fight for her. Shawn, fearful of Christy's threat, "Take yourself from this, young fellow, or I'll maybe add a murder to my deeds to-day," runs in terror. Just as Michael is about to give his blessing to Pegeen and Christy, Mahon, Widow Quin, and a crowd rush in. Christy denies the old man, but he is subdued by the crowd. Pegeen, who declared that she would never renege her pledge to Christy, drops him: "That's it, now the world will see him pandied, and he an ugly liar was playing the off hero, and the fright of men." The crowd shouts jeeringly, "There's the playboy! There's the lad thought he'd rule the roost in Mayo! Slate him now, mister." Christy looks to the Widow Quin for help, but she says that she cannot. Pegeen, furious, shouts to Mahon to take Christy away. But now face to face, the son and the father seem about to fight, and the crowd gleefully cheers them on:

> MAHON [*Making a grab at* CHRISTY.]: Come here to me.
> CHRISTY [*More threateningly.*]: Leave me go, I'm saying.
> MAHON: I will, maybe, when your legs is limping, and your back is blue.
> CROWD: Keep it up, the two of you.

As Christy and Mahon fight, Christy chases his father and hits him again. Believing him to be dead, the crowd vows to hang Christy. Taking pity on him, Widow Quin tries again to woo him, but Christy says that he still prefers Pegeen. Hastily, Christy is draped in a petticoat, an insult to his manhood. Left alone when Widow Quin goes for help, Pegeen and the crowd rush in and drop a noose around Christy's neck. As the crowd ineptly drags Christy from the room to hang him, he struggles (less than manfully) by holding onto a chair leg for dear life. In the midst of this tumult, Mahon appears and, grimly loosening

Christy, says, "My son and myself will be going our own way, and we'll have great times from this out telling stories of the villainy of Mayo, and the fools is here." Christy, chagrined but in high spirits, cries out, "Ten thousand blessings upon all that's here, for you've turned me a likely gaffer in the end of all, the way I'll go romancing through a romping lifetime from this hour to the dawning of the Judgement Day." Realizing that she will now have to wed a silly man, Pegeen boxes Shawn on the ear and laments, "Oh my grief, I've lost him surely. I've lost the only Playboy of the Western World."

The Western World in the title refers to the west of Ireland, in rural County Mayo where the action takes place. When Synge capitalizes the word, he is also leveling criticism at Western civilization in its broadest sense. On the opening night of *The Playboy of the Western World* at the Abbey Theatre, members of the audience, many of whom were Catholic and political nationalists and aware of Synge's previous satires, were openly hostile to the satire. They were rowdy and called out pejoratively. Yeats called the police in order to keep things from getting out of hand that night. Succeeding performances were also treated with disrespect, but the play attracted audiences and was a success. The day after the premiere in January 1907, Synge wrote to Molly Allgood, "I feel like old Maurya [the mother who loses her sons in *Riders to the Sea*] today. 'It's four fine plays I have, though it was a hard birth I had with everyone of them and they coming into the world.'"

After Synge's death, Yeats continued to support his literary reputation, though his plays were seldom produced in Ireland. Synge's work was sporadically produced in England, however, where George Bernard Shaw was among his chief advocates. In the early 1960s Synge was rediscovered and brought to prominence again, even in Ireland. Synge's influence is most important in the development of Irish drama, particularly the work of Sean O'Casey, Brendan Behan, Brian Friel, and, most recently, Martin McDonagh.

Film

The Playboy of the Western World (1962), directed by Brian Desmond Hurst, with Siobhan McKenna and Gary Raymond.

The Playboy of the Western World

PREFACE

In writing "The Playboy of the Western World," as in my other plays, I have used one or two words only that I have not heard among the country people of Ireland, or spoken in my own nursery before I could read the newspapers. A certain number of the phrases I employ I have heard also from herds and fishermen along the coast from Kerry to Mayo or from beggar-women and ballad-singers nearer Dublin; and I am glad to acknowledge how much I owe to the folk-imagination of these fine people. Any one who has lived in real intimacy with the Irish peasantry will know that the wildest sayings and ideas in this play are tame indeed, compared with the fancies one may hear in any little hillside cabin in Geesala, or Carraroe, or Dingle Bay. All art is a collaboration; and there is little doubt that in the happy ages of literature, striking and beautiful phrases were as ready to the story-teller's or the playwright's hand, as the rich cloaks and dresses of his time. It is probable that when the Elizabethan dramatist took his ink-horn and sat down to his work he used many phrases that he had just heard, as he sat at dinner, from his mother or his children. In Ireland, those of us who know the people have the same privilege. When I was writing "The Shadow of the Glen," some years ago, I got more aid than any learning could have given me from a chink in the floor of the old Wicklow house where I was staying, that let me hear what was being said by the servant girls in the kitchen. This matter, I think, is of importance, for in countries where the imagination of the people, and the language they use, is rich and living, it is possible for a writer to be rich and copious in his words, and at the same time to give the reality, which is the root of all poetry, in a comprehensive and natural form. In the modern literature of towns, however, richness is found only in sonnets, or prose poems, or in one or two elaborate books that are far away from the profound and common interests of life. One has, on one side, Mallarmé and Huysmans producing this literature; and on the other, Ibsen and Zola dealing with the reality of life in joyless and pallid works. On the stage one must have reality, and one must have joy; and that is why the intellectual modern drama has failed, and people have grown sick of the false joy of the musical comedy, that has been given them in place of the rich joy found only in what is superb and wild in reality. In a good play every speech should be as fully flavoured as a nut or apple, and such speeches cannot be written by any one who works among people who have shut their lips on poetry. In Ireland, for a few years more, we have a popular imagination that is fiery, and magnificent, and tender; so that those of us who wish to write start with a chance that is not given to writers in places where the springtime of the local life has been forgotten, and the harvest is a memory only, and the straw has been turned into bricks.

J. M. S.
21st January 1907.

PERSONS IN THE PLAY

CHRISTOPHER MAHON
OLD MAHON, his father, a squatter
MICHAEL JAMES FLAHERTY [called MICHAEL JAMES], a publican
MARGARET FLAHERTY [called PEGEEN MIKE], his daughter
WIDOW QUIN, a woman of about thirty
SHAWN KEOGH, her cousin, a young farmer
PHILLY CULLEN AND JIMMY FARRELL, small farmers
SARA TANSEY, SUSAN BRADY, AND HONOR BLAKE, village girls
A BELLMAN
SOME PEASANTS

The action takes place near a village, on a wild coast of Mayo. The first Act passes on an evening of autumn, the other two Acts on the following day.

ACT I

Country public house or shebeen, very rough and untidy. There is a sort of counter on the right with shelves, holding many bottles and jugs, just seen above it. Empty barrels stand near the counter. At back, a little to left of counter, there is a door into the open air, then, more to the left, there is a settle with shelves above it, with more jugs, and a table beneath a window. At the left there is a large open fire-place, with turf fire, and a small door into inner room. PEGEEN, *a wild-looking but fine girl, of about twenty, is writing at table. She is dressed in the usual peasant dress.*

PEGEEN [*Slowly as she writes.*]: Six yards of stuff for to make a yellow gown. A pair of lace boots with lengthy heels on them and brassy eyes. A hat is suited for a wedding-day. A fine-tooth comb. To be sent with three barrels of porter in Jimmy Farrell's creel cart on the evening of the coming Fair to Mister Michael James Flaherty. With the best compliments of this season. Margaret Flaherty.

SHAWN KEOGH [*A fat and fair young man comes in as she signs, looks around awkwardly, when he sees she is alone.*]: Where's himself?

PEGEEN [*Without looking at him.*]: He's coming. [*She directs letter.*] To Mister Sheamus Mulroy, Wine and Spirit Dealer, Castlebar.

SHAWN [*Uneasily.*]: I didn't see him on the road.

PEGEEN: How would you see him [*licks stamp and puts it on letter*] and it dark night this half-hour gone by?

SHAWN [*Turning towards door again.*]: I stood a while outside wondering would I have a right to pass on or to walk in and see you, Pegeen Mike [*comes to fire*], and I could hear the cows breathing and sighing in the stillness of the air, and not a step moving any place from this gate to the bridge.

PEGEEN [*Putting letter in envelope.*]: It's above at the crossroads he is, meeting Philly Cullen and a couple more are going along with him to Kate Cassidy's wake.

SHAWN [*Looking at her blankly.*]: And he's going that length in the dark night.

PEGEEN [*Impatiently.*]: He is surely, and leaving me lonesome on the scruff of the hill. [*She gets up and*

Burgess Meredith, Mildred Natwick, and Eithne Dunne in The Playboy of the Western World, *directed by Guthrie McClintic, the Booth Theatre, New York, 1946.*

puts envelope on dresser, then winds clock.] Isn't it long the nights are now, Shawn Keogh, to be leaving a poor girl with her own self counting the hours to the dawn of day?

SHAWN [*With awkward humour.*]: If it is, when we're wedded in a short while you'll have no call to complain, for I've little will to be walking off to wakes or weddings in the darkness of the night.

PEGEEN [*With rather scornful good humour.*]: You're making mighty certain, Shaneen, that I'll wed you now.

SHAWN: Aren't we after making a good bargain, the way we're only waiting these days on Father Reilly's dispensation from the bishops, or the Court of Rome.

PEGEEN [*Looking at him teasingly, washing up at dresser.*]: It's a wonder, Shaneen, the Holy Father'd be taking notice of the likes of you; for if I was him I wouldn't bother with this place where you'll meet none but Red Linahan, has a squint in his eye, and Patcheen is lame in his heel, or the mad Mulrannies were driven from California and they lost in their wits. We're a queer lot these times to go troubling the Holy Father on his sacred seat.

SHAWN [*Scandalized.*]: If we are, we're as good this place as another, maybe, and as good these times as we were for ever.

PEGEEN [*With scorn.*]: As good is it? Where now will you meet the like of Daneen Sullivan knocked the eye from a peeler; or Marcus Quin, God rest him, got six months for maiming ewes, and he a great warrant to tell stories of holy Ireland till he'd have the old women shedding down tears about their feet. Where will you find the like of them, I'm saying?

SHAWN [*Timidly.*]: If you don't, it's a good job, maybe; for [*with peculiar emphasis on the words*] Father Reilly has small conceit to have that kind walking around and talking to the girls.

PEGEEN [*Impatiently throwing water from basin out of the door.*]: Stop tormenting me with Father Reilly [*imitating his voice*] when I'm asking only what way I'll pass these twelve hours of dark, and not take my death with the fear.

[*Looking out of door.*]

SHAWN [*Timidly.*]: Would I fetch you the Widow Quin, maybe?

PEGEEN: Is it the like of that murderer? You'll not, surely.

SHAWN [*Going to her, soothingly.*]: Then I'm thinking himself will stop along with you when he sees you taking on; for it'll be a long night-time with great darkness, and I'm after feeling a kind of fellow above in the furzy ditch, groaning wicked like a maddening dog, the way it's good cause you have, maybe, to be fearing now.

PEGEEN [*Turning on him sharply.*]: What's that? Is it a man you seen?

SHAWN [*Retreating.*]: I couldn't see him at all; but I heard him groaning out, and breaking his heart. It should have been a young man from his words speaking.

PEGEEN [*Going after him.*]: And you never went near to see was he hurted or what ailed him at all?

SHAWN: I did not, Pegeen Mike. It was a dark, lonesome place to be hearing the like of him.

PEGEEN: Well, you're a daring fellow, and if they find his corpse stretched above in the dews of dawn, what'll you say then to the peelers, or the Justice of the Peace?

SHAWN [*Thunderstruck.*]: I wasn't thinking of that. For the love of God, Pegeen Mike, don't let on I was speaking of him. Don't tell your father and the men is coming above; for if they heard that story they'd have great blabbing this night at the wake.

PEGEEN: I'll maybe tell them, and I'll maybe not.

SHAWN: They are coming at the door. Will you whisht, I'm saying?

PEGEEN: Whisht yourself.

[*She goes behind counter.* MICHAEL JAMES, *fat, jovial publican, comes in followed by* PHILLY CULLEN, *who is thin and mistrusting, and* JIMMY FARRELL, *who is fat and amorous, about forty-five.*]

MEN [*Together.*]: God bless you! The blessing of God on this place!

PEGEEN: God bless you kindly.

MICHAEL [*To* MEN, *who go to the counter.*]: Sit down now, and take your rest. [*Crosses to* SHAWN *at the fire.*] And how is it you are, Shawn Keogh? Are you coming over the sands to Kate Cassidy's wake?

SHAWN: I am not, Michael James. I'm going home the short cut to my bed.

PEGEEN [*Speaking across the counter.*]: He's right, too, and have you no shame, Michael James, to be quitting off for the whole night, and leaving myself lonesome in the shop?

MICHAEL [*Good-humouredly.*]: Isn't it the same whether I go for the whole night or a part only? and I'm thinking it's a queer daughter you are if you'd have me crossing backward through the Stooks of the Dead Women, with a drop taken.

PEGEEN: If I am a queer daughter, it's a queer father'd be leaving me lonesome these twelve hours of dark, and I piling the turf with the dogs barking, and the calves mooing, and my own teeth rattling with the fear.

JIMMY [*Flatteringly.*]: What is there to hurt you, and you a fine, hardy girl would knock the head of any two men in the place?

PEGEEN [*Working herself up.*]: Isn't there the harvest boys with their tongues red for drink, and the ten tinkers is camped in the east glen, and the thousand militia—bad cess to them!—walking idle through the land. There's lots surely to hurt me, and I won't stop alone in it, let himself do what he will.

MICHAEL: If you're that afeard, let Shawn Keogh stop along with you. It's the will of God, I'm thinking, himself should be seeing to you now. [*They all turn on* SHAWN.]

SHAWN [*In horrified confusion.*]: I would and welcome, Michael James, but I'm afeard of Father Reilly; and what at all would the Holy Father and the Cardinals of Rome be saying if they heard I did the like of that?

MICHAEL [*With contempt.*]: God help you! Can't you sit in by the hearth with the light lit and herself beyond in the room? You'll do that surely, for I've heard tell there's a queer fellow above, going mad or getting his death, maybe, in the gripe of the ditch, so she'd be safer this night with a person here.

SHAWN [*With plaintive despair.*]: I'm afeard of Father Reilly, I'm saying. Let you not be tempting me, and we near married itself.

PHILLY [*With cold contempt.*]: Lock him in the west room. He'll stay then and have no sin to be telling to the priest.

MICHAEL [*To* SHAWN, *getting between him and the door.*]: Go up now.

SHAWN [*At the top of his voice.*]: Don't stop me, Michael James. Let me out of the door, I'm saying, for the love of the Almighty God. Let me out. [*Trying to dodge past him.*] Let me out of it, and may God grant you His indulgence in the hour of need.

MICHAEL [*Loudly.*]: Stop your noising, and sit down by the hearth. [*Gives him a push and goes to counter laughing.*]

SHAWN [*Turning back, wringing his hands.*]: Oh, Father Reilly, and the saints of God, where will I hide myself to-day? Oh, St Joseph and St Patrick and St Brigid and St James, have mercy on me now!

[SHAWN *turns round, sees door clear, and makes a rush for it.*]

MICHAEL [*Catching him by the coat-tail.*]: You'd be going, is it?

SHAWN [*Screaming.*]: Leave me go, Michael James, leave me go, you old Pagan, leave me go, or I'll get the curse of the priests on you, and of the scarlet-coated bishops of the Courts of Rome.

[*With a sudden movement he pulls himself out of his coat, and disappears out of the door, leaving his coat in* MICHAEL'*s hands.*]

MICHAEL [*Turning round, and holding up coat.*]: Well, there's the coat of a Christian man. Oh, there's sainted glory this day in the lonesome west; and by the will of God I've got you a decent man, Pegeen, you'll have no call to be spying after if you've a score of young girls, maybe, weeding in your fields.

PEGEEN [*Taking up the defence of her property.*]: What right have you to be making game of a poor fellow for minding the priest, when it's your own the fault is, not paying a penny pot-boy to stand along with me and give me courage in the doing of my work.

[*She snaps the coat away from him, and goes behind counter with it.*]

MICHAEL [*Taken aback.*]: Where would I get a pot-boy? Would you have me send the bell-man screaming in the streets of Castlebar?

SHAWN [*Opening the door a chink and putting in his head, in a small voice.*]: Michael James!

MICHAEL [*Imitating him.*]: What ails you?

SHAWN: The queer dying fellow's beyond looking over the ditch. He's come up, I'm thinking, stealing your hens. [*Looks over his shoulder.*] God help me, he's following me now [*he runs into room*], and if he's heard what I said, he'll be having my life, and I going home lonesome in the darkness of the night.

[*For a perceptible moment they watch the door with curiosity. Someone coughs outside. Then* CHRISTY MAHON, *a slight young man, comes in very tired and frightened and dirty.*]

CHRISTY [*In a small voice.*]: God save all here!

MEN: God save you kindly!

CHRISTY [*Going to the counter.*]: I'd trouble you for a glass of porter, woman of the house. [*He puts down coin.*]

PEGEEN [*Serving him.*]: You're one of the tinkers, young fellow, is beyond camped in the glen?

CHRISTY: I am not; but I'm destroyed walking.

MICHAEL [*Patronizingly.*]: Let you come up then to the fire. You're looking famished with the cold.

CHRISTY: God reward you. [*He takes up his glass and goes a little way across to the left, then stops and looks about him.*] Is it often the polis do be coming into this place, master of the house?

MICHAEL: If you'd come in better hours, you'd have seen 'Licensed for the Sale of Beer and Spirits, to be Consumed on the Premises,' written in white letters above the door, and what would the polis want spying on me, and not a decent house within four miles, the way every living Christian is a bona fide, saving one widow alone?

CHRISTY [*With relief.*]: It's a safe house, so.

[*He goes over to the fire, sighing and moaning. Then he sits down, putting his glass beside him, and begins gnawing a turnip, too miserable to feel the others staring at him with curiosity.*]

MICHAEL [*Going after him.*]: Is it yourself is fearing the polis? You're wanting, maybe?
CHRISTY: There's many wanting.
MICHAEL: Many, surely, with the broken harvest and the ended wars. [*He picks up some stockings, etc., that are near the fire, and carries them away furtively.*] It should be larceny, I'm thinking?
CHRISTY [*Dolefully.*]: I had it in my mind it was a different word and a bigger.
PEGEEN: There's a queer lad. Were you never slapped in school, young fellow, that you don't know the name of your deed?
CHRISTY [*Bashfully.*]: I'm slow at learning, a middling scholar only.
MICHAEL: If you're a dunce itself, you'd have a right to know that larceny's robbing and stealing. Is it for the like of that you're wanting?
CHRISTY [*With a flash of family pride.*]: And I the son of a strong farmer [*with a sudden qualm*], God rest his soul, could have bought up the whole of your old house a while since, from the butt of his tail-pocket, and not have missed the weight of it gone.
MICHAEL [*Impressed.*]: If it's not stealing, it's maybe something big.
CHRISTY [*Flattered.*]: Aye; it's maybe something big.
JIMMY: He's a wicked-looking young fellow. Maybe he followed after a young woman on a lonesome night.
CHRISTY [*Shocked.*]: Oh, the saints forbid, mister; I was all times a decent lad.
PHILLY [*Turning on* JIMMY.]: You're a silly man, Jimmy Farrell. He said his father was a farmer a while since, and there's himself now in a poor state. Maybe the land was grabbed from him, and he did what any decent man would do.
MICHAEL [*To* CHRISTY, *mysteriously.*]: Was it bailiffs?
CHRISTY: The divil a one.
MICHAEL: Agents?
CHRISTY: The divil a one.
MICHAEL: Landlords?
CHRISTY [*Peevishly.*]: Ah, not at all, I'm saying. You'd see the like of them stories on any little paper of a Munster town. But I'm not calling to mind any person, gentle, simple, judge or jury, did the like of me.

[*They all draw nearer with delighted curiosity.*]

PHILLY: Well, that lad's a puzzle-the-world.
JIMMY: He'd beat Dan Davies's circus, or the holy missioners making sermons on the villainy of man. Try him again, Philly.
PHILLY: Did you strike golden guineas out of solder, young fellow, or shilling coins itself?
CHRISTY: I did not, mister, not sixpence nor a farthing coin.
JIMMY: Did you marry three wives maybe? I'm told there's a sprinkling have done that among the holy Luthers of the preaching north.
CHRISTY [*Shyly.*]: I never married with one, let alone with a couple or three.
PHILLY: Maybe he went fighting for the Boers, the like of the man beyond, was judged to be hanged, quartered, and drawn. Were you off east, young fellow, fighting bloody wars for Kruger and the freedom of the Boers?
CHRISTY: I never left my own parish till Tuesday was a week.
PEGEEN [*Coming from counter.*]: He's done nothing, so. [*To* CHRISTY.] If you didn't commit murder or a bad, nasty thing; or false coining, or robbery, or butchery, or the like of them, there isn't anything that would be worth your troubling for to run from now. You did nothing at all.
CHRISTY [*His feelings hurt.*]: That's an unkindly thing to be saying to a poor orphaned traveller, has a prison behind him, and hanging before, and hell's gap gaping below.
PEGEEN [*With a sign to the men to be quiet.*]: You're only saying it. You did nothing at all. A soft lad the like of you wouldn't slit the wind pipe of a screeching sow.
CHRISTY [*Offended.*]: You're not speaking the truth.
PEGEEN [*In mock rage.*]: Not speaking the truth, is it? Would you have me knock the head of you with the butt of the broom?
CHRISTY [*Twisting round on her with a sharp cry of horror.*]: Don't strike me. I killed my poor father, Tuesday was a week, for doing the like of that.
PEGEEN [*With blank amazement.*]: Is it killed your father?
CHRISTY [*Subsiding.*]: With the help of God I did, surely, and that the Holy Immaculate Mother may intercede for his soul.
PHILLY [*Retreating with* JIMMY.]: There's a daring fellow.
JIMMY: Oh, glory be to God!
MICHAEL [*With great respect.*]: That was a hanging crime, mister honey. You should have had good reason for doing the like of that.
CHRISTY [*In a very reasonable tone.*]: He was a dirty man, God forgive him, and he getting old and crusty, the way I couldn't put up with him at all.
PEGEEN: And you shot him dead?

CHRISTY [*Shaking his head.*]: I never used weapons. I've no licence, and I'm a law-fearing man.

MICHAEL: It was with a hilted knife maybe? I'm told, in the big world, it's bloody knives they use.

CHRISTY [*Loudly, scandalized.*]: Do you take me for a slaughter-boy?

PEGEEN: You never hanged him, the way Jimmy Farrell hanged his dog from the licence, and had it screeching and wriggling three hours at the butt of a string, and himself swearing it was a dead dog, and the peelers swearing it had life?

CHRISTY: I did not, then. I just riz the loy and let fall the edge of it on the ridge of his skull, and he went down at my feet like an empty sack, and never let a grunt or groan from him at all.

MICHAEL [*Making a sign to* PEGEEN *to fill* CHRISTY'*s glass.*]: And what way weren't you hanged, mister? Did you bury him then?

CHRISTY [*Considering.*]: Aye. I buried him then. Wasn't I digging spuds in the field?

MICHAEL: And the peelers never followed after you the eleven days that you're out?

CHRISTY [*Shaking his head.*]: Never a one of them, and I walking forward facing hog, dog, or divil on the highway of the road.

PHILLY [*Nodding wisely.*]: It's only with a common weekday kind of a murderer them lads would be trusting their carcass, and that man should be a great terror when his temper's roused.

MICHAEL: He should then. [*To* CHRISTY.] And where was it, mister honey, that you did the deed?

CHRISTY [*Looking at him with suspicion.*]: Oh, a distant place, master of the house, a windy corner of high, distant hills.

PHILLY [*Nodding with approval.*]: He's a close man, and he's right, surely.

PEGEEN: That'd be a lad with the sense of Solomon to have for a pot-boy, Michael James, if it's the truth you're seeking one at all.

PHILLY: The peelers is fearing him, and if you'd that lad in the house there isn't one of them would come smelling around if the dogs itself were lapping poteen from the dung-pit of the yard.

JIMMY: Bravery's a treasure in a lonesome place, and a lad would kill his father, I'm thinking, would face a foxy divil with a pitchpike on the flags of hell.

PEGEEN: It's the truth they're saying, and if I'd that lad in the house, I wouldn't be fearing the loos'ed khaki cutthroats, or the walking dead.

CHRISTY [*Swelling with surprise and triumph.*]: Well, glory be to God!

MICHAEL [*With deference*]: Would you think well to stop here and be pot-boy, mister honey, if we gave you good wages, and didn't destroy you with the weight of work.

SHAWN [*Coming forward uneasily.*]: That'd be a queer kind to bring into a decent, quiet household with the like of Pegeen Mike.

PEGEEN [*Very sharply.*]: Will you whisht? Who's speaking to you?

SHAWN [*Retreating.*]: A bloody-handed murderer the like of . . .

PEGEEN [*Snapping at him.*]: Whisht, I am saying; we'll take no fooling from your like at all. [*To* CHRISTY, *with a honeyed voice.*] And you, young fellow, you'd have a right to stop, I'm thinking, for we'd do our all and utmost to content your needs.

CHRISTY [*Overcome with wonder.*]: And I'd be safe this place from the searching law?

MICHAEL: You would, surely. If they're not fearing you, itself, the peelers in this place is decent, drouthy poor fellows, wouldn't touch a cur dog and not give warning in the dead of night.

PEGEEN [*Very kindly and persuasively.*]: Let you stop a short while anyhow. Aren't you destroyed walking with your feet in bleeding blisters, and your whole skin needing washing like a Wicklow sheep.

CHRISTY [*Looking round with satisfaction.*]: It's a nice room, and if it's not humbugging me you are, I'm thinking that I'll surely stay.

JIMMY [*Jumps up.*]: Now, by the grace of God, herself will be safe this night, with a man killed his father holding danger from the door, and let you come on, Michael James, or they'll have the best stuff drunk at the wake.

MICHAEL [*Going to the door with men.*]: And begging your pardon, mister, what name will we call you, for we'd like to know?

CHRISTY: Christopher Mahon.

MICHAEL: Well, God bless you, Christy, and a good rest till we meet again when the sun'll be rising to the noon of day.

CHRISTY: God bless you all.

MEN: God bless you.

[*They go out, except* SHAWN, *who lingers at the door.*]

SHAWN [*To* PEGEEN.]: Are you wanting me to stop along with you and keep you from harm?

PEGEEN [*Gruffly.*]: Didn't you say you were fearing Father Reilly?

SHAWN: There'd be no harm staying now, I'm thinking, and himself in it too.

PEGEEN: You wouldn't stay when there was need for you, and let you step off nimble this time when there's none.

SHAWN: Didn't I say it was Father Reilly . . .

PEGEEN: Go on, then, to Father Reilly [*in a jeering tone*], and let him put you in the holy brotherhoods, and leave that lad to me.

SHAWN: If I meet the Widow Quin . . .

PEGEEN: Go on, I'm saying, and don't be waking this place with your noise. [*She hustles him out and bolts door.*] That lad would wear the spirits from the saints of peace. [*Bustles about, then takes off her apron and pins it up in the window as a blind,* CHRISTY *watching her timidly. Then she comes to him and speaks with bland good humour.*] Let you stretch out now by the fire, young fellow. You should be destroyed travelling.

CHRISTY [*Shyly again, drawing off his boots.*]: I'm tired surely, walking wild eleven days, and waking fearful in the night.

[*He holds up one of his feet, feeling his blisters, and looking at them with compassion.*]

PEGEEN [*Standing beside him, watching him with delight.*]: You should have had great people in your family, I'm thinking, with the little, small feet you have, and you with a kind of a quality name, the like of what you'd find on the great powers and potentates of France and Spain.

CHRISTY [*With pride.*]: We were great, surely, with wide and windy acres of rich Munster land.

PEGEEN: Wasn't I telling you, and you a fine, handsome young fellow with a noble brow?

CHRISTY [*With a flush of delighted surprise.*]: Is it me?

PEGEEN: Aye. Did you never hear that from the young girls where you come from in the west or south?

CHRISTY [*With venom.*]: I did not, then. Oh, they're bloody liars in the naked parish where I grew a man.

PEGEEN: If they are itself, you've heard it these days, I'm thinking, and you walking the world telling out your story to young girls or old.

CHRISTY: I've told my story no place till this night, Pegeen Mike, and it's foolish I was here, maybe, to be talking free; but you're decent people, I'm thinking, and yourself a kindly woman, the way I wasn't fearing you at all.

PEGEEN [*Filling a sack with straw.*]: You've said the like of that, maybe, in every cot and cabin where you've met a young girl on your way.

CHRISTY [*Going over to her, gradually raising his voice.*]: I've said it nowhere till this night, I'm telling you; for I've seen none the like of you the eleven long days I am walking the world, looking over a low ditch or a high ditch on my north or south, into stony, scattered fields, or scribes of bog, where you'd see young, limber girls, and fine, prancing women making laughter with the men.

PEGEEN: If you weren't destroyed travelling, you'd have as much talk and streeleen, I'm thinking, as Owen Roe O'Sullivan or the poets of the Dingle Bay; and I've heard all times it's the poets are your like—fine, fiery fellows with great rages when their temper's roused.

CHRISTY [*Drawing a little nearer to her.*]: You've a power of rings, God bless you, and would there be any offence if I was asking are you single now?

PEGEEN: What would I want wedding so young?

CHRISTY [*With relief.*]: We're alike so.

PEGEEN [*She puts sack on settle and beats it up.*]: I never killed my father. I'd be afeard to do that, except I was the like of yourself with blind rages tearing me within, for I'm thinking you should have had great tussling when the end was come.

CHRISTY [*Expanding with delight at the first confidential talk he has ever had with a woman.*]: We had not then. It was a hard woman was come over the hill; and if he was always a crusty kind, when he'd a hard woman setting him on, not the divil himself or his four fathers could put up with him at all.

PEGEEN [*With curiosity.*]: And isn't it a great wonder that one wasn't fearing you?

CHRISTY [*Very confidentially.*]: Up to the day I killed my father, there wasn't a person in Ireland knew the kind I was, and I there drinking, waking, eating, sleeping, a quiet, simple poor fellow with no man giving me heed.

PEGEEN [*Getting a quilt out of cupboard and putting it on the sack.*]: It was the girls were giving you heed, maybe, and I'm thinking it's most conceit you'd have to be gaming with their like.

CHRISTY [*Shaking his head, with simplicity.*]: Not the girls itself, and I won't tell you a lie. There wasn't any one heeding me in that place saving only the dumb beasts of the field. [*He sits down at fire.*]

PEGEEN [*With disappointment.*]: And I thinking you should have been living the like of a king of Norway or the eastern world.

[*She comes and sits beside him after placing bread and mug of milk on the table.*]

CHRISTY [*Laughing piteously.*]: The like of a king, is it? And I after toiling, moiling, digging, dodging from the dawn till dusk; with never a sight of joy or sport saving only when I'd be abroad in the dark night poaching rabbits on hills, for I was a divil to poach, God forgive me [*very naïvely*], and I near got six months for going with a dung fork and stabbing a fish.

PEGEEN: And it's that you'd call sport, is it, to be abroad in the darkness with yourself alone?

CHRISTY: I did, God help me, and there I'd be as happy as the sunshine of St Martin's Day, watching the light passing the north or the patches of fog, till I'd hear a rabbit starting to screech and I'd go running in the furze. Then, when I'd my full share, I'd come walking down where you'd see the ducks and geese stretched sleeping on the highway of the road, and before I'd pass the dunghill, I'd hear himself snoring out—a loud, lonesome snore he'd be making all times, the while he was sleeping; and he a man'd be raging all times, the while he was waking, like a gaudy officer you'd hear cursing and damning and swearing oaths.

PEGEEN: Providence and Mercy, spare us all!

CHRISTY: It's that you'd say surely if you seen him and he after drinking for weeks, rising up in the red dawn, or before it maybe, and going out into the yard as naked as an ash-tree in the moon of May, and shying clods against the visage of the stars till he'd put the fear of death into the banbhs and the screeching sows.

PEGEEN: I'd be well-nigh afeard of that lad myself, I'm thinking. And there was no one in it but the two of you alone?

CHRISTY: The divil a one, though he'd sons and daughters walking all great states and territories of the world, and not a one of them, to this day, but would say their seven curses on him, and they rousing up to let a cough or sneeze, maybe, in the deadness of the night.

PEGEEN [*Nodding her head.*]: Well, you should have been a queer lot. I never cursed my father the like of that, though I'm twenty and more years of age.

CHRISTY: Then you'd have cursed mine, I'm telling you, and he a man never gave peace to any, saving when he'd get two months or three, or be locked in the asylums for battering peelers or assaulting men [*with depression*], the way it was a bitter life he led me till I did up a Tuesday and halve his skull.

PEGEEN [*Putting her hand on his shoulder.*]: Well, you'll have peace in this place, Christy Mahon, and none to trouble you, and it's near time a fine lad like you should have your good share of the earth.

CHRISTY: It's time surely, and I a seemly fellow with great strength in me and bravery of . . .

[*Someone knocks.*]

CHRISTY [*Clinging to* PEGEEN.]: Oh, glory! it's late for knocking, and this last while I'm in terror of the peelers, and the walking dead.

[*Knocking again.*]

PEGEEN: Who's there?

VOICE [*Outside.*]: Me.

PEGEEN: Who's me?

VOICE: The Widow Quin.

PEGEEN [*Jumping up and giving him the bread and milk.*]: Go on now with your supper, and let on to be sleepy, for if she found you were such a warrant to talk, she'd be stringing gabble till the dawn of day.

[*He takes bread and sits shyly with his back to the door.*]

PEGEEN [*Opening door, with temper.*]: What ails you, or what is it you're wanting at this hour of the night?

WIDOW QUIN [*Coming in a step and peering at* CHRISTY.]: I'm after meeting Shawn Keogh and Father Reilly below, who told me of your curiosity man, and they fearing by this time he was maybe roaring, romping on your hands with drink.

PEGEEN [*Pointing to* CHRISTY.]: Look now is he roaring, and he stretched out drowsy with his supper and his mug of milk. Walk down and tell that to Father Reilly and to Shaneen Keogh.

WIDOW QUIN [*Coming forward.*]: I'll not see them again, for I've their word to lead that lad forward for to lodge with me.

PEGEEN [*In blank amazement.*]: This night is it?

WIDOW QUIN [*Going over.*]: This night. "It isn't fitting," says the priesteen, "to have his likeness lodging with an orphaned girl." [*To* CHRISTY.] God save you, mister!

CHRISTY [*Shyly.*]: God save you kindly!

WIDOW QUIN [*Looking at him with half amused curiosity.*]: Well, aren't you a little smiling fellow? It should have been great and bitter torments did rouse your spirits to a deed of blood.

CHRISTY [*Doubtfully.*]: It should, maybe.

WIDOW QUIN: It's more than "maybe" I'm saying, and it'd soften my heart to see you sitting so simple with your cup and cake, and you fitter to be saying your catechism than slaying your da.

PEGEEN [*At counter, washing glasses.*]: There's talking when any'd see he's fit to be holding his head high with the wonders of the world. Walk on from this, for I'll not have him tormented, and he destroyed travelling since Tuesday was a week.

WIDOW QUIN [*Peaceably.*]: We'll be walking surely when his supper's done, and you'll find we're great company, young fellow, when it's of the like of you and me you'd hear the penny poets singing in an August Fair.

CHRISTY [*Innocently.*]: Did you kill your father?

PEGEEN [*Contemptuously.*]: She did not. She hit himself with a worn pick, and the rusted poison did corrode his blood the way he never overed it, and died after. That was a sneaky kind of murder did win small glory with the boys itself.

[*She crosses to* CHRISTY'*s left.*]

WIDOW QUIN [*With good humour.*]: If it didn't, maybe all knows a widow woman has buried her children and destroyed her man is a wiser comrade for a young lad than a girl, the like of you, who'd go helter-skeltering after any man would let you a wink upon the road.

PEGEEN [*Breaking out into wild rage.*]: And you'll say that, Widow Quin, and you gasping with the rage you had racing the hill beyond to look on his face.

WIDOW QUIN [*Laughing derisively.*]: Me, is it? Well, Father Reilly has cuteness to divide you now. [*She pulls* CHRISTY *up.*] There's great temptation in a man did slay his da, and we'd best be going, young fellow; so rise up and come with me.

PEGEEN [*Seizing his arm.*]: He'll not stir. He's pot-boy in this place, and I'll not have him stolen off and kidnapped while himself's abroad.

WIDOW QUIN: It'd be a crazy pot-boy'd lodge him in the shebeen where he works by day, so you'd have a right to come on, young fellow, till you see my little houseen, a perch off on the rising hill.

PEGEEN: Wait till morning, Christy Mahon. Wait till you lay eyes on her leaky thatch is growing more pasture for her buck goat than her square of fields, and she without a tramp itself to keep in order her place at all.

WIDOW QUIN: When you see me contriving in my little gardens, Christy Mahon, you'll swear the Lord God formed me to be living lone, and that there isn't my match in Mayo for thatching, or mowing, or shearing a sheep.

PEGEEN [*With noisy scorn.*]: It's true the Lord God formed you to contrive indeed. Doesn't the world know you reared a black ram at your own breast, so that the Lord Bishop of Connaught felt the elements of a Christian, and he eating it after in a kidney stew? Doesn't the world know you've been seen shaving the foxy skipper from France for a threepenny-bit and a sop of grass tobacco would wring the liver from a mountain goat you'd meet leaping the hills?

WIDOW QUIN [*With amusement.*]: Do you hear her now, young fellow? Do you hear the way she'll be rating at your own self when a week is by?

PEGEEN [*To* CHRISTY.]: Don't heed her. Tell her to go on into her pigsty and not plague us here.

WIDOW QUIN: I'm going; but he'll come with me.

PEGEEN [*Shaking him.*]: Are you dumb, young fellow?

CHRISTY [*Timidly to* WIDOW QUIN.]: God increase you; but I'm pot-boy in this place, and it's here I liefer stay.

PEGEEN [*Triumphantly.*]: Now you have heard him, and go on from this.

WIDOW QUIN [*Looking round the room.*]: It's lonesome this hour crossing the hill, and if he won't come along with me, I'd have a right maybe to stop this night with yourselves. Let me stretch out on the settle, Pegeen Mike; and himself can lie by the hearth.

PEGEEN [*Short and fiercely.*]: Faith, I won't. Quit off or I will send you now.

WIDOW QUIN [*Gathering her shawl up.*]: Well, it's a terror to be aged a score. [*To* CHRISTY.] God bless you now, young fellow, and let you be wary, or there's right torment will await you here if you go romancing with her like, and she waiting only, as they bade me say, on a sheepskin parchment to be wed with Shawn Keogh of Killakeen.

CHRISTY [*Going to* PEGEEN *as she bolts door.*]: What's that she's after saying?

PEGEEN: Lies and blather, you've no call to mind. Well, isn't Shawn Keogh an impudent fellow to send up spying on me? Wait till I lay hands on him. Let him wait, I'm saying.

CHRISTY: And you're not wedding him at all?

PEGEEN: I wouldn't wed him if a bishop came walking for to join us here.

CHRISTY: That God in glory may be thanked for that.

PEGEEN: There's your bed now. I've put a quilt upon you I'm after quilting a while since with my own two hands, and you'd best stretch out now for your sleep, and may God give you a good rest till I call you in the morning when the cocks will crow.

CHRISTY [*As she goes to inner room.*]: May God and Mary and St Patrick bless you and reward you for your kindly talk. [*She shuts the door behind her. He settles his bed slowly, feeling the quilt with immense satisfaction.*] Well, it's a clean bed and soft with it, and it's great luck and company I've won me in the end of time—two fine women fighting for the likes of me—till I'm thinking this night wasn't I a foolish fellow not to kill my father in the years gone by.

CURTAIN

ACT II

Scene as before. Brilliant morning light. CHRISTY, *looking bright and cheerful, is cleaning a girl's boots.*

CHRISTY [*To himself, counting jugs on dresser.*]: Half a hundred beyond. Ten there. A score that's above. Eighty jugs. Six cups and a broken one. Two plates. A power of glasses. Bottles, a schoolmaster'd be hard set to count, and enough in them, I'm thinking, to drunken all the wealth and wisdom of the county Clare. [*He puts down the boot *carefully.*] There's her boots now, nice and decent for her evening use, and isn't it grand brushes she has? [*He puts them down and goes by degrees to the looking-glass.*] Well, this'd be a fine place to be my whole life talking out with swearing Christians, in place of my old dogs and cat; and I stalking around, smoking my pipe and drinking my fill, and never a day's work but drawing a cork an odd time, or wiping a glass, or rinsing out a shiny tumbler for a decent man. [*He takes the looking-glass from the wall and puts it on the back of a chair; then sits down in front of it and begins washing his face.*] Didn't I know rightly, I was handsome, though it was the divil's own mirror we had beyond, would twist a squint across an angel's brow; and I'll be growing fine from this day, the way I'll have a soft lovely skin on me and won't be the like of the clumsy young fellows do be ploughing all times in the earth and dung. [*He starts.*] Is she coming again? [*He looks out.*] Stranger girls. God help me, where'll I hide myself away and my long neck naked to the world? [*He looks out.*] I'd best go to the room maybe till I'm dressed again.

[*He gathers up his coat and the looking-glass, and runs into the inner room. The door is pushed open, and* SUSAN BRADY *looks in, and knocks on door.*]

SUSAN: There's nobody in it.

[*Knocks again.*]

NELLY [*Pushing her in and following her, with* HONOR BLAKE *and* SARA TANSEY.]: It'd be early for them both to be out walking the hill.

SUSAN: I'm thinking Shawn Keogh was making game of us, and there's no such man in it at all.

HONOR [*Pointing to straw and quilt.*]: Look at that. He's been sleeping there in the night. Well, it'll be a hard case if he's gone off now, the way we'll never set our eyes on a man killed his father, and we after rising early and destroying ourselves running fast on the hill.

NELLY: Are you thinking them's his boots?

SARA [*Taking them up.*]: If they are, there should be his father's track on them. Did you never read in the papers the way murdered men do bleed and drip?

SUSAN: Is that blood there, Sara Tansey?

SARA [*Smelling it.*]: That's bog water, I'm thinking; but it's his own they are, surely, for I never seen the like of them for whitey mud, and red mud, and turf on them, and the fine sands of the sea. That man's been walking, I'm telling you.

[*She goes down right, putting on one of his boots.*]

SUSAN [*Going to window.*]: Maybe he's stolen off to Belmullet with the boots of Michael James, and you'd have a right so to follow after him, Sara Tansey, and you the one yoked the ass-cart and drove ten miles to set your eyes on the man bit the yellow lady's nostril on the northern shore. [*She looks out.*]

SARA [*Running to window, with one boot on.*]: Don't be talking, and we fooled to-day. [*Putting on the other boot.*] There's a pair do fit me well and I'll be keeping them for walking to the priest, when you'd be ashamed this place, going up winter and summer with nothing worth while to confess at all.

HONOR [*Who has been listening at door.*]: Whisht! there's someone inside the room. [*She pushes door a chink open.*] It's a man.

[SARA *kicks off boots and puts them where they were. They all stand in a line looking through chink.*]

SARA: I'll call him. Mister! Mister! [*He puts in his head.*] Is Pegeen within?

CHRISTY [*Coming in as meek as a mouse, with the looking-glass held behind his back.*]: She's above on the cnuceen, seeking the nanny goats, the way she'd have a sup of goats' milk for to colour my tea.

SARA: And asking your pardon, is it you's the man killed his father?

CHRISTY [*Sidling toward the nail where the glass was hanging.*]: I am, God help me!

SARA [*Taking eggs she has brought.*]: Then my thousand welcomes to you, and I've run up with a brace of duck's eggs for your food to-day. Pegeen's ducks is no use, but these are the real rich sort. Hold out your hand and you'll see it's no lie I'm telling you.

CHRISTY [*Coming forward shyly, and holding out his left hand.*]: They're a great and weighty size.

SUSAN: And I run up with a pat of butter, for it'd be a poor thing to have you eating your spuds dry, and you after running a great way since you did destroy your da.

CHRISTY: Thank you kindly.

HONOR: And I brought you a little cut of a cake, for you should have a thin stomach on you, and you that length walking the world.

NELLY: And I brought you a little laying pullet—boiled and all she is—was crushed at the fall of night by the curate's car. Feel the fat of the breast, mister.

CHRISTY: It's bursting, surely.

[*He feels it with the back of his hand, in which he holds the presents.*]

SARA: Will you pinch it? Is your right hand too sacred for to use at all? [*She slips round behind him.*] It's a glass he has. Well, I never seen to this day a man with a looking-glass held to his back. Them that kills their fathers is a vain lot surely.

[*Girls giggle.*]

CHRISTY [*Smiling innocently and piling presents on glass.*]: I'm very thankful to you all to-day. . . .

WIDOW QUIN [*Coming in quickly, at door.*]: Sara Tanşey, Susan Brady, Honor Blake! What in glory has you here at this hour of day?

GIRLS [*Giggling.*]: That's the man killed his father.

WIDOW QUIN [*Coming to them.*]: I know well it's the man; and I'm after putting him down in the sports below for racing, leaping, pitching, and the Lord knows what.

SARA [*Exuberantly.*]: That's right, Widow Quin. I'll bet my dowry that he'll lick the world.

WIDOW QUIN: If you will, you'd have a right to have him fresh and nourished in place of nursing a feast. [*Taking presents.*] Are you fasting or fed, young fellow?

CHRISTY: Fasting, if you please.

WIDOW QUIN [*Loudly.*]: Well, you're the lot. Stir up now and give him his breakfast. [*To* CHRISTY.] Come here to me [*she puts him on bench beside her while the girls make tea and get his breakfast*], and let you tell us your story before Pegeen will come, in place of grinning your ears off like the moon of May.

CHRISTY [*Beginning to be pleased.*]: It's a long story; you'd be destroyed listening.

WIDOW QUIN: Don't be letting on to be shy, a fine, gamy, treacherous lad the like of you. Was it in your house beyond you cracked his skull?

CHRISTY [*Shy but flattered.*]: It was not. We were digging spuds in his cold, sloping, stony, divil's patch of a field.

WIDOW QUIN: And you went asking money of him, or making talk of getting a wife would drive him from his farm?

CHRISTY: I did not, then; but there I was, digging and digging, and "You squinting idiot," says he, "let you walk down now and tell the priest you'll wed the Widow Casey in a score of days."

WIDOW QUIN: And what kind was she?

CHRISTY [*With horror.*]: A walking terror from beyond the hills, and she two score and five years, and two hundred-weights and five pounds in the weighing scales, with a limping leg on her, and a blinded eye, and she a woman of noted misbehaviour with the old and young.

GIRLS [*Clustering round him, serving him.*]: Glory be.

WIDOW QUIN: And what did he want driving you to wed with her? [*She takes a bit of the chicken.*]

CHRISTY [*Eating with growing satisfaction.*]: He was letting on I was wanting a protector from the harshness of the world, and he without a thought the whole while but how he'd have her hut to live in and her gold to drink.

WIDOW QUIN: There's maybe worse than a dry hearth and a widow woman and your glass at night. So you hit him then?

CHRISTY [*Getting almost excited.*]: I did not. "I won't wed her," says I, "when all know she did suckle me for six weeks when I came into the world, and she a hag this day with a tongue on her has the crows and seabirds scattered, the way they wouldn't cast a shadow on her garden with the dread of her curse."

WIDOW QUIN [*Teasingly.*]: That one should be right company.

SARA [*Eagerly.*]: Don't mind her. Did you kill him then?

CHRISTY: "She's too good for the like of you," says he, "and go on now or I'll flatten you out like a crawling beast has passed under a dray." "You will not if I can help it," says I. "Go on," says he, "or I'll have the divil making garters of your limbs tonight." "You will not if I can help it," says I. [*He sits up brandishing his mug.*]

SARA: You were right surely.

CHRISTY [*Impressively.*]: With that the sun came out between the cloud and the hill, and it shining green in my face. "God have mercy on your soul," says he, lifting a scythe. "Or on your own," says I, raising the loy.

SUSAN: That's a grand story.

HONOR: He tells it lovely.

CHRISTY [*Flattered and confident, waving bone.*]: He gave a drive with the scythe, and I gave a lep to the east. Then I turned around with my back to the north, and I hit a blow on the ridge of his skull, laid him stretched out, and he split to the knob of his gullet.

[*He raises the chicken bone to his Adam's apple.*]

GIRLS [*Together.*]: Well, you're a marvel! Oh, God bless you! You're the lad, surely!

SUSAN: I'm thinking the Lord God sent him this road to make a second husband to the Widow Quin, and she with a great yearning to be wedded, though all dread her here. Lift him on her knee, Sara Tansey.

WIDOW QUIN: Don't tease him.

SARA [*Going over to dresser and counter very quickly and getting two glasses and porter.*]: You're heroes, surely, and let you drink a supeen with your arms linked like the outlandish lovers in the sailor's song. [*She links their arms and gives them the glasses.*] There now. Drink a health to the wonders of the western world, the pirates, preachers, poteen-makers, with the jobbing jockies; parching peelers, and the juries fill their stomachs selling judgments of the English law. [*Brandishing the bottle.*]

WIDOW QUIN: That's a right toast, Sara Tansey. Now, Christy.

[*They drink with their arms linked, he drinking with his left hand, she with her right. As they are drinking,* PEGEEN MIKE *comes in with a milk-can and stands aghast. They all spring away from* CHRISTY. *He goes down left.* WIDOW QUIN *remains seated.*]

PEGEEN [*Angrily to* SARA.]: What is it you're wanting?

SARA [*Twisting her apron.*]: An ounce of tobacco.

PEGEEN: Have you tuppence?

SARA: I've forgotten my purse.

PEGEEN: Then you'd best be getting it and not be fooling us here. [*To the* WIDOW QUIN, *with more elaborate scorn.*] And what is it you're wanting, Widow Quin?

WIDOW QUIN [*Insolently.*]: A penn'orth of starch.

PEGEEN [*Breaking out.*]: And you without a white shift or a shirt in your whole family since the drying of the flood. I've no starch for the like of you, and let you walk on now to Killamuck.

WIDOW QUIN [*Turning to* CHRISTY, *as she goes out with the girls.*]: Well, you're mighty huffy this day, Pegeen Mike, and you, young fellow, let you not forget the sports and racing when the noon is by. [*They go out.*]

PEGEEN [*Imperiously.*]: Fling out that rubbish and put them cups away. [CHRISTY *tidies away in great haste.*] Shove in the bench by the wall. [*He does so.*] And hang that glass on the nail. What disturbed it at all?

CHRISTY [*Very meekly.*]: I was making myself decent only, and this a fine country for young lovely girls.

PEGEEN [*Sharply.*]: Whisht your talking of girls.

[*Goes to counter on right.*]

CHRISTY: Wouldn't any wish to be decent in a place . . .

PEGEEN: Whisht, I'm saying.

CHRISTY [*Looks at her face for a moment with great misgivings, then as a last effort takes up a loy, and goes towards her, with feigned assurance.*]: It was with a loy the like of that I killed my father.

PEGEEN [*Still sharply.*]: You've told me that story six times since the dawn of day.

CHRISTY [*Reproachfully.*]: It's a queer thing you wouldn't care to be hearing it and them girls after walking four miles to be listening to me now.

PEGEEN [*Turning round astonished.*]: Four miles?

CHRISTY [*Apologetically.*]: Didn't himself say there were only bona fides living in the place?

PEGEEN: It's bona fides by the road they are, but that lot came over the river lepping the stones. It's not three perches when you go like that, and I was down this morning looking on the papers the post-boy does have in his bag. [*With meaning and emphasis.*] For there was great news this day, Christopher Mahon.

[*She goes into room on left.*]

CHRISTY [*Suspiciously.*]: Is it news of my murder?

PEGEEN [*Inside.*]: Murder, indeed.

CHRISTY [*Loudly.*]: A murdered da?

PEGEEN [*Coming in again and crossing right.*]: There was not, but a story filled half a page of the hanging of a man. Ah, that should be a fearful end, young fellow, and it worst of all for a man destroyed his da; for the like of him would get small mercies, and when it's dead he is they'd put him in a narrow grave, with cheap sacking wrapping him round, and pour down quicklime on his head, the way you'd see a woman pouring any frish-frash from a cup.

CHRISTY [*Very miserably.*]: Oh, God help me. Are you thinking I'm safe? You were saying at the fall of night I was shut of jeopardy and I here with yourselves.

PEGEEN [*Severely.*]: You'll be shut of jeopardy no place if you go talking with a pack of wild girls the like of them do be walking abroad with the peelers, talking whispers at the fall of night.

CHRISTY [*With terror.*]: And you're thinking they'd tell?

PEGEEN [*With mock sympathy.*]: Who knows, God help you?

CHRISTY [*Loudly.*]: What joy would they have to bring hanging to the likes of me?

PEGEEN: It's queer joys they have, and who knows the thing they'd do, if it'd make the green stones cry itself to think of you swaying and swiggling at the butt of a rope, and you with a fine, stout neck, God bless you! the way you'd be a half an hour, in great anguish, getting your death.

CHRISTY [*Getting his boots and putting them on.*]: If there's that terror of them, it'd be best, maybe, I went on wandering like Esau or Cain and Abel on the sides of Neifin or the Erris plain.

PEGEEN [*Beginning to play with him.*]: It would, maybe, for I've heard the circuit judges this place is a heartless crew.

CHRISTY [*Bitterly.*]: It's more than judges this place is a heartless crew. [*Looking up at her.*] And isn't it a poor thing to be starting again, and I a lonesome fellow will be looking out on women and girls the way the needy fallen spirits do be looking on the Lord?

PEGEEN: What call have you to be that lonesome when there's poor girls walking Mayo in their thousands now?

CHRISTY [*Grimly.*]: It's well you know what call I have. It's well you know it's a lonesome thing to be passing small towns with the lights shining sideways when the night is down, or going in strange places with a dog noising before you and a dog noising behind, or drawn to the cities where you'd hear a voice kissing and talking deep love in every shadow of the ditch, and you passing on with an empty, hungry stomach failing from your heart.

PEGEEN: I'm thinking you're an odd man, Christy Mahon. The oddest walking fellow I ever set my eyes on to this hour to-day.

CHRISTY: What would any be but odd men and they living lonesome in the world?

PEGEEN: I'm not odd, and I'm my whole life with my father only.

CHRISTY [*With infinite admiration.*]: How would a lovely, handsome woman the like of you be lonesome when all men should be thronging around to hear the sweetness of your voice, and the little infant children should be pestering your steps, I'm thinking, and you walking the roads.

PEGEEN: I'm hard set to know what way a coaxing fellow the like of yourself should be lonesome either.

CHRISTY: Coaxing?

PEGEEN: Would you have me think a man never talked with the girls would have the words you've spoken to-day? It's only letting on you are to be lonesome, the way you'd get around me now.

CHRISTY: I wish to God I was letting on; but I was lonesome all times, and born lonesome, I'm thinking, as the moon of dawn. [*Going to door.*]

PEGEEN [*Puzzled by his talk.*]: Well, it's a story I'm not understanding at all why you'd be worse than another, Christy Mahon, and you a fine lad with the great savagery to destroy your da.

CHRISTY: It's little I'm understanding myself, saving only that my heart's scalded this day, and I going off stretching out the earth between us, the way I'll not be waking near you another dawn of the year till the two of us do arise to hope or judgment with the saints of God, and now I'd best be going with my wattle in my hand, for hanging is a poor thing [*turning to go*], and it's little welcome only is left me in this house to-day.

PEGEEN [*Sharply.*]: Christy. [*He turns round.*] Come here to me. [*He goes towards her.*] Lay down that switch and throw some sods on the fire. You're pot-boy in this place, and I'll not have you mitch off from us now.

CHRISTY: You were saying I'd be hanged if I stay.

PEGEEN [*Quite kindly at last.*]: I'm after going down and reading the fearful crimes of Ireland for two weeks or three, and there wasn't a word of your murder. [*Getting up and going over to the counter.*] They've likely not found the body. You're safe so with ourselves.

CHRISTY [*Astonished, slowly.*]: It's making game of me you were [*following her with fearful joy*], and I can stay so, working at your side, and I not lonesome from this mortal day.

PEGEEN: What's to hinder you staying, except the widow woman or the young girls would inveigle you off?

CHRISTY [*With rapture.*]: And I'll have your words from this day filling my ears, and that look is come upon you meeting my two eyes, and I watching you loafing around in the warm sun, or rinsing your ankles when the night is come.

PEGEEN [*Kindly, but a little embarrassed.*]: I'm thinking you'll be a loyal young lad to have working around, and if you vexed me a while since with your leaguing with the girls, I wouldn't give a thraneen for a lad hadn't a mighty spirit in him and a gamy heart.

[SHAWN KEOGH *runs in carrying a cleeve on his back, followed by the* WIDOW QUIN.]

SHAWN [*To* PEGEEN.]: I was passing below, and I seen your mountainy sheep eating cabbages in Jimmy's field. Run up or they'll be bursting surely.

PEGEEN: Oh, God mend them!

[*She puts a shawl over her head and runs out.*]

CHRISTY [*Looking from one to the other. Still in high spirits.*]: I'd best go to her aid maybe. I'm handy with ewes.

WIDOW QUIN [*Closing the door.*]: She can do that much, and there is Shaneen has long speeches for to tell you now.

[*She sits down with an amused smile.*]

SHAWN [*Taking something from his pocket and offering it to* CHRISTY.]: Do you see that, mister?

CHRISTY [*Looking at it.*]: The half of a ticket to the Western States!

SHAWN [*Trembling with anxiety.*]: I'll give it to you and my new hat [*pulling it out of hamper*]; and my breeches with the double seat [*pulling it out*]; and my new coat is woven from the blackest shearings for three miles around [*giving him the coat*]; I'll give you the whole of them, and my blessing, and the blessing of Father Reilly itself, maybe, if you'll quit from this and leave us in the peace we had till last night at the fall of dark.

CHRISTY [*With a new arrogance.*]: And for what is it you're wanting to get shut of me?

SHAWN [*Looking to the* WIDOW *for help.*]: I'm a poor scholar with middling faculties to coin a lie, so I'll tell you the truth, Christy Mahon. I'm wedding with Pegeen beyond, and I don't think well of having a clever fearless man the like of you dwelling in her house.

CHRISTY [*Almost pugnaciously.*]: And you'd be using bribery for to banish me?

SHAWN [*In an imploring voice.*]: Let you not take it badly, mister honey; isn't beyond the best place for you, where you'll have golden chains and shiny coats and you riding upon hunters with the ladies of the land.

[*He makes an eager sign to the* WIDOW QUIN *to come to help him.*]

WIDOW QUIN [*Coming over.*]: It's true for him, and you'd best quit off and not have that poor girl setting her mind on you, for there's Shaneen thinks she wouldn't suit you, though all is saying that she'll wed you now.

[CHRISTY *beams with delight.*]

SHAWN [*In terrified earnest.*]: She wouldn't suit you, and she with the divil's own temper the way you'd be strangling one another in a score of days. [*He makes the movement of strangling with his hands.*] It's the like of me only that she's fit for; a quiet simple fellow wouldn't raise a hand upon her if she scratched itself.

WIDOW QUIN [*Putting* SHAWN'*s hat on* CHRISTY.]: Fit them clothes on you anyhow, young fellow, and he'd maybe loan them to you for the sports. [*Pushing him towards inner door.*] Fit them on and you can give your answer when you have them tried.

CHRISTY [*Beaming, delighted with the clothes.*]: I will then. I'd like herself to see me in them tweeds and hat.

[*He goes into room and shuts the door.*]

SHAWN [*In great anxiety.*]: He'd like herself to see them. He'll not leave us, Widow Quin. He's a score of divils in him the way it's well-nigh certain he will wed Pegeen.

WIDOW QUIN [*Jeeringly.*]: It's true all girls are fond of courage and do hate the like of you.

SHAWN [*Walking about in desperation.*]: Oh, Widow Quin, what'll I be doing now? I'd inform again him, but he'd burst from Kilmainham and he'd be sure and certain to destroy me. If I wasn't so God-fearing, I'd near have courage to come behind him and run a pike into his side. Oh, it's a hard case to be an orphan and not to have your father that you're used to, and you'd easy kill and make yourself a hero in the sight of all. [*Coming up to her.*] Oh, Widow Quin, will you find me some contrivance when I've promised you a ewe?

WIDOW QUIN: A ewe's a small thing, but what would you give me if I did wed him and did save you so?

SHAWN [*With astonishment.*]: You?

WIDOW QUIN: Aye. Would you give me the red cow you have and the mountainy ram, and the right of way across your rye path, and a load of dung at Michaelmas, and turbary upon the western hill?

SHAWN [*Radiant with hope.*]: I would, surely, and I'd give you the wedding-ring I have, and the loan of a new suit, the way you'd have him decent on the wedding-day. I'd give you two kids for your dinner, and a gallon of poteen, and I'd call the piper on the long car to your wedding from Crossmolina or from Ballina. I'd give you . . .

WIDOW QUIN: That'll do, so, and let you whisht, for he's coming now again.

[CHRISTY *comes in very natty in the new clothes.* WIDOW QUIN *goes to him admiringly.*]

WIDOW QUIN: If you seen yourself now, I'm thinking you'd be too proud to speak to at all, and it'd be a pity surely to have your like sailing from Mayo to the western world.

CHRISTY [*As proud as a peacock.*]: I'm not going. If this is a poor place itself, I'll make myself contented to be lodging here.

[WIDOW QUIN *makes a sign to* SHAWN *to leave them.*]

SHAWN: Well, I'm going measuring the racecourse while the tide is low, so I'll leave you the garments and my blessing for the sports to-day. God bless you!

[*He wriggles out.*]

WIDOW QUIN [*Admiring* CHRISTY.]: Well, you're mighty spruce, young fellow. Sit down now while you're quiet till you talk with me.

CHRISTY [*Swaggering.*]: I'm going abroad on the hillside for to seek Pegeen.

WIDOW QUIN: You'll have time and plenty for to seek Pegeen, and you heard me saying at the fall of night the two of us should be great company.

CHRISTY: From this out I'll have no want of company when all sorts is bringing me their food and clothing [*he swaggers to the door, tightening his belt*], the way they'd set their eyes upon a gallant orphan cleft his father with one blow to the breeches belt. [*He opens door, then staggers back.*] Saints of Glory! Holy angels from the throne of light!
WIDOW QUIN [*Going over.*]: What ails you?
CHRISTY: It's the walking spirit of my murdered da!
WIDOW QUIN [*Looking out.*]: Is it that tramper?
CHRISTY [*Wildly.*]: Where'll I hide my poor body from that ghost of hell?

[*The door is pushed open, and old* MAHON *appears on threshold.* CHRISTY *darts in behind door.*]

WIDOW QUIN [*In great amazement.*]: God save you, my poor man.
MAHON [*Gruffly.*]: Did you see a young lad passing this way in the early morning or the fail of night?
WIDOW QUIN: You're a queer kind to walk in not saluting at all.
MAHON: Did you see the young lad?
WIDOW QUIN [*Stiffly.*]: What kind was he?
MAHON: An ugly young streeler with a murderous gob on him, and a little switch in his hand. I met a tramper seen him coming this way at the fall of night.
WIDOW QUIN: There's harvest hundreds do be passing these days for the Sligo boat. For what is it you're wanting him, my poor man?
MAHON: I want to destroy him for breaking the head on me with the clout of a loy. [*He takes off a big hat, and shows his head in a mass of bandages and plaster, with some pride.*] It was he did that, and amn't I a great wonder to think I've traced him ten days with that rent in my crown?
WIDOW QUIN [*Taking his head in both hands and examining it with extreme delight.*]: That was a great blow. And who hit you? A robber maybe?
MAHON: It was my own son hit me, and he the divil a robber, or anything else, but a dirty, stuttering lout.
WIDOW QUIN [*Letting go his skull and wiping her hands in her apron.*]: You'd best be wary of a mortified scalp, I think they call it, lepping around with that wound in the splendour of the sun. It was a bad blow, surely, and you should have vexed him fearful to make him strike that gash in his da.
MAHON: Is it me?
WIDOW QUIN [*Amusing herself.*]: Aye. And isn't it a great shame when the old and hardened do torment the young?
MAHON [*Raging.*]: Torment him is it? And I after holding out with the patience of a martyred saint till there's nothing but destruction on, and I'm driven out in my old age with none to aid me.
WIDOW QUIN [*Greatly amused.*]: It's a sacred wonder the way that wickedness will spoil a man.
MAHON: My wickedness, is it? Amn't I after saying it is himself has me destroyed, and he a lier on walls, a talker of folly, a man you'd see stretched the half of the day in the brown ferns with his belly to the sun.
WIDOW QUIN: Not working at all?
MAHON: The divil a work, or if he did itself, you'd see him raising up a haystack like the stalk of a rush, or driving our last cow till he broke her leg at the hip, and when he wasn't at that he'd be fooling over little birds he had—finches and felts—or making mugs at his own self in the bit of a glass we had hung on the wall.
WIDOW QUIN [*Looking at* CHRISTY.]: What way was he so foolish? It was running wild after the girls maybe?
MAHON [*With a shout of derision.*]: Running wild, is it? If he seen a red petticoat coming swinging over the hill, he'd be off to hide in the sticks, and you'd see him shooting out his sheep's eyes between the little twigs and the leaves, and his two ears rising like a hare looking out through a gap. Girls, indeed!
WIDOW QUIN: It was drink maybe?
MAHON: And he a poor fellow would get drunk on the smell of a pint. He'd a queer rotten stomach, I'm telling you, and when I gave him three pulls from my pipe a while since, he was taken with contortions till I had to send him in the ass-cart to the females' nurse.
WIDOW QUIN [*Clasping her hands.*]: Well, I never, till this day, heard tell of a man the like of that!
MAHON: I'd take a mighty oath you didn't, surely, and wasn't he the laughing joke of every female woman where four baronies meet, the way the girls would stop their weeding if they seen him coming the road to let a roar at him, and call him the loony of Mahon's?
WIDOW QUIN: I'd give the world and all to see the like of him. What kind was he?
MAHON: A small, low fellow.
WIDOW QUIN: And dark?
MAHON: Dark and dirty.
WIDOW QUIN [*Considering.*]: I'm thinking I seen him.
MAHON [*Eagerly.*]: An ugly young blackguard.
WIDOW QUIN: A hideous, fearful villain, and the spit of you.
MAHON: What way is he fled?
WIDOW QUIN: Gone over the hills to catch a coasting steamer to the north or south.
MAHON: Could I pull up on him now?
WIDOW QUIN: If you'll cross the sands below where the tide is out, you'll be in it as soon as himself, for he had to go round ten miles by the top of the

bay. [*She points to the door.*] Strike down by the head beyond and then follow on the roadway to the north and east.

[MAHON *goes abruptly.*]

WIDOW QUIN [*Shouting after him.*]: Let you give him a good vengeance when you come up with him, but don't put yourself in the power of the law, for it'd be a poor thing to see a judge in his black cap reading out his sentence on a civil warrior the like of you. [*She swings the door to and looks at* CHRISTY, *who is cowering in terror, for a moment, then she bursts into a laugh.*] Well, you're the walking Playboy of the Western World, and that's the poor man you had divided to his breeches belt.

CHRISTY [*Looking out; then, to her.*]: What'll Pegeen say when she hears that story? What'll she be saying to me now?

WIDOW QUIN: She'll knock the head of you, I'm thinking, and drive you from the door. God help her to be taking you for a wonder, and you a little schemer making up a story you destroyed your da.

CHRISTY [*Turning to the door, nearly speechless with rage, half to himself.*]: To be letting on he was dead, and coming back to his life, and following after me like an old weasel tracing a rat, and coming in here laying desolation between my own self and the fine women of Ireland, and he a kind of carcass that you'd fling upon the sea. . . .

WIDOW QUIN [*More soberly.*]: There's talking for a man's one only son.

CHRISTY [*Breaking out.*]: His one son, is it? May I meet him with one tooth and it aching, and one eye to be seeing seven and seventy divils in the twists of the road, and one old timber leg on him to limp into the scalding grave. [*Looking out.*] There he is now crossing the strands, and that the Lord God would send a high wave to wash him from the world.

WIDOW QUIN [*Scandalized.*]: Have you no shame? [*Putting her hand on his shoulder and turning him round.*] What ails you? Near crying, is it?

CHRISTY [*In despair and grief.*]: Amn't I after seeing the love-light of the star of knowledge shining from her brow, and hearing words would put you thinking on the holy Brigid speaking to the infant saints, and now she'll be turning again, and speaking hard words to me, like an old woman with a spavindy ass she'd have, urging on a hill.

WIDOW QUIN: There's poetry talk for a girl you'd see itching and scratching, and she with a stale stink of poteen on her from selling in the shop.

CHRISTY [*Impatiently.*]: It's her like is fitted to be handling merchandise in the heavens above, and what'll I be doing now, I ask you, and I a kind of wonder was jilted by the heavens when a day was by.

[*There is a distant noise of girls' voices.* WIDOW QUIN *looks from window and comes to him, hurriedly.*]

WIDOW QUIN: You'll be doing like myself, I'm thinking, when I did destroy my man, for I'm above many's the day, odd times in great spirits, abroad in the sunshine, darning a stocking or stitching a shift; and odd times again looking out on the schooners, hookers, trawlers is sailing the sea, and I thinking on the gallant hairy fellows are drifting beyond, and myself long years living alone.

CHRISTY [*Interested.*]: You're like me, so.

WIDOW QUIN: I am your like, and it's for that I'm taking a fancy to you, and I with my little houseen above where there'd be myself to tend you, and none to ask were you a murderer or what at all.

CHRISTY: And what would I be doing if I left Pegeen?

WIDOW QUIN: I've nice jobs you could be doing—gathering shells to make a whitewash for our hut within, building up a little goose-house, or stretching a new skin on an old curagh I have, and if my hut is far from all sides, it's there you'll meet the wisest old men, I tell you, at the corner of my wheel, and it's there yourself and me will have great times whispering and hugging. . . .

VOICES [*Outside, calling far away.*]: Christy! Christy Mahon! Christy!

CHRISTY: Is it Pegeen Mike?

WIDOW QUIN: It's the young girls, I'm thinking, coming to bring you to the sports below, and what is it you'll have me to tell them now?

CHRISTY: Aid me for to win Pegeen. It's herself only that I'm seeking now. [WIDOW QUIN *gets up and goes to window.*] Aid me for to win her, and I'll be asking God to stretch a hand to you in the hour of death, and lead you short cuts through the Meadows of Ease, and up the floor of heaven to the Footstool of the Virgin's Son.

WIDOW QUIN: There's praying!

VOICES [*Nearer.*]: Christy! Christy Mahon!

CHRISTY [*With agitation.*]: They're coming. Will you swear to aid and save me, for the love of Christ?

WIDOW QUIN [*Looks at him for a moment.*]: If I aid you, will you swear to give me a right of way I want, and a mountainy ram, and a load of dung at Michaelmas, the time that you'll be master here?

CHRISTY: I will, by the elements and stars of night.

WIDOW QUIN: Then we'll not say a word of the old fellow, the way Pegeen won't know your story till the end of time.

CHRISTY: And if he chances to return again?

WIDOW QUIN: We'll swear he's a maniac and not your da. I could take an oath I seen him raving on the sands to-day.

[*Girls run in.*]

SUSAN: Come on to the sports below. Pegeen says you're to come.
SARA TANSEY: The lepping's beginning, and we've a jockey's suit to fit upon you for the mule race on the sands below.
HONOR: Come on, will you?
CHRISTY: I will then if Pegeen's beyond.
SARA: She's in the boreen making game of Shaneen Keogh.
CHRISTY: Then I'll be going to her now.

[*He runs out, followed by the girls.*]

WIDOW QUIN: Well, if the worst comes in the end of all, it'll be great game to see there's none to pity him but a widow woman, the like of me, has buried her children and destroyed her man. [*She goes out.*]

CURTAIN

ACT III

Scene as before. Later in the day. JIMMY *comes in, slightly drunk.*

JIMMY [*Calls.*]: Pegeen! [*Crosses to inner door.*] Pegeen Mike! [*Comes back again into the room.*] Pegeen! [PHILLY *comes in in the same state.—To* PHILLY.] Did you see herself?
PHILLY: I did not; but I sent Shawn Keogh with the ass-cart for to bear him home. [*Trying cupboards, which are locked.*] Well, isn't he a nasty man to get into such staggers at a morning wake; and isn't herself the divil's daughter for locking, and she so fussy after that young gaffer, you might take your death with drouth and none to heed you?
JIMMY: It's little wonder she'd be fussy, and he after bringing bankrupt ruin on the roulette man, and the trick-o'-the-loop man, and breaking the nose of the cockshot-man, and winning all in the sports below, racing, lepping, dancing, and the Lord knows what! He's right luck, I'm telling you.
PHILLY: If he has, he'll be rightly hobbled yet, and he not able to say ten words without making a brag of the way he killed his father, and the great blow he hit with the loy.
JIMMY: A man can't hang by his own informing, and his father should be rotten by now.

[*Old* MAHON *passes window slowly.*]

PHILLY: Supposing a man's digging spuds in that field with a long spade, and supposing he flings up the two halves of that skull, what'll be said then in the papers and the courts of law?
JIMMY: They'd say it was an old Dane, maybe, was drowned in the flood. [*Old* MAHON *comes in and sits down near door listening.*] Did you never hear tell of the skulls they have in the city of Dublin, ranged out like blue jugs in a cabin of Connaught?
PHILLY: And you believe that?
JIMMY [*Pugnaciously.*]: Didn't a lad see them and he after coming from harvesting in the Liverpool boat? "They have them there," says he, "making a show of the great people there was one time walking the world. White skulls and black skulls and yellow skulls, and some with full teeth, and some haven't only but one."
PHILLY: It was no lie, maybe, for when I was a young lad there was a graveyard beyond the house with the remnants of a man who had thighs as long as your arm. He was a horrid man, I'm telling you, and there was many a fine Sunday I'd put him together for fun, and he with shiny bones, you wouldn't meet the like of these days in the cities of the world.
MAHON [*Getting up.*]: You wouldn't, is it? Lay your eyes on that skull, and tell me where and when there was another the like of it, is splintered only from the blow of a loy.
PHILLY: Glory be to God! And who hit you at all?
MAHON [*Triumphantly.*]: It was my own son hit me. Would you believe that?
JIMMY: Well, there's wonders hidden in the heart of man!
PHILLY [*Suspiciously.*]: And what way was it done?
MAHON [*Wandering about the room.*]: I'm after walking hundreds and long scores of miles, winning clean beds and the fill of my belly four times in the day, and I doing nothing but telling stories of that naked truth. [*He comes to them a little aggressively.*] Give me a supeen and I'll tell you now.

[WIDOW QUIN *comes in and stands aghast behind him. He is facing* JIMMY *and* PHILLY, *who are on the left.*]

JIMMY: Ask herself beyond. She's the stuff hidden in her shawl.
WINDOW QUIN [*Coming to* MAHON *quickly.*]: You here, is it? You didn't go far at all?
MAHON: I seen the coasting steamer passing, and I got a drouth upon me and a cramping leg, so I said: "The divil go along with him," and turned again. [*Looking under her shawl.*] And let you give

me a supeen, for I'm destroyed travelling since Tuesday was a week.

WIDOW QUIN [*Getting a glass, in a cajoling tone.*]: Sit down then by the fire and take your ease for a space. You've a right to be destroyed indeed, with your walking, and fighting, and facing the sun. [*Giving him poteen from a stone jar she has brought in.*] There now is a drink for you, and may it be to your happiness and length of life.

MAHON [*Taking glass greedily, and sitting down by fire.*]: God increase you!

WIDOW QUIN [*Taking men to the right stealthily.*]: Do you know what? That man's raving from his wound to-day, for I met him a while since telling a rambling tale of a tinker had him destroyed. Then he heard of Christy's deed, and he up and says it was his son had cracked his skull. Oh, isn't madness a fright, for he'll go killing someone yet, and he thinking it's the man has struck him so?

JIMMY [*Entirely convinced.*]: It's a fright surely. I knew a party was kicked in the head by a red mare, and he went killing horses a great while, till he eat the insides of a clock and died after.

PHILLY [*With suspicion.*]: Did he see Christy?

WIDOW QUIN: He didn't. [*With a warning gesture.*] Let you not be putting him in mind of him, or you'll be likely summoned if there's murder done. [*Looking round at* MAHON.] Whisht! He's listening. Wait now till you hear me taking him easy and unravelling all. [*She goes to* MAHON.] And what way are you feeling, mister? Are you in contentment now?

MAHON [*Slightly emotional from his drink.*]: I'm poorly only, for it's a hard story the way I'm left to-day, when it was I did tend him from his hour of birth, and he a dunce never reached his second book, the way he'd come from school, many's the day, with his legs lamed under him, and he blackened with his beatings like a tinker's ass. It's a hard story, I'm saying, the way some do have their next and nighest raising up a hand of murder on them, and some is lonesome getting their death with lamentation in the dead of night.

WIDOW QUIN [*Not knowing what to say.*]: To hear you talking so quiet, who'd know you were the same fellow we seen pass to-day?

MAHON: I'm the same surely. The wrack and ruin of threescore years; and it's a terror to live that length, I tell you, and to have your sons going to the dogs against you, and you wore out scolding them, and skelping them, and God knows what.

PHILLY [*To* JIMMY.]: He's not raving. [*To* WIDOW QUIN.] Will you ask him what kind was his son?

WIDOW QUIN [*To* MAHON, *with a peculiar look.*]: Was your son that hit you a lad of one year and a score maybe, a great hand at racing and lepping and licking the world?

MAHON [*Turning on her with a roar of rage.*]: Didn't you hear me say he was the fool of men, the way from this out he'll know the orphan's lot, with old and young making game of him, and they swearing, raging, kicking at him like a mangy cur.

[*A great burst of cheering outside, some way off.*]

MAHON [*Putting his hands to his ears.*]: What in the name of God do they want roaring below?

WIDOW QUIN [*With the shade of a smile.*]: They're cheering a young lad, the champion Playboy of the Western World.

[*More cheering.*]

MAHON [*Going to window.*]: It'd split my heart to hear them, and I with pulses in my brain-pan for a week gone by. Is it racing they are?

JIMMY [*Looking from door.*]: It is, then. They are mounting him for the mule race will be run upon the sands. That's the playboy on the winkered mule.

MAHON [*Puzzled.*]: That lad, is it? If you said it was a fool he was, I'd have laid a mighty oath he was the likeness of my wandering son. [*Uneasily, putting his hand to his head.*] Faith, I'm thinking I'll go walking for to view the race.

WIDOW QUIN [*Stopping him, sharply.*]: You will not. You'd best take the road to Belmullet, and not be dilly-dallying in this place where there isn't a spot you could sleep.

PHILLY [*Coming forward.*]: Don't mind her. Mount there on the bench and you'll have a view of the whole. They're hurrying before the tide will rise, and it'd be near over if you went down the pathway through the crags below.

MAHON [*Mounts on bench,* WIDOW QUIN *beside him.*]: That's a right view again the edge of the sea. They're coming now from the point. He's leading. Who is he at all?

WIDOW QUIN: He's the champion of the world, I tell you, and there isn't a ha'p'orth isn't falling lucky to his hands to-day.

PHILLY [*Looking out, interested in the race.*]: Look at that. They're pressing him now.

JIMMY: He'll win it yet.

PHILLY: Take your time, Jimmy Farrell. It's too soon to say.

WIDOW QUIN [*Shouting.*]: Watch him taking the gate. There's riding.

JIMMY [*Cheering.*]: More power to the young lad!

MAHON: He's passing the third.

JIMMY: He'll lick them yet.

WIDOW QUIN: He'd lick them if he was running races with a score itself.

MAHON: Look at the mule he has, kicking the stars.

WIDOW QUIN: There was a lep! [*Catching hold of* MAHON *in her excitement.*] He's fallen? He's mounted again! Faith, he's passing them all!

JIMMY: Look at him skelping her!

PHILLY: And the mountain girls hooshing him on!

JIMMY: It's the last turn! The post's cleared for them now!

MAHON: Look at the narrow place. He'll be into the bogs! [*With a yell.*] Good rider! He's through it again!

JIMMY: He's neck and neck!

MAHON: Good boy to him! Flames, but he's in!

[*Great cheering, in which all join.*]

MAHON [*With hesitation.*]: What's that? They're raising him up. They're coming this way. [*With a roar of rage and astonishment.*] It's Christy, by the stars of God! I'd know his way of spitting and he astride the moon.

[*He jumps down and makes a run for the door, but* WIDOW QUIN *catches him and pulls him back.*]

WIDOW QUIN: Stay quiet, will you? That's not your son. [*To* JIMMY.] Stop him, or you'll get a month for the abetting of manslaughter and be fined as well.

JIMMY: I'll hold him.

MAHON [*Struggling.*]: Let me out! Let me out, the lot of you, till I have my vengeance on his head to-day.

WIDOW QUIN [*Shaking him, vehemently.*]: That's not your son. That's a man is going to make a marriage with the daughter of this house, a place with fine trade, with a licence, and with poteen too.

MAHON [*Amazed.*]: That man marrying a decent and a moneyed girl! Is it mad yous are? Is it in a crazy-house for females that I'm landed now?

WIDOW QUIN: It's mad yourself is with the blow upon your head. That lad is the wonder of the western world.

MAHON: I see it's my son.

WIDOW QUIN: You seen that you're mad. [*Cheering outside.*] Do you hear them cheering him in the zigzags of the road? Aren't you after saying that your son's a fool, and how would they be cheering a true idiot born?

MAHON [*Getting distressed.*]: It's maybe out of reason that that man's himself. [*Cheering again.*] There's none surely will go cheering him. Oh, I'm raving with a madness that would fright the world! [*He sits down with his hand to his head.*] There was one time I seen ten scarlet divils letting on they'd cork my spirit in a gallon can; and one time I seen rats as big as badgers sucking the lifeblood from the butt of my lug; but I never till this day confused that dribbling idiot with a likely man. I'm destroyed surely.

WIDOW QUIN: And who'd wonder when it's your brain-pan that is gaping now?

MAHON: Then the blight of the sacred drouth upon myself and him, for I never went mad to this day, and I not three weeks with the Limerick girls drinking myself silly and parlatic from the dusk to dawn. [*To* WIDOW QUIN, *suddenly.*] Is my visage astray?

WIDOW QUIN: It is, then. You're a sniggering maniac, a child could see.

MAHON [*Getting up more cheerfully.*]: Then I'd best be going to the union beyond, and there'll be a welcome before me, I tell you [*with great pride*], and I a terrible and fearful case, the way that there I was one time, screeching in a straightened waistcoat, with seven doctors writing out my sayings in a printed book. Would you believe that?

WIDOW QUIN: If you're a wonder itself, you'd best be hasty, for them lads caught a maniac one time and pelted the poor creature till he ran out, raving and foaming, and was drowned in the sea.

MAHON [*With philosophy.*]: It's true mankind is the divil when your head's astray. Let me out now and I'll slip down the boreen, and not see them so.

WIDOW QUIN [*Showing him out.*]: That's it. Run to the right, and not a one will see. [*He runs off.*]

PHILLY [*Wisely.*]: You're at some gaming, Widow Quin; but I'll walk after him and give him his dinner and a time to rest, and I'll see then if he's raving or as sane as you.

WIDOW QUIN [*Annoyed.*]: If you go near that lad, let you be wary of your head, I'm saying. Didn't you hear him telling he was crazed at times?

PHILLY: I heard him telling a power; and I'm thinking we'll have right sport before night will fall. [*He goes out.*]

JIMMY: Well, Philly's a conceited and foolish man. How could that madman have his senses and his brain-pan slit? I'll go after them and see him turn on Philly now.

[*He goes;* WIDOW QUIN *hides poteen behind counter. Then hubbub outside.*]

VOICES: There you are! Good jumper! Grand lepper! Darlint boy! He's the racer! Bear him on, will you!

[CHRISTY *comes in, in jockey's dress, with* PEGEEN MIKE, SARA, *and other* GIRLS *and* MEN.]

PEGEEN [*To* CROWD.]: Go on now, and don't destroy him, and he drenching with sweat. Go along, I'm saying, and have your tug-of-warring till he's dried his skin.

CROWD: Here's his prizes! A bagpipes! A fiddle was played by a poet in the years gone by! A flat and three-thorned blackthorn would lick the scholars out of Dublin town!

CHRISTY [*Taking prizes from the* MEN.]: Thank you kindly, the lot of you. But you'd say it was little only I did this day if you'd seen me a while since striking my one single blow.

TOWN CRIER [*Outside ringing a bell.*]: Take notice, last event of this day! Tug-of-warring on the green below! Come on, the lot of you! Great achievements for all Mayo men!

PEGEEN: Go on and leave him for to rest and dry. Go on, I tell you, for he'll do no more.

[*She hustles crowd out;* WIDOW QUIN *following them.*]

MEN [*Going.*]: Come on, then. Good luck for the while!

PEGEEN [*Radiantly, wiping his face with her shawl.*]: Well, you're the lad, and you'll have great times from this out when you could win that wealth of prizes, and you sweating in the heat of noon!

CHRISTY [*Looking at her with delight.*]: I'll have great times if I win the crowning prize I'm seeking now, and that's your promise that you'll wed me in a fortnight, when our banns is called.

PEGEEN [*Backing away from him.*]: You've right daring to go ask me that, when all knows you'll be starting to some girl in your own townland, when your father's rotten in four months, or five.

CHRISTY [*Indignantly.*]: Starting from you, is it? [*He follows her.*] I will not, then, and when the airs is warming, in four months or five, it's then yourself and me should be pacing Neifin in the dews of night, the times sweet smells do be rising, and you'd see a little, shiny new moon, maybe sinking on the hills.

PEGEEN [*Looking at him playfully.*]: And it's that kind of a poacher's love you'd make, Christy Mahon, on the sides of Neifin, when the night is down?

CHRISTY: It's little you'll think if my love's a poacher's, or an earl's itself, when you'll feel my two hands stretched around you, and I squeezing kisses on your puckered lips, till I'd feel a kind of pity for the Lord God is all ages sitting lonesome in His golden chair.

PEGEEN: That'll be right fun, Christy Mahon, and any girl would walk her heart out before she'd meet a young man was your like for eloquence, or talk at all.

CHRISTY [*Encouraged.*]: Let you wait, to hear me talking, till we're astray in Erris, when Good Friday's by, drinking a sup from a well, and making mighty kisses with our wetted mouths, or gaming in a gap of sunshine, with yourself stretched back unto your necklace, in the flowers of the earth.

PEGEEN [*In a low voice, moved by his tone.*]: I'd be nice so, is it?

CHRISTY [*With rapture.*]: If the mitred bishops seen you that time, they'd be the like of the holy prophets, I'm thinking, do be straining the bars of paradise to lay eyes on the Lady Helen of Troy, and she abroad, pacing back and forward, with a nosegay in her golden shawl.

PEGEEN [*With real tenderness.*]: And what is it I have, Christy Mahon, to make me fitting entertainment for the like of you, that has such poet's talking, and such bravery of heart.

CHRISTY [*In a low voice.*]: Isn't there the light of seven heavens in your heart alone, the way you'll be an angel's lamp to me from this out, and I abroad in the darkness, spearing salmons in the Owen or the Carrowmore?

PEGEEN: If I was your wife I'd be along with you those nights, Christy Mahon, the way you'd see I was a great hand at coaxing bailiffs, or coining funny nicknames for the stars of night.

CHRISTY: You, is it? Taking your death in the hailstones, or in the fogs of dawn.

PEGEEN: Yourself and me would shelter easy in a narrow bush [*with a qualm of dread*]; but we're only talking, maybe, for this would be a poor, thatched place to hold a fine lad is the like of you.

CHRISTY [*Putting his arm round her.*]: If I wasn't a good Christian, it's on my naked knees I'd be saying my prayers and paters to every jackstraw you have roofing your head, and every stony pebble is paving the laneway to your door.

PEGEEN [*Radiantly.*]: If that's the truth I'll be burning candles from this out to the miracles of God that have brought you from the south to-day, and I with my gowns bought ready, the way that I can wed you, and not wait at all.

CHRISTY: It's miracles, and that's the truth. Me there toiling a long while, and walking a long while, not knowing at all I was drawing all times nearer to this holy day.

PEGEEN: And myself, a girl, was tempted often to go sailing the seas till I'd marry a Jew-man, with ten kegs of gold, and I not knowing at all there was the like of you drawing nearer, like the stars of God.

CHRISTY: And to think I'm long years hearing women talking that talk, to all bloody fools, and this the first time I've heard the like of your voice talking sweetly for my own delight.

PEGEEN: And to think it's me is talking sweetly, Christy Mahon, and I the fright of seven townlands for my biting tongue. Well, the heart's a wonder; and, I'm thinking, there won't be our like in Mayo, for gallant lovers, from this hour to-day. [*Drunken singing is heard outside.*] There's my father coming from the wake, and when he's had his sleep we'll tell him, for he's peaceful then.

[*They separate.*]

MICHAEL [*Singing outside.*]:
The jailer and the turnkey
They quickly ran us down,
And brought us back as prisoners
Once more to Cavan town.

[*He comes in supported by Shawn.*]

There we lay bewailing
All in a prison bound. . . .

[*He sees* CHRISTY. *Goes and shakes him drunkenly by the hand, while* PEGEEN *and* SHAWN *talk on the left.*]

MICHAEL [*To* CHRISTY.]: The blessing of God and the holy angels on your head, young fellow. I hear tell you're after winning all in the sports below; and wasn't it a shame I didn't bear you along with me to Kate Cassidy's wake, a fine, stout lad, the like of you, for you'd never see the match of it for flows of drink, the way when we sunk her bones at noonday in her narrow grave, there were five men, aye, and six men, stretched out retching speechless on the holy stones.

CHRISTY [*Uneasily, watching* PEGEEN.]: Is that the truth?

MICHAEL: It is, then; and aren't you a louty schemer to go burying your poor father unbeknownst when you'd a right to throw him on the crupper of a Kerry mule and drive him westwards, like holy Joseph in the days gone by, the way we could have given him a decent burial, and not have him rotting beyond, and not a Christian drinking a smart drop to the glory of his soul?

CHRISTY [*Gruffly.*]: It's well enough he's lying, for the likes of him.

MICHAEL [*Slapping him on the back.*]: Well, aren't you a hardened slayer? It'll be a poor thing for the household man where you go sniffing for a female wife; and [*pointing to* SHAWN] look beyond at that shy and decent Christian I have chosen for my daughter's hand, and I after getting the gilded dispensation this day for to wed them now.

CHRISTY: And you'll be wedding them this day, is it?

MICHAEL [*Drawing himself up.*]: Aye. Are you thinking, if I'm drunk itself, I'd leave my daughter living single with a little frisky rascal is the like of you?

PEGEEN [*Breaking away from* SHAWN.]: Is it the truth the dispensation's come?

MICHAEL [*Triumphantly.*]: Father Reilly's after reading it in gallous Latin, and 'It's come in the nick of time,' says he; 'so I'll wed them in a hurry, dreading that young gaffer who'd capsize the stars.'

PEGEEN [*Fiercely.*]: He's missed his nick of time, for it's that lad, Christy Mahon, that I'm wedding now.

MICHAEL [*Loudly, with horror.*]: You'd be making him a son to me, and he wet and crusted with his father's blood?

PEGEEN: Aye. Wouldn't it be a bitter thing for a girl to go marrying the like of Shaneen, and he a middling kind of a scarecrow, with no savagery or fine words in him at all?

MICHAEL [*Gasping and sinking on a chair.*]: Oh, aren't you a heathen daughter to go shaking the fat of my heart, and I swamped and drownded with the weight of drink? Would you have them turning on me the way that I'd be roaring to the dawn of day with the wind upon my heart? Have you not a word to aid me, Shaneen? Are you not jealous at all?

SHAWN [*In great misery.*]: I'd be afeard to be jealous of a man did slay his da.

PEGEEN: Well, it'd be a poor thing to go marrying your like. I'm seeing there's a world of peril for an orphan girl, and isn't it a great blessing I didn't wed you before himself came walking from the west or south?

SHAWN: It's a queer story you'd go picking a dirty tramp up from the highways of the world.

PEGEEN [*Playfully.*]: And you think you're a likely beau to go straying along with the shiny Sundays of the opening year, when it's sooner on a bullock's liver you'd put a poor girl thinking than on the lily or the rose?

SHAWN: And have you no mind of my weight of passion, and the holy dispensation, and the drift of heifers I'm giving, and the golden ring?

PEGEEN: I'm thinking you're too fine for the like of me, Shawn Keogh of Killakeen, and let you go off till you'd find a radiant lady with droves of bullocks on the plains of Meath, and herself bedizened in the diamond jewelleries of Pharaoh's ma. That'd be your match, Shaneen. So God save you now! [*She retreats behind* CHRISTY.]

SHAWN: Won't you hear me telling you . . . ?

CHRISTY [*With ferocity.*]: Take yourself from this, young fellow, or I'll maybe add a murder to my deeds to-day.

MICHAEL [*Springing up with a shriek.*]: Murder is it? Is it mad yous are? Would you go making murder in this place, and it piled with poteen for our drink to-night? Go on to the foreshore if it's fighting you want, where the rising tide will wash all traces from the memory of man.

[*Pushing* SHAWN *towards* CHRISTY.]

SHAWN [*Shaking himself free, and getting behind* MICHAEL.]: I'll not fight him, Michael James. I'd liefer live a bachelor, simmering in passions to the end of time, than face a lepping savage the like of him has descended from the Lord knows where. Strike him yourself, Michael James, or you'll lose my drift of heifers and my blue bull from Sneem.

MICHAEL: Is it me fight him, when it's father-slaying he's bred to now? [*Pushing* SHAWN.] Go on, you fool, and fight him now.

SHAWN [*Coming forward a little.*]: Will I strike him with my hand?

MICHAEL: Take the loy is on your western side.

SHAWN: I'd be afeard of the gallows if I struck with that.

CHRISTY [*Taking up the loy.*]: Then I'll make you face the gallows or quit off from this.

[SHAWN *flies out of the door.*]

CHRISTY: Well, fine weather be after him [*going to* MICHAEL, *coaxingly*], and I'm thinking you wouldn't wish to have that quaking blackguard in your house at all. Let you give us your blessing and hear her swear her faith to me, for I'm mounted on the spring-tide of the stars of luck, the way it'll be good for any to have me in the house.

PEGEEN [*At the other side of* MICHAEL.]: Bless us now, for I swear to God I'll wed him, and I'll not renege.

MICHAEL [*Standing up in the centre, holding on to both of them.*]: It's the will of God, I'm thinking, that all should win an easy or a cruel end, and it's the will of God that all should rear up lengthy families for the nurture of the earth. What's a single man, I ask you, eating a bit in one house and drinking a sup in another, and he with no place of his own, like an old braying jackass strayed upon the rocks? [*To* CHRISTY.] It's many would be in dread to bring your like into their house for to end them, maybe, with a sudden end; but I'm a decent man of Ireland, and I liefer face the grave untimely and I seeing a score of grandsons growing up little gallant swearers by the name of God, than go peopling my bedside with puny weeds the like of what you'd breed, I'm thinking, out of Shaneen Keogh. [*He joins their hands.*] A daring fellow is the jewel of the world, and a man did split his father's middle with a single clout should have the bravery of ten, so may God and Mary and St Patrick bless you, and increase you from this mortal day.

CHRISTY and PEGEEN. Amen, O Lord!

[*Hubbub outside. Old* MAHON *rushes in, followed by all the crowd, and* WIDOW QUIN. *He makes a rush at* CHRISTY, *knocks him down, and begins to beat him.*]

PEGEEN [*Dragging back his arm.*]: Stop that, will you? Who are you at all?

MAHON: His father, God forgive me!

PEGEEN [*Drawing back.*]: Is it rose from the dead?

MAHON: Do you think I look so easy quenched with the tap of a loy? [*Beats* CHRISTY *again.*]

PEGEEN [*Glaring at* CHRISTY.]: And it's lies you told, letting on you had him slitted, and you nothing at all.

CHRISTY [*Catching* MAHON*'s stick.*]: He's not my father. He's a raving maniac would scare the world. [*Pointing to* WIDOW QUIN.] Herself knows it is true.

CROWD: You're fooling, Pegeen! The Widow Quin seen him this day, and you likely knew! You're a liar!

CHRISTY [*Dumbfounded.*]: It's himself was a liar, lying stretched out with an open head on him, letting on he was dead.

MAHON: Weren't you off racing the hills before I got my breath with the start I had seeing you turn on me at all?

PEGEEN: And to think of the coaxing glory we had given him, and he after doing nothing but hitting a soft blow and chasing northward in a sweat of fear. Quit off from this.

CHRISTY [*Piteously.*]: You've seen my doings this day, and let you save me from the old man; for why would you be in such a scorch of haste to spur me to destruction now?

PEGEEN: It's there your treachery is spurring me, till I'm hard set to think you're the one I'm after lacing in my heart-strings half an hour gone by. [*To* MAHON.] Take him on from this, for I think bad the world should see me raging for a Munster liar, and the fool of men.

MAHON: Rise up now to retribution, and come on with me.

CROWD [*Jeeringly.*]: There's the playboy! There's the lad thought he'd rule the roost in Mayo! Slate him now, mister.

CHRISTY [*Getting up in shy terror.*]: What is it drives you to torment me here, when I'd asked the thunders of the might of God to blast me if I ever did hurt to any saving only that one single blow.

MAHON [*Loudly.*]: If you didn't, you're a poor good-for-nothing, and isn't it by the like of you the sins of the whole world are committed?

CHRISTY [*Raising his hands.*]: In the name of the Almighty God. . .

MAHON: Leave troubling the Lord God. Would you have Him sending down droughts, and fevers, and the old hen and the cholera morbus?

CHRISTY [*To* WIDOW QUIN.]: Will you come between us and protect me now?

WIDOW QUIN: I've tried a lot, God help me, and my share is done.

CHRISTY [*Looking round in desperation.*]: And I must go back into my torment is it, or run off like a vagabond straying through the unions with the dust of August making mudstains in the gullet of my throat; or the winds of March blowing on me till I'd take an oath I felt them making whistles of my ribs within?

SARA: Ask Pegeen to aid you. Her like does often change.

CHRISTY: I will not, then, for there's torment in the splendour of her like, and she a girl any moon of midnight would take pride to meet, facing southwards on the heaths of Keel. But what did I want crawling forward to scorch my understanding at her flaming brow?

PEGEEN [*To* MAHON, *vehemently, fearing she will break into tears.*]: Take him on from this or I'll set the young lads to destroy him here.

MAHON [*Going to him, shaking his stick.*]: Come on now if you wouldn't have the company to see you skelped.

PEGEEN [*Half laughing, through her tears.*]: That's it, now the world will see him pandied, and he an ugly liar was playing off the hero, and the fright of men.

CHRISTY [*To* MAHON, *very sharply.*]: Leave me go!

CROWD: That's it. Now, Christy. If them two set fighting, it will lick the world.

MAHON [*Making a grab at* CHRISTY.]: Come here to me.

CHRISTY [*More threateningly.*]: Leave me go, I'm saying.

MAHON: I will, maybe, when your legs is limping, and your back is blue.

CROWD: Keep it up, the two of you. I'll back the old one. Now the playboy.

CHRISTY [*In low and intense voice.*]: Shut your yelling, for if you're after making a mighty man of me this day by the power of a lie, you're setting me now to think if it's a poor thing to be lonesome it's worse, maybe, go mixing with the fools of earth.

[MAHON *makes a movement towards him.*]

CHRISTY [*Almost shouting.*]: Keep off . . . lest I do show a blow unto the lot of you would set the guardian angels winking in the clouds above.

[*He swings round with a sudden rapid movement and picks up a loy.*]

CROWD [*Half frightened, half amused.*]: He's going mad! Mind yourselves! Run from the idiot!

CHRISTY: If I am an idiot, I'm after hearing my voice this day saying words would raise the top-knot on a poet in a merchant's town. I've won your racing, and your lepping, and . . .

MAHON: Shut your gullet and come on with me.

CHRISTY: I'm going, but I'll stretch you first.

[*He runs at old* MAHON *with the loy, chases him out of the door, followed by* CROWD *and* WIDOW QUIN. *There is a great noise outside, then a yell, and dead silence for a moment.* CHRISTY *comes in, half dazed, and goes to fire.*]

WIDOW QUIN [*Coming in hurriedly, and going to him.*] They're turning again you. Come on, or you'll be hanged, indeed.

CHRISTY: I'm thinking, from this out, Pegeen'll be giving me praises, the same as in the hours gone by.

WIDOW QUIN [*Impatiently.*]: Come by the back door. I'd think bad to have you stifled on the gallows tree.

CHRISTY [*Indignantly.*]: I will not, then. What good'd be my lifetime if I left Pegeen?

WIDOW QUIN: Come on, and you'll be no worse than you were last night; and you with a double murder this time to be telling to the girls.

CHRISTY: I'll not leave Pegeen Mike.

WIDOW QUIN [*Impatiently.*]: Isn't there the match of her in every parish public, from Binghamstown unto the plain of Meath? Come on, I tell you, and I'll find you finer sweethearts at each waning moon.

CHRISTY: It's Pegeen I'm seeking only, and what'd I care if you brought me a drift of chosen females, standing in their shifts itself, maybe, from this place to the eastern world?

SARA [*Runs in, pulling off one of her petticoats.*]: They're going to hang him. [*Holding out petticoat and shawl.*] Fit these upon him, and let him run off to the east.

WIDOW QUIN: He's raving now; but we'll fit them on him, and I'll take him in the ferry to the Achill boat.

CHRISTY [*Struggling feebly.*]: Leave me go, will you? when I'm thinking of my luck to-day, for she will wed me surely, and I a proven hero in the end of all.

[*They try to fasten petticoat round him.*]

WIDOW QUIN: Take his left hand and we'll pull him now. Come on, young fellow.

CHRISTY [*Suddenly starting up.*]: You'll be taking me from her? You're jealous, is it, of her wedding me? Go on from this.

[*He snatches up a stool, and threatens them with it.*]

WIDOW QUIN [*Going.*]: It's in the madhouse they should put him, not in jail, at all. We'll go by the back door to call the doctor, and we'll save him so.

[*She goes out, with* SARA, *through inner room. Men crowd in the doorway.* CHRISTY *sits down again by the fire.*]

MICHAEL [*In a terrified whisper.*]: Is the old lad killed surely?

PHILLY: I'm after feeling the last gasps quitting his heart.

[*They peer in at* CHRISTY.]

MICHAEL [*With a rope.*]: Look at the way he is. Twist a hangman's knot on it, and slip it over his head, while he's not minding at all.

PHILLY: Let you take it, Shaneen. You're the soberest of all that's here.

SHAWN: Is it me to go near him, and he the wickedest and worst with me? Let you take it, Pegeen Mike.

PEGEEN: Come on, so.

[*She goes forward with the others, and they drop the double hitch over his head.*]

CHRISTY: What ails you?

SHAWN [*Triumphantly, as they pull the rope tight on his arms.*]: Come on to the peelers, till they stretch you now.

CHRISTY: Me!

MICHAEL: If we took pity on you the Lord God would, maybe, bring us ruin from the law to-day, so you'd best come easy, for hanging is an easy and a speedy end.

CHRISTY: I'll not stir. [*To* PEGEEN.] And what is it you'll say to me, and I after doing it this time in the face of all?

PEGEEN: I'll say, a strange man is a marvel, with his mighty talk; but what's a squabble in your back yard, and the blow of a loy, have taught me that there's a great gap between a gallous story and a dirty deed. [*To men.*] Take him on from this, or the lot of us will be likely put on trial for his deed to-day.

CHRISTY [*With horror in his voice.*]: And it's yourself will send me off, to have a horny-fingered hangman hitching slip-knots at the butt of my ear.

MEN [*Pulling rope.*]: Come on, will you?

[*He is pulled down on the floor.*]

CHRISTY [*Twisting his legs round the table.*] Cut the rope, Pegeen, and I'll quit the lot of you, and live from this out, like the madman of Keel, eating muck and green weeds on the faces of the cliffs.

PEGEEN: And leave us to hang, is it, for a saucy liar, the like of you? [*To men.*] Take him on, out from this.

SHAWN: Pull a twist on his neck, and squeeze him so.

PHILLY: Twist yourself. Sure he cannot hurt you, if you keep your distance from his teeth alone.

SHAWN: I'm afeard of him. [*To* PEGEEN.] Lift a lighted sod, will you, and scorch his leg.

PEGEEN [*Blowing the fire with a bellows.*]: Leave go now, young fellow, or I'll scorch your shins.

CHRISTY: You're blowing for to torture me. [*His voice rising and growing stronger.*] That's your kind, is it? Then let the lot of you be wary, for, if I've to face the gallows, I'll have a gay march down, I tell you, and shed the blood of some of you before I die.

SHAWN [*In terror.*]: Keep a good hold, Philly. Be wary, for the love of God. For I'm thinking he would liefest wreak his pains on me.

CHRISTY [*Almost gaily.*]: If I do lay my hands on you, it's the way you'll be at the fall of night, hanging as a scarecrow for the fowls of hell. Ah, you'll have a gallous jaunt, I'm saying, coaching out through limbo with my father's ghost.

SHAWN [*To* PEGEEN.]: Make haste, will you? Oh, isn't he a holy terror, and isn't it true for Father Reilly, that all drink's a curse that has the lot of you so shaky and uncertain now?

CHRISTY: If I can wring a neck among you, I'll have a royal judgment looking on the trembling jury in the courts of law. And won't there be crying out in Mayo the day I'm stretched upon the rope, with ladies in their silks and satins snivelling in their lacy kerchiefs, and they rhyming songs and ballads on the terror of my fate?

[*He squirms round on the floor and bites* SHAWN'*s leg.*]

SHAWN [*Shrieking.*]: My leg's bit on me. He's the like of a mad dog, I'm thinking, the way that I will surely die.

CHRISTY [*Delighted with himself.*]: You will, then, the way you can shake out hell's flags of welcome for my coming in two weeks or three, for I'm thinking Satan hasn't many have killed their da in Kerry, and in Mayo too.

[*Old* MAHON *comes in behind on all fours and looks on unnoticed.*]

MEN [*To* PEGEEN.]: Bring the sod, will you?

PEGEEN [*Coming over.*]: God help him so. [*Burns his leg.*]

CHRISTY [*Kicking and screaming.*]: Oh, glory be to God!

[*He kicks loose from the table, and they all drag him towards the door.*]

JIMMY [*Seeing old* MAHON.]: Will you look what's come in?

[*They all drop* CHRISTY *and run left.*]

CHRISTY [*Scrambling on his knees face to face with old* MAHON.]: Are you coming to be killed a third time, or what ails you now?

MAHON: For what is it they have you tied?

CHRISTY: They're taking me to the peelers to have me hanged for slaying you.

MICHAEL [*Apologetically.*]: It is the will of God that all should guard their little cabins from the treachery of law, and what would my daughter be doing if I was ruined or was hanged itself?

MAHON [*Grimly, loosening* CHRISTY.]: It's little I care if you put a bag on her back, and went picking cockles till the hour of death; but my son and myself will be going our own way, and we'll have great times from this out telling stories of the villainy of Mayo, and the fools is here. [*To* CHRISTY, *who is freed.*] Come on now.

CHRISTY: Go with you, is it? I will then, like a gallant captain with his heathen slave. Go on now and I'll see you from this day stewing my oatmeal and washing my spuds, for I'm master of all fights from now. [*Pushing* MAHON.] Go on, I'm saying.

MAHON: Is it me?

CHRISTY: Not a word out of you. Go on from this.

MAHON [*Walking out and looking back at* CHRISTY *over his shoulder.*]: Glory be to God! [*With a broad smile.*] I am crazy again. [*Goes.*]

CHRISTY: Ten thousand blessings upon all that's here, for you've turned me a likely gaffer in the end of all, the way I'll go romancing through a romping lifetime from this hour to the dawning of the Judgment Day. [*He goes out.*]

MICHAEL: By the will of God, we'll have peace now for our drinks. Will you draw the porter, Pegeen?

SHAWN [*Going up to her.*]: It's a miracle Father Reilly can wed us in the end of all, and we'll have none to trouble us when his vicious bite is healed.

PEGEEN [*Hitting him a box on the ear.*]: Quit my sight. [*Putting her shawl over her head and breaking out into wild lamentations.*] Oh, my grief, I've lost him surely. I've lost the only Playboy of the Western World.

CURTAIN

Susan Glaspell

Susan Glaspell (1876–1948) was born in Davenport, Iowa, into a middle-class family whose values alternately attracted and repelled her. After graduating from Drake University in Davenport, she set herself up as an independent writer in Davenport and Chicago. She was twenty-nine when she began a romance with George Cram Cook, a married man, whom she later married in 1913. Cook, known as "Jig," was a man of many careers—college teacher, sculptor, writer—none of which was successful. Their marriage was tempestuous, due largely to Cook's alcoholism and promiscuity, but it proved a great catalyst for Glaspell's creativity and career. Much of her writing is autobiographical, and her fiction and drama often focus on marital conflict. *Fidelity* (1915), for example, is a patently autobiographical novel that justifies her adulterous relationship with Cook before they married. In *Woman's Honor*, a short play written three years later, six women compete to save the life of a man who chivalrously refuses to defend himself against a charge of murder. In a production of the play, Glaspell chose to act the part of the Cheated One, the woman who complains that the man she married kept her from enjoying her best years. Though *Woman's Honor* projects a picture of what Glaspell's private life may have become when she was age forty-two, it is a satire of Henrik Ibsen's *A Doll's House*, in which Nora defends a woman's honor to her uncomprehending husband.

Glaspell and Cook moved from Chicago to Greenwich Village, New York, and then Provincetown, Massachusetts. Together they wrote and produced *Suppressed Desires* (1914), a one-act play that pokes ironic fun at psychoanalysis. The following year they founded the Provincetown Players and the Playwrights' Theater, the latter an experimental theater that had far-reaching effects on American drama and literature. The Provincetown Players quickly evolved into an intensely creative group that eventually included the playwright Eugene O'Neill; the poets Edna St. Vincent Millay and e. e. cummings; the fiction writers Floyd Dell, Edna Ferber, and Sherwood Anderson; and the journalist John Reed. Within a few years, Glaspell, Cook, and their circle had established a new style of American drama based on the psychology of character, derived mainly from naturalism and August Strindberg's *Miss Julie* and *The Father*, and to a lesser extent, Henrik Ibsen's problem plays, especially *A Doll's House.*

Glaspell wrote a number of one-act plays for the Provincetown Players, including *Trifles* (1916), today her most widely anthologized work. Praised for its naturalistic dialogue and psychological insight, *Trifles* is also considered a feminist icon because of its depiction of female intuition overcoming male "expertise." In the play, Minnie Wright has been arrested for murdering her husband by strangling him in their bed in his sleep. While Sheriff Peters, a neighbor named Mr. Hale, and the district attorney search vainly for clues to the murder, Mrs. Peters and Mrs. Hale find signs that reveal John Wright's brutal cruelty toward his wife, and they suppress the evidence, without which Minnie cannot be charged. Glaspell revised *Trifles* as a short story, under the title "A Jury of Her Peers" (1918).

Other Glaspell plays produced by the Provincetown Players include *Close the Book* (1917) and *A Woman's Honor* (1918), along with the full-length plays *Bernice* (1919), *Inheritors* (1921), and *The Verge* (1921). *Bernice,* Glaspell's first three-act play, continues her focus on the themes of adultery and death, in this case exploring the effects of a wife's suicide because of an unfaithful husband.

In 1922 Glaspell and Cook traveled to Greece, where they lived until his death two years later. She returned to Provincetown and tried to come to terms with his death. The result was an appreciative biography, *The Road to the Temple* (1927), and an edition of his poems in English and Greek. In time, she began a relationship with Norman Matson, a writer, with whom she collaborated on the play *The Comic Artist* (1928). In 1929 she published *Fugitive's Return,* a novel based on her life in Greece, and in 1930 another play, *Alison's House,* based in part on the life of Emily Dickinson. Although *Alison's House* opened to negative reviews and attracted small audiences, it unexpectedly won the Pulitzer Prize for Drama, a prize that had only once before been given to a woman. She followed this with a novel, *Ambrose Holt and Family* (1931), which advocates birth control and defends the political and moral arguments of Margaret Sanger, a rewrite of Glaspell's 1922 play, *Chains of Dew.* The novel tells the story of Nora Powers, an independent woman working for a social cause, who has an adulterous affair with Seymore Standish, an affluent banker with literary ambitions. The story ends when Nora outgrows Standish and allows him to return to his wife. The name and character of Nora is an allusion to Nora Helmer, Henrik Ibsen's independent woman in *A Doll's House.* Glaspell gained her own independence when her eight-year relationship with Matson ended and he left her for a younger woman.

At fifty-six, Glaspell lost her creative spirit and filled some of her time between 1934 and 1936 working for a unit of the Federal Theatre Project in the Midwest. She returned to Provincetown, and there she eventually rallied, writing three novels: *The Morning Is Near Us* (1939), *Norma Ashe* (1942), and *Judd Rankin's Daughter* (1945). At seventy-one, she died of cancer, aggravated by alcoholism.

The Verge, a three-act play written when she was forty-five, expresses Glaspell's deepest inner conflicts of self and reflects the questions of self-worth that plagued her in real life. Weighted with the symbolic influences of Freudian psychoanalysis, the play focuses on Claire Archer, an artist on the verge of a nervous breakdown, who is caught between competing claims on her life: a husband, Harry, who is supercilious and patronizing, and a lover, Dick Demming, whom she does not love. She is emotionally estranged from her daughter, Elizabeth, whom she cast off as a child and whom she still can find no maternal feeling for. Depressed, she agonizes over the chaos in her life and her inability to control her creative talent. She spends most of her time in a glass greenhouse, where she can control the environment to a limited extent by hybridizing new kinds of plants: the Edge Vine, characterized by a distorted shape, and Breath of

Life, a flower without fragrance. When she is not in the greenhouse, Claire spends time in a room at the top of a distorted tower, reached only by a set of spiral stairs. Claire's only hope seems to be Tom Edgeworthy, a dashing aviator, to whom she reaches out for affection and passionate love. At a particularly cruel moment when a snowstorm freezes the greenhouse, Edgeworthy admits that he cannot love Claire. Surrounded by what she sees is a hostile unloving world, Claire snaps. Tom returns to tell her that he loves her, but she sees him now as a hindrance, and in a frenzy she kills him. She is discovered haltingly singing the hymn "Nearer My God to Thee" as the curtain descends.

Glaspell is still a marginal figure in the dramatic history of the United States, best remembered for her role in founding the Provincetown Players. The collective talent of this group overpowered Glaspell, and it must have been cold comfort to her when she was called the "mother" of modern American theater. She was eclipsed by her contemporaries: O'Neill, who became the leading playwright of pre–World War II America and the only U.S. dramatist to win a Nobel Prize; Edna Ferber, who became a best-selling novelist, noted for *Show Boat;* and John Reed, who became a hero of the political left when he espoused Communism and wrote about the Russian Revolution of 1917. At various points in their careers, some members of the Provincetown Players were deeply engaged in politics and social reform, and though Glaspell generally steered clear of politics, she strongly advocated women's rights. After her death, Glaspell and her plays and stories were largely forgotten; nevertheless, since the 1970s, she has been steadily regaining both recognition as an artist and respect for her unique body of work.

The Verge

PERSONS OF THE PLAY

ANTHONY
HARRY ARCHER, Claire's husband
HATTIE, the maid
CLAIRE
DICK, Richard Demming
TOM EDGEWORTHY
ELIZABETH, Claire's daughter
ADELAIDE, Claire's sister
DR EMMONS

ACT I

The Curtain lifts on a place that is dark, save for a shaft of light from below which comes up through an open trap-door in the floor. This slants up and strikes the long leaves and the huge brilliant blossom of a strange plant whose twisted stem projects from right front. Nothing is seen except this plant and its shadow. A violent wind is heard. A moment later a buzzer. It buzzes once long and three short. Silence. Again the buzzer. Then from below—his shadow blocking the light, comes ANTHONY, *a rugged man past middle life;—he emerges from the stairway into the darkness of the room. Is dimly seen taking up a phone.*

ANTHONY: Yes, Miss Claire?— I'll see. [*he brings a thermometer to the stairway for light, looks sharply, then returns to the phone*] It's down to forty-nine. The plants are in danger— [*with great relief and approval*] Oh, that's fine! [*hangs up the receiver*] Fine!

[*He goes back down the stairway, closing the trap-door upon himself, and the curtain is drawn upon darkness and wind. It opens a moment later on the greenhouse in the sunshine of a snowy morning. The snow piled outside is at times blown through the air. The frost has made patterns on the glass as if—as Plato would have it—the patterns inherent in abstract nature and behind all life had to come out, not only in the creative heart within, but in the creative cold on the other side of the glass. And the wind makes patterns of sound around the glass house.*

The back wall is low; the glass roof slopes sharply up. There is an outside door, a little toward the right. From outside two steps lead down to it. At left a glass partition and a door into the inner room. One sees a little way into this room. At right there is no dividing wall save large plants and vines, a narrow aisle between shelves of plants leads off.

This is not a greenhouse where plants are being displayed, nor the usual workshop for the growing of them, but a place for experiment with plants, a laboratory.

At the back grows a strange vine. It is arresting rather than beautiful. It creeps along the low wall, and one branch gets a little way up the glass. You might see the form of a cross in it, if you happened to think it that way. The leaves of this vine are not the form that leaves have been. They are at once repellent and significant.

ANTHONY *is at work preparing soil—mixing, sifting. As the wind tries the door he goes anxiously to the thermometer, nods as if reassured and returns to his work. The buzzer sounds. He starts to answer the telephone, remembers something, halts and listens sharply. It does not buzz once long and three short. Then he returns to his work. The buzzer goes on and on in impatient jerks which mount in anger. Several times* ANTHONY *is almost compelled by this insistence, but the thing that holds him back is stronger. At last, after a particularly mad splutter, to which* ANTHONY *longs to make retort, the buzzer gives it up.* ANTHONY *goes on preparing soil.*

A moment later the glass door swings violently in, snow blowing in, and also MR HARRY ARCHER, *wrapped in a rug.*]

ANTHONY: Oh, please close the door, sir.

HARRY: Do you think I'm not trying to? [*he holds it open to say this*]

ANTHONY: But please *do*. This stormy air is not good for the plants.

HARRY: I suppose it's just the thing for me! Now, what do you mean, Anthony, by not answering the phone when I buzz for you?

ANTHONY: Miss Claire—Mrs Archer told me not to.

HARRY: Told you not to answer me?

ANTHONY: Not you especially—nobody but her.

HARRY: Well, I like her nerve—and yours.

ANTHONY: You see, she thought it took my mind from my work to be interrupted when I'm out here. And so it does. So she buzzes once long and— Well, she buzzes her way, and all other buzzing—

HARRY: May buzz.

ANTHONY [*nodding gravely*]: She thought it would be better for the flowers.

HARRY: I am not a flower—true, but I too need a little attention—and a little heat. Will you please tell me why the house is frigid?

ANTHONY: Miss Claire ordered all the heat turned out here. [*patiently explaining it to* MISS CLAIRE'*s speechless husband*] You see the roses need a great deal of heat.

HARRY [*reading the thermometer*]: The roses have seventy-three I have forty-five.

ANTHONY: Yes, the roses need seventy-three.

HARRY: Anthony, this is an outrage!

ANTHONY: I think it is myself; when you consider what we paid for the heating plant—but as long as it is defective—Why, Miss Claire would never have done what she has if she hadn't looked out for her plants in just such ways as this. Have you forgotten that Breath of Life is about to flower?

HARRY: And where's my breakfast about to flower?—that's what I want to know.

ANTHONY: Why, Miss Claire got up at five o'clock to order the heat turned off from the house.

HARRY: I see you admire her vigilance.

ANTHONY: Oh, I do. [*fervently*] I do. Harm was near, and that woke her up.

HARRY: And what about the harm to— [*tapping his chest*] Do roses get pneumonia?

ANTHONY: Oh, yes—yes, indeed they do. Why, Mr Archer, look at Miss Claire herself. Hasn't she given her heat to the roses?

HARRY [*pulling the rug around him, preparing for the blizzard*]: She has the fire within.

ANTHONY [*delighted*]: Now isn't that true! How well you said it. [*with a glare for this appreciation,* HARRY *opens the door. It blows away from him*] Please do close the door!

HARRY [*furiously*]: You think it is the aim of my life to hold it open?

ANTHONY [*getting hold of it*]: Growing things need an even temperature. [*while saying this he gets the man out into the snow*]

[ANTHONY *consults the thermometer, not as pleased this time as he was before. He then looks minutely at two of the plants—one is a rose, the other a flower without a name because it has not long enough been a flower. Peers into the hearts of them. Then from a drawer under a shelf, takes two paper bags, puts one over each of these flowers, closing them down at the bottom. Again the door blows wildly in, also* HATTIE, *a maid with a basket.*]

ANTHONY: What do you mean—blowing in here like this? Mrs Archer has ordered—

HATTIE: Mr Archer has ordered breakfast served here. [*she uncovers the basket and takes out an electric toaster*]

ANTHONY: *Breakfast*—here? *Eat*—here? Where plants grow?

HATTIE: The plants won't poison him, will they? [*at a loss to know what to do with things, she puts the toaster under the strange vine at the back, whose leaves lift up against the glass which has frost leaves on the outer side*]

ANTHONY [*snatching it away*]: You—you think you can *cook eggs* under the Edge Vine?

The Verge *was produced at the Provincetown Theatre, New York City, in 1921, with Margaret Wycherly, Henry O'Neill, Louis Hallet, Harold West, and Edward B. Reese.*

HATTIE: I guess Mr Archer's eggs are as important as a vine. I guess my work's as important as yours.

ANTHONY: There's a million people like you—and like Mr Archer. In all the world there is only one Edge Vine.

HATTIE: Well, maybe one's enough. It don't look like nothin', anyhow.

ANTHONY: And you've not got the wit to know that that's why it's the Edge Vine.

HATTIE: You want to look out, Anthony. You talk nutty. Everybody says so.

ANTHONY: Miss Claire don't say so.

HATTIE: No, because she's—

ANTHONY: You talk too much!

[*Door opens, admitting* HARRY; *after looking around for the best place to eat breakfast, moves a box of earth from the table.*]

HARRY: Just give me a hand, will you, Hattie?

[*They bring it to the open space and he and* HATTIE *arrange breakfast things,* HATTIE *with triumphant glances at the distressed* ANTHONY.]

ANTHONY [*deciding he must act*]: Mr Archer, this is not the place to eat breakfast!

HARRY: Dead wrong, old boy. The place that has heat is the place to eat breakfast. [*to* HATTIE] Tell the other gentlemen—I heard Mr Demming up, and Mr Edgeworthy, if he appears, that as long as it is such a pleasant morning, we're having breakfast outside. To the conservatory for coffee. [HATTIE *giggles, is leaving*] And let's see, have we got everything? [*takes the one shaker, shakes a little pepper on his hand. Looks in vain for the other shaker*] And tell Mr Demming to bring the salt.

ANTHONY: But Miss Claire will be very angry.

HARRY: I am very angry. Did I choose to eat my breakfast at the other end of a blizzard?

ANTHONY [*an exclamation of horror at the thermometer*]: The temperature is falling. I must report. [*he punches the buzzer, takes up the phone*] Miss Claire? It is Anthony. A terrible thing has happened. Mr Archer—what? Yes, a terrible thing.—Yes, it is about Mr Archer.—No—no, not dead. But here. He is here. Yes, he is well, he seems well, but he is eating his breakfast. Yes, he is having breakfast served out here—for himself, and the other gentlemen are to come too.—Well, he seemed to be annoyed because the heat had been turned off from the house. But the door keeps opening—this stormy wind blowing right over the plants. The temperature has already fallen.—Yes, yes. I thought you would want to come.

[ANTHONY *opens the trap-door and goes below.* HARRY *looks disapprovingly down into this openness at his feet, returns to his breakfast.* ANTHONY *comes up, bearing a box.*]

HARRY [*turning his face away*]: Phew! What a smell.

ANTHONY: Yes. Fertilizer has to smell.

HARRY: Well, it doesn't have to smell up my breakfast!

ANTHONY [*with a patient sense of order*]: The smell belongs here. [*he and the smell go to the inner room*]

[*The outer door opens just enough to admit* CLAIRE*—is quickly closed. With* CLAIRE *in a room another kind of aliveness is there.*]

CLAIRE: What are you doing here?

HARRY: Getting breakfast. [*all the while doing so*]

CLAIRE: I'll not have you in my place!

HARRY: If you take all the heat then you have to take me.

CLAIRE: I'll show you how I have to take you. [*with her hands begins scooping upon him the soil* ANTHONY *has prepared*]

HARRY [*jumping up, laughing, pinning down her arms, putting his arms around her*]: Claire—be decent. What harm do I do here?

CLAIRE: You pull down the temperature.

HARRY: Not after I'm in.

CLAIRE: And you told Tom and Dick to come and make it uneven.

HARRY: Tom and Dick are our guests. We can't eat where it's warm and leave them to eat where it's cold.

CLAIRE: I don't see why not.

HARRY: You only see what you want to see.

CLAIRE: That's not true. I wish it were. No; no, I don't either. [*she is disturbed—that troubled thing which rises from within, from deep, and takes* CLAIRE. *She turns to the Edge Vine, examines. Regretfully to* ANTHONY, *who has come in with a plant*] It's turning back, isn't it?

ANTHONY: Can you be sure yet, Miss Claire?

CLAIRE: Oh yes—it's had its chance. It doesn't want to be—what hasn't been.

HARRY [*who has turned at this note in her voice. Speaks kindly*]: Don't take it so seriously, Claire. [CLAIRE *laughs*]

CLAIRE: No, I suppose not. But it *does* matter—and why should I pretend it doesn't, just because I've failed with it?

HARRY: Well, I don't want to see it get you—it's not important enough for that.

CLAIRE [*in her brooding way*]: Anything is important enough for that—if it's important at all. [*to the vine*] I thought you were out, but you're—going back home.

ANTHONY: But you're doing it this time, Miss Claire. When Breath of Life opens—and we see its heart—

[CLAIRE *looks toward the inner room. Because of intervening plants they do not see what is seen from the front—a plant like caught motion, and of a greater transparency than plants have had. Its leaves, like waves that curl, close around a heart that's not seen. This plant stands by itself in what, because of the arrangement of things about it, is a hidden place. But nothing is between it and the light.*]

CLAIRE: Yes, if the heart has [*a little laugh*] held its own, then Breath of Life is alive in its otherness. But Edge Vine is running back to what it broke out of.

HARRY: Come, have some coffee, Claire.

[ANTHONY *returns to the inner room, the outer door opens.* DICK *is hurled in.*]

CLAIRE [*going to the door, as he gasps for breath before closing it*]: How dare you make my temperature uneven! [*she shuts the door and leans against it*]

DICK: Is that what I do?

[*A laugh, a look between them, which is held into significance.*]

HARRY [*who is not facing them*]: Where's the salt?

DICK: Oh, I fell down in the snow. I must have left the salt where I fell. I'll go back and look for it.

CLAIRE: And change the temperature? We don't need salt.

HARRY: You don't need salt, Claire. But we eat eggs.

CLAIRE: I must tell you I don't like the idea of any food being eaten here, where things have their own way to go. Please eat as little as possible, and as quickly.

HARRY: A hostess calculated to put one at one's ease.

CLAIRE [*with no ill-nature*]: I care nothing about your ease. Or about Dick's ease.

DICK: And no doubt that's what makes you so fascinating a hostess.

CLAIRE: Was I a fascinating hostess last night, Dick? [*softly sings*] "Oh, night of love—" [*from the Barcorole of "Tales of Hoffman"*]

HARRY: We've got to have salt.

[*He starts for the door.* CLAIRE *slips in ahead of him, locks it, takes the key. He marches off, right.*]

CLAIRE [*calling after him*]: That end's always locked.

DICK: Claire darling, I wish you wouldn't say those startling things. You do get away with it, but I confess it gives me a shock—and really, it's unwise.

CLAIRE: Haven't you learned that the best place to hide is in the truth? [*as* HARRY *returns*] Why won't you believe me, Harry, when I tell you the truth—about doors being locked?

HARRY: Claire, it's selfish of you to keep us from eating salt just because you don't eat salt.

CLAIRE [*with one of her swift changes*]: Oh, Harry! Try your egg without salt. Please—please try it without salt! [*an intensity which seems all out of proportion to the subject*]

HARRY: An egg demands salt.

CLAIRE: "An egg demands salt." Do you know, Harry, why you are such an unseasoned person? "An egg demands salt."

HARRY: Well, it doesn't always get it.

CLAIRE: But your spirit gets no lift from the salt withheld.

HARRY: Not an inch of lift. [*going back to his breakfast*]

CLAIRE: And pleased—so pleased with itself, for getting no lift. Sure, it is just the right kind of spirit—because it gets no lift. [*more brightly*] But, Dick, you must have tried your egg without salt.

DICK: I'll try it now. [*he goes to the breakfast table*]

CLAIRE: You must have tried and tried things. Isn't that the way one leaves the normal and gets into the byways of perversion?

HARRY: Claire.

DICK [*pushing back his egg*]: If so, I prefer to wait for the salt.

HARRY: Claire, there is a *limit.*

CLAIRE: Precisely what I had in mind. To perversion too there is a limit. So—the fortifications are unassailable. If one ever does get out, I suppose it is—quite unexpectedly, and perhaps—a bit terribly.

HARRY: Get out where?

CLAIRE [*with a bright smile*]: Where you, darling, will never go.

HARRY: And from which you, darling, had better beat it.

CLAIRE: I wish I could. [*to herself*] No—no I don't either.

[*Again this troubled thing turns her to the plant. She puts by themselves the two which* ANTHONY *covered with paper bags. Is about to remove these papers.* HARRY *strikes a match.*]

CLAIRE [*turning sharply*]: You can't smoke here. The plants are not used to it.

HARRY: Then I should think smoking would be just the thing for them.

CLAIRE: There is design.

HARRY [*to* DICK]: Am I supposed to be answered? I never can be quite sure at what moment I am answered.

[*They both watch* CLAIRE, *who has uncovered the plants and is looking intently into the flowers. From a drawer she takes some tools. Very carefully gives the rose pollen to an unfamiliar flower—rather wistfully unfamiliar, which stands above on a small shelf near the door of the inner room.*]

DICK: What is this you're doing, Claire?
CLAIRE: Pollenizing. Crossing for fragrance.
DICK: It's all rather mysterious, isn't it?
HARRY: And Claire doesn't make it any less so.
CLAIRE: Can I make life any less mysterious?
HARRY: If you know what you are doing, why can't you tell Dick?
DICK: Never mind. After all, why should I be told? [*he turns away*]

[*At that she wants to tell him. Helpless, as one who cannot get across a stream, starts uncertainly.*]

CLAIRE: I want to give fragrance to Breath of Life [*faces the room beyond the wall of glass*] —the flower I have created that is outside what flowers have been. What has gone out should bring fragrance from what it has left. But no definite fragrance, no limiting enclosing thing. I call the fragrance I am trying to create Reminiscence. [*her hand on the pot of the wistful little flower she has just given pollen*] Reminiscent of the rose, the violet, arbutus—but a new thing—itself. Breath of Life may be lonely out in what hasn't been. Perhaps some day I can give it reminiscence.
DICK: I see, Claire.
CLAIRE: I wonder if you do.
HARRY: Now, Claire, you're going to be gay to-day, aren't you? These are Tom's last couple of days with us.
CLAIRE: That doesn't make me especially gay.
HARRY: Well, you want him to remember you as yourself, don't you?
CLAIRE: I would like him to. Oh—I would like him to!
HARRY: Then be amusing. That's really you, isn't it, Dick?
DICK: Not quite all of her—I should say.
CLAIRE [*gaily*]: Careful, Dick. Aren't you indiscreet? Harry will be suspecting that I am your latest strumpet.
HARRY: Claire! What language you use! A person knowing you only by certain moments could never be made to believe you are a refined woman.
CLAIRE: True, isn't it, Dick?
HARRY: It would be a good deal of a lark to let them listen in at times—then tell them that here is the flower of New England!
CLAIRE: Well, if this is the flower of New England, then the half has never been told.
DICK: About New England?
CLAIRE: I thought I meant that. Perhaps I meant—about me.
HARRY [*going on with his own entertainment*]: Explain that this is what came of the men who made the laws that made New England, that here is the flower of those gentlemen of culture who—
DICK: Moulded the American mind!
CLAIRE: Oh! [*it is pain*]
HARRY: Now what's the matter?
CLAIRE: I want to get away from them!
HARRY: Rest easy, little one—you do.
CLAIRE: I'm not so sure—that I do. But it *can* be done! We need not be held in forms moulded for us. There is outness—and otherness.
HARRY: Now, Claire—I didn't mean to start anything serious.
CLAIRE: No; you never mean to do that. I want to break it up! I tell you, I want to break it up! If it were all in pieces, we'd be [*a little laugh*] shocked to aliveness [*to* DICK] —wouldn't we? There would be strange new comings together—mad new comings together, and we would know what it is to be born, and then we might know—that we are. Smash it. [*her hand is near an egg*] As you'd smash an egg. [*she pushes the egg over the edge of the table and leans over and looks, as over a precipice*]
HARRY [*with a sigh*]: Well, all you've smashed is the egg, and all that amounts to is that now Tom gets no egg. So that's that.
CLAIRE [*with difficulty, drawing herself back from the fascination of the precipice*]: You think I can't smash anything? You think life can't break up, and go outside what it was? Because you've gone dead in the form in which you found yourself, you think that's all there is to the whole adventure? And that is called sanity. And made a virtue—to lock one in. You never worked with things that grow! Things that take a sporting chance—go mad—that sanity mayn't lock them in—from life untouched—from life—that waits. [*she turns toward the inner room*] Breath of Life. [*she goes in there*]
HARRY: Oh, I wish Claire wouldn't be strange like that. [*helplessly*] What is it? What's the matter?
DICK: It's merely the excess of a particularly rich temperament.
HARRY: But it's growing on her. I sometimes wonder if all this [*indicating the place around him*] is a good thing. It would be all right if she'd just do what she did in the beginning—make the flowers as good as possible of their kind. That's an awfully nice thing for a woman to do—raise flowers. But there's something about this—changing things into other things—putting things together and making queer new things—this—
DICK: Creating?
HARRY: Give it any name you want it to have—it's unsettling for a woman. They say Claire's a shark at it, but what's the good of it, if it gets her? What

is the good of it, anyway? Suppose we can produce new things. Lord—look at the one ones we've got. [*looks outside; turns back*] Heavens, what a noise the wind does make around this place. [*but now it is not all the wind, but* TOM EDGEWORTHY, *who is trying to let himself in at the locked door, their backs are to him*] I want my *egg.* You can't eat an egg without salt. I must say I don't get Claire lately. I'd like to have Charlie Emmons see her—he's fixed up a lot of people shot to pieces in the war. Claire needs something to tone her nerves *up*. You think it would irritate her?

DICK: She'd probably get no little entertainment out of it.

HARRY: Yes, dog-gone her, she would. [TOM *now makes more heroic measures to make himself heard at the door*] Funny—how the wind can fool you. Now by not looking around I could imagine—why, I could imagine anything. Funny, isn't it, about imagination? And Claire says I haven't got any!

DICK: It would make an amusing drawing—what the wind makes you think is there. [*first makes forms with his hands, then levelling the soil prepared by* ANTHONY, *traces lines with his finger*] Yes, really—quite jolly.

[TOM, *after a moment of peering in at them, smiles, goes away.*]

HARRY: You're another one of the queer ducks, aren't you? Come now—give me the dirt. Have you queer ones really got anything—or do you just put it over on us that you have? [DICK *smiles, draws on*] Not saying anything, eh? Well, I guess you're wise there. If you keep mum—how are we going to prove there's nothing there?

DICK: I don't keep mum. I draw.

HARRY: Lines that don't make anything—how can they tell you anything? Well, all I ask is, don't make Claire queer. Claire's a first water good sport—really, so don't encourage her to be queer.

DICK: Trouble is, if you're queer enough to be amusing, it might—open the door to queerness.

HARRY: Now don't say things like that to Claire.

DICK: I don't have to.

HARRY: Then *you* think she's queer, do you? Queer as you are, you think she's queer. I would like to have Dr Emmons come out. [*after a moment of silently watching* DICK, *who is having a good time with his drawing*] You know, frankly, I doubt if you're a good influence for Claire. [DICK *lifts his head ever so slightly*] Oh, I don't worry a bit about—things a husband might worry about. I suppose an intellectual woman—and for all Claire's hate of her ancestors, she's got the bug herself. Why, she has times of boring into things until she doesn't know you're there. What do you think I caught her doing the other day? Reading Latin. Well—a woman that reads Latin needn't worry a husband much.

DICK: They said a good deal in Latin.

HARRY: But I was saying, I suppose a woman who lives a good deal in her mind never does have much—well, what you might call passion. [*uses the word as if it shouldn't be used. Brows knitted, is looking ahead, does not see* DICK*'s face. Turning to him with a laugh*] I suppose you know pretty much all there is to know about women?

DICK: Perhaps one or two details have escaped me.

HARRY: Well, for that matter, you might know all there is to know about women and not know much about Claire. But now about [*does not want to say passion again*] —oh, feeling—Claire has a certain—well, a certain—

DICK: Irony?

HARRY: Which is really more—more—

DICK: More fetching, perhaps.

HARRY: Yes! Than the thing itself. But of course—you wouldn't have much of a thing that you have irony about.

DICK: Oh—wouldn't you! I mean—a man might.

HARRY: I'd like to talk to Edgeworthy about Claire. But it's not easy to talk to Tom about Claire—or to Claire about Tom.

DICK [*alert*]: They're very old friends, aren't they?

HARRY: Why—yes, they are. Though they've not been together much of late years, Edgeworthy always going to the ends of the earth to—meditate about something. I must say I don't get it. If you have a place—that's the place for you to be. And he did have a place—best kind of family connections, and it was a very good business his father left him. Publishing business—in good shape, too, when old Edgeworthy died. I wouldn't call Tom a great success in life—but Claire does listen to what he says.

DICK: Yes, I've noticed that.

HARRY: So, I'd like to get him to tell her to quit this queer business of making things grow that never grew before.

DICK: But are you sure that's what he would tell her? Isn't he in the same business himself?

HARRY: Why, he doesn't raise anything.

[TOM *is again at the door.*]

DICK: Anyway, I think he might have some idea that we can't very well reach each other.

HARRY: Damn nonsense. What have we got intelligence for?

DICK: To let each other alone, I suppose. Only we haven't enough to do it.

[TOM *is now knocking on the door with a revolver.* HARRY *half turns, decides to be too intelligent to turn.*]

HARRY: Don't tell me I'm getting nerves. But the way some of you people talk is enough to make even an aviator jumpy. Can't reach each other! Then we're fools. If I'm here and you're there, why can't we reach each other?

DICK: Because I am I and you are you.

HARRY: No wonder your drawing's queer. A man who can't reach another man—

[TOM *here reaches them by pointing the revolver in the air and firing it.* DICK *digs his hand into the dirt.* HARRY *jumps to one side, fearfully looks around.* TOM, *with a pleased smile to see he at last has their attention, moves the handle to indicate he would be glad to come in.*]

HARRY: Why—it's Tom! What the—? [*going to the door*] He's locked out. And Claire's got the key. [*goes to the inner door, tries it*] And she's locked in! [*trying to see her in there*] Claire! Claire! [*returning to the outer door*] Claire's got the key—and I can't get to Claire. [*makes a futile attempt at getting the door open without a key, goes back to inner door—peers, pounds*] Claire! Are you there? Didn't you hear the revolver? Has she gone down the cellar? [*tries the trap-door*] Bolted! Well, I love the way she keeps people locked out!

DICK: And in.

HARRY [*getting angry, shouting at the trap-door*]: Didn't you hear the revolver? [*going to* TOM] Awfully sorry, old man, but— [*in astonishment to* DICK] He can't hear me. [TOM, *knocking with the revolver to get their attention, makes a gesture of inquiry with it*] No—no—no! Is he asking if he shall shoot himself? [*shaking his head violently*] Oh, no—no! Um—*um!*

DICK: Hardly seems a man would shoot himself because he can't get to his breakfast.

HARRY: I'm coming to believe people would do anything! [TOM *is making another inquiry with the revolver*] *No!* not here. Don't shoot yourself. [*trying hard to get the word through*] *Shoot* yourself. I mean—don't. [*petulantly to* DICK] It's ridiculous that you can't make a man understand you when he looks right at you like that. [*turning back to* TOM] Read my lips. Lips. I'm saying—Oh damn. Where is Claire? All right—I'll explain it with motions. We wanted the salt . . . [*going over it to himself*] and Claire wouldn't let us go out for it on account of the temperature. Salt. Temperature. [*takes his egg-cup to the door, violent motion of shaking in salt*] But—no [*shakes his head*] No salt. [*he then takes the thermometer, a flower pot, holds them up to* TOM] On account of the temperature. Tem-per-a— [TOM *is not getting it*] Oh—well, what can you do when a man don't *get* a thing? [TOM *seems to be preparing the revolver for action.* HARRY *pounds on the inner door*] Claire! Do you want Tom to shoot himself?

[*As he looks in there, the trap-door lifts, and* CLAIRE *comes half-way up.*]

CLAIRE: Why, what is Tom doing out there, with a revolver?

HARRY: He is about to shoot himself because you've locked him out from his breakfast.

CLAIRE: He must know more interesting ways of destroying himself. [*bowing to* TOM] Good morning. [*from his side of the glass* TOM *bows and smiles back*] Isn't it strange—our being in here—and he being out there?

HARRY: Claire, have you no ideas of hospitality? Let him in!

CLAIRE: In? Perhaps that isn't hospitality.

HARRY: Well, whatever hospitality is, what is out there is snow—and wind—and our guest—who was asked to come here for his breakfast. To think a man has to *say* such things.

CLAIRE: I'm going to let him in. Though I like his looks out there. [*she takes the key from her pocket*]

HARRY: Thank heaven the door's coming open. Somebody can go for salt, and we can have our eggs.

CLAIRE: And open the door again—to let the salt in? No. If you insist on salt, tell Tom now to go back and get it. It's a stormy morning and there'll be just one opening of the door.

HARRY: How can we tell him what we can't make him hear? And why does he think we're holding this conversation instead of letting him in?

CLAIRE: It would be interesting to know. I wonder if he'll tell us?

HARRY: Claire! Is this any time to wonder anything?

CLAIRE: Give up the idea of salt for your egg and I'll let him in. [*holds up the key to* TOM *to indicate that for her part she is quite ready to let him in*]

HARRY: I want my egg!

CLAIRE: Then ask him to bring the salt. It's quite simple.

[HARRY *goes through another pantomime with the egg-cup and the missing shaker.* CLAIRE, *still standing half-way down cellar, sneezes.* HARRY, *growing all the while less amiable, explains with thermometer and flower-pot that there can only be one opening of the door.* TOM *looks interested, but unenlightened. But suddenly he smiles, nods, vanishes.*]

HARRY: Well, thank heaven [*exhausted*] that's over.

CLAIRE [*sitting on the top step*]: It was all so queer. He locked out on his side of the door. You locked in on yours. Looking right at each other and—

HARRY [*in mockery*]: And me trying to tell him to kindly fetch the salt!

CLAIRE: Yes.

HARRY [*to* DICK]: Well, I didn't do so bad a job, did I? Quite an idea, explaining our situation with the thermometer and the flower-pot. That was really an apology for keeping him out there. Heaven knows—some explanation was in order. [*he is watching, and sees* TOM *coming*] Now there he is, Claire. And probably pretty well fed up with the weather.

[CLAIRE *goes to the door, stops before it. She and* TOM *look at each other through the glass. Then she lets him in.*]

TOM: And now I am in. For a time it seemed I was not to be in. But after I got the idea that you were keeping me out there to see if I could get the idea—it would be too humiliating for a wall of glass to keep one from understanding. [*taking it from his pocket*] So there's the other thermometer. Where do you want it? [CLAIRE *takes it*]

CLAIRE: And where's the pepper?

TOM [*putting it on the table*]: And here's the pepper.

HARRY: Pepper?

TOM: When Claire sneezed I knew—

CLAIRE: Yes, I knew if I sneezed you would bring the pepper.

TOM: Funny how one always remembers the salt, but the pepper gets overlooked in preparations. And what is an egg without pepper?

HARRY [*nastily*]: There's your egg, Edgeworthy. [*pointing to it on the floor*] Claire decided it would be a good idea to smash everything, so she began with your egg.

TOM [*looking at his egg*]: The idea of smashing everything is really more intriguing than an egg.

HARRY: Nice that you feel that way about it.

CLAIRE [*giving* TOM *his coffee*]: You want to hear something amusing? I married Harry because I thought he would smash something.

HARRY: Well, that was an error in judgment.

CLAIRE: I'm such a naive trusting person [HARRY *laughs*—CLAIRE *gives him a surprised look, continues simply*]. Such a guileless soul that I thought flying would do something to a man. But it didn't take us out. We just took it in.

TOM: It's only our own spirit can take us out.

HARRY: Whatever you mean by out.

CLAIRE [*after looking intently at* TOM, *and considering it*]: But our own spirit is not something on the loose. Mine isn't. It has something to do with what I do. To fly. To be free in air. To look from above on the world of all my days. Be where man has never been! Yes—wouldn't you think the spirit could get the idea? The earth grows smaller. I am leaving. What are they—running around down there? Why do they run around down there? Houses? Houses are funny lines and down-going slants—houses are vanishing slants. I am alone. Can I breathe this rarer air? Shall I go higher? Shall I go too high? I am loose. I am out. But no; man flew, and returned to earth the man who left it.

HARRY: And jolly well likely not to have returned at all if he'd had those flighty notions while operating a machine.

CLAIRE: Oh, Harry! [*not lightly asked*] Can't you see it would be better not to have returned than to return the man who left it?

HARRY: I have some regard for human life.

CLAIRE: Why, no—I am the one who has the regard for human life. [*more lightly*] That was why I swiftly divorced my stuck-in-the-mud artist and married—the man of flight. But I merely passed from a stick-in-the-mud artist to a—

DICK: Stick-in-the-air aviator?

HARRY: Speaking of your stick-in-the-mud artist, as you romantically call your first blunder, isn't his daughter—and yours—due here to-day?

CLAIRE: I knew something was disturbing me. Elizabeth. A daughter is being delivered unto me this morning. I have a feeling it will be more painful than the original delivery. She has been, as they quaintly say, educated; prepared for her place in life.

HARRY: And fortunately Claire has a sister who is willing to give her young niece that place.

CLAIRE: The idea of giving anyone a place in life.

HARRY: Yes! The very idea!

CLAIRE: Yes! [*as often, the mocking thing gives true expression to what lies sombrely in her*] The war. There was another gorgeous chance.

HARRY: Chance for what? I call you, Claire. I ask you to say what you mean.

CLAIRE: I don't know—precisely. If I did—there'd be no use saying it. [*at* HARRY'*s impatient exclamation she turns to* TOM]

TOM [*nodding*]: The only thing left worth saying is the thing we can't say.

HARRY: Help!

CLAIRE: Yes. But the war didn't help. Oh, it was a stunning chance! But fast as we could—scuttled right back to the trim little thing we'd been shocked out of.

HARRY: You bet we did—showing our good sense.

CLAIRE: Showing our incapacity—for madness.

HARRY: Oh, come now, Claire—snap out of it. You're not really trying to say that capacity for madness is a good thing to *have?*

CLAIRE [*in simple surprise*]: Why yes, of course.

DICK: But I should say the war did leave enough madness to give you a gleam of hope.

CLAIRE: Not the madness that—breaks through. And it was—a stunning chance! Mankind massed to kill. We have failed. We are through. We will destroy. Break this up—it can't go farther. In the air above—in the sea below—it is to kill! All we had thought we were—we aren't. We were shut in with what wasn't so. Is there one ounce of energy has not gone to this killing? Is there one love not torn in two? Throw it in! Now? Ready? Break up. Push. Harder. Break up. And then—and then—But we didn't say—"And then—" The spirit didn't take the tip.

HARRY: Claire! Come now [*looking to the others for help*] —let's talk of something else.

CLAIRE: Plants do it. The big leap—it's called. Explode their species—because something in them knows they've gone as far as they can go. Something in them knows they're shut in to just that. So—go mad—that life may not be prisoned. Break themselves up into crazy things—into lesser things, and from the pieces—may come one sliver of life with vitality to find the future. How beautiful. How brave.

TOM [*as if he would call her from too far—or would let her know he has gone with her*]: Claire!

CLAIRE [*her eyes turning to him*]: Why should we mind lying under the earth? We who have no such initiative—no proud madness? Why think it death to lie under life so flexible—so ruthless and ever-renewing?

ANTHONY [*from the door of the inner room*]: Miss Claire?

CLAIRE [*after an instant*]: Yes? [*she goes with him, as they disappear his voice heard,* "show me now . . . want those violets bedded"]

HARRY: Oh, this has got to *stop.* I've got to—put a stop to it some way. Why, Claire used to be the best sport a man ever played around with. I can't stand it to see her getting hysterical.

TOM: That was not hysterical.

HARRY: What was it then—I want to know?

TOM: It was—a look.

HARRY: Oh, I might have known I'd get no help from either of you. Even you, Edgeworthy—much as she thinks of you—and fine sort as I've no doubt you are, you're doing Claire no good—encouraging her in these queer ways.

TOM: I couldn't change Claire if I would.

HARRY: And wouldn't if you could.

TOM: No. But you don't have to worry about me. I'm going away in a day or two. And I shall not be back.

HARRY: Trouble with you is, it makes little difference whether you're here or away. Just the fact of your existence does encourage Claire in this—this way she's going.

TOM [*with a smile*]: But you wouldn't ask me to go so far as to stop my existence? Though I would do that for Claire—if it were the way to help her.

HARRY: By Jove, you say that as if you meant it.

TOM: Do you think I would say anything about Claire I didn't mean?

HARRY: You think a lot of her, don't you? [TOM *nods*] You don't mean [*a laugh letting him say it*] —that you're—in love with Claire!

TOM: In love? Oh, that's much too easy. Certainly I do love Claire.

HARRY: Well, you're a cool one!

TOM: Let her be herself. Can't you see she's troubled?

HARRY: Well, what is there to trouble Claire? Now I ask you. It seems to me she has everything.

TOM: She's left so—open. Too exposed. [*as* HARRY *moves impatiently*] Please don't be annoyed with me. I'm doing my best at saying it. You see Claire isn't hardened into one of those forms she talks about. She's too—aware. Always pulled toward what could be—tormented by the lost adventure.

HARRY: Well, there's danger in all that. Of course there's danger.

TOM: But you can't help that.

HARRY: Claire was the best fun a woman could be. Is yet—at times.

TOM: Let her be—at times. As much as she can and will. She does need that. Don't keep her from it by making her feel you're holding her in it. Above all, don't try to stop what she's doing here. If she can do it with plants, perhaps she won't have to do it with herself.

HARRY: Do what?

TOM [*low, after a pause*]: Break up what exists. Open the door to destruction in the hope of—a door on the far side of destruction.

HARRY: Well, you give me the willies. [*moves around in irritation, troubled. To* ANTHONY, *who is passing through with a sprayer*] Anthony, have any arrangements been made about Miss Claire's daughter?

ANTHONY: I haven't heard of any arrangements.

HARRY: Well, she'll have to have some heat in her room. We can't all live out here.

ANTHONY: Indeed you cannot. It is not good for the plants.

HARRY: I'm going where I can *smoke.* [*goes out*]

DICK [*lightly, but fascinated by the idea*]: You think there is a door on the—hinter side of destruction?

TOM: How can one tell—where a door may be? One thing I want to say to you—for it is about you. [*regards* DICK *and not with his usual impersonal contemplation*] I don't think Claire should have—any door closed to her. [*pause*] You know, I think, what I mean. And perhaps you can guess how it hurts to say it. Whether it's—mere escape within,—rather shameful escape within, or the wild hope of that door through, it's— [*suddenly all human*] Be good to her! [*after a difficult moment, smiles*] Going away for ever is like dying, so one can say things.

DICK: Why do you do it—go away for ever?

TOM: I haven't succeeded here.

DICK: But you've tried the going away before.

TOM: Never knowing I would not come back. So that wasn't going away. My hope is that this will be like looking at life from outside life.

DICK: But then you'll not be in it.

TOM: I haven't been able to look at it while in it.

DICK: Isn't it more important to be in it than to look at it?

TOM: Not what I mean by look.

DICK: It's hard for me to conceive of—loving Claire and going away from her for ever.

TOM: Perhaps it's harder to do than to conceive of.

DICK: Then why do it?

TOM: It's my only way of keeping her.

DICK: I'm afraid I'm like Harry now. I don't get you.

TOM: I suppose not. Your way is different. [*with calm, with sadness—not with malice*] But I shall have her longer. And from deeper.

DICK: I know that.

TOM: Though I miss much. Much. [*the buzzer.* TOM *looks around to see if anyone is coming to answer it, then goes to the phone*] Yes? . . . I'll see if I can get her. [*to* DICK] Claire's daughter has arrived. [*looking in the inner room—returns to phone*] I don't see her. [*catching a glimpse of* ANTHONY *off right*] Oh, Anthony, where's Miss Claire? Her daughter has arrived.

ANTHONY: She's working at something very important in her experiments.

DICK: But isn't her daughter one of her experiments?

ANTHONY [*after a baffled moment*]: Her daughter is finished.

TOM [*at the phone*]: Sorry—but I can't get to Claire. She appears to have gone below. [ANTHONY *closes the trap-door*] I did speak to Anthony, but he says that Claire is working at one of her experiments and that her daughter is finished. I don't know how to make her hear—I took the revolver back to the house. Anyway you will remember Claire doesn't answer the revolver. I hate to reach Claire when she doesn't want to be reached. Why, of course—a daughter is very important, but oh, that's too bad. [*putting down the receiver*] He says the girl's feelings are hurt. Isn't that annoying? [*gingerly pounds on the trap-door. Then with the other hand. Waits.* ANTHONY *has a gentle smile for the gentle tapping—nods approval as* TOM *returns to the phone*] She doesn't come up. Indeed I did—with both fists—Sorry.

ANTHONY: Please, you won't try again to disturb Miss Claire, will you?

DICK: Her daughter is here, Anthony. She hasn't seen her daughter for a year.

ANTHONY: Well, if she got along without a mother for a year— [*goes back to his work*]

DICK [*smiling after* ANTHONY]: Plants are queer. Perhaps it's safer to do it with pencil [*regards* TOM] —or with pure thought. Things that grow in the earth—

TOM [*nodding*]: I suppose because we grew in the earth.

DICK: I'm always shocked to find myself in agreement with Harry, but I too am worried about Claire—and this. [*looking at the plants*]

TOM: It's her best chance.

DICK: Don't you hate to go away to India—for ever—leaving Claire's future uncertain?

TOM: You're cruel now. And you knew that you were being cruel.

DICK: Yes, I like the lines of your face when you suffer.

TOM: The lines of yours when you're causing suffering—I don't like them.

DICK: Perhaps that's your limitation.

TOM: I grant you it may be. [*They are silent*] I had an odd feeling that you and I sat here once before, long ago, and that we were plants. And you were a beautiful plant, and I—I was a very ugly plant. I confess it surprised me—finding myself so ugly a plant.

[*A young girl is seen outside.* HARRY *gets the door open for her and brings* ELIZABETH *in.*]

HARRY: There's heat here. And two of your mother's friends. Mr Demming—Richard Demming—the artist—and I think you and Mr Edgeworthy are old friends.

[ELIZABETH *comes forward. She is the creditable young American—well built, poised, 'cultivated', so sound an expression of the usual as to be able to meet the world with assurance—assurance which training has made rather graceful. She is about seventeen—and mature. You feel solid things behind her.*]

TOM: I knew you when you were a baby. You used to kick a great deal then.

ELIZABETH [*laughing, with ease*]: And scream, I haven't a doubt. But I've stopped that. One does, doesn't one? And it was you who gave me the idol.

TOM: Proselytizing, I'm afraid.

ELIZABETH: I beg—? Oh—*yes* [*laughing cordially*] I *see.* [*she doesn't*] I dressed the idol up in my doll's clothes. They fitted perfectly—the idol was just the size of my doll Ailine. But mother didn't like the idol that way, and tore the clothes getting them off. [*to* HARRY, *after looking around*] Is mother here?

HARRY [*crossly*]: Yes, she's here. Of course she's here. And she must know you're here. [*after looking in the inner room he goes to the trap-door and makes a great noise*]

ELIZABETH: Oh—*please.* Really—it doesn't make the least difference.

HARRY: Well, all I can say is, your manners are better than your mother's.

ELIZABETH: But you see I don't do anything interesting, so I have to have good manners. [*lightly, but leaving the impression there is a certain superiority in not doing anything interesting. Turning cordially to* DICK] My father was an artist.

DICK: Yes, I know.

ELIZABETH: He was a portrait painter. Do you do portraits?

DICK: Well, not the kind people buy.

ELIZABETH: They bought father's.

DICK: Yes, I know he did that kind.

HARRY [*still irritated*]: Why, you don't do portraits.

DICK: I did one of you the other day. You thought it was a milk-can.

ELIZABETH [*laughing delightedly*]: No? Not really? Did you think—How *could* you think— [*as* HARRY *does not join the laugh*] Oh, I beg your pardon. I—Does mother grow beautiful roses now?

HARRY: No, she does not.

[*The trap-door begins to move.* CLAIRE*'s head appears.*]

ELIZABETH: Mother! It's been so long— [*she tries to overcome the difficulties and embrace her mother*]

CLAIRE [*protecting a box she has*]: Careful, Elizabeth. We mustn't upset the lice.

ELIZABETH [*retreating*]: Lice? [*but quickly equal even to lice*] Oh—*yes.* You take it—them—off plants, don't you?

CLAIRE: I'm putting them on certain plants.

ELIZABETH [*weakly*]: Oh, I thought you took them off.

CLAIRE [*calling*]: Anthony! [*he comes*] The lice. [*he takes them from her*]

[CLAIRE, *who has not fully ascended, looks at* ELIZABETH, *hesitates, then suddenly starts back down the stairs.*]

HARRY [*outraged*]: Claire! [*slowly she re-ascends—sits on the top step. After a long pause in which he has waited for* CLAIRE *to open a conversation with her daughter*] Well, and what have you been doing at school all this time?

ELIZABETH: Oh—studying.

CLAIRE: Studying what?

ELIZABETH: Why—the things one studies, mother.

CLAIRE: Oh! The things one studies. [*looks down cellar again*]

DICK [*after another wait*]: And what have you been doing besides studying?

ELIZABETH: Oh—the things one does. Tennis and skating and dancing and—

CLAIRE: The things one does.

ELIZABETH: Yes. All the things. The—the things one does. Though I haven't been in school these last few months, you know. Miss Lane took us to Europe.

TOM: And how did you like Europe?

ELIZABETH [*capably*]: Oh, I thought it was awfully amusing. All the girls were quite mad about Europe. Of course, I'm glad I'm an American.

CLAIRE: Why?

ELIZABETH [*laughing*]: Why—mother! Of course one is glad one is an American. All the girls—

CLAIRE [*turning away*]: O—h! [*a moan under the breath*]

ELIZABETH: Why, mother—aren't you well?

HARRY: Your mother has been working pretty hard at all this.

ELIZABETH: Oh, I do so want to know all about it? Perhaps I can help you! I think it's just awfully amusing that you're doing something. One does nowadays, doesn't one?—if you know what I mean. It was the war, wasn't it, made it the thing to do something?

DICK [*slyly*]: And you thought, Claire, that the war was lost.

ELIZABETH: The *war*? *Lost*! [*her capable laugh*] Fancy our losing a war! Miss Lane says we should give *thanks*. She says we should each do some expressive thing—you know what I mean? And that this is the *keynote* of the age. Of course, one's own kind of thing. Like mother—growing flowers.

CLAIRE: You think that is one's own kind of thing?

ELIZABETH: Why, of course I do, mother. And so does Miss Lane. All the girls—

CLAIRE [*shaking her head as if to get something out*]: S-hoo.

ELIZABETH: What is it, mother?

CLAIRE: A fly shut up in my ear—"All the girls!"

ELIZABETH [*laughing*]: Mother was always so amusing. So *different*—if you know what I mean. Vacations I've lived mostly with Aunt Adelaide, you know.

CLAIRE: My sister who is fitted to rear children.

HARRY: Well, somebody has to do it.

ELIZABETH: And I do love Aunt Adelaide, but I think its going to be awfully amusing to be around with mother now—and help her with her work. Help do some useful beautiful thing.

CLAIRE: I am not doing any useful beautiful thing.

ELIZABETH: Oh, but you are, mother. Of course you are. Miss Lane says so. She says it is your splendid heritage gives you this impulse to do a beautiful thing for the race. She says you are doing in your way what the great teachers and preachers behind you did in theirs.

CLAIRE [*who is good for little more*]: Well, all I can say is, Miss Lane is stung.

ELIZABETH: Mother! What a thing to say of Miss *Lane*. [*from this slipping into more of a little girl manner*] Oh, she gave me a spiel one day about living up to the men I come from.

[CLAIRE *turns and regards her daughter*.]

CLAIRE: You'll do it, Elizabeth.

ELIZABETH: Well, I don't know. Quite a job, I'll say. Of course, I'd have to do it in my way. I'm not going to teach or preach or be a stuffy person. But now that— [*she here becomes the product of a superior school*] values have shifted and such sensitive new things have been liberated in the world—

CLAIRE [*low*]: Don't use those words.

ELIZABETH: Why—why not?

CLAIRE: Because you don't know what they mean.

ELIZABETH: Why, of course I know what they mean!

CLAIRE [*turning away*]: You're—stepping on the plants.

HARRY [*hastily*]: Your mother has been working awfully hard at all this.

ELIZABETH: Well, now that I'm here you'll let me help you, won't you, mother?

CLAIRE [*trying for control*]: You needn't—bother.

ELIZABETH: But I *want* to. Help add to the wealth of the world.

CLAIRE: Will you please get it out of your head that I am adding to the wealth of the world!

ELIZABETH: But, mother—of course you are. To produce a new and better kind of plant—

CLAIRE: They may be new. I don't give a damn whether they're better.

ELIZABETH: But—but what are they then?

CLAIRE [*as if choked out of her*]: They're different.

ELIZABETH [*thinks a minute, then laughs triumphantly*]: But what's the use of making them different if they aren't better?

HARRY: A good square question, Claire. Why don't you answer it?

CLAIRE: I don't have to answer it.

HARRY: Why not give the girl a fair show? You never have, you know. Since she's interested, why not tell her what it is you're doing?

CLAIRE: She is not interested.

ELIZABETH: But I am, mother. Indeed I am. I do want awfully to understand what you are doing, and help you.

CLAIRE: You can't help me, Elizabeth.

HARRY: Why not let her try?

CLAIRE: Why do you ask me to do that? This is my own thing. Why do you make me feel I should— [*goes to* ELIZABETH] I will be good to you, Elizabeth. We'll go around together. I haven't done it, but— you'll see. We'll do gay things. I'll have a lot of beaus around for you. Anything else. Not—this is—Not this.

ELIZABETH: As you like, mother, of course. I just would have been so glad to—to share the thing that interests you. [*hurt borne with good breeding and a smile*]

HARRY: Claire! [*which says, "How can you?"*]

CLAIRE [*who is looking at* ELIZABETH]: Yes, I will try.

TOM: *I* don't think so. As Claire says—anything else.

ELIZABETH: Why, of course—I don't at all want to intrude.

HARRY: It'll do Claire good to take someone in. To get down to brass tacks and actually say what she's driving at.

CLAIRE: Oh—*Harry*. But yes—I will try. [*does try, but no words come. Laughs*] When you come to say it it's not—One would rather not nail it to a cross of words— [*laughs again*] with brass tacks.

HARRY [*affectionately*]: But I want to see you put things into words, Claire, and realize just where you are.

CLAIRE [*oddly*]: You think that's a—good idea?

ELIZABETH [*in her manner of holding the world capably in her hands*]: Now let's talk of something else. I hadn't the least idea of making mother feel badly.

CLAIRE [*desperately*]: No, we'll go on. Though I don't know—where we'll end. I can't answer for that. These plants— [*beginning flouderingly*] Perhaps they are less beautiful—less sound—than the plants from which they diverged. But they have found—otherness. [*laughs a little shrilly*] If you know—what I mean.

TOM: Claire—stop this! [*To* HARRY] This is wrong.

CLAIRE [*excitedly*]: No; I'm going on. They have been shocked out of what they were—into something they were not; they've broken from the forms in which they found themselves. They are alien. Outside. That's it, outside; if you—know what I mean.

ELIZABETH [*not shocked from what she is*]: But of course, the object of it all is to make them better plants. Otherwise, what would be the sense of doing it?

CLAIRE [*not reached by* ELIZABETH]: Out there— [*giving it with her hands*] lies all that's not been touched— lies life that waits. Back here—the old pattern, done again, again and again. So long done it doesn't even know itself for a pattern—in immensity. But this—has invaded. Crept a little way into—what wasn't. Strange lines in life unused. And when you make a pattern new you know a pattern's made with life. And then you know that anything may be—if only you know how to reach it. [*this has taken form, not easily, but with great struggle between feeling and words*]

HARRY [*cordially*]: Now I begin to get you, Claire. I never knew before why you called it the Edge Vine.

CLAIRE: I should destroy the Edge Vine. It isn't—over the edge. It's running, back to—"all the girls." It's a little afraid of Miss Lane. [*looking sombrely at it*] You are out, but you are not alive.

ELIZABETH: Why, it looks all right, mother.

CLAIRE: Didn't carry life with it from the life it left. Dick—you know what I mean. At least you ought to. [*her ruthless way of not letting anyone's feelings stand in the way of truth*] Then destroy it for me! It's hard to do it—with the hands that made it.

DICK: But what's the point in destroying it, Claire?

CLAIRE [*impatiently*]: I've told you. It cannot create.

DICK: But you say you can go on producing it, and it's interesting in form.

CLAIRE: And you think I'll stop with that? Be shut in—with different life—that can't creep on? [*after trying to put destroying hands upon it*] It's hard to—get past what we've done. Our own dead things—block the way.

TOM: But you're doing it this next time, Claire. [*nodding to the inner room*] In there!

CLAIRE [*turning to that room*]: I'm not sure.

TOM: But you told me Breath of Life has already produced itself. Doesn't that show it has brought life from the life it left?

CLAIRE: But timidly, rather—wistfully. A little homesick. If it is less sure this time, then it is going back to—Miss Lane. But if the pattern's clearer now, then it has made friends of life that waits. I'll know to-morrow.

ELIZABETH: You know, something tells me this is *wrong*.

CLAIRE: The hymn-singing ancestors are tuning up.

ELIZABETH: I don't know what you mean by that, mother but—

CLAIRE: But we will now sing, "Nearer, my God, to Thee: Nearer to—"

ELIZABETH [*laughingly breaking in*]: Well, I don't care. Of course you can make fun at me, but something does tell me this is wrong. To do what—what—

DICK: What God did?

ELIZABETH: Well—yes. Unless you do it to make them better—to do it just to *do* it—that doesn't seem right to me.

CLAIRE [*roughly*]: "Right to you!" And that's all you know of adventure—and of anguish. Do you know it is you—world of which you're so true a flower—makes me have to leave? You're there to hold the door shut! Because you're young and of a gayer world, you think I can't *see* them—those old men? Do you know why you're so sure of yourself? Because you can't *feel*. Can't feel—the limitless—out there—a sea just over the hill. I will not stay with you! [*buries her hands in the earth around the Edge Vine. But suddenly steps back from it as she had from* ELIZABETH] And I will not stay with you! [*grasps it as we grasp what we would kill, is trying to pull it up. They all step forward in horror.* ANTHONY *is drawn in by this harm to the plant*]

ANTHONY: Miss Claire! Miss Claire! The work of years!

CLAIRE: May only make a prison! [*struggling with* HARRY, *who is trying to stop her*] You think I too will die on the edge? [*she has thrown him away, is now struggling with the vine*] Why did I make you? To get past you! [*as she twists it*] Oh yes, I know you have thorns! The Edge Vine should have thorns. [*with a long tremendous pull for deep roots, she has it up. As she holds the torn roots*] Oh, I have loved you so! You took me where I hadn't been.

ELIZABETH [*who has been looking on with a certain practical horror*]: Well, I'd say it would be better not to go there!

CLAIRE: Now I know what you are for! [*flings her arm back to strike* ELIZABETH *with the Edge Vine*]

HARRY [*wresting it from her*]: Claire! Are you mad?

CLAIRE: No, I'm not mad. I'm—too sane! [*pointing to* ELIZABETH—*and the words come from mighty roots*] To think that object ever moved my belly and sucked my breast! [ELIZABETH *hides her face as if struck*]

HARRY [*going to* ELIZABETH, *turning to* CLAIRE]: This is atrocious! You're cruel.

[*He leads* ELIZABETH *to the door and out. After an irresolute moment in which he looks from* CLAIRE *to* TOM, DICK *follows.* ANTHONY *cannot bear to go. He stoops to take the Edge Vine from the floor.* CLAIRE'*s gesture stops him. He goes into the inner room.*]

CLAIRE [*kicking the Edge Vine out of her way, drawing deep breaths, smiling*]: O-h. How good I feel! Light! [*a movement as if she could fly*] Read me something, Tom dear. Or say something pleasant—about God. But be very careful what you say about him! I have a feeling—he's not far off.

CURTAIN

ACT II

Late afternoon of the following day. CLAIRE *is alone in the tower—a tower which is thought to be round but does not complete the circle. The back is curved, then jagged lines break from that, and the front is a queer bulging window—in a curve that leans. The whole structure is as if given a twist by some terrific force—like something wrong. It is lighted by an old-fashioned watchman's lantern hanging from the ceiling; the innumerable pricks and slits in the metal throw a marvellous pattern on the curved wall—like some masonry that hasn't been.*

There are no windows at back, and there is no door save an opening in the floor. The delicately distorted rail of a spiral staircase winds up from below. CLAIRE *is seen through the huge ominous window as if shut into the tower. She is lying on a seat at the back looking at a book of drawings. To do this she has left the door of her lantern a little open—and her own face is clearly seen.*

A door is heard opening below; laughing voices, CLAIRE *listens, not pleased.*

ADELAIDE [*voice coming up*]: Dear—dear, why do they make such twisting steps.

HARRY: Take your time, most up now. [HARRY'*s head appears, he looks back.*] Making it all right?

ADELAIDE: I can't tell yet. [*laughingly*] No, I don't think so.

HARRY [*reaching back a hand for her*]: The last lap—is the bad lap.

[ADELAIDE *is up, and occupied with getting her breath.*]

HARRY: Since you wouldn't come down, Claire, we thought we'd come up.

ADELAIDE [*as* CLAIRE *does not greet her*]: I'm sorry to intrude, but I have to see you, Claire. There are things to be arranged. [CLAIRE *volunteering nothing about arrangements,* ADELAIDE *surveys the tower. An unsympathetic eye goes from the curves to the lines which diverge. Then she looks from the window*] Well, at least you have a view.

HARRY: This is the first time you've been up here?

ADELAIDE: Yes, in the five years you've had the house I was never asked up here before.

CLAIRE [*amiably enough*]: You weren't asked up here now.

ADELAIDE: Harry asked me.

CLAIRE: It isn't Harry's tower. But never mind—since you don't like it—it's all right.

ADELAIDE [*her eyes again rebuking the irregularities of the tower*]: No, I confess I do not care for it. A round tower should go on being round.

HARRY: Claire calls this the thwarted tower. She bought the house because of it. [*going over and sitting by her, his hand on her ankle*] Didn't you, old girl? She says she'd like to have known the architect.

ADELAIDE: Probably a tiresome person too incompetent to make a perfect tower.

CLAIRE: Well, now he's disposed of, what next?

ADELAIDE [*sitting down in a manner of capably opening a conference*]: Next, Elizabeth, and you, Claire. Just what is the matter with Elizabeth?

CLAIRE [*whose voice is cool, even, as if herself is not really engaged by this*]: Nothing is the matter with her. She is a tower that is a tower.

ADELAIDE: Well, is that anything against her?

CLAIRE: She's just like one of her father's portraits. They never interested me. Nor does she. [*looks at the drawings which do interest her*]

ADELAIDE: A mother cannot cast off her own child simply because she does not interest her!

CLAIRE [*an instant raising cool eyes to* ADELAIDE]: Why can't she?

ADELAIDE: Because it would be monstrous!

CLAIRE: And why can't she be monstrous—if she has to be?

ADELAIDE: You don't have to be. That's where I'm out of patience with you Claire. You are really a particularly intelligent, competent person, and it's time for you to call a halt to this nonsense and be the woman you were meant to be!

CLAIRE [*holding the book up to see another way*]: What inside dope have you on what I was meant to be?

ADELAIDE: I know what you came from.

CLAIRE: Well, isn't it about time somebody got loose from that? What I came from made you, so—

ADELAIDE [*stiffly*]: I see.

CLAIRE: So—you being such a tower of strength, why need I too be imprisoned in what I came from?

ADELAIDE: It isn't being imprisoned. Right there is where you make your mistake, Claire. Who's in a tower—in an unsuccessful tower? Not I. I go about in the world—free, busy, happy. Among people, I have no time to think of myself.

CLAIRE: No.

ADELAIDE: No. My family. The things that interest them; from morning till night it's—

CLAIRE: Yes, I know you have a large family, Adelaide; five and Elizabeth makes six.

ADELAIDE: We'll speak of Elizabeth later. But if you would just get out of yourself and enter into other people's lives—

CLAIRE: Then I would become just like you. And we should all be just alike in order to assure one another that we're all just right. But since you and Harry and Elizabeth and ten million other people bolster each other up, why do you especially need me?

ADELAIDE [*not unkindly*]: We don't need you as much as you need us.

CLAIRE [*a wry face*]: I never liked what I needed.

HARRY: I am convinced I am the worst thing in the world for you, Claire.

CLAIRE [*with a smile for his tactics, but shaking her head*]: I'm afraid you're not. I don't know—perhaps you are.

ADELAIDE: Well, what is it you want, Claire?

CLAIRE [*simply*]: You wouldn't know if I told you.

ADELAIDE: That's rather arrogant.

HARRY: Yes, take a chance, Claire. I have been known to get an idea—and Adelaide quite frequently gets one.

CLAIRE [*the first resentment she has shown*]: You two feel very superior, don't you?

ADELAIDE: I don't think we are the ones who are feeling superior.

CLAIRE: Oh, yes, you are. Very superior to what you think is my feeling of superiority, comparing my—isolation with your "heart of humanity." Soon we will speak of the beauty of common experiences, of the—Oh, I could say it all before we come to it.

HARRY: Adelaide came up here to help you, Claire.

CLAIRE: Adelaide came up here to lock me in. Well, she can't do it.

ADELAIDE [*gently*]: But can't you see that one may do that to one's self?

CLAIRE [*thinks of this, looks suddenly tired—then smiles*]: Well, at least I've changed the keys.

HARRY: "Locked in." Bunkum. Get that out of your head, Claire. Who's locked in? Nobody that I know of, we're all free Americans. Free as air.

ADELAIDE: I wish you'd come and hear one of Mr Morley's sermons, Claire. You're very old-fashioned if you think sermons are what they used to be.

CLAIRE [*with interest*]: And do they still sing "Nearer, my God, to Thee"?

ADELAIDE: They do, and a noble old hymn it is. It would do you no harm at all to sing it.

CLAIRE [*eagerly*]: Sing it to me, Adelaide. I'd like to hear you sing it.

ADELAIDE: It would be sacrilege to sing it to you in this mood.

CLAIRE [*falling back*]: Oh, I don't know. I'm not so sure God would agree with you. That would be one on you, wouldn't it?

ADELAIDE: It's easy to feel one's self set apart!

CLAIRE: No, it isn't.

ADELAIDE [*beginning anew*]: It's a new age, Claire. Spiritual values—

CLAIRE: Spiritual values! [*in her brooding way*] So you have pulled that up. [*with cunning*] Don't think I don't know what it is you do.

ADELAIDE: Well, what do I do? I'm sure I have no idea what you're talking about.

HARRY [*affectionately, as* CLAIRE *is looking with intentness at what he does not see*]: What does she do, Claire?

CLAIRE: It's rather clever, what she does. Snatching the phrase— [*a movement as if pulling something up*] standing it up between her and—the life that's there. And by saying it enough—"We have life! We have life! We have life!" Very good come-back at one who would really be—"Just so! *We* are that. Right this way, please—" That, I suppose is what we mean by needing each other. All join in the chorus, "This is it! This is it! This is it!" And anyone who won't join is to be—visited by relatives. [*regarding* ADELAIDE *with curiosity*] Do you really think that anything is going on in you?

ADELAIDE [*stiffly*]: I am not one to hold myself up as a perfect example of what the human race may be.

CLAIRE [*brightly*]: Well, that's good.

HARRY: Claire!

CLAIRE: Humility's a *real* thing—not just a fine name for laziness.

HARRY: Well, Lord A'mighty, you can't call Adelaide lazy.

CLAIRE: She stays in one place because she hasn't the energy to go anywhere else.

ADELAIDE [*as if the last word in absurdity has been said*]: *I* haven't energy?

CLAIRE [*mildly*]: You haven't any energy at all, Adelaide. That's why you keep so busy.

ADELAIDE: *Well*—Claire's nerves are in a worse state than I had realized.

CLAIRE: So perhaps we'd better look at Blake's drawings. [*takes up the book*]

ADELAIDE: It would be all right for me to look at Blake's drawings. You'd better look at the Sistine Madonna. [*affectionately, after she has watched* CLAIRE*'s face a moment*] What is it, Claire? Why do you shut yourself out from us?

CLAIRE: I told you. Because I do not want to be shut in with you.

ADELAIDE: All of this is not very pleasant for Harry.

HARRY: I want Claire to be *gay*.

CLAIRE: Funny—you should want that. [*speaks unwillingly, a curious, wistful unwillingness*] Did you ever say a preposterous thing, then go trailing after the thing you've said and find it wasn't so preposterous? Here is the circle we are in. [*describes a big circle*] Being gay. It shoots little darts through the circle, and a minute later—gaiety all gone, and you looking through that little hole the gaiety left.

ADELAIDE [*going to her, as she is still looking through that little hole*]: Claire, dear, I wish I could make you feel how much I care for you. [*simply, with real feeling*] You can call me all the names you like—dull, commonplace, lazy—that *is* a new idea, I confess, but the rest of our family's gone now, and the love that used to be there between us all—the only place for it now is between you and me. You were so much loved, Claire. You oughtn't to try and get away from a world in which you are so much loved. [*to* HARRY] Mother—father—all of us, always loved Claire best. We always loved Claire's queer gaiety. Now you've got to hand it to us for that, as the children say.

CLAIRE [*moved, but eyes shining with a queer bright loneliness*]: But never one of you—once—looked with me through the little pricks the gaiety made—never one of you—once, looked with me at the queer light that came in through the pricks.

ADELAIDE: And can't you see, dear, that it's better for us we didn't? And that it would be better for you now if you would just resolutely look somewhere else? You must see yourself that you haven't the poise of people who are held—well, within the circle, if you choose to put it that way. There's something about being in that main body, having one's roots in the big common experiences, gives a calm which you have missed. That's why I want you to take Elizabeth, forget yourself, and—

CLAIRE: I do want calm. But mine would have to be a calm I—worked my way to. A calm all prepared for me—would stink.

ADELAIDE [*less sympathetically*]: I know you have to be yourself, Claire. But I don't admit you have a right to hurt other people

HARRY: I think Claire and I had better take a nice long trip.

ADELAIDE: Now why don't you?

CLAIRE: I am taking a trip.

ADELAIDE: Well, Harry isn't, and he'd like to go and wants you to go with him. Go to Paris and get yourself some awfully good-looking clothes—and have one grand fling at the gay world. You really love that, Claire, and you've been awfully dull lately. I think that's the whole trouble.

HARRY: I think so too.

ADELAIDE: This sober business of growing plants—

CLAIRE: Not sober—it's mad.

ADELAIDE: All the more reason for quitting it.

CLAIRE: But madness that is the only chance for sanity.

ADELAIDE: Come, come, now—let's not juggle words.

CLAIRE [*springing up*]: How dare you say that to me, Adelaide. You who are such a liar and thief and whore with words!

ADELAIDE [*facing her, furious*]: How *dare* you—

HARRY: Of course not, Claire. You have the most preposterous way of using words.

CLAIRE: I respect words.

ADELAIDE: Well, you'll please respect me enough not to dare use certain words to me!

CLAIRE: Yes, I do dare. I'm tired of what you do—you and all of you. Life—experience—values—calm—sensitive words which raise their heads as indications. And you *pull them up*—to decorate your stagnant little minds—and think that makes you—And because you have pulled that word from the life that grew it you won't let one who's honest, and aware, and troubled, try to reach through to—to what she doesn't know is there. [*she is moved, excited, as if a cruel thing has been done*] Why did you come here?

ADELAIDE: To try and help you. But I begin to fear I can't do it. It's pretty egotistical to claim that what so many people are, is wrong.

[CLAIRE, *after looking intently at* ADELAIDE, *slowly, smiling a little, describes a circle. With deftly used hands makes a quick vicious break in the circle which is there in the air.*]

HARRY [*going to her, taking her hands*]: It's getting close to dinner-time. You were thinking of something else, Claire, when I told you Charlie Emmons was coming to dinner to-night. [*answering her look*] Sure—he is a neurologist, and I want him to see you. I'm perfectly honest with you—cards all on the table, you know that. I'm hoping if you like him—and he's the best scout in the world, that he can help you. [*talking hurriedly against the stillness which follows her look from him to* ADELAIDE, *where she sees between them an 'understanding' about her*] Sure you need help, Claire. Your nerves are a little on the blink—from all you've been doing. No use making a mystery of it—or a tragedy. Emmons is a cracker-jack, and naturally I want you to get a move on yourself and be happy again.

CLAIRE [*who has gone over to the window*]: And this neurologist can make me happy?

HARRY: Can make you well—and then you'll be happy.

ADELAIDE [*in the voice of now fixing it all up*]: And I had just an idea about Elizabeth. Instead of working with mere plants, why not think of Elizabeth as a plant and—

[CLAIRE, *who has been looking out of the window, now throws open one of the panes that swings out—or seems to, and calls down in great excitement.*]

CLAIRE: Tom! *Tom!* Quick! Up here! I'm in trouble!

HARRY [*going to the window*]: That's a rotten thing to do, Claire! You've frightened him.

CLAIRE: Yes, how fast he can run. He was deep in thought and I stabbed right through.

HARRY: Well, he'll be none too pleased when he gets up here and finds there was no reason for the stabbing!

[*They wait for his footsteps,* HARRY *annoyed,* ADELAIDE *offended, but stealing worried looks at* CLAIRE, *who is looking fixedly at the place in the floor where* TOM *will appear.—Running footsteps.*]

TOM [*his voice getting there before he does*]: Yes, Claire—yes—yes— [*as his head appears*] What is it?

CLAIRE [*at once presenting him and answering his question*]: My sister.

TOM [*gasping*]: Oh,—why—is that all? I mean—how do you do? Pardon, I [*panting*] came up—rather hurriedly.

HARRY: If you want to slap Claire, Tom, I for one have no objection.

CLAIRE: Adelaide has the most interesting idea, Tom. She proposes that I take Elizabeth and roll her in the gutter. Just let her lie there until she breaks up into—

ADELAIDE: *Claire!* I don't see how—even in fun—pretty vulgar fun—you can speak in those terms of a pure young girl. I'm beginning to think I had better take Elizabeth.

CLAIRE: Oh, I've thought that all along.

ADELAIDE: And I'm also beginning to suspect that—oddity may be just a way of shifting responsibility.

CLAIRE [*cordially interested in this possibility*]: Now you know—that might be.

ADELAIDE: A mother who does not love her own child! You are an unnatural woman, Claire.

CLAIRE: Well, at least it saves me from being a natural one.

ADELAIDE: Oh—I know, you think you have a great deal! But let me tell you, you've missed a great deal! You've never known the faintest stirring of a mother's love.

CLAIRE: That's not true.

HARRY: No. Claire loved our boy.

CLAIRE: I'm glad he didn't live.

HARRY [*low*]: Claire!

CLAIRE: I loved him. Why should I want him to live?

HARRY: Come, dear, I'm sorry I spoke of him—when you're not feeling well.

CLAIRE: I'm feeling all right. Just because I'm seeing something, it doesn't mean I'm sick.

HARRY: Well, let's go down now. About dinner-time. I shouldn't wonder if Emmons were here. [*as* ADELAIDE *is starting down stairs*] Coming, Claire?

CLAIRE: No.

HARRY: But it's time to go down for dinner.

CLAIRE: I'm not hungry.

HARRY: But we have a guest. Two guests—Adelaide's staying too.

CLAIRE: Then you're not alone.

HARRY: But I invited Dr Emmons to meet you.

CLAIRE [*her smile flashing*]: Tell him I am violent to-night.

HARRY: Dearest—how can you joke about such things!

CLAIRE: So you do think they're serious?

HARRY [*irritated*]: No, I do not! But I want you to come down for dinner!

ADELAIDE: Come, come, Claire; you know quite well this is not the sort of thing one does.

CLAIRE: Why go on saying one doesn't, when you are seeing one does? [*to* TOM] Will you stay with me a while? I want to purify the tower.

[ADELAIDE *begins to disappear.*]

HARRY: Fine time to choose for a *tête-à-tête.* [*as he is leaving*] I'd think more of you, Edgeworthy, if you refused to humour Claire in her ill-breeding.

ADELAIDE [*her severe voice coming from below*]: It is not what she was taught.

CLAIRE: No, it's not what I was taught. [*laughing rather timidly*] And perhaps you'd rather have your dinner?

TOM: No.

CLAIRE: We'll get something later. I want to talk to you. [*but she does not—laughs*] Absurd that I should feel bashful with you. Why am I so awkward with words when I go to talk to you?

TOM: The words know they're not needed.

CLAIRE: No, they're not needed. There's something underneath—an open way—down below the way that words can go. [*rather desperately*] It is there, isn't it?

TOM: Oh, yes, it is there.

CLAIRE: Then why do we never—go it?

TOM: If we went it, it would not be there.

CLAIRE: Is that true? How terrible, if that is true.

TOM: Not terrible, wonderful—that it should—of itself—be there.

CLAIRE [*with the simplicity that can say anything*]: I want to go it, Tom, I'm lonely up on top here. Is it that I have more faith than you, or is it only that I'm greedier? You see, you don't know [*her reckless laugh*] what you're missing. You don't know how I could love you.

TOM: Don't, Claire; that isn't—how it is—between you and me.

CLAIRE: But why can't it be—every way—between you and me?

TOM: Because we'd lose—the open way. [*the quality of his denial shows how strong is his feeling for her*] With anyone else—not with you.

CLAIRE: But you are the only one I want. The only one—all of me wants.

TOM: I know; but that's the way it is.

CLAIRE: You're cruel.

TOM: Oh, Claire, I'm trying so hard to—save it for us. Isn't it our beauty and our safeguard that underneath our separate lives, no matter where we may be, with what other, there is this open way between us? That's so much more than anything we could bring to being.

CLAIRE: Perhaps. But—it's different with me. I'm not—all spirit.

TOM [*his hand on her*]: Dear!

CLAIRE: No, don't touch me—since [*moving*] you're going away to-morrow? [*he nods*] For—always? [*his head just moves assent*] India is just another country. But there are undiscovered countries.

TOM: Yes, but we are so feeble we have to reach our country through the actual country lying nearest. Don't you do that yourself, Claire? Reach your country through the plants' country?

CLAIRE: My country? You mean—outside?

TOM: No, I don't think it that way.

CLAIRE: Oh, yes, you do.

TOM: Your country is the inside, Claire. The innermost. You are disturbed because you lie too close upon the heart of life.

CLAIRE [*restlessly*]: I don't know; you can think it one way—or another. No way says it, and that's good—at least it's not shut up in saying. [*she is looking at her enclosing hand, as if something is shut up there*]

TOM: But also, you know, things may be freed by expression. Come from the unrealized into the fabric of life.

CLAIRE: Yes, but why does the fabric of life have to—freeze into its pattern? It should [*doing it with her hands*] flow. [*then turning like an unsatisfied child to him*] But I wanted to talk to you.

TOM: You are talking to me. Tell me about your flower that never was before—your Breath of Life.

CLAIRE: I'll know to-morrow. You'll not go until I know?

TOM: I'll try to stay.

CLAIRE: It seems to me, if it has—then I have, integrity in— [*smiles, it is as if the smile lets her say it*] otherness. I don't want to die on the edge!

TOM: Not you!

CLAIRE: Many do. It's what makes them too smug in allness—those dead things on the edge, died, distorted—trying to get through. Oh—don't think I don't see—The Edge Vine! [*a pause, then swiftly*] Do you know what I mean? Or do you think I'm just a fool, or crazy?

TOM: I think I know what you mean, and you know I don't think you are a fool, or crazy.

CLAIRE: Stabbed to awareness—no matter where it takes you, isn't that more than a safe place to stay? [*telling him very simply despite the pattern of pain in her voice*] Anguish may be a thread—making patterns that haven't been. A thread—blue and burning.

TOM [*to take her from what even he fears for her*]: But you were telling me about the flower you breathed to life. What is your Breath of Life?

CLAIRE [*an instant playing*]: It's a secret. A secret?—it's a trick. Distilled from the most fragile flowers there are. It's only air—pausing—playing; except, far in, one stab of red, its quivering heart—that asks a question. But here's the trick—I bred the air—form to strength. The strength shut up behind us I've sent—far out. [*troubled*] I'll know tomorrow. And I have another gift for Breath of Life; some day—though days of work lie in between—some day I'll give it reminiscence. Fragrance that is—no one thing in here but—reminiscent. [*silence, she raises wet eyes*] We need the haunting beauty from the life we've left. I need that. [*he takes her hands and breathes her name*] Let me reach my country with you. I'm not a plant. After all, they don't—accept me. Who does—accept me? Will you?

TOM: My dear—dear, dear, Claire—you move me so! You stand alone in a clearness that breaks my heart. [*her hands move up his arms. He takes them to hold them from where they would go—though he can hardly do it*] But you've asked what you yourself could answer best. We'd only stop in the country where everyone stops.

CLAIRE: We might come through—to radiance.

TOM: Radiance is an enclosing place.

CLAIRE: Perhaps radiance lighting forms undreamed. [*her reckless laugh*] I'd be willing to—take a chance, I'd rather lose than never know.

TOM: No, Claire. Knowing you from underneath, I know you couldn't bear to lose.

CLAIRE: Wouldn't men say you were a fool!

TOM: They would.

CLAIRE: And perhaps you are. [*he smiles a little*] I feel so desperate, because if only I could—show you what I am, you might see I could have without losing. But I'm a stammering thing with you.

TOM: You do show me what you are.

CLAIRE: I've known a few moments that were life. Why don't they help me now? One was in the air.—I was up with Harry—flying—high. It was about four months before David was born—the doctor was furious—pregnant women are supposed to keep to earth. We were going fast—I *was* flying—I had left the earth. And then—within me, movement, for the first time—stirred to life far in air—movement within. The man unborn, he too, would fly. And so—I always loved him. He was movement—and wonder. In his short life were many flights. I never told anyone about the last one. His little bed was by the window—he wasn't four years old. It was night, but him not asleep. He saw the morning star—you know—the morning star. Brighter—stranger—reminiscent—and a promise. He pointed—"Mother," he asked me, "what is there—beyond the stars?" A baby, a sick baby—the morning star. Next night—the finger that pointed was— [*suddenly bites her own finger*] But, yes, I am glad. He would always have tried to move and too much would hold him. Wonder would die—and he'd laugh at soaring. [*looking down, sidewise*] Though I liked his voice. So I wish you'd stay near me—for I like your voice, too.

TOM: Claire! That's [*choked*] almost too much.

CLAIRE [*one of her swift glances—canny, almost practical*]: Well, I'm glad if it is. How can I make it more? [*but what she sees brings its own change*] I know what it is you're afraid of. It's because I have so much—yes, why shouldn't I say it?—passion. You feel that in me, don't you? You think it would swamp everything. But that isn't all there is to me.

TOM: Oh, I know it! My dearest—why, it's because I know it! You think I *am*—a fool?

CLAIRE: It's a thing that's—sometimes more than I am. And yet I—I am more than it is.

TOM: I know. I know about you.

CLAIRE: I don't know that you do. Perhaps if you really knew about me—you wouldn't go away.

TOM: You're making me suffer, Claire.

CLAIRE: I know I am. I want to. Why shouldn't you suffer? [*now seeing it more clearly than she has ever seen it*] You know what I think about you? You're afraid of suffering, and so you stop this side—in what you persuade yourself is suffering. [*waits, then sends it straight*] You know—how it is—with me and Dick? [*as she sees him suffer*] Oh, no, I don't want to hurt you! Let it be you! I'll teach you—you needn't scorn it. It's rather wonderful.

TOM: Stop that, Claire! That isn't you.

CLAIRE: Why are you so afraid—of letting me be low—if that is low? You see [*cannily*] I believe in beauty. I have the faith that can be bad as well as good. And you know why I have the faith? Because sometimes—from my lowest moments—beauty has opened as the sea. From a cave I saw immensity.

My love, you're going away—
Let me tell you how it is with me;
I want to touch you—somehow touch you once before I die—
Let me tell you how it is with me.
I do not want to work,
I want to be;
Do not want to make a rose or make a poem—
Want to lie upon the earth and know. [*closes her eyes*]
Stop doing that!—words going into patterns;
They do it sometimes when I let come what's there.
Thoughts take pattern—then the pattern is the thing.
But let me tell you how it is with me. [*it flows again*]
All that I do or say—it is to what it comes from,—
A drop lifted from the sea.
I want to lie upon the earth and know.
But—scratch a little dirt and make a flower;
Scratch a bit of brain—something like a poem.
[*covering her face*]
Stop *doing* that. Help me stop doing that!

TOM [*and from the place where she had carried him*]:
Don't talk at all. Lie still and know—
And know that I am knowing.

CLAIRE:
Yes; but we are so weak we have to talk;
To talk—to touch.
Why can't I rest in knowing I would give my life to reach you?
That has—all there is.
But I must—put my timid hands upon you,
Do something about infinity.
Oh, let what will flow into us,
And fill us full—and leave us still.
Wring me dry,
And let me fill again with life more pure.
To know—to feel,
And do nothing with what I feel and know—
That's being good. That's nearer God.
[*drenched in the feeling that has flowed through her—but surprised—helpless*] Why, I said your thing, didn't I? Opened my life to bring you to me, and what came—is what sends you away.

TOM: No! What came is what holds us together. What came is what saves us from ever going apart. [*brokenly*] My beautiful one. You—you brave flower of all our knowing.

CLAIRE: I am not a flower. I am too torn. If you have anything—help me. Breathe. Breathe the healing oneness, and let me know in calm. [*with a sob his head rests upon her*]

CLAIRE [*her hands on his head, but looking far*]: Beauty—you pure one thing. Breathe—Let me know in calm. Then—trouble me, trouble me, for other moments—in farther calm. [*slow, motionless, barely articulate*]

TOM [*as she does not move he lifts his head. And even as he looks at her, she does not move, nor look at him*]: Claire— [*his hand out to her, a little afraid*] You went away from me then. You are away from me now.

CLAIRE: Yes, and I could go on. But I will come back. [*it is hard to do. She brings much with her*] That, too, I will give you—my by-myself-ness. That's the uttermost I can give. I never thought—to try to give it. But let us do it—the great sacrilege! Yes! [*excited, she rises; she has his hands, and bring him up beside her*] Let us take the mad chance! Perhaps it's the only way to save—what's there. How do we know? How can we know? Risk. Risk everything. From all that flows into us, let it rise! All that we never thought to use to make a moment—let it flow into what could be! Bring all into life between us—or send all down to death! Oh, do you know what I am doing? Risk, risk everything, why are you so afraid to lose? What holds you from me? Test all. Let it live or let it die. It is our chance—our chance to bear—what's there. My dear one—I will love you so. With all of me. I am not afraid now—of—all of me. Be generous. Be unafraid. Life is for *life*—though it cuts us from the farthest life. How can I make you know that's true? All that we're open to— [*hesitates, shudders*] But yes—I will, I will risk the life that waits. Perhaps only he who gives his loneliness—shall find. You never keep by holding. [*gesture of giving*] To the uttermost. And it is gone—or it is there. You do not know and—that makes the moment—[*music has begun—a phonograph downstairs; they do not heed it*] Just as I would cut my wrists—[*holding them out*] Yes, perhaps this lesser thing will tell it—would cut my wrists and let the blood flow out till all is gone if my last drop would make—would make— [*looking at them fascinated*] I want to see it doing that! Let me give my last chance for life to—

[*He snatches her—they are on the brink of their moment; now that there are no words the phonograph from downstairs is louder. It is playing languorously the Barcarole; they become conscious of this—they do not want to be touched by the love song.*]

CLAIRE: Don't listen. That's nothing. This isn't that. [*fearing*] I tell you—it isn't that. Yes, I know—that's amorous—enclosing. I know—a little place. This isn't that. [*her arms going around him—all the lure of 'that' while she pleads against it as it comes up to them*] We will come out—to radiance—in far places [*admitting, using*] Oh, then let it be that! Go with it. Give up— the otherness. I will! And in the giving up—perhaps a door—we'd never find by searching. And if it's no more—than all have known, I only say it's worth the allness! [*her arms wrapped round him*] My love—my love—let go your pride in loneliness and let me give you joy!

TOM [*drenched in her passion, but fighting*]: It's *you.* [*in anguish*] You rare thing untouched—not—not into this—not back into this—by me—lover of your apartness.

[*She steps back. She sees he cannot. She stands there, before what she wanted more than life, and almost had, and lost. A long moment. Then she runs down the stairs.*]

CLAIRE [*her voice coming up*]: Harry! Choke that phonograph! If you want to be lewd—do it yourselves! You tawdry things—you cheap little lewd cowards. [*a door heard opening below*] Harry! If you don't stop that music, I'll kill myself. [*far down, steps on stairs*]

HARRY: Claire, what *is* this?

CLAIRE: Stop that phonograph or I'll—

HARRY: Why, of course I'll stop it. What—what is there to get so excited about? Now—now just a minute, dear. It'll take a minute.

[CLAIRE *comes back upstairs, dragging steps, face ghastly. The amorous song still comes up, and louder now that doors are open. She and* TOM *do not look at one another. Then, on a languorous swell the music comes to a grating stop. They do not speak or move. Quick footsteps—*HARRY *comes up.*]

HARRY: What in the world were you saying, Claire? Certainly you could have asked me more quietly to turn off the Victrola. Though what harm was it doing you—way up here? [*a sharp little sound from* CLAIRE; *she checks it, her hand over her mouth.* HARRY *looks from her to* TOM] Well, I think you two would better have had your dinner. Won't you come down now and have some?

CLAIRE [*only now taking her hand from her mouth*]: Harry, tell him to come up here—that insanity man. I—want to ask him something.

HARRY: "Insanity man!" How absurd. He's a nerve specialist. There's a vast difference.

CLAIRE: Is there? Anyway, ask him to come up here. Want to—ask him something.

TOM [*speaking with difficulty*]: Wouldn't it be better for us to go down there?

CLAIRE: No. So nice up here! Everybody—up here!

HARRY [*worried*]: You'll—be yourself, will you, Claire? [*She checks a laugh, nods.*] I think he can help you.

CLAIRE: Want to ask him to—help me.

HARRY [*as he is starting down*]: He's here as a guest to-night, you know, Claire.

CLAIRE: I suppose a guest can—help one.

TOM [*when the silence rejects it*]: Claire, you must know, it's because it is so much, so—

CLAIRE: Be still. There isn't anything to say.

TOM [*torn—tortured*]: If it only weren't *you*!

CLAIRE: Yes,—so you said. If it weren't. I suppose I wouldn't be so—interested! [*hears them starting up below—keeps looking at the place where they will appear*]

[HARRY *is heard to call,* "Coming, Dick?" *and* DICK'S *voice replies,* "In a moment or two." ADELAIDE *comes first.*]

ADELAIDE [*as her head appears*]: Well, these stairs should keep down weight. You missed an awfully good dinner, Claire. And kept Mr Edgeworthy from a good dinner.

CLAIRE: Yes. We missed our dinner. [*her eyes do not leave the place where* DR EMMONS *will come up*]

HARRY [*as he and* EMMONS *appear*]: Claire, this is—

CLAIRE: Yes, I know who he is. I want to ask you—

ADELAIDE: Let the poor man get his breath before you ask him anything. [*he nods, smiles, looks at* CLAIRE *with interest. Careful not to look too long at her, surveys the tower*]

EMMONS: Curious place.

ADELAIDE: Yes; it lacks form, doesn't it?

CLAIRE: What do you mean? How *dare* you?

[*It is impossible to ignore her agitation; she is backed against the curved wall, as far as possible from them.* HARRY *looks at her in alarm, then in resentment at* TOM, *who takes a step nearer* CLAIRE.]

HARRY [*trying to be light*]: Don't take it so hard, Claire.

CLAIRE [*to* EMMONS]: It must be very interesting—helping people go insane.

ADELAIDE: Claire! How preposterous.

EMMONS [*easily*]: I hope that's not precisely what we do.

ADELAIDE [*with the smile of one who is going to "cover it"*]: Trust Claire to put it in the unique and—amusing way.

CLAIRE: Amusing? You are amused? But it doesn't matter. [*to the doctor*] I think it is very kind of you—helping people go insane. I suppose they have all sorts of reasons for having to do it—reasons why they can't stay sane any longer. But tell me, how do they do it? It's not so easy to—get out. How do so many manage it?

EMMONS: I'd like immensely to have a talk with you about all this some day.

ADELAIDE: Certainly this is not the time, Claire.

CLAIRE: The time? When you—can't go any farther—isn't that that—

ADELAIDE [*capably taking the whole thing into matter-of-factness*]: What I think is, Claire has worked too long with plants. There's something—not quite sound about making one thing into another thing. What we need is unity. [*from* CLAIRE *something like a moan*] Yes, dear, we do need it. [*to the doctor*] I can't say that I believe in making life *over* like this. I don't think the new species are worth it. At least I don't believe in it for Claire. If one is an intense, sensitive person—

CLAIRE: Isn't there any way to *stop* her? Always—always smothering it with the word for it?

EMMONS [*soothingly*]: But she can't smother it. Anything that's really there—she can't hurt with words.

CLAIRE [*looking at him with eyes too bright*]: Then you don't see it either. [*angry*] Yes, she can hurt it! Piling it up—always piling it up—between us and—What there. Clogging the way—always. [*to* EMMONS] I want to cease to know! That's all I ask. Darken it. Darken it. If you came to help me, strike me blind!

EMMONS: You're really all tired out, aren't you? Oh, we've got to get you rested.

CLAIRE: They—deny it saying they have it; and he [*half looks at* TOM*—quickly looks away*] —others, deny it—afraid of losing it. We're in the *way*. Can't you see the dead stuff piled in the path? [*Pointing.*]

DICK [*voice coming up*]: Me too?

CLAIRE [*staring at the path, hearing his voice a moment after it has come*]: Yes, Dick—you too. Why not—you too. [*after he has come up*] What is there any more than you are?

DICK [*embarrassed by the intensity, but laughing*]: A question not at all displeasing to me. Who can answer it?

CLAIRE [*more and more excited*]: Yes! Who can answer it? [*going to him, in terror*] Let me go with you—and be with you—and know nothing else!

ADELAIDE [*gasping*]: Why—!

HARRY: Claire! This is going a little too—

CLAIRE: Far? But you have to go far to— [*clinging to* DICK] Only a place to hide your head—what else is there to hope for? I can't stay with them—piling it up! Always—piling it up! I can't get through to—he won't let me through to—what I don't know is there! [DICK *would help her regain herself*] Don't push me away! Don't—don't stand me up, I will go back—to the worst we ever were! Go back—and remember—what we've tried to forget!

ADELAIDE: It's time to stop this by force—if there's no other way. [*the doctor shakes his head*]

CLAIRE: All I ask is to die in the gutter with everyone spitting on me. [*changes to a curious weary smiling quiet*] Still, why should they bother to do that?

HARRY [*brokenly*]: You're sick, Claire. There's no denying it. [*look at* EMMONS, *who nods*]

ADELAIDE: Something to quiet her—to stop it.

CLAIRE [*throwing her arms around* DICK]: You, Dick. Not them. Not—any of them.

DICK: Claire, you are overwrought. You must—

HARRY [*to* DICK, *as if only now realizing that phase of it*]: I'll tell you one thing, you'll answer to me for this! [*he starts for* DICK*—is restrained by* EMMONS, *chiefly by his grave shake of the head. With* HARRY'S *move to them,* DICK *has shielded* CLAIRE]

CLAIRE: Yes—hold me. Keep me. You have mercy! You will have mercy. Anything—everything—that will let me be nothing!

CURTAIN

ACT III

In the greenhouse, the same as Act I. ANTHONY *is bedding small plants where the Edge Vine grew. In the inner room the plant like caught motion glows as from a light within.* HATTIE, *the Maid, rushes in from outside.*

ANTHONY [*turning angrily*]: You are not what this place—

HATTIE: Anthony, come in the house. I'm afraid. Mr Archer, I never saw him like this. He's talking to Mr Demming—something about Mrs Archer.

ANTHONY [*who in spite of himself is disturbed by her agitation*]: And if it is, it's no business of yours.

HATTIE: You don't know how he *is*. I went in the room and—

ANTHONY: Well, he won't hurt you, will he?

HATTIE: How do I know who he'll hurt—a person's whose— [*seeing how to get him*] Maybe he'll hurt Mrs Archer.

ANTHONY [*startled, then smiles*]: No; he won't hurt Miss Claire.

HATTIE: What do you know about it?—out here in the plant house?

ANTHONY: And I don't want to know about it. This is a very important day for me. It's Breath of Life I'm thinking of today—not you and Mr Archer.

HATTIE: Well, suppose he does something to Mr Demming?

ANTHONY: Mr Demming will have to look out for himself, I am at work. [*resuming work*]

HATTIE: Don't you think I ought to tell Mrs Archer that—

ANTHONY: You let her alone! This is no day for her to be bothered by you. At eleven o'clock [*looks at watch*] she comes out here—to Breath of Life.

HATTIE [*with greed for gossip*]: Did you see any of them when they came downstairs last night?

ANTHONY: I was attending to my own affairs.

HATTIE: They was all excited. Mr Edgeworthy—he went away. He was gone all night, I guess. I saw him coming back just as the milkman woke me up. Now he's packing his things. *He* wanted to get to Mrs Archer too—just a little while ago. But she won't open her door for none of them. I can't even get in to do her room.

ANTHONY: Then do some other room—and leave me alone in this room.

HATTIE [*a little afraid of what she is asking*]: Is she *sick*, Anthony—or what? [*vindicating herself, as he gives her a look*] The doctor, he stayed here late. But she'd locked herself in. I heard Mr Archer—

ANTHONY: You heard too much! [*he starts for the door, to make her leave, but* DICK *rushes in. Looks around wildly, goes to the trap-door, finds it locked*]

ANTHONY: What are you doing here?

DICK: Trying not to be shot—if you must know. This is the only place I can think of—till he comes to his senses and I can get away. Open that, will you? Rather—ignominious—but better be absurd than be dead.

HATTIE: Has he got the revolver?

DICK: Gone for it. Thought I wouldn't sit there till he got back. [*to* ANTHONY] Look here—don't you get the idea? Get me some place where he can't come.

ANTHONY: It is not what this place is for.

DICK: Any place is for saving a man's life.

HATTIE: Sure, Anthony. Mrs Archer wouldn't want Mr Demming shot.

DICK: That's right, Anthony. Miss Claire will be angry at you if you get me shot. [*he makes for the door of the inner room*]

ANTHONY: You can't go in there. It's locked.

[HARRY *rushes in from outside.*]

HARRY: I thought so! [*he has the revolver.* HATTIE *screams*]

ANTHONY: Now, Mr Archer, if you'll just stop and think, you'll know Miss Claire wouldn't want Mr Demming shot.

HARRY: You think that can stop me? You think you can stop me? [*raising the revolver*] A dog that—

ANTHONY [*keeping squarely between* HARRY *and* DICK]: Well, you can't shoot him in here. It is not good for the plants. [HARRY *is arrested by this reason*] And especially not today. Why, Mr Archer, Breath of Life may flower today. It's years Miss Claire's been working for this day.

HARRY: I never thought to see this day!

ANTHONY: No, did you? Oh, it will be a wonderful day. And how she has worked for it. She has an eye that sees what isn't right in what looks right. Many's the time I've thought—Here the form is set—and then she'd say, "We'll try this one," and it had—what I hadn't known was there. She's like that.

HARRY: I've always been pleased, Anthony, at the way you've worked with Miss Claire. This is hardly the time to stand there eulogizing her. And she's [*can hardly say it*] things you don't know she is.

ANTHONY [*proudly*]: Oh, I know that! You think I could work with her and not know she's more than I know she is?

HARRY: Well, if you love her you've got to let me shoot the dirty dog that drags her down!

ANTHONY: Not in here. Not today. More than like you'd break the glass. And Breath of Life's in there.

HARRY: Anthony, this is pretty clever of you—but—

ANTHONY: I'm not clever. But I know how easy it is to turn life back. No, I'm not clever at all [CLAIRE *has appeared and is looking in from outside*], but I do know—there are things you mustn't hurt. [*he sees her*] Yes, here's Miss Claire. [*She comes in. She is looking immaculate.*]

CLAIRE: From the gutter I rise again, refreshed. One does, you know. Nothing is fixed—not even the gutter. [*smilingly to* HARRY *and refusing to notice revolver or agitation*] How did you like the way I entertained the nerve specialist?

HARRY: Claire! You can *joke* about it?

CLAIRE [*taking the revolver from the hand she has shocked to limpness*]: Whom are you trying to make hear?

HARRY: I'm trying to make the world hear that [*pointing*] there stands a dirty dog who—

CLAIRE: Listen, Harry. [*turning to* HATTIE, *who is over by the tall plants at right, not wanting to be shot but not wanting to miss the conversation*] You can do my room now, Hattie. [HATTIE *goes*] If you're thinking of shooting Dick, you can't shoot him while he's backed up against that door.

ANTHONY: Just what I told them, Miss Claire. Just what I told them.

CLAIRE: And for that matter, it's quite dull of you to have any idea of shooting him.

HARRY: I may be dull—I know you think I am—but I'll show you that I've enough of the man in me to—

CLAIRE: To make yourself ridiculous? If I ran out and hid my head in the mud, would you think you had to shoot the mud?

DICK [*stung out of fear*]: That's pretty cruel!

CLAIRE: Well, would you rather be shot?

HARRY: So you just said it to protect him!

CLAIRE: I change it to grass. [*nodding to* DICK] Grass. If I hid my face in the grass, would you have to burn the grass?

HARRY: Oh, Claire, how *can* you? When you know how I love you—and how I'm suffering?

CLAIRE [*with interest*]: Are you suffering?

HARRY: Haven't you *eyes?*

CLAIRE: I should think it would—do something to you.

HARRY: God! Have you no heart? [*the door opens.* TOM *comes in*]

CLAIRE [*scarcely saying it*]: Yes, I have a heart.

TOM [*after a pause*]: I came to say good-bye.

CLAIRE: God! Have you no heart? Can't you at least wait till Dick is shot?

TOM: Claire! [*now sees the revolver in her hand that is turned from him. Going to her*] Claire!

CLAIRE: And even you think this is so important? [*carelessly raises the revolver, and with her left hand out flat, tells* TOM *not to touch her*] Harry thinks it important he shoot Dick, and Dick thinks it important not to be shot, and you think I mustn't shoot anybody—even myself—and can't any of you see that none of that is as important as—where revolvers can't reach? [*putting revolver where there is no Edge Vine*] I shall never shoot myself. I'm too interested in destruction to cut it short by shooting. [*after looking from one to the other, laughs. Pointing*] One—two—three. You-love-me. But why do you bring it out here?

ANTHONY [*who has resumed work*]: It is not what this place is for.

CLAIRE: No this place is for the destruction that can get through.

ANTHONY: Miss Claire, it is eleven. At eleven we are to go in and see—

CLAIRE: Whether it has gone through. But how can we go—with Dick against the door?

ANTHONY: He'll have to move.

CLAIRE: And be shot?

HARRY [*irritably*]: Oh, he'll not be shot. Claire can spoil anything.

[DICK *steps away from the door;* CLAIRE *takes a step nearer it.*]

CLAIRE [*halting*]: Have I spoiled everything? I don't want to go in there.

ANTHONY: We're going in together, Miss Claire. Don't you remember? Oh [*looking resentfully at the others*] don't let any little thing spoil it for you—the work of all those days—the hope of so many days.

CLAIRE: Yes—that's it.

ANTHONY: You're afraid you haven't done it?

CLAIRE: Yes, but—afraid I have.

HARRY [*cross, but kindly*]: That's just nervousness, Claire. I've had the same feeling myself about making a record in flying.

CLAIRE [*curiously grateful*]: You have, Harry?

HARRY [*glad enough to be back in a more usual world*]: Sure. I've been afraid to know, and almost as afraid of having done it as of not having done it.

[CLAIRE *nods, steps nearer, then again pulls back.*]

CLAIRE: I can't go in there. [*she almost looks at* TOM] Not today.

ANTHONY: But, Miss Claire, there'll be things to see today we can't see tomorrow.

CLAIRE: You bring it in here!

ANTHONY: In—out from its own place? [*she nods*] And—where they are? [*again she nods. Reluctantly he goes to the door*] I will not look into the heart. No one must know before you know.

[*In the inner room, his head a little turned away, he is seen very carefully to lift the plant which glows from within. As he brings it in, no one looks at it.* HARRY *takes a box of seedlings from a stand and puts them on the floor, that the newcomer may have a place.*]

ANTHONY: Breath of Life is here, Miss Claire.

[CLAIRE *half turns, then stops.*]

CLAIRE: Look—and see—what you see.
ANTHONY: No one should see what you've not seen.
CLAIRE: I can't see—until I know.

[ANTHONY *looks into the flower.*]

ANTHONY [*agitated*]: Miss Claire!
CLAIRE: It has come through?
ANTHONY: It has gone on.
CLAIRE: Stronger?
ANTHONY: Stronger, surer.
CLAIRE: And more fragile?
ANTHONY: And more fragile.
CLAIRE: Look deep. No—turning back?
ANTHONY [*after a searching look*]: The form is set. [*he steps back from it*]
CLAIRE: Then it is—out. [*from where she stands she turns slowly to the plant*] You weren't. You are.
ANTHONY: But come and see, Miss Claire.
CLAIRE: It's so much more than—I'd see.
HARRY: Well, I'm going to see. [*looking into it*] I never saw anything like that before! There seems something alive—inside this outer shell.
DICK [*he too looking in and he has an artist's manner of a hand up to make the light right*]: It's quite new in form. It—says something about form.
HARRY [*cordially to* CLAIRE, *who stands apart*]: So you've really put it over. Well, well,—congratulations. It's a good deal of novelty, I should say, and I've no doubt you'll have a considerable success with it—people always like something new. I'm mighty glad—after all your work, and I hope it will—set you up.
CLAIRE [*low—and like a machine*]: Will you all—go away?

[ANTHONY *goes—into the other room.*]

HARRY: Why—why, yes. But—oh, Claire! Can't you take some pleasure in your work? [*as she stands there very still*] Emmons says you need a good long rest—and I think he's right.
TOM: Can't this help you, Claire? Let this be release. This—breath of the uncaptured.
CLAIRE [*and though speaking, she remains just as still*]: Breath of the uncaptured?

You are a novelty.
Out?
You have been brought in.
A thousand years from now, when you are but a form too long repeated,
Perhaps the madness that gave you birth will burst again,
And from the prison that is you will leap pent queernesses
To make a form that hasn't been—
To make a person new.
And this we call creation. [*very low, her head not coming up*]
Go away!

[TOM *goes;* HARRY *hesitates, looking in anxiety at* CLAIRE. *He starts to go, stops, looks at* DICK, *from him to* CLAIRE. *But goes. A moment later* DICK *moves near* CLAIRE; *stands uncertainly, then puts a hand upon her. She starts, only then knowing he is there.*]

CLAIRE [*a slight shrinking away, but not really reached*]: Um, um.

[*He goes.* CLAIRE *steps nearer her creation. She looks into what hasn't been. With her breath, and by a gentle moving of her hands, she fans it to fuller openness. As she does this* TOM *returns and from outside is looking in at her. Softly he opens the door and comes in. She does not know that he is there. In the way she looks at the flower he looks at her.*]

TOM: Claire. [*she lifts her head*] As you stood there, looking into the womb you breathed to life, you were beautiful to me beyond any other beauty. You were life and its reach and its anguish. I can't go away from you. I will never go away from you. It shall all be—as you wish. I can go with you where I could not go alone. If this is delusion, I want that delusion. It's more than any reality I could attain. [*as she does not move*] Speak to me, Claire. You—are glad?
CLAIRE [*from far*]: Speak to you? [*pause*] Do I know who you are?
TOM: I think you do.
CLAIRE: Oh, yes. I love you. That's who you are. [*waits again*] But why are you something—very far away?
TOM: Come nearer.
CLAIRE: Nearer? [*feeling it with her voice*] Nearer. But I think I am going—the other way.
TOM: No, Claire—come to me. Did you understand, dear? I am not going away.
CLAIRE: You're not going away?
TOM: Not without you, Claire. And you and I will be together. Is that—what you wanted?

CLAIRE: Wanted? [*as if wanting is something that harks far back. But the word calls to her passion*] Wanted! [*a sob, hands out, she goes to him. But before his arms can take her, she steps back*] Are you trying to pull me down into what I wanted? Are you here to make me stop?

TOM: How can you ask that? I love you because it is not in you to stop.

CLAIRE: And loving me for that—would stop me? Oh, help me see it! It is so important that I see it.

TOM: It is important. It is our lives.

CLAIRE: And more than that. I cannot see it because it is so much more than that.

TOM: Don't try to see all that it is. From peace you'll see a little more.

CLAIRE: Peace? [*troubled as we are when looking at what we cannot see clearly*] What is peace? Peace is what the struggle knows in moments very far apart. Peace—that is not a place to rest. Are you resting? What are you? You who'd take me from what I am to something else?

TOM: I thought you knew, Claire.

CLAIRE: I know—what you pass for. But are you beauty? Beauty is that only living pattern—the trying to take pattern. Are you trying?

TOM: Within myself, Claire. I never thought you doubted that.

CLAIRE: Beauty is it. [*she turns to Breath of Life, as if to learn it there, but turns away with a sob*] If I cannot go to you now—I will always be alone.

[TOM *takes her in his arms. She is shaken, then comes to rest.*]

TOM: Yes—rest. And then—come into joy. You have so much life for joy.

CLAIRE [*raising her head, called by promised gladness*]: We'll run around together. [*lovingly he nods*] Up hills. All night on hills.

TOM [*tenderly*]: All night on hills.

CLAIRE: We'll go on the sea in a little boat.

TOM: On the sea in a little boat.

CLAIRE: But—there are other boats on other seas. [*drawing back from him, troubled*] There are other boats on other seas.

TOM [*drawing her back to him*]: My dearest—not now, not now.

CLAIRE [*her arms going round him*]: Oh, I would love those hours with you. I want them. I want you! [*they kiss—but deep in her is sobbing*] Reminiscence. [*her hand feeling his arm as we touch what we would remember*] Reminiscence. [*with one of her swift changes steps back from him*] How dare you pass for what you're not? We are tired, and so we think it's you. Stop with you. Don't get through—to what you're in the way of. Beauty is not something you say about beauty.

TOM: I say little about beauty, Claire.

CLAIRE: Your life says it. By standing far off you pass for it. Smother it with a life that passes for it. But beauty— [*getting it from the flower*] Beauty is the humility breathed from the shame of succeeding.

TOM: But it may all be within one's self, dear.

CLAIRE [*drawn by this, but held, and desperate because she is held*]: When I have wanted you with all my wanting—why must I distrust you now? When I love you—with all of me, why do I know that only you are worth my hate?

TOM: It's the fear of easy satisfactions. I love you for it.

CLAIRE [*over the flower*]: Breath of Life—you here? Are you lonely—Breath of Life?

TOM: Claire—hear me! Don't go where we can't go. As there you made a shell for life within, make for yourself a life in which to live. It must be so.

CLAIRE: As you made for yourself a shell called beauty?

TOM: What is there for you, if you'll have no touch with what we have?

CLAIRE: What is there? There are the dreams we haven't dreamed. There is the long and flowing pattern. [*she follows that, but suddenly and as if blindly goes to him*] I am tired. I am lonely. I'm afraid. [*he holds her, soothing. But she steps back from him*] And because we are tired—lonely—and afraid, we stop with you. Don't get through—to what you're in the way of.

TOM: Then you don't love me?

CLAIRE: I'm fighting for my chance. I don't know—which chance. [*Is drawn to the other chance, to Breath of Life. Looks into it as if to look through to the uncaptured. And through this life just caught comes the truth she chants.*]

I've wallowed at a coarse man's feet,
I'm sprayed with dreams we've not yet come to.
I've gone so low that words can't get there,
I've never pulled the mantle of my fears
around me
And called it loneliness—And called it God.
Only with life that waits have I kept faith.

[*with effort raising her eyes to the man*]

And only you have ever threatened me.

TOM [*coming to her, and with strength now*]: And I will threaten you. I'm here to hold you from where I know you cannot go. You're trying what we can't do.

CLAIRE: What else is there worth trying?

TOM: I love you, and I will keep you—from fartherness—from harm. You are mine, and you will stay with me! [*roughly*] You hear me? You will stay with me!

CLAIRE [*her head on his breast, in ecstasy of rest. Drowsily*]: You can keep me?

TOM: Darling! I can keep you. I will keep you—safe.

CLAIRE [*troubled by the word, but barely able to raise her head*]: Safe?

TOM [*bringing her to rest again*]: Trust me, Claire.

CLAIRE [*not lifting her head, but turning it so she sees Breath of Life*]: Now can I trust—what is? [*suddenly pushing him roughly away*] No! I will beat my life to pieces in the struggle to—

TOM: To *what,* Claire?

CLAIRE: Not to stop it by seeming to have it. [*with fury*] I will keep my life low—low—that I may never stop myself—or anyone—with the thought it's what *I* have. I'd rather be the steam rising from the manure than be a thing called beautiful! [*with sight too clear*] Now I know who you are. It is you puts out the breath of life. Image of beauty—*You fill the place—should be a gate.* [*in agony*] Oh, that it is *you*—fill the place—should be a gate! My darling! That it should be you who— [*her hands moving on him*] Let me tell you something. Never was loving strong as my loving of you! Do you know that? Oh, know that! Know it now! [*her arms go around his neck*] Hours with you—I'd give my life to have! That it should be you— [*he would loosen her hands, for he cannot breathe. But when she knows she is choking him, that knowledge is fire burning its way into the last passion*] It *is* you. It is you.

TOM [*words coming from a throat not free*]: Claire! What are you doing? [*then she knows what she is doing*]

CLAIRE [*to his resistance*]: No! You are *too much!* You are *not enough.* [*still wanting not to hurt her, he is slow in getting free. He keeps stepping backward trying, in growing earnest, to loosen her hands. But he does not loosen them before she has found the place in his throat that cuts off breath. As he gasps*] Breath of Life—my gift—to you!

[*She has pushed him against one of the plants at right as he sways, strength she never had before pushes him over backward, just as they have struggled from sight. Violent crash of glass is heard.*]

TOM [*faint smothered voice*]: *No.* I'm—hurt.

CLAIRE [*in the frenzy and agony of killing*]: Oh, gift! Oh, gift! [*there is no sound.*]

CLAIRE [*rises—steps back—is seen now; is looking down*]: Gift.

[*Like one who does not know where she is, she moves into the room—looks around. Takes a step toward Breath of Life; turns and goes quickly to the door. Stops, as if stopped. Sees the revolver where the Edge Vine was. Slowly goes to it. Holds it as if she cannot think what it is for. Then raises it high and fires above through the place in the glass left open for ventilation.* ANTHONY *comes from the inner room. His eyes go from her to the body beyond.* HARRY *rushes in from outside.*]

HARRY: Who fired that?

CLAIRE: I did. Lonely.

[*Seeing* ANTHONY*'s look,* HARRY*'s eyes follow it.*]

HARRY: Oh! What? What? [DICK *comes running in*] Who? Claire!

[DICK *sees—goes to* TOM.]

CLAIRE: Yes. I did it. MY—Gift.

HARRY: Is he—? He isn't—? He isn't—?

[*Tries to go in there. Cannot—there is the sound of broken glass, of a position being changed—then* DICK *reappears.*]

DICK [*his voice in jerks*]: It's—it's no use, but I'll go for a doctor.

HARRY: No—no. Oh, I suppose— [*falling down beside* CLAIRE*—his face against her*] My darling! How can I save you now?

CLAIRE [*speaking each word very carefully*]: Saved—myself.

ANTHONY: I did it. Don't you see? I didn't want so many around. Not—what this place is for.

HARRY [*snatching at this but lets it go*]: She wouldn't let— [*looking up at* CLAIRE*—then quickly hiding his face*] And—don't you see?

CLAIRE: Out. [*a little like a child's pleased surprise*] Out.

[DICK *stands there, as if unable to get to the door—his face distorted, biting his hand.*]

ANTHONY: Miss Claire! You can do anything—won't you try?

CLAIRE: Reminiscence? [*speaking the word as if she has left even that, but smiles a little*]

[ANTHONY *takes Reminiscence, the flower she was breeding for fragrance for Breath of Life—holds it out to her. But she has taken a step forward, past them all.*]

CLAIRE: Out. [*as if feeling her way*]
Nearer,

[*Her voice now feeling the way to it.*]

Nearer—

[*Voice almost upon it.*]

—my *God,*

[*Falling upon it with surprise.*]

to Thee,

[*Breathing it.*]

Nearer—to Thee,
E'en though it be—

[*A slight turn of the head toward the dead man she loves—a mechanical turn just as far the other way.*]

a cross

That

[*Her head going down.*]

raises me;

[*Her head slowly coming up—singing it.*]

Still all my song shall be,
Nearer, my—

[*Slowly the curtain begins to shut her out. The last word heard is the final* Nearer—*a faint breath from far.*]

CURTAIN

Eugene O'Neill

Eugene Gladstone O'Neill (1888–1953) was born in a hotel room in New York City's theater district, the son of a prominent actor. His father, James O'Neill, was best known for his leading role in his own production of Alexander Dumas's melodramatic *The Count of Monte Cristo*. It is unclear if James was born in the United States or Ireland, but it is certain that he was fiercely Irish, Catholic, autocratic, and alcoholic, traits that he passed on to Eugene, with whom he was never on easy terms. Eugene O'Neill's mother, Ella Quinlan, was a devout Catholic who was consumed by a lifelong sense of guilt over the death of her baby in 1885. After O'Neill's birth three years later, she became addicted to morphine. Although she eventually overcame her addiction, mother and son felt the burden of this knowledge, and O'Neill always had an uneasy relationship with her. Like Ella's, O'Neill's spiritual life was complicated; brought up a Catholic and educated in Catholic schools, he lost his faith as a teenager, a decision that tormented him the rest of his life. O'Neill also had a difficult relationship with his brother, James, a hopeless alcoholic, who followed his father as an actor of modest success.

O'Neill's conflicted feelings about his father, mother, and brother provided him with the resource for many of his plays, especially *Long Day's Journey Into Night*. While he was writing it in 1940, O'Neill explained to George Jean Nathan, a literary critic and friend, that his idea for this most autobiographical play was "the story of one day, 8 A.M. to midnight, in the life of a family of four—father, mother and two sons—back in 1912,—a day in which things occur which evoke the whole past of the family and reveal every aspect of its interrelationships. A deeply tragic play, but without any violent dramatic action. At the final curtain, there they still are, trapped within each other by the past, each guilty and at the same time innocent, scorning, loving, pitying each other, understanding and yet not understanding at all, forgiving but still doomed never to be able to forget."

At eighteen, O'Neill rebelled against his father and mother, veering toward personal disaster. Through his father's influence he attended Princeton University in 1906, but although he evidently had a brilliant intellect, he seems to have preferred drinking and womanizing to formal study, and he was dismissed after a year. Three years later he fell briefly in love with twenty-year-old Kathleen Jenkins. Soon tiring of the relationship, O'Neill nevertheless agreed to a secret marriage because Kathleen was pregnant, but afterward he ran away when his father, without knowing why his son wanted to leave, arranged to send him on a gold-hunting exploration in the jungles of Central America. When O'Neill returned to New York, he ignored Kathleen, who had borne their child. They were eventually divorced in 1912, and O'Neill again sought to escape by booking passage on a freighter bound for Buenos Aires.

When he was thirty, O'Neill married Agnes Boulton, a writer of fiction. But early on the marriage suffered from O'Neill's jealousy, alcoholism, and intense work habits. By 1926 O'Neill was bored with his marriage and, in a fit of depression over his career, began a romance with the actress Carlotta Monterrey, née Hazel Tharsing. He divorced Boulton and married Monterrey in 1929. Though tempestuous and messy on both sides, the marriage lasted twenty-six years. Near the end of his life, O'Neill wrote to Carlotta praising her as the woman "who has endured my rotten nerves, my lack of stability, [and] my cussedness in general."

When he finally returned to New York, O'Neill frequented a rough waterfront bar called Jimmy the Priest's, which provided the setting for his later plays, especially *Anna Christie* and *The Iceman Cometh.* During this period, O'Neill lived from day-to-day, drinking heavily and sometimes working as a merchant seaman. These experiences gave him material for many of his plays that deal with sailors and the sea, but he was also depressed and attempted suicide.

His spirits were partly lifted when he came under the spell of the Abbey Theatre (the Irish National Theatre) during its 1911 engagement in New York City. O'Neill was cool toward John Millington Synge's *The Playboy of the Western World*, but he sat through as many performances of Henrik Ibsen's *Hedda Gabler* as he could. Years later, he wrote *Servitude*, a play based on Ibsen's *A Doll's House,* which explores what happens to Nora Torvald in her quest for independence.

Near the end of 1912, O'Neill developed tuberculosis, and it was during his recuperation that he began to think seriously of becoming a playwright. He now read Greek tragedy, along with the works of Henrik Ibsen, George Bernard Shaw, John Millington Synge, and William Butler Yeats. Most of all he recognized a kindred spirit in August Strindberg; and in *The Father, Miss Julie*, and *The Dance of Death*, O'Neill saw echoes of his own life—the struggle of the inner spirit against external social pressure, strained relationships, unhappiness with women, and family conflict. This burst of intellectual stimulation gave O'Neill a sense of what he eventually called the Faust-Mephistopheles personality, or one who suffers the separateness of the soul and the outer personality. The constant conflict of attempting to reconcile these general ideas became recurring themes for his plays.

O'Neill's decision to become a playwright was certainly motivated in part by his conflict with his father, but self-analysis provided him with sources for characters who might vicariously exorcise his own inner demons. Years later, when he was thirty-six and the successful author of *Desire Under the Elms*, O'Neill explained, "Playwrights are either intuitively keenly analytical psychologists—or they aren't good playwrights. I'm trying to be one. To me, Freud only means uncertain conjectures and explanations about truths of the emotional past of mankind that every dramatist has clearly sensed since real drama began. . . . I respect Freud's work tremendously—but I'm not an addict. Whatever of Freudianism is in *Desire* must have walked right in 'through my unconscious.'" O'Neill's genius lay in his ability to transform his personal life into an art that is universal.

In 1913 O'Neill received permission to study playwriting at Harvard University, and though he did well, he was only able to complete a one-act play. He left after a year, lured by the bohemian life of Greenwich Village. There he set himself up as a playwright and, at his father's expense, published *Thirst and Other One-Act Plays* in 1915. The next year, he fell in with the Provincetown

Players, a group of enthusiastic young writers and playwrights filled with a desire to revolutionize American literature. Co-founded by Susan Glaspell (1876–1948) and George Cram Cook (1873–1924) at their home in Provincetown, Massachusetts, the group shifted its productions to Greenwich Village in the winter of 1916, where O'Neill met them. The Players gave O'Neill a platform for developing his skills and ideas. He wrote and acted among a formidable company that included poets Edna St. Vincent Millay (1892–1950) and e. e. cummings (1894–1962); authors Floyd Dell (1887–1964), Edna Ferber (1887–1968), and Sherwood Anderson (1876–1941); and journalist John Reed (1887–1920), whose lover (and wife), Louise Bryant, O'Neill had an affair with. The Provincetown Players produced O'Neill's first-performed one-act play *Bound East for Cardiff* (1916), in which he had a role, *In the Zone* (1917), and *The Moon of the Caribbees* (1918), among others. These plays often draw heavily on O'Neill's years of wandering with the merchant marine. They are short and lack fully developed characters or thematic depth, but they show O'Neill's raw literary and theatrical power.

O'Neill was entrepreneurial, and when he grew impatient with Cook and Glaspell's inchoate style of management, he founded his own experimental theater, the Greenwich Village Players, which he eventually merged with the Provincetown Players in 1923. Under the aegis of this company, O'Neill exerted more control than he otherwise might have had over his plays, and what he could not accomplish at Princeton and Harvard, he learned to do in a theater of his own making. Among the best of his productions during this period was *The Emperor Jones* (1920), most of which is a dramatic monologue by Brutus Jones, an African American turned Caribbean tyrant, who is overthrown and now wanders in circles in the jungle, delving deeply into his personal and racial past. This play marked one of the first times that a black actor played the protagonist for the Broadway theater. Also notable was *The Hairy Ape* (1922), an adaptation of the beauty and the beast story, which contrasts a coal-stoker on a cruise ship with a society woman.

O'Neill's first important full-length play, *Beyond the Horizon* (1920), won the Pulitzer Prize for Drama. O'Neill called it an American tragedy because of its elemental family strife, which contrasts two unhappy brothers of a New England farming family. Robert Mayo, a dreamy young man who longs to go to sea, makes an unhappy marriage and remains on the farm. The more pragmatic brother, Andrew, leaves home, travels the world, and prospers financially but not spiritually. The title refers to Robert's despairing notion that only in death will he be able to sail beyond the horizon. One of the play's most striking features is its defiantly American dialogue, which catches the rhythms of rural New England speech. *Beyond the Horizon* set a pattern for O'Neill, who worked in a contentiously American idiom by creating specifically located characters and settings. O'Neill was deeply interested in history and defended "the worth of the scorned traditional past in American History," which he understood as a means for probing universal moral issues and conflicting obligations.

Anna Christie (1921), which earned him his second Pulitzer Prize is set in a barroom, where Anna meets and falls in love with a sailor, Mat Burke. Disillusioned when he discovers that Anna is a prostitute, Burke runs off to sea.

O'Neill followed up with *The First Man* (1922), about a scientist whose work is lost because he cannot accept the intrusion of a child in his marriage, and *Welded* (1924), which pits a husband against his wife, both locked in a struggle of love and hate, which bears strong resemblance to that in Strindberg's *The Father. Marco Millions* (1928) was an unsuccessful play, noteworthy for its portrayal of Marco Polo as a man of ideals who succumbs to materialism and greed.

Like Strindberg, O'Neill experimented with expressionism, particularly in *All God's Chillun Got Wings* (1924), *The Great God Brown* (1926), and *Dynamo* (1929). Though it was a critical disaster, *The Great God Brown* portrays an artist who is defeated by a materialistic world. In it, the actors wear masks that served the purpose of blurring and distorting the relationship of inner and outer being. The leading character, Dion Anthony, seems to reflect O'Neill's state of mind concerning his career and his marriage to Carlotta. Anthony, an architect whose talent is unappreciated and appropriated without compensation, turns inward, becoming alcoholic and self-destructive. Despite this negativism, *The Great God Brown* was O'Neill's favorite play.

Strange Interlude (1928), which earned O'Neill his third Pulitzer Prize, stands out because of its length: some seven hours for production. It sold more than 100,000 copies, but it had only a modest theatrical run. It is really two plays, weaving together the external action with the internal states of mind that affect the characters' actions: We hear both what the characters say to each other and what they are really thinking. The play takes its title from the line "Our lives are merely strangely dark interludes in the electrical display of God the Father." *Mourning Becomes Electra* (1931) is O'Neill's trilogy, based on *The Orestia* (458 B.C.) of Aeschylus (525–456 B.C.), in which Greek attributes are replaced with American historical events, characters, and setting. *Days Without End* (1934) again splits the internal and external aspects of character, going so far as to have the protagonist's inner and outer states portrayed by different actors.

In 1936, O'Neill was awarded the Nobel Prize for Literature, but he was too ill to attend the ceremony. O'Neill suffered from Parkinson's disease, and his health, ravaged by alcoholism and bouts of depression, was already in a serious decline. His acceptance statement stressed his belief that American theater had come of age and now rivaled that of Europe's. O'Neill acknowledged his debt to Strindberg, affirming that his "influence runs clearly through more than a few of my plays and is plain for everyone to see."

During the period that followed, O'Neill worked on many projects but finished only *The Iceman Cometh* (1946), a long, rambling play about the dissolution of Theodore Hickman, "Hickey," a seemingly resolute traveling salesman who serves as a false savior for the denizens of Harry Hope's bar. The play has obvious Christian allusions, but it offers no hope for redemption; and when Hickey arrives, it is to tell his friends that he has killed his loving wife.

O'Neill was fifty-three when he completed *Long Day's Journey Into Night*, but he would not allow its production until after his death. Ironically, as he suspected, it was recognized as one of his major plays, and he was posthumously awarded his fourth Pulitzer Prize in 1957. One reason for O'Neill's reluctance to produce the play in his lifetime is that it is the most autobiographical of his works and represents an attempt to make peace with his ghosts, something he could not do. O'Neill's character, Edmund Tyrone, the younger son (and O'Neill's alter ego), says that when he becomes a poet, he will be faithful to realism. The rest of the Tyrone family includes the father who is an actor, a mother who is a morphine addict, and a younger brother who is alcoholic. Other posthumously produced plays include *Hughie* (completed in 1942), *Moon for the Misbegotten* (completed in 1947), and *A Touch of the Poet* (completed in 1947). These four plays were intended to be part of a cycle of eleven "history" plays depicting the rise of American civilization and its decline into a slough of greed and materialism that disastrously alters the ability to nurture love. O'Neill's working title for this project was "A Tale of Possessors and Self-Dispossessed," and for various reasons—his health, politics, the World War—he was against producing any of the plays until the entire cycle was completed.

Desire Under the Elms (1924) is a naturalistic play in the style of Strindberg's *The Father* and *Miss Julie*, presenting a toughly realistic critique of the established American-Victorian-Puritan ethic. The characters exhibit conflicting states of inner and outer turmoil, also influenced by Strindberg, and the realistic setting contrasts sharply with the psychological anguish and instability of the characters. The story, which showcases the rivalry of a father and his sons, as well as sibling rivalry, is a filtering of O'Neill's own family conflict.

In order to deepen the tragic underpinnings of *Desire Under the Elms*, O'Neill alluded frequently to *Hippolytus* (428 B.C.), a tragedy by Euripides (484–406 B.C.), about Phaedra, the second wife of the Greek king Theseus, who unhappily falls in love with her stepson Hippolytus. When Hippolytus coldly rejects her, she commits suicide and leaves a note claiming that Hippolytus tried to rape her. Theseus curses his son, who is mortally injured in a chariot accident. Tragically, Hippolytus is reconciled with Theseus just before he dies.

While loosely following Euripides' tragedy for the story of the Cabot family, O'Neill created a peculiarly American setting—a New England farm—with the characters speaking in the dialect of working farmers. The American elms of the title, large graceful trees that tower over the worn farmhouse, suggest nature's cradle for a family that is at the brink of spiritual exhaustion: "Two enormous elms are on each side of the house. They bend their trailing branches down over the roof. They appear to protect and at the same time subdue. There is a sinister maternity in their aspect, a crushing jealous absorption. They have developed from their intimate contact with the life of man in the house an appalling humaneness. They brood oppressively over the house. They are like exhausted women resting their sagging breasts and hands and hair on its roof, and when it rains their tears trickle down monotonously and rot on the shingles." These oppressive elms are symbolic of the corrosive power of women, the rot of Freudian oedipal conflict, and an environment that no longer nurtures.

The action pits Ephraim Cabot against his three sons, Simeon, Peter, and, particularly, Eben, the youngest. Central to the conflict is Abbie Putnam, the father's third wife, a woman Eben's age, whom he marries not so much because he is lustful, but because he wants to produce an heir so that his older children will be denied the inheritance of the farm. Ephraim is a mean man, scornful of anyone or anything delicate and poetic. Eben is the opposite of his flinty, calculating father, and he has a literary bent. Eben's mother originally owned the farm, but at her death it went to Ephraim Cabot. Eben resents this and wants his inheritance, and he sees the old man's new wife as a threat to his future. In order to regain his lost farm, Eben craftily buys out his older half-brothers with money stolen from Cabot's hoard. Suddenly freed from the drudgery of the farm, the brothers are gleeful. But instead of saying good-bye in a kindly fashion, they defiantly throw rocks through the parlor windows and set out for goldfields of California.

At home, Cabot tries to impregnate his young wife, but he is impotent. The conflict intensifies when Eben and Abbie, sexually attracted to each other, finally make love. When Abbie becomes pregnant by Eben, the child is passed off as Cabot's, though he will not admit how this could be so. Neighbors are more knowing, but the old man's stern Old Testament authority holds sway over the timid younger generation, who are afraid to make the true situation public. Unable to live under these circumstances, Eben plans to leave for the West, and Abbie, unable to bear the guilt of her unfulfilled commitment to Eben, tells him that she will kill the baby in order to prove her love for him. Eben rejects her love and stalks off, not hearing her say, "I'll prove t' ye! I'll prove I love ye better'n . . . Better'n everythin' else in the world!"

Abbie fulfills her promise, but the act is meant to show that she loves Eben and hates Cabot. Horrified by her crime, Eben accuses Abbie of wanting to blame him for the murder and so steal the farm. When the sheriff arrives to take Abbie to jail, Eben softens and declares that he loves her and that he too is responsible for the baby's death. Cabot, smarting from the revelation that his son and wife have committed adultery, stoically takes it all in. He says good-bye to Eben with a "trace of grudging admiration" before defiantly marching off to the barn. As they prepare to go to the jail, the sun rises, illuminating the house and the elms. Eben takes Abbie's hand, and attempting to be kindly, says, "Sun's a-rizin'. Purty, hain't it?"

Desire Under the Elms is O'Neill's first mature play to demonstrate in his own voice his tragic sense of life. Its depiction of intense family relationships established a theme that would be carried through in many American plays, especially those of Susan Glaspell, Arthur Miller, Tennessee Williams, Edward Albee, and Marsha Norman. Sam Shepard's *Buried Child*, which deals with family strife, illicit love, and a murdered child, may be interpreted as a response to O'Neill's *Desire Under the Elms*. In Sweden, O'Neill's reputation approaches Strindberg's, and he has influenced Ingmar Bergman's films and interpretation of drama.

Film

Desire Under the Elms (1958), directed by Delbert Mann, with Burl Ives, Anthony Perkins, Sophia Loren, and Frank Overton. Screenplay by Irwin Shaw. Paramount.

Desire Under the Elms

CHARACTERS
EPHRAIM CABOT
SIMEON
PETER } his sons
EBEN
ABBIE PUTNAM
YOUNG GIRL, two FARMERS, the FIDDLER, a SHERIFF, and other folk from the neighboring farms

The action of the entire play takes place in, and immediately outside of, the Cabot farmhouse in New England, in the year 1850. The south end of the house faces front to a stone wall with a wooden gate at center opening on a country road. The house is in good condition but in need of paint. Its walls are a sickly grayish, the green of the shutters faded. Two enormous elms are on each side of the house. They bend their trailing branches down over the roof. They appear to protect and at the same time subdue. There is a sinister maternity in their aspect, a crushing, jealous absorption. They have developed from their intimate contact with the life of man in the house an appalling humaneness. They brood oppressively over the house. They are like exhausted women resting their sagging breasts and hands and hair on its roof, and when it rains their tears trickle down monotonously and rot on the shingles.

There is a path running from the gate around the right corner of the house to the front door. A narrow porch is on this side. The end wall facing us has two windows in its upper story, two larger ones on the floor below. The two upper are those of the father's bedroom and that of the brothers. On the left, ground floor, is the kitchen—on the right, the parlor, the shades of which are always drawn down.

PART I

Scene 1

Exterior of the Farmhouse. It is sunset of a day at the beginning of summer in the year 1850. There is no wind and everything is still. The sky above the roof is suffused with deep colors, the green of the elms glows, but the house is in shadow, seeming pale and washed out by contrast.

A door opens and EBEN CABOT *comes to the end of the porch and stands looking down the road to the right. He has a large bell in his hand and this he swings mechanically, awakening a deafening clangor. Then he puts his hands on his hips and stares up at the sky. He sighs with a puzzled awe and blurts out with halting appreciation*

EBEN: God! Purty! [*His eyes fall and he stares about him frowningly. He is twenty-five, tall and sinewy. His face is well-formed, good-looking, but its expression is resentful and defensive. His defiant, dark eyes remind one of a wild animal's in captivity. Each day is a cage in which he finds himself trapped but inwardly unsubdued. There is a fierce repressed vitality about him. He has black hair, mustache, a thin curly trace of beard. He is dressed in rough farm clothes. He spits on the ground with intense disgust, turns and goes back into the house.* SIMEON *and* PETER *come in from their work in the fields. They are tall men, much older than their half-brother* (SIMEON *is thirty-nine and* PETER *thirty-seven*)*, built on a squarer, simpler model, fleshier in body, more bovine and homelier in face, shrewder and more practical. Their shoulders stoop a bit from years of farm work. They clump heavily along in their clumsy thick-soled boots caked with earth. Their clothes, their faces, hands, bare arms and throats are earth-stained. They smell of earth. They stand together for a moment in front of the house and, as if with the one impulse, stare dumbly up at the sky, leaning on their hoes. Their faces have a compressed, unresigned expression. As they look upward, this softens.*]

SIMEON [*grudgingly*]: Purty.

PETER: Ay-eh.

SIMEON [*suddenly*]: Eighteen years ago.

PETER: What?

SIMEON: Jenn. My woman. She died.

PETER: I'd fergot.

SIMEON: I rec'lect—now an' agin. Makes it lonesome. She'd hair long's a hoss' tail—an' yaller like gold!

PETER: Waal—she's gone. [*this with indifferent finality—then after a pause*] They's gold in the West, Sim.

SIMEON [*still under the influence of sunset—vaguely*]: In the sky?

PETER: Waal—in a manner o' speakin'—thar's the promise. [*growing excited*] Gold in the sky—in the West—Golden Gate—Californi-a!—Goldest West!—fields o' gold!

SIMEON [*excited in his turn*]: Fortunes layin' just atop o' the ground waitin' t' be picked! Solomon's mines, they says! [*For a moment they continue looking up at the sky—then their eyes drop.*]

PETER [*with sardonic bitterness*]: Here—it's stones atop o' the ground—stones atop o' stones—makin' stone walls—year atop o' year—him 'n' yew 'n' me 'n' then Eben—makin' stone walls fur him to fence us in!

SIMEON: We've wuked. Give our strength. Give our years. Plowed 'em under in the ground— [*he stamps rebelliously*] —rottin'—makin' soil for his crops! [*a pause*] Waal—the farm pays good for hereabouts.

PETER: If we plowed in Californi-a, they'd be lumps o' gold in the furrow!

SIMEON: Californi-a's t'other side o' earth, a'most. We got t' calc'late—

PETER [*after a pause*]: 'Twould be hard fur me, too, to give up what we've 'arned here by our sweat. [*A pause.* EBEN *sticks his head out of the dining-room window, listening.*]

SIMEON: Ay-eh. [*a pause*] Mebbe—he'll die soon.

PETER [*doubtfully*]: Mebbe.

SIMEON: Mebbe—fur all we knows—he's dead now.

PETER: Ye'd need proof.

SIMEON: He's been gone two months—with no word.

PETER: Left us in the fields an evenin' like this. Hitched up an' druv off into the West. That's plumb onnateral. He hain't never been off this farm 'ceptin' t' the village in thirty year or more, not since he married Eben's maw. [*A pause. Shrewdly*] I calc'late we might git him declared crazy by the court.

SIMEON: He skinned 'em too slick. He got the best o' all on 'em. They'd never b'lieve him crazy. [*a pause*] We got t' wait—till he's under ground.

EBEN [*with a sardonic chuckle*]: Honor thy father! [*They turn, startled, and stare at him. He grins, then scowls.*] I pray he's died. [*They stare at him. He continues matter-of-factly.*] Supper's ready.

SIMEON AND PETER [*together*]: Ay-eh.

EBEN [*gazing up at the sky*]: Sun's downin' purty.

SIMEON AND PETER [*pointing*]: Ay-eh. They's gold in the West.

EBEN [*pointing*]: Ay-eh. Yonder atop o' the hill pasture, ye mean?

SIMEON AND PETER [*together*]: In Californi-a!

EBEN: Hunh? [*stares at them indifferently for a second, then drawls*] Waal—supper's gittin' cold. [*He turns back into kitchen.*]

SIMEON [*startled—smacks his lips*]: I air hungry!

PETER [*sniffing*]: I smells bacon!

SIMEON [*with hungry appreciation*]: Bacon's good!

PETER [*in same tone*]: Bacon's bacon! [*They turn, shouldering each other, their bodies bumping and rubbing together as they hurry clumsily to their food, like two friendly oxen toward their evening meal. They disappear around the right corner of house and can be heard entering the door.*]

THE CURTAIN FALLS

Scene 2

The color fades from the sky. Twilight begins. The interior of the kitchen is now visible. A pine table is at center, a cook-stove in the right rear corner, four rough wooden chairs, a tallow candle on the table. In the middle of the rear wall is fastened a big advertizing poster with a ship in full sail and the word "California" in big letters. Kitchen utensils hang from nails. Everything is neat and in order but the atmosphere is of a men's camp kitchen rather than that of a home.

Places for three are laid. EBEN *takes boiled potatoes and bacon from the stove and puts them on the table, also a loaf of bread and a crock of water.* SIMEON *and* PETER *shoulder in, slump down in their chairs without a word.* EBEN *joins them. The three eat in silence for a moment, the two elder as naturally unrestrained as beasts of the field,* EBEN *picking at his food without appetite, glancing at them with a tolerant dislike.*

Walter Huston as Cabot and Mary Morris as Abbie in Desire Under the Elms, *directed by Robert Edmond Jones, Greenwich Village Theatre, New York, 1924.*

SIMEON [*suddenly turns to* EBEN]: Looky here! Ye'd oughtn't t' said that, Eben.

PETER: 'Twa'n't righteous.

EBEN: What?

SIMEON: Ye prayed he'd died.

EBEN: Waal—don't yew pray it? [*a pause*]

PETER: He's our Paw.

EBEN [*violently*]: Not mine!

SIMEON [*dryly*]: Ye'd not let no one else say that about yer Maw! Ha! [*He gives one abrupt sardonic guffaw.* PETER *grins.*]

EBEN [*very pale*]: I meant—I hain't his'n—I hain't like him—he hain't me!

PETER [*dryly*]: Wait till ye've growed his age!

EBEN [*intensely*]: I'm Maw—every drop o' blood! [*A pause. They stare at him with indifferent curiosity.*]

PETER [*reminiscently*]: She was good t' Sim 'n' me. A good Step-maw's scurse.

SIMEON: She was good t' everyone.

EBEN [*greatly moved, gets to his feet and makes an awkward bow to each of them—stammering*]: I be thankful t' ye. I'm her—her heir. [*He sits down in confusion.*]

PETER [*after a pause—judicially*]: She was good even t' him.

EBEN [*fiercely*]: An' fur thanks he killed her!

SIMEON [*after a pause*]: No one never kills nobody. It's allus somethin'. That's the murderer.

EBEN: Didn't he slave Maw t' death?

PETER: He's slaved himself t' death. He's slaved Sim 'n' me 'n' yew t' death—on'y none o' us hain't died—yit.

SIMEON: It's somethin'—drivin' him—t' drive us!

EBEN [*vengefully*]: Waal—I hold him t' jedgment! [*then scornfully*] Somethin'! What's somethin'?

SIMEON: Dunno.

EBEN [*sardonically*]: What's drivin' yew to Californi-a, mebbe? [*They look at him in surprise.*] Oh, I've heerd ye! [*then, after a pause*] But ye'll never go t' the gold fields!

PETER [*assertively*]: Mebbe!

EBEN: Whar'll ye git the money?

PETER: We kin walk. It's an a'mighty ways—Californi-a—but if yew was t' put all the steps we've walked on this farm end t' end we'd be in the moon!

EBEN: The Injuns'll skulp ye on the plains.

SIMEON [*with grim humor*]: We'll mebbe make 'em pay a hair fur a hair!

EBEN [*decisively*]: But t'ain't that. Ye won't never go because ye'll wait here fur yer share o' the farm, thinkin' allus he'll die soon.

SIMEON [*after a pause*]: We've a right.

PETER: Two thirds belongs t' us.

EBEN [*jumping to his feet*]: Ye've no right! She wa'n't yewr Maw! It was her farm! Didn't he steal it from her? She's dead. It's my farm.

SIMEON [*sardonically*]: Tell that t' Paw—when he comes! I'll bet ye a dollar he'll laugh—fur once in his life. Ha! [*He laughs himself in one single mirthless bark.*]

PETER [*amused in turn, echoes his brother*]: Ha!

SIMEON [*after a pause*]: What've ye got held agin us, Eben? Year arter year it's skulked in yer eye—somethin'.

PETER: Ay-eh.

EBEN: Ay-eh. They's somethin'. [*suddenly exploding*] Why didn't ye never stand between him 'n' my Maw when he was slavin' her to her grave—t' pay her back fur the kindness she done t' yew? [*There is a long pause. They stare at him in surprise.*]

SIMEON: Waal—the stock'd got t' be watered.

PETER: 'R they was woodin' t' do.

SIMEON: 'R plowin'.

PETER: 'R hayin'.

SIMEON: 'R spreadin' manure.

PETER: 'R weedin'.

SIMEON: 'R prunin'.

PETER: 'R milkin'.

EBEN [*breaking in harshly*]: An' makin' walls—stone atop o' stone—makin' walls till yer heart's a stone ye heft up out o' the way o' growth onto a stone wall t' wall in yer heart!

SIMEON [*matter-of-factly*]: We never had no time t' meddle.

PETER [*to* EBEN]: Yew was fifteen afore yer Maw died— an' big fur yer age. Why didn't ye never do nothin'?

EBEN [*harshly*]: They was chores t' do, wa'n't they? [*a pause—then slowly*] It was on'y arter she died I come to think o' it. Me cookin'—doin' her work—that made me know her, suffer her sufferin'—she'd come back t' help—come back t' bile potatoes—come back t' fry bacon—come back t' bake biscuits—come back all cramped up t' shake the fire, an' carry ashes, her eyes weepin' an' bloody with smoke an' cinders same's they used t' be. She still comes back—stands by the stove thar in the evenin'—she can't find it nateral sleepin' an' restin' in peace. She can't git used t' bein' free—even in her grave.

SIMEON: She never complained none.

EBEN: She'd got too tired. She'd got too used t' bein' too tired. That was what he done. [*with vengeful passion*] An' sooner'r later, I'll meddle. I'll say the thin's I didn't say then t' him! I'll yell 'em at the top o' my lungs. I'll see t' it my Maw gits some rest an' sleep in her grave! [*He sits down again, relapsing into a brooding silence. They look at him with a queer indifferent curiosity.*]

PETER [*after a pause*]: Whar in tarnation d'ye s'pose he went, Sim?

SIMEON: Dunno. He druv off in the buggy, all spick an' span, with the mare all breshed an' shiny, druv off clackin' his tongue an' wavin' his whip. I remember it right well. I was finishin' plowin', it was spring an' May an' sunset, an' gold in the West, an' he druv off into it. I yells "Whar ye goin', Paw?" an' he hauls up by the stone wall a jiffy. His old snake's eyes was glitterin' in the sun like he'd been drinkin' a jugful an' he says with a mule's grin: "Don't ye run away till I come back!"

PETER: Wonder if he knowed we was wantin' fur Californi-a?

SIMEON: Mebbe. I didn't say nothin' and he says, lookin' kinder queer an' sick: "I been hearin' the hens cluckin' an' the roosters crowin' all the durn day. I been listenin' t' the cows lowin' an' everythin' else kickin' up till I can't stand it no more. It's spring an' I'm feelin' damned," he says. "Damned like an old bare hickory tree fit on'y fur burnin'," he says. An' then I calc'late I must've looked a mite hopeful, fur he adds real spry and vicious: "But don't git no fool idee I'm dead. I've sworn t' live a hundred an' I'll do it, if on'y t' spite yer sinful greed! An' now I'm ridin' out t' learn God's message t' me in the spring, like the prophets done. An' yew git back t' yer plowin'," he says. An' he druv off singin' a hymn. I thought he was drunk—'r I'd stopped him goin'.

EBEN [*scornfully*]: No, ye wouldn't! Ye're scared o' him. He's stronger—inside—than both o' ye put together!

PETER [*sardonically*]: An' yew—be yew Samson?

EBEN: I'm gittin' stronger. I kin feel it growin' in me—growin' an' growin'—till it'll bust out—! [*He gets up and puts on his coat and a hat. They watch him, gradually breaking into grins.* EBEN *avoids their eyes sheepishly.*] I'm goin' out fur a spell—up the road.

PETER: T' the village?

SIMEON: T' see Minnie?

EBEN [*defiantly*]: Ay-eh!

PETER [*jeeringly*]: The Scarlet Woman!

SIMEON: Lust—that's what's growin' in ye!

EBEN: Waal—she's purty!

PETER: She's been purty fur twenty year!

SIMEON: A new coat o' paint'll make a heifer out of forty.

EBEN: She hain't forty!

PETER: If she hain't, she's teeterin' on the edge.

EBEN [*desperately*]: What d'yew know—

PETER: All they is . . . Sim knew her—an' then me arter—

SIMEON: An' Paw kin tell yew somethin' too! He was fust!

EBEN: D'ye mean t' say he . . . ?

SIMEON [*with a grin*]: Ay-eh! We air his heirs in everythin'!

EBEN [*intensely*]: That's more to it. That grows on it! It'll bust soon! [*then violently*] I'll go smash my fist in her face! [*He pulls open the door in rear violently.*]

SIMEON [*with a wink at Peter—drawlingly*]: Mebbe—but the night's wa'm—purty—by the time ye git thar mebbe ye'll kiss her instead!

PETER: Sart'n he will! [*They both roar with coarse laughter.* EBEN *rushes out and slams the door—then the outside front door—comes around the corner of the house and stands still by the gate, staring up at the sky.*]

SIMEON [*looking after him*]: Like his Paw.

PETER: Dead spit an' image!

SIMEON: Dog'll eat dog!

PETER: Ay-eh. [*Pause. With yearning*] Mebbe a year from now we'll be in Californi-a.

SIMEON: Ay-eh. [*A pause. Both yawn.*] Let's git t' bed. [*He blows out the candle. They go out door in rear.* EBEN *stretches his arms up to the sky—rebelliously*]

EBEN: Waal—thar's a star, an' somewhar's they's him an' here's me, an' thar's Min up the road—in the same night. What if I does kiss her? She's like t'night, she's soft 'n' wa'm, her eyes kin wink like a star, her mouth's wa'm, her arms're wa'm, she smells like a wa'm plowed field, she's purty . . . Ay-eh! By God A'mighty she's purty, an' I don't give a damn how many sins she's sinned afore mine or who she's sinned 'em with, my sin's as purty as any one on 'em! [*He strides off down the road to the left.*]

Scene 3

It is the pitch darkness just before dawn. EBEN *comes in from the left and goes around to the porch, feeling his way, chuckling bitterly and cursing half-aloud to himself.*

EBEN: The cussed old miser! [*He can be heard going in the front door. There is a pause as he goes upstairs, then a loud knock on the bedroom door of the brothers.*] Wake up!

SIMEON [*startledly*]: Who's thar?

EBEN [*pushing open the door and coming in, a lighted candle in his hand. The bedroom of the brothers is revealed. Its ceiling is the sloping roof. They can stand upright only close to the center dividing wall of the upstairs.* SIMEON *and* PETER *are in a double bed, front.* EBEN'*s cot is to the rear.* EBEN *has a mixture of silly grin and vicious scowl on his face.*]: I be!

PETER [*angrily*]: What in hell's-fire . . . ?

EBEN: I got news fur ye! Ha! [*He gives one abrupt sardonic guffaw.*]

SIMEON [*angrily*]: Couldn't ye hold it til we'd got our sleep?

EBEN: It's nigh sunup. [*then explosively*] He's gone an' married agen!

SIMEON AND PETER [*explosively*]: Paw?

EBEN: Got himself hitched to a female 'bout thirty-five—an' purty, they says . . .

SIMEON [*aghast*]: It's a durn lie!

PETER: Who says?

SIMEON: They been stringin' ye!

EBEN: Think I'm a dunce, do ye? The hull village says. The preacher from New Dover, he brung the news—told it t' our preacher—New Dover, that's whar the old loon got himself hitched—that's whar the woman lived—

PETER [*no longer doubting—stunned*]: Waal . . . !

SIMEON [*the same*]: Waal . . . !

EBEN [*sitting down on a bed—with vicious hatred*]: Ain't he a devil out o' hell? It's jest t' spite us—the damned old mule!

PETER [*after a pause*]: Everythin'll go t' her now.

SIMEON: Ay-eh. [*a pause—dully*] Waal—if it's done—

PETER: It's done us. [*pause—then persuasively*] They's gold in the fields o' Californi-a, Sim. No good a-stayin' here now.

SIMEON: Jest what I was a-thinkin'. [*then with decision*] S'well fust's last! Let's light out and git this mornin'.

PETER: Suits me.

EBEN: Ye must like walkin'.

SIMEON [*sardonically*]: If ye'd grow wings on us we'd fly thar!

EBEN: Ye'd like ridin' better—on a boat, wouldn't ye? [*fumbles in his pocket and takes out a crumpled sheet of foolscap*] Waal, if ye sign this ye kin ride on a boat. I've had it writ out an' ready in case ye'd ever go. It says fur three hundred dollars t' each ye agree yewr shares o' the farm is sold t' me. [*They look suspiciously at the paper. A pause.*]

SIMEON [*wonderingly*]: But if he's hitched agen—

PETER: An' whar'd yew git that sum o' money, anyways?

EBEN [*cunningly*]: I know whar it's hid. I been waitin'—Maw told me. She knew whar it lay fur years, but she was waitin' . . . It's her'n—the money he hoarded from her farm an' hid from Maw. It's my money by rights now.

PETER: Whar's it hid?

EBEN [*cunningly*]: Whar yew won't never find it without me. Maw spied on him—'r she'd never knowed. [*A pause. They look at him suspiciously, and he at them.*] Waal, is it fa'r trade?

SIMEON: Dunno.

PETER: Dunno.

SIMEON [*looking at window*]: Sky's grayin'.

PETER: Ye better start the fire, Eben.

SIMEON: An' fix some vittles.

EBEN: Ay-eh. [*then with a forced jocular heartiness*] I'll git ye a good one. If ye're startin' t' hoof it t' Californi-a ye'll need somethin' that'll stick t' yer ribs. [*He turns to the door, adding meaningly*] But ye kin ride on a boat if ye'll swap. [*He stops at the door and pauses. They stare at him.*]

SIMEON [*suspiciously*]: Whar was ye all night?

EBEN [*defiantly*]: Up t' Min's. [*then slowly*] Walkin' thar, fust I felt's if I'd kiss her; then I got a-thinkin' o' what ye'd said o' him an' her an' I says, I'll bust her nose fur that! Then I got t' the village an' heerd the news an' I got madder'n hell an' run all the way t' Min's not knowin' what I'd do— [*He pauses—then sheepishly but more defiantly*] Waal—when I seen her, I didn't hit her—nor I didn't kiss her nuther—I begun t' beller like a calf an' cuss at the same time, I was so durn mad—an' she got scared—an' I jest grabbed holt an' tuk her! [*proudly*] Yes, siree! I tuk her. She may've been his'n—and your'n, too—but she's mine now!

SIMEON [*dryly*]: In love, air yew?

EBEN [*with lofty scorn*]: Love! I don't take no stock in sech slop!

PETER [*winking at* SIMEON]: Mebbe Eben's aimin' t' marry, too.

SIMEON: Min'd make a true faithful he'pmeet! [*They snicker.*]

EBEN: What do I care fur her—'ceptin' she's round an' wa'm? The p'int is she was his'n—an' now she b'longs t' me! [*He goes to the door—then turns—rebelliously*] An' Min hain't sech a bad un. They's worse'n Min in the world, I'll bet ye! Wait'll we see this cow the Old Man's hitched t'! She'll beat Min, I got a notion! [*He starts to go out.*]

SIMEON [*suddenly*]: Mebbe ye'll try t' make her your'n, too?

PETER: Ha! [*He gives a sardonic laugh of relish at this idea.*]

EBEN [*spitting with disgust*]: Her—here—sleepin' with him—stealin' my Maw's farm! I'd as soon pet a skunk 'r kiss a snake! [*He goes out. The two stare after him suspiciously. A pause. They listen to his steps receding.*]

PETER: He's startin' the fire.

SIMEON: I'd like t' ride t' Californi-a—but—

PETER: Min might o' put some scheme in his head.

SIMEON: Mebbe it's all a lie 'bout Paw marryin'. We'd best wait an' see the bride.

PETER: An' don't sign nothin' till we does!

SIMEON: Nor till we've tested it's good money! [*then with a grin*] But if Paw's hitched we'd be sellin' Eben somethin' we'd never git nohow!

PETER: We'll wait an' see. [*then with sudden vindictive anger*] An' till he comes, let's yew 'n' me not wuk a lick, let Eben tend to thin's if he's a mind t', let's us just sleep an' eat an' drink likker, an' let the hull damned farm go t' blazes!

SIMEON [*excitedly*]: By God, we've 'arned a rest! We'll play rich fur a change. I hain't a-going to stir outa bed till breakfast's ready.

PETER: An' on the table!

SIMEON [*after a pause—thoughtfully*]: What d'ye calc'late she'll be like—our new Maw? Like Eben thinks?

PETER: More'n' likely.

SIMEON [*vindictively*]: Waal—I hope she's a she-devil that'll make him wish he was dead an' livin' in the pit o' hell fur comfort!

PETER [*fervently*]: Amen!

SIMEON [*imitating his father's voice*]: "I'm ridin' out t' learn God's message t' me in the spring like the prophets done," he says. I'll bet right then an' thar he knew plumb well he was goin' whorin', the stinkin' old hypocrite!

Scene 4

Same as Scene 2—shows the interior of the kitchen with a lighted candle on table. It is gray dawn outside. SIMEON *and* PETER *are just finishing their breakfast.* EBEN *sits before his plate of untouched food, brooding frowningly.*

PETER [*glancing at him rather irritably*]: Lookin' glum don't help none.

SIMEON [*sarcastically*]: Sorrowin' over his lust o' the flesh!

PETER [*with a grin*]: Was she yer fust?

EBEN [*angrily*]: None o' yer business. [*a pause*] I was thinkin' o' him. I got a notion he's gittin' near—I kin feel him comin' on like yew kin feel malaria chill afore it takes ye.

PETER: It's too early yet.

SIMEON: Dunno. He'd like t' catch us nappin'—jest t' have somethin' t' hoss us 'round over.

PETER [*mechanically gets to his feet.* SIMEON *does the same.*]: Waal—let's git t' wuk. [*They both plod mechanically toward the door before they realize. Then they stop short.*]

SIMEON [*grinning*]: Ye're a cussed fool, Pete—and I be wuss! Let him see we hain't wukin'! We don't give a durn!

PETER [*as they go back to the table*]: Not a damned durn! It'll serve t' show him we're done with him. [*They sit down again.* EBEN *stares from one to the other with surprise.*]

SIMEON [*grins at him*]: We're aimin' t' start bein' lilies o' the field.

PETER: Nary a toil 'r spin 'r lick o' wuk do we put in!

SIMEON: Ye're sole owner—till he comes—that's what ye wanted. Waal, ye got t' be sole hand, too.

PETER: The cows air bellerin'. Ye better hustle at the milkin'.

EBEN [*with excited joy*]: Ye mean ye'll sign the paper?

SIMEON [*dryly*]: Mebbe.

PETER: Mebbe.

SIMEON: We're considerin'. [*peremptorily*] Ye better git t' wuk.

EBEN [*with queer excitement*]: It's Maw's farm agen! It's my farm! Them's my cows! I'll milk my durn fingers off fur cows o' mine! [*He goes out door in rear, they stare after him indifferently.*]

SIMEON: Like his Paw.

PETER: Dead spit 'n' image!

SIMEON: Waal—let dog eat dog! [EBEN *comes out of front door and around the corner of the house. The sky is beginning to grow flushed with sunrise.* EBEN *stops by the gate and stares around him with glowing, possessive eyes. He takes in the whole farm with his embracing glance of desire.*]

EBEN: It's purty! It's damned purty! It's mine! [*He suddenly throws his head back boldly and glares with hard, defiant eyes at the sky.*] Mine, d'ye hear? Mine! [*He turns and walks quickly off left, rear, toward the barn. The two brothers light their pipes.*]

SIMEON [*putting his muddy boots up on the table, tilting back his chair, and puffing defiantly*]: Waal—this air solid comfort—fur once.

PETER: Ay-eh. [*He follows suit. A pause. Unconsciously they both sigh.*]

SIMEON [*suddenly*]: He never was much o' a hand at milkin', Eben wa'n't.

PETER [*with a snort*]: His hands air like hoofs! [*a pause*]

SIMEON: Reach down the jug thar! Let's take a swaller. I'm feelin' kind o' low.

PETER: Good idee! [*He does so—gets two glasses—they pour out drinks of whisky.*] Here's t' the gold in Californi-a!

SIMEON: An' luck t' find it! [*They drink—puff resolutely—sigh—take their feet down from the table.*]

PETER: Likker don't 'pear t' sot right.

SIMEON: We hain't used t' it this early. [*A pause. They become very restless.*]

PETER: Gittin' close in this kitchen.

SIMEON [*with immense relief*]: Let's git a breath o' air. [*They arise briskly and go out rear—appear around house and stop by the gate. They stare up at the sky with a numbed appreciation.*]

PETER: Purty!

SIMEON: Ay-eh. Gold's t' the East now.

PETER: Sun's startin' with us fur the Golden West.

SIMEON [*staring around the farm, his compressed face tightened, unable to conceal his emotion*]: Waal—it's our last mornin'—mebbe.

PETER [*the same*]: Ay-eh.

SIMEON [*stamps his foot on the earth and addresses it desperately*]: Waal—ye've thirty year o' me buried in ye—spread out over ye—blood an' bone an' sweat—rotted away—fertilizin' ye—richin' yer soul—prime manure, by God, that's what I been t' ye!

PETER: Ay-eh! An' me!

SIMEON: An' yew, Peter. [*He sighs—then spits.*] Waal—no use'n cryin' over spilt milk.

PETER: They's gold in the West—an' freedom, mebbe. We been slaves t' stone walls here.

SIMEON [*defiantly*]: We hain't nobody's slaves from this out—nor no thin's slaves nuther. [*a pause—restlessly*] Speakin' o' milk, wonder how Eben's managin'?

PETER: I s'pose he's managin'.

SIMEON: Mebbe we'd ought t' help—this once.

PETER: Mebbe. The cows knows us.

SIMEON: An' likes us. They don't know him much.

PETER: An' the hosses, an' pigs, an' chickens. They don't know him much.

SIMEON: They knows us like brothers—an' likes us! [*proudly*] Hain't we raised 'em t' be fust-rate, number one prize stock?

PETER: We hain't—not no more.

SIMEON [*dully*]: I was fergittin'. [*then resignedly*] Waal, let's go help Eben a spell an' git waked up.

PETER: Suits me. [*They are starting off down left, rear, for the barn when* EBEN *appears from there hurrying toward them, his face excited.*]

EBEN [*breathlessly*]: Waal—har they be! The old mule an' the bride! I seen 'em from the barn down below at the turnin'.

PETER: How could ye tell that far?

EBEN: Hain't I as far-sight as he's near-sight? Don't I know the mare 'n' buggy, an' two people settin' in it? Who else . . . ? An' I tell ye I kin feel 'em a-comin', too! [*He squirms as if he had the itch.*]

PETER [*beginning to be angry*]: Waal—let him do his own unhitchin'!

SIMEON [*angry in his turn*]: Let's hustle in an' git our bundles an' be a-goin' as he's a-comin'. I don't want never t' step inside the door agen arter he's back. [*They both start back around the corner of the house.* EBEN *follows them.*]

EBEN [*anxiously*]: Will ye sign it afore ye go?

PETER: Let's see the color o' the old skinflint's money an' we'll sign. [*They disappear left. The two brothers clump upstairs to get their bundles.* EBEN *appears in the kitchen, runs to window, peers out, comes back and pulls up a strip of flooring in under stove, takes out a canvas bag and puts it on table, then sets the floorboard back in place. The two brothers appear a moment after. They carry old carpet bags.*]

EBEN [*puts his hand on bag guardingly*]: Have ye signed?

SIMEON [*shows paper in his hand*]: Ay-eh. [*greedily*] Be that the money?

EBEN [*opens bag and pours out pile of twenty-dollar gold pieces*]: Twenty-dollar pieces—thirty on 'em. Count 'em. [*Peter does so, arranging them in stacks of five, biting one or two to test them.*]

PETER: Six hundred. [*He puts them in bag and puts it inside his shirt carefully.*]

SIMEON [*handing paper to* EBEN]: Har ye be.

EBEN [*after a glance, folds it carefully and hides it under his shirt—gratefully*]: Thank yew.

PETER: Thank yew fur the ride.

SIMEON: We'll send ye a lump o' gold fur Christmas. [*A pause.* EBEN *stares at them and they at him.*]

PETER [*awkwardly*]: Waal—we're a-goin'.

SIMEON: Comin' out t' the yard?

EBEN: No. I'm waitin' in here a spell. [*Another silence. The brothers edge awkwardly to door in rear—then turn and stand.*]

SIMEON: Waal—good-by.

PETER: Good-by.

EBEN: Good-by. [*They go out. He sits down at the table, faces the stove and pulls out the paper. He looks from it to the stove. His face, lighted up by the shaft of sunlight from the window, has an expression of trance. His lips move. The two brothers come out to the gate.*]

PETER [*looking off toward barn*]: Thar he be—unhitchin'.

SIMEON [*with a chuckle*]: I'll bet ye he's riled!

PETER: An' thar she be.

SIMEON: Let's wait 'n' see what our new Maw looks like.

PETER [*with a grin*]: An' give him our partin' cuss!

SIMEON [*grinning*]: I feel like raisin' fun. I feel light in my head an' feet.

PETER: Me, too. I feel like laffin' till I'd split up the middle.

SIMEON: Reckon it's the likker?

PETER: No. My feet feel itchin' t' walk an' walk—an' jump high over thin's—an'. . . .

SIMEON: Dance? [*a pause*]

PETER [*puzzled*]: It's plumb onnateral.

SIMEON [*a light coming over his face*]: I calc'late it's 'cause school's out. It's holiday. Fur once we're free!

PETER [*dazedly*]: Free?

SIMEON: The halter's broke—the harness is busted—the fence bars is down—the stone walls air crumblin' an' tumblin'! We'll be kickin' up an' tearin' away down the road!

PETER [*drawing a deep breath—oratorically*]: Anybody that wants this stinkin' old rock-pile of a farm kin hev it. T'ain't our'n, no sirree!

SIMEON [*takes the gate off its hinges and puts it under his arm*]: We harby 'bolishes shet gates, an' open gates, an' all gates, by thunder!

PETER: We'll take it with us fur luck an' let 'er sail free down some river.

SIMEON [*as a sound of voices comes from left, rear*]: Har they comes! [*The two brothers congeal into two stiff, grim-visaged statues.* EPHRAIM CABOT *and* ABBIE PUTNAM *come in.* CABOT *is seventy-five, tall and gaunt, with great, wiry, concentrated power, but stoop-shouldered from toil. His face is as hard as if it were hewn out of a boulder, yet there is a weakness in it, a petty pride in its own narrow strength. His eyes are small, close together, and extremely near-sighted, blinking continually in the effort to focus on objects, their stare having a straining, ingrowing quality. He is dressed in his dismal black Sunday suit.* ABBIE *is thirty-five, buxom, full of vitality. Her round face is pretty but marred by its rather gross sensuality. There is strength and obstinacy in her jaw, a hard determination in her eyes, and about her whole personality the same unsettled, untamed, desperate quality which is so apparent in* EBEN.]

CABOT [*as they enter—a queer strangled emotion in his dry cracking voice*]: Har we be t' hum, Abbie.

ABBIE [*with lust for the word*]: Hum! [*her eyes gloating on the house without seeming to see the two stiff figures at the gate*] It's purty—purty! I can't b'lieve it's r'ally mine.

CABOT [*sharply*]: Yewr'n? Mine! [*He stares at her penetratingly. She stares back. He adds relentingly*] Our'n—mebbe! It was lonesome too long. I was growin' old in the spring. A hum's got t' hev a woman.

ABBIE [*her voice taking possession*]: A woman's got t' hev a hum!

CABOT [*nodding uncertainly*]: Ay-eh. [*then irritably*] Whar be they? Ain't thar nobody about—'r wukin'—'r nothin'?

ABBIE [*sees the brothers. She returns their stare of cold appraising contempt with interest—slowly*]: Thar's two men loafin' at the gate an' starin' at me like a couple o' strayed hogs.

CABOT [*straining his eyes*]: I kin see 'em—but I can't make out. . . .

SIMEON: It's Simeon.

PETER: It's Peter.

CABOT [*exploding*]: Why hain't ye wukin'?

SIMEON [*dryly*]: We're waintin' t' welcome ye hum—yew an' the bride!

CABOT [*confusedly*]: Huh? Waal—this be yer new Maw, boys. [*She stares at them and they at her.*]

SIMEON [*turns away and spits contemptuously*]: I see her!

PETER [*spits also*]: An' I see her!

ABBIE [*with the conqueror's conscious superiority*]: I'll go in an' look at *my* house. [*She goes slowly around to porch.*]

SIMEON [*with a snort*]: *Her* house!

PETER [*calls after her*]: Ye'll find Eben inside. Ye better not tell him it's *yewr* house.

ABBIE [*mouthing the name*]: Eben. [*then quietly*] I'll tell Eben.

CABOT [*with a contemptuous sneer*]: Ye needn't heed Eben. Eben's a dumb fool—like his Maw—soft an' simple!

SIMEON [*with his sardonic burst of laughter*]: Ha! Eben's a chip o' yew—spit 'n' image—hard 'n' bitter's a hickory tree! Dog'll eat dog. He'll eat ye yet, old man!

CABOT [*commandingly*]: Ye git t' wuk!

SIMEON [*as* ABBIE *disappears in house—winks at* PETER *and says tauntingly*]: So that thar's our new Maw, be it? Whar in hell did ye dig her up? [*He and* PETER *laugh.*]

PETER: Ha! Ye'd better turn her in the pen with the other sows. [*They laugh uproariously, slapping their thighs.*]

CABOT [*so amazed at their effrontery that he stutters in confusion*]: Simeon! Peter! What's come over ye? Air ye drunk?

SIMEON: We're free, old man—free o' yew an' the hull damned farm! [*They grow more and more hilarious and excited.*]

PETER: An' we're startin' out fur the gold fields o' Californi-a!

SIMEON: Ye kin take this place an' burn it!

PETER: An' bury it—fur all we cares!

SIMEON: We're free, old man! [*He cuts a caper.*]

PETER: Free! [*He gives a kick in the air.*]

SIMEON [*in a frenzy*]: Whoop.

PETER: Whoop! [*They do an absurd Indian war dance about the old man, who is petrified between rage and the fear that they are insane.*]

SIMEON: We're free as Injuns! Lucky we don't skulp ye!

PETER: An' burn yer barn an' kill the stock!

SIMEON: An' rape yer new woman! Whoop! [*He and* PETER *stop their dance, holding their sides, rocking with wild laughter.*]

CABOT [*edging away*]: Lust fur gold—fur the sinful, easy gold o' Californi-a! It's made ye mad!

SIMEON [*tauntingly*]: Wouldn't ye like us to send ye back some sinful gold, ye old sinner?

PETER: They's gold besides what's in Californi-a! [*He retreats back beyond the vision of the old man and takes the bag of money and flaunts it in the air above his head, laughing.*]

SIMEON: And sinfuller, too!

PETER: We'll be voyagin' on the sea! Whoop! [*He leaps up and down.*]

SIMEON: Livin' free! Whoop! [*He leaps in turn.*]

CABOT [*suddenly roaring with rage*]: My cuss on ye!

SIMEON: Take our'n in trade fur it! Whoop!

CABOT: I'll hev ye both chained up in the asylum!

PETER: Ye old skinflint! Good-by!

SIMEON: Ye old blood sucker! Good-by!

CABOT: Go afore I . . . !

PETER: Whoop! [*He picks a stone from the road. Simeon does the same.*]

SIMEON: Maw'll be in the parlor.

PETER: Ay-eh! One! Two!

CABOT [*frightened*]: What air ye . . . ?

PETER: Three! [*They both throw, the stones hitting the parlor window with a crash of glass, tearing the shade.*]

SIMEON: Whoop!

PETER: Whoop!

CABOT [*in a fury now, rushing toward them*]: If I kin lay hands on ye—I'll break yer bones fur ye! [*But they beat a capering retreat before him,* SIMEON *with the gate still under his arm.* CABOT *comes back, panting with impotent rage. Their voices as they go off take up the song of the gold-seekers to the old tune of "Oh, Susannah!"*]

"I jumped aboard the Liza ship,
And traveled on the sea,
And every time I thought of home

I wished it wasn't me!
Oh! Californi-a,
That's the land fur me!
I'm off to Californi-a!
With my wash bowl on my knee."

[*In the meantime, the window of the upper bedroom on right is raised and* ABBIE *sticks her head out. She looks down at* CABOT—*with a sigh of relief.*]

ABBIE: Waal—that's the last o' them two, hain't it? [*He doesn't answer. Then in possessive tones*] This here's a nice bedroom, Ephraim. It's a r'al nice bed. Is it my room, Ephraim?

CABOT [*grimly—without looking up*]: Our'n! [*She cannot control a grimace of aversion and pulls back her head slowly and shuts the window. A sudden horrible thought seems to enter* CABOT'*s head.*] They been up to somethin'! Mebbe—mebbe they've pizened the stock—'r somethin'! [*He almost runs off down toward the barn. A moment later the kitchen door is slowly pushed open and* ABBIE *enters. For a moment she stands looking at* EBEN. *He does not notice her at first. Her eyes take him in penetratingly with a calculating appraisal of his strength as against hers. But under this her desire is dimly awakened by his youth and good looks. Suddenly he becomes conscious of her presence and looks up. Their eyes meet. He leaps to his feet, glowering at her speechlessly.*]

ABBIE [*in her most seductive tones which she uses all through this scene*]: Be you—Eben? I'm Abbie—[*She laughs.*] I mean, I'm yer new Maw.

EBEN [*viciously*]: No, damn ye!

ABBIE [*as if she hadn't heard—with a queer smile*]: Yer Paw's spoke a lot o' yew. . . .

EBEN: Ha!

ABBIE: Ye mustn't mind him. He's an old man [*A long pause. They stare at each other.*] I don't want t' pretend playin' Maw t' ye, Eben. [*admiringly*] Ye're too big an' too strong fur that. I want t' be frens with ye. Mebbe with me fur a fren ye'd find ye'd like livin' here better. I kin make it easy fur ye with him, mebbe. [*with a scornful sense of power*] I calc'late I kin git him t' do most anythin' fur me.

EBEN [*with bitter scorn*]: Ha! [*They stare again,* EBEN *obscurely moved, physically attracted to her—in forced stilted tones*] Yew kin go t' the devil!

ABBIE [*calmly*]: If cussin' me does ye good, cuss all ye've a mind t'. I'm all prepared t' have ye agin me—at fust. I don't blame ye nuther. I'd feel the same at any stranger comin' t' take my Maw's place. [*He shudders. She is watching him carefully.*] Yew must've cared a lot fur yewr Maw, didn't ye? My Maw died afore I'd growed. I don't remember her none. [*a pause*] But yew won't hate me long, Eben. I'm not the wust in the world—an' yew an' me've got a lot in common. I kin tell that by lookin' at ye. Waal—I've had a hard life, too—oceans o' trouble an' nuthin' but wuk fur reward. I was a orphan early an' had t' wuk fur others in other folks' hums. Then I married an' he turned out a drunken spreer an' so he had to wuk fur others an' me too agen in other folks' hums, an' the baby died, an' my husband got sick an' died too, an' I was glad sayin' now I'm free fur once, on'y I diskivered right away all I was free fur was t' wuk agen in other folks' hums, doin' other folks' wuk till I'd most give up hope o' ever doin' my own wuk in my own hum, an' then your Paw come. . . . [CABOT *appears returning from the barn. He comes to the gate and looks down the road the brothers have gone. A faint strain of their retreating voices is heard:* "Oh, Californi-a! That's the place for me." *He stands glowering, his fist clenched, his face grim with rage.*]

EBEN [*fighting against his growing attraction and sympathy—harshly*]: An' bought yew—like a harlot! [*She is stung and flushes angrily. She has been sincerely moved by the recital of her troubles. He adds furiously*] An' the price he's payin' ye—this farm—was my Maw's, damn ye!—an' mine now!

ABBIE [*with a cool laugh of confidence*]: Yewr'n? We'll see 'bout that! [*then strongly*] Waal—what if I did need a hum? What else'd I marry an old man like him fur?

EBEN [*maliciously*]: I'll tell him ye said that!

ABBIE [*smiling*]: I'll say ye're lyin' a-purpose—an' he'll drive ye off the place!

EBEN: Ye devil!

ABBIE [*defying him*]: This be my farm—this be my hum—this be my kitchen!

EBEN [*furiously, as if he were going to attack her*]: Shut up, damn ye!

ABBIE [*walks up to him—a queer coarse expression of desire in her face and body—slowly*]: An' upstairs—that be my bedroom—an' my bed! [*He stares into her eyes, terribly confused and torn. She adds softly*] I hain't bad nor mean—'ceptin' fur an enemy—but I got t' fight fur what's due me out o' life, if I ever 'spect t' git it. [*then putting her hand on his arm—seductively*] Let's yew 'n' me be frens, Eben.

EBEN [*stupidly—as if hypnotized*]: Ay-eh. [*then furiously flinging off her arm*] No, ye durned old witch! I hate ye! [*He rushes out the door.*]

ABBIE [*looks after him smiling satisfiedly—then half to herself, mouthing the word*]: Eben's nice. [*She looks at the table, proudly.*] I'll wash up *my* dishes now. [EBEN *appears outside, slamming the door behind him. He comes around corner, stops on seeing his father, and stands staring at him with hate.*]

CABOT [*raising his arms to heaven in the fury he can no longer control*]: Lord God o' Hosts, smite the undutiful sons with Thy wust cuss!

EBEN [*breaking in violently*]: Yew 'n' yewr God! Allus cussin' folks—allus naggin' em!

CABOT [*oblivious to him—summoningly*]: God o' the old! God o' the lonesome!

EBEN [*mockingly*]: Naggin' His sheep t' sin! T' hell with yewr God! [CABOT *turns. He and* EBEN *glower at each other.*]

CABOT [*harshly*]: So it's yew. I might've knowed it. [*shaking his finger threateningly at him*] Blasphemin' fool! [*then quickly*] Why hain't ye t' wuk?

EBEN: Why hain't yew? They've went. I can't wuk it all alone.

CABOT [*contemptuously*]: Nor noways! I'm wuth ten o' ye yit, old's I be! Ye'll never be more'n half a man! [*then, matter-of-factly*] Waal—let's git t' the barn. [*They go. A last faint note of the "Californi-a" song is heard from the distance.* ABBIE *is washing her dishes.*]

THE CURTAIN FALLS

PART II

Scene 1

The exterior of the farmhouse, as in Part I—a hot Sunday afternoon two months later. ABBIE, *dressed in her best, is discovered sitting in a rocker at the end of the porch. She rocks listlessly, enervated by the heat, staring in front of her with bored, half-closed eyes.*

EBEN *sticks his head out of his bedroom window. He looks around furtively and tries to see—or hear—if anyone is on the porch, but although he has been careful to make no noise,* ABBIE *has sensed his movement. She stops rocking, her face grows animated and eager, she waits attentively.* EBEN *seems to feel her presence, he scowls back his thoughts of her and spits with exaggerated disdain—then withdraws back into the room.* ABBIE *waits, holding her breath as she listens with passionate eagerness for every sound within the house.*

EBEN *comes out. Their eyes meet. His falter, he is confused, he turns away and slams the door resentfully. At this gesture,* ABBIE *laughs tantalizingly, amused but at the same time piqued and irritated. He scowls, strides off the porch to the path and starts to walk past her to the road with a grand swagger of ignoring her existence. He is dressed in his store suit, spruced up, his face shines from soap and water.* ABBIE *leans forward on her chair, her eyes hard and angry now, and, as he passes her, gives a sneering, taunting chuckle.*

EBEN [*stung—turns on her furiously*]: What air yew cacklin' 'bout?

ABBIE [*triumphant*]: Yew!

EBEN: What about me?

ABBIE: Ye look all slicked up like a prize bull.

EBEN [*with a sneer*]: Waal—ye hain't so durned purty yerself, be ye? [*They stare into each other's eyes, his held by hers in spite of himself, hers glowingly possessive. Their physical attraction becomes a palpable force quivering in the hot air.*]

ABBIE [*softly*]: Ye don't mean that, Eben. Ye may think ye mean it, mebbe, but ye don't. Ye can't. It's agin nature, Eben. Ye been fightin' yer nature ever since the day I come—tryin' t' tell yerself I hain't purty t' ye. [*She laughs a low humid laugh without taking her eyes from his. A pause—her body squirms desirously—she murmurs languorously*] Hain't the sun strong an' hot? Ye kin feel it burnin' into the earth —Nature—makin' thin's grow—bigger 'n' bigger —burnin' inside ye—makin' ye want t' grow— into somethin' else—till ye're jined with it—an' it's your'n—but it owns ye, too—an' makes ye grow bigger—like a tree—like them elums— [*She laughs again softly, holding his eyes. He takes a step toward her, compelled against his will.*] Nature'll beat ye, Eben. Ye might's well own up t' it fust 's last.

EBEN [*trying to break from her spell—confusedly*]: If Paw'd hear ye goin' on. . . . [*resentfully*] But ye've made such a damned idjit out o' the old devil. . . ! [ABBIE *laughs.*]

ABBIE: Waal—hain't it easier fur yew with him changed softer?

EBEN [*defiantly*]: No. I'm fightin' him—fightin' yew— fightin' fur Maw's rights t' her hum! [*This breaks her spell for him. He glowers at her.*] An' I'm onto ye. Ye hain't foolin' me a mite. Ye're aimin' t' swaller up everythin' an' make it your'n. Waal, you'll find I'm a heap sight bigger hunk nor yew kin chew! [*He turns from her with a sneer.*]

ABBIE [*trying to regain her ascendancy—seductively*]: Eben!

EBEN: Leave me be! [*He starts to walk away.*]

ABBIE [*more commandingly*]: Eben!

EBEN [*stops—resentfully*]: What d'ye want?

ABBIE [*trying to conceal a growing excitement*]: Whar air ye goin'?

EBEN [*with malicious nonchalance*]: Oh—up the road a spell.

ABBIE: T' the village?

EBEN [*airily*]: Mebbe.

ABBIE [*excitedly*]: T' see that Min, I s'pose?

EBEN: Mebbe.

ABBIE [*weakly*]: What d'ye want t' waste time on her fur?

EBEN [*revenging himself now—grinning at her*]: Ye can't beat Nature, didn't ye say? [*He laughs and again starts to walk away.*]

ABBIE [*bursting out*]: An ugly old hake!

EBEN [*with a tantalizing sneer*]: She's purtier'n yew be!

ABBIE: That every wuthless drunk in the country has . . .

EBEN [*tauntingly*]: Mebbe—but she's better'n yew. She owns up fa'r 'n' squar' t' her doin's.

ABBIE [*furiously*]: Don't ye dare compare . . .

EBEN: She don't go sneakin' an' stealin'—what's mine.

ABBIE [*savagely seizing on his weak point*]: Your'n? Yew mean—my farm?

EBEN: I mean the farm yew sold yerself fur like any other old whore—my farm!

ABBIE [*stung—fiercely*]: Ye'll never live t' see the day when even a stinkin' weed on it'll belong t' ye! [*then in a scream*] Git out o' my sight! Go on t' yer slut—disgracin' yer Paw 'n' me! I'll git yer Paw t' horsewhip ye off the place if I want t'! Ye're only livin' here 'cause I tolerate ye! Git along! I hate the sight o' ye! [*She stops, panting and glaring at him.*]

EBEN [*returning her glance in kind*]: An' I hate the sight o' yew! [*He turns and strides off up the road. She follows his retreating figure with concentrated hate. Old* CABOT *appears coming up from the barn. The hard, grim expression of his face has changed. He seems in some queer way softened, mellowed. His eyes have taken on a strange, incongruous dreamy quality. Yet there is no hint of physical weakness about him—rather he looks more robust and younger.* ABBIE *sees him and turns away quickly with unconcealed aversion. He comes slowly up to her.*]

CABOT [*mildly*]: War yew an' Eben quarrelin' agen?

ABBIE [*shortly*]: No.

CABOT: Ye was talkin' a'mighty loud. [*He sits down on the edge of porch.*]

ABBIE [*snappishly*]: If ye heerd us they hain't no need askin' questions.

CABOT: I didn't hear what ye said.

ABBIE [*relieved*]: Waal—it wa'n't nothin' t' speak on.

CABOT [*after a pause*]: Eben's queer.

ABBIE [*bitterly*]: He's the dead spit 'n' image o' yew!

CABOT [*queerly interested*]: D'ye think so, Abbie? [*after a pause, ruminatingly*] Me 'n' Eben's allus fit 'n' fit. I never could b'ar him noways. He's so thunderin' soft—like his Maw.

ABBIE [*scornfully*]: Ay-eh! 'Bout as soft as yew be!

CABOT [*as if he hadn't heard*]: Mebbe I been too hard on him.

ABBIE [*jeeringly*]: Waal—ye're gittin' soft now—soft as slop! That's what Eben was sayin'.

CABOT [*his face instantly grim and ominous*]: Eben was sayin'? Waal, he'd best not do nothin' t' try me 'r he'll soon diskiver . . . [*A pause. She keeps her face turned away. His gradually softens. He stares up at the sky.*] Purty, hain't it?

ABBIE [*crossly*]: I don't see nothin' purty.

CABOT: The sky. Feels like a wa'm field up thar.

ABBIE [*sarcastically*]: Air yew aimin' to' buy up over the farm too? [*She snickers contemptuously.*]

CABOT [*strangely*]: I'd like t' own my place up thar. [*a pause*] I'm gittin' old, Abbie. I'm gittin' ripe on the bough. [*A pause. She stares at him mystified. He goes on.*] It's allus lonesome cold in the house—even when it's bilin' hot outside. Hain't yew noticed?

ABBIE: No.

CABOT: It's wa'm down t' the barn—nice smellin' an' warm—with the cows. [*a pause*] Cows is queer.

ABBIE: Like yew?

CABOT: Like Eben. [*a pause*] I'm gittin' t' feel resigned t' Eben—jest as I got t' feel 'bout his Maw. I'm gettin' t' learn to b'ar his softness—jest like her'n. I calc'late I c'd a'most take t' him—if he wa'n't sech a dumb fool! [*a pause*] I s'pose it's old age a-creepin' in my bones.

ABBIE [*indifferently*]: Waal—ye hain't dead yet.

CABOT [*roused*]: No. I hain't, yew bet—not by a hell of a sight—I'm sound 'n' tough as hickory! [*then moodily*] But arter three score and ten the Lord warns ye t' prepare. [*a pause*] That's why Eben's come in my head. Now that his cussed sinful brothers is gone their path t' hell, they's no one left but Eben.

ABBIE [*resentfully*]: They's me, hain't they? [*agitatedly*] What's all this sudden likin' ye've tuk to Eben? Why don't ye say nothin' 'bout me? Hain't I yer lawful wife?

CABOT [*simply*]: Ay-eh. Ye be. [*A pause—he stares at her desirously—his eyes grow avid—then with a sudden movement he seizes her hands and squeezes them, declaiming in a queer camp meeting preacher's tempo*] Yew air my Rose o' Sharon! Behold, yew air fair; yer eyes air doves; yer lips air like scarlet; yer two breasts air like two fawns; yer navel be like a round goblet; yer belly be like a heap o' wheat. . . . [*He covers her hand with kisses. She does not seem to notice. She stares before her with hard angry eyes.*]

ABBIE [*jerking her hands away—harshly*]: So ye're plannin' t' leave the farm t' Eben, air ye?

CABOT [*dazedly*]: Leave . . . ? [*then with resentful obstinacy*] I hain't a-givin' it t' no one!

ABBIE [*remorselessly*]: Ye can't take it with ye.

CABOT [*thinks a moment—then reluctantly*]: No, I calc'late not. [*after a pause—with a strange passion*] But if I could, I would, by the Etarnal! 'R if I could, in my dyin' hour, I'd set it afire an' watch it burn—this house an' every ear o' corn an' every tree down t' the last blade o' hay! I'd sit an' know it was all a-dying with me an' no one else'd ever own what was mine, what I'd made out o' nothin' with my own sweat 'n' blood! [*a pause—then he adds with a queer affection*] 'Ceptin' the cows. Them I'd turn free.

ABBIE [*harshly*]: An' me?

CABOT [*with a queer smile*]: Ye'd be turned free, too.

ABBIE [*furiously*]: So that's the thanks I git fur marryin' ye—t' have ye change kind to Eben who hates ye, an' talk o' turnin' me out in the road.

CABOT [*hastily*]: Abbie! Ye know I wa'n't . . .

ABBIE [*vengefully*]: Just let me tell ye a thing or two 'bout Eben! Whar's he gone? T' see that harlot, Min! I tried fur t' stop him. Disgracin' yew an' me—on the Sabbath, too!

CABOT [*rather guiltily*]: He's a sinner—nateral-born. It's lust eatin' his heart.

ABBIE [*enraged beyond endurance—wildly vindictive*]: An' his lust fur me! Kin ye find excuses fur that?

CABOT [*stares at her—after a dead pause*]: Lust—fur yew?

ABBIE [*defiantly*]: He was tryin' t' make love t' me—when ye heerd us quarrelin'.

CABOT [*stares at her—then a terrible expression of rage comes over his face—he springs to his feet shaking all over.*]: By the A'mighty God—I'll end him!

ABBIE [*frightened now for* EBEN]: No! Don't ye!

CABOT [*violently*]: I'll git the shotgun an' blow his soft brains t' the top o' them elums!

ABBIE [*throwing her arms around him*]: No! Ephraim!

CABOT [*pushing her away violently*]: I will, by God!

ABBIE [*in a quieting tone*]: Listen, Ephraim. 'Twa'n't nothin' bad—on'y a boy's foolin'—'twa'n't meant serious—jest jokin' an' teasin'. . . .

CABOT: Then why did ye say—lust?

ABBIE: It must hev sounded wusser'n I meant. An' I was mad at thinkin'—ye'd leave him the farm.

CABOT [*quieter but still grim and cruel*]: Waal then, I'll horsewhip him off the place if that much'll content ye.

ABBIE [*reaching out and taking his hand*]: No. Don't think o' me! Ye mustn't drive him off. 'Tain't sensible. Who'll ye get to help ye on the farm? They's no one hereabouts.

CABOT [*considers this—then nodding his appreciation*]: Ye got a head on ye. [*then irritably*] Waal, let him stay. [*He sits down on the edge of the porch. She sits beside him. He murmurs contemptuously*] I oughtn't t' git riled so—at that 'ere fool calf. [*a pause*] But har's the p'int. What son o' mine'll keep on here t' the farm—when the Lord does call me? Simeon an' Peter air gone t' hell—an Eben's follerin' 'em.

ABBIE: They's me.

CABOT: Ye're on'y a woman.

ABBIE: I'm yewr wife.

CABOT: That hain't me. A son is me—my blood—mine. Mine ought t' git mine. An' then it's still mine—even though I be six foot under. D'ye see?

ABBIE [*giving him a look of hatred*]: Ay-eh. I see. [*She becomes very thoughtful, her face growing shrewd, her eyes studying* CABOT *craftily.*]

CABOT: I'm gittin' old—ripe on the bough. [*then with a sudden forced reassurance*] Not but what I hain't a hard nut t' crack even yet—an' fur many a year t' come! By the Etarnal, I kin break most o' the young fellers's backs at any kind o' work any day o' the year!

ABBIE [*suddenly*]: Mebbe the Lord'll give *us* a son.

CABOT [*turns and stares at her eagerly*]: Ye mean—a son—t' me 'n' yew?

ABBIE [*with a cajoling smile*]: Ye're a strong man yet, hain't ye? 'Tain't noways impossible, be it? We know that. Why d'ye stare so? Hain't ye never thought o' that afore? I been thinkin' o' it all along. Ay-eh—an' I been prayin' it'd happen, too.

CABOT [*his face growing full of joyous pride and a sort of religious ecstasy*]: Ye been prayin', Abbie?—fur a son?—t' us?

ABBIE: Ay-eh. [*with a grim resolution*] I want a son now.

CABOT [*excitedly clutching both of her hands in his*]: It'd be the blessin' o' God, Abbie—the blessin' o' God A'mighty on me—in my old age—in my lonesomeness! They hain't nothin' I wouldn't do fur ye then, Abbie. Ye'd hev on'y t' ask it—anythin' ye'd a mind t'!

ABBIE [*interrupting*]: Would ye will the farm t' me then—t' me an' it?

CABOT [*vehemently*]: I'd do anythin' ye axed, I tell ye! I swar it! May I be everlastin' damned t' hell if I wouldn't! [*He sinks to his knees pulling her down with him. He trembles all over with the fervor of his hopes.*] Pray t' the Lord agen, Abbie. It's the Sabbath! I'll jine ye! Two prayers air better nor one. "An' God hearkened unto Rachel"! An' God hearkened unto Abbie! Pray, Abbie! Pray fur him to hearken! [*He bows his head, mumbling. She pretends to do likewise but gives him a side glance of scorn and triumph.*]

Scene 2

About eight in the evening. The interior of the two bedrooms on the top floor is shown. EBEN *is sitting on the side of his bed in the room on the left. On account of the heat he has taken off everything but his undershirt and pants. His feet are bare. He faces front, brooding moodily, his chin propped on his hands, a desperate expression on his face.*

In the other room CABOT *and* ABBIE *are sitting side by side on the edge of their bed, an old four-poster with feather mattress. He is in his night shirt, she in her nightdress. He is still in the queer, excited mood into which the notion of a son has thrown him. Both rooms are lighted dimly and flickeringly by tallow candles.*

CABOT: The farm needs a son.

ABBIE: I need a son.

CABOT: Ay-eh. Sometimes ye air the farm an' sometimes the farm be yew. That's why I clove t' ye in my lonesomeness. [*A pause. He pounds his knee with his fist.*] Me an' the farm has got t' beget a son!

ABBIE: Ye'd best go t' sleep. Ye're gittin' thin's all mixed.

CABOT [*with an impatient gesture*]: No, I hain't. My mind's clear's a well. Ye don't know me, that's it. [*He stares hopelessly at the floor.*]

ABBIE [*indifferently*]: Mebbe. [*In the next room* EBEN *gets up and paces up and down distractedly.* ABBIE *hears him. Her eyes fasten on the intervening wall with concentrated attention.* EBEN *stops and stares. Their hot glances seem to meet through the wall. Unconsciously he stretches out his arms for her and she half rises. Then aware, he mutters a curse at himself and flings himself face downward on the bed, his clenched fists above his head, his face buried in the pillow.* ABBIE *relaxes with a faint sigh but her eyes remain fixed on the wall; she listens with all her attention for some movement from* EBEN.]

CABOT [*suddenly raises his head and looks at her—scornfully*]: Will ye ever know me—'r will any man 'r woman? [*shaking his head*] No. I calc'late 'twa'n't t' be. [*He turns away.* ABBIE *looks at the wall. Then, evidently unable to keep silent about his thoughts, without looking at his wife, he puts out his hand and clutches her knee. She starts violently, looks at him, sees he is not watching her, concentrates again on the wall and pays no attention to what he says.*] Listen, Abbie. When I come here fifty odd year ago—I was jest twenty an' the strongest an' hardest ye ever seen—ten times as strong an' fifty times as hard as Eben. Waal—this place was nothin' but fields o' stones. Folks laughed when I tuk it. They couldn't know what I knowed. When ye kin make corn sprout out o' stones, God's livin' in yew! They wa'n't strong enuf fur that! They reckoned God was easy. They laughed. They don't laugh no more. Some died hereabouts. Some went West an' died. They're all under ground—fur follerin' arter an easy God. God hain't easy. [*He shakes his head slowly.*] An' I growed hard. Folks kept allus sayin' he's a hard man like 'twas sinful t' be hard, so's at last I said back at 'em: Waal then, by thunder, ye'll git me hard an' see how ye like it! [*then suddenly*] But I give in t' weakness once. 'Twas arter I'd been here two year. I got weak—despairful—they was so many stones. They was a party leavin', givin' up, goin' West. I jined 'em. We tracked on 'n' on. We come t' broad medders, plains, whar the soil was black an' rich as gold. Nary a stone. Easy. Ye'd on'y to plow an' sow an' then set an' smoke yer pipe an' watch thin's grow. I could o' been a rich man—but somethin' in me fit me an' fit me—the voice o' God sayin': "This hain't wuth nothin' t' Me. Git ye back t' hum!" I got afeerd o' that voice an' I lit out back t' hum here, leavin' my claim an' crops t' whoever'd a mind t' take em. Ay-eh. I actooly give up what was rightful mine! God's hard, not easy! God's in the stones! Build my church on a rock—out o' stones an' I'll be in them! That's what He meant t' Peter! [*He sighs heavily—a pause.*] Stones. I picked 'em up an' piled 'em into walls. Ye kin read the years o' my life in them walls, every day a hefted stone, climbin' over the hills up and down, fencin' in the fields that was mine, whar I'd made thin's grow out o' nothin'—like the will o' God, like the servant o' His hand. It wa'n't easy. It was hard an' He made me hard fur it. [*He pauses.*] All the time I kept gittin' lonesomer. I tuk a wife. She bore Simeon an' Peter. She was a good woman. She wuked hard. We was married twenty year. She never knowed me. She helped but she never knowed what she was helpin'. I was allus lonesome. She died. After that it wa'n't so lonesome fur a spell. [*a pause*] I lost count o' the years. I had no time t' fool away countin' 'em. Sim an' Peter helped. The farm growed. It was all mine! When I thought o' that I didn't feel lonesome. [*a pause*] But ye can't hitch yer mind t' one thin' day an' night. I tuk another wife—Eben's Maw. Her folks was contestin' me at law over my deeds t' the farm—my farm! That's why Eben keeps a-talkin' his fool talk o' this bein' his Maw's farm. She bore Eben. She was purty—but soft. She tried t' be hard. She couldn't. She never knowed me nor nothin'. It was lonesomer 'n hell with her. After a matter o' sixteen odd years, she died. [*a pause*] I lived with the boys. They hated me 'cause I was hard. I hated them 'cause they was soft. They coveted the farm without knowin' what it meant. It made me bitter 'n wormwood. It aged me—them coveting what I'd made fur mine. Then this spring the call come—the voice o' God cryin' in my wilderness, in my lonesomeness—t' go out an' seek an' find! [*turning to her with strange passion*] I sought ye an' I found ye! Yew air my Rose o' Sharon! Yer eyes air like . . . [*She has turned a blank face, resentful eyes to his. He stares at her for a moment—then harshly*] Air ye any the wiser fur all I've told ye?

ABBIE [*confusedly*]: Mebbe.

CABOT [*pushing her away from him—angrily*]: Ye don't know nothin'—nor never will. If ye don't hev a son t' redeem ye . . . ! [*This in a tone of cold threat.*]

ABBIE [*resentfully*]: I prayed, hain't I?

CABOT [*bitterly*]: Pray agen—fur understandin'!

ABBIE [*a veiled threat in her tone*]: Ye'll have a son out o' me, I promise ye.

CABOT: How kin ye promise?

ABBIE: I got second-sight, mebbe. I kin foretell. [*She gives a queer smile.*]

CABOT: I believe ye have. Ye give me the chills sometimes. [*He shivers.*] It's cold in this house. It's oneasy. They's thin's pokin' about in the dark—in the corners. [*He pulls on his trousers, tucking in his night shirt, and pulls on his boots.*]

ABBIE [*surprised*]: Whar air ye goin'?

CABOT [*queerly*]: Down whar it's restful—whar it's warm—down t' the barn. [*bitterly*] I kin talk t' the cows. They know. They know the farm an' me. They'll give me peace. [*He turns to go out the door.*]

ABBIE [*a bit frightenedly*]: Air ye ailin' tonight, Ephraim?

CABOT: Growin'. Growin' ripe on the bough. [*He turns and goes, his boots clumping down the stairs.* EBEN *sits up with a start, listening.* ABBIE *is conscious of his movement and stares at the wall.* CABOT *comes out of the house around the corner and stands by the gate, blinking at the sky. He stretches up his hands in a tortured gesture.*] God A'mighty, call from the dark! [*He listens as if expecting an answer. Then his arms drop, he shakes his head and plods off toward the barn.* EBEN *and* ABBIE *stare at each other through the wall.* EBEN *sighs heavily and* ABBIE *echoes it. Both become terribly nervous, uneasy. Finally* ABBIE *gets up and listens, her ear to the wall. He acts as if he saw every move she was making, he becomes resolutely still. She seems driven into a decision—goes out the door in rear determinedly. His eyes follow her. Then as the door of his room is opened softly, he turns away, waits in an attitude of strained fixity.* ABBIE *stands for a second staring at him, her eyes burning with desire. Then with a little cry she runs over and throws her arms about his neck, she pulls his head back and covers his mouth with kisses. At first, he submits dumbly; then he puts his arms about her neck and returns her kisses, but finally, suddenly aware of his hatred, he hurls her away from him, springing to his feet. They stand speechless and breathless, panting like two animals.*]

ABBIE [*at last—painfully*]: Ye shouldn't, Eben—ye shouldn't—I'd make ye happy!

EBEN [*harshly*]: I don't want t' be happy—from yew!

ABBIE [*helplessly*]: Ye do, Eben! Ye do! Why d'ye lie?

EBEN [*viciously*]: I don't take t' ye, I tell ye! I hate the sight o' ye!

ABBIE [*with an uncertain troubled laugh*]: Waal, I kissed ye anyways—an' ye kissed back—yer lips was burnin'—ye can't lie 'bout that! [*intensely*] If ye don't care, why did ye kiss me back—why was yer lips burnin'?

EBEN [*wiping his mouth*]: It was like pizen on 'em. [*then tauntingly*] When I kissed ye back, mebbe I thought 'twas someone else.

ABBIE [*wildly*]: Min?

EBEN: Mebbe.

ABBIE [*torturedly*]: Did ye go t' see her? Did ye r'ally go? I thought ye mightn't. Is that why ye throwed me off jest now?

EBEN [*sneeringly*]: What if it be?

ABBIE [*raging*]: Then ye're a dog, Eben Cabot!

EBEN [*threateningly*]: Ye can't talk that way t' me!

ABBIE [*with a shrill laugh*]: Can't I? Did ye think I was in love with ye—a weak thin' like yew! Not much! I on'y wanted ye fur a purpose o' my own—an' I'll hev ye fur it yet 'cause I'm stronger'n yew be!

EBEN [*resentfully*]: I knowed well it was on'y part o' yer plan t' swaller everythin'!

ABBIE [*tauntingly*]: Mebbe!

EBEN [*furious*]: Git out o' my room!

ABBIE: This air my room an' ye're on'y hired help!

EBEN [*threateningly*]: Git out afore I murder ye!

ABBIE [*quite confident now*]: I hain't a mite afeerd. Ye want me, don't ye? Yes, ye do! An' yer Paw's son'll never kill what he wants! Look at yer eyes! They's lust fur me in 'em, burnin' 'em up! Look at yer lips now! They're tremblin' an' longin' t' kiss me, an' yer teeth t' bite! [*He is watching her now with a horrible fascination. She laughs a crazy triumphant laugh.*] I'm a-goin' t' make all o' this hum my hum! They's one room hain't mine yet, but it's a-goin' t' be tonight. I'm a-goin' down now an' light up! [*She makes him a mocking bow.*] Won't ye come courtin' me in the best parlor, Mister Cabot?

EBEN [*staring at her—horribly confused—dully*]: Don't ye dare! It hain't been opened since Maw died an' was laid out thar! Don't ye . . . ! [*But her eyes are fixed on his so burningly that his will seems to wither before hers. He stands swaying toward her helplessly.*]

ABBIE [*holding his eyes and putting all her will into her words as she backs out the door*]: I'll expect ye afore long, Eben.

EBEN [*stares after her for a while, walking toward the door. A light appears in the parlor window. He murmurs*]: In the parlor? [*This seems to arouse connotations for he comes back and puts on his white shirt, collar, half ties the tie mechanically, puts on coat, takes his hat, stands barefooted looking about him in bewilderment, mutters wonderingly*] Maw! Whar air yew? [*then goes slowly toward the door in rear*]

Scene 3

A few minutes later. The interior of the parlor is shown. A grim, repressed room like a tomb in which the family has been interred alive. ABBIE *sits on the edge of the horsehair sofa. She has lighted all the candles and the room is revealed in all its preserved ugliness. A change has come over the woman. She looks awed and frightened now, ready to run away.*

The door is opened and EBEN *appears. His face wears an expression of obsessed confusion. He stands staring at her, his arms hanging disjointedly from his shoulders, his feet bare, his hat in his hand.*

ABBIE [*after a pause—with a nervous, formal politeness*]: Won't ye set?

EBEN [*dully*]: Ay-eh. [*Mechanically he places his hat carefully on the floor near the door and sits stiffly beside her on the edge of the sofa. A pause. They both remain rigid, looking straight ahead with eyes full of fear.*]

ABBIE: When I fust come in—in the dark—they seemed somethin' here.

EBEN [*simply*]: Maw.

ABBIE: I kin still feel—somethin'.

EBEN: It's Maw.

ABBIE: At fust I was feered o' it. I wanted t' yell an' run. Now—since yew come—seems like it's growin' soft an' kind t' me. [*addressing the air—queerly*] Thank yew.

EBEN: Maw allus loved me.

ABBIE: Mebbe it knows I love yew, too. Mebbe that makes it kind t' me.

EBEN [*dully*]: I dunno. I should think she'd hate ye.

ABBIE [*with certainty*]: No. I kin feel it don't—not no more.

EBEN: Hate ye fur stealin' her place—here in her hum—settin' in her parlor whar she was laid—[*He suddenly stops, staring stupidly before him.*]

ABBIE: What is it, Eben?

EBEN [*in a whisper*]: Seems like Maw didn't want me t' remind ye.

ABBIE [*excitedly*]: I knowed, Eben! It's kind t' me! It don't b'ar me no grudges fur what I never knowed an' couldn't help!

EBEN: Maw b'ars him a grudge.

ABBIE: Waal, so does all o' us.

EBEN: Ay-eh. [*with passion*] I does, by God!

ABBIE [*taking one of his hands in hers and patting it*]: Thar! Don't git riled thinkin' o' him. Think o' yer Maw who's kind t' us. Tell me about yer Maw, Eben.

EBEN: They hain't nothin' much. She was kind. She was good.

ABBIE [*putting one arm over his shoulder. He does not seem to notice—passionately*]: I'll be kind an' good t' ye!

EBEN: Sometimes she used t' sing fur me.

ABBIE: I'll sing fur ye!

EBEN: This was her hum. This was her farm.

ABBIE: This is my hum! This is my farm!

EBEN: He married her t' steal 'em. She was soft an' easy. He couldn't 'preciate her.

ABBIE: He can't 'preciate me!

EBEN: He murdered her with his hardness.

ABBIE: He's murderin' me!

EBEN: She died. [*a pause*] Sometimes she used to sing fur me. [*He bursts into a fit of sobbing.*]

ABBIE [*both her arms around him—with wild passion*]: I'll sing fur ye! I'll die fur ye! [*In spite of her overwhelming desire for him, there is a sincere maternal love in her manner and voice—a horribly frank mixture of lust and mother love.*] Don't cry, Eben! I'll take yer Maw's place! I'll be everythin' she was t' ye! Let me kiss ye, Eben! [*She pulls his head around. He makes a bewildered pretense of resistance. She is tender.*] Don't be afeered! I'll kiss ye pure, Eben—same 's if I was a Maw t' ye—an' ye kin kiss me back 's if yew was my son—my boy—sayin' good-night t' me! Kiss me, Eben. [*They kiss in restrained fashion. Then suddenly wild passion overcomes her. She kisses him lustfully again and again and he flings his arms about her and returns her kisses. Suddenly, as in the bedroom, he frees himself from her violently and springs to his feet. He is trembling all over, in a strange state of terror.* ABBIE *strains her arms toward him with fierce pleading.*] Don't ye leave me, Eben! Can't ye see it hain't enuf—lovin' ye like a Maw—can't ye see it's got t' be that an' more—much more—a hundred times more—fur me t' be happy—fur yew t' be happy?

EBEN [*to the presence he feels in the room*]: Maw! Maw! What d'ye want? What air ye tellin' me?

ABBIE: She's tellin' ye t' love me. She knows I love ye an' I'll be good t' ye. Can't ye feel it? Don't ye know? She's tellin' ye t' love me, Eben!

EBEN: Ay-eh. I feel—mebbe she—but—I can't figger out —why—when ye've stole her place—here in her hum—in the parlor whar she was—

ABBIE [*fiercely*]: She knows I love ye!

EBEN [*his face suddenly lighting up with a fierce, triumphant grin*]: I see it! I sees why. It's her vengeance on him—so's she kin rest quiet in her grave!

ABBIE [*wildly*]: Vengeance o' God on the hull o' us! What d'we give a durn? I love ye, Eben! God knows I love ye! [*She stretches out her arms for him.*]

EBEN [*throws himself on his knees beside the sofa and grabs her in his arms—releasing all his pent-up passion*]: An' I love yew, Abbie!—now I kin say it! I been dyin' fur want o' ye—every hour since ye come! I love ye! [*Their lips meet in a fierce, bruising kiss.*]

Scene 4

Exterior of the farmhouse. It is just dawn. The front door at right is opened and EBEN *comes out and walks around to the gate. He is dressed in his working clothes. He seems changed. His face wears a bold and confident expression, he is grinning to himself with evident satisfaction. As he gets near the gate, the window of the parlor is heard opening and the shutters are flung back and* ABBIE *sticks her head out. Her hair tumbles over her shoulders in dissarray, her face is flushed, she looks at* EBEN *with tender, languorous eyes and calls softly*

ABBIE: Eben. [*as he turns—playfully*] Jest one more kiss afore ye go. I'm goin' t' miss ye fearful all day.

EBEN: An' me yew, ye kin bet! [*He goes to her. They kiss several times. He draws away, laughingly*] Thar. That's enuf, hain't it? Ye won't hev none left fur next time.

ABBIE: I got a million o' 'em left fur yew! [*then a bit anxiously*] D'ye r'ally love me, Eben?

EBEN [*emphatically*]: I like ye better'n any gal I ever knowed! That's gospel!

ABBIE: Likin' hain't lovin'.

EBEN: Waal then—I love ye. Now air yew satisfied?

ABBIE: Ay-eh, I be. [*She smiles at him adoringly.*]

EBEN: I better git t' the barn. The old critter's liable t' suspicion an' come sneakin' up.

ABBIE [*with a confident laugh*]: Let him! I kin allus pull the wool over his eyes. I'm goin' t' leave the shutters open and let in the sun 'n' air. This room's been dead long enuf. Now it's goin' t' be my room!

EBEN [*frowning*]: Ay-eh.

ABBIE [*hastily*]: I meant—our room.

EBEN: Ay-eh.

ABBIE: We made it our'n last night, didn't we? We give it life—our lovin' did. [*a pause*]

EBEN [*with a strange look*]: Maw's gone back t' her grave. She kin sleep now.

ABBIE: May she rest in peace! [*then tenderly rebuking*] Ye oughtn't t' talk o' sad thin's—this mornin'.

EBEN: It jest come up in my mind o' itself.

ABBIE: Don't let it. [*He doesn't answer. She yawns.*] Waal, I'm a-goin' t' steal a wink o' sleep. I'll tell the Old Man I hain't feelin' pert. Let him git his own vittles.

EBEN: I see him comin' from the barn. Ye better look smart an' git upstairs.

ABBIE: Ay-eh. Good-by. Don't ferget me. [*She throws him a kiss. He grins—then squares his shoulders and awaits his father confidently.* CABOT *walks slowly up from the left, staring up at the sky with a vague face.*]

EBEN [*jovially*]: Mornin', Paw. Star-gazin' in daylight?

CABOT: Purty, hain't it?

EBEN [*looking around him possessively*]: It's a durned purty farm.

CABOT: I mean the sky.

EBEN [*grinning*]: How d'ye know? Them eyes o' your'n can't see that fur. [*This tickles his humor and he slaps his thigh and laughs.*] Ho-ho! That's a good un!

CABOT [*grimly sarcastic*]: Ye're feelin' right chipper, hain't ye? Whar'd ye steal the likker?

EBEN [*good-naturedly*]: 'Tain't likker. Jest life. [*suddenly holding out his hand—soberly*] Yew 'n' me is quits. Let's shake hands.

CABOT [*suspiciously*]: What's come over ye?

EBEN: Then don't. Mebbe it's jest as well. [*a moment's pause*] What's come over me? [*queerly*] Didn't ye feel her passin'—goin' back t' her grave?

CABOT [*dully*]: Who?

EBEN: Maw. She kin rest now an' sleep content. She's quits with ye.

CABOT [*confusedly*]: I rested. I slept good—down with the cows. They know how t' sleep. They're teachin' me.

EBEN [*suddenly jovial again*]: Good fur the cows! Waal—ye better git t' work.

CABOT [*grimly amused*]: Air yew bossin' me, ye calf?

EBEN [*beginning to laugh*]: Ay-eh! I'm bossin' yew. Ha-ha-ha! See how ye like it! Ha-ha-ha! I'm the prize rooster o' this roost. Ha-ha-ha! [*He goes off toward the barn laughing.*]

CABOT [*looks after him with scornful pity*]: Soft-headed. Like his Maw. Dead spit 'n' image. No hope in him! [*He spits with contemptuous disgust.*] A born fool! [*then matter-of-factly*] Waal—I'm gittin' peckish. [*He goes toward door.*]

THE CURTAIN FALLS

PART III

Scene 1

A night in late spring the following year. The kitchen and the two bedrooms upstairs are shown. The two bedrooms are dimly lighted by a tallow candle in each. EBEN *is sitting on the side of the bed in his room, his chin propped on his fists, his face a study of the struggle he is making to understand his conflicting emotions. The noisy laughter and music from below where a kitchen dance is in progress annoy and distract him. He scowls at the floor.*

In the next room a cradle stands beside the double bed.

In the kitchen all is festivity. The stove has been taken down to give more room to the dancers. The chairs, with wooden benches added, have been pushed back against the walls. On these are seated, squeezed in tight against one another, farmers and their wives and their young folks of both sexes from the neighboring farms. They are all chattering and laughing loudly. They evidently have some secret joke in common. There is no end of winking, of nudging, of meaning nods of the head toward CABOT *who, in a state of extreme hilarious excitement increased by the amount he has drunk, is standing near the rear door where there is a small keg of whisky and serving drinks to all the men. In the left corner, front, dividing the attention with her husband,* ABBIE *is sitting in a rocking chair, a shawl wrapped about her shoulders. She is very pale, her face is thin and drawn, her eyes are fixed anxiously on the open door in rear as if waiting for someone.*

The musician is tuning up his fiddle, seated in the far right corner. He is a lanky young fellow with a long, weak face. His pale eyes blink incessantly and he grins about him slyly with a greedy malice.

ABBIE [*suddenly turning to a* YOUNG GIRL *on her right*]: Whar's Eben?

YOUNG GIRL [*eyeing her scornfully*]: I dunno, Mrs. Cabot. I hain't seen Eben in ages. [*meaningly*] Seems like he's spent most o' his time t' hum since yew come.

ABBIE [*vaguely*]: I tuk his Maw's place.

YOUNG GIRL: Ay-eh. So I've heard. [*She turns away to retail this bit of gossip to her mother sitting next to her.* ABBIE *turns to her left to a big stoutish middle-aged* MAN *whose flushed face and starting eyes show the amount of "likker" he has consumed.*]

ABBIE: Ye hain't seen Eben, hev ye?

MAN: No, I hain't. [*Then he adds with a wink*] If yew hain't, who would?

ABBIE: He's the best dancer in the county. He'd ought t' come an' dance.

MAN [*with a wink*]: Mebbe he's doin' the dutiful an' walkin' the kid t' sleep. It's a boy, hain't it?

ABBIE [*nodding vaguely*]: Ay-eh—born two weeks back—purty's a picter.

MAN: They all is—t' their Maws. [*then in a whisper, with a nudge and a leer*] Listen, Abbie—if ye ever git tired o' Eben, remember me! Don't fergit now! [*He looks at her uncomprehending face for a second—then grunts disgustedly.*] Waal—guess I'll likker agin. [*He goes over and joins* CABOT, *who is arguing noisily with an old farmer over cows. They all drink.*]

ABBIE [*this time appealing to nobody in particular*]: Wonder what Eben's a-doin'? [*Her remark is repeated down the line with many a guffaw and titter until it reaches the fiddler. He fastens his blinking eyes on* ABBIE.]

FIDDLER [*raising his voice*]: Bet I kin tell ye, Abbie, what Eben's doin'! He's down t' the church offerin' up prayers o' thanksgivin'. [*They all titter expectantly.*]

A MAN: What fur? [*another titter*]

FIDDLER: 'Cause unto him a— [*he hesitates just long enough*] —brother is born! [*A roar of laughter. They all look from* ABBIE *to* CABOT. *She is oblivious, staring at the door.* CABOT, *although he hasn't heard the words, is irritated by the laughter and steps forward, glaring about him. There is an immediate silence.*]

CABOT: What're ye all bleatin' about—like a flock o' goats? Why don't ye dance, damn ye? I axed ye here t' dance—t' eat, drink an' be merry—an' thar ye set cacklin' like a lot o' wet hens with the pip! Ye've swilled my likker an' guzzled my vittles like hogs, hain't ye? Then dance fur me, can't ye? That's fa'r an' squar', hain't it? [*A grumble of resentment goes around but they are all evidently in too much awe of him to express it openly.*]

FIDDLER [*slyly*]: We're waitin' fur Eben. [*a suppressed laugh*]

CABOT [*with a fierce exultation*]: T' hell with Eben! Eben's done fur now! I got a new son! [*his mood switching with drunken suddenness*] But ye needn't t' laugh at Eben, none o' ye! He's my blood, if he be a dumb fool. He's better nor any o' yew! He kin do a day's work a'most up t' what I kin—an' that'd put any o' yew pore critters t' shame!

FIDDLER: An' he kin do a good night's work, too! [*a roar of laughter*]

CABOT: Laugh, ye damn fools! Ye're right jist the same, Fiddler. He kin work day an' night too, like I kin, if need be!

OLD FARMER [*from behind the keg where he is weaving drunkenly back and forth—with great simplicity*]: They hain't many t' touch ye, Ephraim—a son at seventy-six. That's a hard man fur ye! I be on'y sixty-eight an' I couldn't do it. [*a roar of laughter in which* CABOT *joins uproariously*]

CABOT [*slapping him on the back*]: I'm sorry fur ye, Hi. I'd never suspicion sech weakness from a boy like yew!

OLD FARMER: An' I never reckoned yew had it in ye nuther, Ephraim. [*There is another laugh.*]

CABOT [*suddenly grim*]: I got a lot in me—a hell of a lot—folks don't know on. [*turning to the fiddler*] Fiddle 'er up, durn ye! Give 'em somethin' t' dance t'! What air ye, an ornament? Hain't this a celebration? Then grease yer elbow an' go it!

FIDDLER [*seizes a drink which the old farmer holds out to him and downs it*]: Here goes! [*He starts to fiddle "Lady of the Lake." Four young fellows and four girls form in two lines and dance a square dance. The fiddler shouts directions for the different movements, keeping his words in the rhythm of the music and interspersing them with jocular personal remarks to the dancers themselves. The people seated along the walls stamp their feet and clap their hands in unison.* CABOT *is especially active in this respect. Only* ABBIE *remains apathetic, staring at the door as if she were alone in a silent room.*]

FIDDLER: Swing your partner t' the right! That's it, Jim! Give her a b'ar hug! Her Maw hain't lookin'. [*laughter*] Change partners! That suits ye, don't it, Essie, now ye got Reub afore ye? Look at her redden up, will ye? Waal, life is short an' so's love, as the feller says. [*laughter*]

CABOT [*excitedly, stamping his foot*]: Go it, boys! Go it, gals!

FIDDLER [*with a wink at the others*]: Ye're the spryest seventy-six ever I sees, Ephraim! Now if ye'd on'y good eyesight . . . ! [*Suppressed laughter. He gives* CABOT *no chance to retort but roars*] Promenade! Ye're walkin' like a bride down the aisle, Sarah! Waal, while they's life they's allus hope, I've heerd tell. Swing your partner to the left! Gosh A'mighty, look at Johnny Cook high-steppin'! They hain't goin' t' be much strength left fur howin' in the corn lot t'morrow. [*laughter*]

CABOT: Go it! Go it! [*Then suddenly, unable to restrain himself any longer, he prances into the midst of the dancers, scattering them, waving his arms about wildly.*] Ye're all hoofs! Git out o' my road! Give me room! I'll show ye dancin'. Ye're all too soft! [*He pushes them roughly away. They crowd back toward the walls, muttering, looking at him resentfully.*]

FIDDLER [*jeeringly*]: Go it, Ephraim! Go it! [*He starts "Pop, Goes the Weasel," increasing the tempo with every verse until at the end he is fiddling crazily as fast as he can go.*]

CABOT [*starts to dance, which he does very well and with tremendous vigor. Then he begins to improvise, cuts incredibly grotesque capers, leaping up and cracking his heels together, prancing around in a circle with body bent in an Indian war dance, then suddenly straightening up and kicking as high as he can with both legs. He is like a monkey on a string. And all the while he intersperses his antics with shouts and derisive comments.*]: Whoop! Here's dancin' fur ye! Whoop! See that! Seventy-six, if I'm a day! Hard as iron yet! Beatin' the young 'uns like I allus done! Look at me! I'd invite ye t' dance on my hundredth birthday on'y ye'll all be dead by then. Ye're a sickly generation! Yer hearts air pink, not red! Yer veins is full o' mud an' water! I be the on'y man in the county! Whoop! See that! I'm a Injun! I've killed Injuns in the West afore ye was born—an' skulped 'em too! They's a arrer wound on my backside I c'd show ye! The hull tribe chased me. I outrun 'em all—with the arrer stuck in me! An' I tuk vengeance on 'em. Ten eyes fur an eye, that was my motter! Whoop! Look at me! I kin kick the ceilin' off the room! Whoop!

FIDDLER [*stops playing—exhaustedly*]: God A'mighty, I got enuf. Ye got the devil's strength in ye.

CABOT [*delightedly*]: Did I beat yew, too? Waal, ye played smart. Hev a swig. [*He pours whisky for himself and fiddler. They drink. The others watch* CABOT *silently with cold, hostile eyes. There is a dead pause. The fiddler rests.* CABOT *leans against the keg, panting, glaring around him confusedly. In the room above,* EBEN *gets to his feet and tiptoes out the door in rear, appearing a moment later in the other bedroom. He moves silently, even frightenedly, toward the cradle and stands there looking down at the baby. His face is as vague as his reactions are confused, but there is a trace of tenderness, of interested discovery. At the same moment that he reaches the cradle,* ABBIE *seems to sense something. She gets up weakly and goes to* CABOT.]

ABBIE: I'm goin' up t' the baby.

CABOT: [*with real solicitation*]: Air ye able fur the stairs? D'ye want me t' help ye, Abbie?

ABBIE: No. I'm able. I'll be down agen soon.

CABOT: Don't ye git wore out! He needs ye, remember—our son does! [*He grins affectionately, patting her on the back. She shrinks from his touch.*]

ABBIE [*dully*]: Don't—tech me. I'm goin'—up. [*She goes.* CABOT *looks after her. A whisper goes around the room.* CABOT *turns. It ceases. He wipes his forehead streaming with sweat. He is breathing pantingly.*]

CABOT: I'm a-goin' out t' git fresh air. I'm feelin' a mite dizzy. Fiddle up thar! Dance, all o' ye! Here's likker fur them as wants it. Enjoy yerselves. I'll be back. [*He goes, closing the door behind him.*]

FIDDLER [*sarcastically*]: Don't hurry none on our account! [*A suppressed laugh. He imitates* ABBIE.] Whar's Eben? [*more laughter*]

A WOMAN [*loudly*]: What's happened in this house is plain as the nose on yer face! [ABBIE *appears in the doorway upstairs and stands looking in surprise and adoration at* EBEN *who does not see her.*]

A MAN: Ssshh! He's li'ble t' be listenin' at the door. That'd be like him. [*Their voices die to an intensive whispering. Their faces are concentrated on this gossip. A noise as of dead leaves in the wind comes from the room.* CABOT *has come out from the porch and stands by the gate, leaning on it, staring at the sky blinkingly.* ABBIE *comes across the room silently.* EBEN *does not notice her until quite near.*]

EBEN [*starting*]: Abbie!

ABBIE: Ssshh! [*She throws her arms around him. They kiss—then bend over the cradle together.*] Ain't he purty?—dead spit 'n' image o' yew!

EBEN [*pleased*]: Air he? I can't tell none.

ABBIE: E-zactly like!

EBEN [*frowningly*]: I don't like this. I don't like lettin' on what's mine's his'n. I been doin' that all my life. I'm gittin' t' the end o' b'arin' it!

ABBIE [*putting her finger on his lips*]: We're doin' the best we kin. We got t' wait. Somethin's bound t' happen. [*She puts her arms around him.*] I got t' go back.

EBEN: I'm goin' out. I can't b'ar it with the fiddle playin' an' the laughin'.

ABBIE: Don't git feelin' low. I love ye, Eben. Kiss me. [*He kisses her. They remain in each other's arms.*]

CABOT [*at the gate, confusedly*]: Even the music can't drive it out—somethin'. Ye kin feel it droppin' off the elums, climbin' up the roof, sneakin' down the chimney, pokin' in the corners! They's no peace in houses, they's no rest livin' with folks. Somethin's always livin' with ye. [*with a deep sigh*] I'll go t' the barn an' rest a spell. [*He goes wearily toward the barn.*]

FIDDLER [*tuning up*]: Let's celebrate the old skunk gittin' fooled! We kin have some fun now he's went. [*He starts to fiddle "Turkey in the Straw." There is real merriment now. The young folks get up to dance.*]

Scene 2

*A half hour later—Exterior—*EBEN *is standing by the gate looking up at the sky, an expression of dumb pain bewildered by itself on his face.* CABOT *appears, returning from the barn, walking wearily, his eyes on the ground. He sees* EBEN *and his whole mood immediately changes. He becomes excited, a cruel, triumphant grin comes to his lips, he strides up and slaps* EBEN *on the back. From within comes the whining of the fiddle and the noise of stamping feet and laughing voices.*

CABOT: So har ye be!

EBEN [*startled, stares at him with hatred for a moment—then dully*]: Ay-eh.

CABOT [*surveying him jeeringly*]: Why hain't ye been in t' dance? They was all axin' fur ye.

EBEN: Let 'em ax!

CABOT: They's a hull passel o' purty gals.

EBEN: T' hell with 'em!

CABOT: Ye'd ought t' be marryin' one o' 'em soon.

EBEN: I hain't marryin' no one.

CABOT: Ye might 'arn a share o' a farm that way.

EBEN [*with a sneer*]: Like yew did, ye mean? I hain't that kind.

CABOT [*stung*]: Ye lie! 'Twas yer Maw's folks aimed t' steal my farm from me.

EBEN: Other folks don't say so. [*after a pause—defiantly*] An' I got a farm, anyways!

CABOT [*derisively*]: Whar?

EBEN [*stamps a foot on the ground*]: Har!

CABOT [*throws his head back and laughs coarsely*]: Ho-ho! Ye hev, hev ye? Waal, that's a good un!

EBEN [*controlling himself—grimly*]: Ye'll see!

CABOT [*stares at him suspiciously, trying to make him out—a pause—then with scornful confidence*]: Ay-eh. I'll see. So'll ye. It's ye that's blind—blind as a mole underground. [EBEN *suddenly laughs, one short sardonic bark:* Ha. *A pause.* CABOT *peers at him with renewed suspicion.*] What air ye hawin' 'bout? [EBEN *turns away without answering.* CABOT *grows angry.*] God A'mighty, yew air a dumb dunce! They's nothin' in that thick skull o' your'n but noise—like a empty keg it be! [EBEN *doesn't seem to hear.* CABOT'*s rage grows.*] Yewr farm! God A'mighty! If ye wa'n't a born donkey ye'd know ye'll never own stick nor stone on it, specially now arter him bein' born. It's his'n, I tell ye—his'n arter I die—but I'll live a hundred jest t' fool ye all—an' he'll be growed then—yewr age a'most! [EBEN *laughs again his sardonic* Ha. *This drives* CABOT *into a fury.*] Ha? Ye think ye kin git 'round that someways, do ye? Waal, it'll be her'n, too—Abbie's—ye won't git 'round her—she knows yer tricks—she'll be too much fur ye—she wants the farm her'n—she was afeerd o' ye—she told me ye was sneakin' 'round tryin' t' make love t' her t' git her on yer side . . . ye . . . ye mad fool, ye! [*He raises his clenched fits threateningly.*]

EBEN [*is confronting him, choking with rage*]: Ye lie, ye old skunk! Abbie never said no sech thing!

CABOT [*suddenly triumphant when he sees how shaken* EBEN *is*]: She did. An' I says, I'll blow his brains t' the top o' them elums—an' she says no, that hain't sense, who'll ye git t' help ye on the farm in his place—an' then she says yew'n me ought t' have a son—I know' we kin, she says—an' I says, if we do, ye kin have anythin' I've got ye've a mind t'. An' she says, I wants Eben cut off so's this farm'll be mine when ye die! [*with terrible gloating*] An' that's what's happened, hain't it? An' the farm's her'n! An' the dust o' the road—that's your'n! Ha! Now who's hawin'?

EBEN [*has been listening, petrified with grief and rage—suddenly laughs wildly and brokenly*]: Ha-ha-ha! So that's her sneakin' game—all along!—like I suspicioned at fust—t' swaller it all—an' me, too. . . ! [*madly*] I'll murder her! [*He springs toward the porch, but* CABOT *is quicker and gets in between.*]

CABOT: No, ye don't!

EBEN: Git out o' my road! [*He tries to throw* CABOT *aside. They grapple in what becomes immediately a murderous struggle. The old man's concentrated strength is too much for* EBEN. CABOT *gets one hand on his throat and presses him back across the stone wall. At the same moment,* ABBIE *comes out on the porch. With a stifled cry she runs toward them.*]

ABBIE: Eben! Ephraim! [*She tugs at the hand on* EBEN'*s throat.*] Let go, Ephraim! Ye're chokin' him!

CABOT [*removes his hand and flings* EBEN *sideways full length on the grass, gasping and choking. With a cry,* ABBIE *kneels beside him, trying to take his head on her lap, but he pushes her away.* CABOT *stands looking down with fierce triumph.*]: Ye needn't t've fret, Abbie, I wa'n't aimin' t' kill him. He hain't wuth hangin' fur—not by a hell of a sight! [*more and more triumphantly*] Seventy-six an' him not thirty yit—an' look whar he be fur thinkin' his Paw was easy! No, by God, I hain't easy! An' him upstairs, I'll raise him t' be like me! [*He turns to leave them.*] I'm goin' in an' dance!—sing an' celebrate! [*He walks to the porch—then turns with a great grin.*]

I don't calc'late it's left in him, but if he gits pesky, Abbie, ye jest sing out. I'll come a-runnin' an' by the Etarnal, I'll put him across my knee an' birch him! Ha-ha-ha! [*He goes into the house laughing. A moment later his loud* "whoop" *is heard.*]

ABBIE [*tenderly*]: Eben. Air ye hurt? [*She tries to kiss him, but he pushes her violently away and struggles to a sitting position.*]

EBEN [*gaspingly*]: T' hell—with ye.

ABBIE [*not believing her ears*]: It's me, Eben—Abbie—don't ye know me?

EBEN [*glowering at her with hatred*]: Ay-eh—I know ye—now! [*He suddenly breaks down, sobbing weakly.*]

ABBIE [*fearfully*]: Eben—what's happened t' ye—why did ye look at me 's if ye hated me?

EBEN [*violently, between sobs and gasps*]: I do hate ye! Ye're a whore—a damn trickin' whore!

ABBIE [*shrinking back horrified*]: Eben! Ye don't know what ye're sayin'!

EBEN [*scrambling to his feet and following her—accusingly*]: Ye're nothin' but a stinkin' passel o' lies! Ye've been lyin' t' me every word ye spoke, day an' night, since we fust—done it. Ye've kept sayin' ye loved me. . . .

ABBIE [*frantically*]: I do love ye! [*She takes his hand, but he flings hers away.*]

EBEN [*unheeding*]: Ye've made a fool o' me—a sick, dumb fool—a-purpose! Ye've been on'y playin' yer sneakin', stealin' game all along—gittin' me t' lie with ye so's ye'd hev a son he'd think was his'n, an' makin' him promise he'd give ye the farm and let me eat dust, if ye did git him a son! [*staring at her with anguished, bewildered eyes*] They must be a devil livin' in ye! T'ain't human t' be as bad as that be!

ABBIE [*stunned—dully*]: He told yew . . . ?

EBEN: Hain't it true? It hain't no good in yew lyin'.

ABBIE [*pleadingly*]: Eben, listen—ye must listen—it was long ago—afore we done nothin'—yew was scornin' me—goin' t' see Min—when I was lovin' ye—an' I said it t' him t' git vengeance on ye!

EBEN [*unheedingly—with tortured passion*]: I wish ye was dead! I wish I was dead along with ye afore this come! [*ragingly*] But I'll git my vengeance too! I'll pray Maw t' come back t' help me—t' put her cuss on yew an' him!

ABBIE [*brokenly*]: Don't ye, Eben! Don't ye! [*She throws herself on her knees before him, weeping.*] I didn't mean t' do bad t' ye! Fergive me, won't ye?

EBEN [*not seeming to hear her—fiercely*]: I'll git squar' with the old skunk—an' yew! I'll tell him the truth 'bout the son he's so proud o'! Then I'll leave ye here t' pizen each other—with Maw comin' out o' her grave at nights—an' I'll go t' the gold fields o' Californi-a whar Sim an' Peter be!

ABBIE [*terrified*]: Ye won't—leave me? Ye can't!

EBEN [*with fierce determination*]: I'm a-goin', I tell ye! I'll git rich thar an' come back an' fight him fur the farm he stole—an' I'll kick ye both out in the road—t' beg an' sleep in the woods—an' yer son along with ye—t' starve an' die! [*He is hysterical at the end.*]

ABBIE [*with a shudder—humbly*]: He's yewr son, too, Eben.

EBEN [*torturedly*]: I wish he never was born! I wish he'd die this minit! I wish I'd never sot eyes on him! It's him—yew havin' him—a-purpose t' steal—that's changed everythin'!

ABBIE [*gently*]: Did ye believe I loved ye—afore he come?

EBEN: Ay-eh—like a dumb ox!

ABBIE: An' ye don't believe no more?

EBEN: B'lieve a lyin' thief! Ha!

ABBIE [*shudders—then humbly*]: An' did yer r'ally love me afore?

EBEN [*brokenly*]: Ay-eh—an' ye was trickin' me!

ABBIE: An' ye don't love me now!

EBEN [*violently*]: I hate ye, I tell ye!

ABBIE: An' ye're truly goin' West—goin' t' leave me—all account o' him being born?

EBEN: I'm a-goin' in the mornin'—or may God strike me t' hell!

ABBIE [*after a pause—with a dreadful cold intensity—slowly*]: If that's what his comin's done t' me—killin' yewr love—takin' yew away—my on'y joy—the on'y joy I ever knowed—like heaven t' me—purtier'n heaven—then I hate him, too, even if I be his Maw!

EBEN [*brokenly*]: Lies! Ye love him! He'll steal the farm fur ye! [*brokenly*] But t'ain't the farm so much—not no more—it's yew foolin' me—gittin' me t' love ye—lyin' yew loved me—jest t' git a son t' steal!

ABBIE [*distractedly*]: He won't steal! I'd kill him fust! I do love ye! I'll prove t' ye . . . !

EBEN [*harshly*]: T'ain't no use lyin' no more. I'm deaf t' ye! [*He turns away.*] I hain't seein' ye agen. Good-by!

ABBIE [*pale with anguish*]: Hain't ye even goin' t' kiss me—not once—arter all we loved?

EBEN [*in a hard voice*]: I hain't wantin' t' kiss ye never agen! I'm wantin' t' forgit I ever sot eyes on ye!

ABBIE: Eben!—ye mustn't—wait a spell—I want t' tell ye. . .

EBEN: I'm a-goin' in t' git drunk. I'm a-goin' t' dance.

ABBIE [*clinging to his arm—with passionate earnestness*]: If I could make it—'s if he'd never come up between us—if I could prove t' ye I wa'n't schemin' t' steal from ye—so's everythin' could be jest the same with us, lovin' each other jest the same, kissin' an' happy the same's we've been happy afore he come—if I could do it—ye'd love me agen, wouldn't ye? Ye'd kiss me agen? Ye wouldn't never leave me, would ye?

EBEN [*moved*]: I calc'late not. [*then shaking her hand off his arm—with a bitter smile*] But ye hain't God, be ye?

ABBIE [*exultantly*]: Remember ye've promised! [*then with strange intensity*] Mebbe I kin take back one thin' God does!

EBEN [*peering at her*]: Ye're gittin' cracked, hain't ye? [*then going towards door*] I'm a-goin' t' dance.

ABBIE [*calls after him intensely*]: I'll prove t' ye! I'll prove I love ye better'n . . . [*He goes in the door, not seeming to hear. She remains standing where she is, looking after him—then she finishes desperately*] Better'n everythin' else in the world!

Scene 3

Just before dawn in the morning—shows the kitchen and CABOT*'s bedroom. In the kitchen, by the light of a tallow candle on the table,* EBEN *is sitting, his chin propped on his hands, his drawn face blank and expressionless. His carpet-bag is on the floor beside him. In the bedroom, dimly lighted by a small whale-oil lamp,* CABOT *lies asleep.* ABBIE *is bending over the cradle, listening, her face full of terror yet with an undercurrent of desperate triumph. Suddenly, she breaks down and sobs, appears about to throw herself on her knees beside the cradle; but the old man turns restlessly, groaning in his sleep, and she controls herself, and, shrinking away from the cradle with a gesture of horror, backs swiftly toward the door in rear and goes out. A moment later she comes into the kitchen and, running to* EBEN*, flings her arms about his neck and kisses him wildly. He hardens himself, he remains unmoved and cold, he keeps his eyes straight ahead.*

ABBIE [*hysterically*]: I done it, Eben! I told ye I'd do it! I've proved I love ye—better'n everythin'—so's ye can't never doubt me no more!

EBEN [*dully*]: Whatever ye done, it hain't no good now.

ABBIE [*wildly*]: Don't ye say that! Kiss me, Eben, won't ye? I need ye t' kiss me arter what I done! I need ye t' say ye love me!

EBEN [*kisses her without emotion—dully*]: That's fur good-by. I'm a-goin' soon.

ABBIE: No! No! Ye won't go—not now!

EBEN [*going on with his own thoughts*]: I been a-thinkin'—an' I hain't goin' t' tell Paw nothin'. I'll leave Maw t' take vengeance on ye. If I told him, the old skunk'd jest be stinkin' mean enuf to take it out on that baby. [*his voice showing emotion in spite of him*] An' I don't want nothin' bad t' happen t' him. He hain't t' blame fur yew. [*He adds with a certain queer pride*] An' he looks like me! An' by God, he's mine! An' some day I'll be a-comin' back an' . . . !

ABBIE [*too absorbed in her own thoughts to listen to him—pleadingly*]: They's no cause fur ye t' go now—they's no sense—it's all the same's it was—they's nothin' come b'tween us now—arter what I done!

EBEN [*Something in her voice arouses him. He stares at her a bit frightenedly.*]: Ye look mad, Abbie. What did ye do?

ABBIE: I—I killed him, Eben.

EBEN [*amazed*]: Ye killed him?

ABBIE [*dully*]: Ay-eh.

EBEN [*recovering from his astonishment—savagely*]: An' serves him right! But we got t' do somethin' quick t' make it look s'if the old skunk'd killed himself when he was drunk. We kin prove by 'em all how drunk he got.

ABBIE [*wildly*]: No! No! Not him! [*laughing distractedly*] But that's what I ought t' done, hain't it? I oughter killed him instead! Why didn't ye tell me?

EBEN [*appalled*]: Instead? What d'ye mean?

ABBIE: Not him.

EBEN [*his face grown ghastly*]: Not—not that baby!

ABBIE [*dully*]: Ay-eh!

EBEN [*falls to his knees as if he'd been struck—his voice trembling with horror*]: Oh, God A'mighty! A'mighty God! Maw, whar was ye, why didn't ye stop her?

ABBIE [*simply*]: She went back t' her grave that night we fust done it, remember? I hain't felt her about since. [*A pause.* EBEN *hides his head in his hands, trembling all over as if he had the ague. She goes on dully.*] I left the piller over his little face. Then he killed himself. He stopped breathin'. [*She begins to weep softly.*]

EBEN [*rage beginning to mingle with grief*]: He looked like me. He was mine, damn ye!

ABBIE [*slowly and brokenly*]: I didn't want t' do it. I hated myself fur doin' it. I loved him. He was so purty—dead spit 'n' image o' yew. But I loved yew more—an' yew was goin' away—far off whar I'd never see ye agen, never kiss ye, never feel ye pressed agin me agen—an' ye said ye hated me fur havin' him—ye said ye hated him an' wished he was dead—ye said if it hadn't been fur him comin' it'd be the same's afore between us.

EBEN [*unable to endure this, springs to his feet in a fury, threatening her, his twitching fingers seeming to reach out for her throat*]: Ye lie! I never said—I never dreamed ye'd—I'd cut off my head afore I'd hurt his finger!

ABBIE [*piteously, sinking on her knees*]: Eben, don't ye look at me like that—hatin' me—not after what I done fur ye—fur us—so's we could be happy agen—

EBEN [*furiously now*]: Shut up, or I'll kill ye! I see yer game now—the same old sneakin' trick—ye're aimin' t' blame me fur the murder ye done!

ABBIE [*moaning—putting her hands over her ears*]: Don't ye, Eben! Don't ye! [*She grasps his legs.*]

EBEN [*his mood suddenly changing to horror, shrinks away from her*]: Don't ye tech me! Ye're pizen! How could ye—t' murder a pore little critter—Ye must've swapped yer soul t' hell! [*suddenly raging*] Ha! I kin see why ye done it! Not the lies ye jest told—but 'cause ye wanted t' steal agen—steal the last thin' ye'd left me—my part o' him—no, the hull o' him—ye saw he looked like me—ye knowed he was all mine—an' ye couldn't b'ar it—I know ye! Ye killed him fur bein' mine! [*All this has driven him almost insane. He makes a rush past her for the door—then turns—shaking both fists at her, violently*] But I'll take vengeance now! I'll git the Sheriff! I'll tell him everythin'! Then I'll sing "I'm off to Californi-a!" an' go—gold—Golden Gate—gold sun—fields o' gold in the West! [*This last he half shouts, half croons incoherently, suddenly breaking off passionately.*] I'm a-goin' fur the Sheriff t' come an' git ye! I want ye tuk away, locked up from me! I can't stand t' luk at ye! Murderer an' thief 'r not, ye still tempt me! I'll give ye up t' the Sheriff! [*He turns and runs out, around the corner of house, panting and sobbing, and breaks into a swerving sprint down the road.*]

ABBIE [*struggling to her feet, runs to the door, calling after him*]: I love ye, Eben! I love ye! [*She stops at the door weakly, swaying, about to fall.*] I don't care what ye do—if ye'll on'y love me agen! [*She falls limply to the floor in a faint.*]

Scene 4

About an hour later. Same as Scene 3. Shows the kitchen and CABOT*'s bedroom. It is after dawn. The sky is brilliant with the sunrise. In the kitchen,* ABBIE *sits at the table, her body limp and exhausted, her head bowed down over her arms, her face hidden. Upstairs,* CABOT *is still asleep but awakens with a start. He looks toward the window and gives a snort of surprise and irritation—throws back the covers and begins hurriedly pulling on his clothes. Without looking behind him, he begins talking to* ABBIE*, whom he supposes beside him.*

CABOT: Thunder 'n' lightnin', Abbie! I hain't slept this late in fifty year! Looks 's if the sun was full riz a'most. Must've been the dancin' an' likker. Must be gittin' old. I hope Eben's t' wuk. Ye might've tuk the trouble t' rouse me, Abbie. [*He turns—sees no one there—surprised*] Waal—whar air she? Gittin' vittles, I calc'late. [*He tiptoes to the cradle and peers down—proudly*] Mornin', sonny. Purty's a picter! Sleepin' sound. He don't beller all night like most o' 'em. [*He goes quietly out the door in rear—a few moments later enters kitchen—sees* ABBIE*—with satisfaction*] So thar ye be. Ye got any vittles cooked?

ABBIE [*without moving*]: No.

CABOT [*coming to her, almost sympathetically*]: Ye feelin' sick?

ABBIE: No.

CABOT [*pats her on shoulder. She shudders.*]: Ye'd best lie down a spell. [*half jocularly*] Yer son'll be needin' ye soon. He'd ought t' wake up with a gnashin' appetite, the sound way he's sleepin.'

ABBIE [*shudders—then in a dead voice*]: He hain't never goin' t' wake up.

CABOT [*jokingly*]: Takes after me this mornin'. I hain't slept so late in . . .

ABBIE: He's dead.

CABOT [*stares at her—bewilderedly*]: What . . .

ABBIE: I killed him.

CABOT [*stepping back from her—aghast*]: Air ye drunk—'r crazy—'r . . . !

ABBIE [*suddenly lifts her head and turns on him—wildly*]: I killed him, I tell ye! I smothered him. Go up an' see if ye don't b'lieve me! [CABOT *stares at her a second, then bolts out the rear door, can be heard bounding up the stairs, and rushes into the bedroom and over to the cradle.* ABBIE *has sunk back lifelessly into her former position.* CABOT *puts his hand down on the body in the crib. An expression of fear and horror comes over his face.*]

CABOT [*shrinking away—trembling*]: God A'mighty! God A'mighty. [*He stumbles out the door—in a short while returns to the kitchen—comes to* ABBIE*, the stunned expression still on his face—hoarsely*] Why did ye do it? Why? [*As she doesn't answer, he grabs her violently by the shoulder and shakes her.*] I ax ye why ye done it! Ye'd better tell me 'r . . . !

ABBIE [*gives him a furious push which sends him staggering back and springs to her feet—with wild rage and hatred*]: Don't ye dare tech me! What right hev ye t' question me 'bout him? He wa'n't yewr son! Think I'd have a son by yew? I'd die fust! I hate the sight o' ye an' allus did! It's yew I should've murdered, if I'd had good sense! I hate ye! I love Eben. I did from the fust. An' he was Eben's son—mine an' Eben's—not your'n!

CABOT [*stands looking at her dazedly—a pause—finding his words with an effort—dully*]: That was it—what I felt—pokin' 'round the corners—while ye lied—holdin' yerself from me—sayin' ye'd a'ready conceived— [*He lapses into crushed silence—then with a strange emotion*] He's dead, sart'n. I felt his heart. Pore little critter! [*He blinks back one tear, wiping his sleeve across his nose.*]

ABBIE [*hysterically*]: Don't ye! Don't ye! [*She sobs unrestrainedly.*]

CABOT [*with a concentrated effort that stiffens his body into a rigid line and hardens his face into a stony mask—through his teeth to himself*]: I got t' be—like a stone—a rock o' jedgment! [*A pause. He gets complete control over himself—harshly*] If he was Eben's, I be glad he air gone! An' mebbe I suspicioned it all along. I felt they was somethin' onnateral—somewhars—the house got so lonesome—an' cold—drivin' me down t' the barn—t' the beasts o' the field. . . . Ay-eh. I must've suspicioned—somethin'. Ye didn't fool me—not altogether, leastways—I'm too old a bird—growin' ripe on the bough. . . . [*He becomes aware he is wandering, straightens again, looks at* ABBIE *with a cruel grin.*] So ye'd liked t' hev murdered me 'stead o' him, would ye? Waal, I'll live to a hundred! I'll live t' see ye hung! I'll deliver ye up t' the jedgment o' God an' the law! I'll git the Sheriff now. [*starts for the door*]

ABBIE [*dully*]: Ye needn't. Eben's gone fur him.

CABOT [*amazed*]: Eben—gone fur the Sheriff?

ABBIE: Ay-eh.

CABOT: T' inform agen ye?

ABBIE: Ay-eh.

CABOT [*considers this—a pause—then in a hard voice*]: Waal, I'm thankful fur him savin' me the trouble. I'll git t' wuk. [*He goes to the door—then turns—in a voice full of strange emotion*] He'd ought t' been my son, Abbie. Ye'd ought t' loved me. I'm a man. If ye'd loved me, I'd never told no Sheriff on ye no matter what ye did, if they was t' brile me alive!

ABBIE [*defensively*]: They's more to it nor yew know, makes him tell.

CABOT [*dryly*]: Fur yewr sake, I hope they be. [*He goes out—comes around to the gate—stares up at the sky. His control relaxes. For a moment he is old and weary. He murmurs despairingly*] God A'mighty, I be lonesomer'n ever! [*He hears running footsteps from the left, immediately is himself again.* EBEN *runs in, panting exhaustedly, wild-eyed and mad looking. He lurches through the gate.* CABOT *grabs him by the shoulder.* EBEN *stares at him dumbly.*] Did ye tell the Sheriff?

EBEN [*nodding stupidly*]: Ay-eh.

CABOT [*gives him a push away that sends him sprawling—laughing with withering contempt*]: Good fur ye! A prime chip o' yer Maw ye be! [*He goes toward the barn, laughing harshly.* EBEN *scrambles to his feet. Suddenly* CABOT *turns—grimly threatening*] Git off this farm when the Sheriff takes her—or, by God, he'll have t' come back an' git me fur murder, too! [*He stalks off.* EBEN *does not appear to have heard him. He runs to the door and comes into the kitchen.* ABBIE *looks up with a cry of anguished joy.* EBEN *stumbles over and throws himself on his knees beside her—sobbing brokenly*]

EBEN: Fergive me!

ABBIE [*happily*]: Eben! [*She kissed him and pulls his head over against her breast.*]

EBEN: I love ye! Fergive me!

ABBIE [*ecstatically*]: I'd fergive ye all the sins in hell fur saying' that! [*She kisses his head, pressing it to her with a fierce passion of possession.*]

EBEN [*brokenly*]: But I told the Sheriff. He's comin' fur ye!

ABBIE: I kin b'ar what happens t' me—now!

EBEN: I woke him up. I told him. He says, wait till I git dressed. I was waiting. I got to thinkin' o' yew. I got to thinkin' how I'd loved ye. It hurt like somethin' was bustin' in my chest an' head. I got t' cryin'. I knowed sudden I loved ye yet, an' allus would love ye!

ABBIE [*caressing his hair—tenderly*]: My boy, hain't ye?

EBEN: I begun t' run back. I cut across the fields an' through the woods. I though ye might have time t' run away—with me—an'. . . .

ABBIE [*shaking her head*]: I got t' take my punishment—t' pay fur my sin.

EBEN: Then I want t' share it with ye.

ABBIE: Ye didn't do nothin'.

EBEN: I put it in yer head. I wisht he was dead! I as much as urged ye t' do it!

ABBIE: No. It was me alone!

EBEN: I'm as guilty as yew be! He was the child o' our sin.

ABBIE [*lifting her head as if defying God*]: I don't repent that sin! I hain't askin' God t' fergive that!

EBEN: Nor me—but it led up t' the other—an' the murder ye did, ye did 'count o' me—an' it's my murder, too, I'll tell the Sheriff—an' if ye deny it, I'll say we planned it t'gether—an' they'll all b'lieve me, fur they suspicion everythin' we've done, an' it'll seem likely an' true to 'em. An' it is true—way down. I did help ye—somehow.

ABBIE [*laying her head on his—sobbing*]: No! I don't want yew t' suffer!

EBEN: I got t' pay fur my part o' the sin! An' I'd suffer wuss leavin' ye, goin' West, thinkin' o' ye day an' night, bein' out when yew was in— [*lowering his voice*] 'R bein' alive when yew was dead. [*a pause*] I want t' share with ye, Abbie—prison 'r death 'r hell 'r anythin'! [*He looks into her eyes and forces a trembling smile.*] If I'm sharin' with ye, I won't feel lonesome, leastways.

ABBIE [*weakly*]: Eben! I won't let ye! I can't let ye!

EBEN [*kissing her—tenderly*]: Ye can't he'p yerself. I got ye beat fur once!

ABBIE [*forcing a smile—adoringly*]: I hain't beat—s'long's I got ye!

EBEN [*hears the sound of feet outside*]: Ssshh! Listen! They've come t' take us!

ABBIE: No, it's him. Don't give him no chance to fight ye, Eben. Don't say nothin'—no matter what he says. An' I won't, neither. [*It is* CABOT. *He comes up from the barn in a great state of excitement and strides into the house and then into the kitchen.* EBEN *is kneeling beside* ABBIE, *his arm around her, hers around him. They stare straight ahead.*]

CABOT [*stares at them, his face hard. A long pause—vindictively*]: Ye make a slick pair o' murderin' turtle doves! Ye'd ought t' be both hung on the same limb an' left thar t' swing in the breeze an' rot—a warnin' t' old fools like me t' b'ar their lonesomeness alone—an' fur young fools like ye t' hobble their lust. [*A pause. The excitement returns to his face, his eyes snap, he looks a bit crazy.*] I couldn't work today. I couldn't take no interest. T' hell with the farm. I'm leavin' it! I've turned the cows an' other stock loose. I've druv 'em into the woods whar they kin be free! By freein' 'em, I'm freein' myself! I'm quittin' here today! I'll set fire t' house an' barn an' watch 'em burn, an' I'll leave yer Maw t' haunt the ashes, an' I'll will the fields back t' God, so that nothin' human kin never touch 'em! I'll be a-goin' to Californi-a—t' jine Simeon an' Peter—true sons o' mine if they be dumb fools—an' the Cabots'll find Solomon's Mines t'gether! [*He suddenly cuts a mad caper.*] Whoop! What was the song they sung? "Oh, Californi-a! That's the land fur me." [*He sings this—then gets on his knees by the floorboard under which the money was hid.*] An' I'll sail thar on one o' the finest clippers I kin find! I've got the money! Pity ye didn't know whar this was hidden so's ye could steal . . . [*He has pulled up the board. He stares—feels—stares again. A pause of dead silence. He slowly turns, slumping into a sitting position on the floor, his eyes like those of a dead fish, his face the sickly green of an attack of nausea. He swallows painfully several times—forces a weak smile at last.*] So—ye did steal it!

EBEN [*emotionlessly*]: I swapped it t' Sim an' Peter fur their share o' the farm—t' pay their passage t' Californi-a.

CABOT [*with one sardonic*]: Ha! [*He begins to recover. Gets slowly to his feet—strangely*] I calc'late God give it to 'em—not yew! God's hard, not easy! Mebbe they's easy gold in the West, but it hain't God's gold. It hain't fur me. I kin hear His voice warnin' me agen t' be hard an' stay on my farm. I kin see His hand usin' Eben t' steal t' keep me from weakness. I kin feel I be in the palm o' His hand, His fingers guidin' me. [*A pause—then he mutters sadly*] It's a-goin' t' be lonesomer now than ever it war afore—an' I'm gittin' old, Lord—ripe on the bough. . . . [*then stiffening*] Waal—what d'ye want? God's lonesome, hain't He? God's hard an' lonesome! [*A pause. The sheriff with two men comes up the road from the left. They move cautiously to the door. The sheriff knocks on it with the butt of his pistol.*]

SHERIFF: Open in the name o' the law! [*They start.*]

CABOT: They've come fur ye. [*He goes to the rear door.*] Come in, Jim! [*The three men enter.* CABOT *meets them in doorway.*] Jest a minit, Jim. I got 'em safe here. [*The* SHERIFF *nods. He and his companions remain in the doorway.*]

EBEN [*suddenly calls*]: I lied this mornin', Jim. I helped her do it. Ye kin take me, too.

ABBIE [*brokenly*]: No!

CABOT: Take 'em both. [*He comes forward—stares at* EBEN *with a trace of grudging admiration.*] Purty good—fur yew! Waal, I got t' round up the stock. Good-by.

EBEN: Good-by.

ABBIE: Good-by. [CABOT *turns and strides past the men—comes out and around the corner of the house, his shoulders squared, his face stony, and stalks grimly toward the barn. In the meantime the* SHERIFF *and men have come into the room.*]

SHERIFF [*embarrassedly*]: Waal—we'd best start.

ABBIE: Wait [*turns to* EBEN] I love ye, Eben.

EBEN: I love ye, Abbie. [*They kiss. The three men grin and shuffle embarrassedly.* EBEN *takes* ABBIE'S *hand. They go out the door in rear, the men following, and come from the house, walking hand in hand to the gate.* EBEN *stops there and points to the sunrise sky.*] Sun's a-rizin'. Purty, hain't it?

ABBIE: Ay-eh. [*They both stand for a moment looking up raptly in attitudes strangely aloof and devout.*]

SHERIFF [*looking around at the farm enviously—to his companion*]: It's a jim-dandy farm, no denyin'. Wished I owned it!

THE CURTAIN FALLS

THORNTON WILDER

Thornton Wilder (1897–1975) was born in Madison, Wisconsin, but his family moved about due to his father's appointments as the American Consul in Hong Kong and Shanghai (1906–1911). Before he was eighteen, Wilder had crossed the Pacific Ocean four times. As might be expected, Wilder's education was eclectic: He attended Hong Kong schools, public school in Berkeley, California, and an Anglican mission school four hundred miles from Shanghai. Wilder first attended Oberlin College, but for his junior year, his father insisted that he transfer to Yale University, where he graduated in 1920. For a year he studied archeology in Rome, and it was there that he began to write his first novel, *The Cabala*, which was not completed until 1926.

Wilder's father, Amos, held a Ph.D. from Yale University in political science, worked as a professional journalist, and was a newspaper owner. His mother, Isabella Niven Thornton, was brilliant, but she was denied the chance to attend Barnard College because her father did not believe in the education of women. She was the most important woman in Wilder's life, and at twenty he wrote her an admiring letter proposing marriage. Wilder never married, and he conducted his personal life so discreetly that he seems never to have had any romantic attachments to either women or men.

Though the Wilder family suffered from the dislocation of foreign travel and the conflicts of a cold marriage, Thornton remained on good terms with his mother and father. He was always close with his siblings, Amos, Janet, and especially Isabel, who also never married and who gave up her own writing career to serve as her brother's executive administrator. The strength and responsibility of family bondings are a prominent theme in Wilder's writing, as is a strong commitment to Christian morality, imbued by his family's Protestant Congregationalism.

When Wilder revealed an inclination to become a writer, his father called him home from Rome, where he was studying architecture, and coerced him into becoming a teacher. Wilder obeyed but also kept on developing his skills as a writer. While teaching at Lawrenceville, a smart prep school in New Jersey, Wilder made his literary debut with *Cabala* (1926), a novel that describes the decline of a family of Italian nobles before the start World War I, and with *The Trumpet Shall Sound* (also 1926), a play inspired by Ben Jonson's *The Alchemist* (1610). Neither was successful. However, the following year his novel *The Bridge of San Luis Rey* was a best-seller and won the Pulitzer Prize for Literature for 1927. The novel's story concerns a group of Peruvian travelers who spend the night at an inn before crossing the bridge at San Luis Rey, on their way to Lima. Each of the novel's five travelers are about to come to terms with his or her own suffering when they begin to cross the bridge the next morning. As they cross the bridge, noted as the strongest bridge in all of Peru, it fails and the travelers perish. Despite the prospect of tragedy in *The Bridge of San Luis Rey*, Wilder seems to say that people have to act on principle and live with the expectation of a future. The inexorability of fate is one of Wilder's favorite themes, and he repeated it in variation, especially in *Our Town* and *The Skin of Our Teeth.*

In 1930 Wilder published *The Woman of Andros,* inspired by *Andria, the Maid of Andros,* by the Roman playwright Terence (185?–159 B.C.). Originally a farce, Wilder's version is a serious and sentimental story about how to accept one's fate and celebrate life despite its sorrows. A later novel, *Heaven Is My Destination* (1935), is a send-up of a traveling bible salesman, George Brush, who tries to set right the wrongs of the world. When that fails, Brush takes the low road and behaves like an ordinary hypocrite. The novel's comic irony was not well received, and Wilder was criticized for being irreverent rather than satirical. Subsequent novels include *The Ides of March* (1948), a historical novel about the last months of Julius Caesar's life, culminating in his murder; *The Eighth Day* (1967), a story about lost faith and redemption that resembles John Bunyan's *Pilgrim's Progress;* and *Theosophilus North,* published when Wilder was eighty-six, a rambling series of stories about a man who would like to become a saint, but never quite manages to pull it off. It is generally acknowledged that the latter's intent was to sum up his life and that the character of North is Wilder's own.

As a playwright, Wilder was not immediately successful. After the poor showing of *Trumpets Shall Sound* in 1926, he published two collections of one-act plays, *The Angel That Troubled the Waters and Other Plays* (1928) and *The Long Christmas Dinner and Other Plays* (1931), but they were also failures. After that, Wilder concentrated on writing fiction and was eventually drawn back to the theater in 1937 at the urging of Jed Harris, a Broadway producer and friend from Yale. At Harris's request, Wilder adapted Henrik Ibsen's *A Doll's House* (1937), which had a modest New York run. This encouraged him, and in 1938 he completed the Pulitzer Prize–winning *Our Town,* which he was writing while doing the Ibsen adaptation.

After *Our Town,* Wilder finished *The Merchant of Yonkers* (1938). Though the title alludes to Shakespeare's *The Merchant of Venice* (1598), the play is really an adaptation of Molière's *The Miser* (1668). Horace Vandergelder, the title character, is a miserly businessman who exemplifies the work ethic and the search for the American dream. He is challenged by Dolly Gallagher Levi, a widow, a devotee of the carpe diem theme, who loves life and its pleasures. "Nature is never completely satisfactory and must be corrected," Dolly says. "Well, I'm with you artists. Life as it is is never quite interesting enough for me—I'm bored, Mr. Kemper, with life as it is—and so I do things. I put my hand in here, and I put my hand in there, and I watch and I listen—and often I'm very amused." Vandergelder wants a wife who will be a kind of employee, but he is taken in hand by Dolly, who transforms him. The idea was a good one, but the play failed. Wilder revised it, and it was successfully produced as *The Matchmaker* in 1954 and again, as a film, in 1958. When it was adapted as a musical by Jerry Herman and Michael Stewart, it achieved monumental success as *Hello Dolly!,* both in the theater (1963) and on film (1969).

The Skin of Our Teeth (1942), which won Wilder his third Pulitzer Prize, best shows the modernist influence of Gertrude Stein on Wilder's drama. The two met in 1934 when Wilder invited her to lecture at the University of Chicago, where he was teaching. Their friendship modernized his literary attitudes, and he admitted that before he met her, he was a slowpoke and a plodder who was still stuck in the literal 19th century. From Stein, Wilder learned that through deep observation and detachment, the simplicity and power of ordinary life could be used for serious art. "She assumes," Wilder wrote in the introduction to the published volume of her Chicago lecture, "that the attentive listener will bring, from a store of observation and reflection, the concrete illustration of her generalization."

The Skin of Our Teeth is an extended allegory of the fall from innocence in the Garden of Eden and the fate of modern humanity, then in the midst of World War II. The play is presented as a vaudeville, a technique Wilder felt complemented its quick shifts of setting, time, and action. The play links a series of sequences juxtaposed in time, taking place in Excelsior, New Jersey (beginning about 1940), and during the Ice Age, the Flood, and the aftermath of a devastating war. The play borrows liberally from elements of Bertolt Brecht's Epic Theater, using signs, screen projections, and practical scenery to foster Wilder's message that humanity can survive the greatest travails, particularly the suburban Antrobus family, who is meant to be a typical American middle-class family. The action ends in a mixture of conflicting sentiments. The younger generation suffers a moral degeneration: Henry Antrobus, the son, already the murderer of his brother, becomes a Fascist; Gladys, the daughter, is unwed and pregnant; and Lily Sabina, the family maid, becomes a selfish opportunist. Only the older generation, George and Mrs. Antrobus, more experienced and very tired, begin to put the world in order. Sabina ends the play by walking to the edge of apron and talking the audience: "You go home. The end of the play isn't written yet. Mr. and Mrs. Antrobus! Their heads are full of plans, and they're as confident as the first day they began—and they told me to tell you: good night."

The play has many subtle autobiographical elements in it, notably Wilder's definition of marriage, which might have derived from that of his parents: "I didn't marry you because you were perfect," says Mrs. Antrobus. "I didn't even marry you because I loved you. I married you because you gave me a promise. [*She takes off her ring and looks at it.*] That promise made up for your faults. Two imperfect people got married and it was the promise that made the marriage." Wilder acted the part of George Antrobus, which his friend Glenway Wescott thought showed that Wilder *was* Antrobus.

The Alcestiad (1955) is Wilder's Christian version of Euripides' *Alcestis* (438 B.C.), in which Alcestis offers to sacrifice herself in place of her husband, Ademetus. She ultimately finds her salvation with the god Apollo, whom she always wanted to serve. The character suggests Wilder's mother, and her devotion to Christian morality in the guise of Apollo.

Beginning in 1957, Wilder wrote a series of plays under the title *The Seven Deadly Sins*, of which *Bernice* (Pride), *The Wreck on the Five-Twenty-Five* (Sloth), and *Someone from Assisi* (Lust) were produced. In 1962, *Plays for Bleeker Street*, a series of short plays named after the street in Greenwich Village in which the theater was located, met with small success. *The Long Christmas Dinner* was produced in 1961 as an opera, with a libretto by Wilder and music by Paul Hindemith (1895–1963).

Our Town is Wilder's most successful play. It has been so ingrained in the American psyche that it was enshrined on a United States postage stamp in 1997. A sentimental evocation of an ideal small town in New England, the play recalls a vision of the past that never existed but that some feel *ought* to have existed. Critics of *Our Town* complained that the play portrayed a world that was unlike the United States, where problems of prejudice, poverty, social injustice, and labor unrest abound. Wilder rejoined that: "*Our Town* is not offered as a picture of life in a New Hampshire village; or as a speculation about the conditions of life after death (that element I took from Dante's *Purgatory*). It is an attempt to find value above all price for the smallest events in our daily life. I have made the claim as preposterous as possible, for I have set the village against the largest dimensions of time and place." *Our Town* owes much to Edgar Lee Masters's *Spoon River Anthology* (1915), which incorporates a series of biographies told by the residents of Spoon River from the cemetery in which they are buried. It also owes its brief scenic sequences to Gertrude Stein's notion of breaking down narrative into small units that have no beginning or ending.

Our Town focuses on the residents of Grover's Corners, New Hampshire, primarily the Gibbs and Webb families, as they live through a cycle of life, growth, and death over the course of fourteen years: Act I (May 7, 1901), Act II (July 7, 1904), Act III (February 7, 1899, and summer 1913). In Act III, Emily has died in childbirth in 1913, but she returns for one last visit to Grover's Corners. As she walks through her house on the day of her twelfth birthday in 1899, she realizes that the past may be viewed but not relived. Cognizant now of the utter separation of life and death, she returns to the underworld saying, "Good-by Good-by, world. Good-by Grover's Corners." It is a poignant moment during which a good soul is finally laid to rest.

Despite its elegiac tone and its preoccupation with death, *Our Town* strikes a chord of optimism in the face of the suffering of the Great Depression (1929–1939) and the peril of world war in Europe and Asia. This sense that "life abides" is typical of Wilder and evident as early as *The Bridge at San Luis Rey.*

The Greek influence on Wilder is present in *Our Town* in the character of the Stage Manager, who acts as a choragus, and in the characters of Professor Willard and Editor Webb, who function as if they are members of the chorus. The bare stage setting is a stylistic device that offsets the homespun ideal of Grover's Corners and the realistic portrayal of the characters. Despite this opposition of old and new, audiences find this play accessible because the characters and their style of language are so easily recognizable.

Wilder's use of modern techniques to tell stories that reinforce traditional social values has never met with universal acclaim. Critics have argued that he should have been more avant-garde or flamboyant. Tennessee Williams told the story of Wilder seeing a performance of *A Streetcar Named Desire* and complaining that a demure Southern woman like Stella could never marry a brute like Stanley Kowalski; this remark led Williams to dismiss Wilder as old-maidish and ignorant of the power of passion. Of course, Wilder's learning was deep, and he admitted that he wrote in the tradition of great literature, inspired by classical Greek drama and continental European literature. Yet, he also admired groundbreaking contemporaries like James Joyce and Gertrude

Stein, with whom he discussed co-authoring a novel. His wide range of literary interests is best seen in *American Characteristics* (1979), a collection of essays compiled after his death that, along with Arthur Miller's theater essays, constitutes perhaps the most important discussions of drama by an American playwright.

Wilder seems to have left relatively few dramatic heirs, although the plays of Wendy Wasserstein and Marsha Norman carry forward his sense of elegiac acceptance of fate in a harried world. Arthur Miller has used the omniscient Stage Manager for his tragedy *A View From the Bridge*. And Sam Shepard turned *Our Town* upsidedown in *Buried Child,* a vision of the Midwestern heartland of the United States in disarray and decrepitude.

In the film version of *Our Town,* Wilder agreed with the producer, Sol Lessser, that there ought to be a happy ending. "In the first place," Wilder wrote, "I think Emily should live. I've always thought so. In a movie you see people so *close* to that a different relation is established. In the theater they are halfway abstractions in an allegory; in the movie they are very concrete. So insofar as the play is a generalized allegory, she dies—we die—they die; insofar as it's a concrete happening it's not important that she die; it's even disproportionately cruel that she die."

Film

Our Town (1940), directed by Sam Wood, with Frank Craven, William Holden, Martha Scott, Faye Bainter, Guy Kibbee, and Thomas Mitchell. Musical score by Aaron Copland. Wilder received credit as screenwriter. Principal Artists.

Our Town (1977), directed by Franklin J. Schaffer (made for television), with Ned Beatty, Sada Thompson, Ronny Cox, Glynnis O'Connor, Robby Benson, Hal Holbrook, and John Houseman. Mastervision, Inc.

Our Town

CHARACTERS (in the order of their appearance)

STAGE MANAGER
DR. GIBBS
JOE CROWELL
HOWIE NEWSOME
MRS. GIBBS
MRS. WEBB
GEORGE GIBBS
REBECCA GIBBS
WALLY WEBB
EMILY WEBB
PROFESSOR WILLARD
MR. WEBB
WOMAN IN THE BALCONY
MAN IN THE AUDITORIUM
LADY IN THE BOX
SIMON STIMSON
MRS. SOAMES
CONSTABLE WARREN
SI CROWELL
THREE BASEBALL PLAYERS
SAM CRAIG
JOE STODDARD

The entire play takes place in Grover's Corners, New Hampshire.

ACT I

No curtain.

No scenery.

The audience, arriving, sees an empty stage in half-light.

Presently the STAGE MANAGER, *hat on and pipe in mouth, enters and begins placing a table and three chairs downstage left, and a table and three chairs downstage right. He also places a low bench at the corner of what will be the Webb house, left.*

"Left" and "right" are from the point of view of the actor facing the audience. "Up" is toward the back wall.

As the house lights go down he has finished setting the stage and leaning against the right proscenium pillar watches the late arrivals in the audience.

When the auditorium is in complete darkness he speaks:

STAGE MANAGER: This play is called "Our Town." It was written by Thornton Wilder; produced and directed by A. . . . (or: produced by A. . . . ; directed by B. . . . .). In it you will see Miss C. . . . ; Miss D. . . . ; Miss E. . . . ; and Mr. F. . . . ; Mr. G. . . . ; Mr. H. . . . ; and many others. The name of the town is Grover's Corners, New Hampshire—just across the Massachusetts line: latitude 42 degrees 40 minutes; longitude 70 degrees 37 minutes. The First Act shows a day in our town. The day is May 7, 1901. The time is just before dawn.

A rooster crows.

The sky is beginning to show some streaks of light over in the East there, behind our mount'in. The morning star always gets wonderful bright the minute before it has to go,—doesn't it?

He stares at it for a moment, then goes upstage.

Well, I'd better show you how our town lies. Up here—

That is: parallel with the back wall.

is Main Street. Way back there is the railway station; tracks go that way. Polish Town's across the tracks, and some Canuck families.

Toward the left.

Over there is the Congregational Church; across the street's the Presbyterian. Methodist and Unitarian are over there. Baptist is down in the holla' by the river. Catholic Church is over beyond the tracks. Here's the Town Hall and Post Office combined; jail's in the basement. Bryan once made a speech from these very steps here. Along here's a row of stores. Hitching posts and horse blocks in front of them. First automobile's going to come along in about five years—belonged to Banker Cartwright, our richest citizen . . . lives in the big white house up on the hill. Here's the grocery store and here's Mr. Morgan's drugstore. Most everybody in town manages to look into those two stores once a day. Public School's over yonder. High School's still farther over. Quarter of nine mornings, noontimes, and three o'clock afternoons, the hull town can hear the yelling and screaming from those schoolyards.

He approaches the table and chairs downstage right.

This is our doctor's house,—Doc Gibbs. This is the back door.

Two arched trellises, covered with vines and flowers, are pushed out, one by each proscenium pillar.

There's some scenery for those who think they have to have scenery. This is Mrs. Gibbs' garden. Corn . . . peas . . . beans . . . hollyhocks . . . heliotrope . . . and a lot of burdock.

Crosses the stage.

In those days our newspaper come out twice a week—the Grover's Corners *Sentinel*—and this is Editor Webb's house. And this is Mrs. Webb's garden. Just like Mrs. Gibbs', only it's got a lot of sunflowers, too.

He looks upward, center stage.

Right here . . . 's a big butternut tree.

He returns to his place by the right proscenium pillar and looks at the audience for a minute.

Nice town, y'know what I mean? Nobody very remarkable ever comes of it, s'far as we know. The earliest tombstones in the cemetery up there on the mountain say 1670–1680—they're Grovers and Cartwrights and Gibbses and Herseys—same names as are around here now.

Well, as I said: it's about dawn. The only lights on in town are in a cottage over by the tracks where a Polish mother's just had twins. And in the Joe Crowell house, where Joe Junior's getting up so as to deliver the paper. And in the depot, where Shorty Hawkins is gettin' ready to flag the 5:45 for Boston.

A train whistle is heard. The STAGE MANAGER *takes out his watch and nods.*

Naturally, out in the country—all around—there've been lights on for some time, what with milkin's and so on. But town people sleep late. So—another day's begun.

There's Doc Gibbs comin' down Main Street now, comin' back from that baby case. And here's his wife comin' downstairs to get breakfast.

MRS. GIBBS, *a plump, pleasant woman in the middle thirties, comes "downstairs" right. She pulls up an imaginary window shade in her kitchen and starts to make a fire in her stove.*

Elizabeth Hartman as Emily, Henry Fonda as the Stage Manager, and Harvey Evans as George in Our Town, *directed by Donald Driver, ANTA Theatre, 1969.*

Doc Gibbs died in 1930. The new hospital's named after him. Mrs. Gibbs died first—long time ago, in fact. She went out to visit her daughter, Rebecca, who married an insurance man in Canton, Ohio, and died there—pneumonia—but her body was brought back here. She's up in the cemetery there now—in with a whole mess of Gibbses and Herseys—she was Julia Hersey 'fore she married Doc Gibbs in the Congregational Church over there. In our town we like to know the facts about everybody.

There's Mrs. Webb, coming downstairs to get her breakfast, too.—That's Doc Gibbs. Got that call at half past one this morning. And there comes Joe Crowell, Jr., delivering Mr. Webb's *Sentinel.*

DR. GIBBS *has been coming along Main Street from the left. At the point where he would turn to approach his house, he stops, sets down his—imaginary—black bag, takes off his hat, and rubs his face with fatigue, using an enormous handkerchief.*

MRS. WEBB, *a thin, serious, crisp woman, has entered her kitchen, left, tying on an apron. She goes through the motions of putting wood into a stove, lighting it, and preparing breakfast.*

Suddenly, JOE CROWELL, JR., *eleven, starts down Main Street from the right, hurling imaginary newspapers into doorways.*

JOE CROWELL, JR.: Morning, Doc Gibbs.
DR. GIBBS: Morning, Joe.
JOE CROWELL, JR.: Somebody been sick, Doc?
DR. GIBBS: No. Just some twins born over in Polish Town.
JOE CROWELL, JR.: Do you want your paper now?
DR. GIBBS: Yes, I'll take it.—Anything serious goin' on in the world since Wednesday?
JOE CROWELL, JR.: Yessir. My schoolteacher, Miss Foster, 's getting married to a fella over in Concord.
DR. GIBBS: I declare.—How do you boys feel about that?
JOE CROWELL, JR.: Well, of course, it's none of my business—but I think if a person starts out to be a teacher, she ought to stay one.
DR. GIBBS: How's your knee, Joe?
JOE CROWELL, JR.: Fine, Doc, I never think about it at all. Only like you said, it always tells me when it's going to rain.
DR. GIBBS: What's it telling you today? Goin' to rain?
JOE CROWELL, JR.: No, sir.
DR. GIBBS: Sure?
JOE CROWELL, JR.: Yessir.
DR. GIBBS: Knee ever make a mistake?
JOE CROWELL, JR.: No, sir.

JOE *goes off.* DR. GIBBS *stands reading his paper.*

STAGE MANAGER: Want to tell you something about that boy Joe Crowell there. Joe was awful bright—graduated from high school here, head of his class. So he got a scholarship to Massachusetts Tech. Graduated head of his class there, too. It was all wrote up in the Boston paper at the time. Goin' to be a great engineer, Joe was. But the war broke out and he died in France.—All that education for nothing.
HOWIE NEWSOME [*Off left*]: Giddap, Bessie! What's the matter with you today?
STAGE MANAGER: Here comes Howie Newsome, deliverin' the milk.

HOWIE NEWSOME, *about thirty, in overalls, comes along Main Street from the left, walking beside an invisible horse and wagon and carrying an imaginary rack with milk bottles. The sound of clinking milk bottles is heard. He leaves some bottles at* MRS. WEBB*'s trellis, then, crossing the stage to* MRS. GIBBS'*, he stops center to talk to* DR. GIBBS.

HOWIE NEWSOME: Morning, Doc.
DR. GIBBS: Morning, Howie.
HOWIE NEWSOME: Somebody sick?
DR. GIBBS: Pair of twins over to Mrs. Goruslawski's.
HOWIE NEWSOME: Twins, eh? This town's gettin' bigger every year.
DR. GIBBS: Goin' to rain, Howie?
HOWIE NEWSOME: No, no. Fine day—that'll burn through. Come on, Bessie.
DR. GIBBS: Hello Bessie. [*He strokes the horse, which has remained up center.*] How old is she, Howie?
HOWIE NEWSOME: Going on seventeen. Bessie's all mixed up about the route ever since the Lockharts stopped takin' their quart of milk every day. She wants to leave 'em a quart just the same—keeps scolding me the hull trip.

He reaches MRS. GIBBS' *back door. She is waiting for him.*

MRS. GIBBS: Good morning, Howie.
HOWIE NEWSOME: Morning, Mrs. Gibbs. Doc's just comin' down the street.
MRS. GIBBS: Is he? Seems like you're late today.
HOWIE NEWSOME: Yes. Somep'n went wrong with the separator. Don't know what 'twas. [*He passes* DR. GIBBS *up center.*] Doc!
DR. GIBBS: Howie!
MRS. GIBBS [*Calling upstairs*]: Children! Children! Time to get up.
HOWIE NEWSOME: Come on, Bessie!

He goes off right.

MRS. GIBBS: George! Rebecca!

DR. GIBBS arrives at his back door and passes through the trellis into his house.

MRS. GIBBS: Everything all right, Frank?
DR. GIBBS: Yes. I declare—easy as kittens.
MRS. GIBBS: Bacon'll be ready in a minute. Set down and drink your coffee. You can catch a couple hours' sleep this morning, can't you?
DR. GIBBS: Hm! . . . Mrs. Wentworth's coming at eleven. Guess I know what's it's about, too. Her stummick ain't what it ought to be.
MRS. GIBBS: All told, you won't get more'n three hours' sleep. Frank Gibbs, I don't know what's goin' to become of you. I do wish I could get you to go away someplace and take a rest. I think it would do you good.
MRS. WEBB: Emileeee! Time to get up! Wally! Seven o'clock!
MRS. GIBBS: I declare, you got to speak to George. Seems like something's come over him lately. He's no help to me at all. I can't even get him to cut me some wood.
DR. GIBBS [*Washing and drying his hands at the sink. MRS. GIBBS is busy at the stove*]: Is he sassy to you?
MRS. GIBBS: No. He just whines! All he thinks about is that baseball—George! Rebecca! You'll be late for school.
DR. GIBBS: M-m-m . . .
MRS. GIBBS: George!
DR. GIBBS: George, look sharp!
GEORGE'S VOICE: Yes, Pa!
DR. GIBBS [*As he goes off the stage*]: Don't you hear your mother calling you? I guess I'll go upstairs and get forty winks.
MRS. WEBB: Walleee! Emileee! You'll be late for school! Walleee! You wash yourself good or I'll come up and do it myself.
REBECCA GIBBS' VOICE: Ma! What dress shall I wear?
MRS. GIBBS: Don't make a noise. Your father's been out all night and needs his sleep. I washed and ironed the blue gingham for you special.
REBECCA: Ma, I hate that dress.
MRS. GIBBS: Oh, hush-up-with-you.
REBECCA: Every day I go to school dressed like a sick turkey.
MRS. GIBBS: Now, Rebecca, you always look *very* nice.
REBECCA: Mama, George's throwing soap at me.
MRS. GIBBS: I'll come and slap the both of you,—that's what I'll do.

A factory whistle sounds. The CHILDREN dash in and take their places at the tables. Right, GEORGE, about sixteen, and REBECCA, eleven. Left, EMILY and WALLY, same ages. They carry strapped schoolbooks.

STAGE MANAGER: We've got a factory in our town too—hear it? Makes blankets. Cartwrights own it and it brung 'em a fortune.
MRS. WEBB: Children! Now I won't have it. Breakfast is just as good as any other meal and I won't have you gobbling like wolves. It'll stunt your growth,—that's a fact. Put away your book, Wally.
WALLY: Aw, Ma! By ten o'clock I got to know all about Canada.
MRS. WEBB: You know the rule's well as I do—no books at table. As for me, I'd rather have my children healthy than bright.
EMILY: I'm both, Mama: you know I am. I'm the brightest girl in school for my age. I have a wonderful memory.
MRS. WEBB: Eat your breakfast.
WALLY: I'm bright, too, when I'm looking at my stamp collection.
MRS. GIBBS: I'll speak to your father about it when he's rested. Seems to me twenty-five cents a week's enough for a boy your age. I declare I don't know how you spend it all.
GEORGE: Aw, Ma,—I gotta lotta things to buy.
MRS. GIBBS: Strawberry phosphates—that's what you spend it on.
GEORGE: I don't see how Rebecca comes to have so much money. She has more'n a dollar.
REBECCA [*Spoon in mouth, dreamily*]: I've been saving it up gradual.
MRS. GIBBS: Well, dear, I think it's a good thing to spend some every now and then.
REBECCA: Mama, do you know what I love most in the world—do you?—Money.
MRS. GIBBS: Eat your breakfast.
THE CHILDREN: Mama, there's first bell.—I gotta hurry.—I don't want any more.—I gotta hurry.

The CHILDREN rise, seize their books and dash out through the trellises. They meet, down center, and chattering, walk to Main Street, then turn left.

The STAGE MANAGER goes off, unobtrusively, right.

MRS. WEBB: Walk fast, but you don't have to run. Wally, pull up your pants at the knee. Stand up straight, Emily.
MRS. GIBBS: Tell Miss Foster I send her my best congratulations—can you remember that?
REBECCA: Yes, Ma.
MRS. GIBBS: You look real nice, Rebecca. Pick up your feet.
ALL: Good-by.

MRS. GIBBS *fills her apron with food for the chickens and comes down to the footlights.*

MRS. GIBBS: Here, chick, chick, chick. No, go away, you. Go away. Here, chick, chick, chick. What's the matter with *you*? Fight, fight, fight,—that's all you do. Hm . . . *you* don't belong to me. Where'd you come from? [*She shakes her apron.*] Oh, don't be so scared. Nobody's going to hurt you.

MRS. WEBB *is sitting on the bench by her trellis, stringing beans.*

Good morning, Myrtle. How's your cold?

MRS. WEBB: Well, I still get that tickling feeling in my throat. I told Charles I didn't know as I'd go to choir practice tonight. Wouldn't be any use.

MRS. GIBBS: Have you tried singing over your voice?

MRS. WEBB: Yes, but somehow I can't do that and stay on the key. While I'm resting myself I thought I'd string some of these beans.

MRS. GIBBS [*Rolling up her sleeves as she crosses the stage for a chat*]: Let me help you. Beans have been good this year.

MRS. WEBB: I've decided to put up forty quarts if it kills me. The children say they hate 'em, but I notice they're able to get 'em down all winter.

Pause. Brief sound of chickens cackling.

MRS. GIBBS: Now, Myrtle. I've got to tell you something, because if I don't tell somebody I'll burst.

MRS. WEBB: Why, Julia Gibbs!

MRS. GIBBS: Here, give me some more of those beans. Myrtle, did one of those secondhand-furniture men from Boston come to see you last Friday?

MRS. WEBB: No-o.

MRS. GIBBS: Well, he called on me. First I thought he was a patient wantin' to see Dr. Gibbs. 'N he wormed his way into my parlor, and, Myrtle Webb, he offered me three hundred and fifty dollars for Grandmother Wentworth's highboy, as I'm sitting here!

MRS. WEBB: Why, Julia Gibbs!

MRS. GIBBS: He did! That old thing! Why, it was so big I didn't know where to put it and I almost give it to Cousin Hester Wilcox.

MRS. WEBB: Well, you're going to take it, aren't you?

MRS. GIBBS: I don't know.

MRS. WEBB: You don't know—three hundred and fifty dollars! What's come over you?

MRS. GIBBS: Well, if I could get the Doctor to take the money and go away someplace on a real trip, I'd sell it like that.—Y'know, Myrtle, it's been the dream of my life to see Paris, France.—Oh, I don't know. It sounds crazy, I suppose, but for years I've been promising myself that if we ever had the chance—

MRS. WEBB: How does the doctor feel about it?

MRS. GIBBS: Well, I did beat about the bush a little and said that if I got a legacy—that's the way I put it—I'd make him take me somewhere.

MRS. WEBB: M-m-m . . . What did he say?

MRS. GIBBS: You know how he is. I haven't heard a serious word out of him since I've known him. No, he said, it might make him discontented with Grover's Corners to go traipsin' about Europe; better let well enough alone, he says. Every two years he makes a trip to the battlefields of the Civil War and that's enough treat for anybody, he says.

MRS. WEBB: Well, Mr. Webb just *admires* the way Dr. Gibbs knows everything about the Civil War. Mr. Webb's a good mind to give up Napoleon and move over to the Civil War, only Dr. Gibbs being one of the greatest experts in the country just makes him despair.

MRS. GIBBS: It's a fact! Dr. Gibbs is never so happy as when he's at Antietam or Gettysburg. The times I've walked over those hills, Myrtle, stopping at every bush and pacing it all out, like we were going to buy it.

MRS. WEBB: Well, if that secondhand man's really serious about buyin' it, Julia, you sell it. And then you'll get to see Paris, all right. Just keep droppin' hints from time to time—that's how I got to see the Atlantic Ocean, y'know.

MRS. GIBBS: Oh, I'm sorry I mentioned it. Only it seems to me that once in your life before you die you ought to see a country where they don't talk in English and don't even want to.

The STAGE MANAGER *enters briskly from the right. He tips his hat to the ladies, who nod their heads.*

STAGE MANAGER: Thank you, ladies. Thank you very much.

MRS. GIBBS *and* MRS. WEBB *gather up their things, return into their homes and disappear.*

Now we're going to skip a few hours. But first we want a little more information about the town, kind of a scientific account, you might say. So I've asked Professor Willard of our State University to sketch in a few details of our past history here. Is Professor Willard here?

PROFESSOR WILLARD, *a rural savant, pince-nez on a wide satin ribbon, enters from the right with some notes in his hand.*

May I introduce Professor Willard of our State University. A few brief notes, thank you, Professor,—unfortunately our time is limited.

PROFESSOR WILLARD: Grover's Corners . . . let me see . . . Grover's Corners lies on the old Pleistocene granite of the Appalachian range. I may say it's some of the oldest land in the world. We're very proud of that. A shelf of Devonian basalt crosses it with vestiges of Mesozoic shale, and some sandstone outcroppings; but that's all more recent: two hundred, three hundred million years old.
Some highly interesting fossils have been found . . . I may say: unique fossils . . . two miles out of town, in Silas Peckham's cow pasture. They can be seen at the museum in our University at any time—that is, at any reasonable time. Shall I read some of Professor Gruber's notes on the meteorological situation—mean precipitation, et cetera?

STAGE MANAGER: Afraid we won't have time for that, Professor. We might have a few words on the history of man here.

PROFESSOR WILLARD: Yes . . . anthropological data: Early Amerindian stock. Cotahatchee tribes . . . no evidence before the tenth century of this era . . . hm . . . now entirely disappeared . . . possible traces in three families. Migration toward the end of the seventeenth century of English brachiocephalic blue-eyed stock . . . for the most part. Since then some Slav and Mediterranean—

STAGE MANAGER: And the population, Professor Willard?

PROFESSOR WILLARD: Within the town limits: 2,640.

STAGE MANAGER: Just a moment, Professor.

He whispers into the professor's ear.

PROFESSOR WILLARD: Oh, yes, indeed?—The population, *at the moment*, is 2,642. The Postal District brings in 507 more, making a total of 3,149. —Mortality and birth rates: constant.—By MacPherson's gauge: 6.032.

STAGE MANAGER: Thank you very much, Professor. We're all very much obliged to you, I'm sure.

PROFESSOR WILLARD: Not at all, sir; not at all.

STAGE MANAGER: This way, Professor, and thank you again.

Exit PROFESSOR WILLARD.

Now the political and social report: Editor Webb.—Oh, Mr. Webb?

MRS. WEBB *appears at her back door.*

MRS. WEBB: He'll be here in a minute. . . . He just cut his hand while he was eatin' an apple.

STAGE MANAGER: Thank you, Mrs. Webb.

MRS. WEBB: Charles! Everybody's waitin'.

Exit MRS. WEBB.

STAGE MANAGER: Mr. Webb is Publisher and Editor of the Grover's Corners *Sentinel.* That's our local paper, y'know.

MR. WEBB *enters from his house, pulling on his coat. His finger is bound in a handkerchief.*

MR. WEBB: Well . . . I don't have to tell you that we're run here by a Board of Selectmen.—All males vote at the age of twenty-one. Women vote indirect. We're lower middle class: sprinkling of professional men . . . ten per cent illiterate laborers. Politically, we're eighty-six per cent Republicans; six per cent Democrats; four per cent Socialists; rest, indifferent. Religiously, we're eighty-five per cent Protestants; twelve per cent Catholics; rest, indifferent.

STAGE MANAGER: Have you any comments, Mr. Webb?

MR. WEBB: Very ordinary town, if you ask me. Little better behaved than most. Probably a lot duller. But our young people here seem to like it well enough. Ninety per cent of 'em graduating from high school settle down right here to live—even when they've been away to college.

STAGE MANAGER: Now, is there anyone in the audience who would like to ask Editor Webb anything about the town?

WOMAN IN THE BALCONY: Is there much drinking in Grover's Corners?

MR. WEBB: Well, ma'am, I wouldn't know what you'd call *much.* Satiddy nights the farmhands meet down in Ellery Greenough's stable and holler some. We've got one or two town drunks, but they're always having remorses every time an evangelist comes to town. No, ma'am, I'd say likker ain't a regular thing in the home here, except in the medicine chest. Right good for snake bite, y'know—always was.

BELLIGERENT MAN AT BACK OF AUDITORIUM: Is there no one in town aware of—

STAGE MANAGER: Come forward, will you, where we can all hear you—What were you saying?

BELLIGERENT MAN: Is there no one in town aware of social injustice and industrial inequality?

MR. WEBB: Oh, yes, everybody is—somethin' terrible. Seems like they spend most of their time talking about who's rich and who's poor.

BELLIGERENT MAN: Then why don't they do something about it?

He withdraws without waiting for an answer.

MR. WEBB: Well, I dunno. . . . I guess we're all hunting like everybody else for a way the diligent and sensible can rise to the top and the lazy and quarrelsome can sink to the bottom. But it ain't easy to find. Meanwhile, we do all we can to help those that can't help themselves and those that can we leave alone.—Are there any other questions?

LADY IN A BOX: Oh, Mr. Webb? Mr. Webb, is there any culture or love of beauty in Grover's Corners?

MR. WEBB: Well, ma'am, there ain't much—not in the sense you mean. Come to think of it, there's some girls that play the piano at High School Commencement; but they ain't happy about it. No, ma'am, there isn't much culture; but maybe this is the place to tell you that we've got a lot of pleasures of a kind here: we like the sun comin' up over the mountain in the morning, and we all notice a good deal about the birds. We pay a lot of attention to them. And we watch the change of the seasons; yes, everybody knows about them. But those other things—you're right, ma'am—there ain't much.—*Robinson Crusoe* and the Bible; and Handel's "Largo," we all know that; and Whistler's "Mother"—those are just about as far as we go.

LADY IN A BOX: So I thought. Thank you, Mr. Webb.

STAGE MANAGER: Thank you, Mr. Webb.

MR. WEBB *retires.*

Now, we'll go back to the town. It's early afternoon. All 2,642 have had their dinners and all the dishes have been washed.

MR. WEBB, *having removed his coat, returns and starts pushing a lawn mower to and fro beside his house.*

There's an early-afternoon calm in our town: a buzzin' and a hummin' from the school buildings; only a few buggies on Main Street—the horses dozing at the hitching posts; you all remember what it's like. Doc Gibbs is in his office, tapping people and making them say "ah." Mr. Webb's cuttin' his lawn over there; one man in ten thinks it's a privilege to push his own lawn mower. No, sir. It's later than I thought. There are the children coming home from school already.

Shrill girls' voices are heard, off left. EMILY *comes along Main Street, carrying some books. There are some signs that she is imagining herself to be a lady of startling elegance.*

EMILY: I *can't,* Lois. I've go to go home and help my mother. I *promised.*

MR. WEBB: Emily, walk simply. Who do you think you are today?

EMILY: Papa, you're terrible. One minute you tell me to stand up straight and the next minute you call me names. I just don't listen to you.

She gives him an abrupt kiss.

MR. WEBB: Golly, I never got a kiss from such a great lady before.

He goes out of sight. EMILY *leans over and picks some flowers by the gate of her house.*

GEORGE GIBBS *comes careening down Main Street. He is throwing a ball up to dizzying heights, and waiting to catch it again. This sometimes requires his taking six steps backward. He bumps into an* OLD LADY *invisible to us.*

GEORGE: Excuse me, Mrs. Forrest.

STAGE MANAGER [*As* MRS. FORREST.]: Go out and play in the fields, young man. You got no business playing baseball on Main Street.

GEORGE: Awfully sorry, Mrs. Forrest.—Hello, Emily.

EMILY: H'lo.

GEORGE: You made a fine speech in class.

EMILY: Well . . . I was really ready to make a speech about the Monroe Doctrine, but at the last minute Miss Corcoran made me talk about the Louisiana Purchase instead. I worked an awful long time on both of them.

GEORGE: Gee, it's funny, Emily. From my window up there I can just see your head nights when you're doing your homework over in your room.

EMILY: Why, can you?

GEORGE: You certainly do stick to it, Emily. I don't see how you can sit still that long. I guess you like school.

EMILY: Well, I always feel it's something you have to go through.

GEORGE: Yeah.

EMILY: I don't mind it really. It passes the time.

GEORGE: Yeah.—Emily, what do you think? We might work out a kinda telegraph from your window to mine; and once in a while you could give me a kinda hint or two about one of those algebra problems. I don't mean the answers, Emily, of course not . . . just some little hint . . .

EMILY: Oh, I think *hints* are allowed.—So—ah—if you get stuck, George, you whistle to me; and I'll give you some hints.

GEORGE: Emily, you're just naturally bright, I guess.

EMILY: I figure that it's just the way a person's born.

GEORGE: Yeah. But, you see, I want to be a farmer, and my Uncle Luke says whenever I'm ready I can come over and work on his farm and if I'm any good I can just gradually have it.

EMILY: You mean the house and everything?

Enter MRS. WEBB *with a large bowl and sits on the bench, by her trellis.*

GEORGE: Yeah. Well, thanks . . . I better be getting out to the baseball field. Thanks for the talk, Emily.—Good afternoon, Mrs. Webb.

MRS. WEBB: Good afternoon, George.

GEORGE: So long, Emily.

EMILY: So long, George.

MRS. WEBB: Emily, come and help me string these beans for the winter. George Gibbs let himself have a real conversation, didn't he? Why, he's growing up. How old would George be?

EMILY: I don't know.

MRS. WEBB: Let's see. He must be almost sixteen.

EMILY: Mama, I made a speech in class today and I was very good.

MRS. WEBB: You must recite it to your father at supper. What was it about?

EMILY: The Louisiana Purchase. It was like silk off a spool. I'm going to make speeches all my life.—Mama, are these big enough?

MRS. WEBB: Try and get them a little bigger if you can.

EMILY: Mama, will you answer me a question, serious?

MRS. WEBB: Seriously, dear—not serious.

EMILY: Seriously,—will you?

MRS. WEBB: Of course, I will.

EMILY: Mama, am I good looking?

MRS. WEBB: Yes, of course you are. All my children have got good features; I'd be ashamed if they hadn't.

EMILY: Oh, Mama, that's not what I mean. What I mean is: am I *pretty?*

MRS. WEBB: I've already told you, yes. Now that's enough of that. You have a nice young pretty face. I never heard of such foolishness.

EMILY: Oh, Mama, you never tell us the truth about anything.

MRS. WEBB: I *am* telling you the truth.

EMILY: Mama, were *you* pretty?

MRS. WEBB: Yes, I was, if I do say it. I was the prettiest girl in town next to Mamie Cartwright.

EMILY: But, Mama, you've got to say *some*thing about me. Am I pretty enough . . . to get anybody . . . to get people interested in me?

MRS. WEBB: Emily, you make me tired. Now stop it. You're pretty enough for all normal purposes.—Come along now and bring that bowl with you.

EMILY: Oh, Mama, you're no help at all.

STAGE MANAGER: Thank you. Thank you! That'll do. We'll have to interrupt again here. Thank you, Mrs. Webb; thank you, Emily.

MRS. WEBB *and* EMILY *withdraw.*

These are some more things we want to explore about this town.

He comes to the center of the stage. During the following speech the lights gradually dim to darkness, leaving only a spot on him.

I think this is a good time to tell you that the Cartwright interests have just begun building a new bank in Grover's Corners—had to go to Vermont for the marble, sorry to say. And they've asked a friend of mine what they should put in the cornerstone for people to dig up . . . a thousand years from now. . . . Of course, they've put in a copy of the *New York Times* and a copy of Mr. Webb's *Sentinel*. . . . We're kind of interested in this because some scientific fellas have found a way of painting all that reading matter with a glue—silicate glue—that'll make it keep a thousand—two thousand years.

We're putting in a Bible . . . and the Constitution of the United States—and a copy of William Shakespeare's plays. What do you say, folks? What do you think?

Y'know—Babylon once had two million people in it, and all we know about 'em is the names of the kings and same copies of wheat contracts . . . and contracts for the sale of slaves. Yet every night all those families sat down to supper, and the father cam home from his work, and the smoke went up the chimney,—same as here. And even in Greece and Rome, all we know about the *real* life of the people is what we can piece together out of the joking poems and the comedies they wrote for the theatre back then.

So I'm going to have a copy of this play put in the cornerstone and the people a thousand years from now'll know a few simple facts about us—more than the Treaty of Versailles and the Lindbergh flight.

See what I mean?

So—people a thousand years from now—this is the way we were in the provinces north of New York at the beginning of the twentieth century.—This is the way we were: in our growing up and in our marrying and in our living and in our dying.

A choir partially concealed in the orchestra pit has begun singing "Blessed Be the Tie That Binds." SIMON STIMSON *stands directing them.*

Two ladders have been pushed onto the stage; they serve as indication of the second story in the GIBBS *and* WEBB *houses.* GEORGE *and* EMILY *mount them, and apply themselves to their schoolwork.*

DR. GIBBS *has entered and is seated in his kitchen reading.*

Well!—good deal of time's gone by. It's evening. You can hear choir practice going on in the Congregational Church. The children are at home doing their schoolwork. The day's running down like a tired clock.

SIMON STIMSON: Now look here, everybody. Music come into the world to give pleasure.—Softer! Softer! Get it out of your heads that music's only good when it's loud. You leave loudness to the Methodists. You couldn't beat 'em, even if you wanted to. Now again. Tenors!

GEORGE: Hssst! Emily!

EMILY: Hello.

GEORGE: Hello!

EMILY: I can't work at all. The moonlight's so *terrible.*

GEORGE: Emily, did you get the third problem?

EMILY: Which?

GEORGE: The *third?*

EMILY: Why, yes, George—that's the easiest of them all.

GEORGE: I don't see it. Emily, can you give me a hint?

EMILY: I'll tell you one thing: the answer's in yards.

GEORGE: ! ! ! In yards? How do you mean?

EMILY: In *square* yards.

GEORGE: Oh . . . in square yards.

EMILY: Yes, George, don't you see?

GEORGE: Yeah.

EMILY: In square yards of *wallpaper*.

GEORGE: Wallpaper,—oh, I see. Thanks a lot, Emily.

EMILY: You're welcome. My, isn't the moonlight *terrible*? And choir practice going on.—I think if you hold your breath you can hear the train all the way to Contoocook. Hear it?

GEORGE: M-m-m—What do you know!

EMILY: Well, I guess I better go back and try to work.

GEORGE: Good night, Emily. And thanks.

EMILY: Good night, George.

SIMON STIMSON: Before I forget it: how many of you will be able to come in Tuesday afternoon and sing at Fred Hersey's wedding?—show your hands. That'll be fine; that'll be right nice. We'll do the same music we did for Jane Trowbridge's last month.

—Now we'll do: "Art Thou Weary; Art Thou Languid?" It's a question, ladies and gentlemen, make it talk. Ready.

DR. GIBBS: Oh, George, can you come down a minute?

GEORGE: Yes, Pa.

He descends the ladder.

DR. GIBBS: Make yourself comfortable, George; I'll only keep you a minute. George, how old are you?

GEORGE: I? I'm sixteen, almost seventeen.

DR. GIBBS: What do you want to do after school's over?

GEORGE: Why, you know, Pa. I want to be a farmer on Uncle Luke's farm.

DR. GIBBS: You'll be willing, will you, to get up early and milk and feed the stock . . . and you'll be able to hoe and hay all day?

GEORGE: Sure, I will. What are you . . . what do you mean, Pa?

DR. GIBBS: Well, George, while I was in my office today I heard a funny sound . . . and what do you think it was? It was your mother chopping wood. There you see your mother—getting up early; cooking meals all day long; washing and ironing;—and still she has to go out in the back yard and chop wood. I suppose she just got tired of asking you. She just gave up and decided it was easier to do it herself. And you eat her meals, and put on the clothes she keeps nice for you, and you run off and play baseball,—like she's some hired girl we keep around the house but that we don't like very much. Well, I knew all I had to do was call your attention to it. Here's a handkerchief, son. George, I've decided to raise your spending money twenty-five cents a week. Not, of course, for chopping wood for your mother, because that's a present you give her, but because you're getting older—and I imagine there are lots of things you must find to do with it.

GEORGE: Thanks, Pa.

DR. GIBBS: Let's see—tomorrow's your payday. You can count on it—Hmm. Probably Rebecca'll feel she ought to have some more too. Wonder what could have happened to your mother. Choir practice never was as late as this before.

GEORGE: It's only half past eight, Pa.

DR. GIBBS: I don't know why she's in that old choir. She hasn't any more voice than an old crow. . . . Traipsin' around the streets at this hour of the night . . . Just about time you retired, don't you think?
GEORGE: Yes, Pa.

GEORGE *mounts to his place on the ladder.*
Laughter and good nights can be heard on stage left and presently MRS. GIBBS, MRS. SOAMES *and* MRS. WEBB *come down Main Street. When they arrive at the corner of the stage they stop.*

MRS. SOAMES: Good night, Martha. Good night, Mr. Foster.
MRS. WEBB: I'll tell Mr. Webb; I *know* he'll want to put it in the paper.
MRS. GIBBS: My, it's late!
MRS. SOAMES: Good night, Irma.
MRS. GIBBS: Real nice choir practice, wa'n't it? Myrtle Webb! Look at that moon, will you! Tsk-tsk-tsk. Potato weather, for sure.

They are silent a moment, gazing up at the moon.

MRS. SOAMES: Naturally I didn't want to say a word about it in front of those others, but now we're alone—really, it's the worst scandal that ever was in this town!
MRS. GIBBS: What?
MRS. SOAMES: Simon Stimson!
MRS. GIBBS: Now, Louella!
MRS. SOAMES: But, Julia! To have the organist of a church *drink* and *drunk* year after year. You know he was drunk tonight.
MRS. GIBBS: Now, Louella! We all know about Mr. Stimson, and we all know about the troubles he's been through, and Dr. Ferguson knows too, and if Dr. Ferguson keeps him on there in his job the only thing the rest of us can do is just not to notice it.
MRS. SOAMES: *Not to notice it!* But it's getting worse.
MRS. WEBB: No, it isn't, Louella. It's getting better. I've been in that choir twice as long as you have. It doesn't happen anywhere near so often. . . . My, I hate to go to bed on a night like this.—I better hurry. Those children'll be sitting up till all hours. Good night, Louella.

They all exchange good nights. She hurries downstage, enters her house and disappears.

MRS. GIBBS: Can you get home safe, Louella?
MRS. SOAMES: It's as bright as day. I can see Mr. Soames scowling at the window now. You'd think we'd been to a dance the way the menfolk carry on.

More good nights. MRS. GIBBS *arrives at her home and passes througb the trellis into the kitchen.*

MRS. GIBBS: Well, we had a real good time.
DR. GIBBS: You're late enough.
MRS. GIBBS: Why, Frank, it ain't any later 'n usual.
DR. GIBBS: And you stopping at the corner to gossip with a lot of hens.
MRS. GIBBS: Now, Frank, don't be grouchy. Come out and smell the heliotrope in the moonlight.

They stroll out arm in arm along the footlights.

Isn't that wonderful? What did you do all the time I was away?
DR. GIBBS: Oh, I read—as usual. What were the girls gossiping about tonight?
MRS. GIBBS: Well, believe me, Frank—there is something to gossip about.
DR. GIBBS: Hmm! Simon Stimson far gone, was he?
MRS. GIBBS: Worst I've ever seen him. How'll that end, Frank? Dr. Ferguson can't forgive him forever.
DR. GIBBS: I guess I know more about Simon Stimson's affairs than anybody in this town. Some people ain't made for small-town life. I don't know how that'll end; but there's nothing we can do but just leave it alone. Come, get in.
MRS. GIBBS: No, not yet . . . Frank, I'm worried about you.
DR. GIBBS: What are you worried about?
MRS. GIBBS: I think it's my duty to make plans for you to get a real rest and change. And if I get that legacy, well, I'm going to insist on it.
DR. GIBBS: Now, Julia, there's no sense in going over that again.
MRS. GIBBS: Frank, you're just *unreasonable!*
DR. GIBBS [*Starting into the house*]: Come on, Julia, it's getting late. First thing you know you'll catch cold. I gave George a piece of my mind tonight. I reckon you'll have your wood chopped for a while anyway. No, no, start getting upstairs.
MRS. GIBBS: Oh, dear. There's always so many things to pick up, seems like. You know, Frank, Mrs. Fairchild always locks her front door every night. All those people up that part of town do.
DR. GIBBS [*Blowing out the lamp*]: They're all getting citified, that's the trouble with them. They haven't got nothing fit to burgle and everybody knows it.

They disappear. REBECCA *climbs up the ladder beside* GEORGE.

GEORGE: Get out, Rebecca. There's only room for one at this window. You're always spoiling everything.
REBECCA: Well, let me look just a minute.

GEORGE: Use your own window.

REBECCA: I did, but there's no moon there. . . . George, do you know what I think, do you? I think maybe the moon's getting nearer and nearer and there'll be a big 'splosion.

GEORGE: Rebecca, you don't know anything. If the moon were getting nearer, the guys that sit up all night with telescopes would see it first and they'd tell about it, and it'd be in all the newspapers.

REBECCA: George, is the moon shining on South America, Canada and half the whole world?

GEORGE: Well—prob'ly is.

The STAGE MANAGER *strolls on. Pause. The sound of crickets is heard.*

STAGE MANAGER: Nine thirty. Most of the lights are out. No, there's Constable Warren trying a few doors on Main Street. And here comes Editor Webb, after putting his newspaper to bed.

MR. WARREN, *an elderly policeman, comes along Main Street from the right,* MR. WEBB *from the left.*

MR. WEBB: Good evening, Bill.

CONSTABLE WARREN: Evenin', Mr. Webb.

MR. WEBB: Quite a moon!

CONSTABLE WARREN: Yepp.

MR. WEBB: All quiet tonight?

CONSTABLE WARREN: Simon Stimson is rolling around a little. Just saw his wife movin' out to hunt for him so I looked the other way—there he is now.

SIMON STIMSON *comes down Main Street from the left, only a trace of unsteadiness in his walk.*

MR. WEBB: Good evening, Simon . . . Town seems to have settled down for the night pretty well. . . .

SIMON STIMSON *comes up to him and pauses a moment and stares at him, swaying slightly.*

Good evening . . . Yes, most of the town's settled down for the night, Simon. . . . I guess we better do the same. Can I walk along a ways with you?

SIMON STIMSON *continues on his way without a word and disappears at the right.*

Good night.

CONSTABLE WARREN: I don't know how that's goin' to end, Mr. Webb.

MR. WEBB: Well, he's seen a peck of trouble, one thing after another. . . . Oh, Bill . . . if you see my boy smoking cigarettes, just give him a word, will you? He thinks a lot of you, Bill.

CONSTABLE WARREN: I don't think he smokes no cigarettes, Mr. Webb. Leastways, not more'n two or three a year.

MR. WEBB: Hm . . . I hope not.—Well, good night, Bill.

CONSTABLE WARREN: Good night, Mr. Webb. *Exit.*

MR. WEBB: Who's that up there? Is that you, Myrtle?

EMILY: No, it's me, Papa.

MR. WEBB: Why aren't you in bed?

EMILY: I don't know. I just can't sleep yet, Papa. The moonlight's so *won*-derful. And the smell of Mrs. Gibbs' heliotrope. Can you smell it?

MR. WEBB: Hm . . . Yes. Haven't any troubles on your mind, have you, Emily?

EMILY: *Troubles,* Papa? *No.*

MR. WEBB: Well, enjoy yourself, but don't let your mother catch you. Good night, Emily.

EMILY: Good night, Papa.

MR. WEBB *crosses into the house, whistling "Blessed Be the Tie That Binds" and disappears.*

REBECCA: I never told you about that letter Jane Crofut got from her minister when she was sick. He wrote Jane a letter and on the envelope the address was like this: It said: Jane Crofut; The Crofut Farm; Grover's Corners; Sutton County; New Hampshire; United States of America.

GEORGE: What's funny about that?

REBECCA: But listen, it's not finished: the United States of America; Continent of North America; Western Hemisphere; the Earth; the Solar System; the Universe; the Mind of God—that's what it said on the envelope.

GEORGE: What do you know!

REBECCA: And the postman brought it just the same.

GEORGE: What do you know!

STAGE MANAGER: That's the end of the First Act, friends. You can go and smoke now, those that smoke.

ACT II

The tables and chairs of the two kitchens are still on the stage.

The ladders and the small bench have been withdrawn.

The STAGE MANAGER *has been at his accustomed place watching the audience return to its seats.*

STAGE MANAGER: Three years have gone by. Yes, the sun's come up over a thousand times. Summers and winters have cracked the mountains a little bit more and the rains have brought down some of the dirt.

Some babies that weren't even born before have begun talking regular sentences already; and a number of people who thought they were right young and spry have noticed that they can't bound up a flight of stairs like they used to, without their heart fluttering a little.

All that can happen in a thousand days.

Nature's been pushing and contriving in other ways, too: a number of young people fell in love and got married.

Yes, the mountain got bit away a few fractions of an inch; millions of gallons of water went by the mill; and here and there a new home was set up under a roof.

Almost everybody in the world gets married,—you know what I mean? In our town there aren't hardly any exceptions. Most everybody in the world climbs into their graves married.
The First Act was called the Daily Life. This act is called Love and Marriage. There's another act coming after this: I reckon you can guess what that's about.

So: It's three years later. It's 1904. It's July 7th, just after High School Commencement. That's the time most of our young people jump up and get married.

Soon as they've passed their last examinations in solid geometry and Cicero's Orations, looks like they suddenly feel themselves fit to be married.

It's early morning. Only this time it's been raining. It's been pouring and thundering. Mrs. Gibbs' garden, and Mrs. Webb's here: drenched. All those bean poles and pea vines: drenched. All yesterday over there on Main Street, the rain looked like curtains being blown along.

Hm . . . it may begin again any minute. There! You can hear the 5:45 for Boston.

MRS. GIBBS *and* MRS. WEBB *enter their kitchen and start the day as in the First Act.*

And there's Mrs. Gibbs and Mrs. Webb come down to make breakfast, just as though it were an ordinary day. I don't have to point out to the women in my audience that those ladies they see before them, both of those ladies cooked three meals a day—one of 'em for twenty years, the other for forty—and no summer vacation. They brought up two children apiece, washed, cleaned the house,—and *never a nervous breakdown.*

It's like what one of those Middle West poets said: You've got to love life to have life, and you've got to have life to love life. . . . It's what they call a vicious circle.

HOWIE NEWSOME [*Off stage left*]: Giddap, Bessie!

STAGE MANAGER: Here comes Howie Newsome delivering the milk. And there's Si Crowell delivering the papers like his brother before him.

SI CROWELL *has entered hurling imaginary newspapers into doorways;* HOWIE NEWSOME *has come along Main Street with Bessie.*

SI CROWELL: Morning, Howie.

HOWIE NEWSOME: Morning, Si.—Anything in the papers I ought to know?

SI CROWELL: Nothing much, except we're losing about the best baseball pitcher Grover's Corners ever had—George Gibbs.

HOWIE NEWSOME: Reckon he is.

SI CROWELL: He could hit and run bases, too.

HOWIE NEWSOME: Yep. Mighty fine ball player.—Whoa! Bessie! I guess I can stop and talk if I've a mind to!

SI CROWELL: I don't see how he could give up a thing like that just to get married. Would you, Howie?

HOWIE NEWSOME: Can't tell, Si. Never had no talent that way.

CONSTABLE WARREN *enters. They exchange good mornings.*

You're up early, Bill.

CONSTABLE WARREN: Seein' if there's anything I can do to prevent a flood. River's been risin' all night.

HOWIE NEWSOME: Si Crowell's all worked up here about George Gibbs' retiring from baseball.

CONSTABLE WARREN: Yes, sir; that's the way it goes. Back in '84 we had a player, Si—even George Gibbs couldn't touch him. Name of Hank Todd. Went down to Maine and become a parson. Wonderful ball player.—Howie, how does the weather look to you?

HOWIE NEWSOME: Oh, 'tain't bad. Think maybe it'll clear up for good.

CONSTABLE WARREN *and* SI CROWELL *continue on their way.*

HOWIE NEWSOME *brings the milk first to* MRS. GIBBS' *house. She meets him by the trellis.*

MRS. GIBBS: Good morning, Howie. Do you think it's going to rain again?

HOWIE NEWSOME: Morning, Mrs. Gibbs. It rained so heavy, I think maybe it'll clear up.
MRS. GIBBS: Certainly hope it will.
HOWIE NEWSOME: How much did you want today?
MRS. GIBBS: I'm going to have a houseful of relations, Howie. Looks to me like I'll need three-a-milk and two-a-cream.
HOWIE NEWSOME: My wife says to tell you we both hope they'll be very happy, Mrs. Gibbs. Know they *will*.
MRS. GIBBS: Thanks a lot, Howie. Tell your wife I hope she gits there to the wedding.
HOWIE NEWSOME: Yes, she'll be there; she'll be there if she kin.

HOWIE NEWSOME *crosses to* MRS. WEBB*'s house.*

Morning, Mrs. Webb.
MRS. WEBB: Oh, good morning, Mr. Newsome. I told you four quarts of milk, but I hope you can spare me another.
HOWIE NEWSOME: Yes'm . . . and the two of cream.
MRS. WEBB: Will it start raining again, Mr. Newsome?
HOWIE NEWSOME: Well. Just sayin' to Mrs. Gibbs as how it may lighten up. Mrs. Newsome told me to tell you as how we hope they'll both be very happy, Mrs. Webb. Know they *will*.
MRS. WEBB: Thank you, and thank Mrs. Newsome and we're counting on seeing you at the wedding.
HOWIE NEWSOME: Yes, Mrs. Webb. We hope to git there. Couldn't miss that. Come on, Bessie.

Exit HOWIE NEWSOME. DR. GIBBS *descends in shirt sleeves, and sits down at his breakfast table.*

DR. GIBBS: Well, Ma, the day has come. You're losin' one of your chicks.
MRS. GIBBS: Frank Gibbs, don't you say another word. I feel like crying every minute. Sit down and drink your coffee.
DR. GIBBS: The groom's up shaving himself—only there ain't an awful lot to shave. Whistling and singing, like he's glad to leave us.—Every now and then he says "I do" to the mirror, but it don't sound convincing to me.
MRS. GIBBS: I declare, Frank, I don't know how he'll get along. I've arranged his clothes and seen to it he's put warm things on,—Frank! they're too *young*. Emily won't think of such things. He'll catch his death of cold within a week.
DR. GIBBS: I was remembering my wedding morning, Julia.
MRS. GIBBS: Now don't start that, Frank Gibbs.
DR. GIBBS: I was the scaredest young fella in the State of New Hampshire. I thought I'd make a mistake for sure. And when I saw you comin' down that aisle I thought you were the prettiest girl I'd ever seen, but the only trouble was that I'd never seen you before. There I was in the Congregational Church marryin' a total stranger.
MRS. GIBBS: And how do you think I felt!—Frank, weddings are perfectly awful things. Farces,—that's what they are! [*She puts a plate before him.*] Here, I've made something for you.
DR. GIBBS: Why, Julia Hersey—French toast!
MRS. GIBBS: 'Tain't hard to make and I had to do *some*thing.

Pause. DR. GIBBS *pours on the syrup.*

DR. GIBBS: How'd you sleep last night, Julia?
MRS. GIBBS: Well, I heard a lot of the hours struck off.
DR. GIBBS: Ye-e-s! I get a shock every time I think of George setting out to be a family man—that great gangling thing!—I tell you Julia, there's nothing so terrifying in the world as a *son*. The relation of father and son is the darndest, awkwardest—
MRS. GIBBS: Well, mother and daughter's no picnic, let me tell you.
DR. GIBBS: They'll have a lot of troubles, I suppose, but that's none of our business. Everybody has a right to their own troubles.
MRS. GIBBS [*At the table, drinking her coffee, meditatively*]: Yes . . . people are meant to go through life two by two. 'Tain't natural to be lonesome.

Pause. DR. GIBBS *starts laughing.*

DR. GIBBS: Julia, do you know one of the things I was scared of when I married you?
MRS. GIBBS: Oh, go along with you!
DR. GIBBS: I was afraid we wouldn't have material for conversation more'n'd last us a few weeks.

Both laugh.

I was afraid we'd run out and eat our meals in silence, that's a fact.—Well, you and I been conversing for twenty years now without any noticeable barren spells.
MRS. GIBBS: Well,—good weather, bad weather—'tain't very choice, but I always find something to say. [*She goes to the foot of the stairs.*] Did you hear Rebecca stirring around upstairs?
DR. GIBBS: No. Only day of the year Rebecca hasn't been managing everybody's business up there. She's hiding in her room.—I got the impression she's crying.
MRS. GIBBS: Lord's sakes!—This has got to stop.—Rebecca! Rebecca! Come and get your breakfast.

GEORGE *comes rattling down the stairs, very brisk.*

GEORGE: Good morning, everybody. Only five more hours to live.

Makes the gesture of cutting his throat, and a loud "k-k-k," and starts through the trellis.

MRS. GIBBS: George Gibbs, where are you going?
GEORGE: Just stepping across the grass to see my girl.
MRS. GIBBS: Now, George! You put on your overshoes. It's raining torrents. You don't go out of this house without you're prepared for it.
GEORGE: Aw, Ma. It's just a *step!*
MRS. GIBBS: George! You'll catch your death of cold and cough all through the service.
DR. GIBBS: George, do as your mother tells you!

DR. GIBBS *goes upstairs.* GEORGE *returns reluctantly to the kitchen and pantomimes putting on overshoes.*

MRS. GIBBS: From tomorrow on you can kill yourself in all weathers, but while you're in my house you'll live wisely, thank you.—Maybe Mrs. Webb isn't used to callers at seven in the morning.—Here, take a cup of coffee first.
GEORGE: Be back in a minute. [*He crosses the stage, leaping over the puddles.*] Good morning, Mother Webb.
MRS. WEBB: Goodness! You frightened me!—Now, George, you can come in a minute out of the wet, but you know I can't ask you in.
GEORGE: Why not—?
MRS. WEBB: George, you know's well as I do: the groom can't see his bride on his wedding day, not until he sees her in church.
GEORGE: Aw!—that's just a superstition.—Good morning, Mr. Webb.

Enter MR. WEBB.

MR. WEBB: Good morning, George.
GEORGE: Mr. Webb, you don't believe in that superstition, do you?
MR. WEBB: There's a lot of common sense in some superstitions, George.

He sits at the table, facing right.

MRS. WEBB: Millions have folla'd it, George, and you don't want to be the first to fly in the face of custom.
GEORGE: How is Emily?
MRS. WEBB: She hasn't waked up yet. I haven't heard a sound out of her.
GEORGE: Emily's *asleep*!!!
MRS. WEBB: No wonder! We were up 'til all hours, sewing and packing. Now I'll tell you what I'll do; you set down here a minute with Mr. Webb and drink this cup of coffee; and I'll go upstairs and see she doesn't come down and surprise you. There's some bacon too; but don't be long about it.

Exit MRS. WEBB. *Embarrassed silence.* MR. WEBB *dunks doughnuts in his coffee. More silence.*

MR. WEBB [*Suddenly and loudly*]: Well George, how are you?
GEORGE [*Startled, choking over his coffee*]: Oh, fine, I'm fine. *Pause.* Mr. Webb, what sense could there be in a superstition like that?
MR. WEBB: Well, you see,—on her wedding morning a girl's head's apt to be full of . . . clothes and one thing and another. Don't you think that's probably it?
GEORGE: Ye-e-s. I never thought of that.
MR. WEBB: A girl's apt to be a mite nervous on her wedding day.

Pause.

GEORGE: I wish a fellow could get married without all that marching up and down.
MR. WEBB: Every man that's ever lived has felt that way about it, George; but it hasn't been any use. It's the womenfolk who've built up weddings, my boy. For a while now the women have it all their own. A man looks pretty small at a wedding, George. All those good women standing shoulder to shoulder making sure that the knot's tied in a mighty public way.
GEORGE: But . . . you *believe* in it, don't you, Mr. Webb?
MR. WEBB [*With alacrity*]: Oh, yes; *oh, yes.* Don't you misunderstand me, my boy. Marriage is a wonderful thing,—wonderful thing. And don't you forget that, George.
GEORGE: No, sir.—Mr. Webb, how old were you when you got married?
MR. WEBB: Well, you see: I'd been to college and I'd taken a little time to get settled. But Mrs. Webb—she wasn't much older than what Emily is. Oh, age hasn't much to do with it, George,—not compared with . . . uh . . . other things.
GEORGE: What were you going to say, Mr. Webb?
MR. WEBB: Oh, I don't know.—Was I going to say something?

Pause.

George, I was thinking the other night of some advice my father gave me when I got married. Charles, he said, Charles, start out early showing who's boss, he said. Best thing to do is to give an order, even if it don't make sense; just so she'll learn to obey. And he said: if anything about your wife irritates you—her conversation, or anything—just get up and leave the house. That'll make it clear to her, he said. And, oh, yes! he said, never, *never* let your wife know how much money you have, never.

GEORGE: Well, Mr. Webb . . . I don't think I could . . .

MR. WEBB: So I took the opposite of my father's advice and I've been happy ever since. And let that be a lesson to you, George, never to ask advice on personal matters.—George, are you going to raise chickens on your farm?

GEORGE: What?

MR. WEBB: Are you going to raise chickens on your farm?

GEORGE: Uncle Luke's never been much interested, but I thought—

MR. WEBB: A book came into my office the other day, George, on the Philo System of raising chickens. I want you to read it. I'm thinking of beginning in a small way in the back yard, and I'm going to put an incubator in the cellar—

Enter MRS. WEBB.

MRS. WEBB: Charles, are you talking about that old incubator again? I thought you two'd be talking about things worth while.

MR. WEBB [*Bitingly*]: Well, Myrtle, if you want to give the boy some good advice, I'll go upstairs and leave you alone with him.

MRS. WEBB [*Pulling* GEORGE *up*]: George, Emily's got to come downstairs and eat her breakfast. She sends you her love but she doesn't want to lay eyes on you. Good-by.

GEORGE: Good-by.

GEORGE *crosses the stage to his own home, bewildered and crestfallen. He slowly dodges a puddle and disappears into his house.*

MR. WEBB: Myrtle, I guess you don't know about that older superstition.

MRS. WEBB: What do you mean, Charles?

MR. WEBB: Since the cave men: no bridegroom should see his father-in-law on the day of the wedding, or near it. Now remember that.

Both leave the stage.

STAGE MANAGER: Thank you very much, Mr. and Mrs. Webb.—Now I have to interrupt again here. You see, we want to know how all this began—this wedding, this plan to spend a lifetime together. I'm awfully interested in how big things like that begin.

You know how it is: you're twenty-one or twenty-two and you make some decisions; then whisssh! you're seventy: you've been a lawyer for fifty years, and that white-haired lady at your side has eaten over fifty thousand meals with you.

How do such things begin?

George and Emily are going to show you now the conversation they had when they first knew that . . . that . . . as the saying goes . . . they were meant for one another. But before they do it I want you to try and remember what it was like to have been very young. And particularly the days when you were first in love; when you were like a person sleepwalking, and you didn't quite see the street you were in, and didn't quite hear everything that was said to you. You're just a little bit crazy. Will you remember that please?

Now they'll be coming out of high school at three o'clock. George has just been elected President of the Junior Class, and as it's June, that means he'll be President of the Senior Class all next year. And Emily's just been elected Secretary and Treasurer. I don't have to tell you how important that is.

He places a board across the backs of two chairs, which he takes from those at the GIBBS *family's table. He brings two high stools from the wings and places them behind the board. Persons sitting on the stools will be facing the audience. This is the counter of* MR. MORGAN'S *drugstore. The sounds of young people's voices are heard off left.*

Yepp,—there they are coming down Main Street now.

EMILY, *carrying an armful of—imaginary—schoolbooks, comes along Main Street from the left.*

EMILY: I can't, Louise. I've go to go home. Good-by. Oh, Ernestine! Ernestine! Can you come over tonight and do Latin? Isn't that Cicero the worst thing—! Tell your mother you *have* to. G'by. G'by, Helen. G'by, Fred.

GEORGE, *also carrying books, catches up with her.*

GEORGE: Can I carry your books home for you, Emily?
EMILY [*Coolly.*]: Why . . . uh . . . Thank you. It isn't far.

She gives them to him.

GEORGE: Excuse me a minute, Emily.—Say, Bob, if I'm a little late, start practice anyway. And give Herb some long high ones.
EMILY: Good-by, Lizzy.
GEORGE: Good-by, Lizzy.—I'm awfully glad you were elected, too, Emily.
EMILY: Thank you.

They have been standing on Main Street, almost against the back wall. They take the first steps toward the audience when GEORGE *stops and says:*

GEORGE: Emily, why are you mad at me?
EMILY: I'm not mad at you.
GEORGE: You've been treating me so funny lately.
EMILY: Well, since you ask me, I might as well say it right out, George,—

She catches sight of a teacher passing.

Good-by, Miss Corcoran.
GEORGE: Good-by, Miss Corcoran.—Wha—what is it?
EMILY [*Not scoldingly; finding it difficult to say*]: I don't like the whole change that's come over you in the last year. I'm sorry if that hurts your feelings, but I've got to—tell the truth and shame the devil.
GEORGE: A *change*?—Wha—what do you mean?
EMILY: Well, up to a year ago I used to like you a lot. And I used to watch you as you did everything . . . because we'd been friends so long . . . and then you began spending all your time at *baseball* . . . and you never stopped to speak to anybody any more. Not even to your own family you didn't . . . and, George, it's a fact, you've got awful conceited and stuck-up, and all the girls say so. They may not say so to your face, but that's what they say about you behind your back, and it hurts me to hear them say it, but I've got to agree with them a little. I'm sorry if it hurts your feelings . . . but I can't be sorry I said it.
GEORGE: I . . . I'm glad you said it, Emily. I never thought that such thing was happening to me. I guess it's hard for a fella not to have faults creep into his character.

They take a step or two in silence, then stand still in misery.

EMILY: I always expect a man to be perfect and I think he should be.
GEORGE: Oh . . . I don't think it's possible to be perfect, Emily.
EMILY: Well, my *father* is, and as far as I can see *your* father is. There's no reason an earth why you shouldn't be, too.
GEORGE: Well, I feel it's the other way round. That men aren't naturally good; but girls are.
EMILY: Well, you might as well know right now that I'm not perfect. It's not as easy for a girl to be perfect as a man, because we girls are more—more—nervous.—Now I'm sorry I said all that about you. I don't know what made me say it.
GEORGE: Emily,—
EMILY: Now I can see it's not the truth at all. And I suddenly feel that it isn't important, anyway.
GEORGE: Emily . . . would you like an ice-cream soda, or something, before you go home?
EMILY: Well, thank you. . . . I would.

They advance toward the audience and make an abrupt right turn, opening the door of MORGAN'S *drugstore. Under strong emotion,* EMILY *keeps her face down.* GEORGE *speaks to some passers-by.*

GEORGE: Hello, Stew,—how are you?—Good afternoon, Mrs. Slocum.

The STAGE MANAGER, *wearing spectacles and assuming the role of* MR. MORGAN, *enters abruptly from the right and stands between the audience and the counter of his soda fountain.*

STAGE MANAGER: Hello, George. Hello, Emily.—What'll you have?—Why, Emily Webb,—what you been crying about?
GEORGE [*He gropes for an explanation*]: She . . . she just got an awful scare, Mr. Morgan. She almost got run over by that hardware-store wagon. Everybody says the Tom Huckins drives like a crazy man.
STAGE MANAGER [*Drawing a drink of water*]: Well, now! You take a drink of water, Emily. You look all shook up. I tell you, you've got to look both ways before you cross Main Street these days. Gets worse every year.—What'll you have?
EMILY: I'll have a strawberry phosphate, thank you, Mr. Morgan.
GEORGE: No, no, Emily. Have an ice-cream soda with me. Two strawberry ice-cream sodas, Mr. Morgan.
STAGE MANAGER [*Working the faucets*]: Two strawberry ice-cream sodas, yes sir. Yes, sir. There are a hundred and twenty-five horses in Grover's Corners this minute I'm talking to you. State Inspector was in here yesterday. And now they're bringing in these auto-mo-biles, the best thing to do is to just

stay home. Why, I can remember when a dog could go to sleep all day in the middle of Main Street and nothing come along to disturb him. [*He sets the imaginary glasses before them.*] There they are. Enjoy 'em. [*He sees a customer, right.*] Yes, Mrs. Ellis. What can I do for you? [*He goes out right.*]

EMILY: They're so expensive.

GEORGE: No, no,—don't you think of that. We're celebrating our election. And then do you know what else I'm celebrating?

EMILY: N-no.

GEORGE: I'm celebrating because I've got a friend who tells me all the things that ought to be told me.

EMILY: George, *please* don't think of that. I don't know why I said it. It's not true. You're—

GEORGE: No, Emily, you stick to it. I'm glad you spoke to me like you did. But you'll *see*: I'm going to change so quick—you bet I'm going to change. And, Emily, I want to ask you a favor.

EMILY: What?

GEORGE: Emily, if I go away to State Agriculture College next year, will you write me a letter once in a while?

EMILY: I certainly will. I certainly will, George . . .

Pause. They start sipping the sodas through the straws.

It certainly seems like being away three years you'd get out of touch with things. Maybe letters from Grover's Corners wouldn't be so interesting after a while. Grover's Corners isn't a very important place when you think of all—New Hampshire; but I think it's a very nice town.

GEORGE: The day wouldn't come when I wouldn't want to know everything that's happening here. I know *that's* true, Emily.

EMILY: Well, I'll try to make my letters interesting.

Pause.

GEORGE: Y'know. Emily, whenever I meet a farmer I ask him if he thinks it's important to go to Agriculture School to be a good farmer.

EMILY: Why, George—

GEORGE: Yeah, and some of them say that it's even a waste of time. You can get all those things, anyway, out of the pamphlets the government sends out. And Uncle Luke's getting old,—he's about ready for me to start in taking over his farm tomorrow, if I could.

EMILY: My!

George: And, like you say, being gone all that time . . . in other places and meeting other people . . . Gosh, if anything like that can happen I don't want to go away. I guess new people aren't any better than old ones. I'll bet they almost never are. Emily . . . I feel that you're as good a friend as I've got. I don't need to go and meet the people in other towns.

EMILY: But, George, maybe it's very important for you to go, and learn all that about—cattle judging and soils and those things. . . . Of course, I don't know.

GEORGE [*After a pause, very seriously*]: Emily, I'm going to make up my mind right now. I won't go. I'll tell Pa about it tonight.

EMILY: Why, George, I don't see why you have to decide right now. It's a whole year away.

GEORGE: Emily, I'm glad you spoke to me about that . . . that fault in my character. What you said was right; but there was *one* thing wrong in it, and that was when you said that for a year I wasn't noticing people, and . . . you, for instance. Why, you say you were watching me when I did everything . . . I was doing the same about you all the time. Why, sure,—I always thought about you as one of the chief people I thought about. I always made sure where you were sitting on the bleachers, and who you were with, and for three days now I've been trying to walk home with you; but something's always got in the way. Yesterday I was standing over against the wall waiting for you, and you walked home with *Miss Corcoran.*

EMILY: George! . . . Life's awful funny! How could I have known that? Why, I thought—

GEORGE: Listen, Emily, I'm going to tell you why I'm not going to Agriculture School. I think that once you've found a person that you're very fond of . . . I mean a person who's fond of you, too, and likes you enough to be interested in your character . . . Well, I think that's just as important as college is, and even more so. That's what I think.

EMILY: I think it's awfully important, too.

GEORGE: Emily.

EMILY: Y-yes, George.

GEORGE: Emily, if I *do* improve and make a big change . . . would you be . . . I mean: *could* you be . . .

EMILY: I . . . I am now; I always have been.

GEORGE [*Pause*]: So I guess this is an important talk we've been having.

EMILY: Yes . . . Yes.

GEORGE [*Takes a deep breath and straightens his back*]: Wait just a minute and I'll walk you home.

With mounting alarm he digs into his pockets for the money. The STAGE MANAGER *enters, right.* GEORGE, *deeply embarrassed, but direct, says to him:*

Mr. Morgan, I'll have to go home and get the money to pay you for this. It'll only take me a minute.

STAGE MANAGER [*Pretending to be affronted*]: What's that? George Gibbs, do you mean to tell me—!

GEORGE: Yes, but I had reasons, Mr. Morgan.—Look, here's my gold watch to keep until I come back with the money.

STAGE MANAGER: That's all right. Keep your watch. I'll trust you.

GEORGE: I'll be back in five minutes.

STAGE MANAGER: I'll trust you ten years, George,—not a day over.—Got all over your shock, Emily?

EMILY: Yes, thank you, Mr. Morgan. It was nothing.

GEORGE [*Taking up the books from the counter*]: I'm ready.

They walk in grave silence across the stage and pass through the trellis at the Webbs' back door and disappear.

The STAGE MANAGER *watches them go out, then turns to the audience, removing his spectacles.*

STAGE MANAGER: Well,—

He claps his hands as a signal.

Now we're ready to get on with the wedding.

He stands waiting while the set is prepared for the next scene.

STAGEHANDS *remove the chairs, tables and trellises from the Gibbs and Webb houses.*

They arrange the pews for the church in the center of the stage. The congregation will sit facing the back wall. The aisle of the church starts at the center of the back wall and comes toward the audience.

A small platform is placed against the back wall on which the STAGE MANAGER *will stand later, playing the minister.*

The image of a stained-glass window is cast from a lantern slide upon the back wall.

When all is ready the STAGE MANAGER *strolls to the center of the stage, down front, and, musingly, addresses the audience.*

There are a lot of things to be said about a wedding; there are a lot of thoughts that go on during a wedding. We can't get them all into one wedding, naturally, and especially not into a wedding at Grover's Corners, where they're awfully plain and short.

In this wedding I play the minister. That gives me the right to say a few more things about it. For a while now, the play gets pretty serious. Y'see, some churches say that marriage is a sacrament. I don't quite know what that means, but I can guess. Like Mrs. Gibbs said a few minutes ago: People were made to live two-by-two.

This is a good wedding, but people are so put together that even at a good wedding there's a lot of confusion way down deep in people's minds and we thought that that ought to be in our play, too.

The real hero of this scene isn't on the stage at all, and you know who that is. It's like what one of those European fellas said: every child born into the world is nature's attempt to make a perfect human being. Well, we've seen nature pushing and contriving for some time now. We all know that nature's interested in quantity; but I think she's interested in quality, too,—that's why I'm in the ministry.

And don't forget all the other witnesses at this wedding,—the ancestors. Millions of them. Most of them set out to live two-by-two, also. Millions of them.

Well, that's all my sermon. 'Twan't very long, anyway.

The organ starts playing Handel's "Largo". The congregation streams into the church and sits in silence. Church bells are heard.

MRS. GIBBS *sits in the front row, the first seat on the aisle, the right section; next to her are* REBECCA *and* DR. GIBBS. *Across the aisle* MRS. WEBB, WALLY *and* MR. WEBB. *A small choir takes its place, facing the audience under the stained-glass window.*

MRS. WEBB, *on the way to her place, turns back and speaks to the audience.*

MRS. WEBB: I don't know why on earth I should be crying. I suppose there's nothing to cry about. It came over me at breakfast this morning; there was Emily eating her breakfast as she's done for seventeen years and now she's going off to eat it in someone else's house. I suppose that's it.

And Emily! She suddenly said: I can't eat another mouthful, and she put her head down on the table and *she* cried. [*She starts toward her seat in the church, but turns back and adds*:] Oh, I've got to say it: you know, there's something downright cruel about sending our girls out into marriage this way.

I hope some of her girl friends have told her a thing or two. It's cruel, I know, but I couldn't bring myself to say anything. I went into it blind as a bat myself. [*In half-amused exasperation*.] The whole world's wrong, that's what's the matter. There they come.

She hurries to her place in the pew. GEORGE *starts to come down the right aisle of the theatre, through the audience.*

Suddenly THREE MEMBERS *of his baseball team appear by the right proscenium pillar and start whistling and catcalling to him. They are dressed for the ball field.*

THE BASEBALL PLAYERS: Eh, George, George! Hast—yaow! Look at him, fellas—he looks scared to death. Yaow! George, don't look so innocent, you old geezer. We know what you're thinking. Don't disgrace the team, big boy. Whoo-oo-oo.

STAGE MANAGER: All right! All right! That'll do. That's enough of that.

Smiling, he pushes them off the stage. They lean back to shout a few more catcalls.

There used to be an awful lot of that kind of thing at weddings in the old days,—Rome, and later. We're more civilized now,—so they say.

The choir starts singing "Love Divine, All Love Excelling—." GEORGE *has reached the stage. He stares at the congregation a moment, then takes a few steps of withdrawal, toward the right proscenium pillar. His mother, from the front row, seems to have felt his confusion. She leaves her seat and comes down the aisle quickly to him.*

MRS. GIBBS: George! George! What's the matter?

GEORGE: Ma, I don't want to grow old. Why's everybody pushing me so?

MRS. GIBBS: Why, George . . . you wanted it.

GEORGE: No, Ma, listen to me—

MRS. GIBBS: No, no, George,—you're a man now.

GEORGE: Listen, Ma,—for the last time I ask you. . . All I want to do is be a fella—

MRS. GIBBS: George! If anyone should hear you! Now stop. Why, I'm ashamed of you!

GEORGE [*He comes to himself and looks over the scene*]: What? Where's Emily!

MRS. GIBBS: [*Relieved*]: George! You gave me such a turn.

GEORGE: Cheer up, Ma. I'm getting married.

MRS. GIBBS: Let me catch my breath a minute.

GEORGE [*Comforting her*]: Now, Ma, you save Thursday nights. Emily and I are coming over to dinner every Thursday night . . . you'll see. Ma, what are you crying for? Come on; we've got to get ready for this.

MRS. GIBBS, *mastering her emotion, fixes his tie and whispers to him.*

In the meantime, EMILY, *in white and wearing her wedding veil, has come through the audience and mounted onto the stage. She too draws back, frightened, when she sees the congregation in the church. The choir begins: "Blessed Be the Tie That Binds."*

EMILY: I never felt so alone in my whole life. And George over there, looking so . . . ! I *hate* him. I wish I were dead. Papa! Papa!

MR. WEBB [*Leaves his seat in the pews and comes toward her anxiously*]: Emily! Emily! Now don't get upset. . . .

EMILY: But, Papa,—I don't want to get married. . . .

MR. WEBB: Sh—sh—Emily. Everything's all right.

EMILY: Why can't I stay for a while just as I am? Let's go away,—

MR. WEBB: No, no, Emily. Now stop and think a minute.

EMILY: Don't you remember that you used to say,—all the time you used to say—all the time: that I was *your* girl! There must be lots of places we can go to. I'll work for you. I could keep house.

MR. WEBB: Sh . . . You mustn't think of such things. You're just nervous, Emily. [*He turns and calls:*] George! George! Will you come here a minute? [*He leads her toward* GEORGE.] Why you're marrying the best young fellow in the world. George is a fine fellow.

EMILY: But Papa,—

MRS. GIBBS *returns unobtrusively to her seat.* MR. WEBB *has one arm around his daughter. He places his hand on* GEORGE'*s shoulder.*

MR. WEBB: I'm giving away my daughter, George. Do you think you can take care of her?

GEORGE: Mr. Webb, I want to . . . I want to try. Emily, I'm going to do my best. I love you, Emily. I need you.

EMILY: Well, if you love me, help me. All I want is someone to love me.

GEORGE: I will, Emily. Emily, I'll try.

EMILY: And I mean for *ever*. Do you hear? For ever and ever.

They fall into each other's arms. The March from Lohengrin *is heard.*

The STAGE MANAGER, *as* CLERGYMAN, *stands on the box, up center.*

MR. WEBB: Come, they're waiting for us. Now you know it'll be all right. Come, quick.

GEORGE *slips away and takes his place beside the* STAGE MANAGER-CLERGYMAN. EMILY *proceeds up the aisle on her father's arm.*

STAGE MANAGER: Do you, George, take this woman, Emily, to be your wedded wife, to have . . .

MRS. SOAMES has been sitting in the last row of the congregation. She now turns to her neighbors and speaks in a shrill voice. Her chatter drowns out the rest of the clergyman's words.

MRS. SOAMES: Perfectly lovely wedding! Loveliest wedding I ever saw. Oh, I do love a good wedding, don't you? Doesn't she make a lovely bride?

GEORGE: I do.

STAGE MANAGER: Do you, Emily, take this man, George, to be your wedded husband,—

Again his further words are covered by those of MRS. SOAMES.

MRS. SOAMES: Don't know *when* I've seen such a lovely wedding. But I always cry. Don't know why it is, but I always cry. I just like to see young people happy, don't you? Oh, I think it's lovely.

The ring. The kiss. The stage is suddenly arrested into silent tableau.

The STAGE MANAGER, his eyes on the distance, as though to himself:

STAGE MANAGER: I've married over two hundred couples in my day. Do I believe in it? I don't know. M. . . . marries N. . . . millions of them. The cottage, the go-cart, the Sunday-afternoon drives in the Ford, the first rheumatism, the grandchildren, the second rheumatism, the deathbed, the reading of the will,—

He now looks at the audience for the first time, with a warm smile that removes any sense of cynicism from the next line.

Once in a thousand times it's interesting.

—Well, lets have Mendelssohn's "Wedding March"!

The organ picks up the March. The BRIDE and GROOM come down the aisle, radiant, but trying to be very dignified.

MRS. SOAMES: Aren't they a lovely couple? Oh, I've never been to such a nice wedding. I'm sure they'll be happy. I always say: *happiness,* that's the great thing! The important thing is to be happy.

The BRIDE and GROOM reach the steps leading into the audience. A bright light is thrown upon them. They descend into the auditorium and run up the aisle joyously.

STAGE MANAGER: That's all the Second Act, folks. Ten minutes' intermission.

CURTAIN

ACT III

During the intermission the audience has seen the STAGEHANDS arranging the stage. On the right-hand side, a little right of the center, ten or twelve ordinary chairs have been placed in three openly spaced rows facing the audience.

These are graves in the cemetery.

Toward the end of the intermission the ACTORS enter and take their places. The front row contains: toward at center of the stage, an empty chair; then MRS. GIBBS; SIMON STIMSON. The second row contains, among others, MRS. SOAMES. The third row has WALLY WEBB.

The dead do not turn their heads or their eyes to right or left, but they sit in a quiet without stiffness. When they speak their tone is matter-of-fact, without sentimentality and, above all, without lugubriousness.

The STAGE MANAGER takes his accustomed place and waits for the house lights to go down.

STAGE MANAGER: This time nine years have gone by, friends—summer, 1913. Gradual changes in Grover's Corners. Horses are getting rarer. Farmers coming into town in Fords. Everybody locks their house doors now at night. Ain't been any burglars in town yet, but everybody's heard about 'em. You'd be surprised, though—on the whole, things don't change much around here.

This is certainly an important part of Grover's Corners. It's on a hilltop—a windy hilltop—lots of sky, lots of clouds,—often lots of sun and moon and stars. You come up here, on a fine afternoon and you can see range on range of hills—awful blue they are—up there by Lake Sunapee and Lake Winnipesaukee . . . and way up, if you've got a glass, you can see the White Mountains and Mt. Washington—where North Conway and Conway is. And, of course, our favorite mountain, Mt. Monadnock, 's right here—and all these towns that lie around it: Jaffrey, 'n East Jaffrey, 'n Peterborough, 'n Dublin; and

Then pointing down in the audience.

there, quite a ways down, is Grover's Corners. Yes, beautiful spot up here. Mountain laurel and li-lacks. I often wonder why people like to be buried in Woodlawn and Brooklyn when they might pass the same time up here in New Hampshire. Over there—

Pointing to stage left.

are the old stones,—1670, 1680. Strong-minded people that come a long way to be independent. Summer people walk around there laughing at the funny words on the tombstones . . . it don't do any harm. And genealogists come up from Boston—get paid by city people for looking up their ancestors. They want to make sure they're Daughters of the American Revolution and of the *Mayflower*. . . . Well, I guess that don't do any harm, either. Wherever you come near the human race, there's layers and layers of nonsense. . . .

Over there are some Civil War veterans. Iron flags on their graves . . . New Hampshire boys . . . had a notion that the Union ought to be kept together, though they'd never seen more than fifty miles of it themselves. All they knew was the name, friends—the United States of America. The United States of America. And they went and died about it.

This here is the new part of the cemetery. Here's your friend Mrs. Gibbs. 'N let me see—Here's Mr. Stimson, organist at the Congregational Church. And Mrs. Soames who enjoyed the wedding so—you remember? Oh, and a lot of others. And Editor Webb's boy, Wallace, whose appendix burst while he was on a Boy Scout trip to Crawford Notch.

Yes, an awful lot of sorrow has sort of quieted down up here. People just wild with grief have brought their relatives up to this hill. We all know how it is . . . and then time . . . and sunny days . . . and rainy days . . . 'n snow . . . We're all glad they're in a beautiful place and we're coming up here ourselves when our fit's over.

Now there are some things we all know, but we don't take'm out and look at'm very often. We all know that *something* is eternal. And it ain't houses and it ain't names, and it ain't earth, and it ain't even the stars . . . everybody knows in their bones that *something* is eternal, and that something has to do with human beings. All the greatest people ever lived have been telling us that for five thousand years and yet you'd be surprised how people are always losing hold of it. There's something way down deep that's eternal about every human being.

Pause.

You know as well as I do that the dead don't stay interested in us living people for very long. Gradually, gradually, they lose hold of the earth . . . and the ambitions they had . . . and the pleasures they had . . . and the things they suffered . . . and the people they loved. They get weaned away from earth—that's the way I put it,—weaned away.

And they stay here while the earth part of 'em burns away, burns out; and all that time they slowly get indifferent to what's goin' on in Grover's Corners.

They're waitin'. They're waitin' for something that they feel is comin'. Something important, and great. Aren't they waitin' for the eternal part in them to come out clear?
Some of the things they're going to say maybe'll hurt your feelings—but that's the way it is: mother'n daughter . . . husband 'n wife . . . enemy 'n enemy . . . money 'n miser . . . all those terribly important things kind of grow pale around here. And what's left when memory's gone, and your identity, Mrs. Smith?

He looks at the audience a minute, then turns to the stage.

Well! There are some *living* people. There's Joe Stoddard, our undertaker, supervising a new-made grave. And here comes a Grover's Corners boy, that left town to go out West.

JOE STODDARD *has hovered about in the background.* SAM CRAIG *enters left, wiping his forehead from the exertion. He carries an umbrella and strolls front.*

SAM CRAIG: Good afternoon, Joe Stoddard.

JOE STODDARD: Good afternoon, good afternoon. Let me see now: do I know you?

SAM CRAIG: I'm Sam Craig.

JOE STODDARD: Gracious sakes' alive! Of all people! I should'a knowed you'd be back for the funeral. You've been away a long time, Sam.

SAM CRAIG: Yes, I've been away over twelve years. I'm in business out in Buffalo now, Joe. But I was in the East when I got news of my cousin's death, so I thought I'd combine things a little and come and see the old home. You look well.

JOE STODDARD: Yes, yes, can't complain. Very sad, our journey today, Samuel.

SAM CRAIG: Yes.

JOE STODDARD: Yes, yes. I always hate to supervise when a young person is taken. They'll be here in a few minutes now. I had to come here early today—my son's supervisin' at the home.

SAM CRAIG [*Reading stones*]: Old Farmer McCarty, I used to do chores for him—after school. He had the lumbago.

JOE STODDARD: Yes, we brought Farmer McCarty here a number of years ago now.

SAM CRAIG [*Staring at* MRS. GIBB*'s knees*]: Why, this is my Aunt Julia . . . I'd forgotten that she'd . . . of course, of course.

JOE STODDARD: Yes, Doc Gibbs lost his wife two-three years ago . . . about this time. And today's another pretty bad blow for him, too.

MRS. GIBBS [*To* SIMON STIMSON: *in an even voice*]: That's my sister Carey's boy, Sam . . . Sam Craig.

SIMON STIMSON: I'm always uncomfortable when *they're* around.

MRS. GIBBS: Simon.

SAM CRAIG: Do they choose their own verses much, Joe?

JOE STODDARD: No . . . not usual. Mostly the bereaved pick a verse.

SAM CRAIG: Doesn't sound like Aunt Julia. There aren't many of those Hersey sisters left now. Let me see: where are . . . I wanted to look at my father's and mother's . . .

JOE STODDARD: Over there with the Craigs . . . Avenue F.

SAM CRAIG [*Reading* SIMON STIMSON*'s epitaph*]: He was organist at church, wasn't he?—Hm, drank a lot, we used to say.

JOE STODDARD: Nobody was supposed to know about it. He'd seen a peck of trouble. [*Behind his hand.*] Took his own life, y' know?

SAM CRAIG: Oh, did he?

JOE STODDARD: Hung himself in the attic. They tried to hush it up, but of course it got around. He chose his own epy-taph. You can see it there. It ain't a verse exactly.

SAM CRAIG: Why, it's just some notes of music—what is it?

JOE STODDARD: Oh, I wouldn't know. It was wrote up in the Boston papers at the time.

SAM CRAIG: Joe, what did she die of?

JOE STODDARD: Who?

SAM CRAIG: My cousin.

JOE STODDARD: Oh, didn't you know? Had some trouble bringing a baby into the world. 'Twas her second, though. There's a little boy 'bout four years old.

SAM CRAIG [*Opening his umbrella*]: The grave's going to be over there?

JOE STODDARD: Yes, there ain't much more room over here among the Gibbses, so they're opening up a whole new Gibbs section over by Avenue B. You'll excuse me now. I see they're comin'.

From left to center, at the back of the stage, comes a procession. FOUR MEN *carry a casket, invisible to us. All the rest are under umbrellas. One can vaguely see:* DR. GIBBS, GEORGE, *the* WEBBS, *etc. They gather about a grave in the back center of the stage, a little to the left of center.*

MRS. SOAMES: Who is it, Julia?

MRS. GIBBS [*Without raising her eyes*]: My daughter-in-law, Emily Webb.

MRS. SOAMES [*A little surprised, but no emotion*]: Well, I declare! The road up here must have been awful muddy. What did she die of, Julia?

MRS. GIBBS: In childbirth.

MRS. SOAMES: Childbirth. [*Almost with a laugh.*] I'd forgotten all about that. My, wasn't life awful—[*With a sigh.*] and wonderful.

SIMON STIMSON [*With a sideways glance.*]: Wonderful, was it?

MRS. GIBBS: Simon! Now, remember!

MRS. SOAMES: I remember Emily's wedding. Wasn't it a lovely wedding! And I remember her reading the class poem at Graduation Exercises. Emily was one of the brightest girls ever graduated from High School. I've heard Principal Wilkins say so time after time. I called on them at their new farm, just before I died. Perfectly beautiful farm.

A WOMAN FROM AMONG THE DEAD: It's on the same road we lived on.

A MAN AMONG THE DEAD: Yepp, right smart farm.

They subside. The group by the grave starts singing "Blessed Be the Tie That Binds."

A WOMAN AMONG THE DEAD: I always liked that hymn. I was hopin' they'd sing a hymn.

Pause. Suddenly EMILY *appears from among the umbrellas. She is wearing a white dress. Her hair is down her back and tied by a white ribbon like a little girl. She comes slowly, gazing wonderingly at the dead, a little dazed. She stops halfway and smiles faintly. After looking at the mourners for a moment, she walks slowly to the vacant chair beside* MRS. GIBBS *and sits down.*

EMILY [*To them all, quietly, smiling*]: Hello.

MRS. SOAMES: Hello, Emily.

A MAN AMONG THE DEAD: Hello, M's Gibbs.

EMILY [*Warmly*]: Hello, Mother Gibbs.

MRS. GIBBS: Emily.

EMILY: Hello. [*With surprise.*] It's raining.

Her eyes drift back to the funeral company.

MRS. GIBBS: Yes . . . They'll be gone soon, dear. Just rest yourself.

EMILY: It seems thousands and thousands of years since I . . . Papa remembered that that was my favorite hymn.

Oh, I wish I'd been here a long time. I don't like being new here.—How do you do, Mr. Stimson?

SIMON STIMSON: How do you do, Emily.

EMILY *continues to took about her with a wondering smile; as though to shut out from her mind the thought of the funeral company she starts speaking to* MRS. GIBBS *with a touch of nervousness.*

EMILY: Mother Gibbs, George and I have made that farm into just the best place you ever saw. We thought of you all the time. We wanted to show you the new barn and a great long ce-ment drinking fountain for the stock. We bought that out of the money you left us.

MRS. GIBBS: I did?

EMILY: Don't you remember, Mother Gibbs—the legacy you left us? Why, it was over three hundred and fifty dollars.

MRS. GIBBS: Yes, yes, Emily.

EMILY: Well, there's a patent device on the drinking fountain so that it never overflows, Mother Gibbs, and it never sinks below a certain mark they have there. It's fine. [*Her voice tails off and her eyes return to the funeral group.*]

It won't be the same to George without me, but it's a lovely farm. [*Suddenly she looks directly at* MRS. GIBBS.] Live people don't understand, do they?

MRS. GIBBS: No, dear—not very much.

EMILY: They're sort of shut up in little boxes, aren't they? I feel as though I knew them last a thousand years ago . . . My boy is spending the day at Mrs. Carter's. [*She sees* MR. CARTER *among the dead.*] Oh, Mr. Carter, my little boy is spending the day at your house.

MR. CARTER: Is he?

EMILY: Yes, he loves it there.—Mother Gibbs, we have a Ford, too. Never gives any trouble. I don't drive, though. Mother Gibbs, when does this feeling go away?—Of being . . . one of *them?* How long does it . . . ?

MRS. GIBBS: Sh! dear. Just wait and be patient.

EMILY [*With a sigh*]: I know.—Look they're finished. They're going.

MRS. GIBBS: Sh—.

The umbrellas leave the stage. DR. GIBBS *has come over to his wife's grave and stands before it a moment.* EMILY *looks up at his face.* MRS. GIBBS *does not raise her eyes.*

EMILY: Look! Father Gibbs is bringing some of my flowers to you. He looks just like George, doesn't he? Oh, Mother Gibbs, I never realized before how troubled and how . . . how in the dark live persons are. Look at him. I loved him so. From morning till night, that's all they are—troubled.

DR. GIBBS *goes off.*

THE DEAD: Little cooler than it was.—Yes, that rain's cooled it off a little. Those northeast winds always do the same thing, don't they? If it isn't a rain, it's a three-day blow.—

A patient calm falls on the stage. The STAGE MANAGER *appears at his proscenium pillar, smoking.* EMILY *sits up abruptly with an idea.*

EMILY: But, Mother Gibbs, one can go back; one can go back there again . . . into living. I feel it. I know it. Why just then for a moment I was thinking about . . . about the farm . . . and for a minute I *was* there, and my baby was on my lap as plain as day.

MRS. GIBBS: Yes, of course you can.

EMILY: I can go back there and live all those days over again . . . why not?

MRS. GIBBS: All I can say is, Emily, don't.

EMILY [*She appeals urgently to the* STAGE MANAGER]: But it's true, isn't it? I can go and live . . . back there . . . again.

STAGE MANAGER: Yes, some have tried—but they soon come back here.

MRS. GIBBS: Don't do it, Emily.

MRS. SOAMES: Emily, don't. It's not what you think it'd be.

EMILY: But I won't live over a sad day. I'll choose a happy one—I'll choose the day I first knew that I loved George. Why should that be painful?

THEY *are silent. Her question turns to the* STAGE MANAGER.

STAGE MANAGER: You not only live it; but you watch yourself living it.

EMILY: Yes?

STAGE MANAGER: And as you watch it, you see the thing that they—down there—never know. You see the future. You know what's going to happen afterwards.

EMILY: But is that—painful? Why?

MRS. GIBBS: That's not the only reason why you shouldn't do it, Emily. When you've been here longer you'll see that our life here is to forget all that, and think only of what's ahead, and be ready for what's ahead. When you've been here longer you'll understand.

EMILY [*Softly*]: But, Mother Gibbs, how can I *ever* forget that life? It's all I know. It's all I had.

MRS. SOAMES: Oh, Emily. It isn't wise. Really, it isn't.

EMILY: But it's a thing I must know for myself. I'll choose a happy day, anyway.

MRS. GIBBS: *No!*—At least, choose an unimportant day. Choose the least important day in your life. It will be important enough.

EMILY [*To herself*]: Then it can't be since I was married; or since the baby was born. [*To the* STAGE MANAGER, *eagerly.*] I can choose a birthday at least, can't I?—I choose my twelfth birthday.

STAGE MANAGER: All right. February 11th, 1899. A Tuesday.—Do you want any special time of day?

EMILY: Oh, I want the whole day.

STAGE MANAGER: We'll begin at dawn. You remember it had been snowing for several days; but it had stopped the night before, and they had begun clearing the roads. The sun's coming up.

EMILY [*With a cry; rising*]: There's Main Street . . . why, that's Mr. Morgan's drugstore before he changed it! . . . And there's the livery stable.

The stage at no time in this act has been very dark; but now the left half of the stage gradually becomes very bright—the brightness of a crisp winter morning. EMILY *walks toward Main Street.*

STAGE MANAGER: Yes, it's 1899. This is fourteen years ago.

EMILY: Oh, that's the town I knew as a little girl. And, *look*, there's the old white fence that used to be around our house. Oh, I'd forgotten that! Oh, I love it so! Are they inside?

STAGE MANAGER: Yes, your mother'll be coming downstairs in a minute to make breakfast.

EMILY [*Softly*]: Will she?

STAGE MANAGER: And you remember: your father had been away for several days; he came back on the early-morning train.

EMILY: No . . . ?

STAGE MANGER: He'd been back to his college to make a speech—in western New York, at Clinton.

EMILY: Look! There's Howie Newsome. There's our policeman. But he's *dead*; he *died*.

The voices of HOWIE NEWSOME, CONSTABLE WARREN *and* JOE CROWELL, JR., *are heard at the left of the stage.* EMILY *listens in delight.*

HOWIE NEWSOME: Whoa, Bessie!—Bessie! 'Morning, Bill.

CONSTABLE WARREN: Morning, Howie.

HOWIE NEWSOME: You're up early.

CONSTABLE WARREN: Been rescuin' a party; darn near froze to death, down by Polish Town thar. Got drunk and lay out in the snowdrifts. Thought he was in bed when I shook'm.

EMILY: Why, there's Joe Crowell . . .

JOE CROWELL: Good morning, Mr. Warren. 'Morning, Howie.

MRS. WEBB *has appeared in her kitchen, but* EMILY *does not see her until she calls.*

MRS. WEBB: Chil-*dren!* Wally! Emily! . . . Time to get up!

EMILY: Mama, I'm here! Oh! how young Mama looks! I didn't know Mama was ever that young.

MRS. WEBB: You can come and dress by the kitchen fire, if you like; but hurry.

HOWIE NEWSOME *has entered along Main Street and brings the milk to* MRS. WEBB*'s door.*

Good morning, Mr. Newsome. Whhhh—it's cold.

HOWIE NEWSOME: Ten below by my barn, Mrs. Webb.

MRS. WEBB: Think of it! Keep yourself wrapped up.

She takes her bottles in, shuddering.

EMILY [*With an effort*]: Mama, I can't find my blue hair ribbon anywhere.

MRS. WEBB: Just open your eyes, dear, that's all. I laid it out for you special—on the dresser, there. If it were a snake it would bite you.

EMILY: Yes, yes . . .

She puts her hand on her heart. MR. WEBB *comes along Main Street, where he meets* CONSTABLE WARREN. *Their movements and voices are increasingly lively in the sharp air.*

MR. WEBB: Good morning, Bill.

CONSTABLE WARREN: Good morning, Mr. Webb. You're up early.

MR. WEBB: Yes, just been back to my old college in New York State. Been any trouble here?

CONSTABLE WARREN: Well, I was called up this mornin' to rescue a Polish fella—darn near froze to death he was.

MR. WEBB: We must get it in the paper.

CONSTABLE WARREN: 'Twan't much.

EMILY [*Whispers*]: Papa.

MR. WEBB *shakes the snow off his feet and enters his house.* CONSTABLE WARREN *goes off, right.*

MR. WEBB: Good morning, Mother.

Mrs. Webb: How did it go, Charles?

MR. WEBB: Oh, fine, I guess. I told'm a few things.—Everything all right here?

MR. WEBB: Yes—can't think of anything that's happened, special. Been right cold. Howie Newsome says it's ten below over to his barn.

MR. WEBB: Yes, well, it's colder than that at Hamilton College. Students' ears are falling off. It ain't Christian.—Paper have any mistakes in it?

MRS. WEBB: None that I noticed. Coffee's ready when you want it. [*He starts upstairs.*] Charles! Don't forget; it's Emily's birthday. Did you remember to get her something?

MR. WEBB [*Patting his pocket*]: Yes, I've got something here. [*Calling up the stairs.*] Where's my girl? Where's my birthday girl?

He goes off left.

MRS. WEBB: Don't interrupt her now, Charles. You can see her at breakfast. She's slow enough as it is. Hurry up, children! It's seven o'clock. Now, I don't want to call you again.

EMILY [*Softly, more in wonder than in grief*]: I can't bear it. They're so young and beautiful. Why did they ever have to get old? Mama, I'm here. I'm grown up. I love you all, everything.—I can't look at everything hard enough.

She looks questioningly at the STAGE MANAGER, *saying or suggesting: "Can I go in?" He nods briefly. She crosses to the inner door to the kitchen, left of her mother, and as though entering the room, says, suggesting the voice of a girl of twelve:*

Good morning, Mama.

MRS. WEBB [*Crossing to embrace and kiss her; in her characteristic matter-of-fact manner*]: Well, now, dear, a very happy birthday to my girl and many happy returns. There are some surprises waiting for you on the kitchen table.

EMILY: Oh, Mama, you *shouldn't* have. [*She throws an anguished glance at the stage manager.*] I can't—I can't.

MRS. WEBB [*Facing the audience, over her stove*]: But birthday or no birthday, I want you to eat your breakfast good and slow. I want you to grow up and be a good strong girl.

That in the blue paper is from your Aunt Carrie; and I reckon you can guess who brought the post-card album. I found it on the doorstep when I brought in the milk—George Gibbs . . . must have come over in the cold pretty early . . . right nice of him.

EMILY [*To herself*]: Oh, George! I'd forgotten that. . . .

MRS. WEBB: Chew that bacon good and slow. It'll help keep you warm on a cold day.

EMILY [*With mounting urgency*]: Oh, Mama, just look at me one minute as though you really saw me. Mama, fourteen years have gone by. I'm dead. You're a grandmother, Mama. I married George Gibbs, Mama. Wally's dead, too. Mama, his appendix burst on a camping trip to North Conway. We felt just terrible about it—don't you remember? But, just for a moment now we're all together. Mama, just for a moment we're happy. *Let's look at one another.*

MRS. WEBB: That in the yellow paper is something I found in the attic among your grandmother's things. You're old enough to wear it now, and I thought you'd like it.

EMILY: And this is from you. Why, Mama, it's just lovely and it's just what I wanted. It's beautiful!

She flings her arms around her mother's neck. Her MOTHER *goes on with her cooking, but is pleased.*

MRS. WEBB: Well, I hoped you'd like it. Hunted all over. Your Aunt Norah couldn't find one in Concord, so I had to send all the way to Boston. [*Laughing.*]
Wally has something for you, too. He made it at manual-training class and he's very proud of it. Be sure you make a big fuss about it.—Your father has a surprise for you, too; don't know what it is myself. Sh—here he comes.

MR. WEBB [*Off stage*]: Where's my girl? Where's my birthday girl?

EMILY [*In a loud voice to the stage manager*]: I can't. I can't go on. It goes so fast. We don't have time to look at one another.

She breaks down sobbing. The lights dim on the left half of the stage. MRS. WEBB *disappears.*

I didn't realize. So all that was going on and we never noticed. Take me back—up the hill—to my grave. But first: Wait! One more look.

Good-by, Good-by, world. Good-by, Grover's Corners . . . Mama and Papa. Good-by to clocks ticking . . . and Mama's sunflowers. And food and coffee. And new-ironed dresses and hot baths . . . and sleeping and waking up. Oh, earth, you're too wonderful for anybody to realize you.

She looks toward the stage manager and asks abruptly, through her tears:

Do any human beings ever realize life while they live it?—every, every minute?

STAGE MANAGER: No. [*Pause.*] The saints and poets, maybe—they do some.

EMILY: I'm ready to go back.

She returns to her chair beside MRS. GIBBS. *Pause.*

MRS. GIBBS: Were you happy?

EMILY: No . . . I should have listened to you. That's all human beings are! Just blind people.

MRS. GIBBS: Look, it's clearing up. The stars are coming out.

EMILY: Oh, Mr. Stimson, I should have listened to them.

SIMON STIMSON [*With mounting violence; bitingly*]: Yes, now you know. Now you know! That's what it was to be alive. To move about in a cloud of ignorance; to go up and down trampling on the feelings of those . . . of those about you. To spend and waste time as though you had a million years. To be always at the mercy of one self-centered passion, or another. Now you know—that's the happy existence you wanted to go back to. Ignorance and blindness.

MRS. GIBBS [*Spiritedly*]: Simon Stimson, that ain't the whole truth and you know it. Emily, look at that star. I forget its name.

A MAN AMONG THE DEAD: My boy Joel was a sailor,—knew 'em all. He'd set on the porch evenings and tell 'em all by name. Yes, sir, wonderful!

ANOTHER MAN AMONG THE DEAD: A star's mighty good company.

A WOMAN AMONG THE DEAD: Yes. Yes, 'tis.

SIMON STIMSON: Here's one of *them* coming.

THE DEAD: That's funny. 'Tain't no time for one of them to be here.— Goodness sakes.

EMILY: Mother Gibbs, it's George.

MRS. GIBBS: Sh, dear. Just rest yourself.

EMILY: It's George.

GEORGE *enters from the left, and slowly comes toward them.*

A MAN FROM AMONG THE DEAD: And my boy, Joel, who knew the stars—he used to say it took millions of years for that speck o' light to git to the earth. Don't seem like a body could believe it, but that's what he used to say—millions of years.

GEORGE *sinks to his knees then falls full length at* EMILY'S *feet.*

A WOMAN AMONG THE DEAD: Goodness! That ain't no way to behave!

MRS. SOAMES: He ought to be home.

EMILY: Mother Gibbs?

MRS. GIBBS: Yes, Emily?

EMILY: They don't understand, do they?

MRS. GIBBS: No, dear. They don't understand.

The STAGE MANAGER *appears at the right, one hand on a dark curtain which he slowly draws across the scene. In the distance a clock is heard striking the hour very faintly.*

STAGE MANAGER: Most everybody's asleep in Grover's Corners. There are a few lights on: Shorty Hawkins, down at the depot, has just watched the Albany train go by. And at the livery stable somebody's setting up late and talking.—Yes, it's clearing up. There are the stars—doing their old, old crisscross journeys in the sky. Scholars haven't settled the matter yet, but they seem to think there are no living beings up there. Just chalk . . . or fire. Only this one is straining away, straining away all the time to make something of itself. The strain's so bad that every sixteen hours everybody lies down and gets a rest. [*He winds his watch.*] Hm. . . . Eleven o'clock in Grover's Corners.—You get a good rest, too. Good night.

THE END

Bertolt Brecht

Bertolt Brecht (1898–1956) was born in Augsburg, Germany, into a middle-class family whose situation and values he rejected. A critic of bourgeois society from an early age, throughout his life he would bear the imprint of a Marxist-Communist point of view. Brecht intended to study medicine, but after having served as a medical orderly in World War I, he became increasingly mordant and nihilistic, probably the result of the horror of trench warfare.

Brecht had an overpowering personality, and many who were associated with him regarded him as a tyrant. He overpowered weaker friends and expected their collaboration, but he seldom gave credit to those who worked with him. He worked closely with his three lovers Elisabeth Hauptmann, Margarete Steffin, and Ruth Berlau, and they seem to have been instrumental in the creation of his most important female characters. Their contributions are only now being assessed and appreciated, however.

At first, Brecht worked within the traditional conventions of the theater and poetry. *Baal* (1918) is an intensely poetic drama, and *Drums in the Night* (1922) is structured as a problem play in the style of Henrik Ibsen. But Brecht soon changed, partly because of his desire to evolve a new style of theater of social and political criticism. Along with Erwin Piscator (1893–1966), a director and also a Marxist, Brecht set out to subvert traditional theater. In 1924, with Piscator's help, Brecht modernized Christopher Marlowe's tragedy *Edward II* (ca. 1592), an Elizabethan chronicle play. Brecht's innovations for this play included scene-by-scene subtitles, describing the action of the kind used in silent movies.

The following year, Brecht wrote *Man Is Man* (1925), a piece leading to the development of his ideas of an "epic theater" that used distancing devices intended to force the audience to confront a play's ideas rather than become emotionally involved with the action. The play was ornamented with printed summary projections, a half-curtain, half-masks for actors, songs accompanying the action, and visible backstage equipment. Two years later, Brecht joined Piscator in a theater company in Berlin that was dedicated to producing plays that criticized middle-class values and were sympathetic to Marxist communism. At this time, Brecht was working on an adaptation of *The Good Soldier Schweik,* a satirical novel by Jaroslav Hašek (1883–1923) about a good-natured but hapless common soldier, whose misadventures satirize the stupidity of war and government bureaucracy. In 1930 Brecht collaborated with Piscator and the artist George Grosz (1893–1959) for the production.

Brecht's first success came with *The Threepenny Opera* (1928), his longest-running production and probably the most successful play of the 1920s in Germany. Brecht's collaborator for the translation of John Gay's text was Elisabeth Hauptmann; Kurt Weill (1900–1950) wrote the music. Brecht and Weill had already collaborated on the musical score for the opera *The Rise and Fall of the*

City of Mahagonny (1927, revised 1930) and would continue to collaborate on several theater pieces, including the ballet-cantata *The Seven Deadly Sins* (1933).

As Brecht became well known, his influence as an innovator grew, particularly in terms of the technical and methodological innovations that make up Epic Theater. The stage, Brecht said, should be used to preach ideas and morality. It ought to be unencumbered by elaborate settings and props. Lighting must be clear (and white) so that the audience can see what is on stage. Costumes should be ordinary clothes (if possible) so that the actors and the characters that they portray are seen as people. He favored narrating action over showing action. He also preferred montage and loosely connected scenes, and shied away from the tightly knit plots of Henrik lbsen. In theory, Brecht's ideas were firm, but in practice, he was pragmatic; and photographs of his productions show that he did not rigidly follow his own dicta.

Brecht hated Adolf Hitler (1889–1945), and in the early 1930s depicted the stupidity of fascism and militarism. A production of *The Measures Taken* was interrupted by the Berlin police; Brecht was charged with treason, but he was not arrested.

In 1933, Brecht left Germany for Switzerland, and then moved to Copenhagen. He lived there until 1939, and safely continued his attacks on the Nazi regime. *The Resistible Rise of Arturo Ui* (1941) is a ferocious satire on the life of Hitler, and *The Private Life of the Master Race* (produced in 1945) is a documentary drama in twenty-four scenes describing Nazi oppression. When Germany invaded Poland in 1939, Brecht moved back to Switzerland, then to Sweden, and then to New York City and Los Angeles (1941–1947), where he lived out the war.

Brecht's six years in the United States were marginally productive, and he achieved no theatrical success. He worked in Hollywood, but was unhappy. With Fritz Lang he wrote an anti-Nazi story that was the basis for Lang's film *Hangman Must Also Die* (1943), but he aborted other projects. Before Brecht returned to Germany in 1947, Charles Laughton, the actor, produced an English version of *The Life of Galileo*, which Brecht had written in 1938. Brecht and Laughton collaborated on the translation, and Laughton portrayed Galileo (1564–1642). Like Galileo, whose observations of the universe threatened the authority of the Catholic Church, Brecht saw himself as oppressed by his criticism of society and politics. In spite of Laughton's star stature, *The Life of Galileo* was not well received when produced in New York City, possibly because of Brecht's association with communism. Brecht was called to testify before the House Un-American Activities Committee about his association with communism. He said that he was not a Communist, but this was a lie.

After returning to East Berlin in 1947, then under Communist control, Brecht established the Berliner Ensemble, an organization dedicated to realizing his concepts of Epic Theater. Brecht's support of the repressive East German Communist regime during a political uprising disappointed many of his admirers in Europe and the United States, who thought he should have acted on principle. The Communists rewarded him with the Stalin Peace Prize (1955), and Brecht, then fifty-five, went to Moscow to receive it.

Brecht's plays are political, and much of his material, such as the early *Edward II*, is taken from history. *Mother Courage and Her Children* (1939), one of his mature plays, is a historical drama set during the Thirty Years' War (1618–1648) between the Protestants and Catholics in central Europe, especially Poland. The choice of this subject is probably an allusion to the outbreak of war and Hitler's invasion of Poland in 1939. But it is also a direct criticism of brutality and false heroism, and the greed of capitalism that thrives on war. Mother Courage, the protagonist, operates a canteen and follows the Protestant army until she is captured by the Catholics. She loses her children: Swiss Cheese, an honest but simple son; Kattrin, a beautiful but dumb daughter; and Eilif, a brutally efficient soldier. Alone, she barely stops to mourn Kattrin's death, and as she harnesses herself to her wagon, she says, "Yes, I'll manage, there's not much in it now. I must get back into business." The question that Brecht poses, and leaves for his audience to ponder, is whether one should empathize with the person of Mother Courage or see in her unfeeling capitalism that thrives on war.

The Good Woman of Setzuan (1943), a play of ten episodes and five songs, is a parable about the double-sidedness of human beings, something like Robert Louis Stevenson's *Dr. Jekyll and Mr. Hyde* (1898), crossed with the biblical story of Lot. The play's chief character is Shen Te, a common prostitute whose character and hospitality impresses three gods when they visit Earth looking for a good person. When they leave, the gods give her some money that she uses to set up a small business. The drive to succeed leads Shen Te to invent a male alter ego, Shui Ta, who is ruthless and avaricious. Alternating between the female and male sides of her personality, Shen Te begins a lifelong pattern of behavior that obscures her inner goodness: succeeding by exploiting others. When Shen Te finally complicates her life to the point of despair, she is again judged by the gods, who fail to understand her needs. When she pleads for help and understanding for her dual life, the gods retreat into heaven. In an epilogue, the audience is asked to help resolve Shen Te's problems. This direct appeal to the audience is an element of Epic Theater and an inherent part of Brecht's attempt to use theater to effect social and political change. For Brecht there is neither god nor heaven, and responsibility for personal and social relationships resides in the individual and the here and now.

Many of Brecht's ideas for Epic Theater were first successfully used in *The Threepenny Opera*. The structure is a series of scenes arbitrarily assembled into two acts. The scenery is sparse and suggestive rather than detailed, and subtitles offer slogans reinforcing the action. The musical play is an adaptation of John Gay's *The Beggar's Opera* (1728). Gay called his play a ballad-opera because in it dialogue was interspersed with songs set to folk melodies and current popular tunes. Gay meant to satirize political corruption, showing that there is no difference between vice in high and low places. His subject may have been suggested by Jonathan Swift, whose idea was to write a satiric pastoral about the thieves and whores of Newgate Prison in London. Brecht's satire is an attack on middle-class society, which he saw as exploiting the working class. Its more scathing tone suits Brecht's German personality, and contrasts with the light comic touches of Gay's English personality.

Brecht's intention for *Threepenny Opera* was to attack the bourgeoisie by exposing its inherent immorality, greed, and corruption. When he transposed middle-class and capitalist values to the criminal classes, Brecht implied that criminals are a phenomenon of middle-class and capitalist corruption. In his "Notes" to *The Threepenny Opera,* Brecht wrote, "The bandit Macheath must be played as a bourgeois phenomenon. The bourgeois fascination for bandits rests on the fallacy: that a bandit is not a bourgeois. This misconception is the child of another misconception: that a bourgeois is not a bandit." Mr. Peachum, Polly's father and the ringleader of London's beggars and thieves, is presented as a middle-class entrepreneur. Polly Peachum is a sweet thing capable of directing a thriving criminal organization. The whores are presented as working women, and their occupation as another aspect of greedy capitalism. What Brecht did not fathom was that the popularity of Macheath and Polly would make criminals into heroes. Consequently, his success tended to obscure rather than crystallize his political and philosophical messages.

Middle-class audiences enjoyed the satire and were generally immune to Brecht's Marxism. Brecht expanded the scenario of the play in a film version (1931), which he hoped would increase his audience. But the film softened his message, and he sued the producers for control of the material. He lost. Brecht switched genres and in 1933 published *Threepenny Opera* as a novel. It was not successful, either.

Brecht's importance to modern and contemporary drama is twofold. First, the technical elements of epic theater, once avant-garde, have become standard. Second, Brecht's use of history as a framework to anchor his plots and themes in the real world, and especially to highlight political and moral dilemmas, can be found in the works of many subsequent writers. Brechtian drama has influenced such diverse playwrights as Arthur Miller (*All My Sons*), Wole Soyinka (*The Lion and the Jewel*), Lorraine Hansberry (*A Raisin in the Sun*), and Sam Shepard (*Buried Child*).

Film

The Three Penny Opera (1962), directed by Wolfgang Staudte, with Curt Jurgens, Hildegarde Neff, Gert Frobe, June Ritchie, Lino Venuta, and Sammy Davis, Jr. Dubbed in English. Embassy Pictures.

The Threepenny Opera (1931), directed by G. W. Pabst, with Lotte Lenya, and Rudolph Forster. German with English subtitles. Seymour Nebenzel for Nero-Film.

The Threepenny Opera

TRANSLATED BY RALPH MANHEIM

CHARACTERS

MACHEATH, nicknamed Mackie the Knife
JONATHAN JEREMIAH PEACHUM, proprietor of the firm "The Beggar's Friend"
CELIA PEACHUM, his wife
POLLY PEACHUM, his daughter
BROWN, chief of police in London
LUCY, his daughter
GINNY JENNY
SMITH
THE REVEREND KIMBALL
FILCH
A BALLAD SINGER, THE GANG, BEGGARS, WHORES, CONSTABLES

PROLOGUE

Market Day in Soho

Beggars are begging, thieves thieving, whores whoring. A ballad singer sings a Moritat.

THE MORITAT OF MACKIE THE KNIFE

And the shark he has his teeth and
There they are for all to see.
And Macheath he has his knife but
No one knows where it may be.

When the shark has had his dinner
There is blood upon his fins.
But Macheath he has his gloves on:
They say nothing of his sins.

All along the Thames Embankment
People fall down with a smack.
And it is not plague or cholera:
Word's around that Mac is back.

On a blue and balmy Sunday
Someone drops dead in the Strand.
And a man slips round the corner.
People say: Macheath's on hand.

And Schmul Meyer still is missing
Like many another rich young man.
And Macheath has got his money.
Try to prove *that* if you can!

PEACHUM *with his wife and daughter stroll across the stage from left to right.*

Jenny Towler was discovered
With a jackknife in her breast.
And Macheath strolls down the dockside
Knows no more than all the rest.

Where is Alphonse Glite the coachman?
Was he stabbed or drowned or shot?
Maybe someone knows the answer.
As for Mackie, he does not.

One old man and seven children
Burnt to cinders in Soho.
In the crowd is Captain Mackie who
Is not asked and does not know.

And the widow not yet twenty
(Everybody calls her Miss)
Woke up and was violated.
What did Mackie pay for this?

There is a burst of laughter from the whores, and a man steps out from among them and walks quickly across the stage and exit.

GINNY JENNY: Look! That was Mackie the Knife!

ACT I

1

IN ORDER TO COMBAT THE INCREASING HARDHEARTEDNESS OF MEN, MR. J. PEACHUM, MAN OF BUSINESS, HAS OPENED A SHOP WHERE THE POOREST OF THE POOR MAY ACQUIRE AN APPEARANCE THAT WILL TOUCH THE STONIEST OF HEARTS

The Wardrobe Room of Jonathan Jeremiah Peachum's Establishment for Beggars

PEACHUM'S MORNING ANTHEM

Wake up, you old Image of Gawd!
Get on with your sinful backsliding!
Continue to perpetrate fraud!
Jehovah will do the providing!

Go barter your brother, you bear!
Sell your wife at an auction, you lout!
You think Our Lord God isn't there?
On Judgment Day you will find out.

PEACHUM [*to the audience*]: Something new—that's what we *must* have. My business is too difficult. You see, my business is trying to arouse human pity. There are a few things that'll move people to pity, a few, but the trouble is, when they've been used several times, they no longer work. Human beings have the horrid capacity of being able to make themselves heartless at will. So it happens, for instance, that a man who sees another man on the street corner with only a stump for an arm will be so shocked the first time that he'll give him sixpence. But the second time it'll be only a threepenny bit. And if he sees him a third time, he'll hand him over cold-bloodedly to the police. It's the same with these spiritual weapons.

A large board is let down from the flies and on it is written: "It is more blessed to give than to receive."

What's the use of the finest and most stirring sayings painted on the most enticing boards if they get used up so quickly? There are four or five sayings in the Bible that really touch the heart. But when they're used up, one's daily bread's just gone. Take that one there: "Give and it shall be given unto you"—how threadbare it has become in the three weeks we've had it. Always something new must be offered. We can fall back on the Bible again, but how often can *that* be done?

There is a knock. PEACHUM *opens the door, and a young man named* FILCH *enters.*

FILCH: Peachum & Co.?
PEACHUM: Peachum.
FILCH: Then you're the owner of the firm called "The Beggars' Friend"? I was sent to you. Oh, those sayings! What an investment! I suppose you've got a whole library of such things? Well, that's something quite different! Fellows like us—we'd never get an idea like that, and not being properly educated, how could business ever flourish?
PEACHUM: Your name?
FILCH: Well, you see, Mr. Peachum, I've had bad luck ever since I was a boy. My mother was a drunkard, my father a gambler. From an early age I had to fend for myself. And without the loving hand of a mother to guide me I sank deeper and deeper into the morass of the great city. I never knew a father's care or the blessings of a contented home. So now you see me . . .
PEACHUM: So now I see you . . .
FILCH [*confused*]: . . . see me . . . completely destitute, a prey to my own desires.
PEACHUM: Like a wreck on the high seas, and so on. Tell me, wreck, in which district do you recite this nursery rhyme?
FILCH: What do you mean, Mr. Peachum?
PEACHUM: Of course, you deliver this speech in public?
FILCH: Yes, you see, Mr. Peachum, there was a nasty little incident yesterday in Highland Street. I was standing quietly and miserably at the corner, hat in hand, not meaning any harm. . . .
PEACHUM [*turning over the pages of a notebook*]: Highland Street. Yes. That's the one. You're the crawling blackleg that Honey and Sam caught yesterday. You had the impertinence to solicit passers-by in District 10. We let it go at a good beating, as we took it you didn't know where God lives. But if you let yourself be seen there again, we shall have to use the saw. Understand?
FILCH: Please, Mr. Peachum, please! What can I *do* then, Mr. Peachum? The gentlemen really beat me black and blue, and then they gave me your business card. If I was to take off my coat, you'd think you was looking at a mackerel.
PEACHUM: My young friend, if you don't look like a flounder, my people were a sight too easy with you. This young sprout comes along and imagines that if he sticks out his paws he'll be all set for a juicy steak. What would you say if someone took the best trout out of your pond?
FILCH: But you see, Mr. Peachum—I haven't got a pond.
PEACHUM: Well, licenses are only granted to professionals. [*He points in a businesslike way to a large map of London.*] London is divided into fourteen districts. Everyone wishing to ply the begging-trade in any one of them has to have a license from Jonathan Jeremiah Peachum and Company. My God, anyone could come along—"a prey to his own desires"!
FILCH: Mr. Peachum. Only a few shillings stand between me and total ruin. I *must* be able to do something with two shillings in hand. . . .
PEACHUM: One pound.
FILCH: Mr. Peachum! [FILCH *points beseechingly at a poster which reads: "Shut not your ears to misery."*]

PEACHUM *points to a curtain in front of a showcase, on which is written: "Give and it shall be given unto you."*

FILCH: Ten shillings.
PEACHUM: And fifty per cent of the weekly takings. Including outfit, seventy per cent.
FILCH: And please, what does the outfit consist of?
PEACHUM: The firm decides that.

FILCH: Well, what district can I start on?

PEACHUM: Top half of Baker Street. That'll be a bit cheaper. It's only fifty per cent there, including outfit.

FILCH: Thank you. [*He pays.*]

PEACHUM: Your full name?

FILCH: Charles Filch.

PEACHUM: Correct. [*Shouts.*] Mrs. Peachum!

MRS. PEACHUM *enters.*

This is Filch. Number 314, Upper Baker Street. I'll enter it myself. Of course, you would want to start now, just before the Coronation—the chance of a lifetime to earn a little money. Outfit C for you. [*He draws back the linen curtain in front of a showcase in which are standing five wax models.*]

FILCH: What's that?

PEACHUM: These are the five basic types of misery best adapted to touching the human heart. The sight of them induces that unnatural state of mind in which a man is actually willing to give money away.

Outfit A: Victim of the Progress of Modern Traffic. The Cheerful Cripple, always good-tempered— [*He demonstrates it.*] —always carefree, effect heightened by a mutilated arm.

Outfit B: Victim of the Art of War. The Troublesome Twitcher, annoys passers-by, his job is to arouse disgust— [*He demonstrates it.*] —modified by medals.

Outfit C: Victim of the Industrial Boom. The Pitiable Blind, or the High School of the Art of Begging. [PEACHUM *displays him, advancing unsteadily toward* FILCH. *At the moment when he bumps into* FILCH, *the latter screams with horror.* PEACHUM *stops instantly, gazes at him in amazement, and suddenly roars:*] He feels pity! You'll never make a beggar—not in a lifetime. That sort of behavior is only fit for the passers-by! Then it's Outfit D!—Celia, you've been drinking again! And now you can't see out of your eyes. Number 136 has been complaining about his neck-rag. How often must I tell you a gentleman will not have filthy clothing next to his skin. Number 136 has paid for a brand-new costume. The stains—the only thing about it capable of awakening pity—were to be put on by neatly ironing in paraffin wax! Never trouble to think! Always have to do everything oneself. [*To* FILCH:] Undress and put this on, but keep it in good condition!

FILCH: And what happens to my things?

PEACHUM: Property of the firm. Outfit E: Young man who's seen better days, preferably one who "never thought he would come down to this."

FILCH: Oh, so you're using that too. Why can't *I* have the better days outfit?

PEACHUM: Because nobody believes in his own misery, my boy. If you've got the stomach-ache and say so, it only sounds disgusting. Anyway, it's not for you to ask questions. Just put these things on.

FILCH: Aren't they rather dirty?

PEACHUM *gives him a piercing glance.*

I'm sorry, Mr. Peachum, I'm sorry.

MRS. PEACHUM: Get a move on, sonny, I'm not going to hold your trousers till Christmas.

FILCH [*suddenly with great determination*]: But I'm not going to take my shoes off! Not for anything. I'd rather chuck the whole thing. They were the only present I had from my poor mother, and never, never, however low I may have fallen . . .

MRS. PEACHUM: Don't talk rubbish. I know you've got dirty feet.

FILCH: Well, where do you expect me to wash my feet? In the middle of winter?

MRS. PEACHUM *leads him behind a folding screen, then sits down left and begins ironing candle-grease into a suit.*

PEACHUM: Where's your daughter?

MRS. PEACHUM: Polly? Upstairs.

PEACHUM: Was that man here again yesterday? The one who always comes when I'm out?

MRS. PEACHUM: Don't be so suspicious, Jonathan! There isn't a finer gentleman alive, and the Captain takes quite an interest in our Polly.

PEACHUM: Um.

MRS. PEACHUM: And if I can see an inch before my nose, Polly is fond of him too.

PEACHUM: There you go, Celia! Throwing your daughter around as if I were a millionaire! So she's going to marry! And do you think our miserable business would last another week if the filthy customers had only *our* legs to look at? A husband! He'd soon have us in his clutches. That he would. Do you think your daughter would be any better than you at keeping her mouth shut in bed?

MRS. PEACHUM: You've got a nice opinion of your daughter!

PEACHUM: The worst! The very worst! She is nothing but a mass of sensuality.

MRS. PEACHUM: Well, she certainly doesn't get that from you!

PEACHUM: Marry! My daughter should be to me what bread is to the starving. [*He thumbs through the Bible.*] That's actually written somewhere in the Bible. Marriage is a disgusting business anyhow. I'll soon beat the marriage out of her.

MRS. PEACHUM: Jonathan, you're just ignorant.

PEACHUM: Ignorant! What's his name, then—this *gentleman*?

MRS. PEACHUM: People just call him always "The Captain."

PEACHUM: So you haven't even asked him his name! Very nice!

MRS. PEACHUM: Well, we wouldn't be so ill-bred as to ask him for his birth certificate; him being such a gentleman, inviting us to the Octopus Hotel for a little hop.

PEACHUM: Where!

MRS. PEACHUM: To the Octopus. For a little hop.

PEACHUM: Captain? Octopus Hotel? I see—

MRS. PEACHUM: The gentleman never touched me and my daughter except with kid gloves on.

PEACHUM: Kid gloves!

MRS. PEACHUM: Now I come to think of it, he always has gloves on—white ones, white kid gloves.

PEACHUM: Ah! White kid gloves and a stick with an ivory handle and spats over his patent leather shoes and a nice polite manner and a scar . . .

MRS. PEACHUM: On his neck. How do you know all this about him?

FILCH *comes out.*

FILCH: Mr. Peachum, could you give me a few tips on what to do? I always like to have a system and not go at things haphazard.

MRS. PEACHUM: He wants a system!

PEACHUM: He can be an idiot. Come back this evening at six and you'll be given the necessaries. Now, get out!

FILCH: Thank you, Mr. Peachum, thank you very much. [*Exit.*]

PEACHUM: Fifty per cent!—And now I'll tell you who this gentleman with the kid glove is—he's Mackie the Knife!

He runs up the stairs into POLLY'*s bedroom.*

MRS. PEACHUM: Lord save us! Mackie the Knife! Jesus, Mary and Joseph! Polly! Where's Polly!

PEACHUM *comes slowly downstairs.*

PEACHUM: Polly? Polly hasn't been home. Her bed's not touched.

MRS. PEACHUM: Then she's been having supper with that wool merchant. I'm certain of it, Jonathan.

PEACHUM: For our sake, I hope it was the wool merchant.

MR. *and* MRS. PEACHUM *step in front of the curtain and sing. Song illumination: a golden light. The organ is lit up. Three lights come down on a bar from above, and on a board is written:*

THE I-FOR-ONE SONG

PEACHUM: I for one
Like to spend the night at home and in my bed.
She prefers fun:
Does she think the Lord keeps busy pouring manna on her head?

MRS. PEACHUM: Such is the moon over Soho
Such is that magic "Can you feel my heart beating" spell
Oh, it's "Whither thou goest, I will go with thee, Johnny"
And the new moon's shining on the asphodel.

PEACHUM: I for one
Like to do what has a purpose and a goal.
They prefer fun:
After which of course they end up in the hole.

BOTH: So where is their moon over Soho?
What's left of their confounded "Can you feel my heart beating" spell?
Where now is their "Whither thou goest, I will go with thee, Johnny!"
For the old moon's waning and you're shot to hell!

2

DEEP IN THE HEART OF SOHO, MACKIE THE KNIFE CELEBRATES HIS WEDDING WITH POLLY PEACHUM, DAUGHTER OF THE KING OF THE BEGGARS

An Empty Stable

MATTHEW [*nicknamed* "MONEY MATTHEW," *carrying a lantern and pointing a revolver round the stable*]: Hi! Hands up, if anyone's there!

MACHEATH *enters and walks round by the front of the stage.*

MACHEATH: Well? Is anyone here?

MATTHEW: Not a soul. We can have our marriage here safe enough.

POLLY [*enters in a wedding dress*]: But this is a stable!

MACHEATH: Sit down on the crib for a while, Polly. [*To the audience:*] Today, in this stable, my marriage to Miss Polly Peachum will be celebrated; she has followed me for love, in order to share the rest of my life with me.

MATTHEW: A lot of people in London will be saying this is the riskiest thing you've ever done, luring Mr. Peachum's only child out of his own house.

MACHEATH: Who *is* Mr. Peachum?

MATTHEW: He himself would say he was the poorest man in London.

POLLY: But you're not thinking of having our marriage here? It's just a nasty, common stable. You can't invite the clergyman here. And besides, it isn't even ours. We really ought not to begin our new life with a burglary, Mac. This is the happiest day of our lives!

MACHEATH: Dearest child, everything shall be as you wish. Not a stone shall touch your little feet. The furnishings are on the way at this very moment.

MATTHEW: Here comes the furniture!

There is a sound of heavy wagons arriving. Half a dozen men enter, carrying furniture, carpets, crockery, etc., and soon the stable is transformed into an over-ornate living room.[1*]

MACHEATH: Junk!

The men place their presents down on the left, congratulate the bride, and report to the bridegroom.[2]

JACOB [*nicknamed* "HOOK-FINGER JACOB"]: Here's luck! At 14 Ginger Street there were some people on the second floor. We had to smoke 'em out.

ROBERT [*nicknamed* "ROBERT THE SAW"]: Good luck! A copper in the Strand got in our way.

MACHEATH: Amateurs!

ED: We did what we could, but three people in the West End are goners. Good luck!

MACHEATH: Amateurs and bunglers!

JIMMY: An old gentleman got something he wasn't expecting. I don't think it's serious. Luck!

MACHEATH: My orders were: bloodshed to be avoided. It makes me quite sick when I think of it. *You'll* never make businessmen. Cannibals—but never businessmen!

WALTER [*nicknamed* "WALLY THE WEEPER"]: Good luck! Half an hour ago, madam, that harpsichord still belonged to the Dutchess of Somerset!

POLLY: Whatever furniture is this?

MACHEATH: How do you like it, Polly?

POLLY [*crying*]: All those poor people, just for a few bits of furniture!

MACHEATH: And what furniture! Junk! You're right to be angry. A rosewood harpsichord—and a Renaissance sofa. That's unforgivable. And where's a table?

WALTER: A table?

They lay planks across the feeding troughs.

POLLY: Oh, Mac, I'm so unhappy. Let's hope anyhow the clergyman won't come!

MATTHEW: But he will. *We* told him the way quite clearly.

WALTER [*pushes forward the improvised table*]: A table!

MACHEATH [*seeing* POLLY *crying*]: My wife is upset. And where are the other chairs? A harpsichord and no chairs! Never trouble to think. How often does it happen that I have a wedding? Shut your trap, Weeper! How often does it happen, I'm asking, that I leave anything to you? It makes my wife unhappy from the start.

ED: Dear Polly . . .

MACHEATH [*knocking his hat from his head*[3]]: "Dear Polly!" I'll knock your head into your guts with your "dear Polly," you sewer rat! Whoever heard the like— "dear Polly"! Maybe you've slept with her?

POLLY: But Mac . . .

ED: I swear that . . . !

WALTER: Madam, if there's anything more you'd like here, we'll go out again . . .

MACHEATH: A rosewood harpsichord and no chairs! [*Laughs.*] What do you say to that, as the bride?

POLLY: Well, it could be worse.

MACHEATH: Two chairs and a sofa, and the bridal pair sits on the ground.

POLLY: Yes, that's a fine thing.

MACHEATH [*sharply*]: Saw the legs off the harpsichord! Come on! Come on!

Four of the men saw the legs off the harpsichord and sing:

Bill Lawgen and Mary Syer
They were spliced last Tuesday night by law!
Where the bride's gown came from he did not
know
She'd no name for her man but So and So
And yet they got a license from the Registrar!
(A toast!)

WALTER: And so, all's well that ends well. We have another bench, madam.

MACHEATH: Might I now request you gentlemen to take off your rags and dress yourselves respectably? After all, this isn't the wedding of a nobody. And Polly, may I ask you to get busy with the grub hampers?

POLLY: Is that the wedding breakfast? Is it all stolen, Mac?

MACHEATH: Of course, of course.

POLLY: I'd like to know what you'd do if there was a knock on the door and the sheriff came in!

---

*Numerals in the text refer to Brecht's "Notes" to the play, which may be found in this volume, beginning on p. 912.

MACHEATH: Then I'd show you what your husband *can* do.

MATTHEW: Not a chance of it today. All the police are lining the streets. The Queen's coming to town for the Coronation on Friday.

POLLY: Two knives and fourteen forks! A knife for each chair!

MACHEATH: What a wash out! That's the work of apprentices, not trained men. Haven't you any idea of style? You ought to be able to tell the difference between Chippendale and Louis Quatorze.

The rest of the gang now return, wearing smart evening dress, but their behavior during the rest of the scene is unfortunately not in keeping with their attire.

WALTER: We wanted to bring the most valuable things. Look at that wood! The material is absolutely first-class.

MATTHEW: Sssst! Permit me, Captain . . .

MACHEATH: Come here, Polly.

The two of them pose for congratulations.

MATTHEW: Permit me, Captain, on behalf of all, on the happiest day of your life, the springtide of your career—its turning point, one might say—to offer you our heartiest congratulations and . . . so forth. It's horrible—this gassy talk. Well, anyway— [*Shakes* MACHEATH*'s hand.*] —chin up, boys!

MACHEATH: Thank you. That was very nice of you, Matthew.

MATTHEW [*shaking* POLLY*'s hand, after having patted* MACHEATH *affectionately on the back*]: Ah, it's spoken from the heart! Well, keep your head up, old man, I mean— [*Grinning.*] —as far as your head's concerned never let it droop.

Roars of laughter from the men. MACHEATH *suddenly catches hold of* MATTHEW *and gently jerks him to the floor.*

MACHEATH: Hold your trap. Keep your dirty jokes for your Kitty: she's the right slut for them.

POLLY: Mac, don't be so common.

MATTHEW: I object to you calling Kitty a slut . . . [*Stands up with difficulty.*]

MACHEATH: Oh! You object, do you?

MATTHEW: And what's more, I never have dirty jokes for her. I respect Kitty far too much for that. Which maybe you can't understand, being made the way you are. And you ought to know about dirty jokes! You think Lucy hasn't told me the things you've said to her? I'm a kid-gloves gent compared to that.

MACHEATH *gives him a look.*

JACOB: Stop it. This is a wedding! [*They pull him back.*]

MACHEATH: A fine wedding, eh, Polly? To see these gutter-rats all round you on the day of your marriage! You never thought your husband would be let down by his friends like this. That'll teach you.

POLLY: I think it's nice.

ROBERT: Tripe! No one's letting you down. A little difference of opinion can happen any time. Your Kitty is as good as anyone else. Now come on with the wedding present, my boy.

ALL: Come on, get on with it!

MATTHEW [*offended*]: There!

POLLY: Oh! A wedding present! How sweet of you, Mr. Money Matthew! Look, Mac, what a lovely nightdress!

MATTHEW: Another dirty joke, eh, Captain?

MACHEATH: All right, now. Didn't want to offend you on this festive occasion.

WALTER: Well, and what about this? Chippendale! [*He uncovers an immense Chippendale grandfather clock.*]

MACHEATH: Quatorze.

POLLY: It's wonderful. I'm so happy. I can't find words, your kindness is so fantastic. A shame we haven't a home for it, isn't it Mac?

MACHEATH: Think of it as a beginning. All beginnngs are difficult. Many thanks, Walter. Now clear the stuff away—food.

JACOB [*while the others are laying the table*]: Of course, I've forgotten to bring anything. [*Emphatically to* POLLY:] Believe me, young lady, I feel very embarrassed.

POLLY: Don't mention it, Mr. Hook-Finger Jacob.

JACOB: All the boys throw their presents around and I stand here with nothing. Put yourself in my place. But this always happens to me! I could tell you of some fixes I've been in! Boy! You wouldn't believe them! The other day I met Ginny Jenny and said to her, "Now look, you old cow," I said . . .

He suddenly sees MACHEATH *standing behind him and walks away without a word.*

MACHEATH: [*leads* POLLY *to her seat*]: This is the finest food you'll get anywhere today, Polly. Shall we start?

They all sit down to the wedding breakfast.[4]

ED [*pointing to the service*]: Lovely plates, Savoy Hotel.

JACOB: The egg mayonnaise is from Selfridge's. We had a jar of goose liver too. But on the way here Jimmy ate it out of spite. He said he had an empty belly.

WALTER: Respectable people don't say "belly."

JIMMY: And, Ed, don't gobble your eggs so, today of all days!

MACHEATH: Can't someone sing something? Something delightful?

MATTHEW [*choking with laughter*]: Something delightful! That's a proper word! [*Under* MACHEATH*'s annihilating glance, he sits down, embarrassed.*]

MACHEATH [*knocking a dish out of someone's hand*]: As a matter of fact, I didn't wish to start eating yet. Instead of this "On-with-the-food-and-into-the-trough" exhibition from you men, I'd have preferred something festive. Other people always do some such thing on a day like this.

JACOB: What sort of thing?

MACHEATH: Must I think of everything myself? I'm not asking for an opera here. But you might have arranged something more than eating and telling dirty jokes—well, a day like this just shows how far one can count on one's friends.

POLLY: The smoked salmon's wonderful, Mac.

ED: I bet you've never ate salmon like it. Mac has it every day. You're in the honeypot all right. I always said Mac'll make a fine match for a girl with a feeling for higher things. I said so to Lucy yesterday.

POLLY: Lucy? Who is Lucy, Mac?

JACOB [*embarrassed*]: Lucy? Well, you know, you mustn't take it so seriously.

MATTHEW *has stood up and is making furious gestures behind* POLLY *to silence* JACOB.

POLLY [*sees him*]: Are you wanting something? The salt? What were you going to say, Mr. Jacob?

JACOB: Oh nothing. Nothing at all. I really wasn't going to say anything. I'll be getting my tongue burnt.

MACHEATH: What have you got in your hand, Jacob?

JACOB: A knife, Captain.

MACHEATH: And what have you got on your plate?

JACOB: A trout, Captain.

MACHEATH: I see. And with the knife, I believe, you are eating the trout. That is unheard of, Jacob. Have you ever seen such a thing, Polly? Eating fish with a knife! A person who does that is a pig, do you understand me, Jacob? Try to learn!—You'll have a lot to do, Polly, before you can teach such oafs to behave like gentlemen. Do you even know what the word means: a gentleman?

WALTER: I know the difference from a woman!

POLLY: Oh, Mr. Walter!

MACHEATH: Well, don't you want to sing a song? Nothing to brighten up the day a bit? It's to be just another damn, sad, ordinary, dirty day like any other? And is anyone keeping watch at the door? Maybe you'd like me to do that? Perhaps I should stand guard at the door, today of all days, so you can stuff yourselves here at my expense?

WALTER [*sullenly*]: What do you mean: at my expense?

JIMMY: Shut up, Wally. I'll go out. Who'd come here anyway? [*Exit.*]

JACOB: It'd be funny if all the wedding guests were copped today!

JIMMY [*bursts in*]: Captain, the coppers!

WALTER: Tiger Brown!

MATTHEW: Garn, it's the Reverend Kimball.

KIMBALL *enters.*

ALL [*shout*]: Good evening, Reverend Kimball!

KIMBALL: Well, well, well, so I've found you at last! In a little hut I find you; a small place, indeed, but your own.

MACHEATH: The Duke of Devonshire's.

POLLY: How do you do, your Reverence. I'm so happy you've come, on the happiest day of our lives . . .

MACHEATH: I request an anthem for the Reverend Kimball.

MATTHEW: How about "Bill Lawgen and Mary Syer"?

JACOB: That's right, "Bill Lawgen" should do.

KIMBALL: It would be pleasing to hear your voices raised in song, my men.

MATTHEW: Let's begin, gents.

Three of the men stand up and sing, hesitating, flat and uncertain.

WEDDING SONG FOR POORER PEOPLE

Bill Lawgen and Mary Syer
They were spliced last Tuesday night by law!
(I give you Bill and Mary, Gawd bless 'em!)
Where the bride's gown came from he did not
 know
She'd no name for her man but So and So
And yet they got a license from the Registrar!
(A toast!)

Do you know what your good wife does? No!
Will you let her go on doing it? No!
(I give you Bill and Mary, Gawd bless 'em!)
Billy Lawgen said to me: Its fine
So long as just one part of her is mine.
(The swine!)

MACHEATH: Is that all? Paltry!

MATTHEW [*choking again*]: Paltry! Just the right word, gents. Paltry!

MACHEATH: Hold your trap!

MATTHEW: Well, I meant—no life, no swing, nothing!

POLLY: Gentlemen, if nobody will do anything, I myself will sing a little song as best I can, and in it I'm going to imitate a girl I once saw in a little bar in Soho. She was the washing-up skivvy, and I must tell you that everyone laughed at her, and then one day she spoke to the customers and told them the things I am going to sing to you now. So this is the little bar—you must imagine it being filthy dirty—and she stood behind it from morning to night. There's her slop pail and that's the cloth she used for drying the glasses. Where you are sitting, sat the men who laughed at her. You can laugh, too, so that everything is just as it was; but if you can't, then you needn't. [*She begins, pretending to wash glasses and muttering to herself.*] Now one of you must say—you for instance, Mr. Walter— [*Pointing at* WALTER:] —"And when is your ship coming home, Jenny?"

WALTER: And when is your ship coming home, Jenny?

POLLY: And another says—you, perhaps: "Do you still wash up the glasses, Pirate Jenny."

MATTHEW: Do you still wash up the glasses, Pirate Jenny?

POLLY: Yes, and now I'll begin.

Song illumination: golden light. The organ is lit up. Three lights on a bar come front above, and on a board is written:

PIRATE JENNY

Gentlemen, today you see me washing up the glasses
And making up the beds and cleaning.
When you give me p'raps a penny, I will curtsey rather well.
When you see my tatty clothing and this tatty old hotel
P'raps you little guess with whom you're dealing.
One fine afternoon there will be shouting from the harbor.
Folk will ask: what's the reason for that shout?
They will see me smiling while I rinse the glasses
And will say: what has she to smile about?
And a ship with eight sails and
With fifty great cannon
Sails in to the quay.

They say: go and wipe your glasses, my girl
And their pennies are thrown to me.
And I thank them for the pennies and I do the beds up right
(Though nobody is going to sleep in them that night)
And they haven't the least idea who I may be.
One fine afternoon there will be roaring from the harbor.
Folk will ask: what's the reason for that roar?
They will see me standing just beside the window
And will say: now what's she sneering for?
And the ship with eight sails and
With fifty great cannon
Will shoot up the town.

Gentlemen, I fear this puts an end to your laughter
For your walls, they will all cave in.
And this whole fair city will be razed to the ground.
Just one tatty old hotel will survive safe and sound.
Folk will ask what special person dwells therein.
And all night long round this hotel there will be shouting.
Folk will ask: why was it this they'd spare?
Folk will see me leave the place the following morning
And will say: so that's who was in there!
And the ship with eight sails and
With fifty great cannon
Will run flags up the mast.

And a hundred men will come ashore before it's noon
And will go where it's dark and chill.
And every man they find, they will drag along the street
And they'll clap him in chains and lay him at my feet
And they'll ask: now which of these are we to kill?
And when the clock strikes noon it will be still down by the harbor.
When folk ask: now just who has got to die?
You will hear me say at that point: All of them!
And when their heads fall, I'll say: Whoopee!
And the ship with eight sails and
With fifty great cannon
Will sail off with me.

MATTHEW: Very nice, comic, eh? How she does it, the young lady!

MACHEATH: What d'you mean: *nice*? That's art, not nice. You did it wonderfully, Polly. But before such swine—pardon me, your Reverence—there's no point, it's wasted. [*In an undertone to* POLLY:] Anyway, I don't approve of your doing this play-acting, kindly drop it in future.

Loud laughter at the table. The gang are making fun of the parson.

What have you got in your hand, your Reverence?

JACOB: Two knives, Captain.

MACHEATH: And what have you got on your plate, your Reverence?

KIMBALL: Smoked salmon, I think.

MACHEATH: And with the knife, I believe, you're eating the salmon?

JACOB: Have you ever seen the like, eating fish with a knife! A person who does that is nothing more than a . . .

MACHEATH: Pig. Understand me, Jacob? That'll teach you.

JIMMY [*bursting in*]: Captain! The coppers! It's the sheriff himself.

WALTER: Brown! Tiger Brown!

MACHEATH: Yes, Tiger Brown it is. It's Tiger Brown, Sheriff of London and pillar of the Old Bailey, who is about to enter Captain Macheath's poor little abode. Now you'll learn something!

The gang creep away.

JACOB: It's the gallows for us.

BROWN *enters.*

MACHEATH: Hello, Jacky!

BROWN: Hello, Mac! Now I haven't got much time, I must leave in a minute. Do you *have* to pick on somebody else's stable? *Another* burglary.

MACHEATH: But Jacky, it's so convenient. I'm delighted you could come to partake of old Mac's wedding breakfast. May I introduce my wife, Polly, née Peachum. Polly, this is Tiger Brown. Eh, old man? [*Slaps him on the back.*] And these are my friends, Jacky. You've probably seen them all before.

BROWN [*in embarrassment*]: I'm here in my private capacity, Mac.

MACHEATH: So are they. [*He calls them. They come, hands up.*] Hi, Jacob!

BROWN: That's Hook-Finger Jacob, he's a dirty skunk.

MACHEATH: Here! Jimmy! Robert! Walter!

BROWN: Well, we'll forget it for today.

MACHEATH: Hi, Ed! Matthew!

BROWN: Sit down, gentlemen, sit down.

ALL: Thank you, sir.

BROWN: Happy to meet the charming wife of my old friend Mac.

POLLY: Don't mention it, sir.

MACHEATH: Sit yourself down, you old rascal, and start in on the whisky! Polly! Gentlemen! Today you see in your midst a man whom our sovereign's inscrutable wisdom has chosen to set high over his fellow men, and who yet has remained through fair weather and foul my friend. You all know who I mean, and you, too, know who I mean, Brown. Ah, Jacky, do you remember when you were a soldier and I was a soldier and we served together in India? Jacky, old man, shall we sing them the "Song of the Heavy Cannon"? [*They sit side by side on the table.*]

Song illumination: a golden light. The organ is lit up. Three lights come down from above on a bar, and on a board is written:

THE SONG OF THE HEAVY CANNON

John was a soldier and so was James
And George became a sergeant in short order.
But the army is not interested in names:
They were soon marching north to the border.
What soldiers live on
Is heavy cannon
From the Cape to Cutch Behar.
If it should rain one night
And they should chance to sight
Pallid or swarthy faces
Of uncongenial races
They'll maybe chop them up to make some
beefsteak tartare.

Now John was rather cold at night
And James, he found the whisky "rather hot, sir."
But George said: "Everything's all right
For the army simply cannot go to pot, sir."
What soldiers live on
Is heavy cannon
From the Cape to Cutch Behar.
If it should rain one night
And they should chance to sight
Pallid or swarthy faces
Of uncongenial races
They'll maybe chop them up to make some
beefsteak tartare.

John's gone west and James is dead
And George is missing and barmy.
Blood, however, is still blood-red:
They're recruiting again for the army.

As they all sit there, they march in time with their feet.

What soldiers live on
Is heavy cannon
From the Cape to Cutch Behar.
If it should rain one night
And they should chance to sight
Pallid or swarthy faces
Of uncongenial races
They'll maybe chop them up to make some
beefsteak tartare.

MACHEATH: We were boyhood friends, and though the great tides of life have swept us far apart, although our professional interests are quite different—some might even say diametrically opposed—our friendship has survived it all.

That'll teach you something. Castor and Pollux, Hector and Andromache, and so forth. Seldom have I, the simple hold-up man—well, you know what I mean—seldom have I undertaken the smallest job without giving my friend Brown a share of the proceeds (a considerable share, Brown) as a token and a proof of my unswerving loyalty to him. And seldom has the all-powerful Sheriff—take that knife out of your mouth, Jacob—organized a raid without previously giving a little tip-off to me, the friend of his youth. Well . . . and so on, and so on . . . it's all a matter of give and take. That'll teach you. [*He takes* BROWN *by the arm.*] Well, Jacky, I'm glad you've come. That's what I call real friendship. [*A pause while* BROWN *sorrowfully regards a carpet.*] Genuine Shiraz.

BROWN: From the Oriental Carpet Company.

MACHEATH: We get all our carpets there. Do you know, I had to have you here today, Jacky. I hope you don't feel too uncomfortable, being in the position you are.

BROWN: You know, Mac, I can't refuse you anything. But I must be going. I've got so much on my mind. If the least thing should go wrong at the Coronation . . .

MACHEATH: Jacky, you know my father-in-law is a repulsive old swine. If he were to raise some sort of stink about me, are there any records in Scotland Yard that could be used against me?

BROWN: In Scotland Yard there is not the slightest thing against you, Mac.

MACHEATH: Of course not.

BROWN: I saw to that. Good night.

MACHEATH: Aren't you all going to stand up?

BROWN [*to* POLLY]: All the best!

Exit BROWN *accompanied by* MACHEATH.

JACOB [*who meanwhile with* MATTHEW *and* WALTER *has been conferring with* POLLY]: I must admit I couldn't repress certain trepidations when I heard Tiger Brown was coming!

MATTHEW: You know, miss, we have our contacts with the highest authorities.

WALTER: Yes. Mac always has an extra iron in the fire which the likes of us haven't a glimmering of. But we have our little irons in the fire too. Gentlemen, it's half past nine.

MATTHEW: And now—the high spot.

All retire to the back, behind a hanging carpet which conceals something. MACHEATH *enters.*

MACHEATH: What's up now?

MATTHEW: Another little surprise, Captain.

Behind the carpet they sing "The Wedding Song for Poorer People," very softly and full of feeling. However, when they get to the end of the first verse, MATTHEW *tears down the carpet and they sing on, bawling at the top of their voices and beating time on a bed which stands behind.*

MACHEATH: Thank you, friends, thank you.

WALTER: And now the unobtrusive departure.

The gang exeunt.

MACHEATH: And now sentiment must come into its own, for otherwise man becomes a mere slave to his work. Sit down, Polly.

Music.

Do you see the moon over Soho?

POLLY: I see it dearest. Can you feel my heart beating, beloved?

MACHEATH: I can feel it, beloved.

POLLY: Whither thou goest, I shall go with thee.

MACHEATH: And where thou stayest, there too shall I stay.

Both sing:

MACHEATH: And if there's no license or Registrar
Nor lovely flowers to make you a crown
POLLY: And if I don't know exactly who you are
Or where I got hold of this gown:
BOTH: The platter from which you are eating your bread
Don't you keep it long, throw it down
For love lasts forever (or not so long)
In many and many a town.

3

FOR PEACHUM, WHO KNOWS THE HARDNESS OF THE WORLD, THE LOSS OF HIS DAUGHTER MEANS NOTHING LESS THAN TOTAL RUIN

Peachum's Establishment for Beggars

Right, PEACHUM *and* MRS. PEACHUM. *In the doorway stands* POLLY, *in hat and coat, a small suitcase in her hand.*

MRS. PEACHUM: Married? First we load her fore and aft with dresses and hats and gloves and parasols, and when she's cost as much as a sailing ship to rig out, she flings herself in the gutter like a rotten tomato. Have you really gone and got married?

Song illumination: golden light. The organ is lit up. Three lights come down on a bar, and on a board is written:

IN A LITTLE SONG POLLY GIVES HER PARENTS A HINT OF HER MARRIAGE WITH THE GANGSTER MACHEATH

When I was a girl, and an innocent girl
(I was innocent once as were you)
I thought that perhaps I might interest some fellow
And so I must know just what to do.
And if he's a rich fellow
And if he's a nice fellow
And his collar is as white as snow
And if he knows how he should treat a real lady
Then I must tell him: No.
That way I can hold my head up high
And be a lady comme il faut.
Yes, the moon shines bright until it's day!
Yes, the boat is launched and duly sails away!
And that's just how far things go.
For one must not rush a fellow off his feet!
No, one must be cold and very slow.
For, hey presto, so much might happen!
The only word to use is: No.

The first man who came was a man from Kent
Who was all that a man should be.
The second, oh, he had three schooners in the harbor
And the third one was crazy for me.
And as they were rich men
And as they were nice men
And their collars were as white as snow
And as they knew how they should treat a real lady
I had to say to each one: No.
That way I could hold my head up high
And be a lady comme il faut.
Yes, the moon shone bright till it was day!
Yes, the boat was launched and duly sailed away!
And that's how far things could go.
For one must not rush a fellow off his feet!
No, I must be cold and very slow.
For, hey presto, so much might happen!
But not if I should whisper: No.

And yet one afternoon (and that day the sky was blue)
Came someone who did not ask.
And he hung his bowler hat upon the nail inside my bedroom
And applied himself to his task.
And as he was not rich
And as he was not nice
And even his Sunday collar was black as a crow
And as he didn't know how he should treat a real lady
I could not tell him: No.
This way I couldn't hold my head up high
Or be a lady comme il faut.
Oh, the moon shone bright the whole night long
But the boat was tied up good and strong
And it all had to be just so.
For a man must simply rush us off our feet
And one really needn't be so cold or slow.
For, hey presto, it had to happen:
I could not tell that someone No.

PEACHUM: So now she's become a crook's hussy! *Very* nice. That's lovely.

MRS. PEACHUM: If you're already so immoral as to marry at all, why must it be a horse thief and a footpad? That'll cost you dear some day! I should have seen it coming. Even as a child she had a head as swollen as the Queen of England.

PEACHUM: So she really got married.

MRS. PEACHUM: Yes. Yesterday afternoon at five o'clock.

PEACHUM: To a notorious criminal! Come to think of it, it shows great courage in the man. If I have to give away my daughter, the last support of my old age, my house will fall in and my last dog will desert me. Why, I couldn't give away the dirt under my fingernails without risking death from starvation. If the three of us can get through the winter on one log of wood, we may live to see next year. We *may*.

MRS. PEACHUM: What are you thinking of? This is our reward for everything, Jonathan. I shall go mad. Everything is going round in my head. I can't stand any more. Oh! [*She faints.*] A glass of brandy!

PEACHUM: There! See what you've done to your mother. Quick! A crook's trollop, that's fine, that's charming. Strange how the old lady has taken it to heart.

POLLY *returns with a bottle of brandy.*

The last consolation left for your poor mother!

POLLY: Go on, you can give her two glasses. *My* mother can carry twice as much when she's not herself. That'll put her on her legs again. [*During the whole of this scene she has a radiantly happy expression on her face.*]

MRS. PEACHUM [*revives*]: Oh! Now she's showing her wicked false sympathy and solicitude again!

Five men enter.[5]

BEGGAR: I must complain most strongly. Because this place is a pigsty. Because this isn't a proper stump, but just a mess, and I won't waste my money on it.

PEACHUM: What do you want? It's as good as the others, only you don't keep it clean.

BEGGAR: All right—then why don't I earn as much as the others? No, you can't put that over on me. [*Hurls the stump away.*] I might as well cut off my real leg, if I wanted such junk.

PEACHUM: Well, what *do* you want? What can *I* do about it if people have hearts of granite. I can't make you five stumps! In ten minutes I can make such a wreck out of any man that a dog would howl if he saw him. What can I do if *people* won't howl? There, take another stump, if one's not enough for you. But look after your things.

BEGGAR: That'll have to do.

PEACHUM [*tries a false arm on another beggar*]: Leather is no good, Celia. Rubber is more repulsive. [*To the third:*] The bruise is going down, and it's your last. Now we can start all over again. [*Examining the fourth.*] Of course, natural scabs are never the same as artificial ones. [*To the fifth:*] What's happened to you? You've been eating again. You'll have to be made an example of.

BEGGAR: Mr. Peachum, I really haven't eaten much, my fat's unnatural, I can't help it.

PEACHUM: Neither can I. You're dismissed. [*Turning his back to the second beggar.*] Between "giving people a shock" and "getting on their nerves" there's obviously a difference, my friend. I need artists. Today, only artists give people the right sort of shock. If you'd work properly, your public would be forced to appreciate you. But that never occurs to you. So naturally I cannot extend your engagement.

The beggars exeunt.

POLLY: Please consider him. Is he handsome? No. But he makes a living. He offers me an existence. He's a first-class burglar, a farsighted and experienced street robber. I could tell you exactly what he's got saved up. A few more successful enterprises and we can retire to a little house in the country, just like that Mr. Shakespeare father admires so much.

PEACHUM: Well then, it's all quite simple. You're married. What do you do when you're married? Don't bother to think. You get a divorce. Eh? Is that so hard to arrange?

POLLY: I don't know what you mean.

MRS. PEACHUM: Divorce.

POLLY: But I love him, how can I think of divorce?

MRS. PEACHUM: Polly, aren't you ashamed of yourself?

POLLY: Mother, if you've ever been in love . . .

MRS. PEACHUM: Love! Those damned books you've been reading have turned your head. Polly, *everyone* does it!

POLLY: Then I shall be an exception.

MRS. PEACHUM: I'll beat your bottom, you exception!

POLLY: All mothers do that, but it's no use. Because love is greater than a beaten bottom!

MRS. PEACHUM: Polly, don't try my patience too far.

POLLY: I won't let you rob me of my love!

MRS. PEACHUM: Another word, and you'll get a box on the ears.

POLLY: Love is the greatest thing in the world!

MRS. PEACHUM: And that fellow has several women. When he's hanged, there'll be half a dozen of them reporting as widows, each probably with a brat in her arms.—Oh, Jonathan!

PEACHUM: Hanged! How did you come to think of hanging? It's a good idea! Go outside, Polly.

Exit POLLY.

You're right. The idea's worth forty pounds.

MRS. PEACHUM: I know what you mean. Tell the sheriff.

PEACHUM: Of course. Besides, this way we get him hanged free. . . . It'll be two birds with one stone. Only we've got to find out where he's hiding.

MRS. PEACHUM: I can tell you, my dear. He's with his whores.

PEACHUM: But they won't give him up.

MRS. PEACHUM: Leave it to me. Money rules the world. I'll go straight to Wapping and talk to the girls. If this fine gentleman meets a single one of them two hours from now, he's a goner.

POLLY [*who has been listening behind the door*]: My dear Mama, you can save yourself the trouble. Before Mac would speak to such a woman, he'd give himself up to the police. And if he went to the police, the Sheriff would offer him a cocktail, and over a cigar they'd discuss a certain business in this street where things aren't quite as they should be either. For, dear Papa, the Sheriff was very merry at my wedding.

PEACHUM: What's the name of this Sheriff?

POLLY: His name is Brown. But you'd only know him as Tiger Brown. Because all who are afraid of him call him Tiger Brown. But my husband, you see, calls him Jacky. They were boyhood friends.

PEACHUM: I see, they're friends, are they? The Sheriff and the number one criminal. Then they're probably the only friends in this fine city.

POLLY [*rhapsodically*]: Whenever they had a cocktail together, they'd stroke each other's cheek and say,

"If you'll have another, I'll have another." And whenever one went out, the other's eyes grew moist and he'd say, "Whither thou goest, I will go too." There's nothing against Mac in Scotland Yard.

PEACHUM: I see. Between Tuesday evening and Thursday morning, Mr. Macheath—surely a much married gentleman—has enticed my daughter Polly Peachum from her parental home under the pretext of marriage. Before this week is over, this will be sufficient to bring him to the death he so richly deserves. "Mr. Macheath, you once had white kid gloves and a stick with an ivory handle and a scar on your neck and you frequented the Octopus Hotel. All that remains is your scar, the least valuable of your distinguishing marks, and henceforth you will frequent only prison cells, and soon you won't frequent anywhere . . ."

MRS. PEACHUM: Oh, Jonathan, you'll never succeed, for it's Mackie the Knife you're dealing with. They say he's the greatest criminal in London. He takes what he wants.

PEACHUM: Who is Mackie the Knife? Polly, get ready, we're going to the Sheriff of London. And *you're* going to Wapping.

MRS. PEACHUM: To his whores.

PEACHUM: For the wickedness of the world is so great you have to run your legs off to avoid having them stolen from under you.

POLLY: And I, Papa, will be very glad to shake Mr. Brown by the hand again.

All three walk to the front of the stage and to song illumination sing the first finale. On the board is written:

FIRST THREEPENNY-FINALE
ON THE UNCERTAINTY OF HUMAN CIRCUMSTANCES

POLLY: There's a thing I want to try:
Once in this my dark existence
To reward a man's persistence.
Do you think I aim too high?

PEACHUM [*with a Bible in his hands*]: The right to happiness is fundamental:
Men live so little time and die alone.
Nor is it altogether incidental
That they want bread to eat and not a stone.
The right to happiness is fundamental.
And yet how great would be the innovation
Should someone claim and get that right—hooray!
The thought appeals to my imagination!
But this old world of ours ain't built that way.

MRS. PEACHUM: How I wish I could supply
Philanthropical assistance
To relieve your dark existence
But one must not aim so high.

PEACHUM: To be a good man—what a nice idea!
And give the poor your money? That is fine!
When all mankind is good, His Kingdom's near!
Who would not like to bask in Light Divine?
To be a good man—what a nice idea!
But there's the little problem of subsistence:
Supplies are scarce and human beings base.
Who would not like a peaceable existence?
But this old world is not that kind of place.

POLLY AND MRS. PEACHUM:

I fear he's right, { my / your } dear old dad:

The world is poor and men are bad.

PEACHUM: Of course, he's right, your dear old dad:
The world is poor and men are bad.
An earthly paradise might be arranged
If this old world of ours could but be changed
But that can never be arranged.
Your brother might be fond of you
But if the meat supply won't do
He'd cut you down right where you stood.
(We'd all be loyal if we could.)
Your good wife might be fond of you
But if your love for her won't do
She'd cut you down right where you stood.
(We'd all be grateful if we could.)
Your children might be fond of you
But if your pension would not do
They'd cut you down right where you stood.
(We'd all be human if we could.)

POLLY AND MRS. PEACHUM: We do not mind confessing
The whole thing is depressing.
The world is poor and men are bad
And we have nothing more to add.

PEACHUM: There is of course no more to add.
The world is poor and men are bad.
We would be good, instead of base
But this old world is not that kind of place.

ALL THREE: We take no comfort from your bunk
For everything's a heap of junk.

PEACHUM: The world is poor and men are bad
There is of course no more to add.

ALL THREE: We do not mind confessing
The whole thing is depressing.
We take no comfort from your bunk
For everything's a heap of junk.

ACT II

1

THURSDAY AFTERNOON. MACKIE THE KNIFE TAKES LEAVE OF HIS WIFE BEFORE FLEEING ACROSS HIGHGATE MOOR TO ESCAPE HIS FATHER-IN-LAW

The Stable

POLLY [*enters*]: Mac! Mac! Don't be afraid, it's me.

MACHEATH [*lying on a bed*]: What's the matter? What are you looking like that for, Polly?

POLLY: I've just been to see Brown, and my father was there too, and they're plotting to catch you. My father threatened something terrible, and Brown stuck up for you at first; but he gave in later, and he thinks you ought to disappear for a while. Mac, you must pack quickly!

MACHEATH: What! Pack? Nonsense! Come here, Polly! We're going to do something quite different from packing.

POLLY: No, Mac, we can't now. I'm so frightened. They were talking about hanging all the time.

MACHEATH: I don't like it, Polly, when you're moody! There's nothing against *me* in Scotland Yard.

POLLY: No, perhaps there wasn't. But today there's a terrible lot. Listen, I've brought the list of charges with me. I don't know whether I shall get through it, it's endless: you've killed two shopkeepers, and committed more than thirty burglaries, twenty-three street robberies, arsons, attempted murders, forgeries, perjuries—and all in eighteen months. You're a terrible person, Mac. And in Winchester you seduced two sisters, both under the age of consent.

MACHEATH: They told me they were twenty-one. And what did Brown say?

He stands up slowly and walks to the right along the footlights, whistling.

POLLY: He caught me up in the corridor and said he couldn't do anything more for you. Oh, Mac! [*She throws her arms around his neck.*]

MACHEATH: Well then, if I *must* go, you'll have to take over the business.

POLLY: Don't talk of business now. I can't bear it! Mac, kiss your Polly again and swear that as far as she is concerned you'll never, never . . .

MACHEATH [*interrupts her and leads her to the table, where he pushes her down into a chair*]: These are the account books. Listen carefully. This is a list of the staff. [*Reads.*] Hook-Finger Jacob, a year and a half in business; let's see what he's brought in. One, two, three, four, five gold watches. Not much, but it's good skilled work.—Don't sit on my lap. I'm not in the mood now. And here's Walter—Wally the Weeper—an unreliable swine. Fences stuff on his own account. Three weeks grace for him, then the gallows. Simply report him to Brown.

POLLY [*sobbing*]: Simply report him to Brown.

MACHEATH: Jimmy the Second, an impudent customer—profitable but impudent. Pinches sheets from under the finest female backsides in the land. Give him a rise.

POLLY: I'll give him a rise.

MACHEATH: Robert—call him Robert the Saw—a petty thief without a trace of genius. He won't end on the gallows, he'll never come to anything.

POLLY: Never come to anything.

MACHEATH: Otherwise carry on the same as before: get up at seven, wash, take one bath a day, and so forth.

POLLY: You're right, Mac, I shall just have to set my teeth and keep an eye on the business. What's yours is mine, isn't it, Mackie? But, Mac, what about your rooms? Shall I give them up? I'm horrified at the rent!

MACHEATH: No, I need them.

POLLY: But why? They only cost us money.

MACHEATH: You seem to think I'm never going to come back.

POLLY: What do you mean? You can take them again![6] Mac . . . Mac, I can't stand it any longer. I look at your lips and I don't hear what you're saying. Will you be true to me, Mac?

MACHEATH: Of course I'll be true to you. I'll repay like with like. Do you think I don't love you? It's just that I look further ahead.

POLLY: I'm so glad, Mac. You think of me when they're after you like bloodhounds . . .

When he hears the word "bloodhounds," MACHEATH *stiffens, stands up, crosses to the right, takes off his coat and starts washing his hands.*

MACHEATH [*hurriedly*]: Send all the profits to Jack Poole's banking house in Manchester. Between ourselves, it's only a question of weeks before I switch to banking exclusively. It's safer as well as more profitable. In two weeks at the most the money must be out of this business. And then you'll go to Brown and hand the whole list of names to the police. In four weeks at the most, all this scum of the earth will be standing their trial at the Old Bailey.

POLLY: But Mac! How can you look them in the eye when you're going to double-cross them like this and have them as good as hanged? Can you still shake them by the hand?

MACHEATH: Who? Money Matthew, Hook-Finger Jacob, Robert the Saw, Wally the Weeper . . . those jailbirds?

Enter the gang.

Gentlemen, I'm very glad to see you.

POLLY: . . . gentlemen.

MATTHEW: Captain, I've got the plans for the Coronation here. There's a day of good hard work ahead of us. The Archbishop of Canterbury arrives in half an hour.

MACHEATH: When?

MATTHEW: Five-thirty. We must go at once, Captain.

MACHEATH: Yes, you must go at once.

ROBERT: What do you mean: *you*?

MACHEATH: As far as I'm concerned, I'm afraid I've got to take a short trip to the country.

ROBERT: What? Are they going to nab you?

MATTHEW: And just when the Coronation's coming off! A Coronation without you will be soup without a spoon.

MACHEATH: Shut your mouth. I'm handing over the management of the business to my wife for a short time.—Polly! [*He pushes her to the front and then retires to the back, where he watches her.*]

POLLY: Men, I think our Captain can go away without having to worry. We shall get along fine, eh?

MATTHEW: I've got nothing to say. But I don't know if a woman . . . at a time like this . . . I'm not saying anything against *you*, ma'am . . .

MACHEATH [*from the back*]: What do you say to that, Polly?

POLLY: You've made a good start, you son of a bitch! [*Screaming.*] Of course you're not saying anything against me, or these gentlemen here would long ago have had your trousers off and tanned your bottom. Isn't that so, gentlemen?

A short pause, then they all clap like mad.

JACOB: She's all right!

WALTER: Bravo! Out new captain knows the answers! Hurrah for Polly!

ALL: Hurrah for Polly!

MACHEATH: It's a shame I can't be in London for the Coronation. It'll be a gold mine. Every house empty during the day, and at night all the best people drunk. That reminds me, Matthew—you drink too much. Last week you made it obvious that it was you that set fire to the children's hospital at Greenwich. If this happens again, you're sacked. Who set fire to the children's hospital?

MATTHEW: I did.

MACHEATH [*to the others*]: Who set it on fire?

THE FIVE OTHERS: You did, Captain.

MACHEATH: Who did?

MATTHEW [*sullenly*]: You did. This way, the likes of me will never come up in the world.

MACHEATH [*with a gesture of hanging*]: You'll come up all right, if you try to compete with me. Did you ever hear of an Oxford professor letting all his scientific mistakes be made by some assistant? Of course not: he takes the credit for them himself.

ROBERT: Ma'am, now you're in command while your husband's away . . . payday every Thursday, ma'am.

POLLY: Every Thursday, men!

Exit gang.

MACHEATH: And now, good-bye, my love. Keep fresh, and don't forget to make up every day, just as if I were there.

POLLY: And you, Mac, promise me you'll never look at another woman, and that you'll leave London at once. Believe me, your little Polly doesn't say this out of jealousy, but because it's important.

MACHEATH: But, Polly, why should I bother with secondhand goods? I love only you. When it's dark enough I shall start out, get my black stallion from . . . oh, some stable or other, and before you can see the moon from your window, I shall be far beyond Highgate Moor.

POLLY: Oh, Mac, don't tear my heart from my body. Stay with me and let us be happy.

MACHEATH: But I have to tear my own heart from my body, for I have to go and no one knows when I shall return.

POLLY: It lasted such a little while, Mac.

MACHEATH: And now it is over?

POLLY: Mac, last night I had a dream. I was looking out of the window and I heard laughter in the street, and when I looked up I saw our moon, and the moon was quite thin, like a penny that's all worn away. Don't forget me, Mac, in the strange cities.

MACHEATH: Of course I shall never forget you, Polly. Kiss me, Polly.

POLLY: Good-bye, Mac.

MACHEATH: Good-bye, Polly. [*As he exits:*]
For love lasts forever (or not so long)
In ever so many a town.

POLLY [*alone*]: And he never will come back again!
[*She sings:*]
Sweet while it lasted
And now it is over.
Tear out your heart
Say "Good-bye, good Polly!"
What use is your weeping
(Blessed Virgin, restore me)
When it's plain my mother
Knew all this before me!

The bells ring.

The Queen is now in London on her way.
Where shall we be on Coronation Day?

INTERLUDE

MRS. PEACHUM *and* GINNY JENNY *step out in front of the curtain.*

MRS. PEACHUM: So if you see Mackie the Knife in the next few days, run to the nearest copper and report him. You'll get ten shillings for it.
GINNY JENNY: But do you think we'll see him if the police are after him? When the hunt starts, he won't be wasting any time with us.
MRS. PEACHUM: Let me tell you this, Jenny: if all London were after him, Macheath is not the man to give up his old habits.

She sings:

THE BALLAD OF SEXUAL SUBMISSIVENESS

Now here's a man who fights old Satan's battle:
The butcher, he! All other men, mere cattle!
He is a shark with all the world to swim in!
What gets him down? What gets 'em all down?
Women.
He may not want to, but he'll acquiesce
For such is sexual submissiveness.
He does not heed the Bible nor the Statute Book.
He says he is an egomaniac.
If women look at him, he won't look back
For girls can murder with a look.
His fortitude by daylight is surprising
But when the night is falling, he is rising.

And many saw the tragic fall of many:
The great Macheath fell into Harlot Jenny.
Those who stood by might swear his sins were scarlet
But when they died, who buried them? Some harlot.
They may not want to, but they acquiesce
For such is sexual submissiveness.
Some read the Bible; others take a Law Degree;
Some join the Church and some attack the State:
While some remove the celery from their plate
And then devise a theory.
By evening all are busy moralizing
But when the night is falling, they are rising.

2

THE CORONATION BELLS HAVE NOT YET RUNG OUT AND MACKIE THE KNIFE IS ALREADY AMONG HIS WHORES AT WAPPING. THE GIRLS BETRAY HIM. IT IS THURSDAY EVENING

A Brothel in Wapping

An ordinary evening. The whores, mostly in their shifts, are quietly ironing, playing draughts, washing themselves: a middle-class idyll.[7] JENNY *sits alone on one side.* HOOK-FINGER JACOB *is reading the newspaper without anyone paying the slightest attention to him. In fact, he is rather in the way.*

JACOB: He won't come today.
WHORE: Won't he?
JACOB: I don't think he'll *ever* come again.
WHORE: That would be a pity.
JACOB: Would it? If I know him, he's out of the city by this time. Up and away!

Enter MACHEATH. *He hangs his hat on a nail and sits on the sofa behind the table.*

MACHEATH: My coffee, please!
VIXEN [*repeats astounded*]: "My coffee, please!"
JACOB [*horrified*]: Why aren't you in Highgate?
MACHEATH: Today is Thursday. I cannot let such trifles disturb my habits. [*He throws his charge-sheet on the floor.*] Besides, it's raining.
GINNY JENNY [*reads the charge-sheet*]: "In the name of the Queen, Captain Macheath is herewith charged with triple . . . "
JACOB [*snatching it from her*]: Am I there too?
MACHEATH: Of course, the whole staff.
GINNY JENNY [*to another whore*]: Look, here are the charges. [*Pause.*] Mac, give me your hand. [*He holds out his hand as he drinks from a coffee cup in the other.*]
DOLLY: Yes, Jenny, read his hand.

She holds forward a paraffin lamp.

MACHEATH: A rich legacy?
GINNY JENNY: No, not a rich legacy.

BETTY: Why are you looking at him like that, Jenny? It's enough to give anyone the shivers.
MACHEATH: A long journey in the near future?
GINNY JENNY: No, not a long journey.
VIXEN: What do you see then?
MACHEATH: Only good news, please! No bad!
GINNY JENNY: Oh well! I see a narrow strip of darkness there and a little love. And then I see a large T, which means the treachery of a woman. Then I see . . .
MACHEATH: Stop. I'd like to have a few details about the narrow strip of darkness and the treachery: for example, the name of the treacherous woman.
GINNY JENNY: I can only see that it begins with J.
MACHEATH: Then it's wrong. It begins with P.
GINNY JENNY: Mac, when the Coronation bells ring out from Westminster, you'll have a bad time of it.
MACHEATH: Go on. [JACOB *laughs raucously.*] What's the matter? [*He goes across to* JACOB, *and reads.*] Quite wrong, there were only three.
JACOB [*laughs*]: That's just it.
MACHEATH: Nice underwear you have here.
WHORE: From the cradle to the coffin, underwear comes first.
OLD WHORE: I never use silk. The gentlemen immediately think you're ill.

GINNY JENNY *edges stealthily out of the door.*

SECOND WHORE [*to* GINNY JENNY]: Where are you going, Jenny?
GINNY JENNY: You'll see. [*Exit.*]
MOLLY: But plain linen puts them off.
OLD WHORE: I've had great success with plain linen.
VIXEN: That's because the gentlemen feel at home with it.
MACHEATH [*to* BETTY]: Have you still got the black braid?
BETTY: Yes, still the black braid.
MACHEATH: And what sort of underwear do you have, my dear?
SECOND WHORE: Oh, I'm so ashamed, I can't bring 'em to my room, my aunt hates men. And in doorways, you know, you just can't have on underwear.

JACOB *laughs.*

MACHEATH: Finished?
JACOB: No, I'm just at the "rapes."
MACHEATH [*again sitting on the sofa*]: But where's Jenny got to? Ladies, long before my star rose over this town . . .
VIXEN: Long before my star rose over this town . . .
MACHEATH: I lived in the poorest circumstances with one of you fair ladies. And though I am Mackie the Knife now, in my present happiness I shall never forget the companions of my darker days: above all Jenny, whom I loved the best of all the girls. Listen!

As MACHEATH *sings,* GINNY JENNY *stands outside the window right and beckons to* CONSTABLE SMITH. *Then* MRS. PEACHUM *joins her. All three stand under the street lamp and look into the house.*

THE BALLAD OF THE FANCY MAN

MACHEATH:
Once on a time—who knows how long ago?—
We shared a home together, I and she.
My head and her abdomen turned the trick.
I protected her and she supported me.
(Some say it's different, but I say it's slick.)
And when a wooer came I crept out of our bed
And got myself a schnapps and showed myself
well-bred.
When he shelled out, I said: Auf Wiedersehn
If any time you'd care to, come again!
For half a year we had no cause to roam
For that bordello was our home from home.

Enter GINNY JENNY *through the door: behind her,* SMITH.

GINNY JENNY:
At that same time—it's rather long ago—
He took the bloom off our relationship.
For when the cash was short, he bawled me out.
One day he yelled: I'm going to pawn your slip!
(A slip is nice but one can do without.)
And then—you know how 'tis— I felt a certain
pique.
I asked him more than once: how did he have the
cheek?
Then he would pummel me, would my good pal
And I would end up in the hospital.
Life was all honey from the honeycomb
In that bordello which was home from home.

BOTH TOGETHER, ALTERNATELY
BOTH: And at that time—long, long, long, long ago—[8]
HE: (To think of it just now gives me a lift)
SHE: By day alone could we two sport and play
HE: For night was usually her working shift.
(The night is usual, but there's also the day.)
SHE: One day I felt beneath my heart a young
Macheath.
HE: We then and there agreed: I should lie
underneath.
SHE: An unborn child, you know, so often crushes.
HE: At that, *this* child was destined for the rushes.
BOTH: Though that bordello was our home from home
In half a year we were constrained to roam.

Dance. MACHEATH *picks up his swordstick: she hands him his hat; and he is still dancing when* SMITH *lays a hand on his shoulder.*

MACHEATH: Has this rat hole still got only one exit?

SMITH *attempts to handcuff* MACHEATH. MACHEATH *pushes against his chest, so that he stumbles over backward. Then* MACHEATH *jumps out of the window. But outside are* MRS. PEACHUM *and other policemen.*

MACHEATH [*calmly and very politely*]: Good evening, madam.

MRS. PEACHUM: My dear Mr. Macheath! My husband always says: "The greatest heroes in history have always tripped up over little obstacles."

MACHEATH: May I inquire how your husband is?

MRS. PEACHUM: Better—now. Well, you can take your leave of these ladies. Officers, take Mr. Macheath to his new lodgings. [*He is led off.* MRS. PEACHUM *speaks through the window.*] The gentleman will be living henceforth at the Old Bailey. If you should wish to visit him, ladies, you will always find him at home. I knew he'd be here with his whores! I will settle the bill. Farewell, ladies. [*Exit.*]

GINNY JENNY: Hey Jacob! Something's happened.

JACOB [*who, on account of his intensive reading, has noticed nothing*]: Where's Mac?

GINNY JENNY: The coppers were here!

JACOB: No! And here was I quietly reading . . . boys, boys, boys! [*Exit.*]

3

BETRAYED BY THE WHORES, MACHEATH IS FREED FROM PRISON THROUGH THE LOVE OF ANOTHER WOMAN

Prison in the Old Bailey. A Barred Cage.

Enter BROWN.

BROWN: I hope my men don't catch him! Dear God, I hope he's beyond Highgate Moor thinking of his old friend Jacky! But he's thoughtless, like all men. If they should bring him in now, and he were to look at me with those faithful friendly eyes, I couldn't stand it. Thank God, there's a moon: once he's out in the country, he'll find his way all right. [*Noise outside.*] What's that? Oh God, they've got him.

MACHEATH [*tied with heavy ropes and guarded by six constables, enters proudly*]: Well, my minions, here we are again! Back in our old home. [*He sees* BROWN, *who has retreated to the farthest corner of the cell.*]

BROWN [*after a long pause, under the fearful gaze of his former friend*]: Mac, I didn't do it . . . I did everything I could . . . don't look at me like that, Mac . . . I can't bear it . . . Your silence is terrible! [*He shouts at a constable.*] Don't pull at that rope, you swine! Say something, Mac. Say something to your old friend Jacky! Lighten his darkness, I beseech you . . . [*He rests his head against the wall and weeps.*] He doesn't think me worth a word. [*Exit.*]

MACHEATH: That miserable Brown! That evil conscience incarnate! And a creature like that is made Sheriff of London! Lucky I didn't bawl him out. I'd intended doing something of the sort. But then I thought a good, piercing, punishing stare would send the shivers down his back. It worked. I looked at him and he wept bitterly. I got that trick from the Bible.

Re-enter SMITH *with handcuffs.*

Well, Mr. Jailer, I suppose those are the heaviest you could find? With your permission, I should like a more comfortable pair. [*He takes out his check book.*]

SMITH: Certainly, Captain, we have them here at all prices. It depends what you want to pay. From one to ten guineas.

MACHEATH: How much do none cost?

SMITH: Fifty.

MACHEATH [*writes out a check*]: The devil of it is, all that business with Lucy will come out. And when Brown hears what I've done to his daughter behind his friendly back, he'll turn into a real tiger for the first time in his life.

SMITH: You've made your bed: lie on it.

MACHEATH: I'll bet that trollop is waiting outside.
I shall have a fine time from now till the execution.
So, gentlemen, is this what you'd call living?
Take no offence if Mackie disagrees.
While still a babe I heard with grave misgiving:
None but the well-to-do can take at ease.

Song illumination: golden light. The organ is illuminated. Three lights come down on a bar from above—and on the board is written:

THE SECRET OF GRACIOUS LIVING[9]

Great praise is always lavished on great thinkers
Who think of books (but do not think of dinner)
In some old shack where even rats grow thinner—
I can't abide such solitary stinkers!
For Simple Living simply does not pay

And I'd be glad to hear the last of it.
From here to Rome no turtledove or tit
Would live on such a menu for one day.
Let 'em keep their freedom! Let 'em keep their
fleas!
Only the well-to-do can take their ease.

Those brave adventurers whose quaint addiction
Is Truth and Freedom in and out of season
And risking their own necks for no good reason
(Materials for adventurous non-fiction):
See how they waste the wintry evenings
napping
Then silently with wintry wife to bed
Their solemn thoughts three thousand years ahead
And both their ears agog for cheers and clapping!
Let 'em keep their bravery! I've a better wheeze:
None but the well-to-do can take their ease.

In spring I ask: could there be something to it?
Could not Macheath be great and solitary?
But then the year works round to January
And I reply: My boy, you'll live to rue it.
Poverty makes you sad as well as wise
And bravery mingles danger with the fame.
Poor, lonely, wise and brave—in heaven's name!
Good-bye to greatness! I return the prize
With this my repartee of repartees:
None but the well-to-do can take their ease.

Enter LUCY.

LUCY: You miserable wretch, you! How can you look me in the face after all that has happened between us?

MACHEATH: Lucy, have you no heart? When you see your own husband in this condition?

LUCY: My husband! You brute! So you think I know nothing about what you've been up to with Miss Peachum? I could scratch your eyes out!

MACHEATH: Lucy, seriously, you're not so silly as to be jealous of Polly?

LUCY: So you're not married to her, you beast?

MACHEATH: Married! That's a good one! I visit a certain house. I talk to her. Now and then I give her a sort of kiss, and the silly bitch runs around boasting that she's married to me. My darling Lucy, I'll do anything to reassure you; if you really do believe she and I are married—well and good. What more can a gentleman say? He cannot say more.

LUCY: Oh, Mac, I only want to become an honest woman.

MACHEATH: If you think you'll become an honest woman by being married to me—good. What more can a gentleman say?

Enter POLLY.

POLLY: Where's my husband? Oh, Mac, there you are. You needn't be ashamed of me. After all, I am your wife.

LUCY: Oh, you miserable fiend!

POLLY: Mackie in prison! Why didn't you escape across Highgate Moor? You told me you wouldn't go to those women any more. I knew what they'd do to you; but I didn't say anything; I believed you. Mac, I'll stick with you to the death.—Not a word, Mac, not a look. Oh, Mac, think how your Polly's suffering!

LUCY: Oh, the trollop!

POLLY: What's that, Mac? Who is that woman? Tell her who I am. Am I not your wife? Look at me, am I not your wife?

LUCY: You treacherous swine, have you got two wives, you monster?

POLLY: Say something, Mac. Am I not your wife? Haven't I done everything for you? When I entered the state of matrimony I was pure and innocent, you know that. Didn't you hand over the gang to me? And I did everything as we arranged, and I was to tell Jacob to . . .

MACHEATH: If you two would shut your traps for five minutes I could explain the whole thing.

LUCY: No, I will not shut my trap. I can't stand it, it's more than flesh and blood can stand.

POLLY: Yes, my love, it's clear that woman there . . .

LUCY: That woman!

POLLY: . . . that woman has a certain physical priority. At least to all outward appearances, my love. Such aggravation is enough to drive one mad.

LUCY: Aggravation! That's rich! What have you gone and picked up? This dirty slut! So that's your great conquest! That's your beauty of Soho!

Song illumination: a golden light. The organ is it up. Three lights come down on a bar from above and on a board is written:

THE JEALOUSY DUET

LUCY: Come right out, Old Soho's beauty queen!
Let me see those legs they call so pretty!
I should delight to recite the praises
Of the fairest figure in our city!
You might, it is true, produce quite an effect on
Mackie!
POLLY: Oh I might? Oh I might?
LUCY: If the whole idea were not so wacky!
POLLY: Is that right? Is that right?
LUCY: He has better things to do
POLLY: Has he better things to do?

LUCY: Than to try his hand on you.
POLLY: Than to try his hand on me?
LUCY: Ha ha ha ha ha, it can't be fun
To get mixed up with such a one!
POLLY: Very well, let's wait and see.
LUCY: Very well, let's wait and see.
TOGETHER: Polly / Lucy } loves Mac
I actually adore him.
He loves me back:
All other women bore him.
A man will not dissever
A bond that lasts forever
To please some filthy creature!
Ludicrous!
POLLY: Yes, they call me Soho's beauty queen!
When they see these legs, they call them pretty!
LUCY: But do they?
POLLY: They all delight to recite the praises
Of the fairest figure in our city!
LUCY: Shit-pot!
POLLY: Shit-pot yourself!
I have, please observe, produced quite an effect on Mackie!
LUCY: Oh you have? Oh you have?
POLLY: And it's you, my dear, who are so wacky!
LUCY: So it's me? So it's me?
POLLY: Who, if either hand were free
LUCY: Who, if either hand were free?
POLLY: Would not try that hand on me?
LUCY: Would not try that hand on you?
POLLY: Ha ha ha ha ha! But as for you
Who'd dip his spoon in such a stew?
LUCY: Very well, lets wait and see.
POLLY: Very well, let's wait and see.
TOGETHER: Lucy / Polly } loves Mac
I actually adore him.
He loves her back:
All other women bore him.
A man will not dissever
A bond that lasts forever
To please some filthy creature!
Ludicrous!

MACHEATH: And now, dear Lucy, be calm. This is just a trick of Polly's. She wants to make trouble. They're going to hang me, and she wants to be able to call herself my widow. Really, Polly, this is not the right moment.
POLLY: You have the heart to deny me?
MACHEATH: And you have the heart to chatter about me being married to you? Why, Polly, must you add to my misery? [*Shakes his head reproachfully.*] Polly, Polly!
LUCY: Really, Miss Peachum, you're making a show of yourself. Quite apart from the fact that it's monstrous of you to excite a poor gentleman in this plight!
POLLY: The simplest rules of decorum, my dear madam, would teach you, I believe, that a person should behave with somewhat more restraint toward a gentleman in the presence of his wife.
MACHEATH: Seriously, Polly, that's really carrying a joke too far.
LUCY: And if you, my good madam, want to start a row in the prison here, I shall find myself compelled to summon a warder to show you the door. I should be sorry to have to do it, Miss Peachum.
POLLY: Mrs.! Mrs.! Mrs. Macheath! Permit me to tell you this—Miss!—these airs don't suit you in the least! My duty compels me to remain with my husband.
LUCY: What do you say to that? What do you say? She won't go! She stands there and waits to be thrown out! Shall I speak more plainly?
POLLY: You—shut your filthy mouth, you slut, or I'll give you a smack in the chops, dear Miss!
LUCY: I'll have you kicked out, Miss Insolence! It's no use mincing words with you. You don't understand delicacy.
POLLY: You and your delicacy! I'm compromising my own dignity! And I'm too good for that . . . I am! [*She weeps loudly.*]
LUCY: Well, look at my stomach, you trollop! Aren't your eyes open yet?
POLLY: Oh! That! I suppose you're hoping to make something out of it? You should never have let yourself in for it, you fine lady!
MACHEATH: Polly!
POLLY [*sobbing*]: This is really too much, Mac, this shouldn't have happened. I just don't know what I shall do!

Enter MRS. PEACHUM.

MRS. PEACHUM: I knew it. She's with her fancy man. Come here this minute, you filthy trollop. When your man's hanged, you can hang yourself with him. A fine way to behave to your poor old mother: she has to come and fetch you out of prison. So, he has two at a time—that Nero!
POLLY: Leave me alone, mama, you don't know . . .
MRS. PEACHUM: Come home this minute!
LUCY: Listen to that, your mama has to tell you how to behave.
MRS. PEACHUM: Quick march!
POLLY: Wait! I must just . . . I must just say something to him . . . really . . . it's very important.

MRS. PEACHUM [*gives her a box on the ears*]: And that's important too—now—quick march.

POLLY: Oh! Mac! [*She is dragged off by* MRS. PEACHUM.]

MACHEATH: Lucy, you behaved wonderfully. Of course, I was sorry for her. That's why I couldn't treat the silly bitch as she deserved. You thought at first there was some truth in what she said? Am I right?

LUCY: Yes, I did think so, dearest.

MACHEATH: Had it been true, her mother would never have got me into this mess. A mother behaves like that only to a seducer, never to a son-in-law.

LUCY: It makes me so happy, when you speak like that from the heart. I love you so much, I'd almost rather see you hanged than in the arms of another girl. Isn't it extraordinary?

MACHEATH: Lucy, I'd like to owe my life to you.

LUCY: It's wonderful, the way you say that. Say it again!

MACHEATH: Lucy, I'd like to owe my life to you.

LUCY: Shall I escape with you, dearest?

MACHEATH: Well, it'll be difficult to hide if we escape together. But as soon as the search is over, I'll have you fetched—by express post, too, as you can imagine!

LUCY: How can I help you?

MACHEATH: Bring me my hat and stick.

LUCY *exits and returns with his hat and stick and throws them into his cell.*

MACHEATH: Lucy, the fruit of our love which you carry beneath your heart will forever bind us together.

Exit LUCY.

SMITH *enters, goes into the cage and says to* MACHEATH:

SMITH: Give me that stick.

After a short chase in which SMITH, *armed with a chair and crowbar, drives* MACHEATH *before him,* MACHEATH *leaps over the bars. Constables pursue him.*

BROWN [*off*]: Hello, Mac! Mac, please answer! It's Jacky. Mac, please be kind and answer, I can't bear it! [*Enters.*] Mackie! What's up? He's gone. Thank God! [*He sits down on the bench.*]

Enter PEACHUM.

PEACHUM [*to* SMITH]: My name is Peachum. I have come to claim the forty pounds reward offered for the capture of the bandit Macheath. [*He appears in front of the cage.*] Hey! Is that Mr. Macheath there?

BROWN *remains silent.*

Ah! So the other gentlemen has gone out for a little walk? I come here to visit a criminal and whom do I find but Mr. Brown! Tiger Brown in, and his friend Macheath out.

BROWN [*groaning*]: Mr. Peachum, it's not my fault.

PEACHUM: Of course not, how could it be? You would never be so . . . as to get yourself into this situation . . . would you, Brown?

BROWN: Mr. Peachum, I am beside myself.

PEACHUM: I believe you. You must feel horrible, Brown.

BROWN: Yes, this feeling of helplessness is crushing. The boys do just what they like! It's terrible, terrible!

PEACHUM: Wouldn't you like to lie down a little? Just shut your eyes and behave as though nothing had happened. Imagine you're lying in a lovely green meadow with little white clouds overhead. The main thing is to get this nasty affair out of your mind. Everything that's happened, and above all what's still to come.

BROWN [*uneasily*]: What do you mean?

PEACHUM: It's wonderful the way you're taking it. If I were in your position, I'd simply collapse and go to bed and drink hot tea. And I'd arrange to have a nice cool hand stroking my forehead.

BROWN: Damn you! I can't help it if a man escapes! The police can't do anything!

PEACHUM: Oh! So the police can't do anything. You don't think we shall have Mr. Macheath back here again?

BROWN *shrugs his shoulders.*

Then what's going to happen to you, Brown, will be a horrible injustice. Of course, people will say that the police shouldn't have let him escape.—No, I can't quite see that brilliant Coronation procession yet.

BROWN: What do you mean?

PEACHUM: I might remind you of an historic instance, which, although it aroused considerable excitement in its time, fourteen hundred years B.C., is unknown to the larger public of today. When the Egyptian king Rameses the Second died, the chief of police of Nineveh, or it may have been Cairo, was guilty of some petty injustice toward the lower classes. Even at that time the results were terrible. The coronation procession of the new queen, Semiramis, was, as the history books state, "a succession of catastrophes caused by the all too lively participation of the lower classes." The historians are far too squeamish to describe what

Semiramis had done to her chief of police. I only remember vaguely; but there was talk of snakes which she nourished at his bosom.
BROWN: Really?
PEACHUM: The Lord be with you, Brown. [*Exit.*]
BROWN: Now only an iron hand will do any good! Sergeant, a conference! Emergency!

Curtain. MACHEATH *and* GINNY JENNY *step in front of the curtain and sing. Song illumination.*

SECOND THREEPENNY-FINALE

MACHEATH: Now all you gentlemen who wish to lead us
Who teach us to desist from mortal sin
Your prior obligation is to feed us:
When we've had lunch, your preaching can begin.
All you who love your paunch and our propriety
Take note of this one thing (for it is late):
You may proclaim, good sirs, your fine philosophy
But till you feed us, right and wrong can wait!
Or is it only those who have the money
Can enter in the land of milk and honey?
VOICE OFF: What does a man live by?
MACHEATH: What does a man live by? By resolutely
Ill-treating, beating, cheating, eating some other bloke!
A man can only live by absolutely
Forgetting he's a man like other folk!
CHORUS OFF: So, gentlemen, do not be taken in:
Men live exclusively by mortal sin.
GINNY JENNY: All you who say what neckline is decreed us
And who decide when ogling is a sin
Your prior obligation is to feed us
When we've had lunch, your preaching can begin.
You who insist upon your pleasure and our shame
Take note of this one thing (for it is late):
Your fine philosophy, good sirs, you may proclaim
But till you feed us, right and wrong can wait!
Or is it only those who have the money
Can enter in the land of milk and honey?
VOICE OFF: What does a man live by?
GINNY JENNY: What does a man live by? By resolutely
Ill-treating, beating, cheating, eating some other bloke!
A man can only live by absolutely
Forgetting he's a man like other folk!
CHORUS OFF: So, gentlemen, do not be taken in:
Men live exclusively by mortal sin.

ACT III

1

THE SAME NIGHT PEACHUM PREPARES FOR ACTION. BY MEANS OF A DEMONSTRATION OF MISERY HE HOPES TO DISORGANIZE THE CORONATION PROCESSION

The Wardrobe Room of Peachum's Establishment

The beggars are painting boards with such inscriptions as "I gave my eye for my king," etc.

PEACHUM: Gentlemen, at this very hour, in our eleven branches between Drury Lane and Wapping, there are one thousand four hundred and thirty-two men like you working on such boards as these in order to be present at the Coronation of our Queen.
MRS. PEACHUM: Come on, come on! If you won't work, you can't beg. You hope to be a blind man, and you can't even write a proper K! That's supposed to be child's handwriting, not an old man's!

Exit PEACHUM. *Roll of drums.*

BEGGAR: There's a guard of honor lining up! Little do they dream that today, the grandest day of their military lives, they've got to deal with us!
FILCH [*enters and announces*]: Here comes a dozen benighted birds, Mrs. Peachum. They say they're to be given their money here.

Enter the whores.

GINNY JENNY: My dear madam . . .
MRS. PEACHUM: Well, well, well, you look as though you've all fallen off your perches! I suppose you've come for the money for your Macheath? You'll get nothing. Understand? Nothing.
GINNY JENNY: And what are we to understand by that, madam?
MRS. PEACHUM: Bursting into my room in the middle of the night! Coming to a respectable house at three in the morning! You'd do better to sleep off the effects of business. You look like skim milk.
GINNY JENNY: So we're not to get our contractual fee for having Mr. Macheath nabbed, madam?
MRS. PEACHUM: Quite correct. In fact, you'll get something you don't like, instead of your blood money.
GINNY JENNY: And why, madam?
MRS. PEACHUM: Because your wonderful Mr. Macheath has vanished again into thin air. That's why. Now get out of my decent house, ladies.
GINNY JENNY: That's the limit. Don't you try that on with us! I give you fair warning, not with us!

MRS. PEACHUM: Filch, the ladies want to be shown out.

FILCH *approaches the girls.* GINNY JENNY *pushes him away.*

GINNY JENNY: I'd advise you to keep your dirty mouth shut . . . or!

Enter PEACHUM.

PEACHUM: What's the matter? I hope you haven't given them any money. Well, what's the matter, ladies? Is Mr. Macheath in prison or is he not?
GINNY JENNY: Leave me in peace with your Mr. Macheath. You're not a patch on him. I had to send a gentleman away tonight because I wanted to cry on my pillow every time I thought how I had sold that real gentleman to you. Yes, ladies, and what do you think happened this morning? Not an hour ago, when I had just cried myself to sleep, I heard a whistle, and there in the street below stood the gentleman I'd been crying for, and he asked me to throw the key down to him: he wished to forget the wrong I had done him—in my arms. He's the last gentleman left in London, ladies. And if our colleague Suky Tawdry isn't with us now, it's because he went from me to her, to comfort her as well.
PEACHUM [*to himself*]: Suky Tawdry . . .
GINNY JENNY: So now you know. You're dirt compared to him. You lowdown informers!
PEACHUM: Filch, run quickly to the nearest police station and say Mr. Macheath is staying with Miss Suky Tawdry.

Exit FILCH.

But ladies, why are we quarreling? Your money will be paid, of course. My dear Celia, wouldn't it be better if you went and made the ladies a nice cup of coffee, instead of insulting them?
MRS. PEACHUM: Suky Tawdry!

She sings the third verse of the "Ballad of Sexual Submissiveness."

Now here's a man who toward the gallow races.
The quicklime's bought that will rub out his traces.
He's dead the minute hangmen do their duty.
And what's his mind on now, this chap? Some
    beauty.
Here at the gallows' foot he'll acquiesce
For such is sexual submissiveness.
He's had it. He's been sold. He marches to his
    doom.
He's seen the money in a female's hand
And he begins to understand
That woman's orifice will be his tomb.
His self-reproaches are uncompromising
But, as the night is falling, he is rising.

Exit MRS. PEACHUM.

PEACHUM: Come on, come on! You'd all be rotting in the sewers of Wapping if I hadn't spent sleepless nights working out how to extract a few pence from your poverty. And I did work out something: that the rich of the earth indeed create misery, but they cannot bear to see it. They are weaklings and fools just like you. As long as they have enough to eat and can grease their floors with butter so that even the crumbs that fall from their tables grow fat, they can't look with indifference on a man collapsing from hunger—although, of course, it must be in front of *their* house that he collapses.

Re-enter MRS. PEACHUM *with a tray full of coffee cups.*

MRS. PEACHUM: You can come to the shop tomorrow and fetch your money: but *after* the Coronation.
GINNY JENNY: Mrs. Peachum, you leave me speechless.
PEACHUM: Fall in! We assemble in an hour outside Buckingham Palace. Quick march!

The beggars fall in.

FILCH [*bursts in*]: The coppers! I never got as far as the station. The coppers are here already!
PEACHUM: Hide yourselves. [*To* MRS. PEACHUM:] Get the orchestra ready! And when you hear me say "harmless," understand me, *harmless* . . .
MRS. PEACHUM: Harmless? I don't understand a thing.
PEACHUM: Of course you don't understand a thing. So when I say "harmless" . . .

There is a knocking on the door.

Thank God, that's the password, *harmless*, then play some sort of music. Now get out.

Exit MRS. PEACHUM. *The beggars, excepting a girl with the board* A VICTIM OF MILITARY DESPOTISM, *hide with their things behind the clothes racks on the right.*

Enter BROWN *with constables.*

BROWN: And now, Mr. Beggars' Friend, we take action! Handcuff him, Smith. Ah, so those are a few of your charming notices. [*To the girl:*] "A Victim of Military Despotism"—is that you, my dear?

PEACHUM: Good morning, Brown, good morning. Slept well?
BROWN: Eh?
PEACHUM: Morning, Brown.
BROWN: Is he speaking to me? Does he know any of you? I don't think I have the pleasure of your acquaintance.
PEACHUM: Haven't you? Morning, Brown.
BROWN: Knock his hat off, Smith.

SMITH *does so.*

PEACHUM: Listen, Brown, since your way leads *past* my house—I said *past*, Brown—I can now ask you to put a certain Macheath under lock and key.
BROWN: The man is mad. Smith, stop laughing. Tell me, Smith, how is it possible that this notorious criminal is allowed at large in London?
PEACHUM: Because he's your friend, Brown.
BROWN: Who?
PEACHUM: Mackie the Knife. Not me, I'm not a criminal. I'm just a poor man, Brown. You can't treat me badly. Listen, Brown. You are on the verge of the worst hour of your life. Would you like a cup of coffee? [*To the whores:*] Girls, give the gentleman a drink, that's not the way to behave. We're all friends here. We all obey the law. The law is simply and solely made for the exploitation of those who do not understand it or of those who, for naked need, cannot obey it. And whoever would pick up the crumbs of this exploitation must strictly obey the law.
BROWN: You think our judges are bribable?
PEACHUM: On the contrary, sir, on the contrary! Our judges are totally unbribable: no amount of money can bribe them to dispense justice.

A second roll of drums.

Departure of the troops to line the route!
Departure of the poorest of the poor half an hour later!

BROWN: Quite right, Mr. Peachum. Departure of the poorest of the poor in half an hour. They're departing for their winter quarters in prison. [*To the constables:*] Well, boys, round 'em up. All the patriots you can find here. [*To the beggars:*] Have you ever heard of Tiger Brown? Tonight, Mr. Peachum, I have found the solution and, I may add, I have saved a friend from death. I shall simply smoke out your whole nest. Then I shall lock you all up for—yes, what *for*? For street-begging! You seem to have warned me that you were going to bother me and the Queen with your beggars. These beggars I shall now arrest. That'll teach you something.
PEACHUM: All very fine—but what beggars?
BROWN: These cripples here. Smith, we'll take the patriotic gentlemen with us right away.
PEACHUM: Brown, I can save you from overstepping your duty. Thank God you came to me! Of course you can arrest these few people, they are *harmless, harmless . . .*

Music starts and plays a few introductory bars of "The Song of the Futility of all Human Endeavor."

BROWN: What's that?
PEACHUM: Music. They play as well as they can. "The Song of Futility." Don't you know it? That'll teach you something!

Song illumination: golden light. The organ is lit up. Three lights come down from above on a bar, and on a board is written:

THE SONG OF THE FUTILITY OF ALL HUMAN ENDEAVOR

A man lives by his head.
That head will not suffice.
Just try it: you will find your head
Will scarce support two lice.
　　For the task assigned them
　　Men aren't smart enough or sly.
　　Any rogue can blind them
　　With a clever lie.
Go make yourself a plan
And be a shining light.
Then make yourself a second plan
For neither will come right.
　　For the situation
　　Men aren't bad enough or vile.
　　Human aspiration
　　Only makes me smile.
Go running after luck
But don't you run too fast:
We all are running after luck
And luck is running last.
　　For the real conditions
　　Men are more demanding than is meet.
　　Their ideal ambitions
　　Are one great big cheat.

PEACHUM: Your plan was ingenious, Brown, but impracticable. All you can arrest here are a few young people who arranged a small fancy-dress ball to celebrate the Coronation of their Queen. But when the really poor ones come—there's not a single one here now—you'll see they'll come in thousands. That's the trouble. You've forgotten the monstrous number of the poor. If they were to stand there in front of the Abbey, it wouldn't be a very cheerful sight. They don't look very nice. Do you know what erysipelas is, Brown? Well, think now of a hundred people with erysipelas on their faces. And then these mutilated creatures at the door of the Abbey? We would rather avoid that, Brown. You say the police will make short work of us poor people. But you don't believe it yourself. What will it look like if six hundred poor cripples have to be knocked down with your truncheons because of the Coronation? It will look bad. Enough to make one sick. I feel ill, Brown, just to think of it. A chair, please.

BROWN [*to* SMITH]: This is a threat. It's blackmail. We can't do anything to this man. In the interest of the public order we can't do anything to this man. Such a thing has never happened before!

PEACHUM: It has happened now, Brown. I'll tell you something: you can do what you like to the Queen of England, but just try and tread on the toes of the poorest man in London and we'll do you brown, Mr. Brown.

BROWN: Then I'm to arrest Mackie the Knife? Arrest him? You can talk! You've got to catch your man before you can arrest him.

PEACHUM: When you say that, I cannot contradict you. So I shall produce him for you. We'll see if there's any morality left! Jenny, where is Mr. Macheath staying?

GINNY JENNY: With Suky Tawdry, at 621 Oxford Street.

BROWN: Smith, go at once to 621 Oxford Street, Suky Tawdry's flat, arrest Macheath and bring him to the Old Bailey. In the meantime I must change into my full-dress uniform. On occasions like this, I have to wear full dress.

PEACHUM: Brown, if he's not hanged by six . . .

BROWN: Oh, Mackie, it didn't work. [*Exit* BROWN *with constables.*]

PEACHUM [*calling after him*]: That's taught you something, Brown.

A third roll of drums.

Drums—the third time! A fresh plan of campaign!
New destination: the Old Bailey! Quick march!

Exeunt the beggars.

PEACHUM [*sings*]: Since men are just no good
Pick up a piece of wood
And hit them on the head with it!
Then maybe they'll be good.
For the human function
They'll be good when they are dead.
So without compunction
Hit them on the head!

In front of the curtain appears GINNY JENNY *with a hurdy-gurdy. She sings:*

THE SONG OF SOLOMON

King Solomon was very wise
So what's his history?
He came to view this world with scorn
And curse the hour he was born
Declaring all is vanity.
King Solomon was very wise
But long before the day was out
The consequence was clear, alas!
And wisdom 'twas that brought him to this pass:
A man is better off without.

You saw Queen Cleopatra too
And what her talents were.
Oh, it was quite a life she led
Until her past caught up with her!
Two emperors joined her in bed:
Such goings-on in Babylon!
But long before the day was out
The consequence was clear, alas!
Her very beauty brought her to this pass:
A woman's better off without.

And Julius Caesar: he was brave.
His fame shall never cease.
He sat like God on an altarpiece
And then they tore him limb from limb
And Brutus helped to slaughter him.
Old Julius was very brave
But long before the day was out
The consequence was clear, alas!
His bravery 'twas what brought him to this pass:
A man is better off without.

You know the inquisitive Bertolt Brecht.
His songs—you loved them so.
But when too oft he asked where from
The riches of the rich did come
You made him pack his bag and go.
Oh how inquisitive was Brecht!
But long before the day was out
The consequence was clear, alas!
Inquisitiveness had brought him to this pass:
A man is better off without.

And here you see our friend Macheath.
His life is now at stake.
So long as he was rational
And took whate'er there was to take
His fame was international.
But then he got emotional
And though the day is not yet out

The consequence is clear, alas!
Emotion 'twas that brought him to this pass:
A man is better off without.

2
The Battle for Possession[10]

An Attic Bedroom in the Old Bailey

SMITH: Miss, Mrs. Polly Macheath would like to speak to you.
LUCY: Mrs. Macheath? Show her in.

Enter POLLY.

POLLY: Good morning, madam. Madam, good morning!
LUCY: What can I do for you?
POLLY: You recognize me again?
LUCY: Of course I recognize you.
POLLY: I've come to beg pardon for my behavior yesterday.
LUCY: Very interesting.
POLLY: I have no excuse at all for my behavior yesterday, except—my unhappiness.
LUCY: I see.
POLLY: You must forgive me. I was very upset yesterday by Mr. Macheath's behavior. He really shouldn't have placed us in such a position, don't you agree? You can tell him so, when you see him.
LUCY: I—I—don't see him.
POLLY: You *do* see him.
LUCY: I do *not* see him.
POLLY: I'm sorry.
LUCY: He is very fond of you.
POLLY: Oh no, he loves you, I know that all right.
LUCY: You're very kind.
POLLY: But a man always fears a woman who loves him too much. And the natural result is that he neglects that woman and avoids her. I saw at first glance that he was bound to you in some way which I naturally couldn't guess.
LUCY: Do you mean that, honestly?
POLLY: Certainly. Of course. Very honestly.
LUCY: Dear Miss Peachum, we have both loved him too much!
POLLY: Perhaps that was it. [*Pause.*] And now, I'll explain how it came about. Ten days ago I saw Mr. Macheath for the first time in the Octopus Hotel. My mother was there too. Later—that is, the day before yesterday—we were married. Yesterday I discovered the police wanted him for a great many crimes. And today I don't know what will happen. So you see, twelve days ago I wouldn't have dreamed I could ever fall for a man. [*Pause.*]
LUCY: I quite understand, Miss Peachum.
POLLY: Mrs. Macheath.
LUCY: Mrs. Macheath.
POLLY: And, indeed, during the last few hours I have been thinking a lot about this fellow. It's not so simple. For, you see, Miss Brown, I have every reason to envy you his behavior toward you the other day. When I had to leave—coerced, I must admit, by my mama—he showed not the slightest regret. But perhaps he hasn't got a heart, just a stone in its place. What do you think, Lucy?
LUCY: Dear Miss Peachum, I am not quite sure if the fault lies entirely with Mr. Macheath. Perhaps you should have kept to your own sort, Miss Peachum.
POLLY: Mrs. Macheath.
LUCY: Mrs. Macheath.
POLLY: You're quite right—or at least I ought to have kept everything, as my father says, "on a business basis."
LUCY: Of course.
POLLY [*weeps*]: He is all that I have.
LUCY: My dear, this is a misfortune that can happen to the cleverest woman. But you are legally his wife, comfort yourself with that. Child, I can't bear to go on seeing you so depressed. May I offer you a little something?
POLLY: A little what?
LUCY: A little something to eat?
POLLY: Oh, yes, please! A little something to eat!

Exit LUCY.

[*To herself:*] The silly little fool!
LUCY [*returning with coffee and cakes*]: Now that'll be enough.
POLLY: You really give yourself too much trouble. [*Pause. She eats.*] A lovely picture you have of him. When did he bring it?
LUCY: What do you mean—bring it?
POLLY [*innocently*]: I meant, when did be bring it up here.
LUCY: He didn't bring it.
POLLY: Didn't he give it to you right here in this room?
LUCY: He never was in this room.
POLLY: I see. But there would have been nothing in that. The paths of fate are already terribly complicated!
LUCY: Don't talk such tripe all the time. You came here to spy around!
POLLY: You know where he is, don't you?
LUCY: I? Don't *you* know?
POLLY: Tell me where he is this minute!

LUCY: I haven't the slightest idea.

POLLY: Then you don't know where he is? Word of honor?

LUCY: No, I don't. And you don't know either?

POLLY: No! This is monstrous! [POLLY *laughs and* LUCY *weeps.*] He has two responsibilities now and he's run out on both of us!

LUCY: I can't bear it any longer. Oh, Polly, it's so awful!

POLLY [*happily*]: But I'm so glad that at the ending of this tragedy I've found a friend like you. Have some more? Another cake?

LUCY: Some more! Oh, Polly, don't be so kind to me. Really I don't deserve it! Oh, Polly, men aren't worth it!

POLLY: Of course men aren't worth it. But what can one do?

LUCY: I'll come clean. Will you be angry with me, Polly?

POLLY: What?

LUCY: It's not real.

POLLY: What isn't?

LUCY: This! [*She points to her stomach.*] I did it all for that crook!

POLLY [*laughs*]: It was a trick. Wonderful! You are a little fool! Listen—you want Mackie? I'll give him to you. Take him when you find him.

There is a sound of voices and steps outside.

What's that?

LUCY [*at the window*]: It's Mackie! They've caught him again.

POLLY [*collapses*]: Then all is over!

Enter MRS. PEACHUM.

MRS. PEACHUM: Ah, Polly, so here you are. Change your dress. Your husband's going to be hanged. I've brought your widow's weeds.

POLLY *starts to undress and puts on the widow's weeds.*

You'll look lovely as a widow! Now cheer up a bit.

3

5 A.M. FRIDAY. MACKIE THE KNIFE, WHO ONCE MORE WENT BACK TO HIS WHORES, HAS AGAIN BEEN BETRAYED BY THEM. HE IS NOW ABOUT TO BE HANGED

The Death Cell

The bells of the City are ringing. Constables bring MACHEATH, *handcuffed, into the cell.*

SMITH: In here with him. The bells have rung once already. [*To* MACHEATH:] Try and behave like a man. I don't know how you manage to look so washed out. I should think you must be ashamed of yourself! [*To the other constables:*] When the bells ring for the third time—that'll be at six o'clock—he must be already hanged. Get everything ready.

A CONSTABLE: Every street in Newgate has been jammed with people for the last quarter of an hour. It's impossible to get through.

SMITH: Extraordinary! How do they know already?

CONSTABLE: If it goes on like this, the whole of London will know in half an hour. Those who were going to the Coronation will all come here instead. The Queen will have to drive through empty streets.

SMITH: That's why we shall have to hurry. If we're through by six, people can be back on the Coronation route by seven. Get on with it.

MACHEATH: Hi, Smith! What's the time?

SMITH: Haven't you got eyes? Four minutes past five.

MACHEATH: Four minutes past five.

As SMITH *shuts the door of the cell from the outside,* BROWN *enters.*

BROWN [*questioning* SMITH, *with his back to the cell*]: Is he there?

SMITH: You want to see him?

BROWN: No, no, no, for God's sake, manage it all yourself. [*Exit.*]

MACHEATH [*suddenly bursting into a soft and rapid torrent of speech*]: Listen, Smith, I won't say a thing, not a thing, about bribery, don't worry. I know all about that. If you let yourself be bribed, you'll at least have to get out of the country. You'd have to do that. And you'll also need money to live on for the rest of your life. A thousand pounds, will that do? Don't speak! In twenty minutes I'll let you know if you can have that thousand pounds by midday. I'm not mentioning anyone's feelings. Go outside and think it over carefully. Life is short and so is money. And I'm not sure I can raise any. But let anyone in here who wants to see me.

SMITH [*slowly*]: You're talking nonsense, Mr. Macheath. [*He withdraws to the side of the stage.*]

MACHEATH [*sings, softly and very quickly*]: Hark to the voice that pleads for pity, hark!
Macheath lies here—beneath no hawthorn tree
Nor under elms but in a dungeon dark.
He was struck down by angry Fate's decree.
God grant you all may hear what he doth say!
Him thickest walls surround and chains entwine.
Do you not ask, my friends, where he hath strayed?
When he is dead, brew elderberry wine!
But while he still doth live, lend him your aid.
Or must his martyrdom endure for aye?[11]

MATTHEW *and* JACOB *appear in the passage.* SMITH *intercepts them on their way to* MACHEATH.

SMITH: We-e-ll, my boys! You look like a gutted herring!

MATTHEW: Now the Captain's away, it's I who have to get the ladies pregnant—so, when they're arrested, they can plead "Not responsible for their actions." One needs the physique of a stallion for this job. Can I speak with the Captain?

SMITH *lets them pass, then exit.*

MACHEATH: Five twenty-five. You've taken your time.

JACOB: Well, after all . . .[12]

MACHEATH: After all, after all, I'm going to be hanged, man! But I've no time to argue with you. Five twenty-eight. How much can you draw out of your private deposits immediately?

MATTHEW: At five o'clock in the morning?

JACOB: Is it really as bad as all that?

MACHEATH: Four hundred pounds? Can you manage that?

JACOB: Well, and what about us? That's all there is.

MACHEATH: Are you going to be hanged, or am I?

MATTHEW [*excitedly*]: Did we sleep with Suky Tawdry instead of making ourselves scarce? Did we sleep with Suky Tawdry or did you?

MACHEATH: Shut your gob. I'll soon be sleeping somewhere else than with that trollop. Five thirty.

JACOB: I suppose we'll have to do it, Matthew.

SMITH [*enters*]: Mr. Brown told me to ask what you'd like for—breakfast.

MACHEATH: Leave me alone! [*To* MATTHEW:] Will you or won't you? [*To* SMITH:] Asparagus.

MATTHEW: I'm certainly not going to be shouted at!

MACHEATH: I'm not shouting at you! It's only because . . . Now, Matthew, are you going to let me be hanged?

MATTHEW: Of course we won't let you be hanged. Whoever suggested that? But that's all. Four hundred pounds is all there is. One's allowed to say that, I suppose.

MACHEATH: Five thirty-eight.

JACOB: Hurry, Matthew, or it'll be too late.

MATTHEW: If we can only get through. The streets are jammed. This riff-raff!

MACHEATH: If you're not here by five minutes to six, you'll never see me again. [*Shouts.*] You'll never see me again . . . !

SMITH: They're off. Well, how goes it? [*He makes a gesture of paying out money.*]

MACHEATH: Four hundred.

SMITH *walks away, shrugging his shoulders.*

MACHEATH [*calling after him*]: I must speak to Brown.

SMITH [*as the constable enters*]: You've got the soap?

CONSTABLE: It's not the right sort.

SMITH: You'll be able to set the thing up in ten minutes.

CONSTABLE: But the trap isn't working yet.

SMITH: It *must* work, the bells have rung the second time.

CONSTABLE: This is a hell of a place!

MACHEATH [*sings*]: Alas, he's fallen from his high estate.
All his affairs have gone from bad to worse.
Oh ye who recognize nor God nor Fate
But place your bets upon your own fat purse
You'd better rescue him or, well-a-day,
Hell drag you all down to that dungeon grim.
Run then unto the Queen for your Macheath.
Tell her the pass he's come to. Say of him:
That man of sorrows, Queen, has fangs for teeth.
Or must his martyrdom endure for aye?

Enter POLLY.

SMITH: I can't let you in. Your number's sixteen. It's not your turn yet.

POLLY: What do you mean: my number's sixteen? I am his wife. I must speak to him!

SMITH: Then five minutes at the most.

POLLY: What do you mean, five minutes! That's ridiculous. Five minutes! You just can't say that. It's not as simple as all that. This is good-bye forever. And there's such a lot that has to be said between man and wife . . . Where is he?

SMITH: Well, can't you see him?

POLLY: Oh yes. Thank you!

MACHEATH: Polly!

POLLY: Yes, Mackie, here I am.

MACHEATH: Yes, of course.

POLLY: How are you? Very done up? It's hard.

MACHEATH: Yes, and what will *you* do? What will become of you?

POLLY: Oh, our business is doing very well. That's the least of our troubles. Mackie, are you very nervous? Who *was* your father? There's so much you haven't told me. I don't understand it at all: you were really always quite healthy.

MACHEATH: Polly, can't you help me out?

POLLY: Of course.

MACHEATH: With money, I mean. I talked to the warder here . . .

POLLY [*slowly*]: The money has gone to Southampton.

MACHEATH: And you haven't any?

POLLY: No, I haven't any. But do you know, Mac, perhaps I could speak to someone . . . maybe the Queen herself! [*She breaks down.*] Oh, Mackie!

SMITH [*pulling* POLLY *away*]: Got your thousand pounds?
POLLY: Good luck, Mac, take care of yourself! Never forget me! [*Exit.*]

SMITH *and a constable bring on a table with a plate of asparagus on it.*

SMITH: Is the asparagus tender?
CONSTABLE: It is. [*Exit.*]

BROWN *enters and walks over to* SMITH.

BROWN: What does he want, Smith? I'm glad you waited for me with the table. We'll take it with us, so he'll see what consideration we have for him. [*They both carry the table into the cell. Exit* SMITH. *Pause.*] Hello, Mac. Here's your asparagus. Won't you try a little?
MACHEATH: Don't trouble yourself, Mr. Brown, there are other people who will do me the last honors.[13]
BROWN: But Mackie!
MACHEATH: I should like the account! Forgive me if, in the meanwhile, I eat. After all, this is my last meal! [*He eats.*]
BROWN: Good appetite! Oh, Mac, you wound me as with a red-hot iron!
MACHEATH: The account, sir, please! No sentimentality.
BROWN [*sighing, draws a little notebook out of a pocket*]: I have brought it, Mac. Here is the account for the last six months.
MACHEATH [*scathingly*]: I see. So you've only come to get your money out of me.
BROWN: Mac, you know that's not true . . . !
MACHEATH: All right, you shan't be the loser. What do I owe you? But please let me have a detailed statement. Life has made me mistrustful . . . And you're the one who ought to know why.
BROWN: Mac, when you speak like that, I can't think straight.

There is a loud banging behind.

SMITH [*off*]: All right, that will hold.
MACHEATH: The account, Brown.
BROWN: Very well—if you insist, there are the rewards for the arrests you or your people made possible. You received from the Government in all . . .
MACHEATH: Three murderers at forty pounds each makes a hundred and twenty pounds. A quarter of that for you is thirty pounds, which we owe you.
BROWN: Yes—yes—but I really don't know, Mac, at the last minute, as it were, if we can . . .
MACHEATH: Please cut out the slop. Thirty pounds. And the one in Dover eight pounds.
BROWN: But why only eight pounds, for there was . . .
MACHEATH: Do you believe me or do you not? So for the last half year there's thirty-eight pounds due to you.
BROWN [*sobbing loudly*]: A life-time together . . . I knew your every thought . . .
BOTH: . . . by just looking in your eyes.
MACHEATH: Three years in India—Johnny and James were both on the scene—five years in London and this is all the thanks I get. [*He shows what he will look like when hanged.*]

Here hangs Macheath who ne'er a soul did
  wrong:
A former friend his former friend betrays.
And hanging by a rope a fathom long
His neck can tell him what his bottom weighs.

BROWN: Mac, if you're going to treat me like this . . . ! Who attacks my honor attacks me! [*He runs angrily out of the cage.*]
MACHEATH: Your honor?
BROWN: Yes, my honor! Smith, begin! Let the people in! [*To* MACHEATH:] Excuse me, please.
SMITH [*entering hurriedly, to* MACHEATH]: I can still get you away, but in one minute it'll be too late. Have you got the money?
MACHEATH: Yes, as soon as the boys get back.
SMITH: There's no sign of them. Well—that's off.

People are admitted: PEACHUM, MRS. PEACHUM, POLLY, LUCY, *the whores, the* REVEREND KIMBALL, MATTHEW *and* JACOB.

GINNY JENNY: They didn't want to let us in, but I told them: if you don't take your something heads out of my way, you'll get to know Ginny Jenny better than you like!
PEACHUM: I am his father-in-law. Pardon me, which of those present is Mr. Macheath?
MACHEATH [*presents himself*]: Macheath.
PEACHUM [*walks past the cage*]: Fate, Mr. Macheath, has decreed that you should become my son-in-law without my knowing you. The circumstances in which I meet you for the first time are very tragic. Mr. Macheath, you once had white kid gloves, a stick with an ivory handle, and a scar on your neck, and you frequented the Octopus Hotel. There remains the scar on your neck, which is probably the least valuable of your distinguishing marks, and now you only frequent jails, and very soon you won't frequent anywhere . . .

POLLY *walks sobbing past the cage and stands right.*

MACHEATH: What a pretty dress you're wearing.

MATTHEW *and* JACOB *come past the cage and stand right.*

MATTHEW: We couldn't get through because of the crowd. But we ran so fast I thought Jacob was going to have a stroke. If you don't believe us . . .
MACHEATH: What do the men say? Have they got good places?
MATTHEW: There, Captain, we knew you'd understand. Look, we don't get a Coronation every day. The men have to earn when they can. They ask to be remembered to you.
JACOB: Kindly.
MRS. PEACHUM [*walks past the cage and stands right*]: Mr. Macheath, who would have thought of this when a week ago we had a little dance together at the Octopus Hotel?
MACHEATH: Yes, a little dance.
MRS. PEACHUM: But here on earth below Fate is cruel.
BROWN [*to the* REVEREND KIMBALL *at the back*]: And with this man I stood at Azerbaijan, shoulder to shoulder, under withering fire!
GINNY JENNY [*comes to the cage*]: Us Drury Lane girls are in a terrible fix. Not a soul's gone to the Coronation; they all want to see you. [*She stands right.*]
MACHEATH: To see me.
SMITH: Come on! Six o'clock. [*He lets him out of the cage.*]
MACHEATH: We will not keep the people waiting. Ladies and gentlemen, you see here the vanishing representative of a vanishing class. We bourgeois artisans, who work with honest jimmies on the cash boxes of small shopkeepers, are being swallowed up by large concerns backed by banks. What is a picklock to a bank share? What is the burgling of a bank to the founding of a bank? What is the murder of a man to the employment of a man? Fellow citizens, I herewith take my leave of you. I thank you all for coming. Some of you have been very close to me. That Jenny should have given me up astonishes me greatly. It is a clear proof that the world will always be the same. The concurrence of several unfortunate circumstances has brought about my fall. Good—I fall.

Song illumination: golden light. The organ is lit up. Three lights come down from above on a bar and on a board is written:

BALLAD IN WHICH MACHEATH BEGS PARDON OF ALL

All you who will live long and die in bed
Pray harden not your hearts against us others
And do not grin behind your beards, my brothers,
When you behold us hung till we are dead.
Nor do not curse because we came a cropper.
Be not, as was the Law to us, unkind:
Not every Christian has a lawful mind.
Your levity, my friends, is most improper.
O brother men, let us a lesson be
And pray to God that He may pardon me.

And now the stormwinds with the rain conspire
To wash the flesh we once did overnourish
And ravens gouge our eyes out with a flourish,
These eyes which see so much and more desire.
We were not always virtuous, alas,
That's why you'll see us hanging by the neck
For every greedy bird of prey to peck
As were we horses' offal on the grass.
So, brother men, let us a warning be
And pray to God that He may pardon me.

The wenches with their bosoms showing
To catch the eye of men with yearnings
The urchins just behind them going
In hopes to filch their sinful earnings
The outlaws, bandits, burglars, gunmen
All Christian souls that love a brawl
Abortionists and pimps and fun-men
I cry them mercy one and all.

Except the coppers—sons of bitches—
For every evening, every morning
Those lice came creeping from their niches
And frequently without a warning.
Police! My epidermis itches!
But for today I'll let that fall
Pretend I love the sons of bitches
And cry them mercy one and all.

O, I could smash their ugly faces
And crush them with an iron maul!
But one can't always hold the aces.
I cry them mercy one and all.

SMITH: If you please, Mr. Macheath.
MRS. PEACHUM: Polly and Lucy, stand by your husband in his last hour.
MACHEATH: Ladies, whatever may have been between us . . .
SMITH [*leads him off*]: Come on!

Passage to the Gallows

All exeunt through the doors left. These doors are set in the wings. Then they re-enter from the other side of the stage, all carrying hurricane lamps. When MACHEATH *is standing on the gallows,* PEACHUM *speaks.*

PEACHUM: So, gentlemen, to this point we have come.
You all can see what Captain Mackie's fate is.
Which proves that in the whole of Christendom
Nothing is granted any of us gratis.
But lest you jump to the conclusion
That we are parties to the deal, and in collusion,
Macheath will *not* be hanged till he is dead.
We have devised another end instead.

You all will hear (yes, all; it's rather loud)
Mercy give Justice quite a dreadful hiding.
This is an opera, and we mean to do you proud.
The Royal Messenger will make his entrance—
riding.

On the board is written:

The Arrival of the Mounted Messenger

THIRD THREEPENNY-FINALE

CHORUS: Hark, who comes? The Royal Messenger riding comes!

Riding high, BROWN *enters as the messenger.*

BROWN [*recitative*]: On the occasion of her Coronation, our Gracious Queen commands that one Captain Macheath shall at once be released. [*All cheer.*] At the same time he is raised to the permanent ranks of the nobility. [*Cheers.*] The castle of Marmarel and a pension of ten thousand pounds a year are his as long as he shall live, while to all happy couples here our great Queen presents her very cordial congratulations.

MACHEATH: A rescue! A rescue! I was sure of it. Where the need is greatest, there will God's help be nearest.

POLLY: A rescue! A rescue! My dearest Mackie has been rescued. I am so happy.

MRS. PEACHUM: So, now the whole thing has a happy end! How calm and peaceful would our life be always if a messenger came from the king whenever we wanted.

PEACHUM: Therefore all remain standing where you are now and sing the chorale of the poorest of the poor, of whose difficult life you have shown us something today. In reality their end is generally bad. Mounted messengers from the Queen come far too seldom, and if you kick a man he kicks you back again. Therefore never be too eager to combat injustice.

All sing to the organ and walk forward.

Combat injustice but in moderation:
Such things will freeze to death if left alone.
Remember: this whole vale of tribulation
Is black as pitch and cold as any stone.

Lillian Hellman

Lillian Florence Hellman (1905–1984) was an only child, born in New Orleans into an upper-middle-class family that prefigures the character relationships in many of her plays. Her father was a German Jew whose family had immigrated in the 1840s and had gone into the merchandising business. Her mother was descended from an established Alabama family. It was a daring marriage at the time, and there were difficulties, but it proved to be successful.

Until she was sixteen, Lillian Hellman lived half of the year with her spinster aunts, her father's sisters, in New Orleans, and the other half with her parents on the Upper West Side of Manhattan in New York City. Hellman said that, as a result of these shifts in residences, she was indifferent to school and "wanted to be left alone to read by myself." At nineteen, she dropped out of New York University and took a job with the publisher Horace Liveright, then the proprietor of a dynamic and avant-garde publishing house, whose authors included James Joyce, T. S. Eliot, e. e. cummings, Dorothy Parker, and Eugene O'Neill. While working at Liveright, Hellman met Arthur Kober, whom she married. They later moved to Hollywood, where she read manuscripts and soon became part of the Hollywood writers' scene.

By 1932, when Hellman divorced Kober, she had already established a relationship with Dashiell Hammett, author of best-selling detective novels such as *The Maltese Falcon* (1930) and *The Thin Man* (1932). Her longtime relationship with Hammett was difficult. Often they lived separate lives and endured the consequences of alcoholism and infidelity. They never married, but he was her lover and mentor until his death in 1961. Hammett dedicated *The Thin Man* to Hellman and used her as the model for Nora Charles, its witty heroine. Like Nora Charles, Hellman was an alcoholic. Unlike Nora, who is nonchalant and cheerful, Hellman admitted that she was often acerbic, irritable, and given to quick mood changes. Hammett encouraged Hellman's decision to write for the theater and helped to make a success of her first play, *The Children's Hour,* in 1934. She dedicated the published edition of the play to "D. Hammett with thanks." The play, about two young school mistresses whose lives are destroyed by a student's malicious lie that they are lesbians, brought Hellman immediate acclaim.

Her second play, *Days to Come* (1936), focuses on the themes of corruption and infidelity. In it, factory-owner Andrew Rodman calls in strikebreakers because he is under pressure to satisfy his stockholders. This plot is further complicated when Julie, his wife, falls in love with the chief labor organizer, Joe Whelan, and an innocent child is murdered by a mob of angry workers. Eventually, Julie admits her adultery, and Rodman admits his indebtedness. The strike is resolved and the marriage fails, though when Julie offers to divorce

Andrew, he declines, saying that they can just go on as they are for the rest of their lives "for days to come." The play closed after six performances.

The Little Foxes (1939) and *Another Part of the Forest* (1946) were probably derived from family stories. Both plays are about the Hubbards, a rapacious family of Southern merchants, whose fortunes depend on dishonesty and exploitation. *The Little Foxes* takes place in the deep South about 1900, as Regina Giddens, foreseeing a business opportunity for modernizing, schemes with her brothers, Ben and Oscar Hubbard, to build a new cotton factory. Her necessary share of the funds, however, belongs to her husband, Horace. When Horace's scruples prevent him from providing the money, Regina aggravates his delicate heart condition and looks away while he dies reaching for his medicine. With the way clear, Regina and Ben cheat Oscar out of part of his share. Hardly expecting any conflict with her daughter, Alexandra, Regina is unexpectedly rebuffed and thwarted when Alexandra suspects her of complicity in Horace's death. Brother Ben, ever alert for chinks in Regina's armor, decides that he might be able to use this information to undermind her. The play ends as the once compliant Alexandra confronts Regina:

> REGINA: I'd like to keep you with me, but I won't make you stay. Too many people used to make me do too many things. No, I won't make you stay.
> ALEXANDRA: You couldn't, Mama, because I want to leave here. As I've never wanted anything in my life before. Because now I understand what Papa was trying to tell me. [*Pause*] All in one day: Addie said there were people who ate the earth and other people who stood around and watched them do it. And just now Uncle Ben said the same thing. Really, he said the same thing. [*Tensely*] Well, tell him for me, Mama, I'm not going to stand around and watch you do it. Tell him I'll be fighting as hard as he'll be fighting [*rises*] some place where people don't just stand around and watch.

Another Part of the Forest (1946) takes place in a small Alabama town that is the home of the Hubbard family, about twenty years before *The Little Foxes*. The Hubbards are riddled with unhappiness. Marcus, the father, suffers from the memory of betraying a troop of Confederate soldiers. His mad wife, Lavinia, torments him with her knowledge of his guilt. Their daughter, Regina, is in love with a former Confederate officer, who wants to go to Brazil. Ben, the older son, is a swindler, and Oscar, the second son, wants money to go to New Orleans to live with a whore, whom he claims to love. When the trickery ends, the father is exposed, Regina loses her fiancé, Oscar's whore spits in his face, and Ben becomes the power in the family and declares that Regina must marry Horace Giddens, a man she disdains.

Between her writing of these two Hubbard plays, Hellman took on political themes in her other work in response to the war raging in Europe. She said she wrote first about people, however. "I've never been interested in political messages," she claimed in 1959, "so it is hard for me to believe I wrote them. Like every other writer, I use myself and the time I live in." In 1941 Hellman wrote *Watch on the Rhine*, about the evils of Nazism and the idealism necessary to fight them. The story takes place in Washington, D.C., in the home of the socially prominent Fanny Farrelly, whose moral judgment will be tested when she witnesses a murder. Her daughter has returned from Germany with her husband, Kurt Müller, a member of the anti-Nazi resistance. Müller is found out by Count Teck De Brancovis, a houseguest who threatens to reveal his identity, and Müller kills him. When put to the test, Farrelly and her son David make the moral decision to help, and they refuse to turn Müller over to the police. Müller heroically bids farewell to his family, who remain in Washington, while he returns to Germany, knowing that he will probably be killed. As a play, *Watch on the Rhine*, produced before the United States entered World War II, was a modest success, but as a film in 1943, written by Hellman and Hammett, it excited American patriotism at a low time during World War II.

The Searching Wind (1944) is also set in Washington, D.C. Told in flashbacks, it depicts the consequences of three key moments leading up to war: Mussolini's takover of Italy in 1922, the rise of Adolf Hitler in 1933, and peace negotiations in Paris just before the outbreak of war. Besides the political tension, there is also the tension of romantic intrigue. Alex Hazen and Cassie Bowman, the chief characters, have followed separate lives and careers; he an ambassador, she a teacher. But they have remained lovers for twenty-two years, and now in this time of international crisis they acknowledge their long-held secret. Bowman says to her, "You know, when you don't think you're bad, then you have a hard time seeing you did things for a bad reason, and you fool yourself that way. You don't do anything for just one reason. It all gets mixed up and—maybe the hardest thing in the world is to see yourself straight. . . . Oh, I don't want to see another generation of people like us who didn't know what they were doing or why they did it. We were frivolous people." Bowman speaks as if she is a stand-in for Hellman, and the lines are probably a reflection of Hellman's own personal and political code.

In 1949 Hellman adapted and directed Emmanuel Robles' *Montserrat*, a historical play about the revolution in Venezuela in 1813, led by Simón Bolívar. The play failed, however. In the following two years, she wrote *The Autumn Garden* while living with Hammett at their farm in Pleasantville, New York. This was probably the happiest time in her life with Hammett, though he was suffering from acute alcoholism and writer's block. Now forty-four, Hellman took as her theme in this play one's mellowing in middle age and the embarrassment of reassessing one's life. It is a comedy set in Constance Tuckerman's home on the Gulf of Mexico, where Tuckerman is entertaining a house full of guests and waiting for the arrival of Nick Denery, a painter who jilted her many years before. When Denery arrives with his wealthy wife, he systematically begins deflating the egos of all the other guests, callously exposing their self-deceptions. When Constance looks at herself in Denery's portrait of her, which depicts her in a cheap dress, looking old, she has a moment of revelation. Only Sophie, Constance's eighteen-year-old niece, seems to have a future, and she takes it by heading out for France, where she was raised. Ben Griggs, probably based on the fifty-seven-year-old Hammett, sees himself honestly as being used-up—a man who frittered his life away and is now unable to write. Of all her plays, Hellman liked this one best, and she again dedicated it to Hammett.

A year later, Hellman and Hammett's idyll ended when they were called to testify before the U.S. House Un-American Activities Committee to "name names" of suspected Communists. Hammett indeed had ties to the Communist Party; and Hellman was criticized for authoring a pro-Russian film, *The North Star,* in 1943, even though Russia and the United States were allies. Hellman refused to cooperate. With eloquence and steely nerves, she wrote that to "hurt innocent people whom I knew many years ago in order to save myself is to me, inhuman and indecent and dishonorable. I cannot and will not cut my conscience to fit this year's fashions." Hellman was released from testifying. Hammett also refused to testify, and he was sentenced to six months in jail. As a casualty of the Communist scare, Hellman was blacklisted, and she did not work again in Hollywood until 1966. Ironically, she returned to Broadway, where she authored the plays upon which her reputation rests.

Despite the failure of *Montserrat*, Hellman continued to stage adaptations of European drama and literature that appealed to her political and moral sensibilities. She achieved critical success with *The Lark* (1955), her adaptation of Jean Anouilh's *L'Alouette* (1953), a play about Joan of Arc. Hellman seems to have identified with Joan and characterized the meek Maid of Orléans as the feisty and sincere woman she saw herself to be. *Candide* (1956) is a musical adaptation of Voltaire's *Candide* (1759), the satirical novel about a naïve man who learns that the world is not what he imagined. With lyrics by Richard Wilbur and music by Leonard Bernstein, Hellman's *Candide* was a critical success but a failure with audiences. Hellman said that she was never really committed to the project, and there was much bickering among the collaborators during and after the production. As audiences changed, *Candide* was revived and staged as an opera, where it has found a popular niche in the repertory of the New York City Opera, although little of Hellman's libretto remains.

When she was fifty-four, Hellman wrote *Toys in the Attic*, a story set in New Orleans, where a young man attempts to rid himself of his possessive sisters and grapples with the effects of miscegenation. The play draws on Hellman's family, particularly her two aunts Jenny and Hannah Hellman, the spinsters with whom she spent much of her youth in New Orleans. The character Julian Berniers has been doted upon by his two spinster sisters, who live vicariously through him. When Julian unexpectedly arrives with Lily Prine, his wife, and a considerable amount of money, the sisters' lives change drastically. Carrie, the younger sister, becomes unhinged. In order to keep Julian dependent, she convinces Lily, who is sweet but not smart, to call Julian's business partner, Warkins, and tell him that Julian and Mrs. Warkins are meeting secretly. Julian is actually meeting with her in order to help her pay off an old debt that will enable her to escape her husband. Warkins is irate and arranges to have Julian beaten and robbed and to have his wife's face slashed. In the end, no one is unscathed, and love proves to be more destructive than constructive.

Hellman's last play was *My Mother, My Father and Me.* (1963), an adaptation of Burt Blechman's *How Much*? It was a failure. At fifty-seven, Hellman, unhappy with her sagging reputation in the 1960s, stopped writing for the theater and wrote about herself. With a series of memoirs completed in 1979, which she called *Three*, including *An Unfinished Woman,* and *Pentimento*, her career took a successful turn. Long reticent about her personal life, Hellman was praised for her candor, but things soured when it was revealed that her some of her memoirs were fictionalized. Hellman's response was to remain silent. She, in turn, is the semi-fictionalized main character of William Luce's *Lillian* (1986), and she also appears as a character in *Cakewalk* (1993), a play by Peter Feibleman, her companion in later life.

Hellman was twenty-nine when she achieved her first success with *The Children's Hour*. The story is loosely based on a crime story in William Roughead's anthology, *Bad Companions* (1931), describing the 1810 trial of Miss Marianne Woods and Miss Jane Prie, who operated a boarding school in Scotland and were accused of improper sexual conduct. Hellman's play concerns the relationship of two teachers, Martha Dobie and Karen Wright, who operate a private boarding school in a converted farmhouse in Lancet, Massachusetts. When they are accused of lesbianism by the malicious Mary Tilford, niece of the school's benefactor, Amelia Tilford, the scandal wrecks the school. Though they have been close friends, Martha, Karen, and Joe Cardin, Karen's fiancé, are forced to reevaluate their relationships with unfortunate consequences.

Though outwardly supportive, Joe Cardin secretly believes that there might have been some truth to the lie. When he says to Karen, "It means that we've got to start putting this whole business behind us now. *Now* Karen. What you've done, you've done—and that's that." When Karen responds, "What *I've* done?" Cardin tries to gloss over his mistake, but Karen knows what is on his mind. Hoping to start over, Cardin suggests that they live in Vienna and escape the sordidness of their situation, but Karen says that running away isn't the answer because "every word will have a new meaning. You think we'll be able to run away from that? Woman, child, love, lawyer—no words that we can use in safety any more. [*Laughs bitterly*] Sick, high-tragic people. That's what we'll be."

This scene is reminiscent of the final act of Henrik Ibsen's *A Doll's House,* when Nora confronts Torvald for his failure to defend her honor against scadal. As in that conflict, Hellman has Karen acknowledge that Cardin has failed her:

> KAREN [*Suddenly*]: I want you to say it now.
> CARDIN: I don't know what you're talking about.
> KAREN: Yes, you do. We've both known for a long time. I knew surely the day we lost the case. I was watching your face in court. It was ashamed—and sad at being ashamed. Say it now, Joe. Ask it now.
> CARDIN: I have nothing to ask. Nothing— [*Quickly*] All right. Is it—was it ever—
> KAREN [*puts her hand over his mouth*]: No. Martha and I have never touched each other.

As this point, and with great resolve, Karen says, "Now go and sit down, Joe. I have things to say. They're all mixed up and I must get them clear." Karen explains the impossibility of their relationship, and ends by saying "It's what we can't have now. Go home, darling." As he leaves, Joe says, "I'll be coming back," but Karen, waiting until he has gone, says with finality, "No, you won't. Never, darling."

Once Joe leaves, Martha enters, and Karen explains to her that Joe thought they were lovers. Martha's response is "We aren't like that," but unable to hold back, she admits that she loves Karen: "I have loved you the way they said." Horrified, Karen tells her to stop, but Martha bitterly expresses her resentment and her love, until Karen suggests that Martha go and lie down. Martha "looks around the room, slowly, carefully" and exits. Moments later, Karen hears the shot announcing Martha's suicide. Depressed, Karen has scarcely any time for reflection or grief when Mrs. Tilford arrives and admits that she has discovered Mary Tilford has lied. Karen, however, is inconsolable, and the play ends mournfully.

The Children's Hour is antiromantic, with no relief or catharsis, but only the stark realism of unhappiness caused by lies and deception. Its structure shows Hellman's indebtedness to the "problem play," in which characters' lives are blasted by scandal. Hellman follows Ibsen's pattern of introducing a problem, having it discussed rather than showing action, and then allowing it to come to a conclusion that is generally without a satisfactory resolution. She may also have been influenced by Dashiell Hammett's antiromantic realism in his detective novels, all of which depend heavily on motives based on lies, mistrust, and deception.

Hellman always denied that the play's theme is lesbianism, although it is obvious in the text. (The play was banned in Boston, Chicago, and London.) In an interview with Harry Gilroy in 1952, she explained that the primary theme of *The Children's Hour* is the "big lie." "It's the result of her [Mary Tilford's] lie," Hellman said, "that make her so dreadful—this is not a play about lesbianism but about a lie. The bigger the lie the better, as always." When Hellman wrote the first of two filmscripts for *The Children's Hour,* in 1936 (retitled *These Three*), she was unequivocal about the big lie but replaced the lesbianism with heterosexual betrayal. Instead of having Mary Tilford accuse Martha and Karen of being lesbians, she reports that Joe Cardin was seen in bed with Martha. Hellman's second filmscript for the 1962 version of *The Children's Hour* restores the lesbian conflict.

Film

The Children's Hour (1936), directed by William Wyler, with Merle Oberon, Miriam Hopkins, Joel McCrea, Bonita Granville, Catherine Doucet, Margaret Hamilton, and Walter Brennan. Screenplay by Lillian Hellman. Samuel Goldwyn.

The Children's Hour (1962), directed by William Wyler, with Audrey Hepburn, Shirley McLaine, James Garner, Miriam Hopkins, and Faye Bainter. Screenplay by Lillian Hellman. United Artists/Mirisch.

The Children's Hour

CHARACTERS

PEGGY ROGERS
MRS. LILY MORTAR
EVELYN MUNN
HELEN BURTON
LOIS FISHER
CATHERINE
ROSALIE WELLS
MARY TILFORD
KAREN WRIGHT
MARTHA DOBIE
DOCTOR JOSEPH CARDIN
AGATHA
MRS. AMELIA TILFORD
A GROCERY BOY

SCENE

ACT I Living room of the Wright-Dobie School. Late afternoon in April.
ACT II Scene I. Living room at MRS. TILFORD's. A few hours later.
Scene II. The same. Later that evening.
ACT III The same as Act I. November.

ACT I

SCENE. *A room in the Wright-Dobie School for girls, a converted farm-house eighteen miles from the town of Lancet. It is a comfortable, unpretentious room used as an afternoon study-room and at all other times as the living room.*

A large door Left Center faces the audience. There is a single door Right. Against both back walls are bookcases. A large desk is at Right; a table, two sofas, and eight or ten chairs.

It is early in an afternoon in April.

AT RISE: MRS. LILY MORTAR *is sitting in a large chair Right Center, with her head back and her eyes closed. She is a plump, florid woman of forty-five with obviously touched-up hair. Her clothes are too fancy for a classroom.*

Seven girls, from twelve to fourteen years old, are informally grouped on chairs and sofa. Six of them are sewing with no great amount of industry on pieces of white material. One of the others, EVELYN MUNN, *is using her scissors to trim the hair* of ROSALIE, *who sits, nervously, in front of her. She has* ROSALIE'S *head bent back at an awkward angle and is enjoying herself.*

The eighth girl, PEGGY ROGERS, *is sitting in a higher chair than the others. She is reading aloud from a book. She is bored and she reads in a singsong, tired voice.*

PEGGY [*reading*]: "It is twice blest; it blesseth him that gives and him that takes: 'tis mightiest in the mightiest; it becomes the throned monarch better than his crown; his sceptre shows the force of temporal power, the attribute to awe and majesty, wherein . . ." [MRS. MORTAR *suddenly opens her eyes and stares at the haircutting. The children make efforts to warn* EVELYN. PEGGY *raises her voice until she is shouting*] "doth sit the dread and fear of kings; but mercy is above . . ."

MRS. MORTAR: Evelyn! What are you doing?

EVELYN [*inanely. She lisps*]: Uh-nothing, Mrs. Mortar.

MRS. MORTAR: You are certainly doing something. You are ruining the scissors for one thing.

PEGGY [*loudly*]: "But mercy is above. It . . ."

MRS. MORTAR: Just a moment, Peggy. It is very unfortunate that you girls cannot sit quietly with your sewing and drink in the immortal words of the immortal bard. [*She sighs*] Evelyn, go back to your sewing.

EVELYN: I can't get the hem thtraight. Honeth, I've been trying for three weekth, but I jutht can't do it.

MRS. MORTAR: Helen, please help Evelyn with the hem.

HELEN [*rises, holding up the garment* EVELYN *has been working on. It is soiled and shapeless, and so much has been cut off that it is now hardly large enough for a child of five. Giggling*]: She can't ever wear *that*, Mrs. Mortar.

MRS. MORTAR [*vaguely*]: Well, try to do something with it. Make some handkerchiefs or something. Be clever about it. Women must learn these tricks. [*To* PEGGY] Continue. "Mightiest in the mightiest."

PEGGY: "'Tis mightiest in the mightiest; it becomes the throned monarch better than his crown; his sceptre—his sceptre shows the force of temporal power, the attribute to awe and majesty, wherein—

LOIS [*from the back of the room chants softly and monotonously through the previous speech*]: Ferebam, ferebas, ferebat, ferebamus, ferebatis, fere, fere—

CATHERINE [*two seats away, the book propped in front of her*]: Ferebant.

LOIS: Ferebamus, ferebatis, fere*bant*.

MRS. MORTAR: Who's doing that?

PEGGY [*the noise ceases. She hurries on*]: "Wherein doth sit the dread and fear of kings; but mercy is above this sceptred sway, it is enthroned in the hearts of kings, it is an attribute to God himself—"

MRS. MORTAR [*sadly, reproachfully*]: Peggy, can't you imagine yourself as Portia? Can't you read the lines with some feeling, some pity? [*Dreamily*] Pity. Ah! As Sir Henry said to me many's the time, pity makes the actress. Now, why can't *you* feel pity?

PEGGY: I guess I feel pity.

LOIS: Ferebamus, ferebatis, fere—fere—fere—

CATHERINE: Fere*bant*, stupid.

MRS. MORTAR: How many people in this room are talking? Peggy, read the line again. I'll give you the cue.

PEGGY: What's a cue?

MRS. MORTAR: A cue is a line or word given the actor or actress to remind them of their next speech.

HELEN [*softly*]: To remind *him* or *her*.

ROSALIE [*a fattish girl with glasses*]: Weren't you ever in the movies, Mrs. Mortar?

MRS. MORTAR: I had many offers, my dear. But the cinema is a shallow art. It has no—no— [*Vaguely*] no fourth dimension. Now, Peggy, if you would only try to submerge yourself in this problem. You are pleading for the life of a man. [*She rises and there are faint sighs from the girls, who stare at her with blank, bored faces. She recites hammily, with gestures*] "But mercy is above this sceptred sway; it is enthroned in the hearts of kings, it is an attribute to God himself; and earthly power doth then show likest God's when mercy seasons justice."

LOIS [*almost singing it*]: Utor, fruor, fungor, potior, and vescor take the dative.

CATHERINE: Take the *ablative*.

LOIS: Oh, dear. Utor, fruor, fung—

MRS. MORTAR [*to* LOIS, *with sarcasm*]: You have something to tell the class?

LOIS [*apologetically*]: We've got a Latin exam this afternoon.

Iris Man, Kim Hunter, and Mary Finney (all standing) in The Children's Hour, *directed by Herman Shumlin, Maxine Elliott's Theatre, New York, 1934.*

MRS. MORTAR: And you intend to occupy the sewing and elocution hour learning what should have been learnt yesterday?

CATHERINE [*wearily*]: It takes her more than yesterday to learn it.

MRS. MORTAR: Well, I cannot allow you to interrupt us like this.

CATHERINE: But we're finished sewing.

LOIS [*admiringly*]: I bet you were good at Latin, Mrs. Mortar.

MRS. MORTAR [*conciliated*]: Long ago, my dear, long ago. Now, take your book over by the window and don't disturb our enjoyment of Shakespeare. [CATHERINE *and* LOIS *rise, go to window, stand mumbling and gesturing*] Let us go back again. "It is an attribute of—"[*At this point the door opens far enough to let* MARY TILFORD, *clutching a slightly faded bunch of wild flowers, squeeze cautiously in. She is fourteen, neither pretty nor ugly. She is an undistinguished-looking girl, except for the sullenly dissatisfied expression on her face*] "And earthly power doth then show likest God's when mercy seasons justice. We do pray for mercy, and that same prayer doth teach—"

PEGGY [*happily*]: You've skipped three lines.

MRS. MORTAR: In my entire career I've never missed a line.

PEGGY: But you did skip three lines. [*Goes to* MRS. MORTAR *with book*] See?

MRS. MORTAR [*seeing* MARY *sidling along wall toward other end of the room, turns to her to avoid* PEGGY *and the book*]: Mary!

HELEN [*in whisper to* MARY]: You're going to catch it now.

MRS. MORTAR: Mary!

MARY: Yes, Mrs. Mortar?

MRS. MORTAR : This is a pretty time to be coming to your sewing class, I must say. Even if you have no interest in your work you might at least remember that you owe me a little courtesy. Courtesy is breeding. Breeding is an excellent thing. [*Turns to class*] Always remember that.

ROSALIE: Please, Mrs. Mortar, can I write that down?

MRS. MORTAR: Certainly. Suppose you all write it down.

PEGGY: But we wrote it down last week.

[MARY *giggles*.]

MRS. MORTAR: Mary, I am still awaiting your explanation. Where have you been?

MARY: I took a walk.

MRS. MORTAR: So you took a walk. And may I ask, young lady, are we in the habit of taking walks when we should be at our classes?

MARY: I am sorry, Mrs. Mortar, I went to get you these flowers. I thought you would like them and I didn't know it would take so long to pick them.

MRS. MORTAR [*flattered*]: Well, well.

MARY [*almost in tears*]: You were telling us last week how much you liked flowers, and I thought that I would bring you some and—

MRS. MORTAR: That was very sweet of you, Mary; I always like thoughtfulness. But you must not allow anything to interfere with your classes. Now run along, dear, and get a vase and some water to put my flowers in. [MARY *turns, sticks out her tongue at* HELEN, *says: "A-a-a," and exits Left*] You may put that book away, Peggy. I am sure your family need never worry about your going on the stage.

PEGGY: I don't want to go on the stage. I want to be a lighthouse-keeper's wife.

MRS. MORTAR: Well, I certainly hope you won't read to him.

[*The laughter of the class pleases her.* PEGGY *sits down among the other girls, who are making a great show of doing nothing.* MRS. MORTAR *returns to her chair, puts her head back, closes her eyes.*]

CATHERINE: How much longer, O Cataline, are you going to abuse our patience? [*To* LOIS] Now translate it, and for goodness' sakes try to get it right this time.

MRS. MORTAR [*for no good reason*]: "One master passion in the breast, like Aaron's serpent, swallows all the rest."

[*She and* LOIS *are murmuring during* KAREN WRIGHT'*s entrance.* KAREN *is an attractive woman of twenty-eight, casually pleasant in manner, without sacrifice of warmth or dignity. She smiles at the girls, goes to the desk. With her entrance there is an immediate change in the manner of the girls: they are fond of her and they respect her. She gives* MORTAR, *whose quotation has reached her, an annoyed look.*]

LOIS: "Quo usque tandem ab*u*tere. . . . "

KAREN [*automatically*]: "Ab*u*tere." [*Opens drawer in desk*] What's happened to your hair, Rosalie?

ROSALIE: It got cut, Miss Wright.

KAREN [*smiling*]: I can see that. A new style? Looks as though it has holes in it.

EVELYN [*giggling*]: I didn't mean to do it that bad, Mith Wright, but Rothalie'th got funny hair. I thaw a picture in the paper, and I wath trying to do it that way.

ROSALIE [*feels her hair, looks pathetically at* KAREN]: Oh, what shall I do, Miss Wright? [*Gesturing*] It's long here, and it's short here and—

KAREN: Never mind. Come up to my room later and I'll see if I can fix it for you.
MRS. MORTAR: And hereafter we'll have no more haircutting.
KAREN: Helen, have you found your bracelet?
HELEN: No, I haven't, and I've looked everywhere.
KAREN: Have another look. It must be in your room somewhere.

[MARY *comes in Right, with her flowers in a vase. When she sees* KAREN, *she loses some of her assurance.* KAREN *looks at the flowers in surprise.*]

MARY: Good afternoon, Miss Wright. [*Sits down, looks at* KAREN, *who is staring hard at the flowers.*]
KAREN: Hello, Mary.
MRS. MORTAR [*fluttering around*]: Peggy has been reading Portia for us.

[PEGGY *sighs.*]

KAREN [*smiling*]: Peggy doesn't like Portia?
MRS. MORTAR: I don't think she quite appreciates it, but—
KAREN [*patting* PEGGY *on the head*]: Well, I didn't either. I don't think I do yet. Where'd you get those flowers, Mary?
MRS. MORTAR: She picked them for me. [*Hurriedly*] It made her a little late to class, but she heard me say I loved flowers, and she went to get them for me. [*With a sigh*] The first wild flowers of the season.
KAREN: But not the very first, are they, Mary?
MARY: I don't know.
KAREN: Where did you get them?
MARY: Near Conway's cornfield, I think.
KAREN: It wasn't necessary to go so far. There was a bunch exactly like this in the garbage can this morning.
MRS. MORTAR [*after a second*]: Oh, I can't believe it! What a nasty thing to do! [*To* MARY] And I suppose you have just as fine an excuse for being an hour late to breakfast this morning, and last week— [*To* KAREN] I haven't wanted to tell you these things before, but—
KAREN [*hurriedly, as a bell rings off stage*]: There's the bell.
LOIS [*walking toward door*]: Ad, ab, ante, in, de, inter, con, post, præ— [*Looks up at* KAREN] I *can't* seem to remember the rest.
KAREN: Præ, pro, sub, super. Don't worry, Lois. You'll come out all right. [LOIS *smiles, exits.* MARY *attempts to make a quick exit*] Wait a minute, Mary. [*Reluctantly* MARY *turns back as the girls file out.* KAREN *moves the small chairs, clearing the room as she talks*] Mary, I've had the feeling—and I don't think I'm wrong—that the girls here were happy; that they liked Miss Dobie and me, that they liked the school. Do you think that's true?
MARY: Miss Wright, I have to get my Latin book.
KAREN: I thought it was true until you came here a year ago. I don't think you're very happy here, and I'd like to find out why. [*Looks at* MARY, *waits for an answer, gets none, shakes her head*] Why, for example, do you find it necessary to lie to us so often?
MARY [*without looking up*]: I'm not lying. I went out walking and I saw the flowers and they looked pretty and I didn't know it was so late.
KAREN [*impatiently*]: Stop it, Mary! I'm not interested in hearing that foolish story again. I *know* you got the flowers out of the garbage can. What I do want to know is why you feel you have to lie out of it.
MARY [*beginning to whimper*]: I *did* pick the flowers near Conway's. You never believe me. You believe everybody but me. It's always like that. Everything I say you fuss at me about. Everything I do is wrong.
KAREN: You know that isn't true. [*Goes to* MARY, *puts her arm around her, waits until the sobbing has stopped*] Look, Mary, look at me. [*Raises* MARY'*s face with her hand*] Let's try to understand each other. If you feel that you *have* to take a walk, or that you just *can't* come to class, or that you'd like to go into the village by yourself, come and tell me—I'll try and understand. [*Smiles*] I don't say that I'll always agree that you should do exactly what you want to do, but I've had feelings like that, too—everybody has—and I won't be unreasonable about yours. But this way, this kind of lying you do, makes everything wrong.
MARY [*looking steadily at* KAREN]: I got the flowers near Conway's cornfield.
KAREN [*looks at* MARY, *sighs, moves back toward desk and stands there for a moment*]: Well, there doesn't seem to be any other way with you; you'll have to be punished. Take your recreation periods alone for the next two weeks. No horseback-riding and no hockey. Don't leave the school grounds for any reason whatsoever. Is that clear?
MARY [*carefully*]: Saturday, too?
KAREN: Yes.
MARY: But you said I could go to the boat-races.
KAREN: I'm sorry, but you can't go.
MARY: I'll tell my grandmother. I'll tell her how everybody treats me here and the way I get punished for every little thing I do. I'll tell her, I'll—
MRS. MORTAR: Why, I'd slap her hands!
KAREN [*turning back from door, ignoring* MRS. MORTAR'*s speech. To* MARY]: Go upstairs, Mary.
MARY: I don't feel well.
KAREN [*wearily*]: Go upstairs now.

MARY: I've got a pain. I've had it all morning. It hurts right here. [*Pointing vaguely in the direction of her heart*] Really it does.

KAREN: Ask Miss Dobie to give you some hot water and bicarbonate of soda.

MARY: It's a bad pain. I've never had it before.

KAREN: I don't think it can be very serious.

MARY: My heart! It's my heart! It's stopping or something. I can't breathe. [*She takes a long breath and falls awkwardly to the floor.*]

KAREN [*sighs, shakes her head, kneels beside* MARY. *To* MRS. MORTAR]: Ask Martha to phone Joe.

MRS. MORTAR [*going out*]: Do you think—? Heart trouble is very serious in a child.

[KAREN *picks* MARY *up from the floor and carries her off Right. After a moment* MARTHA DOBIE *enters Center. She is about the same age as* KAREN. *She is a nervous, high-strung woman.*]

KAREN [*enters Right*]: Did you get Joe?

MARTHA [*nodding*]: What happened to her? She was perfectly well a few hours ago.

KAREN: She probably still is. I told her she couldn't go to the boat-races and she had a heart attack.

MARTHA: Where is she?

KAREN: In there. Mortar's with her.

MARTHA: Anything really wrong with her?

KAREN: I doubt it. [*Sits down at desk and begins to mark papers*] She's a problem, that kid. Her latest trick was kidding your aunt out of a sewing lesson with those faded flowers we threw out. Then she threatened to go to her grandmother with some tale about being mistreated.

MARTHA: And, please God, Grandma would believe her and take her away.

KAREN: Which would give the school a swell black eye. But we ought to do something.

MARTHA: How about having a talk with Mrs. Tilford?

KAREN [*smiling*]: You want to do it? [MARTHA *shakes her head*] I hate to do it. She's been so nice to us. [*Shrugging her shoulders*] Anyway, it wouldn't do any good. She's too crazy about Mary to see her faults very clearly—and the kid knows it.

MARTHA: How about asking Joe to say something to her? She'd listen to him.

KAREN: That would be admitting that we can't do the job ourselves.

MARTHA: Well, we can't, and we might as well admit it. We've tried everything we can think of. She's had more attention than any other three kids put together. And we still haven't the faintest idea what goes on inside her head.

KAREN: She's a strange girl.

MARTHA: That's putting it mildly.

KAREN [*laughs*]: It's funny. We always talk about the child as if she were a grown woman.

MARTHA: It's not so funny. There's something the matter with the kid. That's been true ever since the first day she came. She causes trouble here; she's bad for the other girls. I don't know what it is—it's a feeling I've got that it's wrong somewhere—

KAREN: All right, all right, we'll talk it over with Joe. Now what about our other pet nuisance?

MARTHA [*laughs*]: My aunt the actress? What's she been up to now?

KAREN: Nothing unusual. Last night at dinner she was telling the girls about the time she lost her trunks in Butte, Montana, and how she gave her best performance of Rosalind during a hurricane. Today in the kitchen you could hear her on what Sir Henry said to her.

MARTHA: Wait until she does Hedda Gabler standing on a chair. Sir Henry taught her to do it that way. He said it was a test of great acting.

KAREN: You must have had a gay childhood.

MARTHA [*bitterly*]: Oh, I did. I did, indeed. God, how I used to hate all that—

KAREN: Couldn't we get rid of her soon, Martha? I hate to make it hard on you, but she really ought not to be here.

MARTHA [*after a moment*]: I know.

KAREN: We can scrape up enough money to send her away. Let's do it.

MARTHA [*goes to her, affectionately pats her head*]: You've been very patient about it. I'm sorry and I'll talk to her today. It'll probably be a week or two before she can be ready to leave. Is that all right?

KAREN: Of course. [*Looks at her watch*] Did you get Joe himself on the phone?

MARTHA: He was already on his way. Isn't he always on his way over here?

KAREN [*laughs*]: Well, I'm going to marry him some day, you know.

MARTHA [*looking at her*]: You haven't talked of marriage for a long time.

KAREN: I've talked of it with Joe.

MARTHA: Then you *are* thinking about it—soon?

KAREN: Perhaps when the term is over. By that time we ought to be out of debt, and the school should be paying for itself.

MARTHA [*nervously playing with a book on the table*]: Then we won't be taking our vacation together?

KAREN: Of course we will. The three of us.

MARTHA: I had been looking forward to some place by the lake—just you and me—the way we used to at college.

KAREN [*cheerfully*]: Well, now there will be three of us. That'll be fun, too.

MARTHA [*after a pause*]: Why haven't you told me this before?

KAREN: I'm not telling you anything we haven't talked about often.

MARTHA: But your talking about it as *soon* now.

KAREN: I'm glad to be able to. I've been in love with Joe a long time. [MARTHA *crosses to window and stands looking out, her back to* KAREN. KAREN *finishes marking papers and rises*] It's a big day for the school. Rosalie's finally put an "l" in could.

MARTHA [*in a dull, bitter tone, not turning from window*]: You really *are* going to leave, aren't you?

KAREN: I'm not going to leave, and you know it. Why do you say things like that? We agreed a long time ago that my marriage wasn't going to make any difference to the school.

MARTHA: But it will. You know it will. It can't help it.

KAREN: That's nonsense. Joe doesn't want me to give up here.

MARTHA [*turning from window*]: I don't understand you. It's been so damned hard building this thing up, slaving and going without things to make ends meet—think of having a winter coat without holes in the lining again!—and now when we're getting on our feet, you're all ready to let it go to hell.

KAREN: This is a silly argument, Martha. Let's quit it. You haven't listened to a word I've said. I'm not getting married tomorrow, and when I do, it's not going to interfere with my work here. You're making something out of nothing.

MARTHA: It's going to be hard going on alone afterward.

KAREN: For God's sake, do you expect me to give up my marriage?

MARTHA: I don't mean that, but it's so—

[*Door Center opens and* DOCTOR JOSEPH CARDIN *comes in. He is a large, pleasant-looking, carelessly dressed man of about thirty-five.*]

CARDIN: Hello, darling. Hi, Martha. What's the best news?

MARTHA: Hello, Joe.

KAREN: We tried to get you on the phone. Come in and look at your little cousin.

CARDIN: Sure. What's the matter with her now? I stopped at Vernie's on the way over to look at that little black bull he bought. He's a baby! There's going to be plenty of good breeding done in these hills.

KAREN: You'd better come and see her. She says she has a pain in her heart. [*Goes out Right.*]

CARDIN [*stopping to light a cigarette*]: Our little Mary pops up in every day's dispatches.

MARTHA [*impatiently*]: Go and see her. Heart attacks are nothing to play with.

CARDIN [*looks at her*]: Never played with one in my life.

[*Exits Right.*]

[MARTHA *walks around room and finally goes to stare out window.*]

[MRS. MORTAR *enters Right.*]

MRS. MORTAR: *I* was asked to leave the room. [MARTHA *pays no attention*] It seems that I'm not wanted in the room during the examination.

MARTHA [*over her shoulder*]: What difference does it make?

MRS. MORTAR: What difference does it make? Why, it was a deliberate snub.

MARTHA: There's very little pleasure in watching a man use a stethoscope.

MRS. MORTAR: Isn't it natural that the child should have me with her? Isn't it natural that an older woman should be present? [*No answer*] Very well, if you are so thick-skinned that you don't resent these things—

MARTHA: What are you talking about? Why, in the name of heaven, should *you* be with her?

MRS. MORTAR: It—it's customary for an older woman to be present during an examination.

MARTHA [*laughs*]: Tell that to Joe. Maybe he'll give you a job as duenna for his office.

MRS. MORTAR [*reminiscently*]: It was I who saved Delia Lampert's life the time she had that heart attack in Buffalo. We almost lost her that time. Poor Delia! We went over to London together. She married Robert Laffonne. Not seven months later he left her and ran away with Eve Cloun, who was playing the Infant Phenomenon in Birmingham—

MARTHA: Console yourself. If you've seen one heart attack, you've seen them all.

MRS. MORTAR: So you don't resent your aunt being snubbed and humiliated?

MARTHA: Oh, Aunt Lily!

MRS. MORTAR: Karen is consistently rude to me, and you know it.

MARTHA: I know that she is very polite to you, and—what's more important—very patient.

MRS. MORTAR: Patient with me? *I*, who have worked my fingers to the bone!

MARTHA: Don't tell yourself that too often, Aunt Lily; you'll come to believe it.

MRS. MORTAR: I *know* it's true. Where could you have gotten a woman of my reputation to give these children voice lessons, elocution lessons? Patient with me! Here I've donated my services—

MARTHA: I was under the impression you were being paid.

MRS. MORTAR: That small thing! I used to earn twice that for one performance.

MARTHA: The gilded days. It was very extravagant of them to pay you so much. [*Suddenly tired of the whole thing*] You're not very happy here, are you, Aunt Lily?

MRS. MORTAR: Satisfied enough, I guess, for a poor relation.

MARTHA [*makes a motion of distaste*]: But you don't like the school or the farm or—

MRS. MORTAR: I told you at the beginning you shouldn't have bought a place like this. Burying yourself on a farm! You'll regret it.

MARTHA: We like it here. [*After a moment*] Aunt Lily, you've talked about London for a long time. Would you like to go over?

MRS. MORTAR [*with a sigh*]: It's been twenty years, and I shall never live to see it again.

MARTHA: Well, you can go any time you like. We can spare the money now, and it will do you a lot of good. You pick out the boat you want and I'll get the passage. [*She has been talking rapidly, anxious to end the whole thing*] Now that's all fixed. You'll have a grand time seeing all your old friends, and if you live sensibly I ought to be able to let you have enough to get along on. [*She begins to gather books, notebooks, and pencils.*]

MRS. MORTAR [*slowly*]: So you want me to leave?

MARTHA: That's not the way to put it. You've wanted to go ever since I can remember.

MRS. MORTAR: You're trying to get rid of me.

MARTHA: That's it. We don't want you around when we dig up the buried treasure.

MRS. MORTAR: So? You're turning me out? At my age! Nice, grateful girl you are.

MARTHA: Oh, my God, how can anybody deal with you? You're going where you want to go, and we'll be better off alone. That suits everybody. You complain about the farm, you complain about the school, you complain about Karen, and now you have what you want and you're still looking for something to complain about.

MRS. MORTAR [*with dignity*]: Please do not raise your voice.

MARTHA: You ought to be glad I don't do worse.

MRS. MORTAR: I absolutely refuse to be shipped off three thousand miles away. I'm not going to England. I shall go back to the stage. I'll write to my agents tomorrow, and as soon as they have something good for me—

MARTHA: The truth is I'd like you to leave soon. The three of us can't live together, and it doesn't make any difference whose fault it is.

MRS. MORTAR: You wish me to go tonight?

MARTHA: Don't act, Aunt Lily. Go as soon as you've found a place you like. I'll put the money in the bank for you tomorrow.

MRS. MORTAR: You think I'd take your money? I'd rather scrub floors first.

MARTHA: I imagine you'll change your mind.

MRS. MORTAR: I should have known by this time that the wise thing is to stay out of your way when *he's* in the house.

MARTHA: What are you talking about now?

MRS. MORTAR: Never mind. I should have known better. You always take your spite out on me.

MARTHA: Spite? [*Impatiently*] Oh, don't let's have any more of this today. I'm tired. I've been working since six o'clock this morning.

MRS. MORTAR: Any day that he's in the house is a bad day.

MARTHA: When *who* is in the house?

MRS. MORTAR: Don't think you're fooling me, young lady. I wasn't born yesterday.

MARTHA: Aunt Lily, the amount of disconnected unpleasantness that goes on in your head could keep a psychologist busy for years. Now go take your nap.

MRS. MORTAR: I know what I know. Every time that man comes in this house, you have a fit. It seems like you just can't stand the idea of them being together. God knows what you'll do when they get married. You're jealous of him, that's what it is.

MARTHA [*her voice is tense and the previous attitude of good-natured irritation is gone*]: I'm very fond of Joe, and you know it.

MRS. MORTAR: You're fonder of Karen, and I know that. And it's unnatural, just as unnatural as it can be. You don't like their being together. You were always like that even as a child. If you had a little girl friend, you always got mad when she liked anybody else. Well, you'd better get a beau of your own now—a woman of your age.

MARTHA: The sooner you get out of here, the better. Your vulgarities are making me sick and I won't stand for them any longer. I want you to leave—

[*At this point there is a sound outside the large doors Center.* MARTHA *breaks off, angry and ashamed. After a moment she crosses to the door and opens it.* EVELYN *and* PEGGY *are to be seen on the staircase. For a second she stands still as they stop and look at her. Then, afraid that her anger with her aunt will color anything she might say to the children, she crosses the room again and stands with her back to them.*]

MARTHA: What were you doing outside the door?

EVELYN [*hurriedly*]: We were going upthtairth, Mith Dobie.

PEGGY: We came down to see how Mary was.

MARTHA: And you stopped long enough to see how we were. Did you deliberately listen?

PEGGY: We didn't mean to. We heard voices and we couldn't help—

MRS. MORTAR [*fake social tone*]: Eavesdropping is something nice young ladies just don't do.

MARTHA [*turning to face the children*]: Go upstairs now. We'll talk about this later. [*Slowly shuts door as they begin to climb the stairs.*]

MRS. MORTAR: You mean to say you're not going to do anything about that? [*No answer. She laughs nastily*] That's the trouble with these new-fangled notions of discipline and—

MARTHA [*thoughtfully*]: You know, it's really bad having you around children.

MRS. MORTAR: What exactly does that mean?

MARTHA: It means that I don't like them hearing the things you say. Oh, I'll "do something about it," but the truth is that this is their home, and things shouldn't be said in it that they can't hear. When you're at your best, you're not for tender ears.

MRS. MORTAR: So now it's my fault, is it? Just as I said, whenever he's in the house you think you can take it out on me. You've got to have some way to let out steam and—

[*Door opens Right and* CARDIN *comes in.*]

MARTHA: How is Mary?

[MRS. MORTAR, *head in air, gives* MARTHA *a malicious half-smile and makes what she thinks is majestic exit Center.*]

MRS. MORTAR: Good day, Joseph.

CARDIN: What's the matter with the Duchess? [*Nods at door Center.*]

MARTHA: Just keeping her hand in, in case Sir Henry's watching her from above. What about Mary?

CARDIN: Nothing. Absolutely nothing.

MARTHA [*sighs*]: I thought so.

CARDIN: I could have managed a better faint than that when I was six years old.

MARTHA: Nothing the matter with her at all, then?

CARDIN [*laughs*]: No, ma'am, not a thing. Just a little something she thought up.

MARTHA: But it's such a silly thing to do. She knew we'd have you in. [*Sighs*] Maybe she's not so bright. Any idiots in your family, Joe? Any inbreeding?

CARDIN: Don't blame her on me. It's another side of the family. [*Laughs*] You can look at Aunt Amelia and tell: old New England stock; never married out of Boston; still thinks honor is honor and dinner's at eight thirty. Yes, ma'am, we're a proud old breed.

MARTHA: The Jukes were an old family, too. Look, Joe, have you any idea what is the matter with Mary? I mean, has she always been like this?

CARDIN: She's always been a honey. Aunt Amelia's spoiling hasn't helped any, either.

MARTHA: We're reaching the end of our rope with her. This kind of thing—

CARDIN [*looking at her*]: Aren't you taking this too seriously?

MARTHA [*after a second*]: I guess I am. But you stay around kids long enough and you won't know what to take seriously, either. But I do think somebody ought to talk to Mrs. Tilford about her.

CARDIN: You wouldn't be meaning me now, would you, Miss Dobie?

MARTHA: Well, Karen and I were talking about it this afternoon and—

CARDIN: Listen, friend, I'm marrying Karen, but I'm not writing Mary Tilford in the contract. [MARTHA *moves slightly.* CARDIN *takes her by the shoulders and turns her around to face him again. His face is grave, his voice gentle*] Forget Mary for a minute. You and I have got something to fight about. Every time anything's said about marrying—about Karen marrying me—you— [*She winces*] There it is. I'm fond of you. I always thought you liked me. What is it? I know how fond you are of Karen, but our marriage oughtn't to make a great deal of difference—

MARTHA [*pushing his hands from her shoulders*]: God damn you. I wish— [*She puts her face in her hands.* CARDIN *watches her in silence, mechanically lighting a cigarette. When she takes her hands from her face, she holds them out to him. Contritely*] Joe, please, I'm sorry. I'm a fool, a nasty, bitter—

CARDIN [*takes her hands in one of his, patting them with his other hand*]: Aw, shut up. [*He puts an arm around her, and she leans her head against his lapel. They are standing like that when* KAREN *comes in Right.*]

MARTHA [*to* KAREN, *as she wipes her eyes*]: Your friend's got a nice shoulder to weep on.

KAREN: He's an admirable man in every way. Well, the angel child is now putting her clothes back on.

MARTHA: The angel child's influence is abroad even while she's unconscious. Her room-mates were busy listening at the door while Aunt Lily and I were yelling at each other.

KAREN: We'll have to move those girls away from one another.

[*A bell rings from the rear of the house.*]

MARTHA: That's my class. I'll send Peggy and Evelyn down. You talk to them.

KAREN: All right. [*As* MARTHA *exits Center,* KAREN *goes toward door Right. As she passes* CARDIN *she kisses him*] Mary!

[MARY *opens door, comes in, stands buttoning the neck of her dress.*]

CARDIN [*to* MARY]: How's it feel to be back from the grave?
MARY: My heart hurts.
CARDIN [*laughing. To* KAREN]: Science has failed. Try a hairbrush.
MARY: It's *my* heart, and it hurts.
KAREN: Sit down.
MARY: I want to see my grandmother. I want to—

[EVELYN *and* PEGGY *timidly enter Center.*]

KAREN: Sit down, girls, I want to talk to you.
PEGGY: We're awfully sorry, really. We just didn't think and—
KAREN: I'm sorry too, Peggy. [*Thoughtfully*] You and Evelyn never used to do things like this. We'll have to separate you three.
EVELYN: Ah, Mith Wright, we've been together almotht a year.
KAREN: It was evidently too long. Now, don't let's talk about it. Peggy, you will move into Lois's room, and Lois will move in with Evelyn. Mary will go in with Rosalie.
MARY: Rosalie hates me.
KAREN: That's a very stupid thing to say. I can't imagine Rosalie hating anyone.
MARY [*starting to cry*]: And it's all because I had a pain. If anybody else was sick they'd be put to bed and petted. You're always mean to me. I get blamed and punished for everything. [*To* CARDIN] I do, Cousin Joe. All the time for everything.

[MARY *by now is crying violently and as* KAREN *half moves toward her,* CARDIN, *who has been frowning, picks* MARY *up and puts her down on the couch.*]

CARDIN: You've been unpleasant enough to Miss Wright. Lie here until you've stopped working yourself into a fit. [*Picks up his hat and bag, smiles at* KAREN] I've got to go now. She's not going to hurt herself crying. The next time she faints, I'd wait until she got tired lying on the floor. [*Passing* MARY, *he pats her head. She jerks away from him.*]
KAREN: Wait a minute. I'll walk to the car with you. [*To girls*] Go up now and move your things. Tell Lois to get her stuff ready.

[*She and* CARDIN *exit Center. A second after the door is closed,* MARY *springs up and throws a cushion at the door.*]

EVELYN: Don't do that. She'll hear you.
MARY: Who cares if she does? [*Kicks table*] And she can hear that, too.

[*Small ornament falls off table and breaks on floor.* EVELYN *and* PEGGY *gasp, and* MARY'*s bravado disappears for a moment.*]

EVELYN [*frightened*]: Now what are you going to do?
PEGGY [*stooping down in a vain effort to pick up the pieces*]: You'll get the devil now. Dr. Cardin gave it to Miss Wright. I guess it was kind of a lover's gift. People get awfully angry about a lover's gift.
MARY: Oh, leave it alone. She'll never know we did it.
PEGGY: *We* didn't do it. You did it yourself.
MARY: And what will you do if I say *we* did do it? [*Laughs*] Never mind, I'll think of something else. The wind could've knocked it over.
EVELYN: Yeh. She'th going to believe that one.
MARY: Oh, stop worrying about it. I'll get out of it.
EVELYN: Did you really have a pain?
MARY: I fainted, didn't I?
PEGGY: I wish I could faint sometimes. I've never even worn glasses, like Rosalie.
MARY: A lot it'll get you to faint.
EVELYN: What did Mith Wright do to you when the clath left?
MARY: Told me I couldn't go to the boat-races.
EVELYN: Whew!
PEGGY: But we'll remember everything that happens and we'll give you all the souvenirs and things.
MARY: I won't let you go if I can't go. But I'll find some way to go. What were *you* doing?
PEGGY: I guess we shouldn't have done it, really. We came down to see what was happening to you, but the doors were closed and we could hear Miss Dobie and Mortar having an awful row. Then Miss Dobie opens the door and there we were.
MARY: And a lot of crawling and crying you both did too, I bet.
EVELYN: We were thort of thorry about lithening. I gueth it wathn't—
MARY: Ah, you're always sorry about everything. What were they saying?
PEGGY: What was who saying?
MARY: Dobie and Mortar, silly.
PEGGY [*evasively*]: Just talking, I guess.
EVELYN: Fighting, you mean.
MARY: About what?
EVELYN: Well, they were talking about Mortar going away to England and—
PEGGY: You know, it really wasn't very nice to've listened, and I think it's worse to tell.
MARY: You do, do you? You just don't tell me and see what happens.

[PEGGY *sighs.*]

EVELYN: Mortar got awful thore at that and thaid they juth wanted to get rid of her, and then they thtarted talking about Dr. Cardin.
MARY: What about him?
PEGGY: We'd better get started moving; Miss Wright will be back first thing we know.
MARY [*fiercely*]: Shut up! Go on, Evelyn.
EVELYN: They're going to be married.
MARY: Everybody knows that.
PEGGY: But everybody doesn't know that Miss Dobie doesn't want them to get married. How do you like that?

[*The door opens and* ROSALIE WELLS *sticks her head in.*]

ROSALIE: I have a class soon. If you're going to move your things—
MARY: Close that door, you idiot. [ROSALIE *closes door, stands near it*] What do you want?
ROSALIE: I'm trying to tell you. If you're going to move your things—not that I want you in with me—you'd better start right now. Miss Wright's coming in a minute.
MARY: Who cares if she is?
ROSALIE [*starts for door*]: I'm just telling you for your own good.
PEGGY [*getting up*]: We're coming.
MARY: No. Let Rosalie move our things.
ROSALIE: You crazy?
PEGGY [*nervously*]: It's all right. Evelyn and I'll get your things. Come on, Evelyn.
MARY: Trying to get out of telling me, huh? Well, you won't get out of it that way. Sit down and stop being such a sissy. Rosalie, you go on up and move my things and don't say a word about our being down here.
ROSALIE: And who was your French maid yesterday, Mary Tilford?
MARY [*laughing*]: You'll do for today. Now go on, Rosalie, and fix our things.
ROSALIE: You crazy?
MARY: And the next time we go into town, I'll let you wear my gold locket and buckle. You'll like that, won't you, Rosalie?
ROSALIE [*draws back, moves her hands nervously*]: I don't know what you're talking about.
MARY: Oh, I'm not talking about anything in particular. You just run along now and remind me the next time to get my buckle and locket for you.
ROSALIE [*stares at her a moment*]: All right, I'll do it this time, but just 'cause I got a good disposition. But don't think you're going to boss me around, Mary Tilford.
MARY [*smiling*]: No, indeed. [ROSALIE *starts for door*] And get the things done neatly, Rosalie. Don't muss my white linen bloomers—

[*The door slams as* MARY *laughs.*]

EVELYN: Now what do you think of that? What made her tho agreeable?
MARY: Oh, a little secret we got. Go on, now, what else did they say?
PEGGY: Well, Mortar said that Dobie was jealous of them, and that she was like that when she was a little girl, and that she'd better get herself a beau of her own because it was unnatural, and that she never wanted anybody to like Miss Wright, and that was unnatural. Boy! Did Miss Dobie get sore at that!
EVELYN: Then we didn't hear any more. Peggy dropped a book.
MARY: What'd she mean Dobie was jealous?
PEGGY: What's unnatural?
EVELYN: Un for not. Not natural.
PEGGY: It's funny, because everybody gets married.
MARY: A lot of people don't—they're too ugly.
PEGGY [*jumps up, claps her hand to her mouth*]: Oh, my God! Rosalie'll find that copy of *Mademoiselle de Maupin*. She'll blab like the dickens.
MARY: Ah, she won't say a word.
EVELYN: Who getth the book when we move?
MARY: You can have it. That's what I was doing this morning—finishing it. There's one part in it—
PEGGY: What part?

[MARY *laughs.*]

EVELYN: Well, what wath it?
MARY: Wait until you read it.
EVELYN: Don't forget to give it to me.
PEGGY: It's a shame about being moved. I've got to go in with Helen, and she blows her nose all night. Lois told me.
MARY: It was a dirty trick making us move. She just wants to see how much fun she can take away from me. She hates me.
PEGGY: No, she doesn't, Mary. She treats you just like the rest of us—almost better.
MARY: That's right, stick up for your crush. Take her side against mine.
PEGGY: I didn't mean it that way.
EVELYN [*looks at her watch*]: We'd better get upthtairth.
MARY: I'm not going.
PEGGY: Rosalie isn't so bad.
EVELYN: What you going to do about the vathe?
MARY: I don't care about Rosalie and I don't care about the vase. I'm not going to be here.

EVELYN and PEGGY [*together*]: Not going to be here! What do you mean?

MARY [*calmly*]: I'm going home.

PEGGY: Oh, Mary—

EVELYN: You can't do that.

MARY: Can't I? You just watch. [*Begins to walk around the room*] I'm not staying here. I'm going home and tell Grandma I'm not staying any more. [*Smiles to herself*] I'll tell her I'm not happy. They're scared of Grandma—She helped 'em when they first started, you know—and when she tells 'em something, believe me, they'll sit up and listen. They can't get away with treating me like this, and they don't have to think they can.

PEGGY [*appalled*]: You just going to walk out like that?

EVELYN: What you going to tell your grandmother?

MARY: Oh, who cares? I'll think of something to tell her. I can always do it better on the spur of the moment.

PEGGY: She'll send you right back.

MARY: You let me worry about that. Grandma's very fond of me, on account my father was her favorite son. I can manage *her* all right.

PEGGY: I don't think you ought to go, really, Mary. It's just going to make an awful lot of trouble.

EVELYN: What'th going to happen about the vathe?

MARY: Say I did it—it doesn't make a bit of difference any more to me. Now listen, you two got to help. They won't miss me before dinner if you make Rosalie shut the door and keep it shut. Now, I'll go through the field to French's, and then I can get the bus to Homestead.

EVELYN: How you going to get to the thtreet-car?

MARY: Taxi, idiot.

PEGGY: How are you going to get out of here in the first place?

MARY: I'm going to walk out. You know where the front door is, or are you too dumb even for that? Well, I'm going right out that front door.

EVELYN: Gee, I wouldn't have the nerve.

MARY: Of course you wouldn't. You'd let 'em do anything to you they want. Well, they can't do it to me. Who's got any money?

EVELYN: Not me. Not a thent.

MARY: I've got to have at least a dollar for the taxi and a dime for the bus.

EVELYN: And where you going to find it?

PEGGY: See? Why don't you just wait until your allowance comes Monday, and then you can go any place you want. Maybe by that time—

MARY: I'm going today. *Now.*

EVELYN: You can't *walk* to Lanthet.

MARY [*goes to* PEGGY]: You've got money. You've got two dollars and twenty-five cents.

PEGGY: I—I—

MARY: Go get it for me.

PEGGY: No! No! I won't get it for you.

EVELYN: You can't have *that* money, Mary—

MARY: Get it for me.

PEGGY [*cringes, her voice is scared*]: I won't. I won't. Mamma doesn't send me much allowance—not half as much as the rest of you get—I saved this so long—you took it from me last time—

EVELYN: Ah, she wantth that bithycle tho bad.

PEGGY: I haven't gone to the movies, I haven't had any candy, I haven't had anything the rest of you get all the time. It took me so long to save that and I—

MARY: Go upstairs and get me the money.

PEGGY [*hysterically, backing away from her*]: I won't. I won't. I won't.

[MARY *makes a sudden move for her, grabs her left arm, and jerks it back, hard and expertly.* PEGGY *screams softly.* EVELYN *tries to take* MARY'*s arm away. Without releasing her hold on* PEGGY, MARY *slaps* EVELYN'*s face.* EVELYN *begins to cry.*]

MARY: Just say when you've had enough.

PEGGY [*softly, stifling*]: All—all right—I'll get it.

[MARY *smiles, nods her head as the Curtain falls.*]

ACT II

Scene 1

SCENE. *Living room at* MRS. TILFORD'*s. It is a formal room, without being cold or elegant. The furniture is old, but excellent. The exit to the hall is Left; glass doors Right lead to a dining room that cannot be seen.*

AT RISE: *Stage is empty. Voices are heard in the hall.*

AGATHA [*off-stage*]: What are you doing here? Well, come on in—don't stand there gaping at me. Have they given you a holiday or did you just decide you'd get a better dinner here? [AGATHA *enters Left, followed by* MARY. AGATHA *is a sharp-faced maid, not young, with a querulous voice*] Can't you even say hello?

MARY: Hello, Agatha. You didn't give me a chance. Where's Grandma?

AGATHA: Why aren't you in school? Look at your face and clothes. Where have you been?

MARY: I got a little dirty coming home. I walked part of the way through the woods.

AGATHA: Why didn't you put on your middy blouse and your old brown coat?

MARY: Oh, stop asking me questions. Where's Grandma?

AGATHA: Where ought any clean person be at this time of day? She's taking a bath.

MARY: Is anybody coming for dinner?

AGATHA: She didn't say anything about you coming.

MARY: How could she, stupid? She didn't know.

AGATHA: Then what are you doing here?

MARY: Leave me alone. I don't feel well.

AGATHA: Why don't you feel well? Who ever heard of a person going for a walk in the woods when they didn't feel well?

MARY: Oh, leave me alone. I came home because I was sick.

AGATHA: You look all right.

MARY: But I don't feel all right. [*Whining*] I can't even come home without everybody nagging at me.

AGATHA: Don't think you're fooling me, young lady. You might pull the wool over some people's eyes, but—I bet you've been up to something again. [*Stares suspiciously at* MARY, *who says nothing*] Well, you wait right here till I tell your grandmother. And if you feel so sick, you certainly won't want any dinner. A good dose of rhubarb and soda will fix you up. [*Exits Left.*]

[MARY *makes a face in the direction* AGATHA *has gone and stops sniffling. She looks nervously around the room, then goes to a low mirror and tries several experiments with her face in an attempt to make it look sick and haggard.*]

[MRS. TILFORD, *followed by* AGATHA, *enters Left.* MRS. TILFORD *is a large, dignified woman in her sixties, with a pleasant, strong face.*]

AGATHA [*to* MRS. TILFORD, *as she follows her into the room*]: Why didn't you put some cold water on your chest? Do you want to catch your death of cold at your age? Did you have to hurry so?

MRS. TILFORD: Mary, what are you doing home?

[MARY *rushes to her and buries her head in* MRS. TILFORD*'s dress, crying.* MRS. TILFORD *lets her cry for a moment while she pats her head, then puts an arm around the child and leads her to a sofa.*]

MRS. TILFORD: Never mind, dear; now stop crying and tell me what is the matter.

MARY [*gradually stops crying, fondling* MRS. TILFORD*'s hand*]: It's so good to see you, Grandma. You didn't come to visit me all last week.

MRS. TILFORD: I couldn't, dear. But I was coming tomorrow.

MARY: I missed you so. [*Smiling up at* MRS. TILFORD] I was awful homesick.

MRS. TILFORD: I'm glad that's all it was. I was frightened when Agatha said you were not well.

AGATHA: Did I say that? I said she needed a good dose of rhubarb and soda. Most likely she only came home for Wednesday night fudge cake.

MRS. TILFORD: We all get homesick. But how did you get here? Did Miss Karen drive you over?

MARY: I—I walked most of the way, and then a lady gave me a ride and— [*Looks timidly at* MRS. TILFORD.]

AGATHA: Did she have to walk through the woods in her very best coat?

MRS. TILFORD: Mary! Do you mean you left without permission?

MARY [*nervously*]: I ran away, Grandma. They didn't know—

MRS. TILFORD: That was a very bad thing to do, and they'll be worried. Agatha, phone Miss Wright and tell her Mary is here. John will drive her back before dinner.

MARY [*as* AGATHA *starts toward telephone*]: No, Grandma, don't do that. Please don't do that. Please let me stay.

MRS. TILFORD: But, darling, you can't leave school any time you please.

MARY: Oh, please, Grandma, don't send me back right away. You don't know how they'll punish me.

MRS. TILFORD: I don't think they'll be that angry. Come, you're acting like a foolish little girl.

MARY [*hysterically, as she sees* AGATHA *about to pick up the telephone*]: Grandma! Please! I can't go back! I can't. They'll kill me! They will, Grandma! They'll kill me!

[MRS. TILFORD *and* AGATHA *stare at* MARY *in amazement. She puts her head in* MRS. TILFORD*'s lap and sobs.*]

MRS. TILFORD [*motioning with a hand for* AGATHA *to leave the room*]: Never mind phoning now, Agatha.

AGATHA: If you're going to let her—

[MRS. TILFORD *repeats the gesture.* AGATHA *exits Right, with offended dignity.*]

MRS. TILFORD: Stop crying, Mary.

MARY [*raising her head from* MRS. TILFORD*'s lap*]: It's so nice here, Grandma.

MRS. TILFORD: I'm glad you like being home with me, but at your age you can hardly— [*More seriously*] What made you say such a terrible thing about Miss Wright and Miss Dobie? You know they wouldn't hurt you.

MARY: Oh, but they would. They—I— [*Breaks off, looks around as if hunting for a clue to her next word; then dramatically*] I fainted today!

MRS. TILFORD [*alarmed*]: Fainted?

MARY: Yes, I did. My heart—I had a pain in my heart. I couldn't help having a pain in my heart, and when I fainted right in class, they called Cousin

Joe and he said I didn't. He said it was maybe only that I ate my breakfast too fast and Miss Wright blamed me for it.

MRS. TILFORD [*relieved*]: I'm sure if Joseph said it wasn't serious, it wasn't.

MARY: But I did have a pain in my heart—honest.

MRS. TILFORD: Have you still got it?

MARY: I guess I haven't got it much any more, but I feel a little weak, and I was so scared of Miss Wright being so mean to me just because I was sick.

MRS. TILFORD: Scared of Karen? Nonsense. It's perfectly possible that you had a pain, but if you had really been sick your Cousin Joseph would certainly have known it. It's not nice to frighten people by pretending to be sick when you aren't.

MARY: I didn't *want* to be sick, but I'm always getting punished for everything.

MRS. TILFORD [*gently*]: You mustn't imagine things like that, child, or you'll grow up to be a very unhappy woman. I'm not going to scold you any more for coming home this time, though I suppose I should. Run along upstairs and wash your face and change your dress, and after dinner John will drive you back. Run along.

MARY [*happily*]: I can stay for dinner?

MRS. TILFORD: Yes.

MARY: Maybe I could stay till the first of the week. Saturday's your birthday and I could be here with you.

MRS. TILFORD: We don't celebrate my birthday, dear. You'll have to go back to school after dinner.

MARY: But— [*She hesitates, then goes up to* MRS. TILFORD *and puts her arms around the older woman's neck. Softly*] How much do you love me?

MRS. TILFORD [*smiling*]: As much as all the words in all the books in all the world.

MARY: Remember when I was little and you used to tell me that right before I went to sleep? And it was a rule nobody could say another single word after you finished? You used to say: "Wor-rr-ld," and then I had to shut my eyes tight.

MRS. TILFORD: And sometimes you were naughty and didn't shut them.

MARY: I miss you an awful lot, Grandma.

MRS. TILFORD: And I miss you, but I'm afraid my Latin is too rusty—you'll learn it better in school.

MARY: But couldn't I stay out the rest of this term? After the summer maybe I won't mind it so much. I'll study hard, honest, and—

MRS. TILFORD: You're an earnest little coaxer, but it's out of the question. Back you go tonight. [*Gives* MARY *a playful slap*] Let's not have any more talk about it now, and let's have no more running away from school ever.

MARY [*slowly*]: Then I really have to go back there tonight?

MRS. TILFORD: Of course.

MARY: You don't love me. You don't care whether they kill me or not.

MRS. TILFORD: Mary.

MARY: You don't! You don't! You don't care what happens to me.

MRS. TILFORD [*sternly*]: But I *do* care that you're talking this way.

MARY [*meekly*]: I'm sorry I said that, Grandma. I didn't mean to hurt your feelings. [*Puts her arms around* MRS. TILFORD*'s neck*] Forgive me?

MRS. TILFORD: What made you talk like that?

MARY [*in a whisper*]: I'm scared, Grandma, I'm scared. They'll do dreadful things to me.

MRS. TILFORD: Dreadful? Nonsense. They'll punish you for running away. You deserve to be punished.

MARY: It's not that. It's not anything I do. It never is. They—they just punish me anyhow, just like they got something against me. I'm afraid of them, Grandma.

MRS. TILFORD: That's ridiculous. What have they ever done to you that is so terrible?

MARY: A lot of things—all the time. Miss Wright says I can't go to the boat-races and— [*Realizing the inadequacy of this reply, she breaks off, hesitates, hunting for a more telling reply, and finally stammers*] It's—it's after what happened today.

MRS. TILFORD: You mean something else besides your naughtiness in pretending to faint and then running away?

MARY: I *did* faint. I didn't pretend. They just said that to make me feel bad. Anyway, it wasn't anything that I did.

MRS. TILFORD: What was it, then?

MARY: I can't tell you.

MRS. TILFORD: Why?

MARY [*sulkily*]: Because you're just going to take their part.

MRS. TILFORD [*a little annoyed*]: Very well. Now run upstairs and get ready for dinner.

MARY: It was—it was all about Miss Dobie and Mrs. Mortar. They were talking awful things and Peggy and Evelyn heard them and Miss Dobie found out, and then they made us move our rooms.

MRS. TILFORD: What has that to do with you? I don't understand a word you're saying.

MARY: They made us move our rooms. They said we couldn't be together any more. They're afraid to have us near them, that's what it is, and they're taking it out on me. They're scared of you.

MRS. TILFORD: For a little girl you're imagining a lot of big things. Why should they be scared of me? Am I such an unpleasant old lady?

MARY: They're afraid you'll find out.
MRS. TILFORD: Find out what?
MARY [*vaguely*]: Things.
MRS. TILFORD: Run along, Mary. I hope you'll get more coherent as you get older.
MARY [*slowly starting for door*]: All right. But there're a lot of things. They have secrets or something, and they're afraid I'll find out and tell you.
MRS. TILFORD: There's not necessarily anything wrong with people having secrets.
MARY [*coming back in the room again*]: But they've got funny ones. Peggy and Evelyn heard Mrs. Mortar telling Miss Dobie that she was jealous of Miss Wright marrying Cousin Joe.
MRS. TILFORD: You shouldn't repeat things like that.
MARY: But that's what she said, Grandma. She said it was unnatural for a girl to feel that way.
MRS. TILFORD: What?
MARY: I'm just telling you what she said. She said there was something funny about it, and that Miss Dobie had always been like that, even when she was a little girl, and that it was unnatural—
MRS. TILFORD: Stop using that silly word, Mary.
MARY [*vaguely realizing that she is on the right track, hurries on*]: But that was the word *she* kept using, Grandma, and then they got mad and told Mrs. Mortar she'd have to get out.
MRS. TILFORD: That was probably not the reason at all.
MARY [*nodding vigorously*]: I bet it was, because honestly, Miss Dobie does get cranky and mean every time Cousin Joe comes, and today I heard her say to him: "God damn you," and then she said she was just a jealous fool and—
MRS. TILFORD: You have picked up some very fine words, haven't you, Mary?
MARY: That's just what she said, Grandma, and one time Miss Dobie was crying in Miss Wright's room, and Miss Wright was trying to stop her, and she said that all right, maybe she wouldn't get married right away if—
MRS. TILFORD: How do you know all this?
MARY: We couldn't help hearing because they—I mean Miss Dobie—was talking awful loud, and their room is right next to ours.
MRS. TILFORD: Whose room?
MARY: Miss Wright's room, I mean, and you can just ask Peggy and Evelyn whether we didn't hear. Almost always Miss Dobie comes in after we go to bed and stays a long time. I guess that's why they want to get rid of us—of me—because we hear things. That's why they're making us move our room, and they punish me all the time for—
MRS. TILFORD: For eavesdropping, I should think. [*She has said this mechanically. With nothing definite in her mind, she is making an effort to conceal the fact that* MARY'*s description of the life at school has shocked her*] Well, now I think we've had enough gossip, don't you? Dinner's almost ready, and I can't eat with a girl who has such a dirty face.
MARY [*softly*]: I've heard other things, too.
MRS. TILFORD [*abstractedly*]: What? What did you say?
MARY: I've heard other things. Plenty of other things, Grandma.
MRS. TILFORD: What things?
MARY: Bad things.
MRS. TILFORD: Well, what were they?
MARY: I can't tell you.
MRS. TILFORD: Mary, you're annoying me very much. If you have anything to say, then say it and stop acting silly.
MARY: I mean I can't say it out loud.
MRS. TILFORD: There couldn't possibly be anything so terrible that you couldn't say it out loud. Now either tell the truth or be still.
MARY: Well, a lot of things I don't understand. But it's awful, and sometimes they fight and then they make up, and Miss Dobie cries and Miss Wright gets mad, and then they make up again, and there are funny noises and we get scared.
MRS. TILFORD: Noises? I suppose you girls have a happy time imagining a murder.
MARY: And we've seen things, too. Funny things. [*Sees the impatience of her grandmother*] I'd tell you, but I got to whisper it.
MRS. TILFORD: Why must you whisper it?
MARY: I don't know. I just got to. [*Climbs on the sofa next to* MRS. TILFORD *and begins whispering. At first the whisper is slow and hesitant, but it gradually works itself up to fast, excited talking. In the middle of it* MRS. TILFORD *stops her.*]
MRS. TILFORD [*trembling*]: Do you know what you're saying? [*Without answering,* MARY *goes back to the whispering until the older woman takes her by the shoulders and turns her around to stare in her face*] Mary? *Are you telling me the truth?*
MARY: Honest, honest. You just ask Peggy and Evelyn and— [*After a moment* MRS. TILFORD *gets up and begins to pace about the room. She is no longer listening to* MARY, *who keeps up a running fire of conversation*] They know too. And maybe there're other kids who know, but we've always been frightened and so we didn't ask, and one night I was going to go and find out, but I got scared and we went to bed early so we wouldn't hear, but sometimes I couldn't help it, but we never talked about it much, because we thought they'd find out and—Oh, Grandma, don't make me go back to that awful place.
MRS. TILFORD [*abstractedly*]: What? [*Starts to move about again.*]

MARY: Don't make me go back to that place. I just couldn't stand it any more. Really, Grandma, I'm so unhappy there, and if only I could stay out the rest of the term, why, then—

MRS. TILFORD [*makes irritated gesture*]: Be still a minute. [*After a moment*] No, you won't have to go back.

MARY [*surprised*]: Honest?

MRS. TILFORD: Honest.

MARY [*hugging* MRS. TILFORD]: You're the nicest, loveliest grandma in all the world. You—you're not mad a me?

MRS. TILFORD: I'm not mad at you. Now go upstairs and get ready for dinner. [MARY *kisses her and runs happily out Left.* MRS. TILFORD *stands staring after her for a long moment; then, very slowly, she puts on her eyeglasses and crosses to the phone. She dials a number*] Is Miss Wright—is Miss Wright in? [*Waits a second, hurriedly puts down the receiver*] Never mind, never mind. [*Dials another number*] Dr. Cardin, please. Mrs. Tilford. [*She remains absolutely motionless while she waits. When she does speak, her voice is low and tense*] Joseph? Joseph? Can you come to see me right away? Yes, I'm perfectly well. No, but it's important, Joseph, very important. I must see you right away. I—I can't tell you over the phone. Can't you come sooner? It's not about Mary's fainting—I said it's not about Mary, Joseph; in one way it's about Mary— [*Suddenly quiet*] But will the hospital take so long? Very well, Joseph, make it as soon as you can. [*Hangs up the receiver, sits for a moment undecided. Then, taking a breath, she dials another number*] Mrs. Munn, please. This is Mrs. Tilford. Miriam? This is Amelia Tilford. I have something to tell you—something very shocking, I'm afraid—something about the school and Evelyn and Mary—

CURTAIN

Scene 2

SCENE. *The same as Scene 1. The curtain has been lowered to mark the passing of a few hours.*

AT RISE: MARY *is lying on the floor playing with a puzzle.* AGATHA *appears lugging blankets and pillows across the room. Almost at the door, she stops and gives* MARY *an annoyed look.*

AGATHA: And see to it that she doesn't get my good quilt all dirty, and let her wear your green pajamas.

MARY: Who?

AGATHA: Who? Don't you ever keep your ears open? Rosalie Wells is coming over to spend the night with you.

MARY: You mean she's going to sleep *here?*

AGATHA: You heard me.

MARY: What for?

AGATHA: Do I know all the crazy things that are happening around here? Your grandmother phones Mrs. Wells all the way to New York, three dollars and eighty-five cents and families starving, and Mrs. Wells wanted to know if Rosalie could stay here until tomorrow.

MARY [*relieved*]: Oh. Couldn't Evelyn Munn come instead?

AGATHA: Sure. We'll have the whole town over to entertain you.

MARY: I won't let Rosalie Wells wear my new pajamas.

AGATHA [*exits as the front door-bell rings*]: Don't tell me what you won't do. You'll act like a lady for once in your life. [*Off-stage*] Come on in, Rosalie. Just go on in there and make yourself at home. Have you had your dinner?

ROSALIE [*off-stage*]: Good evening. Yes'm.

AGATHA [*off-stage*]: Hang up your pretty coat. Have you had your bath?

ROSALIE [*off-stage*]: Yes, ma'am. This morning.

AGATHA [*off-stage*]: Well, you better have another one.

[*She is climbing the stairs as* ROSALIE *comes into the room.* MARY, *lying in front of the couch, is hidden from her. Gingerly* ROSALIE *sits down on a chair.*]

MARY [*softly*]: Whoooooo. [ROSALIE *jumps*] Whoooooo. [ROSALIE, *frightened, starts hurriedly for the door.* MARY *sit up, laughs*] You're a goose.

ROSALIE [*belligerently*]: Oh, so it's you. Well, who likes to hear funny noises at night? You could have been a werewolf.

MARY: A werewolf wouldn't want you.

ROSALIE: You know everything, don't you? [MARY *laughs.* ROSALIE *comes over, stands staring at puzzle*] Isn't it funny about school?

MARY: What's funny about it?

ROSALIE: Don't act like you can come home every night.

MARY: Maybe I can from now on. [*Rolls over on her back luxuriously*] Maybe I'm never going back.

ROSALIE: Am I going back? I don't want to stay home.

MARY: What'll you give to know?

ROSALIE: Nothing. I'll ask Mamma.

MARY: Will you give me a free T. L. if I tell you?

ROSALIE [*thinks for a moment*]: All right. Lois Fisher told Helen that you were very smart.

MARY: That's an old one. I won't take it.

ROSALIE: You got to take it.

MARY: Nope.

ROSALIE [*laughs*]: You don't know, anyway.

MARY: I know what I heard, and I know Grandma phoned your mother in New York to come and get you right away. You're just going to spend the night here. I wish Evelyn could come instead of you.

ROSALIE: But what's happened? Peggy and Helen and Evelyn and Lois went home tonight, too. Do you think somebody's got scarlet fever or something?

MARY: No.

ROSALIE: Do *you* know what it is? How'd you find out? [*No answer*] You're always pretending you know everything. You're just faking. [*Flounces away*] Never mind, don't bother telling me. I think curiosity is very unladylike, anyhow. I have no concern with your silly secrets.

MARY: Suppose I told you that I just may have said that you were in on it?

ROSALIE: In on what?

MARY: The secret. Suppose I told you that I *may have* said that you told me about it?

ROSALIE: Why, Mary Tilford! You can't do a thing like that. I didn't tell you about anything. [MARY *laughs*] Did you tell your grandmother such a thing?

MARY: Maybe.

ROSALIE: Did you?

MARY: Maybe.

ROSALIE: Well, I'm going right up to your grandmother and tell her I didn't tell you anything—whatever it is. You're just trying to get me into trouble and I'm not going to let you. [*Starts for door.*]

MARY: Wait a minute, I'll come with you.

ROSALIE: What for?

MARY: I want to tell her about Helen Burton's bracelet.

ROSALIE [*sits down suddenly*]: What about it?

MARY: Just that you stole it.

ROSALIE: Shut up. I didn't do any such thing.

MARY: Yes, you did.

ROSALIE [*tearfully*]: You made it up. You're always making things up.

MARY: You can't call me a fibber, Rosalie Wells. That's a kind of a dare and I won't take a dare. I guess I'll go tell Grandma, anyway. Then she can call the police and they'll come for you and you'll spend the rest of your life in one of those solitary prisons and you'll get older and older, and when you're very old and can't see anymore, they'll let you out maybe with a big sign on your back saying you're a thief, and your mother and father will be dead and you won't have any place to go and you'll beg on the streets—

ROSALIE: I didn't steal anything. I borrowed the bracelet and I was going to put it back as soon as I'd worn it to the movies. I never meant to keep it.

MARY: Nobody'll believe that, least of all the police. You're just a common, ordinary thief. Stop that bawling. You'll have the whole house down here in a minute.

ROSALIE: You won't tell? Say you won't tell.

MARY: Am I a fibber?

ROSALIE: No.

MARY: Then say: "I apologize on my hands and knees."

ROSALIE: I apologize on my hands and knees. Let's play with the puzzle.

MARY: Wait a minute. Say: "From now on, I, Rosalie Wells, am the vassal of Mary Tilford and will do and say whatever she tells me under the solemn oath of a knight."

ROSALIE: I won't say that. That's the worse oath there is. [MARY *starts for the door*] Mary! Please don't—

MARY: Will you swear it?

ROSALIE [*sniffling*]: But then you could tell me to do anything.

MARY: And you'd have to do it. Say it quick or I'll—

ROSALIE [*hurriedly*]: From now on, I, Rosalie Wells, am the vassal of Mary Tilford and will do and say whatever she tells me under the solemn oath of a knight. [*She gasps, and sits up straight as* MRS. TILFORD *enters.*]

MARY: Don't forget that.

MRS. TILFORD: Good evening, Rosalie, you're looking very well.

ROSALIE: Good evening, Mrs. Tilford.

MARY: She's getting fatter every day.

MRS. TILFORD [*abstractedly*]: Then it's very becoming. [*Door-bell rings*] That must be Joseph. Mary, take Rosalie into the library. There's some fruit and milk on the table. Be sure you're both fast asleep by half past ten. [*Leans down, kisses them both.* ROSALIE *starts to exit Right, sees* MARY, *stops and hesitates.*]

MARY: Go on, Rosalie. [*Waits until* ROSALIE *reluctantly exits*] Grandma.

MRS. TILFORD: Yes?

MARY: Grandma, Cousin Joe'll say I've got to go back. He'll say I really wasn't—

[CARDIN *enters and she runs from the room.*]

CARDIN: Hello, Amelia. [*Looks curiously at the fleeing* MARY] Mary home, eh?

MRS. TILFORD [*watching* MARY *as she leaves*]: Hello, Joseph. Sit down. [*He sits down, looks at her curiously, waits for her to speak*] Whisky?

CARDIN: Please. How are you feeling? Headaches again?

MRS. TILFORD [*puts drink on table*]: No.

CARDIN: Those are good powders. Bicarbonate of soda and water. Never hurt anybody yet.

MRS. TILFORD: Yes. How have you been, Joseph?

CARDIN: My good health is monotonous.

MRS. TILFORD [*vaguely, sparring for time*]: I haven't seen you the last few weeks. Agatha misses you for Sunday dinners.

CARDIN: I've been busy. We're getting the results from the mating-season right about now.

MRS. TILFORD: Did I take you away from a patient?

CARDIN: No. I was at the hospital.

MRS. TILFORD: How's it getting on?

CARDIN: Just the same. No money, badly equipped, a lousy laboratory, everybody growling at everybody else—Amelia, you didn't bring me here to talk about the hospital. We're talking like people waiting for the muffins to be passed around. What's the matter with you?

MRS. TILFORD: I—I have something to tell you.

CARDIN: Well, out with it.

MRS. TILFORD: It's a very hard thing to say, Joseph.

CARDIN: Hard for you to say to *me*? [*No answer*] Don't be worried about Mary. I guessed that she ran home to tell you about her faint. It was caused by nothing but bad temper and was very clumsily managed, at that. Amelia, she's terribly spoilt—

MRS. TILFORD: I heard about the faint. That's not what is worrying me.

CARDIN [*gently*]: Are you in some trouble?

MRS. TILFORD: We all are in trouble. Bad trouble.

CARDIN: We? Me, you mean? Nothing's the matter with me.

MRS. TILFORD: When did you last see Karen?

CARDIN: Today. This afternoon.

MRS. TILFORD: Oh. Not since seven o'clock?

CARDIN: What's happened since seven o'clock?

MRS. TILFORD: Joseph, you've been engaged to Karen for a long time. Are your plans any more definite than they were a year ago?

CARDIN: You can get ready to buy the wedding present. We'll have the wedding here, if you don't mind. The smell of clean little girls and boiled linen would worry me.

MRS. TILFORD: Why has Karen decided so suddenly to make it definite?

CARDIN: She has not suddenly decided anything. The school is pretty well on its feet, and now that Mrs. Mortar is leaving—

MRS. TILFORD: I've heard about their putting Mrs. Mortar out.

CARDIN: Putting her out? Well, maybe. But a nice sum for a trip and a promise that a good niece will support you the rest of your life is an enviable way of being put out.

MRS. TILFORD [*slowly*]: Don't you find it odd, Joseph, that they want so much to get rid of that silly, harmless woman?

CARDIN: I don't know what you're talking about, but it isn't odd at all. Lily Mortar is not a harmless woman, although God knows she's silly enough. She's a nasty, tiresome, spoilt old bitch. If you're forming a Mortar Welfare Society, you're wasting your time. [*Gets up, puts down his glass*] It's not like you to waste your time. Now, what's it that's really on your mind?

MRS. TILFORD: You must not marry Karen.

CARDIN [*shocked, he grins*]: You're a very impertinent lady. Why must I— [*imitates her*] not marry Karen?

MRS. TILFORD: Because there's something wrong with Karen—something horrible.

[*The door-bell is heard to ring loud and long.*]

CARDIN: I don't think I can allow you to say things like that, Amelia.

MRS. TILFORD: I have good reason for saying it. [*Breaks off as she hears voices off-stage*] Who is that?

KAREN [*off-stage*]: Mrs. Tilford, Agatha. Is she in?

AGATHA [*off-stage*]: Yes'm. Come on in.

MRS. TILFORD: I won't have her here.

CARDIN [*angrily*]: What are you talking about?

MRS. TILFORD: I won't have her here.

CARDIN [*picks up his hat*]: Then you don't want me here either. [*Turns to face* KAREN, *who, with* MARTHA, *has rushed in*] Darling, what—?

KAREN [*stops when she sees him, puts her hand over her eyes*]: Is it a joke, Joe?

MARTHA [*with great force to* MRS. TILFORD]: We've come to find out what you are doing.

CARDIN [*kissing* KAREN]: What is it?

KAREN: It's crazy! It's crazy! What did she do it for?

CARDIN: What are you talking about? What do you mean?

MRS. TILFORD: You shouldn't have come here.

CARDIN: What is all this? What's happened?

KAREN: I tried to reach you. Hasn't she told you?

CARDIN: Nobody's told me anything. I haven't heard anything but wild talk. What is it, Karen? [*She starts to speak, then dumbly shakes her head*] What's happened, Martha?

MARTHA [*violently*]: An insane asylum has been let loose. How do we know what's happened?

CARDIN: What was it?

KAREN: We didn't know what it was. Nobody would talk to us, nobody would tell us anything.

MARTHA: I'll tell you, I'll tell you. You see if you can make any sense out of it. At dinner-time Mrs. Munn's chauffeur said that Evelyn must be sent home right away. At half past seven Mrs. Burton arrived to tell us that she wanted Helen's things packed and that she'd wait outside because she didn't want to enter a place like ours.

Five minutes later the Wells's butler came for Rosalie.

CARDIN: What was it?

MARTHA: It was a madhouse. People rushing in and out, the children being pushed into cars—

KAREN [*quiet now, takes his hand*]: Mrs. Rogers finally told us.

CARDIN: What? What?

KAREN: That—that Martha and I are—in love with each other. In love with each other. Mrs. Tilford told them.

CARDIN [*for a moment stands staring at her incredulously. Then he walks across the room, stares out of the window, and finally turns to* MRS. TILFORD]: Did you tell them that?

MRS. TILFORD: Yes.

CARDIN: Are you sick?

MRS. TILFORD: You know I'm not sick.

CARDIN [*snapping the words out*]: Then what did you do it for?

MRS. TILFORD [*slowly*]: Because it's true.

KAREN [*incredulously*]: You think it's true, then?

MARTHA: You fool! You damned, vicious—

KAREN: Do you realize what you're saying?

MRS. TILFORD: I realize it very well. And—

MARTHA: You realize nothing, nothing, nothing.

MRS. TILFORD: And that's why I don't think you should have come here. [*Quietly, with a look at* MARTHA] I shall not call you names, and I will not allow you to call me names. It comes to this: I can't trust myself to talk about it with you now or ever.

KAREN: What's she talking about, Joe? What's she mean? What is she trying to do to us? What is everybody doing to us?

MARTHA [*softly, as though to herself*]: Pushed around. We're being pushed around by crazy people. [*Shakes herself slightly*] That's an awful thing. And we're standing here— [CARDIN *puts his arm around* KAREN, *walks with her to the window. They stand there together*] We're standing here taking it. [*Suddenly with violence*] Didn't you know we'd come here? Were we supposed to lie down and grin while you kicked us around with these lies?

MRS. TILFORD: This can't do any of us any good, Miss Dobie.

MARTHA [*scornfully imitating her*]: "This can't do any of us any good." Listen, listen. Try to understand this: you're not playing with paper dolls. We're human beings, see? It's our lives you're fooling with. *Our* lives. That's serious business for us. Can you understand that?

MRS. TILFORD [*for the first time she speaks angrily*]: I can understand that, and I understand a lot more. *You've* been playing with a lot of children's lives, and that's why I stopped you. [*More calmly*] I know how serious this is for you, how serious it is for all of us.

CARDIN [*bitterly*]: I don't think you do know.

MRS. TILFORD: I wanted to avoid this meeting because it can't do any good. You came here to find out if I had made the charge. You've found out. Let's end it there. *I don't want you in this house.* I'm sorry this had to be done to you, Joseph.

CARDIN: I don't like your sympathy.

MRS. TILFORD: Very well. There's nothing I mean to do, nothing I want to do. There's nothing anybody can do.

CARDIN [*carefully*]: You have already done a terrible thing.

MRS. TILFORD: I have done what I had to do. What they are may possibly be their own business. It becomes a great deal more than that when children are involved.

KAREN [*wildly*]: It's not true. Not a word of it is true; can't you understand that?

MRS. TILFORD: There won't be any punishment for either of you. But there mustn't be any punishment for me, either—and that's what this meeting is. This—this thing is your own. Go away with it. I don't understand it and I don't want any part of it.

MARTHA [*slowly*]: So you thought we would go away?

MRS. TILFORD: I think that's best for you.

MARTHA: There must be something we can do to you, and, whatever it is, we'll find it.

MRS. TILFORD: That will be very unwise.

KAREN: You are right to be afraid.

MRS. TILFORD: I am not afraid, Karen.

CARDIN: But you *are* old—and you *are* irresponsible.

MRS. TILFORD [*hurt*]: You know that's not true.

KAREN [*goes to her*]: I don't want to have anything to do with your mess, do you hear me? It makes me feel dirty and sick to be forced to say this, but here it is: there isn't a single word of truth in anything you've said. We're standing here defending ourselves—and against what? Against a lie. A great, awful lie.

MRS. TILFORD: I'm sorry that I can't believe that.

KAREN: Damn you!

CARDIN: But you can believe this: they've worked eight long years to save enough money to buy that farm, to start that school. They did without everything that young people ought to have. You wouldn't know about that. That school meant things to them: self-respect, and bread and butter, and honest work. Do you know what it is to try so hard for anything? Well, now it's gone. [*Suddenly hits the side of the table with his hand*] What the hell did you do it for?

MRS. TILFORD [*softly*]: It had to be done.

CARDIN: Righteousness is a great thing.

MRS. TILFORD [*gently*]: I know how you must feel.

CARDIN: You don't know anything about how I feel. And you don't know how they feel, either.
MRS. TILFORD: I've loved you as much as I loved my own boys. I wouldn't have spared them; I couldn't spare you.
CARDIN [*fiercely*]: I believe you.
MARTHA: What is there to do to you? What can we do to you? There must be something—something that makes you feel the way we do tonight. You don't want any part of this, you said. But you'll get a part. More than you bargained for. [*Suddenly*] Listen: are you willing to stand by everything you've said tonight?
MRS. TILFORD: Yes.
MARTHA: All right. That's fine. But don't get the idea we'll let you whisper this lie: you made it and you'll come out with it. Shriek it to your town of Lancet. We'll *make* you shriek it—and we'll make you do it in a court room. [*Quietly*] Tomorrow, Mrs. Tilford, you will have a libel suit on your hands.
MRS. TILFORD: That will be very unwise.
KAREN: Very unwise—for you.
MRS. TILFORD: It is you I am thinking of. I am frightened for you. It was wrong of you to brazen it out here tonight; it would be criminally foolish of you to brazen it out in public. That can bring you nothing but pain. I am an old woman, Miss Dobie, and I have seen too many people, out of pride, act on that pride. In the end they punish themselves.
MARTHA: And you feel that you are too old to be punished? That we should spare you?
MRS. TILFORD: You know that is not what I meant.
CARDIN [*turns from the window*]: So you took a child's word for it?
MARTHA [*looks at him, shakes her head*]: I knew it, too.
KAREN: That is really where you got it? I can't believe—it couldn't be. Why, she's a child.
MARTHA: She's not a child any longer.
KAREN: Oh, my God, it all fits so well now. That girl has hated us for a long time. We never knew why, we never could find out. There didn't seem to be any reason—
MARTHA: There wasn't any reason. She hates everybody and everything.
KAREN: Your Mary's a strange girl, a bad girl. There's something very awful the matter with her.
MRS. TILFORD: I was waiting for you to say that, Miss Wright.
KAREN: I'm telling you the truth. We should have told it to you long ago. [*Stops, sighs*] It's no use.
MARTHA: Where is she? Bring her out here and let us hear what she has to say.
MRS. TILFORD: You cannot see her.
CARDIN: Where is she?
MRS. TILFORD: I won't have that, Joseph.
CARDIN: I'm going to talk to her.
MRS. TILFORD: *I won't have her go through that again.* [*To* KAREN *and* MARTHA] You came here demanding explanations. It was I who should have asked them from you. You attack me, you attack Mary. I've told you I didn't mean you any harm. I still don't. You claim that it isn't true; it may be natural that you should say that, but I *know* that it is true. No matter what you say, you know very well I wouldn't have acted until I was absolutely sure. All I wanted was to get those children away. That has been done. There won't be any talk about it or about you—I'll see to that. You have been in my house long enough. Get out.
KAREN [*gets up*]: The wicked very young, and the wicked very old. Let's go home.
CARDIN: Sit down. [*To* MRS. TILFORD] When two people come here with their lives spread on the table for you to cut to pieces, then the only honest thing to do is to give them a chance to come out whole. Are you honest?
MRS. TILFORD: I've always thought so.
CARDIN: Then where is Mary? [*After a moment she moves her head to door Right. Quickly* CARDIN *goes to the door and opens it*] Mary! Come here.

[*After a moment* MARY *appears, stands nervously near door. Her manner is shy and afraid.*]

MRS. TILFORD [*gently*]: Sit down, dear, and don't be afraid.
MARTHA [*her lips barely moving*]: Make her tell the truth.
CARDIN [*walking about in front of* MARY]: Look: everybody lies all the time. Sometimes they have to, sometimes they don't. I've lied to myself for a lot of different reasons, but there was never a time when, if I'd been given a second chance, I wouldn't have taken back the lie and told the truth. You're lucky if you ever get that chance. I'm telling you this because I'm about to ask you a question. Before you answer the question, I want to tell you that if you've l—if you made a mistake, you must take this chance and say so. You won't be punished for it. Do you get all that?
MARY [*timidly*]: Yes, Cousin Joe.
CARDIN [*grimly*]: All right, let's get started. Were you telling your grandmother the truth this afternoon? The exact truth about Miss Wright and Miss Dobie?
MARY [*without hesitation*]: Oh, yes.

[KAREN *sighs deeply,* MARTHA, *her fists closed tight, turns her back to the child.* CARDIN *smiles as he looks at* MARY.]

CARDIN: All right, Mary, that was your chance; you passed it up. [*Pulls up a chair, sits down in front of her*] Now let's find out things.

MRS. TILFORD: She's told you. Aren't you through?

CARDIN: Not by a long shot. You've started something, and I'm going to finish it for you. Will you answer some more questions,Mary?

MARY: Yes, Cousin Joe.

MARTHA : Stop that sick sweet tone.

[MRS. TILFORD *half rises;* CARDIN *motions her back.*]

CARDIN: Why don't you like Miss Dobie and Miss Wright?

MARY: Oh, I do like them. They just don't like me. They never have liked me.

CARDIN: How do you know?

MARY: They're always picking on me. They're always punishing me for everything that happens. No matter what happens, it's always me.

CARDIN: Why do you think they do that?

MARY: Because—because they're—because they—[*Stops, turns*] Grandma, I—

CARDIN: All right, we'll skip that one. Did you get punished today?

MARY: Yes, and it was just because Peggy and Evelyn heard them and so they took it out on me.

KAREN: That's a lie.

CARDIN: Sssh. Heard what, Mary?

MARY: Mrs. Mortar told Miss Dobie that there was something funny about her. She said that she had a funny feeling about Miss Wright, and Mrs. Mortar said that was unnatural. That was why we got punished, just because—

KAREN: That was not the reason they got punished.

MRS. TILFORD [*to* MARTHA]: Miss Dobie?

MARTHA: My aunt is a stupid woman. What she said was unpleasant; it was said to annoy me. It meant nothing more than that.

MARY: And, Cousin Joe, she said every time you came to the school Miss Dobie got jealous, and that she didn't want you to get married.

MARTHA [*to* CARDIN]: She said that, too. For God's sake, can't you see what's happening? This—this child is taking little things, little family things, and making them have meanings that— [*Stops, suddenly regards Mary with a combination of disgust and interest*] Where did you learn so much in so little time?

CARDIN: What do you think Mrs. Mortar meant by all that, Mary?

MRS. TILFORD: Stop it, Joseph!

MARY: I don't know, but it was always kind of funny and she always says things like that and all the girls would talk about it when Miss Dobie went and visited Miss Wright late at night—

KAREN [*angrily*]: And we go to the movies at night and sometimes we read at night and sometimes we drink tea at night. Those are guilty things, too, Mrs. Tilford.

MARY: And there are always funny sounds and we'd stay awake and listen because we couldn't help hearing and I'd get frightened because the sounds were like—

MARTHA: Be still!

KAREN [*with violence*]: No, no. You don't want her still now. What else did you hear?

MARY: Grandma, I—

MRS. TILFORD [*bitterly to* CARDIN]: You are trying to make her name it, aren't you?

CARDIN [*ignoring her, speaks to* MARY]: Go on.

MARY: I don't know; there were just sounds.

CARDIN: But what did you think they were? Why did they frighten you?

MARY [*weakly*]: I don't know.

CARDIN [*smiles at* MRS. TILFORD]: She doesn't know.

MARY [*hastily*]: I saw things, too. One night there was so much noise I thought somebody was sick or something and I looked through the keyhole and they were kissing and saying things and then I got scared because it was different sort of and I—

MARTHA [*her face distorted, turns to* MRS. TILFORD]: That child—that child is sick.

KAREN: Ask her again how she could see us.

CARDIN: How could you see Miss Dobie and Miss Wright?

MARY: I—I—

MRS. TILFORD: Tell him what you whispered to me.

MARY: It was at night and I was leaning down by the keyhole.

KAREN: *There's no keyhole on my door.*

MRS. TILFORD: What?

KAREN: There—is—no—keyhole—on—my—door.

MARY [*quickly*]: It wasn't her room, Grandma, it was the other room, I guess. It was *Miss Dobie's* room. I saw them through the keyhole in Miss Dobie's room.

CARDIN: How did you know anybody was in Miss Dobie's room?

MARY: I told you, I told you. Because we heard them. Everybody heard them—

MARTHA : I share a room with my aunt. It is on the first floor at the other end of the house. It is impossible to hear anything from there. [*To* CARDIN] Tell her to come and see for herself.

MRS. TILFORD [*her voice shaken*]: What is this, Mary? Why did you say you saw through a keyhole? *Can* you hear from your room—?

MARY [*starts to cry*]: Everybody is yelling at me. I don't know what I'm saying with everybody mixing me all up. I did see it! I did see it!

MRS. TILFORD: *What* did you see? *Where* did you see it? I want the truth, now. The truth, whatever it is.

CARDIN [*gets up, moves his chair back*]: We can go home. We are finished here. [*Looks around*] It's not a pleasant place to be.

MRS. TILFORD [*angrily*]: Stop that crying, Mary. Stand up.

[MARY *gets up, head down, still crying hysterically.* MRS. TILFORD *goes and stands directly in front of her.*]

MRS. TILFORD: *I want the truth.*

MARY: All—all right.

MRS. TILFORD: What is the truth?

MARY: It was Rosalie who saw them. I just said it was me so I wouldn't have to tattle on Rosalie.

CARDIN [*wearily*]: Oh, my God!

MARY: It *was* Rosalie, Grandma, she told us all about it. She said she had read about it in a book and she knew. [*Desperately*] You ask Rosalie. You just ask Rosalie. She'll tell you. We used to talk about it all the time. That's the truth, that's the honest truth. She said it was when the door was open once and she told us all about it. I was just trying to save Rosalie, and everybody jumps on me.

MRS. TILFORD [*to* CARDIN]: Please wait a minute. [*Goes to library door*] Rosalie!

CARDIN: You're giving yourself an awful beating, Amelia, and you deserve whatever you get.

MRS. TILFORD [*stands waiting for* ROSALIE, *passes her hand over her face*]: I don't know. I don't know, any more. Maybe it's what I do deserve. [*As* ROSALIE, *frightened, appears at the door, making bows to everybody, she takes the child gently by the hand, brings her down Center, talking nervously*] I'm sorry to keep you up so late, Rosalie. You must be tired. [*Speaks rapidly*] Mary says there's been a lot of talk in the school lately about Miss Wright and Miss Dobie. Is that true?

ROSALIE: I—I don't know what you mean.

MRS. TILFORD: That things have been said among you girls.

ROSALIE [*wide-eyed, frightened*]: What things? I never—I—I—

KAREN [*gently*]: Don't be frightened.

MRS. TILFORD: What was the talk about, Rosalie?

ROSALIE [*utterly bewildered*]: I don't know what she means, Miss Wright.

KAREN: Rosalie, Mary has told her grandmother that certain things at school have been—er—puzzling you girls. You, particularly.

ROSALIE: History puzzles me. I guess I'm not very good at history, and Helen helps me sometimes, if that—

KAREN: No, that's not what she meant. She says that you told her that you saw certain—certain acts between Miss Dobie and myself. She says that once, when the door was open, you saw us kissing each other in a way that— [*Unable to bear the child's look, she turns her back*] women don't kiss one another.

ROSALIE: Oh, Miss Wright, I didn't, didn't, I didn't. I *never* said such a thing.

MRS. TILFORD [*grimly*]: That's true, my dear?

ROSALIE: I never saw any such thing. Mary always makes things up about me and everybody else. [*Starts to weep in excitement*] I never said any such thing ever. Why, I never even could have thought of—

MARY [*staring at her, speaks very slowly*]: Yes, you did, Rosalie. You're just trying to get out of it. I remember just when you said it. I remember it, because it was the day Helen Burton's bracelet was—

ROSALIE [*stands fascinated and fearful, looking at* MARY]: I never did. I—I—you're just—

MARY: It was the day Helen's bracelet was stolen, and nobody knew who did it, and Helen said that if her mother found out, she'd have the thief put in jail.

KAREN [*puzzled, as are the others, by the sudden change in* ROSALIE'*s manner*]: There's nothing to cry about. You must help us by telling the truth. Why, what's the matter, Rosalie?

MARY: Grandma, there's something I've got to tell you that—

ROSALIE [*with a shrill cry*]: Yes. Yes. I did see it. I told Mary. What Mary said was right. I said it, I said it— [*Throws herself on the couch, weeping hysterically;* MARTHA *stands leaning against the door;* KAREN, CARDIN *and* MRS. TILFORD *are staring at* ROSALIE; MARY *slowly sits down as the Curtain falls.*]

ACT III

SCENE. *The same as Act I. Living room of the school.*

AT RISE: *The room has changed. It is not dirty, but it is dull and dark and uncared for. The windows are tightly shut, the curtains tightly drawn.* KAREN *is sitting in a large chair, Right Center, feet flat on floor.* MARTHA *is lying on the couch, her face buried against the pillows, her back to* KAREN. *It is a minute or two after the rise of the curtain before either speaks.*

MARTHA: It's cold in here.

KAREN: Yes.

MARTHA: What time is it?

KAREN: I don't know. What's the difference?

MARTHA: None. I was hoping it was time for my bath.

KAREN: Take it early today.

MARTHA [*laughs*]: Oh, I couldn't do that. I look forward all day to that bath. It's my last touch with the full life. It makes me feel important to know that there's one thing ahead of me, one thing I've *got* to do. You ought to get yourself something like that. I tell you, at five o'clock every day you comb your hair. How's that? It's better for you, take my word. You wake up in the morning and you say to yourself, the day's not entirely empty, life is rich and full; at five o'clock I'll comb my hair.

[They fall back into silence. A moment later the phone rings. Neither of them pays the slightest attention to it. But the ringing becomes too insistent. KAREN *rises, takes the receiver off, goes back to her chair and sits down.]*

KAREN: It's raining.
MARTHA: Hungry?
KAREN: No. You?
MARTHA: No, but I'd like to be hungry again. Remember how much we used to eat at college?
KAREN: That was ten years ago.
MARTHA: Well, maybe we'll be hungry in another ten years. It's cheaper this way.
KAREN: What's the old thing about time being more nourishing than bread?
MARTHA: Yeah? Maybe.
KAREN: Joe's late today. What time is it?
MARTHA *[turns again to lie on her side]*: We've been sitting here for eight days asking each other the time. Haven't you heard? There isn't any time any more.
KAREN: It's been days since we've been out of this house.
MARTHA: Well, we'll have to get off these chairs sooner or later. In a couple of months they'll need dusting.
KAREN: What'll we do when we get off?
MARTHA: God knows.
KAREN *[almost in a whisper]*: It's awful.
MARTHA: Let's not talk about it. *[After a moment]* What about eggs for dinner?
KAREN: All right.
MARTHA: I'll make some potatoes with onions, the way you used to like them.
KAREN: It's a week ago Thursday. It never seemed real until the last day. It seems real enough now, all right.
MARTHA: Now and forever after.
KAREN *[suddenly]*: Let's go out.
MARTHA *[turns over, stares at her]*: Where to?
KAREN: We'll take a walk.
MARTHA: Where'll we walk?
KAREN: Why shouldn't we take a walk? We won't see anybody, and suppose we do, what of it? We'll jus—
MARTHA *[slowly gets up]*: Come on. We'll go through the park.
KAREN: They might see us. *[They stand looking at each other]* Let's not go. *[*MARTHA *goes back, lies down again]* We'll go tomorrow.
MARTHA *[laughs]*: Stop kidding yourself.
KAREN: But Joe says we've got to go out. He says that all the people who don't think it's true will begin to wonder if we keep hiding this way.
MARTHA: If it makes you feel better to think there *are* such people, go ahead.
KAREN: He says we ought to go into town and go shopping and act as though—
MARTHA: Shopping? That's a sound idea. There aren't three stores in Lancet that would sell us anything. Hasn't he heard about the ladies' clubs and their meetings and their circulars and their visits and their—
KAREN *[softly]*: Don't tell him.
MARTHA *[gently]*: I won't. *[There are footsteps in the hall, and the sound of something being dragged]* There's our friend.

[A GROCERY BOY *appears lugging a box. He brings it into the room, stands staring at them, giggles a little. Walks toward* KAREN, *stops, examines her. She sits tense, looking away from him. Without taking his eyes from* KAREN, *he speaks.]*

GROCERY BOY: I knocked on the kitchen door but nobody answered.
MARTHA: You said that yesterday. All right. Thanks. Good-bye.
KAREN *[unable any longer to stand the stare]*: Make him stop it.
GROCERY BOY: Here are the things. *[Giggles, moves toward* MARTHA, *stands looking at her. Suddenly* MARTHA *thrusts her hand in the air.]*
MARTHA: I've got eight fingers, see? I'm a freak.
GROCERY BOY *[giggling]*: There's a car comin' here. *[Gets no answer, starts backing out of door, still looking. Familiarly]* Good-bye. *[Exits.]*
MARTHA *[bitterly]*: You still think we should go into town?
KAREN: I don't know. I don't know about anything any more. *[After a moment]* Martha, Martha, Martha—
MARTHA *[gently]*: What is it, Karen?
KAREN: What are we going to do? It's all so cold and unreal and—It's like that dark hour of the night when, half awake, you struggle through the black mess you've been dreaming. Then, suddenly, you wake up and you see your own bed or your own nightgown and you know you're back again in a solid world. But now it's all the nightmare; there is no solid world. Oh. Martha, *why* did it happen? *What* happened? What are we doing here like this?
MARTHA: Waiting.

KAREN: For what?
MARTHA: I don't know.
KAREN: We've got to get out of this place. I can't stand it any more.
MARTHA: You'll be getting married soon. Everything will be all right then.
KAREN [*vaguely*]: Yes.
MARTHA [*looks up at the tone*]: What is it?
KAREN: Nothing.
MARTHA: There mustn't be anything wrong between you and Joe. Never.
KAREN [*without conviction*]: Nothing's wrong. [*As foot steps are heard in the hall, her face lights up*] There's Joe now.

[MRS. MORTAR, *small suitcase in hand, stands in the doorway, her face pushed coyly forward.*]

MRS. MORTAR: And here I am. Hello, hello.
MARTHA [*she has turned over on her back and is staring at her aunt. She speaks to* KAREN]: The Duchess, isn't it? Returned at long last. [*Too jovially*] Come on in. We're delighted to see you. Are you tired from your journey? Is there something I can get you?
MRS. MORTAR [*surprised*]: I'm very glad to see you both, and [*looks around*] I'm very glad to see the old place again. How is everything?
MARTHA: Everything's fine. We're splendid, thank you. You're just in time for tea.
MRS. MORTAR: You know, I should like some tea, if it isn't too much trouble.
MARTHA: No trouble at all. Some small sandwiches and a little brandy?
MRS. MORTAR [*puzzled finally*]: Why, Martha.
MARTHA: Where the hell have you been?
MRS. MORTAR: Around, around. I had a most interesting time. Things—
MARTHA: Why didn't you answer my telegrams?
MRS. MORTAR: Things have changed in the theater—drastically changed, I might say.
MARTHA: *Why didn't you answer my telegrams?*
MRS. MORTAR: Oh, Martha, there's your temper again.
MARTHA: Answer me and don't bother about my temper.
MRS. MORTAR [*nervously*]: I was moving around a great deal. [*Conversationally*] You know, I think it will throw a very revealing light on the state of the new theater when I tell you that the Lyceum in Rochester now has a toilet back stage.
MARTHA: To hell with the toilet in Rochester. Where were you?
MRS. MORTAR: Moving around, I tell you.
KAREN: What difference does it all make now?
MRS. MORTAR: Karen is quite right. Let bygones be bygones. As I was saying, there's an effete something in the theater now, and that accounts for—
MARTHA [*to* KAREN]: Isn't she wonderful? [*To* MRS. MORTAR] Why did you refuse to come back here and testify for us?
MRS. MORTAR: Why, Martha, I didn't refuse to come back at all. That's the wrong way to look at it. I was on a tour; that's a moral obligation, you know. Now don't let's talk about unpleasant things any more. I'll go up and unpack a few things; tomorrow's plenty of time to get my trunk.
KAREN [*laughs*]: Things have changed here, you know.
MARTHA: She doesn't know. She expected to walk right up to a comfortable fire and sit down and she very carefully waited until the whole thing was over. [*Leans forward, speaking to* MRS. MORTAR] Listen, Karen Wright and Martha Dobie brought a libel suit against a woman called Tilford because her grandchild had accused them of having what the judge called "sinful sexual knowledge of one another." [MRS. MORTAR *holds up her hand in protest, and* MARTHA *laughs*] Don't like that, do you? Well, a great part of the defense's case was based on remarks made by Lily Mortar, actress in the toilets of Rochester, against her niece, Martha. And a greater part of the defense's case rested on the telling fact that Mrs. Mortar would not appear in court to deny or explain those remarks. Mrs. Mortar had a moral obligation to the theater. As you probably read in the papers, we lost the case.
MRS. MORTAR: I didn't think of it that way, Martha. It couldn't have done any good for all of us to get mixed up in that unpleasant notoriety—[*Sees* MARTHA*'s face. Hastily*] But now that you've explained it, why, I do see it your way, and I'm sorry I didn't come back. But now that I am here, I'm going to stand shoulder to shoulder with you. I know what you've gone through, but the body and heart *do* recover, you know. I'll be here working right along with you and we'll—
MARTHA: There's an eight o'clock train. Get on it.
MRS. MORTAR: Martha.
MARTHA: You've come back to pick the bones dry. Well, there aren't even bones anymore. There's nothing here for you.
MRS. MORTAR [*sniffling a little*]: How can you talk to me like that?
MARTHA: Because I hate you. I've always hated you.
MRS. MORTAR [*gently*]: God will punish you for that.
MARTHA: He's been doing all right.
MRS. MORTAR: When you wish to apologize, I will be temporarily in my room. [*Starts to exit, almost bumps into* CARDIN, *steps back with dignity*] How do you do?
CARDIN [*laughs*]: Look who's here. A little late, aren't you?

MRS. MORTAR: So it's you. Now, I call *that* loyal. A lot of men wouldn't still be here. They would have felt—

MARTHA: Get out of here.

KAREN [*opening door*]: I'll call you when it's time for your train.

[MRS. MORTAR *looks at her, exits.*]

CARDIN: Now, what do you think brought her back?

KAREN: God knows.

MARTHA: I know. She was broke.

CARDIN [*pats* MARTHA *on the shoulder*]: Don't let her worry you this time, Martha. We'll give her some money and get rid of her. [*Pulls* KAREN *to him*] Been out today, darling?

KAREN: We started to go out.

CARDIN [*shakes his head*]: Feel all right?

[KAREN *leans over to kiss him. Almost imperceptibly he pulls back.*]

KAREN: Why did you do that?

MARTHA: Karen.

CARDIN: Do what?

KAREN: Draw back that way.

CARDIN [*laughs, kisses her*]: If we sit around here much longer, we'll all be bats. I sold my place today to Foster.

KAREN: You did what?

CARDIN: We're getting married this week. Then we're going away—all three of us.

KAREN: You can't leave here. I won't have you do this for me. What about the hospital and—

CARDIN: Shut up, darling, it's all fixed. We're going to Vienna and we're going quick. Fischer wrote that I can have my old place back.

KAREN: No! No! I'm not going to let you.

CARDIN: It's already done. Fischer can't pay me much, but it'll be enough for the three of us. Plenty if we live cheap.

MARTHA: I couldn't go with you, Joe.

CARDIN: Nonsense, Martha, we're all going. We're going to have fun again.

KAREN [*slowly*]: You don't want to go back to Vienna.

CARDIN: No.

KAREN: Then why?

CARDIN: Look: I don't want to go to Vienna; I'd rather have stayed here. But then you don't want to go to Vienna; you'd rather have stayed here. Well, to hell with that. We *can't* stay here, and Vienna offers enough to eat and sleep and drink beer on. Now don't object any more, please, darling. All right?

KAREN: All right.

MARTHA: I can't go. It's better for all of us if I don't.

CARDIN [*puts his arm around her*]: Not now. You stay with us now. Later on, if you want it that way. All right?

MARTHA [*smiles*]: All right.

CARDIN: Swell. I'll buy you good coffee cakes and take you both to Ischl for a honeymoon.

MARTHA [*picking up grocery box, she starts for door*]: A big coffee cake with a lot of raisins. It would be nice to like something again. [*Exits.*]

CARDIN [*with a slightly forced heartiness*]: I'll be going back with a pretty girl who belongs to me. I'll show you off all over the place—to Dr. Engelhardt, and the nurse at the desk, and to the fat gal in the cake shop, and to Fischer. [*Laughs*] The last time I saw him was at the railroad station. He took me back of the baggage car. [*With an imitation of an accent*] "Joseph," he said, "you'll be a good doctor; I would trust you to cut up my Minna. But you're not a great doctor, and you never will be. Go back where you were born and take care of your sick. Leave the fancy work to the others." I came home.

KAREN: You'll be coming home again some day.

CARDIN: No. Let's not talk about it. [*After a moment*] You'll need some clothes?

KAREN: A few. Oh, your Dr. Fischer was so right. This is where you belong.

CARDIN: I need an overcoat and a suit. You'll need a lot of things—heavy things. It's cold there now, much colder than you'd expect—

KAREN: I've done this to you. I've taken you away from everything you want.

CARDIN: But it's lovely in the mountains, and that's where we'll go for a month.

KAREN: They—*they've* done it. They've taken away every chance we had. Everything we wanted, everything we were going to be.

CARDIN: And we've got to stop talking like that. [*Takes her by the shoulder*] We've got a chance. But it's just one chance, and if we miss it we're done for. It means that we've got to start putting the whole business behind us now. *Now,* Karen. What you've done, you've done—and that's that.

KAREN: What *I've* done?

CARDIN [*impatiently*]: What's been done to you.

KAREN: What did you mean? [*When there is no answer*] What did you mean when you said: "What you've done"?

CARDIN [*shouting*]: Nothing. Nothing. [*Then very quietly*] Karen, there are a lot of people in this world who've had bad trouble in their lives. We're three of those people. We could sit around the rest of our lives and exist on that trouble, until in the end we had nothing else and we'd want nothing else. That's something I'm not coming to and I'm not going to let you come to.

KAREN: I know. I'm sorry. [*After a moment*] Joe, can we have a baby right away?

CARDIN [*vaguely*]: Yes, I guess so. Although we won't have much money now.

KAREN: You used to want one right away. You always said that was the way you wanted it. There's some reason for your changing.

CARDIN: My God, we *can't* go on like this. Everything I say to you is made to mean something else. We don't talk like people any more. Oh, let's get out of here as fast as we can.

KAREN [*as though she is finishing the sentence for him*]: And every word will have a new meaning. You think we'll be able to run away from that? Woman, child, love, lawyer—no words that we can use in safety any more. [*Laughs bitterly*] Sick, high-tragic people. That's what we'll be.

CARDIN [*gently*]: No, we won't, darling. Love is casual—that's the way it should be. We must find that out all over again. We must learn again to live and love like other people.

KAREN: It won't work.

CARDIN: What?

KAREN: The two of us together.

CARDIN [*sharply*]: Stop talking like that.

KAREN: It's true. [*Suddenly*] I want you to say it now.

CARDIN: I don't know what you're talking about.

KAREN: Yes, you do. We've both known for a long time. I knew surely the day we lost the case. I was watching your face in court. It was ashamed—and sad at being ashamed. Say it now, Joe. Ask it now.

CARDIN: I have nothing to ask. Nothing— [*Quickly*] All right. Is it—was it ever—

KAREN [*puts her hand over his mouth*]: No. Martha and I have never touched each other. [*Pulls his head down on her shoulder*] That's all right, darling. I'm glad you asked. I'm not mad a bit, really.

CARDIN: I'm sorry, Karen, I'm sorry. I didn't mean to hurt you, I—

KAREN: I know. You wanted to wait until it was all over, you really never wanted to ask at all. You didn't know for sure; you thought there might be just a little truth in it all. [*With great feeling*] You've been good to me and loyal. You're a fine man. [*Afraid of tears, she pats him, walks away*] Now go and sit down, Joe. I have things to say. They're all mixed up and I must get them clear.

CARDIN: Don't let's talk any more. Let's forget and go ahead.

KAREN [*puzzled*]: Go ahead?

CARDIN: Yes, Karen.

KAREN: You believe me, then?

CARDIN: Of course I believe you. I only had to hear you say it.

KAREN: No, no, no. That isn't the way things work. Maybe you believe me. I'd never know whether you did or not. You'd never know whether you did, either. We couldn't do it that way. Can't you see what would happen? We'd be hounded by it all our lives. I'd be frightened, always, and in the end my own fright would make me—would make me hate you. [*Sees slight movement he makes*] Yes, it would; I know it would. I'd hate you for what I thought I'd done to you. And I'd hate myself, too. It would grow and grow until we'd be ruined by it. [*Sees him about to speak*] Ah, Joe, you've seen all that yourself. You knew it first.

CARDIN [*softly*]: I didn't mean it that way; I don't now.

KAREN [*smiles*]: You're still trying to spare me, still trying to tell yourself that we might be all right again. But we won't be all right. Not ever, ever, ever. I don't know all the reasons why. Look, I'm standing here. I haven't changed. [*Holds out her hands*] My hands look just the same, my face is the same, even my dress is old. We're in a room we've been in so many times before; you're sitting where you always sit; it's nearly time for dinner. I'm like everybody else. I can have all the things that everybody has. I can have you and a baby, and I can go to market, and we can go to the movies, and people will talk to me and— [*Suddenly notices the pain in his face*] Oh, I'm sorry. I mustn't talk like that. That couldn't be true any more.

CARDIN: It could be, Karen. We'll make it be like that.

KAREN: No. That's only what we'd like to have had. It's what we can't have now. Go home, darling.

CARDIN [*with force*]: Don't talk like that. No matter what it is, we can't leave each other. I can't leave you—

KAREN: Joe, Joe. Let's do it now and quick; it will be too hard later on.

CARDIN: No, no, no. We love each other. [*His voice breaks*] I'd give anything not to have asked questions, Karen.

KAREN: It had to be asked sooner or later—and answered. You're a good man—the best I'll ever know—and you've been better to me than— But it's no good now, for either of us; you can see that.

CARDIN: It can be. You say I helped you. Help me now; help me to be strong and good enough to— [*Goes toward her with his arms out*] Karen!

KAREN [*drawing back*]: No, Joe! [*Then, as he stops*] Will you do something for me?

CARDIN: No. I won't—

KAREN: Will you—will you go away for two days—a day—and think this all over by yourself—away from me and love and pity? Will you? And then decide.

CARDIN [*after a long pause*]: Yes, if you want, but it won't make any difference. We will—

KAREN: Don't say anything. Please go now. [*She sits down, smiles, closes her eyes. For a moment he stands looking at her, then slowly puts on his hat*] And all my heart goes with you.

CARDIN [*at door, leaving*]: I'll be coming back. [*Exits, slowly, reluctantly, closing door.*]

KAREN [*a moment after he has gone*]: No, you won't. Never, darling. [*Stays as she is until* MARTHA *enters Right.*]

MARTHA [*goes to lamp, lights it*]: It gets dark so early now. [*Sits down, stretches, laughs*] Cooking always makes me feel better. Well, I guess we'll have to give the Duchess some dinner. When the hawks descend, you've got to feed 'em. Where's Joe? [*No answer*] Where's Joe?

KAREN: Gone.

MARTHA: A patient? Will he be back in time for dinner?

KAREN: No.

MARTHA [*watching her*]: We'll save dinner for him, then. Karen! What's the matter?

KAREN [*in a dull tone*]: He won't be back any more.

MARTHA [*speaking slowly and carefully*]: You mean he won't be back any more tonight.

KAREN: He won't be back at all.

MARTHA [*quickly, walks to* KAREN]: What happened? [KAREN *shakes her head*] What happened, Karen?

KAREN: He thought that we had been lovers.

MARTHA [*tensely*]: I don't believe you.

[*Wearily* KAREN *turns her head away.*]

KAREN: All right.

MARTHA [*automatically*]: I don't believe it. He's never said a word all these months, all during the trial— [*Suddenly grabs* KAREN *by the shoulder, shakes her*] Didn't you tell him? For God's sake, didn't you tell him it wasn't true?

KAREN: Yes.

MARTHA: He didn't believe you?

KAREN: I guess he believed me.

MARTHA [*angrily*]: Then what have you done?

KAREN: What had to be done.

MARTHA: It's all wrong. It's silly. He'll be back in a little while and you'll clear it all up— [*Realizes why that can't be, covers her mouth with her hand*] Oh, God, I wanted that for you so much.

KAREN: Don't. I feel sick to my stomach.

MARTHA [*goes to couch opposite Karen, puts her head in her arms*] What's happened to us? What's really happened to us?

KAREN: I don't know. I want to be sleepy. I want to go to sleep.

MARTHA: Go back to Joe. He's strong; he'll understand. It's too much for you this way.

KAREN [*irritably*]: Stop talking about it. Let's pack and get out of here. Let's take the train in the morning.

MARTHA: The train to where?

KAREN: I don't know. Some place; any place.

MARTHA: A job? Money?

KAREN: In a big place we could get something to do.

MARTHA: They'd know about us. We've been famous.

KAREN: A small town, then.

MARTHA: They'd know more about us.

KAREN [*as a child would say it*]: Isn't there anywhere to go?

MARTHA: No. There'll never be any place for us to go. We're bad people. We'll sit. We'll be sitting the rest of our lives wondering what's happened to us. You think this scene is strange? Well, get used to it; we'll be here for a long time. [*Suddenly pinches* KAREN *on the arm*] Let's pinch each other sometimes. We can tell whether we're still living.

KAREN [*shivers, listlessly gets up, starts making a fire in the fireplace*]: But this isn't a new sin they tell us we've done. Other people aren't destroyed by it.

MARTHA: They are the people who believe in it, who want it, who've chosen it. We aren't like that. We don't love each other. [*Suddenly stops, crosses to fireplace, stands looking abstractedly at* KAREN. *Speaks casually*] I don't love you. We've been very close to each other, of course. I've loved you like a friend, the way thousands of women feel about other women.

KAREN [*only half listening*]: Yes.

MARTHA: Certainly that doesn't mean anything. There's nothing wrong about that. It's perfectly natural that I should be fond of you, that I should—

KAREN [*listlessly*]: Why are you saying all this to me?

MARTHA: Because I love you.

KAREN [*vaguely*]: Yes, of course.

MARTHA: I love you that way—maybe the way they said I loved you. I don't know. [*Waits, gets no answer, kneels down next to* KAREN] Listen to me!

KAREN: What?

MARTHA: *I have loved you the way they said.*

KAREN: You're crazy.

MARTHA: There's always been something wrong. Always—as long as I can remember. But I never knew it until all this happened.

KAREN [*for the first time looks up, horrified*]: Stop it!

MARTHA: You're afraid of hearing it; I'm more afraid than you.

KAREN [*puts her hands over her ears*]: I won't listen to you.

MARTHA: Take your hands down. [*Leans over, pulls* KAREN'*s hands away*] You've got to know it. I can't keep it any longer. I've got to tell you how guilty I am.

KAREN [*deliberately*]: You are guilty of nothing.

MARTHA: I've been telling myself that since the night we heard the child say it; I've been praying I could convince myself of it. I can't, I can't any longer. It's there. I don't know how, I don't know why. But I did love you. I do love you. I resented your marriage; maybe because I wanted you; maybe I wanted you all along; maybe I couldn't call it by a name; maybe it's been there ever since I first knew you—

KAREN [*tensely*]: It's a lie. You're telling yourself a lie. We never thought of each other that way.

MARTHA [*bitterly*]: No, of course *you* didn't. But who says I didn't? I never felt that way about anybody but you. I've never loved a man— [*Stops. Softly*] I never knew why before. Maybe it's that.

KAREN [*carefully*]: You are tired and sick.

MARTHA [*as though she were talking to herself*]: It's funny; it's all mixed up. There's something in you, and you don't know it and you don't do anything about it. Suddenly a child gets bored and lies— and there you are, seeing it for the first time. [*Closes her eyes*] I don't know. It all seems to come back to *me*. In some way I've ruined your life. I've ruined my own. I didn't even *know*. [*Smiles*] There's a big difference between us now, Karen. I feel all dirty and— [*Puts out her hand, touches* KAREN's *head*] I can't stay with you any more, darling.

KAREN [*in a shaken, uncertain tone*]: All this isn't true. You've never said it; we'll forget it by tomorrow—

MARTHA: Tomorrow? That's a funny word. Karen, we would have had to invent a new language, as children do, without words like tomorrow.

KAREN [*crying*]: Go and lie down, Martha. You'll feel better.

[MARTHA *looks around the room, slowly, carefully. She is very quiet. Exits Right, stands at door for a second looking at* KAREN, *then slowly shuts the door behind her.*]

[KAREN *sits alone without moving. There is no sound in the house until, a few minutes after* MARTHA's *exit, a shot is heard. The sound of the shot should not be too loud or too strong. For a few seconds after the noise has died out,* KAREN *does not move. Then, suddenly, she springs from the chair, crosses the room, pulls open door Right. Almost at the same moment footsteps are heard on the staircase.*]

MRS. MORTAR: What was that? Where is it? [*Enters door Center, frightened, aimlessly moving about*] Karen! Martha! Where are you? I heard a shot. What was— [*Stops as she sees* KAREN *reappear Right. Walks toward her, still talking. Stops when she sees* KAREN's *face*] What—what is it? [KAREN *moves her hands, shakes her head slightly, passes* MRS. MORTAR, *and goes toward window.* MRS. MORTAR *stares at her for a moment, rushes past her through door Right. Left alone,* KAREN *leans against the window.* MRS. MORTAR *re-enters crying. After a minute*] What shall we do? What shall we do?

KAREN [*in a toneless voice*]: Nothing.

MRS. MORTAR: We've got to get a doctor—right away. [*Goes to phone, nervously, fumblingly starts to dial.*]

KAREN [*without turning*]: There isn't any use.

MRS. MORTAR: We've got to do something. Oh, it's awful. Poor Martha. I don't know what we can do— [*Puts phone down, collapses in chair, sobs quietly*] You think she's dea—

KAREN: Yes.

MRS. MORTAR: Poor, poor Martha. I can't realize it's true. Oh, how could she—she was so—I don't know what— [*Looks up, still crying, surprised*] I'm— I'm frightened.

KAREN: Don't cry.

MRS. MORTAR: I can't help it. How can I help it? [*Gradually the sobs cease, and she sits rocking herself*] I'll never forgive myself for the last words I said to her. But I was good to her, Karen, and you know God will excuse me for that once. I always tried to do everything I could. [*Suddenly*] Suicide's a sin. [*No answer. Timidly*] Shouldn't we call somebody to—

KAREN: In a little while.

MRS. MORTAR: She shouldn't have done it, she shouldn't have done it. It was because of all this awful business. She would have got a job and started all over again—she was just worried and sick and—

KAREN: That isn't the reason she did it.

MRS. MORTAR: What—why—?

KAREN [*wearily*]: What difference does it make now?

MRS. MORTAR [*reproachfully*]: You're not crying.

KAREN: No.

MRS. MORTAR: What will happen to me? I haven't anything. Poor Martha—

KAREN: She was very good to you; she was good to us all.

MRS. MORTAR: Oh, I know she was, Karen, and I was good to her too. I did everything I could. I—I haven't any place to go. [*After a few seconds of silence*] I'm afraid. It seems so queer—in the next room. [*Shivers.*]

KAREN: Don't be afraid.

MRS. MORTAR: It's different for you. You're young.

KAREN: Not any more.

[*The sound of the door-bell ringing.* MRS. MORTAR *jumps.* KAREN *doesn't move. It rings again.*]

MRS. MORTAR [*nervous*]: Who is it? [*The bell rings again*] Shall I answer it? [KAREN *shrugs*] I think we'd better. [*Exits down the hall through Center doors. Returns in a minute followed by* MRS. TILFORD's *maid,* AGATHA, *who stands in the door*] It's a woman. [*No answer*] It's a woman to see you, Karen. [*Getting no answer, she turns to* AGATHA] You can't come in now; we've had a—we've had trouble here.

AGATHA: Miss Karen, I've *got* to speak to you.

KAREN [*turns slowly, mechanically*]: Agatha.

AGATHA [*goes to* KAREN]: Please, Miss Karen. We've tried so hard to get you. I been phoning here all the time. Trying to get you. Phoning and phoning. Please, please let her come in. Just for a minute, Miss Karen. Please—

MRS. MORTAR: Who wants to come in here?

AGATHA: Mrs. Tilford. [*Looks at* KAREN] Don't you feel well? [KAREN *shakes her head*] You ain't mad at *me?*

MRS. MORTAR: That woman can't come in here. She caused all—

KAREN: I'm not mad at you, Agatha.

AGATHA: Can I—can I get you something?

KAREN: No.

AGATHA: You poor child. You look like you got a pain somewhere. [*Hesitates, takes* KAREN'*s hands*] I only came cause she's so bad off. She's got to see you, Miss Karen, she's just got to. She's been sittin' outside in the car, hoping you'd come out. She can't get Dr. Joe. He—he won't talk to her any more. I wouldn't a come—I always been on your side—but she's sick. If only you could see her, you'd let her come for just a minute.

KAREN: I couldn't do that, Agatha.

AGATHA: I don't blame you. But I had to tell you. She's old. It's going to kill her.

KAREN [*bitterly*]: Kill her? Where is Mrs. Tilford?

AGATHA: Outside.

KAREN: All right.

AGATHA [*presses* KAREN'*s arm*]: You always been a good girl. [*Hurriedly exits.*]

MRS. MORTAR: You going to allow that woman to come in here? With Martha lying there? How can you be so feelingless? [*She starts to cry*] I won't stay and see it. I won't have anything to do with it. I'll never let that woman— [*Rushes sobbing from the room.*]

[*A second after,* MRS. TILFORD *appears in the doorway Center. Her face, her walk, her voice have changed. She is feeble.*]

MRS. TILFORD: Karen, let me come in.

[*Without turning,* KAREN *bows her head.* MRS. TILFORD *enters, stands staring at the floor.*]

KAREN: Why have you come here?

MRS. TILFORD: I had to come. [*Stretches out her hand to* KAREN, *who does not turn. She drops her hand*] I know *now;* I know it wasn't true.

KAREN: What?

MRS. TILFORD [*carefully*]: I know it wasn't true, Karen.

KAREN [*stares at her, shudders*]: You know it wasn't true? I don't care what you know. It doesn't matter any more. If that's what you had to say, you've said it. Go away.

MRS. TILFORD [*puts her hand to her throat*]: I've *got* to tell you.

KAREN: I don't want to hear you.

MRS. TILFORD: Last Tuesday Mrs. Wells found a bracelet in Rosalie's room. The bracelet had been hidden for several months. We found out that Rosalie had taken the bracelet from another girl, and that Mary— [*Closes her eyes*] that Mary knew that and used it to force Rosalie into saying that she had seen you and Miss Dobie together. I—I've talked to Mary. I've found out. [KAREN *suddenly begins to laugh, high and sharp*] Don't do that, Karen. I have only a little more to say, I've talked to Judge Potter. He will make all arrangements. There will be a public apology and an explanation. The damage suit will be paid to you in full and—and any more that you will be kind enough to take from me. I—I must see that you won't suffer any more.

KAREN: We're not going to suffer any more. Martha is dead. [MRS. TILFORD *gasps, shakes her head as though to shake off the truth, feebly falls into a chair, and covers her face.* KAREN *watches her for a minute*] So you've come here to relieve your conscience? Well, I won't be your confessor. It's choking you, is it? [*Violently*] And you want to stop the choking, don't you? You've done a wrong and you have to right that wrong or you can't rest your head again. You want to be "just," don't you, and you wanted us to help you be just? You've come to the wrong place for help. You want to be a "good" woman again, don't you? [*Bitterly*] Oh, I know. You told us that night you had to do what you did. Now you "have" to do this. A public apology and money paid, and you can sleep again and eat again. That done and there'll be peace for you. You're old, and the old are callous. Ten, fifteen years left for you. But what of me? It's a whole life for me. A whole God-damned life. [*Suddenly quiet, points to door Right*] And what of her?

MRS. TILFORD [*she is crying*]: You are still living.

KAREN: Yes. I guess so.

MRS. TILFORD [*with a tremendous effort to control herself*]: I didn't come here to relieve myself. I swear to God I didn't. I came to try—to try anything. I knew there wasn't any relief for me, Karen, and that there never would be again. [*Tensely*] But what I am or why I came doesn't matter. The only thing that matters is you and— You, now.

KAREN: There's nothing for me.

MRS. TILFORD: Oh, let's try to make something for you. You're young and I—I can help you.

KAREN [*smiles*]: You can help me?

MRS. TILFORD [*with great feeling*]: Take whatever I can give you. Take it for yourself and use it for yourself. It won't bring me peace, if that's what's worrying you. [*Smiles*] Those ten or fifteen years you talk about! They will be bad years.

KAREN: I'm tired, Mrs. Tilford. [*Almost tenderly*] You will have a hard time ahead, won't you?

MRS. TILFORD: Yes.

KAREN: Mary?

MRS. TILFORD: I don't know.

KAREN: You can send her away.

MRS. TILFORD : No. I could never do that. Whatever she does, it must be to me and no one else. She's— she's—

KAREN: Yes. Your very own, to live with the rest of your life. [*For a moment she watches* MRS. TILFORD'S *face*] It's over for me now, but it will never end for you. She's harmed us both, but she's harmed you more, I guess. [*Sits down beside* MRS. TILFORD] I'm sorry.

MRS. TILFORD [*clings to her*]: Then you'll try for yourself.

KAREN: All right.

MRS. TILFORD: You and Joe.

KAREN: No. We're not together anymore.

MRS. TILFORD [*looks up at her*]: Did I do that, too?

KAREN: I don't think anyone did anything, any more.

MRS. TILFORD [*makes a half-movement to rise*]: I'll go to him right away.

KAREN: No, it's better now the way it is.

MRS. TILFORD: But he must know what I know, Karen. You must go back to him.

KAREN [*smiles*]: No, not any more.

MRS. TILFORD : You must, you must— [*Sees her face, hesitates*] Perhaps later, Karen?

KAREN: Perhaps.

MRS. TILFORD [*after a moment in which they both sit silent*]: Come away from here now, Karen. [KAREN *shakes her head*] You can't stay with— [*Moves her hand toward door Right.*]

KAREN: When she is buried, then I will go.

MRS. TILFORD: You'll be all right?

KAREN: I'll be all right, I suppose. Good-bye, now.

[*They both rise.* MRS. TILFORD *speaks, pleadingly.*]

MRS. TILFORD: You'll let me help you? You'll let me try?

KAREN: Yes, if it will make you feel better.

MRS. TILFORD [*with great feeling*]: Oh, yes, oh, yes, Karen.

[*Unconsciously* KAREN *begins to walk toward the window.*]

KAREN [*suddenly*]: Is it nice out?

MRS. TILFORD: It's been cold. [KAREN *opens the window slightly, sits on the ledge.* MRS. TILFORD *with surprise*] It seems a little warmer, now.

KAREN: It feels very good.

[*They smile at each other.*]

MRS. TILFORD: You'll write me some time?

KAREN: If I ever have anything to say. Good-bye, now.

MRS. TILFORD: You will have. I know it. Good-bye, my dear. [KAREN *smiles, shakes her head as* MRS. TILFORD *exits. She does not turn, but a minute later she raises her hand.*]

KAREN: Good-bye.

CURTAIN

SAMUEL BECKETT

Samuel Barclay Beckett (1906–1989) was born in Dublin into a prosperous Anglo-Irish family. His parents were strictly Protestant, but Beckett lost his faith, and as a young man he abandoned religion for a vision of a universe of blind chance. Beckett's parents were not affectionate, and his mother and father lived separate lives in the same household. Beckett had love/hate relationships with both of them. His father was often not at home and seldom saw his son. Beckett claimed that his father beat him, but it was really his mother who used corporal punishment to curb his stubbornness. Of his mother, he wrote to a friend, "I am whatever her savage loving has made me." This family life may account for his disparaging portrayals of marriage, particularly his negative images of women, in his fiction and plays.

mistake

As an adult Beckett was capable of compassion and generosity, but when he attended Trinity College, Dublin, he was known for being scholarly and standoffish. After graduating, Beckett traveled to Paris, where he worked as a teacher of English at the École Normale. Once there, he joined the literary avant-garde and was introduced to James Joyce (1882–1941), who included him in his circle of friends. Joyce was then writing the novel *Finnegan's Wake,* and Beckett assisted in translating some of its "Anna Livia Plurabelle" sections into French. Years later, he again briefly helped Joyce with the manuscript, which was not published until 1939.

Beckett was deeply influenced by Joyce's prose style, his use of parody and satire, his love for punning, and his distortions of words and phrases. He was also influenced by the French writer Marcel Proust (1871–1922), and in 1931 Beckett wrote a study of Proust's *Remembrance of Things Past* (1913–1927).

Beckett briefly returned to Dublin to teach at Trinity College, but after 1932, he chose to live as an expatriate in France, making Paris his primary residence. He became so immersed in French culture that he composed many of his works in French rather than in English, including *Waiting For Godot* and *Endgame.* During World War II, Beckett remained in France, endured the Nazi occupation, and worked for the French Resistance until 1943. Then he moved to an unoccupied zone, where he lived austerely, working in a small agricultural village in southeastern France until the war was over. The wartime experience deeply unsettled him, and his works reflect the devastation, cultural confusion, and bleak expectations that followed World War II.

Beckett's first love was not theater but fiction: "Theater for me, " he wrote, "is mainly recreation from working on the novel." But in whatever genre he wrote, Beckett's view of the human condition was enigmatic and intense: He was by nature private, taciturn, and austere, and his worldview was grim. His plays and novels are invariably about unhappy people who are difficult to comprehend. When Hamm, the central character of *Endgame,* asks Clov, "Did you ever have an instant of happiness?"; Clov replies, "Not to my knowledge." When

Hamm says, "You weep, and weep, for nothing, so as not to laugh, and little by little . . . you begin to grieve," he may be speaking for Beckett.

Beckett's use of language links him with a nonfigurative style pioneered by Gertrude Stein. Characters in a Beckett play often speak in everyday language, without colorful expressions and shading of imagery. The dialogue consists mainly of staccato sentences, often based on a question-and-answer format, as in this example from *Endgame:*

NAGG: I've lost me tooth.
NELL: When?
NAGG: I had it yesterday.
NELL [*elegiac*]: Ah yesterday. [*They turn painfully towards each other.*]
NAGG: Can you see me?
NELL: Hardly. And you?
NAGG: What?

Another of his stylistic language patterns is the stop and start, separated by a pause:

HAMM: I feel a little queer.
[*Pause.*]
Clov!
CLOV: Yes.
HAMM: Have you not had enough?
CLOV: Yes!
[*Pause.*]
Of what?
HAMM: Of this . . . this . . . thing.
CLOV: I always had.
[*Pause.*]
Not you?
HAMM [*gloomily*]: Then there's no reason for it to change.
CLOV: It may end.
[*Pause.*]
All life long the same questions, the same answers.

The stark simplicity leaves some viewers confused; others find poetry in exchanges such as these.

Waiting for Godot, Beckett's first play, successfully premiered in 1953 in Paris, where it shocked some audiences because of its stark minimalism. It aroused similar reactions when it was produced to sell-out audiences in London (in English) in 1955. In the United States, *Waiting for Godot* was first produced in Miami in 1956 and failed; a few months later it was a great success on Broadway.

Because of its mixture of humor and despair, Beckett subtitled *Waiting for Godot* "a tragicomedy." The play's sparse setting includes only a road and tree, and the action is nearly static. The play opens with the appearance of two tramps, Estragon (called Gogo) and Vladimir (called Didi), who superficially resemble characters from film comedy—Charles Chaplin's Little Tramp, Laurel and Hardy, or Buster Keaton. Gogo and Didi, a couple for fifty years, are waiting for the imminent arrival of Mr. Godot. The waiting continues when they are told by a young boy, Godot's messenger, that Godot will not come that day, but if they wait, he will surely arrive tomorrow. Having nothing to do and in despair, Estragon tries to hang himself but fails. The tramps are surprised by the appearance of another pair of travelers who are middle class: Pozzo, whose manner is burly and aggressive, and his servant, Lucky, whose manner is servile and humble. Lucky is tied to Pozzo by a rope tied around his neck, and Pozzo brandishes a whip. The pair are on a journey without a known destination. In the second act, Gogo and Didi awaken and begin the day chatting and waiting. Pozzo and Lucky reappear, but now Pozzo is blind and Lucky leads rather than follows. The play ends when Gogo says to Didi, "Well? Shall we go?" to which Didi answers, "Yes, let's go." But neither of them moves.

Krapp's Last Tape (1958) is a long monologue, written in English, in which Krapp, the play's only character, talks to himself and listens to recordings of himself that he has accumulated for forty-five years. Surrounded by his tapes, listening, Krapp comments disdainfully about his earlier self. "Just been listening to the stupid bastard I took myself for thirty years ago." The title of the play reflects Beckett's scatological sense of humor, suggesting degeneracy of Krapp's mind and the hopelessness of his life. As an allegory of modern life, the play portrays Beckett's vision of the irrationality and disorientation of ordinary life. As with most of Beckett's characters, who are usually misfits or outcasts, Krapp's speech is built on repetition and discontinuity. The play may also be a response to Maurice Maeterlinck (1862–1949), the French playwright, who advocated a new drama accentuating thought rather than action, something to bridge the gap between the poetic expression of the text and the actor portraying the character. Maeterlinck said in his essay "The Tragic in Daily Life" (1896), "I have come to believe that an old man sitting in his armchair, simply waiting by his lamp, listening unconsciously to all the eternal laws which reign around his house. . . . I have come to believe that this unmoving old man is living in reality a deeper, more human and more universal life than the lover who strangles his mistress, [or] the captain who wins victory." Beckett's static character in *Krapp's Last Tape* seems to prove Maeterlinck's point that the essence of drama lies in its depiction of mind and feeling rather than action and crisis.

Happy Days (1962), also written in English and first performed in Greenwich Village, is one of Beckett's marriage plays. Its central characters are a wife and husband who simply endure each other's company. The setting is simple: they appear to live in a desert, and in Act I, Winnie is buried in a mound of sand, talking nonstop while her husband, Willie, sits off to the side where she can see him. He appears to be listening and occasionally contributes a few words to the conversation. In Act II, Winnie is buried up to her neck in sand, and Willie is absent. She rattles on because she fears that if she stops the world will end. Then Willie, dressed in morning clothes, appears and crawls towards Winnie, while she sings the lyric of a popular tune ending, "Every touch of fingers/Tells me what I know,/Says for you,/It's true,/You love me so!"

In *Play* (1963), three characters appear onstage encased in three funeral urns from which only their heads show. Their heads face forward, rigidly held by the neck of each urn. In this position, the characters recite all of the dialogue twice.

Not I (1972) is a Beckett play that resembles a surrealist painting. The stage is bare except for a large mouth that hovers in air, from which is heard the voice of a woman who begins speaking before the curtain rises and continues speaking after it comes down. This disembodied female voice, Mouth, talks nonstop, describing her life from birth to age seventy. Section 1 begins with Mouth saying, " . . . out . . . into this world . . . this world . . . tiny little thing . . . before its time . . . in a godfor—. . .what?" Section 4 ends with Mouth saying, "April morning . . . face in the grass . . . nothing but larks . . . pick it up—" Downstage from Mouth, stands Auditor, a mysterious, sexless figure who may or may not be listening. Auditor makes four gestures in the entire play, which serve as divisions. The title is derived from the fact that Mouth refers to herself as "she," and not "I."

Beckett wrote *That Time* (1974) about a white-haired character named Listener, whose face is all that the audience sees. He sits and listens to his inner life talk to his outer life. Like Krapp in *Krapp's Last Tape,* who listens to tape recordings of himself, Listener hears his past life repeated until he seems to achieve a smile that may indicate a sense of serenity.

Rockaby (1979) is another one-character play, in which a lonely woman, W, sits in a slowly moving rocking chair. She is dressed in a black sequined evening dress and wears a frivolous hat. As she rocks, W listens to the voice of V, which may be her inner life speaking, until she falls asleep.

Plays that Beckett wrote in the final decade of his life include *Footfalls* (1981), in which a woman in her forties, named May, paces the stage and talks to her ninety-year-old (offstage) mother; and *Catastrophe* (1982), dedicated to Vaclav Havel, the Czech playwright, a sketch about a dictatorial director instructing an actor, suggesting Havel's ordeal when he was imprisoned by the Czechoslovakian Communist regime for crimes against the state. (Ironically, Havel is now president of the Czech Republic.)

Beckett's stories and novels include *Murphy* (1932); the trilogy *Molloy* (1951), *Malone Dies* (1951), and *The Unnameable* (1953); *Watt* (1953); *From an Abandoned Work* (1956); *How It Is* (1964); *Imagination Dead Imagine* (1965); and *Company* (1970). Some of his short stories are collected in *More Pricks Than Kicks* (1934). He also wrote the radio play *All That Fall* (1957), the television plays *Ghost Trio* (1975) and *. . . but the clouds . . .* (1976), and a movie titled *Film* (1964), about a man fleeing from or being pursued by himself. *Film* was shot in New York City and provided Beckett with his only trip there, which he disliked. He never again visited the United States.

Beckett's *Endgame* (1957) premiered in London (in English). (It was paired with *Act Without Words* (1957), a short mime, which still accompanies it in text form but is rarely performed.) The play is plotless, its atmosphere is unsettling, and its tone is melancholy: "You're on earth, there's no cure for that!" says Hamm, the central character. Emotional conflict is created through the conversations of two sets of complementary characters, all disabled. The first is a married couple: Nagg, the husband/father, and Nell, the wife/mother, live in separate garbage cans, from which they talk at each other, without listening. They cannot leave the cans because they have no legs. The other couple is their son,

Hamm, and his caretaker, Clov. Hamm is blind, paralyzed, and confined to a wheelchair. He is cared for by Clov, who is lame and walks only with difficulty.

The action concerns Hamm's attempts to free himself from Nagg, Nell, and Clov. He is supposed to be an artist. Hamm tries to tell a story, but has great difficulty in sustaining a coherent narrative. He may, in fact, be telling the story of how Clov came to live with the family and became a kind of son to him, but one is never sure of his truthfulness or accuracy. To confound matters, his story is constantly being interrupted by his own lapses of memory and by comments from Nagg and Clov. At one point, Hamm complains, "There are days like that, one isn't inspired. [*Pause.*] Nothing you can do about it, just wait for it to come. [*Pause.*] No forcing, no forcing, it's fatal."

The garbage cans take on added symbolism of degeneration and death as Nagg is reduced to mumbling incoherently, unheard by Nell, who is dead. This unhappy couple are similar to Winnie and Willie, who were portrayed in *Happy Days.* Unhappy couples such these are, perhaps, derived from Beckett's memories of his parents, whom he did not like.

Clov, after saying that he will leave, finally makes his exit and is thanked by Hamm for his services. Hamm tries to finish his story, but the best he can do is to cover his head with a bloodstained handkerchief. The play ends in stalemate; a sly reference to the title *Endgame,* which refers to the final part of a chess game in which very few moves are available and a win or a draw is imminent.

Beckett's aim as a minimalist is to restore purity of art, design, and integrity. His idea is to strip away ornamentation and restore the power of the underlying structure. Consequently, in *Endgame* and in his other plays, there are few props, only basic lighting, no music, and few actors. In fact, as Beckett matured, he deliberately minimized the number of characters in his plays, and in the later plays there is often only a single character. His abstraction cuts away familiar ornamentations and leaves only bare essentials. In a Beckett play, there is no plot in the ordinary sense: Action occurs, but the formula of introduction, exposition, rising action, and climax is not observed. Like Proust and Joyce, Beckett was fond of allusion and wrote extensively in a stream of consciousness style. All of these literary and theatrical techniques link Beckett with the Theater of the Absurd and establish him as a master practitioner of the genre. Despite the difficulty of Beckett's work, he achieved a kind of cult status and was greatly admired for his daring style. He was awarded the Nobel Prize for Literature in 1969. Characteristically, he would not violate his code of privacy by accepting the award in Stockholm in person.

Beckett's influence can be seen in Harold Pinter, David Mamet, and Sam Shepard, whose plays share his vision of bleakness and disorientation that render ordinary life absurd. Pinter was befriended by Beckett, and he has publicly acknowledged his belief that Beckett was the finest playwright of his time.

Endgame

A Play in One Act

THE CHARACTERS
NAGG
NELL
HAMM
CLOV

Bare interior.

Grey light.

Left and right back, high up, two small windows, curtains drawn.

Front right, a door. Hanging near door, its face to wall, a picture.

Front left, touching each other, covered with an old sheet, two ashbins.

Center, in an armchair on castors, covered with an old sheet, HAMM.

Motionless by the door, his eyes fixed on HAMM, CLOV. *Very red face.*

Brief tableau.

CLOV *goes and stands under window left. Stiff, staggering walk. He looks up at window left. He turns and looks at window right. He goes and stands under window right. He looks up at window right. He turns and looks at window left. He goes out, comes back immediately with a small step-ladder, carries it over and sets it down under window left, gets up on it, draws back curtain. He gets down, takes six steps (for example) towards window right, goes back for ladder, carries it over and sets it down under window right, gets up on it, draws back curtain. He gets down, takes three steps towards window left, goes back for ladder, carries it over and sets it down under window left, gets up on it, looks out of window. Brief laugh. He gets down, takes one step towards window right, goes back for ladder, carries it over and sets it down under window right, gets up on it, looks out of window. Brief laugh. He gets down, goes with ladder towards ashbins, halts, turns, carries back ladder and sets it down under window right, goes to ashbins, removes sheet covering them, folds it over his arm. He raises one lid, stoops and looks into bin. Brief laugh. He closes lid. Same with other bin. He goes to* HAMM, *removes sheet covering him, folds it over his arm. In a dressing-gown, a stiff toque on his head, a large bloodstained handkerchief over his face, a whistle hanging from his neck, a rug over his knees, thick socks on his feet,* HAMM *seems to be asleep.* CLOV *looks him over. Brief laugh. He goes to door, halts, turns towards auditorium.*

CLOV [*fixed gaze, tonelessly*]: Finished, it's finished, nearly finished, it must be nearly finished.

[*Pause.*]

Grain upon grain, one by one, and one day, suddenly, there's a heap, a little heap, the impossible heap.

[*Pause.*]

I can't be punished any more.

[*Pause.*]

I'll go now to my kitchen, ten feet by ten feet by ten feet, and wait for him to whistle me.

[*Pause.*]

Nice dimensions, nice proportions, I'll lean on the table, and look at the wall, and wait for him to whistle me.

[*He remains a moment motionless, then goes out. He comes back immediately, goes to window right, takes up the ladder and carries it out. Pause.* HAMM *stirs. He yawns under the handkerchief. He removes the handkerchief from his face. Very red face. Black glasses.*]

HAMM: Me—

[*he yawns*]

—to play.

[*He holds the handkerchief spread out before him.*]

Old stancher!

[*He takes off his glasses, wipes his eyes, his face, the glasses, puts them on again, folds the handkerchief and puts it back neatly in the breast-pocket of his dressing-gown. He clears his throat, joins the tips of his fingers.*]

Can there be misery—

[*he yawns*]

—loftier than mine? No doubt. Formerly. But now?

[*Pause.*]

My father?

[*Pause.*]

My mother?

[*Pause.*]

My . . . dog?

[*Pause.*]

Oh I am willing to believe they suffer as much as such creatures can suffer. But does that mean their sufferings equal mine? No doubt.

[*Pause.*]

No, all is a—

[*he yawns*]

—bsolute,

[*proudly*]

the bigger a man is the fuller he is.

[*Pause. Gloomily.*]

And the emptier.

[*He sniffs.*]

Clov!

[*Pause.*]

No, alone.

[*Pause.*]

What dreams! Those forests!

[*Pause.*]

Enough, it's time it ended, in the shelter too.

[*Pause.*]

And yet I hesitate, I hesitate to . . . to end. Yes, there it is, it's time it ended and yet I hesitate to—

[*he yawns*]

—to end.

[*Yawns.*]

God, I'm tired, I'd be better off in bed.

[*He whistles. Enter* CLOV *immediately. He halts beside the chair.*]

You pollute the air!

[*Pause.*]

Get me ready, I'm going to bed.
CLOV: I've just got you up.
HAMM: And what of it?
CLOV: I can't be getting you up and putting you to bed every five minutes, I have things to do.

[*Pause.*]

HAMM: Did you ever see my eyes?
CLOV: No.
HAMM: Did you never have the curiosity, while I was sleeping, to take off my glasses and look at my eyes?
CLOV: Pulling back the lids?

[*Pause.*]

No.
HAMM: One of these days I'll show them to you.

[*Pause.*]

It seems they've gone all white.

[*Pause.*]

What time is it?
CLOV: The same as usual.
HAMM: [*gesture towards window right*]: Have you looked?
CLOV: Yes.
HAMM: Well?
CLOV: Zero.
HAMM: It'd need to rain.
CLOV: It won't rain.

[*Pause.*]

HAMM: Apart from that, how do you feel?

CLOV: I don't complain.
HAMM: You feel normal?
CLOV [*irritably*]: I tell you I don't complain.
HAMM: I feel a little queer.

[*Pause.*]

Clov!
CLOV: Yes.
HAMM: Have you not had enough?
CLOV: Yes!

[*Pause.*]

Of what?
HAMM: Of this . . . this . . . thing.
CLOV: I always had.

[*Pause.*]

Not you?
HAMM [*gloomily*]: Then there's no reason for it to change.
CLOV: It may end.

[*Pause.*]

All life long the same questions, the same answers.
HAMM: Get me ready.

[CLOV *does not move.*]

Go and get the sheet.

[CLOV *does not move.*]

Clov!
CLOV: Yes.
HAMM: I'll give you nothing more to eat.
CLOV: Then we'll die.
HAMM: I'll give you just enough to keep you from dying. You'll be hungry all the time.
CLOV: Then we won't die.

[*Pause.*]

I'll go and get the sheet.

[*He goes towards the door.*]

HAMM: No!

[CLOV *halts.*]

I'll give you one biscuit per day.

[*Pause.*]

One and a half.

[*Pause.*]

Why do you stay with me?
CLOV: Why do you keep me?
HAMM: There's no one else.
CLOV: There's nowhere else.

[*Pause.*]

HAMM: You're leaving me all the same.
CLOV: I'm trying.
HAMM: You don't love me.
CLOV: No.
HAMM: You loved me once.
CLOV: Once!
HAMM: I've made you suffer too much.

[*Pause.*]

Haven't I?
CLOV: It's not that.
HAMM [*shocked*]: I haven't made you suffer too much?
CLOV: Yes!
HAMM [*relieved*]: Ah you gave me a fright!

[*Pause. Coldly.*]

Forgive me.

[*Pause. Louder.*]

I said, Forgive me.
CLOV: I heard you.

[*Pause.*]

Have you bled?

HAMM: Less.

[*Pause.*]

Is it not time for my pain-killer?
CLOV: No.

[*Pause.*]

HAMM: How are your eyes?
CLOV: Bad.
HAMM: How are your legs?

CLOV: Bad.
HAMM: But you can move.
CLOV: Yes.
HAMM [*violently*]: Then move!

[CLOV *goes to back wall, leans against it with his forehead and hands.*]

Where are you?
CLOV: Here.
HAMM: Come back!

[CLOV *returns to his place beside the chair.*]

Where are you?
CLOV: Here.
HAMM: Why don't you kill me?
CLOV: I don't know the combination of the cupboard.

[*Pause.*]

HAMM: Go and get two bicycle-wheels.
CLOV: There are no more bicycle-wheels.
HAMM: What have you done with your bicycle?
CLOV: I never had a bicycle.
HAMM: The thing is impossible.
CLOV: When there were still bicycles I wept to have one. I crawled at your feet. You told me to go to hell. Now there are none.
HAMM: And your rounds? When you inspected my paupers. Always on foot?
CLOV: Sometimes on horse.

[*The lid of one of the bins lifts and the hands of* NAGG *appear, gripping the rim. Then his head emerges. Nightcap. Very white face.* NAGG *yawns, then listens.*]

I'll leave you, I have things to do.

HAMM: In your kitchen?
CLOV: Yes.
HAMM: Outside of here it's death.

[*Pause.*]

All right, be off.

[*Exit* CLOV. *Pause.*]

We're getting on.
NAGG: Me pap!
HAMM: Accursed progenitor!
NAGG: Me pap!
HAMM: The old folks at home! No decency left! Guzzle, guzzle, that's all they think of.

[*He whistles. Enter* CLOV. *He halts beside the chair.*]

Well! I thought you were leaving me.
CLOV: Oh not just yet, not just yet.
NAGG: Me pap!
HAMM: Give him his pap.
CLOV: There's no more pap.
HAMM [*to* NAGG]: Do you hear that? There's no more pap. You'll never get any more pap.
NAGG: I want me pap!
HAMM: Give him a biscuit.

[*Exit* CLOV.]

Accursed fornicator! How are your stumps?
NAGG: Never mind me stumps.

[*Enter* CLOV *with biscuit.*]

CLOV: I'm back again, with the biscuit.

[*He gives biscuit to* NAGG *who fingers it, sniffs it.*]

NAGG [*plaintively*]: What is it?
CLOV: Spratt's medium.
NAGG [*as before*]: It's hard! I can't!
HAMM: Bottle him!

[CLOV *pushes* NAGG *back into the bin, closes the lid.*]

CLOV [*returning to his place beside the chair*]: If age but knew!
HAMM: Sit on him!
CLOV: I can't sit.
HAMM: True. And I can't stand.
CLOV: So it is.
HAMM: Every man his speciality.

[*Pause.*]

No phone calls?

[*Pause.*]

Don't we laugh?
CLOV [*after reflection*]: I don't feel like it.
HAMM [*after reflection*]: Nor I.

[*Pause.*]

Clov!
CLOV: Yes.
HAMM: Nature has forgotten us.
CLOV: There's no more nature.
HAMM: No more nature! You exaggerate.

CLOV: In the vicinity.
HAMM: But we breathe, we change! We lose our hair, our teeth! Our bloom! Our ideals!
CLOV: Then she hasn't forgotten us.
HAMM: But you say there is none.
CLOV [*sadly*]: No one that ever lived ever thought so crooked as we.
HAMM: We do what we can.
CLOV: We shouldn't.

[*Pause.*]

HAMM: You're a bit of all right, aren't you?
CLOV: A smithereen.

[*Pause.*]

HAMM: This is slow work.

[*Pause.*]

Is it not time for my pain-killer?
CLOV: No.

[*Pause.*]

I'll leave you, I have things to do.
HAMM: In your kitchen?
CLOV: Yes.
HAMM: What, I'd like to know.
CLOV: I look at the wall.
HAMM: The wall! And what do you see on your wall? Mene, mene? Naked bodies?
CLOV: I see my light dying.
HAMM: Your light dying! Listen to that! Well, it can die just as well here, *your* light. Take a look at me and then come back and tell me what you think of *your* light.

[*Pause.*]

CLOV: You shouldn't speak to me like that.

[*Pause.*]

HAMM [*coldly*]: Forgive me.

[*Pause. Louder.*]

I said, Forgive me.
CLOV: I heard you.

[*The lid of* NAGG's *bin lifts. His hands appear, gripping the rim. Then his head emerges. In his mouth the biscuit. He listens.*]

HAMM: Did your seeds come up?
CLOV: No.
HAMM: Did you scratch round them to see if they had sprouted?
CLOV: They haven't sprouted.
HAMM: Perhaps it's still too early.
CLOV: If they were going to sprout they would have sprouted.

[*Violently.*]

They'll never sprout!

[*Pause.* NAGG *takes biscuit in his hand.*]

HAMM: This is not much fun.

[*Pause.*]

But that's always the way at the end of the day, isn't it, Clov?
CLOV: Always.
HAMM: It's the end of the day like any other day, isn't it, Clov?
CLOV: Looks like it.

[*Pause.*]

HAMM [*anguished*]: What's happening, what's happening?
CLOV: Something is taking its course.

[*Pause.*]

HAMM: All right, be off.

[*He leans back in his chair, remains motionless.* CLOV *does not move, heaves a great groaning sigh.* HAMM *sits up.*]

I thought I told you to be off.
CLOV: I'm trying.

[*He goes to door, halts.*]

Ever since I was whelped.

[*Exit* CLOV.]

HAMM: We're getting on.

[*He leans back in his chair, remains motionless.* NAGG *knocks on the lid of the other bin. Pause. He knocks harder. The lid lifts and the hands of* NELL *appear, gripping the rim. Then her head emerges. Lace cap. Very white face.*]

NELL: What is it, my pet?

[*Pause.*]

Time for love?
NAGG: Were you asleep?
NELL: Oh no!
NAGG: Kiss me.
NELL: We can't.
NAGG: Try.

[*Their heads strain towards each other, fail to meet, fall apart again.*]

NELL: Why this farce, day after day?

[*Pause.*]

NAGG: I've lost me tooth.
NELL: When?
NAGG: I had it yesterday.
NELL [*elegiac*]: Ah yesterday!

[*They turn painfully towards each other.*]

NAGG: Can you see me?
NELL: Hardly. And you?
NAGG: What?
NELL: Can you see me?
NAGG: Hardly.
NELL: So much the better, so much the better.
NAGG: Don't say that.

[*Pause.*]

Our sight has failed.
NELL: Yes.

[*Pause. They turn away from each other.*]

NAGG: Can you hear me?
NELL: Yes. And you?
NAGG: Yes.

[*Pause.*]

Our hearing hasn't failed.
NELL: Our what?
NAGG: Our hearing.
NELL: No.

[*Pause.*]

Have you anything else to say to me?
NAGG: Do you remember—
NELL: No.
NAGG: When we crashed on our tandem and lost our shanks.

[*They laugh heartily.*]

NELL: It was in the Ardennes.

[*They laugh less heartily.*]

NAGG: On the road to Sedan.

[*They laugh still less heartily.*]

Are you cold?
NELL: Yes, perished. And you?
NAGG: [*Pause.*]

I'm freezing.

[*Pause.*]

Do you want to go in?
NELL: Yes.
NAGG: Then go in.

[NELL *does not move.*]

Why don't you go in?
NELL: I don't know.

[*Pause.*]

NAGG: Has he changed your sawdust?
NELL: It isn't sawdust.

[*Pause. Wearily.*]

Can you not be a little accurate, Nagg?
NAGG: Your sand then. It's not important.
NELL: It is important.

[*Pause.*]

NAGG: It was sawdust once.
NELL: Once!
NAGG: And now it's sand.

[*Pause.*]

From the shore.

[*Pause. Impatiently.*]

Now it's sand he fetches from the shore.

NELL: Now it's sand.
NAGG: Has he changed yours?
NELL: No.
NAGG: Nor mine.

[*Pause.*]

I won't have it!

[*Pause. Holding up the biscuit.*]

Do you want a bit?
NELL: No.

[*Pause.*]

Of what?
NAGG: Biscuit. I've kept you half.

[*He looks at the biscuit. Proudly.*]

Three quarters. For you. Here.

[*He proffers the biscuit.*]

No?

[*Pause.*]

Do you not feel well?
HAMM [*wearily*]: Quiet, quiet, you're keeping me awake.

[*Pause.*]

Talk softer.

[*Pause.*]

If I could sleep I might make love. I'd go into the woods. My eyes would see . . . the sky, the earth. I'd run, run, they wouldn't catch me.

[*Pause.*]

Nature!

[*Pause.*]

There's something dripping in my head.

[*Pause.*]

A heart, a heart in my head.

[*Pause.*]

NAGG [*soft*]: Do you hear him? A heart in his head!

[*He chuckles cautiously.*]

NELL: One mustn't laugh at those things, Nagg. Why must you always laugh at them?
NAGG: Not so loud!
NELL [*without lowering her voice*]: Nothing is funnier than unhappiness, I grant you that. But—
NAGG [*shocked*]: Oh!
NELL: Yes, yes, it's the most comical thing in the world. And we laugh, we laugh, with a will, in the beginning. But it's always the same thing. Yes, it's like the funny story we have heard too often, we still find it funny, but we don't laugh any more.

[*Pause.*]

Have you anything else to say to me?
NAGG: No.
NELL: Are you quite sure?

[*Pause.*]

Then I'll leave you.
NAGG: Do you not want your biscuit?

[*Pause.*]

I'll keep it for you.

[*Pause.*]

I thought you were going to leave me.
NELL: I am going to leave you.
NAGG: Could you give me a scratch before you go?
NELL: No.

[*Pause.*]

Where?
NAGG: In the back.
NELL: No.

[*Pause.*]

Rub yourself against the rim.
NAGG: It's lower down. In the hollow.
NELL: What hollow?
NAGG: The hollow!

[*Pause.*]

Could you not?

[*Pause.*]

Yesterday you scratched me there.
NELL [*elegiac*]: Ah yesterday!
NAGG: Could you not?

[*Pause.*]

Would you like me to scratch you?

[*Pause.*]

Are you crying again?
NELL: I was trying.

[*Pause.*]

HAMM: Perhaps it's a little vein.

[*Pause.*]

NAGG: What was that he said?
NELL: Perhaps it's a little vein.
NAGG: What does that mean?

[*Pause.*]

That means nothing.

[*Pause.*]

Will I tell you the story of the tailor?
NELL: No.

[*Pause.*]

What for?
NAGG: To cheer you up.
NELL: It's not funny.
NAGG: It always made you laugh.

[*Pause.*]

The first time I thought you'd die.
NELL: It was on Lake Como.

[*Pause.*]

One April afternoon.

[*Pause.*]

Can you believe it?
NAGG: What?
NELL: That we once went out rowing on Lake Como.

[*Pause.*]

One April afternoon.
NAGG: We had got engaged the day before.
NELL: Engaged!
NAGG: You were in such fits that we capsized. By rights we should have been drowned.
NELL: It was because I felt happy.
NAGG [*indignant*]: It was not, it was not, it was my story and nothing else. Happy! Don't you laugh at it still? Every time I tell it. Happy!
NELL: It was deep, deep. And you could see down to the bottom. So white. So clean.
NAGG: Let me tell it again.

[RACONTEUR'*s voice.*]

An Englishman, needing a pair of striped trousers in a hurry for the New Year festivities, goes to his tailor who takes his measurements.

[TAILOR'*s voice.*]

"That's the lot, come back in four days, I'll have it ready." Good. Four days later.

[TAILOR'*s voice.*]

"So sorry, come back in a week, I've made a mess of the seat." Good, that's all right, a neat seat can be very ticklish. A week later.

[TAILOR'*s voice.*]

"Frightfully sorry, come back in ten days, I've made a hash of the crotch." Good, can't be helped, a snug crotch is always a teaser. Ten days later.

[TAILOR'*s voice.*]

"Dreadfully sorry, come back in a fortnight, I've made a balls of the fly." Good, at a pinch, a smart fly is a stiff proposition.

[*Pause. Normal voice.*]

I never told it worse.

[*Pause. Gloomy.*]

I tell this story worse and worse.

[*Pause.* RACONTEUR'*s voice.*]

Well, to make it short, the bluebells are blowing and he ballockses the buttonholes.

[CUSTOMER's *voice.*]

"God damn you to hell, Sir, no, it's indecent, there are limits! In six days, do you hear me, six days, God made the world. Yes Sir, no less Sir, the WORLD! And you are not bloody well capable of making me a pair of trousers in three months!"

[TAILOR's *voice, scandalized.*]

"But my dear Sir, my dear Sir, look—

[*disdainful gesture, disgustedly*]

—at the world—

[*pause*]

and look—

[*loving gesture, proudly*]

—at my TROUSERS!"

[*Pause. He looks at* NELL *who has remained impassive, her eyes unseeing, breaks into a high forced laugh, cuts it short, pokes his head towards* NELL, *launches his laugh again.*]

HAMM: Silence!

[NAGG *starts, cuts short his laugh.*]

NELL: You could see down to the bottom.
HAMM [*exasperated*]: Have you not finished? Will you never finish?

[*With sudden fury.*]

Will this never finish?

[NAGG *disappears into his bin, closes the lid behind him.* NELL *does not move. Frenziedly.*]

My kingdom for a nightman!

[*He whistles. Enter* CLOV.]

Clear away this muck! Chuck it in the sea!

[CLOV *goes to bins, halts.*]

NELL: So white.
HAMM: What? What's she blathering about!

[CLOV *stoops, takes* NELL's *hand, feels her pulse.*]

NELL [*to* CLOV]: Desert!

[CLOV *lets go her hand, pushes her back in the bin, closes the lid.*]

CLOV [*returning to his place beside the chair*]: She has no pulse.
HAMM: What was she drivelling about?
CLOV: She told me to go away, into the desert.
HAMM: Damn busybody! Is that all?
CLOV: No.
HAMM: What else?
CLOV: I didn't understand.
HAMM: Have you bottled her?
CLOV: Yes.
HAMM: Are they both bottled?
CLOV: Yes.
HAMM: Screw down the lids.

[CLOV *goes towards door.*]

Time enough.

[CLOV *halts.*]

My anger subsides, I'd like to pee.
CLOV [*with alacrity*]: I'll go and get the catheter.

[*He goes towards door.*]

HAMM: Time enough.

[CLOV *halts.*]

Give me my pain-killer.
CLOV: It's too soon.

[*Pause.*]

It's too soon on top of your tonic, it wouldn't act.
HAMM: In the morning they brace you up and in the evening they calm you down. Unless it's the other way round.

[*Pause.*]

That old doctor, he's dead naturally?
CLOV: He wasn't old.
HAMM: But he's dead?
CLOV: Naturally.

[*Pause.*]

You ask *me* that?

[*Pause.*]

HAMM: Take me for a little turn.

[CLOV *goes behind the chair and pushes it forward.*]

Not too fast!

[CLOV *pushes chair.*]

Right round the world!

[CLOV *pushes chair.*]

Hug the walls, then back to the center again.

[CLOV *pushes chair.*]

I was right in the center, wasn't I?
CLOV [*pushing*]: Yes.
HAMM: We'd need a proper wheel-chair. With big wheels. Bicycle wheels!

[*Pause.*]

Are you hugging?
CLOV [*pushing*]: Yes.
HAMM [*groping for wall*]: It's a lie! Why do you lie to me?
CLOV [*bearing closer to wall*]: There! There!
HAMM: Stop!

[CLOV *stops chair close to back wall.* HAMM *lays his hand against wall.*]

Old wall!

[*Pause.*]

Beyond is the . . . other hell.

[*Pause. Violently.*]

Closer! Closer! Up against!
CLOV: Take away your hand.

[HAMM *withdraws his hand.* CLOV *rams chair against wall.*]

There!

[HAMM *leans towards wall, applies his ear to it.*]

HAMM: Do you hear?

[*He strikes the wall with his knuckles.*]

Do you hear? Hollow bricks!

[*He strikes again.*]

All that's hollow!

[*Pause. He straightens up. Violently.*]

That's enough. Back!
CLOV: We haven't done the round.
HAMM: Back to my place!

[CLOV *pushes chair back to center.*]

Is that my place?
CLOV: Yes, that's your place.
HAMM: Am I right in the center?
CLOV: I'll measure it.
HAMM: More or less! More or less!
CLOV [*moving chair slightly*]: There!
HAMM: I'm more or less in the center?
CLOV: I'd say so.
HAMM: You'd say so! Put me right in the center!
CLOV: I'll go and get the tape.
HAMM: Roughly! Roughly!

[CLOV *moves chair slightly.*]

Bang in the center!
CLOV: There!

[*Pause.*]

HAMM: I feel a little too far to the left.

[CLOV *moves chair slightly.*]

Now I feel a little too far to the right.

[CLOV *moves chair slightly.*]

I feel a little too far forward.

[CLOV *moves chair slightly.*]

Now I feel a little too far back.

[CLOV *moves chair slightly.*]

Don't stay there,

[*i.e. behind the chair*]

you give me the shivers.

[CLOV *returns to his place beside the chair.*]

CLOV: If I could kill him I'd die happy.

[*Pause.*]

HAMM: What's the weather like?
CLOV: As usual.
HAMM: Look at the earth.
CLOV: I've looked.
HAMM: With the glass?
CLOV: No need of the glass.
HAMM: Look at it with the glass.
CLOV: I'll go and get the glass.

[*Exit* CLOV.]

HAMM: No need of the glass!

[*Enter* CLOV *with telescope.*]

CLOV: I'm back again, with the glass.

[*He goes to window right, looks up at it.*]

I need the steps.
HAMM: Why? Have you shrunk?

[*Exit* CLOV *with telescope.*]

I don't like that, I don't like that.

[*Enter* CLOV *with ladder, but without telescope.*]

CLOV: I'm back again, with the steps.

[*He sets down ladder under window right, gets up on it, realizes he has not the telescope, gets down.*]

I need the glass.

[*He goes towards door.*]

HAMM [*violently*]: But you have the glass!
CLOV [*halting, violently*]: No, I haven't the glass!

[*Exit* CLOV.]

HAMM: This is deadly.

[*Enter* CLOV *with telescope. He goes towards ladder.*]

CLOV: Things are livening up.

[*He gets up on ladder, raises the telescope, lets it fall.*]

I did it on purpose.

[*He gets down, picks up the telescope, turns it on auditorium.*]

I see . . . a multitude . . . in transports . . . of joy.

[*Pause.*]

That's what I call a magnifier.

[*He lowers the telescope, turns towards* HAMM.]

Well? Don't we laugh?
HAMM [*after reflection*]: I don't.
CLOV [*after reflection*]: Nor I.

[*He gets up on ladder, turns the telescope on the without.*]

Let's see.

[*He looks, moving the telescope.*]

Zero . . .

[*he looks*]

. . . zero.

[*he looks*]

. . . and zero.
HAMM: Nothing stirs. All is—
CLOV: Zer—
HAMM [*violently*]: Wait till you're spoken to!

[*Normal voice.*]

All is . . . all is . . . all is what?

[*Violently.*]

All is what?
CLOV: What all is? In a word? Is that what you want to know? Just a moment.

[*He turns the telescope on the without, looks, lowers the telescope, turns towards* HAMM.]

Corpsed.

[*Pause.*]

Well? Content?
HAMM: Look at the sea.
CLOV: It's the same.
HAMM: Look at the ocean!

[CLOV *gets down, takes a few steps towards window left, goes back for ladder, carries it over and sets it down under window left, gets up on it, turns the telescope on the without, looks at length. He starts, lowers the telescope, examines it, turns it again on the without.*]

CLOV: Never seen anything like that!
HAMM [*anxious*]: What? A sail? A fin? Smoke?
CLOV [*looking*]: The light is sunk.
HAMM [*relieved*]: Pah! We all knew that.
CLOV [*looking*]: There was a bit left.
HAMM: The base.
CLOV [*looking*]: Yes.
HAMM: And now?
CLOV [*looking*]: All gone.
HAMM: No gulls?
CLOV [*looking*]: Gulls!
HAMM: And the horizon? Nothing on the horizon?
CLOV [*lowering the telescope, turns towards* HAMM, *exasperated*]: What in God's name could there be on the horizon?

[*Pause.*]

HAMM: The waves, how are the waves?
CLOV: The waves?

[He *turns the telescope on the waves.*]

Lead.
HAMM: And the sun?
CLOV [*looking*]: Zero.
HAMM: But it should be sinking. Look again.
CLOV [*looking*]: Damn the sun.
HAMM: Is it night already then?
CLOV [*looking*]: No.
HAMM: Then what is it?
CLOV [*looking*]: Gray.

[*Lowering the telescope, turning towards* HAMM, *louder.*]

Gray!

[*Pause. Still louder.*]

GRRAY!

[*Pause. He gets down, approaches* HAMM *from behind, whispers in his ear.*]

HAMM [*starting*]: Gray! Did I hear you say gray?
CLOV: Light black. From pole to pole.
HAMM: You exaggerate.

[*Pause.*]

Don't stay there, you give me the shivers.

[CLOV *returns to his place beside the chair.*]

CLOV: Why this farce, day after day?
HAMM: Routine. One never knows.

[*Pause.*]

Last night I saw inside my breast. There was a big sore.
CLOV: Pah! You saw your heart.
HAMM: No, it was living.

[*Pause. Anguished.*]

Clov!
CLOV: Yes.
HAMM: What's happening?
CLOV: Something is taking its course.

[*Pause.*]

HAMM: Clov!
CLOV [*impatiently*]: What is it?
HAMM: We're not beginning to . . . to . . . mean something?
CLOV: Mean something? You and I, mean something!

[*Brief laugh.*]

Ah that's a good one!
HAMM: I wonder.

[*Pause.*]

Imagine if a rational being came back to earth, wouldn't he be liable to get ideas into his head if he observed us long enough.

[*Voice of* RATIONAL BEING.]

Ah, good, now I see what it is, yes, now I understand what they're at!

[CLOV *starts, drops the telescope and begins to scratch his belly with both hands. Normal voice.*]

And without going so far as that, we ourselves . . .

[*with emotion*]

. . . we ourselves . . . at certain moments . . .

[*Vehemently.*]

To think perhaps it won't all have been for nothing!
CLOV [*anguished, scratching himself*]: I have a flea!
HAMM: A flea! Are there still fleas?

CLOV: On me there's one.

[*Scratching.*]

Unless it's a crablouse.
HAMM [*very perturbed*]: But humanity might start from there all over again! Catch him, for the love of God!
CLOV: I'll go and get the powder.

[*Exit Clov.*]

HAMM: A flea! This is awful! What a day!

[*Enter* CLOV *with a sprinkling-tin.*]

CLOV: I'm back again, with the insecticide.
HAMM: Let him have it!

[CLOV *loosens the top of his trousers, pulls it forward and shakes powder into the aperture. He stoops, looks, waits, starts, frenziedly shakes more powder, stoops, looks, waits.*]

CLOV: The bastard!
HAMM: Did you get him?
CLOV: Looks like it.

[*He drops the tin and adjusts his trousers.*]

Unless he's laying doggo.
HAMM: Laying! Lying you mean. Unless he's *lying* doggo.
CLOV: Ah? One says lying? One doesn't say laying?
HAMM: Use your head, can't you. If he was laying we'd be bitched.
CLOV: Ah.

[*Pause.*]

What about that pee?
HAMM: I'm having it.
CLOV: Ah that's the spirit, that's the spirit!

[*Pause.*]

HAMM [*with ardour*]: Let's go from here, the two of us! South! You can make a raft and the currents will carry us away, far away, to other . . . mammals!
CLOV: God forbid!
HAMM: Alone, I'll embark alone! Get working on that raft immediately. Tomorrow I'll be gone for ever.
CLOV [*hastening towards door*]: I'll start straight away.
HAMM: Wait!

[CLOV *halts.*]

Will there be sharks, do you think?
CLOV: Sharks? I don't know. If there are there will be.

[*He goes towards door.*]

HAMM: Wait!

[CLOV *halts.*]

Is it not yet time for my pain-killer?
CLOV [*violently*]: No!

[*He goes towards door.*]

HAMM: Wait!

[CLOV *halts.*]

How are your eyes?
CLOV: Bad.
HAMM: But you can see.
CLOV: All I want.
HAMM: How are your legs?
CLOV: Bad.
HAMM: But you can walk.
CLOV: I come . . . and go.
HAMM: In my house.

[*Pause. With prophetic relish.*]

One day you'll be blind, like me. You'll be sitting there, a speck in the void, in the dark, for ever, like me.

[*Pause.*]

One day you'll say to yourself, I'm tired, I'll sit down, and you'll go and sit down. Then you'll say, I'm hungry, I'll get up and get something to eat. But you won't get up. You'll say, I shouldn't have sat down, but since I have I'll sit on a little longer, then I'll get up and get something to eat. But you won't get up and you won't get anything to eat.

[*Pause.*]

You'll look at the wall a while, then you'll say, I'll close my eyes, perhaps have a little sleep, after that I'll feel better, and you'll close them. And when you open them again there'll be no wall any more.

[*Pause.*]

Infinite emptiness will be all around you, all the resurrected dead of all the ages wouldn't fill it, and there you'll be like a little bit of grit in the middle of the steppe.

[*Pause.*]

Yes, one day you'll know what it is, you'll be like me, except that you won't have anyone with you, because you won't have had pity on anyone and because there won't be anyone left to have pity on.

[*Pause.*]

CLOV: It's not certain.

[*Pause.*]

And there's one thing you forget.
HAMM: Ah?
CLOV: I can't sit down.
HAMM [*impatiently*]: Well you'll lie down then, what the hell! Or you'll come to a standstill, simply stop and stand still, the way you are now. One day you'll say, I'm tired, I'll stop. What does the attitude matter?

[*Pause.*]

CLOV: So you all want me to leave you.
HAMM: Naturally.
CLOV: Then I'll leave you.
HAMM: You can't leave us.
CLOV: Then I won't leave you.

[*Pause.*]

HAMM: Why don't you finish us?

[*Pause.*]

I'll tell you the combination of the cupboard if you promise to finish me.
CLOV: I couldn't finish you.
HAMM: Then you won't finish me.

[*Pause.*]

CLOV: I'll leave you, I have things to do.
HAMM: Do you remember when you came here?
CLOV: No. Too small, you told me.
HAMM: Do you remember your father.
CLOV [*wearily*]: Same answer.

[*Pause.*]

You've asked me these questions millions of times.
HAMM: I love the old questions.

[*With fervour.*]

Ah the old questions, the old answers, there's nothing like them!

[*Pause.*]

It was I was a father to you.
CLOV: Yes.

[*He looks at* HAMM *fixedly.*]

You were that to me.
HAMM: My house a home for you.
CLOV: Yes.

[*He looks about him.*]

This was that for me.
HAMM [*proudly*]: But for me,

[*gesture towards himself*]

no father. But for Hamm,

[*gesture towards surroundings*]

no home.

[*Pause.*]

CLOV: I'll leave you.
HAMM: Did you ever think of one thing?
CLOV: Never.
HAMM: That here we're down in a hole.

[*Pause.*]

But beyond the hills? Eh? Perhaps it's still green. Eh?

[*Pause.*]

Flora! Pomona!

[*Ecstatically.*]

Ceres!

[*Pause.*]

Perhaps you won't need to go very far.
CLOV: I can't go very far.

[*Pause.*]

I'll leave you.
HAMM: Is my dog ready?
CLOV: He lacks a leg.
HAMM: Is he silky?
CLOV: He's a kind of Pomeranian.
HAMM: Go and get him.
CLOV: He lacks a leg.
HAMM: Go and get him!

[*Exit* CLOV.]

We're getting on.

[*Enter* CLOV *holding by one of its three legs a black toy dog.*]

CLOV: Your dogs are here.

[*He hands the dog to* HAMM *who feels it, fondles it.*]

HAMM: He's white, isn't he?
CLOV: Nearly.
HAMM: What do you mean, nearly? Is he white or isn't he?
CLOV: He isn't.

[*Pause.*]

HAMM: You've forgotten the sex.
CLOV [*vexed*]: But he isn't finished. The sex goes on at the end.

[*Pause.*]

HAMM: You haven't put on his ribbon.
CLOV [*angrily*]: But he isn't finished, I tell you! First you finish your dog and then you put on his ribbon!

[*Pause.*]

HAMM: Can he stand?
CLOV: I don't know.
HAMM: Try.

[*He hands the dog to* CLOV *who places it on the ground.*]

Well?
CLOV: Wait!

[*He squats down and tries to get the dog to stand on its three legs fails, lets it go. The dog falls on its side.*]

HAMM [*impatiently*]: Well?
CLOV: He's standing.
HAMM [*groping for the dog*]: Where? Where is he?

[CLOV *holds up the dog in a standing position.*]

CLOV: There.

[*He takes* HAMM*'s hand and guides it towards the dog's head.*]

HAMM [*his hand on the dog's head*]: Is he gazing at me?
CLOV: Yes.
HAMM [*proudly*]: As if he were asking me to take him for a walk?
CLOV: If you like.
HAMM [*as before*]: Or as if he were begging me for a bone.

[*He withdraws his hand.*]

Leave him like that, standing there imploring me.

[CLOV *straightens up. The dog falls on its side.*]

CLOV: I'll leave you.
HAMM: Have you had your visions?
CLOV: Less.
HAMM: Is Mother Pegg's light on?
CLOV: Light! How could anyone's light be on?
HAMM: Extinguished!
CLOV: Naturally it's extinguished. If it's not on it's extinguished.
HAMM: No, I mean Mother Pegg.
CLOV: But naturally she's extinguished!

[*Pause.*]

What's the matter with you today?
HAMM: I'm taking my course.

[*Pause.*]

Is she buried?
CLOV: Buried! Who would have buried her?
HAMM: You.
CLOV: Me! Haven't I enough to do without burying people?
HAMM: But you'll bury me.
CLOV: No I won't bury you.

[*Pause.*]

HAMM: She was bonny once, like a flower of the field.

[*With reminiscent leer.*]

And a great one for the men!
CLOV: We too were bonny—once. It's a rare thing not to have been bonny—once.

[*Pause.*]

HAMM: Go and get the gaff.

[CLOV *goes to door, halts.*]

CLOV: Do this, do that, and I do it. I never refuse. Why?
HAMM: You're not able to.
CLOV: Soon I won't do it any more.
HAMM: You won't be able to any more.

[*Exit* CLOV.]

Ah the creatures, the creatures, everything has to be explained to them.

[*Enter* CLOV *with gaff.*]

CLOV: Here's your gaff. Stick it up.

[*He gives the gaff to* HAMM *who, wielding it like a punt-pole, tries to move his chair.*]

HAMM: Did I move?
CLOV: No.

[HAMM *throws down the gaff.*]

HAMM: Go and get the oilcan.
CLOV: What for?
HAMM: To oil the castors.
CLOV: I oiled them yesterday.
HAMM: Yesterday! What does that mean? Yesterday!
CLOV [*violently*]: That means that bloody awful day, long ago, before this bloody awful day. I use the words you taught me. If they don't mean anything any more, teach me others. Or let me be silent.

[*Pause.*]

HAMM: I once knew a madman who thought the end of the world had come. He was a painter—and engraver. I had a great fondness for him. I used to go and see him, in the asylum. I'd take him by the hand and drag him to the window. Look! There! All that rising corn! And there! Look! The sails of the herring fleet! All that loveliness!

[*Pause.*]

He'd snatch away his hand and go back into his corner. Appalled. All he had seen was ashes.

[*Pause.*]

He alone had been spared.

[*Pause.*]

Forgotten.

[*Pause.*]

It appears the case is . . . was not so . . . so unusual.
CLOV: A madman? When was that?
HAMM: Oh way back, way back, you weren't in the land of the living.
CLOV: God be with the days!

[*Pause.* HAMM *raises his toque.*]

HAMM: I had a great fondness for him.

[*Pause. He puts on his toque again.*]

He was a painter—and engraver.
CLOV: There are so many terrible things.
HAMM: No, no, there are not so many now.

[*Pause.*]

Clov!
CLOV: Yes.
HAMM: Do you not think this has gone on long enough?
CLOV: Yes!

[*Pause.*]

What?
HAMM: This . . . this . . . thing.
CLOV: I've always thought so.

[*Pause.*]

You not?
HAMM [*gloomily*]: Then it's a day like any other day.
CLOV: As long as it lasts.

[*Pause.*]

All life long the same inanities.
HAMM: I can't leave you.
CLOV: I know. And you can't follow me.

[*Pause.*]

HAMM: If you leave me how shall I know?
CLOV [*briskly*]: Well you simply whistle me and if I don't come running it means I've left you.

[*Pause.*]

HAMM: You won't come and kiss me goodbye?
CLOV: Oh I shouldn't think so.

[*Pause.*]

HAMM: But you might be merely dead in your kitchen.
CLOV: The result would be the same.
HAMM: Yes, but how would I know, if you were merely dead in your kitchen?
CLOV: Well . . . sooner or later I'd start to stink.
HAMM: You stink already. The whole place stinks of corpses.
CLOV: The whole universe.
HAMM [*angrily*]: To hell with the universe.

[*Pause.*]

Think of something.
CLOV: What?
HAMM: An idea, have an idea.

[*Angrily.*]

A bright idea!
CLOV: Ah good.

[*He starts pacing to and fro, his eyes fixed on the ground, his hands behind his back. He halts.*]

The pains in my legs! It's unbelievable! Soon I won't be able to think any more.
HAMM: You won't be able to leave me.

[CLOV *resumes his pacing.*]

What are you doing?
CLOV: Having an idea.

[*He paces.*]

Ah!

[*He halts.*]

HAMM: What a brain!

[*Pause.*]

Well?
CLOV: Wait!

[*He meditates. Not very convinced.*]

Yes . . .

[*Pause. More convinced.*]

Yes!

[*He raises his head.*]

I have it! I set the alarm.

[*Pause.*]

HAMM: This is perhaps not one of my bright days, but frankly—
CLOV: You whistle me. I don't come. The alarm rings. I'm gone. It doesn't ring. I'm dead.

[*Pause.*]

HAMM: Is it working?

[*Pause. Impatiently.*]

The alarm, is it working?
CLOV: Why wouldn't it be working?
HAMM: Because it's worked too much.
CLOV: But it's hardly worked at all.
HAMM [*angrily*]: Then because it's worked too little!
CLOV: I'll go and see.

[*Exit* CLOV. *Brief ring of alarm off. Enter* CLOV *with alarm-clock. He holds it against* HAMM*'s ear and releases alarm. They listen to it ringing to the end. Pause.*]

Fit to wake the dead! Did you hear it?
HAMM: Vaguely.
CLOV: The end is terrific!
HAMM: I prefer the middle.

[*Pause.*]

Is it not time for my pain-killer?
CLOV: No!

[*He goes to door, turns.*]

I'll leave you.
HAMM: It's time for my story. Do you want to listen to my story.
CLOV: No.
HAMM: Ask my father if he wants to listen to my story.

[CLOV *goes to bins, raises the lid of* NAGG*'s, stoops, looks into it. Pause. He straightens up.*]

CLOV: He's asleep.

HAMM: Wake him.

[CLOV *stoops, wakes* NAGG *with the alarm. Unintelligible words.* CLOV *straightens up.*]

CLOV: He doesn't want to listen to your story.
HAMM: I'll give him a bon-bon.

[CLOV *stoops. As before.*]

CLOV: He wants a sugar-plum.
HAMM: He'll get a sugar-plum.

[CLOV *stoops. As before.*]

CLOV: It's a deal.

[*He goes towards door.* NAGG*'s hands appear, gripping the rim. Then the head emerges.* CLOV *reaches door, turns.*]

Do you believe in the life to come?
HAMM: Mine was always that.

[*Exit* CLOV.]

Got him that time!
NAGG: I'm listening.
HAMM: Scoundrel! Why did you engender me?
NAGG: I didn't know.
HAMM: What? What didn't you know?
NAGG: That it'd be you.

[*Pause.*]

You'll give me a sugar-plum?
HAMM: After the audition.
NAGG: You swear?
HAMM: Yes.
NAGG: On what?
HAMM: My honor.

[*Pause. They laugh heartily.*]

NAGG: Two.
HAMM: One.
NAGG: One for me and one for—
HAMM: One! Silence!

[*Pause.*]

Where was I?

[*Pause. Gloomily.*]

It's finished, we're finished.

[*Pause.*]

Nearly finished.

[*Pause.*]

There'll be no more speech.

[*Pause.*]

Something dripping in my head, ever since the fontanelles.

[*Stifled hilarity of* NAGG.]

Splash, splash, always on the same spot.

[*Pause.*]

Perhaps it's a little vein.

[*Pause.*]

A little artery.

[*Pause. More animated.*]

Enough of that, it's story time, where was I?

[*Pause. Narrative tone.*]

The man came crawling towards me, on his belly. Pale, wonderfully pale and thin, he seemed on the point of—

[*Pause. Normal tone.*]

No, I've done that bit.

[*Pause. Narrative tone.*]

I calmly filled my pipe—the meerschaum, lit it with . . . let us say a vesta, drew a few puffs. Aah!

[*Pause.*]

Well, what is it *you* want?

[*Pause.*]

It was an extra-ordinarily bitter day, I remember, zero by the thermometer. But considering it was Christmas Eve there was nothing . . . extra-ordinary about that. Seasonable weather, for once in a way.

[*Pause.*]

Well, what ill wind blows you my way? He raised his face to me, black with mingled dirt and tears.

[*Pause. Normal tone.*]

That should do it.

[*Narrative tone.*]

No no, don't look at me, don't look at me. He dropped his eyes and mumbled something, apologies I presume.

[*Pause.*]

I'm a busy man, you know, the final touches, before the festivities, you know what it is.

[*Pause. Forcibly.*]

Come on now, what is the object of this invasion?

[*Pause.*]

It was a glorious bright day, I remember, fifty by the heliometer, but already the sun was sinking down into the . . . down among the dead.

[*Normal tone.*]

Nicely put, that.

[*Narrative tone.*]

Come on now, come on, present your petition and let me resume my labors.

[*Pause. Normal tone.*]

There's English for you. Ah well . . .

[*Narrative tone.*]

It was then he took the plunge. It's my little one, he said. Tsstss, a little one, that's bad. My little boy, he said, as if the sex mattered. Where did he come from? He named the hole. A good half-day, on horse. What are you insinuating? That the place is still inhabited? No no, not a soul, except himself and the child—assuming he existed. I enquired about the situation at Kov, beyond the gulf. Not a sinner. Good. And you expect me to believe you have left your little one back there, all alone, and alive into the bargain? Come now!

[*Pause.*]

It was a howling wild day, I remember, a hundred by the anenometer. The wind was tearing up the dead pines and sweeping them . . . away.

[*Pause. Normal tone.*]

A bit feeble, that.

[*Narrative tone.*]

Come on, man, speak up, what is you want from me, I have to put up my holly.

[*Pause.*]

Well to make it short it finally transpired that what he wanted from me was . . . bread for his brat? Bread? But I have no bread, it doesn't agree with me. Good. Then perhaps a little corn?

[*Pause. Normal tone.*]

That should do it.

[*Narrative tone.*]

Corn, yes, I have corn, it's true, in my granaries. But use your head. I give you some corn, a pound, a pound and a half, you bring it back to your child and you make him—if he's still alive—a nice pot of porridge,

[NAGG *reacts*]

a nice pot and a half of porridge, full of nourishment. Good. The colors come back into his little cheeks—perhaps. And then?

[*Pause.*]

I lost patience.

[*Violently.*]

Use your head, can't you, use your head, you're on earth, there's no cure for that!

[*Pause.*]

It was an exceedingly dry day, I remember, zero by the hygrometer. Ideal weather, for my lumbago.

[*Pause. Violently.*]

But what in God's name do you imagine? That the earth will awake in spring? That the rivers and seas will run with fish again? That there's manna in heaven still for imbeciles like you?

[*Pause.*]

Gradually I cooled down, sufficiently at least to ask him how long he had taken on the way. Three whole days. Good. In what condition he had left the child. Deep in sleep.

[*Forcibly.*]

But deep in what sleep, deep in what sleep already?

[*Pause.*]

Well to make it short I finally offered to take him into my service. He had touched a chord. And then I imagined already that I wasn't much longer for this world.

[*He laughs. Pause.*]

Well?

[*Pause.*]

Well? Here if you were careful you might die a nice natural death, in peace and comfort.

[*Pause.*]

Well?

[*Pause.*]

In the end he asked me would I consent to take in the child as well—if he were still alive.

[*Pause.*]

It was the moment I was waiting for.

[*Pause.*]

Would I consent to take in the child . . .

[*Pause.*]

I can see him still, down on his knees, his hands flat on the ground, glaring at me with his mad eyes, in defiance of my wishes.

[*Pause. Normal tone.*]

I'll soon have finished with this story.

[*Pause.*]

Unless I bring in other characters.

[*Pause.*]

But where would I find them?

[*Pause.*]

Where would I look for them?

[*Pause. He whistles. Enter* CLOV.]

Let us pray to God.
NAGG: Me sugar-plum!
CLOV: There's a rat in the kitchen!
HAMM: A rat! Are there still rats?
CLOV: In the kitchen there's one.
HAMM: And you haven't exterminated him?
CLOV: Half. You disturbed us.
HAMM: He can't get away?
CLOV: No.
HAMM: You'll finish him later. Let us pray to God.
CLOV: Again!
NAGG: Me sugar-plum!
HAMM: God first!

[*Pause.*]

Are you right?
CLOV [*resigned*]: Off we go.
HAMM [*to* NAGG]: And you?
NAGG [*clasping his hands, closing his eyes in a gabble*]: Our Father which art—
HAMM: Silence! In silence! Where are your manners?

[*Pause.*]

Off we go.

[*Attitudes of prayer. Silence. Abandoning his attitude, discouraged.*]

Well?
CLOV [*abandoning his attitude*]: What a hope! And you?
HAMM: Sweet damn all!

[*To* NAGG.]

And you?
NAGG: Wait!

[*Pause. Abandoning his attitude.*]

Nothing doing!

HAMM: The bastard! He doesn't exist!

CLOV: Not yet.

NAGG: Me sugar-plum!

HAMM: There are no more sugar-plums!

[*Pause.*]

NAGG: It's natural. After all I'm your father. It's true if it hadn't been me it would have been someone else. But that's no excuse.

[*Pause.*]

Turkish Delight, for example, which no longer exists, we all know that, there is nothing in the world I love more. And one day I'll ask you for some, in return for a kindness, and you'll promise it to me. One must live with the times.

[*Pause.*]

Whom did you call when you were a tiny boy, and were frightened, in the dark? Your mother? No. Me. We let you cry. Then we moved you out of earshot, so that we might sleep in peace.

[*Pause.*]

I was asleep, as happy as a king, and you woke me up to have me listen to you. It wasn't indispensable, you didn't really need to have me listen to you. Besides I didn't listen to you.

[*Pause.*]

I hope the day will come when you'll really need to have me listen to you, and need to hear my voice, any voice.

[*Pause.*]

Yes, I hope I'll live till then, to hear you calling me like when you were a tiny boy, and were frightened, in the dark, and I was your only hope.

[*Pause.* NAGG *knocks on lid of* NELL*'s bin. Pause.*]

Nell!

[*Pause. He knocks, louder. Pause. Louder.*]

Nell!

[*Pause.* NAGG *sinks back into his bin, closes the lid behind him. Pause.*]

HAMM: Our revels now are ended.

[*He gropes for the dog.*]

The dog's gone.

CLOV: He's not a real dog, he can't go.

HAMM [*groping*]: He's not there.

CLOV: He's lain down.

HAMM: Give him up to me.

[CLOV *picks up the dog and gives it to* HAMM. HAMM *holds it in his arms. Pause.* HAMM *throws away the dog.*]

Dirty brute!

[CLOV *begins to pick up the objects lying on the ground.*]

What are you doing?

CLOV: Putting things in order.

[*He straightens up. Fervently.*]

I'm going to clear everything away!

[*He starts picking up again.*]

HAMM: Order!

CLOV [*straightening up*]: I love order. It's my dream. A world where all would be silent and still and each thing in its last place, under the last dust.

[*He starts picking up again.*]

HAMM [*exasperated*]: What in God's name do you think you are doing?

CLOV [*straightening up*]: I'm doing my best to create a little order.

HAMM: Drop it!

[CLOV *drops the objects he has picked up.*]

CLOV: After all, there or elsewhere.

[*He goes towards door.*]

HAMM [*irritably*]: What's wrong with your feet?

CLOV: My feet?

HAMM: Tramp! Tramp!

CLOV: I must have put on my boots.

HAMM: Your slippers were hurting you?

[*Pause.*]

CLOV: I'll leave you.
HAMM: No!
CLOV: What is there to keep me here?
HAMM: The dialogue.

[*Pause.*]

I've got on with my story.

[*Pause.*]

I've got on with it well.

[*Pause. Irritably.*]

Ask me where I've got to.
CLOV: Oh, by the way, your story?
HAMM [*surprised*]: What story?
CLOV: The one you've been telling yourself all your days.
HAMM: Ah you mean my chronicle?
CLOV: That's the one.

[*Pause.*]

HAMM [*angrily*]: Keep going, can't you, keep going!
CLOV: You've got on with it, I hope.
HAMM [*modestly*]: Oh not very far, not very far.

[*He sighs.*]

There are days like that, one isn't inspired.

[*Pause.*]

Nothing you can do about it, just wait for it to come.

[*Pause.*]

No forcing, no forcing, it's fatal.

[*Pause.*]

I've got on with it a little all the same.

[*Pause.*]

Technique, you know.

[*Pause. Irritably.*]

I say I've got on with it a little all the same.
CLOV [*admiringly*]: Well I never! In spite of everything you were able to get on with it!
HAMM [*modestly*]: Oh not very far, you know, not very far, but nevertheless, better than nothing.
CLOV: Better than nothing! Is it possible?
HAMM: I'll tell you how it goes. He comes crawling on his belly—
CLOV: Who?
HAMM: What?
CLOV: Who do you mean, he?
HAMM: Who do I mean! Yet another.
CLOV: Ah him! I wasn't sure.
HAMM: Crawling on his belly, whining for bread for his brat. He's offered a job as gardener. Before—

[CLOV *bursts out laughing.*]

What is there so funny about that?
CLOV: A job as gardener!
HAMM: Is that what tickles you?
CLOV: It must be that.
HAMM: It wouldn't be the bread?
CLOV: Or the brat.

[*Pause.*]

HAMM: The whole thing is comical, I grant you that. What about having a good guffaw the two of us together?
CLOV [*after reflection*]: I couldn't guffaw again today.
HAMM [*after reflection*]: Nor I.

[*Pause.*]

I continue then. Before accepting with gratitude he asks if he may have his little boy with him.
CLOV: What age?
HAMM: Oh tiny.
CLOV: He would have climbed the trees.
HAMM: All the little odd jobs.
CLOV: And then he would have grown up.
HAMM: Very likely.

[*Pause.*]

CLOV: Keep going, can't you, keep going!
HAMM: That's all. I stopped there.

[*Pause.*]

CLOV: Do you see how it goes on.
HAMM: More or less.
CLOV: Will it not soon be the end?
HAMM: I'm afraid it will.
CLOV: Pah! You'll make up another.
HAMM: I don't know.

[*Pause.*]

I feel rather drained.

[*Pause.*]

The prolonged creative effort.

[*Pause.*]

If I could drag myself down to the sea! I'd make a pillow of sand for my head and the tide would come.

CLOV: There's no more tide.

[*Pause.*]

HAMM: Go and see is she dead.

[CLOV *goes to bins, raises the lid of* NELL*'s, stoops, looks into it. Pause.*]

CLOV: Looks like it.

[*He closes the lid, straightens up.* HAMM *raises his toque. Pause. He puts it on again.*]

HAMM [*with his hand to his toque*]: And Nagg?

[CLOV *raises lid of* NAGG*'s bin, stoops, looks into it. Pause.*]

CLOV: Doesn't look like it.

[*He closes the lid, straightens up.*]

HAMM [*letting go his toque*]: What's he doing?

[CLOV *raises lid of* NAGG*'s bin, stoops, looks into it. Pause.*]

CLOV: He's crying.

[*He closes lid, straightens up.*]

HAMM: Then he's living.

[*Pause.*]

Did you ever have an instant of happiness?

CLOV: Not to my knowledge.

[*Pause.*]

HAMM: Bring me under the window.

[CLOV *goes towards chair.*]

I want to feel the light on my face.

[CLOV *pushes chair.*]

Do you remember, in the beginning, when you took me for a turn? You used to hold the chair too high. At every step you nearly tipped me out.

[*With senile quaver.*]

Ah great fun, we had, the two of us, great fun.

[*Gloomily.*]

And then we got into the way of it.

[CLOV *stops the chair under window right.*]

There already?

[*Pause. He tilts back his head.*]

Is it light?

CLOV: It isn't dark.

HAMM [*angrily*]: I'm asking you is it light.

CLOV: Yes.

[*Pause.*]

HAMM: The curtain isn't closed?

CLOV: No.

HAMM: What window is it?

CLOV: The earth.

HAMM: I knew it!

[*Angrily.*]

But there's no light there! The other!

[CLOV *pushes chair towards window left.*]

The earth!

[CLOV *stops the chair under window left.* HAMM *tilts back his head.*]

That's what I call light!

[*Pause.*]

Feels like a ray of sunshine.

[*Pause.*]

No?
CLOV: No.
HAMM: It isn't a ray of sunshine I feel on my face?
CLOV: No.

[*Pause.*]

HAMM: Am I very white?

[*Pause. Angrily.*]

I'm asking you am I very white!
CLOV: Not more so than usual.

[*Pause.*]

HAMM: Open the window.
CLOV: What for?
HAMM: I want to hear the sea.
CLOV: You wouldn't hear it.
HAMM: Even if you opened the window?
CLOV: No.
HAMM: Then it's not worth while opening it?
CLOV: No.
HAMM [*violently*]: Then open it!

[CLOV *gets up on the ladder, opens the window. Pause.*]

Have you opened it?
CLOV: Yes.

[*Pause.*]

HAMM: You swear you've opened it?
CLOV: Yes.

[*Pause.*]

HAMM: Well . . . !

[*Pause.*]

It must be very calm.

[*Pause. Violently.*]

I'm asking you is it very calm!
CLOV: Yes.
HAMM: It's because there are no more navigators.

[*Pause.*]

You haven't much conversation all of a sudden. Do you not feel well?
CLOV: I'm cold.
HAMM: What month are we?

[*Pause.*]

Close the window, we're going back.

[CLOV *closes the window, gets down, pushes the chair back to its place, remains standing behind it, head bowed.*]

Don't stay there, you give me the shivers!

[CLOV *returns to his place beside the chair.*]

Father!

[*Pause. Louder.*]

Father!

[*Pause.*]

Go and see did he hear me.

[CLOV *goes to* NAGG'*s bin, raises the lid, stoops. Unintelligible words.* CLOV *straightens up.*]

CLOV: Yes.
HAMM: Both times?

[CLOV *stoops. As before.*]

CLOV: Once only.
HAMM: The first time or the second?

[CLOV *stoops. As before.*]

CLOV: He doesn't know.
HAMM: It must have been the second.
CLOV: We'll never know.

[*He closes lid.*]

HAMM: Is he still crying?
CLOV: No.
HAMM: The dead go fast.

[*Pause.*]

What's he doing?
CLOV: Sucking his biscuit.
HAMM: Life goes on.

[CLOV *returns to his place beside the chair.*]

Give me a rug, I'm freezing.
CLOV: There are no more rugs.

[*Pause.*]

HAMM: Kiss me.

[*Pause.*]

Will you not kiss me?
CLOV: No.
HAMM: On the forehead.
CLOV: I won't kiss you anywhere.

[*Pause.*]

HAMM [*holding out his hand*]: Give me your hand at least.

[*Pause.*]

Will you not give me your hand?
CLOV: I won't touch you.

[*Pause.*]

HAMM: Give me the dog.

[CLOV *looks round for the dog.*]

No!
CLOV: Do you not want your dog?
HAMM: No.
CLOV: Then I'll leave you.
HAMM: [*head bowed, absently*]: That's right.

[CLOV *goes to door, turns.*]

CLOV: If I don't kill that rat he'll die.
HAMM [*as before*]: That's right.

[*Exit* CLOV. *Pause.*]

Me to play.

[*He takes out his handkerchief, unfolds it, holds it spread out before him.*]

We're getting on.

[*Pause.*]

You weep, and weep, for nothing, so as not to laugh, and little by little. . . . you begin to grieve.

[*He folds the handkerchief, puts it back in his pocket, raises his head.*]

All those I might have helped.

[*Pause.*]

Helped!

[*Pause.*]

Saved.

[*Pause.*]

Saved!

[*Pause.*]

The place was crawling with them!

[*Pause. Violently.*]

Use your head, can't you, use your head, you're on earth, there's no cure for that!

[*Pause.*]

Get out of here and love one another! Lick your neighbor as yourself!

[*Pause. Calmer.*]

When it wasn't bread they wanted it was crumpets.

[*Pause. Violently.*]

Out of my sight and back to your petting parties!

[*Pause.*]

All that, all that!

[*Pause.*]

Not even a real dog!

[*Calmer.*]

The end is in the beginning and yet you go on.

[*Pause.*]

Perhaps I could go on with my story, end it and begin another.

[*Pause.*]

Perhaps I could throw myself out on the floor.

[*He pushes himself painfully off his seat, falls back again.*]

Dig my nails into the cracks and drag myself forward with my fingers.

[*Pause.*]

It will be the end and there I'll be, wondering what can have brought it on and wondering what can have . . .

[*he hesitates*]

. . . why it was so long coming.

[*Pause.*]

There I'll be, in the old shelter, alone against the silence and . . .

[*he hesitates*]

. . . the stillness. If I can hold my peace, and sit quiet, it will be all over with sound, and motion, all over and done with.

[*Pause.*]

I'll have called my father and I'll have called my . . .

[*he hesitates*]

. . . my son. And even twice, or three times, in case they shouldn't have heard me, the first time, or the second.

[*Pause.*]

I'll say to myself, He'll come back.

[*Pause.*]

And then?

[*Pause.*]

And then?

[*Pause.*]

He couldn't, he has gone too far.

[*Pause.*]

And then?

[*Pause. Very agitated.*]

All kinds of fantasies! That I'm being watched! A rat! Steps! Breath held and then . . .

[*He breathes out.*]

Then babble, babble, words, like the solitary child who turns himself into children, two, three, so as to be together, and whisper together, in the dark.

[*Pause.*]

Moment upon moment, pattering down, like the millet grains of . . .

[*he hesitates*]

. . . that old Greek, and all life long you wait for that to mount up to a life.

[*Pause. He opens his mouth to continue, renounces.*]

Ah let's get it over!

[*He whistles. Enter* CLOV *with alarm-clock. He halts beside the chair.*]

What? Neither gone nor dead?
CLOV: In spirit only.
HAMM: Which?
CLOV: Both.
HAMM: Gone from me you'd be dead.
CLOV: And vice versa.
HAMM: Outside of here it's death!

[*Pause.*]

And the rat?
CLOV: He's got away.
HAMM: He can't go far.

[*Pause. Anxious.*]

Eh?
CLOV: He doesn't need to go far.

[*Pause.*]

HAMM: Is it not time for my pain-killer?
CLOV: Yes.
HAMM: Ah! At last! Give it to me! Quick!

[*Pause.*]

CLOV: There's no more pain-killer.

[*Pause.*]

HAMM [*appalled*]: Good. . . !

[*Pause.*]

No more pain-killer!
CLOV: No more pain-killer. You'll never get any more pain-killer.

[*Pause.*]

HAMM: But the little round box. It was full!
CLOV: Yes. But now it's empty. [*Pause.* CLOV *starts to move about the room. He is looking for a place to put down the alarm-clock.*]
HAMM [*soft*]: What'll I do?

[*Pause. In a scream.*]

What'll I do?

[CLOV *sees the picture, takes it down, stands it on the floor with its face to the wall, hangs up the alarm-clock in its place.*]

What are you doing?
CLOV: Winding up.
HAMM: Look at the earth.
CLOV: Again!
HAMM: Since it's calling to you.
CLOV: Is your throat sore?

[*Pause.*]

Would you like a lozenge?

[*Pause.*]

No.

[*Pause.*]

Pity.

[CLOV *goes, humming towards window right, halts before it, looks up at it.*]

HAMM: Don't sing.
CLOV [*turning towards* HAMM]: One hasn't the right to sing any more?
HAMM: No.
CLOV: Then how can it end?
HAMM: You want it to end?
CLOV: I want to sing.
HAMM: I can't prevent you.

[*Pause.* CLOV *turns towards window right.*]

CLOV: What did I do with that steps?

[*He looks around for ladder.*]

You didn't see that steps?

[*He sees it.*]

Ah, about time.

[*He goes towards window left.*]

Sometimes I wonder if I'm in my right mind. Then it passes over and I'm as lucid as before.

[*He gets up on ladder, looks out of window.*]

Christ, she's under water!

[*He looks.*]

How can that be?

[*He pokes forward his head, his hand above his eyes.*]

It hasn't rained.

[*He wipes the pane, looks. Pause.*]

Ah what a fool I am! I'm on the wrong side!

[*He gets down, takes a few steps towards window right.*]

Under water!

[*He goes back for ladder.*]

What a fool I am!

[*He carries ladder towards window right.*]

Sometimes I wonder if I'm in my right senses. Then it passes off and I'm as intelligent as ever.

[*He sets down ladder under window right, gets up on it, looks out of window. He turns towards* HAMM.]

Any particular sector you fancy? Or merely the whole thing?

HAMM: Whole thing.
CLOV: The general effect? Just a moment.

[*He looks out of window. Pause.*]

HAMM: Clov.
CLOV [*absorbed*]: Mmm.
HAMM: Do you know what it is?
CLOV [*as before*]: Mmm.
HAMM: I was never there.

[*Pause.*]

Clov!
CLOV [*turning towards* HAMM, *exasperated*]: What is it?
HAMM: I was never there.
CLOV: Lucky for you.

[*He looks out of window.*]

HAMM: Absent, always. It all happened without me. I don't know what's happened.

[*Pause.*]

Do you know what's happened?

[*Pause.*]

Clov!
CLOV [*turning towards* HAMM, *exasperated*]: Do you want me to look at this muckheap, yes or no?
HAMM: Answer me first.
CLOV: What?
HAMM: Do you know what's happened?
CLOV: When? Where?
HAMM [*violently*]: When! What's happened? Use your head, can't you! What has happened?
CLOV: What for Christ's sake does it matter?

[*He looks out of window.*]

HAMM: I don't know.

[*Pause.* CLOV *turns towards* HAMM.]

CLOV [*harshly*]: When old Mother Pegg asked you for oil for her lamp and you told her to get out to hell, you knew what was happening then, no?

[*Pause.*]

You know what she died of, Mother Pegg? Of darkness.
HAMM [*feebly*]: I hadn't any.
CLOV [*as before*]: Yes, you had.

[*Pause.*]

HAMM: Have you the glass?
CLOV: No, it's clear enough as it is.
HAMM: Go and get it.

[*Pause.* CLOV *casts up his eyes, brandishes his fists. He loses balance, clutches on to the ladder. He starts to get down, halts.*]

CLOV: There's one thing I'll never understand.

[*He gets down.*]

Why I always obey you. Can you explain that to me?
HAMM: No . . . Perhaps it's compassion.

[*Pause.*]

A kind of great compassion.

[*Pause.*]

Oh you won't find it easy, you won't find it easy.

[*Pause.* CLOV *begins to move about the room in search of the telescope.*]

CLOV: I'm tired of our goings on, very tired.

[*He searches.*]

You're not sitting on it?

[*He moves the chair, looks at the place where it stood, resumes his search.*]

HAMM [*anguished*]: Don't leave me there!

[*Angrily* CLOV *restores the chair to its place.*]

Am I right in the center?
CLOV: You'd need a microscope to find this—

[*He sees the telescope.*]

Ah, about time.

[*He picks up the telescope, gets up on the ladder, turns the telescope on the without.*]

HAMM: Give me the dog.
CLOV [*looking*]: Quiet!

HAMM [*angrily*]: Give me the dog!

[CLOV *drops the telescope, clasps his hands to his head. Pause. He gets down precipitately, looks for the dog, sees it, picks it up, hastens towards* HAMM *and strikes him violently on the head with the dog.*]

CLOV: There's your dog for you!

[*The dog falls to the ground. Pause.*]

HAMM: He hit me!
CLOV: You drive me mad, I'm mad!
HAMM: If you must hit me, hit me with the axe.

[*Pause.*]

Or with the gaff, hit me with the gaff. Not with the dog. With the gaff. Or with the axe.

[CLOV *picks up the dog and gives it to* HAMM *who takes it in his arms.*]

CLOV [*imploringly*]: Let's stop playing!
HAMM: Never!

[*Pause.*]

Put me in my coffin.
CLOV: There are no more coffins.
HAMM: Then let it end!

[CLOV *goes towards ladder.*]

With a bang!

[CLOV *gets up on ladder, gets down again, looks for telescope, sees it, picks it up, gets up ladder, raises telescope.*]

Of darkness! And me? Did anyone ever have pity on me?
CLOV [*lowering the telescope, turning towards* HAMM]: What?

[*Pause.*]

Is it me you're referring to?
HAMM [*angrily*]: An aside, ape! Did you never hear an aside before?

[*Pause.*]

I'm warming up for my last soliloquy.
CLOV: I warn you. I'm going to look at this filth since it's an order. But it's the last time.

[*He turns the telescope on the without.*]

Let's see.

[*He moves the telescope.*]

Nothing . . . nothing . . . good . . . good . . . nothing . . . goo—

[*He starts, lowers the telescope, examines it, turns it again on the without. Pause.*]

Bad luck to it!
HAMM: More complications!

[CLOV *gets down.*]

Not an underplot, I trust.

[CLOV *moves ladder nearer window, gets up on it, turns telescope on the without.*]

CLOV [*dismayed*]: Looks like a small boy!
HAMM [*sarcastic*]: A small . . . boy!
CLOV: I'll go and see.

[*He gets down, drops the telescope, goes towards door, turns.*]

I'll take the gaff.

[*He looks for the gaff, sees it, picks it up, hastens towards door.*]

HAMM: No!

[CLOV *halts.*]

CLOV: No? A potential procreator?
HAMM: If he exists he'll die there or he'll come here. And if he doesn't . . .

[*Pause.*]

CLOV: You don't believe me? You think I'm inventing?

[*Pause.*]

HAMM: It's the end, Clov, we've come to the end. I don't need you any more.

[*Pause.*]

CLOV: Lucky for you.

[*He goes towards door.*]

HAMM: Leave me the gaff.

[CLOV *gives him the gaff, goes towards door, halts, looks at alarm-clock, takes it down, looks round for a better place to put it, goes to bins, puts it on lid of* NAGG's *bin. Pause.*]

CLOV: I'll leave you.

[*He goes towards door.*]

HAMM: Before you go . . .

[CLOV *halts near door.*]

. . . say something.
CLOV: There is nothing to say.
HAMM: A few words . . . to ponder . . . in my heart.
CLOV: Your heart!
HAMM: Yes.

[*Pause. Forcibly.*]

Yes!

[*Pause.*]

With the rest, in the end, the shadows, the murmurs, all the trouble, to end up with.

[*Pause.*]

Clov . . . He never spoke to me. Then, in the end, before he went, without my having asked him, he spoke to me. He said . . .
CLOV [*despairingly*]: Ah. . . !
HAMM: Something . . . from your heart.
CLOV: My heart!
HAMM: A few words . . . from your heart.

[*Pause.*]

CLOV [*fixed gaze, tonelessly, towards auditorium*]: They said to me, That's love, yes, yes, not a doubt, now you see how—
HAMM: Articulate!
CLOV [*as before*]: How easy it is. They said to me, That's friendship, yes, yes, no question, you've found it. They said to me, Here's the place, stop, raise your head and look at all that beauty. That order! They said to me, Come now, you're not a brute beast, think upon these things and you'll see how all becomes clear. And simple! They said to me, What skilled attention they get, all these dying of their wounds.
HAMM: Enough!
CLOV [*as before*]: I say to myself—sometimes, Clov, you must learn to suffer better than that if you want them to weary of punishing you—one day. I say to myself—sometimes, Clov, you must be there better than that if you want them to let you go—one day. But I feel too old, and too far, to form new habits. Good, it'll never end, I'll never go.

[*Pause.*]

Then one day, suddenly, it ends, it changes, I don't understand, it dies, or it's me, I don't understand, that either. I ask the words that remain—sleeping, waking, morning, evening. They have nothing to say.

[*Pause.*]

I open the door of the cell and go. I am so bowed I only see my feet, if I open my eyes, and between my legs a little trail of black dust. I say to myself that the earth is extinguished, though I never saw it lit.

[*Pause.*]

It's easy going.

[*Pause.*]

When I fall I'll weep for happiness.

[*Pause. He goes towards door.*]

HAMM: Clov!

[CLOV *halts, without turning.*]

Nothing.

[CLOV *moves on.*]

Clov!

[CLOV *halts, without turning.*]

CLOV: This is what we call making an exit.
HAMM: I'm obliged to you, Clov. For your services.
CLOV [*turning, sharply*]: Ah pardon, it's I am obliged to you.
HAMM: It's we are obliged to each other.

[*Pause.* CLOV *goes towards door.*]

One thing more.

[CLOV *halts.*]

A last favor.

[*Exit* CLOV.]

Cover me with the sheet.

[*Long pause.*]

No? Good.

[*Pause.*]

Me to play.

[*Pause. Wearily.*]

Old endgame lost of old, play and lose and have done with losing.

[*Pause. More animated.*]

Let me see.

[*Pause.*]

Ah yes!

[*He tries to move the chair, using the gaff as before. Enter* CLOV, *dressed for the road. Panama hat, tweed coat, raincoat over his arm, umbrella, bag. He halts by the door and stands there, impassive and motionless, his eyes fixed on* HAMM, *till the end.* HAMM *gives up.*]

Good.

[*Pause.*]

Discard.

[*He throws away the gaff, makes to throw away the dog, thinks better of it.*]

Take it easy.

[*Pause.*]

And now?

[*Pause.*]

Raise hat.

[*He raises his toque.*]

Peace to our . . . arses.

[*Pause.*]

And put on again.

[*He puts on his toque.*]

Deuce.

[*Pause. He takes off his glasses.*]

Wipe.

[*He takes out his handkerchief and, without unfolding it, wipes his glasses.*]

And put on again.

[*He puts on his glasses, puts back the handkerchief in his pocket.*]

We're coming. A few more squirms like that and I'll call.

[*Pause.*]

A little poetry.

[*Pause.*]

You prayed—

[*Pause. He corrects himself.*]

You CRIED for night; it comes—

[*Pause. He corrects himself.*]

It FALLS: now cry in darkness.

[*He repeats, chanting.*]

You cried for night; it falls: now cry in darkness.

[*Pause.*]

Nicely put, that.

[*Pause.*]

And now?

[*Pause.*]

Moments for nothing, now as always, time was never and time is over, reckoning closed and story ended.

[*Pause. Narrative tone.*]

If he could have his child with him. . . .

[*Pause.*]

It was the moment I was waiting for.

[*Pause.*]

You don't want to abandon him? You want him to bloom while you are withering? Be there to solace your last million last moments?

[*Pause.*]

He doesn't realize, all he knows is hunger, and cold, and death to crown it all. But you! You ought to know what the earth is like, nowadays. Oh I put him before his responsibilities.

[*Pause. Normal tone.*]

Well, there we are, there I am, that's enough.

[*He raises the whistle to his lips, hesitates, drops it. Pause.*]

Yes, truly!

[*He whistles. Pause. Louder. Pause.*]

Good.

[*Pause.*]

Father!

[*Pause. Louder.*]

Father!

[*Pause.*]

Good.

[*Pause.*]

We're coming.

[*Pause.*]

And to end up with?

[*Pause.*]

Discard.

[*He throws away the dog. He tears the whistle from his neck.*]

With my compliments.

[*He throws whistle towards auditorium. Pause. He sniffs. Soft.*]

Clov!

[*Long pause.*]

No? Good.

[*He takes out the handkerchief.*]

Since that's the way we're playing it . . .

[*he unfolds handkerchief*]

. . . let's play it that way . . .

[*he unfolds*]

. . . and speak no more about it . . .

[*he finishes unfolding*]

. . . speak no more.

[*He holds handkerchief spread out before him.*]

Old stancher!

[*Pause.*]

You . . . remain.

[*Pause. He covers his face with handkerchief, lowers his arms to armrests, remains motionless.*]

[*Brief tableau.*]

CURTAIN

EUGÈNE IONESCO

Eugène Ionesco (1912–1994) was born of mixed European parentage in Slatina, a provincial town in Romania. His Romanian father was a municipal official, and his French mother was the daughter of an engineer. Throughout his youth, Ionesco's family moved alternately between Romania and France, where his father studied law. His family was troubled, and in 1916 Ionesco's father abandoned his family in France, returned to Romania, secretly divorced his wife, and later forced the children to return to Bucharest. Ionesco identified with his mother, whom he saw as a victim. Later in life, however, his associations with women were more ambiguous, and this is reflected in the unflattering portrayals of women in his plays.

Ionesco recalled that his childhood dreams were haunted by a dark and menacing figure, mostly likely a manifestation of his dominant father, an opportunist who shifted allegiances with the times: first collaborating with the Germans during World War I, then supporting the fascist Romanian government and the Nazis during World War II, and finally switching allegiance to the Communist regime in 1945. Such a sinister, chameleon-like figure often appears in Ionesco's plays, usually projecting aspects of menace and hostility that one associates with a totalitarian government impinging on the rights of individuals.

Ionesco's choice of profession met with parental disdain. His father had wanted him to do something useful with his life, such as following a career in law enforcement, but Ionesco decided to study French literature at the University of Bucharest in 1928.

At twenty-four, he married Rodica Burileanu, with whom he maintained a difficult marriage, which lasted until his death. In 1938 Ionesco obtained a teaching post in Paris, and he and Rodica left Bucharest to escape the rise of fascism there. At the start of World War II, the Ionescos had to return to Romania but were allowed to reenter France in 1942. They lived unhappily in Marseilles under the Vichy collaborationist government. When the war was over, they returned to Paris, where Eugène worked as a proofreader, until he made his reputation as a playwright. Ionesco became a French citizen in 1958.

Having seen firsthand the effects of Romanian and Nazi political tyranny and authoritarianism, Ionesco was repelled by any form of totalitarianism. He was an adversary of communism and socialism, and his plays may be read as critiques of the political views of Bertold Brecht. "I dislike Brecht," Ionesco wrote in "Brief Notes for Radio," "just because he is didactic and ideological. He is not primitive, he is elementary. He is simple, not simplistic. He does not give us matter for thought, he is himself the reflection and illusion of an ideology. Brechtian man is incomplete and often he is merely a puppet. . . . Brecht's human beings are conditioned solely by social factors, interpreted, moreover in one particular way . . . the struggle of classes. . . . So to reduce all the problems of society to this is to belittle society and mankind. . . . What obsesses me personally, what interests me profoundly, what I am committed to is the problem of the human condition as a whole, in its social and nonsocial aspects."

Ionesco's suffering during World War I, and later World War II, left him with a sense of foreboding of death, a sense of social oppression, and a pessimistic attitude toward life in general. His sense of social oppression led him to revile the bourgeois values of hard work and materialism, which he portrayed as forces actually bound to destroy individual happiness. His criticism of the middle class was also inspired by his admiration for Charles Chaplin's character of the Little Tramp, the small man who battles against the big world. Ionesco's plays often mocked the clichés and social conventions of contemporary life.

Ionesco's portrayal of the confusion of the modern world and the futility of existence identifies him as an Absurdist, that is, one who deliberately uses art to confound everyday situations and thus seeks a deeper meaning. In keeping with his iconoclastic outlook, his plays are plotless: a deliberate break with the Aristotelian rules of time, place, and unity. It is the interactions between the characters rather than their actions that matter. Like Franz Kafka (1883–1924), one of his literary heroes, Ionesco tended to construct fantastic parables or tales rather than realistic stories. In "Experience of the Theatre" (1958), Ionesco wrote: "I have always considered imaginative truth to be more profound, more loaded with significance, than everyday reality. Realism, socialist or not, never looks beyond reality. It narrows it down, diminishes it, falsifies it, and leaves out of account the obsessive truths that are most fundamental to us: love, death, and wonder. . . . Everything we dream is 'realizable.' Reality does not have to be: it is simply what it is. It is the dreamer, the thinker or the scientist who is the revolutionary; it is he who tries to change the world."

At thirty-six, Ionesco wrote *The Bald Soprano* (1948) and at once revealed his idea of the "anti-play." According to Ionesco, the play came to him as he attempted to learn English through self-study, and the gap between knowing and understanding a new language enlightened his sense of modern life's absurdity. The play opens with the sound of a clock striking seventeen in the home of the Smiths, banal people who are ridiculous in their complacency and conformity. For example, the middle-class Smiths and their guests, the Martins, speak to each other in stilted phrases and clichéd statements of the kind found in a manual of English. As the play ends, their dialogue is reduced to gibberish:

> MRS. SMITH: Mice have lice, lice haven't mice.
> MRS. MARTIN: Don't ruche my brooch!
> MR. MARTIN: Don't smooch the brooch!
> MR. SMITH: Groom the goose, don't goose the groom.

Even the title *The Bald Soprano* is deliberately misleading and opaque. There is a brief exchange on this subject, but it is a non sequitur:

> FIRE CHIEF: Speaking of that—the bald soprano? [*General silence, embarrassment.*]
> MRS. SMITH: She always wears her hair in the same style.
> FIRE CHIEF: Ah! Then goodbye, ladies and gentlemen.

The Lesson (1951), subtitled "A Comic Drama," is a parody of education, perhaps a fantasy built on Ionesco's own academic career, and an allegory of educators in a totalitarian world. The story focuses on the professor, ruled by his iron-willed maid, who stabs his young female pupil during the course of a private lesson because she cannot understand him. When the pupil is dead, the professor is calmed by the maid:

> PROFESSOR [*sobbing*]: I didn't kill her on purpose!
> MAID: Are you sorry at least?
> PROFESSOR: Oh, yes, Marie, I swear it to you!
> MAID: I can't help feeling sorry for you! Ah! You're a good boy in spite of everything! I'll try to fix this.

As they prepare to remove the body, the maid reassures the professor by taking "out an armband with an insignia, perhaps the Nazi swastika" and says to the professor, "Wait, if you're afraid, wear this, then you won't have anything more to be afraid of."

Ionesco next wrote about old age and the desire to make sense of a life. In *The Chairs: A Tragic Farce* (1952), the Old Man and the Old Woman, he about ninety-five, she about ninety-four, invite guests to their home, which is in a tower surrounded by water. At the Old Woman's urging, the Old Man is to offer his message on the meaning of life. As empty chairs fill the room, the Old Man and the Old Woman behave as if the chairs are filled with attentive guests; even the Emperor attends. Unsure of his ability to present the message himself, the Old Man has engaged an orator. When he finally appears, he is dressed like a "typical painter or poet of the nineteenth century" and moves like an automaton. Before committing double suicide by leaping out of windows at opposite sides of the room, the Old Man and Old Woman console themselves:

> OLD MAN: We will leave some traces, for we are people and not cities.
> OLD MAN AND OLD WOMAN [*together*]: We will have a street named after us.

However, when they are gone and the Orator begins, he cannot speak. He makes the signs of a deaf mute and coughs the sounds, "He, mme, mm, mm. Ju, gou, hou, hou. Heu. Heu, gu, gou, gueue." In frustration he writes "Angelfood" on a blackboard.

In *Amédée, or How to Get Rid of It* (1954), Ionesco described the absurd situation of Amédée and Madeleine Buccinonni, who have a corpse in their apartment that they cannot get rid of. A year later he produced *Jack, or the Submission: A Naturalistic Comedy*, which parodies clichés of conventional theater; in this play all of the characters are named Jack, Jacqueline, Robert, or Roberta. In 1956 he satirized literary critics (especially the French critic, Roland Barthes) in *The Shepherd's Chameleon*, followed by *The Future Is in Eggs* (1957) and *The Killer* (1959).

The Killer is set in a world in which there are no social or political problems because anyone resisting the routine of life is killed. Life in this radiant city of the future is without serious threats to order, and Ionesco's character, Berenger, faces it with awe. Berenger's attitude changes, however, as he tries to find the mysterious killer who is terrorizing the city and who has murdered Mlle. Dany, with whom Berenger had been in love. Berenger's search leads him through a world that resembles a strange version of the Emerald City in *The Wizard of Oz.* He learns that Dany's killer is an idiot dwarf, and he tries to reason with him. Failing, Berenger realizes that his humanism will not allow him to kill the dwarf. While he waits for the killer to approach him, the play ends abruptly. The character of Berenger suggests a central sanity around which hallucinatory and absurd actions of other people—and the world in general—dizzily swirl. Berenger is by turns naïve and knowing, and his refusal to succumb to the insanity around him (such as by killing the dwarf) is emblematic of the plight of the artist who endures isolation. It is often suggested that Berenger is the fictional persona of Ionesco, and he wrote several more plays with characters of the same name, including *Rhinoceros.*

Other Ionesco plays include *Exit the King* and *A Stroll in the Air,* both produced in 1962; his *Hunger and Thirst* (1966), is a satire of Bertolt Brecht's work and explores one's hunger to break down the stability of middle-class life and search for novelty, along with one's thirst of never quite achieving satisfaction. *Killing Game* (1970) is about a community invaded by a mysterious disease that kills all the inhabitants. Ionesco's *Macbett* (1972) is his adaptation of Shakespeare's *Macbeth. The Man with the Valises* (1975) is a dream play about a spiritual exile, a man who always has his bags packed and is eternally traveling. *Journeys Among the Dead* (1980) is a sequence of twenty-seven segments or scenes that Ionesco wrote about a character named Jean, who seems to be Ionesco's alter ego. It is an unsettling play, more autobiography than fiction, and it shows Ionesco smarting from the decline of his own reputation and the rising prestige of Samuel Beckett, who had been awarded the Nobel Prize in 1969.

In addition to his plays, Ionesco wrote several volumes of prose, including a collection of essays on theater, *Notes and Counter Notes* (1961); memoirs titled *Fragments of a Journal* (1967), *Present Past Past Present* (1968), and *Discoveries* (1969); and a novel, *The Hermit* (1973).

In 1970 he was awarded France's highest academic honor when he was elected to the Académie Française. Ionesco had always chided intellectuals for their fuzzy logic and had called them "the real plague of intellectual life," but he accepted the honor with grace.

Ionesco was forty-seven when *Rhinoceros* (1959) was produced, and it brought him international fame, especially in England and the United States. Its premiere in London was directed by Orson Welles and starred Laurence Olivier as Berenger. *Rhinoceros* may be understood as a political allegory, showing the extent to which people will conform or will change political affiliations in order to move with the times. The play captures in atmosphere and essence the key forces in Ionesco's life: his changeling father, the rise of fascism in Romania, the shame of the Nazi occupation of France during World War II, and the Communist domination of Eastern Europe and China.

Ionesco's political arguments concerning *Rhinoceros* address the stress an individual endures to maintain personal integrity in the face of political pressure.

According to Ionesco, rhinoceritis is an "attack of collective hysteria and the epidemic that works beneath the surface of reason" that turns the people of a small provincial town into rhinoceroses, first one at a time, then almost en masse. Only Berenger, the protagonist, does not succumb to the rhinoceros disease. Like Job, Berenger is advised by friends to admit his faults and change; he is studied, berated, and challenged until he is alone. As the action nears its climax, Berenger and Daisy promise to reject joining the rhinoceros herd:

> BERENGER: Well, in spite of everything, I swear to you I'll never give in, never!
> DAISY [*she rises, goes to* BERENGER, *puts her arms around his neck*]: My poor darling, I'll help you to resist—to the very end.
> BERENGER: Will you be capable of it?
> DAISY: I give you my word. You can trust me.

Of course, when Berenger turns his back to her, she deserts him for the herd. Berenger is shocked and says, "Daisy! Daisy! Where are you, Daisy? You can't do that to me! . . . Come back, my dear! You haven't even had your lunch." Though he nearly succumbs to the desire to become a rhinoceros, Berenger resolutely declares, "Oh well, too bad! I'll take on the whole of them! I'll put up a fight against the lot of them, the whole lot of them! I'm the last man left, and I'm staying that way until the end. I'm not capitulating!" Berenger has gone to the brink but does not fall.

Ionesco called attention to the question of reality versus illusion when Jean asks Berenger, "Instead of squandering all of your spare money on drink, isn't it better to buy a ticket for an interesting play? Do you know anything about the avant garde theatre there's so much talk about? Have you seen Ionesco's plays?" The remark is not merely self-aggrandizement, but a satirical twist, calling attention to the absurdity of a fictional character discussing a "real" play. Ironically, Ionesco became a character in his autobiographical play *Journey to the Homes of the Dead* (1981), which was staged by Roger Planchon, an avowed Marxist, as *Ionesco* in 1982.

Ionesco's interest in the illusions and absurdities of life links him with Luigi Pirandello, especially with Pirandello's *Six Characters in Search of an Author.* In his memoir *Present Past Past Present,* Ionesco said, "I am not quite sure whether I am dreaming or remembering, whether I have lived my life or dreamed it. Just as dreams do, memory makes me profoundly aware of the unreality, the evanescence of the world, a fleeting image in the moving water, colored smoke." Like Pirandello, Ionesco made fiction and nonsense seem real, and the combined influence of these playwrights can be seen in the plays of Edward Albee, Harold Pinter, Tom Stoppard, and Sam Shepard.

Film

Rhinoceros (1974), directed by Tom O'Horgan, with Zero Mostel, Gene Wilder, Karen Black, Robert Weil, and Joe Silver. American Film Theater.

Rhinoceros

A Play in Three Acts and Four Scenes

TRANSLATED BY DEREK PROUSE

CHARACTERS

JEAN
BERENGER
THE WAITRESS
THE GROCER
THE GROCER'S WIFE
THE OLD GENTLEMAN
THE LOGICIAN
THE HOUSEWIFE
THE CAFÉ PROPRIETOR
DAISY
MR. PAPILLON
DUDARD
BOTARD
MRS. BOEUF
A FIREMAN
THE LITTLE OLD MAN
THE LITTLE OLD MAN'S WIFE
And a lot of Rhinoceros heads

ACT I

The scene is a square in a small provincial town. Up-stage a house composed of a ground floor and one storey. The ground floor is the window of a grocer's shop. The entrance is up two or three steps through a glass-paned door. The word EPICERIE is written in bold letters above the shop window. The two windows on the first floor are the living quarters of the grocer and his wife. The shop is up-stage, but slightly to the left, not far from the wings. In the distance a church steeple is visible above the grocer's house. Between the shop and the left of the stage there is a little street in perspective. To the right, slightly at an angle, is the front of a café. Above the café, one floor with a window; in front, the café terrace; several chairs and tables reach almost to centre stage. A dusty tree stands near the terrace chairs. Blue sky; harsh light; very white walls. The time is almost mid-day on a Sunday in summertime. JEAN *and* BERENGER *will sit at one of the terrace tables.*

[*The sound of church bells is heard, which stop a few moments before the curtain rises. When the curtain rises, a woman carrying a basket of provisions under one arm and a cat under the other crosses the stage in silence from right to left. As she does so, the* GROCER'S WIFE *opens her shop door and watches her pass.*]

GROCER'S WIFE: Oh that woman gets on my nerves! [*To her husband who is in the shop:*] Too stuck-up to buy from us nowadays. [*The* GROCER'S WIFE *leaves; the stage is empty for a few moments.*]

[JEAN *enters right, at the same time as* BERENGER *enters left.* JEAN *is very fastidiously dressed: brown suit, red tie, stiff collar, brown hat. He has a reddish face. His shoes are yellow and well-polished.* BERENGER *is unshaven and hatless, with unkempt hair and creased clothes; everything about him indicates negligence. He seems weary, half-asleep; from time to time he yawns.*]

JEAN [*advancing from right*]: Oh, so you managed to get here at last, Berenger!

BERENGER [*advancing from left*]: Morning, Jean!

JEAN: Late as usual, of course. [*He looks at his wrist watch.*] Our appointment was for 11:30. And now it's practically midday.

BERENGER: I'm sorry. Have you been waiting long?

JEAN: No, I've only just arrived myself, as you saw.

[*They go and sit at one of the tables on the café terrace.*]

BERENGER: In that case I don't feel so bad, if you've only just . . .

JEAN: It's different with me. I don't like waiting; I've no time to waste. And as you're never on time, I come late on purpose—at a time when I presume you'll be there.

BERENGER: You're right . . . quite right, but . . .

JEAN: Now don't try to pretend you're ever on time!

BERENGER: No, of course not . . . I wouldn't say that.

[JEAN *and* BERENGER *have sat down.*]

JEAN: There you are, you see!

BERENGER: What are you drinking?

JEAN: You mean to say you've got a thirst even at this time in the morning?

BERENGER: It's so hot and dry.

JEAN: The more you drink the thirstier you get, popular science tells us that . . .

BERENGER: It would be less dry, and we'd be less thirsty, if they'd invent us some scientific clouds in the sky.

JEAN [*studying* BERENGER *closely*]: That wouldn't help you any. You're not thirsty for water, Berenger . . .

BERENGER: I don't understand what you mean.

JEAN: You know perfectly well what I mean. I'm talking about your parched throat. That's a territory that can't get enough!

BERENGER: To compare my throat to a piece of land seems . . .

JEAN [*interrupting him*]: You're in a bad way, my friend.

BERENGER: In a bad way? You think so?

JEAN: I'm not blind, you know. You're dropping with fatigue. You've gone without your sleep again, you yawn all the time, you're dead-tired . . .

BERENGER There is something the matter with my hair . . .

JEAN: You reek of alcohol.

BERENGER: I have got a bit of a hang-over, it's true!

JEAN: It's the same every Sunday morning—not to mention the other days of the week.

BERENGER: Oh no, it's less frequent during the week, because of the office . . .

JEAN: And what's happened to your tie? Lost it during your orgy, I suppose!

BERENGER [*putting his hand to his neck*]: You're right. That's funny! Whatever could I have done with it?

JEAN [*taking a tie out of his coat pocket*]: Here, put this one on.

BERENGER: Oh thank you, that is kind. [*He puts on the tie.*]

JEAN [*while* BERENGER *is unskillfully tying his tie*]: Your hair's all over the place.

[BERENGER *runs his fingers through his hair.*]

Here, here's a comb! [*He takes a comb from his other pocket.*]

BERENGER [*taking the comb*]: Thank you. [*He vaguely combs his hair.*]

JEAN: You haven't even shaved! Just take a look at yourself!

[*He takes a mirror from his inside pocket, hands it to* BERENGER, *who looks at himself; as he does so, he examines his tongue.*]

BERENGER: My tongue's all coated.

JEAN [*taking the mirror and putting it back in his pocket*]: I'm not surprised! [*He takes back the comb as well, which* BERENGER *offers to him, and puts it in his pocket.*] You're heading for cirrhosis, my friend.

BERENGER [*worried*]: Do you think so?

JEAN [*to* BERENGER, *who wants to give him back his tie*]: Keep the tie, I've got plenty more.

BERENGER [*admiringly*]: You always look so immaculate.

JEAN [*continuing his inspection of* BERENGER]: Your clothes are all crumpled, they're a disgrace! Your

Zero Mostel, Eli Wallach, Anne Jackson, and Morris Carnovsky in Rhinoceros, *directed by Joseph Anthony, the Longacre Theatre, New York, 1961.*

shirt is downright filthy, and your shoes . . . [BERENGER *tries to hide his feet under the table.*] Your shoes haven't been touched. What a mess you're in! And look at your shoulders . . .

BERENGER: What's the matter with my shoulders?

JEAN: Turn round! Come on, turn round! You've been leaning against some wall. [BERENGER *holds his hand out docilely to* JEAN.] No, I haven't got a brush with me; it would make my pockets bulge. [*Still docile,* BERENGER *flicks his shoulders to get rid of the white dust;* JEAN *averts his head.*] Heavens! Where did you get all that from?

BERENGER: I don't remember.

JEAN: It's a positive disgrace! I feel ashamed to be your friend.

BERENGER: You're very hard on me . . .

JEAN: I've every reason to be.

BERENGER: Listen, Jean. There are so few distractions in this town—I get so bored. I'm not made for the work I'm doing . . . every day at the office, eight hours a day—and only three weeks' holiday a year! When Saturday night comes round I feel exhausted and so—you know how it is—just to relax . . .

JEAN: My dear man, everybody has to work. I spend eight hours a day in the office the same as everyone else. And I only get three weeks off a year, but even so you don't catch me . . . Will-power, my good man!

BERENGER: But everybody hasn't got as much will-power as you have. I can't get used to it. I just can't get used to life.

JEAN: Everybody has to get used to it. Or do you consider yourself some superior being?

BERENGER: I don't pretend to be . . .

JEAN [*interrupting him*]: I'm just as good as you are; I think with all due modesty I may say I'm better. The superior man is the man who fulfils his duty.

BERENGER: What duty?

JEAN: His duty . . . His duty as an employee, for example.

BERENGER: Oh yes, his duty as an employee . . .

JEAN: Where did your debauch take place last night? If you can remember!

BERENGER: We were celebrating Auguste's birthday, our friend Auguste . . .

JEAN: Our friend Auguste? Nobody invited me to our friend Auguste's birthday . . .

[*At this moment a noise is heard, far off, but swiftly approaching, of a beast panting in its headlong course, and of a long trumpeting.*]

BERENGER: I couldn't refuse. It wouldn't have been nice . . .

JEAN: Did I go there?

BERENGER: Well, perhaps it was because you weren't invited.

WAITRESS [*coming out of café*]: Good morning, gentlemen. Can I get you something to drink?

[*The noise becomes very loud.*]

JEAN [*to* BERENGER, *almost shouting to make himself heard above the noise which he has not become conscious of*]: True, I was not invited. That honour was denied me. But in any case, I can assure you, that even if I had been invited, I would not have gone, because . . .

[*The noise has become intense.*]

What's going on?

[*The noise of a powerful, heavy animal, galloping at great speed is heard very close; the sound of panting.*]

Whatever is it?

WAITRESS: Whatever is it?

[BERENGER, *still listless without appearing to hear anything at all, replies tranquilly to* JEAN *about the invitation; his lips move but one doesn't hear what he says;* JEAN *bounds to his feet, knocking his chair over as he does so, looks off left pointing, whilst* BERENGER, *still a little dopey, remains seated.*]

JEAN: Oh, a rhinoceros!

[*The noise made by the animal dies away swiftly and one can already hear the following words. The whole of this scene must be played very fast, each repeating in swift succession: 'Oh, a rhinoceros!'*]

WAITRESS: Oh, a rhinoceros!

GROCER'S WIFE [*sticks her head out of her shop doorway*]: Oh, a rhinoceros! [*To her husband still inside the shop:*] Quick, come and look; it's a rhinoceros!

[*They are all looking off left after the animal.*]

JEAN: It's rushing straight ahead, brushing up against the shop windows.

GROCER [*in his shop*]: Whereabouts?

WAITRESS [*putting her hands on her hips*]: Well!

GROCER'S WIFE [*to her husband who is still in shop*]: Come and look!

[*At this moment the* GROCER *puts his head out.*]

GROCER: Oh, a rhinoceros!

LOGICIAN [*entering quickly left*]: A rhinoceros going full-tilt on the opposite pavement!

[*All these speeches from the time when* JEAN *says "Oh, a rhinoceros" are practically simultaneous. A woman is heard crying "Ah!" She appears. She runs to the centre-stage; it is a* HOUSEWIFE *with a basket on her arm; once arrived centre- stage she drops her basket; the contents scatter all over the stage, a bottle breaks, but she does not drop her cat.*]

HOUSEWIFE: Ah! Oh!

[*An elegant* OLD GENTLEMAN *comes from left stage, after the* HOUSEWIFE, *rushes into the* GROCER*'s shop, knocks into the* GROCER *and his* WIFE, *whilst the* LOGICIAN *installs himself against the back wall on the left of the grocery entrance.* JEAN *and the* WAITRESS, *standing, and* BERENGER, *still apathetically seated, together form another group. At the same time, coming from the left, cries of 'Oh' and 'Ah' and the noise of people running have been heard. The dust raised by the animal spreads over the stage.*]

CAFÉ PROPRIETOR [*sticking his head out of the first-floor window*]: What's going on?
OLD GENTLEMAN [*disappearing behind the* GROCER *and his* WIFE]: Excuse me, please!

[*The* OLD GENTLEMAN *is elegantly dressed, with white spats, a soft hat and an ivory-handled cane; the* LOGICIAN, *propped up against the wall has a little grey moustache, an eyeglass, and is wearing a straw hat.*]

GROCER'*s* WIFE [*jostled and jostling her husband; to the* OLD GENTLEMAN]: Watch out with that stick!
GROCER: Look where you're going, can't you!

[*The head of the* OLD GENTLEMAN *is seen behind the* GROCER *and his* WIFE.]

WAITRESS [*to the* PROPRIETOR]: A rhinoceros!
PROPRIETOR [*to the* WAITRESS *from his window*]: You're seeing things. [*He sees the rhinoceros:*] Well, I'll be . . . !
HOUSEWIFE: Ah!

[*The "Ohs" and "Ahs" from off-stage form a background accompaniment to her "Ah." She has dropped her basket, her provisions and the bottle, but has nevertheless kept tight hold of her cat which she carries under her other arm.*]

There, they frightened the poor pussy!
PROPRIETOR [*still looking off left, following the distant course of the animal as the noises fade; hooves, trumpetings, etc.*]:

[BERENGER *sleepily averts his head a little on account of the dust, but says nothing; he simply makes a grimace.*]

Well, of all things!
JEAN [*also averting his head a little, but very much awake*]: Well, of all things! [*He sneezes.*]
HOUSEWIFE [*she is centre-stage but turned towards left; her provisions scattered on the ground round her*]: Well of all things! [*She sneezes.*]

[*The* OLD GENTLEMAN, GROCER'*s* WIFE *and* GROCER *up-stage re-opening the glass door of the* GROCER*'s shop that the* OLD GENTLEMAN *has closed behind him.*]

ALL THREE: Well, of all things!
JEAN: Well, of all things! [*To* BERENGER:] Did you see that?

[*The noise of the rhinoceros and its trumpeting are now far away; the people are still staring after the animal, all except for* BERENGER *who is still apathetically seated.*]

ALL [*except* BERENGER]: Well, of all things!
BERENGER [*to* JEAN]: It certainly looked as if it was a rhinoceros. It made plenty of dust. [*He takes out a handkerchief and blows his nose.*]
HOUSEWIFE: Well, of all things! Gave me such a scare.
GROCER [*to the* HOUSEWIFE]: Your basket . . . and all your things . . .
OLD GENTLEMAN [*approaching the lady and bending to pick up her things scattered about the stage. He greets her gallantly, raising his hat.*]
PROPRIETOR: Really, these days, you never know . . .
WAITRESS: Fancy that!
OLD GENTLEMAN [*to the* HOUSEWIFE]: May I help you pick up your things?
HOUSEWIFE [*to the* OLD GENTLEMAN]: Thank you, how very kind! Do put on your hat. Oh, it gave me such a scare!
LOGICIAN: Fear is an irrational thing. It must yield to reason.
WAITRESS: It's already out of sight.
OLD GENTLEMAN [*to the* HOUSEWIFE *and indicating the* LOGICIAN]: My friend is a logician.
JEAN [*to* BERENGER]: Well, what did you think of that?
WAITRESS: Those animals can certainly travel!
HOUSEWIFE [*to the* LOGICIAN]: Very happy to meet you!
GROCER'*s* WIFE [*to the* GROCER]: That'll teach her to buy her things from somebody else!
JEAN [*to the* PROPRIETOR *and the* WAITRESS]: What did you think of that?
HOUSEWIFE: I still didn't let my cat go.
PROPRIETOR [*shrugging his shoulders, at window*]: You don't often see that!

HOUSEWIFE [*to the* LOGICIAN *and the* OLD GENTLEMAN *who is picking up her provisions*]: Would you hold him a moment!
WAITRESS [*to* JEAN]: First time I've seen that!
LOGICIAN [*to the* HOUSEWIFE, *taking the cat in his arms*]: It's not spiteful, is it?
PROPRIETOR [*to* JEAN]: Went past like a comet!
HOUSEWIFE [*to the* LOGICIAN]: He wouldn't hurt a fly. [*To the others:*] What happened to my wine?
GROCER [*to the* HOUSEWIFE]: I've got plenty more.
JEAN [*to* BERENGER]: Well, what did you think of that?
GROCER [*to the* HOUSEWIFE]: And good stuff, too!
PROPRIETOR [*to the* WAITRESS]: Don't hang about! Look after these gentlemen! [*He indicates* BERENGER *and* JEAN. *He withdraws.*]
BERENGER [*to* JEAN]: What did I think of what?
GROCER'S WIFE [*to the* GROCER]: Go and get her another bottle!
JEAN [*to* BERENGER]: Of the rhinoceros, of course! What did you think I meant?
GROCER [*to the* HOUSEWIFE]: I've got some first-class wine, in unbreakable bottles! [*He disappears into his shop.*]
LOGICIAN [*stroking the cat in his arms*]: Puss, puss, puss.
WAITRESS [*to* BERENGER *and* JEAN]: What are you drinking?
BERENGER: Two pastis.
WAITRESS: Two pastis—right! [*She walks to the café entrance.*]
HOUSEWIFE [*picking up her things with the help of the* OLD GENTLEMAN]: Very kind of you, I'm sure.
WAITRESS: Two pastis! [*She goes into café.*]
OLD GENTLEMAN [*to the* HOUSEWIFE]: Oh, please don't mention it, it's a pleasure.

[*The* GROCER'S WIFE *goes into shop.*]

LOGICIAN [*to the* OLD GENTLEMAN *and the* HOUSEWIFE *picking up the provisions*]: Replace them in an orderly fashion.
JEAN [*to* BERENGER]: Well, what did you think about it?
BERENGER [*to* JEAN, *not knowing what to say*]: Well . . . nothing . . . it made a lot of dust . . .
GROCER [*coming out of shop with a bottle of wine; to the* HOUSEWIFE]: I've some good leeks as well.
LOGICIAN [*still stroking the cat*]: Puss, puss, puss.
GROCER [*to the* HOUSEWIFE]: It's a hundred francs a litre.
HOUSEWIFE [*paying the* GROCER, *then to the* OLD GENTLEMAN *who has managed to put everything back in the basket*]: Oh, you are kind! Such a pleasure to come across the old French courtesy. Not like the young people today!
GROCER [*taking money*]: You should buy from me. You wouldn't even have to cross the street, and you wouldn't run the risk of these accidents. [*He goes back into his shop.*]
JEAN [*who has sat down and is still thinking of the rhinoceros*]: But you must admit it's extraordinary.
OLD GENTLEMAN [*taking off his hat, and kissing the* HOUSEWIFE'S *hand*]: It was a great pleasure to meet you!
HOUSEWIFE [*to the* LOGICIAN]: Thank you very much for holding my cat.

[*The* LOGICIAN *gives the* HOUSEWIFE *back her cat. The* WAITRESS *comes back with drinks.*]

WAITRESS: Two pastis!
JEAN [*to* BERENGER]: You're incorrigible!
OLD GENTLEMAN [*to the* HOUSEWIFE]: May I accompany you part of the way?
BERENGER [*to* JEAN, *and pointing to the* WAITRESS *who goes back into the café*]: I asked for mineral water. She's made a mistake.

[JEAN, *scornful and disbelieving, shrugs his shoulders.*]

HOUSEWIFE [*to the* OLD GENTLEMAN]: My husband's waiting for me, thank you. Perhaps some other time . . .
OLD GENTLEMAN [*to the* HOUSEWIFE]: I sincerely hope so, Madame.
HOUSEWIFE [*to the* OLD GENTLEMAN]: So do I! [*She gives him a sweet look as she leaves left.*]
BERENGER: The dust's settled . . .

[JEAN *shrugs his shoulders again.*]

OLD GENTLEMAN [*to the* LOGICIAN, *and looking after the* HOUSEWIFE]: Delightful creature!
JEAN [*to* BERENGER]: A rhinoceros! I can't get over it!

[*The* OLD GENTLEMAN *and the* LOGICIAN *move slowly right and off. They chat amiably.*]

OLD GENTLEMAN [*to the* LOGICIAN, *after casting a last fond look after the* HOUSEWIFE]: Charming, isn't she?
LOGICIAN [*to the* OLD GENTLEMAN]: I'm going to explain to you what a syllogism is.
OLD GENTLEMAN: Ah yes, a syllogism.
JEAN [*to* BERENGER]: I can't get over it! It's unthinkable!

[BERENGER *yawns.*]

LOGICIAN: A syllogism consists of a main proposition, a secondary one, and a conclusion.

OLD GENTLEMAN: What conclusion?

[*The* LOGICIAN *and the* OLD GENTLEMAN *go out.*]

JEAN: I just can't get over it.

BERENGER: Yes, I can see you can't. Well, it was a rhinoceros—all right, so it was a rhinoceros! It's miles away by now . . . miles away . . .

JEAN: But you must see it's fantastic! A rhinoceros loose in the town, and you don't bat an eyelid! It shouldn't be allowed!

[BERENGER *yawns.*]

Put your hand in front of your mouth!

BERENGER: Yais . . . yais . . . It shouldn't be allowed. It's dangerous. I hadn't realized. But don't worry about it, it won't get us here.

JEAN: We ought to protest to the Town Council! What's the Council there for?

BERENGER [*yawning, then quickly putting his hand to his mouth*]: Oh excuse me . . . perhaps the rhinoceros escaped from the zoo.

JEAN: You're day-dreaming.

BERENGER: But I'm wide awake.

JEAN: Awake or asleep, it's the same thing.

BERENGER: But there is some difference.

JEAN: That's not the point.

BERENGER: But you just said being awake and being asleep were the same thing . . .

JEAN: You didn't understand. There's no difference between dreaming awake and dreaming asleep.

BERENGER: I do dream. Life is a dream.

JEAN: You're certainly dreaming when you say the rhinoceros escaped from the zoo . . .

BERENGER: I only said: perhaps.

JEAN: . . . because there's been no zoo in our town since the animals were destroyed in the plague . . . ages ago . . .

BERENGER [*with the same indifference*]: Then perhaps it came from a circus.

JEAN: What circus are you talking about?

BERENGER: I don't know . . . some travelling circus.

JEAN: You know perfectly well that the Council banned all travelling performers from the district . . . There haven't been any since we were children.

BERENGER [*trying unsuccessfully to stop yawning*]: In that case, maybe it's been hiding ever since in the surrounding swamps?

JEAN: The surrounding swamps! The surrounding swamps! My poor friend, you live in a thick haze of alcohol.

BERENGER [*naïvely*]: That's very true . . . it seems to mount from my stomach . . .

JEAN: It's clouding your brain! Where do you know of any surrounding swamps? Our district is known as 'little Castille' because the land is so arid.

BERENGER [*surfeited and pretty weary*]: How do I know, then? Perhaps it's been hiding under a stone? . . . Or maybe it's been nesting on some withered branch?

JEAN: If you think you're being witty, you're very much mistaken! You're just being a bore with . . . with your stupid paradoxes. You're incapable of talking seriously!

BERENGER: Today, yes, only today . . . because of . . . because *of* . . . [*He indicates his head with a vague gesture.*]

JEAN: Today the same as any other day!

BERENGER: Oh, not quite as much.

JEAN: Your witticisms are not very inspired.

BERENGER: I wasn't trying to be . . .

JEAN [*interrupting him*]: I can't bear people to try and make fun of me!

BERENGER [*hand on his heart*]: But my dear Jean, I'd never allow myself to . . .

JEAN [*interrupting him*]: My dear Berenger, you are allowing yourself . . .

BERENGER: Oh no, never. I'd never allow myself to.

JEAN: Yes, you would; you've just done so.

BERENGER: But how could you possibly think . . .

JEAN [*interrupting him*]: I think what is true!

BERENGER: But I assure you . . .

JEAN [*interrupting him*]: . . . that you were making fun of me!

BERENGER: You really can be obstinate, sometimes.

JEAN: And now you're calling me a mule into the bargain. Even you must see how insulting you're being.

BERENGER: It would never have entered my mind.

JEAN: You have no mind!

BERENGER: All the more reason why it would never enter it.

JEAN: There are certain things which enter the minds of even people without one.

BERENGER: That's impossible.

JEAN: And why, pray, is it impossible?

BERENGER: Because it's impossible.

JEAN: Then kindly explain to me why it's impossible, as you seem to imagine you can explain everything.

BERENGER: I don't imagine anything of the kind.

JEAN: Then why do you act as if you do? And, I repeat, why are you being so insulting to me?

BERENGER: I'm not insulting you. Far from it. You know what tremendous respect I have for you.

JEAN: In that case, why do you contradict me, making out that it's not dangerous to let a rhinoceros go racing about in the middle of the town—

particularly on a Sunday morning when the streets are full of children . . . and adults, too . . .

BERENGER: A lot of them are in church. They don't run any risk . . .

JEAN [*interrupting him*]: If you will allow me to finish . . . and at market time, too.

BERENGER: I never said it wasn't dangerous to let a rhinoceros go racing about the town. I simply said I'd personally never considered the danger. It had never crossed my mind.

JEAN: You never consider anything.

BERENGER: All right, I agree. A rhinoceros roaming about is not a good thing.

JEAN: It shouldn't be allowed.

BERENGER: I agree. It shouldn't be allowed. It's a ridiculous thing all right! But it's no reason for you and me to quarrel. Why go on at me just because some wretched perissodactyle happens to pass by. A stupid quadruped not worth talking about. And ferocious into the bargain. And which has already disappeared, which doesn't exist any longer. We're not going to bother about some animal that doesn't exist. Let's talk about something else, Jean, please; [*He yawns.*] there are plenty of other subjects for conversation. [*He takes his glass:*] To you!

[*At this moment the* LOGICIAN *and the* OLD GENTLEMAN *come back on stage from left; they walk over, talking as they go, to one of the tables on the café terrace, some distance from* BERENGER *and* JEAN, *behind and to the right of them.*]

JEAN: Put that glass back on the table! You're not to drink it.

[JEAN *takes a large swallow from his own pastis and puts back the glass, half-empty, on the table.* BERENGER *continues to hold his glass, without putting it down, and without daring to drink from it either.*]

BERENGER [*timidly*]: There's no point in leaving it for the proprietor. [*He makes as if to drink.*]

JEAN: Put it down, I tell you!

BERENGER: Very well.

[*He is putting the glass back on the table when* DAISY *passes. She is a young blonde typist and she crosses the stage from right to left. When he sees her,* BERENGER *rises abruptly, and in doing so makes an awkward movement; the glass falls and splashes* JEAN'S *trousers.*]

Oh, there's Daisy!

JEAN: Look out! How clumsy you are!

BERENGER: That's Daisy . . . I'm so sorry . . . [*He hides himself out of sight of* DAISY.] I don't want her to see me in this state.

JEAN: Your behaviour's unforgivable, absolutely unforgivable! [*He looks in the direction of* DAISY, *who it just disappearing.*] Why are you afraid of that young girl?

BERENGER: Oh, be quiet, please be quiet!

JEAN: She doesn't look an unpleasant person!

BERENGER [*coming back to* JEAN, *now that* DAISY *has gone*]: I must apologize once more for . . .

JEAN: You see what comes of drinking, you can no longer control your movements, you've no strength left in your hands, you're besotted and fagged out. You're digging your own grave, my friend, you're destroying yourself.

BERENGER: I don't like the taste of alcohol much. And yet if I don't drink, I'm done for; it's as if I'm frightened, and so I drink not to be frightened any longer.

JEAN: Frightened of what?

BERENGER: I don't know exactly. It's a sort of anguish difficult to describe. I feel out of place in life, among people, and so I take to drink. That calms me down and relaxes me so I can forget.

JEAN: You try to escape from yourself!

BERENGER: I'm so tired, I've been tired for years. It's exhausting to drag the weight of my own body about . . .

JEAN: That's alcoholic neurasthenia, drinker's gloom . . .

BERENGER [*continuing*]: I'm conscious of my body all the time, as if it were made of lead, or as if I were carrying another man around on my back. I can't seem to get used to myself. I don't even know if I *am* me. Then as soon as I take a drink, the lead slips away and I recognize myself, I become me again.

JEAN: That's just being fanciful. Look at me, Berenger, I weigh more than you do. And yet I feel light, light as a feather! [*He flaps his arms as if about to fly. The* OLD GENTLEMAN *and the* LOGICIAN *have come back and have taken a few steps on stage deep in talk. At this moment they are passing by* JEAN *and* BERENGER. JEAN'S *arm deals the* OLD GENTLEMAN *a sharp knock which precipitates him into the arms of the* LOGICIAN.]

LOGICIAN: An example of a syllogism . . . [*He is knocked.*] Oh!

OLD GENTLEMAN [*to* JEAN]: Look out! [*To the* LOGICIAN:] I'm so sorry.

JEAN [*to the* OLD GENTLEMAN]: I'm so sorry.

LOGICIAN [*to the* OLD GENTLEMAN]: No harm done.

OLD GENTLEMAN [*to* JEAN]: No harm done.

[*The* OLD GENTLEMAN *and the* LOGICIAN *go and sit at one of the terrace tables a little to the right and behind* JEAN *and* BERENGER.]

BERENGER [*to* JEAN]: You certainly are strong.

JEAN: Yes, I'm strong. I'm strong for several reasons. In the first place I'm strong because I'm naturally strong, and secondly I'm strong because I have moral strength. I'm also strong because I'm not riddled with alcohol. I don't wish to offend you, my dear Berenger, but I feel I must tell you that it's alcohol which weighs so heavy on you.

LOGICIAN [*to the* OLD GENTLEMAN]: Here is an example of a syllogism. The cat has four paws. Isidore and Fricot both have four paws. Therefore Isidore and Fricot are cats.

OLD GENTLEMAN [*to the* LOGICIAN]: My dog has got four paws.

LOGICIAN [*to the* OLD GENTLEMAN]: Then it's a cat.

BERENGER [*to* JEAN]: I've barely got the strength to go on living. Maybe I don't even want to.

OLD GENTLEMAN [*to the* LOGICIAN, *after deep reflection*]: So then logically speaking, my dog must be a cat?

LOGICIAN [*to the* OLD GENTLEMAN]: Logically, yes. But the contrary is also true.

BERENGER [*to* JEAN]: Solitude seems to oppress me. And so does the company of other people.

JEAN [*to* BERENGER]: You contradict yourself. What oppresses you—solitude, or the company of others? You consider yourself a thinker, yet you're devoid of logic.

OLD GENTLEMAN [*to the* LOGICIAN]: Logic is a very beautiful thing.

LOGICIAN [*to the* OLD GENTLEMAN]: As long as it is not abused.

BERENGER [*to* JEAN]: Life is an abnormal business.

JEAN: On the contrary. Nothing could be more natural, and the proof is that people go on living.

BERENGER: There are more dead people than living. And their numbers are increasing. The living are getting rarer.

JEAN: The dead don't exist, there's no getting away from that! . . . Ah! Ah . . . ! [*He gives a huge laugh.*] Yet you're oppressed by them, too? How can you be oppressed by something that doesn't exist?

BERENGER: I sometimes wonder if I exist myself.

JEAN: You don't exist, my dear Berenger, because you don't think. Start thinking, then you will.

LOGICIAN [*to the* OLD GENTLEMAN]: Another syllogism. All cats die. Socrates is dead. Therefore Socrates is a cat.

OLD GENTLEMAN: And he's got four paws. That's true. I've got a cat named Socrates.

LOGICIAN: There you are, you see . . .

JEAN [*to* BERENGER]: Fundamentally you're just a bluffer. And a liar. You say that life doesn't interest you. And yet there's somebody who does.

BERENGER: Who?

JEAN: Your little friend from the office who just went past. You're very fond of her!

OLD GENTLEMAN [*to the* LOGICIAN]: So Socrates was a cat, was he?

LOGICIAN: Logic has just revealed the fact to us.

JEAN [*to* BERENGER]: You didn't want her to see you in your present state. [BERENGER *makes a gesture.*] That proves you're not indifferent to everything. But how can you expect Daisy to be attracted to a drunkard?

LOGICIAN [*to the* OLD GENTLEMAN]: Let's get back to our cats.

OLD GENTLEMAN [*to the* LOGICIAN]: I'm all ears.

BERENGER [*to* JEAN]: In any case, I think she's already got her eye on someone.

JEAN: Oh, who?

BERENGER: Dudard. An office colleague, qualified in law, with a big future in the firm—and in Daisy's affections. I can't hope to compete with him.

LOGICIAN [*to the* OLD GENTLEMAN]: The cat Isidore has four paws.

OLD GENTLEMAN: How do you know?

LOGICIAN: It's stated in the hypothesis.

BERENGER [*to* JEAN]: The Chief thinks a lot of him. Whereas I've no future, I've no qualifications. I don't stand a chance.

OLD GENTLEMAN [*to the* LOGICIAN]: Ah! In the hypothesis.

JEAN [*to* BERENGER]: So you're giving up, just like that . . . ?

BERENGER: What else can I do?

LOGICIAN [*to the* OLD GENTLEMAN]: Fricot also has four paws. So how many paws have Fricot and Isidore?

OLD GENTLEMAN: Separately or together?

JEAN [*to* BERENGER]: Life is a struggle, it's cowardly not to put up a fight!

LOGICIAN [*to the* OLD GENTLEMAN]: Separately or together, it all depends.

BERENGER [*to* JEAN]: What can I do? I've nothing to put up a fight with.

JEAN: Then find yourself some weapons, my friend.

OLD GENTLEMAN [*to the* LOGICIAN, *after painful reflection*]: Eight, eight paws.

LOGICIAN: Logic involves mental arithmetic, you see.

OLD GENTLEMAN: It certainly has many aspects!

BERENGER [*to* JEAN]: Where can I find the weapons?

LOGICIAN [*to the* OLD GENTLEMAN]: There are no limits to logic.

JEAN: Within yourself. Through your own will.

BERENGER: What weapons?

LOGICIAN [*to the* OLD GENTLEMAN]: I'm going to show you . . .

JEAN [*to* BERENGER]: The weapons of patience and culture, the weapons of the mind. [BERENGER *yawns.*] Turn yourself into a keen and brilliant intellect. Get yourself up to the mark!

BERENGER: How do I get myself up to the mark?

LOGICIAN [*to the* OLD GENTLEMAN]: If I take two paws away from these cats—how many does each have left?

OLD GENTLEMAN: That's not so easy.

BERENGER [*to* JEAN]: That's not so easy.

LOGICIAN [*to the* OLD GENTLEMAN]: On the contrary, it's simple.

OLD GENTLEMAN [*to the Logician*]: It may be simple for you, but not for me.

BERENGER [*to* JEAN]: It may be simple for you, but not for me.

LOGICIAN [*to the* OLD GENTLEMAN]: Come on, exercise your mind. Concentrate!

JEAN [*to* BERENGER]: Come on, exercise your will. Concentrate!

OLD GENTLEMAN [*to the* LOGICIAN]: I don't see how.

BERENGER [*to* JEAN]: I really don't see how.

LOGICIAN [*to the* OLD GENTLEMAN]: You have to be told everything.

JEAN [*to* BERENGER]: You have to be told everything.

LOGICIAN [*to the* OLD GENTLEMAN]: Take a sheet of paper and calculate. If you take six paws from the two cats, how many paws are left to each cat?

OLD GENTLEMAN: Just a moment . . . [*He calculates on a sheet of paper which he takes from his pocket.*]

JEAN: This is what you must do: dress yourself properly, shave every day, put on a clean shirt.

BERENGER: The laundry's so expensive . . .

JEAN: Cut down on your drinking. This is the way to come out: wear a hat, a tie like this, a well-cut suit, shoes well polished.

[*As he mentions the various items of clothing he points self-contentedly to his own hat, tie and shoes.*]

OLD GENTLEMAN [*to the* LOGICIAN]: There are several possible solutions.

LOGICIAN [*to the* OLD GENTLEMAN]: Tell me.

BERENGER [*to* JEAN]: Then what do I do? Tell me . . .

LOGICIAN [*to the* OLD GENTLEMAN]: I'm listening.

BERENGER [*to* JEAN]: I'm listening.

JEAN: You're a timid creature, but not without talent.

BERENGER: I've got talent, me?

JEAN: So use it. Put yourself in the picture. Keep abreast of the cultural and literary events of the times.

OLD GENTLEMAN [*to the* LOGICIAN]: One possibility is: one cat could have four paws and the other two.

BERENGER [*to* JEAN]: I get so little spare time!

LOGICIAN [*to the* OLD GENTLEMAN]: You're not without talent. You just needed to exercise it.

JEAN: Take advantage of what free time you *do* have. Don't just let yourself drift.

OLD GENTLEMAN: I've never had the time. I was an official, you know.

LOGICIAN: One can always find time to learn.

JEAN [*to* BERENGER]: One can always find time.

BERENGER [*to* JEAN]: It's too late now.

OLD GENTLEMAN [*to the* LOGICIAN]: It's a bit late in the day for me.

JEAN [*to* BERENGER]: It's never too late.

LOGICIAN [*to the* OLD GENTLEMAN]: It's never too late.

JEAN [*to* BERENGER]: You work eight hours a day, like me and everybody else, but not on Sundays, nor in the evening, nor for three weeks in the summer. That's quite sufficient, with a little method.

LOGICIAN [*to the* OLD GENTLEMAN]: Well, what about the other solutions? Use a little method, a little method!

[*The* OLD GENTLEMAN *starts to calculate anew.*]

JEAN [*to* BERENGER]: Look, instead of drinking and feeling sick, isn't it better to be fresh and eager, even at work? And you can spend your free time constructively.

BERENGER: How do you mean?

JEAN: By visiting museums, reading literary periodicals, going to lectures. That'll solve your troubles, it will develop your mind. In four weeks you'll be a cultured man.

BERENGER: You're right!

OLD GENTLEMAN [*to the* LOGICIAN]: There could be one cat with five paws . . .

JEAN [*to* BERENGER]: You see, you even think so yourself!

OLD GENTLEMAN [*to the* LOGICIAN]: And one cat with one paw. But would they still be cats, then?

LOGICIAN [*to the* OLD GENTLEMAN]: Why not?

JEAN [*to* BERENGER]: Instead of squandering all your spare money on drink, isn't it better to buy a ticket for an interesting play? Do you know anything about the avant-garde theatre there's so much talk about? Have you seen Ionesco's plays?

BERENGER [*to* JEAN]: Unfortunately, no. I've only heard people talk about them.

OLD GENTLEMAN [*to the* LOGICIAN]: By taking two of the eight paws away from the two cats . . .

JEAN [*to* BERENGER]: There's one playing now. Take advantage of it.

OLD GENTLEMAN [*to the* LOGICIAN]: . . . we could have one cat with six paws . . .

BERENGER: It would be an excellent initiation into the artistic life of our times.

OLD GENTLEMAN [*to the* LOGICIAN]: We could have one cat with no paws at all.

BERENGER: You're right, perfectly right. I'm going to put myself into the picture, like you said.

LOGICIAN [*to the* OLD GENTLEMAN]: In that case, one cat would be specially privileged.

BERENGER [*to* JEAN]: I will, I promise you.

JEAN: You promise yourself, that's the main thing.

OLD GENTLEMAN: And one under-privileged cat deprived of all paws.

BERENGER: I make myself a solemn promise, I'll keep my word to myself.

LOGICIAN: That would be unjust, and therefore not logical.

BERENGER: Instead of drinking, I'll develop my mind. I feel better already. My head already feels clearer.

JEAN: You see!

OLD GENTLEMAN [*to the* LOGICIAN]: Not logical?

BERENGER: This afternoon I'll go to the museum. And I'll book two seats for the theatre this evening. Will you come with me?

LOGICIAN [*to the* OLD GENTLEMAN]: Because Logic means Justice.

JEAN [*to* BERENGER]: You must persevere. Keep up your good resolutions.

OLD GENTLEMAN [*to the* LOGICIAN]: I get it. Justice . . .

BERENGER [*to* JEAN]: I promise you, and I promise myself. Will you come to the museum with me this afternoon?

JEAN [*to* BERENGER]: I have to take a rest this afternoon; it's in my programme for the day.

OLD GENTLEMAN: Justice is one more aspect of Logic.

BERENGER [*to* JEAN]: But you will come with me to the theatre this evening?

JEAN: No, not this evening.

LOGICIAN [*to the* OLD GENTLEMAN]: Your mind is getting clearer!

JEAN [*to* BERENGER]: I sincerely hope you'll keep up your good resolutions. But this evening I have to meet some friends for a drink.

BERENGER: For a drink?

OLD GENTLEMAN [*to the* LOGICIAN]: What's more, a cat with no paws at all . . .

JEAN [*to* BERENGER]: I've promised to go. I always keep my word.

OLD GENTLEMAN [*to the* LOGICIAN]: . . . wouldn't be able to run fast enough to catch mice.

BERENGER [*to* JEAN]: Ah, now it's you that's setting me a bad example! You're going out drinking.

LOGICIAN [*to the* OLD GENTLEMAN]: You're already making progress in logic.

[A sound of rapid galloping is heard approaching again, trumpeting and the sound of rhinoceros hooves and pantings; this time the sound comes from the opposite direction approaching from backstage to front, in the left wings.]

JEAN [*furiously to* BERENGER]: It's not a habit with me, you know. It's not the same as with you. With you . . . you're . . . it's not the same thing at all . . .

BERENGER: Why isn't it the same thing?

JEAN [*shouting over the noise coming from the café*]: I'm no drunkard, not me!

LOGICIAN [*shouting to the* OLD GENTLEMAN]: Even with no paws a cat must catch mice. That's in it's nature.

BERENGER [*shouting very loudly*]: I didn't mean you were a drunkard. But why would it make me one any more than you, in a case like that?

OLD GENTLEMAN [*shouting to the* LOGICIAN]: What's in the cat's nature?

JEAN [*to* BERENGER]: Because there's moderation in all things. I'm a moderate person, not like you!

LOGICIAN [*to the* OLD GENTLEMAN, *cupping his hands to his ears*]: What did you say? [*Deafening sounds drown the words of the four characters.*]

BERENGER [*to* JEAN, *cupping his hands to his ears*]: What about me, what? What did you say?

JEAN [*roaring*]: I said that . . .

OLD GENTLEMAN [*roaring*]: I said that . . .

JEAN [*suddenly aware of the noises which are now very near*]: Whatever's happening?

LOGICIAN: What is going on?

JEAN [*rises, knocking his chair over as he does so; looks towards left wings where the noises of the passing rhinoceros are coming from*]: Oh, a rhinoceros!

LOGICIAN [*rising, knocking over his chair*]: Oh, a rhinoceros!

OLD GENTLEMAN [*doing the same*]: Oh, a rhinoceros!

BERENGER [*still seated, but this time, taking more notice*]: Rhinoceros! In the opposite direction!

WAITRESS [*emerging with a tray and glasses*]: What is it? Oh, a rhinoceros! [*She drops the tray, breaking the glasses.*]

PROPRIETOR [*coming out of the café*]: What's going on?

WAITRESS [*to the* PROPRIETOR]: A rhinoceros!

LOGICIAN: A rhinoceros, going full-tilt on the opposite pavement!

GROCER [*coming out of his shop*]: Oh, a rhinoceros!

JEAN: Oh, a rhinoceros!

GROCER'S WIFE [*sticking her head through the upstairs window of shop*]: Oh, a rhinoceros!

PROPRIETOR: It's no reason to break the glasses.

JEAN: It's rushing straight ahead, brushing up against the shop windows.

DAISY [*entering left*]: Oh, a rhinoceros!

BERENGER [*noticing* DAISY]: Oh, Daisy!

[Noise of people fleeing, the same "Ohs" and "Ahs" as before.]

WAITRESS: Well, of all things!
PROPRIETOR [*to the* WAITRESS]: You'll be charged up for those!

[BERENGER *tries to make himself scarce, not to be seen by* DAISY. *The* OLD GENTLEMAN, *the* LOGICIAN, *the* GROCER *and his* WIFE *move to centre-stage and say together:*]

ALL: Well, of all things!
JEAN AND BERENGER: Well, of all things!

[*A piteous mewing is heard, then an equally piteous cry of a woman.*]

ALL: Oh!

[*Almost at the same time, and as the noises are rapidly dying away the* HOUSEWIFE *appears without her basket but holding the blood-stained corpse of her cat in her arms.*]

HOUSEWIFE [*wailing*]: It ran over my cat, it ran over my cat!
WAITRESS: It ran over her cat!

[*The* GROCER, *his* WIFE (*at the window*), *the* OLD GENTLEMAN, DAISY *and the* LOGICIAN *crowd round the* HOUSEWIFE, *saying*]:

ALL: What a tragedy, poor little thing!
OLD GENTLEMAN: Poor little thing!
DAISY AND WAITRESS: Poor little thing!
GROCER'S WIFE [*at the window*]:
OLD GENTLEMAN:
LOGICIAN: } Poor little thing!
PROPRIETOR [*to the* WAITRESS, *pointing to the broken glasses and the upturned chairs*]: Don't just stand there! Clear up the mess!

[JEAN *and* BERENGER *also rush over to the* HOUSEWIFE *who continues to lament, her dead cat in her arms.*]

WAITRESS [*moving to the café terrace to pick up the broken glasses and the chairs, and looking over her shoulder at the* HOUSEWIFE]: Oh, poor little thing!
PROPRIETOR [*pointing, for the* WAITRESS*'s benefit, to the debris*]: Over there, over there!
OLD GENTLEMAN [*to the* GROCER]: Well, what do you think of that?
BERENGER [*to the* HOUSEWIFE]: You mustn't cry like that, it's too heartbreaking!
DAISY [*to* BERENGER]: Were you there, Mr. Berenger? Did you see it?
BERENGER [*to* DAISY]: Good morning, Miss Daisy, you must excuse me, I haven't had a chance to shave . . .
PROPRIETOR [*supervising the clearing up of the debris, then glancing towards the* HOUSEWIFE]: Poor little thing!
WAITRESS [*clearing up the mess, her back to the* HOUSEWIFE]: Poor little thing!

[*These remarks must obviously be made very rapidly, almost simultaneously.*]

GROCER'S WIFE [*at window*]: That's going too far!
JEAN: That's going too far!
HOUSEWIFE [*lamenting, and cradling the dead cat in her arms*]: My poor little pussy, my poor little cat.
OLD GENTLEMAN [*to the* HOUSEWIFE]: What can you do, dear lady, cats are only mortal.
LOGICIAN: What do you expect, Madame? All cats are mortal! One must accept that.
HOUSEWIFE [*lamenting*]: My little cat, my poor little cat.
PROPRIETOR [*to the* WAITRESS *whose apron is full of broken glass*]: Throw that in the dustbin! [*He has picked up the chairs.*] You owe me a thousand francs.
WAITRESS [*moving into the café*]: All you think of is money!
GROCER'S WIFE [*to the* HOUSEWIFE; *from window*]: Don't upset yourself!
OLD GENTLEMAN [*to the* HOUSEWIFE]: Don't upset yourself, dear lady!
GROCER'S WIFE [*from window*]: It's very upsetting a thing like that!
HOUSEWIFE: My little cat, my little cat!
DAISY: Yes, it's very upsetting a thing like that.
OLD GENTLEMAN [*supporting the* HOUSEWIFE, *and guiding her to a table on the terrace followed by the others*]: Sit down here, dear lady.
JEAN [*to the* OLD GENTLEMAN]: Well, what do you think of that?
GROCER [*to the* LOGICIAN]: Well, what do you think of that?
GROCER'S WIFE [*to* DAISY, *from window*]: Well, what do you think of that?
PROPRIETOR [*to the* WAITRESS, *who comes back while they are installing the weeping* HOUSEWIFE *at one of the terrace tables, still cradling her dead cat*]: A glass of water for the lady.
OLD GENTLEMAN [*to the* HOUSEWIFE]: Sit down, dear lady!
JEAN: Poor woman!
GROCER'S WIFE [*from window*]: Poor cat!
BERENGER [*to the* WAITRESS]: Better give her a brandy.
PROPRIETOR [*to the* WAITRESS]: A brandy! [*Pointing to* BERENGER:] This gentleman is paying!
WAITRESS [*going into the café*]: One brandy, right away!
HOUSEWIFE [*sobbing*]: I don't want any, I don't want any!
GROCER: It went past my shop a little while ago.

JEAN [*to the* GROCER]: It wasn't the same one!
GROCER [*to* JEAN]: But I could have . . .
GROCER'S WIFE: Yes it was, it was the same one.
DAISY: Did it go past twice, then?
PROPRIETOR: I think it was the same one.
JEAN: No, it was not the same rhinoceros. The one that went by first had two horns on its nose, it was an Asiatic rhinoceros; this only had one, it was an African rhinoceros!

[*The* WAITRESS *appears with a glass of brandy and takes it to the* HOUSEWIFE.]

OLD GENTLEMAN: Here's a drop of brandy to pull you together.
HOUSEWIFE [*in tears*]: No . . . o . . . o . . .
BERENGER [*suddenly unnerved, to* JEAN]: You're talking nonsense . . . How could you possibly tell about the horns? The animal flashed past at such speed, we hardly even saw it . . .
DAISY [*to the* HOUSEWIFE]: Go on, it will do you good!
OLD GENTLEMAN [*to* BERENGER]: Very true. It did go fast.
PROPRIETOR [*to the* HOUSEWIFE]: Just have a taste, it's good.
BERENGER [*to* JEAN]: You had no time to count its horns . . .
GROCER'S WIFE [*to the* WAITRESS, *from window*]: Make her drink it.
BERENGER [*to* JEAN]: What's more, it was travelling in a cloud of dust.
DAISY [*to the* HOUSEWIFE]: Drink it up.
OLD GENTLEMAN [*to the* HOUSEWIFE]: Just a sip, dear little lady . . . be brave . . .

[*The* WAITRESS *forces her to drink it by putting the glass to her lips; the* HOUSEWIFE *feigns refusal, but drinks all the same.*]

WAITRESS: There, you see!
GROCER'S WIFE [*from her window*] AND DAISY: There, you see!
JEAN [*to* BERENGER]: I don't have to grope my way through a fog. I can calculate quickly, my mind is clear!
OLD GENTLEMAN [*to the* HOUSEWIFE]: Better now?
BERENGER [*to* JEAN]: But it had its head thrust down.
PROPRIETOR [*to the* HOUSEWIFE]: Now wasn't that good?
JEAN [*to* BERENGER]: Precisely, one could see all the better.
HOUSEWIFE [*after having drunk*]: My little cat!
BERENGER [*irritated*]: Utter nonsense!
GROCER'S WIFE [*to the* HOUSEWIFE, *from window*]: I've got another cat you can have.
JEAN [*to* BERENGER]: What me? You dare to accuse me of talking nonsense?
HOUSEWIFE [*to the* GROCER'S WIFE]: I'll never have another! [*She weeps, cradling her cat.*]
BERENGER [*to* JEAN]: Yes, absolute, blithering nonsense!
PROPRIETOR [*to the* HOUSEWIFE]: You have to accept these things!
JEAN [*to* BERENGER]: I've never talked nonsense in my life!
OLD GENTLEMAN [*to the* HOUSEWIFE]: Try and be philosophic about it!
BERENGER [*to* JEAN]: You're just a pretentious show-off— [*Raising his voice:*] a pedant!
PROPRIETOR [*to* JEAN *and* BERENGER]: Now, gentlemen!
BERENGER [*to* JEAN, *continuing*]: . . . and what's more, a pedant who's not certain of his facts because in the first place it's the Asiatic rhinoceros with only one horn on its nose, and it's the African with two . . .

[*The other characters leave the* HOUSEWIFE *and crowd round* JEAN *and* BERENGER *who argue at the top of their voices.*]

JEAN [*to* BERENGER]: You're wrong, it's the other way about!
HOUSEWIFE [*left alone*]: He was so sweet!
BERENGER: Do you want to bet?
WAITRESS: They want to make a bet!
DAISY [*to* BERENGER]: Don't excite yourself, Mr. Berenger.
JEAN [*to* BERENGER]: I'm not betting with you. If anybody's got two horns, it's you! You Asiatic Mongol!
WAITRESS: Oh!
GROCER'S WIFE [*from window to her husband*]: They're going to have a fight!
GROCER [*to his* WIFE]: Nonsense, it's just a bet!
PROPRIETOR [*to* JEAN *and* BERENGER]: We don't want any scenes here!
OLD GENTLEMAN: Now look . . . What kind of rhinoceros has one horn on its nose? [*To the* GROCER:] You're a tradesman, you should know.
GROCER'S WIFE [*to her husband*]: Yes, you should know!
BERENGER [*to* JEAN]: I've got no horns. And I never will have.
GROCER [*to the* OLD GENTLEMAN]: Tradesmen can't be expected to know everything.
JEAN [*to* BERENGER]: Oh yes, you have!
BERENGER [*to* JEAN]: I'm not Asiatic either. And in any case, Asiatics are people the same as everyone else . . .
WAITRESS: Yes, Asiatics are people the same as we are . . .
OLD GENTLEMAN [*to the* PROPRIETOR]: That's true!

PROPRIETOR [*to the* WAITRESS]: Nobody's asking for your opinion!

DAISY [*to the* PROPRIETOR]: She's right. They're people the same as we are.

[*The* HOUSEWIFE *continues to lament throughout this discussion.*]

HOUSEWIFE: He was so gentle, just like one of us.

JEAN [*beside himself*]: They're yellow!

[*The* LOGICIAN, *a little to one side between the* HOUSEWIFE *and the group which has formed round* JEAN *and* BERENGER, *follows the controversy attentively, without taking part.*]

Good-bye gentlemen! [*To* BERENGER:] You, I will not deign to include!

HOUSEWIFE: He was devoted to us! [*She sobs.*]

DAISY: Now listen a moment, Mr. Berenger, and you, too, Mr. Jean . . .

OLD GENTLEMAN: I once had some friends who were Asiatics! But perhaps they weren't real ones . . .

PROPRIETOR: I've known some real ones.

WAITRESS [*to the* GROCER'S WIFE]: I had an Asiatic friend once.

HOUSEWIFE [*still sobbing*]: I had him when he was a little kitten.

JEAN [*still quite beside himself*]: They're yellow, I tell you, bright yellow!

BERENGER [*to* JEAN]: Whatever they are, you're bright red!

GROCER'S WIFE [*from window*]
AND WAITRESS: Oh!

PROPRIETOR: This is getting serious!

HOUSEWIFE: He was so clean. He always used his tray.

JEAN [*to* BERENGER]: If that's how you feel, it's the last time you'll see me. I'm not wasting my time with a fool like you.

HOUSEWIFE: He always made himself understood.

[JEAN *goes off right, very fast and furious . . . but doubles back before making his final exit.*]

OLD GENTLEMAN [*to the* GROCER]: There are white Asiatics as well, and black and blue, and even some like us.

JEAN [*to* BERENGER]: You drunkard!

[*Everybody looks at him in consternation.*]

BERENGER [*to* JEAN]: I'm not going to stand for that!

ALL [*looking in* JEAN'S *direction*]: Oh!

HOUSEWIFE: He could almost talk—in fact he did.

DAISY [*to* BERENGER]: You shouldn't have made him angry.

BERENGER [*to* DAISY]: It wasn't my fault.

PROPRIETOR [*to the* WAITRESS]: Go and get a little coffin for the poor thing . . .

OLD GENTLEMAN [*to* BERENGER]: I think you're right. It's the Asiatic rhinoceros with two horns and the African with one . . .

GROCER: But he was saying the opposite.

DAISY [*to* BERENGER]: You were both wrong!

OLD GENTLEMAN [*to* BERENGER]: Even so, you were right.

WAITRESS [*to the* HOUSEWIFE]: Come with me, we're going to put him in a little box.

HOUSEWIFE [*sobbing desperately*]: No, never!

GROCER: If you don't mind my saying so, I think Mr. Jean was right.

DAISY [*turning to the* HOUSEWIFE]: Now, you must be reasonable!

[DAISY *and the* WAITRESS *lead the* HOUSEWIFE, *with her dead cat, towards the café entrance.*]

OLD GENTLEMAN [*to* DAISY *and the* WAITRESS]: Would you like me to come with you?

GROCER: The Asiatic rhinoceros has one horn and the African rhinoceros has two. And vice versa.

DAISY [*to the* OLD GENTLEMAN]: No, don't you bother.

[DAISY *and the* WAITRESS *enter the café leading the inconsolable* HOUSEWIFE.]

GROCER'S WIFE [*to the* GROCER, *from window*]: Oh you always have to be different from everybody else!

BERENGER [*aside, whilst the others continue to discuss the horns of the rhinoceros*]: Daisy was right, I should never have contradicted him.

PROPRIETOR [*to the* GROCER'S WIFE]: Your husband's right, the Asiatic rhinoceros has two horns and the African one must have two, and vice versa.

BERENGER [*aside*]: He can't stand being contradicted. The slightest disagreement makes him fume.

OLD GENTLEMAN [*to the* PROPRIETOR]: You're mistaken, my friend.

PROPRIETOR [*to the* OLD GENTLEMAN]: I'm very sorry, I'm sure.

BERENGER [*aside*]: His temper's his only fault.

GROCER'S WIFE [*from window, to the* OLD GENTLEMAN, *the* PROPRIETOR *and the* GROCER]: Maybe they're both the same.

BERENGER [*aside*]: Deep down, he's got a heart of gold; he's done me many a good turn.

PROPRIETOR [*to the* GROCER'S WIFE]: If the one has two horns, then the other must have one.

OLD GENTLEMAN: Perhaps it's the other with two and the one with one.

BERENGER [*aside*]: I'm sorry I wasn't more accommodating. But why is he so obstinate? I didn't want to exasperate him. [*To the others:*] He's always making fantastic statements! Always trying to dazzle people with his knowledge. He never will admit he's wrong.

OLD GENTLEMAN [*to* BERENGER]: Have you any proof?

BERENGER: Proof of what?

OLD GENTLEMAN: Of the statement you made just now which started the unfortunate row with your friend.

GROCER [*to* BERENGER]: Yes, have you any proof?

OLD GENTLEMAN [*to* BERENGER]: How do you know that one of the two rhinoceroses has one horn and the other two? And which is which?

GROCER'S WIFE: He doesn't know any more than we do.

BERENGER: In the first place we don't know that there were two. I myself believe there was only one.

PROPRIETOR: Well, let's say there were two. Does the single-horned one come from Asia?

OLD GENTLEMAN: No. It's the one from Africa with two, I think.

PROPRIETOR: Which is two-horned?

GROCER: It's not the one from Africa.

GROCER'S WIFE: It's not easy to agree on this.

OLD GENTLEMAN: But the problem must be cleared up.

LOGICIAN [*emerging from his isolation*]: Excuse me gentlemen for interrupting. But that is not the question. Allow me to introduce myself . . .

HOUSEWIFE [*coming out of the café in tears*]: He's a logician.

PROPRIETOR: Oh! A logician, is he?

OLD GENTLEMAN [*introducing the* LOGICIAN *to* BERENGER]: My friend, the Logician.

BERENGER: Very happy to meet you.

LOGICIAN [*continuing*]: Professional Logician; my card. [*He shows his card.*]

BERENGER: It's a great honour.

GROCER: A great honour for all of us.

PROPRIETOR: Would you mind telling us then, sir, if the African rhinoceros is single-horned . . .

OLD GENTLEMAN: Or bicorned . . .

GROCER'S WIFE: And is the Asiatic rhinoceros bicorned . . .

GROCER: Or unicorned.

LOGICIAN: Exactly, that is not the question. Let me make myself clear.

GROCER: But it's still what we want to find out.

LOGICIAN: Kindly allow me to speak, gentlemen.

OLD GENTLEMAN: Let him speak!

GROCER'S WIFE [*to the* GROCER, *from window*]: Give him a chance to speak.

PROPRIETOR: We're listening, sir.

LOGICIAN [*to* BERENGER]: I'm addressing you in particular. And all the others present as well.

GROCER: Us as well . . .

LOGICIAN: You see, you have got away from the problem which instigated the debate. In the first place you were deliberating whether or not the rhinoceros which passed by just now was the same one that passed by earlier, or whether it was another. That is the question to decide.

BERENGER: Yes, but how?

LOGICIAN: Thus: you may have seen on two occasions a single rhinoceros bearing a single horn . . .

GROCER [*repeating the words, as if to understand better*]: On two occasions a single rhinoceros . . .

PROPRIETOR [*doing the same*]: Bearing a single horn . . .

LOGICIAN: . . . or you may have seen on two occasions a single rhinoceros with two horns.

OLD GENTLEMAN [*repeating the words*]: A single rhinoceros with two horns on two occasions . . .

LOGICIAN: Exactly. Or again, you may have seen one rhinoceros with one horn, and then another also with a single horn.

GROCER'S WIFE [*from window*]: Ha, ha . . .

LOGICIAN: Or again, an initial rhinoceros with two horns, followed by a second with two horns . . .

PROPRIETOR: That's true.

LOGICIAN: Now, if you had seen . . .

GROCER: If we'd seen . . .

OLD GENTLEMAN: Yes, if we'd seen . . .

LOGICIAN: If on the first occasion you had seen a rhinoceros with two horns . . .

PROPRIETOR: With two horns . . .

LOGICIAN: And on the second occasion, a rhinoceros with one horn . . .

GROCER: With one horn . . .

LOGICIAN: That wouldn't be conclusive either.

OLD GENTLEMAN: Even that wouldn't be conclusive.

PROPRIETOR: Why not?

GROCER'S WIFE: Oh, I don't get it at all.

GROCER: Shoo! Shoo!

[*The* GROCER'S WIFE *shrugs her shoulders and withdraws from her window.*]

LOGICIAN: For it is possible that since its first appearance, the rhinoceros may have lost one of its horns, and that the first and second transit were still made by a single beast.

BERENGER: I see, but . . .

OLD GENTLEMAN [*interrupting* BERENGER]: Don't interrupt!

LOGICIAN: It may also be that two rhinoceroses both with two horns may each have lost a horn.

OLD GENTLEMAN: That is possible.

PROPRIETOR: Yes, that's possible.

GROCER: Why not?

BERENGER: Yes, but in any case . . .

OLD GENTLEMAN [*to* BERENGER]: Don't interrupt.

LOGICIAN: If you could prove that on the first occasion you saw a rhinoceros with one horn, either Asiatic or African . . .

OLD GENTLEMAN: Asiatic or African . . .

LOGICIAN: And on the second occasion a rhinoceros with two horns . . .

GROCER: One with two . . .

LOGICIAN: No matter whether African or Asiatic . . .

OLD GENTLEMAN: African or Asiatic . . .

LOGICIAN: . . . we could then conclude that we were dealing with two different rhinoceroses, for it is hardly likely that a second horn could grow sufficiently in a space of a few minutes to be visible on the nose of a rhinoceros.

OLD GENTLEMAN: It's hardly likely.

LOGICIAN [*enchanted with his discourse*]: That would imply one rhinoceros either Asiatic or African . . .

OLD GENTLEMAN: Asiatic or African . . .

LOGICIAN: . . . and one rhinoceros either African or Asiatic.

PROPRIETOR: African or Asiatic.

GROCER: Er . . . yais.

LOGICIAN: For good logic cannot entertain the possibility that the same creature be born in two places at the same time . . .

OLD GENTLEMAN: Or even successively.

LOGICIAN [*to* OLD GENTLEMAN]: Which was to be proved.

BERENGER [*to* LOGICIAN]: That seems clear enough, but it doesn't answer the question.

LOGICIAN [*to* BERENGER, *with a knowledgeable smile*]: Obviously, my dear sir, but now the problem is correctly posed.

OLD GENTLEMAN: It's quite logical. Quite logical.

LOGICIAN [*raising his hat*]: Good-bye, gentlemen.

[*He retires, going out left, followed by the* OLD GENTLEMAN.]

OLD GENTLEMAN: Good-bye, gentlemen. [*He raises his hat and follows the* LOGICIAN *out.*]

GROCER: Well, it may be logical . . .

[*At this moment the* HOUSEWIFE *comes out of the café in deep mourning, and carrying a box; she is followed by* DAISY *and the* WAITRESS *as if for a funeral. The* cortège *moves towards the right exit.*]

. . . it may be logical, but are we going to stand for our cats being run down under our very eyes by one-horned rhinoceroses *or* two, whether they're Asiatic *or* African? [*He indicates with a theatrical gesture the* cortège *which is just leaving.*]

PROPRIETOR: He's absolutely right! We're not standing for our cats being run down by rhinoceroses or anything else!

GROCER: We're not going to stand for it!

GROCER'S WIFE [*sticking her head round the shop door, to her husband*]: Are you coming in? The customers will be here any minute.

GROCER [*moving to the shop*]: No, we're not standing for it.

BERENGER: I should never have quarrelled with Jean! [*To the* PROPRIETOR:] Get me a brandy! A double!

PROPRIETOR: Coming up! [*He goes into the café for the brandy.*]

BERENGER [*alone*]: I never should have quarrelled with Jean. I shouldn't have got into such a rage!

[*The* PROPRIETOR *comes out carrying a large glass of brandy.*]

I feel too upset to go to the museum. I'll cultivate my mind some other time. [*He takes the glass of brandy and drinks it.*]

CURTAIN

ACT II

Scene 1

A government office, or the office of a private concern—such as a large firm of law publications. Up-stage centre, a large double door, above which a notice reads: "Chef du Service." Up-stage left, near to the Head of the Department's door, stands DAISY'S *little table with a typewriter. By the left wall, between a door which leads to the staircase and* DAISY'S *table, stands another table on which the time sheets are placed, which the employees sign on arrival. The door leading to the staircase is down-stage left. The top steps of the staircase can be seen, the top of a stair-rail and a small landing. In the foreground, a table with two chairs. On the table: printing proofs, an inkwell, pens; this is the table where* BOTARD *and* BERENGER *work;* BERENGER *will sit on the left chair,* BOTARD *on the right. Near to the right wall, another bigger, rectangular table, also covered with papers, proofs, etc.*

Two more chairs stand at each end of this table—more elegant and imposing chairs. This is the table of DUDARD *and* MR. BOEUF. DUDARD *will sit on the chair next to the wall, the other employees facing him. He acts as Deputy-Head. Between the up-stage door and the right wall, there is a window. If the theatre has an orchestra pit it would be preferable to have simply a window frame in front of the stage, facing the auditorium. In the right-hand corner, up-stage, a coat-stand, on which grey blouses or old coats are hung. The coat-stand could also be placed down-stage, near to the right wall.*

On the walls are rows of books and dusty documents. On the back wall, left, above the shelves, there are signs: "Jurisprudence," "Codes"; on the right-hand wall which can be slightly on an angle, the signs read: "Le Journal Officiel," "Lois fiscales." Above the Head of the Department's door a clock registers three minutes past nine.

When the curtain rises, DUDARD *is standing near his chair, his right profile to the auditorium; on the other side of the desk, left profile to the auditorium, is* BOTARD; *between them, also near to the desk, facing the auditorium, stands the Head of the Department;* DAISY *is near to the Chief, a little up-stage of him. She holds some sheets of typing paper. On the table round which the three characters stand, a large open newspaper lies on the printing proofs.*

When the curtain rises the characters remain fixed for a few seconds in position for the first line of dialogue. They make a tableau vivant. *The same effect marks the beginning of the first act.*

The Head of the Department is about forty, very correctly dressed: dark blue suit, a rosette of the Legion of Honour, starched collar, black tie, large brown moustache. He is MR. PAPILLON.

DUDARD, *thirty-five years old; grey suit; he wears black lustrine sleeves to protect his coat. He may wear spectacles. He is a quite tall, young employee with a future. If the Department Head became the Assistant Director he would take his place:* BOTARD *does not like him.*

BOTARD: *former schoolteacher; short, he has a proud air, and wears a little white moustache; a brisk sixty year-old: [he knows everything, understands everything, judges everything]. He wears a Basque beret, and wears a long grey blouse during working hours; spectacles on a longish nose; a pencil behind his ear; he also wears protective sleeves at work.*

DAISY: *young blonde.*

Later, MRS. BOEUF: *a large woman of some forty to fifty years old, tearful, and breathless.*

[*As the curtain rises, the characters therefore are standing motionless around the table, right; the Chief with index finger pointing to the newspaper;* DUDARD, *with his hand extended in* BOTARD*'s direction, seems to be saying: 'so you see!'* BOTARD, *hands in the pocket of his blouse, wears an incredulous smile and seems to say: 'You won't take me in.'* DAISY, *with her typing paper in her hand seems, from her look, to be supporting* DUDARD. *After a few brief seconds,* BOTARD *starts the attack.*]

BOTARD: It's all a lot of made-up nonsense.

DAISY: But I saw it, I saw the rhinoceros!

DUDARD: It's in the paper, in black and white, you can't deny that.

BOTARD [*with an air of the greatest scorn*]: Pfff!

DUDARD: It's all here; it's down here in the dead cats column! Read it for yourself, Chief.

PAPILLON: 'Yesterday, just before lunch time, in the church square of our town, a cat was trampled to death by a pachyderm!'

DAISY: It wasn't exactly in the church square.

PAPILLON: That's all it says. No other details.

BOTARD: Pfff!

DUDARD: Well, that's clear enough.

BOTARD: I never believe journalists. They're all liars. I don't need them to tell me what to think; I believe what I see with my own eyes. Speaking as a former teacher, I like things to be precise, scientifically valid; I've got a methodical mind.

DUDARD: What's a methodical mind got to do with it?

DAISY [*to* BOTARD]: I think it's stated very precisely, Mr. Botard.

BOTARD: You call that precise? And what, pray, does it mean by a pachyderm? What does the editor of a dead cats column understand by a pachyderm? He doesn't say. And what does he mean by a cat?

DUDARD: Everybody knows what a cat is.

BOTARD: Does it concern a male cat or a female? What breed was it? And what colour? The colour bar is something I feel strongly about. I hate it.

PAPILLON: What has the colour bar to do with it, Mr. Botard? It's quite beside the point.

BOTARD: Please forgive me, Mr. Papillon. But you can't deny that the colour problem is one of the great stumbling blocks of our time.

DUDARD: I know that, we all know that, but it has nothing to do with . . .

BOTARD: It's not an issue to be dismissed lightly, Mr. Dudard. The course of history has shown that racial prejudice . . .

DUDARD: I tell you it doesn't enter into it.

BOTARD: I'm not so sure.

PAPILLON: The colour bar is not the issue at stake.

BOTARD: One should never miss an occasion to denounce it.

DAISY: But we told you that none of us is in favour of the colour bar. You're obscuring the issue; it's simply a question of a cat being run over by a pachyderm—in this case, a rhinoceros.

BOTARD: I'm a Northerner myself. Southerners have got too much imagination. Perhaps it was merely a flea run over by a mouse. People make mountains out of molehills.

PAPILLON [*to* DUDARD]: Let us try and get things clear. Did you yourself, with your own eyes, see a rhinoceros strolling through the streets of the town?

DAISY: It didn't stroll, it ran.

DUDARD: No, I didn't see it personally. But a lot of very reliable people . . . !

BOTARD [*interrupting him*]: It's obvious they were just making it up. You put too much trust in these journalists; they don't care what they invent to sell their wretched newspapers and please the bosses they serve! And you mean to tell me they've taken you in—you, a qualified man of law! Forgive me for laughing! Ha! Ha! Ha!

DAISY: But I saw it, I saw the rhinoceros. I'd take my oath on it.

BOTARD: Get away with you! And I thought you were a sensible girl!

DAISY: Mr. Botard, I can see straight! And I wasn't the only one; there were plenty of other people watching.

BOTARD: Pfff! They were probably watching something else! A few idlers with nothing to do, work-shy loafers!

DUDARD: It happened yesterday, Sunday.

BOTARD: I work on Sundays as well. I've no time for priests who do their utmost to get you to church, just to prevent you from working, and earning your daily bread by the sweat of your brow.

PAPILLON [*indignant*]: Oh!

BOTARD: I'm sorry, I didn't mean to offend you. The fact that I despise religion doesn't mean I don't esteem it highly. [*To* DAISY:] In any case, do you know what a rhinoceros looks like?

DAISY: It's a . . . it's a very big, ugly animal.

BOTARD: And you pride yourself on your precise thinking! The rhinoceros, my dear young lady . . .

PAPILLON: There's no need to start a lecture on the rhinoceros here. We're not in school.

BOTARD: That's a pity.

[*During these last speeches* BERENGER *is seen climbing the last steps of the staircase; he opens the office door cautiously; as he does so one can read the notice on it: "Editions de Droit."*]

PAPILLON: Well! It's gone nine, Miss Daisy; put the time sheets away. Too bad about the late-comers.

[DAISY *goes to the little table, left, on which the time sheets are placed, at the same moment as* BERENGER *enters.*]

BERENGER [*entering, whilst the others continue their discussion, to* DAISY]: Good morning, Miss Daisy. I'm not late, am I?

BOTARD [*to* DUDARD *and* PAPILLON]: I campaign against ignorance wherever I find it . . . !

DAISY [*to* BERENGER]: Hurry up, Mr. Berenger.

BOTARD: . . . in palace or humble hut!

DAISY [*to* BERENGER]: Quick! Sign the time sheet!

BERENGER: Oh thank you! Has the Boss arrived?

DAISY [*a finger on her lips*]: Shh! Yes, he's here.

BERENGER: Here already? [*He hurries to sign the time sheet.*]

BOTARD [*continuing*]: No matter where! Even in printing offices.

PAPILLON [*to* BOTARD]: Mr. Botard, I consider . . .

BERENGER [*signing the sheet, to* DAISY]: But it's not ten past . . .

PAPILLON [*to* BOTARD]: I consider you have gone too far.

DUDARD [*to* PAPILLON]: I think so too, sir.

PAPILLON [*to* BOTARD]: Are you suggesting that Mr. Dudard, my colleague and yours, a law graduate and a first-class employee, is ignorant?

BOTARD: I wouldn't go so far as to say that, but the teaching you get at the university isn't up to what you get at the ordinary schools.

PAPILLON [*to* DAISY]: What about that time sheet?

DAISY [*to* PAPILLON]: Here it is, sir. [*She hands it to him.*]

BOTARD [*to* DUDARD]: There's no clear thinking at the universities, no encouragement for practical observation.

DUDARD [*to* BOTARD]: Oh come now!

BERENGER [*to* PAPILLON]: Good morning, Mr. Papillon. [*He has been making his way to the coat-rack behind the Chief's back and around the group formed by the three characters; there he takes down his working overall or his well-worn coat, and hangs up his street coat in its place; he changes his coat by the coat-rack, then makes his way to his desk, from the drawer of which he takes out his black protective sleeves, etc.*] Morning, Mr. Papillon! Sorry I was almost late. Morning Dudard! Morning, Mr. Botard.

PAPILLON: Well Berenger, did you see the rhinoceros by any chance?

BOTARD [*to* DUDARD]: All you get at the universities are effete intellectuals with no practical knowledge of life.

DUDARD [*to* BOTARD]: Rubbish!

BERENGER [*continuing to arrange his working equipment with excessive zeal as if to make up for his late arrival; in a natural tone to* PAPILLON]: Oh yes, I saw it all right.

BOTARD [*turning round*]: Pfff!

DAISY: So you see, I'm not mad after all.

BOTARD [*ironic*]: Oh, Mr. Berenger says that out of chivalry—he's a very chivalrous man even if he doesn't look it.

DUDARD: What's chivalrous about saying you've seen a rhinoceros?

BOTARD: A lot—when it's said to bolster up a fantastic statement by Miss Daisy. Everybody is chivalrous to Miss Daisy, it's very understandable.

PAPILLON: Don't twist the facts, Mr. Botard. Mr. Berenger took no part in the argument. He's only just arrived.

BERENGER [*to* DAISY]: But you did see it, didn't you? We both did.

BOTARD: Pfff! It's possible that Mr. Berenger thought he saw a rhinoceros. [*He makes a sign behind* BERENGER*'s back to indicate he drinks.*] He's got such a vivid imagination! Anything's possible with him!

BERENGER: I wasn't alone when I saw the rhinoceros! Or perhaps there were two rhinoceroses.

BOTARD: He doesn't even know how many he saw.

BERENGER: I was with my friend Jean! And other people were there, too.

BOTARD [*to* BERENGER]: I don't think you know what you're talking about.

DAISY: It was a unicorned rhinoceros.

BOTARD: Pff! They're in league, the two of them, to have us on.

DUDARD [*to* DAISY]: I rather think it had two horns, from what I've heard!

BOTARD: You'd better make up your minds.

PAPILLON [*looking at the time*]: That will do, gentlemen, time's getting on.

BOTARD: Did you see one rhinoceros, Mr. Berenger, or two rhinoceroses?

BERENGER: Well, it's hard to say!

BOTARD: You don't know. Miss Daisy saw one unicorned rhinoceros. What about your rhinoceros, Mr. Berenger, if indeed there was one, did it have one horn or two?

BERENGER: Exactly, that's the whole problem.

BOTARD: And it's all very dubious.

DAISY: Oh!

BOTARD: I don't mean to be offensive. But I don't believe a word of it. No rhinoceros has ever been seen in this country!

DAISY: There's a first time for everything.

BOTARD: It has never been seen! Except in school-book illustrations. Your rhinoceroses are a flower of some washerwoman's imagination.

BERENGER: The word "flower" applied to a rhinoceros seems a bit out of place.

DUDARD: Very true.

BOTARD [*continuing*]: Your rhinoceros is a myth!

DAISY: A myth?

PAPILLON: Gentlemen I think it is high time we started to work.

BOTARD [*to* DAISY]: A myth—like flying saucers.

DUDARD: But nevertheless a cat was trampled to death—that you can't deny.

BERENGER: I was a witness to that.

DUDARD [*pointing to* BERENGER]: In front of witnesses.

BOTARD: Yes, and what a witness!

PAPILLON: Gentlemen, gentlemen!

BOTARD [*to* DUDARD]: An example of collective psychosis, Mr. Dudard. Just like religion—the opiate of the people!

DAISY: Well I believe flying saucers exist!

BOTARD: Pfff!

PAPILLON [*firmly*]: That's quite enough. There's been enough gossip! Rhinoceros or no rhinoceros, saucers or no saucers, work must go on! You're not paid to waste your time arguing about real or imaginary animals.

BOTARD: Imaginary!

DUDARD: Real!

DAISY: Very real!

PAPILLON: Gentlemen, I remind you once again that we are in working hours. I am putting an end to this futile discussion.

BOTARD [*wounded and ironic*]: Very well, Mr. Papillon. You are the Chief. Your wishes are our commands.

PAPILLON: Get on, gentlemen. I don't want to be forced to make a deduction from your salaries! Mr. Dudard, how is your report on the alcoholic repression law coming along?

DUDARD: I'm just finishing it off, sir.

PAPILLON: Then do so. It's very urgent. Mr. Berenger and Mr. Botard, have you finished correcting the proofs for the wine trade control regulations?

BERENGER: Not yet, Mr. Papillon. But they're well on the way.

PAPILLON: Then finish off the corrections together. The printers are waiting. And Miss Daisy, you bring the letters to my office for signature. Hurry up and get them typed.

DAISY: Very good, Mr. Papillon.

[DAISY *goes and types at her little desk.* DUDARD *sits at his desk and starts to work.* BERENGER *and* BOTARD *sit at their little tables in profile to the auditorium.* BOTARD, *his back to the staircase, seems in a bad temper.* BERENGER *is passive and limp; he spreads the proofs on the table, passes the manuscript to* BOTARD; BOTARD *sits down grumbling, whilst* PAPILLON *exits banging the door loudly.*]

PAPILLON: I shall see you shortly, gentlemen. [*Goes out.*]

BERENGER [*reading and correcting whilst* BOTARD *checks the manuscript with a pencil*]: Laws relating to the control of proprietary wine produce . . . [*He corrects.*] control with one L . . . [*He corrects.*] proprietary . . . one P, proprietary . . . The controlled wines of the Bordeaux region, the lower sections of the upper slopes . . .

BOTARD: I haven't got that! You've skipped a line.

BERENGER: I'll start again. The Wine Control!

DUDARD [*to* BERENGER *and* BOTARD]: Please don't read so loud. I can't concentrate with you shouting at the tops of your voices.

BOTARD [*to* DUDARD, *over* BERENGER'*s head, resuming the recent discussion, whilst* BERENGER *continues the corrections on his own for a few moments; he moves his lips noiselessly as he reads*]: It's all a hoax.

DUDARD: What's all a hoax?

BOTARD: Your rhinoceros business, of course. You've been making all this propaganda to get these rumours started!

DUDARD [*interrupting his work*]: What propaganda?

BERENGER [*breaking in*]: No question of any propaganda.

DAISY [*interrupting her typing*]: Do I have to tell you again, I saw it . . . I actually saw it, and others did, too.

DUDARD [*to* BOTARD]: You make me laugh! Propaganda! Propaganda for what?

BOTARD [*to* DUDARD]: Oh you know more about that than I do. Don't make out you're so innocent.

DUDARD [*getting angry*]: At any rate, Mr. Botard, I'm not in the pay of any furtive underground organization.

BOTARD: That's an insult, I'm not standing for that . . . [*Rises.*]

BERENGER [*pleading*]: Now, now, Mr. Botard . . .

DAISY [*to* DUDARD, *who has also risen*]: Now, now, Mr. Dudard . . .

BOTARD: I tell you it's an insult.

[MR. PAPILLON'*s door suddenly opens.*] BOTARD *and* DUDARD *sit down again quickly;* MR. PAPILLON *is holding the time sheet in his hand; there is silence at his appearance.*]

PAPILLON: Is Mr. Boeuf not in today?

BERENGER [*looking around*]: No, he isn't. He must be absent.

PAPILLON: Just when I needed him. [*To* DAISY:] Did he let anyone know he was ill or couldn't come in?

DAISY: He didn't say anything to me.

PAPILLON [*opening his door wide, and coming in*]: If this goes on I shall fire him. It's not the first time he's played me this trick. Up to now I haven't said anything, but it's not going on like this. Has anyone got the key to his desk?

[*At this moment* MRS. BOEUF *enters. She has been seen during the last speech coming up the stairs. She bursts through the door, out of breath, apprehensive.*]

BERENGER: Oh here's Mrs. Boeuf.

DAISY: Morning, Mrs. Boeuf.

MRS. BOEUF: Morning, Mr. Papillon. Good morning everyone.

PAPILLON: Well, where's your husband? What's happened to him? Is it too much trouble for him to come any more?

MRS. BOEUF [*breathless*]: Please excuse him, my husband I mean . . . he went to visit his family for the week-end. He's got a touch of flu.

PAPILLON: So he's got a touch of flu, has he?

MRS. BOEUF [*handing a paper to* PAPILLON]: He says so in the telegram. He hopes to be back on Wednesday . . . [*Almost fainting.*] Could I have a glass of water . . . and sit down a moment . . .

[BERENGER *takes his own chair centre-stage, on which she flops.*]

PAPILLON [*to* DAISY]: Give her a glass of water.

DAISY: Yes, straightaway! [*She goes to get her a glass of water, and gives it to her during the following speeches.*]

DUDARD [*to* PAPILLON]: She must have a weak heart.

PAPILLON: It's a great nuisance that Mr. Boeuf can't come. But that's no reason for you to go to pieces.

MRS. BOEUF [*with difficulty*]: It's not . . . it's . . . well I was chased here all the way from the house by a rhinoceros . . .

BERENGER: How many horns did it have?

BOTARD [*guffawing*]: Don't make me laugh!

DUDARD [*indignant*]: Give her a chance to speak!

MRS. BOEUF [*making a great effort to be exact, and pointing in the direction of the staircase*]: It's down there, by the entrance. It seemed to want to come upstairs.

[*At this moment a noise is heard. The staircase steps are seen to crumble under an obviously formidable weight. From below an anguished trumpeting is heard. As the dust clears after the collapse of the staircase, the staircase landing is seen to be hanging in space.*]

DAISY: My God!

MRS. BOEUF [*seated, her hand on her heart*]: Oh! Ah!

[BERENGER *runs to administer to* MRS. BOEUF, *patting her cheeks and making her drink.*]

BERENGER: Keep calm!

[*Meanwhile* PAPILLON, DUDARD *and* BOTARD *rush left, jostling each other in their efforts to open the door, and stand covered in dust on the landing; the trumpetings continue to be heard.*]

DAISY [*to* MRS. BOEUF]: Are you feeling better now, Mrs. Boeuf?

PAPILLON [*on the landing*]: There it is! Down there! It is one!

BOTARD: I can't see a thing. It's an illusion.

DUDARD: Of course it's one, down there, turning round and round.

DUDARD: It can't get up here. There's no staircase any longer.
BOTARD: It's most strange. What can it mean?
DUDARD [*turning towards* BERENGER]: Come and look. Come and have a look at your rhinoceros.
BERENGER: I'm coming.

[BERENGER *rushes to the landing, followed by* DAISY *who abandons* MRS. BOEUF.]

PAPILLON [*to* BERENGER]: You're the rhinoceros expert—take a good look.
BERENGER: I'm no rhinoceros expert . . .
DAISY: Oh look at the way it's going round and round. It looks as if it was in pain . . . what can it want?
DUDARD: It seems to be looking for someone. [*To* BOTARD:] Can you see it now?
BOTARD [*vexed*]: Yes, yes, I can see it.
DAISY [*to* PAPILLON]: Perhaps we're all seeing things. You as well . . .
BOTARD: I never see things. Something is definitely down there.
DUDARD [*to* BOTARD]: What do you mean, something?
PAPILLON [*to* BERENGER]: It's obviously a rhinoceros. That's what you saw before, isn't it? [*To* DAISY:] And you, too?
DAISY: Definitely.
BERENGER: It's got two horns. It's an African rhinoceros, or Asiatic rather. Oh! I don't know whether the African rhinoceros has one horn or two.
PAPILLON: It's demolished the staircase—and a good thing, too! When you think how long I've been asking the management to install stone steps in place of that worm-eaten old staircase.
DUDARD: I sent a report a week ago, Chief.
PAPILLON: It was bound to happen, I knew that. I could see it coming, and I was right.
DAISY [*to* PAPILLON, *ironically*]: As always.
BERENGER [*to* DUDARD *and* PAPILLON]: Now look, are two horns a characteristic of the Asiatic rhinoceros or the African? And is one horn a characteristic of the African or the Asiatic one . . . ?
DAISY: Poor thing, it keeps on trumpeting and going round and round. What does it want? Oh, it's looking at us! [*To the rhinoceros.*] Puss, puss, puss . . .
DUDARD: I shouldn't try to stroke it, it's probably not tame . . .
PAPILLON: In any case, it's out of reach.

[*The rhinoceros gives a horrible trumpeting.*]

DAISY: Poor thing!
BERENGER [*to* BOTARD, *still insisting*]: You're very well informed, don't you think that the ones with two horns are . . .
PAPILLON: What are you rambling on about, Berenger? You're still a bit under the weather, Mr. Botard was right.
BOTARD: How can it be possible in a civilized country . . . ?
DAISY [*to* BOTARD]: All right. But does it exist or not?
BOTARD: It's all an infamous plot! [*With a political orator's gesture he points to* DUDARD, *quelling him with a look.*] It's all your fault!
DUDARD: Why mine, rather than yours?
BOTARD [*furious*]: Mine? It's always the little people who get the blame. If I had my way . . .
PAPILLON: We're in a fine mess with no staircase.
DAISY [*to* BOTARD *and* DUDARD]: Calm down, this is no time to quarrel!
PAPILLON: It's all the management's fault.
DAISY: Maybe. But how are we going to get down?
PAPILLON [*joking amorously and caressing* DAISY'S *cheek*]: I'll take you in my arms and we'll float down together.
DAISY [*rejecting* PAPILLON'S *advances*]: You keep your horny hands off my face, you old pachyderm!
PAPILLON: I was only joking!

[*Meanwhile the rhinoceros has continued its trumpeting.* MRS. BOEUF *has risen and joined the group. For a few moments she stares fixedly at the rhinoceros turning round and round below; suddenly she lets out a terrible cry.*]

MRS. BOEUF: My God! It can't be true!
BERENGER [*to* MRS. BOEUF]: What's the matter?
MRS. BOEUF: It's my husband. Oh Boeuf, my poor Boeuf, what's happened to you?
DAISY [*to* MRS. BOEUF]: Are you positive?
MRS. BOEUF: I recognize him, I recognize him!

[*The rhinoceros replies with a violent but tender trumpeting.*]

PAPILLON: Well! That's the last straw. This time he's fired for good!
DUDARD: Is he insured?
BOTARD [*aside*]: I understand it all now . . .
DAISY: How can you collect insurance in a case like this?
MRS. BOEUF [*fainting into* BERENGER'S *arms*]: Oh! My God!
BERENGER: Oh!
DAISY: Carry her over here!

[BERENGER, *helped by* DUDARD *and* DAISY, *installs* MRS. BOEUF *in a chair.*]

DUDARD [*while they are carrying her*]: Don't upset yourself, Mrs. Boeuf.
MRS. BOEUF: Ah! Oh!

DAISY: Maybe it can all be put right . . .
PAPILLON [*to* DUDARD]: Legally, what can be done?
DUDARD: You need to get a solicitor's advice.
BOTARD [*following the procession, raising his hands to heaven*]: It's the sheerest madness! What a society!

[*They crowd round* MRS. BOEUF, *pinching her cheeks; she opens her eyes, emits an "Ah" and closes them again; they continue to pinch her cheeks as* BOTARD *speaks:*]

You can be certain of one thing: I shall report this to my union. I don't desert a colleague in the hour of need. It won't be hushed up.
MRS. BOEUF [*coming to*]: My poor darling, I can't leave him like that, my poor darling. [*A trumpeting is heard.*] He's calling me. [*Tenderly*] He's calling me.
DAISY: Feeling better now, Mrs. Boeuf?
DUDARD: She's picking up a bit.
BOTARD [*to* MRS. BOEUF]: You can count on the union's support. Would you like to become a member of the committee?
PAPILLON: Work's going to be delayed again. What about the post, Miss Daisy?
DAISY: I want to know first how we're going to get out of here.
PAPILLON: It is a problem. Through the window.

[*They all go to the window with the exception of* MRS. BOEUF *slumped in her chair and* BOTARD *who stays centre-stage.*]

BOTARD: I know where it came from.
DAISY [*at window*]: It's too high.
BERENGER: Perhaps we ought to call the firemen, and get them to bring ladders!
PAPILLON: Miss Daisy, go to my office and telephone the fire brigade. [*He makes as if to follow her.*]

[DAISY *goes out up-stage and one hears her voice on the telephone say: "Hello, hello, is that the Fire Brigade?" followed by a vague sound of telephone conversation.*]

MRS. BOEUF [*rising suddenly*]: I can't desert him, I can't desert him now!
PAPILLON: If you want to divorce him . . . you'd be perfectly justified.
DUDARD: You'd be the injured party.
MRS. BOEUF: No! Poor thing! This is not the moment for that. I won't abandon my husband in such a state.
BOTARD: You're a good woman.
DUDARD [*to* MRS. BOEUF]: But what are you going to do?

[*She runs left towards the landing.*]

BERENGER: Watch out!
MRS. BOEUF: I can't leave him, I can't leave him now!
DUDARD: Hold her back!
MRS. BOEUF: I'm taking him home!
PAPILLON: What's she trying to do?
MRS. BOEUF [*preparing to jump; on the edge of the landing*]: I'm coming my darling, I'm coming!
BERENGER: She's going to jump.
BOTARD: It's no more than her duty.
DUDARD: She can't do that.

[*Everyone with the exception of* DAISY, *who is still telephoning, is near to* MRS. BOEUF *on the landing; she jumps;* BERENGER *who tries to restrain her, is left with her skirt in his hand.*]

BERENGER: I couldn't hold her back. [*The rhinoceros is heard from below, tenderly trumpeting.*]
VOICE OF MRS. BOEUF: Here I am, my sweet, I'm here now.
DUDARD: She landed on his back in the saddle.
BOTARD: She's a good rider.
VOICE OF MRS. BOEUF: Home now, dear, let's go home.
DUDARD: They're off at a gallop.

[DUDARD, BOTARD, BERENGER, PAPILLON *come back on-stage and go to the window.*]

BERENGER: They're moving fast.
DUDARD [*to* PAPILLON]: Ever done any riding?
PAPILLON: A bit . . . a long time ago . . . [*Turning to the up-stage door, to* DUDARD:] Is she still on the telephone?
BERENGER [*following the course of the rhinoceros*]: They're already a long way off. They're out of sight.
DAISY [*coming on-stage*]: I had trouble getting the firemen.
BOTARD [*as if concluding an interior monologue*]: A fine state of affairs!
DAISY: . . . I had trouble getting the firemen!
PAPILLON: Are there fires all over the place, then?
BERENGER: I agree with Mr. Botard. Mrs. Boeuf's attitude is very moving; she's a woman of feeling.
PAPILLON: It means one employee less, who has to be replaced.
BERENGER: Do you really think he's no use to us any more?
DAISY: No, there aren't any fires, the firemen have been called out for other rhinoceroses.
BERENGER: For other rhinoceroses?
DAISY: Yes, other rhinoceroses. They've been reported all over the town. This morning there were seven, now there are seventeen.
BOTARD: What did I tell you?

DAISY: As many as thirty-two have been reported. They're not official yet, but they're bound to be confirmed soon.
BOTARD [*less certain*]: Pff!! They always exaggerate.
PAPILLON: Are they coming to get us out of here?
BERENGER: I'm hungry . . . !
DAISY: Yes, they're coming; the firemen are on the way.
PAPILLON: What about the work?
DUDARD: It looks as if it's out of our hands.
PAPILLON: We'll have to make up the lost time.
DUDARD: Well, Mr. Botard, do you still deny all rhinocerotic evidence?
BOTARD: Our union is against your dismissing Mr. Boeuf without notice.
PAPILLON: It's not up to me; we shall see what conclusions they reach at the enquiry.
BOTARD [*to* DUDARD]: No, Mr. Dudard, I do not deny the rhinocerotic evidence. I never have.
DUDARD: That's not true.
DAISY: Oh no, that's not true.
BOTARD: I repeat I have never denied it. I just wanted to find out exactly where it was all leading. Because I know my own mind. I'm not content to simply state that a phenomenon exists. I make it my business to understand and explain it. At least I could explain it if . . .
DUDARD: Then explain it to us.
DAISY: Yes, explain it, Mr. Botard.
PAPILLON: Explain it, when your colleagues ask you.
BOTARD: I will explain it . . .
DUDARD: We're all listening.
DAISY: I'm most curious.
BOTARD: I will explain it . . . one day . . .
DUDARD: Why not now?
BOTARD [*menacingly; to* MR. PAPILLON]: We'll go into the explanation later, in private. [*To everyone:*] I know the whys and the wherefores of this whole business . . .
DAISY: What whys?
BERENGER: What wherefores?
DUDARD: I'd give a lot to know these whys and wherefores . . .
BOTARD [*continuing; with a terrible air*]: And I also know the names of those responsible. The names of the traitors. You can't fool me. I'll let you know the purpose and the meaning of this whole plot! I'll unmask the perpetrators!
BERENGER: But who'd want to . . .
DUDARD [*to* BOTARD]: You're evading the question, Mr. Botard.
PAPILLON: Let's have no evasions.
BOTARD: Evading? What, me?
DAISY: Just now you accused us of suffering from hallucinations.
BOTARD: Just now, yes. Now the hallucination has become a provocation.
DUDARD: And how do you consider this change came about?
BOTARD: It's an open secret, gentlemen. Even the man in the street knows about it. Only hypocrites pretend not to understand.

[*The noise and hooting of a fire-engine is heard. The brakes are abruptly applied just under the window.*]

DAISY: That's the firemen!
BOTARD: There're going to be some big changes made; they won't get away with it as easily as that.
DUDARD: That doesn't mean anything, Mr. Botard. The rhinoceroses exist, and that's that. That's all there is to it.
DAISY [*at the window, looking down*]: Up here, firemen!

[*A bustling is heard below, commotion, engine noises.*]

VOICE OF FIREMAN: Put up the ladder!
BOTARD [*to* DUDARD]: I hold the key to all these happenings, an infallible system of interpretation.
PAPILLON: I want you all back in the office this afternoon.

[*The fireman's ladder is placed against the window.*]

BOTARD: Too bad about the office, Mr. Papillon.
PAPILLON: I don't know what the management will say!
DUDARD: These are exceptional circumstances.
BOTARD [*pointing to the window*]: They can't force us to come back this way. We'll have to wait till the staircase is repaired.
DUDARD: If anyone breaks a leg, it'll be the management's responsibility.
PAPILLON: That's true.

[*A fireman's helmet is seen, followed by the* FIREMAN.]

BERENGER [*to* DAISY *pointing to the window*]: After you, Miss Daisy.
FIREMAN: Come on, Miss.

[*The fireman takes* DAISY *in his arms; she steps astride the window and disappears with him.*]

DUDARD: Good-bye Miss Daisy. See you soon.
DAISY [*disappearing*]: See you soon, good-bye!
PAPILLON [*at window*]: Telephone me tomorrow morning, Miss Daisy. You can come and type the letters at my house. [*To* BERENGER:] Mr. Berenger, I draw your attention to the fact that we are not

on holiday, and that work will resume as soon as possible. [*To the other two:*] You hear what I say, gentlemen?
DUDARD: Of course, Mr. Papillon.
BOTARD: They'll go on exploiting us till we drop, of course.
FIREMAN [*reappearing at window*]: Who's next?
PAPILLON [*to all three of them*]: Go on!
DUDARD: After you, Mr. Papillon.
BERENGER: After you, Chief.
BOTARD: You first, of course.
PAPILLON [*to* BERENGER]: Bring me Miss Daisy's letters. There, on the table.

[BERENGER *goes and gets the letters, brings them to* PAPILLON.]

FIREMAN: Come on, hurry up. We've not got all day. We've got other calls to make.
BOTARD: What did I tell you?

[PAPILLON, *the letters under his arm, steps astride the window.*]

PAPILLON [*to the* FIREMAN]: Careful of the documents! [*Turning to the others:*] Good-bye, gentlemen.
DUDARD: Good-bye, Mr. Papillon.
BERENGER: Good-bye, Mr. Papillon.
PAPILLON [*he has disappeared; one hears him say*]: Careful of my papers. Dudard! Lock up the offices!
DUDARD [*shouting*]: Don't you worry, Mr. Papillon. [*To* BOTARD:] After you, Mr. Botard.
BOTARD: I am about to descend, gentlemen. And I am going to take this matter up immediately with the proper authorities. I'll get to the bottom of this so-called mystery. [*He moves to window.*]
DUDARD [*to* BOTARD]: I thought it was all perfectly clear to you!
BOTARD [*astride the window*]: Your irony doesn't affect me. What I'm after are the proofs and the documents—yes, proof positive of your treason.
DUDARD: That's absurd . . .
BOTARD: Your insults . . .
DUDARD [*interrupting him*]: It's you who are insulting me . . .
BOTARD [*disappearing*]: I don't insult. I merely prove.
VOICE OF FIREMAN: Come on there!
DUDARD [*to* BERENGER]: What are you doing this afternoon? Shall we meet for a drink?
BERENGER: Sorry, I can't. I'm taking advantage of this afternoon off to go and see my friend Jean. I do want to make it up with him, after all. We got carried away. It was all my fault.

[*The* FIREMAN'*s head reappears at the window.*]

FIREMAN: Come along there!
BERENGER [*pointing to the window*]: After you.
DUDARD: After you.
BERENGER: Oh no, after you.
DUDARD: No, I insist, after you.
BERENGER: No, please, after you, after you.
FIREMAN: Hurry up!
DUDARD: After you, after you.
BERENGER: No, after you, after you.

[*They climb through the window together. The fireman helps them down, as the curtain falls.*]

CURTAIN

Scene 2

JEAN'*s house. The layout is roughly the same as Act II, Scene 1. That is to say, the stage is divided into two. To the right, occupying three-quarters or four-fifths of the stage, according to size, is* JEAN'*s bedroom. Up-stage, a chair or an armchair, on which* BERENGER *will sit. Right centre, a door leading to* JEAN'*s bathroom. When* JEAN *goes in to wash, the noise of a tap is heard, and that of the shower. To the left of the room, a partition divides the stage in two. Centre-stage, the door leading to the stairs. If a less realistic, more stylized* décor *is preferred, the door may be placed without a partition. To the left is the staircase; the top steps are visible, leading to* JEAN'*s flat, the banister and the landing. At the back, on the landing level, is the door to the neighbour's flat. Lower down, at the back, there is a glass door, over which is written: "Concierge."*

[*When the curtain rises,* JEAN *is in bed, lying under the blanket, his back to the audience. One hears him cough. After a few moments* BERENGER *is seen, climbing the top steps of the staircase. He knocks at the door;* JEAN *does not answer.* BERENGER *knocks again.*]

BERENGER: Jean! [*He knocks again.*] Jean!

[*The door at the end of the landing opens slightly, and a little old man with a white goatee appears.*]

OLD MAN: What is it?
BERENGER: I want to see Jean. I am a friend of his.
OLD MAN: I thought it was me you wanted. My name's Jean as well, but it's the other one you want.
VOICE OF OLD MAN'S WIFE [*from within the room*]: Is it for us?
OLD MAN [*turning to his wife who is not seen*]: No, for the other one.
BERENGER [*knocking*]: Jean!

OLD MAN: I didn't see him go out. But I saw him last night. He looked in a bad temper.

BERENGER: Yes, I know why; it was my fault.

OLD MAN: Perhaps he doesn't feel like opening the door to you. Try again.

VOICE OF OLD MAN'S WIFE: Jean, don't stand gossiping, Jean!

BERENGER [*knocking*]: Jean!

OLD MAN [*to his wife*]: Just a moment. Oh dear, dear . . . [*He closes the door and disappears.*]

JEAN [*still lying down, his back to the audience, in a hoarse voice*]: What is it?

BERENGER: I've dropped by to see you, Jean.

JEAN: Who is it?

BERENGER: It's me, Berenger. I hope I'm not disturbing you.

JEAN: Oh it's you, is it? Come in!

BERENGER [*trying to open the door*]: The door's locked.

JEAN: Just a moment. Oh dear, dear . . . [JEAN *gets up in a pretty bad temper. He is wearing green pyjamas, his hair is tousled.*] Just a moment. [*He unlocks the door.*] Just a moment. [*He goes back to bed, gets under the blanket.*] Come in!

BERENGER [*coming in*]: Hello Jean!

JEAN [*in bed*]: What time is it? Aren't you at the office?

BERENGER: You're still in bed; you're not at the office, then? Sorry if I'm disturbing you.

JEAN [*still with his back turned*]: Funny, I didn't recognize your voice.

BERENGER: I didn't recognize yours either.

JEAN [*still with his back turned*]: Sit down!

BERENGER: Aren't you feeling well?

[JEAN *replies with a grunt.*]

You know, Jean, it was stupid of me to get so upset yesterday over a thing like that.

JEAN: A thing like what?

BERENGER: Yesterday . . .

JEAN: When yesterday? Where yesterday?

BERENGER: Don't you remember? It was about that wretched rhinoceros.

JEAN: What rhinoceros?

BERENGER: The rhinoceros, or rather, the two wretched rhinoceroses we saw.

JEAN: Oh yes, I remember . . . How do you know they were wretched?

BERENGER: Oh I just said that.

JEAN: Oh. Well let's not talk any more about it.

BERENGER: That's very nice of you.

JEAN: Then that's that.

BERENGER: But I would like to say how sorry I am for being so insistent . . . and so obstinate . . . and getting so angry . . . in fact . . . I acted stupidly.

JEAN: That's not surprising with you.

BERENGER: I'm very sorry.

JEAN: I don't feel very well. [*He coughs.*]

BERENGER: That's probably why you're in bed. [*With a change of tone:*] You know, Jean, as it turned out, we were both right.

JEAN: What about?

BERENGER: About . . . well, you know, the same thing. Sorry to bring it up again, but I'll only mention it briefly. I just wanted you to know that in our different ways we were both right. It's been proved now. There are some rhinoceroses in the town with two horns and some with one.

JEAN: That's what I told you! Well, that's just too bad.

BERENGER: Yes, too bad.

JEAN: Or maybe it's all to the good; it depends.

BERENGER [*continuing*]: In the final analysis it doesn't much matter which comes from where. The important thing, as I see it, is the fact that they're there at all, because . . .

JEAN [*turning and sitting on his unmade bed, facing* BERENGER]: I don't feel well, I don't feel well at all!

BERENGER: Oh I am sorry! What do you think it is?

JEAN: I don't know exactly, there's something wrong somewhere . . .

BERENGER: Do you feel weak?

JEAN: Not at all. On the contrary, I feel full of beans.

BERENGER: I meant just a passing weakness. It happens to everybody.

JEAN: It never happens to me.

BERENGER: Perhaps you're too healthy then. Too much energy can be a bad thing. It unsettles the nervous system.

JEAN: My nervous system is in perfect order. [*His voice has become more and more hoarse.*] I'm sound in mind and limb. I come from a long line of . . .

BERENGER: I know you do. Perhaps you've just caught a chill. Have you got a temperature?

JEAN: I don't know. Yes, probably I have a touch of fever. My head aches.

BERENGER: Just a slight migraine. Would you like me to leave you alone?

JEAN: No, stay. You don't worry me.

BERENGER: Your voice is hoarse, too.

JEAN: Hoarse?

BERENGER: A bit hoarse, yes. That's why I didn't recognize it.

JEAN: Why should I be hoarse? My voice hasn't changed; it's yours that's changed!

BERENGER: Mine?

JEAN: Why not?

BERENGER: It's possible. I hadn't noticed.

JEAN: I sometimes wonder if you're capable of noticing anything. [*Putting his hand to his forehead.*] Actually it's my forehead that hurts. I must have given it a knock. [*His voice is even hoarser.*]

BERENGER: When did you do that?

JEAN: I don't know. I don't remember it happening.

BERENGER: But it must have hurt you.
JEAN: I must have done it while I was asleep.
BERENGER: The shock would have wakened you up. You must have just dreamed you knocked yourself.
JEAN: I never dream . . .
BERENGER [*continuing*]: Your headache must have come on while you were asleep. You've forgotten you dreamed, or rather you only remember subconsciously.
JEAN: Subconsciously, me? I'm master of my own thoughts, my mind doesn't wander. I think straight, I always think straight.
BERENGER: I know that. I haven't made myself clear.
JEAN: Then make yourself clearer. And you needn't bother to make any of your unpleasant observations to me.
BERENGER: One often has the impression that one has knocked oneself when one has a headache. [*Coming closer to* JEAN.] If you'd really knocked yourself, you'd have a bump. [*Looking at* JEAN.] Oh, you've got one, you do have a bump, in fact.
JEAN: A bump?
BERENGER: Just a tiny one.
JEAN: Where?
BERENGER [*pointing to* JEAN'*s forehead*]: There, it starts just above your nose.
JEAN: I've no bump. We've never had bumps in my family.
BERENGER: Have you got a mirror?
JEAN: That's the limit! [*Touching his forehead.*] I can feel something. I'm going to have a look, in the bathroom. [*He gets up abruptly and goes to the bathroom.* BERENGER *watches him as he goes. Then, from the bathroom:*] It's true, I have got a bump. [*He comes back; his skin has become greener.*] So you see I did knock myself
BERENGER: You don't look well, your skin is quite green.
JEAN: You seem to delight in saying disagreeable things to me. Have you taken a look at yourself lately?
BERENGER: Forgive me. I didn't mean to upset you.
JEAN [*very hoarse*]: That's hard to believe.
BERENGER: Your breathing's very heavy. Does your throat hurt?

[JEAN *goes and sits on his bed again.*]

If your throat hurts, perhaps it's a touch of quinsy.
JEAN: Why should I have a touch of quinsy?
BERENGER: It's nothing to be ashamed of—I sometimes get it. Let me feel your pulse. [*He rises and takes* JEAN'*s pulse.*]
JEAN [*in an even hoarser voice*]: Oh, it'll pass.
BERENGER: Your pulse is normal. You needn't get alarmed.
JEAN: I'm not alarmed in the slightest—why should I be?
BERENGER: You're right. A few days' rest will put you right.
JEAN: I've no time to rest. I must go and buy some food.
BERENGER: There's not much the matter with you, if you're hungry. But even so, you ought to take a few days' rest. It's wise to take care. Has the doctor been to see you?
JEAN: I don't need a doctor.
BERENGER: Oh but you ought to get the doctor.
JEAN: You're not going to get the doctor because I don't want the doctor. I can look after myself.
BERENGER: You shouldn't reject medical advice.
JEAN: Doctors invent illnesses that don't exist.
BERENGER: They do it in good faith—just for the pleasure of looking after people.
JEAN: They invent illnesses, they invent them, I tell you.
BERENGER: Perhaps they do—but after they invent them they cure them.
JEAN: I only have confidence in veterinary surgeons. There!
BERENGER [*who has released* JEAN'*s wrist, now takes it up again*]: Your veins look swollen. They're jutting out.
JEAN: It's a sign of virility.
BERENGER: Of course it's a sign of health and strength. But . . .

[*He examines* JEAN'*s forearm more closely, until* JEAN *violently withdraws it.*]

JEAN: What do you think you're doing—scrutinizing me as if I were some strange animal?
BERENGER: It's your skin . . .
JEAN: What's my skin got to do with you? I don't go on about your skin, do I?
BERENGER: It's just that . . . it seems to be changing colour all the time. It's going green. [*He tries to take* JEAN'*s hand.*] It's hardening as well.
JEAN [*withdrawing his hand again*]: Stop mauling me about! What's the matter with you? You're getting on my nerves.
BERENGER [*to himself*]: Perhaps it's more serious than I thought. [*To* JEAN:] We must get the doctor. [*He goes to the telephone.*]
JEAN: Leave that thing alone. [*He darts over to* BERENGER *and pushes him.* BERENGER *staggers.*] You mind your own business.
BERENGER: All right. It was for your own good.
JEAN [*coughing and breathing noisily*]: I know better than you what's good for me.

BERENGER: You're breathing very hard.

JEAN: One breathes as best one can. You don't like the way I breathe, and I don't like the way you breathe. Your breathing's too feeble, you can't even hear it; it's as if you were going to drop dead any moment.

BERENGER: I know I'm not as strong as you.

JEAN: I don't keep trying to get you to the doctor, do I? Leave people to do as they please.

BERENGER: Don't get angry with me. You know very well I'm your friend.

JEAN: There's no such thing as friendship. I don't believe in your friendship.

BERENGER: That's a very hurtful thing to say.

JEAN: There's nothing for you to get hurt about.

BERENGER: My dear Jean . . .

JEAN: I'm not your dear Jean.

BERENGER: You're certainly in a very misanthropic mood today.

JEAN: Yes, I am misanthropic, very misanthropic indeed. I like being misanthropic.

BERENGER: You're probably still angry with me over our silly quarrel yesterday. I admit it was my fault. That's why I came to say I was sorry . . .

JEAN: What quarrel are you talking about?

BERENGER: I told you just now. You know, about the rhinoceros.

JEAN [*not listening to* BERENGER]: It's not that I hate people. I'm just indifferent to them—or rather, they disgust me; and they'd better keep out of my way, or I'll run them down.

BERENGER: You know very well that I shall never stand in your way.

JEAN: I've got one aim in life. And I'm making straight for it.

BERENGER: I'm sure you're right. But I feel you're passing through a moral crisis.

[*JEAN has been pacing the room like a wild beast in a cage, from one wall to the other.* BERENGER *watches him, occasionally stepping aside to avoid him.* JEAN*'s voice has become more and more hoarse.*]

You mustn't excite yourself, it's bad for you.

JEAN: I felt uncomfortable in my clothes; now my pyjamas irritate me as well. [*He undoes his pyjama jacket and does it up again.*]

BERENGER: But whatever's the matter with your skin?

JEAN: Can't you leave my skin alone? I certainly wouldn't want to change it for yours.

BERENGER: It's gone like leather.

JEAN: That makes it more solid. It's weatherproof.

BERENGER: You're getting greener and greener.

JEAN: You've got colour mania today. You're seeing things, you've been drinking again.

BERENGER: I did yesterday, but not today.

JEAN: It's the result of all your past debauches.

BERENGER: I promised you to turn over a new leaf. I take notice when friends like you give me advice. And I never feel humiliated—on the contrary!

JEAN: I don't care what you feel. Brrr . . .

BERENGER: What did you say?

JEAN: I didn't say anything. I just went Brrrr . . . because I felt like it.

BERENGER [*looking fixedly at* JEAN]: Do you know what's happened to Boeuf? He's turned into a rhinoceros.

JEAN: What happened to Boeuf?

BERENGER: He's turned into a rhinoceros.

JEAN [*fanning himself with the flaps of his jacket*]: Brrr . . .

BERENGER: Come on now, stop joking.

JEAN: I can puff if I want to, can't I? I've every right . . . I'm in my own house.

BERENGER: I didn't say you couldn't.

JEAN: And I shouldn't if I were you. I feel hot, I feel hot. Brrr . . . Just a moment. I must cool myself down.

BERENGER [*whilst* JEAN *darts to the bathroom*]: He must have a fever.

[JEAN *is in the bathroom, one hears him puffing, and also the sound of a running tap.*]

JEAN [*off*]: Brrr . . .

BERENGER: He's got the shivers. I'm jolly well going to 'phone the doctor. [*He goes to the telephone again then comes back quickly when he hears* JEAN*'s voice.*]

JEAN [*off*]: So old Boeuf turned into a rhinoceros, did he? Ah, ah, ah . . . ! He was just having you on, he'd disguised himself. [*He pokes his head round the bathroom door. He is very green. The bump over his nose is slightly larger.*] He was just disguised.

BERENGER [*walking about the room, without seeing* JEAN]: He looked very serious about it, I assure you.

JEAN: Oh well, that's his business.

BERENGER [*turning to* JEAN *who disappears again into the bathroom*]: I'm sure he didn't do it on purpose. He didn't want to change.

JEAN [*off*]: How do you know?

BERENGER: Well, everything led one to suppose so.

JEAN: And what if he did do it on purpose? Eh? What if he did it on purpose?

BERENGER: I'd be very surprised. At any rate, Mrs. Boeuf didn't seem to know about it . . .

JEAN [*in a very hoarse voice*]: Ah, ah, ah! Fat old Mrs. Boeuf. She's just a fool!

BERENGER: Well fool or no fool . . .

JEAN [*he enters swiftly, takes off his jacket, and throws it on the bed.* BERENGER *discreetly averts his gaze.* JEAN, *whose back and chest are now green, goes back into the bathroom. As he walks in and out*]: Boeuf never let his wife know what he was up to . . .

BERENGER: You're wrong there, Jean—it was a very united family.

JEAN: Very united, was it? Are you sure? Hum, hum, Brr . . .

BERENGER [*moving to the bathroom, where* JEAN *slams the door in his face*]: Very united. And the proof is that . . .

JEAN [*from within*]: Boeuf led his own private life. He had a secret side to him deep down which he kept to himself.

BERENGER: I shouldn't make you talk, it seems to upset you.

JEAN: On the contrary, it relaxes me.

BERENGER: Even so, let me call the doctor, I beg you.

JEAN: I absolutely forbid it. I can't stand obstinate people.

[JEAN *comes back into the bedroom.* BERENGER *backs away a little scared, for* JEAN *is greener than ever and speaks only with difficulty. His voice is unrecognizable.*]

Well, whether he changes into a rhinoceros on purpose or against his will, he's probably all the better for it.

BERENGER: How can you say a thing like that? Surely you don't think . . .

JEAN: You always see the black side of everything. It obviously gave him great pleasure to turn into a rhinoceros. There's nothing extraordinary in that.

BERENGER: There's nothing extraordinary in it, but I doubt if it gave him much pleasure.

JEAN: And why not, pray?

BERENGER: It's hard to say exactly why; it's just something you feel.

JEAN: I tell you it's not as bad as all that. After all, rhinoceroses are living creatures the same as us; they've got as much right to life as we have!

BERENGER: As long as they don't destroy ours in the process. You must admit the difference in mentality.

JEAN [*pacing up and down the room, and in and out of the bathroom*]: Are you under the impression that our way of life is superior?

BERENGER: Well at any rate, we have our own moral standards which I consider incompatible with the standards of these animals.

JEAN: Moral standards! I'm sick of moral standards! We need to go beyond moral standards!

BERENGER: What would you put in their place?

JEAN [*still pacing*]: Nature!

BERENGER: Nature?

JEAN: Nature has its own laws. Morality's against Nature.

BERENGER: Are you suggesting we replace our moral laws by the law of the jungle?

JEAN: It would suit me, suit me fine.

BERENGER: You say that. But deep down, no one . . .

JEAN [*interrupting him, pacing up and down*]: We've got to build our life on new foundations. We must get back to primeval integrity.

BERENGER: I don't agree with you at all.

JEAN [*breathing noisily*]: I can't breathe.

BERENGER: Just think a moment. You must admit that we have a philosophy that animals don't share, and an irreplaceable set of values, which it's taken centuries of human civilization to build up . . .

JEAN [*in the bathroom*]: When we've demolished all that, we'll be better off!

BERENGER: I know you don't mean that seriously. You're joking! It's just a poetic fancy.

JEAN: Brrr. [*He almost trumpets.*]

BERENGER: I'd never realized you were a poet.

JEAN [*comes out of the bathroom*]: Brrr. [*He trumpets again.*]

BERENGER: That's not what you believe fundamentally—I know you too well. You know as well as I do that mankind . . .

JEAN [*interrupting him*]: Don't talk to me about mankind!

BERENGER: I mean the human individual, humanism . . .

JEAN: Humanism is all washed up! You're a ridiculous old sentimentalist. [*He goes into the bathroom.*]

BERENGER: But you must admit that the mind . . .

JEAN [*from the bathroom*]: Just clichés! You're talking rubbish!

BERENGER: Rubbish!

JEAN [*from the bathroom in a very hoarse voice, difficult to understand*]: Utter rubbish!

BERENGER: I'm amazed to hear you say that, Jean, really! You must be out of your mind. You wouldn't like to be a rhinoceros yourself, now would you?

JEAN: Why not? I'm not a victim of prejudice like you.

BERENGER: Can you speak more clearly? I didn't catch what you said. You swallowed the words.

JEAN [*still in the bathroom*]: Then keep your ears open.

BERENGER: What?

JEAN: Keep your cars open. I said what's wrong with being a rhinoceros? I'm all for change.

BERENGER: It's not like you to say a thing like that . . .

[BERENGER *stops short, for* JEAN's *appearance is truly alarming.* JEAN *has become, in fact, completely green. The bump on his forehead is practically a rhinoceros horn.*]

Oh! You really must be out of your mind!

[JEAN *dashes to his bed, throws the covers on the floor, talking in a fast and furious gabble, and making very weird sounds.*]

You mustn't get into such a state—calm down! I hardly recognize you any more.

JEAN [*hardly distinguishable*]: Hot . . . far too hot! Demolish the lot, clothes itch, they itch! [*He drops his pyjama trousers.*]

BERENGER: What are you doing? You're not yourself! You're generally so modest!

JEAN: The swamps! The swamps!

BERENGER: Look at me! Can't you see me any longer? Can't you hear me?

JEAN: I can hear you perfectly well! I can see you perfectly well!

[*He lunges towards* BERENGER, *head down.* BERENGER *gets out of the way.*]

BERENGER: Watch out!

JEAN [*puffing noisily*]: Sorry! [*He darts at great speed into the bathroom.*]

BERENGER [*makes as if to escape by the door left, then comes back and goes into the bathroom after* JEAN, *saying*]: I really can't leave him like that—after all he is a friend. [*From the bathroom:*] I'm going to get the doctor! It's absolutely necessary, believe me!

JEAN [*from the bathroom*]: No!

BERENGER [*from the bathroom*]: Calm down, Jean, you're being ridiculous! Oh, your horn's getting longer and longer—you're a rhinoceros!

JEAN [*from the bathroom*]: I'll trample you, I'll trample you down! [*A lot of noise comes from the bathroom, trumpetings, objects falling, the sound of a shattered mirror; then* BERENGER *reappears, very frightened; he closes the bathroom door with difficulty against the resistance that is being made from inside.*]

BERENGER [*pushing against the door*]: He's a rhinoceros, he's a rhinoceros!

[BERENGER *manages to close the door. As he does so, his coat is pierced by a rhinoceros horn. The door shakes under the animal's constant pressure and the din continues in the bathroom; trumpetings are heard, interspersed with indistinct phrases such as: "I'm furious! The swine!" etc.* BERENGER *rushes to the door right.*]

I never would have thought it of him—never!

[*He opens the staircase door and goes and knocks at the landing door; he bangs repeatedly on it with his fist.*]

There's a rhinoceros in the building! Get the police!

OLD MAN [*poking his head out*]: What's the matter?

BERENGER: Get the police! There's a rhinoceros in the house!

VOICE OF OLD MAN'S WIFE: What are you up to, Jean? Why are you making all that noise?

OLD MAN [*to his wife*]: I don't know what he's talking about. He's seen a rhinoceros.

BERENGER: Yes, here in the house. Get the police!

OLD MAN: What do you think you're up to, disturbing people like that. What a way to behave! [*He shuts the door in his face.*]

BERENGER [*rushing to the stairs*]: Porter, porter, there's a rhinoceros in the house, get the police! Porter!

[*The upper part of the porter's lodge is seen to open; the head of a rhinoceros appears.*]

Another!

[BERENGER *rushes upstairs again. He wants to go back into* JEAN'S *room, hesitates, then makes for the door of the* OLD MAN *again. At this moment the door of the room opens to reveal two rhinoceros heads.*]

Oh, my God!

[BERENGER *goes back into* JEAN'S *room where the bathroom door is still shaking. He goes to the window which is represented simply by the frame, facing the audience. He is exhausted, almost fainting; he murmurs.*]

My God! Oh my God!

[*He makes a gigantic effort, and manages to get astride the window (that is, towards the audience) but gets back again quickly, for at the same time, crossing the orchestra pit at great speed, move a large number of rhinoceros heads in line.* BERENGER *gets back with all speed, looks out of the window for a moment.*]

There's a whole herd of them in the street now! An army of rhinoceroses, surging up the avenue . . . ! [*He looks all around.*] Where can I get out? Where can I get out? If only they'd keep to the middle of the road! They're all over the pavement as well. Where can I get out? Where can I get out?

[*Distracted, he goes from door to door and to the window, whilst the bathroom door continues to shake and* JEAN *continues to trumpet and hurl incomprehensible insults. This continues for some moments; whenever* BERENGER *in his disordered attempts to escape reaches the door of the Old People's flat or the stairway, he is greeted by rhinoceros heads which trumpet and cause him to beat a hasty retreat. He goes to the window for the last time and looks out.*]

A whole herd of them! And they always said the rhinoceros was a solitary animal! That's not true, that's a conception they'll have to revise! They've smashed up all the public benches. [*He wrings his hands.*] What's to be done?

[*He goes once more to the various exits, but the spectacle of the rhinoceros halts him. When he gets back to the bathroom door it seems about to give way.* BERENGER *throws himself against the back wall, which yields; the street is visible in the background; he flees, shouting:*]

Rhinoceros! Rhinoceros!

[*Noises. The bathroom door is on the point of yielding.*]

CURTAIN

ACT III

The arrangement is roughly the same as in the previous scene. It is BERENGER'*s room, which bears a striking resemblance to that of* JEAN. *Only certain details, one or two extra pieces of furniture, reveal that it is a different room. Staircase to the left, and landing. Door at the end of the landing. There is no porter's lodge. Up-stage is a divan.*

An armchair, and a little table with a telephone. Perhaps an extra telephone, and a chair. Window up-stage, open. A window frame in the foreground.

BERENGER *is lying on his divan, his back to the audience.* BERENGER *is lying fully dressed. His head is bandaged. He seems to be having a bad dream, and writhes in his sleep.*

BERENGER: No. [*Pause*] Watch out for the horns! [*Pause*]

[*The noise of a considerable number of rhinoceroses is heard passing under the up-stage window.*]

No! [*He falls to the floor still fighting with what he has seen in his dream, and wakes up. He puts his hand to his head with an apprehensive air, then moves to the mirror and lifts his bandage, as the noises fade away. He heaves a sigh of relief when he sees he has no bump. He hesitates, goes to the divan, lies down, and instantly gets up again. He goes to the table where he takes up a bottle of brandy and a glass, and is about to pour himself a drink. Then after a short internal struggle he replaces the bottle and glass.*] Now, now, where's your will-power! [*He wants to go back to his divan, but the rhinoceroses are heard again under the up-stage window. The noises stop; he goes to the little table, hesitates a moment, then with a gesture of "Oh what's it matter!" he pours himself a glass of brandy which he downs at one go. He puts the bottle and glass back in place. He coughs. His cough seems to worry him; he coughs again and listens hard to the sound. He looks at himself again in the mirror, coughing, then opens the window; the panting of the animals becomes louder; he coughs again.*] No, it's not the same! [*He calms down, shuts the window, feels his bandaged forehead, goes to his divan, and seems to fall asleep.*]

[DUDARD *is seen mounting the top stairs; he gets to the landing and knocks on* BERENGER'*s door.*]

BERENGER [*starting up*]: What is it?
DUDARD: I've dropped by to see you, Berenger.
BERENGER: Who is it?
DUDARD: It's me.
BERENGER: Who's me?
DUDARD: Me, Dudard.
BERENGER: Ah, it's you, come in!
DUDARD: I hope I'm not disturbing you. [*He tries to open the door.*] The door's locked.
BERENGER: Just a moment. Oh dear, dear! [*He opens the door.* DUDARD *enters.*]
DUDARD: Hello Berenger.
BERENGER: Hello Dudard, what time is it?
DUDARD: So, you're still barricaded in your room! Feeling any better, old man?
BERENGER: Forgive me, I didn't recognize your voice. [*Goes to open the window.*] Yes, yes, I think I'm a bit better.
DUDARD: My voice hasn't changed. I recognized yours easily enough.
BERENGER: I'm sorry, I thought that . . . you're right, your voice is quite normal. Mine hasn't changed either, has it?
DUDARD: Why should it have changed?
BERENGER: I'm not a bit . . . a bit hoarse, am I?
DUDARD: Not that I notice.
BERENGER: That's good. That's very reassuring.
DUDARD: Why, what's the matter with you?
BERENGER: I don't know—does one ever know? Voices can suddenly change—they do change, alas!
DUDARD: Have you caught cold, as well?
BERENGER: I hope not . . . I sincerely hope not. But do sit down, Dudard, take a seat. Sit in the armchair.
DUDARD [*sitting in the armchair*]: Are you still feeling a bit off colour? Is your head still bad? [*He points to* BERENGER'*s bandage.*]

BERENGER: Oh yes, I've still got a headache. But there's no bump, I haven't knocked myself . . . have I? [*He lifts the bandage, shows his forehead to* DUDARD.]

DUDARD: No, there's no bump as far as I can see.

BERENGER: I hope there never will be. Never.

DUDARD: If you don't knock yourself, why should there be?

BERENGER: If you really don't want to knock yourself, you don't.

DUDARD: Obviously. One just has to take care. But what's the matter with you? You're all nervous and agitated. It must be your migraine. You just stay quiet and you'll feel better.

BERENGER: Migraine! Don't talk to me about migraines! Don't talk about them!

DUDARD: It's understandable that you've got a migraine after all that emotion.

BERENGER: I can't seem to get over it!

DUDARD: Then it's not surprising you've got a headache.

BERENGER [*darting to the mirror, lifting the bandage*]: Nothing there . . . You know, it can all start from something like that.

DUDARD: What can all start?

BERENGER: I'm frightened of becoming someone else.

DUDARD: Calm yourself, now, and sit down. Dashing up and down the room like that can only make you more nervous.

BERENGER: You're right, I must keep calm. [*He goes and sits down.*] I just can't get over it, you know.

DUDARD: About Jean you mean?—I know.

BERENGER: Yes, Jean, of course—and the others, too.

DUDARD: I realize it must have been a shock to you.

BERENGER: Well, that's not surprising, you must admit.

DUDARD: I suppose so, but you mustn't dramatize the situation; it's no reason for you to . . .

BERENGER: I wonder how you'd have felt. Jean was my best friend. Then to watch him change before my eyes, and the way he got so furious!

DUDARD: I know. You felt let down; I understand. Try and not think about it.

BERENGER: How can I help thinking about it? He was such a warm-hearted person, always so human! Who'd have thought it of him! We'd known each other for . . . for donkey's years. He was the last person I'd have expected to change like that. I felt more sure of him than of myself! And then to do that to me!

DUDARD: I'm sure he didn't do it specially to annoy you!

BERENGER: It seemed as if he did. If you'd seen the state he was in . . . the expression on his face . . .

DUDARD: It's just that you happened to be with him at the time. It would have been the same no matter who was there.

BERENGER: But after all our years together he might have controlled himself in front of me.

DUDARD: You think everything revolves round you, you think that everything that happens concerns you personally; you're not the centre of the universe, you know.

BERENGER: Perhaps you're right. I must try to re-adjust myself, but the phenomenon in itself is so disturbing. To tell the truth, it absolutely shatters me. What can be the explanation?

DUDARD: For the moment I haven't found a satisfactory explanation. I observe the facts, and I take them in. They exist, so they must have an explanation. A freak of Nature, perhaps, some bizarre caprice, an extravagant joke, a game—who knows?

BERENGER: Jean was very proud, of course. I'm not ambitious at all. I'm content to be what I am.

DUDARD: Perhaps he felt an urge for some fresh air, the country, the wide-open spaces . . . perhaps he felt a need to relax. I'm not saying that's any excuse . . .

BERENGER: I understand what you mean, at least I'm trying to. But you know—if someone accused me of being a bad sport, or hopelessly middle class, or completely out of touch with life, I'd still want to stay as I am.

DUDARD: We'll all stay as we are, don't worry. So why get upset over a few cases of rhinoceritis. Perhaps it's just another disease.

BERENGER: Exactly! And I'm frightened of catching it.

DUDARD: Oh stop thinking about it. Really, you attach too much importance to the whole business. Jean's case isn't symptomatic, he's not a typical case—you said yourself he was proud. In my opinion—if you'll excuse me saying this about your friend—he was far too excitable, a bit wild, an eccentric. You mustn't base your judgments on exceptions. It's the average case you must consider.

BERENGER: I'm beginning to see daylight. You see, you couldn't explain this phenomenon to me. And yet you just provided me with a plausible explanation. Yes, of course, he must have been in a critical condition to have got himself into that state. He must have been temporarily unbalanced. And yet he gave his reasons for it, he'd obviously given it a lot of thought, and weighed the pros and cons . . . And what about Boeuf then, was he mad, too . . . ? and what about all the others . . . ?

DUDARD: There's still the epidemic theory. It's like influenza. It's not the first time there's been an epidemic.

BERENGER: There's never been one like this. And what if it's come from the colonies?

DUDARD: In any case you can be sure that Boeuf and the others didn't do what they did—become what they became—just to annoy you. They wouldn't have gone to all that trouble.

BERENGER: That's true, that makes sense, it's a reassuring thought . . . or on the other hand, perhaps that makes it worse? [*Rhinoceroses are heard, galloping under the up-stage window.*] There, you hear that? [*He darts to the window.*]

DUDARD: Oh, why can't you leave them alone!

[BERENGER *closes the window again.*]

They're not doing you any harm. Really, you're obsessed by them! It's not good for you. You're wearing yourself out. You've had one shock, why look for more? You just concentrate on getting back to normal.

BERENGER: I wonder if I really am immune?

DUDARD: In any case it's not fatal. Certain illnesses are good for you. I'm convinced this is something you can cure if you want to. They'll get over it, you'll see.

BERENGER: But it's bound to have certain after-effects! An organic upheaval like that can't help but leave . . .

DUDARD: It's only temporary, don't you worry.

BERENGER: Are you absolutely certain?

DUDARD: I think so, yes, I suppose so.

BERENGER: But if one really doesn't want to, really doesn't want to catch this thing, which after all is a nervous disease—then you don't catch it, you simply don't catch it! Do you feel like a brandy? [*He goes to the table where the bottle stands.*]

DUDARD: Not for me, thank you, I never touch it. But don't mind me if you want some—you go ahead, don't worry about me. But watch out it doesn't make your headache worse.

BERENGER: Alcohol is good for epidemics. It immunizes you. It kills influenza microbes, for instance.

DUDARD: Perhaps it doesn't kill all microbes. They don't know about rhinoceritis yet.

BERENGER: Jean never touched alcohol. He just pretended to. Maybe that's why he . . . perhaps that explains his attitude. [*He offers a full glass to* DUDARD:] You're sure you won't?

DUDARD: No, no, never before lunch, thank you.

[BERENGER *empties his glass, continues to hold it, together with the bottle, in his hands; he coughs.*]

You see, you can't take it. It makes you cough.

BERENGER [*worried*]: Yes, it did make me cough. How did I cough?

DUDARD: Like everyone coughs when they drink something a bit strong.

BERENGER [*moving to put the glass and bottle back on the table*]: There wasn't anything odd about it, was there? It *was* a real human cough?

DUDARD: What are you getting at? It was an ordinary human cough. What other sort of cough could it have been?

BERENGER: I don't know . . . Perhaps an animal's cough . . . Do rhinoceroses cough?

DUDARD: Look, Berenger, you're being ridiculous, you invent difficulties for yourself, you ask yourself the weirdest questions . . . I remember you said yourself that the best protection against the thing was will-power.

BERENGER: Yes, I did.

DUDARD: Well then, prove you've got some.

BERENGER: I have, I assure you . . .

DUDARD: Prove it to yourself—now, don't drink any more brandy. You'll feel more sure of yourself then.

BERENGER: You deliberately misunderstand me. I told you the only reason I take it is because it keeps the worst at bay; I'm doing it quite deliberately. When the epidemic's over, then I shall stop drinking. I'd already decided that before the whole business began. I'm just putting it off for the time being!

DUDARD: You're inventing excuses for yourself.

BERENGER: Do you think I am . . . ? In any case, that's got nothing to do with what's happening now.

DUDARD: How do we know?

BERENGER [*alarmed*]: Do you really think so? You think that's how the rot sets in? I'm not an alcoholic. [*He goes to the mirror and examines himself.*] Do you think, by any chance . . . [*He touches his face, pats his bandaged forehead.*] Nothing's changed; it hasn't done any harm so it must have done good . . . or it's harmless at any rate.

DUDARD: I was only joking. I was just teasing you. You see the black side of everything—watch out, or you'll become a neurotic. When you've got over your shock completely and you can get out for a breath of fresh air, you'll feel better—you'll see! All these morbid ideas will vanish.

BERENGER: Go out? I suppose I'll have to. I'm dreading the moment. I'll be bound to meet some of them . . .

DUDARD: What if you do? You only have to keep out of their way. And there aren't as many as all that.

BERENGER: I see them all over the place. You'll probably say that's being morbid, too.

DUDARD: They don't attack you. If you leave them alone, they just ignore you. You can't say they're spiteful. They've even got a certain natural innocence, a sort of frankness. Besides I walked right along the avenue to get to you today. I got here safe and sound, didn't I? No trouble at all.

BERENGER: Just the sight of them upsets me. It's a nervous thing. I don't get angry—no, it doesn't pay to get angry, you never know where it'll lead to, I watch out for that. But it does something to me, here! [*He points to his heart*.] I get a tight feeling inside.

DUDARD: I think you're right to a certain extent to have some reaction. But you go too far. You've no sense of humour, that's your trouble, none at all. You must learn to be more detached, and try and see the funny side of things.

BERENGER: I feel responsible for everything that happens. I feel involved, I just can't be indifferent.

DUDARD: Judge not lest ye be judged. If you start worrying about everything that happens you'd never be able to go on living.

BERENGER: If only it had happened somewhere else, in some other country, and we'd just read about it in the papers, one could discuss it quietly, examine the question from all points of view and come to an objective conclusion. We could organize debates with professors and writers and lawyers, and blue-stockings and artists and people. And the ordinary man in the street, as well—it would be very interesting and instructive. But when you're involved yourself, when you suddenly find yourself up against the brutal facts you can't help feeling directly concerned—the shock is too violent for you to stay cool and detached. I'm frankly surprised, I'm very very surprised. I can't get over it.

DUDARD: Well I'm surprised, too. Or rather I was. Now I'm starting to get used to it.

BERENGER: Your nervous system is better balanced than mine. You're lucky. But don't you agree it's all very unfortunate . . .

DUDARD [*interrupting him*]: I don't say it's a good thing. And don't get the idea that I'm on the rhinoceroses' side . . .

[*More sounds of rhinoceroses passing, this time under the down-stage window-frame*.]

BERENGER [*with a start*]: There they are, there they are again! Oh, it's no use, I just can't get used to them. Maybe it's wrong of me, but they obsess me so much in spite of myself, I just can't sleep at night. I get insomnia. I doze a bit in the daytime out of sheer exhaustion.

DUDARD: Take some sleeping tablets.

BERENGER: That's not the answer. If I sleep, it's worse. I dream about them, I get nightmares.

DUDARD: That's what comes of taking things too seriously. You get a kick out of torturing yourself—admit it!

BERENGER: I'm no masochist, I assure you.

DUDARD: Then face the facts and get over it. This is the situation and there's nothing you can do about it.

BERENGER: That's fatalism.

DUDARD: It's common sense. When a thing like this happens there's bound to be a reason for it. That's what we must find out.

BERENGER [*getting up*]: Well, I don't want to accept the situation.

DUDARD: What else can you do? What are your plans?

BERENGER: I don't know for the moment. I must think it over. I shall write to the papers; I'll draw up manifestos; I shall apply for an audience with the mayor—or his deputy, if the mayor's too busy.

DUDARD: You leave the authorities to act as they think best! I'm not sure if morally you have the right to butt in. In any case, I still think it's not all that serious. I consider it's silly to get worked up because a few people decide to change their skins. They just didn't feel happy in the ones they had. They're free to do as they like.

BERENGER: We must attack the evil at the roots.

DUDARD: The evil! That's just a phrase! Who knows what is evil and what is good? It's just a question of personal preferences. You're worried about your own skin—that's the truth of the matter. But you'll never become a rhinoceros, really you won't . . . you haven't got the vocation!

BERENGER: There you are, you see! If our leaders and fellow citizens all think like you, they'll never take any action.

DUDARD: You wouldn't want to ask for help from abroad, surely? This is an internal affair, it only concerns our country,

BERENGER: I believe in international solidarity . . .

DUDARD: You're a Don Quixote. Oh, I don't mean that nastily, don't be offended! I'm only saying it for your own good, because you really need to calm down.

BERENGER: You're right, I know—forgive me. I get too worked up. But I'll change, I will change. I'm sorry to keep you all this time listening to my ramblings. You must have work to do. Did you get my application for sick leave?

DUDARD: Don't worry about that. It's all in order. In any case, the office hasn't resumed work.

BERENGER: Haven't they repaired the staircase yet? What negligence! That's why everything goes so badly.

DUDARD: They're repairing it now. But it's slow work. It's not easy to find the workmen. They sign on and work for a couple of days, then don't turn up any more. You never see them again. Then you have to look for others.

BERENGER: And they talk about unemployment! At least I hope we're getting a stone staircase.

DUDARD: No, it's wood again, but new wood this time.

BERENGER: Oh! The way these organizations stick to the old routine. They chuck money down the drain but when it's needed for something really useful they pretend they can't afford it. I bet Mr. Papillon's none too pleased. He was dead set on having a stone staircase. What's he say about it?

DUDARD: We haven't got a Chief any more. Mr. Papillon's resigned.

BERENGER: It's not possible!

DUDARD: It's true, I assure you.

BERENGER: Well, I'm amazed . . . Was it on account of the staircase?

DUDARD: I don't think so. Anyway that wasn't the reason he gave.

BERENGER: Why was it then? What got into him?

DUDARD: He's retiring to the country.

BERENGER: Retiring? He's not the age. He might still have become the Director.

DUDARD: He's given it all up! Said he needed a rest.

BERENGER: I bet the management's pretty upset to see him go; they'll have to replace him. All your diplomas should come in useful—you stand a good chance.

DUDARD: I suppose I might as well tell you . . . it's really rather funny—the fact is, he turned into a rhinoceros.

[*Distant rhinoceros noises.*]

BERENGER: A rhinoceros!!!! Mr. Papillon a rhinoceros! I can't believe it! I don't think it's funny at all! Why didn't you tell me before?

DUDARD: Well you know you've no sense of humour. I didn't want to tell you . . . I didn't want to tell you because I knew very well you wouldn't see the funny side, and it would upset you. You know how impressionable you are!

BERENGER [*raising his arms to heaven*]: Oh that's awful . . . Mr. Papillon! And he had such a good job.

DUDARD: That proves his metamorphosis was sincere.

BERENGER: He couldn't have done it on purpose. I'm certain it must have been involuntary.

DUDARD: How can we tell? It's hard to know the real reasons for people's decisions.

BERENGER: He must have made a mistake. He'd got some hidden complexes. He should have been psychoanalysed.

DUDARD: Even if it's a case of dissociation it's still very revealing. It was his way of sublimating himself.

BERENGER: He let himself be talked into it, I feel sure.

DUDARD: That could happen to anybody!

BERENGER [*alarmed*]: To anybody? Oh no, not to you it couldn't—could it? And not to me!

DUDARD: We must hope not.

BERENGER: Because we don't want to . . . that's so, isn't it? Tell me, that *is* so, isn't it?

DUDARD: Yes, yes, of course . . .

BERENGER [*a little calmer*]: I still would have thought Mr. Papillon would have had the strength to resist. I thought he had a bit more character! Particularly as I fail to see where his interest lay—what possible material or moral interest . . .

DUDARD: It was obviously a disinterested gesture on his part.

BERENGER: Obviously. There were extenuating circumstances . . . or were they aggravating? Aggravating, I should think, because if he did it from choice . . . You know, I feel sure that Botard must have taken a very poor view of it—what did he think of his Chief's behaviour?

DUDARD: Oh poor old Botard was quite indignant, absolutely outraged. I've rarely seen anyone so incensed.

BERENGER: Well for once I'm on his side. He's a good man after all. A man of sound common sense. And to think I misjudged him.

DUDARD: He misjudged you, too.

BERENGER: That proves how objective I'm being now. Besides, you had a pretty bad opinion of him yourself.

DUDARD: I wouldn't say I had a bad opinion. I admit I didn't often agree with him. I never liked his scepticism, the way he was always so incredulous and suspicious. Even in this instance I didn't approve of him entirely.

BERENGER: This time for the opposite reasons.

DUDARD: No, not exactly—my own reasoning and my judgment are a bit more complex than you seem to think. It was because there was nothing precise or objective about the way Botard argued. I don't approve of the rhinoceroses myself, as you know—not at all, don't go thinking that! But Botard's attitude was too passionate, as usual, and therefore over-simplified. His stand seems to me entirely dictated by hatred of his superiors. That's where he gets his inferiority complex and his resentment. What's more he talks in clichés, and commonplace arguments leave me cold.

BERENGER: Well forgive me, but this time I'm in complete agreement with Botard. He's somebody worthwhile.

DUDARD: I don't deny it, but that doesn't mean anything.

BERENGER: He's a very worthwhile person—and they're not easy to find these days. He's down-to-earth, with four feet planted firmly on the ground—I mean, both feet. I'm in complete agreement with him, and I'm proud of it. I shall congratulate him when I see him. I deplore Mr. Papillon's action; it was his duty not to succumb.

DUDARD: How intolerant you are! Maybe Papillon felt the need for a bit of relaxation after all these years of office life.

BERENGER [*ironically*]: And you're too tolerant, far too broadminded!

DUDARD: My dear Berenger, one must always make an effort to understand. And in order to understand a phenomenon and its effects you need to work back to the initial causes, by honest intellectual effort. We must try to do this because, after all, we are thinking beings. I haven't yet succeeded, as I told you, and I don't know if I shall succeed. But in any case one has to start out favourably disposed—or at least, impartial; one has to keep an open mind—that's essential to a scientific mentality. Everything is logical. To understand is to justify.

BERENGER: You'll be siding with the rhinoceroses before long.

DUDARD: No, no, not at all. I wouldn't go that far. I'm simply trying to look the facts unemotionally in the face. I'm trying to be realistic. I also contend that there is no real evil in what occurs naturally. I don't believe in seeing evil in everything. I leave that to the inquisitors.

BERENGER: And you consider all this natural?

DUDARD: What could be more natural than a rhinoceros?

BERENGER: Yes, but for a man to turn into a rhinoceros is abnormal beyond question.

DUDARD: Well, of course, that's a matter of opinion . . .

BERENGER: It is beyond question, absolutely beyond question!

DUDARD: You seem very sure of yourself. Who can say where the normal stops and the abnormal begins? Can you personally define these conceptions of normality and abnormality? Nobody has solved this problem yet, either medically or philosophically. You ought to know that.

BERENGER: The problem may not be resolved philosophically—but in practice it's simple. They may prove there's no such thing as movement . . . and then you start walking . . . [*He starts walking up and down the room.*] . . . and you go on walking, and you say to yourself, like Galileo, "E pur si muove" . . .

DUDARD: You're getting things all mixed up! Don't confuse the issue. In Galileo's case it was the opposite: theoretic and scientific thought proving itself superior to mass opinion and dogmatism.

BERENGER [*quite lost*]: What does all that mean? Mass opinion, dogmatism—they're just words! I may be mixing everything up in my head but you're losing yours. You don't know what's normal and what isn't any more. I couldn't care less about Galileo . . . I don't give a damn about Galileo.

DUDARD: You brought him up in the first place and raised the whole question, saying that practice always had the last word. Maybe it does, but only when it proceeds from theory! The history of thought and science proves that.

BERENGER [*more and more furious*]: It doesn't prove anything of the sort! It's all gibberish, utter lunacy!

DUDARD: There again we need to define exactly what we mean by lunacy . . .

BERENGER: Lunacy is lunacy and that's all there is to it! Everybody knows what lunacy is. And what about the rhinoceroses—are they practice or are they theory?

DUDARD: Both!

BERENGER: How do you mean—both?

DUDARD: Both the one and the other, or one or the other. It's a debatable point!

BERENGER: Well in that case . . . I refuse to think about it!

DUDARD: You're getting all het up. Our opinions may not exactly coincide but we can still discuss the matter peaceably. These things should be discussed.

BERENGER [*distracted*]: You think I'm getting all het up, do you? I might be Jean. Oh no, no, I don't want to become like him. I mustn't be like him. [*He calms down.*] I'm not very well up in philosophy. I've never studied; you've got all sorts of diplomas. That's why you're so at ease in discussion, whereas I never know what to answer—I'm so clumsy. [*Louder rhinoceros noises passing first under the up-stage window and then the down-stage.*] But I do feel you're in the wrong . . . I feel it instinctively—no, that's not what I mean, it's the rhinoceros which has instinct—I feel it intuitively, yes, that's the word, intuitively.

DUDARD: What do you understand by "intuitive"?

BERENGER: Intuitively means . . . well, just like that! I feel it, just like that. I think your excessive tolerance, and your generous indulgence . . . believe me, they're really only weakness . . . just blind spots . . .

DUDARD: You're innocent enough to think that.

BERENGER: You'll always be able to dance rings round me. But, you know what? I'm going to try and get hold of the Logician . . .

DUDARD: What logician?

BERENGER: The Logician, the philosopher, a logician, you know . . . you know better than I do what a logician is. A logician I met, who explained to me . . .

DUDARD: What did he explain to you?

BERENGER: He explained that the Asiatic rhinoceroses were African and the African ones Asiatic.
DUDARD: I don't follow you.
BERENGER: No . . . no . . . he proved the contrary—that the African ones were Asiatic and the Asiatic ones . . . I know what I mean. That's not what I wanted to say. But you'll get on very well with him. He's your sort of person, a very good man, a very subtle mind, brilliant.

[Increasing noises from the rhinoceroses. The words of the two men are drowned by the animals passing under the windows; for a few moments the lips of DUDARD *and* BERENGER *are seen to move without any words being heard.]*

There they go again! Will they never stop! *[He runs to the up-stage window.]* Stop it! Stop it! You devils!

[The rhinoceroses move away. BERENGER *shakes his fist after them.]*

DUDARD *[seated]*: I'd be happy to meet your Logician. If he can enlighten me on these obscure and delicate points, I'd be only too delighted.
BERENGER *[as he runs to the down-stage window]*: Yes, I'll bring him along, he'll talk to you. He's a very distinguished person, you'll see. [To *the rhinoceroses, from the window.]* You devils! *[Shakes his fist as before.]*
DUDARD: Let them alone. And be more polite. You shouldn't talk to people like that . . .
BERENGER *[still at the window]*: There they go again!

[A boater pierced by a rhinoceros horn emerges from the orchestra pit under the window and passes swiftly from left to right.]

There's a boater impaled on a rhinoceros horn. Oh, it's the Logician's hat! It's the Logician's! That's the bloody limit! The Logician's turned into a rhinoceros!
DUDARD: That's no reason to be coarse!
BERENGER: Dear Lord, who can you turn to—who? I ask you! The Logician a rhinoceros!
DUDARD *[going to the window]*: Where is he?
BERENGER *[pointing]*: There, that one there, you see!
DUDARD: He's the only rhinoceros in a boater! That makes you think. You're sure it's your Logician?
BERENGER: The Logician . . . a rhinoceros!!!
DUDARD: He's still retained a vestige of his old individuality.
BERENGER *[shakes his fist again at the straw-hatted rhinoceros, which has disappeared]*: I'll never join up with you! Not me!
DUDARD: If he was a genuine thinker, as you say, he couldn't have got carried away. He must have weighed all the pros and cons before deciding.
BERENGER *[still shouting after the ex-Logician and the other rhinoceroses who have moved away]*: I'll never join up with you!
DUDARD *[settling into the armchair]*: Yes, that certainly makes you think!

*[*BERENGER *closes the down-stage window; goes to the up-stage window where other rhinoceroses are passing, presumably making a tour of the house. He opens the window and shouts:]*

BERENGER: No, I'll never join up with you!
DUDARD *[aside, in his armchair]*: They're going round and round the house. They're playing! Just big babies!

*[*DAISY *has been seen mounting the top stairs. She knocks on* BERENGER*'s door. She is carrying a basket.]*

There's somebody at the door, Berenger!

[He takes BERENGER, *who is still at the window, by the sleeve.]*

BERENGER *[shouting after the rhinoceroses]*: It's a disgrace, masquerading like this, a disgrace!

DUDARD: There's someone knocking, Berenger, can't you hear?

BERENGER: Open, then, if you want to! *[He continues to watch the rhinoceroses whose noise is fading away.]*

*[*DUDARD *goes to open the door.]*

DAISY *[Coming in]*: Morning, Mr. Dudard.
DUDARD: Oh, it's you, Miss Daisy.
DAISY: Is Berenger here, is he any better?
DUDARD: How nice to see you, my dear. Do you often visit Berenger?
DAISY: Where is he?
DUDARD *[pointing]*: There.
DAISY: He's all on his own, poor thing. And he's not very well at the moment, somebody has to give him a hand.
DUDARD: You're a good friend, Miss Daisy.
DAISY: That's just what I am, a good friend.
DUDARD: You've got a warm heart.
DAISY: I'm a good friend, that's all.
BERENGER *[turning, leaving the window open]*: Oh Miss Daisy! How kind of you to come, how very kind!

DUDARD: It certainly is.

BERENGER: Did you know, Miss Daisy, that the Logician is a rhinoceros?

DAISY: Yes, I did. I caught sight of him in the street as I arrived. He was running very fast for someone his age! Are you feeling any better, Mr. Berenger?

BERENGER: My head's still bad! Still got a headache! Isn't it frightful? What do you think about it?

DAISY: I think you ought to be resting . . . you should take things quietly for a few more days.

DUDARD [*to* BERENGER *and* DAISY]: I hope I'm not disturbing you!

BERENGER [*to* DAISY]: I meant about the Logician . . .

DAISY [*to* DUDARD]: Why should you be? [*To* BERENGER:] Oh, about the Logician? I don't think anything at all!

DUDARD [*to* DAISY]: I thought I might be in the way!

DAISY [*to* BERENGER]: What do you expect me to think? [*To both:*] I've got some news for you: Botard's a rhinoceros!

DUDARD: Well, well!

BERENGER: I don't believe it. He was against it. You must be mistaken. He protested. Dudard has just been telling me. Isn't that so, Dudard?

DUDARD: That is so.

DAISY: I know he was against it. But it didn't stop him turning, twenty-four hours after Mr. Papillon.

DUDARD: Well, he must have changed his mind! Everybody has the right to do that.

BERENGER: Then obviously anything can happen!

DUDARD [*to* BERENGER]: He was a very good man according to you just now.

BERENGER [*to* DAISY]: I just can't believe you. They must have lied to you.

DAISY: I saw him do it.

BERENGER: Then he must have been lying; he was just pretending.

DAISY: He seemed very sincere; sincerity itself.

BERENGER: Did he give any reasons?

DAISY: What he said was: we must move with the times! Those were his last human words.

DUDARD [*to* DAISY]: I was almost certain I'd meet you here, Miss Daisy.

BERENGER: . . . Move with the times! What a mentality! [*He makes a wide gesture.*]

DUDARD [*to* DAISY]: Impossible to find you anywhere else, since the office closed.

BERENGER [*continuing, aside*]: What childishness! [*He repeats the same gesture.*]

DAISY [*to* DUDARD]: If you wanted to see me, you only had to telephone.

DUDARD [*to* DAISY]: Oh you know me, Miss Daisy, I'm discretion itself.

BERENGER: But now I come to think it over, Botard's behaviour doesn't surprise me. His firmness was only a pose. Which doesn't stop him from being a good man, of course. Good men make good rhinoceroses, unfortunately. It's because they are so good that they get taken in.

DAISY: Do you mind if I put this basket on the table? [*She does so.*]

BERENGER: But he was a good man with a lot of resentment. . .

DUDARD [*to* DAISY, *and hastening to help her with the basket*]: Excuse me, excuse us both, we should have given you a hand before.

BERENGER [*continues*]: . . . He was riddled with hatred for his superiors, and he'd got an inferiority complex . . .

DUDARD [*to* BERENGER]: Your argument doesn't hold water, because the example he followed was the Chief's, the very instrument of the people who exploited him, as he used to say. No, it seems to me that with him it was a case of community spirit triumphing over his anarchic impulses.

BERENGER: It's the rhinoceroses which are anarchic, because they're in the minority.

DUDARD: They are, it's true—for the moment.

DAISY: They're a pretty big minority, and getting bigger all the time. My cousin's a rhinoceros now, and his wife. Not to mention leading personalities like the Cardinal de Retz . . .

DUDARD: A prelate!

DAISY: Mazarin.

DUDARD: This is going to spread to other countries, you'll see.

BERENGER: And to think it all started with us!

DAISY: . . . and some of the aristocracy. The Duke of St. Simon.

BERENGER [*with uplifted arms*]: All our great names!

DAISY: And others, too. Lots of others. Maybe a quarter of the whole town.

BERENGER: We're still in the majority. We must take advantage of that. We must do something before we're inundated.

DUDARD: They're very potent, very.

DAISY: Well for the moment, let's eat. I've brought some food.

BERENGER: You're very kind, Miss Daisy.

DUDARD [*aside*]: Very kind indeed.

BERENGER: I don't know how to thank you.

DAISY [*to* DUDARD]: Would you care to stay with us?

DUDARD: I don't want to be a nuisance.

DAISY: Whatever do you mean, Mr. Dudard? You know very well we'd love you to stay.

DUDARD: Well, you know, I'd hate to be in the way . . .

BERENGER: Of course, stay, Dudard. It's always a pleasure to talk to you.

DUDARD: As a matter of fact I'm in a bit of a hurry. I have an appointment.

BERENGER: Just now you said you had nothing to do.

DAISY [*unpacking her basket*]: You know, I had a lot of trouble finding food. The shops have been plundered; they just devour everything. And a lot of the shops are closed. It's written up outside: "Closed on account of transformation."

BERENGER: They should be all rounded up in a big enclosure, and kept under strict supervision.

DUDARD: That's easier said than done. The animals' protection league would be the first to object.

DAISY: And besides everyone has a close relative or a friend among them, and that would make it even more difficult.

BERENGER: So everybody's mixed up in it!

DUDARD: Everybody's in the same boat!

BERENGER: But how can people be rhinoceroses? It doesn't bear thinking about! [*To* DAISY:] Shall I help you lay the table?

DAISY: No, don't bother. I know where the plates are. [*She goes to a cupboard and takes out the plates.*]

DUDARD [*aside*]: She's obviously very familiar with the place . . .

DAISY [*to* DUDARD]: I'm laying for three—all right? You are staying with us?

BERENGER [*to* DUDARD]: Yes, of course you're staying.

DAISY [*to* BERENGER]: You get used to it, you know. Nobody seems surprised any more to see herds of rhinoceroses galloping through the streets. They just stand aside, and then carry on as if nothing had happened.

DUDARD: It's the wisest course to take.

BERENGER: Well I can't get used to it.

DUDARD [*reflectively*]: I wonder if one oughtn't to give it a try?

DAISY: Well right now, let's have lunch.

BERENGER: I don't see how a legal man like yourself can . . .

[*A great noise of rhinoceroses travelling very fast is heard outside. Trumpets and drums are also heard.*]

What's going on?

[*They rush to the down-stage window.*]

What is it?

[*The sound of a wall crumbling is heard. Dust covers part of the stage, enveloping, if possible, the characters. They are heard speaking through it.*]

BERENGER: You can't see a thing! What's happening?

DUDARD: You can't see, but you can hear all right.

BERENGER: That's no good!

DAISY: The plates will be all covered in dust.

BERENGER: How unhygienic!

DAISY: Let's hurry up and eat. We won't pay any attention to them.

[*The dust disperses.*]

BERENGER [*pointing into the auditorium*]: They've demolished the walls of the Fire Station.

DUDARD: That's true, they've demolished them!

DAISY [*who after moving from the window to near the table holding the plate which she is endeavouring to clean, rushes to join the other two*]: They're coming out.

BERENGER: All the firemen, a whole regiment of rhinoceroses, led by drums.

DAISY: They're pouring up the streets!

BERENGER: It's gone too far, much too far!

DAISY: More rhinoceroses are streaming out of the courtyard.

BERENGER: And out of the houses . . .

DUDARD: And the windows as well!

DAISY: They're joining up with the others.

[*A man comes out of the landing door left and dashes downstairs at top speed; then another with a large horn on his nose; then a woman wearing an entire rhinoceros head.*]

DUDARD: There aren't enough of us left any more.

BERENGER: How many with one horn, and how many with two?

DUDARD: The statisticians are bound to be compiling statistics now. There'll be plenty of erudite controversy you can be sure!

BERENGER: They can only calculate approximately. It's all happening so fast. It leaves them no time. No time to calculate.

DAISY: The best thing is to let the statisticians get on with it. Come and eat, my dear. That'll calm you down. You'll feel better afterwards. [To DUDARD:] And you, too.

[*They move away from the window.* DAISY *takes* BERENGER's *arm; he allows himself to be led docilely.* DUDARD *suddenly halts.*]

DUDARD: I don't feel very hungry—or rather, to be frank, I don't like tinned food very much. I feel like eating outside on the grass.

BERENGER: You mustn't do that. Think of the risk!

DUDARD: But really I don't want to put you to the trouble.

BERENGER: But we've already told you . . .

DUDARD [*interrupting* BERENGER]: I really mean it.

DAISY [*to* DUDARD]: Of course if you really don't want to stay, we can't force you . . .

DUDARD: I didn't mean to offend you.

BERENGER [*to* DAISY]: Don't let him go, he mustn't go.

DAISY: I'd like him to stay . . . but people must do as they please.

BERENGER [*to* DUDARD]: Man is superior to the rhinoceros.

DUDARD: I didn't say he wasn't. But I'm not with you absolutely either. I don't know; only experience can tell.

BERENGER [*to* DUDARD]: You're weakening too, Dudard. It's just a passing phase which you'll regret.

DAISY: If it's just a passing phase then there's no great danger.

DUDARD: I feel certain scruples! I feel it's my duty to stick by my employers and my friends, through thick and thin.

BERENGER: It's not as if you were married to them.

DUDARD: I've renounced marriage. I prefer the great universal family to the little domestic one.

DAISY [*softly*]: We shall miss you a lot, Dudard, but we can't do anything about it.

DUDARD: It's my duty to stick by them; I have to do my duty.

BERENGER: No you're wrong, your duty is to . . . you don't see where your real duty lies . . . your duty is to oppose them, with a firm, clear mind.

DUDARD: I shall keep my mind clear. [*He starts to move round the stage in circles.*] As clear as ever it was. But if you're going to criticize, it's better to do so from the inside. I'm not going to abandon them. I won't abandon them.

DAISY: He's very good-hearted.

BERENGER: He's too good-hearted. [*To* DUDARD, *then dashing to the door:*] You're too good-hearted, you're human. [*To* DAISY:] Don't let him go. He's making a mistake. He's human.

DAISY: What can I do?

[DUDARD *opens the door and runs off; he goes down the stairs at top speed followed by* BERENGER *who shouts after him from the landing.*]

BERENGER: Come back, Dudard! We're fond of you, don't go! It's too late! [*He comes back.*] Too late!

DAISY: We couldn't do anything. [*She closes the door behind* BERENGER, *who darts to the down-stage window.*]

BERENGER: He's joined up with them. Where is he now?

DAISY [*moving to the window*]: With them.

BERENGER: Which one is he?

DAISY: You can't tell. You can't recognize him any more.

BERENGER: They all look alike, all alike. [*To* DAISY:] He *did* hesitate. You should have held him back by force.

DAISY: I didn't dare to.

BERENGER: You should have been firmer with him, you should have insisted; he was in love with you, wasn't he?

DAISY: He never made me any official declaration.

BERENGER: Everybody knew he was. He's done this out of thwarted love. He was a shy man. He wanted to make a big gesture to impress you. Don't you feel like going after him?

DAISY: Not at all. Or I wouldn't be here!

BERENGER [*looking out of the window*]: You can see nothing but them in the street. [*He darts to the up-stage window.*] Nothing but them! You were wrong, Daisy. [*He looks through the down-stage window again.*] Not a single human being as far as the eye can see. They're all over the street. Half with one horn and half with two, and that's the only distinction!

[*Powerful noises of moving rhinoceroses are heard, but somehow it is a musical sound. On the up-stage wall stylized heads appear and disappear; they become more and more numerous from now on until the end of the play. Towards the end they stay fixed for longer and longer, until eventually they fill the entire back wall, remaining static. The heads, in spite of their monstrous appearance, seem to become more and more beautiful.*]

You don't feel let down, do you, Daisy? There's nothing you regret?

DAISY: No, no.

BERENGER: I want so much to be a comfort to you. I love you, Daisy; don't ever leave me.

DAISY: Shut the window, darling. They're making such a noise. And the dust is rising even up to here. Everything will get filthy.

BERENGER: Yes, you're right. [*He closes the down-stage window and* DAISY *closes the up-stage one. They meet centre-stage.*] I'm not afraid of anything as long as we're together. I don't care what happens. You know, Daisy, I thought I'd never be able to fall in love again. [*He takes her hands, strokes her arms.*]

DAISY: Well you see, everything is possible.

BERENGER: I want so much to make you happy. Do you think you can be happy with me.

DAISY: Why not? If you're happy, then I'll be happy, too. You say nothing scares you, but you're really frightened of everything. What can possibly happen to us?

BERENGER [*stammering*]: My love, my dear love . . . let me kiss your lips. I never dreamed I could still feel such tremendous emotion!

DAISY: You must be more calm and more sure of yourself, now.

BERENGER: I am; let me kiss you.

DAISY: I'm very tired, dear. Stay quiet and rest yourself. Sit in the armchair.

[BERENGER, *led by* DAISY, *sits in the armchair.*]

BERENGER: There was no point in Dudard quarrelling with Botard, as things turned out.

DAISY: Don't think about Dudard any more. I'm here with you. We've no right to interfere in other people's lives.

BERENGER: But you're interfering in mine. You know how to be firm with me.

DAISY: That's not the same thing; I never loved Dudard.

BERENGER: I see what you mean. If he'd stayed he'd always have been an obstacle between us. Ah, happiness is such an egotistical thing!

DAISY: You have to fight for happiness, don't you agree?

BERENGER: I adore you, Daisy; I admire you as well.

DAISY: Maybe you won't say that when you get to know me better.

BERENGER: The more I know you the better you seem; and you're so beautiful, so very beautiful. [*More rhinoceroses are heard passing.*] Particularly compared to them . . . [*He points to the window.*] You probably think that's no compliment, but they make you seem more beautiful than ever . . .

DAISY: Have you been good today? You haven't had any brandy?

BERENGER: Oh yes, I've been good.

DAISY: Is that the truth?

BERENGER: Yes, it's the truth I assure you.

DAISY: Can I believe you, I wonder?

BERENGER [*a little flustered*]: Oh yes, you must believe me.

DAISY: Well all right then, you can have a little glass. It'll buck you up.

[BERENGER *is about to leap up.*]

You stay where you are, dear. Where's the bottle?

BERENGER [*pointing to it*]: There, on the little table.

DAISY [*going to the table and getting the bottle and glass*]: You've hidden it well away.

BERENGER: It's out of the way of temptation.

DAISY [*pours a small glass and gives it to* BERENGER]: You've been a good boy. You're making progress.

BERENGER: I'll make a lot more now I'm with you.

DAISY [*handing him the glass*]: Here you are. That's your reward.

BERENGER [*downing it at one go*]: Thank you. [*He holds up his empty glass to* DAISY.]

DAISY: Oh no, dear. That's enough for this morning. [*She takes his glass, puts it back on the table with the bottle.*] I don't want it to make you ill. [*She comes back to him.*] How's your head feel now?

BERENGER: Much better, darling.

DAISY: Then we'll take off the bandage. It doesn't suit you at all.

BERENGER: Oh no, don't touch it.

DAISY: Nonsense, we'll take it off now.

BERENGER: I'm frightened there might be something underneath.

DAISY [*removing the bandage in spite of his protests*]: Always frightened, aren't you, always imagining the worst! There's nothing there, you see. Your forehead's as smooth as a baby's.

BERENGER [*feeling his brow*]: You're right; you're getting rid of my complexes. [DAISY *kisses him on the brow.*] What should I do without you?

DAISY: I'll never leave you alone again.

BERENGER: I won't have any more fears now I'm with you.

DAISY: I'll keep them all at bay.

BERENGER: We'll read books together. I'll become clever.

DAISY: And when there aren't so many people about we'll go for long walks.

BERENGER: Yes, along the Seine, and in the Luxembourg Gardens . . .

DAISY: And to the Zoo.

BERENGER: I'll be brave and strong. I'll keep you safe from harm.

DAISY: You won't need to defend me, silly! We don't wish anyone any harm. And no one wishes us any, my dear.

BERENGER: Sometimes one does harm without meaning to, or rather one allows it to go unchecked. I know you didn't like poor old Mr. Papillon very much—but perhaps you shouldn't have spoken to him so harshly that day when Boeuf turned into a rhinoceros. You needn't have told him he had such horny hands.

DAISY: But it was true—he had!

BERENGER: I know he had, my dear. But you could have said so less bluntly and not hurt his feelings so much. It had a big effect on him.

DAISY: Do you think so?

BERENGER: He didn't show it—he was too proud for that—but the remark certainly went home. It must have influenced his decision. Perhaps you might have been the means of saving him.

DAISY: I couldn't possibly foresee what was going to happen to him . . . besides he was so ill-mannered.

BERENGER: For my own part, I shall never forgive myself for not being nicer to Jean. I never managed to give him a really solid proof of the friendship I felt for him. I wasn't sufficiently understanding with him.

DAISY: Don't worry about it. You did all you could. Nobody can do the impossible. There's no point in reproaching yourself now. Stop thinking about all those people. Forget about them. You must forget all those bad memories.

BERENGER: But they keep coming back to me. They're very real memories.

DAISY: I never knew you were such a realist—I thought you were more poetic. Where's your imagination? There are many sides to reality. Choose the one that's best for you. Escape into the world of the imagination.

BERENGER: It's easy to say that!

DAISY: Aren't I enough for you?

BERENGER: Oh yes, more than enough!

DAISY: You'll spoil everything if you go on having a bad conscience. Everybody has their faults, but you and I have got less than a lot of people.

BERENGER: Do you really think so?

DAISY: We're comparatively better than most. We're good, both of us.

BERENGER: That's true, you're good and I'm good. That's true.

DAISY: Well then we have the right to live. We even owe ourselves a duty to be happy in spite of everything. Guilt is a dangerous symptom. It shows a lack of purity.

BERENGER: You're right, it can lead to that . . . [*He points to the window under which the rhinoceroses are passing and to the up-stage wall where another rhinoceros head appears.*] . . . a lot of them started like that!

DAISY: We must try and not feel guilty any more.

BERENGER: How right you are, my wonderful love . . . You're all my happiness; the light of my life . . . We are together, aren't we? No one can separate us. Our love is the only thing that's real. Nobody has the right to stop us from being happy —in fact, nobody could, could they?

[*The telephone rings.*]

Who could that be?

DAISY [*fearful*]: Don't answer.

BERENGER: Why not?

DAISY: I don't know. I just feel it's better not to.

BERENGER: It might be Mr. Papillon, or Botard, or Jean or Dudard ringing to say they've had second thoughts. You did say it was probably only a passing phase.

DAISY: I don't think so. They wouldn't have changed their minds so quickly. They've not had time to think it over. They're bound to give it a fair trial.

BERENGER: Perhaps the authorities have decided to take action at last; maybe they're ringing to ask our help in whatever measures they've decided to adopt.

DAISY: I'd be surprised if it was them.

[*The telephone rings again.*]

BERENGER: It is the authorities, I tell you, I recognize the ring—a long drawn-out ring, I can't ignore an appeal from them. It can't be anyone else. [*He picks up the receiver.*] Hallo? [*Trumpetings are heard coming from the receiver.*] You hear that? Trumpeting! Listen!

[DAISY *puts the telephone to her ear, is shocked by the sound, quickly replaces the receiver.*]

DAISY [*frightened*]: What's going on?

BERENGER: They're playing jokes now.

DAISY: Jokes in bad taste!

BERENGER: You see! What did I tell you?

DAISY: You didn't tell me anything.

BERENGER: I was expecting that; it was just what I'd predicted.

DAISY: You didn't predict anything. You never do. You can only predict things after they've happened.

BERENGER: Oh yes, I can; I can predict things all right.

DAISY: That's not nice of them—in fact it's very nasty. I don't like being made fun of.

BERENGER : They wouldn't dare make fun of you. It's me they're making fun of.

DAISY: And naturally I come in for it as well because I'm with you. They're taking their revenge. But what have we done to them?

[*The telephone rings again.*]

Pull the plug out.

BERENGER: The telephone authorities say you mustn't.

DAISY: Oh you never dare to do anything—and you say you could defend me!

BERENGER [*darting to the radio*]: Let's turn on the radio for the news!

DAISY: Yes, we must find out how things stand!

[*The sound of trumpeting comes from the radio.* BERENGER *peremptorily switches it off. But in the distance other trumpetings, like echoes, can be heard.*]

Things are getting really serious! I tell you frankly, I don't like it! [*She is trembling.*]

BERENGER [*very agitated*]: Keep calm! Keep calm!

DAISY: They've taken over the radio stations!

BERENGER [*agitated and trembling*]: Keep calm, keep calm!

[DAISY *runs to the up-stage window, then to the down-stage window and looks out;* BERENGER *does the same in the opposite order, then the two come and face each other centre-stage.*]

DAISY: It's no joke any longer. They mean business!

BERENGER: There's only them left now; nobody but them. Even the authorities have joined them.

[*They cross to the windows as before, and meet again centre-stage.*]

DAISY: Not a soul left anywhere.

BERENGER: We're all alone, we're left all alone.

DAISY: That's what you wanted.

BERENGER: You mean that's what you wanted!

DAISY: It was you!

BERENGER: You!

[*Noises come from everywhere at once. Rhinoceros heads fill the up-stage wall. From left and right in the house, the noise of rushing feet and the panting breath of the animals. But all these disquieting sounds are nevertheless somehow rhythmical, making a kind of music. The loudest noises of all come from above; a noise of stamping. Plaster falls from the ceiling. The house shakes violently.*]

DAISY: The earth's trembling! [*She doesn't know where to run.*]

BERENGER: No, that's our neighbours, the Perissodactyles! [*He shakes his fist to left and right and above.*] Stop it! You're preventing us from working! Noise is forbidden in these flats! Noise is forbidden!

DAISY: They'll never listen to you!

[*However the noise does diminish, merely forming a sort of musical background.*]

BERENGER [*he, too, is afraid*]: Don't be frightened, my dear. We're together—you're happy with me, aren't you? It's enough that I'm with you, isn't it? I'll chase all your fears away.

DAISY: Perhaps it's all our own fault.

BERENGER: Don't think about it any longer. We mustn't start feeling remorse. It's dangerous to start feeling guilty. We must just live our lives, and be happy. We have the right to be happy. They're not spiteful, and we're not doing them any harm. They'll leave us in peace. You just keep calm and rest. Sit in the armchair. [*He leads her to the armchair.*] Just keep calm! [DAISY *sits in the armchair.*] Would you like a drop of brandy to pull you together?

DAISY: I've got a headache.

BERENGER [*taking up his bandage and binding* DAISY*'s head*]: I love you, my darling. Don't you worry, they'll get over it. It's just a passing phase.

DAISY: They won't get over it. It's for good.

BERENGER: I love you. I love you madly.

DAISY [*taking off the bandage*]: Let things just take their course. What can we do about it?

BERENGER: They've all gone mad. The world is sick. They're all sick.

DAISY: We shan't be the ones to cure them.

BERENGER: How can we live in the same house with them?

DAISY [*calming down*]: We must be sensible. We must adapt ourselves and try and get on with them.

BERENGER: They can't understand us.

DAISY: They must. There's no other way.

BERENGER: Do you understand them?

DAISY: Not yet. But we must try to understand the way their minds work, and learn their language.

BERENGER: They haven't got a language! Listen . . . do you call that a language?

DAISY: How do you know? You're no polyglot!

BERENGER: We'll talk about it later. We must have lunch first.

DAISY: I'm not hungry any more. It's all too much. I can't take any more.

BERENGER: But you're the strong one. You're not going to let it get you down. It's precisely for your courage that I admire you so.

DAISY: You said that before.

BERENGER: Do you feel sure of my love?

DAISY: Yes, of course.

BERENGER: I love you so.

DAISY: You keep saying the same thing, my dear.

BERENGER: Listen, Daisy, there *is* something we can do. We'll have children, and our children will have children—it'll take time, but together we can regenerate the human race.

DAISY: Regenerate the human race?

BERENGER: It happened once before.

DAISY: Ages ago. Adam and Eve . . . They had a lot of courage.

BERENGER: And we, too, can have courage. We don't need all that much. It happens automatically with time and patience.

DAISY: What's the use?

BERENGER: Of course we can—with a little bit of courage.

DAISY: I don't want to have children—it's a bore.

BERENGER: How can we save the world, if you don't?

DAISY: Why bother to save it?

BERENGER: What a thing to say! Do it for me, Daisy. Let's save the world.

DAISY: After all, perhaps it's we who need saving. Perhaps we're the abnormal ones.

BERENGER: You're not yourself, Daisy, you've got a touch of fever.

DAISY: There aren't any more of our kind about anywhere, are there?

BERENGER: Daisy, you're not to talk like that!

[DAISY *looks all around at the rhinoceros heads on the walls, on the landing door, and now starting to appear along the footlights.*]

DAISY: Those are the real people. They look happy. They're content to be what they are. They don't look insane. They look very natural. They were right to do what they did.
BERENGER [*clasping his hands and looking despairingly at* DAISY]: We're the ones who are doing right, Daisy, I assure you.
DAISY: That's very presumptuous of you!
BERENGER: You know perfectly well I'm right.
DAISY: There's no such thing as absolute right. It's the world that's right—not you and me.
BERENGER: I *am* right, Daisy. And the proof is that you understand me when I speak to you.
DAISY: What does that prove?
BERENGER: The proof is that I love you as much as it's possible for a man to love a woman.
DAISY: Funny sort of argument!
BERENGER: I don't understand you any longer, Daisy. You don't know what you're saying, darling. Think of our love! Our love . . .
DAISY: I feel a bit ashamed of what you call love—this morbid feeling, this male weakness. And female, too. It just doesn't compare with the ardour and the tremendous energy emanating from all these creatures around us.
BERENGER: Energy! You want some energy, do you? I can let you have some energy! [*He slaps her face.*]
DAISY: Oh! I never would have believed it possible . . . [*She sinks into the armchair.*]
BERENGER: Oh forgive me, my darling, please forgive me! [*He tries to embrace her, she evades him.*] Forgive me, my darling. I didn't mean it. I don't know what came over me, losing control like that!
DAISY: It's because you've run out of arguments, that's why.
BERENGER: Oh dear! In the space of a few minutes we've gone through twenty-five years of married life.
DAISY: I pity you. I understand you all too well . . .
BERENGER [*as* DAISY *weeps*]: You're probably right that I've run out of arguments. You think they're stronger than me, stronger than us. Maybe they are.
DAISY: Indeed they are.
BERENGER: Well, in spite of everything, I swear to you I'll never give in, never!
DAISY [*she rises, goes to* BERENGER, *puts her arms round his neck*]: My poor darling, I'll help you to resist—to the very end.
BERENGER: Will you be capable of it?
DAISY: I give you my word. You can trust me.

[*The rhinoceros noises have become melodious.*]

Listen, they're singing!
BERENGER: They're not singing, they're roaring.
DAISY: They're singing.
BERENGER: They're roaring, I tell you.
DAISY: You're mad, they're singing.
BERENGER: You can't have a very musical ear, then.
DAISY: You don't know the first thing about music, poor dear—and look, they're playing as well, and dancing.
BERENGER: You call that dancing?
DAISY: It's their way of dancing. They're beautiful.
BERENGER: They're disgusting!
DAISY: You're not to say unpleasant things about them. It upsets me.
BERENGER: I'm sorry. We're not going to quarrel on their account.
DAISY: They're like gods.
BERENGER: You go too far, Daisy; take a good look at them.
DAISY: You mustn't be jealous, my dear.

[*She goes to* BERENGER *again and tries to embrace him. This time it is* BERENGER *who frees himself.*]

BERENGER: I can see our opinions are directly opposed. It's better not to discuss the matter.
DAISY: Now you mustn't be nasty.
BERENGER: Then don't you be stupid!
DAISY [*to* BERENGER, *who turns his back on her. He looks at himself closely in the mirror*]: It's no longer possible for us to live together.

[*As* BERENGER *continues to examine himself in the mirror she goes quietly to the door, saying:*]

He isn't very nice, really, he isn't very nice. [*She goes out, and is seen slowly descending the stairs.*]
BERENGER [*still looking at himself in the mirror*]: Men aren't so bad-looking, you know. And I'm not a particularly handsome specimen! Believe me, Daisy! [*He turns round.*] Daisy! Daisy! Where are you, Daisy? You can't do that to me! [*He darts to the door.*] Daisy! [*He gets to the landing and leans over the banister.*] Daisy! Come back! Come back, my dear! You haven't even had your lunch. Daisy, don't leave me alone! Remember your promise! Daisy! Daisy! [*He stops calling, makes a despairing gesture, and comes back into the room.*] Well, it was obvious we weren't getting along together. The home was broken up. It just wasn't working out. But she shouldn't have left like that with no explanation. [*He looks all around.*] She didn't even leave a message. That's no way to behave. Now I'm all

on my own. [*He locks the door carefully, but angrily.*] But they won't get me. [*He carefully closes the windows.*] You won't get me! [*He addresses all the rhinoceros heads.*] I'm not joining you; I don't understand you! I'm staying as I am. I'm a human being. A human being. [*He sits in the armchair.*] It's an impossible situation. It's my fault she's gone. I meant everything to her. What'll become of her? That's one more person on my conscience. I can easily picture the worst, because the worst can easily happen. Poor little thing left all alone in this world of monsters! Nobody can help me find her, nobody, because there's nobody left.

[*Fresh trumpetings, hectic racings, clouds of dust.*]

I can't bear the sound of them any longer, I'm going to put cotton wool in my cars. [*He does so, and talks to himself in the mirror.*] The only solution is to convince them—but convince them of what? Are the changes reversible, that's the point? Are they reversible? It would be a labour of Hercules, far beyond me. In any case, to convince them you'd have to talk to them. And to talk to them I'd have to learn their language. Or they'd have to learn mine. But what language do I speak? What is my language? Am I talking French? Yes, it must be French. But what is French? I call it French if I want, and nobody can say it isn't—I'm the only one who speaks it. What am I saying? Do I understand what I'm saying? Do I? [He *crosses to the middle of the room.*] And what if it's true what Daisy said, and they're the ones in the right? [*He turns back to the mirror.*] A man's not ugly to look at, not ugly at all! [*He examines himself, passing his hand over his face.*] What a funny-looking thing! What do I look like? What? [*He darts to a cupboard, takes out some photographs which he examines.*] Photographs! Who are all these people? Is it Mr. Papillon—or is it Daisy? And is that Botard or Dudard or Jean? Or is it me? [*He rushes to the cupboard again and takes out two or three pictures.*] Now I recognize me: that's me, that's me! [*He hangs the pictures on the back wall, beside the rhinoceros heads.*] That's me, that's me!

[*When he hangs the pictures one sees that they are of an old man, a huge woman, and another man. The ugliness of these pictures is in contrast to the rhinoceros heads which have become very beautiful.* BERENGER *steps back to contemplate the pictures.*]

I'm not good-looking, I'm not good-looking. [*He takes down the pictures, throws them furiously to the ground, and goes over to the mirror.*] They're the good-looking ones. I was wrong! Oh, how I wish I was like them! I haven't got any horns, more's the pity. A smooth brow looks so ugly. I need one or two horns to give my sagging face a lift. Perhaps one will grow and I needn't be ashamed any more—than I could go and join them. But it will never grow! [*He looks at the palms of his hands.*] My hands are so limp—oh, why won't they get rough! [*He takes his coat off, undoes his shirt to look at his chest in the mirror.*] My skin is so slack. I can't stand this white, hairy body. Oh I'd love to have a hard skin in that wonderful dull green colour—a skin that looks decent naked without any hair on it, like theirs! [*He listens to the trumpetings.*] Their song is charming—a bit raucous perhaps, but it does have charm! I wish I could do it! [*He tries to imitate them.*] Ahh, Ahh, Brr! No, that's not it! Try again, louder! Ahh, Ahh, Brr! No, that's not it, it's too feeble, it's got no drive behind it. I'm not trumpeting at all; I'm just howling. Ahh, Ahh, Brr. There's a big difference between howling and trumpeting. I've only myself to blame; I should have gone with them while there was still time. Now it's too late! Now I'm a monster, just a monster. Now I'll never become a rhinoceros, never, never! I've gone past changing. I want to, I really do, but I can't, I just can't. I can't stand the sight of me. I'm too ashamed! [*He turns his back on the mirror.*] I'm so ugly! People who try to hang on to their individuality always come to a bad end! [*He suddenly snaps out of it.*] Oh well, too bad! I'll take on the whole of them! I'll put up a fight against the lot of them, the whole lot of them! I'm the last man left, and I'm staying that way until the end. I'm not capitulating!

CURTAIN

TENNESSEE WILLIAMS

Thomas Lanier ("Tennessee") Williams (1911–1983) was born in Columbus, Mississippi. He spent his early years in small southern towns and his adolescence in St. Louis, Missouri. Williams's family life was characterized by family tension and the mutual hostility of his parents. Edwina, his mother, was a Southern belle, given to exaggeration, and Cornelius Coffin, his father, was an alcoholic businessman. Williams's most enduring emotional and financial support came from his mother's parents, Walter Daikin, an Episcopal minister, and his wife Rosina (called Rose), for whom Williams's sister, Rose, was named.

Williams was an average student at the University of Missouri, but parental pressure forced him to withdraw. He returned home to work for three years in the branch of the shoe company his father managed, escaping the drudgery of the job by writing poetry, short stories, and one-act plays. Underweight and tortured by parental conflicts, Williams was briefly hospitalized in 1935 for a heart ailment that was later rediagnosed as emotional exhaustion. Williams always referred to this incident as his first heart attack, and he suffered from the fear of a heart attack, which he later came to call "cardiac neurosis," throughout his life. But with his great drive to survive, he recovered quickly, left home to live with his grandfather Daikin, kept on writing, and returned to college, finally graduating from the University of Iowa in 1938.

With a college degree, no steady income, and an intense desire to become a writer, Williams traveled. Being on the move helped him to exorcize his nervous energy, and near-incessant travel became a lifelong pattern. In 1939, when the traveling stopped momentarily, Williams settled briefly in New Orleans, and there he liberated his repressed sexuality, changed his name to Tennessee, and came out as a homosexual. Thirty-six years later, in his *Memoirs* (1975), Williams admitted that realizing his homosexuality was crucial to his identity and his creativity. "I was late coming out," he said, "and when I did it was with one hell of a bang."

Many of Williams's plays have their roots in his tragic sense of a world in which moral values are in violent juxtaposition. He found an appropriate model in Henrik Ibsen's problem plays, which culminate in the disclosure of long-buried guilt, particularly in plays such as *Ghosts.* He was impressed with August Strindberg's *Miss Julie,* probably because its subject reflected his own sense of sexual frustration and family conflict. From Anton Chekhov, he learned that characters' feelings and words are more important than what they do. Williams was impressed by *The Cherry Orchard* and *The Sea Gull.* He carried a picture of Chekhov with him on his travels and hung it over his writing desk. In the verse of poet Hart Crane (1899–1932), Williams found a hero who was a homosexual like himself. But Crane's conflicted sexuality, which led him to commit suicide at thirty-two, was a reminder to Williams of his own sense of fatality. In the sexually charged novels of D. H. Lawrence (1885–1930), Williams found a modern author, many of whose themes matched his own; it is one of those "hideous [books] by that insane Mr. Lawrence" that Amanda Wingfield, the protagonist of Williams's *The Glass Menagerie,* refuses to allow in her house.

In the 1930s Williams had a number of plays produced in St. Louis, and in 1939 he won a national playwriting prize for a group of his one-act plays. In 1940 he moved to New York for the production of *Battle of Angels,* a full-length play about a sexually hysterical religious fanatic. The play failed in Boston, but it eventually was redrafted as *Orpheus Descending* (1957). On the strength of his failed play and the efforts of his literary agent, Audrey Wood, Williams got work as a screenwriter in Hollywood. While there, in 1943, he wrote an early draft of *The Glass Menagerie.* Two years later, *The Glass Menagerie* won the New York Drama Critics' Circle Award, and Williams's career as a playwright was set. *You Touched Me!* (1946), co-authored with Donald Windham, followed, but it was not a success. A collection of one-act plays written over the previous decade, *27 Wagons Full of Cotton,* was published the same year.

Williams's *A Streetcar Named Desire* was produced in 1947 and was awarded the Pulitzer Prize for Drama in 1948. The title refers to an actual New Orleans streetcar line, with street destinations named Desire and Cemeteries, a bit of serendipity that Williams sardonically called the intersection of love and death. The play's protagonist, Blanche DuBois, is a southern belle of thirty, who has lost a family home to debt. She comes to stay in New Orleans with her sister, Stella, who has married beneath her. Stella's husband, Stanley Kowalski, is a handsome, sexy, and brutish man. Blanche openly disdains Stanley's coarseness, and she weaves illusions about her own gentility that Stella accepts as true. Stanley distrusts Blanche, and he discovers that she has a reputation for promiscuity and even lost her position as a teacher because of an affair with a student. While Stella is in the hospital where she delivers their baby, Stanley remains at home where he brutally shreds Blanche's version of reality: "I've been on to you from the start! Not once did you pull any wool over this boy's eye! You come in here and sprinkle the place with powder and spray perfume and cover the light bulb with a paper lantern, and lo and behold the place has turned into Egypt and you are the Queen of the Nile! Sitting on your throne and swilling down my liquor! I say—*Ha!—Ha!* Do you hear me? *Ha—ha—ha!*" When menace turns physical, Stanley attacks Blanche and, carrying her "inert figure" to the bed, says, "We've had this date with each other from the beginning!"

The experience crushes Blanche, and she finally loses her sanity. In the final scene, Stanley is deceitfully cunning about what happened, and he encourages Stella to have Blanche committed to an asylum. As Blanche is taken off by attendants, she says, "Whoever you are—I have always depended on the kindness of strangers." Years after the play's production, Williams acknowledged his deep personal identification with the character of Blanche, declaring "I am Blanche DuBois." Stella's cry, "What have I done to my sister? Oh God, what have I done to my sister?" is probably Williams's anguished cry for his own guilt for the condition of his sister, Rose.

Other important Williams plays—*Summer and Smoke* (1948), *The Rose Tattoo* (1951), and *Camino Real* (1953), an anti-fascist drama—followed quickly. *Cat on a Hot Tin Roof* (1955), another winner of the Pulitzer Prize, focuses on a Southern scion, Brick, who is saved from self-destruction by his sensuous wife, Maggie "the Cat," who helps him exorcize what the family regards as an unnatural attachment to a dead male friend. In *Orpheus Descending* (1957), the chief character, Valentine Xavier (pronounced "savior"), is an itinerant musician whose sexual appeal to women leads to disaster.

In Williams's *Suddenly, Last Summer* (1958), Catherine, a young woman, acts as a lure for her homosexual cousin, Sebastian Veneble. She nearly goes insane as she recalls how Sebastian was killed by local street-boys, who "devoured parts of him." Violet Veneble, Sebastian's forbidding and steely mother, refuses to acknowledge Sebastian's lifestyle, and to protect Sebastian's name, she threatens Catherine with a lobotomy.

Sweet Bird of Youth (1959) is Williams's serious yet campy exploration of the fall and rise of an aging film star Alexandra del Lago, who depends on the services of Chance Wayne, a gigolo. Williams wrote *Period of Adjustment* (1960), a domestic comedy about the American Dream and fear of homosexuality. His *The Night of the Iguana* (1961) is set in a Mexican seaside hotel, a favorite vacation place for Williams. Here, the Reverend Shannon, a defrocked Episcopalian priest, can find no relief from guilt in either alcohol or quick sex; only Hannah Jelkes, a disillusioned spinster, has the capacity to offer Shannon a chance for resurrection, but he hasn't the strength to accept it.

Williams's plays after 1963 are generally criticized as being seriously flawed as a result of his frenetic lifestyle and his alcohol and drug dependency. *The Milk Train Doesn't Stop Here Anymore* (1963), *The Gnädiges Fraulein* (1966), *The Seven Descents of Myrtle* (1968), *In the Bar of the Tokyo Hotel* (1969), and *Small-Craft Warnings* (1972) were not successful. Even *Outcry* (1973), a revision of *The Two-Character Play* (1967), which Williams considered his most important play after *A Street Car Named Desire,* was greeted with critical disdain. *Outcry* concerns a brother and sister team of professional actors, Felice and Clare, who suffer from paranoia and guilt as they perform before a hostile audience. The play has no action and is a stylized dialogue spoken by two people, who seem to speak as if they are one person. It was probably Williams's cry for help in fighting his personal demons, but critics and audiences only saw Williams in disarray, milking aspects of his tortured family relationships with his sister Rose. His later plays, such as *Vieux Carrée* (1978) and *A Lovely Sunday for Creve Coeur* (1979), were also unsuccessful.

In 1980 Williams returned to the theme of insanity in *Clothes for a Summer Hotel: A Ghost Play,* about Zelda and F. Scott Fitzgerald. Zelda, who is confined to a psychiatric hospital, accuses Scott of having abused and thwarted her creative imagination for his own purposes; her character, another in a line of long-suffering Southern women, seems a personification of Williams's feelings of guilt about the lobotomy of his sister Rose, whom he was supporting in a psychiatric hospital.

Williams's collections of short stories and poems—*Hard Candy* (1954), *In the Winter of Cities* (1956), *The Knightly Quest: A Novella and Four Stories* (1966), and *Eight Mortal Ladies Possessed* (1974)—provide insights into his life and plays. He also wrote two novels, *The Roman Spring of Mrs. Stone* (1950) and *Moise and the Age of Reason* (1975), and a collection of essays, *Where I Live* (1978). Williams's only successful original film script is *Baby Doll* (1956), although he was involved in adapting at least fifteen of his plays for the screen. (Williams's dealings with Hollywood were difficult, but most of his income came from screenwriting and residuals.)

Williams openly discussed his untidy life in his *Memoirs*, sometimes so candidly that he alienated even his friends and professional colleagues. He wrote with bravado often laced with self-deprecation about his neurosis, his sexual maladjustment, his homosexuality, and his anxiety about health, which he carried over into his plays.

The Glass Menagerie (1944) sets the pattern and theme for Williams's later dramas. It is substantially autobiographical. Tom Wingfield, the narrator, is Williams's persona; Amanda Wingfield, the faded Southern belle, is Williams's mother, Edwina; the long-gone father, Amanda's husband, is based on his father, Cornelius; and Laura, a young lame woman, is based on Williams's sister Rose, an unstable woman, who at age thirty, was lobotomized, which left her in a perpetual mental twilight. Williams was forever guilty about what happened to Rose, and her portrayal in *The Glass Menagerie* is the first (and most successful) of her many appearances in his plays and stories. Ironically, this personal experience that Williams transformed into *The Glass Menagerie* was lost on his family. In his *Memoirs*, Williams related that when Edwina met Laurette Taylor, the actress who portrayed Amanda in the original production, she was asked, "Well, Mrs. Williams . . . how did you like yourself?" to which Edwina innocently responded, "Myself?"

In the "Production Notes" for *The Glass Menagerie*, Williams pointed out that he found Strindberg's and Ibsen's sense of theatrical realism conventional and outdated. Instead, he adopted Eugene O'Neill's penetrating psychological portrayal of character and action in which memory and real time blend into one another; in fact, Williams called this a memory play. Telling his story as flashbacks allows Tom Wingfield to break down the planes of reality. As a dreamer and a failed poet whose life is unfulfilled, Tom relates the events that finally led him to run away from home. Now older, and perhaps wiser, his elegiac tone comes across as being honest, yet there is some lingering doubt as to whether Tom is indeed a reliable narrator.

The Glass Menagerie takes place about 1936 or 1937, the time when *Gone with the Wind* was the literary rage and the town of Guernica was destroyed during the Spanish Civil War. The Wingfields' apartment is out of the mainstream of history, however, though it is on the brink of a social and personal cataclysm. The apartment is at a dead end, located in the rear of the building, where its windows face a murky alley filled with garbage and clotheslines, as well as the marquee of movie theaters, the garish lights of which illuminate the apartment within. Also outside is the Paradise Dance Hall, from which the sound of the song "The World Is Waiting for the Sunrise!"drifts into the apartment—one of the play's many ironies because no sunrise, metaphorical or figurative, will occur here.

The action focuses on the experiences that precipitate Laura's decline into spinsterhood and Tom's own escape from the boundaries of the Wingfield apartment. Laura, twenty-three, lame and plain-looking, is bullied by Amanda, her mother, who wants her to have a romance and marry. Amanda, oblivious to the fact of her declined social status, is relentless and overbearing, but well-meaning; she never realizes the damage she causes to Laura or Tom.

Laura finds solace in tending her collection of glass animals, the glass menagerie. When Tom brings home Jim O'Connor, a work friend, to meet Laura, Amanda gets carried away with enthusiasm. Scene 7 is meant to be both emotionally brutal and romantic, as indicated by the fact that the action is lighted by candlelight.

Though Laura remembers Jim from high school, and has long held a secret crush on him, Jim recalls her only faintly. Shyly, she responds to Jim, though he is not too smart ("Unicorns—aren't they extinct in the modern world?") and talks brashly about the money he says he will make in the future ("I believe in the future of television"). Laura shows Jim her glass animals and allows him to hold her favorite, a tiny glass unicorn. Jim encourages Laura to dance, but when he swings her into motion, they bump the unicorn sitting on a table and it breaks. Jim feels tenderness for Laura—he holds her and kisses her on the lips—but then tells her, "I've—got strings on me. Laura, I've—been going steady . . . Well—right away from the start it was—love!"

Stunned, Laura struggles silently with her misery: "She bites her lip which was trembling and then bravely smiles. She opens her hand again on the broken glass figure. Then she gently takes his hand and raises it level with her own. She carefully places the unicorn in the palm of his hand, then pushes his finger closed upon it." When Amanda bursts in carrying lemonade, she is not unaware of the stress in the room but thinks that it suggests love blossoming: "Mmm, just breathe that air! So fresh, and the moon's so pretty! I'll skip back out—I know where my place is when young folks are having a—serious conversation!" Amanda's bravado diminishes when Jim abruptly tells her of his steady girl, which she registers by "bravely grimacing."

As the play ends, Tom says that he will go to the movies. But Amanda scathingly tells him: "That's right, now that you've had us make such fools of ourselves. The effort, the preparations, all the expense! The new floor lamp, the rug, the clothes for Laura! All for what? To entertain some other girl's fiancé! Go to the movies, go! Don't think about us, a mother deserted, an unmarried sister who's crippled and has no job! Don't let anything interfere with your selfish pleasure! Just go, go, go—to the movies!" Tom smashes his glass of lemonade on the floor and plunges out of the room onto the fire escape, slamming the door as he leaves. Laura screams with fright. At this point the action separates the past from the present: Tom, the narrator, stands on the fire escape, his face illuminated by moonlight, but inside carrying on a conversation that cannot be heard, Amanda comforts Laura, who looks up at her and smiles. Laura bends over the candelabra while Tom delivers his final lines: "Oh, Laura, Laura, I tried to leave you behind me, but I am more faithful than I intended to be! I reach for a cigarette, I cross the street, I run into the movies or a bar, I buy a drink, I speak to the nearest stranger—anything that can blow your candles out!" Then Tom delivers a kind of benediction: "For nowadays the world is lit by lightning! Blow out your candles, Laura—and so goodbye. . . . " Laura blows the candles out.

Williams's "Notes" on the use of a screen device, music, and lighting show the influence of Bertolt Brecht's and Erwin Piscator's concept of Epic Theater.

Williams was attracted to Brecht's drama, but not his political or social themes. He used the screen device in order to create a poetic effect, and he explained that "the legend or image upon the screen will strengthen the effect of what is merely allusion in the writing and allow the primary point to be made more simply and lightly than if the entire responsibility were on the spoken lines." For example, just as Amanda begins to speak in Scene 1, the message "Ou sont les neiges d'antan?" (Where are the snows of yesteryear?) appears. When Amanda tells about her gentlemen callers, an image of Amanda as a young girl appears on the screen. The opposition of the character and image allows the audience to share Tom's version of Amanda. Ironically, the original production of the play did not use screen devices. He later admitted that the omission did not diminish the play's effectiveness, but he let the messages on the screen stand in the published text. Williams also called for removing the play's opening transparent exterior wall, the so-called fourth wall, which Strindberg had advocated in the "Preface" to *Miss Julie*. This wall is not brought down again until Tom's final speech.

Williams's influence can be traced throughout contemporary playwriting. He is greatly appreciated for his artistry, his fluency of dialogue, and his controlled pace of action. His daring use of such themes as sexual promiscuity, castration, prostitution, drug abuse, alcoholism, and racism opened the theater to a renewed sense of drama especially advocated by Strindberg. The clash of opposites and the survival of the fit are particularly influential and admired by Edward Albee, John Osborne, David Mamet, Sam Shepard, and Marsha Norman.

Film

The Glass Menagerie (1950), directed by Irving Rapper, with Gertrude Lawrence, Jane Wyman, Kirk Douglas, and Arthur Kennedy. Williams received credit for the screenplay. Warner Brothers.

The Glass Menagerie (1950), directed by Anthony Harvey, with Katharine Hepburn, Sam Waterston, Michael Moriarity, and Joanna Miles. ABC Saturday Night Movie.

The Glass Menagerie (1987), directed by Paul Newman, with Joanne Woodward, Karen Allen, John Malkovich, and James Naughton. Cineplex Odeon Films (Burtt Harris).

The Glass Menagerie

Nobody, not even the rain, has such small hands.
—E. E. CUMMINGS

THE CHARACTERS

AMANDA WINGFIELD, the mother

A little woman of great but confused vitality clinging frantically to another time and place. Her characterization must be carefully created, not copied from type. She is not paranoiac, but her life is paranoia. There is much to admire in AMANDA, and as much to love and pity as there is to laugh at. Certainly she has endurance and a kind of heroism, and though her foolishness makes her unwittingly cruel at times, there is tenderness in her slight person.

LAURA WINGFIELD, her daughter

AMANDA, having failed to establish contact with reality, continues to live vitally in her illusions, but LAURA's situation is even graver. A childhood illness has left her crippled, one leg slightly shorter than the other, and held in a brace. This defect need not be more than suggested on the stage. Stemming from this, LAURA's separation increases till she is like a piece of her own glass collection, too exquisitely fragile to move from the shelf.

TOM WINGFIELD, her son

And the narrator of the play. A poet with a job in a warehouse. His nature is not remorseless, but to escape from a trap he has to act without pity.

JIM O'CONNOR, the gentleman caller

A nice, ordinary, young man.

SCENE: *An Alley in St. Louis*

Part I. Preparation for a Gentleman Caller.
Part II. The Gentleman calls.

Time: Now and the Past.

PRODUCTION NOTES

Being a "memory play," *The Glass Menagerie* can be presented with unusual freedom of convention. Because of its considerably delicate or tenuous material, atmospheric touches and subtleties of direction play a particularly important part. Expressionism and all other unconventional techniques in drama have only one valid aim, and that is a closer approach to truth. When a play employs unconventional techniques, it is not, or certainly shouldn't be, trying to escape its responsibility of dealing with reality, or interpreting experience, but is actually or should be attempting to find a closer approach, a more penetrating and vivid expression of things as they are. The straight realistic play with its genuine Frigidaire and authentic ice-cubes, its characters who speak exactly as its audience speaks, corresponds to the academic landscape and has the same virtue of a photographic likeness. Everyone should know nowadays the unimportance of the photographic in art: that truth, life, or reality is an organic thing which the poetic imagination can represent or suggest, in essence, only through transformation, through changing into other forms than those which were merely present in appearance.

These remarks are not meant as a preface only to this particular play. They have to do with a conception of a new, plastic theatre which must take the place of the exhausted theatre of realistic conventions if the theatre is to resume vitality as a part of our culture.

THE SCREEN DEVICE: There is *only one important difference between the original and the acting version of the play* and that is the *omission* in the latter of the device that I tentatively included in my *original* script. This device was the use of a screen on which were projected magic-lantern slides bearing images or titles. I do not regret the omission of this device from the original Broadway production. The extraordinary power of Miss Taylor's performance made it suitable to have the utmost simplicity in the physical production. But I think it may be interesting to some readers to see how this device was conceived. So I am putting it into the published manuscript. These images and legends, projected from behind, were cast on a section of wall between the front-room and diningroom areas, which should be indistinguishable from the rest when not in use.

The purpose of this will probably be apparent. It is to give accent to certain values in each scene. Each scene contains a particular point (or several) which is structurally the most important. In an episodic play, such as this, the basic structure or narrative line may be obscured from the audience; the effect may seem fragmentary rather than architectural. This may not be the fault of the play so much as a lack of attention in the audience. The legend or image upon the screen will strengthen the effect of what is merely allusion in the writing and allow the primary point to be made more simply and lightly than if the entire responsibility were on the spoken lines. Aside from this structural value, I think the screen will have a definite emotional appeal, less definable but just as important. An imaginative producer or director may invent many other uses for this device than those indicated in the present script. In fact the possibilities of the device seem much larger to me than the instance of this play can possibly utilize.

THE MUSIC: Another extra-literary accent in this play is provided by the use of music. A single recurring tune, "The Glass Menagerie," is used to give emotional emphasis to suitable passages. This tune is like circus music, not when you are on the grounds or in the immediate vicinity of the parade, but when you are at some distance and very likely thinking of something else. It seems under those circumstances to continue almost interminably and it weaves in and out of your preoccupied consciousness; then it is the lightest, most delicate music in the world and perhaps the saddest. It expresses the surface vivacity of life with the underlying strain of immutable and inexpressible sorrow. When you look at a piece of delicately spun glass you think of two things: how beautiful it is and how easily it can be broken. Both of those ideas should be woven into the recurring tune, which dips in and out of the play as if it were carried on a wind that changes. It serves as a thread of connection and allusion between the narrator with his separate point in time and space and the subject of his story. Between each episode it returns as reference to the emotion, nostalgia, which is the first condition of the play. It is primarily Laura's music and therefore comes out most clearly when the play focuses upon her and the lovely fragility of glass which is her image.

THE LIGHTING: The lighting in the play is not realistic. In keeping with the atmosphere of memory, the stage is dim. Shafts of light are focused on selected areas or actors, sometimes in contradistinction to what is the apparent center. For instance, in the quarrel scene between Tom and Amanda, in which Laura has no active part, the clearest pool of light is on her figure. This is also true of the supper scene, when her silent figure on the sofa should remain the visual center. The light upon Laura should be distinct from the others, having a peculiar pristine clarity such as light used in early religious portraits of female saints or madonnas. A certain correspondence to light in religious paintings, such as El Greco's, where the figures are radiant in atmosphere that is relatively dusky, could be effectively used throughout the play. (It will also permit a more effective use of the screen.) A free, imaginative use of light can be of enormous value in giving a mobile, plastic quality to plays of a more or less static nature.

Tennessee Williams

Eddie Dowling, Laurette Taylor, Anthony Ross, and Julie Haydon in The Glass Menagerie, *directed by Eddie Dowling and Margo Jones, the Playhouse Theatre, New York, 1945.*

SCENE 1

The Wingfield apartment is in the rear of the building, one of those vast hive-like conglomerations of cellular living-units that flower as warty growths in overcrowded urban centers of lower middle-class population and are symptomatic of the impulse of this largest and fundamentally enslaved section of American society to avoid fluidity and differentiation and to exist and function as one interfused mass of automatism.

The apartment faces an alley and is entered by a fire escape, a structure whose name is a touch of accidental poetic truth, for all of these huge buildings are always burning with the slow and implacable fires of human desperation. The fire escape is part of what we see—that is, the landing of it and steps descending from it.

The scene is memory and is therefore nonrealistic. Memory takes a lot of poetic license. It omits some details; others are exaggerated, according to the emotional value of the articles it touches, for memory is seated predominantly in the heart. The interior is therefore rather dim and poetic.

At the rise of the curtain, the audience is faced with the dark, grim rear wall of the Wingfield tenement. This building is flanked on both sides by dark, narrow alleys which run into murky canyons of tangled clotheslines, garbage cans, and the sinister latticework of neighboring fire escapes. It is up and down these side alleys that exterior entrances and exits are made during the play. At the end of TOM'S *opening commentary, the dark tenement wall slowly becomes transparent and reveals the interior of the ground-floor Wingfield apartment.*

Nearest the audience is the living room, which also serves as a sleeping room for LAURA, *the sofa unfolding to make her bed. Just beyond, separated from the living room by a wide arch or second proscenium with transparent faded portieres (or second curtain), is the dining room. In an old-fashioned whatnot in the living room are seen scores of transparent glass animals. A blown-up photograph of the father hangs on the wall of the living room, to the left of the archway. It is the face of a very handsome young man in a doughboy's First World War cap. He is gallantly smiling, ineluctably smiling, as if to say "I will be smiling forever."*

Also hanging on the wall, near the photograph, are a typewriter keyboard chart and a Gregg shorthand diagram. An upright typewriter on a small table stands beneath the charts.

The audience hears and sees the opening scene in the dining room through both the transparent fourth wall of the building and the transparent gauze portieres of the dining-room arch. It is during this revealing scene that the fourth wall slowly ascends, out of sight. This transparent exterior wall is not brought down again until the very end of the play, during TOM'S *final speech.*

The narrator is an undisguised convention of the play. He takes whatever license with dramatic convention is convenient to his purposes.

TOM *enters, dressed as a merchant sailor, and strolls across to the fire escape. There he stops and lights a cigarette. He addresses the audience.*

TOM: Yes, I have tricks in my pocket, I have things up my sleeve. But I am the opposite of a stage magician. He gives you illusion that has the appearance of truth. I give you truth in the pleasant disguise of illusion.

To begin with, I turn back time. I reverse it to that quaint period, the thirties, when the huge middle class of America was matriculating in a school for the blind. Their eyes had failed them, or they had failed their eyes, and so they were having their fingers pressed forcibly down on the fiery Braille alphabet of a dissolving economy.

In Spain there was revolution. Here there was only shouting and confusion. In Spain there was Guernica. Here there were disturbances of labor, sometimes pretty violent, in otherwise peaceful cities such as Chicago, Cleveland, Saint Louis . . .

This is the social background of the play.

[*Music begins to play.*]

The play is memory. Being a memory play, it is dimly lighted, it is sentimental, it is not realistic. In memory everything seems to happen to music. That explains the fiddle in the wings.

I am the narrator of the play, and also a character in it. The other characters are my mother, Amanda, my sister, Laura, and a gentleman caller who appears in the final scenes. He is the most realistic character in the play, being an emissary from a world of reality that we were somehow set apart from. But since I have a poet's weakness for symbols, I am using this character also as a symbol; he is the long-delayed but always expected something that we live for.

There is a fifth character in the play who doesn't appear except in this larger-than-life-size photograph over the mantel. This is our father who left us a long time ago. He was a telephone man who fell in love with long distances; he gave up his job with the telephone company and skipped the light fantastic out of town . . .

The last we heard of him was a picture postcard from Mazatlan, on the Pacific coast of Mexico, containing a message of two words: "Hello—Goodbye!" and no address.

I think the rest of the play will explain itself. . . .

[AMANDA'S *voice becomes audible through the portieres.*]

[*Legend on screen:* "Ou sont les neiges."]

[TOM *divides the portieres and enters the dining room.* AMANDA *and* LAURA *are seated at a drop-leaf table. Eating is indicated by gestures without food or utensils.* AMANDA *faces the audience.* TOM *and* LAURA *are seated in profile. The interior has lit up softly and through the scrim we see* AMANDA *and* LAURA *seated at the table.*]

AMANDA [*calling*]: Tom?

TOM: Yes, Mother.

AMANDA: We can't say grace until you come to the table!

TOM: Coming, Mother. [*He bows slightly and withdraws, reappearing a few moments later in his place at the table.*]

AMANDA [*to her son*]: Honey, don't *push* with your *fingers*. If you have to push with something, the thing to push with is a crust of bread. And chew—chew! Animals have secretions in their stomachs which enable them to digest food without mastication, but human beings are supposed to chew their food before they swallow it down. Eat food leisurely, son, and really enjoy it. A well-cooked meal has lots of delicate flavors that have to be held in the mouth for appreciation. So chew your food and give your salivary glands a chance to function!

[TOM *deliberately lays his imaginary fork down and pushes his chair back from the table.*]

TOM: I haven't enjoyed one bite of this dinner because of your constant directions on how to eat it. It's you that make me rush through meals with your hawklike attention to every bite I take. Sickening—spoils my appetite—all this discussion of—animals' secretion—salivary glands—mastication!

AMANDA [*lightly*]: Temperament like a Metropolitan star!

[TOM *rises and walks toward the living room.*]

You're not excused from the table.

TOM: I'm getting a cigarette.

AMANDA: You smoke too much.

[LAURA *rises.*]

LAURA: I'll bring in the blanc mange.

[TOM *remains standing with his cigarette by the portieres.*]

AMANDA [*rising*]: No, sister, no, sister—you be the lady this time and I'll be the darky.

LAURA: I'm already up.

AMANDA: Resume your seat, little sister—I want you to stay fresh and pretty—for gentlemen callers!

LAURA [*sitting down*]: I'm not expecting any gentlemen callers.

AMANDA [*crossing out to the kitchenette, airily*]: Sometimes they come when they are least expected! Why, I remember one Sunday afternoon in Blue Mountain—

[*She enters the kitchenette.*]

TOM: I know what's coming!

LAURA: Yes. But let her tell it.

TOM: Again?

LAURA: She loves to tell it.

[AMANDA *returns with a bowl of dessert.*]

AMANDA: One Sunday afternoon in Blue Mountain—your mother received—*seventeen!*—gentlemen callers! Why, sometimes there weren't chairs enough to accommodate them all. We had to send the nigger over to bring in folding chairs from the parish house.

TOM [*remaining at the portieres*]: How did you entertain those gentlemen callers?

AMANDA: I understood the art of conversation!

TOM: I bet you could talk.

AMANDA: Girls in those days *knew* how to talk, I can tell you.

TOM: Yes?

[*Image on screen:* AMANDA as a girl on a porch, greeting callers.]

AMANDA: They knew how to entertain their gentlemen callers. It wasn't enough for a girl to be possessed of a pretty face and a graceful figure—although I wasn't slighted in either respect. She also needed to have a nimble wit and a tongue to meet all occasions.

TOM: What did you talk about?

AMANDA: Things of importance going on in the world! Never anything coarse or common or vulgar.

[*She addresses* TOM *as though he were seated in the vacant chair at the table though he remains by the portieres. He plays this scene as though reading from a script.*]

My callers were gentlemen—all! Among my callers were some of the most prominent young planters of the Mississippi Delta—planters and sons of planters!

[TOM *motions for music and a spot of light on* AMANDA. *Her eyes lift, her face glows, her voice becomes rich and elegiac.*]

[*Screen legend*: "Ou sont les neiges d'antan?"]

There was young Champ Laughlin who later became vice-president of the Delta Planters Bank. Hadley Stevenson who was drowned in Moon Lake and left his widow one hundred and fifty thousand in Government bonds. There were the Cutrere brothers, Wesley and Bates. Bates was one of my bright particular beaux! He got in a quarrel with that wild Wainwright boy. They shot it out on the floor of Moon Lake Casino. Bates was shot through the stomach. Died in the ambulance on his way to Memphis. His widow was also well provided-for, came into eight or ten thousand acres, that's all. She married him on the rebound—never loved her—carried my picture on him the night he died! And there was that boy that every girl in the Delta had set her cap for! That beautiful, brilliant young Fitzhugh boy from Greene County!

TOM: What did he leave his widow?

AMANDA: He never married! Gracious, you talk as though all of my old admirers had turned up their toes to the daisies!

TOM: Isn't this the first you've mentioned that still survives?

AMANDA: That Fitzhugh boy went North and made a fortune—came to be known as the Wolf of Wall Street! He had the Midas touch, whatever he touched turned to gold! And I could have been Mrs. Duncan J. Fitzhugh, mind you! But—I picked your *father!*

LAURA [*rising*]: Mother, let me clear the table.

AMANDA: No, dear, you go in front and study your typewriter chart. Or practice your shorthand a little. Stay fresh and pretty!—It's almost time for our gentlemen callers to start arriving. [*She flounces girlishly toward the kitchenette.*] How many do you suppose we're going to entertain this afternoon?

[TOM *throws down the paper and jumps up with a groan.*]

LAURA [*alone in the dining room*]: I don't believe we're going to receive any, Mother.

AMANDA [*reappearing, airily*]: What? No one—not one? You must be joking!

[LAURA *nervously echoes her laugh. She slips in a fugitive manner through the half-open portieres and draws them gently behind her. A shaft of very clear light is thrown on her face against the faded tapestry of the curtains. Faintly the music of "The Glass Menagerie" is heard as she continues, lightly:*]

Not one gentleman caller? It can't be true! There must be a flood, there must have been a tornado!

LAURA: It isn't a flood, it's not a tornado, Mother. I'm just not popular like you were in Blue Mountain. . . .

[TOM *utters another groan.* LAURA *glances at him with a faint, apologetic smile. Her voice catches a little:*]

Mother's afraid I'm going to be an old maid.

[*The scene dims out with the "Glass Menagerie" music.*]

SCENE 2

On the dark stage the screen is lighted with the image of blue roses. Gradually LAURA*'s figure becomes apparent and the screen goes out. The music subsides.*

LAURA *is seated in the delicate ivory chair at the small claw-foot table. She wears a dress of soft violet material for a kimono—her hair is tied back from her forehead with a ribbon. She is washing and polishing her collection of glass.* AMANDA *appears on the fire escape steps. At the sound of her ascent,* LAURA *catches her breath, thrusts the bowl of ornaments away, and seats herself stiffly before the diagram of the typewriter keyboard as though it held her spellbound. Something has happened to* AMANDA. *It is written in her face as she climbs to the landing: a look that is grim and hopeless and a little absurd. She has on one of those cheap or imitation velvety-looking cloth coats with imitation fur collar. Her hat is five or six years old, one of those dreadful cloche hats that were worn in the late Twenties, and she is clutching an enormous black patent-leather pocketbook with nickel clasps and initials. This is her full-dress outfit, the one she usually wears to the D.A.R. Before entering she looks through the door. She purses her lips, opens her eyes very wide, rolls them upward and shakes her head. Then she slowly lets herself in the door. Seeing her mother's expression* LAURA *touches her lips with a nervous gesture.*

LAURA: Hello, Mother, I was— [*She makes a nervous gesture toward the chart on the wall.* AMANDA *leans against the shut door and stares at* LAURA *with a martyred look.*]

AMANDA: Deception? Deception? [*She slowly removes her hat and gloves, continuing the sweet suffering stare. She lets the hat and gloves fall on the floor—a bit of acting.*]

LAURA [*shakily*]: How was the D.A.R. meeting?

[AMANDA *slowly opens her purse and removes a dainty white handkerchief which she shakes out delicately and delicately touches so her lips and nostrils.*]

Didn't you go to the D.A.R. meeting, Mother?

AMANDA [*faintly, almost inaudibly*]: —No.—No. [*then more forcibly*:] I did not have the strength —to go to the D.A.R. In fact, I did not have the courage! I wanted to find a hole in the ground and hide myself in it forever! [*She crosses slowly to the wall and removes the diagram of the typewriter keyboard. She holds it in front of her for a second, staring at it sweetly and sorrowfully—then bites her lips and tears it in two pieces.*]

LAURA [*faintly*]: Why did you do that, Mother?

[AMANDA *repeats the same procedure with the chart of the Gregg Alphabet.*]

Why are you—

AMANDA: Why? Why? How old are you, Laura?

LAURA: Mother, you know my age.

AMANDA: I thought that you were an adult; it seems that I was mistaken. [*She crosses slowly to the sofa and sinks down and stares at* LAURA.]

LAURA: Please don't stare at me, Mother.

[AMANDA *closes her eyes and lowers her head. There is a ten-second pause.*]

AMANDA: What are we going to do, what is going to become of us, what is the future?

[*There is another pause.*]

LAURA: Has something happened, Mother?

[AMANDA *draws a long breath, takes out the handkerchief again, goes through the dabbing process.*]

Mother, has—something happened?

AMANDA: I'll be all right in a minute, I'm just bewildered— [*She hesitates.*] —by life. . . .

LAURA: Mother, I wish that you would tell me what's happened!

AMANDA: As you know, I was supposed to be inducted into my office at the DA.R. this afternoon.

[*Screen image*: A swarm of typewriters.]

But I stopped off at Rubicam's Business College to speak to your teachers about your having a cold and ask them what progress they thought you were making down there.

LAURA: Oh. . . .

AMANDA: I went to the typing instructor and introduced myself as your mother. She didn't know who you were. "Wingfield," she said, "We don't have any such student enrolled at the school!" I assured her she did, that you had been going to classes since early in January.

"I wonder," she said, "If you could be talking about that terribly shy little girl who dropped out of school after only a few days' attendance?"

"No," I said, "Laura, my daughter, has been going to school every day for the past six weeks!"

"Excuse me," she said. She took the attendance book out and there was your name, unmistakably printed, and all the dates you were absent until they decided that you had dropped out of school. I still said, "No, there must have been some mistake! There must have been some mix-up in the records!"

And she said, "No—I remember her perfectly now. Her hands shook so that she couldn't hit the right keys! The first time we gave a speed test, she broke down completely—was sick at the stomach and almost had to be carried into the wash room! After that morning she never showed up any more. We phoned the house but never got any answer"—While I was working at Famous–Barr, I suppose, demonstrating those—

[*She indicates a brassiere with her hands.*]

Oh! I felt so weak I could barely keep on my feet! I had to sit down while they got me a glass of water! Fifty dollars' tuition, all of our plans—my hopes and ambitions for you—just gone up the spout, just gone up the spout like that.

[LAURA *draws a long breath and gets awkwardly to her feet. She crosses to the Victrola and winds it up.*]

What are you doing?

LAURA: Oh! [*She releases the handle and returns to her seat.*]

AMANDA: Laura, where have you been going when you've gone out pretending that you were going to business college?

LAURA: I've just been going out walking.

AMANDA: That's not true.

LAURA: It is. I just went walking.

AMANDA: Walking? Walking? In winter? Deliberately courting pneumonia in that light coat? Where did you walk to, Laura?

LAURA: All sorts of places—mostly in the park.

AMANDA: Even after you'd started catching that cold?

LAURA: It was the lesser of two evils, Mother.

[*Screen image*: Winter scene in a park.]

I couldn't go back there. I—threw up—on the floor!

AMANDA: From half past seven till after five every day you mean to tell me you walked around in the park, because you wanted to make me think that you were still going to Rubicam's Business College?

LAURA: It wasn't as bad as it sounds. I went inside places to get warmed up.

AMANDA: Inside where?

LAURA: I went in the art museum and the bird houses at the Zoo. I visited the penguins every day! Sometimes I did without lunch and went to the movies. Lately I've been spending most of my afternoons in the Jewel Box, that big glass house where they raise the tropical flowers.

AMANDA: You did all this to deceive me, just for deception? [LAURA *looks down*.] Why?

LAURA: Mother, when you're disappointed, you get that awful suffering look on your face, like the picture of Jesus' mother in the museum!

AMANDA: Hush!

LAURA: I couldn't face it.

[*There is a pause. A whisper of strings is heard. Legend on screen*: "The Crust of Humility."]

AMANDA [*hopelessly fingering the huge pocketbook*]: So what are we going to do the rest of our lives? Stay home and watch the parades go by? Amuse ourselves with the glass menagerie, darling? Eternally play those worn-out phonograph records your father left as a painful reminder of him? We won't have a business career—we've given that up because it gave us nervous indigestion! [*She laughs wearily*.] What is there left but dependency all our lives? I know so well what becomes of unmarried women who aren't prepared to occupy a position. I've seen such pitiful cases in the South—barely tolerated spinsters living upon the grudging patronage of sister's husband or brother's wife!—stuck away in some little mousetrap of a room—encouraged by one in-law to visit another—little birdlike women without any nest— eating the crust of humility all their life!

Is that the future that we've mapped out for ourselves? I swear it's the only alternative I can think of! [*She pauses*.] It isn't a very pleasant alternative, is it? [*She pauses again*.] Of course—some girls *do marry*.

[LAURA *twists her hands nervously*.]

Haven't you ever liked some boy?

LAURA: Yes. I liked one once. [*She rises*.] I came across his picture a while ago.

AMANDA [*with some interest*]: He gave you his picture?

LAURA: No, it's in the yearbook.

AMANDA [*disappointed*]: Oh—a high school boy.

[*Screen image*: JIM as the high school hero bearing a silver cup.]

LAURA: Yes. His name was Jim. [*She lifts the heavy annual from the claw-toot table*.] Here he is in *The Pirates of Penzance*.

AMANDA [*absently*]: The what?

LAURA: The operetta the senior class put on. He had a wonderful voice and we sat across the aisle from each other Mondays, Wednesdays and Fridays in the Aud. Here he is with the silver cup for debating! See his grin?

AMANDA [*absently*]: He must have had a jolly disposition.

LAURA: He used to call me—Blue Roses.

[*Screen image*: Blue roses.]

AMANDA: Why did he call you such a name as that?

LAURA: When I had that attack of pleurosis—he asked me what was the matter when I came back. I said pleurosis—he thought that I said Blue Roses! So that's what he always called me after that. Whenever he saw me, he'd holler, "Hello, Blue Roses!" I didn't care for the girl that he went out with. Emily Meisenbach. Emily was the best-dressed girl at Soldan. She never struck me, though, as being sincere . . . It says in the Personal Section—they're engaged. That's—six years ago! They must be married by now.

AMANDA: Girls that aren't cut out for business careers usually wind up married to some nice man. [*She gets up with a spark of revival*.] Sister, that's what you'll do!

[LAURA *utters a startled, doubtful laugh. She reaches quickly for a piece of glass.*]

LAURA: But, Mother—
AMANDA: Yes? [*She goes over to the photograph.*]
LAURA [*in a tone of frightened apology*]: I'm—crippled!
AMANDA: Nonsense! Laura, I've told you never, never to use that word. Why, you're not crippled, you just have a little defect—hardly noticeable, even! When people have some slight disadvantage like that, they cultivate other things to make up for it—develop charm—and vivacity—and—*charm!* That's all you have to do! [*She turns again to the photograph.*] One thing your father had *plenty of*—was *charm!*

[*The scene fades out with music.*]

SCENE 3

Legend on screen: "After the fiasco—"

TOM *speaks from the fire escape landing.*

TOM: After the fiasco at Rubicam's Business College, the idea of getting a gentleman caller for Laura began to play a more and more important part in Mother's calculations. It became an obsession. Like some archetype of the universal unconscious, the image of the gentleman caller haunted our small apartment. . . .

[*Screen image*: A young man at the door of a house with flowers.]

An evening at home rarely passed without some allusion to this image, this specter, this hope. . . . Even when he wasn't mentioned, his presence hung in Mother's preoccupied look and in my sister's frightened, apologetic manner—hung like a sentence passed upon the Wingfields!

Mother was a woman of action as well as words. She began to take logical steps in the planned direction. Late that winter and in the early spring—realizing that extra money would be needed to properly feather the nest and plume the bird—she conducted a vigorous campaign on the telephone, roping in subscribers to one of those magazines for matrons called *The Homemaker's Companion*, the type of journal that features the serialized sublimations of ladies of letters who think in terms of delicate cuplike breasts, slim, tapering waists, rich, creamy thighs, eyes like wood smoke in autumn, fingers that soothe and caress like strains of music, bodies as powerful as Etruscan sculpture.

[*Screen image*: The cover of a glamor magazine.]

[AMANDA *enters with the telephone on a long extension cord. She is spotlighted in the dim stage.*]

AMANDA: Ida Scott? This is Amanda Wingfield! We *missed* you at the DA.R. last Monday! I said to myself: She's probably suffering with that sinus condition! How is that sinus condition?

Horrors! Heaven have mercy!—You're a Christian martyr, yes, that's what you are, a Christian martyr!

Well, I just now happened to notice that your subscription to the *Companion*'s about to expire! Yes, it expires with the next issue, honey!—just when that wonderful new serial by Bessie Mae Hopper is getting off to such an exciting start. Oh, honey, it's something that you can't miss! You remember how *Gone with the Wind* took everybody by storm? You simply couldn't go out if you hadn't read it. All everybody *talked* was Scarlett O'Hara. Well, this is a book that critics already compare to *Gone with the Wind*. It's the *Gone with the Wind* of the post-World-War generation!—What?—Burning?—Oh, honey, don't let them burn, go take a look in the oven and I'll hold the wire! Heavens—I think she's hung up!

[*The scene dims out.*]

[*Legend on screen*: "You think I'm in love with Continental Shoemakers?"]

[*Before the lights come up again, the violent voices of* TOM *and* AMANDA *are heard. They are quarreling behind the portieres. In front of them stands* LAURA *with clenched hands and panicky expression. A clear pool of light is on her figure throughout this scene.*]

TOM: What in Christ's name am I—
AMANDA [*shrilly*]: Don't you use that—
TOM: —supposed to do!
AMANDA: —expression! Not in my—
TOM: Ohhh!
AMANDA: —presence! Have you gone out of your senses?
TOM: I have, that's true, *driven* out!
AMANDA: What is the matter with you, you—big—big—IDIOT!
TOM: Look!—I've got *no thing*, no single thing—

AMANDA: Lower your voice!
TOM: —in my life here that I can call my OWN! Everything is—
AMANDA: Stop that shouting!
TOM: Yesterday you confiscated my books! You had the nerve to—
AMANDA: I took that horrible novel back to the library—yes! That hideous book by that insane Mr. Lawrence.

[TOM *laughs wildly.*]

I cannot control the output of diseased minds or people who cater to them—

[TOM *laughs still more wildly.*]

BUT I WON'T ALLOW SUCH FILTH BROUGHT INTO MY HOUSE! No, no, no, no, no!
TOM: House, house! Who pays rent on it, who makes a slave of himself to—
AMANDA [*fairly screeching*]: Don't you DARE to—
TOM: No, no, *I* mustn't say things! *I've* got to just—
AMANDA: Let me tell you—
TOM: I don't want to hear any more!

[*He tears the portieres open. The dining-room area is lit with a turgid smokey red glow. Now we see* AMANDA; *her hair is in metal curlers and she is wearing a very old bathrobe, much too large for her slight figure, a relic of the faithless Mr. Wingfield. The upright typewriter now stands on the drop-leaf table, along with a wild disarray of manuscripts. The quarrel was probably precipitated by* AMANDA'S *interruption of* TOM'S *creative labor. A chair lies overthrown on the floor. Their gesticulating shadows are cast on the ceiling by the fiery glow.*]

AMANDA: You *will* hear more, you—
TOM: No, I won't hear more, I'm going out!
AMANDA: You come right back in—
TOM: Out, out, out! Because I'm—
AMANDA: Come back here, Tom Wingfield! I'm not through talking to you!
TOM: Oh, go—
LAURA [*desperately*]: —TOM!
AMANDA: You're going to listen, and no more insolence from you! I'm at the end of my patience!

[*He comes back toward her.*]

TOM: What do you think I'm at? Aren't I supposed to have any patience to reach the end of, Mother? I know, I know. It seems unimportant to you, what I'm *doing*—what I *want* to do—having a little *difference* between them! You don't think that—
AMANDA: I think you've been doing things that you're ashamed of. That's why you act like this. I don't believe that you go every night to the movies. Nobody goes to the movies night after night. Nobody in their right minds goes to the movies as often as you pretend to. People don't go to the movies at nearly midnight, and movies don't let out at two A.M. Come in stumbling. Muttering to yourself like a maniac! You get three hours' sleep and then go to work. Oh, I can picture the way you're doing down there. Moping, doping, because you're in no condition.
TOM [*wildly*]: No, I'm in no condition!
AMANDA: What right have you got to jeopardize your job? Jeopardize the security of us all? How do you think we'd manage if you were—
TOM: Listen! You think I'm crazy about the *warehouse?* [*He bends fiercely toward her slight figure.*] You think I'm in love with the Continental Shoemakers? You think I want to spend fifty-five *years* down there in that—*celotex interior!*—with—*fluorescent*—*tubes!* Look! I'd rather somebody picked up a crowbar and battered out my brains—than go back mornings! I *go!* Every time you come in yelling that Goddamn *"Rise and Shine!" "Rise and Shine!"* I say to myself, "How *lucky dead* people are!" But I get up. I *go!* For sixty-five dollars a month I give up all that I dream of doing and being *ever!* And you say self—*self's* all I ever think of. Why, listen, if self is what I thought of, Mother, I'd be where he is—GONE! [*He points to his father's picture.*] As far as the system of transportation reaches! [*He starts past her. She grabs his arm.*] Don't grab at me, Mother!
AMANDA: Where are you going?
TOM: I'm going to the *movies!*
AMANDA: I don't believe that lie!

[TOM *crouches toward her, overtowering her tiny figure. She backs away, gasping.*]

TOM: I'm going to opium dens! Yes, opium dens, dens of vice and criminals' hangouts, Mother. I've joined the Hogan Gang, I'm a hired assassin, I carry a tommy gun in a violin case! I run a string of cat houses in the Valley! They call me Killer, Killer Wingfield, I'm leading a double-life, a simple, honest warehouse worker by day, by night a dynamic *czar* of the *underworld, Mother*. I go to gambling casinos, I spin away fortunes on the roulette table! I wear a patch over one eye and a false mustache, sometimes I put on green whiskers. On those occasions they call me—*El Diablo!* Oh, I could tell you many things to make you sleepless! My enemies plan to dynamite this place. They're going to blow us all sky-high some night! I'll be glad, very happy, and so will you! You'll go up, up on a broomstick, over Blue Mountain with seventeen gentlemen callers! You ugly—babbling old—*witch*. . . .

[*He goes through a series of violent, clumsy movements, seizing his overcoat, lunging to the door, pulling it fiercely open. The women watch him, aghast. His arm catches in the sleeve of the coat as he struggles to pull it on. For a moment he is pinioned by the bulky garment. With an outraged groan he tears the coat off again, splitting the shoulder of it, and hurls it across the room. It strikes against the shelf of* LAURA's *glass collection, and there is a tinkle of shattering glass.* LAURA *cries out as if wounded.*]

[*Music.*]

[*Screen legend*: "The Glass Menagerie."]

LAURA [*shrilly*]: *My glass!*—menagerie. . . . [*She covers her face and turns away.*]

[*But* AMANDA *is still stunned and stupefied by the "ugly witch" so that she barely notices this occurrence. Now she recovers her speech.*]

AMANDA [*in an awful voice*]: I won't speak to you—until you apologize!

[*She crosses through the portieres and draws them together behind her.* TOM *is left with* LAURA. LAURA *clings weakly to the mantel with her face averted.* TOM *stares at her stupidly for a moment. Then he crosses to the shelf. He drops awkwardly on his knees to collect the fallen glass, glancing at* LAURA *as if he would speak but couldn't.*]

["*The Glass Menagerie" music steals in as the scene dims out.*]

SCENE 4

The interior of the apartment is dark. There is a faint light in the alley. A deep-voiced bell in a church is tolling the hour of five.

TOM *appears at the top of the alley. After each solemn boom of the bell in the tower, he shakes a little noisemaker or rattle as if to express the tiny spasm of man in contrast to the sustained power and dignity of the Almighty. This and the unsteadiness of his advance make it evident that he has been drinking. As he climbs the few steps to the fire escape landing light steals up inside.* LAURA *appears in the front room in a nightdress. She notices that* TOM's *bed is empty.* TOM *fishes in his pockets for his door key, removing a motley assortment of articles in the search, including a shower of movie ticket stubs and an empty bottle. At last he finds the key, but just as he is about to insert it, it slips from his fingers. He strikes a match and crouches below the door.*

TOM [*bitterly*]: One crack—and it falls through!

[LAURA *opens the door.*]

LAURA: Tom! Tom, what are you doing?
TOM: Looking for a door key.
LAURA: Where have you been all this time?
TOM: I have been to the movies.
LAURA: All this time at the movies?
TOM: There was a very long program. There was a Garbo picture and a Mickey Mouse and a travelogue and a newsreel and a preview of coming attractions. And there was an organ solo and a collection for the Milk Fund—simultaneously—which ended up in a terrible fight between a fat lady and an usher!
LAURA [*innocently*]: Did you have to stay through everything?
TOM: Of course! And, oh, I forgot! There was a big stage show! The headliner on this stage show was Malvolio the Magician. He performed wonderful tricks, many of them, such as pouring water back and forth between pitchers. First it turned to wine and then it turned to beer and then it turned to whisky. I know it was whisky it finally turned into because he needed somebody to come up out of the audience to help him, and I came up—both shows! It was Kentucky Straight Bourbon. A very generous fellow, he gave souvenirs. [*He pulls from his back pocket a shimmering rainbow-colored scarf.*] He gave me this. This is his magic scarf. You can have it, Laura. You wave it over a canary cage and you get a bowl of goldfish. You wave it over the goldfish bowl and they fly away canaries. . . . But the wonderfullest trick of all was the coffin trick. We nailed him into a coffin and he got out of the coffin without removing one nail. [*He has come inside.*] There is a trick that would come in handy for me—get me out of this two-by-four situation! [*He flops onto the bed and starts removing his shoes.*]
LAURA: Tom—shhh!
TOM: What're you shushing me for?
LAURA: You'll wake up Mother.
TOM: Goody, goody! Pay 'er back for all those "Rise an' Shines." [*He lies down, groaning.*] You know it don't take much intelligence to get yourself into a nailed-up coffin, Laura. But who in hell ever got himself out of one without removing one nail?

[*As if in answer, the father's grinning photograph lights up. The scene dims out.*]

[*Immediately following, the church bell is heard striking six. At the sixth stroke the alarm clock goes off in* AMANDA'*s room, and after a few moments we hear her calling: "Rise and Shine! Rise and Shine!* LAURA, *go tell your brother to rise and shine!"*]

TOM [*sitting up slowly*]: I'll rise—but I won't shine.

[*The light increases.*]

AMANDA: Laura, tell your brother his coffee is ready.

[LAURA *slips into the front room.*]

LAURA: Tom!—It's nearly seven. Don't make Mother nervous.

[*He stares at her stupidly.*]

[*beseechingly:*] Tom, speak to Mother this morning. Make up with her, apologize, speak to her!

TOM: She won't to me. It's her that started not speaking.

LAURA: If you just say you're sorry she'll start speaking.

TOM: Her not speaking—is that such a tragedy?

LAURA: Please—please!

AMANDA [*calling from the kitchenette*]: Laura, are you going to do what I asked you to do, or do I have to get dressed and go out myself?

LAURA: Going, going—soon as I get on my coat!

[*She pulls on a shapeless felt hat with a nervous, jerky movement, pleadingly glancing at* TOM. *She rushes awkwardly for her coat. The coat is one of* AMANDA'*s, inaccurately made-over, the sleeves too short for* LAURA.]

Butter and what else?

AMANDA [*entering from the kitchenette*]: Just butter. Tell them to charge it.

LAURA: Mother, they make such faces when I do that.

AMANDA: Sticks and stones can break our bones, but the expression on Mr. Garfinkel's face won't harm us! Tell your brother his coffee is getting cold.

LAURA [*at the door*]: Do what I asked you, will you, will you, Tom?

[*He looks sullenly away.*]

AMANDA: Laura, go now or just don't go at all!

LAURA [*rushing out*]: Going—going!

[*A second later she cries out.* TOM *springs up and crosses to the door.* TOM *opens the door.*]

TOM: Laura?

LAURA: I'm all right. I slipped, but I'm all right.

AMANDA [*peering anxiously after her*]: If anyone breaks a leg on those fire-escape steps, the landlord ought to be sued for every cent he possesses! [*She shuts the door. Now she remembers she isn't speaking to* TOM *and returns to the other room.*]

[*As* TOM *comes listlessly for his coffee, she turns her back to him and stands rigidly facing the window on the gloomy gray vault of the areaway. Its light on her face with its aged but childish features is cruelly sharp, satirical as a Daumier print.*]

[*The music of "Ave Maria," is heard softly.*]

[TOM *glances sheepishly but sullenly at her averted figure and slumps at the table. The coffee is scalding hot; he sips it and gasps and spits it back in the cup. At his gasp,* AMANDA *catches her breath and half turns. Then she catches herself and turns back to the window.* TOM *blows on his coffee, glancing sidewise at his mother. She clears her throat.* TOM *clears his. He starts to rise, sinks back down again, scratches his head, clears his throat again.* AMANDA *coughs.* TOM *raises his cup in both hands to blow on it, his eyes staring over the rim of it at his mother for several moments. Then he slowly sets the cup down and awkwardly and hesitantly rises from the chair.*]

TOM [*hoarsely*]: Mother. I—I apologize, Mother.

[AMANDA *draws a quick, shuddering breath. Her face works grotesquely. She breaks into childlike tears.*]

I'm sorry for what I said, for everything that I said, I didn't mean it.

AMANDA [*sobbingly*]: My devotion has made me a witch and so I make myself hateful to my children!

TOM: *No*, you *don't*.

AMANDA: I worry so much, don't sleep, it makes me nervous!

TOM [*gently*]: I understand that.

AMANDA: I've had to put up a solitary battle all these years. But you're my right-hand bower! Don't fall down, don't fail!

TOM [*gently*]: I try, Mother.

AMANDA [*with great enthusiasm*]: Try and you will *succeed!* [*The notion makes her breathless.*] Why, you—you're just *full* of natural endowments! Both of my children—they're *unusual* children! Don't you think I know it? I'm so—*proud!* Happy and—feel I've—so much to be thankful for but—promise me one thing, son!

TOM: What, Mother?

AMANDA: Promise, son, you'll—never be a drunkard!
TOM [*turns to her grinning*]: I will never be a drunkard, Mother.
AMANDA: That's what frightened me so, that you'd be drinking! Eat a bowl of Purina!
TOM: Just coffee, Mother.
AMANDA: Shredded wheat biscuit?
TOM: No. No, Mother, just coffee.
AMANDA: You can't put in a day's work on an empty stomach. You've got ten minutes—don't gulp! Drinking too hot liquids makes cancer of the stomach. . . . Put cream in.
TOM: No, thank you.
AMANDA: To cool it.
TOM: No! No, thank you, I want it black.
AMANDA: I know, but it's not good for you. We have to do all that we can to build ourselves up. In these trying times we live in, all that we have to cling to is—each other. . . . That's why it's so important to— Tom, I— I sent out your sister so I could discuss something with you. If you hadn't spoken I would have spoken to you. [*She sits down.*]
TOM [*gently*]: What is it, Mother, that you want to discuss?
AMANDA: *Laura!*

[TOM *puts his cup down slowly.*]

[*Legend on screen*: "LAURA" *Music: "The Glass Menagerie."*]

TOM: —Oh.—Laura . . .
AMANDA [*touching his sleeve*]: You know how Laura is. So quiet but—still water runs deep! She notices things and I think she—broods about them.

[TOM *looks up.*]

A few days ago I came in and she was crying.
TOM: What about?
AMANDA: You.
TOM: Me?
AMANDA: She has an idea that you're not happy here.
TOM: What gave her that idea?
AMANDA: What gives her any idea? However, you do act strangely. I—I'm not criticizing, understand *that!* I know your ambitions do not lie in the warehouse, that like everybody in the whole wide world—you've had to—make sacrifices, but—Tom—Tom—life's not easy, it calls for—Spartan endurance! There's so many things in my heart that I cannot describe to you! I've never told you but I—*loved* your father. . . .
TOM [*gently*]: I know that, Mother.
AMANDA: And you—when I see you taking after his ways! Staying out late—and—well, you *had* been drinking the night you were in that—terrifying condition! Laura says that you hate the apartment and that you go out nights to get away from it! Is that true, Tom?
TOM: No. You say there's so much in your heart that you can't describe to me. That's true of me, too. There's so much in my heart that I can't describe to *you!* So let's respect each other's—
AMANDA: But, why—*why*, Tom—are you always so *restless?* Where do you *go* to, nights?
TOM: I—go to the movies.
AMANDA: Why do you go to the movies so much, Tom?
TOM: I go to the movies because—I like adventure. Adventure is something I don't have much of at work, so I go to the movies.
AMANDA: But, Tom, you go to the movies *entirely* too *much!*
TOM: I like a lot of adventure.

[AMANDA *looks baffled, then hurt. As the familiar inquisition resumes,* TOM *becomes hard and impatient again.* AMANDA *slips back into her querulous attitude toward him.*]

[*Image on screen:* A sailing vessel with Jolly Roger.]

AMANDA: Most young men find adventure in their careers.
TOM: Then most young men are not employed in a warehouse.
AMANDA: The world is full of young men employed in warehouses and offices and factories.
TOM: Do all of them find adventure in their careers?
AMANDA: They do or they do without it! Not everybody has a craze for adventure.
TOM: Man is by instinct a lover, a hunter, a fighter, and none of those instincts are given much play at the warehouse!
AMANDA: Man is by instinct! Don't quote instinct to me! Instinct is something that people have got away from! It belongs to animals! Christian adults don't want it!
TOM: What do Christian adults want, then, Mother?
AMANDA: Superior things! Things of the mind and the spirit! Only animals have to satisfy instincts! Surely your aims are somewhat higher than theirs! Than monkeys—pigs—
TOM: I reckon they're not.
AMANDA: You're joking. However, that isn't what I wanted to discuss.
TOM [*rising*]: I haven't much time.
AMANDA [*pushing his shoulders*]: Sit down.

TOM: You want me to punch in red at the warehouse, Mother?

AMANDA: You have five minutes. I want to talk about Laura.

[*Screen legend*: "Plans and Provisions."]

TOM: All right! What about Laura?

AMANDA: We have to be making some plans and provisions for her. She's older than you, two years, and nothing has happened. She just drifts along doing nothing. It frightens me terribly how she just drifts along.

TOM: I guess she's the type that people call home girls.

AMANDA: There's no such type, and if there is, it's a pity! That is unless the home is hers, with a husband!

TOM: What?

AMANDA: Oh, I can see the handwriting on the wall as plain as I see the nose in front of my face! It's terrifying! More and more you remind me of your father! He was out all hours without explanation! —Then *left! Goodbye!* And me with the bag to hold. I saw that letter you got from the Merchant Marine. I know what you're dreaming of. I'm not standing here blindfolded. [*She pauses.*] Very well, then. Then *do* it! But not till there's somebody to take your place.

TOM: What do you mean?

AMANDA: I mean that as soon as Laura has got somebody to take care of her, married, a home of her own, independent—why, then you'll be free to go wherever you please, on land, on sea, whichever way the wind blows you! But until that time you've got to look out for your sister. I don't say me because I'm old and don't matter! I say for your sister because she's young and dependent.

I put her in business college—a dismal failure! Frightened her so it made her sick at the stomach. I took her over to the Young People's League at the church. Another fiasco. She spoke to nobody, nobody spoke to her. Now all she does is fool with those pieces of glass and play those worn-out records. What kind of a life is that for a girl to lead?

TOM: What can I do about it?

AMANDA: Overcome selfishness! Self, self, self is all that you ever think of!

[TOM *springs up and crosses to get his coat. It is ugly and bulky. He pulls on a cap with earmuffs.*]

Where is your muffler? Put your wool muffler on!

[*He snatches it angrily from the closet, tosses it around his neck and pulls both ends tight.*]

Tom! I haven't said what I had in mind to ask you.

TOM: I'm too late to—

AMANDA [*catching his arm—very importunately; then shyly*]: Down at the warehouse, aren't there some—nice young men?

TOM: No!

AMANDA: There *must* be—*some . . .*

TOM: Mother— [*He gestures.*]

AMANDA: Find out one that's clean-living—doesn't drink and ask him out for sister!

TOM: What?

AMANDA: For *sister!* To *meet!* Get *acquainted!*

TOM [*stamping to the door*]: Oh, my *go-osh!*

AMANDA: Will you?

[*He opens the door. She says, imploringly:*]

Will you?

[*He starts down the fire escape.*]

Will you? *Will* you, dear?

TOM: [*calling back*]: *Yes!*

[AMANDA *closes the door hesitantly and with a troubled but faintly hopeful expression.*]

[*Screen image:* The cover of a glamor magazine.]

[*The spotlight picks up* AMANDA *at the phone.*]

AMANDA: Ella Cartwright? This is Amanda Wingfield! How are you, honey? How is that kidney condition?

[*There is a five-second pause.*]

Horrors!

[*There is another pause.*]

You're a Christian martyr, yes, honey, that's what you are, a Christian martyr! Well, I just now happened to notice in my little red book that your subscription to the *Companion* has just run out! I knew that you wouldn't want to miss out on the wonderful serial starting in this new issue. It's by Bessie Mae Hopper, the first thing she's written since *Honeymoon for Three.* Wasn't that a strange and interesting story? Well, this one is even lovelier, I believe. It has a sophisticated, society background. It's all about the horsey set on Long Island!

[*The light fades out.*]

SCENE 5

Legend on the screen: "Annunciation."

Music is heard as the light slowly comes on.

It is early dusk of a spring evening. Supper has just been finished in the Wingfield apartment. AMANDA *and* LAURA, *in light-colored dresses, are removing dishes from the table in the dining room, which is shadowy, their movements formalized almost as a dance or ritual, their moving forms as pale and silent as moths.* TOM, *in white shirt and trousers, rises from the table and crosses toward the fire escape.*

AMANDA [*as he passes her*]: Son, will you do me a favor?

TOM: What?

AMANDA: Comb your hair! You look so pretty when your hair is combed!

[TOM *slouches on the sofa with the evening paper. Its enormous headline reads: "Franco Triumphs."*]

There is only one respect in which I would like you to emulate your father.

TOM: What respect is that?

AMANDA: The care he always took of his appearance. He never allowed himself to look untidy.

[*He throws down the paper and crosses to the fire escape.*]

Where are you going?

TOM: I'm going out to smoke.

AMANDA: You smoke too much. A pack a day at fifteen cents a pack. How much would that amount to in a month? Thirty times fifteen is how much, Tom? Figure it out and you will be astounded at what you could save. Enough to give you a night-school course in accounting at Washington U.! Just think what a wonderful thing that would be for you, son!

[TOM *is unmoved by the thought.*]

TOM: I'd rather smoke. [*He steps out on the landing, letting the screen door slam.*]

AMANDA [*sharply*]: I know! That's the tragedy of it. . . . [*Alone, she turns to look at her husband's picture.*]

[*Dance music: "The World Is Waiting for the Sunrise!"*]

TOM [*to the audience*]: Across the alley from us was the Paradise Dance Hall. On evenings in spring the windows and doors were open and the music came outdoors. Sometimes the lights were turned out except for a large glass sphere that hung from the ceiling. It would turn slowly about and filter the dusk with delicate rainbow colors. Then the orchestra played a waltz or a tango, something that had a slow and sensuous rhythm. Couples would come outside, to the relative privacy of the alley. You could see them kissing behind ash pits and telephone poles. This was the compensation for lives that passed like mine, without any change or adventure. Adventure and change were imminent in this year. They were waiting around the corner for all these kids. Suspended in the mist over Berchtesgaden, caught in the folds of Chamberlain's umbrella. In Spain there was Guernica! But here there was only hot swing music and liquor, dance halls, bars, and movies, and sex that hung in the gloom like a chandelier and flooded the world with brief, deceptive rainbows. . . . All the world was waiting for bombardments!

[AMANDA *turns from the picture and comes outside.*]

AMANDA [*sighing*]: A fire escape landing's a poor excuse for a porch. [*She spreads a newspaper on a step and sits down, gracefully and demurely as if she were settling into a swing on a Mississippi veranda.*] What are you looking at?

TOM: The moon.

AMANDA: Is there a moon this evening?

TOM: It's rising over Garfinkel's Delicatessen.

AMANDA: So it is! A little silver slipper of a moon. Have you made a wish on it yet?

TOM: Um-hum.

AMANDA: What did you wish for?

TOM: That's a secret.

AMANDA: A secret, huh? Well, I won't tell mine either. I will be just as mysterious as you.

TOM: I bet I can guess what yours is.

AMANDA: Is my head so transparent?

TOM: You're not a sphinx.

AMANDA: No, I don't have secrets. I'll tell you what I wished for on the moon. Success and happiness for my precious children! I wish for that whenever there's a moon, and when there isn't a moon, I wish for it, too.

TOM: I thought perhaps you wished for a gentleman caller.

AMANDA: Why do you say that?

TOM: Don't you remember asking me to fetch one?

AMANDA: I remember suggesting that it would be nice for your sister if you brought home some nice young man from the warehouse. I think that I've made that suggestion more than once.

TOM: Yes, you have made it repeatedly.

AMANDA: Well?
TOM: We are going to have one.
AMANDA: *What?*
TOM: A gentleman caller!

[*The annunciation is celebrated with music.*]

[AMANDA *rises.*]

[*Image on screen:* A caller with a bouquet.]

AMANDA: You mean you have asked some nice young man to come over?
TOM: Yep. I've asked him to dinner.
AMANDA: You really did?
TOM: I did!
AMANDA: You did, and did he—*accept?*
TOM: He did!
AMANDA: Well, well—well, well! That's—lovely!
TOM: I thought that you would be pleased.
AMANDA: It's definite then?
TOM: Very definite.
AMANDA: Soon?
TOM: Very Soon.
AMANDA: For heaven's sake, stop putting on and tell me some things, will you?
TOM: What things do you want me to tell you?
AMANDA: *Naturally* I would like to know when he's *coming!*
TOM: He's coming tomorrow.
AMANDA: *Tomorrow?*
TOM: Yep. Tomorrow.
AMANDA: But, Tom!
TOM: Yes, Mother?
AMANDA: Tomorrow gives me no time!
TOM: Time for what?
AMANDA: Preparations! Why didn't you phone me at once, as soon as you asked him, the minute that he accepted? Then, don't you see, I could have been getting ready!
TOM: You don't have to make any fuss.
AMANDA: Oh, Tom, Tom, Tom, of course I have to make a fuss! I want things nice, not sloppy! Not thrown together. I'll certainly have to do some fast thinking, won't I?
TOM: I don't see why you have to think at all.
AMANDA: You just don't know. We can't have a gentleman caller in a pigsty! All my wedding silver has to be polished, the monogrammed table linen ought to be laundered! The windows have to be washed and fresh curtains put up. And how about clothes? We have to *wear* something, don't we?
TOM: Mother, this boy is no one to make a fuss over!
AMANDA: Do you realize he's the first young man we've introduced to your sister? It's terrible, dreadful, disgraceful that poor little sister has never received a single gentleman caller! Tom, come inside! [*She opens the screen door.*]
TOM: What for?
AMANDA: I want to ask you some things.
TOM: If you're going to make such a fuss, I'll call it off, I'll tell him not to come!
AMANDA: You certainly won't do anything of the kind. Nothing offends people worse than broken engagements. It simply means I'll have to work like a Turk! We won't be brilliant, but we will pass inspection. Come on inside.

[TOM *follows her inside, groaning.*]

Sit down.
TOM: Any particular place you would like me to sit?
AMANDA: Thank heavens I've got that new sofa! I'm also making payments on a floor lamp I'll have sent out! And put the chintz covers on, they'll brighten things up! Of course I'd hoped to have these walls re-papered. . . . What is the young man's name?
TOM: His name is O'Connor.
AMANDA: That, of course, means fish—tomorrow is Friday! I'll have that salmon loaf—with Durkee's dressing! What does he do? He works at the warehouse?
TOM: Of course! How else would I—
AMANDA: Tom, he—doesn't drink?
TOM: Why do you ask me that?
AMANDA: Your father *did!*
TOM: Don't get started on that!
AMANDA: He *does* drink, then?
TOM: Not that I know of!
AMANDA: Make sure, be certain! The last thing I want for my daughter's a boy who drinks!
TOM: Aren't you being a little bit premature? Mr. O'Connor has not yet appeared on the scene!
AMANDA: But will tomorrow. To meet your sister, and what do I know about his character? Nothing! Old maids are better off than wives of drunkards!
TOM: Oh, my God!
AMANDA: Be still!
TOM [*leaning forward to whisper*]: Lots of fellows meet girls whom they don't marry!
AMANDA: Oh, talk sensibly, Tom—and don't be sarcastic! [*She has gotten a hairbrush.*]
TOM: What are you doing?
AMANDA: I'm brushing that cowlick down! [*She attacks his hair with the brush.*] What is this young man's position at the warehouse?
TOM [*submitting grimly to the brush and the interrogation*]: This young man's position is that of a shipping clerk, Mother.
AMANDA: Sounds to me like a fairly responsible job, the sort of a job *you* would be in if you just had

more *get-up*. What is his salary? Have you any idea?

TOM: I would judge it to be approximately eighty-five dollars a month.

AMANDA: Well—not princely, but—

TOM: Twenty more than I make.

AMANDA: Yes, how well I know! But for a family man, eighty-five dollars a month is not much more than you can just get by on. . . .

TOM: Yes, but Mr. O'Connor is not a family man.

AMANDA: He might be, mightn't he? Some time in the future?

TOM: I see. Plans and provisions.

AMANDA: You are the only young man that I know of who ignores the fact that the future becomes the present, the present the past, and the past turns into everlasting regret if you don't plan for it!

TOM: I will think that over and see what I can make of it.

AMANDA: Don't be supercilious with your mother! Tell me some more about this—what do you call him?

TOM: James D. O'Connor. The D. is for Delaney.

AMANDA: Irish on *both* sides! *Gracious!* And doesn't drink?

TOM: Shall I call him up and ask him right this minute?

AMANDA: The only way to find out about those things is to make discreet inquiries at the proper moment. When I was a girl in Blue Mountain and it was suspected that a young man drank, the girl whose attentions he had been receiving, if any girl *was*, would sometimes speak to the minister of his church, or rather her father would if her father was living, and sort of feel him out on the young man's character. That is the way such things are discreetly handled to keep a young woman from making a tragic mistake!

TOM: Then how did you happen to make a tragic mistake?

AMANDA: That innocent look of your father's had everyone fooled! He *smiled*—the world was *enchanted!* No girl can do worse than put herself at the mercy of a handsome appearance! I hope that Mr. O'Connor is not too good-looking

TOM: No, he's not too good-looking. He's covered with freckles and hasn't too much of a nose.

AMANDA: He's not right-down homely, though?

TOM: Not right-down homely. Just medium homely, I'd say.

AMANDA: Character's what to look for in a man.

TOM: That's what I've always said, Mother.

AMANDA: You've never said anything of the kind and I suspect you would never give it a thought.

TOM: Don't be so suspicious of me.

AMANDA: At least I hope he's the type that's up and coming.

TOM: I think he really goes in for self-improvement.

AMANDA: What reason have you to think so?

TOM: He goes to night school.

AMANDA [*beaming*]: Splendid! What does he do, I mean study?

TOM: Radio engineering and public speaking!

AMANDA: Then he has visions of being advanced in the world! Any young man who studies public speaking is aiming to have an executive job some day! And radio engineering? A thing for the future! Both of these facts are very illuminating. Those are the sort of things that a mother should know concerning any young man who comes to call on her daughter. Seriously or—not.

TOM: One little warning. He doesn't know about Laura. I didn't let on that we had dark ulterior motives. I just said, why don't you come and have dinner with us? He said okay and that was the whole conversation.

AMANDA: I bet it was! You're eloquent as an oyster. However, he'll know about Laura when he gets here. When he sees how lovely and sweet and pretty she is, he'll thank his lucky stars he was asked to dinner.

TOM: Mother, you mustn't expect too much of Laura.

AMANDA: What do you mean?

TOM: Laura seems all those things to you and me because she's ours and we love her. We don't even notice she's crippled any more.

AMANDA: Don't say crippled! You know that I never allow that word to be used!

TOM: But face facts, Mother. She is and—that's not all—

AMANDA: What do you mean "not all"?

TOM: Laura is very different from other girls.

AMANDA: I think the difference is all to her advantage.

TOM: Not quite all—in the eyes of others—strangers—she's terribly shy and lives in a world of her own and those things make her seem a little peculiar to people outside the house.

AMANDA: Don't say peculiar.

TOM: Face the facts. She is.

[*The dance hall music changes to a tango that has a minor and somewhat ominous tone.*]

AMANDA: In what way is she peculiar—may I ask?

TOM [*gently*]: She lives in a world of her own—a world of little glass ornaments, Mother. . . .

[*He gets up.* AMANDA *remains holding the brush, looking at him, troubled.*]

She plays old phonograph records and—that's about all— [*He glances at himself in the mirror and crosses to the door.*]

AMANDA [*sharply*]: Where are you going?

TOM: I'm going to the movies. [*He goes out the screen door.*]

AMANDA: Not to the movies, every night to the movies! [*She follows quickly to the screen door.*] I don't believe you always go to the movies!

[*He is gone.* AMANDA *looks worriedly after him for a moment. Then vitality and optimism return and she turns from the door, crossing to the portieres.*]

Laura! Laura!

[LAURA *answers from the kitchenette.*]

LAURA: Yes, Mother.

AMANDA: Let those dishes go and come in front!

[LAURA *appears with a dish towel.* AMANDA *speaks to her gaily.*]

Laura, come here and make a wish on the moon!

[*Screen image:* The Moon.]

LAURA [*entering*]: Moon—moon?

AMANDA: A little silver slipper of a moon. Look over your left shoulder, Laura, and make a wish!

[LAURA *looks faintly puzzled as if called out of sleep.* AMANDA *seizes her shoulders and turns her at an angle by the door.*]

Now! Now, darling, *wish!*

LAURA: What shall I wish for, Mother?

AMANDA [*her voice trembling and her eyes suddenly filling with tears*]: Happiness! Good fortune!

[*The sound of the violin rises and the stage dims out.*]

SCENE 6

The light comes up on the fire escape landing. TOM *is leaning against the grill, smoking.*

[*Screen image:* The high school hero.]

TOM: And so the following evening I brought Jim home to dinner. I had known Jim slightly in high school. In high school Jim was a hero. He had tremendous Irish good nature and vitality with the scrubbed and polished look of white chinaware. He seemed to move in a continual spotlight. He was a star in basketball, captain of the debating club, president of the senior class and the glee club, and he sang the male lead in the annual light operas. He was always running or bounding, never just walking. He seemed always at the point of defeating the law of gravity. He was shooting with such velocity through his adolescence that you would logically expect him to arrive at nothing short of the White House by the time he was thirty. But Jim apparently ran into more interference after his graduation from Soldan. His speed had definitely slowed. Six years after he left high school he was holding a job that wasn't much better than mine.

[*Screen image:* The Clerk.]

He was the only one at the warehouse with whom I was on friendly terms. I was valuable to him as someone who could remember his former glory, who had seen him win basketball games and the silver cup in debating. He knew of my secret practice of retiring to a cabinet of the washroom to work on poems when business was slack in the warehouse. He called me Shakespeare. And while the other boys in the warehouse regarded me with suspicious hostility, Jim took a humorous attitude toward me. Gradually his attitude affected the others, their hostility wore off and they also began to smile at me as people smile at an oddly fashioned dog who trots across their path at some distance.

I knew that Jim and Laura had known each other at Soldan, and I had heard Laura speak admiringly of his voice. I didn't know if Jim remembered her or not. In high school Laura had been as unobtrusive as Jim had been astonishing. If he did remember Laura, it was not as my sister, for when I asked him to dinner, he grinned and said, "You know, Shakespeare, I never thought of you as having folks!"

He was about to discover that I did . . .

[*Legend on screen:* "The accent of a coming foot."]

[*The light dims out on* TOM *and comes up in the Wingfield living room—a delicate lemony light. It is about five on a Friday evening of late spring which comes "scattering poems in the sky."*]

[AMANDA *has worked like a Turk in preparation for the gentleman caller. The results are astonishing. The new floor lamp with its rose silk shade is in place, a colored paper lantern conceals the broken light fixture in the ceiling, new billowing white curtains are at the windows, chintz covers are on the chairs and sofa, a pair of new sofa pillows make their initial appearance. Open boxes and tissue paper are scattered on the floor.*]

[LAURA *stands in the middle of the room with lifted arms while* AMANDA *crouches before her, adjusting the hem of a new dress, devout and ritualistic. The dress is colored and designed by memory. The arrangement of* LAURA*'s hair is changed; it is softer and more becoming. A fragile, unearthly prettiness has come out in* LAURA*: she is like a piece of translucent glass touched by light, given a momentary radiance, not actual, not lasting.*]

AMANDA [*impatiently*]: Why are you trembling?
LAURA: Mother, you've made me so nervous!
AMANDA: How have I made you nervous?
LAURA: By all this fuss! You make it seem so important!
AMANDA: I don't understand you, Laura. You couldn't be satisfied with just sitting home, and yet whenever I try to arrange something for you, you seem to resist it. [*She gets up.*] Now take a look at yourself. No, wait! Wait just a moment—I have an idea!
LAURA: What is it now?

[AMANDA *produces two powder puffs which she wraps in handkerchiefs and stuffs in* LAURA*'s bosom.*].

LAURA: Mother, what are you doing?
AMANDA: They call them "Gay Deceivers"!
LAURA: I won't wear them!
AMANDA: You will!
LAURA: Why should I?
AMANDA: Because, to be painfully honest, your chest is flat.
LAURA: You make it seem like we were setting a trap.
AMANDA: All pretty girls are a trap, a pretty trap, and men expect them to be.

[*Legend on screen:* "A pretty trap."]

Now look at yourself, young lady. This is the prettiest you will ever be! [*She stands back to admire* LAURA.] I've got to fix myself now! You're going to be surprised by your mother's appearance!

[AMANDA *crosses through the portieres, humming gaily.* LAURA *moves slowly to the long mirror and stares solemnly at herself. A wind blows the white curtains inward in a slow, graceful motion and with a faint, sorrowful sighing.*]

AMANDA [*from somewhere behind the portieres*]: It isn't dark enough yet.

[LAURA *turns slowly before the mirror with a troubled look.*]

[*Legend on screen*: "This is my sister: Celebrate her with strings!" *Music plays.*]

AMANDA [*laughing, still not visible*]: I'm going to show you something. I'm going to make a spectacular appearance!
LAURA: What is it, Mother?
AMANDA: Possess your soul in patience—you will see! Something I've resurrected from that old trunk! Styles haven't changed so terribly much after all. . . . [*She parts the portieres.*] Now just look at your mother! [*She wears a girlish frock of yellowed voile with a blue silk sash. She carries a bunch of jonquils—the legend of her youth is nearly revived. Now she speaks feverishly:*] This is the dress in which I led the cotillion. Won the cakewalk twice at Sunset Hill, wore one Spring to the Governor's Ball in Jackson! See how I sashayed around the ballroom, Laura? [*She raises her skirt and does a mincing step around the room.*] I wore it on Sundays for my gentlemen callers! I had it on the day I met your father. . . . I had malaria fever all that Spring. The change of climate from East Tennessee to the Delta—weakened resistance. I had a little temperature all the time—not enough to be serious—just enough to make me restless and giddy! Invitations poured in—parties all over the Delta! "Stay in bed," said Mother, "you have a fever!"—but I just wouldn't. I took quinine but kept on going, going! Evenings, dances! Afternoons, long, long rides! Picnics—lovely! So lovely, that country in May—all lacy with dogwood, literally flooded with jonquils! That was the spring I had the craze for jonquils. Jonquils became an absolute obsession. Mother said, "Honey, there's no more room for jonquils." And still I kept on bringing in more jonquils. Whenever, wherever I saw them, I'd say, "Stop! Stop! I see jonquils!" I made the young men help me gather the jonquils! It was a joke, Amanda and her jonquils. Finally there were no more vases to hold them, every available space was filled with jonquils. No vases to hold them? All right, I'll hold them myself! And then I— [*She stops in front of the picture. Music plays.*] met your father! Malaria fever and jonquils and then—this—boy. . . . [*She switches on the rose-colored lamp.*] I hope they get here before it starts to rain. [*She crosses the room and places the jonquils in a bowl on the table.*] I gave your brother a little extra change so he and Mr. O'Connor could take the service car home.
LAURA [*with an altered look*]: What did you say his name was?
AMANDA: O'Connor.

LAURA: What is his first name?
AMANDA: I don't remember. Oh, yes, I do. It was—Jim!

[LAURA *sways slightly and catches hold of a chair.*]

[*Legend on screen:* "Not Jim!"]

LAURA [*faintly*]: Not—Jim!
AMANDA: Yes, that was it, it was Jim! I've never known a Jim that wasn't nice!

[*The music becomes ominous.*]

LAURA: Are you sure his name is Jim O'Connor?
AMANDA: Yes. Why?
LAURA: Is he the one that Tom used to know in high school?
AMANDA: He didn't say so. I think he just got to know him at the warehouse.
LAURA: There was a Jim O'Connor we both knew in high school— [*then, with effort*] If that is the one that Tom is bringing to dinner—you'll have to excuse me, I won't come to the table.
AMANDA: What sort of nonsense is this?
LAURA: You asked me once if I'd ever liked a boy. Don't you remember I showed you this boy's picture?
AMANDA: You mean the boy you showed me in the yearbook?
LAURA: Yes, that boy.
AMANDA: Laura, Laura, were you in love with that boy?
LAURA: I don't know, Mother. All I know is I couldn't sit at the table if it was him!
AMANDA: It won't be him! It isn't the least bit likely. But whether it is or not, you will come to the table. You will not be excused.
LAURA: I'll have to be, Mother.
AMANDA: I don't intend to humor your silliness, Laura. I've had too much from you and your brother, both! So just sit down and compose yourself till they come. Tom has forgotten his key so you'll have to let them in, when they arrive.
LAURA [*panicky*]: Oh, Mother—*you* answer the door!
AMANDA [*lightly*]: I'll be in the kitchen—busy!
LAURA: Oh, Mother, please answer the door, don't make me do it!
AMANDA [*crossing into the kitchenette*]: I've got to fix the dressing for the salmon. Fuss, fuss—silliness! —over a gentleman caller!

[*The door swings shut.* LAURA *is left alone.*]

[*Legend on screen:* "Terror!"]

[*She utters a low moan and turns off the lamp—sits stiffly on the edge of the sofa, knotting her fingers together.*]

[*Legend on screen:* "The Opening of a Door!"]

[TOM *and* JIM *appear on the fire escape steps and climb to the landing. Hearing them approach,* LAURA *rises with a panicky gesture. She retreats to the portieres. The doorbell rings.* LAURA *catches her breath and touches her throat. Low drums sound.*]

AMANDA [*calling*]: Laura, sweetheart! The door!

[LAURA *stares at it without moving.*]

JIM: I think we just beat the rain.
TOM: Uh-huh. [*He rings again, nervously.* JIM *whistles and fishes for a cigarette.*]
AMANDA [*very, very gaily*]: Laura, that is your brother and Mr. O'Connor! Will you let them in, darling?

[LAURA *crosses toward the kitchenette door.*]

LAURA [*breathlessly*]: Mother—you go to the door!

[AMANDA *steps out of the kitchenette and stares furiously at* LAURA. *She points imperiously at the door.*]

LAURA: Please, please!
AMANDA [*in a fierce whisper*]: What is the matter with you, you silly thing?
LAURA [*desperately*]: Please, you answer it, *please!*
AMANDA: I told you I wasn't going to humor you, Laura. Why have you chosen this moment to lose your mind?
LAURA: Please, please, please, you go!
AMANDA: You'll have to go to the door because I can't!
LAURA [*despairingly*]: I can't either!
AMANDA: *Why?*
LAURA: I'm *sick!*
AMANDA: I'm sick, too—of your nonsense! Why can't you and your brother be normal people? Fantastic whims and behavior!

[TOM *gives a long ring.*]

Preposterous goings on! Can you give me one reason— [*She calls out lyrically.*] *Coming! Just one second!*—why you should be afraid to open a door? Now you answer it, Laura!
LAURA: Oh, oh, oh . . . [*She returns through the portieres, darts to the Victrola, winds it frantically and turns it on.*]

AMANDA: Laura Wingfield, you march right to that door!
LAURA: *Yes—yes, Mother!*

[*A faraway, scratchy rendition of "Dardanella" softens the air and gives her strength to move through it. She slips to the door and draws it cautiously open.* TOM *enters with the caller,* JIM O'CONNOR.]

TOM: Laura, this is Jim. Jim, this is my sister, Laura.
JIM [*stepping inside*]: I didn't know that Shakespeare had a sister!
LAURA [*retreating, stiff and trembling, from the door*]: How—how do you do?
JIM [*heartily, extending his hand*]: Okay!

[LAURA *touches it hesitantly with hers.*]

JIM: Your hand's *cold*, Laura!
LAURA: Yes, well—I've been playing the Victrola. . . .
JIM: Must have been playing classical music on it! You ought to play a little hot swing music to warm you up!
LAURA: Excuse me—I haven't finished playing the Victrola. . . . [*She turns awkwardly and hurries into the front room. She pauses a second by the Victrola. Then she catches her breath and darts through the portieres like a frightened deer.*]
JIM [*grinning*]: What was the matter?
TOM: Oh—with Laura? Laura is—terribly shy.
JIM: Shy, huh? It's unusual to meet a shy girl nowadays. I don't believe you ever mentioned you had a sister.
TOM: Well, now you know. I have one. Here is the *Post Dispatch*. You want a piece of it?
JIM: Uh-huh.
TOM: What piece? The comics?
JIM: Sports! [*He glances at it.*] Ole Dizzy Dean is on his bad behavior.
TOM [*uninterested*]: Yeah? [*He lights a cigarette and goes over to the fire-escape door.*]
JIM: Where are *you* going?
TOM: I'm going out on the terrace.
JIM [*going after him*]: You know, Shakespeare—I'm going to sell you a bill of goods!
TOM: What goods?
JIM: A course I'm taking.
TOM: Huh?
JIM: In public speaking! You and me, we're not the warehouse type.
TOM: Thanks—that's good news. But what has public speaking got to do with it?
JIM: It fits you for—executive positions!
TOM: Awww.
JIM: I tell you it's done a helluva lot for me.

[*Image on screen*: Executive at his desk.]

TOM: In what respect?
JIM: In every! Ask yourself what is the difference between you an' me and men in the office down front? Brains?—No!—Ability?—No! Then what? Just one little thing—
TOM: What is that one little thing?
JIM: Primarily it amounts to—social poise! Being able to square up to people and hold your own on any social level!
AMANDA [*from the kitchenette*]: Tom?
TOM: Yes, Mother?
AMANDA: Is that you and Mr. O'Connor?
TOM: Yes, Mother.
AMANDA: Well, you just make yourselves comfortable in there.
TOM: Yes, Mother.
AMANDA: Ask Mr. O'Connor if he would like to wash his hands.
JIM: Aw, no—no—thank you—I took care of that at the warehouse. Tom—
TOM: Yes?
JIM: Mr. Mendoza was speaking to me about you.
TOM: Favorably?
JIM: What do you think?
TOM: Well—
JIM: You're going to be out of a job if you don't wake up.
TOM: I am waking up—
JIM: You show no signs.
TOM: The signs are interior.

[*Image on screen*: The sailing vessel with the Jolly Roger again.]

TOM: I'm planning to change. [*He leans over the fire-escape rail, speaking with quiet exhilaration. The incandescent marquees and signs of the first-run movie houses light his face from across the alley. He looks like a voyager.*] I'm right at the point of committing myself to a future that doesn't include the warehouse and Mr. Mendoza or even a night-school course in public speaking.
JIM: What are you gassing about?
TOM: I'm tired of the movies.
JIM: Movies!
TOM: Yes, movies! Look at them— [*a wave toward the marvels of Grand Avenue*] All of those glamorous people—having adventures—hogging it all, gobbling the whole thing up! You know what happens? People go to the *movies* instead of *moving!* Hollywood characters are supposed to have all the adventures for everybody in America, while everybody in America sits in a dark room and

watches them have them! Yes, until there's a war. That's when adventure becomes available to the masses! *Everyone's* dish, not only Gable's! Then the people in the dark room come out of the dark room to have some adventures themselves—goody, goody! It's our turn now, to go to the South Sea Island—to make a safari—to be exotic, far-off! But I'm not patient. I don't want to wait till then. I'm tired of the *movies* and I am *about* to *move!*

JIM [*incredulously*]: Move?

TOM: Yes.

JIM: When?

TOM: Soon!

JIM: Where? Where?

[*The music seems to answer the question, while* TOM *thinks it over. He searches in his pockets.*]

TOM: I'm starting to boil inside. I know I seem dreamy, but inside—well, I'm boiling! Whenever I pick up a shoe, I shudder a little thinking how short life is and what I am doing! Whatever that means, I know it doesn't mean shoes—except as something to wear on a traveler's feet! [*He finds what he has been searching for in his pockets and holds out a paper to* JIM.] Look—

JIM: What?

TOM: I'm a member.

JIM [*reading*]: The Union of Merchant Seamen.

TOM: I paid my dues this month, instead of the light bill.

JIM: You will regret it when they turn the lights off.

TOM: I won't be here.

JIM: How about your mother?

TOM: I'm like my father. The bastard son of a bastard! Did you notice how he's grinning in his picture in there? And he's been absent going on sixteen years!

JIM: You're just talking, you drip. How does your mother feel about it?

TOM: Shhh! Here comes Mother! Mother is not acquainted with my plans!

AMANDA [*coming through the portieres*]: Where are you all?

TOM: On the terrace, Mother.

[*They start inside. She advances to them.* TOM *is distinctly shocked at her appearance. Even* JIM *blinks a little. He is making his first contact with girlish Southern vivacity and in spite of the night-school course in public speaking is somewhat thrown off the beam by the unexpected outlay of social charm. Certain responses are attempted by* JIM *but are swept aside by* AMANDA'*s gay laughter and chatter.* TOM *is embarrassed but after the first shock* JIM *reacts very warmly. He grins and chuckles, is altogether won over.*]

[*Image on screen*: Amanda as a girl.]

AMANDA [*coyly smiling, shaking her girlish ringlets*]: Well, well, well, so this is Mr. O'Connor. Introductions entirely unnecessary. I've heard so much about you from my boy. I finally said to him, Tom—good gracious!—why don't you bring this paragon to supper? I'd like to meet this nice young man at the warehouse!—instead of just hearing him sing your praises so much! I don't know why my son is so stand-offish—that's not Southern behavior!

Let's sit down and—I think we could stand a little more air in here! Tom, leave the door open. I felt a nice fresh breeze a moment ago. Where has it gone to? Mmm, so warm already! And not quite summer, even. We're going to burn up when summer really gets started. However, we're having—we're having a very light supper. I think light things are better fo' this time of year. The same as light clothes are. Light clothes an' light food are what warm weather calls fo'. You know our blood gets so thick during th' winter—it takes a while fo' us to *adjust* ou'selves!—when the season changes . . . It's come so quick this year. I wasn't prepared. All of a sudden—heavens! Already summer! I ran to the trunk an' pulled out this light dress—terribly old! Historical almost! But feels so good—so good an' co-ol, y' know. . . .

TOM: Mother—

AMANDA: Yes, honey?

TOM: How about—supper?

AMANDA: Honey, you go ask Sister if supper is ready! You know that Sister is in full charge of supper! Tell her you hungry boys are waiting for it. [*to* JIM] Have you met Laura?

JIM: She—

AMANDA: Let you in? Oh, good, you've met already! It's rare for a girl as sweet an' pretty as Laura to be domestic! But Laura is, thank heavens, not only pretty but also very domestic. I'm not at all. I never was a bit. I never could make a thing but angel-food cake. Well, in the South we had so many servants. Gone, gone, gone. All vestige of gracious living! Gone completely! I wasn't prepared for what the future brought me. All of my gentlemen callers were sons of planters and so of course I assumed that I would be married to one and raise my family on a large piece of land with plenty of servants. But man proposes—and woman accepts the proposal! To vary that old, old saying a little bit—I married no planter! I married a man who worked for the telephone company! That gallantly smiling gentleman over there! [*She points to the picture.*] A telephone man who—fell in love with long-distance! Now he travels and I don't even know where! But what am I going on for about my—tribulations? Tell me yours—I hope you don't have any! Tom?

TOM [*returning*]: Yes, Mother?

AMANDA: Is supper nearly ready?

TOM: It looks to me like supper is on the table.

AMANDA: Let me look— [*She rises prettily and looks through the portieres.*] Oh, lovely! But where is Sister?

TOM: Laura is not feeling well and she says that she thinks she'd better not come to the table.

AMANDA: What? Nonsense! Laura? Oh, Laura!

LAURA [*from the kitchenette, faintly*]: Yes, Mother.

AMANDA: You really must come to the table. We won't be seated until you come to the table! Come in, Mr. O'Connor. You sit over there, and I'll . . . Laura? Laura Wingfield! You're keeping us waiting, honey! We can't say grace until you come to the table!

[*The kitchenette door is pushed weakly open and* LAURA *comes in. She is obviously quite faint, her lips trembling, her eyes wide and staring. She moves unsteadily toward the table.*]

[*Screen legend*: "Terror!"]

[*Outside a summer storm is coming on abruptly. The white curtains billow inward at the windows and there is a sorrowful murmur from the deep blue dusk.*]

[LAURA *suddenly stumbles; she catches at a chair with a faint moan.*]

TOM: Laura!

AMANDA: Laura!

[*There is a clap of thunder.*]

[*Screen legend:* "Ah!"]

[*despairingly*] Why, Laura, you *are* ill, darling! Tom, help your sister into the living room, dear! Sit in the living room, Laura—rest on the sofa. Well! [*to* JIM *as* TOM *helps his sister to the sofa in she living room*] Standing over the hot stove made her ill! I told her that it was just too warm this evening, but—

[TOM *comes back to the table.*]

Is Laura all right now?

TOM: Yes.

AMANDA: What *is* that? Rain? A nice cool rain has come up! [*She gives* JIM *a frightened look.*] I think we may—have grace—now . . .
[TOM *looks at her stupidly.*] Tom, honey—you say grace!

TOM: Oh . . . "For these and all thy mercies—"

[*They bow their heads,* AMANDA *stealing a nervous glance at* JIM. *In the living room* LAURA, *stretched on the sofa, clenches her hand to her lips, to hold back a shuddering sob.*]

God's Holy Name be praised—

[*The scene dims out.*]

SCENE 7

It is half an hour later. Dinner is just being finished in the dining room, LAURA *is still huddled upon the sofa, her feet drawn under her, her head resting on a pale blue pillow, her eyes wide and mysteriously watchful. The new floor lamp with its shade of rose-colored silk gives a soft, becoming light to her face, bringing out the fragile, unearthly prettiness which usually escapes attention. From outside there is a steady murmur of rain, but it is slackening and soon stops; the air outside becomes pale and luminous as the moon breaks through the clouds. A moment after the curtain rises, the lights in both rooms flicker and go out.*

JIM: Hey, there, Mr. Light Bulb!

[AMANDA *laughs nervously.*]

[*Legend on screen:* "Suspension of a public service."]

AMANDA: Where was Moses when the lights went out? Ha-ha. Do you know the answer to that one, Mr. O'Conner?

JIM: No, Ma'am, what's the answer?

AMANDA: In the dark!

[JIM *laughs appreciatively.*]

Everybody sit still. I'll light the candles. Isn't it lucky we have them on the table? Where's a match? Which of you gentlemen can provide a match?

JIM: Here.

AMANDA: Thank you, Sir.

JIM: Not at all, Ma'am!

AMANDA [*as she lights the candles*]: I guess the fuse has burnt out. Mr. O'Connor, can you tell a burnt-out fuse? I know I can't and Tom is a total loss when it comes to mechanics.

[*They rise from the table and go into the kitchenette, from where their voices are heard.*]

Oh, be careful you don't bump into something. We don't want our gentleman caller to break his neck. Now wouldn't that be a fine howdy-do?

JIM: Ha-ha! Where is the fuse-box?

AMANDA: Right here next to the stove. Can you see anything?

JIM: Just a minute.

AMANDA: Isn't electricity a mysterious thing? Wasn't it Benjamin Franklin who tied a key to a kite? We live in such a mysterious universe, don't we? Some people say that science clears up all the mysteries for us. In my opinion it only creates more! Have you found it yet?

JIM: No, Ma'am. All these fuses look okay to me.

AMANDA: Tom!

TOM: Yes, Mother?

AMANDA: That light bill I give you several days ago. The one I told you we got the notices about?

[*Legend on screen:* "Ha!"]

TOM: Oh—yeah.

AMANDA: You didn't neglect to pay it by any chance?

TOM: Why, I—

AMANDA: Didn't! I might have known it!

JIM: Shakespeare probably wrote a poem on that light bill, Mrs. Wingfield.

AMANDA: I might have known better than to trust him with it! There's such a high price for negligence in this world!

JIM: Maybe the poem will win a ten-dollar prize.

AMANDA: We'll just have to spend the remainder of the evening in the nineteenth century, before Mr. Edison made the Mazda lamp!

JIM: Candlelight is my favorite kind of light.

AMANDA: That shows you're romantic! But that's no excuse for Tom. Well, we got through dinner. Very considerate of them to let us get through dinner before they plunged us into everlasting darkness, wasn't it, Mr. O'Connor?

JIM: Ha-ha!

AMANDA: Tom, as a penalty for your carelessness you can help me with the dishes.

JIM: Let me give you a hand.

AMANDA: Indeed you will not!

JIM: I ought to be good for something.

AMANDA: Good for something? [*Her tone is rhapsodic.*] *You?* Why, Mr. O'Connor, nobody, *nobody's* given me this much entertainment in years—as you have!

JIM: Aw, now, Mrs. Wingfield!

AMANDA: I'm not exaggerating, not one bit! But Sister is all by her lonesome. You go keep her company in the parlor! I'll give you this lovely old candelabrum that used to be on the altar at the Church of the Heavenly Rest. It was melted a little out of shape when the church burnt down. Lightning struck it one spring. Gypsy Jones was holding a revival at the time and he intimated that the church was destroyed because the Episcopalians gave card parties.

JIM: Ha-ha.

AMANDA: And how about you coaxing Sister to drink a little wine? I think it would be good for her! Can you carry both at once?

JIM: Sure. I'm Superman!

AMANDA: Now, Thomas, get into this apron!

[JIM *comes into the dining room, carrying the candelabrum, its candles lighted, in one hand and a glass of wine in the other. The door of the kitchenette swings closed on* AMANDA'S *gay laughter; the flickering light approaches the portieres.* LAURA *sits up nervously as* JIM *enters. She can hardly speak from the almost intolerable strain of being alone with a stranger.*]

[*Screen legend:* "I don't suppose you remember me at all!"]

[*At first, before* JIM'S *warmth overcomes her paralyzing shyness,* LAURA'S *voice is thin and breathless, as though she had just run up a steep flight of stairs.* JIM'S *attitude is gently humorous. While the incident is apparently unimportant, it is to* LAURA *the climax of her secret life.*]

JIM: Hello there, Laura.

LAURA [*faintly*]: Hello.

[*She clears her throat.*]

JIM: How are you feeling now? Better?

LAURA: Yes. Yes, thank you.

JIM: This is for you. A little dandelion wine. [*He extends the glass toward her with extravagant gallantry.*]

LAURA: Thank you.

JIM: Drink it—but don't get drunk!

[*He laughs heartily.* LAURA *takes the glass uncertainly; she laughs shyly.*]

Where shall I set the candles?

LAURA: Oh—oh, anywhere . . .

JIM: How about here on the floor? Any objections?

LAURA: No.
JIM: I'll spread a newspaper under to catch the drippings. I like to sit on the floor. Mind if I do?
LAURA: Oh, no.
JIM: Give me a pillow?
LAURA: What?
JIM: A pillow!
LAURA: Oh . . . [*She hands him one quickly.*]
JIM: How about you? Don't you like to sit on the floor?
LAURA: Oh—yes.
JIM: Why don't you, then?
LAURA: I—will.
JIM: Take a pillow!

[LAURA *does. She sits on the floor on the other side of the candelabrum.* JIM *crosses his legs and smiles engagingly at her.*] I can't hardly see you sitting way over there.

LAURA: I can—see you.
JIM: I know, but that's not fair, I'm in the limelight.

[LAURA *moves her pillow closer.*]

Good! Now I can see you! Comfortable?
LAURA: Yes.
JIM: So am I. Comfortable as a cow! Will you have some gum?
LAURA: No, thank you.
JIM: I think that I will indulge, with your permission. [*He musingly unwraps a stick of gum and holds it up.*] Think of the fortune made by the guy that invented the first piece of chewing gum. Amazing, huh? The Wrigley Building is one of the sights of Chicago—I saw it when I went up to the Century of Progress. Did you take in the Century of Progress?
LAURA: No, I didn't.
JIM: Well, it was quite a wonderful exposition. What impressed me most was the Hall of Science. Gives you an idea of what the future will be in America, even more wonderful than the present time is! [*There is a pause.* JIM *smiles at her.*] Your brother tells me you're shy. Is that right, Laura?
LAURA: I—don't know.
JIM: I judge you to be an old-fashioned type of girl. Well, I think that's a pretty good type to be. Hope you don't think I'm being too personal—do you?
LAURA [*hastily, out of embarrassment*]: I believe I *will* take a piece of gum, if you—don't mind. [*clearing her throat*] Mr. O'Connor, have you—kept up with your singing?
JIM: Singing? Me?
LAURA: Yes. I remember what a beautiful voice you had.
JIM: When did you hear me sing?

[LAURA *does not answer, and in the long pause which follows a man's voice is heard singing offstage.*]

VOICE:
O blow, ye winds, heigh-ho,
A-roving I will go!
I'm off to my love
With a boxing glove—
Ten thousand miles away!

JIM: You say you've heard me sing?
LAURA: Oh, yes! Yes, very often . . . I—don't suppose—you remember me—at all?
JIM [*smiling doubtfully*]: You know I have in idea I've seen you before. I had that idea soon as you opened the door. It seemed almost like I was about to remember your name. But the name that I started to call you—wasn't a name! And so I stopped myself before I said it.
LAURA: Wasn't it—Blue Roses?
JIM [*springing up, grinning*]: Blue Roses! My gosh, yes—Blue Roses! That's what I had on my tongue when you opened the door! Isn't it funny what tricks your memory plays? I didn't connect you with high school somehow or other. But that's where it was; it was high school. I didn't even know you were Shakespeare's sister! Gosh, I'm sorry.
LAURA: I didn't expect you to. You—barely knew me!
JIM: But we did have a speaking acquaintance, huh?
LAURA: Yes, we—spoke to each other.
JIM: When did you recognize me?
LAURA: Oh, right away!
JIM: Soon as I came in the door?
LAURA: When I heard your name I thought it was probably you. I knew that Tom used to know you a little in high school. So when you came in the door—well, then I was—sure.
JIM: Why didn't you *say* something, then?
LAURA [*breathlessly*]: I didn't know what to say, I was—too surprised!
JIM: For goodness' sakes! You know, this sure is funny!
LAURA: Yes! Yes, isn't it, though . . .
JIM: Didn't we have a class in something together?
LAURA: Yes, we did.
JIM: What class was that?
LAURA: It was—singing—chorus!
JIM: Aw!
LAURA: I sat across the aisle from you in the Aud.
JIM: Aw.
LAURA: Mondays, Wednesdays, and Fridays.
JIM: Now I remember—you always came in late.
LAURA: Yes, it was so hard for me, getting upstairs. I had that brace on my leg—it clumped so loud!
JIM: I never heard any clumping.
LAURA [*wincing at the recollection*]: To me it sounded like—thunder!

JIM: Well, well, well, I never even noticed.

LAURA: And everybody was seated before I came in. I had to walk in front of all those people. My seat was in the back row. I had to go clumping all the way up the aisle with everyone watching!

JIM: You shouldn't have been self-conscious.

LAURA: I know, but I was. It was always such a relief when the singing started.

JIM: Aw, yes, I've placed you now! I used to call you Blue Roses. How was it that I got started calling you that?

LAURA: I was out of school a little while with pleurosis. When I came back you asked me what was the matter. I said I had pleurosis—you thought I said *Blue Roses*. That's what you always called me after that!

JIM: I hope you didn't mind.

LAURA: Oh, no—I liked it. You see, I wasn't acquainted with many—people. . . .

JIM: As I remember you sort of stuck by yourself.

LAURA: I—I—never have had much luck at—making friends.

JIM: I don't see why you wouldn't.

LAURA: Well, I—started out badly.

JIM: You mean being—

LAURA: Yes, it sort of—stood between me—

JIM: You shouldn't have let it!

LAURA: I know, but it did, and—

JIM: You were shy with people!

LAURA: I tried not to be but never could—

JIM: Overcome it?

LAURA: No, I—I never could!

JIM: I guess being shy is something you have to work out of kind of gradually.

LAURA [*sorrowfully*]: Yes—I guess it—

JIM: Takes time!

LAURA: Yes—

JIM: People are not so dreadful when you know them. That's what you have to remember! And everybody has problems, not just you, but practically everybody has got some problems. You think of yourself as having the only problems, as being the only one who is disappointed. But just look around you and you will see lots of people as disappointed as you are. For instance, I hoped when I was going to high school that I would be further along at this time, six years later, than I am now. You remember that wonderful write-up I had in *The Torch?*

LAURA: Yes! [*She rises and crosses to the table.*]

JIM: It said I was bound to succeed in anything I went into!

[LAURA *returns with the high school yearbook.*]

Holy Jeez! *The Torch!*

[*He accepts it reverently. They smile across the book with mutual wonder.* LAURA *crouches beside him and they begin to turn the pages.* LAURA*'s shyness is dissolving in his warmth.*]

LAURA: Here you are in *The Pirates of Penzance!*

JIM [*wistfully*]: I sang the baritone lead in that operetta.

LAURA [*raptly*]: So—*beautifully!*

JIM [*protesting*]: Aw—

LAURA: Yes, yes—beautifully—beautifully!

JIM: You heard me?

LAURA: All three times!

JIM: No!

LAURA: Yes!

JIM: All three performances?

LAURA [*looking down*]: Yes.

JIM: Why?

LAURA: I—wanted to ask you to—autograph my program. [*She takes the program from the back of the yearbook and shows it to him.*]

JIM: Why didn't you ask me to?

LAURA: You were always surrounded by your own friends so much that I never had a chance to.

JIM: You should have just—

LAURA: Well, I—thought you might think I was—

JIM: Thought I might think you was—what?

LAURA: Oh—

JIM [*with reflective relish*]: I was beleaguered by females in those days.

LAURA: You were terribly popular!

JIM: Yeah—

LAURA: You had such a—friendly way—

JIM: I was spoiled in high school.

LAURA: Everybody—liked you!

JIM: Including you?

LAURA: I—yes, I—did, too— [*She gently closes the book in her lap.*]

JIM: Well, well, well! Give me that program, Laura.

[*She hands it to him. He signs it with a flourish.*]

There you are—better late than never!

LAURA: Oh, I—what a—surprise!

JIM: My signature isn't worth very much right now. But some day—maybe—it will increase in value! Being disappointed is one thing and being discouraged is something else. I am disappointed but I am not discouraged. I'm twenty-three years old. How old are you?

LAURA: I'll be twenty-four in June.

JIM: That's not old age!

LAURA: No, but—

JIM: You finished high school?

LAURA [*with difficulty*]: I didn't go back.

JIM: You mean you dropped out?

LAURA: I made bad grades in my final examinations. [*She rises and replaces the book and the program on the table. Her voice is strained.*] How is—Emily Meisenbach getting along?
JIM: Oh, that kraut-head!
LAURA: Why do you call her that?
JIM: That's what she was.
LAURA: You're not still—going with her?
JIM: I never see her.
LAURA: It said the "Personal" section that you were—engaged!
JIM: I know, but I wasn't impressed by that—propaganda!
LAURA: It wasn't—the truth?
JIM: Only in Emily's optimistic opinion!
LAURA: Oh—

[*Legend:* "What have you done since high school?"]

[JIM *lights a cigarette and leans indolently back on his elbows smiling at* LAURA *with a warmth and charm which lights her inwardly with altar candles. She remains by the table, picks up a piece from the glass menagerie collection, and turns it in her hands to cover her tumult.*]

JIM [*after several reflective puffs on his cigarette*]: What have you done since high school?

[*She seems not to hear him.*]

Huh?

[LAURA *looks up.*]

I said what have you done since high school, Laura?
LAURA: Nothing much.
JIM: You must have been doing something these six long years.
LAURA: Yes.
JIM: Well, then, such as what?
LAURA: I took a business course at business college—
JIM: How did that work out?
LAURA: Well, not very—well—I had to drop out, it gave me—indigestion—

[JIM *laughs gently.*]

JIM: What are you doing now?
LAURA: I don't do anything—much. Oh, please don't think I sit around doing nothing! My glass collection takes up a good deal of time. Glass is something you have to take good care of.
JIM: What did you say—about glass?
LAURA: Collection I said—I have one— [*She clears her throat and turns away again, acutely shy.*]
JIM [*abruptly*]: You know what I judge to be the trouble with you? Inferiority complex! Know what that is? That's what they call it when someone low-rates himself! I understand it because I had it, too. Although my case was not so aggravated as yours seems to be. I had it until I took up public speaking, developed my voice, and learned that I had an aptitude for science. Before that time I never thought of myself as being outstanding in any way whatsoever! Now I've never made a regular study of it, but I have a friend who says I can analyze people better than doctors that make a profession of it. I don't claim that to be necessarily true, but I can sure guess a person's psychology, Laura! [*He takes out his gum.*] Excuse me, Laura. I always take it out when the flavor is gone. I'll use this scrap of paper to wrap it in. I know how it is to get it stuck on a shoe. [*He wraps the gum in paper and puts it in his pocket.*] Yep—that's what I judge to be your principal trouble. A lack of confidence in yourself as a person. You don't have the proper amount of faith in yourself. I'm basing that fact on a number of your remarks and also on certain observations I've made. For instance that clumping you thought was so awful in high school. You say that you even dreaded to walk into class. You see what you did? You dropped out of school, you gave up an education because of a clump, which as far as I know was practically non-existent! A little physical defect is what you have. Hardly noticeable even! Magnified thousands of times by imagination! You know what my strong advice to you is? Think of yourself *superior* in some way!
LAURA: In what way would I think?
JIM: Why, man alive, Laura! Just look about you a little. What do you see? A world full of common people! All of 'em born and all of 'em going to die! Which of them has one-tenth of your good points! Or mine! Or anyone else's, as far as that goes—gosh! Everybody excels in some one thing. Some in many! [*He unconsciously glances at himself in the mirror.*] All you've got to do is discover in *what!* Take me, for instance. [*He adjusts his tie at the mirror.*] My interest happens to lie in electrodynamics. I'm taking a course in radio engineering at night school, Laura, on top of a fairly responsible job at the warehouse. I'm taking that course and studying public speaking.
LAURA: Ohhhh.
JIM: Because I believe in the future of television! [*Turning his back to her.*] I wish to be ready to go up right along with it. Therefore I'm planning to get in on the ground floor. In fact I've already made the right connections and all that remains is for the industry itself to get under way! Full steam—[*His eyes are starry.*] *Knowledge*—Zzzzzp! *Money*—

Zzzzzzp!—*Power!* That's the cycle democracy is built on!

[*His attitude is convincingly dynamic.* LAURA *stares at him, even her shyness eclipsed in her absolute wonder. He suddenly grins.*]

I guess you think I think a lot of myself!

LAURA: No—o-o-o, I—

JIM: Now how about you? Isn't there something you take more interest in than anything else?

LAURA: Well, I do—as I said—have my—glass collection—

[*A peal of girlish laughter rings from the kitchenette.*]

JIM: I'm not right sure I know what you're talking about. What kind of glass is it?

LAURA: Little articles of it, they're ornaments mostly! Most of them are little animals made out of glass, the tiniest little animals in the world. Mother calls them a glass menagerie! Here's an example of one, if you'd like to see it! This one is one of the oldest. It's nearly thirteen.

[*Music:* "The Glass Menagerie."]

[*He stretches out his hand.*]

Oh, be careful—if you breathe, it breaks!

JIM: I'd better not take it. I'm pretty clumsy with things.

LAURA: Go on, I trust you with him! [*She places the piece in his palm.*] There now—you're holding him gently! Hold him over the light, he loves the light! You see how the light shines through him?

JIM: It sure does shine!

LAURA: I shouldn't be partial, but he is my favorite one.

JIM: What kind of a thing is this one supposed to be?

LAURA: Haven't you noticed the single horn on his forehead?

JIM: A unicorn, huh?

LAURA: Mmmm-hmmm!

JIM: Unicorns—aren't they extinct in the modern world?

LAURA: I know!

JIM: Poor little fellow, he must feel sort of lonesome.

LAURA [*smiling*]: Well, if he does, he doesn't complain about it. He stays on a shelf with some horses that don't have horns and all of them seem to get along nicely together.

JIM: How do you know?

LAURA [*lightly*]: I haven't heard any arguments among them!

JIM [*grinning*]: No arguments, huh? Well, that's a pretty good sign! Where shall I set him?

LAURA: Put him on the table. They all like a change of scenery once in a while!

JIM: Well, well, well, well— [*He places the glass piece on the table, then raises his arms and stretches.*] Look how big my shadow is when I stretch!

LAURA: Oh, oh, yes—it stretches across the ceiling!

JIM [*crossing to the door*]: I think it's stopped raining. [*He opens the fire-escape door and the background music changes to a dance tune.*] Where does the music come from?

LAURA: From the Paradise Dance Hall across the alley.

JIM: How about cutting the rug a little, Miss Wingfield?

LAURA: Oh, I—

JIM: Or is your program filled up? Let me have a look at it. [*He grasps an imaginary card.*] Why, every dance is taken! I'll just have to scratch some out.

[*Waltz music:* "La Golondrina."]

Ahhh, a waltz! [*He executes some sweeping turns by himself, then holds his arms toward* LAURA.]

LAURA [*breathlessly*]: I—can't dance!

JIM: There you go, that inferiority stuff!

LAURA: I've never danced in my life!

JIM: Come on, try!

LAURA: Oh, but I'd step on you!

JIM: I'm not made out of glass.

LAURA: How—how—how do we start?

JIM: Just leave it to me. You hold your arms out a little.

LAURA: Like this?

JIM [*taking her in his arms*]: A little bit higher. Right. Now don't tighten up, that's the main thing about it—relax.

LAURA [*laughing breathlessly*]: It's hard not to.

JIM: Okay.

LAURA: I'm afraid you can't budge me.

JIM: What do you bet I can't? [*He swings her into motion.*]

LAURA: Goodness, yes, you can!

JIM: Let yourself go, now, Laura, just let yourself go.

LAURA: I'm—

JIM: Come on!

LAURA: —trying!

JIM: Not so stiff—easy does it!

LAURA: I know but I'm—

JIM: Loosen th' backbone! There now, that's a lot better.

LAURA: Am I?

JIM: Lots, lots better! [*He moves her about the room in a clumsy waltz.*]

LAURA: Oh, my!

JIM: Ha-ha!
LAURA: Oh, my goodness!
JIM: Ha-ha-ha!

[*They suddenly bump into the table, and the glass piece on it falls to the floor.* JIM *stops the dance.*]

What did we hit on?
LAURA: Table.
JIM: Did something fall off it? I think—
LAURA: Yes.
JIM: I hope that it wasn't the little glass horse with the horn!
LAURA: Yes. [*She stoops to pick it up.*]
JIM: Aw, aw, aw. Is it broken?
LAURA: Now it is just like all the other horses.
JIM: It's lost its—
LAURA: Horn! It doesn't matter. Maybe it's a blessing in disguise.
JIM: You'll never forgive me. I bet that that was your favorite piece of glass.
LAURA: I don't have favorites much. It's no tragedy, Freckles. Glass breaks so easily. No matter how careful you are. The traffic jars the shelves and things fall off them.
JIM: Still I'm awfully sorry that I was the cause.
LAURA [*smiling*]: I'll just imagine he had an operation. The horn was removed to make him feel less—freakish!

[*They both laugh.*]

Now he will feel more at home with the other horses, the ones that don't have horns. . . .
JIM: Ha-ha, that's very funny! [*Suddenly he is serious.*] I'm glad to see that you have a sense of humor. You know—you're—well—very different! Surprisingly different from anyone else I know! [*His voice becomes soft and hesitant with a genuine feeling.*] Do you mind me telling you that?

[LAURA *is abashed beyond speech.*]

I mean it in a nice way—

[LAURA *nods shyly, looking away.*]

You make me feel sort of—I don't know how to put it! I'm usually pretty good at expressing things, but—this is something that I don't know how to say!

[LAURA *touches her throat and clears it—turns the broken unicorn in her hands. His voice becomes softer.*]

Has anyone ever told you that you were pretty?

[*There is a pause, and the music rises slightly.* LAURA *looks up slowly, with wonder, and shakes her head.*]

Well, you are! In a very different way from anyone else. And all the nicer because of the difference, too.

[*His voice becomes low and husky.* LAURA *turns away, nearly faint with the novelty of her emotions.*]

I wish that you were my sister. I'd teach you to have some confidence in yourself. The different people are not like other people, but being different is nothing to be ashamed of. Because other people are not such wonderful people. They're one hundred times one thousand. You're one times one! They walk all over the earth. You just stay here. They're common as—weeds, but—you—well, you're—*Blue Roses!*

[*Image on screen:* Blue Roses.]

[*The music changes.*]

LAURA: But blue is wrong for—roses. . . .
JIM: It's right for you! You're—pretty!
LAURA: In what respect am I pretty?
JIM: In all respects—believe me! Your eyes—your hair—are pretty! Your hands are pretty! [*He catches hold of her hand.*] You think I'm making this up because I'm invited to dinner and have to be nice. Oh, I could do that! I could put on an act for you, Laura, and say lots of things without being very sincere. But this time I am. I'm talking to you sincerely. I happened to notice you had this inferiority complex that keeps you from feeling comfortable with people. Somebody needs to build your confidence up and make you proud instead of shy and turning away and—blushing. Somebody—ought to—*kiss* you, Laura!

[*His hand slips slowly up her arm to her shoulder as the music swells tumultuously. He suddenly turns her about and kisses her on the lips. When he releases her,* LAURA *sinks on the sofa with a bright, dazed look.* JIM *backs away and fishes in his pocket for a cigarette.*]

[*Legend on screen:* "A souvenir."]

Stumblejohn!

[*He lights the cigarette, avoiding her look. There is a peal of girlish laughter from* AMANDA *in the kitchenette.*

LAURA *slowly raises and opens her hand. It still contains the little broken glass animal. She looks at it with a tender, bewildered expression.*]

Stumblejohn! I shouldn't have done that—that was way off the beam. You don't smoke, do you?

[*She looks up, smiling, not hearing the question. He sits beside her rather gingerly. She looks as him speechlessly—waiting. He coughs decorously and moves a little farther aside as he considers the situation and senses her feelings, dimly, with perturbation. He speak gently.*]

Would you—care for a—mint?

[*She doesn't seem to hear him but her look grows brighter even.*]

Peppermint? Life Saver? My pocket's a regular drugstore—wherever I go. . . . [*He pops a mint in his mouth. Then he gulps and decides to make a clean breast of it. He speaks slowly and gingerly.*] Laura, you know, if I had a sister like you, I'd do the same thing as Tom. I'd bring out fellows and—introduce her to them. The right type of boys—of a type to—appreciate her. Only—well—he made a mistake about me. Maybe I've got no call to be saying this. That may not have been the idea in having me over. But what if it was? There's nothing wrong about that. The only trouble is that in my case—I'm not in a situation to—do the right thing. I can't take down your number and say I'll phone. I can't call up next week and—ask for a date. I thought I had better explain the situation in case you—misunderstood it and—I hurt your feelings. . . .

[*There is a pause. Slowly, very slowly,* LAURA*'s look changes, her eyes returning slowly from his to the glass figure in her palm.* AMANDA *utters another gay laugh in the kitchenette.*]

LAURA [*faintly*]: You—won't—call again?
JIM: No, Laura, I can't. [*He rises from the sofa.*] As I was just explaining, I've—got strings on me. Laura, I've—been going steady! I go out all the time with a girl named Betty. She's a home-girl like you, and Catholic, and Irish, and in a great many ways we—get along fine. I met her last summer on a moonlight boat trip up the river to Alton, on the *Majestic*. Well—right away from the start it was—love!

[*Legend:* Love!]

[LAURA *sways slightly forward and grips the arm of the sofa. He fails to notice, now enrapt in his own comfortable being.*]

Being in love has made a new man of me!

[*Leaning stiffly forward, clutching the arm of the sofa,* LAURA *struggles visibly with her storm. But* JIM *is oblivious; she is a long way off.*]

The power of love is really pretty tremendous! Love is something that—changes the whole world, Laura!

[*The storm abates a little and* LAURA *leans back. He notices her again.*]

It happened that Betty's aunt took sick, she got a wire and had to go to Centralia. So Tom—when he asked me to dinner—I naturally just accepted the invitation, not knowing that you—that he—that I— [*He stops awkwardly.*] Huh—I'm a stumblejohn!

[*He flops back on the sofa. The holy candles on the altar of* LAURA*'s face have been snuffed out. There is a look of almost infinite desolation.* JIM *glances at her uneasily.*]

I wish that you would—say something.

[*She bites her lip which was trembling and then bravely smiles. She opens her hand again on the broken glass figure. Then she gently takes his hand and raises it level with her own. She carefully places the unicorn in the palm of his hand, then pushes his finger closed upon it.*]

What are you—doing that for? You want me to have him? Laura?

[*She nods.*]

What for?
LAURA: A—souvenir. . . .

[*She rises unsteadily and crouches beside the Victrola to wind it up.*]

[*Legend on screen*: "Things have a way of turning out so badly!" *Or image:* "Gentleman caller waving good-bye—gaily."]

[*At this moment* AMANDA *rushes brightly back into the living room. She bears a pitcher of fruit punch in an old-fashioned cut-glass pitcher, and a plate of macaroons. The plate has a gold border and poppies painted on it.*]

AMANDA: Well, well, well! Isn't the air delightful after the shower? I've made you children a little liquid refreshment.

[*She turns gaily to* JIM.] Jim, do you know that song about lemonade?

"Lemonade, lemonade
Made in the shade and stirred with a spade—
Good enough for any old maid!"

JIM [*uneasily*]: Ha-ha! No—I never heard it.

AMANDA: Why, Laura! You look so serious!

JIM: We were having a serious conversation.

AMANDA: Good! Now you're better acquainted!

JIM [*uncertainly*]: Ha-ha! Yes.

AMANDA: You modern young people are much more serious-minded than my generation. I was so gay as a girl!

JIM: You haven't changed, Mrs. Wingfield.

AMANDA: Tonight I'm rejuvenated! The gaiety of the occasion, Mr. O'Connor! [*She tosses her head with a peal of laughter, spilling some lemonade.*] Oooo! I'm baptizing myself!

JIM: Here—let me—

AMANDA [*setting the pitcher down*]: There now. I discovered we had some maraschino cherries. I dumped them in, juice and all!

JIM: You shouldn't have gone to that trouble, Mrs. Wingfield.

AMANDA: Trouble, trouble? Why, it was loads of fun! Didn't you hear me cutting up in the kitchen? I bet your ears were burning! I told Tom how outdone with him I was for keeping you to himself so long a time! He should have brought you over much, much sooner! Well, now that you've found your way, I want you to be a very frequent caller! Not just occasional but all the time. Oh, we're going to have a lot of gay times together! I see them coming! Mmm, just breathe that air! So fresh, and the moon's so pretty! I'll skip back out—I know where my place is when young folks are having a—serious conversation!

JIM: Oh, don't go out, Mrs. Wingfield. The fact of the matter is I've got to be going.

AMANDA: Going, now? You're joking! Why, it's only the shank of the evening, Mr. O'Connor!

JIM: Well, you know how it is.

AMANDA: You mean you're a young workingman and have to keep workingmen's hours. We'll let you off early tonight. But only on the condition that next time you stay later. What's the best night for you? Isn't Saturday night the best night for you workingmen?

JIM: I have a couple of time-clocks to punch, Mrs. Wingfield. One at morning, another one at night!

AMANDA: My, but you *are* ambitious! You work at night, too?

JIM: No, Ma'am, not work but—Betty!

[*He crosses deliberately to pick up his hat. The band at the Paradise Dance Hall goes into a tender waltz.*]

AMANDA: Betty? Betty? Who's—Betty?

[*There is an ominous cracking sound in the sky.*]

JIM: Oh, just a girl. The girl I go steady with!

[*He smiles charmingly. The sky falls.*]

[*Legend*: "The Sky Falls."]

AMANDA [*a long-drawn exhalation*]: Ohhhh . . . Is it a serious romance, Mr. O'Connor?

JIM: We're going to be married the second Sunday in June.

AMANDA: Ohhhh—how nice! Tom didn't mention that you were engaged to be married.

JIM: The cat's not out of the bag at the warehouse yet. You know how they are. They call you Romeo and stuff like that. [*He stops at the oval mirror to put on his hat. He carefully shapes the brim and the crown to give a discreetly dashing effect.*] It's been a wonderful evening, Mrs. Wingfield. I guess this is what they mean by Southern hospitality.

AMANDA: It really wasn't anything at all.

JIM: I hope it don't seem like I'm rushing off. But I promised Betty I'd pick her up at the Wabash depot, an' by the time I get my jalopy down there her train'll be in. Some women are pretty upset if you keep 'em waiting.

AMANDA: Yes, I know—the tyranny of women! [*She extends her hand.*] Goodbye, Mr. O'Connor. I wish you luck—and happiness—and success! All three of them, and so does Laura! Don't you, Laura?

LAURA: Yes!

JIM [*taking* LAURA'*s hand*]: Goodbye, Laura. I'm certainly going to treasure that souvenir. And don't you forget the good advice I gave you. [*He raises his voice to a cheery shout.*] So long, Shakespeare! Thanks again, ladies. Good night!

[*He grins and ducks jauntily out. Still bravely grimacing,* AMANDA *closes the door on the gentleman caller. Then she turns back to the room with a puzzled expression. She and* LAURA *don't dare to face each other.* LAURA *crouches beside the Victrola to wind it.*]

AMANDA [*faintly*]: Things have a way of turning out so badly. I don't believe that I would play the Victrola. Well, well—well! Our gentleman caller was engaged to be married! [*She raises her voice.*] Tom!

TOM [*from the kitchenette*]: Yes, Mother?

AMANDA: Come in here a minute. I want to tell you something awfully funny.

TOM [*entering with a macaroon and a glass of the lemonade*]: Has the gentleman caller gotten away already?

AMANDA: The gentleman caller has made an early departure. What a wonderful joke you played on us!

TOM: How do you mean?

AMANDA: You didn't mention that he was engaged to be married.

TOM: Jim? Engaged?

AMANDA: That's what he just informed us.

TOM: I'll be jiggered! I didn't know about that.

AMANDA: That seems very peculiar.

TOM: What's peculiar about it?

AMANDA: Didn't you call him your best friend down at the warehouse?

TOM: He is, but how did I know?

AMANDA: It seems extremely peculiar that you wouldn't know your best friend was going to be married!

TOM: The warehouse is where I work, not where I know things about people!

AMANDA: You don't know things anywhere! You live in a dream; you manufacture illusions!

[*He crosses to the door.*]

Where are you going?

TOM: I'm going to the movies.

AMANDA: That's right, now that you've had us make such fools of ourselves. The effort, the preparations, all the expense! The new floor lamp, the rug, the clothes for Laura! All for what? To entertain some other girl's fiancé! Go to the movies, go! Don't think about us, a mother deserted, an unmarried sister who's crippled and has no job! Don't let anything interfere with your selfish pleasure! Just go, go, go—to the movies!

TOM: All right, I will! The more you shout about my selfishness to me the quicker I'll go, and I won't go to the movies!

AMANDA: Go, then! Go to the moon—you selfish dreamer!

[TOM *smashes his glass on the floor. He plunges out on the fire-escape, slamming the door.* LAURA *screams in fright. The dance-hall music becomes louder.* TOM *stands on the fire escape, gripping the rail. The moon breaks through the storm clouds, illuminating his face.*]

[*Legend on screen:* "And so goodbye . . . "]

[TOM*'s closing speech is timed with what is happening inside the house. We see, as though through soundproof glass, that* AMANDA *appears to be making a comforting speech to* LAURA, *who is huddled upon the sofa. Now that we cannot hear the mother's speech, her silliness is gone and she has dignity and tragic beauty.* LAURA*'s hair hides her face until, at the end of the speech, she lifts her head to smile at her mother.* AMANDA*'s gestures are slow and graceful, almost dancelike, as she comforts her daughter. At the end of her speech she glances a moment at the father's picture—then withdraws through the portieres. At the close of* TOM*'s speech,* LAURA *blows out the candles, ending the play.*]

TOM: I didn't go to the moon, I went much further—for time is the longest distance between two places. Not long after that I was fired for writing a poem on the lid of a shoe-box. I left Saint Louis. I descended the steps of this fire escape for a last time and followed, from then on, in my father's footsteps, attempting to find in motion what was lost in space. I traveled around a great deal. The cities swept about me like dead leaves, leaves that were brightly colored but torn away from the branches. I would have stopped, but I was pursued by something. It always came upon me unawares, taking me altogether by surprise. Perhaps it was a familiar bit of music. Perhaps it was only a piece of transparent glass. Perhaps I am walking along a street at night, in some strange city, before I have found companions. I pass the lighted window of a shop where perfume is sold. The window is filled with pieces of colored glass, tiny transparent bottles in delicate colors, like bits of a shattered rainbow. Then all at once my sister touches my shoulder. I turn around and look into her eyes. Oh, Laura, Laura, I tried to leave you behind me, but I am more faithful than I intended to be! I reach for a cigarette, I cross the street, I run into the movies or a bar, I buy a drink, I speak to the nearest stranger —anything that can blow your candles out!

[LAURA *bends over the candles.*]

For nowadays the world is lit by lightning! Blow out your candles, Laura—and so goodbye. . . .

[*She blows the candles out.*]

Arthur Miller

Arthur Asher Miller (1915) was born and raised in New York City, where his family enjoyed middle-class comfort. His father, Isidore, barely literate, immigrated from Poland at the age of twelve but became the owner of a successful coat and suit manufacturing business. This business collapsed during the Great Depression (1929–1939), and the family's economic circumstances were much reduced. Miller's mother, Augusta, was sympathetic and intelligent, but Miller has suggested that she was weak and burdened by the weight of her marriage, especially when the family's fortunes turned. He seems to have had ambivalent feelings about Augusta and, in many plays, portrays wives and mothers as compliant characters. Miller's older brother, Kermit, who was handsome and seemingly more talented than Arthur, was the object of some sibling rivalry, a theme that appears in much of Miller's work.

Miller was raised as an orthodox Jew, but eventually abandoned his faith. The influence of his religious training did provide him with a deep sense of the dilemmas involved in making moral choices. Like Bertolt Brecht, Miller views playwriting as a social and ethical mission; he has said that in all of his plays he tries "to involve questions of right and wrong." Unlike Brecht, however, Miller was never a propagandist for Marxist or socialist idealogy. Briefly attracted in his twenties to socialism as a viable means of alleviating economic inequalities, Miller was soon disillusioned and rejected these early beliefs. Miller was, however, deeply affected by the social and economic adversity caused by the Great Depression, the rise of fascism, and political demagoguery in Europe and the United States.

Before he enrolled at the University of Michigan in 1934, Miller worked at various low-level jobs, which gave him an enduring sense of blue-collar life. At Michigan, he intended to study journalism, but he distinguished himself by writing plays, several of which won scholarship awards. After college, Miller dedicated himself to professional writing, working for the Federal Theater Project, and later, writing scripts for major radio networks. His radio work paid well, but he continued to write for the theater without much success. His chief inspiration during this period came from Henrik Ibsen, the social moralist, and Clifford Odets (1906–1963), who, he said, gave him a strong sense of how proletarian social drama might become a powerful force in his own vision of theater. Before Miller found his own voice, the major work of his early period was a historical play about the Spanish conquest of Mexico and the contest between Hernando Cortez and Montezuma, which was never produced. Miller seems also to have been impressed by Thornton Wilder, first through the production of Wilder's version of Ibsen's *A Doll's House* as produced by Jed Harris for the Group Theatre. Wilder's *Our Town* might have reinforced Miller's idea of the fluidity of time, which he later called "timebending."

In 1940 Miller married Mary Grace Slattery, with whom he had lived since leaving Michigan. Though Miller was a lapsed Jew and she a lapsed Catholic, both families disapproved of the marriage. The marriage endured for a time, but its stability diminished as Miller's success as a playwright increased, and they were divorced in 1956. At twenty-nine, Miller published the book *Situation Normal* (1944), a work of nonfiction on life in army camps during World War II. The same year, he produced the play *The Man Who Had All the Luck,* a story about David Beeves, who fears failure and feels guilty about success. David survives his loses, but his brother fails to overcome the well-meaning attention of his father. Both works were unsuccessful. Even after it had closed, however, *The Man Who Had All the Luck* was cited by the Theater Guild, and Miller was noted as a promising playwright. A year later he published the novel *Focus,* whose protagonist, Lawrence Newman, suffers anti-Semitic attacks in New York City because he looks Jewish, when in fact he is not.

All My Sons (1947), Miller's first successful play, is a problem play using profiteering during World War II to reveal the price of maintaining moral integrity and the cost of losing it. The play was immediately recognized and criticized as being "Ibsenesque," which Miller accepted with good graces because he had found his dramatic voice—realism. Miller was thirty-four when *Death of a Salesman* (1949) won the Pulitzer Prize for Drama.

Like *All My Sons*, *Death of a Salesman* is a problem play dealing with the ruthlessness of modern business and the American's preoccupation with material success at the expense of personal dignity. The Loman family is Miller's vision of the American family in the grip of unfulfilled dreams and constant demand for money. At sixty, Willy Loman's productive working life is ending and with it his life as a man. Linda, his devoted wife, looks on lovingly, just making sure the bills are paid. Their grown sons, Biff and Happy, are failures wracked by sibling rivalry. Willy kills himself under the delusion that his insurance money will make his family happy, but his dream is unfulfilled. The sons bicker at Willy's grave, and Linda, uncomprehending and in a state of emotional lethargy, addresses Willy as if he were alive, reminding him that the mortgage has been paid and they are now "free." Miller has long contended that Willy's ability to face his failures and take action raises him above his ordinary life and makes him a "modern" tragic hero. This has been a contentious question of sustained critical debate since 1949.

Miller's next work, an homage to Ibsen, was an adaptation of *An Enemy of the People* (1950). Its subject is what happens to an ethical though somewhat muddleheaded man when he is faced with a moral dilemma of calling to account a town that is the site of a lucrative spa he discovers is a health hazard. Miller's depiction of Dr. Stockmann seems a stand-in for himself as a playwright whose goal is to tell the truth with no regard for public approbation. Miller wrote, "It is the question of whether one's vision of the truth ought to be a source of guilt at a time when the mass of men condemn it as a dangerous and devilish lie."

The Crucible (1953) is based on the historical record of the Salem, Massachusetts, witch trials of 1642. Miller acknowledges that he used the history detailed by Marion Starkey in her study, *The Devil in Massachusetts* (1950), as his chief resource. In *Timebends* (1987), his autobiography, Miller writes, "Over weeks, a living connection [developed] between myself and Salem, and between Salem and Washington. . . . for whatever else they might be, I saw that the hearings in Washington were profoundly ritualistic. . . . the Salem prosecution was actually on more solid legal ground since the defendant, if guilty of familiarity with the Unclean One, had broken a law against the practice of witchcraft, a civil and religious offense; whereas the offender against HUAC could not be accused of any such violation but only of a spiritual crime, subservience to a political enemy's desires and ideology."

During this period of political turmoil, Miller also wrote two one-act plays, *Memory of Two Mondays* (1955), which recalls the time he worked in a warehouse, and *A View from the Bridge* (1955), about a Brooklyn longshoreman whose love for his niece results in unintended catastrophe. The original version of *A View from the Bridge* is particularly noteworthy because it is modeled on Greek tragedy, although Miller later revised it more conventionally. It is a cautionary tale of what happens when a man sacrifices his honor and moral integrity, just as Miller was refusing to do before the House of Representatives Un-American Activities Committee. In the play, Eddie Carbone, the protagonist, betrays Rudolpho and Marco, both illegal aliens, to the immigration authority. When his guilt is exposed in full view of the neighborhood, Eddie shouts at Marco, "Wipin' the neighborhood with my name like a dirty rag! I want my name, Marco." But it is too late for Eddie: the shame of his action is indelible. As a personal statement, Miller makes it clear that he will neither betray his friends nor be willing to lose his name. The action is narrated by a lawyer, Alfieri, who recalls the choragus of the chorus in Greek tragedy and the Stage Manager of Wilder's *Our Town*.

For nine years, during his divorce from Mary Grace Slattery and his marriage to Marilyn Monroe, which lasted from 1956 to 1961, Miller produced no plays for the theater. He began a new surge of creativity when he began a relationship with Inge Morath, an Austrian photographer, whom he married in 1962. Ironically, Miller met Morath when she was photographing on the set of *The Misfits*, a film with a screenplay by Miller and staring Monroe. His divorce from Monroe and its aftermath provided Miller with the story for his most autobiographical play, *After the Fall* (1964). Miller argued that his characters in *After the Fall* are literary creations, but they match the facts of his life. Through the character of Quentin, a lawyer, Miller chronicles the trials of a man and the three loves of his life: his failed first marriage to Louise (Mary Grace Slattery), his second disastrous marriage to Maggie (Marilyn Monroe), and his romance with Helga (Inga Morath).

Incident at Vichy (1964) is an examination of the oppression of the Jews in France during the Vichy Republic, whose authorities collaborated with the Nazis from 1940 to 1945. The action centers on an Austrian nobleman's altruistic gesture of giving his passport to a Jewish psychoanalyst. *The Price* (1968)) contrasts the lives of the Franz brothers, who have chosen different paths in response to their father's needs. Victor has become a policeman in order to help out the family; Walter has gone to college and become a wealthy surgeon. The brothers meet to sort out the family furniture and possessions after the death of the parents, renew their sibling rivalry, and learn that Victor cannot change the stern logic of Walter's belief that our lives are guided by illusion and denial. *The Creation of the*

World and Other Business (1972) retells the story of Adam and Eve, their expulsion from Paradise, and their son Cain's murder of his brother Abel.

The Archbishop's Ceiling (1977) examines the problem of writers' integrity and ethical conduct while living under a repressive political regime in Eastern Europe before the fall of Communism. The title refers to a hidden listening device used to detect subversive behavior in an apartment that once belonged to an archbishop. *The American Clock: A Vaudeville* (1984) is a series of vignettes portraying the experience of an American Jewish family, based in part on Studs Terkel's *Hard Times* (1970), a collection of interviews with people about their experience during the Depression years.

In his eighties, Miller's creativity was invigorated, and he continues to explore the topics that have most intrigued him. *Some Kind of Love Story* (1990) is a murder mystery in which the investigator falls for a woman who is a fantasist. Miller's only comedy *The Ride Down Mount Morgan* (1991), satirizes Lyman, a man with two wives; one is proper, restrained, and middle-aged, the other young, sexy, and passionate. *Broken Glass* (1993) explores the ethical consequences of the Holocaust for American and American-Jewish families. Along with *After the Fall* and *Incident at Vichy, Broken Glass* completes a trilogy of plays dealing with fate, the elusiveness of ethical conduct, and the Jewish experience in the twentieth century. *The Last Yankee* (1993) contrasts two married couples, one working class and the other white collar, who meet in a mental hospital where the wives are trying to piece their lives together. Miller calls this play a comedy about tragedy, arising out of "the absurdity of people constantly comparing themselves to others." The full-length *Mr. Peter's Connections* (1998) is a kind of memory play, "comedic in spirit" but not in substance, about a retired airline pilot, sitting in an unused nightclub, musing about people in his life, especially the women he has known.

Miller's critical writing, collected in *The Theater Essays of Arthur Miller* (1971, rev. 1995), is important for understanding Miller's creative and philosophical endeavors. "Tragedy and the Common Man," "The American Theater," "On Social Plays," "The Family in Modern Drama," "About Theater Language," and "Ibsen and the Modern Drama" are perhaps Miller's most important essays, constituting what many critics believe to be the most important commentary on American drama in the twentieth century.

Miller has had only a small interest in film, having written only four screenplays: *The Misfits* (1961), *Playing for Time* (made for television, 1961), *Everybody Wins* (1990), and his adaptation of *The Crucible* (1996). In addition to the novel *Focus,* Miller also published a collection of short stories, *I Don't Need You Anymore* (1967), and the novel *Homely Girl* (1992), the story of a murdered daughter seen as a young girl and as a young woman.

All My Sons (1947), Miller's first successful play, took two years to write and premiered when he was thirty-two. Miller later called the play Greco-Ibsen in style for two reasons: First, because it keeps the tradition of the classical unities of time (the action is completed in a single day—morning, evening, and early morning), place (there is a single unified setting of the house and its garden), and action (events lead to the inexorable revelation of the truth); and second, because *All My Sons* is a problem play that Miller said concentrates on "hard actions, irrevocable deeds" that lead logically to a crisis in which "sentiment is never confused with the action it conceals." In the "Introduction" to the *Collected Plays,* Miller wrote, "I wanted then to write so that people of common sense would mistake my play for life itself and not be required to lend it some poetic license before it could be believed. I wanted to make the moral world as real and evident as the immoral one so splendidly is."

The idea of *All My Sons* came from an anecdote Miller overheard about a family that was destroyed when a daughter turned her father in to the authorities for selling faulty machinery to the army. Using this story as a prompt, Miller devised a story that embodies his primary dramatic themes: the inability to tell right from wrong, father-son conflict, the Depression, the American Dream, sibling rivalry, and consequences of the Fall. The central figure is Joe Keller, a man of sixty-one, who knowingly sold defective airplane engines to the military during World War II that caused the crash of twenty-one planes. Though uneducated, Keller was motivated by the American Dream and has become a model American businessman. But when his moral resolve is tested, Keller's ego and love prove too weak, and he is ruined. "You lay forty years into a business," Joe says, "and they knock you out in five minutes, what could I do, let them take forty years, let them take my life away?" So Joe lies to his family and evades responsibility for his actions, allowing his business partner, Deever, to go to jail for a crime of which he, too, is guilty.

The Keller family is the prototype of the many families Miller creates who suffer the dilemmas brought on by the competing forces of self-awareness and stubborn reality. The members of the family suffer the painful revelation of hidden truth. Everyone knows a portion of the truth, though it is not fully revealed to all until the climax (as is expected in a well-made play). Then it is clear that Keller cravenly let Deever take the fall; he has lied to the family and himself; Kate admits Larry is dead; and Ann (Larry's fiancée, who now loves Chris) learns that the townspeople have always known Keller's guilt but have never spoken it aloud.

The setting, Keller's home and yard in "an American town," is perhaps a sly reference to Thornton Wilder's Grover's Corners in *Our Town* (1938). But if Wilder's town has an elegiac quality and its dead are laid to rest with an aura of serious sentimentality, Miller's town (somewhere in Ohio or Michigan) is rife with the consequences of bad deeds.

Act I begins on a beautiful Sunday morning in August 1946 or '47 after a tempestuous wind has toppled an apple tree (a tree planted to commemorate Larry). Its presence and the wreck it has caused remain visible throughout the act as a silent testament to the play's theme and action. It is a reminder of the war that cannot be evaded, since both Keller and Kate favor Larry, and Kate is zealously guarding her unrealistic dreams that Larry is alive, although he has been missing in action for three years. She willfully holds onto this belief even when it means damaging Chris's chance of happiness with Ann, whom Chris wants to marry. Kate, referred to as Mother in the script, is the first of Miller's long-suffering wives, guarding the truth when it ought to be revealed. Miller describes her as being subject to "uncontrolled inspirations," which may be interpreted as a euphemism for "the capacity for lying, and an overwhelming capacity for love."

Act II begins as Chris removes the dead tree, which signifies the process of clearing the way for the truth of Keller's guilt to emerge. George Deever, Ann's brother, now a lawyer, arrives believing that Keller is guilty of selling the faulty engines. His anger leads Kate to blurt out to Chris that Larry is alive, "because if he's dead, your father killed him." This sets the stage for the son to confront the father:

> CHRIS: Then why didn't you tell them?
> KELLER: It was too late. . . . Chris . . . Chris, I did it for you, it was a chance and I took it for you. I'm sixty-one years old, when would I have another chance to make something for you? Sixty-one years old you don't get another chance, do ya? . . .
> CHRIS: What the hell do you mean, you did it for me? Don't you have a country? Don't you live in the world? What the hell are you?

Despairing for a satisfactory response to the revelation and recognizing the truth, Chris runs off.

Act III finds Kate waiting for Chris to return home in the early morning. Jim Bayliss, the cynical but honest doctor who lives in the "usual darkness" of an unhappy marriage, says to Kate that Chris is such a moralist he doesn't know how to lie like the rest of them. It takes a certain talent, he says. Then saying aloud that he knows the truth about Keller, Kate admits the lie. When Keller appears, he asks Kate, "What am I, a stranger? I thought I had a family here. What happened to my family?" Kate responds by saying that there's something bigger than family, to which Keller says, "If there's something bigger than that I'll put a bullet in my head." Ann now reveals her secret, that she has always known that Larry killed himself. She produces a letter in which Larry acknowledges Keller's dastardly act and his own impending suicide. Chris returns saying that he is no longer the stern moralist. Claiming that he is practical now, he shouts that the world is gone mad: "This is a zoo, a zoo!"

Keller, gruff to the end, says, "What's clean? Half the Goddamn country is gotta go if I go!" At this point, Chris reads Larry's letter aloud, and Keller, crushed, holds it in his hand. In a moment of recognition, he says, "Sure, he was my son. But I think to him they were all my sons. And I guess they were, I guess they were." Kate, who still doesn't understand the fullness of the moment, says to Chris, "The war is over! Didn't you hear?—it's over!" But Chris, once again the stern moralist, says to Keller, "You can be better! Once and for all you can know there's a universe of people outside and you're responsible to it, and unless you know that you threw away your son because that's why he died." Keller meanwhile runs into the house and, having realized that there is something bigger than business, wife, sons, and family, he shoots himself. Chris runs into the house, and Ann runs up the driveway. Then Chris comes out of the house stunned; he holds Kate, but she lets go and stands on the porch alone saying, "Shhh."

All My Sons is a typical example of Miller's tendency to examine characters as they work their way through conflict "in real life," in contrast to the Absurdist playwrights, who he says create cartoons, not characters. Miller admires Samuel Beckett because of his steadfast attempt to project a meaningless world without pity. But as heir to the European styles of realism and naturalism, particularly the plays of Henrik Ibsen, Miller also believes that social drama is the ongoing heart of the theater and that Beckett's antisocial drama will be less enduring.

Themes that Miller has steadfastly explored over his career include the corrupting influence of money, the conflict between private and public responsibility, and the power of guilt. Miller's plays are distinctly American, and he follows the pattern of using American characters and places for his plays. In turn, Miller's influence radiates in the plays of Peter Shaefer, Edward Albee, John Osborne, Tom Stoppard, Sam Shepard, and David Mamet. After O'Neill, Miller and Tennessee Williams are generally acclaimed as the major playwrights of the United States in the twentieth century.

Film

All My Sons (1948), directed by Irving Reis, with Edward G. Robinson, Burt Lancaster, Mady Christians, Louisa Horton, and Howard Duff. Universal (and Universal International).

All My Sons (1986), directed by John Power, with James Whitmore, Aidan Quinn, Joan Allen, and Michael Learned. (A production adapted for television.)

All My Sons

CHARACTERS

JOE KELLER, a factory owner
KATE KELLER, his wife
CHRIS KELLER, their son
ANN DEEVER, their house-guest
GEORGE DEEVER, her brother
DR. JIM BAYLISS, friend of the Kellers
SUE BAYLISS, his wife
FRANK LUBEY, LYDIA LUBEY } the KELLERS' next-door neighbors
BERT, a neighborhood eight-year-old

SYNOPSIS OF SCENES

ACT I The back yard of the KELLER home in the outskirts of an American town. August of our era.
ACT II Scene, as before. The same evening, as twilight falls.
ACT III Scene, as before. Two o'clock the following morning.

ACT I

The back yard of the KELLER *home in the outskirts of an American town. August of our era.*

The stage is hedged on right and left by tall, closely planted poplars which lend the yard a secluded atmosphere. Upstage is filled with the back of the house and its open, unroofed porch which extends into the yard some six feet. The house is two stories high and has seven rooms. It would have cost perhaps fifteen thousand in the early twenties when it was built. Now it is nicely painted, looks tight and comfortable, and the yard is green with sod, here and there plants whose season is gone. At the right, beside the house, the entrance of the driveway can be seen, but the poplars cut off view of its continuation downstage. In the left corner, downstage, stands the four-foot high stump of a slender apple tree whose upper trunk and branches lie toppled beside it, fruit still clinging to its branches.

Downstage right is a small, trellised arbor, shaped like a seashell, with a decorative bulb hanging from its forward-curving roof. Garden chairs and a table are scattered about. A garbage pail on the ground next to the porch steps, a wire leaf-burner near it.

ON THE RISE: *It is early Sunday morning.* JOE KELLER *is sitting in the sun reading the want ads of the Sunday paper, the other sections of which lie neatly on the ground beside him. Behind his back, inside the arbor,* DOCTOR JIM BAYLISS *is reading part of the paper at the table.*

KELLER *is nearing sixty. A heavy man of stolid mind and build, a business man these many years, but with the imprint of the machine-shop worker and boss still upon him. When he reads, when he speaks, when he listens, it is with the terrible concentration of the uneducated man for whom there is still wonder in many commonly known things, a man whose judgments must be dredged out of experience and a peasant-like common sense. A man among men.*

DOCTOR BAYLISS *is nearing forty. A wry self-controlled man, an easy talker, but with a wisp of sadness that clings even to his self-effacing humor.*

AT CURTAIN, JIM *is standing at left, staring at the broken tree. He taps a pipe on it, blows through the pipe, feels in his pockets for tobacco, then speaks.*

JIM: Where's your tobacco?

KELLER: I think I left it on the table. [JIM *goes slowly to table on the arbor at right, finds a pouch, and sits there on the bench, filling his pipe.*] Gonna rain tonight.

JIM: Paper says so?

KELLER: Yeah, right here.

JIM: Then it can't rain.

[FRANK LUBEY *enters, from right, through a small space between the poplars.* FRANK *is thirty-two but balding. A pleasant, opinionated man, uncertain of himself, with a tendency toward peevishness when crossed, but always wanting it pleasant and neighborly. He rather saunters in, leisurely, nothing to do. He does not notice* JIM *in the arbor. On his greeting,* JIM *does not bother looking up.*]

FRANK: Hya.

KELLER: Hello, Frank. What's doin'?

FRANK: Nothin'. Walking off my breakfast. [*Looks up at the sky.*] That beautiful? Not a cloud.

KELLER [*looks up*]: Yeah, nice.

FRANK: Every Sunday ought to be like this.

KELLER [*indicating the sections beside him*]: Want the paper?

FRANK: What's the difference, it's all bad news. What's today's calamity?

KELLER: I don't know, I don't read the news part any more. It's more interesting in the want ads.

FRANK: Why, you trying to buy something?

KELLER: No, I'm just interested. To see what people want, y'know? For instance, here's a guy is lookin' for two Newfoundland dogs. Now what's he want with two Newfoundland dogs?

FRANK: That is funny.

KELLER: Here's another one. Wanted—Old Dictionaries. High prices paid. Now what's a man going to do with an old dictionary?

FRANK: Why not? Probably a book collector.

KELLER: You mean he'll make a living out of that?

FRANK: Sure, there's a lot of them.

KELLER [*shakes his head*]: All the kind of business goin' on. In my day, either you were a lawyer, or a doctor, or you worked in a shop. Now . . .

FRANK: Well, I was going to be a forester once.

KELLER: Well, that shows you; in my day, there was no such thing. [*Scanning the page, sweeping it with his hand.*] You look at a page like this you realize how ignorant you are. [*Softly, with wonder, as he scans page.*] Psss!

FRANK [*noticing tree*]: Hey, what happened to your tree?

Beth Merrill, John Forsythe, Sidney Blackmur, and Peggy Meredith in All My Sons, *directed by Elia Kazan, the Coronet Theatre, New York, 1947.*

KELLER: Ain't that awful? The wind must've got it last night. You heard the wind, didn't you?

FRANK: Yeah, I got a mess in my yard, too. [*Goes to tree.*] What a pity. [*Turns to* KELLER.] What'd Kate say?

KELLER: They're all asleep yet. I'm just waiting for her to see it.

FRANK [*struck*]: You know?—It's funny.

KELLER: What?

FRANK: Larry was born in August. He'd been twenty-seven this month. And his tree blows down.

KELLER [*touched*]: I'm surprised you remember his birthday, Frank. That's nice.

FRANK: Well, I'm working on his horoscope.

KELLER: How can you make him a horoscope? That's for the future, ain't it?

FRANK: Well, what I'm doing is this, see. Larry was reported missing on November 25th, right?

KELLER: Yeah?

FRANK: Well, we assume that if he was killed it was on November 25th. Now, what Kate wants . . .

KELLER: Oh, Kate asked you to make a horoscope?

FRANK: Yeah, what she wants to find out is whether November 25th was a favorable day for Larry.

KELLER: What is that, favorable day?

FRANK: Well, a favorable day for a person is a fortunate day, according to his stars. In other words it would be practically impossible for him to have died on his favorable day.

KELLER: Well, was that his favorable day? —November 25th?

FRANK: That's what I'm working on to find out. It takes time! See, the point is, if November 25th was his favorable day, then it's completely possible he's alive somewhere, because . . . I mean it's possible. [*He notices* JIM *now.* JIM *is looking at him as though at an idiot. To* JIM*—with an uncertain laugh.*] I didn't even see you.

KELLER [*to* JIM]: Is he talkin' sense?

JIM: Him? He's all right. He's just completely out of his mind, that's all.

FRANK [*peeved*]: The trouble with you is, you don't *believe* in anything.

JIM: And your trouble is that you believe in *anything*. *You* didn't see my kid this morning, did you?

FRANK: No.

KELLER: Imagine? He walked off with his thermometer. Right out of his bag.

JIM [*gets up*]: What a problem. One look at a girl and he takes her temperature. [*Goes to driveway, looks upstage toward street.*]

FRANK: That boy's going to be a real doctor; he's smart.

JIM: Over my dead body he'll be a doctor. A good beginning, too.

FRANK: Why? It's an honorable profession.

JIM [*looks at him tiredly*]: Frank, will you stop talking like a civics book? [KELLER *laughs.*]

FRANK: Why, I saw a movie a couple of weeks ago, reminded me of you. There was a doctor in that picture . . .

KELLER: Don Ameche!

FRANK: I think it was, yeah. And he worked in his basement discovering things. That's what you ought to do; you could help humanity, instead of . . .

JIM: I would love to help humanity on a Warner Brothers salary.

KELLER [*points at him, laughing*]: That's very good, Jim.

JIM [*looks toward house*]: Well, where's the beautiful girl was supposed to be here?

FRANK [*excited*]: Annie came?

KELLER: Sure, sleepin' upstairs. We picked her up on the one o'clock train last night. Wonderful thing. Girl leaves here, a scrawny kid. Couple of years go by, she's a regular woman. Hardly recognized her, and she was running in and out of this yard all her life. That was a very happy family used to live in your house, Jim.

JIM: Like to meet her. The block can use a pretty girl. In the whole neighborhood there's not a damned thing to look at. [*Enter* SUE, JIM*'s wife, from left. She is rounding forty, an overweight woman who fears it. On seeing her* JIM *wryly adds:*] . . . Except my wife, of course.

SUE [*in same spirit*]: Mrs. Adams is on the phone, you dog.

JIM [*to* KELLER]: Such is the condition which prevails, [*Going to his wife.*] my love, my light. . . .

SUE: Don't sniff around me. [*Points to their house, left.*] And give her a nasty answer. I can smell her perfume over the phone.

JIM: What's the matter with her now?

SUE: I don't know, dear. She sounds like she's in terrible pain—unless her mouth is full of candy.

JIM: Why don't you just tell her to lay down?

SUE: She enjoys it more when you tell her to lay down. And when are you going to see Mr. Hubbard?

JIM: My dear; Mr. Hubbard is not sick, and I have better things to do than to sit there and hold his hand.

SUE: It seems to me that for ten dollars you could hold his hand.

JIM [*to* KELLER]: If your son wants to play golf tell him I'm ready. [*Going left.*] Or if he'd like to take a trip around the world for about thirty years. [*He exits left.*]

KELLER: Why do you needle him? He's a doctor, women are supposed to call him up.

SUE: All I said was Mrs. Adams is on the phone. Can I have some of your parsley?

KELLER: Yeah, sure. [*She goes left to parsley box and pulls some parsley.*] You were a nurse too long, Susie. You're too . . . too . . . realistic.

SUE [*laughing, points at him*]: Now you said it! [*Enter* LYDIA LUBEY *from right. She is a robust, laughing girl of twenty-seven.*]

LYDIA: Frank, the toaster . . . [*Sees the others.*] Hya.

KELLER: Hello!

LYDIA [*to* FRANK]: The toaster is off again.

FRANK: Well, plug it in, I just fixed it.

LYDIA [*kindly, but insistently*]: Please, dear, fix it back like it was before.

FRANK: I don't know why you can't learn to turn on a simple thing like a toaster! [FRANK *exits right.*]

SUE [*laughs*]: Thomas Edison.

LYDIA [*apologetically*]: He's really very handy. [*She sees broken tree.*] Oh, did the wind get your tree?

KELLER: Yeah, last night.

LYDIA: Oh, what a pity. Annie get in?

KELLER: She'll be down soon. Wait'll you meet her, Sue, she's a knockout.

SUE: I should've been a man. People are always introducing me to beautiful women. [*To* JOE.] Tell her to come over later; I imagine she'd like to see what we did with her house. And thanks. [SUE *exits left.*]

LYDIA: Is she still unhappy, Joe?

KELLER: Annie? I don't suppose she goes around dancing on her toes, but she seems to be over it.

LYDIA: She going to get married? Is there anybody . . . ?

KELLER: I suppose . . . say, it's a couple years already. She can't mourn a boy forever.

LYDIA: It's so strange . . . Annie's here and not even married. And I've got three babies. I always thought it'd be the other way around.

KELLER: Well, that's what a war does. I had two sons, now I got one. It changed all the tallies. In my day when you had sons it was an honor. Today a doctor could make a million dollars if he could figure out a way to bring a boy into the world without a trigger finger.

LYDIA: You know, I was just reading . . . [*Enter* CHRIS KELLER *from house, stands in doorway.*]

LYDIA: Hya, Chris . . . [FRANK *shouts from off right.*]

FRANK: Lydia, come in here! If you want the toaster to work don't plug in the malted mixer.

LYDIA [*embarrassed, laughs*]: Did I . . . ?

FRANK: And the next time I fix something don't tell me I'm crazy! Now come in here!

LYDIA [*to* KELLER]: I'll never hear the end of this one.

KELLER [*calling to* FRANK]: So what's the difference? Instead of toast have a malted!

LYDIA: Sh! sh! [*She exits right laughing.*]

[CHRIS *watches her off. He is thirty-two; like his father, solidly built, a listener. A man capable of immense affection and loyalty. He has a cup of coffee in one hand, part of a doughnut in other.*]

KELLER: You want the paper?

CHRIS: That's all right, just the book section. [*He bends down and pulls out part of paper on porch floor.*]

KELLER: You're always reading the book section and you never buy a book.

CHRIS [*coming down to settee*]: I like to keep abreast of my ignorance. [*He sits on settee.*]

KELLER: What is that, every week a new book comes out?

CHRIS: Lot of new books.

KELLER: All different.

CHRIS: All different.

KELLER [*shakes his head, puts knife down on bench, takes oil-stone up to the cabinet*]: Psss! Annie up yet?

CHRIS: Mother's giving her breakfast in the dining-room.

KELLER [*crosses, downstage of stool, looking at broken tree*]: See what happened to the tree?

CHRIS [*without looking up*]: Yeah.

KELLER: What's Mother going to say? [BERT *runs on from driveway. He is about eight. He jumps on stool, then on* KELLER'*s back.*]

BERT: You're finally up.

KELLER [*swinging him around and putting him down*]: Ha! Bert's here! Where's Tommy? He's got his father's thermometer again.

BERT: He's taking a reading.

CHRIS: What!

BERT: But it's only oral.

KELLER: Oh, well, there's no harm in oral. So what's new this morning, Bert?

BERT: Nothin'. [*He goes to broken tree, walks around it.*]

KELLER: Then you couldn't've made a complete inspection of the block. In the beginning, when I first made you a policeman you used to come in every morning with something new. Now, nothin's ever new.

BERT: Except some kids from Thirtieth Street. They started kicking a can down the block, and I made them go away because you were sleeping.

KELLER: Now you're talkin', Bert. Now you're on the ball. First thing you know I'm liable to make you a detective.

BERT [*pulls him down by the lapel and whispers in his ear*]: Can I see the jail now?

KELLER: Seein' the jail ain't allowed, Bert. You know that.

BERT: Aw, I betcha there isn't even a jail. I don't see any bars on the cellar windows.

KELLER: Bert, on my word of honor, there's a jail in the basement. I showed you my gun, didn't I?

BERT: But that's a hunting gun.

KELLER: That's an arresting gun!

BERT: Then why don't you ever arrest anybody? Tommy said another dirty word to Doris yesterday, and you didn't even demote him.

KELLER [*he chuckles and winks at* CHRIS *who is enjoying all this*]: Yeah, that's a dangerous character, that Tommy. [*Beckons him closer.*] What word does he say?

BERT [*backing away quickly in great embarrassment*]: Oh, I can't say that.

KELLER [*grabs him by the shirt and pulls him back*]: Well, gimme an idea.

BERT: I can't. It's not a nice word.

KELLER: Just whisper it in my ear. I'll close my eyes. Maybe I won't even hear it.

BERT [*on tiptoe, puts his lips to* KELLER*'s ear, then in unbearable embarrassment steps back*]: I can't Mr. Keller.

CHRIS [*laughing*]: Don't make him do that.

KELLER: Okay, Bert. I take your word. Now go out, and keep both eyes peeled.

BERT [*interested*]: For what?

KELLER: For what! Bert, the whole neighborhood is depending on you. A policeman don't ask questions. Now peel them eyes!

BERT [*mystified, but willing*]: Okay. [*He runs off right back of arbor*].

KELLER [*calling after him*]: And mum's the word Bert.

BERT [*stops and sticks his head thru the arbor*]: About what?

KELLER: Just in general. Be v-e-r-y careful.

BERT [*nods in bewilderment*]: Okay. [BERT *exits downstage right.*]

KELLER [*laughs*]: I got all the kids crazy!

CHRIS: One of these days, they'll all come in here and beat your brains out.

KELLER: What's she going to say? Maybe we ought to tell her before she sees it.

CHRIS: She saw it.

KELLER: How could she see it? I was the first one up. She was still in bed.

CHRIS: She was out here when it broke.

KELLER: When?

CHRIS: About four this morning. [*Indicating window above them.*] I heard it cracking and I woke up and looked out. She was standing right here when it cracked.

KELLER: What was she doing out here four in the morning?

CHRIS: I don't know. When it cracked she ran back into the house and cried in the kitchen.

KELLER: Did you talk to her?

CHRIS: No, I . . . I figured the best thing was to leave her alone.

[*Pause.*]

KELLER [*deeply touched*]: She cried hard?

CHRIS: I could hear her right through the floor of my room.

KELLER [*slight pause*]: What was she doing out here at that hour? [CHRIS *silent. An undertone of anger showing.*] She's dreaming about him again. She's walking around at night.

CHRIS: I guess she is.

KELLER: She's getting just like after he died. [*Slight pause.*] What's the meaning of that?

CHRIS: I don't know the meaning of it. [*Slight pause.*] But I know one thing, Dad. We've made a terrible mistake with Mother.

KELLER: What?

CHRIS: Being dishonest with her. That kind of thing always pays off, and now it's paying off.

KELLER: What do you mean, dishonest?

CHRIS: You know Larry's not coming back and I know it. Why do we allow her to go on thinking that we believe with her?

KELLER: What do you want to do, argue with her?

CHRIS: I don't want to argue with her, but it's time she realized that nobody believes Larry is alive any more. [KELLER *simply moves away, thinking, looking at the ground.*] Why shouldn't she dream of him, walk the nights waiting for him? Do we contradict her? Do we say straight out that we have no hope any more? That we haven't had any hope for years now?

KELLER [*frightened at the thought*]: You can't say that to her.

CHRIS: We've got to say it to her.

KELLER: How're you going to prove it? Can you prove it?

CHRIS: For God's sake, three years! Nobody comes back after three years. It's insane.

KELLER: To you it is, and to me. But not to her. You can talk yourself blue in the face, but there's no body and there's no grave, so where are you?

CHRIS: Sit down, Dad. I want to talk to you.

KELLER [*looks at him searchingly a moment, and sitting . . .*]: The trouble is the Goddam newspapers. Every month some boy turns up from nowhere, so the next one is going to be Larry, so . . .

CHRIS: All right, all right, listen to me. [*Slight pause.* KELLER *sits on settee.*] You know why I asked Annie here, don't you?

KELLER [*he knows, but . . .*]: Why?

CHRIS: You know.

KELLER: Well, I got an idea, but . . . What's the story?

CHRIS: I'm going to ask her to marry me. [*Slight pause.*]

KELLER [*nods*]: Well, that's only your business, Chris.

CHRIS: You know it's not only my business.
KELLER: What do you want me to do? You're old enough to know your own mind.
CHRIS [*asking, annoyed*]: Then it's all right, I'll go ahead with it?
KELLER: Well, you want to be sure your Mother isn't going to . . .
CHRIS: Then it isn't just my business.
KELLER: I'm just sayin'. . . .
CHRIS: Sometimes you infuriate me, you know that? Isn't it your business, too, if I tell this to Mother and she throws a fit about it? You have such a talent for ignoring things.
KELLER: I ignore what I gotta ignore. The girl is Larry's girl . . .
CHRIS: She's not Larry's girl.
KELLER: From Mother's point of view he is not dead and you have no right to take his girl. [*Slight pause.*] Now you can go on from there if you know where to go, but I'm tellin' you I don't know where to go. See? I don't know. Now what can I do for you?
CHRIS: I don't know why it is, but every time I reach out for something I want, I have to pull back because other people will suffer. My whole bloody life, time after time after time.
KELLER: You're a considerate fella, there's nothing wrong in that.
CHRIS: To hell with that.
KELLER: Did you ask Annie yet?
CHRIS: I wanted to get this settled first.
KELLER: How do you know she'll marry you? Maybe she feels the same way Mother does?
CHRIS: Well, if she does, then that's the end of it. From her letters I think she's forgotten him. I'll find out. And then we'll thrash it out with Mother? Right? Dad, don't avoid me.
KELLER: The trouble is, you don't see enough women. You never did.
CHRIS: So what? I'm not fast with women.
KELLER: I don't see why it has to be Annie. . . .
CHRIS: Because it is.
KELLER: That's a good answer, but it don't answer anything. You haven't seen her since you went to war. It's five years.
CHRIS: I can't help it. I know her best. I was brought up next door to her. These years when I think of someone for my wife, I think of Annie. What do you want, a diagram?
KELLER: I don't want a diagram . . . I . . . I'm . . . She thinks he's coming back, Chris. You marry that girl and you're pronouncing him dead. Now what's going to happen to Mother? Do you know? I don't! [*Pause.*]
CHRIS: All right, then, Dad.
Keller [*thinking* CHRIS *has retreated*]: Give it some more thought.
CHRIS: I've given it three years of thought. I'd hoped that if I waited, Mother would forget Larry and then we'd have a regular wedding and everything happy. But if that can't happen here, then I'll have to get out.
KELLER: What the hell is *this?*
CHRIS: I'll get out. I'll get married and live some place else. Maybe in New York.
KELLER: Are you crazy?
CHRIS: I've been a good son too long, a good sucker. I'm through with it.
KELLER: You've got a business here, what the hell is this?
CHRIS: The business! The business doesn't inspire me.
KELLER: Must you be inspired?
CHRIS: Yes. I like it an hour a day. If I have to grub for money all day long at least at evening I want it beautiful. I want a family, I want some kids, I want to build something I can give myself to. Annie is in the middle of that. Now . . . where do I find it?
KELLER: You mean . . . [*Goes to him.*] Tell me something, you mean you'd leave the business?
CHRIS: Yes. On this I would.
KELLER [*pause*]: Well . . . you don't want to think like that.
CHRIS: Then help me stay here.
KELLER: All right, but . . . but don't think like that. Because what the hell did I work for? That's only for you, Chris, the whole shootin'-match is for you!
CHRIS: I know that, Dad. Just you help me stay here.
KELLER [*puts a fist up to* CHRIS' *jaw*]: But don't think that way, you hear me?
CHRIS: I am thinking that way.
KELLER [*lowering his hand*]: I don't understand you, do I?
CHRIS: No, you don't. I'm a pretty tough guy.
KELLER: Yeah. I can see that. [MOTHER *appears on porch. She is in her early fifties, a woman of uncontrolled inspirations, and an overwhelming capacity for love.*]
MOTHER: Joe?
CHRIS [*going toward porch*]: Hello, Mom.
MOTHER [*indicating house behind her. To* KELLER]: Did you take a bag from under the sink?
KELLER: Yeah. I put it in the pail.
MOTHER: Well, get it out of the pail. That's my potatoes. [CHRIS *bursts out laughing—goes up into alley.*]
KELLER [*laughing*]: I thought it was garbage.
MOTHER: Will you do me a favor, Joe? Don't be helpful.
KELLER: I can afford another bag of potatoes.

MOTHER: Minnie scoured that pail in boiling water last night. It's cleaner than your teeth.

KELLER: And I don't understand why, after I worked forty years and I got a maid, why I have to take out the garbage.

MOTHER: If you would make up your mind that every bag in the kitchen isn't full of garbage you wouldn't be throwing out my vegetables. Last time it was the onions. [CHRIS *comes on, hands her bag.*]

KELLER: I don't like garbage in the house.

MOTHER: Then don't eat. [*She goes into the kitchen with bag.*]

CHRIS: That settles you for today.

KELLER: Yeah, I'm in last place again. I don't know, once upon a time I used to think that when I got money again I would have a maid and my wife would take it easy. Now I got money, and I got a maid, and my wife is workin' for the maid. [*He sits in one of the chairs.* MOTHER *comes out on last line. She carries a pot of stringbeans.*]

MOTHER: It's her day off, what are you crabbing about?

CHRIS [*to* MOTHER]: Isn't Annie finished eating?

MOTHER [*looking around preoccupiedly at yard*]: She'll be right out. [*Moves.*] That wind did some job on this place. [*Of the tree.*] So much for that, thank God.

KELLER [*indicating chair beside him*]: Sit down, take it easy.

MOTHER [*she presses her hand to top of her head*]: I've got such a funny pain on the top of my head.

CHRIS: Can I get you an aspirin?

MOTHER [*picks a few petals off ground, stands there smelling them in her hand, then sprinkles them over plants*]: No more roses. It's so funny . . . everything decides to happen at the same time. This month is his birthday; his tree blows down, Annie comes. Everything that happened seems to be coming back. I was just down the cellar, and what do I stumble over? His baseball glove. I haven't seen it in a century.

CHRIS: Don't you think Annie looks well?

MOTHER: Fine. There's no question about it. She's a beauty . . . I still don't know what brought her here. Not that I'm not glad to see her, but . . .

CHRIS: I just thought we'd all like to see each other again. [MOTHER *just looks at him, nodding ever so slightly—almost as though admitting something.*] And I wanted to see her myself.

MOTHER [*her nods halt. To* KELLER]: The only thing is I think her nose got longer. But I'll always love that girl. She's one that didn't jump into bed with somebody else as soon as it happened with her fella.

KELLER [*as though that were impossible for* ANNIE]: Oh, what're you . . . ?

MOTHER: Never mind. Most of them didn't wait till the telegrams were opened. I'm just glad she came, so you can see I'm not *completely* out of my mind. [*Sits, and rapidly breaks stringbeans in the pot.*]

CHRIS: Just because she isn't married doesn't mean she's been mourning Larry.

MOTHER [*with an undercurrent of observation*]: Why then isn't she?

CHRIS [*a little flustered*]: Well . . . it could've been any number of things.

MOTHER [*directly at him*]: Like what, for instance?

CHRIS [*embarrassed, but standing his ground*]: I don't know. Whatever it is. Can I get you an aspirin? [MOTHER *puts her hand to her head.*]

MOTHER [*she gets up and goes aimlessly toward the trees on rising*]: It's not like a headache.

KELLER: You don't sleep, that's why. She's wearing out more bedroom slippers than shoes!

MOTHER: I had a terrible night. [*She stops moving.*] I never had a night like that.

CHRIS [*looks at* KELLER]: What was it, Mom? Did you dream?

MOTHER: More, more than a dream.

CHRIS [*hesitantly*]: About Larry?

MOTHER: I was fast asleep, and . . . [*Raising her arm over the audience.*] Remember the way he used to fly low past the house when he was in training? When we used to see his face in the cockpit going by? That's the way I saw him. Only high up. Way, way up, where the clouds are. He was so real I could reach out and touch him. And suddenly he started to fall. And crying, crying to me . . . Mom, Mom! I could hear him like he was in the room. Mom! . . . it was his voice! If I could touch him I knew I could stop him, if I could only . . . [*Breaks off, allowing her outstretched hand to fall.*] I woke up and it was so funny . . . The wind . . . it was like the roaring of his engine. I came out here . . . I must've still been half asleep. I could hear that roaring like he was going by. The tree snapped right in front of me . . . and I like . . . came awake. [*She is looking at tree. She suddenly realizes something, turns with a reprimanding finger shaking slightly at* KELLER.] See? We should never have planted that tree. I said so in the first place; It was too soon to plant a tree for him.

CHRIS [*alarmed*]: Too soon!

MOTHER [*angering*]: We rushed into it. Everybody was in such a hurry to bury him. I said not to plant it yet. [*To* KELLER.] I *told* you to . . . !

CHRIS: Mother, Mother! [*She looks into his face.*] The wind blew it down. What significance has that got? What are you talking about? Mother, please . . . Don't go through it all again, will you? It's no good, it doesn't accomplish anything. I've been thinking y'know?—maybe we ought to put our minds to forgetting him?

MOTHER: That's the third time you've said that this week.

CHRIS: Because it's not right; we never took up our lives again. We're like at a railroad station waiting for a train that never comes in.

MOTHER [*presses top of her head*]: Get me an aspirin, heh?

CHRIS: Sure, and let's break out of this, heh, Mom? I thought the four of us might go out to dinner a couple of nights, maybe go dancing out at the shore.

MOTHER: Fine. [*To* KELLER.] We can do it tonight.

KELLER: Swell with me!

CHRIS: Sure, let's have some fun. [*To* MOTHER.] You'll start with this aspirin. [*He goes up and into house with new spirit. Her smile vanishes.*]

MOTHER [*with an accusing undertone*]: Why did he invite her here?

KELLER: Why does that bother you?

MOTHER: She's been in New York three and a half years, why all of a sudden . . . ?

KELLER: Well, maybe . . . maybe he just wanted to see her . . .

MOTHER: Nobody comes seven hundred miles "just to see."

KELLER: What do you mean? He lived next door to the girl all his life, why shouldn't he want to see her again? [MOTHER *looks at him critically.*] Don't look at me like that, he didn't tell me any more than he told you.

MOTHER [*a warning and a question*]: He's not going to marry her.

KELLER: How do you know he's even thinking of it?

MOTHER: It's got that about it.

KELLER [*sharply watching her reaction*]: Well? So what?

MOTHER [*alarmed*]: What's going on here, Joe?

KELLER: Now listen, kid . . .

MOTHER [*avoiding contact with him*]: She's not his girl, Joe; she knows she's not.

KELLER: You can't read her mind.

MOTHER: Then why is she still single? New York is full of men, why isn't she married? [*Pause.*] Probably a hundred people told her she's foolish, but she's waited.

KELLER: How do you know why she waited?

MOTHER: She knows what I know, that's why. She's faithful as a rock. In my worst moments, I think of her waiting, and I know again that I'm right.

KELLER: Look, it's a nice day. What are we arguing for!

MOTHER [*warningly*]: Nobody in this house dast take her faith away, Joe. Strangers might. But not his father, not his brother.

KELLER [*exasperated*]: What do you want me to do? What do you want?

MOTHER: I want you to act like he's coming back. Both of you. Don't think I haven't noticed you since Chris invited her. I won't stand for any nonsense.

KELLER: But, Kate . . .

MOTHER: Because if he's not coming back, then I'll kill myself! Laugh. Laugh at me. [*She points to tree.*] But why did that happen the very night she came back? Laugh, but there are meanings in such things. She goes to sleep in his room and his memorial breaks in pieces. Look at it; look. [*She sits on bench at his left.*] Joe . . .

KELLER: Calm yourself.

MOTHER: Believe with me, Joe. I can't stand all alone.

KELLER: Calm yourself.

MOTHER: Only last week a man turned up in Detroit, missing longer than Larry. You read it yourself.

KELLER: All right, all right, calm yourself.

MOTHER: You above all have got to believe, you . . .

KELLER [*rises*]: Why me above all?

MOTHER: . . . Just don't stop believing . . .

KELLER: What does that mean, me above all? [BERT *comes rushing on from left.*]

BERT: Mr. Keller! Say, Mr. Keller . . . [*Pointing up driveway.*] Tommy just said it again!

KELLER [*not remembering any of it*]: Said what? . . . Who? . . .

BERT: The dirty word.

KELLER: Oh. Well . . .

BERT: Gee, aren't you going to arrest him? I warned him.

MOTHER [*with suddenness*]: Stop that, Bert. Go home. [BERT *backs up, as she advances.*] There's no jail here.

KELLER [*as though to say, "Oh-what-the-hell-let-him-believe-there-is."*]: Kate . . .

MOTHER [*turning on* KELLER, *furiously*]: There's no jail here! I want you to stop that jail business! [*He turns, shamed, but peeved.*]

BERT [*past her to* KELLER]: He's right across the street.

MOTHER: Go home, Bert. [BERT *turns around and goes up driveway. She is shaken. Her speech is bitten off, extremely urgent.*] I want you to stop that, Joe. That whole jail business!

KELLER [*alarmed, therefore angered*]: Look at you, look at you shaking.

MOTHER [*trying to control herself, moving about clasping her hands*]: I can't help it.

KELLER: What have I got to hide? What the hell is the matter with you, Kate?

MOTHER: I didn't say you had anything to hide, I'm just telling you to stop it; Now stop it! [*As* ANN *and* CHRIS *appear on porch.* ANN *is twenty-six, gentle but despite herself capable of holding fast to what she knows.* CHRIS *opens door for her.*]

ANN: Hya, Joe! [*She leads off a general laugh that is not self-conscious because they know one another too well.*]

CHRIS [*bringing* ANN *down, with an outstretched, chivalric arm*]: Take a breath of that air, kid. You never get air like that in New York.

MOTHER [*genuinely overcome with it*]: Annie, where did you get that dress!

ANN: I couldn't resist. I'm taking it right off before I ruin it. [*Swings around.*] How's that for three weeks' salary?

MOTHER [*to* KELLER]: Isn't she the most . . . ? [*To* ANN.] It's gorgeous, simply gor . . .

CHRIS [*to* MOTHER]: No kidding, now, isn't she the prettiest gal you ever saw?

MOTHER [*Caught short by his obvious admiration, she finds herself reaching out for a glass of water and aspirin in his hand, and . . .*]: You gained a little weight, didn't you, darling? [*She gulps pill and drinks.*]

ANN: It comes and goes.

KELLER: Look how nice her legs turned out!

ANN [*she runs to fence, left*]: Boy, the poplars got thick, didn't they?

KELLER [*moves upstage to settee and sits*]: Well, it's three years, Annie. We're gettin' old, kid.

MOTHER: How does Mom like New York? [ANN *keeps looking through trees.*]

ANN [*a little hurt*]: Why'd they take our hammock away?

KELLER: Oh, no, it broke. Couple of years ago.

MOTHER: What broke? He had one of his light lunches and flopped into it.

ANN [*she laughs and turns back toward* JIM*'s yard . . .*]: Oh, excuse me! [JIM *has come to fence and is looking over it. He is smoking a cigar. As she cries out, he comes on around on stage.*]

JIM: How do you do. [*To* CHRIS.] She looks very intelligent!

CHRIS: Ann, this is Jim . . . Doctor Bayliss.

ANN [*shaking* JIM*'s hand*]: Oh sure, he writes a lot about you.

JIM: Don't believe it. He likes everybody. In the Battalion he was known as Mother McKeller.

ANN: I can believe it . . . You know——? [*To* MOTHER.] It's so strange seeing him come out of that yard. [*To* CHRIS.] I guess I never grew up. It almost seems that Mom and Pop are in there now. And you and my brother doing Algebra, and Larry trying to copy my home-work. Gosh, those dear dead days beyond recall.

JIM: Well, I hope that doesn't mean you want me to move out?

SUE [*calling from off left*]: Jim, come in here! Mr. Hubbard is on the phone!

JIM: I told you I don't want . . .

SUE [*commandingly sweet*]: Please, dear! Please!!

JIM [*resigned*]: All right, Susie, [*Trailing off.*] all right, all right . . . [*To* ANN.] I've only met you, Ann, but if I may offer you a piece of advice—When you marry, never—even in your mind—never count your husband's money.

SUE: [*from off*]: Jim?!

JIM: At once! [*Turns and goes left.*] At once. [*He exits left.*]

MOTHER [ANN *is looking at her. She speaks meaningfully*]: I told her to take up the guitar. It'd be a common interest for them. [*They laugh.*] Well, he loves the guitar!

ANN [*as though to overcome* MOTHER, *she becomes suddenly lively, crosses to* KELLER *on settee, sits on his lap*]: Let's eat at the shore tonight! Raise some hell around here, like we used to before Larry went!

MOTHER [*emotionally*]: You think of him! You see? [*Triumphantly.*] She thinks of him!

ANN [*with an uncomprehending smile*]: What do you mean, Kate?

MOTHER: Nothing. Just that you . . . remember him, he's in your thoughts.

ANN: That's a funny thing to say; how could I help remembering him?

MOTHER [*it is drawing to a head the wrong way for her; she starts anew. She rises and comes to* ANN]: Did you hang up your things?

ANN: Yeah . . . [*To* CHRIS.] Say, you've sure gone in for clothes. I could hardly find room in the closet.

MOTHER: No, don't you remember? That's Larry's room.

ANN: You mean . . . they're Larry's?

MOTHER: Didn't you recognize them?

ANN [*slowly rising, a little embarrassed*]: Well, it never occurred to me that you'd . . . I mean the shoes are all shined.

MOTHER: Yes, dear. [*Slight pause.* ANN *can't stop staring at her.* MOTHER *breaks it by speaking with the relish of gossip, putting her arm around* ANN *and walking stage left with her.*] For so long I've been aching for a nice conversation with you, Annie. Tell me something.

ANN: What?

MOTHER: I don't know. Something nice.

Chris [*wryly*]: She means do you go out much?

MOTHER: Oh, shut up.

KELLER: And are any of them serious?

MOTHER [*laughing, sits, in her chair*]: Why don't you both choke?

KELLER: Annie, you can't go into a restaurant with that woman any more. In five minutes thirty-nine strange people are sitting at the table telling her their life story.

MOTHER: If I can't ask Annie a personal question . . .

KELLER: Askin' is all right, but don't beat her over the head. You're beatin' her, you're beatin' her. [*They are laughing.*]

ANN [*to* MOTHER. *Takes pan of beans off stool, puts them on floor under chair and sits*]: Don't let them bulldoze you. Ask me anything you like. What do you want to know, Kate? Come on, let's gossip.

MOTHER [*to* CHRIS *and* KELLER]: She's the only one is got any sense. [*To* ANN.] Your mother . . . She's not getting a divorce, heh?

ANN: No, she's calmed down about it now. I think when he gets out they'll probably live together. In New York, of course.

MOTHER: That's fine. Because your father is still . . . I mean he's a decent man after all is said and done.

ANN: I don't care. She can take him back if she likes.

MOTHER: And you? You . . . [*Shakes her head negatively.*] . . . go out much? [*Slight pause.*]

ANN [*delicately*]: You mean am I still waiting for him?

MOTHER: Well, no, I don't expect you to wait for him but . . .

ANN [*kindly*]: But that's what you mean, isn't it?

MOTHER: . . . Well . . . yes.

ANN: Well, I'm not, Kate.

MOTHER [*faintly*]: You're not?

ANN: Isn't it ridiculous? You don't really imagine he's . . . ?

MOTHER: I know, dear, but don't say it's ridiculous, because the papers were full of it; I don't know about New York, but there was half a page about a man missing even longer than Larry, and he turned up from Burma.

CHRIS [*coming to* ANN]: He couldn't have wanted to come home very badly, Mom.

MOTHER: Don't be so smart.

CHRIS: You can have a helluva time in Burma.

ANN [*rises and swings around in back of* CHRIS]: So I've heard.

CHRIS: Mother, I'll bet you money that you're the only woman in the country who after three years is still . . .

MOTHER: You're sure?

CHRIS: Yes, I am.

MOTHER: Well, if you're sure then you're sure. [*She turns her head away an instant.*] They don't say it on the radio but I'm sure that in the dark at night they're still waiting for their sons.

CHRIS: Mother, you're absolutely—

MOTHER [*waving him off*]: Don't be so damned smart! Now stop it! [*Slight pause.*] There are just a few things you *don't* know. All of you. And I'll tell you one of them, Annie. Deep, deep in your heart you've always been waiting for him.

ANN [*resolutely*]: No, Kate.

MOTHER [*with increasing demand*]: But deep in your heart, Annie!

CHRIS: She ought to know, shouldn't she?

MOTHER: Don't let them tell you what to think. Listen to your heart. Only your heart.

ANN: Why does your heart tell you he's alive?

MOTHER: Because he has to be.

ANN: But why, Kate?

MOTHER [*going to her*]: Because certain things have to be, and certain things can never be. Like the sun has to rise, it has to be. That's why there's God. Otherwise anything could happen. But there's God, so certain things can never happen. I would know, Annie—just like I knew the day he [*indicates* CHRIS.] went into that terrible battle. Did he write me? Was it in the papers? No, but that morning I couldn't raise my head off the pillow. Ask Joe. Suddenly, I knew. I knew! And he was nearly killed that day. Ann, you *know* I'm right!

ANN [*she stands there in silence, then turns trembling, going upstage*]: No, Kate.

MOTHER: I have to have some tea. [FRANK *appears from left, carrying ladder.*]

FRANK: Annie! [*Coming down.*] How are you, gee whiz!

ANN [*taking his hand*]: Why, Frank, you're losing your hair.

KELLER: He's got responsibility.

FRANK: Gee whiz!

KELLER: Without Frank the stars wouldn't know when to come out.

FRANK [*laughs. To* ANN]: You look more womanly. You've matured. You . . .

KELLER: Take it easy, Frank, you're a married man.

ANN [*as they laugh*]: You still haberdashering?

FRANK: Why not? Maybe I too can get to be president. How's your brother? Got his degree, I hear.

ANN: Oh, George has his own office now!

FRANK: Don't say! [*Funereally.*] And your dad? Is he . . . ?

ANN [*abruptly*]: Fine. I'll be in to see Lydia.

FRANK [*sympathetically*]: How about it, does Dad expect a parole soon?

ANN [*with growing ill-ease*]: I really don't know, I . . .

FRANK [*staunchly defending her father for her sake*]: I mean because I feel, y'know, that if an intelligent man like your father is put in prison, there ought to be a law that says either you execute him, or let him go after a year.

CHRIS [*interrupting*]: Want a hand with that ladder, Frank?

FRANK [*taking cue*]: That's all right, I'll . . . [*picks up ladder*] I'll finish the horoscope tonight, Kate. [*Embarrassed.*] See you later, Ann, you look wonderful. [*He exits right. They look at* ANN.]

ANN [*to* CHRIS, *sits slowly on stool*]: Haven't they stopped talking about Dad?

CHRIS [*comes down and sits on arm of chair*]: Nobody talks about him any more.

KELLER [*rises and comes to her*]: Gone and forgotten, kid.

ANN: Tell me. Because I don't want to meet anybody on the block if they're going to . . .

CHRIS: I don't want you to worry about it.

ANN [*to* KELLER]: Do they still remember the case, Joe? Do they talk about you?

KELLER: The only one still talks about it is my wife.

MOTHER: That's because you keep on playing policeman with the kids. All their parents hear out of you is jail, jail, jail.

KELLER: Actually what happened was that when I got home from the penitentiary the kids got very interested in me. You know kids. I was [*Laughs.*] like the expert on the jail situation. And as time passed they got it confused and . . . I ended up a detective. [*Laughs.*]

MOTHER: Except that *they* didn't get it confused. [*To* ANN.] He hands out police badges from the Post Toasties boxes. [*They laugh.*]

ANN [*wondrously at them, happily. She rises and comes to* KELLER, *putting her arm around his shoulder*]: Gosh, it's wonderful to hear you laughing about it.

CHRIS: Why, what'd you expect?

ANN: The last thing I remember on this block was one word—"Murderers!" Remember that, Kate? . . . Mrs. Hammond standing in front of our house and yelling that word . . . She's still around, I suppose?

MOTHER: They're all still around.

KELLER: Don't listen to her. Every Saturday night the whole gang is playin' poker in this arbor. All the ones who yelled murderer takin' my money now.

MOTHER: Don't, Joe, she's a sensitive girl, don't fool her. [*To* ANN.] They still remember about Dad. It's different with him— [*Indicates* JOE.] —he was exonerated, your father's still there. That's why I wasn't so enthusiastic about your coming. Honestly, I know how sensitive you are, and I told Chris, I said . . .

KELLER: Listen, you do like I did and you'll be all right. The day I come home, I got out of my car;—but not in front of the house . . . on the corner. You should've been here, Annie, and you too, Chris; you'd-a seen something. Everybody knew I was getting out that day; the porches were loaded. Picture it now; none of them believed I was innocent. The story was, I pulled a fast one getting myself exonerated. So I get out of my car, and I walk down the street. But very slow. And with a smile. The beast! I was the beast; the guy who sold cracked cylinder heads to the Army Air Force; the guy who made twenty-one P-40's crash in Australia. Kid, walkin' down the street that day I was guilty as hell. Except I wasn't, and there was a court paper in my pocket to prove I wasn't, and I walked . . . past . . . the porches. Result? Fourteen months later I had one of the best shops in the state again, a respected man again; bigger than ever.

CHRIS [*with admiration*]: Joe McGuts.

KELLER [*now with great force*]: That's the only way you lick 'em is guts! [*To* ANN.] The worst thing you did was to move away from here. You made it tough for your father when he gets out. That's why I tell you, I'd like to see him move back right on this block.

MOTHER [*pained*]: How could they move back?

KELLER: It ain't gonna end *till* they move back! [*To* ANN.] Till people play cards with him again, and talk with him, and smile with him—you play cards with a man you know he can't be a murderer. And the next time you write him I like you to tell him just what I said. [ANN *simply stares at him.*] You hear me?

ANN [*surprised*]: Don't you hold anything against him?

KELLER: Annie, I never believed in crucifying people.

ANN [*mystified*]: But he was your partner, he dragged you through the mud . . .

KELLER: Well, he ain't my sweetheart, but you gotta forgive, don't you?

ANN: You, either, Kate? Don't you feel any . . . ?

KELLER [*to* ANN]: The next time you write Dad . . .

ANN: I don't write him.

KELLER [*struck*]: Well every now and then you . . .

ANN [*a little ashamed, but determined*]: No, I've *never* written to him. Neither has my brother. [*To* CHRIS.] Say, do you feel this way, too?

CHRIS: He murdered twenty-one pilots.

KELLER: What the hell kinda talk is that?

MOTHER: That's not a thing to say about a man.

ANN: What else can you say? When they took him away I followed him, went to him every visiting day. I was crying all the time. Until the news came about Larry. Then I realized. It's wrong to pity a man like that. Father or no father, there's only one way to look at him. He knowingly shipped out parts that would crash an airplane. And how do you know Larry wasn't one of them?

MOTHER: I was waiting for that. [*Going to her.*] As long as you're here, Annie, I want to ask you never to say that again.

ANN: You surprise me. I thought you'd be mad at him.

MOTHER: What your father did had nothing to do with Larry. Nothing.

ANN: But we can't know that.

MOTHER [*striving for control*]: As long as you're here!

ANN [*perplexed*]: But, Kate . . .

MOTHER: Put that out of your head!

KELLER: Because . . .

MOTHER [*quickly to* KELLER]: That's all, that's enough. [*Places her hand on her head.*] Come inside now, and have some tea with me. [*She turns and goes up steps.*]

KELLER [*to* ANN]: The one thing you . . .

MOTHER [*sharply*]: He's not dead, so there's no argument! Now come!

KELLER [*angrily*]: In a minute! [MOTHER *turns and goes into house.*] Now look, Annie . . .

CHRIS: All right, Dad, forget it.

KELLER: No, she dasn't feel that way. Annie . . .

CHRIS: I'm sick of the whole subject, now cut it out.

KELLER: You want her to go on like this? [*To* ANN.] Those cylinder heads went into P-40's only. What's the matter with you? You know Larry never flew a P-40.

CHRIS: So who flew those P-40's, pigs?

KELLER: The man was a fool, but don't make a murderer out of him. You got no sense? Look what it does to her! [*To* ANN.] Listen, you gotta appreciate what was doin' in that shop in the war. The both of you! It was a madhouse. Every half hour the Major callin' for cylinder heads, they were whippin' us with the telephone. The trucks were hauling them away hot, damn near. I mean just try to see it human, see it human. All of a sudden a batch comes out with a crack. That happens, that's the business. A fine, hairline crack. All right, so . . . so he's a little man, your father, always scared of loud voices. What'll the Major say?—Half a day's production shot. . . . What'll I say? You know what I mean? Human. [*He pauses.*] So he takes out his tools and he . . . covers over the cracks. All right . . . that's bad, it's wrong, but that's what a little man does. If I could have gone in that day I'd a told him—junk 'em, Herb, we can afford it. But alone he was afraid. But I know he meant no harm. He believed they'd hold up a hundred percent. That's a mistake, but it ain't murder. You mustn't feel that way about him. You understand me? It ain't right.

ANN [*she regards him a moment*]: Joe, let's forget it.

KELLER: Annie, the day the news came about Larry he was in the next cell to mine . . . Dad. And he cried, Annie . . . he cried half the night.

ANN [*touched*]: He shoulda cried all night. [*Slight pause.*]

KELLER [*almost angered*]: Annie, I do not understand why you . . . !

CHRIS [*breaking in—with nervous urgency*]: Are you going to stop it?!

ANN: Don't yell at him. He just wants everybody happy.

KELLER [*clasps her around waist, smiling*]: That's my sentiments. Can you stand steak?

CHRIS: And champagne!

KELLER: Now you're operatin'! I'll call Swanson's for a table! Big time tonight. Annie!

ANN: Can't scare me.

KELLER [*to* CHRIS, *pointing at* ANN]: I like that girl. Wrap her up. [*They laugh. Goes up porch.*] You got nice legs, Annie! . . . I want to see everybody drunk tonight. [*Pointing to* CHRIS.] Look at him, he's blushin'! [*He exits, laughing, into house.*]

CHRIS [*calling after him*]: Drink your tea, Casanova. [*He turns to* ANN.] Isn't he a great guy?

ANN: You're the only one I know who loves his parents!

CHRIS: I know. It went out of style, didn't it?

ANN [*with a sudden touch of sadness*]: It's all right. It's a good thing. [*She looks about.*] You know? It's lovely here. The air is sweet.

CHRIS [*hopefully*]: You're not sorry you came?

ANN: Not sorry, no. But I'm . . . not going to stay . . .

CHRIS: Why?

ANN: In the first place, your mother as much as told me to go.

CHRIS: Well . . .

ANN: You saw that . . . and then you . . . you've been kind of . . .

CHRIS: What?

ANN: Well . . . kind of embarrassed ever since I got here.

CHRIS: The trouble is I planned on kind of sneaking up on you over a period of a week or so. But they take it for granted that we're all set.

ANN: I knew they would. Your mother anyway.

CHRIS: How did you know?

ANN: From *her* point of view, why else would I come?

CHRIS: Well . . . would you want to? [ANN *studies him.*] I guess you know this is why I asked you to come.

ANN: I guess this is why I came.

CHRIS: Ann, I love you. I love you a great deal. [*Finally.*] I love you [*Pause. She waits.*] I have no imagination . . . that's all I know to tell you. [ANN, *waiting, ready.*] I'm embarrassing you. I didn't want to tell it to you here. I wanted some place we'd never been; a place where we'd be brand new to each other. . . . You feel it's wrong here, don't you? This yard, this chair? I want you to be ready for me. I don't want to win you away from anything.

ANN [*putting her arms around him*]: Oh, Chris, I've been ready a long, long time!

CHRIS: Then he's gone forever. You're sure.

ANN: I almost got married two years ago.

CHRIS: . . . why didn't you?

ANN: You started to write to me . . . [*Slight pause.*]

CHRIS: You felt something that far back?

ANN: Every day since!

CHRIS: Ann, why didn't you let me know?

ANN: I was waiting for you Chris. Till then you never wrote. And when you did, what did you say? You sure can be ambiguous, you know.

CHRIS [*he looks towards house, then at her, trembling*]: Give me a kiss, Ann. Give me a . . . [*They kiss.*] God, I kissed you, Annie, I kissed Annie. How long, how long I've been waiting to kiss you!

ANN: I'll never forgive you. Why did you wait all these years? All I've done is sit and wonder if I was crazy for thinking of you.

CHRIS: Annie, we're going to live now! I'm going to make you so happy. [*He kisses her, but without their bodies touching.*]

ANN [*a little embarrassed*]: Not like that you're not.

CHRIS: I kissed you . . .

ANN: Like Larry's brother. Do it like you, Chris. [*He breaks away from her abruptly.*] What is it, Chris?

CHRIS: Let's drive some place . . . I want to be alone with you.

ANN: No . . . what is it, Chris, your mother?

CHRIS: No . . . nothing like that . . .

ANN: Then what's wrong? . . . Even in your letters, there was something ashamed.

CHRIS: Yes. I suppose I have been. But it's going from me.

ANN: You've got to tell me—

CHRIS: I don't know how to start. [*He takes her hand. He speaks quietly, factually at first.*]

ANN: It wouldn't work this way. [*Slight pause.*]

CHRIS: It's all mixed up with so many other things. . . . You remember, overseas, I was in command of a company?

ANN: Yeah, sure.

CHRIS: Well, I lost them.

ANN: How many?

CHRIS: Just about all.

ANN: Oh, gee!

CHRIS: It takes a little time to toss that off. Because they weren't just men. For instance, one time it'd been raining several days and this kid came to me, and gave me his last pair of dry socks. Put them in my pocket. That's only a little thing . . . but . . . that's the kind of guys I had. They didn't die; they killed themselves for each other. I mean that exactly; a little more selfish and they'd've been here today. And I got an idea—watching them go down. Everything was being destroyed, see, but it seemed to me that one new thing was made. A kind of . . . responsibility. Man for man. You understand me?—To show that, to bring that on to the earth again like some kind of a monument and everyone would feel it standing there, behind him, and it would make a difference to him. [*Pause.*] And then I came home and it was incredible. I . . . there was no meaning in it here; the whole thing to them was a kind of a—bus accident. I went to work with Dad, and that rat-race again. I felt . . . what you said . . . ashamed somehow. Because nobody was changed at all. It seemed to make suckers out of a lot of guys. I felt wrong to be alive, to open the bank-book, to drive the new car, to see the new refrigerator. I mean you can take those things out of a war, but when you drive that car you've got to know that it came out of the love a man can have for a man, you've got to be a little better because of that. Otherwise what you have is really loot, and there's blood on it. I didn't want to take any of it. And I guess that included you.

ANN: And you still feel that way?

CHRIS: I want you now, Annie.

ANN: Because you mustn't feel that way any more. Because you have a right to whatever you have. Everything, Chris, understand that? To me, too . . . And the money, there's nothing wrong in your money. Your father put hundreds of planes in the air, you should be proud. A man should be paid for that . . .

CHRIS: Oh Annie, Annie . . . I'm going to make a fortune for you!

KELLER [*offstage*]: Hello . . . Yes. Sure.

ANN [*laughing softly*]: What'll I do with a fortune . . . ? [*They kiss.* KELLER *enters from house.*]

KELLER [*thumbing toward house*]: Hey, Ann, your brother . . . [*They step apart shyly.* KELLER *comes down, and wryly . . .*] What is this, Labor Day?

CHRIS [*waving him away, knowing the kidding will be endless*]: All right, all right . . .

ANN: You shouldn't burst out like that.

KELLER: Well, nobody told me it was Labor Day. [*Looks around.*] Where's the hot dogs?

CHRIS [*loving it*]: All right. You said it once.

KELLER: Well, as long as I know it's Labor Day from now on, I'll wear a bell around my neck.

ANN [*affectionately*]: He's so subtle!

CHRIS: George Bernard Shaw as an elephant.

KELLER: George—hey, you kissed it out of my head—your brother's on the phone.

ANN [*surprised*]: My brother?

KELLER: Yeah, George. Long distance.

ANN: What's the matter, is anything wrong?

KELLER: I don't know, Kate's talking to him. Hurry up, she'll cost him five dollars.

ANN [*She takes a step upstage, then comes down toward* CHRIS.]: I wonder if we ought to tell your mother yet? I mean I'm not very good in an argument.

CHRIS: We'll wait till tonight. After dinner. Now don't get tense, just leave it to me.

KELLER: What're you telling her?

CHRIS: Go ahead, Ann. [*With misgivings,* ANN *goes up and into house.*] We're getting married, Dad. [KELLER *nods indecisively.*] Well, don't you say anything?

KELLER [*distracted*]: I'm glad, Chris, I'm just . . . George is calling from Columbus.

CHRIS: Columbus!

KELLER: Did Annie tell you he was going to see his father today?

CHRIS: No, I don't think she knew anything about it.

KELLER [*asking uncomfortably*]: Chris! You . . . you think you know her pretty good?

CHRIS [*hurt and apprehensive*]: What kind of a question . . . ?

KELLER: I'm just wondering. All these years George don't go to see his father. Suddenly he goes . . . and she comes here.

CHRIS: Well, what about it?

KELLER: It's crazy, but it comes to my mind. She don't hold nothin' against me, does she?

CHRIS [*angry*]: I don't know what you're talking about.

KELLER [*a little more combatively*]: I'm just talkin'. To his last day in court the man blamed it all on me; and this is his daughter. I mean if she was sent here to find out something?

CHRIS [*angered*]: Why? What is there to find out?

ANN [*on phone, offstage*]: Why are you so excited, George? What happened there?

KELLER: I mean if they want to open up the case again, for the nuisance value, to hurt us?

CHRIS: Dad . . . how could you think that of her?

ANN [*still on phone*]: But what did he say to you, for God's sake?

[*Together.*]

KELLER: It couldn't be, heh. You know.

CHRIS: Dad, you amaze me . . .

KELLER [*breaking in*]: All right, forget it, forget it. [*With great force, moving about.*] I want a clean start for you, Chris. I want a new sign over the plant—Christopher Keller, Incorporated.

CHRIS [*a little uneasily*]: J. O. Keller is good enough.

KELLER: We'll talk about it. I'm going to build you a house, stone, with a driveway from the road. I want you to spread out, Chris, I want you to use what I made for you . . . [*He is close to him now.*] . . . I mean, with joy, Chris, without shame . . . with joy.

CHRIS [*touched*]: I will, Dad.

KELLER [*with deep emotion*]: . . . Say it to me.

CHRIS: Why?

KELLER: Because sometimes I think you're . . . ashamed of the money.

CHRIS: No, don't feel that.

KELLER: Because it's good money, there's nothing wrong with that money.

CHRIS [*a little frightened*]: Dad, you don't have to tell me this.

KELLER [*with overriding affection and self-confidence now. He grips* CHRIS *by the back of the neck, and with laughter between his determined jaws*]: Look, Chris, I'll go to work on Mother for you. We'll get her so drunk tonight we'll all get married! [*Steps away, with a wide gesture of his arm.*] There's gonna be a wedding, kid, like there never was seen! Champagne, tuxedoes . . . !

[*He breaks off as* ANN*'s voice comes out loud from the house where she is still talking on phone.*]

ANN: Simply because when you get excited you don't control yourself. . . . [MOTHER *comes out of house.*] Well, what did he tell you for God's sake? [*Pause.*] All right, come then. [*Pause.*] Yes, they'll all be here. Nobody's running away from you. And try to get hold of yourself, will you? [*Pause.*] All right, all right. Goodbye. [*There is a brief pause as* ANN *hangs up receiver, then comes out of kitchen.*]

CHRIS: Something happen?

KELLER: He's coming here?

ANN: On the seven o'clock. He's in Columbus. [*To* MOTHER.] I told him it would be all right.

KELLER: Sure, fine! Your father took sick?

ANN [*mystified*]: No, George didn't say he was sick. I . . . [*Shaking it off.*] I don't know, I suppose it's something stupid, you know my brother . . . [*She comes to* CHRIS.] Let's go for a drive, or something . . .

CHRIS: Sure. Give me the keys, Dad.

MOTHER: Drive through the park. It's beautiful now.

CHRIS: Come on, Ann. [*To them.*] Be back right away.

ANN [*as she and* CHRIS *exit up driveway*]: See you. [MOTHER *comes down toward* KELLER, *her eyes fixed on him.*]

KELLER: Take your time. [*To* MOTHER.] What does George want?

MOTHER: He's been in Columbus since this morning with Steve. He's gotta see Annie right away, he says.

KELLER: What for?

MOTHER: I don't know. [*She speaks with warning.*] He's a lawyer now, Joe. George is a lawyer. All these years he never even sent a postcard to Steve. Since he got back from the war, not a postcard.

KELLER: So what?

MOTHER [*her tension breaking out*]: Suddenly he takes an airplane from New York to see him. An airplane!

KELLER: Well? So?

MOTHER [*trembling*]: Why?

KELLER: I don't read minds. Do you?

MOTHER: Why, Joe? What has Steve suddenly got to tell him that he takes an airplane to see him?

KELLER: What do I care what Steve's got to tell him?

MOTHER: You're sure, Joe?

KELLER [*frightened, but angry*]: Yes, I'm sure.

MOTHER [*she sits stiffly in a chair*]: Be smart now, Joe. The boy is coming. Be smart.

KELLER [*desperately*]: Once and for all, did you hear what I said? I said I'm sure!

MOTHER [*she nods weakly*]: All right, Joe. [*He straightens up.*] Just . . . be smart. [KELLER, *in hopeless fury, looks at her, turns around, goes up to porch and into house, slamming screen door violently behind him.* MOTHER *sits in chair downstage, stiffly, staring, seeing.*]

ACT II

As twilight falls, that evening.

On the rise, CHRIS *is discovered at right, sawing the broken-off tree, leaving stump standing alone. He is dressed in good pants, white shoes, but without a shirt. He disappears with tree up the alley when* MOTHER *appears on porch. She comes down and stands watching him. She has on a dressing-gown, carries a tray of grape-juice drink in a pitcher, and glasses with sprigs of mint in them.*

MOTHER [*calling up alley*]: Did you have to put on good pants to do that? [*She comes downstage and puts tray on table in the arbor. Then looks around uneasily, then feels pitcher for coolness.* CHRIS *enters from alley brushing off his hands.*] You notice there's more light with that thing gone?

CHRIS: Why aren't you dressing?

MOTHER: It's suffocating upstairs. I made a grape drink for Georgie. He always liked grape. Come and have some.

CHRIS [*impatiently*]: Well, come on, get dressed. And what's Dad sleeping so much for? [*He goes to table and pours a glass of juice.*]

MOTHER: He's worried. When he's worried he sleeps. [*Pauses. Looks into his eyes.*] We're dumb, Chris. Dad and I are stupid people. We don't know anything. You've got to protect us.

CHRIS: You're silly; what's there to be afraid of?

MOTHER: To his last day in court Steve never gave up the idea that Dad made him do it. If they're going to open the case again I won't live through it.

CHRIS: George is just a damn fool, Mother. How can you take him seriously?

MOTHER: That family hates us. Maybe even Annie. . . .

CHRIS: Oh, now, Mother . . .

MOTHER: You think just because you like everybody, they like you!

CHRIS: All right, stop working yourself up. Just leave everything to me.

MOTHER: When George goes home tell her to go with him.

CHRIS [*non-committally*]: Don't worry about Annie.

MOTHER: Steve is her father, too.

CHRIS: Are you going to cut it out? Now, come.

MOTHER [*going upstage with him*]: You don't realize how people can hate, Chris, they can hate so much they'll tear the world to pieces. . . . [ANN, *dressed up, appears on porch.*]

CHRIS: Look! She's dressed already. [*As he and* MOTHER *mount porch.*] I've just got to put on a shirt.

ANN [*in a preoccupied way*]: Are you feeling well, Katie?

MOTHER: What's the difference, dear. There are certain people, y'know, the sicker they get the longer they live. [*She goes into house.*]

CHRIS: You look nice.

ANN: We're going to tell her tonight.

CHRIS: Absolutely, don't worry about it.

ANN: I wish we could tell her now. I can't stand scheming. My stomach gets hard.

CHRIS: It's not scheming, we'll just get her in a better mood.

MOTHER [*offstage, in the house*]: Joe, are you going to sleep all day!

ANN [*laughing*]: The only one who's relaxed is your father. He's fast asleep.

CHRIS: I'm relaxed.

ANN: Are you?

CHRIS: Look. [*He holds out his hand and makes it shake.*] Let me know when George gets here. [*He goes into the house. She moves aimlessly, then is drawn toward tree stump. She goes to it, hesitantly touches broken top in the hush of her thoughts. Offstage* LYDIA *calls, "Johnny! Come get your supper!"* SUE *enters from left, and calls, seeing* ANN.]

SUE: Is my husband . . . ?

ANN [*turns, startled*]: Oh!

SUE: I'm terribly sorry.

ANN: It's all right, I . . . I'm a little silly about the dark.

SUE [*looks about*]: It is getting dark.

ANN: Are you looking for your husband?

SUE: As usual. [*Laughs tiredly.*] He spends so much time here, they'll be charging him rent.

ANN: Nobody was dressed so he drove over to the depot to pick up my brother.

SUE: Oh, your brother's in?

ANN: Yeah, they ought to be here any minute now. Will you have a cold drink?

SUE: I will, thanks. [ANN *goes to table and pours.*] My husband. Too hot to drive me to beach.—Men are like little boys; for the neighbors they'll always cut the grass.

ANN: People like to do things for the Kellers. Been that way since I can remember.

SUE: It's amazing. I guess your brother's coming to give you away, heh?

ANN [*giving her drink*]: I don't know. I suppose.

SUE: You must be all nerved up.

ANN: It's always a problem getting yourself married, isn't it?

SUE: That depends on your shape, of course. I don't see why you should have had a problem.

ANN: I've had chances—

SUE: I'll bet. It's romantic . . . it's very unusual to me, marrying the brother of your sweetheart.

ANN: I don't know. I think it's mostly that whenever I need somebody to tell me the truth I've always thought of Chris. When he tells you something you know it's so. He relaxes me.

SUE: And he's got money. That's important, you know.

ANN: It wouldn't matter to me.

SUE: You'd be surprised. It makes all the difference. I married an interne. On my salary. And that was bad, because as soon as a woman supports a man he owes her something. You can never owe somebody without resenting them. [ANN *laughs.*] That's true, you know.

ANN: Underneath, I think the doctor is very devoted.

SUE: Oh, certainly. But it's bad when a man always sees the bars in front of him. Jim thinks he's in jail all the time.

ANN: Oh . . .

SUE: That's why I've been intending to ask you a small favor, Ann . . . it's something very important to me.

ANN: Certainly, if I can do it.

SUE: You can. When you take up housekeeping, try to find a place away from here.

ANN: Are you fooling?

SUE: I'm very serious. My husband is unhappy with Chris around.

ANN: How is that?

SUE: Jim's a successful doctor. But he's got an idea he'd like to do medical research. Discover things. You see?

ANN: Well, isn't that good?

SUE: Research pays twenty-five dollars a week minus laundering the hair shirt. You've got to give up your life to go into it.

ANN: How does Chris?

SUE [*with growing feeling*]: Chris makes people want to be better than it's possible to be. He does that to people.

ANN: Is that bad?

SUE: My husband has a family, dear. Every time he has a session with Chris he feels as though he's compromising by not giving up everything for research. As though Chris or anybody else isn't compromising. It happens with Jim every couple of years. He meets a man and makes a statue out of him.

ANN: Maybe he's right. I don't mean that Chris is a statue, but . . .

SUE: Now darling, you know he's not right.

ANN: I don't agree with you. Chris . . .

SUE: Let's face it, dear. Chris is working with his father, isn't he? He's taking money out of that business every week in the year.

ANN: What of it?

SUE: You ask me what of it?

ANN: I certainly do ask you.[*She seems about to burst out.*] You oughtn't cast aspersions like that, I'm surprised at you.

SUE: You're surprised at me!

ANN: He'd never take five cents out of that plant if there was anything wrong in it.

SUE: You know that.

ANN: I know it. I resent everything you've said.

SUE [*moving toward her*]: You know what I resent, dear?

ANN: Please, I don't want to argue.

SUE: I resent living next door to the Holy Family. It makes me look like a bum, you understand?

ANN: I can't do anything about that.

SUE: Who is he to ruin a man's life? Everybody knows Joe pulled a fast one to get out of jail.

ANN: That's not true!

SUE: Then why don't you go out and talk to people? Go on, talk to them. There's not a person on the block who doesn't know the truth.

ANN: That's a lie. People come here all the time for cards and . . .

SUE: So what? They give him credit for being smart. I do, too, I've got nothing against Joe. But if Chris wants people to put on the hair shirt let him take off his broadcloth. He's driving my husband crazy with that phony idealism of his, and I'm at the end of my rope on it! [CHRIS *enters on porch, wearing shirt and tie now. She turns quickly, hearing. With a smile.*] Hello, darling. How's Mother?

CHRIS: I thought George came.

SUE: No, it was just us.

CHRIS [*coming down to them*]: Susie, do me a favor, heh? Go up to Mother and see if you can calm her. She's all worked up.

SUE: She still doesn't know about you two?

CHRIS [*laughs a little*]: Well, she senses it, I guess. You know my mother.

SUE [*going up to porch*]: Oh, yeah, she's psychic.

CHRIS: Maybe there's something in the medicine chest.

SUE: I'll give her one of everything. [*On porch.*] Don't worry about Kate; couple of drinks, dance her around a little . . . she'll love Ann. [*To* ANN.] Because you're the female version of him. [CHRIS *laughs.*] Don't be alarmed, I said version. [*She goes into house.*]

CHRIS: Interesting woman, isn't she?

ANN: Yeah, she's very interesting.

CHRIS: She's a great nurse, you know, she . . .

ANN [*in tension, but trying to control it*]: Are you still doing that?

CHRIS [*sensing something wrong, but still smiling*]: Doing what?

ANN: As soon as you get to know somebody you find a distinction for them. How do you know she's a great nurse?

CHRIS: What's the matter, Ann?

ANN: The woman hates you. She despises you!

CHRIS: Hey . . . what's hit you?

ANN: Gee, Chris . . .

CHRIS: What happened here?

ANN: You never . . . Why didn't you tell me?

CHRIS: Tell you what?

ANN: She says they think Joe is guilty.

CHRIS: What difference does it make what they think?

ANN: I don't care what they think, I just don't understand why you took the trouble to deny it. You said it was all forgotten.

CHRIS: I didn't want you to feel there was anything wrong in you coming here, that's all. I know a lot of people think my father was guilty, and I assumed there might be some question in your mind.

ANN: But I never once said I suspected him.

CHRIS: Nobody says it.

ANN: Chris, I know how much you love him, but it could never . . .

CHRIS: Do you think I could forgive him if he'd done that thing?

ANN: I'm not here out of a blue sky, Chris. I turned my back on my father, if there's anything wrong here now . . .

CHRIS: I know that, Ann.

ANN: George is coming from Dad, and I don't think it's with a blessing.

CHRIS: He's welcome here. You've got nothing to fear from George.

ANN: Tell me that . . . just tell me that.

CHRIS: The man is innocent, Ann. Remember he was falsely accused once and it put him though hell. How would you behave it you were faced with the same thing again? Annie, believe me, there's nothing wrong for you here, believe me, kid.

ANN: All right, Chris, all right. [*They embrace as* KELLER *appears quietly on porch.* ANN *simply studies him.*]

KELLER: Every time I come out here it looks like Playland!

[*They break and laugh in embarrassment.*]

CHRIS: I thought you were going to shave?

KELLER [*sitting on bench*]: In a minute. I just woke up, I can't see nothin'.

ANN: You look shaved.

KELLER: Oh, no. [*Massages his jaw.*] Gotta be extra special tonight. Big night, Annie. So how's it feel to be a married woman?

ANN [*laughs*]: I don't know, yet.

KELLER [*to* CHRIS]: What's the matter, you slippin'? [*He takes a little box of apples from under the bench as they talk.*]

CHRIS: The great roué!

KELLER: What is that, roué?

CHRIS: It's French.

KELLER: Don't talk dirty. [*They laugh.*]

CHRIS [*to* ANN]: You ever meet a bigger ignoramus?

KELLER: Well, somebody's got to make a living.

ANN [*as they laugh*]: That's telling him.

KELLER: I don't know, everybody's gettin' so Goddam educated in this country there'll be nobody to take away the garbage. [*They laugh.*] It's gettin' so the only dumb ones left are the bosses.

ANN: You're not so dumb, Joe.

KELLER: I know, but you go into our plant, for instance. I got so many lieutenants, majors and colonels that I'm ashamed to ask somebody to sweep the floor. I gotta be careful I'll insult somebody. No kiddin'. It's a tragedy: you stand on the street today and spit, you're gonna hit a college man.

CHRIS: Well, don't spit.

KELLER [*breaks apple in half, passing it to* ANN *and* CHRIS]: I mean to say, it's comin' to a pass. [*He takes a breath.*] I been thinkin', Annie . . . your brother, George. I been thinkin' about your brother George. When he comes I like you to *brooch* something to him.

CHRIS: Broach.

KELLER: What's the matter with brooch?

CHRIS [*smiling*]: It's not English.

KELLER: When I went to night school it was brooch.

ANN [*laughing*]: Well, in day school it's broach.

KELLER: Don't surround me, will you? Seriously, Ann . . . You say he's not well. George, I been thinkin', why should he knock himself out in New York with that cut-throat competition, when I got so many friends here; I'm very friendly with some big lawyers in town. I could set George up here.

ANN: That's awfully nice of you, Joe.

KELLER: No, kid, it ain't nice of me. I want you to understand me. I'm thinking of Chris. [*Slight pause.*] See . . . this is what I mean. You get older, you want to feel that you . . . accomplished something. My only accomplishment is my son. I ain't brainy. That's all I accomplished. Now, a year, eighteen months, your father'll be a free man. Who is he going to come to Annie? His baby. You. He'll come, old, mad, into your house.

ANN: That can't matter any more, Joe.

KELLER: I don't want that hate to come between us. [*Gestures between* CHRIS *and himself.*]

ANN: I can only tell you that that could never happen.

KELLER: You're in love now, Annie, but believe me, I'm older than you and I know—a daughter is a daughter, and a father is a father. And it could happen. [*He pauses.*] I like you and George to go to him in prison and tell him. . . . "Dad, Joe wants to bring you into the business when you get out."
ANN [*surprised, even shocked*]: You'd have him as a partner?
KELLER: No, no partner. A good job. [*Pause. He sees she is shocked, a little mystified. He gets up, speaks more nervously.*] I want him to know, Annie . . . while he's sitting there I want him to know that when he gets out he's got a place waitin' for him. It'll take his bitterness away. To know you got a place . . . it sweetens you.
ANN: Joe, you owe him nothing.
KELLER: I owe him a good kick in the teeth, but he's your father. . . .
CHRIS: Then kick him in the teeth! I don't want him in the plant, so that's that! You understand? And besides, don't talk about him like that. People misunderstand you!
KELLER: And I don't understand why she has to crucify the man.
CHRIS: Well, it's her father, if she feels . . .
KELLER: No, no. . . .
CHRIS [*almost angrily*]: What's it to you? Why . . . ?
KELLER [*a commanding outburst in his high nervousness*]: A father is a father! [*As though the outburst had revealed him, he looks about, wanting to retract it. His hand, goes to his cheek.*] I better . . . I better shave. [*He turns and a smile is on his face. To* ANN.] I didn't mean to yell at you, Annie.
ANN: Let's forget the whole thing, Joe.
KELLER: Right. [*To* CHRIS.] She's likable.
CHRIS [*a little peeved at the man's stupidity*]: Shave, will you?
KELLER: Right again.

[*As he turns to porch* LYDIA *comes hurrying from her house, right.*]

LYDIA: I forgot all about it . . . [*Seeing* CHRIS *and* ANN.] Hya. [*To* JOE.] I promised to fix Kate's hair for tonight. Did she comb it yet?
KELLER: Always a smile, hey, Lydia?
LYDIA: Sure, why not?
KELLER [*going up on porch*]: Come on up and comb my Katie's hair. [LYDIA *goes up on porch.*] She's got a big night, make her beautiful.
LYDIA: I will.
KELLER [*he holds door open for her and she goes into kitchen. To* CHRIS *and* ANN]: Hey, that could be a song. [*He sings softly.*]
"Come on up and comb my Katie's hair . . .
Oh, come on up, 'cause she's my lady fair—"
[*To* ANN.] How's that for one year of night school? [*He continues, singing as he goes into kitchen.*]
"Oh, come on up, come on up, and comb my lady's hair—"

[JIM BAYLISS *rounds corner of driveway, walking rapidly.* JIM *crosses to* CHRIS, *motions him up and pulls him down to stage left, excitedly.* KELLER *stands just inside kitchen door, watching them.*]

CHRIS: What's the matter? Where is he?
JIM: Where's your mother?
CHRIS: Upstairs, dressing.
ANN [*crossing to them rapidly*]: What happened to George?
JIM: I asked him to wait in the car. Listen to me now. Can you take some advice? [*They wait.*] Don't bring him in here.
ANN: Why?
JIM: Kate is in bad shape, you can't explode this in front of her.
ANN: Explode what?
JIM: You know why he's here, don't try to kid it away. There's blood in his eye; drive him somewhere and talk to him alone.

[ANN *turns to go up drive, takes a couple of steps, sees* KELLER *and stops. He goes quietly on into house.*]

CHRIS [*shaken, and therefore angered*]: Don't be an old lady.
JIM: He's come to take her home. What does that mean? [*To* ANN.] You know what that means. Fight it out with him some place else.
ANN [*she comes back down toward* CHRIS]: I'll drive . . . him somewhere.
CHRIS [*goes to her*]: No.
JIM: Will you stop being an idiot?
CHRIS: Nobody's afraid of him here. Cut that out! [*He starts for driveway, but is brought up short by* GEORGE, *who enters there.* GEORGE *is* CHRIS' *age, but a paler man, now on the edge of his self-restraint. He speaks quietly, as though afraid to find himself screaming. An instant's hesitation and* CHRIS *steps up to him, hand extended, smiling.*] Helluva way to do; what're you sitting out there for?
GEORGE: Doctor said your mother isn't well, I . . .
CHRIS: So what? She'd want to see you, wouldn't she? We've been waiting for you all afternoon. [*He puts his hand on* GEORGE'S *arm, but* GEORGE *pulls away, coming across toward* ANN.]
ANN [*touching his collar*]: This is filthy, didn't you bring another shirt? [GEORGE *breaks away from her, and moves down and left, examining the yard. Door opens, and he turns rapidly, thinking it is* KATE, *but it's* SUE. *She looks at him, he turns away and moves on*

left, to fence. He looks over it at his former home. SUE *comes down stage.*]

SUE [*annoyed*]: How about the beach, Jim?

JIM: Oh, it's too hot to drive.

SUE: How'd you get to the station—Zeppelin?

CHRIS: This is Mrs. Bayliss, George. [*Calling, as* GEORGE *pays no attention, staring at house off left.*] George! [GEORGE *turns.*] Mrs. Bayliss.

SUE: How do you do.

GEORGE [*removing his hat*]: You're the people who bought our house, aren't you?

SUE: That's right. Come and see what we did with it before you leave.

GEORGE [*he walks down and away from her*]: I liked it the way it was.

SUE [*after a brief pause*]: He's frank, isn't he?

JIM [*pulling her off left*]: See you later. . . . Take it easy, fella. [*They exit, left.*]

CHRIS [*calling after them*]: Thanks for driving him! [*Turning to* GEORGE.] How about some grape juice? Mother made it especially for you.

GEORGE [*with forced appreciation*]: Good old Kate, remembered my grape juice.

CHRIS: You drank enough of it in this house. How've you been, George?—Sit down.

GEORGE [*he keeps moving*]: It takes me a minute. [*Looking around.*] It seems impossible.

CHRIS: What?

GEORGE: I'm back here.

CHRIS: Say, you've gotten a little nervous, haven't you?

GEORGE: Yeah, toward the end of the day. What're you, big executive now?

CHRIS: Just kind of medium. How's the law?

GEORGE: I don't know. When I was studying in the hospital it seemed sensible, but outside there doesn't seem to be much of a law. The trees got thick didn't they? [*Points to stump.*] What's that?

CHRIS: Blew down last night. We had it there for Larry. You know.

GEORGE: Why, afraid you'll forget him?

CHRIS [*starts for* GEORGE]: Kind of a remark is that?

ANN [*breaking in, putting a restraining hand on* CHRIS]: When did you start wearing a hat?

GEORGE [*discovers hat in his hand*]: Today. From now on I decided to look like a lawyer, anyway. [*He holds it up to her.*] Don't you recognize it?

ANN: Why? Where . . . ?

GEORGE: Your father's . . . he asked me to wear it.

ANN: . . . How is he?

GEORGE: He got smaller.

ANN: Smaller?

GEORGE: Yeah, little. [*Holds out his hand to measure.*] He's a little man. That's what happens to suckers, you know. It's good I went to him in time—another year there'd be nothing left but his smell.

CHRIS: What's the matter, George, what's the trouble?

GEORGE: The trouble? The trouble is when you make suckers out of people once, you shouldn't try to do it twice.

CHRIS: What does that mean?

GEORGE [*to* ANN]: You're not married yet, are you?

ANN: George, will you sit down and stop—?

GEORGE: Are you married yet?

ANN: No, I'm not married yet.

GEORGE: You're not going to marry him.

ANN: Why am I not going to marry him?

GEORGE: Because his father destroyed your family.

CHRIS: Now look, George . . .

GEORGE: Cut it short, Chris. Tell her to come home with me. Let's not argue, you know what I've got to say.

CHRIS: George, you don't want to be the voice of God, do you?

GEORGE: I'm . . .

CHRIS: That's been your trouble all your life, George, you dive into things. What kind of a statement is that to make? You're a big boy now.

GEORGE: I'm a big boy now.

CHRIS: Don't come bulling in here. If you've got something to say, be civilized about it.

GEORGE: Don't civilize me!

ANN: Shhh!

CHRIS [*ready to hit him*]: Are you going to talk like a grown man or aren't you?

ANN [*quickly, to forestall an outburst*]: Sit down, dear. Don't be angry, what's the matter? [*He allows her to seat him, looking at her.*] Now what happened? You kissed me when I left, now you . . .

GEORGE [*breathlessly*]: My life turned upside down since then. I couldn't go back to work when you left. I wanted to go to Dad and tell him you were going to be married. It seemed impossible not to tell him. He loved you so much . . . . [*He pauses.*] Annie . . . we did a terrible thing. We can never be forgiven. Not even to send him a card at Christmas. I didn't see him once since I got home from the war! Annie, you don't know what was done to that man. You don't know what happened.

ANN [*afraid*]: Of course I know.

GEORGE: You can't know, you wouldn't be here. Dad came to work that day. The night foreman came to him and showed him the cylinder heads . . . they were coming out of the process with defects. There was something wrong with the process. So Dad went directly to the phone and called here and told Joe to come down right away. But the morning passed. No sign of Joe. So Dad called again. By this time he had over a hundred defectives. The Army was screaming for stuff and Dad didn't have anything to ship. So Joe told him . . .

on the phone he told him to weld, cover up the cracks in any way he could, and ship them out.

CHRIS: Are you through now?

GEORGE [*surging up at him*]: I'm not through now! [*Back to* ANN.] Dad was afraid. He wanted Joe there if he was going to do it. But Joe can't come down . . . he's sick. Sick! He suddenly gets the flu! Suddenly! But he promised to take responsibility. Do you understand what I'm saying? On the telephone you can't have responsibility! In a court you can always deny a phone call and that's exactly what he did. They knew he was a liar the first time, but in the appeal they believed that rotten lie and now Joe is a big shot and your father is the patsy. [*He gets up.*] Now what're you going to do? Eat his food, sleep in his bed? Answer me; what're you going to do?

CHRIS: What're you going to do, George?

GEORGE: He's too smart for me, I can't prove a phone call.

CHRIS: Then how dare you come in here with that rot?

ANN: George, the court . . .

GEORGE: The court didn't know your father! But you know him. You know in your heart Joe did it.

CHRIS [*whirling him around*]: Lower your voice or I'll throw you out of here!

GEORGE: She knows. She knows.

CHRIS [*to* ANN]: Get him out of here, Ann. Get him out of here.

ANN: George, I know everything you've said. Dad told that whole thing in court, and they . . .

GEORGE [*almost a scream*]: The court did not know him, Annie!

ANN: Shhh!—But he'll say anything, George. You know how quick he can lie.

GEORGE [*turning to* CHRIS *with deliberation*]: I'll ask you something, and look me in the eye when you answer me.

CHRIS: I'll look you in the eye.

GEORGE: You know your father. . .

CHRIS: I know him well.

GEORGE: And he's the kind of boss to let a hundred and twenty-one cylinder heads be repaired and shipped out of his shop without even knowing about it?

CHRIS: He's that kind of boss.

GEORGE: And that's the same Joe Keller who never left his shop without first going around to see that all the lights were out.

CHRIS [*with growing anger*]: The same Joe Keller.

GEORGE: The same man who knows how many minutes a day his workers spend in the toilet.

CHRIS: The same man.

GEORGE: And my father, that frightened mouse who'd never buy a shirt without somebody along—that man would dare do such a thing on his own?

CHRIS: On his own. And because he's a frightened mouse this is another thing he'd do;—throw the blame on somebody else because he's not man enough to take it himself. He tried it in court but it didn't work, but with a fool like you it works!

GEORGE: Oh, Chris, you're a liar to yourself!

ANN [*deeply shaken*]: Don't talk like that!

CHRIS [*sits facing* GEORGE]: Tell me, George. What happened? The court record was good enough for you all these years, why isn't it good now? Why did you believe it all these years?

GEORGE [*after a slight pause*]: Because you believed it. . . . That's the truth, Chris. I believed everything, because I thought you did. But today I heard it from his mouth. From his mouth it's altogether different than the record. Anyone who knows him, and knows your father, will believe it from his mouth. Your Dad took everything we have. I can't beat that. But she's one item he's not going to grab. [*He turns to* ANN.] Get your things. Everything they have is covered with blood. You're not the kind of a girl who can live with that. Get your things.

CHRIS: Ann . . . you're not going to believe that, are you?

ANN [*she goes to him*]: You know it's not true, don't you?

GEORGE: How can he tell you? It's his father. [*To* CHRIS.] None of these things ever even cross your mind?

CHRIS: Yes, they crossed my mind. Anything can cross your mind!

GEORGE: He *knows*, Annie. He knows!

CHRIS: The Voice of God!

GEORGE: Then why isn't your name on the business? Explain that to her!

CHRIS: What the hell has that got to do with . . . ?

GEORGE: Annie, why isn't his name on it?

CHRIS: Even when I don't own it!

GEORGE: Who're you kidding? Who gets it when he dies? [*To* ANN.] Open your eyes, you know the both of them, isn't that the first thing they'd do, the way they love each other?—J. O. Keller & Son? [*Pause.* ANN *looks from him to* CHRIS.] I'll settle it. Do you want to settle it, or are you afraid to?

CHRIS: . . . What do you mean?

GEORGE: Let me go up and talk to your father. In ten minutes you'll have the answer. Or are you afraid of the answer?

CHRIS: I'm not afraid of the answer. I know the answer. But my mother isn't well and I don't want a fight here now.

GEORGE: Let me go to him.

CHRIS: You're not going to start a fight here now.

GEORGE [*to* ANN]: What more do you want!!! [*There is a sound of footsteps in the house.*]

ANN [*turns her head suddenly toward the house*]: Someone's coming.

CHRIS [*to* GEORGE, *quietly*]: You won't say anything now.

ANN: You'll go soon. I'll call a cab.

GEORGE: You're coming with me.

ANN: And don't mention marriage, because we haven't told her yet.

GEORGE: You're coming with me.

ANN: You understand? Don't . . . George, you're not going to start anything now! [*She hears footsteps.*] Shsh! [MOTHER *enters on porch. She is dressed almost formally, her hair is fixed. They are all turned toward her. On seeing* GEORGE *she raises both hands, comes down toward him.*]

MOTHER: Georgie, Georgie.

GEORGE [*he has always liked her*]: Hello, Kate.

MOTHER [*she cups his face in her hands*]: They made an old man out of you. [*Touches his hair.*] Look, you're gray.

GEORGE [*her pity, open and unabashed, reaches into him, and he smiles sadly*]: I know, I . . .

MOTHER: I told you when you went away, don't try for medals.

GEORGE [*he laughs, tiredly*]: I didn't try, Kate. They made it very easy for me.

MOTHER [*actually angry*]: Go on. You're all alike. [*To* ANN.] Look at him, why did you say he's fine? He looks like a ghost.

GEORGE [*relishing her solicitude*]: I feel all right.

MOTHER: I'm sick to look at you. What's the matter with your mother, why don't she feed you?

ANN: He just hasn't any appetite.

MOTHER: If he ate in my house he'd have an appetite. [*To* ANN.] I pity your husband! [*To* GEORGE.] Sit down. I'll make you a sandwich.

GEORGE [*sits with an embarrassed laugh*]: I'm really not hungry.

MOTHER: Honest to God, it breaks my heart to see what happened to all the children. How we worked and planned for you, and you end up no better than us.

GEORGE [*with deep feeling for her*]: You . . . you haven't changed at all, you know that, Kate?

MOTHER: None of us changed, Georgie. We all love you. Joe was just talking about the day you were born and the water got shut off. People were carrying basins from a block away—a stranger would have thought the whole neighborhood was on fire! [*They laugh. She sees the juice. To* ANN.] Why didn't you give him some juice!

ANN [*defensively*]: I offered it to him.

MOTHER [*scoffingly*]: You offered it to him! [*Thrusting glass into* GEORGE*'s hand.*] Give it to him! [*To* GEORGE, *who is laughing.*] And now you're going to sit here and drink some juice . . . and look like something!

GEORGE [*sitting*]: Kate, I feel hungry already.

CHRIS [*proudly*]: She could turn Mahatma Ghandi into a heavyweight!

MOTHER [*to* CHRIS, *with great energy*]: Listen, to hell with the restaurant! I got a ham in the icebox, and frozen strawberries, and avocados, and . . .

ANN: Swell, I'll help you!

GEORGE: The train leaves at eight-thirty, Ann.

MOTHER [*to* ANN]: You're leaving?

CHRIS: No, Mother, she's not . . .

ANN [*breaking through it, going to* GEORGE]: You hardly got here; give yourself a chance to get acquainted again.

CHRIS: Sure, you don't even know us any more.

MOTHER: Well, Chris, if they can't stay, don't . . .

CHRIS: No, it's just a question of George, Mother, he planned on . . .

GEORGE [*he gets up politely, nicely, for* KATE*'s sake*]: Now wait a minute, Chris . . .

CHRIS [*smiling and full of command, cutting him off*]: If you want to go, I'll drive you to the station now, but if you're staying, no arguments while you're here.

MOTHER [*at last confessing the tension*]: Why should he argue? [*She goes to him, and with desperation and compassion, stroking his hair.*] Georgie and us have no argument. How could we have an argument, Georgie? We all got hit by the same lightning, how can you . . . ? Did you see what happened to Larry's tree, Georgie? [*She has taken his arm, and unwillingly he moves across stage with her.*] Imagine? While I was dreaming of him in the middle of the night, the wind came along and . . . [LYDIA *enters on porch. As soon as she sees him.*]

LYDIA: Hey, Georgie! Georgie! Georgie! Georgie! Georgie! [*She comes down to him eagerly. She has a flowered hat in her hand, which* KATE *takes from her as she goes to* GEORGE.]

GEORGE [*They shake hands eagerly, warmly.*]: Hello, Laughy. What'd you do, grow?

LYDIA: I'm a big girl now.

MOTHER [*taking hat from her*]: Look what she can do to a hat!

ANN: [*to* LYDIA, *admiring the hat*]: Did you make that?

MOTHER: In ten minutes! [*She puts it on.*]

LYDIA [*fixing it on her head*]: I only rearranged it.

GEORGE: You still make your own clothes?

CHRIS [*of* MOTHER]: Ain't she classy! All she needs now is a Russian wolfhound.

MOTHER [*moving her head from left to right*]: It feels like somebody is sitting on my head.

ANN: No, it's beautiful, Kate.

MOTHER [*kisses* LYDIA—*to* GEORGE]: She's a genius! You should've married her. [*They laugh.*] This one can feed you!

LYDIA [*strangely embarrassed*]: Oh, stop that, Kate.

GEORGE [*to* LYDIA]: Didn't I hear you had a baby?

MOTHER: You don't hear so good. She's got three babies.

GEORGE [*a little hurt by it—to* LYDIA]: No kidding, three?

LYDIA: Yeah, it was one, two, three—You've been away a long time, Georgie.

GEORGE: I'm beginning to realize.

MOTHER [*to* CHRIS *and* GEORGE]: The trouble with you kids is you *think* too much.

LYDIA: Well, we think, too.

MOTHER: Yes, but not all the time.

GEORGE [*with almost obvious envy*]: They never took Frank, heh?

LYDIA [*a little apologetically*]: No, he was always one year ahead of the draft.

MOTHER: It's amazing. When they were calling boys twenty-seven Frank was just twenty-eight, when they made it twenty-eight he was just twenty-nine. That's why he took up astrology. It's all in when you were born, it just goes to show.

CHRIS: What does it go to show?

MOTHER [*to* CHRIS]: Don't be so intelligent. Some superstitions are very nice! [*To* LYDIA.] Did he finish Larry's horoscope?

LYDIA: I'll ask him now, I'm going in. [*To* GEORGE, *a little sadly, almost embarrassed.*] Would you like to see my babies? Come on.

GEORGE: I don't think so, Lydia.

LYDIA [*understanding*]: All right. Good luck to you, George.

GEORGE: Thanks. And to you . . . And Frank. [*She smiles at him, turns and goes off right to her house.* GEORGE *stands staring after her.*]

LYDIA [*as she runs off*]: Oh, Frank!

MOTHER [*reading his thoughts*]: She got pretty, heh?

GEORGE [*sadly*]: Very pretty.

MOTHER [*as a reprimand*]: She's beautiful, you damned fool!

GEORGE [*looks around longingly; and softly, with a catch in his throat*]: She makes it seem so nice around here.

MOTHER [*shaking her finger at him*]: Look what happened to you because you wouldn't listen to me! I told you to marry that girl and stay out of the war!

GEORGE [*laughs at himself*]: She used to laugh too much.

MOTHER: And you didn't laugh enough. While you were getting mad about Fascism, Frank was getting into her bed.

GEORGE [*to* CHRIS]: He won the war, Frank.

CHRIS: All the battles.

MOTHER [*in pursuit of this mood*]: The day they started the draft, Georgie, I told you you loved that girl.

CHRIS [*laughs*]: And truer love hath no man!

MOTHER: I'm smarter than any of you.

GEORGE [*laughing*]: She's wonderful!

MOTHER: And now you're going to listen to me, George. You had big principles, Eagle Scouts the three of you; so now I got a tree, and this one, [*Indicating* CHRIS.] when the weather gets bad he can't stand on his feet; and that big dope, [*Pointing to* LYDIA'*s house.*] next door who never reads anything but Andy Gump has three children and his house paid off. Stop being a philosopher, and look after yourself. Like Joe was just saying—you move back here, he'll help you get set, and I'll find you a girl and put a smile on your face.

GEORGE: Joe? Joe wants me here?

ANN [*eagerly*]: He asked me to tell you, and I think it's a good idea.

MOTHER: Certainly. Why must you make believe you hate us? Is that another principle?—that you have to hate us? You don't hate us, George, I know you, you can't fool me, I diapered you. [*Suddenly to* ANN.] You remember Mr. Marcy's daughter?

ANN: [*laughing, to* GEORGE]: She's got you hooked already!

[GEORGE *laughs, is excited.*]

MOTHER: You look her over, George; you'll see she's the most beautiful . . .

CHRIS: She's got warts, George.

MOTHER [*to* CHRIS]: She hasn't got warts! [*To* GEORGE.] So the girl has a little beauty mark on her chin . . .

CHRIS: And two on her nose.

MOTHER: You remember. Her father's the retired police inspector.

CHRIS: Sergeant, George.

MOTHER: He's a very kind man!

CHRIS: He looks like a gorilla.

MOTHER [*to* GEORGE]: He never shot anybody! [*They all burst out laughing, as* KELLER *appears in doorway.* GEORGE *rises abruptly, stares at* KELLER, *who comes rapidly down to him.*]

KELLER [*the laughter stops. With strained joviality*]: Well! Look who's here! [*Extending his hand.*] Georgie, good to see ya.

GEORGE [*shakes hands—somberly*]: How're you, Joe?

KELLER: So-so. Gettin' old. You comin' out to dinner with us?

GEORGE: No, got to be back in New York.

ANN: I'll call a cab for you. [*She goes up into the house.*]

KELLER: Too bad you can't stay, George. Sit down. [*To* MOTHER.] He looks fine.

MOTHER: He looks terrible.

KELLER: That's what I said, you look terrible, George. [*They laugh.*] I wear the pants and she beats me with the belt.

GEORGE: I saw your factory on the way from the station. It looks like General Motors.

KELLER: I wish it was General Motors, but it ain't. Sit down, George. Sit down. [*Takes cigar out of his pocket.*] So you finally went to see your father, I hear?
GEORGE: Yes, this morning. What kind of stuff do you make now?
KELLER: Oh, little of everything. Pressure cookers, an assembly for washing machines. Got a nice, flexible plant now. So how'd you find Dad? Feel all right?
GEORGE [*searching* KELLER, *he speaks indecisively*]: No, he's not well, Joe.
KELLER [*lighting his cigar*]: Not his heart again, is it?
GEORGE: It's everything, Joe. It's his soul.
KELLER [*blowing out smoke*]: Uh huh—
CHRIS: How about seeing what they did with your house?
KELLER: Leave him be.
GEORGE [*to* CHRIS, *indicating* KELLER]: I'd like to talk to him.
KELLER: Sure, he just got here. That's the way they do, George. A little man makes a mistake and they hang him by the thumbs; the big ones become ambassadors. I wish you'd-a told me you were going to see Dad.
GEORGE [*studying him*]: I didn't know you were interested.
KELLER: In a way, I am. I would like him to know, George, that as far as I'm concerned, any time he wants, he's got a place with me. I would like him to know that.
GEORGE: He hates your guts, Joe. Don't you know that?
GEORGE: I imagined it. But that can change, too.
MOTHER: Steve was never like that.
GEORGE: He's like that now. He'd like to take every man who made money in the war and put him up against a wall.
CHRIS: He'll need a lot of bullets.
GEORGE: And he'd better not get any.
KELLER: That's a sad thing to hear.
GEORGE [*with bitterness dominant*]: Why? What'd you expect him to think of you?
KELLER [*the force of his nature rising, but under control*]: I'm sad to see he hasn't changed. As long as I know him, twenty-five years, the man never learned how to take the blame. You know that, George.
GEORGE [*he does*]: Well, I . . .
KELLER: But you do know it. Because the way you come in here you don't look like you remember it. I mean like in 1937 when we had the shop on Flood Street. And he damn near blew us all up with that heater he left burning for two days without water. He wouldn't admit that was his fault, either. I had to fire a mechanic to save his face. You remember that.
GEORGE: Yes, but . . .
KELLER: I'm just mentioning it, George. Because this is just another one of a lot of things. Like when he gave Frank that money to invest in oil stock.
GEORGE [*distressed*]: I know that, I . . .
KELLER [*driving in, but restrained*]: But it's good to remember those things, kid. The way he cursed Frank because the stock went down. Was that Frank's fault? To listen to him Frank was a swindler. And all the man did was give him a bad tip.
GEORGE [*gets up, moves away*]: I know those things . . .
KELLER: Then remember them, remember them. [ANN *comes out of house.*] There are certain men in the world who rather see everybody hung before they'll take blame. You understand me, George? [*They stand facing each other,* GEORGE *trying to judge him.*]
ANN [*coming downstage*]: The cab's on its way. Would you like to wash?
MOTHER [*with the thrust of hope*]: Why must he go? Make the midnight, George.
KELLER: Sure, you'll have dinner with us!
ANN: How about it? Why not? We're eating at the lake, we could have a swell time.
GEORGE [*long pause, as he looks at* ANN, CHRIS, KELLER, *then back to her*]: All right.
MOTHER: Now you're talking.
CHRIS: I've got a shirt that'll go right with that suit.
MOTHER: Size fifteen and a half, right, George?
GEORGE: Is Lydia . . . ? I mean—Frank and Lydia coming?
MOTHER: I'll get you a date that'll make her look like a . . .

[*She starts upstage.*]

GEORGE [*laughs*]: No, I don't want a date.
CHRIS: I know somebody just for you! Charlotte Tanner! [*He starts for the house.*]
KELLER: Call Charlotte, that's right.
MOTHER: Sure, call her up. [CHRIS *goes into house.*]
ANN: You go up and pick out a shirt and tie.
GEORGE [*he stops, looks around at them and the place*]: I never felt at home anywhere but here. I feel so . . . [*He nearly laughs, and turns away from them.*] Kate, you look so young, you know? You didn't change at all. It . . . rings an old bell. [*Turns to* KELLER.] You too, Joe, you're amazingly the same. The whole atmosphere is.
KELLER: Say, I ain't got time to get sick.
MOTHER: He hasn't been laid up in fifteen years . . .
KELLER: Except my flu during the war.
MOTHER: Huhh?
KELLER: My flu, when I was sick during . . . the war.

MOTHER: Well, sure . . . [*To* GEORGE.] I meant except for that flu. [GEORGE *stands perfectly still.*] Well, it slipped my mind, don't look at me that way. He wanted to go to the shop but he couldn't lift himself off the bed. I thought he had pneumonia.
GEORGE: Why did you say he's never . . . ?
KELLER: I know how you feel, kid, I'll never forgive myself. If I could've gone in that day I'd never allow Dad to touch those heads.
GEORGE: She said you've never been sick.
MOTHER: I said he was sick, George.
GEORGE [*going to* ANN]: Ann, didn't you hear her say . . . ?
MOTHER: Do you remember every time you were sick?
GEORGE: I'd remember pneumonia. Especially if I got it just the day my partner was going to patch up cylinder heads . . . What happened that day, Joe?
FRANK [*enters briskly from driveway, holding* LARRY'S *horoscope in his hand. He comes to* KATE]: Kate! Kate!
MOTHER: Frank, did you see George?
FRANK [*extending his hand*]: Lydia told me, I'm glad to . . . you'll have to pardon me. [*Pulling* MOTHER *over right.*] I've got something amazing for you, Kate, I finished Larry's horoscope.
MOTHER: You'd be interested in this, George. It's wonderful the way he can understand the . . . .
CHRIS [*entering from house*]: George, the girl's on the phone . . .
MOTHER [*desperately*]: He finished Larry's horoscope!
CHRIS: Frank, can't you pick a better time than this?
FRANK: The greatest men who ever lived believed in the stars!
CHRIS: Stop filling her head with that junk!
FRANK: Is it junk to feel that there's a greater power than ourselves? I've studied the stars of his life! I won't argue with you, I'm telling you. Somewhere in this world your brother is alive!
MOTHER [*instantly to* CHRIS]: Why isn't it possible?
CHRIS: Because it's insane.
FRANK: Just a minute now. I'll tell you something and you can do as you please. Just let me say it. He was supposed to have died on November twenty-fifth. But November twenty-fifth was his favorable day.
CHRIS: Mother!
MOTHER: Listen to him!
FRANK: It was a day when everything good was shining on him, the kind of day he should've married on. You can laugh at a lot of it, I can understand you laughing. But the odds are a million to one that a man won't die on his favorable day. That's known, that's known, Chris!
MOTHER: Why isn't it possible, why isn't it possible, Chris!
GEORGE [*to* ANN]: Don't you understand what she's saying? She just told you to go. What are you waiting for now?
CHRIS: Nobody can tell her to go. [*A car horn is heard.*]
MOTHER [*to* FRANK]: Thank you, darling, for your trouble. Will you tell him to wait, Frank?
FRANK [*as he goes*]: Sure thing.
MOTHER [*calling out*]: They'll be right out, driver!
CHRIS: She's not leaving, Mother.
GEORGE: You heard her say it, he's never been sick!
MOTHER: He misunderstood me, Chris! [CHRIS *looks at her, struck.*]
GEORGE [*to* ANN]: He simply told your father to kill pilots, and covered himself in bed!
CHRIS: You'd better answer him, Annie. Answer him.
MOTHER: I packed your bag, darling . . .
CHRIS: What?
MOTHER: I packed your bag. All you've got to do is close it.
ANN: I'm not closing anything. He asked me here and I'm staying till he tells me to go. [*To* GEORGE.] Till Chris tells me!
CHRIS: That's all! Now get out of here, George!
MOTHER [*to* CHRIS]: But if that's how he feels . . .
CHRIS: That's all, nothing more till Christ comes, about the case or Larry as long as I'm here! [*To* ANN.] Now get out of here, George!
GEORGE [*to* ANN]: You tell me. I want to hear you tell me.
ANN: Go, George! [*They disappear up the driveway,* ANN *saying "Don't take it that way, Georgie! Please don't take it that way."*]

[CHRIS *turns to his mother.*]

CHRIS: What do you mean, you packed her bag? How dare you pack her bag?
MOTHER: Chris . . .
CHRIS: How dare you pack her bag?
MOTHER: She doesn't belong here.
CHRIS: Then I don't belong here.
MOTHER: She's Larry's girl.
CHRIS: And I'm his brother and he's dead, and I'm marrying his girl.
MOTHER: Never, never in this world!
KELLER: You lost your mind?
MOTHER: You have nothing to say!
KELLER [*cruelly*]: I got plenty to say. Three and a half years you been talking like a maniac—
MOTHER [*she smashes him across the face*]: Nothing. You have nothing to say. Now I say. He's coming back, and everybody has got to wait.
CHRIS: Mother, Mother . . .
MOTHER: Wait, wait . . .
CHRIS: How long? How long?

MOTHER [*rolling out of her*]: Till he comes; forever and ever till he comes!

CHRIS [*as an ultimatum*]: Mother, I'm going ahead with it.

MOTHER: Chris, I've never said no to you in my life, now I say no!

CHRIS: You'll never let him go till I do it.

MOTHER: I'll never let him go and you'll never let him go . . . !

CHRIS: I've let him go. I've let him go a long . . .

MOTHER [*with no less force, but turning from him*]: Then let your father go. [*Pause.* CHRIS *stands transfixed.*]

KELLER: She's out of her mind.

MOTHER: Altogether! [*To* CHRIS, *but not facing them.*] Your brother's alive, darling, because if he's dead, your father killed him. Do you understand me now? As long as you live, that boy is alive. God does not let a son be killed by his father. Now you see, don't you? Now you see. [*Beyond control she hurries up and into house.*]

KELLER [CHRIS *has not moved. He speaks insinuatingly, questioningly*]: She's out of her mind.

CHRIS [*a broken whisper*]: Then . . . you did it?

KELLER [*the beginning of plea in his voice*]: He never flew a P-40—

CHRIS [*struck. Deadly*]: But the others.

KELLER [*insistently*]: She's out of her mind. [*He takes a step toward* CHRIS, *pleadingly.*]

CHRIS [*unyielding*]: Dad . . . you did it?

KELLER: He never flew a P-40, what's the matter with you?

CHRIS [*still asking, and saying*]: Then you did it. To the others.

[*Both hold their voices down.*]

KELLER [*afraid of him, his deadly insistence*]: What's the matter with you? What the hell is the matter with you?

CHRIS [*quietly, incredibly*]: How could you do that? How?

KELLER: What's the matter with you?

CHRIS: Dad . . . Dad, you killed twenty-one men!

KELLER: What, killed?

CHRIS: You killed them, you murdered them.

KELLER [*as though throwing his whole nature open before* CHRIS]: How could I kill anybody?

CHRIS: Dad! Dad!

KELLER [*trying to hush him*]: I didn't kill anybody!

CHRIS: Then explain it to me. What did you do? Explain it to me or I'll tear you to pieces!

KELLER [*horrified at his overwhelming fury*]: Don't Chris, don't . . .

CHRIS: I want to know what you did, now what did you do? You had a hundred and twenty cracked engine-heads, now what did you do?

KELLER: If you're going to hang me then I . . .

CHRIS: I'm listening, God Almighty, I'm listening!

KELLER [*their movements now are those of subtle pursuit and escape.* KELLER *keeps a step out of* CHRIS' *range as he talks*]: You're a boy, what could I do! I'm in business, a man is in business; a hundred and twenty cracked, you're out of business; you got a process, the process don't work you're out of business; you don't know how to operate, your stuff is no good; they close you up, they tear up your contracts, what the hell's it to them? You lay forty years into a business and they knock you out in five minutes, what could I do, let them take forty years, let them take my life away? [*His voice cracking.*] I never thought they'd install them. I swear to God. I thought they'd stop 'em before anybody took off.

CHRIS: Then why'd you ship them out?

KELLER: By the time they could spot them I thought I'd have the process going again, and I could show them they needed me and they'd let it go by. But weeks passed and I got no kick-back, so I was going to tell them.

CHRIS: They why didn't you tell them?

KELLER: It was too late. The paper, it was all over the front page, twenty-one went down, it was too late. They came with handcuffs into the shop, what could I do? [*He sits on bench at center.*] Chris . . . Chris, I did it for you, it was a chance and I took it for you. I'm sixty-one years old, when would I have another chance to make something for you? Sixty-one years old you don't get another chance, do ya?

CHRIS: You even knew they wouldn't hold up in the air.

KELLER: I didn't say that . . .

CHRIS: But you were going to warn them not to use them . . .

KELLER: But that don't mean . . .

CHRIS: It means you knew they'd crash.

KELLER: It don't mean that.

CHRIS: Then you *thought* they'd crash.

Keller: I was afraid maybe . . .

CHRIS: You were afraid maybe! God in heaven, what kind of a man are you? Kids were hanging in the air by those heads. You knew that!

KELLER: For you, a business for you!

CHRIS [*with burning fury*]: For me! Where do you live, where have you come from? For me!—I was dying every day and you were killing my boys and you did it for me? What the hell do you think I was thinking of, the Goddamn business? Is that as far as your mind can see, the business? What is that, the world—the business? What the hell do you mean, you did it for me? Don't you have a country? Don't you live in the world? What the hell are you? You're not even an animal, no animal kills his own, what are you? What must I do to you? I ought to tear the tongue out of your mouth, what must I do? [*With his fist he pounds down upon his father's shoulder. He stumbles away, covering his face as he weeps.*] What must I do, Jesus God, what must I do?

KELLER: Chris . . . My Chris . . .

ACT III

Two o'clock the following morning, MOTHER *is discovered on the rise, rocking ceaselessly in a chair, staring at her thoughts. It is an intense, slight, sort of rocking. A light shows from upstairs bedroom, lower floor windows being dark. The moon is strong and casts its bluish light. Presently* JIM, *dressed in jacket and hat, appears from the left, and seeing her, goes up beside her.*

JIM: Any news?

MOTHER: No news.

JIM [*gently*]: You can't sit up all night, dear, why don't you go to bed?

MOTHER: I'm waiting for Chris. Don't worry about me, Jim, I'm perfectly all right.

JIM: But it's almost two o'clock.

MOTHER: I can't sleep. [*Slight pause.*] You had an emergency?

JIM [*tiredly*]: Somebody had a headache and thought he was dying. [*Slight pause.*] Half of my patients are quite mad. Nobody realizes how many people are walking around loose, and they're cracked as coconuts. Money. Money-money-money-money. You say it long enough it doesn't mean anything. [*She smiles, makes a silent laugh.*] Oh, how I'd love to be around when that happens!

MOTHER [*shakes her head*]: You're so childish, Jim! Sometimes you are.

JIM [*looks at her a moment*]: Kate. [*Pause.*] What happened?

KATE: I told you. He had an argument with Joe. Then he got in the car and drove away.

JIM: What kind of an argument?

MOTHER: An argument, Joe . . . he was crying like a child, before.

JIM: They argued about Ann?

MOTHER [*slight hesitation*]: No, not Ann. Imagine? [*Indicates lighted window above.*] She hasn't come out of that room since he left. All night in that room.

JIM [*looks at window, then at her*]: What'd Joe do, tell him?

MOTHER [*she stops rocking*]: Tell him what?

JIM: Don't be afraid, Kate, I know. I've always known.

MOTHER: How?

JIM: It occurred to me a long time ago.

MOTHER: I always had the feeling that in the back of his head, Chris . . . almost knew. I didn't think it would be such a shock.

JIM [*gets up*]: Chris would never know how to live with a thing like that. It takes a certain talent . . . for lying. You have it, and I do. But not him.

MOTHER: What do you mean . . . he's not coming back?

JIM: Oh, no, he'll come back. We all come back, Kate. These private little revolutions always die. The compromise is always made. In a peculiar way. Frank is right—every man does have a star. The star is one's honesty. And you spend your life groping for it, but once it's out it never lights again. I don't think he went very far. He probably just wanted to be alone to watch his star go out.

MOTHER: Just as long as he comes back.

JIM: I wish he wouldn't, Kate. One year I simply took off, went to New Orleans; for two months I lived on bananas and milk, and studied a certain disease. It was beautiful. And then she came, and she cried. And I went back home with her. And now I live in the usual darkness: I can't find myself; it's even hard sometimes to remember the kind of man I wanted to be. I'm a good husband; Chris is a good son—he'll come back. [KELLER *comes out on porch in dressing-gown and slippers. He goes upstage—to alley.* JIM *goes to him.*]

JIM: I have a feeling he's in the park. I'll look around for him. Put her to bed, Joe; this is no good for what she's got. [JIM *exits up driveway.*]

KELLER [*coming down*]: What does he want here?

MOTHER: His friend is not home.

KELLER [*his voice is husky. Comes down to her*]: I don't like him mixing in so much.

MOTHER: It's too late, Joe. He knows.

KELLER [*apprehensively*]: How does he know?

MOTHER: He guessed a long time ago.

KELLER: I don't like that.

MOTHER [*laughs dangerously, quietly into the line*]: What you don't like . . .

KELLER: Yeah, what I don't like.

MOTHER: You can't bull yourself through this one, Joe, you better be smart now. This thing—this thing is not over yet.

KELLER [*indicating lighted window above*]: And what is she doing up there? She don't come out of the room.

MOTHER: I don't know, what is she doing? Sit down, stop being mad. You want to live? You better figure out your life.

KELLER: She don't know, does she?

MOTHER: She saw Chris storming out of here. It's one and one—she knows how to add.

KELLER: Maybe I ought to talk to her?

MOTHER: Don't ask me, Joe.

KELLER [*almost an outburst*]: Then who do I ask? But I don't think she'll do anything about it.

MOTHER: You're asking me again.

KELLER: I'm askin' you. What am I, a stranger? I thought I had a family here. What happened to my family?

MOTHER: You've got a family. I'm simply telling you that I have no strength to think anymore.

KELLER: You have no strength. The minute there's trouble you have no strength.

MOTHER: Joe, you're doing the same thing again; all your life whenever there's trouble you yell at me and you think that settles it.

KELLER: Then what do I do? Tell me, talk to me, what do I do?

MOTHER: Joe . . . I've been thinking this way. If he comes back . . .

KELLER: What do you mean "if"? . . . he's comin' back!

MOTHER: I think if you sit him down and you . . . explain yourself. I mean you ought to make it clear to him that you know you did a terrible thing. [*Not looking into his eyes.*] I mean if he saw that you realize what you did. You see?

KELLER: What ice does that cut?

MOTHER [*a little fearfully*]: I mean if you told him that you want to pay for what you did.

KELLER [*sensing . . . quietly*]: How can I pay?

MOTHER: Tell him . . . you're willing to go to prison. [*Pause.*]

KELLER [*struck, amazed*]: I'm willing to . . . ?

MOTHER [*quickly*]: You wouldn't go, he wouldn't ask you to go. But if you told him you wanted to, if he could feel that you wanted to pay, maybe he would forgive you.

KELLER: He would forgive me! For what?

MOTHER: Joe, you know what I mean.

KELLER: I don't know what you mean! You wanted money, so I made money. What must I be forgiven? You wanted money, didn't you?

MOTHER: I didn't want it that way.

KELLER: I didn't want it that way, either! What difference is it what you want? I spoiled the both of you. I should've put him out when he was ten like I was put out, and made him earn his keep. Then he'd know how a buck is made in this world. Forgiven! I could live on a quarter a day myself, but I got a family so I . . .

MOTHER: Joe, Joe . . . it don't excuse it that you did it for the family.

KELLER: It's got to excuse it!

MOTHER: There's something bigger than the family to him.

KELLER: Nothin' is bigger!

MOTHER: There is to him.

KELLER: There's nothin' he could do that I wouldn't forgive. Because he's my son. Because I'm his father and he's my son.

MOTHER: Joe, I tell you . . .

KELLER: Nothin's bigger than that. And you're goin' to tell him, you understand? I'm his father and he's my son, and if there's something bigger than that I'll put a bullet in my head!

MOTHER: You stop that!

KELLER: You heard me. Now you know what to tell him. [*Pause. He moves from her—halts.*] But he wouldn't put me away though . . . He wouldn't do that . . . Would he?

MOTHER: He loved you, Joe, you broke his heart.

KELLER: But to put me away . . .

MOTHER: I don't know. I'm beginning to think we don't really know him. They say in the war he was such a killer. Here he was always afraid of mice. I don't know him. I don't know what he'll do.

KELLER: Goddamn, if Larry was alive he wouldn't act like this. He understood the way the world is made. He listened to me. To him the world had a forty-foot front, it ended at the building line. This one, everything bothers him. You make a deal, overcharge two cents, and his hair falls out. He don't understand money. Too easy, it came too easy. Yes sir. Larry. That was a boy we lost. Larry. Larry. [*He slumps on chair in front of her.*] What am I gonna do, Kate . . .

MOTHER: Joe, Joe, please . . . you'll be all right, nothing is going to happen . . .

KELLER [*desperately, lost*]: For you, Kate, for both of you, that's all I ever lived for . . .

MOTHER: I know, darling, I know . . . [ANN *enters from house. They say nothing, waiting for her to speak.*]

ANN: Why do you stay up? I'll tell you when he comes.

KELLER [*rises, goes to her*]: You didn't eat supper, did you? [*To* MOTHER.] Why didn't you make her eat something?

MOTHER: Sure, I'll . . .

ANN: Never mind. Kate, I'm all right. [*They are unable to speak to each other.*] There's something I want to tell you. [*She starts, then halts.*] I'm not going to do anything about it. . . .

MOTHER: She's a good girl! [*To* KELLER.] You see? She's a . . .

ANN: I'll do nothing about Joe, but you're going to do something for me. [*Directly to* MOTHER.] You made Chris feel guilty with me. Whether you wanted to or not, you've crippled him in front of me. I'd like you to tell him that Larry is dead and that you know it. You understand me? I'm not going out of here alone. There's no life for me that way. I want you to set him free. And then I promise you, everything will end, and we'll go away, and that's all.

KELLER: You'll do that. You'll tell him.

ANN: I know what I'm asking, Kate. You had two sons. But you've only got one now.

KELLER: You'll tell him . . .

ANN: And you've got to say it to him so he knows you mean it.

MOTHER: My dear, if the boy was dead, it wouldn't depend on my words to make Chris know it. . . . The night he gets into your bed, his heart will dry up. Because he knows and you know. To his dying day he'll wait for his brother! No, my dear, no such thing. You're going in the morning, and you're going alone. That's your life, that's your lonely life.

[*She goes to porch, and starts in.*]

ANN: Larry is dead, Kate.

MOTHER [*she stops*]: Don't speak to me.

ANN: I said he's dead. I know! He crashed off the coast of China November twenty-fifth! His engine didn't fail him. But he died. I know . . .

MOTHER: How did he die? You're lying to me. If you know, how did he die?

ANN: I loved him. You know I loved him. Would I have looked at anyone else if I wasn't sure? That's enough for you.

MOTHER [*moving on her*]: What's enough for me? What're you talking about? [*She grasps* ANN's *wrists.*]

ANN: You're hurting my wrists.

MOTHER: What are you talking about! [*Pause. She stares at* ANN *a moment, then turns and goes to* KELLER.]

ANN: Joe, go in the house . . .

KELLER: Why should I . . .

ANN: Please go.

KELLER: Lemme know when he comes. [KELLER *goes into house.*]

MOTHER [*she sees* ANN *take a letter from her pocket*]: What's that?

ANN: Sit down . . . [MOTHER *moves left to chair, but does not sit.*] First you've got to understand. When I came, I didn't have any idea that Joe . . . I had nothing against him or you. I came to get married. I hoped . . . So I didn't bring this to hurt you. I thought I'd show it to you only if there was no other way to settle Larry in your mind.

MOTHER: Larry? [*Snatches letter from* ANN's *hand.*]

ANN: He wrote it to me just before he— [MOTHER *opens and begins to read letter.*] I'm not trying to hurt you, Kate. You're making me do this, now remember you're—— Remember. I've been so lonely, Kate . . . I can't leave here alone again. [*A long, low moan comes from* MOTHER's *throat as she reads.*] You made me show it to you. You wouldn't believe me. I told you a hundred times, why wouldn't you believe me!

MOTHER: Oh, my God . . .

ANN [*with pity and fear*]: Kate, please, please . . .

MOTHER: My God, my God . . .

ANN: Kate, dear, I'm so sorry . . . I'm so sorry. [CHRIS *enters from driveway. He seems exhausted.*]

CHRIS: What's the matter . . . ?

ANN: Where were you? . . . you're all perspired. [MOTHER *doesn't move.*] Where were you?

CHRIS: Just drove around a little. I thought you'd be gone.

ANN: Where do I go? I have nowhere to go.

CHRIS [*to* MOTHER]: Where's Dad?

ANN: Inside lying down.

CHRIS: Sit down, both of you. I'll say what there is to say.

MOTHER: I didn't hear the car . . .

CHRIS: I left it in the garage.

MOTHER: Jim is out looking for you.

CHRIS: Mother . . . I'm going away. There are a couple of firms in Cleveland, I think I can get a place. I mean, I'm going away for good. [*To* ANN *alone.*] I know what you're thinking Annie. It's true. I'm yellow. I was made yellow in this house because I suspected my father and I did nothing about it, but if I knew that night when I came home what I know now, he'd be in the district attorney's office by this time, and I'd have brought him there. Now if I look at him, all I'm able to do is cry.

MOTHER: What are you talking about? What else can you do?

CHRIS: I could jail him! I could jail him, if I were human any more. But I'm like everybody else now. I'm practical now. You made me practical.

MOTHER: But you have to be.

CHRIS: The cats in that alley are practical, the bums who ran away when we were fighting were practical. Only the dead ones weren't practical. But now I'm practical, and I spit on myself. I'm going away. I'm going now.

ANN [*goes up to stop him*]: I'm coming with you . . .

CHRIS: No, Ann.

ANN: Chris, I don't ask you to do anything about Joe.

CHRIS: You do, you do . . .

ANN: I swear I never will.

CHRIS: In your heart you always will.

ANN: Then do what you have to do!

CHRIS: Do what? What is there to do? I've looked all night for a reason to make him suffer.

ANN: There's reason, there's reason!

CHRIS: What? Do I raise the dead when I put him behind bars? Then what'll I do it for? We used to shoot a man who acted like a dog, but honor was real there, you were protecting something. But here? This is the land of the great big dogs, you don't love a man here, you eat him! That's the principle; the only one we live by—it just happened to kill a few people this time, that's all. The world's that way, how can I take it out on him? What sense does that make? This is a zoo, a zoo!

ANN [*to* MOTHER]: You know what he's got to do! Tell him!

MOTHER: Let him go.

ANN: I won't let him go. You'll tell him what he's got to do . . .

MOTHER: Annie!

ANN: Then I will! [KELLER *enters from house.* CHRIS *sees him, goes down right near arbor.*]

KELLER: What's the matter with you? I want to talk to you.

CHRIS: I've got nothing to say to you.

KELLER [*taking his arm*]: I want to talk to you!

CHRIS [*pulling violently away from him*]: Don't do that, Dad. I'm going to hurt you if you do that. There's nothing to say, so say it quick.

KELLER: Exactly what's the matter? What's the matter? You got too much money? Is that what bothers you?

CHRIS [*with an edge of sarcasm*]: It bothers me.

KELLER: If you can't get used to it, then throw it away. You hear me? Take every cent and give it to charity, throw it in the sewer. Does that settle it? In the sewer, that's all. You think I'm kidding? I'm tellin' you what to do, if it's dirty then burn it. It's your money, that's not my money. I'm a dead man, I'm an old dead man, nothing's mine. Well, talk to me!—what do you want to do!

CHRIS: It not what I want to do. It's what you want to do.

KELLER: What should I want to do? [CHRIS *is silent.*] Jail? You want me to go to jail? If you want me to go, say so! Is that where I belong?—then tell me so! [*Slight pause.*] What's the matter, why can't you tell me? [*Furiously.*] You say everything else to me, say that! [*Slight pause.*] I'll tell you why you can't say it. Because you know I don't belong there. Because you know! [*With growing emphasis and passion, and a persistent tone of desperation.*] Who worked for nothin' in that war? When they work for nothin', I'll work for nothin'. Did they ship a gun or a truck outa Detroit before they got their price? Is that clean? It's dollars and cents, nickels and dimes; war and peace, it's nickels and dimes, what's clean? Half the Goddamn country is gotta go if I go! That's why you can't tell me.

CHRIS: That's exactly why.

KELLER: Then . . . why am *I* bad?

CHRIS: *I* know you're no worse than most men but I thought you were better. I never saw you as a man. I saw you as my father. [*Almost breaking.*] I can't look at you this way, I can't look at myself! [*He turns away unable to face* KELLER. ANN *goes quickly to* MOTHER, *takes letter from her and starts for* CHRIS. MOTHER *instantly rushes to intercept her.*]

MOTHER: Give me that!

ANN: He's going to read it! [*She thrusts letter into* CHRIS' *hand.*] Larry. He wrote it to me the day he died . . .

KELLER: Larry!?

MOTHER: Chris, it's not for you. [*He starts to read.*] Joe . . . go away . . .

KELLER [*mystified, frightened*]: Why'd she say, Larry, what . . . ?

MOTHER [*She desperately pushes him toward alley, glancing at* CHRIS.]: Go to the street Joe, go to the street! [*She comes down beside* KELLER.] Don't Chris . . . [*Pleading from her whole soul.*] Don't tell him . . .

CHRIS [*quietly*]: Three and one half years . . . talking, talking. Now you tell me what you must do . . . This is how he died, now tell me where you belong.

KELLER [*pleading*]: Chris, a man can't be a Jesus in this world!

CHRIS: I know all about the world. I know the whole crap story. Now listen to this, and tell me what a man's got to be! [*Reads.*] "My dear Ann: . . ." You listening? He wrote this the day he died. Listen, don't cry . . . listen! "My dear Ann: It is impossible to put down the things I feel. But I've got to tell you something. Yesterday they flew in a load of papers from the States and I read about Dad and your father being convicted. I can't express myself. I can't tell you how I feel—I can't bear to live any more. Last night I circled the base for twenty minutes before I could bring myself in. How could he have done that? Every day three or four men never come back and he sits back there doing business . . . I don't know how to tell you what I feel . . . I can't face anybody . . . I'm going out on a mission in a few minutes. They'll probably report me missing. If they do, I want you to know that you mustn't wait for me. I tell you, Ann, if I had him here now I could kill him—" [KELLER *grabs letter from* CHRIS' *hand and reads it.*] [*After a long pause.*] Now blame the world. Do you understand that letter?

KELLER [*he speaks almost inaudibly*]: I think I do. Get the car, I'll put on my jacket. [*He turns and starts slowly for the house.* MOTHER *rushes to intercept him.*]

MOTHER: Why are you going? You'll sleep, why are you going?

KELLER: I can't sleep here. I'll feel better if I go.

MOTHER: You're so foolish. Larry was your son too, wasn't he? You know he'd never tell you to do this.

KELLER [*looking at letter in his hand*]: Then what is this if it isn't telling me? Sure, he was my son. But I think to him they were all my sons. And I guess they were, I guess they were. I'll be right down. [*Exits into house.*]

MOTHER [*to* CHRIS, *with determination*]: You're not going to take him!

CHRIS: I'm taking him.

MOTHER: It's up to you, if you tell him to stay he'll stay. Go and tell him!

CHRIS: Nobody could stop him now.

MOTHER: You'll stop him! How long will he live in prison?—are you trying to kill him?

CHRIS [*holding out letter*]: I thought you read this!

MOTHER [*of* LARRY, *the letter*]: The war is over! Didn't you hear?—it's over!

CHRIS: Then what was Larry to you? A stone that fell into the water? It's not enough for him to be sorry. Larry didn't kill himself to make you and Dad sorry.

MOTHER: What more can we be!

CHRIS: You can be better! Once and for all you can know there's a universe of people outside and you're responsible to it, and unless you know that you threw away your son because that's why he died.

[*A shot is heard in the house. They stand frozen for a brief second.* CHRIS *starts for porch, pauses at step, turns to* ANN.]

CHRIS: Find Jim! [*He goes on into the house and* ANN *runs up driveway.* MOTHER *stands alone, transfixed.*]

MOTHER [*softly, almost moaning*]: Joe . . . Joe . . . Joe . . . Joe . . . [CHRIS *comes out of house, down to* MOTHER'*s arms.*]

CHRIS [*almost crying*]: Mother, I didn't mean to . . .

MOTHER: Don't dear. Don't take it on yourself. Forget now. Live. [CHRIS *stirs as if to answer.*] Shhh . . . [*She puts his arms down gently and moves towards porch.*] Shhh . . . [*As she reaches porch steps she begins sobbing, as the curtain falls.*]

Edward Albee

Edward Franklin Albee III was born in 1928 in Washington, D.C., and adopted in infancy by an affluent family who owned the Keith-Albee theater circuit, a chain of vaudeville theaters. He was an only child and suffered through an unhappy youth, fraught with constant conflict between his passive father, Reed, and his domineering and abrasive mother, Frances, who was twenty-three years younger than her husband. Before her marriage, Frances had been a successful fashion model, but she was particularly unsuited to the role of wife and mother. She serves as Edward Albee's model for the predatory woman in virtually all of his plays, and he finally faced her directly in *Three Tall Women,* when he was sixty-four. Frances and Reed Albee are the source of Albee's obsessive portrayal of threatening women and weak men, engaged in a constant battle of the sexes.

Albee hated school, and although he started at Trinity College, he never finished. At nineteen, his formal education ceased, and he settled in Greenwich Village in New York City, where, for almost ten years, he lived with his lover, William Flanagan, a writer. From the time he left home, Albee never relied on his family's wealth, but worked at many menial jobs in order to maintain his independence. He intended to be a poet and found his voice as a playwright only at thirty, when he finished writing *The Zoo Story.*

Albee's plays show the influence of Eugène Ionesco and Samuel Beckett. He shares their sense of pessimism and futility of understanding the nature of existence, even though he does not share Beckett's minimalism or oblique style of language. Albee's language is robust, even baroque, and his characters are never at a loss for words. He has closer affinities with Ionesco and accepts his argument that if drama is to edify, it must disturb and terrify the audience. In his essay "Which Theatre Is Absurd?" (1962), Albee argues that realistic theater is actually absurd because it is falsely reassuring; on the contrary, the Theatre of the Absurd shows the world as it is—bereft of moral, religious, and social structures that make sense. An Albee play is usually a discussion, sometimes conducted in a drawing room, and is essentially plotless. His usual action—argument–counterargument–violent response—is characteristic of the work of Harold Pinter, who is closely linked with Beckett.

The Zoo Story was successfully produced in Berlin and off Broadway. This was followed with a one-act play, *The Death of Bessie Smith* (1960), based on the death of the famed blues singer in 1937, from injuries sustained in a car crash, because a hospital in Memphis refused to admit her for treatment. The timing of the play, in 1960, is usually taken as evidence of Albee's political beliefs and support of the civil rights movement. His work avoids political or large social issues, however, and, in this play, Smith's death is actually peripheral to the conflict between a bigoted Southern nurse, who will not overcome her intolerance, and a liberal intern, who, incredulously, courts her.

Albee continued his assault on the myth of the American culture with *The American Dream* (1959–1960), a satire of a contemporary family that is modeled on Ionesco's *The Bald Soprano* (1948). The characters have no names, but are referred to by type—Daddy, Mommy, Grandma, and Young Man—and all speak in clichés. The plot concerns the problems of Mommy and Daddy, who are sterile but want to replace their adopted child, who has died. When the Young Man unexpectedly appears and announces that he will replace the dead child because he will do anything for money, they accept him. *The American Dream* is a dramatic portrayal of Albee's family—the mother and father he did not like and the maternal grandmother he loved.

Albee's *The Sandbox* (1960) is a continuation of *The American Dream*, named for the sandbox that Mommy and Daddy store Grandma in until she is summoned by the Angel of Death, who is again the Young Man. Grandma's death signifies the loss of the past and the prospect of an unsatisfying future, dominated by Mommy and Daddy's mindless bickering.

Albee joked that *Who's Afraid of Virginia Woolf?* (1962), his first full-length play, was so successful that it freed him from the task of having to write *Son of Who's Afraid of Virginia Woolf?* In the tradition of August Strindberg's psychological probing of character, *Who's Afraid of Virginia Woolf?* is an allegory that savages the American middle class and its dreams of success. The chief characters are George and Martha (as in Washington), the false parents of an imaginary child, whom they call the "little bugger." The marriage, as presented in Act I (titled "Fun and Games"), is a typical Albee battle of love, hate, and sadomasochism. George tells the story of a boy (himself) who shot his mother and later killed his father in an automobile accident. Martha takes Nick, a guest, to her bedroom to make love, while George and Nick's wife, Honey, wait downstairs. At the end of Act III (titled "The Exorcism"), George and Martha, exhausted and hung over, are finally fully aware that the "little bugger" is dead. At this moment of anguished but relative peace, George softly hums the nursery rhyme "Who's Afraid of the Big Bad Wolf," and Martha answers, "I . . . am . . . George," and George nods slowly. The reference to Virginia Woolf, whose madness ended in suicide, closes the play.

Albee examined his sexuality, his despair over the hypocrisy of the Catholic Church, and the elusiveness of spiritual ease in *Tiny Alice* (1964), a play whose title may refer to Lewis Carroll's *Alice's Adventures in Wonderland* (although it is also a homosexual term for a tight anus). Albee's Miss Alice, the richest woman in the world, is a femme fatale who seduces Brother Julian, a lay priest (Albee's pun). Julian, unable to resist temptation, believes that Miss Alice in the flesh is the mystical vision of a mother/god figure he calls Tiny Alice. Once he is seduced, the predatory Miss Alice abandons him, and her lawyer shoots him. Julian dies unabsolved, in the posture of Jesus Christ on the cross. Critics of *Tiny Alice* were baffled by its philosophical mysticism and bemused by the scatological slang of the play's title.

Albee was thirty-eight when *A Delicate Balance* (1966), his problem play in the style of Henrik Ibsen, was awarded a Pulitzer Prize for Drama. As in *The American Dream* and *Who's Afraid of Virginia Woolf?*, Albee's target in this play is the discordant relationship between a weak husband, Tobias, and a strong-willed wife, Agnes—an affluent middle-aged couple enduring a marriage without love, passion, or sex. Their daughter Julia is home attending to her fourth divorce. Claire, Agnes's sister, is also a guest; she is an alcoholic whose sharp wit and humor cannot provide her with enough confidence to make her life a success. The delicate balance these four maintain is disrupted when Edna and Harry, Agnes's and Tobias's closest friends, are struck with a moment of abject fear and temporarily move into the house. Agnes, who has always held the marriage together, shows how tired she is, and Tobias, free from Agnes's authority, no longer pretends that he is master of his house. Since the action of *A Delicate Balance* takes place between Good Friday and Easter Sunday, it seems to suggest that people living in bad faith are incapable of renewing that faith.

Box (1970) and *Quotations from Chairman Mao Tse Tung* (1970) are Albee plays that have neither plot nor action. *Box* (1970), similar to Samuel Beckett's *Not I* (1972), is a monologue about death, spoken by an old woman who is not seen. *Quotations from Chairman Mao Tse Tung* is really a staged reading in which the characters stand and deliver speeches that are wholly separate from each other. Chairman Mao reads about Imperialism from the *Red Book;* the Old Woman recites "Over the Hill to the Poor-House," by Irish poet William Carleton; and the Long-Winded Lady talks about death, before announcing "Good heavens, no; *I* have nothing to die for." A fourth character is the Minister, but he remains silent, presumably because he has nothing to say. The theme of both plays suggests spiritual fragmentation and alienation of people from each other and from the simple joy of humanity.

All Over (1971) is an allegory about death inspired by Jean-Paul Sartre's *No Exit* (1944). The protagonist is the Husband, a dying man who is attended in his large bedroom by his adulterous Wife, his grown Daughter and Son, his Mistress, his Best Friend (who is the Wife's lover), a Doctor, and a Nurse. It is a story without love or the hope of redemption, and all of the characters are at each other's throats. *Seascape* (1975) is an Albee parody of Darwinian evolution and a contrast of experience and innocence. The setting is an ocean beach, where a middle-aged couple, Nancy and Charlie, sit and examine their lives: Nancy wants to be more daringly vivacious, but Charlie wants to let things be. Suddenly, two human-sized green lizards, Leslie and Sarah, come out of the sea, determined to leave the ooze and become more highly developed. As the foursome chat about life, death, and human emotion, Nancy and Charlie give the innocent Sarah and Leslie a lesson in human anger, sorrow, and frustration; however, they remain on the beach. Despite *Seascape*'s poor critical reviews and very limited run, it was awarded a Pulitzer Prize for Drama.

From 1976 to 1993, Albee had no clear successes. Plays during this period include *Listening* (1976), an allegory of Eden that takes place in a classical garden with a dry fountain surrounded by a stone wall, and *The Lady from Dubuque* (1980) about Jo, a woman of thirty dying of cancer, attended by her husband, mother, and friends. *The Man Who Had Three Arms* (1982) concerns a character, named Himself, who berates the audience and then cries "Stay with me. . . . Don't leave me alone!" The violence and self-loathing—which recall many of Albee's male characters, especially Jerry in *The Zoo Story* and Tobias in *A Delicate Balance*—may reveal Albee's depressed spirits at a low point in his career.

When he was sixty-six, Albee returned to prominence with *Three Tall Women* (1992) and earned a third Pulitzer Prize for Drama. It is an autobiographical play, focusing on Albee's mother, about whom he writes, "I felt no need for revenge. We had managed to make each other very unhappy over the years. . . . It is true I did not like her much, could not abide her prejudices, her loathings, her paranoias, but I did admire her pride and sense of self." Albee's scheme in *Three Tall Women* is to conflate past and present, showing the life of A, the protagonist, at the ages of twenty-six, fifty-two, and ninety-two as she loses her energy and evolves into a vicious, mean-spirited old woman. Her twenty-three-year-old son, Albee's stand-in, sits silently at her bedside and watches her with tacit satisfaction.

Throughout his career Albee also adapted other literary works (primarily about unhappy people) for the stage. He was attracted to the despair of a man without a future in Herman Melville's "Bartleby, the Scrivener" (1853), which he adapted as an opera, *Bartleby*, in 1961. Four years later he adapted Carson McCullers's novel *The Ballad of the Sad Café* (1951), the story of a woman's unrequited love for a dwarf, who ends up running off with her sleazy husband. The following year he modified James Purdy's novel *Malcolm* (1959), the story of an innocent boy of fifteen, who finds hell instead of heaven while looking for his lost father. In 1981 Albee adapted Vladimir Nabokov's novel *Lolita*, a satire of an author who is seduced by a teenager, which portrays the enervation and moral vacuity of the American Dream. All of these were failures, but they show Albee's unremitting criticism of the American Dream and his observations of the breakdown of intimate relationships and moral conduct.

Because Albee could not find an American producer for *The Zoo Story*, the play was first produced in 1959 in Berlin in German. The next year it was presented off Broadway, at the Provincetown Playhouse, Eugene O'Neill's old theater. Though only one act, *The Zoo Story* explores in microcosm the issues of conformity and nonconformity, love and hate, suicide and murder, manhood and sexual ambiguity, and loss of religious faith and the illusion of reality. Its autobiographical associations suggest that Albee was working out his personal difficulties with his parents, as he rejected his comfortable middle-class upbringing and explored his homosexuality. Peter and Jerry, the opposing characters, represent two competing elements of Albee's character, the stifled conformist and the artist/renegade.

Albee has suggested that he was inspired to write *The Zoo Story* by Tennessee Williams's *Suddenly, Last Summer* (1958), another tale of repressed homosexuality that ends in violence and death. But unquestionably, *The Zoo Story* is an Absurdist drama in the style of Ionesco's *The Bald Soprano* (1948), which Albee knew and perhaps saw when it premiered on Broadway in 1958. Following Absurdist conventions, the action of *The Zoo Story* includes a random encounter, incongruous dialogue, and an underlying tension that turns swiftly into unexpected violent disaster.

Peter, with a set career, a good job in publishing, and a conventional family, represents mainstream social values. His opposite, Jerry, has no career, no job, and no family; he is unsure of his sexuality, frustrated, and driven obsessively to seek some satisfaction that remains elusive. At the opening, Jerry, a stranger, approaches Peter in Central Park and engages him in a long and increasingly personal conversation. At one point, Jerry says to Peter, "You don't *have* to listen. Nobody is holding you here; remember that. Keep that in your mind." Peter responds by saying, "I know that," but he cannot cease listening, just as the Wedding Guest in Samuel Taylor Coleridge's "The Rime of the Ancient Mariner" has to listen to the crazed Mariner. Jerry describes at length his fear of women and his homosexual experience when he was fifteen, and he tells of a love/hate relationship with his landlady and her black dog, the gatekeepers of his hell. Jerry is sure that he is the object of the landlady's lust, but he is not reliable on the subject of love. He is more believable when he speaks in anger, "First, I'll kill the dog with kindness, and if that doesn't work . . . I'll just kill him." But when the poisoned dog recovers, Jerry says, "I loved the dog now, and I wanted him to love me. I had tried to love, and I had tried to kill, and both had been unsuccessful by themselves. . . . and I don't really know why I expected the dog to understand anything, much less my motivations."

Peter cannot comprehend that Jerry's story is a plea for help and love. When Peter starts to leave, Jerry begins to tickle him until he begins to laugh hysterically. Peter stays, but Jerry purposely antagonizes him, punching and pushing him, all the while mocking him: "You have everything in the world you want; you've told me about your home, and your family, and *your own* little zoo. You have everything, and now you want this bench. Are these the things men fight for? Tell me, Peter, is this bench, this iron and this wood, is this your honor? Is this the thing in the world you'd fight for? Can you think of anything more absurd?" Flabbergasted, Peter does not fight but calls for the police, then feels impotent and gets angrier. Jerry throws a knife at Peter's feet and commands him to pick it up. When Peter has the knife in his hands, Jerry "charges PETER and impales himself on the knife." With this act, the mystery of what happened at the zoo is ironically revealed, and Jerry says, "Peter . . . Peter? . . . Peter . . . thank you. I came unto you and you have comforted me. Dear Peter," suggesting a parody of Christ and the apostle Peter, who died for Christ. Albee disingenuously denied any connection, however: "In *The Zoo Story,* I named two characters Peter and Jerry. I know two people named Peter and Jerry. But then the learned papers started coming in, and of course Jerry is supposed to be Jesus . . . which is more interesting, I suppose, to the public than the truth."

Albee battered the illusion of self-sufficiency and the smugness of moral rectitude and materialism, and he showed his characters desperately seeking to connect despite their fears and self-contempt. Albee's theme links him with Eugene O'Neill, Tennessee Williams, and Arthur Miller. His style borrows from the Absurdism of Eugène Ionesco and Samuel Beckett. Albee's influence may be seen in Sam Shepard's *Buried Child,* which alludes to the imaginary child in *Whose Afraid of Virginia Woolf?*

The Zoo Story

THE PLAYERS

PETER, a man in his early forties, neither fat nor gaunt, neither handsome nor homely. He wears tweeds, smokes a pipe, carries horn-rimmed glasses. Although he is moving into middle age, his dress and his manner would suggest a man younger.

JERRY, a man in his late thirties, not poorly dressed, but carelessly. What was once a trim and lightly muscled body has begun to go to fat; and while he is no longer handsome, it is evident that he once was. His fall from physical grace should not suggest debauchery; he has, to come closest to it, a great weariness.

THE SCENE. It is Central Park; a Sunday afternoon in summer; the present. There are two park benches, one toward either side of the stage; they both face the audience. Behind them: foliage, trees, sky. At the beginning, Peter is seated on one of the benches.

Stage Directions: As the curtain rises, PETER *is seated on the bench stage-right. He is rea]ding a book. He stops reading, cleans his glasses, goes back to reading.* JERRY *enters.*

JERRY: I've been to the zoo. [PETER *doesn't notice*] I said, I've been to the zoo. MISTER, I'VE BEEN TO THE ZOO!

PETER: Hm? . . . What? . . . I'm sorry, were you talking to me?

JERRY: I went to the zoo, and then I walked until I came here. Have I been walking north?

PETER [*Puzzled*]: North? Why . . . I . . . I think so. Let me see.

JERRY [*Pointing past the audience*]: Is that Fifth Avenue?

PETER: Why yes; yes, it is.

JERRY: And what is that cross street there; that one, to the right?

PETER: That? Oh, that's Seventy-fourth Street.

JERRY: And the zoo is around Sixty-fifth Street; so, I've been walking north.

PETER [*Anxious to get back to his reading*]: Yes; it would seem so.

JERRY: Good old north.

PETER [*Lightly, by reflex*]: Ha, ha.

JERRY [*After a slight pause*]: But not due north.

PETER: I . . . well, no, not due north; but, we . . . call it north. It's northerly.

JERRY [*Watches as* PETER, *anxious to dismiss him, prepares his pipe*]: Well, boy; *you're* not going to get lung cancer, are you?

PETER [*Looks up, a little annoyed, then smiles*]: No, sir. Not from this.

JERRY: No, sir. What you'll probably get is cancer of the mouth, and then you'll have to wear one of those things Freud wore after they took one whole side of his jaw away. What do they call those things?

PETER [*Uncomfortable*]: A prosthesis?

JERRY: The very thing! A prosthesis. You're an educated man, aren't you? Are you a doctor?

PETER: Oh, no; no. I read about it somewhere; *Time* magazine, I think. [*He turns to his book*]

JERRY: Well, *Time* magazine isn't for blockheads.

PETER: No, I suppose not.

JERRY [*After a pause*]: Boy, I'm glad that's Fifth Avenue there.

PETER [*Vaguely*]: Yes.

JERRY: I don't like the west side of the park much.

PETER: Oh? [*Then slightly wary, but interested*] Why?

JERRY [*Offhand*]: I don't know.

PETER: Oh. [*He returns to his book*]

JERRY [*He stands for few seconds, looking at* PETER, *who finally looks up again, puzzled*]: Do you mind if we talk?

PETER [*Obviously minding*]: Why . . . no, no.

JERRY: Yes you do; you do.

PETER [*Puts his book down, his pipe out and away, smiling*]: No, really; I don't mind.

JERRY: Yes you do.

PETER [*Finally decided*]: No; I don't mind at all, really.

JERRY: It's . . . it's a nice day.

PETER [*Stares unnecessarily at the sky*]: Yes. Yes, it is; lovely.

JERRY: I've been to the zoo.

PETER: Yes, I think you said so . . . didn't you?

JERRY: You'll read about it in the papers tomorrow, if you don't see it on your TV tonight. You have TV, haven't you?

PETER: Why yes, we have two; one for the children.

JERRY: You're married!

PETER [*With pleased emphasis*]: Why, certainly.

JERRY: It isn't a law, for God's sake.

PETER: No . . . no, of course not.

JERRY: And you have a wife?

PETER [*Bewildered by the seeming lack of communication*]: Yes!

JERRY: And you have children.

PETER: Yes; two.

JERRY: Boys?

PETER: No, girls . . . both girls.

JERRY: But you wanted boys.

PETER: Well . . . naturally, every man wants a son, but . . .

JERRY [*Lightly mocking*]: But that's the way the cookie crumbles?

PETER [*Annoyed*]: I wasn't going to say that.
JERRY: And you're not going to have any more kids, are you?
PETER [*A bit distantly*]: No. No more. [*Then back, and irksome*] Why did you say that? How would you know about that?
JERRY: The way you cross your legs, perhaps; something in the voice. Or maybe I'm just guessing. Is it your wife?
PETER [*Furious*]: That's none of your business! [*A silence*] Do you understand? [JERRY *nods.* PETER *is quiet now*] Well, you're right. We'll have no more children.
JERRY [*Softly*]: That *is* the way the cookie crumbles.
PETER [*Forgiving*]: Yes . . . I guess so.
JERRY: Well, now; what else?
PETER: What were you saying about the zoo . . . that I'd read about it, or see . . . ?
JERRY: I'll tell you about it, soon. Do you mind if I ask you questions?
PETER: Oh, not really.
JERRY: I'll tell you why I do it; I don't talk to many people—except to say like: give me a beer, or where's the john, or what time does the feature go on, or keep your hands to yourself, buddy. You know—things like that.
PETER: I must say I don't . . .
JERRY: But every once in a while I like to talk to somebody, really *talk;* like to get to know somebody, know all about him.
PETER [*Lightly laughing, still a little uncomfortable*]: And am I the guinea pig for today?
JERRY: On a sun-drenched Sunday afternoon like this? Who better than a nice married man with two daughters and . . . uh . . . a dog? [PETER *shakes his head*] No? Two dogs. [PETER *shakes his head again*] Hm. No dogs? [PETER *shakes his head, sadly*] Oh, that's a shame. But you look like an animal man. CATS? [PETER *nods his head, ruefully*] Cats! But, that can't be your idea. No, sir. Your wife and daughters? [PETER *nods his head*] Is there anything else I should know?
PETER [*He has to clear his throat*]: There are . . . there are two parakeets. One . . . uh . . . one for each of my daughters.
JERRY: Birds.

Donald Davis and Ben Piazza in The Zoo Story, *directed by Richard Burr, Billy Rose Theatre, New York, 1968.*

PETER: My daughters keep them in a cage in their bedroom.

JERRY: Do they carry disease? The birds.

PETER: I don't believe so.

JERRY: That's too bad. If they did you could set them loose in the house and the cats could eat them and die, maybe. [PETER *looks blank for a moment, then laughs*] And what else? What do you do to support your enormous household?

PETER: I . . . uh . . . I have an executive position with a . . . a small publishing house. We . . . uh . . . we publish textbooks.

JERRY: That sounds nice; very nice. What do you make?

PETER [*still cheerful*]: Now look here!

JERRY: Oh, come on.

PETER: Well, I make around eighteen thousand a year, but I don't carry more than forty dollars at any one time . . . in case you're a . . . a holdup man . . . ha, ha, ha.

JERRY [*Ignoring the above*]: Where do you live? [PETER *is reluctant*] Oh, look; I'm not going to rob you, and I'm not going to kidnap your parakeets, your cats, or your daughters.

PETER [*Too loud*]: I live between Lexington and Third Avenue, on Seventy-fourth Street.

JERRY: That wasn't so hard, was it?

PETER: I didn't mean to seem . . . ah . . . it's that you don't really carry on a conversation; you just ask questions. And I'm . . . I'm normally . . . uh . . . reticent. Why do you just stand there?

JERRY: I'll start walking around in a little while, and eventually I'll sit down. [*Recalling*] Wait until you see the expression on his face.

PETER: What? Whose face? Look here; is this something about the zoo?

JERRY [*Distantly*]: The what?

PETER: The zoo; the zoo. Something about the zoo.

JERRY: The zoo?

PETER: You've mentioned it several times.

JERRY [*Still distant, but returning abruptly*]: The zoo? Oh, yes; the zoo. I was there before I came here. I told you that. Say, what's the dividing line between upper-middle-middle-class and lower-upper-middle-class?

PETER: My dear fellow, I . . .

JERRY: Don't my dear fellow me.

PETER [*Unhappily*]: Was I patronizing? I believe I was; I'm sorry. But, you see, your question about the classes bewildered me.

JERRY: And when you're bewildered you become patronizing?

PETER: I . . . I don't express myself too well, sometimes. [*He attempts a joke on himself*] I'm in publishing, not writing.

JERRY [*Amused, but not at the humor*]: So be it. The truth *is: I* was being patronizing.

PETER: Oh, now; you needn't say that.

[*It is at this point that* JERRY *may begin to move about the stage with slowly increasing determination and authority, but pacing himself, so that the long speech about the dog comes at the high point of the arc*]

JERRY: All right. Who are your favorite writers? Baudelaire and J. P. Marquand?

PETER [*wary*]: Well, I like a great many writers; I have a considerable . . . catholicity of taste, if I may say so. Those two men are fine, each in his way. [*Warming up*] Baudelaire, of course . . . uh . . . is by far the finer of the two, but Marquand has a place . . . in our . . . uh . . . national . . .

JERRY: Skip it.

PETER: I . . . sorry.

JERRY: Do you know what I did before I went to the zoo today? I walked all the way up Fifth Avenue from Washington Square; all the way.

PETER: Oh; you live in the Village! [*This seems to enlighten* PETER]

JERRY: No, I don't. I took the subway down to the Village so I could walk all the way up Fifth Avenue to the zoo. It's one of those things a person has to do; sometimes a person has to go a very long distance out of his way to come back a short distance correctly.

PETER [*Almost pouting*]: Oh, I thought you lived in the Village.

JERRY: What were you trying to do? Make sense out of things? Bring order? The old pigeonhole bit? Well, that's easy; I'll tell you. I live in a four-story brownstone roominghouse on the upper West Side between Columbus Avenue and Central Park West. I live on the top floor; rear; west. It's a laughably small room, and one of my walls is made of beaverboard; this beaverboard separates my room from another laughably small room, so I assume that the two rooms were once one room, a small room, but not necessarily laughable. The room beyond my beaverboard wall is occupied by a colored queen who always keeps his door open; well, not always but *always* when he's plucking his eyebrows, which he does with Buddhist concentration. This colored queen has rotten teeth, which is rare, and he has a Japanese kimono, which is also pretty rare; and he wears this kimono to and from the john in the hall, which is pretty frequent. I mean, he goes to the john a lot. He never bothers me, and he never brings anyone up to his room. All he does is pluck his eyebrows, wear his kimono and go to the john. Now, the two front rooms on my floor are a little larger, I guess; but they're pretty small, too. There's a Puerto Rican family in one of them, a husband, a wife, and some kids; I don't know how many. These people entertain a lot. And in the other front room, there's somebody living there, but I don't know who it is. I've never seen who it is. Never. Never ever.

PETER [*Embarrassed*]: Why . . . why do you live there?

JERRY [*From a distance again*]: I don't know.

PETER: It doesn't sound like a very nice place . . . where you live.

JERRY: Well, no; it isn't an apartment in the East Seventies. But, then again, I don't have one wife, two daughters, two cats and two parakeets. What I do have, I have toilet articles, a few clothes, a hot plate that I'm not supposed to have, a can opener, one that works with a key, you know; a knife, two forks, and two spoons, one small, one large; three plates, a cup, a saucer, a drinking glass, two picture frames, both empty, eight or nine books, a pack of pornographic playing cards, regular deck, an old Western Union typewriter that prints nothing but capital letters, and a small strongbox without a lock which has in it . . . what? Rocks! Some rocks . . . sea-rounded rocks I picked up on the beach when I was a kid. Under which . . . weighed down . . . are some letters . . . please letters . . . please why don't you do this, and please when will you do that letters. And when letters, too. When will you write? When will you come? When? These letters are from more recent years.

PETER [*Stares glumly at his shoes, then*]: About those two empty picture frames . . . ?

JERRY: I don't see why they need any explanation at all. Isn't it clear? I don't have pictures of anyone to put in them.

PETER: Your parents . . . perhaps . . . a girl friend . . .

JERRY: You're a very sweet man, and you're possessed of a truly enviable innocence. But good old Mom and good old Pop are dead . . . you know? . . . I'm broken up about it, too . . . I mean really. BUT. That particular vaudeville act is playing the cloud circuit now, so I don't see how I can look at them, all neat and framed. Besides, or, rather, to be pointed about it, good old Mom walked out on good old Pop when I was ten and a half years old; she embarked on an adulterous turn of our southern states . . . a journey of a year's duration . . . and her most constant companion . . . among others, among many others . . . was a Mr. Barleycorn. At least, that's what good old Pop told me after he went down . . . came back . . . brought her body north. We'd received the news between Christmas and New Year's, you see, that good old Mom had parted with the ghost in some dump in Alabama. And, without the ghost . . . she was less welcome. I mean, what was she? A stiff . . . a northern stiff. At any rate, good old Pop celebrated the New Year for an even two weeks and then slapped into the front of a somewhat moving city omnibus, which sort of cleaned things out family-wise. Well no; then there was Mom's sister, who was given neither to sin nor the consolations of the bottle. I moved in on her, and my memory of her is slight excepting I remember still that she did all things dourly: sleeping, eating, working, praying. She dropped dead on the stairs to her apartment, my apartment then, too, on the afternoon of my high school graduation. A terribly middle-European joke, if you ask me.

PETER: Oh, my; oh, my.

JERRY: Oh, your what? But that was a long time ago, and I have no feeling about any of it that I care to admit to myself. Perhaps you can see, though, why good old Mom and good old Pop are frameless. What's your name? Your first name?

PETER: I'm Peter.

JERRY: I'd forgotten to ask you. I'm Jerry.

PETER [*With a slight, nervous laugh*]: Hello, Jerry.

JERRY [*Nods his hello*]: And let's see now; what's the point of having a girl's picture, especially in two frames? I have two picture frames, you remember. I never see the pretty little ladies more than once, and most of them wouldn't be caught in the same room with a camera. It's odd, and I wonder if it's sad.

PETER: The girls?

JERRY: No. I wonder if it's sad that I never see the little ladies more than once. I've never been able to have sex with, or, how is it put? . . . make love to anybody more than once. Once; that's it. . . . Oh, wait; for a week and a half, when I was fifteen . . . and I hang my head in shame that puberty was late . . . I was a h-o-m-o-s-e-x-u-a-l. I mean, I was queer . . . [*Very fast*] . . . queer, queer, queer . . . with bells ringing, banners snapping in the wind. And for those eleven days, I met at least twice a day with the park superintendent's son . . . a Greek boy, whose birthday was the same as mine, except he was a year older. I think I was very much in love . . . maybe just with sex. But that was the jazz of a very special hotel, wasn't it? And now; oh, do I love the little ladies; really, I love them. For about an hour.

PETER: Well, it seems perfectly simple to me. . . .

JERRY [*Angry*]: Look! Are you going to tell me to get married and have parakeets?

PETER [*Angry himself*]: Forget the parakeets! And stay single if you want to. It's no business of mine. I didn't start this conversation in the . . .

JERRY: All right, all right. I'm sorry. All right? You're not angry?
PETER [*Laughing*]: No, I'm not angry.
JERRY [*Relieved*]: Good. [*Now back to his previous tone*] Interesting that you asked me about the picture frames. I would have thought that you would have asked me about the pornographic playing cards.
PETER [*With a knowing smile*]: Oh, I've seen those cards.
JERRY: That's not the point. [*Laughs*] I suppose when you were a kid you and your pals passed them around, or you had a pack of your own.
PETER: Well, I guess a lot of us did.
JERRY: And you threw them away just before you got married.
PETER: Oh, now; look here. I didn't *need* anything like that when I got older.
JERRY: No?
PETER [*Embarrassed*]: I'd rather not talk about these things.
JERRY: So? Don't. Besides, I wasn't trying to plumb your post-adolescent sexual life and hard times; what I wanted to get at is the value difference between pornographic playing cards when you're a kid, and pornographic playing cards when you're older. It's that when you're a kid you use the cards as a substitute for a real experience, and when you're older you use real experience as a substitute for the fantasy. But I imagine you'd rather hear about what happened at the zoo.
PETER [*Enthusiastic*]: Oh, yes; the zoo. [*Then, awkward*] That is . . . if you . . .
JERRY: Let me tell you about why I went . . . well, let me tell you some things. I've told you about the fourth floor of the roominghouse where I live. I think the rooms are better as you go down, floor by floor. I guess they are; I don't know. I don't know any of the people on the third and second floors. Oh, wait! I do know that there's a lady living on the third floor, in the front. I know because she cries all the time. Whenever I go out or come back in, whenever I pass her door, I always hear her crying, muffled, but . . . very determined. Very determined indeed. But the one I'm getting to, and all about the dog, is the landlady. I don't like to use words that are too harsh in describing people. I don't like to. But the landlady is a fat, ugly, mean, stupid, unwashed, misanthropic, cheap, drunken bag of garbage. And you may have noticed that I very seldom use profanity, so I can't describe her as well as I might.
PETER: You describe her . . . vividly.
JERRY: Well, thanks. Anyway, she has a dog, and I will tell you about the dog, and she and her dog are the gatekeepers of my dwelling. The woman is bad enough; she leans around in the entrance hall, spying to see that I don't bring in things or people, and when she's had her midafternoon pint of lemon-flavored gin she always stops me in the hall, and grabs ahold of my coat or my arm, and she presses her disgusting body up against me to keep me in a corner so she can talk to me. The smell of her body and her breath . . . you can't imagine it . . . and somewhere, somewhere in the back of that pea-sized brain of hers, an organ developed just enough to let her eat, drink, and emit, she has some foul parody of sexual desire. And I, Peter, I am the object of her sweaty lust.
PETER: That's disgusting. That's . . . horrible.
JERRY: But I have found a way to keep her off. When she talks to me, when she presses herself to my body and mumbles about her room and how I should come there, I merely say: but, Love; wasn't yesterday enough for you, and the day before? Then she puzzles, she makes slits of her tiny eyes, she sways a little, and then, Peter . . . and it is at this moment that I think I might be doing some good in that tormented house . . . a simple-minded smile begins to form on her unthinkable face, and she giggles and groans as she thinks about yesterday and the day before; as she believes and relives what never happened. Then, she motions to that black monster of a dog she has, and she goes back to her room. And I am safe until our next meeting.
PETER: It's so . . . unthinkable. I find it hard to believe that people such as that really *are*.
JERRY [*Lightly mocking*]: It's for reading about, isn't it?
PETER [*Seriously*]: Yes.
JERRY: And fact is better left to fiction. You're right, Peter. Well, what I have been meaning to tell you about is the dog; I shall, now.
PETER [*Nervously*]: Oh, yes; the dog.
JERRY: Don't go. You're not thinking of going, are you?
PETER: Well . . . no, I don't think so.
JERRY [*As if to a child*]: Because after I tell you about the dog, do you know what then? Then . . . then I'll tell you about what happened at the zoo.
PETER [*Laughing faintly*]: You're . . . you're full of stories, aren't you?
JERRY: You don't *have* to listen. Nobody is holding you here; remember that. Keep that in your mind.
PETER [*Irritably*]: I know that.
JERRY: You do? Good.

[*The following long speech, it seems to me, should be done with a great deal of action, to achieve a hypnotic effect on* PETER, *and on the audience, too. Some specific actions have been suggested, but the director and the actor playing* JERRY *might best work it out for themselves*]

ALL RIGHT. [*As if reading from a huge billboard*] THE STORY OF JERRY AND THE DOG! [*Natural again*] What I am going to tell you has something to do with how sometimes it's necessary to go a long distance out of the way in order to come back a short distance correctly; or, maybe I only think that it has something to do with that. But, it's why I went to the zoo today, and why I walked north . . . northerly, rather . . . until I came here. All right. The dog, I think I told you, is a black monster of a beast: an oversized head, tiny, tiny ears, and eyes . . . bloodshot, infected, maybe; and a body you can see the ribs through the skin. The dog is black, all black; all black except for the bloodshot eyes, and . . . yes . . . and an open sore on its . . . *right* forepaw; that is red, too. And, oh yes; the poor monster, and I do believe it's an old dog . . . it's certainly a misused one . . . almost always has an erection . . . of sorts. That's red, too. And . . . what else? . . . oh, yes; there's a gray-yellow-white color, too, when he bares his fangs. Like this: Grrrrrrr! Which is what he did when he saw me for the first time . . . the day I moved in. I worried about that animal the very first minute I met him. Now, animals don't take to me like Saint Francis had birds hanging off him all the time. What I mean is: animals are indifferent to me . . . like people [*He smiles slightly*] . . . most of the time. But this dog wasn't indifferent. From the very beginning he'd snarl and then go for me, to get one of my legs. Not like he was rabid, you know; he was sort of a stumbly dog, but he wasn't half-assed, either. It was a good, stumbly run; but I always got away. He got a piece of my trouser leg, look, you can see right here, where it's mended; he got that the second day I lived there; but, I kicked free and got upstairs fast, so that was that. [*Puzzles*] I still don't know to this day how the other roomers manage it, but you know what I *think:* I think it had to do only with me. Cozy. So. Anyway, this went on for over a week, whenever I came in; but never when I went out. That's funny. Or, it *was* funny. I could pack up and live in the street for all the dog cared. Well, I thought about it up in my room one day, one of the times after I'd bolted upstairs, and I made up my mind. I decided: First, I'll kill the dog with kindness, and if that doesn't work . . . I'll just kill him. [PETER *winces*] Don't react, Peter; just listen. So, the next day I went out and bought a bag of hamburgers, medium rare, no catsup, no onion; and on the way home I threw away all the rolls and kept just the meat.

[*Action for the following, perhaps*]

When I got back to the roominghouse the dog was waiting for me. I half opened the door that led into the entrance hall, and there he was; waiting for me. It figured. I went in, very cautiously, and I had the hamburgers, you remember; I opened the bag, and I set the meat down about twelve feet from where the dog was snarling at me. Like so! He snarled; stopped snarling; sniffed; moved slowly; then faster; then faster toward the meat. Well, when he got to it he stopped, and he looked at me. I smiled; but tentatively, you understand. He turned his face back to the hamburgers, smelled, sniffed some more, and then . . . RRRAAAAGGGGGHHHH, like that . . . he tore into them. It was as if he had never eaten anything in his life before, except like garbage. Which might very well have been the truth. I don't think the landlady ever eats anything but garbage. But. He ate all the hamburgers, almost all at once, making sounds in his throat like a woman. *Then,* when he'd finished the meat, the hamburger, and tried to eat the paper, too, he sat down and smiled. I think he smiled; I know cats do. It was a very gratifying few moments. Then, BAM, he snarled and made for me again. He didn't get me this time, either. So, I got upstairs, and I lay down on my bed and started to think about the dog again. To be truthful, I was offended, and I was damn mad, too. It was six perfectly good hamburgers with not enough pork in them to make it disgusting. I was offended. But, after a while, I decided to try it for a few more days. If you think about it, this dog had what amounted to an antipathy toward me; really. And, I wondered if I mightn't overcome this antipathy. So, I tried it for five more days, but it was always the same: snarl, sniff; move; faster; stare; gobble; RAAGGGHHH; smile; snarl; BAM. Well, now; by this time Columbus Avenue was strewn with hamburger rolls and I was less offended than disgusted. So, I decided to kill the dog.

[PETER *raises a hand in protest*]

Oh, don't be so alarmed, Peter; I didn't succeed. The day I tried to kill the dog I bought only one hamburger and what I thought was a murderous portion of rat poison. When I bought the hamburger I asked the man not to bother with the roll, all I wanted was the meat. I expected some reaction from him, like: we don't sell no hamburgers without rolls; or, wha' d'ya wanna do, eat it out'a ya han's? But no; he smiled benignly, wrapped up the hamburger in waxed paper, and said: A bite for ya pussy-cat? I wanted to say: No, not really; it's part of a plan to poison a dog I know. But, you

can't say "a dog I know" without sounding funny; so I said, a little too loud, I'm afraid, and too formally: YES, A BITE FOR MY PUSSY-CAT. People looked up. It always happens when I try to simplify things; people look up. But that's neither hither nor thither. So. On my way back to the roominghouse, I kneaded the hamburger and the rat poison together between my hands, at that point feeling as much sadness as disgust. I opened the door to the entrance hall, and there the monster was, waiting to take the offering and then jump me. Poor bastard; he never learned that the moment he took to smile before he went for me gave me time enough to get out of range. BUT, there he was; malevolence with an erection, waiting. I put the poison patty down, moved toward the stairs and watched. The poor animal gobbled the food down as usual, smiled, which made me almost sick, and then, BAM. But, I sprinted up the stairs, as usual, and the dog didn't get me, as usual. AND IT CAME TO PASS THAT THE BEAST WAS DEATHLY ILL. I knew this because he no longer attended me, and because the landlady sobered up. She stopped me in the hall the same evening of the attempted murder and confided the information that God had struck her puppy-dog a surely fatal blow. She had forgotten her bewildered lust, and her eyes were wide open for the first time. They looked like the dog's eyes. She sniveled and implored me to pray for the animal. I wanted to say to her: Madam, I have myself to pray for, the colored queen, the Puerto Rican family, the person in the front room whom I've never seen, the woman who cries deliberately behind her closed door, and the rest of the people in all roominghouses, everywhere; besides, Madam, I don't understand how to pray.
But . . . to simplify things . . . I told her I would pray. She looked up. She said that I was a liar, and that I probably wanted the dog to die. I told her, and there was so much truth here, that I didn't want the dog to die. I didn't, and not just because I'd poisoned him. I'm afraid that I must tell you I wanted the dog to live so that I could see what our new relationship might come to.

[PETER *indicates his increasing displeasure and slowly growing antagonism*]

Please understand, Peter; that sort of thing is important. You must believe me; it *is* important. We have to know the effect of our actions. [*Another deep sigh*] Well, anyway; the dog recovered. I have no idea why, unless he was a descendant of the puppy that guarded the gates of hell or some such resort. I'm not up on my mythology. [*He pronounces the word myth-o-*logy] Are you?

[PETER *sets to thinking, but* JERRY *goes on*]

At any rate, and you've missed the eight-thousand-dollar question, Peter; at any rate, the dog recovered his health and the landlady recovered her thirst, in no way altered by the bow-wow's deliverance. When I came home from a movie that was playing on Forty-second Street, a movie I'd seen, or one that was very much like one or several I'd seen, after the landlady told me puppykins was better, I was so hoping for the dog to be waiting for me. I was . . . well, how would you put it . . . enticed? . . . fascinated? . . . no, I don't think so . . . heart-shatteringly anxious, that's it; I was heart-shatteringly anxious to confront my friend again.

[PETER *reacts scoffingly*]

Yes, Peter; friend. That's the only word for it. I was heart-shatteringly et cetera to confront my doggy friend again. I came in the door and advanced, unafraid, to the center of the entrance hall. The beast was there . . . looking at me. And, you know, he looked better for his scrape with the nevermind. I stopped; I looked at him; he looked at me. I think . . . I think we stayed a long time that way . . . still, stone-statue . . . just looking at one another. I looked more into his face than he looked into mine. I mean, I can concentrate longer at looking into a dog's face than a dog can concentrate at looking into mine, or into anybody else's face, for that matter. But during that twenty seconds or two hours that we looked into each other's face, we made contact. Now, here is what I had wanted to happen: I loved the dog now, and I wanted him to love me. I had tried to love, and I had tried to kill, and both had been unsuccessful by themselves. I hoped . . . and I don't really know why I expected the dog to understand anything, much less my motivations . . . I hoped that the dog would understand.

[PETER *seems to be hypnotized*]

It's just . . . it's just that . . . [JERRY *is abnormally tense, now*] . . . it's just that if you can't deal with people, you have to make a start somewhere. WITH ANIMALS! [*Much faster now, and like a conspirator*] Don't you see? A person has to have some way of dealing with SOMETHING. If not with people . . . if not with people . . . SOMETHING.

With a bed, with a cockroach, with a mirror . . . no, that's too hard, that's one of the last steps. With a cockroach, with a . . . with a . . . with a carpet, a roll of toilet paper . . . no, not that, either . . . that's a mirror, too; always check bleeding. You see how hard it is to find things? With a street corner, and too many lights, all colors reflecting on the oily-wet streets . . . with a wisp of smoke, a wisp . . . of smoke . . . with . . . with pornographic playing cards, with a strongbox . . . WITHOUT A LOCK . . . with love, with vomiting, with crying, with fury because the pretty little ladies aren't pretty little ladies, with making money with your body which is an act of love and I could prove it, with howling because you're alive; with God. How about that? WITH GOD WHO IS A COLORED QUEEN WHO WEARS A KIMONO AND PLUCKS HIS EYEBROWS, WHO IS A WOMAN WHO CRIES WITH DETERMINATION BEHIND HER CLOSED DOOR . . . with God who, I'm told, turned his back on the whole thing some time ago . . . with . . . some day, with people. [JERRY *sighs the next word heavily*] People. With an idea; a concept. And where better, where ever better in this humiliating excuse for a jail, where better to communicate one single, simple-minded idea than in an entrance hall? Where? It would be A START! Where better to make a beginning . . . to understand and just possibly be understood . . . a beginning of an understanding, than with . . .

[*Here* JERRY *seems to fall into almost grotesque fatigue*]

. . . than with A DOG. Just that; a dog.

[*Here there is a silence that might be prolonged for a moment or so; then* JERRY *wearily finishes his story*]

A dog. It seemed like a perfectly sensible idea. Man is a dog's best friend, remember. So: the dog and I looked at each other. I longer than the dog. And what I saw then has been the same ever since. Whenever the dog and I see each other we both stop where we are. We regard each other with a mixture of sadness and suspicion, and then we feign indifference. We walk past each other safely; we have an understanding. It's very sad, but you'll have to admit that it is an understanding. We had made many attempts at contact, and we had failed. The dog has returned to garbage, and I to solitary but free passage. I have not returned. I mean to say, I have *gained* solitary free passage, if that much further loss can be said to be gain. I have learned that neither kindness nor cruelty by themselves, independent of each other, creates any effect beyond themselves; and I have learned that the two combined, together, at the same time, are the teaching emotion. And what is gained is loss. And what has been the result: the dog and I have attained a compromise; more of a bargain, really. We neither love nor hurt because we do not try to reach each other. And, *was* trying to feed the dog an act of love? And, perhaps, was the dog's attempt to bite me *not* an act of love? If we can so misunderstand, well then, why have we invented the word love in the first place?

[*There is silence.* JERRY *moves to* PETER*'s bench and sits down beside him. This is the first time* JERRY *has sat down during the play*]

The Story of Jerry and the Dog: the end.

[PETER *is silent*]

Well, Peter? [JERRY *is suddenly cheerful*] Well, Peter? Do you think I could sell that story to the *Reader's Digest* and make a couple of hundred bucks for *The Most Unforgettable Character I've Ever Met?* Huh?

[JERRY *is animated, but* PETER *is disturbed*]

Oh, come on now, Peter; tell me what you think.

PETER [*Numb*]: I . . . I don't understand what . . . I don't think I . . . [*Now, almost tearfully*] Why did you tell me all of this?

JERRY: Why not?

PETER: I DON'T UNDERSTAND!

JERRY [*Furious, but whispering*]: That's a lie.

PETER: No. No, it's not.

JERRY [*Quietly*]: I tried to explain it to you as I went along. I went slowly; it all has to do with . . .

PETER: I DON'T WANT TO HEAR ANY MORE. I don't understand you, or your landlady, or her dog. . . .

JERRY: *Her* dog! I thought it was my . . . No. No, you're right. It *is* her dog. [*Looks at* PETER *intently, shaking his head*] I don't know what I was thinking about; of course you don't understand. [*In a monotone, wearily*] I don't live in your block; I'm not married to two parakeets, or whatever your setup is. I am a *permanent transient,* and my home is the sickening roominghouses on the West Side of New York City, which is the greatest city in the world. Amen.

PETER: I'm . . . I'm sorry; I didn't mean to . . .

JERRY: Forget it. I suppose you don't quite know what to make of me, eh?

PETER [*A joke*]: We get all kinds in publishing. [*Chuckles*]

JERRY: You're a funny man. [*He forces a laugh*] You know that? You're a very . . . a richly comic person.

PETER [*Modestly, but amused*]: Oh, now, not really. [*Still chuckling*]

JERRY: Peter, do I annoy you, or confuse you?

PETER [*Lightly*]: Well, I must confess that this wasn't the kind of afternoon I'd anticipated.

JERRY: You mean, I'm not the gentleman you were expecting.

PETER: I wasn't expecting anybody.

JERRY: No, I don't imagine you were. But I'm here, and I'm not leaving.

PETER [*Consulting his watch*]: Well, you may not be, but I must be getting home soon.

JERRY: Oh, come on; stay a while longer.

PETER: I really should get home; you see . . .

JERRY [*Tickles* PETER*'s ribs with his fingers*]: Oh, come on.

PETER [*He is very ticklish; as* JERRY *continues to tickle him his voice becomes falsetto*]: No, I . . . OHHHHH! Don't do that. Stop, Stop. Ohhh, no, no.

JERRY: Oh, come on.

PETER [*As* JERRY *tickles*]: Oh, hee, hee, hee. I must go. I . . . hee, hee, hee. After all, stop, stop, hee, hee, hee, after all, the parakeets will be getting dinner ready soon. Hee, hee. And the cats are setting the table. Stop, stop, and, and . . . [PETER *is beside himself now*] . . . and we're having . . . hee, hee . . . uh . . . ho, ho, ho.

[JERRY *stops tickling* PETER, *but the combination of the tickling and his own mad whimsy has* PETER *laughing almost hysterically. As his laughter continues, then subsides,* JERRY *watches him, with a curious fixed smile*]

JERRY: Peter?

PETER: Oh, ha, ha, ha, ha, ha. What? What?

JERRY: Listen, now.

PETER: Oh, ho, ho. What . . . what is it, Jerry? Oh, my.

JERRY [*Mysteriously*]: Peter, do you want to know what happened at the zoo?

PETER: Ah, ha, ha. The what? Oh, yes; the zoo. Oh, ho, ho. Well I had my own zoo there for a moment with . . . hee, hee, the parakeets getting dinner ready, and the . . . ha, ha, whatever it was, the . . .

JERRY [*Calmly*]: Yes, that was very funny, Peter. I wouldn't have expected it. But do you want to hear about what happened at the zoo, or not?

PETER: Yes. Yes, by all means; tell me what happened at the zoo. Oh, my. I don't know what happened to me.

JERRY: Now I'll let you in on what happened at the zoo; but first, I should tell you why I went to the zoo. I went to the zoo to find out more about the way people exist with animals, and the way animals exist with each other, and with people too. It probably wasn't a fair test, what with everyone separated by bars from everyone else, the animals for the most part from each other, and always the people from the animals. But, if it's a zoo, that's the way it is. [*He pokes* PETER *on the arm*] Move over.

PETER [*Friendly*]: I'm sorry, haven't you enough room? [*He shifts a little*]

JERRY [*Smiling slightly*]: Well, all the animals are there, and all the people are there, and it's Sunday and all the children are there. [*He pokes* PETER *again*] Move over.

PETER [*Patiently, still friendly*]: All right.

[*He moves some more, and* JERRY *has all the room he might need*]

JERRY: And it's a hot day, so all the stench is there, too, and all the balloon sellers, and all the ice cream sellers, and all the seals are barking, and all the birds are screaming. [*Pokes* PETER *harder*] Move over!

PETER [*Beginning to be annoyed*]: Look here, you have more than enough room! [*But he moves more, and is now fairly cramped at one end of the bench*]

JERRY: And I am there, and it's feeding time at the lions' house, and the lion keeper comes into the lion cage, one of the lion cages, to feed one of the lions. [*Punches* PETER *on the arm, hard*] MOVE OVER!

PETER [*Very annoyed*]: I can't move over any more, and stop hitting me. What's the matter with you?

JERRY: Do you want to hear the story? [*Punches* PETER*'s arm again*]

PETER [*Flabbergasted*]: I'm not so sure! I certainly don't want to be punched in the arm.

JERRY [*Punches* PETER*'s arm again*]: Like that?

PETER: Stop it! What's the matter with you?

JERRY: I'm crazy, you bastard.

PETER: That isn't funny.

JERRY: Listen to me, Peter. I want this bench. You go sit on the bench over there, and if you're good I'll tell you the rest of the story.

PETER [*Flustered*]: But . . . whatever for? What *is* the matter with you? Besides, I see no reason why I should give up this bench. I sit on this bench almost every Sunday afternoon, in good weather. It's secluded here; there's never anyone sitting here, so I have it all to myself.

JERRY [*Softly*]: Get off this bench, Peter; I want it.

PETER [*Almost whining*]: No.

JERRY: I said I want this bench, and I'm going to have it. Now get over there.

PETER: People can't have everything they want. You should know that; it's a rule; people can have some of the things they want, but they can't have everything.

JERRY [*Laughs*]: Imbecile! You're slow-witted!

PETER: Stop that!

JERRY: You're a vegetable! Go lie down on the ground.

PETER [*Intense*]: Now *you* listen to me. I've put up with you all afternoon.

JERRY: Not really.

PETER: LONG ENOUGH. I've put up with you long enough. I've listened to you because you seemed . . . well, because I thought you wanted to talk to somebody.

JERRY: You put things well; economically, and, yet . . . oh, what is the word I want to put justice to your . . . JESUS, you make me sick . . . get off here and give me my bench.

PETER: MY BENCH!

JERRY [*Pushes* PETER *almost, but not quite, off the bench*]: Get out of my sight.

PETER [*Regaining his position*]: God da . . . mn you. That's enough! I've had enough of you. I will not give up this bench; you can't have it, and that's that. Now, go away.

[JERRY *snorts but does not move*]

Go away, I said.

[JERRY *does not move*]

Get away from here. If you don't move on . . . you're a bum . . . that's what you are . . . If you don't move on, I'll get a policeman here and make you go.

[JERRY *laughs, stays*]

I warn you, I'll call a policeman.

JERRY [*Softly*]: You won't find a policeman around here; they're all over on the west side of the park chasing fairies down from trees or out of the bushes. That's all they do. That's their function. So scream your head off; it won't do you any good.

PETER: POLICE! I warn you, I'll have you arrested. POLICE! [*Pause*] I said POLICE! [*Pause*] I feel ridiculous.

JERRY: You look ridiculous: a grown man screaming for the police on a bright Sunday afternoon in the park with nobody harming you. If a policeman *did* fill his quota and come sludging over this way he'd probably take you in as a nut.

PETER [*With disgust and impotence*]: Great God, I just came here to read, and now you want me to give up the bench. You're mad.

JERRY: Hey, I got news for you, as they say. I'm on your precious bench, and you're never going to have it for yourself again.

PETER [*Furious*]: Look, you; get off my bench. I don't care if it makes any sense or not. I want this bench to myself; I want you OFF IT!

JERRY [*Mocking*]: Aw . . . look who's mad.

PETER: GET OUT!

JERRY: No.

PETER: I WARN YOU!

JERRY: Do you know how ridiculous you look *now?*

PETER [*His fury and self-consciousness have possessed him*]: It doesn't matter. [*He is almost crying*] GET AWAY FROM MY BENCH!

JERRY: Why? You have everything in the world you want; you've told me about your home, and your family, and *your own* little zoo. You have everything, and now you want this bench. Are these the things men fight for? Tell me, Peter, is this bench, this iron and this wood, is this your honor? Is this the thing in the world you'd fight for? Can you think of anything more absurd?

PETER: Absurd? Look, I'm not going to talk to you about honor, or even try to explain it to you. Besides, it isn't a question of honor; but even if it were, you wouldn't understand.

JERRY [*Contemptuously*]: You don't even know what you're saying, do you? This is probably the first time in your life you've had anything more trying to face than changing your cats' toilet box. Stupid! Don't you have any idea, not even the slightest, what other people *need?*

PETER: Oh, boy, listen to you; well, you don't need this bench. That's for sure.

JERRY: Yes; yes, I do.

PETER [*Quivering*]: I've come here for years; I have hours of great pleasure, great satisfaction, right here. And that's important to a man. I'm a responsible person, and I'm a GROWNUP. This is my bench, and you have no right to take it away from me.

JERRY: Fight for it, then. Defend yourself; defend your bench.

PETER: You've *pushed* me to it. Get up and fight.

JERRY: Like a man?

PETER [*Still angry*]: Yes, like a man, if you insist on mocking me even further.

JERRY: I'll have to give you credit for one thing: you *are* a vegetable, and a slightly nearsighted one, I think . . .

PETER: THAT'S ENOUGH . . .

JERRY: . . . but, you know, as they say on TV all the time—you know—and I mean this, Peter, you have a certain dignity; it surprises me . . .

PETER: STOP!

JERRY [*Rises lazily*]: Very well, Peter, we'll battle for the bench, but we're not evenly matched.

[*He takes out and clicks open an ugly-looking knife*]

PETER [*Suddenly awakening to the reality of the situation*]: You *are* mad! You're stark raving mad! YOU'RE GOING TO KILL ME!

[*But before* PETER *has time to think what to do,* JERRY *tosses the knife at* PETER'*s feet*]

JERRY: There you go. Pick it up. You have the knife and we'll be more evenly matched.

PETER [*Horrified*]: No!

JERRY [*Rushes over to* PETER, *grabs him by the collar;* PETER *rises; their faces almost touch*]: Now you pick up that knife and you fight with me. You fight for your self-respect; you fight for that goddamned bench.

PETER [*Struggling*]: No! Let . . . let go of me! He . . . Help!

JERRY [*Slaps* PETER *on each "fight"*]: You fight, you miserable bastard; fight for that bench; fight for your parakeets; fight for your cats, fight for your two daughters; fight for your wife; fight for your manhood, you pathetic little vegetable. [*Spits in* PETER'*s face*] You couldn't even get your wife with a male child.

PETER [*Breaks away, enraged*]: It's a matter of genetics, not manhood, you . . . you monster.

[*He darts down, picks up the knife and backs off a little; he is breathing heavily*]

I'll give you one last chance; get out of here and leave me alone!

[*He holds the knife with a firm arm, but far in front of him, not to attack, but to defend*]

JERRY [*Sighs heavily*]: So be it!

[*With a rush he charges* PETER *and impales himself on the knife. Tableau: For just a moment, complete silence,* JERRY *impaled on the knife at the end of* PETER'*s still firm arm. Then* PETER *screams, pulls away, leaving the knife in* JERRY. JERRY *is motionless, on point. Then he, too, screams, and it must be the sound of an infuriated and fatally wounded animal. With the knife in him, he stumbles back to the bench that* PETER *had vacated. He crumbles there, sitting, facing* PETER, *his eyes wide in agony, his mouth open*]

PETER [*Whispering*]: Oh my God, oh my God, oh my God. . . .

[*He repeats these words many times, very rapidly*]

JERRY [JERRY *is dying; but now his expression seems to change. His features relax, and while his voice varies, sometimes wrenched with pain, for the most part he seems removed from his dying. He smiles*]: Thank you, Peter. I mean that, now; thank you very much.

[PETER'*s mouth drops open. He cannot move; he is transfixed*]

Oh, Peter, I was so afraid I'd drive you away. [*He laughs as best he can*] You don't know how afraid I was you'd go away and leave me. And now I'll tell you what happened at the zoo. I think . . . I think this is what happened at the zoo . . . I think. I think that while I was at the zoo I decided that I would walk north . . . northerly, rather . . . until I found you . . . or somebody . . . and I decided that I would talk to you . . . I would tell you things . . . and things that I would tell you would . . . Well, here we are. You see? Here we *are*. But . . . I don't know . . . could I have planned all this? No . . . no, I couldn't have. But I think I did. And now I've told you what you wanted to know, haven't I? And now you know all about what happened at the zoo. And now you know what you'll see in your TV, and the face I told you about . . . you remember . . . the face I told you about . . . my face, the face you see right now. Peter . . . Peter? . . . Peter . . . thank you. I came unto you [*He laughs, so faintly*] and you have comforted me. Dear Peter.

PETER [*Almost fainting*]: Oh my God!

JERRY: You'd better go now. Somebody might come by, and you don't want to be here when anyone comes.

PETER [*Does not move, but begins to weep*]: Oh my God, oh my God.

JERRY [*Most faintly, now; he is very near death*]: You won't be coming back here any more, Peter; you've been dispossessed. You've lost your bench, but you've defended your honor. And Peter, I'll tell you something now; you're not really a vegetable; it's all right, you're an animal. You're an animal, too. But you'd better hurry now, Peter. Hurry, you'd better go . . . see?

[JERRY *takes a handkerchief and with great effort and pain wipes the knife handle clean of fingerprints*]

Hurry away, Peter.

[PETER *begins to stagger away*]

Wait . . . wait, Peter. Take your book . . . book. Right here . . . beside me . . . on your bench . . . my bench, rather. Come . . . take your book.

[PETER *starts for the book, but retreats*]

Hurry . . . Peter.

[PETER *rushes to the bench, grabs the book, retreats*]

Very good, Peter . . . very good. Now . . . hurry away.

[PETER *hesitates for a moment, then flees, stage left*]

Hurry away . . . [*His eyes are closed now*] Hurry away, your parakeets are making the dinner . . . the cats . . . are setting the table . . .

PETER [*Off stage*]: [*A pitiful howl*] OH MY GOD!

JERRY [*His eyes still closed, he shakes his head and speaks; a combination of scornful mimicry and supplication*]: Oh . . . my . . . God.

[*He is dead*]

CURTAIN

LORRAINE HANSBERRY

Lorraine Hansberry (1930–1965) was born in Chicago to a middle-class black family. Her father, a successful businessman who died early, was a civil rights activist, and through him she became acquainted with Paul Robeson (1898–1976), the singer and actor, W. E. B. Du Bois (1868–1963), the eminent scholar of black history and culture, and Langston Hughes, the poet and writer.

Because she was impatient with school, Hansberry never finished a degree, though she attended classes at the University of Wisconsin and the New School for Social Research in New York City. Most important to her intellectual development was the year she spent studying African history under the tutelage of Du Bois, the intellectual leader of black awareness in the United States. This experience committed her to becoming a political activist working for civil rights reform and black equality. She was twenty-one when she began writing for *Freedom,* a magazine advocating Marxist-Communist doctrine published by Paul Robeson. From 1951 to 1955, Hansberry worked as journalist and editor, an experience that greatly influenced the development of her literary ideas and writing style.

Hansberry met Robert Nemiroff while on a pro–civil rights picket line at New York University, and they were married in 1953. Although white, Nemiroff was committed to civil rights and social equality for blacks. Nemiroff's financial success as a popular songwriter and his enthusiastic encouragement allowed Hansberry to be a full-time writer.

Hansberry was twenty-nine when *A Raisin in the Sun* (1959) became the first play written by a black woman produced on Broadway. Its success also brought to prominence Lloyd Richards, the director, and the cast of actors including Sidney Poitier, Claudia McNeill, and Ruby Dee. Richards's role was crucial for focusing the action and characterizations of the play. Hansberry allowed him to play a creative directorial role akin to that of Konstantin Stanislavsky when Stanislavsky directed the plays of Anton Chekhov. (Richards was later instrumental in developing the talent of August Wilson.) In 1960 Hansberry wrote the screenplay for the film version of *A Raisin in the Sun,* one of the first Hollywood films to portray a black middle-class family.

Hansberry's only other complete play, *The Sign in Sidney Brustein's Window* (1964), is about Greenwich Village life and seems to be drawn from Hansberry's marriage to Nemiroff. In the play Hansberry attempts to deal with the lost spirit of 1950s liberalism. The action concerns a mixed marriage between Sidney Brustein, a Jewish publisher of a neighborhood newspaper, and his wife, Iris, an actress of Greek descent. Iris has two sisters: one a high-class call girl (Gloria) and the other a housewife. Gloria's lover, Alton Scales, is a black political activist who commits suicide when he learns that she is a prostitute. The sign in the window refers to Brustein's support for a reform political candidate who sells out to the bosses once he is elected. The outcome of the action is pessimistic. Though

Sidney and Iris remain a couple, Sidney's idealism is ravaged, and Iris leaves the theater for the security of working in the field of commercial advertisements. The play was not a success, and tragically, Hansberry died of duodenal cancer at the age of thirty-five on the day of its closing performance.

Les Blancs (1965) is an unfinished Hansberry play that Nemiroff reworked and produced in 1970. Hansberry's idea was to create a black version of Jean Genet's *Les Negres* (1960), a nihilistic play about black characters who perform a play in which they enact their feeling toward whites. *Les Blancs* is a play about the Kikuyu people of East Africa and the Mau Mau insurrection against British colonialism that led to the creation of the independent nation of Kenya. In this play within a play, a group of blacks present a clown show, during which they vent their feelings of hatred for whites before a white audience. Apparently, Hansberry meant for the action to be an Absurdist drama, but Broadway audiences felt that the play's anticolonialism was aimed too broadly at them, and it was not a success.

About a year before her death, Hansberry and Nemiroff were secretly divorced, though they continued to collaborate. As Hansberry's literary executor until his death in 1991, Nemiroff chose to be extraordinarily protective of Hansberry's private life, their stormy relationship, and her bisexuality. Nemiroff's main homage to Hansberry, *To Be Young, Gifted, and Black* (1969), is a compilation of the playwright's letters, diaries, and scenes from her plays. It was originally published as a play, but in book form it has been a mainstay of Hansberry's artistic and philosophical legacy. Among Hansberry's comments in *To Be Young, Gifted, and Black* is her explanation of the role of the American playwright:

> The problem is that there are great plays and lousy plays and reasonably good plays; when the artist achieves a force of art which is commensurate with his message—he hooks us. . . . Of course, whatever is said must be said through the living arguments of human beings in conflict with other human beings, with themselves, with abstractions which seem to them to be "their society." Of course! But, that narrows nothing and enlarges everything. The more swiftly that American drama comes to believe that my dramatic experience will be larger when I know *why* the pathetic chap has turned to alcohol and not merely that he has; why to heroin; why to prostitution, despair, decadent preoccupations—the more swiftly, I insist, our drama will gain more meaningful stature. The fact of the matter is that we are all surrounded by the elements of profound tragedy in contemporary life, no less than were Shakespeare and the Greeks, but that thus far we (the dramatists, all of us, I think) are still confounded by its elusive properties and colossal dimensions.

A Raisin in the Sun takes its name from a line in Langston Hughes's poem "Harlem: A Dream Deferred" (1951), which is presented as the epigraph for the play. The play is set in a black neighborhood in Chicago sometime between 1945 and 1959. It was a time of relative complacency in the United States, and Hansberry's play appears just as this era is coming to an end and the United States was entering a period of social and political turmoil—the war in Vietnam, the civil rights movement, and the black power movement.

A Raisin in the Sun draws upon Hansberry's own experience. When her mother and father tried to purchase a home in a white neighborhood in Chicago in 1938, they were blocked from doing so. Her father took the matter to court and won the case. The Hansberrys moved into the house and lived there several years, despite intimidation and harassment. The theme was pertinent and realistic, and Hansberry had been advocating black activism since her work with Robeson's *Freedom,* and now she had found her voice in the theater. The plight and stress of blacks seeking to get out of the segregated neighborhoods and integrate became an issue in the middle-class theater of Broadway. In a letter responding to a reluctant admirer of *A Raisin in the Sun,* Hansberry explained that her plays were social plays dealing with problems of American blacks: "We must come out of the ghettoes of America, because the ghettoes are killing us; not only in our dreams, as Mama says, but our very bodies. . . . As for changing 'the hearts of individuals'—I am glad the American nation did not wait for the hearts of individual slave owners to change to abolish the slave system—for I suspect that I should still be running around on a plantation as a slave. And that really would not do."

A Raisin in the Sun appeals to the American dream of working toward a better life, but it also suggests that the middle-class drive to achieve material success may be marred by schemes for getting rich, false ideals, and social oppression. The characters in the play are emblematic of these middle-class people wanting to better themselves and having to face the test of this challenge.

In Act I, Lena Younger, Mama, a woman in her early sixties, is waiting for the payout of the life insurance carried by her dead husband. The combined loss of a husband and father has understandably left the family unsettled, particularly because the insurance money seems to offer a tantalizing chance for change. Mama, who is deeply moral, tries to understand the difference between the generations in her family and their aspirations. Ruth, her daughter-in-law, is disturbed because she is pregnant and has not told her husband, Walter Lee. She lets it slip to Mama that she has consulted an abortionist because she feels that they cannot afford to keep the child she is carrying. Walter Lee is upset because Mama will not give him any of the insurance money, which he wants to invest in a liquor store. He is resentful that Mama is against the idea on principle. At thirty-five, Walter Lee views her denial as a perpetual sentence to servility, a dead-end job as a chauffeur for a rich white man. When Mama lets Walter Lee know that Ruth is pregnant and thinking about an abortion, he is stunned and speechless. Mama is appalled at her son's inability to act decisively and to tell Ruth she must not have an abortion.

Act II begins with Beneatha, Walter Lee's sister, dressed in the Nigerian costume her friend Joseph Asagai bought her, readying for a theater date with George Murchison, a well-to-do, college-educated black who is thoroughly assimilated. Beneatha is mocked by Walter Lee, who parodies an African warrior: "FLAMING SPEAR! HOT DAMN! . . . . THE LION IS WAKING." Though he is drunk, he suddenly takes on the qualities of a warrior and "the Southside chauffeur has assumed unexpected majesty," which fades when Murchison enters.

Murchison is unimpressed with both Walter Lee's behavior and Beneatha's dress, which he thinks is inappropriate, and he insists that she change her clothing. Beneatha lashes out at him, saying that she hates "assimilationist

Negroes," but she leaves to change clothes. While she is gone, Walter Lee mocks and insults Murchison, who finally says to him, "You're all wacked up with bitterness, man." Ruth tries to soothe Walter Lee by telling him, "Honey . . . life don't have to be like this. I mean sometimes people can do things so that things are better." The moment of tenderness doesn't last, however, for Mama comes in and tells how she has gone to place a down payment on a house in the white neighborhood of Clybourne Park. Ruth is jubilant, but Walter says, "So you butchered up dream of mine—you—who always talking 'bout your children's dreams."

A few weeks pass, and the family is packed and nearly ready to move. Mama learns that Walter Lee is not working and is spending time at a bar instead. In order to show her love and trust, Mama gives him sixty-five hundred dollars, the balance of insurance to deposit in the bank; three thousand in a checking account and three thousand in an account for Beneatha's medical school tuition. Walter Lee takes the money, but the expression in his voice as he talks about his dreams for the future indicates that he has his own plans for Mama's money.

A week later, Karl Lindner, an agent for the Clybourne Park homeowners' association, arrives and offers to return the Youngers' down payment (and more) if they will agree not to buy the house. Lindner tries to make his offer seem reasonable, but it is really ugly racism: "It is a matter of the people of Clybourne Park believing, rightly or wrongly, as I say, that for the happiness of all concerned that our Negro families are happier when they live in their *own* communities." Walter Lee orders Lindner out, and the family finds a new sense of solidarity. There is a small celebration and Walter Lee, Ruth, and Travis give Mama a set of new gardening tools and a gardening hat, the first presents she ever received "without its being Christmas." Their happiness fades when Bobo, a friend, appears to tell Walter Lee that Willy Harris, with whom Walter Lee invested Mama's money, has run off. As the impact of his failure becomes apparent, Walter Lee turns frantic with fear and grief until he "starts to pound the floor with his fists, sobbing wildly." Mama, unnaturally calm at first, cries out to God for strength.

An hour later, at the start of Act III, the apartment is filled with packing crates, but the family is listless and solemn. Beneatha greets Asagai and lets out her feelings of frustration while Walter Lee listens from the next room. Beneatha and Asagai argue over the future:

> BENEATHA: . . . All your talk and dreams about Africa and Independence. Independence and then what? What about all the crooks and petty thieves and just plain idiots who will come to power to steal and plunder the same before—only now they will be black and do it in the name of the new Independence—You cannot answer that.
>
> ASAGAI [*shouting over her*]: *I live the answer!* [*Pause.*] In my village at home it is the exceptional man who can even read a newspaper . . . or who ever *sees* a book at all. I will go home and much of what I will have to say will seem strange to the people of my village. . . . But I will teach and work and things will happen, slowly and swiftly. At times it will seem that nothing changes at all . . . and then again . . . the sudden dramatic events which make history leap into the future. And then quiet again.

Beneatha cannot accept Asagai's offer of marriage and life in Nigeria, and just as Asagai leaves, Walter Lee enters. Beneatha hisses at him as he runs out of the apartment, "I look at you and I see the final triumph of stupidity in the world." Mama, lost and trying to regain her sense of command, suggests that they give up the house and unpack. But Ruth, with great sense of purpose, says that they must fight on: "Lena—I'll work. . . . I'll work twenty hours a day in all the kitchens in Chicago. . . . I'll strap my baby on my back if I have to . . . but we got to move. . . . We got to get out of here." When Walter Lee returns and cynically explains that he has arranged to accept the buy-out from the Clybourne Park Association, Mama begins to cry:

> WALTER: Don't cry, Mama. Understand. That white man is going to walk in that door able to write checks for more money than we ever had. It's important to him and I'm going to help him . . . I'm going to put on the show, Mama.
>
> MAMA: Son—I come from five generations of people who was slaves and sharecroppers—but ain't nobody in my family never let nobody pay 'em no money that was a way of telling us we wasn't fit to walk the earth. We ain't never been that poor. [*Raising her eyes and looking at him*] We ain't never been dead inside.

Realizing the truth of what Mama has said, Walter Lee breaks down. Beneatha calls him a "toothless rat" and says that he is no brother of hers, but Mama cautions her to love him just the same: "There is always something left to love. And if you ain't learned that, you ain't learned nothing."

The moving men and Lindner arrive at the same time. Walter Lee, having learned his lesson, tells Lindner that "we are very proud and that this is—this is my son, who makes the sixth generation of our family in this country, and that we have all thought about your offer and we have decided to move into our house because my father—my father—he earned it."

Hansberry does not leave the audience with a simple happy ending. The play's mood shifts from harsh realism to guarded optimism. The family coheres and sets out to break the color line when it leaves its crowded apartment in the ghetto of Southside Chicago for its house in a white neighborhood. Mama's final gesture after the furniture is moved out is to return to the old apartment's kitchen in search of her favorite houseplant. This is supposed to be taken as a hopeful sign for a very uncertain future.

Hansberry is honored among playwrights, but she is an especially strong influence on black American playwrights Amiri Baraka, Lonnie Elder III, Alice Childress, Ed Bullins, Ntozake Shange, and, most importantly, August Wilson.

Film

A Raisin in the Sun (1961), directed by Daniel Petrie, with Sidney Poitier, Claudia McNeill, Ruby Dee, Diana Sands, and Louis Gossett, Jr. Screenplay by Hansberry. Columbia Pictures.

A Raisin in the Sun (1988), directed by Bill Duke, with Danny Glover, Starletta DuPois, Kimble Joyner, Kim Yancy, Esther Rolle, and Lou Ferguson. American Playhouse/NBLA Productions.

A Raisin in the Sun

CHARACTERS

RUTH YOUNGER
TRAVIS YOUNGER
WALTER LEE YOUNGER (BROTHER)
BENEATHA YOUNGER
LENA YOUNGER (MAMA)
JOSEPH ASAGAI
GEORGE MURCHISON
KARL LINDNER
BOBO
MOVING MEN

The action of the play is set in Chicago's Southside, sometime between World War II and the present.

ACT I	Scene 1	Friday morning
	Scene 2	The following morning
ACT II	Scene 1	Later, the same day
	Scene 2	Friday night, a few weeks later
	Scene 3	Saturday, moving day, one week later
ACT III	An hour later	

What happens to a dream deferred?
Does it dry up
Like a raisin in the sun?
Or fester like a sore—

And then run?
Does it stink like rotten meat?
Or crust and sugar over—
Like a syrupy sweet?

Maybe it just sags
Like heavy load.

Or does it explode?

—LANGSTON HUGHES[1]

ACT I

Scene 1

The YOUNGER *living room would be a comfortable and well-ordered room if it were not for a number of indestructible contradictions to this state of being. Its furnishings are typical and undistinguished and their primary feature now is that they have clearly had to accommodate the living of too many people for too many years—and they are tired. Still, we can see that at some time, a time probably no longer remembered by the family (except perhaps for* MAMA), *the furnishings of this room were actually selected with care and love and even hope—and brought to this apartment and arranged with taste and pride.*

That was a long time ago. Now the once loved pattern of the couch upholstery has to fight to show itself from under acres of crocheted doilies and couch covers which have themselves finally come to be more important than the upholstery. And here a table or a chair has been moved to disguise the worn places in the carpet; but the carpet has fought back by showing its weariness, with depressing uniformity, elsewhere on its surface.

Weariness has, in fact, won in this room. Everything has been polished, washed, sat on, used, scrubbed too often. All pretenses but living itself have long since vanished from the very atmosphere of this room.

Moreover, a section of this room, for it is not really a room unto itself, though the landlord's lease would make it seem so, slopes backward to provide a small kitchen area, where the family prepares the meals that are eaten in the living room proper, which must also serve as dining room. The single window that has been provided for these "two" rooms is located in this kitchen area. The sole natural light the family may enjoy in the course of a day is only that which fights its way through this little window.

At left, a door leads to a bedroom which is shared by MAMA *and her daughter,* BENEATHA. *At right, opposite, is a second room (which in the beginning of the life of this apartment was probably a breakfast room), which serves as a bedroom for* WALTER *and his wife,* RUTH.

Time: Sometime between World War II and the present.

Place: Chicago's Southside.

At rise: It is morning dark in the living room. TRAVIS *is asleep on the make-down bed at center. An alarm clock sounds from within the bedroom at right, and presently* RUTH *enters from that room and closes the door behind her.*

---

[1]From "Dream Deferred." Copyright 1951 by Langston Hughes. Reprinted from *The Panther and the Lash* by Langston Hughes, by permission of Alfred A. Knopf, Inc.

She crosses sleepily toward the window. As she passes her sleeping son she reaches down and shakes him a little. At the window she raises the shade and a dusky Southside morning light comes in feebly. She fills a pot with water and puts it on to boil. She calls to the boy, between yawns, in a slightly muffled voice.

RUTH *is about thirty. We can see that she was a pretty girl, even exceptionally so, but now it is apparent that life has been little that she expected, and disappointment has already begun to hang in her face. In a few years, before thirty-five even, she will be known among her people as a "settled woman."*

She crosses to her son and gives him a good, final, rousing shake.

RUTH: Come on now, boy, it's seven thirty! [*Her son sits up at last, in a stupor of sleepiness.*] I say hurry up, Travis! You ain't the only person in the world got to use a bathroom! [*The child, a sturdy, handsome little boy of ten or eleven, drags himself out of the bed and almost blindly takes his towels and "today's clothes" from drawers and a closet, and goes out to the bathroom, which is in an outside hall and which is shared by another family or families on the same floor.* RUTH *crosses to the bedroom door at right and opens it and calls in to her husband.*] Walter Lee! . . . It's after seven thirty! Lemme see you do some waking up in there now! [*She waits.*] You better get up from there, man! It's after seven thirty I tell you. [*She waits again.*] All right, you just go ahead and lay there and next thing you know Travis be finished and Mr. Johnson'll be in there and you'll be fussing and cussing round here like a mad man! And be late too! [*She waits, at the end of patience.*] Walter Lee—it's time for you to get up!

[*She waits another second and then starts to go into the bedroom, but is apparently satisfied that her husband has begun to get up. She stops, pulls the door to, and returns to the kitchen area. She wipes her face with a moist cloth and runs her fingers through her sleep-disheveled hair in a vain effort and ties an apron around her housecoat. The bedroom door at right opens and her husband stands in the doorway in his pajamas, which are rumpled and mismated. He is a lean, intense young man in his middle thirties, inclined to quick nervous movements and erratic speech habits—and always in his voice there is a quality of indictment.*]

Ruby Dee, Sidney Poitier, and Diana Sands in A Raisin in the Sun, *directed by Lloyd Richards, the Ethel Barrymore Theatre, 1959.*

WALTER: Is he out yet?
RUTH: What you mean *out*? He ain't hardly got in there good yet.
WALTER [*wandering in, still more oriented to sleep than to a new day*]: Well, what was you doing all that yelling for if I can't even get in there yet? [*Stopping and thinking*] Check coming today?
RUTH: They *said* Saturday and this is just Friday and I hopes to God you ain't going to get up here first thing this morning and start talking to me 'bout no money—'cause I 'bout don't want to hear it.
WALTER: Something the matter with you this morning?
RUTH: No—I'm just sleepy as the devil. What kind of eggs you want?
WALTER: Not scrambled. [RUTH *starts to scramble eggs.*] Paper come? [RUTH *points impatiently to the rolled up* Tribune *on the table, and he gets it and spreads it out and vaguely reads the front page.*] Set off another bomb yesterday.
RUTH [*maximum indifference*]: Did they?
WALTER [*looking up*]: What's the matter with you?
RUTH: Ain't nothing the matter with me. And don't keep asking me that this morning.
WALTER: Ain't nobody bothering you. [*Reading the news of the day absently again*] Say Colonel McCormick is sick.
RUTH [*affecting tea-party interest*]: Is he now? Poor thing.
WALTER [*sighing and looking at his watch*]: Oh, me. [*He waits.*] Now what is that boy doing in that bathroom all this time? He just going to have to start getting up earlier. I can't be being late to work on account of him fooling around in there.
RUTH [*turning on him*]: Oh, no he ain't going to be getting up no earlier no such thing! It ain't his fault that he can't get to bed no earlier nights 'cause he got a bunch of crazy good-for-nothing clowns sitting up running their mouths in what is supposed to be his bedroom after ten o'clock at night. . . .
WALTER: That's what you mad about, ain't it? The things I want to talk about with my friends just couldn't be important in your mind, could they?

He rises and finds a cigarette in her handbag on the table and crosses to the little window and looks out, smoking and deeply enjoying this first one.

RUTH [*almost matter of factly, a complaint too automatic to deserve emphasis*]: Why you always got to smoke before you eat in the morning?
WALTER [*at the window*]: Just look at 'em down there. . . . Running and racing to work . . . [*he turns and faces his wife and watches her a moment at the stove, and then, suddenly*] You look young this morning, baby.
RUTH [*indifferently*]: Yeah?
WALTER: Just for a second—stirring them eggs. It's gone now—just for a second it was—you looked real young again. [*Then, drily*] It's gone now—you look like yourself again.
RUTH: Man, if you don't shut up and leave me alone.
WALTER [*looking out to the street again*]: First thing a man ought to learn in life is not to make love to no colored woman first thing in the morning. You all some evil people at eight o'clock in the morning.

[TRAVIS *appears in the hall doorway, almost fully dressed and quite wide awake now, his towels and pajamas across his shoulders. He opens the door and signals for his father to make the bathroom in a hurry.*]

TRAVIS [*watching the bathroom*]: Daddy, come on!

[WALTER *gets his bathroom utensils and flies out to the bathroom.*]

RUTH: Sit down and have your breakfast, Travis.
TRAVIS: Mama, this is Friday. [*Gleefully*] Check coming tomorrow, huh?
RUTH: You get your mind off money and eat your breakfast.
TRAVIS [*eating*]: This is the morning we supposed to bring the fifty cents to school.
RUTH: Well, I ain't got no fifty cents this morning.
TRAVIS: Teacher say we have to.
RUTH: I don't care what teacher say. I ain't got it. Eat your breakfast, Travis.
TRAVIS: I *am* eating.
RUTH: Hush up now and just eat!

The boy gives her an exasperated look for her lack of understanding, and eats grudgingly.

TRAVIS: You think Grandmama would have it?
RUTH: No! And I want you to stop asking your grandmother for money, you hear me?
TRAVIS [*outraged*]: Gaaaleee! I don't ask her, she just gimme it sometimes!
RUTH: Travis Willard Younger—I got too much on me this morning to be—
TRAVIS: Maybe Daddy—
RUTH: *Travis!*

The boy hushes abruptly. They are both quiet and tense for several seconds.

TRAVIS [*presently*]: Could I maybe go carry some groceries in front of the supermarket for a little while after school then?
RUTH: Just hush, I said. [TRAVIS *jabs his spoon into his cereal bowl viciously, and rests his head in anger upon*

his fists.] If you through eating, you can get over there and make up your bed.

[*The boy obeys stiffly and crosses the room, almost mechanically, to the bed and more or less carefully folds the covering. He carries the bedding into his mother's room and returns with his books and cap.*]

TRAVIS [*sulking and standing apart from her unnaturally*]: I'm gone.

RUTH [*looking up from the stove to inspect him automatically*]: Come *here.* [*He crosses to her and she studies his head.*] If you don't take this comb and fix this here head, you better! [TRAVIS *puts down his books with a great sigh of oppression, and crosses to the mirror. His mother mutters under her breath about his "slubbornness."*] But to march out of here with that head looking just like chickens slept in it! I just don't know where you get your slubborn ways. . . . And get your jacket, too. Looks chilly out this morning.

TRAVIS [*with conspicuously brushed hair and jacket*]: I'm gone.

RUTH: Get carfare and milk money— [*waving one finger*] —and not a single penny for no caps, you hear me?

TRAVIS [*with sullen politeness*]: Yes'm.

He turns in outrage to leave. His mother watches after him as in his frustration he approaches the door almost comically. When she speaks to him her voice has become a very gentle tease.

RUTH [*mocking; as she thinks he would say it*]: Oh, Mama makes me so mad sometimes, I don't know what to do! [*She waits and continues to his back as he stands stock-still in front of the door.*] I wouldn't kiss that woman good-bye for nothing in this world this morning! [*The boy finally turns around and rolls his eyes at her, knowing the mood has changed and he is vindicated; he does not, however, move toward her yet.*] Not for nothing in this world! [*She finally laughs aloud at him and holds out her arms to him and we see that it is a way between them, very old and practiced. He crosses to her and allows her to embrace him warmly but keeps his face fixed with masculine rigidity. She holds him back from her presently and looks at him and runs her fingers over the features of his face. With utter gentleness—*] Now—whose little old angry man are you?

TRAVIS [*the masculinity and gruffness start to fade at last*]: Aw gaalee—Mama . . .

RUTH [*mimicking*]: Aw—gaaaaalleeeee, Mama! [*She pushes him, with rough playfulness and finality, toward the door.*] Get on out of here or you going to be late.

TRAVIS [*in the face of love, new aggressiveness*]: Mama, could I please go carry groceries?

RUTH: Honey, it's starting to get so cold evenings.

WALTER [*coming in from the bathroom and drawing a make-believe gun from a make-believe holster and shooting at his son*]: What is it he wants to do?

RUTH: Go carry groceries after school at the supermarket.

WALTER: Well, let him go . . .

TRAVIS [*quickly, to the ally*]: I *have* to—she won't gimme the fifty cents. . . .

WALTER [*to his wife only*]: Why not?

RUTH [*simply, and with flavor*]: 'Cause we don't have it.

WALTER [*to* RUTH *only*]: What you tell the boy things like that for? [*Reaching down into his pants with a rather important gesture*] Here, son—

He hands the boy the coin, but his eyes are directed to his wife's. TRAVIS *takes the money happily.*

TRAVIS: Thanks, Daddy.

He starts out. RUTH *watches both of them with murder in her eyes.* WALTER *stands and stares back at her with defiance, and suddenly reaches into his pocket again on an afterthought.*

WALTER [*without even looking at his son, still staring hard at his wife*]: In fact, here's another fifty cents. . . . Buy yourself some fruit today—or take a taxicab to school or something!

TRAVIS: Whoopee—

He leaps up and clasps his father around the middle with his legs, and they face each other in mutual appreciation; slowly WALTER LEE *peeks around the boy to catch the violent rays from his wife's eyes and draws his head back as if shot.*

WALTER: You better get down now—and get to school, man.

TRAVIS [*at the door*]: O.K. Good-bye. [*He exits.*]

WALTER [*after him, pointing with pride*]: That's *my* boy. [*She looks at him in disgust and turns back to her work.*] You know what I was thinking 'bout in the bathroom this morning?

RUTH: No.

WALTER: How come you always try to be so pleasant!

RUTH: What is there to be pleasant 'bout!

WALTER: You want to know what I was thinking 'bout in the bathroom or not!

RUTH: I know what you thinking 'bout.

WALTER [*ignoring her*]: 'Bout what me and Willy Harris was talking about last night.

RUTH [*immediately—a refrain*]: Willy Harris is a good-for-nothing loud mouth.

WALTER: Anybody who talks to me has got to be a good-for-nothing loud mouth, ain't he? And what you know about who is just a good-for-nothing loud mouth? Charlie Atkins was just a "good-for-nothing loud mouth" too, wasn't he! When he wanted me to go in the dry-cleaning business with him. And now—he's grossing a hundred thousand a year. A hundred thousand dollars a year! You still call *him* a loud mouth!

RUTH [*bitterly*]: Oh, Walter Lee. . . . [*She folds her head on her arms over the table.*]

WALTER [*rising and coming to her and standing over her*]: You tired, ain't you? Tired of everything. Me, the boy, the way we live—this beat-up hole—everything. Ain't you? [*She doesn't look up, doesn't answer.*] So tired—moaning and groaning all the time, but you wouldn't do nothing to help, would you? You couldn't be on my side that long for nothing, could you?

RUTH: Walter, please leave me alone.

WALTER: A man needs for a woman to back him up. . . .

RUTH: Walter—

WALTER: Mama would listen to you. You know she listen to you more than she do me and Bennie. She think more of you. All you have to do is just sit down with her when you drinking your coffee one morning and talking 'bout things like you do and— [*he sits down beside her and demonstrates graphically what he thinks her methods and tone should be*]—you just sip your coffee, see, and say easy like that you been thinking 'bout that deal Walter Lee is so interested in, 'bout the store and all, and sip some more coffee, like what you saying ain't really that important to you—And the next thing you know, she be listening good and asking you questions and when I come home—I can tell her the details. This ain't no fly-by-night proposition, baby. I mean we figured it out, me and Willy and Bobo.

RUTH [*with a frown*]: Bobo?

WALTER: Yeah. You see, this little liquor store we got in mind cost seventy-five thousand and we figured the initial investment on the place be 'bout thirty thousand, see. That be ten thousand each. Course, there's a couple of hundred you got to pay so's you don't spend your life just waiting for them clowns to let your license get approved—

RUTH: You mean graft?

WALTER [*frowning impatiently*]: Don't call it that. See there, that just goes to show you what women understand about the world. Baby, don't *nothing* happen for you in this world 'less you pay *somebody* off!

RUTH: Walter, leave me alone! [*She raises her head and stares at him vigorously—then says, more quietly*] Eat your eggs, they gonna be cold.

WALTER [*straightening up from her and looking off*]: That's it. There you are. Man say to his woman: I got me a dream. His woman say: Eat your eggs. [*Sadly, but gaining in power*] Man say: I got to take hold of this here world, baby! And a woman will say: Eat your eggs and go to work. [*Passionately now*] Man say: I got to change my life, I'm choking to death, baby! And his woman say— [*in utter anguish as he brings his fists down on his thighs*] —Your eggs is getting cold!

RUTH [*softly*]: Walter, that ain't none of our money.

WALTER [*not listening at all or even looking at her*]: This morning, I was lookin' in the mirror and thinking about it. . . . I'm thirty-five years old; I been married eleven years and I got a boy who sleeps in the living room— [*very, very quietly*] —and all I got to give him is stories about how rich white people live. . . .

RUTH: Eat your eggs, Walter.

WALTER: *Damn my eggs . . . damn all the eggs that ever was!*

RUTH: Then go to work.

WALTER [*looking up at her*]: See—I'm trying to talk to you 'bout myself— [*shaking his head with the repetition*] —and all you can say is eat them eggs and go to work.

RUTH [*wearily*]: Honey, you never say nothing new. I listen to you every day, every night and every morning, and you never say nothing new. [*Shrugging.*] So you would rather *be* Mr. Arnold than be his chauffeur. So— I would *rather* be living in Buckingham Palace.

WALTER: That is just what is wrong with the colored woman in this world. . . . Don't understand about building their men up and making 'em feel like they somebody. Like they can do something.

RUTH [*drily, but to hurt*]: There *are* colored men who do things.

WALTER: No thanks to the colored woman.

RUTH: Well, being a colored woman, I guess I can't help myself none.

She rises and gets the ironing board and sets it up and attacks a huge pile of rough-dried clothes, sprinkling them in preparation for the ironing and then rolling them into tight fat balls.

WALTER [*mumbling*]: We one group of men tied to a race of women with small minds.

His sister BENEATHA *enters. She is about twenty, as slim and intense as her brother. She is not as pretty as her sister-in-law, but her lean, almost intellectual face has a handsomeness of its own. She wears a bright-red flannel nightie, and her thick hair stands wildly about her head. Her speech is a mixture of many things; it is different from the rest of the family's insofar as education has permeated her sense of English—and perhaps the Midwest rather than the South has finally—at last—won out in her inflection; but not altogether, because over all of it is a soft slurring and transformed use of vowels which is the decided influence of the Southside. She passes through the room without looking at either* RUTH *or* WALTER *and goes to the outside door and looks, a little blindly, out to the bathroom. She sees that it has been lost to the Johnsons. She closes the door with a sleepy vengeance and crosses to the table and sits down a little defeated.*

BENEATHA: I am going to start timing those people.

WALTER: You should get up earlier.

BENEATHA [*her face in her hands; she is still fighting the urge to go back to bed*]: Really—would you suggest dawn? Where's the paper?

WALTER [*pushing the paper across the table to her as he studies her almost clinically, as though he has never seen her before*]: You a horrible-looking chick at this hour.

BENEATHA [*drily*]: Good morning, everybody.

WALTER [*senselessly*]: How is school coming?

BENEATHA [*in the same spirit*]: Lovely. Lovely. And you know, biology is the greatest. [*Looking up at him.*] I dissected something that looked just like you yesterday.

WALTER: I just wondered if you've made up your mind and everything.

BENEATHA [*gaining in sharpness and impatience*]: And what did I answer yesterday morning—and the day before that?

RUTH [*from the ironing board, like someone disinterested and old*]: Don't be so nasty, Bennie.

BENEATHA [*still to her brother*]: And the day before that and the day before that!

WALTER [*defensively*]: I'm interested in you. Something wrong with that? Ain't many girls who decide—

WALTER and BENEATHA [*in unison*]: —"to be a doctor."

Silence.

WALTER: Have we figured out yet just exactly how much medical school is going to cost?

RUTH: Walter Lee, why don't you leave that girl alone and get out of here to work?

BENEATHA [*exits to the bathroom and bangs on the door*]: Come on out of there, please! [*She comes back into the room.*]

WALTER [*looking at his sister intently*]: You know the check is coming tomorrow.

BENEATHA [*turning on him with a sharpness all her own*]: That money belongs to Mama, Walter, and it's for her to decide how she wants to use it. I don't care if she wants to buy a house or a rocket ship or just nail it up somewhere and look at it. It's hers. Not ours—*hers.*

WALTER [*bitterly*]: Now ain't that fine! You just got your mother's interest at heart, ain't you, girl? You such a nice girl—but if Mama got that money she can always take a few thousand and help you through school too—can't she?

BENEATHA: I have never asked anyone around here to do anything for me!

WALTER: No! And the line between asking and just accepting when the time comes is big and wide—ain't it!

BENEATHA [*with fury*]: What do you want from me, Brother—that I quit school or just drop dead, which!

WALTER: I don't want nothing but for you to stop acting holy 'round here. Me and Ruth done made some sacrifices for you—why can't you do something for the family?

RUTH: Walter, don't be dragging me in it.

WALTER: You are in it—Don't you get up and go work in somebody's kitchen for the last three years to help put clothes on her back?

RUTH: Oh, Walter—that's not fair. . . .

WALTER: It ain't that nobody expects you to get on your knees and say thank you, Brother; thank you, Ruth; thank you, Mama—and thank you, Travis, for wearing the same pair of shoes for two semesters—

BENEATHA [*dropping to her knees*]: Well—I *do*—all right?—thank everybody . . . and forgive me for ever wanting to be anything at all . . . forgive me, forgive me!

Ruth: Please stop it! Your mama'll hear you.

WALTER: Who the hell told you you had to be a doctor? If you so crazy 'bout messing 'round with sick people—then go be a nurse like other women—or just get married and be quiet. . . .

BENEATHA: Well—you finally got it said. . . . It took you three years but you finally got it said. Walter, give up; leave me alone—it's Mama's money.

WALTER: *He was my father, too!*

BENEATHA: So what? He was mine, too—and Travis' grandfather—but the insurance money belongs to Mama. Picking on me is not going to make her give it to you to invest in any liquor stores—[*underbreath, dropping into a chair*] —and I for one say, God bless Mama for that!

WALTER [*to* RUTH]: See—did you hear? Did you hear!

RUTH: Honey, please go to work.

WALTER: Nobody in this house is ever going to understand me.

BENEATHA: Because you're a nut.

WALTER: Who's a nut?

BENEATHA: You—you are a nut. Thee is mad, boy.

WALTER [*looking at his wife and his sister from the door, very sadly*]: The world's most backward race of people, and that's a fact.

BENEATHA [*turning slowly in her chair*]: And then there are all those prophets who would lead us out of the wilderness— [WALTER *slams out of the house*] into the swamps!

RUTH: Bennie, why you always gotta be pickin' on your brother? Can't you be a little sweeter sometimes?

[*Door opens.* WALTER *walks in.*]

WALTER [*to* RUTH]: I need some money for carfare.

RUTH [*looks at him, then warms; teasing, but tenderly*]: Fifty cents? [*She goes to her bag and gets money.*] Here, take a taxi.

[WALTER *exits.* MAMA *enters. She is a woman in her early sixties, full-bodied and strong. She is one of those women of a certain grace and beauty who wear it so unobtrusively that it takes a while to notice. Her dark-brown face is surrounded by the total whiteness of her hair, and, being a woman who has adjusted to many things in life and overcome many more, her face is full of strength. She has, we can see, wit and faith of a kind that keep her eyes lit and full of interest and expectancy. She is, in a word, a beautiful woman. Her bearing is perhaps most like the noble bearing of the women of the Hereros of Southwest Africa—rather as if she imagines that as she walks she still bears a basket or a vessel upon her head. Her speech, on the other hand, is as careless as her carriage is precise—she is inclined to slur everything—but her voice is perhaps not so much quiet as simply soft.*]

MAMA: Who that 'round here slamming doors at this hour?

She crosses through the room, goes to the window, opens it, and brings in a feeble little plant growing doggedly in a small pot on the window sill. She feels the dirt and puts it back out.

RUTH: That was Walter Lee. He and Bennie was at it again.

MAMA: My children and they tempers. Lord, if this little old plant don't get more sun than it's been getting it ain't never going to see spring again. [*She turns from the window.*] What's the matter with you this morning, Ruth? You looks right peaked. You aiming to iron all them things? Leave some for me. I'll get to 'em this afternoon. Bennie honey, it's too drafty for you to be sitting 'round half dressed. Where's your robe?

BENEATHA: In the cleaners.

MAMA: Well, go get mine and put it on.

BENEATHA: I'm not cold, Mama, honest.

MAMA: I know—but you so thin. . . .

BENEATHA [*irritably*]: Mama, I'm not cold.

MAMA [*seeing the make-down bed as* TRAVIS *has left it*]: Lord have mercy, look at that poor bed. Bless his heart—he tries, don't he?

[*She moves to the bed* TRAVIS *has sloppily made up.*]

RUTH: No—he don't half try at all 'cause he knows you going to come along behind him and fix everything. That's just how come he don't know how to do nothing right now—you done spoiled that boy so.

MAMA: Well—he's a little boy. Ain't supposed to know 'bout housekeeping. My baby, that's what he is. What you fix for his breakfast this morning?

RUTH [*angrily*]: I feed my son, Lena!

MAMA: I ain't meddling— [*underbreath; busy bodyish*] —I just noticed all last week he had cold cereal, and when it starts getting this chilly in the fall a child ought to have some hot grits or something when he goes out in the cold—

RUTH [*furious*]: I gave him hot oats—is that all right!

MAMA: I ain't meddling. [*Pause.*] Put a lot of nice butter on it? [RUTH *shoots her an angry look and does not reply.*] He likes lots of butter.

RUTH [*exasperated*]: Lena—

MAMA [*to* BENEATHA; MAMA *is inclined to wander conversationally sometimes*]: What was you and your brother fussing 'bout this morning?

BENEATHA: It's not important, Mama.

[*She gets up and goes to look out at the bathroom, which is apparently free, and she picks up her towels and rushes out.*]

MAMA: What was they fighting about?

RUTH: Now you know as well as I do.

MAMA [*shaking her head*]: Brother still worrying hisself sick about that money?

RUTH: You know he is.

MAMA: You had breakfast?

RUTH: Some coffee.

MAMA: Girl, you better start eating and looking after yourself better. You almost thin as Travis.

RUTH: Lena—

MAMA: Un-hunh?

RUTH: What are you going to do with it?

MAMA: Now don't you start, child. It's too early in the morning to be talking about money. It ain't Christian.

RUTH: It's just that he got his heart set on that store—

MAMA: You mean that liquor store that Willy Harris want him to invest in?

RUTH: Yes—

MAMA: We ain't no business people, Ruth. We just plain working folks.

RUTH: Ain't nobody business people till they go into business. Walter Lee say colored people ain't never going to start getting ahead till they start gambling on some different kinds of things in the world—investments and things.

MAMA: What done got into you, girl? Walter Lee done finally sold you on investing.

RUTH: No. Mama, something is happening between Walter and me. I don't know what it is—but he needs something—something I can't give him any more. He needs this chance, Lena.

MAMA [*frowning deeply*]: But liquor, honey—

RUTH: Well—like Walter say—I spec people going to always be drinking themselves some liquor.

MAMA: Well—whether they drinks it or not ain't none of my business. But whether I go into business selling it to 'em *is,* and I don't want that on my ledger this late in life. [*Stopping suddenly and studying her daugher-in-law*] Ruth Younger, what's the matter with you today? You look like you could fall over right there.

RUTH: I'm tired.

MAMA: Then you better stay home from work today.

RUTH: I can't stay home. She'd be calling up the agency and screaming at them, "My girl didn't come in today—send me somebody! My girl didn't come in!" Oh, she just have a fit . . .

MAMA: Well, let her have it. I'll just call her up and say you got the flu—

RUTH [*laughing*]: Why the flu?

MAMA: 'Cause it sounds respectable to 'em. Something white people get, too. They know 'bout the flu. Otherwise they think you been cut up or something when you tell 'em you sick.

RUTH: I got to go in. We need the money.

MAMA: Somebody would of thought my children done all but starved to death the way they talk about money here late. Child, we got a great big old check coming tomorrow.

RUTH [*sincerely, but also self-righteously*]: Now that's your money. It ain't got nothing to do with me. We all feel like that—Walter and Bennie and me—even Travis.

MAMA [*thoughtfully, and suddenly very far away*]: Ten thousand dollars—

RUTH: Sure is wonderful.

MAMA: Ten thousand dollars.

RUTH: You know what you should do, Miss Lena? You should take yourself a trip somewhere. To Europe or South America or someplace—

MAMA [*throwing up her hands at the thought*]: Oh, child!

RUTH: I'm serious. Just pack up and leave! Go on away and enjoy yourself some. Forget about the family and have yourself a ball for once in your life—

MAMA [*drily*]: You sound like I'm just about ready to die. Who'd go with me? What I look like wandering 'round Europe by myself?

RUTH: Shoot—these here rich white women do it all the time. They don't think nothing of packing up they suitcases and piling on one of them big steamships and—swoosh!—they gone, child.

MAMA: Something always told me I wasn't no rich white woman.

RUTH: Well—what are you going to do with it then?

MAMA: I ain't rightly decided. [*Thinking. She speaks now with emphasis.*] Some of it got to be put away for Beneatha and her schoolin'—and ain't nothing going to touch that part of it. Nothing. [*She waits several seconds, trying to make up her mind about something, and looks at* RUTH *a little tentatively before going on.*] Been thinking that we maybe could meet the notes on a little old two-story somewhere, with a yard where Travis could play in the summertime, if we use part of the insurance for a down payment and everybody kind of pitch in. I could maybe take on a little day work again, few days a week—

RUTH [*studying her mother-in-law furtively and concentrating on her ironing, anxious to encourage without seeming to*]: Well, Lord knows, we've put enough rent into this here rat trap to pay for four houses by now. . . .

MAMA [*Looking up at the words "rat trap" and then looking around and leaning back and sighing—in a suddenly reflective mood—*]: "Rat trap"—yes, that's all it is. [*Smiling*] I remember just as well the day me and Big Walter moved in here. Hadn't been married but two weeks and wasn't planning on living here no more than a year. [*She shakes her head at the dissolved dream*] We was going to set away, little by little, don't you know, and buy a little place out in Morgan Park. We had even picked out the house. [*Chuckling a little*] Looks right dumpy today. But Lord, child, you should know all the dreams I had 'bout buying that house and fixing it up and making me a little garden in the back— [*She waits and stops smiling*] And didn't none of it happen. [*Dropping her hands in a futile gesture*]

RUTH [*Keeps her head down, ironing*]: Yes, life can be a barrel of disappointments, sometimes.

MAMA: Honey, Big Walter would come in here some nights back then and slump down on that couch there and just look at the rug, and look at me and look at the rug and then back at me—and I'd know he was down then . . . really down. [*After a second very long and thoughtful pause; she is seeing back to times that only she can see*] And then, Lord, when I lost that baby—little Claude—I almost thought I was going to lose Big Walter too. Oh, that man grieved hisself! He was one man to love his children.

RUTH: Ain't nothin' can tear at you like losin' your baby.

MAMA: I guess that's how come that man finally worked hisself to death like he done. Like he was fighting his own war with this here world that took his baby from him.

RUTH: He sure was a fine man, all right. I always liked Mr. Younger.

MAMA: Crazy 'bout his children! God knows there was plenty wrong with Walter Younger—hard-headed, mean, kind of wild with women—plenty wrong with him. But he sure loved his children. Always wanted them to have something—be something. That's where Brother gets all these notions, I reckon. Big Walter used to say, he'd get right wet in the eyes sometimes, lean his head back with the water standing in his eyes and say, "Seem like God didn't see fit to give the black man nothing but dreams—but He did give us children to make them dreams seem worth while." [*She smiles*] He could talk like that, don't you know.

RUTH: Yes, he sure could. He was a good man, Mr. Younger.

MAMA: Yes, a fine man—just couldn't never catch up with his dreams, that's all.

[BENEATHA *comes in, brushing her hair and looking up to the ceiling, where the sound of a vacuum cleaner has started up*]

BENEATHA: What could be so dirty on that woman's rugs that she has to vacuum them every single day?

RUTH: I wish certain young women 'round here who I could name would take inspiration about certain rugs in a certain apartment I could also mention.

BENEATHA [*shrugging*]: How much cleaning can a house need, for Christ's sakes.

MAMA [*not liking the Lord's name used thus*]: Bennie!

RUTH: Just listen to her—just listen!

BENEATHA: Oh, God!

MAMA: If you use the Lord's name just one more time—

BENEATHA [*a bit of a whine*]: Oh, Mama—

RUTH: Fresh—just fresh as salt, this girl!

BENEATHA [*drily*]: Well—if the salt loses its savor—

MAMA: Now that will do. I just ain't going to have you 'round here reciting the scriptures in vain—you hear me?

BENEATHA: How did I manage to get on everybody's wrong side by just walking into a room?

RUTH: If you weren't so fresh—

BENEATHA: Ruth, I'm twenty years old.

MAMA: What time you be home from school today?

BENEATHA: Kind of late. [*With enthusiasm*] Madeline is going to start my guitar lessons today.

MAMA *and* RUTH *look up with the same expression.*

MAMA: Your *what* kind of lessons?

BENEATHA: Guitar.

RUTH: Oh, Father!

MAMA: How come you done taken it in your mind to learn to play the guitar?

BENEATHA: I just want to, that's all.

MAMA [*smiling*]: Lord, child, don't you know what to do with yourself? How long it going to be before you get tired of this now—like you got tired of that little play-acting group you joined last year? [*Looking at* RUTH] And what was it the year before that?

RUTH: The horseback-riding club for which she bought that fifty-five-dollar riding habit that's been hanging in the closet ever since!

MAMA [*to* BENEATHA]: Why you got to flit so from one thing to another, baby?

BENEATHA [*sharply*]: I just want to learn to play the guitar. Is there anything wrong with that?

MAMA: Ain't nobody trying to stop you. I just wonders sometimes why you has to flit so from one thing to another all the time. You ain't never done nothing with all that camera equipment you brought home—

BENEATHA: I don't flit! I—I experiment with different forms of expression—

RUTH: Like riding a horse?

BENEATHA: —People have to express themselves one way or another.

MAMA: What is it you want to express?

BENEATHA [*angrily*]: Me! [MAMA *and* RUTH *look at each other and burst into raucous laughter.*] Don't worry—I don't expect you to understand.

MAMA [*to change the subject*]: Who you going out with tomorrow night?

BENEATHA [*with displeasure*]: George Murchison again.

MAMA [*pleased*]: Oh—you getting a little sweet on him?

RUTH: You ask me, this child ain't sweet on nobody but herself— [*Underbreath*] Express herself!

They laugh.

BENEATHA: Oh—I like George all right, Mama. I mean I like him enough to go out with him and stuff, but—

RUTH [*for devilment*]: What does *and stuff* mean?

BENEATHA: Mind your own business.

MAMA: Stop picking at her now, Ruth. [*A thoughtful pause, and then a suspicious sudden look at her daughter as she turns in her chair for emphasis*] What *does* it mean?

BENEATHA [*wearily*]: Oh, I just mean I couldn't ever really be serious about George. He's—he's so shallow.

RUTH: Shallow—what do you mean he's shallow? He's *rich!*

MAMA: Hush, Ruth.

BENEATHA: I know he's rich. He knows he's rich, too.

RUTH: Well—what other qualities a man got to have to satisfy you, little girl?

BENEATHA: You wouldn't even begin to understand. Anybody who married Walter could not possibly understand.

MAMA [*outraged*]: What kind of way is that to talk about your brother?

BENEATHA: Brother is a flip—let's face it.

MAMA [*to* RUTH, *helplessly*]: What's a flip?

RUTH [*glad to add kindling*]: She's saying he's crazy.

BENEATHA: Not crazy. Brother isn't really crazy yet—he—he's an elaborate neurotic.

MAMA: Hush your mouth!

BENEATHA: As for George. Well. George looks good—he's got a beautiful car and he takes me to nice places and, as my sister-in-law says, he is probably the richest boy I will ever get to know and I even like him sometimes—but if the Youngers are sitting around waiting to see if their little Bennie is going to tie up the family with the Murchisons, they are wasting their time.

RUTH: You mean you wouldn't marry George Murchison if he asked you someday? That pretty, rich thing? Honey, I knew you was odd—

BENEATHA: No I would not marry him if all I felt for him was what I feel now. Besides, George's family wouldn't really like it.

MAMA: Why not?

BENEATHA: Oh, Mama—The Murchisons are honest-to-God-real-*live*–rich colored people, and the only people in the world who are more snobbish than rich white people are rich colored people. I thought everybody knew that. I've met Mrs. Murchison. She's a scene!

MAMA: You must not dislike people 'cause they well off, honey.

BENEATHA: Why not? It makes just as much sense as disliking people 'cause they are poor, and lots of people do that.

RUTH [*a wisdom-of-the-ages manner; to* MAMA]: Well, she'll get over some of this—

BENEATHA: Get over it? What are you talking about, Ruth? Listen, I'm going to be a doctor. I'm not worried about who I'm going to marry yet—if I ever get married.

MAMA and RUTH: *If!*

MAMA: Now, Bennie—

BENEATHA: Oh, I probably will . . . but first I'm going to be a doctor, and George, for one, still think's that's pretty funny. I couldn't be bothered with that, I am going to be a doctor and everybody around here better understand that!

MAMA [*kindly*]: 'Course you going to be a doctor, honey, God willing.

BENEATHA [*drily*]: God hasn't got a thing to do with it.

MAMA: Beneatha—that just wasn't necessary.

BENEATHA: Well—neither is God. I get sick of hearing about God.

MAMA: Beneatha!

BENEATHA: I mean it! I'm just tired of hearing about God all the time. What has He got to do with anything? Does He pay tuition?

MAMA: You 'bout to get your fresh little jaw slapped!

RUTH: That's just what she needs, all right!

BENEATHA: Why? Why can't I say what I want to around here, like everybody else?

MAMA: It don't sound nice for a young girl to say things like that—you wasn't brought up that way. Me and your father went to trouble to get you and Brother to church every Sunday.

BENEATHA: Mama, you don't understand. It's all a matter of ideas, and God is just one idea I don't accept. It's not important, I am not going out and be immoral or commit crimes because I don't believe in God. I don't even think about it. It's just that I get tired of Him getting credit for all the things the human race achieves through its own stubborn effort. There simply is no blasted God—there is only man and it is he who makes miracles!

MAMA *absorbs this speech, studies her daughter and rises slowly and crosses to* BENEATHA *and slaps her powerfully across the face. After, there is only silence and the daughter drops her eyes from her mother's face, and* MAMA *is very tall before her.*

MAMA: Now—you say after me, in my mother's house there is still God. [*There is a long pause and* BENEATHA *stares at the floor wordlessly.* MAMA *repeats the phrase with precision and cool emotion.*] In my mother's house there is still God.

BENEATHA: In my mother's house there is still God.

A long pause.

MAMA [*walking away from* BENEATHA, *too disturbed for triumphant posture; stopping and turning back to her daughter*]: There are some ideas we ain't going to have in this house. Not long as I am at the head of this family.

BENEATHA: Yes, ma'am.

[MAMA *walks out of the room.*]

RUTH [*almost gently, with profound understanding*]: You think you a woman, Bennie—but you still a little girl. What you did was childish—so you got treated like a child.

BENEATHA: I see. [*Quietly*] I also see that everybody thinks it's all right for Mama to be a tyrant. But all the tyranny in the world will never put a God in the heavens! [*She picks up her books and goes out.*]

RUTH [*goes to* MAMA'*s door*]: She said she was sorry.

MAMA [*coming out, going to her plant*]: They frightens me, Ruth. My children.

RUTH: You got good children, Lena. They just a little off sometimes—but they're good.

MAMA: No—there's something come down between me and them that don't let us understand each other and I don't know what it is. One done almost lost his mind thinking 'bout money all the time and the other done commence to talk about things I can't seem to understand in no form or fashion. What is it that's changing, Ruth?

RUTH [*soothingly, older than her years*]: Now . . . you taking it all too seriously. You just got strong-willed children and it takes a strong woman like you to keep 'em in hand.

MAMA [*looking at her plant and sprinkling a little water on it*]: They spirited all right, my children. Got to admit they got spirit—Bennie and Walter. Like this little old plant that ain't never had enough sunshine or nothing—and look at it. . . .

She has her back to RUTH *who has had to stop ironing and lean against something and put the back of her hand to her forehead.*

RUTH [*trying to keep* MAMA *from noticing*]: You . . . sure . . . loves that little old thing, don't you? . . .

MAMA: Well, I always wanted me a garden like I used to see sometimes at the back of the houses down home. This plant is close as I ever got to having one. [*She looks out of the window as she replaces the plant.*] Lord, ain't nothing as dreary as the view from this window on a dreary day, is there? Why ain't you singing this morning, Ruth? Sing that "No Ways Tired." That song always lifts me up so— [*She turns at last to see that* RUTH *has slipped quietly into a chair, in a state of semiconsciousness.*] Ruth! Ruth honey—what's the matter with you . . . Ruth!

CURTAIN

Scene 2

It is the following morning; a Saturday morning, and house cleaning is in progress at the YOUNGERS. *Furniture has been shoved hither and yon and* MAMA *is giving the kitchen-area walls a washing down.* BENEATHA, *in dungarees, with a handkerchief tied around her face, is spraying insecticide into the cracks in the walls. As they work, the radio is on and a Southside disc-jockey program is inappropriately filling the house with a rather exotic saxophone blues.* TRAVIS, *the sole idle one, is leaning on his arms, looking out of the window.*

TRAVIS: Grandmama, that stuff Bennie is using smells awful. Can I go downstairs, please?

MAMA: Did you get all them chores done already? I ain't see you doing much.

TRAVIS: Yes'm—finished early. Where did Mama go this morning?

MAMA [*looking at* BENEATHA]: She had to go on a little errand.

TRAVIS: Where?

MAMA: To tend to her business.

TRAVIS: Can I go outside then?

MAMA: Oh, I guess so. You better stay right in front of the house, though . . . and keep a good lookout for the postman.

TRAVIS: Yes'm. [*He starts out and decides to give his* AUNT BENEATHA *a good swat on the legs as he passes her*] Leave them poor little old cockroaches alone, they ain't bothering you none.

[*He runs as she swings the spray gun at him both viciously and playfully.* WALTER *enters from the bedroom and goes to the phone.*]

MAMA: Look out there, girl, before you be spilling some of that stuff on that child!

TRAVIS [*teasing*]: That's right—look out now!

[*He exits.*]

BENEATHA [*drily*]: I can't imagine that it would hurt him—it has never hurt the roaches.

MAMA: Well, little boys' hides ain't as tough as Southside roaches.

WALTER [*into phone*]: Hello—Let me talk to Willy Harris.

MAMA: You better get over there behind the bureau. I seen one marching out of there like Napoleon yesterday.

WALTER: Hello, Willy? It ain't come yet. It'll be here in a few minutes. Did the lawyer give you the papers?

BENEATHA: There's really only one way to get rid of them, Mama—

MAMA: How?

BENEATHA: Set fire to this building.
WALTER: Good. Good. I'll be right over.
BENEATHA: Where did Ruth go, Walter?
WALTER: I don't know.

[*He exits abruptly.*]

BENEATHA: Mama, where did Ruth go?
MAMA [*looking at her with meaning*]: To the doctor, I think.
BENEATHA: The doctor? What's the matter? [*They exchange glances.*] You don't think—
MAMA [*with her sense of drama*]: Now I ain't saying what I think. But I ain't never been wrong 'bout a women neither.

[*The phone rings.*]

BENEATHA [*at the phone*]: Hay-lo . . . [*Pause, and a moment of recognition*] Well—when did you get back! . . . And how was it? . . . Of course I've missed you—in my way . . . This morning? No . . . house cleaning and all that and Mama hates it if I let people come over when the house is like this . . . You *have?* Well, that's different . . . What is it—Oh, what the hell, come on over . . . Right, see you then.

[*She hangs up.*]

MAMA [*who has listened vigorously, as is her habit*]: Who is that you inviting over here with this house looking like this? You ain't got the pride you was born with!
BENEATHA: Asagai doesn't care how houses look, Mama—he's an intellectual.
MAMA: *Who?*
BENEATHA: Asagai—Joseph Asagai. He's an African boy I met on campus. He's been studying in Canada all summer.
MAMA: What's his name?
BENEATHA: Asagai, Joseph. Ah-sah-guy . . . He's from Nigeria.
MAMA: Oh, that's the little country that was founded by slaves way back. . . .
BENEATHA: No, Mama—that's Liberia.
MAMA: I don't think I never met no African before.
BENEATHA: Well, do me a favor and don't ask him a whole lot of ignorant questions about Africans. I mean, do they wear clothes and all that—
MAMA: Well, now, I guess if you think we so ignorant 'round here maybe you shouldn't bring your friends here—
BENEATHA: It's just that people ask such crazy things. All anyone seems to know about when it comes to Africa is Tarzan—
MAMA [*indignantly*]: Why should I know anything about Africa?
BENEATHA: Why do you give money at church for the missionary work?
MAMA: Well, that's to help save people.
BENEATHA: You mean to save them from *heathenism*—
MAMA [*innocently*]: Yes.
BENEATHA: I'm afraid they need more salvation from the British and the French.

[RUTH *comes in forlornly and pulls off her coat with dejection. They both turn to look at her.*]

RUTH [*dispiritedly*]: Well, I guess from all the happy faces—everybody knows.
BENEATHA: You pregnant?
MAMA: Lord have mercy, I sure hope it's a little old girl. Travis ought to have a sister.

BENEATHA *and* RUTH *give her a hopeless look for this grandmotherly enthusiasm.*

BENEATHA: How far along are you?
RUTH: Two months.
BENEATHA: Did you mean to? I mean did you plan it or was it an accident?
MAMA: What do you know about planning or not planning?
BENEATHA: Oh, Mama.
RUTH [*wearily*]: She's twenty years old, Lena.
BENEATHA: Did you plan it, Ruth?
RUTH: Mind your own business.
BENEATHA: It is my business—where is he going to live, on the *roof?* [*There is silence following the remark as the three women react to the sense of it.*] Gee—I didn't mean that, Ruth, honest. Gee, I don't feel like that at all. I—I think it is wonderful.
RUTH [*dully*]: Wonderful.
BENEATHA: Yes—really.
MAMA [*looking at* RUTH, *worried*]: Doctor say everything going to be all right?
RUTH [*far away*]: Yes—she says everything is going to be fine. . . .
MAMA [*immediately suspicious*]: "She"—What doctor you went to?

RUTH *folds over, near hysteria.*

MAMA [*worriedly hovering over* RUTH]: Ruth honey—what's the matter with you—you sick?

RUTH *has her fists clenched on her thighs and is fighting hard to suppress a scream that seems to be rising in her.*

BENEATHA: What's the matter with her, Mama?

MAMA [*working her fingers in* RUTH's *shoulder to relax her*]: She be all right. Women gets right depressed sometimes when they get her way. [*Speaking softly, expertly, rapidly*] Now you just relax. That's right . . . just lean back, don't think 'bout nothing at all . . . nothing at all—

RUTH: I'm all right. . . .

The glassy-eyed look melts and then she collapses into a fit of heavy sobbing. The bell rings.

BENEATHA: Oh, my God—that must be Asagai.

MAMA [*to* RUTH]: Come on now, honey. You need to lie down and rest awhile . . . then have some nice hot food.

[*They exit,* RUTH's *weight on her mother-in-law.* BENEATHA, *herself profoundly disturbed, opens the door to admit a rather dramatic-looking young man with a large package.*]

ASAGAI: Hello, Alaiyo—

BENEATHA [*holding the door open and regarding him with pleasure*]: Hello . . . [*Long pause*] Well—come in. And please excuse everything. My mother was very upset about my letting anyone come here with the place like this.

ASAGAI [*coming into the room*]: You look disturbed too. . . . Is something wrong?

BENEATHA [*still at the door, absently*]: Yes. . . we've all got acute ghetto-itus. [*She smiles and comes toward him, finding a cigarette and sitting.*] So—sit down! How was Canada?

ASAGAI [*a sophisticate*]: Canadian.

BENEATHA [*looking at him*]: I'm very glad you are back.

ASAGAI [*looking back at her in turn*]: Are you really?

BENEATHA: Yes—very.

ASAGAI: Why—you were quite glad when I went away. What happened?

BENEATHA: You went away.

ASAGAI: Ahhhhhhhh.

BENEATHA: Before—you wanted to be so serious before there was time.

ASAGAI: How much time must there be before one knows what one feels?

BENEATHA [*stalling this particular conversation; her hands pressed together, in a deliberately childish gesture*]: What did you bring me?

ASAGAI [*handing her the package*]: Open it and see.

BENEATHA [*eagerly opening the package and drawing out some records and the colorful robes of a Nigerian woman*]: Oh, Asagai! . . . You got them for me! . . . How beautiful . . . and the records too! [*She lifts out the robes and runs to the mirror with them and holds the drapery up in front of herself.*]

ASAGAI [*coming to her at the mirror*]: I shall have to teach you how to drape it properly. [*He flings the material about her for the moment and stands back to look at her.*] Ah—*Oh-pay-gay-day, oh-gbah-mu-shay.* [*A Yoruba exclamation for admiration*] You wear it well . . . very well . . . mutilated hair and all.

BENEATHA [*turning suddenly*]: My hair—what's wrong with my hair?

ASAGAI [*shrugging*]: Were you born with it like that?

BENEATHA [*reaching up to touch it*]: No . . . of course not. [*She looks back to the mirror, disturbed.*]

ASAGAI [*smiling*]: How then?

BENEATHA: You know perfectly well how . . . as crinkly as yours . . . that's how.

ASAGAI: And it is ugly to you that way?

BENEATHA [*quickly*]: Oh, no—not ugly . . . [*More slowly, apologetically*] But it's so hard to manage when it's well—raw.

ASAGAI: And so to accommodate that—you mutilate it every week?

BENEATHA: It's not mutilation!

ASAGAI [*laughing aloud at her seriousness*]: Oh . . . please! I am only teasing you because you are so very serious about these things. [*He stands back from her and folds his arms across his chest as he watches her pulling at her hair and frowning in the mirror.*] Do you remember the first time you met me at school? . . . [*He laughs.*] You came up to me and you said—and I thought you were the most serious little thing I had ever seen—you said: [*He imitates her.*] "Mr. Asagai—I want very much to talk with you. About Africa. You see, Mr. Asagai, I am looking for my *identity!*" [*He laughs.*]

BENEATHA [*turning to him, not laughing*]: Yes— [*Her face is quizzical, profoundly disturbed.*]

ASAGAI [*still teasing and reaching out and taking her face in his hands and turning her profile to him*]: Well . . . it is true that this is not so much a profile of a Hollywood queen as perhaps a queen of the Nile— [*A mock dismissal of the importance of the question*] But what does it matter? Assimilationism is so popular in your country.

BENEATHA [*wheeling, passionately, sharply*]: I am not an assimilationist!

ASAGAI [*the protest hangs in the room for a moment and* ASAGAI *studies her, his laughter fading*]: Such a serious one. [*There is a pause.*] So—you like the robes? You must take excellent care of them—they are from my sister's personal wardrobe.

BENEATHA [*with incredulity*]: You—you sent all the way home—for me?

ASAGAI [*with charm*]: For you—I would do much more. . . . Well, that is what I came for. I must go.

BENEATHA: Will you call me Monday?

ASAGAI: Yes . . . We have a great deal to talk about. I mean about identity and time and all that.

BENEATHA: Time?

ASAGAI: Yes. About how much time one needs to know what one feels.

BENEATHA: You never understood that there is more than one kind of feeling which can exist between a man and a woman—or, at least, there should be.

ASAGAI [*shaking his head negatively but gently*]: No. Between a man and a woman there need be only one kind of feeling. I have that for you. . . . Now even . . . right this moment. . . .

BENEATHA: I know—and by itself—it won't do. I can find that anywhere.

ASAGAI: For a woman it should be enough.

BENEATHA: I know—because that's what it says in all the novels that men write. But it isn't. Go ahead and laugh—but I'm not interested in being someone's little episode in America or— [*with feminine vengeance*] —one of them! [ASAGAI *has burst into laughter again.*] That's funny as hell, huh!

ASAGAI: It's just that every American girl I have known has said that to me. White—black—in this you are all the same. And the same speech, too!

BENEATHA [*angrily*]: Yuk, yuk, yuk!

ASAGAI: It's how you can be sure that the world's most liberated women are not liberated at all. You all talk about it too much!

[MAMA *enters and is immediately all social charm because of the presence of a guest.*]

BENEATHA: Oh—Mama—this is Mr. Asagai.

MAMA: How do you do?

ASAGAI [*total politeness to an elder*]: How do you do, Mrs. Younger. Please forgive me for coming at such an outrageous hour on a Saturday.

MAMA: Well, you are quite welcome. I just hope you understand that our house don't always look like this. [*Chatterish*] You must come again. I would love to hear all about— [*not sure of the name*] —your country. I think it's so sad the way our American Negroes don't know nothing about Africa 'cept Tarzan and all that. And all that money they pour into these churches when they ought to be helping you people over there drive out them French and Englishmen done taken away your land.

The mother flashes a slightly superior look at her daughter upon completion of the recitation.

ASAGAI [*taken aback by this sudden and acutely unrelated expression of sympathy*]: Yes . . . yes. . . .

MAMA [*smiling at him suddenly and relaxing and looking him over*]: How many miles is it from here to where you come from?

ASAGAI: Many thousands.

MAMA [*looking at him as she would* WALTER]: I bet you don't half look after yourself, being away from your mama either. I spec you better come 'round here from time to time and get yourself some decent home-cooked meals. . . .

ASAGAI [*moved*]: Thank you. Thank you very much. [*They are all quiet, then—*] Well . . . I must go. I will call you Monday, Alaiyo.

MAMA: What's that he call you?

ASAGAI: Oh—"Alaiyo." I hope you don't mind. It is what you would call a nickname, I think. It is a Yoruba word. I am a Yoruba.

MAMA [*looking at* BENEATHA]: I—I thought he was from—

ASAGAI [*understanding*]: Nigeria is my country. Yoruba is my tribal origin—

BENEATHA: You didn't tell us what Alaiyo means . . . for all I know, you might be calling me Little Idiot or something. . . .

ASAGAI: Well . . . let me see . . . I do not know how just to explain it. . . . The sense of a thing can be so different when it changes languages.

BENEATHA: You're evading.

ASAGAI: No—really it is difficult. . . . [*Thinking*] It means . . . it means One for Whom Bread—Food—Is Not Enough. [*He looks at her.*] Is that all right?

BENEATHA [*understanding, softly*]: Thank you.

MAMA [*looking from one to the other and not understanding any of it*]: Well . . . that's nice. . . . You must come see us again—Mr.—

ASAGAI: Ah-sah-guy . . .

MAMA: Yes . . . Do come again.

ASAGAI: Good-bye. [*He exits.*]

MAMA [*after him*]: Lord, that's a pretty thing just went out here! [*Insinuatingly, to her daughter*] Yes, I guess I see why we done commence to get so interested in Africa 'round here. Missionaries my aunt Jenny! [*She exits.*]

BENEATHA: Oh, Mama! . . .

[*She picks up the Nigerian dress and holds it up to her in front of the mirror again. She sets the headdress on haphazardly and then notices her hair again and clutches at it and then replaces the headdress and frowns at herself. Then she starts to wriggle in front of the mirror as she thinks a Nigerian woman might.* TRAVIS *enters and regards her.*]

TRAVIS: You cracking up?

BENEATHA: Shut up.

She pulls the headdress off and looks at herself in the mirror and clutches at her hair again and squinches her eyes as if trying to imagine something. Then, suddenly, she gets her raincoat and kerchief and hurriedly prepares for going out.

MAMA [*coming back into the room*]: She's resting now. Travis, baby, run next door and ask Miss Johnson to please let me have a little kitchen cleanser. This here can is empty as Jacob's kettle.

TRAVIS: I just come in.

MAMA: Do as you told. [*He exits and she looks at her daughter.*] Where you going?

BENEATHA [*halting at the door*]: To become a queen of the Nile!

[*She exits in a breathless blaze of glory.* RUTH *appears in the bedroom doorway.*]

MAMA: Who told you to get up?

RUTH: Ain't nothing wrong with me to be lying in no bed for. Where did Bennie go?

MAMA [*drumming her fingers*]: Far as I could make out—to Egypt. [RUTH *just looks at her.*] What time is it getting to?

RUTH: Ten twenty. And the mailman going to ring that bell this morning just like he done every morning for the last umpteen years.

[TRAVIS *comes in with the cleanser can.*]

TRAVIS: She say to tell you that she don't have much.

MAMA [*angrily*]: Lord, some people I could name sure is tightfisted! [*Directing her grandson*] Mark two cans of cleanser down on the list there. If she that hard up for kitchen cleanser, I sure don't want to forget to get her none!

RUTH: Lena—maybe the woman is just short on cleanser—

MAMA [*not listening*]: —Much baking powder as she done borrowed from me all these years, she could of done gone into the baking business!

The bell sounds suddenly and sharply and all three are stunned—serious and silent—mid-speech. In spite of all the other conversations and distractions of the morning, this is what they have been waiting for, even TRAVIS, *who looks helplessly from his mother to his grandmother.* RUTH *is the first to come to life again.*

RUTH [*to* TRAVIS]: *Get down them steps, boy!*

[TRAVIS *snaps to life and flies out to get the mail.*]

MAMA [*her eyes wide, her hand to her breast*]: You mean it done really come?

RUTH [*excitedly*]: Oh, Miss Lena!

MAMA [*collecting herself*]: Well . . . I don't know what we all so excited about 'round here for. We known it was coming for months.

RUTH: That's a whole lot different from having it come and being able to hold it in your hands . . . a piece of paper worth ten thousand dollars. . . . [TRAVIS *bursts back into the room. He holds the envelope high above his head, like a little dancer, his face is radiant and he is breathless. He moves to his grandmother with sudden slow ceremony and puts the envelope into her hands. She accepts it, and then merely holds it and looks at it.*] Come on! Open it . . . Lord have mercy, I wish Walter Lee was here!

TRAVIS: Open it, Grandmama!

MAMA [*staring at it*]: Now you all be quiet. It's just a check.

RUTH: *Open it. . . .*

MAMA [*still staring at it*]: Now don't act silly. . . . We ain't never been no people to act silly 'bout no money—

RUTH [*swiftly*]: We ain't never had none before—*open it!*

MAMA *finally makes a good strong tear and pulls out the thin blue slice of paper and inspects it closely. The boy and his mother study it raptly over* MAMA'*s shoulders.*

MAMA: *Travis!* [*She is counting off with doubt.*] Is that the right number of zeros.

TRAVIS: Yes'm . . . ten thousand dollars. Gaalee, Grandmama, you rich.

MAMA [*She holds the check away from her, still looking at it. Slowly her face sobers into a mask of unhappiness*]: Ten thousand dollars. [*She hands it to* RUTH.] Put it away somewhere, Ruth. [*She does not look at* RUTH; *her eyes seem to be seeing something somewhere very far off.*] Ten thousand dollars they give you. Ten thousand dollars.

TRAVIS: [*to his mother, sincerely*]: What's the matter with Grandmama—don't she want to be rich?

RUTH [*distractedly*]: You go on out and play now, baby. [TRAVIS *exits.* MAMA *starts wiping dishes absently, humming intently to herself.* RUTH *turns to her, with kind exasperation.*] You're gone and got yourself upset.

MAMA [*not looking at her*]: I spec if it wasn't for you all . . . I would just put that money away or give it to the church or something.

RUTH: Now what kind of talk is that. Mr. Younger would just be plain mad if he could hear you talking foolish like that.

MAMA [*stopping and staring off*]: Yes . . . he sure would. [*Sighing*] We got enough to do with that money, all right. [*She halts then, and turns and looks at her daughter-in-law hard;* RUTH *avoids her eyes and* MAMA *wipes her hands with finality and starts to speak firmly to* RUTH.] Where did you go today, girl?

RUTH: To the doctor.

MAMA [*impatiently*]: Now, Ruth . . . you know better than that. Old Doctor Jones is strange enough in his way but there ain't nothing 'bout him make somebody slip and call him "she"—like you done this morning.

RUTH: Well, that's what happened—my tongue slipped.

MAMA: You went to see that woman, didn't you?

RUTH [*defensively, giving herself away*]: What woman you talking about?

MAMA [*angrily*]: That woman who—

[WALTER *enters in great excitement.*]

WALTER: Did it come?

MAMA [*quietly*]: Can't you give people a Christian greeting before you start asking about money?

WALTER [*to* RUTH]: Did it come? [RUTH *unfolds the check and lays it quietly before him, watching him intently with thoughts of her own.* WALTER *sits down and grasps it close and counts off the zeros.*] Ten thousand dollars— [*He turns suddenly, frantically to his mother and draws some papers out of his breast pocket.*] Mama—look. Old Willy Harris put everything on paper—

MAMA: Son—I think you ought to talk to your wife. . . . I'll go on out and leave you alone if you want—

WALTER: I can talk to her later—Mama, look—

MAMA: Son—

WALTER: WILL SOMEBODY PLEASE LISTEN TO ME TODAY!

MAMA [*quietly*]: I don't 'low no yellin' in this house, Walter Lee, and you know it— [WALTER *stares at them in frustration and starts to speak several times.*] And there ain't going to be no investing in no liquor stores. I don't aim to have to speak on that again.

A long pause.

WALTER: Oh—so you don't aim to have to speak on that again? So *you* have decided. . . . [*Crumpling his papers*] Well, *you* tell that to my boy tonight when you put him to sleep on the living-room couch. . . . [*Turning to* MAMA *and speaking directly to her*] Yeah—and tell it to my wife, Mama, tomorrow when she has to go out of here to look after somebody else's kids. And tell it to *me,* Mama, every time we need a new pair of curtains and I have to watch *you* go out and work in somebody's kitchen. Yeah, you tell me then!

[WALTER *starts out.*]

RUTH: Where you going?

WALTER: I'm going out!

RUTH: Where?

WALTER: Just out of this house somewhere—

RUTH [*getting her coat*]: I'll come too.

WALTER: I don't want you to come!

RUTH: I got something to talk to you about, Walter.

WALTER: That's too bad.

MAMA [*still quietly*]: Walter Lee— [*She waits and he finally turns and looks at her.*] Sit down.

WALTER: I'm a grown man, Mama.

MAMA: Ain't nobody said you wasn't grown. But you still in my house and my presence. And as long as you are—you'll talk to your wife civil. Now sit down.

RUTH [*suddenly*]: Oh, let him go on out and drink himself to death! He makes me sick to my stomach! [*She flings her coat against him.*]

WALTER: [*violently*]: And you turn mine too, baby! [RUTH *goes into their bedroom and slams the door behind her.*] That was my greatest mistake—

MAMA [*still quietly*]: Walter, what is the matter with you?

WALTER: Matter with me? Ain't nothing the matter with *me!*

MAMA: Yes there is. Something eating you up like a crazy man. Something more than me not giving you this money. The past few years I been watching it happen to you. You get all nervous acting and kind of wild in the eyes— [WALTER *jumps up impatiently at her words.*] I said sit there now, I'm talking to you!

WALTER: Mama—I don't need no nagging at me today.

MAMA: Seem like you getting to a place where you always tied up in some kind of knot about something. But if anybody ask you 'bout it you just yell at 'em and bust out the house and go out and drink somewheres. Walter Lee, people can't live with that. Ruth's a good, patient girl in her way—but you getting to be too much. Boy, don't make the mistake of driving that girl away from you.

WALTER: Why—what she do for me?

MAMA: She loves you.

WALTER: Mama—I'm going out. I want to go off somewhere and be by myself for a while.

MAMA: I'm sorry 'bout your liquor store, son. It just wasn't the thing for us to do. That's what I want to tell you about—

WALTER: I got to go out, Mama— [*He rises.*]

MAMA: It's dangerous, son.

WALTER: What's dangerous?

MAMA: When a man goes outside his home to look for peace.

WALTER: [*beseechingly*]: Then why can't there never be no peace in this house then?

MAMA: You done found it in some other house?

WALTER: No—there ain't no woman! Why do women always think there's a woman somewhere when a man gets restless. [*Coming to her*] Mama—Mama—I want so many things. . . .

MAMA: Yes, son—

WALTER: I want so many things that they are driving me kind of crazy. . . . Mama—look at me.

MAMA: I'm looking at you. You a good-looking boy. You got a job, a nice wife, a fine boy and—

WALTER: A job. [*Looks at her*] Mama, a job? I open and close car doors all day long. I drive a man around in his limousine and I say, "Yes, sir; no, sir; very good, sir; shall I take the Drive, sir?" Mama, that ain't no kind of job . . . that ain't nothing at all. [*Very quietly*] Mama, I don't know if I can make you understand.

MAMA: Understand what, baby?

WALTER: [*quietly*]: Sometimes it's like I can see the future stretched out in front of me—just plain as day. The future, Mama. Hanging over there at the edge of my days. Just waiting for me—a big, looming blank space—full of *nothing*. Just waiting for *me*. [*Pause*] Mama—sometimes when I'm downtown and I pass them cool, quiet-looking restaurants where them white boys are sitting back and talking 'bout things . . . sitting there turning deals worth millions of dollars . . . sometimes I see guys don't look much older than me—

MAMA: Son—how come you talk so much 'bout money?

WALTER: [*with immense passion*]: Because it is life, Mama!

MAMA [*quietly*]: Oh— [*Very quietly*] So now it's life. Money is life. Once upon a time freedom used to be life—now it's money. I guess the world really do change. . . .

WALTER: No—it was always money, Mama. We just didn't know about it.

MAMA: No . . . something has changed. [*She looks at him.*] You something new, boy. In my time we was worried about not being lynched and getting to the North if we could and how to stay alive and still have a pinch of dignity too. . . . Now here come you and Beneatha—talking 'bout things we ain't never even thought about hardly, me and your daddy. You ain't satisfied or proud of nothing we done. I mean that you had a home; that we kept you out of trouble till you was grown; that you don't have to ride to work on the back of nobody's streetcar—You my children—but how different we done become.

WALTER: You just don't understand, Mama, you just don't understand.

MAMA: Son—do you know your wife is expecting another baby? [WALTER *stands, stunned, and absorbs what his mother has said.*] That's what she wanted to talk to you about. [WALTER *sinks down into a chair.*] This ain't for me to be telling—but you ought to know. [*She waits.*] I think Ruth is thinking 'bout getting rid of that child.

WALTER: [*slowly understanding*]: No—no—Ruth wouldn't do that.

MAMA: When the world gets ugly enough—a woman will do anything for her family. *The part that's already living.*

WALTER: You don't know Ruth, Mama, if you think she would do that.

[RUTH *opens the bedroom door and stands there a little limp.*]

RUTH [*beaten*]: Yes I would too, Walter. [*Pause*] I gave her a five-dollar down payment.

There is total silence as the man stares at his wife and the mother stares at her son.

MAMA [*presently*]: Well— [*Tightly*] Well—son, I'm waiting to hear you say something. . . . I'm waiting to hear how you be your father's son. Be the man he was. . . . [*Pause*] Your wife say she going to destroy your child. And I'm waiting to hear you talk like him and say we a people who give children life, not who destroys them— [*She rises.*] I'm waiting to see you stand up and look like your daddy and say we done give up one baby to poverty and that we ain't going to give up nary another one. . . . I'm waiting.

WALTER: Ruth—

MAMA: If you a son of mine, tell her! [WALTER *turns, looks at her and can say nothing. She continues, bitterly.*] You . . . you are a disgrace to your father's memory. Somebody get me my hat.

CURTAIN

ACT II

Scene 1

Time: Later the same day.

At rise: RUTH *is ironing again. She has the radio going. Presently* BENEATHA*'s bedroom door opens and* RUTH*'s mouth falls and she puts down the iron in fascination.*

RUTH: What have we got on tonight!

BENEATHA [*emerging grandly from the doorway so that we can see her thoroughly robed in the costume* ASAGAI *brought*]: You are looking at what a well-dressed Nigerian woman wears— [*She parades for* RUTH*, her hair completely hidden by the headdress; she is coquettishly fanning herself with an ornate oriental fan, mistakenly more like Butterfly than any Nigerian that ever *was.*] Isn't it beautiful? [*She promenades to the radio and, with an arrogant flourish, turns off the good loud blues that is playing.*] Enough of this assimilationist junk! [RUTH *follows her with her eyes as she goes to the phonograph and puts on a record and turns and waits ceremoniously for the music to come up. Then, with a shout—*] OCOMOGOSIAY!

RUTH *jumps. The music comes up, a lovely Nigerian melody.* BENEATHA *listens, enraptured, her eyes far away—"back to the past." She begins to dance.* RUTH *is dumfounded.*

RUTH: What kind of dance is that?
BENEATHA: A folk dance.
RUTH [*Pearl Bailey*]: What kind of folks do that, honey?
BENEATHA: It's from Nigeria. It's a dance of welcome.
RUTH: Who you welcoming?
BENEATHA: The men back to the village.
RUTH: Where they been?
BENEATHA: How should I know—out hunting or something. Anyway, they are coming back now. . . .
RUTH: Well, that's good.
BENEATHA [*with the record*]:

Alundi, alundi
Alundi alunya
Jop pu a jeepua
Ang gu soooooooooo

Ai yai yae . . .
Ayehaye—alundi . . .

[WALTER *comes in during this performance; he has obviously been drinking. He leans against the door heavily and watches his sister, at first with distaste. Then his eyes look off—"back to the past"—as he lifts both his fists to the roof, screaming.*]

WALTER: YEAH . . . AND ETHIOPIA STRETCH FORTH HER HANDS AGAIN! . . .
RUTH [*drily, looking at him*]: Yes—and Africa sure is claiming her own tonight. [*She gives them both up and starts ironing again.*]
WALTER: [*all in a drunken, dramatic shout*]: Shut up! . . . I'm digging them drums . . . them drums move me! . . . [*He makes his weaving way to his wife's face and leans in close to her.*] In my *heart of hearts*— [*he thumps his chest*] —I am much warrior!
RUTH [*without even looking up*]: In your heart of hearts you are much drunkard.
WALTER: [*coming away from her and starting to wander around the room, shouting*]: Me and Jomo . . . [*Intently, in his sister's face. She has stopped dancing to watch him in this unknown mood.*] That's my man, Kenyatta. [*Shouting and thumping his chest*] FLAMING SPEAR! HOT DAMN! [*He is suddenly in possession of an imaginary spear and actively spearing enemies all over the room.*] OCOMOGOSIAY . . . THE LION IS WAKING. . . . OWIMOWEH! [*He pulls his shirt open and leaps up on a table and gestures with his spear. The bell rings.* RUTH *goes to answer.*]
BENEATHA [*to encourage* WALTER, *thoroughly caught up with this side of him*]: OCOMOGOSIAY, FLAMING SPEAR!
WALTER [*on the table, very far gone, his eyes pure glass sheets; he sees what we cannot, that he is a leader of his people, a great chief, a descendant of Chaka, and that the hour to march has come*]: Listen, my black broth—ers—
BENEATHA: OCOMOGOSIAY!
WALTER: —Do you hear the waters rushing against the shores of the coastlands—
BENEATHA: OCOMOGOSIAY!
WALTER: —Do you hear the screeching of the cocks in yonder hills beyond where the chiefs meet in council for the coming of the mighty war—
BENEATHA: OCOMOGOSIAY!
WALTER: —Do you hear the beating of the wings of the birds flying low over the mountains and the low places of our land—

[RUTH *opens the door.* GEORGE MURCHISON *enters.*]

BENEATHA: OCOMOGOSIAY!
WALTER: —Do you hear the singing of the women, singing the war songs of our fathers to the babies in the great houses . . . singing the sweet war songs? OH, DO YOU HEAR, MY BLACK BROTHERS!
BENEATHA [*completely gone*]: We hear you, Flaming Spear—
WALTER: Telling us to prepare for the greatness of the time— [*To* GEORGE] Black Brother! [*He extends his hand for the fraternal clasp.*]
GEORGE: Black Brother, hell!
RUTH [*having had enough, and embarrassed for the family*]: Beneatha, you got company—what's the matter with you? Walter Lee Younger, get down off that table and stop acting like a fool. . . .

[WALTER *comes down off the table suddenly and makes a quick exit to the bathroom.*]

RUTH: He's had a little to drink. . . . I don't know what her excuse is.
GEORGE: [*to* BENEATHA]: Look honey, we're going *to* the theater—we're not going to be *in* it . . . so go change, huh?

RUTH: You expect this boy to go out with you looking like that?

BENEATHA [*looking at* GEORGE]: That's up to George. If he's ashamed of his heritage—

GEORGE: Oh, don't be so proud of yourself, Bennie—just because you look eccentric.

BENEATHA: How can something that's natural be eccentric?

GEORGE: That's what being eccentric means—being natural. Get dressed.

BENEATHA: I don't like that, George.

RUTH: Why must you and your brother make an argument out of everything people say?

BENEATHA: Because I hate assimilationist Negroes!

RUTH: Will somebody please tell me what assimila-whoever means!

GEORGE: Oh, it's just a college girl's way of calling people Uncle Toms—but that isn't what it means at all.

RUTH: Well, what does it mean?

BENEATHA [*cutting* GEORGE *off and staring at him as she replies to* RUTH]: It means someone who is willing to give up his own culture and submerge himself completely in the dominant, and in this case, *oppressive* culture!

GEORGE: Oh, dear, dear, dear! Here we go! A lecture on the African past! On our Great West African Heritage! In one second we will hear all about the great Ashanti empires; the great Songhay civilizations; and the great sculpture of Bénin—and then some poetry in the Bantu—and the whole monologue will end with the word *heritage!* [*Nastily*] Let's face it, baby, your heritage is nothing but a bunch of raggedy-assed spirituals and some grass huts!

BENEATHA: *Grass huts!* [RUTH *crosses to her and forcibly pushes her toward the bedroom.*] See there . . . you are standing there in your splendid ignorance talking about people who were the first to smelt iron on the face of the earth! [RUTH *is pushing her through the door.*] The Ashanti were performing surgical operations when the English— [RUTH *pulls the door to, with* BENEATHA *on the other side, and smiles graciously at* GEORGE. BENEATHA *opens the door and shouts the end of the sentence defiantly at* GEORGE] —were still tattooing themselves with blue dragons. . . . [*She goes back inside.*]

RUTH: Have a seat, George. [*They both sit.* RUTH *folds her hands rather primly on her lap, determined to demonstrate the civilization of the family.*] Warm, ain't it? I mean for September. [*Pause*] Just like they always say about Chicago weather: If it's too hot or cold for you, just wait a minute and it'll change. [*She smiles happily at this cliché of clichés.*] Everybody say it's got to do with them bombs and things they keep setting off. [*Pause*] Would you like a nice cold beer?

GEORGE: No, thank you. I don't care for beer. [*He looks at his watch.*] I hope she hurries up.

RUTH: What time is the show?

GEORGE: It's an eight-thirty curtain. That's just Chicago, though. In New York standard curtain time is eight forty. [*He is rather proud of this knowledge.*]

RUTH [*properly appreciating it*]: You get to New York a lot?

GEORGE: [*offhand*]: Few times a year.

RUTH: Oh—that's nice. I've never been to New York.

[WALTER *enters. We feel he has relieved himself, but the edge of unreality is still with him.*]

WALTER: New York ain't got nothing Chicago ain't. Just a bunch of hustling people all squeezed up together—being "Eastern." [*He turns his face into a screw of displeasure.*]

GEORGE: Oh—you've been?

WALTER: *Plenty* of times.

RUTH [*shocked at the lie*]: Walter Lee Younger!

WALTER: [*staring her down*]: Plenty! [*Pause*] What we got to drink in this house? Why don't you offer this man some refreshment? [*To* GEORGE] They don't know how to entertain people in this house, man.

GEORGE: Thank you—I don't really care for anything.

WALTER [*feeling his head; sobriety coming*]: Where's Mama?

RUTH: She ain't come back yet.

WALTER [*looking* MURCHISON *over from head to toe, scrutinizing his carefully casual tweed sports jacket over cashmere V-neck sweater over soft eyelet shirt and tie, and soft slacks, finished off with white buckskin shoes*]: Why all you college boys wear them fairyish-looking white shoes?

RUTH: Walter Lee!

[GEORGE MURCHISON *ignores the remark.*]

WALTER: [*to* RUTH]: Well, they look crazy as hell—white shoes, cold as it is.

RUTH [*crushed*]: You have to excuse him—

WALTER: No he don't! Excuse me for what? What you always excusing me for! I'll excuse myself when I needs to be excused! [*A pause*] They look as funny as them black knee socks Beneatha wears out of here all the time.

RUTH: It's the college *style,* Walter.

WALTER: Style, hell. She looks like she got burnt legs or something!

RUTH: Oh, Walter—

WALTER [*an irritable mimic*]: Oh, Walter! Oh, Walter! [*To* MURCHISON] How's your old man making out? I understand you all going to buy that big hotel on the Drive? [*He finds a beer in the refrigerator, wanders over to* MURCHISON, *sipping and wiping his lips with the back of his hand, and straddling a chair backwards to talk to the other man.*] Shrewd move. Your old man is all right, man. [*Tapping his head and half winking for emphasis*] I mean he knows how to operate. I mean he thinks *big*, you know what I mean, I mean for a *home*, you know? But I think he's kind of running out of ideas now. I'd like to talk to him. Listen, man, I got some plans that could turn this city upside down. I mean I think like he does. *Big*. Invest big, gamble big, hell, lose *big* if you have to, you know what I mean. It's hard to find a man on this whole Southside who understands my kind of thinking—you dig? [*He scrutinizes* MURCHISON *again, drinks his beer, squints his eyes and leans in close, confidential, man to man.*] Me and you ought to sit down and talk sometimes, man. Man, I got me some ideas. . . .

MURCHISON [*with boredom*]: Yeah—sometimes we'll have to do that, Walter.

WALTER [*understanding the indifference, and offended*]: Yeah—well, when you get the time, man. I know you a busy little boy.

RUTH: Walter, please—

WALTER: [*bitterly, hurt*]: I know ain't nothing in this world as busy as you colored college boys with your fraternity pins and white shoes. . . .

RUTH [*covering her face with humiliation*]: Oh, Walter Lee—

WALTER: I see you all the time—with the books tucked under your arms—going to your [*British A—a mimic*] "clahsses." And for what! What the hell you learning over there? Filling up your heads—[*counting off on his fingers*] —with the sociology and the psychology—but they teaching you how to be a man? How to take over and run the world? They teaching you how to run a rubber plantation or a steel mill? Naw—just to talk proper and read books and wear white shoes. . . .

GEORGE: [*looking at him with distaste, a little above it all*]: You're all wacked up with bitterness, man.

WALTER: [*intently, almost quietly, between the teeth, glaring at the boy*]: And you—ain't you bitter, man? Ain't you just about had it yet? Don't you see no stars gleaming that you can't reach out and grab? You happy?—You contented son-of-a-bitch—you happy? You got it made? Bitter? Man, I'm a volcano. Bitter? Here I am a giant—surrounded by ants! Ants who can't even understand what it is the giant is talking about.

RUTH [*passionately and suddenly*]: Oh, Walter—ain't you with nobody!

WALTER: [*violently*]: No! 'Cause ain't nobody with me! Not even my own mother!

RUTH: Walter, that's a terrible thing to say!

[BENEATHA *enters, dressed for the evening in a cocktail dress and earrings.*]

GEORGE: Well—hey, you look great.

BENEATHA: Let's go, George. See you all later.

RUTH: Have a nice time.

GEORGE: Thanks. Good night. [*To* WALTER, *sarcastically*] Good night, *Prometheus.* [BENEATHA *and* GEORGE *exit.*]

WALTER: [*to* RUTH]: Who is Prometheus?

RUTH: I don't know. Don't worry about it.

WALTER: [*in fury, pointing after* GEORGE]: See there—they get to a point where they can't insult you man to man—they got to talk about something ain't nobody never heard of!

RUTH: How do you know it was an insult? [*To humor him*] Maybe Prometheus is a nice fellow.

WALTER: Prometheus! I bet there ain't even no such thing! I bet that simple-minded clown—

RUTH: Walter— [*She stops what she is doing and looks at him.*]

WALTER: [*yelling*]: Don't start!

RUTH: Start what?

WALTER: Your nagging! Where was I? Who was I with? How much money did I spend?

RUTH [*plaintively*]: Walter Lee—why don't we just try to talk about it. . . .

WALTER: [*not listening*]: I been out talking with people who understand me. People who care about the things I got on my mind.

RUTH [*wearily*]: I guess that means people like Willy Harris.

WALTER: Yes, people like Willy Harris.

RUTH [*with a sudden flash of impatience*]: Why don't you all just hurry up and go into the banking business and stop talking about it!

WALTER: Why? You want to know why? 'Cause we all tied up in a race of people that don't know how to do nothing but moan, pray and have babies!

The line is too bitter even for him and he looks at her and sits down.

RUTH: Oh, Walter . . . [*Softly*] Honey, why can't you stop fighting me?

WALTER: [*without thinking*]: Who's fighting you? Who even cares about you?

This line begins the retardation of his mood.

RUTH: Well— [*She waits a long time, and then with resignation starts to put away her things.*] I guess I might as well go on to bed. . . . [*More or less to herself*] I don't know where we lost it . . . but we have. . . . [*Then, to him*] I—I'm sorry about this new baby, Walter. I guess maybe I better go on and do what I started . . . I guess I just didn't realize how bad things was with us . . . I guess I just didn't really realize— [*She starts out to the bedroom and stops.*] You want some hot milk?

WALTER: Hot milk?

RUTH: Yes—hot milk.

WALTER: Why hot milk?

RUTH: 'Cause after all that liquor you come home with you ought to have something hot in your stomach.

WALTER: I don't want no milk.

RUTH: You want some coffee then?

WALTER: No, I don't want no coffee. I don't want nothing hot to drink. [*Almost plaintively*] Why you always trying to give me something to eat?

RUTH [*standing and looking at him helplessly*]: What else can I give you, Walter Lee Younger?

She stands and looks at him and presently turns to go out again. He lifts his head and watches her going away from him in a new mood which began to emerge when he asked her "Who cares about you?"

WALTER: It's been rough, ain't it, baby? [*She hears and stops but does not turn around and he continues to her back.*] I guess between two people there ain't never as much understood as folks generally thinks there is. I mean like between me and you— [*She turns to face him.*] How we gets to the place where we scared to talk softness to each other. [*He waits, thinking hard himself.*] Why you think it got to be like that? [*He is thoughtful, almost as a child would be.*] Ruth, what is it gets into people ought to be close?

RUTH: I don't know, honey. I think about it a lot.

WALTER: On account of you and me, you mean? The way things are with us. The way something done come down between us.

RUTH: There ain't so much between us, Walter. . . . Not when you come to me and try to talk to me. Try to be with me . . . a little even.

WALTER: [*total honesty*]: Sometimes . . . sometimes . . . I don't even know how to try.

RUTH: Walter—

WALTER: Yes?

RUTH [*coming to him, gently and with misgiving, but coming to him*]: Honey . . . life don't have to be like this. I mean sometimes people can do things so that things are better. . . . You remember how we used to talk when Travis was born . . . about the way we were going to live . . . the kind of house . . . [*She is stroking his head.*] Well, it's all starting to slip away from us. . . .

[MAMA *enters, and* WALTER *jumps up and shouts at her.*]

WALTER: Mama, where have you been?

MAMA: My—them steps is longer than they used to be. Whew! [*She sits down and ignores him.*] How you feeling this evening, Ruth?

RUTH *shrugs, disturbed some at having been prematurely interrupted and watching her husband knowingly.*

WALTER: Mama, where have you been all day?

MAMA [*still ignoring him and leaning on the table and changing to more comfortable shoes*]: Where's Travis?

RUTH: I let him go out earlier and he ain't come back yet. Boy, is he going to get it!

WALTER: Mama!

MAMA [*as if she has heard him for the first time*]: Yes, son?

WALTER: Where did you go this afternoon?

MAMA: I went downtown to tend to some business that I had to tend to.

WALTER: What kind of business?

MAMA: You know better than to question me like a child, Brother.

WALTER [*rising and bending over the table*] Where were you, Mama? [*Bringing his fists down and shouting*] Mama, you didn't go do something with that insurance money, something crazy?

[*The front door opens slowly, interrupting him, and* TRAVIS *peeks his head in, less than hopefully.*]

TRAVIS: [*to his mother*]: Mama, I—

RUTH: "Mama I" nothing! You're going to get it, boy! Get on in that bedroom and get yourself ready!

TRAVIS: But I—

MAMA: Why don't you all never let the child explain hisself.

RUTH: Keep out of it now, Lena.

MAMA *clamps her lips together, and* RUTH *advances toward her son menacingly.*

RUTH: A thousand times I have told you not to go off like that—

MAMA [*holding out her arms to her grandson*]: Well—at least let me tell him something. I want him to be the first one to hear. . . . Come here, Travis. [*The boy obeys, gladly.*] Travis— [*she takes him by the shoulder and looks into his face*] —you know that money we got in the mail this morning?

Travis Yes'm—

MAMA: Well—what do you think your grandmama gone and done with that money?

TRAVIS: I don't know, Grandmama.

MAMA [*putting her finger on his nose for emphasis*]: She went out and she bought you a house! [*The explosion comes from* WALTER *at the end of the revelation and he jumps up and turns away from all of them in a fury.* MAMA *continues, to* TRAVIS] You glad about the house? It's going to be yours when you get to be a man.

TRAVIS: Yeah—I always wanted to live in a house.

MAMA: All right, gimme some sugar then— [TRAVIS *puts his arms around her neck as she watches her son over the boy's shoulder. Then, to* TRAVIS, *after the embrace*] Now when you say your prayers tonight, you thank God and your grandfather—'cause it was him who give you the house—in his way.

RUTH [*taking the boy from* MAMA *and pushing him toward the bedroom*]: Now you get out of here and get ready for your beating.

TRAVIS: Aw, Mama—

RUTH: Get on in there— [*Closing the door behind him and turning radiantly to her mother-in-law*] So you went and did it!

MAMA [*quietly, looking at her son with pain*]: Yes, I did.

RUTH [*raising both arms classically*]: Praise God! [*Looks at* WALTER *a moment, who says nothing. She crosses rapidly to her husband.*] Please, honey—let me be glad . . . you be glad too. [*She has laid her hands on his shoulders, but he shakes himself free of her roughly, without turning to face her.*] Oh, Walter . . . a home . . . a home . . . a home. [*She comes back to* MAMA] Well—where is it? How big is it? How much it going to cost?

MAMA: Well—

RUTH: When we moving?

MAMA [*smiling at her*]: First of the month.

RUTH [*throwing back her head with jubilance*]: *Praise God!*

MAMA [*tentatively, still looking at her son's back turned against her and* RUTH]: It's—it's a nice house too. . . . [*She cannot help speaking directly to him. An imploring quality in her voice, her manner, makes her almost like a girl now.*] Three bedrooms—nice big one for you and Ruth. . . . Me and Beneatha still have to share our room, but Travis have one of his own—and [*with difficulty*] I figure if the—new baby—is a boy, we could get one of them double-decker outfits. . . . And there's a yard with a little patch of dirt where I could maybe get to grow me a few flowers. . . . And a nice big basement. . . .

RUTH: Walter honey, be glad—

MAMA [*still to his back, fingering things on the table*]: 'Course I don't want to make it sound fancier than it is. . . . It's just a plain little old house—but it's made good and solid—and it will be *ours*. Walter Lee—it makes a difference in a man when he can walk on floors that belong to *him*. . . .

RUTH: Where is it?

MAMA [*frightened at this telling*]: Well—well—it's out there in Clybourne Park—

RUTH's radiance fades abruptly, and WALTER finally turns slowly to face his mother with incredulity and hostility.

RUTH: Where?

MAMA [*matter-of-factly*]: Four o six Clybourne Street, Clybourne Park.

RUTH: Clybourne Park? Mama, there ain't no colored people living in Clybourne Park.

MAMA [*almost idiotically*]: Well, I guess there's going to be some now.

WALTER: [*bitterly*]: So that's the peace and comfort you went out and bought for us today!

MAMA [*raising her eyes to meet his finally*]: Son—I just tried to find the nicest place for the least amount of money for my family.

RUTH [*trying to recover from the shock*]: Well—well—'course I ain't one never been 'fraid of no crackers, mind you—but—well, wasn't there no other houses nowhere?

MAMA: Them houses they put up for colored in them areas way out all seem to cost twice as much as other houses. I did the best I could.

RUTH [*struck senseless with the news, in its various degrees of goodness and trouble, she sits a moment, her fists propping her chin in thought, and then she starts to rise, bringing her fists down with vigor, the radiance spreading from cheek to cheek again*]: Well—well!—All I can say is—if this is my time in life—*my time*—to say goodbye— [*and she builds with momentum as she starts to circle the room with an exuberant, almost tearfully happy release*] —to these Goddamned cracking walls!— [*she pounds the walls*] —and these marching *roaches!*— [*she wipes at an imaginary army of marching roaches*] —and this cramped little closet which ain't now or never was no kitchen! . . . then I say it loud and good, *Hallelujah! and good-bye misery . . . . I don't never want to see your ugly face again!* [*She laughs joyously, having practically destroyed the apartment, and flings her arms up and lets them come down happily, slowly, reflectively, over her abdomen, aware for the first time perhaps that the life therein pulses with happiness and not despair.*] Lena?

MAMA [*moved, watching her happiness*]: Yes, honey?

RUTH [*looking off*]: Is there—is there a whole lot of sunlight?

MAMA [*understanding*]: Yes, child, there's a whole lot of sunlight.

Long pause.

RUTH [*collecting herself and going to the door of the room* TRAVIS *is in*]: Well—I guess I better see 'bout Travis. [*To* MAMA] Lord, I sure don't feel like whipping nobody today! [*She exits.*]

MAMA [*the mother and son are left alone now and the mother waits a long time, considering deeply, before she speaks*]: Son—you—you understand what I done, don't you? [WALTER *is silent and sullen.*] I—I just seen my family falling apart today . . . just falling to pieces in front of my eyes. . . . We couldn't of gone on like we was today. We was going backwards 'stead of forwards—talking 'bout killing babies and wishing each other was dead. . . . When it gets like that in life—you just got to do something different, push on out and do something bigger. . . . [*She waits.*] I wish you say something, son . . . I wish you'd say how deep inside you you think I done the right thing—

WALTER: [*crossing slowly to his bedroom door and finally turning there and speaking measuredly*]: What you need me to say you done right for? *You* the head of this family. You run our lives like you want to. It was your money and you did what you wanted with it. So what you need for me to say it was all right for? [*Bitterly, to hurt her as deeply as he knows is possible*] So you butchered up a dream of mine—you—who always talking 'bout your children's dreams. . . .

MAMA: Walter Lee—

[*He just closes the door behind him.* MAMA *sits alone, thinking heavily.*]

CURTAIN

Scene 2

Time: Friday night, a few weeks later.

At rise: Packing crates mark the intention of the family to move. BENEATHA *and* GEORGE *come in, presumably from an evening out again.*

GEORGE: O.K. . . . O.K., whatever you say. . . . [*They both sit on the couch. He tries to kiss her. She moves away.*] Look, we've had a nice evening; let's not spoil it, huh? . . .

He again turns her head and tries to nuzzle in and she turns away from him, not with distaste but with momentary lack of interest; in a mood to pursue what they were talking about.

BENEATHA: I'm *trying* to talk to you.

GEORGE: We always talk.

BENEATHA: Yes—and I love to talk.

GEORGE [*exasperated; rising*]: I know it and I don't mind it sometimes . . . I want you to cut it out, see—The moody stuff. I mean. I don't like it. You're a nice-looking girl . . . all over. That's all you need, honey, forget the atmosphere. Guys aren't going to go for the atmosphere—they're going to go for what they see. Be glad for that. Drop the Garbo routine. It doesn't go with you. As for myself, I want a nice— [*groping*] —simple [*thoughtfully*] —sophisticated girl . . . not a poet—O.K.?

She rebuffs him again and he starts to leave.

BENEATHA: Why are you angry?

GEORGE: Because this is stupid! I don't go out with you to discuss the nature of "quiet desperation" or to hear all about your thoughts—because the world will go on thinking what it thinks regardless—

BENEATHA: Then why read books? Why go to school?

GEORGE [*with artificial patience, counting on his fingers*]: It's simple. You read books—to learn facts—to get grades—to pass the course—to get a degree. That's all—it has nothing to do with thoughts.

A long pause.

BENEATHA: I see. [*A longer pause as she looks at him*] Good night, George.

GEORGE *looks at her a little oddly, and starts to exit. He meets* MAMA *coming in.*

GEORGE: Oh—hello, Mrs. Younger.

MAMA: Hello, George, how you feeling?

GEORGE: Fine—fine, how are you?

MAMA: Oh, a little tired. You know them steps can get you after a day's work. You all have a nice time tonight?

GEORGE: Yes—a fine time. Well, good night.

MAMA: Good night. [*He exits.* MAMA *closes the door behind her.*] Hello, honey. What you sitting like that for?

BENEATHA: I'm just sitting.

MAMA: Didn't you have a nice time?

BENEATHA: No.

MAMA: No? What's the matter?

BENEATHA: Mama, George is a fool—honest. [*She rises.*]

MAMA [*hustling around unloading the packages she has entered with; she stops*]: Is he, baby?

BENEATHA: Yes.

BENEATHA *makes up* TRAVIS' *bed as she talks.*

MAMA: You sure?

BENEATHA: Yes.

MAMA: Well—I guess you better not waste your time with no fools.

BENEATHA *looks up at her mother, watching her put groceries in the refrigerator. Finally she gathers up her things and starts into the bedroom. At the door she stops and looks back at her mother.*

BENEATHA: Mama—

MAMA: Yes, baby—

BENEATHA: Thank you.

MAMA: For what?

BENEATHA: For understanding me this time.

[*She exits quickly and the mother stands, smiling a little, looking at the place where* BENEATHA *just stood.* RUTH *enters.*]

RUTH: Now don't you fool with any of this stuff, Lena—

MAMA: Oh, I just thought I'd sort a few things out.

The phone rings. RUTH *answers.*

RUTH [*at the phone*]: Hello—Just a minute. [*Goes to the door*] Walter, it's Mrs. Arnold. [*Waits. Goes back to the phone. Tense*] Hello. Yes, this is his wife speaking . . . He's lying down now. Yes . . . well, he'll be in tomorrow. He's been very sick. Yes—I know we should have called, but we were so sure he'd be able to come in today. Yes—yes, I'm very sorry. Yes . . . Thank you very much. [*She hangs up.* WALTER *is standing in the doorway of the bedroom behind her.*] That was Mrs. Arnold.

WALTER: [*indifferently*]: Was it?

RUTH: She said if you don't come in tomorrow that they are getting a new man. . . .

WALTER: Ain't that sad—ain't that crying sad.

RUTH: She said Mr. Arnold has had to take a cab for three days. . . . Walter, you ain't been to work for three days! [*This is a revelation to her.*] Where you been, Walter Lee Younger? [WALTER *looks at her and starts to laugh.*] You're going to lose your job.

WALTER: That's right . . .

RUTH: Oh, Walter, and with your mother working like a dog everyday—

WALTER: That's sad too—Everything is sad.

MAMA: What you been doing for these three days, son?

WALTER: Mama—you don't know all the things a man what got leisure can find to do in this city. . . . What's this—Friday night? Well—Wednesday I borrowed Willy Harris' car and I went for a drive . . . just me and myself and I drove and drove . . . Way out . . . way past South Chicago, and I parked the car and I sat and looked at the steel mills all day long. I just sat in the car and looked at them big black chimneys for hours. Then I drove back and I went to the Green Hat. [*Pause*] And Thursday—Thursday I borrowed the car again and I got in it and I pointed it the other way and I drove the other way—for hours—way, way up to Wisconsin, and I looked at the farms. I just drove and looked at the farms. Then I drove back and I went to the Green Hat. [*Pause*] And today—today I didn't get the car. Today I just walked. All over the South side. And I looked at the Negroes and they looked at me and finally I just sat down on the curb at Thirty-ninth and South Parkway and I just sat there and watched the Negroes go by. And then I went to the Green Hat. You all sad? You all depressed? And you know where I am going right now—

[RUTH *goes out quietly.*]

MAMA: Oh, Big Walter, is this the harvest of our days?

WALTER: You know what I like about the Green Hat? [*He turns the radio on and a steamy, deep blues pours into the room.*] I like this little cat they got there who blows a sax. . . . He blows. He talks to me. He ain't but 'bout five feet tall and he's got a conked head and his eyes is always closed and he's all music—

MAMA [*rising and getting some papers out of her handbag*]: Walter—

WALTER: And there's this other guy who plays the piano . . . and they got a sound. I mean they can work on some music. . . . They got the best little combo in the world in the Green Hat. . . . You can just sit there and drink and listen to them three men play and you realize that don't nothing matter worth a damn, but just being there—

MAMA: I've helped do it to you, haven't I, son? Walter, I been wrong.

WALTER: Naw—you ain't never been wrong about nothing, Mama.

MAMA: Listen to me, now. I say I been wrong, son. That I been doing to you what the rest of the world been doing to you. [*She stops and he looks up slowly at her and she meets his eyes pleadingly.*] Walter—what you ain't never understood is that I ain't got nothing, don't own nothing, ain't never really wanted nothing that wasn't for you. There ain't nothing as precious to me. . . . There ain't nothing worth holding on to, money, dreams, nothing else—if it means—if it means it's going to destroy my boy. [*She puts her papers in front of him and he watches her without speaking or moving.*] I paid the man thirty-five hundred dollars down on the house. That leaves sixty-five hundred dollars. Monday morning I want you to take this money and take three thousand dollars and put it in a savings account for Beneatha's medical schooling. The rest you put in a checking account—with your name on it. And from now on any penny that come out of it or that go in it is for you to look after. For you to decide. [*She drops her hands a little helplessly.*] It ain't much, but it's all I got in the world and I'm putting it in your hands. I'm telling you to be the head of this family from now on like you supposed to be.

WALTER: [*stares at the money*]: You trust me like that, Mama?

MAMA: I ain't never stop trusting you. Like I ain't never stop loving you.

[*She goes out, and* WALTER *sits looking at the money on the table as the music continues in its idiom, pulsing in the room. Finally, in a decisive gesture, he gets up, and, in mingled joy and desperation, picks up the money. At the same moment,* TRAVIS *enters for bed.*]

TRAVIS: What's the matter, Daddy? You drunk?

WALTER: [*sweetly, more sweetly than we have ever known him*]: No, Daddy ain't drunk. Daddy ain't going to never be drunk again. . . .

TRAVIS: Well, good night, Daddy.

The Father has come from behind the couch and leans over, embracing his son.

WALTER: Son, I feel like talking to you tonight.

TRAVIS: About what?

WALTER: Oh, about a lot of things. About you and what kind of man you going to be when you grow up. . . . Son—son, what do you want to be when you grow up?

TRAVIS: A bus driver.

WALTER: [*laughing a little*]: A what? Man, that ain't nothing to want to be!

TRAVIS: Why not?

WALTER: 'Cause, man—it ain't big enough—you know what I mean.

TRAVIS: I don't know then. I can't make up my mind. Sometimes Mama asks me that too. And sometimes when I tell her I just want to be like you—she says she don't want me to be like that and sometimes she says she does. . . .

WALTER: [*gathering him up in his arms*]: You know what, Travis? In seven years you going to be seventeen years old. And things is going to be very different with us in seven years, Travis. . . . One day when you are seventeen I'll come home—home from my office downtown somewhere—

TRAVIS: You don't work in no office, Daddy.

WALTER: No—but after tonight. After what your daddy gonna do tonight, there's going to be offices—a whole lot of offices. . . .

TRAVIS: What you gonna do tonight, Daddy?

WALTER: You wouldn't understand yet, son, but your daddy's gonna make a transaction . . . a business transaction that's going to change our lives. . . . That's how come one day when you 'bout seventeen years old I'll come home and I'll be pretty tired, you know what I mean, after a day of conferences and secretaries getting things wrong the way they do . . . 'cause an executive's life is hell, man— [*The more he talks, the farther away he gets.*] And I'll pull the car up on the driveway . . . just a plain black Chrysler, I think, with white walls—no—black tires. More elegant. Rich people don't have to be flashy . . . though I'll have to get something a little sportier for Ruth—maybe a Cadillac convertible to do her shopping in. . . . And I'll come up the steps to the house and the gardener will be clipping away at the hedges and he'll say, "Good evening, Mr. Younger." And I'll say, "Hello, Jefferson, how are you this evening?" And I'll go inside and Ruth will come downstairs and meet me at the door and we'll kiss each other and she'll take my arm and we'll go up to your room to see you sitting on the floor with the catalogues of all the great schools in America around you. . . . All the great schools in the world! And—and I'll say, all right son—it's your seventeenth birthday, what is it you've decided? . . . Just tell me where you want to go to school and you'll *go.* Just tell me, what it is you want to be—and you'll *be* it. . . . Whatever you want to be—Yessir! [*He holds his arms open for* TRAVIS.] You just name it, son . . . [TRAVIS *leaps into them.*] and I hand you the world!

WALTER'*s voice has risen in pitch and hysterical promise and on the last line he lifts* TRAVIS *high.*

BLACKOUT

Scene 3

Time: Saturday, moving day, one week later.

Before the curtain rises, RUTH'*s voice, a strident, dramatic church alto cuts through the silence.*

It is, in the darkness a triumphant surge, a penetrating statement of expectation: "Oh, Lord, I don't feel no ways tired! Children, oh, glory hallelujah!"

As the curtain rises we see that RUTH *is alone in the living room, finishing up the family's packing. It is moving day. She is nailing crates and tying cartons.* BENEATHA *enters, carrying a guitar case, and watches her exuberant sister-in-law.*

RUTH: Hey!

BENEATHA [*putting away the case*]: Hi.

RUTH [*pointing at a package*]: Honey—look in that package there and see what I found on sale this morning at the South Center. [RUTH *gets up and moves to the package and draws out some curtains.*] Lookahere—hand-turned hems!

BENEATHA: How do you know the window size out there?

RUTH [*who hadn't thought of that*]: Oh—Well, they bound to fit something in the whole house. Anyhow, they was too good a bargain to pass up. [RUTH *slaps her head, suddenly remembering something.*] Oh, Bennie—I meant to put a special note on that carton over there. That's your mamma's good china and she wants 'em to be very careful with it.

BENEATHA: I'll do it.

BENEATHA *finds a piece of paper and starts to draw large letters on it.*

RUTH: You know what I'm going to do soon as I get in that new house?

BENEATHA: What?

RUTH: Honey—I'm going to run me a tub of water up to here. . . . [*With her fingers practically up to her nostrils*] And I'm going to get in it—and I am going to sit . . . and sit . . . and sit in that hot water and the first person who knocks to tell *me* to hurry up and come out—

BENEATHA: Gets shot at sunrise.

RUTH [*laughing happily*]: You said it, sister! [*Noticing how large* BENEATHA *is absent-mindedly making the note*] Honey, they ain't going to read that from no airplane.

BENEATHA [*laughing herself*]: I guess I always think things have more emphasis if they are big, somehow.

RUTH: [*looking up at her and smiling*]: You and your brother seem to have that as a philosophy of life. Lord, that man—done changed so 'round here. You know—you know what we did last night? Me and Walter Lee?

BENEATHA: What?

RUTH: [*smiling to herself*]: We went to the movies. [*Looking at* BENEATHA *to see if she understands*] We went to the movies. You know the last time me and Walter went to the movies together?

BENEATHA: No.

RUTH: Me neither. That's how long it been. [*Smiling again*] But we went last night. The picture wasn't much good, but that didn't seem to matter. We went—and we held hands.

BENEATHA: Oh, Lord!

RUTH: We held hands—and you know what?

BENEATHA: What?

RUTH: When we come out of the show it was late and dark and all the stores and things was closed up . . . and it was kind of chilly and there wasn't many people on the streets . . . and we was still holding hands, me and Walter.

BENEATHA: You're killing me.

[WALTER *enters with a large package. His happiness is deep in him; he cannot keep still with his new-found exuberance. He is singing and wiggling and snapping his fingers. He puts his package in a corner and puts a phonograph record, which he has brought in with him, on the record player. As the music comes up he dances over to* RUTH *and tries to get her to dance with him. She gives in at last to his raunchiness and in a fit of giggling allows herself to be drawn into his mood and together they deliberately burlesque an old social dance of their youth.*]

BENEATHA [*regarding them a long time as they dance, then drawing in her breath for a deeply exaggerated comment which she does not particularly mean*]: Talk about—olddddddddd–fashioneddddddd—Negroes!

WALTER: [*stopping momentarily*]: What kind of Negroes?

He says this in fun. He is not angry with her today, nor with anyone. He starts to dance with his wife again.

BENEATHA: Old-fashioned.

WALTER: [*as he dances with* RUTH]: You know, when these *New Negroes* have their convention— [*pointing at his sister*] —that is going to be the chairman of the Committee on Unending Agitation. [*He goes on dancing, then stops.*] Race, race, race! . . . Girl, I do believe you are the first person in the history of the entire human race to successfully brainwash yourself. [BENEATHA *breaks up and he goes on dancing. He stops again, enjoying his tease.*] Damn, even the N double A C P takes a holiday sometimes! [BENEATHA *and* RUTH *laugh. He dances with* RUTH *some more and starts to laugh and stops and pantomimes someone over an operating table.*] I can just see that chick someday looking down at some poor cat on an operating table before she starts to slice him, saying . . . [*pulling his sleeves back maliciously*] "By the way, what are your views on civil rights down there? . . ."

He laughs at her again and starts to dance happily. The bell sounds.

BENEATHA: Sticks and stones may break my bones but . . . words will never hurt me!

[BENEATHA *goes to the door and opens it as* WALTER *and* RUTH *go on with the clowning.* BENEATHA *is somewhat surprised to see a quiet-looking middle-aged white man in a business suit holding his hat and a briefcase in his hand and consulting a small piece of paper.*]

MAN: Uh—how do you do, miss. I am looking for a Mrs.— [*he looks at the slip of paper*] Mrs. Lena Younger?

BENEATHA [*smoothing her hair with slight embarrassment*]: Oh—yes, that's my mother. Excuse me. [*She closes the door and turns to quiet the other two.*] Ruth! Brother! Somebody's here. [*Then she opens the door. The man casts a curious quick glance at all of them.*] Uh—come in please.

MAN [*coming in*]: Thank you.

BENEATHA: My mother isn't here just now. Is it business?

MAN: Yes . . . well, of a sort.

WALTER: [*freely, the Man of the House*]: Have a seat. I'm Mrs. Younger's son. I look after most of her business matters.

RUTH *and* BENEATHA *exchange amused glances.*

MAN [*regarding* WALTER, *and sitting*]: Well—my name is Karl Lindner . . .

WALTER: [*stretching out his hand*]: Walter Younger. This is my wife— [RUTH *nods politely*] —and my sister.

LINDNER: How do you do.

WALTER: [*amiably, as he sits himself easily on a chair, leaning with interest forward on his knees and looking expectantly into the newcomer's face*]: What can we do for you, Mr. Lindner!

LINDNER [*some minor shuffling of the hat and briefcase on his knees*]: Well—I am a representative of the Clybourne Park Improvement Association—

WALTER: [*pointing*]: Why don't you sit your things on the floor?

LINDNER: Oh—yes. Thank you. [*He slides the briefcase and hat under the chair.*] And as I was saying—I am from the Clybourne Park Improvement Association and we have had it brought to our attention at the last meeting that you people—or at least your mother—has bought a piece of residential property at— [*he digs for the slip of paper again*] —four o six Clybourne Street. . . .

WALTER: That's right. Care for something to drink? Ruth, get Mr. Lindner a beer.

LINDNER [*upset for some reason*]: Oh—no, really. I mean thank you very much, but no thank you.

RUTH [*innocently*]: Some coffee?

LINDNER: Thank you, nothing at all.

BENEATHA *is watching the man carefully.*

LINDNER: Well, I don't know how much you folks know about our organization. [*He is a gentle man; thoughtful and somewhat labored in his manner.*] It is one of those community organizations set up to look after—oh, you know, things like block upkeep and special projects and we also have what we call our New Neighbors Orientation Committee. . . .

BENEATHA [*drily*]: Yes—and what do they do?

LINDNER [*turning a little to her and then returning the main force to* WALTER]: Well—it's what you might call a sort of welcoming committee, I guess. I mean they, we, I'm the chairman of the committee—go around and see the new people who move into the neighborhood and sort of give them the lowdown on the way we do things out in Clybourne Park.

BENEATHA [*with appreciation of the two meanings, which escape* RUTH *and* WALTER]: Uh-huh.

LINDNER: And we also have the category of what the association calls— [*he looks elsewhere*] —uh—special community problems. . . .

BENEATHA: Yes—and what are some of those?

WALTER: Girl, let the man talk.

LINDNER [*with understated relief*]: Thank you. I would sort of like to explain this thing in my own way. I mean I want to explain to you in a certain way.

WALTER: Go ahead.

LINDNER: Yes. Well. I'm going to try to get right to the point. I'm sure we'll all appreciate that in the long run.

BENEATHA: Yes.

LINDNER: Well—

WALTER: Be still now!

LINDNER: Well—

RUTH [*still innocently*]: Would you like another chair—you don't look comfortable.

LINDNER [*more frustrated than annoyed*]: No, thank you very much. Please. Well—to get right to the point I— [*a great breath, and he is off at last*] I am sure you people must be aware of some of the incidents which have happened in various parts of the city when colored people have moved into certain areas— [BENEATHA *exhales heavily and starts tossing a piece of fruit up and down in the air.*] Well—because we have what I think is going to be a unique type of organization in American community life—not only do we deplore that kind of thing—but we are trying to do something about it. [BENEATHA *stops tossing and turns with a new and quizzical interest to the man.*] We feel— [*gaining confidence in his mission because of the interest in the faces of the people he is talking to*] —we feel that most of the trouble in this world, when you come right down to it— [*he hits his knee for emphasis*] —most of the trouble exists because people just don't sit down and talk to each other.

RUTH [*nodding as she might in church, pleased with the remark*]: You can say that again, mister.

LINDNER [*more encouraged by such affirmation*]: That we don't try hard enough in this world to understand the other fellow's problem. The other guy's point of view.

RUTH: Now that's right.

BENEATHA *and* WALTER *merely watch and listen with genuine interest.*

LINDNER: Yes—that's the way we feel out in Clybourne Park. And that's why I was elected to come here this afternoon and talk to you people. Friendly like, you know, the way people should talk to each other and see if we couldn't find some way to work this thing out. As I say, the whole business is a matter of *caring* about the other fellow. Anybody can see that you are a nice family of folks, hard-working and honest I'm sure. [BENEATHA *frowns slightly, quizzically, her head tilted regarding him.*] Today everybody knows what it means to be on the outside of *something.* And of course, there is always somebody who is out to take the advantage of people who don't always understand.

WALTER: What do you mean?

LINDNER: Well—you see our community is made up of people who've worked hard as the dickens for years to build up that little community. They're not rich and fancy people; just hardworking, honest people who don't really have much but those little homes and a dream of the kind of community they want to raise their children in. Now, I don't say we are perfect and there is a lot wrong in some of the things they want. But you've got to admit that a man, right or wrong, has the right to want to have the neighborhood he lives in a certain kind of way. And at the moment the overwhelming majority of our people out there feel that people get along better, take more of a common interest in the life of the community, when they share a common background. I want you to believe me when I tell you that race prejudice simply doesn't enter into it. It is a matter of the people of Clybourne Park believing, rightly or wrongly, as I say, that for the happiness of all concerned that our Negro families are happier when they live in their *own* communities.

BENEATHA [*with a grand and bitter gesture*]: This, friends, is the Welcoming Committee!

WALTER: [*dumbfounded, looking at* LINDNER]: Is this what you came marching all the way over here to tell us?

LINDNER: Well, now we've been having a fine conversation. I hope you'll hear me all the way through.

WALTER: [*tightly*]: Go ahead, man.

LINDNER: You see—in the face of all things I have said, we are prepared to make your family a very generous offer. . . .

BENEATHA: Thirty pieces and not a coin less!

WALTER: Yeah?

LINDNER [*putting on his glasses and drawing a form out of the briefcase*]: Our association is prepared, through the collective effort of our people, to buy the house from you at a financial gain to your family.

RUTH: Lord have mercy, ain't this the living gall!

WALTER: All right, you through?

LINDNER: Well, I want to give you the exact terms of the financial arrangement—

WALTER: We don't want to hear no exact terms of no arrangements. I want to know if you got any more to tell us 'bout getting together?

LINDNER [*taking off his glasses*]: Well—I don't suppose that you feel. . . .

WALTER: Never mind how I feel—you got any more to say 'bout how people ought to sit down and talk to each other? . . . Get out of my house, man. [*He turns his back and walks to the door.*]

LINDNER [*looking around at the hostile faces and reaching and assembling his hat and briefcase*]: Well—I don't understand why you people are reacting this way. What do you think you are going to gain by moving into a neighborhood where you just aren't wanted and where some elements—well—people can get awful worked up when they feel that their whole way of life and everything they've ever worked for is threatened.

WALTER: Get out.

LINDNER [*at the door, holding a small card*]: Well—I'm sorry it went like this.

WALTER: Get out.

LINDNER [*almost sadly, regarding* WALTER]: You just can't force people to change their hearts, son.

[*He turns and puts his card on a table and exits.* WALTER *pushes the door to with stinging hatred, and stands looking at it.* RUTH *just sits and* BENEATHA *just stands. They say nothing.* MAMA *and* TRAVIS *enter.*]

MAMA: Well—this all the packing got done since I left out of here this morning. I testify before God that my children got all the energy of the dead. What time the moving men due?

BENEATHA: Four o'clock. You had a caller, Mama. [*She is smiling, teasingly.*]

MAMA: Sure enough—who?

BENEATHA [*her arms folded saucily*]: The Welcoming Committee.

WALTER *and* RUTH *giggle.*

MAMA [*innocently*]: Who?

BENEATHA: The Welcoming Committee. They said they're sure going to be glad to see you when you get there.

WALTER [*devilishly*]: Yeah, they said they can't hardly wait to see your face.

Laughter.

MAMA [*sensing their facetiousness*]: What's the matter with you all?

WALTER: Ain't nothing the matter with us. We just telling you 'bout the gentleman who came to see you this afternoon. From the Clybourne Park Improvement Association.

MAMA: What he want?

RUTH [*in the same mood as* BENEATHA *and* WALTER]: To welcome you, honey.

WALTER: He said they can't hardly wait. He said the one thing they don't have, that they just *dying* to have out there is a fine family of colored people! [*To* RUTH *and* BENEATHA] Ain't that right!

RUTH *and* BENEATHA [*mockingly*]: Yeah! He left his card in case—

They indicate the card, and MAMA *picks it up and throws it on the floor—understanding and looking off as she draws her chair up to the table on which she has put her plant and some sticks and some cord.*

MAMA: Father, give us strength. [*Knowingly—and without fun*] Did he threaten us?

BENEATHA: Oh—Mama—they don't do it like that any more. He talked Brotherhood. He said everybody ought to learn how to sit down and hate each other with good Christian fellowship.

She and WALTER *shake hands to ridicule the remark.*

MAMA [*sadly*]: Lord, protect us. . . .

RUTH: You should hear the money those folks raised to buy the house from us. All we paid and then some.

BENEATHA: What they think we going to do—eat 'em?

RUTH: No, honey, marry 'em.

MAMA [*shaking her head*]: Lord, Lord, Lord. . . .

RUTH: Well—that's the way the crackers crumble. Joke.

BENEATHA [*laughingly noticing what her mother is doing*]: Mama, what are you doing?

MAMA: Fixing my plant so it won't get hurt none on the way. . . .

BENEATHA: Mama, you going to take *that* to the new house?

MAMA: Uh-huh—

BENEATHA: That raggedy-looking old thing?

MAMA [*stopping and looking at her*]: It expresses *me*.

RUTH [*with delight, to* BENEATHA]: So there, Miss Thing!

WALTER *comes to* MAMA *suddenly and bends down behind her and squeezes her in his arms with all his strength. She is overwhelmed by the suddenness of it and, though delighted, her manner is like that of* RUTH *with* TRAVIS.

MAMA: Look out now, boy! You make me mess up my thing here!

WALTER: [*his face lit, he slips down on his knees beside her, his arms still about her*]: Mama . . . you know what it means to climb up in the chariot?

MAMA [*gruffly, very happy*]: Get on away from me now. . . .

RUTH [*near the gift-wrapped package, trying to catch* WALTER'S *eye*]: Psst—

WALTER: What the old song say, Mama. . . .

RUTH: Walter—Now? [*She is pointing at the package.*]

WALTER [*speaking the lines, sweetly, playfully, in his mother's face*]:

I got wings . . . you got wings . . .
All God's children got wings . . .

MAMA: Boy—get out of my face and do some work. . . .

WALTER:

When I get to heaven gonna put on my wings.
Gonna fly all over God's heaven . . .

BENEATHA [*teasingly, from across the room*]: Everybody talking 'bout heaven ain't going there!

WALTER: [*to* RUTH, *who is carrying the box across to them*]: I don't know, you think we ought to give her that. . . . Seems to me she ain't been very appreciative around here.

MAMA [*eyeing the box, which is obviously a gift*]: What is that?

WALTER: [*taking it from* RUTH *and putting it on the table in front of* MAMA]: Well—what you all think? Should we give it to her?

RUTH: Oh—she was pretty good today.

MAMA: I'll good you— [*She turns her eyes to the box again.*]

BENEATHA: Open it, Mama.

She stands up, looks at it, turns and looks at all of them, and then presses her hands together and does not open the package.

WALTER [*sweetly*]: Open it, Mama. It's for you. [MAMA *looks in his eyes. It is the first present in her life without its being Christmas. Slowly she opens her package and lifts out, one by one, a brand-new sparkling set of gardening tools.* WALTER *continues, prodding*] Ruth made up the note—read it . . .

MAMA [*picking up the card and adjusting her glasses*]: "To our own Mrs. Miniver—Love from Brother, Ruth, and Beneatha." Ain't that lovely. . . .

TRAVIS [*tugging at his father's sleeve*]: Daddy, can I give her mine now?

WALTER: All right, son. [TRAVIS *flies to get his gift*] Travis didn't want to go in with the rest of us, Mama. He got his own. [*Somewhat amused*] We don't know what it is. . . .

TRAVIS [*racing back in the room with a large hatbox and putting it in front of his grandmother*]: Here!

MAMA: Lord have mercy, baby. You done gone and bought your grandmother a hat?

TRAVIS: [*very proud*]: Open it!

She does and lifts out an elaborate, but very elaborate, wide gardening hat, and all the adults break up at the sight of it.

RUTH: Travis, honey, what is that?

TRAVIS [*who thinks it is beautiful and appropriate*]: It's a gardening hat! Like the ladies always have on in the magazines when they work in their gardens.

BENEATHA [*giggling fiercely*]: Travis—we were trying to make Mama Mrs. Miniver—not Scarlett O'Hara!

MAMA [*indignantly*]: What's the matter with you all! This here is a beautiful hat! [*Absurdly*] I always wanted me one just like it!

She pops it on her head to prove it to her grandson, and the hat is ludicrous and considerably oversized.

RUTH: Hot dog! Go, Mama!

WALTER [*doubled over with laughter*]: I'm sorry, Mama—but you look like you ready to go out and chop you some cotton sure enough!

They all laugh except MAMA, *out of deference to* TRAVIS' *feelings.*

MAMA [*gathering the boy up to her*]: Bless your heart—this is the prettiest hat I ever owned— [WALTER, RUTH, *and* BENEATHA *chime in noisily, festively and insincerely congratulating* TRAVIS *on his gift.*] What are we all standing around here for? We ain't finished packin' yet. Bennie, you ain't packed one book.

The bell rings.

BENEATHA: That couldn't be the movers . . . it's not hardly two good yet—

[BENEATHA *goes into her room.* MAMA *starts for door.*]

WALTER [*turning, stiffening*]: Wait—wait—I'll get it. [*He stands and looks at the door.*]

MAMA: You expecting company, son?

WALTER [*just looking at the door*]: Yeah—yeah. . . .

MAMA *looks at* RUTH, *and they exchange innocent and unfrightened glances.*

MAMA [*not understanding*]: Well, let them in, son.

BENEATHA [*from her room*]: We need some more string.

MAMA: Travis—you run to the hardware and get me some string cord.

[MAMA *goes out and* WALTER *turns and looks at* RUTH. TRAVIS *goes to a dish for money.*]

RUTH: Why don't you answer the door, man?

WALTER [*suddenly bounding across the floor to her*]: 'Cause sometimes it hard to let the future begin! [*Stooping down in her face.*]

I got wings! You got wings!
All God's children got wings!

[*He crosses to the door and throws it open. Standing there is a very slight little man in a not too prosperous business suit and with haunted frightened eyes and a hat pulled down tightly, brim up, around his forehead.* TRAVIS *passes between the men and exits.* WALTER *leans deep in the man's face, still in his jubilance.*]

When I get to heaven gonna put on my wings.
Gonna fly all over God's heaven . . .

The little man just stares at him.

Heaven—

[*Suddenly he stops and looks past the little man into the empty hallway.*] Where's Willy, man?

BOBO: He ain't with me.

WALTER: [*not disturbed*]: Oh—come on in. You know my wife.

BOBO [*dumbly, taking off his hat*]: Yes—h'you, Miss Ruth.

RUTH [*quietly, a mood apart from her husband already, seeing* BOBO]: Hello, Bobo.

WALTER: You right on time today. . . . Right on time. That's the way! [*He slaps* BOBO *on his back.*] Sit down . . . lemme hear.

RUTH *stands stiffly and quietly in back of them, as though somehow she senses death, her eyes fixed on her husband.*

BOBO [*his frightened eyes on the floor, his hat in his hands*]: Could I please get a drink of water, before I tell you about it, Walter Lee?

WALTER does not take his eyes off the man. RUTH goes blindly to the tap and gets a glass of water and brings it to BOBO.

WALTER: There ain't nothing wrong, is there?
BOBO: Lemme tell you—
WALTER: Man—didn't nothing go wrong?
BOBO: Lemme tell you—Walter Lee. [*Looking at* RUTH *and talking to her more than to* WALTER] You know how it was. I got to tell you how it was. I mean first I got tell you how it was all the way . . . I mean about the money I put in, Walter Lee. . . .
WALTER [*with taut agitation*]: What about the money you put in?
BOBO: Well—it wasn't much as we told you—me and Willy— [*He stops.*] I'm sorry, Walter. I got a bad feeling about it. I got a real bad feeling about it. . . .
WALTER: Man, what you telling me about all this for? . . . Tell me what happened in Springfield. . . .
BOBO: Springfield.
RUTH [*like a dead woman*]: What was supposed to happen in Springfield?
BOBO [*to her*]: This deal that me and Walter went into with Willy—Me and Willy was going to go down to Springfield and spread some money 'round so's we wouldn't have to wait so long for the liquor license. . . . That's what we were going to do. Everybody said that was the way you had to do, you understand, Miss Ruth?
WALTER: Man—what happened down there?
BOBO [*a pitiful man, near tears*]: I'm trying to tell you, Walter.
WALTER [*screaming at him suddenly*]: THEN TELL ME, GOD DAMMIT . . . WHAT'S THE MATTER WITH YOU?
BOBO: Man . . . I didn't go to no Springfield, yesterday.
WALTER [*halted, life hanging in the moment*]: Why not?
BOBO [*the long way, the hard way to tell*]: 'Cause I didn't have no reasons to. . . .
WALTER: Man, what are you talking about!
BOBO: I'm talking about the fact that when I got to the train station yesterday morning—eight o'clock like we planned . . . Man—*Willy didn't never show up.*
WALTER: Why . . . where was he . . . where is he?
BOBO: That's what I'm trying to tell you . . . I don't know . . . I waited six hours . . . I called his house . . . and I waited . . . six hours . . . I waited in that train station six hours . . . [*Breaking into tears*] That was all the extra money I had in the world. . . . [*Looking up at* WALTER *with the tears running down his face*] Man, *Willy is gone.*
WALTER: Gone, what you mean Willy is gone? Gone where? You mean he went by himself. You mean he went off to Springfield by himself—to take care of getting the license— [*Turns and looks anxiously at* RUTH] You mean maybe he didn't want too many people in on the business down there? [*Looks to* RUTH *again, as before*] You know Willy got his own ways. [*Looks back to* BOBO] Maybe you was late yesterday and he just went on down there without you. Maybe—maybe—he's been callin' you at home tryin' to tell you what happened or something. Maybe—maybe—he just got sick. He's somewhere—he's got to be somewhere. We just got to find him—me and you got to find him. [*Grabs* BOBO *senselessly by the collar and starts to shake him*] We got to!
BOBO [*in sudden angry, frightened agony*]: What's the matter with you, Walter! *When a cat take off with your money he don't leave you no maps!*
WALTER: [*turning madly, as though he is looking for* WILLY *in the very room*]: Willy! . . . Willy . . . don't do it. . . . Please don't do it . . . Man, not with that money . . . Man, please not with that money . . . Oh, God . . . Don't let it be true. . . . [*He is wandering around, crying out for* WILLY *and looking for him or perhaps for help from God.*] Man . . . I trusted you . . . Man, I put my life in your hands. . . . [*He starts to crumple down on the floor as* RUTH *just covers her face in horror.* MAMA *opens the door and comes into the room, with* BENEATHA *behind her.*] Man . . . [*He starts to pound the floor with his fists, sobbing wildly.*] *That money is made out of my father's flesh. . . .*
BOBO [*standing over him helplessly*]: I'm sorry, Walter. . . . [*Only* WALTER'S *sobs reply.* BOBO *puts on his hat.*] I had my life staked on this deal, too. . . . [*He exits.*]
MAMA [*to* WALTER]: Son— [*She goes to him, bends down to him, talks to his bent head.*] Son . . . Is it gone? Son, I gave you sixty-five hundred dollars. Is it gone? All of it? Beneatha's money too?
WALTER [*lifting his head slowly*] Mama . . . I never . . . went to the bank at all. . . .
MAMA [*not wanting to believe him*]: You mean . . . your sister's school money . . . you used that too . . . Walter? . . . .
WALTER: Yessss! . . . All of it. . . . It's all gone. . . .

There is total silence. RUTH *stands with her face covered with her hands;* BENEATHA *leans forlornly against a wall, fingering a piece of red ribbon from the mother's gift.* MAMA *stops and looks at her son without recognition and then, quite without thinking about it, starts to beat him senselessly in the face.* BENEATHA *goes to them and stops it.*

BENEATHA: Mama!

MAMA *stops and looks at both of her children and rises slowly and wanders vaguely, aimlessly away from them.*

MAMA: I seen . . . him . . . night after night . . . come in . . . and look at that rug . . . and then look at me . . . the red showing in his eyes . . . the veins moving in his head . . . . I seen him grow thin and old before he was forty . . . working and working and working like somebody's old horse . . . killing himself . . . and you—you give it all away in a day. . . .

BENEATHA: Mama—

MAMA: Oh, God. . . . [*She looks up to Him.*] Look down here—and show me the strength.

BENEATHA: Mama—

MAMA [*plaintively*]: Strength. . . .

BENEATHA [*plaintively*]: Mama. . . .

MAMA: Strength!

CURTAIN

ACT III

An hour later.

At curtain, there is a sullen light of gloom in the living room, gray light not unlike that which began the first scene of ACT I. At left we can see WALTER *within his room, alone with himself. He is stretched out on the bed, his shirt out and open, his arms under his head. He does not smoke, he does not cry out, he merely lies there, looking up at the ceiling, much as if he were alone in the world.*

In the living room BENEATHA *sits at the table, still surrounded by the now almost ominous packing crates. She sits looking off. We feel that this is a mood struck perhaps an hour before, and it lingers now, full of the empty sound of profound disappointment. We see on a line from her brother's bedroom the sameness of their attitudes. Presently the bell rings and* BENEATHA *rises without ambition or interest in answering. It is* ASAGAI, *smiling broadly, striding into the room with energy and happy expectation and conversation.*

ASAGAI: I came over . . . I had some free time. I thought I might help with the packing. Ah, I like the look of packing crates! A household in preparation for a journey! It depresses some people . . . but for me . . . it is another feeling. Something full of the flow of life, do you understand? Movement, progress . . . It makes me think of Africa.

BENEATHA: Africa!

ASAGAI: What kind of a mood is this? Have I told you how deeply you move me?

BENEATHA: He gave away the money, Asagai. . . .

ASAGAI: Who gave away what money?

BENEATHA: The insurance money. My brother gave it away.

ASAGAI: Gave it away?

BENEATHA: He made an investment! With a man even Travis wouldn't have trusted.

ASAGAI: And it's gone?

BENEATHA: Gone!

ASAGAI: I'm very sorry. . . . And you, now?

BENEATHA: Me? . . . Me? . . . Me I'm nothing. . . . Me. When I was very small . . . we used to take our sleds out in the wintertime and the only hills we had were the ice-covered stone steps of some houses down the street. And we used to fill them in with snow and make them smooth and slide down them all day . . . and it was very dangerous you know . . . far too steep . . . and sure enough one day a kid named Rufus came down too fast and hit the sidewalk . . . and we saw his face just split open right there in front of us. . . . And I remember standing there looking at his bloody open face thinking that was the end of Rufus. But the ambulance came and they took him to the hospital and they fixed the broken bones and they sewed it all up . . . and the next time I saw Rufus he just had a little line down the middle of his face. . . . I never got over that. . . .

WALTER *sits up, listening on the bed. Throughout this scene it is important that we feel his reaction at all times, that he visibly respond to the words of his sister and* ASAGAI.

ASAGAI: What?

BENEATHA: That was what one person could do for another, fix him up—sew up the problem, make him all right again. That was the most marvelous thing in the world. . . . I wanted to do that. I always thought it was the one concrete thing in the world that a human being could do. Fix up the sick, you know—and make them whole again. This was truly being God. . . .

ASAGAI: You wanted to be God?

BENEATHA: No—I wanted to cure. It used to be so important to me. I wanted to cure. It used to matter. I used to care. I mean about people and how their bodies hurt. . . .

ASAGAI: And you've stopped caring?

BENEATHA: Yes—I think so.

ASAGAI: Why?

WALTER *rises, goes to the door of his room and is about to open it, then stops and stands listening, leaning on the door jamb.*

BENEATHA: Because it doesn't seem deep enough, close enough to what ails mankind—I mean this thing of sewing up bodies or administering drugs. Don't you understand? It was a child's reaction to the world. I thought that doctors had the secret to all the hurts. . . . That's the way a child sees things—or an idealist.

ASAGAI: Children see things very well sometimes—and idealists even better.

BENEATHA: I know that's what you think. Because you are still where I left off—you still care. This is what you see for the world, for Africa. You with the dreams of the future will patch up all Africa—you are going to cure the Great Sore of colonialism with Independence—

ASAGAI: Yes!

BENEATHA: Yes—and you think that one word is the penicillin of the human spirit: "Independence!" But then what?

ASAGAI: That will be the problem for another time. First we must get there.

BENEATHA: And where does it end?

ASAGAI: End? Who even spoke of an end? To life? To living?

BENEATHA: An end to misery!

ASAGAI: [*smiling*]: You sound like a French intellectual.

BENEATHA: No! I sound like a human being who just had her future taken right out of her hands! While I was sleeping in my bed in there, things were happening in this world that directly concerned me—and nobody asked me, consulted me—they just went out and did things—and changed my life. Don't you see there isn't any real progress, Asagai, there is only one large circle that we march in, around and around, each of us with our own little picture—in front of us—our own little mirage that we think is the future.

ASAGAI: That is the mistake.

BENEATHA: What?

ASAGAI: What you just said—about the circle. It isn't a circle—it is simply a long line—as in geometry, you know, one that reaches into infinity. And because we cannot see the end—we also cannot see how it changes. And it is very odd but those who see the changes are called "idealists"—and those who cannot, or refuse to think, they are the "realists." It is very strange, and amusing too, I think.

BENEATHA: You—you are almost religious.

ASAGAI: Yes . . . I think I have the religion of doing what is necessary in the world—and of worshipping man—because he is so marvelous, you see.

BENEATHA: Man is foul! And the human race deserves its misery!

ASAGAI: You see: *you* have become the religious one in the old sense. Already, and after such a small defeat, you are worshipping despair.

BENEATHA: From now on, I worship the truth—and the truth is that people are puny, small, and selfish. . . .

ASAGAI: Truth? Why is it that you despairing ones always think that only you have the truth? I never thought to see *you* like that. You! Your brother made a stupid, childish mistake—and you are grateful to him. So that now you can give up the ailing human race on account of it. You talk about what good is struggle; what good is anything? Where are we all going? And why are we bothering?

BENEATHA: *And you cannot answer it!* All your talk and dreams about Africa and Independence. Independence and then what? What about all the crooks and petty thieves and just plain idiots who will come into power to steal and plunder the same as before—only now they will be black and do it in the name of the new Independence—You cannot answer that.

ASAGAI [*shouting over her*]: *I live the answer!* [*Pause.*] In my village at home it is the exceptional man who can even read a newspaper . . . or who ever *sees* a book at all. I will go home and much of what I will have to say will seem strange to the people of my village. . . . But I will teach and work and things will happen, slowly and swiftly. At times it will seem that nothing changes at all . . . and then again . . . the sudden dramatic events which make history leap into the future. And then quiet again. Retrogression even. Guns, murder, revolution. And I even will have moments when I wonder if the quiet was not better than all that death and hatred. But I will look about my village at the illiteracy and disease and ignorance and I will not wonder long. And perhaps . . . perhaps I will be a great man. . . . I mean perhaps I will hold on to the substance of truth and find my way always with the right course . . . and perhaps for it I will be butchered in my bed some night by the servants of the empire. . . .

BENEATHA: *The martyr!*

ASAGAI: . . . or perhaps I shall live to be a very old man, respected and esteemed in my new nation. . . . And perhaps I shall hold office and this is what I'm trying to tell you, Alaiyo; perhaps the things I believe now for my country will be wrong and outmoded, and I will not understand and do terrible things to have things my way or merely to keep my power. Don't you see that there will be young men and women, not British soldiers then, but my own black countrymen . . . to step out of the shadows some evening and slit my then useless throat? Don't you see they have always been there . . . that they always will be. And that such a thing as my own death will be an advance? They who might kill me even . . . actually replenish me!

BENEATHA: Oh, Asagai, I know all that.

ASAGAI: Good! Then stop moaning and groaning and tell me what you plan to do.

BENEATHA: Do?

ASAGAI: I have a bit of a suggestion.

BENEATHA: What?

ASAGAI [*rather quietly for him*]: That when it is all over—that you come home with me—

BENEATHA [*slapping herself on the forehead with exasperation born of misunderstanding*]: Oh—Asagai—at this moment you decide to be romantic!

ASAGAI: [*quickly understanding and misunderstanding*]: My dear, young creature of the New World—I do not mean across the city—I mean across the ocean; home—to Africa.

BENEATHA [*slowly understanding and turning to him with murmured amazement*]: To—to Nigeria?

ASAGAI: Yes! . . . [*Smiling and lifting his arms playfully*] Three hundred years later the African Prince rose up out of the seas and swept the maiden back across the middle passage over which her ancestors had come—

BENEATHA [*unable to play*]: Nigeria?

ASAGAI: Nigeria. Home. [*Coming to her with genuine romantic flippancy.*] I will show you our mountains and our stars; and give you cool drinks from gourds and teach you the old songs and the ways of our people—and, in time, we will pretend that—[*very softly*] —you have only been away for a day—

She turns her back to him, thinking. He swings her around and takes her full in his arms in a long embrace which proceeds to passion.

BENEATHA [*pulling away*]: You're getting me all mixed up—

ASAGAI: Why?

BENEATHA: Too many things—too many things have happened today. I must sit down and think. I don't know what I feel about anything right this minute. [*She promptly sits down and props her chin on her fist.*]

ASAGAI: [*charmed*]: All right, I shall leave you. No—don't get up. [*Touching her, gently, sweetly*] Just sit awhile and think. . . . Never be afraid to sit awhile and think. [*He goes to door and looks at her.*] How often I have looked at you and said, "Ah—so this is what the New World hath finally wrought. . . ."

[*He exits.* BENEATHA *sits on alone. Presently* WALTER *enters from his room and starts to rummage through things, feverishly looking for something. She looks up and turns in her seat.*]

BENEATHA [*hissingly*]: Yes—just look at what the New World hath wrought! . . . Just look! [*She gestures with bitter disgust.*] There he is! *Monsieur le petit bourgeois noir*—himself! There he is—Symbol of a Rising Class! Entrepreneur! Titan of the system! [WALTER *ignores her completely and continues frantically and destructively looking for something and hurling things to floor and tearing things out of their place in his search.* BENEATHA *ignores the eccentricity of his actions and goes on with the monologue of insult.*] Did you dream of yachts on Lake Michigan, Brother? Did you see yourself on that Great Day sitting down at the Conference Table, surrounded by all the mighty bald-headed men in America? All halted, waiting, breathless, waiting for your pronouncements on industry? Waiting for you—Chairman of the Board? [WALTER *finds what he is looking for—a small piece of white paper—and pushes it in his pocket and puts on his coat and rushes out without even having looked at her. She shouts after him.*] I look at you and I see the final triumph of stupidity in the world!

[*The door slams and she returns to just sitting again.* RUTH *comes quickly out of* MAMA'*s room.*]

RUTH: Who was that?

BENEATHA: Your husband.

RUTH: Where did he go?

BENEATHA: Who knows—maybe he has an appointment at U.S. Steel.

RUTH [*anxiously, with frightened eyes*]: You didn't say nothing bad to him, did you?

BENEATHA: Bad? Say anything bad to him? No—I told him he was a sweet boy and full of dreams and everything is strictly peachy keen, as the ofay kids say!

[MAMA *enters from her bedroom. She is lost, vague, trying to catch hold, to make some sense of her former command of the world, but it still eludes her. A sense of waste overwhelms her gait; a measure of apology rides on her shoulders. She goes to her plant, which has remained on the table, looks at it, picks it up and takes it to the window sill and sits it outside, and she stands and looks at it a long moment. Then she closes the window, straightens her body with effort and turns around to her children.*]

MAMA: Well—ain't it a mess in here, though? [*A false cheerfulness, a beginning of something*] I guess we all better stop moping around and get some work done. All this unpacking and everything we got to do. [RUTH *raises her head slowly in response to the sense of the line; and* BENEATHA *in similar manner turns very slowly to look at her mother.*] One of you all better call the moving people and tell 'em not to come.

RUTH: Tell 'em not to come?

MAMA: Of course, baby. Ain't no need in 'em coming all the way here and having to go back. They charges for that too. [*She sits down, fingers to her brow, thinking.*] Lord, ever since I was a little girl, I always remembers people saying, "Lena—Lena Eggleston, you aims too high all the time. You needs to slow down and see life a little more like it is. Just slow down some." That's what they always used to say down home—"Lord, that Lena Eggleston is a high-minded thing. She'll get her due one day!"

RUTH: No, Lena. . . .

MAMA: Me and Big Walter just didn't never learn right.

RUTH: Lena, no! We gotta go. Bennie—tell her. . . . [*She rises and crosses to* BENEATHA *with her arms outstretched.* BENEATHA *doesn't respond.*] Tell her we can still move . . . the notes ain't but a hundred and twenty-five a month. We got four grown people in this house—we can work. . . .

MAMA [*to herself*]: Just aimed too high all the time—

RUTH [*turning and going to* MAMA *fast—the words pouring out with urgency and desperation*]: Lena—I'll work. . . . I'll work twenty hours a day in all the kitchens in Chicago. . . . I'll strap my baby on my back if I have to and scrub all the floors in America and wash all the sheets in America if I have to—but we got to move. . . . We got to get out of here. . . .

MAMA *reaches out absently and pats* RUTH*'s hand.*

MAMA: No—I see things differently now. Been thinking 'bout some of the things we could do to fix this place up some. I seen a second-hand bureau over on Maxwell Street just the other day that could fit right there. [*She points to where the new furniture might go.* RUTH *wanders away from her.*] Would need some new handles on it and then a little varnish and then it look like something brand-new. And—we can put up them new curtains in the kitchen. . . . Why this place be looking fine. Cheer us all up so that we forget trouble ever came. . . . [*To* RUTH] And you could get some nice screens to put up in your room round the baby's bassinet. . . . [*She looks at both of them, pleadingly.*] Sometimes you just got to know when to give up some things . . . and hold on to what you got.

[WALTER *enters from the outside, looking spent and leaning against the door, his coat hanging from him.*]

MAMA: Where you been, son?

WALTER [*breathing hard*]: Made a call.

MAMA: To who, son?

WALTER: To The Man.

MAMA: What man, baby?

WALTER: The Man, Mama. Don't you know who The Man is?

RUTH: Walter Lee?

WALTER: *The Man.* Like the guys in the streets say—The Man. Captain Boss—Mistuh Charley . . . Old Captain Please Mr. Bossman . . .

BENEATHA [*suddenly*]: Lindner!

WALTER: That's right! That's good. I told him to come right over.

BENEATHA [*fiercely, understanding*]: For what? What do you want to see him for!

WALTER: [*looking at his sister*]: We going to do business with him.

MAMA: What you talking 'bout, son?

WALTER: Talking 'bout life, Mama. You all always telling me to see life like it is. Well—I laid in there on my back today . . . and I figured it out. Life just like it is. Who gets and who don't get. [*He sits down with his coat on and laughs.*] Mama, you know it's all divided up. Life is. Sure enough. Between the takers and the "tooken." [*He laughs.*] I've figured it out finally. [*He looks around at them.*] Yeah. Some of us always getting "tooken." [*He laughs.*] People like Willy Harris, they don't never get "tooken." And you know why the rest of us do? 'Cause we all mixed up. Mixed up bad. We get to looking 'round for the right and the wrong; and we worry about it and cry about it and stay up nights trying to figure out 'bout the wrong and the right of things all the time. . . . And all the time, man, them takers is out there operating, just taking and taking. Willy Harris? Shoot—Willy Harris don't even count. He don't even count in the big scheme of things. But I'll say one thing for old Willy Harris . . . he's taught me something. He's taught me to keep my eye on what counts in this world. Yeah— [*shouting out a little*]. Thanks, Willy!

RUTH: What did you call that man for, Walter Lee?

WALTER: Called him to tell him to come on over to the show. Gonna put on a show for the man. Just what he wants to see. You see, Mama, the man came here today and he told us that them people out there where you want us to move—well they so upset they willing to pay us not to move out there. [*He laughs again.*] And—and oh, Mama—you would of been proud of the way me and Ruth and Bennie acted. We told him to get out . . . Lord have mercy! We told the man to get out. Oh, we was some proud folks this afternoon, yeah. [*He lights a cigarette.*] We were still full of that old-time stuff. . . .

RUTH [*coming toward him slowly*]: You talking 'bout taking them people's money to keep us from moving in that house?

WALTER: I ain't just talking 'bout it, baby—I'm telling you that's what's going to happen.

BENEATHA: Oh, God! Where is the bottom! Where is the real honest-to-God bottom so he can't go any farther!

WALTER: See—that's old stuff. You and that boy that was here today. You all want everybody to carry a flag and a spear and sing some marching songs, huh? You wanna spend your life looking into things and trying to find the right and the wrong part, huh? Yeah. You know what's going to happen to that boy someday—he'll find himself sitting in a dungeon, locked in forever—and the takers will have the key! Forget it, baby! There ain't no causes—there ain't nothing but taking in this world, and he who takes most is smartest—and it don't make a damn bit of difference *how.*

MAMA: You making something inside me cry, son. Some awful pain inside me.

WALTER: Don't cry, Mama. Understand. That white man is going to walk in that door able to write checks for more money than we ever had. It's important to him and I'm going to help him . . . I'm going to put on the show, Mama.

MAMA: Son—I come from five generations of people who was slaves and sharecroppers—but ain't nobody in my family never let nobody pay 'em no money that was a way of telling us we wasn't fit to walk the earth. We ain't never been that poor. [*Raising her eyes and looking at him*] We ain't never been that dead inside.

BENEATHA: Well—we are dead now. All the talk about dreams and sunlight that goes on in this house. All dead.

WALTER: What's the matter with you all! I didn't make this world! It was give to me this way! Hell, yes, I want me some yachts someday! Yes, I want to hang some real pearls 'round my wife's neck. Ain't she supposed to wear no pearls? Somebody tell me—tell me, who decides which women is suppose to wear pearls in this world. I tell you I am a *man*—and I think my wife should wear some pearls in this world!

This last line hangs a good while and WALTER *begins to move about the room. The word "Man" has penetrated his consciousness; he mumbles it to himself repeatedly between strange agitated pauses as he moves about.*

MAMA: Baby, how you going to feel on the inside?

WALTER: Fine! . . . Going to feel fine . . . a man. . . .

MAMA: You won't have nothing left then, Walter Lee.

WALTER: [*coming to her*]: I'm going to feel fine, Mama. I'm going to look that son-of-a-bitch in the eyes and say— [*he falters*] —and say, "All right, Mr. Lindner— [*he falters even more*] —that's your neighborhood out there. You got the right to keep it like you want. You got the right to have it like you want. Just write the check and—the house is yours." And, and I am going to say— [*His voice almost breaks.*] And you—you people just put the money in my hand and you won't have to live next to this bunch of stinking niggers! . . . [*He straightens up and moves away from his mother, walking around the room.*] Maybe—maybe I'll just get down on my black knees. . . . [*He does so;* RUTH *and* BENNIE *and* MAMA *watch him in frozen horror.*] Captain, Mistuh, Bossman. [*He starts crying.*] A-hee-hee-hee! [*Wringing his hands in profoundly anguished imitation*] Yassssuh! Great White Father, just gi' ussen de money, fo' God's sake, and we's ain't gwine come out deh and dirty up yo' white folks neighborhood. . . .

[*He breaks down completely, then gets up and goes into the bedroom.*]

BENEATHA: That is not a man. That is nothing but a toothless rat.

MAMA: Yes—death done come in this here house. [*She is nodding, slowly, reflectively.*] Done come walking in my house. On the lips of my children. You what supposed to be my beginning again. You—what supposed to be my harvest. [*To* BENEATHA] You—you mourning your brother?

BENEATHA: He's no brother of mine.

MAMA: What you say?

BENEATHA: I said that that individual in that room is no brother of mine.

MAMA: That's what I thought you said. You feeling like you better than he is today? [BENEATHA *does not answer.*] Yes? What you tell him a minute ago? That he wasn't a man? Yes? You give him up for me? You done wrote his epitaph too—like the rest of the world? Well, who give you the privilege?

BENEATHA: Be on my side for once! You saw what he just did, Mama! You saw him—down on his knees. Wasn't it you who taught me—to despise any man who would do that. Do what he's going to do.

MAMA: Yes—I taught you that. Me and your daddy. But I thought I taught you something else too . . . I thought I taught you to love him.

BENEATHA: Love him? There is nothing left to love.

MAMA: There is always something left to love. And if you ain't learned that, you ain't learned nothing. [*Looking at her*] Have you cried for that boy today?

I don't mean for yourself and for the family 'cause we lost the money. I mean for him; what he been through and what it done to him. Child, when do you think is the time to love somebody the most; when they done good and made things easy for everybody? Well then, you ain't through learning—because that ain't the time at all. It's when he's at his lowest and can't believe in hisself 'cause the world done whipped him so. When you starts measuring somebody, measure him right, child, measure him right. Make sure you done taken into account what hills and valleys he come through before he got to wherever he is.

[TRAVIS *bursts into the room at the end of the speech, leaving the door open.*]

TRAVIS: Grandmama—the moving men are downstairs! The truck just pulled up.

MAMA [*turning and looking at him*]: Are they, baby? They downstairs?

[*She sighs and sits.* LINDNER *appears in the doorway. He peers in and knocks lightly, to gain attention, and comes in. All turn to took at him.*]

LINDNER [*hat and briefcase in hand*]: Uh—hello . . .

RUTH *crosses mechanically to the bedroom door and opens it and lets it swing open freely and slowly as the lights come up on* WALTER *within, still in his coat, sitting at the far corner of the room. He looks up and out through the room to* LINDER.

RUTH: He's here.

A long minute passes and WALTER *slowly gets up.*

LINDNER [*coming to the table with efficiency, putting his briefcase on the table and starting to unfold papers and unscrew fountain pens*]: Well, I certainly was glad to hear from you people. [WALTER *has begun the trek out of the room, slowly and awkwardly, rather like a small boy, passing the back of his sleeve across his mouth from time to time.*] Life can really be so much simpler than people let it be most of the time. Well—with whom do I negotiate? You, Mrs. Younger, or your son here? [MAMA *sits with her hands folded on her lap and her eyes closed as* WALTER *advances.* TRAVIS *goes close to* LINDNER *and looks at the papers curiously.*] Just some official papers, sonny.

RUTH: Travis, you go downstairs.

MAMA [*opening her eyes and looking into* WALTER'*s*]: No. Travis, you stay right here. And you make him understand what you doing, Walter Lee. You teach him good. Like Willy Harris taught you. You show where our five generations done come to. Go ahead, son—

WALTER [*looks down into his boy's eyes;* TRAVIS *grins at him merrily and* WALTER *draws him beside him with his arm lightly around his shoulders*]: Well, Mr. Lindner. [BENEATHA *turns away.*] We called you—[*there is a profound, simple groping quality in his speech*] —because, well, me and my family— [*He looks around and shifts from one foot to the other.*] Well—we are very plain people. . . .

LINDNER: Yes—

WALTER: I mean—I have worked as a chauffeur most of my life—and my wife here, she does domestic work in people's kitchens. So does my mother. I mean—we are plain people. . . .

LINDNER: Yes, Mr. Younger—

WALTER [*really like a small boy, looking down at his shoes and then up at the man*]: And—uh—well, my father, well, he was a laborer most of his life.

LINDNER [*absolutely confused*]: Uh, yes—

WALTER [*looking down at his toes once again*]: My father almost beat a man to death once because this man called him a bad name or something, you know what I mean?

LINDNER: No, I'm afraid I don't.

WALTER [*finally straightening up*]: Well, what I mean is that we come from people who had a lot of pride. I mean—we are very proud people. And that's my sister over there and she's going to be a doctor—and we are very proud—

LINDNER: Well—I am sure that is very nice, but—

WALTER [*starting to cry and facing the man eye to eye*]: What I am telling you is that we called you over here to tell you that we are very proud and that this is—this is my son, who makes the sixth generation of our family in this country, and that we have all thought about your offer and we have decided to move into our house because my father—my father—he earned it. [MAMA *has her eyes closed and is rocking back and forth as though she were in church, with her head nodding the amen yes.*] We don't want to make no trouble for nobody or fight no causes—but we will try to be good neighbors. That's all we got to say. [*He looks the man absolutely in the eyes.*] We don't want your money. [*He turns and walks away from the man.*]

LINDNER [*looking around at all of them*]: I take it then that you have decided to occupy.

BENEATHA: That's what the man said.

LINDNER [*to* MAMA *in her reverie*]: Then I would like to appeal to you, Mrs. Younger. You are older and wiser and understand things better I am sure . . .

MAMA [*rising*]: I am afraid you don't understand. My son said we was going to move and there ain't nothing left for me to say. [*Shaking her head with double meaning*] You know how these young folks is nowadays, mister. Can't do a thing with 'em. Good-bye.

LINDNER [*folding up his materials*]: Well—if you are that final about it. . . . There is nothing left for me to say. [*He finishes. He is almost ignored by the family, who are concentrating on* WALTER LEE. *At the door* LINDER *halts and looks around.*] I sure hope you people know what you're doing. [*He shakes his head and exits.*]

RUTH [*looking around and coming to life*]: Well, for God's sake—if the moving men are here—LET'S GET THE HELL OUT OF HERE!

MAMA [*into action*]: Ain't it the truth! Look at all this here mess. Ruth, put Travis' good jacket on him. . . . Walter Lee, fix your tie and tuck your shirt in, you look just like somebody's hoodlum. Lord have mercy, where is my plant? [*She flies to get it amid the general bustling of the family, who are deliberately trying to ignore the nobility of the past moment.*] You all start on down. . . . Travis child, don't go empty-handed. . . . Ruth, where did I put that box with my skillets in it? I want to be in charge of it myself. . . . I'm going to make us the biggest dinner we ever ate tonight. . . . Beneatha, what's the matter with them stockings? Pull them things up, girl. . . .

[*The family starts to file out as two moving men appear and begin to carry out the heavier pieces of furniture, bumping into the family as they move about.*]

BENEATHA: Mama, Asagai—asked me to marry him today and go to Africa—

MAMA [*in the middle of her getting-ready activity*]: He did? You ain't old enough to marry nobody—[*Seeing the moving men lifting one of her chairs precariously*] Darling, that ain't no bale of cotton, please handle it so we can sit in it again. I had that chair twenty-five years. . . .

The movers sigh with exasperation and go on with their work.

BENEATHA [*girlishly and unreasonably trying to pursue the conversation*]: To go to Africa, Mama—be a doctor in Africa. . . .

MAMA [*distracted*]: Yes, baby—

WALTER: Africa! What he want you to go to Africa for?

BENEATHA: To practice there. . . .

WALTER: Girl, if you don't get all them silly ideas out your head! You better marry yourself a man with some loot. . . .

BENEATHA [*angrily, precisely as in the first scene of the play*]: What have you got to do with who I marry!

WALTER: Plenty. Now I think George Murchison—

[*He and* BENEATHA *go out yelling at each other vigorously;* BENEATHA *is heard saying that she would not marry* GEORGE MURCHISON *if he were Adam and she were Eve, etc. The anger is loud and real till their voices diminish.* RUTH *stands at the door and turns to* MAMA *and smiles knowingly.*]

MAMA [*fixing her hat at last*]: Yeah—they something all right, my children. . . .

RUTH: Yeah—they're something. Let's go, Lena.

MAMA [*stalling, starting to look around at the house*]: Yes—I'm coming. Ruth—

RUTH: Yes?

MAMA [*quietly, woman to woman*]: He finally come into his manhood today, didn't he? Kind of like a rainbow after the rain. . . .

RUTH [*biting her lip lest her own pride explode in front of* MAMA]: Yes, Lena.

WALTER'S *voice calls for them raucously.*

MAMA [*waving* RUTH *out vaguely*]: All right, honey—go on down. I be down directly.

[RUTH *hesitates, then exits.* MAMA *stands, at last alone in the living room, her plant on the table before her as the lights start to come down. She looks around at all the walls and ceilings and suddenly, despite herself, while the children call below, a great heaving thing rises in her and she puts her fist to her mouth, takes a final desperate look, pulls her coat about her, pats her hat and goes out. The lights dim down. The door opens and she comes back in, grabs her plant, and goes out for the last time.*]

CURTAIN

Harold Pinter

Harold Pinter (1930–) was born in London, where his father, Hyman (Jack), was a tailor in the women's garment industry, and his mother, Frances, was a housewife. Pinter's grandparents emigrated to England from Poland and Russia in about 1900 and settled in the Jewish enclave of Hackney, a middle-class section of East London, where he was raised. It is from this milieu, Pinter says, that he derived his respect for literature and reading. Though he lost his faith as a teenager, Pinter has not escaped the lasting effects of his Jewish heritage.

In 1939, when World War II began, Pinter's parents sent him to Cornwall, 300 miles from home. It was a formative experience. Pinter, an only child, describes himself as being especially morose during this period of separation from his doting parents. He returned to London in 1940, but he and his mother again left to escape the Nazi blitz of London. Over the course of the war, the young Pinter was evacuated two more times, yet he still experienced firsthand the intense bombing of his East End neighborhood.

These experiences of separation and war indelibly marked Pinter's artistic imagination, imbuing his work with a sense of dislocation and powerlessness, of love withheld, and of the pain associated with separation or betrayal. The settings of his plays often suggest an atmosphere of destruction, deprivation, and oppression. Pinter's favorite scenes are usually closed or confined rooms, basements, or old farmhouses, many filled with the cast-off junk of modern life.

Pinter was not unhappy with school, but he did not attend college. At sixteen he wanted to become an actor; and he briefly attended London's Royal Academy of Dramatic Arts, but was put off by its pretension. Two years later, still without any real prospects, he enrolled in the Central School of Dramatics, but again dropped out. Through perseverance, he was able to get work as a radio actor for the BBC in 1950, which started his career. He also began writing poetry.

During this time, Pinter was called to do national service in the British armed forces; he resisted, however, on the grounds that he was a pacifist and a conscientious objector. Twice he was brought to court and fined for his defiance of authority and his beliefs. Pinter's fierce opposition to the military and political oppression became important thematic choices for his plays from the 1970s on.

From 1950 to 1960 Pinter worked as a professional actor, touring with a regional Shakespearean acting company, and later with a classical company, sometimes using the stage name David Baron, the surname of his paternal grandmother. Pinter seems to have had a fondness for calling himself by other names, and when he first started publishing his poems and other writings, he signed them Harold da Pinta or Pinta, derived from a misspelling of the family name.

In 1953 Pinter met Vivien Merchant, a successful actress among touring companies, and they were married in 1956. It was a tempestuous marriage, partly because of their life in the theater and Merchant's chronic alcoholism. Besides being his muse, she originated many of his important female characters, including roles in *The Room, The Homecoming,* and *Old Times.* After six years, as Pinter's fame increased and Merchant's became dependent on his plays, the marriage soured. For seven years (1962–1969), Pinter had an affair with television journalist Joan Bakewell and then began a passionate relationship with Lady Antonia Fraser, a historian and biographer, who was also married at the time. In 1975 he left Merchant, and after a messy divorce in 1980, he married Lady Antonia.

Though he is not often forthcoming about his literary influences, Pinter is indebted to the plays of the Absurdists and minimalists that emerged in the 1950s, when Pinter was in his early twenties. Pinter shares with Beckett a sense of simplicity, reducing place and setting to a minimum, and using stylized repetitive dialogue interspersed with pauses. Like a Beckett play, a Pinter play is neither well made nor filled with fully formed characters. A typical Pinter character is one whose life has atrophied, who is unable to make decisions, and who seems to have no outside interests, no enduring opinions about events, history, or politics, nor a vision of God or the universe. He has said, "I'm convinced that what happens in my plays could happen anywhere, at any time, in any place, although the events may seem unfamiliar at first glance. If you press me for a definition, I'd say that what goes on in my plays is realistic, but what I'm doing is not realism." Eventually Pinter befriended Beckett, and after 1959, Beckett was an unofficial commentator on his plays. In 1967 Pinter called Beckett the finest playwright then writing.

Pinter's first play, *The Room,* was written at the request of a friend studying drama at Bristol University and was produced there in 1957. *The Room* is a one-act play centering on a chattering old woman and her ominously silent husband. After a series of encounters, recalling the patterns of Eugène Ionesco, the husband, Bert Hudd, violently attacks Riley, a mysterious blind black man, who has come from the basement with a message for Rose, the wife, to "come home." When it was produced again by the Bristol Old Vic, it was noticed by Harry Hobson, the *Sunday Times* drama critic; this eventually helped Pinter get his first London production in 1958, *The Birthday Party.*

Pinter's third play, *The Dumb Waiter,* was translated into German and premiered in Frankfurt, Germany, in 1959, not opening in London until a year later. The title is a pun: The characters are waiting in a basement room of a restaurant for a message that will arrive in a dumbwaiter, their means of communicating with the outside world. Gus and Ben, two murderers for hire, each with a macabre sense of humor, wait for the call from someone unknown to kill their next victim. The message, delivered through the dumbwaiter after Gus leaves the room, orders Ben to kill the first person who enters the room. When Gus reenters, Ben prepares to shoot him, and the play ends.

After writing several radio plays, later adapted for the stage, Pinter had his first success with *The Caretaker* (1960), which had a run of 444 performances before largely baffled audiences. The action is set in a decrepit junk-filled room in a ramshackle house, cared for by Aston, unemployed and left slow-witted by electroshock treatments. He takes in Davies, a tramp, but just as Davies is about to take up residence, Mike, Aston's brother, appears, and when he sees that Mike is the stronger brother, Davies makes an effort to befriend him. Mike callously rejects him, however, and now friendless, Davies leaves to go on the road to nowhere, again.

The Lover (1963) contrasts Sarah as a wife and whore. She is Richard's wife, but their marriage often works best when they make believe they are committing adultery with each other. *The Lover* ends as Sarah and Richard seduce each other. The following exchange of dialogue is typical of Pinter:

> SARAH: . . . Aren't you sweet? I've never seen you before after sunset. My husband's at a late-night conference. Yes, you look different. Why are you wearing this strange suit, and this tie? You usually wear something else, don't you. Take off your jacket. Mmmnn? Would you like me to change? Would you like me to change clothes? Shall I? Would you like that?
> *Silence. She is very close to him.*
> RICHARD: Yes.
> *Pause*
> Change.
> *Pause*
> Change.
> *Pause*
> Change your clothes.
> *Pause*
> You lovely whore.

The Lover was produced with *The Dwarfs,* a stage version of a novel that Pinter had been writing since 1949. Len, *The Dwarfs'* protagonist, is a manic-depressive who seeks truth. He sees dwarfs who revile him, but when he rids himself of their presence in his dreams, he loses his imagination.

Pinter's *The Homecoming* (1965) attacks the sanctity of the family. It is a sardonically grotesque play about Teddy, a college professor, who unexpectedly returns to London with his wife, Ruth, to meet his family of misfit men: his father, Max, an aggressive butcher; his uncle, Sam, a weak-willed chauffeur; and his brothers—Lenny, a pimp, and Joey, an unsuccessful boxer. Despite Teddy's feeling that he and Ruth are menaced by the family, they do not leave. When Lenny and Joey make love to Ruth, Teddy and Max look on passively. Finally, Teddy gathers enough courage to leave, but Ruth remains, seemingly satisfied that she can be both mother and whore to the family. The men hover around her, while Sam lies unnoticed on the floor, having suffered a stroke.

Pinter was forty, and his marriage to Merchant was coming apart, when he finished *Landscape* (1968), a play about the utter irreconcilability of a married couple. The stage directions explain that "Duff refers to Beth, but does not appear to hear her voice. Beth never looks at Duff and does not appear to hear his voice. Both characters are relaxed, in no sense rigid." Like characters in Beckett's *Happy Days* (1962), Beth and Duff talk in separated but parallel monologues about memories of love and their betrayal of each other. One of Duff's memories is of seeing a couple, which may have been Beth and her lover, making love by a pond, though he cannot be sure.

Silence (1969) again mirrors Pinter's unsettled marital life, focusing on the unfulfilled lives and failed relationships of three characters from their twenties to their seventies. *Old Times* (1971), a memory play, suggests that because the past can be invented, memory is not trustworthy. The action takes place in a remodeled farmhouse, where Kate and her husband, Deeley, are waiting for Anna, Kate's roommate of twenty years before. There is a competition for friendship and dominance, partly of a sexual nature and partly of a social nature, as Kate tries to recall what Anna was like then and what she will be like now. Although Deeley may or may not have had an affair with Anna, he is upset by the hint that Kate and Anna might have been lovers. He is also very jealous of their friendship. In the end, however, Deeley resolves his conflicts by insisting that nothing really matters and that old times have no relation to the present.

No Man's Land (1975) is Pinter's version of T. S. Eliot's "The Love Song of J. Alfred Prufrock" (1917), reiterating that there are no love songs, nor are there friendships. The setting is Hirst's sparsely furnished West London apartment, where he brings Spooner, a slovenly dressed man of about sixty. Spooner offers his friendship, but Hirst, also about sixty, rejects it. As Hirst's memories flood his imagination to the point of drowning, it becomes evident that Hirst seduced Spooner's wife. Spooner does not understand. The conversation ends when Hirst finally says that he wishes to change the subject for the last time, and the wish is taken literally. As the curtain falls, Hirst sits silently, and Spooner says, "You are in no man's land. Which never moves, which never changes, which never grows older, but which remains forever icy and silent." After a moment of silence, Hirst responds, "I'll drink to that."

Pinter's *Betrayal,* produced when he was fifty, explores many kinds of betrayal—of husbands and wives, of lovers, of friends, and of oneself. Pinter was in the midst of his divorce from Merchant as he was writing the play, and the action of *Betrayal* is a fairly autobiographical account of his relationship with Joan Bakewell. The play's nine scenes, presented in reverse chronological order from 1977 to 1966, focus on Jerry's love affair with Emma, the wife of his best friend, Robert. As the story opens, Jerry and Emma are discussing their seven-year affair and Emma's news that she and Robert are separating because she has just learned that *he* has been unfaithful to *her.* This conversation is contrasted with a scene (set four years earlier) in which Emma tells Robert about her affair with Jerry, and in which neither bothered to mention it to Jerry. In fact, in the opening scene, Emma has lied to Jerry, telling him that Robert learned of their affair only the evening before. When the play ends, Jerry is upset, not because he committed adultery, not because his lover was his best friend's wife, but because his best friend betrayed him by never telling him that he knew what was going on.

After *Betrayal,* Pinter did not write a major play until 1993, but spent his time working on filmscripts. His short plays, such as *One for the Road* (1984), *Mountain Language* (1988), *Party Time* (1991), and *The New World Order* (1991), reflect his developing interest in international political affairs and criticize torture, oppression, and the abuse of power.

Moonlight (1993) was Pinter's first full-length play in fifteen years, even though it is only about seventy-five minutes in duration. The play has many similarities to Arthur Miller's *Death of a Salesman,* particularly its use of shifting time sequences to show a family's inability to establish an equanimity. Its protagonist is Andy, a retired civil servant in his fifties, dying, bedridden, and unable to sleep, who complains that fate has mocked him. Bel, his wife, is serene, but she loves without tenderness and is largely self-sufficient. Both Andy and Bel have betrayed each other by having affairs with the same woman, and they essentially live separate lives. Their sons, Jake and Fred, the latter bedridden with a nameless disease, are unemployed and more intent on bantering with each other and complaining about their inheritance than caring for their father. Bridget, Bel's and Andy's deceased sixteen-year-old daughter, asks for peace in the family, but it is not possible.

In 1996, Pinter's one-act play *Ashes to Ashes* explored current political abuse and memories of the Holocaust. The setting is a large, sparsely furnished room in a country house, in which an authoritarian man questions a long-suffering woman. The relation between Devlin, the man, and Rebecca, the woman, is unclear: They may be married or lovers. What is clear, however, is that he is cruel, unloving, and voyeuristic, and that she has the qualities of both whore and mother. Though they begin with a question-and-answer sequence about Rebecca's sexuality, the conversation deepens as Rebecca recalls memories of her lost baby and people willfully walking to their deaths into the sea, which suggests the Holocaust: "They took us to the trains . . . ," she says. ". . . They were taking the babies away . . . And we got on the train . . . And we arrived at this place . . ."

Pinter has also written screenplays and won most of the major international film awards, except an Oscar. Like Tennessee Williams, Pinter derives a large portion of his income from films. Pinter is especially good at adapting novels, among which are L. P. Hartley's *The Go-Between* (1970), John Fowles's *The French Lieutenant's Woman* (1981), Margaret Atwood's *The Handmaid's Tale* (1990), and Franz Kafka's *The Trial* (1993). He has adapted several of his plays for film, notably *The Birthday Party* (1968) and *Betrayal* (1982).

The Birthday Party (1958), Pinter's first full-length play, received only one positive review—from Harold Hobson, the *Sunday Times* drama critic—before it closed at the end of one week. Six years later, when it was revived and praised, Pinter commented that his play did not change; rather, the audience did. *The Birthday* epitomizes a Pinter play, and its characters are typical for him—an unhappy wife, a bored husband, a clownish loner who has trouble making his presence felt, a burly antagonist, and a sexy young woman. These characters are presented flatly, having no fully defined past, few clearly defined relationships, and a certain emotional distance. None of them is ever happy, and they are all in some way socially, emotionally, and sexually dysfunctional.

Pinter's style of language in *The Birthday Party* is also quintessential, marked by the use of pauses and rapid-fire conversation to convey anxiety and emotion, or the lack of it. Its plot may owe its inspiration to Ernest Hemingway's short story "The Killers" (1926), in which a boxer who refused to throw a fight waits stoically for hired killers to find him. Pinter was fond of the story and knew it as a Hollywood *film noire* directed by Robert Siodmak in 1946.

The plot blends realism with manic activity that is paced like a vaudeville comedy act turned deadly serious. Events happen and they are not controlled. Act I opens in the dining room of the seaside boarding house of Petey and Meg

Boles, where Stanley Webber, a scruffy young man, has been staying. He is evidently hiding from someone whom he has betrayed, living as if he is in jail, although Petey and Meg treat him like a son. When Meg flirts with Stanley, he pushes her away. Stanley is also unresponsive to Lulu, a buxom young woman in her twenties, who lives nearby. When Nat Goldberg, a sinister Jew, and Seamus McCann, a loutish Catholic Irishman, show up, Stanley is visibly upset because they have obviously come for him. Stanley asks them to leave, but they intend to complete their appointed task.

The birthday party takes place in Act II. Meg insists that it is Stanley's birthday, though it is not, and Goldberg and McCann give him a party. During the course of the evening, they interrogate Stanley mercilessly, without expecting any answers. As everyone drinks and gets a bit drunk, Goldberg flirts with Lulu, who welcomes his advances. During a game of blind man's buff, Stanley has a breakdown and begins to giggle uncontrollably.

Act III begins the morning after the party. When Stanley finally appears, dressed and clean-shaven, Goldberg and McCann taunt him, but he stands stooped and mute. They barrage him with words, non sequiturs, bits and pieces of ideas, songs, and slogans, until Stanley utters sounds, "Ug-gug . . . uh-gug . . . eeehhh-gag." Petey watches helplessly as Goldberg and McCann take Stanley away. Ineffectually and in a broken voice, Petey says, "Stan, don't let them tell you what to do!" When Meg comes in, he lies and tells her that Stanley is still sleeping. She can only think of the wonderful party of the night before.

Pinter's themes are the unresolvable conflicts between memory and reality, the inability of individuals to communicate meaningfully, the attraction and repulsion of sexual desire and lust, and the deep emotional and physical brutality that people inflict. Pinter's work shares many similarities with that of his contemporaries, such as Alan Ayckbourn, Edward Albee, and Simon Gray, several of whose plays Pinter has directed.

Pinter's tightness, sparseness, and brutality are often contrasted with Tom Stoppard's flowing elegance, baroque wit, and sprawling plot structure. David Mamet's work clearly shows Pinter's influence, especially in his style of language, though the speech of his characters in such plays as *American Buffalo, Speed the Plow*, or *Glengarry Glen Ross* is coarser and more profane. Sam Shepard's blend of comedy and mystery focuses on misfit characters, who tend to be more talkative and more overtly dysfunctional than Pinter's.

Film

The Birthday Party (1968), directed by William Friedkin, with Robert Shaw, Patrick Magee, Sidney Tafler, Dandy Nichols, and Moultrie Kelsall. Screenplay by Harold Pinter. Palomar.

The Birthday Party

PETEY, a man in his sixties
MEG, a woman in her sixties
STANLEY, a man in his late thirties
LULU, a girl in her twenties
GOLDBERG, a man in his fifties
MCCANN, a man of thirty

ACT I — A morning in summer
ACT II — Evening of the same day
ACT III — The next morning

ACT I

The living-room of a house in a seaside town. A door leading to the hall down left. Back door and small window up left. Kitchen hatch, centre back. Kitchen door up right. Table and chairs, centre.

PETEY *enters from the door on the left with a paper and sits at the table. He begins to read.* MEG*'s voice comes through the kitchen hatch.*

MEG: Is that you, Petey?

Pause.

Petey, is that you?

Pause.

Petey?
PETEY: What?
MEG: Is that you?
PETEY: Yes, it's me.
MEG: What? [*Her face appears at the hatch.*] Are you back?
PETEY: Yes.
MEG: I've got your cornflakes ready. [*She disappears and reappears.*] Here's your cornflakes.

He rises and takes the plate from her, sits at the table, props up the paper and begins to eat. MEG *enters by the kitchen door.*

Are they nice?
PETEY: Very nice.
MEG: I thought they'd be nice. [*She sits at the table.*] You got your paper?
PETEY: Yes.
MEG: Is it good?
PETEY: Not bad.
MEG: What does it say?
PETEY: Nothing much.
MEG: You read me out some nice bits yesterday.
PETEY: Yes, well, I haven't finished this one yet.
MEG: Will you tell me when you come to something good?
PETEY: Yes.

Pause.

MEG: Have you been working hard this morning?
PETEY: No. Just stacked a few of the old chairs. Cleaned up a bit.
MEG: Is it nice out?
PETEY: Very nice.

Pause.

MEG: Is Stanley up yet?
PETEY: I don't know. Is he?
MEG: I don't know. I haven't seen him down yet.
PETEY: Well then, he can't be up.
MEG: Haven't you seen him down?
PETEY: I've only just come in.
MEG: He must be still asleep.

She looks round the room, stands, goes to the sideboard and takes a pair of socks from a drawer, collects wool and a needle and goes back to the table.

What time did you go out this morning, Petey?
PETEY: Same time as usual.
MEG: Was it dark?
PETEY: No, it was light.
MEG [*beginning to darn*]: But sometimes you go out in the morning and it's dark.
PETEY: That's in the winter.
MEG: Oh, in winter.
PETEY: Yes, it gets light later in winter.
MEG: Oh.

Pause.

What are you reading?
PETEY: Someone's just had a baby.
MEG: Oh, they haven't! Who?
PETEY: Some girl.

MEG: Who, Petey, who?
PETEY: I don't think you'd know her.
MEG: What's her name?
PETEY: Lady Mary Splatt.
MEG: I don't know her.
PETEY: No.
MEG: What is it?
PETEY [*studying the paper*]: Er—a girl.
MEG: Not a boy?
PETEY: No.
MEG: Oh, what a shame. I'd be sorry. I'd much rather have a little boy.
PETEY: A little girl's all right.
MEG: I'd much rather have a little boy.

Pause.

PETEY: I've finished my cornflakes.
MEG: Were they nice?
PETEY: Very nice.
MEG: I've got something else for you.
PETEY: Good.

She rises, takes his plate and exits into the kitchen. She then appears at the hatch with two pieces of fried bread on a plate.

MEG: Here you are, Petey.

He rises, collects the plate, looks at it, sits at the table. MEG *re-enters.*

Is it nice?
PETEY: I haven't tasted it yet.
MEG: I bet you don't know what it is.
PETEY: Yes, I do.
MEG: What is it, then?
PETEY: Fried bread.
MEG: That's right.

He begins to eat.
She watches him eat.

PETEY: Very nice.
MEG: I knew it was.
PETEY [*turning to her*]: Oh, Meg, two men came up to me on the beach last night.
MEG: Two men?
PETEY: Yes. They wanted to know if we could put them up for a couple of nights.
MEG: Put them up? Here?
PETEY: Yes.
MEG: How many men?
PETEY: Two.
MEG: What did you say?
PETEY: Well, I said I didn't know. So they said they'd come round to find out.

The Birthday Party, *Booth Theatre, New York, 1967.*

MEG: Are they coming?
PETEY: Well, they said they would.
MEG: Had they heard about us, Petey?
PETEY: They must have done.
MEG: Yes, they must have done. They must have heard this was a very good boarding house. It is. This house is on the list.
PETEY: It is.
MEG: I know it is.
PETEY: They might turn up today. Can you do it?
MEG: Oh, I've got that lovely room they can have.
PETEY: You've got a room ready?
MEG: I've got the room with the armchair all ready for visitors.
PETEY: You're sure?
MEG: Yes, that'll be all right then, if they come today.
PETEY: Good.

She takes the socks etc. back to the sideboard drawer.

MEG: I'm going to wake that boy.
PETEY: There's a new show coming to the Palace.
MEG: On the pier?
PETEY: No. The Palace, in the town.
MEG: Stanley could have been in it, if it was on the pier.
PETEY: This is a straight show.
MEG: What do you mean?
PETEY: No dancing or singing.
MEG: What do they do then?
PETEY: They just talk.

Pause.

MEG: Oh.
PETEY: You like a song eh, Meg?
MEG: I like listening to the piano. I used to like watching Stanley play the piano. Of course, he didn't sing. [*Looking at the door.*] I'm going to call that boy.
PETEY: Didn't you take him up his cup of tea?
MEG: I always take him up his cup of tea. But that was a long time ago.
PETEY: Did he drink it?
MEG: I made him. I stood there till he did. I'm going to call him. [*She goes to the door.*] Stan! Stanny! [*She listens.*] Stan! I'm coming up to fetch you if you don't come down! I'm coming up! I'm going to count three! One! Two! Three! I'm coming to get you! [*She exits and goes upstairs. In a moment, shouts from* STANLEY, *wild laughter from* MEG. PETEY *takes his plate to the hatch. Shouts. Laughter.* PETEY *sits at the table. Silence. She returns.*] He's coming down. [*She is panting and arranges her hair.*] I told him if he didn't hurry up he'd get no breakfast.
PETEY: That did it, eh?
MEG: I'll get his cornflakes.

MEG *exits to the kitchen.* PETEY *reads the paper.* STANLEY *enters. He is unshaven, in his pyjama jacket and wears glasses. He sits at the table.*

PETEY: Morning, Stanley.
STANLEY: Morning.

Silence. MEG *enters with the bowl of cornflakes, which she sets on the table.*

MEG: So he's come down at last, has he? He's come down at last for his breakfast. But he doesn't deserve any, does he, Petey? [STANLEY *stares at the cornflakes.*] Did you sleep well?
STANLEY: I didn't sleep at all.
MEG: You didn't sleep at all? Did you hear that, Petey? Too tired to eat your breakfast, I suppose? Now you eat up those cornflakes like a good boy. Go on.

He begins to eat.

STANLEY: What's it like out today?
PETEY: Very nice.
STANLEY: Warm?
PETEY: Well, there's a good breeze blowing.
STANLEY: Cold?
PETEY: No, no, I wouldn't say it was cold.
MEG: What are the cornflakes like, Stan?
STANLEY: Horrible.
MEG: Those flakes? Those lovely flakes? You're a liar, a little liar. They're refreshing. It says so. For people when they get up late.
STANLEY: The milk's off.
MEG: It's not. Petey ate his, didn't you, Petey?
PETEY: That's right.
MEG: There you are then.
STANLEY: All right, I'll go on to the second course.
MEG: He hasn't finished the first course and he wants to go on to the second course!
STANLEY: I feel like something cooked.
MEG: Well, I'm not going to give it to you.
PETEY: Give it to him.
MEG [*sitting at the table, right*]: I'm not going to.

Pause.

STANLEY: No breakfast.

Pause.

All night long I've been dreaming about this breakfast.
MEG: I thought you said you didn't sleep.

STANLEY: Day-dreaming. All night long. And now she won't give me any. Not even a crust of bread on the table.

Pause.

Well, I can see I'll have to go down to one of those smart hotels on the front.
MEG [*rising quickly*]: You won't get a better breakfast there than here.

She exits to the kitchen. STANLEY *yawns broadly.* MEG *appears at the hatch with a plate.*

Here you are. You'll like this.

PETEY *rises, collects the plate, brings it to the table, puts it in front of* STANLEY, *and sits.*

STANLEY: What's this?
PETEY: Fried bread.
MEG [*entering*]: Well, I bet you don't know what it is.
STANLEY: Oh yes I do.
MEG: What?
STANLEY: Fried bread.
MEG: He knew.
STANLEY: What a wonderful surprise.
MEG: You didn't expect that, did you?
STANLEY: I bloody well didn't.
PETEY [*rising*]: Well, I'm off.
MEG: You going back to work?
PETEY: Yes.
MEG: Your tea! You haven't had your tea!
PETEY: That's all right. No time now.
MEG: I've got it made inside.
PETEY: No, never mind. See you later. Ta-ta, Stan.
STANLEY: Ta-ta.

PETEY *exits, left.*

Tch, tch, tch, tch.
MEG [*defensively*]: What do you mean?
STANLEY: You're a bad wife.
MEG: I'm not. Who said I am?
STANLEY: Not to make your husband a cup of tea. Terrible.
MEG: He knows I'm not a bad wife.
STANLEY: Giving him sour milk instead.
MEG: It wasn't sour.
STANLEY: Disgraceful.
MEG: You mind your own business, anyway. [STANLEY *eats.*] You won't find many better wives than me, I can tell you. I keep a very nice house and I keep it clean.
STANLEY: Whoo!
MEG: Yes! And this house is very well known, for a very good boarding house for visitors.
STANLEY: Visitors? Do you know how many visitors you've had since I've been here?
MEG: How many?
STANLEY: One.
MEG: Who?
STANLEY: Me! I'm your visitor.
MEG: You're a liar. This house is on the list.
STANLEY: I bet it is.
MEG: I know it is.

He pushes his plate away and picks up the paper.

Was it nice?
STANLEY: What?
MEG: The fried bread.
STANLEY: Succulent.
MEG: You shouldn't say that word.
STANLEY: What word?
MEG: That word you said.
STANLEY: What, succulent—?
MEG: Don't say it!
STANLEY: What's the matter with it?
MEG: You shouldn't say that word to a married woman.
STANLEY: Is that a fact?
MEG: Yes.
STANLEY: Well, I never knew that.
MEG: Well, it's true.
STANLEY: Who told you that?
MEG: Never you mind.
STANLEY: Well, if I can't say it to a married woman who can I say it to?
MEG: You're bad.
STANLEY: What about some tea?
MEG: Do you want some tea? [STANLEY *reads the paper.*] Say please.
STANLEY: Please.
MEG: Say sorry first.
STANLEY: Sorry first.
MEG: No. Just Sorry.
STANLEY: Just sorry!
MEG: You deserve the strap.
STANLEY: Don't do that!

She takes his plate and ruffles his hair as she passes. STANLEY *exclaims and throws her arm away. She goes into the kitchen. He rubs his eyes under his glasses and picks up the paper. She enters.*

I brought the pot in.
STANLEY [*absently*]: I don't know what I'd do without you.
MEG: You don't deserve it though.

STANLEY: Why not?
MEG [*pouring the tea, coyly*]: Go on. Calling me that.
STANLEY: How long has that tea been in the pot?
MEG: It's good tea. Good strong tea.
STANLEY: This isn't tea. It's gravy!
MEG: It's not.
STANLEY: Get out of it. You succulent old washing bag.
MEG: I am not! And it isn't your place to tell me if I am!
STANLEY: And it isn't your place to come into a man's bedroom and—wake him up.
MEG: Stanny! Don't you like your cup of tea of a morning—the one I bring you?
STANLEY: I can't drink this muck. Didn't anyone ever tell you to warm the pot, at least?
MEG: That's good strong tea, that's all.
STANLEY [*putting his head in his hands*]: Oh God, I'm tired.

Silence. MEG *goes to the sideboard, collects a duster, and vaguely dusts the room, watching him. She comes to the table and dusts it.*

Not the bloody table!

Pause.

MEG: Stan?
STANLEY: What?
MEG [*shyly*]: Am I really succulent?
STANLEY: Oh, you are. I'd rather have you than a cold in the nose any day.
MEG: You're just saying that.
STANLEY [*violently*]: Look, why don't you get this place cleared up! It's a pigsty. And another thing, what about my room? It needs sweeping. It needs papering. I need a new room!
MEG [*sensual, stroking his arm*]: Oh, Stan, that's a lovely room. I've had some lovely afternoons in that room.

He recoils from her hand in disgust, stands and exits quickly by the door on the left. She collects his cup and the teapot and takes them to the hatch shelf. The street door slams. STANLEY *returns.*

MEG: Is the sun shining? [*He crosses to the window, takes a cigarette and matches from his pyjama jacket, and lights his cigarette.*] What are you smoking?
STANLEY: A cigarette.
MEG: Are you going to give me one?
STANLEY: No.
MEG: I like cigarettes. [*He stands at the window, smoking. She crosses behind him and tickles the back of his neck.*] Tickle, tickle.
STANLEY [*pushing her*]: Get away from me.
MEG: Are you going out?
STANLEY: Not with you.
MEG: But I'm going shopping in a minute.
STANLEY: Go.
MEG: You'll be lonely, all by yourself.
STANLEY: Will I?
MEG: Without your old Meg. I've got to get things in for the two gentlemen.

A pause. STANLEY *slowly raises his head. He speaks without turning.*

STANLEY: What two gentlemen?
MEG: I'm expecting visitors.

He turns.

STANLEY: What?
MEG: You didn't know that, did you?
STANLEY: What are you talking about?
MEG: Two gentlemen asked Petey if they could come and stay for a couple of nights. I'm expecting them. [*She picks up the duster and begins to wipe the cloth on the table.*]
STANLEY: I don't believe it.
MEG: It's true.
STANLEY [*moving to her*]: You're saying it on purpose.
MEG: Petey told me this morning.
STANLEY [*grinding his cigarette*]: When was this? When did he see them?
MEG: Last night.
STANLEY: Who are they?
MEG: I don't know.
STANLEY: Didn't he tell you their names?
MEG: No.
STANLEY [*pacing the room*]: Here? They wanted to come here?
MEG: Yes, they did. [*She takes the curlers out of her hair.*]
STANLEY: Why?
MEG: This house is on the list.
STANLEY: But who are they?
MEG: You'll see when they come.
STANLEY [*decisively*]: They won't come.
MEG: Why not?
STANLEY [*quickly*]: I tell you they won't come. Why didn't they come last night, if they were coming?
MEG: Perhaps they couldn't find the place in the dark. It's not easy to find in the dark.
STANLEY: They won't come. Someone's taking the Michael. Forget all about it. It's a false alarm. A false alarm. [*He sits at the table.*] Where's my tea?
MEG: I took it away. You didn't want it.
STANLEY: What do you mean, you took it away?

MEG: I took it away.
STANLEY: What did you take it away for?
MEG: You didn't want it!
STANLEY: Who said I didn't want it?
MEG: You did!
STANLEY: Who gave you the right to take away my tea?
MEG: You wouldn't drink it.

STANLEY *stares at her.*

STANLEY [*quietly*]: Who do you think you're talking to?
MEG [*uncertainly*]: What?
STANLEY: Come here.
MEG: What do you mean?
STANLEY: Come over here.
MEG: No.
STANLEY: I want to ask you something. [MEG *fidgets nervously. She does not go to him.*] Come on. [*Pause.*] All right. I can ask it from here just as well. [*Deliberately.*] Tell me, Mrs Boles, when you address yourself to me, do you ever ask yourself who exactly you are talking to? Eh?

Silence. He groans, his trunk falls forward, his head falls into his hands.

MEG [*in a small voice*]: Didn't you enjoy your breakfast, Stan? [*She approaches the table.*] Stan? When are you going to play the piano again? [STANLEY *grunts.*] Like you used to? [STANLEY *grunts.*] I used to like watching you play the piano. When are you going to play it again?
STANLEY: I can't, can I?
MEG: Why not?
STANLEY: I haven't got a piano, have I?
MEG: No, I meant like when you were working. That piano.
STANLEY: Go and do your shopping.
MEG: But you wouldn't have to go away if you got a job, would you? You could play the piano on the pier.

He looks at her, then speaks airily.

STANLEY: I've . . . er . . . I've been offered a job, as a matter of fact.
MEG: What?
STANLEY: Yes. I'm considering a job at the moment.
MEG: You're not.
STANLEY: A good one, too. A night club. In Berlin.
MEG: Berlin?
STANLEY: Berlin. A night club. Playing the piano. A fabulous salary. And all found.
MEG: How long for?
STANLEY: We don't stay in Berlin. Then we go to Athens.
MEG: How long for?
STANLEY: Yes. Then we pay a flying visit to . . . er . . . whatsisname. . . .
MEG: Where?
STANLEY: Constantinople. Zagreb. Vladivostock. It's a round the world tour.
MEG [*sitting at the table*]: Have you played the piano in those places before?
STANLEY: Played the piano? I've played the piano all over the world. All over the country. [*Pause.*] I once gave a concert.
MEG: A concert?
STANLEY [*reflectively*]: Yes. It was a good one, too. They were all there that night. Every single one of them. It was a great success. Yes. A concert. At Lower Edmonton.
MEG: What did you wear?
STANLEY [*to himself*]: I had a unique touch. Absolutely unique. They came up to me. They came up to me and said they were grateful. Champagne we had that night, the lot. [*Pause.*] My father nearly came down to hear me. Well, I dropped him a card anyway. But I don't think he could make it. No, I—I lost the address, that was it. [*Pause.*] Yes. Lower Edmonton. Then after that, you know what they did? They carved me up. Carved me up. It was all arranged, it was all worked out. My next concert. Somewhere else it was. In winter. I went down there to play. Then, when I got there, the hall was closed, the place was shuttered up, not even a caretaker. They'd locked it up. [*Takes off his glasses and wipes them on his pyjama jacket.*] A fast one. They pulled a fast one. I'd like to know who was responsible for that. [*Bitterly.*] All right, Jack, I can take a tip. They want me to crawl down on my bended knees. Well I can take a tip . . . any day of the week. [*He replaces his glasses, then looks at* MEG.] Look at her. You're just an old piece of rock cake, aren't you? [*He rises and leans across the table to her.*] That's what you are, aren't you?
MEG: Don't you go away again, Stan. You stay here. You'll be better off. You stay with your old Meg. [*He groans and lies across the table.*]Aren't you feeling well this morning, Stan. Did you pay a visit this morning?

He stiffens, then lifts himself slowly, turns to face her and speaks lightly, casually.

STANLEY: Meg. Do you know what?
MEG: What?
STANLEY: Have you heard the latest?
MEG: No.
STANLEY: I'll bet you have.
MEG: I haven't.
STANLEY: Shall I tell you?

MEG: What latest?
STANLEY: You haven't heard it?
MEG: No.
STANLEY [*advancing*]: They're coming today.
STANLEY: They're coming in a van.
MEG: Who?
STANLEY: And do you know what they've got in that van?
MEG: What?
STANLEY: They've got a wheelbarrow in that van.
MEG [*breathlessly*]: They haven't.
STANLEY: Oh yes they have.
MEG: You're a liar.
STANLEY [*advancing upon her*]: A big wheelbarrow. And when the van stops they wheel it out, and they wheel it up the garden path, and then they knock at the front door.
MEG: They don't.
STANLEY: They're looking for someone.
MEG: They're not.
STANLEY: They're looking for someone. A certain person.
MEG [*hoarsely*]: No, they're not!
STANLEY: Shall I tell you who they're looking for?
MEG: No!
STANLEY: You don't want me to tell you?
MEG: You're a liar!

A sudden knock on the front door. LULU'*s voice: Ooh-ooh!* MEG *edges past* STANLEY *and collects her shopping bag.* MEG *goes out.* STANLEY *sidles to the door and listens.*

VOICE [*through letter box*]: Hullo, Mrs Boles . . .
MEG: Oh, has it come?
VOICE: Yes, it's just come.
MEG: What, is that it?
VOICE: Yes. I thought I'd bring it round.
MEG: Is it nice?
VOICE: Very nice. What shall I do with it?
MEG: Well, I don't . . . [*Whispers.*]
VOICE: No, of course not . . . [*Whispers.*]
MEG. All right, but . . . [*Whispers.*]
VOICE: I won't . . . [*Whispers.*] Ta-ta, Mrs Boles.

STANLEY *quickly sits at the table. Enter* LULU.

LULU: Oh, hullo.
STANLEY: Ay-ay.
LULU: I just want to leave this in here.
STANLEY: Do. [LULU *crosses to the sideboard and puts a solid, round parcel upon it.*] That's a bulky object.
LULU: You're not to touch it.
STANLEY: Why would I want to touch it?
LULU: Well, you're not to, anyway.

LULU *walks upstage.*

LULU: Why don't you open the door? It's all stuffy in here.

She opens the back door.

STANLEY [*rising*]: Stuffy? I disinfected the place this morning.
LULU [*at the door*]: Oh, that's better.
STANLEY: I think it's going to rain to-day. What do you think?
LULU: I hope so. You could do with it.
STANLEY: Me! I was in the sea at half past six.
LULU: Were you?
STANLEY: I went right out to the headland and back before breakfast. Don't you believe me!

She sits, takes out a compact and powders her nose.

LULU [*offering him the compact*]: Do you want to have a look at your face? [STANLEY *withdraws from the table.*] You could do with a shave, do you know that? [STANLEY *sits, right at the table.*] Don't you ever go out? [*He does not answer.*] I mean, what do you do, just sit around the house like this all day long? [*Pause.*] Hasn't Mrs Boles got enough to do without having you under her feet all day long?
STANLEY: I always stand on the table when she sweeps the floor.
LULU: Why don't you have a wash? You look terrible.
STANLEY: A wash wouldn't make any difference.
LULU [*rising*]: Come out and get a bit of air. You depress me, looking like that.
STANLEY: Air? Oh, I don't know about that.
LULU: It's lovely out. And I've got a few sandwiches.
STANLEY: What sort of sandwiches?
LULU: Cheese.
STANLEY: I'm a big eater, you know.
LULU: That's all right. I'm not hungry.
STANLEY [*abruptly*]: How would you like to go away with me?
LULU: Where.
STANLEY: Nowhere. Still, we could go.
LULU: But where could we go?
STANLEY: Nowhere. There's nowhere to go. So we could just go. It wouldn't matter.
LULU: We might as well stay here.
STANLEY: No. It's no good here.
LULU: Well, where else is there?
STANLEY: Nowhere.
LULU: Well, that's a charming proposal. [*He gets up.*] Do you have to wear those glasses?
STANLEY: Yes.
LULU: So you're not coming out for a walk?
STANLEY: I can't at the moment.
LULU: You're a bit of a washout, aren't you?

She exits, left. STANLEY *stands. He then goes to the mirror and looks in it. He goes into the kitchen, takes off his glasses and begins to wash his face. A pause. Enter, by the back door,* GOLDBERG *and* MCCANN. MCCANN *carries two suitcases,* GOLDBERG *a briefcase. Thy halt inside the door, then walk downstage.* STANLEY, *wiping his face, glimpses their backs through the hatch.* GOLDBERG *and* MCCANN *look round the room.* STANLEY *slips on his glasses, idles through the kitchen door and out of the back door.*

MCCANN: Is this it?
GOLDBERG: This is it.
MCCANN: Are you sure?
GOLDBERG: Sure I'm sure.

Pause.

MCCANN: What now?
GOLDBERG: Don't worry yourself, McCann. Take a seat.
MCCANN: What about you?
GOLDBERG: What about me?
MCCANN: Are you going to take a seat?
GOLDBERG: We'll both take a seat. [MCCANN *puts down the suitcase and sits at the table, left.*] Sit back, McCann. Relax. What's the matter with you? I bring you down for a few days to the seaside. Take a holiday. Do yourself a favour. Learn to relax, McCann, or you'll never get anywhere.
MCCANN: Ah sure, I do try, Nat.
GOLDBERG [*sitting at the table, right*]: The secret is breathing. Take my tip. It's a well-known fact. Breathe in, breathe out, take a chance, let yourself go, what can you lose? Look at me. When I was an apprentice yet, McCann, every second Friday of the month my Uncle Barney used to take me to the seaside, regular as clockwork. Brighton, Canvey Island, Rottingdean—Uncle Ramey wasn't particular. After lunch on Shabbuss we'd go and sit in a couple of deck chairs—you know, the ones with canopies—we'd have a little paddle, we'd watch the tide coming in, going out, the sun coming down—golden days, believe me, McCann. [*Reminiscent.*] Uncle Barney. Of course, he was an impeccable dresser. One of the old school. He had a house just outside Basingstoke at the time. Respected by the whole community. Culture? Don't talk to me about culture. He was an all-round man, what do you mean? He was a cosmopolitan.
MCCANN: Hey, Nat. . . .
GOLDBERG [*reflectively*]: Yes. One of the old school.
MCCANN: Nat. How do we know this is the right house?
GOLDBERG: What?
MCCANN: How do we know this is the right house?
GOLDBERG: What makes you think it's the wrong house?
MCCANN: I didn't see a number on the gate.
GOLDBERG: I wasn't looking for a number.
MCCANN: No?
GOLDBERG [*settling in the armchair*]: You know one thing Uncle Barney taught me? Uncle Barney taught me that the word of a gentleman is enough. That's why, when I had to go away on business I never carried any money. One of my sons used to come with me. He used to carry a few coppers. For a paper, perhaps, to see how the M.C.C. was getting on overseas. Otherwise my name was good. Besides, I was a very busy man.
MCCANN: What about this, Nat? Isn't it about time someone came in?
GOLDBERG: McCann, what are you so nervous about? Pull yourself together. Everywhere you go these days it's like a funeral.
MCCANN: That's true.
GOLDBERG: True? Of course it's true. It's more than true. It's a fact.
MCCANN: You may be right.
GOLDBERG: What is it, McCann? You don't trust me like you did in the old days?
MCCANN: Sure I trust you, Nat.
GOLDBERG: But why is it that before you do a job you're all over the place, and when you're doing the job you're as cool as a whistle?
MCCANN: I don't know, Nat. I'm just all right once I know what I'm doing. When I know what I'm doing, I'm all right.
GOLDBERG: Well, you do it very well.
MCCANN: Thank you, Nat.
GOLDBERG: You know what I said when this job came up. I mean naturally they approached me to take care of it. And you know who I asked for?
MCCANN: Who?
GOLDBERG: You.
MCCANN: That was very good of you, Nat.
GOLDBERG: No, it was nothing. You're a capable man, McCann.
MCCANN: That's a great compliment, Nat, coming from a man in your position.
GOLDBERG: Well, I've got a position, I won't deny it.
MCCANN: You certainly have.
GOLDBERG: I would never deny that I had a position.
MCCANN: And what a position!
GOLDBERG: It's not a thing I would deny.
MCCANN: Yes, it's true, you've done a lot for me. I appreciate it.
GOLDBERG: Say no more.
MCCANN: You've always been a true Christian.
GOLDBERG: In a way.

MCCANN: No, I just thought I'd tell you that I appreciate it.
GOLDBERG: It's unnecessary to recapitulate.
MCCANN: You're right there.
GOLDBERG: Quite unnecessary.

Pause. MCCANN *leans forward.*

MCCANN: Hey Nat, just one thing. . . .
GOLDBERG: What now?
MCCANN: This job—no, listen—this job, is it going to be like anything we've ever done before?
GOLDBERG: Tch, tch, tch.
MCCANN: No, just tell me that. Just that, and I won't ask any more.

GOLDBERG *sighs, stands, goes behind the table, ponders, looks at* MCCANN, *and then speaks in a quiet, fluent, official tone.*

GOLDBERG: The main issue is a singular issue and quite distinct from your previous work. Certain elements, however, might well approximate in points of procedure to some of your other activities. All is dependent on the attitude of our subject. At all events, McCann, I can assure you that the assignment will be carried out and the mission accomplished with no excessive aggravation to you or myself. Satisfied?
MCCANN: Sure. Thank you, Nat.

MEG *enters, left.*

GOLDBERG: Ah, Mrs Boles?
MEG: Yes?
GOLDBERG: We spoke to your husband last night. Perhaps he mentioned us? We heard that you kindly let rooms for gentlemen. So I brought my friend along with me. We were after a nice place, you understand. So we came to you. I'm Mr Goldberg and this is Mr McCann.
MEG: Very pleased to meet you.

They shake hands.

GOLDBERG: We're pleased to meet you, too.
MEG: That's very nice.
GOLDBERG: You're right. How often do you meet someone it's a pleasure to meet?
MCCANN: Never.
GOLDBERG: But today it's different. How are you keeping, Mrs Boles?
MEG: Oh, very well, thank you.
GOLDBERG: Yes? Really?
MEG: Oh yes, really.
GOLDBERG: I'm glad.

GOLDBERG *sits at the table, right.*

GOLDBERG: Well, so what do you say? You can manage to put us up, eh, Mrs Boles?
MEG: Well, it would have been easier last week.
GOLDBERG: It would, eh?
MEG: Yes.
GOLDBERG: Why? How many have you got here at the moment?
MEG: Just one at the moment.
GOLDBERG: Just one?
MEG: Yes. Just one. Until you came.
GOLDBERG: And your husband, of course?
MEG: Yes, but he sleeps with me.
GOLDBERG: What does he do, your husband?
MEG: He's a deck-chair attendant.
GOLDBERG: Oh, very nice.
MEG: Yes, he's out in all weathers.

She begins to take her purchases from her bag.

GOLDBERG: Of course. And your guest? Is he a man?
MEG: A man?
GOLDBERG: Or a woman?
MEG: No. A man.
GOLDBERG: Been here long?
MEG: He's been here about a year now.
GOLDBERG: Oh yes. A resident. What's his name?
MEG: Stanley Webber.
GOLDBERG: Oh yes? Does he work here?
MEG: He used to work. He used to be a pianist. In a concert party on the pier.
GOLDBERG: Oh yes? On the pier, eh? Does he play a nice piano?
MEG: Oh, lovely. [*She sits at the table.*] He once gave a concert.
GOLDBERG: Oh? Where?
MEG [*falteringly*]: In . . . a big hall. His father gave him champagne. But then they locked the place up and he couldn't get out. The caretaker had gone home. So he had to wait until the morning before he could get out. [*With confidence.*] They were very grateful. [*Pause.*] And then they all wanted to give him a tip. And so he took the tip. And then he got a fast train and he came down here.
GOLDBERG: Really?
MEG: Oh yes. Straight down.

Pause.

MEG: I wish he could have played tonight.
GOLDBERG: Why tonight?

Meg: It's his birthday today.
Goldberg: His birthday?
Meg: Yes. Today. But I'm not going to tell him until tonight.
Goldberg: Doesn't he know it's his birthday?
Meg: He hasn't mentioned it.
Goldberg [*thoughtfully*]: Ah! Tell me. Are you going to have a party?
Meg: A party?
Goldberg: Weren't you going to have one?
Meg [*her eyes wide*]: No.
Goldberg: Well, of course, you must have one. [*He stands.*] We'll have a party, eh? What do you say?
Meg: Oh yes!
Goldberg: Sure. We'll give him a party. Leave it to me.
Meg: Oh, that's wonderful, Mr Gold—
Goldberg: Berg.
Meg: Berg.
Goldberg: You like the idea?
Meg: Oh, I'm so glad you came today.
Goldberg: If we hadn't come today we'd have come tomorrow. Still, I'm glad we came today. Just in time for his birthday.
Meg: I wanted to have a party. But you must have people for a party.
Goldberg: And now you've got McCann and me. McCann's the life and soul of any party.
McCann: What?
Goldberg: What do you think of that, McCann? There's a gentleman living here. He's got a birthday today, and he's forgotten all about it. So we're going to remind him. We're going to give him a party.
McCann: Oh, is that a fact?
Meg: Tonight.
Goldberg: Tonight.
Meg: I'll put on my party dress.
Goldberg: And I'll get some bottles.
Meg: And I'll invite Lulu this afternoon. Oh, this is going to cheer Stanley up. It will. He's been down in the dumps lately.
Goldberg: We'll bring him out of himself.
Meg: I hope I look nice in my dress.
Goldberg: Madam, you'll look like a tulip.
Meg: What colour?
Goldberg: ~~Er—well, I'll~~ have to see the dress first.
McCann: Could I go up to my room?
Meg: Oh, I've put you both together. Do you mind being both together?
Goldberg: I don't mind. Do you mind, McCann?
McCann: No.
Meg: What time shall we have the party?
Goldberg: Nine o'clock.
McCann [*at the door*]: Is this the way?
Meg [*rising*]: I'll show you. If you don't mind coming upstairs.
Goldberg: With a tulip? It's a pleasure.

Meg and Goldberg exit laughing, followed by McCann. Stanley appears at the window. He enters by the back door. He goes to the door on the left, opens it and listens. Silence. He walks to the table. He stands. He sits, as Meg enters. She crosses and hangs her shopping bag on a hook. He lights a match and watches it burn.

Stanley: Who is it?
Meg: The two gentlemen.
Stanley: What two gentlemen?
Meg: The ones that were coming. I just took them to their room. They were thrilled with their room.
Stanley: They've come?
Meg: They're very nice, Stan.
Stanley: Why didn't they come last night?
Meg: They said the beds were wonderful.
Stanley: Who are they?
Meg [*sitting*]: They're very nice, Stanley.
Stanley: I said, who are they?
Meg: I've told you, the two gentlemen.
Stanley: I didn't think they'd come.

He rises and walks to the window.

Meg: They have. They were here when I came in.
Stanley: What do they want here?
Meg: They want to stay.
Stanley: How long for?
Meg: They didn't say.
Stanley [*turning*]: But why here? Why not somewhere else?
Meg: This house is on the list.
Stanley [*coming down*]: What are they called? What are their names?
Meg: Oh, Stanley, I can't remember.
Stanley: They told you, didn't they? Or didn't they tell you?
Meg: Yes, they. . . .
Stanley: Then what are they? Come on. Try to remember.
Meg: Why, Stan? Do you know them?
Stanley: How do I know if I know them until I know their names?
Meg: Well . . . he told me, I remember.
Stanley: Well?

She thinks.

Meg: Gold—something.
Stanley: Goldsomething?
Meg: Yes. Gold. . . .
Stanley: Yes?

MEG: Goldberg.
STANLEY: Goldberg?
MEG: That's right. That was one of them.

STANLEY *slowly sits at the table, left.*

Do you know them?

STANLEY *does not answer.*

Stan, they won't wake you up, I promise. I'll tell them they must be quiet.

STANLEY *sits still.*

They won't be here long, Stan. I'll still bring you up your early morning tea.

STANLEY *sits still.*

You mustn't be sad today. It's your birthday.

A pause.

STANLEY [*dumbly*]: Uh?
MEG: It's your birthday, Stan. I was going to keep it a secret until tonight.
STANLEY: No.
MEG: It is. I've brought you a present. [*She goes to the side-board, picks up the parcel, and places it on the table in front of him.*] Here. Go on. Open it.
STANLEY: What's this?
MEG: It's your present.
STANLEY: This isn't my birthday, Meg.
MEG: Of course it is. Open your present.

He stares at the parcel, slowly stands, and opens it. He takes out a boy's drum.

STANLEY [*flatly*]: It's a drum. A boy's drum.
MEG [*tenderly*]: It's because you haven't got a piano. [*He stares at her, then turns and walks towards the door, left.*] Aren't you going to give me a kiss? [*He turns sharply, and stops. He walks back towards her slowly. He stops at her chair, looking down upon her. Pause. His shoulders sag, he bends and kisses her on the cheek.*] There are some sticks in there. [STANLEY *looks into the parcel. He takes out two drumsticks. He taps them together. He looks at her.*]
STANLEY: Shall I put it round my neck?

She watches him, uncertainly. He hangs the drum around his neck, taps it gently with the sticks, then marches round the table, beating it regularly. MEG, *pleased, watches him. Still beating it regularly, he begins to go round the table a second time. Halfway round the beat becomes erratic, uncontrolled.* MEG *expresses dismay. He arrives at her chair, banging the drum, his face and the drumbeat now savage and possessed.*

CURTAIN

ACT II

MCCANN *is sitting at the table tearing a sheet of newspaper into five equal strips. It is evening. After a few moments* STANLEY *enters from the left. He stops upon seeing* MCCANN, *and watches him. He then walks towards the kitchen, stops, and speaks.*

STANLEY: Evening.
MCCANN: Evening.

Chuckles are heard from outside the back door, which is open.

STANLEY: Very warm tonight. [*Returns towards the back door, and back.*] Someone out there?

MCCANN *tears another length of paper.* STANLEY *goes into the kitchen and pours a glass of water. He drinks it looking through the hatch. He puts the glass down, comes out of the kitchen and walks quickly towards the door, left.* MCCANN *rises and intercepts him.*

MCCANN: I don't think we've met.
STANLEY: No, we haven't.
MCCANN: My name's McCann.
STANLEY: Staying here long?
MCCANN: Not long. What's your name?
STANLEY: Webber.
MCCANN: I'm glad to meet you, sir. [*He offers his hand.* STANLEY *takes it, and* MCCANN *holds the grip.*] Many happy returns of the day. [STANLEY *withdraws his hand. They face each other.*] Were you going out?
STANLEY: Yes.
MCCANN: On your birthday?
STANLEY: Yes. Why not?
MCCANN: But they're holding a party here for you tonight.
STANLEY: Oh really? That's unfortunate.
MCCANN: Ah no. It's very nice.

Voices from outside the back door.

STANLEY: I'm sorry. I'm not in the mood for a party tonight.
MCCANN: Oh, is that so? I'm sorry.
STANLEY: Yes, I'm going out to celebrate quietly, on my own.
MCCANN: That's a shame.

They stand.

STANLEY: Well, if you'd move out of my way—
MCCANN: But everything's laid on. The guests are expected.
STANLEY: Guests? What guests?
MCCANN: Myself for one. I had the honour of an invitation.

MCCANN *begins to whistle "The Mountains of Morne."*

STANLEY [*moving away*]: I wouldn't call it an honour, would you? It'll just be another booze-up.

STANLEY *joins* MCCANN *in whistling "The Mountains of Morne." During the next five lines the whistling is continuous, one whistling while the other speaks, and both whistling together.*

MCCANN: But it is an honour.
STANLEY: I'd say you were exaggerating.
MCCANN: Oh no. I'd say it was an honour.
STANLEY: I'd say that was plain stupid.
MCCANN: Ah no.

They stare at each other.

STANLEY: Who are the other guests?
MCCANN: A young lady.
STANLEY: Oh yes? And . . . ?
MCCANN: My friend.
STANLEY: Your friend?
MCCANN: That's right. It's all laid on.

STANLEY *walks round the table towards the door.* MCCANN *meets him.*

STANLEY: Excuse me.
MCCANN: Where are you going?
STANLEY: I want to go out.
MCCANN: Why don't you stay here?

STANLEY *moves away, to the right of the table.*

STANLEY: So you're down here on holiday?
MCCANN: A short one. [STANLEY *picks up a strip of paper.* MCCANN *moves in.*] Mind that.
STANLEY: What is it?
MCCANN: Mind it. Leave it.
STANLEY: I've got a feeling we've met before.
MCCANN: No we haven't.
STANLEY: Ever been anywhere near Maidenhead?
MCCANN: No.
STANLEY: There's a Fuller's teashop. I used to have my tea there.
MCCANN: I don't know it.
STANLEY: And a Boots Library. I seem to connect you with the High Street.
MCCANN: Yes?
STANLEY: A charming town, don't you think?
MCCANN: I don't know it.
STANLEY: Oh no. A quiet, thriving community. I was born and brought up there. I lived well away from the main road.
MCCANN: Yes?

Pause.

STANLEY: You're here on a short stay?
MCCANN: That's right.
STANLEY: You'll find it very bracing.
MCCANN: Do you find it bracing?
STANLEY: Me? No. But you will. [*He sits at the table.*] I like it here, but I'll be moving soon. Back home. I'll stay there too, this time. No place like home. [*He laughs.*] I wouldn't have left, but business calls. Business called, and I had to leave for a bit. You know how it is.
MCCANN [*sitting at the table, left*]: You in business?
STANLEY: No. I think I'll give it up. I've got a small private income, you see. I think I'll give it up. Don't like being away from home. I used to live very quietly—played records, that's about all. Everything delivered to the door. Then I started a little private business, in a small way, and it compelled me to come down here—kept me longer than I expected. You never get used to living in someone else's house. Don't you agree? I lived so quietly. You can only appreciate what you've had when things change. That's what they say, isn't it? Cigarette?
MCCANN: I don't smoke.

STANLEY *lights a cigarette. Voices from the back.*

STANLEY: Who's out there?
MCCANN: My friend and the man of the house.
STANLEY: You know what? To look at me, I bet you wouldn't think I'd led such a quiet life. The lines on my face, eh? It's the drink. Been drinking a bit down here. But what I mean is . . . you know how it is . . . away from your own . . . all wrong, of course . . . I'll be all right when I get back . . . but what I mean is, the way some people look at me you'd think I was a different person. I suppose I have changed, but I'm still the same man that I always was. I mean, you wouldn't think, to look at me, really . . . I mean, not really, that I was the sort of bloke to—to cause any trouble, would you? [MCCANN *looks at him.*] Do you know what I mean?

MCCANN: No. [*As* STANLEY *picks up a strip of paper.*] Mind that.
STANLEY [*quickly*]: Why are you down here?
MCCANN: A short holiday.
STANLEY: This is a ridiculous house to pick on. [*He rises.*]
MCCANN: Why?
STANLEY: Because it's not a boarding house. It never was.
MCCANN: Sure it is.
STANLEY: Why did you choose this house?
MCCANN: You know, sir, you're a bit depressed for a man on his birthday.
STANLEY [*sharply*]: Why do you call me sir?
MCCANN: You don't like it?
STANLEY [*to the table*]: Listen. Don't call me sir.
MCCANN: I won't, if you don't like it.
STANLEY [*moving away*]: No. Anyway, this isn't my birthday.
MCCANN: No?
STANLEY: No. It's not till next month.
MCCANN: Not according to the lady.
STANLEY: Her? She's crazy. Round the bend.
MCCANN: That's a terrible thing to say.
STANLEY [*to the table*]: Haven't you found that out yet? There's a lot you don't know. I think someone's leading you up the garden path.
MCCANN: Who would do that?
STANLEY [*leaning across the table*]: That woman is mad!
MCCANN: That's slander.
STANLEY: And you don't know what you're doing.
MCCANN: Your cigarette is near that paper.

Voices from the back.

STANLEY: Where the hell are they? [*Stubbing his cigarette.*] Why don't they come in? What are they doing out there?
MCCANN: You want to steady yourself.

STANLEY *crosses to him and grips his arm.*

STANLEY [*urgently*]: Look—
MCCANN: Don't touch me.
STANLEY: Look. Listen a minute.
MCCANN: Let go my arm.
STANLEY: Look. Sit down a minute.
MCCANN [*savagely, hitting his arm*]: Don't do that!

STANLEY *backs across the stage, holding his arm.*

STANLEY: Listen. You knew what I was talking about before, didn't you?
MCCANN: I don't know what you're at at all.
STANLEY: It's a mistake! Do you understand?
MCCANN: You're in a bad state, man.
STANLEY [*whispering, advancing*]: Has he told you anything? Do you know what you're here for? Tell me. You needn't be frightened of me. Or hasn't he told you?
MCCANN: Told me what?
STANLEY [*hissing*]: I've explained to you, damn you, that all those years I lived in Basingstoke I never stepped outside the door.
MCCANN: You know, I'm flabbergasted with you.
STANLEY [*reasonably*]: Look. You look an honest man. You're being made a fool of, that's all. You understand? Where do you come from?
MCCANN: Where do you think?
STANLEY: I know Ireland very well. I've many friends there. I love that country and I admire and trust its people. I trust them. They respect the truth and they have a sense of humour. I think their policemen are wonderful. I've been there. I've never seen such sunsets. What about coming out to have a drink with me? There's a pub down the road serves draught Guinness. Very difficult to get in these parts— [*He breaks off. The voices draw nearer.* GOLDBERG *and* PETEY *enter from the back door.*]
GOLDBERG [*as he enters*]: A mother in a million. [*He sees* STANLEY.] Ah.
PETEY: Oh hullo, Stan. You haven't met Stanley, have you, Mr Goldberg?
GOLDBERG: I haven't had the pleasure.
PETEY: Oh well, this is Mr Goldberg, this is Mr Webber.
GOLDBERG: Pleased to meet you.
PETEY: We were just getting a bit of air in the garden.
GOLDBERG: I was telling Mr Boles about my old mum. What days. [*He sits at the table, right.*] Yes. When I was a youngster, of a Friday, I used to go for a walk down the canal with a girl who lived down my road. A beautiful girl. What a voice that bird had! A nightingale, my word of honour. Good? Pure? She wasn't a Sunday school teacher for nothing. Anyway, I'd leave her with a little kiss on the cheek—I never took liberties—we weren't like the young men these days in those days. We knew the meaning of respect. So I'd give her a peck and I'd bowl back home. Humming away I'd be, past the children's playground. I'd tip my hat to the toddlers, I'd give a helping hand to a couple of stray dogs, everything came natural. I can see it like yesterday. The sun falling behind the dog stadium. Ah! [*He leans back contentedly.*]
MCCANN: Like behind the town hall.
GOLDBERG: What town hall?
MCCANN: In Carrikmacross.
GOLDBERG: There's no comparison. Up the street, into my gate, inside the door, home. "Simey!" my old

mum used to shout, "quick before it gets cold." And there on the table what would I see? The nicest piece of gefilte fish you could wish to find on a plate.

McCANN: I thought your name was Nat.

GOLDBERG: She called me Simey.

PETEY: Yes, we all remember our childhood.

GOLDBERG: Too true. Eh, Mr Webber, what do you say? Childhood. Hot water bottles. Hot milk. Pancakes. Soap suds. What a life.

Pause.

PETEY [*rising from the table*]: Well, I'll have to be off.

GOLDBERG: Off?

PETEY: It's my chess night.

GOLDBERG: You're not staying for the party?

PETEY: No, I'm sorry, Stan. I didn't know about it till just now. And we've got a game on. I'll try and get back early.

GOLDBERG: We'll save some drink for you, all right? Oh, that reminds me. You'd better go and collect the bottles.

McCANN: Now?

GOLDBERG: Of course, now. Time's getting on. Round the corner, remember? Mention my name.

PETEY: I'm coming your way.

GOLDBERG: Beat him quick and come back, Mr Boles.

PETEY: Do my best. See you later, Stan.

PETEY *and* McCANN *go out, left.* STANLEY *moves to the centre.*

GOLDBERG: A warm night.

STANLEY [*turning*]: Don't mess me about!

GOLDBERG: I beg your pardon?

STANLEY [*moving downstage*]: I'm afraid there's been a mistake. We're booked out. Your room is taken. Mrs Boles forgot to tell you. You'll have to find somewhere else.

GOLDBERG: Are you the manager here?

STANLEY: That's right.

GOLDBERG: Is it a good game?

STANLEY: I run the house. I'm afraid you and your friend will have to find other accommodation.

GOLDBERG [*rising*]: Oh, I forgot, I must congratulate you on your birthday. [*Offering his hand.*] Congratulations.

STANLEY [*ignoring hand*]: Perhaps you're deaf.

GOLDBERG: No, what makes you think that? As a matter of fact, every single one of my senses is at its peak. Not bad going, eh? For a man past fifty. But a birthday, I always feel, is a great occasion, taken too much for granted these days. What a thing to celebrate—birth! Like getting up in the morning. Marvellous! Some people don't like the idea of getting up in the morning. I've heard them. Getting up in the morning, they say, what is it? Your skin's crabby, you need a shave, your eyes are full of muck, your mouth is like a boghouse, the palms of your hands are full of sweat, your nose is clogged up, your feet stink, what are you but a corpse waiting to be washed? Whenever I hear that point of view I feel cheerful. Because I know what it is to wake up with the sun shining, to the sound of the lawnmower, all the little birds, the smell of the grass, church bells, tomato juice—

STANLEY: Get out.

Enter McCANN, *with bottles.*

Get that drink out. These are unlicensed premises.

GOLDBERG: You're in a terrible humour today, Mr Webber. And on your birthday too, with the good lady getting her strength up to give you a party.

McCANN *puts the bottles on the sideboard.*

STANLEY: I told you to get those bottles out.

GOLDBERG: Mr Webber, sit down a minute.

STANLEY: Let me—just make this clear. You don't bother me. To me, you're nothing but a dirty joke. But I have a responsibility towards the people in this house. They've been down here too long. They've lost their sense of smell. I haven't. And nobody's going to take advantage of them while I'm here. [*A little less forceful.*] Anyway, this house isn't your cup of tea. There's nothing here for you, from any angle, any angle. So why don't you just go, without any more fuss?

GOLDBERG: Mr Webber, sit down.

STANLEY: It's no good starting any kind of trouble.

GOLDBERG: Sit down.

STANLEY: Why should I?

GOLDBERG: If you want to know the truth, Webber, you're beginning to get on my breasts.

STANLEY: Really? Well, that's—

GOLDBERG: Sit down.

STANLEY: No.

GOLDBERG *sighs, and sits at the table right.*

GOLDBERG: McCann.

McCANN: Nat?

GOLDBERG: Ask him to sit down.

McCANN: Yes, Nat. [McCANN *moves to* STANLEY.] Do you mind sitting down?

STANLEY: Yes, I do mind.

McCANN: Yes now, but—it'd be better if you did.

STANLEY: Why don't you sit down?

McCANN: No, not me—you.

STANLEY: No thanks.

Pause.

MCCANN: Nat.
GOLDBERG: What?
MCCANN: He won't sit down.
GOLDBERG: Well, ask him.
MCCANN: I've asked him.
GOLDBERG: Ask him again.
MCCANN [*to* STANLEY]: Sit down.
STANLEY: Why?
MCCANN: You'd be more comfortable.
STANLEY: So would you.

Pause.

MCCANN: All right. If you will I will.
STANLEY: You first.

MCCANN *slowly sits at the table, left.*

MCCANN. Well?
STANLEY: Right. Now you've both had a rest you can get out!
MCCANN [*rising*]: That's a dirty trick! I'll kick the shite out of him!
GOLDBERG [*rising*]: No! I have stood up.
MCCANN: Sit down again!
GOLDBERG: Once I'm up I'm up.
STANLEY: Same here.
MCCANN [*moving to* STANLEY]: You've made Mr Goldberg stand up.
STANLEY [*his voice rising*]: It'll do him good!
MCCANN: Get in that seat.
GOLDBERG: McCann.
MCCANN: Get down in that seat!
GOLDBERG [*crossing to him*]: Webber. [*Quietly.*] SIT DOWN. [*Silence.* STANLEY *begins to whistle "The Mountains of Morne." He strolls casually to the chair at the table. They watch him. He stops whistling. Silence. He sits.*]
STANLEY: You'd better be careful.
GOLDBERG: Webber, what were you doing yesterday?
STANLEY: Yesterday?
GOLDBERG: And the day before. What did you do the day before that?
STANLEY: What do you mean?
GOLDBERG: Why are you wasting everybody's time, Webber? Why are you getting in everybody's way?
STANLEY: Me? What are you—
GOLDBERG: I'm telling you, Webber. You're a washout. Why are you getting on everybody's wick? Why are you driving that old lady off her conk?
MCCANN: He likes to do it!
GOLDBERG: Why do you behave so badly, Webber? Why do you force that old man out to play chess?
STANLEY: Me?
GOLDBERG: Why do you treat that young lady like a leper? She's not the leper, Webber!
STANLEY: What the—
GOLDBERG: What did you wear last week, Webber? Where do you keep your suits?
MCCANN: Why did you leave the organization?
GOLDBERG: What would your old mum say, Webber?
MCCANN: Why did you betray us?
GOLDBERG: You hurt me, Webber. You're playing a dirty game.
MCCANN: That's a Black and Tan fact.
GOLDBERG: Who does he think he is?
MCCANN: Who do you think you are?
STANLEY: You're on the wrong horse.
GOLDBERG: When did you come to this place?
STANLEY: Last year.
GOLDBERG: Where did you come from?
STANLEY: Somewhere else.
GOLDBERG: Why did you come here?
STANLEY: My feet hurt!
GOLDBERG: Why did you stay?
STANLEY: I had a headache!
GOLDBERG: Did you take anything for it?
STANLEY: Yes.
GOLDBERG: What?
STANLEY: Fruit salts!
GOLDBERG: Enos or Andrews?
STANLEY: En— An—
GOLDBERG: Did you stir properly? Did they fizz?
STANLEY: Now, now, wait, you—
GOLDBERG: Did they fizz? Did they fizz or didn't they fizz?
MCCANN: He doesn't know!
GOLDBERG: You don't know. When did you last have a bath?
STANLEY: I have one every—
GOLDBERG: Don't lie.
MCCANN: You betrayed the organization. I know him!
STANLEY: You don't!
GOLDBERG: What can you see without your glasses?
STANLEY: Anything.
GOLDBERG: Take off his glasses.

MCCANN *snatches his glasses and as* STANLEY *rises, reaching for them, takes his chair downstage centre, below the table,* STANLEY *stumbling as he follows.* STANLEY *clutches the chair and stays bent over it.*

Webber, you're a fake. [*They stand on each side of the chair.*] When did you last wash up a cup?
STANLEY: The Christmas before last.
GOLDBERG: Where?
STANLEY: Lyons Corner House.
GOLDBERG: Which one?
STANLEY: Marble Arch.

GOLDBERG: Where was your wife?
STANLEY: In—
GOLDBERG: Answer.
STANLEY [*turning, crouched*]: What wife?
GOLDBERG: What have you done with your wife?
MCCANN: He's killed his wife!
GOLDBERG: Why did you kill your wife?
STANLEY [*sitting, his back to the audience*]: What wife?
MCCANN: How did he kill her?
GOLDBERG: How did you kill her?
MCCANN: You throttled her.
GOLDBERG: With arsenic.
MCCANN: There's your man!
GOLDBERG: Where's your old mum?
STANLEY: In the sanatorium.
MCCANN: Yes!
GOLDBERG: Why did you never get married?
MCCANN: She was waiting at the porch.
GOLDBERG: You skeddadled from the wedding.
MCCANN: He left her in the lurch.
GOLDBERG: You left her in the pudding club.
MCCANN: She was waiting at the church.
GOLDBERG: Webber! Why did you change your name?
STANLEY: I forgot the other one.
GOLDBERG: What's your name now?
STANLEY: Joe Soap.
GOLDBERG: You stink of sin.
MCCANN: I can smell it.
GOLDBERG: Do you recognise an external force?
STANLEY: What?
GOLDBERG: Do you recognise an external force?
MCCANN: That's the question!
GOLDBERG: Do you recognise an external force, responsible for you, suffering for you?
STANLEY: It's late.
GOLDBERG: Late! Late enough! When did you last pray?
MCCANN: He's sweating!
GOLDBERG: When did you last pray?
MCCANN: He's sweating!
GOLDBERG: Is the number 846 possible or necessary?
STANLEY: Neither.
GOLDBERG: Wrong! Is the number 846 possible or necessary?
STANLEY: Both.
GOLDBERG: Wrong! It's necessary but not possible.
STANLEY: Both.
GOLDBERG: Wrong! Why do you think the number 846 is necessarily possible?
STANLEY: Must be.
GOLDBERG: Wrong! It's only necessarily necessary! We admit possibility only after we grant necessity. It is possible because necessary but by no means necessary through possibility. The possibility can only be assumed after the proof of necessity.
MCCANN: Right!
GOLDBERG: Right? Of course right! We're right and you're wrong, Webber, all along the line.
MCCANN: All along the line!
GOLDBERG: Where is your lechery leading you?
MCCANN: You'll pay for this.
GOLDBERG: You stuff yourself with dry toast.
MCCANN: You contaminate womankind.
GOLDBERG: Why don't you pay the rent?
MCCANN: Mother defiler!
GOLDBERG: Why do you pick your nose?
MCCANN: I demand justice!
GOLDBERG: What's your trade?
MCCANN: What about Ireland?
GOLDBERG: What's your trade?
STANLEY: I play the piano.
GOLDBERG: How many fingers do you use?
STANLEY: No hands!
GOLDBERG: No society would touch you. Not even a building society.
MCCANN: You're a traitor to the cloth.
GOLDBERG: What do you use for pyjamas?
STANLEY: Nothing.
GOLDBERG: You verminate the sheet of your birth.
MCCANN: What about the Albigensenist heresy?
GOLDBERG: Who watered the wicket in Melbourne?
MCCANN: What about the blessed Oliver Plunkett?
GOLDBERG: Speak up, Webber. Why did the chicken cross the road?
STANLEY: He wanted to—he wanted to—he wanted to. . . .
MCCANN: He doesn't know!
GOLDBERG: Why did the chicken cross the road?
STANLEY: He wanted to—he wanted to. . . .
GOLDBERG: Why did the chicken cross the road?
STANLEY: He wanted. . . .
MCCANN: He doesn't know. He doesn't know which came first!
GOLDBERG: Which came first?
MCCANN: Chicken? Egg? Which came first?
GOLDBERG AND MCCANN: Which came first? Which came first? Which came first?

STANLEY *screams.*

GOLDBERG: He doesn't know. Do you know your own face?
MCCANN: Wake him up. Stick a needle in his eye.
GOLDBERG: You're a plague, Webber. You're an overthrow.
MCCANN: You're what's left!
GOLDBERG: But we've got the answer to you. We can sterilise you.
MCCANN: What about Drogheda?
GOLDBERG: Your bite is dead. Only your pong is left.
MCCANN: You betrayed our land.
GOLDBERG: You betray our breed.

MCCANN: Who are you, Webber?
GOLDBERG: What makes you think you exist?
MCCANN: You're dead.
GOLDBERG: You're dead. You can't live, you can't think, you can't love. You're dead. You're a plague gone bad. There's no juice in you. You're nothing but an odour!

Silence. They stand over him. He is crouched in the chair. He looks up slowly and kicks GOLDBERG *in the stomach.* GOLDBERG *falls.* STANLEY *stands.* MCCANN *seizes a chair and lifts it above his head.* STANLEY *seizes a chair and covers his head with it.* MCCANN *and* STANLEY *circle.*

GOLDBERG: Steady, McCann.
STANLEY [*circling*]: Uuuuuhhhhh!
MCCANN: Right, Judas.
GOLDBERG [*rising*]: Steady, McCann.
MCCANN: Come on!
STANLEY: Uuuuuuuhhhhh!
MCCANN: He's sweating.
STANLEY: Uuuuuhhhhh!
GOLDBERG: Easy, McCann.
MCCANN: The bastard sweatpig is sweating.

A loud drumbeat off left, descending the stairs. GOLDBERG *takes the chair from* STANLEY. *They put the chairs down. They stop still. Enter* MEG, *in evening dress, holding sticks and drum.*

MEG: I brought the drum down. I'm dressed for the party.
GOLDBERG: Wonderful.
MEG: You like my dress?
GOLDBERG: Wonderful. Out of this world.
MEG: I know. My father gave it to me. [*Placing drum on table.*] Doesn't it make a beautiful noise?
GOLDBERG: It's a fine piece of work. Maybe Stan'll play us a little tune afterwards.
MEG: Oh yes. Will you, Stan?
STANLEY: Could I have my glasses?
GOLDBERG: Ah yes. [*He holds his hand out to* MCCANN. MCCANN *passes him his glasses.*] Here they are. [*He holds them out for* STANLEY, *who reaches for them.*] Here they are. [STANLEY *takes them.*] Now. What have we got here? Enough to scuttle a liner. We've got four bottles of Scotch and one bottle of Irish.
MEG: Oh, Mr Goldberg, what should I drink?
GOLDBERG: Glasses, glasses first. Open the Scotch, McCann.
MEG [*at the sideboard*]: Here's my very best glasses in here.
MCCANN: I don't drink Scotch.
GOLDBERG: You've got the Irish.
MEG [*bringing the glasses*]: Here they are.
GOLDBERG: Good. Mrs Boles, I think Stanley should pour the toast, don't you?
MEG: Oh yes. Come on, Stanley. [STANLEY *walks slowly to the table.*] Do you like my dress, Mr Goldberg?
GOLDBERG: It's out on it's own. Turn yourself round a minute. I used to be in the business. Go on, walk up there.
MEG: Oh no.
GOLDBERG: Don't be shy. [*He slaps her bottom.*]
MEG: Oooh!
GOLDBERG: Walk up the boulevard. Let's have a look at you. What a carriage. What's your opinion, McCann? Like a Countess, nothing less. Madam, now turn about and promenade to the kitchen. What a deportment!
MCCANN [*to* STANLEY]: You can pour my Irish too.
GOLDBERG: You look like a Gladiola.
MEG: Stan, what about my dress?
GOLDBERG: One for the lady, one for the lady. Now madam—your glass.
MEG: Thank you.
GOLDBERG: Lift your glasses, ladies and gentlemen. We'll drink a toast.
MEG: Lulu isn't here.
GOLDBERG: It's past the hour. Now—who's going to propose the toast? Mrs Boles, it can only be you.
MEG: Me?
GOLDBERG: Who else?
MEG: But what do I say?
GOLDBERG: Say what you feel. What you honestly feel. [MEG *looks uncertain.*] It's Stanley's birthday. Your Stanley. Look at him. Look at him and it'll come. Wait a minute, the light's too strong. Let's have proper lighting. McCann, have you got your torch?
MCCANN [*bringing a small torch from his pocket*]: Here.
GOLDBERG: Switch out the light and put on your torch. [MCCANN *goes to the door, switches off the light, comes back, shines the torch on* MEG. *Outside the window there is still a faint light.*] Not on the lady, on the gentleman! You must shine it on the birthday boy. [MCCANN *shines the torch in* STANLEY'*s face.*] Now, Mrs Boles, it's all yours.

Pause.

MEG: I don't know what to say.
GOLDBERG: Look at him. Just look at him.
MEG: Isn't the light in his eyes?
GOLDBERG: No, no. Go on.
MEG: Well—It's very, very nice to be here tonight, in my house, and I want to propose a toast to Stanley, because it's his birthday, and he's lived here for a long while now, and he's my Stanley now. And I think he's a good boy, although sometimes he's bad. [*An appreciative laugh from*

GOLDBERG.] And he's the only Stanley I know, and I know him better than all the world, although he doesn't think so. [*"Hear—hear" from* GOLDBERG.] Well, I could cry because I'm so happy, having him here and not gone away, on his birthday, and there isn't anything I wouldn't do for him, and all you good people here tonight. . . . [*She sobs.*]

GOLDBERG: Beautiful! A beautiful speech. Put the light on, McCann. [MCCANN *goes to the door.* STANLEY *remains still.*] That was a lovely toast. [*The light goes on.* LULU *enters from the door, left.* GOLDBERG *comforts* MEG.] Buck up now. Come on, smile at the birdy. That's better. Ah, look who's here.

MEG: Lulu.

GOLDBERG: How do you do, Lulu? I'm Nat Goldberg.

LULU: Hallo.

GOLDBERG: Stanley, a drink for your guest. You just missed the toast, my dear, and what a toast.

LULU: Did I?

GOLDBERG: Stanley, a drink for your guest. Stanley. [STANLEY *hands a glass to* LULU.] Right. Now raise your glasses. Everyone standing up? No, not you, Stanley. You must sit down.

MCCANN: Yes, that's right. He must sit down.

GOLDBERG: You don't mind sitting down a minute? We're going to drink to you.

MEG: Come on!

LULU: Come on!

STANLEY *sits in a chair at the table.*

GOLDBERG: Right. Now Stanley's sat down. [*Taking the stage.*] Well, I want to say first that I've never been so touched to the heart as by the toast we've just heard. How often, in this day and age, do you come across real, true warmth? Once in a lifetime. Until a few minutes ago, ladies and gentlemen, I, like all of you, was asking the same question. What's happened to the love, the bonhomie, the unashamed expression of affection of the day before yesterday, that our mums taught us in the nursery?

MCCANN: Gone with the wind.

GOLDBERG: That's what I thought, until today. I believe in a good laugh, a day's fishing, a bit of gardening. I was very proud of my old greenhouse, made out of my own spit and faith. That's the sort of man I am. Not size but quality. A little Austin, tea in Fullers, a library book from Boots, and I'm satisfied. But just now, I say just now, the lady of the house said her piece and I for one am knocked over by the sentiments she expressed. Lucky is the man who's at the receiving end, that's what I say. [*Pause.*] How can I put it to you? We all wander on our tod through this world. It's a lonely pillow to kip on. Right!

LULU [*admiringly*]: Right!

GOLDBERG: Agreed. But tonight, Lulu, McCann, we've known a great fortune. We've heard a lady extend the sum total of her devotion, in all its pride, plume and peacock, to a member of her own living race. Stanley, my heartfelt congratulations. I wish you, on behalf of us all, a happy birthday. I'm sure you've never been a prouder man than you are today. Mazoltov! And may we only meet at Simchahs! [LULU *and* MEG *applaud.*] Turn out the light, McCann, while we drink the toast.

LULU: That was a wonderful speech.

MCCANN *switches out the light, comes back and shines the torch in* STANLEY'*s face. The light outside the window is fainter.*

GOLDBERG: Lift your glasses. Stanley—happy birthday.

MCCANN: Happy birthday.

LULU: Happy birthday.

MEG: Many happy returns of the day, Stan.

GOLDBERG: And well over the fast.

They all drink.

MEG [*kissing him*]: Oh, Stanny. . . .

GOLDBERG: Lights!

MCCANN: Right! [*He switches on the lights.*]

MEG: Clink my glass, Stan.

LULU: Mr Goldberg—

GOLDBERG. Call me Nat.

MEG [*to* MCCANN]: You clink my glass.

LULU [*to* GOLDBERG]: You're empty. Let me fill you up.

GOLDBERG: It's a pleasure.

LULU: You're a marvellous speaker, Nat, you know that? Where did you learn to speak like that?

GOLDBERG: You liked it, eh?

LULU: Oh yes!

GOLDBERG: Well, my first chance to stand up and give a lecture was at the Ethical Hall, Bayswater. A wonderful opportunity. I'll never forget it. They were all there that night. Charlotte Street was empty. Of course, that's a good while ago.

LULU: What did you speak about?

GOLDBERG: The Necessary and the Possible. It went like a bomb. Since then I always speak at weddings.

STANLEY *is still.* GOLDBERG *sits left of the table.* MEG *joins* MCCANN *downstage, right,* LULU *is downstage, left.* MCCANN *pours more Irish from the bottle, which he carries, into his glass.*

MEG: Let's have some of yours.

MCCANN: In that?

MEG: Yes.
MCCANN: Are you used to mixing them?
MEG: No.
MCCANN: Give me your glass.

MEG sits on a shoe-box, downstage, right. LULU, at the table, pours more drink for GOLDBERG and herself, and gives GOLDBERG his glass.

GOLDBERG: Thank you.
MEG [*to* MCCANN]: Do you think I should?
GOLDBERG: Lulu, you're a big bouncy girl. Come and sit on my lap.
MCCANN: Why not?
LULU: Do you think I should?
GOLDBERG: Try it.
MEG [*sipping*]: Very nice.
LULU: I'll bounce up to the ceiling.
MCCANN: I don't know how you can mix that stuff.
GOLDBERG: Take a chance.
MEG [*to* MCCANN]: Sit down on this stool.

LULU sits on GOLDBERG's lap.

MCCANN: This?
GOLDBERG: Comfortable?
LULU: Yes thanks.
MCCANN [*sitting*]: It's comfortable.
GOLDBERG: You know, there's a lot in your eyes.
LULU: And in yours, too.
GOLDBERG: Do you think so?
LULU [*giggling*]: Go on!
MCCANN [*to* MEG]: Where'd you get it?
MEG: My father gave it to me.
LULU: I didn't know I was going to meet you here tonight.
MCCANN [*to* MEG]: Ever been to Carrikmacross?
MEG [*drinking*]: I've been to King's Cross.
LULU: You came right out of the blue, you know that?
GOLDBERG [*as she moves*]: Mind how you go. You're cracking a rib.
MEG [*standing*]: I want to dance! [LULU *and* GOLDBERG *look into each other's eyes.* MCCANN *drinks.* MEG *crosses to* STANLEY.] Stanley. Dance. [STANLEY *sits still.* MEG *dances round the room alone, then comes back to* MCCANN, *who fills her glass. She sits.*]
LULU [*to* GOLDBERG]: Shall I tell you something?
GOLDBERG: What?
LULU: I trust you.
GOLDBERG [*lifting his glass*]: Gesundheit.
LULU: Have you got a wife?
GOLDBERG: I had a wife. What a wife. Listen to this. Friday, of an afternoon, I'd take myself for a little constitutional, down over the park. Eh, do me a favour, just sit on the table a minute, will you? [LULU *sits on the table. He stretches and continues.*] A little constitutional. I'd say hullo to the little boys, the little girls—I never made distinctions—and then back I'd go, back to my bungalow with the flat roof. "Simey," my wife used to shout, "quick, before it gets cold!" And there on the table what would I see? The nicest piece of rollmop and pickled cucumber you could wish to find on a plate.
LULU: I thought your name was Nat.
GOLDBERG: She called me Simey.
LULU: I bet you were a good husband.
GOLDBERG: You should have seen her funeral.
LULU: Why?
GOLDBERG [*draws in his breath and wags head*]: What a funeral.
MEG [*to* MCCANN]: My father was going to take me to Ireland once. But then he went away by himself.
LULU [*to* GOLDBERG]: Do you think you knew me when I was a little girl?
GOLDBERG: Were you a nice little girl?
LULU: I was.
MEG: I don't know if he went to Ireland.
GOLDBERG: Maybe I played piggy-back with you.
LULU: Maybe you did.
MEG: He didn't take me.
GOLDBERG: Or pop goes the weasel.
LULU: Is that a game?
GOLDBERG: Sure it's a game!
MCCANN: Why didn't he take you to Ireland?
LULU: You're tickling me!
GOLDBERG: You should worry.
LULU: I've always liked older men. They can soothe you.

They embrace.

MCCANN: I know a place. Roscrea. Mother Nolan's.
MEG: There was a night-light in my room, when I was a little girl.
MCCANN: One time I stayed there all night with the boys. Singing and drinking all night.
MEG: And my Nanny used to sit up with me, and sing songs to me.
MCCANN: And a plate of fry in the morning. Now where am I?
MEG: My little room was pink. I had a pink carpet and pink curtains, and I had musical boxes all over the room. And they played me to sleep. And my father was a very big doctor. That's why I never had any complaints. I was cared for, and I had little sisters and brothers in other rooms, all different colours.
MCCANN: Tullamore, where are you?
MEG [*to* MCCANN]: Give us a drop more.

MCCANN [*filling her glass and singing*]: Glorio, Glorio, to the bold Fenian men!
MEG: Oh, what a lovely voice.
GOLDBERG: Give us a song, McCann.
LULU: A love song!
MCCANN [*reciting*]: The night that poor Paddy was stretched, the boys they all paid him a visit.
GOLDBERG: A love song!
MCCANN [*in a full voice, sings*]:

Oh, the Garden of Eden has vanished, they say,
But I know the lie of it still.
Just turn to the left at the foot of Ben Clay
And stop when halfway to Coote Hill.
It's there you will find it, I know sure enough,
And it's whispering over to me:
Come back, Paddy Reilly, to Bally-James-Duff,
Come home, Paddy Reilly, to me!

LULU [*to* GOLDBERG]: You're the dead image of the first man I ever loved.
GOLDBERG: It goes without saying.
MEG [*rising*]: I want to play a game!
GOLDBERG: A game?
LULU: What game?
MEG: Any game.
LULU [*jumping up*]: Yes, let's play a game.
GOLDBERG: What game?
MCCANN: Hide and seek.
LULU: Blind man's buff.
MEG: Yes!
GOLDBERG: You want to play blind man's buff?
LULU AND MEG: Yes!
GOLDBERG: All right. Blind man's buff. Come on! Everyone up! [*Rising.*] McCann. Stanley—Stanley!
MEG: Stanley. Up.
GOLDBERG: What's the matter with him?
MEG [*bending over him*]: Stanley, were going to play a game. Oh, come on, don't be sulky, Stan.
LULU: Come on.

STANLEY *rises.* MCCANN *rises.*

GOLDBERG: Right! Now—who's going to be blind first?
LULU: Mrs Boles.
MEG: Not me.
GOLDBERG: Of course you.
MEG: Who, me?
LULU [*taking her scarf from her neck*]: Here you are.
MCCANN: How do you play this game?
LULU [*tying her scarf round* MEG's *eyes*]: Haven't you ever played blind man's buff? Keep still, Mrs Boles. You mustn't be touched. But you can't move after she's blind. You must stay where you are after she's blind. And if she touches you then you become blind. Turn round. How many fingers am I holding up?
MEG: I can't see.
LULU: Right.
GOLDBERG: Right! Everyone move about. McCann. Stanley. Now stop. Now still. Off you go!

STANLEY *is downstage, right,* MEG *moves about the room.* GOLDBERG *fondles* LULU *at arm's length.* MEG *touches* MCCANN.

MEG: Caught you!
LULU: Take off your scarf.
MEG: What lovely hair!
LULU [*untying the scarf*]: There.
MEG: It's you!
GOLDBERG: Put it on, McCann.
LULU [*trying it on* MCCANN]: There. Turn round. How many fingers am I holding up?
MCCANN: I don't know.
GOLDBERG: Right! Everyone move about. Right. Stop! Still!

MCCANN *begins to move.*

MEG: Oh, this is lovely!
GOLDBERG: Quiet! Tch, tch, tch. Now—all move again. Stop! Still!

MCCANN *moves about.* GOLDBERG *fondles* LULU *at arm's length.* MCCANN *draws near* STANLEY. *He stretches his arm and touches* STANLEY'S *glasses.*

MEG: It's Stanley!
GOLDBERG [*to* LULU]: Enjoying the game?
MEG: It's your turn, Stan.

MCCANN *takes off the scarf.*

MCCANN [*to* STANLEY]: I'll take your glasses.

MCCANN *takes* STANLEY'S *glasses.*

MEG: Give me the scarf.
GOLDBERG [*holding* LULU]: Tie his scarf, Mrs Boles.
MEG: That's what I'm doing. [*To* STANLEY.] Can you see my nose?
GOLDBERG: He can't. Ready? Right! Everyone move. Stop! And still!

STANLEY *stands blindfold.* MCCANN *backs slowly across the stage to the left. He breaks* STANLEY'S *glasses, snapping the frames.* MEG *is downstage, left,* LULU *and* GOLDBERG *upstage centre, close together.* STANLEY *begins to move, very slowly, across the stage to the left.* MCCANN *picks up the drum and places it sideways in* STANLEY'S *path.*

STANLEY walks into the drum and falls over with his foot caught in it.

MEG: Ooh!
GOLDBERG: Sssh!

STANLEY rises. He begins to move towards MEG, dragging the drum on his foot. He reaches her and stops. His hands move towards her and they reach her throat. He begins to strangle her. MCCANN and GOLDBERG rush forward and throw him off.

BLACKOUT

There is now no light at all through the window. The stage is in darkness.

LULU: The lights!
GOLDBERG: What's happened?
LULU: The lights!
MCCANN: Wait a minute.
GOLDBERG: Where is he?
MCCANN: Let go of me!
GOLDBERG: Who's this?
LULU: Someone's touching me!
MCCANN: Where is he?
MEG: Why has the light gone out?
GOLDBERG: Where's your torch? [*MCCANN shines the torch in GOLDBERG's face.*] Not on me! [*MCCANN shifts the torch. It is knocked from his hand and falls. It goes out.*]
MCCANN: My torch!
LULU: Oh God!
GOLDBERG: Where's your torch? Pick up your torch!
MCCANN: I can't find it.
LULU: Hold me. Hold me.
GOLDBERG: Get down on your knees. Help him find the torch.
LULU: I can't.
MCCANN: It's gone.
MEG: Why has the light gone out?
GOLDBERG: Everyone quiet! Help him find the torch.

Silence. Grunts from MCCANN and GOLDBERG on their knees. Suddenly there is a sharp, sustained rat-a-tat with a stick on the side of the drum from the back of the room. Silence. Whimpers from LULU.

GOLDBERG: Over here. McCann!
MCCANN: Here.
GOLDBERG: Come to me, come to me. Easy. Over there.

GOLDBERG and MCCANN move up left of the table. STANLEY moves down right of the table. LULU suddenly perceives him moving towards her, screams and faints.

GOLDBERG and MCCANN turn and stumble against each other.

GOLDBERG: What is it?
MCCANN: Who's that?
GOLDBERG: What is it?

In the darkness STANLEY picks up LULU and places her on *the table.*

MEG: It's Lulu!

GOLDBERG and MCCANN move downstage, right.

GOLDBERG: Where is she?
MCCANN: She fell.
GOLDBERG: Where?
MCCANN: About here.
GOLDBERG: Help me pick her up.
MCCANN [*moving downstage, left*]: I can't find her.
GOLDBERG: She must be somewhere.
MCCANN: She's not here.
GOLDBERG [*moving downstage, left*]: She must be.
MCCANN: She's gone.

MCCANN finds the torch on the floor, shines it on the table and STANLEY. LULU is lying spread-eagled on the table, STANLEY bent over her. STANLEY, as soon as the torchlight hits him, begins to giggle. GOLDBERG and MCCANN move towards him. He backs, giggling, the torch on his face. They follow him upstage, left. He backs against the hatch, giggling. The torch draws closer. His giggle rises and grows as he flattens himself against the wall. Their figures converge upon him.

CURTAIN

ACT III

The next morning. PETEY enters, left, with a newspaper and sits at the table. He begins to read. MEG's voice comes through the kitchen hatch.

MEG: Is that you, Stan? [*Pause.*] Stanny?
PETEY: Yes?
MEG: Is that you?
PETEY: It's me.
MEG [*appearing at the hatch*]: Oh, it's you. I've run out of cornflakes.
PETEY: Well, what else have you got?
MEG: Nothing.
PETEY: Nothing?
MEG: Just a minute. [*She leaves the hatch and enters by the kitchen door.*] You got your paper?
PETEY: Yes.

MEG: Is it good?
PETEY: Not bad.
MEG: The two gentlemen had the last of the fry this morning.
PETEY: Oh, did they?
MEG: There's some tea in the pot though. [*She pours tea for him.*] I'm going out shopping in a minute. Get you something nice. I've got a splitting headache.
PETEY [*reading*]: You slept like a log last night.
MEG: Did I?
PETEY: Dead out.
MEG: I must have been tired. [*She looks about the room and sees the broken drum in the fireplace.*] Oh, look. [*She rises and picks it up.*] The drum's broken. [PETEY *looks up.*] Why is it broken?
PETEY: I don't know.

She hits it with her hand.

MEG: It still makes a noise.
PETEY: You can always get another one.
MEG [*sadly*]: It was probably broken in the party. I don't remember it being broken though, in the party. [*She puts it down.*] What a shame.
PETEY: You can always get another one, Meg.
MEG: Well, at least he did have it on his birthday, didn't he? Like I wanted him to.
PETEY [*reading*]: Yes.
MEG: Have you seen him down yet? [PETEY *does not answer.*] Petey.
PETEY: What?
MEG: Have you seen him down?
PETEY: Who?
MEG: Stanley.
PETEY: No.
MEG: Nor have I. That boy should be up. He's late for his breakfast.
PETEY: There isn't any breakfast.
MEG: Yes, but he doesn't know that. I'm going to call him.
PETEY [*quickly*]: No, don't do that, Meg. Let him sleep.
MEG: But you say he stays in bed too much.
PETEY: Let him sleep . . . this morning. Leave him.
MEG: I've been up once, with his cup of tea. But Mr McCann opened the door. He said they were talking. He said he'd made him one. He must have been up early. I don't know what they were talking about. I was surprised. Because Stanley's usually fast asleep when I wake him. But he wasn't this morning. I heard him talking. [*Pause.*] Do you think they know each other? I think they're old friends. Stanley had a lot of friends. I know he did. [*Pause.*] I didn't give him his tea. He'd already had one. I came down again and went on with my work. Then, after a bit, they came down to breakfast. Stanley must have gone to sleep again.

Pause.

PETEY: When are you going to do your shopping, Meg?
MEG: Yes, I must. [*Collecting the bag.*] I've got a rotten headache. [*She goes to the back door, stops suddenly and turns.*] Did you see what's outside this morning?
PETEY: What?
MEG: That big car.
PETEY: Yes.
MEG: It wasn't there yesterday. Did you . . . did you have a look inside it?
PETEY: I had a peep.
MEG [*coming down tensely, and whispering*]: Is there anything in it?
PETEY: In it?
MEG: Yes.
PETEY: What do you mean, in it?
MEG: Inside it.
PETEY: What sort of thing?
MEG: Well . . . I mean . . . is there . . . is there a wheelbarrow in it?
PETEY: A wheelbarrow?
MEG: Yes.
PETEY: I didn't see one.
MEG: You didn't? Are you sure?
PETEY: What would Mr Goldberg want with a wheelbarrow?
MEG: Mr Goldberg?
PETEY: It's his car.
MEG [*relieved*]: His car? Oh, I didn't know it was his car.
PETEY: Of course it's his car.
MEG: Oh, I feel better.
PETEY: What are you on about?
MEG: Oh, I do feel better.
PETEY: You go and get a bit of air.
MEG: Yes, I will. I will. I'll go and get the shopping. [*She goes towards the back door. A door slams upstairs. She turns.*] It's Stanley! He's coming down—what am I going to do about his breakfast? [*She rushes into the kitchen.*] Petey, what shall I give him? [*She looks through the hatch.*] There's no cornflakes. [*They both gaze at the door. Enter* GOLDBERG. *He halts at the door, as he meets their gaze, then smiles.*]
GOLDBERG: A reception committee!
MEG: Oh, I thought it was Stanley.
GOLDBERG: You find a resemblance?
MEG: Oh no. You look quite different.
GOLDBERG [*coming into the room*]: Different build, of course.

MEG [*entering from the kitchen*]: I thought he was coming down for his breakfast. He hasn't had his breakfast yet.

GOLDBERG: Your wife makes a very nice cup of tea, Mr Boles, you know that?

PETEY: Yes, she does sometimes. Sometimes she forgets.

MEG: Is he coming down?

GOLDBERG: Down? Of course he's coming down. On a lovely sunny day like this he shouldn't come down? He'll be up and about in next to no time. [*He sits at the table.*] And what a breakfast he's going to get.

MEG: Mr Goldberg.

GOLDBERG: Yes?

MEG: I didn't know that was your car outside.

GOLDBERG: You like it?

MEG: Are you going to go for a ride?

GOLDBERG [*to* PETEY]: A smart car, eh?

PETEY: Nice shine on it all right.

GOLDBERG: What is old is good, take my tip. There's room there. Room in the front, and room in the back. [*He strokes the teapot.*] The pot's hot. More tea, Mr Boles?

PETEY: No thanks.

GOLDBERG [*pouring tea*]: That car? That car's never let me down.

MEG: Are you going to go for a ride?

GOLDBERG *does not answer, drinks his tea.*

MEG: Well, I'd better be off now. [*She moves to the back door, and turns.*] Petey, when Stanley comes down. . . .

PETEY: Yes?

MEG: Tell him I won't be long.

PETEY: I'll tell him.

MEG [*vaguely*]: I won't be long. [*She exits.*]

GOLDBERG [*sipping his tea*]: A good woman. A charming woman. My mother was the same. My wife was identical.

PETEY: How is he this morning?

GOLDBERG: Who?

PETEY: Stanley. Is he any better?

GOLDBERG [*a little uncertainly*]: Oh . . . a little better, I think, a little better. Of course, I'm not really qualified to say, Mr Boles. I mean, I haven't got the . . . the qualifications. The best thing would be if someone with the proper . . . mnn . . . qualifications . . . was to have a look at him. Someone with a few letters after his name. It makes all the difference.

PETEY: Yes.

GOLDBERG: Anyway, Dermot's with him at the moment. He's . . . keeping him company.

PETEY: Dermot?

GOLDBERG: Yes.

PETEY: It's a terrible thing.

GOLDBERG [*sighs*]: Yes. The birthday celebration was too much for him.

PETEY: What came over him?

GOLDBERG [*sharply*]: What came over him? Breakdown, Mr Boles. Pure and simple. Nervous breakdown.

PETEY: But what brought it on so suddenly?

GOLDBERG [*rising, and moving upstage*]: Well, Mr Boles, it can happen in all sorts of ways. A friend of mine was telling me about it only the other day. We'd both been concerned with another case—not entirely similar, of course, but . . . quite alike, quite alike. [*He pauses.*] Anyway, he was telling me, you see, this friend of mine, that sometimes it happens gradual—day by day it grows and grows and grows . . . day by day. And then other times it happens all at once. Poof! Like that! The nerves break. There's no guarantee how it's going to happen, but with certain people . . . it's a foregone conclusion.

PETEY: Really?

GOLDBERG: Yes. This friend of mine—he was telling me about it—only the other day. [*He stands uneasily for a moment, then brings out a cigarette case and takes a cigarette.*] Have an Abdullah.

PETEY: No, no, I don't take them.

GOLDBERG: Once in a while I treat myself to a cigarette. An Abdullah, perhaps, or a . . . [*He snaps his fingers.*]

PETEY: What a night. [GOLDBERG *lights his cigarette with a lighter.*] Came in the front door and all the lights were out. Put a shilling in the slot, came in here and the party was over.

GOLDBERG [*coming downstage*]: You put a shilling in the slot?

PETEY: Yes.

GOLDBERG: And the lights came on.

PETEY: Yes, then I came in here.

GOLDBERG [*with a short laugh*]: I could have sworn it was a fuse.

PETEY [*continuing*]: There was dead silence. Couldn't hear a thing. So I went upstairs and your friend—Dermot—met me on the landing. And he told me.

GOLDBERG [*sharply*]: Who?

PETEY: Your friend—Dermot.

GOLDBERG [*heavily*]: Dermot. Yes. [*He sits.*]

PETEY: They get over it sometimes though, don't they? I mean, they can recover from it, can't they?

GOLDBERG: Recover? Yes, sometimes they recover, in one way or another.

PETEY: I mean, he might have recovered by now, mightn't he?

GOLDBERG: It's conceivable. Conceivable.

PETEY *rises and picks up the teapot and cup.*

PETEY: Well, if he's no better by lunchtime I'll go and get hold of a doctor.
GOLDBERG [*briskly*]: It's all taken care of, Mr Boles. Don't worry yourself.
PETEY [*dubiously*]: What do you mean? [*Enter* MCCANN *with two suitcases.*] All packed up?

PETEY *takes the teapot and cups into the kitchen.* MCCANN *crosses left and puts down the suitcases. He goes up to the window and looks out.*

GOLDBERG: Well? [MCCANN *does not answer.*] McCann. I asked you well.
MCCANN [*without turning*]: Well what?
GOLDBERG: What's what? [MCCANN *does not answer.*]
MCCANN [*turning to look at* GOLDBERG, *grimly*]: I'm not going up there again.
GOLDBERG: Why not?
MCCANN: I'm not going up there again.
GOLDBERG: What's going on now?
MCCANN [*moving down*]: He's quiet now. He stopped all that . . . talking a while ago.

PETEY *appears at the kitchen hatch, unnoticed.*

GOLDBERG: When will he be ready?
MCCANN [*sullenly*]: You can go up yourself next time.
GOLDBERG: What's the matter with you?
MCCANN [*quietly*]: I gave him. . . .
GOLDBERG: What?
MCCANN: I gave him his glasses.
GOLDBERG: Wasn't he glad to get them back?
MCCANN: The frames are bust.
GOLDBERG: How did that happen?
MCCANN: He tried to fit the eyeholes into his eyes. I left him doing it.
PETEY [*at the kitchen door*]: There's some Sellotape somewhere. We can stick them together.

GOLDBERG *and* MCCANN *turn to see him. Pause.*

GOLDBERG: Sellotape? No, no, that's all right, Mr Boles. It'll keep him quiet for the time being, keep his mind off other things.
PETEY [*moving downstage*]: What about a doctor?
GOLDBERG: It's all taken care of.

MCCANN *moves over right to the shoe-box, and takes out a brush and brushes his shoes.*

PETEY [*moves to the table*]: I think he needs one.
GOLDBERG: I agree with you. It's all taken care of. We'll give him a bit of time to settle down, and then I'll take him to Monty.
PETEY: You're going to take him to a doctor?
GOLDBERG [*staring at him*]: Sure. Monty.

Pause. MCCANN *brushes his shoes.*

So Mrs Boles has gone out to get us something nice for lunch?
PETEY: That's right.
GOLDBERG: Unfortunately we may be gone by then.
PETEY: Will you?
GOLDBERG: By then we may be gone.

Pause.

PETEY: Well, I think I'll see how my peas are getting on, in the meantime.
GOLDBERG: The meantime?
PETEY: While we're waiting.
GOLDBERG: Waiting for what? [PETEY *walks towards the back door.*] Aren't you going back to the beach?
PETEY: No, not yet. Give me a call when he comes down, will you, Mr Goldberg?
GOLDBERG [*earnestly*]: You'll have a crowded beach today . . . on a day like this. They'll be lying on their backs, swimming out to sea. My life. What about the deck-chairs? Are the deck-chairs ready?
PETEY: I put them all out this morning.
GOLDBERG: But what about the tickets? Who's going to take the tickets?
PETEY: That's all right. That'll be all right. Mr Goldberg. Don't you worry about that. I'll be back.

He exits. GOLDBERG *rises, goes to the window and looks after him.* MCCANN *crosses to the table, left, sits, picks up the paper and begins to tear it into strips.*

GOLDBERG: Is everything ready?
MCCANN: Sure.

GOLDBERG *walks heavily, brooding, to the table. He sits right of it noticing what* MCCANN *is doing.*

GOLDBERG: Stop doing that!
MCCANN: What?
GOLDBERG: Why do you do that all the time? It's childish, it's pointless. It's without a solitary point.
MCCANN: What's the matter with you today?
GOLDBERG: Questions, questions. Stop asking me so many questions. What do you think I am?

MCCANN *studies him. He then folds the paper, leaving the strips inside.*

McCANN: Well?

Pause. GOLDBERG *leans back in the chair, his eyes closed.*

McCANN: Well?
GOLDBERG [*with fatigue*]: Well what?
McCANN: Do we wait or do we go and get him?
GOLDBERG [*slowly*]: You want to go and get him?
McCANN: I want to get it over.
GOLDBERG: That's understandable.
McCANN: So do we wait or do we go and get him?
GOLDBERG [*interrupting*]: I don't know why, but I feel knocked out. I feel a bit . . . It's uncommon for me.
McCANN: Is that so?
GOLDBERG: It's unusual.
McCANN [*rising swiftly and going behind* GOLDBERG*'s chair. Hissing*]: Let's finish and go. Let's get it over and go. Get the thing done. Let's finish the bloody thing. Let's get the thing done and go!

Pause.

Will I go up?

Pause.

Nat!

GOLDBERG *sits humped.* McCANN *slips to his side.*

Simey!
GOLDBERG [*opening his eyes, regarding* McCANN]: What—did—you—call—me?
McCANN: Who?
GOLDBERG [*murderously*]: Don't call me that! [*He seizes* McCANN *by the throat.*] NEVER CALL ME THAT!
McCANN [*writhing*]: Nat, Nat, Nat, NAT! I called you Nat. I was asking you, Nat. Honest to God. Just a question, that's all, just a question, do you see, do you follow me?
GOLDBERG [*jerking him away*]: What question?
McCANN: Will I go up?
GOLDBERG [*violently*]: Up? I thought you weren't going to go up there again?
McCANN: What do you mean? Why not?
GOLDBERG: You said so!
McCANN: I never said that!
GOLDBERG: No?
McCANN [*from the floor, to the room at large*]: Who said that? I never said that! I'll go up now!

He jumps up and rushes to the door, left.

GOLDBERG: Wait!

He stretches his arms to the arms of the chair.

Come here.

McCANN *approaches him very slowly.*

I want your opinion. Have a look in my mouth.

He opens his mouth wide.

Take a good look.

McCANN *looks.*

You know what I mean?

McCANN *peers.*

You know what? I've never lost a tooth. Not since the day I was born. Nothing's changed. [*He gets up.*] That's why I've reached my position, McCann. Because I've always been as fit as a fiddle. All my life I've said the same. Play up, play up, and play the game. Honour thy father and thy mother. All along the line. Follow the line, the line, McCann, and you can't go wrong. What do you think, I'm a self-made man? No! I sat where I was told to sit. I kept my eye on the ball. School? Don't talk to me about school. Top in all subjects. And for why? Because I'm telling you, I'm telling you, follow my line? Follow my mental? Learn by heart. Never write down a thing. And don't go too near the water.
And you'll find—that what I say is true.
Because I believe that the world . . . [*Vacant.*]. . . .
Because I believe that the world . . . [*Desperate.*]. . . .
BECAUSE I BELIEVE THAT THE WORLD. . . [*Lost.*]. . . .

He sits in chair.

Sit down, McCann, sit here where I can look at you.

McCANN *kneels in front of the table.*

[*Intensely, with growing certainty.*] My father said to me, Benny, Benny, he said, come here. He was dying. I knelt down. By him day and night. Who else was there? Forgive, Benny, he said, and let live. Yes, Dad. Go home to your wife. I will, Dad. Keep an eye open for low-lives, for schnorrers and for layabouts. He didn't mention names. I lost my life in the service of others, he said, I'm not ashamed. Do your duty and keep your observations. Always bid good morning to the neighbours. Never, never forget your family, for they are the rock, the constitution and the core! If you're ever in any difficulties Uncle Barney will see you in the clear. I knelt down. [*He kneels, facing* MCCANN.] I swore on the good book. And I knew the word I had to remember—Respect! Because McCann— [*Gently.*] Seamus—who came before your father? His father. And who came before him? Before him? . . . [*Vacant—triumphant.*] Who came before your father's father but your father's father's mother! Your great-gran-granny.

Silence. He slowly rises.

And that's why I've reached my position, McCann. Because I've always been as fit as a fiddle. My motto. Work hard and play hard. Not a day's illness.

GOLDBERG *sits.*

GOLDBERG: All the same, give me a blow. [*Pause.*] Blow in my mouth.

MCCANN *stands, puts his hands on his knees, bends, and blows in* GOLDBERG*'s mouth.*

One for the road.

MCCANN *blows again in his mouth.* GOLDBERG *breathes deeply, smiles.*

GOLDBERG: Right!

Enter LULU. MCCANN *looks at them, and goes to the door.*

MCCANN [*at the door*]: I'll give you five minutes. [*He exits.*]
GOLDBERG: Come over here.
LULU: What's going to happen?
GOLDBERG: Come over here.
LULU: No, thank you.
GOLDBERG: What's the matter? You got the needle to Uncle Natey?
LULU: I'm going.
GOLDBERG: Have a game of pontoon first, for old time's sake.
LULU: I've had enough games.
GOLDBERG: A girl like you, at your age, at your time of health, and you don't take to games?
LULU: You're very smart.
GOLDBERG: Anyway, who says you don't take to them?
LULU: Do you think I'm like all the other girls?
GOLDBERG: Are all the other girls like that, too?
LULU: I don't know about any other girls.
GOLDBERG: Nor me. I've never touched another woman.
LULU [*distressed*]: What would my father say, if he knew? And what would Eddie say?
GOLDBERG: Eddie?
LULU: He was my first love, Eddie was. And whatever happened, it was pure. With him! He didn't come into my room at night with a briefcase!
GOLDBERG: Who opened the briefcase, me or you? Lulu, schmulu, let bygones be bygones, do me a turn. Kiss and make up.
LULU: I wouldn't touch you.
GOLDBERG: And today I'm leaving.
LULU: You're leaving?
GOLDBERG: Today.
LULU [*with growing anger*]: You used me for a night. A passing fancy.
GOLDBERG: Who used who?
LULU: You made use of me by cunning when my defences were down.
GOLDBERG: Who took them down?
LULU: That's what you did. You quenched your ugly thirst. You taught me things a girl shouldn't know before she's been married at least three times!
GOLDBERG: Now you're a jump ahead! What are you complaining about?

Enter MCCANN *quickly.*

LULU: You didn't appreciate me for myself. You took all those liberties only to satisfy your appetite. Oh Nat, why did you do it?
GOLDBERG: You wanted me to do it, Lulula, so I did it.
MCCANN: That's fair enough. [*Advancing.*] You had a long sleep, Miss.
LULU [*backing upstage left*]: Me?
MCCANN: Your sort, you spend too much time in bed.
LULU: What do you mean?
MCCANN: Have you got anything to confess?
LULU: What?
MCCANN [*savagely*]: Confess!
LULU: Confess what?
MCCANN: Down on your knees and confess!
LULU: What does he mean?
GOLDBERG: Confess. What can you lose?
LULU: What, to him?
GOLDBERG: He's only been unfrocked six months.
MCCANN: Kneel down, woman, and tell me the latest!
LULU [*retreating to the back door*]: I've seen everything that's happened. I know what's going on. I've got a pretty shrewd idea.
MCCANN [*advancing*]: I've seen you hanging about the Rock of Cashel, profaning the soil with your goings-on. Out of my sight!

LULU: I'm going.

She exits. MCCANN *goes to the door, left, and goes out. He ushers in* STANLEY, *who is dressed in a dark well cut suit and white collar. He holds his broken glasses in his hand. He is clean-shaven.* MCCANN *follows and closes the door.* GOLDBERG *meets* STANLEY, *seats him in a chair.*

GOLDBERG: How are you, Stan?

Pause.

Are you feeling any better?

Pause.

What's the matter with your glasses?

GOLDBERG *bends to look.*

They're broken. A pity.

STANLEY *stares blankly at the floor.*

MCCANN [*at the table*]: He looks better, doesn't he?
GOLDBERG: Much better.
MCCANN: A new man.
GOLDBERG: You know what we'll do?
MCCANN: What?
GOLDBERG: We'll buy him another pair.

They begin to woo him, gently and with relish. During the following sequence STANLEY *shows no reaction. He remains, with no movement, where he sits.*

MCCANN: Out of our own pockets.
GOLDBERG: It goes without saying. Between you and me, Stan, it's about time you had a new pair of glasses.
MCCANN: You can't see straight.
GOLDBERG: It's true. You've been cockeyed for years.
MCCANN: Now you're even more cockeyed.
GOLDBERG: He's right. You've gone from bad to worse.
MCCANN: Worse than worse.
GOLDBERG: You need a long convalescence.
MCCANN: A change of air.
GOLDBERG: Somewhere over the rainbow.
MCCANN: Where angels fear to tread.
GOLDBERG: Exactly.
MCCANN: You're in a rut.
GOLDBERG: You look anaemic.
MCCANN: Rheumatic.
GOLDBERG: Myopic.
MCCANN: Epileptic.
GOLDBERG: You're on the verge.
MCCANN: You're a dead duck.
GOLDBERG: But we can save you.
MCCANN: From a worse fate.
GOLDBERG: True.
MCCANN: Undeniable.
GOLDBERG: From now on, we'll be the hub of your wheel.
MCCANN: We'll renew your season ticket.
GOLDBERG: We'll take tuppence off your morning tea.
MCCANN: We'll give you a discount on all inflammable goods.
GOLDBERG: We'll watch over you.
MCCANN: Advise you.
GOLDBERG: Give you proper care and treatment.
MCCANN: Let you use the club bar.
GOLDBERG: Keep a table reserved.
MCCANN: Help you acknowledge the fast days.
GOLDBERG: Bake you cakes.
MCCANN: Help you kneel on kneeling days.
GOLDBERG: Give you a free pass.
MCCANN: Take you for constitutionals.
GOLDBERG: Give you hot tips.
MCCANN: We'll provide the skipping rope.
GOLDBERG: The vest and pants.
MCCANN: The ointment.
GOLDBERG: The hot poultice.
MCCANN: The fingerstall.
GOLDBERG: The abdomen belt.
MCCANN: The ear plugs.
GOLDBERG: The baby powder.
MCCANN: The back scratcher.
GOLDBERG: The spare tyre.
MCCANN: The stomach pump.
GOLDBERG: The oxygen tent.
MCCANN: The prayer wheel.
GOLDBERG: The plaster of Paris.
MCCANN: The crash helmet.
GOLDBERG: The crutches.
MCCANN: A day and night service.
GOLDBERG: All on the house.
MCCANN: That's it.
GOLDBERG: We'll make a man of you.
MCCANN: And a woman.
GOLDBERG: You'll be re-orientated.
MCCANN: You'll be rich.
GOLDBERG: You'll be adjusted.
MCCANN: You'll be our pride and joy.
GOLDBERG: You'll be a mensch.
MCCANN: You'll be a success.
GOLDBERG: You'll be integrated.
MCCANN: You'll give orders.
GOLDBERG: You'll make decisions.
MCCANN: You'll be a magnate.
GOLDBERG: A statesman.

McCANN: You'll own yachts.
GOLDBERG: Animals.
McCANN: Animals.

GOLDBERG *looks at* McCANN.

GOLDBERG: I said animals. [*He turns back to* STANLEY.] You'll be able to make or break, Stan. By my life. [*Silence.* STANLEY *is still.*] Well? What do you say?

STANLEY'*s head lifts very slowly and turns in* GOLDBERG'*s direction.*

GOLDBERG: What do you think? Eh, boy?

STANLEY *begins to clench and unclench his eyes.*

McCANN: What's your opinion, sir? Of this prospect, sir?
GOLDBERG: Prospect. Sure. Sure it's a prospect.

STANLEY'*s hands clutching his glasses begins to tremble.*

What's your opinion of such a prospect? Eh, Stanley?

STANLEY *concentrates, his mouth opens, he attempts to speak, fails and emits sounds from his throat.*

STANLEY: Uh-gug . . . uh-gug . . . eeehhh-gag . . . [*On the breath.*] Caahh . . . caahh. . . .

They watch him. He draws a long breath which shudders down his body. He concentrates.

GOLDBERG: Well, Stanny boy, what do you say, eh?

They watch. He concentrates. His head lowers, his chin draws into his chest, he crouches.

STANLEY: Ug-gughh . . . uh-gughhh. . . .
McCANN: What's your opinion, sir?
STANLEY: Caaahhh . . . caaahhh. . . .
McCANN: Mr Webber! What's your opinion?
GOLDBERG: What do you say, Stan? What do you think of the prospect?
McCANN: What's your opinion of the prospect?

STANLEY'*s body shudders, relaxes, his head drops, he becomes still again, stooped.* PETEY *enters from door, downstage, left.*

GOLDBERG: Still the same old Stan. Come with us. Come on, boy.
McCANN: Come along with us.
PETEY: Where are you taking him?

They turn. Silence.

GOLDBERG: We're taking him to Monty.
PETEY: He can stay here.
GOLDBERG: Don't be silly.
PETEY: We can look after him here.
GOLDBERG: Why do you want to look after him?
PETEY: He's my guest.
GOLDBERG: He needs special treatment.
PETEY: We'll find someone.
GOLDBERG: No. Monty's the best there is. Bring him, McCann.

They help STANLEY *out of the chair. They all three move towards the door, left.*

PETEY: Leave him alone!

They stop. GOLDBERG *studies him.*

GOLDBERG [*insidiously*]: Why don't you come with us, Mr Boles?
McCANN: Yes, why don't you come with us?
GOLDBERG: Come with us to Monty. There's plenty of room in the car.

PETEY *makes no move. They pass him and reach the door.* McCANN *opens the door and picks up the suitcases.*

PETEY [*broken*]: Stan, don't let them tell you what to do!

They exit.

Silence. PETEY *stands. The front door slams. Sound of a car starting. Sound of a car going away. Silence.* PETEY *slowly goes to the table. He sits on a chair, left. He picks up the paper and opens it. The strips fall to the floor. He looks down at them.* MEG *comes past the window and enters by the back door.* PETEY *studies the front page of the paper.*

MEG [*coming downstage*]: The car's gone.
PETEY: Yes.
MEG: Have they gone?
PETEY: Yes.
MEG: Won't they be in for lunch?
PETEY: No.
MEG: Oh, what a shame. [*She puts her bag on the table.*] It's hot out. [*She hangs her coat on a hook.*] What are you doing?
PETEY: Reading.
MEG: Is it good?
PETEY: All right.

She sits by the table.

MEG: Where's Stan?

Pause.

Is Stan down yet, Petey?
PETEY: No . . . he's. . . .
MEG: Is he still in bed?
PETE: Yes, he's . . . still asleep.
MEG: Still? He'll be late for his breakfast.
PETEY: Let him . . . sleep.

Pause.

MEG: Wasn't it a lovely party last night?
PETEY: I wasn't there.
MEG: Weren't you?
PETEY: I came in afterwards.
MEG: Oh.

Pause.

It was a lovely party. I haven't laughed so much for years. We had dancing and singing. And games. You should have been there.
PETEY: It was good, eh?

Pause.

MEG: I was the belle of the ball.
PETEY: Were you?
MEG: Oh yes. They all said I was.
PETEY: I bet you were, too.
MEG: Oh, it's true. I was.

Pause.

I know I was.

CURTAIN

Wole Soyinka

Akinwande Oluwole Soyinka (1934–) was born in Abeokuta, a provincial city in Western Nigeria, which was then a British colony. Soyinka's parents belonged to the Yoruba tribe, but they were Christian converts. Ayo, his father, was a school headmaster, and Eniola, his mother (called "Wild Christian"), was an early advocate for the rights of Nigerian women. Both parents were stern, and in response Soyinka was stubborn, rebellious, and strongly opinionated—traits for which he is still known. These characteristics probably led him to resolve the clash of cultures by adopting the Yoruba spiritual tradition and forsaking his Anglican faith.

Soyinka's education was based on the British colonial model, and after he graduated from parsonage school in Abeokuta, he completed a two-year course of study at the University College in Ibadan, then the capital of Western Nigeria. He finished his education at Leeds University in England. Soyinka was already an active writer at Leeds, and after graduation he took a job as play-reader at the Royal Court Theatre in London, where he learned theater production firsthand. He finished his education and married an English woman, from whom he was divorced three years later. Soyinka was apparently troubled by the prospect of assimilation and not entirely prepared to reject his heritage. There was a moment, though he has not described it, when he freed himself from his Anglophilia and clearly saw himself as a black writer who is a Yoruban and a Nigerian.

Soyinka's vision of being a Yoruban playwright conflicts with critics who would label him as an "African" playwright. He is not a supporter of Negritude, the pan-African literary movement that seeks to establish an African identity in literature and the arts. Instead, Soyinka advocates Yoruba nativism derived from the worship of Ogun, the Yoruba god of iron, war, and hunting, who, Soyinka maintains, is his personal source of artistic vision. He has said that in some way all of his plays and other writings incorporate ritual related to Ogun or other Yoruba deities. In "The Fourth Stage: Drama and the Revolutionary Ideal" (1976), Soyinka argued that the transition from unknowing to self-awareness comes through Yoruba ritual, and in "Neo-Tarzanism: The Aesthetic Illusion" (1976) he advocated "selective eclecticism," a concept that supports a mix of history and myth, borrowing from many cultural sources, including the era of African colonization.

While still in England, Soyinka wrote his first play, based on his preparation for returning to Nigeria. *The Swamp-Dwellers* (1958) looks at the problems of Igwezu, a citified young man who returns to the family farm and stubbornly complains that the land is too swampy to produce good crops. Even when he is advised by a wise beggar, Ogun in human form, that the swamp is not what it seems, he does not listen. He wanders off back to the city, but the old beggar stands and waits.

Soyinka's second play, *The Invention* (1959), was staged at the Royal Court Theatre. It is a brief political satire about what happens in South Africa when a missile explodes and the people all lose their skin pigmentation. Soyinka's attack on apartheid is an example of the social and political moralism that eventually became his chief aim in drama.

In 1959 Soyinka returned to Nigeria under the auspices of a Rockefeller Foundation grant to research Nigerian drama, folklore, and myth. He used the opportunity to reacquaint himself with his homeland and to have his play *The Lion and the Jewel* produced in Ibadan. Though he was only twenty-four, he was honored with a commission to write a tribute to Nigerian independence from England. Soyinka's play *A Dance of the Forests* (1960) is the first of many to take English and European models and recast them with subjects taken from Yoruban history, folklore, and social mores. There are parallels to Shakespeare's *A Midsummer Night's Dream* in *A Dance of the Forests,* which concerns the rivalry between two gods, Ogun and Eshuoro. Eshuoro, a god of fate and mischief, contests the punishment of Demoke, a carver and poet. Demoke has murdered his apprentice out of jealousy and is hiding in the forest, where he is accompanied by Adenbi, a corrupt court orator, and Rola, a prostitute who caused a scandal resulting in two deaths. In the forest, the trio meets Obanji, the forest father god, masquerading as an ordinary man. Obanji leads them through the ritual of the dead until they admit their guilt and are transformed. In the new dawn, Demoke, Adenbi, and Rola, no longer guilt-ridden, begin the transition to self-awareness and take part in an elaborate dance that signifies a chance for a productive future. *A Dance of the Forests* satisfied the mood of the people of the new Nigeria. It signified Soyinka's personal artistic journey and defined his role as a Yoruban Nigerian playwright.

Soyinka's most widely produced play is the comic satire *The Trials of Brother Jero* (1960). In its single act, Soyinka depicts the machinations of Jero, a self-proclaimed Christian prophet, with a small following, living in Lagos, Nigeria's largest city. Brother Jero is adept at exploiting simpletons, such as Chume, with whose wife Jero is having an affair. Chume wants Jero to grant him dispensation to beat his wife, but when he finds out that he is cuckolded he tries to beat Jero and goes berserk. A less popular sequel, *Jero's Metamorphosis,* was produced in 1973. This time, Chume, restored to sanity, is again tricked by Brother Jero. Both plays rely heavily on current events, which provide Soyinka with opportunities to pick his targets and keep them in the limelight.

In 1965 Soyinka published a novel, *The Interpreters,* and had two plays produced, *Kongi's Harvest* in Lagos and *The Road* in London. *Kongi's Harvest* is satire aimed at the political conflicts between the old and new Nigeria. Its subject concerns what happens when an elected official seeks to subvert the tribal chieftains and create a dictatorship. Contrasted here are Kongi, a modern dictator, and Oba Danlola, the old tyrannical king who is being forced to sanctify Kongi's ascension by allowing him the honor of eating the first yam. Danlola submits, but Kongi's triumph is mitigated when the first yam is replaced with the severed head of one of his adversaries. The play is an obvious warning to Nigeria's leadership. It labeled Soyinka as a threat to the regime, and he was jailed for several months.

The Road is a bitter attack on Nigerian society and its failure to keep tradition as a unifying force in contemporary life. The protagonist, the Professor, is a quixotic lay preacher who confuses Christian and Yoruba ritual. Pushed out of his church because of his obsessive quest for the knowledge of death without dying, the Professor operates a squalid truck stop and junkyard next to the church. He is portrayed as a roadside casualty of modern life, without benefit of ritual and tradition, whose quest ends when he is accidentally stabbed in a scuffle and dies without realizing his foolishness.

In 1963 Soyinka became more serious as democracy in Nigeria was threatened by a militaristic government. His response was *The Strong Breed* (1963), a tragedy about the ritual in Yoruban culture of using the scapegoat. The plot hinges on the Yoruba New Year tradition that requires each community to exorcize its guilt through human sacrifice. When Eman, the protagonist, realizes that Ifada, a young crippled boy, has been chosen the local scapegoat, he refuses to permit the townspeople to use him. In the ensuing argument, Eman is made a scapegoat instead. He resists, but he is lured into a trap and killed. This break in the ritual is a disgrace for the village, and the play is Soyinka's unmistakable warning that broken ritual can only bring misery to a community—or to a nation that abandons its past for corrupt modern political and social imperatives. The play takes its name from Eman's vision of his dead father, whose remonstrance, "Ours is a strong breed that can take this boat to the river year after year and wax stronger on it," Eman fails to heed.

Because of his defense of political freedom and traditional values, Soyinka was a threat to the dictatorial government in Nigeria. During the Nigerian civil war (1966–1970), he supported the secessionist state of Biafra, and he was again jailed by the Nigerian government in 1967. He was acquitted and released in 1969, but he was left with an indelible pessimism. In the aftermath of the civil war and his imprisonment, Soyinka vented his anger in a play, *Madmen and Specialists* (1970); a memoir, *The Man Died* (1972); a collection of poems, *A Shuttle in the Crypt* (1972); and *The Bacchae of Euripides: A Communion Rite* (1973), an adaptation of the Greek tragedy, which was obviously influenced by Nigeria's political turmoil.

Soyinka's most important play after his break with the Nigerian ruling elite is *Death and the King's Horseman,* produced in 1976. The story is based on a Yoruba custom, which demands that the king's horseman commit suicide when the old king dies. In the play, when Elesin Oba, the king's horseman, is on his way to his ritual death, he sees a beautiful young woman and asks to make love to her as his final act on earth. While this is happening, Simon Pilkings, the British District Officer, arbitrarily prohibits the suicide because he thinks it is a barbaric custom. A Yoruban sergeant is sent to arrest Elesin, but he is detained by the village women until the lovemaking is consummated. Pilkings finds Elesin and arrests him. Elesin's British-educated son, Olunde, is dismayed that his father has not fulfilled the ritual, and he takes his place. Elesin blames the British and denies that he lost his will to complete the suicide ritual. But when Elesin learns that Olunde is dead, he kills himself. The play is Soyinka's stern warning that Nigerian society will suffer remorselessly if ritual can be so distorted that the young must die in place of the old. This is a reversal of the conflict in *The Strong Breed,* in which the young refuse to keep the old rituals, but the outcome is still unnerving in its pessimism.

Soyinka was dismayed that critics of *Death and the King's Horseman* in Europe and the United States generally failed to understand the nature of this African tragedy. He surmised that, even in 1975, whites still could not fathom an African tragedy in which the protagonists are black and the minor characters are white. In an author's note included in the published text (1976), Soyinka cautioned any would-be producer of this play against changing the playwright's vision and failing to elicit "the play's threnodic essence." When a production of *Death and the King's Horseman* that Soyinka approved of received poor reviews, however, Soyinka was angered. In an interview at the time, he was asked by Henry Louis Gates, Jr., "Do you think the response which your play elicited from these reviewers would be the same if the play had been by Brecht?" Soyinka responded, "Of course not. There is definitely more than an overtone of racism in some of the language used. The very idea that somebody from Africa, from the ex-colonial jungle, should (1) come and challenge their theatrical ideas in such a demanding way and (2) even propose the idea of an African tragedy in which whites supply the comic relief: that is very clearly there."

After 1976 Soyinka's work became topical, basically responding to Nigerian or African issues. His *Opera Wonyosi* (1977) is a Nigerian version of Bertolt Brecht's *The Threepenny Opera. Requiem for a Futurologist,* published in 1985, is a political satire about two con artists who vie over predicting the future. It is a thinly disguised attack on the dictators of the Nigerian government and the gullibility of the Nigerian people. Soyinka's *Play of Giants* (1984), based on Jean Genet's *The Balcony* (1956), a play about men indulging in fantasy in a brothel, satirizes Idi Amin, the tyrant of Uganda. Soyinka has his protagonist take hostages at the United Nations in New York City in order to extort money, a fantasy that plays uneasily in the modern world. These plays are a marked contrast to *The Lion and The Jewel,* completed when Soyinka was twenty-five and more hopeful.

The Lion and the Jewel (1959) is Soyinka's first full-length play and the best example of the wide range of European drama he adroitly manages to incorporate into his own unmistakable voice. Like John Millington Synge's *The Playboy of the Western World,* which satirized the Irish, Soyinka intended *The Lion and the Jewel* to satirize both the Nigerians and the colonial English. And like Synge's, Soyinka's play was not well received when it was produced in Ibadan or in London (1966).

The Lion and the Jewel compares the legacy of British colonialism with Yoruba culture by contrasting attitudes of social pretension and sexual conduct in a Nigerian village. It presents a battle of the sexes that pits youth against age. Lakunle is a twenty-three-year-old school teacher who has adopted British ways and calls himself a modern African. His false sense of self-importance is clear to most of the villagers, and he is an object of mockery. Sidi, the woman he wants to marry, not so politely tells him:

> You are dressed like him
> You look like him
> You speak his tongue
> You think like him
> You're just as clumsy

In your Lagos ways—
You'll do for him!

Ironically, Sidi is also the subject of mockery. Though she is the jewel of the village and the embodiment of sexual vitality, she is exceedingly vain. Her photograph has been published in a magazine in Lagos, the capital. She is proud that she has posed in exotic, if not sexually compromising, positions, yet she is unaware of being compromised. Lakunle's rival for Sidi is Baroka, the Bale, or village chief. Crafty old Baroka is the lion of the village. Though he is sixty, he is still lustful, and he wants to add Sidi to his harem. Recognizing Sidi's vanity and naïveté, Baroka's strategy for seducing her is to claim falsely that he is impotent. The result is inevitable. When Sidi visits him to gloat and scoff at him, she is overwhelmed by his flattery and his palm wine; when he promises to put her picture on local stamps, she finds him irresistible. Sidi fails to understand until it is too late that when she loses her virginity, she loses her local stardom. She becomes very angry, but thinking it over, she selfishly decides to take advantage of the situation and marry Baroka. At least, she reasons, he is the Bale, he is an avid lover, and she will have the prestige of being the youngest (and favorite) wife.

Lakunle tries to explain to Sidi that because she is no longer a virgin there is no need to pay her bride-price, and he offers her a monogamous Western-style marriage. Sidi is unimpressed, and her rejection of Lakunle reaffirms his lowly status. Before Sidi goes off to her wedding, Sadiku, Baroka's head wife, blesses her and invokes the fertility gods to give her many children. This suggests that Sidi's choice is the correct one for Yorubans. Even with this culture's imperfections, it is still seen to be superior to the threadbare Western ways and to the vestiges of British colonialism. Lakunle cannot (and probably never will) understand why he has been rejected, and his reasoning shows his obtuseness and his shallowness:

"Man takes the fallen woman by the hand"
And ever after they live happily.
Moreover, I will admit,
It solves the problem of her bride-price too.
A man must live or fall by his true
Principles. That, I had sworn,
Never to pay.

Lost in the festivities celebrating Sidi's marriage to Baroka, Lakunle is last seen making a pass at another young woman.

Despite Soyinka's prominence and reputation, his plays are not produced frequently in Europe or the United States. He is obviously frustrated by this, but he is undaunted in his outspokenness and defense of human rights. Soyinka is a moralist and a severe critic of political demagoguery and human rights abuses. He was exiled from Nigeria from 1970 to 1975, but returned to Ibadan to teach for fifteen years. His criticism of the Nigerian government has not brought him peace, and when threatened by the government, he again went into a voluntary exile in 1994. He now lives abroad as a kind of wandering Nigerian, criticizing the Nigerian government and its abuse of human rights. At present, Soyinka's home is a secret, and interviews with him concerning *The Open Sore of a Continent:*

A Personal Narrative of the Nigerian Crisis (1996) are often conducted in places like airports or by telephone.

Soyinka was awarded the Nobel Prize for Literature in 1986. His acceptance speech, "The Past Must Address Its Present," is a restatement of his artistic credo and a sharp commentary on the need for African writers to use the past, including the evils of colonialism, as a cultural and historical legacy for literature. This attitude sets him at odds with another of Nigeria's great writers (and Soyinka's schoolmate), Chinua Achebe, who is unforgiving about the effects of colonialism and is a leader of the Negritude movement. Achebe's remarks about Soyinka's award reveal his distance from Soyinka and the pride of African literary achievement. "This is the year of Wole Soyinka's Nobel Prize. . . . One of us has proved that we can beat the white man at his own game. That is wonderful for us and for the white man. But now we must turn away and play our own game."

The Lion and the Jewel

CHARACTERS

SIDI, the Village Belle
LAKUNLE, school teacher
BAROKA, the "Bale" of Ilujinle
SADIKU, his head wife
THE FAVOURITE
VILLAGE GIRLS
A WRESTLER
A SURVEYOR
SCHOOLBOYS
ATTENDANTS ON THE "BALE"
MUSICIAN, DANCERS, MUMMERS,
PRISONERS, TRADERS, THE VILLAGE.

MORNING

A clearing on the edge of the market, dominated by an immense 'odan' tree. It is the village centre. The wall of the bush school flanks the stage on the right, and a rude window opens on to the stage from the wall. There is a chant of the "Arithmetic Times" issuing from this window. It begins a short while before the action begins. SIDI *enters from left, carrying a small pail of water on her head. She is a slim girl with plaited hair. A true village belle. She balances the pail on her head with accustomed ease. Around her is wrapped the familiar broad cloth which is folded just above her breasts, leaving the shoulders bare.*

Almost as soon as she appears on the stage, the schoolmaster's face also appears at the window. (The chanting continues—"Three times two are six," "Three times three are nine," etc.) The teacher LAKUNLE, *disappears. He is replaced by two of his pupils, aged roughly eleven, who make a buzzing noise at* SIDI, *repeatedly clapping their hands across the mouth.* LAKUNLE *now re-appears below the window and makes for* SIDI, *stopping only to give the boys admonitory whacks on the head before they can duck. They vanish with a howl and he shuts the window on them. The chanting dies away. The schoolmaster is nearly twenty-three. He is dressed in an old-style English suit, threadbare but not ragged, clean but not ironed, obviously a size or two too small. His tie is done in a very small knot, disappearing beneath a shiny black waistcoat. He wears twenty-three-inch-bottom trousers, and blanco-white tennis shoes.*

LAKUNLE: Let me take it.
SIDI: No.
LAKUNLE: Let me. [*Seizes the pail. Some water spills on him.*]
SIDI [*delighted*]: There. Wet for your pains.
Have you no shame?
LAKUNLE: That is what the stewpot said to the fire.
Have you no shame—at your age
Licking my bottom? But she was tickled
Just the same.
SIDI: The school teacher is full of stories
This morning. And now, if the lesson
Is over, may I have the pail?
LAKUNLE: No. I have told you not to carry loads
On your head. But you are as stubborn
As an illiterate goat. It is bad for the spine.
And it shortens your neck, so that very soon
You will have no neck at all. Do you wish to look
Squashed like my pupils' drawings?

SIDI: Why should that worry me? Haven't you sworn
That my looks do not affect your love?
Yesterday, dragging your knees in the dust
You said, Sidi, if you were crooked or fat,
And your skin was scaly like a . . .
LAKUNLE: Stop!
SIDI: I only repeat what you said.
LAKUNLE: Yes, and I will stand by every word I spoke.
But must you throw away your neck on that account?
Sidi, it is so unwomanly. Only spiders
Carry loads the way you do.
SIDI [*huffily, exposing the neck to advantage*]:
Well, it is my neck, not your spider.
LAKUNLE [*looks, and gets suddenly agitated*]:
And look at that! Look, look at that!

[*Makes a general sweep in the direction of her breasts.*]

Who was it talked of shame just now?
How often must I tell you, Sidi, that
A grown-up girl must cover up her . . .
Her . . . shoulders? I can see quite . . . quite
A good portion of—that! And so I imagine
Can every man in the village. Idlers
All of them, good-for-nothing shameless men
Casting their lustful eyes where
They have no business . . .
SIDI: Are you at that again? Why, I've done the fold
So high and so tight, I can hardly breathe.
And all because you keep at me so much.
I have to leave my arms so I can use them . . .
Or don't you know that?
LAKUNLE: You could wear something.
Most modest women do. But you, no.
You must run about naked in the streets.
Does it not worry you . . . the bad names,
The lewd jokes, the tongue-licking noises
Which girls, uncovered like you,
Draw after them?
SIDI: This is too much. Is it you, Lakunle,
Telling me that I make myself common talk?
When the whole world knows of the madman
Of Ilujinle, who calls himself a teacher!
Is it Sidi who makes the men choke
In their cups, or you, with your big loud words
And no meaning? You and your ragged books
Dragging your feet to every threshold
And rushing them out again as curses
Greet you instead of welcome. Is it Sidi
They call a fool—even the children—
Or you with your fine airs and little sense!
LAKUNLE [*first indignant, then recovers composure*]:
For that, what is a jewel to pigs?
If now I am misunderstood by you
And your race of savages, I rise above taunts
And remain unruffled.

The Lion and the Jewel, *production directed by Jonathan Wilson, the Court Theatre, Chicago, 1990.*

SIDI [*furious, shakes both fists at him*]:
O . . . oh, you make me want to pulp your brain.
LAKUNLE [*retreats a little, but puts her aside with a very lofty gesture*]:
A natural feeling, arising out of envy;
For, as a woman, you have a smaller brain
Than mine.
SIDI [*madder still*]:
Again! I'd like to know
Just what gives you these thoughts
Of manly conceit.
LAKUNLE [*very, very patronizing*]: No, no. I have fallen for that trick before.
You can no longer draw me into arguments
Which go above your head.
SIDI [*can't find the right words, chokes back*]:
Give me the pail now. And if you ever dare
To stop me in the streets again . . .
LAKUNLE: Now, now, Sidi . . .
SIDI: Give it or I'll . . .
LAKUNLE [*holds on to her*]:
Please, don't be angry with me.
I didn't mean you in particular.
And anyway, it isn't what I say.
The scientists have proved it. It's in my books.
Women have a smaller brain than men
That's why they are called the weaker sex.
SIDI [*throws him off*]:
The weaker sex, is it?
Is it a weaker breed who pounds the yam
Or bends all day to plant the millet
With a child strapped to her back?
LAKUNLE: That is all part of what I say.
But don't you worry. In a year or two
You will have machines which will do
Your pounding, which will grind your pepper
Without it getting in your eyes.
SIDI: O-oh. You really mean to turn
The whole world upside down.
LAKUNLE: The world? Oh, that. Well, maybe later.
Charity, they say, begins at home.
For now, it is this village I shall turn
Inside out. Beginning with that crafty rogue,
Your past master of self-indulgence—Baroka.
SIDI: Are you still on about the Bale?
What has he done to you?
LAKUNLE: He'll find out. Soon enough, I'll let him know.
SIDI: These thoughts of future wonders—do you buy them
Or merely go mad and dream of them?
LAKUNLE: A prophet has honour except
In his own home. Wise men have been called mad
Before me and after, many more shall be
So abused. But to answer you, the measure
Is not entirely of my own coinage.
What I boast is known in Lagos, that city
Of magic, in Badagry where Saro women bathe
In gold, even in smaller towns less than
Twelve miles from here . . .
SIDI: Well go there. Go to these places where
Women would understand you
If you told them of your plans with which
You oppress me daily. Do you not know
What name they give you here?
Have you lost shame completely that jeers
Pass you over.
LAKUNLE: No. I have told you no. Shame belongs
Only to the ignorant.
SIDI: Well, I am going.
Shall I take the pail or not?
LAKUNLE: Not till you swear to marry me.

[*Takes her hand, instantly soulful.*]

Sidi, a man must prepare to fight alone.
But it helps if he has a woman
To stand by him, a woman who . . .
Can understand . . . like you.
SIDI: I do?
LAKUNLE: Sidi, my love will open your mind
Like the chaste leaf in the morning, when
The sun first touches it.
SIDI: If you start that I will run away.
I had enough of that nonsense yesterday.
LAKUNLE: Nonsense? Nonsense? Do you hear?
Does anybody listen? Can the stones
Bear to listen to this? Do you call it
Nonsense that I poured the waters of my soul
To wash your feet?
SIDI: You did what!
LAKUNLE: Wasted! Wasted! Sidi, my heart
Bursts into flowers with my love.
But you, you and the dead of this village
Trample it with feet of ignorance.
SIDI [*shakes her head in bafflement*]:
If the snail finds splinters in his shell
He changes house. Why do you stay?
LAKUNLE: Faith. Because I have faith.
Oh Sidi, vow to me your own undying love
And I will scorn the jibes of these bush minds
Who know no better. Swear, Sidi,
Swear you will be my wife and I will
Stand against earth, heaven, and the nine
Hells . . .
SIDI: Now there you go again.
One little thing
And you must chirrup like a cockatoo.
You talk and talk and deafen me
With words which always sound the same
And make no meaning.
I've told you, and I say it again

I shall marry you today, next week
Or any day you name.
But my bride-price must first be paid.
Aha, now you turn away.
But I tell you, Lakunle, I must have
The full bride-price. Will you make me
A laughing-stock? Well, do as you please.
But Sidi will not make herself
A cheap bowl for the village spit.
LAKUNLE: On my head let fall their scorn.
SIDI: They will say I was no virgin
That I was forced to sell my shame
And marry you without a price.
LAKUNLE: A savage custom, barbaric, out-dated,
Rejected, denounced, accursed,
Excommunicated, archaic, degrading,
Humiliating, unspeakable, redundant.
Retrogressive, remarkable, unpalatable.
SIDI: Is the bag empty? Why did you stop?
LAKUNLE: I own only the Shorter Companion
Dictionary, but I have ordered
The Longer One—you wait!
SIDI: Just pay the price.
LAKUNLE [*with a sudden shout*]:
An ignoble custom, infamous, ignominious
Shaming our heritage before the world.
Sidi, I do not seek a wife
To fetch and carry,
To cook and scrub,
To bring forth children by the gross . . .
SIDI: Heaven forgive you! Do you now scorn
Child-bearing in a wife?
LAKUNLE: Of course I do not. I only mean . . .
Oh Sidi, I want to wed
Because I love,
I seek a life-companion . . .

[*Pulpit-declamatory.*]

"And the man shall take the woman
And the two shall be together
As one flesh."
Sidi, I seek a friend in need.
An equal partner in my race of life.
SIDI [*attentive no more. Deeply engrossed in counting the beads on her neck*]:
Then pay the price.
LAKUNLE: Ignorant girl, can you not understand?
To pay the price would be
To buy a heifer off the market stall.
You'd be my chattel, my mere property.
No, Sidi! [*Very tenderly.*]
When we are wed, you shall not walk or sit
Tethered, as it were, to my dirtied heels.
Together we shall sit at table
—Not on the floor—and eat,
Not with fingers, but with knives
And forks, and breakable plates
Like civilized beings.
I will not have you wait on me
Till I have dined my fill.
No wife of mine, no lawful wedded wife
Shall eat the leavings off my plate—
That is for the children.
I want to walk beside you in the street,
Side by side and arm in arm
Just like the Lagos couples I have seen
High-heeled shoes for the lady, red paint
On her lips. And her hair is stretched
Like a magazine photo. I will teach you
The waltz and we'll both learn the foxtrot
And we'll spend the week-end in night-clubs at Ibadan.
Oh I must show you the grandeur of towns
We'll live there if you like or merely pay visits.
So choose. Be a modern wife, look me in the eye
And give me a little kiss—like this.

[*Kisses her.*]

SIDI [*backs away*]:
No, don't! I tell you I dislike
This strange unhealthy mouthing you perform.
Every time, your action deceives me
Making me think that you merely wish
To whisper something in my ear.
Then comes this licking of my lips with yours.
It's so unclean. And then,
The sound you make—"Pyout!"
Are you being rude to me?
LAKUNLE [*wearily*]: It's never any use.
Bush-girl you are, bush-girl you'll always be;
Uncivilized and primitive—bush-girl!
I kissed you as all educated men—
And Christians—kiss their wives.
It is the way of civilized romance.
SIDI [*lightly*]: A way you mean, to avoid
Payment of lawful bride-price
A cheating way, mean and miserly.
LAKUNLE [*violently*]: It is not.

[SIDI *bursts out laughing.* LAKUNLE *changes his tone to a soulful one, both eyes dreamily shut.*]

Romance is the sweetening of the soul
With fragrance offered by the stricken heart.
SIDI [*looks at him in wonder for a while*]:
Away with you. The village says you're mad,
And I begin to understand.
I wonder that they let you run the school.
You and your talk. You'll ruin your pupils too
And then they'll utter madness just like you.

[*Noise off-stage.*]

There are people coming
Give me the bucket or they'll jeer.

[*Enter a crowd of youths and drummers, the girls being in various stages of excitement.*]

FIRST GIRL: Sidi, he has returned. He came back just as he said he would.
SIDI: Who has?
FIRST GIRL: The stranger. The man from the outside world. The clown who fell in the river for you.

[*They all burst out laughing.*]

SIDI: The one who rode on the devil's own horse?
SECOND GIRL: Yes, the same. The stranger with the one-eyed box.

[*She demonstrates the action of a camera amidst admiring titters.*]

THIRD GIRL: And he brought his new horse right into the village square this time. This one has only two feet. You should have seen him. B-r-r-r-r.

[*Runs around the platform driving an imaginary motor-bike.*]

SIDI: And has he brought . . . ?
FIRST GIRL: The images? He brought them all. There was hardly any part of the village which does not show in the book.

[*Clicks the imaginary shutter.*]

SIDI: The book? Did you see the book?
Had he the precious book
That would bestow upon me
Beauty beyond the dreams of a goddess?
For so he said.
The book which would announce
This beauty to the world—
Have you seen it?
THIRD GIRL: Yes, yes, he did. But the Bale is still feasting his eyes on the images. Oh, Sidi, he was right. You *are* beautiful. On the cover of the book is an image of you from here [*touches the top of her head*] to here [*her stomach*]. And in the middle leaves, from the beginning of one leaf right across to the end of another, is one of you from head to toe. Do you remember it? It was the one for which he made you stretch your arms towards the sun. [*Rapturously.*] Oh, Sidi, you looked as if, at that moment, the sun himself had been your lover.

[*They all gasp with pretended shock at this blasphemy and one slaps her playfully on the buttocks.*]

FIRST GIRL: The Bale is jealous, but he pretends to be proud of you. And when this man tells him how famous you are in the capital, he pretends to be pleased, saying how much honour and fame you have brought to the village.
SIDI [*with amazement*]: Is not Baroka's image in the book at all?
SECOND GIRL [*contemptuous*]: Oh yes, it is. But it would have been much better for the Bale if the stranger had omitted him altogether. His image is in a little corner somewhere in the book, and even that corner he shares with one of the village latrines.
SIDI: Is that the truth? Swear! Ask Ogun to
Strike you dead.
GIRL: Ogun strike me dead if I lie.
SIDI: If that is true, then I am more esteemed
Than Bale Baroka,
The Lion of Ilujinle.
This means that I am greater than
The Fox of the Undergrowth,
The living god among men . . .
LAKUNLE [*peevishly*]: And devil among women.
SIDI: Be silent, you.
You are merely filled with spite.
LAKUNLE: I know him for what he is. This is
Divine justice that a mere woman
Should outstrip him in the end.
SIDI: Be quiet;
Or I swear I'll never speak to you again.

[*Affects sudden coyness.*]

In fact, I am not so sure I'll want to wed
you now.
LAKUNLE: Sidi!
SIDI: Well, why should I?
Known as I am to the whole wide world,
I would demean my worth to wed
A mere village school teacher.
LAKUNLE [*in agony*]: Sidi!
SIDI: And one who is too mean
To pay the bride-price like a man.
LAKUNLE: Oh, Sidi, don't!
SIDI [*plunging into an enjoyment of* LAKUNLE'S *misery*]:
Well, don't you know?
Sidi is more important even than the Bale.
More famous than that panther of the trees.
He is beneath me now—
Your fearless rake, the scourge of womanhood!
But now,
He shares the corner of the leaf
With the lowest of the low—
With the dug-out village latrine!

While I—How many leaves did my own image take?
FIRST GIRL: Two in the middle and . . .
SIDI: No, no. Let the school teacher count!
How many were there, teacher-man?
LAKUNLE: Three leaves.
SIDI [*threateningly*]: One leaf for every heart that I shall break.
Beware!

[*Leaps suddenly into the air.*]

Hurray! I'm beautiful!
Hurray for the wandering stranger!
CROWD: Hurray for the Lagos man!
SIDI [*wildly excited*]: I know. Let us dance the dance of the lost Traveller.
SHOUTS: Yes, let's.
SIDI: Who will dance the devil-horse?
You, you, you and you.

[*The four girls fall out.*]

A python. Who will dance the snake?
Ha ha! Your eyes are shifty and your ways are sly.

[*The selected youth is pushed out amidst jeers.*]

The stranger. We've got to have the being
From the mad outer world . . . You there,
No, you have never felt the surge
Of burning liquor in your milky veins.
Who can we pick that knows the walk of drunks?
You? . . . No, the thought itself
Would knock you out as sure as wine . . . Ah!

[*Turns round slowly to where* LAKUNLE *is standing with a kindly, fatherly smile for the children at play.*]

Come on book-worm, you'll play his part.
LAKUNLE: No, no. I've never been drunk in all my life.
SIDI: We know. But your father drank so much,
He must have drunk your share, and that
Of his great grandsons.
LAKUNLE [*tries to escape*]: I won't take part.
SIDI: You must.
LAKUNLE: I cannot stay. It's nearly time to take
Primary four in Geography.
SIDI [*goes over to the window and throws it open*]:
Did you think your pupils would remain in school
Now that the stranger has returned?
The village is on holiday, you fool.
LAKUNLE [*as they drag him towards the platform*]:
No, no. I won't. This foolery bores me.
It is a game of idiots. I have work of more importance.

SIDI [*bending down over* LAKUNLE *who has been seated forcibly on the platform*]:
You are dressed like him
You look like him
You speak his tongue
You think like him
You're just as clumsy
In your Lagos ways—
You'll do for him!

[*This chant is taken up by all and they begin to dance round* LAKUNLE, *speaking the words in a fast rhythm. The drummers join in after the first time, keeping up a steady beat as the others whirl round their victim. They go faster and faster and chant faster and faster with each round. By the sixth or seventh,* LAKUNLE *has obviously had enough.*]

LAKUNLE [*raising his voice above the din*]:
All right! I'll do it.
Come now, let's get it over with.

[*A terrific shout and a clap of drums.* LAKUNLE *enters into the spirit of the dance with enthusiasm. He takes over from* SIDI, *stations his cast all over the stage as the jungle, leaves the right top-stage clear for the four girls who are to dance the motor-car. A mime follows of the visitor's entry into Ilujinle, and his short stay among the villagers. The four girls crouch on the floor, as four wheels of a car.* LAKUNLE *directs their spacing, then takes his place in the middle, and sits on air. He alone does not dance. He does realistic miming. Soft throbbing drums, gradually swelling in volume, and the four "wheels" begin to rotate the upper halves of their bodies in perpendicular circles.* LAKUNLE *clowning the driving motions, obviously enjoying this fully. The drums gain tempo, faster, faster, faster. A sudden crash of drums and the girls quiver and dance the stall. Another effort at rhythm fails, and the "stalling wheels" give a corresponding shudder, finally, and let their faces fall on to their laps.* LAKUNLE *tampers with a number of controls, climbs out of the car and looks underneath it. His lips indicate that he is swearing violently. Examines the wheels, pressing them to test the pressure, betrays the devil in him by seizing his chance to pinch the girls' bottoms. One yells and bites him on the ankle. He climbs hurriedly back into the car, makes a final attempt to re-start it, gives it up and decides to abandon it. Picks up his camera and his helmet, pockets a flask of whisky from which he takes a swig, before beginning the trek. The drums resume beating, a different, darker tone and rhythm, varying with the journey. Full use of "gangan" and "iya ilu." The 'trees' perform a subdued and unobtrusive dance on the same spot. Details as a snake slithering out of the branches and poising over* LAKUNLE*'s head when he leans against a tree for a rest. He flees, restoring his nerves shortly after by a swig. A monkey drops suddenly in his path and gibbers at him before scampering off. A roar comes from somewhere, etc.*

His nerves go rapidly and he recuperates himself by copious draughts. He is soon tipsy, battles violently with the undergrowth and curses silently as he swats the flies off his tortured body.

Suddenly, from somewhere in the bush comes the sound of a girl singing. The Traveller shakes his head but the sound persists. Convinced he is suffering from sun-stroke, he drinks again. His last drop, so he tosses the bottle in the direction of the sound, only to be rewarded by a splash, a scream and a torrent of abuse, and finally, silence again. He tip-toes, clears away the obstructing growth, blinks hard and rubs his eyes. Whatever he has seen still remains. He whistles softly, unhitches his camera and begins to jockey himself into a good position for a take. Backwards and forwards, and his eyes are so closely glued to the lens that he puts forward a careless foot and disappears completely. There is a loud splash and the invisible singer alters her next tone to a sustained scream. Quickened rhythm and shortly afterwards, amidst sounds of splashes, SIDI *appears on the stage, with a piece of cloth only partially covering her.* LAKUNLE *follows a little later, more slowly, trying to wring out the water from his clothes. He has lost all his appendages except the camera.* SIDI *has run right across the stage, and returns a short while later, accompanied by the* VILLAGERS. *The same cast has disappeared and re-forms behind* SIDI *as the* VILLAGERS. *They are in an ugly mood, and in spite of his protests, haul him off to the town centre, in front of the "Odan" tree.*

Everything comes to a sudden stop as BAROKA *the Bale, wiry, goateed, tougher than his sixty-two years, himself emerges at this point from behind the tree. All go down, prostrate or kneeling with the greetings of "Kabiyesi" "Baba" etc. All except* LAKUNLE *who begins to sneak off.*]

BAROKA: Akowe. Teacher wa. Misita Lakunle.

[*As the others take up the cry "Misita Lakunle" he is forced to stop. He returns and bows deeply from the waist.*]

LAKUNLE: A good morning to you sir.
BAROKA: Guru morin guru morin, ngh-hn! That is
All we get from "alakowe." You call at his house
Hoping he sends for beer, but all you get is
Guru morin. Will guru morin wet my throat?
Well, well, our man of knowledge, I hope you have no
Query for an old man today.
LAKUNLE: No complaints.
BAROKA: And we are not feuding in something
I have forgotten.
LAKUNLE: Feuding sir? I see no cause at all.
BAROKA: Well, the play was much alive until I came.
And now everything stops, and you were leaving
Us. After all, I knew the story and I came in
Right on cue. It makes me feel as if I was
Chief Baseje.
LAKUNLE: One hardly thinks the Bale would have the time
For such childish nonsense.
BAROKA: A-ah Mister Lakunle. Without these things you call
Nonsense, a Bale's life would be pretty dull.
Well, now that you say I am welcome, shall we
Resume your play?

[*Turns suddenly to his attendants.*]

Seize him!
LAKUNLE [*momentarily baffled*]: What for? What have I done?
BAROKA: You tried to steal our village maidenhead
Have you forgotten? If he has, serve him a slap
To wake his brain.

[*An uplifted arm being proffered,* LAKUNLE *quickly recollects and nods his head vigorously. So the play is back in performance. The Villagers gather round threatening, clamouring for his blood.* LAKUNLE *tries bluff, indignation, appeasement in turn. At a sudden signal from the Bale, they throw him down prostrate on his face. Only then does the Chief begin to show him sympathy, appear to understand the Stranger's plight, and pacify the villagers on his behalf. He orders dry clothes for him, seats him on his right and orders a feast in his honour. The Stranger springs up every second to take photographs of the party, but most of the time his attention is fixed on* SIDI *dancing with abandon. Eventually he whispers to the Chief, who nods in consent, and* SIDI *is sent for. The Stranger arranges* SIDI *in all sorts of magazine postures and takes innumerable photographs of her. Drinks are pressed upon him; he refuses at first, eventually tries the local brew with skepticism, appears to relish it, and drinks profusely. Before long, however, he leaves the party to be sick. They clap him on the back as he goes out, and two drummers who insist on dancing round him nearly cause the calamity to happen on the spot. However, he rushes out with his hand held to the mouth.* LAKUNLE's *exit seems to signify the end of the mime. He returns almost at once and the others discard their roles.*]

SIDI [*delightedly*]: What did I say? You played him to the bone,
A court jester would have been the life for you,
Instead of school.

[*Points contemptuously to the school.*]

BAROKA: And where would the village be, robbed of
Such wisdom as Mister Lakunle dispenses
Daily? Who would tell us where we go wrong?
Eh, Mister Lakunle?

SIDI [*hardly listening, still in the full grip of her excitement*]:
Who comes with me to find the man?
But Lakunle, you'll have to come and find sense
In his clipping tongue. You see book-man
We cannot really do
Without your head.

[LAKUNLE *begins to protest, but they crowd him and try to bear him down. Suddenly he breaks free and takes to his heels with all the women in full pursuit.* BAROKA *is left sitting by himself—his wrestler, who accompanied him on his entry, stands a respectful distance away—staring at the flock of women in flight. From the folds of his agbada he brings out his copy of the magazine and admires the heroine of the publication. Nods slowly to himself.*]

BAROKA: Yes, yes . . . it is five full months since last
I took a wife . . . five full months . . .

NOON

A road by the market. Enter SIDI, *happily engrossed in the pictures of herself in the magazine.* LAKUNLE *follows one or two paces behind carrying a bundle of firewood which* SIDI *has set out to obtain. They are met in the centre by* SADIKU, *who has entered from the opposite side.* SADIKU *is an old woman, with a shawl over her head.*

SADIKU: Fortune is with me. I was going to your house to see you.
SIDI [*startled out of her occupation*]: What! Oh, it is you, Sadiku.
SADIKU: The Lion sent me. He wishes you well.
SIDI: Thank him for me.

[*Then excitedly.*]

Have you seen these?
Have you seen these images of me
Wrought by the man from the capital city?
Have you felt the gloss? [*Caresses the page.*]
Smoother by far than the parrot's breast.
SADIKU: I have. I have. I saw them as soon as the city man came . . . Sidi, I bring a message from my lord. [*Jerks her head at* LAKUNLE.] Shall we draw aside a little?
SIDI: Him? Pay no more heed to that
Than you would a eunuch.
SADIKU: Then, in as few words as it takes to tell,
Baroka wants you for a wife.
LAKUNLE [*bounds forward, dropping the wood*]:
What! The greedy dog!
Insatiate camel of a foolish, doting race;
Is he at his tricks again?
SIDI: Be quiet, 'Kunle. You get so tiresome.
The message is for me, not you.
LAKUNLE [*down on his knees at once. Covers* SIDI'*s hands with kisses*]:
My Ruth, my Rachel, Esther, Bathsheba
Thou sum of fabled perfections
From Genesis to the Revelations
Listen not to the voice of this infidel . . .
SIDI [*snatches her hand away*]:
Now that's your other game;
Giving me funny names you pick up
In your wretched books.
My name is Sidi. And now, let me be.
My name is Sidi, and I am beautiful.
The stranger took my beauty
And placed it in my hands.
Here, here it is. I need no funny names
To tell me of my fame.
Loveliness beyond the jewels of a throne—
That is what he said.
SADIKU [*gleefully*]: Well, will you be Baroka's own jewel? Will you be his sweetest princess, soothing him on weary nights? What answer shall I give my lord?
SIDI [*wags her finger playfully at the woman*]:
Ha ha. Sadiku of the honey tongue.
Sadiku, head of the Lion's wives.
You'll make no prey of Sidi with your wooing tongue
Not this Sidi whose fame has spread to Lagos
And beyond the seas.

[LAKUNLE *beams with satisfaction and rises.*]

SADIKU: Sidi, have you considered what a life of bliss awaits you? Baroka swears to take no other wife after you. Do you know what it is to be the Bale's last wife? I'll tell you. When he dies—and that should not be long; even the Lion has to die sometime—well, when he does, it means that you will have the honour of being the senior wife of the new Bale. And just think, until Baroka dies, you shall be his favourite. No living in the outhouses for you, my girl. Your place will always be in the palace; first as the latest bride, and afterwards, as the head of the new harem . . . It is a rich life, Sidi. I know. I have been in that position for forty-one years.
SIDI: You waste your breath.
Why did Baroka not request my hand
Before the stranger
Brought his book of images?
Why did the Lion not bestow his gift
Before my face was lauded to the world?
Can you not see? Because he sees my worth
Increased and multiplied above his own;
Because he can already hear

The ballad-makers and their songs
In praise of Sidi, the incomparable,
While the Lion is forgotten.
He seeks to have me as his property
Where I must fade beneath his jealous hold.
Ah, Sadiku,
The school-man here has taught me certain things
And my images have taught me all the rest.
Baroka merely seeks to raise his manhood
Above my beauty
He seeks new fame
As the one man who has possessed
The jewel of Ilujinle!

SADIKU [*shocked, bewildered, incapable of making any sense of* SIDI'*s words*]: But Sidi, are you well? Such nonsense never passed your lips before. Did you not sound strange, even in your own hearing? [*Rushes suddenly at* LAKUNLE.] Is this your doing, you popinjay? Have you driven the poor girl mad at last? Such rubbish . . . I will beat your head for this!

LAKUNLE [*retreating in panic*]: Keep away from me, old hag.

SIDI: Sadiku, let him be.
Tell your lord that I can read his mind,
That I will none of him.
Look—judge for yourself.

[*Opens the magazine and points out the pictures.*]

He's old. I never knew till now,
He was that old . . .

[*During the rest of her speech,* SIDI *runs her hand over the surface of the relevant part of the photographs, tracing the contours with her fingers.*]

. . . To think I took
No notice of my velvet skin.
How smooth it is!
And no man ever thought
To praise the fulness of my breasts . . .

LAKUNLE [*laden with guilt and full of apology*]:
Well, Sidi, I did think . . .
But somehow it was not the proper thing.

SIDI [*ignores the interruption*]:
See I hold them to the warm caress

[*Unconsciously pushes out her chest.*]

Of a desire-filled sun.

[*Smiles mischievously.*]

There's a deceitful message in my eyes
Beckoning insatiate men to certain doom.
And teeth that flash the sign of happiness,
Strong and evenly, beaming full of life.
Be just, Sadiku,
Compare my image and your lord's—
An age of difference!
See how the water glistens on my face
Like the dew-moistened leaves on a Harmattan morning
But he—his face is like a leather piece
Torn rudely from the saddle of his horse,

[SADIKU *gasps.*]

Sprinkled with the musty ashes
From a pipe that is long over-smoked.
And this goat-like tuft
Which I once thought was manly;
It is like scattered twists of grass—
Not even green—
But charred and lifeless, as after a forest fire!
Sadiku, I am young and brimming; he is spent.
I am the twinkle of a jewel
But he is the hind-quarters of a lion!

SADIKU [*recovering at last from helpless amazement*]: May Sango restore your wits. For most surely some angry god has taken possession of you. [*Turns around and walks away. Stops again as she remembers something else.*] Your ranting put this clean out of my head. My lord says that if you would not be his wife, would you at least come to supper at his house tonight. There is a small feast in your honour. He wishes to tell you how happy he is that the great capital city has done so much honour to a daughter of Ilujinle. You have brought great fame to your people.

SIDI: Ho ho! Do you think that I was only born
Yesterday?
The tales of Baroka's little suppers,
I know all.
Tell your lord that Sidi does not sup with
Married men.

SADIKU: They are lies, lies. You must not believe everything you hear. Sidi, would I deceive you? I swear to you . . .

SIDI: Can you deny that
Every woman who has supped with him one night,
Becomes his wife or concubine the next.

LAKUNLE: Is it for nothing he is called the Fox?

SADIKU [*advancing on him*]: You keep out of this, or so Sango be my witness . . .

LAKUNLE [*retreats just a little, but continues to talk*]:
His wiliness is known even in the larger towns.
Did you never hear
Of how he foiled the Public Works attempt
To build the railway through Ilujinle.

SADIKU: Nobody knows the truth of that. It is all
hearsay.
SIDI: I love hearsays. Lakunle, tell me all.
LAKUNLE: Did you not know it? Well sit down and
listen.
My father told me, before he died. And few men
Know of this trick—oh he's a die-hard rogue
Sworn against our progress . . . yes . . . it
was . . . somewhere here
The track should have been laid just along
The outskirts. Well, the workers came, in fact
It was prisoners who were brought to do
The harder part . . . to break the jungle's back . . .

[*Enter the prisoners, guarded by two warders. A white surveyor examines his map (khaki helmet, spats, etc.) The foreman runs up with his camp stool, table etc., erects the umbrella over him and unpacks the usual box of bush comforts—soda siphon, whisky bottle and geometric sandwiches. His map consulted, he directs the sweat team where to work. They begin felling, matchet swinging, log dragging, all to the rhythm of the work gang's metal percussion (rod on gong or rude triangle, etc.) The two performers are also the song leaders and the others fill the chorus. "N'ijo itoro," "Amuda el 'ebe l'aiya" "Gbe je on'ipa" etc.*]

LAKUNLE: They marked the route with stakes, ate
Through the jungle and began the tracks. Trade,
Progress, adventure, success, civilization,
Fame, international conspicuousity . . . it was
All within the grasp of Ilujinle . . .

[*The wrestler enters, stands horrified at the sight and flees. Returns later with the Bale himself who soon assesses the situation. They disappear. The work continues, the surveyor occupies himself with the fly-whisk and whisky. Shortly after, a bull-roarer is heard. The prisoners falter a little, pick up again. The bull-roarer continues on its way, nearer and farther, moving in circles, so that it appears to come from all round them. The foreman is the first to break and then the rest is chaos. Sole survivor of the rout is the surveyor who is too surprised to move.*

BAROKA *enters a few minutes later accompanied by some attendants and preceded by a young girl bearing a calabash bowl. The surveyor, angry and threatening, is prevailed upon to open his gift. From it he reveals a wad of pound notes and kola nuts. Mutual understanding is established. The surveyor frowns heavily, rubs his chin and consults his map. Re-examines the contents of the bowl, shakes his head.* BAROKA *adds more money, and a coop of hens. A goat follows, and more money. This time "truth" dawns on him at last, he has made a mistake. The track really should go the other way. What an unfortunate error, discovered just in time! No, no, no possibility of a mistake this time, the track should be much further away. In fact (scooping up the soil) the earth is most unsuitable, couldn't possibly support the weight of a railway engine. A gourd of palm wine is brought to seal the agreement and a kola nut is broken.* BAROKA*'s men help the surveyor pack and they leave with their arms round each other followed by the surveyor's booty.*]

LAKUNLE [*as the last of the procession disappears, shakes his fist at them, stamping on the ground*]:
Voluptuous beast! He loves this life too well
To bear to part from it. And motor roads
And railways would do just that, forcing
Civilization at his door. He foresaw it
And he barred the gates, securing fast
His dogs and horses, his wives and all his
Concubines . . . ah, yes . . . all those concubines
Baroka has such a selective eye, none suits him
But the best . . .

[*His eyes truly light up.* SIDI *and* SADIKU *snigger, tip-toe offstage.*]

. . . Yes, one must grant him that.
Ah, I sometimes wish I led his kind of life.
Such luscious bosoms make his nightly pillow.
I am sure he keeps a time-table just as
I do at school. Only way to ensure fair play.
He must be healthy to keep going as he does.
I don't know what the women see in him. His eyes
Are small and always red with wine. He must
Possess some secret . . . No! I do not envy him!
Just the one woman for me. Alone I stand
For progress, with Sidi my chosen soul-mate,
the one
Woman of my life . . . Sidi! Sidi where are you?

[*Rushes out after them, returns to fetch the discarded firewood and runs out again.*]

●

[BAROKA *in bed, naked except for baggy trousers, calf-length. It is a rich bedroom covered in animal skins and rugs. Weapons round the wall. Also a strange machine, a most peculiar contraption with a long lever. Kneeling beside the bed is* BAROKA*'s current* FAVOURITE, *engaged in plucking the hairs from his armpit. She does this by first massaging the spot around the selected hair very gently with her forefinger. Then, with hardly a break, she pulls out the hair between her finger and the thumb with a sudden sharp movement.* BAROKA *twitches slightly with each pull. Then an aspirated "A-ah," and a look of complete beatitude spreads all over his face.*]

FAVOURITE: Do I improve my lord?

BAROKA: You are still somewhat over-gentle with the pull
As if you feared to hurt the panther of the trees.
Be sharp and sweet
Like the swift sting of a vicious wasp
For there the pleasure lies—the cooling aftermath.
FAVOURITE: I'll learn, my lord.
BAROKA: You have not time, my dear.
Tonight I hope to take another wife.
And the honour of this task, you know,
Belongs by right to my latest choice.
But—A-ah—Now that was sharp.
It had in it the scorpion's sudden sting
Without its poison.
It was an angry pull; you tried to hurt
For I had made you wrathful with my boast.
But now your anger flows in my blood-stream.
How sweet it is! A-ah! That was sweeter still.
I think perhaps that I shall let you stay,
The sole out-puller of my sweat-bathed hairs.
Ach!

[*Sits up suddenly and rubs the sore point angrily.*]

Now that had far more pain than pleasure
Vengeful creature, you did not caress
The area of extraction long enough!

[*Enter* SADIKU. *She goes down on her knees at once and bows her head into her lap.*]

Aha! Here comes Sadiku.
Do you bring some balm,
To soothe the smart of my misused armpit?
Away, you enemy!

[*Exit the* FAVOURITE.]

SADIKU: My lord . . .
BAROKA: You have my leave to speak.
What did she say?
SADIKU: She will not, my lord. I did my best, but she will have none of you.
BAROKA: It follows the pattern—a firm refusal
At the start. Why will she not?
SADIKU: That is the strange part of it. She say's you're much too old. If you ask me, I think that she is really off her head. All this excitement of the books has been too much for her.
BAROKA [*springs to his feet*]:
She says . . . That I am old
That I am much too old? Did a slight
Unripened girl say this of me?
SADIKU: My lord, I heard the incredible words with my ears, and I thought the world was mad.
BAROKA: But is it possible, Sadiku? Is this right?
Did I not, at the festival of Rain,
Defeat the men in the log-tossing match?
Do I not still with the most fearless ones,
Hunt the leopard and the boa at night
And save the farmers' goats from further harm?
And does she say I'm old?
Did I not, to announce the Harmattan,
Climb to the top of the silk-cotton tree,
Break the first pod, and scatter tasselled seeds
To the four winds—and this but yesterday?
Do any of my wives report
A failing in my manliness?
The strongest of them all
Still wearies long before the Lion does!
And so would she, had I the briefest chance
To teach this unfledged birdling
That lacks the wisdom to embrace
The rich mustiness of age . . . if I could once . . .
Come hither, soothe me, Sadiku
For I am wroth at heart.

[*Lies back on the bed, staring up as before.* SADIKU *takes her place at the foot of the bed and begins to tickle the soles of his feet.* BAROKA *turns to the left suddenly, reaches down the side, and comes up with a copy of the magazine. Opens it and begins to study the pictures. He heaves a long sigh.*]

That is good, Sadiku, very good.

[*He begins to compare some pictures in the book, obviously his own and* SIDI'*s. Flings the book away suddenly and stares at the ceiling for a second or two. Then, unsmiling.*]

Perhaps it is as well, Sadiku.
SADIKU: My lord, what did you say?
BAROKA: Yes, faithful one, I say it is as well.
The scorn, the laughter and the jeers
Would have been bitter.
Had she consented and my purpose failed,
I would have sunk with shame.
SADIKU: My lord, I do not understand.
BAROKA: The time has come when I can fool myself
No more. I am no man, Sadiku. My manhood
Ended near a week ago.
SADIKU: The gods forbid.
BAROKA: I wanted Sidi because I still hoped—
A foolish thought I know, but still—I hoped
That, with a virgin young and hot within,
My failing strength would rise and save my pride.

[SADIKU *begins to moan.*]

A waste of hope. I knew it even then.
But it's a human failing never to accept

The worst; and so I pandered to my vanity.
When manhood must, it ends.
The well of living, tapped beyond its depth,
Dries up, and mocks the wastrel in the end.
I am withered and unsapped, the joy
Of ballad-mongers, the aged butt
Of youth's ribaldry.

SADIKU [*tearfully*]: The Gods must have mercy yet.

BAROKA [*as if suddenly aware of her presence, starts up*]:
I have told this to no one but you,
Who are my eldest, my most faithful wife.
But if you dare parade my shame before the
world . . .

[SADIKU *shakes her head in protest and begins to stroke the soles of his feet with renewed tenderness.* BAROKA *sighs and falls back slowly.*]

How irritable I have grown of late
Such doubts to harbour of your loyalty . . .
But this disaster is too much for one
Checked thus as I upon the prime of youth.
That rains that blessed me from my birth
Number a meagre sixty-two;
While my grandfather, that man of teak,
Fathered two sons, late on sixty-five.
But Okiki, my father beat them all
Producing female twins at sixty-seven.
Why then must I, descendant of these lions
Forswear my wives at a youthful sixty-two
My veins of life run dry, my manhood gone!

[*His voice goes drowsy;* SADIKU *sighs and moans and caresses his feet. His face lights up suddenly with rapture.*]

Sango bear witness! These weary feet
Have felt the loving hands of much design
In women.
My soles have felt the scratch of harsh,
Gravelled hands.
They have borne the heaviness of clumsy,
Gorilla paws.
And I have known the tease of tiny,
Dainty hands,
Toy-like hands that tantalized
My eager senses,
Promised of thrills to come
Remaining
Unfulfilled because the fingers
Were too frail
The touch too light and faint to pierce
The incredible thickness of my soles.
But thou Sadiku, thy plain unadorned hands
Encase a sweet sensuality which age
Will not destroy. A-ah,
Oyayi! Beyond a doubt Sadiku,
Thou art the queen of them all.

[*Falls asleep.*]

NIGHT

The village centre. SIDI *stands by the Schoolroom window, admiring her photos as before. Enter* SADIKU *with a longish bundle. She is very furtive. Unveils the object which turns out to be a carved figure of the Bale, naked and in full detail. She takes a good look at it, bursts suddenly into derisive laughter, sets the figure standing in front of the tree.* SIDI *stares in utter amazement.*

SADIKU: So we did for you too did we? We did for you in the end. Oh high and mighty lion, have we really scotched you? A—ya-ya-ya . . . we women undid you in the end. I was there when it happened to your father, the great Okiki. I did for him, I, the youngest and freshest of the wives. I killed him with my strength. I called him and he came at me, but no, for him, this was not like other times. I, Sadiku, was I not flame itself and he the flax on old women's spindles? I ate him up! Race of mighty lions, we always consume you, at our pleasure we spin you, at our whim we make you dance; like the foolish top you think the world revolves around you . . . fools! fools! . . . it is you who run giddy while we stand still and watch, and draw your frail thread from you, slowly, till nothing is left but a runty old stick. I scotched Okiki, Sadiku's unopened treasure-house demanded sacrifice, and Okiki came with his rusted key. Like a snake he came at me, like a rag he went back, a limp rag, smeared shame. . . . [*Her ghoulish laugh re-possesses her.*] Ah, take warning my masters, we'll scotch you in the end . . . [*With a yell she leaps up, begins to dance round the tree, chanting.*]
Take warning, my masters
We'll scotch you in the end.

[SIDI *shuts the window gently, comes out,* SADIKU, *as she comes round again, gasps and is checked in mid-song.*]

SADIKU: Oh it is you my daughter. You should have chosen a better time to scare me to death. The hour of victory is no time for any woman to die.

SIDI: Why? What battle have you won?

SADIKU: Not me alone girl. You too. Every woman. Oh my daughter, that I have lived to see this day . . . To see him fizzle with the drabbest puff of a mis-primed "sakabula."

[*Resumes her dance.*]

Take warning, my masters
We'll scotch you in the end.

SIDI: Wait Sadiku. I cannot understand.

SADIKU: You will my girl. You will.
Take warning my masters . . .

SIDI: Sadiku, are you well?

SADIKU: Ask no questions my girl. Just join my victory dance. Oh Sango my lord, who of us possessed your lightning and ran like fire through that lion's tail . . .

SIDI [*holds her firmly as she is about to go off again*]:
Stop your loose ranting. You will not
Move from here until you make some sense.

SADIKU: Oh you are troublesome. Do you promise to tell no one?

SIDI: I swear it. Now tell me quickly.

[*As* SADIKU *whispers, her eyes widen.*]

O-ho-o-o-o-!
But Sadiku, if he knew the truth, why
Did he ask me to . . .

[*Again* SADIKU *whispers.*]

Ha ha! Some hope indeed. Oh Sadiku
I suddenly am glad to be a woman.

[*Leaps in the air.*]

We won! We won! Hurray for womankind!

[*Falls in behind* SADIKU.]

Take warning, my masters
We'll scotch you in the end. [LAKUNLE *enters unobserved.*]

LAKUNLE: The full moon is not yet, but
The women cannot wait.
They must go mad without it.

[*The dancing stops.* SADIKU *frowns.*]

SADIKU: The scarecrow is here. Begone fop! This is the world of women. At this moment our star sits in the centre of the sky. We are supreme. What is more, we are about to perform a ritual. If you remain, we will chop you up, we will make you the sacrifice.

LAKUNLE: What is the hag gibbering?

SADIKU [*advances menacingly*]: You less than man, you less than the littlest woman, I say begone!

LAKUNLE [*nettled*]: I will have you know that I am a man
As you will find out if you dare
To lay a hand on me.

SADIKU [*throws back her head in laughter*]: You a man? Is Baroka not more of a man than you? And if he is no longer a man, then what are you? [LAKUNLE, *understanding the meaning, stands rooted, shocked.*] Come on, dear girl, let him look on if he will. After all, only *men* are barred from watching this ceremony.
Take warning, my masters
We'll . . .

SIDI: Stop. Sadiku stop. Oh such an idea
Is running in my head. Let me to the palace for
This supper he promised me. Sadiku, what a way
To mock the devil. I shall ask forgiveness
For my hasty words . . . No need to change
My answer and consent to be his bride—he might
Suspect you've told me. But I shall ask a month
To think on it.

SADIKU [*somewhat doubtful*]: Baroka is no child you know, he will know I have betrayed him.

SIDI: No, he will not. Oh Sadiku let me go.
I long to see him thwarted, to watch his longing
His twitching hands which this time cannot
Rush to loosen his trouser cords.

SADIKU: You will have to match the fox's cunning.
Use your bashful looks and be truly repentant.
Goad him my child, torment him until he weeps for shame.

SIDI: Leave it to me. He will never suspect you of deceit.

SADIKU [*with another of her energetic leaps*]: Yo-rooo o!
Yo-rororo o!
Shall I come with you?

SIDI: Will that be wise? You forget
We have not seen each other.

SADIKU: Away then. Away woman. I shall bide here.
Haste back and tell Sadiku how the no-man is.
Away, my lovely child.

LAKUNLE [*he has listened with increasing horror*]:
No, Sidi, don't. If you care
One little bit for what I feel,
Do not go to torment the man.
Suppose he knows that you have come to jeer—
And he will know, if he is not a fool—
He is a savage thing, degenerate
He would beat a helpless woman if he could . . .

SIDI [*running off gleefully*]: Ta-raa school teacher. Wait here for me.

LAKUNLE [*stamps his foot helplessly*]:
Foolish girl! . . . And this is all your work.
Could you not keep a secret?
Must every word leak out of you
As surely as the final drops
Of mother's milk
Oozed from your flattened breast
Generations ago?

SADIKU: Watch your wagging tongue, unformed creature!

LAKUNLE: If any harm befalls her . . .
SADIKU: Woman though she is, she can take better care of herself than you can of her. Fancy a thing like you actually wanting a girl like that, all to your little self. [*Walks round him and looks him up and down.*] Ah! Oba Ala is an accommodating god. What a poor figure you cut!
LAKUNLE: I wouldn't demean myself to bandy words
With a woman of the bush.
SADIKU: At this moment, your betrothed is supping with the Lion.
LAKUNLE [*pleased at the use of the word "Betrothed"*]:
Well, we are not really betrothed as yet,
I mean, she is not promised yet.
But it will come in time, I'm sure.
SADIKU [*bursts into her cackling laughter*]:
The bride-price, is that paid?
LAKUNLE: Mind your own business.
SADIKU: Why don't you do what other men have done. Take a farm for a season. One harvest will be enough to pay the price, even for a girl like Sidi. Or will the smell of the wet soil be too much for your delicate nostrils?
LAKUNLE: I said mind your own business.
SADIKU: A—a—ah. It is true what they say then. You are going to convert the whole village so that no one will ever pay the bride-price again. Ah, you're a clever man. I must admit that it is a good way for getting out of it, but don't you think you'd use more time and energy that way than you would if . . .
LAKUNLE [*with conviction*]:
Within a year or two, I swear,
This town shall see a transformation
Bride-price will be a thing forgotten
And wives shall take their place by men.
A motor road will pass this spot.
And bring the city ways to us.
We'll buy saucepans for all the women
Clay pots are crude and unhygienic
No man shall take more wives than one
That's why they're impotent too soon.
The ruler shall ride cars, not horses
Or a bicycle at the very least.
We'll burn the forest, cut the trees
Then plant a modern park for lovers
We'll print newspapers every day
With pictures of seductive girls.
The world will judge our progress by
The girls that win beauty contests.
While Lagos builds new factories daily
We only play "ayo" and gossip.
Where is our school of Ballroom dancing?
Who here can throw a cocktail party?
We must be modern with the rest
Or live forgotten by the world
We must reject the palm wine habit
And take to tea, with milk and sugar.

[*Turns on* SADIKU *who has been staring at him in terror. She retreats, and he continues to talk down at her as they go round, then down and off-stage,* LAKUNLE*'s hectoring voice trailing away in the distance.*]

This is my plan, you withered face
And I shall start by teaching you.
From now you shall attend my school
And take your place with twelve-year olds.
For though you're nearly seventy,
Your mind is simple and unformed.
Have you no shame that at your age,
You neither read nor write nor think?
You spend your days as senior wife,
Collecting brides for Baroka.
And now because you've sucked him dry,
You send my Sidi to his shame. . . .

[*The scene changes to* BAROKA*'s bedroom. On the left in a one-knee-on-floor posture, two men are engaged in a kind of wrestling, their arms clasped round each other's waist, testing the right moment to leave. One is* BAROKA, *the other a short squat figure of apparent muscular power. The contest is still in the balanced stage. In some distant part of the house,* SIDI*'s voice is heard lifted in the familiar general greeting, addressed to no one in particular.*]

SIDI: A good day to the head and people
Of this house.

[BAROKA *lifts his head, frowns as if he is trying to place the voice.*]

A good day to the head and people
Of this house.

[BAROKA *now decides to ignore it and to concentrate on the contest.* SIDI*'s voice draws progressively nearer. She enters nearly backwards, as she is still busy admiring the room through which she has just passed. Gasps on turning round to see the two men.*]

BAROKA [*without looking up*]: Is Sadiku not at home then?
SIDI [*absent-mindedly*]: Hm?
BAROKA: I asked, is Sadiku not at home?
SIDI [*recollecting herself, she curtsys quickly*]:
I saw no one, Baroka.
BAROKA: No one? Do you mean there was no one
To bar unwanted strangers from my privacy?
SIDI [*retreating*]: The house . . . seemed . . . empty.
BAROKA: Ah, I forget. This is the price I pay
Once every week, for being progressive.

Prompted by the school teacher, my servants
Were prevailed upon to form something they call
The Palace Workers' Union. And in keeping
With the habits—I am told—of modern towns,
This is their day off.

SIDI [*seeing that* BAROKA *seems to be in a better mood; she becomes somewhat bolder. Moves forward—saucily*]:
Is this also a day off
For Baroka's wives?

BAROKA [*looks up sharply, relaxes and speaks with a casual voice*]:
No, the madness has not gripped them—yet.
Did you not meet with one of them?
SIDI: No, Baroka. There was no one about.
BAROKA: Not even Ailatu, my favourite?
Was she not at her usual place,
Beside my door?
SIDI [*absently. She is deeply engrossed in watching the contest*]:
Her stool is there. And I saw
The slippers she was embroidering.
BAROKA: Hm. Hm. I think I know
Where she'll be found. In a dark corner
Sulking like a slighted cockroach.
By the way, look and tell me
If she left her shawl behind.

[*So as not to miss any part of the tussle, she moves backwards, darts a quick look round the door and back again.*]

SIDI: There is a black shawl on the stool.
BAROKA [*a regretful sigh*]:
Then she'll be back tonight. I had hoped
My words were harsh enough
To free me from her spite for a week or more.
SIDI: Did Ailatu offend her husband?
BAROKA: Offend? My armpit still weeps blood
For the gross abuse I suffered from one
I called my favourite.
SIDI [*in a disappointed voice*]: Oh. Is that all?
BAROKA: Is that not enough? Why child?
What more could the woman do?
SIDI: Nothing. Nothing, Baroka. I thought perhaps—
Well—young wives are known to be—
Forward—sometimes—to their husbands.
BAROKA: In an ill-kept household perhaps. But not
Under Baroka's roof. And yet,
Such are the sudden spites of women
That even I cannot foresee them all.
And child—if I lose this little match
Remember that my armpit
Burns and itches turn by turn.

[SIDI *continues watching for some time, then clasps her hand over her mouth as she remembers what she should have done to begin with. Doubtful how to proceed, she hesitates for some moments, then comes to a decision and kneels.*]

SIDI: I have come, Bale, as a repentant child.
BAROKA: What?
SIDI [*very hesitantly, eyes to the floor, but she darts a quick look up when she thinks the Bale isn't looking*]:
The answer which I sent to the Bale
Was given in a thoughtless moment . . . .
BAROKA: Answer, child? To what?
SIDI: A message brought by . . .
BAROKA [*groans and strains in a muscular effort*]:
Will you say that again? It is true that for supper
I did require your company. But up till now
Sadiku has brought no reply.
SIDI [*amazed*]: But the other matter! Did not the Bale
Send . . . did Baroka not send . . . ?
BAROKA [*with sinister encouragement*]:
What did Baroka not, my child?
SIDI [*cowed, but angry, rises*]:
It is nothing, Bale. I only hope
That I am here at the Bale's invitation.
BAROKA [*as if trying to understand, he frowns as he looks at her*]:
A-ah, at last I understand. You think
I took offence because you entered
Unannounced?
SIDI: I remember that the Bale called me
An unwanted stranger.
BAROKA: That could be expected. Is a man's bedroom
To be made naked to any flea
That chances to wander through?

[SIDI *turns away, very hurt.*]

Come, come my child. You are too quick
To feel aggrieved. Of course you are
More than welcome. But I expected Ailatu
To tell me you were here.

[SIDI *curtsys briefly with her back to* BAROKA. *After a while, she turns round. The mischief returns to her face.* BAROKA*'s attitude of denial has been a set-back but she is now ready to pursue her mission.*]

SIDI: I hope the Bale will not think me
Forward. But, like everyone, I had thought
The Favourite was a gentle woman.
BAROKA: And so had I.
SIDI [*slyly*]: One would hardly think that *she*
Would give offence without a cause
Was the Favourite . . . in some way . . .
Dissatisfied . . . with her lord and husband?

[*With a mock curtsy, quickly executed as* BAROKA *begins to look up.*]

BAROKA [*slowly turns toward her*]:
Now that
Is a question which I never thought to hear
Except from a school teacher. Do you think
The Lion has such leisure that he asks
The whys and wherefores of a woman's
Squint?

[SIDI *steps back and curtsys. As before, and throughout this scene, she is easily cowed by* BAROKA*'s change of mood, all the more easily as she is, in any case, frightened by her own boldness.*]

SIDI: I meant no disrespect . . .
BAROKA [*gently*]: I know. [*Breaks off.*] Christians on my
Father's shrines, child!
Do you think I took offence? A—aw
Come in and seat yourself. Since you broke in
Unawares, and appear resolved to stay,
Try, if you can, not to make me feel
A humorless old ram. I allow no one
To watch my daily exercise, but as we say,
The woman gets lost in the woods one day
And every wood deity dies the next.

[SIDI *curtsys, watches and moves forward warily, as if expecting the two men to spring apart too suddenly.*]

SIDI: I think he will win.
BAROKA: Is that a wish, my daughter?
SIDI: No, but— [*Hesitates, but boldness wins.*]
If the tortoise cannot tumble
It does not mean that he can stand.

[BAROKA *looks at her, seemingly puzzled.* SIDI *turns away, humming.*]

BAROKA: When the child is full of riddles, the mother
Has one water-pot the less.

[SIDI *tiptoes to* BAROKA*'s back and pulls asses' ears at him.*]

SIDI: I think he will win.
BAROKA: He knows he must. Would it profit me
To pit my strength against a weakling?
Only yesterday, this son of—I suspect—
A python for a mother, and fathered beyond doubt
By a blubber-bottomed baboon,

[*The complimented man grins.*]

Only yesterday, he nearly
Ploughed my tongue with my front teeth
In a friendly wrestling bout.
WRESTLER [*encouraged, makes an effort*]: Ugh Ugh.
SIDI [*bent almost over them. Genuinely worried*]:
Oh! Does it hurt?
BAROKA: Not yet . . . but, as I was saying
I change my wrestlers when I have learnt
To throw them. I also change my wives
When I have learnt to tire them.
SIDI: And is this another . . . changing time
For the Bale?
BAROKA: Who knows? Until the finger nails
Have scraped the dust, no one can tell
Which insect released his bowels.

[SIDI *grimaces in disgust and walks away. Returns as she thinks up a new idea.*]

SIDI: A woman spoke to me this afternoon.
BAROKA: Indeed. And does Sidi find this
unusual—
That a woman speak with her in the afternoon?
SIDI [*stamping*]: No. She had the message of a
go-between.
BAROKA: Did she? Then I rejoice with you.

[SIDI *stands biting her lips.* BAROKA *looks at her, this time with deliberate appreciation.*]

And now I think of it, why not?
There must be many men who
Build their loft to fit your height.
SIDI [*unmoving, pointedly*]:
Her message came from one
With many lofts.
BAROKA: Ah! Such is the greed of men.
SIDI: If Baroka were my father
[*aside*] —which many would take him to be—

[*Makes a rude sign.*]

Would he pay my dowry to this man
And give his blessings?
BAROKA: Well, I must know his character.
For instance, is the man rich?
SIDI: Rumour has it so.
BAROKA: Is he repulsive?
SIDI: He is old. [BAROKA *winces.*]
BAROKA: Is he mean and miserly?
SIDI: To strangers—no. There are tales
Of his open-handedness, which are never
Quite without a motive. But his wives report
—To take one little story—
How he grew the taste for ground corn
And pepper—because he would not pay
The price of snuff!

[*With a sudden burst of angry energy,* BAROKA *lifts his opponent and throws him over his shoulder.*]

BAROKA: A lie! The price of snuff
Had nothing to do with it.
SIDI [*too excited to listen*]: You won!
BAROKA: By the years on my beard, I swear
They slander me!
SIDI [*excitedly*]: You won. You won!

[*She breaks into a kind of shoulder dance and sings.*]

Yokolu Yokolu. Ko ha tan bi
Iyawo gb'oko san'le
Oko yo 'ke . . .

[*She repeats this throughout* BAROKA*'s protests.* BAROKA *is pacing angrily up and down. The defeated man, nursing a hip, goes to the corner of the room and lifts out a low "ako" bench. He sits on the floor, and soon,* BAROKA *joins him; using only their arms now, they place their elbows on the bench and grip hands.* BAROKA *takes his off again, replaces it, takes it off again and so on during the rest of his outburst.*]

BAROKA: This means nothing to me of course.
Nothing!
But I know the ways of women, and I know
Their ruinous tongues.
Suppose that, as a child—only suppose—
Suppose then, that as a child, I—
And remember, I only use myself
To illustrate the plight of many men . . .
So, once again, suppose that as a child
I grew to love "tanfiri"—with a good dose of
pepper
And growing old, I found that—
Sooner than die away, my passion only
Bred itself upon each mouthful of
Ground corn and pepper I consumed.
Now, think child, would it be seemly
At my age, and the father of children,
To be discovered, in public
Thrusting fistfuls of corn and pepper
In my mouth? Is it not wise to indulge
In the little masquerade of a dignified
Snuff-box?—But remember, I only make
A pleading for this prey of women's
Malice. I feel his own injustice,
Being myself, a daily fellow-sufferer!

[BAROKA *seems to realize for the first time that* SIDI *has paid no attention to his explanation. She is, in fact, still humming and shaking her shoulders. He stares questioningly at her.* SIDI *stops, somewhat confused and embarrassed, points sheepishly to the wrestler.*]

SIDI: I think this time he will win.

[BAROKA*'s grumbling subsides slowly. He is now attentive to the present bout.*]

BAROKA: Now let us once again take up
The questioning. [*Almost timidly.*] Is this man
Good and kindly.
SIDI: They say he uses well
His dogs and horses.
BAROKA [*desperately*]:
Well is he fierce then? Reckless!
Does the bush cow run to hole
When he hears his beaters' Hei-ei-wo-rah!
SIDI: There are heads and skins of leopards
Hung around his council room.
But the market is also
Full of them.
BAROKA: Is he not wise? Is he not sagely?
Do the young and old not seek
His counsel?
SIDI: The Fox is said to be wise
So cunning that he stalks and dines on
New-hatched chickens.
BAROKA [*more and more desperate*]:
Does he not beget strength on wombs?
Are his children not tall and stout-limbed?
SIDI: Once upon a time.
BAROKA: Once upon a time?
What do you mean, girl?
SIDI: Just once upon a time.
Perhaps his children have of late
Been plagued with shyness and refuse
To come into the world. Or else
He is so tired with the day's affairs
That at night, he turns his buttocks
To his wives. But there have been
No new reeds cut by his servants,
No new cots woven.
And his household gods are starved
For want of child-naming festivities
Since the last two rains went by.
BAROKA: Perhaps he is a frugal man.
Mindful of years to come,
Planning for a final burst of life, he
Husbands his strength.
SIDI [*giggling. She is actually stopped, half-way, by giggling at the cleverness of her remark*]:
To husband his wives surely ought to be
A man's first duties—at all times.
BAROKA: My beard tells me you've been a pupil,
A most diligent pupil of Sadiku.
Among all shameless women,
The sharpest tongues grow from that one
Peeling bark—Sadiku, my faithful lizard!

[*Growing steadily warmer during this speech, he again slaps down his opponent's arm as he shouts* "SADIKU."]

SIDI [*backing away, aware that she has perhaps gone too far and betrayed knowledge of the "secret"*]:
I have learnt nothing of anyone.

BAROKA: No more. No more.
Already I have lost a wrestler
On your account. This town-bred daring
Of little girls, awakes in me
A seven-horned devil of strength.
Let one woman speak a careless word
And I can pin a wriggling—Bah!

[*Lets go the man's arm. He has risen during the last speech but held on to the man's arm, who is forced to rise with him.*]

The tappers should have called by now.
See if we have a fresh gourd by the door.

[*The wrestler goes out.* BAROKA *goes to sit on the bed,* SIDI *eyeing him, doubtfully.*]

What an ill-tempered man I daily grow
Towards. Soon my voice will be
The sand between two grinding stones.
But I have my scattered kindliness
Though few occasions serve to herald it.
And Sidi, my daughter, you do not know
The thoughts which prompted me
To ask the pleasure that I be your host
This evening, I would not tell Sadiku,
Meaning to give delight
With the surprise of it. Now, tell me, child
Can you guess a little at this thing?

SIDI: Sadiku told me nothing.

BAROKA: You are hasty with denial. For how indeed
Could Sadiku, since I told her
Nothing of my mind, But, my daughter,
Did she not, perhaps . . . invent some tale?
For I know Sadiku loves to be
All-knowing.

SIDI: She said no more, except the Bale
Begged my presence.

BAROKA [*rises quickly to the bait*]:
Begged? Bale Baroka begged?

[*Wrestler enters with gourd and calabash-cups.* BAROKA *relapses.*]

Ah! I see you love to bait your elders.
One way the world remains the same,
The child still thinks she is wiser than
The cotton head of age.
Do you think Baroka deaf or blind
To little signs? But let that pass.
Only, lest you fall victim to the schemes
Of busy women, I will tell you this—
I know Sadiku plays the match-maker
Without the prompting. If I look
On any maid, or call her name
Even in the course of harmless, neighbourly
Well-wishing—How fares your daughter?
—Is your sister now recovered from her
Whooping cough?—How fast your ward
Approaches womanhood! Have the village lads
Begun to gather at your door?—
Or any word at all which shows I am
The thoughtful guardian of the village health,
If it concerns a woman, Sadiku straightway
Flings herself into the role of go-between
And before I even don a cap, I find
Yet another stranger in my bed!

SIDI: It seems a Bale's life
Is full of great unhappiness.

BAROKA: I do not complain. No, my child
I accept the sweet and sour with
A ruler's grace. I lose my patience
Only when I meet with
The new immodesty with women.
Now, my Sidi, you have not caught
This new and strange disease, I hope.

SIDI [*curtsying*]: The threading of my smock—
Does Baroka not know the marking
Of the village loom?

BAROKA: But will Sidi, the pride of mothers,
Will she always wear it?

SIDI: Will Sidi, the proud daughter of Baroka,
Will she step out naked?

[*A pause.* BAROKA *surveys* SIDI *in an almost fatherly manner and she bashfully drops her eyes.*]

BAROKA: To think that once I thought,
Sidi is the eye's delight, but
She is vain, and her head
Is feather-light, and always giddy
With a trivial thought. And now
I find her deep and wise beyond her years.

[*Reaches under his pillow, brings out the now familiar magazine, and also an addressed envelope. Retains the former and gives her the envelope.*]

Do you know what this means?
The trim red piece of paper
In the corner?

SIDI: I know it. A stamp. Lakunle receives
Letters from Lagos marked with it.

BAROKA [*obviously disappointed*]:
Hm. Lakunle. But more about him
Later. Do you know what it means—
This little frippery?

SIDI [*very proudly*]:
Yes. I know that too. Is it not a tax on
The habit of talking with paper?
BAROKA: Oh. Oh. I see you dip your hand
Into the pockets of the school teacher
And retrieve it bulging with knowledge.

[*Goes to the strange machine, and pulls the lever up and down.*]

Now this, not even the school teacher can tell
What magic this performs. Come nearer,
It will not bite.
SIDI: I have never seen the like.
BAROKA: The work dear child, of the palace blacksmiths
Built in full secrecy. All is not well with it—
But I will find the cause and then Ilujinle
Will boast its own tax on paper, made with
Stamps like this. For long I dreamt it
And here it stands, child of my thoughts.
SIDI [*wonder-struck*]: You mean . . . this will work some day?
BAROKA: Ogun has said the word. And now my girl
What think you of that image on the stamp
This spiderwork of iron, wood and mortar?
SIDI: Is it not a bridge?
BAROKA: It is a bridge. The longest—so they say
In the whole country. When not a bridge,
You'll find a print of groundnuts
Stacked like pyramids,
Or palm trees, or cocoa-trees, and farmers
Hacking pods, and workmen
Felling trees and tying skinned logs
Into rafts. A thousand thousand letters
By road, by rail, by air,
From one end of the world to another,
And not one human head among them;
Not one head of beauty on the stamp?
SIDI: But I once saw Lakunle's letter
With a head of bronze.
BAROKA: A figurehead, my child, a lifeless work
Of craft, with holes for eyes, and coldness
For the warmth of life and love
In youthful cheeks like yours,
My daughter . . .

[*Pauses to watch the effect on* SIDI.]

. . . Can you see it, Sidi?
Tens of thousands of these dainty prints
And each one with this legend of Sidi.

[*Flourishes the magazine, open in the middle.*]

The village goddess, reaching out
Towards the sun, her lover.
Can you see it, my daughter!

[SIDI *drowns herself totally in the contemplation, takes the magazine but does not even look at it. Sits on the bed.*]

BAROKA [*very gently*]:
I hope you will not think it too great
A burden, to carry the country's mail
All on your comeliness.

[*Walks away, an almost business-like tone.*]

Our beginnings will
Of course be modest. We shall begin
By cutting stamps for our own village alone.
As the schoolmaster himself would say—
Charity begins at home.

[*Pause. Faces* SIDI *from nearly the distance of the room.*]

For a long time now,
The town-dwellers have made up tales
Of the backwardness of Ilujinle
Until it hurts Baroka, who holds
The welfare of his people deep at heart.
Now, if we do this thing, it will prove more
Than any single town has done!

[*The wrestler, who has been listening open-mouthed, drops his cup in admiration.* BAROKA, *annoyed, realizing only now in fact that he is still in the room, waves him impatiently out.*]

I do not hate progress, only its nature
Which makes all roofs and faces look the same.
And the wish of one old man is
That here and there,

[*Goes progressively towards* SIDI, *until he bends over her, then sits beside her on the bed.*]

Among the bridges and the murderous roads,
Below the humming birds which
Smoke the face of Sango, dispenser of
The snake-tongue lightning; between this moment
And the reckless broom that will be wielded
In these years to come, we must leave
Virgin plots of lives, rich decay
And the tang of vapour rising from
Forgotten heaps of compost, lying
Undisturbed . . . But the skin of progress
Masks, unknown, the spotted wolf of sameness . . .

Does sameness not revolt your being,
My daughter?

[SIDI *is capable only of a bewildered nod, slowly.*]

BAROKA [*sighs, hands folded piously on his lap*]:
I find my soul is sensitive, like yours,
Indeed, although there is one—no more think I—
One generation between yours and mine,
Our thoughts fly crisply through the air
And meet, purified, as one.
And our first union
Is the making of this stamp.
The one redeeming grace on any paper-tax
Shall be your face. And mine,
The soul behind it all, worshipful
Of Nature for her gift of youth
And beauty to our earth. Does this
Please you, my daughter?

SIDI: I can no longer see the meaning, Baroka.
Now that you speak
Almost like the school teacher, except
Your words fly on a different path,
I find . . .

BAROKA: It is a bad thing, then, to sound
Like your school teacher?

SIDI: No Bale, but words are like beetles
Boring at my ears, and my head
Becomes a jumping bean. Perhaps after all,
As the school teacher tells me often,

[*Very miserably.*]

I have a simple mind.

BAROKA [*pats her kindly on the head*]:
No, Sidi, not simple, only straight and truthful
Like a fresh-water reed. But I do find
Your school teacher and I are much alike.
The proof of wisdom is the wish to learn
Even from children. And the haste of youth
Must learn its temper from the gloss
Of ancient leather, from a strength
Knit close along the grain. The school teacher
And I, must learn one from the other.
Is this not right?

[*A tearful nod.*]

BAROKA: The old must flow into the new, Sidi,
Not blind itself or stand foolishly
Apart. A girl like you must inherit
Miracles which age alone reveals.
Is this not so?

SIDI: Everything you say, Bale,
Seems wise to me.

BAROKA: Yesterday's wine alone is strong and blooded, child,
And though the Christians' holy book denies
The truth of this, old wine thrives best
Within a new bottle. The coarseness
Is mellowed down, and the rugged wine
Acquires a full and rounded body . . .
Is this not so—my child?

[*Quite overcome,* SIDI *nods.*]

BAROKA: Those who know little of Baroka think
His life one pleasure-living course.
But the monkey sweats, my child,
The monkey sweats,
It is only the hair upon his back
Which still deceives the world . . .

[SIDI'*s head falls slowly on the Bale's shoulder. The Bale remains in his final body-weighed-down-by-burdens-of-State attitude.*

Even before the scene is completely shut off a crowd of dancers burst in at the front and dance off at the opposite side without slackening pace. In their brief appearance it should be apparent that they comprise a group of female dancers pursuing a masked male. Drumming and shouts continue quite audibly and shortly afterwards. They enter and re-cross the stage in the same manner.

The shouts fade away and they next appear at the market clearing. It is now full evening. LAKUNLE *and* SADIKU *are still waiting for* SIDI'*s return. The traders are beginning to assemble one by one, ready for the evening market. Hawkers pass through with oil-lamps beside their ware. Food sellers enter with cooking-pots and foodstuffs, set up their "adogan" or stone hearth and build a fire.*

All this while, LAKUNLE *is pacing wretchedly,* SADIKU *looks on placidly.*]

LAKUNLE [*he is pacing furiously*]:
He's killed her.
I warned you. You know him,
And I warned you.

[*Goes up all the approaches to look.*]

She's been gone half the day. It will soon
Be daylight. And still no news.
Women have disappeared before.
No trace. Vanished. Now we know how.

[*Checks, turns round.*]

And why!
Mock an old man, will you? So?
You can laugh? Ha ha! You wait.

I'll come and see you
Whipped like a dog. Baroka's head wife
Driven out of the house for plotting
With a girl.

[*Each approaching footstep brings* LAKUNLE *to attention, but it is only a hawker or a passer-by. The wrestler passes.* SADIKU *greets him familiarly. Then, after he has passed, some signifiicance of this breaks on* SADIKU *and she begins to look a little puzzled.*]

LAKUNLE: I know he has dungeons. Secret holes
Where a helpless girl will lie
And rot for ever. But not for nothing
Was I born a man. I'll find my way
To rescue her. She little deserves it, but
I shall risk my life for her.

[*The mummers can now be heard again, distantly.* SADIKU *and* LAKUNLE *become attentive as the noise approaches,* LAKUNLE *increasingly uneasy. A little, but not too much notice is paid by the market people.*]

What is that?
SADIKU: If my guess is right, it will be mummers.

[*Adds slyly.*]

Somebody must have told them the news.
LAKUNLE: What news?

[SADIKU *chuckles darkly and comprehension breaks on the School teacher.*]

Baroka! You dared . . . ?
Woman, is there no mercy in your veins?
He gave you children, and he stood
Faithfully by you and them.
He risked his life that you may boast
A warrior-hunter for your lord . . . But you—
You sell him to the rhyming rabble
Gloating in your disloyalty . . .
SADIKU [*calmly dips her hand in his pocket*]:
Have you any money?
LAKUNLE [*snatching out her hand*]:
Why? What? . . . Keep away, witch! Have you
Turned pickpocket in your dotage?
SADIKU: Don't be a miser. Will you let them go without giving you a special performance?
LAKUNLE: If you think I care for their obscenity . . .
SADIKU [*wheedling*]: Come on, school teacher. They'll expect if of you . . . The man of learning . . . the young sprig of foreign wisdom . . . You must not demean yourself in their eyes . . . you must give them money to perform for your lordship . . .

[*Re-enter the mummers, dancing straight through (more centrally this time) as before. Male dancer enters first, pursued by a number of young women and other choral idlers. The man dances in tortured movements. He and about half of his pursuers have already danced off-stage on the opposite side when* SADIKU *dips her hand briskly in* LAKUNLE's *pocket, this time with greater success. Before* LAKUNLE *can stop her, she has darted to the drummers and pressed a coin apiece on their foreheads, waving them to possession of the floor. Tilting their heads backwards, they drum her praises.* SADIKU *denies the credit, points to* LAKUNLE *as the generous benefactor. They transfer their attention to him where he stands biting his lips at the trick. The other dancers have now been brought back and the drummers resume the beat of the interrupted dance. The treasurer removes the coins from their foreheads and places them in a pouch. Now begins the dance of virility which is of course none other than the* BAROKA *story. Very athletic movements. Even in his prime, "*BAROKA*" is made a comic figure, held in a kind of tolerant respect by his women. At his decline and final downfall, they are most unsparing in their taunts and tantalizing motions.* SADIKU *has never stopped bouncing on her toes through the dance, now she is done the honour of being invited to join at the kill. A dumb show of bashful refusals, then she joins them, reveals surprising agility for her age, to the wild enthusiasm of the rest who surround and spur her on.*

*With "*BAROKA*" finally scotched, the crowd dances away to their incoming movement, leaving* SADIKU *to dance on oblivious of their departure. The drumming becomes more distant and she unwraps her eyelids. Sighs, looks around her and walks contentedly towards* LAKUNLE. *As usual he has enjoyed the spectacle in spite of himself, showing especial relish where "*BAROKA*" gets the worst of it from his women.* SADIKU *looks at him for a moment while he tries to replace his obvious enjoyment with disdain. She shouts "Boo" at him, and breaks into a dance movement, shakes a sudden leg at* LAKUNLE.]

SADIKU: Sadiku of the duiker's feet . . . that's what the men used to call me. I could twist and untwist my waist with the smoothness of a water snake . . .
LAKUNLE: No doubt. And you are still just as slippery.
I hope Baroka kills you for this.
When he finds out what your wagging tongue
Has done to him, I hope he beats you
Till you choke on your own breath . . .

[SIDI *bursts in, she has been running all the way. She throws herself on the ground against the tree and sobs violently, beating herself on the ground.*]

SADIKU [*on her knees beside her*]: Why, child. What is the matter?

SIDI [*pushes her off*]:
Get away from me. Do not touch me.
LAKUNLE [*with a triumphant smile, he pulls* SADIKU *away and takes her place*]: Oh, Sidi, let me kiss your tears . . .
SIDI [*pushes him so hard that he sits down abruptly*]:
Don't touch me.
LAKUNLE [*dusting himself*]:
He must have beaten her.
Did I not warn you both?
Baroka is a creature of the wilds,
Untutored, mannerless, devoid of grace.

[SIDI *only cries all the more, beats on the ground with clenched fists and stubs her toes in the ground.*]

Chief though he is,
I shall kill him for this . . .
No. Better still, I shall demand
Redress from the central courts.
I shall make him spend
The remainder of his wretched life
In prison—with hard labour.
I'll teach him
To beat defenceless women
SIDI: [*lifting her head*]:
Fool! You little fools! It was a lie.
The frog. The cunning frog!
He lied to you, Sadiku.
SADIKU: Sango forbid!
SIDI: He told me . . . afterwards, crowing.
It was a trick.
He knew Sadiku would not keep it to herself,
That I, or maybe other maids would hear of it
And go to mock his plight.
And how he laughed!
How his frog-face croaked and croaked
And called me little fool!
Oh how I hate I him! How I loathe
And long to kill the man!
LAKUNLE [*retreating*]: But Sidi, did he . . . ? I mean . . .
Did you escape?

[*Louder sobs from* SIDI.]

Speak, Sidi, this is agony.
Tell me the worst; I'll take it like a man.
Is it the fright which effects you so,
Or did he . . . ? Sidi, I cannot bear the thought.
The words refuse to form.
Do not unman me, Sidi. Speak
Before I burst in tears.
SADIKU [*raises* SIDI*'s chin in her hand*]:
Sidi, are you a maid or not?

[SIDI *shakes her head violently and bursts afresh in tears.*]

LAKUNLE: The Lord forbid!
SADIKU: Too late for prayers. Cheer up. It happens to the best of us.
LAKUNLE: Oh heavens, strike me dead!
Earth, open up and swallow Lakunle.
For he no longer has the wish to live.
Let the lightning fall and shrivel me
To dust and ashes . . .

[*Recoils.*]

No, that wish is cowardly. This trial is my own.
Let Sango and his lightning keep out of this. It
Is my cross, and let it not be spoken that
In the hour of need, Lakunle stood
Upon the scales and was proved wanting.
My love is selfless—the love of spirit
Not of flesh.

[*Stands over* SIDI.]

Dear Sidi, we shall forget the past.
This great misfortune touches not
The treasury of my love.
But you will agree, it is only fair
That we forget the bride-price totally
Since you no longer can be called a maid.
Here is my hand; if on these terms,
You'll be my cherished wife.
We'll take an oath, between us three
That this shall stay
A secret to our dying days . . .

[*Takes a look at* SADIKU *and adds quickly.*]

Oh no, a secret even after we're dead and gone.
And if Baroka dares to boast of it,
I'll swear he is a liar—and swear by Sango too!

[SIDI *raises herself slowly, staring at* LAKUNLE *with unbelieving eyes. She is unsmiling, her face a puzzle.*]

SIDI: You would? You would marry me?
LAKUNLE [*puffs out his chest*]: Yes.

[*Without a change of expression,* SIDI *dashes suddenly off the stage.*]

SADIKU: What on earth has got into her?
LAKUNLE: I wish I knew
She took off suddenly
Like a hunted buck.

[*Looks off-stage.*]

I think—yes, she is,

She is going home.
Sadiku, will you go?
Find out if you can
What she plans to do.

[SADIKU *nods and goes.* LAKUNLE *walks up and down.*]

And now I know I am the biggest fool
That ever walked this earth.
There are women to be found
In every town or village in these parts,
And every one a virgin.
But I obey my books.

[*Distant music. Light drums, flutes, box-guitars, "sekere."*]

"Man takes the fallen woman by the hand"
And ever after they live happily.
Moreover, I will admit,
It solves the problem of her bride-price too.
A man must live or fall by his true
Principles. That, I had sworn,
Never to pay.

[*Enter* SADIKU.]

SADIKU: She is packing her things. She is gathering her clothes and trinkets together, and oiling herself as a bride does before her wedding.

LAKUNLE: Heaven help us! I am not impatient.
Surely she can wait a day or two at least.
There is the asking to be done,
And then I have to hire a praise-singer,
And such a number of ceremonies
Must firstly be performed.

SADIKU: Just what I said but she only laughed at me and called me a . . . a . . . what was it now . . . a bra . . . braba . . . brabararian. It serves you right. It all comes of your teaching. I said what about the asking and the other ceremonies. And she looked at me and said, leave all that nonsense to savages and brabararians.

LAKUNLE: But I must prepare myself.
I cannot be
A single man one day and a married one the next.
It must come gradually.
I will not wed in haste.
A man must have time to prepare,
To learn to like the thought.
I must think of my pupils too:
Would they be pleased if I were married
Not asking their consent . . . ?

[*The singing group is now audible even to him.*]

What is that? The musicians?
Could they have learnt so soon?

SADIKU: The news of a festivity travels fast. You ought to know that.

LAKUNLE: The goddess of malicious gossip
Herself must have a hand in my undoing.
The very spirits of the partial air
Have all conspired to blow me, willy-nilly
Down the slippery slope of grim matrimony.
What evil have I done . . . ? Ah, here they come!

[*Enter crowd and musicians.*]

Go back. You are not needed yet. Nor ever.
Hence parasites, you've made a big mistake.
There is no one getting wedded; get you home.

[SIDI *now enters. In one hand she holds a bundle, done up in a richly embroidered cloth: in the other the magazine. She is radiant, jewelled, lightly clothed, and wears light leather-thong sandals. They all go suddenly silent except for the long-drawn O-Ohs of admiration. She goes up to* LAKUNLE *and hands him the book.*]

SIDI: A present from Sidi.
I tried to tear it up
But my fingers were too frail.

[*To the crowd.*]

Let us go.

[*To* LAKUNLE.]

You may come too if you wish,
You are invited.

LAKUNLE [*lost in the miracle of transformation*]:
Well I should hope so indeed
Since I am to marry you.

SIDI [*turns round in surprise*]:
Marry who . . . ? You thought . . .
Did you really think that you, and I . . .
Why, did you think that after him,
I could endure the touch of another man?
I who have felt the strength,
The perpetual youthful zest
Of the panther of the trees?
And would I choose a watered-down,
A beardless version of unripened man?

LAKUNLE [*bars her way*]:
I shall not let you.
I shall protect you from yourself.

SIDI [*gives him a shove that sits him down again, hard against the tree base*]:
Out of my way, book-nourished shrimp.
Do you see what strength he has given me?

That was not bad. For a man of sixty,
It was the secret of God's own draught
A deed for drums and ballads.
But you, at sixty, you'll be ten years dead!
In fact, you'll not survive your honeymoon . . .
Come to my wedding if you will. If not . . .

[*She shrugs her shoulders. Kneels down at* SADIKU*'s feet.*]

Mother of brides, your blessing . . .

SADIKU [*lays her hand on* SIDI*'s head*]: I invoke the fertile gods. They will stay with you. May the time come soon when you shall be as round-bellied as a full moon in a low sky.

SIDI [*hands her the bundle*]:
Now bless my worldly goods.

[*Turns to the musicians.*]

Come, sing to me of seeds
Of children, sired of the lion stock.

[*The Musicians resume their tune.* SIDI *sings and dances.*]

Mo te'ni. Mo te'ni.
Mo te'ni. Mo te'ni.
Sun mo mi, we mo mi
Sun mo mi, fa mo mi
Yarabi lo m'eyi t'o le d'omo . . .

[*Festive air, fully pervasive. Oil lamps from the market multiply as traders desert their stalls to join them. A young girl flaunts her dancing buttocks at* LAKUNLE *and he rises to the bait.* SADIKU *gets in his way as he gives chase. Tries to make him dance with her.* LAKUNLE *last seen, having freed himself of* SADIKU*, clearing a space in the crowd for the young girl.*

The crowd repeat the song after SIDI.]

Tolani Tolani
T'emi ni T'emi ni
Sun mo mi, we mo mi
Sun mo mi, fa mo mi
Yarabi lo m'eyi t'o le d'omo.

Tom Stoppard

Tom Stoppard (1937–   ), now an assimilated Englishman, was born Tomas Straussler in Gottwaldov (formerly Zlin), Czechoslovakia. His father, Eugene, a medical doctor employed by an international shoe company, moved the family to Singapore shortly before World War II began in Europe. When the Asian war began, Stoppard's mother, Martha, took him and his brother to India, where they lived in Darjeeling. His father, who remained behind, was killed. When his mother remarried in 1946, the family took the name of her new husband, Stoppard.

Because Stoppard was educated in English-speaking schools in Singapore and India, he adopted English as his first language and Czech as his second. He was nine when the family relocated to England, and he finished his formal education in Yorkshire. Stoppard did not attend college but went to work as a reporter. He has romanticized this choice by saying he made it to emulate one of his literary heroes, Ernest Hemingway, who began his career as a reporter. Eventually, Stoppard became a drama and film critic, a position that proved to be the basis for his development as a playwright. If Stoppard did not attend a university, he has gone about his career systematically, developing his own course of study and building into his plays a knowledge of politics, landscape gardening, biography, mathematics, and moral philosophy. Stoppard is especially fond of historical drama, and he often mixes fictional and real people in his plots. He also likes to use the device of the play within the play, which allows him to mix levels of reality to the point of controlled confusion.

Stoppard is a private person, and not much is known about his life, except what he freely but glibly admits in interviews. He is on good terms with his family and employs his brother as his accountant. He was married in 1965 to Jose Ingle, with whom he had two sons. They were divorced in 1972. He then married Miriam Moore-Robinson, a physician and author, and they also have two sons. Stoppard's success allows him to live well in an English country house in Sussex, which he used as the model for the setting of *Arcadia* (1994).

Stoppard has said that he was first inspired to write plays by John Osborne's *Look Back in Anger* (1956). Unlike Osborne, Stoppard recognized that his own voice was not one of anger but of parody and satire. Stoppard favors themes that contrast reality and illusion, and his preferred characters are often spies, actors, philosophers, artists, and writers, who allow him to depict contradictory points of view through which the real world loses its surety and veers off into uncertainty.

When he was twenty-six, *Walk on the Water* (1963), Stoppard's first satire, was produced on BBC television, and he continued to write for the BBC from 1964 to 1972, long after his first play, *Rosencrantz & Guildenstern Are Dead* (1967), became a hit.

Stoppard admires the Absurdist plays of Samuel Beckett, Eugène Ionesco, and the Polish playwright Slawomir Mrozek, whose play *Tango* he adapted for a British audience (1966). In 1973 he translated Frederico Garcia Lorca's *The House of Bernarda Alba;* in 1979 he adapted Arthur Schnitzler's satire of Viennese middle-class society, *The Vast Country* (1911), retitled *Undiscovered Country.* In 1997 he adapted Anton Chekhov's *The Seagull.* Stoppard is an admirer of spy novels, in particular John Le Carré's *The Spy Who Came in from the Cold* (1963) and Graham Greene's *The Human Factor* (1978), for which he wrote the film script in 1979. Stoppard says that he is drawn to the oppositions and double acts of spies such as Alec Leamas, the protagonist of Le Carré's book. He used Leamas as the inspiration for *Hapgood* (1988), a play about a woman spy, code-named "Mother," who is probably a triple agent.

The Real Inspector Hound (1968) is Stoppard's parody of a police murder mystery in the style of Agatha Christie. As usual with a Stoppard play, the plot is a baroque mixture including a play within the play. The central characters are Moon, a second-string drama critic who hates the first-string critic, and Birdboot, another drama critic who is in love with an actress in the play they are watching. Illogically, Birdboot and Moon become part of the action of the play and take the roles of the characters. While trying to solve the mystery of the murder, they are murdered by Puckeridge, a third-string critic.

The same year, Stoppard revised *Walk on the Water* as *Enter a Free Man* (1968), a farcical send-up of post–World War II British working-class society about a would-be inventor, George Riley, who spends most of his time in a local pub. Stoppard's protagonist is not a modern tragic hero but a dreamer hoping to be free so he can invent something useful—something beyond his grasp because his ideas are crazy and wildly impractical. The play is notable for its skillful borrowing from such plays as Robert Bolt's *Flowering Cherry* (1957), Arthur Miller's *Death of a Salesman* (1949), and N. F. Simpson's *A Oneway Pendulum* (1959).

Jumpers (1972) combines a bedroom farce, a murder mystery, and a satire of academic life. The term "jumpers" refers to the followers of Sir Achibold Jumper, a philosophical gymnast who jumps from idea to idea with seeming indifference. (The choreography of the play calls for actors to do acrobatics and make human pyramids.) Early in the play, one of the jumpers, a professor of logic, is shot and killed, perhaps by Dotty Moore, a onetime musical hall singer (named after a real-life singer), who suffers from dementia. George, Dotty's husband, is an ethical philosopher named after the real-life analytical philosopher G. E. Moore, author of *Principia Ethica* (1903). George is an academic philosopher, bogged down by silly jargon, who tries to prove that God does not exist. Though he fails at writing an essay on the subject, he succeeds in a practical experiment: He shoots an arrow into the air assuming that it will never reach its destination, but inexplicably it kills his pet rabbit, Thumper. The moment of revelation when he realizes what he has done leads George to the conclusion that though the world is chaotic, the existence of God is knowable by intuition.

Travesties (1974) is a distortion of the historical moment in 1918 when the novelist James Joyce and a minor British diplomat named Henry Carr were both living in Zurich, where they worked in a production of Oscar Wilde's

The Importance of Being Earnest. Stoppard adds to this situation by including in the cast the Russian revolutionary Vladimir Lenin and the Romanian surrealist poet Tristan Tzara, who were also living in Zurich at the time but had no contact with Joyce or Carr. As the play within the play unfolds, Joyce, Lenin, Tzara, and Carr play double roles as characters in *The Importance of Being Earnest:* Tzara, for example, is Jack/Ernest, and Joyce is Lady Bracknell. In the debate over the question of art, Joyce, perhaps speaking for Stoppard, says, "An artist is the magician put among men to gratify—capriciously—their urge for immortality. The temples are built and brought down around him, continuously and contiguously from Troy, to the field of Flanders. If there is any meaning in any of it, it is what survives as art." The seriousness of Joyce's statement is undermined, however, when he ends the speech by playing magician and pulling a rabbit out of his hat.

Night and Day (1978), Stoppard's dark comedy in the style of a well-made play, takes its title from Cole Porter's song. The theme concerns the conflicting responsibility of the press and the ethics of political reporting in Kambawe, a mythical African state. Pitted against each other are a seasoned reporter, an idealistic young reporter who favors "prose" to "facts," and a capitalist and his bored, unfaithful wife. The situation ends badly: The idealistic reporter is killed in search of a story, the seasoned reporter becomes more cynical, the capitalist juggles his morality, and his wife accurately points out the stupidity of what has happened, though to no avail.

Stoppard's *The Real Thing* (1982) takes its title from Henry James's short story of the same name, which depicts the irony of perception occurring when an artist uses models from the lower classes to successfully convey the illusion of aristocrats.

Stoppard says that *The Real Thing* (1982) is as close to a love story as he wished to write, and it probably is based on his situation in the late 1960s and early 1970s, when his first marriage broke down and his second marriage began. Though *The Real Thing*'s theme is the conflict between married love and infidelity, the play also focuses on the integrity of the artist in a world of opportunism. Like Stoppard, Henry, the protagonist, is a playwright whose life and plays intersect. His art and life are confused until he realizes that his marriage to Annie, his second wife, is "the real thing." Henry probably also speaks for Stoppard when he says that carnal knowledge "is what lovers trust each other with. Knowledge of each other, not of the flesh but through the flesh, knowledge of self, the real him, the real her, *in extremis,* the mask slipped from the face. Every other version of oneself is on offer to the public. We share our vivacity, grief, sulks, anger, joy . . . we hand it out to anybody who happens to be standing around, to friends and family with a momentary sense of indecency perhaps, to strangers without hesitation. Our lovers share with us the passing trade. But in pairs we insist that we give ourselves to each other. . . . Personal, final, uncompromised. Knowing, being known. I revere that."

Arcadia (1994) makes fun of nineteenth-century romanticism and modern literary criticism. It is a kind of play within a play; the action takes place in the room in an English country house both from 1809 to 1812 and in the present. *Arcadia* is inspired by Thomas Love Peacock's novel *Headlong Hall* (1815), itself a parody about the romantic poets Samuel Taylor Coleridge, Percy Bysshe Shelley, and Lord Byron, and the art and design of landscape architecture. Stoppard's title refers to the theme *et in Arcadia ego,* a reference to the presence of death in the midst of an Edenic environment.

Stoppard's *Invention of Love,* produced in 1997, is an imaginary biography of the English poet A. E. Housman (1859–1936), best known for his volume of poems *A Shropshire Lad* (1896). The play begins as Housman, recently dead, discusses his life with Charon, the ferryman, as he is carried across the river Styx to the underworld. Along the way Housman meets himself as a young man and several old companions, with whom he discusses his career and the unrequited homosexual love that inspired his famous volume of poems. In particular, he meets Oscar Wilde, whose exuberant expressions of homosexual love and trial for gross indecency cost him his career. Wilde says to Housman, "You are right to be a scholar. A scholar is all scruple, an artist is none. The artist must lie, cheat, deceive, be untrue to nature and contemptuous of history. I made my life into my art and it was an unqualified success. . . . I lived at the turning point of the world where everything was waking up new—the New Drama, the New Novel, New Journalism, New Hedonism, New Paganism, even the New Woman. Where were you," he asks the young Housman, "when all of this was happening?" Housman responds, "At home." In the end, as Wilde is carried across the river, young Housman stands on the shore of the Styx and says, "How lucky to find myself standing on this empty shore, with the indifferent waters at my feet."

Other works by Stoppard include *Lord Malquist and Mr. Moon* (1966), his only novel, which parodies James Joyce's *Ulysses* and takes place in London on the day of Winston Churchill's funeral; *Every Good Boy Deserves a Favour* (1977), a pair of monologues about Russian dissidents accompanied by a symphony orchestra; and *Dogg's Hamlet, Cahoots Macbeth* (both 1979), two plays performed together—the former a fifteen-minute version of *Hamlet,* and the latter a surrealistic blend of Shakespeare's play and Eastern European politics under Communist domination.

Rosencrantz & Guildenstern Are Dead, produced in 1967, links Stoppard to the plays of Shakespeare and Oscar Wilde, both of whose influence he freely admits. The play's extensive use of parody and satire was natural to Stoppard, and they became his preferred modes for exploring his favorite themes—the tangled consequences of probability, free will, and the play within the play.

The inspiration for *Rosencrantz & Guildenstern Are Dead* may have come from Francis Fergusson's *The Idea of a Theatre* (1949), in which he says that modern realism might have its origin in the theater of Shakespeare "at the point where Hamlet meets Rosencrantz and Guildenstern: the non-committal 'center' of human awareness, the 'middle' of Fortune's favors, where the beggarly body looks sure and solid and all motivations which might lead to wider awarenesses look shadowy and deluded." Though not a realist, Stoppard seems to have used Fergusson's idea in an absurd sense, and in his version Rosencrantz and Guildenstern find that while they are at the center of the action, they have no sense of awareness of it. Critics have noticed that Stoppard's two hapless courtiers may be parodies of Samuel Beckett's characters of Vladimir (Didi) and Estragon (Gogo), the two tramps in *Waiting for Godot*. Though Beckett's characters have a future while they are endlessly waiting for Godot, Rosencrantz and

Guildenstern (their names are abbreviated to Ros and Guil in the text) are dead men even before the action begins. Beckett's characters speak haltingly in pause-filled dialogue, but Stoppard's characters banter endlessly. In general, Stoppard prefers fast-paced action closer to the British musical hall comedy, whereas the action of Beckett's characters tends toward inertia.

Act I begins with Ros and Guil traveling to Elsinore, where they have been summoned by King Claudius for some reason they cannot guess. Along the way, Ros is defying the law of probability by flipping coins in an unending succession of heads. Guil, who is betting against Ros, cannot believe his bad luck and keeps betting that the law of probability will inevitably make him a winner. It does not. The appearance of the troupe of tragedians on their way to the court provides Ros and Guil with a moment of respite, but they are baffled by the Player, who offers them a choice of sexual services of a young boy, Alfred, or a performance by the troupe. The Player announces, "We'll stoop to anything," a sly sexual innuendo also hinting that the actor is never out of costume, always looking for a role, and always looking for money. Appalled, Ros and Guil go to court, where they meet Claudius, who, not caring who is Ros or who is Guil (a recurring gag), instructs them to spy on Hamlet and find out why he is acting strangely. Ros and Guil are not eager spies, but they feel that they must follow the king's request. Guil says, "We've been caught up. Your smallest action sets off another somewhere else, and is set off by it. Keep an eye open, an ear cocked. Tread warily, follow instructions. We'll be all right." Ros asks, "For how long?" and Guil responds, "Till events have played themselves out," which, of course, the audience knows will be their death.

In Act II, Hamlet mocks the hapless Ros and Guil, and they know it. Ros says, "I think we can say he made us look ridiculous." Guil says, "He caught us on the wrong foot once or twice, perhaps, but I thought we gained some ground." Ros, oblivious to the dramatic irony of his reply, says, "He murdered us."

Hamlet instructs the tragedians to play *The Murder of Gonzago,* by which he hopes to expose the murderous Claudius, but during the dress rehearsal, Ros and Guil become dimly aware that they are looking at themselves as characters in the play, and they become upset. Neither knows that what they are viewing is the beginning and middle of *their* story (it is also the middle of Stoppard's play), nor that it is mirroring *their* lives. Ros and Guil cannot separate the play from life, and when the Player directs the Spies to die, Guil says, "No, no, no . . . you've got it all wrong . . . you can't act death." Stoppard's inspiration for this parody of characters and actors arguing about how to play a role seems to be Luigi Pirandello's *Six Characters in Search of an Author.* When Guil and Ros attempt to correct the plays, they are rebuffed: "Don't you see?!" cries the Player. "We're *actors*—we're the opposite of people!" Ros and Guil, confused, back off.

Act III opens with Ros and Guil at sea, in pitch darkness, accompanying Hamlet to England. During the voyage, Hamlet steals their letter of instruction and rewrites it to arrange for their deaths instead of his own. There are three barrels on the ship's deck, and when pirates attack, Hamlet jumps into the left barrel, Ros and Guil take the middle barrel, and the Player takes the right one. When the fighting fades, Ros and Guil appear from the right barrel, and the Player appears from the left barrel. Hamlet is missing. Ros and Guil's concern is that they have lost their charge. They wonder if he is dead or not, and they bicker over whether to go on. "But don't you understand," Guil explains to the Player. "We've had our instructions—the whole thing's pointless without him." Despairingly, Guil moans, "We've travelled too far, and our momentum has taken over; we move idly towards eternity, without possibility of reprieve or hope of explanation." When they open Claudius's letter (as rewritten by Hamlet) and read their fate, they are shocked and baffled. "Who are *we*?" Ros and Guil ask the players, who emerge from a barrel and form a menacing circle around them. The Player's answer, "You are Rosencrantz and Guildenstern. That's enough." However, this provokes Guil to say, "No—it is not enough. To be told so little—to such an end—and still, finally, to be denied an explanation—." Furious and frustrated, Guil snatches the Player's knife and stabs him. The Player enacts a death scene, but springing back to life, informs Guil that the knife blade is retractable. The irony is that when Ros and Guil die, it will be irrevocable.

Just before the end, Ros and Guil whine about destiny:

> ROS: Couldn't we just stay put? I mean no one is going to come on and drag us off. . . . they'll just have to wait. We're still young . . . fit . . . we've got years. . . .
> *Pause. No answer*
> [*A cry.*] We've done nothing wrong! We didn't harm anyone. Did we?
> GUIL: I can't remember.
> ROS *pulls himself together.*
> ROS: All right, then. I don't care. I've had enough. To tell you the truth, I'm relieved.
> *And he disappears from view.*

Guil, not realizing he is alone, says, "There must have been a moment, at the beginning, where we could have said—no. But we somehow missed it." Finally realizing that he is alone, he calls out "Rosen—?" Then, doubting his own identity, he calls out his own name, "Guil—?" He says, "We'll know better next time," and he, too, disappears. The final irony is that as Guil vanishes, the stage lights come up revealing the last act of *Hamlet,* in which there is a tableau of the court of Claudius strewn with corpses.

Stoppard's success in combining multiple resources in *Rosencrantz & Guildenstern* showed how artfully he mastered the art of satire and parody. More than any other contemporary playwright, Stoppard shares with Wilde the capacity for presenting characters who reveal themselves as being silly without meaning to be, being serious without cause, and being dense when insight is required.

Stoppard's plays are often contrasted with those of Harold Pinter: Stoppard's plays are filled with rapid and confusing changes of action; Pinter's are slow-moving and essentially plotless. Stoppard's dialogue is baroque, roiling with puns, jokes, and allusions; Pinter's is terse and generally lacking metaphors. Stoppard's characters are arch but capable of tenderness or even love; Pinter's almost always mix comedy with brutality. Stoppard, for all of his comedy, is always alluding to something serious, and though his characters are often presented as lacking insight, they are, after all, sympathetic.

Film

Rosencrantz & Guildenstern Are Dead (1990), written and directed by Tom Stoppard, with Gary Oldman, Tim Roth, Richard Dreyfuss, and Ian Glenn. Hobo/Brandenberg.

Rosencrantz & Guildenstern Are Dead

ROSENCRANTZ
GUILDENSTERN
THE PLAYER
ALFRED
TRAGEDIANS
HAMLET
OPHELIA
CLAUDIUS
GERTRUDE
POLONIUS
SOLDIER
HORATIO
COURTIERS, AMBASSADORS, SOLDIERS, AND ATTENDANTS

ACT I

Two ELIZABETHANS *passing the time in a place without any visible character.*

They are well dressed—hats, cloaks, sticks and all.

Each of them has a large leather money bag.

GUILDENSTERN*'s bag is nearly empty.*

ROSENCRANTZ*'s bag is nearly full.*

The reason being: they are betting on the toss of a coin, in the following manner: GUILDENSTERN [*hereafter* "GUIL"] *takes a coin out of his bag, spins it, letting it fall.* ROSENCRANTZ [*hereafter* "ROS"] *studies it, announces it as "heads"* [*as it happens*] *and puts it into his own bag. Then they repeat the process. They have apparently been doing this for some time.*

The run of "heads" is impossible, yet ROS *betrays no surprise at all—he feels none. However, he is nice enough to feel a little embarrassed at taking so much money off his friend. Let that be his character note.*

GUIL *is well alive to the oddity of it. He is not worried about the money, but he is worried by the implications; aware but not going to panic about it—his character note.*

GUIL *sits.* ROS *stands* [*he does the moving, retrieving coins*]. GUIL *spins.* ROS *studies coin.*

ROS: Heads.

He picks it up and puts it in his bag. The process is repeated.

Heads.

Again.

Heads.

Again.

Heads.

Again.

Heads.

GUIL [*flipping a coin*]: There is an art to the building up of suspense.

ROS: Heads.

GUIL [*flipping another*]: Though it can be done by luck alone.

ROS: Heads.

GUIL: If that's the word I'm after.

ROS [*raises his head at* GUIL]: Seventy-six—love.

GUIL *gets up but has nowhere to go. He spins another coin over his shoulder without looking at it, his attention being directed at his environment or lack of it.*

Heads.

GUIL: A weaker man might be moved to re-examine his faith, if in nothing else at least in the law of probability. [*He slips a coin over his shoulder as he goes to look upstage.*]

ROS: Heads.

GUIL, *examining the confines of the stage, flips over two more coins as he does so, one by one of course.* ROS *announces each of them as "heads."*

GUIL [*musing*]: The law of probability, it has been oddly asserted, is something to do with the proposition that if six monkeys [*he has surprised himself*] . . . if six monkeys were . . .

ROS: Game?

GUIL: Were they?

ROS: Are you?

GUIL [*understanding*]: Game. [*Flips a coin.*] The law of averages, if I have got this right, means that if six monkeys were thrown up in the air for long enough they would land on their tails about as often as they would land on their——

ROS: Heads. [*He picks up the coin.*]

GUIL: Which even at first glance does not strike one as a particularly rewarding speculation, in either sense, even without the monkeys. I mean you wouldn't *bet* on it. I mean *I* would, but *you* wouldn't. . . . [*As he flips a coin.*]

ROS: Heads.

GUIL: Would you? [*Flips a coin.*]

ROS: Heads.

Repeat.

Heads. [*He looks up at* GUIL*—embarrassed laugh.*] Getting a bit of a bore, isn't it?

GUIL [*coldly*]: A bore?

ROS: Well . . .

GUIL: What about the suspense?

ROS [*innocently*]: What suspense?

Small pause.

GUIL: It must be the law of diminishing returns . . . I feel the spell about to be broken. [*Energizing himself somewhat. He takes out a coin, spins it high, catches it, turns it over on to the back of his other hand, studies the coin—and tosses it to* ROS. *His energy deflates and he sits.*] Well, it was an even chance . . . if my calculations are correct.

ROS: Eighty-five in a row—beaten the record!

GUIL: Don't be absurd.

ROS: Easily!

GUIL [*angry*]: Is that *it,* then? Is that all?

ROS: What?

GUIL: A new record? Is that as far as you are prepared to go?

ROS: Well . . .

GUIL: No questions? Not even a pause?

ROS: You spun them yourself.

GUIL: Not a flicker of doubt?

ROS [*aggrieved, aggressive*]: Well, I won—didn't I?

GUIL [*approaches him—quieter*]: And if you'd lost? If they'd come down against you, eighty-five times, one after another, just like that?

ROS [*dumbly*]: Eighty-five in a row? *Tails?*

GUIL: Yes! What would you think?

ROS [*doubtfully*]: Well . . . . [*Jocularly.*] Well, I'd have a good look at your coins for a start!

GUIL [*retiring*]: I'm relieved. At least we can still count on self-interest as a predictable factor. . . . I suppose it's the last to go. Your capacity for trust made me wonder if perhaps . . . you, alone . . . [*He turns on him suddenly, reaches out a hand.*] Touch.

ROS *clasps his hand.* GUIL *pulls him up to him.*

GUIL [*more intensely*]: We have been spinning coins together since— [*He releases him almost as violently.*] This is not the first time we have spun coins!

ROS: Oh no—we've been spinning coins for as long as I remember.

GUIL: How long is that?

ROS: I forget. Mind you—eighty-five times!

GUIL: Yes?

ROS: It'll take some beating, I imagine.

GUIL: Is *that* what you imagine? Is that it? No *fear?*

ROS: Fear?

GUIL [*in fury—flings a coin on the ground*]: *Fear!* The crack that might flood your brain with light!

ROS: Heads. . . . [*He puts it in his bag.*]

GUIL *sits despondently. He takes a coin, spins it, lets it fall between his feet. He looks at it, picks it up, throws it to* ROS, *who puts it in his bag.*

GUIL *takes another coin, spins it, catches it, turns it over on to his other hand, looks at it, and throws it to* ROS, *who puts it in his bag.*

GUIL *takes a third coin, spins it, catches it in his right hand, turns it over onto his left wrist, lobs it in the air, catches it with his left hand, raises his left leg, throws the coin up under it, catches it and turns it over on the top of his head, where it sits.* ROS *comes, looks at it, puts it in his bag.*

ROS: I'm afraid——

GUIL: So am I.

ROS: I'm afraid it isn't your day.

GUIL: I'm afraid it is.

Small pause.

ROS: Eighty-nine.

GUIL: It must be indicative of something, besides the redistribution of wealth. [*He muses.*] List of possible explanations. One: I'm willing it. Inside where nothing shows, I am the essence of a man spinning double-headed coins, and betting against himself in private atonement for an unremembered past. [*He spins a coin at* ROS.]

ROS: Heads.

GUIL: Two: time has stopped dead, and the single experience of one coin being spun once has been repeated ninety times. . . . [*He flips a coin, looks at it, tosses it to* ROS.] On the whole, doubtful. Three: divine intervention, that is to say, a good turn from above concerning him, cf. children of Israel, or retribution from above concerning me, cf. Lot's wife. Four: a spectacular vindication of the principle that each individual coin spun individually [*he spins one*] is as likely to come down heads as tails and therefore should cause no surprise each individual time it does. [*It does. He tosses it to* ROS.]

ROS: I've never known anything like it!

GUIL: And a syllogism: One, he has never known anything like it. Two, he has never known anything to write home about. Three, it is nothing to write home about. . . . Home . . . What's the first thing you remember?

ROS: Oh, let's see. . . . The first thing that comes into my head, you mean?

GUIL: No—the first thing you remember.

ROS: Ah. [*Pause.*] No, it's no good, it's gone. It was a long time ago.

GUIL [*patient but edged*]: You don't get my meaning. What is the first thing after all the things you've forgotten?

ROS: Oh I see. [*Pause.*] I've forgotten the question.

GUIL *leaps up and paces.*

GUIL: Are you happy?

ROS: What?

GUIL: Content? At ease?

ROS: I suppose so.

GUIL: What are you going to do now?

ROS: I don't know. What do you want to do?

GUIL: I have no desires. None. [*He stops pacing dead.*] There was a messenger . . . that's right. We were sent for. [*He wheels at* ROS *and raps out:*] Syllogism the second: One, probability is a factor which operates within natural forces. Two, probability is not operating as a factor. Three, we are now within un-, sub- or supernatural forces. Discuss. [ROS *is suitably startled. Acidly.*] Not too heatedly.

ROS: I'm sorry I—What's the matter with you?

GUIL: The scientific approach to the examination of phenomena is a defence against the pure emotion of fear. Keep tight hold and continue while there's time. Now—counter to the previous syllogism: tricky one, follow me carefully, it may prove a comfort. If we postulate, and we just have, that within un-, sub- or supernatural forces *the probability is* that the law of probability will not operate as a factor, then we must accept that the probability of the *first* part will not operate as a factor, in which case the law of probability *will* operate as a factor within un-, sub- or supernatural forces. And since it obviously hasn't been doing so, we can take it that we are not held within un-, sub- or supernatural forces after all; in all probability, that is. Which is a great relief to me personally. [*Small pause.*] Which is all very well, except that—— [*He continues with slight hysteria, under control.*] We have been spinning coins together since I don't know when, and in all that time [if it *is* all that time] I don't suppose either of us was more than a couple of gold pieces up or down. I hope that doesn't sound surprising because its very unsurprisingness is something I am trying to keep hold of. The equanimity of your average tosser of coins depends upon a law, or rather a tendency, or let us say a probability, or at any rate a mathematically calculable chance, which ensures that he will not upset himself by losing too much nor upset his opponent by winning too often. This made for a kind of harmony and a kind of confidence. It related the fortuitous and the ordained into a reassuring union which we recognized as nature. The sun came up about as often as it went down, in the long run, and a coin showed heads about as often as it showed tails. Then a messenger arrived. We had been sent for. Nothing else happened. Ninety-two coins spun consecutively have come down heads ninety-two consecutive times . . . and for the last three minutes on the wind of a windless day I have heard the sound of drums and flute. . . .

ROS [*cutting his fingernails*]: Another curious scientific phenomenon is the fact that the fingernails grow after death, as does the beard.

GUIL: What?

ROS [*loud*]: Beard!

GUIL: But you're not dead.

ROS [*irritated*]: I didn't say they *started* to grow after death! [*Pause, calmer.*] The fingernails also grow before birth, though *not* the beard.

GUIL: *What?*

ROS [*shouts*]: Beard! What's the matter with you? [*Reflectively.*] The toenails, on the other hand, never grow at all.

GUIL [*bemused*]: The toenails never grow at all?

ROS: Do they? It's a funny thing—I cut my fingernails all the time, and every time I think to cut them, they need cutting. Now, for instance. And yet, I never, to the best of my knowledge, cut my toenails. They ought to be curled under my feet by now, but it doesn't happen. I never think about them. Perhaps I cut them absent-mindedly, when I'm thinking of something else.

GUIL [*tensed up by this rambling*]: Do you remember the first thing that happened today?

ROS [*promptly*]: I woke up, I suppose. [*Triggered.*] Oh—I've got it now—that man, a foreigner, he woke us up——

GUIL: A messenger. [*He relaxes, sits.*]

ROS: That's it—pale sky before dawn, a man standing on his saddle to bang on the shutters—shouts—What's all the row about?! Clear off!—But then he called our names. You remember that—this man woke us up.

GUIL: Yes.

ROS: We were sent for.

GUIL: Yes.

ROS: That's why we're here. [*He looks round, seems doubtful, then the explanation.*] Travelling.

GUIL: Yes.

ROS [*dramatically*]: It was urgent—a matter of extreme urgency, a royal summons, his very words: official business and no questions asked—lights in the stable-yard, saddle up and off headlong and hotfoot across the land, our guides outstripped in breakneck pursuit of our duty! Fearful lest we come too late!!

Small pause.

GUIL: Too late for what?
ROS: How do I know? We haven't got there yet.
GUIL: Then what are we doing here, I ask myself.
ROS: You might well ask.
GUIL: We better get on.
ROS: You might well think.
GUIL: We better get on.
ROS [*actively*]: Right! [*Pause.*] On where?
GUIL: Forward.
ROS [*forward to footlights*]: Ah. [*Hesitates.*] Which way do we—— [*He turns round.*] Which way did we——?
GUIL: Practically starting from scratch. . . . An awakening, a man standing on his saddle to bang on the shutters, our names shouted in a certain dawn, a message, a summons . . . A new record for heads and tails. We have not been . . . picked out . . . simply to be abandoned . . . set loose to find our own way. . . . We are entitled to some direction. . . . I would have thought.
ROS [*alert, listening*]: I say——! I say——
GUIL: Yes?
ROS: I can hear—I thought I heard—music.

GUIL *raises himself.*

GUIL: Yes?
ROS: Like a band. [*He looks around, laughs embarrassedly, expiating himself.*] It sounded like—a band. Drums.
GUIL: Yes.
ROS [*relaxes*]: It couldn't have been real.
GUIL: "The colours red, blue and green are real. The colour yellow is a mystical experience shared by everybody"—demolish.
ROS [*at edge of stage*]: It must have been thunder. Like drums . . .

By the end of the next speech, the band is faintly audible.

GUIL: A man breaking his journey between one place and another at a third place of no name, character, population or significance, sees a unicorn cross his path and disappear. That in itself is startling, but there are precedents for mystical encounters of various kinds, or to be less extreme, a choice of persuasions to put it down to fancy; until—"My God," says a second man, "I must be dreaming, I thought I saw a unicorn." At which point, a dimension is added that makes the experience as alarming as it will ever be. A third witness, you understand, adds no further dimension but only spreads it thinner, and a fourth thinner still, and the more witnesses there are the thinner it gets and the more reasonable it becomes until it is as thin as reality, the name we give to the common experience. . . . "Look, look!" recites the crowd. "A horse with an arrow in its forehead! It must have been mistaken for a deer."
ROS [*eagerly*]: I knew all along it was a band.
GUIL [*tiredly*]: He knew all along it was a band.
ROS: Here they come!
GUIL [*at the last moment before they enter—wistfully*]: I'm sorry it wasn't a unicorn. It would have been nice to have unicorns.

The TRAGEDIANS *are six in number, including a small* BOY [ALFRED]. *Two pull and push a cart piled with props and belongings. There is also a* DRUMMER, *a* HORN-PLAYER *and a* FLAUTIST. *The* SPOKESMAN [*"the* PLAYER*"*] *has no instrument. He brings up the rear and is the first to notice them.*

PLAYER: Halt!

The group turns and halts.

[*Joyously.*] An audience!

ROS *and* GUIL *half rise.*

Don't move!

They sink back. He regards them fondly.

Perfect! A lucky thing we came along.
ROS: For us?
PLAYER: Let us hope so. But to meet two gentlemen on the road—we would not hope to meet them off it.
ROS: No?
PLAYER: Well met, in fact, and just in time.
ROS: Why's that?
PLAYER: Why, we grow rusty and you catch us at the very point of decadence—by this time tomorrow we might have forgotten everything we ever knew. That's a thought, isn't it? [*He laughs generously.*] We'd be back where we started—improvising.
ROS: Tumblers, are you?
PLAYER: We can give you a tumble if that's your taste, and times being what they are. . . . Otherwise, for a jingle of coin we can do you a selection of gory romances, full of fine cadence and corpses, pirated from the Italian; and it doesn't take much to make a jingle—even a single coin has music in it.

They all flourish and bow, raggedly.

Tragedians, at your command.

Ros and Guil have got to their feet.

ROS: My name is Guildenstern, and this is Rosencrantz.

Guil confers briefly with him.

[*Without embarrassment.*] I'm sorry—*his* name's Guildenstern, and *I'm* Rosencrantz.

PLAYER: A pleasure. We've played to bigger, of course, but quality counts for something. I recognized you at once——

ROS: And who are we?

PLAYER: —as fellow artists.

ROS: I thought we were gentlemen.

PLAYER: For some of us it is performance, for others, patronage. They are two sides of the same coin, or, let us say, being as there are so many of us, the same side of two coins. [*Bows again.*] Don't clap too loudly—it's a very old world.

ROS: What is your line?

PLAYER: Tragedy, sir. Deaths and disclosures, universal and particular, denouements both unexpected and inexorable, transvestite melodrama on all levels including the suggestive. We transport you into a world of intrigue and illusion . . . clowns, if you like, murderers—we can do you ghosts and battles, on the skirmish level, heroes, villains, tormented lovers—set pieces in the poetic vein; we can do you rapiers or rape or both, by all means, faithless wives and ravished virgins—*flagrante delicto* at a price, but that comes under realism for which there are special terms. Getting warm, am I?

ROS [*doubtfully*]: Well, I don't know. . . .

PLAYER: It costs little to watch, and little more if you happen to get caught up in the action, if that's your taste and times being what they are.

ROS: What are they?

PLAYER: Indifferent.

ROS: Bad?

PLAYER: Wicked. Now what precisely is your pleasure? [*He turns to the* TRAGEDIANS.] Gentlemen, disport yourselves.

The TRAGEDIANS *shuffle into some kind of line.*

There! See anything you like?

ROS [*doubtful, innocent*]: What do they do?

PLAYER: Let your imagination run riot. They are beyond surprise.

ROS: And how much?

PLAYER: To take part?

ROS: To watch.

PLAYER: Watch what?

ROS: A private performance.

PLAYER: How private?

ROS: Well, there are only two of us. Is that enough?

PLAYER: For an audience, disappointing. For voyeurs, about average.

ROS: What's the difference?

PLAYER: Ten guilders.

ROS [*horrified*]: Ten *guilders!*

PLAYER: I mean eight.

ROS: Together?

PLAYER: Each. I don't think you understand—

ROS: What are you *saying?*

PLAYER: What am I saying—seven.

ROS: Where have you *been?*

PLAYER: Roundabout. A nest of children carries the custom of the town. Juvenile companies, they are the fashion. But they cannot match our repertoire . . . we'll stoop to anything if that's your bent. . . .

He regards ROS *meaningfully but* ROS *returns the stare blankly.*

ROS: They'll grow up.

PLAYER [*giving up*]: There's one born every minute. [*To* TRAGEDIANS:] On-ward!

The TRAGEDIANS *start to resume their burdens and their journey.* GUIL *stirs himself at last.*

GUIL: Where are you going?

PLAYER: Ha-alt!

They halt and turn.

Home, sir.

GUIL: Where from?

PLAYER: Home. We're travelling people. We take our chances where we find them.

GUIL: It was chance, then?

PLAYER: Chance?

GUIL: You found us.

PLAYER: Oh yes.

GUIL: You were looking?

PLAYER: Oh no.

GUIL: Chance, then.

PLAYER: Or fate.

GUIL: Yours or ours?

PLAYER: It could hardly be one without the other.

GUIL: Fate, then.

PLAYER: Oh yes. We have no control. Tonight we play to the court. Or the night after. Or to the tavern. Or not.

GUIL: Perhaps I can use my influence.

PLAYER: At the tavern?

GUIL: At the court. I would say I have some influence.

PLAYER: Would you say so?
GUIL: I have influence yet.
PLAYER: Yet what?

GUIL *seizes the* PLAYER *violently.*

GUIL: I have influence!

The PLAYER *does not resist.* GUIL *loosens his hold.*

[*More calmly.*] You said something—about getting caught up in the action——

PLAYER [*gaily freeing himself*]: I did!—I did! You're quicker than your friend. . . . [*Confidingly.*] Now for a handful of guilders I happen to have a private and uncut performance of *The Rape of the Sabine Women*—or rather woman, or rather Alfred——[*Over his shoulder.*] Get your skirt on, Alfred——

The BOY *starts struggling into a female robe.*

. . . and for eight you can participate.

GUIL *backs,* PLAYER *follows.*

. . . taking either part.

GUIL *backs.*

. . . or both for ten.

GUIL *tries to turn away,* PLAYER *holds his sleeve.*

. . . with encores——

GUIL *smashes the* PLAYER *across the face. The* PLAYER *recoils.* GUIL *stands trembling.*

[*Resigned and quiet.*] Get your skirt off, Alfred. . . .

ALFRED *struggles out of his half-on robe.*

GUIL [*shaking with rage and fright*]: It could have been—it didn't have to be *obscene*. . . . It could have been—a bird out of season, dropping bright-feathered on my shoulder. . . . It could have been a tongueless dwarf standing by the road to point the way. . . . I was *prepared*. But it's this, is it? No enigma, no dignity, nothing classical, portentous, only this—a comic pornographer and a rabble of prostitutes. . . .

PLAYER [*acknowledging the description with a sweep of his hat, bowing; sadly*]: You should have caught us in better times. We were purists then. [*Straightens up.*] On-ward.

The PLAYERS *make to leave.*

ROS [*his voice has changed: he has caught on*]: Excuse me!

PLAYER: Ha-alt!

They halt.

A-al-l-fred!

ALFRED *resumes the struggle. The* PLAYER *comes forward.*

ROS: You're not—ah—exclusively players, then?
PLAYER: We're inclusively players, sir.
ROS: So you give—exhibitions?
PLAYER: Performances, sir.
ROS: Yes, of course. There's more money in that, is there?
PLAYER: There's more trade, sir.
ROS: Times being what they are.
PLAYER: Yes.
ROS: Indifferent.
PLAYER: Completely.
ROS: You know I'd no idea——
PLAYER: No——
ROS: I mean, I've *heard* of—but I've never actually——
PLAYER: No.
ROS: I mean, what exactly do you *do?*
PLAYER: We keep to our usual stuff, more or less, only inside out. We do on stage the things that are supposed to happen off. Which is a kind of integrity, if you look on every exit being an entrance somewhere else.
ROS [*nervy, loud*]: Well, I'm not really the type of man who—no, but don't hurry off—sit down and tell us about some of the things people ask you to do——

The PLAYER *turns away.*

PLAYER: On-ward!
ROS: Just a minute!

They turn and look at him without expression.

Well, all right—I wouldn't mind seeing—just an idea of the kind of— [*Bravely.*] What will you do for that? [*And tosses a single coin on the ground between them.*]

The PLAYER *spits at the coin, from where he stands.*
The TRAGEDIANS *demur, trying to get at the coin. He kicks and cuffs them back.*

On!

ALFRED *is still half in and out of his robe. The* PLAYER *cuffs him.*

[*To* ALFRED:] What are you playing at?

ROS *is shamed into fury.*

ROS: Filth! Disgusting—I'll report you to the authorities—*perverts!* I know your game all right, it's all filth!

The PLAYERS *are about to leave.* GUIL *has remained detached.*

GUIL [*casually*]: Do you like a bet?

The TRAGEDIANS *turn and look interested. The* PLAYER *comes forward.*

PLAYER: What kind of bet did you have in mind?

GUIL *walks half the distance towards the* PLAYER, *stops with his foot over the coin.*

GUIL: Double or quits.
PLAYER: Well . . . heads.

GUIL *raises his foot. The* PLAYER *bends. The* TRAGEDIANS *crowd round. Relief and congratulations. The* PLAYER *picks up the coin.* GUIL *throws him a second coin.*

GUIL: Again?

Some of the TRAGEDIANS *are for it, others against.*

GUIL: Evens.

The PLAYER *nods and tosses the coin.*

GUIL: Heads.

It is. He picks it up.

Again.

GUIL *spins coin.*

PLAYER: Heads.

It is. PLAYER *picks up coin. He has two coins again. He spins one.*

GUIL: Heads.

It is. GUIL *picks it up. Then tosses it immediately.*

PLAYER [*fractional hesitation*]: Tails.

But it's heads. GUIL *picks it up.* PLAYER *tosses down his last coin by way of paying up, and turns away.* GUIL *doesn't pick it up; he puts his foot on it.*

GUIL: Heads.
PLAYER: No!

Pause. The TRAGEDIANS *are against this.*

[*Apologetically.*] They don't like the odds.
GUIL [*lifts his foot, squats; picks up the coin still squatting; looks up*]: You were right—heads. [*Spins it, slaps his hand on it, on the floor.*] Heads I win.
PLAYER: No.
GUIL [*uncovers coin*]: Right again. [*Repeat.*] Heads I win.
PLAYER: No.
GUIL [*uncovers coin*]: And right again. [*Repeat.*] Heads I win.
PLAYER: *No!*

He turns away, the TRAGEDIANS *with him.* GUIL *stands up, comes close.*

GUIL: Would you believe it? [*Stands back, relaxes, smiles.*] Bet me the year of my birth doubled is an odd number.
PLAYER: *Your* birth——!
GUIL: If you don't trust me don't bet with me.
PLAYER: Would you trust *me?*
GUIL: *Bet* me then.
PLAYER: My birth?
GUIL: Odd numbers you win.
PLAYER: You're on——

The TRAGEDIANS *have come forward, wide awake.*

GUIL: Good. Year of your birth. Double it. Even numbers I win, odd numbers I lose.

Silence. An awful sigh as the TRAGEDIANS *realize that any number doubled is even. Then a terrible row as they object. Then a terrible silence.*

PLAYER: We have no money.

GUIL *turns to him.*

GUIL: Ah. Then what *have* you got?

The PLAYER *silently brings* ALFRED *forward.* GUIL *regards* ALFRED *sadly.*

Was it for this?

PLAYER: It's the best we've got.
GUIL [*looking up and around*]: Then the times are bad indeed.

The PLAYER *starts to speak, protestation, but* GUIL *turns on him viciously.*

The very *air* stinks.

The PLAYER *moves back.* GUIL *moves down to the footlights and turns.*

Come here, Alfred.

ALFRED *moves down and stands, frightened and small.*

[*Gently.*] Do you lose often?
ALFRED: Yes, sir.
GUIL: Then what could you have left to lose?
ALFRED: Nothing, sir.

Pause. GUIL *regards him.*

GUIL: Do you like being . . . an actor?
ALFRED: No, sir.

GUIL *looks around, at the audience.*

GUIL: You and I, Alfred—we could create a dramatic precedent here.

And ALFRED, *who has been near tears, starts to sniffle.*

Come, come, Alfred, this is no way to fill the theatres of Europe.

The PLAYER *has moved down, to remonstrate with* ALFRED. GUIL *cuts him off again.*

[*Viciously.*] Do you know any good plays?
PLAYER: Plays?
ROS [*coming forward, faltering shyly*]: Exhibitions. . . .
GUIL: I thought you said you were actors.
PLAYER [*dawning*]: Oh. Oh well, we *are.* We are. But there hasn't been much call——
GUIL: You lost. Well then—one of the Greeks, perhaps? You're familiar with the tragedies of antiquity, are you? The great homicidal classics? Matri, patri, fratri, sorrori, uxori and it goes without saying——
ROS: Saucy——
GUIL: —Suicidal—hm? Maidens aspiring to godheads——
ROS: And vice versa——
GUIL: Your kind of thing, is it?
PLAYER: Well, no, I can't say it is, really. We're more of the blood, love and rhetoric school.
GUIL: Well, I'll leave the choice to you, if there is anything to choose between them.
PLAYER: They're hardly divisible, sir—well, I can do you blood and love without the rhetoric, and I can do you blood and rhetoric without the love, and I can do you all three concurrent or consecutive, but I can't do you love and rhetoric without the blood. Blood is compulsory—they're all blood, you see.
GUIL: Is that what people want?
PLAYER: It's what we do. [*Small pause. He turns away.*]

GUIL *touches* ALFRED *on the shoulder.*

GUIL [*wry, gentle*]: Thank you; we'll let you know.

The PLAYER *has moved upstage.* ALFRED *follows.*

PLAYER [*to* TRAGEDIANS]: Thirty-eight!
ROS [*moving across, fascinated and hopeful*]: *Position?*
PLAYER: Sir?
ROS: One of your—tableaux?
PLAYER: No, sir.
ROS: Oh.
PLAYER [*to the* TRAGEDIANS, *now departing with their cart, already taking various props off it*]: Entrances there and there [*indicating upstage*].

The PLAYER *has not moved his position for his last four lines. He does not move now.* GUIL *waits.*

GUIL: Well . . . aren't you going to change into your costume?
PLAYER: I never change out of it, sir.
GUIL: Always in character.
PLAYER: That's it.

Pause.

GUIL: Aren't you going to—come *on?*
PLAYER: I *am* on.
GUIL: But if you *are* on, you can't *come* on. *Can* you?
PLAYER: I *start* on.
GUIL: But it hasn't *started.* Go on. We'll look out for you.
PLAYER: I'll give you a wave.

He does not move. His immobility is now pointed, and getting awkward. Pause. ROS *walks up to him till they are face to face.*

ROS: Excuse me.

Pause. The PLAYER *lifts his downstage foot. It was covering* GUIL*'s coin.* ROS *puts his foot on the coin. Smiles.*

Thank you.

The PLAYER *turns and goes.* ROS *has bent for the coin.*

GUIL [*moving out*]: Come on.
ROS: I say—that was lucky.
GUIL [*turning*]: What?
ROS: It was tails.

He tosses the coin to GUIL *who catches it. Simultaneously—a lighting change sufficient to alter the exterior mood into interior, but nothing violent.*

And OPHELIA *runs on in some alarm, holding up her skirts—followed by* HAMLET.

OPHELIA *has been sewing and she holds the garment. They are both mute.* HAMLET, *with his doublet all unbraced, no hat upon his head, his stockings fouled, ungartered and downgyved to his ankle, pale as his shirt, his knees knocking each other . . . and with a look so piteous, he takes her by the wrist and holds her hard, then he goes to the length of his arm, and with his other hand over his brow, falls to such perusal of her face as he would draw it. . . . At last, with a little shaking of his arm, and thrice his head waving up and down, he raises a sigh so piteous and profound that it does seem to shatter all his bulk and end his being. That done he lets her go, and with his head over his shoulder turned, he goes out backwards without taking his eyes off her . . . she runs off in the opposite direction.*

ROS *and* GUIL *have frozen.* GUIL *unfreezes first. He jumps at* ROS.

GUIL: Come on!

But a flourish—enter CLAUDIUS *and* GERTRUDE, *attended.*

CLAUDIUS: Welcome, dear Rosencrantz . . . [*he raises a hand at* GUIL *while* ROS *bows*—GUIL *bows late and hurriedly*] . . . and Guildenstern.

He raises a hand at ROS *while* GUIL *bows to him*—ROS *is still straightening up from his previous bow and halfway up he bows down again. With his head down, he twists to look at* GUIL, *who is on the way up.*

Moreover that we did much long to see you,
The need we have to use you did provoke
Our hasty sending.

ROS *and* GUIL *still adjusting their clothing for* CLAUDIUS'S *presence.*

Something have you heard
Of Hamlet's transformation, so call it,
Sith nor th'exterior nor the inward man
Resembles that it was. What it should be,
More than his father's death, that thus hath put him,
So much from th'understanding of himself,
I cannot dream of. I entreat you both
That, being of so young days brought up with him
And sith so neighboured to his youth and haviour
That you vouchsafe your rest here in our court
Some little time, so by your companies
To draw him on to pleasures, and to gather
So much as from occasion you may glean,
Whether aught to us unknown afflicts him thus,
That opened lies within our remedy.

GERTRUDE: Good [*fractional suspense*] gentlemen . . .

They both bow.

He hath much talked of you,
And sure I am, two men there is not living
To whom he more adheres. If it will please you
To show us so much gentry and goodwill
As to expand your time with us awhile
For the supply and profit of our hope,
Your visitation shall receive such thanks
As fits a king's remembrance.

ROS: Both your majesties
Might, by the sovereign power you have of us,
Put your dread pleasures more into command
Than to entreaty.

GUIL: But we both obey,
And here give up ourselves in the full bent
To lay our service freely at your feet,
To be commanded.

CLAUDIUS: Thanks, Rosencrantz [*turning to* ROS *who is caught unprepared, while* GUIL *bows*] and gentle Guildenstern [*turning to* GUIL *who is bent double*].

GERTRUDE [*correcting*]: Thanks Guildenstern [*turning to* ROS, *who bows as* GUIL *checks upward movement to bow too—both bent double, squinting at each other*] . . . and gentle Rosencrantz [*turning to* GUIL, *both straightening up*—GUIL *checks again and bows again*].
And I beseech you instantly to visit
My too much changed son. Go, some of you,
And bring these gentlemen where Hamlet is.

Two ATTENDANTS *exit backwards, indicating that* ROS *and* GUIL *should follow.*

GUIL: Heaven make our presence and our practices
Pleasant and helpful to him.

GERTRUDE: Ay, amen!

ROS *and* GUIL *move towards a downstage wing. Before they get there,* POLONIUS *enters. They stop and bow to him. He nods and hurries upstage to* CLAUDIUS. *They turn to look at him.*

POLONIUS: The ambassadors from Norway, my good lord, are joyfully returned.
CLAUDIUS: Thou still hast been the father of good news.
POLONIUS: Have I, my lord? Assure you, my good liege,
I hold my duty as I hold my soul,
Both to my God and to my gracious King;
And I do think, or else this brain of mine
Hunts not the trail of policy so sure
As it hath used to do, that I have found
The very cause of Hamlet's lunacy. . . .

Exeunt—leaving ROS *and* GUIL.

ROS: I want to go home.
GUIL: Don't let them confuse you.
ROS: I'm out of my step here—
GUIL: We'll soon be home and high—dry and home—I'll——
ROS: It's all over my *depth*——
GUIL: —I'll hie you home and——
ROS: —out of my head——
GUIL: —dry you high and——
ROS [*cracking, high*]: —over my step over my head body!—I tell you it's all stopping to a death, it's boding to a depth, stepping to a head, it's all heading to a dead stop——
GUIL [*the nursemaid*]: There! . . . and we'll soon be home and dry . . . and *high* and dry. . . . [*Rapidly.*] Has it ever happened to you that all of a sudden and for no reason at all you haven't the faintest idea how to spell the word—"wife"—or "house"—because when you write it down you just can't remember ever having seen those letters in that order before . . . ?
ROS: I remember——
GUIL: Yes?
ROS: I remember when there were no questions.
GUIL: There were always questions. To exchange one set for another is no great matter.
ROS: Answers, yes. There were answers to everything.
GUIL: You've forgotten.
ROS [*flaring*]: I haven't forgotten—how I used to remember my own name—and yours, oh *yes!* There were answers everywhere you *looked*. There was no question about it—people knew who I was and if they didn't they asked and I told them.
GUIL: You did, the trouble is, each of them is . . . plausible, without being instinctive. All your life you live so close to truth, it becomes a permanent blur in the corner of your eye, and when something nudges it into outline it is like being ambushed by a grotesque. A man standing in his saddle in the half-lit half-alive dawn banged on the shutters and called two names. He was just a hat and a cloak levitating in the grey plume of his own breath, but when he called we came. That much is certain—we came.
ROS: Well I can tell you I'm sick to death of it. I don't care one way or another, so why don't you make up your mind.
GUIL: We can't afford anything quite so arbitrary. Nor did we come all this way for a christening. All *that*—preceded us. But we are comparatively fortunate; we might have been left to sift the whole field of human nomenclature, like two blind men looting a bazaar for their own portraits. . . . At least we are presented with alternatives.
ROS: Well as from now——
GUIL: —But not choice.
ROS: You made me look ridiculous in there.
GUIL: I looked just as ridiculous as you did.
ROS [*an anguished cry*]: Consistency is all I ask!
GUIL [*low, wry rhetoric*]: Give us this day our daily mask.
ROS [*a dying fall*]: I want to go home. [*Moves.*] Which way did we come in? I've lost my sense of direction.
GUIL: The only beginning is birth and the only end is death—if you can't count on that, what can you count on?

They connect again.

ROS: We don't owe anything to anyone.
GUIL: We've been caught up. Your smallest action sets off another somewhere else, and is set off by it. Keep an eye open, an ear cocked. Tread warily, follow instructions. We'll be all right.
ROS: For how long?
GUIL: Till events have played themselves out. There's a logic at work—it's all done for you, don't worry. Enjoy it. Relax. To be taken in hand and led, like being a child again, even without the innocence, a child—it's like being given a prize, an extra slice of childhood when you least expect it, as a prize for being good, or compensation for never having had one. . . . Do I contradict myself?
ROS: I can't remember. . . . What have we got to go on?
GUIL: We have been briefed. Hamlet's transformation. What do you recollect?
ROS: Well, he's changed, hasn't he? The exterior and inward man fails to resemble——
GUIL: Draw him on to pleasures—glean what afflicts him.
ROS: Something more than his father's death——
GUIL: He's always talking about us—there aren't two people living whom he dotes on more than us.

ROS: We cheer him up—find out what's the matter——
GUIL: Exactly, it's a matter of asking the right questions and giving away as little as we can. It's a game.
ROS: And then we can go?
GUIL: And receive such thanks as fits a king's remembrance.
ROS: I like the sound of that. What do you think he means by remembrance?
GUIL: He doesn't forget his friends.
ROS: Would you care to estimate?
GUIL: Difficult to say, really—some kings tend to be amnesiac, others I suppose—the opposite, whatever that is. . . .
ROS: Yes—but——
GUIL: Elephantine . . . ?
ROS: Not how long—how much?
GUIL: *Retentive*—he's a very retentive king, a royal retainer. . . .
ROS: What are you playing at?
GUIL: Words, words. They're all we have to go on.

Pause.

ROS: Shouldn't we be doing something—constructive?
GUIL: What did you have in mind? . . . A short, blunt human pyramid . . . ?
ROS: We could go.
GUIL: Where?
ROS: After him.
GUIL: Why? They've got us placed now—if we start moving around, we'll all be chasing each other all night.

Hiatus.

ROS [*at footlights*]: How very intriguing! [*Turns.*] I feel like a spectator—an appalling business. The only thing that makes it bearable is the irrational belief that somebody interesting will come on in a minute. . . .
GUIL: See anyone?
ROS: No. You?
GUIL: No. [*At footlights.*] What a fine persecution—to be kept intrigued without ever quite being enlightened. . . . [*Pause.*] We've had no practice.
ROS: We could play at questions.
GUIL: What good would that do?
ROS: Practice!
GUIL: Statement! One—love.
ROS: Cheating!
GUIL: How?
ROS: I hadn't started yet.
GUIL: Statement. Two—love.
ROS: Are you counting that?
GUIL: What?
ROS: Are you counting that?
GUIL: Foul! No repetitions. Three—love. First game to . . .
ROS: I'm not going to play if you're going to be like that.
GUIL: Whose serve?
ROS: Hah?
GUIL: Foul! No grunts. Love—one.
ROS: Whose go?
GUIL: Why?
ROS: Why not?
GUIL: What for?
ROS: Foul! No synonyms! One—all.
GUIL: What in God's name is going on?
ROS: Foul! No rhetoric. Two—one.
GUIL: What does it all add up to?
ROS: Can't you guess?
GUIL: Were you addressing me?
ROS: Is there anyone else?
GUIL: Who?
ROS: How would I know?
GUIL: Why do you ask?
ROS: Are you serious?
GUIL: Was that rhetoric?
ROS: No.
GUIL: Statement! Two—all. Game point.
ROS: What's the matter with you today?
GUIL: When?
ROS: What?
GUIL: Are you deaf?
ROS: Am I dead?
GUIL: Yes or no?
ROS: Is there a choice?
GUIL: Is there a God?
ROS: Foul! No *non sequiturs*, three—two, one game all.
GUIL [*seriously*]: What's your name?
ROS: What's yours?
GUIL: I asked you first.
ROS: Statement. One—love.
GUIL: What's your name when you're at home?
ROS: What's yours?
GUIL: When I'm at home?
ROS: Is it different at home?
GUIL: What home?
ROS: Haven't you got one?
GUIL: Why do you ask?
ROS: What are you driving at?
GUIL [*with emphasis*]: What's your name?!
ROS: Repetition. Two—love. Match point to me.
GUIL [*seizing him violently*]: WHO DO YOU THINK YOU ARE?
ROS: Rhetoric! Game and match! [*Pause.*] Where's it going to end?
GUIL: That's the question.
ROS: It's *all* questions.
GUIL: Do you think it matters?

ROS: Doesn't it matter to you?
GUIL: Why should it matter?
ROS: What does it matter why?
GUIL [*teasing gently*]: Doesn't it *matter* why it matters?
ROS [*rounding on him*]: What's the *matter* with you?

Pause.

GUIL: It doesn't matter.
ROS [*voice in the wilderness*]: . . . What's the game?
GUIL: What are the rules?

Enter HAMLET *behind, crossing the stage, reading a book—as he is about to disappear* GUIL *notices him.*

GUIL [*sharply*]: Rosencrantz!
ROS [*jumps*]: What!

HAMLET *goes. Triumph dawns on them, they smile.*

GUIL: There! How was that?
ROS: Clever!
GUIL: Natural?
ROS: Instinctive.
GUIL: Got it in your head?
ROS: I take my hat off to you.
GUIL: Shake hands.

They do.

ROS: Now I'll try you—Guil—!
GUIL: —Not yet—catch me unawares.
ROS: Right.

They separate. Pause. Aside to GUIL.

Ready?
GUIL [*explodes*]: Don't be stupid.
ROS: Sorry.

Pause.

GUIL [*snaps*]: Guildenstern!
ROS [*jumps*]: What?

He is immediately crestfallen, GUIL *is disgusted.*

GUIL: Consistency is all I ask!
ROS [*quietly*]: Immortality is all I seek. . . .
GUIL [*dying fall*]: Give us this day our daily week. . . .

Beat.

ROS: Who was that?
GUIL: Didn't you know him?
ROS: He didn't know me.
GUIL: He didn't see you.
ROS: I didn't see him.
GUIL: We shall see. I *hardly* knew him, he's changed.
ROS: You could see that?
GUIL: Transformed.
ROS: How do you know?
GUIL: Inside and out.
ROS: I see.
GUIL: He's not himself.
ROS: He's changed.
GUIL: I could see that.

Beat.

Glean what afflicts him.
ROS: Me?
GUIL: Him.
ROS: How?
GUIL: Question and answer. Old ways are the best ways.
ROS: He's afflicted.
GUIL: You question, I'll answer.
ROS: He's not himself, you know.
GUIL: I'm him, you see.

Beat.

ROS: Who am I then?
GUIL: You're yourself.
ROS: And he's you?
GUIL: Not a bit of it.
ROS: Are you afflicted?
GUIL: That's the idea. Are you ready?
ROS: Let's go back a bit.
GUIL: I'm afflicted.
ROS: I see.
GUIL: Glean what afflicts me.
ROS: Right.
GUIL: Question and answer.
ROS: How should I begin?
GUIL: Address me.
ROS: My dear Guildenstern!
GUIL [*quietly*]: You've forgotten—haven't you?
ROS: My dear Rosencrantz!
GUIL [*great control*]: I don't think you quite understand. What we are attempting is a hypothesis in which *I* answer for *him*, while *you* ask me questions.
ROS: Ah! Ready?
GUIL: You know what to do?
ROS: What?
GUIL: Are you stupid?
ROS: Pardon?
GUIL: Are you deaf?
ROS: Did you speak?
GUIL [*admonishing*]: Not now——

ROS: Statement.
GUIL [*shouts*]: Not now! [*Pause.*] If I had any doubts, or rather hopes, they are dispelled. What could we possibly have in common except our situation? [*They separate and sit.*] Perhaps he'll come back this way.
ROS: Should we go?
GUIL: Why?

Pause.

ROS [*starts up. Snaps fingers*]: Oh! You mean—you pretend to be *him*, and I ask you questions!
GUIL [*dry*]: Very good.
ROS: You had me confused.
GUIL: I could see I had.
ROS: How should I begin?
GUIL: Address me.

They stand and face each other, posing.

ROS: My honoured Lord!
GUIL: My dear Rosencrantz!

Pause.

ROS: Am I pretending to be you, then?
GUIL: Certainly not. If you like. Shall we continue?
ROS: Question and answer.
GUIL: Right.
ROS: Right. My honoured lord!
GUIL: My dear fellow!
ROS: How are you?
GUIL: Afflicted!
ROS: Really? In what way?
GUIL: Transformed.
ROS: Inside or out?
GUIL: Both.
ROS: I see. [*Pause.*] Not much new there.
GUIL: Go into details. *Delve.* Probe the background, establish the situation.
ROS: So—so your uncle is the king of Denmark?!
GUIL: And my father before him.
ROS: His father before him?
GUIL: No, my father before him.
ROS: But surely——
GUIL: You might well ask.
ROS: Let me get it straight. Your father was king. You were his only son. Your father dies. You are of age. Your uncle becomes king.
GUIL: Yes.
ROS: Unorthodox.
GUIL: Undid me.
ROS: Undeniable. Where were you?
GUIL: In Germany.
ROS: Usurpation, then.
GUIL: He slipped in.
ROS: Which reminds me.
GUIL: Well, it would.
ROS: I don't want to be personal.
GUIL: It's common knowledge.
ROS: Your mother's marriage.
GUIL: He slipped in.

Beat.

ROS [*lugubriously*]: His body was still warm.
GUIL: So was hers.
ROS: Extraordinary.
GUIL: Indecent.
ROS: Hasty.
GUIL: Suspicious.
ROS: It makes you think.
GUIL: Don't think I haven't thought of it.
ROS: And with her husband's brother.
GUIL: They were close.
ROS: She went to him——
GUIL: —Too close——
ROS: —for comfort.
GUIL: It looks bad.
ROS: It adds up.
GUIL: Incest to adultery.
ROS: Would you go so far?
GUIL: Never.
ROS: To sum up: your father, whom you love, dies, you are his heir, you come back to find that hardly was the corpse cold before his young brother popped onto his throne and into his sheets, thereby offending both legal and natural practice. Now why exactly are you behaving in this extraordinary manner?
GUIL: I can't imagine! [*Pause.*] But all that is well known, common property. Yet he sent for us. And we did come.
ROS [*alert, ear cocked*]: I say! I heard music——
GUIL: We're here.
ROS: —Like a band—I thought I heard a band.
GUIL: Rosencrantz . . .
ROS [*absently, still listening*]: What?

Pause, short.

GUIL [*gently wry*]: Guildenstern . . .
ROS [*irritated by the repetition*]: *What?*
GUIL: Don't you discriminate at all?
ROS [*turning dumbly*]: Wha'?

Pause.

GUIL: Go and see if he's there.
ROS: Who?
GUIL: There.

ROS *goes to an upstage wing, looks, returns, formally making his report.*

ROS: Yes.
GUIL: What is he doing?

ROS *repeats movement.*

ROS: Talking.
GUIL: To himself?

ROS *starts to move.* GUIL *cuts in impatiently.*

Is he alone?
ROS: No.
GUIL: Then he's not talking to himself, is he?
ROS: Not *by* himself. . . . Coming this way, I think. [*Shiftily.*] Should we go?
GUIL: Why? We're marked now.

HAMLET *enters, backwards, talking, followed by* POLONIUS, *upstage.* ROS *and* GUIL *occupy the two downstage corners looking upstage.*

HAMLET: . . . for you yourself, sir, should be as old as I am if like a crab you could go backward.
POLONIUS [*aside*]: Though this be madness, yet there is method in it. Will you walk out of the air, my lord?
HAMLET: Into my grave.
POLONIUS: Indeed, that's out of the air.

HAMLET *crosses to upstage exit,* POLONIUS *asiding unintelligibly until——*

My lord, I will take my leave of you.
HAMLET: You cannot take from me anything that I will more willingly part withal—except my life, except my life, except my life. . . .
POLONIUS [*crossing downstage*]: Fare you well, my lord. [*To* ROS:] You go to seek Lord Hamlet? There he is.
ROS [*to* POLONIUS]: God save you sir.

POLONIUS *goes.*

GUIL [*calls upstage to* HAMLET]: My honoured lord!
ROS: My most dear lord!

HAMLET *centred upstage, turns to them.*

HAMLET: My excellent good friends! How dost thou Guildenstern? [*Coming downstage with an arm raised to* ROS, GUIL *meanwhile bowing to no greeting.* HAMLET *corrects himself. Still to* ROS:] Ah Rosencrantz!

They laugh good-naturedly at the mistake. They all meet midstage, turn upstage to walk, HAMLET *in the middle, arm over each shoulder.*

HAMLET: Good lads how do you both?

BLACKOUT

ACT II

HAMLET, ROS *and* GUIL *talking, the continuation of the previous scene. Their conversation, on the move, is indecipherable at first. The first intelligible line is* HAMLET*'s, coming at the end of a short speech—see Shakespeare Act II, scene ii.*

HAMLET: S'blood, there is something in this more than natural, if philosophy could find it out.

A flourish from the TRAGEDIANS' *band.*

GUIL: There are the players.
HAMLET: Gentlemen, you are welcome to Elsinore. Your hands, come then. [*He takes their hands.*] The appurtenance of welcome is fashion and ceremony. Let me comply with you in this garb, lest my extent to the players (which I tell you must show fairly outwards) should more appear like entertainment than yours.You are welcome. [*About to leave.*] But my uncle-father and aunt-mother are deceived.
GUIL: In what, my dear lord?
HAMLET: I am but mad north north-west; when the wind is southerly I know a hawk from a handsaw.

POLONIUS *enters as* GUIL *turns away.*

POLONIUS: Well be with you gentlemen.
HAMLET [*to* ROS]: Mark you, Guildenstern [*uncertainly to* GUIL] and you too; at each ear a hearer. That great baby you see there is not yet out of his swaddling clouts. . . . [*He takes* ROS *upstage with him, talking together.*]
POLONIUS: My Lord! I have news to tell you.
HAMLET [*releasing* ROS *and mimicking*]: My lord, I have news to tell you. . . . When Roscius was an actor in Rome . . .

ROS *comes downstage to rejoin* GUIL.

POLONIUS [*as he follows* HAMLET out]: The actors are come hither my lord.
HAMLET: Buzz, buzz.

Exeunt HAMLET *and* POLONIUS.

ROS *and* GUIL *ponder. Each reluctant to speak first.*

GUIL: Hm?
ROS: Yes?
GUIL: What?
ROS: I thought you . . .
GUIL: No.
ROS: Ah.

Pause.

GUIL: I think we can say we made some headway.
ROS: You think so?
GUIL: I think we can say that.
ROS: I think we can say he made us look ridiculous.
GUIL: We played it close to the chest of course.
ROS [*derisively*]: "Question and answer. Old ways are the best ways"! He was scoring off us all down the line.
GUIL: He caught us on the wrong foot once or twice, perhaps, but I thought we gained some ground.
ROS [*simply*]: He murdered us.
GUIL: He might have had the edge.
ROS [*roused*]: Twenty-seven—three, and you think he might have had the edge?! He *murdered* us.
GUIL: What about our evasions?
ROS: Oh, our evasions were lovely. "Were you sent for?" he says. "My lord, we were sent for. . . ." I didn't know where to put myself.
GUIL: He had six rhetoricals——
ROS: It was question and answer, all right. Twenty-seven questions he got out in ten minutes, and answered three. I was waiting for you to *delve.* "When is he going to start *delving*?" I asked myself.
GUIL: —And two repetitions.
ROS: Hardly a leading question between us.
GUIL: We got his *symptoms*, didn't we?
ROS: Half of what he said meant something else, and the other half didn't mean anything at all.
GUIL: Thwarted ambition—a sense of grievance, that's my diagnosis.
ROS: Six rhetorical and two repetition, leaving nineteen, of which we answered fifteen. And what did we get in return? He's depressed! . . . Denmark's a prison and he'd rather live in a nutshell; some shadow-play about the nature of ambition, which never got down to cases, and finally one direct question which might have led somewhere, and led in fact to his illuminating claim to tell a hawk from a handsaw.

Pause.

GUIL: When the wind is southerly.
ROS: And the weather's clear.
GUIL: And when it isn't he can't.
ROS: He's at the mercy of the elements. [*Licks his finger and holds it up—facing audience.*] Is that southerly?

They stare at audience.

GUIL: It doesn't *look* southerly. What made you think so?
ROS: I didn't *say* I think so. It could be northerly for all I know.
GUIL: I wouldn't have thought so.
ROS: Well, if you're going to be dogmatic.
GUIL: Wait a minute—we came from roughly south according to a rough map.
ROS: I see. Well, which way did we come in? [GUIL *looks round vaguely.*] Roughly.
GUIL [*clears his throat*]: In the morning the sun would be easterly. I think we can assume that.
ROS: That it's morning?
GUIL: If it is, and the sun is over *there* [*his right as he faces the audience*] for instance, *that* [*front*] would be northerly. On the other hand, if it is not morning and the sun is over *there* [*his left*] . . . *that* . . . [*lamely*] would *still* be northerly. [*Picking up.*] To put it another way, if we came from down there [*front*] and it is morning, the sun would be up there [*his left*], and if it is actually over *there* [*his right*] and it's still morning, we must have come from up *there* [*behind him*], and if *that* is southerly [*his left*] and the sun is really over *there* [*front*], then it's the afternoon. However, if none of these is the case——
ROS: Why don't you go and have a look?
GUIL: Pragmatism?!—is that all you have to offer? You seem to have no conception of where we stand! You won't find the answer written down for you in the bowl of a compass—I can tell you that. [*Pause.*] Besides, you can never tell this far north—it's probably dark out there.
ROS: I merely suggest that the position of the sun, if it is out, would give you a rough idea of the time; alternatively, the clock, if it is going, would give you a rough idea of the position of the sun. I forget which you're trying to establish.
GUIL: I'm trying to establish the direction of the wind.
ROS: There isn't any wind. *Draught*, yes.
GUIL: In that case, the origin. Trace it to its source and it might give us a rough idea of the way we came in—which might give us a rough idea of south, for further reference.
ROS: It's coming up through the floor. [*He studies the floor.*] That can't be south, can it?
GUIL: That's not a direction. Lick your toe and wave it around a bit.

ROS *considers the distance of his foot.*

ROS: No, I think you'd have to lick it for me.

Pause.

GUIL: I'm prepared to let the whole matter drop.
ROS: Or I could lick yours, of course.
GUIL: No thank you.
ROS: I'll even wave it around for you.
GUIL [*down* ROS*'s throat*]: What in God's name is the matter with you?
ROS: Just being friendly.
GUIL [*retiring*]: Somebody might come in. It's what we're counting on, after all. Ultimately.

Good pause.

ROS: Perhaps they've all trampled each other to death in the rush. . . . Give them a shout. Something provocative. *Intrigue* them.
GUIL: Wheels have been set in motion, and they have their own pace, to which we are . . . condemned. Each move is dictated by the previous one—that is the meaning of order. If we start being arbitrary it'll just be a shambles: at least, let us hope so. Because if we happened, just happened to discover, or even suspect, that our spontaneity was part of their order, we'd know that we were lost. [*He sits.*] A Chinaman of the T'ang Dynasty—and, by which definition, a philosopher—dreamed he was a butterfly, and from that moment he was never quite sure that he was not a butterfly dreaming it was a Chinese philosopher. Envy him; in his two-fold security.

A good pause. ROS *leaps up and bellows at the audience.*

ROS: Fire!

GUIL *jumps up.*

GUIL: Where?
ROS: It's all right—I'm demonstrating the misuse of free speech. To prove that it exists. [*He regards the audience, that is the direction, with contempt—and other directions, then front again.*] Not a move. They should burn to death in their shoes. [*He takes out one of his coins. Spins it. Catches it. Looks at it. Replaces it.*]
GUIL: What was it?
ROS: What?
GUIL: Heads or tails?
ROS: Oh. I didn't look.
GUIL: Yes you did.
ROS: Oh, did I? [*He takes out a coin, studies it.*] Quite right—it rings a bell.
GUIL: What's the last thing you remember?
ROS: I don't wish to be reminded of it.
GUIL: We cross our bridges when we come to them and burn them behind us, with nothing to show for our progress except a memory of the smell of smoke, and a presumption that once our eyes watered.

ROS *approaches him brightly, holding a coin between finger and thumb. He covers it with his other hand, draws his fists apart and holds them for* GUIL. GUIL *considers them. Indicates the left hand,* ROS *opens it to show it empty.*

ROS: No.

Repeat process. GUIL *indicates left hand again.* ROS *shows it empty.*

Double bluff!

*Repeat process—*GUIL *taps one hand, then the other hand, quickly.* ROS *inadvertently shows that both are empty.* ROS *laughs as* GUIL *turns upstage.* ROS *stops laughing, looks around his feet, pats his clothes, puzzled.*

POLONIUS *breaks that up by entering upstage followed by the* TRAGEDIANS *and* HAMLET.

POLONIUS [*entering*]: Come sirs.
HAMLET: Follow him, friends. We'll hear a play tomorrow. [*Aside to the* PLAYER, *who is the last of the* TRAGEDIANS:] Dost thou hear me, old friend? Can you play *The Murder of Gonzago?*
PLAYER: Ay, my lord.
HAMLET: We'll ha't tomorrow night. You could for a need study a speech of some dozen or sixteen lines which I would set down and insert in't, could you not?
PLAYER: Ay, my lord.
HAMLET: Very well. Follow that lord, and look you mock him not.

The PLAYER *crossing downstage, notes* ROS *and* GUIL. *Stops.* HAMLET *crossing downstage addresses them without pause.*

HAMLET: My good friends, I'll leave you till tonight. You are welcome to Elsinore.
ROS: Good, my lord.

HAMLET *goes.*

GUIL: So you've caught up.
PLAYER [*coldly*]: Not yet, sir.

GUIL: Now mind your tongue, or we'll have it out and throw the rest of you away, like a nightingale at a Roman feast.
ROS: Took the very words out of my mouth.
GUIL: You'd be *lost* for words.
ROS: You'd be tongue-tied.
GUIL: Like a mute in a monologue.
ROS: Like a nightingale at a Roman feast.
GUIL: Your diction will go to pieces.
ROS: Your lines will be cut.
GUIL: To dumbshows.
ROS: And dramatic pauses.
GUIL: You'll never *find* your tongue.
ROS: Lick your lips.
GUIL: Taste your tears.
ROS: Your breakfast.
GUIL: You won't know the difference.
ROS: There won't be any.
GUIL: We'll take the very words out of your mouth.
ROS: So you've caught on.
GUIL: So you've caught up.
PLAYER [*tops*]: Not yet! [*Bitterly.*] You left us.
GUIL: Ah! I'd forgotten—you performed a dramatic spectacle on the way. Yes, I'm sorry we had to miss it.
PLAYER [*bursts out*]: We can't look each other in the face! [*Pause, more in control.*] You don't understand the humiliation of it—to be tricked out of the single assumption which makes our existence viable—that somebody is *watching*. . . . The plot was two corpses gone before we caught sight of ourselves, stripped naked in the middle of nowhere and pouring ourselves down a bottomless well.
ROS: Is *that* thirty-eight?
PLAYER [*lost*]: There we were—demented children mincing about in clothes that no one ever wore, speaking as no man ever spoke, swearing love in wigs and rhymed couplets, killing each other with wooden swords, hollow protestations of faith hurled after empty promises of vengeance—and every gesture, every pose, vanishing into the thin unpopulated air. We ransomed our dignity to the clouds, and the uncomprehending birds listened. [*He rounds on them.*] Don't you see?! We're *actors*—we're the opposite of people! [*They recoil nonplussed, his voice calms.*] Think, in your head, *now*, think of the most . . . *private* . . . *secret* . . . *intimate* thing you have ever done secure in the knowledge of its privacy. . . . [*He gives them—and the audience—a good pause.* ROS *takes on a shifty look.*] Are you thinking of it? [*He strikes with his voice and his head.*] *Well, I saw you do it!*

ROS *leaps up, dissembling madly.*

ROS: You never! It's a lie! [*He catches himself with a giggle in a vacuum and sits down again.*]
PLAYER: We're actors. . . . We pledged our identities, secure in the conventions of our trade, that someone would be watching. And then, gradually, no one was. We were caught, high and dry. It was not until the murderer's long soliloquy that we were able to look around; frozen as we were in profile, our eyes searched you out, first confidently, then hesitantly, then desperately as each patch of turf, each log, every exposed corner in every direction proved uninhabited, and all the while the murderous King addressed the horizon with his dreary interminable guilt. . . . Our heads began to move, wary as lizards, the corpse of unsullied Rosalinda peeped through his fingers, and the King faltered. Even then, habit and a stubborn trust that our audience spied upon us from behind the nearest bush, forced our bodies to blunder on long after they had emptied of meaning, until like runaway carts they dragged to a halt. No one came forward. No one shouted at us. The silence was unbreakable, it imposed itself upon us; it was obscene. We took off our crowns and swords and cloth of gold and moved silent on the road to Elsinore.

Silence. Then GUIL *claps solo with slow measured irony.*

GUIL: Brilliantly re-created—if these eyes could weep! . . . Rather strong on metaphor, mind you. No criticism—only a matter of taste. And so here you are—with a vengeance. That's a figure of speech . . . isn't it? Well let's say we've made up for it, for you may have no doubt whom to thank for your performance at the court.
ROS: We are counting on you to take him out of himself. You are the pleasures which we draw him on to— [*he escapes a fractional giggle but recovers immediately*] and by that I don't mean your usual filth; you can't treat royalty like people with normal perverted desires. They know nothing of that and you know nothing of them, to your mutual survival. So give him a good clean show suitable for all the family, or you can rest assured you'll be playing the tavern tonight.
GUIL: Or the night after.
ROS: Or not.
PLAYER: We already have an entry here. And always have had.
GUIL: You've played for him before?
PLAYER: Yes, sir.
ROS: And what's *his* bent?
PLAYER: Classical.
ROS: Saucy!

GUIL: What will you play?
PLAYER: *The Murder of Gonzago.*
GUIL: Full of fine cadence and corpses.
PLAYER: Pirated from the Italian. . . .
ROS: What is it about?
PLAYER: It's about a King and Queen. . . .
GUIL: Escapism! What else?
PLAYER: Blood——
GUIL: —Love and rhetoric.
PLAYER: Yes. [*Going.*]
GUIL: Where are you going?
PLAYER: I can come and go as I please.
GUIL: You're evidently a man who knows his way around.
PLAYER: I've been here before.
GUIL: We're still finding our feet.
PLAYER: I should concentrate on not losing your heads.
GUIL: Do you speak from knowledge?
PLAYER: Precedent.
GUIL: You've been here before.
PLAYER: And I know which way the wind is blowing.
GUIL: Operating on two levels, are we?! How clever! I expect it comes naturally to you, being in the business so to speak.

The PLAYER'S *grave face does not change. He makes to move off again.* GUIL *for the second time cuts him off.*

The truth is, we value your company, for want of any other. We have been left so much to our own devices—after a while one welcomes the uncertainty of being left to other people's.
PLAYER: Uncertainty is the normal state. You're nobody special.

He makes to leave again. GUIL *loses his cool.*

GUIL: But for God's sake what are we supposed to *do*?!
PLAYER: Relax. Respond. That's what people do. You can't go through life questioning your situation at every turn.
GUIL: But we don't know what's going on, or what to do with ourselves. We don't know how to *act*.
PLAYER: Act natural. You know why you're here at least.
GUIL: We only know what we're told, and that's little enough. And for all we know it isn't even true.
PLAYER: For all anyone knows, nothing is. Everything has to be taken on trust; truth is only that which is taken to be true. It's the currency of living. There may be nothing behind it, but it doesn't make any difference so long as it is honoured. One acts on assumptions. What do you assume?
ROS: Hamlet is not himself, outside or in. We have to glean what afflicts him.
GUIL: He doesn't give much away.
PLAYER: Who does, nowadays?
GUIL: He's—melancholy.
PLAYER: Melancholy?
ROS: Mad.
PLAYER: How is he mad?
ROS: Ah. [*To* GUIL:] How is he mad?
GUIL: More morose than mad, perhaps.
PLAYER: Melancholy.
GUIL: Moody.
ROS: He has moods.
PLAYER: Of moroseness?
GUIL: Madness. And yet.
ROS: Quite.
GUIL: For instance.
ROS: He talks to himself, which might be madness.
GUIL: If he didn't talk sense, which he does.
ROS: Which suggests the opposite.
PLAYER: Of what?

Small pause.

GUIL: I think I have it. A man talking sense to himself is no madder than a man talking nonsense not to himself.
ROS: Or just as mad.
GUIL: Or just as mad.
ROS: And he does both.
GUIL: So there you are.
ROS: Stark raving sane.

Pause.

PLAYER: Why?
GUIL: Ah. [*To* ROS:] Why?
ROS: Exactly.
GUIL: Exactly what?
ROS: Exactly why.
GUIL: Exactly why *what*?
ROS: What?
GUIL: *Why*?
ROS: Why what, exactly?
GUIL: Why is he mad?!
ROS: *I* don't know!

Beat.

PLAYER: The old man thinks he's in love with his daughter.
ROS [*appalled*]: Good God! We're out of our depth here.
PLAYER: No, no, no—*he* hasn't got a daughter—the old man thinks he's in love with *his* daughter.

ROS: The old man is?
PLAYER: Hamlet, in love with the old man's daughter, the old man thinks.
ROS: Ha! It's beginning to make sense! Unrequited passion!

The PLAYER *moves.*

GUIL: [*Fascist.*] Nobody leaves this room! [*Pause, lamely.*] Without a *very* good reason.
PLAYER: Why not?
GUIL: All this strolling about is getting too arbitrary by half—I'm rapidly losing my grip. From now on reason will prevail.
PLAYER: I have lines to learn.
GUIL: Pass!

The PLAYER *passes into one of the wings.* ROS *cups his hands and shouts into the opposite one.*

ROS: Next!

But no one comes.

GUIL: What did you expect?
ROS: Something . . . someone . . . nothing.

They sit facing front.

Are you hungry?
GUIL: No, are you?
ROS [*thinks*]: No. You remember that coin?
GUIL: No.
ROS: I think I lost it.
GUIL: What coin?
ROS: I don't remember exactly.

Pause.

GUIL: Oh, that coin . . . clever.
ROS: I can't remember how I did it.
GUIL: It probably comes natural to you.
ROS: Yes, I've got a show-stopper there.
GUIL: Do it again.

Slight pause.

ROS: We can't afford it.
GUIL: Yes, one must think of the future.
ROS: It's the normal thing.
GUIL: To have one. One is, after all, having it all the time . . . now . . . and now . . . and now. . . .
ROS: It could go on for ever. Well, not for *ever,* I suppose. [*Pause.*] Do you ever think of yourself as actually *dead,* lying in a box with a lid on it?
GUIL: No.
ROS: Nor do I, really. . . . It's silly to be depressed by it. I mean one thinks of it like being *alive* in a box, one keeps forgetting to take into account the fact that one is *dead* . . . which should make all the difference . . . shouldn't it? I mean, you'd never *know* you were in a box, would you? It would be just like being *asleep* in a box. Not that I'd like to sleep in a box, mind you, not without any air—you'd wake up dead, for a start, and then where would you be? Apart from inside a box. That's the bit I don't like, frankly. That's why I don't think of it. . . .

GUIL *stirs restlessly, pulling his cloak round him.*

Because you'd be helpless, wouldn't you? Stuffed in a box like that, I mean you'd be in there for ever. Even taking into account the fact that you're dead, it isn't a pleasant thought. *Especially* if you're dead, really . . . *ask* yourself, if I asked you straight off—I'm going to stuff you in this box now, would you rather be alive or dead? Naturally, you'd prefer to be alive. Life in a box is better than no life at all. I expect. You'd have a chance at least. You could lie there thinking—well, at least I'm not dead! In a minute someone's going to bang on the lid and tell me to come out. [*Banging the floor with his fists.*] "Hey you, whatsyername! Come out of there!"
GUIL [*jumps up savagely*]: You don't have to flog it to death!

Pause.

ROS: I wouldn't think about it, if I were you. You'd only get depressed. [*Pause.*] Eternity is a terrible thought. I mean, where's it going to end? [*Pause, then brightly.*] Two early Christians chanced to meet in Heaven. "Saul of Tarsus yet!" cried one. "What are *you* doing here?!" . . . "Tarsus-Schmarsus," replied the other, "I'm Paul already." [*He stands up restlessly and flaps his arms.*] They don't care. We count for nothing. We could remain silent till we're green in the face, they wouldn't come.
GUIL: Blue, red.
ROS: A Christian, a Moslem and a Jew chanced to meet in a closed carriage. . . . "Silverstein!" cried the Jew. "Who's your friend?" . . . "His name's Abdullah," replied the Moslem, "but he's no friend of mine since he became a convert." [*He leaps up again, stamps his foot and shouts into the wings.*] All right, we know you're in there! Come out talking! [*Pause.*] We have no control. None at

all . . . [*He paces.*] Whatever became of the moment when one first knew about death? There must have been one, a moment, in childhood when it first occurred to you that you don't go on for ever. It must have been shattering—stamped into one's memory. And yet I can't remember it. It never occurred to me at all. What does one make of that? We must be born with an intuition of mortality. Before we know the words for it, before we know that there are words, out we come, bloodied and squalling with the knowledge that for all the compasses in the world, there's only one direction, and time is its only measure. [*He reflects, getting more desperate and rapid.*] A Hindu, a Buddhist and a lion-tamer chanced to meet, in a circus on the Indo-Chinese border. [*He breaks out.*] They're taking us for granted! Well, I won't stand for it! In future, notice will be taken. [*He wheels again to face into the wings.*] Keep out, then! I forbid anyone to enter! [*No one comes. Breathing heavily.*] That's better. . . .

Immediately, behind him a grand procession enters, principally CLAUDIUS, GERTRUDE, POLONIUS *and* OPHELIA. CLAUDIUS *takes* ROS*'s elbow as he passes and is immediately deep in conversation: the context is Shakespeare Act III, scene i.* GUIL *still faces front as* CLAUDIUS, ROS, *etc., pass upstage and turn.*

GUIL: Death followed by eternity . . . the worst of both worlds. It *is* a terrible thought.

He turns upstage in time to take over the conversation with CLAUDIUS. GERTRUDE *and* ROS *head downstage.*

GERTRUDE: Did he receive you well?
ROS: Most like a gentleman.
GUIL [*returning in time to take it up*]: But with much forcing of his disposition.
ROS [*a flat lie and he knows it and shows it, perhaps catching* GUIL*'s eye*]: Niggard of question, but of our demands most free in his reply.
GERTRUDE: Did you assay him to any pastime?
ROS: Madam, it so fell out that certain players
We o'erraught on the way: of these we told him
And there did seem in him a kind of joy
To hear of it. They are here about the court,
And, as I think, they have already order
This night to play before him.
POLONIUS: 'Tis most true
And he beseeched me to entreat your Majesties
To hear and see the matter.
CLAUDIUS: With all my heart, and it doth content me
To hear him so inclined.
Good gentlemen, give him a further edge
And drive his purpose into these delights.
ROS: We shall, my lord.
CLAUDIUS [*leading out procession*]:
Sweet Gertrude, leave us, too,
For we have closely sent for Hamlet hither,
That lie, as t'were by accident, may here
Affront Ophelia. . . .

Exeunt CLAUDIUS *and* GERTRUDE.

ROS [*peevish*]: Never a moment's peace! In and out, on and off, they're coming at us from all sides.
GUIL: You're never satisfied.
ROS: Catching us on the trot. . . . Why can't *we* go by *them?*
GUIL: What's the difference?
ROS: I'm going.

ROS *pulls his cloak round him.* GUIL *ignores him. Without confidence* ROS *heads upstage. He looks out and comes back quickly.*

He's coming.
GUIL: What's he doing?
ROS: Nothing.
GUIL: He must be doing something.
ROS: Walking.
GUIL: On his hands?
ROS: No, on his feet.
GUIL: Stark naked?
ROS: Fully dressed.
GUIL: Selling toffee apples?
ROS: Not that I noticed.
GUIL: You could be wrong?
ROS: I don't think so.

Pause.

GUIL: I can't for the life of me see how we're going to get into conversation.

HAMLET *enters upstage, and pauses, weighing up the pros and cons of making his quietus.*
ROS *and* GUIL *watch him.*

ROS: Nevertheless, I suppose one might say that this was a chance. . . . One might well . . . accost him. . . . Yes, it definitely looks like a chance to me. . . . Something on the lines of a direct informal approach . . . man to man . . . straight from the shoulder. . . . Now look here, what's it all about . . . sort of thing. Yes. Yes, this looks like one to be grabbed with both hands, I should say . . . if I were asked. . . . No point in looking at a gift horse till you see the whites of its eyes, etcetera. [*He has moved towards* HAMLET *but his nerve fails. He returns.*] We're overawed, that's our trouble.

When it comes to the point we succumb to their personality. . . .

OPHELIA *enters, with prayerbook, a religious procession of one.*

HAMLET: Nymph, in thy orisons be all my sins remembered.

At his voice she has stopped for him, he catches her up.

OPHELIA: Good my lord, how does your honour for this many a day?
HAMLET: I humbly thank you—well, well, well.

They disappear talking into the wing.

ROS: It's like living in a public park!
GUIL: Very impressive. Yes, I thought your direct informal approach was going to stop this thing dead in its tracks there. If I might make a suggestion—shut up and sit down. Stop being perverse.
ROS [*near tears*]: I'm not going to stand for it!

A FEMALE FIGURE, *ostensibly the* QUEEN, *enters.* ROS *marches up behind her, puts his hands over her eyes and says with a desperate frivolity.*

ROS: Guess who?!
PLAYER [*having appeared in a downstage corner*]: Alfred!

ROS *lets go, spins around. He has been holding* ALFRED, *in his robe and blond wig.* PLAYER *is in the downstage corner still.* ROS *comes down to that exit. The* PLAYER *does not budge. He and* ROS *stand toe to toe.*

ROS: Excuse me.

The PLAYER *lifts his downstage foot.* ROS *bends to put his hand on the floor. The* PLAYER *lowers his foot.* ROS *screams and leaps away.*

PLAYER [*gravely*]: I beg your pardon.
GUIL [*to* ROS]: What did he do?
PLAYER: I put my foot down.
ROS: My hand was on the floor!
GUIL: You put your hand under his foot?
ROS: I——
GUIL: What for?
ROS: I thought—— [*Grabs* GUIL.] Don't leave me!

He makes a break for an exit. A TRAGEDIAN *dressed as a* KING *enters.* ROS *recoils, breaks for the opposite wing. Two cloaked* TRAGEDIANS *enter.* ROS *tries again but another* TRAGEDIAN *enters, and* ROS *retires to midstage. The* PLAYER *claps his hands matter-of-factly.*

PLAYER: Right! We haven't got much time.
GUIL: What are you doing?
PLAYER: Dress rehearsal. Now if you two wouldn't mind just moving back . . . there . . . good. . . . [*To* TRAGEDIANS:] Everyone ready? And for goodness' sake, remember what we're doing. [*To* ROS *and* GUIL:] We always use the same costumes more or less, and they forget what they are supposed to be *in* you see. . . . Stop picking your nose, Alfred. When Queens have to they do it by a cerebral process passed down in the blood. . . . Good. Silence! Off we go!
PLAYER-KING: Full thirty times hath Phoebus' cart——

PLAYER *jumps up angrily.*

PLAYER: No, no, no! Dumbshow first, your confounded majesty! [*To* ROS *and* GUIL] They're a bit out of practice, but they always pick up wonderfully for the deaths—it brings out the poetry in them.
GUIL: How nice.
PLAYER: There's nothing more unconvincing than an unconvincing death.
GUIL: I'm sure.

PLAYER *claps his hands.*

PLAYER: Act One—moves now.

The mime. Soft music from a recorder. PLAYER-KING and PLAYER-QUEEN *embrace. She kneels and makes a show of protestation to him. He takes her up, declining his head upon her neck. He lies down. She, seeing him asleep, leaves him.*

GUIL: What is the dumbshow for?
PLAYER: Well, it's a device, really—it makes the action that follows more or less comprehensible; you understand, we are tied down to a language which makes up in obscurity what it lacks in style.

The mime [*continued*]*—enter another. He takes off the* SLEEPER's *crown, kisses it. He has brought in a small bottle of liquid. He pours the poison in the* SLEEPER's *ear, and leaves him. The* SLEEPER *convulses heroically, dying.*

ROS: Who was that?
PLAYER: The King's brother and uncle to the Prince.
GUIL: Not exactly fraternal.
PLAYER: Not exactly avuncular, as time goes on.

The QUEEN *returns, makes passionate action, finding the* KING *dead. The* POISONER *comes in again, attended by two others (the two in cloaks). The* POISONER *seems to console with her. The dead body is carried away. The*

POISONER woos the QUEEN with gifts. She seems harsh awhile but in the end accepts his love. End of mime, at which point, the wail of a woman in torment and OPHELIA appears, wailing, closely followed by HAMLET in a hysterical state, shouting at her, circling her, both midstage.

HAMLET: Go to, I'll no more on't; it hath made me mad!

She falls on her knees weeping.

I say we will have no more marriage! [*His voice drops to include the TRAGEDIANS, who have frozen.*] Those that are married already [*he leans close to the PLAYER-QUEEN and POISONER, speaking with quiet edge*] all but one shall live. [*He smiles briefly at them without mirth, and starts to back out, his parting shot rising again.*] The rest shall keep as they are. [*As he leaves, OPHELIA tottering upstage, he speaks into her ear a quick clipped sentence.*] To a nunnery, go.

He goes out. OPHELIA falls on to her knees upstage, her sobs barely audible. A slight silence.

PLAYER-KING: Full thirty times hath Phoebus' cart——

CLAUDIUS enters with POLONIUS and goes over to OPHELIA and lifts her to her feet. The TRAGEDIANS jump back with heads inclined.

CLAUDIUS: Love? His affections do not that way tend,
Or what he spake, though it lacked form a little,
Was not like madness. There's something
In his soul o'er which his melancholy sits on
Brood, and I do doubt the hatch and the
Disclose will be some danger; which for to
Prevent I have in quick determination thus set
It down: he shall with speed to England . . .

Which carries the three of them—CLAUDIUS, POLONIUS, OPHELIA—out of sight. The PLAYER moves, clapping his hands for attention.

PLAYER: Gentle*men*! [*They look at him.*] It doesn't seem to be coming. We are not getting it at all. [*To* GUIL:] What did you think?
GUIL: What was I supposed to think?
PLAYER [*to* TRAGEDIANS]: You're not getting across!

ROS had gone halfway up to OPHELIA; he returns.

ROS: That didn't look like love to me.
GUIL: Starting from scratch again . . .
PLAYER [*to* TRAGEDIANS]: It was a *mess.*
ROS [*to* GUIL]: It's going to be chaos on the night.
GUIL: Keep back—we're spectators.
PLAYER: Act Two! Positions!
GUIL: Wasn't that the end?
PLAYER: Do you call that an ending?—with practically everyone on his feet? My goodness no—over your dead body.
GUIL: How am I supposed to take that?
PLAYER: Lying down. [*He laughs briefly and in a second has never laughed in his life.*] There's a design at work in all art—surely you know that? Events must play themselves out to aesthetic, moral and logical conclusion.
GUIL: And what's that, in this case?
PLAYER: It never varies—we aim at the point where everyone who is marked for death dies.
GUIL: Marked?
PLAYER: Between "just desserts" and "tragic irony" we are given quite a lot of scope for our particular talent. Generally speaking, things have gone about as far as they can possibly go when things have got about as bad as they reasonably get. [*He switches on a smile.*]
GUIL: Who decides?
PLAYER [*switching off his smile*]: *Decides?* It is *written.*

He turns away. GUIL grabs him and spins him back violently.

[*Unflustered.*] Now if you're going to be subtle, we'll miss each other in the dark. I'm referring to oral tradition. So to speak.

GUIL releases him.

We're tragedians, you see. We follow directions—there is no *choice* involved. The bad end unhappily, the good unluckily. That is what tragedy means. [*Calling.*] Positions!

The TRAGEDIANS have taken up positions for the continuation of the mime: which in this case means a love scene, sexual and passionate, between the QUEEN and the POISONER/KING.

PLAYER: Go!

The lovers begin. The PLAYER contributes a breathless commentary for ROS and GUIL.

Having murdered his brother and wooed the widow—the poisoner mounts the throne! Here we see him and his queen give rein to their unbridled passion! She little knowing that the man she holds in her arms——!
ROS: Oh, I say—here—really! You can't do that!
PLAYER: Why not?

ROS: Well, really—I mean, people want to be *entertained*—they don't come expecting sordid and gratuitous filth.

PLAYER: You're wrong—they do! Murder, seduction and incest—what do you want—*jokes?*

ROS: I want a good story, with a beginning, middle and end.

PLAYER [*to* GUIL]: And you?

GUIL: I'd prefer art to mirror life, if it's all the same to you.

PLAYER: It's all the same to me, sir. [*To the grappling* LOVERS:] All right, no need to indulge yourselves. [*They get up. To* GUIL:] I come on in a minute. Lucianus, nephew to the king! [*Turns his attention to the* TRAGEDIANS.] Next!

They disport themselves to accommodate the next piece of mime, which consists of the PLAYER *himself exhibiting an excitable anguish* [*choreographed, stylized*] *leading to an impassioned scene with the* QUEEN [*cf. "The Closet Scene," Shakespeare Act III, scene iv*] *and a very stylized reconstruction of a* POLONIUS *figure being stabbed behind the arras* [*the murdered* KING *to stand in for* POLONIUS] *while the* PLAYER *himself continues his breathless commentary for the benefit of* ROS *and* GUIL.

PLAYER: Lucianus, nephew to the king . . . usurped by his uncle and shattered by his mother's incestuous marriage . . . loses his reason . . . throwing the court into turmoil and disarray as he alternates between bitter melancholy and unrestricted lunacy . . . staggering from the suicidal [*a pose*] to the homicidal [*here he kills* "POLONIUS"] . . . he at last confronts his mother and in a scene of provocative ambiguity— [*a somewhat oedipal embrace*] begs her to repent and recant—— [*He springs up, still talking*] The King—— [*he pushes forward* the POISONER/KING] tormented by guilt—haunted by fear—decides to despatch his nephew to England—and entrusts this undertaking to two smiling accomplices—friends—courtiers—to two spies——

He has swung round to bring together the POISONER/KING *and the two cloaked* TRAGEDIANS; *the latter kneel and accept a scroll from the* KING.

—giving them a letter to present to the English court——! And so they depart—on board ship——

The two SPIES *position themselves on either side of the* PLAYER, *and the three of them sway gently in unison, the motion of a boat; and then the* PLAYER *detaches himself.*

—and they arrive——

One SPY *shades his eyes at the horizon.*

—and disembark—and present themselves before the English king—— [*He wheels round.*] The English king——

An exchange of headgear creates the ENGLISH KING *from the remaining player—that is, the* PLAYER *who played the original murdered king.*

But where is the Prince? Where indeed? The plot has thickened—a twist of fate and cunning has put into their hands a letter that seals their deaths!

The two SPIES *present their letter; the* ENGLISH KING *reads it and orders their deaths. They stand up as the* PLAYER *whips off their cloaks preparatory to execution.*

Traitors hoist by their own petard?—or victims of the gods?—we shall never know!

The whole mime has been fluid and continuous but now ROS *moves forward and brings it to a pause. What brings* ROS *forward is the fact that under their cloaks the two* SPIES *are wearing coats identical to those worn by* ROS *and* GUIL, *whose coats are now covered by their cloaks.* ROS *approaches "his"* SPY *doubtfully. He does not quite understand why the coats are familiar.* ROS *stands close, touches the coat, thoughtfully. . . .*

ROS: Well, if it isn't——! No, wait a minute, don't tell me—it's a long time since—where was it? Ah, this is taking me back to—when was it? I know you, don't I? I never forget a face— [*he looks into the* SPY's *face*] . . . not that I know yours, that is. For a moment I thought—no, I don't know you, do I? Yes, I'm afraid you're quite wrong. You must have mistaken me for someone else.

GUIL *meanwhile has approached the other* SPY, *brow creased in thought.*

PLAYER [*to* GUIL]: Are you familiar with this play?

GUIL: No.

PLAYER: A slaughterhouse—eight corpses all told. It brings out the best in us.

GUIL [*tense, progressively rattled during the whole mime and commentary*]: You!—What do *you* know about *death?*

PLAYER: It's what the actors do best. They have to exploit whatever talent is given to them, and their talent is dying. They can die heroically, comically, ironically, slowly, suddenly, disgustingly, charmingly, or from a great height. My own talent is more general. I extract significance from melodrama, a significance which it does not in fact contain; but occasionally, from out of this matter, there escapes a thin beam of light that, seen at the right angle, can crack the shell of mortality.

ROS: Is that all they can do—die?

PLAYER: No, no—they kill beautifully. In fact some of them kill even better than they die. The rest die better than they kill. They're a team.

ROS: Which ones are which?

PLAYER: There's not much in it.

GUIL [*fear, derision*]: Actors! The mechanics of cheap melodrama! That isn't *death!* [*More quietly.*] You scream and choke and sink to your knees, but it doesn't bring death home to anyone—it doesn't catch them unawares and start the whisper in their skulls that says—"One day you are going to die." [*He straightens up.*] You die so many times; how can you expect them to believe in your death?

PLAYER: On the contrary, it's the only kind they do believe. They're conditioned to it. I had an actor once who was condemned to hang for stealing a sheep—or a lamb, I forget which—so I got permission to have him hanged in the middle of a play—had to change the plot a bit but I thought it would be effective, you know—and you wouldn't believe it, he just *wasn't* convincing! It was impossible to suspend one's disbelief—and what with the audience jeering and throwing peanuts, the whole thing was a *disaster!*—he did nothing but cry all the time—right out of character—just stood there and cried. . . . Never again.

In good humour he has already turned back to the mime: the two SPIES *awaiting execution at the hands of the* PLAYER, *who takes his dagger out of his belt.*

Audiences know what to expect, and that is all that they are prepared to believe in. [*To the* SPIES:] Show!

The SPIES *die at some length, rather well.*

The light has begun to go, and it fades as they die, and as GUIL *speaks.*

GUIL: No, no, no . . . you've got it all wrong . . . you can't act death. The *fact* of it is nothing to do with seeing it happen—it's not gasps and blood and falling about—that isn't what makes it death. It's just a man failing to reappear, that's all—now you see him, now you don't, that's the only thing that's real: here one minute and gone the next and never coming back—an exit, unobtrusive and unannounced, a disappearance gathering weight as it goes on, until, finally, it is heavy with death.

The two SPIES *lie still, barely visible. The* PLAYER *comes forward and throws the* SPIES' *cloaks over their bodies.* ROS *starts to clap, slowly.*

BLACKOUT

A second of silence, then much noise. Shouts . . . "The King rises!" . . . "Give o'er the play!" . . . and cries for "Lights, lights, lights!"

When the light comes, after a few seconds, it comes as a sunrise.

The stage is empty save for two cloaked figures sprawled on the ground in the approximate positions last held by the dead SPIES. *As the light grows, they are seen to be* ROS *and* GUIL, *and to be resting quite comfortably.* ROS *raises himself on his elbows and shades his eyes as he stares into the auditorium. Finally:*

ROS: That must be east, then. I think we can assume that.

GUIL: I'm assuming nothing.

ROS: No, it's all right. That's the sun. East.

GUIL [*looks up*]: Where?

ROS: I watched it come up.

GUIL: No . . . it was light all the time, you see, and you opened your eyes very, very slowly. If you'd been facing back there you'd be swearing *that* was east.

ROS [*standing up*]: You're a mass of prejudice.

GUIL: I've been taken in before.

ROS [*looks out over the audience*]: Rings a bell.

GUIL: They're waiting to see what we're going to do.

ROS: Good old east.

GUIL: As soon as we make a move they'll come pouring in from every side, shouting obscure instructions, confusing us with ridiculous remarks, messing us about from here to breakfast and getting our names wrong.

ROS *starts to protest but he has hardly opened his mouth before:*

CLAUDIUS [*off stage—with urgency*]: Ho, Guildenstern!

GUIL *is still prone. Small pause.*

ROS AND GUIL: You're wanted. . . .

GUIL *furiously leaps to his feet as* CLAUDIUS *and* GERTRUDE *enter. They are in some desperation.*

CLAUDIUS: Friends both, go join you with some further aid: Hamlet in madness hath Polonius slain, and from his mother's closet hath he dragged him. Go seek him out; speak fair and bring the body into the chapel. I pray you haste in this. [*As he and* GERTRUDE *are hurrying out.*] Come Gertrude, we'll call up our wisest friends and let them know both what we mean to do. . . .

They've gone. ROS *and* GUIL *remain quite still.*

GUIL: Well . . .
ROS: Quite . . .
GUIL: Well, well.
ROS: Quite, quite. [*Nods with spurious confidence.*] Seek him out. [*Pause.*] Etcetera.
GUIL: Quite.
ROS: Well. [*Small pause.*] Well, that's a step in the right direction.
GUIL: You didn't like him?
ROS: Who?
GUIL: Good God, I hope more tears are shed for *us!* . . .
ROS: Well, it's *progress,* isn't it? Something positive. Seek him out. [*Looks round without moving his feet.*] Where does one begin . . . ? [*Takes one step towards the wings and halts.*]
GUIL: Well, that's a step in the right direction.
ROS: You think so? He could be anywhere.
GUIL: All right—you go that way, I'll go this way.
ROS: Right.

They walk towards opposite wings. ROS *halts.*

No.

GUIL *halts.*

You go this way—I'll go that way.
GUIL: All right.

They march towards each other, cross. ROS *halts.*

ROS: Wait a minute.

GUIL *halts.*

I think we should stick together. He might be violent.
GUIL: Good point. I'll come with you.

GUIL *marches across to* ROS. *They turn to leave.* ROS *halts.*

ROS: No, I'll come with *you.*
GUIL: Right.

They turn, march across to the opposite wing. ROS *halts.* GUIL *halts.*

ROS: I'll come with *you, my* way.
GUIL: All right.

They turn again and march across. ROS *halts.* GUIL *halts.*

ROS: I've just thought. If we both go, he could come *here.* That would be stupid, wouldn't it?
GUIL: All right—I'll stay, you go.
ROS: Right.

GUIL *marches to midstage.*

I say.

GUIL *wheels and carries on marching back towards* ROS, *who starts marching downstage. They cross.* ROS *halts.*

I've just thought.

GUIL *halts.*

We ought to stick together; he might be violent.
GUIL: Good point.

GUIL *marches down to join* ROS. *They stand still for a moment in their original positions.*

Well, at last we're getting somewhere.

Pause.

Of course, he might not come.
ROS [*airily*]: Oh, he'll come.
GUIL: We'd have some explaining to do.
ROS: He'll come. [*Airily wanders upstage.*] Don't worry—take my word for it— [*Looks out—is appalled.*] He's coming!
GUIL: What's he doing?
ROS: Walking.
GUIL: Alone?
ROS: No.
GUIL: Not walking?
ROS: No.
GUIL: Who's with him?
ROS: The old man.
GUIL: Walking?
ROS: No.
GUIL: Ah. That's an opening if ever there was one. [*And is suddenly galvanized into action.*] Let him walk into the trap!
ROS: What trap?
GUIL: You stand there! Don't let him pass!

He positions ROS *with his back to one wing, facing* HAMLET'S *entrance.*

GUIL *positions himself next to* ROS, *a few feet away, so that they are covering one side of the stage, facing the opposite side.* GUIL *unfastens his belt.* ROS *does the same. They join the two belts, and hold them taut between them.* ROS*'s trousers slide slowly down.*

HAMLET *enters opposite, slowly, dragging* POLONIUS*'s body. He enters upstage, makes a small arc and leaves by the same side, a few feet downstage.*

ROS *and* GUIL, *holding the belts taut, stare at him in some bewilderment.*

HAMLET *leaves, dragging the body. They relax the strain on the belts.*

ROS: That was close.
GUIL: There's a limit to what two people can do.

They undo the belts: ROS *pulls up his trousers.*

ROS [*worriedly—he walks a few paces towards* HAMLET*'s exit*]: He *was* dead.
GUIL: Of course he's dead!
ROS [*turns to* GUIL]: Properly.
GUIL [*angrily*]: Death's death, isn't it?

ROS *falls silent. Pause.*

Perhaps he'll come back this way.

ROS *starts to take off his belt.*

No, no, no!—if we can't learn by experience, what else have we got?

ROS *desists.*
Pause.

ROS: Give him a shout.
GUIL: I thought we'd been into all that.
ROS [*shouts*]: Hamlet!
GUIL: Don't be absurd.
ROS [*shouts*]: Lord Hamlet!

HAMLET *enters.* ROS *is a little dismayed.*

What have you done, my lord, with the dead body?
HAMLET: Compounded it with dust, whereto 'tis kin.
ROS: Tell us where 'tis, that we may take it thence and bear it to the chapel.
HAMLET: Do not believe it.
ROS: Believe what?
HAMLET: That I can keep your counsel and not mine own. Besides, to be demanded of a sponge, what replication should be made by the son of a king?
ROS: Take you me for a sponge, my lord?
HAMLET: Ay, sir, that soaks up the King's countenance, his rewards, his authorities. But such officers do the King best service in the end. He keeps them, like an ape, in the corner of his jaw, first mouthed, to be last swallowed. When he needs what you have gleaned, it is but squeezing you and, sponge, you shall be dry again.
ROS: I understand you not, my lord,
HAMLET: I am glad of it: a knavish speech sleeps in a foolish ear.
ROS: My lord, you must tell us where the body is and go with us to the King.
HAMLET: The body is with the King, but the King is not with the body. The King is a thing——
GUIL: A thing, my lord——?
HAMLET: Of nothing. Bring me to him.

HAMLET *moves resolutely towards one wing. They move with him, shepherding. Just before they reach the exit,* HAMLET, *apparently seeing* CLAUDIUS *approaching from off stage, bends low in a sweeping bow.* ROS *and* GUIL, *cued by* HAMLET, *also bow deeply—a sweeping ceremonial bow with their cloaks swept round them.* HAMLET, *however, continues the movement into an about-turn and walks off in the opposite direction.* ROS *and* GUIL, *with their heads low, do not notice.*

No one comes on. ROS *and* GUIL *squint upwards and find that they are bowing to nothing.*

CLAUDIUS *enters behind them. At first words they leap up and do a double-take.*

CLAUDIUS: How now? What hath befallen?
ROS: Where the body is bestowed, my lord, we cannot get from him.
CLAUDIUS: But where is he?
ROS [*fractional hesitation*]: Without, my lord; guarded to know your pleasure.
CLAUDIUS [*moves*]: Bring him before us.

This hits ROS *between the eyes but only his eyes show it. Again his hesitation is fractional. And then with great deliberation he turns to* GUIL.

ROS: Ho! Bring in the lord.

Again there is a fractional moment in which ROS *is smug,* GUIL *is trapped and betrayed.* GUIL *opens his mouth and closes it.*

The situation is saved: HAMLET, *escorted, is marched in just as* CLAUDIUS *leaves.* HAMLET *and his* ESCORT *cross the stage and go out, following* CLAUDIUS.

Lighting changes to Exterior.

ROS [*moves to go*]: All right, then?
GUIL [*does not move; thoughtfully*]: And yet it doesn't seem enough; to have breathed such

significance. Can that be all? And why us?—anybody would have done. And we have contributed nothing.

ROS: It was a trying episode while it lasted, but they've done with us now.

GUIL: Done what?

ROS: I don't pretend to have understood. Frankly, I'm not very interested. If they won't tell us, that's their affair. [*He wanders upstage towards the exit.*] For my part, I'm only glad that that's the last we've seen of him— [*And he glances off stage and turns front, his face betraying the fact that* HAMLET *is there.*]

GUIL: I knew it wasn't the end. . . .

ROS [*high*]: What else?!

GUIL: We're taking him to England. What's he doing?

ROS *goes upstage and returns.*

ROS: Talking.

GUIL: To himself?

ROS *makes to go,* GUIL *cuts him off.*

Is he alone?

ROS: No, he's with a soldier.

GUIL: Then he's not talking to himself, is he?

ROS: Not *by* himself. . . . Should we go?

GUIL: Where?

ROS. Anywhere.

GUIL: Why?

ROS *puts up his head listening.*

ROS: There it is again. [*In anguish.*] All I ask is a change of ground!

GUIL [*coda*]: Give us this day our daily round. . . .

HAMLET *enters behind them, talking with a soldier in arms.* ROS *and* GUIL *don't look round.*

ROS: They'll have us hanging about till we're dead. At least. And the weather will change. [*Looks up.*] The spring can't last for ever.

HAMLET: Good sir, whose powers are these?

SOLDIER: They are of Norway, sir.

HAMLET: How purposed, sir, I pray you?

SOLDIER: Against some part of Poland.

HAMLET: Who commands them, sir?

SOLDIER: The nephew to old Norway, Fortinbras.

ROS: We'll be cold. The summer won't last.

GUIL: It's autumnal.

ROS [*examining the ground*]: No leaves.

GUIL: Autumnal—nothing to do with leaves. It is to do with a certain brownness at the edges of the day. . . . Brown is creeping up on us, take my word for it. . . . Russets and tangerine shades of old gold flushing the very outside edge of the senses . . . deep shining ochres, burnt umber and parchments of baked earth—reflecting on itself and through itself, filtering the light. At such times, perhaps, coincidentally, the leaves might fall, somewhere, by repute. Yesterday was blue, like smoke.

ROS [*head up, listening*]: I got it again then.

They listen—faintest sound of TRAGEDIANS' *band.*

HAMLET: I humbly thank you, sir.

SOLDIER: God by you, sir. [*Exit.*]

ROS *gets up quickly and goes to* HAMLET.

ROS: Will it please you go, my lord?

HAMLET: I'll be with you straight. Go you a little before.

HAMLET *turns to face upstage.* ROS *returns down.* GUIL *faces front, doesn't turn.*

GUIL: Is he there?

ROS: Yes.

GUIL: What's he doing?

ROS *looks over his shoulder.*

ROS: Talking.

GUIL: To himself?

ROS: Yes.

Pause. ROS *makes to leave.*

ROS: He *said* we can go. Cross my heart.

GUIL: I like to know where I am. Even if I don't know where I am, I like to know *that.* If we go there's no knowing.

ROS: No knowing what?

GUIL: If we'll ever come back.

ROS: We don't want to come back.

GUIL: That may very well be true, but do we want to go?

ROS: We'll be free.

GUIL: I don't know. It's the same sky.

ROS: We've come this far.

He moves towards exit. GUIL *follows him.*

And besides, anything could happen yet.

They go.

BLACKOUT

ACT III

Opens in pitch darkness.

Soft sea sounds.

After several seconds of nothing, a voice from the dark . . .

GUIL: Are you there?
ROS: Where?
GUIL [*bitterly*]: A flying start. . . .

Pause.

ROS: Is that you?
GUIL: Yes.
ROS: How do you know?
GUIL [*explosion*]: Oh-for-God's-sake!
ROS: We're not finished, then?
GUIL: Well, we're here, aren't we?
ROS: Are we? I can't see a thing.
GUIL: You can still *think*, can't you?
ROS: I think so.
GUIL. You can still *talk*.
ROS: What should I say?
GUIL: Don't bother. You can *feel*, can't you?
ROS: Ah! There's life in me yet!
GUIL: What are you feeling?
ROS: A leg. Yes, it feels like my leg.
GUIL: How does it feel?
ROS: Dead.
GUIL: Dead?
ROS [*panic*]: I can't feel a thing!
GUIL: Give it a pinch! [*Immediately he yelps.*]
ROS: Sorry.
GUIL: Well, that's cleared that up.

Longer pause: the sound builds a little and identifies itself—the sea. Ship timbers, wind in the rigging, and then shouts of sailors calling obscure but inescapably nautical instructions from all directions, far and near: A short list:

Hard a larboard!
Let go the stays!
Reef down me hearties!
Is that you, cox'n?
Hel-llo! Is that you?
Hard a port!
Easy as she goes!
Keep her steady on the lee!
Haul away, lads!

[*Snatches of sea shanty maybe.*]

Fly the jib!
Tops'l up, me maties!

When the point has been well made and more so.

ROS: We're on a boat. [*Pause.*] Dark, isn't it?
GUIL: Not for night.
ROS: No, not for *night*.
GUIL: Dark for day.

Pause.

ROS: Oh yes, it's dark for *day*.
GUIL: We must have gone north, of course.
ROS: Off course?
GUIL: Land of the midnight sun, that is.
ROS: Of course.

Some sailor sounds.

A lantern is lit upstage—in fact by HAMLET.

The stage lightens disproportionately—

Enough to see:

ROS *and* GUIL *sitting downstage.*

Vague shapes of rigging, etc., behind.

I think it's getting light.
GUIL: Not for night.
ROS: This far north.
GUIL: Unless we're off course.
ROS [*small pause*]: Of course.

A better light—Lantern? Moon? . . . Light.

Revealing, among other things, three large man-sized casks on deck, upended, with lids. Spaced but in line. Behind and above—a gaudy striped umbrella, on a pole stuck into the deck, tilted so that we do not see behind it—one of those huge six-foot-diameter jobs. Still dim upstage. ROS *and* GUIL *still facing front.*

ROS: Yes, it's lighter than it was. It'll be night soon. This far north. [*Dolefully.*] I suppose we'll have to go to sleep. [*He yawns and stretches.*]
GUIL: Tired?
ROS: No . . . I don't think I'd take to it. Sleep all night, can't see a thing all day. . . . Those eskimos must have a quiet life.
GUIL: Where?
ROS: What?
GUIL: I thought you—— [*Relapses.*] I've lost all capacity for disbelief. I'm not sure that I could even rise to a little gentle scepticism.

Pause.

ROS: Well, shall we stretch our legs?
GUIL: I don't feel like stretching my legs.
ROS: I'll stretch them for you, if you like.
GUIL: No.
ROS: We could stretch each other's. That way we wouldn't have to go anywhere.
GUIL [*pause*]: No, somebody might come in.
ROS: In where?
GUIL: Out here.
ROS: In out here?
GUIL: On deck.

ROS *considers the floor: slaps it.*

ROS: Nice bit of planking, that.
GUIL: Yes, I'm very fond of boats myself. I like the way they're—contained. You don't have to worry about which way to go, or whether to go at all—the question doesn't arise, because you're on a *boat,* aren't you? Boats are safe areas in the game of tag . . . the players will hold their positions until the music starts. . . . I think I'll spend most of my life on boats.
ROS: Very healthy.

ROS *inhales with expectation, exhales with boredom.* GUIL *stands up and looks over the audience.*

GUIL: One is free on a boat. For a time. Relatively.
ROS: What's it like?
GUIL: Rough.

ROS *joins him. They look out over the audience.*

ROS: I think I'm going to be sick.

GUIL *licks a finger, holds it up experimentally.*

GUIL: Other side, I think.

ROS *goes upstage: Ideally a sort of upper deck joined to the downstage lower deck by short steps. The umbrella being on the upper deck.* ROS *pauses by the umbrella and looks behind it.* GUIL *meanwhile has been resuming his own theme—looking out over the audience——*

Free to move, speak, extemporise, and yet. We have not been cut loose. Our truancy is defined by one fixed star, and our drift represents merely a slight change of angle to it: we may seize the moment, toss it around while the moments pass, a short dash here, an exploration there, but we are brought round full circle to face again the single immutable fact—that we, Rosencrantz and Guildenstern, bearing a letter from one king to another, are taking Hamlet to England.

By which time, ROS *has returned, tiptoeing with great import, teeth clenched for secrecy, gets to* GUIL, *points surreptitiously behind him—and a tight whisper:*

ROS: I say—*he's there!*
GUIL [*unsurprised*]: What's he doing?
ROS: Sleeping.
GUIL: It's all right for him.
ROS: What is?
GUIL: He can sleep.
ROS: It's all right for him.
GUIL: He's got us now.
ROS: He can sleep.
GUIL: It's all done for him.
ROS: He's got us.
GUIL: And we've got nothing. [*A cry.*] All I ask is our common due!
ROS: For those in peril on the sea. . . .
GUIL: Give us this day our daily cue.

Beat, pause. Sit. Long pause.

ROS [*after shifting, looking around*]: What now?
GUIL: What do you mean?
ROS: Well, nothing is happening.
GUIL: We're on a boat.
ROS: I'm aware of that.
GUIL [*angrily*]: Then what do you expect? [*Unhappily.*] We act on scraps of information . . . sifting half-remembered directions that we can hardly separate from instinct.

ROS *puts a hand into his purse, then both hands behind his back, then holds his fists out.*
GUIL *taps one fist.*
ROS *opens it to show a coin.*
He gives it to GUIL.
He puts his hand back into his purse. Then both hands behind his back, then holds his fists out.
GUIL *taps one.*
ROS *opens it to show a coin. He gives it to* GUIL.
Repeat.
Repeat.
GUIL *getting tense. Desperate to lose.*
Repeat.
GUIL *taps a hand, changes his mind, taps the other, and* ROS *inadvertently reveals that he has a coin in both fists.*

GUIL: You had money in both hands.
ROS [*embarrassed*]: Yes.
GUIL: Every time?
ROS: Yes.

GUIL: What's the point of that?
ROS [*pathetic*]: I wanted to make you happy.

Beat.

GUIL: How much did he give you?
ROS: Who?
GUIL: The King. He gave us some money.
ROS: How much did he give you?
GUIL: I asked you first.
ROS: I got the same as you.
GUIL: He wouldn't discriminate between us.
ROS: How much did you get?
GUIL: The same.
ROS: How do you know?
GUIL: You just told me—how do *you* know?
ROS: He wouldn't discriminate between us.
GUIL: Even if he could.
ROS: Which he never could.
GUIL: He couldn't even be sure of mixing us up.
ROS: Without mixing us up.
GUIL [*turning on him furiously*]: Why don't you say something original! No wonder the whole thing is so stagnant! You don't take me up on anything—you just repeat it in a different order.
ROS: I can't think of anything original. I'm only good in support.
GUIL: I'm sick of making the running.
ROS [*humbly*]: It must be your dominant personality. [*Almost in tears.*] Oh, what's going to become of us!

And GUIL *comforts him, all harshness gone.*

GUIL: Don't cry . . . it's all right . . . there . . . there, I'll see we're all right.
ROS: But we've got nothing to go on, we're out on our own.
GUIL: We're on our way to England—we're taking Hamlet there.
ROS: What for?
GUIL: What for? Where have you been?
ROS: When? [*Pause.*] We won't know what to do when we get there.
GUIL: We take him to the King.
ROS: Will *he* be there?
GUIL: No—the king of England.
ROS: He's expecting us?
GUIL: No.
ROS: He won't know what we're playing at. What are we going to *say?*
GUIL: We've got a letter. You remember the letter.
ROS. Do I?
GUIL: Everything is explained in the letter. We count on that.
ROS: Is that it, then?
GUIL: What?
ROS: We take Hamlet to the English king, we hand over the letter—what then?
GUIL: There may be something in the letter to keep us going a bit.
ROS: And if not?
GUIL: Then that's it—we're finished.
ROS: At a loose end?
GUIL: Yes.

Pause.

ROS: Are there likely to be loose ends? [*Pause.*] Who is the English king?
GUIL: That depends on when we get there.
ROS: What do you think it says?
GUIL: Oh . . . greetings. Expressions of loyalty. Asking of favours, calling in of debts. Obscure promises balanced by vague threats. . . . Diplomacy. Regards to the family.
ROS: And about Hamlet?
GUIL: Oh yes.
ROS: And us—the full background?
GUIL: I should say so.

Pause.

ROS: So we've got a letter which explains everything.
GUIL: You've got it.

ROS *takes that literally. He starts to pat his pockets, etc.*

What's the matter?
ROS: The letter.
GUIL: Have you got it?
ROS [*rising fear*]: Have I? [*Searches frantically.*] Where would I have put it?
GUIL: You can't have lost it.
ROS: I must have!
GUIL: That's odd—I thought he gave it to me.

ROS *looks at him hopefully.*

ROS: Perhaps he did.
GUIL: But you seemed so sure it was *you* who hadn't got it.
ROS [*high*]: It *was* me who hadn't got it!
GUIL: But if he gave it to me there's no reason why you should have had it in the first place, in which case I don't see what all the fuss is about you *not* having it.
ROS [*pause*]: I admit it's confusing.
GUIL: This is all getting rather undisciplined. . . . The boat, the night, the sense of isolation and uncertainty . . . all these induce a loosening of the concentration. We must not lose control. Tighten up. Now. Either you have lost the letter

or you didn't have it to lose in the first place, in which case the King never gave it to you, in which case he gave it to me, in which case I would have put it into my inside top pocket, in which case [*calmly producing the letter*] . . . it will be . . . here. [*They smile at each other.*] We mustn't drop off like that again.

Pause. ROS *takes the letter gently from him.*

ROS: Now that we have found it, why were we looking for it?
GUIL [*thinks*]: We thought it was lost.
ROS: Something else?
GUIL: No.

Deflation.

ROS: Now we've lost the tension.
GUIL: What tension?
ROS: What was the last thing I said before we wandered off?
GUIL: When was that?
ROS [*helplessly*]: I can't remember.
GUIL [*leaping up*]: What a shambles! We're just not getting anywhere.
ROS [*mournfully*]: Not even England. I don't believe in it anyway.
GUIL: What?
ROS: England.
GUIL: Just a conspiracy of cartographers, you mean?
ROS: I mean I don't believe it! [*Calmer.*] I have no image. I try to picture us arriving, a little harbour perhaps . . . roads . . . inhabitants to point the way . . . horses on the road . . . riding for a day or a fortnight and then a palace and the English king. . . . That would be the logical kind of thing. . . . But my mind remains a blank. No. We're slipping off the map.
GUIL: Yes . . . yes. . . . [*Rallying.*] But you don't believe anything till it happens. And it *has* all happened. Hasn't it?
ROS: We drift down time, clutching at straws. But what good's a brick to a drowning man?
GUIL: Don't give up, we can't be long now.
ROS: We might as well be dead. Do you think death could possibly be a boat?
GUIL: No, no, no . . . Death is . . . not. Death isn't. You take my meaning. Death is the ultimate negative. Not-being. You can't not-be on a boat.
ROS: I've frequently not been on boats.
GUIL: No, no, no—what you've been is not on boats.
ROS: I wish I was dead. [*Considers the drop.*] I could jump over the side. That would put a spoke in their wheel.
GUIL: Unless they're counting on it.
ROS: I shall remain on board. That'll put a spoke in their wheel. [*The futility of it, fury.*] All right! We don't question, we don't doubt. We perform. But a line must be drawn somewhere, and I would like to put it on record that I have no confidence in England. Thank you. [*Thinks about this.*] And even if it's true, it'll just be another shambles.
GUIL: I don't see why.
ROS [*furious*]: He won't know what we're talking about.—What are we going to *say?*
GUIL: We say—Your majesty, we have arrived!
ROS [*kingly*]: And who are you?
GUIL: We are Rosencrantz and Guildenstern.
ROS [*barks*]: Never heard of you!
GUIL: Well, we're nobody special——
ROS [*regal and nasty*]: What's your game?
GUIL: We've got our instructions——
ROS: First I've heard of it——
GUIL [*angry*]: Let me finish—— [*Humble.*] We've come from Denmark.
ROS: What do you want?
GUIL: Nothing—we're delivering Hamlet——
ROS: Who's he?
GUIL [*irritated*]: You've heard of *him*——
ROS: Oh, I've heard of him all right and I want nothing to do with it.
GUIL: But——
ROS: You march in here without so much as a by-your-leave and expect me to take in every lunatic you try to pass off with a lot of unsubstantiated——
GUIL: We've got a letter——

ROS *snatches it and tears it open.*

ROS [*efficiently*]: I see . . . I see . . . well, this seems to support your story such as it is—it is an exact command from the king of Denmark, for several different reasons, importing Denmark's health and England's too, that on the reading of this letter, without delay, I should have Hamlet's head cut off——!

GUIL *snatches the letter.* ROS, *double-taking, snatches it back.* GUIL *snatches it half back. They read it together, and separate.*

Pause.

They are well downstage looking front.

ROS: The sun's going down. It will be dark soon.
GUIL: Do you think so?
ROS: I was just making conversation. [*Pause.*] We're his *friends.*
GUIL: How do you know?
ROS: From our young days brought up with him.
GUIL: You've only got their word for it.

ROS: But that's what we depend on.

GUIL: Well, yes, and then again no. [*Airily.*] Let us keep things in proportion. Assume, if you like, that they're going to kill him. Well, he is a man, he is mortal, death comes to us all, etcetera, and consequently he would have died anyway, sooner or later. Or to look at it from the social point of view—he's just one man among many, the loss would be well within reason and convenience. And then again, what is so terrible about death? As Socrates so philosophically put it, since we don't know what death is, it is illogical to fear it. It might be . . . very nice. Certainly it is a release from the burden of life, and, for the godly, a haven and a reward. Or to look at it another way—we are little men, we don't know the ins and outs of the matter, there are wheels within wheels, etcetera—it would be presumptuous of us to interfere with the designs of fate or even of kings. All in all, I think we'd be well advised to leave well alone. Tie up the letter—there—neatly—like that.—They won't notice the broken seal, assuming you were in character.

ROS: But what's the point?

GUIL: Don't apply logic.

ROS: He's done nothing to us.

GUIL: Or justice.

ROS: It's awful.

GUIL: But it could have been worse. I was beginning to think it was. [*And his relief comes out in a laugh.*]

Behind them HAMLET *appears from behind the umbrella. The light has been going. Slightly.* HAMLET *is going to the lantern.*

ROS: The position as I see it, then. We, Rosencrantz and Guildenstern, from our young days brought up with him, awakened by a man standing on his saddle, are summoned, and arrive, and are instructed to glean what afflicts him and draw him on to pleasures, such as a play, which unfortunately, as it turns out, is abandoned in some confusion owing to certain nuances outside our appreciation—which, among other causes, results in, among other effects, a high, not to say, homicidal, excitement in Hamlet, whom we, in consequence, are escorting, for his own good, to England. Good. We're on top of it now.

HAMLET *blows out the lantern. The stage goes pitch black. The black resolves itself to moonlight, by which* HAMLET *approaches the sleeping* ROS *and* GUIL. *He extracts the letter and takes it behind his umbrella; the light of his lantern shines through the fabric,* HAMLET *emerges again with a letter, and replaces it, and retires, blowing out his lantern.*

Morning comes.

ROS *watches it coming—from the auditorium. Behind him is a gay sight. Beneath the re-tilted umbrella, reclining in a deck-chair, wrapped in a rug, reading a book, possibly smoking, sits* HAMLET.

ROS *watches the morning come, and brighten to high noon.*

ROS: I'm assuming nothing. [*He stands up.* GUIL *wakes.*] The position as I see it, then. That's west unless we're off course, in which case it's night; the King gave me the same as you, the King gave you the same as me; the King never gave me the letter, the King gave you the letter, we don't know what's in the letter; we take Hamlet to the English king, it depending on when we get there who he is, and we hand over the letter, which may or may not have something in it to keep us going, and if not, we are finished and at a loose end, if they have loose ends. We could have done worse. I don't think we missed any chances. . . . Not that we're getting much help. [*He sits down again. They lie down—prone.*] If we stopped breathing we'd vanish.

The muffled sound of a recorder. They sit up with disproportionate interest.

GUIL: Here we go.

ROS: Yes, but what?

They listen to the music.

GUIL [*excitedly*]: Out of the void, finally, a sound; while on a boat [admittedly] outside the action [admittedly] the perfect and absolute silence of the wet lazy slap of water against water and the rolling creak of timber—breaks; giving rise at once to the speculation or the assumption or the hope that something is about to happen; a pipe is heard. One of the sailors has pursed his lips against a woodwind, his fingers and thumb governing, shall we say, the ventages, whereupon, giving it breath, let us say, with his mouth, it, the pipe, discourses, as the saying goes, most eloquent music. A thing like that, it could change the course of events. [*Pause.*] Go and see what it is.

ROS: It's someone playing on a pipe.

GUIL: Go and find him.

ROS: And then what?

GUIL: I don't know—request a tune.

ROS: What for?

GUIL: Quick—before we lose our momentum.

ROS: Why!—something is happening. It had quite escaped my attention!

He listens: Makes a stab at an exit. Listens more carefully: Changes direction.

GUIL *takes no notice.*

ROS *wanders about trying to decide where the music comes from. Finally he tracks it down—unwillingly—to the middle barrel. There is no getting away from it. He turns to* GUIL *who takes no notice.* ROS, *during this whole business, never quite breaks into articulate speech. His face and his hands indicate his incredulity. He stands gazing at the middle barrel. The pipe plays on within. He kicks the barrel. The pipe stops. He leaps back towards* GUIL. *The pipe starts up again. He approaches the barrel cautiously. He lifts the lid. The music is louder. He slams down the lid. The music is softer. He goes back towards* GUIL. *But a drum starts, muffled. He freezes. He turns. Considers the left-hand barrel. The drumming goes on within, in time to the flute. He walks back to* GUIL. *He opens his mouth to speak. Doesn't make it. A lute is heard. He spins round at the third barrel. More instruments join in. Until it is quite inescapable that inside the three barrels, distributed, playing together a familiar tune which has been heard three times before, are the* TRAGEDIANS.

They play on.

ROS *sits beside* GUIL. *They stare ahead.*

The tune comes to an end.

Pause.

ROS: I thought I heard a band. [*In anguish.*] Plausibility is all I presume!

GUIL [*coda*]: Call us this day our daily tune. . . .

The lid of the middle barrel flies open and the PLAYER'*s head pops out.*

PLAYER: Aha! All in the same boat, then! [*He climbs out. He goes round banging on the barrels.*] Everybody out!

Impossibly, the TRAGEDIANS *climb out of the barrels. With their instruments, but not their cart. A few bundles. Except* ALFRED. *The* PLAYER *is cheerful.*

[*To* ROS:] Where are we?

ROS: Travelling.

PLAYER: Of course, we haven't got there yet.

ROS: Are we all right for England?

PLAYER: You look all right to me. I don't think they're very particular in England. Al-l-fred!

ALFRED *emerges from the* PLAYER'*s barrel.*

GUIL: What are you doing here?

PLAYER: Travelling. [*To* TRAGEDIANS:] Right—blend into the background!

The TRAGEDIANS *are in costume* [*from the mime*]: *A King with crown,* ALFRED *as Queen, Poisoner and the two cloaked figures.*

They blend.

[*To* GUIL:] Pleased to see us? [*Pause.*] You've come out of it very well, so far.

GUIL: And you?

PLAYER: In disfavour. Our play offended the King.

GUIL: Yes.

PLAYER: Well, he's a second husband himself. Tactless, really.

ROS: It was quite a good play nevertheless.

PLAYER: We never really got going—it was getting quite interesting when they stopped it.

Looks up at HAMLET.

That's the way to travel. . . .

GUIL: What were you doing in there?

PLAYER: Hiding. [*Indicating costumes.*] We had to run for it just as we were.

ROS: Stowaways.

PLAYER: Naturally—we didn't get paid, owing to circumstances ever so slightly beyond our control, and all the money we had we lost betting on certainties. Life is a gamble, at terrible odds—if it was a bet you wouldn't take it. Did you know that any number doubled is even?

ROS: Is it?

PLAYER: We learn something every day, to our cost. But we troupers just go on and on. Do you know what happens to old actors?

ROS: What?

PLAYER: Nothing. They're still acting. Surprised, then?

GUIL: What?

PLAYER: Surprised to see us?

GUIL: I knew it wasn't the end.

PLAYER: With practically everyone on his feet. What do you make of it, so far?

GUIL: We haven't got much to go on.

PLAYER: You speak to him?

ROS: It's possible.

GUIL: But it wouldn't make any difference.

ROS: But it's possible.

GUIL: Pointless.

ROS: It's allowed.

GUIL: Allowed, yes. We are not restricted. No boundaries have been defined, no inhibitions imposed. We have, for the while, secured, or blundered into, our release, for the while. Spontaneity and whim are the order of the day. Other wheels are turning but they are not our concern. We can breathe. We can relax. We can do what we like and say what we like to whomever we like, without restriction.

ROS: Within limits, of course.

GUIL: Certainly within limits.

HAMLET *comes down to footlights and regards the audience. The others watch but don't speak.* HAMLET *clears his throat noisily and spits into the audience. A split second later he claps his hand to his eye and wipes himself. He goes back upstage.*

ROS: A compulsion towards philosophical introspection is his chief characteristic, if I may put it like that. It does not mean he is mad. It does not mean he isn't. Very often, it does not mean anything at all. Which may or may not be a kind of madness.
GUIL: It really boils down to symptoms. Pregnant replies, mystic allusions, mistaken identities, arguing his father is his mother, that sort of thing; intimations of suicide, forgoing of exercise, loss of mirth, hints of claustrophobia not to say delusions of imprisonment; invocations of camels, chameleons, capons, whales, weasels, hawks, handsaws—riddles, quibbles and evasions; amnesia, paranoia, myopia; day-dreaming, hallucinations; stabbing his elders, abusing his parents, insulting his lover, and appearing hatless in public—knock-kneed, droop-stockinged and sighing like a love-sick schoolboy, which at his age is coining on a bit strong.
ROS: And talking to himself.
GUIL: And talking to himself.

ROS *and* GUIL *move apart together.*

Well, where has that got us?
ROS: He's the Player.
GUIL: His play offended the King——
ROS: —offended the King——
GUIL: —who orders his arrest——
ROS: —orders his arrest——
GUIL: —so he escapes to England——
ROS: On the boat to which he meets——
GUIL: Guildenstern and Rosencrantz taking Hamlet——
ROS: —who also offended the King——
GUIL: —and killed Polonius——
ROS: —offended the King in a variety of ways——
GUIL: —to England. [*Pause.*] That seems to be it.

ROS *jumps up.*

ROS: Incidents! All we get is incidents! Dear God, is it too much to expect a little sustained action?!

And on the word, the PIRATES *attack. That is to say: Noise and shouts and rushing about.* "Pirates."

Everyone visible goes frantic. HAMLET *draws his sword and rushes downstage.* GUIL, ROS *and* PLAYER *draw swords and rush upstage. Collision.* HAMLET *turns back up. They turn back down. Collision. By which time there is general panic right upstage. All four charge upstage with* ROS, GUIL *and* PLAYER *shouting:*

At last!
To arms!
Pirates!
Up there!
Down there!
To my sword's length!
Action!

All four reach the top, see something they don't like, waver, run for their lives downstage:

HAMLET, *in the lead, leaps into the left barrel.* PLAYER *leaps into the right barrel.* ROS *and* GUIL *leap into the middle barrel. All closing the lids after them.*

The lights dim to nothing while the sound of fighting continues. The sound fades to nothing. The lights come up. The middle barrel [ROS's *and* GUIL's] *is missing.*

The lid of the right-hand barrel is raised cautiously, the heads of ROS *and* GUIL *appear.*

The lid of the other barrel [HAMLET's] *is raised. The head of the* PLAYER *appears.*

All catch sight of each other and slam down lids.

Pause.

Lids raised cautiously.

ROS [*relief*]: They've gone. [*He starts to climb out.*] That was close. I've never thought quicker.

They are all three out of barrels. GUIL *is wary and nervous.* ROS *is light-headed. The* PLAYER *is phlegmatic. They note the missing barrel.*

ROS *looks round.*

ROS: Where's——?

The PLAYER *takes off his hat in mourning.*

PLAYER: Once more, alone—on our own resources.
GUIL [*worried*]: What do you mean? Where is he?
PLAYER: Gone.
GUIL: Gone where?
PLAYER: Yes, we were dead lucky there. If that's the word I'm after.
ROS [*not a pick up*]: Dead?
PLAYER: Lucky.
ROS [*he means*]: Is he dead?
PLAYER: Who knows?
GUIL [*rattled*]: He's not coming back?
PLAYER: Hardly.
ROS: He's dead then. He's dead as far as we're concerned.

PLAYER: Or we are as far as he is. [*He goes and sits on the floor to one side.*] Not too bad, is it?
GUIL [*rattled*]: But he can't—we're supposed to be—we've got a *letter*—we're going to England with a letter for the King——
PLAYER: Yes, that much seems certain. I congratulate you on the unambiguity of your situation.
GUIL: But you don't understand—it contains—we've had our instructions—the whole thing's pointless without him.
PLAYER: Pirates could happen to anyone. Just deliver the letter. They'll send ambassadors from England to explain. . . .
GUIL [*worked up*]: Can't you see—the pirates left us home and high—dry and home—drome——[*Furiously.*] The pirates left us high and dry!
PLAYER [*comforting*]: There . . .
GUIL [*near tears*]: Nothing will be resolved without him. . . .
PLAYER: There . . . !
GUIL: We need Hamlet for our release!
PLAYER: There!
GUIL: What are we supposed to do?
PLAYER: This.

He turns away, lies down if he likes. ROS *and* GUIL *apart.*

ROS: Saved again.
GUIL: Saved for what?

ROS *sighs.*

ROS: The sun's going down. [*Pause.*] It'll be night soon. [*Pause.*] If that's west. [*Pause.*] Unless we've——
GUIL [*shouts*]: Shut up! I'm sick of it! Do you think conversation is going to help us now?
ROS [*hurt, desperately ingratiating*]: I—I bet you all the money I've got the year of my birth doubled is an odd number.
GUIL [*moan*]: No-o.
ROS: *Your* birth!

GUIL *smashes him down.*

GUIL [*broken*]: We've travelled too far, and our momentum has taken over; we move idly towards eternity, without possibility of reprieve or hope of explanation.
ROS: Be happy—if you're not even *happy* what's so good about surviving? [*He picks himself up.*] We'll be all right. I suppose we just go on.
GUIL: Go where?
ROS: To England.
GUIL: England! *That's* a dead end. I never believed in it anyway.
ROS: All we've got to do is make our report and that'll be that. Surely.
GUIL: I don't *believe* it—a shore, a harbour, say—and we get off and we stop someone and say—Where's the King?—And he says, Oh, you follow that road there and take the first left and——[*Furiously.*] I don't believe any of it!
ROS: It doesn't sound very plausible.
GUIL: And even if we came face to face, what do we say?
ROS: We say—We've arrived!
GUIL [*kingly*]: And who are you?
ROS: We are Guildenstern and Rosencrantz.
GUIL: Which is which?
ROS: Well, I'm—You're——
GUIL: What's it all about?——
ROS: Well, we were bringing Hamlet—but then some pirates——
GUIL: I don't begin to understand. Who are all these people, what's it got to do with me? You turn up out of the blue with some cock and bull story——
ROS [*with letter*]: We have a letter——
GUIL [*snatches it, opens it*]: A letter—yes—that's true. That's something . . . a letter . . . [*Reads.*] "As England is Denmark's faithful tributary . . . as love between them like the palm might flourish, etcetera . . . that on the knowing of this contents, without delay of any kind, should those bearers, Rosencrantz and Guildenstern, put to sudden death——"

He double-takes. ROS *snatches the letter.* GUIL *snatches it back.* ROS *snatches it half back. They read it again and look up.*

The PLAYER *gets to his feet and walks over to his barrel and kicks it and shouts into it.*

PLAYER: They've gone! It's all over!

One by one the PLAYERS *emerge, impossibly, from the barrel, and form a casually menacing circle round* ROS *and* GUIL, *who are still appalled and mesmerised.*

GUIL [*quietly*]: Where we went wrong was getting on a boat. We can move, of course, change direction, rattle about, but our movement is contained within a larger one that carries us along as inexorably as the wind and current. . . .
ROS: They had it in for us, didn't they? Right from the beginning. Who'd have thought that we were so important?
GUIL: But why? Was it all for this? Who are we that so much should converge on our little deaths? [*In anguish to the* PLAYER:] Who are *we?*
PLAYER: You are Rosencrantz and Guildenstern. That's enough.

GUIL: No—it is not enough. To be told so little—to such an end—and still, finally, to be denied an explanation——

PLAYER: In our experience, most things end in death.

GUIL [*fear, vengeance, scorn*]: Your experience!—*Actors!*

He snatches a dagger from the PLAYER*'s belt and holds the point at the* PLAYER*'s throat: the* PLAYER *backs and* GUIL *advances, speaking more quietly.*

I'm talking about death—and you've never experienced *that.* And you cannot *act* it. You die a thousand casual deaths—with none of that intensity which squeezes out life . . . and no blood runs cold anywhere. Because even as you die you know that you will come back in a different hat. But no one gets up after *death*—there is no applause—there is only silence and some second-hand clothes, and that's—*death*——

And he pushes the blade in up to the hilt. The PLAYER *stands with huge, terrible eyes, clutches at the wound as the blade withdraws: he makes small weeping sounds and falls to his knees, and then right down.*

While he is dying, GUIL*, nervous, high, almost hysterical, wheels on the* TRAGEDIANS—

If we have a destiny, then so had he—and if this is ours, then that was his—and if there are no explanations for us, then let there be none for him——

The TRAGEDIANS *watch the* PLAYER *die: they watch with some interest. The* PLAYER *finally lies still. A short moment of silence. Then the* TRAGEDIANS *start to applaud with genuine admiration. The* PLAYER *stands up, brushing himself down.*

PLAYER [*modestly*]: Oh, come, come, gentlemen—no flattery—it was merely competent——

The TRAGEDIANS *are still congratulating him. The* PLAYER *approaches* GUIL*, who stands rooted, holding the dagger.*

PLAYER: What did you think? [*Pause.*] You see, it *is* the kind they do believe in—it's what is expected.

He holds his hand out for the dagger. GUIL *slowly puts the point of the dagger on to the* PLAYER*'s hand, and pushes . . . the blade slides back into the handle. The* PLAYER *smiles, reclaims the dagger.*

For a moment you thought I'd—cheated.

ROS *relieves his own tension with loud nervy laughter.*

ROS: Oh, very good! *Very* good! Took me in completely—didn't he take you in completely—[*claps his hands*]. Encore! Encore!

PLAYER [*activated, arms spread, the professional*]: Deaths for all ages and occasions! Deaths by suspension, convulsion, consumption, incision, execution, asphyxiation and malnutrition—! Climactic carnage, by poison and by steel—! Double deaths by duel—! Show!—

ALFRED*, still in his* QUEEN*'s costume, dies by poison: the* PLAYER*, with rapier, kills the "*KING*" and duels with a fourth* TRAGEDIAN*, inflicting and receiving a wound. The two remaining* TRAGEDIANS*, the two "*SPIES*" dressed in the same coats as* ROS *and* GUIL*, are stabbed, as before. And the light is fading over the deaths which take place right upstage.*

[*Dying amid the dying—tragically; romantically.*] So there's an end to that—it's commonplace: light goes with life, and in the winter of your years the dark comes early. . . .

GUIL [*tired, drained, but still an edge of impatience; over the mime*]: No . . . no . . . not for *us,* not like that. Dying is not romantic, and death is not a game which will soon be over . . . Death is not anything . . . death is not . . . It's the absence of presence, nothing more . . . the endless time of never coming back . . . a gap you can't see, and when the wind blows through it, it makes no sound. . . .

The light has gone upstage. Only GUIL *and* ROS *are visible as* ROS*'s clapping falters to silence.*

Small pause.

ROS: That's it, then, is it?

No answer. He looks out front.

The sun's going down. Or the earth's coming up, as the fashionable theory has it.

Small pause.

Not that it makes any difference.

Pause.

What was it all about? When did it begin?

Pause. No answer.

Couldn't we just stay put? I mean no one is going to come on and drag us off. . . . They'll just have to wait. We're still young . . . fit . . . we've got years. . . .

Pause. No answer.

[*A cry.*] We've done nothing wrong! We didn't harm anyone. Did we?

GUIL: I can't remember.

ROS *pulls himself together.*

ROS: All right, then. I don't care. I've had enough. To tell you the truth, I'm relieved.

And he disappears from view. GUIL *does not notice.*

GUIL: Our names shouted in a certain dawn . . . a message . . . a summons . . . There must have been a moment, at the beginning, where we could have said—no. But somehow we missed it. [*He looks round and sees he is alone.*]

Rosen—?
Guil—?

He gathers himself.

Well, we'll know better next time. Now you see me, now you— [*and disappears*].

Immediately the whole stage is lit up, revealing, upstage, arranged in the approximate positions last held by the dead TRAGEDIANS, *the tableau of court and corpses which is the last scene of* HAMLET.

That is: The KING, QUEEN, LAERTES *and* HAMLET *all dead.* HORATIO *holds* HAMLET. FORTINBRAS *is there.*

So are two AMBASSADORS *from England.*

AMBASSADOR: The sight is dismal;
and our affairs from England come too late.
The ears are senseless that should give us hearing
to tell him his commandment is fulfilled,
that Rosencrantz and Guildenstern are dead.
Where should we have our thanks?

HORATIO: Not from his mouth,
had it the ability of life to thank you:
He never gave commandment for their death.
But since, so jump upon this bloody question,
you from the Polack wars, and you from England,
are here arrived, give order that these bodies
high on a stage be placed to the view;
and let me speak to the yet unknowing world
how these things came about: so shall you hear
of carnal, bloody and unnatural acts,
of accidental judgments, casual slaughters,
of deaths put on by cunning and forced cause,
and, in this upshot, purposes mistook
fallen on the inventors' heads: all this can I
truly deliver.

But during the above speech, the play fades out, overtaken by dark and music.

SAM SHEPARD

Sam Shepard (1943–) was born Samuel Shepard Rogers VII at Fort Sheridan, Illinois, a military base near Chicago. At the time, his father, Samuel, was an Army Air Corps bomber pilot serving in Europe. His mother, Jane Schook, reared Sam while her husband was at war. After Samuel returned, the young Shepard, called Steve to distinguish him from his father, moved with his family from base to base until his father left the service in 1949. They finally settled in southern California, but his father's drinking and violent behavior led to the family's disintegration, and his father deserted the family when Shepard was in high school.

This family experience is an important element in Shepard's creative life. The father-son conflict, never fully reconciled, is a constant theme, and the character of the father as a swaggering alcoholic heavy often reappears in Shepard's plays. At twenty, Shepard legally changed his name in order to hurt his father, even though it meant breaking seven generations of family tradition. In general, Shepard's female characters are weak, and his portrayal of mothers as uncaring and unfaithful is probably a sign of his ambiguous and often negative feelings toward his own mother.

After a few semesters at a community college, Shepard joined an acting group in order to get away from home, and he toured the United States for most of 1962. He left the group in New York City and settled in the Beat community of the East Village. At nineteen, Shepard was addicted to drugs, dreaming of making it as a rock and roll drummer, and attracted to the avant-garde theater. In the essay "American Experimental Theatre: Then and Now" (1977), Shepard wrote that during this formative time, "the influence of the sixties and the off-off Broadway Theatre and the Lower East Side was a combination of hallucinogenic drugs, the effect of those drugs on the perceptions of those I came in contact with, the effect of those drugs on my own perceptions, the Viet Nam war, and all the rest of it, which is now gone. The only thing which still remains and still persists as the single most important idea is the idea of consciousness."

Shepard is primarily an improvisational playwright, and he is contemptuous of mainstream theater and playwrights whose plays are "carefully planned and regurgitated." Nevertheless, Shepard adopted many of the Absurdists' dramatic characteristics (fragmented reality, non sequiturs, lack of decorum, boorishness, scatological humor, and disdain for middle-class social attitudes). Most important, he is keyed into the theories of Antonin Artaud (1896–1948), whose concept of the Theater of Cruelty is based on the premise that savage, erotic, and ritualized action onstage will create a dramatic experience, awakening a spectator to sublime ideas and great myths.

Shepard was twenty-one when his one-act plays *Cowboys* and *The Rock Garden* were produced in 1964 by Theater Genesis, an early off-off Broadway group, under the direction of Ralph Cook, its founder. Both plays received negative reviews, but in the following years, 1965 and 1966, *Chicago, Icarus's Mother,* and *Red Cross* established Shepard in the off-off Broadway theater. At twenty-four, he completed *La Turista* (1967), a two-act satire about a dysfunctional couple, Kent and his wife, Salem, named after popular cigarettes. They visit Mexico, where Kent suffers sunburn, dysentery, and Salem's infidelity, until he finally "gets out" by leaping through the rear wall of the stage. Three years later, *Operation Sidewinder* (1970), Shepard's first venture not produced off-off Broadway, was performed at the Vivian Beaumont Theater at Lincoln Center. Traditional audiences were baffled by the convoluted plot that deals with what happens when an Air Force computer designed to find UFOs is disguised as a sidewinder (rattlesnake) and is mistaken by local Hopi Indians as a snake god. It was a critical disaster, and another Shepard play was not produced on Broadway until the revival of *Buried Child* in 1996.

Shepard married O-Lan Johnson in 1969, but by 1971 their marriage was failing, and he was living with poet Patti Smith. Much of this experience is filtered into *Mad Dog Blues* and *Cowboy Mouth* (both 1971), which were not successes. Disappointed, Shepard reconciled with O-Lan and went to live in London, where he tried to conquer his drug addiction. He continued writing and in 1972 finished *The Tooth of Crime,* a satire of television westerns such as *Gunsmoke* and *Ponderosa* and the rock and roll mystique. Its protagonist, Hoss, is a rock and roll hero, dressed in black leather, who cavorts with Becky, his girlfriend, is served drugs by Doc, and is driven to suicide by a younger singer-gangster named Crow.

Shepard returned to the United States in 1974 and settled in San Francisco, where he began a long association with the Magic Theater under the direction of Joseph Chaikin, the founder of the Open Theater in New York City (1964). In 1976 Shepard had three plays produced, the first of which, *Suicide in B-Flat: A Mysterious Overture,* is a *film noire*–style mystery about the suicide of a jazz pianist, named Niles, who unexpectedly improvises his return to life. *The Sad Lament of Pecos Bill On the Eve of Killing His Wife* (1976), a collaboration with Catherine Stone, is a folk opera in which all the roles are sung. *Angel City* (1976), a pun on Los Angeles, is a Hollywood satire in the style of Ionesco's *Rhinoceros,* about a scriptwriter who tries desperately to resist Hollywood greed. Though Shepard's character, Rabbit Brown, has good intentions, he succumbs to Hollywood's allure and turns into a slimy green lizard.

Despite his skepticism about Hollywood's foibles at this time, Shepard started acting and writing for Hollywood films. For his portrayal of Chuck Yeager, the daring test pilot, Shepard received an Oscar nomination in 1983 for best supporting actor in the film *The Right Stuff.* During this period, Shepard's marriage ended in divorce, and in 1984 he began living with the actress Jessica Lange, with whom he has three children.

In 1977 Shepard began a series of plays about wildly dysfunctional families, which are heavily autobiographical. His *The Curse of the Starving Class* opened the series with an examination of a family in Southern California selling their farm to real estate hustlers. The characters are only starving figuratively; however, they are cursed with greed, alcoholism, infidelity, and the inability to communicate love. The chief conflict is duplicity: Weston, the father, and Ella, the mother, have each decided to sell the farm without telling the other. During the process, Ella is seduced by her attorney, Weston runs off to Mexico with the money from the sale, and Emma, their daughter, is blown up in the family car by thugs. Wesley, their son and probable stand-in for Shepard, tries to carry on, but his future is uncertain.

In 1978 Shepard wrote *Seduced,* a send-up of Howard Hughes, the enigmatic billionaire who had died in 1976. With *Buried Child* (1978) and *True West* (1980), he returned to his acerbic view of the American family. *True West* is a surrealistic version of the story of Cain and Abel (Genesis 4:1–15) and the parable of the Prodigal Son (Luke 15:11–32). Shepard has said that the two brothers in *True West* are really parts of the same person, each the alter ego of the other. The sons are still on good terms with their mother, but their father, an alcoholic, has abandoned them. As the play opens, Austin, the younger brother, a successful Hollywood writer, is at his mother's house in southern California trying to finish a project for the sleazy producer Saul Kimmer. Lee, his older brother, who is a vagrant, a thief, and an alcoholic, appears and mocks Austin's middle-class values. With bravado, Lee plays golf with Kimmer and cons him into reading a script, as yet unwritten, which is plainly dumb, about a "true" western adventure. Lee then forces Austin to help him write it, and in the process, they switch roles. Austin builds a monstrous rage, and when he gets the chance, he attempts to strangle Lee. Just then, Mom, a silly woman, appears, tells the sons "You boys shouldn't fight in the house," and leaves. Alone again in the wrecked kitchen of their mother's house, the brothers face each other, and the action ends unresolved.

Fool for Love (1983), the third play in the family series, reiterates the theme of the sinning father. It concerns the love affair of Eddie and May, who are half-siblings. Tired of Eddie's machismo, cowboy delusions, and infidelities, May has run away and is working as a short-order cook, when he finds her at the edge of the Mojave Desert. During their confrontation, they are observed by the mysterious Old Man, who is revealed to be their father—the "fool for love"—who loved two women and had two families. The Old Man says, "It was the same love, just got split in two that's all." Unable to reconcile, Eddie and May separate and the Old Man crumples under the weight of his foolishness.

A Lie of the Mind (1985) continues Shepard's family cycle by showcasing two troubled families, one in California and the other in Montana. The play's title derives from the protagonist's inability to separate reality from illusion. Unfortunately, Jake imagines that Beth, an actress, is unfaithful because she acts a role in which she loves another man. In anger, Jake beats her savagely but then remorsefully complains that his life is lost without her. In a delirium, Jake dredges up the memory that he indirectly killed his father, an Air Force pilot who ran away from home. Jake has never told his mother about this, and now, dressed in his father's flight jacket and medals, he drapes himself with the flag that draped his father's coffin and runs off to Beth's house in Montana, where he finds Beth in the care of his brother Frankie. Briefly reunited with her, Jake leaves to go somewhere where he can be alone.

After *A Lie of the Mind,* Shepard concentrated on his Hollywood career and did not write a new play until *States of Shock* (1991), which marked a return to his hallucinatory improvisational style of the 1960s. The play has five familiar Shepard characters: the Colonel, a maniacal veteran; his buddy, Stubbs, a man in a wheelchair, who says he is rotting from the inside out; a waitress named Glory Bee; the White Man, who masturbates when chowder is spilled in his lap; and the White Woman, who ignores the White Man and encourages the Colonel to beat Stubbs. It was another critical failure.

Shepard's *Simpatico*, a play in three acts, follows the rivalry between Vinnie, a man in his forties who is hiding in a small room in Cucamonga, California, and Carter, a successful horse-dealer in Kentucky. Besides a long friendship, Vinnie and Carter share a woman, Rosie, who was once married to Vinnie, but who abandoned him for Carter. The men also share the guilt of blackmailing a racing official, Simms, by photographing him in a sexual act with Rosie, who says that it was her idea. Now, years later, Vinnie, broke and alcoholic, restores himself by trying to divest himself of his guilt—giving away the photographs (except to Carter), which nobody wants. Fearful that exposure of the crime and the photographs will destroy his business, Carter succumbs to desperation and alcohol. When the action ends, the two men have traded places.

Buried Child, Shepard's second play in his family cycle, is generally regarded as Shepard's most accessible play and was awarded the Pulitzer Prize for Drama in 1979, a sign of approbation from the mainstream theatrical establishment. As is usual in Shepard's work, this is a family gone irredeemably off-kilter. The family's Illinois farm has not been plowed in thirty-five years and is meant to symbolize America's lost Eden. Beyond the screened porch are elm trees, a reminder of the ravaged family in Eugene O'Neill's *Desire Under the Elms* (1923), which, like Shepard's play, focuses on a father/son rivalry and one son's desire to claim his inheritance. In O'Neill's play, the patriarch takes a young wife who falls in love with the youngest son. When his wife and his son have a child, the old man is deceived. The lovers suffer guilt, and the wife, unable to bear the thought of separation from the old man's son, kills the child. In Shepard's play, the wife bears a child that is not her husband's, but she has the husband kill the child. It is weakly hinted that the father of the murdered child might be the husband's oldest son, which adds the taboo of incest.

Shepard also ties *Buried Child* to Luke's parable of the Prodigal Son. The return of the Prodigal Son was meant to be an occasion for rejoicing: When the wayward son kneels before his father and says, "Father, I have sinned against heaven and you; I no longer deserve to be called your son," the father responds by saying, "Quick! Bring out the finest robe, and put it on him; put a ring on his finger and shoes on his feet." And when the older brother, who had remained faithful, complains about not being rewarded, the father says, "You are with me always, and everything I have is yours. But we had to celebrate and rejoice! This brother of yours was dead, and has come back to life. He was lost, and is found."

In Shepard's version, many allusions to Luke's parable appear, slightly distorted. For instance, there are two prodigal sons. The first is Tilden, Dodge and Halie's oldest son, who has returned after twenty years, suffering from too much sun and chronic alcoholism. He says to Dodge that he had nowhere else to go and so came home, but Dodge says, "You're a grown man. You shouldn't be needing your parents at your age. It's unnatural. There's nothing we can do for you now anyway. Couldn't you make a living down there? Couldn't you find some way to make a living? Support yourself? What'd'ya come back here for?"

The second prodigal son is Tilden's son, Vince, twenty-two, who was raised by Dodge and Halie and who has not seen them or his father in six years. When Vince appears, Tilden merely makes eye contact with him, and Dodge refuses to acknowledge who he is: "Stop calling me Grandpa will ya'! It's sickening. 'Grandpa.' I'm nobody's Grandpa!" Bradley, the brother who remained at home, is a crude man who foolishly cut off his own leg, a symbol of castration. The fine robe that the prodigal is wrapped in is transposed by Shepard into a grimy blanket, stained with Dodge's spittle and coughed-up blood. When Dodge dies, Vince wraps himself in this blanket as a symbol of his inheritance. In *Buried Child,* Shepard has each son in some way diminish the power of his father: Bradley ruthlessly cuts Dodge's hair when he is asleep, Vince steps over Dodge's dead body and assumes his place, and Tilden unburies the secret that Dodge murdered Halie's child.

Unlike the family in Shepard's *The Curse of the Starving Class,* the Illinois family in *Buried Child* has kept the farm but lives in a seedy farmhouse. Dodge, the patriarch, is a nasty man in his seventies, suffering from alcoholism and illness. Covered with a grimy blanket, he reclines on a sleazy couch in the living room, watching television. Halie, the matriarch in her mid-sixties, lives upstairs. They talk long-distance, shouting at each other, but neither one really listens to the other. The farmhouse is their prison, for Dodge is infirm and seldom leaves, and it is the place where his guilt lies buried. He yells at Tilden, who wanders about in the fields, "Don't go outside. There's nothing out there." Of course, since his guilt *is* out there, Tilden will eventually bring it in.

Instead of a renewal, Shepard's farm family rapidly falls apart. Halie has stayed away all night and returns, accompanied by Father Dewis and wearing different clothing. Dodge reveals that the buried child was Halie's, but not his, and despite her plea to "shut up," he admits, "I killed it. I drowned it. Just like the runt of the litter. Just drowned it." At this moment, Vince crashes through the screened porch in a drunken stupor and falls flat on his face, an act that seems to indicate his place in this mockery of a family. Dodge, now unburdened of his guilt, divides his worldly goods and dies, and no one cares. Vince makes sure that Dodge is dead, and as he covers the body, he is already dreaming of how he will resurrect the farm. Shelly, his girlfriend, tells him that it is time to leave, but Vince says, "I just inherited a house. . . . I've gotta carry on the line. I've gotta see to it that things keep rolling." Shelly just stares at Vince, sets down his saxophone, and then resolutely exits.

Vince is asked by Father Dewis to help his grandmother, who has suffered a breakdown, but Vince coolly responds, "My Grandmother? There's nobody else in this house. Except for you. And you're leaving aren't you." When Dewis leaves, Vince lies down on the sofa and stares at the ceiling, listening to Halie as she calls down to Dodge to tell him that the field is filled with corn as tall as a man. While Vince listens, he is unaware that Tilden is now in the house holding the corpse of a child "wrapped in muddy, rotten cloth." Slowly, Tilden walks upstairs with his gift for Halie, while she, still speaking to Dodge, says, with unintended irony, "You can't force a thing to grow. You can't interfere with it. It's all hidden. It's all unseen. You just gotta wait til it pops up out of the ground. Tiny little shoot. Tiny little white shoot. All hairy and fragile. Strong though. Strong enough to break the earth even. It's a miracle, Dodge. I've never seen a crop like this in my whole life. Maybe it's the sun. Maybe it's that's it. Maybe it's the sun."

Though Shepard's plays are interesting, he has not won over the critics, who in Shepard's words treat him with "bemused condescension or outright indignance," praising him for his facility with words but complaining "when is he going to stop playing around and give us a really MAJOR NEW AMERICAN PLAY." *Buried Child*, probably Shepard's most conventional play, depicts universal themes that affect family relationships and tie them to a place. But it is his unrelenting mining of personal experience that situates him among the modern playwrights, from August Strindberg through Eugene O'Neill, Tennessee Williams, and on to Edward Albee.

Buried Child

While the rain of your fingertips falls,
while the rain of your bones falls,
and your laughter and marrow fall down,
you come flying.

PABLO NERUDA

CHARACTERS

DODGE, in his seventies
HALIE, his wife, mid-sixties
TILDEN, their oldest son
BRADLEY, their next oldest son, an amputee
VINCE, Tilden's son
SHELLY, Vince's girlfriend
FATHER DEWIS, a Protestant minister

ACT I

SCENE. *Day. Old wooden staircase down left with pale, frayed carpet laid down on the steps. The stairs lead off stage left up into the wings with no landing. Up right is an old, dark green sofa with the stuffing coming out in spots. Stage right of the sofa is an upright lamp with a faded yellow shade and a small night table with several small bottles of pills on it. Down right of the sofa, with the screen facing the sofa, is a large, old-fashioned brown T.V. A flickering blue light comes from the screen, but no image, no sound. In the dark, the light of the lamp and the T.V. slowly brighten in the black space. The space behind the sofa, upstage, is a large, screened-in porch with a board floor. A solid interior door to stage right of the sofa, leading into the room on stage; and another screen door up left, leading from the porch to the outside. Beyond that are the shapes of dark elm trees.*

Gradually the form of DODGE *is made out, sitting on the couch, facing the T.V., the blue light flickering on his face. He wears a well-worn T-shirt, suspenders, khaki work pants and brown slippers. He's covered himself in an old brown blanket. He's very thin and sickly looking, in his late seventies. He just stares at the T.V. More light fills the stage softly. The sound of light rain.* DODGE *slowly tilts his head back and stares at the ceiling for a while, listening to the rain. He lowers his head again and stares at the T.V. He turns his head slowly to the left and stares at the cushion of the sofa next to the one he's sitting on. He pulls his left arm out from under the blanket, slides his hand under the cushion, and pulls out a bottle of whiskey. He looks down left toward the staircase, listens, them uncaps the bottle, takes a long swig and caps it again. He puts the bottle back under the cushion and stares at the T.V. He starts to cough slowly and softly. The coughing gradually builds. He holds one hand to his mouth and tries to stifle it. The coughing gets louder, then suddenly stops when he hears the sound of his wife's voice coming from the top of the staircase.*

HALIE'S VOICE: Dodge?

[DODGE *just stares at the T.V. Long pause. He stifles two short coughs.*]

HALIE'S VOICE: Dodge! You want a pill, Dodge?

[*He doesn't answer. Takes the bottle out again and takes another long swig. Puts the bottle back, stares at T.V., pulls blanket up around his neck.*]

HALIE'S VOICE: You know what it is, don't you? It's the rain! Weather. That's it. Every time. Every time you get like this, it's the rain. No sooner does the rain start then you start. [*pause*] Dodge?

[*He makes no reply. Pulls a pack of cigarettes out from his sweater and lights one. Stares at T.V. Pause.*]

HALIE'S VOICE: You should see it coming down up here. Just coming down in sheets. Blue sheets. The bridge is pretty near flooded. What's it like down there? Dodge?

[DODGE *turns his head back over his left shoulder and takes a look out through the porch. He turns back to the T.V.*]

DODGE [*to himself*]: Catastrophic.
HALIE'S VOICE: What? What'd you say, Dodge?
DODGE [*louder*]: It looks like rain to me! Plain old rain!
HALIE'S VOICE: Rain? Of course it's rain! Are you having a seizure or something! Dodge? [*pause*] I'm coming down there in about five minutes if you don't answer me!
DODGE: Don't come down.
HALIE'S VOICE: What!
DODGE [*louder*]: Don't come down!

[*He has another coughing attack. Stops.*]

HALIE'S VOICE: You should take a pill for that! I don't see why you just don't take a pill. Be done with it once and for all. Put a stop to it.

[*He takes bottle out again. Another swig. Returns bottle.*]

HALIE'S VOICE: It's not Christian, but it works. It's not necessarily Christian, that is. We don't know. There's some things the ministers can't even answer. I, personally, can't see anything wrong with it. Pain is pain. Pure and simple. Suffering is a different matter. That's entirely different. A pill seems as good an answer as any. Dodge? [*pause*] Dodge, are you watching baseball?
DODGE: No.
HALIE'S VOICE: What?
DODGE [*louder*]: No!
HALIE'S VOICE: What're you watching? You shouldn't be watching anything that'll get you excited! No horse racing!
DODGE: They don't race on Sundays.
HALIE'S VOICE: What?
DODGE [*louder*]: They don't race on Sundays!
HALIE'S VOICE: Well they shouldn't race on Sundays.
DODGE: Well they don't!
HALIE'S VOICE: Good. I'm amazed they still have that kind of legislation. That's amazing.
DODGE: Yeah, it's amazing.
HALIE'S VOICE: What?

Buried Child, *directed by Robert Woodruff, with Ed Seamon (far left) as Dodge, directed by Robert Woodruff, Circle Repertory Theatre, New York.*

DODGE [*louder*]: It is amazing!

HALIE'S VOICE: It is. It truly is. I would've thought these days they'd be racing on Christmas even. A big flashing Christmas tree right down at the finish line.

DODGE [*shakes his head*]: No.

HALIE'S VOICE: They used to race on New Year's! I remember that.

DODGE: They never raced on New Year's!

HALIE'S VOICE: Sometimes they did.

DODGE: They never did!

HALIE'S VOICE: Before we were married they did!

[DODGE *waves his hand in disgust at the staircase. Leans back in sofa. Stares at T.V.*]

HALIE'S VOICE: I went once. With a man.

DODGE [*mimicking her*]: Oh, a "man."

HALIE'S VOICE: What?

DODGE: Nothing!

HALIE'S VOICE: A wonderful man. A breeder.

DODGE: A what?

HALIE'S VOICE: A breeder! A horse breeder! Thoroughbreds.

DODGE: Oh, Thoroughbreds. Wonderful.

HALIE'S VOICE: That's right. He knew everything there was to know.

DODGE: I bet he taught you a thing or two huh? Gave you a good turn around the old stable!

HALIE'S VOICE: Knew everything there was to know about horses. We won bookoos of money that day.

DODGE: What?

HALIE'S VOICE: Money! We won every race I think.

DODGE: Bookoos?

HALIE'S VOICE: Every single race.

DODGE: Bookoos of money?

HALIE'S VOICE: It was one of those kind of days.

DODGE: New Year's!

HALIE'S VOICE: Yes! It might've been Florida. Or California! One of those two.

DODGE: Can I take my pick?

HALIE'S VOICE: It was Florida!

DODGE: Aha!

HALIE'S VOICE: Wonderful! Absolutely wonderful! The sun was just gleaming. Flamingos. Bougainvilleas. Palm trees.

DODGE [*to himself, mimicking her*]: Bougainvilleas. Palm trees.

HALIE'S VOICE: Everything was dancing with life! There were all kinds of people from everywhere. Everyone was dressed to the nines. Not like today. Not like they dress today.

DODGE: When was this anyway?

HALIE'S VOICE: This was long before I knew you.

DODGE: Must've been.

HALIE'S VOICE: Long before. I was escorted.

DODGE: To Florida?

HALIE'S VOICE: Yes. Or it might've been California. I'm not sure which.

DODGE: All that way you were escorted?

HALIE'S VOICE: Yes.

DODGE: And he never laid a finger on you I suppose? [*long silence*] Halie?

[*No answer. Long pause.*]

HALIE'S VOICE: Are you going out today?

DODGE [*gesturing toward rain*]: In this?

HALIE'S VOICE: I'm just asking a simple question.

DODGE: I rarely go out in the bright sunshine, why would I go out in this?

HALIE'S VOICE: I'm just asking because I'm not doing any shopping today. And if you need anything you should ask Tilden.

DODGE: Tilden's not here!

HALIE'S VOICE: He's in the kitchen.

[DODGE *looks toward stage left, then back toward T.V.*]

DODGE: All right.

HALIE'S VOICE: What?

DODGE [*louder*]: All right!

HALIE'S VOICE: Don't scream. It'll only get your coughing started.

DODGE: All right.

HALIE'S VOICE: Just tell Tilden what you want and he'll get it. [*pause*] Bradley should be over later.

DODGE: Bradley?

HALIE'S VOICE: Yes. To cut your hair.

DODGE: My hair? I don't need my hair cut!

HALIE'S VOICE: It won't hurt!

DODGE: I don't need it!

HALIE'S VOICE: It's been more than two weeks Dodge.

DODGE: I don't need it!

HALIE'S VOICE: I have to meet Father Dewis for lunch.

DODGE: You tell Bradley that if he shows up here with those clippers, I'll kill him!

HALIE'S VOICE: I won't be very late. No later than four at the very latest.

DODGE: You tell him! Last time he left me almost bald! And I wasn't even awake! I was sleeping! I woke up and he'd already left!

HALIE'S VOICE: That's not my fault!

DODGE: You put him up to it!

HALIE'S VOICE: I never did!

DODGE: You did too! You had some fancy, stupid meeting planned! Time to dress up the corpse for company! Lower the ears a little! Put up a little front! Surprised you didn't tape a pipe to my mouth while you were at it! That woulda' looked nice! Huh? A pipe? Maybe a bowler hat! Maybe a copy of The Wall Street Journal casually placed on my lap!

HALIE'S VOICE: You always imagine the worst things of people!

DODGE: That's not the worst! That's the least of the worst!

HALIE'S VOICE: I don't need to hear it! All day long I hear things like that and I don't need to hear more.

DODGE: You better tell him!

HALIE'S VOICE: You tell him yourself! He's your own son. You should be able to talk to your own son.

DODGE: Not while I'm sleeping! He cut my hair while I was sleeping!

HALIE'S VOICE: Well he won't do it again.

DODGE: There's no guarantee.

HALIE'S VOICE: I promise he won't do it without your consent.

DODGE [*after pause*]: There's no reason for him to even come over here.

HALIE'S VOICE: He feels responsible.

DODGE: For my hair?

HALIE'S VOICE: For your appearance.

DODGE: My appearance is out of his domain! It's even out of mine! In fact, it's disappeared! I'm an invisible man!

HALIE'S VOICE: Don't be ridiculous.

DODGE: He better not try it. That's all I've got to say.

HALIE'S VOICE: Tilden will watch out for you.

DODGE: Tilden won't protect me from Bradley!

HALIE'S VOICE: Tilden's the oldest. He'll protect you.

DODGE: Tilden can't even protect himself!

HALIE'S VOICE: Not so loud! He'll hear you. He's right in the kitchen.

DODGE [*yelling off left*]: Tilden!

HALIE'S VOICE: Dodge, what are you trying to do?

DODGE [*yelling off left*]: Tilden, get in here!

HALIE'S VOICE: Why do you enjoy stirring things up?

DODGE: I don't enjoy anything!

HALIE'S VOICE: That's a terrible thing to say.

DODGE: Tilden!

HALIE'S VOICE: That's the kind of statement that leads people right to the end of their rope.

DODGE: Tilden!

HALIE'S VOICE: It's no wonder people turn to Christ!

DODGE: TILDEN!!

HALIE'S VOICE: It's no wonder the messengers of God's word are shouted down in public places!

DODGE: TILDEN!!!!

[DODGE *goes into a violent, spasmodic coughing attack as* TILDEN *enters from stage left, his arms loaded with fresh ears of corn.* TILDEN *is* DODGE'S *oldest son, late forties, wears heavy construction boots, covered with mud, dark green work pants, a plaid shirt and a faded brown windbreaker. He has a butch haircut, wet from the rain. Something about him is profoundly burned out and displaced. He stops center stage with the ears of corn in his arms and just stares at* DODGE *until he slowly finishes his coughing attack.* DODGE *looks up at him slowly. He stares at the corn. Long pause as they watch each other.*]

HALIE'S VOICE: Dodge, if you don't take that pill nobody's going to force you.

[*The two men ignore the voice.*]

DODGE [*to* TILDEN]: Where'd you get that?

TILDEN: Picked it.

DODGE: You picked all that?

[TILDEN *nods.*]

DODGE: You expecting company?

TILDEN: No.

DODGE: Where'd you pick it from?

TILDEN: Right out back.

DODGE: Out back where?

TILDEN: Right out in back.

DODGE: There's nothing out there!

TILDEN: There's corn.

DODGE: There hasn't been corn out there since about nineteen thirty-five! That's the last time I planted corn out there!

TILDEN: It's out there now.

DODGE [*yelling at stairs*]: Halie!

HALIE'S VOICE: Yes dear!

DODGE: Tilden's brought a whole bunch of corn in here! There's no corn out in back is there?

TILDEN [*to himself*]: There's tons of corn.

HALIE'S VOICE: Not that I know of!

DODGE: That's what I thought.

HALIE'S VOICE: Not since about nineteen thirty-five!

DODGE [*to* TILDEN]: That's right. Nineteen thirty-five.

TILDEN: It's out there now.

DODGE: You go and take that corn back to wherever you got it from!

TILDEN [*after pause, staring at* DODGE]: It's picked. I picked it all in the rain. Once it's picked you can't put it back.

DODGE: I haven't had trouble with neighbors here for fifty-seven years. I don't even know who the neighbors are! And I don't wanna know! Now go put that corn back where it came from!

[TILDEN *stares at* DODGE *then walks slowly over to him and dumps all the corn on* DODGE'S *lap and steps back.* DODGE *stares at the corn then back to* TILDEN. *Long pause.*]

DODGE: Are you having trouble here, Tilden! Are you in some kind of trouble?

TILDEN: I'm not in any trouble.
DODGE: You can tell me if you are. I'm still your father.
TILDEN: I know you're still my father.
DODGE: I know you had a little trouble back in New Mexico. That's why you came out here.
TILDEN: I never had any trouble.
DODGE: Tilden, your mother told me all about it.
TILDEN: What'd she tell you?

[TILDEN *pulls some chewing tobacco out of his jacket and bites off a plug.*]

DODGE: I don't have to repeat what she told me! She told me all about it!
TILDEN: Can I bring my chair in from the kitchen?
DODGE: What?
TILDEN: Can I bring in my chair from the kitchen?
DODGE: Sure. Bring your chair in.

[TILDEN *exits left.* DODGE *pushes all the corn off his lap onto the floor. He pulls the blanket off angrily and tosses it at one end of the sofa, pulls out the bottle and takes another swig.* TILDEN *enters again from left with a milking stool and a pail.* DODGE *hides the bottle quickly under the cushion before* TILDEN *sees it.* TILDEN *sets the stool down by the sofa, sits on it, puts the pail in front of him on the floor.* TILDEN *starts picking up the ears of corn one at a time and husking them. He throws the husks and silk in the center of the stage and drops the ears into the pail each time he cleans one. He repeats this process as they talk.*]

DODGE [*after pause*]: Sure is nice-looking corn.
TILDEN: It's the best.
DODGE: Hybrid?
TILDEN: What?
DODGE: Some kinda fancy hybrid?
TILDEN: You planted it. I don't know what it is.
DODGE [*pause*]: Tilden, look, you can't stay here forever. You know that, don't you?
TILDEN [*spits in spittoon*]: I'm not.
DODGE: I know you're not. I'm not worried about that. That's not the reason I brought it up.
TILDEN: What's the reason?
DODGE: The reason is I'm wondering what you're gonna do.
TILDEN: You're not worried about me, are you?
DODGE: I'm not worried about you.
TILDEN: You weren't worried about me when I wasn't here. When I was in New Mexico.
DODGE: No, I wasn't worried about you then either.
TILDEN: You shoulda worried about me then.
DODGE: Why's that? You didn't do anything down there, did you?
TILDEN: I didn't do anything.
DODGE: Then why should I have worried about you?
TILDEN: Because I was lonely.
DODGE: Because you were lonely?
TILDEN: Yeah. I was more lonely than I've ever been before.
DODGE: Why was that?
TILDEN [*pause*]: Could I have some of that whiskey you've got?
DODGE: What whiskey? I haven't got any whiskey.
TILDEN: You've got some under the sofa.
DODGE: I haven't got anything under the sofa! Now mind your own damn business! Jesus God, you come into the house outa the middle of nowhere, haven't heard or seen you in twenty years and suddenly you're making accusations.
TILDEN: I'm not making accusations.
DODGE: You're accusing me of hoarding whiskey under the sofa!
TILDEN: I'm not accusing you.
DODGE: You just got through telling me I had whiskey under the sofa!
HALIE'S VOICE: Dodge?
DODGE [*to* TILDEN]: Now she knows about it!
TILDEN: She doesn't know about it.
HALIE'S VOICE: Dodge, are you talking to yourself down there?
DODGE: I'm talking to Tilden!
HALIE'S VOICE: Tilden's down there?
DODGE: He's right here!
HALIE'S VOICE: What?
DODGE [*louder*]: He's right here!
HALIE'S VOICE: What's he doing?
DODGE [*to* TILDEN]: Don't answer her.
TILDEN [*to* DODGE]: I'm not doing anything wrong.
DODGE: I know you're not.
HALIE'S VOICE: What's he doing down there!
DODGE [*to* TILDEN]: Don't answer.
TILDEN: I'm not.
HALIE'S VOICE: Dodge!

[*The men sit in silence.* DODGE *lights a cigarette.* TILDEN *keeps husking corn, spits tobacco now and then in spittoon.*]

HALIE'S VOICE: Dodge! He's not drinking anything, is he? You see to it that he doesn't drink anything! You've gotta watch out for him. It's our responsibility. He can't look after himself anymore, so we have to do it. Nobody else will do it. We can't just send him away somewhere. If we had lots of money we could send him away. But we don't. We never will. That's why we have to stay healthy. You and me. Nobody's going to look after us. Bradley can't look after us. Bradley can hardly look after himself. I was always hoping that Tilden would look out for Bradley when they got older. After Bradley lost his leg. Tilden's the oldest. I always thought he'd be the one to take responsibility. I had no idea in the world that Tilden would be so much trouble. Who would've dreamed. Tilden was an All-American, don't forget. Don't forget that. Fullback. Or quarterback. I forget which.

TILDEN [*to himself*]: Fullback. [*still husking*]

HALIE'S VOICE: Then when Tilden turned out to be so much trouble, I put all my hopes on Ansel. Of course Ansel wasn't as handsome, but he was smart. He was the smartest probably. I think he probably was. Smarter than Bradley, that's for sure. Didn't go and chop his leg off with a chain saw. Smart enough not to go and do that. I think he was smarter than Tilden too. Especially after Tilden got in all that trouble. Doesn't take brains to go to jail. Anybody knows that. Course then when Ansel died that left us all alone. Same as being alone. No different. Same as if they'd all died. He was the smartest. He could've earned lots of money. Lots and lots of money.

[HALIE *enters slowly from the top of the staircase as she continues talking. Just her feet are seen at first as she makes her way down the stairs, a step at a time. She appears dressed completely in black, as though in mourning. Black handbag, hat with a veil, and pulling on elbow length black gloves. She is about sixty-five with pure white hair. She remains absorbed in what she's saying as she descends the stairs and doesn't really notice the two men who continue sitting there as they were before she came down, smoking and husking.*]

HALIE: He would've took care of us, too. He would've seen to it that we were repaid. He was like that. He was a hero. Don't forget that. A genuine hero. Brave. Strong. And very intelligent. Ansel could've been a great man. One of the greatest. I only regret that he didn't die in action. It's not fitting for a man like that to die in a motel room. A soldier. He could've won a medal. He could've been decorated for valor. I've talked to Father Dewis about putting up a plaque for Ansel. He thinks it's a good idea. He agrees. He knew Ansel when he used to play basketball. Went to every game. Ansel was his favorite player. He even recommended to the City Council that they put up a statue of Ansel. A big, tall statue with a basketball in one hand and a rifle in the other. That's how much he thinks of Ansel.

[HALIE *reaches the stage and begins to wander around, still absorbed in pulling on her gloves, brushing lint off her dress and continuously talking to herself as the men just sit.*]

HALIE: Of course, he'd still be alive today if he hadn't married into the Catholics. The Mob. How in the world he never opened his eyes to that is beyond me. Just beyond me. Everyone around him could see the truth. Even Tilden. Tilden told him time and again. Catholic women are the Devil incarnate. He wouldn't listen. He was blind with love. Blind. I knew. Everyone knew. The wedding was more like a funeral. You remember? All those Italians. All that horrible black, greasy hair. The smell of cheap cologne. I think even the priest was wearing a pistol. When he gave her the ring I knew he was a dead man. I knew it. As soon as he gave her the ring. But then it was the honeymoon that killed him. The honeymoon. I knew he'd never come back from the honeymoon. I kissed him and he felt like a corpse. All white. Cold. Icy blue lips. He never used to kiss like that. Never before. I knew then that she'd cursed him. Taken his soul. I saw it in her eyes. She smiled at me with that Catholic sneer of hers. She told me with her eyes that she'd murder him in his bed. Murder my son. She told me. And there was nothing I could do. Absolutely nothing. He was going with her, thinking he was free. Thinking it was love. What could I do? I couldn't tell him she was a witch. I couldn't tell him that. He'd have turned on me. Hated me. I couldn't stand him hating me and then dying before he ever saw me again. Hating me in his death bed. Hating me and loving her! How could I do that? I had to let him go. I had to. I watched him leave. I watched him throw gardenias as he helped her into the limousine. I watched his face disappear behind the glass.

[*She stops abruptly and stares at the corn husks. She looks around the space as though just waking up. She turns and looks hard at* TILDEN *and* DODGE *who continue sitting calmly. She looks again at the corn husks.*]

HALIE [*pointing to the husks*]: What's this in my house! [*kicks husks*] What's all this!

[TILDEN *stops husking and stares at her.*]

HALIE [*to* DODGE]: And you encourage him!

[DODGE *pulls blanket over him again.*]

DODGE: You're going out in the rain?

HALIE: It's not raining.

[TILDEN *starts husking again.*]

DODGE: Not in Florida it's not.

HALIE: We're not in Florida!

DODGE: It's not raining at the race track.

HALIE: Have you been taking those pills? Those pills always make you talk crazy. Tilden, has he been taking those pills?

TILDEN: He hasn't took anything.

HALIE [*to* DODGE]: What've you been taking?

DODGE: It's not raining in California or Florida or the race track. Only in Illinois. This is the only place it's raining. All over the rest of the world it's bright golden sunshine.

[HALIE *goes to the night table next to the sofa and checks the bottle of pills.*]

HALIE: Which ones did you take? Tilden, you must've seen him take something.

TILDEN: He never took a thing.

HALIE: Then why's he talking crazy?

TILDEN: I've been here the whole time.

HALIE: Then you've both been taking something!

TILDEN: I've just been husking the corn.

HALIE: Where'd you get that corn anyway? Why is the house suddenly full of corn?

DODGE: Bumper crop!

HALIE [*moving center*]: We haven't had corn here for over thirty years.

TILDEN: The whole back lot's full of corn. Far as the eye can see.

DODGE [*to* HALIE]: Things keep happening while you're upstairs, ya know. The world doesn't stop just because you're upstairs. Corn keeps growing. Rain keeps raining.

HALIE: I'm not unaware of the world around me! Thank you very much. It so happens that I have an over-all view from the upstairs. The back yard's in plain view of my window. And there's no corn to speak of. Absolutely none!

DODGE: Tilden wouldn't lie. If he says there's corn, there's corn.

HALIE: What's the meaning of this corn Tilden!

TILDEN: It's a mystery to me. I was out in back there. And the rain was coming down. And I didn't feel like coming back inside. I didn't feel the cold so much. I didn't mind the wet. So I was just walking. I was muddy but I didn't mind the mud so much. And I looked up. And I saw this stand of corn. In fact I was standing in it. So, I was standing in it.

HALIE: There isn't any corn outside, Tilden! There's no corn! Now, you must've either stolen this corn or you bought it.

DODGE: He doesn't have any money.

HALIE [*to* TILDEN]: So you stole it!

TILDEN: I didn't steal it. I don't want to get kicked out of Illinois. I was kicked out of New Mexico and I don't want to get kicked out of Illinois.

HALIE: You're going to get kicked out of this house, Tilden, if you don't tell me where you got that corn!

[TILDEN *starts crying softly to himself but keeps husking corn. Pause.*]

DODGE [*to* HALIE]: Why'd you have to tell him that? Who cares where he got the corn? Why'd you have to go and tell him that?

HALIE [*to* DODGE]: It's your fault you know! You're the one that's behind all this! I suppose you thought it'd be funny! Some joke! Cover the house with corn husks. You better get this cleaned up before Bradley sees it.

DODGE: Bradley's not getting in the front door!

HALIE [*kicking husks, striding back and forth*]: Bradley's going to be very upset when he sees this. He doesn't like to see the house in disarray. He can't stand it when one thing is out of place. The slightest thing. You know how he gets.

DODGE: Bradley doesn't even live here!

HALIE: It's his home as much as ours. He was born in this house!

DODGE: He was born in a hog wallow.

HALIE: Don't you say that! Don't you ever say that!

DODGE: He was born in a goddamn hog wallow! That's where he was born and that's where he belongs! He doesn't belong in this house!

HALIE [*she stops*]: I don't know what's come over you, Dodge. I don't know what in the world's come over you. You've become an evil man. You used to be a good man.

DODGE: Six of one, a half dozen of another.

HALIE: You sit here day and night, festering away! Decomposing! Smelling up the house with your putrid body! Hacking your head off till all hours of the morning! Thinking up mean, evil, stupid things to say about your own flesh and blood!

DODGE: He's not my flesh and blood! My flesh and blood's buried in the back yard!

[*They freeze. Long pause. The men stare at her.*]

HALIE [*quietly*]: That's enough, Dodge. That's quite enough. I'm going out now. I'm going to have lunch with Father Dewis. I'm going to ask him about a monument. A statue. At least a plaque.

[*She crosses to the door up right. She stops.*]

HALIE: If you need anything, ask Tilden. He's the oldest. I've left some money on the kitchen table.

DODGE: I don't need anything.

HALIE: No, I suppose not. [*she opens the door and looks out through porch*] Still raining. I love the smell just after it stops. The ground. I won't be too late.

[*She goes out door and closes it. She's still visible on the porch as she crosses toward stage left screen door. She stops in the middle of the porch, speaks to* DODGE *but doesn't turn to him.*]

HALIE: Dodge, tell Tilden not to go out in the back lot anymore. I don't want him back there in the rain.
DODGE: You tell him. He's sitting right here.
HALIE: He never listens to me Dodge. He's never listened to me in the past.
DODGE: I'll tell him.
HALIE: We have to watch him just like we used to now. Just like we always have. He's still a child.
DODGE: I'll watch him.
HALIE: Good.

[*She crosses to screen door, left, takes an umbrella off a hook and goes out the door. The door slams behind her. Long pause.* TILDEN *husks corn, stares at pail.* DODGE *lights a cigarette, stares at T.V.*]

TILDEN [*still husking*]: You shouldn't a told her that.
DODGE [*staring at T.V.*]: What?
TILDEN: What you told her. You know.
DODGE: What do you know about it?
TILDEN: I know. I know all about it. We all know.
DODGE: So what difference does it make? Everybody knows, everybody's forgot.
TILDEN: She hasn't forgot.
DODGE: She should've forgot.
TILDEN: It's different for a woman. She couldn't forget that. How could she forget that?
DODGE: I don't want to talk about it!
TILDEN: What do you want to talk about?
DODGE: I don't want to talk about anything! I don't want to talk about troubles or what happened fifty years ago or thirty years ago or the race track or Florida or the last time I seeded the corn! I don't want to talk!
TILDEN: You don't wanna die do you?
DODGE: No, I don't wanna die either.
TILDEN: Well, you gotta talk or you'll die.
DODGE: Who told you that?
TILDEN: That's what I know. I found that out in New Mexico. I thought I was dying but I just lost my voice.
DODGE: Were you with somebody?
TILDEN: I was alone. I thought I was dead.
DODGE: Might as well have been. What'd you come back here for?
TILDEN: I didn't know where to go.
DODGE: You're a grown man. You shouldn't be needing your parents at your age. It's unnatural. There's nothing we can do for you now anyway. Couldn't you make a living down there? Couldn't you find some way to make a living? Support yourself? What'd'ya come back here for? You expect us to feed you forever?
TILDEN: I didn't know where else to go.
DODGE: I never went back to my parents. Never. Never even had the urge. I was independent. Always independent. Always found a way.
TILDEN: I didn't know what to do. I couldn't figure anything out.
DODGE: There's nothing to figure out. You just forge ahead. What's there to figure out?

[TILDEN *stands.*]

TILDEN: I don't know.
DODGE: Where are you going?
TILDEN: Out back.
DODGE: You're not supposed to go out there. You heard what she said. Don't play deaf with me!
TILDEN: I like it out there.
DODGE: In the rain?
TILDEN: Especially in the rain. I like the feeling of it. Feels like it always did.
DODGE: You're supposed to watch out for me. Get me things when I need them.
TILDEN: What do you need?
DODGE: I don't need anything! But I might. I might need something any second. Any second now. I can't be left alone for a minute!

[DODGE *starts to cough.*]

TILDEN: I'll be right outside. You can just yell.
DODGE [*between coughs*]: No! It's too far! You can't go out there! It's too far! You might not ever hear me!
TILDEN [*moving to pills*]: Why don't you take a pill? You want a pill?

[DODGE *coughs more violently, throws himself back against sofa, clutches his throat.* TILDEN *stands by helplessly.*]

DODGE: Water! Get me some water!

[TILDEN *rushes off left.* DODGE *reaches out for the pills, knocking some bottles to the floor, coughing in spasms. He grabs a small bottle, takes out pills and swallows them.* TILDEN *rushes back on with a glass of water.* DODGE *takes it and drinks, his coughing subsides.*]

TILDEN: You all right now?

[DODGE *nods. Drinks more water.* TILDEN *moves in closer to him.* DODGE *sets glass of water on the night table. His coughing is almost gone.*]

TILDEN: Why don't you lay down for a while? Just rest a little.

[TILDEN *helps* DODGE *lay down on the sofa. Covers him with blanket.*]

DODGE: You're not going outside are you?
TILDEN: No.
DODGE: I don't want to wake up and find you not here.
TILDEN: I'll be here.

[TILDEN *tucks blanket around* DODGE.]

DODGE: You'll stay right here?
TILDEN: I'll stay in my chair.
DODGE: That's not a chair. That's my old milking stool.
TILDEN: I know.
DODGE: Don't call it a chair.
TILDEN: I won't.

[TILDEN *tries to take* DODGE*'s baseball cap off.*]

DODGE: What're you doing! Leave that on me! Don't take that offa me! That's my cap!

[TILDEN *leaves the cap on* DODGE.]

TILDEN: I know.
DODGE: Bradley'll shave my head if I don't have that on. That's my cap.
TILDEN: I know it is.
DODGE: Don't take my cap off.
TILDEN: I won't.
DODGE: You stay right here now.
TILDEN [*sits on stool*]: I will.
DODGE: Don't go outside. There's nothing out there.
TILDEN: I won't.
DODGE: Everything's in here. Everything you need. Money's on the table. T.V. Is the T.V. on?
TILDEN: Yeah.
DODGE: Turn it off! Turn the damn thing off! What's it doing on?
TILDEN [*shuts off T.V., light goes out*]: You left it on.
DODGE: Well turn it off.
TILDEN [*sits on stool again*]: It's off.
DODGE: Leave it off.
TILDEN: I will.
DODGE: When I fall asleep you can turn it on.
TILDEN: Okay.
DODGE: You can watch the ball game. Red Sox. You like the Red Sox don't you?
TILDEN: Yeah.
DODGE: You can watch the Red Sox. Pee Wee Reese. Pee Wee Reese. You remember Pee Wee Reese?
TILDEN: No.
DODGE: Was he with the Red Sox?
TILDEN: I don't know.
DODGE: Pee Wee Reese. [*falling asleep*] You can watch the Cardinals. You remember Stan Musial.
TILDEN: No.
DODGE: Stan Musial. [*falling into sleep*] Bases loaded. Top a' the sixth. Bases loaded. Runner on first and third. Big fat knuckle ball. Floater. Big as a blimp. Cracko! Ball just took off like a rocket. Just pulverized. I marked it. Marked it with my eyes. Straight between the clock and the Burma Shave ad. I was the first kid out there. First kid. I had to fight hard for that ball. I wouldn't give it up. They almost tore the ears right off me. But I wouldn't give it up.

[DODGE *falls into deep sleep.* TILDEN *just sits staring at him for a while. Slowly he leans toward the sofa, checking to see if* DODGE *is well asleep. He reaches slowly under the cushion and pulls out the bottle of booze.* DODGE *sleeps soundly.* TILDEN *stands quietly, staring at* DODGE *as he uncaps the bottle and takes a long drink. He caps the bottle and sticks it in his hip pocket. He looks around at the husks on the floor and then back to* DODGE. *He moves center stage and gathers an armload of corn husks then crosses back to the sofa. He stands holding the husks over* DODGE *and looking down at him he gently spreads the corn husks over the whole length of* DODGE*'s body. He stands back and looks at* DODGE. *Pulls out bottle, takes another drink, returns bottle to his hip pocket. He gathers more husks and repeats the procedure until the floor is clean of corn husks and* DODGE *is completely covered in them except for his head.* TILDEN *takes another long drink, stares at* DODGE *sleeping then quietly exits stage left. Long pause as the sound of rain continues.* DODGE *sleeps on. The figure of* BRADLEY *appears up left, outside the screen porch door. He holds a wet newspaper over his head as a protection from the rain. He seems to be struggling with the door then slips and almost falls to the ground.* DODGE *sleeps on, undisturbed.*]

BRADLEY: Sonuvabitch! Sonuvagoddamnbitch!

[BRADLEY *recovers his footing and makes it through the screen door onto the porch. He throws the newspaper down, shakes the water out of his hair, and brushes the rain off of his shoulders. He is a big man dressed in a gray sweat shirt, black suspenders, baggy dark blue pants and black janitor's shoes. His left leg is wooden, having been amputated above the knee. He walks with an exaggerated, almost mechanical limp. The squeaking sounds of leather and metal accompany his walk coming from the harness and hinges of the false leg. His arms and shoulders are extremely powerful and muscular due to a lifetime dependency on the upper torso doing all the work for the legs. He is about five years younger than* TILDEN. *He moves laboriously to the stage right door and enters, closing the door behind him. He doesn't notice* DODGE *at first. He moves toward the staircase.*]

BRADLEY [*calling to upstairs*]: Mom!

[*He stops and listens. Turns upstage and sees* DODGE *sleeping. Notices corn husks. He moves slowly toward sofa. Stops next to pail and looks into it. Looks at husks.* DODGE *stays asleep. Talks to himself.*]

BRADLEY: What in the hell is this?

[*He looks at* DODGE*'s sleeping face and shakes his head in disgust. He pulls out a pair of black electric hair clippers from his pocket. Unwinds the cord and crosses to the lamp. He jabs his wooden leg behind the knee, causing it to bend at the joint and awkwardly kneels to plug the cord into a floor outlet. He pulls himself to his feet again by using the sofa as leverage. He moves to* DODGE*'s head and again jabs his false leg. Goes down on one knee. He violently knocks away some of the corn husks then jerks off* DODGE*'s baseball cap and throws it down center stage.* DODGE *stays asleep.* BRADLEY *switches on the clippers. Lights start dimming.* BRADLEY *cuts* DODGE*'s hair while he sleeps. Lights dim slowly to black with the sound of clippers and rain.*]

ACT II

SCENE. *Same set as ACT I. Night. Sounds of rain.* DODGE *still asleep on sofa. His hair is cut extremely short and in places the scalp is cut and bleeding. His cap is still center stage. All the corn and husks, pail and milking stool have been cleared away. The lights come up to the sound of a young girl laughing off stage left.* DODGE *remains asleep.* SHELLY *and* VINCE *appear up left outside the screen porch door sharing the shelter of* VINCE*'s overcoat above their heads.* SHELLY *is about nineteen, black hair, very beautiful. She wears tight jeans, high heels, purple T-shirt and a short rabbit fur coat. Her makeup is exaggerated and her hair has been curled.* VINCE *is* TILDEN*'s son, about twenty-two, wears a plaid shirt, jeans, dark glasses, cowboy boots and carries a black saxophone case. They shake the rain off themselves as they enter the porch through the screen door.*

SHELLY [*laughing, gesturing to house*]: This is it? I don't believe this is it!
VINCE: This is it.
SHELLY: This is the house?
VINCE: This is the house.
SHELLY: I don't believe it!
VINCE: How come?
SHELLY: It's like a Norman Rockwell cover or something.
VINCE: What's a' matter with that? It's American.
SHELLY: Where's the milkman and the little dog? What's the little dog's name? Spot. Spot and Jane. Dick and Jane and Spot.
VINCE: Knock it off.
SHELLY: Dick and Jane and Spot and Mom and Dad and Junior and Sissy!

[*She laughs. Slaps her knee.*]

VINCE: Come on! It's my heritage. What dya' expect?

[*She laughs more hysterically, out of control.*]

SHELLY: "And Tuffy and Toto and Dooda and Bonzo all went down one day to the corner grocery store to buy a big bag of licorice for Mr. Marshall's pussy cat!"

[*She laughs so hard she falls to her knees holding her stomach.* VINCE *stands there looking at her.*]

VINCE: Shelly will you get up!

[*She keeps laughing. Staggers to her feet. Turning in circles holding her stomach.*]

SHELLY [*continuing her story in kid's voice*]: "Mr. Marshall was on vacation. He had no idea that the four little boys had taken such a liking to his little kitty cat."
VINCE: Have some respect would ya'!
SHELLY [*trying to control herself*]: I'm sorry.
VINCE: Pull yourself together.
SHELLY [*salutes him*]: Yes sir.

[*She giggles.*]

VINCE: Jesus Christ, Shelly.
SHELLY [*pause, smiling*]: And Mr. Marshall—
VINCE: Cut it out.

[*She stops. Stands there staring at him. Stifles a giggle.*]

VINCE [*after pause*]: Are you finished?
SHELLY: Oh brother!
VINCE: I don't wanna go in there with you acting like an idiot.
SHELLY: Thanks.
VINCE: Well, I don't.
SHELLY: I won't embarrass you. Don't worry.
VINCE: I'm not worried.
SHELLY: You are too.
VINCE: Shelly look, I just don't wanna go in there with you giggling your head off. They might think something's wrong with you.

SHELLY: There is.
VINCE: There is not!
SHELLY: Something's definitely wrong with me.
VINCE: There is not!
SHELLY: There's something wrong with you too.
VINCE: There's nothing wrong with me either!
SHELLY: You wanna know what's wrong with you?
VINCE: What?

[SHELLY *laughs.*]

VINCE [*crosses back left toward screen door*]: I'm leaving!
SHELLY [*stops laughing*]: Wait! Stop! Stop! [VINCE *stops*] What's wrong with you is that you take the situation too seriously.
VINCE: I just don't want to have them think that I've suddenly arrived out of the middle of nowhere completely deranged.
SHELLY: What do you want them to think then?
VINCE [*pause*]: Nothing. Let's go in.

[*He crosses porch toward stage right interior door.* SHELLY *follows him. The stage right door opens slowly.* VINCE *sticks his head in, doesn't notice* DODGE *sleeping. Calls out toward staircase.*]

VINCE: Grandma!

[SHELLY *breaks into laughter, unseen behind* VINCE. VINCE *pulls his head back outside and pulls door shut. We hear their voices again without seeing them.*]

SHELLY'S VOICE [*stops laughing*]: I'm sorry. I'm sorry Vince. I really am. I really am sorry. I won't do it again. I couldn't help it.
VINCE'S VOICE: It's not all that funny.
SHELLY'S VOICE: I know it's not. I'm sorry.
VINCE'S VOICE: I mean this is a tense situation for me! I haven't seen them for over six years. I don't know what to expect.
SHELLY'S VOICE: I know. I won't do it again.
VINCE'S VOICE: Can't you bite your tongue or something?
SHELLY'S VOICE: Just don't say "Grandma," okay? [*she giggles, stops*] I mean if you say "Grandma" I don't know if I can stop myself.
VINCE'S VOICE: Well try!
SHELLY'S VOICE: Okay. Sorry.

[*Door opens again.* VINCE *sticks his head in then enters.* SHELLY *follows behind him.* VINCE *crosses to staircase, sets down saxophone case and overcoat, looks up staircase.* SHELLY *notices* DODGE'S *baseball cap. Crosses to it. Picks it up and puts it on her head.* VINCE *goes up the stairs and disappears at the top.* SHELLY *watches him then turns and sees* DODGE *on the sofa. She takes off the baseball cap.*]

VINCE'S VOICE [*from above stairs*]: Grandma!

[SHELLY *crosses over to* DODGE *slowly and stands next to him. She stands at his head, reaches out slowly and touches one of the cuts. The second she touches his head,* DODGE *jerks up to a sitting position on the sofa, eyes open.* SHELLY *gasps.* DODGE *looks at her, sees his cap in her hands, quickly puts his hand to his bare head. He glares at* SHELLY *then whips the cap out of her hands and puts it on.* SHELLY *backs away from him.* DODGE *stares at her.*]

SHELLY: I'm uh—with Vince.

[DODGE *just glares at her.*]

SHELLY: He's upstairs.

[DODGE *looks at the staircase then back to* SHELLY.]

SHELLY [*calling upstairs*]: Vince!
VINCE'S VOICE: Just a second!
SHELLY: You better get down here!
VINCE'S VOICE: Just a minute! I'm looking at the pictures.

[DODGE *keeps staring at her.*]

SHELLY [*to* DODGE]: We just got here. Pouring rain on the freeway so we thought we'd stop by. I mean Vince was planning on stopping anyway. He wanted to see you. He said he hadn't seen you in a long time.

[*Pause.* DODGE *just keeps staring at her.*]

SHELLY: We were going all the way through to New Mexico. To see his father. I guess his father lives out there. We thought we'd stop by and see you on the way. Kill two birds with one stone, you know? [*she laughs,* DODGE *stares, she stops laughing*] I mean Vince has this thing about his family now. I guess it's a new thing with him. I kind of find it hard to relate to. But he feels it's important. You know. I mean he feels he wants to get to know you all again. After all this time.

[*Pause.* DODGE *just stares at her. She moves nervously to staircase and yells up to* VINCE.]

SHELLY: Vince will you come down here please!

[VINCE *comes half way down the stairs.*]

VINCE: I guess they went out for a while.

[SHELLY *points to sofa and* DODGE. VINCE *turns and sees* DODGE. *He comes all the way down staircase and crosses to* DODGE. SHELLY *stays behind near staircase, keeping her distance.*]

VINCE: Grandpa?

[DODGE *looks up at him, not recognizing him.*]

DODGE: Did you bring the whiskey?

[VINCE *looks back at* SHELLY *then back to* DODGE.]

VINCE: Grandpa, it's Vince. I'm Vince. Tilden's son. You remember?

[DODGE *stares at him.*]

DODGE: You didn't do what you told me. You didn't stay here with me.
VINCE: Grandpa, I haven't been here until just now. I just got here.
DODGE: You left. You went outside like we told you not to do. You went out there in back. In the rain.

[VINCE *looks back at* SHELLY. *She moves slowly toward sofa.*]

SHELLY: Is he okay?
VINCE: I don't know. [*takes off his shades*] Look, Grandpa, don't you remember me? Vince. Your Grandson.

[DODGE *stares at him then takes off his baseball cap.*]

DODGE [*points to his head*]: See what happens when you leave me alone? See that? That's what happens.

[VINCE *looks at his head.* VINCE *reaches out to touch his head.* DODGE *slaps his hand away with the cap and puts it back on his head.*]

VINCE: What's going on Grandpa? Where's Halie?
DODGE: Don't worry about her. She won't be back for days. She says she'll be back but she won't be. [*he starts laughing*] There's life in the old girl yet! [*stops laughing*]
VINCE: How did you do that to your head?
DODGE: I didn't do it! Don't be ridiculous!
VINCE: Well who did then?

[*Pause.* DODGE *stares at* VINCE.]

DODGE: Who do you think did it? Who do you think?

[SHELLY *moves toward* VINCE.]

SHELLY: Vince, maybe we oughta' go. I don't like this. I mean this isn't my idea of a good time.
VINCE [*to* SHELLY]: Just a second. [*to* DODGE] Grandpa, look, I just got here. I just now got here. I haven't been here for six years. I don't know anything that's happened.

[*Pause,* DODGE *stares at him.*]

DODGE: You don't know anything?
VINCE: No.
DODGE: Well that's good. That's good. It's much better not to know anything. Much, much better.
VINCE: Isn't there anybody here with you?

[DODGE *turns slowly and looks off to stage left.*]

DODGE: Tilden's here.
VINCE: No, Grandpa, Tilden's in New Mexico. That's where I was going. I'm going out there to see him.

[DODGE *turns slowly back to* VINCE.]

DODGE: Tilden's here.

[VINCE *backs away and joins* SHELLY. DODGE *stares at them.*]

SHELLY: Vince, why don't we spend the night in a motel and come back in the morning? We could have breakfast. Maybe everything would be different.
VINCE: Don't be scared. There's nothing to be scared of. He's just old.
SHELLY: I'm not scared!
DODGE: You two are not my idea of the perfect couple!
SHELLY [*after pause*]: Oh really? Why's that?
VINCE: Shh! Don't aggravate him.
DODGE: There's something wrong between the two of you. Something not compatible.
VINCE: Grandpa, where did Halie go? Maybe we should call her.
DODGE: What are you talking about? Do you know what you're talking about? Are you just talking for the sake of talking? Lubricating the gums?
VINCE: I'm trying to figure out what's going on here!
DODGE: Is that it?
VINCE: Yes. I mean I expected everything to be different.

DODGE: Who are you to expect anything? Who are you supposed to be?
VINCE: I'm Vince! Your Grandson!
DODGE: Vince. My Grandson.
VINCE: Tilden's son.
DODGE: Tilden's son, Vince.
VINCE: You haven't seen me for a long time.
DODGE: When was the last time?
VINCE: I don't remember.
DODGE: You don't remember?
VINCE: No.
DODGE: You don't remember. How am I supposed to remember if you don't remember?
SHELLY: Vince, come on. This isn't going to work out.
VINCE [*to* SHELLY]: Just take it easy.
SHELLY: I'm taking it easy! He doesn't even know who you are!
VINCE [*crossing toward* DODGE]: Grandpa, look—
DODGE: Stay where you are! Keep your distance!

[VINCE *stops. Looks back at* SHELLY *then to* DODGE.]

SHELLY: Vince, this is really making me nervous. I mean he doesn't even want us here. He doesn't even like us.
DODGE: She's a beautiful girl.
VINCE: Thanks.
DODGE: Very Beautiful Girl.
SHELLY: Oh my God.
DODGE [*to* SHELLY]: What's your name?
SHELLY: Shelly.
DODGE: Shelly. That's a man's name isn't it?
SHELLY: Not in this case.
DODGE [*to* VINCE]: She's a smart-ass too.
SHELLY: Vince! Can we go?
DODGE: She wants to go. She just got here and she wants to go.
VINCE: This is kind of strange for her.
DODGE: She'll get used to it. [*to* SHELLY] What part of the country do you come from?
SHELLY: Originally?
DODGE: That's right. Originally. At the very start.
SHELLY: L.A.
DODGE: L.A. Stupid country.
SHELLY: I can't stand this Vince! This is really unbelievable!
DODGE: It's stupid! L.A. is stupid! So is Florida! All those Sunshine States. They're all stupid. Do you know why they're stupid?
SHELLY: Illuminate me.
DODGE: I'll tell you why. Because they're full of smart-asses! That's why.

[SHELLY *turns her back to* DODGE, *crosses to staircase and sits on bottom step.*]

DODGE [*to* VINCE]: Now she's insulted.
VINCE: Well you weren't very polite.
DODGE: She's insulted! Look at her! In my house she's insulted! She's over there sulking because I insulted her!
SHELLY [*to* VINCE]: This is really terrific. This is wonderful. And you were worried about me making the right first impression!
DODGE [*to* VINCE]: She's a fireball isn't she? Regular fireball. I had some a' them in my day. Temporary stuff. Never lasted more than a week.
VINCE: Grandpa—
DODGE: Stop calling me Grandpa will ya'! It's sickening. "Grandpa." I'm nobody's Grandpa!

[DODGE *starts feeling around under the cushion for the bottle of whiskey.* SHELLY *gets up from the staircase.*]

SHELLY [*to* VINCE]: Maybe you've got the wrong house. Did you ever think of that? Maybe this is the wrong address!
VINCE: It's not the wrong address! I recognize the yard.
SHELLY: Yeah but do you recognize the people? He says he's not your Grandfather.
DODGE [*digging for bottle*]: Where's that bottle!
VINCE: He's just sick or something. I don't know what's happened to him.
DODGE: Where's my goddamn bottle!

[DODGE *gets up from sofa and starts tearing the cushions off it and throwing them downstage, looking for the whiskey.*]

SHELLY: Can't we just drive on to New Mexico? This is terrible, Vince! I don't want to stay here. In this house. I thought it was going to be turkey dinners and apple pie and all that kinda stuff.
VINCE: Well I hate to disappoint you!
SHELLY: I'm not disappointed! I'm fuckin' terrified! I wanna' go!

[DODGE *yells toward stage left.*]

DODGE: Tilden! Tilden!

[DODGE *keeps ripping away at the sofa looking for his bottle, he knocks over the night stand with the bottles.* VINCE *and* SHELLY *watch as he starts ripping the stuffing out of the sofa.*]

VINCE: [*to* SHELLY]: He's lost his mind or something. I've got to try to help him.
SHELLY: You help him! I'm leaving!

[SHELLY *starts to leave. Vince grabs her. They struggle as* DODGE *keeps ripping away at the sofa and yelling.*]

DODGE: Tilden! Tilden get your ass in here! Tilden!
SHELLY: Let go of me!
VINCE: You're not going anywhere! You're going to stay right here!
SHELLY: Let go of me you sonuvabitch! I'm not your property!

[*Suddenly* TILDEN *walks on from stage left just as he did before. This time his arms are full of carrots.* DODGE, VINCE *and* SHELLY *stop suddenly when they see him. They all stare at* TILDEN *as he crosses slowly center stage with the carrots and stops.* DODGE *sits on sofa, exhausted.*]

DODGE [*panting, to* TILDEN]: Where in the hell have you been?
TILDEN: Out back.
DODGE: Where's my bottle?
TILDEN: Gone.

[TILDEN *and* VINCE *stare at each other.* SHELLY *backs away.*]

DODGE [*to* TILDEN]: You stole my bottle!
VINCE [*to* TILDEN]: Dad?

[TILDEN *just stares at* VINCE.]

DODGE: You had no right to steal my bottle! No right at all!
VINCE [*to* TILDEN]: It's Vince. I'm Vince.

[TILDEN *stares at* VINCE *then looks at* DODGE *then turns to* SHELLY.]

TILDEN [*after pause*]: I picked these carrots. If anybody wants any carrots, I picked 'em.
SHELLY [*to* VINCE]: This is your father?
VINCE [*to* TILDEN]: Dad, what're you doing here?

[TILDEN *just stares at* VINCE, *holding carrots,* DODGE *pulls the blanket back over himself.*]

DODGE [*to* TILDEN]: You're going to have to get me another bottle! You gotta get me a bottle before Halie comes back! There's money on the table. [*points to stage left kitchen*]
TILDEN [*shaking his head*]: I'm not going down there. Into town.

[SHELLY *crosses to* TILDEN. TILDEN *stares at her.*]

SHELLY [*to* TILDEN]: Are you Vince's father?
TILDEN [*to* SHELLY]: Vince?
SHELLY [*pointing to* VINCE]: This is supposed to be your son! Is he your son? Do you recognize him! I'm just along for the ride here. I thought everybody knew each other!

[TILDEN *stares at* VINCE. DODGE *wraps himself up in the blanket and sits on sofa staring at the floor.*]

TILDEN: I had a son once but we buried him.

[DODGE *quickly looks at* TILDEN. SHELLY *looks to* VINCE.]

DODGE: You shut up about that! You don't know anything about that!
VINCE: Dad, I thought you were in New Mexico. We were going to drive down there and see you.
TILDEN: Long way to drive.
DODGE [*to* TILDEN]: You don't know anything about that! That happened before you were born! Long before!
VINCE: What's happened, Dad? What's going on here? I thought everything was all right. What's happened to Halie?
TILDEN: She left.
SHELLY [*to* TILDEN]: Do you want me to take those carrots for you?

[TILDEN *stares at her. She moves in close to him. Holds out her arms.* TILDEN *stares at her arms then slowly dumps the carrots into her arms.* SHELLY *stands there holding the carrots.*]

TILDEN [*to* SHELLY]: You like carrots?
SHELLY: Sure. I like all kinds of vegetables.
DODGE [*to* TILDEN]: You gotta get me a bottle before Halie comes back!

[DODGE *hits sofa with his fist.* VINCE *crosses up to* DODGE *and tries to console him.* SHELLY *and* TILDEN *stay facing each other.*]

TILDEN [*to* SHELLY]: Back yard's full of carrots. Corn. Potatoes.
SHELLY: You're Vince's father, right?
TILDEN: All kinds of vegetables. You like vegetables?
SHELLY [*laughs*]: Yeah. I love vegetables.
TILDEN: We could cook these carrots ya' know. You could cut 'em up and we could cook 'em.
SHELLY: All right.
TILDEN: I'll get you a pail and a knife.
SHELLY: Okay.
TILDEN: I'll be right back. Don't go.

[TILDEN *exits off stage left.* SHELLY *stands center, arms full of carrots.* VINCE *stands next to* DODGE. SHELLY *looks toward* VINCE *then down at the carrots.*]

DODGE [*to* VINCE]: You could get me a bottle. [*pointing off left*] There's money on the table.

VINCE: Grandpa why don't you lay down for a while?

DODGE: I don't wanna lay down for a while! Every time I lay down something happens! [*whips off his cap, points at his head*] Look what happens! That's what happens! [*pulls his cap back on*] You go lie down and see what happens to you! See how you like it! They'll steal your bottle! They'll cut your hair! They'll murder your children! That's what'll happen.

VINCE: Just relax for a while.

DODGE [*pause*]: You could get me a bottle ya' know. There's nothing stopping you from getting me a bottle.

SHELLY: Why don't you get him a bottle, Vince? Maybe it would help everybody identify each other.

DODGE [*pointing to* SHELLY]: There, see? She thinks you should get me a bottle.

[VINCE *crosses to* SHELLY.]

VINCE: What're you doing with those carrots.

SHELLY: I'm waiting for your father.

DODGE: She thinks you should get me a bottle!

VINCE: Shelly put the carrots down will ya'! We gotta deal with the situation here! I'm gonna need your help.

SHELLY: I'm helping.

VINCE: You're only adding to the problem! You're making things worse! Put the carrots down!

[VINCE *tries to knock the carrots out of her arms. She turns away from him, protecting the carrots.*]

SHELLY: Get away from me! Stop it!

[VINCE *stands back from her. She turns to him still holding the carrots.*]

VINCE [*to* SHELLY]: Why are you doing this! Are you trying to make fun of me? This is my family you know!

SHELLY: You coulda' fooled me! I'd just as soon not be here myself. I'd just as soon be a thousand miles from here. I'd rather be anywhere but here. You're the one who wants to stay. So I'll stay. I'll stay and I'll cut the carrots. And I'll cook the carrots. And I'll do whatever I have to do to survive. Just to make it through this.

VINCE: Put the carrots down Shelly.

[TILDEN *enters from left with pail, milking stool and a knife. He sets the stool and pail center stage for* SHELLY. SHELLY *looks at* VINCE *then sits down on stool, sets the carrots on the floor and takes the knife from* TILDEN. *She looks at* VINCE *again then picks up a carrot, cuts the ends off, scrapes it and drops it in pail. She repeats this,* VINCE *glares at her. She smiles.*]

DODGE: She could get me a bottle. She's the type a' girl that could get me a bottle. Easy. She'd go down there. Slink up to the counter. They'd probably give her two bottles for the price of one. She could do that.

[SHELLY *laughs. Keeps cutting carrots.* VINCE *crosses up to* DODGE, *looks at him.* TILDEN *watches* SHELLY'*s hands. Long pause.*]

VINCE [*to* DODGE]: I haven't changed that much. I mean physically. Physically I'm just about the same. Same size. Same weight. Everything's the same.

[DODGE *keeps staring at* SHELLY *while* VINCE *talks to him.*]

DODGE: She's a beautiful girl. Exceptional.

[VINCE *moves in front of* DODGE *to block his view of* SHELLY. DODGE *keeps craning his head around to see her as* VINCE *demonstrates tricks from his past.*]

VINCE: Look. Look at this. Do you remember this? I used to bend my thumb behind my knuckles. You remember? I used to do it at the dinner table.

[VINCE *bends a thumb behind his knuckles for* DODGE *and holds it out to him.* DODGE *takes a short glance then looks back at* SHELLY. VINCE *shifts position and shows him something else.*]

VINCE: What about this?

[VINCE *curls his lips back and starts drumming on his teeth with his fingernails making little tapping sounds.* DODGE *watches a while.* TILDEN *turns toward the sound.* VINCE *keeps it up. He sees* TILDEN *taking notice and crosses to* TILDEN *as he drums on his teeth.* DODGE *turns T.V. on. Watches it.*]

VINCE: You remember this Dad?

[VINCE *keeps on drumming for* TILDEN. TILDEN *watches a while, fascinated, then turns back to* SHELLY. VINCE *keeps up the drumming on his teeth, crosses back to* DODGE *doing it.* SHELLY *keeps working on carrots, talking to* TILDEN.]

SHELLY [*to* TILDEN]: He drives me crazy with that sometimes.

VINCE [*to* DODGE]: I know! Here's one you'll remember. You used to kick me out of the house for this one.

[VINCE *pulls his shirt out of his belt and holds it tucked under his chin with his stomach exposed. He grabs the flesh on either side of his belly button and pushes it in and out to make it look like a mouth talking. He watches his belly button and makes a deep sounding cartoon voice to synchronize with the movement. He demonstrates it to* DODGE *then crosses down to* TILDEN *doing it. Both* DODGE *and* TILDEN *take short, uninterested glances then ignore him.*]

VINCE [*deep cartoon voice*]: "Hello. How are you? I'm fine. Thank you very much. It's so good to see you looking well this fine Sunday morning. I was going down to the hardware store to fetch a pail of water."

SHELLY: Vince, don't be pathetic will ya'!

[VINCE *stops. Tucks his shirt back in.*]

SHELLY: Jesus Christ. They're not gonna play. Can't you see that?

[SHELLY *keeps cutting carrots.* VINCE *slowly moves toward* TILDEN. TILDEN *keeps watching* SHELLY. DODGE *watches T.V.*]

VINCE [*to* SHELLY]: I don't get it. I really don't get it. Maybe it's me. Maybe I forgot something.

DODGE [*from sofa*]: You forgot to get me a bottle! That's what you forgot. Anybody in this house could get me a bottle. Anybody! But nobody will. Nobody understands the urgency! Peelin' carrots is more important. Playin' piano on your teeth! Well I hope you all remember this when you get up in years. When you find yourself immobilized. Dependent on the whims of others.

[VINCE *moves up toward* DODGE. *Pause as he looks at him.*]

VINCE: I'll get you a bottle.

DODGE: You will?

VINCE: Sure.

[SHELLY *stands holding knife and carrot.*]

SHELLY: You're not going to leave me here are you?

VINCE [*moving to her*]: You suggested it! You said, "why don't I go get him a bottle." So I'll go get him a bottle!

SHELLY: But I can't stay here.

VINCE: What is going on! A minute ago you were ready to cut carrots all night!

SHELLY: That was only if you stayed. Something to keep me busy, so I wouldn't be so nervous. I don't want to stay here alone.

DODGE: Don't let her talk you out of it! She's a bad influence. I could see it the minute she stepped in here.

SHELLY [*to* DODGE]: You were asleep!

TILDEN [*to* SHELLY]: Don't you want to cut carrots anymore?

SHELLY: Sure. Sure I do.

[SHELLY *sits back down on stool and continues cutting carrots. Pause.* VINCE *moves around, stroking his hair, staring at* DODGE *and* TILDEN. VINCE *and* SHELLY *exchange glances.* DODGE *watches T.V.*]

VINCE: Boy! This is amazing. This is truly amazing. [*keeps moving around*] What is this anyway? Am I in a time warp or something? Have I committed an unpardonable offence? It's true, I'm not married. [SHELLY *looks at him, then back to carrots*] But I'm also not divorced. I have been known to plunge into sinful infatuation with the Alto Saxophone. Sucking on number 5 reeds deep into the wee, wee hours.

SHELLY: Vince, what are you doing that for? They don't care about any of that. They just don't recognize you, that's all.

VINCE: How could they not recognize me! How in the hell could they not recognize me! I'm their son!

DODGE [*watching T.V.*]: You're no son of mine. I've had sons in my time and you're not one of 'em.

[*Long pause.* VINCE *stares at* DODGE *then looks at* TILDEN. *He turns to* SHELLY.]

VINCE: Shelly, I gotta go out for a while. I just gotta go out. I'll get a bottle and I'll come right back. You'll be o.k. here. Really.

SHELLY: I don't know if I can handle this, Vince.

VINCE: I just gotta think or something. I don't know. I gotta put this all together.

SHELLY: Can't we just go?

VINCE: No! I gotta find out what's going on.

SHELLY: Look, you think you're bad off, what about me? Not only don't they recognize me but I've never seen them before in my life. I don't know who these guys are. They could be anybody!

VINCE: They're not anybody!

SHELLY: That's what you say.

VINCE: They're my family for Christ's sake! I should know who my own family is! Now give me a break. It won't take that long. I'll just go out and I'll come right back. Nothing'll happen. I promise.

[SHELLY *stares at him. Pause.*]

SHELLY: All right.
VINCE: Thanks. [*he crosses up to* DODGE] I'm gonna go out now, Grandpa, and I'll pick you up a bottle. Okay?
DODGE: Change of heart huh? [*pointing off left*] Money's on the table. In the kitchen.

[VINCE *moves toward* SHELLY.]

VINCE [*to* SHELLY]: You be all right?
SHELLY [*cutting carrots*]: Sure. I'm fine. I'll just keep real busy while you're gone.

[VINCE *looks at* TILDEN *who keeps staring down at* SHELLY'*s hands.*]

DODGE: Persistence see? That's what it takes. Persistence. Persistence, fortitude and determination. Those are the three virtues. You stick with those three and you can't go wrong.
VINCE [*to* TILDEN]: You want anything, Dad?
TILDEN [*looks up at* VINCE]: Me?
VINCE: From the store? I'm gonna get Grandpa a bottle.
TILDEN: He's not supposed to drink. Halie wouldn't like it.
VINCE: He wants a bottle.
TILDEN: He's not supposed to drink.
DODGE [*to* VINCE]: Don't negotiate with him! Don't make any transactions until you've spoken to me first! He'll steal you blind!
VINCE [*to* DODGE]: Tilden says you're not supposed to drink.
DODGE: Tilden's lost his marbles! Look at him! He's around the bend. Take a took at him.

[VINCE *stares at* TILDEN. TILDEN *stares at* SHELLY'*s hands as she keeps cutting carrots.*]

DODGE: Now look at me. Look here at me!

[VINCE *looks back to* DODGE.]

DODGE: Now, between the two of us, who do you think is more trustworthy? Him or me? Can you trust a man who keeps bringing in vegetables from out of nowhere? Take a look at him.

[VINCE *looks back at* TILDEN.]

SHELLY: Go get the bottle, Vince.
VINCE [*to* SHELLY]: You sure you'll be all right?
SHELLY: I'll be fine. I feel right at home now.
VINCE: You do?
SHELLY: I'm fine. Now that I've got the carrots everything is all right.
VINCE: I'll be right back.

[VINCE *crosses stage left.*]

DODGE: Where are you going?
VINCE: I'm going to get the money.
DODGE: Then where are you going?
VINCE: Liquor store.
DODGE: Don't go anyplace else. Don't go off some place and drink. Come right back here.
VINCE: I will.

[VINCE *exits stage left.*]

DODGE [*calling after* VINCE]: You've got responsibility now! And don't go out the back way either! Come out through this way! I wanna' see you when you leave! Don't go out the back!
VINCE'*s* VOICE [*off left*]: I won't!

[DODGE *turns and looks at* TILDEN *and* SHELLY.]

DODGE: Untrustworthy. Probably drown himself if he went out the back. Fall right in a hole. I'd never get my bottle.
SHELLY: I wouldn't worry about Vince. He can take care of himself.
DODGE: Oh he can, huh? Independent.

[VINCE *comes on again from stage left with two dollars in his hand. He crosses stage right past* DODGE.]

DODGE [*to* VINCE]: You got the money?
VINCE: Yeah. Two bucks.
DODGE: Two bucks. Two bucks is two bucks. Don't sneer.
VINCE: What kind do you want?
DODGE: Whiskey! Gold Star Sour Mash. Use your own discretion.
VINCE: Okay.

[VINCE *crosses to stage right door. Opens it. Stops when he hears* TILDEN.]

TILDEN [*to* VINCE]: You drove all the way from New Mexico?

[VINCE *turns and looks at* TILDEN. *They stare at each other.* VINCE *shakes his head, goes out the door, crosses porch and exits out screen door.* TILDEN *watches him go. Pause.*]

SHELLY: You really don't recognize him? Either one of you?

[TILDEN *turns again and stares at* SHELLY*'s hands as she cuts carrots.*]

DODGE [*watching T.V.*]: Recognize who?
SHELLY: Vince.
DODGE: What's to recognize?

[DODGE *lights a cigarette, coughs slightly and stares at T.V.*]

SHELLY: It'd be cruel if you recognized him and didn't tell him. Wouldn't be fair.

[DODGE *just stares at T.V., smoking.*]

TILDEN: I thought I recognized him. I thought I recognized something about him.
SHELLY: You did?
TILDEN: I thought I saw a face inside his face.
SHELLY: Well it was probably that you saw what he used to look like. You haven't seen him for six years.
TILDEN: I haven't?
SHELLY: That's what he says.

[TILDEN *moves around in front of her as she continues with carrots.*]

TILDEN: Where was it I saw him last?
SHELLY: I don't know. I've only known him for a few months. He doesn't tell me everything.
TILDEN: He doesn't?
SHELLY: Not stuff like that.
TILDEN: What does he tell you?
SHELLY: You mean in general?
TILDEN: Yeah.

[TILDEN *moves around behind her.*]

SHELLY: Well he tells me all kinds of things.
TILDEN: Like what?
SHELLY: I don't know! I mean I can't just come right out and tell you how he feels.
TILDEN: How come?

[TILDEN *keeps moving around her slowly in a circle.*]

SHELLY: Because it's stuff he told me privately!
TILDEN: And you can't tell me?
SHELLY: I don't even know you!
DODGE: Tilden, go out in the kitchen and make me some coffee! Leave the girl alone.
SHELLY [*to* DODGE]: He's all right.

[TILDEN *ignores* DODGE, *keeps moving around* SHELLY. *He stares at her hair and coat.* DODGE *stares at T.V.*]

TILDEN: You mean you can't tell me anything?
SHELLY: I can tell you some things. I mean we can have a conversation.
TILDEN: We can?
SHELLY: Sure. We're having a conversation right now.
TILDEN: We are?
SHELLY: Yes. That's what we're doing.
TILDEN: But there's certain things you can't tell me, right?
SHELLY: Right.
TILDEN: There's certain things I can't tell you either.
SHELLY: How come?
TILDEN: I don't know. Nobody's supposed to hear it.
SHELLY: Well, you can tell me anything you want to.
TILDEN: I can?
SHELLY: Sure.
TILDEN: It might not be very nice.
SHELLY: That's all right. I've been around.
TILDEN: It might be awful.
SHELLY: Well, can't you tell me anything nice?

[TILDEN *stops in front of her and stares at her coat.* SHELLY *looks back at him. Long pause.*]

TILDEN [*after pause*]: Can I touch your coat?
SHELLY: My coat? [*she looks at her coat then back to* TILDEN] Sure.
TILDEN: You don't mind?
SHELLY: No. Go ahead.

[SHELLY *holds her arm out for* TILDEN *to touch.* DODGE *stays fixed on T.V.* TILDEN *moves in slowly toward* SHELLY, *staring at her arm. He reaches out very slowly and touches her arm, feels the fur gently then draws his hand back.* SHELLY *keeps her arm out.*]

SHELLY: It's rabbit.
TILDEN: Rabbit.

[*He reaches out again very slowly and touches the fur on her arm then pulls back his hand again.* SHELLY *drops her arm.*]

SHELLY: My arm was getting tired.
TILDEN: Can I hold it?
SHELLY [*pause*]: The coat? Sure.

[SHELLY *takes off her coat and hands it to* TILDEN. TILDEN *takes it slowly, feels the fur then puts it on.* SHELLY *watches as* TILDEN *strokes the fur slowly. He smiles at her. She goes back to cutting carrots.*]

SHELLY: You can have it if you want.
TILDEN: I can?
SHELLY: Yeah. I've got a raincoat in the car. That's all I need.

TILDEN: You've got a car?
SHELLY: Vince does.

[TILDEN *walks around stroking the fur and smiling at the coat.* SHELLY *watches him when he's not looking.* DODGE *sticks with T.V., stretches out on sofa wrapped in blanket.*]

TILDEN [*as he walks around*]: I had a car once! I had a white car! I drove. I went everywhere. I went to the mountains. I drove in the snow.
SHELLY: That must've been fun.
TILDEN [*still moving, feeling coat*]: I drove all day long sometimes. Across the desert. Way out across the desert. I drove past towns. Anywhere. Past palm trees. Lightning. Anything. I would drive through it. I would drive through it and I would stop and I would look around and I would drive on. I would get back in and drive! I loved to drive. There was nothing I loved more. Nothing I dreamed of was better than driving.
DODGE [*eyes on T.V.*]: Pipe down would ya'!

[TILDEN *stops. Stares at* SHELLY.]

SHELLY: Do you do much driving now?
TILDEN: Now? Now? I don't drive now.
SHELLY: How come?
TILDEN: I'm grown up now.
SHELLY: Grown up?
TILDEN: I'm not a kid.
SHELLY: You don't have to be a kid to drive.
TILDEN: It wasn't driving then.
SHELLY: What was it?
TILDEN: Adventure. I went everywhere.
SHELLY: Well you can still do that.
TILDEN: Not now.
SHELLY: Why not?
TILDEN: I just told you. You don't understand anything. If I told you something you wouldn't understand it.
SHELLY: Told me what?
TILDEN: Told you something that's true.
SHELLY: Like what?
TILDEN: Like a baby. Like a little tiny baby.
SHELLY: Like when you were little?
TILDEN: If I told you you'd make me give your coat back.
SHELLY: I won't. I promise. Tell me.
TILDEN: I can't. Dodge won't let me.
SHELLY: He won't hear you. It's okay.

[*Pause.* TILDEN *stares at her. Moves slightly toward her.*]

TILDEN: We had a baby. [*motioning to* DODGE] He did. Dodge did. Could pick it up with one hand. Put it in the other. Little baby. Dodge killed it.

[SHELLY *stands.*]

TILDEN: Don't stand up. Don't stand up!

[SHELLY *sits again.* DODGE *sits up on sofa and looks at them*]

TILDEN: Dodge drowned it.
SHELLY: Don't tell me anymore! Okay?

[TILDEN *moves closer to her.* DODGE *takes more interest.*]

DODGE: Tilden? You leave that girl alone!
TILDEN [*pays no attention*]: Never told Halie. Never told anybody. Just drowned it.
DODGE [*shuts off T.V.*]: Tilden!
TILDEN: Nobody could find it. Just disappeared. Cops looked for it. Neighbors. Nobody could find it.

[DODGE *struggles to get up from sofa.*]

DODGE: Tilden, what're you telling her! Tilden!

[DODGE *keeps struggling until he's standing.*]

TILDEN: Finally everybody just gave up. Just stopped looking. Everybody had a different answer. Kidnap. Murder. Accident. Some kind of accident.

[DODGE *struggles to walk toward* TILDEN *and falls.* TILDEN *ignores him.*]

DODGE: Tilden you shut up! You shut up about it!

[DODGE *starts coughing on the floor.* SHELLY *watches him from the stool.*]

TILDEN: Little tiny baby just disappeared. It's not hard. It's so small. Almost invisible.

[SHELLY *makes a move to help* DODGE. TILDEN *firmly pushes her back down on the stool.* DODGE *keeps coughing.*]

TILDEN: He said he had his reasons. Said it went a long way back. But he wouldn't tell anybody.
DODGE: Tilden! Don't tell her anything! Don't tell her!
TILDEN: He's the only one who knows where it's buried. The only one. Like a secret buried treasure. Won't tell any of us. Won't tell me or mother or even Bradley. Especially Bradley. Bradley tried to force it out of him but he wouldn't tell. Wouldn't even tell why he did it. One night he just did it.

[DODGE'S *coughing subsides.* SHELLY *stays on stool staring at* DODGE. TILDEN *slowly takes* SHELLY'S *coat off and holds it out to her. Long pause.* SHELLY *sits there trembling.*]

TILDEN: You probably want your coat back now.

[SHELLY *stares at coat but doesn't move to take it. The sound of* BRADLEY'S *leg squeaking is heard off left. The others on stage remain still.* BRADLEY *appears up left outside the screen door wearing a yellow rain slicker. He enters through screen door, crosses porch to stage right door and enters stage. Closes door. Takes off rain slicker and shakes it out. He sees all the others and stops.* TILDEN *turns to him.* BRADLEY *stares at* SHELLY. DODGE *remains on floor.*]

BRADLEY: What's going on here? [*motioning to* SHELLY] Who's that?

[SHELLY *stands, moves back away from* BRADLEY *as he crosses toward her. He stops next to* TILDEN. *He sees coat in* TILDEN'S *hand and grabs it away from him.*]

BRADLEY: Who's she supposed to be?
TILDEN: She's driving to New Mexico.

[BRADLEY *stares at her.* SHELLY *is frozen.* BRADLEY *limps over to her with the coat in his fist. He stops in front of her.*]

BRADLEY [*to* SHELLY, *after pause*]: Vacation?

[SHELLY *shakes her head "no," trembling.*]

BRADLEY [*to* SHELLY, *motioning to* TILDEN]: You taking him with you?

[SHELLY *shakes her head "no."* BRADLEY *crosses back to* TILDEN.]

BRADLEY: You oughta'. No use leaving him here. Doesn't do a lick a' work. Doesn't raise a finger. [*stopping, to* TILDEN] Do ya'? [*to* SHELLY] 'Course he used to be an All American. Quarterback or Fullback or somethin'. He tell you that?

[SHELLY *shakes her head "no."*]

BRADLEY: Yeah, he used to be a big deal. Wore lettermen's sweaters. Had medals hanging all around his neck. Real purty. Big deal. [*he laughs to himself, notices* DODGE *on floor, crosses to him, stops*] This one too. [*to* SHELLY] You'd never think it to look at him would ya'? All bony and wasted away.

[SHELLY *shakes her head again.* BRADLEY *stares at her, crosses back to her, clenching the coat in his fist. He stops in front of* SHELLY.]

BRADLEY: Women like that kinda' thing don't they?
SHELLY: What?
BRADLEY: Importance. Importance in a man?
SHELLY: I don't know.
BRADLEY: Yeah. You know, you know. Don't give me that. [*moves closer to* SHELLY] You're with Tilden?
SHELLY: No.
BRADLEY [*turning to* TILDEN]: Tilden! She with you?

[TILDEN *doesn't answer. Stares at floor.*]

BRADLEY: Tilden!

[TILDEN *suddenly bolts and runs off up stage left.* BRADLEY *laughs. Talks to* SHELLY. DODGE *starts moving his lips silently as though talking to someone invisible on the floor.*]

BRADLEY [*laughing*]: Scared to death! He was always scared!

[BRADLEY *stops laughing. Stares at* SHELLY.]

BRADLEY: You're scared too, right? [*laughs again*] You're scared and you don't even know me. [*stops laughing*] You don't gotta be scared.

[SHELLY *looks at* DODGE *on the floor.*]

SHELLY: Can't we do something for him?
BRADLEY [*looking at* DODGE]: We could shoot him. [*laughs*] We could drown him! What about drowning him?
SHELLY: Shut up!

[BRADLEY *stops laughing. Moves in closer to* SHELLY. *She freezes.* BRADLEY *speaks slowly and deliberately.*]

BRADLEY: Hey! Missus. Don't talk to me like that. Don't talk to me in that tone a' voice. There was a time when I had to take that tone a' voice from pretty near everyone. [*motioning to* DODGE] Him, for one! Him and that half brain that just ran outa' here. They don't talk to me like that now. Not any more. Everything's turned around now. Full circle. Isn't that funny?
SHELLY: I'm sorry.
BRADLEY: Open your mouth.
SHELLY: What?
BRADLEY [*motioning for her to open her mouth*]: Open up.

[*She opens her mouth slightly.*]

BRADLEY: Wider.

[*She opens her mouth wider.*]

BRADLEY: Keep it like that.

[*She does. Stares at* BRADLEY. *With his free hand he puts his fingers into her mouth. She tries to pull away.*]

BRADLEY: Just stay put!

[*She freezes. He keeps his fingers in her mouth. Stares at her. Pause. He pulls his hand out. She closes her mouth, keeps her eyes on him.* BRADLEY *smiles. He looks at* DODGE *on the floor and crosses over to him.* SHELLY *watches him closely.* BRADLEY *stands over* DODGE *and smiles at* SHELLY. *He holds her coat up in both hands over* DODGE, *keeps smiling at* SHELLY. *He looks down at* DODGE *then drops the coat so that it lands on* DODGE *and covers his head.* BRADLEY *keeps his hands up in the position of holding the coat, looks over at* SHELLY *and smiles. The lights black out.*]

ACT III

SCENE. *Same set. Morning. Bright sun. No sound of rain. Everything has been cleared up again. No sign of carrots. No pail. No stool.* VINCE*'s saxophone case and overcoat are still at the foot of the staircase.* BRADLEY *is asleep on the sofa under* DODGE*'s blanket. His head toward stage left.* BRADLEY*'s wooden leg is leaning against the sofa right by his head. The shoe is left on it. The harness hangs down.* DODGE *is sitting on the floor, propped up against the T.V. set facing stage left wearing his baseball cap.* SHELLY*'s rabbit fur coat covers his chest and shoulders. He stares off toward stage left. He seems weaker and more disoriented. The lights rise slowly to the sound of birds and remain for a while in silence on the two men.* BRADLEY *sleeps very soundly.* DODGE *hardly moves.* SHELLY *appears from stage left with a big smile, slowly crossing toward* DODGE *balancing a steaming cup of broth in a saucer.* DODGE *just stares at her as she gets closer to him.*

SHELLY [*as she crosses*]: This is going to make all the difference in the world, Grandpa. You don't mind me calling you Grandpa do you? I mean I know you minded when Vince called you that but you don't even know him.

DODGE: He skipped town with my money ya' know. I'm gonna hold you as collateral.

SHELLY: He'll be back. Don't you worry.

[*She kneels down next to* DODGE *and puts the cup and saucer in his lap.*]

DODGE: It's morning already! Not only didn't I get my bottle but he's got my two bucks!

SHELLY: Try to drink this, okay? Don't spill it.

DODGE: What is it?

SHELLY: Beef bouillon. It'll warm you up.

DODGE: Bouillon! I don't want any goddamn bouillon! Get that stuff away from me!

SHELLY: I just got through making it.

DODGE: I don't care if you just spent all week making it! I ain't drinking it!

SHELLY: Well, what am I supposed to do with it then? I'm trying to help you out. Besides, it's good for you.

DODGE: Get it away from me!

[SHELLY *stands up with cup and saucer.*]

DODGE: What do you know what's good for me anyway?

[*She looks at* DODGE *then turns away from him, crossing to staircase, sits on bottom step and drinks the bouillon.* DODGE *stares at her.*]

DODGE: You know what'd be good for me?

SHELLY: What?

DODGE: A little massage. A little contact.

SHELLY: Oh no. I've had enough contact for a while. Thanks anyway.

[*She keeps sipping bouillon, stays sitting. Pause as* DODGE *stares at her.*]

DODGE: Why not? You got nothing better to do. That fella's not gonna be back here. You're not expecting him to show up again are you?

SHELLY: Sure. He'll show up. He left his horn here.

DODGE: His horn? [*laughs*] You're his horn!

SHELLY: Very funny.

DODGE: He's run off with my money? He's not coming back. There.

SHELLY: He'll be back.

DODGE: You're a funny chicken, you know that?

SHELLY: Thanks.

DODGE: Full of faith. Hope. Faith and hope. You're all alike you hopers. If it's not God then it's a man. If it's not a man then it's a woman. If it's not a woman then it's the land or the future of some kind. Some kind of future.

[*Pause.*]

SHELLY [*looking toward porch*]: I'm glad it stopped raining.

DODGE [*looks toward porch then back to her*]: That's what I mean. See, you're glad it stopped raining. Now you think everything's gonna be different. Just 'cause the sun comes out.

SHELLY: It's already different. Last night I was scared.

DODGE: Scared a' what?

SHELLY: Just scared.

DODGE: Bradley? [*looks at* BRADLEY] He's a push-over. 'Specially now. All ya' gotta' do is take his leg and throw it out the back door. Helpless. Totally helpless.

[SHELLY *turns and stares at* BRADLEY'*s wooden leg then looks at* DODGE. *She sips bouillon.*]

SHELLY: You'd do that?

DODGE: Me? I've hardly got the strength to breathe.

SHELLY: But you'd actually do it if you could?

DODGE: Don't be so easily shocked, girlie. There's nothing a man can't do. You dream it up and he can do it. Anything.

SHELLY: You've tried I guess.

DODGE: Don't sit there sippin' your bouillon and judging me! This is my house!

SHELLY: I forgot.

DODGE: You forgot? Whose house did you think it was?

SHELLY: Mine.

[DODGE *just stares at her. Long pause. She sips from cup.*]

SHELLY: I know it's not mine but I had that feeling.

DODGE: What feeling?

SHELLY: The feeling that nobody lives here but me. I mean everybody's gone. You're here, but it doesn't seem like you're supposed to be. [*pointing to* BRADLEY] Doesn't seem like he's supposed to be here either. I don't know what it is. It's the house or something. Something familiar. Like I know my way around here. Did you ever get that feeling?

[DODGE *stares at her in silence. Pause.*]

DODGE: No. No, I never did.

[SHELLY *gets up. Moves around space holding cup.*]

SHELLY: Last night I went to sleep up there in that room.

DODGE: What room?

SHELLY: That room up there with all the pictures. All the crosses on the wall.

DODGE: Halie's room?

SHELLY: Yeah. Whoever "Halie" is.

DODGE: She's my wife.

SHELLY: So you remember her?

DODGE: Whad'ya mean! 'Course I remember her! She's only been gone for a day—half a day. However long it's been.

SHELLY: Do you remember her when her hair was bright red? Standing in front of an apple tree?

DODGE: What is this, the third degree or something! Who're you to be askin' me personal questions about my wife!

SHELLY: You never look at those pictures up there?

DODGE: What pictures!

SHELLY: Your whole life's up there hanging on the wall. Somebody who looks just like you. Somebody who looks just like you used to look.

DODGE: That isn't me! That never was me! This is me. Right here. This is it. The whole shootin' match, sittin' right in front of you.

SHELLY: So the past never happened as far as you're concerned?

DODGE: The past? Jesus Christ. The past. What do you know about the past?

SHELLY: Not much. I know there was a farm.

[*Pause.*]

DODGE: A farm?

SHELLY: There's a picture of a farm. A big farm. A bull. Wheat. Corn.

DODGE: Corn?

SHELLY: All the kids are standing out in the corn. They're all waving these big straw hats. One of them doesn't have a hat.

DODGE: Which one was that?

SHELLY: There's a baby. A baby in a woman's arms. The same woman with the red hair. She looks lost standing out there. Like she doesn't know how she got there.

DODGE: She knows! I told her a hundred times it wasn't gonna' be the city! I gave her plenty a' warning.

SHELLY: She's looking down at the baby like it was somebody else's. Like it didn't even belong to her.

DODGE: That's about enough outa' you! You got some funny ideas. Some damn funny ideas. You think just because people propagate they have to love their offspring? You never seen a bitch eat her puppies? Where are you from anyway?

SHELLY: L.A. We already went through that.

DODGE: That's right, L.A. I remember.

SHELLY: Stupid country.

DODGE: That's right! No wonder.

[*Pause.*]

SHELLY: What's happened to this family anyway?

DODGE: You're in no position to ask! What do you care? You some kinda' Social Worker?

SHELLY: I'm Vince's friend.

DODGE: Vince's friend! That's rich. That's really rich. "Vince"! "Mr. Vince"! "Mr. Thief" is more like it! His name doesn't mean a hoot in hell to me. Not a tinkle in the well. You know how many kids I've spawned? Not to mention Grand kids and Great Grand kids and Great Great Grand kids after them?

SHELLY: And you don't remember any of them?

DODGE: What's to remember? Halie's the one with the family album. She's the one you should talk to. She'll set you straight on the heritage if that's what you're interested in. She's traced it all the way back to the grave.

SHELLY: What do you mean?

DODGE: What do you think I mean? How far back can you go? A long line of corpses! There's not a living soul behind me. Not a one. Who's holding me in their memory? Who gives a damn about bones in the ground?

SHELLY: Was Tilden telling the truth?

[DODGE *stops short. Stares at* SHELLY. *Shakes his head. He looks off stage left.*]

SHELLY: Was he?

[DODGE*'s tone changes drastically.*]

DODGE: Tilden? [*turns to* SHELLY, *calmly*] Where is Tilden?

SHELLY: Last night. Was he telling the truth about the baby?

[*Pause.*]

DODGE [*turns toward stage left*]: What's happened to Tilden? Why isn't Tilden here?

SHELLY: Bradley chased him out.

DODGE [*looking at* BRADLEY *asleep*]: Bradley? Why is he on my sofa? [*turns back to* SHELLY] Have I been here all night? On the floor?

SHELLY: He wouldn't leave. I hid outside until he fell asleep.

DODGE: Outside? Is Tilden outside? He shouldn't be out there in the rain. He'll get himself into trouble. He doesn't know his way around here anymore. Not like he used to. He went out West and got himself into trouble. Got himself into bad trouble. We don't want any of that around here.

SHELLY: What did he do?

[*Pause.*]

DODGE [*quietly stares at* SHELLY]: Tilden? He got mixed up. That's what he did. We can't afford to leave him alone. Not now.

[*Sound of* HALIE *laughing comes from off left.* SHELLY *stands, looking in direction of voice, holding cup and saucer, doesn't know whether to stay or run.*]

DODGE [*motioning to* SHELLY]: Sit down! Sit back down!

[SHELLY *sits. Sound of* HALIE*'s laughter again.*]

DODGE [*to* SHELLY *in a heavy whisper, pulling coat up around him*]: Don't leave me alone now! Promise me? Don't go off and leave me alone. I need somebody here with me. Tilden's gone now and I need someone. Don't leave me! Promise!

SHELLY [*sitting*]: I won't.

[HALIE *appears outside the screen porch door, up left with* FATHER DEWIS. *She is wearing a bright yellow dress, no hat, white gloves and her arms are full of yellow roses.* FATHER DEWIS *is dressed in traditional black suit, white clerical collar and shirt. He is a very distinguished grey haired man in his sixties. They are both slightly drunk and feeling giddy. As they enter the porch through the screen door,* DODGE *pulls the rabbit fur coat over his head and hides.* SHELLY *stands again.* DODGE *drops the coat and whispers intensely to* SHELLY. *Neither* HALIE *nor* FATHER DEWIS *are aware of the people inside the house.*]

DODGE [*to* SHELLY *in a strong whisper*]: You promised!

[SHELLY *sits on stairs again.* DODGE *pulls coat back over his head.* HALIE *and* FATHER DEWIS *talk on the porch as they cross toward stage right interior door.*]

HALIE: Oh Father! That's terrible! That's absolutely terrible. Aren't you afraid of being punished?

[*She giggles.*]

DEWIS: Not by the Italians. They're too busy punishing each other.

[*They both break out in giggles.*]

HALIE: What about God?

DEWIS: Well, prayerfully, God only hears what he wants to. That's just between you and me of course. In our heart of hearts we know we're every bit as wicked as the Catholics.

[*They giggle again and reach the stage right door.*]

HALIE: Father, I never heard you talk like this in Sunday sermon.
DEWIS: Well, I save all my best jokes for private company. Pearls before swine you know.

[*They enter the room laughing and stop when they see* SHELLY. SHELLY *stands.* HALIE *closes the door behind* FATHER DEWIS. DODGE*'s voice is heard under the coat, talking to* SHELLY.]

DODGE [*under coat, to* SHELLY]: Sit down, sit down! Don't let 'em buffalo you!

[SHELLY *sits on stair again.* HALIE *looks at* DODGE *on the floor then looks at* BRADLEY *asleep on sofa and sees his wooden leg. She lets out a shriek of embarrassment for* FATHER DEWIS.]

HALIE: Oh my gracious! What in the name of Judas Priest is going on in this house!

[*She hands over the roses to* FATHER DEWIS.]

HALIE: Excuse me Father.

[HALIE *crosses to* DODGE, *whips the coat off him and covers the wooden leg with it.* BRADLEY *stays asleep.*]

HALIE: You can't leave this house for a second without the Devil blowing in through the front door!
DODGE: Gimme back that coat! Gimmie back that goddamn coat before I freeze to death!
HALIE: You're not going to freeze! The sun's out in case you hadn't noticed!
DODGE: Gimme back that coat! That coat's for live flesh not dead wood!

[HALIE *whips the blanket off* BRADLEY *and throws it on* DODGE. DODGE *covers his head again with blanket.* BRADLEY*'s amputated leg can be faked by having half of it under a cushion of the sofa. He's fully clothed.* BRADLEY *sits up with a jerk when the blanket comes off him.*]

HALIE [*as she tosses blanket*]: Here! Use this! It's yours anyway! Can't you take care of yourself for once!
BRADLEY [*yelling at* HALIE]: Gimme that blanket! Gimme back that blanket! That's my blanket!

[HALIE *crosses back toward* FATHER DEWIS *who just stands there with the roses.* BRADLEY *thrashes helplessly on the sofa trying to reach blanket.* DODGE *hides himself deeper in blanket.* SHELLY *looks on from staircase, still holding cup and saucer.*]

HALIE: Believe me, Father, this is not what I had in mind when I invited you in.
DEWIS: Oh, no apologies please. I wouldn't be in the ministry if I couldn't face real life.

[*He laughs self-consciously.* HALIE *notices* SHELLY *again and crosses over to her.* SHELLY *stays sitting.* HALIE *stops and stares at her.*]

BRADLEY: I want my blanket back! Gimme my blanket!

[HALIE *turns toward* BRADLEY *and silences him.*]

HALIE: Shut up, Bradley! Right this minute! I've had enough!

[BRADLEY *slowly recoils, lies back down on sofa, turns his back toward* HALIE *and whimpers softly.* HALIE *directs her attention to* SHELLY *again. Pause.*]

HALIE [*to* SHELLY]: What're you doing with my cup and saucer?
SHELLY [*looking at cup, back to* HALIE]: I made some bouillon for Dodge.
HALIE: For Dodge?
SHELLY: Yeah.
HALIE: Well, did he drink it?
SHELLY: No.
HALIE: Did you drink it?
SHELLY: Yes.

[HALIE *stares at her. Long pause. She turns abruptly away from* SHELLY *and crosses back to* FATHER DEWIS.]

HALIE: Father, there's a stranger in my house. What would you advise? What would be the Christian thing?
DEWIS [*squirming*]: Oh, well. . . . I . . . I really—
HALIE: We still have some whiskey, don't we?

[DODGE *slowly pulls the blanket down off his head and looks toward* FATHER DEWIS. SHELLY *stands.*]

SHELLY: Listen, I don't drink or anything. I just—

[HALIE *turns toward* SHELLY *viciously.*]

HALIE: You sit back down!

[SHELLY *sits again on stair.* HALIE *turns again to* DEWIS.]

HALIE: I think we have plenty of whiskey left! Don't we Father?
DEWIS: Well, yes. I think so. You'll have to get it. My hands are full.

[HALIE *giggles. Reaches into* DEWIS'S *pockets, searching for bottle. She smells the roses as she searches.* DEWIS *stands stiffly.* DODGE *watches* HALIE *closely as she looks for bottle.*]

HALIE: The most incredible things, roses! Aren't they incredible, Father?

DEWIS: Yes. Yes they are.

HALIE: They almost cover the stench of sin in this house. Just magnificent! The smell. We'll have to put some at the foot of Ansel's statue. On the day of the unveiling.

[HALIE *finds a silver flask of whiskey in* DEWIS'S *vest pocket. She pulls it out.* DODGE *looks on eagerly.* HALIE *crosses to* DODGE, *opens the flask and takes a sip.*]

HALIE [*to* DODGE]: Ansel's getting a statue, Dodge. Did you know that? Not a plaque but a real live statue. A full bronze. Tip to toe. A basketball in one hand and a rifle in the other.

BRADLEY [*his back to* HALIE]: He never played basketball!

HALIE: You shut up, Bradley! You shut up about Ansel! Ansel played basketball better than anyone! And you know it! He was an All American! There's no reason to take the glory away from others.

[HALIE *turns away from* BRADLEY, *crosses back toward* DEWIS *sipping on the flask and smiling.*]

HALIE [*to* DEWIS]: Ansel was a great basketball player. One of the greatest.

DEWIS: I remember Ansel.

HALIE: Of course! You remember. You remember how he could play. [*she turns toward* SHELLY] Of course, nowadays they play a different brand of basketball. More vicious. Isn't that right, dear?

SHELLY: I don't know.

[HALIE *crosses to* SHELLY, *sipping on flask. She stops in front of* SHELLY.]

HALIE: Much, much more vicious. They smash into each other. They knock each other's teeth out. There's blood all over the court. Savages.

[HALIE *takes the cup from* SHELLY *and pours whiskey into it.*]

HALIE: They don't train like they used to. Not at all. They allow themselves to run amuck. Drugs and women. Women mostly.

[HALIE *hands the cup of whiskey back to* SHELLY *slowly.* SHELLY *takes it.*]

HALIE: Mostly women. Girls. Sad, pathetic little girls. [*she crosses back to* FATHER DEWIS] It's just a reflection of the times, don't you think Father? An indication of where we stand?

DEWIS: I suppose so, yes.

HALIE: Yes. A sort of a bad omen. Our youth becoming monsters.

DEWIS: Well, I uh—

HALIE: Oh you can disagree with me if you want to, Father. I'm open to debate. I think argument only enriches both sides of the question don't you? [*she moves toward* DODGE] I suppose, in the long run, it doesn't matter. When you see the way things deteriorate before your very eyes. Everything running down hill. It's kind of silly to even think about youth.

DEWIS: No, I don't think so. I think it's important to believe in certain things.

HALIE: Yes. Yes, I know what you mean. I think that's right. I think that's true. [*she looks at* DODGE] Certain basic things. We can't shake certain basic things. We might end up crazy. Like my husband. You can see it in his eyes. You can see how mad he is.

[DODGE *covers his head with the blanket again.* HALIE *takes a single rose from* DEWIS *and moves slowly over to* DODGE.]

HALIE: We can't not believe in something. We can't stop believing. We just end up dying if we stop. Just end up dead.

[HALIE *throws the rose gently onto* DODGE'S *blanket. It lands between his knees and stays there. Long pause as* HALIE *stares at the rose.* SHELLY *stands suddenly.* HALIE *doesn't turn to her but keeps staring at rose.*]

SHELLY [*to* HALIE]: Don't you wanna' know who I am! Don't you wanna know what I'm doing here! I'm not dead!

[SHELLY *crosses toward* HALIE. HALIE *turns slowly toward her.*]

HALIE: Did you drink your whiskey?

SHELLY: No! And I'm not going to either!

HALIE: Well that's a firm stand. It's good to have a firm stand.

SHELLY: I don't have any stand at all. I'm just trying to put all this together.

[HALIE *laughs and crosses back to* DEWIS.]

HALIE [*to* DEWIS]: Surprises, surprises! Did you have any idea we'd be returning to this?
SHELLY: I came here with your Grandson for a little visit! A little innocent friendly visit.
HALIE: My Grandson?
SHELLY: Yes! That's right. The one no one remembers.
HALIE [*to* DEWIS]: This is getting a little far fetched.
SHELLY: I told him it was stupid to come back here. To try to pick up from where he left off.
HALIE: Where was that?
SHELLY: Wherever he was when he left here! Six years ago! Ten years ago! Whenever it was. I told him nobody cares.
HALIE: Didn't he listen?
SHELLY: No! No he didn't. We had to stop off at every tiny little meatball town that he remembered from his boyhood! Every stupid little donut shop he ever kissed a girl in. Every Drive-In. Every Drag Strip. Every football field he ever broke a bone on.
HALIE [*suddenly alarmed, to* DODGE]: Where's Tilden?
SHELLY: Don't ignore me!
HALIE: Dodge! Where's Tilden gone?

[SHELLY *moves violently toward* HALIE.]

SHELLY [*to* HALIE]: I'm talking to you!

[BRADLEY *sits up fast on the sofa,* SHELLY *backs away.*]

BRADLEY [*to* SHELLY]: Don't you yell at my mother!
HALIE: Dodge! [*she kicks* DODGE] I told you not to let Tilden out of your sight! Where's he gone to?
DODGE: Gimme a drink and I'll tell ya'.
DEWIS: Halie, maybe this isn't the right time for a visit.

[HALIE *crosses back to* DEWIS.]

HALIE [*to* DEWIS]: I never should've left. I never, never should've left! Tilden could be anywhere by now! Anywhere! He's not in control of his faculties. Dodge knew that. I told him when I left here. I told him specifically to watch out for Tilden.

[BRADLEY *reaches down, grabs* DODGE*'s blanket and yanks it off him. He lays down on sofa and pulls the blanket over his head.*]

DODGE: He's got my blanket again! He's got my blanket!
HALIE [*turning to* BRADLEY]: Bradley! Bradley, put that blanket back!

[HALIE *moves toward* BRADLEY. SHELLY *suddenly throws the cup and saucer against the stage right door.* DEWIS *ducks. The cup and saucer smash into pieces.* HALIE *stops, turns toward* SHELLY. *Everyone freezes.* BRADLEY *slowly pulls his head out from under blanket, looks toward stage right door, then to* SHELLY. SHELLY *stares at* HALIE. DEWIS *cowers with roses.* SHELLY *moves slowly toward* HALIE. *Long pause.* SHELLY *speaks softly.*]

SHELLY [*to* HALIE]: I don't like being ignored. I don't like being treated like I'm not here. I didn't like it when I was a kid and I still don't like it.
BRADLEY [*sitting up on sofa*]: We don't have to tell you anything, girl. Not a thing. You're not the police are you? You're not the government. You're just some prostitute that Tilden brought in here.
HALIE: Language! I won't have that language in my house!
SHELLY [*to* BRADLEY]: You stuck your hand in my mouth and you call me a prostitute!
HALIE: Bradley! Did you put your hand in her mouth? I'm ashamed of you. I can't leave you alone for a minute.
BRADLEY: I never did. She's lying!
DEWIS: Halie, I think I'll be running along now. I'll just put the roses in the kitchen.

[DEWIS *moves toward stage left.* HALIE *stops him.*]

HALIE: Don't go now, Father! Not now.
BRADLEY: I never did anything, mom! I never touched her! She propositioned me! And I turned her down. I turned her down flat!

[SHELLY *suddenly grabs her coat off the wooden leg and takes both the leg and coat down stage, away from* BRADLEY.]

BRADLEY: Mom! Mom! She's got my leg! She's taken my leg! I never did anything to her! She's stolen my leg!

[BRADLEY *reaches pathetically in the air for his leg.* SHELLY *sets it down for a second, puts on her coat fast and picks the leg up again.* DODGE *starts coughing softly.*]

HALIE [*to* SHELLY]: I think we've had about enough of you young lady. Just about enough. I don't know where you came from or what you're doing here but you're no longer welcome in this house.
SHELLY [*laughs, holds leg*]: No longer welcome!
BRADLEY: Mom! That's my leg! Get my leg back! I can't do anything without my leg.

[BRADLEY *keeps making whimpering sounds and reaching for his leg.*]

HALIE: Give my son back his leg. Right this very minute!

[DODGE *starts laughing softly to himself in between coughs.*]

HALIE [*to* DEWIS]: Father, do something about this would you! I'm not about to be terrorized in my own house!

BRADLEY: Gimme back my leg!

HALIE: Oh, shut up Bradley! Just shut up! You don't need your leg now! Just lay down and shut up!

[BRADLEY *whimpers. Lays down and pulls blanket around him. He keeps one arm outside blanket, reaching out toward his wooden leg.* DEWIS *cautiously approaches* SHELLY *with the roses in his arms.* SHELLY *clutches the wooden leg to her chest as though she's kidnapped it.*]

DEWIS [*to* SHELLY]: Now, honestly dear, wouldn't it be better to try to talk things out? To try to use some reason?

SHELLY: There isn't any reason here! I can't find a reason for anything.

DEWIS: There's nothing to be afraid of. These are all good people. All righteous people.

SHELLY: I'm not afraid!

DEWIS: But this isn't your house. You have to have some respect.

SHELLY: You're the strangers here, not me.

HALIE: This has gone far enough!

DEWIS: Halie, please. Let me handle this.

SHELLY: Don't come near me! Don't anyone come near me. I don't need any words from you. I'm not threatening anybody. I don't even know what I'm doing here. You all say you don't remember Vince, okay, maybe you don't. Maybe it's Vince that's crazy. Maybe he's made this whole family thing up. I don't even care anymore. I was just coming along for the ride. I thought it'd be a nice gesture. Besides, I was curious. He made all of you sound familiar to me. Every one of you. For every name, I had an image. Every time he'd tell me a name, I'd see the person. In fact, each of you was so clear in my mind that I actually believed it was you. I really believed when I walked through that door that the people who lived here would turn out to be the same people in my imagination. But I don't recognize any of you. Not one. Not even the slightest resemblance.

DEWIS: Well you can hardly blame others for not fulfilling your hallucination.

SHELLY: It was no hallucination! It was more like a prophecy. You believe in prophecy, don't you?

HALIE: Father, there's no point in talking to her any further. We're just going to have to call the police.

BRADLEY: No! Don't get the police in here. We don't want the police in here. This is our home.

SHELLY: That's right. Bradley's right. Don't you usually settle your affairs in private? Don't you usually take them out in the dark? Out in the back?

BRADLEY: You stay out of our lives! You have no business interfering!

SHELLY: I don't have any business period. I got nothing to lose.

[*She moves around, staring at each of them.*]

BRADLEY: You don't know what we've been through. You don't know anything!

SHELLY: I know you've got a secret. You've all got a secret. It's so secret in fact, you're all convinced it never happened.

[HALIE *moves to* DEWIS.]

HALIE: Oh, my God, Father!

DODGE [*laughing to himself*]: She thinks she's going to get it out of us. She thinks she's going to uncover the truth of the matter. Like a detective or something.

BRADLEY: I'm not telling her anything! Nothing's wrong here! Nothing's ever been wrong! Everything's the way it's supposed to be! Nothing ever happened that's bad! Everything is all right here! We're all good people!

DODGE: She thinks she's gonna suddenly bring everything out into the open after all these years.

DEWIS [*to* SHELLY]: Can't you see that these people want to be left in peace? Don't you have any mercy? They haven't done anything to you.

DODGE: She wants to get to the bottom of it. [*to* SHELLY] That's it, isn't it? You'd like to get right down to bedrock? You want me to tell ya'? You want me to tell ya' what happened? I'll tell ya'. I might as well.

BRADLEY: No! Don't listen to him. He doesn't remember anything!

DODGE: I remember the whole thing from start to finish. I remember the day he was born.

[*Pause.*]

HALIE: Dodge, if you tell this thing—if you tell this, you'll be dead to me. You'll be just as good as dead.

DODGE: That won't be such a big change, Halie. See this girl, this girl here, she wants to know. She wants to know something more. And I got this feeling that it doesn't make a bit a' difference. I'd sooner tell it to a stranger than anybody else.

BRADLEY [*to* DODGE]: We made a pact! We made a pact between us! You can't break that now!

DODGE: I don't remember any pact.

BRADLEY [*to* SHELLY]: See, he doesn't remember anything. I'm the only one in the family who remembers. The only one. And I'll never tell you!

SHELLY: I'm not so sure I want to find out now.

DODGE [*laughing to himself*]: Listen to her! Now she's runnin' scared!

SHELLY: I'm not scared!

[DODGE *stops laughing, long pause.* DODGE *stares at her.*]

DODGE: You're not huh? Well, that's good. Because I'm not either. See, we were a well established family once. Well established. All the boys were grown. The farm was producing enough milk to fill Lake Michigan twice over. Me and Halie here were pointed toward what looked like the middle part of our life. Everything was settled with us. All we had to do was ride it out. Then Halie got pregnant again. Outa' the middle a' nowhere, she got pregnant. We weren't planning on havin' any more boys. We had enough boys already. In fact, we hadn't been sleepin' in the same bed for about six years.

HALIE [*moving toward stairs*]: I'm not listening to this! I don't have to listen to this!

DODGE [*stops* HALIE]: Where are you going! Upstairs! You'll just be listenin' to it upstairs! You go outside, you'll be listenin' to it outside. Might as well stay here and listen to it.

[HALIE *stays by stairs.*]

BRADLEY: If I had my leg you wouldn't be saying this. You'd never get away with it if I had my leg.

DODGE [*pointing to* SHELLY]: She's got your leg. [*laughs*] She's gonna keep your leg too. [*to* SHELLY] She wants to hear this. Don't you?

SHELLY: I don't know.

DODGE: Well even if ya' don't I'm gonna' tell ya'. [*pause*] Halie had this kid. This baby boy. She had it. I let her have it on her own. All the other boys I had had the best doctors, best nurses, everything. This one I let her have by herself. This one hurt real bad. Almost killed her, but she had it anyway. It lived, see. It lived. It wanted to grow up in this family. It wanted to be just like us. It wanted to be a part of us. It wanted to pretend that I was its father. She wanted me to believe in it. Even when everyone around us knew. Everyone. All our boys knew. Tilden knew.

HALIE: You shut up! Bradley, make him shut up!

BRADLEY: I can't.

DODGE: Tilden was the one who knew. Better than any of us. He'd walk for miles with that kid in his arms. Halie let him take it. All night sometimes. He'd walk all night out there in the pasture with it. Talkin' to it. Singin' to it. Used to hear him singing to it. He'd make up stories. He'd tell that kid all kinds a' stories. Even when he knew it couldn't understand him. Couldn't understand a word he was sayin'. Never would understand him. We couldn't let a thing like that continue. We couldn't allow that to grow up right in the middle of our lives. It made everything we'd accomplished look like it was nothin'. Everything was cancelled out by this one mistake. This one weakness.

SHELLY: So you killed him?

DODGE: I killed it. I drowned it. Just like the runt of a litter. Just drowned it.

[HALIE *moves toward* BRADLEY.]

HALIE [*to* BRADLEY]: Ansel would've stopped him! Ansel would've stopped him from telling these lies! He was a hero! A man! A whole man! What's happened to the men in this family! Where are the men!

[*Suddenly* VINCE *comes crashing through the screen porch door up left, tearing it off its hinges. Everyone but* DODGE *and* BRADLEY *back away from the porch and stare at* VINCE *who has landed on his stomach on the porch in a drunken stupor. He is singing loudly to himself and hauls himself slowly to his feet. He has a paper shopping bag full of empty booze bottles. He takes them out one at a time as he sings and smashes them at the opposite end of the porch, behind the solid interior door, stage right.* SHELLY *moves slowly toward stage right, holding wooden leg and watching* VINCE.]

VINCE [*singing loudly as he hurls bottles*]: "From the Halls of Montezuma to the Shores of Tripoli. We will fight our country's battles on the land and on the sea."

[*He punctuates the words "Montezuma," "Tripoli," "battles" and "sea" with a smashed bottle each. He stops throwing for a second, stares toward stage right of the porch, shades his eyes with his hand as though looking across to a battle field, then cups his hands around his mouth and yells across the space of the porch to an imaginary army. The others watch in terror and expectation.*]

VINCE [*to imagined Army*]: Have you had enough over there! 'Cause there's a lot more here where that came from! [*pointing to paper bag full of bottles*] A helluva lot more! We got enough over here to blow ya' from here to Kingdomcome!

[*He takes another bottle, makes high whistling sound of a bomb and throws it toward stage right porch. Sound of bottle smashing against wall. This should be the actual smashing of bottles and not tape sound. He keeps yelling and heaving bottles one after another.* VINCE *stops for a while, breathing heavily from exhaustion. Long silence as the others watch him.* SHELLY *approaches tentatively in* VINCE'S *direction, still holding* BRADLEY'S *wooden leg.*]

SHELLY [*after silence*]: Vince?

[VINCE *turns toward her. Peers through screen.*]

VINCE: Who? What? Vince who? Who's that in there?

[VINCE *pushes his face against the screen from the porch and stares in at everyone.*]

DODGE: Where's my goddamn bottle!
VINCE [*looking in at* DODGE]: What? Who is that?
DODGE: It's me! Your Grandfather! Don't play stupid with me! Where's my two bucks!
VINCE: Your two bucks?

[HALIE *moves away from* DEWIS, *upstage, peers out at* VINCE, *trying to recognize him.*]

HALIE: Vincent? Is that you, Vincent?

[SHELLY *stares at* HALIE *then looks out at* VINCE.]

VINCE [*from porch*]: Vincent who? What is this! Who are you people?
SHELLY [*to* HALIE]: Hey, wait a minute. Wait a minute! What's going on?
HALIE [*moving closer to porch screen*]: We thought you were a murderer or something. Barging in through the door like that.
VINCE: I am a murderer! Don't underestimate me for a minute! I'm the Midnight Strangler! I devour whole families in a single gulp!

[VINCE *grabs another bottle and smashes it on the porch.* HALIE *backs away.*]

SHELLY [*approaching* HALIE]: You mean you know who he is?
HALIE: Of course I know who he is! That's more than I can say for you.
BRADLEY [*sitting up on sofa*]: You get off our front porch you creep! What're you doing out there breaking bottles? Who are these foreigners anyway! Where did they come from?
VINCE: Maybe I should come in there and break them!
HALIE [*moving toward porch*]: Don't you dare! Vincent, what's got into you! Why are you acting like this?
VINCE: Maybe I should come in there and usurp your territory!

[HALIE *turns back toward* DEWIS *and crosses to him.*]

HALIE [*to* DEWIS]: Father, why are you just standing around here when everything's falling apart? Can't you rectify this situation?

[DODGE *laughs, coughs.*]

DEWIS: I'm just a guest here, Halie. I don't know what my position is exactly. This is outside my parish anyway.

[VINCE *starts throwing more bottles as things continue.*]

BRADLEY: If I had my leg I'd rectify it! I'd rectify him all over the goddamn highway! I'd pull his ears out if I could reach him!

[BRADLEY *sticks his fist through the screening of the porch and reaches out for* VINCE, *grabbing at him and missing.* VINCE *jumps away from* BRADLEY'S *hand.*]

VINCE: Aaaah! Our lines have been penetrated! Tentacled animals! Beasts from the deep!

[VINCE *strikes out at* BRADLEY'S *hand with a bottle.* BRADLEY *pulls his hand back inside.*]

SHELLY: Vince! Knock it off will ya'! I want to get out of here!

[VINCE *pushes his face against screen, looks in at* SHELLY.]

VINCE [*to* SHELLY]: Have they got you prisoner in there, dear? Such a sweet young thing too. All her life in front of her. Nipped in the bud.
SHELLY: I'm coming out there, Vince! I'm coming out there and I want us to get in the car and drive away from here. Anywhere. Just away from here.

[SHELLY *moves toward* VINCE'S *saxophone case and overcoat. She sets down the wooden leg, downstage left and picks up the saxophone case and overcoat.* VINCE *watches her through the screen.*]

VINCE [*to* SHELLY]: We'll have to negotiate. Make some kind of a deal. Prisoner exchange or something. A few of theirs for one of ours. Small price to pay if you ask me.

[SHELLY *crosses toward stage right door with overcoat and case.*]

SHELLY: Just go and get the car! I'm coming out there now. We're going to leave.
VINCE: Don't come out here! Don't you dare come out here!

[SHELLY *stops short of the door, stage right.*]

SHELLY: How come?
VINCE: Off limits! Verboten! This is taboo territory. No man or woman has ever crossed the line and lived to tell the tale!
SHELLY: I'll take my chances.

[SHELLY *moves to stage right door and opens it.* VINCE *pulls out a big folding hunting knife and pulls open the blade. He jabs the blade into the screen and starts cutting a hole big enough to climb through.* BRADLEY *cowers in a corner of the sofa as* VINCE *rips at the screen.*]

VINCE [*as he cuts screen*]: Don't come out here! I'm warning you! You'll disintegrate!

[DEWIS *takes* HALIE *by the arm and pulls her toward staircase.*]

DEWIS: Halie, maybe we should go upstairs until this blows over.
HALIE: I don't understand it. I just don't understand it. He was the sweetest little boy!

[DEWIS *drops the roses beside the wooden leg at the foot of the staircase then escorts* HALIE *quickly up the stairs.* HALIE *keeps looking back at* VINCE *as they climb the stairs.*]

HALIE: There wasn't a mean bone in his body. Everyone loved Vincent. Everyone. He was the perfect baby.
DEWIS: He'll be all right after a while. He's just had a few too many that's all.
HALIE: He used to sing in his sleep. He'd sing. In the middle of the night. The sweetest voice. Like an angel. [*she stops for a moment*] I used to lie awake listening to it. I used to lie awake thinking it was all right if I died. Because Vincent was an angel. A guardian angel. He'd watch over us. He'd watch over all of us.

[DEWIS *takes her all the way up the stairs. They disappear above.* VINCE *is now climbing through the porch screen onto the sofa.* BRADLEY *crashes off the sofa, holding tight to his blanket, keeping it wrapped around him.* SHELLY *is outside on the porch.* VINCE *holds the knife in his teeth once he gets the hole wide enough to climb through.* BRADLEY *starts crawling slowly toward his wooden leg, reaching out for it.*]

DODGE [*to* VINCE]: Go ahead! Take over the house! Take over the whole goddamn house! You can have it! It's yours. It's been a pain in the neck ever since the very first mortgage. I'm gonna die any second now. Any second. You won't even notice. So I'll settle my affairs once and for all.

[*As* DODGE *proclaims his last will and testament,* VINCE *climbs into the room, knife in mouth, and strides slowly around the space, inspecting his inheritance. He casually notices* BRADLEY *as he crawls toward his leg.* VINCE *moves to the leg and keeps pushing it with his foot so that it's out of* BRADLEY*'s reach then goes on with his inspection. He picks up the roses and carries them around smelling them.* SHELLY *can be seen outside on the porch, moving slowly center and staring in at* VINCE. VINCE *ignores her.*]

DODGE: The house goes to my Grandson, Vincent. All the furnishings, accoutrements and paraphernalia therein. Everything tacked to the walls or otherwise resting under this roof. My tools—namely my band saw, my skill saw, my drill press, my chain saw, my lathe, my electric sander, all go to my eldest son, Tilden. That is, if he ever shows up again. My shed and gasoline powered equipment, namely my tractor, my dozer, my hand tiller plus all the attachments and riggings for the above mentioned machinery, namely my spring tooth harrow, my deep plows, my disk plows, my automatic fertilizing equipment, my reaper, my swathe, my seeder, my John Deere Harvester, my post hole digger, my jackhammer, my lathe—[*to himself*] Did I mention my lathe? I already mentioned my lathe—my Bennie Goodman records, my harnesses, my bits, my halters, my brace, my rough rasp, my forge, my welding equipment, my shoeing nails, my levels and bevels, my milking stool—no, not my milking stool—my hammers and chisels, my hinges, my cattle gates, my barbed wire, self-tapping augers, my horse hair ropes and all related materials are to be pushed into a gigantic heap and set ablaze in the very center of my fields. When the blaze is at its highest, preferably on a cold, windless night, my body is to be pitched into the middle of it and burned til nothing remains but ash.

[*Pause.* VINCE *takes the knife out of his mouth and smells the roses. He's facing toward audience and doesn't turn around to* SHELLY. *He folds up knife and pockets it.*]

SHELLY [*from porch*]: I'm leaving, Vince. Whether you come or not, I'm leaving.

VINCE [*smelling roses*]: Just put my horn on the couch there before you take off.

SHELLY [*moving toward hole in screen*]: You're not coming?

[VINCE *stays downstage, turns and looks at her.*]

VINCE: I just inherited a house.

SHELLY [*through hole, from porch*]: You want to stay here?

VINCE [*as he pushes* BRADLEY'*s leg out of reach*]: I've gotta carry on the line. I've gotta see to it that things keep rolling.

[BRADLEY *looks up at him from floor, keeps pulling himself toward his leg.* VINCE *keeps moving it.*]

SHELLY: What happened to you Vince? You just disappeared.

VINCE [*pause, delivers speech front*]: I was gonna run last night. I was gonna run and keep right on running. I drove all night. Clear to the Iowa border. The old man's two bucks sitting right on the seat beside me. It never stopped raining the whole time. Never stopped once. I could see myself in the windshield. My face. My eyes. I studied my face. Studied everything about it. As though I was looking at another man. As though I could see his whole race behind him. Like a mummy's face. I saw him dead and alive at the same time. In the same breath. In the windshield, I watched him breathe as though he was frozen in time. And every breath marked him. Marked him forever without him knowing. And then his face changed. His face became his father's face. Same bones. Same eyes. Same nose. Same breath. And his father's face changed to his Grandfather's face. And it went on like that. Changing. Clear on back to faces I'd never seen before but still recognized. Still recognized the bones underneath. The eyes. The breath. The mouth. I followed my family clear into Iowa. Every last one. Straight into the Corn Belt and further. Straight back as far as they'd take me. Then it all dissolved. Everything dissolved.

[SHELLY *stares at him for a while then reaches through the hole in the screen and sets the saxophone case and* VINCE'*s overcoat on the sofa. She looks at* VINCE *again.*]

SHELLY: Bye Vince.

[*She exits left off the porch.* VINCE *watches her go.* BRADLEY *tries to make a lunge for his wooden leg.* VINCE *quickly picks it up and dangles it over* BRADLEY'*s head like a carrot.* BRADLEY *keeps making desperate grabs at the leg.* DEWIS *comes down the staircase and stops half way, staring at* VINCE *and* BRADLEY. VINCE *looks up at* DEWIS *and smiles. He keeps moving backwards with the leg toward upstage left as* BRADLEY *crawls after him.*]

VINCE [*to* DEWIS *as he continues torturing* BRADLEY]: Oh, excuse me Father. Just getting rid of some of the vermin in the house. This is my house now, ya' know? All mine. Everything. Except for the power tools and stuff. I'm gonna get all new equipment anyway. New plows, new tractor, everything. All brand new. [VINCE *teases* BRADLEY *closer to the up left corner of the stage.*] Start right off on the ground floor.

[VINCE *throws* BRADLEY'*s wooden leg far offstage left.* BRADLEY *follows his leg off stage, pulling himself along on the ground, whimpering. As* BRADLEY *exits* VINCE *pulls the blanket off him and throws it over his own shoulder. He crosses toward* DEWIS *with the blanket and smells the roses.* DEWIS *comes to the bottom of the stairs.*]

DEWIS: You'd better go up and see your Grandmother.

VINCE [*looking up stairs, back to* DEWIS]: My Grandmother? There's nobody else in this house. Except for you. And you're leaving aren't you?

[DEWIS *crosses toward stage right door. He turns back to* VINCE.]

DEWIS: She's going to need someone. I can't help her. I don't know what to do. I don't know what my position is. I just came in for some tea. I had no idea there was any trouble. No idea at all.

[VINCE *just stares at him.* DEWIS *goes out the door, crosses porch and exits left.* VINCE *listens to him leaving. He smells roses, looks up the staircase then smells roses again. He turns and looks upstage at* DODGE. *He crosses up to him and bends over looking at* DODGE'*s open eyes.* DODGE *is dead. His death should have come completely unnoticed.* VINCE *lifts the blanket, then covers his head. He sits on the sofa, smelling roses and staring at* DODGE'*s body. Long pause.* VINCE *places the roses on* DODGE'*s chest then lays down on the sofa, arms folded behind his head, staring at the ceiling. His body is in the same relationship to* DODGE'*s. After a while* HALIE'*s voice is heard coming from above the staircase. The lights start to dim almost imperceptibly as* HALIE *speaks.* VINCE *keeps staring at the ceiling.*]

HALIE'S VOICE: Dodge? Is that you Dodge? Tilden was right about the corn you know. I've never seen such corn. Have you taken a look at it lately? Tall as a man already. This early in the year. Carrots too. Potatoes. Peas. It's like a paradise out there, Dodge. You oughta' take a look. A miracle. I've never seen it like this. Maybe the rain did something. Maybe it was the rain.

[As HALIE *keeps talking offstage,* TILDEN *appears from stage left, dripping with mud from the knees down. His arms and hands are covered with mud. In his hands he carries the corpse of a small child at chest level, staring down at it. The corpse mainly consists of bones wrapped in muddy, rotten cloth. He moves slowly downstage toward the staircase, ignoring* VINCE *on the sofa.* VINCE *keeps staring at the ceiling as though* TILDEN *wasn't there. As* HALIE'S VOICE *continues,* TILDEN *slowly makes his way up the stairs. His eyes never leave the corpse of the child. The lights keep fading.*]

HALIE'S VOICE: Good hard rain. Takes everything straight down deep to the roots. The rest takes care of itself. You can't force a thing to grow. You can't interfere with it. It's all hidden. It's all unseen. You just gotta wait til it pops up out of the ground. Tiny little shoot. Tiny little white shoot. All hairy and fragile. Strong though. Strong enough to break the earth even. It's a miracle, Dodge. I've never seen a crop like this in my whole life. Maybe it's the sun. Maybe that's it. Maybe it's the sun.

[TILDEN *disappears above. Silence. Lights go to black.*]

August Wilson

August Wilson (1945–) was born Frederick August Kittel into a poor working-class family living in the Hill section of Pittsburgh, a ghetto neighborhood. Wilson's father was a white man born in Germany, and his mother, Daisy Wilson, was an African American from North Carolina. When Kittel abandoned his family of six children, Daisy worked as a housecleaner in order to keep the family intact; even after she remarried, to David Bedford. Betrayed by his white father and suffering the indignities of racism, Wilson took his mother's maiden name in order to identify more completely with the African-American side of his heritage. Wilson is deeply resentful of racial injustice, and this has inspired him to make strong claims for the validity of African-American experience as the source for themes and situations in his plays.

Wilson dropped out of high school at fifteen, an act of conscience and rebellion that his mother and stepfather disapproved of. Wilson says that he left because of racial insults, but he apparently did not like school, and he was never interested in returning. In place of formal education, Wilson's schooling took place in the streets, where he worked at menial jobs in food stores and restaurants. He lived at home until he was eighteen; he was then drafted into the Army, but was discharged after one year.

By the age of twenty, Wilson was publishing poetry in local black literary magazines. He has said that in 1965 he had an epiphany listening to a recording by blues singer Bessie Smith, which led him to see more contexts for life than he had seen in mainstream literature. In 1968, with Rob Penny, a friend and early mentor, Wilson cofounded the Black Horizon Theater in the Hill section of Pittsburgh. During this time, Wilson supported the Black Muslim movement and married Brenda Burton, a Black Muslim, in 1969. They had a daughter in 1970, but it was a troubled marriage that ended in a bitter divorce in 1972. Wilson later married Judy Oliver, a social worker from Minneapolis, but in 1981 this marriage also ended in divorce. He has since remarried and is now living in Seattle.

The Black Horizon Theater provided the foundation for Wilson's sense of being a playwright. The company was strongly influenced by the poet and playwright Amiri Imamu Baraka (1934), who had also changed his name, from Everett Leroi Jones, in order to identify with his black heritage. Baraka's literary platform is a call for revolution, and his rhetoric is especially clear in his *Four Black Revolutionary Plays* (1969), which opens with the statement, "Unless you killing white people, killing the shit they've built, don't read this shit, you won't like it, and it sure won't like you." Along with Baraka's raw power as a playwright, Wilson was impressed by his ability to incorporate jazz rhythms into his dialogue and to catch the speech rhythms of African American street talk and regional vernacular. For Wilson, his use of this language taps into the African-American imagination and art. Wilson takes his characters from the lower classes, from which he comes, and he disdains the middle classes, whether African American or white.

At first, Wilson was satisfied with producing and directing plays, but after seeing *Sizwe Bansi Is Dead* (1972), by South African playwright Athol Fugard, he decided to try his hand at playwriting and to tell the African-American experience from the point of view of an African American. In 1978, Claude Purdy, a friend who was directing a black theater group, invited Wilson to St. Paul, Minnesota. There, he continued writing and searching for his voice, until Purdy brought to his attention a selection of paintings and collages by Romare Bearden (1911–1988), who was a native of Pittsburgh and had lived in the Hill. Through Wilson's close study of Bearden's *The Prevalence of Ritual,* a series that includes *Conjur Woman, Conjur Woman As an Angel, Baptism,* and *Tidings* (or his study of Bearden's works in a 1971 show at the Museum of Modern Art in New York City—it is not clear), he took Bearden as his chief model for the African-American artist. Wilson wrote, "I was then a thirty-two-year-old poet who had taken his aesthetic from the blues but was unsure how to turn it into a narrative that would encompass all the elements of culture and tradition—what [James] Baldwin so eloquently called 'the field of manners and ritual of intercourse' that sustains black American life." Suddenly, Wilson realized that jazz music, the blues, and Baraka's militancy were too narrow for expressing his sense of the African-American experience. He wrote that after seeing Bearden's work, he knew it was possible that black life could be "presented on its own terms, on a grand and epic scale, with all richness and fullness, in a language that was vibrant and which, made attendant to everyday life, ennobled it, affirmed its value, and exalted its presence."

However, it took five years for Wilson to get his first play, *Jitney* (1982), staged in Pittsburgh, where it was unsuccessful. In the same year, Wilson's *Ma Rainey's Black Bottom* was accepted at the National Playwrights Conference at the Eugene O'Neill Theater Center in New London, Connecticut. Lloyd Richards, then dean of the Yale Drama School and artistic director of the Yale Repertory Theater and the Eugene O'Neill Center, recognized Wilson's talent. (Richards's ability as a talent-spotter is formidable, and it was his direction that was largely responsible for the success of Lorraine Hansberry's *A Raisin in the Sun* in 1959.) Since then, Richards has nurtured Wilson and directed almost all of his major plays, and Wilson sees his relationship with Richards as one of surrogate son and theatrical mentor.

Ma Rainey's Black Bottom, first produced in 1984, is a mixture of history and fiction, inspired by the life and songs of Ma Rainey (1886–1939), an early blues singer who was called "Queen of the Blues." (The "black bottom" in the title refers to a popular dance in the 1920s.) The play's action takes place in 1927, when Rainey is about to record for a white record company in Chicago. The focus of the action is not on Rainey but on the four members of her band, Toledo, Cutler, Slow Drag, and especially Levee, the trumpet player, who has the black male warrior spirit that Wilson admires. When Levee unsuccessfully tries to sell his own music to Sturdyvant, the white producer, he loses Rainey's support and his own job. In a wave of uncontrolled frustration, Levee cracks, and when Toledo, who represents religious faith and reason, accidentally steps on his shoes,

Levee stabs him to death. It is an inappropriate action and is aimed at the wrong man, but the conflict and its outcome signal Wilson's own anger over the economic repression of African Americans.

Fences (first produced in 1987 and winner of the Pulitzer Prize for Drama) owes its inspiration to Wilson's stepfather, David Bedford, who murdered a man when he attempted a robbery and who subsequently served more than twenty years in prison. Wilson only learned this story after Bedford died in 1969, and the play is partly a homage to a man who wanted Wilson to better himself but did not live to see it. Many, however, have noticed that *Fences* may be interpreted as an African-American version of Arthur Miller's *Death of a Salesman.*

Fences, set in 1957, takes place in the Hill section of Pittsburgh, where Troy Maxon, a failed baseball player—who mastered the game while serving a fifteen-year sentence for murder—now a garbage collector, attempts to deal with the discomfort of his unhappy marriage to Rose and his disquieting relationship with their son, Cory. Troy is a dutiful but unfaithful husband, whose swaggering is contrasted with the strong Christian morality and suffering of his wife. Rose forgives Troy, and when his mistress dies she adopts Troy's illegitimate daughter, Raynell. Troy intransigently keeps his son Cory from accepting a college football scholarship because he did not go to college and he was unable to fulfill his dream of being a baseball player in the white-dominated professional sport twenty years earlier. The deep antagonism between father and son results in Cory's complete alienation, and he leaves home. Seven years later, on the day of Troy's funeral, Cory returns and listens to Rose affirm Troy's essential goodness: "You can't be nobody but who you are." Cory tries to sing his father's song about a dog named blue ("Blue laid down and died like a man") as an act of forgiveness, and Gabriel, Troy's mentally incompetent brother, tries to blow his horn to warn St. Peter to open the gates of heaven. Unable to make it sound, he dances Troy into heaven, an act of reconciliation, signifying Wilson's feeling for this frustrated and angry man who was powerless to achieve his dream for himself. The title takes its meaning from the fences that Troy builds: The fence he actually constructs to define the plot on which his house sits, and the fences that separate him from Rose, Cory, and himself.

Wilson's favorite play, *Joe Turner's Come and Gone* (1986), was inspired by Bearden's work and by the blues. In Bearden's "Mill Hand's Lunch Bucket" (1978), Wilson saw the figure of a man whom he liked and made him into Harald Loomis, the protagonist of *Joe Turner's Come and Gone,* a title taken from the blues song "Joe Turner." (In folklore, Joe Turner, perhaps a real person, was a white bounty hunter who used African-American men as slaves long after the emancipation.) In the play, Loomis has worked on Turner's chain gang for seven years, during which his wife, Martha Pentecost, left for Pittsburgh. When the action begins, it is 1911; Loomis has returned to Pittsburgh with his daughter, Zonia, desperately searching for Martha in order to start his life over. His search leads him to Bynum Walker, a conjur man, who represents African-American history and who points Loomis in the direction he must follow to achieve salvation and reconciliation. When Martha finally arrives, Loomis finds that her Christianity does not sway him. He gives Zonia to Martha to raise, then in a frenzy, he denies Christ, lacerates his chest, and baptizes his body in his own blood. This act enables Loomis to find his selfhood, but as the play ends, he faces an uncertain future.

Wilson's play *Two Trains Running* (1992) is inspired by Bearden's painting "The Family Dinner" and by a blues song about trains running in opposite directions, neither of which is a satisfactory choice: "Two trains running, neither one going my way. One running by night, one running by day." The action is set in Pittsburgh, in a homey restaurant, symbolically situated across the street from Lutz's meat market and West's funeral home. The time is 1969, a period of unrest in the United States, during the Vietnam War, when African Americans protested the war and racism and debated black nationalism. There is a casual reference to a black nationalist rally that sets the mood of the world around the diner. Memphis Lee, the restaurant's owner, came north in 1936, after being swindled out of a piece of property by an unscrupulous white man. He has never returned to reclaim his heritage. When the diner is condemned by the city, Memphis gets a large payment and seeks advice from Aunt Ester, a "322-year-old" conjur woman, who embodies the history of African Americans in the United States. She makes him realize that he must go back to the South and face his past in order to have a future.

Seven Guitars (1995), set in the 1940s, continues Wilson's portrayal of the African-American underclass. It celebrates the life of a hustler, the blues guitarist Floyd "Schoolboy" Barton, who is victimized by the corrupt white-controlled music industry and his own greed. Floyd is a ladies' man and a jailbird, who is killed when he steals money to get his guitar out of hock. When the action begins, Floyd is dead, and his story evolves from the tales that his friends tell about him and themselves. There are seven characters, each symbolically suggesting a guitar, and their stories about racism and economic and political repression form the substance of the blues that embodies Floyd's and their lives.

The Piano Lesson (first produced in 1987 and winner of the Pulitzer Prize for Drama) is Wilson's most unified and well-plotted play. It explores the theme that one must respect and preserve family history in order to survive the present and provide for the future. Bearden's "Piano Lesson," a collage that shows two women at a piano, inspired this play. Wilson transforms the painting's figures into Berniece Charles and her daughter, Maretha, and has made the piano a symbol of African-American cultural history.

The play commingles realism and supernaturalism; the people and the piano are realistically portrayed, along with the ghost of a white man that haunts the piano. The struggle of the family to exorcize the ghost is the crux of the action. The shift from realism to mystical wrestling with the ghost of the past is both culturally meaningful and dramatically believable and allows Wilson to make his point that modern African Americans must wrestle with the past controlled by whites in order to realize freedom and self-esteem. Significantly, this play is dedicated to Wilson's five brothers and sisters, and it has been suggested that the story of *The Piano Lesson* is Wilson's own attempt to deal with his family's past.

Though it is set during the Great Depression of the 1930s, a time of general economic deprivation, *The Piano Lesson* is Wilson's only play about African Americans who have attained economic stability. The situation seems loosely drawn from Wilson's family's experience: The characters Berniece, thirty-five, and Maretha, eleven, have traveled north from Mississippi to make a new life in Pittsburgh. Three years earlier, Berniece was widowed when her husband, Crawley, was killed during a robbery. Now she shares a house with her Uncle Doaker, forty-seven, who is a cook on a railroad line. Berniece is dour and nurses resentment toward her brother Boy Willie, age thirty, whom she blames for her husband's death. Berniece works as a housecleaner for rich white people and lives on the edge of solvency. She is courted by Avery, an elevator operator turned minister, but she accepts only his friendship.

The most opulent piece of furniture in Berniece's otherwise spartan home is a piano carved by her grandfather, Willie Boy, a master carpenter but a slave, showing the history of the family. The piano was paid for by the slave master, Sutter, by selling Mama Berniece and her son Papa Boy Charles, who became Berniece's father. The piano came into the Charles family's possession when Papa Boy stole it from the Sutters, but he was killed for his effort. The piano's deep spiritual power enthralls Berniece, and she will not play it, partly because it was the cause of her father's death. Though she allows Maretha to play the piano, she does not tell her its story, and by not doing so she deprives her daughter of the richness of her family history and her heritage.

Berniece's orderly life is disrupted by the visit of Boy Willie, his friend Lymon, and a truck filled with watermelons that they hope to sell in order to make enough money to buy a piece of land belonging to the Sutter family in Mississippi. Boy Willie is as exuberant as Berniece is restrained, and when he needs more money to buy his land, he insists that the piano be sold. He does not see it as a symbol but as an object with economic value. He says, "If my daddy had seen where he could have traded that piano in for some land of his own, it wouldn't be sitting up here now." He does not take into account Sutter's ghost hovering over the piano.

The Piano Lesson climaxes when three things happen almost simultaneously: Boy Willie attempts to move the piano out of the house; Uncle Wining Boy, Doaker's musician brother, appears drunk and begins to play a blues song on it; and Avery attempts to exorcize Sutter's ghost with a Christian ritual. Boy Willie parodies the ritual, but when he does so, the ghost attacks him, and they wrestle. The spell is only broken and Sutter's ghost exorcized when Berniece begins to play the piano, calling out the names of their ancestors: "I want you to help me/Mama Berniece/I want you to help me/Mama Esther/. . . I want you to help me/Mama Ola." Freed from Sutter's ghost by the music, Boy Willie stands and realizes the power of the music and the family's heritage. In her newfound voice, Berniece sings, "Thank you." Her life is changed because she is free to tell her story to Maretha, and perhaps to marry Avery. Boy Willie agrees to leave the piano with Berniece, and he returns to Mississippi to start a new life on the ancestral land.

Wilson claims that he has purposefully not read Shakespeare, Ibsen, Shaw, or the major American playwrights, especially Eugene O'Neill, Tennessee Williams, and Arthur Miller. He claims the influence of such writers as Langston Hughes, Arna Bontemps, Zora Neale Hurston, Ralph Ellison, and James Baldwin. Wilson's stake as an African-American playwright does seem built on a platform that separates him, at least theoretically, from the traditional influences of

European and American drama, which have largely ignored African Americans in the United States. Like the early nineteenth-century American writers who sought to establish a distinctly American voice in literature and the fine arts, Wilson wants to depict experience as seen through African-American eyes. It is Wilson's intention to complete a cycle of ten plays that he calls a "grand dramatic design providing a panoramic view of the American black experience since the days of Lincoln." The project resembles Eugene O'Neill's incomplete scheme to depict the rise of American civilization and its decline into a slough of materialism and greed.

The Piano Lesson

Gin my cotton
Sell my seed
Buy my baby
Everything she need

—SKIP JAMES

DOAKER
BOY WILLIE
LYMON
BERNIECE
MARETHA
AVERY
WINING BOY
GRACE

THE SETTING. *The action of the play takes place in the kitchen and parlor of the house where* DOAKER CHARLES *lives with his niece,* BERNIECE, *and her eleven-year-old daughter,* MARETHA. *The house is sparsely furnished, and although there is evidence of a woman's touch, there is a lack of warmth and vigor.* BERNIECE *and* MARETHA *occupy the upstairs rooms.* DOAKER*'s room is prominent and opens onto the kitchen. Dominating the parlor is an old upright piano. On the legs of the piano, carved in the manner of African sculpture, are mask-like figures resembling totems. The carvings are rendered with a grace and power of invention that lifts them out of the realm of craftsmanship and into the realm of art. At left is a staircase leading to the upstairs.*

ACT I

Scene 1

[*The lights come up on the* CHARLES *household. It is five o'clock in the morning. The dawn is beginning to announce itself, but there is something in the air that belongs to the night. A stillness that is a portent, a gathering, a coming together of something akin to a storm. There is a loud knock at the door.*]

BOY WILLIE [*Off stage, calling.*]: Hey, Doaker . . . Doaker! [*He knocks again and calls.*] Hey, Doaker! Hey, Berniece! Berniece!

[DOAKER *enters from his room. He is a tall, thin man of forty-seven, with severe features, who has for all intents and purposes retired from the world though he works full-time as a railroad cook.*]

DOAKER: Who is it?

BOY WILLIE: Open the door, nigger! It's me . . . Boy Willie!

DOAKER: Who?

BOY WILLIE: Boy Willie! Open the door!

[DOAKER *opens the door and* BOY WILLIE *and* LYMON *enter.* BOY WILLIE *is thirty years old. He has an infectious grin and a boyishness that is apt for his name. He is brash and impulsive, talkative and somewhat crude in speech and manner.* LYMON *is twenty-nine.* BOY WILLIE*'s partner, he talks little, and then with a straightforwardness that is often disarming.*]

DOAKER: What you doing up here?

BOY WILLIE: I told you, Lymon. Lymon talking about you might be sleep. This is Lymon. You remember Lymon Jackson from down home? This my Uncle Doaker.

DOAKER: What you doing up here? I couldn't figure out who that was. I thought you was still down in Mississippi.

BOY WILLIE: Me and Lymon selling watermelons. We got a truck out there. Got a whole truckload of watermelons. We brought them up here to sell. Where's Berniece? [*Calls.*] Hey, Berniece!

DOAKER: Berniece up there sleep.

BOY WILLIE: Well, let her get up. [*Calls.*] Hey, Berniece!

DOAKER: She got to go to work in the morning.

BOY WILLIE: Well she can get up and say hi. It's been three years since I seen her. [*Calls.*] Hey, Berniece! It's me . . . Boy Willie.

DOAKER: Berniece don't like all that hollering now. She got to work in the morning.

BOY WILLIE: She can go on back to bed. Me and Lymon been riding two days in that truck . . . the least she can do is get up and say hi.

DOAKER [*Looking out the window.*]: Where you all get that truck from?

BOY WILLIE: It's Lymon's. I told him let's get a load of watermelons and bring them up here.

LYMON: Boy Willie say he going back, but I'm gonna stay. See what it's like up here.

BOY WILLIE: You gonna carry me down there first.

LYMON: I told you I ain't going back down there and take a chance on that truck breaking down again. You can take the train. Hey, tell him Doaker, he can take the train back. After we sell them watermelons he have enough money he can buy him a whole railroad car.

DOAKER: You got all them watermelons stacked up there no wonder the truck broke down. I'm surprised you made it this far with a load like that. Where you break down at?

BOY WILLIE: We broke down three times! It took us two and a half days to get here. It's a good thing we picked them watermelons fresh.

LYMON: We broke down twice in West Virginia. The first time was just as soon as we got out of Sunflower. About forty miles out she broke down. We got it going and got all the way to West Virginia before she broke down again.

BOY WILLIE: We had to walk about five miles for some water.

LYMON: It got a hole in the radiator but it runs pretty good. You have to pump the brakes sometime before they catch. Boy Willie have his door open and be ready to jump when that happens.

BOY WILLIE: Lymon think that's funny. I told the nigger I give him ten dollars to get the brakes fixed. But he thinks that funny.

LYMON: They don't need fixing. All you got to do is pump them till they catch.

Epatha Merkerson and Charles Dutton in The Piano Lesson, *directed by Lloyd Richards, Walter Kerr Theatre, New York, 1989.*

[BERNIECE *enters on the stairs. Thirty-five years old, with an eleven-year-old daughter, she is still in mourning for her husband after three years.*]

BERNIECE: What you doing all that hollering for?

BOY WILLIE: Hey, Berniece. Doaker said you was sleep. I said at least you could get up and say hi.

BERNIECE: It's five o'clock in the morning and you come in here with all this noise. You can't come like normal folks. You got to bring all that noise with you.

BOY WILLIE: Hell, I ain't done nothing but come in and say hi. I ain't got in the house good.

BERNIECE: That's what I'm talking about. You start all that hollering and carry on as soon as you hit the door.

BOY WILLIE: Aw hell, woman, I was glad to see Doaker. You ain't had to come down if you didn't want to. I come eighteen hundred miles to see my sister I figure she might want to get up and say hi. Other than that you can go back upstairs. What you got, Doaker? Where your bottle? Me and Lymon want a drink. [*To* BERNIECE.] This is Lymon. You remember Lymon Jackson from down home.

LYMON: How you doing, Berniece. You look just like I thought you looked.

BERNIECE: Why you all got to come in hollering and carrying on? Waking the neighbors with all that noise.

BOY WILLIE: They can come over and join the party. We fixing to have a party. Doaker, where your bottle? Me and Lymon celebrating. The Ghosts of the Yellow Dog got Sutter.

BERNIECE: Say what?

BOY WILLIE: Ask Lymon, they found him the next morning. Say he drowned in his well.

DOAKER: When this happen, Boy Willie?

BOY WILLIE: About three weeks ago. Me and Lymon was over in Stoner County when we heard about it. We laughed. We thought it was funny. A great big old three-hundred-and-forty-pound man gonna fall down his well.

LYMON: It remind me of Humpty Dumpty.

BOY WILLIE: Everybody say the Ghosts of the Yellow Dog pushed him.

BERNIECE: I don't want to hear that nonsense. Somebody down there pushing them people in their wells.

DOAKER: What was you and Lymon doing over in Stoner County?

BOY WILLIE: We was down there working. Lymon got some people down there.

LYMON: My cousin got some land down there. We was helping him.

BOY WILLIE: Got near about a hundred acres. He got it set up real nice. Me and Lymon was down there chopping down trees. We was using Lymon's truck to haul the wood. Me and Lymon used to haul wood all around them parts. [*To* BERNIECE.] Me and Lymon got a truckload of watermelons out there.

[BERNIECE *crosses to the window to the parlor.*]

Doaker, where your bottle? I know you got a bottle stuck up in your room. Come on, me and Lymon want a drink.

[DOAKER *exits into his room.*]

BERNIECE: Where you all get that truck from?

BOY WILLIE: I told you it's Lymon's.

BERNIECE: Where you get the truck from, Lymon?

LYMON: I bought it.

BERNIECE: Where he get that truck from, Boy Willie?

BOY WILLIE: He told you he bought it. Bought it for a hundred and twenty dollars. I can't say where he got that hundred and twenty dollars from . . . but he bought that old piece of truck from Henry Porter. [*To* LYMON.] Where you get that hundred and twenty dollars from, nigger?

LYMON: I got it like you get yours. I know how to take care of money.

[DOAKER *brings a bottle and sets it on the table.*]

BOY WILLIE: Aw hell, Doaker got some of that good whiskey. Don't give Lymon none of that. He ain't used to good whiskey. He liable to get sick.

LYMON: I done had good whiskey before.

BOY WILLIE: Lymon bought that truck so he have him a place to sleep. He down there wasn't doing no work or nothing. Sheriff looking for him. He bought that truck to keep away from the sheriff. Got Stovall looking for him too. He down there sleeping in that truck ducking and dodging both of them. I told him come on let's go up and see my sister.

BERNIECE: What the sheriff looking for you for, Lymon?

BOY WILLIE: The man don't want you to know all his business. He's my company. He ain't asking you no questions.

LYMON: It wasn't nothing. It was just a misunderstanding.

BERNIECE: He in my house. You say the sheriff looking for him, I wanna know what he looking for him for. Otherwise you all can go back out there and be where nobody don't have to ask you nothing.

LYMON: It was just a misunderstanding. Sometimes me and the sheriff we don't think alike. So we just got crossed on each other.

BERNIECE: Might be looking for him about that truck. He might have stole that truck.

BOY WILLIE: We ain't stole no truck, woman. I told you Lymon bought it.

DOAKER: Boy Willie and Lymon got more sense than to ride all the way up here in a stolen truck with a load of watermelons. Now they might have stole them watermelons, but I don't believe they stole that truck.

BOY WILLIE: You don't even know the man good and you calling him a thief. And we ain't stole them watermelons either. Them old man Pitterford's watermelons. He give me and Lymon all we could load for ten dollars.

DOAKER: No wonder you got them stacked up out there. You must have five hundred watermelons stacked up out there.

BERNIECE: Boy Willie, when you and Lymon planning on going back?

BOY WILLIE: Lymon say he staying. As soon as we sell them watermelons I'm going on back.

BERNIECE [*Starts to exit up the stairs.*]: That's what you need to do. And you need to do it quick. Come in here disrupting the house. I don't want all that loud carrying on around here. I'm surprised you ain't woke Maretha up.

BOY WILLIE: I was fixing to get her now. [*Calls.*] Hey, Maretha!

DOAKER: Berniece don't like all that hollering now.

BERNIECE: Don't you wake that child up!

BOY WILLIE: You going up there . . . wake her up and tell her her uncle's here. I ain't seen her in three years. Wake her up and send her down here. She can go back to bed.

BERNIECE: I ain't waking that child up . . . and don't you be making all that noise. You and Lymon need to sell them watermelons and go on back.

[BERNIECE *exits up the stairs.*]

BOY WILLIE: I see Berniece still try to be stuck up.

DOAKER: Berniece alright. She don't want you making all that noise. Maretha up there sleep. Let her sleep until she get up. She can see you then.

BOY WILLIE: I ain't thinking about Berniece. You hear from Wining Boy? You know Cleotha died?

DOAKER: Yeah, I heard that. He come by here about a year ago. Had a whole sack of money. He stayed here about two weeks. Ain't offered nothing. Berniece asked him for three dollars to buy some food and he got mad and left.

LYMON: Who's Wining Boy?

BOY WILLIE: That's my uncle. That's Doaker's brother. You heard me talk about Wining Boy. He play piano. He done made some records and everything. He still doing that, Doaker?

DOAKER: He made one or two records a long time ago. That's the only ones I ever known him to make. If you let him tell it he a big recording star.

BOY WILLIE: He stopped down home about two years ago. That's what I hear. I don't know. Me and Lymon was up on Parchman Farm doing them three years.

DOAKER: He don't never stay in one place. Now, he been here about eight months ago. Back in the winter. Now, you subject not to see him for another two years. It's liable to be that long before he stop by.

BOY WILLIE: If he had a whole sack of money you liable never to see him. You ain't gonna see him until he get broke. Just as soon as that sack of money is gone you look up and he be on your doorstep.

LYMON [*Noticing the piano.*]: Is that the piano?

BOY WILLIE: Yeah . . . look here, Lymon. See how it got all cash money. He don't know I found out the most Stovall how it's carved up real nice and polished and everything? You never find you another piano like that.

LYMON: Yeah, that look real nice.

BOY WILLIE: I told you. See how it's polished? My mama used to polish it every day. See all them pictures carved on it? That's what I was talking about. You can get a nice price for that piano.

LYMON: That's all Boy Willie talked about the whole trip up here. I got tired of hearing him talk about the piano.

BOY WILLIE: All you want to talk about is women. You ought to hear this nigger, Doaker. Talking about all the women he gonna get when he get up here. He ain't had none down there but he gonna get a hundred when he get up here.

DOAKER: How your people doing down there, Lymon?

LYMON: They alright. They still there. I come up here to see what it's like up here. Boy Willie trying to get me to go back and farm with him.

BOY WILLIE: Sutter's brother selling the land. He say he gonna sell it to me. That's why I come up here. I got one part of it. Sell them watermelons and get me another part. Get Berniece to sell that piano and I'll have the third part.

DOAKER: Berniece ain't gonna sell that piano.

BOY WILLIE: I'm gonna talk to her. When she see I got a chance to get Sutter's land she'll come around.

DOAKER: You can put that thought out your mind. Berniece ain't gonna sell that piano.

BOY WILLIE: I'm gonna talk to her. She been playing on it?

DOAKER: You know she won't touch that piano. I ain't never known her to touch it since Mama Ola died. That's over seven years now. She say it got blood on it. She got Maretha playing on it though. Say Maretha can go on and do everything she can't do. Got her in an extra school down at the Irene Kaufman Settlement House. She want Maretha to grow up and be a schoolteacher. Say she good enough she can teach on the piano.

BOY WILLIE: Maretha don't need to be playing on no piano. She can play on the guitar.

DOAKER: How much land Sutter got left?

BOY WILLIE: Got a hundred acres. Good land. He done sold it piece by piece, he kept the good part for himself. Now he got to give that up. His brother come down from Chicago for the funeral . . . he up there in Chicago got some kind of business with soda fountain equipment. He anxious to sell the land, Doaker. He don't want to be bothered with it. He called me to him and said cause of how long our families done known each other and how we been good friends and all, say he wanted to sell the land to me. Say he'd rather see me with it than Jim Stovall. Told me he'd let me have it for two thousand dollars cash money. He don't know I found out the most Stovall would give him for it was fifteen hundred dollars. He trying to get that extra five hundred out of me telling me he doing me a favor. I thanked him just as nice. Told him what a good man Sutter was and how he had my sympathy and all. Told him to give me two weeks. He said he'd wait on me. That's why I come up here. Sell them watermelons. Get Berniece to sell that piano. Put them two parts with the part I done saved. Walk in there. Tip my hat. Lay my money down on the table. Get my deed and walk on out. This time I get to keep all the cotton. Hire me some men to work it for me. Gin my cotton. Get my seed. And I'll see you again next year. Might even plant some tobacco or some oats.

DOAKER: You gonna have a hard time trying to get Berniece to sell that piano. You know Avery Brown from down there don't you? He up here now. He followed Berniece up here trying to get her to marry him after Crawley got killed. He been up here about two years. He call himself a preacher now.

BOY WILLIE: I know Avery. I know him from when he used to work on the Willshaw place. Lymon know him too.

DOAKER: He after Berniece to marry him. She keep telling him no but he won't give up. He keep pressing her on it.

BOY WILLIE: Avery think all white men is bigshots. He don't know there some white men ain't got as much as he got.

DOAKER: He supposed to come past here this morning. Berniece going down to the bank with him to see if he can get a loan to start his church. That's why I know Berniece ain't gonna sell that piano. He tried to get her to sell it to help him start his church. Sent the man around and everything.

BOY WILLIE: What man?

DOAKER: Some white fellow was going around to all the colored people's houses looking to buy up musical instruments. He'd buy anything. Drums. Guitars. Harmonicas. Pianos. Avery sent him past here. He looked at the piano and got excited. Offered her a nice price. She turned him down and got on Avery for sending him past. The man kept on her about two weeks. He seen where she wasn't gonna sell it, he gave her his number and told her if she ever wanted to sell it to call him first. Say he'd go one better than what anybody else would give her for it.

BOY WILLIE: How much he offer her for it?

DOAKER: Now you know me. She didn't say and I didn't ask. I just know it was a nice price.

LYMON: All you got to do is find out who he is and tell him somebody else wanna buy it from you. Tell him you can't make up your mind who to sell it to, and if he like Doaker say, he'll give you anything you want for it.

BOY WILLIE: That's what I'm gonna do. I'm gonna find out who he is from Avery.

DOAKER: It ain't gonna do you no good. Berniece ain't gonna sell that piano.

BOY WILLIE: She ain't got to sell it. I'm gonna sell it. I own just as much of it as she does.

BERNIECE [*Offstage, hollers.*]: Doaker! Go on get away. Doaker!

DOAKER [*Calling.*]: Berniece?

[DOAKER *and* BOY WILLIE *rush to the stairs,* BOY WILLIE *runs up the stairs, passing* BERNIECE *as she enters, running.*]

DOAKER: Berniece, what's the matter? You alright? What's the matter?

[BERNIECE *tries to catch her breath. She is unable to speak.*]

DOAKER: That's alright. Take your time. You alright. What's the matter? [*He calls.*] Hey, Boy Willie?

BOY WILLIE [*Offstage.*]: Ain't nobody up here.

BERNIECE: Sutter . . . Sutter's standing at the top of the steps.

DOAKER [*Calls.*]: Boy Willie!

[LYMON *crosses to the stairs and looks up.* BOY WILLIE *enters from the stairs.*]

BOY WILLIE: Hey Doaker, what's wrong with her? Berniece, what's wrong? Who was you talking to?

DOAKER: She say she seen Sutter's ghost standing at the top of the stairs.

BOY WILLIE: Seen what? Sutter? She ain't seen no Sutter.

BERNIECE: He was standing right up there.

BOY WILLIE [*Entering on the stairs.*]: That's all in Berniece's head. Ain't nobody up there. Go on up there, Doaker.

DOAKER: I'll take your word for it. Berniece talking about what she seen. She say Sutter's ghost standing at the top of the steps. She ain't just make all that up.

BOY WILLIE: She up there dreaming. She ain't seen no ghost.

LYMON: You want a glass of water, Berniece? Get her a glass of water, Boy Willie.

BOY WILLIE: She don't need no water. She ain't seen nothing. Go on up there and look. Ain't nobody up there but Maretha.

DOAKER: Let Berniece tell it.

BOY WILLIE: I ain't stopping her from telling it.

DOAKER: What happened, Berniece?

BERNIECE: I come out my room to come back down here and Sutter was standing there in the hall.

BOY WILLIE: What he look like?

BERNIECE: He look like Sutter. He look like he always look.

BOY WILLIE: Sutter couldn't find his way from Big Sandy to Little Sandy. How he gonna find his way all the way up here to Pittsburgh? Sutter ain't never even heard of Pittsburgh.

DOAKER: Go on, Berniece.

BERNIECE: Just standing there with the blue suit on.

BOY WILLIE: The man ain't never left Marlin County when he was living . . . and he's gonna come all the way up here now that he's dead?

DOAKER: Let her finish. I want to hear what she got to say.

BOY WILLIE: I'll tell you this. If Berniece had seen him like she think she seen him she'd still be running.

DOAKER: Go on, Berniece. Don't pay Boy Willie no mind.

BERNIECE: He was standing there . . . had his hand on top of his head. Look like he might have thought if he took his hand down his head might have fallen off.

LYMON: Did he have on a hat?

BERNIECE: Just had on that blue suit . . . I told him to go away and he just stood there looking at me . . . calling Boy Willie's name.

BOY WILLIE: What he calling my name for?

BERNIECE: I believe you pushed him in the well.

BOY WILLIE: Now what kind of sense that make? You telling me I'm gonna go out there and hide in the weeds with all them dogs and things he got around there . . . I'm gonna hide and wait till I catch him looking down his well just right . . . then I'm gonna run over and push him in. A great big old three-hundred-and-forty-pound man.

BERNIECE: Well, what he calling your name for?

BOY WILLIE: He bending over looking down his well, woman . . . how he know who pushed him? It could have been anybody. Where was you when Sutter fell in his well? Where was Doaker? Me and Lymon was over in Stoner County. Tell her, Lymon. The Ghosts of the Yellow Dog got Sutter. That's what happened to him.

BERNIECE: You can talk all that Ghosts of the Yellow Dog stuff if you want. I know better.

LYMON: The Ghosts of the Yellow Dog pushed him. That's what the people say. They found him in his well and all the people say it must be the Ghosts of the Yellow Dog. Just like all them other men.

BOY WILLIE: Come talking about he looking for me. What he come all the way up here for? If he looking for me all he got to do is wait. He could have saved himself a trip if he looking for me. That ain't nothing but in Berniece's head. Ain't no telling what she liable to come up with next.

BERNIECE: Boy Willie, I want you and Lymon to go ahead and leave my house. Just go on somewhere. You don't do nothing but bring trouble with you everywhere you go. If it wasn't for you Crawley would still be alive.

BOY WILLIE: Crawley what? I ain't had nothing to do with Crawley getting killed. Crawley three time seven. He had his own mind.

BERNIECE: Just go on and leave. Let Sutter go somewhere else looking for you.

BOY WILLIE: I'm leaving. Soon as we sell them watermelons. Other than that I ain't going nowhere. Hell, I just got here. Talking about Sutter looking for me. Sutter was looking for that piano. That's what he was looking for. He had to die to find out where that piano was at . . . If I was you I'd get rid of it. That's the way to get rid of Sutter's ghost. Get rid of that piano.

BERNIECE: I want you and Lymon to go on and take all this confusion out of my house!

BOY WILLIE: Hey, tell her, Doaker. What kind of sense that make? I told you, Lymon, as soon as Berniece see me she was gonna start something. Didn't I tell you that? Now she done made up that story about Sutter just so she could tell me to leave her house. Well, hell, I ain't going nowhere till I sell them watermelons.

BERNIECE: Well why don't you go out there and sell them! Sell them and go on back!

BOY WILLIE: We waiting till the people get up.

LYMON: Boy Willie say if you get out there too early and wake the people up they get mad at you and won't buy nothing from you.

DOAKER: You won't be waiting long. You done let the sun catch up with you. This the time everybody be getting up around here.

BERNIECE: Come on, Doaker, walk up here with me. Let me get Maretha up and get her started. I got to get ready myself. Boy Willie, just go on out there and sell them watermelons and you and Lymon leave my house. [BERNIECE *and* DOAKER *exit up the stairs.*]

BOY WILLIE [*Calling after them.*]: If you see Sutter up there . . . tell him I'm down here waiting on him.

LYMON: What if she see him again?

BOY WILLIE: That's all in her head. There ain't no ghost up there. [*Calls.*] Hey, Doaker . . . I told you ain't nothing up there.

LYMON: I'm glad he didn't say he was looking for me.

BOY WILLIE: I wish I would see Sutter's ghost. Give me a chance to put a whupping on him.

LYMON: You ought to stay up here with me. You be down there working his land . . . he might come looking for you all the time.

BOY WILLIE: I ain't thinking about Sutter. And I ain't thinking about staying up here. You stay up here. I'm going back and get Sutter's land. You think you ain't got to work up here. You think this the land of milk and honey. But I ain't scared of work. I'm going back and farm every acre of that land.

[DOAKER *enters from the stairs.*]

I told you there ain't nothing up there, Doaker. Berniece dreaming all that.

DOAKER: I believe Berniece seen something. Berniece level-headed. She ain't just made all that up. She say Sutter had on a suit. I don't believe she ever seen Sutter in a suit. I believe that's what he was buried in, and that's what Berniece saw.

BOY WILLIE: Well, let her keep on seeing him then. As long as he don't mess with me.

[DOAKER *starts to cook his breakfast.*]

I heard about you, Doaker. They say you got all the women looking out for you down home. They be looking to see you coming. Say you got a different one every two weeks. Say they be fighting one another for you to stay with them. [*To* LYMON.] Look at him, Lymon. He know it's true.

DOAKER: I ain't thinking about no women. They never get me tied up with them. After Coreen I ain't got no use for them. I stay up on Jack Slattery's place when I be down there. All them women want is somebody with a steady payday.

BOY WILLIE: That ain't what I hear. I hear every two weeks the women all put on their dresses and line up at the railroad station.

DOAKER: I don't get down there but once a month. I used to go down there every two weeks but they keep switching me around. They keep switching all the fellows around.

BOY WILLIE: Doaker can't turn that railroad loose. He was working the railroad when I was walking around crying for sugartit. My mama used to brag on him.

DOAKER: I'm cooking now, but I used to line track. I pieced together the Yellow Dog stitch by stitch. Rail by rail. Line track all up around there. I lined track all up around Sunflower and Clarksdale. Wining Boy worked with me. He helped put in some of that track. He'd work it for six months and quit. Go back to playing piano and gambling.

BOY WILLIE: How long you been with the railroad now?

DOAKER: Twenty-seven years. Now, I'll tell you something about the railroad. What I done learned after twenty-seven years. See, you got North. You got West. You look over here you got South. Over there you got East. Now, you can start from anywhere. Don't care where you at. You got to go one of them four ways. And whichever way you decide to go they got a railroad that will take you there. Now, that's something simple. You think anybody would be able to understand that. But you'd be surprised how many people trying to go North get on a train going West. They think the train's supposed to go where they going rather than where it's going.

Now, why people going? Their sister's sick. They leaving before they kill somebody . . . and they sitting across from somebody who's leaving to keep from getting killed. They leaving cause they can't get satisfied. They going to meet someone. I wish I had a dollar for every time that someone wasn't at the station to meet them. I done seen that a lot. In between the time they sent the telegram and the time the person get there . . . they done forgot all about them.

They got so many trains out there they have a hard time keeping them from running into each other. Got trains going every whichaway. Got people on all of them. Somebody going where somebody just left. If everybody stay in one place I believe this would be a better world. Now what I done learned after twenty-seven years of railroading is this . . . if the train stays on the track . . . it's going to get where it's going. It might not be where you going. If it ain't, then all you got to do is sit and wait cause the train's coming back to get you. The train don't never stop. It'll come back every time. Now I'll tell you another thing . . .

BOY WILLIE: What you cooking over there, Doaker? Me and Lymon's hungry.

DOAKER: Go on down there to Wylie and Kirkpatrick to Eddie's restaurant. Coffee cost a nickel and you can get two eggs, sausage, and grits for fifteen cents. He even give you a biscuit with it.

BOY WILLIE: That look good what you got. Give me a little piece of that grilled bread.

DOAKER: Here . . . go on take the whole piece.

BOY WILLIE: Here you go, Lymon . . . you want a piece?

[*He gives* LYMON *a piece of toast.* MARETHA *enters from the stairs.*]

BOY WILLIE: Hey, sugar. Come here and give me a hug. Come on give Uncle Boy Willie a hug. Don't be shy. Look at her, Doaker. She done got bigger. Ain't she got big?

DOAKER: Yeah, she getting up there.

BOY WILLIE: How you doing, sugar?

MARETHA: Fine.

BOY WILLIE: You was just a little old thing last time I seen you. You remember me, don't you? This your Uncle Boy Willie from down South. That there's Lymon. He my friend. We come up here to sell watermelons. You like watermelons?

[MARETHA *nods.*]

We got a whole truckload out front. You can have as many as you want. What you been doing?

MARETHA: Nothing.

BOY WILLIE: Don't be shy now. Look at you getting all big. How old is you?

MARETHA: Eleven. I'm gonna be twelve soon.

BOY WILLIE: You like it up here? You like the North?

MARETHA: It's alright.

BOY WILLIE: That there's Lymon. Did you say hi to Lymon?

MARETHA: Hi.

LYMON: How you doing? You look just like your mama. I remember you when you was wearing diapers.

BOY WILLIE: You gonna come down South and see me? Uncle Boy Willie gonna get him a farm. Gonna get a great big old farm. Come down there and I'll teach you how to ride a mule. Teach you how to kill a chicken, too.

MARETHA: I seen my mama do that.

BOY WILLIE: Ain't nothing to it. You just grab him by his neck and twist it. Get you a real good grip and then you just wring his neck and throw him in the pot. Cook him up. Then you got some good eating. What you like to eat? What kind of food you like?

MARETHA: I like everything . . . except I don't like no black-eyed peas.

BOY WILLIE: Uncle Doaker tell me your mama got you playing that piano. Come on play something for me.

[BOY WILLIE *crosses over to the piano followed by* MARETHA.]

Show me what you can do. Come on now. Here . . . Uncle Boy Willie give you a dime . . . show me what you can do. Don't be bashful now. That dime say you can't be bashful.

[MARETHA *plays. It is something any beginner first learns.*]

Here, let me show you something.

[BOY WILLIE *sits and plays a simple boogie-woogie.*]

See that? See what I'm doing? That's what you call the boogie-woogie. See now . . . you can get up and dance to that. That's how good it sound. It sound like you wanna dance. You can dance to that. It'll hold you up. Whatever kind of dance you wanna do you can dance to that right there. See that? See how it go? Ain't nothing to it. Go on you do it.

MARETHA: I got to read it on the paper.

BOY WILLIE: You don't need no paper. Go on. Do just like that there.

BERNIECE: Maretha! You get up here and get ready to go so you be on time. Ain't no need you trying to take advantage of company.

MARETHA: I got to go.

BOY WILLIE: Uncle Boy Willie gonna get you a guitar. Let Uncle Doaker teach you how to play that. You don't need to read no paper to play the guitar. Your mama told you about that piano? You know how them pictures got on there?

MARETHA: She say it just always been like that since she got it.

BOY WILLIE: You hear that, Doaker? And you sitting up here in the house with Berniece.

DOAKER: I ain't got nothing to do with that. I don't get in the way of Berniece's raising her.

BOY WILLIE: You tell your mama to tell you about that piano. You ask her how them pictures got on there. If she don't tell you I'll tell you.

BERNIECE: Maretha!

MARETHA: I got to get ready to go.
BOY WILLIE: She getting big, Doaker. You remember her, Lymon?
LYMON: She used to be real little.

[There is a knock on the door. DOAKER *goes to answer it.* AVERY *enters. Thirty-eight years old, honest and ambitious, he has taken to the city like a fish to water, finding in it opportunities for growth and advancement that did not exist for him in the rural South. He is dressed in a suit and tie with a gold cross around his neck. He carries a small Bible.]*

DOAKER: Hey, Avery, come on in. Berniece upstairs.
BOY WILLIE: Look at him . . . look at him . . . he don't know what to say. He wasn't expecting to see me.
AVERY: Hey, Boy Willie. What you doing up here?
BOY WILLIE: Look at him, Lymon.
AVERY: Is that Lymon? Lymon Jackson?
BOY WILLIE: Yeah, you know Lymon.
DOAKER: Berniece be ready in a minute, Avery.
BOY WILLIE: Doaker say you a preacher now. What . . . we supposed to call you Reverend? You used to be plain old Avery. When you get to be a preacher, nigger?
LYMON: Avery say he gonna be a preacher so he don't have to work.
BOY WILLIE: I remember when you was down there on the Willshaw place planting cotton. You wasn't thinking about no Reverend then.
AVERY: That must be your truck out there. I saw that truck with them watermelons, I was trying to figure out what it was doing in front of the house.
BOY WILLIE: Yeah, me and Lymon selling watermelons. That's Lymon's truck.
DOAKER: Berniece say you all going down to the bank.
AVERY: Yeah, they give me a half day off work. I got an appointment to talk to the bank about getting a loan to start my church.
BOY WILLIE: Lymon say preachers don't have to work. Where you working at, nigger?
DOAKER: Avery got him one of them good jobs. He working at one of them skyscrapers downtown.
AVERY: I'm working down there at the Gulf Building running an elevator. Got a pension and everything. They even give you a turkey on Thanksgiving.
LYMON: How you know the rope ain't gonna break? Ain't you scared the rope's gonna break?
AVERY: That's steel. They got steel cables hold it up. It take a whole lot of breaking to break that steel. Naw, I ain't worried about nothing like that. It ain't nothing but a little old elevator. Now, I wouldn't get in none of them airplanes. You couldn't pay me to do nothing like that.
LYMON: That be fun. I'd rather do that than ride in one of them elevators.
BOY WILLIE: How many of them watermelons you wanna buy?
AVERY: I thought you was gonna give me one seeing as how you got a whole truck full.
BOY WILLIE: You can get one, get two. I'll give you two for a dollar.
AVERY: I can't eat but one. How much are they?
BOY WILLIE: Aw, nigger, you know I'll give you a watermelon. Go on, take as many as you want. Just leave some for me and Lymon to sell.
AVERY: I don't want but one.
BOY WILLIE: How you get to be a preacher, Avery? I might want to be a preacher one day. Have everybody call me Reverend Boy Willie.
AVERY: It come to me in a dream. God called me and told me he wanted me to be a shepherd for his flock. That's what I'm gonna call my church . . . The Good Shepherd Church of God in Christ.
DOAKER: Tell him what you told me. Tell him about the three hobos.
AVERY: Boy Willie don't want to hear all that.
LYMON: I do. Lots a people say your dreams can come true.
AVERY: Naw. You don't want to hear all that.
DOAKER: Go on. I told him you was a preacher. He didn't want to believe me. Tell him about the three hobos.
AVERY: Well, it come to me in a dream. See . . . I was sitting out in this railroad yard watching the trains go by. The train stopped and these three hobos got off. They told me they had come from Nazareth and was on their way to Jerusalem. They had three candles. They gave me one and told me to light it . . . but to be careful that it didn't go out. Next thing I knew I was standing in front of this house. Something told me to go knock on the door. This old woman opened the door and said they had been waiting on me. Then she led me into this room. It was a big room and it was full of all kinds of different people. They looked like anybody else except they all had sheep heads and was making noise like sheep make. I heard somebody call my name. I looked around and there was these same three hobos. They told me to take off my clothes and they give me a blue robe with gold thread. They washed my feet and combed my hair. Then they showed me these three doors and told me to pick one.

I went through one of them doors and that flame leapt off that candle and it seemed like my whole head caught fire. I looked around and there was four or five other men standing there with these same blue robes on. Then we heard a voice tell us to look out across this valley. We looked out and saw the valley was full of wolves. The voice told us that these sheep people that I had seen in the other room had to go over to the other side of this valley and somebody had to take them. Then I heard another voice say, "Who shall I send?" Next thing I knew I said, "Here I am. Send me." That's when I met Jesus. He say, "If you go, I'll go with you." Something told me to say, "Come on. Let's go." That's when I woke up. My head still felt like it was on fire . . . but I had a peace about myself that was hard to explain. I knew right then that I had been filled with the Holy Ghost and called to be a servant of the Lord. It took me a while before I could accept that. But then a lot of little ways God showed me that it was true. So I became a preacher.

LYMON: I see why you gonna call it the Good Shepherd Church. You dreaming about them sheep people. I can see that easy.

BOY WILLIE: Doaker say you sent some white man past the house to look at that piano. Say he was going around to all the colored people's houses looking to buy up musical instruments.

AVERY: Yeah, but Berniece didn't want to sell that piano. After she told me about it . . . I could see why she didn't want to sell it.

BOY WILLIE: What's this man's name?

AVERY: Oh, that's a while back now. I done forgot his name. He give Berniece a card with his name and telephone number on it, but I believe she throwed it away.

[BERNIECE *and* MARETHA *enter from the stairs.*]

BERNIECE: Maretha, run back upstairs and get my pocketbook. And wipe that hair grease off your forehead. Go ahead, hurry up.

[MARETHA *exits up the stairs.*]

How you doing, Avery? You done got all dressed up. You look nice. Boy Willie, I thought you and Lymon was going to sell them watermelons.

BOY WILLIE: Lymon done got sleepy. We liable to get some sleep first.

LYMON: I ain't sleepy.

DOAKER: As many watermelons as you got stacked up on that truck out there, you ought to have been gone.

BOY WILLIE: We gonna go in a minute. We going.

BERNIECE: Doaker. I'm gonna stop down there on Logan Street. You want anything?

DOAKER: You can pick up some ham hocks if you going down there. See if you can get the smoked ones. If they ain't got that get the fresh ones. Don't get the ones that got all that fat under the skin. Look for the long ones. They nice and lean. [*He gives her a dollar.*] Don't get the short ones lessen they smoked. If you got to get the fresh ones make sure that they the long ones. If they ain't got them smoked then go ahead and get the short ones.

[*Pause.*]

You may as well get some turnip greens while you down there. I got some buttermilk . . . if you pick up some cornmeal I'll make me some cornbread and cook up them turnip greens.

[MARETHA *enters from the stairs.*]

MARETHA: We gonna take the streetcar?

BERNIECE: Me and Avery gonna drop you off at the settlement house. You mind them people down there. Don't be going down there showing your color. Boy Willie, I done told you what to do. I'll see you later, Doaker.

AVERY: I'll be seeing you again, Boy Willie.

BOY WILLIE: Hey, Berniece . . . what's the name of that man Avery sent past say he want to buy the piano?

BERNIECE: I knew it. I knew it when I first seen you. I knew you was up to something.

BOY WILLIE: Sutter's brother say he selling the land to me. He waiting on me now. Told me he'd give me two weeks. I got one part. Sell them watermelons get me another part. Then we can sell that piano and I'll have the third part.

BERNIECE: I ain't selling that piano, Boy Willie. If that's why you come up here you can just forget about it. [*To* DOAKER.] Doaker, I'll see you later. Boy Willie ain't nothing but a whole lot of mouth. I ain't paying him no mind. If he come up here thinking he gonna sell that piano then he done come up here for nothing.

[BERNIECE, AVERY, *and* MARETHA *exit the front door.*]

BOY WILLIE: Hey, Lymon! You ready to go sell these watermelons.

[BOY WILLIE *and* LYMON *start to exit. At the door* BOY WILLIE *turns to* DOAKER.]

Hey, Doaker . . . if Berniece don't want to sell that piano . . . I'm gonna cut it in half and go on and sell my half.

[BOY WILLIE *and* LYMON *exit.*]

[*The lights go down on the scene.*]

Scene 2

[*The lights come up on the kitchen. It is three days later.* WINING BOY *sits at the kitchen table. There is a half-empty pint bottle on the table.* DOAKER *busies himself washing pots.* WINING BOY *is fifty-six years old.* DOAKER*'s older brother, he tries to present the image of a successful musician and gambler, but his music, his clothes, and even his manner of presentation are old. He is a man who looking back over his life continues to live it with an odd mixture of zest and sorrow.*]

WINING BOY: So the Ghosts of the Yellow Dog got Sutter. That just go to show you I believe I always lived right. They say every dog gonna have his day and time it go around it sure come back to you. I done seen that a thousand times. I know the truth of that. But I'll tell you outright . . . if I see Sutter's ghost I'll be on the first thing I find that got wheels on it.

[DOAKER *enters from his room.*]

DOAKER: Wining Boy!

WINING BOY: And I'll tell you another thing . . . Berniece ain't gonna sell that piano.

DOAKER: That's what she told him. He say he gonna cut it in half and go on and sell his half. They been around here three days trying to sell them watermelons. They trying to get out to where the white folks live but the truck keep breaking down. They go a block or two and it break down again. They trying to get out to Squirrel Hill and can't get around the corner. He say soon as he can get that truck empty to where he can set the piano up in there he gonna take it out of here and go sell it.

WINING BOY: What about them boys Sutter got? How come they ain't farming that land?

DOAKER: One of them going to school. He left down there and come North to school. The other one ain't got as much sense as that frying pan over yonder. That is the dumbest white man I ever seen. He'd stand in the river and watch it rise till it drown him.

WINING BOY: Other than seeing Sutter's ghost how's Berniece doing?

DOAKER: She doing alright. She still got Crawley on her mind. He been dead three years but she still holding on to him. She need to go out here and let one of these fellows grab a whole handful of whatever she got. She act like it done got precious.

WINING BOY: They always told me any fish will bite if you got good bait.

DOAKER: She stuck up on it. She think it's better than she is. I believe she messing around with Avery. They got something going. He a preacher now. If you let him tell it the Holy Ghost sat on his head and heaven opened up with thunder and lightning and God was calling his name. Told him to go out and preach and tend to his flock. That's what he gonna call his church. The Good Shepherd Church.

WINING BOY: They had that joker down in Spear walking around talking about he Jesus Christ. He gonna live the life of Christ. Went through the Last Supper and everything. Rented him a mule on Palm Sunday and rode through the town. Did everything . . . talking about he Christ. He did everything until they got up to that crucifixion part. Got up to that part and told everybody to go home and quit pretending. He got up to the crucifixion part and changed his mind. Had a whole bunch of folks come down there to see him get nailed to the cross. I don't know who's the worse fool. Him or them. Had all them folks come down there . . . even carried the cross up this little hill. People standing around waiting to see him get nailed to the cross and he stop everything and preach a little sermon and told everybody to go home. Had enough nerve to tell them to come to church on Easter Sunday to celebrate his resurrection.

DOAKER: I'm surprised Avery ain't thought about that. He trying every little thing to get him a congregation together. They meeting over at his house till he get him a church.

WINING BOY: Ain't nothing wrong with being a preacher. You got the preacher on one hand and the gambler on the other. Sometimes there ain't too much difference in them.

DOAKER: How long you been in Kansas City?

WINING BOY: Since I left here. I got tied up with some old gal down there. [*Pause.*] You know Cleotha died.

DOAKER: Yeah, I heard that last time I was down there. I was sorry to hear that.

WINING BOY: One of her friends wrote and told me. I got the letter right here. [*He takes the letter out of his pocket.*] I was down in Kansas City and she wrote and told me Cleotha had died. Name of Willa Bryant. She say she know cousin Rupert.

[*He opens the letter and reads.*]

Dear Wining Boy: I am writing this letter to let you know Miss Cleotha Holman passed on Saturday the first of May she departed this world in the loving arms of her sister Miss Alberta Samuels. I know you would want to know this and am writing as a friend of Cleotha. There have been many hardships since last you seen her but she survived them all and to the end was a good woman whom I hope have God's grace and is in His Paradise. Your cousin Rupert Bates is my friend also and he give me your address and I pray this reaches you about Cleotha. Miss Willa Bryant. A friend. [*He folds the letter and returns it to his pocket.*]

They was nailing her coffin shut by the time I heard about it. I never knew she was sick. I believe it was that yellow jaundice. That's what killed her mama.

DOAKER: Cleotha wasn't but forty-some.

WINING BOY: She was forty-six. I got ten years on her. I met her when she was sixteen. You remember I used to run around there. Couldn't nothing keep me still. Much as I loved Cleotha I loved to ramble. Couldn't nothing keep me still. We got married and we used to fight about it all the time. Then one day she asked me to leave. Told me she loved me before I left. Told me, Wining Boy, you got a home as long as I got mine. And I believe in my heart I always felt that and that kept me safe.

DOAKER: Cleotha always did have a nice way about her.

WINING BOY: Man that woman was something. I used to thank the Lord. Many a night I sat up and looked out over my life. Said, well, I had Cleotha. When it didn't look like there was nothing else for me, I said, thank God, at least I had that. If ever I go anywhere in this life I done known a good woman. And that used to hold me till the next morning.

[*Pause.*] What you got? Give me a little nip. I know you got something stuck up in your room.

DOAKER: I ain't seen you walk in here and put nothing on the table. You done sat there and drank up your whiskey. Now you talking about what you got.

WINING BOY: I got plenty money. Give me a little nip.

[DOAKER *carries a glass into his room and returns with it half-filled. He sets it on the table in front of* WINING BOY.]

WINING BOY: You hear from Coreen?

DOAKER: She up in New York. I let her go from my mind.

WINING BOY: She was something back then. She wasn't too pretty but she had a way of looking at you made you know there was a whole lot of woman there. You got married and snatched her out from under us and we all got mad at you.

DOAKER: She up in New York City. That's what I hear.

[*The door opens and* BOY WILLIE *and* LYMON *enter.*]

BOY WILLIE: Aw hell . . . look here! We was just talking about you. Doaker say you left out of here with a whole sack of money. I told him we wasn't going see you till you got broke.

WINING BOY: What you mean broke? I got a whole pocketful of money.

DOAKER: Did you all get that truck fixed?

BOY WILLIE: We got it running and got halfway out there on Centre and it broke down again. Lymon went out there and messed it up some more. Fellow told us we got to wait till tomorrow to get it fixed. Say he have it running like new. Lymon going back down there and sleep in the truck so the people don't take the watermelons.

LYMON: Lymon nothing. You go down there and sleep in it.

BOY WILLIE: You was sleeping in it down home, nigger! I don't know nothing about sleeping in no truck.

LYMON: I ain't sleeping in no truck.

BOY WILLIE: They can take all the watermelons. I don't care. Wining Boy, where you coming from? Where you been?

WINING BOY: I been down in Kansas City.

BOY WILLIE: You remember Lymon? Lymon Jackson.

WINING BOY: Yeah, I used to know his daddy.

BOY WILLIE: Doaker say you don't never leave no address with nobody. Say he got to depend on your whim. See when it strike you to pay a visit.

WINING BOY: I got four or five addresses.

BOY WILLIE: Doaker say Berniece asked you for three dollars and you got mad and left.

WINING BOY: Berniece try and rule over you too much for me. That's why I left. It wasn't about no three dollars.

BOY WILLIE: Where you getting all these sacks of money from? I need to be with you. Doaker say you had a whole sack of money . . . turn some of it loose.

WINING BOY: I was just fixing to ask you for five dollars.

BOY WILLIE: I ain't got no money. I'm trying to get some. Doaker tell you about Sutter? The Ghosts of the Yellow Dog got him about three weeks ago. Berniece done seen his ghost and everything. He right upstairs. [*Calls.*] Hey Sutter! Wining Boy's here. Come on, get a drink!

WINING BOY: How many that make the Ghosts of the Yellow Dog done got?

BOY WILLIE: Must be about nine or ten, eleven or twelve. I don't know.

DOAKER: You got Ed Saunders. Howard Peterson. Charlie Webb.

WINING BOY: Robert Smith. That fellow that shot Becky's boy . . . say he was stealing peaches . . .

DOAKER: You talking about Bob Mallory.

BOY WILLIE: Berniece say she don't believe all that about the Ghosts of the Yellow Dog.

WINING BOY: She ain't got to believe. You go ask them white folks in Sunflower County if they believe. You go ask Sutter if he believe. I don't care if Berniece believe or not. I done been to where the Southern cross the Yellow Dog and called out their names. They talk back to you, too.

LYMON: What they sound like? The wind or something?

BOY WILLIE: You done been there for real, Wining Boy?

WINING BOY: Nineteen thirty. July of nineteen thirty I stood right there on that spot. It didn't look like nothing was going right in my life. I said everything can't go wrong all the time . . . let me go down there and call on the Ghosts of the Yellow Dog, see if they can help me. I went down there where them two railroads cross each other . . . I stood right there on that spot and called out their names. They talk back to you, too.

LYMON: People say you can ask them questions. They talk to you like that?

WINING BOY: A lot of things you got to find out on your own. I can't say how they talked to nobody else. But to me it just filled me up in a strange sort of way to be standing there on that spot. I didn't want to leave. It felt like the longer I stood there the bigger I got. I seen the train coming and it seem like I was bigger than the train. I started not to move. But something told me to go ahead and get on out the way. The train passed and I started to go back up there and stand some more. But something told me not to do it. I walked away from there feeling like a king. Went on and had a stroke of luck that run on for three years. So I don't care if Berniece believe or not. Berniece ain't got to believe. I know cause I been there. Now Doaker'll tell you about the Ghosts of the Yellow Dog.

DOAKER: I don't try and talk that stuff with Berniece. Avery got her all tied up in that church. She just think it's a whole lot of nonsense.

BOY WILLIE: Berniece don't believe in nothing. She just think she believe. She believe in anything if it's convenient for her to believe. But when that convenience run out then she ain't got nothing to stand on.

WINING BOY: Let's not get on Berniece now. Doaker tell me you talking about selling that piano.

BOY WILLIE: Yeah . . . hey, Doaker, I got the name of that man Avery was talking about. The man what's fixing the truck gave me his name. Everybody know him. Say he buy up anything you can make music with. I got his name and his telephone number. Hey, Wining Boy, Sutter's brother say he selling the land to me. I got one part. Sell them watermelons get me the second part. Then . . . soon as I get them watermelons out that truck I'm gonna take and sell that piano and get the third part.

DOAKER: That land ain't worth nothing no more. The smart white man's up here in these cities. He cut the land loose and step back and watch you and the dumb white man argue over it.

WINING BOY: How you know Sutter's brother ain't sold it already? You talking about selling the piano and the man's liable to sold the land two or three times.

BOY WILLIE: He say he waiting on me. He say he give me two weeks. That's two weeks from Friday. Say if I ain't back by then he might gonna sell it to somebody else. He say he wanna see me with it.

WINING BOY: You know as well as I know the man gonna sell the land to the first one walk up and hand him the money.

BOY WILLIE: That's just who I'm gonna be. Look, you ain't gotta know he waiting on me. I know. Okay. I know what the man told me. Stoval already done tried to buy the land from him and he told him no. The man say he waiting on me . . . he waiting on me. Hey, Doaker . . . give me a drink. I see Wining Boy got his glass.

[DOAKER *exits into his room.*]

Wining Boy, what you doing in Kansas City? What they got down there?

LYMON: I hear they got some nice-looking women in Kansas City. I sure like to go down there and find out.

WINING BOY: Man, the women down there is something else.

[DOAKER *enters with a bottle of whiskey. He sets it on the table with some glasses.*]

DOAKER: You wanna sit up here and drink up my whiskey, leave a dollar on the table when you get up.

BOY WILLIE: You ain't doing nothing but showing your hospitality. I know we ain't got to pay for your hospitality.

WINING BOY: Doaker say they had you and Lymon down on the Parchman Farm. Had you on my old stomping grounds.

BOY WILLIE: Me and Lymon was down there hauling wood for Jim Miller and keeping us a little bit to sell. Some white fellows tried to run us off of it. That's when Crawley got killed. They put me and Lymon in the penitentiary.

LYMON: They ambushed us right there where that road dip down and around that bend in the creek. Crawley tried to fight them. Me and Boy Willie got away but the sheriff got us. Say we was stealing wood. They shot me in my stomach.

BOY WILLIE: They looking for Lymon down there now. They rounded him up and put him in jail for not working.

LYMON: Fined me a hundred dollars. Mr. Stovall come and paid my hundred dollars and the judge say I got to work for him to pay him back his hundred dollars. I told them I'd rather take my thirty days but they wouldn't let me do that.

BOY WILLIE: As soon as Stovall turned his back, Lymon was gone. He down there living in that truck dodging the sheriff and Stovall. He got both of them looking for him. So I brought him up here.

LYMON: I told Boy Willie I'm gonna stay up here. I ain't going back with him.

BOY WILLIE: Ain't nobody twisting your arm to make you go back. You can do what you want to do.

WINING BOY: I'll go back with you. I'm on my way down there. You gonna take the train? I'm gonna take the train.

LYMON: They treat you better up here.

BOY WILLIE: I ain't worried about nobody mistreating me. They treat you like you let them treat you. They mistreat me I mistreat them right back. Ain't no difference in me and the white man.

WINING BOY: Ain't no difference as far as how somebody supposed to treat you. I agree with that. But I'll tell you the difference between the colored man and the white man. Alright. Now you take and eat some berries. They taste real good to you. So you say I'm gonna go out and get me a whole pot of these berries and cook them up to make a pie or whatever. But you ain't looked to see them berries is sitting in the white fellow's yard. Ain't got no fence around them. You figure anybody want something they'd fence it in. Alright. Now the white man come along and say that's my land. Therefore everything that grow on it belong to me. He tell the sheriff, "I want you to put this nigger in jail as a warning to all the other niggers. Otherwise first thing you know these niggers have everything that belong to us."

BOY WILLIE: I'd come back at night and haul off his whole patch while he was sleep.

WINING BOY: Alright. Now Mr. So and So, he sell the land to you. And he come to you and say, "John, you own the land. It's all yours now. But them is my berries. And come time to pick them I'm gonna send my boys over. You got the land . . . but them berries, I'm gonna keep them. They mine." And he go and fix it with the law that them is his berries. Now that's the difference between the colored man and the white man. The colored man can't fix nothing with the law.

BOY WILLIE: I don't go by what the law say. The law's liable to say anything. I go by if it's right or not. It don't matter to me what the law say. I take and look at it for myself.

LYMON: That's why you gonna end up back down there on the Parchman Farm.

BOY WILLIE: I ain't thinking about no Parchman Farm. You liable to go back before me.

LYMON: They work you too hard down there. All that weeding and hoeing and chopping down trees. I didn't like all that.

WINING BOY: You ain't got to like your job on Parchman. Hey, tell him, Doaker, the only one got to like his job is the waterboy.

DOAKER: If he don't like his job he need to set that bucket down.

BOY WILLIE: That's what they told Lymon. They had Lymon on water and everybody got mad at him cause he was lazy.

LYMON: That water was heavy.

BOY WILLIE: They had Lymon down there singing: [*Sings.*]

O Lord Berta Berta O Lord gal oh-ah
O Lord Berta Berta O Lord gal well

[LYMON *and* WINING BOY *join in.*]

Go 'head marry don't you wait on me oh-ah
Go 'head marry don't you wait on me well
Might not want you when I go free oh-ah
Might not want you when I go free well

BOY WILLIE: Come on, Doaker. Doaker know this one.

[As DOAKER *joins in the men stamp and clap to keep time. They sing in harmony with great fervor and style.*]

O Lord Berta Berta O Lord gal oh-ah
O Lord Berta Berta O Lord gal well

Raise them up higher, let them drop on down oh-ah
Raise them up higher, let them drop on down well
Don't know the difference when the sun go down oh-ah
Don't know the difference when the sun go down well

Berta in Meridan and she living at ease oh-ah
Berta in Meridan and she living at ease well

I'm on old Parchman, got to work or leave oh-ah
I'm on old Parchman, got to work or leave well

O Alberta, Berta, O Lord gal oh-ah
O Alberta, Berta, O Lord gal well

When you marry, don't marry no farming man oh-ah
When you marry, don't marry no farming man well
Everyday Monday, hoe handle in your hand oh-ah
Everyday Monday, hoe handle in your hand well

When you marry, marry a railroad man, oh-ah
When you marry, marry a railroad man, well
Everyday Sunday, dollar in your hand oh-ah
Everyday Sunday, dollar in your hand well

O Alberta, Berta, O Lord gal oh-ah
O Alberta, Berta, O Lord gal well

BOY WILLIE: Doaker like that part. He like that railroad part.

LYMON: Doaker sound like Tangleye. He can't sing a lick.

BOY WILLIE: Hey, Doaker, they still talk about you down on Parchman. They ask me, "You Doaker Boy's nephew?" I say, "Yeah, me and him is family." They treated me alright soon as I told them that. Say, "Yeah, he my uncle."

DOAKER: I don't never want to see none of them niggers no more.

BOY WILLIE: I don't want to see them either. Hey, Wining Boy, come on play some piano. You a piano player, play some piano. Lymon wanna hear you.

WINING BOY: I give that piano up. That was the best thing that ever happened to me, getting rid of that piano. That piano got so big and I'm carrying it around on my back. I don't wish that on nobody. See, you think it's all fun being a recording star. Got to carrying that piano around and man did I get slow. Got just like molasses. The world just slipping by me and I'm walking around with that piano. Alright. Now, there ain't but so many places you can go. Only so many road wide enough for you and that piano. And that piano get heavier and heavier. Go to a place and they find out you play piano, the first thing they want to do is give you a drink, find you a piano, and sit you right down. And that's where you gonna be for the next eight hours. They ain't gonna let you get up! Now, the first three or four years of that is fun. You can't get enough whiskey and you can't get enough women and you don't never get tired of playing that piano. But that only last so long. You look up one day and you hate the whiskey, and you hate the women, and you hate the piano. But that's all you got. You can't do nothing else. All you know how to do is play that piano. Now, who am I? Am I me? Or am I the piano player? Sometime it seem like the only thing to do is shoot the piano player cause he the cause of all the trouble I'm having.

DOAKER: What you gonna do when your troubles get like mine?

LYMON: If I knew how to play it, I'd play it. That's a nice piano.

BOY WILLIE: Whoever playing better play quick. Sutter's brother say he waiting on me. I sell them watermelons. Get Berniece to sell that piano. Put them two parts with the part I done saved . . .

WINING BOY: Berniece ain't gonna sell that piano. I don't see why you don't know that.

BOY WILLIE: What she gonna do with it? She ain't doing nothing but letting it sit up there and rot. That piano ain't doing nobody no good.

LYMON: That's a nice piano. If I had it I'd sell it. Unless I knew how to play like Wining Boy. You can get a nice price for that piano.

DOAKER: Now I'm gonna tell you something, Lymon don't know this . . . but I'm gonna tell you why me and Wining Boy say Berniece ain't gonna sell that piano.

BOY WILLIE: She ain't got to sell it! I'm gonna sell it! Berniece ain't got no more rights to that piano than I do.

DOAKER: I'm talking to the man . . . let me talk to the man. See, now . . . to understand why we say that . . . to understand about that piano . . . you got to go back to slavery time. See, our family was owned by a fellow named Robert Sutter. That was Sutter's grandfather. Alright. The piano was owned by a fellow named Joel Nolander. He was one of the Nolander brothers from down in Georgia. It was coming up on Sutter's wedding anniversary and he was looking to buy his wife . . . Miss Ophelia was her name . . . he was looking to buy her an anniversary present. Only thing with him . . . he ain't had no money. But he had some niggers. So he asked Mr. Nolander to see if maybe he could trade off some of his niggers for that piano. Told him he would give him one and a half niggers for it. That's the way he told him. Say he could have one full grown and one half grown. Mr. Nolander agreed only he say he had to pick them. He didn't want Sutter to give him just any old nigger. He say he wanted to have the pick of the litter. So Sutter lined up his niggers and Mr. Nolander looked them over and out of the whole bunch he picked my grandmother . . . her name was Berniece . . .

same like Berniece . . . and he picked my daddy when he wasn't nothing but a little boy nine years old. They made the trade off and Miss Ophelia was so happy with that piano that it got to be just about all she would do was play on that piano.

WINING BOY: Just get up in the morning, get all dressed up and sit down and play on that piano.

DOAKER: Alright. Time go along. Time go along. Miss Ophelia got to missing my grandmother . . . the way she would cook and clean the house and talk to her and what not. And she missed having my daddy around the house to fetch things for her. So she asked to see if maybe she could trade back that piano and get her niggers back. Mr. Nolander said no. Said a deal was a deal. Him and Sutter had a big falling out about it and Miss Ophelia took sick to the bed. Wouldn't get out of the bed in the morning. She just lay there. The doctor said she was wasting away.

WINING BOY: That's when Sutter called our granddaddy up to the house.

DOAKER: Now, our granddaddy's name was Boy Willie. That's who Boy Willie's named after . . . only they called him Willie Boy. Now, he was a worker of wood. He could make you anything you wanted out of wood. He'd make you a desk. A table. A lamp. Anything you wanted. Them white fellows around there used to come up to Mr. Sutter and get him to make all kinds of things for them. Then they'd pay Mr. Sutter a nice price. See, everything my granddaddy made Mr. Sutter owned cause he owned him. That's why when Mr. Nolander offered to buy him to keep the family together Mr. Sutter wouldn't sell him. Told Mr. Nolander he didn't have enough money to buy him. Now . . . am I telling it right, Wining Boy?

WINING BOY: You telling it.

DOAKER: Sutter called him up to the house and told him to carve my grandmother and my daddy's picture on the piano for Miss Ophelia. And he took and carved this . . . [DOAKER *crosses over to the piano.*]

See that right there? That's my grandmother, Berniece. She looked just like that. And he put a picture of my daddy when he wasn't nothing but a little boy the way he remembered him. He made them up out of his memory. Only thing . . . he didn't stop there. He carved all this. He got a picture of his mama . . . Mama Esther . . . and his daddy, Boy Charles.

WINING BOY: That was the first Boy Charles.

DOAKER: Then he put on the side here all kinds of things. See that? That's when him and Mama Berniece got married. They called it jumping the broom. That's how you got married in them days. Then he got here when my daddy was born . . . and here he got Mama Esther's funeral . . . and down here he got Mr. Nolander taking Mama Berniece and my daddy away down to his place in Georgia. He got all kinds of things what happened with our family. When Mr. Sutter seen the piano with all them carvings on it he got mad. He didn't ask for all that. But see . . . there wasn't nothing he could do about it. When Miss Ophelia seen it . . . she got excited. Now she had her piano and her niggers too. She took back to playing it and played on it right up till the day she died. Alright . . . now see, our brother Boy Charles . . . that's Berniece and Boy Willie's daddy . . . he was the oldest of us three boys. He's dead now. But he would have been fifty-seven if he had lived. He died in 1911 when he was thirty-one years old. Boy Charles used to talk about that piano all the time. He never could get it off his mind. Two or three months go by and he be talking about it again. He be talking about taking it out of Sutter's house. Say it was the story of our whole family and as long as Sutter had it . . . he had us. Say we was still in slavery. Me and Wining Boy tried to talk him out of it but it wouldn't do any good. Soon as he quiet down about it he'd start up again. We seen where he wasn't gonna get it off his mind . . . so, on the Fourth of July, 1911 . . . when Sutter was at the picnic what the county give every year . . . me and Wining Boy went on down there with him and took that piano out of Sutter's house. We put it on a wagon and me and Wining Boy carried it over into the next county with Mama Ola's people. Boy Charles decided to stay around there and wait until Sutter got home to make it look like business as usual.

Now, I don't know what happened when Sutter came home and found that piano gone. But somebody went up to Boy Charles's house and set it on fire. But he wasn't in there. He must have seen them coming cause he went down and caught the 3:57 Yellow Dog. He didn't know they was gonna come down and stop the train. Stopped the train and found Boy Charles in the boxcar with four of them hobos. Must have got mad when they couldn't find the piano cause they set the boxcar afire and killed everybody. Now, nobody know who done that. Some people say it was Sutter cause it was his piano. Some people say it was Sheriff Carter. Some people say it was Robert Smith and Ed Saunders. But don't nobody know for sure. It was about two months after that that Ed Saunders fell down his well. Just upped and fell down his well for no reason. People say it was the ghost of them men who burned up in the boxcar that pushed him in his well. They started calling them the Ghosts of the Yellow Dog. Now, that's how all that got started and that why we say Berniece ain't gonna sell that piano. Cause her daddy died over it.

BOY WILLIE: All that's in the past. If my daddy had seen where he could have traded that piano in for some land of his own, it wouldn't be sitting up here now. He spent his whole life farming on somebody else's land. I ain't gonna do that. See, he couldn't do no better. When he come along he ain't had nothing he could build on. His daddy ain't had nothing to give him. The only thing my daddy had to give me was that piano. And he died over giving me that. I ain't gonna let it sit up there and rot without trying to do something with it. If Berniece can't see that, then I'm gonna go ahead and sell my half. And you and Wining Boy know I'm right.

DOAKER: Ain't nobody said nothing about who's right and who's wrong. I was just telling the man about the piano. I was telling him why we say Berniece ain't gonna sell it.

LYMON: Yeah, I can see why you say that now. I told Boy Willie he ought to stay up here with me.

BOY WILLIE: You stay! I'm going back! That's what I'm gonna do with my life! Why I got to come up here and learn to do something I don't know how to do when I already know how to farm? You stay up here and make your own way if that's what you want to do. I'm going back and live my life the way I want to live it.

[WINING BOY *gets up and crosses to the piano.*]

WINING BOY: Let's see what we got here. I ain't played on this thing for a while.

DOAKER: You can stop telling that. You was playing on it the last time you was through here. We couldn't get you off of it. Go on and play something.

[WINING BOY *sits down at the piano and plays and sings. The song is one which has put many dimes and quarters in his pocket, long ago, in dimly remembered towns and way stations. He plays badly, without hesitation, and sings in a forceful voice.*]

WINING BOY: [*Singing.*]

I am a rambling gambling man
I gambled in many towns
I rambled this wide world over
I rambled this world around
I had my ups and downs in life
And bitter times I saw
But I never knew what misery was
Till I lit on old Arkansas.

I started out one morning
to meet that early train
He said, "You better work for me
I have some land to drain.
I'll give you fifty cents a day,
Your washing, board and all
And you shall be a different man
In the state of Arkansas."

I worked six months for the rascal
Joe Herrin was his name
He fed me old corn dodgers
They was hard as any rock
My tooth is all got loosened
And my knees begin to knock
That was the kind of hash I got
In the state of Arkansas.

Traveling man
I've traveled all around this world
Traveling man
I've traveled from land to land
Traveling man
I've traveled all around this world
Well it ain't no use
writing no news
I'm a traveling man.

[*The door opens and* BERNIECE *enters with* MARETHA.]

BERNIECE: Is that . . . Lord, I know that ain't Wining Boy sitting there.

WINING BOY: Hey, Berniece.

BERNIECE: You all had this planned. You and Boy Willie had this planned.

WINING BOY: I didn't know he was gonna be here. I'm on my way down home. I stopped by to see you and Doaker first.

DOAKER: I told the nigger he left out of here with that sack of money, we thought we might never see him again. Boy Willie say he wasn't gonna see him till he got broke. I looked up and seen him sitting on the doorstep asking for two dollars. Look at him laughing. He know it's the truth.

BERNIECE: Boy Willie, I didn't see that truck out there. I thought you was out selling watermelons.

BOY WILLIE: We done sold them all. Sold the truck too.

BERNIECE: I don't want to go through none of your stuff. I done told you to go back where you belong.

BOY WILLIE: I was just teasing you, woman. You can't take no teasing?

BERNIECE: Wining Boy, when you get here?

WINING BOY: A little while ago. I took the train from Kansas City.

BERNIECE: Let me go upstairs and change and then I'll cook you something to eat.

BOY WILLIE: You ain't cooked me nothing when I come.

BERNIECE: Boy Willie, go on and leave me alone. Come on, Maretha, get up here and change your clothes before you get them dirty.

[BERNIECE *exits up the stairs, followed by* MARETHA.]

WINING BOY: Maretha sure getting big, ain't she, Doaker. And just as pretty as she want to be. I didn't know Crawley had it in him.

[BOY WILLIE *crosses to the piano.*]

BOY WILLIE: Hey, Lymon . . . get up on the other side of this piano and let me see something.

WINING BOY: Boy Willie, what is you doing?

BOY WILLIE: I'm seeing how heavy this piano is. Get up over there, Lymon.

WINING BOY: Go on and leave that piano alone. You ain't taking that piano out of here and selling it.

BOY WILLIE: Just as soon as I get them watermelons out that truck.

WINING BOY: Well, I got something to say about that.

BOY WILLIE: This my daddy's piano.

WINING BOY: He ain't took it by himself. Me and Doaker helped him.

BOY WILLIE: He died by himself. Where was you and Doaker at then? Don't come telling me nothing about this piano. This is me and Berniece's piano. Am I right, Doaker?

DOAKER: Yeah, you right.

BOY WILLIE: Let's see if we can lift it up, Lymon. Get a good grip on it and pick it up on your end. Ready? Lift!

[*As they start to move the piano, the sound of* SUTTER'S GHOST *is heard.* DOAKER *is the only one to hear it. With difficulty they move the piano a little bit so it is out of place.*]

BOY WILLIE: What you think?

LYMON: It's heavy . . . but you can move it. Only it ain't gonna be easy.

BOY WILLIE: It wasn't that heavy to me. Okay, let's put it back.

[*The sound of* SUTTER'S GHOST *is heard again. They all hear it as* BERNIECE *enters on the stairs.*]

BERNIECE: Boy Willie . . . you gonna play around with me one too many times. And then God's gonna bless you and West is gonna dress you. Now set that piano back over there. I done told you a hundred times I ain't selling that piano.

BOY WILLIE: I'm trying to get me some land, woman. I need that piano to get me some money so I can buy Sutter's land.

BERNIECE: Money can't buy what that piano cost. You can't sell your soul for money. It won't go with the buyer. It'll shrivel and shrink to know that you ain't taken on to it. But it won't go with the buyer.

BOY WILLIE: I ain't talking about all that, woman. I ain't talking about selling my soul. I'm talking about trading that piece of wood for some land. Get something under your feet. Land the only thing God ain't making no more of. You can always get you another piano. I'm talking about some land. What you get something out the ground from. That's what I'm talking about. You can't do nothing with that piano but sit up there and look at it.

BERNIECE: That's just what I'm gonna do. Wining Boy, you want me to fry you some pork chops?

BOY WILLIE: Now, I'm gonna tell you the way I see it. The only thing that make that piano worth something is them carvings Papa Willie Boy put on there. That's what make it worth something. That was my great-grandaddy. Papa Boy Charles brought that piano into the house. Now, I'm supposed to build on what they left me. You can't do nothing with that piano sitting up here in the house. That's just like if I let them watermelons sit out there and rot. I'd be a fool. Alright now, if you say to me, Boy Willie, I'm using that piano. I give out lessons on it and that help me make my rent or whatever. Then that be something else. I'd have to go on and say, well, Berniece using that piano. She building on it. Let her go on and use it. I got to find another way to get Sutter's land. But Doaker say you ain't touched that piano the whole time it's been up here. So why you wanna stand in my way? See, you just looking at the sentimental value. See, that's good. That's alright. I take my hat off whenever somebody say my daddy's name. But I ain't gonna be no fool about no sentimental value. You can sit up here and look at the piano for the next hundred years and it's just gonna be a piano. You can't make more than that. Now I want to get Sutter's land with that piano. I get Sutter's land and I can go down and cash in the crop and get my seed. As long as I got the land and the seed then I'm alright. I can always get me a little something else. Cause that land give back to you. I can make me another crop and cash that in. I still got the land and the seed. But that piano don't put out nothing else. You ain't got nothing working for you. Now, the kind of man my daddy was he would have understood that. I'm sorry you can't see it that way. But that's why I'm gonna take that piano out of here and sell it.

BERNIECE: You ain't taking that piano out of my house. [*She crosses to the piano.*] Look at this piano. Look at it. Mama Ola polished this piano with her tears for seventeen years. For seventeen years she rubbed on it till her hands bled. Then she rubbed the blood in . . . mixed it up with the rest of the blood on it. Every day that God breathed life into her body she rubbed and cleaned and polished and prayed over it. "Play something for me, Berniece. Play something for me, Berniece." Every day. "I cleaned it up for you, play something for me, Berniece." You always talking about your daddy but you ain't never stopped to look at what his foolishness cost your mama. Seventeen years' worth of cold nights and an empty bed. For what? For a piano? For a piece of wood? To get even with somebody? I look at you and you're all the same. You, Papa Boy Charles, Wining Boy, Doaker, Crawley . . . you're all alike. All this thieving and killing and thieving and killing. And what it ever lead to? More killing and more thieving. I ain't never seen it come to nothing. People getting burned up. People getting shot. People falling down their wells. It don't never stop.

DOAKER: Come on now, Berniece, ain't no need in getting upset.

BOY WILLIE: I done a little bit of stealing here and there, but I ain't never killed nobody. I can't be speaking for nobody else. You all got to speak for yourself, but I ain't never killed nobody.

BERNIECE: You killed Crawley just as sure as if you pulled the trigger.

BOY WILLIE: See, that's ignorant. That's downright foolish for you to say something like that. You ain't doing nothing but showing your ignorance. If the nigger was here I'd whup his ass for getting me and Lymon shot at.

BERNIECE: Crawley ain't knew about the wood.

BOY WILLIE: We told the man about the wood. Ask Lymon. He knew all about the wood. He seen we was sneaking it. Why else we gonna be out there at night? Don't come telling me Crawley ain't knew about the wood. Them fellows come up on us and Crawley tried to bully them. Me and Lymon seen the sheriff with them and give in. Wasn't no sense in getting killed over fifty dollars' worth of wood.

BERNIECE: Crawley ain't knew you stole that wood.

BOY WILLIE: We ain't stole no wood. Me and Lymon was hauling wood for Jim Miller and keeping us a little bit on the side. We dumped our little bit down there by the creek till we had enough to make a load. Some fellows seen us and we figured we better get it before they did. We come up there and got Crawley to help us load it. Figured we'd cut him in. Crawley trying to keep the wolf from his door . . . we was trying to help him.

LYMON: Me and Boy Willie told him about the wood. We told him some fellows might be trying to beat us to it. He say let me go back and get my thirty-eight. That's what caused all the trouble.

BOY WILLIE: If Crawley ain't had the gun he'd be alive today.

LYMON: We had it about half loaded when they come up on us. We seen the sheriff with them and we tried to get away. We ducked around near the bend in the creek . . . but they was down there too. Boy Willie say let's give in. But Crawley pulled out his gun and started shooting. That's when they started shooting back.

BERNIECE: All I know is Crawley would be alive if you hadn't come up there and got him.

BOY WILLIE: I ain't had nothing to do with Crawley getting killed. That was his own fault.

BERNIECE: Crawley's dead and in the ground and you still walking around here eating. That's all I know. He went off to load some wood with you and ain't never come back.

BOY WILLIE: I told you, woman . . . I ain't had nothing to do with . . .

BERNIECE: He ain't here, is he? He ain't here! [BERNIECE *hits* BOY WILLIE.] I said he ain't here. Is he?

[BERNIECE *continues to hit* BOY WILLIE, *who doesn't move to defend himself, other than back up and turning his head so that most of the blows fall on his chest and arms.*]

DOAKER [*Grabbing* BERNIECE.]: Come on, Berniece . . . let it go, it ain't his fault.

BERNIECE: He ain't here, is he? Is he?

BOY WILLIE: I told you I ain't responsible for Crawley.

BERNIECE: He ain't here.

BOY WILLIE: Come on now, Berniece . . . don't do this now. Doaker get her. I ain't had nothing to do with Crawley . . .

BERNIECE: You come up there and got him!

BOY WILLIE: I done told you now. Doaker, get her. I ain't playing.

DOAKER: Come on. Berniece.

[MARETHA *is heard screaming upstairs. It is a scream of stark terror.*]

MARETHA: Mama! . . . Mama! [*The lights go down to black. End of Act I.*]

ACT II

Scene 1

[*The lights come up on the kitchen. It is the following morning.* DOAKER *is ironing the pants to his uniform. He has a pot cooking on the stove at the same time. He is singing a song. The song provides him with the rhythm for his work and he moves about the kitchen with the ease born of many years as a railroad cook.*]

DOAKER:

Gonna leave Jackson Mississippi
and go to Memphis
and double back to Jackson
Come on down to Hattiesburg
Change cars on the Y. D.
coming through the territory to
Meridian
and Meridian to Greenville
and Greenville to Memphis
I'm on my way and I know where

Change cars on the Katy
Leaving Jackson
and going through Clarksdale
Hello Winona!
Courtland!
Bateville!
Como!
Senitobia!
Lewisberg!
Sunflower!
Glendora!
Sharkey!
And double back to Jackson
Hello Greenwood
I'm on my way Memphis
Clarksdale
Moorhead
Indianola
Can a highball pass through?
Highball on through sir
Grand Carson!
Thirty First Street Depot
Fourth Street Depot
Memphis!

[WINING BOY *enters carrying a suit of clothes.*]

DOAKER: I thought you took that suit to the pawnshop?

WINING BOY: I went down there and the man tell me the suit is too old. Look at this suit. This is one hundred percent silk! How a silk suit gonna get too old? I know what it was he just didn't want to give me five dollars for it. Best he wanna give me is three dollars. I figure a silk suit is worth five dollars all over the world. I wasn't gonna part with it for no three dollars so I brought it back.

DOAKER: They got another pawnshop up on Wylie.

WINING BOY: I carried it up there. He say he don't take no clothes. Only thing he take is guns and radios. Maybe a guitar or two. Where's Berniece?

DOAKER: Berniece still at work. Boy Willie went down there to meet Lymon this morning. I guess they got that truck fixed, they been out there all day and ain't come back yet. Maretha scared to sleep up there now. Berniece don't know, but I seen Sutter before she did.

WINING BOY: Say what?

DOAKER: About three weeks ago. I had just come back from down there. Sutter couldn't have been dead more than three days. He was sitting over there at the piano. I come out to go to work . . . and he was sitting right there. Had his hand on top of his head just like Berniece said. I believe he broke his neck when he fell in the well. I kept quiet about it. I didn't see no reason to upset Berniece.

WINING BOY: Did he say anything? Did he say he was looking for Boy Willie?

DOAKER: He was just sitting there. He ain't said nothing. I went on out the door and left him sitting there. I figure as long as he was on the other side of the room everything be alright. I don't know what I would have done if he had started walking toward me.

WINING BOY: Berniece say he was calling Boy Willie's name.

DOAKER: I ain't heard him say nothing. He was just sitting there when I seen him. But I don't believe Boy Willie pushed him in the well. Sutter here cause of that piano. I heard him playing on it one time. I thought it was Bernice but then she don't play that kind of music. I come out here and ain't seen nobody, but them piano keys was moving a mile a minute. Berniece need to go on and get rid of it. It ain't done nothing but cause trouble.

WINING BOY: I agree with Berniece. Boy Charles ain't took it to give it back. He took it cause he figure he had more right to it than Sutter did. If Sutter can't understand that . . . then that's just the way that go. Sutter dead and in the ground . . . don't care where his ghost is. He can hover around and play on the piano all he want. I want to see him carry it out the house. That's what I want to see. What time Berniece get home? I don't see how I let her get away from me this morning.

DOAKER: You up there sleep. Berniece leave out of here early in the morning. She out there in Squirrel

Hill cleaning house for some bigshot down there at the steel mill. They don't like you to come late. You come late they won't give you your carfare. What kind of business you got with Berniece?

WINING BOY: My business. I ain't asked you what kind of business you got.

DOAKER: Berniece ain't got no money. If that's why you was trying to catch her. She having a hard enough time trying to get by as it is. If she go ahead and marry Avery . . . he working every day . . . she go ahead and marry him they could do alright for themselves. But as it stands she ain't got no money.

WINING BOY: Well, let me have five dollars.

DOAKER: I just give you a dollar before you left out of here. You ain't gonna take my five dollars out there and gamble and drink it up.

WINING BOY: Aw, nigger, give me five dollars. I'll give it back to you.

DOAKER: You wasn't looking to give me five dollars when you had that sack of money. You wasn't looking to throw nothing my way. Now you wanna come in here and borrow five dollars. If you going back with Boy Willie you need to be trying to figure out how you gonna get train fare.

WINING BOY: That's why I need the five dollars. If I had five dollars I could get me some money.

[DOAKER *goes into his pocket.*]

Make it seven.

DOAKER: You take this five dollars . . . and you bring my money back here too.

[BOY WILLIE *and* LYMON *enter. They are happy and excited. They have money in all of their pockets and are anxious to count it.*]

DOAKER: How'd you do out there?

BOY WILLIE: They was lining up for them.

LYMON: Me and Boy Willie couldn't sell them fast enough. Time we got one sold we'd sell another.

BOY WILLIE: I seen what was happening and told Lymon to up the price on them.

LYMON: Boy Willie say charge them a quarter more. They didn't care. A couple of people give me a dollar and told me to keep the change.

BOY WILLIE: One fellow bought five. I say now what he gonna do with five watermelons? He can't eat them all. I sold him the five and asked him did he want to buy five more.

LYMON: I ain't never seen nobody snatch a dollar fast as Boy Willie.

BOY WILLIE: One lady asked me say, "Is they sweet?" I told her say, "Lady, where we grow these watermelons we put sugar in the ground." You know, she believed me. Talking about she had never heard of that before. Lymon was laughing his head off. I told her, "Oh, yeah, we put the sugar right in the ground with the seed." She say, "Well, give me another one." Them white folks is something else . . . ain't they, Lymon?

LYMON: Soon as you holler watermelons they come right out their door. Then they go and get their neighbors. Look like they having a contest to see who can buy the most.

WINING BOY: I got something for Lymon.

[WINING BOY *goes to get his suit.* BOY WILLIE *and* LYMON *continue to count their money.*]

BOY WILLIE: I know you got more than that. You ain't sold all them watermelons for that little bit of money.

LYMON: I'm still looking. That ain't all you got either. Where's all them quarters?

BOY WILLIE: You let me worry about the quarters. Just put the money on the table.

WINING BOY [*Entering with his suit.*]: Look here, Lymon . . . see this? Look at his eyes getting big. He ain't never seen a suit like this. This is one hundred percent silk. Go ahead . . . put it on. See if it fit you.

[LYMON *tries the suit coat on.*]

Look at that. Feel it. That's one hundred percent genuine silk. I got that in Chicago. You can't get clothes like that nowhere but New York and Chicago. You can't get clothes like that in Pittsburgh. These folks in Pittsburgh ain't never seen clothes like that.

LYMON: This is nice, feel real nice and smooth.

WINING BOY: That's a fifty-five-dollar suit. That's the kind of suit the bigshots wear. You need a pistol and a pocketful of money to wear that suit. I'll let you have it for three dollars. The women will fall out their windows they see you in a suit like that. Give me three dollars and go on and wear it down the street and get you a woman.

BOY WILLIE: That looks nice, Lymon. Put the pants on. Let me see it with the pants.

[LYMON *begins to try on the pants.*]

WINING BOY: Look at that . . . see how it fits you? Give me three dollars and go on and take it. Look at that, Doaker . . . don't he look nice?

DOAKER: Yeah . . . that's a nice suit.

WINING BOY: Got a shirt to go with it. Cost you an extra dollar. Four dollars you got the whole deal.

LYMON: How this look, Boy Willie?

BOY WILLIE: That look nice . . . if you like that kind of thing. I don't like them dress-up kind of clothes. If you like it, look real nice.

WINING BOY: That's the kind of suit you need for up here in the North.

LYMON: Four dollars for everything? The suit and the shirt?

WINING BOY: That's cheap. I should be charging you twenty dollars. I give you a break cause you a homeboy. That's the only way I let you have it for four dollars.

LYMON [*Going into his pocket.*]: Okay . . . here go the four dollars.

WINING BOY: You got some shoes? What size you wear?

LYMON: Size nine.

WINING BOY: That's what size I got! Size nine. I let you have them for three dollars.

LYMON: Where they at? Let me see them.

WINING BOY: They real nice shoes, too. Got a nice tip to them. Got pointy toe just like you want. [WINING BOY *goes to get his shoes.*]

LYMON: Come on, Boy Willie, let's go out tonight. I wanna see what it looks like up here. Maybe we go to a picture show. Hey, Doaker, they got picture shows up here?

DOAKER: The Rhumba Theater. Right down there on Fullerton Street. Can't miss it. Got the speakers outside on the sidewalk. You can hear it a block away. Boy Willie know where it's at. [DOAKER *exits into his room.*]

LYMON: Let's go to the picture show, Boy Willie. Let's go find some women.

BOY WILLIE: Hey, Lymon, how many of them watermelons would you say we got left? We got just under a half a load . . . right?

LYMON: About that much. Maybe a little more.

BOY WILLIE: You think that piano will fit up in there?

LYMON: If we stack them watermelons you can sit it up in the front there.

BOY WILLIE: I'm gonna call that man tomorrow.

WINING BOY [*Returns with his shoes.*]: Here you go . . . size nine. Put them on. Cost you three dollars. That's a Florsheim shoe. That's the kind Staggerlee wore.

LYMON [*Trying on the shoes.*]: You sure these size nine?

WINING BOY: You can look at my feet and see we wear the same size. Man, you put on that suit and them shoes and you got something there. You ready for whatever's out there. But is they ready for you? With them shoes on you be the King of the Walk. Have everybody stop to look at your shoes. Wishing they had a pair. I'll give you a break. Go on and take them for two dollars.

[LYMON *pays* WINING BOY *two dollars.*]

LYMON: Come on, Boy Willie . . . let's go find some women. I'm gonna go upstairs and get ready. I'll be ready to go in a minute. Ain't you gonna get dressed?

BOY WILLIE: I'm gonna wear what I got on. I ain't dressing up for these city niggers.

[LYMON *exits up the stairs.*]

That's all Lymon think about is women.

WINING BOY: His daddy was the same way. I used to run around with him. I know his mama too. Two strokes back and I would have been his daddy! His daddy's dead now . . . but I got the nigger out of jail one time. They was fixing to name him Daniel and walk him through the Lion's Den. He got in a tussle with one of them white fellows and the sheriff lit on him like white on rice. That's how the whole thing come about between me and Lymon's mama. She knew me and his daddy used to run together and he got in jail and she went down there and took the sheriff a hundred dollars. Don't get me to lying about where she got it from. I don't know. The sheriff *looked at that hundred dollars and turned his nose up*. Told her, say, "That ain't gonna do him no good. You got to put another hundred on top of that." She come up *there and got me where I was playing at this saloon* . . . said she had all but fifty dollars and asked me if I could help. Now the way I figured it . . . without that fifty dollars the sheriff was gonna turn him over to Parchman. The sheriff turn him over to Parchman it be three years before anybody see him again. Now I'm gonna say it right . . . I will give anybody fifty dollars to keep them out of jail for three years. I give her the fifty dollars and she told me to come over to the house. I ain't asked her. I figure if she was nice enough to invite me I ought to go. I ain't had to say a word. She invited me over just as nice. Say, "Why don't you come over to the house?" She ain't had to say nothing else. Them words rolled off her tongue just as nice. I went on down there and sat about three hours. Started to leave and changed my mind. She grabbed hold to me and say, "Baby, it's all night long." That was one of the shortest nights I have ever spent on this earth! I could have used another eight hours. Lymon's daddy didn't even say nothing to me when he got out. He just looked at me funny. He had a good notion something had happened between me an' her. L. D. Jackson. That was one bad-luck nigger. Got killed at some dance. Fellow walked in and shot him thinking he was somebody else.

[DOAKER *enters from his room.*]

Hey, Doaker, you remember L. D. Jackson?

DOAKER: That's Lymon's daddy. That was one bad-luck nigger.

BOY WILLIE: Look like you ready to railroad some.

DOAKER: Yeah, I got to make that run.

[LYMON *enters from the stairs. He is dressed in his new suit and shoes, to which he has added a cheap straw hat.*]

LYMON: How I look?

WINING BOY: You look like a million dollars. Don't he look good, Doaker? Come on, let's play some cards. You wanna play some cards?

BOY WILLIE: We ain't gonna play no cards with you. Me and Lymon gonna find some women. Hey, Lymon, don't play no cards with Wining Boy. He'll take all your money.

WINING BOY [*To* LYMON.]: You got a magic suit there. You can get you a woman easy with that suit . . . but you got to know the magic words. You know the magic words to get you a woman?

LYMON: I just talk to them to see if I like them and they like me.

WINING BOY: You just walk right up to them and say, "If you got the harbor I got the ship." If that don't work ask them if you can put them in your pocket. The first thing they gonna say is, "It's too small." That's when you look them dead in the eye and say, "Baby, ain't nothing small about me." If that don't work then you move on to another one. Am I telling him right, Doaker?

DOAKER: That man don't need you to tell him nothing about no women. These women these days ain't gonna fall for that kind of stuff. You got to buy them a present. That's what they looking for these days.

BOY WILLIE: Come on, I'm ready. You ready, Lymon? Come on, let's go find some women.

WINING BOY: Here, let me walk out with you. I wanna see the women fall out their window when they see Lymon.

[*They all exit and the lights go down on the scene.*]

Scene 2

[*The lights come up on the kitchen. It is late evening of the same day.* BERNIECE *has set a tub for her bath in the kitchen. She is heating up water on the stove. There is a knock at the door.*]

BERNIECE: Who is it?

AVERY: It's me, Avery.

[BERNIECE *opens the door and lets him in.*]

BERNIECE: Avery, come on in. I was just fixing to take my bath.

AVERY: Where Boy Willie? I see that truck out there almost empty. They done sold almost all them watermelons.

BERNIECE: They was gone when I come home. I don't know where they went off to. Boy Willie around here about to drive me crazy.

AVERY: They sell them watermelons . . . he'll be gone soon.

BERNIECE: What Mr. Cohen say about letting you have the place?

AVERY: He say he'll let me have it for thirty dollars a month. I talked him out of thirty-five and he say he'll let me have it for thirty.

BERNIECE: That's a nice spot next to Benny Diamond's store.

AVERY: Berniece . . . I be at home and I get to thinking you up here an' I'm down there. I get to thinking how that look to have a preacher that ain't married. It makes for a better congregation if the preacher was settled down and married.

BERNIECE: Avery . . . not now. I was fixing to take my bath.

AVERY: You know how I feel about you, Berniece. Now . . . I done got the place from Mr. Cohen. I get the money from the bank and I can fix it up real nice. They give me a ten cents a hour raise down there on the job . . . now Berniece, I ain't got much in the way of comforts. I got a hole in my pockets near about as far as money is concerned. I ain't never found no way through life to a woman I care about like I care about you. I need that. I need somebody on my bond side. I need a woman that fits in my hand.

BERNIECE: Avery, I ain't ready to get married now.

AVERY: You too young a woman to close up, Berniece.

BERNIECE: I ain't said nothing about closing up. I got a lot of woman left in me.

AVERY: Where's it at? When's the last time you looked at it?

BERNIECE [*Stunned by his remark.*]: That's a nasty thing to say. And you call yourself a preacher.

AVERY: Anytime I get anywhere near you . . . you push me away.

BERNIECE: I got enough on my hands with Maretha. I got enough people to love and take care of.

AVERY: Who you got to love you? Can't nobody get close enough to you. Doaker can't half say nothing to you. You jump all over Boy Willie. Who you got to love you, Bernicce?

BERNIECE: You trying to tell me a woman can't be nothing without a man. But you alright, huh? You can just walk out of here without me—without a woman—and still be a man. That's alright. Ain't nobody gonna ask you, "Avery, who you got to love you?" That's alright for you. But everybody gonna be worried about Berniece. "How Berniece gonna take care of herself? How she gonna raise that child without a man? Wonder what she do with herself. How she gonna live like that?" Everybody got all kinds of questions for Berniece. Everybody telling me I can't be a woman unless I got a man. Well, you tell me, Avery—you know—how much woman am I?

AVERY: It wasn't me, Berniece. You can't blame me for nobody else. I'll own up to my own shortcomings. But you can't blame me for Crawley or nobody else.

BERNIECE: I ain't blaming nobody for nothing. I'm just stating the facts.

AVERY: How long you gonna carry Crawley with you, Berniece? It's been over three years. At some point you got to let go and go on. Life's got all kinds of twists and turns. That don't mean you stop living. That don't mean you cut yourself off from life. You can't go through life carrying Crawley's ghost with you. Crawley's been dead three years. Three years, Berniece.

BERNIECE: I know how long Crawley's been dead. You ain't got to tell me that. I just ain't ready to get married right now.

AVERY: What is you ready for, Berniece? You just gonna drift along from day to day. Life is more than making it from one day to another. You gonna look up one day and it's all gonna be past you. Life's gonna be gone out of your hands—there won't be enough to make nothing with. I'm standing here now, Berniece—but I don't know how much longer I'm gonna be standing here waiting on you.

BERNIECE: Avery, I told you . . . when you get your church we'll sit down and talk about this. I got too many other things to deal with right now. Boy Willie and the piano . . . and Sutter's ghost. I thought I might have been seeing things, but Maretha done seen Sutter's ghost, too.

AVERY: When this happen, Berniece?

BERNIECE: Right after I came home yesterday. Me and Boy Willie was arguing about the piano and Sutter's ghost was standing at the top of the stairs. Maretha scared to sleep up there now. Maybe if you bless the house he'll go away.

AVERY: I don't know, Berniece. I don't know if I should fool around with something like that.

BERNIECE: I can't have Maretha scared to go to sleep up there. Seem like if you bless the house he would go away.

AVERY: You might have to be a special kind of preacher to do something like that.

BERNIECE: I keep telling myself when Boy Willie leave he'll go on and leave with him. I believe Boy Willie pushed him in the well.

AVERY: That's been going on down there a long time. The Ghosts of the Yellow Dog been pushing people in their wells long before Boy Willie got grown.

BERNIECE: Somebody down there pushing them people in their wells. They ain't just upped and fell. Ain't no wind pushed nobody in their well.

AVERY: Oh, I don't know. God works in mysterious ways.

BERNIECE: He ain't pushed nobody in their wells.

AVERY: He caused it to happen. God is the Great Causer. He can do anything. He parted the Red Sea. He say I will smite my enemies. Reverend Thompson used to preach on the Ghosts of the Yellow Dog as the hand of God.

BERNIECE: I don't care who preached what. Somebody down there pushing them people in their wells. Somebody like Boy Willie. I can see him doing something like that. You ain't gonna tell me that Sutter just upped and fell in his well. I believe Boy Willie pushed him so he could get his land.

AVERY: What Doaker say about Boy Willie selling the piano?

BERNIECE: Doaker don't want no part of that piano. He ain't never wanted no part of it. He blames himself for not staying behind with Papa Boy Charles. He washed his hands of that piano a long time ago. He didn't want me to bring it up here—but I wasn't gonna leave it down there.

AVERY: Well, it seems to me somebody ought to be able to talk to Boy Willie.

BERNIECE: You can't talk to Boy Willie. He been that way all his life. Mama Ola had her hands full trying to talk to him. He don't listen to nobody. He just like my daddy. He get his mind fixed on something and can't nobody turn him from it.

AVERY: You ought to start a choir at the church. Maybe if he seen you was doing something with it—if you told him you was gonna put it in my church—maybe he'd see it different. You ought to put it down in the church and start a choir. The Bible say "Make a joyful noise unto the Lord." Maybe if Boy Willie see you was doing something with it he'd see it different.

BERNIECE: I done told you I don't play on that piano. Ain't no need in you to keep talking this choir stuff. When my mama died I shut the top on that piano and I ain't never opened it since. I was only playing it for her. When my daddy died seem like all her life went into that piano. She used to have me playing on it . . . had Miss Eula come in and teach me . . . say when I played it she could hear my daddy talking to her. I used to think them pictures came alive and walked through the house. Sometime late at night I could hear my mama talking to them. I said that wasn't gonna happen to me. I don't play that piano cause I don't want to wake them spirits. They never be walking around in this house.

AVERY: You got to put all that behind you, Berniece.

BERNIECE: I got Maretha playing on it. She don't know nothing about it. Let her go on and be a schoolteacher or something. She don't have to carry all of that with her. She got a chance I didn't have. I ain't gonna burden her with that piano.

AVERY: You got to put all of that behind you, Berniece. That's the same thing like Crawley. Everybody got stones in their passway. You got to step over them or walk around them. You picking them up and carrying them with you. All you got to do is set them down by the side of the road. You ain't got to carry them with you. You can walk over there right now and play that piano. You can walk over there right now and God will walk over there with you. Right now you can set that sack of stones down by the side of the road and walk away from it. You don't have to carry it with you. You can do it right now. [AVERY *crosses over to the piano and raises the lid.*]

Come on, Berniece . . . set it down and walk away from it. Come on, play "Old Ship of Zion." Walk over here and claim it as an instrument of the Lord. You can walk over here right now and make it into a celebration.

[BERNIECE *moves toward the piano.*]

BERNIECE: Avery . . . I done told you I don't want to play that piano. Now or no other time.

AVERY: The Bible say, "The Lord is my refuge . . . and my strength!" With the strength of God you can put the past behind you, Berniece. With the strength of God you can do anything! God got a bright tomorrow. God don't ask what you done . . . God ask what you gonna do. The strength of God can move mountains! God's got a bright tomorrow for you . . . all you got to do is walk over here and claim it.

BERNIECE: Avery, just go on and let me finish my bath. I'll see you tomorrow.

AVERY: Okay, Berniece. I'm gonna go home. I'm gonna go home and read up on my Bible. And tomorrow . . . if the good Lord give me strength tomorrow . . . I'm gonna come by and bless the house . . . and show you the power of the Lord. [AVERY *crosses to the door.*]

It's gonna be alright, Berniece. God say he will soothe the troubled waters. I'll come by tomorrow and bless the house.

[*The lights go down to black.*]

Scene 3

[*Several hours later. The house is dark.* BERNIECE *has retired for the night.* BOY WILLIE *enters the darkened house with* GRACE.]

BOY WILLIE: Come on in. This my sister's house. My sister live here. Come on, I ain't gonna bite you.

GRACE: Put some light on. I can't see.

BOY WILLIE: You don't need to see nothing, baby. This here is all you need to see. All you need to do is see me. If you can't see me you can feel me in the dark. How's that, sugar? [*He attempts to kiss her.*]

GRACE: Go on now . . . wait!

BOY WILLIE: Just give me one little old kiss.

GRACE [*Pushing him away.*]: Come on, now. Where I'm gonna sleep at?

BOY WILLIE: We got to sleep out here on the couch. Come on, my sister don't mind. Lymon come back he just got to sleep on the floor. He run off with Dolly somewhere he better stay there. Come on, sugar.

GRACE: Wait now . . . you ain't told me nothing about no couch. I thought you had a bed. Both of us can't sleep on that little old couch.

BOY WILLIE: It don't make no difference. We can sleep on the floor. Let Lymon sleep on the couch.

GRACE: You ain't told me nothing about no couch.

BOY WILLIE: What difference it make? You just wanna be with me.

GRACE: I don't want to be with you on no couch. Ain't you got no bed?

BOY WILLIE: You don't need no bed, woman. My granddaddy used to take women on the backs of horses. What you need a bed for? You just want to be with me.

GRACE: You sure is country. I didn't know you was this country.

BOY WILLIE: There's a lot of things you don't know about me. Come on, let me show you what this country boy can do.

GRACE: Let's go to my place. I got a room with a bed if Leroy don't come back there.

BOY WILLIE: Who's Leroy? You ain't said nothing about no Leroy.

GRACE: He used to be my man. He ain't coming back. He gone off with some other gal.

BOY WILLIE: You let him have your key?

GRACE: He ain't coming back.

BOY WILLIE: Did you let him have your key?

GRACE: He got a key but he ain't coming back. He took off with some other gal.

BOY WILLIE: I don't wanna go nowhere he might come. Let's stay here. Come on, sugar. [*He pulls her over to the couch.*] Let me heist your hood and check your oil. See if your battery needs charged. [*He pulls her to him. They kiss and tug at each other's clothing. In their anxiety they knock over a lamp.*]

BERNIECE: Who's that . . . Wining Boy?

BOY WILLIE: It's me . . . Boy Willie. Go on back to sleep. Everything's alright. [*To* GRACE.] That's my sister. Everything's alright, Berniece. Go on back to sleep.

BERNIECE: What you doing down there? What you done knocked over?

BOY WILLIE: It wasn't nothing. Everything's alright. Go on back to sleep. [*To* GRACE.] That's my sister. We alright. She gone back to sleep.

[*They begin to kiss.* BERNIECE *enters from the stairs dressed in a nightgown. She cuts on the light.*]

BERNIECE: Boy Willie, what you doing down here?

BOY WILLIE: It was just that there lamp. It ain't broke. It's okay. Everything's alright. Go on back to bed.

BERNIECE: Boy Willie, I don't allow that in my house. You gonna have to take your company someplace else.

BOY WILLIE: It's alright. We ain't doing nothing. We just sitting here talking. This here is Grace. That's my sister Berniece.

BERNIECE: You know I don't allow that kind of stuff in my house.

BOY WILLIE: Allow what? We just sitting here talking.

BERNIECE: Well, your company gonna have to leave. Come back and talk in the morning.

BOY WILLIE: Go on back upstairs now.

BERNIECE: I got an eleven-year-old girl upstairs. I can't allow that around here.

BOY WILLIE: Ain't nobody said nothing about that. I told you we just talking.

GRACE: Come on . . . let's go to my place. Ain't nobody got to tell me to leave but once.

BOY WILLIE: You ain't got to be like that, Berniece.

BERNIECE: I'm sorry, Miss. But he know I don't allow that in here.

GRACE: You ain't got to tell me but once. I don't stay nowhere I ain't wanted.

BOY WILLIE: I don't know why you want to embarrass me in front of my company.

GRACE: Come on, take me home.

BERNIECE: Go on, Boy Willie. Just go on with your company.

[BOY WILLIE *and* GRACE *exit.* BERNIECE *puts the light on in the kitchen and puts on the teakettle. Presently there is a knock at the door.* BERNIECE *goes to answer it.* BERNIECE *opens the door.* LYMON *enters.*]

LYMON: How you doing, Berniece? I thought you'd be asleep. Boy Willie been back here?

BERNIECE: He just left out of here a minute ago.

LYMON: I went out to see a picture show and never got there. We always end up doing something else. I was with this woman she just wanted to drink up all my money. So I left her there and came back looking for Boy Willie.

BERNIECE: You just missed him. He just left out of here.

LYMON: They got some nice-looking women in this city. I'm gonna like it up here real good. I like seeing them with their dresses on. Got them high heels. I like that. Make them look like they real precious. Boy Willie met a real nice one today. I wish I had met her before he did.

BERNIECE: He come by here with some woman a little while ago. I told him to go on and take all that out of my house.

LYMON: What she look like, the woman he was with? Was she a brown-skinned woman about this high? Nice and healthy? Got nice hips on her?

BERNIECE: She had on a red dress.

LYMON: That's her! That's Grace. She real nice. Laugh a lot. Lot of fun to be with. She don't be trying to put on. Some of these woman act like they the Queen of Sheba. I don't like them kind. Grace ain't like that. She real nice with herself.

BERNIECE: I don't know what she was like. He come in here all drunk knocking over the lamp, and making all kind of noise. I told them to take that somewhere else. I can't really say what she was like.

LYMON: She real nice. I seen her before he did. I was trying not to act like I seen her. I wanted to look at her a while before I said something. She seen me when I come into the saloon. I tried to act like I didn't see her. Time I looked around Boy Willie was talking to her. She was talking to him kept looking at me. That's when her friend Dolly came. I asked her if she wanted to go to the picture show. She told me to buy her a drink while she thought about it. Next thing I knew she done had three drinks talking about she too tired to go. I bought her another drink, then I left. Boy Willie was gone and I thought he might have come back here. Doaker gone, huh? He say he had to make a trip.

BERNIECE: Yeah, he gone on his trip. This is when I can usually get me some peace and quiet, Maretha asleep.

LYMON: She look just like you. Got them big eyes. I remember her when she was in diapers.

BERNIECE: Time just keep on. It go on with or without you. She going on twelve.

LYMON: She sure is pretty. I like kids.

BERNIECE: Boy Willie say you staying . . . what you gonna do up here in this big city? You thought about that?

LYMON: They never get me back down there. The sheriff looking for me. All because they gonna try and make me work for somebody when I don't want to. They gonna try and make me work for Stovall when he don't pay nothing. It ain't like that up here. Up here you more or less do what you want to. I figure I find me a job and try to get set up and then see what the year brings. I tried to do that two or three times down there . . . but it never would work out. I was always in the wrong place.

BERNIECE: This ain't a bad city once you get to know your way around.

LYMON: Up here is different. I'm gonna get me a job unloading boxcars or something. One fellow told me say he know a place. I'm gonna go over there with him next week. Me and Boy Willie finish selling them watermelons I'll have enough money to hold me for a while. But I'm gonna go over there and see what kind of jobs they have.

BERNIECE: You shouldn't have too much trouble finding a job. It's all in how you present yourself. See now, Boy Willie couldn't get no job up here. Somebody hire him they got a pack of trouble on their hands. Soon as they find that out they fire him. He don't want to do nothing unless he do it his way.

LYMON: I know. I told him let's go to the picture show first and see if there was any women down there. They might get tired of sitting at home and walk down to the picture show. He say he wanna look around first. We never did get down there. We tried a couple of places and then we went to this saloon where he met Grace. I tried to meet her before he did but he beat me to her. We left Wining Boy sitting down there running his mouth. He told me if I wear this suit I'd find me a woman. He was almost right.

BERNIECE: You don't need to be out there in them saloons. Ain't no telling what you liable to run into out there. This one liable to cut you as quick as that one shoot you. You don't need to be out there. You start out that fast life you can't keep it up. It makes you old quick. I don't know what them women out there be thinking about.

LYMON: Mostly they be lonely and looking for somebody to spend the night with them. Sometimes it matters who it is and sometimes it don't. I used to be the same way. Now it got to matter. That's why I'm here now. Dolly liable not to even recognize me if she sees me again. I don't like women like that. I like my women to be with me in a nice and easy way. That way we can both enjoy ourselves. The way I see it we the only two people like us in the world. We got to see how we fit together. A woman that don't want to take the time to do that I don't bother with. Used to. Used to bother with all of them. Then I woke up one time with this woman and I didn't know who she was. She was the prettiest woman I had ever seen in my life. I spent the whole night with her and didn't even know it. I had never taken the time to look at her. I guess she kinda knew I ain't never really looked at her. She must have known that cause she ain't wanted to see me no more. If she had wanted to see me I believe we might have got married. How come you ain't married? It seem like to me you would be married. I remember Avery from down home. I used to call him plain old Avery. Now he Reverend Avery. That's kinda funny about him becoming a preacher. I like when he told about how that come to him in a dream about them sheep people and them hobos. Nothing ever come to me in a dream like that. I just dream about women. Can't never seem to find the right one.

BERNIECE: She out there somewhere. You just got to get yourself ready to meet her. That's what I'm trying to do. Avery's alright. I ain't really got nobody in mind.

LYMON: I get me a job and a little place and get set up to where I can make a woman comfortable I might get married. Avery's nice. You ought to go ahead and get married. You be a preacher's wife you won't have to work. I hate living by myself. I didn't want to be no strain on my mama so I left home when I was about sixteen. Everything I tried seem like it just didn't work out. Now I'm trying this.

BERNIECE: You keep trying it'll work out for you.

LYMON: You ever go down there to the picture show?

BERNIECE: I don't go in for all that.

LYMON: Ain't nothing wrong with it. It ain't like gambling and sinning. I went to one down in Jackson once. It was fun.

BERNIECE: I just stay home most of the time. Take care of Maretha.

LYMON: It's getting kind of late. I don't know where Boy Willie went off to. He's liable not to come back. I'm gonna take off these shoes. My feet hurt. Was you in bed? I don't mean to be keeping you up.

BERNIECE: You ain't keeping me up. I couldn't sleep after that Boy Willie woke me up.

LYMON: You got on that nightgown. I likes women when they wear them fancy nightclothes and all. It makes their skin look real pretty.

BERNIECE: I got this at the five-and-ten-cents store. It ain't so fancy.

LYMON: I don't too often get to see a woman dressed like that.

[*There is a long pause.* LYMON *takes off his suit coat.*]

Well, I'm gonna sleep here on the couch. I'm supposed to sleep on the floor but I don't reckon Boy Willie's coming back tonight. Wining Boy sold me this suit. Told me it was a magic suit. I'm gonna put it on again tomorrow. Maybe it bring me a woman like he say. [*He goes into his coat pocket and takes out a small bottle of perfume.*]
I almost forgot I had this. Some man sold me this for a dollar. Say it come from Paris. This is the same kind of perfume the Queen of France wear. That's what he told me. I don't know if it's true or not. I smelled it. It smelled good to me. Here . . . smell it see if you like it. I was gonna give it to Dolly. But I didn't like her too much.

BERNIECE [*Takes the bottle.*]: It smells nice.

LYMON: I was gonna give it to Dolly if she had went to the picture with me. Go on, you take it.

BERNIECE: I can't take it. Here . . . go on you keep it. You'll find somebody to give it to.

LYMON: I wanna give it to you. Make you smell nice. [*He takes the bottle and puts perfume behind* BERNIECE*'s ear.*] They tell me you supposed to put it right here behind your ear. Say if you put it there you smell nice all day.

[BERNIECE *stiffens at his touch.* LYMON *bends down to smell her.*]

There . . . you smell real good now.

[*He kisses her neck.*]

You smell real good for Lymon.

[*He kisses her again.* BERNIECE *returns the kiss, then breaks the embrace and crosses to the stairs. She turns and they look silently at each other.* LYMON *hands her the bottle of perfume.* BERNIECE *exits up the stairs.* LYMON *picks up his suit coat and strokes it lovingly with the full knowledge that it is indeed a magic suit. The lights go down on the scene.*]

Scene 4

[*It is late the next morning. The lights come up on the parlor.* LYMON *is asleep on the sofa.* BOY WILLIE *enters the front door.*]

BOY WILLIE: Hey, Lymon! Lymon, come on get up.

LYMON: Leave me alone.

BOY WILLIE: Come on, get up, nigger! Wake up, Lymon.

LYMON: What you want?

BOY WILLIE: Come on, let's go. I done called the man about the piano.

LYMON: What piano?

BOY WILLIE [*Dumps* LYMON *on the floor.*]: Come on, get up!

LYMON: Why you leave, I looked around and you was gone.

BOY WILLIE: I come back here with Grace, then I went looking for you. I figured you'd be with Dolly.

LYMON: She just want to drink and spend up your money. I come on back here looking for you to see if you wanted to go to the picture show.

BOY WILLIE: I been up at Grace's house. Some nigger named Leroy come by but I had a chair up against the door. He got mad when he couldn't get in. He went off somewhere and I got out of there before he could come back. Berniece got mad when we came here.

LYMON: She say you was knocking over the lamp busting up the place.

BOY WILLIE: That was Grace doing all that.

LYMON: Wining Boy seen Sutter's ghost last night.

BOY WILLIE: Wining Boy's liable to see anything. I'm surprised he found the right house. Come on, I done called the man about the piano.

LYMON: What he say?

BOY WILLIE: He say to bring it on out. I told him I was calling for my sister, Miss Berniece Charles. I told him some man wanted to buy it for eleven hundred dollars and asked him if he would go any better. He said yeah, he would give me eleven hundred and fifty dollars for it if it was the same piano. I described it to him again and he told me to bring it out.

LYMON: Why didn't you tell him to come and pick it up?

BOY WILLIE: I didn't want to have no problem with Berniece. This way we just take it on out there and it be out the way. He want to charge twenty-five dollars to pick it up.

LYMON: You should have told him the man was gonna give you twelve hundred for it.

BOY WILLIE: I figure I was taking a chance with that eleven hundred. If I had told him twelve hundred he might have run off. Now I wish I had told him twelve-fifty. It's hard to figure out white folks sometimes.

LYMON: You might have been able to tell him anything. White folks got a lot of money.

BOY WILLIE: Come on, let's get it loaded before Berniece come back. Get that end over there. All you got to do is pick it up on that side. Don't worry about this side. You wanna stretch you' back for a minute?

LYMON: I'm ready.

BOY WILLIE: Get a real good grip on it now.

[*The sound of* SUTTER'S GHOST *is heard. They do not hear it.*]

LYMON: I got this end. You get that end.
BOY WILLIE: Wait till I say ready now. Alright. You got it good? You got a grip on it?
LYMON: Yeah, I got it. You lift up on that end.
BOY WILLIE: Ready? Lift!

[*The piano will not budge.*]

LYMON: Man, this piano is heavy! It's gonna take more than me and you to move this piano.
BOY WILLIE: We can do it. Come on—we did it before.
LYMON: Nigger—you crazy! That piano weighs five hundred pounds!
BOY WILLIE: I got three hundred pounds of it! I know you can carry two hundred pounds! You be lifting them cotton sacks! Come on lift this piano!

[*They try to move the piano again without success.*]

LYMON: It's stuck. Something holding it.
BOY WILLIE: How the piano gonna be stuck? We just moved it. Slide you' end out.
LYMON: Naw—we gonna need two or three more people. How this big old piano get in the house?
BOY WILLIE: I don't know how it got in the house. I know how it's going out though! You get on this end. I'll carry three hundred and fifty pounds of it. All you got to do is slide your end out. Ready?

[*They switch sides and try again without success.* DOAKER *enters from his room as they try to push and shove it.*]

LYMON: Hey, Doaker . . . how this piano get in the house?
DOAKER: Boy Willie, what you doing?
BOY WILLIE: I'm carrying this piano out the house. What it look like I'm doing? Come on, Lymon, let's try again.
DOAKER: Go on let the piano sit there till Berniece come home.
BOY WILLIE: You ain't got nothing to do with this, Doaker. This my business.
DOAKER: This is my house, nigger! I ain't gonna let you or nobody else carry nothing out of it. You ain't gonna carry nothing out of here without my permission!
BOY WILLIE: This is my piano. I don't need your permission to carry my belongings out of your house. This is mine. This ain't got nothing to do with you.
DOAKER: I say leave it over there till Berniece come home. She got part of it too. Leave it set there till you see what she say.
BOY WILLIE: I don't care what Berniece say. Come on, Lymon. I got this side.
DOAKER: Go on and cut it half in two if you want to. Just leave Berniece's half sitting over there. I can't tell you what to do with your piano. But I can't let you take her half out of here.
BOY WILLIE: Go on, Doaker. You ain't got nothing to do with this. I don't want you starting nothing now. Just go on and leave me alone. Come on, Lymon. I got this end.

[DOAKER *goes into his room.* BOY WILLIE *and* LYMON *prepare to move the piano.*]

LYMON: How we gonna get it in the truck?
BOY WILLIE: Don't worry about how we gonna get it on the truck. You got to get it out the house first.
LYMON: It's gonna take more than me and you to move this piano.
BOY WILLIE: Just lift up on that end, nigger!

[DOAKER *comes to the doorway of his room and stands.*]

DOAKER [*Quietly with authority.*]: Leave that piano set over there till Berniece come back. I don't care what you do with it then. But you gonna leave it sit over there right now.
BOY WILLIE: Alright . . . I'm gonna tell you this, Doaker. I'm going out of here . . . I'm gonna get me some rope . . . find me a plank and some wheels . . . and I'm coming back. Then I'm gonna carry that piano out of here . . . sell it and give Berniece half the money. See . . . now that's what I'm gonna do. And you . . . or nobody else is gonna stop me. Come on, Lymon . . . let's go get some rope and stuff. I'll be back, Doaker.

[BOY WILLIE *and* LYMON *exit. The lights go down on the scene.*]

Scene 5

[*The lights come up.* BOY WILLIE *sits on the sofa, screwing casters on a wooden plank.* MARETHA *is sitting on the piano stool.* DOAKER *sits at the table playing solitaire.*]

BOY WILLIE [*To* MARETHA.]: Then after that them white folks down around there started falling down their wells. You ever seen a well? A well got a wall around it. It's hard to fall down a well. You got to be leaning way over. Couldn't nobody figure out too much what was making these fellows fall down their well . . . so everybody says the Ghosts of the Yellow Dog must have pushed them. That's what everybody called them four men what got burned up in the boxcar.
MARETHA: Why they call them that?

BOY WILLIE: Cause the Yazoo Delta railroad got yellow boxcars. Sometime the way the whistle blow sound like an old dog howling so the people call it the Yellow Dog.

MARETHA: Anybody ever see the Ghosts?

BOY WILLIE: I told you they like the wind. Can you see the wind?

MARETHA: No.

BOY WILLIE: They like the wind you can't see them. But sometimes you be in trouble they might be around to help you. They say if you go where the Southern cross the Yellow Dog . . . you go to where them two railroads cross each other . . . and call out their names . . . they say they talk back to you. I don't know, I ain't never done that. But Uncle Wining Boy he say he been down there and talked to them. You have to ask him about that part.

[BERNIECE *has entered from the front door.*]

BERNIECE: Maretha, you go on and get ready for me to do your hair.

[MARETHA *crosses to the steps.*]

Boy Willie, I done told you to leave my house. [*To* MARETHA.] Go on, Maretha.

[MARETHA *is hesitant about going up the stairs.*]

BOY WILLIE: Don't be scared. Here, I'll go up there with you. If we see Sutter's ghost I'll put a whupping on him. Come on, Uncle Boy Willie going with you.

[BOY WILLIE *and* MARETHA *exit up the stairs.*]

BERNIECE: Doaker—what is going on here?

DOAKER: I come home and him and Lymon was moving the piano. I told them to leave it over there till you got home. He went out and got that board and them wheels. He say he gonna take that piano out of here and ain't nobody gonna stop him.

BERNIECE: I ain't playing with Boy Willie. I got Crawley's gun upstairs. He don't know but I'm through with it. Where Lymon go?

DOAKER: Boy Willie sent him for some rope just before you come in.

BERNIECE: I ain't studying Boy Willie or Lymon—or the rope. Boy Willie ain't taking that piano out this house. That's all there is to it.

[BOY WILLIE *and* MARETHA *enter on the stairs.* MARETHA *carries a hot comb and a can of hair grease.* BOY WILLIE *crosses over and continues to screw the wheels on the board.*]

MARETHA: Mama, all the hair grease is gone. There ain't but this little bit left.

BERNIECE [*Gives her a dollar.*]: Here . . . run across the street and get another can. You come straight back, too. Don't you be playing around out there. And watch the cars. Be careful when you cross the street.

[MARETHA *exits out the front door.*]

Boy Willie, I done told you to leave my house.

BOY WILLIE: I ain't in you' house. I'm in Doaker's house. If he ask me to leave then I'll go on and leave. But consider me done left your part.

BERNIECE: Doaker, tell him to leave. Tell him to go on.

DOAKER: Boy Willie ain't done nothing for me to put him out of the house. I told you if you can't get along just go on and don't have nothing to do with each other.

BOY WILLIE: I ain't thinking about Berniece. [*He gets up and draws a line across the floor with his foot.*] There! Now I'm out of your part of the house. Consider me done left your part. Soon as Lymon come back with that rope. I'm gonna take that piano out of here and sell it.

BERNIECE: You ain't gonna touch that piano.

BOY WILLIE: Carry it out of here just as big and bold. Do like my daddy would have done come time to get Sutter's land.

BERNIECE: I got something to make you leave it over there.

BOY WILLIE: It's got to come better than this thirty-two-twenty.

DOAKER: Why don't you stop all that! Boy Willie, go on and leave her alone. You know how Berniece get. Why you wanna sit there and pick with her?

BOY WILLIE: I ain't picking with her. I told her the truth. She the one talking about what she got. I just told her what she better have.

BERNIECE: That's alright, Doaker. Leave him alone.

BOY WILLIE: She trying to scare me. Hell, I ain't scared of dying. I look around and see people dying every day. You got to die to make room for somebody else. I had a dog that died. Wasn't nothing but a puppy. I picked it up and put it in a bag and carried it up there to Reverend C. L. Thompson's church. I carried it up there and prayed and asked Jesus to make it live like he did the man in the Bible. I prayed real hard. Knelt down and everything. Say ask in Jesus' name. Well, I must have called Jesus' name two hundred times. I called his name till my mouth got sore.

I got up and looked in the bag and the dog still dead. It ain't moved a muscle! I say, "Well, ain't nothing precious." And then I went out and killed me a cat. That's when I discovered the power of death. See, a nigger that ain't afraid to die is the worse kind of nigger for the white man. He can't hold that power over you. That's what I learned when I killed that cat. I got the power of death too. I can command him. I can call him up. The white man don't like to see that. He don't like for you to stand up and look him square in the eye and say, "I got it too." Then he got to deal with you square up.

BERNIECE: That's why I don't talk to him, Doaker. You try and talk to him and that's the only kind of stuff that comes out his mouth.

DOAKER: You say Avery went home to get his Bible?

BOY WILLIE: What Avery gonna do? Avery can't do nothing with me. I wish Avery would say something to me about this piano.

DOAKER: Berniece ain't said about that. Avery went home to get his Bible. He coming by to bless the house see if he can get rid of Sutter's ghost.

BOY WILLIE: Ain't nothing but a house full of ghosts down there at the church. What Avery look like chasing away somebody's ghost?

[MARETHA *enters the front door.*]

BERNIECE: Light that stove and set that comb over there to get hot. Get something to put around your shoulders.

BOY WILLIE: The Bible say an eye for an eye, a tooth for a tooth, and a life for a life. Tit for tat. But you and Avery don't want to believe that. You gonna pass up that part and pretend it ain't in there. Everything else you gonna agree with. But if you gonna agree with part of it you got to agree with all of it. You can't do nothing halfway. You gonna go at the Bible halfway. You gonna act like that part ain't in there. But you pull out the Bible and open it and see what it say. Ask Avery. He a preacher. He'll tell you it's in there. He the Good Shepherd. Unless he gonna shepherd you to heaven with half the Bible.

BERNIECE: Maretha, bring me that comb. Make sure it's hot.

[MARETHA *brings the comb.* BERNIECE *begins to do her hair.*]

BOY WILLIE: I will say this for Avery. He done figured out a path to go through life. I don't agree with it. But he done fixed it so he can go right through it real smooth. Hell, he liable to end up with a million dollars that he done got from selling bread and wine.

MARETHA: OWWWWWWW!

BERNIECE: Be still, Maretha. If you was a boy I wouldn't be going through this.

BOY WILLIE: Don't you tell that girl that. Why you wanna tell her that?

BERNIECE: You ain't got nothing to do with this child.

BOY WILLIE: Telling her you wished she was a boy. How's that gonna make her feel?

BERNIECE: Boy Willie, go on and leave me alone.

DOAKER: Why don't you leave her alone? What you got to pick with her for? Why don't you go on out and see what's out there in the streets? Have something to tell the fellows down home.

BOY WILLIE: I'm waiting on Lymon to get back with that truck. Why don't you go on out and see what's out there in the streets? You ain't got to work tomorrow. Talking about me . . . why don't you go out there? It's Friday night.

DOAKER: I got to stay around here and keep you all from killing one another.

BOY WILLIE: You ain't got to worry about me. I'm gonna be here just as long as it takes Lymon to get back here with that truck. You ought to be talking to Berniece. Sitting up there telling Maretha she wished she was a boy. What kind of thing is that to tell a child? If you want to tell her something tell her about that piano. You ain't even told her about that piano. Like that's something to be ashamed of. Like she supposed to go off and hide somewhere about that piano. You ought to mark down on the calendar the day that Papa Boy Charles brought that piano into the house. You ought to mark that day down and draw a circle around it . . . and every year when it come up throw a party. Have a celebration. If you did that she wouldn't have no problem in life. She could walk around here with her head held high. I'm talking about a big party!

Invite everybody! Mark that day down with a special meaning. That way she know where she at in the world. You got her going out here thinking she wrong in the world. Like there ain't no part of it belong to her.

BERNIECE: Let me take care of my child. When you get one of your own then you can teach it what you want to teach it.

[DOAKER *exits into his room.*]

BOY WILLIE: What I want to bring a child into this world for? Why I wanna bring somebody else into all this for? I'll tell you this . . . If I was Rockefeller I'd have forty or fifty. I'd make one every day. Cause they gonna start out in life with all the advantages. I ain't got no advantages to offer nobody. Many is the time I looked at my daddy and seen him staring off at his hands. I got a little older I know what he was thinking. He sitting there saying, "I got these big old hands but what I'm gonna do with them? Best I can do is make a fifty-acre crop for Mr. Stovall. Got these big old hands capable of doing anything. I can take and build something with these hands. But where's the tools? All I got is these hands. Unless I go out here and kill me somebody and take what they got . . . it's a long row to hoe for me to get something of my own. So what I'm gonna do with these big old hands? What would you do?"

See now . . . if he had his own land he wouldn't have felt that way. If he had something under his feet that belonged to him he could stand up taller. That's what I'm talking about. Hell, the land is there for everybody. All you got to do is figure out how to get you a piece. Ain't no mystery to life. You just got to go out and meet it square on. If you got a piece of land you'll find everything else fall right into place. You can stand right up next to the white man and talk about the price of cotton . . . the weather, and anything else you want to talk about. If you teach that girl that she living at the bottom of life, she's gonna grow up and hate you.

BERNIECE: I'm gonna teach her the truth. That's just where she living. Only she ain't got to stay there. [*To* MARETHA.] Turn you' head over to the other side.

BOY WILLIE: This might be your bottom but it ain't mine. I'm living at the top of life. I ain't gonna just take my life and throw it away at the bottom. I'm in the world like everybody else. The way I see it everybody else got to come up a little taste to be where I am.

BERNIECE: You right at the bottom with the rest of us.

BOY WILLIE: I'll tell you this . . . and ain't a living soul can put a come back on it. If you believe that's where you at then you gonna act that way. If you act that way then that's where you gonna be. It's as simple as that. Ain't no mystery to life. I don't know how you come to believe that stuff. Crawley didn't think like that. He wasn't living at the bottom of life. Papa Boy Charles and Mama Ola wasn't living at the bottom of life. You ain't never heard them say nothing like that. They would have taken a strap to you if they heard you say something like that.

[DOAKER *enters from his room.*]

Hey, Doaker . . . Berniece say the colored folks is living at the bottom of life. I tried to tell her if she think that . . . that's where she gonna be. You think you living at the bottom of life? Is that how you see yourself?

DOAKER: I'm just living the best way I know how. I ain't thinking about no top or no bottom.

BOY WILLIE: That's what I tried to tell Berniece. I don't know where she got that from. That sound like something Avery would say. Avery think cause the white man give him a turkey for Thanksgiving that makes him better than everybody else. That's gonna raise him out of the bottom of life. I don't need nobody to give me a turkey. I can get my own turkey. All you have to do is get out my way. I'll get me two or three turkeys.

BERNIECE: You can't even get a chicken let alone two or three turkeys. Talking about get out your way. Ain't nobody in your way. [*To* MARETHA.] Straighten your head, Maretha! Don't be bending down like that. Hold your head up! [*To* BOY WILLIE.] All you got going for you is talk. You' whole life that's all you ever had going for you.

BOY WILLIE: See now . . . I'll tell you something about me. I done strung along and strung along. Going this way and that. Whatever way would lead me to a moment of peace. That's all I want. To be as easy with everything. But I wasn't born to that. I was born to a time of fire.

The world ain't wanted no part of me. I could see that since I was about seven. The world say it's better off without me. See, Berniece accept that. She trying to come up to where she can prove something to the world. Hell, the world a better place cause of me. I don't see it like Berniece. I got a heart that beats here and it beats just as loud as the next fellow's. Don't care if he black or white. Sometime it beats louder. When it beats louder, then everybody can hear it. Some people get scared of that. Like Berniece. Some people get scared to hear a nigger's heart beating. They think you ought to lay low with that heart. Make it beat quiet and go along with everything the way it is. But my mama ain't birthed me for nothing. So what I got to do? I got to mark my passing on the road. Just like you write on a tree, "Boy Willie was here."

That's all I'm trying to do with that piano. Trying to put my mark on the road. Like my daddy done. My heart say for me to sell that piano and get me some land so I can make a life for myself to live in my own way. Other than that I ain't thinking about nothing Berniece got to say.

[*There is a knock at the door.* BOY WILLIE *crosses to it and yanks it open thinking it is* LYMON. AVERY *enters. He carries a Bible.*]

BOY WILLIE: Where you been, nigger? Aw . . . I thought you was Lymon. Hey, Berniece, look who's here.

BERNIECE: Come on in, Avery. Don't you pay Boy Willie no mind.

BOY WILLIE: Hey . . . Hey, Avery . . . tell me this . . . can you get to heaven with half the Bible?

BERNIECE: Boy Willie . . . I done told you to leave me alone.

BOY WILLIE: I just ask the man a question. He can answer. He don't need you to speak for him. Avery . . . if you only believe on half the Bible and don't want to accept the other half . . . you think God let you in heaven? Or do you got to have the whole Bible? Tell Berniece . . . if you only believe in part of it . . . when you see God he gonna ask you why you ain't believed in the other . . . then he gonna send you straight to Hell.

AVERY: You got to be born again. Jesus say unless a man be born again he cannot come unto the Father and whosoever heareth my words and believeth them not shall be cast into a fiery pit.

BOY WILLIE: That's what I was trying to tell Berniece. You got to believe in it all. You can't go at nothing halfway. She think she going to heaven with half the Bible. [*To* BERNIECE.] You hear that . . . Jesus say you got to believe in it all.

BERNIECE: You keep messing with me.

BOY WILLIE: I ain't thinking about you.

DOAKER: Come on in, Avery, and have a seat. Don't pay neither one of them no mind. They been arguing all day.

BERNIECE: Come on in, Avery.

AVERY: How's everybody in here?

BERNIECE: Here, set this comb back over there on that stove. [*To* AVERY.] Don't pay Boy Willie no mind. He been around here bothering me since I come home from work.

BOY WILLIE: Boy Willie ain't bothering you. Boy Willie ain't bothering nobody. I'm just waiting on Lymon to get back. I ain't thinking about you. You heard the man say I was right and you still don't want to believe it. You just wanna go and make up anythin'. Well there's Avery . . . there's the preacher . . . go on and ask him.

AVERY: Berniece believe in the Bible. She been baptized.

BOY WILLIE: What about that part that say an eye for an eye a tooth for a tooth and a life for a life? Ain't that in there?

DOAKER: What they say down there at the bank, Avery?

AVERY: Oh, they talked to me real nice. I told Berniece . . . they say maybe they let me borrow the money. They done talked to my boss down at work and everything.

DOAKER: That's what I told Berniece. You working every day you ought to be able to borrow some money.

AVERY: I'm getting more people in my congregation every day. Berniece says she gonna be the Deaconess. I get me my church I can get married and settled down. That's what I told Berniece.

DOAKER: That be nice. You all ought to go ahead and get married. Berniece don't need to be by herself. I tell her that all the time.

BERNIECE: I ain't said nothing about getting married. I said I was thinking about it.

DOAKER: Avery get him his church you all can make it nice. [*To* AVERY.] Berniece said you was coming by to bless the house.

AVERY: Yeah, I done read up on my Bible. She asked me to come by and see if I can get rid of Sutter's ghost.

BOY WILLIE: Ain't no ghost in this house. That's all in Berniece's head. Go on up there and see if you see him. I'll give you a hundred dollars if you see him. That's all in her imagination.

DOAKER: Well, let her find that out then. If Avery blessing the house is gonna make her feel better . . . what you got to do with it?

AVERY: Berniece say Maretha seen him too. I don't know, but I found a part in the Bible to bless the house. If he is here then that ought to make him go.

BOY WILLIE: You worse than Berniece believing all that stuff. Talking about . . . if he here. Go on up there and find out. I been up there I ain't seen him. If you reading from that Bible gonna make him leave out of Berniece imagination, well, you might be right. But if you talking about . . .

DOAKER: Boy Willie, why don't you just be quiet? Gettin' all up in the man's business. This ain't got nothing to do with you. Let him go ahead and do what he gonna do.

BOY WILLIE: I ain't stopping him. Avery ain't got no power to do nothing.

AVERY: Oh, I ain't got no power. God got the power! God got power over everything in His creation. God can do anything. God say, "As I commandeth so it shall be." God said, "Let there be light," and there was light. He made the world in six days and rested on the seventh. God's got a wonderful power. He got power over life and death. Jesus raised Lazareth from the dead. They was getting ready to bury him and Jesus told him say, "Rise up and walk." He got up and walked and the people made great rejoicing at the power of God. I ain't worried about him chasing away a little old ghost!

[*There is a knock at the door.* BOY WILLIE *goes to answer it.* LYMON *enters carrying a coil of rope.*]

BOY WILLIE: Where you been? I been waiting on you and you run off somewhere.

LYMON: I ran into Grace. I stopped and bought her drink. She say she gonna go to the picture show with me.

BOY WILLIE: I ain't thinking about no Grace nothing.

LYMON: Hi, Berniece.

BOY WILLIE: Give me that rope and get up on this side of the piano.

DOAKER: Boy Willie, don't start nothing now. Leave the piano alone.

BOY WILLIE: Get that board there, Lymon. Stay out of this, Doaker.

[BERNIECE *exits up the stairs.*]

DOAKER: You just can't take the piano. How you gonna take the piano? Berniece ain't said nothing about selling that piano.

BOY WILLIE: She ain't got to say nothing. Come on, Lymon. We got to lift one end at a time up on the board. You got to watch so that the board don't slide up under there.

LYMON: What we gonna do with the rope?

BOY WILLIE: Let me worry about the rope. You just get up on this side over here with me.

[BERNIECE *enters from the stairs. She has her hand in her pocket where she has Crawley's gun.*]

AVERY: Boy Willie . . . Berniece . . . why don't you all sit down and talk this out now?

BERNIECE: Ain't nothing to talk out.

BOY WILLIE: I'm through talking to Berniece. You can talk to Berniece till you get blue in the face, and it don't make no difference. Get up on that side, Lymon. Throw that rope around there and tie it to the leg.

LYMON: Wait a minute . . . wait a minute, Boy Willie. Berniece got to say. Hey, Berniece . . . did you tell Boy Willie he could take this piano?

BERNIECE: Boy Willie ain't taking nothing out of my house but himself. Now you let him go ahead and try.

BOY WILLIE: Come on, Lymon, get up on this side with me.

[LYMON *stands undecided.*]

Come on, nigger! What you standing there for?

LYMON: Maybe Berniece is right, Boy Willie. Maybe you shouldn't sell it.

AVERY: You all ought to sit down and talk it out. See if you can come to an agreement.

DOAKER: That's what I been trying to tell them. Seem like one of them ought to respect the other one's wishes.

BERNIECE: I wish Boy Willie would go on and leave my house. That's what I wish. Now, he can respect that. Cause he's leaving here one way or another.

BOY WILLIE: What you mean one way or another? What's that supposed to mean? I ain't scared of no gun.

DOAKER: Come on, Berniece, leave him alone with that.

BOY WILLIE: I don't care what Berniece say. I'm selling my half. I can't help it if her half got to go along with it. It ain't like I'm trying to cheat her out of her half. Come on, Lymon.

LYMON: Berniece . . . I got to do this . . . Boy Willie say he gonna give you half of the money . . . say he want to get Sutter's land.

BERNIECE: Go on, Lymon. Just go on . . . I done told Boy Willie what to do.

BOY WILLIE: Here, Lymon . . . put that rope up over there.

LYMON: Boy Willie, you sure you want to do this? The way I figure it . . . I might be wrong . . . but I figure she gonna shoot you first.

BOY WILLIE: She just gonna have to shoot me.

BERNIECE: Maretha, get on out the way. Get her out the way, Doaker.

DOAKER: Go on, do what your mama told you.

BERNIECE: Put her in your room.

[MARETHA *exits to* DOAKER'S *room.* BOY WILLIE *and* LYMON *try to lift the piano. The door opens and* WINING BOY *enters. He has been drinking.*]

WINING BOY: Man, these niggers around here! I stopped down there at Seefus. . . . These folks standing around talking about Patchneck Red's coming. They jumping back and getting off the sidewalk talking about Patchneck Red this and Patchneck Red that. Come to find out . . . you know who they was talking about? Old John D. from up around Tyler! Used to run around with Otis Smith. He got everybody scared of him. Calling him Patchneck Red. They don't know I whupped the nigger's head in one time.

BOY WILLIE: Just make sure that board don't slide, Lymon.

LYMON: I got this side. You watch that side.

WINING BOY: Hey, Boy Willie, what you got? I know you got a pint stuck up in your coat.

BOY WILLIE: Wining Boy, get out the way!

WINING BOY: Hey, Doaker. What you got? Gimme a drink. I want a drink.

DOAKER: It look like you had enough of whatever it was. Come talking about "What you got?" You ought to be trying to find somewhere to lay down.

WINING BOY: I ain't worried about no place to lay down. I can always find me a place to lay down in Berniece's house. Ain't that right, Berniece?

BERNIECE: Wining Boy, sit down somewhere. You been out there drinking all day. Come in here smelling like an old polecat. Sit on down there, you don't need nothing to drink.

DOAKER: You know Berniece don't like all that drinking.

WINING BOY: I ain't disrespecting Berniece. Berniece, am I disrespecting you? I'm just trying to be nice. I been with strangers all day and they treated me like family. I come in here to family and you treat me like a stranger. I don't need your whiskey. I can buy my own. I wanted your company, not your whiskey.

DOAKER: Nigger, why don't you go upstairs and lay down? You don't need nothing to drink.

WINING BOY: I ain't thinking about no laying down. Me and Boy Willie fixing to party. Ain't that right, Boy Willie? Tell him. I'm fixing to play me some piano. Watch this. [WINING BOY *sits down at the piano.*]

BOY WILLIE: Come on, Wining Boy! Me and Lymon fixing to move the piano.

WINING BOY: Wait a minute . . . wait a minute. This a song I wrote for Cleotha. I wrote this song in memory of Cleotha. [*He begins to play and sing.*]

Hey little woman what's the matter with you now
Had a storm last night and blowed the line all
down

Tell me how long
Is I got to wait
Can I get it now
Or must I hesitate

It takes a hesitating stocking in her hesitating shoe
It takes a hesitating woman wanna sing the blues

Tell me how long
Is I got to wait
Can I kiss you now
Or must I hesitate.

BOY WILLIE: Come on, Wining Boy, get up! Get up, Wining Boy! Me and Lymon's fixing to move the piano.

WINING BOY: Naw . . . Naw . . . you ain't gonna move this piano!

BOY WILLIE: Get out the way, Wining Boy.

[WINING BOY, *his back to the piano, spreads his arms out over the piano.*]

WINING BOY: You ain't taking this piano out the house. You got to take me with it!

BOY WILLIE: Get on out the way, Wining Boy! Doaker get him!

[*There is a knock on the door.*]

BERNIECE: I got him, Doaker. Come on, Wining Boy. I done told Boy Willie he ain't taking the piano.

[BERNIECE *tries to take* WINING BOY *away from the piano.*]

WINING BOY: He got to take me with it!

[DOAKER *goes to answer the door.* GRACE *enters.*]

GRACE: Is Lymon here?

DOAKER: Lymon.

WINING BOY: He ain't taking that piano.

BERNIECE: I ain't gonna let him take it.

GRACE: I thought you was coming back. I ain't gonna sit in that truck all day.

LYMON: I told you I was coming back.

GRACE [*Sees* BOY WILLIE.]: Oh, hi, Boy Willie. Lymon told me you was gone back down South.

LYMON: I said he was going back. I didn't say he had left already.

GRACE: That's what you told me.

BERNIECE: Lymon, you got to take your company someplace else.

LYMON: Berniece, this is Grace. That there is Berniece. That's Boy Willie's sister.

GRACE: Nice to meet you. [*To* LYMON.] I ain't gonna sit out in that truck all day. You told me you was gonna take me to the movie.

LYMON: I told you I had something to do first. You supposed to wait on me.

BERNIECE: Lymon, just go on and leave. Take Grace or whoever with you. Just go on get out my house.

BOY WILLIE: You gonna help me move this piano first, nigger!

LYMON [*To* GRACE.]: I got to help Boy Willie move the piano first.

[*Everybody but* GRACE *suddenly senses* SUTTER'*s presence.*]

GRACE: I ain't waiting on you. Told me you was coming right back. Now you got to move a piano. You just like all the other men.

[GRACE *now senses something.*]

Something ain't right here. I knew I shouldn't have come back up in this house. [GRACE *exits.*]

LYMON: Hey, Grace! I'll be right back, Boy Willie.

BOY WILLIE: Where you going, nigger?

LYMON: I'll be back. I got to take Grace home.

BOY WILLIE: Come on, let's move the piano first!

LYMON: I got to take Grace home. I told you I'll be back.

[LYMON *exits.* BOY WILLIE *exits and calls after him.*]

BOY WILLIE: Come on, Lymon! Hey . . . Lymon! Lymon . . . come on!

[*Again, the presence of* SUTTER *is felt.*]

WINING BOY: Hey, Doaker, did you feel that? Hey, Berniece . . . did you get cold? Hey, Doaker . . .

DOAKER: What you calling me for?

WINING BOY: I believe that's Sutter.

DOAKER: Well, let him stay up there. As long as he don't mess with me.

BERNIECE: Avery, go on and bless the house.

DOAKER: You need to bless that piano. That's what you need to bless. It ain't done nothing but cause trouble. If you gonna bless anything go on and bless that.

WINING BOY: Hey, Doaker, if he gonna bless something let him bless everything. The kitchen . . . the upstairs. Go on and bless it all.

BOY WILLIE: Ain't no ghost in this house. He need to bless Berniece's head. That's what he need to bless.

AVERY: Seem like that piano's causing all the trouble. I can bless that. Berniece, put me some water in that bottle.

[AVERY *takes a small bottle from his pocket and hands it to* BERNIECE, *who goes into the kitchen to get water.* AVERY *takes a candle from his pocket and lights it. He gives it to* BERNIECE *as she gives him the water.*]

Hold this candle. Whatever you do make sure it don't go out.

O Holy Father we gather here this evening in the Holy Name to cast out the spirit of one James Sutter. May this vial of water be empowered with thy spirit. May each drop of it be a weapon and a shield against the presence of all evil and may it be a cleansing and blessing of this humble abode.

Just as Our Father taught us how to pray so He say, "I will prepare a table for you in the midst of mine enemies," and in His hands we place ourselves to come unto his presence. Where there is Good so shall it cause Evil to scatter to the Four Winds. [*He throws water at the piano at each commandment.*]

AVERY: Get thee behind me, Satan! Get thee behind the face of Righteousness as we Glorify His Holy Name! Get thee behind the Hammer of Truth that breaketh down the Wall of Falsehood! Father. Father. Praise. Praise. We ask in Jesus' name and call forth the power of the Holy Spirit as it is written. . . . [*He opens the Bible and reads from it.*] I will sprinkle clean water upon thee and ye shall be clean.

BOY WILLIE: All this old preaching stuff. Hell, just tell him to leave.

[AVERY *continues reading throughout* BOY WILLIE'*s outburst.*]

AVERY: I will sprinkle clean water upon you and you shall be clean: from all your uncleanliness, and from all your idols, will I cleanse you. A new heart also will I give you, and a new spirit will I put within you: and I will take out of your flesh the heart of stone, and I will give you a heart of flesh. And I will put my spirit within you, and cause you to walk in my statutes, and ye shall keep my judgments, and do them.

[BOY WILLIE *grabs a pot of water from the stove and begins to fling it around the room.*]

BOY WILLIE: Hey Sutter! Sutter! Get your ass out this house! Sutter! Come on and get some of this water! You done drowned in the well, come on and get some more of this water!

[BOY WILLIE *is working himself into a frenzy as he runs around the room throwing water and calling* SUTTER'*s name.* AVERY *continues reading.*]

BOY WILLIE: Come on, Sutter! [*He starts up the stairs.*] Come on, get some water! Come on, Sutter!

[*The sound of* SUTTER'*s* GHOST *is heard. As* BOY WILLIE *approaches the steps he is suddenly thrown back by the unseen force, which is choking him. As he struggles he frees himself, then dashes up the stairs.*]

BOY WILLIE: Come on, Sutter!

AVERY [*Continuing.*]: A new heart also will I give you and a new spirit will I put within you: and I will take out of your flesh the heart of stone, and I will give you a heart of flesh. And I will put my spirit within you, and cause you to walk in my statutes, and ye shall keep my judgments, and do them.

[*There are loud sounds heard from upstairs as* BOY WILLIE *begins to wrestle with* SUTTER'S GHOST. *It is a life-and-death struggle fraught with perils and faultless terror.* BOY WILLIE *is thrown down the stairs.* AVERY *is stunned into silence.* BOY WILLIE *picks himself up and dashes back upstairs.*]

AVERY: Berniece, I can't do it.

[*There are more sounds heard from upstairs.* DOAKER *and* WINING BOY *stare at one another in stunned disbelief. It is in this moment, from somewhere old, that* BERNIECE *realizes what she must do. She crosses to the piano. She begins to play. The song is found piece by piece. It is an old urge to song that is both a commandment and a plea. With each repetition it gains in strength. It is intended as an exorcism and a dressing for battle. A rustle of wind blowing across two continents.*]

BERNIECE [*Singing.*]:
I want you to help me
I want you to help me
I want you to help me
I want you to help me
I want you to help me
I want you to help me
Mama Berniece
I want you to help me
Mama Esther
I want you to help me
Papa Boy Charles
I want you to help me
Mama Ola
I want you to help me

I want you to help me
I want you to help me
I want you to help me
I want you to help me
I want you to help me
I want you to help me
I want you to help me
I want you to help me

[*The sound of a train approaching is heard. The noise upstairs subsides.*]

BOY WILLIE: Come on, Sutter! Come back, Sutter!

[BERNIECE *begins to chant:*]

BERNIECE:
Thank you.
Thank you.
Thank you.

[*A calm comes over the house.* MARETHA *enters from* DOAKER'S *room.* BOY WILLIE *enters on the stairs. He pauses a moment to watch* BERNIECE *at the piano.*]

BERNIECE:
Thank you.
Thank you.

BOY WILLIE: Wining Boy, you ready to go back down home? Hey, Doaker, what time the train leave?

DOAKER: You still got time to make it.

[MARETHA *crosses and embraces* BOY WILLIE.]

BOY WILLIE: Hey Berniece . . . if you and Maretha don't keep playing on that piano . . . ain't no telling . . . me and Sutter both liable to be back. [*He exits.*]

BERNIECE: Thank you.

[*The lights go down to black.*]

Marsha Norman

Marsha Williams Norman (1947–) was born in Louisville, Kentucky, into a middle-class family. Her father, Billie Williams, was an insurance salesman, and her mother, Bertha, was a stern fundamentalist Methodist, who took care of her ailing mother and neglected her children. Norman apparently still harbors ill feelings toward her mother, but as a well-brought-up Southern woman, she is cautious about expressing them. She is not reticent, however, about acknowledging that she has rejected the Christianity of her mother and father, and she answers firmly that she does not believe in the God of the Bible, though she does believe in spirituality. Norman was greatly influenced by Bubbie, her great-aunt and surrogate mother, and by Grandaddy, her grandfather, who grew up in New Mexico and intrigued her with stories about the West. A lonely child, she has said, "I knew as long as I was reading or playing the piano I was safe. That's still true."

In 1969 Norman married Michael Norman, one of her college professors, but they divorced in 1974. She married Dann C. Byck, a Louisville businessman and theater producer in 1978, but this marriage seemed to have soured by 1981, and Norman came to work in New York City alone. In 1987 she married a third time, to Tim Dykma, an artist, and they have a daughter and a son. This marriage seems the inspiration for Norman's latest play, *Trudy Blue* (1995), in which the protagonist is a middle-aged playwright who has outgrown her husband.

Norman came to playwriting circuitously. She graduated from Agnes Scott College in Decatur, Georgia, a school for women, and then got a job teaching disturbed adolescents at the Kentucky Central State Hospital. In 1973 she moved on to teach at a school for gifted children but also began working as a journalist for the *Louisville Times*. While working on a project for children, she was challenged by Jon Jory, the director of the Louisville Actors Theatre, to write a play, and so she wrote *Getting Out*, which was produced in 1977, when Norman was thirty.

Getting Out concerns the troubled life of Arlene Holsclaw, a woman of twenty-eight fighting to reconcile two disparate personalities competing for dominance of her spirit and life. The Arlene personality, released after serving eight years in an Alabama prison for manslaughter, armed robbery, and kidnapping, has returned to Louisville in order to make herself over and reclaim her child. But when she arrives, she is haunted by Arlie, her deviant personality — played by a second actress—who is suffering from the memory of being sexually abused by her father and rejected by her mother. Faced with the prospect of reverting to her old life, Arlene eventually defeats Arlie and accepts her mother's rejection. The action ends with Arlene making friends with Ruby, a waitress and ex-convict, who will become her mentor. (The conflict of a woman beset by conflicting demands is a theme that Norman explores frequently in subsequent plays.) Arlene is *not* Norman—she is poor white trash and lacks formal education. The character is based on the adolescents Norman worked with at Central State Hospital. Arlie's struggle for selfhood is probably a fictionalized version of Norman's personal conflicts—her desire to become an independent woman, her ill-feelings toward her mother, and her rejection of Christian fundamentalism.

Norman's play *The Laundromat* (1978) contrasts two Southern women, who meet in a dreary laundromat at 3:00 A.M. and form a tender moment of temporary friendship before they separate. Alberta Johnson is an educated widow in her late fifties; Deedee is uneducated and twenty, a bit outgoing and careless, and lives with her unfaithful husband, Joe. As they talk, these women realize the common desperation in their lives. The laundromat setting suggests the public washing of dirty laundry and the inner cleansing of the dirt and grime of life; however, the women do not achieve a breakthrough. When Deedee asks Alberta, "How can you stand it?" Alberta responds, "I can't. [*Pause*] But I have to just the same."

The companion play to *The Laundromat* is *The Pool Hall,* an unconvincing episode involving Willie, a black man in his fifties and the owner of a seedy pool hall, who meets Shooter Stevens, a black radio disc jockey in his late twenties. A key issue of the discussion is why Shooter's father committed suicide. Willie insists that his luck ran out, and though Shooter remains unsatisfied, they achieve a moment of reconciliation and shoot pool man-to-man. This is Norman's only venture with an all-male cast, and it is evident that she works best with women characters searching for self-understanding and personal dignity.

The Holdup (1980) is a satire about the American myth of the Wild West, set in Clovis, New Mexico, in 1914. The protagonist is the Outlaw, also known as Tom, or the Sundance Kid, now a grizzled desperado of fifty who has come looking for Lily, his lover of twenty years before. They have arranged to meet at the old water hole, now a shack in the midst of a wheat farm. But when Lily appears, she is not the saloon girl he remembers but a successful businesswoman and owner of the finest hotel east of Albuquerque. The Outlaw arrives on a horse so decrepit that he has to shoot it; Lily arrives driving her new Buick. When the Outlaw shoots Henry Tucker, a foul-mouthed ranch hand of thirty, who lives at home with Mom, he is so unnerved that he tries to commit suicide with an overdose of morphine. Lily nurses him, and when he recovers, they come to an understanding on Lily's terms, proving she is the more resilient and powerful.

Traveler in the Dark (1984) is about a man who became a surgeon because he was angry with his mother for dying when he was an infant and distanced from his father, a minister who could not help her. Sam Butler's confidence as a surgeon is disturbed by the death of his nurse and close friend, after he had performed an operation to save her life. Confused, he lashes out at his wife, Glory, and their son, Stephen. Though Sam and Glory have been unfaithful to each other, their marriage persevered because of her management, and it is she who emerges as the dominant figure because she has the power of bestowing life. When Sam says, "Glory, if you could . . . hold on a little longer, I want to be a better man," Glory responds, "I can do that Sam. [*He shakes his head, first out of relief, and then in confusion.*] You don't understand, do you? [*He shakes his head no.*] I'd explain it to you if I could, or maybe you'll explain it to me in a week or so, or maybe we'll just love each other anyway and never know." When Sam sweeps away the debris from the ruined garden of his father's house, he is symbolically sweeping away the debris of his inner emotional life. This action seems inspired by Frances Hodgson Burnett's popular children's novel, *The Secret Garden* (1911), which hinges on the main character's ability to return to joy as she restores a derelict garden to its former glory. Six years later, Norman adapted *The Secret Garden* as a Broadway musical.

Norman calls *Sarah and Abraham* (1988) her "marriage play," after the model of Henrik Ibsen. The play retells the story of the biblical Abraham and Sarah, but it is structured as a play within a play in which modern actors begin a production of the traditional story using modern allusions, such as referring to Canaan as Hollywood, Sarah as the woman who cannot bear a child, Abraham as the man who cannot understand how infidelity can interrupt a marriage, and God as the director of the play. The woman's point of view is provided by Virginia Mason, the dramaturge and feminist historian, under whose guidance it is revealed that Sarah was a priestess of the moon who was replaced by Abraham, a priest of the sun. In the play, Abraham's ascendency over Sarah is paralleled by Cliff Wells's ascendency over Kitty, his wife. When the play prepares to move to New York, where Cliff will become a star, Kitty chooses not to go along. Instead, she deliberately leaves her successful career in the theater to become an independent woman and the mother of a child whose paternity she is not sure of because she has had an affair with the play's director, Jack. "I am happy," she says. "Finally, I'm doing something that has to do with me." This echo of Ibsen's Nora Helmer, from *A Doll's House,* unmistakably makes Kitty the true heroine of *Sarah and Abraham,* and it probably reaffirms Norman's personal decision to be a playwright and independent woman.

In 1991 Norman collaborated with composer Lucy Simon on a musical adaptation of Burnett's *The Secret Garden.* It was a noteworthy production because most of the key figures involved in the production—playwright, composer, director, set designer, and several of its producers—were women. Norman rendered a faithful version of the novel for the stage. Mary Lennox, the central character, is an orphan who is sent to England to live with her uncle, Archibald Craven, in his somber Victorian mansion, after the death of her parents in India. There Mary meets her cousin Colin, sickly and crippled. Mary is haunted by the past and generally misbehaves until she discovers a secret garden and attempts to restore it. As she does, her psyche is healed, and she brings joy into the house made sorrowful by the death of Lily, Craven's wife and Colin's mother. Mary's ability to overcome adversity inspires Craven to forget the unhappiness over Lily's death and helps Colin to restore his health. Again Norman's theme is one of regeneration through the character of a woman.

Loving Daniel Boone (1992), written to celebrate Kentucky's bicentennial, gently debunks the myth of Daniel Boone, the man who first settled Kentucky. The protagonist is Florence, a modern woman who is so disappointed with the men in her life that she falls in love with the romantic image of Daniel Boone. Escaping from the present, she travels back to the past, where she joins Boone, makes love to him, and realizes that he is merely a world-weary middle-aged man past his prime. It is not a serious play except that it sends up the myth of the powerful male in American history, which Norman had already done in *The Holdup.*

After the success of *The Secret Garden,* Norman aspired to write Broadway musicals and prepared an adaptation of Michael Powell's 1948 film *The Red Shoes,* this time with composer Julie Styne. In it, Victoria Paige, a ballerina, is fought over by her lover and an impresario. When she cannot meet the demands of either man, she kills herself. It is the kind of material Norman finds congenial, but the 1993 play failed, and in its aftermath, Norman, forty-six, endured a sort of midlife crisis and wrote a play about the end of a marriage, *Trudy Blue.* Ginny, the protagonist, is a middle-aged playwright, oppressed by a complacent marriage and the tyranny of her dead mother's spirit. In *'night, Mother,* Jessie Cates commits suicide, but in *Trudy Blue,* Ginny decides to save herself, and she leaves her husband, Don, to find peace in a hot tub, looking up at the moon. Unlike Ibsen's Nora in *A Doll's House,* Ginny takes her children.

Norman's play *'night, Mother* was awarded the Pulitzer Prize for Drama in 1983, when Norman was thirty-six. It is a problem play about suicide, in the vein of Ibsen's *Hedda Gabler* or August Strindberg's *Miss Julie,* whose title characters find that they have created situations from which they cannot extricate themselves except by death. In *'night, Mother,* Jessie Cates announces to her mother that she will commit suicide, and does it—to our horror. Suicide, said Norman, is Jessie's way of resolving her litany of woes: social (divorced with a wayward son, no ability to hold a job, celibate); emotional (loveless, in conflict with her mother, feeling a sense of unworthiness); health-related (epileptic); personal (plain, generally shy). By contrast, Thelma, her Mama, can make do with what little she has—television, needlework, a weekly manicure, and Jessie to take care of her. She says, "I don't know what I'm here for, but then I don't think about it."

On this fateful night, when Jessie has decided to kill herself at 9:45 P.M., the questions and answers between daughter and mother range from the mundane to the profound. It becomes evident that Jessie does not like cocoa, Mama does not like to cook, and Mama never loved Daddy. Jessie has suffered from epilepsy from childhood, although Mama hid the fact until Jessie was a married woman. The key question that is never asked by either woman is "Do you love me?"

Norman's reluctance to raise this issue may stem from her own inability to reconcile with her mother. When an interviewer shyly asked Norman about exploring her own relationship with her mother, Norman retorted, "You don't think I've done that? . . . Do you think I got this mother out of thin air? . . . Do you think I made this mother up?" From this, one suspects that on a personal level, Jessie's suicide is more than an act of rebellion against her mother, but Norman's way of venting her anger over her own emotional injuries sustained in her childhood and youth.

The setting of the play is a very realistic living room and kitchen. The door to Jessie's bedroom, which the stage directions indicate "opens onto absolute nothingness," holds a central position on the stage and "is the point of all the action." Norman's stage directions indicate that the house is "more comfortable than messy" and that the furnishings must not be taken as a reflection of the taste or intelligence of Mama and Jessie. These are ordinary country people of the lower middle class who live simply. Much is made of eating in *'night, Mother,* but what is eaten can be understood as neither satisfying nor nourishing to the body or the spirit: cupcakes, caramel apples, and candy of all sorts. Jessie, in her late thirties or early forties, is in a sense starving from want of nourishing love and affection.

The unseen men in *'night, Mother* are presented in a negative light. Daddy is remembered as a laconic old man in faded blue denims. Mama says she never loved him, and she was jealous of Jessie's friendship with him. Dawson, Jessie's brother, is unloving and unloved by Jessie and Mama. Ricky, Jessie's son, is an adolescent who is, in turn, unloved by his mother. He is uncontrollable, and he has stolen his mother's jewelry. Cecil, Jessie's former husband, apparently never cared deeply for her, and when he left, Jessie forged a note explaining that he was leaving even though he loved her.

In an interview in 1983, Norman explained that Jessie wants something from Mama but does not know how to get it or take it; finally, she decides that life is not worth living and drops any residual pretense that it will ever be. Norman said, "What Mama does understand, finally, is that there wasn't anything she could do. And so Jessie does win. Mama certainly loses in the battle to keep her alive, but Mama does gain other things in the course of the evening." Norman wants her audience to recognize that Mama and Jessie finally make a connection—"a moment when they actually lived together, when the issues in their lives were standing there with them." Most important, by maintaining that Jessie is a heroine because she knows what she wants and stops at nothing to achieve it, Norman links Jessie in *'night, Mother* to Arthur Miller's Willy Loman in *Death of a Salesman* (1947).

In "Tragedy and the Common Man," Miller argued that a modern American character is tragic when that character "is ready to lay down his life, if need be, to secure one thing—his sense of personal dignity. From Orestes to Hamlet, Medea to Macbeth, the underlying struggle is that of the individual attempting to gain his 'rightful' position in his society. . . . Sometimes he is one who has been displaced from it, sometimes one who seeks to attain it for the first time, but the fateful wound from which the inevitable events spiral is the wound of indignity, and its dominant force is indignation. Tragedy, then, is the consequence of a man's compulsion to evaluate himself justly." Norman's position echoes Miller's, but she believes that an ordinary country woman such as Jessie Cates has to get her story told.

In response to a question by Linda Ginter Brown, Norman was emphatic that the chief object in her plays is to make women more visible in American culture and literature: "Clearly, women in our culture feel invisible. I felt invisible as a girl. That's why I have said so often, you know, I write about people you never see, like *me*. This has got to change! We have got to have our stories told!"

Film

'night, Mother (1986), directed by Tom Moore, with Anne Bancroft, Sissy Spacek, Ed Berke, Carol Robbins, and Jennifer Roosendahl. Screenplay by Marsha Norman. Universal Studios.

'night, Mother

CHARACTERS

JESSIE CATES, in her late thirties or early forties, is pale and vaguely unsteady physically. It is only in the last year that JESSIE has gained control of her mind and body, and tonight she is determined to hold on to that control. She wears pants and a long black sweater with deep pockets, which contain scraps of paper, and there may be a pencil behind her ear or a pen clipped to one of the pockets of the sweater.

As a rule, JESSIE doesn't feel much like talking. Other people have rarely found her quirky sense of humor amusing. She has a peaceful energy on this night, a sense of purpose, but is clearly aware of the time passing moment by moment. Oddly enough, Jessie has never been as communicative or as enjoyable as she is on this evening, but we must know she has not always been this way. There is a familiarity between these two women that comes from having lived together for a long time. There is a shorthand to the talk and a sense of routine comfort in the way they relate to each other physically. Naturally, there are also routine aggravations.

THELMA CATES, "MAMA," is JESSIE's mother, in her late fifties or early sixties. She has begun to feel her age and so takes it easy when she can, or when it serves her purpose to let someone help her. But she speaks quickly and enjoys talking. She believes that things *are* what she says they are. Her sturdiness is more a mental quality than a physical one, finally. She is chatty and nosy, and this is *her* house.

The play takes place in a relatively new house built way out on a country road, with a living room and connecting kitchen, and a center hall that leads off to the bedrooms. A pull cord in the hall ceiling releases a ladder which leads to the attic. One of these bedrooms opens directly onto the hall, and its entry should be visible to everyone in the audience. It should be, in fact, the focal point of the entire set, and the lighting should make it disappear completely at times and draw the entire set into it at others. It is a point of both threat and promise. It is an ordinary door that opens onto absolute nothingness. That door is the point of all the action, and the utmost care should be given to its design and construction.

The living room is cluttered with magazines and needlework catalogues, ashtrays and candy dishes. Examples of MAMA*'s needlework are everywhere—pillows, afghans, and quilts, doilies and rugs, and they are quite nice examples. The house is more comfortable than messy, but there is quite a lot to keep in place here. It is more personal than charming. It is not quaint. Under no circumstances should the set and its dressing make a judgment about the intelligence or taste of* JESSIE *and* MAMA. *It should simply indicate that they are very specific real people who happen to live in a particular part of the country. Heavy accents, which would further distance the audience from* JESSIE *and* MAMA, *are also wrong.*

The time is the present, with the action beginning about 8:15. Clocks onstage in the kitchen and on a table in the living room should run throughout the performance and be visible to the audience.

There will be no intermission.

MAMA *stretches to reach the cupcakes in a cabinet in the kitchen. She can't see them, but she can feel around for them, and she's eager to have one, so she's working pretty hard at it. This may be the most serious exercise* MAMA *ever gets. She finds a cupcake, the coconut-covered, raspberry-and-marshmallow-filled kind known as a snowball, but sees that there's one missing from the package. She calls to* JESSIE, *who is apparently somewhere else in the house.*

MAMA [*Unwrapping the cupcake*]: Jessie, it's the last snowball, sugar. Put it on the list, O.K.? And we're out of Hershey bars, and where's that peanut brittle? I think maybe Dawson's been in it again. I ought to put a big mirror on the refrigerator door. That'll keep him out of my treats, won't it? You hear me, honey? [*Then more to herself*] I hate it when the coconut falls off. Why does the coconut fall off?

[JESSIE *enters from her bedroom, carrying a stack of newspapers*]

JESSIE: We got any old towels?

MAMA: There you are!

JESSIE [*Holding a towel that was on the stack of newspapers*]: Towels you don't want anymore. [*Picking up* MAMA*'s snowball wrapper*] How about this swimming towel Loretta gave us? Beach towel, that's the name of it. You want it? [MAMA *shakes her head no*]

MAMA: What have you been doing in there?

JESSIE: And a big piece of plastic like a rubber sheet or something. Garbage bags would do if there's enough.

MAMA: Don't go making a big mess, Jessie. It's eight o'clock already.

JESSIE: Maybe an old blanket or towels we got in a soap box sometime?

MAMA: I said don't make a mess. Your hair is black enough, hon.

JESSIE [*Continuing to search the kitchen cabinets, finding two or three more towels to add to her stack*]: It's not for my hair, Mama. What about some old pillows anywhere, or a foam cushion out of a yard chair would be real good.

MAMA: You haven't forgot what night it is, have you? [*Holding up her fingernails*] They're all chipped, see? I've been waiting all week, Jess. It's Saturday night, sugar.

JESSIE: I know. I got it on the schedule.

MAMA [*Crossing to the living room*]: You want me to wash 'em now or are you making your mess first? [*Looking at the snowball*] We're out of these. Did I say that already?

JESSIE: There's more coming tomorrow. I ordered you a whole case.

MAMA [*Checking the* TV Guide]: A whole case will go stale, Jessie.

JESSIE: They can go in the freezer till you're ready for them. Where's Daddy's gun?

MAMA: In the attic.

JESSIE: Where in the attic? I looked your whole nap and couldn't find it anywhere.

MAMA: One of his shoeboxes, I think.

JESSIE: Full of shoes. I looked already.

MAMA: Well, you didn't look good enough, then. There's that box from the ones he wore to the hospital. When he died, they told me I could have them back, but I never did like those shoes.

JESSIE [*Pulling them out of her pocket*]: I found the bullets. They were in an old milk can.

MAMA [*As* JESSIE *starts for the hall*]: Dawson took the shotgun, didn't he? Hand me that basket, hon.

JESSIE [*Getting the basket for her*]: Dawson better not've taken that pistol.

MAMA [*Stopping her again*]: Now my glasses, please. [JESSIE *returns to get the glasses*] I told him to take those rubber boots, too, but he said they were for fishing. I told him to take up fishing.

[JESSIE *reaches for the cleaning spray, and cleans* MAMA*'s glasses for her*]

JESSIE: He's just too lazy to climb up there, Mama. Or maybe he's just being smart. That floor's not very steady.

MAMA [*Getting out a piece of knitting*]: It's not a floor at all, hon, it's a board now and then. Measure this for me. I need six inches.

JESSIE [*As she measures*]: Dawson could probably use some of those clothes up there. Somebody should have them. You ought to call the Salvation Army before the whole thing falls in on you. Six inches exactly.

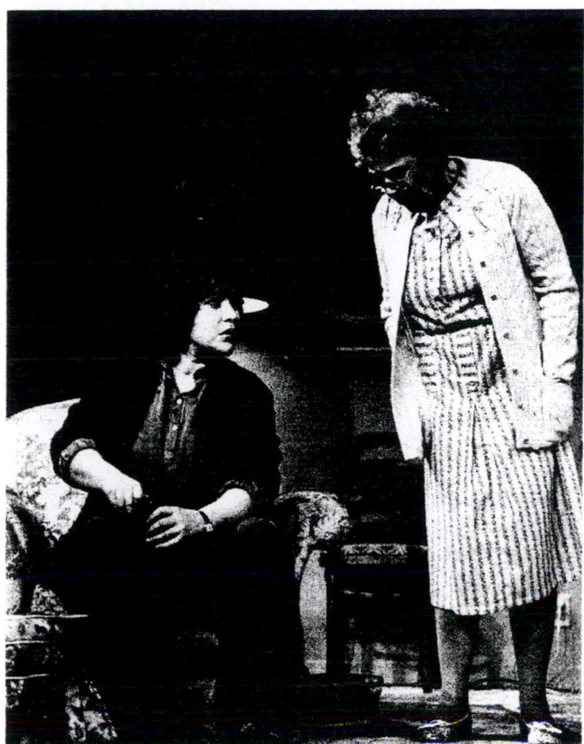

Kathy Bates and Anne Pitniak in 'night, Mother, *directed by Tom Moore, Golden Theatre, New York, 1983.*

MAMA: It's plenty safe! As long as you don't go up there.

JESSIE [*Turning to go again*]: I'm careful.

MAMA: What do you want the gun for, Jess?

JESSIE [*Not returning this time. Opening the ladder in the hall*]: Protection. [*She steadies the ladder as* MAMA *talks*]

MAMA: You take the TV way too serious, hon. I've never seen a criminal in my life. This is way too far to come for what's out here to steal. Never seen a one.

JESSIE [*Taking her first step up*]: Except for Ricky.

MAMA: Ricky is mixed up. That's not a crime.

JESSIE: Get your hands washed. I'll be right back. And get 'em real dry. You dry your hands till I get back or it's no go, all right?

MAMA: I thought Dawson told you not to go up those stairs.

JESSIE [*Going up*]: He did.

MAMA: I don't like the idea of a gun, Jess.

JESSIE [*Calling down from the attic*]: Which shoebox, do you remember?

MAMA: Black.

JESSIE: The box was black?

MAMA: The shoes were black.
JESSIE: That doesn't help much, Mother.
MAMA: I'm not trying to help, sugar. [*No answer*] We don't have anything anybody'd want, Jessie. I mean, I don't even want what we got, Jessie.
JESSIE: Neither do I. Wash your hands. [MAMA *gets up and crosses to stand under the ladder*]
MAMA: You come down from there before you have a fit. I can't come up and get you, you know.
JESSIE: I know.
MAMA: We'll just hand it over to them when they come, how's that? Whatever they want, the criminals.
JESSIE: That's a good idea, Mama.
MAMA: Ricky will grow out of this and be a real fine boy, Jess. But I have to tell you, I wouldn't want Ricky to know we had a gun in the house.
JESSIE: Here it is. I found it.
MAMA: It's just something Ricky's going through. Maybe he's in with some bad people. He just needs some time, sugar. He'll get back in school or get a job or one day you'll get a call and he'll say he's sorry for all the trouble he's caused and invite you out for supper someplace dress-up.
JESSIE [*Coming back down the steps*]: Don't worry. It's not for him, it's for me.
MAMA: I didn't think you would shoot your own boy, Jessie. I know you've felt like it, well, we've all felt like shooting somebody, but we don't do it. I just don't think we need . . .
JESSIE [*Interrupting*]: Your hands aren't washed. Do you want a manicure or not?
MAMA: Yes, I do, but . . .
JESSIE [*Crossing to the chair*]: Then wash your hands and don't talk to me any more about Ricky. Those two rings he took were the last valuable things *I* had, so now he's started in on other people, door to door. I hope they put him away sometime. I'd turn him in myself if I knew where he was.
MAMA: You don't mean that.
JESSIE: Every word. Wash your hands and that's the last time I'm telling you.

[JESSIE *sits down with the gun and starts cleaning it, pushing the cylinder out, checking to see that the chambers and barrel are empty, then putting some oil on a small patch of cloth and pushing it through the barrel with the push rod that was in the box.* MAMA *goes to the kitchen and washes her hands, as instructed, trying not to show her concern about the gun*]

MAMA: I shoulda got you to bring down that milk can. Agnes Fletcher sold hers to somebody with a flea market for forty dollars apiece.
JESSIE: I'll go back and get it in a minute. There's a wagon wheel up there, too. There's even a churn. I'll get it all if you want.
MAMA [*Coming over, now, taking over now*]: What are you doing?
JESSIE: The barrel has to be clean, Mama. Old powder, dust gets in it . . .
MAMA: What for?
JESSIE: I told you.
MAMA [*Reaching for the gun*]: And I told you, we don't get criminals out here.
JESSIE [*Quickly pulling it to her*]: And I told you . . . [*Then trying to be calm*] The gun is for me.
MAMA: Well, you can have it if you want. When I die, you'll get it all, anyway.
JESSIE: I'm going to kill myself, Mama.
MAMA [*Returning to the sofa*]: Very funny. Very funny.
JESSIE: I am.
MAMA: You are not! Don't even say such a thing, Jessie.
JESSIE: How would you know if I didn't say it? You want it to be a surprise? You're lying there in your bed or maybe you're just brushing your teeth and you hear this . . . noise down the hall?
MAMA: Kill yourself.
JESSIE: Shoot myself. In a couple of hours.
MAMA: It must be time for your medicine.
JESSIE: Took it already.
MAMA: What's the matter with you?
JESSIE: Not a thing. Feel fine.
MAMA: You feel fine. You're just going to kill yourself.
JESSIE: Waited until I felt good enough, in fact.
MAMA: Don't make jokes, Jessie. I'm too old for jokes.
JESSIE: It's not a joke, Mama.

[MAMA *watches for a moment in silence*]

MAMA: That gun's no good, you know. He broke it right before he died. He dropped it in the mud one day.
JESSIE: Seems O.K. [*She spins the chamber, cocks the pistol, and pulls the trigger. The gun is not yet loaded, so all we hear is the click, but it will definitely work. It's also obvious that* JESSIE *knows her way around a gun.* MAMA *cannot speak*] I had Cecil's all ready in there, just in case I couldn't find this one, but I'd rather use Daddy's.
MAMA: Those bullets are at least fifteen years old.
JESSIE [*Pulling out another box*]: These are from last week.
MAMA: Where did you get those?
JESSIE: Feed store Dawson told me about.
MAMA: Dawson!

JESSIE: I told him I was worried about prowlers. He said he thought it was a good idea. He told me what kind to ask for.

MAMA: If he had any idea . . .

JESSIE: He took it as a compliment. He thought I might be taking an interest in things. He got through telling me all about the bullets and then he said we ought to talk like this more often.

MAMA: And where was I while this was going on?

JESSIE: On the phone with Agnes. About the milk can, I guess. Anyway, I asked Dawson if he thought they'd send me some bullets and he said he'd just call for me, because he knew they'd send them if he told them to. And he was absolutely right. Here they are.

MAMA: How could he do that?

JESSIE: Just trying to help, Mama.

MAMA: And then I told you where the gun was.

JESSIE [*Smiling, enjoying this joke*]: See? Everybody's doing what they can.

MAMA: You told me it was for protection!

JESSIE: It *is!* I'm still doing your nails, though. Want to try that new Chinaberry color?

MAMA: Well, I'm calling Dawson right now. We'll just see what he has to say about this little stunt.

JESSIE: Dawson doesn't have any more to do with this.

MAMA: He's your brother.

JESSIE: And that's all.

MAMA [*Stands up, moves toward the phone*]: Dawson will put a stop to this. Yes he will. He'll take the gun away.

JESSIE: If you call him, I'll just have to do it before he gets here. Soon as you hang up the phone, I'll just walk in the bedroom and lock the door. Dawson will get here just in time to help you clean up. Go ahead, call him. Then call the police. Then call the funeral home. Then call Loretta and see if *she'll* do your nails.

MAMA: You will not! This is crazy talk, Jessie!

[MAMA *goes directly to the telephone and starts to dial, but* JESSIE *is fast, coming up behind her and taking the receiver out of her hand, putting it back down*]

JESSIE [*Firm and quiet*]: I said no. This is private. Dawson is not invited.

MAMA: Just me.

JESSIE: I don't want anybody else over here. Just you and me. If Dawson comes over, it'll make me feel stupid for not doing it ten years ago.

MAMA: I think we better call the doctor. Or how about the ambulance. You like that one driver, I know. What's his name, Timmy? Get you somebody to talk to.

JESSIE [*Going back to her chair*]: I'm through talking, Mama. You're it. No more.

MAMA: We're just going to sit around like every other night in the world and then you're going to kill yourself? [JESSIE *doesn't answer*] You'll miss. [*Again there is no response*] You'll just wind up a vegetable. How would you like that? Shoot your ear off? You know what the doctor said about getting excited. You'll cock the pistol and have a fit.

JESSIE: I think I can kill myself, Mama.

MAMA: You're not going to kill yourself, Jessie. You're not even upset! [JESSIE *smiles, or laughs quietly, and* MAMA *tries a different approach*] People don't really kill themselves, Jessie. No, mam, doesn't make sense, unless you're retarded or deranged, and you're as normal as they come, Jessie, for the most part. We're all *afraid* to die.

JESSIE: I'm not, Mama. I'm cold all the time, anyway.

MAMA: That's ridiculous.

JESSIE: It's exactly what I want. It's dark and quiet.

MAMA: So is the back yard, Jessie! Close your eyes. Stuff cotton in your ears. Take a nap! It's quiet in your room. I'll leave the TV off all night.

JESSIE: So quiet I don't know it's quiet. So nobody can get me.

MAMA: You don't know what dead is like. It might not be quiet at all. What if it's like an alarm clock and you can't wake up so you can't shut it off. Ever.

JESSIE: Dead is everybody and everything I ever knew, gone. Dead is dead quiet.

MAMA: It's a sin. You'll go to hell.

JESSIE: Uh-huh.

MAMA: You will!

JESSIE: Jesus was a suicide, if you ask me.

MAMA: You'll go to hell just for saying that. Jessie!

JESSIE [*With genuine surprise*]: I didn't know I thought that.

MAMA: Jessie!

[JESSIE *doesn't answer. She puts the now-loaded gun back in the box and crosses to the kitchen. But* MAMA *is afraid she's headed for the bedroom*]

MAMA [*In a panic*]: You can't use my towels! They're my towels. I've had them for a long time. I like my towels.

JESSIE: I asked you if you wanted that swimming towel and you said you didn't.

MAMA: And you can't use your father's gun, either. It's mine now, too. And you can't do it in my house.

JESSIE: Oh, come on.

MAMA: No. You can't do it. I won't let you. The house is in my name.

JESSIE: I have to go in the bedroom and lock the door behind me so they won't arrest you for killing me. They'll probably test your hands for gunpowder, anyway, but you'll pass.

MAMA: Not in my house!

JESSIE: If I'd known you were going to act like this, I wouldn't have told you.

MAMA: How am I supposed to act? Tell you to go ahead? O.K. by me, sugar? Might try it myself. What took you so long?

JESSIE: There's just no point in fighting me over it, that's all. Want some coffee?

MAMA: Your birthday's coming up, Jessie. Don't you want to know what we got you?

JESSIE: You got me dusting powder, Loretta got me a new housecoat, pink probably, and Dawson got me new slippers, too small, but they go with the robe, he'll say. [MAMA *cannot speak*] Right? [*Apparently* JESSIE *is right*] Be back in a minute.

[JESSIE *takes the gun box, puts it on top of the stack of towels and garbage bags, and takes them into her bedroom.* MAMA, *alone for a moment, goes to the phone, picks up the receiver, looks toward the bedroom, starts to dial, and then replaces the receiver in its cradle as* JESSIE *walks back into the room.* JESSIE *wonders, silently. They have lived together for so long there is very rarely any reason for one to ask what the other was about to do*]

MAMA: I started to, but I didn't. I didn't call him.

JESSIE: Good. Thank you.

MAMA [*Starting over, a new approach*]: What's this all about, Jessie?

JESSIE: About?

[JESSIE *now begins the next task she had "on the schedule," which is refilling all the candy jars, taking the empty papers out of the boxes of chocolates, etc.* MAMA *generally snitches when* JESSIE *does this. Not tonight, though. Nevertheless,* JESSIE *offers*]

MAMA: What did I do?

JESSIE: Nothing. Want a caramel?

MAMA [*Ignoring the candy*]: You're mad at me.

JESSIE: Not a bit. I am worried about you, but I'm going to do what I can before I go. We're not just going to sit around tonight. I made a list of things.

MAMA: What things?

JESSIE: How the washer works. Things like that.

MAMA: I know how the washer works. You put the clothes in. You put the soap in. You turn it on. You wait.

JESSIE: You do something else. You don't just wait.

MAMA: Whatever else you find to do, you're still mainly waiting. The waiting's the worst part of it. The waiting's what you pay somebody else to do, if you can.

JESSIE: [*Nodding*]: O.K. Where do we keep the soap?

MAMA: I could find it.

JESSIE: See?

MAMA: If you're mad about doing the wash, we can get Loretta to do it.

JESSIE: Oh now, that might be worth staying to see.

MAMA: She'd never in her life, would she?

JESSIE: Nope.

MAMA: What's the matter with her?

JESSIE: She thinks she's better than we are. She's not.

MAMA: Maybe if she didn't wear that yellow all the time.

JESSIE: The washer repair number is on a little card taped to the side of the machine.

MAMA: Loretta doesn't ever have to come over here again. Dawson can just leave her at home when he comes. And we don't ever have to see Dawson either if he bothers you. Does he bother you?

JESSIE: Sure he does. Be sure you clean out the lint tray every time you use the dryer. But don't ever put your house shoes in, it'll melt the soles.

MAMA: What does Dawson do, that bothers you?

JESSIE: He just calls me Jess like he knows who he's talking to. He's always wondering what I do all day. I mean, I wonder that myself, but it's my day, so it's mine to wonder about, not his.

MAMA: Family is just accident, Jessie. It's nothing personal, hon. They don't mean to get on your nerves. They don't even mean to be your family, they just are.

JESSIE: They know too much.

MAMA: About what?

JESSIE: They know things about you, and they learned it before you had a chance to say whether you wanted them to know it or not. They were there when it happened and it don't belong to them, it belongs to you, only they got it. Like my mail-order bra got delivered to their house.

MAMA: By accident!

JESSIE: All the same . . . they opened it. They saw the little rosebuds on it. [*Offering her another candy*] Chewy mint?

MAMA [*Shaking her head no*]: What do they know about you? I'll tell them never to talk about it again. Is it Ricky or Cecil or your fits or your hair is falling out or you drink too much coffee or you never go out of the house or what?

JESSIE: I just don't like their talk. The account at the grocery is in Dawson's name when you call. The number's on a whole list of numbers on the back cover of the phone book.

MAMA: Well! Now we're getting somewhere. They're none of them ever setting foot in this house again.

JESSIE: It's not them, Mother. I wouldn't kill myself just to get away from them.
MAMA: You leave the room when they come over, anyway.
JESSIE: I stay as long as I can. Besides, it's you they come to see.
MAMA: That's because I stay in the room when they come.
JESSIE: It's not them.
MAMA: Then what is it?
JESSIE [*Checking the list on her note pad*]: The grocery won't deliver on Saturday anymore. And if you want your order the same day, you have to call before ten. And they won't deliver less than fifteen dollars' worth. What I do is tell them what we need and tell them to add on cigarettes until it gets to fifteen dollars.
MAMA: It's Ricky. You're trying to get through to him.
JESSIE: If I thought I could do that, I would stay.
MAMA: Make him sorry he hurt you, then. That's it, isn't it?
JESSIE: He's hurt me, I've hurt him. We're about even.
MAMA: You'll be telling him killing is O.K. with you, you know. Want him to start killing next? Nothing wrong with it. Mom did it.
JESSIE: Only a matter of time, anyway, Mama. When the call comes, you let Dawson handle it.
MAMA: Honey, nothing says those calls are always going to be some new trouble he's into. You could get one that he's got a job, that he's getting married, or how about he's joined the army, wouldn't that be nice?
JESSIE: If you call the Sweet Tooth before you call the grocery, that Susie will take your fudge next door to the grocery and it'll all come out together. Be sure you talk to Susie, though. She won't let them put it in the bottom of a sack like that one time, remember?
MAMA: Ricky could come over, you know. What if he calls us?
JESSIE: It's not Ricky, Mama.
MAMA: Or anybody could call us, Jessie.
JESSIE: Not on Saturday night, Mama.
MAMA: Then what is it? Are you sick? If your gums are swelling again, we can get you to the dentist in the morning.
JESSIE: No. Can you order your medicine or do you want Dawson to? I've got a note to him. I'll add that to it if you want.
MAMA: Your eyes don't look right. I thought so yesterday.
JESSIE: That was just the ragweed. I'm not sick.
MAMA: Epilepsy is sick, Jessie.
JESSIE: It won't kill me. [*A pause*] If it would, I wouldn't have to.
MAMA: You don't *have* to.
JESSIE: No, I don't. That's what I like about it.
MAMA: Well, I won't let you!
JESSIE: It's not up to you.
MAMA: Jessie!
JESSIE: I want to hang a big sign around my neck, like Daddy's on the barn. GONE FISHING.
MAMA: You don't like it here.
JESSIE [*Smiling*]: Exactly.
MAMA: I meant here in my house.
JESSIE: I know you did.
MAMA: You never should have moved back in here with me. If you'd kept your little house or found another place when Cecil left you, you'd have made some new friends at least. Had a life to lead. Had your own things around you. Give Ricky a place to come see you. You never should've come here.
JESSIE: Maybe.
MAMA: But I didn't force you, did I?
JESSIE: If it was a mistake, we made it together. You took me in. I appreciate that.
MAMA: You didn't have any business being by yourself right then, but I can see how you might want a place of your own. A grown woman should . . .
JESSIE: Mama . . . I'm just not having a very good time and I don't have any reason to think it'll get anything but worse. I'm tired. I'm hurt. I'm sad. I feel used.
MAMA: Tired of what?
JESSIE: It all.
MAMA: What does that mean?
JESSIE: I can't say it any better.
MAMA: Well, you'll have to say it better because I'm not letting you alone till you do. What were those other things? Hurt . . . [*Before* JESSIE *can answer*] You had this all ready to say to me, didn't you? Did you write this down? How long have you been thinking about this?
JESSIE: Off and on, ten years. On all the time, since Christmas.
MAMA: What happened at Christmas?
JESSIE: Nothing.
MAMA: So why Christmas?
JESSIE: That's it. On the nose.

[*A pause.* MAMA *knows exactly what* JESSIE *means. She was there, too, after all*]

JESSIE [*Putting the candy sacks away*]: See where all this is? Red hots up front, sour balls and horehound mixed together in this one sack. New packages of toffee and licorice right in back there.
MAMA: Go back to your list. You're hurt by what?
JESSIE [MAMA *knows perfectly well*]: Mama . . .

MAMA: O.K. Sad about what? There's nothing real sad going on right now. If it was after your divorce or something, that would make sense.

JESSIE [*Looking at her list, then opening the drawer*]: Now, this drawer has everything in it that there's no better place for. Extension cords, batteries for the radio, extra lighters, sandpaper, masking tape, Elmer's glue, thumbtacks, that kind of stuff. The mousetraps are under the sink, but you call Dawson if you've got one and let him do it.

MAMA: Sad about what?

JESSIE: The way things are.

MAMA: Not good enough. What things?

JESSIE: Oh, everything from you and me to Red China.

MAMA: I think we can leave the Chinese out of this.

JESSIE [*Crosses back into the living room*]: There's extra light bulbs in a box in the hall closet. And we've got a couple of packages of fuses in the fuse box. There's candles and matches in the top of the broom closet, but if the lights go out, just call Dawson and sit tight. But don't open the refrigerator door. Things will stay cool in there as long as you keep the door shut.

MAMA: I asked you a question.

JESSIE: I read the paper. I don't like how things are. And they're not any better out there than they are in here.

MAMA: If you're doing this because of the newspapers, I can sure fix that!

JESSIE: There's just more of it on TV.

MAMA [*Kicking the television set*]: Take it out, then!

JESSIE: You wouldn't do that.

MAMA: Watch me.

JESSIE: What would you do all day?

MAMA [*Desperately*]: Sing. [JESSIE *laughs*] I would, too. You want to watch? I'll sing till morning to keep you alive, Jessie, please!

JESSIE: No. [*Then affectionately*] It's a funny idea, though. What do you sing?

MAMA [*Has no idea how to answer this*]: We've got a good life here!

JESSIE [*Going back into the kitchen*]: I called this morning and canceled the papers, except for Sunday, for your puzzles; you'll still get that one.

MAMA: Let's get another dog, Jessie! You liked a big dog, now, didn't you? That King dog, didn't you?

JESSIE [*Washing her hands*]: I did like that King dog, yes.

MAMA: I'm so dumb. He's the one run under the tractor.

JESSIE: That makes him dumb, not you.

MAMA: For bringing it up.

JESSIE: It's O.K. Handi-Wipes and sponges under the sink.

MAMA: We could get a new dog and keep him in the house. Dogs are cheap!

JESSIE [*Getting big pill jars out of the cabinet*]: No.

MAMA: Something for you to take care of.

JESSIE: I've had you, Mama.

MAMA [*Frantically starting to fill pill bottles*]: You do too much for me. I can fill pill bottles all day, Jessie, and change the shelf paper and wash the floor when I get through. You just watch me. You don't have to do another thing in this house if you don't want to. You don't have to take care of me, Jessie.

JESSIE: I know that. You've just been letting me do it so I'll have something to do, haven't you?

MAMA [*Realizing this was a mistake*]: I don't do it as well as you. I just meant if it tires you out or makes you feel used . . .

JESSIE: Mama, I know you used to ride the bus. Riding the bus and it's hot and bumpy and crowded and too noisy and more than anything in the world you want to get off and the only reason in the world you don't get off is it's still fifty blocks from where you're going? Well, I can get off right now if I want to, because even if I ride fifty more years and get off then, it's the same place when I step down to it. Whenever I feel like it, I can get off. As soon as I've had enough, it's my stop. I've had enough.

MAMA: You're feeling sorry for yourself!

JESSIE: The plumber's helper is under the sink, too.

MAMA: You're not having a good time! Whoever promised you a good time? Do you think I've had a good time?

JESSIE: I think you're pretty happy, yeah. You have things you like to do.

MAMA: Like what?

JESSIE: Like crochet.

MAMA: I'll teach you to crochet.

JESSIE: I can't do any of that nice work, Mama.

MAMA: Good time don't come looking for you, Jessie. You could work some puzzles or put in a garden or go to the store. Let's call a taxi and go to the A&P!

JESSIE: I shopped you up for about two weeks already. You're not going to need toilet paper till Thanksgiving.

MAMA [*Interrupting*]: You're acting like some little brat, Jessie. You're mad and everybody's boring and you don't have anything to do and you don't like me and you don't like going out and you don't like staying in and you never talk on the phone and you don't watch TV and you're miserable and it's your own sweet fault.

JESSIE: And it's time I did something about it.

MAMA: Not something like killing yourself. Something like . . . buying us all new dishes! I'd like that. Or maybe the doctor would let you get a driver's license now, or I know what let's do right this minute, let's rearrange the furniture.

JESSIE: I'll do that. If you want. I always thought if the TV was somewhere else, you wouldn't get such a glare on it during the day. I'll do whatever you want before I go.

MAMA [*Badly frightened by those words*]: You could get a job!

JESSIE: I took that telephone sales job and I didn't even make enough money to pay the phone bill, and I tried to work at the gift shop at the hospital and they said I made people real uncomfortable smiling at them the way I did.

MAMA: You could keep books. You kept your dad's books.

JESSIE: But nobody ever checked them.

MAMA: When he died, they checked them.

JESSIE: And that's when they took the books away from me.

MAMA: That's because without him there wasn't any business, Jessie!

JESSIE [*Putting the pill bottles away*]: You know I couldn't work. I can't do anything. I've never been around people my whole life except when I went to the hospital. I could have a seizure any time. What good would a job do? The kind of job I could get would make me feel worse.

MAMA: Jessie!

JESSIE: It's true!

MAMA: It's what you think is true!

JESSIE [*Struck by the clarity of that*]: That's right. It's what I think is true.

MAMA [*Hysterically*]: But I can't do anything about that!

JESSIE [*Quietly*]: No. You can't. [MAMA *slumps, if not physically, at least emotionally*] And I can't do anything either, about my life, to change it, make it better, make me feel better about it. Like it better, make it work. But I can stop it. Shut it down, turn it off like the radio when there's nothing on I want to listen to. It's all I really have that belongs to me and I'm going to say what happens to it. And it's going to stop. And I'm going to stop it. So. Let's just have a good time.

MAMA: Have a good time.

JESSIE: We can't go on fussing all night. I mean, I could ask you things I always wanted to know and you could make me some hot chocolate. The old way.

MAMA [*In despair*]: It takes cocoa, Jessie.

JESSIE [*Gets it out of the cabinet*]: I bought cocoa, Mama. And I'd like to have a caramel apple and do your nails.

MAMA: You didn't eat a bite of supper.

JESSIE: Does that mean I can't have a caramel apple?

MAMA: Of course not. I mean . . . [*Smiling a little*] Of course you can have a caramel apple.

JESSIE: I thought I could.

MAMA: I make the best caramel apples in the world.

JESSIE: I know you do.

MAMA: Or used to. And you don't get cocoa like mine anywhere anymore.

JESSIE: It takes time, I know, but . . .

MAMA: The salt is the trick.

JESSIE: Trouble and everything.

MAMA [*Backing away toward the stove*]: It's no trouble. What trouble? You put it in the pan and stir it up. All right. Fine. Caramel apples. Cocoa. O.K.

[JESSIE *walks to the counter to retrieve her cigarettes as* MAMA *looks for the right pan. There are brief nearsmiles, and maybe* MAMA *clears her throat. We have a truce, for the moment. A genuine but nevertheless uneasy one.* JESSIE, *who has been in constant motion since the beginning, now seems content to sit.*

MAMA *starts looking for a pan to make the cocoa, getting out all the pans in the cabinets in the process. It looks like she's making a mess on purpose so* JESSIE *will have to put them all away again.* MAMA *is buying time, or trying to, and entertaining*]

JESSIE: You talk to Agnes today?

MAMA: She's calling me from a pay phone this week. God only knows why. She has a perfectly good Trimline at home.

JESSIE [*Laughing*]: Well, how is she?

MAMA: How is she every day, Jessie? Nuts.

JESSIE: Is she really crazy or just silly?

MAMA: No, she's really crazy. She was probably using the pay phone because she had another little fire problem at home.

JESSIE: Mother . . .

MAMA: I'm serious! Agnes Fletcher's burned down every house she ever lived in. Eight fires, and she's due for a new one any day now.

JESSIE [*Laughing*]: No!

MAMA: Wouldn't surprise me a bit.

JESSIE [*Laughing*]: Why didn't you tell me this before? Why isn't she locked up somewhere?

MAMA: 'Cause nobody ever got hurt, I guess. Agnes woke everybody up to watch the fires as soon as she set 'em. One time she set out porch chairs and served lemonade.

JESSIE [*Shaking her head*]: Real lemonade?

MAMA: The houses they lived in, you knew they were going to fall down anyway, so why wait for it, is all I could ever make out about it. Agnes likes a feeling of accomplishment.

JESSIE: Good for her.

MAMA [*Finding the pan she wants*]: Why are you asking about Agnes? One cup or two?

JESSIE: One. She's your friend. No marshmallows.

MAMA [*Getting the milk, etc.*]: You have to have marshmallows. That's the old way, Jess. Two or three? Three is better.

JESSIE: Three, then. Her whole house burns up? Her clothes and pillows and everything? I'm not sure I believe this.

MAMA: When she was a girl, Jess, not now. Long time ago. But she's still got it in her, I'm sure of it.

JESSIE: She wouldn't burn her house down now. Where would she go? She can't get Buster to build her a new one, he's dead. How could she burn it up?

MAMA: Be exciting, though, if she did. You never know.

JESSIE: You do too know, Mama. She wouldn't do it.

MAMA [*Forced to admit, but reluctant*]: I guess not.

JESSIE: What else? Why does she wear all those whistles around her neck?

MAMA: Why does she have a house full of birds?

JESSIE: I didn't know she had a house full of birds!

MAMA: Well, she does. And she says they just follow her home. Well, I know for a fact she's still paying on the last parrot she bought. You gotta keep your life filled up, she says. She says a lot of stupid things. [JESSIE *laughs*, MAMA *continues, convinced she's getting somewhere*] It's all that okra she eats. You can't just willy-nilly eat okra two meals a day and expect to get away with it. Made her crazy.

JESSIE: She really eats okra twice a day? Where does she get it in the winter?

MAMA: Well, she eats it a lot. Maybe not two meals, but . . .

JESSIE: More than the average person.

MAMA [*Beginning to get irritated*]: I don't know how much okra the average person eats.

JESSIE: Do you know how much okra Agnes eats?

MAMA: No.

JESSIE: How many birds does she have?

MAMA: Two.

JESSIE: Then what are the whistles for?

MAMA: They're not real whistles. Just little plastic ones on a necklace she won playing Bingo, and I only told you about it because I thought I might get a laugh out of you for once even if it wasn't the truth, Jessie. Things don't have to be true to talk about 'em, you know.

JESSIE: Why won't she come over here?

[MAMA *is suddenly quiet, but the cocoa and milk are in the pan now, so she lights the stove and starts stirring*]

MAMA: Well now, what a good idea. We should've had more cocoa. Cocoa is perfect.

JESSIE: Except you don't like milk.

MAMA [*Another attempt, but not as energetic*]: I hate milk. Coats your throat as bad as okra. Something just downright disgusting about it.

JESSIE: It's because of me, isn't it?

MAMA: No, Jess.

JESSIE: Yes, Mama.

MAMA: O.K. Yes, then, but she's crazy. She's as crazy as they come. She's a lunatic.

JESSIE: What is it exactly? Did I say something, sometime? Or did she see me have a fit and's afraid I might have another one if she came over, or what?

MAMA: I guess.

JESSIE: You guess what? What's she ever said? She must've given you some reason.

MAMA: Your hands are cold.

JESSIE: What difference does that make?

MAMA: "Like a corpse," she says, "and I'm gonna be one soon enough as it is."

JESSIE: That's crazy.

MAMA: That's Agnes. "Jessie's shook the hand of death and I can't take the chance it's catching, Thelma, so I ain't comin' over, and you can understand or not, but I ain't comin'. I'll come up the driveway, but that's as far as I go."

JESSIE [*Laughing, relieved*]: I thought she didn't like me! She's scared of me! How about that! Scared of me.

MAMA: I could make her come over here, Jessie. I could call her up right now and she could bring the birds and come visit. I didn't know you ever thought about her at all. I'll tell her she just has to come and she'll come, all right. She owes me one.

JESSIE: No, that's all right. I just wondered about it. When I'm in the hospital, does she come over here?

MAMA: Her kitchen is just a tiny thing. When she comes over here, she feels like . . . [*Toning it down a little*] Well, we all like a change of scene, don't we?

JESSIE [*Playing along*]: Sure we do. Plus there's no birds diving around.

MAMA: I hate those birds. She says I don't understand them. What's there to understand about birds?

JESSIE: Why Agnes likes them, for one thing. Why they stay with her when they could be outside with the other birds. What their singing means. How they fly. What they think Agnes is.

MAMA: Why do you have to know so much about things, Jessie? There's just not that much *to* things that I could ever see.

JESSIE: That you could ever *tell*, you mean. You didn't have to lie to me about Agnes.

MAMA: I didn't lie. You never asked before!

JESSIE: You lied about setting fire to all those houses and about how many birds she has and how much okra she eats and why she won't come over here. If I have to keep dragging the truth out of you, this is going to take all night.

MAMA: That's fine with me. I'm not a bit sleepy.
JESSIE: Mama . . .
MAMA: All right. Ask me whatever you want. Here.

[They come to an awkward stop, as the cocoa is ready and MAMA *pours it into the cups* JESSIE *has set on the table]*

JESSIE *[As* MAMA *takes her first sip]*: Did you love Daddy?

MAMA: No.

JESSIE *[Pleased that* MAMA *understands the rules better now]*: I didn't think so. Were you really fifteen when you married him?

MAMA: The way he told it? I'm sitting in the mud, he comes along, drags me in the kitchen, "She's been there ever since"?

JESSIE: Yes.

MAMA: No. It was a big fat lie, the whole thing. He just thought it was funnier that way. God, this milk in here.

JESSIE: The cocoa helps.

MAMA *[Pleased that they agree on this, at least]*: Not enough, though, does it? You can still taste it, can't you?

JESSIE: Yeah, it's pretty bad. I thought it was my memory that was bad, but it's not. It's the milk, all right.

MAMA: It's a real waste of chocolate. You don't have to finish it.

JESSIE *[Putting her cup down]*: Thanks, though.

MAMA: I should've known not to make it. I knew you wouldn't like it. You never did like it.

JESSIE: You didn't ever love him, or he did something and you stopped loving him, or what?

MAMA: He felt sorry for me. He wanted a plain country woman and that's what he married, and then he held it against me the rest of my life like I was supposed to change and surprise him somehow. Like I remember this one day he was standing on the porch and I told him to get a shirt on and he went in and got one and then he said, real peaceful, but to the point, "You're right, Thelma. If God had meant for people to go around without any clothes on, they'd have been born that way."

JESSIE *[Sees* MAMA*'s hurt]*: He didn't mean anything by that, Mama.

MAMA: He never said a word he didn't have to, Jessie. That was probably all he'd said to me all day, Jessie. So if he said it, there was something to it, but I never did figure that one out. What did that mean?

JESSIE: I don't know. I liked him better than you did, but I didn't know him any better.

MAMA: How could I love him, Jessie. I didn't have a thing he wanted. *[*JESSIE *doesn't answer]* He got his share, though. You loved him enough for both of us. You followed him around like some . . . Jessie, all the man ever did was farm and sit . . . and try to think of somebody to sell the farm to.

JESSIE: Or make me a boyfriend out of pipe cleaners and sit back and smile like the stick man was about to dance and wasn't I going to get a kick out of that. Or sit up with a sick cow all night and leave me a chain of sleepy stick elephants on my bed in the morning.

MAMA: Or just sit.

JESSIE: I liked him sitting. Big old faded blue man in the chair. Quiet.

MAMA: Agnes gets more talk out of her birds than I got from the two of you. He could've had that GONE FISHING sign around his neck in that chair. I saw him stare off at the water. I saw him look at the weather rolling in. I got where I could practically see the boat myself. But you, you knew what he was thinking about and you're going to tell me.

JESSIE: I don't know, Mama! His life, I guess. His corn. His boots. Us. Things. You know.

MAMA: No, I don't know, Jessie! You had those quiet little conversations after supper every night. What were you whispering about?

JESSIE: We weren't whispering, you were just across the room.

MAMA: What did you talk about?

JESSIE: We talked about why black socks are warmer than blue socks. Is that something to go tell Mother? You were just jealous because I'd rather talk to him than wash the dishes with you.

MAMA: I was jealous because you'd rather talk to him than anything! *[*JESSIE *reaches across the table for the small clock and starts to wind it]* If I had died instead of him, he wouldn't have taken you in like I did.

JESSIE: I wouldn't have expected him to.

MAMA: Then what would you have done?

JESSIE: Come visit.

MAMA: Oh, I see. He died and left you stuck with me and you're mad about it.

JESSIE *[Getting up from the table]*: Not anymore. He didn't mean to. I didn't have to come here. We've been through this.

MAMA: He felt sorry for you, too, Jessie, don't kid yourself about that. He said you were a runt and he said it from the day you were born and he said you didn't have a chance.

JESSIE *[Getting the canister of sugar and starting to refill the sugar bowl]*: I know he loved me.

MAMA: What if he did? It didn't change anything.

JESSIE: It didn't have to. I miss him.

MAMA: He never really went fishing, you know. Never once. His tackle box was full of chewing tobacco and all he ever did was drive out to the lake and sit in his car. Dawson told me. And

Bennie at the bait shop, he told Dawson. They all laughed about it. And he'd come back from fishing and all he'd have to show for it was . . . a whole pipe-cleaner *family*—chickens, pigs, a dog with a bad leg—it was creepy strange. It made me sick to look at them and I hid his pipe cleaners a couple of times but he always had more somewhere.

JESSIE: I thought it might be better for you after he died. You'd get interested in things. Breathe better. Change somehow.

MAMA: Into what? The Queen? A clerk in a shoe store? Why should I? Because he said to? Because you said to? [JESSIE *shakes her head*] Well I wasn't here for his entertainment and I'm not here for yours either, Jessie. I don't know what I'm here for, but then I don't think about it. [*Realizing what all this means*] But I bet you wouldn't be killing yourself if he were still alive. That's a fine thing to figure out, isn't it?

JESSIE [*Filling the honey jar now*]: That's not true.

MAMA: Oh no? Then what were you asking about him for? Why did you want to know if I loved him?

JESSIE: I didn't think you did, that's all.

MAMA: Fine then. You were right. Do you feel better now?

JESSIE [*Cleaning the honey jar carefully*]: It feels good to be right about it.

MAMA: It didn't matter whether I loved him. It didn't matter to me and it didn't matter to him. And it didn't mean we didn't get along. It wasn't important. We didn't talk about it. [*Sweeping the pots off the cabinet*] Take all these pots out to the porch!

JESSIE: What for?

MAMA: Just leave me this one pan. [*She jerks the silverware drawer open*] Get me one knife, one fork, one big spoon, and the can opener, and put them out where I can get them. [*Starts throwing knives and forks in one of the pans*]

JESSIE: Don't do that! I just straightened that drawer!

MAMA [*Throwing the pan in the sink*]: And throw out all the plates and cups. I'll use paper. Loretta can have what she wants and Dawson can sell the rest.

JESSIE [*Calmly*]: What are you doing?

MAMA: I'm not going to cook. I never liked it, anyway. I like candy. Wrapped in plastic or coming in sacks. And tuna. I like tuna. I'll eat tuna, thank you.

JESSIE [*Taking the pan out of the sink*]: What if you want to make apple butter? You can't make apple butter in that little pan. What if you leave carrots on cooking and burn up that pan?

MAMA: I don't like carrots.

JESSIE: What if the strawberries are good this year and you want to go picking with Agnes.

MAMA: I'll tell her to bring a pan. You said you would do whatever I wanted! I don't want a bunch of pans cluttering up my cabinets I can't get down to, anyway. Throw them out. Every last one.

JESSIE [*Gathering up the pots*]: I'm putting them all back in. I'm not taking them to the porch. If you want them, they'll be here. You'll bend down and get them, like you got the one for the cocoa. And if somebody else comes over here to cook, they'll have something to cook in, and that's the end of it!

MAMA: Who's going to come cook here?

JESSIE: Agnes.

MAMA: In my pots. Not on your life.

JESSIE: There's no reason why the two of you couldn't just live here together. Be cheaper for both of you and somebody to talk to. And if the birds bothered you, well, one day when Agnes is out getting her hair done, you could take them all for a walk!

MAMA [*As* JESSIE *straightens the silverware*]: So that's why you're pestering me about Agnes. You think you can rest easy if you get me a new babysitter? Well, I don't want to live with Agnes. I barely want to talk with Agnes. She's just around. We go back, that's all. I'm not letting Agnes near this place. You don't get off as easy as that, child.

JESSIE: O.K., then. It's just something to think about.

MAMA: I don't like things to think about. I like things to go on.

JESSIE [*Closing the silverware drawer*]: I want to know what Daddy said to you the night he died. You came storming out of his room and said I could wait it out with him if I wanted to, but you were going to watch *Gunsmoke.* What did he say to you?

MAMA: He didn't have *anything* to say to me, Jessie. That's why I left. He didn't say a thing. It was his last chance not to talk to me and he took full advantage of it.

JESSIE [*After a moment*]: I'm sorry you didn't love him. Sorry for you, I mean. He seemed like a nice man.

MAMA [*As* JESSIE *walks to the refrigerator*]: Ready for your apple now?

JESSIE: Soon as I'm through here, Mama.

MAMA: You won't like the apple, either. It'll be just like the cocoa. You never liked eating at all, did you? Any of it! What have you been living on all these years, toothpaste?

JESSIE [*As she starts to clean out the refrigerator*]: Now, you know the milkman comes on Wednesdays and Saturdays, and he leaves the order blank in an egg box, and you give the bills to Dawson once a month.

MAMA: Do they still make that orangeade?

JESSIE: It's not orangeade, it's just orange.

MAMA: I'm going to get some. I thought they stopped making it. You just stopped ordering it.

JESSIE: You should drink milk.

MAMA: Not anymore, I'm not. That hot chocolate was the last. Hooray.

JESSIE [*Getting the garbage can from under the sink*]: I told them to keep delivering a quart a week no matter what you said. I told them you'd run out of Cokes and you'd have to drink it. I told them I knew you wouldn't pour it on the ground . . .

MAMA [*Finishing her sentence*]: And you told them you weren't going to be ordering anymore?

JESSIE: I told them I was taking a little holiday and to look after you.

MAMA: And they didn't think something was funny about that? You who doesn't go to the front steps? You, who only sees the driveway looking down from a stretcher passed out cold?

JESSIE [*Enjoying this, but not laughing*]: They said it was about time, but why didn't I take you with me? And I said I didn't think you'd want to go, and they said, "Yeah, everybody's got their own idea of vacation."

MAMA: I guess you think that's funny.

JESSIE [*Pulling jars out of the refrigerator*]: You know there never was any reason to call the ambulance for me. All they ever did for me in the emergency room was let me wake up. I could've done that here. Now, I'll just call them out and you say yes or no. I know you like pickles. Ketchup?

MAMA: Keep it.

JESSIE: We've had this since last Fourth of July.

MAMA: Keep the ketchup. Keep it all.

JESSIE: Are you going to drink ketchup from the bottle or what? How can you want your food and not want your pots to cook it in? This stuff will all spoil in here, Mother.

MAMA: Nothing I ever did was good enough for you and I want to know why.

JESSIE: That's not true.

MAMA: And I want to know why you've lived here this long feeling the way you do.

JESSIE: You have no earthly idea how I feel.

MAMA: Well, how could I? You're real far back there, Jessie.

JESSIE: Back where?

MAMA: What's it like over there, where you are? Do people always say the right thing or get whatever they want, or what?

JESSIE: What are you talking about?

MAMA: Why do you read the newspaper? Why don't you wear that sweater I made for you? Do you remember how I used to look, or am I just any old woman now? When you have a fit, do you see stars or what? How did you fall off the horse, really? Why did Cecil leave you? Where did you put my old glasses?

JESSIE [*Stunned by* MAMA*'s intensity*]: They're in the bottom drawer of your dresser in an old Milk of Magnesia box. Cecil left me because he made me choose between him and smoking.

MAMA: Jessie, I know he wasn't that dumb.

JESSIE: I never understood why he hated it so much when it's so good. Smoking is the only thing I know that's always just what you think it's going to be. Just like it was the last time, right there when you want it and real quiet.

MAMA: Your fits made him sick and you know it.

JESSIE: Say seizures, not fits. Seizures.

MAMA: It's the same thing. A seizure in the hospital is a fit at home.

JESSIE: They didn't bother him at all. Except he did feel responsible for it. It *was* his idea to go horseback riding that day. It was his idea I could do *anything* if I just made up my mind to. I fell off the horse because I didn't know how to hold on. Cecil left for pretty much the same reason.

MAMA: He had a girl, Jessie. I walked right in on them in the toolshed.

JESSIE [*After a moment*]: O.K. That's fair. [*Lighting another cigarette*] Was she very pretty?

MAMA: She was Agnes's girl, Carlene. Judge for yourself.

JESSIE [*As she walks to the living room*]: I guess you and Agnes had a good talk about that, huh?

MAMA: I never thought he was good enough for you. They moved here from Tennessee, you know.

JESSIE: What are you talking about? You liked him better than I did. You flirted him out here to build your porch or I'd never even met him at all. You thought maybe he'd help you out around the place, come in and get some coffee and talk to you. God knows what you thought. All that curly hair.

MAMA: He's the best carpenter I ever saw. That little house of yours will still be standing at the end of the world, Jessie.

JESSIE: You didn't need a porch, Mama.

MAMA: All right! I wanted you to have a husband.

JESSIE: And I couldn't get one on my own, of course.

MAMA: How were you going to get husband never opening your mouth to a living soul?

JESSIE: So I was quiet about it, so what?

MAMA: So I should have let you just sit here? Sit like your daddy? Sit here?

JESSIE: Maybe.

MAMA: Well, I didn't think so.

JESSIE: Well, what did you know?

MAMA: I never said I knew much. How was I supposed to learn anything living out here? I didn't know enough to do half the things I did in my life.

Things happen. You do what you can about them and you see what happens next. I married you off to the wrong man, I admit that. So I took you in when he left. I'm sorry.

JESSIE: He wasn't the wrong man.

MAMA: He didn't love you, Jessie, or he wouldn't have left.

JESSIE: He wasn't the wrong man, Mama. I loved Cecil so much. And I tried to get more exercise and I tried to stay awake. I tried to learn to ride a horse. And I tried to stay outside with him, but he always knew I was trying, so it didn't work.

MAMA: He was a selfish man. He told me once he hated to see people move into his houses after he built them. He knew they'd mess them up.

JESSIE: I loved that bridge he built over the creek in back of the house. It didn't have to be anything special, a couple of boards would have been just fine, but he used that yellow pine and rubbed it so smooth . . .

MAMA: He had responsibilities here. He had a wife and son here and he failed you.

JESSIE: Or that baby bed he built for Ricky. I told him he didn't have to spend so much time on it, but he said it had to last, and the thing ended up weighing two hundred pounds and I couldn't move it. I said, "How long does a baby bed have to last, anyway?" But maybe he thought if it was strong enough, it might keep Ricky a baby.

MAMA: Ricky is too much like Cecil.

JESSIE: He is not. Ricky is as much like me as it's possible for any human to be. We even wear the same size pants. These are his, I think.

MAMA: That's just the same size. That's not you're the same person.

JESSIE: I see it on his face. I hear it when he talks. We look out at the world and we see the same thing: Not Fair. And the only difference between us is Ricky's out there trying to get even. And he knows not to trust anybody and he got it straight from me. And he knows not to try to get work, and guess where he got that. He walks around like there's loose boards in the floor, and you know who laid that floor, I did.

MAMA: Ricky isn't through yet. You don't know how he'll turn out!

JESSIE [*Going back to the kitchen*]: Yes I do and so did Cecil. Ricky is the two of us together for all time in too small a space. And we're tearing each other apart, like always, inside that boy, and if you don't see it, then you're just blind.

MAMA: Give him time, Jess.

JESSIE: Oh, he'll have plenty of that. Five years for forgery, ten years for armed assault . . .

MAMA [*Furious*]: Stop that! [*Then pleading*] Jessie, Cecil might be ready to try it again, honey, that happens sometimes. Go downtown. Find him. Talk to him. He didn't know what he had in you. Maybe he sees things different now, but you're not going to know that till you go see him. Or call him up! Right now! He might be home.

JESSIE: And say what? Nothing's changed, Cecil, I'd just like to look at you, if you don't mind? No. He loved me, Mama. He just didn't know how things fall down around me like they do. I think he did the right thing. He gave himself another chance, that's all. But I did beg him to take me with him. I did tell him I would leave Ricky and you and everything I loved out here if only he would take me with him, but he couldn't and I understood that. [*Pause*] I wrote that note I showed you. I wrote it. Not Cecil. I said "I'm sorry, Jessie, I can't fix it all for you." I said I'd always love me, not Cecil. But that's how he felt.

MAMA: Then he should've taken you with him!

JESSIE [*Picking up the garbage bag she has filled*]: Mama, you don't pack your garbage when you move.

MAMA: You will not call yourself garbage, Jessie.

JESSIE [*Taking the bag to the big garbage can near the back door*]: Just a way of saying it, Mama. Thinking about my list, that's all. [*Opening the can, putting the garbage in, then securing the lid*] Well, a little more than that. I was trying to say it's all right that Cecil left. It was . . . a relief in a way. I never was what he wanted to see, so it was better when he wasn't looking at me all the time.

MAMA: I'll make your apple now.

JESSIE: No thanks. You get the manicure stuff and I'll be right there.

[JESSIE *ties up the big garbage bag in the can and replaces the small garbage bag under the sink, all the time trying desperately to regain her calm.* MAMA *watches, from a distance, her hand reaching unconsciously for the phone. Then she has a better idea. Or rather she thinks of the only other thing left and is willing to try it. Maybe she is even convinced it will work*]

MAMA: Jessie, I think your daddy had little . . .

JESSIE [*Interrupting her*]: Garbage night is Tuesday. Put it out as late as you can. The Davis's dogs get in it if you don't. [*Replacing the garbage bag in the can under the sink*] And keep ordering the heavy black bags. It doesn't pay to buy the cheap ones. And I've got all the ties here with the hammers and all. Take them out of the box as soon as you open a new one and put them in this drawer. They'll get lost if you don't, and rubber bands or something else won't work.

MAMA: I think your daddy had fits, too. I think he sat in his chair and had little fits. I read this a long time ago in a magazine, how little fits go, just little blackouts where maybe their eyes don't even close and people just call them "thinking spells."

JESSIE [*Getting the slipcover out of the laundry basket*]: I don't think you want this manicure we've been looking forward to. I washed this cover for the sofa, but it'll take both of us to get it back on.

MAMA: I watched his eyes. I know that's what it was. The magazine said some people don't even know they've had one.

JESSIE: Daddy would've known if he'd had fits, Mama.

MAMA: The lady in this story had kept track of hers and she'd had eighty thousand of them in the last eleven years.

JESSIE: Next time you wash this cover, it'll dry better if you put it on wet.

MAMA: Jessie, listen to what I'm telling you. This lady had anywhere between five and five hundred fits a day and they lasted maybe fifteen seconds apiece, so that out of her life, she'd only lost about two weeks altogether, and she had a full-time secretary job and an IQ of 120.

JESSIE [*Amused by* MAMA*'s approach*]: You want to talk about fits, is that it?

MAMA: Yes. I do. I want to say . . .

JESSIE [*Interrupting*]: Most of the time I wouldn't even know I'd had one, except I wake up with different clothes on, feeling like I've been run over. Sometimes I feel my head start to turn around or hear myself scream. And sometimes there *is* this dizzy stupid feeling a little before it, but if the TV's on, well, it's easy to miss.

[*As* JESSIE *and* MAMA *replace the slipcover on the sofa and the afghan on the chair, the physical struggle somehow mirrors the emotional one in the conversation*]

MAMA: I can tell when you're about to have one. Your eyes get this big! But, Jessie, you haven't . . .

JESSIE [*Taking charge of this*]: What do they look like? The seizures.

MAMA [*Reluctant*]: Different each time, Jess.

JESSIE: O.K. Pick one, then. A good one. I think I want to know now.

MAMA: There's not much to tell. You just . . . crumple, in a heap, like a puppet and somebody cut the strings all at once, or like the firing squad in some Mexican movie, you just slide down the wall, you know. You don't know what happens? How can you not know what happens?

JESSIE: I'm busy.

MAMA: That's not funny.

JESSIE: I'm not laughing. My head turns around and I fall down and then what?

MAMA: Well, your chest squeezes in and out, and you sound like you're gagging, sucking air in and out like you can't breathe.

JESSIE: Do it for me. Make the sound for me.

MAMA: I will not. It's awful-sounding.

JESSIE: Yeah. It felt like it might be. What's next?

MAMA: Your mouth bites down and I have to get your tongue out of the way fast, so you don't bite yourself.

JESSIE: Or you. I bite you, too, don't I?

MAMA: You got me once real good. I had to get a tetanus! But I know what to watch for now. And then you turn blue and the jerks start up. Like I'm standing there poking you with a cattle prod or you're sticking your finger in a light socket as fast as you can . . .

JESSIE: Foaming like a mad dog the whole time.

MAMA: It's bubbling, Jess, not foam like the washer overflowed, for God's sake; it's bubbling like a baby spitting up. I go get a wet washcloth, that's all. And then the jerks slow down and you wet yourself and it's over. Two minutes tops.

JESSIE: How do I get to the bed?

MAMA: How do you think?

JESSIE: I'm too heavy for you now. How do you do it?

MAMA: I call Dawson. But I get you cleaned up before he gets here and I make him leave before you wake up.

JESSIE: You could just leave me on the floor.

MAMA: I want you to wake up someplace nice, O.K.? [*Then making a real effort*] But, Jessie, and this is the reason I even brought this up! You haven't had a seizure for a solid year. A whole year, do you realize that?

JESSIE: Yeah, the phenobarb's about right now, I guess.

MAMA: You bet it is. You might never have another one, ever! You might be through with it for all time!

JESSIE: Could be.

MAMA: You are. I know you are!

JESSIE: I sure am feeling good. I really am. The double vision's gone and my gums aren't swelling. No rashes or anything. I'm feeling as good as I ever felt in my life. I'm even feeling like worrying or getting mad and I'm not afraid it will start a fit if I do, I just go ahead.

MAMA: Of course you do! You can even scream at me, if you want to. I can take it. You don't have to act like you're just visiting here, Jessie. This is your house, too.

JESSIE: The best part is, my memory's back.

MAMA: Your memory's always been good. When couldn't you remember things? You're always reminding me what . . .

JESSIE: Because I've made lists for everything. But now I remember what things mean on my lists. I see "dish towels," and I used to wonder whether I was supposed to wash them, buy them, or look for them because I wouldn't remember where I put them after I washed them, but now I know it means wrap them up, they're a present for Loretta's birthday.

MAMA [*Finished with the sofa now*]: You used to go looking for your lists, too, I've noticed that. You always know where they are now! [*Then suddenly worried*] Loretta's birthday isn't coming up, is it?

JESSIE: I made a list of all the birthdays for you. I even put yours on it. [*A small smile*] So you can call Loretta and remind her.

MAMA: Let's take Loretta to Howard Johnson's and have those fried clams. I *know* you love that clam roll.

JESSIE [*Slight pause*]: I won't be here, Mama.

MAMA: What have we just been talking about? You'll be here. You're well, Jessie. You're starting all over. You said it yourself. You're remembering things and . . .

JESSIE: I won't be here. If I'd ever had a year like this, to think straight and all, before now, I'd be gone already.

MAMA [*Not pleading, commanding*]: No, Jessie.

JESSIE [*Folding the rest of the laundry*]: Yes, Mama. Once I started remembering, I could see what it all added up to.

MAMA: The fits are over!

JESSIE: It's not the fits, Mama.

MAMA: Then it's me for giving them to you, but I didn't do it!

JESSIE: It's not the fits! You said it yourself, the medicine takes care of the fits.

MAMA [*Interrupting*]: Your daddy gave you those fits, Jessie. He passed it down to you like your green eyes and your straight hair. It's not my fault!

JESSIE: So what if he had little fits? It's not inherited. I fell off the horse. It was an accident.

MAMA: The horse wasn't the first time, Jessie. You had a fit when you were five years old.

JESSIE: I did not.

MAMA: You did! You were eating a popsicle and down you went. He gave it to you. It's *his* fault, not mine.

JESSIE: Well, you took your time telling me.

MAMA: How do you tell that to a five-year-old?

JESSIE: What did the doctor say?

MAMA: He said kids have them all the time. He said there wasn't anything to do but wait for another one.

JESSIE: But I didn't have another one.

[*Now there is a real silence*]

JESSIE: You mean to tell me I had fits all the time as a kid and you just told me I fell down or something and it wasn't till I had the fit when Cecil was looking that anybody bothered to find out what was the matter with me?

MAMA: It wasn't *all the time,* Jessie. And they changed when you started to school. More like your daddy's. Oh, that was some swell time, sitting here with the two of you turning off and on like light bulbs some nights.

JESSIE: How many fits did I have?

MAMA: You never hurt yourself. I never let you out of my sight. I caught you every time.

JESSIE: But you didn't tell anybody.

MAMA: It was none of their business.

JESSIE: You were ashamed.

MAMA: I didn't want anybody to know. Least of all you.

JESSIE: Least of all me. Oh, right. That was mine to know, Mama, not yours. Did Daddy know?

MAMA: He thought you were . . . you fell down a lot. That's what he thought. You were careless. Or maybe he thought I beat you. I don't know what he thought. He didn't think about it.

JESSIE: Because you didn't tell him!

MAMA: If I told him about you, I'd have to tell him about him!

JESSIE: I don't like this. I don't like this one bit.

MAMA: I didn't think you'd like it. That's why I didn't tell you.

JESSIE: If I'd known I was an epileptic, Mama, I wouldn't have ridden any horses.

MAMA: Make you feel like a freak, is that what I should have done?

JESSIE: Just get the manicure tray and sit down!

MAMA [*Throwing it to the floor*]: I don't want a manicure!

JESSIE: Doesn't look like you do, no.

MAMA: Maybe I did drop you, you don't know.

JESSIE: If you say you didn't, you didn't.

MAMA [*Beginning to break down*]: Maybe I fed you the wrong thing. Maybe you had a fever sometime and I didn't know it soon enough. Maybe it's a punishment.

JESSIE: For what?

MAMA: I don't know. Because of how I felt about your father. Because I didn't want any more children. Because I smoked too much or didn't eat right when I was carrying you. It has to be something I did.

JESSIE: It does not. It's just a sickness, not a curse. Epilepsy doesn't mean anything. It just is.

MAMA: I'm not talking about the fits here, Jessie! I'm talking about this killing yourself. It has to be me that's the matter here. You wouldn't be doing this if it wasn't. I didn't tell you things or I married you off to the wrong man or I took you in and let your life get away from you or all of it put together. I don't know what I did, but I did it, I know. This is all my fault, Jessie, but I don't know what to do about it now!

JESSIE [*Exasperated at having to say this again*]: It doesn't have anything to do with you!

MAMA: Everything you do has to do with me, Jessie. You can't do *anything*, wash your face or cut your finger, without doing it to me. That's right! You might as well kill me as you, Jessie, it's the same thing. This has to do with me, Jessie.

JESSIE: Then what if it does! What if it has everything to do with you! What if you are all I have and you're not enough? What if I could take all the rest of it if only I didn't have you here? What if the only way I can get away from you for good is to kill myself? What if it is? I can *still* do it!

MAMA [*In desperate tears*]: Don't leave me, Jessie! [JESSIE *stands for a moment, then turns for the bedroom*] No! [*She grabs* JESSIE*'s arm*]

JESSIE [*Carefully taking her arm away*]: I have a box of things I want people to have. I'm just going to go get it for you. You . . . just rest a minute.

[JESSIE *is gone.* MAMA *heads for the telephone, but she can't even pick up the receiver this time and, instead, stoops to clean up the bottles that have spilled out of the manicure tray.*

JESSIE *returns, carrying a box that groceries were delivered in. It probably says Hershey Kisses or Starkist Tuna.* MAMA *is still down on the floor cleaning up, hoping that maybe if she just makes it look nice enough,* JESSIE *will stay*]

MAMA: Jessie, how can I live here without you? I need you! You're supposed to tell me to stand up straight and say how nice I look in my pink dress, and drink my milk. You're supposed to go around and lock up so I know we're safe for the night, and when I wake up, you're supposed to be out there making the coffee and watching me get older every day, and you're supposed to help me die when the time comes. I can't do that by myself, Jessie. I'm not like you, Jessie. I hate the quiet and I don't want to die and I don't want you to go, Jessie. How can I . . . [*Has to stop a moment*] How can I get up every day knowing you had to kill yourself to make it stop hurting and I was here all the time and I never even saw it. And then you gave me this chance to make it better, convince you to stay alive, and I couldn't do it. How can I live with myself after this, Jessie?

JESSIE: I only told you so I could explain it, so you wouldn't blame yourself, so you wouldn't feel bad. There wasn't anything you could say to change my mind. I didn't want you to save me. I just wanted you to know.

MAMA: Stay with me just a little longer. Just a few more years. I don't have that many more to go, Jessie. And as soon as I'm dead, you can do whatever you want. Maybe with me gone, you'll have all the quiet you want, right here in the house. And maybe one day you'll put in some begonias up the walk and get just the right rain for them all summer. And Ricky will be married by then and he'll bring your grandbabies over and you can sneak them a piece of candy when their daddy's not looking and then be real glad when they've gone home and left you to your quiet again.

JESSIE: Don't you see, Mama, everything I do winds up like this. How could I think you would understand? How could I think you would want a manicure? We could hold hands for an hour and then I could go shoot myself? I'm sorry about tonight, Mama, but it's exactly why I'm doing it.

MAMA: If you've got the guts to kill yourself, Jessie, you've got the guts to stay alive.

JESSIE: I know that. So it's really just a matter of where I'd rather be.

MAMA: Look, maybe I can't think of what you should do, but that doesn't mean there isn't something that would help. *You* find it. *You* think of it. You can keep trying. You can get brave and try some more. You don't have to give up!

JESSIE: I'm *not* giving up! This *is* the other thing I'm trying. And I'm sure there are some other things that might work, but *might* work isn't good enough anymore. I need something that *will* work. *This* will work. That's why I picked it.

MAMA: But something might happen. Something that could change everything. Who knows what it might be, but it might be worth waiting for! [JESSIE *doesn't respond*] Try it for two more weeks. We could have more talks like tonight.

JESSIE: No, Mama.

MAMA: I'll pay more attention to you. Tell the truth when you ask me. Let you have your say.

JESSIE: No, Mama! We wouldn't have more talks like tonight, because it's this next part that's made this last part so good, Mama. No, Mama. *This* is how I have my say. This is how I say what I thought about it *all* and I say no. To Dawson and Loretta and the Red Chinese and epilepsy and Ricky and Cecil and you. And me. And hope. I say no! [*Then going to* MAMA *on the sofa*] Just let me go easy, Mama.

MAMA: How can I let you go?

JESSIE: You can because you have to. It's what you've always done.

MAMA: You are my child!

JESSIE: I am what became of your child. [MAMA *cannot answer*] I found an old baby picture of me. And it was somebody else, not me. It was somebody pink and fat who never heard of sick or lonely, somebody who cried and got fed, and reached up and got held and kicked but didn't hurt anybody, and slept whenever she wanted to, just by closing her eyes. Somebody who mainly just laid there and laughed at the colors waving around over her head and chewed on a polka-dot whale and woke up knowing some new trick nearly every day, and rolled over and drooled on the sheet and felt your hand pulling my quilt back up over me. That's who I started out and this is who is left. [*There is no self-pity here*] That's what this is about. It's somebody I lost, all right, it's my own self. Who I never was. Or who I tried to be and never got there. Somebody I waited for who never came. And never will. So, see, it doesn't much matter what else happens in the world or in this house, even. I'm what was worth waiting for and I didn't make it. Me . . . who might have made a difference to me . . . I'm not going to show up, so there's no reason to stay, except to keep you company, and that's . . . not reason enough because I'm not . . . very good company. [*Pause*] Am I.

MAMA [*Knowing she must tell the truth*]: No. And neither am I.

JESSIE: I had this strange little thought, well, maybe it's not so strange. Anyway, after Christmas, after I decided to do this, I would wonder, sometimes, what might keep me here, what might be worth staying for, and you know what it was? It was maybe if there was something I really liked, like maybe if I really liked rice pudding or cornflakes for breakfast or something, that might be enough.

MAMA: Rice pudding is good.

JESSIE: Not to me.

MAMA: And you're not afraid?

JESSIE: Afraid of what?

MAMA: I'm afraid of it, for me, I mean. When my time comes. I know it's coming, but . . .

JESSIE: You don't know when. Like in a scary movie.

MAMA: Yeah, sneaking up on me like some killer on the loose, hiding out in the back yard just waiting for me to have my hands full someday and how am I supposed to protect myself anyhow when I don't know what he looks like and I don't know how he sounds coming up behind me like that or if it will hurt or take very long or what I don't get done before it happens.

JESSIE: You've got plenty of time left.

MAMA: I forget what for, right now.

JESSIE: For whatever happens, I don't know. For the rest of your life. For Agnes burning down one more house or Dawson losing his hair or . . .

MAMA [*Quickly*]: Jessie. I can't just sit here and say O.K., kill yourself if you want to.

JESSIE: Sure you can. You just did. Say it again.

MAMA [*Really startled*]: Jessie! [*Quiet horror*] How dare you! [*Furious*] How dare you! You think you can just leave whenever you want, like you're watching television here? No, you can't, Jessie. You make me feel like a fool for being alive, child, and you are so wrong! I like it here, and I will stay here until they make me go, until they drag me screaming and I mean screeching into my grave, and you're real smart to get away before then because, I mean, honey, you've never heard noise like that in your life. [JESSIE *turns away*] Who am I talking to? You're gone already, aren't you? I'm looking right through you! I can't stop you because you're already gone! I guess you think they'll all have to talk about you now! I guess you think this will really confuse them. Oh yes, ever since Christmas you've been laughing to yourself and thinking, "Boy, are they all in for a surprise." Well, nobody's going to be a bit surprised, sweetheart. This is just like you. Do it the hard way, that's my girl, all right. [JESSIE *gets up and goes into the kitchen, but* MAMA *follows her*] You know who they're going to feel sorry for? Me! How about that! Not you, me! They're going to be *ashamed* of you. Yes. *Ashamed!* If somebody asks Dawson about it, he'll change the subject as fast as he can. He'll talk about how much he has to pay to park his car these days.

JESSIE: Leave me alone.

MAMA: It's the truth!

JESSIE: I should've just left you a note!

MAMA [*Screaming*]: Yes! [*Then suddenly understanding what she has said, nearly paralyzed by the thought of it, she turns slowly to face* JESSIE, *nearly whispering*] No. No. I . . . might not have thought of all the things you've said.

JESSIE: It's O.K., Mama.

[MAMA *is nearly unconscious from the emotional devastation of these last few moments. She sits down at the kitchen table, hurt and angry and desperately afraid. But she looks almost numb. She is so far beyond what is known as pain that she is virtually unreachable and* JESSIE *knows this, and talks quietly, watching for signs of recovery*]

JESSIE [*Washes her hands in the sink*]: I remember you liked that preacher who did Daddy's, so if you want to ask him to do the service, that's O.K. with me.

MAMA [*Not an answer, just a word*]: What.

JESSIE [*Putting on hand lotion as she talks*]: And pick some songs you like or let Agnes pick, she'll know exactly which ones. Oh, and I had your dress cleaned that you wore to Daddy's. You looked real good in that.

MAMA: I don't remember, hon.

JESSIE: And it won't be so bad once your friends start coming to the funeral home. You'll probably see people you haven't seen for years, but I thought about what you should say to get you over that nervous part when they first come in.

MAMA [*Simply repeating*]: Come in.

JESSIE: Take them up to see their flowers, they'd like that. And when they say, "I'm so sorry, Thelma," you just say, "I appreciate your coming, Connie." And then ask how their garden was this summer or what they're doing for Thanksgiving or how their children . . .

MAMA: I don't think I should ask about their children. I'll talk about what they have on, that's always good. And I'll have some crochet work with me.

JESSIE: And Agnes will be there, so you might not have to talk at all.

MAMA: Maybe if Connie Richards does come, I can get her to tell me where she gets that Irish yarn, she calls it. I know it doesn't come from Ireland. I think it just comes with a green wrapper.

JESSIE: And be sure to invite enough people home afterward so you get enough food to feed them all and have some left for you. But don't let anybody take anything home, especially Loretta.

MAMA: Loretta will get all the food set up, honey. It's only fair to let her have some macaroni or something.

JESSIE: No, Mama. You have to be more selfish from now on. [*Sitting at the table with* MAMA] Now, somebody's bound to ask you why I did it and you just say you don't know. That you loved me and you know I loved you and we just sat around tonight like every other night of our lives, and then I came over and kissed you and said, "'Night, Mother," and you heard me close my bedroom door and the next thing you heard was the shot. And whatever reasons I had, well, you guess I just took them with me.

MAMA [*Quietly*]: It was something personal.

JESSIE: Good. That's good, Mama.

MAMA: That's what I'll say, then.

JESSIE: Personal. Yeah.

MAMA: Is that what I tell Dawson and Loretta, too? We sat around, you kissed me, "'Night, Mother"? They'll want to know more, Jessie. They won't believe it.

JESSIE: Well, then, tell them what we did. I filled up the candy jars. I cleaned out the refrigerator. We made some hot chocolate and put the cover back on the sofa. You had no idea. All right? I really think it's better that way. If they know we talked about it, they really won't understand how you let me go.

MAMA: I guess not.

JESSIE: It's private. Tonight is private, yours and mine, and I don't want anybody else to have any of it.

MAMA: O.K., then.

JESSIE [*Standing behind* MAMA *now, holding her shoulders*]: Now, when you hear the shot, I don't want you to come in. First of all, you won't be able to get in by yourself, but I don't want you trying. Call Dawson, then call the police, and then call Agnes. And then you'll need something to do till somebody gets here, so wash the hot-chocolate pan. You wash that pan till you hear the doorbell ring and I don't care if it's an hour, you keep washing that pan.

MAMA: I'll make my calls and then I'll just sit. I won't need something to do. What will the police say?

JESSIE: They'll do that gunpowder test, I guess, and ask you what happened, and by that time, the ambulance will be here and they'll come in and get me and you know how that goes. You stay out here with Dawson and Loretta. You keep Dawson out here. I want the police in the room first, not Dawson, O.K.?

MAMA: What if Dawson and Loretta want me to go home with them?

JESSIE [*Returning to the living room*]: That's up to you.

MAMA: I think I'll stay here. All they've got is Sanka.

JESSIE: Maybe Agnes could come stay with you for a few days.

MAMA [*Standing up, looking into the living room*]: I'd rather be by myself, I think. [*Walking toward the box* JESSIE *brought in earlier*] You want me to give people those things?

JESSIE [*They sit down on the sofa,* JESSIE *holding the box on her lap*]: I want Loretta to have my little calculator. Dawson bought it for himself, you know, but then he saw one he liked better and he couldn't bring both of them home with Loretta counting every penny the way she does, so he gave the first one to me. Be funny for her to have it now, don't you think? And all my house slippers are in a sack for her in my closet. Tell her I know they'll fit and I've never worn any of them, and make sure Dawson hears you tell her that. I'm glad he loves Loretta so much, but I wish he knew not everybody has her size feet.

MAMA [*Taking the calculator*]: O.K.

JESSIE [*Reaching into the box again*]: This letter is for Dawson, but it's mostly about you, so read it if you want. There's a list of presents for you for at least twenty more Christmases and birthdays, so if you want anything special you better add it to this list before you give it to him. Or if you want to be surprised, just don't read that page. This Christmas, you're getting mostly stuff for the house, like a new rug in your bathroom and needlework, but next Christmas, you're really going to cost him next Christmas. I think you'll like it a lot and you'd never think of it.

MAMA: And you think he'll go for it?

JESSIE: I think he'll feel like a real jerk if he doesn't. Me telling him to, like this and all. Now, this number's where you call Cecil. I called it last week and he answered, so I know he still lives there.

MAMA: What do you want me to tell him?

JESSIE: Tell him we talked about him and I only had good things to say about him, but mainly tell him to find Ricky and tell him what I did, and tell Ricky you have something for him, out here, from me, and to come get it. [*Pulls a sack out of the box*]

MAMA [*The sack feels empty*]: What is it?

JESSIE [*Taking it off*]: My watch. [*Putting it in the sack and taking a ribbon out of the sack to tie around the top of it*]

MAMA: He'll sell it!

JESSIE: That's the idea. I appreciate him not stealing it already. I'd like to buy him a good meal.

MAMA: He'll buy dope with it!

JESSIE: Well, then, I hope he gets some good dope with it, Mama. And the rest of this is for you. [*Handing* MAMA *the box now.* MAMA *picks up the things and looks at them*]

MAMA [*Surprised and pleased*]: When did you do all this? During my naps, I guess.

JESSIE: I guess. I tried to be quiet about it. [*As* MAMA *is puzzled by the presents*] Those are just little presents. For whenever you need one. They're not bought presents, just things I thought you might like to look at, pictures or things you think you've lost. Things you didn't know you had, even. You'll see.

MAMA: I'm not sure I want them. They'll make me think of you.

JESSIE: No they won't. They're just things, like a free tube of toothpaste I found hanging on the door one day.

MAMA: Oh. All right, then.

JESSIE: Well, maybe there's one nice present in there somewhere. It's Granny's ring she gave me and I thought you might like to have it, but I didn't think you'd wear it if I gave it to you right now.

MAMA [*Taking the box to a table nearby*]: No. Probably not. [*Turning back to face her*] I'm ready for my manicure, I guess. Want me to wash my hands again?

JESSIE [*Standing up*]: It's time for me to go, Mama.

MAMA [*Starting for her*]: No, Jessie, you've got all night!

JESSIE [*As* MAMA *grabs her*]: No, Mama.

MAMA: It's not even ten o'clock.

JESSIE [*Very calm*]: Let me go, Mama.

MAMA: I can't. You can't go. You can't do this. You didn't say it would be so soon, Jessie. I'm scared. I love you.

JESSIE [*Takes her hands away*]: Let go of me, Mama. I've said everything I had to say.

MAMA [*Standing still a minute*]: You said you wanted to do my nails.

JESSIE [*Taking a small step backward*]: I can't. It's too late.

MAMA: It's not too late!

JESSIE: I don't want you to wake Dawson and Loretta when you call. I want them to still be up and dressed so they can get right over.

MAMA [*As* JESSIE *backs up,* MAMA *moves in on her, but carefully*]: They wake up fast, Jessie, if they have to. They don't matter here, Jessie. You do. I do. We're not through yet. We've got a lot of things to take care of here. I don't know where my prescriptions are and you didn't tell me what to tell Dr. Davis when he calls or how much you want me to tell Ricky or who I call to rake the leaves or . . .

JESSIE: Don't try and stop me, Mama, you can't do it.

MAMA [*Grabbing her again, this time hard*]: I can too! I'll stand in front of this hall and you can't get past me. [*They struggle*] You'll have to knock me down to get away from me, Jessie. I'm not about to let you . . .

[MAMA *struggles with* JESSIE *at the door and in the struggle* JESSIE *gets away from her and*—]

JESSIE [*Almost a whisper*]: 'Night, Mother. [*She vanishes into her bedroom and we hear the door lock just as* MAMA *gets to it*]

MAMA [*Screams*]: Jessie! [*Pounding on the door*] Jessie, you let me in there. Don't you do this, Jessie. I'm not going to stop screaming until you open this door, Jessie. Jessie! Jessie! What if I don't do any of the things you told me to do! I'll tell Cecil what a miserable man he was to make you feel the way he did and I'll give Ricky's watch to Dawson if I feel like it and the only way you can make sure I do what you want is you come out here and make me, Jessie! [*Pounding again*] Jessie! Stop this! I didn't know! I was here with you all the time. How could I know you were so alone?

[*And* MAMA *stops for a moment, breathless and frantic, putting her ear to the door, and when she doesn't hear anything, she stands up straight again and screams once more*]

Jessie! Please!

[*And we hear the shot, and it sounds like an answer, it sounds like No.*

MAMA *collapses against the door, tears streaming down her face, but not screaming anymore. In shock now*]

Jessie, Jessie, child . . . Forgive me. [*Pause*] I thought you were mine.

[*And she leaves the door and makes her way through the living room, around the furniture, as though she didn't know where it was, not knowing what to do. Finally, she goes to the stove in the kitchen and picks up the hot-chocolate pan and carries it with her to the telephone, and holds on to it while she dials the number. She looks down at the pan, holding it tight like her life depended on it. She hears Loretta answer*]

MAMA: Loretta, let me talk to Dawson, honey.

Wendy Wasserstein

Wendy Wasserstein (1950–) was born in Brooklyn, New York, the youngest child of an upper-middle-class Jewish family. Her father, Morris, immigrated from Poland and became successful in the textile business; his patent for velveteen made the family rich. Lola, Wasserstein's mother, also a Polish immigrant, was devoted to her family, but often spent six hours daily practicing jazz dance. Lola expected her four children to get married, have children, and live conventional lives. Wasserstein has not satisfied her mother's plans, however, and her guilt at being, as yet, unmarried, childless, and pursuing an unconventional life is an important factor of her plays, which may be viewed as attempts to reconcile her family's expectations with her decision to live her life on her own terms.

Wasserstein was educated in Brooklyn public schools until she was twelve and then at a private school for girls on Manhattan's East Side. In her teens she appeared on the television program "The Herald Tribune World Youth Forum," on which she discussed current events—about which she now admits to have been more opinionated than knowledgeable. Later, Wasserstein attended Mount Holyoke College in Massachusetts. After graduation, she returned to New York, where she studied playwrighting with Israel Horovitz (1939–) and Joseph Heller (1923–) at the Graduate Center of City University of New York. In 1973 her play *Any Woman Can't* was produced off Broadway and failed, but it showed promise, and she was accepted at the Yale School of Drama, where she studied under Robert Brustein (1927–), the founder of the Yale and American Repertory Theaters.

Wasserstein's responses to contemporary feminism are based on the tension caused by the opposition of the conventional expectations of a middle-class Jewish family and the ambitious Jewish woman's struggles, which do not fit in the mold. Like herself, Wasserstein's women characters are college-educated and associated with elite schools such as Mount Holyoke and Yale; they are articulate and able to support themselves, but they cannot discover a balance between their careers and their personal relationships with men. Her characters are always faced with the dilemma of accepting loneliness or having the stamina to succeed in their interpersonal affairs.

Wasserstein's ambivalence over not having found "Mr. Right" to fulfill her parents' expectations seems an important element in her creative imagination. Her plays often deconstruct the idea of "the right man." Her fictional men are unavailable because they are unfaithful, unworthy, or homosexual. Wasserstein's comedic portrayals of female-male relationship is deliberately superficial, shying away from central issues of passion and romantic love.

Wasserstein's *Uncommon Women and Others* was written while she was studying at the Yale School of Drama in 1975. It was first produced at the O'Neill

Theater Center and, a year later, was produced off Broadway (where it failed after two weeks). It was later filmed for PBS. The play is about eight friends at a women's college, clearly Mount Holyoke College. When the play opens, five of them are meeting, six years after graduation, in order to share their experiences. The action is set in a trendy restaurant, where the women compare their lives, looking for consolation and affirmation that the choices they made were the right ones. The action then shifts to six years earlier, to their senior year. The cast of characters includes Rita, a promiscuous radical feminist; Samantha, a virgin who becomes engaged; Muffet, who wants a perfect husband and marriage but ends up with a career as a corporate lawyer; Kate, portrayed as being cold and an overachiever, who also becomes a lawyer; and Leila, an anthropologist, who marries an Iranian and adopts the Muslim faith. Joining the group is Carter, an eccentric freshman, who is shy and just listens. The eighth participant is Holly Kaplan, who provides a snapshot of the playwright at twenty-six: a woman loving though lonely, dressed in expensive clothes that don't fit because she's overweight, and slightly fearful of the future.

Wasserstein followed up with *Isn't It Romantic* (1981, revised 1983), an autobiographical comedy that affirms her aspiration and dedication to become a playwright and not follow a career in business. The protagonist, Janie Blumberg, is a twenty-eight-year-old Jewish woman from Manhattan who is contrasted with Harriet Cornwall, a Harvard MBA who, emulating her mother, is obsessed with success and insists on making it in the corporate world, even if it means not having a family. Harriet does not have the necessary stamina, however. She begins an affair with her boss, Paul Stuart, a man twice her age who refuses any emotional commitment. Eager to marry, Harriet finds another man and decides to accept the traditional female role: to marry and have children.

Janie, a struggling freelance writer, is appalled. She faces the unrelenting pressure to be traditional and meet the expectations of her Jewish mother and father, Tasha and Simon. But she resists the temptation to conform, even when "Mr. Right" comes along in the character Marty Sterling, a Jewish doctor (her mother's dream come true). Janie's incredulous parents accept her decision with graceful disappointment, and Tasha, without realizing the irony of her response, says to Janie, "I'm a modern woman too, you know. I have my dancing, I have your father, and I have my beautiful grandchild and Ben [her son]. . . . I'm an independent woman—a person in my own right. Am I right, Simon?" Finally alone, Janie decides to unpack her possessions and make herself at home while dancing to "Isn't It Romantic," a nostalgic love song by Richard Rodgers and Lorenz Hart.

Wasserstein was thirty-eight when her play *The Heidi Chronicles* won the Pulitzer Prize for drama. An episodic history play, it follows the career of Heidi Holland through some of the major events of her life, from 1965 to 1987. When the action begins, Heidi is a PhD and professor of art history at Columbia University, specializing in women's art. She is in her forties, single, and feeling middle-aged and melancholy. Her opening monologue is a review of the last twenty-three years of her life, which flash like slides at one of her art history lectures.

In 1965, when Heidi is sixteen, she appears at a high school dance in Chicago; in 1968, at nineteen, she supports Eugene McCarthy's failed presidential bid; in 1970, at twenty-one, she is dragged to a consciousness-raising session for women and lesbians in Ann Arbor, Michigan. At twenty-five, she is finally forced to recognize that Peter Patrone, her best friend, is gay and does not want a woman as a sex partner. In 1974, at twenty-eight, Heidi attends the wedding of another old friend, Scoop Rosenbaum, whom she refused to be serious about because he could never be faithful.

There are other stops as Heidi observes friends who have babies and establish lucrative careers. But the most important moment occurs in 1986, when Heidi addresses her high school class at a reunion in the Plaza Hotel. She begins her speech—titled "Women, Where Are We Going?"—as planned, but in mid-course, she realizes that she is out of sync with the women in the audience. Not sure of herself, or the role or expectations of the modern American woman, she momentarily falters, saying, "It's just that I feel stranded. And I thought the whole point was that we shouldn't feel stranded. I thought the point was we were all in this together."

Heidi consequently makes the decision to become a single parent by adopting a child. She names the baby Judy for the character in the 1948 movie *A Date with Judy,* a corny romantic 1940s film starring Elizabeth Taylor. But Heidi also knows that Judith, the biblical heroine, is the subject of "Judith Decapitating Holifernes," a painting by Artemisia Gentileschi (1593–1653). The lurid depiction of Judith's heroism is, perhaps, a not so subtle warning to the men in her future. Heidi once said to Scoop Rosenbaum, "I can take care of myself, thanks," and she does. It is a remark that many of Wasserstein's women characters make, and it represents her belief in the importance of affirming a sense of self.

The title *The Heidi Chronicles* is a mild parody of Johanna Spryri's *Heidi* (1880), the story of a naive girl, Heidi, whose innate goodness overcomes all obstacles in her life. The novel was adapted in a 1937 film starring Shirley Temple that portrays the stereotype of the cute little girl, which Wasserstein's Heidi is not.

Wasserstein's most recent play, *An American Daughter* (1997), concerns a successful woman and the politics of personal choice. Lyssa Hughes must endure the tribulations of deciding whether she ought to accept the nomination as Surgeon General of the United States and its ensuing public scrutiny. The crux of the problem is not whether Lyssa, a successful doctor of medicine, has the qualifications for the job, but whether she has the correct political and public persona. Lyssa's idealism is tested against her belief in herself and the moral attitudes of others toward issues that have nothing to do with health care policy. Trying to restore her sense of self, Lyssa withdraws her name from consideration because she can neither limit her idealism nor play the power game of modern politics. Contrasted with Lyssa is Judith (the name of the adopted daughter in *The Heidi Chronicles*), who suffers self-doubt during an enactment of the Jewish ritual the Festival of Regrets. Judith regrets that she has not had a child and that, at forty-two, she probably never will, and this makes her feel like a failure.

The Sisters Rosensweig (1992) is Wasserstein's most carefully crafted play, with strong character interactions rather than the casual one-liners of her earlier comedies. It is loosely based on Anton Chekhov's *The Three Sisters* (1901), in which three Russian women yearn for lives that cannot be or for romantic places they cannot go. In contrast, Wasserstein's Jewish-American women characters have all gone somewhere, have had adventures, and are now reuniting to celebrate the fifty-forth birthday of Sara, the oldest. Unlike the dark comedy of Chekhov's *The Three Sisters*, Wasserstein's *The Sisters Rosensweig* is a drawing-room comedy in the style of Noel Coward, George S. Kaufman, and Moss Hart, all of whom Wasserstein mentions in her preface to the play.

Wasserstein, forty-two at the time she wrote the play, said, "For the record, I am the youngest of three sisters, and my oldest sister never dated a faux furrier. However, I have known many actresses whose career opportunities diminish because they made the grievous error of growing older. Therefore I deliberately set out to write smart and funny parts for women over forty." There is also a sly reference to the painting "Three Sisters Playing Chess" by Sofonisba Anguissola (c. 1535–1625), mentioned in *The Heidi Chronicles*, suggesting that the Rosensweig sisters are, after all, playing a game of sibling rivalry.

The play is set in 1991, in the drawing room of a fashionable London apartment, where Sara Goode awaits the arrival of her sisters, Gorgeous and Pfeni. Though the sisters all share their New York and Jewish heritage, they have taken up different vocations and attitudes toward the world. Sara is an expatriate living in London, where she is director of a major international bank. For all of Sara's independence and worldly success—twice on the cover of *Fortune*—she is lonely, involved with the wrong man, and in need of accepting her Jewish family roots. The middle sister, Gorgeous Teitelbaum, is a housewife-cum-radio talk show host, living in Newton, Massachusetts. Loud and brassy, she wears knock-off designer clothing. Gorgeous, a name given to her by her father, is married to an unemployed lawyer, who is trying to write murder mysteries. Gorgeous is as Jewish as Sara is assimilated. Pfeni Rosensweig, the youngest at forty, is unmarried and a successful professional writer and world traveler. She has flown in from Bombay for Sara's birthday. Pfeni, really Penny, took the spelling of her name at the suggestion of Geoffrey Duncan, a bisexual theater director with whom she is in love. It is a hopeless affair, since Geoffrey finally realizes that he prefers men.

A key moment in the opening scene occurs when Pfeni offers a statue of the Hindu god Shiva, destroyer of evil and symbol of hope and rebirth, to Tess Goode, Sara's seventeen-year-old daughter. Tess suggests that the statue be given to her mother: "Can I give this to my mother? My mother's in desperate need of hope and rebirth. I think she's perfectly content to relive her life through me."

Other characters are in need of rebirth too, and the statue is eventually passed from Pfeni to Tess to Sara, and finally to Mervyn Kant (formerly Kantlowitz), a nice Jewish businessman who sells faux furs, and whom Geoffrey brings to Sara's birthday celebration. Mervyn falls for Sara, but at first she remains aloof, preferring her current lover, suave British businessman Nicholas Pym, who himself prefers younger women for lovers. Wistfully, Sara takes Mervyn to bed for a one-night stand, as a way of asserting herself and dispelling her depression over her recent hysterectomy due to an ovarian abscess. Later, she offers him friendship.

The play gently explores the feminist issues of women's roles from a woman's point of view. The characters embody the Rosensweig's family history and values and sibling love and friendship, all of which Wasserstein shares and admires. In the play, these values continue to be passed on as Tess interviews Sara for a class project. Sara complains that Tess is "determined to make her life the opposite of mine," and Pfeni responds: "That's exactly what we set out to do because of our mother."

In the last scene, the mother and daughter reconcile, acknowledging the family's Jewish heritage. Sara has to account for her assimilation, and when she recites the family history to Tess, she acknowledges their spiritual traditions, with seriousness and humor. For Tess, the transmission of the family heritage serves as a symbolic rite of passage, as she assumes her role as a Rosensweig woman who will succeed not because of the men in her life but because of her own intelligence and abilities.

Wasserstein's forte is comedy: she has a natural ear for clever dialogue and a keen sense of humor. She has been compared to Neil Simon, and she is sometimes referred to as the "Queen of Jewish Comedy." Wasserstein's plays are topical, but one question raised by critics is whether or not her topicality will stay the course. In a 1987 interview, Wasserstein complained that when she went back to Mount Holyoke College for a production of *Uncommon Women and Others,* the undergraduates surprised her by telling her that her play was already out of date.

Wasserstein's dedication to exploring women's issues places her in the forefront of playwrights portraying women in contemporary life. Her focus is the urban, middle-class, educated women of the Northeast, which sets her apart from Marsha Norman, whose milieu is often the South and the plight of largely ordinary women of the lower socioeconomic classes.

The Sisters Rosensweig

Tess Goode
Pfeni Rosensweig
Sara Goode
Geoffrey Duncan
Mervyn Kant
Gorgeous Teitelbaum
Tom Valiunus
Nicholas Pym

ACT I

A weekend in late August, 1991.

A sitting room in Queen Anne's Gate, London.

Scene 1

Late morning Friday. The room is decorator "done" with cozy, comfy, but expensive chintz couches, chairs, and window treatments. There is a dining room upstage right and a staircase upstage left leading to the bedrooms. Tess, *seventeen, in blue jeans and a flannel shirt, is listening to* Sara*'s collegiate all-women's singing group doing an a cappella version of "Shine On Harvest Moon." She speaks into a tape recorder.*

Tess: Elongated note on moon. A harvest moon is a full September moon. *The doorbell rings.* Also notice the use of the vernacular, "I ain't had no lovin'."

The doorbell rings.

Sara, *offstage:* Tessie, get the door! *The doorbell rings.*

Tess *lowers the music and races towards the door. Her aunt,* Pfeni, *forty, enters. She carries at least five shopping bags brimming with clothes, gifts, and a laptop computer.* Pfeni *appears younger than her age, and wears comfortable pants and jacket, well known to journalists and world travelers.*

Pfeni: His name was Jesse.
Tess: Aunt Pfeni!
Pfeni: Jesse the Sikh.
Tess: We've been waiting for you. Mother and I had no idea what time you'd be coming.
Pfeni: Blame it all on Jesse. Jesse the Sikh.
Tess: Who?
Pfeni: That was the name of my taxi driver. He was a Sikh. The lion of India.
Tess: My mother says you exaggerate.
Pfeni: He drove me all last night around Bombay until all I could catch was the last plane.
Tess: Well, my mother's going to be delighted you actually showed up.
Pfeni: And you, are you delighted? *They embrace. The music has changed to the all-women's version of "Begin the Beguine." They begin dancing.* What are you listening to?
Tess: My mother's college singing group. This was their signature song. We're doing biographies of our parents' early years for our school summer project. It's pretentious. *Shuts off the music.* I can't wait to leave London and go back home to school.
Pfeni: Did your mother say you could?
Tess: Are you kidding? The woman who named me for Tess of the D'Urbervilles? The only American who is convinced that Harvard and Yale are second-rate institutions. She won't even discuss it.

Sara *enters from upstairs. She is a very handsome woman of fifty-four. Even in the bathrobe she's now wearing, she exudes dignity and authority.*

Sara: Tess, who are you talking to? Hello my baby sister! I didn't know you were here. *Kisses her on the cheek.* Tessie, I never said Harvard and Yale were second-rate institutions. I said they were floundering on their way to being second rate.
Pfeni: It's good to see you, Sara.
Sara: Did you sleep at all on the plane? I was just reading a very good piece in *The Financial Times* about the Russian coup by that friend of yours who won the Overseas Press Award this year. Isn't it time you won that?
Pfeni: Tessie, come here and protect me from your mother.
Tess: My English teacher at Westminster assigned Aunt Pfeni's book for next semester.
Sara: Really? Which one?
Tess: *Life in the Afghan Village.* It's for our women's segment. She says when Aunt Pfeni began using her expertise to write travel columns, she became counterrevolutionary.
Pfeni: Did she tell you who my dentist is?
Sara: Pfeni's books are super. Brilliant. Having a separate category for women's writing is counterrevolutionary.
Tess: Well, it doesn't matter anyway. I'm going to study hairdressing so I can make my way in the world.
Sara: Tessie, my luv, if you want to be a hairdresser, I'll still love you and be very proud of you. Of course the way the economy is going, you'd be far

Christine Estabrook, Jane Alexander, and Madeline Kahn in The Sisters Rosensweig, *Ethel Barrymore Theatre, New York, 1992.*

more practical choosing a less luxury-oriented field.

PFENI: Tessie, have you considered welding?

SARA: Pfeni, you're diverting the argument.

PFENI, *with an accent:* Vell excuse me for living.

SARA: We're discussing Tessie's future! *The phone rings.* Yes, hello. Oh, hello Nick! How nice to hear from you.

TESS, *rolling her eyes:* Oh, God, it's him!

SARA: Could you hold while I take this in the kitchen? Pfeni, please share with Tessie your worldly advice. *Exits.*

TESS: My mother says she worries about me because I'm so much like you. She says you compulsively travel because you have a fear of commitment, and when you do stay in one place, you become emotional and defensive just like me.

PFENI: Tessie, honey, I'm so sorry. I didn't know it was contagious. *Begins rummaging through her shopping bags.* There's a valuable gift for you in one of these.

TESS: Aunt Pfeni, why don't you have any suitcases?

PFENI: Because your grandmother Rita told me that only crazy people travel with shopping bags. So I've made it my personal signature ever since. *Hands a package to* TESS. *It contains a statue of Shiva.* Here it is. This god will destroy all evil and bring you hope, rebirth, and a life-time guarantee that under no circumstances will you grow up to be like me.

TESS: Why does it have so many arms?

PFENI: It's very versatile. Its name is Shiva the destroyer. I found it on Elephanta Island off the coast of Bombay yesterday. A hot tip for where to shop in the Indian Ocean.

TESS: Aunt Pfeni?

PFENI: Niece Tess?

TESS: Can I give this to my mother? My mother's in desperate need of hope and rebirth. I think she's perfectly content to relive her life through me.

SARA *reenters.*

SARA: Good news. Nick Pym's coming to dinner tonight.

TESS: You know, mother, there are homeless people sleeping under Charing Cross Station.

SARA: Do you think Nick Pym would prefer to have my birthday dinner with them?

TESS: Mother, I just don't think it's right to have bourgeois dinner parties with capitalists like Nicholas Pym when people are living in boxes under Charing Cross Station.

SARA, *staring at* TESS: Pfeni, hasn't Tess grown up brilliantly.

TESS: Mother, now you're the one diverting the argument!

SARA: I don't know how it happened, but I've been blessed with a totally beautiful and brilliant daughter. My daughter just happens to be perfect. I tell your Aunt Pfeni to be certain that sometime during her peripatetic life she have at least one child, because the greatest joy of my life is having you.

TESS: Mother, that's sentimental revisionist history! Hermia Cox-Jones's father says you have the biggest balls at the Hong Kong/Shanghai Bank worldwide.

PFENI: Pish-pish.

SARA: Pfeni, there's something very New York about your tone today.

PFENI: Vell, excuse me for living two times.

TESS: What do you mean, New York?

SARA: Well . . .

PFENI: Tessie, many decades and a continent ago, when your mother was a freshman at Radcliffe and I was still living home with your grandparents in Flatbush, Brooklyn, a very nice man named Harry Rose called our house every morning. Mr. Rose was the head salesman at Grampa's Kiddie Tog factory.

SARA: What is your point, Pfeni?

PFENI: Tessie, Mr. Rose liked to catch Grampa to discuss the day's business just when the entire house would be waking up. So every day at seven A.M. I'd rush to pick up the phone just to hear Mr. Rose say, "Hallo, Maury, is that you?" And then I'd answer, "No, Mr. Rose. It's me. Maury's daughter Penny." And he'd always say, "Vell, excuse me for living, Penny, but how could you recognize it was me?"

TESS: So Mr. Harry Rose was New York?

SARA: New York in a way that has very little to do with us. Pfeni's the one who's guilty of revisionist history, my luv. Pfeni's the one who's romanticized a world we never belonged to.

PFENI: I was mistaken. Mr. Rose never called our house every morning. It was Louis Auchincloss.

SARA: You see, Tessie. I told you Pfeni's defensive just like you.

TESS: You have no sense of humor, mother, none.

SARA, *with an accent:* What? You think you're telling me something I don't know. *Smiles.* That was very New York.

TESS: I gotta go. I'm meeting Tom. Can he come to this late dinner too?

PFENI: Who's Tom?

SARA: Who's Tom, Tessie?

TESS: Tom Valiunus is the man I'm currently seeing.

SARA: Tell Pfeni more. She's very good about people.

TESS: Tom's father owns a radio supply store in Liverpool, and he's hoping to go into the business if the economy turns around.

PFENI: That sounds nice.

TESS: Mother doesn't think so.

SARA: I never said that. I just don't know what you have in common with someone who dreams of selling radio parts. And you certainly don't have to chase him through greater Latvia.

TESS: Lithuania. Aunt Pfeni, Tom and I are very committed to the Lithuanian resistance. And because of the coup Tom feels we should be there.

PFENI: Vilnius was once the Jerusalem of Lithuania.

SARA: You're not being very helpful, Pfeni.

PFENI: There's also a good restaurant, the famous and traditional Old Cellar. Also, for plays, check out the Central Theatre of Vilnius.

SARA: That way, Tessie, when they send the tanks in, you and Tom can take in a quick hamburger and a show.

TESS: Mother, that's not funny.

SARA: I know. I have no sense of humor.

TESS: Aunt Pfeni, would you like to join Tom and me for tea today?

SARA: Aunt Pfeni, don't you think it's just slightly irregular for a nice Jewish girl from Connecticut to find her calling in the Lithuanian resistance?

TESS: But I'm not a nice Jewish girl from Connecticut. I'm an expatriate American who's lived in London for five years and the daughter of an atheist.

SARA: This has nothing to do with organized religion.

TESS: Mother, Tom comes from a perfectly balanced and normal family, which is something you've never managed to maintain despite being on the cover of *Fortune* twice. But if you like, I'll tell him that he's not invited to dinner here tonight with the socially acceptable, racist, sexist, and more than likely anti-Semitic Nicholas Pym.

SARA, *quietly:* Tessie, please invite Tom to supper tonight.

TESS, *kissing* SARA *on the cheek:* Tea is at Fortnum's at five.

SARA: Guess who's paying for the tea. I never met a freedom fighter who didn't enjoy a good meal. Pfeni, you must talk to her.

PFENI: I did talk to her.

SARA: She's determined to make her life the opposite of mine.

PFENI: That's exactly what we set out to do because of our mother.

SARA: Yes, but we were right.

PFENI: So, maybe, is Tessie. SARA *starts to move the shopping bags.* Sara, relax. I'll take them down later.

SARA, *picks up the Shiva:* I don't know why Tessie insists on bringing home junk like this from Portobello Road.

PFENI: I brought it from Bombay.

SARA: Oh, it's lovely.

PFENI *gives her the Shiva:* This will destroy all evil and bring you hope and rebirth.

SARA: I'm too old.

PFENI: You're not too old.

SARA: You don't know. You're only forty.

PFENI: Forty is old.

SARA: Oh, Pfeni, I'm so glad you're here.

PFENI: Did you think I'd let Dr. Gorgeous show up for your birthday and not be here?

SARA: Your sister's not just showing up for my birthday. She's leading the Temple Beth El sisterhood on a tour of the crown jewels.

PFENI: But she managed to plan it in time for your birthday.

SARA: True. You're a good sister, Pfeni Rosensweig. Pfeni! God, what an awful name! Why do you keep it? *Sits with* PFENI *on the couch. Puts her feet up on* PFENI.

PFENI: Penny Rosensweig wasn't any better. Now, Sara Goode, on the other hand, is a great name.

SARA: Multiple divorce is a brilliant thing. You get so many names to choose from. But my second was definitely my best. And how nice that there is now a Mrs. Samantha Goode, Mrs. Melissa Goode, Mrs. Pamela Goode, and, as of last year, the twenty-four-year-old Mrs. Sushiro Goode. We could form the Wives of Kenneth Goode Club, with branches in Chicago, New York, London, and Tokyo. Well, never mind. I'm looking forward to us growing old together. Like two old-maid spinsters in a Muriel Spark novel.

PFENI: Sara, that's beyond depressing.

SARA: No it isn't. It could be rather cozy. You could stop traveling, finally settle into the downstairs flat, and grow more and more eccentric, and I could get meaner and crabbier.

PFENI: But I have Geoffrey.

SARA: Well, he can visit us. He's here all the time anyway.

PFENI: Geoffrey says we'll live together when his house is finished.

SARA: That man has no intention of ever living there, when he can enjoy the hospitality of all his friends.

PFENI: Geoffrey adds a little texture to your life.

SARA: I don't need that much texture in my life. You'd be better off getting old with me. Is Geoffrey joining us for dinner tonight?

PFENI: I hope so.

SARA *gets up from the couch:* Good. Maybe he'll solve both our problems and fall madly in love with Tom and lead him on the children's crusade to Vilnius. *Pause.* Indulge me, Pfeni. I told you, I'm an old and bitter woman.

PFENI: You're not old and bitter. You're anticipating an era of hope and rebirth.

SARA: Promise me you'll stay awhile this time. The other night I was singing in the kitchen and Tessie told me to stop. She hates it when I sing now. She says I'm too grown-up and scary to sing. Am I very scary?

PFENI: Terrifying. But what about her summer project? She was listening to your college group when I came in.

SARA: Her thesis is to prove that my early years have no bearing on my present life. Frankly, I can hardly remember my early years. You know what I was thinking about the other night? What happens to the Cannibal King after Ah-rump Da-de-ya-de-day.

PFENI: Sara, you're speaking in tongues.

SARA: The Cannibal King with the big nose ring.

PFENI: Oh, *that* Cannibal King with the big nose ring! *Begins to sing:*

Fell in love with the dusky maid,
And every night in the pale moonlight
This is what she'd say . . .

SARA AND PFENI *begin to play patty-cake.*

SARA AND PFENI, *spoken:*

Ah-rump, Ah-rump, Ah-rump, Da-de-ya-de-day,
Ah-rump, Ah-rump, Ah-rump, Da-de-ya-de-day.

SARA: Now what?

PFENI *begins to sing quickly:*

Let's build a bungalow big enough for two,
Big enough for two, my honey . . .

SARA: Pfeni, that's it. That's it. You're a genius!

PFENI:

Big enough for two,
Big enough for two,
And when we're married, happy we'll be,
Under the bamboo,
Under the bamboo tree.

SARA AND PFENI, SARA *continues to play patty-cake as* PFENI *sings:*

If you'll be M-I-N-E mine
I'll be T-H-I-N-E thine,
And I'll L-O-V-E love you
All the T-I-M-E time.

Let's take an L-A-R-K lark
Into the P-A-R-K park,
And I'll K-I-S-S kiss you
In the D-A-R-K dark.

You are the B-E-S-T best
Of all the R-E-S-T rest,
And I'll L-O-V-E love you
All the T-I-M-E time.

GEOFFREY, *an attractive forty-year-old man in a hip leather jacket and a Sunset in Penang T-shirt, enters the house. He carries an overnight bag and immediately begins applauding.*

GEOFFREY: That was brilliant! Just brilliant! But you must make the recitative even faster, even crisper.

PFENI *waves at him:* Hello, Geoffrey.

GEOFFREY: Hello my luv. And ready, "You are the B-E-S-T best of all the R-E-S-T rest." And one, two, three . . . *Conducts them.*

SARA AND PFENI *very quickly:*

You are the B-E-S-T best
Of all the R-E-S-T rest,
And I'll L-O-V-E love you
All the T-I-M-E time.

GEOFFREY, *applauding:* Bravo! Bravo! Bravo the sisters Rosensweig! *Lifts up* PFENI *and carries her to the downstairs exit.*

SARA *remains on stage looking distractedly out the window.*

Scene 2

Later that afternoon. PFENI *enters from her apartment, which is downstairs.* GEOFFREY *follows her.*

GEOFFREY: The problem with you, Pfeni darling, is that you just don't like women very much.

PFENI: That's not true.

GEOFFREY: Of course it is, luv. Think about it. Women make you feel competitive and insecure.

PFENI: That's nonsense, Geoffrey.

GEOFFREY: It's all right, darling. You can't like everyone.

PFENI: And I suppose that you, on the other hand, are open to people of all sexes, race, and color.

GEOFFREY *starts to sing:* "I am everyday people!" Sly and the Family Stone, 1969.

PFENI: Sara says we should stop seeing each other. She says she and I should grow old together.

GEOFFREY: Pfeni my luv, all you've talked about since you've arrived here is Sara. How guilty you feel that she was ill. How guilty you feel that she's alone. How much you love her. How much you can't bear to be around her. How much you want her praise. How little you care for her opinions.

PFENI: That's not true.

GEOFFREY: All I know is that whenever you're around that woman, you tell me we have to stop seeing each other. My darling, we hardly ever do see each other. I'm always in rehearsal and you're in Timbuktu half the year. It's a bloody brilliant relationship. *Kisses her on the forehead.*

PFENI: Oh my God, my life is stuck. "I've forgotten the Italian for window."

GEOFFREY: Very good! *Three Sisters,* Act III. Now, Pfeni darling, see how worthwhile it's been knowing me. If not for me, you'd still think that *Uncle Vanya* was a Neil Simon play about his pathetic uncle in the Bronx.

PFENI: And now instead I've had a three-year relationship with an internationally renowned director and bisexual.

GEOFFREY: You left out botanist. I read botany at Cambridge. And I also put that "f" betwixt your name. If not for me, you'd be plain and simple Penny Rosensweig.

PFENI: Thank you. I have your "f" to keep me warm.

GEOFFREY: For Christ's sake, Pfeni, if you want to find unconditional love, have a baby. Adopt a red and fuzzy brood of them. Better yet, have artificial insemination. *Lifts up a water glass.* "Hello darling, this is Daddy. Say good morning to your daddy." "Morning, Daddy." Or you could become a lesbian. Most of the really interesting women I know are lesbians.

PFENI: Just tell me one thing? What do you still get out of this?

GEOFFREY: T-shirts from all over the world. Would I be sporting Sunset in Penang if not for you? I've been meaning to ask you, darling, where is Penang?

PFENI: Malaysia. Somerset Maugham lived there.

GEOFFREY: This is what's so wonderful about dating a nice American Jewish girl! You're all so well versed in British colonial history. *Embraces her.* Pfeni, my luv, trust me. I am still very happy with you.

PFENI: You wouldn't like to meet a nice man?

GEOFFREY: I meet nice men all the time. I'm a director.

PFENI: I mean some nice man for you to come home to.

GEOFFREY: I've already done that, my darling, and he left me for Rum-Tum-Tugger.

PFENI: Who?

GEOFFREY: Jordan left me for that chorus boy from *Cats.*

PFENI: But that was ages ago.

GEOFFREY: Exactly. And then I met you at the ballet, and Jordan became England's hottest flatware designer. He's soon to be knighted "Sir Cutlery."

PFENI: But . . .

GEOFFREY: But what? Do you want to know if I have my eye on anyone in my show? Is it true what they say about *The Scarlet Pimpernel?* My darling, I am committed. I've signed exclusively with you. Have I told you I've been offered the animated *Fawlty Towers?* I could fit it in next season between *The Duchess of Malfi* and *Oklahoma!* On the other hand, my film career is nowhere near where it should be. Unfortunately, movies do mean enduring extended time in Los Angeles. Why don't you have your film capital somewhere more civilized, like *Des Moines? Pronounces it as if it were French.*

PFENI: Where?

GEOFFREY: *Des Moines,* Idaho.

PFENI: It's Des Moines. And it's in Iowa. I'll see what I can do.

GEOFFREY: Pfeni, my angel, I wish you knew what a gorgeous person you are.

PFENI: My sister is gorgeous. I'm not.

GEOFFREY: My darling, I can't waste any more time listening to your negativity and self-criticism. You're becoming almost as self-absorbed as I am. Besides, I'm expecting two hundred homeless people who live under Charing Cross Station to arrive here in just a few.

PFENI: To arrive here? At Sara's house?

GEOFFREY: Well, it's not all two hundred of them, actually. It's closer to a small delegation, and I told them to be certain to ring the downstairs bell and not Sara's.

PFENI: That was thoughtful!

GEOFFREY: Tell me what you think, my darling. I have an idea to do this year's homeless benefit at The National as a sort of story theatre. I want to hear their brilliant voices telling the simple human tale of their survival. The theatre's in danger of becoming hopelessly elitist. *The bell rings.* What's that? *The bell rings again.*

PFENI: The bell.

GEOFFREY: But that's not the downstairs bell.

PFENI: No.

GEOFFREY: What should we do?

PFENI: Let's invite your delegation to stay for Sara's birthday party.

The bell rings again.

GEOFFREY: I can't allow these people into Sara's house. They're desperate. They take things. They deserve to kill us for centuries of oppression.

PFENI: Relax. Go downstairs. I'll tell them to meet you down there.

GEOFFREY: Brilliant.

GEOFFREY *exits to the downstairs service entrance.* PFENI *answers the door.* MERV KANT, *a fifty-eight-year-old American in a wrinkled linen suit, stands in the door. He is immediately warm, but surprisingly sexy. He carries a Turnbull & Asser bag.*

MERV: Hi!

PFENI: Mr. Duncan said he'd prefer to meet you and your group downstairs. There's another entrance down the back.

MERV: My group? You mean my combo?

PFENI: You're not English.

MERV: No, and neither are you.

PFENI: Do you live under Charing Cross Station?

MERV: I live over Charing Cross Station, at the Savoy Hotel. May I leave this for Geoff? *Enters.*

PFENI: Who?

MERV: I like to call him Geoff. Drives him crazy. He tells me, "Murf, only someone who rhymes with surf can call me Geoff."

PFENI: Your name is "Murf the Surf"?

MERV: How do you do.

PFENI: Pfeni Rosensweig. I'll get him for you.

MERV: And tell him I went to the Turnbull sale and found the purple shirts we've been searching for. Honey, when I saw that shirt, I was kvelling—like I just discovered the double helix. PFENI, *knocking on the door:* Murf is here to say he just discovered the double helix.

GEOFFREY *comes out.*

MERV: Geoffrey, mazeltov, you've finally come out of the closet.

GEOFFREY: What ho, Sir Murf?

MERV: What ho! *Begins to sing and dance around the room.*

I found the shirt at Turnbull's-a-nanny-nanny-no.
I found the purple shirt at Turnbull's-a-nanny-nanny-no.
And I got one for you and I got one for me.

Gives GEOFFREY *the package.*

A-nanny-nanny-no.

MERV AND GEOFFREY *sing and dance:*

I found the shirts at Turnbull's. A-nanny-nanny-no!

They finish in a big finale.

MERV, *to* PFENI: Honey, I would have gotten one for you, but I didn't know your size.

GEOFFREY: How did you find me here?

MERV: You left a message to meet you at seven.

GEOFFREY: But what about the homeless?

MERV: What about the homeless?

GEOFFREY: I believe I told them to meet me where I thought I'd be seeing you.

MERV: Where's that?

GEOFFREY: Drinks at the Savoy at seven. *Grabs his coat.* Pfeni, offer Sir Murf a drink, and I'll try to head them off. *Kisses her.* Much love, angel. *Exits.*

MERV: So.

PFENI: So.

MERV: Would I like a drink?

PFENI: Would you?

MERV: Not really. Whose house am I in?

PFENI: My sister, Sara's.

MERV: It's very nice. What does her husband do?

PFENI: My sister is the managing director of the Hong Kong/Shanghai Bank Europe.

MERV: Sounds like a smart girl.

PFENI: How did you meet Geoffrey?

MERV: Mutual friends. How did you meet Geoffrey?

PFENI: I sat next to him at *Giselle,* and he asked me to be the mother of his children.

SARA *enters, wearing an apron over pants and a sweater.*

SARA: Pfeni! Who's here? Hello.
MERV: Hi. Hello. Merv Kant.
PFENI: This is an American friend of Geoffrey's.
MERV: And you must be Pfeni's younger sister.
SARA: Ha ha ha. Are you here on holiday?
MERV: I was in Budapest last week with the American Jewish Congress.
SARA: Yes, well, Budapest seems to be quite popular recently.
MERV: And on Sunday we go to Ireland to have brunch with the Rabbi of Dublin.
SARA: Fascinating! Where's your friend Geoffrey?
MERV: He's stood me up for the homeless under Charing Cross Station.
SARA: Yes, they also seem to be quite popular these days.
PFENI: Well, I'd better go meet Tom and Tessie. Would you like to share a taxi, Merv?
MERV *looks at* SARA: No, I'm fine.
SARA: Pfeni, if you're only meeting Tessie now, when will you be home?
PFENI: Soon.
SARA: But you're already two hours late.
PFENI: Sara, doll, soon is soon. *With accent.* Now that was really New York! *Exits,* leaving the door wide open.

SARA *stands by the door, waiting for* MERV *to exit voluntarily.*

MERV: Your sister was just offering me a drink. Some cold water would be perfect. Thanks. SARA *goes to get him a drink.* So you and your sister are from New York!
SARA: My sister is a traveler, and I live right here in Queen Anne's Gate. Here's your water, Mr. Kant.
MERV: Thanks. Your sister tells me you're a brilliant woman.
SARA: I have a few opinions about European common currency. That hardly makes me brilliant.
MERV: Well, you're the first Jewish woman I've met to run a Hong Kong bank.
SARA: I'm the first woman to run a Hong Kong bank, Mr. Kant.
MERV: It used to be Kantlowitz. You're looking at your watch. Would you prefer that I leave?
SARA: I'm just wondering what time my daughter's coming home.
MERV: Relax. I had three children who never came home and they're all fine now. My oldest, Kip, is a semiotics professor at Boston University. That means he screens *Hiroshima, Mon Amour* once a week. The other boy is a radiologist in North Carolina, Chapel Hill, and my baby, Eva, is a forest ranger in Israel. That means she works for the parks department in Haifa. And your daughter?
SARA: We're hoping she'll be up at Oxford next year.
MERV: She wants to stay here for school?
SARA: From what we've heard about the States now, I think it's wise.
MERV: Tell me what "we've heard."
SARA: It's conventional wisdom, really.
MERV: Really?
SARA: Well, obviously what you have is a society in transition. You've got an industrial economy that is rapidly being transformed into a transactional one. And that's exacerbated by a growing disenfranchised class, decaying inner cities, and a bankrupt educational system. Don't misunderstand me, Mr. Kantlowitz . . .
MERV: Kant, like the philosopher.
SARA: In many ways America is a brilliant country. But it's becoming as class-driven a society as this one.
MERV: So you're a hot-shot Jewish lady banker who's secretly a Marxist.
SARA: This is hardly the time to be a Marxist.
MERV: But your sister's right. You are a brilliant woman!
SARA: Excuse me, Mr. Kant, I really should check on my roast.
MERV: Are we having roast beef and Yorkshire pudding? Blimey, I've been hoping for a good old-fashioned, high-cholesterol English meal. I had a banger for breakfast this morning.
SARA *extends her hand:* It was lovely to meet you, Mr. Kant.
MERV: Whenever I come over here, I treat myself to one blow-out meal at Simpson's in the Strand.
SARA: Only Americans eat there. It's a tourist trap.
MERV: That's why I was so delighted when Geoffrey invited me here for dinner tonight.
SARA: Geoffrey did what?
MERV: And I said to myself, "Merv, this way you can avoid that tourist trap Simpson's in the Strand and have a good old-fashioned Anglo-Saxon Jewish meal."
SARA: How intimate are you with Geoffrey, Mr. Kant?
MERV: I'd say we have a close working relationship.
SARA: Oh?
MERV: When Geoffrey's musical *The Scarlet Pimpernel* came to New York last season, there arose during rehearsal an emergency need for signature chartreuse pelts. And while the British production blithely used dyed scarlet fox, the anti-fur lobby in New York pressed into early action. So my services were recommended by Geoffrey's producer, Mr. Bernard Lasker. And that was the beginning of a very beautiful friendship.
SARA: So you're a show biz furrier.

MERV: I was a show biz and novelty furrier. Now I am the world leader in synthetic animal protective covering. And Sara, to this day my one regret is that while the anti-furries were still picketing I didn't have Geoffrey sign over to me a quarter percent of that Pumpernickel. Next year I could be playing in Tokyo, Reykjavik, and forty-seven other cities worldwide.

SARA: Mr. Kant . . .

MERV: Please call me Merv. You call me Mr. Kant and I think I'm your high school principal. My hunch is we're roughly the same age.

SARA: Mr. Merv, today is my fifty-fourth birthday.

MERV: We are the same age. Roughly.

SARA: My sister Pfeni has flown here from Bombay, and my other sister, Gorgeous, is due in shortly from Newton, Massachusetts.

MERV: That's exactly why I want to come to your birthday party. Sounds like there'll be such interesting people here. I can't believe your father named you Sara and your other sister Gorgeous!

SARA: We're not just having a roast, actually. The roast is part of a cassoulet. That calls for beans, lamb, and duck and pork sausage. I don't recall the rules precisely, but if any of those go against your or the Rabbi of Dublin's religious or dietary regimen, you might want to get to Simpson's in the Strand after all.

MERV: And what will I tell Geoffrey?

SARA: That I behaved rather rudely and scared you away.

MERV: Do you tend to do that with men?

SARA: Are you a psychiatrist in addition to a furrier?

MERV: Shhh! Please, synthetic animal covering.

SARA: In answer to your question, yes, some men find me threatening.

MERV: My daughter tells me men find her threatening. Of course, when my daughter isn't in the Haifa parks, she's a captain in the Israeli army.

SARA: And your wife?

MERV: My wife was a Roslyn housewife. She died three years ago.

SARA: I'm sorry.

MERV: So was I. Her name was Helene and she wasn't very threatening, which is probably why my daughter is in the Israeli army. And you?

SARA: Me what?

MERV: Your husband.

SARA: My second is on his fifth wife. My first I've lost track of, and personally I doubt there will be a third.

MERV: So you've closed shop.

SARA: I'm a very busy woman, Mr. Merv. Would you excuse me? *Exits.*

MERV: Of course. Please make myself at home. *Looks at some books on a small table.* Sara, you've gotta lot of books about Disraeli here. Personally, I prefer Adlai Stevenson. Do you still have your Stevenson buttons, Sara? I keep mine with the ones from the Columbia Varsity Show of 1955. I played Madame Chiang Kai-shek. Actually, I think I would like a real drink, thanks. Scotch and water? Why not? *Pours himself a drink from the bar.* You know, I don't think it's particularly true that Jews don't drink. I think it's a myth made up by our mothers to persuade innocent women that Jewish men make superior husbands. In other words, it's worth it to put up with my crankiness, my hypochondria, my opinions on world problems, because I don't drink. *Takes a sip and begins looking through her records.* How about a little music, Sara? You have a lot of LPs. That's nice, I like a girl with LPs. CDs belong in the bank. Of course, I don't have to tell you that. I'm glad to see that you like Frank Sinatra and all the Broadway show tunes. I still cry at *Finian's Rainbow,* or is it *Brigadoon? Takes out two albums as* GORGEOUS, *a very pretty but overdone woman of around forty-six enters through the open door. She wears a fake Chanel suit with too many accessories, and carries imitation Louis Vuitton suitcases. He doesn't notice her.* Which one has "Look to the Rainbow"?

GORGEOUS: "Finian's Rainbow." You must be a friend of Geoffrey's.

MERV: How did you know?

GORGEOUS: All of Geoffrey's friends like musicals.

MERV: And you must be Gorgeous. We were just talking about you.

GORGEOUS: And how I got my name! Well, it's obvious, isn't it! Thanks for leaving the door open. I feel like Elijah.

MERV: I also just met your sister Pfeni.

GORGEOUS: Aren't my sisters fabulous? They're really such funsy people!

MERV: I wouldn't say your sister Sara is "funsy."

GORGEOUS: Maybe you should marry her.

MERV: I've only spent five minutes with her.

GORGEOUS: So what? Some people know at first sight. People call me from the Massachusetts Turnpike because they've just met someone at a rest stop and have fallen in love.

MERV: And you speak to these people?

GORGEOUS: Have you ever been to Boston?

MERV: My son lives there.

GORGEOUS: Well, if you ever listen to the radio when you visit your son, you'd know that everyone calls Dr. Gorgeous. *Begins to sing her theme song.*

Call Dr. Gorgeous, ring, ring, ring,
Call Dr. Gorgeous, ring, ring, ring.

Mimes picking up a phone.

"Hello, I'm Dr. Gorgeous, how can I help you?" Isn't that great! Isn't that funsy! I just have the best time. I'm sorry, I didn't catch your name.

MERV: Mervyn Kant.

GORGEOUS *helps herself to nuts from a dish:* Merlin, let me tell you something. I was a Newton housewife with four wonderful kids. My husband, Henry, is a very prominent attorney. We have a very comfortable lifestyle. In other words, everything was going just great, but I needed just a little sparkle to make it all perfect.

MERV: So you're the sister who did everything right. You married the attorney, you had the children, you moved to the suburbs.

GORGEOUS: Now, don't make me into a cliché. I am much more than that. Merlin, I am one of the first real jugglers. I love nuts and they're just terrible for you. Ucch! I'm so fat! I ate like a pig! Honey, do me a favor, give me one more and then put these on the other table. Sara shouldn't keep things like this around the house. The Dr. Gorgeous Show is hoping to make the leap from radio to cable. You know that absolutely everything shows on television.

MERV: I'm sure you'll have no problem.

GORGEOUS: Sara, who is such a brilliant woman, says I could have a spectacular career in communications. Talking has always come easily to me.

MERV: Yes, you're very natural.

GORGEOUS: In fact, my first show really happened by accident. So many women in the Newton Temple Beth El sisterhood wanted to know how I managed in our frantic modern times to maintain a warm traditional home, that they begged me to give a speech to their local chapter. Well, as it happens, P. S., who should be in the audience but Rabbi Carl Pearlstein, the host of "Newton at Sunrise." Pearlstein was so impressed with my presentation that he invited me on his show.

MERV: I've heard of Pearlstein. Didn't he write *I Learned Everything but Handwriting in First Grade?*

GORGEOUS: Try *Learning to Love Again, Learning to Live Again.* Only twenty-six months on every best-seller list.

MERV: Of course. He was recently indicted.

GORGEOUS: Rabbi Pearlstein is a great man. His accountant was evil.

MERV: I think we use the same one. I'm sorry, please tell me what happened next.

GORGEOUS: I became a regular on Pearlstein's show. Then he was indicted, and the rest is history. Now you just mention Dr. Gorgeous anywhere in suburban Boston, Framingham, Natick, or Lynn, and they all know who I am. Merlin, I am what they call a real middle-aged success story. And I am having a ball. It's really funsy.

MERV: Your husband must be very proud.

GORGEOUS: He is thrilled. And so supportive.

MERV: I have only one more question. When did you become a doctor?

GORGEOUS: You've heard of Dr. Pepper?

MERV: Yes.

GORGEOUS: So I'm Dr. Gorgeous. *Laughs and takes his arm.* Merlin, I loved talking to you. Geoffrey always has the most darling friends, although you're a little older than most of them. But I really must say hello to my sister. You know, my sister Sara is a brilliant woman. But she's also very vulnerable, very loving, very tender. She's had a hard year, she was ill, urgent female trouble, and couldn't come to our mother's funeral. That's why we're all here for her birthday. We're extremely close. *Calls.* Sara! *Turns back to* MERV. I adore my sisters. *Calls her again.* Sara! I'm here. Sara, it's me, Gorgeous.

SARA *enters.*

SARA, *very British*: Hallo Gorgeous!

GORGEOUS *imitates her:* Hallo Sara! *They embrace.* GORGEOUS *looks over* SARA *in her apron.* Well, well, don't you look glamorous!

SARA: Gorgeous, where's Henry?

GORGEOUS: He has a very heavy case load, and he wanted to watch Lily play lacrosse. Merlin here was just telling me what a handsome woman you are. I believe that men really are looking for strong women these days. The decade of the bimbo is over. This is the nineties, Sara. This is the era of the strong but feminine woman. Don't you think so, Merlin?

MERV: I think I should go back to the Savoy to freshen up.

GORGEOUS: Why don't you freshen up downstairs? That's where Geoffrey always goes. *Winks at him.* But I'm sure you knew that.

SARA: I don't think he did, actually. He's Geoffrey's New York furrier.

GORGEOUS: How fabulous! Are they picketing outside?

MERV: I'm afraid, Gorgeous, that you've made me out to be a far more interesting man than I really am.

GORGEOUS: I'm sure you're a very interesting man. Some of the most interesting men I know in Newton, Massachusetts are furriers.

SARA: How many furriers do you know in Newton, Massachusetts exactly?

GORGEOUS: I'm sure there are more than a few.

SARA: Yes, but how many do you actually know?

GORGEOUS: Well, there's mine, Monsieur Joseph of Newton, and Lily's friend Jonah Mazzarelli's father was a furrier at Jordan Marsh. And Henry once did a furrier's bankruptcy.

MERV: Oh, Jesus.

SARA: And all of them, Messieurs Joseph and Mazzarelli and Henry's bankruptcy, are among the most interesting men in Newton!

GORGEOUS: Sara, I'm tired!

SARA: I am asking you to be specific. I am asking you to take responsibility for whatever it is you babble about. Life is serious business, Gorgeous. Life isn't funsy.

GORGEOUS *takes out a gift from a shopping bag:* Happy birthday, Sara. I'll stay with my ladies. *Picks up her suitcase and her purse.*

SARA: Oh, here we go again. At least say hello to Pfeni.

GORGEOUS: Is Pfeni still sleeping with Geoffrey?

SARA: Yes.

GORGEOUS: Then I don't need to see Pfeni.

SARA: Gorgeous!

GORGEOUS: Don't you think it's time she considered someone even remotely available? Don't you think it's time she stopped living her life like she was on an extended junior year abroad?

MERV: Maybe you could help her. You help so many people.

GORGEOUS: That's true. I do. Thank you, Mervyn.

MERV: Thank you for not calling me the magician.

GORGEOUS: I'll stay for dinner if you will.

MERV: Sara?

SARA: I can put the sausage on a different plate.

MERV: Ladies, would you please excuse me. I'm going downstairs to change my shirt.

GORGEOUS: Why don't you use the guest room upstairs? It's much cozier.

MERV: Thank you. Who knows? Tonight could be funsy. *Exits upstairs.*

GORGEOUS: I like him.

SARA: He's a certain type.

GORGEOUS: You've become a hard woman, Sara.

SARA: I can't be surprised about things I already know.

GORGEOUS: Rabbi Pearlstein says he has great hope for you. He says you need a man to make you soft again.

SARA: You know what Tessie says when she can't bear to listen to me for a moment longer? "Mommy, I am going to throw up!" Gorgeous, I am going to throw up!

GORGEOUS: Rabbi Pearlstein is a very wise man.

SARA: Then tell him to concentrate on his income tax. Besides, there is someone in my life. Nick Pym's coming for dinner tonight.

GORGEOUS: Nick Pym is a Nazi.

SARA: Nick Pym can trace his lineage back to the Duke of Marlborough.

GORGEOUS: That's fine, sweetsie, but we can't. He's a philanderer and a Nazi.

SARA: He was a Thatcher M. P. and he dates a few other women.

GORGEOUS: You said he screws a lot of other women.

SARA: I never said that!

GORGEOUS: Well, I didn't hear it at the Safeway in Newton! Who knows, he could be just the ticket. Sara, the experts tell me that after your kind of "procedure" it's very important for you to get back on the saddle.

SARA: In the saddle.

GORGEOUS: You're not the only woman who's been ill. I read in *Newsweek*, it's now at least three in ten.

SARA: Really! That's quite a sisterhood. Even bigger than Hadassah.

GORGEOUS: Female Trouble is going to be the health issue of the decade.

SARA: Female Trouble? There are real words, Gorgeous. Ovarian abscess. Hysterectomy. According to all experts, I am now happily recovered and shall survive.

GORGEOUS: Do you want to share your anger, your rage?

SARA: Actually, I prefer to get on with my life.

GORGEOUS: Rabbi Pearlstein says we should openly discuss our feelings.

SARA: I can't tell you what a comfort it is to live in a country where "our feelings" are openly repressed. End of conversation, Gorgeous!

GORGEOUS: Fine. Have it your way. Achhhh! My feet are killing me. *Slips her shoes off and lies on the couch.* I schlepped twenty ladies through Harrods and up and down Sloane Street. One of them, Mrs. Hershkovitz, her daughter was a counselor at Lily's summer camp, everywhere she goes she has to have another piece of Wedgwood. She's got Wedgwood clocks, Wedgwood bells, Wedgwood napkin holders, and meanwhile her daughter was the biggest dope dealer at Camp Pinehurst.

SARA, *laughing:* I don't know how you do it. I couldn't put up with them.

GORGEOUS: Believe me, Sara, they wouldn't like you either.

SARA: Oh, God, I'm sure not.

GORGEOUS *picks up shoe:* I don't mind, really. The one thing that bothers me is my feet. I told Henry if I get this cable job, the first thing I'm going to do is stop wearing cheap shoes. I'm marching myself right into Saks and treating myself to Bruno Maglis, Ferragamos, and Manulo Blanchikis.

SARA: Manulo who?

GORGEOUS: Manulo Blahnik. Whatever. It's all the brands the ladies in my group tell me are the best. Do you know, those bitches—achh, I shouldn't use that kind of language—what those ladies said to me this morning. "Gorgeous, you're a celebrity now. Why don't you treat yourself to a real Chanel suit? You're such a brilliant and attractive woman, it kills us to see you with an imitation Louis Vuitton purse." Do you know how much one of those Chanel suits costs? Sara, you're my brilliant big sister, when we were growing up, why didn't Daddy tell us about money?

SARA: Because girls weren't supposed to know about money.

GORGEOUS: But you became a banker.

SARA: That's because no one ever called me Gorgeous. *Kisses* GORGEOUS' *forehead and begins to stroke her hair.*

GORGEOUS: I'm so tired, Sara. So very tired. Up a little higher. Mmmm. That feels so good. Remember when Mother stroked our hair?

SARA: I remember coming home with a 99 and her shrieking at me, "Where's the other point?"

GORGEOUS: Mother really missed saying good-bye to you.

SARA: Mother and I had a Female Trouble conflict.

GORGEOUS: She wanted to see us all happy.

SARA: We are happy, Gorgeous. It's just not our mother's kind of happiness. I wonder why Tessie isn't back yet.

GORGEOUS: What time is it?

SARA: Around 7:45.

GORGEOUS: But the sun's just going down.

SARA: "'Tis dark and dreary, this sepulchral isle. This royal throne of kings."

GORGEOUS *stands up and puts on her shoes:* Oh my God! We have to light the candles.

SARA: Why? We have electricity.

GORGEOUS: Sara. It's the Sabbath sundown. Where are your candles?

SARA: I have two Asprey candelabras in the dining room.

GORGEOUS: What about those two on the mantelpiece?

SARA: Majolica. Victorian, I believe, 1893.

GORGEOUS: I need a tichkel for my head.

SARA: I doubt I have that.

GORGEOUS: All right. Just a napkin.

SARA: Cloth or paper?

GORGEOUS: Sara, the sun's going down.

SARA: Here, take this. *Gives her a cloth from India that* PFENI *left on the couch.*

GORGEOUS: Matches?

SARA: Can't we wait for my birthday cake?

GORGEOUS: Sara, remember the Sabbath Day and keep it holy. *Lights the candles.*

SARA: I can't tell you how many Sabbath sundowns have come and gone here without lighting candles. And guess what? The next morning the sun comes right back up again.

GORGEOUS *prays over the candles:* Baruch ahtah adonai! elohenu! melech ha-olam!

TESS *and* TOM, *twenty, a working-class hero with spiked hair and black boots, enter. He cuts off* GORGEOUS*'s prayer.*

TOM: Hello, Mrs. Goode, are you having a seance?

SARA: Hello, Tom. Tessie.

TOM: I love Stonehenge.

GORGEOUS: Shh! *Continues to pray.* Asher! kiddish! shanu b'mitzvosov!

TOM: Why is she wearing a dishtowel on her head?

TESS: Shh.

SARA: Tessie's aunt is performing an ancient tribal ritual.

GORGEOUS *looks at* SARA: Vit zi vahnu! lehadlik nehr!

PFENI *enters:* Tessie, I just went to meet you. Sorry, Gorgeous!

SARA: I told you you'd be late.

GORGEOUS: Sara, I am not finished!

SARA: Tessie, shh! Your aunt isn't finished.

GORGEOUS *completes the prayer:* Shel Shabbas. Amen.

SARA: Finished now?

GORGEOUS: You've become a hard woman, Sara! *Picks up her suitcase and charges upstairs.*

TESS: Mother, how could you do that?

SARA: Do what? What is this to you? If we had a Muslim visiting here, you wouldn't suddenly bow down to Mecca.

TESS: But this is important to Aunt Gorgeous.

SARA: Pfeni, blow out the candles.

PFENI: But Gorgeous just lit them.

SARA: Stop being the good little sister and blow out the goddamned candles! PFENI *blows out the candles. It is suddenly dark in the room.* TESS *runs upstairs.* Drinks here in the sitting room at half-past.

Scene 3

Around 8:30 P.M. Frank Sinatra is playing on the stereo. NICHOLAS PYM, *an extremely well groomed British gentleman of about fifty-eight, enters from the dining room.* TOM *comes down the stairs. They eye each other as* PYM *turns off the Sinatra.* TESS *enters from the kitchen in blue jeans.*

TESS: It's just like my mother to have a dinner party on the night the Soviet Union is falling apart.

TOM: A crowd in Vilnius tore down the statue of Lenin today. It's amazing.

TESS: Mr. Pym, are you aware that fifty years of Soviet occupation has inflicted environmental damage that will cost the people of Lithuania at least one hundred and fifty billion dollars to repair?

NICK PYM: Tell me something, Tessie, where does this passion for the Baltics come from?

TOM: My dad is from Lithuania. And me uncles and me aunties still live there.

NICK PYM: There's a decent old restaurant in Vilnius.

TESS: The Old Cellar. My Aunt Pfeni already told me.

NICK PYM: Tessie, my luv, do you think the state of Kentucky is viable without the United States?

TOM: Lithuania has a culture and people independent from the Soviets.

NICK PYM: So does Kentucky. Think about the Derby.

TESS: If Western culture is to survive at all, Mr. Pym, one has to look beyond the States, England, France, or Germany. As it is, I feel completely irrelevant coming of age as a white European female.

NICK PYM: Tess, dear, I'm terribly sorry.

TESS: It could be worse. I could be a white European male.

Enter SARA *with a tray. She wears elegant hostess clothes.*

SARA: As promised, a few little nibblies.

TESS: Nibblies?

SARA: Hors d'oeuvries. Nick?

NICK PYM: They look marvelous, darling. Tom and Tessie were just sharing with me their excitement over the demise of the Soviet Union.

TESS: Well, mother, everything in Eastern Europe is going to change.

NICK PYM: I'd say it depends on the particular countries, actually. For instance, the Hungarians have always been industrious. This is marvelous cheese, darling!

SARA: New kind of chevre from the place on Wilton Street.

TOM: What's chevre?

SARA: Form of goat, dear. Would you care for some?

TOM: No thanks, Mrs. Goode. I don't much like cheese unless it's yellow. I only eat primary color foods, ma'am.

SARA: When Tessie was in nursery school, her favorite food was sushi. But Tessie's always had a sophisticated palette.

TESS: That's not true, mother. I only eat fish and chips and hamburgers.

MERV *enters singing:* Zip-pa-dee-do-dah, I love my new shirt! Good evening everyone. I'm Merv Kant.

NICK PYM *stands up:* Nick Pym. How do you do.

MERV: And you must be Tessie, and Tom the Lithuanian nationalist. You know, before the Holocaust, Vilnius was home to about 65,000 Jews.

SARA: Can I get you a drink, Merv?

MERV: Tessie, I suspect your mother is one of those hostesses who prefers that a guest not come into a room and immediately bring the conversation around to the Holocaust. I'll have a scotch, please.

NICK PYM: At least it's not English politics, the EEC, or the personal lives of the bloody royals.

MERV: That's true. It could be worse, Sara. I could chat about leopardette—that's my fall leopard line.

TOM: Fantastic.

NICK PYM: Oh, are you a furrier?

SARA: In addition to being Geoffrey's very talented New York furrier, Mr. Kant has recently been visiting Eastern Europe with the American Jewish Confederacy.

MERV: Congress.

NICK PYM: Were they all furriers, too?

MERV *pauses to look at* PYM: No.

NICK PYM: Please tell us, Merv, what did you find on your travels?

MERV: Tessie, do you remember an event in modern history called the Concert of Europe?

TESS: Count Metternich's plan to reestablish stability in Europe after Napoleon. 1815.

TOM: Tessie's really smart, Mrs. Goode. She's the brains in our family. *Nestles* TESS. SARA *turns away.*

MERV *smiles at* SARA: Like mother, like daughter.

TESS: Metternich's goal was nationalism.

SARA, *very quickly:* And, specifically, creating an alliance between England, Austria, Russia, and Prussia.

NICK PYM: Another disastrous European economic community!

SARA: Completely different circumstances, Nick.

MERV: Bankers have to wait. The historians haven't finished. And Tessie, what always goes hand in hand with European nationalism?

TOM: American movies and CNN?

MERV: Sorry, Tom, the answer is anti-Semitism.

NICK PYM: That's a sweeping generalization.

MERV: You asked me what I found on my travels. What I found was sweeping, but unfortunately true. Pick a country—any country, Russia, France, Austria, Hungary—it remains from before Count Metternich to I'm sure centuries from now a soft but never silent refrain. And that, Tessie, is the true concert of Europe. In Britain, of course, it's all handled a little more politely.

NICK PYM: That's bloody nonsense. Jews have been at the financial core of England for generations.

SARA: I always liked Metternich. If I wasn't promised to Disraeli, I think we would have made a rather nice couple.

MERV: But, Sara, do I have a point about England? You're a Jewish woman living in London.

SARA: I really don't have an opinion about this.

TESS: Why not?

SARA: Because this isn't about us, honey.

TOM: I thought Tessie was Jewish.

SARA: She is. But Mr. Kant is really talking about families in Russia and Eastern Europe who are unable to practice their religion.

TOM: I hate the Soviets.

SARA: That aside, if Tessie chooses to practice her religion in England, she perfectly well can.

NICK PYM: For that matter, she could go to the East End for a gefilte sandwich.

SARA: You'd like them, Tom. They're a fish cake, very much like quenelles.

TESS: Mother, would you stop it!

SARA: What am I doing?

TESS: Mother, if you don't leave Tom alone, we're leaving.

GORGEOUS *sweeps into the room. She is in fake Ungaro cocktail wear, with accessories.*

GORGEOUS: Good evening! Good evening!

NICK PYM *rises:* Gorgeous, you look absolutely smashing!

TOM: Maybe she should change her name to Smashing!

GORGEOUS: Well, well, well, this looks like a funsy little group.

NICK PYM: We've been having the most marvelous time chatting about anti-Semitism and the Concert of Europe.

GORGEOUS: Which concert is that? I must have missed it.

SARA: It's all right, Gorgeous. It took place in 1815.

GORGEOUS: You know, I'm taking a music appreciation class now at the Boston Symphony. Why are all those opera singers so overweight? Honestly, I don't know how they breathe, much less sing. Is that goat cheese? Blech. I hate goat cheese. *Kisses* TESS. Tessie, Tessie, you look so beautiful. Isn't my niece beautiful? I'm sorry, I forgot your name.

TOM: Tom.

GORGEOUS: Isn't my niece beautiful, Tom? My daughters are all desperately jealous of Tessie. Of all the cousins she was always the prettiest and the brightest. But I tell them to just make the most of what they've got. I knew girls who were just like Tessie in high school—beautiful, talented, bright—who have had such difficult times in later life. Tessie, carpe diem; now's the time to enjoy.

SARA: Gorgeous, would you like a drink?

GORGEOUS: Did I say something wrong? I'm always saying something wrong.

The lights flash up and down. GEOFFREY *appears on the steps in evening clothes and a plumed hat. He puts on rhinestone glasses.*

GEOFFREY: Ladies and gentlemen! In honor of our kindest innkeeper Sara Goode's birthday, and the collapse this very day of the Soviet Union, my beloved Pfeni Rosensweig and I have prepared an evening's entertainment with a very special guest. Ladies and gentlemen, it is my honor to present to you, after almost a century of hiding in a Santa Monica post office, her royal highness the Grand Duchess Anastasia Rosensweig Romanov.

PFENI *comes down the steps in a ball gown and tiara:* Das Vi Danya.

SARA: Pfeni, that's my good evening gown!

PFENI: Da! I am here to celebrate the name day of my sister Sara Goode Romanov.

GEOFFREY: Don't forget about your other sister, the eminent Petrograd physician, Dr. Gorgeous "Noodles" Romanov.

GORGEOUS: They're always making fun of me, Merv.

GEOFFREY: But stay, gentle "Noodles," who is this Murf that you so spritely call on? And see his amazing technicolor shirt of many colors.

NICK PYM: Bravo, Geoffrey! So many Jewish American men I know, professionals mostly, wear those shirts. Why is that, Merv?

MERV: It's a money-lending uniform.

NICK PYM: Beg your pardon.

MERV: They're so well designed, you'd never know it costs a pound of flesh to get them.

SARA *looks at* PYM *as the room laughs with* MERV: Geoffrey, what's happened to our play?

GORGEOUS *applauding:* We want our play! We want our play!

NICK PYM: Bring on the elves and the faerie sprites!

MERV: Bring on the beautiful dancing girls!

SARA: Bring on the Scarlet Pimpernel!

All shout "Pimpernel! The Pimpernel!"

GEOFFREY *sings:*

They seek him here,
They seek him there,
Those Frenchies seek him everywhere.

ALL *sing:* I knew him well, I knew him well, the Scarlet Pimpernel!

GEOFFREY *gets* TOM *up and puts the plumed hat on him.*

TOM: I love being in your house, Tessie!

GEOFFREY *kneels in front of* SARA: Milady, I have been dispatched twelve days on horseback by your sisters to wish you the happiest, merriest, jolliest birthday ever . . . hip, hip . . .

ALL: Hooray!
GEOFFREY: Hip, hip . . .
ALL: Hooray! Speech . . . speech!
SARA: Thank you. Thank you. I feel truly fortunate tonight to have my beautiful daughter and my family and friends with me. And Geoffrey, my baby sister is right. You do add texture to my life.
GEOFFREY: Long live Sara Goode.
ALL: Long live Sara Goode.
SARA: Long live the Scarlet Pimpernel.
GEOFFREY: And all his touring companies!
ALL: And all his touring companies!
SARA: Dinner is served.
GEOFFREY: "Once more unto the breach, dear friends."

TOM, TESS, GORGEOUS, PFENI, *and* NICK PYM *march behind* GEOFFREY. *They sing:*

They seek him here,
They seek him there,
Those Frenchies seek him everywhere.

GORGEOUS *sings:*

I knew him well!
I knew him well!

They march into the dining room. MERV *stays behind and watches* SARA *as she clears the hors d'oeuvres. He joins in as all the others continue to sing.*

Ding the bells go dong,
Hear the maiden's song,
I knew him well.

MERV: You're not singing.
SARA: I only do show tunes from the fifties.

TOM, TESS, GORGEOUS, PFENI, NICK PYM, GEOFFREY *in the dining room, singing,* MERV *singing directly to* SARA:

The Scarlet Pimpernel!

MERV: Sara, you really know how to throw a good Shabbes!

SARA *looks up from her tray. The lights fade as she joins the others in the dining room. They sit down to a gracious dinner.*

Scene 4

After dinner: around 11:30. GEOFFREY, PFENI, SARA, MERVYN, NICK PYM, TESS, *and* TOM *enter, laughing hysterically, from the dining room.* GORGEOUS *clears the dishes.*

GEOFFREY, *still laughing:* Yes, yes. It's true.
SARA: No.
GEOFFREY, *laughing:* Wait, there's more. So, Danny Kaye. So Danny Kaye dresses up as a customs inspector. And! And Sir Larry! I'm sorry!
TOM: Who's Sir Larry?
SARA: Laurence Olivier, Tom. He was in the movie, *Marathon Man.*
TESS: Mother!
GEOFFREY: So Danny Kaye supposedly dresses up like a customs inspector at the New York airport, and when Sir Larry comes through, he calls him aside into a special room, strips him buck naked, and inspects every single bloody part of him!
SARA: Why? Was he smuggling?
GEOFFREY: Sara, they were, as we say, "very close personal friends."
SARA: Danny Kaye! As in Hans Christian Andersen!
GEOFFREY: And then apparently they went off and spent a very warm and funsy night at the Saint Regis.
SARA: Has this been documented?
GEOFFREY: Who gives a damn?
GORGEOUS, *coming into the room from the dining area carrying four glasses:* Sara, does your crystal go in the dishwasher?
SARA: Gorgeous, please stop. You don't have to do that.
GEOFFREY *looks at his watch:* Well, I'm afraid we must be going.
PFENI: We must?
GEOFFREY: Hollywood people are in town, my darling, and I'm afraid I agreed to meet for late drinks at The Groucho with the producers of *Body Heat.*
TOM: *Body Heat?* You mean Kathleen Turner?
GEOFFREY: Well, it's the stage version. Tommy, I'm the only theatre director who can ignite the stage with true female sexuality.
SARA: Since when are you the expert on female sexuality?
GEOFFREY: Did you see my Cleopatra? Or my Lulu? Love is love, Sara. Gender is merely spare parts. Just ask Danny Kaye.

PFENI *and* GEOFFREY *exit.*

TOM: Isn't it late for a meeting?
MERV: Geoffrey's always working, Tom. He and I once walked right past a shootout on Broadway. The police yelled "Take cover," and Geoffrey asked me if I thought he should do *Showboat* for television.
SARA: That's a musical, Tom.
TESS: Mother.
GORGEOUS, *carrying napkin holders in a gold basket:* It was a great musical, Tom. Here, Sara, I didn't

know where to put this. Everything's put away now. *Puts the basket on the mantelpiece.* You don't have to thank me. It's been such a funsy evening, but I'm exhausted. G'mbye, you lovely people.

ALL: Goodnight.

TOM: Goodnight, Aunt Gorgeous.

GORGEOUS: Goodnight, dear. *Exits up the stairs.*

NICK PYM: I think I'd better be leaving as well.

SARA: You can't stay for another port?

NICK PYM: Darling, you're too kind. But I'm meeting my niece early in the morning.

TESS: Your niece?

MERV: We all love our nieces, Tessie.

NICK PYM: Fabulous, darling. *Gives her a gift.* Happy birthday. Merv. Good-bye, Tom. Good-bye, Tessie. Good luck in Latvia, darling. You know the shocking thing about all this business with the Soviets is one questions what in God's name the entire twentieth century was for. Good night. *Exits.*

TESS: People like him are what's wrong with this country.

SARA: Tessie, that's a ridiculous statement.

TESS: But it's true. The man has no commitments.

SARA: The man doesn't have your commitments.

TESS: Mother, he's dating the best friend of a girl in my class. He's one of those weirdo English bankers who takes sixteen-year-old models to dinner at Annabel's and then goes home alone and puts panty hose over his head and dances to *Parsifal.*

SARA: Tessie, you have no business saying things like that.

TOM: What's *Parsifal?*

SARA: It's a Wagner opera, Tom.

TESS: Come on, Tom.

SARA: Where are you going?

TESS: Upstairs.

TOM: There's a candlelight vigil tomorrow in Hyde Park. We're coordinating.

SARA: And you have to do that now?

TESS: Mother, would you like a rundown of our schedule?

SARA: No, I wouldn't. Good night, dear. Good night, Tom.

TOM: Great party, Mrs. Goode. That stew was brilliant.

SARA: It was a cassoulet, dear. Good night.

They exit upstairs.

MERV: The duck was very bright too. I'd say at least 150 I.Q.

SARA *begins straightening the living room.*

SARA: Aren't you going home to bed too? It's very late.

MERV: Not when I can watch you clean.

SARA: You enjoy watching women clean?

MERV: I enjoy watching women who don't need to clean, clean.

SARA: Actually, I have to clean. The help is on vacation and I like a tidy household.

MERV: Just like your mother.

SARA: My mother never cleaned. When I came home from college, she made an effort and pushed all the laundry under the bed.

MERV: But I bet she was a great cook.

SARA: She never cooked. We all went out to dinner every night at Sparky's family restaurant.

MERV: Was your mother Jewish?

SARA: For a supposedly intelligent man you have a persistently narrow perspective.

MERV: Thank you.

SARA: Excuse me.

MERV: You called me intelligent; I didn't know that you noticed.

SARA: I know you, Merv. You're just like all the other men I went to high school with. You're smart, you're a good provider, you read *The Times* every day, you started running at fifty to recapture your youth, you worry a little too much about your health, you thought about having affairs, but you never actually did it, and now that she's departed, your late wife Roslyn is a saint.

MERV: Her name was Helene. We lived in Roslyn.

SARA: And I'm sure you traveled and I'm sure your children are very nice people, and Merv, if my sisters or I had any sense, we would all have married you too.

MERV: What about Gorgeous? I thought she did marry me. Old Henry sounds like a nice enough guy: lawyer, good father, stays home to watch the kids play lacrosse.

SARA *begins dusting the mantelpiece:* Yes, Henry's wonderful, and I'm sure you're wonderful, and Tom's wonderful. You're all wonderful. *Knocks over the napkin rings.* God damn it, Gorgeous!

MERV: Hey, hey, take it easy. Take it easy.

SARA: You know what really irritates me in life, Merv? When men like you tell women to take it easy because somewhere they believe that all women are innately hysterics.

MERV: Why won't you give me a break?

SARA: Why won't you please just go home! *She starts to cry suddenly. He puts his arm around her.*

MERV: It's all right. I promise.

SARA *laughs slightly and moves away:* Now you're really convinced all women are hysterics. I'm sorry. Really. Tessie says I should take stress tabs.

MERV: You're fine. Let's talk about something else. How 'bout the American class system. Or, I've got a lively topic: Count Metternich and the Concert of Europe. Sadie, my lips haven't formed those words since I was a senior in high school.

SARA: Why did you call me Sadie?

MERV: You called me Mr. Kantlowitz. And Gorgeous called me Merlin the Magician. I figure anything goes in this house.

SARA: My grandfather called me Sadie. Sara was too biblical for him. He hoped I'd grow up to be a singer.

MERV: So you do sing!

SARA: When I was at Radcliffe. I was with a girls' singing group. The Cliffe Clef. I was a Cleffie!

MERV: Can I hear a little?

SARA: Merv, we're too old for this.

MERV: For what?

SARA: You're a very nice man. But you're not my type.

MERV: Sadie, you're not mine either. You're not what I'd call a warm or accessible woman.

SARA: Unlike the wonderful Roslyn.

MERV: Unlike the wonderful Roslyn. Tell me something, when did you figure out that you had all the answers?

SARA: High school. I knew what the teacher was going to ask before she asked it. I knew what was going to become of every girl in my class, and I knew, for some reason, I was different from them.

MERV: You weren't a nice Jewish girl.

SARA: Why do you always come back to that?

MERV: I have a limited repertoire. I'm not as smart as you are, Sadie. I didn't get double 800's on my College Boards.

SARA: When we took those tests, they didn't publish the results.

MERV: But I'm sure the school called your mother just to let her know. What? So I'm right.

SARA: It was no big deal.

MERV: Of course it was a big deal. I'll bet the valedictorian was nowhere as intelligent as you.

SARA: Sonia Kirschenblatt. Went to Bryn Mawr, married an astronomy professor, lives in Princeton, works for educational testing.

MERV: Fuzzy brown hair. Poodle skirts. Started going to Greenwich Village bookstores at sixteen.

SARA: You knew her?

MERV: Her parents had a cabana at the Brighton Beach Baths. I was a cabana boy. I shtupped her the year before she went to Bryn Mawr.

SARA: So Sonia Kirschenblatt went to Bryn Mawr not a virgin.

MERV: It was no big deal.

SARA: Are you kidding? Thirty years ago it was a very big deal.

MERV: Look, thank God she didn't get pregnant or today I'd be an astronomy professor at Princeton. I like talking to you, Sadie. I wish you'd stop pushing the ashtray back and forth and maybe your shoulders could come down from your ears. *Starts to rub her shoulders.* I didn't think they could get any higher. Pretty soon they'll be on the ceiling.

SARA: Merv, do you want to "shtup" me tonight in Queen Anne's Gate, like you did Sonia Kirschenblatt that hot and lusty summer night at the Brighton Beach Baths?

MERV: We did it at Columbia in my dorm room in John Jay Hall.

SARA: They didn't allow women in Columbia rooms then.

MERV: Sonia was a woman of great ingenuity. She didn't get to be valedictorian by being a half-wit.

SARA: But she wasn't so smart, either. She just worked hard. *Gets up from the couch.* Look, Merv, if you're thinking, "I know who this woman is sitting next to me. I grew up with her, with women like her, only sometime in her life she decided to run away. She moved to England, she dyed her hair, she named her daughter Tess and sent her to Westminster. She assimilated beyond her wildest dreams, and now she's lonely and wants to come home," you're being too obvious. Yes, I'm lonely, but I don't want to come home.

MERV: What about connect, Sadie?

SARA: Connect?

MERV: Connect, to another person.

SARA: How many support groups did you join when Roslyn died? I'm sorry, that was cruel.

MERV: No, but it was in surprisingly bad taste. I joined two, plus last year I went on Outward Bound to find myself on a cliff on Prince Edward Island.

SARA: And what did you learn about yourself?

MERV: That I couldn't write poetry. That I couldn't solve the Middle East with a Merv Kant peace plan. That I wasn't a particularly original thinker. And that more than anything I wanted to be in love again.

SARA: To have someone take care of you.

MERV: Listen, my wife wasn't named Roslyn and she wasn't a saint. She drank a little, she was depressed, a little, and she thought she could have been a contender if it wasn't for me. She put me through school, she brought up the children, and finally she got to take art classes at the museum four years before she died. Is that fair to a talented, intelligent woman? Sadie, I've already done having someone take care of me.

SARA: I'm sorry. I guess I'm the one who's being too obvious.

MERV: Thank you.
SARA: You're welcome.
MERV: I still believe there can be happiness in life, Sara. Brief but a moment or two.
SARA: Who's to say what's happy?
MERV: Are you?
SARA: It's not so bad. I'm looking forward to Tessie going to college and selling the house for a cozy flat.
MERV: And sex?
SARA: I miss sex. I always liked sex.
MERV: What about Lord Gefilte?
SARA: You heard Tessie. His taste runs to younger women.
MERV: I think you're gorgeous.
SARA: My sister is Gorgeous.
MERV: No, you are, Sara Rosensweig.
SARA *laughs:* Jesus. No one's called me that in thirty years. *He kisses her somewhat passionately.* I could never love you, Merv. And I'm old enough now and kind enough not to let you love me. But Merv, just for one night I could be Sonia Kirschenblatt at the Brighton Beach Baths and you a Columbia sophomore.
MERV: You think I have the energy of a Columbia sophomore?
SARA: I certainly hope so, Merv.

She starts to lead him up the stairs. He stops suddenly.

MERV: Sadie, I do have one request.
SARA: What?
MERV: Would you sing for me?
SARA: Merv, I . . .
MERV: I'll sing with you. I'm a wonderful singer. I was Mrs. Chiang Kai-shek in the Columbia Varsity Show of 1955.
SARA: So I heard.
MERV: You don't have to do anything fancy. I would just like it very much if I could hear you sing.
SARA: Merv, I have every Sinatra song ever recorded. How 'bout we let Frank sing?
MERV: But he was never a Cliffe Clef.
SARA: Please, Merv, pick a Sinatra song and let's go upstairs.

MERV *puts on "Just the Way You Look Tonight." He begins singing:*

Lovely, don't you ever change,
Keep that breathless charm . . ."
Take it, Sara . . .

SARA, *quietly:* Merv, I just can't sing for you.

MERV *touches her face and begins leading her upstairs, singing:*

Just the way you look tonight.

ACT II

Scene 1

Early Saturday morning. GEOFFREY, *in a Save the Rose T-shirt and turquoise underwear, is dancing and lipsynching to The Four Tops, singing "Sugar Pie Honey Bunch." He does some choreographed spots and turns.*

GEOFFREY:

Sugar Pie Honey Bunch,
You know that I love you,
Can't help myself,
I love you and nobody else.
In and out of my life,
You come and you go,
Leaving only your picture behind,
And I've kissed it a thousand times!

PFENI *comes up from her apartment and stares at him. He notices her.* Ladies and gentlemen, my favorite dancing partner, the lovely and talented "Pfeni"!

They dance together. They are both wonderful dancers. Suddenly PFENI *falls onto the sofa.*

PFENI: Geoffrey, it's six o'clock in the morning.
GEOFFREY: My darling, they'll never pick us for the ice follies if you don't practice. How can anyone be disparaging about American culture when you produced The Temptations, The Miracles, and The Four Tops? Every Holland/Dosier/Holland Motown song is brilliant, simply brilliant. "Sugar Pie Honey Bunch, you know that I love you" is comparable in every way to "Shall I compare thee to a summer's day."
PFENI: Geoffrey . . .
GEOFFREY: In fact, I'd much prefer to be a sugar pie honey bunch than a summer's day. Less elitist.
PFENI: Geoffrey . . . It's 6:12 in the morning.
GEOFFREY: That's the wonderful thing about this music, my angel. It's perfect for any and all social occasions! O.K., Miss U.S.A., for two hundred points, can you name the Four Tops? Time's up. Take it, U.K. Yes, Lady Bracknell. "The Four Tops are Levi Stubbs, Abdul 'Duke' Fakir, Lawrence Payton, and Renaldo 'Obie' Benson. They were all born and raised in Detroit, the Motor City, and the first time they entertained was at a high school graduation party in 1954." Congratulations, Lady Bracknell. You just won a two-week vacation for

two to downtown Detroit and a year's supply of McVittie's digestive biscuits. *Pulls* PFENI *back up.*

PFENI: Geoffrey!

GEOFFREY: Ding! Ding! Ding! Ladies and gentlemen, the interval is now over. Please take your seats. This morning's performance will resume in one minute. *Turns the record back up even louder and begins dancing.*

Baby, I need your loving.
Got to have all your loving . . .

PFENI *turns the music off.*

PFENI: Geoffrey.

GEOFFREY: Come in, Big Ben.

PFENI: Geoffrey, it's now 6:16 in the morning and you're dancing around my big sister's house in your underwear.

GEOFFREY: I didn't want to wake you up.

PFENI: What about Sara?

GEOFFREY: I believe she's otherwise engaged.

PFENI: She is?

GEOFFREY: Your sister is a desirable woman. *Grabs* PFENI. She's related to you.

PFENI: You mean Sara and Merv. That's impossible.

GEOFFREY: Nothing is impossible, my darling. Look at us.

PFENI: I just thought he wasn't her . . .

GEOFFREY: Well, no one thinks you're my . . .

PFENI: Stop it, Geoffrey.

GEOFFREY *embraces her:* Pfeni, I'm a closet heterosexual.

PFENI: Well, I certainly haven't told anyone except my sisters.

GEOFFREY: And what do they think?

PFENI: They both wish they had met you first.

GEOFFREY *kisses* PFENI *on the forehead:* You're a wonderful person, Pfeni Rosensweig. I will never forget you. *Begins walking around the room.* Where is that damned Susie Cooper?

PFENI: Who?

GEOFFREY: I'm taking Jordan to the country this afternoon, and I have to find that plate of his that I loaned to your sister for Boxing Day. He's always nudging me for it. How was I to know it was a limited edition Susie Cooper?

PFENI: Is Jordan still with Rum-Tum-Tugger?

GEOFFREY: Who?

PFENI: The cat.

GEOFFREY: Oh, Ian. Yes, he says he's quite happy with him.

PFENI: That's nice. Is Ian joining you in the country also?

GEOFFREY: Stop it, Pfeni.

PFENI: Stop what?

GEOFFREY: Jordan is my best friend. Stop making our lives more complicated than they already are.

PFENI: Your life isn't complicated. You do exactly what you want.

GEOFFREY: And you don't? My luv, you're the one who's always popping in from Bombay. You're the one who had me up all last night watching the reruns of Kurds hurling themselves into their children's early graves. There I am in bed with the woman I love, knowing she'd rather be in Kurdland. *Starts to sing,*

Come on along and listen to,
the lullaby of Kurdland!

PFENI *cuts him off:* It's Kurdistan. And it's important to see these things.

GEOFFREY: Poor baby. You're so sensitive and vulnerable.

PFENI: I'm fine.

GEOFFREY: There's nothing wrong with that, my darling. I've made a career out of being sensitive and vulnerable.

PFENI: Geoffrey . . .

GEOFFREY: What is it, Pfeni? What is it that you want, my angel, that you're not getting? Do you want to get married? We'll get married. Whenever you leave, I think to myself, "Why is she going again? Pfeni belongs here with me." You are the first person I want to see in the morning and the last person I want to talk to at night. Do you want to have children? Brill. We'll have a troop of them. They'll be running Metro-Goldwyn-Mayer before age seven.

PFENI: But will they be Jewish children?

GEOFFREY: They'll have to be if they're going to run M.G.M.

PFENI: Geoffrey, I'm already forty.

GEOFFREY: Time is on our side, angel. That's the joy of an unconventional life.

PFENI: Some days, Geoffrey, I wish I were you.

GEOFFREY: "Alas, our frailty is the cause, not we. For such as we are made of, such we be."

PFENI: Put on some pants, Geoffrey.

GEOFFREY: What?

PFENI: Just put on some pants.

GEOFFREY: You're much too modest.

PFENI: This is my sister's house.

GEOFFREY: And you think she's never seen a man without pants?

PFENI: She's never seen you without pants.

GEOFFREY: How do you know?

PFENI: Are you sure you're not part of some antifeminist, anti-Semitic plot?

GEOFFREY: What? You expect me to like women *and* Jews?

PFENI: God help me. "If I could only get to Moscow!"

GEOFFREY: I love being with you. Pfeni, what are you working on now?

PFENI: Right now? With you? Here this morning? In Sara's sitting room? Well, as we sit here, I have a new book about gender and class working in a crock pot somewhere in Tajikistan. It's writing itself.

GEOFFREY: You've been talking about that book for years. It's time to move on.

PFENI: I always move on. I'm a travel writer.

GEOFFREY: Pfeni, have you ever heard of a singer named Lilli Lehman?

PFENI: Was she a Marvellette or a Ronnette?

GEOFFREY: She was one of the greatest opera singers of all time.

PFENI: Oh well.

GEOFFREY: But by the time Lilli got around to making records, she was too old and her voice fairly shot. So what's the moral?

PFENI: Record early.

GEOFFREY: Pfeni, I am serious. I've changed address books three times this year because I couldn't bear to cross out any more names. I've lost too many friends. I've seen too many lights that never had their chance to glow burn out overnight. I've tried for years now to make sense of all this, and all I know is life is random and there is no case to be made for a just or loving god. So how then do we proceed? In directing terms, what is the objective? Of course, we must cherish those that we love. That's a given. But just as important, people like you and me have to work even harder to create the best art, the best theatre, the best bloody book about gender and class in Tajikistan that we possibly can. And the rest, the children, the country kitchen, the domestic bliss, we leave to others who will have different regrets. Pfeni, you and I can't idle time.

PFENI: I love you, Geoffrey. I'm not going to travel anymore. I want to stay with you.

Begins to take his hand as GORGEOUS *enters in a flannel nightgown.*

GORGEOUS: Hello. Hello.

GEOFFREY: Good morning!

GORGEOUS: Good morning! I thought I heard noises down here and I was hoping it meant it was time for coffee. Geoffrey, you have fabulous legs! *She hikes up her nightgown and puts her legs beside his.* I noticed because I happen to have great legs, too. Pfeni's ankles are good, but then she gets a little thick in the calves. *Grabs* GEOFFREY*'s knee.* So, Geoffrey, Geoffrey, I can't tell you how excited my ladies were when I told them you agreed to have breakfast at the National with them this morning.

GEOFFREY, *confused:* I did? Brilliant.

GORGEOUS: Even Mrs. Hershkovitz with the Wedgwood said to me, "Well, well, Gorgeous, aren't you connected?" Everyone is always so impressed when I tell them about my sister who writes for the PLO and her famous director boyfriend.

PFENI: I don't write for the PLO. I did an interview with Hanan Ashrawi for my book four years ago.

GORGEOUS: She's a puppet for the PLO.

PFENI: She's a professor at Birzeit University.

GORGEOUS: Have it your way. Geoffrey honey, tell me about your new house. Is it almost finished?

GEOFFREY: Just another month. It's going to be marvelous. It has the most spectacular view of the Thames.

GORGEOUS: Uh-huh. So you and Pfeni will be moving there together soon?

PFENI: Gorgeous!

GORGEOUS: I tell my children that anything is possible if you just hold on to your dreams. You held on to your dreams, Geoffrey. All creative people do. That's why I'm so happy to have you in the family.

TESS, *offstage:* Mom, Mother, are you there? Have you seen my passport?

GORGEOUS: Tessie, darling. Don't come down here. Geoffrey has no clothes on.

GEOFFREY *gets up:* Well, I suppose I'd better go put on my face for Mrs. Hershkowitz.

GORGEOUS: Vitz. She's a Vitz.

GEOFFREY *kisses* PFENI: Good-bye, my darling. *Takes* GORGEOUS*'s hand.* Gorgeous, I look forward to seeing you and your lovely ladies shortly. *Kisses* GORGEOUS*'s hand.* GORGEOUS *curtsies. Then, as he exits, he mutters:* Vitz. She's a Vitz.

GORGEOUS: He really is so much fun! Well, they say companionship is 90% of any marriage. Even the best sex is gone in two years. And I know, because Henry and I had the most delicious sex!

PFENI: What are you doing?

GORGEOUS: What do you mean "What am I doing?" Pfeni, I came down for coffee. Your boyfriend was lounging in his Fruit of the Looms, and I was making pleasant morning conversation.

PFENI: And that's why you asked if we'll be moving in together next month?

GORGEOUS: Sweetsie, be happy I didn't ask about your sex life—about which I am dying to know. Tell me something, does Geoffrey still, you know, with men?

PFENI: You know, what, with men?

GORGEOUS: Pfeni, if you don't know by now, you're really in trouble.

PFENI: Gorgeous, we're living in the midst of a world health crisis!

GORGEOUS: I know that. But there are still safe ways to do it. Even in Newton.

PFENI: I love Geoffrey. As much as I've ever loved any man, and I've had my share. Is Geoffrey every Jewish mother's—never mind Jewish, make it Baptist, Buddhist, Bahai—dream date for their daughter? No, but Gorgeous, I'm not every mother's dream daughter.

GORGEOUS: Sweetsie, don't waste your time rebelling against mother anymore. She's not even here to enjoy it. It's just us now.

PFENI: I'm on deadline.

GORGEOUS: Ucch, sweetsie, why won't you take my advice. You're pretending to be someone you're not! Men, desirable men of any age, aren't interested in eccentric women in their forties. Eccentric women in their twenties is maybe interesting—especially with the big, funsy, way-out hair. Eccentric in their thirties is all right only if you're superthin and arty successful. But wandering around the world alone at forty, Pfeni, you're wandering yourself right out of the marketplace. And don't tell me you have Geoffrey. I know you can't judge a book by its cover, but sweetsie, you're at the wrong library altogether. Pfeni, don't you want what any normal woman wants?

PFENI: I never know what you mean by normal.

GORGEOUS: Pfeni, you and I are people people. We're not like Sara. We need warmth and cuddles and kisses.

PFENI: We sound like puppies.

GORGEOUS: Pfeni. Listen to your other smart big sister. You still have time. Don't waste it. *Strokes her cheek.* You know, your skin is very dry. You should have weekly collagen masks.

PFENI: I should?

GORGEOUS: And it's not too early for Retin A.

Enter TOM *and* TESS *from upstairs.*

TOM: Good morning, Aunt Pfeni. Good morning, Aunt Gorgeous.

GORGEOUS: Well, well, well. Teenagers, teenagers, teenagers.

TESS: Have you seen my Mom?

TOM: We saw her dancing last night with Mr. Mervyn, the furrier.

GORGEOUS: Well, well, well. I guess it was a full house.

TESS: He is a better choice for my mother than Benjamin Disraeli.

TOM: Who's Benjamin Disraeli?

GORGEOUS: A famous Jewish philanthropist. He founded Harrods department store.

PFENI *and* TESS *laugh with* GORGEOUS.

TESS: The furrier was singing Frank Sinatra.

GORGEOUS: Tessie, as your Aunt Pfeni can tell you, a good man is hard to find.

PFENI: Tessie, if my life depended on it, I would never tell you that.

Enter SARA.

SARA: Tell you what? Hello, my sisters. Hello, Tessie. *Goes to get the morning paper.*

TOM: Good morning, Mrs. Goode.

SARA: Good morning, Tom. This is an early family gathering. Have you all had your coffee?

TESS: Mother . . .

SARA: Yes, Tessie, my love.

TESS: Nothing.

GORGEOUS: Well, I'm not shy. How was it?

SARA: How was what?

GORGEOUS *winks:* How was your night?

SARA: Lovely. I spent it with my family and a few close friends. How was your night, Gorgeous?

GORGEOUS: We mean your night after the family and a few close friends.

SARA: Gorgeous, stop winking. You look like you have an astigmatism.

TESS: Mother, you slept with that furrier last night. Everyone here knows that.

SARA: I see.

GORGEOUS: We like him.

TOM: A good man is hard to find.

TESS: Aren't you happy?

GORGEOUS: This is so exciting, honey. I always said to mother, if only Sara would meet a furrier or a dentist.

SARA: Why not a C.P.A.? Gorgeous, I am not going to drive off into the sunset with a man I've had dinner with once.

GORGEOUS: Why not?

TESS: He's too nice?

GORGEOUS: Too warm? Where is he now?

SARA: Have you never heard of "privacy," "discretion"?

GORGEOUS: I just want to see you settled.

SARA: This is it, Gorgeous. Trust me, I'm settled.

GORGEOUS: Tessie, don't you want to see your mother settled with a nice man?

SARA: Gorgeous, you may be the happiest woman in all of Newton. You may even be healing the entire funsy Massachusetts Turnpike! But you are not our mother. Our mother is dead.

GORGEOUS: I am not a stupid woman, Sara!

SARA: Then explain to me why your mind is cluttered with nonsense.

GORGEOUS: Let me tell you something, Sara. Rabbi Pearlstein says you're very troubled because you never grew up to be the woman our mother expected us to be.

SARA: I beg your pardon?

GORGEOUS: Well, I'm sorry things have not worked out as you had hoped. But I can no longer allow you to hurt my feelings because you are so threatened by my pride in my husband, my family, and my accomplishments!

SARA: This is actually quite absurd!

GORGEOUS: Is it quite! Well, you can speak with your la-di-dah British accent, and Pfeni can send my children postcards from every ca-ca-mamie capital in the world, but I know that deep inside both of you wish you were me! Dr. Gorgeous Teitelbaum, a middle-aged West Newton housewife who wears imitation Ferragamo shoes and is very soon to have her own cable call-in talk show! *She trips as she exits.* God damn it! I wish I had a pair of real friggin' Manulo Blahnik, Blanchik, fuck-it shoes! Pardon my French, Tom. *Exits upstairs.*

TOM: That wasn't French, Mrs. Goode.

SARA: Thank you, Tom.

TESS: Mother, we were all having such a nice time down here. We were all so happy for you, and then you came down and spoiled it.

SARA: Well, this is my house.

TESS: Yes, it is. Where do you keep my passport? We're leaving for Vilnius tomorrow morning.

TOM: We want to get there in time for independence.

SARA: Tessie, can we please talk about this quietly after breakfast?

TESS: "Quietly after breakfast" means without Tom. Tom and I are here together.

SARA: Yes, I see. Pfeni, do you have nothing to add to your niece flying off tomorrow?

TESS: Aunt Pfeni flies all over the world.

SARA: But for a reason. You have no bloody reason to fly off to Vilnius during a revolution!

TESS: Let's go, Tom. Just because it's not important to her to have any passion in her life doesn't mean that we can't. *Exits.*

SARA *calls after her:* Don't call me "her," Tessie.

TOM: Mrs. Goode, me mum and me sisters don't get on all the time either. There are twelve of them and good Roman Catholics, Mrs. Goode.

SARA: That's nice.

TOM: Have a nice day, Mrs. Goode. Me dad sings Frank Sinatra too. *Exits.*

SARA: Why couldn't she take up with a lovely boy from the IRA? At least it's close by.

PFENI: Sara, I just want to know one thing.

SARA: What?

PFENI: How was it?

SARA: Oh! How was it? Well, I'd say that furrier has some very special skills.

PFENI: Really! You mean, like synthetic animal covering?

SARA *laughs:* Let's just call it "fun fur."

PFENI: What?

SARA: When you're older.

PFENI: Do you think Gorgeous and Henry have "the most delicious sex"? She's always talking about it.

SARA: Maybe Gorgeous is the smartest one of us all. Maybe if I were "settled," my daughter wouldn't be on the road to being a new-age Emma Goldman.

PFENI: You don't believe that.

SARA: Not for a minute. Please talk to Tessie today. It frightens me how much she's like you.

PFENI: How can I tell Tessie not to go to Vilnius when I was up all last night watching Kurdish refugee evacuations? In some crazy way I wished I could be there.

SARA: But unlike my daughter you're a grown person and a journalist. Why don't you go?

PFENI: I don't do that kind of writing anymore.

SARA: Why not?

PFENI: Don't know. I won't. I don't. Who knows?

SARA: That's a succinct and thoughtful answer.

PFENI: Sara, I had the most unsettling experience last week. Before Bombay I went back to Doubandi, my Afghan village. I wanted to visit the women I'd written about, but when I arrived, I was told that half of them were dead and the rest refugees. And Sara, with every bit of dire information, I became more and more excited to listen.

SARA: I don't understand.

PFENI: Somewhere I need the hardship of the Afghan women and the Kurdish suffering to fill up my life for me. And if I'm that empty, then I might as well continue to wander to the best hotels, restaurants, and poori stands.

SARA: But how are you helping them if you don't tell their stories? Is it morally better to dispatch four-star Karachi hotel reviews?

PFENI: It's wrong for me to use these women.

SARA: Pfeni, real compassion is genuinely rarer than any correct agenda. I'm a pretty good banker, but it's not a passion. You, on the other hand, have a true calling, and the sad and surprisingly weak thing is you're actively trying to avoid it. I think you care too much and you're looking for excuses not to. Tessie says I should have a talk show instead of Gorgeous. "Opinions with Sara Goode." *Returns to reading the paper.*

PFENI *takes* SARA*'s hand:* There is no one I rely on in life more than you. There is no one I am more grateful to than you.

SARA, *moving her hand away:* Pfeni, don't, and I won't.

Enter MERV, *humming "Just the Way You Look Tonight."*

MERV: Good morning.
PFENI: Good morning, Merv. How nice to see you again. I'm afraid I have a deadline.
SARA: I thought you finished "Bombay by Night."
PFENI: Yes, now there's "Bombay by Day." *Exits downstairs.*
MERV: She is a hard-working girl, your sister.
SARA: We're all hard-working girls. So, what's on your agenda?
MERV: My agenda?
SARA, *British:* Your schedule.
MERV: I love the way you say schedule. Say "vitamin."
SARA, *British:* Vitamin.
MERV: Again.
SARA, *giggling:* Vitamin.
MERV: That's adorable. *Kisses her.*
SARA: I have a tennis date this morning. And you?
MERV: Me? I don't have a tennis date this morning.
SARA: I'm just being reasonably clear.
MERV: Isn't it usually the reverse? Aren't most women warm and cozy the morning after and the men reasonably clear?
SARA: I wouldn't know.
MERV: I've never met anyone like you, Sara. You're warm and cold all at the same time. Your face is so familiar and so distant. Sometimes I look at you and see all my mother's photographs of her mother and her mother's entire family.
SARA: Well, it's a look.
MERV: My mother's family had a villa in a spa resort in Poland called Ciechocinek. And the pictures we had were of the family gathered at a picnic. The men waving at the camera or smiling, holding up a cantaloupe! They were sweet, these men, some even handsome, but they couldn't hold a candle to the women. The women in their too-large dresses with their arms folded all had your brilliant eyes—they sparkled even from those curled and faded photographs. Unfortunately, most of them and their families didn't survive. But Sara, when I look into your eyes, I see those women's strength and their intelligence. To me you are a beautiful and most remarkable woman. Why are you laughing? You're like a teenager. I say you're beautiful and you start laughing?
SARA: You want to hear something cuckoo, Merv?
MERV: You cuckoo? You're too "not cuckoo" for your own good.
SARA: I've been to Ciechocinek. I was sent there by the Hong Kong/Shanghai Bank.
MERV: My mother always said it was the Palm Beach of Poland.
SARA: It's now a postmodern, prefab, post-cold-war resort of the gray cinder block variety.
MERV: Thank God there's somewhere for me to retire besides Coral Gables. Sadie . . . *Begins laughing.* Why did the Hong Kong Shanghainese send you to Ciechocinek? Never in my life did I think I'd be asking a woman such a question!
SARA: Someone has to pay to privatize the state industries. Capitalism is expensive, Merv. They were asking for a loan, and I was being reasonably clear.
MERV: I'm sure you were brilliant.
SARA: I was all right. But while I reviewed their detailed proposals for renovating heating services and redistricting agricultural cooperatives, I couldn't help but see it all as a minor triumph for the women with those same sparkling eyes in my mother's faded photographs. Fifty years after the lucky few had escaped with false passports, Esther Malchah's granddaughter Sara was deciding how to put bread on the tables of those who had so blithely driven them all away.
MERV: I want to know you better, Sara. We could spend some pleasant time together. You can meet my children, and I already like Tessie. We're not young, Sara.
SARA: And a good man is hard to find. Mervyn . . .
MERV: "Mervyn." That means you're pulling away again.
SARA: I think you've set your sights on the wrong sister.
MERV: Do you make a practice of spending the night with men you plan to fix up with your sisters?
SARA: I think you and someone like Gorgeous could be quite happy together. You're both very lively.
MERV: What does that mean?
SARA: You have interests in common.
MERV: You mean we're both a little too lively and a little too Jewish. That's what we have in common. Sara, you remind me of my classmates from DeWitt Clinton High School in the Bronx who now pretend as if DeWitt Clinton was a prep school down the Connecticut River right around the bend from Groton or St. Paul's.
SARA: St. Paul's is in New Hampshire and Groton School is in Massachusetts. Groton, Connecticut is a shipbuilding town.
MERV: You would know that.
SARA: I don't see what any of this has to do with you and someone like Gorgeous.
MERV: I'm afraid that you do, or you wouldn't be chasing Lord Gefilte, and Gorgeous and I wouldn't

be quite so happy together. I don't understand what's so wrong with you, Sara. I like you.
SARA: Your world is very different from mine.
MERV: No, it's not. I changed my name from Kantlowitz, and my daughter, the Israeli captain, went to St. Paul's. And where did you come from, Sara?
SARA: Don't proselytize me, Merv.
MERV: Sara, you're an American Jewish woman living in London, working for a Chinese Hong Kong bank, and taking weekends at a Polish resort with a daughter who's running off to Lithuania!
SARA: And who are you? My knight in shining armor? The furrier who came to dinner. Why won't you give up, Merv? I'm a cold, bitter woman who's turned her back on her family, her religion, and her country! And I held so much in. I harbored so much guilt that it all made me ill and capsized in my ovaries. Isn't that the way the old assimilated story goes?
MERV: Why do you dislike me so much?
SARA: I don't dislike you, Merv.
MERV: Then what is your problem, lady?
SARA: "Lady," that's very Brooklyn.
MERV: No, actually, it's very the Bronx. Is it because I remind you too much of home?
SARA: Merv, the home you're talking about is the Bronx, the Brooklyn, the America of forty years ago. It doesn't even exist anymore.
MERV: If it doesn't exist, why the hell are you working so hard to make it go away?
SARA: I didn't have a "you" in my life at sixteen. I'm certainly not going to have a "you" in my life now. You deserve someone who really does know how to throw a good Shabbes. Someone who will make you a "warm and happy home" and show up at holidays and family gatherings in a tasteful but cheery crepe orange suit.
MERV: And you can't, Sara Rosensweig?
SARA: You don't know me as well as you think you do. Orange pales my already far too sallow skin.
MERV *extends his hand:* It was a pleasure to meet you, Sara.
SARA *holds onto his hand:* You're a very nice man.
MERV: Do women like it when a man says, "I'm sorry. You're very nice"?
SARA: No. Especially not when the man has just spent the night.
MERV: You still have all the answers, Sara. *Exits.*

SARA goes to the record player and puts away the Sinatra album. She picks up the Cliffe Clef album and puts it on the record player when the phone rings. She picks up the phone.

SARA: Oh, hello, Nick. Yes, it was a lovely evening. Glynebourne Tuesday would be terrific. Oh, I'm so sorry. Your gift was absolutely brilliant. And Tessie thought it was brilliant as well. Thanks so much. See you Tuesday. Good-bye.

She turns on the record player and picks up a gift box that has remained unwrapped on the window seat. As she sits to open the gift, we hear on the record, "Hi, I'm Sara Rosensweig of Brooklyn, New York and we're the Cliffe Clef of 1959." There are assorted cheers. "Tonight is our concert of Europe." There are assorted laughs. SARA laughs and shrugs her shoulders. "Well, we call it that as a tribute to Metternich, Talleyrand, and other well-known Harvard men." There are more laughs. "Those of us who are graduating this year . . ." There is a whooping cheer, and SARA raises her arm in triumph. "Each has a chance tonight to lead with her favorite song, and this one, ever since freshman year, has been mine." The group begins to sing a cappella "MacNamara's Band." SARA listens. She continues to unwrap the gift. Suddenly she begins to sing a different verse softly:

Oh my name is Moishe Pupick
And I come from Palestine,
I live on bread and honey
And on Manischewitz wine.
Oh my mother makes the best
Gefilte fish in all the land . . .

Her voice cracks.

And I'm the only Yiddish girl
In MacNamara's Band.

SARA is crying as she lifts up a standard tea kettle from the gift box. It's brilliant, Nick. Absolutely fucking brilliant.

Scene 2

Later that afternoon, around 4:00 P.M. PFENI enters from downstairs, with her laptop computer. She sits on the window seat and works. TESS enters carrying a tray with tea cups and a pot of tea. The final bars of the Cliffe Clef's singing "When My Sugar Walks Down the Street" is on the stereo.

TESS: Your tea, madam.
PFENI: Thank you, Tessie. I rely on the kindness of nieces.
TESS: Are you writing something new?
PFENI: I have an idea. And that's a very good thing.

Enter GEOFFREY.

GEOFFREY: I've returned from the Crimea, my darling, and I've missed you so! Could this be little Tessie? Let me look at you. You've grown into a beautiful woman. Oh God, I'm old! How old do I look to you today, Tessie?

TESS: Mmmmm. About seventy.

GEOFFREY: She's a nasty little thing, isn't she? No more ginger cookies for you, young lady.

TESS: I'm going upstairs to pack.

GEOFFREY: Are you really off to the Baltics, then?

TESS: Yes! There's a rally here tonight, and Tom says we'll leave tomorrow. *She runs up the stairs singing:*

All the little birdies go tweet-tweet-tweet!

GEOFFREY: I'm thinking of making a film, *Three Days That Shook the Rosensweigs,* with Dr. Gorgeous making her film debut as Trotsky.

PFENI: I sort of envy Tessie going.

GEOFFREY: But my darling, she's not going anywhere. Trust me, Pfeni, I have an eye for real talent.

PFENI: You're such a bloody snob!

GEOFFREY: Perhaps I was once. But not anymore. I've had my consciousness raised by the full assemblage of the Temple Beth El sisterhood.

PFENI *kisses him:* I take it all back, you're not a snob. You're a saint.

GEOFFREY: I fielded such penetrating questions from Mrs. Ida Hershkovitz as, "Mr. Duncan, I would like to know what exactly your function as director of *The Scarlet Pimpernel* was. You didn't write the story or the music and you don't act. So, from my point of view, you're being paid very good money just to sit there and do nothing."

PFENI: Poor Gorgeous.

GEOFFREY: Gorgeous loves it, darling! She's a star! The most beautiful and well-connected woman in Newton. They've asked me to the States to direct the West Newton Community Center revival of *Milk and Honey.* I suggested we do *Marat/Sade* instead. *Kisses her.* I love that you have no bloody idea what I'm babbling about. Did Jordan ring? He said he'd be by around now.

PFENI: No, he didn't ring. Was Jordan at your talk?

GEOFFREY: I thought the ladies might want to meet him. Royal Jordan flatware is very big in the States these days. *Takes a sip of* PFENI'*s tea and spits it out into the cup.* What's the matter with this tea? Uccch! Undrinkable!

PFENI: Geoffrey, that was mine!

GEOFFREY: "I would give all my fame for a pot of ale and safety."

PFENI: Geoffrey, please sit down. You're making me anxious.

GEOFFREY *sings and dances:*

Oh pretty baby, I can't sit down.
Don't you hear the band a groovin', I can't sit down.
Gotta get your motor movin'.

All right, U.S., for fifty points?

PFENI: "You Can't Sit Down," 1963. The Dovelles.

GEOFFREY: You're the brightest woman I've ever known.

PFENI: No, my sister Sara's the brightest woman you've ever known.

GEOFFREY *finally sits:* Pfeni . . .

PFENI: What is it, Geoffrey? You're beyond manic today.

GEOFFREY: Pfeni, after my speech to the Gorgeous ladies, I drove around London for hours. And then up past the Isle of Dogs and out to Greenwich. And I sat at the water's edge on the bow of the Cutty Sark and thought about us. Mostly about you, actually. Pfeni, I love you. I will always love you. But the truth is, I miss men. What?

PFENI: Nothing.

GEOFFREY: I want us to be the most remarkable friends. The Noel and Gertie of our day.

PFENI: I'm not in the theatre, Geoffrey. I'm a journalist.

GEOFFREY: You know how wonderful I think you are. You must know that the entire time I've been with you, I've never acted out, I've never cheated on you.

PFENI: Really, not even on the Cutty Sark?

GEOFFREY: Bitchiness doesn't become you, darling.

PFENI: I'm sorry.

GEOFFREY: You also don't have to be so bloody polite.

PFENI: The only place I am at home, or even close, is when I'm with you.

GEOFFREY: Pfeni, when I sat next to you at the ballet, it was a dark time in my life. Jordan had just left me, and my friends were becoming increasingly ill.

PFENI: So you thought to yourself, why not try something completely different. Why not get as far away from the hurt and the fear as possible. And there I was seated beside you; pretty, eccentric, and more than just a little bit lonely. You're right. You do have an eye for real talent!

GEOFFREY: Pfeni, don't.

PFENI: Why? Am I being self-indulgent? And maybe even just a little bitchy? Geoffrey, you're the one who said we should get married that very first night. You're the one who said, what beautiful children we'd have just this morning.

GEOFFREY: But we would have beautiful children. Pfeni, my friends need me.

PFENI: I never stopped you from being there for them.
GEOFFREY: I was frightened.
PFENI: And you're not now?

Pause.

GEOFFREY: You really don't understand what it is to have absolutely no idea who you are.
PFENI: What?
GEOFFREY: I thought about this on the bow of the clipper ship. For all your wandering, you're always basically the same—you have your sisters, your point of view, and even in some casual drop-in way, your God. Pfeni, the only time I have a real sense of who I am and where I'm going is when I'm in a darkened theatre and we're making it all up. Starting from scratch. But now I want a real life outside the theatre, too. So maybe I will regret this choice. I know I'll miss you. But I'm an instinctive person, my luv, and speaking to those ladies, it all just clicked. Today this is who I am. I have no other choice. I miss men.
PFENI: It's all right, Geoffrey, I do too. *A car horn is heard.* Jordan.
GEOFFREY: I don't have to go.
PFENI: He's waiting for you.
GEOFFREY: We're in no rush.
PFENI: Please, Geoffrey, just go.
GEOFFREY *kisses her head:* Sugar pie, honey bunch.

Enter SARA *in a tennis outfit.*

SARA: Jordan's outside, Geoffrey. He's looking rather well. He's driving a red Miata convertible. Things must be booming in the flatware design business. I suggested he move into cups and saucers, and we'll all get into business. Pfeni can be in charge of worldwide distribution, Geoffrey, you'll be director of special events, and Jordan can introduce his new line of sheets on Gorgeous's talk show. There, I've solved all of our futures!
GEOFFREY: The thing that no one can appreciate about you, Sara, is you're remarkably sweet. *The horn honks again.* I think I have a crush on all the sisters Rosensweig. *Exits.*
SARA: Maybe he just likes Jewish girls. Do you think I'm too old for a red convertible? Jordan says it works for any age.
PFENI: That's nice.
SARA: What's nice?
PFENI: Whatever Jordan said.
SARA: I thought you never particularly cared for him.
PFENI: He's fine. It's people I don't like very much, Sara.
SARA: Why are you always so hard on yourself? Oh God, it's raining again. I hope Jordan puts his top up.
PFENI: Geoffrey misses men.
SARA: What?
PFENI: Geoffrey just took a drive to the Isle of Dogs and he realized he misses men.
SARA: My poor baby sister.
PFENI: I really don't like people, Sara.
SARA: Pfeni, you're a beautiful and brilliant woman. Next time just don't agree to marry the man you're sitting next to at *Giselle.* See *Swan Lake* instead. C'mon, luvey, have a cup of tea.
PFENI: I need a Brioschi.
SARA: What?
PFENI *sings softly:* "Eat too much, drink too much, take Brioschi, take Brioschi!" Named, I'm sure, for the eminent Dr. Brioschi. One night, when I was around nine, I was watching Rosemary Clooney on "Your Hit Parade" with our mother in Brooklyn. Rosemary was singing some sad love song, and I asked mother what a broken heart felt like. She thought I meant heartburn and told me when I grew up to take Brioschi.
SARA: How do you remember these things?
PFENI: How could I forget? Sara, I don't want to lose Geoffrey and Mommy at the same time. And they don't even make Brioschi anymore!
SARA *embraces* PFENI *as* PFENI *begins to cry:* Yes they do. Shah, Penny, shah!

GORGEOUS *enters, drenched, with an umbrella and a shopping bag. She is wearing only one shoe.*

GORGEOUS: Does it ever stop raining in this country? A person could drown just from walking.
SARA: It was beautiful just a minute ago.
GORGEOUS: That's what's even worse. You never know where you stand. *She gives a Wedgwood gift to* SARA. This is for you, Sara. Thank you very much. I had a lovely stay. I'll just go upstairs and pack my things and be gone in an hour. Mrs. Hershkovitz said I could room with her tonight. Pfeni, if you leave for Bora Bora or Karachi before I come back down, it was great to see you, sweetsie. Your boyfriend was terrific with the ladies this morning. Hold on to him, honey. He's a gem. *Begins going up the stairs.*
SARA: Gorgeous?
GORGEOUS: Yes, Sara.
SARA: What happened to your shoe?
GORGEOUS: What shoe? *Pulls a heel out of her bag.* You call this a shoe? It's a heel. A four-hundred-dollar, imported from Italy, genuine all man-made material goddamned heel!
SARA: Gorgeous, sit down. Have some tea.
GORGEOUS: I'd rather stand. Rabbi Pearlstein says I should finish the tour and come home.
PFENI: You called him?

GORGEOUS: Let me tell you that, thanks to both of you, this has not been an especially enjoyable trip for me. I've spent two days schlepping around London with the sisterhood and two nights having my own sisters tell me everything I do is wrong. Then I decide to treat myself to a little something because I can't bear the stress anymore.

SARA: Gorgeous, I'm—

GORGEOUS: Let me finish. So I go to eight shoe stores on Sloane Street—one nicer than the other. I spread my toes in Tanino Crisci, I slide into the Ferragamos with the bows, and I even clip-clop in royal velvet Manulo Blanchiki frontless, backless mules. And finally, I make my choice—an exquisite pair I know I've seen before on the feet of Fergie or Di or Lady Michael of Kent. They're the softest grosgrain, on the shapeliest heel I've ever seen. I take out my charge card—with tax it comes to two hundred pounds—that's four hundred dollars for a pair of shoes—don't tell me that's insane, I know, but I'm tired and I decide for once I'm worth it.

SARA: Of course!

GORGEOUS: I'm not finished! So I'm walking past Harrods in my new shoes, and for the first time since I arrived here I feel like a person. I debate taking the taxi back to Queen Anne's Gate, and I decide that just because I have shoes like Princess Di, I shouldn't spend like her. So I go into the tube stop at Kensington Station. I get on the escalator, and guess what happens—the shapely goddamned heel gets caught and rips the hell out of my four-hundred-dollar shoe! And all along a blind man with a cup is watching me. And I think to myself, I'm being punished by God because I did not give that man money, even if he is a fake!

SARA: Let me see your shoe, Gorgeous. I have a brilliant cobbler.

GORGEOUS: Sara, even the Sir Isaac Newton of footwear couldn't fix these!

SARA: Let me see it.

GORGEOUS: Sara, there are things in life that you do not have the answers to and one of them is my shoes. *She pulls the remaining pump from her bag.* They are shot, hopeless, kaplooie! *Throws the shoe into the coal bin.*

SARA: Henry will buy you another pair of shoes. I'll call and tell him the brand. *Reaches for the phone.*

GORGEOUS: Put the phone down, Sara.

SARA: Henry will listen to me. What are big sisters for?

GORGEOUS: Henry can't buy me or anyone else in his family a pair of shoes. My dear husband Henry hasn't worked in two years.

SARA: That's ridiculous. He's a lawyer.

GORGEOUS: As a banker there's something going on that you should know about, Sara. It's called a recession.

SARA: But Henry's a Harvard lawyer.

GORGEOUS: And I'm Dr. Gorgeous. Pish-pish.

SARA: I thought he was a partner.

GORGEOUS: Sara, my banker genius sister, the partnership was dissolved.

PFENI: But something will obviously turn up.

GORGEOUS: Sweetsie, they can get someone young and peppy for half the price. I'm going upstairs to pack. I need to rest and go home.

SARA: Maybe I know someone.

GORGEOUS: You don't know anybody! Henry isn't even looking for a job. He's writing mysteries in the basement.

SARA: What?

GORGEOUS: He says he could have been Raymond Chandler or Dashiell Hammett if only he hadn't been brought up in Scarsdale. So now every night at ten he dresses in a trench coat and goes out to prowl around the bars of South End. He comes home at five in the morning and begins typing in the basement until he falls asleep at noon. We pass each other in the hall and he tells me how much it means to him that I am still here. And you know the funniest part of it all? He doesn't even drink. He's out all night having diet Cokes.

SARA: He should see a psychiatrist.

GORGEOUS: I am a psychiatrist.

SARA: You're a lay analyst.

GORGEOUS: Pish-pish. They don't know any more than I do. Stick with Geoffrey, Pfeni. He's handsome, he's rich, and who cares about sex, it goes away after six months anyway. All the ladies fell in love with Geoffrey. Mrs. Hershkovitz thought he was so adorable, she sent over this genuine Wedgwood chachka for him. It cost about as much as my shoes.

SARA: I thought it was for me.

GORGEOUS: Mrs. Hershkovitz sent it over for both of you. Where is Geoffrey?

SARA: He went away for the weekend with Jordan.

PFENI: Geoffrey met Mrs. Hershkovitz and realized he missed men.

GORGEOUS: Sweetsie, don't take it personally.

PFENI: I am so stupid.

GORGEOUS: Sara, tell her none of Rita Rosensweig's daughters are stupid.

SARA: Is stupid. Merv, the world leader in leopardette, isn't here anymore either. I was big and mean and nasty and chased him far away.

GORGEOUS: Why did you do that?

SARA: I don't know, Gorgeous. You just told me there are things in life that I don't have the answers to.

GORGEOUS: Well, did you like him?

SARA: Actually, I had a nice time.
GORGEOUS: Did you tell him that?
SARA: No. I told him he was a very nice man instead.
GORGEOUS AND PFENI *sigh:* Ugh.
GORGEOUS: How did our nice Jewish mother do such a lousy job on us?
SARA: Why is it her fault? She always told me to say thank you, I had a lovely time.
GORGEOUS: Well, it's not Daddy's fault. He called me Gorgeous.
PFENI, *getting up:* Personally, I feel that tea time is over. And we can now move right into wine.
SARA: Such a good baby sister.
GORGEOUS: Very good. And gifted.
PFENI *takes a bottle from the wine rack:* This cab-sauv has a reputation for being rather versatile.
GORGEOUS: Pish-pish.
SARA *giggles:* Double pish-pish.
PFENI *pours them all wine:* What does pish-pish actually mean?
SARA: Gorgeous, have you met my sister the wandering gentile?
GORGEOUS: Pfeni, when Geoffrey told you he missed men, what did you do?
PFENI: I said I missed them, too.

They laugh.

GORGEOUS: Good girl!
SARA: Brilliant girl! Maybe Rita Rosensweig didn't do so badly by us after all.
PFENI *lifts her glass:* To Rita!
GORGEOUS *lifts her glass:* To Rita!
SARA *lifts her glass:* To Rita! And her stunningly brilliant daughters.
GORGEOUS AND PFENI: And her stunningly brilliant daughters. *They sip the wine.* Mmmmm, versatile.
GORGEOUS *sits:* Drinking goes directly to my feet. Does it go to your feet, Pfeni?
PFENI: No, my head. Directly to my head. What about you, Sara?
SARA *sits:* In my hair. I feel it in my hair.
GORGEOUS: I'm exhausted.
PFENI: Me too. Very tired.

They both lie down on SARA. SARA *strokes their foreheads.*

GORGEOUS: Sara, didn't Mama always say you were a shtarker? Maybe you should take care of us now.
PFENI: That would be very nice.
GORGEOUS: Pfeni, do you know what a shtarker is?
PFENI: A person who takes charge. A general in the Cossack army.
SARA: That must be why I'm so popular!

GORGEOUS *kisses* SARA*'s hand.*

GORGEOUS: You have nice hands, Sara. But you should use hot oil treatments. It would loosen your cuticles. What do you think, Pfeni?
PFENI: I think Sara was a starker to that nice Merlin.
SARA: Shtarker. But I really hardly even know him.
GORGEOUS: You could get to know him. Call him.
GORGEOUS AND PFENI, *chanting*: Call him! Call him! Call him!
SARA: Please. Girls, girls, girls. *She holds both their faces in her hands.* My two little sisters! Gorgeous and also Gorgeous. We are—
ALL THREE: The sisters Gorgeous! *They laugh.*
GORGEOUS: You know what I wish with all my heart?
SARA: What?
PFENI: What?
GORGEOUS: I wish that on one of our birthdays, when all the children and men have gone upstairs to sleep . . .
SARA: What men?
GORGEOUS: And we finally sit together, just us three sisters . . .
PFENI: Around the samovar.
GORGEOUS: And we talk about life!
PFENI: And art.
SARA: Pfeni!
GORGEOUS: Thank you, Sara. *Kisses* SARA*'s hand.* That each of us can say at some point that we had a moment of pure, unadulterated happiness! Do you think that's possible, Sara?
SARA: Brief. But a moment or two.
PFENI: I like that.
GORGEOUS: Me too.

Pause.

SARA: Gorgeous, there's something I've been meaning to share with you.
GORGEOUS: What?
SARA: Your neck is very dry.
GORGEOUS: No.
SARA: Don't you think her neck is dry, Pfeni?
PFENI: Let me see. *Touches her.* Oh, yes, very dry!
SARA: Don't you think she should use that special rejuvenation treatment? The deluxe pish-pish one!
PFENI: Oh, that pish-pish rejuvenation treatment! Yes, I think so. *They both suddenly jump on* GORGEOUS *and begin tickling her.* Rabbi Pearlstein says more collagen shots!
GORGEOUS: No! No! Pfeni, stop and you can have my remaining shoe! *Jumps up from the sofa.*
PFENI: I want that shoe. Gorgeous, gimme that shoe! Gorgeous! *Chases* GORGEOUS *upstairs. They are laughing and giggling like children.* Gorgeous!

SARA *remains on the couch, listening and smiling.*

Scene 3

Early Sunday morning. The Clefs singing "And a Nightingale Sang." TOM *and* TESS *come downstairs. They hug, and* TOM *leaves with his bag.* TESS *begins listening to the music. She speaks into her tape recorder.*

TESS: What exactly did the nightingale sing in Berkeley Square? And why not in Hyde Park or Hampstead Heath?

GORGEOUS *enters in an aerobic ensemble.*

GORGEOUS: Hello! Hello! I just finished my morning exercises and I thought I heard activity. Tessie, why don't you listen to more contemporary music? I'll loan you my exercise tapes.

TESS: I'm finishing my summer project. Do you mind if I interview you?

GORGEOUS: Of course.

TESS: Your name is?

GORGEOUS: My name is Dr. Gorgeous Teitelbaum. I am a housewife, mother, and radio personality.

TESS: Tell me about my mother as a girl.

GORGEOUS: Your mother never had a sense of style. Her dolls were always half-naked and mine were perfectly groomed. In fact, I was the one who taught your mother how to pull herself together. I gave her my prescription to dress for success.

TESS: What was that?

GORGEOUS: Accessories!

TESS: What?

GORGEOUS: Accessories are the key to fashion. Tessie, honey, you can wear real junk from Filene's basement, but with the right earrings, bracelet, and scarf you will always be very "too-too." You go into my closet today, pull together an ensemble, practice around the house, and let me check it. That's how I taught my own daughters, and they thanked me for it.

Enter PFENI *carrying her shopping bags and computer.*

TESS: Are you leaving now, Aunt Pfeni?

PFENI: Are you, Niece Tess? Aren't you supposed to be on the road to Vilnius?

TESS: Well, I went with Tom to the rally last night, and everyone was holding hands and singing Lithuanian folk songs. But the more they smiled at me and held my hand, the more apart from it all I became. Aunt Pfeni, are we people who will always be watching and never belong?

PFENI: How did you get to be so young and intelligent?

GORGEOUS: Where are you going now, sweetsie?

PFENI: Back to work. I'm going to a crock pot in Tajikistan.

GORGEOUS: Why did you choose that? I can't even spell it.

PFENI: Well, Gorgeous, if you only write "Bombay by Night" and you make sure to fall in love with men who can never really love you back, one morning you wake up at forty in your big sister's house, and where you should be seems sort of clear. *Kisses* GORGEOUS. Good-bye, Gorgeous.

GORGEOUS: Sunblock, sweetsie.

TESS: But Aunt Pfeni, what if I need you?

PFENI: The best life advice I've ever gotten was from your mother, and the best moisturizer was from your aunt. So the way I see it, they can cover the entire temporal and spiritual world. *She embraces* TESS. Tessie, I'll see you soon.

TESS: When is that?

PFENI: Soon is soon.

The doorbell rings.

GORGEOUS: There's always activity in this house.

PFENI *opens the door.*

MERV *enters, carrying a large box:* Good morning, ladies.

GORGEOUS: Merlin!

MERV: This is such a family of early risers! I'm sorry I can't stay. I have a car waiting outside.

GORGEOUS: Sit down, Merlin, relax, the car knows how to wait. Let Tessie bring you some of Sara's fabulous homemade oatmeal.

MERV: To tell you the truth, I only came because I got a message from Sara that I left my shirt. She said she'd put it by the door.

PFENI: Sara called you!

GORGEOUS: Tessie, get the oatmeal! I know there's something in that box Merlin is carrying and it's bigger than a bread box and furrier than a bear, and he's just waiting for us all to leave so that he can give it to Sara. *Calls.* Sara!!

MERV: It's for you, actually.

GORGEOUS: For me!

MERV *looks at the note:* It says, "For Gorgeous, with love." It was outside on the steps when I arrived.

GORGEOUS: It's from Mrs. Hershkovitz and the sisterhood. "Dearest Gorgeous, no one works harder than you. Isn't it time you had the real thing? Thank you for a job beautifully done." *Opens the box and immediately clutches her heart.* Oh my God! Oh my God! Hold me, Tessie.

PFENI: Tessie, hold your Aunt Gorgeous.

GORGEOUS *pulls a Chanel suit out of the box.*

GORGEOUS: It's the real thing! A genuine Chanel suit! And a purse! and earrings! And even the shoes! They got me the shoes! *She immediately pulls off her aerobic shoes and puts on the Chanels.* The classic pump! 7AA. How did they know 7AA? They're so comfortable! Am I floating! *Walks around the room.* I swear I'm floating. Tessie, pass me the skirt. Merlin, you're a furrier, drape me the scarf. *Puts on the skirt and the jacket over her aerobic gear.*

MERV: This is quality goods! I'm glad they didn't send the ones they sell on the street.

GORGEOUS: I haven't been so happy since the day I found out I made cheerleader and I knew that Sara didn't. *Poses in the full ensemble.* Do I look like Audrey Hepburn? I swear I feel just like Audrey Hepburn.

MERV: You look Gorgeous!

PFENI: Beyond Gorgeous!

GORGEOUS: I need the earrings. *Puts them on.* I am going right now to Claridge's to show Mrs. Hershkovitz and the ladies.

TESS: Right now?

GORGEOUS: Yes, and then I'm going directly to the House of Chanel to return every last piece of this.

PFENI: What?

GORGEOUS: Sweetsie, somebody's got to pay for tuition this fall, and better Chanel than Henry or me. Tessie, put my sneakers and purse in that box. I'll let your Aunt Pfeni drop me off and I'll jog home just for funsy. I wish they sent blue instead of pink, because blue is not my color. Pfeni, we'd better hurry or I'll lose my will power. It's very hard for me to postpone gratification. If I have something in my hand for more than two minutes, I want to keep it or at least eat it. Merlin, I hope you've moved in by the time I get back. *Exits with the box.*

PFENI *calls upstairs:* Sara! Sara! I'm leaving.

TESS: I wish Aunt Gorgeous could keep just the earrings.

PFENI: Sara!!

TESS: Mother!! SARA *comes down.* Mother, look who's here!

SARA: Hello Merv.

MERV: Hello Sara.

PFENI: Tally-ho, Sir Murf! Good-bye, my big sister.

SARA *touches* PFENI'S *face:* I'll miss you.

PFENI: I'm a wandering Jew, Sara. I'll see you soon. *Exits.*

MERV: Sara, can I have my shirt? I've got a lunch date with the rabbi of Dublin.

SARA: Mervyn, you came all the way to Queen Anne's Gate. Please sit a minute.

TESS: Sit down, Merv. I'll get your shirt. *Winks at her mother.*

SARA: Tessie, you've caught your aunt's astigmatism. TESS *runs upstairs.* Would you like a drink?

MERV: Sara, it's eight o'clock in the morning.

SARA: How 'bout a little cassoulet?

MERV: What's on your mind, Sara?

SARA: Do you know how many cabbage rose bouquets are on this wallpaper? Forty-six.

MERV: You had me come all the way to Queen Anne's Gate to tell me this. Sara, I'm a grown man with a plane to catch and you're a very mature and responsible woman. What is it that you want?

SARA: I don't like that "very mature."

MERV: All right. You're a "stunning grownup."

SARA: Merv, I spent yesterday afternoon from teatime until sundown on this sofa counting the roses on the wall and waiting for you to call. And I have to tell you I'm furious with you for putting me in that position.

MERV: But how would I have known you wanted me to call?

SARA: From my very consistently warm and welcoming behavior. Merv, there's nothing I look forward to more on Saturday nights than getting into bed early with a mystery novel and licking all the chocolate from my favorite wheat-meal biscuits. But last night, after my sisters went to bed, the mysteries and the wheat meals were not their usual satisfying company. Merv, I called you because I can't seem to come up with a good enough answer for what's wrong with you. I like you.

MERV: Why?

SARA: Why?

MERV: It's a simple question.

SARA: You're a man who says he wants a grownup.

MERV: You call licking wheat-meal biscuits in bed grownup?

SARA: Maybe sometime you'd like to try it.

MERV: Sara, I think you need someone who's maybe a little more . . .

SARA: What?

MERV: Well, maybe a little less . . .

SARA: Merv, I don't think about us getting married, and I don't even need to get our children together, but sometime I'd really like to hear more about the concert of Europe.

MERV: From a post-industrial Zionist perspective?

SARA: If you're willing to debate it.

MERV: With you that could be difficult.

SARA: Grownups can be difficult.

MERV: But difficult can be engaging. Even surprising. I meant to tell you I had dinner last night at that tourist trap Simpson's in the Strand, and the bubble and squeak was rather good, actually.

SARA: Actually?

MERV: There are real possibilities in life, Sara, even for leftover meat and cabbage. And speaking of cabbage. The Rabbi of Dublin!

SARA: Go, go, go. *Gives him the Shiva statue.* Here, take this on your pilgrimage. It's the god Shiva.

MERV: The destroyer! I'm getting on a plane.

SARA: It'll ward off evil and bring you hope and rebirth.

MERV: You want me to worship pagan imagery?

SARA: I want to stir up your life a little, Mervyn Kantlowitz. Jesus Christ, why did your name have to be Mervyn? *She starts to hit him.* And you're a furrier!

MERV: Good-bye, Sara. *Kisses her.*

SARA: Let me know how you are.

MERV: You still have my shirt.

SARA: Give my regards to the Rabbi.

MERV: Today the rabbi of Dublin. Tomorrow the cantor of Cork. *Exits.*

TESS *enters in* GORGEOUS'*s original pink ensemble with full accessories and heels. She can hardly walk.*

SARA: What are you wearing?

TESS: Aunt Gorgeous says you can't accessorize enough. She said I should practice around the house. I think it's very "too-too."

SARA: I think it's maybe too "too-too" for the Lithuanian resistance.

TESS: I told Tom to go without me.

SARA: Thank you, honey.

TESS: I didn't make this decision for you. I made it for me. You have to have your own life.

SARA: Really, I can't have yours?

TESS: You wouldn't want mine. I don't even know what mine is. Mother, if I've never really been Jewish, and I'm not actually American anymore, and I'm not English or European, then who am I?

SARA: Tessie honey, as a child I was told that when your grandmother Rita was a girl, she was so smart, so competent, so beautiful and brave, that on the day the Cossacks came they were so impressed with her, they ran away.

TESS: I don't understand.

SARA: Everyone always told me, "Sadie, that Tessie of yours is just like Rita." So if Rita could make the Cossacks run away, you are smart enough, and brave enough, and certainly beautiful enough to find your place in the world.

TESS: Thank you, Mommy.

SARA: There are real possibilities in life, Tessie.

TESS: Mother!

SARA: Yes, honey.

TESS: If she was so beautiful, why did they run away?

SARA: I never understood that either. *Sits down on a chair.*

TESS: Can I ask you a few questions for this paper now? It's due tomorrow. *Turns on her tape recorder and kneels beside her mother.* Your name is? I know it's dumb, but we have to ask these things.

Pause.

SARA: My name is Sara Rosensweig. I am the daughter of Rita and Maury Rosensweig. I was born in Brooklyn, New York, August 23, 1937.

TESS: And when did you first sing?

SARA: I made my debut at La Scala at fourteen.

TESS: Mother!

SARA: I first sang at the Hanukah Festival at East Midwood Jewish Center. I played a candle.

TESS: And why did you become a Cliffe Clef?

SARA: Your great-grandfather thought I could be a singer.

TESS: Would you sing something now?

SARA: Honey, it's so early.

TESS: Please sing something. *Begins to sing:*

Shine on, shine on, harvest moon
Up in the sky.

SARA:

I ain't had no loving since January, February, June or July.

TESS: Do it, mother!

SARA *sings:*

Snow time ain't no time to stay outdoors and spoon.

TESS AND SARA *sing:*

So shine on, shine on, harvest moon.

SARA *sings, touching her daughter's face:*

For me and my gal.

END

Drama Theory and Criticism

George Bernard Shaw
The Technical Novelty in Ibsen's Plays

It is a striking and melancholy example of the preoccupation of critics with phrases and formulas to which they have given life by taking them into the tissue of their own living minds, and which therefore seem and feel vital and important to them whilst they are to everybody else the deadest and dreariest rubbish (this is the great secret of academic dryasdust), that to this day they remain blind to a new technical factor in the art of popular stage-play making which every considerable playwright has been thrusting under their noses night after night for a whole generation. This technical factor in the play is the discussion. Formerly you had in what was called a well made play an exposition in the first act, a situation in the second, and unravelling in the third. Now you have exposition, situation, and discussion; and the discussion is the test of the playwright. The critics protest in vain. They declare that discussions are not dramatic, and that art should not be didactic. Neither the playwrights nor the public take the smallest notice of them. The discussion conquered Europe in Ibsen's Doll's House; and now the serious playwright recognizes in the discussion not only the main test of his highest powers, but also the real centre of his play's interest. Sometimes he even takes every possible step to assure the public beforehand that his play will be fitted with that newest improvement.

This was inevitable if the drama was ever again to be raised above the childish demand for fables without morals. Children have a settled arbitrary morality: therefore to them moralizing is nothing but an intolerable platitudinizing. The morality of the grown-up is also very largely a settled morality, either purely conventional and of no ethical significance, like the rule of the road or the rule that when you ask for a yard of ribbon the shopkeeper shall give you thirty-six inches and not interpret the word yard as he pleases, or else too obvious in its ethics to leave any room for discussion: for instance, that if the boots keeps you waiting too long for your shaving water you must not plunge your razor into his throat in your irritation, no matter how great an effort of self-control your forbearance may cost you.

Now when a play is only a story of how a villain tries to separate an honest young pair of betrothed lovers; to gain the hand of the woman by calumny; and to ruin the man by forgery, murder, false witness, and other commonplaces of the Newgate Calendar, the introduction of a discussion would clearly be ridiculous. There is nothing for sane people to discuss; and any attempt to Chadbandize on the wickedness of such crimes is at once resented as, in Milton's phrase, "moral babble."

But this sort of drama is soon exhausted by people who go often to the theatre. In twenty visits one can see every possible change rung on all the available plots and incidents out of which plays of this kind can be manufactured. The illusion of reality is soon lost: in fact it may be doubted whether any adult ever entertains it: it is only to very young children that the fairy queen is anything but an actress. But at the age when we cease to mistake the figures on the stage for *dramatis personae,* and know that they are actors and actresses, the charm of the performer begins to assert itself; and the child who would have been cruelly hurt by being told that the Fairy Queen was only Miss Smith dressed up to look like one, becomes the man who goes to the theatre expressly to see Miss Smith, and is fascinated by her skill or beauty to the point of delighting in plays which would be unendurable to him without her. Thus we get plays "written round" popular performers, and popular performers who give value to otherwise useless plays by investing them with their own attractiveness. But all these enterprises are, commercially speaking, desperately precarious. To begin with, the supply of performers whose attraction is so far independent of the play that their inclusion in the cast sometimes makes the difference between success and failure is too small to enable all our theatres, or even many of them, to depend on their actors rather than on their plays. And to finish with, no actor can make bricks entirely without straw. From Grimaldi to Sothern, Jefferson, and Henry Irving (not to mention living actors) we have had players succeeding once in a lifetime in grafting on to a play which would have perished without them some figure imagined wholly by themselves; but none of them has been able to repeat the feat, nor to save many of the plays in which he has appeared from failure. In the long run nothing can retain the interest of the playgoer after the theatre has lost its illusion for his childhood, and its glamor for his adolescence, but a constant supply of interesting plays; and this is specially true in London, where the expense and trouble of theatregoing have been raised to a point at which it is surprising that sensible people of middle age go to the theatre at all. As a matter of fact, they mostly stay at home.

Now an interesting play cannot in the nature of things mean anything but a play in which problems of conduct and character of personal importance to the audience are raised and suggestively discussed. People have a thrifty sense of taking away something from such plays: they not only have had something for their money, but they retain that something as a permanent possession. Consequently none of the commonplaces of the box office hold good of such plays. In vain does the experienced acting manager declare that people want to be amused and not preached at in the theatre; that they will not stand long speeches; that a play must not contain more than 18,000 words; that it must not begin before nine nor last beyond eleven; that there must be no politics and no religion in it; that breach of these golden rules will drive people to the variety theatres; that there must be a woman of bad character, played by a very attractive actress, in the piece; and so on and so forth. All these counsels are valid for plays in which there is nothing to discuss. They may be disregarded by the playwright who is a moralist and a debater as well as a dramatist. From him, within the inevitable limits set by the clock and by the physical endurance of the human frame, people will stand anything as soon as they are matured enough and cultivated enough to be susceptible to the appeal of his particular form of art. The difficulty at present is that mature and cultivated people do not go to the theatre, just as they do not read penny novelets; and when an attempt is made to cater for them they do not respond to it in time, partly because they have not the habit of playgoing, and partly because it takes too long for them to find out that the new theatre is not like all the other theatres. But when they do at last find their way there, the attraction is not the firing of blank cartridges at one another by actors, nor the pretence of falling down dead that ends the stage combat, nor the simulation of erotic thrills by a pair of stage lovers, nor any of the other tomfooleries called action, but the exhibition and discussion of the character and conduct of stage figures who are made to appear real by the art of the playwright and the performers.

This, then, is the extension of the old dramatic form effected by Ibsen. Up to a certain point in the last act, A Doll's House is a play that might be turned into a very ordinary French drama by the excision of a few lines, and the substitution of a sentimental happy ending for the famous last scene: indeed the very first thing the theatrical wiseacres did with it was to effect exactly this transformation, with the result that the play thus pithed had no success and attracted no notice worth mentioning. But at just that point in the last act, the heroine very unexpectedly (by the wiseacres) stops her emotional acting and says: "We must sit down and discuss all this that has been happening between us." And it was by this new technical feature: this addition of a new movement, as musicians would say, to the dramatic form, that A Doll's House conquered Europe and founded a new school of dramatic art.

Since that time the discussion has expanded far beyond the limits of the last ten minutes of an otherwise "well made" play. The disadvantage of putting the discussion at the end was not only that it came when the audience was fatigued, but that it was necessary to see the play over again, so as to follow the earlier acts in the light of the final discussion, before it became fully intelligible. The practical utility of this book is due to the fact that unless the spectator at an Ibsen play has read the pages referring to it beforehand, it is hardly possible for him to get its bearings at a first hearing if he approaches it, as most spectators still do, with conventional idealist prepossessions. Accordingly, we now have plays, including some of my own, which begin with discussion and end with action, and others in which the discussion interpenetrates the action from beginning to end. When Ibsen invaded England discussion had vanished from the stage; and women could not write plays. Within twenty years women were writing better plays than men; and these plays were passionate arguments from beginning to end. The action of such plays consists of a case to be argued. If the case is uninteresting or stale or badly conducted or obviously trumped up, the play is a bad one. If it is important and novel and convincing, or at least disturbing, the play is a good one. But anyhow the play in which there is no argument and no case no longer counts as serious drama. It may still please the child in us as Punch and Judy does; but nobody nowadays pretends to regard the well made play as anything more than a commercial product which is not in question when modern schools of serious drama are under discussion. Indeed within ten years of the production of A Doll's House in London, audiences had become so derisive of the more obvious and hackneyed features of the methods of Sardou that it became dangerous to resort to them; and playwrights who persisted in "constructing" plays in the old French manner lost ground not for lack of ideas, but because their technique was unbearably out of fashion.

In the new plays, the drama arises through a conflict of unsettled ideals rather than through vulgar attachments, rapacities, generosities, resentments, ambitions, misunderstandings, oddities and so forth as to which no moral question is raised. The conflict is not between clear right and wrong: the villain is as conscientious as the hero, if not more so: in fact, the question which makes the play interesting (when it *is* interesting) is which is the villain and which the hero. Or, to put it another way, there are no villains and no heroes. This strikes the critics mainly as a departure from dramatic art; but it is really the inevitable return to nature which ends all the merely technical fashions. Now the natural is mainly the everyday; and its climaxes must be, if not everyday, at least everylife, if they are to have any importance for the spectator. Crimes, fights, big legacies, fires, shipwrecks, battles, and thunderbolts are mistakes in a play, even when they can be effectively simulated. No doubt they may acquire dramatic interest by putting a character through the test of an emergency; but the test is likely to be too obviously theatrical, because, as the playwright cannot in the nature of things have much experience of such catastrophes, he is forced to substitute a set of conventions or conjectures for the feelings they really produce.

In short, pure accidents are not dramatic: they are only anecdotic. They may be sensational, impressive, provocative, ruinous, curious, or a dozen other things; but they have no specifically dramatic interest. There is no drama in being knocked down or run over. The catastrophe in Hamlet would not be in the least dramatic had Polonius fallen downstairs and broken his neck, Claudius succumbed to delirium tremens, Hamlet forgotten to breathe in the intensity of his philosophic speculation, Ophelia died of Danish measles, Laertes been shot by the palace sentry, and Rosencrantz and Guildenstern drowned in the North Sea. Even as it is, the Queen, who poisons herself by accident, has an air of being polished off to get her out of the way: her death is the one dramatic failure of the piece. Bushels of good paper have been inked in vain by writers who imagined they could produce a tragedy by killing everyone in the last act accidentally. As a matter of fact no accident, however sanguinary, can produce a moment of real drama, though a difference of opinion between husband and wife as to living in town or country might be the beginning of an appalling tragedy or a capital comedy.

It may be said that everything is an accident: that Othello's character is an accident, Iago's character another accident, and the fact that they happened to come together in the Venetian service an even more accidental accident. Also that Torvald Helmer might just as likely have married Mrs. Nickleby as Nora. Granting this trifling for what it is worth, the fact remains that marriage is no more an accident than birth or death: that is, it is expected to happen to everybody. And if every man has a good deal of Torvald Helmer in him, and every woman a good deal of Nora, neither their characters nor their meeting and marrying are accidents. Othello, though entertaining, pitiful, and resonant with the thrills a master of language can produce by mere artistic sonority is certainly much more accidental than A Doll's House; but it is correspondingly less important and interesting to us. It has been kept alive, not by its manufactured misunderstandings and stolen handkerchiefs and the like, nor even by its orchestral verse, but by its exhibition and discussion of human nature, marriage, and jealousy; and it would be a prodigiously better play if it were a serious discussion of the highly interesting problem of how a simple Moorish soldier would get on with a "supersubtle" Venetian lady of fashion if he married her. As it is, the play turns on a mistake; and though a mistake can produce a murder, which is the vulgar substitute for a tragedy, it cannot produce a real tragedy in the modern sense. Reflective people are not more interested in the Chamber of Horrors than in their own homes, nor in murderers, victims, and villains than in themselves; and the moment a man has acquired sufficient reflective power to cease gaping at waxworks, he is on his way to losing interest in Othello, Desdemona, and Iago exactly to the extent to which they become interesting to the police. Cassio's weakness for drink comes much nearer home to most of us than Othello's strangling and throat cutting, or Iago's theatrical confidence trick. The proof is that Shakespear's professional colleagues, who exploited all his sensational devices, and piled up torture on murder and incest on adultery until they had far out-Heroded Herod, are now unmemorable and unplayable. Shakespear survives because he coolly treated the sensational horrors of his borrowed plots as inorganic theatrical accessories, using them simply as pretexts for dramatizing human character as it exists in the normal world. In enjoying and discussing his plays we unconsciously discount the combats and murders: commentators are never so astray (and consequently so ingenious) as when they take Hamlet seriously as a madman, Macbeth as a homicidal Highlander, and impish humorists like Richard and Iago as lurid villains of the Renascence. The plays in which these figures appear could be changed into comedies without altering a hair of their beards. Shakespear, had anyone been intelligent enough to tax him with this, would perhaps have said that most crimes are accidents that happen to people exactly like ourselves, and that Macbeth, under propitious circumstances, would have made an exemplary rector of Stratford, a real criminal being a defective monster, a human accident, useful on the stage only for minor parts such as Don Johns, second murderers, and the like. Anyhow, the fact remains that Shakespear survives by what he has in common with Ibsen, and not by what he has in common with Webster and the rest. Hamlet's surprise at finding that he "lacks gall" to behave in the idealistically conventional manner, and that no extremity of rhetoric about the duty of revenging "a dear father slain" and exterminating the "bloody bawdy villain" who murdered him seems to make any difference in their domestic relations in the palace in Elsinore, still keeps us talking about him and going to the theatre to listen to him, whilst the older Hamlets, who never had any Ibsenist hesitations, and shammed madness, and entangled the courtiers in the arras and burnt them, and stuck hard to the theatrical school of the fat boy in Pickwick ("I wants to make your flesh creep"), are as dead as John Shakespear's mutton.

We have progressed so rapidly on this point under the impulse given to the drama by Ibsen that it seems strange now to contrast him favorably with Shakespear on the ground that he avoided the old catastrophes which left the stage strewn with the dead at the end of an Elizabethan tragedy. For perhaps the most plausible reproach levelled at Ibsen by modern critics of his own school is just that survival of the old school in him which makes the death rate so high in his last acts. Do Oswald Alving, Hedvig Ekdal, Rosmer and Rebecca, Hedda Gabler, Solness, Eyolf, Borkman, Rubeck and Irene die dramatically natural deaths, or are they slaughtered in the classic and Shakespearean manner, partly because the audience expects blood for its money, partly because it is difficult to make people attend seriously to anything except by startling them with some violent calamity? It is so easy to make out a case for either view that I shall not argue the point. The post-Ibsen playwrights apparently think that Ibsen's homicides and suicides were forced. In Tchekov's Cherry Orchard, for example, where the sentimental ideals of our amiable, cultured, Schumann playing propertied class are reduced to dust and ashes by a hand not less deadly than Ibsen's because it is so much more caressing, nothing more violent happens than that the family cannot afford to keep up its old house. In Granville-Barker's plays, the campaign against our society is carried on with all Ibsen's implacability; but the one suicide (in Waste) is unhistorical; for neither Parnell nor Dilke, who were the actual cases in point of the waste which was the subject of the play, killed himself. I myself have been reproached because the characters in my plays "talk but do nothing," meaning that they do not commit felonies. As a matter of fact we have come to see that it is no true *dénouement* to cut the Gordian knot as Alexander did with a stroke of the sword. If people's souls are tied up by law and public opinion it is much more tragic to leave them to wither in these bonds than to end their misery and relieve the salutary compunction of the audience by outbreaks of violence. Judge Brack was, on the whole, right when he said that people dont do such things. If they did, the idealists would be brought to their senses very quickly indeed.

But in Ibsen's plays the catastrophe, even when it seems forced, and when the ending of the play would be more tragic without it, is never an accident; and the play never exists for its sake. His nearest to an accident is the death of little Eyolf, who falls off a pier and is drowned. But this instance only reminds us that there is one good dramatic use for an accident: it can awaken people. When England wept over the deaths of little Nell and Paul Dombey, the strong soul of Ruskin was moved to scorn: to novelists who were at a loss to make their books sell he offered the formula: When at a loss, kill a child. But Ibsen did not kill little Eyolf to manufacture pathos. The surest way to achieve a thoroughly bad performance of Little Eyolf is to conceive it as a sentimental tale of a drowned darling. Its drama lies in the awakening of Allmers and his wife to the despicable quality and detestable rancors of the life they have been idealizing as blissful and poetic. They are so sunk in their dream that the awakening can be effected only by a violent shock. And that is just the one dramatically useful thing an accident can do. It can shock. Hence the accident that befalls Eyolf.

As to the deaths in Ibsen's last acts, they are a sweeping up of the remains of dramatically finished people. Solness's fall from the tower is as obviously symbolic as Phaeton's fall from the chariot of the sun. Ibsen's dead bodies are those of the exhausted or destroyed: he does not kill Hilda, for instance, as Shakespear killed Juliet. He is ruthless enough with Hedvig and Eyolf because he wants to use their deaths to expose their parents; but if he had written Hamlet nobody would have been killed in the last act except perhaps Horatio, whose correct nullity might have provoked Fortinbras to let some of the moral sawdust out of him with his sword. For Shakespearean deaths in Ibsen you must go back to Lady Inger and the plays of his nonage, with which this book is not concerned.

The drama was born of old from the union of two desires: the desire to have a dance and the desire to hear a story. The dance became a rant: the story became a situation. When Ibsen began to make plays, the art of the dramatist had shrunk into the art of contriving a situation. And it was held that the stranger the situation, the better the play. Ibsen saw that, on the contrary, the more familiar the situation, the more interesting the play. Shakespear had put ourselves on the stage but not our situations. Our uncles seldom murder our fathers, and cannot legally marry our mothers; we do not meet witches; our kings are not as a rule stabbed and succeeded by their stabbers; and when we raise money by bills we do not promise to pay pounds of our flesh. Ibsen supplies the want left by Shakespear. He gives us not only ourselves, but ourselves in our own situations. The things that happen to his stage figures are things that happen to us. One consequence is that his plays are much more important to us than Shakespear's. Another is that they are capable both of hurting us cruelly and of filling us with excited hopes of escape from idealistic tyrannies, and with visions of intenser life in the future.

Changes in technique follow inevitably from these changes in the subject matter of the play. When a dramatic poet can give you hopes and visions, such old maxims as that stage-craft is the art of preparation become boyish, and may be left to those unfortunate playwrights who, being unable to make anything really interesting happen on the stage, have to acquire the art of continually persuading the audience that it is going to happen presently. When he can stab people to the heart by shewing them the meanness or cruelty of something they did yesterday and intend to do tomorrow, all the old tricks to catch and hold their attention become the silliest of superfluities. The play called The Murder of Gonzago, which Hamlet makes the players act before his uncle, is artlessly constructed; but it produces a greater effect on Claudius than the Œdipus of Sophocles, because it is about himself. The writer who practises the art of Ibsen therefore discards all the old tricks of preparation, catastrophe, *dénouement,* and so forth without thinking about it, just as a modern rifleman never dreams of providing himself with powder horns, percussion caps, and wads: indeed he does not know the use of them. Ibsen substituted a terrible art of sharpshooting at the audience, trapping them, fencing with them, aiming always at the sorest spot in their consciences. Never mislead an audience, was an old rule. But the new school will trick the spectator into forming a meanly false judgment, and then convict him of it in the next act, often to his grievous mortification. When you despise something you ought to take off your hat to, or admire and imitate something you ought to loathe, you cannot resist the dramatist who knows how to touch these morbid spots in you and make you see that they are morbid. The dramatist knows that as long as he is teaching and saving his audience, he is as sure of their strained attention as a dentist is, or the Angel of the Annunciation. And though he may use all the magic of art to make you forget the pain he causes you or to enhance the joy of the hope and courage he awakens, he is never occupied in the old work of manufacturing interest and expectation with materials that have neither novelty, significance, nor relevance to the experience or prospects of the spectators.

Hence a cry has arisen that the post-Ibsen play is not a play, and that its technique, not being the technique described by Aristotle, is not a technique at all. I will not enlarge on this: the fun poked at my friend Mr. A. B. Walkley in the prologue of Fanny's First Play need not be repeated here. But I may remind him that the new technique is new only on the modern stage. It has been used by preachers and orators ever since speech was invented. It is the technique of playing upon the human conscience; and it has been practised by the playwright whenever the playwright has been capable of it. Rhetoric, irony, argument, paradox, epigram, parable, the rearrangement of haphazard facts into orderly and intelligent situations: these are both the oldest and the newest arts of the drama; and your plot construction and art of preparation are only the tricks of theatrical talent and the shifts of moral sterility, not the weapons of dramatic genius. In the theatre of Ibsen we are not flattered spectators killing an idle hour with an ingenious and amusing entertainment: we are "guilty creatures sitting at a play"; and the technique of pastime is no more applicable than at a murder trial.

The technical novelties of the Ibsen and post-Ibsen plays are, then: first, the introduction of the discussion and its development until it so overspreads and interpenetrates the action that it finally assimilates it, making play and discussion practically identical; and, second, as a consequence of making the spectators themselves the persons of the drama, and the incidents of their own lives its incidents, the disuse of the old stage tricks by which audiences had to be induced to take an interest in unreal people and improbable circumstances, and the substitution of a forensic technique of recrimination, disillusion, and penetration through ideals to the truth, with a free use of all the rhetorical and lyrical arts of the orator, the preacher, the pleader, and the rhapsodist.

August Strindberg

Author's Preface to *Miss Julie*

The theatre has long seemed to me to be, like art in general, a *Biblia pauperum*, a Bible in pictures for those who can't read what is written or printed, and the playwright a lay preacher hawking the ideas of the day in popular form, so popular that the middle classes, the theatre's primary audience, can understand the basic questions without too much effort. And so the theatre has always been a public school for the young, the half-educated, and women, who still possess that primitive capacity for deceiving themselves or letting themselves be deceived, that is to say, are receptive to the illusion, to the playwright's power of suggestion. It seems to me, therefore, in our time, when rudimentary, undeveloped, and fanciful ways of thinking seem to be evolving toward reflection, investigation, and analysis, that the theatre, like religion, is dying out, a form for whose enjoyment we lack the necessary preconditions. Supporting this assertion is the serious theatre crisis now prevailing throughout Europe, especially in those bastions of culture that produced the greatest thinkers of the age, England and Germany, where the art of drama, like most of the other fine arts, is dead.

In other countries people have believed it possible to create a new drama by filling old forms with new contents. For a number of reasons, however, this has failed: in part because there has not been sufficient time to popularize the new ideas, so that the public does not understand the basic questions; in part because partisan politics has stirred up emotions, making dispassionate enjoyment impossible—how can people be objective when their innermost beliefs are offended or when they are subjected in the confines of a theatre to the public pressure of an applauding or hissing audience?; and in part because new forms have not been found for the new contents, so that the new wine has burst the old bottles.

In the following play, instead of trying to do anything new—which is impossible—I have simply modernized the form in accordance with demands I think contemporary audiences make upon this art. Toward this end, I have chosen, or let myself be moved by, a theme that can be said to lie outside partisan politics since the problem of social climbing or falling, or higher or lower, better or worse, man or woman, are, have been, and will be of lasting interest. When I took this theme from a true story I heard told some years ago, which made a strong impression on me, I found it appropriate for tragedy, for it still seems tragic to see someone favored by fortune go under, much more to see a family die out. Perhaps the time will come when we will be so advanced, so enlightened, that we can witness with indifference what now seem the coarse, cynical, heartless dramas life has to offer, when we have closed down those lower, unreliable mechanisms of thought called feelings, because better developed organs of judgment will have found them superfluous and harmful. The fact that the heroine arouses compassion is because we are too weak to resist the fear that the same fate could overtake us. A hypersensitive spectator may not be satisfied with compassion alone, while a man with faith in the future may demand some positive proposals to remedy the evil, in other words, a program of some kind. But for one thing there is no absolute evil. The fall of one family can mean a chance for another family to rise, and the alternation of rising and falling fortunes is one of life's greatest delights since happiness lies only in comparison. And to the man who wants a program to remedy the unpleasant fact that the bird of prey eats the dove and the louse eats the bird of prey I ask: why should it be remedied? Life is not so idiotically mathematical that only the great eat the small; it is just as common for a bee to kill a lion or at least drive it mad.

If my tragedy depresses many people, it is their own fault. When we become as strong as the first French revolutionaries, it will afford nothing but pleasure and relief to witness the thinning out in royal parks of overage, decaying trees that have long stood in the way of others equally entitled to their time in the sun, the kind of relief we feel when we see someone incurably ill die!

Recently, my tragedy *The Father* was criticized for being too sad, as if one should expect cheerful tragedies. People clamor pretentiously for "the joy of life," and theatre managers call for farces, as if the joy of life lay in being silly and depicting people as if they were all afflicted with St. Vitus's dance or imbecility. I find the joy of life in its cruel and powerful struggles, and my enjoyment comes from being able to know something, being able to learn something. That is why I have chosen an unusual case, but one from which we can learn much—in a word an exception, but an important exception which proves the rule—though this will probably offend those who love the conventional and predictable. What will next shock simple minds is that I have not motivated the action in a simple way, nor is there a single point of view. Every event in life—and this is a rather new discovery!—is ordinarily the result of a whole series of more or less deep-lying motives. The spectator, however, usually singles out the one that is either easiest for him to understand or is most advantageous to him personally. Take the case of suicide. "Financial problems," says a businessman. "Unrequited love," says a woman. "Physical illness," says an invalid. "Dashed hopes," says a shipwrecked man. It might be that all or none of these were motives and that the deceased concealed the real motive by advancing a totally different one that would bring the most credit to his memory!

I have motivated Miss Julie's tragic fate by a great number of circumstances: her mother's primary instincts, her father raising her incorrectly, her own nature, and the influence of her fiancé on her weak and degenerate brain. Also, more particularly: the festive atmosphere of midsummer night, her father's absence, her monthly indisposition, her preoccupation with animals, the provocative effect of the dancing, the magical midsummer twilight, the powerfully aphrodisiac influence of flowers, and, finally, the chance that drives the couple together into a room alone—plus the boldness of the aroused man.

My treatment of the subject has thus been neither one-sidedly physiological nor exclusively psychological. I have not put the entire blame on what she inherited from her mother, nor on her monthly indisposition, nor on immorality. I have not even preached morality—this I left to the cook in the absence of a minister.

This multiplicity of motives, it pleases me to assert, is in keeping with the times. And if others have done it before me, then it pleases me that I have not been alone in my "paradoxes," as all discoveries are called.

As for characterization, I have made my people rather "characterless" for the following reasons:

The word *character* has come to mean many things over the course of time. Originally, it must have meant the dominant trait in the soul-complex and was confused with temperament. Later it became the middle-class expression for the automaton, one whose disposition was fixed once and for all or had adapted himself to a particular role in life. In a word, someone who had stopped growing was called a character. In contrast the person who continued to develop, the skillful navigator on the river of life, sailing not with sheets belayed, but veering before the wind to luff again, was called characterless—in a derogatory sense, of course—because he was so difficult to understand, classify, and keep track of. This bourgeois concept of the immobility of the soul was transferred to the stage, which the bourgeoisie has always dominated. There a character became a man who was ready-made; whenever he appeared, he was drunk or comical or sad. The only thing necessary to characterize him was to give him a physical defect—a clubfoot, a wooden leg, a red nose—or have him repeat an expression, such as "that was splendid" or "Barkis is willin'." This simplified view of human character still survives in the great Molière. Harpagon is nothing but a miser although he could have been not only a miser but an excellent financier, or splendid father and good citizen. What is worse is that his "defect" is very advantageous to his son-in-law and daughter, who are his heirs and therefore should not criticize him, even if they have to wait a bit before climbing into bed together. Therefore, I do not believe in simple theatrical characters. And an author's summary judgments of people—this one is stupid, that one brutal, this one jealous, that one stingy—should be challenged by naturalists, who know how rich the soul-complex is and realize that "vice" has a reverse side closely resembling virtue.

As modern characters living in an age of transition more compulsively hysterical than the one that preceded it at least, I have depicted my people as more vacillating and disintegrating than their predecessors, a mixture of the old and the new. If the valet belches something modern from the depths of his ancient slave's soul, it is because I think it not improbable that through newspapers and conversations modern ideas filter down even to the level a servant lives on. There are those who find it wrong in modern drama for characters to speak Darwinism. At the same time they hold up Shakespeare as a model. I would like to remind these critics that the gravedigger in *Hamlet* speaks the fashionable philosophy of the day—Giordano Bruno's (Bacon's)—which is more improbable since there were fewer means then for the spread of ideas than there are now. Besides, "Darwinism" has existed in every age, ever since the description in Genesis of the steps in creation from lower animals to man. It is just that only now have we discovered and formulated it.

My souls (characters) are conglomerates of past and present cultural phases, bits from books and newspapers, scraps of humanity, pieces torn from fine clothes and become rags, patched together as is the human soul. I have also added a little evolutionary history by having the weaker mind steal and repeat words from the stronger. Ideas are induced through the power of suggestion: from other people, from the surroundings (the blood of the greenfinch), and from attributes (the straight razor); and I have inanimate objects (the Count's boots, the bell) serve as agents for *Gedankenübertragung* ["thought transference"]. Finally, I have used "open suggestion," a variation of sleeplike hypnosis, which is now so well known and popularized that it cannot arouse the kind of ridicule or skepticism it would have done in Mesmer's time.

Miss Julie is a modern character. Not that the man-hating half-woman has not existed in all ages but because now that she has been discovered, she has come out in the open to make herself heard. The half-woman is a type who pushes her way ahead, selling herself nowadays for power, decorations, honors, and diplomas, as formerly she used to do for money. The type implies a retrogressive step in evolution, an inferior species who cannot endure. Unfortunately, they are able to pass on their wretchedness; degenerate men seem unconsciously to choose their mates from among them. And so they breed, producing an indeterminate sex for whom life is a torture. Fortunately, the offspring go under either because they are out of harmony with reality or because their repressed instincts break out uncontrollably or because their hopes of achieving equality with men are crushed. The type is tragic, revealing the drama of a desperate struggle against Nature, tragic as the romantic heritage now being dissipated by naturalism, which has a contrary aim: happiness, and happiness belongs only to the strong and skillful species.

But Miss Julie is also: a relic of the old warrior nobility now giving way to a new nobility of nerve and intellect, a victim of her own flawed constitution, a victim of the discord caused in a family by a mother's "crime," a victim of the delusions and conditions of her age—and together these are the equivalent of the concept of Destiny, or Universal Law, of antiquity. Guilt has been abolished by the naturalist, along with God, but the consequences of an action—punishment, imprisonment or the fear of it—that he cannot erase, for the simple reason that they remain, whether he pronounces acquittal or not. Those who have been injured are not as kind and understanding as an unscathed outsider can afford to be. Even if her father felt constrained not to seek revenge, his daughter would wreak vengeance upon herself, as she does here, out of an innate or acquired sense of honor, which the upper classes inherit—from where? From barbarism, from the ancient Aryan home of the race, from medieval chivalry. It is a beautiful thing, but nowadays a hindrance to the survival of the race. It is the nobleman's harikari, which compels him to slit open his own stomach when someone insults him and which survives in a modified form in the duel, that privilege of the nobility. That is why Jean, the servant, lives, while Miss Julie cannot live without honor. The slave's advantage over the nobleman is that he lacks this fatal preoccupation with honor. But in all of us Aryans there is something of the nobleman, or a Don Quixote. And so we sympathize with the suicide, whose act means a loss of honor. We are noblemen enough to be pained when we see the mighty fallen and as superfluous as a corpse, yes, even if the fallen should rise again and make amends through an honorable act. The servant Jean is a race-founder, someone in whom the process of differentiation can be detected. Born the son of a tenant farmer, he has educated himself in the things a gentleman should know. He has been quick to learn, has finely developed senses (smell, taste, sight) and a feeling for what is beautiful. He is already moving up in the world and is not embarrassed about using other people's help. He is alienated from his fellow servants, despising them as parts of a past he has already put behind him. He fears and flees them because they know his secrets, pry into his intentions, envy his rise, and look forward eagerly to his fall. Hence his dual, indecisive nature, vacillating between sympathy for people in high social positions and hatred for those who currently occupy those positions. He is an aristocrat, as he himself says, has learned the secrets of good society, is polished on the surface but coarse beneath, wears a frock coat tastefully but without any guarantee that his body is clean.

He has respect for Miss Julie, but is afraid of Kristine because she knows his dangerous secrets. He is sufficiently callous not to let the night's events disturb his plans for the future. With both a slave's brutality and a master's lack of squeamishness, he can see blood without fainting and shake off misfortune easily. Consequently, he comes through the struggle unscathed and will probably end up an innkeeper. And even if *he* does not become a Rumanian count, his son will become a university student and possibly a county police commissioner.

In any case he has important things to say about the lower classes' view of life—when he is telling the truth, that is, which he often does not do, for he is more interested in saying what is favorable to himself than in telling the truth. When Miss Julie says she assumes the lower classes feel oppressed from above, Jean naturally agrees since it is his intention to win sympathy, but he quickly changes his attitude when he realizes that it is more to his advantage to distance himself from the "rabble."

Apart from the fact that Jean is rising in the world, he is superior to Miss Julie because he is a man. Sexually, he is an aristocrat because of his masculine strength, his more keenly developed senses, and his capacity for taking the initiative. His sense of inferiority is mostly due to the social circumstances in which he happens to be living, and he can probably shed it along with his valet's jacket.

His slave mentality expresses itself in the fearful respect he has for the Count (the boots) and his religious superstition; but he respects the Count mainly as the occupant of the kind of high position to which he himself aspires; and the respect remains even after he has conquered the daughter of the house and seen how empty the lovely shell was.

I do not believe that love in any "higher" sense can exist between two people of such different natures, and so I have Miss Julie's love as something she fabricates in order to protect and excuse herself; and I have Jean suppose himself capable of loving her under other social circumstances. I think it is the same with love as with the hyacinth, which must take root in darkness *before* it can produce a sturdy flower. Here a flower shoots up, blooms, and goes to seed all at once, and that is why it dies so quickly.

Kristine, finally, is a female slave. Years standing over the stove have made her conventional and lethargic; instinctively hypocritical, she uses morality and religion as cloaks and scapegoats. A strong person would not need these because he can either bear his guilt or reason it away. Kristine goes to church as a quick and easy way to unload her household thefts on Jesus and to take on a new charge of innocence. Furthermore, she is a minor character, and I purposely simply sketched her in, as I did the minister and the doctor in *The Father,* because I wanted ordinary people, as country ministers and provincial doctors usually are. If my minor characters seem abstract to some people, it is because ordinary people are abstract to some extent in their occupations. As they carry out their duties, they lose their individuality, showing only one side of themselves, and as long as the spectator has no need to see them from several sides, my abstract depiction of them is probably correct.

As for the dialogue, I have broken with tradition somewhat by not making my characters catechists who ask stupid questions in order to elicit clever replies. I have avoided the symmetrical, mathematical, constructed dialogue of French drama and let characters' minds function irregularly, as they do in a real-life conversation, where no topic of discussion is exhausted entirely and one mind by chance finds a cog in another mind in which to engage. Consequently, the dialogue also wanders, presenting material in the opening scenes that is later taken up, reworked, repeated, expanded, and developed, like the theme in a musical composition.

The plot is serviceable enough, and since it really concerns only two people, I have concentrated on them, including only one minor character, the cook, and having the father's unhappy spirit hover over and behind the action. I have done this because I believe that people of today are most interested in the psychological process. Our inquisitive souls are not satisfied just to see something happen; we want to know how it happened. We want to see the strings, the machinery, examine the double-bottomed box, feel for the seam in the magic ring, look at the cards to see how they are marked.

In this regard I have kept in mind the monographic novels of the brothers Goncourt, which I find more appealing than anything else in contemporary literature.

As for the technical aspects of composition, I have experimented with eliminating act divisions. The reason is that I believe our dwindling capacity for accepting illusion is possibly further disturbed by intermissions, during which the spectator has time to reflect and thereby escape the suggestive influence of the author-hypnotist. My play will probably run an hour and a half, and since people can listen to a lecture, sermon, or conference discussion for just as long or longer, I imagine that a ninety-minute theatre piece will not be too tiring. I tested this concentrated form in 1872 in one of my first plays, *The Outlaw,* although with little success. The first draft was in five acts, and when I noticed the disjointed, restless effect it produced, I burned it. From the ashes rose a single, long, coherent act of fifty pages in print, with a playing time of one hour. And so the form is not new, and I seem to have a feel for it; changing tastes may make it timely. My hope for the future is to so educate audiences that they can sit through a one-act play that lasts an entire evening. But this will require experimentation. Meanwhile, in order to relax tension for the audience and the actors, without breaking the illusion for the audience, I have used three art forms traditionally associated with drama: monologue, mime, and ballet. The original association was with the tragedy of antiquity, monody having become monologue, and chorus, ballet.

Our realists today condemn the monologue as implausible, but if I motivate it, I can make it plausible and use it to advantage. It is perfectly plausible for an orator to pace the floor alone and practice his speech aloud, plausible for an actor to rehearse his lines aloud, for a servant girl to talk to her cat, a mother babble to her baby, an old maid jabber to her parrot, a sleeper talk in his sleep. And in order to give the actor a chance, for once, to work independently, free for a moment of the author's authority, I have sketched in the monologues rather than worked them out in detail. Since it is irrelevant what someone says in his sleep or to a parrot or to a cat, for this has no influence on the action, a talented actor, absorbed in the mood and the situation, perhaps can improvise the monologue more effectively than the author, who cannot determine in advance how much may be spoken, and for how long, before an audience senses that the illusion is broken.

As we know, some Italian theatres have returned to improvisation, producing actors who are creative in their own right, although in accordance with the author's intentions. This could be the beginning of a fertile new art form, something worthy of the name *creative.*

In places where a monologue would be implausible, I have resorted to mime, and here I leave the actor even greater freedom to be creative—and to win independent acclaim. But in order not to try the audience beyond its limits, I have let music—coming from the midsummer dance, and thus believably motivated—exercise its illusion-evoking power during the sections of dumb show. I beg the music director to consider carefully his choice of pieces; the wrong mood may be produced if there are familiar selections from popular dances or operettas, or unusual folk melodies, no matter how ethnographically correct.

The ballet I have indicated cannot be replaced by a so-called "crowd scene" because crowd scenes are always badly acted, with a mob of grimacing idiots trying to use the occasion to appear clever and so disturb the illusion. And since uneducated people do not improvise when they wish to poke fun maliciously but use ready-made material that can take on a double meaning, I did not compose the taunting song they sing. Instead, I used a little-known dance song* I discovered myself in the Stockholm area. The words are only approximately appropriate, but this is intentional, for the slyness (weakness) of the slave does not permit him to make a direct attack. And so the seriousness of the action forbids clowning; there must be no coarse sneering in a situation which closes the lid on a family coffin.

As for the scenery, I have borrowed from impressionist painting the device of making a setting appear cut off and asymmetrical, thus strengthening the illusion. When we see only part of a room and a portion of the furniture, we are left to conjecture, that is to say, our imagination goes to work and complements what is seen. I have also profited by doing away with those tiresome exits through doors because scenery doors, made of canvas, wobble at the slightest touch; they cannot even allow a father to express his anger after a bad dinner by going out and slamming the door behind him "so that the whole house shakes." (In the theatre it wobbles.) I have also confined the action to one setting, both to allow the characters more time to interact with their environment and to break with the tradition of expensive scenery. With only one setting we should be able to demand that it be realistic, but nothing is more difficult than to get a room on stage to look like a room, however easily the scene painter can produce flaming volcanoes and waterfalls. Even if the walls must be of canvas, it is surely time to stop painting shelves and kitchen utensils on them. We have so many other stage conventions in which we are asked to believe, we should not have to strain ourselves trying to believe in painted pots and pans.

---

*The version of the song as it appears in this translation of the play is a free interpretation of the playwright's intention rather than a literal rendering of the actual song he chose (translator).

I have placed the upstage wall and the table diagonally so that the actors can play facing the audience or in half-profile when they sit opposite each other at the table. I saw a diagonal backdrop in a production of *Aïda;* it led the eye out into unknown vistas and did not look simply like a defiant reaction to the boredom of straight lines.

Another perhaps necessary innovation is the removal of footlights. The purpose of this lighting from below is said to be to make the actors' faces fatter, but I ask: why must all actors have fat faces? Does not this lighting obliterate many subtleties in the lower part of the face, especially the jaws, distort the shape of the nose, and cast shadows up over the eyes? Even if this were not so, one thing is certain: actors find it so painful for their eyes that they are unable to use them with full expressiveness. Footlights strike the retina in places usually protected (except in the case of seamen, who have to look at the sun's reflection in the water), and so we seldom see anything but a crude rolling of the eyes, either to the side or up toward the balconies, exposing the whites. Perhaps this also accounts for the tedious habit, especially common among actresses, of blinking eyelashes. And when anyone on stage wants to speak with his eyes, he must resort to staring straight out, thus breaking the wall of the curtain line and coming into direct contact with the audience. Justly or unjustly, this unfortunate practice is called "greeting your friends."

Would not sufficiently strong side lighting (using parabolic reflectors, for example) provide the actor with a new advantage: the strengthening of mime effects through the most expressive asset in his face—the play of his eyes?

I have no illusions about getting the actor to play for the audience rather than with it, although this would be desirable. I cannot hope to see an actor play with his back to the audience throughout an entire important scene, though I wish very much that crucial scenes were staged, not next to the prompter's box, like duets intended to evoke applause, but in places more appropriate to the action. In other words, I call for no revolution, just small modifications, for to really transform the stage into a room where the fourth wall is removed, and consequently a portion of the furniture faces away from the audience, would probably, for the present, produce a disturbing effect.

When it comes to makeup, I dare not hope to be listened to by the ladies, who would rather be beautiful than believable. But the actor might consider whether it is really to his advantage when putting on makeup to fix an abstract character, like a mask, on his face. Picture an actor who has drawn sharp lines of anger between his eyes and then, with that incensed look, has to smile in response to someone else's line. What a terrible grimace there would be as a result! And how would the false forehead attached to his wig, bald as a billiard ball, wrinkle when the old man got angry?

In a modern psychological drama, where the subtlest movements of the soul must be revealed more through the face than through gesture and sound, it would probably be best to experiment with strong side lighting on a small stage, and with actors wearing no makeup, or at least a minimum of it.

If, in addition, we could avoid having the orchestra visible, its lights disturbing, and the musicians' faces turned toward the audience; if the seating in the auditorium were raised so that eye level for the spectator was higher than the hollow of the actor's knee; if we could get rid of stage boxes (behind bull's-eye openings), with their grinning late arrivals from dinners and supper parties; if we could have complete darkness during performances; and, finally, and most importantly, a *small* stage and a *small* auditorium, then perhaps we might see a new drama arise, or at the very least a theatre that was once again a place of entertainment for educated people. While waiting for this theatre, we will just have to go on writing, preparing the repertoire that will one day be needed.

Here is an attempt! If it fails, there is surely time enough for another!

Francis Fergusson
From *The Idea of a Theater*

The Plot of *The Cherry Orchard*

The Cherry Orchard is often accused of having no plot whatever, and it is true that the story gives little indication of the play's content or meaning; nothing happens, as the Broadway reviewers so often point out. Nor does it have a thesis, though many attempts have been made to attribute a thesis to it, to make it into a Marxian tract, or into a nostalgic defense of the old regime. The play does not have much of a plot in either of these accepted meanings of the word, for it is not addressed to the rationalizing mind but to the poetic and histrionic sensibility. It is an imitation of an action in the strictest sense, and it is plotted according to the first meaning of this word which I have distinguished in other contexts: the incidents are selected and arranged to define an action in a certain mode; a complete action, with a beginning, middle, and end in time. Its freedom from the mechanical order of the thesis or the intrigue is the sign of the perfection of Chekhov's realistic art. And its apparently casual incidents are actually composed with most elaborate and conscious skill to reveal the underlying life, and the natural, objective form of the play as a whole.

In *Ghosts*, as I showed, the action is distorted by the stereotyped requirements of the thesis and the intrigue. That is partly a matter of the mode of action which Ibsen was trying to show; a quest "of ethical motivation" which requires some sort of intellectual framework, and yet can have no final meaning in the purely literal terms of Ibsen's theater. *The Cherry Orchard*, on the other hand, is a drama "of pathetic motivation," a theater-poem of the suffering of change; and this mode of action and awareness is much closer to the skeptical basis of modern realism, and to the histrionic basis of all realism. Direct perception before predication is always true, says Aristotle; and the extraordinary feat of Chekhov is to predicate nothing. This he achieves by means of his plot: he selects only those incidents, those moments in his characters' lives, between their rationalized efforts, when they sense their situation and destiny most directly. So he contrives to show the action of the play as a whole—the unsuccessful attempt to cling to the Cherry Orchard—in many diverse reflectors and without propounding any thesis about it.

The slight narrative thread which ties these incidents and characters together for the inquiring mind, is quickly recounted. The family that owns the old estate named after its famous orchard—Lyubov, her brother Gaev, and her daughters Varya and Anya—is all but bankrupt, and the question is how to prevent the bailiffs from selling the estate to pay their debts. Lopahin, whose family were formerly serfs on the estate, is now rapidly growing rich as a businessman, and he offers a very sensible plan: chop down the orchard, divide the property into small lots, and sell them off to make a residential suburb for the growing industrial town nearby. Thus the cash value of the estate could be not only preserved, but increased. But this would not save what Lyubov and her brother find valuable in the old estate; they cannot consent to the destruction of the orchard. But they cannot find, or earn, or borrow the money to pay their debts either; and in due course the estate is sold at auction to Lopahin himself, who will make a very good thing of it. His workmen are hacking at the old trees before the family is out of the house.

The play may be briefly described as a realistic ensemble pathos: the characters all suffer the passing of the estate in different ways, thus adumbrating this change at a deeper and more generally significant level than that of any individual's experience. The action which they all share by analogy, and which informs the suffering of the destined change of the Cherry Orchard, is "to save the Cherry Orchard": that is, each character sees some value in it—economic, sentimental, social, cultural—which he wishes to keep. By means of his plot, Chekhov always focuses attention on the general action: his crowded stage, full of the characters I have mentioned as well as half a dozen hangers-on, is like an implicit discussion of the fatality which concerns them all; but Chekhov does not believe in their ideas, and the interplay he shows among his *dramatis personae* is not so much the play of thought as the alternation of his characters' perceptions of their situation, as the moods shift and the time for decision comes and goes.

Though the action which Chekhov chooses to show on-stage is "pathetic," i.e., suffering and perception, it is complete: the Cherry Orchard is constituted before our eyes, and then dissolved. The first act is a prologue: it is the occasion of Lyubov's return from Paris to try to resume her old life. Through her eyes and those of her daughter Anya, as well as from the complementary perspectives of Lopahin and Trofimov, we see the estate as it were in the round, in its many possible meanings. The second act corresponds to the agon; it is in this act that we become aware of the conflicting values of all the characters, and of the efforts they make (off-stage) to save each one *his* Orchard. The third act corresponds to the pathos and peripety of the traditional tragic form. The occasion is a rather hysterical party which Lyubov gives while her estate is being sold at auction in the nearby town; it ends with Lopahin's announcement, in pride and the bitterness of guilt, that he was the purchaser. The last act is the epiphany: we see the action, now completed, in a new and ironic light. The occasion is the departure of the family: the windows are boarded up, the furniture piled in the corners, and the bags packed. All the characters feel, and the audience sees in a thousand ways, that the wish to save the Orchard has amounted in fact to destroying it; the gathering of its denizens to separation; the homecoming to departure. What this "means" we are not told. But the action is completed, and the poem of the suffering of change concludes in a new and final perception, and a rich chord of feeling.

The structure of each act is based upon a more or less ceremonious social occasion. In his use of the social ceremony—arrivals, departures, anniversaries, parties—Chekhov is akin to James. His purpose is the same: to focus attention on an action which all share by analogy, instead of upon the reasoned purpose of any individual, as Ibsen does in his drama of ethical motivation. Chekhov uses the social occasion also to reveal the individual at moments when he is least enclosed in his private rationalization and most open to disinterested insights. The Chekhovian ensembles may appear superficially to be mere pointless stalemates—too like family gatherings and arbitrary meetings which we know off-stage. So they are. But in his miraculous arrangement the very discomfort of many presences is made to reveal fundamental aspects of the human situation.

That Chekhov's art of plotting is extremely conscious and deliberate is clear the moment one considers the distinction between the stories of his characters as we learn about them, and the moments of their lives which he chose to show directly on-stage. Lopahin, for example, is a man of action like one of the new capitalists in Gorki's plays. Chekhov knew all about him, and could have shown us an exciting episode from his career if he had not chosen to see him only when he was forced to pause and pathetically sense his own motives in a wider context which qualifies their importance. Lyubov has been dragged about Europe for years by her ne'er-do-well lover, and her life might have yielded several sure-fire erotic intrigues like those of the commercial theater. But Chekhov, like all the great artists of modern times, rejected these standard motivations as both stale and false. The actress Arkadina, in *The Seagull*, remarks, as she closes a novel of Maupassant's, "Well, among the French that may be, but here with us there's nothing of the kind, we've no set program." In the context the irony of her remark is deep: she is herself a purest product of the commercial theater, and at that very time she is engaged in a love affair of the kind she objects to in Maupassant. But Chekhov, with his subtle art of plotting, has caught her in a situation, and at a brief moment of clarity and pause, when the falsity of her career is clear to all, even herself.

Thus Chekhov, by his art of plot-making, defines an action in the opposite mode to that of *Ghosts*. Ibsen defines a desperate quest for reasons and for ultimate, intelligible moral values. This action falls naturally into the form of the agon, and at the end of the play Ibsen is at a loss to develop the final pathos, or bring it to an end with an accepted perception. But the pathetic is the very mode of action and awareness which seems to Chekhov closest to the reality of the human situation, and by means of his plot he shows, even in characters who are not in themselves unusually passive, the suffering and the perception of change. The "moment" of human experience which *The Cherry Orchard* presents thus corresponds to that of the Sophoclean chorus, and of the evenings in the *Purgatorio*. *Ghosts* is a fighting play, armed for its sharp encounter with the rationalizing mind, its poetry concealed by its reasons. Chekhov's poetry, like Ibsen's, is behind the naturalistic surfaces; but the form of the play as a whole is "nothing but" poetry in the widest sense: the coherence of the concrete elements of the composition. Hence the curious vulnerability of Chekhov on the contemporary stage: he does not argue, he merely presents; and though his audiences even on Broadway are touched by the time they reach the last act, they are at a loss to say what it is all about.

It is this reticent objectivity of Chekhov also which makes him so difficult to analyze in words: he appeals exclusively to the histrionic sensibility where the little poetry of modern realism is to be found. Nevertheless, the effort of analysis must be made if one is to understand this art at all; and if the reader will bear with me, he is asked to consider one element, that of the scene, in the composition of the second act.

Act II: The Scene as a Basic Element in the Composition

M. Cocteau writes, in his preface to *Les Mariés de la Tour Eiffel:* "The action of my play is in images (*imagée*) while the text is not: I attempt to substitute a 'poetry of the theater' for 'poetry in the theater.' Poetry in the theater is a piece of lace which it is impossible to see at a distance. Poetry of the theater would be coarse lace; a lace of ropes, a ship at sea. *Les Mariés* should have the frightening look of a drop of poetry under the microscope. The *scenes* are integrated like the *words* of a poem."

This description applies very exactly to *The Cherry Orchard:* the larger elements of the composition—the scenes or episodes, the setting and the developing story—are composed in such a way as to make a poetry of the theater; but the "text" as we read it literally, is not. Chekhov's method, as Mr. Stark Young puts it in the preface to his translation of *The Seagull,* "is to take actual material such as we find in life and manage it in such a way that the inner meanings are made to appear. On the surface the life in his plays is natural, possible, and at times in effect even casual."

Mr. Young's translations of Chekhov's plays, together with his beautifully accurate notes, explanations, and interpretations, have made the text of Chekhov at last available for the English-speaking stage, and for any reader who will bring to his reading a little patience and imagination.* Mr. Young shows us what Chekhov means in detail: by the particular words his characters use; by their rhythms of speech; by their gestures, pauses, and bits of stage business. In short, he makes the text transparent, enabling us to see through it to the music of action, the underlying poetry of the composition as a whole—and this is as much as to say that any study of Chekhov (lacking as we do adequate and available productions) must be based upon Mr. Young's work. At this point I propose to take this work for granted; to assume the translucent text; and to consider the role of the setting in the poetic or musical order of Act II.

---

*The quotations from *The Cherry Orchard* are taken from the translation by Stark Young (New York: Samuel French). Copyright, 1947, by Stark Young. All rights reserved. Reprinted by permission of the author and Samuel French.

The second act, as I have said, corresponds to the agon traditional plot scheme: it is here that we see most clearly the divisive purposes of the characters, the contrasts between their views of the Cherry Orchard itself. But the center of interest is not in these individual conflicts, nor in the contrasting visions for their own sake, but in the common fatality which they reveal: the passing of the old estate. The setting, as we come to know it behind the casual surfaces of the text, is one of the chief elements in this poem of change: if Act II were a lyric, instead of an act of a play, the setting would be a crucial word appearing in a succession of rich contexts which endow it with a developing meaning.

Chekhov describes the setting in the following realistic terms. "A field. An old chapel, long abandoned, with crooked walls, near it a well, big stones that apparently were once tombstones, and an old bench. A road to the estate of Gaev can be seen. On one side poplars rise, casting their shadows, the cherry orchard begins there. In the distance a row of telegraph poles; and far, far away, faintly traced on the horizon, is a large town, visible only in the clearest weather. The sun will soon be down."

To make this set out of a cyclorama, flats, cut-out silhouettes, and lighting-effects, would be difficult, without producing that unbelievable but literally intended—and in any case indigestible—scene which modern realism demands; and here Chekhov is uncomfortably bound by the convention of his time. The best strategy in production is that adopted by Robert Edmund Jones in his setting for *The Seagull:* to pay lip service only to the convention of photographic realism, and make the trees, the chapel and all the other elements as simple as possible. The less closely the setting is defined by the carpenter, the freer it is to play the role Chekhov wrote for it: a role which changes and develops in relation to the story. Shakespeare did not have this problem; he could present his setting in different ways at different moments in a few lines of verse:

Alack! the night comes on, and the bleak winds
Do sorely ruffle; for many miles about
There's scarce a bush.

Chekhov, as we shall see, gives his setting life and flexibility in spite of the visible elements on-stage, not by means of the poetry of words but by means of his characters' changing sense of it.

When the curtain rises we see the setting simply as the country at the sentimental hour of sunset. Epihodov is playing his guitar and other hangers-on of the estate are loafing, as is their habit, before supper. The dialogue which starts after a brief pause focuses attention upon individuals in the group: Charlotta, the governess, boasting of her culture and complaining that no one understands her; the silly maid Dunyasha, who is infatuated with Yasha, Lyubov's valet. The scene, as reflected by these characters, is a satirical period-piece like the "Stag at eve" or "The Maiden's Prayer"; and when the group falls silent and begins to drift away (having heard Lyubov, Gaev, and Lopahin approaching along the path) Chekhov expects us to smile at the sentimental clichés which the place and the hour have produced.

But Lyubov's party brings with it a very different atmosphere: of irritation, frustration, and fear. It is here we learn that Lopahin cannot persuade Lyubov and Gaev to put their affairs in order; that Gaev has been making futile gestures toward getting a job and borrowing money; that Lyubov is worried about the estate, about her daughters, and about her lover, who has now fallen ill in Paris. Lopahin, in a huff, offers to leave; but Lyubov will not let him go—"It's more cheerful with you here," she says; and this group in its turn falls silent. In the distance we hear the music of the Jewish orchestra—when Chekhov wishes us to raise our eyes from the people in the foreground to their wider setting, he often uses music as a signal and an inducement. This time the musical entrance of the setting into our consciousness is more urgent and sinister than it was before: we see not so much the peace of evening as the silhouette of the dynamic industrial town on the horizon, and the approach of darkness. After a little more desultory conversation, there is another pause, this time without music, and the foreboding aspect of the scene in silence is more intense.

In this silence Firs, the ancient servant, hurries on with Gaev's coat, to protect him from the evening chill, and we briefly see the scene through Firs's eyes. He remembers the estate before the emancipation of the serfs, when it was the scene of a way of life which made sense to him; and now we become aware of the frail relics of this life: the old gravestones and the chapel "fallen out of the perpendicular."

In sharpest contrast with this vision come the young voices of Anya, Varya, and Trofimov who are approaching along the path. The middle-aged and the old in the foreground are pathetically grateful for this note of youth, of strength, and of hope; and presently they are listening happily (though without agreement or belief) to Trofimov's aspirations, his creed of social progress, and his conviction that their generation is no longer important to the life of Russia. When the group falls silent again, they are all disposed to contentment with the moment; and when Epihodov's guitar is heard, and we look up, we feel the country and the evening under the aspect of hope—as offering freedom from the responsibilities and conflicts of the estate itself:

> (*Epihodov passes by at the back, playing his guitar.*)
> LYUBOV. (*Lost in thought.*) Epihodov is coming—
> ANYA. (*Lost in thought.*) Epihodov is coming.
> GAEV. The sun has set, ladies and gentlemen.
> TROFIMOV. Yes.
> GAEV. (*Not loud and as if he were declaiming.*) Oh, Nature, wonderful, you gleam with eternal radiance, beautiful and indifferent, you, whom we call Mother, combine in yourself both life and death, you give life and take it away.
> VARYA. (*Beseechingly.*) Uncle!

Gaev's false, rhetorical note ends the harmony, brings us back to the present and to the awareness of change on the horizon, and produces a sort of empty stalemate—a silent pause with worry and fear in it.

> (*All sit absorbed in their thoughts. There is only the silence.* FIRS *is heard muttering to himself softly. Suddenly a distant sound is heard, as if from the sky, like the sound of a snapped string, dying away, mournful.*)

This mysterious sound is used like Epihodov's strumming to remind us of the wider scene, but (though distant) it is sharp, almost a warning signal, and all the characters listen and peer toward the dim edges of the horizon. In their attitudes and guesses Chekhov reflects, in rapid succession, the contradictory aspects of the scene which have been developed at more length before us:

> LYUBOV. What's that?
> LOPAHIN. I don't know. Somewhere far off in a mine shaft a bucket fell. But somewhere very far off.
> GAEV. And it may be some bird—like a heron.
> TROFIMOV. Or an owl—
> LYUBOV. (*Shivering.*) It's unpleasant, somehow. (*A pause.*)
> FIRS. Before the disaster it was like that. The owl hooted and the samovar hummed without stopping, both.
> GAEV. Before what disaster?
> FIRS. Before the emancipation.
> (*A pause.*)
> LYUBOV. You know, my friends, let's go. . . .

Lyubov feels the need to retreat, but the retreat is turned into flight when "the wayfarer" suddenly appears on the path asking for money. Lyubov in her bewilderment, her sympathy, and her bad conscience, gives him gold. The party breaks up, each in his own way thwarted and demoralized.

Anya and Trofimov are left on-stage; and, to conclude his theatrical poem of the suffering of change, Chekhov reflects the setting in them:

> ANYA. (*A pause.*) It's wonderful here today!
> TROFIMOV. Yes, the weather is marvelous.
> ANYA. What have you done to me, Petya, why don't I love the cherry orchard any longer the way I used to? I loved it too tenderly; it seemed to me there was not a better place on earth than our orchard.
> TROFIMOV. All Russia is our garden. The earth is immense and beautiful. . . .

The sun has set, the moon is rising with its chill and its ancient animal excitement, and the estate is dissolved in the darkness as Nineveh is dissolved in a pile of rubble with vegetation creeping over it. Chekhov wishes to show the Cherry Orchard as "gone"; but for this purpose he employs not only the literal time-scheme (sunset to moonrise) but, as reflectors, Anya and Trofimov, for whom the present in any form is already gone and only the bodiless future is real. Anya's young love for Trofimov's intellectual enthusiasm (like Juliet's "all as boundless as the sea") has freed her from her actual childhood home, made her feel "at home in the world" anywhere. Trofimov's abstract aspirations give him a chillier and more artificial, but equally complete, detachment not only from the estate itself (he disapproves of it on theoretical grounds) but from Anya (he thinks it would be vulgar to be in love with her). We hear the worried Varya calling for Anya in the distance; Anya and Trofimov run down to the river to discuss the socialistic *Paradiso Terrestre;* and with these complementary images of the human scene, and this subtle chord of feeling, Chekhov ends the act.

The "scene" is only one element in the composition of Act II, but it illustrates the nature of Chekhov's poetry of the theater. It is very clear, I think, that Chekhov is not trying to present us with a rationalization of social change *à la* Marx, or even with a subtler rationalization *à la* Shaw. On the other hand, he is not seeking, like Wagner, to seduce us into one passion. He shows us a moment of change in society, and he shows us a "pathos"; but the elements of his composition are always taken as objectively real. He offers us various rationalizations, various images and various feelings, which cannot be reduced either to one emotion or to one idea: they indicate an action and a scene which is "there" before the rational formulations, or the emotionally charged attitudes, of any of the characters.

The surrounding scene of *The Cherry Orchard* corresponds to the significant stage of human life which Sophocles' choruses reveal, and to the empty wilderness beyond Ibsen's little parlor. We miss, in Chekhov's scene, any fixed points of human significance, and that is why, compared with Sophocles, he seems limited and partial—a bit too pathetic even for our bewildered times. But, precisely because he subtly and elaborately develops the moments of pathos with their sad insights, he sees much more in the little scene of modern realism than Ibsen does. Ibsen's snowpeaks strike us as rather hysterical, but the "stage of Europe" which we divine behind the Cherry Orchard is confirmed by a thousand impressions derived from other sources. We may recognize its main elements in a cocktail party in Connecticut or Westchester: someone's lawn full of voluble people; a dry white clapboard church (instead of an Orthodox chapel) just visible across a field; time passing, and the muffled roar of a four-lane highway under the hill—or we may be reminded of it in the final section of *The Wasteland*, with its twittering voices, its old gravestones and deserted chapel, and its dim crowd on the horizon foreboding change. It is because Chekhov says so little that he reveals so much, providing a concrete basis for many conflicting rationalizations of contemporary social change: by accepting the immediacy and unintelligibility of modern realism so completely, he in some ways transcends its limitations, and prepares the way for subsequent developments in the modern theater.

Chekhov's Histrionic Art: An End and a Beginning

Era già l'ora che volge il disio
    ai naviganti, e intenercisce il core
    lo dì ch'han detto ai dolci amici addio;
e che lo nuovo peregrin d'amore
    punge, se ode squilla di lontano,
    che paia il giorno pianger che si more.

—*Purgatorio*, CANTO VIII*

---

*It was now the hour that turns back the desire of those who sail the seas and melts their heart, that day when they have said to their sweet friends adieu, and that pierces the new pilgrim with love, if from afar he hears the chimes which seem to mourn for the dying day.

The poetry of modern realistic drama is to be found in those inarticulate moments when the human creature is shown responding directly to his immediate situation. Such are the many moments—composed, interrelated, echoing each other—when the waiting and loafing characters in Act II get a fresh sense (one after the other, and each in his own way) of their situation on the doomed estate. It is because of the exactitude with which Chekhov perceives and imitates these tiny responses, that he can make them echo each other, and convey, when taken together, a single action with the scope, the general significance or suggestiveness, of poetry. Chekhov, like other great dramatists, has what might be called an ear for action, comparable to the trained musician's ear for musical sound.

The action which Chekhov thus imitates in his second act (that of lending ear, in a moment of freedom from practical pressures, to impending change) echoes, in its turn, a number of other poets: Laforgue's "poetry of waiting-rooms" comes to mind, as well as other works stemming from the period of hush before the first World War. The poets are to some extent talking about the same thing, and their works, like voices in a continuing colloquy, help to explain each other: hence the justification and the purpose of seeking comparisons. The eighth canto of the *Purgatorio* is widely separated from *The Cherry Orchard* in space and time, but these two poems unmistakably echo and confirm each other. Thinking of them together, one can begin to place Chekhov's curiously non-verbal dramaturgy and understand the purpose and the value of his reduction of the art to histrionic terms, as well as the more obvious limitations which he thereby accepts. For Dante accepts similar limitations at this point but locates the mode of action he shows here at a certain point in his vast scheme.

The explicit co-ordinates whereby Dante places the action of Canto VIII might alone suffice to give one a clue to the comparison with *The Cherry Orchard:* we are in the Valley of Negligent Rulers who, lacking light, unwillingly suffer their irresponsibility, just as Lyubov and Gaev do. The ante-purgatorio is behind us, and purgatory proper, with its hoped-for work, thought, and moral effort, is somewhere ahead, beyond the night which is now approaching. It is the end of the day; and as we wait, watch, and listen, evening moves slowly over our heads, from sunset to darkness to moonrise. Looking more closely at this canto, one can see that Dante the Pilgrim, and the Negligent Rulers he meets, are listening and looking as Chekhov's characters are in Act II: the action is the same; in both a childish and uninstructed responsiveness, an unpremeditated obedience to what is actual, informs the suffering of change. Dante the author, for his elaborate and completely conscious reasons, works here with the primitive histrionic sensibility, he composes with elements sensuously or sympathetically, but not rationally or verbally, defined. The rhythms, the pauses, and the sound effects he employs are strikingly similar to Chekhov's. And so he shows himself—Dante "the new Pilgrim"—meeting this mode of awareness for the first time: as delicately and ignorantly as Gaev when he feels all of a sudden the extent of evening, and before he falsifies this perception with his embarrassing apostrophe to Nature.

If Dante allows himself as artist and as protagonist only the primitive sensibility of the child, the naïf, the natural saint, at this point in the ascent; it is because, like Chekhov, he is presenting a threshold or moment of change in human experience. He wants to show the unbounded potentialities of the psyche before or between the moments when it is morally and intellectually realized. In Canto VIII the pilgrim is both a child, and a child who is changing; later moments of transition are different. Here he is virtually (but for the Grace of God) lost; all the dangers are present. Yet he remains uncommitted and therefore open to finding himself again and more truly. In all of this the parallel to Chekhov is close. But because Dante sees this moment as a moment only in the ascent, Canto VIII is also composed in ways in which Act II of *The Cherry Orchard* is not—ways which the reader of the *Purgatorio* will not understand until he looks back from the top of the mountain. Then he will see the homesickness which informs Canto VIII in a new light, and all of the concrete elements, the snake in the grass, the winged figures that roost at the edge of the valley like night-hawks, will be intelligible to the mind and, without losing their concreteness, take their places in a more general frame. Dante's fiction is laid in the scene beyond the grave, where every human action has its relation to ultimate reality, even though that relation becomes explicit only gradually. But Chekhov's characters are seen in the flesh and in their very secular emotional entanglements: in the contemporary world as anyone can see it—nothing visible beyond the earth's horizon, with its signs of social change. The fatality of the *Zeitgeist* is the ultimate reality in the theater of modern realism; the anagoge is lacking. And though Ibsen and Chekhov are aware of both history and moral effort, they do not know what to make of them—perhaps they reveal only illusory perspectives, "masquerades which time resumes." If Chekhov echoes Dante, it is not because of what he ultimately understood but because of the accuracy with which he saw and imitated that moment of action.

If one thinks of the generation to which Anya and Trofimov were supposed to belong, it is clear that the new motives and reasons which they were to find, after their inspired evening together, were not such as to turn all Russia, or all the world, into a garden. The potentialities which Chekhov presented at that moment of change were not to be realized in the wars and revolutions which followed: what actually followed was rather that separation and destruction, that scattering and destinationless trekking, which he also sensed as possible. But, in the cultivation of the dramatic art after Chekhov, renewals, the realization of hidden potentialities, did follow. In Chekhov's histrionic art, the "desire is turned back" to its very root, to the immediate response, to the movements of the psyche before they are limited, defined, and realized in reasoned purpose. Thus Chekhov revealed hidden potentialities, if not in the life of the time, at least in ways of seeing and showing human life; if not in society, at least in the dramatic art. The first and most generally recognized result of these labors was to bring modern realism to its final perfection in the productions of the Moscow Art Theater and in those who learned from it. But the end of modern realism was also a return to very ancient sources; and in our time the fertilizing effect of Chekhov's humble objectivity may be traced in a number of dramatic forms which cannot be called modern realism at all.

The acting technique of the Moscow Art Theater is so closely connected, in its final development, with Chekhov's dramaturgy, that it would be hard to say which gave the more important clues. Stanislavsky and Nemirovitch-Dantchenko from one point of view, and Chekhov from another, approached the same conception: both were searching for an attitude and a method that would be less hidebound, truer to experience, than the cliché-responses of the commercial theater. The Moscow Art Theater taught the performer to make that direct and total response which is the root of poetry in the widest sense: they cultivated the histrionic sensibility in order to free the actor to realize, in his art, the situations and actions which the playwright had imagined. Chekhov's plays demand this accuracy and imaginative freedom from the performer; and the Moscow Art Theater's productions of his works were a demonstration of the perfection, the reticent poetry, of modern realism. And modern realism of this kind is still alive in the work of many artists who have been more or less directly influenced either by Chekhov or by the Moscow Art Theater. In our country, for instance, there is Clifford Odets; in France, Vildrac and Bernard, and the realistic cinema, of which *Symphonie Pastorale* is a recent example.

But this cultivation of the histrionic sensibility, bringing modern realism to its end and its perfection, also provided fresh access to many other dramatic forms. The Moscow technique, when properly developed and critically understood, enables the producer and performer to find the life in any theatrical form; and before the revolution the Moscow Art Theater had thus revivified *Hamlet, Carmen*, the interludes of Cervantes, Neoclassic comedies of several kinds, and many other works which were not realistic in the modern sense at all. A closely related acting technique underlay Reinhardt's virtuosity; and Copeau, in the Vieux Colombier, used it to renew not only the art of acting but, by that means, the art of play-writing also. I shall return to this development in the last chapter, when I discuss Obey's *Noah*, a play based upon Chekhovian modes of awareness but transcending the limitations of modern realism by means of the Biblical legend.

After periods when great drama is written, great performers usually appear to carry on the life of the theater for a few more generations. Such were the Siddonses and Macreadys who kept the great Shakespearian roles alive after Shakespeare's theater was gone, and such, at a further stage of degeneration, were the mimes of the Commedia dell'Arte, improvising on the themes of Terence and Plautus when the theater had lost most of its meaning. The progress of modern realism from Ibsen to Chekhov looks in some respects like a withering and degeneration of this kind: Chekhov does not demand the intellectual scope, the ultimate meanings, which Ibsen demanded, and to some critics Chekhov does not look like a real dramatist but merely an overdeveloped mime, a stage virtuoso. But the theater of modern realism did not afford what Ibsen demanded, and Chekhov is much the more perfect master of its little scene. If Chekhov drastically reduced the dramatic art, he did so in full consciousness, and in obedience both to artistic scruples and to a strict sense of reality. He reduced the dramatic art to its ancient root, from which new growths are possible.

But the tradition of modern realism is not the only version of the theater in our time. The stage itself, belying the realistic pretense of artlessness and pseudo-scientific truth, is there. Most of the best contemporary play-writing accepts the stage "as stage," and by so doing tries to escape realistic limitations altogether. In the following chapters I propose to sample this effort in several kinds of modern plays.

Luigi Pirandello
Preface to *Six Characters in Search of an Author*

It seems like yesterday but is actually many years ago that a nimble little maidservant entered the service of my art. However, she always comes fresh to the job.

She is called Fantasy.

A little puckish and malicious, if she likes to dress in black no one will wish to deny that she is often positively bizarre and no one will wish to believe that she always does everything in the same way and in earnest. She sticks her hand in her pocket, pulls out a cap and bells, sets it on her head, red as a cock's comb, and dashes away. Here today, there tomorrow. And she amuses herself by bringing to my house—since I derive stories and novels and plays from them—the most disgruntled tribe in the world, men, women, children, involved in strange adventures which they can find no way out of; thwarted in their plans; cheated in their hopes; with whom, in short, it is often torture to deal.

Well, this little maidservant of mine, Fantasy, several years ago, had the bad inspiration or ill-omened caprice to bring a family into my house. I wouldn't know where she fished them up or how, but, according to her, I could find in them the subject for a magnificent novel.

I found before me a man about fifty years old, in a dark jacket and light trousers, with a frowning air and ill-natured, mortified eyes; a poor woman in widow's weeds leading by one hand a little girl of four and by the other a boy of rather more than ten; a cheeky and "sexy" girl, also clad in black but with an equivocal and brazen pomp, all atremble with a lively, biting contempt for the mortified old man and for a young fellow of twenty who stood on one side closed in on himself as if he despised them all. In short, the six characters who are seen coming on stage at the beginning of the play. Now one of them and now another—often beating down one another—embarked on the sad story of their adventures, each shouting his own reasons, and projecting in my face his disordered passions, more or less as they do in the play to the unhappy Manager.

What author will be able to say how and why a character was born in his fantasy? The mystery of artistic creation is the same as that of birth. A woman who loves may desire to become a mother; but the desire by itself, however intense, cannot suffice. One fine day she will find herself a mother without having any precise intimation when it began. In the same way an artist imbibes very many germs of life and can never say how and why, at a certain moment, one of these vital germs inserts itself into his fantasy, there to become a living creature on a plane of life superior to the changeable existence of every day.

I can only say that, without having made any effort to seek them out, I found before me, alive—you could touch them and even hear them breathe—the six characters now seen on the stage. And they stayed there in my presence, each with his secret torment and all bound together by the one common origin and mutual entanglement of their affairs, while I had them enter the world of art, constructing from their persons, their passions, and their adventures a novel, a drama, or at least a story.

Born alive, they wished to live.

To me it was never enough to present a man or a woman and what is special and characteristic about them simply for the pleasure of presenting them; to narrate a particular affair, lively or sad, simply for the pleasure of narrating it; to describe a landscape simply for the pleasure of describing it.

There are some writers (and not a few) who do feel this pleasure and, satisfied, ask no more. They are, to speak more precisely, historical writers.

But there are others who, beyond such pleasure, feel a more profound spiritual need on whose account they admit only figures, affairs, landscapes which have been soaked, so to speak, in a particular sense of life and acquire from it a universal value. These are, more precisely, philosophical writers.

I have the misfortune to belong to these last.

I hate symbolic art in which the presentation loses all spontaneous movement in order to become a machine, an allegory—a vain and misconceived effort because the very fact of giving an allegorical sense to a presentation clearly shows that we have to do with a fable which by itself has no truth either fantastic or direct; it was made for the demonstration of some moral truth. The spiritual need I speak of cannot be satisfied—or seldom, and that to the end of a superior irony . . . as for example in Ariosto—by such allegorical symbolism. This latter starts from a concept, and from a concept which creates or tries to create for itself an image. The former on the other hand seeks in the image—which must remain alive and free throughout—a meaning to give it value.

Now, however much I sought, I did not succeed in uncovering this meaning in the six characters. And I concluded therefore that it was no use making them live.

I thought to myself: "I have already afflicted my readers with hundreds and hundreds of stories. Why should I afflict them now by narrating the sad entanglements of these six unfortunates?"

And, thinking thus, I put them away from me. Or rather I did all I could to put them away.

But one doesn't give life to a character for nothing.

Creatures of my spirit, these six were already living a life which was their own and not mine any more, a life which it was not in my power any more to deny them.

Thus it is that while I persisted in desiring to drive them out of my spirit, they, as if completely detached from every narrative support, characters from a novel miraculously emerging from the pages of the book that contained them, went on living on their own, choosing certain moments of the day to reappear before me in the solitude of my study and coming—now one, now the other, now two together—to tempt me, to propose that I present or describe this scene or that, to explain the effects that could be secured with them, the new interest which a certain unusual situation could provide, and so forth.

For a moment I let myself be won over. And this condescension of mine, thus letting myself go for a while, was enough, because they drew from it a new increment of life, a greater degree of clarity and addition, consequently a greater degree of persuasive power over me. And thus as it became gradually harder and harder for me to go back and free myself from them, it became easier and easier for them to come back and tempt me. At a certain point I actually became obsessed with them. Until, all of a sudden, a way out of the difficulty flashed upon me.

"Why not," I said to myself, "present this highly strange fact of an author who refuses to let some of his characters live though they have been born in his fantasy, and the fact that these characters, having by now life in their veins, do not resign themselves to remaining excluded from the world of art? They are detached from me; live on their own; have acquired voice and movement; have by themselves—in this struggle for existence that they have had to wage with me—become dramatic characters, characters that can move and talk on their own initiative; already see themselves as such; have learned to defend themselves against me; will even know how to defend themselves against others. And so let them go where dramatic characters do go to have life: on a stage. And let us see what will happen."

That's what I did. And, naturally, the result was what it had to be: a mixture of tragic and comic, fantastic and realistic, in a humorous situation that was quite new and infinitely complex, a drama which is conveyed by means of the characters, who carry it within them and suffer it, a drama, breathing, speaking, self-propelled, which seeks at all costs to find the means of its own presentation; and the comedy of the vain attempt at an improvised realization of the drama on stage. First, the surprise of the poor actors in a theatrical company rehearsing a play by day on a bare stage (no scenery, no flats). Surprise and incredulity at the sight of the six characters announcing themselves as such in search of an author. Then, immediately afterward, through that sudden fainting fit of the Mother veiled in black, their instinctive interest in the drama of which they catch a glimpse in her and in the other members of the strange family, an obscure, ambiguous drama, coming about so unexpectedly on a stage that is empty and unprepared to receive it. And gradually the growth of this interest to the bursting forth of the contrasting passions of Father, of Stepdaughter, of Son, of that poor Mother, passions seeking, as I said, to overwhelm each other with a tragic, lacerating fury.

And here is the universal meaning at first vainly sought in the six characters, now that, going on stage of their own accord, they succeed in finding it within themselves in the excitement of the desperate struggle which each wages against the other and all wage against the Manager and the actors, who do not understand them.

Without wanting to, without knowing it, in the strife of their bedeviled souls, each of them, defending himself against the accusations of the others, expresses as his own living passion and torment the passion and torment which for so many years have been the pangs of my spirit: the deceit of mutual understanding irremediably founded on the empty abstraction of the words, the multiple personality of everyone corresponding to the possibilities of being to be found in each of us, and finally the inherent tragic conflict between life (which is always moving and changing) and form (which fixes it, immutable).

Two above all among the six characters, the Father and the Stepdaughter, speak of that outrageous unalterable fixity of their form in which he and she see their essential nature expressed permanently and immutably, a nature that for one means punishment and for the other revenge; and they defend it against the factitious affectations and unaware volatility of the actors, and they try to impose it on the vulgar Manager who would like to change it and adapt it to the so-called exigencies of the theatre.

If the six characters don't all seem to exist on the same plane, it is not because some are figures of first rank and others of the second, that is, some are main characters and others minor ones—the elementary perspective necessary to all scenic or narrative art—nor is it that any are not completely created—for their purpose. They are all six at the same point of artistic realization and on the same level of reality, which is the fantastic level of the whole play. Except that the Father, the Stepdaughter, and also the Son are realized as mind; the Mother as nature; the Boy as a presence watching and performing a gesture and the Baby unaware of it all. This fact creates among them a perspective of a new sort. Unconsciously I had had the impression that some of them needed to be fully realized (artistically speaking), others less so, and others merely sketched in as elements in a narrative or presentational sequence: the most alive, the most completely created, are the Father and the Stepdaughter who naturally stand out more and lead the way, dragging themselves along beside the almost dead weight of the others—first, the Son, holding back; second, the Mother, like a victim resigned to her fate, between the two children who have hardly any substance beyond their appearance and who need to be led by the hand.

And actually! actually they had each to appear in that stage of creation which they had attained in the author's fantasy at the moment when he wished to drive them away.

If I now think about these things, about having intuited that necessity, having unconsciously found the way to resolve it by means of a new perspective, and about the way in which I actually obtained it, they seem like miracles. The fact is that the play was really conceived in one of those spontaneous illuminations of the fantasy when by a miracle all the elements of the mind answer to each other's call and work in divine accord. No human brain, working "in the cold," however stirred up it might be, could ever have succeeded in penetrating far enough, could ever have been in a position to satisfy all the exigencies of the play's form. Therefore the reasons which I will give to clarify the values of the play must not be thought of as intentions that I conceived beforehand when I prepared myself for the job and which I now undertake to defend, but only as discoveries which I have been able to make afterward in tranquillity.

I wanted to present six characters seeking an author. Their play does not manage to get presented—precisely because the author whom they seek is missing. Instead is presented the comedy of their vain attempt with all that it contains of tragedy by virtue of the fact that the six characters have been rejected.

But can one present a character while rejecting him? Obviously, to present him one needs, on the contrary, to receive him into one's fantasy before one can express him. And I have actually accepted and realized the six characters: I have, however, accepted and realized them as rejected: in search of *another* author.

What have I rejected of them? Not themselves, obviously, but their drama, which doubtless is what interests them above all but which did not interest me—for the reasons already indicated.

And what is it, for a character—his drama?

Every creature of fantasy and art, in order to exist, must have his drama, that is, a drama in which he may be a character and for which he *is* a character. This drama is the character's *raison d'être,* his vital function, necessary for his existence.

In these six, then, I have accepted the "being" without the reason for being. I have taken the organism and entrusted to it, not its own proper function, but another more complex function into which its own function entered, if at all, only as a datum. A terrible and desperate situation especially for the two—Father and Stepdaughter—who more than the others crave life and more than the others feel themselves to be characters, that is, absolutely need a drama and therefore their own drama—the only one which they can envisage for themselves yet which meantime they see rejected: an "impossible" situation from which they feel they must escape at whatever cost; it is a matter of life and death. True, I have given them another *raison d'être,* another function: precisely that "impossible" situation, the drama of being in search of an author and rejected. But that this should be a *raison d'être,* that it should have become their real function, that it should be necessary, that it should suffice, they can hardly suppose; for they have a life of their own. If someone were to tell them, they wouldn't believe him. It is not possible to believe that the sole reason for our living should lie in a torment that seems to us unjust and inexplicable.

I cannot imagine, therefore, why the charge was brought against me that the character of the Father was not what it should have been because it stepped out of its quality and position as a character and invaded at times the author's province and took it over. I who understand those who don't quite understand me see that the charge derives from the fact that the character expresses and makes his own a torment of spirit which is recognized as mine. Which is entirely natural and of absolutely no significance. Aside from the fact that this torment of spirit fit the character of the Father derives from causes, and is suffered and lived for reasons that have nothing to do with the drama of my personal experience, a fact which alone removes all substance from the criticism, I want to make it clear that the inherent torment of my spirit is one thing, a torment which I can legitimately—provided that it be organic—reflect in a character, and that the activity of my spirit as revealed in the realized work, the activity that succeeds in forming a drama out of the six characters in search of an author is another thing. If the Father participated in this latter activity, if he competed in forming the drama out of the six characters without an author, then and only then would it by all means be justified to say that he was at times the author himself and therefore not the man he should be. But the Father suffers and does not create his existence as a character in search of an author. He suffers it as an inexplicable fatality and as a situation which he tries with all his powers to rebel against, which he tries to remedy; hence it is that he is a character in search of an author and nothing more, even if he expresses as his own the torment of my spirit. If he, so to speak, assumed some of the author's responsibilities, the fatality would be completely explained. He would, that is to say, see himself accepted, if only as a rejected character, accepted in the poet's heart of hearts, and he would no longer have any reason to suffer the despair of not finding someone to construct and affirm his life as a character. I mean that he would quite willingly accept the *raison d'être* which the author gives him and without regrets would forgo his own, throwing over the Manager and the actors to whom in fact he runs as his only recourse.

There is one character, that of the Mother, who on the other hand does not care about being alive (considering being alive as an end in itself). She hasn't the least suspicion that she is *not* alive. It has never occurred to her to ask how and why and in what manner she lives. In short, she is not aware of being a character inasmuch as she is never, even for a moment, detached from her role. She doesn't know she has a role.

This makes her perfectly organic. Indeed, her role of Mother does not of itself, in its natural essence, embrace mental activity. And she does not exist as a mind. She lives in an endless continuum of feeling and therefore she cannot acquire awareness of her life—that is, of her existence as a character. But with all this, even she, in her own way and for her own ends, seeks an author, and at a certain stage seems happy to have been brought before the Manager. Because she hopes to take life from him, perhaps? No: because she hopes the Manager will have her present a scene with the Son in which she would put so much of her own life. But it is a scene which does not exist, which never has and never could take place. So unaware is she of being a character, that is, of the life that is possible to her, all fixed and determined, moment by moment, in every action, every phrase.

She appears on stage with the other characters but without understanding what the others make her do. Obviously, she imagines that the itch for life with which the husband and the daughter are afflicted and for which she herself is to be found on stage is no more than one of the usual incomprehensible extravagances of this man who is both tortured and torturer and—horrible, most horrible—a new equivocal rebellion on the part of that poor erring girl. The Mother is completely passive. The events of her own life and the values they assume in her eyes, her very character, are all things which are "said" by the others and which she only once contradicts, and that because the maternal instinct rises up and rebels within her to make it clear that she didn't at all wish to abandon either the son or the husband: the Son was taken from her and the husband forced her to abandon him. She is only correcting data; she explains and knows nothing.

In short, she is nature. Nature fixed in the figure of a mother.

This character gave me a satisfaction of a new sort, not to be ignored. Nearly all my critics, instead of defining her, after their habit, as "unhuman"—which seems to be the peculiar and incorrigible characteristic of all my creatures without exception—had the goodness to note "with real pleasure" that at last a *very human* figure had emerged from my fantasy. I explain this praise to myself in the following way: since my poor Mother is entirely limited to the natural attitude of a Mother with no possibility of free mental activity, being, that is, little more than a lump of flesh completely alive in all its functions—procreation, lactation, caring for and loving its young—without any need therefore of exercising her brain, she realizes in her person the true and complete "human type." That must be how it is, since in a human organism nothing seems more superfluous than the mind.

But the critics have tried to get rid of the Mother with this praise without bothering to penetrate the nucleus of poetic values which the character in the play represents. A very human figure, certainly, because mindless, that is, unaware of being what she is or not caring to explain it to herself. But not knowing that she is a character doesn't prevent her from being one. That is her drama in my play. And the most living expression of it comes spurting out in her cry to the Manager, who wants her to think all these things have happened already and therefore cannot now be a reason for renewed lamentations: "No, it's happening now, it's happening always! My torture is not a pretense, signore! I am alive and present, always, in every moment of my torture: it is renewed, alive, and present always!" This she *feels*, without being conscious of it, and feels it therefore as something inexplicable: but she feels it so terribly that she doesn't think it *can* be something to explain either to herself or to others. She feels it and that is that. She feels it is pain and this pain is immediate; she cries it out. Thus she reflects the growing fixity of life in a form—the same thing, which in another way, tortures the Father and the Stepdaughter. In them, mind. In her, nature. The mind rebels and, as best it may, seeks an advantage; nature, if not aroused by sensory stimuli, weeps.

Conflict between life-in-movement and form is the inexorable condition not only of the mental but also of the physical order. The life which in order to exist has become fixed in our corporeal form little by little kills that form. The tears of a nature thus fixed lament the irreparable, continuous aging of our bodies. Hence the tears of the Mother are passive and perpetual. Revealed in three faces, made significant in three distinct and simultaneous dramas, this inherent conflict finds in the play its most complete expression. More: the Mother declares also the particular value of artistic form—a form which does not delimit or destroy its own life and which life does not consume—in her cry to the Manager. If the Father and Stepdaughter began their scene a hundred thousand times in succession, always, at the appointed moment, at the instant when the life of the work of art must be expressed with that cry, it would always be heard, unaltered and unalterable in its form, not as a mechanical repetition, not as a return determined by external necessities, but, on the contrary, alive every time and as new, suddenly born *thus forever!* embalmed alive in its incorruptible form. Hence, always, as we open the book, we shall find Francesca alive and confessing to Dante her sweet sin, and if we turn to the passage a hundred thousand times in succession, a hundred thousand times in succession Francesca will speak her words, never repeating them mechanically, but saying them as though each time were the first time with such living and sudden passion that Dante every time will turn faint. All that lives, by the fact of living, has a form, and by the same token must die—except the work of art which lives forever in so far as it *is* form.

The birth of a creature of human fantasy, a birth which is a step across the threshold between nothing and eternity, can also happen suddenly, occasioned by some necessity. An imagined drama needs a character who does or says a certain necessary thing; accordingly this character is born and is precisely what he had to be. In this way Madame Pace is born among the six characters and seems a miracle, even a trick, realistically portrayed on the stage. It is no trick. The birth is real. The new character is alive not because she was alive already but because she is now happily born as is required by the fact of her being a character—she is obliged to be as she is. There is a break here, a sudden change in the level of reality of the scene, because a character can be born in this way only in the poet's fancy and not on the boards of a stage. Without anyone's noticing it, I have all of a sudden changed the scene: I have gathered it up again into my own fantasy without removing it from the spectator's eyes. That is, I have shown them, instead of the stage, my own fantasy in the act of creating—my own fantasy in the form of this same stage. The sudden and uncontrollable changing of a visual phenomenon from one level of reality to another is a miracle comparable to those of the saint who sets his own statue in motion: it is neither wood nor stone at such a moment. But the miracle is not arbitrary. The stage—a stage which accepts the fantastic reality of the six characters—is no fixed, immutable datum. Nothing in this play exists as given and preconceived. Everything is in the making, is in motion, is a sudden experiment: even the place in which this unformed life, reaching after its own form, changes and changes again contrives to shift position organically. The level of reality changes. When I had the idea of bringing Madame Pace to birth right there on the stage, I felt I could do it and I did it. Had I noticed that this birth was unhinging and silently, unnoticed, in a second, giving another shape, another reality to my scene, I certainly wouldn't have brought it about. I would have been afraid of the apparent lack of logic. And I would have committed an ill-omened assault on the beauty of my work. The fervor of my mind saved me from doing so. For, despite appearances, with their specious logic, this fantastic birth is sustained by a real necessity in mysterious, organic relation with the whole life of the work.

That someone now tells me it hasn't all the value it could have because its expression is not constructed but chaotic, because it smacks of romanticism, makes me smile.

I understand why this observation was made to me: because in this work of mine the presentation of the drama in which the six characters are involved appears tumultuous and never proceeds in an orderly manner. There is no logical development, no concatenation of the events. Very true. Had I hunted it with a lamp I couldn't have found a more disordered, crazy, arbitrary, complicated, in short, romantic way of presenting "the drama in which the six characters are involved." Very true. But I have not presented that drama. I have presented another—and I won't undertake to say again what!—in which, among the many fine things that everyone, according to his tastes, can find, there is a discreet satire on romantic procedures: in the six characters thus excited to the point where they stifle themselves in the roles which each of them plays in a certain drama while I present them as characters in another play which they don't know and don't suspect the existence of, so that this inflammation of their passions—which belongs to the realm of romantic procedures—is humorously "placed," located in the void. And the drama of the six characters presented not as it would have been organized by my fantasy had it been accepted but in this way, as a rejected drama, could not exist in the work except as a "situation," with some little development, and could not come out except in indications, stormily, disorderedly, in violent foreshortenings, in a chaotic manner: continually interrupted, sidetracked, contradicted (by one of its characters), denied, and (by two others) not even seen.

There is a character indeed—he who denies the drama which makes him a character, the Son—who draws all his importance and value from being a character not of the comedy in the making—which as such hardly appears—but from the presentation that I made of it. In short, he is the only one who lives solely as a "character in search of an author"—inasmuch as the author he seeks is not a dramatic author. Even this could not be otherwise. The character's attitude is an organic product of my conception, and it is logical that in the situation it should produce greater confusion and disorder and another element of romantic contrast.

But I had precisely to *present* this organic and natural chaos. And to present a chaos is not at all to present chaotically, that is, romantically. That my presentation is the reverse of confused, that it is quite simple, clear, and orderly, is proved by the clarity which the intrigue, the characters, the fantastic and realistic, dramatic and comic levels of the work have had for every public in the world and by the way in which, for those with more searching vision, the unusual values enclosed within it come out.

Great is the confusion of tongues among men if criticisms thus made find words for their expression. No less great than this confusion is the intimate law of order which, obeyed in all points, makes this work of mine classical and typical and at its catastrophic close forbids the use of words. Though the audience eventually understands that one does not create life by artifice and that the drama of the six characters cannot be presented without an author to give them value with his spirit, the Manager remains vulgarly anxious to know how the thing turned out, and the "ending" is remembered by the Son in its sequence of actual moments, but without any sense and therefore not needing a human voice for its expression. It happens stupidly, uselessly, with the going off of a mechanical weapon on stage. It breaks up and disperses the sterile experiment of the characters and the actors, which has apparently been made without the assistance of the poet.

The poet, unknown to them, as if looking on at a distance during the whole period of the experiment, was at the same time busy creating—with it and of it—his own play.

Karen Malpede
Reflections on *The Verge*

Claire, the heroine of Susan Glaspell's *The Verge,* is not a nice woman. She is self-involved. She ignores everyone else's feelings and all her domestic duties, for the sake of her own work. She has several lovers, whom she teases openly, in front of one another and in front of her adoring husband, Harry Archer. She detests her conventional sister, Adelaide, and is openly cruel to her equally conventional daughter, Elizabeth, toward whom she feels not a shred of maternal solicitude or warmth. In a final, brutal moment she kills Tom Edgeworthy, the only person in the play she truly loves.

Hedda Gabler, the most well-known nasty woman in modern drama, has, at least, the decency to kill herself (and to cut off her line by killing her unborn child) after thoroughly disrupting the lives of those around her. She atones for the "sin of being" and rebels against the captivity of the female in one sudden, wordless, masculine act of firing a pistol into her skull. "People don't do such things," the play's last words belong to Judge Brack, one of Hedda's would-be captors.

Claire survives the murder she commits, arguably gone mad but with the lucidity of madness, her verbal capacity all intact. Claire talks us through her dawning understanding of her actions, much as any tragic hero, surrounded by the bodies of his beloved dead, talks us through his final self-revelation.

Hedda Gabler kills herself because she is trapped, not only by the conventions of the nineteenth-century bourgeois housewife but also by the particularly fierce inner contradiction such conventions serve to enforce. Hedda wants to breathe the exalted air of freedom, but she is afraid to leave the house. Gabler, like many of Ibsen's heroines, displays the restless temperament of the creative personality, but she shows neither a shred of artistic talent nor of artistic discipline. Ultimately, she is doomed by what her author, Ibsen, saw as her own infernal emptiness. In plays by men female characters are never artists, are *never* able, therefore, to create and to reflect upon a destiny uniquely theirs. Male playwrights have been too frightened of the female artist ever to reify her form.

Yet Glaspell's Claire is an artist, passionately, obsessively involved. Claire's need to envision and to make gives the play its driving force; there is no other energy equal to hers, no other need as great. Claire stands at the center of this work as a woman character has seldom stood at the center of a drama; she is not the victim but, instead, the executioner of a great and savage plot. Claire's work is breeding plants, and she is on the verge of creating a new species, "Breath of Life." Her struggle is the creator's struggle from first to last. Everything in her upper-class milieu conspires against her. Every move she makes transgresses the proprieties of her sex and station. Yet she makes every move, takes every chance, is active, restless, ceaselessy involved in her creation. The energy of the play revolves around her not because, like Hedda, she is a parasite, sucking other's lives, but because she is the active source, the vibrant center that attracts.

The plant, of course, is a metaphor for self-creation. If Claire could make a new species, she would have made a new woman—one capable of life on life's own terms, a free, unfettered being. It is a life and death struggle, this one for self-creation; at any moment the soul might turn stagnant, and the life force it animates might wither on the vine. The artist, the creatrix, undertakes this struggle, entwines her every reason for living around it. Breath of Life is the creative spirit, the spectacular ability to bring form and essence into being.

Claire is the woman struggling to create herself as artist, struggling to liberate herself from the two thousand years or more of prohibition against the female creative self. Claire is a revolutionary character in a revolutionary play written by a revolutionary woman.

Claire kills her beloved, Tom, in a final lyric passage of an increasingly lyric play, because he represents to her the false ideal of romantic love that has slain women's independent creative selves since romantic love began.

> TOM: I love you, and I will keep you—from fartherness—from harm. You are mine, and you will stay with me! [*roughly*] You hear me? You will stay with me!
>
> CLAIRE [*her head on his breast, in ecstasy of rest. Drowsily*]: You can keep me?
>
> TOM: Darling! I can keep you. I will keep you—safe.
>
> CLAIRE [*troubled by the word, but barely able to raise her head*]: Safe?
>
> TOM [*bringing her to rest again*]: Trust me, Claire.
>
> CLAIRE [*not lifting her head, but turning so she sees Breath of Life*]: Now I can trust—what is? [*suddenly pushing him roughly away*] No! I will beat my life to pieces in the struggle to . . .
>
> TOM: To *what* Claire?
>
> CLAIRE: Not to stop it by seeming to have it. [*with fury*] I will keep my life low—low—that I may never stop myself—or anyone—with the thought it's what *I* have. I'd rather be the steam rising from the manure than be a thing called beautiful! [*with a sight too clear*] Now I know who you are. It is you who puts out the breath of life. Image of beauty—*You fill the place—should be a gate* [*in agony*] Oh, that is it is *you*—fill the place—should be a gate! My darling! . . . Never was loving strong as my loving of you! Do you know that? Oh, know that! Know it now! [*her arms go round his neck*] Hours with you—I'd give my life to have! That it should be you—[*he would loosen her hands, for he cannot breathe. But when she knows she is*

> *choking him, that knowledge is fire burning its way into the last passion*] It is you. It is you . . .

"No! Your are *too much!* You are *not* enough," Claire screams, as she strangles him. The words in every woman's heart in that most sacred moment, not of death but, rather, of orgasmic union, the knowledge that plunders love in a world in which both partners are not free. "You are *too much!*"—I cannot be myself. "You are *not* enough"—I cannot find myself in you.

Claire could lose herself in love. Claire, the beautiful, vivacious, brilliant, is pursued by love all through the play. Harry, the husband; Tom, the doomed lover, whose love for her was chaste; and Dick, the man with whom she is actually having an affair; the daughter Elizabeth, craving a mother's love—all these people lust after Claire, each would claim her for their own, turn her into an image not herself.

Yet real love is not possible in a world in which the woman is not first of all free to become herself through the act of creation. Human beings make culture in order to know themselves as parts and as reflections of the living world. Insofar as women have been forbidden to make culture,women have also been forbidden knowledge of self in the world. Lacking unique destinies, independently wrought, women have lacked dignity, have ultimately lacked the ability to morally reckon with themselves.

A destiny is found through an act of transgression: one steps outside the accepted norm and suddenly recognizes self as distinct and begins, then, if one is made of heroic mettle, to hold self accountable. All the great tragedies teach us this. Claire is a tragic heroine—one of the first. She is given a transgressive action, and she is given words, by her female author, so that she might reflect on what she's done.

When a whole group of American women began to write plays in the 1920s out of a collective feminist consciousness, they often depicted women killing men. Glaspell's most well-known play, *Trifles,* revolves around this theme, as does Sophie Treadwell's *Machinal,* a Broadway hit in 1928, revived successfully in New York in 1990.

Yet by the 1990s popular culture has bowdlerized any radical metaphoric meaning from women's murderous impulses. Now in commercial films and plays women murder their men, their rapists, or their men's wives, as part of the general violent culture in which we live, in which all conflicts are shown to be satisfactorily dealt with by annihilating one's opponent. Patriarchy justifies the brutality of its rule by spinning tales of the murderous intentions of *the other* (as the Gulf "war," more aptly named "slaughter," gives horrifying proof). That women, if given half the chance, will murder men is a cherished, dirty xlittle patriarchal fantasy, albeit sometimes true.

Glaspell's denouement is no longer a satisfactory model for contemporary women playwrights, who must go beyond the annihilative ending in order to further subvert the plot of a society so bent on violence. But this critique in no way diminishes the power of what Glaspell did or the power of reading, or staging, her play today. *The Verge* remains a great drama, and Claire remains a great and necessary character.

Doris Alexander
Desire Under the Elms

It was grief—grief for his mother—that set off *Desire Under the Elms* in Eugene O'Neill's mind. After her death, he made a note of it with the title "Under the Elms" and the date "1922": "Play of New England—laid on farm in 1850, time of California gold rush—make N.E. farmhouse and elm trees almost characters." It had a "hard" father who has "killed off wives (2) with work," along with "3 sons—all hate him." The old man's "possessive pride" is in the farm because "it is so hard." In his "old age in moment of sensual weakness" he marries a young woman and brings her back to the farm. The "youngest son falls for her" and brings on the tragedy.

The clue to O'Neill's grief lies in the California gold rush setting. Of course, the lust for possession is a central theme, and the gold rush expresses it, but O'Neill might have chosen another symbol for it, and later he did hesitate about whether to make it the Silver City silver rush. California and the gold rush won out because they came straight out of memories of his mother's death journey. At the beginning of January 1922 his mother and his brother Jamie had set out for California. No sooner had they arrived than his mother was felled by a brain tumor. She was dead by February 28.

They had gone to realize the money on a piece of property—suddenly booming in value—his father had bought out there years ago. The pursuit of his father's money had powerful associations for O'Neill. He had always seen it as the gold buried on the island of Monte Cristo in the play that had made his father rich from years of starring in it. After his father died, he had written the family friend George C. Tyler that his mother was putting the estate in order: "The treasures of Monte Cristo are buried deep again in prairie dog gold mines, in unlubricated oil wells," he said, but he hoped that with his mother's capable direction "some dividends may finally accrue from the junk buried on the island of Monte Cristo." The modest allowance from his father during his wild years had always appeared to him a witholding of love, and he had always resented the odd investments in which his father had buried the money. Two of his early plays, *Where the Cross Is Made* (1918) and *Gold* (1920), had dealt with a son madly determined to go after his father's treasure of gold buried on a desert island—gold that ironically is actually "junk." Out of these old associations his mother's fatal pursuit of his father's gold buried in California earth naturally transmuted itself for him into a tragedy of the California gold rush with death at the end.

The plot had come to him with three sons, the number his mother had had, and dominated by the image of a house brooded over by two elm trees and pervaded by memories of two dead mothers. The description of the trees in the play shows that they were meant to express the pull out of the past of those two dead women:

> Two enormous elms are on each side of the house. They bend their trailing branches down over the roof. They appear to protect and at the same time

> subdue. There is a sinister maternity in their aspect, a crushing, jealous absorption. They have developed from their intimate contact with the life of man in the house an appalling humanness. They brood oppressively over the house. They are like exhausted women resting their sagging breasts and hands and hair on its roof, and when it rains their tears trickle down monotonously and rot on the shingles.

The house is of a "sickly grayish" color with faded green shutters under its shingled roof, recalling the house in New London where O'Neill spent his boyhood summers, which also had gray paint and shutters and shingles. The extraordinary thing about the two maternal trees that brood over it and their association with two dead women is that O'Neill had actually had *two* mothers. He himself would draw up a "Diagram" of his early emotional life with three love lines in it: one for his father, and two more close together, one labeled "mother love" and the second labeled "nurse love," connected to the other with a line and the word "meaning." So he had mother love from his actual mother and "nurse love meaning mother love" from his nurse Sarah Sandy. When he broke off both lines in adolescence, he terminated Sarah's with the words "breaking away from nurse as mother value." His two mothers often mingled in his mind. He had called the ship that would get the father's gold in *Where the Cross Is Made* the "Mary Allen," a name just one letter off his mother's name, "Mary Ellen." In *Gold* the name combined both mothers to become the "Sarah Allen." The dead spinster Sarah would be floating in the back of his mind when he wrote the square dance scene for *Desire Under the Elms*, for he had the fiddler call out to one of the guests, "Ye're walkin' like a bride down the aisle, Sarah! Waal, while they's life they's allus hope, I've heerd tell." So the two maternal trees and the two dead mothers of his 1922 plot emerged directly out of the double mother of his infancy, called up by his grief for his actual one.

O'Neill did not spell out the "tragedy" of this first plot, but he must have had in mind the killing of the old man, and the subsequent immolation of the young lovers. It was so much the obvious ending for the love conflict that afterward, when O'Neill discarded it, he had to explain it away by having the woman realize confusedly, "That's what I ought t' done, hain't it?" But the murder of the old man did not interest O'Neill. He tried to prod his thinking on the murderous rivalry of father and son by reading pertinent case histories in one of Wilhelm Stekel's psychoanalytic books. It was early November 1923, and Malcolm Cowley happened to be visiting him in his home at Ridgefield, Connecticut. As Cowley recalled, he talked of plans for a "New England" play and showed him Stekel's book, which, he said, had plots enough for "all the playwrights who ever lived." He pointed out particularly—so Cowley recalled—the case record of a mother who seduced her son and drove him mad. (Actually the case—from *Twelve Essays on Sex and Psychoanalysis*—was closer to O'Neill's plot than Cowley remembered, for the seducing mother was really a stepmother, and the son in it was torn by conflicting thoughts of his good mother and his "whore" stepmother in a manner similar to O'Neill's character.) But Stekel did not bring his idea to life. He needed something more meaningful than the murder of the old man to plunge him into participation.

The plunge came when he woke up on New Year's morning in 1924 with his mind still pervaded by a dream. It gave him, he realized, just the right tragic ending for his play. It added *Desire* to the title, making it "Desire Under the Elms." It added a baby to the characters and changed the tragedy to that of a mother who kills her baby to prove her greater love for its father. Like the first plot, this idea came out of his grief, for it recalls the major tragedy of his mother's life back in 1885, more than three years before he himself was born. His father, James O'Neill, had been on tour in *Monte Cristo* out west and had become desperately lonely for his wife, whom he had left in New York with the two children: Jamie, who was seven, and the baby Edmund. For love of her husband, Mary Ellen O'Neill left the two children with her mother and went out to join him. They had just reached Denver when they received a telegram telling them that the baby Edmund was mortally ill. She took the first train back on March 4, but he died that very day. The older boy had caught the measles, and her mother had carelessly allowed him to infect the baby. She felt that if she had been there she could have kept them apart. She felt she had killed the baby by abandoning him, and she was haunted by guilt for the rest of her life.

Eugene O'Neill had been born into the dead baby's place. All his mother's bereavement had focused—so he wrote in a sketched "family history"—into a "fierce concentration of affection" for him. From that time on, he was her baby. She was still calling him "my baby" after he had a baby son of his own, Shane. She ended a letter to him with love for his wife, his baby, "and the biggest baby of the three, *You*." So he was linked eternally to the dead baby whose place he had taken. When he came to write his autobiographical play *Long Day's Journey into Night*, he actually exchanged names with the dead baby, making the live son "Edmund" and the dead baby himself, "Eugene." His brother Jamie had longed only to follow their mother into the grave, and he had had his wish—had succeeded in drinking himself to death—only a little less than two months before Eugene O'Neill dreamed his New Year's dream. The same wish was in the dream of the dead baby which brought the play to such urgent life for O'Neill that he started in on it at once.

The dream had been fraught with his current feelings for his wife Agnes, who was—so he told her—"mother of the best of me" and whose baby he also was, as her letters to him show. "My own dear big baby," she would write, urging him to take care of himself, or, "You poor, poor dear baby," wanting to take care of him. Somewhere behind the dream of the beloved dead baby had lurked his growing unhappiness as the live baby of Agnes. He had founded his life on his love for her, but their marriage had been "unhappy." He had said so after only two years of it, and after six, abysses of silence had begun to open between them, and more and more frequently destructive quarrels broke out between them. He had always felt uncertain of his wife's love. She had come to him out of a precociously complicated love past that made him doubt her. She herself was chronically jealous, and so she had always instinctively reassured herself of his love by provoking his jealousy. Besides, he had a basic distrust of love because of his traumatic discovery at the age of fifteen that his mother was addicted to morphine. So great had been this shock to his faith in life and love that he had discontinued his mother's love line in his "Diagram" at this point. All that basic distrust had been accentuated in his marriage, blending his feeling for his mother with his feeling for Agnes inextricably.

Blended too were his feelings of guilt toward both his wife and his mother. He was convinced that his own birth had shattered his mother's health and made her vulnerable to addiction when her doctor prescribed morphine. He felt the same guilt in his marriage for all the pain that he caused his wife. So Agnes joined his mother to enter both into the dead mother of his play and into Abbie, the new "Maw." O'Neill drew Eben's overall guilt toward his mother from his own, but the concrete example of it recalls Agnes at the time shortly after their marriage when they lived in her house at Point Pleasant on the New Jersey shore. She knew the house, so he had let her take care of the coal stoves, which—Agnes said—needed "to be shaken down every day and the ashes taken out." Only after some time did he awake to the fact that the work was much too heavy for his fragile wife. Then, remorsefully, he took over. His remorse enters the play as Eben's haunted vision of his mother "come back all cramped up t' shake the fire, an' carry ashes, her eyes weepin' an' bloody with smoke an' cinders same's they used t'be." Agnes enters into the stepmother too. Although O'Neill called this character "Abbie" because it is a typically New England name, he could never have chosen a name so close to his pet name for Agnes, "Aggie," had not Abbie been imbued with his feeling for her. All his distrust of Agnes enters Eben's distrust of Abbie when she first enters his life, and after their union, when it sets off her proof of love by infanticide. The same distrust of Agnes invests Abbie as the betraying wife and pulls O'Neill into the betrayed old man.

O'Neill found that he could use for *Desire Under the Elms* some ideas that he had used for a one-act play back in 1918 called *The Rope.* It had also been a farm play, and he had apparently based it on the story of a real farmer he knew, probably from the Truro area near his Provincetown summer home. O'Neill changed him from the fragile old lunatic of *The Rope* into a powerful patriarch for *Desire Under the Elms* but kept his other features. In both plays he is tall, gaunt, stoop-shouldered, and has very weak eyesight. He quotes scripture, often wrathfully. By hard work he has made his farm extraordinarily valuable for the area, but he is a miser and has an ugly history of driving an earlier wife to death. In *The Rope* he has had a second, much younger wife, who has been flagrantly unfaithful. She became the third wife, Abbie, of *Desire Under the Elms.* In both plays he has a hidden treasure of twenty-dollar gold pieces. The younger son of *Desire Under the Elms* digs it up from under the floorboards to buy out his brother's share in the farm with the boatfare to California. In *The Rope* the coins are attached to a noose the old man has set up in the barn, supposedly for his son to hang himself but actually to shower him with the gold.

O'Neill's most intimate feelings toward his family had gone into *The Rope,* for it is an ironical version of the prodigal son story. During his wild years of wandering, O'Neill saw himself as a prodigal son, and he had longed for the prodigal's fated return to the love of his father. The idea of a return to love became permanently linked for him with his feeling of being the prodigal. When he was coming back to New London from Harvard to see his beloved Beatrice Ashe in the fall of 1914, he told her once to expect her "Prodigal Bridegroom" and another time to expect her "Prodigal Husband." A year before he wrote

The Rope, his own father had literally turned into the prodigal's father, for he had taken that role in *The Wanderer,* a play based on the parable in the Bible. O'Neill had watched him deliver the moving words "For this my son was dead, and is alive again" months before he put them into the mouth of the miser father in his play. Quite naturally all his ambivalent feelings for his own father had gone along with them: all the "resentment & hatred" (so labeled in his "Diagram") that he had felt when his father had exiled him to boarding school, all his longing for the love he had had before, all his later resentment at his father's miserly witholding of his "gold," and all the longing to take it. In the play, the father's gold is actually waiting for his son, if he can triumph over his fear of the invitation to hang himself with the rope.

Although the prodigal's mother has already died in *The Rope,* O'Neill found a way to bring his own mother into the play along with all his distrust of her. She enters in the form of a "soft-minded" child whose commonplace name is actually her own: "Mary." The play opens with the child enacting a little pantomime with her doll strangely expressive of O'Neill's mother with her "baby" Eugene. (In *The Great God Brown* O'Neill would have his protagonist see his mother as a child and himself as her "doll," and have him say, "She played mother and child with me for many years.") He gave the child Mary in *The Rope* his mother's "fierce concentration of affection" for her baby. Startled by a noise, she "quickly snatches up the doll, which she hugs fiercely to her breast," and then she runs to hide. She is very like his picture of his mother Mary in his later autobiographical play *Long Day's Journey into Night,* who "hugs him with a frightened, protective tenderness" and hides herself in the depths of her drug addiction. Indeed, the "soft-minded" child stands in the place of his mother, soft-minded from the drug, and she gives herself away by a curious parody of his mother's gestures. In *Long Day's Journey into Night* he describes them: "Her hands flutter up to pat her hair in their aimless, distracted way." Under the drug, she "settles back in relaxed dreaminess, staring fixedly at nothing. Her arms rest limply along the arms of the chair." The child Mary is first seen "staring fixedly" at her doll, and her "hands flutter about aimlessly in relaxed, flabby gestures"—a combination of his mother's tremor with her limpness under the drug. It is this "mother-child" (O'Neill actually once called Beatrice that) who brings down the father's gold by swinging on the rope that the prodigal son feared to touch. At the play's end she is foolishly tossing the goldpieces one by one into the sea. If there is an "unconscious" substratum in all this, it reads like this: the father's gold (love), ardently desired by the son, goes to the mother, but it is "thrown away" on her, soft-minded as she is from the drug.

Both O'Neill's mother and father, trailing the shapes that they had taken in *The Rope,* pushed their way into *Desire Under the Elms.* The miser father even takes on the same age at the end of the play as O'Neill's father when he died in 1920, seventy-six. He also takes on his actual vitality in his old age. Even as late as 1913, James O'Neill's interviewers were rapturous over "the robust power of his features and the strength—physical and mental—that has made him what he is." An echo of the soft-minded child of *The Rope* sounds in the lines of *Desire Under the Elms* on the dead mother of Eben. His father comments on him: "Soft-headed. Like his Maw." O'Neill's own father had thought that he was out of his head during his wild youth, and had always considered him "a bundle of nerves like his mother." O'Neill was so possessed by this oneness with her, and by thoughts of her death as he wrote, that he had the old man at one point threaten to take his shotgun to his son "an' blow his soft brains t' the top o' them elums!" That gives Eben—and O'Neill with him—a death like his mother's death of brain tumor. It merges his soft brains with hers (at the top of the maternal tree). If O'Neill's parents had haunted *The Rope,* written when they were both alive, they could only do so more intensely in *Desire Under the Elms,* written when they were both dead, his mother after his father, united with the dead baby Edmund in the New London earth.

No wonder, then, that as he wrote, the house with its brooding elms became a haunted house, drenched in past sorrow, pervaded by the memory of the dead mother. The set shows all four rooms of the house with its elms, the sky, and a piece of the road, and O'Neill deliberately contrasted its haunted interior with the freedom and promise of the sky and road. The indoor scenes are all set in the shadows of twilight, dawn, or candlelit night. The dead mother pervades these shifting shadows, first in her kitchen where her son Eben sees her come back "all cramped up" to stand by her stove, and then even more palpably in the tomblike parlor—O'Neill says that it is like a "tomb"—where she was laid out. Even the old man senses the chill of her presence, "droppin' off the elums, climbin' up the roof, sneakin' down the chimney, pokin' in the corners!" By contrast, almost all the outdoor scenes are flooded with golden light. A golden sunset begins the play, and the opening lines link it with the longing for love and the gold in California. It is golden sunrise when the two older brothers break free of the farm and go capering off down the road bound "fur the gold fields o' Californi-a." It is golden sunrise again when Eben and Abbie find love, and it is most intensely golden sunrise at the end of their tragedy when they stand for a moment, transfigured by love and sacrifice, "looking up raptly in attitudes strangely aloof and devout."

No one could have sensed more sharply than Eugene O'Neill the push of all these memories arising to direct his plot, his set, his dialogue. He was used to looking beyond the surface in himself and others. He had chosen the Swedish playwright Strindberg as his "master," because Strindberg had led the way that he wanted to go with dramas that pierced the banal exterior of life to reveal the immense realities—psychological, biological, sociological—that work behind them. O'Neill had selected one of the most difficult of Strindberg's "behind-life" dramas, *The Spook Sonata,* for the very first production of a new theater group he had formed with Kenneth Macgowan and Robert Edmond Jones, and, even though he hated essay-writing, he took the trouble to write an explanation of Strindberg's greatness for the program. It would serve to prepare audiences for coming productions of his own plays by educating them to his intention to cut through surface realism. (*The Spook Sonata* had opened on January 3, 1924, two days after his New Year's dream.) Of course, this was his intention in *Desire Under the Elms.*

After it went on he told his friend George Jean Nathan: "What I think everyone missed in 'Desire' is the quality in it I set most store by—the attempt to give an epic tinge to New England's inhibited life-lust, to make its inexpressiveness poetically expressive, to release it." He was not reproducing New England speech literally; he was "trying," he said, "to write a synthetic dialogue which should be, in a way, the distilled essence of New England." He had his characters speak in powerful fragments and piquant arrangements of New England clichés that convey their inexpressiveness yet become vivid poetry. The two older brothers sum up Eben and his belief that he is "Maw—every drop o' blood!" with an ironic refrain that comes up three times, each with variations:

> SIMEON: Like his Paw.
> PETER: Dead spit an' image!
> SIMEON: Dog'll eat dog!

O'Neill knew that a playwright works "as Beethoven did" (so he declared in an interview) "molding tones, giving them color, new meaning, thus creating music." In the dialogue of *Desire Under the Elms,* O'Neill creates a musical theme and variations on the New England stones beginning with Peter's chant "Here—it's stones atop o' the ground—stones atop o' stones," and going on to Eben's "stone atop o' stone—makin' walls till yer heart's a stone," to reach a climax in the old man's "God's in the stones! Build my church on a rock—out o' stones an' I'll be in them! That's what he meant t' Peter! Stones. I picked 'em up an' piled 'em into walls. Ye kin read the years o' my life in them walls, every day a hefted stone."

Both in action and in words his characters recall the animals they live with. The older brothers come in from work "like two friendly oxen" and move clumsily toward their food, "their bodies bumping and rubbing together." Simeon sees their escape from the farm as if they really were oxen: "The halter's broke—the harness is busted—the fence bars is down—the stone walls air crumblin' an' tumblin'! We'll be kickin' up an' tearin' away down the road!" Going off to visit Min, the village prostitute, young Eben is "all slicked up like a prize bull," and when he takes her for the first time he begins "t' beller like a calf." All the women—Min, Eben's Maw, and Abbie—are called cows. His characters see life as did the ancient agricultural civilizations that created all the mythical cow-mother goddesses and all the bull gods. O'Neill knew them from reading Sir James Frazer's *The Golden Bough* and Carl Jung's analysis of the myth-making unconscious in *The Psychology of the Unconscious,* the psychoanalytic book that had interested him most. He explained, "I never intended that the language of that play should be a record of what the characters actually said. I wanted to express what they felt subconsciously."

Subconsciously, all his characters make the age-old equation of the fertile woman with the fertile land. They see in the cultivation of the earth, just as all the ancient cults did, "the fertilization of the mother." They think of the farm as a woman. Eben says that Min, the prostitute, "smells like a wa'm plowed field," and when he takes her, a woman his father and his brothers have possessed before him, he is making his opening battle to possess his mother's farm. The new stepmother, Abbie, lusting for him, "squirms desirously" under the masculine sun, receiving it as if she were the fertile earth. "Hain't the sun strong an' hot?" she asks Eben pointedly. "Ye kin feel it burnin' into the earth—Nature—

makin' thin's grow—bigger an' bigger—burnin' inside ye—makin' ye want t' grow—into somethin' else." The old man looks upon her directly as the fertile earth that he possesses. He tells her: "Sometimes ye air the farm an' sometimes the farm be yew!" He pounds his fist on his knee, crying, "Me an' the farm has got to beget a son!" Eben takes possession of the farm by possessing Abbie. Coming upon his father right afterward, he reverses their roles and orders the old man to get to work. "Ay-eh! I'm bossin' yew! Ha-ha-ha! See how ye like it! Ha-ha-ha! I'm the prize rooster o' this roost." The primeval life-lust creates mythical overtones in his characters so that their struggle takes on an "epic tinge." He told George Jean Nathan, "It's just that—the poetical (in the broadest and deepest sense) vision illuminating even the most sordid and mean blind alleys of life—which I'm convinced is, and is to be, *my* concern and justification as a dramatist. . . . It's where the poetic is buried deep beneath the dull and crude that one's deep-seeing vision is tested."

Later, asked point-blank what *Desire Under the Elms* was all about, O'Neill answered, "'Desire,' briefly, is a tragedy of the possessive—the pitiful longing of man to build his own heaven here on earth by glutting his sense of power with ownership of land, people, money—but principally the land and other people's lives." He did shape his play with this idea in mind, and saw to it that his principal characters transcended their lust for possession through tragic suffering. But O'Neill himself realized instantly the inadequacy of his own explanation, and he added: "Of course, there's more to it than that, and the above is so crude as to misrepresent, but it's the best I can do."

Actually, the meaning of the play emerged from the directive push of the dead-baby dream working itself out within the channels of his theme of possessiveness. His memories formed no passive reservoir but a shaping force. Abbie is driven toward her tragic apotheosis by the same force that impelled O'Neill's mother toward hers. O'Neill derives her passion to possess the farm out of her bitterly homeless state. Homelessness had been his mother's agony. As a touring actor's wife, she had moved endlessly from one alien hotel room to another. In his "family history," O'Neill said that "her bitterest resentment" against her husband had been "that she never had [a] home." In *Long Day's Journey into Night* she attributes the baby's death to that, declaring, "Women need homes, if they are to be good mothers." Abbie enters the play with a passionate utterance of the word "Hum!" and repeats almost the same words with a New England accent: "A woman's got t' hev a hum!" Within the play logic, she seduces her stepson primarily to get a baby that will give her title to the farm (with lust and pique intermixed). The seduction brings her love, so that when Eben discovers that his baby gives her the farm and furiously rejects her, she proves her greater love for him by killing the baby she loves. Out of the magnitude of her sacrifice for love, she rises to tragic exaltation.

The scenes that deal with the baby's death were shaped by O'Neill's sense of oneness with the dead baby Edmund. He has the old man celebrate the birth of the baby with a square dance at which he flaunts his pride in begetting a son so late in life. The scene was called up in O'Neill by his own birth. In his "family history" he wrote of it: "Husband very proud of his birth (confirmed by stories to me)—44 years old at time." The transfer of that pride from his forty-four-year-old father to one seventy-six is enough to make it grotesque, but it is made far more so by the savage irony with which O'Neill designed these scenes. His picture of the old man dancing in triumph before his neighbors what is actually his disgrace emanated from a witches' brew of self-loathing and hatred in himself set off by this proxy vision of his birth (the birth that had caused—so he believed—his mother's addiction). The same witches' brew must have been boiling up in him twelve years before his dream of the dead baby, when he had tried to kill himself. That had been shortly after he supplied the evidence for his divorce from Kathleen Jenkins late in December 1911. It had been a New York divorce, with adultery the only legal grounds, and so he had had to arrange to be seen in bed with a prostitute by several witnesses. That degrading scene had demonstrated intolerably for him the mess he had made of life and love. After it, he had tried to kill himself with an overdose of sleeping tablets. Somewhere in that rush to die out of the loveless world in which he found himself must have been the desire to become what his brother Edmund had always been, his mother's eternally beloved baby. That desire had created his New Year's dream, and so he merged both the baby's birth and his death with his own. Abbie's words on it are redolent of his own suicide attempt: "I left the piller over his little face. Then he killed himself. He stopped breathin'."

The old suicidal pull drew O'Neill more powerfully now that becoming the dead baby meant joining his mother in the grave. That pull sweeps Eben to his tragic end. His is the greatest triumph over possessiveness and the greatest sacrifice for love. Abbie's sacrifice had aimed at possessing him, but his sacrifice of farm, liberty, and life is directed only at sharing her suffering in "prison 'r death 'r hell." Through Eben's tragic end, O'Neill shares with his mother the guilt for the dead baby that proved her love for his father and at the same time is united to her forever as the dead baby. So powerful was this drive toward a reunion in death that it almost broke into complete expression before the tragic climax of the play during the scene in which Abbie and Eben are joined in love. Within the play logic, he takes her in the parlor haunted by his dead mother because the act revenges his mother on his father. But the union vibrates with overtones of a consummation in death. It takes place in a room that looks like "a tomb in which the family has been interred alive." (O'Neill's whole family was in the grave as he wrote.) Its candles summon up the image of Eben's Maw laid out in death, and he takes his new Maw in her name. This initial union with her foreshadows the ultimate union at the end of the tragedy, when he joins her in death.

Those final moments reveal the ultimate aim of that drive toward death. Logically, the Sheriff (alerted by Eben in his first horror at the murder of the baby before his love triumphs) enters at the last as a mere dramatic device to carry the lovers off at the apotheosis of their sacrifice. Actually he comes out of the very heart of the dream wish. O'Neill gives him a quite unnecessary personal name, which rings out with peculiar insistence in the last few lines of the play. It turns out to be that commonplace name—so redolent of meaning for O'Neill—his father's name, "Jim." It is pronounced three times in the space of a few seconds and emerges yet again in the last words of the play, in which the story logic meets the dream logic: "It's a jim-dandy farm, no denyin'. Wished I owned it!" By joining the mother in death through his protagonist, O'Neill is taken up with her into the eternal custody of a father figure in authority (like James O'Neill, who was usually called "the Governor" among theater friends), and he actually bears O'Neill's father's name, "Jim." The image emerges wordlessly out of O'Neill's earliest image of felicity in love. As a real baby, he had been doubly encircled in love, first in the protective arms of his mother and then along with her, in the greater love of his father, that "indefinite hero" of his infancy (so O'Neill called him in his "Diagram"). The same image had inspired his plays of the son who strives to attain his father's gold by way of a mother ship. Eben is impelled by O'Neill's own longing to join his mother in love and death and so attain eternal custody by his father.

With such a powerful death-urge sweeping through his play, O'Neill might easily have been swept along with it. But he was writing drama, the essence of which is conflict, and so he could struggle against it within his play. He fought out his battle by way of his warring father and son. Their clash represents all the life forces in Eugene O'Neill struggling against the lure of death. O'Neill had been drawn into both characters—in part—because he had a powerful sense of being both father and son at this time. He was living among the stony Connecticut farms of Ridgefield, which called up his boyhood New London, Connecticut, summer home surrounded by fields a long walk over the railroad trestle away from the town. "I have a place at New London where I bury stones in the summer," his father had said of it. Eugene O'Neill had raised chickens as a boy, and now his son Shane repeated him, running about with his pet rooster. His other son from his first marriage, Eugene Jr., had been staying for the Christmas holidays with him just before he dreamed his New Year's dream, and he arranged a ticket for him to see *The Spook Sonata* when he returned to school in New York, just as his own father had arranged New York theater tickets for him when he was a boy at school in Stamford, Connecticut. He also had vivid recollections of his father in his roles as the father of the biblical prodigal son in *The Wanderer* and even more as the patriarch Jacob in the play *Joseph and His Brethren*, in which he had toured from 1913 to 1915. (Echoes of the Joseph story crept into *Desire Under the Elms*, such as in Abbie's advances toward Eben and her revenge when repulsed by accusing the boy, which recall Potiphar's wife with Joseph.) All that winter O'Neill had been reading the Old Testament to himself. He later told Lawrence Langner: "Ridgefield always drove me to hard cider, acidosis, and the Old Testament in the weepy, muddy, slush-and-snow days." He was also writing a "Book of Revelation" adaptation from the New Testament when he dreamed his New Year's dream. (Robert Edmond Jones wanted to use it as a medium for experiment with dance movements as theatrical expression.) Finishing it had kept him from starting in on *Desire Under the Elms* after the dream. When he did begin, on January 15, he fit smoothly into the scripture-quoting old man of his play.

This character had originally been conceived as the most possessive of all, one who could gladly set fire to the farm when he died so as to know that "it was all a-dying with me an' no one else'd ever own what was mine, what I'd made out o' nothin' with my own sweat an' blood!" But, as O'Neill wrote, old Ephraim came virtually to transcend the possessiveness that dominates him because he values the farm, not for itself but for its expression of his own creative power. "When ye kin make corn sprout out o' stones, God's livin' in yew!" he says. Ephraim takes on grandeur because O'Neill's most intimate life philosophy flowed into him. Whereas Eben had been impelled to his tragic destiny by O'Neill's sense of oneness with his mother, Ephraim became impelled by O'Neill's realization that he was also "spit an' image" of his strongwilled father. He had early absorbed the striving spirit that had transformed his father from a poor Irish immigrant file-cutter with a heavy brogue into a prominent actor-manager famous for the beauty of his diction. James O'Neill's anecdotes all stress his enthusiasm for overcoming limitations and triumphing over difficulties. One of his favorites had the dying Charlotte Cushman advising him—after their last tour together—to "work, *work,* WORK!" He made a creed of that "work, *work,* WORK!" He often told of his flat failure when he first stepped into the role of Monte Cristo with no time to rehearse, and of how he got at the part "hammer and tongs" to convert it into success. O'Neill had taken over the striving philosophy of his "Hero Father" (so called in his "Diagram"). At eighteen he had discovered Friedrich Nietzsche's *Thus Spake Zarathustra,* and he went on to reread it almost every year of his life thereafter. Its philosophy of striving to create and live by higher values, he found, blended easily into his heritage from his father. Nietzsche has a dialogue between a diamond and a piece of charcoal over the virtues of hardness and softness, with the diamond being hard as all "creators are hard" and suggesting the new commandment: *"Become hard!"* O'Neill had accepted that commandment, and the *hard,* the *difficult,* became his object. Outlining his ideal program for life, he described it as "years of undisturbed hard and difficult work." In his program explanation of *The Spook Sonata,* he said that they had chosen it because "the difficult is properly our special task." "Easy" was his favorite term of contempt. He insisted: "Truth, in the theatre as in life, is eternally difficult just as the easy is the everlasting lie." He never had forgotten his father's regrets in his old age at missing his opportunity to become a great Shakespearean actor. O'Neill thought that he had given in to the lure of "easy" popularity and money with *Monte Cristo,* and he swore on his deathbed to "remain true to the best that is in me though the heavens fall." He knew he could go on writing one successful *Anna Christie* after another, but he declared scathingly, "It would be too easy!" He meant to follow his dream unswervingly so that "my real significant bit of truth, and the ability to express it, will be conquered in time—not tomorrow nor the next day nor any near, easily-attained period, but after the struggle has been long enough and hard enough to merit victory."

He put this entire creative philosophy into the old man of his play, even to his own way of using the words "hard" and "easy." Ephraim says:

> When I come here fifty odd year ago—I was jest twenty an' the strongest an' hardest ye ever seen—ten times as strong an' fifty times as hard as Eben. Waal—this place was nothin' but fields o' stones. Folks laughed when I tuk it. They couldn't know what I knowed. When ye kin make corn sprout out o'

> stones, God's livin' in yew! They wa'n't strong enuf fur that! They reckoned God was easy. They laughed. They don't laugh no more. . . . They're all underground—fur follerin' arter an easy God. God hain't easy.

As O'Neill rejected easy wealth from repeating plays like *Anna Christie,* Ephraim has rejected the easy money he could have had from farming the fertile lands out west. "I could o' been a rich man—but somethin' in me fit me an' fit me—the voice o' God sayin': 'This hain't wuth nothin' to Me!'" He sums up O'Neill's faith as a creator in four words: "God's hard, not easy!"

O'Neill gave the old man his own loneliness as a creator—his own loneliness as a man. Ephraim is "allus lonesome" because everyone covets the farm he has created "without knowin' what it meant." O'Neill had experienced that loneliness deeply in his marriage. Agnes had felt crushed by his triumph as a writer, which was so much greater than her own. Yet she never could grasp his advice to write only out of the best that was in her, and instead had been turning out easy items for money. The abyss between their viewpoints became ever wider; silence divided them. O'Neill put all the pathos of his own "inexpressiveness" into his lonely and betrayed old New Englander's one effort to break his silence and communicate his deepest thinking to his wife. She does not hear a word of it, absorbed as she is in her own designs. Bitterly, the old man tells her to pray "fur understandin'." He foreshadows O'Neill's words to Agnes when all was over between them: "But what do you understand of me or I of you?"

Into the old man too he put his own realization of his tragic possessiveness—particularly in love. The fiercely repeated "my" and "mine" of his characters came right out of his own self-knowledge. His letters to Agnes call her "My Own" or "Own Sweetheart" or "Own little wife." He had been struggling throughout their marriage to adapt to her need for superficial socializing and to accept the invasions of Ridgefield by her impecunious family or casual friends. He did not feel he had conquered it until they moved to their Bermuda home later, and then he told her: "I love Spithead—and not with my old jealous bitter possessiveness—my old man Cabotism!—but as ours, not mine except as mine is included in ours." He had given old Ephraim Cabot his own possessiveness in love, which echoed his father's. In the "family history" O'Neill describes his father as "morbidly jealous of her, even of her affection for children" when he took his wife from them and Edmund died. O'Neill knew he had within him the same "jealous bitter possessiveness." His sense of himself as "spit an' image" of his father shaped old Ephraim Cabot and determined his end.

So powerful was that sense of his father as a directive ideal working within him that he contradicts Ephraim's history in the play to make him fulfill it. His father had been for him the supreme example of romantic married love. He had held him up as a model to live by when he wrote Agnes from his deathbed of the enduring power of his love for his wife. He had been, O'Neill said, "a husband to marvel at." Despite Ephraim's history of working his former wives to death, O'Neill converts him into a standard and model for love. He says of the dead baby, "He'd ought t' been my son, Abbie. Ye'd ought t' loved me. I'm a man. If ye'd loved me, I'd never told no Sheriff on ye no matter what ye did, if they was t' brile me alive!" (At his father's funeral O'Neill had heard William F. Connor sum up James O'Neill as "a man in every sense and in the noblest interpretation of the word.") It is Ephraim who grudgingly praises Eben for his decision to share Abbie's guilt. "Purty good—fur yew!" he says. Although O'Neill devoted the last moment of his play to his exalted lovers walking "hand in hand" out of life, the most impressive final figure is that of the old man, bereft of love and money, relinquishing an impulse to follow his elder sons to California and going back to work with the words "Waal—what d'ye want? God's lonesome, hain't He? God's hard an' lonesome!" If, in the end, the old man took on the most pronounced epic tinge of all, it was because O'Neill put into him his own philosophy of work, taken up from his father, and it was that philosophy beyond everything else that bound him to life. Through Ephraim all the life forces in Eugene O'Neill triumph over the lure of death. O'Neill knew well how much of himself had gone into this character. He said, "I have always loved Ephraim so much! He's so autobiographical!"

If Eugene O'Neill found a theater ready for this play of adultery and infanticide in 1924 America, he did so only because he had taken care to create the theater for it. He had been the prime mover in resurrecting Jig Cook's Provincetown Playhouse and bringing to it the fresh creative talents of Kenneth Macgowan and Robert Edmond Jones. A flurry of productions in their new theater had actually split the writing of *Desire Under the Elms* into two distinct parts. O'Neill had just finished part one at the end of January when he was swept into rehearsals for no less than four of his plays: *Welded, All God's Chillun Got Wings, The Emperor Jones* (a revival with Paul Robeson, who would also take the lead in *All God's Chillun Got Wings*), and an adaptation of Coleridge's *Rime of the Ancient Mariner* (like his adaptation of the last book of the New Testament, which he called the "Book of Revelation," for Robert Edmond Jones to experiment with dance movement). Not until May 24 could O'Neill get back to *Desire Under the Elms.* He finished it on June 16, 1924, and a week later he was reading it to his partners Kenneth Macgowan and Bobby Jones in a hospital where Jones happened to be "laid up." They decided to open *Desire Under the Elms* that fall in their Greenwich Village theater and fill the smaller Provincetown Playhouse with a revival of four of O'Neill's one-act sea plays combined into a cycle to be called "S.S. Glencairn." Rehearsals got under way October 18. O'Neill found himself, as often before, rushing from play to play, with *Desire Under the Elms* rehearsing all morning and afternoon and "S.S. Glencairn" in the evening.

They were painfully handicapped by lack of time and money. Even a brilliant set designer like Bobby Jones could not, in such short time, create elms redolent of a "sinister maternity" which would participate in the play like characters. (In the opening scene, for instance, they were to glow green to make the house they oppress "pale and washed out by contrast.") Neither the elms nor "the house as character" with its "flow of life from room to room" came through as O'Neill knew they could. He had divided each of the three parts of his play into four quick scenes punctuated by moments of darkness. Unfortunately, in performance, these were extended to intermissions with lights turned up in the theater. Later, he declared, "It ruined my idea in 'Desire Under the Elms,' that lights up business! What I want is black out, curtain down, change made in a few seconds, curtain up, then lights again." In compensation, O'Neill was delighted with Walter Huston's acting in the role of the old man. It was, he said, "exactly what I had in mind." He added: "Walter's work was as fine as any I've seen in a theatre. He was infinitely superior to Mary Morris [as Abbie], who was good in sections but had nothing to contribute but stock acting and pumped emotion when something deeply passionate was demanded. The part carried her a lot of the time. Yet it was Mary who made the biggest hit with the public, who received most publicity and critical praise." They opened on November 11, and the first-night critics did their best to kill the play. Most of them thought it a "gruesome morbid" thing. It was the subscription audiences who turned it into a success.

When they moved uptown to the Earl Carroll Theater in January, the District Attorney of New York, Joab Banton, provoked a sudden run on their box office by attacking the play as obscene and threatening to close it. Later that year, when O'Neill payed his dentist, Dr. Lief, he remarked humorously, "But don't thank me, thank that so-amiable District Attorney! Seriously though, his press-agent work is bad in the long run. It attracts the low-minded, looking for smut, and they are highly disappointed or else laugh wherever they imagine double-meanings." The threat to close was opposed so vigorously by those who saw the play's greatness that Banton finally agreed to submit the question to a play jury, which the Authors League had suggested as a way of getting censorship out of the hands of ignorant officials and into those of people competent to judge. When the jury cleared it, laughingly O'Neill said to Kenneth Macgowan: "All's well what ends in publicity only."

In the midst of the Banton uproar O'Neill had asked his agent, Richard Madden: "Do you have to send in script of 'Desire' to committee to make it eligible for Pulitzer Prize? If so, do so. Of course, I know there's no chance for it, but I *do*, for the sake of principle, want to *make* them pass it up." They did pass it up. The prize went to Sidney Howard's comedy *They Knew What They Wanted*, which had opened at about the same time. Howard's own judgment was better. He had rushed to O'Neill's defense during the Banton threat with a letter to the *New York Times* (December 14, 1924) in which he said, "I only ask to be shown anything produced in the English-speaking theatre of recent generations which is half so fine or true or brave as 'Desire Under the Elms.'" The play ran eleven months in New York and then set out for a road tour.

Macgowan thought that they might avoid trouble by softening the most objectionable words, and O'Neill agreed: "Yes, 'harlot' could substitute for 'whore' and 'femalin' or 'sluttin'' or something of the kind for 'whorin.'" Trouble came anyway. O'Neill told Upton Sinclair, "I hear they have 'pinched' my play 'Desire Under the Elms' in your Holy City, Los Angeles. Well, well, and so many of the pioneers are said to have come from New England! Boston has also barred it." In England, the Lord Chamberlain prohibited any production of it. (It had its first very successful opening in London sixteen years later in the midst of World War II, when O'Neill was astounded that "a war ravaged England should show such an interest in a play like 'Desire.'") Long before that it had been produced all over Europe. O'Neill was fascinated by the "stir raised in Moscow" when the Kamerny Theater produced *Desire Under the Elms*. He told Alexander Berkman, the old anarchist: "It seems they held a public trial of the character 'Abby' in the play on the charge of having murdered a child. An audience of the intellegentsia were the jury." She had been declared innocent unanimously because of the pressure on her of "the curse of private property and inhibited New England morals." Berkman assured him that he was right in taking the trial as a sign of the play's popularity. By chance, O'Neill was able to see the Kamerny production of *Desire Under the Elms* when they brought it to Paris in June 1930. Despite the translation into Russian, O'Neill found that they had captured "the inner spirit" of his work. So brilliant was their production that he felt they had fulfilled his lifelong dream of a "theatre of creative imagination."

American critics had greeted the book *Desire Under the Elms* when it appeared in 1925 far more favorably than the first-night play reviewers had. The Freudian critics grasped the father-son rivalry and praised the play as an illustration of the Oedipus complex. O'Neill remarked, "The Freudian brethren and sisteren seem quite set up about it and, after reading astonishing complexes between the lines of my simplicities, claim it for their own. Well, so some of them did with 'Emperor Jones.' They are hard to shake!" To a student who asked him point-blank if he were dramatizing Freud, O'Neill explained the hypothetical nature of scientific theory: "To me, Freud only means uncertain conjectures and explanations about the truths of the emotional past of mankind that every dramatist has clearly sensed since real drama began. Which, I think, answers your question. I respect Freud's work tremendously—but I'm not an addict!"

By this time most critics found *Desire Under the Elms* worth fighting over and began disputes as to whether Abbie, Eben, or Ephraim was the central character, as to whether the theories of Freud or Jung, or a play by Strindberg or by Ibsen, or specifically *They Knew What They Wanted* by Sidney Howard, were the central source, and as to whether the play meant this or that. Even when the Banton conflict was raging, O'Neill himself was already two plays on. Far too busy to be deflected by what he called "the megaphone men," he carried on unswervingly his pursuit of the real realities.

Thornton Wilder

Some Thoughts on Playwrighting

Four fundamental conditions of the drama separate it from the other arts. Each of these conditions has its advantages and disadvantages, each requires a particular aptitude from the dramatist, and from each there are a number of instructive consequences to be derived. These conditions are:

I. The theater is an art which reposes upon the work of many collaborators;
II. It is addressed to the group-mind;
III. It is based upon a pretense and its very nature calls out a multiplication of pretenses;
IV. Its action takes place in a perpetual present time.

I
THE THEATER IS AN ART WHICH REPOSES UPON THE WORK OF MANY COLLABORATORS.

We have been accustomed to think that a work of art is by definition the product of one governing selecting will. A landscape by Cézanne consists of thousands of brushstrokes each commanded by one mind. *Paradise Lost* and *Pride and Prejudice,* even in cheap frayed copies, bear the immediate and exclusive message of one intelligence. It is true that in musical performance we meet with intervening executants, but the element of intervention is slight compared to that which takes place in drama. Illustrations:

1. One of the finest productions of *The Merchant of Venice* in our time showed Sir Henry Irving as Shylock, a noble, wronged, and indignant being, of such stature that the merchants of Venice dwindled before him into irresponsible schoolboys. He was confronted in court by a gracious, even queenly Portia, Miss Ellen Terry. At the Odéon in Paris, however, Gémier played Shylock as a vengeful and hysterical buffoon, confronted in court by a Portia who was a *gamine* from the Paris streets with a lawyer's quill three feet long over her ear; at the close of the trial scene Shylock was driven screaming about the auditorium, behind the spectators' backs and onto the stage again, in a wild Elizabethan revel. Yet for all their divergences both were admirable productions of the play.

2. If there was ever a play in which fidelity to the author's requirements was essential in the representation of the principal rôle, it would seem to be Ibsen's *Hedda Gabler,* for the play is primarily an exposition of her character. Ibsen's directions read:

> Enter from the left Hedda Gabler. She is a woman of twenty-nine. Her face and figure show great refinement and distinction. Her complexion is pale and opaque. Her steel-gray eyes express an unruffled calm. Her hair is of an attractive medium brown, but is not particularly abundant; and she is dressed in a flowing loose-fitting morning gown.

I once saw Eleonora Duse in this rôle. She was a woman of sixty and made no effort to conceal it. Her complexion was pale and transparent. Her hair was white, and she was dressed in a gown that suggested some medieval empress in mourning. And the performance was very fine.

One may well ask: Why write for the theater at all? Why not work in the novel, where such deviations from one's intentions cannot take place?

There are two answers:

1. The theater presents certain vitalities of its own so inviting and stimulating that the writer is willing to receive them in compensation for this inevitable variation from an exact image.

2. The dramatist through working in the theater gradually learns not merely to take account of the presence of the collaborators, but to derive advantage from them; and he learns, above all, to organize the play in such a way that its strength lies not in appearances beyond his control, but in the succession of events and in the unfolding of an idea, in narration.

The gathered audience sits in a darkened room, one end of which is lighted. The nature of the transaction at which it is gazing is a succession of events illustrating a general idea—the stirring of the idea; the gradual feeding out of information; the shock and counter-shock of circumstances; the flow of action; the interruption of action; the moments of allusion to earlier events; the preparation of surprise, dread, or delight—all that is the author's and his alone.

For reasons to be discussed later—the expectancy of the group-mind, the problem of time on the stage, the absence of the narrator, the element of pretense—the theater carries the art of narration to a higher power than the novel or the epic poem. The theater is unfolding action and in the disposition of events the authors may exercise a governance so complete that the distortions effected by the physical appearance of actors, by the fancies of scene-painters, and the misunderstandings of directors, fall into relative insignificance. It is just because the theater is an art of many collaborators, with the constant danger of grave misinterpretation, that the dramatist learns to turn his attention to the laws of narration, its logic, and its deep necessity of presenting a unifying idea stronger than its mere collection of happenings. The dramatist must be by instinct a storyteller.

There is something mysterious about the endowment of the storyteller. Some very great writers possessed very little of it, and some others, lightly esteemed, possessed it in so large a measure that their books survive down the ages, to the confusion of severer critics. Alexandre Dumas had it to an extraordinary degree; while Melville, for all his splendid quality, had it barely sufficiently to raise his work from the realm of nonfiction. It springs, not, as some have said, from an aversion to general ideas, but from an instinctive coupling of idea and illustration; the idea, for a born storyteller, can only be expressed imbedded in its circumstantial illustration. The myth, the parable, the fable are the fountainhead of all fiction and in them is seen most clearly the didactic, moralizing employment of a story. Modern taste shrinks from emphasizing the central idea that hides behind the fiction, but it exists there nevertheless, supplying the unity to fantasizing, and offering a justification to what otherwise we would repudiate as mere arbitrary contrivance, pretentious lying, or individualistic emotional association-spinning. For all their magnificent intellectual endowment, George Meredith and George Eliot were not born storytellers; they chose fiction as the vehicle for their reflections, and the passing of time is revealing their error in that choice. Jane Austen was pure storyteller and her works are outlasting those of apparently more formidable rivals. The theater is more exacting than the novel in regard to this faculty and its presence constitutes a force which compensates the dramatist for the deviations which are introduced into his work by the presence of his collaborators.

The chief of these collaborators are the actors.

The actor's gift is a combination of three separate faculties or endowments. Their presence to a high degree in any one person is extremely rare, although the ambition to possess them is common. Those who rise to the height of the profession represent a selection and a struggle for survival in one of the most difficult and cruel of the artistic activities. The three endowments that compose the gift are observation, imagination, and physical coordination.

1. An observant and analyzing eye for all modes of behavior about us, for dress and manner, and for the signs of thought and emotion in oneself and in others.

2. The strength of imagination and memory whereby the actor may, at the indication in the author's text, explore his store of observations and represent the details of appearance and the intensity of the emotions—joy, fear, surprise, grief, love, and hatred—and through imagination extend them to intenser degrees and to differing characterizations.

3. A physical coordination whereby the force of these inner realizations may be communicated to voice, face, and body.

An actor must *know* the appearances and the mental states; he must *apply* his knowledge to the rôle; and he must physically *express* his knowledge. Moreover, his concentration must be so great that he can effect this representation under conditions of peculiar difficulty—in abrupt transition from the non-imaginative conditions behind the stage; and in the presence of fellow actors who may be momentarily destroying the reality of the action.

A dramatist prepares the characterization of his personages in such a way that it will take advantage of the actor's gift.

Characterization in a novel is presented by the author's dogmatic assertion that the personage was such, and by an analysis of the personage with generally an account of his or her past. Since in the drama this is replaced by the actual presence of the personage before us and since there is no occasion for the intervening all-knowing author to instruct us as to his or her inner nature, a far greater share is given in a play to (1) highly characteristic utterances and (2) concrete occasions in which the character defines itself under action and (3) a conscious preparation of the text whereby the actor may build upon the suggestions in the rôle according to his own abilities.

Characterization in a play is like a blank check which the dramatist accords to the actor for him to fill in—not entirely blank, for a number of indications of individuality are already there, but to a far less definite and absolute degree than in the novel.

The dramatist's principal interest being the movement of the story, he is willing to resign the more detailed aspects of characterization to the actor and is often rewarded beyond his expectation.

The sleepwalking scene from *Macbeth* is a highly compressed selection of words whereby despair and remorse rise to the surface of indirect confession. It is to be assumed that had Shakespeare lived to see what the genius of Sarah

Siddons could pour into the scene from that combination of observation, self-knowledge, imagination, and representational skill, even he might have exclaimed, "I never knew I wrote so well!"

II
THE THEATER IS AN ART ADDRESSED TO A GROUP-MIND.

Painting, sculpture, and the literature of the book are certainly solitary experiences; and it is likely that most people would agree that the audience seated shoulder to shoulder in a concert hall is not an essential element in musical enjoyment.

But a play presupposes a crowd. The reasons for this go deeper than (1) the economic necessity for the support of the play and (2) the fact that the temperament of actors is proverbially dependent on group attention.

It rests on the fact that (1) the pretense, the fiction, on the stage would fall to pieces and absurdity without the support accorded to it by the crowd, and (2) the excitement induced by pretending a fragment of life is such that it partakes of ritual and festival, and requires a throng.

Similarly, the fiction that royal personages are of a mysteriously different nature from other people requires audiences, levées, and processions for its maintenance. Since the beginnings of society, satirists have occupied themselves with the descriptions of kings and queens in their intimacy and delighted in showing how the prerogatives of royalty become absurd when the crowd is not present to extend to them the enhancement of an imaginative awe.

The theater partakes of the nature of festival. Life imitated is life raised to a higher power. In the case of comedy, the vitality of these pretended surprises, deceptions, and *contretemps* becomes so lively that before a spectator, solitary or regarding himself as solitary, the structure of so much event would inevitably expose the artificiality of the attempt and ring hollow and unjustified; and in the case of tragedy, the accumulation of woe and apprehension would soon fall short of conviction. All actors know the disturbing sensation of playing before a handful of spectators at a dress rehearsal or performance where only their interest in pure craftsmanship can barely sustain them. During the last rehearsals the phrase is often heard: "This play is hungry for an audience."

Since the theater is directed to a group-mind, a number of consequences follow:

1. A group-mind presupposes, if not a lowering of standards, a broadening of the fields of interest. The other arts may presuppose an audience of connoisseurs trained in leisure and capable of being interested in certain rarefied aspects of life. The dramatist may be prevented from exhibiting, for example, detailed representations of certain moments in history that require specialized knowledge in the audience, or psychological states in the personages which are of insufficient general interest to evoke self-identification in the majority. In the Second Part of Goethe's *Faust* there are long passages dealing with the theory of paper money. The exposition of the nature of misanthropy (so much more drastic

than Molière's) in Shakespeare's *Timon of Athens* has never been a success. The dramatist accepts this limitation in subject matter and realizes that the group-mind imposes upon him the necessity of treating material understandable by the larger number.

2. It is the presence of the group-mind that brings another requirement to the theater—forward movement.

Maeterlinck said that there was more drama in the spectacle of an old man seated by a table than in the majority of plays offered to the public. He was juggling with the various meanings in the word "drama." In the sense whereby drama means the intensified concentration of life's diversity and significance he may well have been right; if he meant drama as a theatrical representation before an audience, he was wrong. Drama on the stage is inseparable from forward movement, from action.

Many attempts have been made to present Plato's dialogues, Gobineau's fine series of dialogues, *La Renaissance,* and the *Imaginary Conversations* of Landor, but without success. Through some ingredient in the group-mind, and through the sheer weight of anticipation involved in the dressing-up and the assumption of fictional rôles, an action is required, and an action that is more than a mere progress in argumentation and debate.

III

THE THEATRE IS A WORLD OF PRETENSE.

It lives by conventions: a convention is an agreed-upon falsehood, a permitted lie.

Illustrations: Consider at the first performance of the *Medea,* the passage where Medea meditates the murder of her children. An anecdote from antiquity tells us that the audience was so moved by this passage that considerable disturbance took place.

The following conventions were involved:

1. Medea was played by a man.

2. He wore a large mask on his face. In the lip of the mask was an acoustical device for projecting the voice. On his feet he wore shoes with soles and heels half a foot high.

3. His costume was so designed that it conveyed to the audience, by convention: woman of royal birth and Oriental origin.

4. The passage was in metric speech. All poetry is an "agreed-upon falsehood" in regard to speech.

5. The lines were sung in a kind of recitative. All opera involves this "permitted lie" in regard to speech.

Modern taste would say that the passage would convey much greater pathos if a woman "like Medea" had delivered it—with an uncovered face that exhibited all the emotions she was undergoing. For the Greeks, however, there was no pretense that Medea was on the stage. The mask, the costume, the mode of declamation were a series of signs which the spectator interpreted and reassembled in his own mind. Medea was being re-created within the imagination of each of the spectators.

The history of the theater shows us that in its greatest ages the stage employed the greatest number of conventions. The stage is fundamental pretense and it thrives on the acceptance of that fact and in the multiplication of additional pretenses. When it tries to assert that the personages in the action "really are," really inhabit such-and-such rooms, really suffer such-and-such emotions, it loses rather than gains credibility. The modern world is inclined to laugh condescendingly at the fact that in the plays of Racine and Corneille the gods and heroes of antiquity were dressed like the courtiers under Louis XIV; that in the Elizabethan Age scenery was replaced by placards notifying the audience of the location; and that a whip in the hand and a jogging motion of the body indicated that a man was on horseback in the Chinese theater; these devices did not spring from naïveté, however, but from the vitality of the public imagination in those days and from an instinctive feeling as to where the essential and where the inessential lay in drama.

The convention has two functions:

1. It provokes the collaborative activity of the spectator's imagination; and
2. It raises the action from the specific to the general.

This second aspect is of even greater importance than the first.

If Juliet is represented as a girl "very like Juliet"—it was not merely a deference to contemporary prejudices that assigned this rôle to a boy in the Elizabethan Age—moving about in a "real" house with marble staircases, rugs, lamps, and furniture, the impression is irresistibly conveyed that these events happened to this one girl, in one place, at one moment in time. When the play is staged as Shakespeare intended it, the bareness of the stage releases the events from the particular and the experience of Juliet partakes of that of all girls in love, in every time, place, and language.

The stage continually strains to tell this generalized truth and it is the element of pretense that reinforces it. Out of the lie, the pretense, of the theater proceeds a truth more compelling than the novel can attain, for the novel by its own laws is constrained to tell of an action that "once happened"—"once upon a time."

IV

THE ACTION ON THE STAGE TAKES PLACE IN A PERPETUAL PRESENT TIME.

Novels are written in the past tense. The characters in them, it is true, are represented as living moment by moment their present time, but the constant running commentary of the novelist ("Tess slowly descended into the valley"; "Anna Karenina laughed") inevitably conveys to the reader the fact that these events are long since past and over.

The novel is a past reported in the present. On the stage it is always now. This confers upon the action an increased vitality which the novelist longs in vain to incorporate into his work.

This condition in the theater brings with it another important element:

In the theater we are not aware of the intervening storyteller. The speeches arise from the characters in an apparently pure spontaneity.

A play is what takes place.

A novel is what one person tells us took place.

A play visibly represents pure existing. A novel is what one mind, claiming to omniscience, asserts to have existed.

Many dramatists have regretted this absence of the narrator from the stage, with his point of view, his powers of analyzing the behavior of the characters, his ability to interfere and supply further facts about the past, about simultaneous actions not visible on the stage, and, above *all*, his function of pointing the moral and emphasizing the significance of the action. In some periods of the theater he has been present as chorus, or prologue and epilogue, or as *raisonneur.* But surely this absence constitutes an additional force to the form, as well as an additional tax upon the writer's skill. It is the task of the dramatist so to coordinate his play, through the selection of episodes and speeches, that, though he is himself not visible, his point of view and his governing intention will impose themselves on the spectator's attention, not as dogmatic assertion or motto, but as self-evident truth and inevitable deduction.

Imaginative narration—the invention of souls and destinies—is to a philosopher an all but indefensible activity.

Its justification lies in the fact that the communication of ideas from one mind to another inevitably reaches the point where exposition passes into illustration, into parable, metaphor, allegory, and myth.

It is no accident that when Plato arrived at the height of his argument and attempted to convey a theory of knowledge and a theory of the structure of man's nature, he passed over into storytelling, into the myths of the Cave and the Charioteer; and that the great religious teachers have constantly had recourse to the parable as a means of imparting their deepest intuitions.

The theater offers to imaginative narration its highest possibilities. It has many pitfalls and its very vitality betrays it into service as mere diversion and the enhancement of insignificant matter; but it is well to remember that it was the theater that rose to the highest place during those epochs that aftertime has chosen to call "great ages" and that the Athens of Pericles and the reigns of Elizabeth I, Philip II, and Louis XIV were also the ages that gave to the world the greatest dramas it has known.

Bertolt Brecht

Selected Writings on *The Threepenny Opera*

Notes to *The Threepenny Opera*

The Reading of Plays

There is no reason why John Gay's motto for his *Beggar's Opera*—nos haec novimus esse nihil—should be changed for *The Threepenny Opera.* Its publication represents little more than the promptbook of a play wholly surrendered to theatres, and thus is directed at the expert rather than at the consumer. This doesn't mean that the conversion of the maximum number of readers or spectators into experts is not thoroughly desirable; indeed it is under way.

The Threepenny Opera is concerned with bourgeois conceptions not only as content, by representing them, but also through the manner in which it does so. It is a kind of report on life as any member of the audience would like to see it. Since at the same time, however, he sees a good deal that he has no wish to see; since therefore he sees his wishes not merely fulfilled but also criticised (sees himself not as the subject but as the object), he is theoretically in a position to appoint a new function for the theatre. But the theatre itself resists any alteration of its function, and so it seems desirable that the spectator should read plays whose aim is not merely to be performed in the theatre but to change it: out of mistrust of the theatre. Today we see the theatre being given absolute priority over the actual plays. The theatre apparatus's priority is a priority of means of production. This apparatus resists all conversion to other purposes, by taking any play which it encounters and immediately changing it so that it no longer represents a foreign body within the apparatus—except at those points where it neutralises itself. The necessity to stage the new drama correctly—which matters more for the theatre's sake than for the drama's—is modified by the fact that the theatre can stage anything: it theatres it all down. Of course this priority has economic reasons.

The Principal Characters

The character of JONATHAN PEACHUM is not to be resumed in the stereotyped formula "miser," He has no regard for money. Mistrusting as he does anything that might inspire hope, he sees money as just one more wholly ineffective weapon of defence. Certainly he is a rascal, a theatrical rascal of the old school. His crime lies in his conception of the world. Though it is a conception worthy in its ghastliness of standing alongside the achievements of any of the other great criminals, in making a commodity of human misery he is merely following the trend of the times. To give a practical example, when Peachum takes Filch's money in scene I he does not think of locking it in a cashbox but merely shoves it in his pocket: neither this nor any other money is going to save him. It is pure conscientiousness on his part, and a proof of his general despondency, if he does not just throw it away: he cannot throw away the least trifle. His attitude to a million shillings would be exactly the same. In his view neither his money (or all the money in the world) nor his head (or all the heads in the world) will see him through. And this is the reason why he never works but just wanders round his shop with his hat on his head and his hands in his pockets, checking that nothing is going astray. No truly worried man ever works. It is not meanness on his part if he has his Bible chained to his desk because he is scared someone might steal it. He never looks at his son-in-law before he has got him on the gallows, since no conceivable personal values of any kind could influence him to adopt a different approach to a man who deprives him of his daughter. Mac the Knife's other crimes only concern him in so far as they provide a means of getting rid of him. As for Peachum's daughter, she is like the Bible, just a potential aid. This is not so much repellent as disturbing, once you consider what depths of desperation are implied when nothing in the world is of any use except that minute portion which could help to save a drowning man.

The actress playing POLLY PEACHUM should study the foregoing description of Mr Peachum. She is his daughter.

The bandit MACHEATH must be played as a bourgeois phenomenon. The bourgeoisie's fascination with bandits rests on a misconception: that a bandit is not a bourgeois. This misconception is the child of another misconception: that a bourgeois is not a bandit. Does this mean that they are identical? No: occasionally a bandit is not a coward. The qualification "peaceable" normally attributed to the bourgeois by our theatre is here achieved by Macheath's dislike, as a good businessman, of the shedding of blood except where strictly necessary—for the sake of the business. This reduction of bloodshed to a minimum, this economising, is a business principle; at a pinch Mr Macheath can wield an exceptionally agile blade. He is aware what is due to his legend: a certain romantic aura can further the economies in question if enough care is taken to spread it around. He is punctilious in ensuring that all hazardous, or at any rate bloodcurdling actions by his subordinates get ascribed to himself, and is just as reluctant as any professor to see his assistants put their name to a job. He impresses women less as a handsome man than as a well situated one. There are English drawings of *The Beggar's Opera* which show a short, stocky man of about forty with a head like a radish, a bit bald but not lacking dignity. He is emphatically staid, is without the least sense of humour, while his solid qualities can be gauged from the fact that he thinks more of exploiting his employees than of robbing strangers. With the forces of law and order he is on good terms; his common sense tells him that his own security is closely bound up with that of society. To Mr Macheath the kind of affront to public order with which Peachum menaces the police would be profoundly disturbing. Certainly his relations with the ladies of Turnbridge strike him as demanding justification, but this justification is adequately provided by the special nature of his business. Occasionally he has made use of their purely business relationship to cheer himself up, as any bachelor is entitled to do in moderation; but what he appreciates about this more private aspect is the fact that his regular and pedantically punctual visits to a certain Turnbridge coffee-house are *habits*, whose cultivation and proliferation is perhaps the main objective of his correspondingly bourgeois life.

In any case the actor playing Macheath must definitely not base his interpretation of the part on this frequenting of a disorderly house. It is one of the not uncommon but none the less incomprehensible instances of bourgeois demonism.

As for Macheath's true sexual needs, he naturally would rather satisfy them where he can get certain domestic comforts thrown in, in other words with women who are not entirely without means. He sees his marriage as an insurance for his business. However slight his regard for it, his profession necessitates a temporary absence from the capital, and his subordinates are highly unreliable. When he pictures his future he never for one moment sees himself on the gallows, just quietly fishing the stream on a property of his own.

BROWN the police commissioner is a very modern phenomenon. He is a twofold personality: his private and official natures differ completely. He lives not in spite of this fission but through it. And along with him the whole of society is living through its fission. As a private individual he would never dream of lending himself to what he considers his duty as an official. As a private individual he would not (and must not) hurt a fly. . . . In short, his affection for Macheath is entirely genuine; the fact that it brings certain business advantages does not render it suspect; too bad that life is always throwing mud at everything. . . .

Hints for Actors

As for the communication of this material, the spectator must not be made to adopt the empathetic approach. There must be a process of exchange between spectator and actor, with the latter at bottom addressing himself directly to the spectator despite all the strangeness and detachment. The actor then has to tell the spectator more about his character "than lies in the part," He must naturally adopt the attitude which allows the episode to develop easily. At the same time he must also set up relationships with episodes other than those of the story, not just be the story's servant. In a love scene with Macheath, for instance, Polly is not only Macheath's beloved but also Peachum's daughter. Her relations with the spectator must embrace her criticisms of the accepted notions concerning bandits' women and shopkeepers' daughters.

1.* [p. 323] The actors should refrain from depicting these bandits as a collection of those depressing individuals with red neckerchiefs who frequent places of entertainment and with whom no decent person would drink a glass of beer. They are naturally sedate persons, some of them portly and all without exception good mixers when off duty.

2. [p. 323] This is where the actors can demonstrate the practical use of bourgeois virtues and the close relationship between dishonesty and sentiment.

3. [p. 323] It must be made clear how violently energetic a man needs to be if he is to create a situation in which a worthier attitude (that of a bridegroom) is possible.

4. [p. 324] What has to be shown here is the displaying of the bride, her fleshliness, at the moment of its final apportionment. At the very instant when supply must cease, demand has once again to be stimulated to its peak. The bride is desired all round; the bridegroom then sets the pace. It is, in other words, a thoroughly theatrical event. At the same time it has to be shown that the bride is hardly eating. How often one sees the daintiest creatures wolfing down entire chickens and fishes! Not so brides.

5. [p. 329] In showing such matters as Peachum's business the actors do not need to bother too much about the normal *development of the plot.* It is, however,

*These figures refer to numbered passages in the text of *The Threepenny Opera,* which may be found in this volume, beginning on p. 323.

important that they should present a development rather than an ambience. The actor playing one of the beggars should aim to show the selection of an appropriately effective wooden leg (trying on one, laying it aside, trying another, then going back to the first) in such a way that people decide to see the play a second time at the right moment to catch this turn; nor is there anything to prevent the theatre featuring it on the screens in the background.

6. [p. 332] It is absolutely essential that the spectator should see Miss Polly Peachum as a virtuous and agreeable girl. Having given evidence of her uncalculating love in the second scene, she now demonstrates that practical-mindedness which saves it from being mere ordinary frivolity.

7. [p. 334] These ladies are in undisturbed possession of their means of production. Just for this reason they must give no impression that they are free. Democracy for them does not represent the same freedom as it does for those whose means of production can be taken away from them.

8. [p. 335] This is where those Macheaths who seem least inhibited from portraying his death agony commonly baulk at singing the third verse. They would obviously not reject the sexual theme if a tragedy had been made of it. But in our day and age sexual themes undoubtedly belong in the realm of comedy; for sex life and social life conflict, and the resulting contradiction is comic because it can only be resolved historically, i.e. under a different social order. So the actor must be able to put across a ballad like this in a comic way. It is very important how sexual life is represented on stage, if only because a certain primitive materialism always enters into it. The artificiality and transitoriness of all social superstructures becomes visible.

9. [p. 336] Like other ballades in *The Threepenny Opera* this one contains a few lines from François Villon in the German version by K. L. Ammer. The actor will find that it pays to read Ammer's translation, as it shows the differences between a ballade to be sung and a ballade to be read.

10. [p. 344] This scene is an optional one designed for those Pollys who have a gift for comedy.

11. [p. 345] As he paces round his cell the actor playing Macheath can at this point recapitulate all the ways of walking which he has so far shown the audience. The seducer's insolent way, the hunted man's nervous way, the arrogant way, the experienced way and so on. In the course of this brief stroll he can once again show every attitude adopted by Macheath in the course of these few days.

12. [p. 346] This is where the actor of the epic theatre is careful not to let his efforts to stress Macheath's fear of death and make it dominate the whole message of the Act, lead him to throw away the depiction of *true* friendship which follows. (True friendship is only true if it is kept within limits. The moral victory scored by Macheath's two truest friends is barely diminished by these two gentlemen's subsequent moral defeat, when they are not quick *enough* to hand over their means of existence in order to save their friend.)

13. [p. 347] Perhaps the actor can find some way of showing the following: Macheath quite rightly feels that in his case there has been a gruesome miscarriage of justice. And true enough, if justice were to lead to the

victimisation of any more bandits than it does at present it would lose what little reputation it has.

About the Singing of the Songs

When an actor sings he undergoes a change of function. Nothing is more revolting than when the actor pretends not to notice that he has left the level of plain speech and started to sing. The three levels—plain speech, heightened speech and singing—must always remain distinct, and in no case should heightened speech represent an intensification of plain speech, or singing of heightened speech. In no case therefore should singing take place where words are prevented by excess of feeling. The actor must not only sing but show a man singing. His aim is not so much to bring out the emotional content of his song (has one the right to offer others a dish that one has already eaten oneself?) but to show gestures that are so to speak the habits and usage of the body. To this end he would be best advised not to use the actual words of the text when rehearsing, but common everyday phrases which express the same thing in the crude language of ordinary life. As for the melody, he must not follow it blindly: there is a kind of speaking-against-the-music which can have strong effects, the results of a stubborn, incorruptible sobriety which is independent of music and rhythm. If he drops into the melody it must be an event; the actor can emphasise it by plainly showing the pleasure which the melody gives him. It helps the actor if the musicians are visible during his performance and also if he is allowed to make visible preparation for it (by straightening a chair perhaps or making himself up, etc.). Particularly in the songs it is important that "he who is showing should himself be shown."

Why Does the Mounted Messenger Have to be Mounted?

The Threepenny Opera provides a picture of bourgeois society, not just of "elements of the Lumpenproletariat." This society has in turn produced a bourgeois structure of the world, and thereby a specific view of the world without which it could scarcely hope to survive. There is no avoiding the sudden appearance of the Royal Mounted Messenger if the bourgeoisie is to see its own world depicted. Nor has Mr Peachum any other concern in exploiting society's bad conscience for gain. Workers in the theatre should reflect just why it is so particularly stupid to deprive the messenger of his *mount*, as nearly every modernistic director of the play has done. After all, if a judicial murder is to be shown, there is surely no better way of paying due tribute to the theatre's rôle in bourgeois society than to have the journalist who establishes the murdered man's innocence towed into court by a swan. Is it not a piece of self-evident tactlessness if people persuade the audience to laugh at itself by making something comic of the mounted messenger's sudden appearance? Depriving bourgeois literature of the sudden appearance of some form of mounted messenger would reduce it to a mere depiction of conditions. The mounted messenger guarantees you a truly undisturbed appreciation of even the most intolerable conditions, so it is a *sine qua non* for a literature whose *sine qua non* is that it leads nowhere.

It goes without saying that the third finale must be played with total seriousness and utter dignity.

(1928)

Stage Design for *The Threepenny Opera*

In *The Threepenny Opera* the more different the set's appearance as between acting and songs, the better its design. For the Berlin production (1928) a great fairground organ was placed at the back of the stage, with steps on which the jazz band was lodged, together with coloured lamps that lit up when the orchestra was playing. Right and left of the organ were two big screens for the projection of Neher's drawings, framed in red satin. Each time there was a song its title was projected on them in big letters, and lights were lowered from the grid. So as to achieve the right blend of patina and newness, shabbiness and opulence, the curtain was a small, none too clean piece of calico running on metal wires. For the Paris production (1937) opulence and patina took over. There was a real satin drapery with gold fringes, above and to the side of which were suspended big fairground lamps which were lit during the songs. The curtain had two figures of beggars painted on it, more than life size, who pointed to the title "The Threepenny Opera." Screens with further painted figures of beggars were placed downstage right and left.

Peachum's Beggars' Outfitting Shop

Peachum's shop must be so equipped that the audience is able to grasp the nature of this curious concern. The Paris production had two shop windows in the background containing dummies in beggars' outfits. Inside the shop was a stand from which garments and special headgear were suspended, all marked with white labels and numbers. A small low rack contained a few worn-out shoes, numbered like the garments, of a kind only seen in museums under glass. The Kamerny Theatre in Moscow showed Mr Peachum's clients entering the dressing booths as normal human beings, then leaving them as horrible wrecks.

(c. 1937)

Martin Esslin

Samuel Beckett: The Search for Self

If *Waiting for Godot* shows its two heroes whiling away the time in a succession of desultory, and never-ending, games, Beckett's second play deals with an "endgame," the final game in the hour of death.

Waiting for Godot takes place on a terrifying empty open road, *Endgame* in a claustrophobic interior. *Waiting for Godot* consists of two symmetrical movements that balance each other; *Endgame* has only one act that shows the running down of a mechanism until it comes to a stop. Yet *Endgame*, like *Waiting for Godot*, groups its characters in symmetrical pairs.

In a bare room with two small windows, a blind old man, Hamm, sits in a wheelchair. Hamm is paralysed, and can no longer stand. His servant, Clov, is unable to sit down. In two ash-cans that stand by the wall are Hamm's legless parents, Nagg and Nell. The world outside is dead. Some great catastrophe, of which the four characters in the play are, or believe themselves to be, the sole survivors, has killed all living beings.

Hamm and Clov (ham actor and clown? Hammer and Nail—French *"clou"*?) in some ways resemble Pozzo and Lucky. Hamm is the master, Clov the servant. Hamm is selfish, sensuous, domineering. Clov hates Hamm and wants to leave him, but he must obey his orders. "Do this, do that, and I do it. I never refuse. Why?" Will Clov have the force to leave Hamm? That is the source of the dramatic tension of the play. If he leaves, Hamm must die, as Clov is the only one left who can feed him. But Clov also must die, as there is no one else left in the world, and Hamm's store is the last remaining source of food. If Clov can muster the will power to leave, he will not only kill Hamm but commit suicide. He will thus succeed where Estragon and Vladimir have failed so often.

Hamm fancies himself as a writer—or, rather, as the spinner of a tale of which he composes a brief passage every day. It is a story about a catastrophe that caused the death of large numbers of people. On this particular day, the tale has reached an episode in which the father of a starving child asks Hamm for bread for his child. Finally the father begs Hamm to take in his child, should it still be alive when he gets back to his home. It appears that Clov might well be that very child. He was brought to Hamm when he was too small to remember. Hamm was a father to him, or, as he himself puts it, "But for me . . . no father. But for Hamm . . . no home." The situation in *Endgame* is the reverse of that in Joyce's *Ulysses,* where a father finds a substitute for a lost son. Here a foster son is trying to leave his foster father.

Clov has been trying to leave Hamm ever since he was born, or as he says, "Ever since I was whelped." Hamm is burdened with a great load of guilt. He might have saved large numbers of people who begged him for help. "The place was crawling with them!" One of the neighbours, old Mother Pegg, who was "bonny once, like a flower of the field" and perhaps Hamm's lover, was killed through his cruelty: "When old Mother Pegg asked you for oil for her lamp and you told her to get out to hell . . . you know what she died of, Mother Pegg? Of darkness." Now the supplies in Hamm's own household are running out: the sweets, the flour for the parents' pap, even Hamm's painkiller. The world is running down. "Something is taking its course."

Hamm is childish; he plays with a three-legged toy dog, and he is full of self-pity. Clov serves him as his eyes. At regular intervals he is asked to survey the outside world from the two tiny windows high up in the wall. The right-hand window looks out on land, the left-hand on to the sea. But even the tides have stopped.

Hamm is untidy. Clov is a fanatic of order.

Hamm's parents, in their dustbins, are grotesquely sentimental imbeciles. They lost their legs in an accident while cycling through the Ardennes on their tandem, on the road to Sedan. They remember the day they went rowing on Lake Como—the day after they became engaged—one April afternoon (cf. the love scene in a boat on a lake in *Krapp's Last Tape*), and Nagg, in the tones of an

Edwardian raconteur, retells the funny story that made his bride laugh then and that he has since repeated *ad nauseam.*

Hamm hates his parents. Nell secretly urges Clov to desert Hamm. Nagg, having been awakened to listen to Hamm's tale, scolds him: "Whom did you call when you were a tiny boy, and were frightened in the dark? Your mother? No. Me." But he immediately reveals how selfishly he ignored these calls. "We let you cry. Then we moved out of earshot, so that we might sleep in peace. . . . I hope the day will come when you'll really need to have me listen to you. . . . Yes, I hope I'll live till then, to hear you calling me like when you were a tiny little boy, and were frightened, in the dark, and I was your only hope."

As the end approaches, Hamm imagines what will happen when Clov leaves him. He confirms Nagg's forecast: "There I'll be in the old shelter, alone against the silence and . . . the stillness. . . . I'll have called my father and I'll have called my . . . son," which indicates that he does indeed regard Clov as his son.

For a last time, Clov looks out of the windows with his telescope. He sees something unusual. "A small . . . boy!" But it is not entirely clear whether he has really seen this strange sign of continuing life, "a potential procreator." In some way, this is the turning point. Hamm says, "It's the end, Clov, we've come to the end. I don't need you any more." Perhaps he does not believe that Clov will really be able to leave him. But Clov has finally decided that he will go: "I open the door of the cell and go. I am so bowed I only see my feet, if I open my eyes, and between my legs a little trail of black dust. I say to myself that the earth is extinguished, though I never saw it lit. . . . It's easy going. . . . When I fall I'll weep for happiness." And as blind Hamm indulges in a last monologue of reminiscence and self-pity, Clov appears, dressed for departure in a Panama hat, tweed coat, raincoat over his arm, and listens to Hamm's speech, motionless. When the curtain falls, he is still there. It remains open whether he will really leave.

The final tableau of *Endgame* bears a curious resemblance to the ending of a little-known but highly significant play by the brilliant Russian dramatist and man of the theatre Nikolai Evreinov, which appeared in an English translation as early as 1915—*The Theatre of the Soul.*[1] This one-act play is a monodrama that takes place *inside a human being* and shows the constituent parts of his ego, his emotional self and his rational self, in conflict with each other. The man, Ivanov, is sitting in a café, debating with himself whether to run away with a nightclub singer or go back to his wife. His emotional self urges him to leave, his rational self tries to persuade him of the advantages, moral and material, of staying with his wife. As they come to blows, a bullet pierces the heart that has been beating in the background. Ivanov has shot himself. The rational and emotional selves fall down dead. A third figure, who has been sleeping in the background, gets up. He is dressed in travelling clothes and carries a suitcase. It is the immortal part of Ivanov that now has to move on.

---

[1] Nikolai Evreinov, *The Theatre of the Soul, Monodrama,* trans. M. Potapenko and C. St John (London, 1915).

While it is unlikely that Beckett knew this old and long-forgotten Russian play, the parallels are very striking. Evreinov's monodrama is a purely rational construction designed to present to a cabaret audience what was then the newest psychological trend. Beckett's play springs from genuine depths. Yet the suggestion that *Endgame* may also be a monodrama has much to be said for it. The enclosed space with the two tiny windows through which Clov observes the outside world; the dustbins that hold the suppressed and despised parents, and whose lids Clov is ordered to press down when they become obnoxious; Hamm, blind and emotional; Clov, performing the function of the senses for him—all these might well represent different aspects of a single personality, repressed memories in the subconscious mind, the emotional and the intellectual selves. Is Clov then the intellect, bound to serve the emotions, instincts, and appetites, and trying to free himself from such disorderly and tyrannical masters, yet doomed to die when its connection with the animal side of the personality is severed? Is the death of the outside world the gradual receding of the links to reality that takes place in the process of ageing and dying? Is *Endgame* a monodrama depicting the dissolution of a personality in the hour of death?

It would be wrong to assume that these questions can be definitely answered. *Endgame* certainly was not planned as a sustained allegory of this type. But there are indications that there is an element of monodrama in the play. Hamm describes a memory that is strangely reminiscent of the situation in *Endgame:* "I once knew a madman who thought the end of the world had come. He was a painter—an engraver. . . . I used to go and see him in the asylum. I'd take him by the hand and drag him to the window. Look! There! All that rising corn! And there! Look! The sails of the herring fleet! All that loveliness! . . . He'd snatch away his hand and go back into his corner. Appalled. All he had seen was ashes. . . . He alone had been spared. Forgotten. . . . It appears the case is . . . was not so . . . so unusual." Hamm's own world resembles the delusions of the mad painter. Moreover, what is the significance of the picture mentioned in the stage directions? "Hanging near door, its face to wall, a picture." Is that picture a memory? Is the story a lucid moment in the consciousness of that very painter whose dying hours we witness from behind the scenes of his mind?

Beckett's plays can be interpreted on many levels. *Endgame* may well be a monodrama on one level and a morality play about the death of a rich man on another. But the peculiar psychological reality of Beckett's characters has often been noticed. Pozzo and Lucky have been interpreted as body and mind; Vladimir and Estragon have been seen as so complementary that they might be the two halves of a single personality, the conscious and the subconscious mind. Each of these three pairs—Pozzo-Lucky; Vladimir-Estragon; Hamm-Clov—is linked by a relationship of mutual interdependence, wanting to leave each other, at war with each other, and yet dependent on each other. *"Nec tecum, nec sine te."* This is a frequent situation among people—married couples, for example—but it is also an image of the interrelatedness of the elements within a single personality, particularly if the personality is in conflict with itself.

In Beckett's first play, *Eleutheria,* the basic situation was, superficially, analogous to the relationship between Clov and Hamm. The young hero of that play wanted to leave his family; in the end he succeeded in getting away. In *Endgame*, however, that situation has been deepened into truly universal significance; it has been concentrated and immeasurably enriched precisely by having been freed from all elements of a naturalistic social setting and external plot. The process of contraction, which Beckett described as the essence of the artistic tendency in his essay on Proust, has here been carried out triumphantly. Instead of merely exploring a surface, a play like *Endgame* has become a shaft driven deep down into the core of being; that is why it exists on a multitude of levels, revealing new ones as it is more closely studied. What at first might have appeared as obscurity or lack of definition is later recognized as the very hallmark of the density of texture, the tremendous concentration of a work that springs from a truly creative imagination, as distinct from a merely imitative one.

The force of these considerations is brought out with particular clarity when we are confronted by an attempt to interpret a play like *Endgame* as a mere exercise in conscious or subconscious autobiography. In an extremely ingenious essay[2] Lionel Abel has worked out the thesis that in the characters of Hamm and Pozzo Beckett may have portrayed his literary master, James Joyce, while Lucky and Clov stand for Beckett himself. *Endgame* then becomes an allegory of the relationship between the domineering, nearly blind Joyce and his adoring disciple, who felt himself crushed by his master's overpowering literary influence. Superficially the parallels are striking: Hamm is presented as being at work on an interminable story, Lucky is being made to perform a set piece of thinking, which, Mr Abel argues, is in fact a parody of Joyce's style. Yet on closer reflection this theory surely becomes untenable; not because there may not be a certain amount of truth in it (every writer is bound to use elements of his own experience of life in his work) but because, far from illuminating the full content of a play like *Endgame,* such an interpretation reduces it to a trivial level. If *Endgame* really were nothing but a thinly disguised account of the literary, or even the human, relationship between two particular individuals, it could not possibly produce the impact it has had on audiences utterly ignorant of these particular, very private circumstances. Yet *Endgame* undoubtedly has a very deep and direct impact, which can spring only from its touching a chord in the minds of a very large number of human beings. The problems of the relationship between a literary master and his pupil would be very unlikely to elicit such a response; very few people in the audience would feel directly involved. Admittedly, a play that presented the conflict between Joyce and Beckett openly, or thinly disguised, might arouse the curiosity of audiences who are always eager for autobiographical revelations. But this is just what *Endgame* does *not* do. If it nevertheless arouses profound emotion in its audience, this can be due only to the fact that it is felt to deal with a conflict of a far more universal nature. Once that is seen, it becomes clear that while it is fascinating to argue about the aptness

[2] Lionel Abel, "Joyce the father, Beckett the son," *The New Leader,* New York, 14 December 1959.

of such autobiographical elements, such a discussion leaves the central problem of understanding the play and exploring its many-layered meanings still to be tackled.

As a matter of fact, the parallels are by no means so close: Lucky's speech in *Waiting for Godot*, for example, is anything but a parody of Joyce's style. It is, if anything, a parody of philosophical jargon and scientific double-talk—the very opposite of what either Joyce or Beckett ever wanted to achieve in their writing. Pozzo, on the other hand, who would stand for Joyce, is utterly inartistic in his first persona, and becomes reflective in a melancholy vein only after he has gone blind. And if Pozzo is Joyce, what would be the significance of Lucky's dumbness, which comes at the same time as Pozzo's blindness? The novel that Hamm composes in *Endgame* is characterized by its attempt at scientific exactitude, and there is a clear suggestion that it is not a work of art at all but a thinly disguised vehicle for the expression of Hamm's sense of guilt about his behaviour at the time of the great mysterious calamity, when he refused to save his neighbours. Clov, on the other hand, is shown as totally uninterested in Hamm's "Work in Progress," so that Hamm has to bribe his senile father to listen to it—surely a situation as unlike that of Joyce and Beckett as can be imagined.

The experience expressed in Beckett's plays is of a far more profound and fundamental nature than mere autobiography. They reveal his experience of temporality and evanescence; his sense of the tragic difficulty of becoming aware of one's own self in the merciless process of renovation and destruction that occurs with change in time; of the difficulty of communication between human beings; of the unending quest for reality in a world in which everything is uncertain and the borderline between dream and waking is ever shifting; of the tragic nature of all love relationships and the self-deception of friendship (of which Beckett speaks in the essay on Proust), and so on. In *Endgame* we are also certainly confronted with a very powerful expression of the sense of deadness, of leaden heaviness and hopelessness, that is experienced in states of deep depression: the world outside goes dead for the victim of such states, but inside his mind there is ceaseless argument between parts of his personality that have become autonomous entities.

This is not to say that Beckett gives a clinical description of psychopathological states. His creative intuition explores the elements of experience and shows to what extent all human beings carry the seeds of such depression and disintegration within the deeper layers of their personality. If the prisoners of San Quentin responded to *Waiting for Godot*, it was because they were confronted with *their own experience* of time, waiting, hope, and despair; because they recognized the truth about *their own human relationships* in the sadomasochistic interdependence of Pozzo and Lucky and in the bickering hate-love between Vladimir and Estragon. This is also the key to the wide success of Beckett's plays: to be confronted with concrete projections of the deepest fears and anxieties, which have been only vaguely experienced at a half-conscious level, constitutes a process of catharsis and liberation analogous to the therapeutic effect in psychoanalysis of confronting the subconscious contents of the mind. This is the moment of release from deadening habit, through facing up to the suffering of existence, that Vladimir almost attains in *Waiting for Godot*. This also, probably, is the release that could occur if Clov had the courage to break his bondage to Hamm and venture out into the world, which may not, after all, be so dead as it appeared from within the claustrophobic confines of Hamm's realm. This, in fact, seems to be hinted at by the strange episode of the little boy whom Clov observes in the last stage of *Endgame*. Is this boy a symbol of life outside the closed circuit of withdrawal from reality?

It is significant that in the original, French version, this episode is dealt with in greater detail than in the later, English one. Again Beckett seems to have felt that he had been too explicit. And from an artistic point of view he is surely right; in his type of theatre the half-light of suggestion is more powerful than the overtly symbolical. But the comparison between the two versions is illuminating nevertheless. In the English version, Clov, after expressing surprise at what he has discovered, merely says:

> CLOV [*dismayed*]: Looks like a small boy!
> HAMM [*sarcastic*]: A small . . . boy!
> CLOV: I'll go and see. [*He gets down, drops the telescope, goes towards the door, turns.*] I'll take the gaff. [*He looks for the gaff, sees it, picks it up, hastens towards the door.*]
> HAMM: No!
> [CLOV *halts.*]
> CLOV: No? A potential procreator?
> HAMM: If he exists he'll die there or he'll come here. And if he doesn't . . . [*Pause.*]

In the original, French version, Hamm shows far greater interest in the boy, and his attitude changes from open hostility to resignation.

> CLOV: There is someone there! Someone!
> HAMM: Well, go and exterminate him! [CLOV *gets down from the stool.*] Somebody! [*With trembling voice*] Do your duty! [CLOV *rushes to the door.*] No, don't bother. [CLOV *stops.*] What distance? [CLOV *climbs back on the stool, looks through the telescope.*]
> CLOV: Seventy . . . four metres.
> HAMM: Approaching? Receding?
> CLOV [*continues to look*]: Stationary.
> HAMM: Sex?
> CLOV: What does it matter? [*He opens the window, leans out. Pause. He straightens, lowers the telescope, turns to* HAMM, *frightened.*] Looks like a little boy.
> HAMM: Occupied with?
> CLOV: What?
> HAMM [*violently*]: What is he doing?
> CLOV [*also violently*]: I don't know what he's doing. What little boys used to do. [*He looks through the telescope. Pause. Puts it down, turns to* HAMM.] He seems to be sitting on the ground, with his back against something.
> HAMM: The lifted stone. [*Pause.*] Your eyesight is getting better. [*Pause.*] No doubt he is looking at the house with the eyes of Moses dying.
> CLOV: No.
> HAMM: What is he looking at?
> CLOV [*violently*]: I don't know what he is looking at. [*He raises the telescope. Pause.*

> *Lowers the telescope, turns to* HAMM.] His navel. Or thereabouts. [*Pause.*] Why this cross-examination?
>
> HAMM: Perhaps he is dead.[3]

After this, the French text and the English version again coincide: Clov wants to tackle the newcomer with his gaff, Hamm stops him, and, after a brief moment of doubt as to whether Clov has told him the truth, realizes that the turning point has come: "It's the end, Clov, we've come to the end. I don't need you any more."

The longer, more elaborate version of this episode clearly reveals the religious or quasi-religious symbolism of the little boy; the references to Moses and the lifted stone seem to hint that the first human being, the first sign of life discovered in the outside world since the great calamity when the earth went dead, is not, like Moses, dying within sight of the promised land, but, like Christ the moment after the resurrection, has been newly born into a new life, leaning, a babe, against the lifted stone. Moreover, like the Buddha, the little boy contemplates his navel. And his appearance convinces Hamm that the moment of parting, the final stage of the endgame, has come.

It may well be that the sighting of this little boy—undoubtedly a climactic event in the play—stands for redemption from the illusion and evanescence of time through the recognition, and acceptance, of a higher reality: the little boy contemplates his own navel; that is, he fixes his attention on the great emptiness of nirvana, nothingness, of which Democritus the Abderite has said, in one of Beckett's favourite quotations, "Nothing is more real than nothing."[4]

There is a moment of illumination, shortly before he himself dies, in which Murphy, having played a *game of chess*, experiences a strange sensation: ". . . and Murphy began to see nothing, that colourlessness which is such a rare post-natal treat, being the absence . . . not of *percipere* but of *percipi.* His other senses also found themselves at peace, an unexpected pleasure. Not the numb peace of their own suspension, but the positive peace that comes when the somethings give way, or perhaps simply add up, to the Nothing, than which in the guffaw of the Abderite naught is more real. Time did not cease, that would be asking too much, but the wheels of rounds and pauses did, as Murphy with his head among the armies [i.e. of the chessmen] continued to suck in, through all the posterns of his withered soul, the accidentless One-and-Only, conveniently called Nothing."[5]

Does Hamm, who has shut himself off from the world and killed the rest of mankind by holding on to his material possessions—Hamm, blind, sensual, egocentric—then die when Clov, the rational part of the self, perceives the true reality of the illusoriness of the material world, the redemption and resurrection, the liberation from the wheels of time that lies in union with the "accidentless One-and-Only, conveniently called Nothing"? Or is the discovery of the little boy

---

[3] Beckett, *Fin de Partie* (Paris: Les Editions de Minuit, 1957), pp. 103–5.

[4] Beckett, *Malone Dies*, in *Molloy/Malone Dies/The Unnamble* (London: John Calder, 1959), p. 193.

[5] *Murphy*, p. 246.

merely a symbol of the coming of death—union with nothingness in a different, more concrete sense? Or does the reappearance of life in the outside world indicate that the period of loss of contact with the world has come to an end, that the crisis has passed and that a disintegrating personality is about to find the way back to integration, "the solemn change towards merciless reality in Hamm and ruthless acceptance of freedom in Clov," as the Jungian analyst Dr Metman puts it?[6]

There is no need to try to pursue these alternatives any further; to decide in favour of one would only impair the stimulating coexistence of these and other possible implications. There is, however, an illuminating commentary on Beckett's views about the interrelation between material wants and a feeling of restlessness and futility in the short mime play *Act Without Words I*, which was performed with *Endgame* during its first run. The scene is a desert on to which a man is "flung backwards." Mysterious whistles draw his attention in various directions. A number of more or less desirable objects, notably a carafe of water, are dangled before him. He tries to get the water. It hangs too high. A number of cubes, obviously designed to make it easier for him to reach the water, descend from the flies. But however ingeniously he piles them on top of one another, the water always slides just outside his reach. In the end he sinks into complete immobility. The whistle sounds—but he no longer heeds it. The water is dangled in front of his face—but he does not move. Even the palm tree in the shade of which he has been sitting is whisked off into the flies. He remains immobile, looking at his hands.[7]

Here again we find man flung on to the stage of life, at first obeying the call of a number of impulses, having his attention drawn to the pursuit of illusory objectives by whistles from the wings, but finding peace only when he has learned his lesson and refuses any of the material satisfactions dangled before him. The pursuit of objectives that forever recede as they are attained—inevitably so through the action of time, which changes us in the process of reaching what we crave—can find release only in the recognition of that nothingness which is the only reality. The whistle that sounds from the wings resembles the whistle with which Hamm summons Clov to minister to his material needs. And the final, immobile position of the man in *Act Without Words I* recalls the posture of the little boy in the original version of *Endgame.*

The activity of Pozzo and Lucky, the driver and the driven, always on the way from place to place; the waiting of Estragon and Vladimir, whose attention is always focused on the promise of a coming; the defensive position of Hamm, who has built himself a shelter from the world to hold on to his possessions, are all aspects of the same futile preoccupation with objectives and illusory goals. All movement is disorder. As Clov says, "I love order. It's my dream. A world where all would be silent and still and each thing in its last place, under the last dust."

[6] Eva Metman, "Reflections on Samual Beckett's Plays," *Journal of Analytical Psychology*, London, January 1960, p. 58.
[7] Beckett, *Act Without Words I*, in *Krapp's Last Tape and Other Dramatic Pieces* (New York: Grove Press, 1960).

Eugène Ionesco

From *Notes and Counter Notes: Writings on the Theatre*

Preface to *Rhinoceros*

For an American School Edition with the French Text

In 1938 the writer, Denis de Rougemont, was staying in Germany, at Nuremberg, during a Nazi demonstration. He tells us how he found himself in the midst of a dense crowd awaiting the arrival of Hitler. The people were beginning to show signs of impatience when the Führer and his entourage came in sight, at the far end of an avenue, looking very small in the distance. As they drew near, the narrator watched the crowd, gradually caught up in a kind of hysteria, frenziedly acclaiming the sinister man. The hysteria spread and advanced, with Hitler, like a tide. This delirious enthusiasm first of all astonished the writer. But when the Führer came quite near and all the people round him gave way to the general hysteria, Denis de Rougemont felt the same raging madness in himself, struggling to possess him, a delirium that electrified him. He was on the point of falling under the spell, when something rose from the depth of his being and resisted the rising storm. Denis de Rougemont tells us how uneasy he felt, how terribly alone in the crowd, offering hesitant resistance. His hair stood on end, literally he says, and then he understood what is meant by Holy Terror. Just then it was not his mind that resisted, not arguments formulated in his brain, but his whole being, his whole personality that bridled. There, perhaps, is the starting point of *Rhinoceros;* when one is assailed by arguments, theories, intellectual slogans and all kinds of propaganda, it is probably impossible to give any explanation for this refusal. Later on, discursive reasoning will doubtless lend support to this natural instinctive resistance, this spiritual rejection. So Bérenger is not very sure at the time why he resists rhinoceritis, and this is proof that his resistance is genuine and profound. It may be that Bérenger is a man who, like Denis de Rougemont, is allergic to mass movements and marches of all kinds, military or not. *Rhinoceros* is certainly an anti-Nazi play, yet it is also and mainly an attack on collective hysteria and the epidemics that lurk beneath the surface of reason and ideas but are none the less serious collective diseases passed off as ideologies: once we realize that History has lost its reason, that lying propaganda masks a contradiction between the facts and the ideologies that explain them, once we cast a lucid eye on the world as it is today, this is enough to stop us being taken in by irrational reasons and so help us not to lose our heads.

Indoctrinated champions of several different persuasions have obviously blamed the author for taking up an anti-intellectual attitude and choosing as principal hero a human being who is rather simple. But I considered it was not for me to present an emotional ideological system opposed to the other emotional ideological systems in force today. Quite simply I thought it was my job to reveal the inanity of these terrible systems, what they can lead to, how they stir people up, stupefy them and then reduce them to slavery. It will surely be apparent that the speeches of Botard, of Jean and Dudard are nothing but the pet shibboleths and slogans of various dogmas, concealing beneath a mask of cold objectivity the most irrational and violent pressures. *Rhinoceros* too is an attempt at "demystification."

(November 1960.)

A Note on *Rhinoceros*

In a recent number of *Arts* my critic, and friend notwithstanding, Pierre Marcabru, considers this play to be the "reactionary" expression of an outsider's refusal to join in the human adventure. I must say that the play really was meant to show the Nazification of a country as well as the confusion of a man who, naturally immune to the disease, witnesses the mental metamorphosis of the community in which he lives. Originally "rhinoceritis" was indeed a form of Nazism. Between the two world wars, Nazism was largely invented by the fashionable intellectuals, ideologists and pseudo-intellectuals who spread the doctrine. They were rhinoceroses. Even more than the mob they have the mentality of the mob. They do not think, they recite "intellectual" slogans.

Rhinoceros, which is now being acted in a number of countries, makes a surprisingly strong impression on audiences of every kind. Is it because this play is a vague attack on all sorts of things? This is one reproach leveled at me, though others specially blame me for attacking only Nazi totalitarianism. And is it really refusing the human adventure to stand up to the collective hysteria, even if backed by philosophy, to which whole nations periodically fall victim? Is it not in fact astonishing that the vicissitudes of such a lonely and individualistic character as the hero of my play should appeal to so many people throughout the world? And is it not in our profound isolation, far beyond sophistry and schism, that this universal fraternity finds common ground? In spite of the well-reasoned objections of so many distinguished critics, people have responded sympathetically to my chief character, which would rather seem to prove that it is not this odd man out who is cut off from the human adventure, but our harebrained ideologists instead. I wonder if I have hit upon a new plague of modern times, a strange disease that thrives in different forms but is in principle the same. Automatic systematized thinking, the idolization of ideologies, screens the mind from reality, perverts our understanding and makes us blind. Ideologies too raise the barricades, dehumanize men and make it impossible for them to be *friends notwithstanding;* they get in the way of what we call co-existence, for a rhinoceros can only come to terms with one of his own kind, a sectarian with a member of his particular sect.

I believe Jean-Louis Barrault has caught the meaning of the play and put it over perfectly. The Germans turned it into tragedy, Jean-Louis Barrault into terrible farce and fantastic fable. Both interpretations are valid, exemplary productions of this play.

(*Arts,* January 1961.)

About *Rhinoceros* in the United States

I am delighted that *Rhinoceros* is a popular success in New York, but at the same time surprised and saddened. I was present at only one almost complete rehearsal before the first night. I must admit I was completely baffled. As far as I could see they had turned Bérenger's friend, Jean, a character that is hard, fierce and disturbing, into a comic figure, a *feeble* rhinoceros. It also seemed to me that the production had turned Bérenger himself, an irresolute character, a reluctant hero, allergic to this epidemic of rhinoceritis, into a kind of tough hard-headed intellectual, a kind of unruly revolutionary who knows quite well what he is doing (and though he knows, does not wish to explain the reasons for his attitude). I also saw on the stage some boxing matches that do not figure in the text, introduced by the director. I wonder why? I have often been at odds with my directors: either they are not daring enough and reduce the impact of my plays by not exhausting their full potentialities as the stage demands: or else they adorn the text, overloading it with cheap embellishment and decoration, unnecessary and therefore worthless. I am not writing literature. I am doing something quite different: I am writing drama. I mean that my text is not just dialogue, but also "stage directions." These should be respected as much as the text, they are essential, they are also sufficient. If I gave no indication that Bérenger and Jean should come to blows on the stage and pull each other's noses, it is because I had no desire for them to do so.

I have read the American critics on the play and noticed that everyone agreed the play was funny. Well, it isn't. Although it is a farce, it is above all a tragedy. The production reveals not only an absence of style (as in everything put on in the boulevard theatres of Paris or on Broadway; and in Moscow too, moreover, where the advanced theatre is the old theatre of 1900) but above all intellectual dishonesty. We actually witness a mental transformation in a whole group of people; the old values are degraded and overthrown, new ones emerge and triumph. One man helplessly sees his whole world transformed and can do nothing to stop it: he no longer knows if he is right or wrong; he struggles but without hope; he is the last of his species. He is lost. This is thought to be funny. The New York critics agreed unanimously. Barrault, on the other hand, has made a tragic farce of it: a farce, yes, but an oppressive one. Moretti, the Italian actor who has just died and was one of the greatest actors in the world, made a sad and moving drama of it. Stroux, the director in Düsseldorf, and his leading actor, Karl Maria Schley, turned it into a stark tragedy with no concessions, barely relieved by its cold irony; the Poles made it a weighty play. But Mr. Anthony, acting on the advice of Heaven-knows-who, and certainly not the author, has made it into something funny and anti-conformist. Now there is something too imprecise about conformism. Strictly speaking, my play is not even a satire: it is a fairly objective description of the growth of fanaticism, of the birth of a totalitarianism that grows, propagates, conquers, transforms a whole world and, naturally, being totalitarian, transforms it totally. The play should trace and point the different stages of this phenomenon. I really tried to say this to the American director; I clearly indicated in the few interviews I was able to give that the aim of this play was to denounce, to expose, to show how an ideology gets transformed into idolatry, how it seeps into everything, how it reduces the masses to hysteria, how an idea, which was reasonable enough for discussion at the start, can become monstrous when leaders, then totalitarian dictators, governing islands, acres or continents, use it as a powerful stimulant, a strong dose of which has a malignant and monstrous effect on the "people," turning them into an hysterical mob. I had made it quite clear that I was not attacking conformism, for there is a certain anti-conformism which is conformist in so far as the conformism it attacks is merely something vague. An anti-conformist play may be amusing; an anti-totalitarian play, for example, is not. It cannot be anything else but painful and serious.

Some critics blame me for denouncing evil without saying what good is. I have been reproached for not letting Bérenger say what ideology inspired his resistance. They take this to be a fundamental objection: but it is so easy to rely on a system of thought that is more or less mechanical. If I asked Mr. Walter Kerr, the dramatic critic of the *New York Herald Tribune*, to define his personal philosophy for me, he would be highly embarrassed. And yet it is for him and not for me to find the answer, for him and the other critics, and above all for the audience. Personally I mistrust the intellectuals who for thirty-odd years have done nothing but propagate different forms of rhinoceritis and who merely provide a philosophical justification for those waves of collective hysteria that periodically sweep over whole nations. Is it not the intellectuals who are the inventors of Nazism? If I set up a ready-made ideology in opposition to other ready-made ideologies, which clutter up the brain, I should only be opposing one system of rhinoceric slogans to another. There was once a time when, if someone uttered the words "Jew" or "Bolshevik," people would lower their horns and charge off to kill a Jew or a Bolshevik and anyone accused of compromise with a Jew or a Bolshevik. Nowadays if someone utters the word "bourgeois" or in any part of the wide world, "capitalist Imperialist," everyone charges off just as stupidly, just as blindly, to kill the bourgeois or the capitalist without having the slightest idea what lies behind the insult or why it has been used, without even knowing what kind of person tries to incite others to do his own dirty work or what private motives provoke such monstrous violence. It seems to me absurd to ask a dramatist to produce a bible, a way to salvation; it is absurd to think for a whole world and give it some automatic philosophy: a playwright poses problems. People should think about them, when they are quiet and alone, and try and resolve them for themselves, without constraint; an unworkable solution one has found for oneself is infinitely more valuable than a ready-made ideology that stops men from thinking.

Besides, personally, I have my own answer: if I gave it away it would lose its force; like a key, it would have no further use and become a pass key, another system of slogans leading to a new form of rhinoceritis.

One of the great critics in New York complains that, after destroying one conformism, I put nothing else in its place, leaving him and the audience in a vacuum. That is exactly what I wanted to do. A free man should pull himself out of vacuity on his own, by his own efforts and not by the efforts of other people.[1]

(*Arts*, 1961.)

Geoffrey Borny
The Two *Glass Menageries:* Reading Edition and Acting Edition

I. From Page

The Glass Menagerie was rescued from possible oblivion in December 1944 by the almost unprecedented efforts of the Chicago critics who cajoled audiences to go and see the play. Since its rather faltering first appearance, the play has gone on to become a classic of American theatre. Like all classics it has had built up around it a body of criticism which has done as much to obscure the meaning of the play as to elucidate it. King rightly claims that "*The Glass Menagerie*, though it has achieved a firmly established position in the canon of American plays, is often distorted, if not misunderstood, by readers, directors and audiences."

One of the most enduring, and least endearing, critical standpoints that has guided generations of readers into seeing the play from a point of view different from that intended and created by the playwright has been the almost constant, and often unquestioned, assumption that Williams's strength lies in his ability to depict *realistic* characters and situations. Not surprisingly this same standpoint leads to a devaluation of all the "plastic" or "expressionistic" elements of his playwriting.

The major results of such a view of Williams would not have been quite so harmful had they stayed within the covers of books and articles about Williams. Unfortunately many directors seem to be influenced by the pro-realism critics, and often downplay or cut many of the more overtly expressionistic staging devices suggested by Williams as important for the play's production. Understandably audiences can appreciate only what is presented to them, and what is most often presented by directors of *The Glass Menagerie* is a kind of

[1] *Rhinoceros* has to date had more than a thousand performances in Germany, hundreds in the Americas and in France. Many others in England, Italy, Poland, Japan, Scandinavia, Czechoslovakia, Yugoslavia, Holland, etc. etc. . . . I am amazed at the success of this play. Do people understand it properly? Do they see in it that monstrous phenomenon of "massification"? And while they are all "massifiable," are they also, essentially and in their heart of hearts, all individualists, unique human beings?

sentimental soap opera. An anonymous reviewer of the Broadway revival of the play succinctly sums up the result of ignoring the plastic/expressionistic elements of the play when he claims of Williams that

> his plays are seldom performed with the force, subtlety and imaginative risk-taking they require. Instead they have [been] . . . pushed toward realism, their complex truths dealt with as so much emotional merchandise to be peddled.

I am convinced that any downplaying in production of the expressionist elements in Williams's *Glass Menagerie* results in a trivialization of the play. I wished to see whether or not my thesis could be sustained and the acid test had to be a production of the play. Some of the hoary old critical clichés about the so-called weaknesses of Williams's expressionistic staging devices immediately come under close scrutiny the moment one examines the play in the theatre rather than simply in the study. Long revered critical judgements concerning *The Glass Menagerie* which appear on the face of it to be incontestable, turn out to be either of dubious validity or downright unworkable, when tested in the laboratory of the theatre.

Leacroft came to a similar conclusion concerning the famous drawings for the Tragic, Comic and Satyric scenes that appeared in Serlio's *Achitettura* (1545). When Leacroft tried to move from page to stage he found that the drawings were inconsistent with each other, a thing that no one had noticed before because no one had previously tested them.

> As is so often the case the preparation of a reconstruction—whether in the form of a drawing or a model—draws attention to discrepancies between drawings *which have been reproduced many times by historians without comment.*

Leacroft's comment certainly applies mutatis mutandis to the judgements of critics concerning Williams's use of nonrealistic staging techniques. Gassner's (*Masters of the Drama*) early attitude that "*The Glass Menagerie* was marred only by some preciosity, mainly in the form of stage directions, most of which were eliminated in Eddie Dowling's memorable Broadway production" is echoed, and echoed uncritically, by as important a critic as Styan in his recent three volume work on modern drama:

> From the German director Erwin Piscator he had borrowed the idea of scattering through the play titles and images projected on a screen, and Williams certainly thought of his episodic method as expressionistic. "Expressionism and all other unconventional techniques in drama have only one valid aim, and that is a closer approach to truth." Such devices were not an attempt to escape from reality, but to find "a more penetrating and vivid expression of things as they are." He also believed that they were a step towards "a new, plastic theatre," one replacing "the exhausted theatre of realistic conventions." This was the familiar tune, but in the event, the screen device got in the way of the direct impact of the play's action, and was wisely abandoned.

Styan's dismissive attitude towards those plastic expressionistic elements of Williams's dramaturgy is based on his theoretical predilection for dramas employing realistic techniques of both staging and dramaturgy. Styan thereby "saves" Williams from himself by transforming the American dramatist into a copy of Anton Chekhov:

> The non-realistic framework of the play, in which the son of the family, Tom Wingfield, plays chorus to the scenes of his memory, and even the Piscator devices of expressionistically projected titles and images (dropped in the New York production without damaging the fabric of the play), scarcely disturbed the Chekhovian detail of the main action.

Weales has taken into account the importance of both the realistic and nonrealistic elements of Williams's work:

> [Williams] has never been a realistic playwright . . . but he has always been capable of writing a psychologically valid scene in the American realistic tradition—the breakfast scene in *The Glass Menagerie* for instance. . . . However grounded in realistic surface, the events in Williams' plays . . . take on meaning that transcends psychological realism.

Ten years earlier however, even Weales had implied that Williams's use of nonrealistic techniques was the weaker part of his work and specifically pointed out that it was realism that was central to the American theatrical tradition:

> In the Production Notes to *The Glass Menagerie* he [Williams] makes quite clear that he believes that poetic truth can best be depicted through a transformation that escapes the appearance of reality. Despite his aesthetic stand, he is enough in the tradition of the American theater to ask his characters to move and speak realistically when he wants them to.

Weales's slighting reference to Williams's "aesthetic stand" and Styan's even more dismissive reference to "the familiar tune" echo Gassner's charge of "preciosity." Each of these important critics recognizes that Williams has claimed that he is not a realist, yet all of them undervalue precisely those nonrealistic elements in Williams's work that lie outside the mainstream of the American theatre tradition. Williams is praised whenever his work fits the realistic tradition that Corrigan has called "the theater of verisimilitude [where] the settings, props, and lighting provide an environment for the action." Even as perceptive a critic as Eric Bentley asserts that "Williams can write very well when he writes realistically, when, for example, he writes dialogue based on observation of character; in fact, all his dramatic talent lies in that direction."

In my production of *The Glass Menagerie* I did not wish to challenge the obviously correct view that Williams did in fact write fine realistic dialogue and create convincing characters. Rather I wished to see whether or not the nonrealistic plastic/expressionistic elements so often dismissed by the major critics did have theatrical validity. In effect I wished to test who was the better judge of the play, the critics or the playwright himself.

When embarking on the production I accepted a directorial standpoint that assumed that there is such an entity as *the playwright's play.* With this in mind I tried to follow Williams's stated instructions as closely as possible. I fully accepted the relationship between director and playwright that is so lucidly expressed by Corrigan:

> In the theatre, the playwright must be the primary creator. His intention *must* be expressed in every aspect of production. . . . The chief aim of all the artists of the theatre must always be to realise that attitude toward life expressed by the playwright in his play.

I believe that it is only when a director utilises Williams's specified nonrealistic staging techniques in combination with actors creating their characters through the use of a realistic acting style that the audience can actually experience the play that Williams wrote.

The first thing that faces a director of *The Glass Menagerie* is that there are *two* published versions to choose between. The script that Eddie Dowling used in Chicago and later New York is not the version that is published in Williams's collected works. It is not true as Styan claims that Williams "wisely abandoned" the screen device and the other nonrealistic elements. The truth is that Williams wrote a more "acceptable," because more realistic, version of his play in order to get it performed. He in effect wrote an adaptation of *The Glass Menagerie* for the original performance *but* he chose to have his original play published in his collected works.

The version used by Eddie Dowling in the original production is the so-called Acting Edition published and commented on by the Dramatists Play Service Inc. This version

> differs from the book of the play as first issued by Random House: the dialogue itself has to some extent been revised by the author, and the stage directions likewise. The latter have been drastically changed in order to guide the director and actor.

The Acting Edition certainly is different from the Reading Edition. The director and actors are given a play that is much more realistic than the one published as the Reading Edition and republished in Williams's collected plays. To begin with in the Acting Edition, unlike the Reading Edition, there is no summary description of the characters preceding the play; the expressionistic stage devices are dispensed with; the expressionistic lighting plot is made more realistic; the transition between scenes is made less obviously artificial. When one adds to this the fact that, as Beaurline noted, there are "1100 verbal changes" that transform the characters, we can see that we are dealing with two markedly different plays.

I chose to direct the Reading Edition both because Williams seems to prefer this version and also because I think it is a much finer play than the Acting Edition. The critics who prefer the Acting Edition usually do so because that version is more realistic. Rowland, who made a study of the two versions of *The Glass Menagerie* using the character of Amanda as the focus of his examination, claims that the Amanda of the Acting Edition is

> more gentle, more loving and understanding . . . more conversational, more human, more realistic. . . . We see a more humble and practical Amanda in a more depressing and realistic world. . . . [She speaks] lines that are full of life and realism.

Ultimately Rowland rests his case concerning the "superiority" of the Acting Edition over the Reading Edition on the grounds that the Acting Version is more lifelike:

> The "reading version" gives Laura and Tom a stage companion. The "acting version" gives them a mother.

I don't contest that the Acting Edition may be more lifelike—more realistic or that that version was well received by audiences. What I do contest is the assumption that dramatic art is better the closer it gets to verisimilitude. More precisely it seems to me that the harder one pushes Williams's play towards realism the more one confuses art with life and falsifies the vision of reality that he wished to dramatize. In his production notes to the play Williams explicitly defends expressionism and attacks realism, as a means of expressing reality. Williams, while vindicating the artist and denigrating the photographer, argues strongly that

> reality is an organic thing which the poetic imagination can represent, in essence only through transformation, through changing into other forms than those which were merely present in appearance.

Williams does not see his function as an artist simply in terms of putting life on stage. He follows Aristotle's view that "poetry [art] is something more philosophical and more worthy of serious attention than history; for while poetry is concerned with universal truths, history treats of particular facts." Williams does everything in his power to transcend the particular by using all the nonrealistic techniques he can to break the illusion of reality which is so beloved in the tradition of American realism. The mere accurate description of "a mother" is trivial for Williams who has always claimed that his concern as a dramatist was to master the "necessary trick of rising above the singular to the plural concern, from personal to general import."

Because Williams is so adept at writing realistic dialogue and creating convincingly real characters there is a great danger that the director and actors will emphasize these realistic elements at the cost of the nonrealistic ones. We need constantly in a production of *The Glass Menagerie* to remind ourselves that it is a work of art and not a slice of life. A play is, as Hethmon succinctly puts it, "in its very nature a symbolic representation of an individual action in relation to a system."

There seems to be little problem for critics and directors when dealing with either overtly realistic or overtly symbolic dramas. It is only in plays like *The Glass Menagerie* where realism and nonrealism are mixed, where, as Wimsatt puts it, "the order of images . . . follows or apparently follows the lines of representational necessity or probability, though at the same time a symbolic significance is managed" that problems of interpretation seem to occur.

It should be clear why I chose the Reading Edition in preference to the Acting Edition as the version I wished to direct. The Reading Version has within it a realistic story that is like life and has individual significance but because it is seen through a filter of nonrealistic staging devices and metafictional elements which draw attention to the fact that the play is a play, not a slice of life, the realistic story is made symbolically significant. It moves from the particular to the universal, from history to philosophy, from a representation of men to a representation of an action.

In directing *The Glass Menagerie* Reading Edition I did not undervalue the realistic characterization because any attempt to make symbolic puppets of characters like Amanda, Tom or Laura would be to make a travesty of the play. However, by equally emphasizing the nonrealistic and metafictional elements, I hoped to avoid the trap noted by Juneja when he accurately pointed out that "in *The Glass Menagerie* it is the warm flesh and blood humanity of three dimensional characters that tends to mask the philosophic import of the play."

II. To Stage

Tom, the narrator, immediately sets up the metafictional nature of the play. Williams gives the actor playing Tom the stage direction: "He addresses the audience." This immediately breaks the fourth wall convention so central to realism. The fact that this is a "memory play" also means that historification takes place inducing a kind of alienation effect which controls the possible empathetic response that would otherwise occur. Empathy is inappropriate because it leads to an identification between the audience and the hero or heroine. What Williams requires is a degree of "distance" to allow the audience to see beyond the particular problems of his characters in order to perceive the symbolic truth of the action of the play. It is for this reason that Williams makes Tom both a character in the play and the narrator of the play. In his stage instructions Williams points out that "the narrator is an undisguised convention of the play. He takes whatever licence with dramatic convention is convenient to his purposes." In my production presented in a small proscenium arch theatre, I emphasized this conventional use of the narrator figure by having Tom enter through the audience, click his fingers as a signal for the curtain to rise, and then climb up the fire-escape steps onto the stage itself. The aim of this entrance was to immediately establish for the audience that the theatre, including the auditorium in which they were sitting, was a world that they shared with the narrator. The characters in the play, who are figments of the narrator's memory, all existed only on the stage and so they never entered the auditorium or played directly to the audience. The characters in Tom's "memory play" become distanced and objectified no matter how realistically they are played by the actors because they are seen through the mediating sensibility of the often ironically humorous narrator.

Having Tom click his fingers and "magically" having the curtain rise helped to overcome the first problem of the play. Tom's opening line is difficult for an actor to justify as it appears to be an answer to an implied question from the audience:

> TOM: Yes, I have tricks in my pocket, I have things up my sleeve.

The "trick" of raising the curtain and then the immediate turning to the audience to explain this behaviour overcomes this problem. Immediately the rules of the theatre game that is being played are established. Williams has Tom point out that although he does have all the "tricks" of the theatrical trade he is "the opposite of the stage magician." He gives you illusion that has the appearance of truth. "I give you truth in the pleasant disguise of illusion." Realism, which attempts to create an illusion of reality, has only the surface appearance of truth, but through employing nonrealistic theatrical fictions Williams, through his alter-ego Tom, will depict the truth. This opening speech is a direct attack on the inadequacies of realism and therefore anything that can be legitimately used in actual production to stop audiences reading the play as a slice of life is justifiable. Tom's preference for nonrealism as a mode for embodying truth echoes what Schlueter has called "the phenomenon of self-consciousness which characterizes so much of modern art." She outlines what Williams as an artist dramatizes, namely the bankruptcy of realism as a mode for expressing anything truthful about life:

> While the great tradition of Western literature willingly accepts fiction as reality, the "other tradition" bases itself on the logical possibility that, since fictions are not real—a work of art comes closer to the truth of reality when it does not pretend to be what it is not, but rather declares itself to be what it is.

So Tom begins *The Glass Menagerie* by saying what the play *is*, not life but art. In life time goes relentlessly forward. The world of the play is not bound by such limitations. As Tom points out: "To begin with I can turn back time." What is important to note here is that, in production, the audience is aware of two time scales—the present in which they and the narrator exist and the past in which the other characters exist. Spectators are also made aware that they are present in two places: in a theatre in Armidale and in a slum apartment in St Louis. In life one cannot be in two places at once nor in one place at two times. In art which does not try to be life but draws attention to its own artifice, both things are possible.

In life events are not normally accompanied by music but in Williams's play music not only occurs but, as if to emphasize the artifice of such a convention, Tom is made to draw attention to its use:

> [*Music begins to play.*] The play is memory. Being a memory play, it is dimly lighted, it is sentimental, it is not realistic. In memory everything happens to music. That explains the fiddle in the wings.

We all of us have seen films where the music which we are largely unaware of carries us along on a tide of emotion. We might also remember the effect in Mel Brooks's *Blazing Saddles* where the music's typical emotional evocation of the wide open prairies is undercut when the camera forces us to see the whole of the Count Basie band playing in the middle of the Wild West! Williams's use of music is closer to the Mel Brooks variety. I chose extremely sentimental romantic music for Amanda in several phrases taken from Paganini's Violin Concertos. The idea was to back up Amanda's reveries but at the same time to allow Tom and the nonrealistic stage devices to function as Williams intended them to do by ironically undercutting the scenes in which Amanda waxes lyrical.

In scene 1 we have a perfect example of Williams's ability to give his audience a twofold perspective. He allows the actress playing Amanda to play the character's own reality with honest sentiment while at the same time having Tom as the narrator, and the stage devices reduce this sentiment to sentimentality.

> [*She addresses* TOM *as though he were seated in the vacant chair at the table though he remains at the portieres. He plays this scene as though reading from a script.*]
> My callers were gentleman callers—all! Among my callers were some of the most prominent young planters of the Mississippi Delta—planters and sons of planters! [TOM *motions for music and a spot of light on* AMANDA. *Her eyes lift, her face glows, her voice becomes rich and elegiac.*]
> [SCREEN LEGEND: OÙ SONT LES NEIGES D'ANTAN?] There was young Champ Loughlin.

The first important thing that I noticed in production was that the metafictional elements and expressionistic stage devices paradoxically allowed the actors to play their own roles totally realistically. They had no need to supply any ironic comments on their own behaviour as these were supplied by the narrator and his bag of theatrical tricks. When the play is presented without the ironical undercutting, it either becomes unbearably sentimental or the actors themselves have to include in their own performances some ironical undercutting.

In the scene just quoted I had Tom as the narrator resignedly mouthing a couple of Amanda's lines as she spoke them to indicate that he had heard this "script" so many times that he knew it by heart. The spotlight and romantic music should not come in unnoticed. I had Tom click his fingers again to "magically" produce these theatrical effects. All the while the actress playing Amanda was asked to play the truth of her character. She certainly does not see herself as ridiculous. The screen image is the final, and to my mind perfect, means of deflating Amanda's pretentions. We take the same ironical view of Amanda as Tom does in his memory. These much maligned screen legends are not, as some critics seem to suppose, ponderously serious captions supplying some sort of Brechtian "gestus" for each scene. In this scene the screen legend has a humorous deflating function allowing an audience to see the pathetically romantic pretentiousness of Amanda as Tom remembers her. "Où sont les neiges d'antan?" is a cliché of Romanticism and is intentionally "over-the-top." Amanda's slightly ridiculous behaviour both in the scene quoted and in her later "jonquil" speech reminded me of the histrionic performing of actresses like

Lilian Gish in the early silent films. This gave me the idea of presenting the screen legends in the form of silent film subtitles. While neither the acting style nor the conventions of silent film subtitles were originally meant to be funny, time has made them so. In "memory" they appear laughable. Certainly audiences in Armidale found the use of these legends amusing and therefore were induced to see Amanda in the ironic light of a silent film heroine! The use of silent film subtitles also seemed to reflect Tom's obsession with the movies. When Williams's stage instructions are read without awareness of their ironical overtones they do indeed appear banal. Once one moves from page to stage however their theatrical power is easily realized. A few examples should suffice to illustrate the subtlety of Williams's use of screen legends. In scene 6 Laura learns that the gentleman caller is none other than Jim O'Connor, the boy she has silently loved from schooldays! Now if this is played realistically without any ironic comment it becomes the most clichéd piece of coincidental nonsense. This is precisely what happens in Williams's Acting Edition:

> LAURA: Mother!
> AMANDA: What's the matter now? [*Re-entering room.*]
> LAURA: What did you say his name was?
> AMANDA: O'Connor. Why?
> LAURA: What is his first name?
> AMANDA [*Crosses to armchair R.*]: I don't remember—Oh yes, I do too—it was—Jim! [*Picks up flowers.*]
> LAURA: Oh Mother, not Jim O'Connor?

There is not a note of irony here—all we have is soap-opera. In Williams's Reading Edition we have the following:

> LAURA [*With an altered look.*]: What did you say his name was?
> AMANDA: O'Connor.
> LAURA: What is his first name?
> AMANDA: I don't remember. Oh yes, I do. It was—Jim!
> [LAURA *sways slightly and catches hold of a chair.*]
> [LEGEND ON SCREEN: "NOT JIM!"]
> LAURA: [*Faintly*] Not—Jim!
> AMANDA: Yes, that was it, it was Jim! I've never known a Jim that wasn't nice! [*The music becomes ominous.*]

In this version the soap-opera cliché is not made at all realistic. Rather Williams heightens the level of cliché to a point where it is parody. This is the ironic parodic view of Tom's memory and we experience both its pathos and its bathos. "Not Jim!" like the later legend "Terror!" are so overtly melodramatic that they almost certainly cause a chuckle and the ominous music is a perfect parodic "gilding of the lily."

Laughter is constantly encouraged by Williams's stage devices. A most obvious example occurs when Tom groans:

> You know it don't take much intelligence to get yourself into a nailed up coffin, Laura. But who in hell ever got himself out of one without removing one nail? [*As if in answer, the father's grinning photograph lights up. The scene dims out.*]

In Armidale we used the larger than life picture of the "telephone man who fell in love with long distance" and when the spot on the picture came up on the otherwise darkened stage, it was always greeted with a sympathetic laugh. Often the stage devices that Williams employs are to make the audience laugh in order that they may not weep. Tom's ironic defence against the pain he feels at Laura's situation is almost always laughter. He knows that there is no solution to Laura's problems. No gentleman caller will save her. To emphasize this, in my production I cast an actress who could play Laura as physically not very attractive and as mentally slightly retarded. The brace on her leg was really only a symbol of her being a psychic cripple like Williams's sister Rose who was the model for Laura. No magic "adjustment" as occurred in the film of *The Glass Menagerie* was possible for this Laura. The scene where this Laura, replete with "gay deceivers" padding her brassiere and overdressed in one of Amanda's old ball-gowns examines herself in a mirror, would have been a total tear-jerker without the irony supplied by both the screen legend and the sound effects:

> [LEGEND ON SCREEN: THIS IS MY SISTER: CELEBRATE HER WITH STRINGS! MUSIC PLAYS.]

Tom's voice, heard through the caption, holds back the pain and possible tears by the use of rather bitter irony.

Perhaps the most effective stage device that Williams uses to prevent his audiences from empathising too readily with the characters from Tom's past is The Screen Image. The finest example of this relates to Jim, the gentleman caller. The device allows us to see Jim's character in relation to the whole action of the play which concerns man's need for "illusions."

In scene 5 Amanda and Tom have discussed callers in general and Jim in particular. Amanda has checked him out as a prospective suitor for Laura. Despite Tom's attempts to control Amanda's fantasies this "nice, ordinary, young man" with freckles is turned by her into an ideal suitor for her daughter. His going to night school means for Amanda that

> he has visions of being advanced in the world! Any young man who studies public speaking is aiming to have an executive job some day!

Scene 5 ends with an uncomprehending Laura being asked by an elated Amanda to wish on the moon. A romantic moon is projected as a screen image and the scene dims out to the accompaniment of a violin! Every signal to the audience presages disaster for Amanda's plan. Tom's honest description of Laura's psychic limitations has already shown the audience that she lives "in a world of her own." The screen image of the moon and the sentimental violin, when juxtaposed with Tom's view of Laura, ironically emphasize the fantasy world of Amanda with her pathetic wish for "Happiness! Good Fortune!" At the end of this scene everything is set up for the catastrophe of Jim's visit. It was at this point that I placed the Interval. The idea was to keep the audience in suspense.

Scene 6 begins with Tom giving another of his narrator speeches. As this mirrors the opening of scene 1, I again had him enter from the auditorium. He immediately begins to talk about Mr. O'Connor and a screen image of the expected gentleman caller appears. This is a picture of Jim, the high-school hero. The audience has by now almost come to know Jim, partly because of Tom's description of him but mainly because they have seen pictures of him before. The first picture was in scene 2 at the point when Amanda first gets the idea of marrying Laura off to some unsuspecting gentleman caller:

> [SCREEN IMAGE: JIM AS HIGH SCHOOL HERO BEARING A SILVER CUP.]

In this early picture the actor attempted to show some of the "tremendous Irish good nature and vitality with the scrubbed and polished look of white chinaware" that Tom refers to at the beginning of scene 6.

The second picture of Jim that the audience sees occurs at the beginning of scene 3 when Tom humorously observes:

> Like some archetype of the universal unconscious, the image of the gentleman caller haunted our small apartment. . . .
> [SCREEN IMAGE: A YOUNG MAN AT THE DOOR OF A HOUSE WITH FLOWERS.]

The audience in Armidale immediately recognised that the young man was the same fellow who had earlier appeared carrying a silver cup.

The third picture of Jim appears in scene 5. The scene has opened with the gently blasphemous legend "Annunciation" which of course presages a visitation. Jim may not be God-Almighty, but he does later state: "I'm Superman!" In scene 5 the picture of Jim is a repetition of the one in scene 3:

> TOM: We are going to have one.
> AMANDA: What?
> TOM: A gentleman caller!
> [*The annunciation is celebrated with music.* AMANDA *rises.*]
> [IMAGE ON SCREEN: A CALLER WITH A BOUQUET.]

The picture of Jim, the high-school hero that opens scene 6 is therefore the fourth time we have seen this confident young man. Before his actual arrival however there is one more image of him that ironically cuts this walking example of the American Dream down to size. As someone who "was shooting with such velocity through his adolescence that you would logically expect him to arrive at nothing short of the White House by the time he was thirty," Jim has in fact not lived up to his dreams of success. Tom points out:

> His speed had definitely slowed. Six years after he left High School he was holding a job that wasn't much better than mine. [SCREEN IMAGE: THE CLERK.]

The image we had of Jim in my production was of a harrassed looking clerk checking off a clipboard list amid row upon row of shoeboxes. This image, following the four earlier pictures of Jim in his glory always produced laughter from the audience and prepared the way for them to see that Jim's image of himself which occurs later in scene 6:

[IMAGE ON SCREEN: EXECUTIVE AT HIS DESK.]

was as laughably inflated as Amanda's earlier view of him as an executive. The effect on the audience of Jim's actual "visitation," having seen five pictures of him, was electrifying. With one audience of high-school students the appearance of Jim produced excited mutterings on the theme of "Here he is!" What the screen images had done was to make Jim become what Williams intended him to be, namely "the long-delayed but always expected something that we live for." Instead of being the Redeemer, Jim turns out unintentionally to bring hell rather than heaven to the Wingfield home. The stage devices—the nonrealistic use of lighting, the music, the legends and the screen images, all combine to help the audience to realize that Jim is just as much a dreamer as either Laura or Amanda. As Stein has delightfully pointed out:

> Jim's attempt to play the modern saviour is an abysmal failure. In the after dinner scene, he offers Laura the sacrament—wine and "life-savers," in this case—and a Dale Carnegie version of the Sermon on the Mount—self-help rather than divine help—but to no avail.

The film version and the Acting Edition of *The Glass Menagerie* are both pushed toward realism. Often in productions of the Reading Edition directors follow the critical objections of writers like Gassner and Styan and cut the expressionistic/plastic staging devices from the script. The result is that a realistic portrayal of a particular family is produced. The play becomes a sensitive portrayal of the plight of a few pathetic individuals. This leads to a devaluation of Williams's work. It leads critics like Falk to see Amanda as "an escapist like her daughter . . . [who] also lives unhappily in her cocoon of dreams."

What Williams's nonrealistic stage techniques help an audience to see is that there is in the play no one single absolute reality to which characters can adjust. Jim O'Connor, who in the film version clearly represented reality and helped Laura snap out of her inferiority complex, is shown in the Reading Version to be living in his own Glass Menagerie world. His belief in the illusions of the prevailing American Dream with its success myth are undermined by his actual achievement. He is not an executive but a clerk. It is only in fantasy that his beliefs succor him.

> JIM: *Knowledge*—Zzzzzp! *Money*—Zzzzzp! *Power!* That's the cycle democracy is built on.

The action of Williams's play then is not about a group of misfits who fail to adjust to reality. Jim is "an emissary from *a* world of reality" not *the* world of reality. All the characters in the play live in private illusionary worlds. Williams is presenting an action that is making a universal statement about what he sees as the human condition. Amanda lives "vitally in her illusions" of a past age of jonquils and gentleman callers; Laura lives in a world of glass animals and old records; Jim lives in an illusory world of hopes of success and even Tom lives in the world of art. He escapes to the movies and into the world of writing.

What Esther Merle Jackson has called "The Broken World of Tennessee Williams" can only be realized on stage if the idea of a single absolute and "normal" reality is rejected. This is especially true of *The Glass Menagerie.* Each character in the play creates his or her own subjective reality as a defence against the "horror at the heart of the meaninglessness of existence." The only absolute in Williams's dramatized vision of reality is death: "There is no way to beat the game of *being* as against *non-being,* in which non-being is the predestined victor on realistic levels." Against the awfulness of this absurd reality, symbolized in *The Glass Menagerie* by the alleys outside the Wingfield apartment, the individuals give their lives meaning by using their imaginations to create fragile glass menagerie worlds—worlds that are "truth in the pleasant disguise of illusion."

Given that Williams believes in a vision of reality that is so highly relativistic, in which "no man has a monopoly on right," it is not surprising that he has rejected realism as a means for expressing his vision. The solid mirror of external reality is suitable for expressing a vision of reality where truth is absolute, but not where there are as many truths as there are people. What is surprising is the way that so many critics and even more importantly, so many directors reject, or neglect to follow, Williams's stated nonrealistic intentions. Williams has argued that "truth, life, or reality is an organic thing which the poetic imagination can represent or suggest, in essence, only through transformation, through changing into other forms than those which were merely present in appearance." It seems wilful distortion on the part of critics and directors to neglect the use of the nonrealistic staging devices that facilitate the "transformation" Williams desires, in favour of producing a realistic slice-of-life that presents aspects of reality "merely present in appearance."

Arthur Miller

Ibsen and the Drama of Today

There is one element in Ibsen's method which I do not think ought to be overlooked, let alone dismissed as it so often is nowadays. If his plays, and his method, do nothing else, they reveal the evolutionary quality of life. One is constantly aware, in watching his plays, of process, change, development. I think too many modern plays assume, so to speak, that their duty is merely to show the present countenance rather than to account for what happens. It is therefore wrong to imagine that because his first and sometimes his second acts devote so much time to a studied revelation of antecedent material, his view is static compared to our own. In truth, it is profoundly dynamic, for that enormous past was always heavily documented to the end that the present be comprehended with wholeness, as a moment in a flow of time, and not—as with so many modern plays—as a situation without roots. Indeed, even though I can myself reject other aspects of his work, it nevertheless presents barely and unadorned what I believe is the biggest single dramatic problem, namely, how to dramatize what has gone before. I say this not merely out of technical interest, but because dramatic characters, and the drama itself, can never hope to attain a maximum degree of consciousness unless they contain a viable unveiling of the contrast between past and present, and an awareness of the process by which the present has become what it is. And I say this, finally, because I take it as a truth that the end of drama is the creation of a higher consciousness and not merely a subjective attack upon the audience's nerves and feelings. What is precious in the Ibsen method is its insistence upon valid causation, and this cannot be dismissed as a wooden notion.

This is the "real" in Ibsen's realism for me, for he was, after all, as much a mystic as a realist, which is simply to say that while there are mysteries in life which no amount of analyzing will reduce to reason, it is perfectly realistic to admit and even to proclaim that hiatus as a truth. But the problem is not to make complex what is essentially explainable; it is to make understandable what is complex without distorting and oversimplifying what cannot be explained. I think many of his devices are, in fact, quite arbitrary; that he betrays a Germanic ponderousness at times and a tendency to overprove what is quite clear in the first place. But we could do with more of his basic intention, which was to assert nothing he had not proved, and to cling always to the marvelous spectacle of life forcing one event out of the jaws of the preceding one and to reveal its elemental consistencies with surprise. In other words, I contrast his realism not with the lyrical, which I prize, but with sentimentality, which is always a leak in the dramatic dike. He sought to make a play as weighty and living a fact as the discovery of the steam engine or algebra. This can be scoffed away only at a price, and the price is a living drama.

Some 35 years after these words were written, Arthur Miller once again turned to the question of how one might assess Ibsen's influence today.

I am not scholar enough—or journalist either—to be able to say with any real certainty what Ibsen's influence is today. I have only impressions, which may or may not be accurate.

I don't believe that many of today's playwrights look to his methods as models, but his standing as a modern has nevertheless improved, I think, over the past thirty or forty years. When I began writing plays in the late thirties he was a favourite of the Left for his radical politics and rebellious mind. His work, however, not often performed, was frequently regarded as quaintly methodical onion-peeling. If you had the patience to labour through it an Ibsen play was more like argument in a legal case than an entertainment. Such was the prejudice and ignorance of the time, his most important lack was thought to be the poetic spirit; it was fashionable, as it still is in some places today, to call him more of a carpenter than the visionary architect that Shaw, among others, thought him to be. What the young avant-garde wanted in the thirties, positioned as ever against clunky Broadway realism, was the lyrical voice. Clifford Odets and Sean O'Casey specifically, were the more or less Marxist prophets while Saroyan, a premature or closet absurdist, sang basically for his supper. In the Broadway/West End mainstream Maxwell Anderson and Christopher Fry were trying to wring popular drama from unconventional word usage, reviving even Elizabethan iambics. These were very different writers but they were all attempting to sing the language on the stage, as Yeats had done for a more recondite audience and Eliot, too. All of these were self-conscious artists rather than stage shopsmiths but they would all have no doubt thought that Ibsen's time had passed.

Ibsen's language, lyrical as it may sound in Scandinavia, does not sing in translation, although his ideas often do. Of course they were only Ibsen's realistic social plays that were produced but these became his stamp, his mysticism having been more or less overlooked and his metaphysical side likewise. Probably his more social plays, like the genre itself, are fundamentally optimistic—demanding change, which is itself an upbeat notion and therefore easy to grasp, while his deepest personal thought is the opposite; symbolist, mythic, muffled in pessimism as it surveys the changless sea, the sky, aging, cowardice, the classic brick walls against which philosophy has always broken its head.

It is the quasi-journalistic element therefore which came down to later generations, at least in America. He seemed to write about "issues," rather than circumstance. Especially in the Leftist tide of the thirties his stance was translated into an anti-capitalist militancy, but occasionally his apparent elitism seemed relevant to Fascism. For example, a small controversy developed over whether *An Enemy of the People* had a Fascistic tendency with its admittedly confusing claims for an elite of the intellect which must be trusted to lead ordinary folk. Nowadays the wheel has turned once more and probably something similar is happening now that political correctness is (again) in vogue. But *An Enemy of the People*, it seems to me, is really about Ibsen's belief that there is such a thing as a truth and that it bears something like holiness within it, regardless of the cost its discovery at any one moment entails. And the job of the elite is to guard and explain that holiness without compromise or stint.

For myself, I was deeply stirred by his indignation at the social lies of his time, but it was in his structures that I was thrilled to find his poetry. His plays were models of a stringent economy of means to create immense symphonic images of tragic proportions. It wasn't that things fit together but that *everything* fit together, like a natural organism, a human being, for example, or a rose. His works had an organic intensity making them, or most of them, undeniable. To me he was a reincarnation of the Greek dramatic spirit, especially its obsessive fascination with past transgressions as the seeds of current catastrophe. In this slow unfolding was wonder, even god. Past and present were drawn into a single continuity, and thus a secret moral order was being limned. He and the Greeks were related also through their powerful integrative impulse which, at least in theory, could make possible a total picture of a human being—character sprang from action, and like a spiritual CAT scan the drama could conceivably offer up a human being seen from within and without at the same. (In fact, my *Death of a Salesman* would proceed in that fashion.) Present dilemma was simply the face that the past had left visible. Every catastrophe was the story of how the birds came home to roost, and I still believe that a play without a past is a mere shadow of a play, just as a man or woman whose past is largely blank or ineptly drawn is merely a suggestion of a man or a woman, and a trivialization to boot.

I don't know what exactly has happened to the concept of the past in contemporary dramaturgy, but it is rarely there any more. Things happen, God knows why. Maybe we are just too tired of thinking, or maybe meaning itself has become an excrescence. But most likely it is that we have too often been wrong about what important things mean.

Perhaps it comes down to our loss of confidence in our ability to lay a finger on the inevitable in life; in the name of freedom and poetry it is now customary to declare, in effect, that our existence is itself a surprise and that surprise is the overwhelmingly central principle of life. Or maybe we are just surfeited with entertainment and prefer to lie back and let our brains enjoy a much needed rest.

The triumph of the past-less art is of course the film. A film persona requires no past or any other proof of his existence; he need only be photographed and he is palpably *there.*

The past keeps coming back to our art, however, if only in the parodistic form of the detective or crime story, probably our most popular fictional entertainment. The crime exists, or is about to happen, and we have to move backwards to find out whose general character fits the crime, who has dropped hints of his dire tendency, and so forth. It is the tragic event scrubbed clean of its visionary moral values, its sole job being the engendering of anxiety and fear. (Detective fiction also reassures us about the stability of our civilization, but that's another story.)

The so-called Absurd theater, in a different way, also helped make any obsession with the past seem quaint, and Ibsen with it. The proof of a character's existence was simply his awareness of his ironical situation, that was all and that was enough. Character itself, which surely must mean individuation, smacked of realism, and in its stead were interchangeable stickmen whose individuation lay in their varying attitudes and remarks about the determining force, the situation. Without a past the present, and its anxieties, was all that was left to talk about. And the situation of the stickman is of course so utterly overwhelming—war, or concentration camps, or economic disaster—that what individually he may have had, his will or lack of will, his self-doubt or assurance, his faith or cynicism is squashed out, leaving only the irony of humans continuing to exist at all.

So that the quality we instantly recognized as supremely human was not characterological definition, which requires a history, but its very absence; whatever his personality, it is without significance because it doesn't affect history—that is, his kindness, his dreams of a different kind of life, his love, his devotion to duty or to another human being simply do not matter as he is marched towards the flames. It may be the Holocaust clinched the case for reducing personality to a laughable affectation. I am inclined to believe this to be so, even for people who never think about the events in Eastern Europe directly. The Holocaust—the story of a great nation turned criminal on a vast scale—implicitly defeated us, broke confidence in our claims to being irrevocably in the camp of what was once securely called humanity, and left us with absurdity as the defining human essence.

Again, the concept of a gradually in-gathering, swelling, evidentiary, revelatory explosion is now reserved for thrillers, by and large; but instead of insights we have clues, mechanically dropped most of the time, to both lead us on and astray. We are given, if you will, the skeleton of the Ibsen form without the soul or the flesh.

The revolt—or rather the loss of interest in what is commonly thought of as Ibsenism—also imagines itself to be a revolt against the well-made play, quite as though Ibsen was not himself the first to attack that kind of play. Instead of being well-made his plays are true. That is the difference. They follow the psycho-moral dilemma, not the plot. But we have arrived at a point where, as indicated, the very notion of inevitability is itself highly suspect—in short, no one can know why great events happen, let alone why the shifts and changes in human attitudes take place. Under the rubric of a new freedom and a deeper wisdom we have turned against the rational, claiming the delightful license to simply express feeling and impressions, the more randomly the better to create surprise, the ultimate aesthetic value.

In short, Strindberg has won the philosophical battle with Ibsen and Ibsenism. The poet of instinct and the impromptu, of the paradoxical surprise, his mission is not to save anyone or a society, but simply to rip the habit of hypocrisy from the human heart and cant from the life of the mind. He is the destroying rebel chopping off the ever-growing heads of a thousand-armed dragon, a pessimistic labor to be sure. Ibsen, quite otherwise, is the revolutionary groping for a new system, an optimistic business, for when the old is destroyed, the new construct implies rational decisions, and above all hope.

And who can gainsay Strindberg any more? Apart from the Holocaust are we not witnesses to the implosion of the Soviet Union, the most "rationally" run society, falling in upon itself, a fraud and a farce? And what has survived but old, chaotic, irrational capitalism, blinding itself to its poor behind the glaring lights of its packed store windows, and hiding its spiritual starvation under the shiny bonnets of its marvellous cars? How to rationally account for *this* surprise—the victory of the decadent doomed and the disgrace of the historically "inevitable victors," the "new men" who stand revealed as medieval fief-holders when they were not actual gangsters and killers of the dream?

Compare this awesome moral chaos, this wracking collapse of the comfortably predictable, with Ibsen's methodical unravelling of motives and the interplay of social and psychological causation, all of it speaking of rational control! They cannot jibe, our reality and his. So he must seem outmoded, a picturesque mind out of a more orderly time.

Perhaps that is why he seems to be coming back, at least his prestige as a modern, if not precisely his methods. For while it is purely a sense of the new mood on my part, it does seem that the taste for "real plays" rather than only fun effusions has begun to stir again. Of course, there are still old-fashioned critics who think that anything that has a beginning and end is out of date, but there are young playwrights who would disagree and are looking to life rather than the theater for their inspiration, and life, of course, includes not only surprise but the consequences flowing from our actions or structure, in other words.

Perhaps I ought to add here that in these past dozen years my most Ibsen-influenced play, *All My Sons*, written nearly fifty years ago, is more and more frequently and more widely produced now and the reviewers no longer feel obliged to dismiss its structure as not-modern. I have had to wonder whether this is partly due to the number of investigations of official malfeasance in the papers all the time, and the spectacle of men of stature and social influence being brought down practically every week by revelations excavated from the hidden past. From the heights of Wall Street, the Pentagon, the White House, big business, the same lesson seems to fly out at us—the past lives! As does Ibsen, the master of the explosive force when it bombs in the present, and above all, with the soul-rot that comes of the hypocrisy of its denial.

Needless to say, I have not attempted in this short note to deal with Ibsen as poet and creator of mythic plays, beginning with the opening of his career. For one thing, those plays remain to be interpreted for modern audiences, their mythology having little obvious meaning for most people outside Scandinavia.

Henry Louis Gates, Jr.
The Chitlin Circuit

The setting was the McCarter Theatre, a brick-and-stone edifice on the outskirts of the Princeton University campus. On a hot, sticky evening last June, five hundred members of the Theatre Communications Group—all representatives of serious, which is to say nonprofit, theatre—had gathered for their eleventh biennial national conference. The keynote speech was being delivered by August Wilson, who, at fifty-one, is probably the most celebrated American playwright now writing and is certainly the most accomplished black playwright in this nation's history. Before he said a word, the largely white audience greeted him with a standing ovation.

That was the conference's last moment of unanimity. For here, at this gathering of saints, the dean of American dramatists had come to deliver an unexpected and disturbing polemic. American theatre, Wilson declared, was an instrument of white cultural hegemony, and the recent campaign to integrate and diversify it only made things worse. The spiritual and moral survival of black Americans demanded that they be given a stage of their own. They needed their very own theatres the way they needed sunlight and oxygen. They needed integration the way they needed acid rain.

"There are and have always been two distinct and parallel traditions in black art: that is, art that is conceived and designed to entertain white society, and art that feeds the spirit and celebrates the life of black America," Wilson told his Princeton audience, in a quietly impassioned voice. "The second tradition occurred when the African in the confines of the slave quarters sought to invest his spirit with the strength of his ancestors by conceiving in his art, in his song and dance, a world in which he was the spiritual center." That was the tradition Wilson found to be exemplified by the Black Power movement of the sixties and its cultural arm, the Black Arts scene. Revolutionary Black Arts dramatists such as Ed Bullins and Amiri Baraka were models for authentic black creativity, Wilson maintained, and he placed himself in their direct line of descent.

"His speech was shocking and it was thrilling," recalled Ricardo Khan, the president of the Theatre Communications Group and the artistic director of the country's premier black repertory company, the Crossroads Theatre, in New Brunswick. Wilson is light-skinned, with sparse hair and a close-cropped beard: to some in the audience, he brought to mind Maulana Karenga ("Black art must expose the enemy, praise the people and support the revolution"); to others, Ernst Blofeld ("Hot enough for you, Mr. Bond?"). The black members of the audience started glancing at one another: heads bobbed, a black-power sign was flashed, encouragement was murmured—"Go ahead, brother," "Tell it." Many white audience members, meanwhile, began to shift uneasily, gradually acquiring an expression compounded of pain and puzzlement: *After all we've done for him, this is how he thanks us?* The world of nonprofit theatre is tiny but intense, and, as soon became clear, Wilson's oration was its version of the Simpson verdict.

In the conversational ferment that ensued, almost every conceivable question was given a full airing: Did Wilson's call for an autonomous black theatre amount to separatism? Did race matter to culture, and if so, how much? Was Wilson's salvific notion of the theatre—and his dream of a theatre that would address ordinary black folk—mere romantic delusion? In the course of much high-minded handwringing, practically the only possibility not broached was that a black theatre for the masses *already* existed—just not of an order that anybody in the world of serious theatre had in mind.

What attracted the greatest immediate attention was Wilson's unqualified denunciation of color-blind casting. To cast black actors in "white" plays was, he said, "to cast us in the role of mimics." Worse, for a black actor to walk the stage of Western drama was to collaborate with the culture of racism, "to be in league with a thousand naysayers who wish to corrupt the vigor and spirit of his heart." An all-black production of "Death of a Salesman," say, would "deny us our own humanity."

Not surprisingly, Wilson's stand on this issue has found little acceptance among working black actors, dramatists, and directors. Lloyd Richards—Wilson's longtime director and creative partner—has never thought twice about casting James Earl Jones as Timon of Athens or as Judge Brack in "Hedda Gabler." Wole Soyinka, the Nigerian playwright and Nobel Laureate, staunchly declares, "I can assure you that if 'Death of a Salesman' were performed in Nigeria by an all-Eskimo cast it would have resonances totally outside the mediation of color." What's more surprising is that many stars of the Black Arts firmament are equally dismissive. "If O.J. can play a black man, I don't see any problem with Olivier playing Othello," Amiri Baraka says, with a mordant laugh. And the legendary black playwright and director Douglas Turner Ward claims that many of Sean O'Casey's plays, with their ethos of alienation, actually work better with black actors.

But the dissent on color-blind casting was almost something of a footnote to Wilson's larger brief—that of encouraging the creation of an authentic black theatre. As he saw it, the stakes couldn't be greater. Black theatre could help change the world: it could be "the spearhead of a movement to reignite and reunite our people's positive energy for a political and social change that is reflective of our spiritual truths rather than economic fallacies." The urgency of this creed led to a seemingly self-divided rhetoric. On the one hand, Wilson maintained that "we cannot depend on others," that we must be a "self-determining, self-respecting people." On the other hand, this self-sufficiency was to be subsidized by foundations and government agencies.

If Wilson's rhetoric struck many of his listeners as contradictory—seeming to alternate the balled fist and the outstretched palm—the contradictions only multiplied upon further investigation. August Wilson, born Frederick August Kittel, is in some respects an unlikely spokesman for a new Black Arts movement. He neither looks nor sounds typically black—had he the desire, he could easily pass—and that makes him black first and foremost by self-identification. (His father was a German-American baker in Pittsburgh, where he grew up.) Some see significance in this. The estimable black playwright OyamO, né Charles Gordon, says, "Within our history, many people who are lighter—including the very lightest of us, who can really pass—are sometimes the most angry."

Nor has it escaped comment that Wilson failed to acknowledge his own power and stature within the world of mainstream theatre: his works début at major Broadway theatres, and the white critical establishment has honored them with a cascade of Pulitzer, Drama Desk, and Tony awards. The experimental black playwright Suzan-Lori Parks, whose works include "Venus" and "The Death of the Last Black Man in the Whole Entire World," says, "August can start by having his own acclaimed plays première in black theatres, instead of where they première now. I'm sorry, but he should examine his own house." One historical luminary of black theatre charges that Wilson himself is the problem of which he purports to hold the solution: "Once the white mainstream theatre found a black artistic spokesman, the one playwright who could do no wrong, the money that used to go to autonomous black theatre started to dry up."

And yet, on closer examination, sharply drawn lines of battle begin to blur. Wilson's oration provoked a swingeing rebuttal in *American Theatre* by Robert Brustein, who is the artistic director of the American Repertory Theatre, the drama critic for *The New Republic,* and a longtime sparring partner of Wilson's. Brustein charged Wilson with promoting subsidized separatism: "What next?" he asked. "Separate schools? Separate washrooms? Separate drinking fountains?" With Anna Deavere Smith—herself a paradigm of casting beyond color—serving as the moderator, the men are to continue their debate this Monday, in New York's Town Hall. The critic Paul Goldberger, writing in the *Times* last week, went so far as to declare that "this is shaping up to be the sharpest cultural debate" since the Mapplethorpe controversy. You'd never guess that Brustein and Wilson are in complete agreement on the one subject that agitates them most: the disastrous nature of the donor-driven trend to diversify regional theatres. Brustein dislikes the trend because he believes that it supplants aesthetic considerations with sociological ones. Wilson dislikes it because, as is true of all movement toward integration, it undermines the integrity and strength of autonomous black institutions.

He has a point. George Wolfe, the producer of the Public Theatre, singles out the Lila Wallace–Reader's Digest Fund as having been "incredibly irresponsible" in this regard. He goes on to explain, "It has created a peculiar dynamic where, you know, there was a struggling black theatre that had been nurturing a series of artists and all of a sudden this predominantly white theatre next door is getting a couple of million dollars to invite artists of color into its fold." (To be sure, the officials at the Lila Wallace Fund have also given money to black companies like the Crossroads.) But Wilson wants to take things another step, and create black theatres where they do not currently exist. He believes that any theatre situated in a city with a black population of more than sixty per cent should be converted into a black theatre. White board members and staff would be largely retired in order to insure what he believes to be a cultural and moral imperative: art by, of, and for black people.

Unquestionably, Wilson remains in the grip of a sentimental separatism. (I'll own that it has an emotional grip on me, too, just a rather attenuated one.) He says he has a lot of respect for the "do for self" philosophy of the Nation of Islam; in the early seventies, he was briefly a convert, though mostly in order to keep his Muslim wife company. He's a man who views integration primarily as a destructive force—one that ruined once vital black institutions. He thinks back fondly to an era when we had our own dress shops and businesses, our own Negro Baseball League. This segregated, pre-Brown v. Board of Education era was, he'll tell you, "black America at its strongest and most culturally self-sufficient." From his perspective, separate-but-equal, far from being a perversion of social justice, is an ideal that we should aspire to.

Now, it's one thing to hear this view espoused by Minister Louis Farrakhan and quite another to hear it advanced by August Wilson, a man as lionized as any writer of his generation. It represents a romantic attempt to retrieve an imaginary community in the wake of what seems to be a disintegration of the real one. One of the functions of literature is to bring back the dead, the absent, the train gone by; you might say that cultural nationalism is what happens when the genre of the elegy devolves into ideology, the way furniture might be kilned into charcoal.

Certainly the brutal reductionism of August Wilson's polemics is in stark contrast to his richly textured dramatic oeuvre. Wilson first came to prominence in the mid-eighties, with his fourth play, "Ma Rainey's Black Bottom," which the director Lloyd Richards was able to move from the Yale Repertory Theatre to the Cort Theatre on Broadway. There, his dramatic and verbal imagination galvanized critics, who heralded a major new presence on the American stage. With "Ma Rainey," an ambitious, and still ongoing, cycle of plays came to public notice. Wilson's aim is to explore black American life through plays set during each of the decades of the century; most are situated in a black working-class neighborhood of Pittsburgh. "Joe Turner's Come and Gone" (1986), for example, takes place in 1911, and deals with the sense of cultural loss that accompanied the Great Migration; "The Piano Lesson" (which received the Pulitzer in 1987), set during the Depression, uses a dispute over an inherited piano—once the possession of a slave owner—to show that the past is never quite past. In "Fences" (a 1990 Pulitzer), which opens in the year 1957, the grandiloquently embittered Troy Maxson is a former Negro League baseball player who now works as a garbage man; the trajectory of his own life has made a mockery of the supposed glories of integration.

Wilson's 1990 play "Two Trains Running" takes place in a Pittsburgh luncheonette in the late sixties:

> WOLF: I thought [the jukebox] was just fixed. Memphis, I thought you was gonna get you a new jukebox.
>
> MEMPHIS: I told Zanelli to bring me a new one. That what he say he gonna do. He been saying that for the last year.

If you're black, you can't rely on the Zanellis of the world, as the characters in the play learn to their detriment. But a great deal more than race politics is going on here. An unruly luxuriance of language—an ability to ease between trash talk and near-choral transport—is Wilson's great gift; sometimes you wish he were less generous with that gift, for it can come at the expense of conventional dramaturgic virtues like pacing and the sense of closure. Even when he falters, however, Wilson's work is demanding and complex—at the furthest remove from a cultural manifesto.

But if Wilson's avowed cultural politics is difficult to square with his art, it comes with a venerable history of its own. In 1926, W. E. B. Du Bois, writing in his magazine *The Crisis,* took a dim view of "colored" productions of mainstream plays (they "miss the real path," he warned) and called for a new Negro theatre, for which he laid down "four fundamental principles":

> The plays of a real Negro theatre must be: 1. *About us.* That is, they must have plots which reveal Negro life as it is. 2. *By us.* That is, they must be written by Negro authors who understand from birth and continual association just what it means to be a Negro today. 3. *For us.* That is, the theatre must cater primarily to Negro audiences and be supported and sustained by their entertainment and approval. 4. *Near us.* The theatre must be in a Negro neighborhood near the mass of ordinary Negro people.

What would such a theatre look like? Wilson, of course, directs us to what may seem the most plausible candidate: the dramatic art of the Black Power era. That moment and milieu bring to mind a radicalized, leather-clad generation forging its art in the streets, writing plays fuelled by the masses' righteous rage: revolutionary art by the people and for the people. That's certainly how the illuminati liked to represent their project. Baraka's manifesto for "The Revolutionary Theatre" provides a representative précis: "What we show must cause the blood to rush, so that pre-revolutionary temperaments will be bathed in this blood, and it will cause their deepest souls to move, and they will find themselves tensed and clenched, even ready to die. . . . We will scream and cry, murder, run through the streets in agony, if it means some soul will be moved."

Theatre, precisely because of its supposed potential to mobilize the masses, was always at the forefront of the Black Arts movement. Still, it's a funny thing about cultural movements: as a rule, they consist of a handful of people. (The Aesthetic, the Constructivist, the Futurist movements were devoted largely to declaring themselves, self-consciously, to *be* movements.) And by the late sixties, it was clear that the vitality of Black Arts drama had come to center upon two New York-based theatres: the Negro Ensemble Company (N.E.C.), based downtown, under the direction of Douglas Turner Ward; and the New Lafayette

Theatre, based in Harlem, under the direction of Robert Macbeth. Here was the full flowering of genuine black theatre in this country—the kind that would raise consciousness and temperatures, that promised to make us whole.

"Populist modernism," is a phrase coined by the literary scholar Werner Sollors, characterized the regnant ethos of that time and place—its aspiration to an art of high seriousness that would engage the energies of the masses. But between the ideals of modernism and those of populism, one or the other had to give. OyamO—who, like many more senior luminaries of the Black Arts scene (Baraka and Ed Bullins among them), was affiliated with the blacker and artier New Lafayette—recalls that the Harlem theatre's high-flown airs were accompanied by paltry audiences. "There was a condescending attitude toward this community, buttressed by the fact that it was getting five hundred grand from the Ford Foundation every year," he recalls. And the N.E.C. was similarly provided for. This isn't to say that worthy and important work wasn't created in these theatres; it was. But these companies do provide a textbook example of how quickly beneficence becomes entitlement, and patronage a paycheck.

And so the dirty little secret of the Black Arts movement was that it was a project promoted and sustained largely by the Ford Foundation. Liberal-minded Medicis made it; in the fullness of time, they left it to unmake itself. Ed Bullins, one of the principals of the New Lafayette, remembers how that particular temple—a magnificent structure on 137th Street, which the Ford had converted from a movie house with the help of some tony theatrical architects—was destroyed. He describes a meeting between a visiting program officer from the Ford Foundation and the theatre's board. The visitor noticed that there were no women on the board, and he asked about their absence. Bullins both laughs and groans when he recalls, "And then some great mind from Harlem, an actor, spoke up and said, 'Oh, no, we don't need any women on the board, because every thirty days women go through their period and they get evil.' Then and there, I saw one million dollars start sprouting wings and flapping away through the door."

These days, of course, *all* nonprofit theatre is starved for cash. And yet black theatres are already out there, as someone like Larry Leon Hamlin could tell you. Hamlin is the artistic director of the National Black Theatre Festival, and by his count there are perhaps two hundred and fifty regional black theatres in this country, about forty of which are reasonably active. Of course, most of Wilson's own plays gestated at places like the Huntington Theatre Company or the Yale Rep before they were launched on the Great White Way. I asked Wilson about this apparent contradiction. He explained that the Negro Ensemble Company had fallen into decline by the early eighties: "It was not doing work of the quality that we deserve, and there's no theatre that's since stepped into the breach." Wilson can sound as if he were boycotting black theatres for artistic reasons, which is why some people in the black-theatre world can't decide whether he's their savior or their slayer. "I do good work," he says, his point being that his plays deserve the best conditions he can secure for them. And among white theatres, he says, "the rush is now on to do anything that's black. Largely through my plays, what the theatres have found out is that they had this white audience that was starving to get a little understanding of what was happening with the black population, because they very seldom come into contact with them, so they're curious. The white theatres have discovered that there is a market for that."

The fact that part of Wilson's success owes to the appeal of ethnography is precisely what disturbs some black critics: they suspect that Wilson's work is systematically overrated along those lines. "August is genuinely very gifted," Margo Jefferson, one of those critics, says. "Whites who don't know the world whereof he writes get a sense of vast, existential melodramas, sweeping pageants, and it's very exciting, with his insistence always that these people onstage are the real and genuine black people. What happens with whites is that the race element is signalling them every minute, 'You know nothing about this, you're lucky to be here.'"

So if you're looking for a theatre of black folk, by black folk, and for black folk—a genuinely sequestered cultural preserve—you'll have to cross the extraordinary dramas of August Wilson off your list. Nor would the Black Arts scene, for all its grand aspirations, qualify: the revolution, it's safe to say, will not be subsidized. You could be forgiven for wondering whether such a black popular theatre really exists. But it does, and, if populist modernism is your creed, it will probably turn your stomach. It's called the Chitlin Circuit, and nobody says you have to like it. But everything in God's creation has a reason, and the Chitlin Circuit is no exception. Perhaps OyamO brings us closest to comprehension when he despairingly observes an uncomfortable truth: "A lot of what they call highbrow, progressive, avant-garde theatre is *boring the shit out of people.*" Not to put too fine a point on it.

The setting now is the Sarah Vaughan Concert Hall—built in 1925 as a Masonic temple—on Broad Street, in downtown Newark. It's a chilly, overcast Sunday afternoon, closing in on three o'clock, which is when the matinée performance of Adrian Williamson's play "My Grandmother Prayed for Me" is supposed to begin. In every sense, we're a long way from the Princeton campus, the site of the despond-drenched T.C.G. conference. On the sidewalk, patrons are eating grilled sausages and hot dogs. Older people make their way inside with the assistance of wheelchairs or walkers; younger ones strut about and survey one another appraisingly. There is much to appraise. These people are styling out, many of them having come from church: you see cloudlike tulle, hatbands of the finest grosgrain ribbon, wool suits and pants in neon shades. Women have taken care to match their shoes and handbags; men sport Stetson and Dobbs hats, Kente-cloth cummerbunds and scarves. There's a blue velvet fedora here, electric-blue trousers there, a Superfly hat and overcoat on a man escorting his magenta-clad wife. Bodies are gleaming, moisturized and fragrant; cheeks are lightly powdered, eyes mascaraed. Broad Street is a poor substitute for a models' runway, but it will have to do until the theatre doors open and swallow up this impromptu village. There are nearly three thousand seats in the hall; within several minutes, most of them are occupied.

The Chitlin Circuit dates back to the nineteen-twenties, when the Theater Owners Booking Association brought plays and other forms of entertainment to black audiences throughout the South and the Midwest. Though it had a reputation for lousy pay and demanding scheduling—its acronym, TOBA, was sometimes said to stand for "Tough on Black Asses"—it was the spawning ground for a good number of accomplished black actors, comics, and musicians. TOBA proper had gone into eclipse by the decade's end, yet the tradition it began—that disparagingly named Chitlin Circuit—never entirely died out. Touring black companies would play anywhere—in a theatre if there was one (sometimes they booked space on weekends or late at night, when the boards would otherwise be vacant) or in a school auditorium if there wasn't. Crisscrossing black America, the circuit established an empire of comedy and pathos, the sublime and the ridiculous: a movable feast that enabled blacks to patronize black entertainers. On the whole, these productions were for the moment, not for the ages. They were the kind of melodrama or farce—or as often both—in which nothing succeeded like excess. But the productions were for, by, and about black folks; and their audience wasn't much inclined to check them against their Stanislavsky anyway.

You don't expect anything very fancy from something called the Chitlin Circuit. Wilson—by way of emphasizing the irreducible differences between blacks and whites—had told the T.C.G. members that "in our culinary history we had to make do with the . . . intestines of the pig rather than the loin and the ham and the bacon." The intestines of the pig are the source of the delicacy known as chitlins; it's a good example of how something that was originally eaten of necessity became, as is the way with acquired tastes, a thing actively enjoyed. The same might be said of the Chitlin Circuit, for the circuit is back in full flush, and has been for several years. Black audiences throughout the country flock to halls like the Beacon Theatre in New York, the Strand Theatre in Boston, and the Fox Theatre in Atlanta. Those audiences are basically blue-collar and pink-collar, and not the type to attend traditional theatre, Larry Leon Hamlin adjudges. But, as the saying has it, they know what they like.

The people behind the shows tend not to vaporize about the "emancipatory potentialities" of their work, or about "forging organic links to the community": they'd be out of business if black folks stopped turning up. Instead, they like to talk numbers. Terryl Calloway, who has worked as a New England promoter for some Chitlin Circuit productions, tells me about plays that have grossed twenty million dollars or more. "It's no joke," he says gravely.

"Good afternoon! Are you ready to have a good time?" This is the master of ceremonies warming up the Newark crowd. The play that ensues is a now standard combination of elements; that is, it's basically a melodrama, with abundant comic relief and a handful of gospel songs interspersed.

So what have we turned out to see? It seems that Grandmother—stout of body and of spirit—is doing her best to raise her two grandsons, their mother, Samantha, having fallen into crack addiction and prostitution. (When we first see Samantha, she is trying to steal her mother's television in order to pay for her habit.) The elder boy, Rashad, is devout and studious, but the younger one, Ein, has taken up with bad company; in fact, today is the day that he and his best friend, Stickey, are to be inducted into the Big Guns, a local gang headed by Slow Pimp. When Stickey is killed on the street by a member of a rival gang, Ein sets out, gun in hand, to avenge his death. What's a grandmother to do? Well, pray, for one thing.

Artistically speaking, "My Grandmother Prayed for Me" makes "Good Times" look like Strindberg. The performances are loud and large; most of the gospel is blared by said grandmother with all the interpretative nuance of a car horn. So broad, so coarse, so over-the-top is this production that to render an aesthetic evaluation would seem a sort of category mistake, like asking Julia Child to taste-test chewing tobacco. But it deals with matters that are of immediate concern to the Newark audience, working-class and middle-class alike: gang violence, crack addiction, teen-age pregnancy, deadbeat dads. For this audience, these issues are not *Times* Op-Ed-page fodder, they're the problems of everyday life, as real and close at hand as parking tickets and head colds. It's also true that black America remains disproportionately religious. (Count on a black rap artist—"gangsta" or no—to thank Jesus in his liner notes.) So that's part of it, too.

On my way to the Sarah Vaughan Concert Hall, I bumped into Amiri Baraka, who, when he learned my destination, gave me a gleaming smile and some brotherly advice: "You're about to step into some deep doo-doo." Maybe he's right, and yet I find myself enjoying the spectacle as much as everybody else here. "You lost faith in the church, abandoned your kids, and I even heard you were prostituting," the grandmother tells her daughter. "Let me tell you something. Them drugs ain't nothing but a demon." Samantha's response: "Well, if they a demon, then I'm gon' love hell." People laugh, but they recognize the sound of a lost soul. So the two fabled institutions of the inner city, the pusher and the preacher, must battle for Samantha's soul. There's a similar exchange between the good son and the one going to the bad:

> RASHAD: Those boys you hang with ain't nothing but a bunch of punks. All y'all do is run around these streets beating up on people, robbing people, our black folks at that. . . .
>
> EIN: If we so-called punks, why we got everybody scared of us? I'll tell you why—because we hardcore. We'll smoke anybody that get in our way.
>
> RASHAD: Hardcore? . . . Ain't a thing you out there doing hardcore. Let me tell you what hardcore is: hardcore is going to school, putting your nose in a book getting an education. Hardcore is going to church trying to live your life right for the Lord. Hardcore is going to work everyday, busting your behind providing for a family. Look around you. Grandma provided all of this for us, and she pray for us every day. Now *that's* hardcore.

This doubtless isn't what Wilson has in mind when he speaks of the spiritual fortification and survival that black drama can provide. All the same, the audience is audibly stirred by Rashad's peroration, crying out "Hallelujah!" and "Testify!" The subject of racism—or, for that matter, white people—simply never arises: in the all-black world depicted onstage, the risks and remedies are all much closer to hand.

That's one puzzle. Here's another: If theatre is dying, what do we make of these nearly three thousand black folks gathered in downtown Newark? The phenomenon I'm witnessing has nothing in common with "Tony n' Tina's Wedding," say, or dinner theatre in Westchester, offering "Damn Yankees" over a steak and two veg. It's true that black audiences have always had a predilection for talking back at performances. But more than that is going on in this theatre:

the intensity of engagement is palpable. During some of the gospel numbers, there are members of the audience who stand up and do the Holy Dance by their seats. However crude the script and the production, they're generating the kind of audience communion that most playwrights can only dream of.

In "My Grandmother Prayed for Me," the deus ex machina is pretty literal. When Ein sets off to seek vengeance, his grandma and brother go in search of him, joined by Samantha, who—having been visited by an angel in the shape of a little boy—has seen the light. ("It was this voice, Mama, this voice from Heaven. It told me that Ein and Rashad need a good mama.") The curtain rises on a gang-infested project. It appears that Ein, too, has seen the light and laid down his gun. "I know I haven't had the best things in life," he tells Slow Pimp defiantly, "but God gave me the best grandmother in the world." Slow Pimp doesn't take his defection well, but it's Rashad who catches the first bullet. Next, Slow Pimp turns his gat on the meddling grandmother. She prays for divine intervention and gets it: the gun jams; Slow Pimp is struck by lightning; the angel raises Rashad from the ground. The audience goes wild.

Nobody said it was high culture, but historically this is what a lot of American theatre, particularly before the First World War, was like. Other "ghettoized" theatres, for all their vibrancy, also ignored many of the criteria for serious art—not least the Yiddish theatre, a center of immigrant Jewish life in New York at the end of the nineteenth century and the beginning of the twentieth. The former *Times* theatre critic Frank Rich says, "What we think of as the Yiddish theatre today was essentially popular entertainment for immigrants. There were what we'd now think of as hilarious versions of, say, 'King Lear,' in which King Lear lives. Or there were fairy tales, about an impoverished family arriving on the Lower East Side and ending up on Riverside Drive living high on the hog." (There was also, as he notes, an avant-garde Yiddish theatre, based largely in the Bronx, but that's a different, and more elevated, story.)

The fact that the audience at the Sarah Vaughan Concert Hall is entirely black creates an essential dynamic. I mentioned elements of comic relief: they include a black preacher greedy for Grandma's chicken wings; a randy old man trailing toilet paper from a split seam in the back of his pants; the grandmother herself, whose churchiness is outlandishly caricatured; endless references to Stickey's lapses of personal hygiene. All the very worst stereotypes of the race are on display, larger than life. Here, in this racially sequestered space, a black audience laughs uninhibitedly, whereas the presence of white folks would have engendered a familiar anxiety: *Will they think that's what we're really like?* If this drama were shown on television—on any integrated forum—Jesse Jackson would probably denounce it, the N.A.A.C.P. would demand a boycott, and every soul here would swap his or her finery for sandwich boards in order to picket it. You don't want white people to see this kind of spectacle; you want them to see the noble dramas of August Wilson, where the injuries and injustices perpetrated by the white man are never far from our consciousness. (It should be mentioned that there are far more respectable and well-groomed versions of gospel drama—most notably Vy Higgenson's "Mama I Want to Sing" and its progeny—that have achieved a measure of crossover success, serving mainly as vehicles for some very impressive singing. But they're better regarded as pageants, or revues, than stage plays.) By contrast, these Chitlin Circuit plays carry an invisible racial warning sticker: For domestic consumption only—export strictly prohibited.

For the creators of this theatre, there are other gratifications to be had. "I've never made so much money in my life as I made when I did the forty or so cities we did on the Chitlin Circuit," James Chapmyn, one veteran of the circuit, tells me. And Chapmyn wasn't even one of the top grossers. "The guy that did 'Beauty Shop' probably grossed fifteen to twenty-five million dollars in the Chitlin Circuit," he says. "These plays make enormous money."

Chapmyn is a blunt-featured, odd-shaped man, with a bullet head and a Buddha belly. He's thirty-six, and he grew up in Kansas, the son of a Baptist minister. He tells me that he fell out with his father in his early twenties. "He was adamant in teaching us to stand up for who we are, and who I am happens to be a black gay man. He taught me to tell the truth," Chapmyn says, but adds that his father changed his mind when his son came out. "I just wish you had lied," the minister told his son. A resulting disaffection with the church—and a spell as a homeless person—impelled him to write a play for which he has become widely known; "Our Young Black Men Are Dying and Nobody Seems to Care." His experience with the Chitlin Circuit was decidedly mixed but still memorable.

Chapmyn, like everyone else who has succeeded on the Chitlin Circuit, had to master the dark arts of marketing and promotion; and to do so while bypassing the major media. He genially explains the ground rules: "What has happened in America is that you have a very active African-American theatre audience that doesn't get their information from the arts section in the newspaper, that doesn't read reviews but listens to the radio, gets things stuffed in their bulletins in church, has flyers put on their car when they're nightclubbing. That's how people get to know about black theatre. Buying the arts section ain't going to cut it for us. That audience is not interested in the 'black theatre,' and the black-theatre audience is not interested in reading that information. We use radio quite extensively, because in our community and places we've gone African-Americans listen to radio. In fact, there's kind of an unspoken rule on the Chitlin Circuit: if a city doesn't have a black radio station, then the Chitlin Circuit won't perform there."

But the Chitlin Circuit has a less amiable side; indeed, to judge from some of the tales you hear, many of its most dramatic events occur offstage. The inner-city version of foundation program officers are drug dealers with money to burn, and their influence is unmistakable. "They do everything in cash," Chapmyn says. "At our highest point, I know that after we all got our money, we were still collecting in the neighborhood of a hundred thousand dollars a week. That was cash being given to us, usually in envelopes, by people we didn't know. It was scary." He continues, "When I was in that circuit, I dealt with a lot of people who didn't have anything but beeper numbers, who would call me with hotel numbers, who operated through post-office boxes, who would show up at the time of the show—and most of the time take care of me and my people very well."

Not always, though. "In one city, I think we did three shows, and the receipts after expenses were a hundred and forty thousand dollars," Chapmyn recounts. "My percentage of that was to be sixty-five thousand dollars. I remember the people gave me five thousand and told me that if I wanted the rest I'd have to sue them." He ended up spending the night in jail. "I was so mad I was ready to hurt somebody," he explains. "Somebody is going to tell me that they got my sixty thousand dollars and they ain't going to give it to me? I think I flipped a table over and hit somebody in the face."

Larry Leon Hamlin, too, becomes animated when he talks about the sleazy world of popular theatre. "Contracts have been put out on people," he tells me. "If you are a big-time drug dealer, it's like, 'These plays are making money, and I've got money. I'm going to put out a play.' That drug dealer will write a play who has never written a play before, will direct the play, who has never directed a play before. They get deep with guns." James Chapmyn says he dropped out of the circuit because of the criminal element: "Here I am doing a play about all the things killing African-American men, chief among those things being the violence and the drugs, and I'm doing business with people who are probably using the money they make from drugs to promote my play. I had a fundamental problem with that." Chapmyn, plainly, is a man with a mission of uplift. By contrast, many other stars of the Chitlin Circuit have the more single-minded intent of pleasing an audience: they stoop to conquer.

That might be said, certainly, of the most successful impresario of the Chitlin Circuit, a man named Shelly Garrett. Garrett maintains that his play "Beauty Shop" has been seen by more than twenty million people; that it's the most successful black stage play in American history; and that he himself is "America's No. 1 black theatrical producer, director, and playwright." Shelly Garrett has never met August Wilson; August Wilson has never heard of Shelly Garrett. They are as unacquainted with each other as art and commerce are said to be. (Except for "Fences" and "The Piano Lesson," both of which were profitable, all of August Wilson's plays have lost money.)

Garrett is a handsome man in his early fifties, given to bright-colored sports coats and heavy gold jewelry, and there is about him the unquiet air of a gambler. He was born in Dallas, worked there as a disk jockey, and later moved to Los Angeles to begin an acting career, he didn't make his debut as a dramatist until 1986, with "Snuff and Miniskirts." It played in the Ebony Showcase Theatre, in Los Angeles, for about six weeks. The following year, he staged "Beauty Shop." After running on and off in Los Angeles, that show went on tour, and, as Garrett likes to say, "the rest is history." Garrett had his audience in the palm of his hand and his formula at his fingertips; all that was left was for him to repeat it with slight variation, in plays like "Beauty Shop Part 2," "Living Room," "Barber Shop," and "Laundromat."

"It reminds you of the old commedia-dell'arte stuff," OyamO says of Garrett's approach to theatre. "But it's black, and it's today, and it's loud." He also makes the obvious remark that "if a white man was producing 'Beauty Shop,' they would be lynching it." Still, what Shelly Garrett does has a far better claim to be "community theatre" than what we normally refer to by that name.

Garrett's dramatis personae are as uniform as restaurant place settings: the parts invariably include a mouthy fat woman, a beautiful vamp, a sharp-tongued and swishy gay man, and a handsome black stud, who will ultimately be coupled with the fat woman. Much of the dialogue consists of insults and trash talk. Other options and accessories may be added, to taste; but typically there's a striptease scene, and lots of Teddy Pendergrass on the mixing board. The gay man and the fat woman swap gibes—"play the dozens"—during lulls in the action.

Although Garrett's plays adhere to pretty much the same situational and narrative template, they are not dashed off. "I take so much time in rehearsals and writing these shows," Garrett tells me. "I might rewrite a show forty times, and I take so much time with them and the rehearsals and the delivery of the lines that I just run actors crazy. I run them nuts. But then, at the end, when they get their standing ovation, they love me." A strained chuckle: "Takes them a long time to love me, but finally they do." Garrett prides himself on his professionalism, which lifts him far above the cheesier theatrical realm where drug-pusher auteurs and shakedown artists might freelance. And there's something disarming about his buoyant, show-me-the-money brand of dramaturgy.

Garrett is not the product of anyone's drama workshop; he comes from a world in which the Method refers to a birth-control technique. He has seen almost no "legitimate" theatre, even in its low-end form. "I'm embarrassed to tell people that I've never even seen 'The Wiz.' On Broadway, I've seen 'Les Miz,' 'Cats,' and—What was that black show that had Gregory Hines in it?" His shows play to ordinary black people—the "people on the avenue," as Wilson wistfully puts it—and if these shows are essentially invisible to the white mainstream, so much the better. "But I have things in my show that black people can relate to," Garrett declares. "If you're sitting in that audience and something is happening on that stage that you can absolutely not relate to, why are you even there?"

In "Beauty Shop," Terry (conservative, pretty) is the proprietor of the hair salon; Sylvia (sexy), Margaret (fat), and Chris (gay) are stylists; and Rachel (tall, well dressed) is a customer.

> TERRY: Barbara Dell! Is that man still beating on her?
> SYLVIA: Punching her lights out! It must have been a humdinger 'cause her glasses were *real* dark!
> TERRY: Well, if she's stupid enough to stay there with him, she deserves it!
> RACHEL: I have never understood why a woman just takes that kind of stuff off of a man.
> MARGARET: I can't understand a man raising his hand to *hit* a woman!
> CHRIS: I guess you wouldn't. What man would be *brave* enough to hit *you*?

Despite outrageous caricature, it doesn't seem quite right to call these plays homophobic. The gay characters may be stereotyped, but the bigots aren't treated charitably, either; the queen is always given the last word. "You are an embarrassment to the male gender, to the Y.M.C.A., the Cub Scouts, Boy Scouts, U.S. Army, and . . . Old Spice!" a customer tells Chris in the course of a steadily escalating argument. Chris replies, "Now what you *need* to do is go home and have a little talk with you *mother*! I wasn't *always* gay, I *might* be your *daddy!*" Politically correct it isn't, but neither is it mean-spirited. At the end, the fat woman is rewarded with a desirable man. And occasionally there are even monologues with morals, in which philandering males are put in their place by right-on women.

First and foremost, though, Garrett is a businessman. His production company moves along with him; he refuses to fly, but has a bus that's fully equipped with fax and phone. He's known for his skill in saturating the black press and radio stations. He's also known for the money he makes selling merchandise like T-shirts and programs. He can tell you that his average ticket price is twenty-seven dollars and fifty cents, that he rarely plays a venue with fewer than two thousand seats, that a show he did in Atlanta netted about six hundred thousand dollars a week. (For purposes of comparison, the weekly net of hit "straight" plays—like "Master Class," "Taking Sides," and so forth—is typically between one and two hundred thousand dollars; the weekly net of hit musicals like "Miss Saigon," "Les Misérables," and "Sunset Boulevard" is usually in the neighborhood of five hundred thousand.) In New York, Garrett's "Beauty Shop" had weekly revenues of more than eight hundred thousand, and that was for an eleven-week run, during which the show sold out every week but one. Garrett remembers the time fondly: "They put me up at the Plaza in New York. First black to ever stay at the penthouse of the Plaza. And I was there for three weeks—the penthouse of the Plaza!"

To most people who both take the theatrical arts seriously and aspire to an "organic connection" with the black community, Garrett is a cultural candy man, and his plays the equivalent of caries. Woodie King, Jr., of New York's New Federal Theatre (which has had unusual success in attracting black audiences for black theatre), expresses a widespread sentiment in the world of political theatre when he describes Garrett as "an individual going after our personal riches." He says, "It's not doing anything for any kind of black community. It's not like he's going to make money, then find five deserving women writers and put on their work. It's always going to be about him." It's clear that for dramatists who view themselves as producing work for their community, but depend for their existence on foundation and government support, Garrett is an embarrassment in more ways than one.

"Artistically, I think they're horrible," the Crossroads' Ricardo Khan says of the Chitlin Circuit's carnivalesque productions. "I don't think the acting is good, I don't think the direction is good, I don't think the level of production is good. But I don't put them down for being able to speak to something that people are feeling. I think the reason it's working is that it's making people laugh at themselves, making them feel good, and they're tired of heavy stuff." But his political consciousness rebels at the easy anodyne, the theatregoer's opiate. His own work, he says, aspires to raise consciousness and transform society. He sounds almost discouraged when he adds, "But people don't always want that. Sometimes they just want to have fun."

Nobody wants to see the Chitlin Circuit and the Crossroads converge. But there's something heartening about the spectacle of black drama that pays its own way—even if aficionados of serious theatre find something disheartening about the nature of that drama. So maybe we shouldn't worry so much about those Du Boisian yardsticks of blackness. That way lies heartbreak, or confusion. Wilson and his supporters, to listen to them, would divvy up American culture along the color line, sorting out possessions like an amicably divorcing couple. But, as I insist, Wilson's polemics disserve his poetics.

Indeed, his work is a tribute to a hybrid vigor, as an amalgam of black vernacular, American naturalism, and high modernist influences. (In the history of black drama, perhaps only Baraka's 1964 play "Dutchman" represents as formidable an achievement, and that was explicitly a drama of interracial conflict. By contrast, one of Wilson's accomplishments is to register the ambiguous presence of white folks in a segregated black world—the way you see them nowhere and feel them everywhere.) There's no contradiction in the fact that Wilson revels in the black cadences of the barbershop and the barbecue, on the one hand, and pledges fealty to Aristotle's Poetics, on the other. Wilson may talk about cultural autarky, but, to his credit, he doesn't practice it. Inevitably, the audience for serious plays in this mostly white country is mostly white. Wilson writes serious plays. His audience is mostly white. What's to apologize for?

By all means, let there be "political" art and formalist art, populism and modernism, Baraka and Beckett, but let them jostle and collide in the cultural agora. There will be theatres that are black, and also Latino and Asian, and what you will; but, all told, it's better that they not arise from the edicts of cultural commissioners. Despite all the rhetoric about inclusion, I was struck by the fact that many black playwrights told me they felt that their kind of work—usually more "experimental" than realist—was distinctly unwelcome in most black regional theatres. Suzan-Lori Parks reminds me that she didn't grow up in the 'hood: "I'm not black according to a nationalist definition of black womanhood. . . . We discriminate in our own family." As a working dramatist and director, George Wolfe—who, in the spirit of pluralism, says he welcomes all kinds of theatres, ethnically specific and otherwise—admits unease about the neatly color-coded cultural landscape that Wilson conjures up. "I don't live in the world of absolutes," Wolfe says. "I don't think it's a matter of a black theatre versus an American theatre, a black theatre versus a white theatre. I think we need an American theatre that is of, for, and by us—*all* of us."

You may wonder, then, what happens to that self-divided creed of populist modernism: the dream of an art that combines aesthetic vanguardism with popular engagement—which is to say the elevated black theatre for which Wilson seeks patronage. "People are not busting their ass to go and see this stuff," OyamO says bluntly, "and I keep thinking, if this stuff is so significant, why can't it touch ordinary people?" There's reason to believe that such impatience is beginning to spread. Indeed, maybe the most transgressive move for such black theatre would be to explore that sordid, sullying world of the truly demotic. Ed Bullins, the doyen of black revolutionary theatre, regales me with stories he's heard about Chitlin Circuit entrepreneurs "rolling away at night with suitcases of money"— the shadowy realm of cash-only transactions. But the challenge appeals to him, all the same.

So brace yourself: the Ed Bullins to whom Wilson paid tribute—as one whose dramatic art was hallowed with the blood of proud black warriors—now tells me he's been thinking about entering the Chitlin Circuit himself. Call it populist postmodernism. Somehow, he relishes the idea of a theatre that would be self-supporting, one that didn't just glorify the masses but actually appealed to them. Naturally, though, he'd try to do it a little better. "The idea is to upgrade the production a bit, but go after the same market," he says eagerly. Now, that's a radical thought.

Katherine H. Burkman

The Demeter Myth and Doubling in Marsha Norman's *'night, Mother*

Marsha Norman's Pulitzer Prize–winning play, *'night, Mother,* has been greeted by many critics as a major drama. Robert Brustein notes that the play is "chastely classical in its observance of the unities," and he welcomes Norman as one writing in "a great dramatic tradition" who, "young as she is, has the potential to preserve and revitalize it."[1] Another critic appreciates Norman's dissection of the "mythic relationship between mother and daughter"[2] in the play. Escaping the weaknesses of melodrama, Norman offers a drama that not only leads up to the carefully planned suicide of Jessie Cates, for which Jessie prepares her mother, Thelma, during the play, but one that also leads to a quickened sense of life. Departing from an overt dramatization of a split self in an earlier drama, *Getting Out* (1977), in which the author explored the relationship between Arlene, newly released from prison, and her earlier, juvenile delinquent self, Arlie, Norman offers in *'night, Mother* a dramatization of doubling between mother and daughter that leads to a character integration her earlier heroine sought in vain.

One way of approaching this drama is by looking at its banal surface in the context of the underlying mythic relationships of Demeter and Kore (Persephone), a relationship that offers clues to the mother-daughter relationship in the play. C. G. Jung and C. Kerényi, in their exploration of the Mysteries of Eleusis in *Essays On a Science of Mythology*, suggest an essential oneness of the Demeter and Kore figures in mythology, a oneness that is actually threefold, also embracing the third mythological figure, Hecate. Commenting on the identification of mother and daughter, Jung writes, "Demeter and Kore, mother and daughter, extend the feminine consciousness both upwards and downwards. They add an 'older and younger,' 'stronger and weaker' dimension to it and widen out the narrowly limited conscious mind bound in space and time, giving it intimations of a greater and more comprehensive personality which has a share in the eternal course of things."[3] Much of the power of Norman's play emerges from a mythical identification of mother and daughter that leaves Thelma bereft of the daughter she thought she had possessed but ironically at one with that daughter from whom she has derived new strength and life. More cathartic than depressing, the play reveals a bond between mother and daughter and a mythical sense of their oneness that allows for what Kerényi, commenting on Jung's ideas, calls *"being in death."*[4]

Although Jessie seems like a very different protagonist in her quiet determination and lack of pretension, she is, in some ways, descended from such self-destructive and flamboyant heroines as Ibsen's Hedda Gabler and Strindberg's Miss Julie. Like Hedda and Miss Julie, Jessie is her father's daughter (like Hedda, Jessie kills herself with her father's pistol), and she has identified with his kind of withdrawal: "I want to hang a big sign around my neck, like Daddy's on the barn. GONE FISHING," she explains to her mother. Like Hedda and Miss Julie, Jessie finds some measure of redemption in a suicide that is partly an escape from a world in which she lacks the strength to act with freedom or control; but her suicide also is a way of taking control by embracing a death that affords that freedom and fulfillment denied her in life.

What distinguishes Jessie from these former heroines is her reaching out to her mother in her last hours of life, recognizing her mother's greater appetite for life, arranging for the continued availability of the sweets her mother craves as a consolation for her empty existence but also offering her the more nourishing truths that may sustain her after her daughter's death. As she plays the role of mother to her mother, a role she has assumed after her husband has deserted her and she has moved into her mother's house, Jessie may be understood as both the Kore figure who feels used or raped and the Demeter figure who shares in that sense of loss and has lost the zest for life. As the drama progresses, however, we see not only the reversal of the Demeter-Kore role as daughter plays mother but also the common ground that binds the two, both in their shared sense of being used and in their deep feeling for each other. This kind of mutual participation in an archetype is that Jung suggests rescues the individual from isolation and restores her to wholeness.[5] Only a sense of incipient wholeness allows Jessie's mother to accept her daughter's death, to allow her that freedom, and to understand her choice.

The major difference between Jessie Cates and her mother seems to be a question of appetite. As Jessie readies herself for suicide and attempts to prepare her mother for her life without her, the focus is on food. Mama opens the play with her assertion of appetite.

> MAMA [*Unwrapping the cupcake.*]: Jessie, it's the last snowball, sugar. Put it on the list, O.K.? And we're out of Hershey bars, and where's that peanut brittle? I think maybe Dawson's been in it again. I ought to put a big mirror on the refrigerator door. That'll keep him out of my treats, won't it? You hear me, honey? [*Then more to herself*] I hate it when the coconut falls off. Why does the coconut fall off?

Mama is concerned with not running out of the sweets that sustain and console her in what we soon learn is an arid existence. Significantly, she addresses her daughter as sugar and honey here as well as in subsequent exchanges.

Although Jessie assures her mother that she has ordered a "whole case" of snowballs, she is intent in the opening moments of the drama on preparing for her death by locating her father's gun and collecting enough old towels for the mess her death will make. There is nothing sweet about Jessie as she determines that "garbage bags would do if there's enough." Later, when she tries to explain her failed marriage to her mother and why her husband has chosen to leave her behind, Jessie notes: "You don't pack your garbage when you move." What Jessie has bought in a "feed store" her brother Dawson told her about is bullets, not food.

The question of appetite is at the heart of Mama's choice for life and Jessie's choice for death. When they discuss Jessie's son Ricky, who has become a thief, Mama looks on the bright side and sees Ricky's redemption in terms of food. Ricky, she suggests, may simply be going through a bad period, mixing with the wrong people. "He just needs some time, sugar. He'll get back in school or get a job or one day you'll get a call and he'll say he's sorry for all the trouble he's caused and invite you out for supper someplace dress-up." Such a proposition has no value for Jessie, however, who says, "Those two rings he took were the last valuable things I had," and she insists she would turn him in if she knew where he was. Jessie knows she could choose to live rather than to die, but she lacks the appetite for the choice. She tells her mother that she wondered after her decision at Christmas time to kill herself what might make it worth while staying alive and says, "It was maybe if there was something I really liked, like maybe if I really liked rice pudding or cornflakes for breakfast or something, that might be enough."

Appetite is also a major concern in the Demeter myth for both mother and daughter. When she learns of her daughter's rape by Hades, who has taken her to be queen of the Underworld, Demeter will neither eat nor drink. In the myth, however, the implications of this loss of appetite involve the fertility of the earth itself and the revolution of the seasons. As goddess of the corn, not only does Demeter refrain from eating; she also will not permit the crops to grow, depriving mankind as well as herself of food and the gods of their sacrifices. Only the restoration of her daughter will bring the return of spring. Persephone as Kore, the maiden, also refuses food in the Underworld, but her eating of pomegranate seeds just before her return to her mother ensures her marriage to Hades and her return for three months of each year to his abode.

Here the paradox of the myth may offer a clue to the paradox of the play. The pomegranate, although it ties the Persephone-Kore figure to the Underworld and thus to death, is associated with fertility and sexuality. Geoffrey Grigson describes the fruit as "enclosed by the enlarged calyx—a womb with an opening, a womb packed with seeds of translucent pink . . . The pomegranate, then, is the physical secrecy and portal of the feminine, whether for Aphrodite, or any related goddess of fertility and the sexual."[6] Not just a fruit of the Underworld, the pomegranate is one of Demeter's "fruits of the earth" as well, symbolizing marriage, in this case the marriage of Persephone and Hades for the winter of each year. The fruit is paradoxical in that it ties the daughter figure simultaneously to life on earth and to death in the Underworld—in other words, to life's cycle with its death and rebirth.

Although on one level the play deals with Mama as a Demeter figure trying to rescue her child from death, to talk her out of it, one senses as the play unfolds that on a deeper level it is about the reclamation of the mother from death, that it is about Thelma's rebirth. However, because there is a doubling of mother and daughter in the drama that is similar to its doubling in the myth, one senses at the end of the play a rebirth that combines mother and daughter as aspects of one entity.

Despite differences in Mama and Jessie's appetite for food and life and their different attitudes toward death, Mama fearing that which her daughter seeks to embrace, Norman establishes the similarity between mother and daughter early in the play. When Mama thinks Jessie is looking for her father's gun to protect them from thieves, she says, "We don't have anything anybody'd want, Jessie. I mean, I don't even want what we got, Jessie." Jessie's "Neither do I," of course, has a more ominous meaning because one senses that the "protection" she seeks with the gun is not from thieves but from life even before she announces her intention to commit suicide. Still, neither woman values what she has.

Mother and daughter also share the sense of violation that permeates the Demeter myth. Some versions of the myth depict Demeter as herself raped by Poseidon, lord of the sea, while searching for her violated and kidnapped daughter.[7] In the play, mother and daughter feel violated by their respective husbands. Mama admits to Jessie that she didn't love her husband, who "wanted a plain country woman and that's what he married, and then he held it against me the rest of my life like I was supposed to change and surprise him somehow." Although Jessie did love her husband, she expresses a similar feeling about their relationship, explaining to her mother that it was a "relief" when Cecil left. "I never was what he wanted to see, so it was better when he wasn't looking at me all the time." As Jenny S. Spencer has noted, "Despite differences in personality and coping patterns, the two characters share similar attitudes toward the meaninglessness of their lives, toward the demands of their husbands and children."[8]

Even concerning appetite, one comes to see that the differences between mother and daughter are less profound than they would appear. Rather than having a true appetite for life, Mama's appetite for sweets symbolizes her need for a slave for her death-in-life existence, a way of filling up an emptiness and of hiding from her fear of life and death. One begins to see that she, like Jessie, also is in death's grip.

Although Jessie has no particular fondness for any food, Mama has rejected almost all nourishing foods. In her state of agony over her daughter's announced suicide, she even rejects the proferred sweets that are her main source of consolation if not nourishment, and she insists that she will not cook if Jessie carries through with her plan. She wants her daughter to throw out all but one pan: "I'm not going to cook," she explains, and adds, significantly, "I never liked it, anyway. I like candy. Wrapped in plastic or coming in sacks. And tuna. I like tuna. I'll eat tuna, thank you."

Mama also informs Jessie that she doesn't like carrots, and after making cocoa at her daughter's request, she finds it as undrinkable, because of the milk, as her daughter does. "God, this milk in here," Mama complains, and Jessie agrees; "I thought it was my memory that was bad, but it's not. It's the milk, all right." When Mama tells Jessie she doesn't need to finish it, she might be talking about Jessie's life, which Jessie has decided not to finish.[9] Perhaps it is this shared and symbolic distaste for milk that helps Mama finally to accept and understand Jessie's decision.

Jessie's preparations for her mother's welfare, however, involve milk. She has told the grocer to deliver "a quart a week no matter what you said," she informs Mama, thus insisting on offering her mother the nourishment that she herself rejects, recognizing in her mother a life force that she lacks. Mama's old glasses, it also turns out, are "in an old Milk of Magnesia box," further information she garners from her daughter that suggests Thelma's gaining insight during the play as well as the nourishment that such insight affords her.[10] When she grasps the hot chocolate pan at the end of the play, holding *"it tight like her life depended on it,"* something Jessie has advised her to clean after hearing the shot, calling her son, and waiting for him to arrive, Thelma is doing what she said she would not and could not. She is finding a way to go on, a way pointed out to her by her daughter, who, by taking control of her life by killing herself, has also offered her mother a new sense of life and strength to live it.[11] One shares Mama's feelings of devastation at the end of the play but also feels a sense of her impending renewal.

The seeds of that renewal, like the pomegranate seeds of the myth, involve a quickened sense of life through the gaining of a quickened sense of death; Mama must face that death which Jessie chooses; must, so to speak, taste it, if she is to achieve a reversal of her death-in-life existence and achieve that *"being in death"* that Kerényi suggests is at the center of the Demeter-Kore myth.[12] Explaining her fear of death to her daughter, Mama describes death as "some killer on the loose, hiding out in the back yard just waiting for me to have my hands full someday and how am I supposed to protect myself anyhow when I don't know what he looks like and I don't know how he sounds coming up behind me like that or if it will hurt or take very long or what I don't get done before it happens." Mama might be describing some modern version of Hades, waiting to pounce, violate her, and carry her off to the Underworld.

After this outburst, however, Mama confronts death in her own daughter, whom she now sees is beyond persuasion, "Who am I talking to? You're gone already, aren't you? I'm looking right through you!" Only by coming to see her daughter as gone, unreclaimable, married to Hades, and by experiencing her daughter's acceptance of her own lostness and death can Mama undergo an integration with her daughter that is the only possible source of renewal at hand.

As she battles with Jessie over the impending suicide, partly blaming herself for urging Jessie to move in with her after her divorce, Mama senses in some profound way the doubling of herself and her daughter.

> MAMA: Everything you do has to do with me, Jessie. You can't do *anything*, wash your face or cut your finger, without doing it to me. That's right. You might as well kill me as you, Jessie, it's the same thing. This has to do with me, Jessie.

Here Mama is partly expressing her identification with Jessie as a part of herself—but as that part Jessie is also the antagonist, the killer. Otto Rank has discussed this aspect of doubling in which the double symbolizes death so that encountering one's double is a kind of encounter with one's own mortality. Although doubling, Rank explains, grows out of a narcissistic inability to love others and a fear of death, resisting exclusive self-love leads to the doubling and a projection of hate or fear onto the other self.[13] Mama's slow acceptance of Jessie's decision to die is a movement toward acceptance of her own mortality. That this is a life-giving experience becomes clear as Thelma begins to accept the impending separation and hence the death of her dependency. Mama's expression of identification with Jessie—"This has to do with me Jessie"—is partly an expression of dependency. Realizing Jessie's loneliness—"How could I know you were so alone?" she begs, addressing the now locked door—her final words after she hears the shot display a moment of true recognition. "Jessie, Jessie, child . . . Forgive me. (*Pause*) I thought you were mine."[14] Mother and daughter merge as they separate, the death of one giving life to the other.

Similarly, it is only through an anticipated encounter with death, one that Jessie associates as a merging with her withdrawn father, a gentle and quiet Hades, that Jessie has been able to achieve the independence that she manages at last to pass on to her mother. When Thelma claims possession—"You are my child!"—Jessie explains that she is "what became of your child." She has decided not "to stay" because she feels she has never shown up as a person and that she never will. Again, there is a paradoxical sense of identity here as Jessie, taking control and guiding her mother to acceptance, finally does seem to arrive as a person.

If Jessie were entirely calm as she approached her death, the play might lose some of the tension that comes from her vulnerability that lasts, despite her overall control, until the end; thus both Jessie and Mama experience growth during the play. Learning from her distraught and angry mother that the epilepsy she thought derived from a fall from a horse as an adult had been with her since childhood and was probably inherited from her father, who had similar seizures, Jessie feels that this knowledge was her right, that it was hers to know. She is hurt further to learn from her mother that her husband Cecil had another woman, the daughter of her mother's friend Agnes. Jessie's ability to digest these new hurts without loss of control is a measure of the sense of self she has achieved now that she has decided to protect herself from further hurt through death. Significantly, her seizures, which are like minor descents into the Underworld and represent a loss of control and self, have been brought under control by medication, and it has been more than a year since her last one. No longer overtaken by Hades and violated by him, she is choosing to consummate her union with him.

More information Jessie gains during the drama involves the somewhat comic Hecate figure, Agnes. In the Homeric Hymn to Demeter, the oldest account of the rape of Persephone, there is, according to Kerényi, a doubling not only of Demeter with Persephone but also with the moon goddess Hecate.[15] Hearing the cries of the raped Persephone in her cave, Hecate meets Demeter and together, torches in hand, they seek knowledge of the lost child from the sun. Various versions of the myth, according to Kerényi, depict now Demeter, now Hecate seeking Persephone in the Underworld, these different versions suggesting an underlying unity between the goddesses.[16] Because Hecate also is sometimes portrayed as queen of the Underworld, she may also be identified with Persephone. Despite her slight role in the myth, Kerényi suggests that Hecate may even be its primary goddess on some level.[17] Whether one considers her in her depictions as three-headed like her dog Cerberus, or as having influence over either the three realms of heaven, earth, and sea, or heaven, earth, and the Underworld, she may be understood as one who encompasses the other two figures in the myth.

Agnes, who is only discussed by Jessie and Mama in the play, seems to have more of the crone and witchlike attributes that Hecate has developed over time. Surrounded by birds and living on okra, even in the winter, Agnes is described by Thelma as being "as crazy as they come . . . a lunatic"—hence her lunar aspect or association with the moon. She does not help Thelma with Jessie, avoiding the house when Jessie is home because she associates Jessie with death and she fears that it is catching. But if her avoidance of Jessie seems to preclude her Hecate role on the mythic level of the play's action, her setting fire to her houses may be associated with Hecate as a torch bearer bringing light. Agnes's behavior is akin to Jessie's suicide and is applauded by mother and daughter, although they consider it "crazy." Apparently Agnes has set eight fires already, waking up people so they won't be hurt and serving lemonade. Seeking to rationalize this behavior, Mama explains, "The houses they lived in, you knew they were going to fall down anyway, so why wait for it, is all I could ever make out about it. Agnes likes a feeling of accomplishment." Jessie's "Good for her" indicates her appreciation of Agnes deciding to terminate before termination date, a similar choice to her own, and when she expresses doubt that Agnes would burn down a house now since her dead husband could not build a new one, Mama also appreciates the act: "Be exciting, though, if she did. You never know," is Mama's response.

Although Mama's picture of Agnes surrounded by birds, living on okra, and burning down houses may be an exaggeration, it has some of the festive quality that is associated not only with the torch-bearing Hecate but with Demeter in her role as goddess of the grain. One may liken the burning and rebuilding of houses to the dying and returning moon (Hecate) or the dying and returning corn (Demeter or Persephone). Kerényi reminds us that "Whether it is parched or baked as bread, death by fire is the fate of the grain. Nevertheless, every sort of grain is eternal."[18] In the Demeter myth, Demeter treats the child Demophoön with fire in an attempt to make him immortal, as though he were the grain.[19] Jessie recognizes Agnes's value for her mother, and despite being hurt by what she learns of Agnes's fear of her, she suggests that her mother may like to live with Agnes after she is gone. Thelma, however, doubtless will be able to live alone. In the midst of telling Jessie about Agnes, Thelma insists that three marshmallows are the best way, the "old way" to have hot chocolate. She is imbibing not only Jessie's strength but Agnes's strength as well. She will be the primary goddess among the three in this drama.

Marsha Norman surely did not attempt to make *'night, Mother* a modern version of the Demeter myth. The rhythms and resonance of that myth, however, give the play, despite its great sadness and sense of loss, its quickened sense of life. "Hades," it has been noted, "is the god presiding over our descents, investing the darkness in our lives, our depressions, our anxieties, our emotional upheavals and our grief with the power to bring illumination and renewal."[20] Jessie embraces this god, and it is he that she introduces to her mother, who perhaps is able to see him more clearly through the image of Agnes's fires, a torch that burns to help one find what is lost. Mama learns from Jessie what it is that she used to whisper about after dinner with her withdrawn father—"His life, I guess," Jessie reveals. "His corn. His boots. Us. Things. You know." And now Mama does.

Notes

1. Robert Brustein, "Don't Read This Review!," *New Republic* (2 May 1983), p. 25.
2. Patricia Basworth, "Some Secret Worlds Revealed," *Working Woman* 8 (October 1983): 204.
3. C. G. Jung, "The Psychological Aspects of the Kore," in C. G. Jung and C. Kerényi, *Essays on a Science of Mythology: The Myth of the Divine Child and the Mysteries of Eleusis,* trans. R. F. C. Hull (Princeton: Princeton University Press, 1969), p. 162.
4. C. Kerényi, "Epilegomena: The Miracle of Eleusis," in C. G. Jung and C. Kerényi, *Essays on a Science of Mythology: The Myth of the Divine Child and the Mysteries of Eleusis,* trans. R. F. C. Hull (Princeton: Princeton University Press, 1969), p. 182.
5. Jung, "The Psychological Aspects of the Kore," p. 162.
6. Geoffrey Grigson, *The Goddess of Love: The Birth, Triumph, Death and Return of Aphrodite* (New York: Stein and Day, 1977), p. 202.
7. C. Kerényi, "Kore," in C. G. Jung and C. Kerényi, *Essays on a Science of Mythology: The Myth of the Divine Child and the Mysteries of Eleusis,* trans. R. F. C. Hull (Princeton: Princeton University Press, 1969), p. 123.
8. Jenny S. Spencer, "Norman's *'night, Mother:* Psycho-drama of Female Identity," *Modern Drama* 30, no. 3 (September 1987): 371–72.
9. This idea was suggested in an unpublished paper on *'night, Mother,* written by Linda Brown, 1986.
10. Debbie McCormick, "The Use of Food in *'night, Mother,*" unpublished paper, 1986.
11. Ibid.
12. Kerényi, "Epilegomena: The Miracle of Eleusis," p. 182.
13. Otto Rank, *The Double: A Psychoanalytic Study,* ed. and trans. Harry Tucker, Jr. (Chapel Hill: The University of North Carolina Press, 1971), pp. 71–73.
14. Inexplicably, the otherwise sensitive film version of *'night, Mother* leaves out this crucial line.
15. Kerényi, "Kore," pp. 110–11.
16. Ibid., p. 110.
17. Ibid., p. 113.
18. Ibid., p. 116.
19. Ibid.
20. Arianna Stassinopoulis and Roloff Beny, *The Gods of Greece* (New York: Harry N. Abrams, Inc., 1983), p. 187.

Chronology of Drama, History, and Culture

	Drama	History and Culture
1824		Ludwig van Beethoven's *Ninth Symphony* premiers in Vienna
1828	Henrik Ibsen is born in Skien, Norway	
1837		Queen Victoria is crowned
1839		Giuseppe Verdi's first opera, *Oberto, conte di San Bonifacio,* is staged at La Scala, Milan
1848		Revolutions against established aristocratic governments in Europe occur Karl Marx writes the *Communist Manifesto* Gold is discovered in California
1849	August Strindberg is born in Stockholm	
1850		William Wordsworth dies in Ambleside, England
1852		Napoleon III is declared Emperor of France
1854	Oscar Wilde is born in Dublin	
1856	George Bernard Shaw is born in Dublin	
1859		Charles Darwin publishes *The Origin of Species by Means of Natural Selection*
1860	Anton Chekhov is born in Taganrog, Ukraine	
1861		Abraham Lincoln is inaugurated as 16th president of the United States The U.S. Civil War begins
1862		Count Otto von Bismarck becomes prime minister of Prussia
1865		Abraham Lincoln is assassinated in Washington, D.C.
1867	Luigi Pirandello is born in Agrigento, Sicily	

	Drama	History and Culture
1871	John Millington Synge is born in Dublin	German Empire under Kaiser Wilhelm I is established
1876	Susan Glaspell is born in Davenport, Iowa	Richard Wagner's *Ring* Cycle begins the Bayreuth Festival
1879	Henrik Ibsen's *A Doll's House* is performed in Copenhagen, Denmark	Thomas Edison invents the light bulb
1883		The Brooklyn Bridge is completed
1886		Robert Louis Stevenson's *The Strange Case of Dr. Jekyll and Mr. Hyde* is published
1888	Eugene O'Neill is born in New York City	
1889	August Strindberg's *Miss Julie* is performed in Copenhagen	
1895	Oscar Wilde's *The Importance of Being Earnest* is performed in London	H. G. Wells's *The Time Machine* is published The Eastman Kodak hand camera is introduced First theater showing of a motion picture by Louis and Auguste Lumière (Paris)
1896		First theater showing of a motion picture using Thomas Edison's Kinetoscope, Joseph Armat's Vitascope, and Francis Jenkins's projector (New York City)
1897	Thornton Wilder is born in Madison, Wisconsin	
1898	The Moscow Art Theatre is founded by Konstantin Stanislavsky and Vladimir Nemirovich-Danchenko	
1898	Bertolt Brecht is born in Augsburg, Germany	Marie and Pierre Curie announce the discovery of radium H. G. Wells's *The War of the Worlds* published
1900	Oscar Wilde dies in Paris	The Paris Metro opens Sigmund Freud publishes *The Interpretation of Dreams*
1901		Queen Victoria dies; Edward VII is crowned
1902		Henry James's *The Wings of the Dove* is published
1903		Wilbur and Orville Wright fly the first airplane
1904	Anton Chekhov's *The Cherry Orchard* is produced in Moscow; Chekhov dies in Yalta, Ukraine The Irish National Theatre, or the Abbey Theatre, is founded in Dublin by William Butler Yeats and Lady Augusta Gregory	

	Drama	History and Culture
1905	Lillian Hellman is born in New York City	The first movie theater opens in New York City
1906	Henrik Ibsen dies Samuel Beckett is born in Dublin	Pablo Picasso paints *Demoiselles d'Avignon*
1907	*The Playboy of the Western World* is performed in Dublin	
1909	John Millington Synge dies in Dublin	
1911	Tennessee Williams is born in Columbus, Mississippi	
1912	Eugène Ionesco is born in Slatina, Romania August Strindberg dies in Stockholm	
1913	George Bernard Shaw's *Pygmalion* is produced in Berlin and Vienna	Igor Stravinsky's *Rite of Spring* premieres in Paris
1914		World War I begins
1915	Arthur Miller is born in New York City Provincetown Players is founded by George Cram Cook and Susan Glaspell	
1917		The United States enters World War I Czar Nicholas II of Russia is overthrown; Communists, under Vladimir I. Lenin, establish the Soviet Union
1918		World War I Armistice is signed
1920		Edith Wharton's *The Age of Innocence* is published
1921	Luigi Pirandello's *Six Characters in Search of an Author* is performed in Rome Zonal Gale's *Miss Lulu Bett* is the first play by a woman to win a Pulitzer Prize for Drama Susan Glaspell's *The Verge* is produced in New York City	James Joyce's *Ulysses* is published in Paris
1922		Benito Mussolini transforms Italy into a fascist state The Irish Free State is established
1923	Luigi Pirandello's *Six Characters in Search of an Author* is performed in Paris	
1924	Eugene O'Neill's *Desire Under the Elms* is performed in New York City	Vladimir Lenin dies; Joseph Stalin assumes power in Soviet Union

	Drama	History and Culture
1925		F. Scott Fitzgerald's *The Great Gatsby* is published Virginia Woolf's *Mrs. Dalloway* is published
1926		Ernest Hemingway's *The Sun Also Rises* is published
1928	Edward Albee is born in Washington, D.C. Bertolt Brecht's *The Threepenny Opera* is performed in Berlin	
1929		The New York Stock market crashes, and the Great Depression begins Ernest Hemingway's *A Farewell to Arms* is published
1930	Lorraine Hansberry is born in Chicago Harold Pinter is born in London	
1932		The Empire State Building is completed
1933		Franklin Delano Roosevelt becomes president of the United States Adolph Hitler becomes chancellor of Germany
1934	Wole Soyinka is born in Abeokuta, Nigeria Lillian Hellman's *The Children's Hour* is performed in New York City	
1935	The Federal Theater Project is established as part of the Works Progress Administration	
1936	Luigi Pirandello dies in Rome Eugene O'Neill is awarded the Nobel Prize for Literature	
1937	Tom Stoppard is born in Czechoslovakia	Pablo Picasso paints *Guernica* Jean Renoir produces the film *Grand Illusion*
1938	Thornton Wilder's *Our Town* is produced in New York City	
1939		Hitler invades Poland; World War II begins in Europe David O. Selznick produces *Gone With the Wind*
1941		Japan bombs Pearl Harbor; United States enters World War II Orson Welles's film *Citizen Kane* is produced
1943	Sam Shepard is born on an army base near Chicago	
1944	Tennessee Williams's *The Glass Menagerie* is performed in Chicago	

	Drama	History and Culture
1945	August Wilson is born Pittsburgh, Pennsylvania	Germany capitulates and the war is over in Europe Japan capitulates after atomic bombs are dropped on Hiroshima and Nagasaki Benjamin Britten's opera *Peter Grimes* is premiered
1947	Arthur Miller's *All My Sons* is performed in New York City Marsha Norman is born in Louisville, Kentucky The Actors Studio is founded in New York City	The cold war between the Western democracies and the Soviet Union begins
1948	Susan Glaspell dies in Provincetown, Massachusetts	Mahatma Gandhi is assassinated
1949	The Berliner Ensemble is founded by Bertolt Brecht	George Orwell's *1984* is published Hunt for Communist subversives in United States is begun by Senator Joseph R. McCarthy of Wisconsin; House Un-American Activities Committee begins to search for Communists in the entertainment industry and the arts Mao Zedong establishes the People's Republic of China
1950	Wendy Wasserstein is born in New York City George Bernard Shaw dies at his country home in Devon, England	Korean War begins
1953	Eugene O'Neill dies in Boston Samuel Beckett's *Waiting for Godot* is produced in Paris	Joseph Stalin dies in Moscow
1954	The New York Shakespeare Workshop is founded in New York City by Joseph Papp	
1956	Bertolt Brecht dies in Berlin	
1957	Samuel Beckett's *Endgame* is produced in London and Paris	
1958	Harold Pinter's *The Birthday Party* is produced in London	Charles de Gaulle becomes president of France
1959	Lorraine Hansberry's *A Raisin in the Sun* is produced in New York City Eugène Ionesco's *Rhinoceros* is produced in Paris Edward Albee's *The Zoo Story* is produced in New York City	

	Drama	History and Culture
1961		John Kennedy becomes president of the United States Russian cosmonaut Yuri Gagarin orbits the Earth
1962		John Glenn is the first American to orbit the Earth
1963	Wole Soyinka's *The Lion and the Jewel* is produced in London	John Kennedy is assassinated in Dallas, Texas
1964		President Lyndon Johnson orders air strikes in Vietnam
1965	Lorraine Hansberry dies in New York City	
1967	Tom Stoppard's *Rosencrantz & Guildenstern Are Dead* is produced in London	Nigerian civil war begins
1969	U.S. astronauts Neil Armstrong and Edwin Aldrin walk on the moon	
1970		Nigerian civil war ends
1973		U.S. troops leave Vietnam
1974		President Richard Nixon resigns rather than face impeachment
1978	Sam Shepard's *Buried Child* is produced in San Francisco and New York City	
1983	Marsha Norman's *'night, Mother* is produced in New York City Tennessee Williams dies in New York City	
1984	Lillian Hellman dies in Martha's Vineyard, Massachusetts	Mikhail Gorbachev becomes leader of the Soviet Union
1989	August Wilson's *The Piano Lesson* is produced in New York City Samuel Beckett dies in Paris	
1991		The cold war ends, and the Soviet Union breaks up
1992	Wendy Wasserstein's *The Sisters Rosensweig* is produced in New York City	
1994	Eugène Ionesco dies in Paris	

Glossary

Abbey Theatre Originally the Irish National Theatre, founded by William Butler Yeats and Lady Augusta Gregory in 1899. The group was renamed when it moved to the Abbey Theatre in 1904. Among its artistic directors was John Millington Synge, and all of his plays were first produced there.

Absurd, Theatre of A term coined by critic Martin Esslin in *The Theatre of the Absurd* (1961) to describe the avant-garde theater that portrays unrealistic situations, the futility of understanding the nature of existence, and a world over which there is no control. The earliest play of this kind is Alfred Jarry's *Ubi Roi* (1896), but the chief playwrights of this genre are Samuel Beckett (*Endgame*), Eugène Ionesco (*Rhinoceros*), Harold Pinter (*The Birthday Party*), and Edward Albee (*The Zoo Story*). Characteristics of absurdity are the distortion of chronological time, incongruous action, repetitive dialogue, illogical reasoning, and bitter humor. An absurd play does not tell a story in a traditional way but presents scenes that are often plotless. Scenes are meant to convey images of situations, portraying the complexity and disparity in the chaotic world as it is now. Realism, or verisimilitude, is abandoned in favor of abstraction and symbolism. There is a deliberate attempt to break down conventions; ironically, to confuse in order to enlighten.

act A main division of action in drama, which includes scenes or episodes. In classical Greek theater there were no acts per se; instead, the action was divided into smaller units—usually five episodes in which actors spoke their lines, alternating with dances, song, and dialog performed by the chorus. Classical Greek drama was performed without interruption. The familiar act and scene division was developed during the Elizabethan period, when editors began dividing scenes into larger units. Shakespeare divided his plays into five acts, and he usually defined scene endings with a couplet. Divisions of modern and contemporary plays are eclectic and may range from one to five acts, may have all scenes and no acts, or may have any variation according to the requirements of the playwright and director.

actor A person who acts in a play.

alienation effect see **Epic Theater.**

allegory A story in which the apparent characters and actions refer to another story; the figurative treatment of one subject under the guise of another. For example, abstract notions of virtue (good, evil, fear, chastity, profanity, etc.) may be portrayed by characters who communicate those ideas.

antagonist A character (enemy, rival, or opponent) who creates conflict for the protagonist, or hero.

antecedent action Action that takes place before the opening scene of the play. It is usual for the characters to recapitulate the antecedent action (also called **exposition**) in the opening scene of the first act in order to prepare the audience for what is to come next. Ibsen follows this pattern in *A Doll's House*, but Strindberg advocated letting the action tell itself, as in *Miss Julie*.

apron The part of the stage extending in front of the **proscenium arch.**

arena stage A stage completely surrounded by the audience. Also called **theater-in-the-round.**

atmosphere The mood or tone of the setting, usually accomplished by lighting, music, sound effects, and scenery.

avant-garde A French word that means the most advanced part of an army, the vanguard. It is used to describe literary and artistic innovators who push beyond the traditional or currently accepted modes of form and expression.

ballad-opera A **burlesque** opera, exemplified by John Gay's *The Beggar's Opera* (1728), the inspiration for Bertolt Brecht's *The Threepenny Opera* (1928).

black humor An expression of comedy that is funny in an unpleasant or inappropriate way. It is often used for satiric purposes or for exploiting a grotesque situation. It is used extensively by Eugène Ionesco (*Rhinoceros*), Samuel Beckett (*Endgame*), Harold Pinter (*The Birthday Party*), Edward Albee (*The Zoo Story*), and Sam Shepard (*Buried Child*).

bombast A speech in which a character rants or shouts wildly but does not say much that matters.

bourgeois drama and tragedy A play in which the leading characters are middle class instead of noble or aristocratic as in the case of classical Greek and Shakespearean tragedy. Bourgeois drama is especially favored in the United States and the concept is central to Eugene O'Neill's *Desire Under the Elms* and Arthur Miller's *All My Sons.* Miller suggests that Joe Keller's ability to face his failures raises him above the local problem and so makes him a tragic hero in search of his universal destiny. Also see **Epic Theater.**

box set A three-walled stage setting that resembles a room. This is the preferred set for portraying realism or naturalism on stage because it allows the audience to look in on the action.

burlesque A comedy that is based on wild exaggeration or distortion.

catastrophe The conclusion of a play. It is also called **dénouement.** In modern usage the common meaning of catastrophe is disaster.

character A fictional person, or, the elements of personality.

climax The designation of the turning point in action that leads to **catastrophe** or **dénouement.**

closet drama A play meant to be read, not acted.

comedy A drama in which conflicts of love, social ideas and relationships, satire and ridicule end with a clear, if not happy, resolution. Comedy is usually designed to give pleasure or make people laugh. For the classical Greeks, comedy was based on the actions of the common or ignoble. Their comedy ranged from comedy of manners, and sentimental comedy to farce, slapstick comedy, and burlesque. Modern comedy is eclectic; for example, Anton Chekhov's *The Cherry Orchard* is sentimental but relies on the comic social attitudes of his characters; Oscar Wilde's *The Importance of Being Earnest*, John Millington Synge's *The Playboy of the Western World,* and Wolie Soyinka's *The Lion and the Jewel* are mock-serious satires; Bernard Shaw's *Pygmalion* is a comedy of class distinction and manners. There is also "black" or "sick" comedy, designed to portray depravity and despair. This kind of comedy uses laughter more from contradiction and absurdity than from pleasure, as in Samuel Beckett's *Waiting for Godot* (1953) or Harold Pinter's *The Birthday Party.* Situation comedy depicts family and social conflict, as in Wendy Wasserstein's *The Sisters Rosensweig*.

Comedy of Manners A comedy in which the particular customs, manners, or ideals of a society are held up for examination and fun, often satire, and sometimes savaging, as in black or sick comedy. See Oscar Wilde's *The Importance of Being Earnest*, Bernard Shaw's *Pygmalion,* and Wole Soyinka's *The Lion and the Jewel.*

crisis The point in a plot in classical drama when the hero or heroine cannot turn back and must go on to the climax.

Cruelty, Theater of A type of drama defined by Antonin Artaud (1896–1948) in *Manifesto* (1932) and the collection of essays *Theater and Its Double* (1938). Artaud sought to break down the traditions of Aristotelian structure and defy the structural limitations of naturalism and problem plays such as Ibsen's. Almost fifty years before Artuad, Strindberg had advocated loosening the restrictions between stage and audience. Artuad's idea was to include the audience in the play. This was accomplished in part by developing the theater-in-the-round, a structure in which the stage is surrounded by the audience. Artuad's influence may be observed in Harold Pinter's *The Birthday Party* and Sam Shepard's *Buried Child.*

demonstration According to Bertolt Brecht, a technique for actors designed to keep the audience aware that the actor is playing a role and that the character represented is only a role. This is an element of Brecht's attempt to break with traditional theater and the illusion of verisimilitude, which is a central aspect of **realism** and **naturalism.** See Brecht's *The Threepenny Opera.* It is also called aesthetic distance, **alienation effect,** and disinterestness.

dénouement French for unknotting. It is the final scene or ending; the story ends when misunderstanding and mystery are solved. It is used by Oscar Wilde in *The Importance of Being Earnest* to sort out the confused identity of Jack Worthing.

dialogue What the characters say to one another or to the audience.

diction The quality and manner of speech, often representing the class, education, and quality of a character. Bernard Shaw uses diction to differentiate the social class and education of his characters in *Pygmalion:* Professor Higgins is educated and speaks standard London English, while Eliza Doolittle and her father, Alfred Doolittle, speak the curbside English of the uneducated poor in London. Also see Eugene O'Neill's *Desire Under the Elms* for an example of New England regional diction.

director The person who makes the decisions for translating the playwright's text into action on the stage. The director interprets the playwright's intentions regarding character, action, and setting, and helps the actors fulfill his idea of how the play should be presented. A director may change, edit, rearrange the text, and reinterpret it, without the approval of the playwright.

dramaturge A literary advisor for dramatic productions who assists the playwright with research, rewriting, or developing ideas; assists the director and actors by providing interpretations of characters, actions, and context.

environmental theater A dramatic presentation in which the distinction between the stage and the audience is broken down. The action may take place in areas where the audience is seated.

Epic Theater Developed by Bertolt Brecht in collaboration with Erwin Piscator (1893–1966) in Berlin during the early 1920s. Epic Theater is anti-Aristotelian in the sense that it breaks the convention of unity and concerns common people rather than nobility. It is involved with moral social issues, not the relationship of mortals to gods or the revelation of personal tragic flaws. According to Walter Benjamin's "What is Epic Theater?" (1939), Epic Theater is meant to astonish, not to encourage catharsis or empathy for the protagonist. The task of Epic Theater is to represent conditions affecting the life of the characters that are meant to make the audience think about what is happening and why it is happening. Brecht's plots usually depict class struggle. A play in the Epic Theater mode is structurally designed to be nonrealistic or expressionistic. The traditional act and scene structure of drama may be replaced with a series of episodes, something on the order of a vaudeville show. Scenery is often reduced to essentials; perhaps a bare stage with the stage workings—scaffolds, ropes, and so on—left open for scrutiny. Brecht believed that this drama should exemplify the tenets of Marxism and Communist socialism and should criticize especially the middle-class values of religion, work, family, and politics. Brecht's first successful play in this style is *The Threepenny Opera,* in which he employed extraneous props, such as film screens, placards, and music, which intrude on the action or announce what is going to happen next. Tennessee Williams called for many of the attributes of Epic Theater in the stage directions for *The Glass Menagerie.* **Epic Theatre** is also called **alienation effect,** total theater, and multimedia theater.

epilogue The very end of the play in which a character sums up the action and brings the proceedings to a close.

episode A dramatic scene in Greek classical drama in which actors speak; or a scene or an event in a scene.

existentialism A philosophical school of thought developed after World War II in France by Jean Paul Sartre, Simone de Beauvoir, and others. It is based on the concept that an individual is responsible to him- or herself for moral guidance and social action. Existentialism is also based on the premise that a person must adapt to a situation and make appropriate choices that define the conflicts between personal freedom and quality of life.

exposition The recapitulation of events that takes place before the action of the play begins (also called **antecedent action**). It prepares the audience for the action and conflict that are about to unfold. Exposition is usually descriptive and is reported early in the first act. Henrik Ibsen employed exposition in *A Doll House.* On the contrary, there is no exposition in August Strindberg's *Miss Julie* or Bernard Shaw's *Pygmalion.* Exposition is a key factor in understanding the nature of the characters' quest for an author in Luigi Pirandello's *Six Characters in Search of an Author.* Samuel Beckett purposely obscured exposition in *Endgame* by having Clov tell a story that might not be true. Tennessee Williams's *The Glass Menagerie* begins with a prologue by Tom Wingfield that places the action in time and provides exposition.

expressionism An artistic movement that describes the world as a free associating chain of actions, which often resembles a dream sequence and makes the interior mind visible. In *A Dream Play* (1902), Strindberg attempted to recreate the logic of a dream. Events are loosely connected and relationships are deliberately ambiguous. He suggested that life be reduced to a dream—the action consisting of the disconnected but logical elements of a dream—and time and space conflate. Expressionism tends to be iconoclastic and abstract, showing the world in a purposely distorted way. It is characterized by symbolism, allegory, or nonrepresentational situations that especially influenced Luigi Pirandello, Bertolt Brecht, Eugene O'Neill, Susan Glaspell, Thornton Wilder, Tennessee Williams, Samuel Beckett, Eugène Ionesco, Harold Pinter, Edward Albee, Sam Shepard, and August Wilson. Glaspell's *The Verge* may be the first full-length play in the United States to utilize an expressionistic setting—a ruined stone tower and a glass hothouse in a snow storm—which mirrors the mind of the unhappy protagonist. Pirandello's *Six Characters in Search of an Author* and Wilder's *Our Town* freely mix reality and illusion. In *The Glass Menagerie* Williams employed expressionistic devices, especially the collection of glass animals, which is a symbol for Amanda Wingfield's delicate psyche and the fragility of social and personal relationships.

farce A kind of comic drama that portrays conflict as overblown and exaggerated. It is built on almost unbelievable coincidence, usually involving conflicts of love, family relationships, or politics. Farce usually depends on physical and sensual action for laughter, and it is not meant to be philosophical or intellectual. Its success depends very much on the bravura of the performers. Oscar Wilde's *The Importance of Being Earnest* is an example of **farce** combined with **comedy of manners.**

foil A character whose function is to support or set off another character, usually the protagonist. In Bernard Shaw's *Pygmalion,* Colonel Pickering, who is reserved and considerate, sets off the opposite qualities of character in Henry Higgins. In Anton Chekhov's *The Cherry Orchard,* Trofimov, the eternal student, is the foil for Lopakhin, the peasant who has risen into the middle class by virtue of hard work and business acumen.

folk drama Plays that deal with the lives and customs of country people and that are written by a sophisticated playwright. See John Millington Synge's *The Playboy of the Western World.*

genre A type of literary form such as drama, novel, or short story.

hero or heroine The leading character in a story who is at the center of conflict and most affected by it. In classical Greek tragedy, the hero or heroine is always of high rank and means to do good, but causes unintended harm. A hero or heroine is sometimes confused with **protagonist,** who is not necessarily good. In **bourgeois,** or middle-class, **drama,** heroes and heroines are middle class and unexalted socially or politically.

history play A type of drama mixing history and fiction that tells the story of a real person, or a fictional person involved with real events and people. Also called chronicle play.

lighting Effects used to enhance atmosphere and mood, as in Tennessee Williams's *The Glass Menagerie.* It may accentuate a character's presence or intensify an action, as in Bernard Shaw's *Pygmalion,* when Eliza's fury is contrasted with Higgins's and Pickering's review of how they confounded London society.

melodrama A play characterized by deep sentimentality, morbidity, terror, and mystery. Broadly defined, melodrama stresses plot rather than character development in order to maintain excitement and keep the audience interested. See Lillian Hellman's *The Children's Hour.*

metatheatre A concept of theater defined by Lionel Abel, in *Metatheatre* (1963), who argued the paradox that because a play presents the world as reality, life becomes less real. According to Abel, metatheatre postulates that the playwright presumes the world is a stage because human actions and emotions are theatrical and life is a dream because it cannot be understood. Abel said that Luigi Pirandello used illusion to define the limits of human subjectivity (see *Six Characters in Search of an Author*) and Bertolt Brecht rejected the logic of realism by presenting characters as "puppets" who are obviously not real people (see *Threepenny Opera*).

mise-en-scène French for putting a thing in its place; in this case, enacting the script on the stage, including scenery and props. For playwrights' notes concerning mis-en-scène see Henrik Ibsen's *A Doll's House,* August Strindberg's *Miss Julie,* Bernard Shaw's *Pygmalion,* Susan Glaspell's *The Verge,* and Eugene O'Neill's *Desire Under the Elms.*

naturalism A literary and dramatic movement in literature, drama, and the arts of the late-nineteenth and early-twentieth centuries that is a reaction to **realism.** The chief practioner was the novelist Émile Zola (1840–1902), who pushed the limits of realism by attempting to depict scientific factualness (truth) and psychological analysis to understand motivations and actions. In *The Experimental Novel* (1880), a collection of essays, Zola argued for a literature based on the scientific method of studying of man and nature, psychological analysis of character, and realistic descriptions of scenery (August Strindberg was infused with the desire to deromanticize literature, and he adopted Zola's stern verisimilitude and made it his own.) Zola also advocated using fiction and drama as a medium for improving social justice. Unlike Ibsen, Zola argued that the theater was a means for political and social debate, if not propaganda. Zola's assertion was adopted by Bernard Shaw and Bertolt Brecht. Strindberg's *Miss Julie* is an example of naturalism, and his "Preface" largely defines what Strindberg had in mind.

obligatory scene A scene that is anticipated by the audience and must take place in order to satisfy its audience's expectations. Also called *scène à faire.*

pantomime Action without words; a theatrical entertainment that tells a story through physical movement or dance.

pathos The evocation of pity or tenderness that comes about because something sorrowful has occurred.

play Aristotle defined a play as a work that has the ingredients of plot, character, thought, diction, spectacle, and song. Plot is most important, and it must show unified action. In tragedy there must be a change of fortune, a recognition. According to Clayton Hamilton in *Theory of the Theatre* (1910) a play is "a story devised to be presented by actors on stage before an audience." **Closet drama,**

however, is meant to be read, not performed. In "Some Thoughts on Playwrighting" (1941), Thornton Wilder explained that a play "is a succession of events illustrating a general idea—the stirring of the idea; the gradual feeding out of information; the shock and counter-shock of circumstances; the flow of action; the interruption of action; the moments of allusion to earlier events; the preparation of surprise, dread, or delight."

problem play A version of the **well-made play,** developed by Henrik Ibsen, in which the characters discuss the personal and social ramifications of controversial domestic, social, or psychological concerns. In Ibsen's *A Doll's House* (1879) characters tackle issues of marriage and a woman's right to leave her husband and family. August Strindberg's *Miss Julie* (1889) portrays the problem of Miss Julie's sexual frustration and psychological motivations. Arthur Miller's *All My Sons* (1947) is a problem play about Joe Keller's dilemma in confronting his personal guilt. Other variations of the problem play are Eugene O'Neill's *Desire Under the Elms,* Lillian Hellman's *The Children's Hour,* and Susan Glaspell's *The Verge.* Lorraine Hansberry's *A Raisin in the Sun* portrays characters who must overcome the oppression of racial hatred and social discord in the United States. Marsha Norman's *'night, Mother* explores the problem of coming to terms with oneself.

prologue An introduction that precedes the action. Tennessee Williams' *The Glass Menagerie* begins with a prologue by Tom Wingfield in which he places the action and provides exposition. Also see **exposition.**

proscenium The arch over the stage.

protagonist The leading and most important character in any story; or, the main character in a play who forces or leads the action and conflict. Also see **hero or heroine.**

realism A literary and dramatic movement in the literature and arts of the late-nineteenth and early-twentieth centuries that requires the portrayal of characters in a realistic physical and cultural environment, or, the portrayal of the story in a style that is familiar to the audience. Realistic settings use actual props and create an environment that gives the appearance of being plausibly real. Examples of use of realism are found in Henrik Ibsen's *A Doll's House,* Anton Chekhov's *The Cherry Orchard,* Bernard Shaw's *Pygmalion,* Arthur Miller's *All My Sons,* and Marsha Norman's *'night, Mother.* Also see **naturalism.**

romanticism A movement in the literature and arts of the late-eighteenth and early-nineteenth centuries in which the artist's emotions, impressions, and beliefs become the main sources of art. Romantics tend to be rebellious and struggle against the establishment and current or fashionable attitudes or traditions. Romantic themes include love of nature, idealization of rural life, sentimental melancholy, and affinity for the exotic and bizarre. It is the opposite of **realism** and **naturalism** and a chief resource for **expressionism.**

satire A kind of comedy that makes fun of or exploits personal, social, political, or religious ideas and actions for various purposes such as fun, maliciousness, parody, or philosophical inquiry; satire may aim to correct behavior or social attitudes or customs through ridicule. Examples of satire that poke fun at social attitudes and class consciousness are Anton Chekhov's *The Cherry Orchard,* Bernard Shaw's *Pygmalion,* and Oscar Wilde's *The Importance of Being Earnest.* John Millington Synge's *The Playboy of the Western World* is a satire of Irish life and the universal idea of the hero. Bertolt Brecht's *The Threepenny Opera* is a political satire that ridicules the bourgeoisie. Edward Albee's *The Zoo Story* and Sam Shepard's *Buried Child* are satires of the American dream of worldly success.

sentimentalism Emotion characterized by too much sweetness and softness in response to character or situation. See *The Cherry Orchard* for an example of Anton Chekhov's adroit handling of a sentimental situation.

social realism A type of realistic presentation of character and conflict concerned with social and political ideas; a type of drama approved by the Communist Party of the former Soviet Union to portray politically correct ideology, disparage Western capitalism, and point out the inherent social and personal conflict in European and United States society.

soliloquy A speech delivered by a character, either as a personal monologue or directly to the audience.

stock character A character with little depth, who represents a conventional type or stereotype: such as the young lover, clever servant, old father, long-suffering wife, good mother, whore with a heart of gold, country bumpkin, city slicker, confidant, or the clown.

subtext A concept developed by Russian director Konstantin Stanislavsky (1863–1938) to analyse a character's motivations, actions, and thoughts so that actors may simulate real experiences for their roles. The process as described in *My Life in Art* (1924, rev. 1936); *An Actor Prepares* (1937) tells how an actor can make the shift between herself or himself and the character by understanding the inner life of the character or role.

surrealism A movement in literature, drama, and the arts that emerged in the early 1920s, aimed at upsetting, if not destroying, traditional and conventional art forms and esthetic values. In drama, surrealism is often presented in the guise of a dream, with all of its meanderings and seeming non sequiturs. The manifestos for surrealism written by André Breton beginning in 1924 set the tone of the movement, which is based on idiosyncratic and personal references and symbols that are not always apparent. Breton and his fellow surrealists claimed to be searching for truth, but this could only be accomplished by smashing through the barriers set by tradition and established rules of decorum. Surrealism led to Antonin Artaud's (1896–1948) **Theater of Cruelty.**

suspense The emotion the audience experiences while waiting for something to happen; anxiety or anticipation.

symbolism A movement in literature, art, and drama of the late-nineteenth and early-twentieth centuries that repudiates realism and naturalism. Those employing symbolism avoid the verisimilitude expressed in the conventional theater by their tendency to present characters and their actions in the form of a dream, reverie, mystical experience, or unworldly event or environment. Symbolist drama deliberately confounds the distinction between the unreal and the real, as in Luigi Pirandello's *Six Characters in Search of an Author,* Thornton Wilder's *Our Town,* Tennessee Williams's *The Glass Menagerie,* or Sam Shepard's *Buried Child.*

subplot The line of action that runs parallel to the main plot and subordinate to the main line of action. In Henrik Ibsen's *A Doll's House* the relationship of Kristine Linde and Nils Krogstad functions as a subplot to the main action, which concentrates on Nora and Torvald Helmer.

theater-in-the-round A stage that is surrounded by the audience. The concept of surrounding the actors with an audience was advocated by Antonin Artaud for his 1935 production of his adaptation of Percy Bysshe Shelley's *The Cenci* (1819), a **closet drama.** See also **arena stage.**

thrust stage A stage that projects beyond the **proscenium** and is surrounded by seating on three sides. The part of the stage that is thrust forward is called an **apron.** This is the basic arrangement of the Elizabethan stage.

tragedy A type of drama that depicts human nobility in the face of disaster in a world beyond human control. For the classical Greeks, tragedy, as defined by Aristotle in his *Rhetoric and Poetics,* was the highest form of drama, depicting the noble hero's or heroine's reversal of fortune from a position of high stature and public importance due to a flaw (hamartia) in character. The flaw is usually excessive pride (hubris), intransigence, or stubbornness in the pursuit of idealism. The hero or heroine means to do good or noble actions but causes unintended harm. Once the action has begun, there is no turning back (peripety) and conflict ends when the hero or heroine finally recognizes (anagnorisis) the consequences of his or her action, which results in the **catastrophe,** or a reversal of fortune. Aristotle's prime example of tragedy was Sophocles' *Oedipus Tyranus.* Beginning in the 1920s, both Eugene O'Neill and Arthur Miller redefined tragedy for middle-class audiences in the United States. Miller's essay "Tragedy and the Common Man" (1949) is an important statement on this issue.

tragicomedy Denotes a play combining the qualities of tragedy and comedy and allowing for adaptation of classical Greek rules and models of tragedy. The term seems to have been coined by the Roman playwright Plautus (250–184 B.C.) in *Amphitryon* (186 B.C.), which is a parody of Roman mythology. Sam Shepard's *Buried Child* mingles seriousness and laughter; Eugène Ionesco's *Rhinoceros* pushes the limits of tragicomedy to the point of absurdity; and Samuel Beckett's subtitle for *Waiting for Godot* is "a Tragicomedy."

tragic hero or heroine According to Aristotle (384–322 B.C.) the tragic hero or heroine must be a person of royalty or of the nobility and important in the community. One who means to do good, but causes unintended harm.

unity According to Aristotle, whose *Rhetoric and Poetics* is devoted mainly to an explanation of tragedy, a play ought to have three unified or common elements—a time frame, in which the action is completed in twenty-four hours and action that takes place in the same basic location and leads directly to a **climax.** See **expressionism** and **Theater of the Absurd,** which purposely distort unity.

verisimilitude The appearance of being true or real, an important attribute of **realism** and **naturalism.** Strindberg's concept of **naturalism** called for real-looking stage settings and properties, or those that look plausibly real, something he explained in his "Preface to *Miss Julie.*"

villain A character who is evil or causes premeditated harm and conflict for the hero, heroine, or protagonist. Examples of villains are

Ephraim Cabot in Eugène O'Neill's *Desire Under the Elms* and Mary Tilford in Lillian Hellman's *The Children's Hour,* and Goldberg and McCann in Harold Pinter's *The Birthday Party.*

well-made play A term coined by French critic Francisque Sarcy (1827–1899) that describes the formula of dramatic action developed by Eugene Scribe (1791–1861) and Victorien Sardou (1831–1908). In a well-made play, the plot builds on sustained suspense until the revelation of a secret turns disaster into success for the hero or heroine. It is a play built on the notion of a seesaw: a reversal of action, usually going from a state of unhappiness to happiness. There is an **obligatory scene** in which the conflict in reconciled. Scribe developed the well-made play as a framework for comedy or farce, exposing the silliness of the middle class. Gustav Freytag (1816–1895) used this model in his influential work, *Technique of Drama* (1865), and his structure—**exposition,** conflict, rising action, **crisis,** and **dénouement**—is often the starting point for understanding dramatic structure in drama and literature. Henrik Ibsen, August Strindberg, and George Bernard Shaw were influced by Scribe's formula and Freytag's explication of it (see **problem play**). In Ibsen's *A Doll's House,* Nora's secret and its subsequent revelation are placed in the framework of the well-made play. Oscar Wilde was deeply influenced by Scribe and Sardou, and his play *The Importance of Being Earnest* is a well-made play that satirizes structural origins.

Credits

PLAYS

Henrik Ibsen, *A Doll's House,* translated by Otto Reinert. *An Introductory Anthology* (Boston: Little, Brown and Company, 1961). Copyright © 1977 by Otto Reinert. Reprinted with the permission of the translator.

August Strindberg, *Miss Julie,* translated by Henry Carlson, from *Strindberg: Five Plays.* Copyright © 1983 by The Regents of the University of California. Reprinted with the permission of University of California Press.

Oscar Wilde, *The Importance of Being Earnest* from *The Plays of Oscar Wilde, Volume II* (Boston and London: John W. Luce & Co., 1905). Originally published 1895.

Bernard Shaw, *Pygmalion* from *Bernard Shaw, Plays* (New York: W. H. Wise & Co., 1930). Originally published 1913, 1916.

Anton Chekhov, *The Cherry Orchard,* translated by Constance Garnett (London: Shattow & Windus: 1923).

Luigi Pirandello, *Six Characters in Search of an Author,* translated by Edward Storer (New York: E. P. Dutton, 1922).

John Millington Synge, *Playboy of the Western World* (Dublin: Maunsel & Co., 1907).

Susan Glaspell, *The Verge* (New York: Dodd, Mead and Company, 1921).

Eugene O'Neill, *Desire Under the Elms* from *Selected Plays of Eugene O'Neill.* Copyright 1924 and renewed 1954 by Eugene O'Neill. Reprinted with the permission of Random House, Inc.

Thornton Wilder, *Our Town* (New York: Harper & Row, 1938). Copyright 1938 and renewed © 1957 by Thornton Wilder. Reprinted with the permission of HarperCollins Publishers, Inc.

Lillian Hellman, *The Children's Hour.* Copyright 1934 and renewed © 1962 by Lillian Hellman. Reprinted with the permission of Random House, Inc.

Bertolt Brecht, *The Threepenny Opera,* translated by Ralph Manheim, from John Willett and Ralph Manheim, eds., *Bertolt Brecht Collected Plays, Volume 5.* Copyright 1928 by Gustav Kiepenheuer Verlag, renewed © 1968 by Helene Brecht-Weigel. Translation copyright © 1979 by Stefen S. Brecht. Reprinted with the permission of Arcade Publishing, Inc., New York.

Samuel Beckett, *Endgame.* Copyright © 1958 by Grove Press, renewed 1986 by Samuel Beckett. Reprinted with the permission of Grove/Atlantic, Inc.

Eugène Ionesco, *Rhinoceros,* translated by Derek Prouse. Copyright © 1959, renewed 1987 by Eugène Ionesco. Reprinted with the permission of John Calder Publishers, Ltd.

Tennessee Williams, *The Glass Menagerie* from *The Theatre of Tennessee Williams, Volume 3.* Copyright 1945 by Tennessee Williams and Edwina D. Williams, renewed © 1973 by Tennessee Williams. Reprinted with the permission of Random House, Inc.

Arthur Miller, *All My Sons* from *Arthur Miller's Collected Plays.* Copyright 1947 and renewed © 1975 by Arthur Miller. Reprinted with the permission of Viking Penguin, a division of Penguin Books USA Inc.

Edward Albee, *The Zoo Story* (New York: E. P. Dutton, 1960). Copyright © 1969 and renewed 1987 by Edward Albee. Reprinted with the permission of William Morris Agency. CAUTION: Professionals and amateurs are hereby warned that The ZOO STORY is subject to a royalty. It is fully protected under the copyright laws of the United States of America and of all countries covered by the International Copyright Union (including the Dominion of Canada and the rest of the British Commonwealth), the Berne Convention, as well as all countries with which the United States has reciprocal copyright relations. All rights, including professional/amateur stage rights, motion picture, recitation, lecturing, public reading, radio broadcasting, television, video or sound recording, all other forms of mechanical or electronic reproduction, such as CD-ROM, CD-I, information storage and retrieval systems and photocopying, and the rights of translation into foreign languages, are expressly reserved. Particular emphasis is laid upon the matter of readings, permission for which must be secured from the Author's agent in writing. Inquiries concerning rights should be addressed to William Morris Agency, Inc., 1325 Avenue of the Americas, New York, NY 10019, Attn.: George Lane.

Lorraine Hansberry, *A Raisin in the Sun.* Copyright © 1958 by Robert Nemiroff as an unpublished work. Copyright © 1959, 1966, 1984 by Robert Nemiroff. Reprinted with the permission of Random House, Inc.

Harold Pinter, *The Birthday Party.* Copyright © 1958 and renewed 1978 by Harold Pinter. Reprinted with the permission of Grove/Atlantic, Inc.

Wole Soyinka, *The Lion and the Jewel* from *Collected Plays 2.* Copyright © 1964 by Oxford University Press. Reprinted with the permission of Oxford University Press, Ltd.

Tom Stoppard, *Rosencrantz & Guidenstein Are Dead.* Copyright © 1967 by Tom Stoppard. Reprinted with the permission of Grove/Atlantic, Inc. and Faber and Faber, Ltd.

Sam Shepard, *Buried Child* from *Seven Plays.* Copyright © 1979 by Sam Shepard. Reprinted with the permission of Bantam Books, a division of Bantam Doubleday Dell Publishing Group, Inc.

August Wilson, *The Piano Lesson.* Copyright © 1988, 1990 by August Wilson. Reprinted with the permission of Dutton Signet, a division of Penguin Books USA Inc.

Marsha Norman, *'night, Mother.* Copyright © 1983 by Marsha Norman. Reprinted with the permission of Hill and Wang, a division of Farrar, Straus & Giroux, Inc. CAUTION: Professionals and amateurs are hereby warned that *'night, Mother* by Marsha Norman, being fully protected under the Copyright Laws of the United States and all other countries of the Berne and Universal Copyright Conventions, is subject to a royalty. All rights including, but not limited to, professional, amateur, recording, motion picture, recitation, lecturing, public reading, radio and television broadcasting, and the rights of translation into foreign languages are expressly reserved. All inquiries concerning rights should be addressed to the author's agent, The Tentleff Office, 375 Greenwich Street, Suite 700, New York, NY 10013, Attention: Charmaine Ferenczi. No performance of the play may be given without obtaining in advance the written permission of the agent, and paying the requisite fee.

Wendy Wasserstein, *The Sisters Rosensweig.* Copyright © 1993 by Wendy Wasserstein. Reprinted with the permission of Harcourt Brace and Company.

THEORY AND CRITICISM

George Bernard Shaw, "The Technical Novelty of Ibsen's Plays," from *The Quintessence of Ibsenism* (New York and Boston: Brentano's, 1913).

August Strindberg, "Preface to *Miss Julie,*" translated by Henry Carlson, from *Strindberg: Five Plays,* pp. 50–61. Copyright © 1983 by The Regents of the University of California. Reprinted with the permission of University of California Press.

Francis Fergusson, from "*Ghosts* and *The Cherry Orchard:* The Theater of Modern Realism," Chapter 5 of *The Idea of a Theater,* pp. 161–177. Copyright 1949 Princeton University Press. Reprinted with the permission of the publishers.

Pirand Luigi Pirandello, "Preface to *Six Characters in Search of an Author,*" translated by Eric Bentley, from *Naked Masks: Five Plays* (New York: E. P. Dutton, 1922.)

Karen Malpede, "Reflections on *The Verge*" from Linda Ben-zvi, ed., *Susan Glaspell: Essays on Her Theater and Fiction,* pp. 123–127. Copyright © 1995 by The University of Michigan. Reprinted with the permission of The University of Michigan Press.

Doris Alexander, "Desire Under the Elms" from *Eugene O'Neill's Creative Struggle: The Decisive Decade 1924–1933* (University Park: Penn State Press, 1992), pp. 21–39. Copyright © 1992 by Doris Alexander. Reprinted with the permission of the author.

Thornton Wilder, "Some Thoughts on Playwrighting" from Augusto Centeno, ed., *The Intent of of the Artist.* Copyright 1941 by Princeton University Press. Reprinted with the permission of the publisher.

Bertolt Brecht, "Notes to *The Threepenny Opera*" and "Stage Design for *The Threepenny Opera,*" translated by Ralph Manheim, from John Willett and Ralph Manheim, eds., *The Threepenny Opera* (1994), pp. 90–98. Copyright 1928 by Arvid Englind Teaterforlag a.b., renewed © 1968 by Helene Brecht-Weigel. Translation copyright © 1979 by Stefen S. Brecht. Reprinted with the permission of Arcade Publishing, New York.

Martin Esslin, "Samuel Beckett: The Search for Self" from *The Theatre of the Absurd.* Copyright © 1961, 1968, 1969, 1980 and renewed 1989 by Martin Esslin. Reprinted with the permission of Doubleday, a division of Bantam Doubleday Dell Publishing Group Inc.

Eugène Ionesco, "Preface to *Rhinoceros,*" "Note on *Rhinoceros,*" and "About *Rhinoceros* in the United States," from *Notes and Counter Notes*, translated by Donald Watson, pp. 198–199, 206–207, and 207–211. Copyright © 1964 by Grove Press, Inc. Copyright © 1962 by Editions Gallimard. Reprinted with the permission of Calder Publications, Ltd.

Geoffrey Borney, "The Two *Glass Menageries:* Reading Edition and Acting Edition" from Ortrum Zuber-Skeritt, ed., *Page to Stage: Theater as Translation.* Copyright © 1984 by Editions Rodopi B. V. Reprinted with the permission of the publishers.

Arthur Miller, "Ibsen and the Drama of Today" from James McFarlane, ed., *The Cambridge Companion to Ibsen.* Copyright © 1994. Reprinted with the permission of Cambridge University Press.

Henry Louis Gates, Jr., "The Chitlin Circuit" from *The New Yorker* (February 3, 1997), pp. 44–50. Copyright © 1997 by Henry Louis Gates, Jr. Reprinted with the permission of the author, c/o Janklow & Nesbitt Associates.

Katherine H. Burkman, "The Demeter Myth and Doubling in Marsha Norman's *'night, Mother*" from June Schlueter, ed., *Modern American Drama: The Female Canon* (Fairleigh Dickinson University Press, 1990), pp. 254–263. Copyright © 1990 by Associated University Presses. Reprinted with the permission of the publisher.

PHOTOGRAPHS

P. 13: Henry Grossman.

P. 67: New York Public Library for the Performing Arts.

P. 101: Martha Swope/Time Life Syndication.

P. 144: Billy Rose Theater Collection, New York Public Library for the Performing Arts. Photograph by Van Williams.

P. 200: Eileen Darby.

P. 228: New York Public Library for the Performing Arts.

P. 261: The New York Public Library for the Performing Arts. Brugiere Collection, Lincoln Center.

P. 290: The New York Public Library for the Performing Arts. Friedman-Abeles Collection.

P. 357: The New York Public Library for the Performing Arts. Alfredo Valente Collection.

P. 428: The New York Public Library for the Performing Arts. Friedman-Abeles Collection.

P. 477: Museum of the City of New York.

P. 514: Billy Rose Theater Collection, New York Public Library for the Performing Arts. Photograph by Eileen Darby, Graphic House.

P. 549: Billy Rose Theater Collection, New York Public Library for the Performing Arts. Photograph by Sherwin, Greenberg Associates.

P. 566: The New York Public Library for the Performing Arts. Friedman-Abeles Collection.

P. 610: Henry Grossman.

P. 644: Lisa Ebright/Court Theatre.

P. 716: Billy Rose Theater Collection, New York Public Library for the Performing Arts. Photo by Gerry Goodstein.

P. 753: Billy Rose Theater Collection, New York Public Library for the Performing Arts. Photo by Gerry Goodstein.

P. 795: Richard Feldman.

P. 820: Martha Swope/Time Life Syndication.